July 24–28, 2011
Beijing, China

Association for
Computing Machinery

Advancing Computing as a Science & Profession

SIGIR'11

Proceedings of the 34th International ACM SIGIR Conference on

Research and Development in Information Retrieval

Sponsored by:

ACM SIGIR

Supported by:

Microsoft Research, Baidu, EMC², Google, SOSO, Yahoo!, eBay, HP Labs, IBM Research, Yandex, CIPS, and Universitité de Montréal

Association for
Computing Machinery

Advancing Computing as a Science & Profession

The Association for Computing Machinery
2 Penn Plaza, Suite 701
New York, New York 10121-0701

Notice to Past Authors of ACM-Published Articles
ACM intends to create a complete electronic archive of all articles and/or other material previously published by ACM. If you have written a work that has been previously published by ACM in any journal or conference proceedings prior to 1978, or any SIG Newsletter at any time, and you do NOT want this work to appear in the ACM Digital Library, please inform permissions@acm.org, stating the title of the work, the author(s), and where and when published.

ISBN: 978-1-4503-0934-9

ISBN Print: 978-1-4503-1250-9

Additional copies may be ordered prepaid from:

ACM Order Department
PO Box 30777
New York, NY 10087-0777, USA

Phone: 1-800-342-6626 (USA and Canada)
+1-212-626-0500 (Global)
Fax: +1-212-944-1318
E-mail: acmhelp@acm.org
Hours of Operation: 8:30 am – 4:30 pm ET

Printed in the USA

Preface from the General Chairs

Welcome to the 34th ACM SIGIR conference on research and development in information retrieval, and welcome to Beijing!

The whole Chinese IR community is delighted to host this year's SIGIR conference for the first time in China in the historical and vibrant city of Beijing. The last decade has witnessed the great surge of China's Internet and search engine industry as one of the largest and most active in the world. The SIGIR conferences have also seen increased Chinese participation: the number of full papers from China has reached a record high of 18 this year, while more than half of them have at least one Chinese name as author. This year's SIGIR conference is a significant opportunity to forge stronger ties between the Chinese IR community and the international SIGIR community. We hope that you will enjoy the great technical program as well as the supporting events in connection with the search engine industry in China.

The conference promises to be a success, with a record number of full papers to be presented. The program committee, chaired by Ricardo Baeza-Yates, Tat-Seng Chua and Bruce Croft and helped by 43 area chairs and many reviewers, did a great job in selecting high quality papers that reflect the latest developments in IR. We are equally grateful to all the other committee members: the Posters and Demos chairs Kevyn Collins-Thompson, Gary Geunbae Lee, and Massimo Melucci; the Tutorial chair Yi Zhang; the Workshops chairs Noriko Kando and Luo Si; the Mentoring Program chair Gareth Jones; the Outstanding Paper Award chair Susan Dumais; the Doctoral Consortium chairs Marteen de Rijke and Paul Thomas; the Industrial Track chairs David Carmel and Haifeng Wang; and the Publication chair Zaiqing Nie. We are especially grateful to Jimmy Huang for his active attraction of corporate sponsorship. The conference also benefits from the great help of the Local Organization Committee, chaired by Xiaoming Li. Special thanks go to Hang Li and Ling Huang for their involvement throughout the preparation of this conference.

SIGIR'11 is sponsored by ACM and has received generous financial support from a large number of companies and organizations. To date, Microsoft Research supports at the *Diamond* level; Baidu, EMC, Google, Tencent and Yahoo! provide *Gold* support; eBay is a *Silver* supporter; HP, IBM Research and Yandex take part at the *Bronze* level; while Springer, Now Publishers and Morgan & Claypool exhibit their products. SIGIR'11 is organized in association with the Chinese Information Processing Society. Finally, we are thankful to the University of Montreal for allowing Jian-Yun Nie to devote himself entirely to this conference during the last 6 months, and we thank ACM and the SIGIR Executive Committee for their constant support.

We hope you will enjoy the conference and your visit to Beijing and China.

Wei-Ying Ma
Microsoft Research Asia

Jian-Yun Nie
University of Montreal

Preface from the Program Committee Chairs

Welcome to the 34th ACM SIGIR International Conference on Research and Development in Information Retrieval. The record number of papers in this year's conference represents both the breadth and depth of the research being done in this vibrant field, both in academia and industry. We have done our best to ensure that these papers meet high standards of quality in terms of presentation, citations, and experimental methodology. At the same time, we have tried to be flexible in the application of these criteria in order to accept papers describing novel and innovative work that may be somewhat unconventional.

The conference received 543 full paper submissions this year, with 240 (44%) coming from Asia and Pacific region, 185 (34%) from the Americas, and 112 (21%) from Europe (the rest were "unknown"). Of these papers, 108 (19.9%) were accepted, up from the acceptance rate of 16.7% in last year's conference. The top five countries in terms of accepted papers were the U.S.A. (52), China (18), Germany (7), and then the U.K. and Spain (both 5). In addition, 274 short papers were submitted to the poster track, of which 89 (32.5%) were accepted. In the other categories, there were 15 (42.8%) demonstrations, 8 workshops, and 11 half-day tutorials accepted. In terms of the technical areas that the accepted papers cover, using the primary keyword assigned by the authors, the top five areas are document representation and content analysis (20%), retrieval models and ranking (17%), users and interactive IR (13%), queries and query analysis (11%), and filtering and recommendation (11%). Perhaps the only surprise there is the increase in the number of papers in filtering and recommendation. We believe that the papers at this year's conference provide an excellent cross-section of what is going on in our field. We hope that you find that reading them and listening to the presenters to be a rewarding experience.

SIGIR uses a two-tier double blind review system. For the full papers, the first step is that at least three first-tier reviewers read every paper and provide ratings and comments. Then two additional reviewers, referred to as the primary or secondary area chairs, study those reviews, and introduce their own opinions and summaries where appropriate by making additional comments. In some cases, the area chairs initiate the discussion among the first-tier reviewers to work out any controversial issues or significant differences of opinion. A new step introduced this year was to request author feedback for specific issues in some papers. Another change this year was that final decisions for nearly all papers were made by the two area chairs together with the reviewers. At the program committee meeting in Barcelona, the program chairs and some area chairs went over the reviews, obtained additional input, and made decisions in the few cases where the area chairs had requested more discussion.

The success of the conference depends entirely on the large number of volunteers that every year devotes large amounts of their time to reviewing and organizing. We are grateful to the more than 200 first-tier reviewers (or general program committee), who performed their tasks very well. We also acknowledge the tremendous job done by the Posters Chairs in handling the short papers, and the great work done by the other Chairs with their tasks. We are particularly indebted to the 43 Area Chairs for their willingness to try a new approach that required more effort from them, and for their responsiveness throughout the reviewing process. We also acknowledge the help of Thomas Preuss with support for the ConfMaster reviewing system. Finally, we extend our best wishes to next year's Program Chairs!

Ricardo Baeza-Yates
Yahoo! Research Barcelona
Africa and Europe

Tat-Seng Chua
National University of Singapore
Asia and Pacific

W. Bruce Croft
University of Massachusetts
Americas

Table of Contents

VOLUME 1

Session 1C: Learning to Rank

Session 2A: Personalization

Session 2B: Retrieval Models I

Session 2C: Social Media

Session 3A: Content Analysis

Session 3B: Web IR

Session 3C: Collaborative Filtering I

Session 4A: Users II

Session 4B: Query Analysis II

Session 4C: Communities

Session 5A: Classification

Session 5B: Retrieval Models II

Session 5C: Image Search

Session 6A: Indexing

Session 6B: Web Queries

Session 6C: Collaborative Filtering II

VOLUME 2

Session 8B: Query Suggestions

Session 8C: Linguistic Analysis

Session 9A: Clustering

Session 9B: Effectiveness

Session 9C: Multilingual IR

Session 10A: Efficiency

Session 10B: Recommender Systems

Session 10C: Test Collections

Posters Presentations

Demonstrations

Tutorials

Doctoral Consortium

Industrial Track

SIGIR 2011 Organization

General Co-Chairs:	Wei-Ying Ma (*Microsoft Research Asia, China*) Jian-Yun Nie (*University of Montreal, Canada*)
Program Co-Chairs:	Ricardo Baeza-Yates (*Yahoo! Research, Spain*) Tat-Seng Chua (*National University of Singapore*) W. Bruce Croft (*University of Massachusetts, Amherst, USA*)
Posters and Demos Co-Chairs:	Kevyn Collins-Thompson (*Microsoft Research, USA*) Gary Geunbae Lee (*POSTECH, Korea*) Massimo Melucci (*University of Padua, Italy*)
Tutorial Chair:	Yi Zhang (*University of California, Santa Cruz, USA*)
Workshop Co-Chairs:	Noriko Kando (*National Institute of Informatics, Japan*) Luo Si (*Purdue University, USA*)
Mentor Chair:	Gareth Jones (*Dublin City University, Ireland*)
Outstanding Paper Awards Chair:	Susan Dumais (*Microsoft Research, USA*)
Doctoral Consortium Co-Chairs:	Maarten de Rijke (*University of Amsterdam, The Netherlands*) Paul Thomas (*CSIRO, Australia*)
Industrial Track Co-Chairs:	David Carmel (*IBM Research, Haifa, Israel*) Haifeng Wang (*Baidu, China*)
Sponsorship Chair:	Jimmy Huang (*York University, Canada*)
Publicity Chair:	Kam-Fai Wong (*Chinese University of Hong Kong, China*)
Local Organization Chair:	Xiaoming Li (*Peking University, China*)
Finance Chair:	Hang Li (*Microsoft Research Asia, China*)
Proceedings Chair:	Zaiqing Nie (*Microsoft Research Asia, China*)
Chair of Coordination with Local Societies:	Sheng Li (*Harbin Institute of Technology, China*)
Conference Management:	Racemind (*China*)

SIGIR 2011 Area Chairs

Ricardo Baeza-Yates (*Yahoo! Research, Spain*) - Chair
Tat-Seng Chua (*National University of Singapore, Singapore*) - Chair
W. Bruce Croft (*University of Massachusetts, Amherst, USA*) – Chair

1. Document Representation and Content Analysis
James Allan (*University of Massachusetts Amherst, USA*)
Jamie Callan (*CMU, USA*)
Fernando Diaz (*Yahoo! Research, USA*)
Wessel Kraaij (*Radboud University Nijmegen, The Netherlands*)
Douglas Oard (*University of Maryland, USA*)
Maarten de Rijke (*Universiteit van Amsterdam, The Netherlands*)

2. Queries and Query Analysis
Eugene Agichtein (*Emory University, USA*)
Nick Craswell (*Microsoft Research, USA*)
Evgeniy Gabrilovich (*Yahoo! Research, USA*)
Rosie Jones (*Akamai, USA*)

3. Users and Interactive IR
Nick Belkin (*Rutgers, The State University of New Jersey, USA*)
Susan Dumais (*Microsoft Research, USA*)
Diane Kelly (*University of North Carolina, Chapel Hill, USA*)
Ryen White (*Microsoft Research, USA*)

4. Retrieval Models and Ranking
Norbert Fuhr (*Universität Duisburg-Essen, Germany*)
Djoerd Hiemstra (*University of Twente, The Netherlands*)
Oren Kurland (*Technion, Israel*)
Hang Li (*Microsoft Research Asia, China*)
Tie-Yan Liu (*Microsoft Research Asia, China*)
Donald Metzler (*USC/ISI, USA*)
Luo Si (*Purdue University, USA*)
ChengXiang Zhai (*University of Illinois at Urbana-Champaign, USA*)

5. Search Engine Architectures and Scalability
Alistair Moffat (*University of Melbourne, Australia*)
Fabrizio Silvestri (*ISTI-CNR, Italy*)

6. Filtering and Recommendion
David Carmel (*IBM Research, Israel*)
John Riedl (*University of Minnesota, USA*)
Yi Zhang (*UC Santa Cruz, USA*)

7. Evaluation
Ben Carterette (*University of Delaware, USA*)
Mark Sanderson (*RMIT, Australia*)
Ian Soboroff (*NIST, USA*)
Justin Zobel (*University of Melbourne, Australia*)

8. Web IR and Social Media Search
Soumen Chakrabarti (*Indian Institute of Technology, Bombay, India*)
Yoelle Maarek (*Yahoo! Research, Israel*)
Marc Najork (*Microsoft Research, USA*)
Iadh Ounis (*University of Glasgow, UK*)
Berthier Ribeiro-Neto (*Federal University of Minas Gerais, Brazil*)

9. IR and Structured Data
Mounia Lalmas (*Yahoo! Research, Spain*)
Andrew Trotman (*University of Otago, New Zealand*)
Arjen de Vries (*Centrum Viskunde & Informatica and Delft University of Technology, The Netherlands*)

10. Multimedia IR
Xian-Sheng Hua (*Microsoft Research Asia, China*)
R. Manmatha (*University of Massachusetts Amherst, USA*)

11. Other Applications
Charlie Clarke (*University of Waterloo, Canada*)
Edward Fox (*Virginia Tech, USA*)

SIGIR 2011 Program Committee

Maristella Agosti (*University of Padua, Italy*)
Omar Alonso (*Microsoft, USA*)
Ismail Altingovde (*Bilkent University, Turkey*)
Gianni Amati (*Fondazione Ugo Bordoni, Italy*)
Avi Arampatzis (*Democritus University of Thrace, Greece*)
Paavo Arvola (*University of Tampere Finland, Finland*)
Javed Aslam (*Northeastern University, USA*)
Leif Azzopardi (*University of Glasgow, United Kingdom*)
Ricardo Baeza-Yates (*Yahoo! Research, Spain*)
Peter Bailey (*Microsoft, USA*)
Niranjan Balasubramanian (*University of Massachusetts Amherst, USA*)
Timothy Baldwin (*University of Melbourne, Australia*)
Krisztian Balog (*Norwegian University of Science and Tech., Norway*)
Roberto Basili (*University of Roma, Tor Vergata, Italy*)
Steve Beitzel (*Telcordia Technologies, USA*)
Michael Bendersky (*University of Massachusetts Amherst, USA*)
Paul Bennett (*Microsoft, USA*)
Mikhail Bilenko (*Microsoft Research, USA*)
Gloria Bordogna (*National Research Council of Italy, Italy*)
Mohand Boughanem (*IRIT, University Paul Sabatier, Toulouse, France*)
Giorgio Brajnik (*University of Udine, Italy*)
Martin Braschler (*Zurich University of Applied Sciences, Switzerland*)
Eric Brown (*IBM Research, USA*)
Peter Bruza (*Queensland University of Technology, Australia*)
Chris Buckley (*Sabir Research, USA*)
Stefan Buettcher (*Google, USA*)
Fazli Can (*Bilkent University, Turkey*)
Guihong Cao (*Microsoft, USA*)
Robert Capra (*University of North Carolina at Chapel Hill, USA*)
Ben Carterette (*University of Delaware, USA*)
Vitor Carvalho (*Microsoft, USA*)
Carlos Castillo (*Yahoo! Research, Spain*)
Raman Chandrasekar (*Evri, USA*)
Yi Chang (*Yahoo! Labs, USA*)
Kevin Chang (*University of Illinois at Urbana-Champaign, USA*)
Francine Chen (*FX Palo Alto Laboratory, USA*)
Pu-Jen Cheng (*National Taiwan University, Taiwan*)
Jean-Pierre Chevallet (*Université Grenoble, France*)
Abdur Chowdhury (*Twitter, USA*)
Paul Clough (*University of Sheffield, United Kingdom*)
Jack Conrad (*Thomson Reuters, USA*)
Gordon V. Cormack (*University of Waterloo, Canada*)
Hang Cui (*Google, USA*)
Brian Davison (*Lehigh University, USA*)
Debora Donato (*Yahoo! Labs, USA*)
Antoine Doucet (*University of Caen, France*)
Georges Dupret (*Yahoo! Labs, USA*)
Koji Eguchi (*Kobe University, Japan*)
David Eichmann (*U. Iowa, USA*)
Jonathan Elsas (*CMU, USA*)
David Elsweiler (*Friedrich-Alexander Universitaet Erlangen, Germany*)
Jianping Fan (*UNC-Charlotte, USA*)
Hui Fang (*U. of Delaware, USA*)
Henry Feild (*University of Massachusetts Amherst, USA*)
Shaolei Feng (*Siemens Corporate Research Labs, USA*)
Radu Florian (*IBM Research, USA*)
Martin Franz (*IBM, USA*)
Jim French (*Corporation for National Research Initiatives, USA*)
Luanne Freund (*University of British Columbia, Canada*)
Evgeniy Gabrilovich (*Yahoo, USA*)
Patrick Gallinari (*Université Pierre et Marie Curie - Paris 6, France*)
Bin Gao (*Microsoft Research Asia, China*)
Eric Gaussier (*Université Joseph Fourier, France*)
Fredric Gey (*University of California, Berkeley, USA*)
C. Lee Giles (*Pennsylvania State University, USA*)
Ayse Goker (*City University London, United Kingdom*)
Marcos Goncalves (*UFMG, Brazil*)
Gregory Grefenstette (*Exalead, France*)
Jacek Gwizdka (*Rutgers University, USA*)
Sanda Harabagiu (*USA*)
Donna Harman (*NIST, USA*)
David Harper (*Google Switzerland, Switzerland*)
Ahmed Hassan (*University of Michigan Ann Arbor, USA*)
Claudia Hauff (*TU Delft, Netherlands*)
Daqing He (*University of Pittsburgh, USA*)
William Hersh (*Oregon Health and Science University, USA*)
Timo Honkela (*Helsinki University of Technology, Finland*)
Eric Horvitz (*Microsoft Research, USA*)
Xuanjing Huang (*Fudan University, China*)
Jimmy Huang (*York University, Canada*)
Panos Ipeirotis (*New York University, USA*)
CV Jawahar (*IIIT Hyderabad, India*)
Jiwoon Jeon (*Google, USA*)
Daxin Jiang (*Microsoft Research Asia, China*)
Hideo Joho (*University of Tsukuba, Japan*)
Gareth Jones (*Dublin City University, Ireland*)
Joemon Jose (*University of Glasgow, United Kingdom*)
Vanja Josifovski (*Yahoo! Research, USA*)

Marko Junkkari (*University of Tampere Finland, Finland*)
Jaap Kamps (*University of Amsterdam, Netherlands*)
Noriko Kando (*National Institute of Informatics, Japan*)
Evangelos Kanoulas (*University of Sheffield, United Kingdom*)
David Karger (*MIT, USA*)
Jussi Karlgren (*Gavagai, Sweden*)
Gabriella Kazai (*Microsoft Research Cambridge, United Kingdom*)
Weimao Ke (*Drexel University, USA*)
Qifa Ke (*Microsoft Research, USA*)
Marijn Koolen (*University of Amsterdam, Netherlands*)
Yehuda Koren (*Yahoo! Research Israel, Israel*)
Ravi Kumar (*Yahoo! Research, USA*)
Giridhar Kumaran (*Microsoft Corporation, USA*)
Alberto Laender (*Federal University of Minas Gerais, Brazil*)
Wai Lam (*The Chinese University of Hong Kong, Hong Kong*)
Monica Landoni (*USI, Switzerland*)
Guy Lapalme (*Université de Montréal, Canada*)
Birger Larsen (*Royal School of Library and Information Science Denmark, Denmark*)
Ray Larson (*University of California, Berkeley, USA*)
Victor Lavrenko (*University of Edinburgh, United Kingdom*)
Matthew Lease (*University of Texas at Austin, USA*)
Miro Lehtonen (*University of Helsinki, Finland*)
Jochen Leidner (*Thomson Reuters Global Services, Switzerland*)
Anton Leuski (*University of Southern California, USA*)
David Lewis (*David D. Lewis Consulting, USA*)
Xiao Li (*Microsoft Research, USA*)
Zhisheng Li (*National University of Singapore, Singapore*)
Ee-Peng Lim (*Singapore Management University, Singapore*)
Chin-Yew Lin (*Microsoft Research Asia, China*)
Yi Liu (*Google, USA*)
Ting Liu (*Harbin Institute of Technology, China*)
David Losada (*University of Santiago de Compostela, Spain*)
Jie Lu (*IBM Research, USA*)
Robert Luk (*The Hong Kong Polytechnic University, Hong Kong*)
Yuanhua Lv (*UIUC, USA*)
Yoelle Maarek (*Yahoo! Research, Israel*)
Craig Macdonald (*U. Glasgow, United Kingdom*)
Andrew MacFarlane (*City University London, United Kingdom*)
Prasenjit Majumder (*DAIICT, India*)
Thomas Mandl (*U. Hildesheim, Germany*)
Stephane Marchand-Maillet (*University of Geneva - CS Dept - Viper group, Switzerland*)
James Mayfield (*JHU HLT/COE, USA*)
Paul McNamee (*Johns Hopkins University, USA*)
Tao Mei (*Microsoft Research Asia, China*)
Massimo Melucci (*University of Padua, Italy*)
Natasa Milic-Frayling (*Microsoft Research Ltd, United Kingdom*)
Zhao-yan Ming (*National University of Singapore, Singapore*)
Mandar Mitra (*Indian Statistical Institute, India*)
Vibhu Mittal (*Root-1 Research, USA*)
Marie-Francine Moens (*Katholieke Universiteit Leuven, Belgium*)
Alistair Moffat (*University of Melbourne, Australia*)
Alessandro Moschitti (*University of Trento, Italy*)
Josiane Mothe (*IRIT, Université de Toulouse, France*)
Isabelle Moulinier (*Thomson Reuters, USA*)
Philippe Mulhem (*Laboratoire d'Informatique de Grenoble, France*)
Vanessa Murdock (*Yahoo! Research, Spain*)
Sung HYon Myaeng (*Korea Advanced Institute of Science and Tech, South Korea*)
Gonzalo Navarro (*University of Chile, Chile*)
Michael Nelson (*Old Dominion University, USA*)
Hwee Tou Ng (*National University of Singapore, Singapore*)
Charles Nicholas (*USA*)
Alexandros Ntoulas (*Microsoft Research, USA*)
Giorgio Maria Di Nunzio (*University of Padua, Italy*)
Paul Ogilvie (*LinkedIn, USA*)
Marius Pasca (*Google Inc., USA*)
Gabriella Pasi (*University of Milano-Bicocca, Italy*)
Virgil Pavlu (*Northeastern University, USA*)
Jan Pedersen (*Microsoft Corp., USA*)
Fuchun Peng (*Microsoft, USA*)
Jeremy Pickens (*Catalyst Repository Systems, USA*)
Ari Pirkola (*University of Tampere Finland, Finland*)
Benjamin Piwowarski (*University of Glasgow, United Kingdom*)
John Prager (*IBM Research, USA*)
Tao Qin (*Microsoft Research Asia, China*)
Filip Radlinski (*Microsoft, Canada*)
Hema Raghavan (*IBM Research, USA*)
Vijay Raghavan (*USA*)
Edie Rasmussen (*University of British Columbia, Canada*)
Andreas Rauber (*Vienna University of Technology, Austria*)
Matthew Richardson (*Microsoft Research, USA*)
Soo Young Rieh (*University of Michigan, USA*)
Hae-Chang Rim (*Korea University, South Korea*)
Thomas Roelleke (*Queen Mary University of London, United Kingdom*)
Dmitri Roussinov (*University of Strathclyde, United Kingdom*)
Stefan Rueger (*United Kingdom*)
Tetsuya Sakai (*Microsoft Research Asia, China*)

Ralf Schenkel (*Saarland University, Germany*)
Hinrich Schuetze (*University of Stuttgart, Germany*)
Jangwon Seo (*University of Massachusetts Amherst, USA*)
Chirag Shah (*Rutgers University, USA*)
Rao Shen (*Yahoo!, USA*)
Jialie Shen (*Singapore Management University, Singapore*)
Dou Shen (*Buzz Labs, USA*)
Milad Shokouhi (*Microsoft, United Kingdom*)
David Smith (*University of Massachusetts Amherst, USA*)
Mark Smucker (*University of Waterloo, Canada*)
Aya Soffer (*IBM, Israel*)
Dawei Song (*The Robert Gordon University, United Kingdom*)
Ruihua Song (*Microsoft Research Asia, China*)
Eero Sormunen (*Finland*)
Torsten Suel (*Polytechnic Institute of NYU, USA*)
Krysta Svore (*Microsoft Research, USA*)
John Tait (*Information Retrieval Facility, Austria*)
Simone Teufel (*University of Cambridge, United Kingdom*)
Martin Theobald (*Max-Planck Institute Informatics, Germany*)
James Thom (*RMIT, Australia*)
Paul Thomas (*CSIRO, Australia*)
Paul Thompson (*Dartmouth College, USA*)
Anastasios Tombros (*Queen Mary University of London, United Kingdom*)
Elaine Toms (*Dalhousie University, Canada*)
Andrew Turpin (*University of Melbourne, Australia*)
Howard Turtle (*Syracuse University, USA*)
Antti Ukkonen (*Yahoo! Research Barcelona, Spain*)
Pertti Vakkari (*University of Tampere, Finland*)
Olga Vechtomova (*University of Waterloo, Canada*)
Nina Wacholder (*Rutgers University, USA*)
Jingdong Wang (*Microsoft Research Asia, China*)
Meng Wang (*National University of Singapore, Singapore*)
Kai Wang (*Institute for Infocom Research (I2R), Singapore*)
Qiuyue Wang (*Renmin Univ. of China, China*)
William Webber (*University of Melbourne, Australia*)
Ingmar Weber (*Yahoo! Research Barcelona, Spain*)
Xing Wei (*Microsoft Corp., USA*)
Gerhard Weikum (*Max-Planck Institute for Informatics, Germany*)
Thijs Westerveld (*Teezir Search Solutions, Netherlands*)
Gu Xu (*Microsoft Research Asia, China*)
Xiaobing Xue (*University of Massachusetts, USA*)
Yiming Yang (*Carnegie Mellon University, USA*)
Linjun Yang (*Microsoft Research Asia, China*)
Xing Yi (*University of Massachusetts Amherst, USA*)
Emine Yilmaz (*Microsoft Research Cambridge, United Kingdom*)
Elad Yom-Tov (*Yahoo! Research, USA*)
Masaharu Yoshioka (*Hokkaido University, Japan*)
Markus Zanker (*Alpen-Adria-Universitaet Klagenfurt, Austria*)
Lei Zhang (*Microsoft Research Asia, China*)
Shenghuo Zhu (*NEC Labs America, USA*)
Nivio Ziviani (*Federal University of Minas Gerais, Brazil*)

Posters Committee

Kevyn Collins-Thompson (*Microsoft Research, USA*) - Chair
Gary Geunbae Lee (*POSTECH, Korea*) - Chair
Massimo Melucci (*University of Padua, Italy*) - Chair

Eugene Agichtein (*Emory University, USA*)
Alnur Ali (*Microsoft, USA*)
Omar Alonso (*Microsoft, USA*)
Robin Aly (*University of Twente, The Netherlands*)
Jaime Arguello (*Carnegie Mellon University, USA*)
Azin Ashkan (*University of Waterloo, Canada*)
Javed Aslam (*Northeastern University, USA*)
Hany Azzam (*Queen Mary, University of London, UK*)
Niranjan Balasubramanian (*University of Massachusetts, Amherst, USA*)
Alberto Barrón-Cedeño (*University of Valencia, Spain*)
Michael Bendersky (*University of Massachusetts, Amherst, USA*)
Roi Blanco (*Yahoo! Research, Spain*)
Rui Cai (*Microsoft Research Asia, China*)
Silvia Calegari (*University of Milan-Bicocca, Italy*)
Annalina Caputo (*University of Bari, Italy*)
Ben Carterette (*University of Delaware, USA*)
Marc-Allen Cartright (*University of Massachusetts, Amherst, USA*)
Carlos Castillo (*Yahoo! Research Barcelona, Spain*)
Khe Chai Sim (*National University of Singapore, Singapore*)
Yi Chang (*Yahoo! Research, USA*)
Francine Chen (*FXPAL, USA*)
Yi Chen (*Dublin City University, Ireland*)
Yun Chi (*NEC Laboratories, USA*)
Paul Clough (*University of Sheffield, UK*)
Gao Cong (*Nanyang Technological University, Singapore*)
Bin Cui (*Peking University, China*)
Tonya Custis (*Thomson Reuters, USA*)
Na Dai (*Lehigh University, USA*)
Lorand Dali (*Jozef Stefan Institute, Slovenia*)
Kareem Darwish (*Microsoft, Egypt*)

Emanuele Di Buccio (*University of Padua, Italy*)
Debora Donato (*Yahoo! Labs, USA*)
Georges Dupret (*Yahoo! Labs, USA*)
Miles Efron (*University of Illinois, Urbana-Champaign, USA*)
Koji Eguchi (*Kobe University, Japan*)
Jonathan Elsas (*Carnegie Mellon University, USA*)
Tamer Elsayed (*University of Maryland, USA*)
Jianping Fan (*UNC Charlotte, USA*)
Hui Fang (*University of Delaware, USA*)
Fabio Faria (*University of Campinas, Brazil*)
Ingo Frommholz (*University of Glasgow, UK*)
Xin Fu (*Microsoft, USA*)
Atsushi Fujii (*Tokyo Institute of Technology, Japan*)
Bin Gao (*Microsoft Research Asia, China*)
Wei Gao (*The Chinese University of Hong Kong, China*)
Susan Gauch (*University of Arkansas, USA*)
Shima Gerani (*University of Lugano, Switzerland*)
Brigitte Grau (*LIMSI, France*)
Mark Greenwood (*University of Sheffield, UK*)
Gregory Grefenstette (*Exalead, France*)
Daniel Gruhl (*IBM, USA*)
Guihong Cao (*Microsoft, USA*)
Karl Gyllstrom (*Katholieke Universiteit Leuven, Belgium*)
Preben Hansen (*Swedish Institute of Computer Science, Sweden*)
Donna Harman (*NIST, USA*)
Morgan Harvey (*Strathclyde University, Glasgow, UK*)
Claudia Hauff (*University of Twente, The Netherlands*)
Ben He (*Chinese Academy of Sciences, China*)
Jiyin He (*University of Amsterdam, The Netherlands*)
Andreas Henrich (*University of Bamberg, Germany*)
Katja Hofmann (*University of Amsterdam, The Netherlands*)
Frank Hopfgartner (*University of Glasgow, UK*)
Vivian (Qinmin) Hu (*York University, Canada*)
Meishan Hu (*Nanyang Technological University, Singapore*)
Jimmy Huang (*York University, Canada*)
Yoshiyuki Inagaki (*Yahoo! Labs, USA*)
Giacomo Inches (*UNISI, Switzerland*)
Jagadeesh Jagarlamudi (*University of Maryland, USA*)
Adam Jatowt (*Kyoto University, Japan*)
Daxin Jiang (*Microsoft Research Asia, China*)
Jing Jiang (*Singapore Management University, Singapore*)
Gareth Jones (*Dublin City University, Ireland*)
Joemon Jose (*University of Glasgow, UK*)
Leszek Kaliciak (*Robert Gordon University, UK*)
Jaap Kamps (*University of Amsterdam, The Netherlands*)
Nattiya Kanhabua (*Norwegian University of Science and Technology, Norway*)
Evangelos Kanoulas (*University of Sheffield, UK*)
Maryam Karimzadehgan (*University of Illinois, Urbana-Champaign, USA*)
Mostafa Keikha (*University of Lugano, Switzerland*)
Jin-Dong Kim (*University of Tokyo, Japan*)
Jinyoung Kim (*University of Massachusetts, Amherst, USA*)
Seokhwan Kim (*Pohang University of Science and Technology, Korea*)
Jonathan Koren (*University of California, Santa Cruz, USA*)
Alexander Kotov (*University of Illinois, Urbana-Champaign, USA*)
Donald Kraft (*Louisiana State University, USA*)
Anagha Kulkarni-Joshi (*Carnegie Mellon University, USA*)
Giridhar Kumaran (*Microsoft, USA*)
Oren Kurland (*Technion, Israel*)
Ni Lao (*Carnegie Mellon University, USA*)
Guy Lapalme (*Université de Montréal, Canada*)
Neal Lathia (*University College London, UK*)
Matthew Lease (*University of Texas at Austin, USA*)
Jung-Tae Lee (*Korea University, Korea*)
Yeha Lee (*Pohang University of Science and Technology, Korea*)
Teerapong Leelanupab (*University of Glasgow, UK*)
Xiao Li (*Microsoft Research, USA*)
Elizabeth Liddy (*Syracuse University, USA*)
Xia Lin (*Drexel University, USA*)
Nathan Liu (*Hong Kong University of Science and Technology, China*)
Yi Liu (*Microsoft Research Asia, China*)
Robert Luk (*The Hong Kong Polytechnic University, China*)
Yuanhua Lv (*University of Illinois, Urbana-Champaign, USA*)
Hao Ma (*The Chinese University of Hong Kong, China*)
Craig Macdonald (*University of Glasgow, UK*)
Andrew MacFarlane (*City University London, UK*)
Takuya Maekawa (*NTT, Japan*)
Prasenjit Majumder (*Dhirubhai Ambani Institute of Information and Communication Technology, India*)
Yi Mao (*Microsoft, USA*)
Giorgio Maria Di Nunzio (*University of Padua, Italy*)
Ilya Markov (*UNISI, Switzerland*)
Paul McNamee (*Johns Hopkins University, USA*)
Tao Mei (*Microsoft Research Asia, China*)
Edgar Meij (*University of Amsterdam, The Netherlands*)
Donald Metzler (*University of Southern California, USA*)
Natasa Milic-Frayling (*Microsoft Research Cambridge, UK*)
Zhao-Yan Ming (*National University of Singapore, Singapore*)
Einat Minkov (*University of Haifa, Israel*)
Riccardo Miotto (*University of Padua, Italy*)

Nicola Montecchio (*University of Padua, Italy*)
Yashar Moshfeghi (*University of Glasgow, UK*)
Seung-Hoon Na (*National University of Singapore, Singapore*)
Preslav Nakov (*National University of Singapore, Singapore*)
Michael Nelson (*Old Dominion University, USA*)
Charles Nicholas (*University of Maryland, USA*)
Tae-Gil Noh (*Kyungpook National University, Korea*)
Virgil Pavlu (*Northeastern University, USA*)
Fuchun Peng (*Microsoft, USA*)
Jeremy Pickens (*Catalyst Repository Systems, USA*)
Karen Pinel-Sauvagnat (*IRIT, France*)
Benjamin Piwowarski (*University of Glasgow, UK*)
Tamara Polajnar (*University of Glasgow, UK*)
Luca Pretto (*University of Padua, Italy*)
Diego Puppin (*Google, USA*)
Xiaoguang Qi (*Lehigh University, USA*)
Kira Radinsky (*Technion, Israel*)
Hema Raghavan (*IBM, USA*)
Edie Rasmussen (*University of British Columbia, Canada*)
Henning Rode (*CWI Amsterdam, The Netherlands*)
Haggai Roitman, (*IBM Research – Haifa, Israel*)
Jun Sakuma (*Tokyo Institute of Technology, Japan*)
Kazuhiro Seki (*Kobe University, Japan*)
Jangwon Seo (*University of Massachusetts, Amherst, USA*)
Pavel Serdyukov (*Delft University of Technology, The Netherlands*)
James Shanahan (*Church and Duncan Group, USA*)
Jialie Shen (*Singapore Management University, Singapore*)
Milad Shokouhi (*Microsoft Research, UK*)
Gianmaria Silvello (*University of Padua, Italy*)
Mark Smucker (*University of Waterloo, Canada*)
Vassilios Stathopoulos (*University of Glasgow, UK*)
J. Stephen Downie (*University of Illinois, Urbana-Champaign, USA*)
Juliane Stiller (*Humboldt University, Germany*)
Aixin Sun (*Nanyang Technological University, Singapore*)
Mingxuan Sun (*Georgia Institute of Technology, USA*)
Shanu Sushmita (*University of Glasgow, UK*)
S.M.M. Tahaghoghi (*Microsoft, USA*)
John Tait (*Information Retrieval Facility, Austria*)
Bin Tan (*Amazon, USA*)
Michael Taylor (*Microsoft Research Cambridge, UK*)
Carla Teixeira Lopes (*University of Porto, Portugal*)
Martin Theobald (*Max-Planck Institute Informatics, Germany*)
Ulrich Thiel (*IPSI-Darmstadt, Germany*)
James Thom (*RMIT, Australia*)
Paul Thomas (*CSIRO Australian National University, Australia*)
Paul Thompson (*Dartmouth College, USA*)
Qi Tian (*University of Texas at San Antonio, USA*)
Anastasios Tombros (*Queen Mary, University of London, UK*)
Ricardo Torres (*University of Campinas, Brazil*)
Andrew Trotman (*University of Otago, New Zealand*)
Sarah Tyler (*University of California, Santa Cruz, USA*)
Eduardo Valle (*University of Campinas, Brazil*)
Sumithra Velupillai (*Stockholm University, Sweden*)
Xiaojun Wan (*Peking University, China*)
Changhu Wang (*Microsoft Research Asia, China*)
Jun Wang (*University College London, UK*)
Lidan Wang (*University of Maryland, USA*)
Mengqiu Wang (*Stanford University, USA*)
Taifeng Wang (*Microsoft Research Asia, China*)
Xin-Jing Wang (*Microsoft Research Asia, China*)
William Webber (*University of Melbourne, Australia*)
Wouter Weerkamp (*University of Amsterdam, The Netherlands*)
Tak-Lam Wong (*The Chinese University of Hong Kong, China*)
Jun Xu (*Microsoft Research Asia, China*)
Xiaobing Xue (*University of Massachusetts, Amherst, USA*)
Murat Yakici (*Strathclyde University, Glasgow, UK*)
Hui Yang (*Carnegie Mellon University, USA*)
Jiang-Ming Yang (*Microsoft, China*)
Emine Yilmaz (*Microsoft Research Cambridge, UK*)
Elad Yom-Tov (*Yahoo! Research, USA*)
Minoru Yoshida (*University of Tokyo, Japan*)
Xiaojun Yuan (*SUNY Albany, USA*)
Dell Zhang (*Birkbeck University of London, UK*)
Lei Zhang (*Microsoft Research Asia, China*)
Min Zhang (*Tsinghua University, China*)
Peng Zhang (*Robert Gordon University, Aberdeen, UK*)
Zhongfei Zhang (*SUNY Binghamton, USA*)
Le Zhao (*Carnegie Mellon University, USA*)
Dong Zhou, (*Trinity College Dublin, Ireland*)
Guido Zuccon (*University of Glasgow, UK*)

Demonstrations Committee

Kevyn Collins-Thompson (*Microsoft Research, USA*) - Chair
Gary Geunbae Lee (*POSTECH, Korea*) - Chair
Massimo Melucci (*University of Padua, Italy*) - Chair

Omar Alonso (*Microsoft, USA*)
Steve Beitzel (*Telcordia Technologies, USA*)
Mikhail Bilenko (*Microsoft Research, USA*)
Gloria Bordogna (*CNR - National Research Council of Italy, Italy*)
Mohand Boughanem (*IRIT, University Paul Sabatier, Toulouse, France*)
Carlos Castillo (*Yahoo! Research, Spain*)
Silviu Cucerzan (*Microsoft Research, USA*)
Emanuele Di Buccio (*University of Padua, Italy*)
Giorgio Maria Di Nunzio (*University of Padua, Italy*)
Debora Donato (*Yahoo! Labs, USA*)
Georges Dupret (*Yahoo! Labs, USA*)
Jiwoon Jeon (*Google, USA*)
Joemon Jose (*University of Glasgow, UK*)
Giridhar Kumaran (*Microsoft, USA*)
Jochen Leidner (*Thomson Reuters, Switzerland*)
Chin-Yew Lin (*Microsoft Research Asia, China*)
Ting Liu (*Harbin Institute of Technology, China*)
Vibhu Mittal (*Root-1, USA*)
John Prager (*IBM Research, USA*)
Filip Radlinski (*Microsoft, Canada*)
Hema Raghavan (*IBM Research, USA*)
Chirag Shah (*Rutgers University, USA*)
Rao Shen (*Yahoo!, USA*)
Milad Shokouhi (*Microsoft, UK*)
Anastasios Tombros (*Queen Mary University of London, UK*)
Antti Ukkonen (*Yahoo! Research, Spain*)
Lei Zhang (*Microsoft Research Asia, China*)

Tutorials Committee

Yi Zhang (*UC Santa Cruz, USA*) – Chair

Jing Bai (*Microsoft, USA*)
Xueqi Cheng (*Institute of Computing Technology, Chinese Academy of Science, China*)
Nick Craswell (*Microsoft, USA*)
Cai Deng (*Zhejiang University, China*)
Byron Dom (*Yahoo! Lab, USA*)
Tao Hong (*University of California Santa Cruz, USA*)
Jussi Karlgren (*Swedish Institute of Computer Science, Sweden*)
Birger Larsen (*Royal School of Library and Information Science, Denmark*)
Donald Metzler (*ISI, University of South California, USA*)
Marie-Francine Moens (*Katholieke Universiteit Leuven, Belgium*)
Paul Ogilvie (*LinkedIn, USA*)
Tao Qin (*Microsoft, China*)
Maarten de Rijke (*University of Amsterdam, The Netherlands*)
Ian Ruthven (*University of Strathclyde, UK*)
James G. Shanahan (*Church and Duncan Group, USA*)
Min Zhang (*Tsinghua University, China*)

Workshops Committee

Noriko Kando (*National Institute of Informatics, Japan*) – Chair
Luo Si (*Purdue University, USA*) – Chair

Omar Alonso (*Microsoft, USA*)
Kuang-hua Chen (*National Taiwan University, Taiwan*)
Hazem Elmeleegy (*AT&T Research, USA*)
Hui Fang (*University of Delaware, USA*)
Gareth Jones (*Dublin City University, Ireland*)
Jaana Kekäläinen (*University of Tampere, Finland*)
Mounia Lalmas (*Yahoo! Research, Spain*)
Tetsuya Sakai (*Microsoft Research Asia, China*)
Mark Smucker (*University of Waterloo, Canada*)
Andrew Trotman (*University of Otago, New Zealand*)

Outstanding Paper Awards Committee

Susan T. Dumais (*Microsoft Research, USA*) – Chair

Javed A. Aslam (*Northeastern University, USA*)
Gordon V. Cormack (*University of Waterloo, Canada*)
Brian D. Davison (*Lehigh University, USA*)
David Hawking (*Funnelback and Australian National University, Australia*)
Rong Jin (*Michigan State University, USA*)
Thorsten Joachims (*Cornell University, USA*)
Jussi Karlgren (*Swedish Institute of Computer Science, Sweden*)
Daniel M. Russell (*Google, USA*)
Howard Turtle (*Syracuse University, USA*)

Doctoral Consortium Committee

Maarten de Rijke (*University of Amsterdam, The Netherlands*) - Chair
Paul Thomas (*CSIRO, Australia*) - Chair

Maristella Agosti (*University of Padua, Italy*)
Jamie Callan (*Carnegie Mellon University, USA*)
Charles L.A. Clarke (*University of Waterloo, Canada*)
Julio Gonzalo (*UNED, Spain*)
Franciska de Jong (*University of Twente, The Netherlands*)
Diane Kelly (*University of North Carolina at Chapel Hill, USA*)
Mounia Lalmas (*Yahoo! Research, Spain*)
Marie-Francine Moens (*Katholieke Universiteit Leuven, Belgium*)
Ian Ruthven (*University of Strathclyde, UK*)
Tetsuya Sakai (*Microsoft Research Asia, China*)
Mark Sanderson (*RMIT University, Australia*)
Howard Turtle (*Syracuse University, USA*)
Arjen de Vries (*Centrum Wiskunde & Informatica, The Netherlands*)
ChengXiang Zhai (*University of Illinois at Urbana-Champaign, USA*)
Min Zhang (*Tsinghua University, China*)

Mentoring Committee

Gareth Jones (*Dublin City University, Ireland*) - Chair

B. Barla Cambazoglu (*Yahoo! Research, Spain*)
David Elsweiler (*University of Erlangen, Germany*)
Oren Kurland (*Technion, Israel*)
David Losada (*University of Santiago de Compostela, Spain*)
Jahna Otterbacher (*Illinois Institute of Technology, USA*)
Le Sun (*Institute of Software, Chinese Academy of Sciences, China*)
Bin Wang (*Institute of Computing Technology, Chinese Academy of Sciences, China*)

Local Organization Committee

Xiaoming Li (*Peking University, China*) - Chair

Xueqi Cheng (*Institute of Computing Technology, Chinese Academy of Sciences, China*)
Ling Huang (*Microsoft Research Asia, China*)
Ting Liu (*Harbin Institute of Technology, China*)
Le Sun (*Institute of Software, Chinese Academy of Sciences, China*)
Min Zhang (*Tsinghua University, China*)

SIGIR 2011 Sponsor and Supporters

Sponsor

SIGIR
Special Interest Group
on Information Retrieval

Association for
Computing Machinery
Advancing Computing as a Science & Profession

Corporate Supporters

Diamond

Microsoft Research

Gold

Baidu 百度
EMC²
Google
SOSO 搜搜
YAHOO!

Silver

eBay Research Labs

Bronze

HP Labs
IBM Research
Yandex

Associated Organization

CIPS

Also supported by

Université de Montréal

Exhibitors

Morgan & Claypool Publishers
now the essence of knowledge
Springer the language of science

ILDA: Interdependent LDA Model for Learning Latent Aspects and their Ratings from Online Product Reviews

Samaneh Moghaddam
School of Computing Science
Simon Fraser University
Burnaby, BC, Canada
sam39@cs.sfu.ca

Martin Ester
School of Computing Science
Simon Fraser University
Burnaby, BC, Canada
ester@cs.sfu.ca

ABSTRACT

Today, more and more product reviews become available on the Internet, e.g., product review forums, discussion groups, and Blogs. However, it is almost impossible for a customer to read all of the different and possibly even contradictory opinions and make an informed decision. Therefore, mining online reviews (opinion mining) has emerged as an interesting new research direction. Extracting aspects and the corresponding ratings is an important challenge in opinion mining. An *aspect* is an attribute or component of a product, e.g. 'screen' for a digital camera. It is common that reviewers use different words to describe an aspect (e.g. 'LCD', 'display', 'screen'). A *rating* is an intended interpretation of the user satisfaction in terms of numerical values. Reviewers usually express the rating of an aspect by a set of sentiments, e.g. 'blurry screen'. In this paper we present three probabilistic graphical models which aim to extract aspects and corresponding ratings of products from online reviews. The first two models extend standard PLSI and LDA to generate a rated aspect summary of product reviews. As our main contribution, we introduce *Interdependent Latent Dirichlet Allocation (ILDA)* model. This model is more natural for our task since the underlying probabilistic assumptions (interdependency between aspects and ratings) are appropriate for our problem domain. We conduct experiments on a real life dataset, Epinions.com, demonstrating the improved effectiveness of the *ILDA* model in terms of the likelihood of a held-out test set, and the accuracy of aspects and aspect ratings.

Categories and Subject Descriptors

H.3.3 [**Information Search and Retrieval**]: Text Mining; G.3 [**Mathematics of Computing**]: Probability and Statistics—*statistical computing, multivariate statistics*

General Terms

Algorithms, Design, Experimentation

Keywords

opinion mining, probabilistic graphical models, variational methods, aspect identification, rating prediction

1. INTRODUCTION

Other people's opinions have always been an important piece of information during the decision-making process when buying a new product [13]. Today people like to make their opinions available to strangers via the Internet. As a result, the Web has become an excellent source for gathering consumer opinions [8]. Amazon, Cnet, ZDnet, Rateitall and Epinions are examples of the most important Web resources containing such opinions. However, reading all product reviews to make a good decision will be a time-consuming job. Therefore, mining online product reviews (opinion mining) has emerged as a new research direction.

Some of the review websites ask reviewers to express an overall rating (as stars) for the reviewed item. While these ratings can be helpful in decision making, focusing on just overall ratings may not be sufficient for a user to make decisions. Rated aspect summarization addresses this limitation [10]. Providing aspects (also called product-features) and the corresponding ratings of a product does not only help users gain more insight into the quality of the product, but also enables them to compare different products. The problem definition is illustrated in Figure 1.

Rated aspect summarization consists of two tasks [18]. The first is aspect identification with the goal of finding a set of relevant aspects for the target product. The second task is rating prediction with the goal of providing the user a numeric rating for each aspect. Most of the current works consider aspect identification as main task and treat rating prediction at most as a side task. However, from the user's point of view, having the ratings and aspects together is important in decision making.

During the last decade, many methods have been proposed to detect product aspects in reviews, including statistical approaches and model based techniques. The existing statistical approaches [7, 9, 12, 14] usually apply some constraints on high-frequency noun phrases to identify product aspects. One of the limitations of these methods is that they may produce too many non-aspects and miss low-frequency aspects and their variations [5]. In addition, statistical approaches require the manual tuning of various parameters which makes them hard to port to another dataset. Existing model based techniques [19, 22, 10, 20] overcome the limitations of statistical approaches by automatically learning the model parameters from the data. However, all of

Input

Canon GL2 Mini DVD Camcorder

... excellent zoom ... blurry lcd ... great picture quality ... accurate zooming ... poor battery ... inaccurate screen ... good quality ... affordable price ... poor display ... inadequate battery life... fantastic zoom ... great price ...

Output

Aspect	Head Terms	Rating
zoom	zoom, zooming	5
price	price	4
picture quality	picture quality, quality	4
battery life	battery life, battery	2
screen	screen, lcd, display	1
...		...

Figure 1: Problem Definition

the existing models perform aspect identification and rating prediction in separate steps leading to the accumulation of errors. For example, a separate rating prediction algorithm will rate the sentiment 'long' equally for the aspects 'battery life' and 'shutter lag', although 'long' expresses a positive opinion for 'battery life' but a negative opinion for 'shutter lag'.

Furthermore, most of the current works [19, 18, 11, 5, 20] use the bag-of-words representation of reviews. As shown in [19], representing a document as a mixture of latent topics which generate all words of the document, can mainly be used in document clustering, by finding an overall topic of each document. However, in rated aspect summarization problem, the goal is not to cluster reviews, but to identify aspects and their corresponding ratings. For example, a topic modeling method applied to a collection of digital camera reviews is likely to infer some overall topics for that collection, such as 'Sony digital camera', and 'reviews of Sony'. Though these are valid topics, they do not represent product aspects. A rated aspect summarization model, on the other hand, tries to infer product aspects, such as 'zoom' and 'battery life', from the same collection of reviews. A solution that has been proposed in [10] is to first preprocess the reviews (chunk them into opinion phrases containing of a head term and a sentiment) and then learn models that generate only opinion phrases, not all the words of a review.

In this paper, we propose a series of increasingly sophisticated probabilistic graphical models to jointly identify aspects and predict their ratings from online reviews. The first model is an extension of the PLSI model proposed in [10], and the second model is extending the standard LDA to generate a rated aspect summary of product reviews. We consider these two models as baselines. As our main contribution, we introduce the *Interdependent Latent Dirichlet Allocation (ILDA)* model. We argue that ILDA is most natural for our problem since the underlying probabilistic assumptions (interdependency between aspects and ratings) are appropriate for the problem domain.

Since all of our proposed models are based on the opinion phrases representation of reviews, and no benchmark dataset of opinion phrases is publicly available, we crawled the well-known reviewing website Epinions.com and built a new dataset containing 29,609 opinion phrases in 2,483 reviews from 5 categories. This data set has been made publicly available for research purposes[1]. We conduct experiments on this real life dataset and evaluate the performance of the proposed models according to various criteria: likelihood of the held-out test set, and accuracy of aspect identification and rating prediction.

The remainder of the paper is organized as follows. The next section is devoted to related work. Section 3 introduces the problem statement and discusses our contributions. Section 4 presents three probabilistic graphical models for the considered problem. Section 5 describes the inference algorithms for our proposed models. In Section 6 we report the results of our experimental evaluation. Section 7 concludes the paper with a summary and the discussion of future work.

2. RELATED WORK

Most of the current works on opinion mining have focused on the aspect identification task, and ignored or treated rating prediction as a side problem. However, there are several lines of related work which we will review in this section. We first review some models based on the bag-of-words representation of reviews and then describe a recent work to learn a model from preprocessed reviews (i.e. from opinion phrases).

The authors of [22] assume that words in the same context have similar semantic association. They propose two alternative latent semantic association (LaSA) models for identifying aspects from reviews. The first LaSA model groups words into a set of aspects according to their context in the reviews. Given a word t_i, its context is defined to be composed of all the context units (adjacent sentiments) around t_i in the corpus. The second LaSA model groups words according to their latent semantic structures and context in the review. Given a latent aspect a_i, its semantic structure is defined to be composed of the context units of all the words generated by a_i.

Guo et al. [5] present a probabilistic graphical model for modeling the page-independent content information and the page-dependent layout information of text fragments. One characteristic of their model is that an aspect can be discovered based on the layout format. The authors show that content and layout information can collaborate and improve the performance of aspect identification. However, they ignore the rating prediction task.

In [20] the authors assume that for each review an overall rating and k aspects of the reviewed item are given as input. They first use a boot-strapping algorithm to obtain more related words for each aspect, and then assign each sentence of the review to the aspect whose set of related words has the maximum overlap with that sentence. As their main contribution, they propose a latent rating regression (LRR) model to infer ratings and weights of the given aspects for each review. LRR assumes the overall rating is generated based on the weighted combination of the latent ratings over all the aspects. While they consider the rating prediction task, they do not perform aspect identification and assume that the aspects are given.

Titov et al. in [19] propose a model, based on LDA, for modeling two types of topics in reviews: global topics and local topics. They assumed global topics correspond to a global property of the product in the review, such as its brand, and local topics correlate with the product aspects.

[1] http://www.sfu.ca/~sam39/ILDA/

However, they conclude that representing a document as a mixture of latent topics which generate all words of the document, is not a good choice for the rated aspect summarization problem since the extracted topics are very general. In [18] the same authors extend their proposed model to find the correspondence between the extracted topics and the product aspects. The second model introduces a set of classifiers (sentiment predictors) for each aspect, which is used to find the correspondence between topics and aspects. Note that none of their models generates the rating of aspects.

Recently, Lu et al. [10] show that using preprocessed reviews can improve the ability of models in identifying aspects. The authors assume that each review can be parsed into opinion phrases of the format $< \textit{headterm}, \textit{sentiment} >$, and propose a probabilistic model based on PLSI to identifies major aspects of a product by clustering the head terms. Since our proposed models use preprocessed reviews as input, this method will be the only comparison partner for our work.

There is yet another line of the research in text mining which tries to model the mixture of topics in documents [2, 17, 21]. However, none of these works has tried to model the sentiment related to the topics, thus cannot be applied to our problem. There are also some recent works on sentiment classification which all use some external knowledge (in the form of word lists [23] or training examples [11]) to distinguish positive and negative polarities. Our work is focused more on solving the rated aspect summarization problem in a general way and we propose general models to both decomposing a review into a set of rated aspects and predicting ratings for the identified aspects.

As we mentioned before, there are also some statistical approaches [7, 9, 12, 14] to detect product aspects in reviews. These approaches usually apply some constraints on high-frequency noun phrases to identify product aspects. The main limitation of these methods is that they may produce too many non-aspects and miss low-frequency aspects and their variations [5].

3. PROBLEM DEFINITION

In this section we introduce the problem statement, provide a motivating example for our problem, and discuss our contributions for the considered problem.

3.1 Problem Statement

Let $P = \{P_1, P_2, ..., P_l\}$ be a set of products which can be from different categories, like 'Apple Smartphone', 'Canon Powershot digital camera', 'Denon DVD player', etc. For each product P_i there is a set of reviews $R_i = \{d_1, d_2, ..., d_N\}$. Each review d_j consists of a set of opinion phrases, such as 'great zoom', 'excellent quality', etc. In the following, we define the problem addressed more formally.

Aspect: An aspect is an attribute or component of the product that has been commented on in a review. For example, 'battery life' in the opinion sentence 'The battery life of this camera is too short'.

Rating: A rating is an intended interpretation of the user satisfaction in terms of numerical values. Most of the reviewing websites use ratings (number of stars) in the range from 1 to 5.

Opinion Phrase: An opinion phrase $f =< t, s >$ is a pair of head term t and sentiment s [10]. Usually the head term is an aspect, and the sentiment expresses some opinion towards this aspect, e.g. $< \textit{battery life}, \textit{short} >$.

Review: A review is a bag of opinion phrases $d_j = \{f = < t, s > | f \in d_j\}$.

Problem Definition: Given a set of reviews for product P, the task is to identify the k major aspects of P and to predict the rating of each aspect.

Since different products in a category share many similar aspects, it would also make sense to identify the k major aspects of a product category. However, many products have some unique aspects which usually play an important role in purchase decisions. In addition, different products will have different ratings for one and the same aspect. To consider the product specific aspects and to be able to predict the ratings of aspects for each product, we treat reviews of each product as a separate dataset and identify aspects for each product separately.

3.2 A Motivating Example

A sample rated aspect summary of two camcorders is shown in Table 1. Rated aspect summarization decomposes the review's overall rating into individual ratings for the major aspects so that a user can gain different perspectives towards the target product [10].

Table 1: Rated Aspect Summary of Two Camcorders

Aspects	Camcorder1	Camcorder2
zoom	4	2
sound	1	3
screen	2	4
price	3	3
size	4	2
Overall Rating	3	3

We can see that although two camcorders have the same overall ratings, Camcorder1 has better zooming aspect while Camcorder2 has better screen and sound. This decomposed view of rated aspects clearly provides more detailed information than the overall rating and helps users to make better decisions.

Rated aspect summary can also be used as input for various computer systems: in summarization systems to find sentences which summarize the review more accurately, in recommendation systems to provide explanations for recommendation, and in opinion-based question answering systems to answer opinion-based questions by comparing aspects and ratings of different products.

3.3 Our Contributions

As discussed in the preceding section, our goal is to provide a method to identify aspects and predict their ratings from online product reviews without any human supervision. Therefore, we use probabilistic graphical models, which represent each review as a mixture of latent aspects and ratings. We first extend the proposed model in [10] which is based on Probabilistic Latent Semantic Indexing (PLSI) model [6]. Then we extend the most well-known method for unsupervised modeling of documents, Latent Dirichlet Allocation (LDA) [3] to solve the considered problem. We make simple adaptions on both models for the aspect identification and rating prediction problem and consider them as baseline models. As our main contribution, we propose a novel model, called ILDA, for jointly extracting major product aspects and predicting their ratings from online reviews. Unlike existing graphical models that treat aspect identification and rating prediction as separate tasks [5, 22, 10], ILDA can perform both tasks simultaneously in an unsupervised manner. We argue that considering the interdependency between aspects and ratings improves the performance of the model. To illustrate the importance of this interdependency, consider the following examples: 'low LCD resolution' and 'low price'. The sentiment 'low' expresses a negative opinion for 'LCD resolution', while it is a positive opinion for 'price'. Treating rating prediction as a separate task, both aspects receive equal ratings. We also present algorithms for approximate inference and parameter estimation for the proposed LDA and ILDA models.

We have conducted experiments on a real life dataset from Epinions.com from five product categories. The experimental results show that ILDA consistently outperforms the baseline PLSI and LDA models.

4. PROBABILISTIC GRAPHICAL MODELS

In this section, we first describe our two baseline probabilistic models of reviews, noting their strengths and limitations: A PLSI model, and a multinomial LDA model. Then we introduce a novel model, ILDA, which models the interdependency between aspects and ratings.

All of the following models assume that aspects and their ratings can be represented by multinomial distributions and try to cluster head terms into aspects and sentiments into ratings. As a shortcoming of unsupervised models, the correspondence between identified clusters and the actual aspects or ratings is not explicit.

4.1 PLSI Model

Probabilistic Latent Semantic Indexing (PLSI) [6] has recently been applied to many text mining problems. Lu et al. applied the PLSI model on opinion phrases to identify aspects from reviews [10]. However, as we described in section 2, they used PLSI only for aspect identification, and their model does not generate ratings for the identified aspects. We extend their PLSI model to identify aspects and predict their ratings simultaneously, as shown in Figure 2. Following the standard graphical model formalism, nodes represent random variables and edges indicate possible dependence. Shaded nodes are observed random variables and unshaded nodes are latent random variables. Finally, a box around groups of random variables is a 'plate' which denotes replication. The outer plate represents reviews and the inner plate represents opinion phrases. N and M are the number of product reviews and the number of opinion phrases in each review, respectively. Since M is independent of all the other data generating variables (a and r), its randomness is generally ignored [3].

To extend the PLSI model in [10] for our problem, we add the second row (dependency of the observed sentiment s to the latent rating r, and the latent rating r to the observed review d). For each product P, a PLSI model is generated to associate unobserved aspect a_m and rating r_m with each observation, i.e., with each opinion phrase $f_m =< t_m, s_m >$ in a review $d \in R$. The adapted generative PLSI model can be defined in the following way:

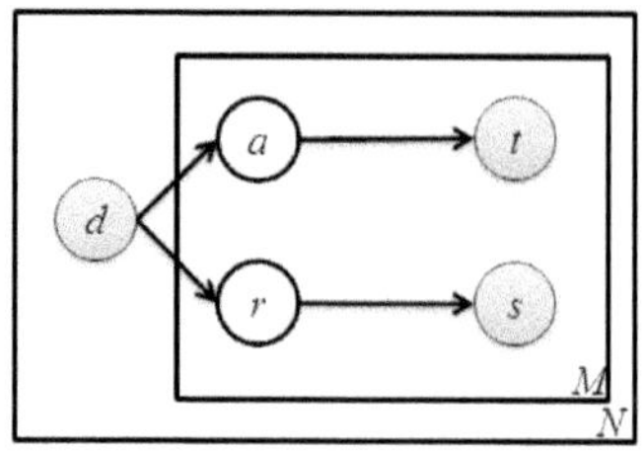

Figure 2: The PLSI Model of Reviews

1. Select a review d from R with probability $P(d)$.
2. For each opinion phrase $< t_m, s_m >$, $m \in \{1, 2, ..., M\}$
   (a) Sample $a_m \sim P(a_m|d)$ and $r_m \sim P(r_m|d)$.
   (b) Sample $t_m \sim P(t_m|a_m)$ and $s_m \sim P(s_m|r_m)$.

Translating this process into a joint probability distribution results in the expression:

$$P(d, \boldsymbol{a}, \boldsymbol{r}, \boldsymbol{t}, \boldsymbol{s}) = P(d) \prod_{m=1}^{M} [P(a_m|d)P(r_m|d)P(t_m|a_m)P(s_m|r_m)] \quad (1)$$

An equivalent symmetric version of the model can be obtained by inverting the conditional probabilities $P(a_m|d) = P(d|a_m)P(a_m)$ and $P(r_m|d) = P(d|r_m)P(r_m)$ with the help of Bayes' rule. Adopting the likelihood principle, $P(d)$ and $P(\boldsymbol{a}, \boldsymbol{r}|d)$ can be determined by maximization of the log-likelihood. The standard procedure for maximum likelihood estimation in latent variable models is the Expectation Maximization (EM) algorithm [4]. EM alternates two steps: expectation (E) step which compute the posterior probabilities for latent variables, and maximization (M) step which update the parameters. The E-step equation for the PLSI model is:

$$P(a_m, r_m|d, t_m, s_m) = \frac{P(d|a_m)P(a_m)P(d|r_m)P(r_m)P(t_m|a_m)P(s_m|r_m)}{\sum_{a,r} P(d|a)P(a)P(d|r)P(r)P(t_m|a)P(s_m|r)} \quad (2)$$

and the M-step formulas are:

$$P(d|a_m) \propto \sum_{r,t,s} P(a_m, r|d, t, s)n(d, t, s) \quad (3)$$

$$P(a_m) \propto \sum_{d,r,t,s} P(a_m, r|d, t, s)n(d, t, s) \quad (4)$$

$$P(d|r_m) \propto \sum_{a,t,s} P(a, r_m|d, t, s)n(d, t, s) \quad (5)$$

$$P(r_m) \propto \sum_{d,a,t,s} P(a, r_m|d, t, s)n(d, t, s) \quad (6)$$

$$P(t_m|a_m) \propto \sum_{d,r,s} P(a_m, r|d, t_m, s)n(d, t_m, s) \quad (7)$$

$$P(s_m|r_m) \propto \sum_{d,a,t} P(a, r_m|d, t, s_m)n(d, t, s_m) \quad (8)$$

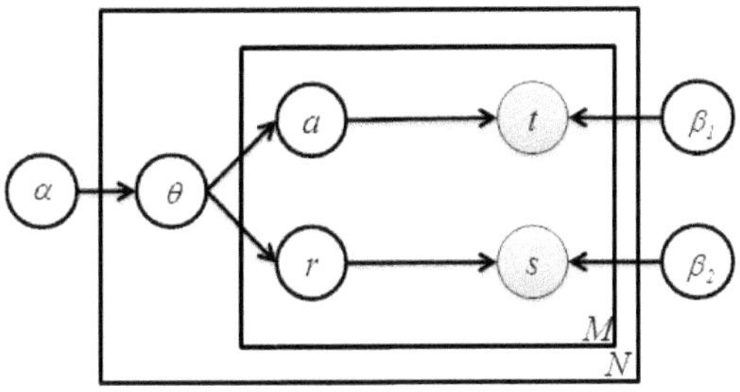

Figure 3: The LDA Model of Reviews

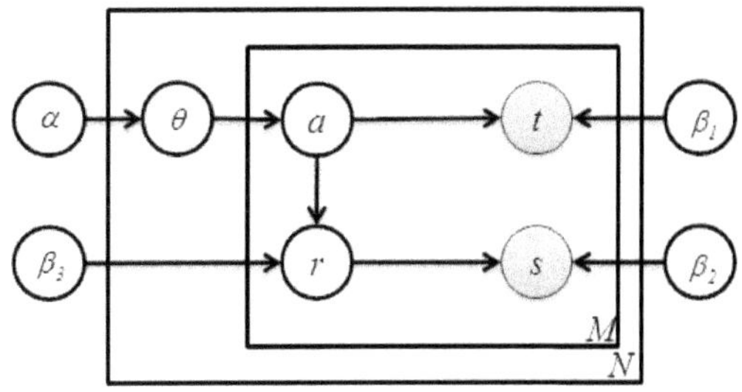

Figure 4: The ILDA Model of Reviews

where $n(d,t,s)$ denotes the frequency of the phrase $< t,s >$ occurred in review d. The EM algorithm obtains a local maximum of the log-likelihood by alternating E-step (2) with M-steps (3)-(8). It is important to note that d is a multinomial random variable with as many possible values as there are training reviews (i.e a dummy index into the list of reviews in the training set) and the PLSI model learns the $P(\boldsymbol{a},\boldsymbol{r}|d,\boldsymbol{t},\boldsymbol{s})$ only for those reviews on which it is trained. For this reason, PLSI is not a well-defined generative model of reviews [3]. Furthermore, the number of PLSI parameters which must be estimated grows linearly with the number of training reviews which causes overfitting. One reasonable approach to avoid overfitting is assigning probability to previously unseen data by marginalizing over seen data [3]. We use this approach to smooth the parameters of the PLSI model for acceptable predictive performance as follows:

$$P(\boldsymbol{t},\boldsymbol{s}) = \sum_{d} \prod_{m=1}^{M} \sum_{a,r} P(d|a,r)p(a,r)P(t_m|a)P(s_m|r) \quad (9)$$

4.2 Multinomial LDA

The Latent Dirichlet Allocation (LDA) model is a generative probabilistic model for collections of discrete data such as text corpora [3]. The basic idea is that each item of a collection is modeled as a finite mixture over an underlying set of latent variables.

The aspect identification and rating prediction problem can be modeled as an extension of LDA (Figure 3). We make a simple adaption to the basic LDA by adding the second row (dependency among s, r, and θ) to the basic LDA model. This model is similar to the GM-LDA model presented in [1] for the annotation of images. In our adapted LDA model a review is assumed to be generated by first choosing a value of θ, and then repeatedly sampling M opinion phrases $< t_m, s_m >$ conditional on the chosen value of θ. Similar to [1], where θ represents the image/caption pairs, in our LDA model we can view θ as a high-level representation of the collection of aspect/rating pairs. For every pair, θ contains the probability of generating that combination of aspect and rating. The variable θ is sampled once per review, and is held fixed during the process of generating opinion phrases for that review. After sampling θ, the latent variables a_m and r_m are sampled independently (conditional independency) and then an opinion phrase $< t_m, s_m >$ is sampled conditional on the sampled a_m and r_m. Our adapted LDA model assumes the following generative process:

1. Sample $\theta \sim Dir(\alpha)$.
2. For each opinion phrase $< t_m, s_m >$, $m \in \{1,2,...,M\}$
   (a) Sample $a_m \sim P(a_m|\theta)$ and $r_m \sim P(r_m|\theta)$
   (b) Sample $t_m \sim P(t_m|a_m,\beta_1)$ and sample $s_m \sim P(s_m|r_m,\beta_2)$

$P(t_m|a_m,\beta_1)$ and $P(s_m|r_m,\beta_2)$ are multinomial distributions conditioned on aspect a_m and rating r_m, respectively. The resulting joint distribution is as follows:

$$P(\boldsymbol{a},\boldsymbol{r},\boldsymbol{t},\boldsymbol{s},\theta|\alpha,\beta_1,\beta_2) = P(\theta|\alpha) \prod_{m=1}^{M} [P(a_m|\theta)P(r_m|\theta)P(t_m|a_m,\beta_1)P(s_m|r_m,\beta_2)] \quad (10)$$

The key inferential problem is to compute the posterior distribution of the latent variables given a review $< \boldsymbol{t},\boldsymbol{s} >$ (collection of M opinion phrases $< t_m, s_m >$):

$$P(\boldsymbol{a},\boldsymbol{r},\theta|\boldsymbol{s},\boldsymbol{t},\alpha,\beta_1,\beta_2) = \frac{P(\boldsymbol{a},\boldsymbol{r},\boldsymbol{t},\boldsymbol{s},\theta|\alpha,\beta_1,\beta_2)}{P(\boldsymbol{t},\boldsymbol{s}|\alpha,\beta_1,\beta_2)} \quad (11)$$

Similar to the basic LDA model, due to the coupling between θ and β's, the conditional distribution of latent variables given observed data is intractable to compute. Although the posterior distribution is intractable for exact inference, a wide variety of approximate inference algorithm can be considered for LDA [3]. In this paper, we use variational inference to compute an approximation for the posterior distribution. The variational inference and parameter estimation of the LDA model will be discussed in Section 5.

The LDA model overcomes both of the PLSI problems (mentioned in Section 4.1) by using a latent random variable θ rather than a large set of individual parameters which are explicitly linked to the training reviews [3]. However, conditional on the latent variable θ, the LDA model generates aspects and ratings independently, and so the dependency between specific aspects and specific ratings is ignored. We will show experimentally that due to the lack of this dependency, the LDA model cannot capture the correspondence between aspects and ratings.

4.3 Interdependent LDA

We introduce *Interdependent Latent Dirichlet Allocation (ILDA)* which models the conditional interdependency between the latent aspects and ratings. As described in section 3.2 and shown in Table 1, different aspects of a product can have different quality and consequently different ratings. As pointed out already, one and the same sentiment word

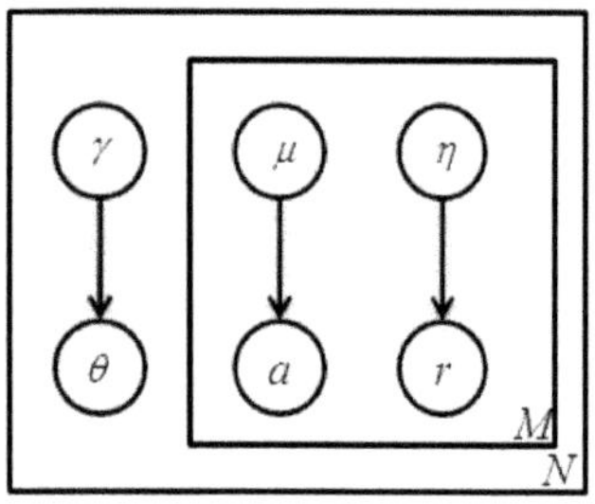

Figure 5: Graphical Model Representation of the Variational Distribution Used to Approximate the Posterior in LDA and ILDA models

may show different opinions for different aspects, and such methods that model aspects and ratings separately miss this interdependency between aspects and expressed sentiments.

We present the ILDA model, shown in Figure 4, to overcome this weakness by jointly modeling latent aspects and ratings. ILDA can be viewed as generative process that first generates an aspect and subsequently generates its rating. In particular, for generating each opinion phrase, ILDA first generates an aspect a_m from an LDA model. Then it generates a rating r_m conditioned on the sampled aspect a_m. Finally, a head term t_m and a sentiment s_m are drawn conditioned on a_m and r_m, respectively. Formally, the k-factor ILDA model assumes the following generative process for a review (collection of opinion phrases):

1. Sample $\theta \sim Dir(\alpha)$.
2. For each opinion phrase $< t_m, s_m >$, $m \in \{1, 2, ..., M\}$
   (a) Sample $a_m \sim Mult(\theta)$
   (b) Sample $r_m \sim P(r_m|a_m, \beta_3)$, a multinomial distribution conditioned on the aspect a_m.
   (c) Sample $t_m \sim P(t_m|a_m, \beta_1)$ and sample $s_m \sim P(s_m|r_m, \beta_2)$

$P(t_m|a_m, \beta_1)$ and $P(s_m|r_m, \beta_2)$ are multinomial distributions conditioned on the aspect a_m and rating r_m, respectively. ILDA thus specifies the following joint distribution:

$$P(\boldsymbol{a}, \boldsymbol{r}, \boldsymbol{t}, \boldsymbol{s}, \theta|\alpha, \beta_1, \beta_2, \beta_3) = P(\theta|\alpha) \prod_{m=1}^{M} [P(a_m|\theta) \\ P(r_m|a_m, \beta_3) P(t_m|a_m, \beta_1) P(s_m|r_m, \beta_2)] \quad (12)$$

The dependency assumption of the ILDA model overcomes the lack of correspondence in the LDA model, where the head terms and sentiments are generated independently, conditional on the latent variable θ. In the ILDA model, the head term is conditional on a generated aspect and the sentiment must be conditional on a rating which is correspondent to that aspect. In fact, the ILDA model captures the phenomenon that the aspect is generated first and then the sentiment rates the aspect.

5. INFERENCE AND ESTIMATION

In this section, we describe approximate inference and parameter estimation for the LDA and ILDA models, adopting a variational method.

Algorithm 1 Variational Inference Algorithm for ILDA

initialize $\mu^0_{mi} := 1/k$ for all i and m
initialize $\eta^0_{mj} := 1/5$ for all j and m
initialize $\gamma^0_i := \alpha_i + M/k$ for all i
repeat
  for $m = 1$ to M **do**
    for $i = 1$ to k **do**
      $\mu^{t+1}_{mi} := \beta_{1ix}\beta_{3iy} \exp(\psi(\gamma^t_i))$
    end for
    normalize μ^{t+1}_{mi} to sum to 1
    for $j = 1$ to 5 **do**
      $\eta^{t+1}_{mj} := \beta_{2zj}\beta_{3wj}$
    end for
    normalize η^{t+1}_{mj} to sum to 1
  end for
  $\gamma^{t+1} := \alpha + \sum_{m=1}^{M} \mu^{t+1}_m$
until convergence

5.1 Variational Inference

Computing the posterior distribution of the latent variables for both LDA and ILDA models is intractable. A common way to obtain a tractable lower bound is to consider simple modifications of the original graphical model [3]. In particular, we simplify these models into the graphical model shown in Figure 5. This model specifies the following variational distribution on the latent variables:

$$Q(\boldsymbol{a}, \boldsymbol{r}, \theta|\boldsymbol{\mu}, \boldsymbol{\eta}, \gamma) = Q(\theta|\gamma) \prod_{m=1}^{M} [Q(a_m|\mu_m) Q(r_m|\eta_m)] \quad (13)$$

where the Dirichlet parameter γ and the multinomial parameters $(\mu_1, ..., \mu_m)$ and $(\eta_1, .., \eta_m)$ are free variational parameters.

To have a good approximation, the KL-divergence between the variational distribution and the true posterior $P(\boldsymbol{a}, \boldsymbol{r}, \theta)$ needs to be minimized. This minimization can be achieved via an iterative method. Taking derivatives of the KL-divergence with respect to variational parameters and setting them equal to zero, we obtain the update equations. The pseudo-code of the variational inference procedure for the ILDA model is presented in Algorithm 1. These update equations are invoked repeatedly until the change in KL-divergence is small.

In Algorithm 1, β_{1ix} is $P(t^x_m = 1|a^i = 1)$ for the appropriate x. Recall that each t_m is a vector with exactly one component equal to one; we can select the unique x such that $t^x_m = 1$. In the same way β_{3iy}, β_{2zj} , and β_{3wj} are $P(\eta^t_{my} = 1|a^i = 1)$, $P(s^z_m = 1|r^j = 1)$, and $P(\mu^t_{mw} = 1|r^j = 1)$ for the appropriate y,z, and w respectively. With the approximate posterior in hand, we can find a lower bound on the joint probability, $P(\boldsymbol{a}, \boldsymbol{r}, \theta)$. In the next Section we use this lower bound to estimate the ILDA parameters.

The variational inference update formulas for the LDA model are as follows[2]:

$$\mu^{t+1}_{mi} := \beta_{1ix} \exp(\psi(\gamma^t_i)) \quad (14)$$

[2]The detailed derivation of the variational EM algorithm for both LDA and ILDA models is available at http://www.sfu.ca/~sam39/ILDA

$$\eta_{mi}^{t+1} := \beta_{2zi} \exp(\psi(\gamma_i^t)) \quad (15)$$

$$\gamma^{t+1} := \alpha + \sum_{m=1}^{M} (\mu_m^{t+1} + \eta_m^{t+1}) \quad (16)$$

5.2 Parameter Estimation

Given a corpus of reviews $R = \{d_1, d_2, ..., d_N\}$ about product P, we want to find parameters α and β's that maximize the (marginal) log likelihood of the data:

$$\ell(\alpha, \beta_1, \beta_2, \beta_3) = \sum_{d=1}^{N} \log P(\boldsymbol{a_d}, \boldsymbol{r_d}, \theta_d | \boldsymbol{s_d}, \boldsymbol{t_d}, \alpha, \beta_1, \beta_2, \beta_3) \quad (17)$$

As we have described, the computation of the posterior distribution of the latent variable given a review is intractable, and therefore we use variational inference to obtain a tractable lower bound on the log likelihood. We can thus find approximate estimates for the ILDA model via an alternative *Variational EM* procedure [3]. The variational EM maximizes the lower bound of the log likelihood with respect to the variational parameters, and then for fixed values of the variational parameters, maximizes the lower bound with respect to the model parameters.

To maximize with respect to each variational parameter, we take derivatives with respect to it and set it to zero. The derivation yields the following iterative algorithm:

1. (E-step) for each review, find the optimizing values of the variational parameters γ^*, μ^*, and η^* (using Algorithm 1).
2. (M-step) Maximize the resulting lower bound on the log likelihood with respect to the model parameters α, β_1, β_2, and β_3.

The variational EM algorithm alternates between these two steps until the bound on the expected log likelihood converges.

The M-step updates for the conditional multinomial parameters β_1 and β_2 in both LDA and ILDA models are as follows:

$$\beta_{1ij} = \sum_{d=1}^{N} \sum_{m=1}^{M_d} \mu_{dmi}^{*} t_{dm}^{j} \quad (18)$$

$$\beta_{2ij} = \sum_{d=1}^{N} \sum_{m=1}^{M_d} \eta_{dmj}^{*} s_{dm}^{i} \quad (19)$$

The M-step update for β_3 in the ILDA model is equal to:

$$\beta_{3ij} = \sum_{d=1}^{N} \sum_{m=1}^{M_d} \eta_{dmj}^{*} \mu_{dmi}^{*} \quad (20)$$

The M-step update for the Dirichlet parameter α is implemented using an efficient Newton-Raphson method in which the Hessian is inverted in linear time [3]. The Newton-Raphson optimization technique finds a stationary point of a function by iterating:

$$\alpha_{new} = \alpha_{old} - H(\alpha_{old})^{-1} g(\alpha_{old}) \quad (21)$$

where $H(\alpha)$ and $g(\alpha)$ are the Hessian matrix and gradient respectively at the point α.

5.3 Smoothing

Overfitting has always been a serious problem when working with conditional distributions [3]. A new review is very likely to contain head terms or sentiments that did not appear in any of the reviews in a training corpus. Maximum likelihood estimate of the multinomial parameters β_1 and β_2 assign zero probability to such head terms or sentiments, and so zero probability to new reviews. The standard approach to dealing with this problem is smoothing the parameters which are dependent to the observed data, by assigning positive probability to all vocabulary items whether or not they are observed in the training set [3]. We deal with this issue, in both the LDA and ILDA models, by treating β_1 and β_2, which are dependent to the observed data, as random matrices whose rows are multinomial parameters for the latent variables a and r. Each row is independently drawn from an exchangeable Dirichlet distribution (a Dirichlet distribution with a single scalar parameter). We now extend our inference procedure to treat $\beta_{1i} \sim \mathit{Dirichlet}(\rho_1, \rho_1, ..., \rho_1)$ and $\beta_{2i} \sim \mathit{Dirichlet}(\rho_2, \rho_2, ..., \rho_2)$ where ρ_1 and ρ_2 are scalar parameters.

A variational approach can again be used to find an approximation to this posterior distribution. We adopt a variational approach that places a separable distribution on the random variables β_1, β_2, θ, a, and r:

$$Q(\boldsymbol{a}, \boldsymbol{r}, \theta, \beta_1, \beta_2 | \boldsymbol{\mu}, \boldsymbol{\eta}, \gamma, \pi_1, \pi_2) = \prod_{i=1}^{K} Dir(\beta_{1i}|\pi_{1i})$$
$$\prod_{i=1}^{5} Dir(\beta_{2i}|\pi_{2i}) \prod_{d=1}^{N} Q_d(\boldsymbol{a}_d, \boldsymbol{r}_d, \theta_d | \boldsymbol{\mu}_d, \boldsymbol{\eta}_d, \gamma_d) \quad (22)$$

where π_1 and π_2 are variational Dirichlet parameters for β_1 and β_2, respectively, and $Q_d(\boldsymbol{a}_d, \boldsymbol{r}_d, \theta_d | \gamma_d, \boldsymbol{\mu}_d, \boldsymbol{\eta}_d)$ is the variational distribution defined in Equation (13). The only change to our M-step algorithm (in both LDA and ILDA models) is to replace the maximization with respect to β_1 and β_2 with the following variational updates:

$$\pi_{1ij} = \rho_1 + \sum_{d=1}^{N} \sum_{m=1}^{M_d} \mu_{dmi}^{*} t_{dm}^{j} \quad (23)$$

$$\pi_{2ij} = \rho_2 + \sum_{d=1}^{N} \sum_{m=1}^{M_d} \eta_{dmj}^{*} s_{dm}^{i} \quad (24)$$

Bayesian methods often assume a noninformative prior which means setting $\rho_1 = 1$ and $\rho_2 = 1$ [1]. Iterating these equations to convergence yields an approximate posterior distribution on β_1, β_2, θ, $\boldsymbol{a}$, and $\boldsymbol{r}$.

5.4 Model Selection

To find the optimal number of aspects we compute the Bayesian Information Criterion (BIC) [16]. BIC is a criterion for model selection among a class of parametric models with different numbers of parameters. When estimating model parameters using maximum likelihood estimation, it is possible to increase the likelihood by adding parameters, which may however result in overfitting. The BIC resolves this problem by introducing a penalty term for the number of parameters in the model.

Let m be the number of opinion phrases in the given test set, k be the number of free parameters to be estimated

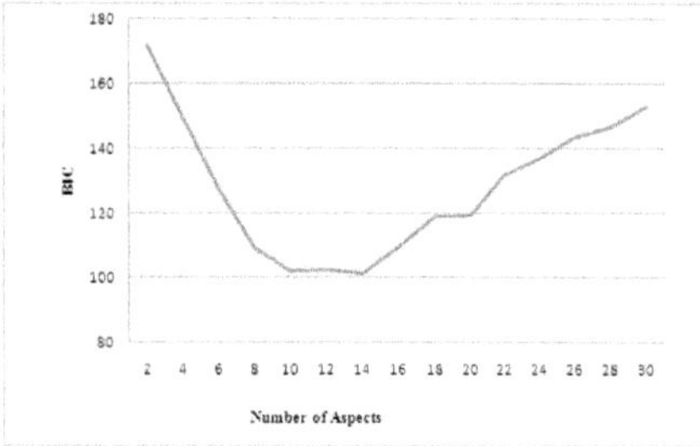

Figure 6: BIC of ILDA for Different Numbers of Aspects (k)

(number of aspects), and $\mathcal{L}$ be the maximized value of the likelihood function for the estimated model. The formula for the BIC is:

$$BIC = -2\ln(\mathcal{L}) + k\ln(m) \quad (25)$$

Given any two learnt models, the model with the lower value of BIC is the one to be preferred. Hence, lower BIC implies either fewer free parameters, better fit, or both. Figure 6 shows BIC values of the ILDA model for one representative product in the digital camera category. For this product, the BIC value of the model reaches its minimum for $k = 14$, i.e. ILDA identifies 14 aspect clusters in the given reviews. For each product, we train models for a range of values of k and pick the model with the optimal k, i.e. lowest BIC.

6. EXPERIMENTAL RESULTS

Since none of the existing benchmark datasets of opinion phrases is publicly available, we had to build a new dataset. We crawled the well-known reviewing website Epinion.com and made the dataset publicly available for research purposes.

We experimentally compare the three models proposed in this paper, i.e. PLSI, LDA, and ILDA. As pointed out already, most of the current works use the bag-of-words representation of reviews, and so cannot be compared to our proposed model which uses the opinion phrases representation. There is only one recent model using the opinion phrases representation [10]. This model identifies the aspects by clustering the head terms, and a separate statistical method is applied on the sentiments to predict their polarity. Our PLSI model is identical to the model of [10] for aspect identification. We also test a simple multinomial model (ML), that treats the head terms and sentiments as independent multinomials, as a simple baseline method.

In the next subsections, we first briefly describe our dataset and then present the evaluation of the models in terms of test set likelihood and accuracy of aspect identification and rating prediction.

6.1 Dataset

We built a crawler to extract reviews from the well-known reviewing website Epinions.com. The dataset contains 2,483 reviews (29,609 opinion phrases) about 40 products from 5 categories: camcorder, cellular phone, digital camera, DVD player, and Mp3 player. For preprocessing, we adopt the technique proposed in [12] to identify opinion phrases in the form of a pair of head term and sentiment. In Table 2, for each category the number of reviews, opinion phrases, and phrases per product (on average) are shown.

Table 2: Statistics of the Dataset

Category	#Reviews	#Opinion Phrases	#Phrases per Product
Camcorder	197	1,694	211.77
Cel. Phone	630	7,642	955.23
Dig. Camera	707	10,435	1304.41
DVD Player	324	3,707	463.32
Mp3 Player	625	6,131	766.41
Overall	2,483	29,609	3701.14

A standard approach for evaluation of graphical models is comparing the achieved likelihoods of a held-out test set. In this paper we evaluate our main proposed model, ILDA, by comparing its obtained likelihood on a held-out test set with the likelihoods achieved by the comparison partners. However, the accuracy of aspect identification and rating prediction cannot be inferred easily by this evaluation. Therefore, to make the evaluation stronger we compute the accuracy of the model's results using a standard measure of clustering. While accuracy evaluation provides more information about the performance of the learned model, it needs a truly labeled test set which makes it subjective in contrast with the likelihood evaluation approach which is completely objective. To this extent, we manually create a set of true aspects and ratings for each product as *gold standard*. We asked some judges to label each opinion phrase with a pair of $< g_a, g_r >$ based on the given head term and corresponding sentiment. g_a is a number showing the aspect cluster of the given head term, and g_r is the rating of the given sentiment with respect to the given head term (considering the correspondence between head term and sentiment). This gold standard is used in the evaluation of aspect identification and rating prediction.

6.2 Test Set Likelihood

We held out 20% of the reviews for testing purposes and used the remaining 80% to learn the model. Our goal is to achieve high likelihood on a held-out test set. Note that, unlike in text modeling problems which learn one model from the whole collection of documents, in rated aspect summarization one independent model is learnt per product. In the following, we present evaluation results for each category which is the average of the results of the products of that category.

To evaluate how well a model fits the data, we computed the *perplexity* of the held-out test set on all models for various values of aspects, k. The perplexity is monotonically decreasing in the likelihood of the test data, and a lower perplexity score indicates better performance [3]. More formally, for a test set of N reviews, the perplexity is:

$$perplexity(R_{test}) = exp\{-\frac{\sum_{d=1}^{N} \log P(\boldsymbol{t}_d, \boldsymbol{s}_d)}{\sum_{d=1}^{N} M_d}\} \quad (26)$$

Figure 7 shows the perplexity of different models for different product categories. As described in sections 4.1 and 5.3, we use smoothing for all models to avoid overfitting. As expected, the latent variable models perform better than the

Table 3: Rand Index of Aspect Identification for Different Models

Category	PLSI	LDA	ILDA
Camcorder	0.59	0.68	0.8
Cellular Phone	0.64	0.76	0.86
Digital Camera	0.65	0.79	0.88
DVD Player	0.62	0.73	0.81
Mp3 Player	0.63	0.74	0.84
Average	0.62	0.74	0.83

Table 4: Rand Index of Rating Prediction for Different Models

Category	PLSI	LDA	ILDA
Camcorder	0.41	0.49	0.68
Cellular Phone	0.48	0.56	0.74
Digital Camera	0.5	0.58	0.76
DVD Player	0.44	0.53	0.71
Mp3 Player	0.45	0.56	0.74
Average	0.46	0.54	0.73

simple Multinomial model (ML). LDA, which suffers from neither of the PLSI problems, consistently performs better. Most notably, ILDA performs much better than either LDA or PLSI and provides better fit which indicates that ILDA models the reviews more accurately.

The major reason for significant performance enhancement of ILDA and LDA compared to PLSI is that they effectively capture the latent semantic association among aspects. Moreover, ILDA consistently outperforms LDA. We believe that this is due to the fact that ILDA captures the interdependency between latent aspects and the sentiments used to rate them. Also, it is notable that all the models perform better when the size of the training dataset is larger (e.g. digital camera category).

6.3 Accuracy of Aspect Identification

In this section , we evaluate the accuracy of identifying the k major aspect clusters in the given test set. Since all of the proposed models are soft clustering techniques, for each head term the cluster with the highest probability is selected as its aspect cluster. For each model, the accuracy of identified aspects is evaluated using the Rand Index [15], a standard measure of clustering similarity often used to compare clusterings against a gold standard.

$$RandIndex(P_i, P_m) = \frac{2(x+y)}{k \times (k-1)} \tag{27}$$

where P_i and P_m represent the clustering produced by an algorithm i and manual labeling, respectively. The agreement of P_i and P_m is checked on their $k \times (k-1)$ pairs of aspects, where k is the number of identified aspects. For each two aspects, P_i and P_m either assign them to the same cluster or to different clusters. In the above equation, x is the number of pairs belonging to the same cluster in both partitions, and y is the number of pairs belonging to different clusters in both partitions.

Table 3 presents the Rand Index (the higher the better) of different models for the optimal numbers of aspects, i.e. for the k with the minimum BIC value for that model. The Rand Index of aspect identification for each category is the average of the Rand Index of its products. Not surprisingly, Table 3 shows that ILDA and LDA achieve better accuracy than PLSI in all of the categories and ILDA clearly outperforms LDA.

6.4 Accuracy of Rating Prediction

For each model, the accuracy of predicted ratings is evaluated using the Rand Index. The Rand Index scores of different models are shown in Table 4. Note that the number of clusters in rating prediction for all models is known and fixed ($k = 5$). Again, for each sentiment the cluster with the highest probability is selected as its rating cluster.

Again, ILDA and LDA achieve better accuracy than PLSI because of capturing the latent semantic association among ratings. Moreover, by capturing the interdependency between latent ratings and the head terms, ILDA outperforms LDA. Note that the gain of ILDA vs. LDA is much larger than the gain of LDA vs. PLSI. In Table 3 and 4 again, all the models perform better for digital camera category which has the largest training set.

7. SUMMARY AND FUTURE WORK

Rated aspect summarization provides very useful information for users to make their purchase decision. However, such summaries are usually unavailable in practice. In this paper we have proposed an unsupervised graphical model, ILDA, that learns a set of product aspects and corresponding ratings from a collection of product reviews that have been preprocessed into a collection of opinion phrases. We performed an experimental evaluation on real life data from the Epinions.com website and compared ILDA against baseline PLSI and LDA models. ILDA clearly outperformed all of the comparison partners in terms of likelihood of the test set, and accuracy of aspect identification and rating prediction. We argue that the major reason for the consistent enhancement is that ILDA better captures the interdependency between latent aspects and ratings.

One of the shortcomings of unsupervised models is that the correspondence between generated clusters and latent variables are not explicit [18]. As future work we plan to investigate the correspondence between identified clusters and real aspects or ratings. Most of the reviewing websites such as Epinions.com provide some additional information on top of the review text and overall rating, including a set of predefined aspects and their ratings, and a rating guideline which shows the intended interpretation of the numerical ratings. Using this prior knowledge may help in establishing these correspondences.

8. REFERENCES

[1] D. M. Blei and M. I. Jordan. Modeling annotated data. In *SIGIR '03*.

[2] D. M. Blei and J. D. Lafferty. Correlated topic models, 2006.

[3] D. M. Blei, A. Y. Ng, and M. I. Jordan. Latent Dirichlet Allocation. *J. Mach. Learn. Res.*, 3:993–1022, 2003.

[4] A. P. Dempster, N. M. Laird, and D. B. Rubin. Maximum likelihood from incomplete data via the EM

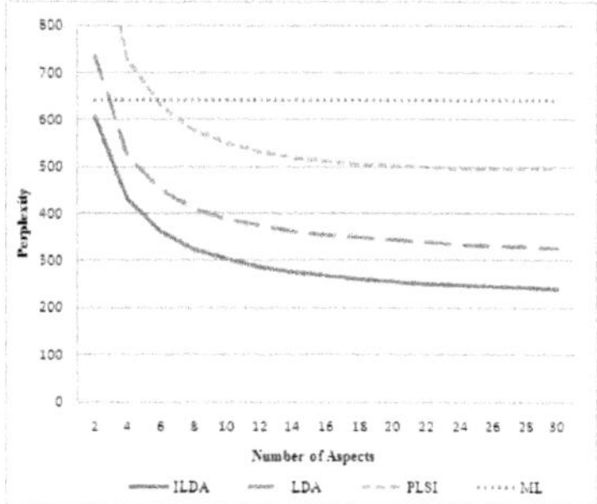

(a) Camcorder

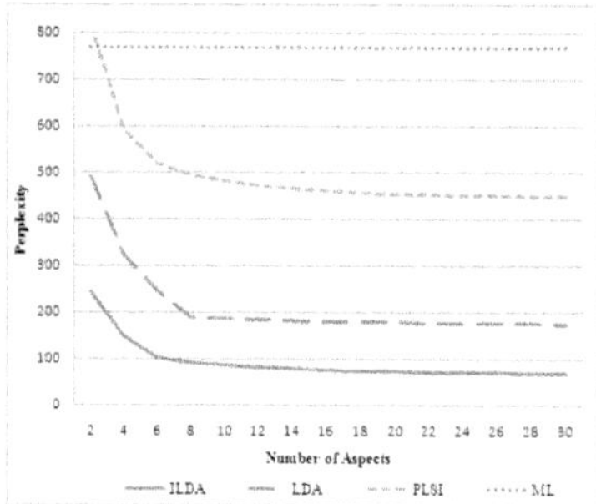

(b) Cellular Phone

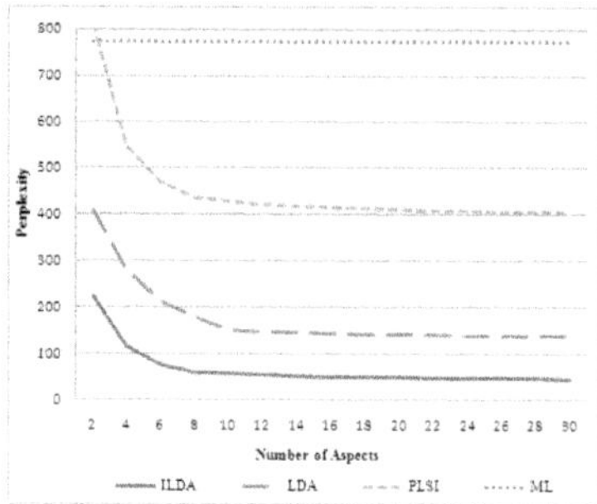

(c) Digital Camera

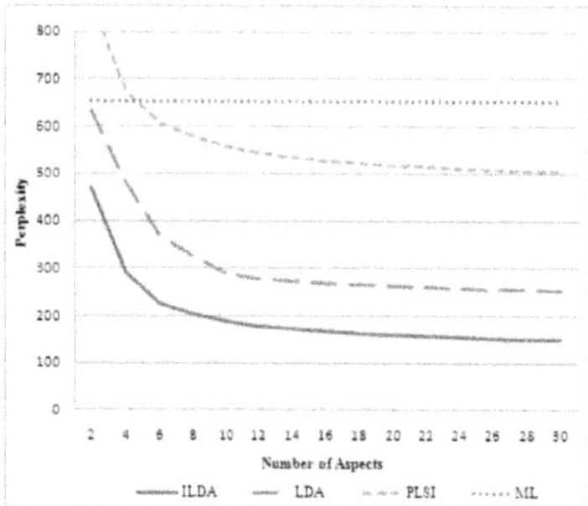

(d) DVD Player

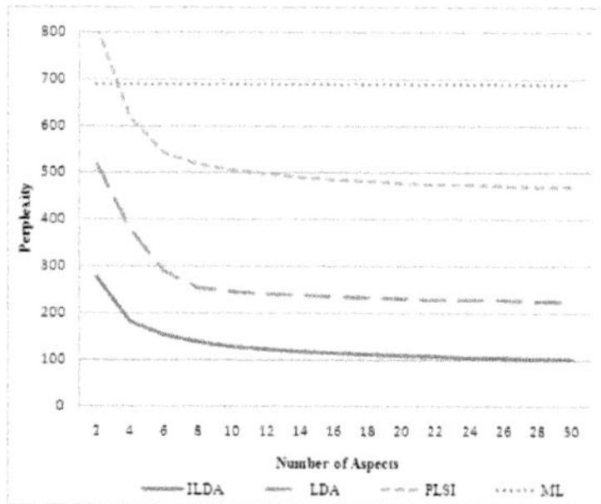

(e) Mp3 Player

Figure 7: Perplexity Results for Multinomial Model (ML), PLSI, LDA, and ILDA for Different Product Categories

algorithm. *Journal of the Royal Statistical Society, series* B, 39(1):1–38, 1977.

[5] H. Guo, H. Zhu, Z. Guo, X. Zhang, and Z. Su. Product feature categorization with multilevel latent semantic association. In *CIKM '09.*

[6] T. Hofmann. Probabilistic Latent Semantic Indexing. In *SIGIR '99.*

[7] M. Hu and B. Liu. Mining and summarizing customer reviews. In *KDD '04.*

[8] M. Hu and B. Liu. Opinion extraction and summarization on the web. In *AAAI'06.*

[9] B. Liu, M. Hu, and J. Cheng. Opinion observer: analyzing and comparing opinions on the web. In *WWW '05.*

[10] Y. Lu, C. Zhai, and N. Sundaresan. Rated aspect summarization of short comments. In *WWW '09.*

[11] Q. Mei, X. Ling, M. Wondra, H. Su, and C. Zhai. Topic sentiment mixture: modeling facets and opinions in weblogs. In *WWW '07.*

[12] S. Moghaddam and M. Ester. Opinion digger: An unsupervised opinion miner from unstructured product reviews. In *CIKM '10.*

[13] B. Pang and L. Lee. Opinion mining and sentiment analysis. *Foundations and Trends in Information Retrieval,* 2(1-2):1–135, 2008.

[14] A.-M. Popescu and O. Etzioni. Extracting product features and opinions from reviews. In *HLT'5.*

[15] W. M. Rand. Objective criteria for the evaluation of clustering methods. *Journal of the American Statistical Association,* 66(336):846–850, 1971.

[16] G. Schwarz. Estimating the dimension of a model. *The Annal of Statistics,* 6(2):461–464, 1978.

[17] E. E. Stephen, S. Fienberg, and J. Lafferty. Mixed membership models of scientific publications. In *Proceedings of the National Academy of Sciences,* 2004.

[18] I. Titov and R. McDonald. A joint model of text and aspect ratings for sentiment summarization. In *Proceedings of ACL-08: HLT.*

[19] I. Titov and R. McDonald. Modeling online reviews with multi-grain topic models. In *WWW '08.*

[20] H. Wang, Y. Lu, and C. Zhai. Latent aspect rating analysis on review text data: a rating regression approach. In *KDD '10.*

[21] X. Wang and A. McCallum. Topics over time: a non-markov continuous-time model of topical trends. In *KDD '06.*

[22] T.-L. Wong, W. Lam, and T.-S. Wong. An unsupervised framework for extracting and normalizing product attributes from multiple web sites. In *SIGIR '08.*

[23] J. Yi, T. Nasukawa, R. Bunescu, and W. Niblack. Sentiment analyzer: Extracting sentiments about a given topic using natural language processing techniques. In *ICDM '03.*

Clickthrough-Based Latent Semantic Models for Web Search

Jianfeng Gao
Microsoft Research
One Microsoft Way
Redmond, WA 98052 USA
jfgao@microsoft.com

Kristina Toutanova
Microsoft Research
One Microsoft Way
Redmond, WA 98052 USA
kristout@microsoft.com

Wen-tau Yih
Microsoft Research
One Microsoft Way
Redmond, WA 98052 USA
scottyih@microsoft.com

ABSTRACT

This paper presents two new document ranking models for Web search based upon the methods of semantic representation and the statistical translation-based approach to information retrieval (IR). Assuming that a query is parallel to the titles of the documents clicked on for that query, large amounts of query-title pairs are constructed from clickthrough data; two latent semantic models are learned from this data. One is a bilingual topic model within the language modeling framework. It ranks documents for a query by the likelihood of the query being a semantics-based translation of the documents. The semantic representation is language independent and learned from query-title pairs, with the assumption that a query and its paired titles share the same distribution over semantic topics. The other is a discriminative projection model within the vector space modeling framework. Unlike Latent Semantic Analysis and its variants, the projection matrix in our model, which is used to map from term vectors into sematic space, is learned discriminatively such that the distance between a query and its paired title, both represented as vectors in the projected semantic space, is smaller than that between the query and the titles of other documents which have no clicks for that query. These models are evaluated on the Web search task using a real world data set. Results show that they significantly outperform their corresponding baseline models, which are state-of-the-art.

Categories and Subject Descriptors

H.3.3 [**Information Storage and Retrieval**]: Information Search and Retrieval; I.2.6 [**Artificial Intelligence**]: *Learning*

General Terms

Algorithms, Experimentation

Keywords

Clickthrough Data, Latent Semantic Analysis, Topic Model, Linear Projection, Translation Model, Web Search

1. INTRODUCTION

Most modern search engines retrieve Web documents by literally matching terms in documents with those in a search query. However, lexical matching methods can be inaccurate due to the language discrepancy between Web documents and search queries [20, 31] i.e., a concept is often expressed using different vocabularies and language styles in documents and queries.

In the last two decades, different latent semantic models have been proposed to address the issue [e.g., 9, 19, 4]. Different terms that occur in a similar context are grouped into the same semantic cluster. Thus, a query and a document, represented as vectors in the lower-dimensional semantic space, can still have a high similarity even if they do not share any term.

An alternative strategy to cope with the problem is the approach based on statistical translation [2]: A query term can be a translation of any word in a document which may be different from, but semantically related to the query term; and the relevance of a document given a query is assumed proportional to the translation probability from the document to the query.

The research goal of this paper is to develop new ranking models for Web search by combining, in a principled way, the methods of semantic representation and statistical translation. Our assumption is that the translation between a query and a document can be modeled more effectively by mapping them into some semantic representations that are language independent than by mapping them at the word level.

Our work is based on two lines of previous research. The first is a set of clickthrough-based translation models for Web search presented and evaluated in [14], which is a significant extension of the original approach [2], motivated by the increasingly large amount of clickthrough data. Following [14], in this study we consider documents and queries as two different "languages" (i.e., the query language and the document language), and construct parallel training data from clickthrough data by pairing a query with the titles of the documents that have clicks for that query[1]. Different from [14], our models are trained to capture the map-

[1] In modern search engines, a Web document is described by multiple fields [14, 31], including title, body, anchor text etc. In our experiments, we only used the title field of a Web document for ranking. In addition to providing simplicity for fast experimentation, our decision is motivated by two factors, as described and empirically justified in [14]. First, titles are more similar to queries both in length and in vocabulary, making the translation model learning more effective. Second, the title field gives a good single-field retrieval result, although it is much shorter than other fields such as anchor and body; thus it can serve as a reasonable baseline in our experiments. Nevertheless, our methods are not limited to the title field, and can be easily applied to the multi-field description.

ping relationships between terms in a document and terms in a query at the sematic level rather than at the word level.

The second line of previous work that lays the foundation of this study is the research on cross-lingual and multi-lingual latent semantic models [11, 25, 27]. In these earlier works, various extensions of Latent Semantic Analysis (LSA) or topic models are developed for applications such as cross-lingual IR [11] and retrieval of parallel Web pages [27]. In this study we investigate a variety of bilingual latent semantic models, which are the extensions and variants of these previous models. In particular, we focus the research on three aspects: (1) the methods of learning semantic representations from clickthrough data, (2) the approaches to incorporating the latent semantic models into proper IR frameworks, and (3) the evaluation of their effectiveness for Web search on a real world data set.

In this paper we present two new document ranking models for Web search, a bilingual topic model and a discriminative projection model. Both models are learned on clickthrough data. The topic model represents a document as a distribution of semantic topics, and is incorporated into the language modeling framework for IR by assuming that a query term is generated from a mixture of these topics. The bilingual topic model learns a semantic representation in such a way that each query and its paired titles, extracted from clickthrough data, share as much as possible the same topic fractions. Unlike the topic model, the projection model, similar to LSA, represents a document as a point in the semantic space. It fits naturally the IR framework based on vector space model (VSM). The relevance of a query and a document is computed as the (cosine) similarity between their vectors in the semantic space. Different from LSA and its variants, our model learns a projection matrix, which maps the term-vector of a document onto a lower-dimensional semantic space, using a supervised learning method. Inspired by the learning-to-rank framework [6], the projection matrix is learned *discriminatively* in such a way that the distance between a query and its paired title, both represented as vectors in a projected semantic space, is smaller than that between the query and the titles of other documents which have no clicks for that query. We evaluated the two new ranking models on the Web search task using a real world data set. Results show that they significantly outperform their corresponding baseline models, which are considered state-of-the-art.

In the rest of the paper, Section 2 reviews related work. Sections 3 and 4 describe in detail the bilingual topic model and the discriminative projection model, respectively. Section 5 presents the experiments. Section 6 concludes the paper.

2. PREVIOUS WORK

This section reviews previous approaches to bridging the lexical gap between queries and documents for IR.

2.1 Statistical Translation Models

The statistical translation based approach is an extension of the language modeling approach to IR [2, 28]. Each document is scored by the likelihood of it translating into a query. Let $\mathbf{q} = q_1 \ldots q_{|\mathbf{q}|}$ be a query and $\mathbf{d} = d_1 \ldots d_{|\mathbf{d}|}$ be a document. A word translation model [2] assumes that both **q** and **d** are bags of words, and that the translation probability of **q** given **d** is computed as

$$P(\mathbf{q}|\mathbf{d}) = \prod_{q \in \mathbf{q}} \sum_{w \in \mathbf{d}} P(q|w)P(w|\mathbf{d}) \quad (1)$$

where $P(w|\mathbf{d})$ is the unigram probability of word w in $\mathbf{d}$, and $P(q|w)$ is the probability of translating w into a query term q.

It is easy to verify that if we only allow a word to be translated into itself, Eq. (1) is reduced to the simple exact term matching that is used by traditional unigram language modeling approaches. To bridge the lexical gap between queries and documents, the translation based approach allows a document to translate any one of its words w to a different but semantically related query term with a nonzero probability.

Unlike latent semantic models, which will be reviewed shortly, the translation-based approach does not map different terms into latent semantic clusters but learns translation relationships directly between a term in a document and a term in a query. A major challenge of this approach is how to estimate the translation probabilities. The ideal training data would be a large amount of query-document pairs, in each of which the document is judged as relevant to the query. Due to the lack of such training data, [2] resorts to some *synthetic* query-document pairs, and [22] simply uses the title-document pairs as substitutes for training data. Since recently, with the growing availability of search logs, it is possible to mine implicit relevance judgments from clickthrough data, and to generate a large amount of *real* query-document pairs for translation model training [14]. Given enough training data, more sophisticated translation models such as phrase models and factored models have also been investigated [14, 23, 26].

2.2 Generative Topic Models

One of the first topic models widely used for IR is Probabilistic Latent Semantic Analysis (PLSA) [19]. Although Hofmann applied PLSA to IR in the VSM framework in the original paper, PLSA is in nature a generative model, and can be more straightforwardly incorporated into the language modeling framework, under which documents are ranked by their probabilities of generating a query. In PLSA, a query, viewed as a short document, is generated from a document using the following process. First, a multinomial distribution $\boldsymbol{\theta}$ of T topics for each document is selected as the most likely topic distribution for the document. Second, a latent topic z is picked for each query term with probability $P(z|\mathbf{d}, \boldsymbol{\theta}) = \theta_z$. Finally, a query term q is generated with probability $P(q|\boldsymbol{\phi}_z)$, where $\boldsymbol{\phi}_z$ is the topic specific word distribution. Assuming that both a document and a query are bag-of-words, the probability of generating the query **q** from the document **d** is

$$P(\mathbf{q}|\mathbf{d}) = \prod_{q \in \mathbf{q}} \sum_{z} P(q|\boldsymbol{\phi}_z)\theta_z. \quad (2)$$

Notice that both Eq. (1) and (2) are in the form of a factored generative model where a query term is generated from a mixture of factors. While in translation models the factors are simply words in a document, in PLSA the factors are hidden topics.

Latent Dirichlet Allocation (LDA) [4] generalizes PLSA to a proper generative model and places Dirichlet priors over the parameters $\boldsymbol{\theta}$ and $\boldsymbol{\phi}$. As a result, in LDA, instead of a single most likely topic vector $\boldsymbol{\theta}$ for a document, a posterior distribution over vectors $\boldsymbol{\theta}$ is used, where the prior is a conjugate Dirichlet prior which is the same for all documents. So, in theory LDA overcomes some problems of PLSA such as overfitting and the issues regarding generating queries from unseen documents [4, 32]. However, whether the theoretical superiority of LDA can be translated into significant empirical improvement over PLSA on realistic applications, such as Web search, remains to be demonstrated.

The effectiveness of LDA for IR is demonstrated in [32] without directly comparing it to PLSA. [17] clarifies the relationship between LDA and PLSA in the context of IR, and concludes that PLSA is a *maximum a posteriori* (MAP) estimated LDA model. [1] shows that MAP inference performs comparably to the best Bayesian inference methods for LDA. Therefore, in our experiments all the topic models are implemented as PLSA, or equivalently, LDA with MAP inference.

Recently, these topic models have been extended to handle cross-lingual or multi-lingual cases, where there are pairs or tuples of corresponding documents in different languages. For example, the Poly-Lingual Topic Model (PLTM) [25] is an extension to LDA that views documents in a tuple as having a shared topic distribution $\boldsymbol{\theta}$. Each of the documents in the tuple uses $\boldsymbol{\theta}$ to select topics z, but could use a different language-specific, word-topic-distribution $\boldsymbol{\phi}_z^L$ to generate words for the topics. Two additional models, Joint PLSA (JPLSA) and Coupled PLSA (CPLSA) are introduced in [27]. JPLSA is a variant of PLTM when documents of different languages share the same word-topic distribution, and MAP inference, instead of Gibbs sampling, is performed. CPLSA extends JPLSA by constraining corresponding documents to have similar fractions of words assigned to each topic according to the posterior distribution of topic assignments, instead of sharing the prior topic distributions. The bilingual topic models discussed in Section 3 are the variants and extensions to these previous models when we strive to effectively learn model parameters on click-through data for the application of Web search.

2.3 Linear Projection Models

One of the most well-known linear projection models for IR is LSA [9]. LSA models the whole document collection using a $n \times d$ document-term matrix $\mathbf{C}$, where n is the number of documents and d is the number of word types, and performs singular value decomposition (SVD) on $\mathbf{C}$. The k biggest singular values are then used to find the $d \times k$ projection matrix. Thus, a document represented by a d-dimensional term vector can be mapped to a k-dimensional concept vector.

Similar to topic models, LSA can also be extended to handle pairs or tuples of parallel or comparable documents. For example, Cross-Language LSA (CL-LSA) [11] applies LSA to concatenated comparable documents from different languages. Oriented Principal Component Analysis (OPCA) [12, 27] solves a generalized Eigen problem by introducing a noise covariance matrix to ensure that comparable documents can be projected closely. Canonical Correlation Analysis (CCA) [30] finds projections that maximize the cross-covariance between the projected vectors. In all these methods, the linear projection is learned without explicitly taking into account how documents are ranked. We will show that learning the projection matrix discriminatively on query-title pairs, using a cost function closely related to the measure of evaluating document ranking, leads to a much more effective model for Web search.

3. BILINGUAL TOPIC MODEL

The bilingual topic model (BLTM) can be viewed as a special case of PLTM [25], where search queries and web documents are assumed to be written in two different languages and MAP inference is used instead of Bayesian inference. BLTM is also a close variant of JPLSA [27].

We assume that a query $\mathbf{q} = q_1 \dots q_{|\mathbf{q}|}$ and its paired title $\mathbf{d} = w_1 \dots w_{|\mathbf{d}|}$ share a common distribution of topics, but use different (probably overlapping) vocabularies to express these topics. The graphical model is shown in Figure 1. Formally, BLTM assumes the following process of generating a query-title pair.

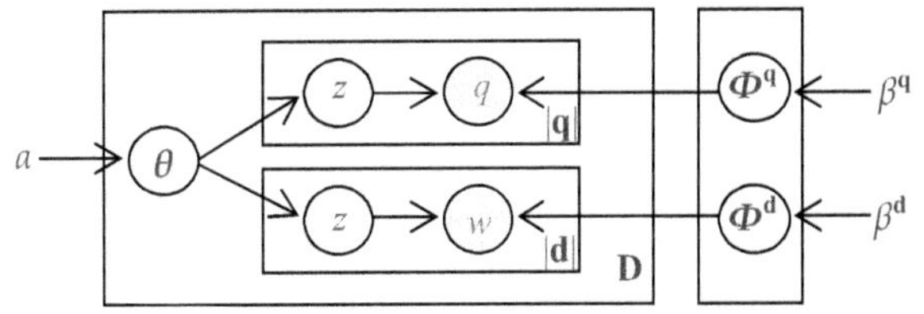

Figure 1: Graphical model for BLTM.

- First, for each topic z, a pair of different word distributions $(\boldsymbol{\phi}_z^{\mathbf{q}}, \boldsymbol{\phi}_z^{\mathbf{d}})$ are selected from a Dirichlet prior with concentration parameter β, where $\boldsymbol{\phi}_z^{\mathbf{q}}$ is a topic-specific query-word distribution, and $\boldsymbol{\phi}_z^{\mathbf{d}}$ a topic-specific title-word distribution. Assuming there are T topics, we have two sets of distributions $\boldsymbol{\phi}^{\mathbf{q}} = (\boldsymbol{\phi}_1^{\mathbf{q}}, \dots, \boldsymbol{\phi}_T^{\mathbf{q}})$ and $\boldsymbol{\phi}^{\mathbf{d}} = (\boldsymbol{\phi}_1^{\mathbf{d}}, \dots, \boldsymbol{\phi}_T^{\mathbf{d}})$.
- Then, for each query and its paired title, a topic distribution $\boldsymbol{\theta}^{\mathbf{q,d}}$ is drawn from a Dirichlet prior with concentration parameter α.
- Each term in the query is then generated by first selecting a topic z according to $\boldsymbol{\theta}^{\mathbf{q,d}}$, and drawing a word from $\boldsymbol{\phi}_z^{\mathbf{q}}$.
- Similarly, each term in the paired title is generated by selecting a topic z according to the same topic distribution $\boldsymbol{\theta}^{\mathbf{q,d}}$, and then drawing a word from $\boldsymbol{\phi}_z^{\mathbf{d}}$.

Thus, the log-likelihood of a corpus of query-title pairs, together with the paired document-topic vectors and word-topic vectors, is

$$\log\left(P(\boldsymbol{\phi}^{\mathbf{q}}|\beta^{\mathbf{q}})P(\boldsymbol{\phi}^{\mathbf{d}}|\beta^{\mathbf{d}}) \prod_{(\mathbf{q},\mathbf{d})} P(\boldsymbol{\theta}|\alpha)P\big((\mathbf{q},\mathbf{d})\big|\boldsymbol{\theta}^{\mathbf{q,d}},\boldsymbol{\phi}^{\mathbf{q}},\boldsymbol{\phi}^{\mathbf{d}}\big) \right) \quad (3)$$

where

$$P\big((\mathbf{q},\mathbf{d})\big|\boldsymbol{\theta}^{\mathbf{q,d}},\boldsymbol{\phi}^{\mathbf{q}},\boldsymbol{\phi}^{\mathbf{d}}\big) = \prod_{q\in\mathbf{q}}\sum_{z} P(q|\,\boldsymbol{\phi}_z^{\mathbf{q}})P(z|\boldsymbol{\theta}^{\mathbf{q,d}}) \cdot \prod_{w\in\mathbf{d}}\sum_{z} P(w|\,\boldsymbol{\phi}_z^{\mathbf{d}})P(z|\boldsymbol{\theta}^{\mathbf{q,d}})$$

Note that since we use MAP estimation, as will be described in Section 3.1, $\boldsymbol{\theta}^{\mathbf{q,d}}$, $\boldsymbol{\phi}^{\mathbf{q}}$ and $\boldsymbol{\phi}^{\mathbf{d}}$ in Eq. (3) are treated as parameters rather than hidden variables, as in the Bayesian inference methods.

3.1 MAP Estimation

We use the standard EM algorithm [10] to estimate the parameters $(\boldsymbol{\theta}^{\mathbf{q,d}}, \boldsymbol{\phi}^{\mathbf{q}}, \boldsymbol{\phi}^{\mathbf{d}})$ of BLTM by maximizing the joint log-likelihood of the parallel corpus and the parameters, as shown in Eq. (3). The derivation of the updates is similar to that described in [7, 8]. In the E-step, the posterior probabilities for each term q in query $\mathbf{q}$ and each term w in its paired title $\mathbf{d}$ are computed for the latent variables z according to:

$$P\big(z\big|q,\boldsymbol{\theta}^{\mathbf{q,d}}\big) = \frac{P\big(q\big|\boldsymbol{\phi}_z^{\mathbf{q}}\big)P(z|\boldsymbol{\theta}^{\mathbf{q,d}})}{\sum_{z'} P\big(q\big|\boldsymbol{\phi}_{z'}^{\mathbf{q}}\big)P(z'|\boldsymbol{\theta}^{\mathbf{q,d}})} \quad (4)$$

$$P\big(z\big|w,\boldsymbol{\theta}^{\mathbf{q,d}}\big) = \frac{P\big(w\big|\boldsymbol{\phi}_z^{\mathbf{d}}\big)P(z|\boldsymbol{\theta}^{\mathbf{q,d}})}{\sum_{z'} P\big(w\big|\boldsymbol{\phi}_{z'}^{\mathbf{d}}\big)P(z'|\boldsymbol{\theta}^{\mathbf{q,d}})} \quad (5)$$

In the M-step, parameters are updated for given posterior probabilities computed in the previous E-step. We treat α, $\beta^{\mathbf{d}}$ and $\beta^{\mathbf{q}}$ as hyperparameters, each corresponding to one Dirichlet prior, and denote Q as the size of the query vocabulary and W the size of title vocabulary. To simplify notation, letting $n(q,\mathbf{q})$ be the frequency of term q in query $\mathbf{q}$, and $n(w,\mathbf{d})$ the frequency of term w in title $\mathbf{d}$, we define $N_{q,z}{}^{\mathbf{q,d}} = n(q,\mathbf{q})P(z|q,\boldsymbol{\theta}^{\mathbf{q,d}})$ and $N_{w,z}{}^{\mathbf{q,d}} = n(w,\mathbf{d})P(z|w,\boldsymbol{\theta}^{\mathbf{q,d}})$. Then, the updates can be written as

$$P(q|\boldsymbol{\phi}_z^{\mathbf{q}}) = \frac{\beta^{\mathbf{q}} - 1 + \sum_{(\mathbf{q,d})} N_{q,z}{}^{\mathbf{q,d}}}{Q\beta^{\mathbf{q}} - Q + \sum_{(\mathbf{q,d}),q'} N_{q',z}{}^{\mathbf{q,d}}} \quad (6)$$

$$P(w|\boldsymbol{\phi}_z^{\mathbf{d}}) = \frac{\beta^{\mathbf{d}} - 1 + \sum_{(\mathbf{q,d})} N_{w,z}{}^{\mathbf{q,d}}}{W\beta^{\mathbf{d}} - W + \sum_{(\mathbf{q,d}),w'} N_{w',z}{}^{\mathbf{q,d}}} \quad (7)$$

$$P(z|\boldsymbol{\theta}^{\mathbf{q,d}}) = \frac{\alpha - 1 + (\sum_q N_{q,z}{}^{\mathbf{q,d}} + \sum_w N_{w,z}{}^{\mathbf{q,d}})}{T\alpha - T + \sum_{z'}(\sum_q N_{q,z'}{}^{\mathbf{q,d}} + \sum_w N_{w,z'}{}^{\mathbf{q,d}})} \quad (8)$$

3.2 Posterior Regularization (PR)

A query and a title, if they are paired, are expected to not only share the same prior distribution over topics but also contain similar fractions of words assigned each topic. Since MAP estimation of the shared topic vector is concerned with explaining the union of tokens in the query and document and can be easily dominated by the longer one of the two, it does not guarantee that each topic z occurs with similar frequency in the query and title. Thus, following [27], we extend BTLM by constraining the paired query and title to have similar fractions of tokens assigned to each topic, and the constraint is enforced on expectation using posterior regularization [13].

BTLM with posterior regularization (BTLM-PR) is a variant of CPLSA [27] with two important modifications. First, while BTLM-PR assumes a pair of query and title to share the same topic distribution $\boldsymbol{\theta}$ as shown in Figure 1, in CPLSA the topic distributions of a pair of documents in two languages are completely independent. Second, CPLSA uses inequality constraints with slack variables to form the constrained space whereas BTLM-PR uses only equality constraints. These modifications not only lead to a mathematically simpler model, thus making the model training faster (e.g., it requires fewer EM iterations), but also significantly improve the retrieval results.

BTLM-PR can be trained using a modified EM algorithm, where in the E-step the posterior distributions of topics computed on a query-title pair $(\mathbf{q},\mathbf{d})$ are *projected* onto a constrained set of distributions, for which the expected fraction of tokens in $\mathbf{q}$ that are assigned topic t is the same as the expected fraction of tokens in $\mathbf{d}$ that are assigned the same topic. The expected counts with respect to this projected posterior distribution are then used in the M-step, which remains the same as Eq. (6) to (8).

In what follows, we describe in detail how the projection is performed. Let $(\mathbf{q},\mathbf{d})$ be a pair of sequences of tokens and their topic assignments, where

$$\mathbf{q} = \{(q_1,\dots,q_{|\mathbf{q}|}),(z_1,\dots,z_{|\mathbf{q}|})\}$$

$$\mathbf{d} = \{(w_1,\dots,w_{|\mathbf{d}|}),(z_1,\dots,z_{|\mathbf{d}|})\}.$$

The projection minimizes the Kullback-Leibler divergence between two sets of distributions $\boldsymbol{P}$ and $\boldsymbol{P}'$, $\mathbf{KL}(\boldsymbol{P}'||\boldsymbol{P})$. Let $\boldsymbol{P}$ denote the set of posterior distributions over hidden topic assignments for the tokens in $\mathbf{q}$ and $\mathbf{d}$, computed by the standard E-step as in Eq. (4) and (5). There are $|\mathbf{q}|$ plus $|\mathbf{d}|$ distributions in this set.

$$\boldsymbol{P} = \{P(z|q,\boldsymbol{\theta}^{\mathbf{q,d}}), P(z|w,\boldsymbol{\theta}^{\mathbf{q,d}})\}.$$

$\boldsymbol{P}'$ is an ideal set of distributions that has the desired property: the expected fraction of each topic is equal in $\mathbf{q}$ and $\mathbf{d}$

$$\boldsymbol{P}' = \{P_{\mathbf{q}}'(z|q), P_{\mathbf{d}}'(z|w)\},$$

such that for each topic

$$\mathbf{E}_{P'_{\mathbf{q}}}\left[\frac{1}{|\mathbf{q}|}\sum_{j=1}^{|\mathbf{q}|}\mathbf{1}(z_j=t)\right] = \mathbf{E}_{P'_{\mathbf{d}}}\left[\frac{1}{|\mathbf{d}|}\sum_{j=1}^{|\mathbf{d}|}\mathbf{1}(z_j=t)\right],$$

where

$$\mathbf{E}_{P'_q}\left[\frac{1}{|\mathbf{q}|}\sum_{j=1}^{|\mathbf{q}|}\mathbf{1}(z_j=t)\right] = \frac{1}{|\mathbf{q}|}\sum_{q\in\mathbf{q}} P'(z=t|q)\text{, and}$$

$$\mathbf{E}_{P'_d}\left[\frac{1}{|\mathbf{d}|}\sum_{j=1}^{|\mathbf{d}|}\mathbf{1}(z_j=t)\right] = \frac{1}{|\mathbf{d}|}\sum_{w\in\mathbf{d}} P'(z=t|w).$$

Now, the projection can be formulated as a constrained optimization problem, where we seek an ideal set of distributions $\boldsymbol{P}'$ that is closest to $\boldsymbol{P}$:

$$\min_{\boldsymbol{P}'\in\boldsymbol{\mathcal{P}}} \mathbf{KL}(\boldsymbol{P}'||\boldsymbol{P}) \quad (9)$$

where $\boldsymbol{\mathcal{P}}$ is a space of distribution sets $\boldsymbol{P}'$ satisfying the constraint:

$$\mathbf{E}_{P'_q}\left[\frac{1}{|\mathbf{q}|}\sum_{j=1}^{|\mathbf{q}|}\mathbf{1}(z_j=t)\right] = \mathbf{E}_{P'_d}\left[\frac{1}{|\mathbf{d}|}\sum_{j=1}^{|\mathbf{d}|}\mathbf{1}(z_j=t)\right], t = 1\dots T.$$

In our case, the valid ideal distribution space $\boldsymbol{\mathcal{P}}$ is non-empty. The problem of Eq. (9) can be solved efficiently in its dual form. For the sake of clarity, we leave the derivation to Appendix A, and only present the result below. The primal solution P' is given in terms of the dual solution λ_t by

$$P'(z=t|q) = \frac{1}{Z_{\lambda,q}} P(z=t|q,\boldsymbol{\theta}^{\mathbf{q,d}}) \exp\left(-\frac{\lambda_t}{|\mathbf{q}|}\right) \quad (10)$$

where $Z_{\lambda,q} = \sum_t P(z=t|q,\boldsymbol{\theta}^{\mathbf{q,d}}) \exp\left(-\frac{\lambda_t}{|\mathbf{q}|}\right)$, and

$$P'(z=t|w) = \frac{1}{Z_{\lambda,w}} P(z=t|w,\boldsymbol{\theta}^{\mathbf{q,d}}) \exp\left(\frac{\lambda_t}{|\mathbf{d}|}\right) \quad (11)$$

where $Z_{\lambda,w} = \sum_t P(z=t|w,\boldsymbol{\theta}^{\mathbf{q,d}}) \exp\left(\frac{\lambda_t}{|\mathbf{d}|}\right)$.

The optimal value of λ_t can be obtained using the gradient ascent algorithm with the update

$$\lambda_t^{new} = \lambda_t^{old} + \epsilon\cdot\mathbf{g}(\lambda_t) \quad (12)$$

where ϵ is the learning rate, and the gradient $\mathbf{g}$ is computed as

$$\mathbf{g}(\lambda_t) = \mathbf{E}_{P'_{\mathbf{q}}}\left[\frac{1}{|\mathbf{q}|}\sum_{j=1}^{|\mathbf{q}|}\mathbf{1}(z_j=t)\right] - \mathbf{E}_{P'_{\mathbf{d}}}\left[\frac{1}{|\mathbf{d}|}\sum_{j=1}^{|\mathbf{d}|}\mathbf{1}(z_j=t)\right] \quad (13)$$

In summary, the projection step is performed for each pair $(\mathbf{q},\mathbf{d})$ in training data as follows. First, parameters $\lambda_t, t = 1\dots T$ are optimized using gradient ascent according to Eq. (12) and (13). Then, the projected probabilities are computed according to Eq. (10) and (11). The modified EM algorithm uses the projected posterior probabilities P' to update the model parameters in the M-step.

3.3 Ranking Documents

In our Web search experiments, we mixed BLTM with the smoothed unigram language model, and used the following document ranking function:

$$P_s(\mathbf{q}|\mathbf{d}) = \prod_{q \in \mathbf{q}} P_s(q|\mathbf{d}) \tag{14}$$

$$P_s(q|\mathbf{d}) = \lambda_1 P(q|C) + (1-\lambda_1) P_{mx}(q|\mathbf{d}) \tag{15}$$

$$P_{mx}(q|\mathbf{d}) = \lambda_2 P(q|\mathbf{d}) + (1-\lambda_2) P_{bltm}(q|\mathbf{d}) \tag{16}$$

$$P_{bltm}(q|\mathbf{d}) = \sum_z P(q|\boldsymbol{\phi}_z^q) P(z|\boldsymbol{\theta}^d) \tag{17}$$

Here, $P(q|C)$ in Eq. (15) and $P(q|\mathbf{d})$ in Eq. (16) are the unsmoothed background model and document model, respectively. λ_1 and λ_2 are tuning parameters with their values between 0 and 1. Notice that letting $\lambda_2 = 1$ reduces the model to a unigram language model with Jelinek-Mercer smoothing [34], which is used as baseline in our experiments. Letting $\lambda_2 = 0$, the document model depends solely on BLTM. Also notice that BLTM in Eq. (17) differs from a topic model of Eq. (2). Although in both models the topics are generated from **d** written in *title language*, the query term q is generated from topic-specific word distributions in *query language* in BLTM. Thus, BLTM can be considered as performing a translation from title to query via hidden topics. In our experiments, we used folding-in with 20 EM iterations to map a document in test data to its corresponding topic vector $\boldsymbol{\theta}^d$.

4. DISCRIMINATIVE PROJECTION MODEL

The discriminative projection model (DPM) maps a sparse, high-dimensional term vector onto a dense, low-dimensional space through a simple matrix multiplication. DPM differs from other linear projection models in the way the projection matrix is learned. In this study we compare DPM to LSA and its variants. Since in our implementation DPM and various LSA models take the same clickthrough data as input and output the projection matrix in the same model form, we start the description of DPM with a brief review of LSA and its variants.

4.1 LSA and its Variants

LSA models the whole document collection using a $n \times d$ document-term matrix $\mathbf{C}$, where n is the number of documents and d is the number of word types. $\mathbf{C}$ is first factored into the product of three matrices using SVD

$$\mathbf{C} = \mathbf{U}\boldsymbol{\Sigma}\mathbf{V}^T \tag{18}$$

where the orthogonal matrices $\mathbf{U}$ and $\mathbf{V}$ are called term and document vectors, respectively, and the diagonal elements of $\boldsymbol{\Sigma}$ are singular values in descending order. Then, a low-rank matrix approximation of $\mathbf{C}$ is generated by retaining only the k biggest singular values in $\boldsymbol{\Sigma}$. Now, a document (or a query) represented by a term vector $\mathbf{D}$ can be mapped to a low-dimensional concept vector $\widehat{\mathbf{D}}$ as

$$\widehat{\mathbf{D}} = \mathbf{A}^T\mathbf{D} \tag{19}$$

where the $d \times k$ matrix $\mathbf{A} = \mathbf{U}_k\boldsymbol{\Sigma}_k^{-1}$ is called the projection matrix. In document search, the relevance score between a query and a document, represented respectively by term vectors $\mathbf{Q}$ and $\mathbf{D}$, is assumed to be proportional to their cosine similarity score of the corresponding concept vectors $\widehat{\mathbf{Q}}$ and $\widehat{\mathbf{D}}$, according to the projection matrix $\mathbf{A}$

$$sim_{\mathbf{A}}(\mathbf{Q},\mathbf{D}) = \frac{\widehat{\mathbf{Q}}\widehat{\mathbf{D}}}{\|\widehat{\mathbf{Q}}\|\|\widehat{\mathbf{D}}\|} \tag{20}$$

Notice that LSA is closely related to principal component analysis (PCA), and can be solved via Eigen-decomposition instead. Let $\mathbf{S}$ be the correlation matrix between terms $\mathbf{S} = \mathbf{C}^{\mathbf{T}}\mathbf{C}$. The projection matrix $\mathbf{A}$ is exactly the top-k Eigen vectors of $\mathbf{S}$. Compared to LSA, the only difference is that PCA solves the Eigen problem on the covariance matrix instead. Because the term vectors are very sparse in practice and the column means are close to zero, $\mathbf{S}$ is in fact very close to the covariance matrix. In our experiments we used PCA to derive the LSA projection matrix.

The objective of LSA is to find the matrix to maximize the variance of the projected vectors. When applied directly to the clickthrough data, queries and title are treated as separate documents and the click information is not used. CL-LSA [11] and OPCA [12, 27] are two variants to LSA, striving to reduce the projected distance between a query and its paired title. Unfortunately, although both variants use the pair information to bias the derivation of the projection matrix, their objective functions are in fact only a coarse approximation to the final ranking measure. We hypothesize that with a large set of training data, the projection matrix can be learned discriminatively by minimizing a loss function that targets the ranking scenario, and thus yields better results. We describe this new projection learning framework in the next section.

4.2 Projection Learning via Siamese Neural Network (S2Net)

The projection matrix in DPM is learned from query-title pairs using S2Net, a newly proposed learning framework that learns discriminatively the projection matrix from pairs of related and unrelated documents. We briefly introduce the model below and interested readers can refer to [33] for more detail.

S2Net treats the raw term vector as the input layer and the mapped concept vector as the output layer. The value of each node in the output layer is a linear sum of all the input nodes, where the weights are associated with the edges. In other words, the network structure is a complete bipartite graph between the input and output layers, and the edge weights are equivalent to the form of a linear projection matrix $\mathbf{A}$, as in Eq. (19). Below, we describe the loss function and training process.

The design of the loss function in S2Net follows the pairwise learning-to-rank paradigm outlined in [6]. Consider a query $\mathbf{q}$ and two documents $\mathbf{d_1}$ and $\mathbf{d_2}$, where $\mathbf{d_1}$ has clicks for $\mathbf{q}$ but $\mathbf{d_2}$ does not. Let $\mathbf{Q}, \mathbf{D}_1$ and $\mathbf{D}_2$ be the term vectors of $\mathbf{q}, \mathbf{d_1}$ and $\mathbf{d_2}$, respectively. We then construct two pairs of term vectors $(\mathbf{Q},\mathbf{D}_1)$ and $(\mathbf{Q},\mathbf{D}_2)$, where the former is preferred and should be ranked higher. Given the model (i.e., the projection matrix) $\mathbf{A}$, let Δ be the difference of the cosine similarity scores of their projected concept vectors, following Eq. (20). Namely, $\Delta = sim_{\mathbf{A}}(\mathbf{Q},\mathbf{D}_1) - sim_{\mathbf{A}}(\mathbf{Q},\mathbf{D}_2)$. Intuitively, we want to learn a model to increase Δ. We use the following logistic loss over Δ, which can be shown to upper bound the pairwise accuracy

$$L(\Delta; \mathbf{A}) = \log(1 + \exp(-\gamma\Delta)) \quad (21)$$

The loss function in Eq. (21) has a shape similar to the hinge loss used in SVMs. Because of the use of the cosine similarity function, we add a scaling factor γ that magnifies Δ from [-2, 2] to a larger range. Empirically, the value of γ makes no difference as long as it is large enough. In the experiments, we set $\gamma = 10$. Because the loss function is differentiable, optimizing the model parameters $\mathbf{A}$ can be done using the gradient-based methods, such as L-BFGS. For the sake of a clean presentation, we leave the gradient derivation to Appendix B.

Given that the optimization problem is not convex, initializing the model from a good projection matrix often helps reduce the training time and may converge to a better local minimum. In our experiments, we always started the model parameters from the LSA matrix. In principle, Eq. (21) can further be regularized by adding a term $\frac{\beta}{2}||\mathbf{A} - \mathbf{A}_0||^2$, which forces the learned model not to deviate too much from the initial model $\mathbf{A}_0$. However, we did not find clear empirical advantage over the simpler *early stop* approach in a preliminary study, which is adopted in the experiments in this paper.

5. EXPERIMENTS

This section evaluates the effectiveness of the models described in Sections 3 and 4 on the Web search application. Instead of presenting a direct comparison between topic modeling and linear projection modeling[2], we focus our experiments on demonstrating that for each type of models, clickthrough data can lead to significant improvements when modeled properly. Thus, we will report the results of the topic models and the linear projection models in separate sections. For each type, we compare our models to their baseline methods, which are considered state-of-the-art in the research community.

5.1 Data Sets and Evaluation Methodology

We evaluated the retrieval models on a large-scale real world data set, called the evaluation data set henceforth. The data set contains 16,510 English queries sampled from one-year query log files of the Microsoft Bing search engine. On average, each query is associated with 15 Web documents (URLs). Each query-title pair has a relevance label. The label is human generated and is on a 5-level relevance scale, 0 to 4, with 4 meaning document $\mathbf{d}$ is the most relevant to query $\mathbf{q}$ and 0 meaning $\mathbf{d}$ is not relevant to $\mathbf{q}$. All the queries and documents are preprocessed as follows. The text is white-space tokenized and lowercased, numbers are retained, and no stemming/inflection is performed.

All the ranking models used in this study (i.e., language models, topic models, VSM and linear projection models) contain free parameters that must be estimated empirically by trial and error. Therefore, we used 2-fold cross validation: A set of results on one half of the data is obtained using the parameter settings optimized on the other half, and the global retrieval results are combined from those of the two sets.

The performance of all the ranking models was measured by mean *Normalized Discounted Cumulative Gain* (NDCG) [21]. We report NDCG scores at truncation levels 1, 3, and 10. We also performed a significance test using the paired *t*-test. Differences are considered statistically significant when the *p*-value is less than 0.05.

In our experiments, the query-title pairs, used for model training, are extracted from one year query log files using a procedure similar to [16]. First of all, a set of query sessions were extracted from the raw log files. A query session consists of a user-issued query and a ranked list of documents, each of which may or may not be clicked by a user. Second, we built for each document a so-called query click field, which consists of a set of query-score pairs $(\mathbf{q}, Score(\mathbf{d}, \mathbf{q}))$, where $\mathbf{q}$ is a unique query string for which the document $\mathbf{d}$ has clicks and $Score(\mathbf{d}, \mathbf{q})$ is a score assigned to $\mathbf{q}$, as defined in Eq. (1) in [16]. Only those pairs whose scores are larger than a threshold were retained. $Score(\mathbf{d}, \mathbf{q})$ could be the number of times the document was clicked on for that query, but it is important to also consider the number of times the page has been shown to the user and the position in the ranked list at which the page was shown. Finally, we formed a set of query-title pairs by aligning the title of the document to each unique query string in the query click field of the same document.

Some previous studies [e.g., 16, 29] show that the query click field, when it is valid, is the most effective for Web search. However, click information is unavailable for many URLs, especially new URLs and tail URLs, leaving their click fields invalid (i.e., the field is either empty or unreliable because of sparseness). In this study, we assume that each document contained in the evaluation data set is either a new URL or a tail URL, thus has no click information (i.e., its click field is invalid). Our research goal is to investigate how to learn the latent semantic models from the popular URLs that have rich click information, and apply the models to improve the retrieval of those tail or new URLs. To this end, in our experiments only the title fields of the Web documents are used for ranking.

From one-year query log files, we were able to generate large amounts of query-title pairs using the procedure described above. For training latent semantic models in this study, we used a randomly sampled subset of 82,834,648 pairs whose documents are popular and have rich click information. We then tested the trained models in ranking the documents in the evaluation data set, which do not have click information. The query-title pairs were pre-processed in the same way as the evaluation data to ensure uniformity.

5.2 Topic Model Results

Table 1 shows the main Web document ranking results using various topic models, tested on the human-labeled evaluation data set via 2-fold cross validation, as described in Section 5.1.

UM (Row 1) is the baseline model, a unigram language model with Jelinek-Mercer smoothing, parameterized by Eq. (14) to (16) with $\lambda_2 = 1$.

[2] Strictly speaking, the results of topic models and linear projection models, reported in Tables 1 and 2 respectively, cannot be compared directly due to three reasons. First, the baseline models, with which the proposed models are combined to achieve the best results, are different. Second, in order to perform S2Net training efficiently for fast experimentation, the vocabulary used in building linear projection models is much smaller than that for topic models. Third, the input term weighting functions for them are different: the topic models use the raw term frequency counts, while the projection models take TFIDF vectors. We leave to future work a direct comparison of topic modeling and linear projection modeling in a more consistent setting, and how to best combine them for Web document ranking.

Rows 2 to 9 are four different topic models, parameterized by Eq. (14) to (17). To improve the efficiency of model training, we pruned the query-title training data by retaining only top 500K high-frequency words. We used 100 topics ($T = 100$) for all the topic models. In order to investigate the relative contributions of the unigram model and the latent semantic model to ranking, we report for each topic model the results using two different settings. One is letting the document model solely depend on the latent semantic model by setting $\lambda_2 = 0$ in Eq. (16). These results are shown in the shaded rows in Table 1. The other is defining the document model as a mixture of the unigram model and the latent semantic model by using a nonzero λ_2 in Eq. (16), tuned via cross-validation. We used folding-in with 20 EM iterations to map each document in the evaluation data set to its corresponding topic vector. In what follows, we describe the four topic models in turn.

PLSA (Rows 2 and 3) is our implementation of the model proposed in [19], and was trained on documents only (i.e., the title side of the query-title pairs). Different from [19], our version of PLSA was learned using MAP estimation, with $\alpha = 1.1$ and $\beta = 1.01$. The model can also be viewed as an approximation to the LDA document model described in [32], which is learned on the TREC document collection via Gibbs sampling.

BLTM (Rows 4 and 5) is the model described in Figure 1, where the model parameters were learned on query-title pairs using MAP estimation, as described in 3.1. We found that the model performance is not very sensitive to the values of the hyperparameters, which were set in our experiments as $\alpha = 1.1$ and $\beta^d = \beta^q = 1.01$. We also found after around 20 EM iterations, the likelihood of the model barely increases.

BLTM-PR (Rows 6 and 7) is BLTM trained using the modified EM algorithm that uses posterior regularization (PR), described in Section 3.2, to constrain the paired query and title not only to share the same prior topic distribution $\boldsymbol{\theta}$, but to also have similar fractions of tokens assigned to each topic. We found that with PR, the EM algorithm takes fewer iterations to converge. In our experiments, the likelihood seems to saturate after 16 iterations.

BLTM-PR-1V (Rows 8 and 9) is a variant of BLTM-PR where we merge the vocabularies in query and title languages and learn topic-specific word distributions over these merged vocabularies. This is suggested in [27], arguing that such a variant not only simplifies the implementation but also sometimes leads to better results. In our experiments, we found that using the merged vocabularies does not bring any significant difference for BLTM, but does lead to some small but significant improvement for BLTM-PR. One possible interpretation is that the same word in a query and document very often has the same topic, which is not used at all by the two-vocabulary version. In particular, for some rare words that may be harmful since there might not be enough data to estimate their topic distributions in queries and titles completely independently. Therefore, we speculate that a hierarchical Bayesian model that encourages matching words in queries and titles to have the same topics, but also allows them to diverge, would be superior to both the single vocabulary and two-vocabulary models. We leave it to future work.

WTM_M1 (Rows 10 and 11) is our implementation of the word translation model described in [14], listed here for comparison. The corresponding ranking function is similar to Eq. (14) to (16). The only difference is that P_{bltm} in Eq. (16) is replaced by the word translation model P_{wtm} defined as

#	Models	NDCG@1	NDCG@3	NDCG@10
1	**UM**	0.308	0.373	0.454
2	**PLSA** ($\lambda_2 = 0$)	0.295	0.371	0.456
3	**PLSA**	0.325	0.391	0.470
4	**BLTM** ($\lambda_2 = 0$)	0.330	0.399	0.476
5	**BLTM**	0.338	0.404	0.479
6	**BLTM-PR** ($\lambda_2 = 0$)	0.334	0.403	0.479
7	**BLTM-PR**	0.342	0.406	0.482
8	**BLTM-PR-1V** ($\lambda_2 = 0$)	0.337	0.403	0.480
9	**BLTM-PR-1V**	0.344	0.407	0.483
10	**WTM_M1** ($\lambda_2 = 0$)	0.332	0.400	0.478
11	**WTM_M1**	0.338	0.404	0.480

Table 1: Web document ranking results using different topic models, tested on the evaluation data set, where only the title field of each document is used.

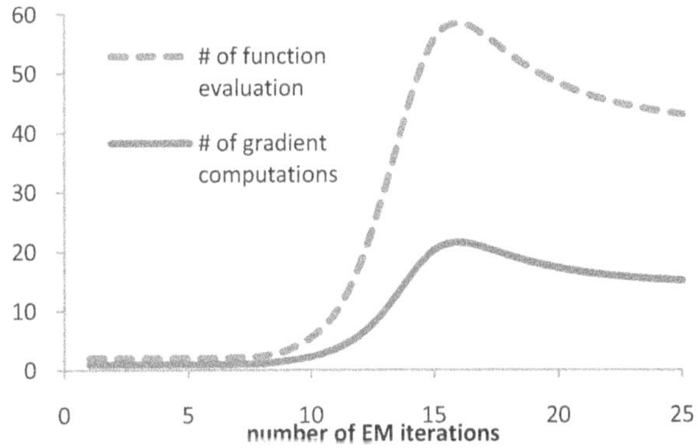

Figure 2: Average number of function evaluations and gradient computations per EM iteration, as a function of the number of the EM iterations, in the projection step for training BLTM-PR.

$$P_{wtm}(q|\mathbf{d}) = \sum_{w \in \mathbf{d}} P(q|w)P(w|\mathbf{d}),$$

where $P(q|w)$ is the word translation probability assigned by IBM-Model-1 [5], trained on query-title pairs using EM.

The results in Table 1 suggest several conclusions. First, using PLSA alone as a document model hurts the ranking performance (Row 2 vs. Row 1). But a linear combination of PLSA and the original document model significantly outperforms the baseline model (Row 3 vs. Row 1). The results are consistent with those previously reported on the TREC collections [32]. Second, using clickthrough data for model training by extending PLSA to BLTM, leads to a significant improvement (Rows 4 and 5 vs. Rows 2 and 3). Third, the performance of BLTM can be further improved by introducing constraints in the EM training to force the paired query and title to share the same proportion of topics (Rows 6 to 9 vs. Rows 4 and 5). The differences among BLTM, BLTM-PR, and BLTM-PR-V1 are statistically significant. Finally, we confirmed the effectiveness of the word translation model. The model performs as well as BLTM, i.e., their results are not significantly different (Rows 10 and 11 vs. Rows 4 and 5). However, both BLTM-PR and BLTM-PR-V1 beat the translation model with a statistically significant margin (Rows 6 to 9 vs. Rows 10 and 11). We also tried combining WTM_M1 with BLTM-PR, but the result is not significantly better than that of BLTM-PR.

The complexity of the training algorithm for BLTM is the same as the EM training for PLSA, which has been well-studied. BLTM-PR uses a modified EM algorithm. Although BLTM-PR needs fewer EM iterations to converge, each iteration is more expensive due to the projection step. The runtime of the projection step is dominated by function evaluations (Eq. (28)), and otherwise the most expensive step is the computation of the gradients (Eq. (13)). Notice that the projection function needs to be called for each query-title pair. Initializing BLTM-PR with a uniform distribution for $\boldsymbol{\theta}$ and $\boldsymbol{\phi}$, Figure 2 plots the average number of function evaluations and gradient computations per EM iteration, as a function of the number of the EM iterations. Both curves show that after 10 EM iterations, the training becomes much slower due to the dramatically increased cost of the projection step, indicating that from this moment EM starts to lead the distribution set far away from the ideal one in terms of KL distance. The cost of projection reduces slightly after 16 iterations when the EM training saturates. In our experiments, we found that training BLTM takes around 30 hours on a commodity 8-core server with 64-GB memory, and training BLTM-PR takes twice as much time. In practice, since the EM algorithm can be easily parallelized, topic model training could be performed much more efficiently on a cluster of computers.

5.3 Linear Projection Model Results

Table 2 shows the main Web document ranking results using various linear projection models, tested on the human-labeled evaluation data set.

VSM (Row 1) is the baseline model, where both documents and queries are represented as term vectors, with the TF-IDF term weighting, and the documents are ranked by the cosine similarity between the query and document vectors.

Rows 2 to 9 are four different linear projection models. All of them have the same model form as that of LSA [9]. To improve the efficiency of model training, we truncated the term vectors based on a vocabulary consisting of only the top 40K high document-frequency (DF) words, where the DF values are calculated based on the clickthrough data. We used 100 dimensions (k=100) for the vectors in semantic space. Similar to topic models, we report a pair of results for each projection model using two different settings. One is ranking documents using the cosine similarity scores in the semantic space, as in Eq. (20). These results are shown in the shaded rows in Table 2. The other is ranking documents based a weighted linear combination of two cosine similarity scores, computed in the original term space and in the projected semantic space, respectively. The linear combination weight is tuned via cross-validation. In what follows, we describe each of these models in turn.

LSA (Rows 2 and 3) is our implementation of the model described in [9]. As described in Section 4.1, we used PCA instead of SVD to compute the matrix. Queries and titles are treated as separate documents; the pair information from the clickthrough data was not used in this model.

CL-LSA (Rows 4 and 5) extends LSA by leveraging the pair information so that the projected distance between a query and its paired title is reduced [11]. In our implementation, each query and its paired title were concatenated first to form a new document. Then, the projection matrix was learned by applying LSA to this new corpus.

OPCA (Rows 6 and 7) leverages the pair information in a more principled way [12, 27] than CL-LSA does. Noticing that

#	Models	NDCG@1	NDCG@3	NDCG@10
1	VSM	0.313	0.379	0.460
2	LSA	0.298	0.372	0.455
3	LSA + VSM	0.330	0.396	0.474
4	CL-LSA	0.298	0.370	0.454
5	CL-LSA + VSM	0.330	0.396	0.474
6	OPCA	0.306	0.373	0.454
7	OPCA + VSM	0.328	0.395	0.473
8	S2Net	0.329	0.401	0.479
9	S2Net + VSM	0.340	0.407	0.483

Table 2: Web document ranking results using different linear projection models, tested on the evaluation data set, where only the title field of each document is used.

solving the Eigen-decomposition problem in PCA is the same as finding the vectors $\boldsymbol{v}$ that maximize the Rayleigh quotient:

$$\frac{\boldsymbol{v}^T \mathbf{S} \boldsymbol{v}}{\boldsymbol{v}^T \boldsymbol{v}} \tag{22}$$

OPCA improves PCA by replacing Eq. (22) with the generalized Rayleigh quotient:

$$\frac{\boldsymbol{v}^T \mathbf{S} \boldsymbol{v}}{\boldsymbol{v}^T \mathbf{N} \boldsymbol{v}} \tag{23}$$

where $\mathbf{N}$ is the noise covariance matrix. The role of $\mathbf{N}$ is to ensure that the variance of the projected vectors of the query and title from the same pair can be minimized. Let $\mathbf{C_Q}$ and $\mathbf{C_D}$ be the document-term matrices of queries and titles, respectively. In addition, column vectors in $\mathbf{C_Q}$ and $\mathbf{C_D}$ correspond respectively to the query and title in the pair when they have the same column index. The noise covariance matrix is constructed as

$$\mathbf{N} = \frac{1}{n}(\mathbf{C_Q} - \mathbf{C_D})^T(\mathbf{C_Q} - \mathbf{C_D}) \tag{24}$$

where n is the number of query-title pairs.

S2Net (Rows 8 and 9) is the learning framework introduced in Section 4.2, where the projection matrix is discriminatively learned using relevant and irrelevant pairs of queries and titles. We first randomly split the clickthrough corpus into two subsets, training (99.5%) and validation (0.5%). For each query, the paired title is treated relevant (positive) and we randomly selected 4 other titles from the data as the irrelevant ones (negative). The pairwise training setting encourages the model to lead to higher similarity scores of positive pairs compared to negative ones of the same query. We stop the training process based on the model performance on the validation set.

Several interesting conclusions can be drawn from the results shown in Table 2. First, when comparing different linear projection models with the VSM baseline (Rows 2, 4, 6 and 9 vs. Row 1), we found that all models except S2Net perform worse than VSM. This is consistent with the observation made by other researchers, which is that using LSA alone can hurt the ranking performance, especially for a very low dimensional concept vector space [24]. This result also justifies the scheme of combining the projection models with VSM. As presented in Table 2, the NDCG scores of the combined models are all better than both VSM and the corresponding projection models. Second, unlike the case of topic models, simply extending LSA to its bilingual version CL-LSA does not lead to any significant improvement (Rows 4 and 5 vs. Rows 2 and 3). Third, by simultaneously minimizing the distance between projected vectors of queries and their paired titles, OPCA does outperform LSA and CL-LSA with a small but statistically significant margin (Row 6 vs. Rows 2 and 4). However, after combining with the term vector model, the differences among these methods are not significant (Row 7 vs. Rows 3 and 5). Finally, the S2Net-trained DPM, when either used alone or combined with the term vector model, outperforms significantly other competing models (Rows 8 and 9 vs. Rows 1 to 7). Its superior results demonstrate that with an objective tightly related to the measure of evaluating document ranking, the discriminative learning approach can be very effective.

S2Net clearly outperforms other linear projection methods, but its training process is, unfortunately, more computationally expensive. Unlike LSA, CL-LSA and OPCA, which can all be solved by Eigen-decomposition, there is no analytic solution that minimizes the loss function in S2Net. In our current implementation, using a cluster of 60 ~ 80 nodes, each training iteration takes 1 to 1.5 hours and the model converges in approximately 40 iterations. The training time scales roughly linearly in terms of the number of dimensions and the number of examples. In contrast, using a commodity 8-core server with 64-GB memory, it typically takes 8 hours or less to derive an LSA, CL-LSA or OPCA model.

6. CONCLUSION

This paper presents two new document ranking models by combining the methods of latent semantic representation and the statistical translation-based approach to IR. We explore various methods of learning the semantic representation that is shared by a query and its paired titles from clickthrough data. Our evaluation on Web search shows that the proposed clickthrough-based latent semantic models significantly outperform both the standard IR models that do not use clickthrough data and those previous clickthrough-based translation models that do not use semantic representation.

In future work, we intend to explore alternative strategies of combining latent semantic models and translation models for IR. For example, we can form query-title corpora, where both the queries and titles are labeled by topics or concepts (e.g., generated using LSA). Then we can align the corpora using word-alignment models and readily compute translation probabilities based on words and topics. Another research area is the modeling of the correlations between topics in document ranking, as suggested in [3]. This is motivated by the observation that a search user may click a document on a topic that is related to, but not the same as, the topic in her query.

7. REFERENCE

[1] Asuncion, A., Welling, M, Smyth, P., and Teh, Y W. 2009. On smoothing and inference for topic models. In *Proceedings of Uncertainty in Artificial Intelligence*, pp. 27-34.

[2] Berger, A., and Lafferty, J. 1999. Information retrieval as statistical translation. In *SIGIR*, pp. 222-229.

[3] Blei, D., and Lafferty, J. 2007. A correlated topic model of science. *The Annals of Applied Statistics*, Vol. 1, No. 1, 17-35.

[4] Blei, D. M., Ng, A. Y., and Jordan, M. J. 2003. Latent Dirichlet allocation. *Journal of Machine Learning Research*, 3: 993-1022.

[5] Brown, P. F., Della Pietra, S. A., Della Pietra, V. J., and Mercer, R. L. 1993. The mathematics of statistical machine translation: parameter estimation. *Computational Linguistics*, 19(2): 263-311.

[6] Burges, C., Shaked, T., Renshaw, E., Lazier, A., Deeds, M., Hamilton, and Hullender, G. 2005. Learning to rank using gradient descent. In *ICML*, pp. 89-96.

[7] Chien, J-T., and Wu, M-S. 2008. Adaptive Bayesian latent semantic analysis. *IEEE Trans on Audio, Speech, and Language Processing*, 16(1): 198-207.

[8] de Freitas, N., and Barnard, K. 2001. Bayesian latent semantic analysis of multimedia databases. *Tech Report TR-2001-15*, University of British Columbia.

[9] Deerwester, S., Dumais, S. T., Furnas, G. W., Landauer, T., and Harshman, R. 1990. Indexing by latent semantic analysis. *Journal of the American Society for Information Science*, 41(6): 391-407

[10] Dempster, A., Laird, N., and Rubin, D. 1977. Maximum likelihood from incomplete data via the EM algorithm. *Journal of the Royal Statistical Society*, 39: 1-38.

[11] Dumais, S. T., Letsche, T. A., Littman, M. L., and Landauer, T. K. 1997. Automatic cross-linguistic information retrieval using latent semantic indexing. In *AAAI-97 Spring Symposium Series: Cross-Language Text and Speech Retrieval*.

[12] Diamantaras, K. I., and Kung, S. Y. 1996. *Principle Component Neural Networks: Theory and Applications*. Wiley-Interscience.

[13] Ganchev, K., Graca, J., Gillenwater, J., and Taskar, B. 2010. Posterior regularization for structured latent variable models. *Journal of Machine Learning Research*, 11 (2010): 2001-2049.

[14] Gao, J., He, X., and Nie, J-Y. 2010. Clickthrough-based translation models for web search: from word models to phrase models. In *CIKM*, pp. 1139-1148.

[15] Gao, J., Wu, Q., Burges, C., Svore, K., Su, Y., Khan, N., Shah, S., and Zhou, H. 2009. Model adaptation via model interpolation and boosting for web search ranking. In *EMNLP*, 505-513.

[16] Gao, J., Yuan, W., Li, X., Deng, K., and Nie, J-Y. 2009. Smoothing clickthrough data for web search ranking. In *SIGIR*.

[17] Girolami, M., and Kaban, A. 2003. On an equivalence between PLSA and LDA. In *SIGIR*, pp. 433-434.

[18] Griffiths, T. L., Tenenbaum, J. B., and Steyvers, M. 2007. Topics in semantic representation. *Psychological Review*, Vol. 114, No. 2, 211-244.

[19] Hofmann, T. 1999. Probabilistic latent semantic indexing. In *SIGIR*, pp. 50-57.

[20] Huang, J., Gao, J., Miao, J., Li, X., Wang, K., and Behr, F. 2010. Exploring web scale language models for search query processing. In *Proc. WWW 2010*, pp. 451-460.

[21] Jarvelin, K. and Kekalainen, J. 2000. IR evaluation methods for retrieving highly relevant documents. In *SIGIR*, pp. 41-48

[22] Jin, R., Hauptmann, A. G., and Zhai, C. 2002. Title language model for information retrieval. In *SIGIR*, pp. 42-48.

[23] Koehn, P., Och, F., and Marcu, D. 2003. Statistical phrase-based translation. In *HLT/NAACL*, pp. 127-133.

[24] Manning, C. D., and Schutze, H. 1999. *Foundations of Statistical Natural Language Processing*. The MIT Press.

[25] Mimno, D., Wallach, H. J., Naradowsky, J., Smith, D. A., and McCallum, A. 2009. Polylingual topic models. In *EMNLP*, pp. 880-889.

[26] Och, F. 2002. *Statistical machine translation: from single-word models to alignment templates*. PhD thesis, RWTH Aachen.

[27] Platt, J., Toutanova, K., and Yih, W. 2010. Translingual document representations from discriminative projections. In *EMNLP*, pp. 251-261.

[28] Ponte, J., and Croft, W. B. 1998. A language model approach to information retrieval. In SIGIR, pp. 275-281.

[29] Svore, K., and Burges, C. 2009. A machine learning approach for improved BM25 retrieval. In *CIKM*.

[30] Vinokourov, A., Shawe-taylor, J., and Cristianini, N. 2003. Inferring a semantic representation of text via cross-language correlation analysis. In *NIPS*, pp. 1473-1480.

[31] Wang, K., Li, X., and Gao, J. 2010. Multi-style language model for web scale information retrieval. In *SIGIR*, pp. 467-474.

[32] Wei, X., and Croft, W. B. 2006. LDA-based document models for ad-hoc retrieval. In *SIGIR*, pp. 178-185.
[33] Yih, W., Toutanova, K., Platt, J., and Meek, C. 2011. Learning discriminative projections for text similarity measures. In *CoNLL*.
[34] Zhai, C., and Lafferty, J. 2001. A study of smoothing methods for language models applied to ad hoc information retrieval. In *SIGIR*, pp. 334-342.

Appendix A: Derivation of the Projection Step in BLTM-PR Training

We derive the forms of the projected posterior probabilities in Eq. (10) and (11), and the gradient of Eq. (13). The derivation follows closely the one presented in [13], and uses the standard Lagrangian duality results.

The corresponding Lagrangian of the constrained optimization problem in Eq. (9) is

$$\max_{\lambda,\mu,\eta} \min_{\boldsymbol{P}'} L(\boldsymbol{P}',\lambda,\mu,\eta)\,, \tag{25}$$

where

$$\begin{aligned} L(\boldsymbol{P}',\lambda,\mu,\eta) &= \mathbf{KL}(\boldsymbol{P}'||\boldsymbol{P}) \\ &+\sum_t \lambda_t\left(\frac{1}{|\mathbf{q}|}\sum_{q\in\mathbf{q}} P'(z=t|q)-\frac{1}{|\mathbf{d}|}\sum_{w\in\mathbf{d}} P'(z=t|w)\right) \\ &+\sum_{q\in\mathbf{q}}\mu_q\left(\sum_t P'(z=t|q)-1\right) \\ &+\sum_{w\in\mathbf{d}}\eta_w\left(\sum_t P'(z=t|w)-1\right) \end{aligned}$$

The Lagrangian includes the equality constraints to ensure that we are in the desired constrained space and that we have valid distributions. A non-negativity constraint on P' can also be added, but this is not necessary as it falls out from the other conditions. The form of $P'(z=t|w)$ can be obtained by setting the derivative of $L(.)$ with respect to P' to zero as

$$\begin{aligned} &\frac{\partial L(\boldsymbol{P}',\lambda,\mu,\eta)}{\partial P'(z=t|q)}=0 \\ &=\log P'(z=t|q)+1-\log P\left(z=t\middle|q,\boldsymbol{\theta}^{\mathbf{q},\mathbf{d}}\right)+\frac{\lambda_t}{|\mathbf{q}|}+\mu_q. \end{aligned}$$

Thus, we have

$$P'(z=t|q)=\frac{P\left(z=t\middle|q,\boldsymbol{\theta}^{\mathbf{q},\mathbf{d}}\right)\exp\left(-\frac{\lambda_t}{|\mathbf{q}|}\right)}{e\cdot\exp\left(-\mu_q\right)}.$$

Since $\sum_t P'(z=t|q)=1$, we get

$$Z_{\lambda,q}=e\cdot\exp\left(-\mu_q\right)=\sum_t P\left(z=t\middle|q,\boldsymbol{\theta}^{\mathbf{q},\mathbf{d}}\right)\exp\left(-\frac{\lambda_t}{|\mathbf{q}|}\right).$$

We end up with the following form

$$P'(z=t|q)=\frac{1}{Z_{\lambda,q}}P\left(z=t\middle|q,\boldsymbol{\theta}^{\mathbf{q},\mathbf{d}}\right)\exp\left(-\frac{\lambda_t}{|\mathbf{q}|}\right) \tag{26}$$

Similarly, we can derive the form of $P'(z=t|w)$ as

$$P'(z=t|w)=\frac{1}{Z_{\lambda,w}}P\left(z=t\middle|w,\boldsymbol{\theta}^{\mathbf{q},\mathbf{d}}\right)\exp\left(\frac{\lambda_t}{|\mathbf{d}|}\right) \tag{27}$$

where

$$Z_{\lambda,w}=\sum_t P\left(z=t\middle|w,\boldsymbol{\theta}^{\mathbf{q},\mathbf{d}}\right)\exp\left(\frac{\lambda_t}{|\mathbf{d}|}\right)$$

Notice that Eq. (26) and (27) are identical to Eq. (10) and (11), respectively. Now, we show how to estimate λ_t. Plugging Eq. (26) and (27) into Eq. (25), we have

$$\begin{aligned} L(\boldsymbol{P}',\lambda) &= \sum_{t,q} P'(z=t|q)\left(-\frac{\lambda_t}{|\mathbf{q}|}-\log Z_{\lambda,q}\right) \\ &+\sum_{t,w} P'(z=t|w)\left(\frac{\lambda_t}{|\mathbf{d}|}-\log Z_{\lambda,w}\right) \\ &+\sum_t \lambda_t\left(\frac{1}{|\mathbf{q}|}\sum_{q\in\mathbf{q}} P'(z=t|q)-\frac{1}{|\mathbf{d}|}\sum_{w\in\mathbf{d}} P'(z=t|w)\right) \\ &=-\sum_q \log Z_{\lambda,q}-\sum_w \log Z_{\lambda,w} \end{aligned} \tag{28}$$

We then use the gradient ascent algorithm to get the optimal λ_t

$$\lambda_t^{new}=\lambda_t^{old}+\epsilon\cdot\mathbf{g}(\lambda_t) \tag{29}$$

where ϵ is the learning rate, and the gradient $\mathbf{g}$ is computed as

$$\begin{aligned} \mathbf{g}(\lambda_t) &= \frac{\partial L(\boldsymbol{P}',\lambda)}{\partial \lambda_t} \\ &= \mathbf{E}_{P'_{\mathbf{q}}}\left[\frac{1}{|\mathbf{q}|}\sum_{j=1}^{|\mathbf{q}|}\mathbf{1}(z_j=t)\right]-\mathbf{E}_{P'_{\mathbf{d}}}\left[\frac{1}{|\mathbf{d}|}\sum_{j=1}^{|\mathbf{d}|}\mathbf{1}(z_j=t)\right] \end{aligned} \tag{30}$$

which is identical to Eq. (13)

Appendix B: Gradient Derivation in S2Net

We derive the gradient of the loss function in Eq. (21) as follows.

$$\mathbf{g}(\mathbf{A})=\frac{\partial L(\Delta;\mathbf{A})}{\partial\mathbf{A}}=\frac{-\gamma}{1+\exp(-\gamma\Delta)}\frac{\partial\Delta}{\partial\mathbf{A}} \tag{31}$$

$$\frac{\partial\Delta}{\partial\mathbf{A}}=\frac{\partial}{\partial\mathbf{A}}sim_{\mathbf{A}}(\mathbf{Q},\mathbf{D}_1)-\frac{\partial}{\partial\mathbf{A}}sim_{\mathbf{A}}(\mathbf{Q},\mathbf{D}_2) \tag{32}$$

$$\frac{\partial}{\partial\mathbf{A}}sim_{\mathbf{A}}(\mathbf{Q},\mathbf{D})=\frac{\partial}{\partial\mathbf{A}}\frac{\widehat{\mathbf{Q}}^T\widehat{\mathbf{D}}}{\|\widehat{\mathbf{Q}}\|\|\widehat{\mathbf{D}}\|}=\frac{\partial}{\partial\mathbf{A}}\frac{(\mathbf{A}^T\mathbf{Q})^T(\mathbf{A}^T\mathbf{D})}{\|\mathbf{A}^T\mathbf{Q}\|\|\mathbf{A}^T\mathbf{D}\|} \tag{33}$$

Breaking it into three parts, we have

$$\frac{\partial}{\partial\mathbf{A}}(\mathbf{A}^T\mathbf{Q})^T(\mathbf{A}^T\mathbf{D})=\boldsymbol{Q}\widehat{\mathbf{D}}^T+\boldsymbol{D}\widehat{\mathbf{Q}}^T \tag{34}$$

$$\frac{\partial}{\partial\mathbf{A}}\frac{\mathbf{1}}{\|\mathbf{A}^T\mathbf{Q}\|}=-\left(\widehat{\mathbf{Q}}^T\widehat{\mathbf{Q}}\right)^{-\frac{3}{2}}\mathbf{Q}\widehat{\mathbf{Q}}^T \tag{35}$$

$$\frac{\partial}{\partial\mathbf{A}}\frac{\mathbf{1}}{\|\mathbf{A}^T\mathbf{D}\|}=-\left(\widehat{\mathbf{D}}^T\widehat{\mathbf{D}}\right)^{-\frac{3}{2}}\mathbf{D}\widehat{\mathbf{D}}^T \tag{36}$$

To simply the notation, let a,b,c be $\widehat{\mathbf{Q}}^T\widehat{\mathbf{D}}$, $1/\|\widehat{\mathbf{Q}}\|$ and $1/\|\widehat{\mathbf{D}}\|$, respectively. Eq. (33) becomes

$$\frac{\partial}{\partial\mathbf{A}}sim_{\mathbf{A}}(\mathbf{Q},\mathbf{D})=-abc^3\mathbf{D}\widehat{\mathbf{D}}^T-acb^3\mathbf{Q}\widehat{\mathbf{Q}}^T+bc\left(\boldsymbol{Q}\widehat{\mathbf{D}}^T+\boldsymbol{D}\widehat{\mathbf{Q}}^T\right)$$

Regularized Latent Semantic Indexing

Quan Wang
MOE-Microsoft Key Laboratory of
Statistics&Information Technology
Peking University, China
v-quwan@microsoft.com

Jun Xu, Hang Li
Microsoft Research Asia
No. 5 Danling Street
Beijing, China
{junxu,hangli}@microsoft.com

Nick Craswell
Microsoft
Bellevue, Washington, USA
nickcr@microsoft.com

ABSTRACT

Topic modeling can boost the performance of information retrieval, but its real-world application is limited due to scalability issues. Scaling to larger document collections via parallelization is an active area of research, but most solutions require drastic steps such as vastly reducing input vocabulary. We introduce Regularized Latent Semantic Indexing (RLSI), a new method which is designed for parallelization. It is as effective as existing topic models, and scales to larger datasets without reducing input vocabulary. RLSI formalizes topic modeling as a problem of minimizing a quadratic loss function regularized by ℓ_1 and/or ℓ_2 norm. This formulation allows the learning process to be decomposed into multiple sub-optimization problems which can be optimized in parallel, for example via MapReduce. We particularly propose adopting ℓ_1 norm on topics and ℓ_2 norm on document representations, to create a model with compact and readable topics and useful for retrieval. Relevance ranking experiments on three TREC datasets show that RLSI performs better than LSI, PLSI, and LDA, and the improvements are sometimes statistically significant. Experiments on a web dataset, containing about 1.6 million documents and 7 million terms, demonstrate a similar boost in performance on a larger corpus and vocabulary than in previous studies.

Categories and Subject Descriptors: H.3.1 [Information Storage and Retrieval]: Content Analysis and Indexing

General Terms: Experimentation

Keywords: Topic Modeling, Regularization, Sparse Methods

1. INTRODUCTION

Recent years have seen significant progress on topic modeling technologies in machine learning, information retrieval, natural language processing, and other related fields. Given a collection of text documents, a topic model represents the relationship between terms and documents through latent topics. A topic is defined as a probability distribution of terms or a cluster of weighted terms. A document is then viewed as a bag of terms generated from a mixture of latent topics. Various topic modeling methods, such as Latent Semantic Indexing (LSI) [10], Probabilistic Latent Semantic Indexing (PLSI) [16], and Latent Dirichlet Allocation (LDA) [3] have been proposed and successfully applied in various settings.

One of the main challenges in topic modeling is scaling to millions or even billions of *documents* while maintaining a representative vocabulary of *terms*, which is necessary in many applications such as web search. A typical approach is to approximate the learning processes of an existing topic model.

In this work, instead of modifying existing methods, we introduce a new topic modeling method that is intrinsically scalable: Regularized Latent Semantic Indexing (RLSI). Topic modeling is formalized as minimization of a quadratic loss function on term-document occurrences regularized by ℓ_1 and/or ℓ_2 norm. Specifically, in RLSI the text collection is represented as a term-document matrix, where each entry represents the occurrence (or tf-idf score) of a term in a document. The term-document matrix is then approximated by the product of two matrices: the term-topic matrix which represents the latent topics with terms and the topic-document matrix which represents the documents with topics. Finally, the quadratic loss function is defined as the squared Frobenius norm of the difference between the term-document matrix and the output of the topic model. Both ℓ_1 norm and ℓ_2 norm may be used for regularization. We particularly propose using ℓ_1 norm on topics and ℓ_2 norm on document representations, which can result in a model with compact and readable topics and useful for retrieval. Note that we call our new method RLSI because it makes use of the same quadratic loss function as LSI. RLSI differs from LSI in that it uses regularization rather than orthogonality to constrain the solutions.

The learning process of RLSI iteratively updates the term-topic matrix given the fixed topic-document matrix, and updates the topic-document matrix given the fixed term-topic matrix. The formulation of RLSI makes it possible to decompose the learning problem into multiple sub-optimization problems and conduct learning in parallel. Specifically, for both the term-topic matrix and the topic-document matrix, the update in each iteration is decomposed into many sub-optimization problems. These may be run in parallel, which is the main reason that RLSI can scale up. We describe our implementation of RLSI in MapReduce [9]. The MapReduce system maps the sub-optimization problems over multiple processors and then merges (reduces) the results from the processors. During this process, documents and terms are distributed and processed automatically.

For probabilistic topic models like LDA and PLSI, the scalability challenge mainly comes from the necessity of simultaneously updating the term-topic matrix to meet the probability distribution assumptions. When the number of terms is large, which is inevitable in real applications, this problem becomes particularly severe. For LSI, the challenge is due to the orthogonality assumption in the for-

SIGIR'11, July 24–28, 2011, Beijing, China.

mulation, and as a result the problem needs to be solved by Singular Value Decomposition (SVD) and thus is hard to be parallelized.

Regularization is a well-known technique in machine learning. In our setting, if we employed ℓ_2 norm on topics and ℓ_1 norm on document representations, RLSI becomes Sparse Coding [19, 25], which is a method used in computer vision and other fields. As far as we know, regularization for topic modeling has not been widely studied, in terms of the performance of different norms or their scalability advantages.

Experimental results on a large web dataset show that 1) RLSI can scale up well and help improve search relevance. Specifically, we show that RLSI can efficiently run on *1.6 million documents and 7 million terms* on 16 distributed machines. In contrast, existing methods on parallelizing LDA were demonstrated on far fewer documents and/or far fewer terms. Experiments on three TREC datasets show that 2) The readability and coherence of RLSI topics is equal or better than those learned by LDA, PLSI and LSI. 3) RLSI topics can be used in retrieval with better performance than LDA, PLSI, and LSI (sometimes statistically significant). 4) The best choice of regularization is ℓ_1 on topics and ℓ_2 on document representations in terms of topic readability and retrieval performance.

2. RELATED WORK

Studies on topic modeling fall into two categories: probabilistic approaches and non-probabilistic (matrix factorization) approaches. In the probabilistic approaches, a topic is defined as a probability distribution over terms and documents are defined as data generated from mixtures of topics. To generate a document, one chooses a distribution over topics. Then, for each term in that document, one chooses a topic according to the topic distribution, and draws a term from the topic according to its term distribution. For example, PLSI [16] and LDA [3] are two widely-used generative models. In the non-probabilistic approaches, the term-document matrix is projected into a K-dimensional topic space in which each axis corresponds to a topic. In the topic space, each document is represented as a linear combination of the K topics. LSI [10] is a representative non-probabilistic model. It decomposes the term-document matrix with SVD under the assumption that topics are orthogonal. See also Non-negative Matrix Factorization (NMF) [17, 18] and Sparse Coding methods [19, 25].

It has been demonstrated that topic modeling is useful for knowledge discovery, relevance ranking in search, and document classification [23, 35]. In fact, topic modeling is becoming one of important technologies in machine learning, information retrieval, and other related fields.

Most efforts to improve topic modeling scalability have modified existing learning methods, such as LDA. Newman, et al. [24] proposed Approximate Distributed LDA (AD-LDA), in which each processor performs a local Gibbs sampling iteration followed by a global update. Two recent papers implemented AD-LDA as PLDA [34] and modified AD-LDA as PLDA+ [21], using MPI [32] and MapReduce [9]. In [2], the authors proposed purely asynchronous distributed LDA algorithms based on Gibbs Sampling or Bayesian inference, called Async-CGB or Async-CVB, respectively. In Async-CGB and Async-CVB, each processor performs a local computation step followed by a step of communicating with other processors. In all the methods, the local processors need to maintain and update a dense term-topic matrix, usually in memory, which becomes a bottleneck for improving the scalability. In this paper, we propose a new topic model learning algorithm which can efficiently scale up to large text corpora. The key ingredient of our method is to make the formulation of learning decomposable and thus make the process of learning parallelizable. In [1, 15], online versions of stochastic LDA were proposed. In this paper, we consider batch learning of topic models, which is a different setting from online learning. For other related work refer to [23, 31, 36].

Regularization is a common technique in machine learning to prevent over-fitting. Typical examples of regularization in machine learning include the use of ℓ_1 and ℓ_2 norms. Regularization via ℓ_1 norm uses the sum of absolute values of parameters and thus has the effect of causing many parameters to be zero and selecting a sparse model as solution [14, 26]. Regularization via ℓ_2 norm, on the other hand, uses the sum of squares of parameters and thus can make a smooth regularization and effectively deal with over-fitting.

Sparse methods have recently received a lot of attention in machine learning community. They aim to learn sparse representations (simple models) hidden in the input data by using ℓ_1 norm regularization. Sparse Coding algorithms [19, 25] are proposed which can be used for discovering basis functions, to capture meta-level features in the input data. One justification to the sparse methods is that human brains have similar sparse mechanism for information processing. For example, when Sparse Coding algorithms are applied to natural images, the learned bases resemble the receptive fields of neurons in the visual cortex [25]. Previous work on sparse methods mainly focused on image processing (e.g., [28]). In this paper we propose using sparse methods (ℓ_1 norm regularization) in topic modeling, particularly to make the learned topics sparse. The use of sparse methods for topic modeling was also proposed very recently by Chen et al. [8]. Their motivation was not to improve scalability and they made an orthogonality assumption (requiring an SVD). In [33], the authors also proposed to discover sparse topics based on a modified version of LDA.

3. SCALABILITY OF TOPIC MODELS

One of the key problems in topic modeling is to improve scalability, to handle millions of documents or even more. As collection size increases, so does vocabulary size, rather than a maximum vocabulary being reached. For example, in the 1.6 million web documents in our experiment, there are more than 7 million unique terms even after pruning the low frequency ones (e.g., with term frequency in the whole collection less than 2). This means that both matrices, term-topic and topic-document, grow as the number of documents increases.

LSI needs to be solved by SVD due to the orthogonality assumption. The time complexity of computing SVD is normally of order $O(\min\{MN^2, NM^2\})$, where M denotes number of rows of the input matrix and N number of columns. Thus, it appears to be very difficult to make LSI scalable and efficient.

For PLSI and LDA, it is necessary to maintain the probability distribution constraints of the term-topic matrix. When the matrix is large, there is a cost for maintaining the probabilistic framework. One possible solution is to reduce the number of terms, but the negative consequence is that it can sacrifice learning accuracy.

How to make existing topic modeling methods scalable is still a challenging problem. In this paper, we adopt a different approach, that is, to develop new methods which can work equally well or even better, but are scalable by design.

4. RLSI

4.1 Problem Formulation

We are given a set of documents $\mathcal{D}$ with size N, containing terms from a vocabulary $\mathcal{V}$ with size M. A document is simply represented as an M-dimensional vector $\boldsymbol{d}$, where the mth entry denotes the score of the mth term, for example, a Boolean value indicating

Table 1: Table of notations.

Notation	Meaning
M	Number of terms in vocabulary
N	Number of documents in collection
K	Number of topics
$\mathbf{D} \in \mathbb{R}^{M\times N}$	Term-document matrix $[\boldsymbol{d}_1, \cdots, \boldsymbol{d}_N]$
$\boldsymbol{d}_n$	The nth document
d_{mn}	Weight of the mth term in document $\boldsymbol{d}_n$
$\mathbf{U} \in \mathbb{R}^{M\times K}$	Term-topic matrix $[\boldsymbol{u}_1, \cdots, \boldsymbol{u}_K]$
$\boldsymbol{u}_k$	The kth topic
u_{mk}	Weight of the mth term in topic $\boldsymbol{u}_k$
$\mathbf{V} \in \mathbb{R}^{K\times N}$	Topic-document matrix $[\boldsymbol{v}_1, \cdots, \boldsymbol{v}_N]$
$\boldsymbol{v}_n$	Representation of $\boldsymbol{d}_n$ in the topic space
v_{kn}	Weight of the kth topic in $\boldsymbol{v}_n$

occurrence, term frequency, tf-idf, or joint probability of the term and document. The N documents in $\mathcal{D}$ are then represented in an $M \times N$ term-document matrix $\mathbf{D} = [\boldsymbol{d}_1, \cdots, \boldsymbol{d}_N]$, in which each row corresponds to a term and each column corresponds to a document.

A topic is defined over terms in the vocabulary and is also represented as an M-dimensional vector $\boldsymbol{u}$, where the mth entry denotes the weight of the mth term in the topic. Intuitively, the terms with larger weights are more indicative to the topic. Suppose that there are K topics in the collection. The K topics can be summarized into an $M \times K$ term-topic matrix $\mathbf{U} = [\boldsymbol{u}_1, \cdots, \boldsymbol{u}_K]$, in which each column corresponds to a topic.

Topic modeling means discovering the latent topics in the document collection as well as modeling the documents by representing them as mixtures of the topics. More precisely, given topics $\boldsymbol{u}_1, \cdots, \boldsymbol{u}_K$, document $\boldsymbol{d}_n$ is succinctly represented as $\boldsymbol{d}_n \approx \sum_{k=1}^{K} v_{kn}\boldsymbol{u}_k = \mathbf{U}\boldsymbol{v}_n$, where v_{kn} denotes the weight of the kth topic $\boldsymbol{u}_k$ in document $\boldsymbol{d}_n$. The larger value of v_{kn}, the more important role topic $\boldsymbol{u}_k$ plays in the document. Let $\mathbf{V} = [\boldsymbol{v}_1, \cdots, \boldsymbol{v}_N]$ be the topic-document matrix, where column $\boldsymbol{v}_n$ stands for the representation of document $\boldsymbol{d}_n$ in the latent topic space. Table 1 gives a summary of notations.

Different topic modeling techniques choose different schemas to model matrices $\mathbf{U}$ and $\mathbf{V}$ and impose different constraints on them. For example, in the generative topic models such as PLSI and LDA, $\boldsymbol{u}_1, \cdots, \boldsymbol{u}_K$ are probability distributions so that $\sum_{m=1}^{M} u_{mk} = 1$ for $k = 1, \cdots, K$; In LSI, topics $\boldsymbol{u}_1, \cdots, \boldsymbol{u}_K$ are orthogonal and thus SVD can be applied.

Regularized Latent Semantic Indexing (RLSI) learns latent topics as well as representations of documents from the given text collections in the following way.

Document $\boldsymbol{d}_n$ is approximated as $\mathbf{U}\boldsymbol{v}_n$ where $\mathbf{U}$ is the term-topic matrix and $\boldsymbol{v}_n$ is the representation of $\boldsymbol{d}_n$ in the latent topic space. The goodness of the approximation is measured by the squared ℓ_2 norm of the difference between $\boldsymbol{d}_n$ and $\mathbf{U}\boldsymbol{v}_n$: $\|\boldsymbol{d}_n - \mathbf{U}\boldsymbol{v}_n\|_2^2$. Furthermore, regularization is made on topics and document representations. Specifically, we suggest ℓ_1 norm regularization on term-topic matrix $\mathbf{U}$ (i.e., topics $\boldsymbol{u}_1, \cdots, \boldsymbol{u}_K$) and ℓ_2 on topic-document matrix $\mathbf{V}$ (i.e., document representations $\boldsymbol{v}_1, \cdots, \boldsymbol{v}_N$) to favor a model with compact and readable topics and useful for retrieval.

Thus, given a text collection $\mathcal{D} = \{\boldsymbol{d}_1, \ldots, \boldsymbol{d}_N\}$, RLSI amounts to solving the following optimization problem:

$$\min_{\mathbf{U},\{\boldsymbol{v}_n\}} \sum_{n=1}^{N} \|\boldsymbol{d}_n - \mathbf{U}\boldsymbol{v}_n\|_2^2 + \lambda_1 \sum_{k=1}^{K} \|\boldsymbol{u}_k\|_1 + \lambda_2 \sum_{n=1}^{N} \|\boldsymbol{v}_n\|_2^2, \tag{1}$$

where $\lambda_1 \geq 0$ is the parameter controlling the regularization on $\boldsymbol{u}_k$: the larger value of λ_1, the more sparse $\boldsymbol{u}_k$; and $\lambda_2 \geq 0$ is the parameter controlling the regularization on $\boldsymbol{v}_n$: the larger value of λ_2, the larger amount of shrinkage on $\boldsymbol{v}_n$.

Algorithm 1 Regularized Latent Semantic Indexing

Require: $\mathbf{D} \in \mathbb{R}^{M\times N}$
1: $\mathbf{V}^{(0)} \in \mathbb{R}^{K\times N} \leftarrow$ random matrix
2: **for** $t = 1 : T$ **do**
3: $\quad\mathbf{U}^{(t)} \leftarrow$ Update$\mathbf{U}$($\mathbf{D}, \mathbf{V}^{(t-1)}$)
4: $\quad\mathbf{V}^{(t)} \leftarrow$ Update$\mathbf{V}$($\mathbf{D}, \mathbf{U}^{(t)}$)
5: **end for**
6: **return** $\mathbf{U}^{(T)}, \mathbf{V}^{(T)}$

In general, the regularization on topics and document representations (the second term and the third term) can be either ℓ_1 norm or ℓ_2 norm. When they are ℓ_2 and ℓ_1 respectively, the method is equivalent to Sparse Coding [19, 25]. When both of them are ℓ_1, the model is similar to the double sparse model proposed in [28][1].

4.2 Regularization Strategy

We propose using the formulation above (i.e., regularization via ℓ_1 norm on topics and ℓ_2 norm on document representations), because in our experience this regularization strategy leads to a model with compact and readable topics and useful for retrieval.

First, ℓ_1 norm regularization on topics has the effect of making them compact. We do this under the assumption that the essence of a topic can be captured via a small number of terms, which is reasonable in practice. In many applications, small and concise topics are more useful. For example, small topics can be interpreted as sets of synonyms, roughly corresponding to the WordNet synsets used in natural language processing.

Second, ℓ_1 norm can make the topics readable, no matter whether it is imposed on topics or document representations, according to our experiments. This has advantages in applications such as text summarization and visualization.

Third, there are four ways of combining ℓ_1 and ℓ_2 norms. We perform retrieval experiments across multiple test collections, showing that better ranking performance is achieved with ℓ_1 norm on topics and ℓ_2 norm on document representations.

Last, in both learning and using of topic models, topic sparsity means that we can efficiently store and process topics. We can also leverage existing techniques on sparse matrix computation [4, 20], which are efficient and scalable.

4.3 Optimization

The optimization Eq. (1) is convex with respect to $\mathbf{U}$ when $\mathbf{V}$ is fixed and convex with respect to $\mathbf{V}$ when $\mathbf{U}$ is fixed. However, it is not convex with respect to both of them. Following the practice in Sparse Coding [19], we optimize the function in Eq. (1) by alternately minimizing it with respect to term-topic matrix $\mathbf{U}$ and topic-document matrix $\mathbf{V}$. This procedure is summarized in Algorithm 1. Note that for simplicity we describe the algorithm when ℓ_1 norm is imposed on topics and ℓ_2 norm on document representations; one can easily extend it to other regularization strategies.

4.3.1 Update of Matrix $\mathbf{U}$

Holding $\mathbf{V} = [\boldsymbol{v}_1, \cdots, \boldsymbol{v}_N]$ fixed, the update of $\mathbf{U}$ amounts to the following optimization problem:

$$\min_{\mathbf{U}} \|\mathbf{D} - \mathbf{U}\mathbf{V}\|_F^2 + \lambda_1 \sum_{m=1}^{M} \sum_{k=1}^{K} |u_{mk}|, \tag{2}$$

where $\|\cdot\|_F$ is the Frobenius norm and u_{mk} is the $(mk)^{th}$ entry of

[1]Note that both Sparse Coding and double sparse model formulate optimization problems in constrained forms instead of regularized forms. The two forms are equivalent.

U. Let $\bar{\boldsymbol{d}}_m = (d_{m1}, \cdots, d_{mN})^T$ and $\bar{\boldsymbol{u}}_m = (u_{m1}, \cdots, u_{mK})^T$ be the column vectors whose entries are those of the mth row of **D** and **U** respectively. Thus, Eq. (2) can be rewritten as

$$\min_{\{\bar{\boldsymbol{u}}_m\}} \sum_{m=1}^{M} \left\|\bar{\boldsymbol{d}}_m - \mathbf{V}^T\bar{\boldsymbol{u}}_m\right\|_2^2 + \lambda_1 \sum_{m=1}^{M} \|\bar{\boldsymbol{u}}_m\|_1 ,$$

which can be decomposed into M optimization problems that can be solved independently, with each corresponding to one row of **U**:

$$\min_{\bar{\boldsymbol{u}}_m} \left\|\bar{\boldsymbol{d}}_m - \mathbf{V}^T\bar{\boldsymbol{u}}_m\right\|_2^2 + \lambda_1 \|\bar{\boldsymbol{u}}_m\|_1 , \qquad (3)$$

for $m = 1, \cdots, M$.

Eq. (3) is an ℓ_1-regularized least squares problem, whose objective function is not differentiable and it is not possible to directly apply gradient-based methods. A number of techniques can be used here, such as interior point method [7], coordinate descent with soft-thresholding [13, 14], Lars-Lasso algorithm [12, 26], and feature-sign search [19]. Here we choose coordinate descent with soft-thresholding.

Let $\bar{\boldsymbol{v}}_k = (v_{k1}, \cdots, v_{kN})^T$ be the column vector whose entries are those of the kth row of **V**, $\mathbf{V}^T{}_{\backslash k}$ the matrix of $\mathbf{V}^T$ with the kth column removed, and $\bar{\boldsymbol{u}}_{m\backslash k}$ the vector of $\bar{\boldsymbol{u}}_m$ with the kth entry removed, and we can rewrite the objective function in Eq.(3) as

$$\begin{aligned} L(\bar{\boldsymbol{u}}_m) &= \left\|\bar{\boldsymbol{d}}_m - \mathbf{V}^T{}_{\backslash k}\bar{\boldsymbol{u}}_{m\backslash k} - u_{mk}\bar{\boldsymbol{v}}_k\right\|_2^2 + \lambda_1 \left\|\bar{\boldsymbol{u}}_{m\backslash k}\right\|_1 + \lambda_1 |u_{mk}| \\ &= u_{mk}^2 \|\bar{\boldsymbol{v}}_k\|_2^2 - 2u_{mk}\left(\bar{\boldsymbol{d}}_m - \mathbf{V}^T{}_{\backslash k}\bar{\boldsymbol{u}}_{m\backslash k}\right)^T \bar{\boldsymbol{v}}_k + \lambda_1 |u_{mk}| + const \\ &= u_{mk}^2 s_{kk} - 2u_{mk}\left(r_{mk} - \sum_{l\neq k} s_{kl}u_{ml}\right) + \lambda_1 |u_{mk}| + const, \end{aligned}$$

where s_{ij} and r_{ij} are the $(ij)^{th}$ entries of $K \times K$ matrix $\mathbf{S} = \mathbf{V}\mathbf{V}^T$ and $M \times K$ matrix $\mathbf{R} = \mathbf{D}\mathbf{V}^T$, respectively, and *const* is a constant with respect to u_{mk}. Then, we can conduct the minimization over u_{mk} while keeping all the u_{ml} fixed for which $l \neq k$. Furthermore, $L(\bar{\boldsymbol{u}}_m)$ is differentiable with respect to u_{mk} except for the point $u_{mk} = 0$. Forcing the partial derivative to be zero leads to

$$u_{mk} = \begin{cases} \dfrac{\left(r_{mk} - \sum_{l\neq k} s_{kl}u_{ml}\right) - \frac{1}{2}\lambda_1}{s_{kk}}, & \text{if } u_{mk} > 0, \\ \dfrac{\left(r_{mk} - \sum_{l\neq k} s_{kl}u_{ml}\right) + \frac{1}{2}\lambda_1}{s_{kk}}, & \text{if } u_{mk} < 0, \end{cases}$$

which can be approximated by the following update rule:

$$u_{mk} \leftarrow \frac{\left(\left|r_{mk} - \sum_{l\neq k} s_{kl}u_{ml}\right| - \frac{1}{2}\lambda_1\right)_+ \operatorname{sign}\left(r_{mk} - \sum_{l\neq k} s_{kl}u_{ml}\right)}{s_{kk}},$$

where $(\cdot)_+$ denotes the hinge function. The algorithm for updating **U** is summarized in Algorithm 2.

4.3.2 *Update of Matrix* V

The update of **V** with **U** fixed is a least squares problem with ℓ_2 norm regularization. It can also be decomposed into N optimization problems, with each corresponding to one $\boldsymbol{v}_n$ and can be solved in parallel:

$$\min_{\boldsymbol{v}_n} \|\boldsymbol{d}_n - \mathbf{U}\boldsymbol{v}_n\|_2^2 + \lambda_2 \|\boldsymbol{v}_n\|_2^2 ,$$

for $n = 1, \cdots, N$. It is a standard ℓ_2-regularized least squares problem (also known as Ridge Regression in statistics) and the solution is:

$$\boldsymbol{v}_n^* = \left(\mathbf{U}^T\mathbf{U} + \lambda_2\mathbf{I}\right)^{-1} \mathbf{U}^T\boldsymbol{d}_n.$$

Algorithm 3 shows the procedure. (If K is large such that the matrix inversion $\left(\mathbf{U}^T\mathbf{U} + \lambda_2\mathbf{I}\right)^{-1}$ is hard, we can employ gradient descent in the update of $\boldsymbol{v}_n$.)

Algorithm 2 UpdateU

Require: $\mathbf{D} \in \mathbb{R}^{M\times N}$, $\mathbf{V} \in \mathbb{R}^{K\times N}$

```
S ← VV^T
R ← DV^T
for m = 1 : M do
    ū_m ← 0
    repeat
        for k = 1 : K do
            w_mk ← r_mk − Σ_{l≠k} s_kl u_ml
            u_mk ← (|w_mk| − ½λ_1)_+ sign(w_mk) / s_kk
        end for
    until convergence
end for
return U
```

Algorithm 3 UpdateV

Require: $\mathbf{D} \in \mathbb{R}^{M\times N}$, $\mathbf{U} \in \mathbb{R}^{M\times K}$

```
Σ ← (U^T U + λ_2 I)^{-1}
Φ ← U^T D
for n = 1 : N do
    v_n ← Σφ_n, where φ_n is the n^th column of Φ
end for
return V
```

4.4 Implementation on MapReduce

MapReduce [9] is a computing model that supports distributed computing on large datasets. MapReduce expresses a computing task as a series of Map and Reduce operations and performs the task by executing the operations in a distributed computing environment. In this paper, we implement RLSI on MapReduce, referred to as Distributed RLSI, as shown in Figure 1. At each iteration the algorithm updates **U** and **V** using the following MapReduce operations:

Map-1 Broadcast $\mathbf{S} = \mathbf{V}\mathbf{V}^T$ and map $\mathbf{R} = \mathbf{D}\mathbf{V}^T$ on m $(m = 1, \cdots, M)$ such that all of the entries in the mth row of **R** are shuffled to the same machine in the form of $\langle m, \bar{\boldsymbol{r}}_m, \mathbf{S}\rangle$, where $\bar{\boldsymbol{r}}_m$ is the column vector whose entries are those of the mth row of **R**.

Reduce-1 Take $\langle m, \bar{\boldsymbol{r}}_m, \mathbf{S}\rangle$ and emit $\langle m, \bar{\boldsymbol{u}}_m\rangle$, where $\bar{\boldsymbol{u}}_m$ is the optimal solution for the mth optimization problem (Eq. (3)). We have $\mathbf{U} = [\bar{\boldsymbol{u}}_1, \cdots, \bar{\boldsymbol{u}}_M]^T$.

Map-2 Broadcast $\boldsymbol{\Sigma} = \left(\mathbf{U}^T\mathbf{U} + \lambda_2\mathbf{I}\right)^{-1}$ and map $\boldsymbol{\Phi} = \mathbf{U}^T\mathbf{D}$ on n $(n = 1, \cdots, N)$ such that the entries in the nth column of $\boldsymbol{\Phi}$ are shuffled to the same machine in the form of $\langle n, \boldsymbol{\phi}_n, \boldsymbol{\Sigma}\rangle$, where $\boldsymbol{\phi}_n$ is the nth column of $\boldsymbol{\Phi}$.

Reduce-2 Take $\langle n, \boldsymbol{\phi}_n, \boldsymbol{\Sigma}\rangle$ and emit $\langle n, \boldsymbol{v}_n = \boldsymbol{\Sigma}\boldsymbol{\phi}_n\rangle$. We have $\mathbf{V} = [\boldsymbol{v}_1, \cdots, \boldsymbol{v}_N]$.

Note that the data partitioning schemas for **R** in Map-1 and for $\boldsymbol{\Phi}$ in Map-2 are different. **R** is split such that entries in the same row (corresponding to one term) are shuffled to the same machine while $\boldsymbol{\Phi}$ is split such that entries in the same column (corresponding to one document) are shuffled to the same machine.

There are a number of large scale matrix multiplication operations in operation Map-1 ($\mathbf{D}\mathbf{V}^T$ and $\mathbf{V}\mathbf{V}^T$) and Map-2 ($\mathbf{U}^T\mathbf{D}$ and $\mathbf{U}^T\mathbf{U}$). These matrix multiplication operations can also be conducted on MapReduce infrastructure efficiently. As example, $\mathbf{D}\mathbf{V}^T$ can be calculated as $\sum_{n=1}^{N} \boldsymbol{d}_n\boldsymbol{v}_n^T$ and thus fully parallelized. For details please refer to [4, 20].

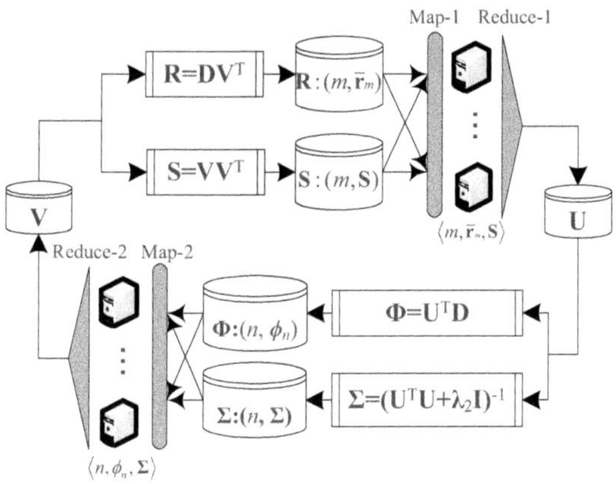

Figure 1: Update of U and V on MapReduce.

4.5 Discussion

We discuss the properties of RLSI with ℓ_1 norm on $\mathbf{U}$ and ℓ_2 norm on $\mathbf{V}$ as example.

4.5.1 Relationship with Other Methods

Despite having better scalability properties, RLSI is closely related to existing topic modeling methods such as LSI, PLSI, and Sparse Coding. In [30], the relationship between LSI and PLSI are discussed, from the view point of loss function and regularization. We describe their framework, so we can describe RLSI in the context of existing approaches. In that framework, topic modeling is considered as a problem of optimizing the following general loss function

$$\min_{(\mathbf{U},\mathbf{V})\in C} \quad \mathcal{B}(\mathbf{D}\|\mathbf{UV}) + \lambda\mathcal{R}(\mathbf{U},\mathbf{V}),$$

where $\mathcal{B}(\cdot\|\cdot)$ is generalized Bregman divergence with non-negative values and is equal to zero if and only if the two inputs are equivalent; $\mathcal{R}(\cdot,\cdot) \geq 0$ is the regularization on the two inputs, C is the solution space; and λ is a coefficient making trade-off between the divergence and regularization.

Different choices of $\mathcal{B}$, $\mathcal{R}$, and C lead to different topic modeling techniques. Table 2 shows the relationship between RLSI and existing methods of LSI, PLSI, and Sparse Coding. (Suppose that we first conduct normalization $\sum_{m,n} d_{mn} = 1$ in PLSI [11].) Viewing topic modeling methods in this framework, the major question is how to conduct regularization as well as optimization to make the learned topics coherent and readable.

4.5.2 Probabilistic and Non-probabilistic Models

Many non-probabilistic topic modeling techniques, such as LSI, Sparse Coding, and RLSI can be translated into a probabilistic framework, as shown in Figure 2.

In the probabilistic framework, columns of the term-topic matrix $\boldsymbol{u}_k$'s are assumed to be independent from each other and columns of the topic-document matrix $\boldsymbol{v}_n$'s are regarded as latent variables. Next, each document $\boldsymbol{d}_n$ is assumed to be generated according to a Gaussian distribution conditioned on $\mathbf{U}$ and $\boldsymbol{v}_n$, i.e., $p(\boldsymbol{d}_n|\mathbf{U},\boldsymbol{v}_n) \propto \exp\left(-\|\boldsymbol{d}_n - \mathbf{U}\boldsymbol{v}_n\|_2^2\right)$. Furthermore, all the pairs $(\boldsymbol{d}_n, \boldsymbol{v}_n)$ are conditionally independent given $\mathbf{U}$.

Different techniques use different priors or constraints on $\boldsymbol{u}_k$'s and $\boldsymbol{v}_n$'s. Table 3 lists the priors or constraints used in LSI, Sparse Coding, and RLSI, respectively. It can be shown that LSI, Sparse Coding, and RLSI can be obtained with Maximum A Posteriori (MAP) Estimation [22]. That is to say, the techniques can be understood in the same framework.

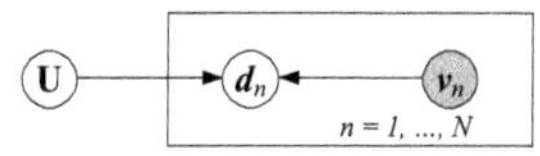

Figure 2: Probabilistic framework for non-probabilistic methods.

Table 3: Priors/constraints in different non-probabilistic methods.

Method	Prior/Constraint on $\boldsymbol{u}_k$	Prior/Constraint on $\boldsymbol{v}_n$
LSI	orthonormality	orthogonality
Sparse Coding	$\|\boldsymbol{u}_k\|_2^2 \leq 1$	$p(\boldsymbol{v}_n) \propto \exp(-\lambda \|\boldsymbol{v}_n\|_1)$
RLSI	$p(\boldsymbol{u}_k) \propto \exp(-\lambda_1 \|\boldsymbol{u}_k\|_1)$	$p(\boldsymbol{v}_n) \propto \exp\left(-\lambda_2 \|\boldsymbol{v}_n\|_2^2\right)$

4.5.3 Scalability Comparison

As explained, several methods for improving the efficiency and scalability of existing topic models, especially LDA have been proposed. Table 4 shows the space and time complexities of AD-LDA [24], Async-CBS, Async-CVB [2], and Distributed RLSI, where AvgDL is the average document length in the collection and γ is the sparsity of topics.

The space complexity of AD-LDA (also Async-CGS and Async-CVB) is of order $\frac{N\times\text{AvgDL}+NK}{P} + MK$, where MK is for storing the term-topic matrix on each processor. For a large text collection, the vocabulary size M will be very large and thus the space complexity will be very high. This will hinder it from being applied to large datasets in real applications.

The space complexity of Distributed RLSI is $\frac{N\times\text{AvgDL}+(1+\gamma)MK+2NK}{P} + K^2$ for updating $\mathbf{U}$ and $\mathbf{V}$, where K^2 is for storing $\mathbf{S}$ or $\mathbf{\Sigma}$, $\frac{(1+\gamma)MK}{P}$ is for storing $\mathbf{U}$ and $\mathbf{R}$ in P processors, and $\frac{2NK}{P}$ is for storing $\mathbf{V}$ and $\mathbf{\Phi}$ in P processors. Since $K \ll M$, it is clear that Distributed RLSI has better scalability. We can reach the same conclusion when comparing Distributed RLSI with other parallel/distributed topic modeling methods. The key is that Distributed RLSI can distribute both terms and documents over P processors. The sparsity on the term-topic matrix can also help save the space in each processor.

The time complexities of different topic modeling methods are also listed. For Distributed RLSI, I is the number of inner iterations in Algorithm 2; T_U and T_V are for the matrix operations in Algorithms 2 and 3 (e.g., $\mathbf{VV}^T$, $\mathbf{DV}^T$, $\mathbf{U}^T\mathbf{U}$, $\mathbf{U}^T\mathbf{D}$, and matrix inversion), respectively:

$$T_U = \max\left\{\frac{\text{AvgDL}\times NK}{P} + nnz(\mathbf{R})\log P, \frac{NK^2}{P} + K^2\log P\right\},$$

$$T_V = \max\left\{\frac{\text{AvgDL}\times \gamma NK}{P} + nnz(\mathbf{\Phi})\log P, \frac{M(\gamma K)^2}{P} + K^2\log P + K^3\right\},$$

where $nnz(\cdot)$ is the number of nonzero entries in the input matrix. For details please refer to [20]. Note that the time complexities of these methods are comparable.

5. RELEVANCE RANKING

Topic models can be used in a wide variety of applications. We apply RLSI to relevance ranking in information retrieval (IR) and evaluate its performance in comparison to existing topic modeling methods. The use of topic modeling techniques such as LSI was proposed in IR many years ago [10]. A more recent paper [35] demonstrated improvements in retrieval performance by applying topic modeling on modern test collections. We do not replicate their precise ranking approach here, since it relies on a probabilistic topic model, but we achieve similar gains.

Table 2: Optimization framework for different topic modeling methods.

Method	$\mathcal{B}(\mathbf{D}\|\mathbf{UV})$	$\mathcal{R}(\mathbf{U},\mathbf{V})$	Constraint on $\mathbf{U}$	Constraint on $\mathbf{V}$
LSI	$\|\mathbf{D}-\mathbf{UV}\|_F^2$	—	$\mathbf{U}^T\mathbf{U}=\mathbf{I}$	$\mathbf{V}\mathbf{V}^T=\mathbf{\Lambda}^2$ ($\mathbf{\Lambda}$ is diagonal)
PLSI	$\sum_{mn}\left(d_{mn}\log\frac{d_{mn}}{(\mathbf{UV})_{mn}}\right)$	—	$\mathbf{U}^T\mathbf{1}=\mathbf{1}$, $u_{mk}\geq 0$	$\mathbf{1}^T\mathbf{V}\mathbf{1}=1$, $v_{kn}\geq 0$
Sparse Coding	$\|\mathbf{D}-\mathbf{UV}\|_F^2$	$\sum_n\|\boldsymbol{v}_n\|_1$	$\|\boldsymbol{u}_k\|_2^2\leq 1$	—
RLSI	$\|\mathbf{D}-\mathbf{UV}\|_F^2$	$\sum_k\|\boldsymbol{u}_k\|_1$, $\sum_n\|\boldsymbol{v}_n\|_2^2$	—	—

Table 4: Complexity of parallel/distributed topic models.

Method	Space complexity	Time complexity (per iter)
AD-LDA	$\frac{N\times\text{AvgDL}+NK}{P}+MK$	$\frac{NK\times\text{AvgDL}}{P}+MK\log P$
Async-CGS	$\frac{N\times\text{AvgDL}+NK}{P}+2MK$	$\frac{NK\times\text{AvgDL}}{P}+MK\log P$
Async-CVB	$\frac{N\times\text{AvgDL}+2NK}{P}+4MK$	$\frac{MK}{P}+MK\log P$
Distributed RLSI	$\frac{N\times\text{AvgDL}+(1+\gamma)MK+2NK}{P}+K^2$	$\frac{IMK^2+NK^2}{P}+T_U+T_V$

The advantage of incorporating topic modeling in relevance ranking is to reduce "term mismatch". Traditional relevance models, such as VSM [29] and BM25 [27], are all based on term matching. The term mismatch problem arises when the authors of documents and the users of search system use different terms to describe the same concepts, and thus relevant documents get low relevance scores. For example, if a query contains the term "airplane" but a relevant document instead contains the term "aircraft", then there is a mismatch and the document may not be easily distinguished from an irrelevant one. In the topic space, however, it is very likely that the two terms are in the same topic, and thus the use of matching score in the topic space can help improve relevance ranking. In practice it is beneficial to combine topic matching scores with term matching scores, to leverage both broad topic matching and specific term matching.

To do so, given a query and document, we must calculate their matching scores in both term space and topic space. For query q, we represent it in the topic space:

$$\boldsymbol{v}_q = \arg\min_{\boldsymbol{v}} \|\boldsymbol{q}-\mathbf{U}\boldsymbol{v}\|_2^2 + \lambda_2\|\boldsymbol{v}\|_2^2,$$

where vector $\boldsymbol{q}$ is the tf-idf representation of query q in the term space[2]. Similarly, for document d (and its tf-idf representation $\boldsymbol{d}$ in the term space) we represent it in the topic space as $\boldsymbol{v}_d$. The matching score between the query and the document in the topic space is, then, calculated as the cosine similarity between $\boldsymbol{v}_q$ and $\boldsymbol{v}_d$:

$$s_{topic}(q,d) = \frac{\langle \boldsymbol{v}_q, \boldsymbol{v}_d\rangle}{\|\boldsymbol{v}_q\|_2 \cdot \|\boldsymbol{v}_d\|_2}. \quad (4)$$

The topic matching score $s_{topic}(q,d)$ is combined with the conventional term matching score $s_{term}(q,d)$, for final relevance ranking. There are several ways to conduct the combination. A simple and effective approach is to use a linear combination. The final relevance ranking score $s(q,d)$ is:

$$s(q,d) = \alpha s_{topic}(q,d) + (1-\alpha)s_{term}(q,d), \quad (5)$$

where $\alpha \in [0,1]$ is the coefficient. $s_{term}(q,d)$ can be calculated with any of the conventional relevance models such as VSM and BM25.

Another combination approach is to incorporate the topic matching score as a feature in a learning to rank model, e.g., LambdaRank [5]. In this paper, we use both approaches in our experiments.

[2]Using $\boldsymbol{v}_q = \arg\min_{\boldsymbol{v}} \|\boldsymbol{q}-\mathbf{U}\boldsymbol{v}\|_2^2+\lambda_2\|\boldsymbol{v}\|_1$ if ℓ_1 norm is imposed on $\mathbf{V}$

Table 5: Dataset statistics.

Dataset	AP	WSJ	OHSUMED	Web dataset
# terms	83,541	106,029	26,457	7,014,881
# documents	29,528	45,305	14,430	1,562,807
# queries	250	250	106	10,680

6. EXPERIMENTS

We have conducted experiments to compare different RLSI regularization strategies, to compare RLSI with existing methods, and to test scalability and retrieval performance of RLSI using several datasets.

6.1 Experimental Settings

Our three TREC datasets were AP, WSJ, and OHSUMED, which have been widely used in relevance ranking experiments. We also used a large real-world web dataset from a commercial web search engine, containing about 1.6 million documents and 10 thousand queries. Each dataset consists of a document collection, a set of queries, and relevance judgments on some documents with respect to each query. For all four datasets, only the retrieved documents were included and a standard list of stop words was removed. For the Web dataset, we further discarded the terms whose frequencies in the whole dataset are less than two. Table 5 gives some statistics on the datasets.

In AP and WSJ the relevance judgments are at two levels: "relevant" or "irrelevant". In OHSUMED, the relevance judgments are at three levels: "definitely relevant", "partially relevant", and "not relevant". In the Web dataset, there are five levels: "perfect", "excellent", "good", "fair", and "bad". In the experiments of retrieval performance, we used MAP and NDCG at the positions of 1, 3, 5, and 10 for evaluating retrieval performance. In calculating MAP, we consider "definitely relevant" and "partially relevant" in OHSUMED, and "perfect", "excellent", and "good" in Web dataset as "relevant".

In the experiments on TREC datasets (Section 6.2 and Section 6.3), no validation set was used since we only had small query sets, making it difficult to hold out a validation set of meaningful size in each case. Instead, we chose to evaluate each model in a predefined grid of parameters, showing its performance under the best parameter choices. In the experiments on the Web dateset (Section 6.4), the queries were randomly split into training/validation/test sets, with 6000/2000/2680 queries, respectively. We trained the ranking models with the training set, selected the best models with the validation set, and evaluated the performances of the methods with the test set.

The experiments on AP, WSJ, and OHSUMED were conducted on a server with Intel Xeon 2.33GHZ CPU, 16GB RAM. The experiments on the Web dataset were conducted on a distributed system and the Distributed RLSI was implemented with SCOPE language [6].

6.2 Regularization in RLSI

Our comparison of different RLSI regularization strategies was

Table 7: Performance of the RLSI variants.

	Readability	Compactness	Retrieval performance
RLSI ($U\ell_1$-$V\ell_2$)	√	√	√
RLSI ($U\ell_2$-$V\ell_1$)	√	×	×
RLSI ($U\ell_1$-$V\ell_1$)	√	√	×
RLSI ($U\ell_2$-$V\ell_2$)	×	×	×

carried out on AP, WSJ, and OHSUMED datasets. Regularization on **U** and **V** via either ℓ_1 or ℓ_2 norm gives us four RLSI variants: RLSI ($U\ell_1$-$V\ell_2$), RLSI ($U\ell_2$-$V\ell_1$), RLSI ($U\ell_1$-$V\ell_1$), and RLSI ($U\ell_2$-$V\ell_2$), where RLSI ($U\ell_1$-$V\ell_2$) means, for example, applying ℓ_1 norm on **U** and ℓ_2 norm on **V**. Parameters K, λ_1, λ_2, and α were respectively set in ranges of $[10, 50]$, $[0.01, 1]$, $[0.01, 1]$, and $[0.1, 1]$ for all variants.

We first compared the RLSI variants in terms of topic readability, by looking at the contents of topics they generated. As example, Table 6 shows 10 topics (randomly selected) and the average topic compactness (AvgComp) on AP dataset, for all four RLSI variants, when $K = 20$ and λ_1 and λ_2 are the optimal parameters for the retrieval experiment described next. Here, average topic compactness is defined as average ratio of terms with non-zero weights per topic. For each topic, its top 5 weighted terms are shown. From the results, we have found that 1) If ℓ_1 norm is imposed on either **U** or **V**, RLSI can always discover readable topics; 2) Without ℓ_1 norm regularization (i.e., RLSI($U\ell_2$-$V\ell_2$)), many topics are not readable; 3) If ℓ_1 norm is only imposed on **V** (i.e. RLSI ($U\ell_2$-$V\ell_1$)), then the discovered topics are not compact or sparse (e.g., AvgComp = 1). We also conducted the same experiments on WSJ and OHSUMED and observed similar phenomena. The examining topics on them are not shown due to space limitation.

We also compared the RLSI variants in terms of retrieval performance. Specifically, for each of the RLSI variants, we combined topic matching scores ($s_{topic}(q, d)$ in Eq. (5)) with term matching scores given by conventional IR models of VSM or BM25. Since BM25 performed better than VSM on AP and WSJ, and VSM performed better than BM25 on OHSUMED, we combined the topic matching scores with BM25 on AP and WSJ, and with VSM on OHSUMED. The methods we tested were denoted as "BM25+RLSI ($U\ell_1$-$V\ell_2$)", "BM25+RLSI ($U\ell_2$-$V\ell_1$)", "BM25+RLSI ($U\ell_1$-$V\ell_1$)", "BM25+RLSI ($U\ell_2$-$V\ell_2$)", etc. Figures 3, 4, and 5 show the retrieval performance of RLSI variants achieved by the best parameter setting on AP, WSJ, and OHSUMED, respectively. From the results, we can see that 1) All of these methods can improve over the baseline and in most cases the improvement is statistically significant (t-test, p-value < 0.05); 2) Among the RLSI variants, RLSI ($U\ell_1$-$V\ell_2$) performs best and RLSI ($U\ell_2$-$V\ell_2$) performs worst.

Table 7 summarizes the experimental results in terms of topic readability, topic compactness, and retrieval performance. From the result, we can see that in RLSI, ℓ_1 norm regularization is essential for discovering readable topics, and the discovered topics will also be compact if ℓ_1 norm is imposed on **U**. Furthermore, between the two RLSI variants with good topic readability and compactness, i.e., RLSI ($U\ell_1$-$V\ell_2$) and RLSI ($U\ell_1$-$V\ell_1$), RLSI ($U\ell_1$-$V\ell_2$) performs better in improving retrieval performance. Thus we conclude that it is a better practice to apply ℓ_1 norm on **U** and ℓ_2 norm on **V** in RLSI, for achieving good topic readability, topic compactness, and retrieval performance.

We will use RLSI ($U\ell_1$-$V\ell_2$) in the following experiments and denote it as RLSI for simplicity.

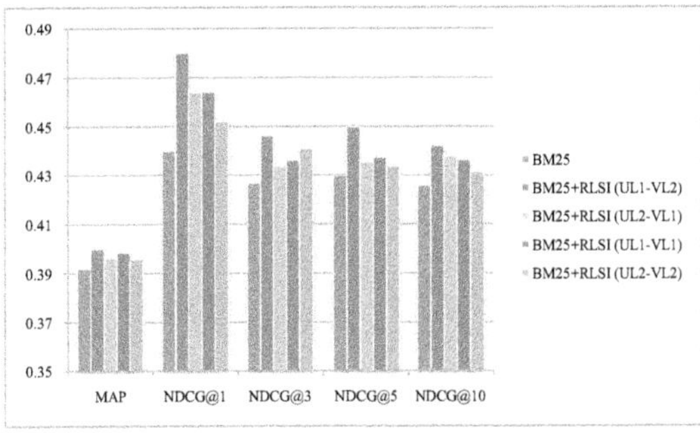

Figure 3: Retrieval performance of RLSI variants on AP.

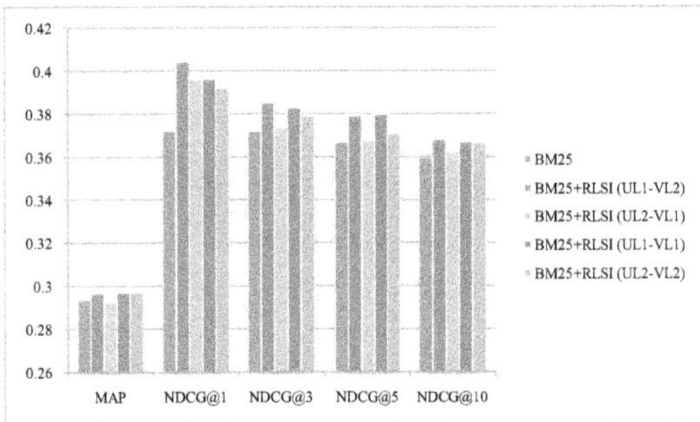

Figure 4: Retrieval performance of RLSI variants on WSJ.

6.3 Comparison of Topic Models

In this experiment, we compared RLSI with LDA, PLSI, and LSI on AP, WSJ, and OHSUMED datasets.

We first compared RLSI with LDA, PLSI, and LSI in terms of topic readability, by looking at the topics they generated. We made use of the tools available on Internet for creating the baselines[3]. The number of topics K was again set to 20 for all the methods. In RLSI, λ_1 and λ_2 were the optimal parameters used in Section 6.2 (i.e., $\lambda_1 = 0.5$ and $\lambda_2 = 1.0$). For LDA, PLSI, and LSI, there was no additional parameter to tune.

Table 8 shows 10 randomly selected topics discovered by RLSI, LDA, PLSI, and LSI and the average topic compactness (AvgComp) on AP dataset. For each topic, its top 5 weighted terms are shown. From the results, we have found 1) RLSI can discover readable and compact (e.g., AvgComp = 0.0075) topics; 2) PLSI and LDA can discover coherent and readable topics as expected, however the discovered topics are not compact (e.g., AvgComp = 0.9534 and AvgComp = 1, respectively); 3) LDA performs better than PLSI. There is some redundancy in the topics discovered by PLSI; 4) The topics discovered by LSI were hard to understand, and this may be due to its orthogonality assumption. We also conducted the same experiments on WSJ and OHSUMED and observed similar phenomena. The results on them are not shown due to space limitation.

We also tested the performance of RLSI in terms of retrieval performance, in comparison to LSI, PLSI, LDA. The experimental settings was similar to that of used in Section 6.2. Parameters K and α were respectively set in ranges of $[10, 50]$ and $[0.1, 1]$ for all four methods, and parameters λ_1 and λ_2 in RLSI were respectively set in ranges of $[0.01, 1]$ and $[0.01, 1]$. Figures 6, 7, and 8 show retrieval performance achieved by the best parameter setting on AP, WSJ, and OHSUMED, respectively. From the results, we can see that

[3]LSI: `http://tedlab.mit.edu/~dr/SVDLIBC/`; PLSI: `http://www.lemurproject.org/`; LDA: `http://www.cs.princeton.edu/~blei/lda-c/`

Table 6: Topics discovered by RLSI variants from AP dataset.

	Topic 1	Topic 2	Topic 3	Topic 4	Topic 5	Topic 6	Topic 7	Topic 8	Topic 9	Topic 10
	opec	africa	aid	school	noriega	percent	plane	israeli	nuclear	bush
	oil	south	virus	student	panama	billion	crash	palestinian	soviet	dukakis
RLSI ($U\ell_1$-$V\ell_2$)	cent	african	infect	teacher	panamanian	rate	flight	israel	treaty	campaign
AvgComp = 0.0075	barrel	angola	test	educate	delval	0	air	arab	missile	quayle
	price	apartheid	patient	college	canal	trade	airline	plo	weapon	bentsen
	nuclear	court	noriega	africa	cent	israeli	dukakis	student	plane	percent
	treaty	judge	panama	south	opec	palestinian	bush	school	crash	billion
RLSI ($U\ell_2$-$V\ell_1$)	missile	prison	panamanian	african	oil	israel	jackson	teacher	flight	rate
AvgComp = 1	weapon	trial	delval	angola	barrel	arab	democrat	educate	air	0
	soviet	sentence	canal	apartheid	price	plo	campaign	college	airline	trade
	court	plane	dukakis	israeli	africa	soviet	school	yen	cent	noriega
	prison	crash	bush	palestinian	south	treaty	student	trade	opec	panama
RLSI ($U\ell_1$-$V\ell_1$)	judge	air	jackson	israel	african	missile	teacher	dollar	oil	panamanian
AvgComp = 0.0197	sentence	flight	democrat	arab	angola	nuclear	educate	market	barrel	delval
	trial	airline	campaign	plo	apartheid	gorbachev	college	japan	price	canal
	dukakis	palestinian	soviet	school	africa	dukakis	soviet	drug	percent	soviet
	oil	israeli	noriega	student	south	bush	treaty	cent	billion	israeli
RLSI ($U\ell_2$-$V\ell_2$)	opec	israel	panama	bakker	iran	democrat	student	police	price	missile
AvgComp = 1	cent	arab	drug	trade	african	air	nuclear	student	trade	israel
	bush	plo	quake	china	dukakis	jackson	missile	percent	cent	treaty

Table 8: Topics discovered by RLSI, LDA, PLSI, and LSI from AP dataset.

	Topic 1	Topic 2	Topic 3	Topic 4	Topic 5	Topic 6	Topic 7	Topic 8	Topic 9	Topic 10
	opec	africa	aid	school	noriega	percent	plane	israeli	nuclear	bush
	oil	south	virus	student	panama	billion	crash	palestinian	soviet	dukakis
RLSI	cent	african	infect	teacher	panamanian	rate	flight	israel	treaty	campaign
AvgComp = 0.0075	barrel	angola	test	educate	delval	0	air	arab	missile	quayle
	price	apartheid	patient	college	canal	trade	airline	plo	weapon	bentsen
	soviet	school	dukakis	party	year	water	price	court	air	iran
	nuclear	student	democrat	govern	new	year	year	charge	plane	iranian
LDA	union	year	campaign	minister	time	fish	market	case	flight	ship
AvgComp = 1	state	educate	bush	elect	television	animal	trade	judge	crash	iraq
	treaty	university	jackson	nation	film	0	percent	attorney	airline	navy
	company	israeli	year	year	bush	court	soviet	year	plane	year
	million	iran	state	state	dukakis	charge	treaty	state	flight	state
PLSI	share	israel	new	new	democrat	attorney	missile	new	airline	new
AvgComp = 0.9534	billion	palestinian	nation	nation	campaign	judge	nuclear	nation	crash	people
	stock	arab	govern	0	republican	trial	gorbachev	govern	air	nation
	soviet	567	0	earthquake	drug	0	israel	yen	urgent	student
	percent	234	yen	quake	school	dukakis	israeli	dukakis	oil	school
LSI	police	0	dollar	richter	test	bush	student	bush	opec	noriega
AvgComp = 1	govern	percent	percent	scale	court	jackson	palestinian	dollar	dukakis	panama
	state	12	tokyo	damage	dukakis	dem	africa	jackson	cent	teacher

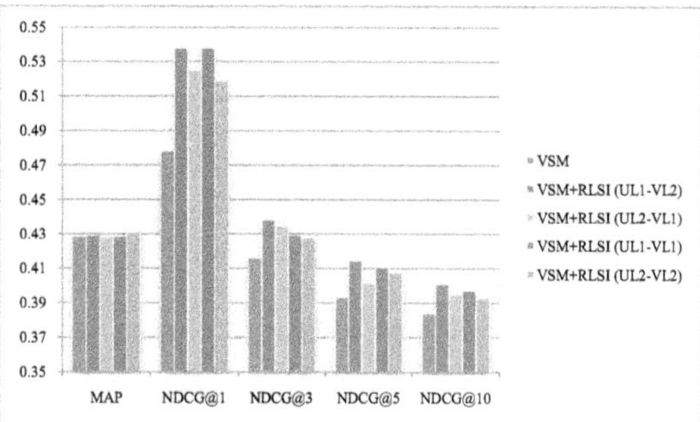

Figure 5: Retrieval performance of RLSI variants on OHSUMED.

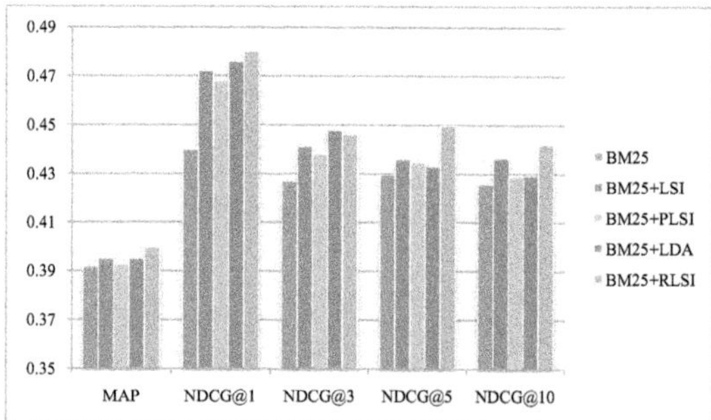

Figure 6: Retrieval performance on AP.

RLSI can *significantly* improve the baseline (t-test, p-value < 0.05), going beyond the simple term matching paradigm. Among the different topic modeling methods, RLSI performs slightly better than the other methods, and sometimes the improvements are statistically significant (t-test, p-value < 0.05). We conclude that RLSI is a proper choice for combining topic matching and term matching.

6.4 Experiment on Web Dataset

We tested the scalability of RLSI using a large real-world web

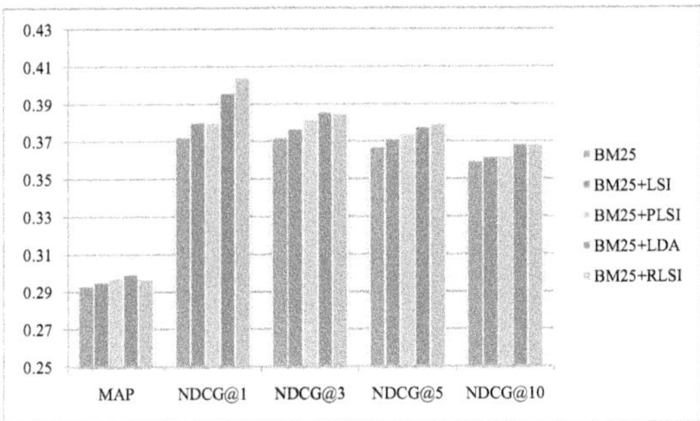

Figure 7: Retrieval performance on WSJ.

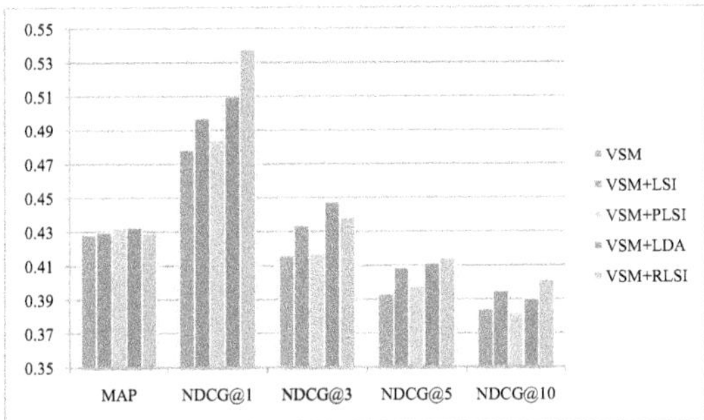

Figure 8: Retrieval performance on OHSUMED.

dataset. Table 9 lists the sizes of popular datasets used to evaluate existing distributed/parallel topic models, as well as the size of our Web dataset. We can see that the number of terms in Web dataset is much larger (about 35 times of the number of terms in Wiki-200T), which hinders the scaling up of existing parallel/distributed topic models, as they need to keep the dense term-topic matrix in memory on each processor. Distributed RLSI, on the other hand, can distribute the terms and documents over processors and thus can handle the Web dataset effectively and efficiently. (Note that it is difficult for us to re-implement existing parallel topic modeling methods, because most of them require special computing infrastructures and the development costs of the methods are high.)

In our experiments, the number of topics K was set to 500, λ_1 and λ_2 were again set to 0.5 and 1.0 respectively. It took about 1.5 hours for Distributed RLSI to complete an iteration on the MapReduce system with 16 processors. Table 10 shows 10 randomly sampled topics and the overall topic compactness on the Web dataset. We can see that the topics obtained by RLSI are compact and readable.

Next, we tested retrieval performance of Distributed RLSI. We randomly split the queries into training/validation/test sets, with 6000/2000/2680 queries, respectively. We took LambdaRank [5] as the baseline. There are 16 features used in the LambdaRank model, including BM25, PageRank, and Query-Exact-Match. In our methods, the topic matching scores by RLSI were used as a new feature in LambdaRank, denoted as "LambdaRank+RLSI". Figure 9 shows the results on the test set, indicating that topics discovered by RLSI allowed "LambdaRank+RLSI" to significantly (t-test, p-value < 0.01) outperform the baseline method of LambdaRank.

Finally, since other papers reduced input vocabulary size, we tested the effect of reducing the vocabulary size in RLSI. Specifically, we removed the terms whose total term frequency is less than 100 from the Web dataset obtaining a new dataset with 222,904 terms. We applied RLSI on the new dataset with parameters $K = 500, \lambda_1 = 0.5$ and $\lambda_2 = 1.0$. We then created a LambdaRank

Table 9: Size of datasets.

Dataset	# docs	# terms	Applied algorithms
NIPS	1,500	12,419	Async-CVB, Async-CGS, PLDA
Wiki-200T	2,122,618	200,000	PLDA+
PubMed	8,200,000	141,043	AD-LDA, Async-CVB, Async-CGS
Web dataset	1,562,807	7,014,881	Distributed RLSI

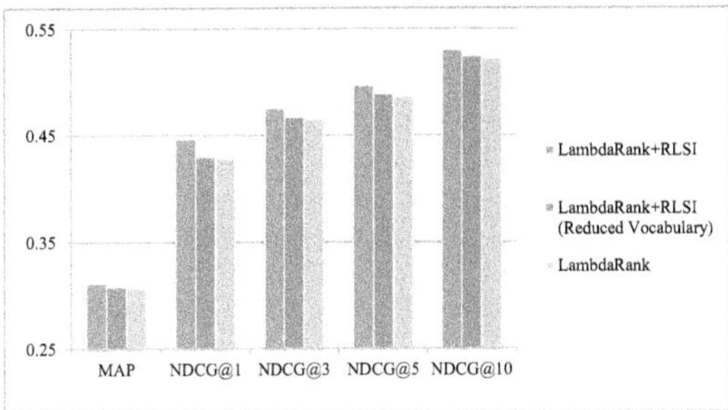

Figure 9: Retrieval performance on Web dataset.

model with topic matching scores as a feature, denoted as "LambdaRank+RLSI (Reduced Vocabulary)". Figure 9 shows the retrieval performance of "LambdaRank+RLSI (Reduced Vocabulary)" on the test set. The result indicates that reducing the vocabulary size will sacrifice learning accuracy of RLSI and consequently hurt the retrieval performance. We conducted t-tests on the differences between "LambdaRank+RLSI (Reduced Vocabulary)" and "LambdaRank+RLSI" and found that the difference is statistically significant (p-value < 0.01). We observed the same trends on the TREC datasets for RLSI and LDA, but we do not report the details due to space limitation.

7. CONCLUSIONS

In this paper, we have studied topic modeling from the viewpoint of enhancing scalability and retrieval performance. We have proposed a new method for topic modeling, called Regularized Latent Semantic Indexing (RLSI). RLSI formalizes topic modeling as minimization of a quadratic loss function with a regularization (either ℓ_1 or ℓ_2 norm). Although similar techniques have been used in other fields, such as sparse coding in computer vision, this is the first comprehensive study of regularization for topic modeling, as far as we know. It is exactly the formulation of RLSI that makes its optimization process decomposable, and thus scalable. Specifically, RLSI replaces the orthogonality constraint or probability distribution constraints with regularization. Therefore, RLSI can be more easily implemented in a parallel and/or distributed computing environment, such as MapReduce. We presented a specific algorithm for running RLSI on MapReduce.

In our experiments we tested different variants of RLSI and confirmed that the sparse topic regularization and smooth document regularization is the best choice from the viewpoint of overall performance. Specifically the ℓ_1 norm on topics (making topics sparse) and ℓ_2 norm on document representations gave the best readability and retrieval performance.

Experimental results on TREC data and large scale web data show that RLSI is better than or comparable with existing methods such as LSI, PLSI, and LDA in terms of readability of topics and accuracy in relevance ranking. We have also demonstrated that RLSI can scale up to large document collection with 1.6 million documents and 7 million terms, which is very difficult for exiting methods. Most previous papers reduced the input vocabulary size to tens of thousands of terms. As far as we know, this is the largest

Table 10: Topics discovered by RLSI from Web dataset (AvgComp = 0.0035).

Topic 1	Topic 2	Topic 3	Topic 4	Topic 5	Topic 6	Topic 7	Topic 8	Topic 9	Topic 10
casino	mortgage	wheel	cheap	login	christian	google	obj	spywar	friend
poker	loan	rim	flight	password	bible	web	pdf	anti	myspace
slot	credit	tire	hotel	username	church	yahoo	endobj	sun	music
game	estate	truck	student	registration	god	host	stream	virus	comment
vegas	bank	car	travel	email	jesus	domain	xref	adwar	photo

size which the topic modeling methods can handle so far. We have also verified that RLSI can help improve web search relevance.

As future work, we plan to further enhance the scale of experiments to process even larger datasets. We also want to further study the theoretical properties of RLSI and new applications of RLSI.

8. REFERENCES

[1] L. AlSumait, D. Barbara, and C. Domeniconi. On-line lda: Adaptive topic models for mining text streams with applications to topic detection and tracking. In *ICDM*, 2008.

[2] A. Asuncion, P. Smyth, and M. Welling. Asynchronous distributed estimation of topic models for document analysis. *Statistical Methodology*, 2011.

[3] D. Blei, A. Y. Ng, and M. I. Jordan. Latent dirichlet allocation. *JMLR*, 3:993–1022, 2003.

[4] A. Buluc and J. R. Gilbert. Challenges and advances in parallel sparse matrix-matrix multiplication. In *ICPP*, pages 503–510, 2008.

[5] C. J. Burges, R. Ragno, and Q. V. Le. Learning to rank with nonsmooth cost functions. In *NIPS 19*, 2007.

[6] R. Chaiken, B. Jenkins, P.-A. Larson, B. Ramsey, D. Shakib, S. Weaver, and J. Zhou. Scope: Easy and efficient parallel processing of massive data sets. *VLDB Endow.*, 1:1265–1276, 2008.

[7] S. S. Chen, D. L. Donoho, and M. A. Saunders. Atomic decomposition by basis pursuit. *SISC*, 20:33–61, 1998.

[8] X. Chen, B. Bai, Y. Qi, Q. Lin, and J. Carbonell. Sparse latent semantic analysis. In *NIPS Workshop*, 2010.

[9] J. Dean, S. Ghemawat, and G. Inc. Mapreduce: simplified data processing on large clusters. In *OSDI*, 2004.

[10] S. Deerwester, S. T. Dumais, G. W. Furnas, T. K. Landauer, and R. Harshman. Indexing by latent semantic analysis. *J AM SOC INFORM SCI*, 41:391–407, 1990.

[11] C. Ding, T. Li, and W. Peng. On the equivalence between non-negative matrix factorization and probabilistic latent semantic indexing semantic indexing. *COMPUT STAT DATA AN*, 52:3913–3927, 2008.

[12] B. Efron, T. Hastie, I. Johnstone, and R. Tibshirani. Least angle regression. *ANN STAT*, 32:407–499, 2004.

[13] J. Friedman, T. Hastie, H. Hofling, and R. Tibshirani. Pathwise coordinate optimization. *ANN APPL STAT*, 1:302–332, 2007.

[14] W. J. Fu. Penalized regressions: The bridge versus the lasso. *J COMPUT GRAPH STAT*, 7:397–416, 1998.

[15] M. D. Hoffman, D. M. Blei, and F. Bach. Online learning for latent dirichlet allocation. In *NIPS*, 2010.

[16] T. Hofmann. Probabilistic latent semantic indexing. In *SIGIR*, pages 50–57, 1999.

[17] D. D. Lee and H. S. Seung. Learning the parts of objects with nonnegative matrix factorization. *Nature*, 401:391–407, 1999.

[18] D. D. Lee and H. S. Seung. Algorithms for non-negative matrix factorization. In *NIPS 13*, pages 556–562. 2001.

[19] H. Lee, A. Battle, R. Raina, and A. Y. Ng. Efficient sparse coding algorithms. In *NIPS*, pages 801–808. 2007.

[20] C. Liu, H. chih Yang, J. Fan, L.-W. He, and Y.-M. Wang. Distributed nonnegative matrix factorization for web-scale dyadic data analysis on mapreduce. In *WWW*, pages 681–690, 2010.

[21] Z. Liu, Y. Zhang, and E. Y. Chang. Plda+: Parallel latent dirichlet allocation with data placement and pipeline processing. In *TIST*, 2010.

[22] J. Mairal, F. Bach, J. Ponce, G. Sapiro, and A. Zisserman. Supervised dictionary learning. In *NIPS 21*, pages 1033–1040. 2009.

[23] D. M. Mimno and McCallum. Organizing the oca: Learning faceted subjects from a library of digital books. In *JCDL*, pages 376–385, 2007.

[24] D. Newman, A. Asuncion, P. Smyth, and M. Welling. Distributed inference for latent dirichlet allocation. In *NIPS*, 2008.

[25] B. A. Olshausen and D. J. Fieldt. Sparse coding with an overcomplete basis set: a strategy employed by v1. *VISION RES*, 37:3311–3325, 1997.

[26] M. Osborne, B. Presnell, and B. Turlach. A new approach to variable selection in least squares problems. *IMA J NUMER ANAL*, 2000.

[27] S. E. Robertson, S. Walker, S. Jones, M. Hancock-Beaulieu, and M. Gatford. Okapi at trec-3. In *TREC'3*, 1994.

[28] R. Rubinstein, M. Zibulevsky, and M. Elad. Double sparsity: Learning sparse dictionaries for sparse signal approximation. *IEEE T SIGNAL PROCES*, pages 1553–1564, 2008.

[29] G. Salton, A. Wong, and C. S. Yang. A vector space model for automatic indexing. *Commun. ACM*, 18:613–620, 1975.

[30] A. P. Singh and G. J. Gordon. A unified view of matrix factorization models. In *ECMLPKDD*, pages 358–373, 2008.

[31] A. Smola and S. Narayanamurthy. An architecture for parallel topic models. *Proc. VLDB Endow.*, 3:703–710, 2010.

[32] R. Thakur and R. Rabenseifner. Optimization of collective communication operations in mpich. *INT J HIGH PERFORM C*, 19:49–66, 2005.

[33] C. Wang and D. M. Blei. Decoupling sparsity and smoothness in the discrete hierachical dirichlet process. In *NIPS*, 2009.

[34] Y. Wang, H. Bai, M. Stanton, W. yen Chen, and E. Y. Chang. Plda: Parallel latent dirichlet allocation for large-scale applications. In *AAIM*, pages 301–314, 2009.

[35] X. Wei and B. W. Croft. Lda-based document models for ad-hoc retrieval. In *SIGIR*, pages 178–185, 2006.

[36] F. Yan, N. Xu, and Y. A. Qi. Parallel inference for latent dirichlet allocation on graphics processing units. In *NIPS*, pages 2134–2142, 2009.

Multimedia Answering: Enriching Text QA with Media Information

Liqiang Nie, Meng Wang, Zheng-Jun Zha, Guangda Li and Tat-Seng Chua
School of Computing
National University of Singapore
{nieliqiang, eric.mengwang, junzzustc}@gmail.com
{g0701808, chuats}@nus.edu.sg

ABSTRACT

Existing community question-answering forums usually provide only textual answers. However, for many questions, pure texts cannot provide intuitive information, while image or video contents are more appropriate. In this paper, we introduce a scheme that is able to enrich text answers with image and video information. Our scheme investigates a rich set of techniques including question/answer classification, query generation, image and video search reranking, etc. Given a question and the community-contributed answer, our approach is able to determine which type of media information should be added, and then automatically collects data from Internet to enrich the textual answer. Different from some efforts that attempt to directly answer questions with image and video data, our approach is built based on the community-contributed textual answers and thus it is more feasible and able to deal with more complex questions. We have conducted empirical study on more than 3,000 QA pairs and the results demonstrate the effectiveness of our approach.

Categories and Subject Descriptors

H.3.3 [**Information Search and Retrieval**]: Retrieval models; H.3.5 [**Information Systems**]: Information Storage and Retrieval

General Terms

Algorithms, Experimentation, Performance

Keywords

Question answering, CQA, medium selection, reranking

1. INTRODUCTION

Question answering (QA) is defined as the task of automatically providing a precise answer to a natural language question posed by users [28, 26, 11, 32]. Typically, given a question, an ideal QA system is expected to find answer from certain corpuses (such as the Wide World Web) using information retrieval and natural language processing techniques. Despite great progress and encouraging results have been reported, traditional automated QA still faces challenges that are not easy to tackle, such as the deep understanding of complex questions and the sophisticated syntactic, semantic and contextual processing to generate answers. It is found that, in most cases, automated approach cannot obtain results that are as good as those generated by manual processing [2, 12].

Along with the proliferation and improvement of underlying communication technologies, community question answering (cQA) has emerged as an extremely popular alternative to finding information online, owning to the following facts. First, information seekers are able to post their specific questions on any topic and obtain answers provided by other participants. By leveraging community efforts, they are able to get better answers than simply using search engine to find them. Second, in comparison with automated QA systems, cQA usually receives answers with better quality as they are generated based on human intelligence. Third, over times, a tremendous number of QA pairs have been accumulated in their repositories, and it facilitates the preservation and retrieval of answered questions. The most well-known Internet cQA system is Yahoo! Answers (Y!A), which contains more than 1 billion QA pairs as at Oct 2009, contributed by the general public.

Despite great success has been achieved, existing cQA forums mostly provide only textual answers, as shown in Figure 1. However, a picture is worth a thousand words. In many cases, the questions cannot be well explained using only texts, and it will be much better to visualize the answers with images and videos. Figure 1 (a) illustrates such an example: for the question "*How do you cook beef in gravy*", the answer is described by several long sentences. However, users still can hardly grasp the process. Clearly, it will be much better if there is an accompanying video describing the process. Therefore, the textual answers in cQA can be significantly enhanced by adding multimedia contents, and it will provide answer seekers with better experience.

Actually in cQA corpuses, there are already many answers that directly embed hyperlinks to images or videos from which the users can get supplementary information in media form. For example, for the question "*What are the best steps to take in order to repent*", the best answer on Y!A is a URL that leads information seekers to YouTube

SIGIR'11, July 24–28, 2011, Beijing, China.

Figure 1: Examples of Question-Answering on popular cQA corpuses. (a) An example on Yahoo! Answer; (b) an example on Answerbag; and (c) an example on MetaFilter.

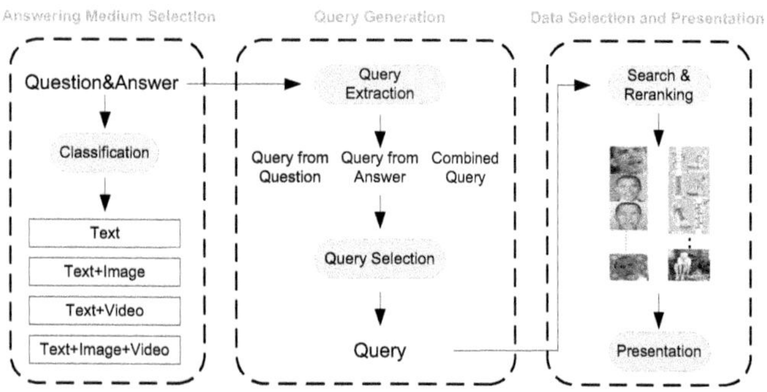

Figure 2: The schematic illustration of the proposed multimedia answering scheme.

[1]. This indicates that many answers can be enhanced by leveraging multimedia information. However, existing cQA forums do not provide adequate support on using media information.

In this work, we propose a multimedia answering scheme that is able to find appropriate image or video information to complement the community-contributed textual answers in cQA. It explores a rich set of techniques, including question/answering classification, query extraction and classification, image and video search reranking, etc. As shown in Figure 2, the scheme consists of three main components:

(1) Answer medium selection. In this work, we consider the following four cases[2] for answer media: (a) only text, i.e., the original textual answers are sufficient; (b) text + image, i.e., image information needs to be added; (c) text + video, i.e., only video information is to be added; and (d) text + image + video, i.e., we add both image and video information. We regard it as a QA pair classification problem, that is, given a question and its community-contributed answer in cQA corpus, we classify it into one of the above four classes.

(2) Multimedia query generation. In order to collect multimedia data from the web, we generate queries from each QA pair. Here we generate three types of queries from (a) question, (b) answer, and (c) both question and answer. We then choose one from the three queries by learning a classification model.

(3) Multimedia data selection and presentation. Based on the generated queries, we collect image and video data with multimedia search engines. We then perform reranking and duplicate removal to obtain a set of accurate and representative samples for presentation together with the textual answers.

It is worth mentioning that there already exist several efforts dedicated to research on automatically answering questions with multimedia data, i.e., the so-called Multimedia Question Answering (MMQA). For example, Yang et al. [36] proposed to extend text-based QA technology to support factoid QA in news video. A photo-based QA system for finding information about physical objects was presented in [37]. Li et al. [20] explored how to leverage YouTube video collections as a source to automatically find videos to describe cooking techniques. But these approaches usually work on certain narrow domains and can hardly be generalized to handle general questions in broad domains. This is due to the fact that, in order to accomplish automatic MMQA, we first need to understand questions, which is not an easy task. Our proposed approach in this work does not aim to directly answer the questions, and instead we enrich the community-contributed answers with multimedia content. Our strategy splits the large gap between question and multimedia answer into two smaller gaps, i.e., the gap between question and textual answer and the gap between textual answer and multimedia answer. In our scheme, the first gap is bridged by the crowd sourcing intelligence of community members, and thus we can focus on solving the second gap. Therefore, our scheme can also be viewed as an approach that accomplishes the MMQA problem by jointly exploring human and computer. Figure 3 demonstrates the difference between the conventional MMQA approaches and an MMQA framework based on our scheme. It is worth noting that, although the proposed approach is automated, we can also further involve human interactions. For example, our approach can provide a set of candidate images and videos based on textual answers, and answerers then can manually choose several candidates for final presentation.

The contributions of this work can be summarized as follows:

(1) To the best of our knowledge, this is the first work on automatically enriching textual answers with image and video data for better QA experience. Different from the conventional MMQA research that aims to automatically generate multimedia answers with given questions, our approach is built based on the community-contributed answers, and it can thus deal with more general questions and achieve better performance.

(2) We investigate the prediction of appropriate answer medium. Here we want to predict whether a textual answer should or should not be enriched with multimedia information, and which kind of media data should be added.

[1]http://www.youtube.com/watch?v=zJCzrTnfPn0

[2]Here we have not considered audio because our studies show that very few users would like to answer questions using this kind medium in cQA, as most speech content can be presented in text form.

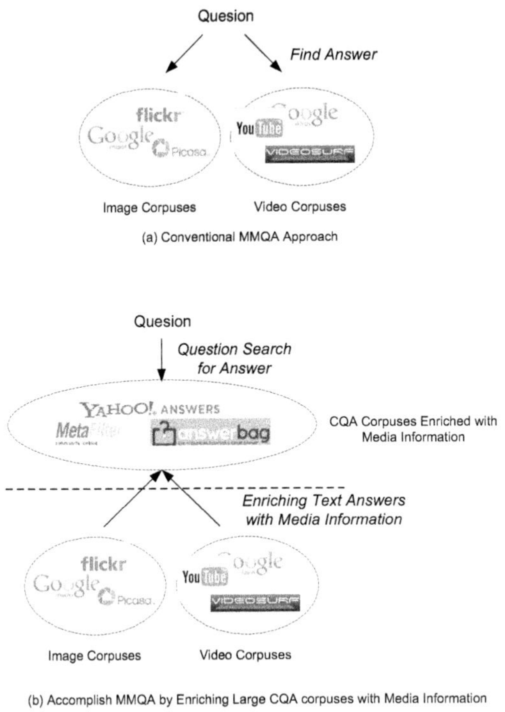

Figure 3: The differences of the conventional MMQA approaches and MMQA based on our scheme. (a) Conventional MMQA aims to seek multimedia answers from online corpuses. (b) Our proposed scheme enriches textual answers in large cQA corpuses with image and video information (this process can be offline), and then, for a user-provided question, we can perform question search to find multimedia answers in the cQA corpuses.

(3) We propose a method to generate queries from QA pairs for multimedia search and perform query-dependent reranking for image and video data obtained from search engines by analyzing visual features.

The rest of the paper is organized as follows. Section 2 briefly reviews the related work. In Section 3 and 4, we introduce the answer medium selection and query generation components, respectively. We then introduce the media data selection and presentation approach in Section 5. Experimental results and analysis are presented in section 6, followed by the conclusion and future work in section 7.

2. RELATED WORK

The research on QA can be traced back to the 1960s, and early QA systems were mainly natural language interfaces to expert systems that were tailored to specific domains. Text Retrieval Conference (TREC) evaluations established a QA track in the late 1990s [1], and it generates extensive research interests in textual QA, such as Open-Domain QA [28], Restricted-Domain QA [26], Definitional QA [11] and List QA [32]. However, despite the great progress achieved, automatic QA still has difficulties in answering complex and realistic questions. Along with the blooming of Web 2.0, cQA becomes an alternative approach. It is a large and diverse question-answer forum, acting not only as a corpus for sharing technical knowledge but also a place where one can seek advice and opinions [2, 12]. However, nearly all existing cQA systems, such as Yahoo! Answer, Answerbag and Ask Metafilter, only support pure text-based answers, which may not provide intuitive and sufficient information.

Some research works have been conducted on multimedia QA, which aims to answer questions using multimedia data. An early system named VideoQA was presented in [36]. This system extends the text based QA technology to support factoid QA in news video by leveraging visual contents of news video as well as the text transcripts. Following this work, several video QA systems were proposed and most of them rely on the use of text transcript derived from video OCR (Optical Character Recognition) and ASR (Automatic Speech Recognition) outputs [8, 33, 18, 34]. Li et al. [21] presented a solution on "how-to" QA by leveraging community-contributed texts and videos. Kacmarcik et al. [17] explored a method of creating a non-text input mode for QA that relies on specially annotated virtual photographs. An image-based QA approach was introduced in [37], which mainly focuses on finding information about physical objects. Chua et al. [9] in 2009 proposed an approach to extend text based QA research to multimedia QA to tackle a range of factoid, definition and "how-to" QA in a common framework. Their system was designed to find multimedia answers from web-scale media resources such as Flicker and YouTube. However, literature regarding multimedia QA is still relatively sparse. As mentioned in Section 1, automatic multimedia QA only works in specific domains and can hardly handle complex questions. Different from the above mentioned works, our approach is built based on cQA. Instead of directly collecting multimedia data for answering questions, our method only finds images and videos to enrich the textual answers provided by humans. This makes our approach able to deal with more general questions and achieve better performance.

3. ANSWER MEDIUM SELECTION

As introduced in Section 1, the first component of our scheme is answer medium selection, as we first need to determine whether we need to and if so which type of medium we should add to enrich the textual answers. For some questions, such as "*what day is President Obama's birthday*", using pure textual answers is sufficient. But we need to add image or video information for some other questions. For example, for the question, "*who is Obama*", it is better to add images to complement the textual answer, whereas we should add videos for answering the question "*how to cook beef*". We regard the answer medium selection as a QA pair classification task, i.e., given a question and textual answer, we classify it into the following four classes of answer medium combinations: (1) only text; (2) text + image; (3) text + video; and (4) text + image + video. For the "only text" class, we do not need to perform more operations, and for the other cases we will need to collect appropriate data by the other two components.

There are some existing research efforts on question classification. Li and Roth [22] developed a machine learning approach that uses the SNoW learning architecture to classify questions into five coarse classes and 50 finer classes. They used lexical and syntactic features such as part-of-speech tags, chunks and head chunks together with two semantic features: named entities and semantically related words to represent the questions. Zhang and Lee [39] used

Interrogative Word	Category
be, can, will, have, when, be there, how+adj/adv	Text
what, where, which, why, how to, who, etc.	Need further classification

Table 1: A question can be judged to be answered with pure text if the interrogative word falls into a list. Otherwise, we perform classification for selecting answer medium.

linear SVMs with all possible question word grams to perform question classification. Arguello et al. [6] have investigated selecting medium type as well as search sources for a query. But there is no work on classifying QA pair according their best answer medium types. This task is more challenging as we are dealing with real data on the web, including many complex and multi-sentence questions and answers, and we need to extract rules to connect QA texts and the best answer medium types. We accomplish the task by first analyzing the question and answer separately and then combining the results.

3.1 Question-Based Classification

Since many questions contain multiple sentences (actually our statistics on Y!A show that at least 1/5 of the questions contain more than two sentences) and some of the sentences are uninformative, we first employ the method in [30] to extract the core sentence from each question.

The classification is accomplished in two steps. First, we categorize the questions based on the interrogatives (some starting words and ending words), and for some questions we can directly derive that they should be answered with text. Second, for the rest questions, we perform classification using a naive Bayes classifier.

We first introduce the categorization based on interrogative words. Questions can mainly be categorized into the following classes based on interrogative words: yes/no class (such as "*Does Java support VoIP*"), choice class (such as "*Which country is bigger, Canada or America*"), quantity class (such as "*When is the Chinese New Year*"), enumeration class (such as "*Names of the 3 wise men from the East who came to venerate Jesus Christ*"), and description class (such as "*What are the steps required to edit, publish and distribute a book*"). For example, a question will be categorized to the "quantity" class if the interrogative is "how+adj/adv" or "when". For the "yes/no", "choice" and "quantity" questions, we categorize them into the class of answering with only text; while the "enumeration" and "description" questions can need "text+image", "text+video" or "text+image+video answers". Therefore, given a question, we first judge whether it should use only textual answer based on the interrogative word. If not, we further perform classification with a Naive Bayes classifier. Table 1 shows the heuristics. For building the Naive Bayes classifier, we extract a set of text features, including bigram text features, head words and a list of class-specific related words[3].

[3]Actually we have also investigated other features such as unigram and trigram. Empirical study demonstrates that the combination of bigram, head words and the class-specific related words is able to achieve promising performance while maintaining good generalization ability.

Categories	Class-Specific Related Word List
Text	name, population, period, times, country, height, website, birthday, age, date, rate, distance, speed, religions, number, etc
Text+Image	colour, pet, clothes, look like, who, image, pictures, appearance, largest, band, photo, surface, capital, figure, what is a, symbol, whom, logo, place, etc.
Text+Video	How to, how do, how can, invented, story, film, tell, songs, music, recipe, differences, ways, steps, dance, first, said, etc.
Text+Both	president, king, prime minister, kill, issue, nuclear, earthquake, singer, battle, event, war, happened, etc.

Table 2: Representative class-specific related words. "Text+Both" stands for "Text+Image+Video".

Here head word is referred to as the word specifying the object that the question seeks.The semantics of head words play an important role in deciding answer medium. For instance, for the question "*what year did the cold war end*", the head word is "year", based on which we can judge that the sought-after answer is a simple date. Therefore, it is reasonable to use textual answer medium. We adopt the method in [16], but the key difference is that we do not use post fix as it better fit our answer medium classification task.

We also extract a list of class-specific related words in a semi-automatic way. We first estimate the appearing frequency of each phrase in the positive samples of each class, and collect all the phrases that have the frequencies above a threshold (we empirically set the threshold to 3 in this work). We then manually refine the list based on human's understanding. Examples of class-specific related words for each class is given in Table 2.

3.2 Answer-Based Classification

Besides question, the answer with rich text can also be an important information clue. For example, for the question "*how do you cook beef in gravy*", we may find a textual answer as "*cut it up, put in oven proof dish ...*". Then we can judge that the question can be better answered with a video clip as the textual answer contains many verbs and describes a dynamic process.

For answer classification, we extract bigram text features and verbs[4]. The verbs in the answer will be useful for judging whether the question can be answered with video content. Intuitively, if a textual answer contains many complex verbs, it is more likely to describe a dynamic process and thus it has high probability to be well answered by videos. Therefore, verb can be an important clue.

Based on the bigram text features and verbs, we again build a Naive Bayes classifier with a set of training data, and then perform a four-class classification with the model. The classification results are linearly combined with those of question-based classification.

[4]Actually we have investigated other features such as unigram and visually descriptive nouns. Empirical study demonstrates that the combination of bigram and verbs shows promising performance and good generalization ability.

4. MULTIMEDIA QUERY GENERATION

To collect relevant image and video data from the web, we need to generate appropriate queries from text QA pairs before performing search on multimedia search engines. We accomplish the task with two steps. The first step is query extraction. Text questions and answers are usually complex sentences. But frequently search engines do not perform well with queries that are long and verbose. Therefore, we need to extract a set of informative keywords from questions and answers for querying. The second step is query selection. This is because we can generate different queries: one from question, one from answer, and one from the combination of question and answer. Which one is the most informative depends on the question: some QA pairs embed the useful query terms in their questions, such as "*What does Disneyland tickets look like*"; some hide the helpful key words in their answers, such as the QA pair "*Q: What is the capital of Thailand; A: Bangkok*"; and some should combine question and answer to generate useful query, such as the QA pair "*Q: Who is the man in the moon; A: astronaut*", for which both of the "astronaut" and the "moon" are functional words.

For each QA pair, we will generate three queries. First, we convert question to query, i.e., we convert a grammatically correct interrogative sentence into one of the potential syntactically correct declarative sentences or meaningful phrases. We directly employ the method in [4]. Second, we identify several key concepts from verbose answer which will have the most impact on effectiveness. Here we employ the method in [7]. Finally, we combine the two queries that are generated from question and answer respectively. Therefore, we obtain three queries, and the next step is selecting one from them.

The query selection is formulated as a three-class classification task, since we need to choose one from the three queries that are generated from the question, answer and the combination of question and answer. We adopt the following features:

(1) POS Histogram. We use POS tagger to assign part-of-speech to each word of both question and answer. Here we employ the Stanford Log-linear Part Of-Speech Tagger and 36 POS are identified[5] . For both question and answer, we then generate a 36-dimensional histogram, in which each bin counts the number of words belonging to a corresponding category of part-of-speech.

(2) Retrieval effectiveness. This is because for certain queries, existing image and video search engines cannot return satisfactory results. We adopt the method proposed in [10], which defines a clarity score for a query based on the KL divergence between the query and collection language models. We can generate 6-dimensional retrieval effectiveness features in all (three queries and search is performed on image and video search engines).

Therefore, for each QA pair, we can extract 42-dimensional features. Based on the extracted features, we train an SVM classifier with a labeled training set for classification, i.e., selecting one from the three queries.

[5]They are: RB, DT, RP, RBR, RBS, LS, VBN, VB, VBP, PRP, MD, SYM, VBZ, IN, VBG, POS, EX, VBD, LRB, UH, NNS, NNP, JJ, RRB, TO,JJS, JJR, FW, NN, NNPS, PDT, WP, WDT, CC, CD, and WRB.

5. MULTIMEDIA DATA SELECTION AND PRESENTATION

We perform search using the generated queries to collect image and video data with Google image and video search engines respectively. However, commercial search engines, such as Google, Yahoo and Bing, usually index web images and videos using textual information, such as titles, ALT text and surrounding texts on web pages. But frequently the text information does not fully describe content of the images and videos, and this fact can severely degrade the search relevance of web images and videos. Reranking is an approach to improving search relevance by mining the visual information of images and videos. Existing reranking algorithms can mainly be categorized into two approaches, one is pseudo relevance feedback [27, 35, 23] and the other one is graph-based reranking [25, 15, 31]. The pseudo relevance feedback approach regards top results as relevant ones and then collects some samples that are assumed to be irrelevant. A classification or ranking model is learned based on the pseudo relevant and irrelevant samples and the model is then used to rerank the images. The graph-based reranking approach assumes that the relevant images lie on a manifold in visual feature space. Generally, the approach constructs a graph where the vertices are images or videos and the edges reflect their pairwise similarities. Here we adopt the graph-based reranking method in [15]. We re-state the equation from [15] as,

$$r^j_{(k)} = \alpha \sum_{i \in B_j} r^i_{(k-1)} W_{ij} + (1-\alpha) r^j_{(0)} \tag{1}$$

where $r^j_{(k)}$ stands for the state probability of node j in the k-th round of iterations, α is a parameter that satisfies $0 \leq \alpha < 1$, and W_{ij} is the similarity between the i-th and j-th samples. Here $r^i_{(0)}$ is the initial relevance score of the sample at the i-th position, which is heuristically estimated as

$$r^i_{(0)} = \frac{N-i}{N(N-1)/2} \qquad i = 1, 2...N \tag{2}$$

For images, we directly estimate their similarity based on their Euclidean distance

$$W_{ij} = \exp(-\frac{||x_i - x_j||^2}{\sigma^2}) \tag{3}$$

The parameter σ is simply set to the median of the Euclidean distance of all image pairs.

For videos, we first perform shot boundary detection and then extract a key-frame from each shot using the method in [38]. Considering two videos $(v_{i,1}, ..., v_{i,m})$ and $(v_{j,1}, ..., v_{j,n})$, which contain m and n key-frames respectively, we employ average distance [24] of all cross-video key-frame pairs for similarity estimation, i.e.,

$$W_{ij} = \exp(-\frac{\sum_{i=1}^{m}\sum_{j=1}^{n} ||v_{1,i} - v_{2,j}||^2}{\sigma^2}) \tag{4}$$

Similarly, the parameter σ is simply set to the median of the Euclidean distance of all video pairs.

However, a problem with existing reranking methods is that they usually use features extracted from the whole images or video frames and they overlooked that many queries are actually person-related. Clearly, for person-related queries, it is more reasonable to use facial features instead of global visual features for reranking. For question-answering, our

Category	Distribution
Text	45%
Text+Image	24%
Text+Video	22%
Text+Image+Video	9%

Table 3: The distribution of the expected answer medium types labeled by humans.

Question-based classification with different features	Accuracy
Bigram	69.02%
Bigram+Head	73.60%
Bigram+Related	71.43%
Bigram+Related+Head	**74.38%**

Table 4: The performance of question-based classification with different features. Related means class-specific related words.

statistics show that more than 1/4 of the QA pairs in our data set are about person. Therefore, in this work we propose a query-depentdent reranking approach. We first decide whether a query is person-related or not, and then we use different features for reranking.

We establish the following rules to judge whether a query is person-related:

(1) If the given question starts by interrogative words who or whom, then it is categorized as person-related.

(2) We perform morphological analysis on the given question to extract information on Part-of-Speech, verb-phrase and noun-phrase. We then extract the main core terms (the strongest noun or noun phrase), followed by the other possible key terms. Following that, we employ the Name Entity extractor to identify names of persons, organizations and possible objects in the question. If a person's name appears in the query as the core term, the query is categorized as person-related.

If a query is person-related, we perform face detection for each image and video key-frame. If an image or a key-frame does not contain faces, it will be not considered in reranking (it is reasonable as we will only consider images and frames that contain faces for person-related queries). If faces are found in images or key-frames, we extract the 256 dimensional Local Binary Pattern features [5] from the largest faces of images or video frames. More specifically, the method works as follows. For person-unrelated queries, we extract 428-dimensional global visual features, including 225-D block-wise color moments generated from 5-by-5 fixed partition of the image, 128-D wavelet texture, and 75-D edge direction histogram.

After reranking, visually similar images or videos may be ranked together. Thus we perform a duplicate removal step to avoid information redundancy. We check the ranking list from top to bottom, and if an image or video is close to a sample that appears above it, we remove it. More specifically, we remove the i-th image or video if there exists $j < i$ that satisfies $W_{ij} > T$. Here we empirically set T to 0.8 throughout the work.

Answer-based classification with different features	Accuracy
Bigram	54.71%
Bigram+Verb	**57.39%**

Table 5: The performance of answer-based classification with different features.

Classification Method	Accuracy
Question-Based Classification	74.38%
Answer-Based Classification	57.39%
Linear combination	**78.29%**

Table 6: Results of linear fusion for answer medium selection.

After duplicate removal, we keep the top 10 images and top 2 videos (keeping which kind of media data depend on the classification results of answer medium selection). When presenting videos, we not only provide videos but also illustrate the key-frames to help users quickly understand the video content as well as easily browse the videos.

6. EXPERIMENTS

6.1 Experimental Settings

We randomly select 5,000 questions and their corresponding answers from the dataset used in [29], which contains 4,483,032 questions and their answers from Y!A. Here we use the best answer that is determined by the asker or the community voting[6]. Inspired by [19, 13], we first classify all the questions in cQA into two categories: conversational and informational. Since conversational questions usually only seek personal opinions or judgments, such as "*Anybody watch the Bears game last night*", in this work we only consider informational questions. In our work, there are 3333 informational questions among the 5000 questions. The questions and answers in our dataset cover a wide range of topics, including travel, life, education, etc.

Our answer medium selection and query selection need training data, and thus we split the 3333 QA pairs into two parts, a training set that contains 2666 QA pairs and a testing set of the remaining 667 QA pairs. The classifiers for answer medium selection and query selection are trained with the training set and evaluated on the testing set.

6.2 Evaluation of Answer Medium Selection

We first evaluate our answer medium selection approach. The ground truths are established by humans. Five human labelers were involved in the process. For every question, each labeler categorized it into one of the following four classes (text, text+image, text+video, text+image+video), and then voting was performed to obtain the final ground truth. For the cases that there are two classes having the same number of ballots, a discussion is carried out among

[6] There are also many research efforts on ranking community-contributed answers or selecting the best answer by machine learning and NLP technologies [29, 14, 3]. These methods can also been integrated with our work and we only need to change the best answer for each question.

Text
1. How many pairs of shoes were found when Imelda Marcos left the presidential palace in 1986?
2. When is the second generation mini cooper coming out?
3. What year was the movie Mustang Sally made?
4. what is speed limit on on california freeways?
5. Is the abbrevation for Mathematics - 'Maths' or 'Math'? Please give me a grammatically correct answer.
Text+Image
1. who won the 1992 Alice Springs cup?
2. Anybody have a picture of Anthropologie's edwarian overcoat?
3. What is the symbol of the Democratic Party?
4. What are 5 manufacturing plants around the world for reebok?
5. Largest and the highest bridge in Asia?
Text+Video
1. Does anyone have an easy recipe for butternut squash soup?
2. How do I remove wax from my refrigerator??? Please help!!!?
3. I want to go 2 for studies abroad so plz tell me the procedure how to get through it plzzzzz.?
4. What is the best way to become an Ebay Powerseller?
5. Exactly what steps do I take to get more space in my mail box?
Text+Image+Video
1. Which President had his old war horse grazing on the White House lawn?
2. What is the largest earthquake (magnitude) to strike the U.S.?
3. What was the worst event that happened in the U.S. other than wars?
4. America Drops Nuclear Bomb On Japan?
5. Who is the most popular Asian singer in Western countries like US and UK??

Table 7: The representative questions for each answer medium class. Here we do not illustrate the answers because several answers are fairly long.

Category	Ground Truth Distribution
Answer	29%
Question	49%
Combination	22%

Table 8: The Ground truth distribution for Query selection.

Classification with Different Features	Accuracy
POS Histogram	66.17%
Retrieval Effectiveness	59.41%
POS Histogram+Retrieval Effectiveness	**71.27%**

Table 9: The classification performance for query selection with different features

the labelers to decide the final ground truths. Table 3 illustrates the distribution of the four classes. We can see that, more than 50% of the questions can best be answered by adding multimedia contents instead of using purely text. This also demonstrates that our multimedia answering approach is highly desired.

For the component of medium selection, we first investigate different feature combinations for the question and answer analysis. The results are illustrated in Tables 4 and 5, respectively. It is worth noting that the stop-words are not removed for question classification since some stop-words also play an important part in question classification. But for answering classification, stop words are removed. Stemming is performed for both question and answer. From the results we can see that, for both of the two classifiers, integrating all of the introduced features is better than only part of them.

We linearly fuse the two classifiers with a grid search with optimal weighting. Table 6 illustrates the classification accuracies when combining question-based classification and answer-based classification. It can be observed that question-based classification achieves better results than answer-based classification. But fusing the classifiers is able to achieve significantly better performance with a final classification accuracy of 78.29%. Table 7 presents representative examples of classified questions for each category.

6.3 Evaluation of Query Generation

Now we evaluate the retrieval effectiveness of our query generation and selection approach. The ground truth was also obtained by the five human labelers. For every QA pair, each labeler selected one from the three queries, which are generated from the question, answer and the combination of question and answer, which will provide best information to retrieve relevant multimedia answers. These labelers are allowed to perform search on the web to compare the query effectiveness. Voting was performed to obtain the final ground truth. The distribution of the three classes is illustrated in Table 8.

We adopt SVM with RBF kernel, and the parameters, including radius parameter and the weighting parameter that modulates the regularizer term and loss term, are established with 5-fold cross-validation. Table 9 illustrates the classification results. Our approach that integrates POS histogram and retrieval effectiveness features achieves an accuracy of 71.27%.

In order to evaluate our query-dependent strategy, we first randomly selected 25 queries from the person-related ones. For each query, the top 150 images or videos are collected for reranking. We adopt NDCG@10 as our performance evaluation metric, which is estimated by

$$NDCG@n = \frac{DCG}{IDCG} = \frac{(rel_1 + \sum_{i=2}^{n} \frac{rel_i}{\log_2 i})}{IDCG} \quad (5)$$

where rel_i is the relevance score of i-th image or video in the ranking list, $IDCG$ is the normalizing factor that equals to the DCG of an ideal ordering. Each image or video is labeled to be very relevant (score 2), relevant (score 1) or irrelevant (score 0) to a query by the voting of the five human labelers.

6.4 Evaluation of Reranking

Figures 4 and 5 illustrate the average performance comparison of our approach and the conventional method that

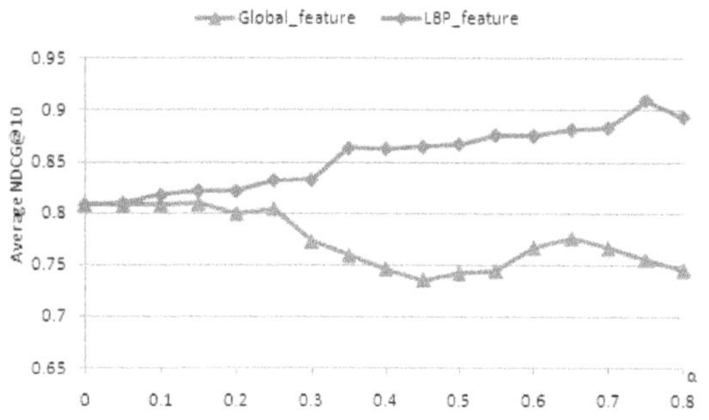

Figure 4: The image search reranking performance comparison of using global features and LBP features for person-related queries.

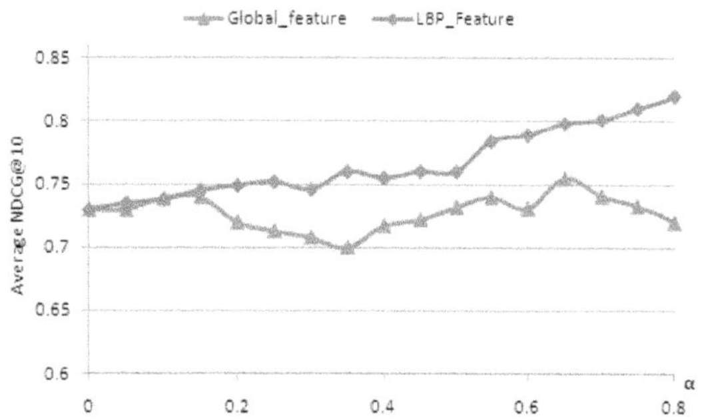

Figure 5: The video search reranking performance comparison of using global features and LBP features for person-related queries.

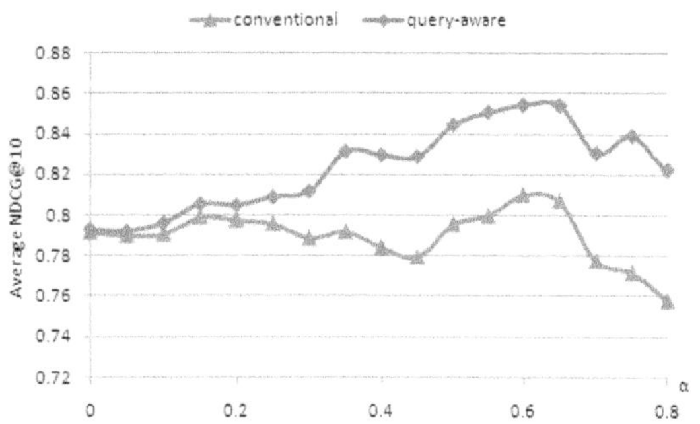

Figure 6: The image search reranking performance comparison of using our method and using the conventional method.

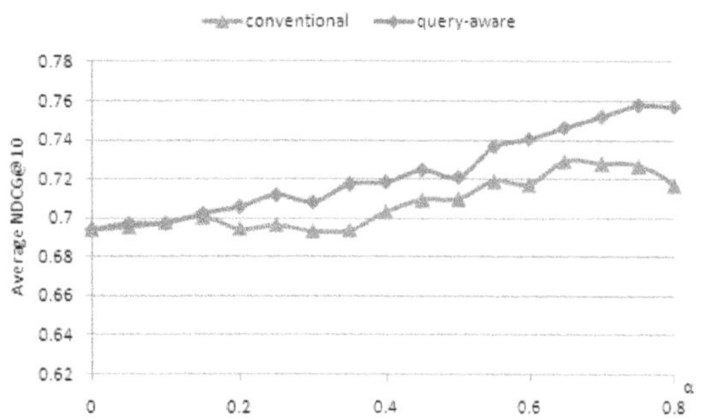

Figure 7: The video search reranking performance comparison of using our method and using the conventional method.

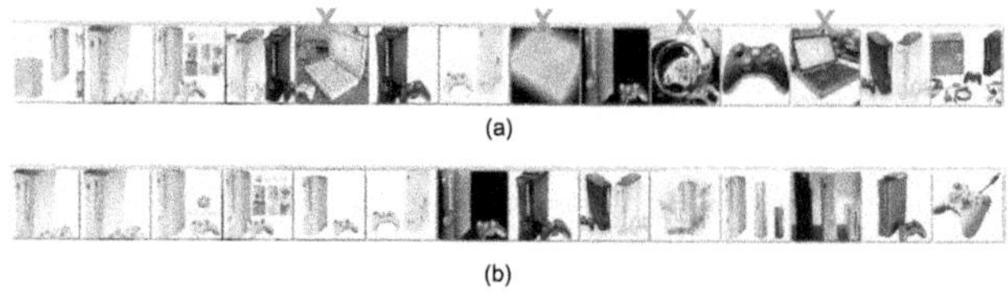

Figure 8: The non-person related image search reranking results for the query "X-Box360". (a)The top images before reranking; (b) the top images after reranking

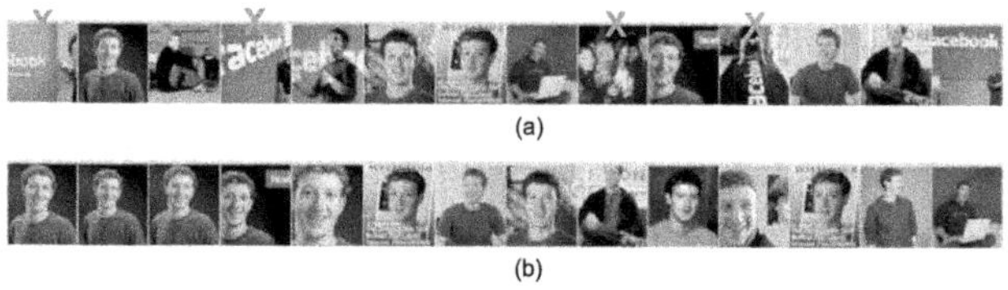

Figure 9: The person-related image search reranking results for the query "Facebook CEO". (a) The top images before reranking; (b) the top images after reranking

uses only global features for the 25 person-related queries. Here we have illustrated the performance with different values of the parameter α. Smaller α means more original ranking information is kept in reranking. When α equals 0, the reranked list will be identical to the original ranking list obtained by the text-based search. We can see that, our approach consistently outperforms the method that uses global features. This demonstrates that it is more reasonable to use facial features for person-related queries.

We then randomly selected 100 queries from image and video class, respectively. Figures 6 and 7 illustrate the average performance comparison. For our query-dependent method, we use global features and facial features for non-person-related and person-related queries respectively. While the conventional method only employ global features regardless the query oriented. Our approach significantly outperforms the conventional methods. We can see that, our approach can effectively improve search relevance when α varies in a wide range. Throughout our rest experiments, we set α as 0.65 and 0.8 for image and video reranking, respectively.

We illustrate the top results before and after reranking for two example queries shown in Figures 8 and 9, one about object and one about person. Figure 8(a) shows the top 14 results before reranking about "X-Box360", while (b) shows the top 14 results after reranking based on global features. Similarly, Figures 9(a) and (b) presents the top results before and after reranking with respect to person-related query "Facebook CEO". We can see that several less relevant results, marked with "X", are removed from top positions after reranking.

After reranking we perform duplicate removal and present the images or/and videos together with the textual answers, depending on the results of answer medium selection. Figure 10 shows the multimedia answer for 3 example queries.

6.5 Subjective Test of Multimedia Answering

Finally, we conduct a user study with 20 volunteers that

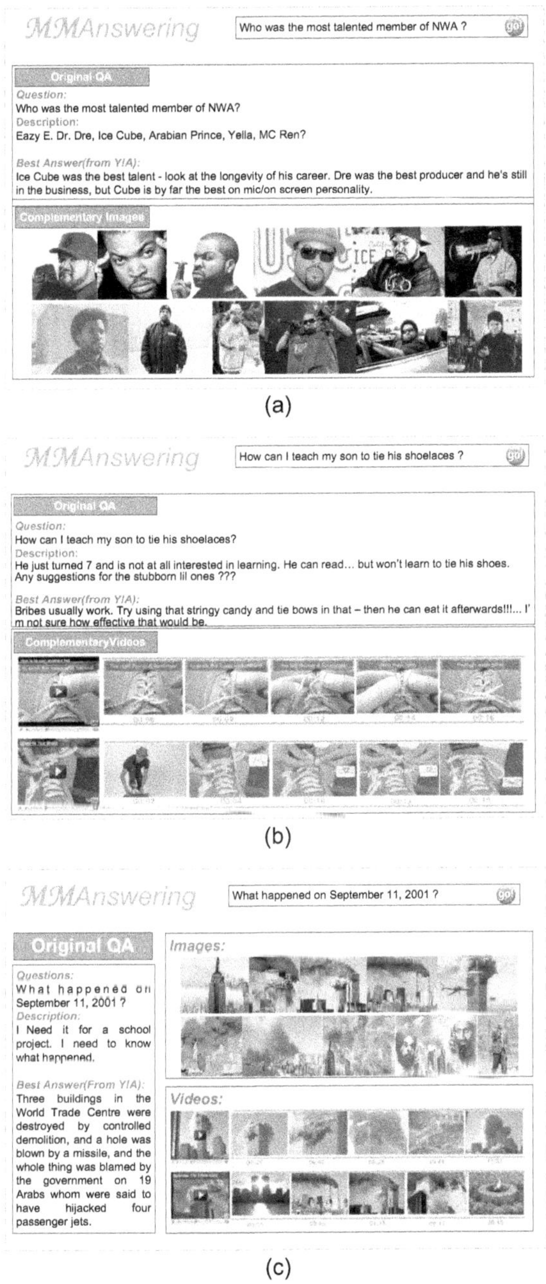

Figure 10: Results of multimedia answering for 3 example queries, "the most talented member of NWA", "tie shoelace", and "September 11". Our scheme answers the three questions with text + image, text + video, and text + image + video, respectively.

Prefer multimedia answer	Neutral	Prefer Original textual answer
45.3%	**51.5%**	3.2%

Table 10: Statistics of the comparison of our multimedia answer and the original textual answer.

Prefer multimedia answer	Neutral	Prefer Original textual answer
82.4%	11.8%	5.8%

Table 11: Statistics of the comparison of our multimedia answer and the original textual answer with exclusion of questions where only text-based answers are sufficient.

frequently use Y!A to evaluate the usability of our application. The users are asked to freely compare the conventional textual answers and our multimedia answers for different questions, and provide their ratings of the 2 systems. We adopt the following quantization approach: score 1 is assigned to the worse scheme and the other scheme is assigned with score 1, 2 and 3 if it is comparable, better and much better than this one, respectively. The average rating scores are illustrated in Figure 11. We can clearly see the preference of users towards the multimedia answering. We also perform an analysis of variance (ANOVA) test. The F-statistic of scheme factor is 18.11 and it can be derived that $p = 1.3154e-004$. This indicates that the difference of the two schemes is significant. The F-statistic of user factor is 1.0 and it can be derived that $p > 0.5$, and this indicates that the difference among users is statistically insignificant.

We then conducted a more detailed study. For each question in the testing set, we simultaneously demonstrate the conventional best answer and the multimedia answer generated by our approach. Each user is asked to choose the preferred one. Table 10 presents the statistical results. We can see that, in about 45.3% of the cases users prefer our answer and only in 3.2% of the cases they prefer the original answers. But there are 51.5% neutral cases. This is because there are many questions that are classified to be answered by only texts, and for these questions our answer and the original textual answer are the same. If we exclude such questions, i.e., we only consider questions of which the original answer and our answer are different, then the statistics will turn to Table 11. We can see that for more than 82.4% of the questions, users will prefer the multimedia answers, i.e., the added image or video data are helpful. For cases that users prefer original textual answers, it is mainly due to the irrelevant image or video content. For several questions, the added image and video content are not only irrelevant to the question and answer but also distractive, and this thus degrades users' experience.

7. CONCLUSION AND FUTURE WORK

In this work, we have proposed a scheme to enrich text QA with media Information. For a given QA pair from cQA, our scheme first predicts which medium is appropriate to enrich the original textual answer. Next, it automatically generates a query based on the QA knowledge, and retrieves relevant image and video from search engines. Finally, query-dependent reranking and duplicate removal are performed to obtain a set of images and videos for presentation along with the original textual answer.

To our knowledge, this is the first work on enriching textual answer with multimedia information, and there is a lot of future work along this research direction. We will further improve the answer medium selection and query selection performance. We will also investigate methods to boost the relevance of the finally selected images and videos, as irrel-

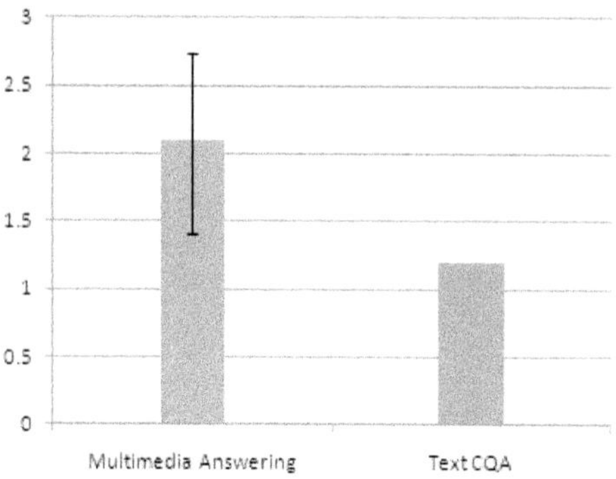

Figure 11: The mean ratings and variance of text cQA and multimedia answering.

evant multimedia content may degrade user experience. We also plan to conduct a more comprehensive user study on a larger dataset.

8. ACKNOWLEDGEMENT

We would like to acknowledge the support of "NExT Research Center" funded by MDA, Singapore, under the research grant: WBS:R-252-300-001-490.

9. REFERENCES

[1] Trec: The text retrieval conference. see http://trec.nist.gov/.

[2] L. A. Adamic, J. Zhang, E. Bakshy, and M. S. Ackerman. Knowledge sharing and yahoo answers: everyone knows something. In *Proceedings of International World Wide Web Conference*, 2008.

[3] E. Agichtein, C. Castillo, D. Donato, A. Gionis, and G. Mishne. Finding high-quality content in social media. In *Proceedings of International Conference on Web Search and Web Data Mining*, 2008.

[4] E. Agichtein, S. Lawrence, and L. Gravano. Learning search engine specific query transformations for question answering. In *Proceedings of International World Wide Web Conference*, 2001.

[5] T. Ahonen, A. Hadid, and M. Pietikainen. Face recognition with local binary patterns. *Proceedings of European Conference on Computer Vision*, 2004.

[6] J. Arguello, F. Diaz, J. Callan, and J. F. Crespo. Sources of evidence for vertical selection. In *Proceedings of ACM International SIGIR conference*, 2009.

[7] M. Bendersky and W. B. Croft. Discovering key concepts in verbose queries. In *Proceedings of ACM International SIGIR conference*, 2008.

[8] J. Cao and J. Jay F. Nunamaker. Question answering on lecture videos: A multifaceted approach. *Proceedings of International Joint Conference on Digital Libraries*, 2004.

[9] T.-S. Chua, R. Hong, G. Li, and J. Tang. From text question-answering to multimedia qa on web-scale media resources. In *Proceedings of ACM workshop on Large-Scale Multimedia Retrieval and Mining*, 2009.

[10] S. Cronen-Townsend, Y. Zhou, and W. B. Croft. Predicting query performance. In *Proceedings of ACM International SIGIR conference*, 2002.

[11] H. Cui, M.-Y. Kan, and T.-S. Chua. Soft pattern matching models for definitional question answering. *ACM Transactions on Information Systems*, 2007.

[12] Z. Gyongyi, G. Koutrika, J. Pedersen, and H. Garcia-Molina. Questioning yahoo! answers. Technical report, Stanford InfoLab, 2007.

[13] F. M. Harper, D. Moy, and J. A. Konstan. Facts or friends?: distinguishing informational and conversational questions in social qa sites. In *Proceedings of International Conference on Human Factors in Computing Systems*, 2009.

[14] F. M. Harper, D. Raban, S. Rafaeli, and J. A. Konstan. Predictors of answer quality in online qa sites. In *Proceedings of International Conference on Human Factors in Computing Systems*, 2008.

[15] W. H. Hsu, L. S. Kennedy, and S.-F. Chang. Video search reranking through random walk over document-level context graph. In *Proceedings of ACM International Conference on Multimedia*, 2007.

[16] Z. Huang, M. Thint, and Z. Qin. Question classification using head words and their hypernyms. In *Proceedings of International Conference on Empirical Methods in Natural Language Processing*, 2008.

[17] G. Kacmarcik. Multi-modal question-answering: Questions without keyboards. Asia Federation of Natural Language Processing, 2005.

[18] Y.-S. Lee, Y.-C. Wu, and J.-C. Yang. Bvideoqa: Online english/chinese bilingual video question answering. *American Society for Information Science and Technology*, 2009.

[19] B. Li, Y. Liu, A. Ram, E. V. Garcia, and E. Agichtein. Exploring question subjectivity prediction in community qa. In *Proceedings of ACM International SIGIR conference*, 2008.

[20] G. Li, R. Hong, Y.-T. Zheng, S. Yan, and T.-S. Chua. Learning cooking techniques from youtube. In *Advances in Multimedia Modeling*. 2010.

[21] G. Li, H. Li, Z. Ming, R. Hong, S. Tang, and T.-S. Chua. Question answering over community contributed web video. *IEEE Multimedia*, 2010.

[22] X. Li and D. Roth. Learning question classifiers. In *Proceedings of International Conference on Computational Linguistics*, 2002.

[23] Y. Liu, T. Mei, X.-S. Hua, J. Tang, X. Wu, and S. Li. Learning to video search rerank via pseudo preference feedback. In *International Conference on Multimedia & Expo*, 2008.

[24] J. T. R. H. Meng Wang, Xian-Sheng Hua. Beyond distance measurement: Constructing neighborhood similarity for video annotation. *IEEE Transactions on Multimedia*, 2009.

[25] X.-S. H. H.-J. Z. Meng Wang, Kuiyuan Yang. Towards relevant and diverse search of social images. *IEEE Transactions on Multimedia*, 2010.

[26] D. Mollá and J. L. Vicedo. Question answering in restricted domains: An overview. *Computational Linguistics*, 2007.

[27] A. P. Natsev, M. R. Naphade, and J. TešiĆ. Learning the semantics of multimedia queries and concepts from a small number of examples. In *Proceedings of ACM International Conference on Multimedia*, 2005.

[28] S. A. Quarteroni and S. Manandhar. Designing an interactive open domain question answering system. *Journal of Natural Language Engineering*, 2008.

[29] M. Surdeanu, M. Ciaramita, and H. Zaragoza. Learning to rank answers on large online QA collections. In *Proceedings of the Association for Computational Linguistics*, 2008.

[30] A. Tamura, H. Takamura, and M. Okumura. Classification of multiple-sentence questions. In *Natural Language Processing*. 2005.

[31] X. Tian, L. Yang, J. Wang, Y. Yang, X. Wu, and X.-S. Hua. Bayesian video search reranking. In *Proceeding of ACM International Conference on Multimedia*, 2008.

[32] R. C. Wang, N. Schlaefer, W. W. Cohen, and E. Nyberg. Automatic set expansion for list question answering. In *Proceedings of International Conference on Empirical Methods in Natural Language Processing*, 2008.

[33] Y.-C. Wu, C.-H. Chang, and Y.-S. Lee. Cross-language video question/answering system. *Proceedings of International Symposium on Multimedia Software Engineering*, 2004.

[34] Y.-C. Wu and J.-C. Yang. A robust passage retrieval algorithm for video question answering. *IEEE Transactions on Circuits and Systems for Video Technology*, 2008.

[35] R. Yan, A. Hauptmann, and R. Jin. Multimedia search with pseudo-relevance feedback. In *Proceedings of International Conference on Image and Video Retrieval*, 2003.

[36] H. Yang, T.-S. Chua, S. Wang, and C.-K. Koh. Structured use of external knowledge for event-based open domain question answering. In *Proceedings of ACM International SIGIR Conference*, 2003.

[37] T. Yeh, J. J. Lee, and T. Darrell. Photo-based question answering. In *Proceeding of ACM International Conference on Multimedia*, 2008.

[38] H. Zhang, A. Kankanhalli, and S. W. Smoliar. Automatic partitioning of full-motion video. *Multimedia Systems*, 1993.

[39] J. Zhang, R. Lee, and Y. J. Wang. Support vector machine classifications for microarray expression data set. *Proceedings of International Conference on Computational Intelligence and Multimedia Applications*, 2003.

Enhancing Multi-Label Music Genre Classification Through Ensemble Techniques

Chris Sanden
Mathematics and Computer Science
University of Lethbridge
Lethbridge, AB Canada T1K 3M4
sanden@cs.uleth.ca

John Z. Zhang
Mathematics and Computer Science
University of Lethbridge
Lethbridge, AB Canada T1K 3M4
zhang@cs.uleth.ca

ABSTRACT

In the field of Music Information Retrieval (MIR), multi-label genre classification is the problem of assigning one or more genre labels to a music piece. In this work, we propose a set of ensemble techniques, which are specific to the task of multi-label genre classification. Our goal is to enhance classification performance by combining multiple classifiers. In addition, we also investigate some existing ensemble techniques from machine learning. The effectiveness of these techniques is demonstrated through a set of empirical experiments and various related issues are discussed. To the best of our knowledge, there has been limited work on applying ensemble techniques to multi-label genre classification in the literature and we consider the results in this work as our initial efforts toward this end. The significance of our work has two folds: (1) proposing a set of ensemble techniques specific to music genre classification and (2) shedding light on further research along this direction.

Categories and Subject Descriptors

H.5.5 [**Sound and Music Computing**]: Methodologies and techniques; H.3 [**Information Storage and Retrieval**]: Information search and retrieval

General Terms

Experimentation, Performance

Keywords

Music Information Retrieval (MIR), genre classification, multi-label classification, ensemble techniques

1. INTRODUCTION

For the past decade, digital music collections have been growing enormously in volume, due to advances in technologies, such as storage capacity, network transmission, data compression, information retrieval, etc. The rapid rise in music downloading has created a major shift in the music industry away from physical media formats to electronic distributions. Large on-line music providers now offer catalogs that contain millions of songs. At present, these catalogs are commonly accessed through *textual meta-data*, such as *genre*, *style*, *mood*, *artist*, etc. While this meta-data is rich and descriptive, it is difficult to maintain and in many cases is not comprehensive, due to the ambiguity and subjectivity that is introduced in the annotation process [13]. Therefore, manual annotation is insufficient and ineffective when facing large volumes of music.

Music Information Retrieval (*MIR*) is an emerging area of interdisciplinary research that is engaged in the design and implementation of algorithmic approaches to manage digital music collections [6]. Various tasks, such as music classification, recommendation, fingerprinting, play-list generation, etc., are studied in MIR. In our work, we study the problem of automatic music genre classification. As a fundamental task of MIR, automatic genre classification has attracted considerable attention for many reasons. For instance, music genres have historically been used as categorical descriptions to organize music collections. While no universally accepted definition of genres exists, a genre can be described by the common characteristics shared by its members. These characteristics are related to the instrumentation, harmonic content, rhythmic structures, etc. [23] However, as McKay [11] indicates, there is some controversy regarding the current state of automatic genre classification with some works proposing that it be abandoned in favor of a more general similarity search problem. It has also been suggested that only limited agreement can be achieved among human annotators when classifying music by genres. This imposes an unavoidable ceiling on the performance of automatic genre classification. Moreover, the time and expertise needed to manually classify a corpus of music poses serious obstacles to generating quality ground-truth, against which classification performance can be evaluated. To further complicate matters, the understanding of existing genres can change with time, which can necessitate the re-annotation of ground truth [11].

Despite these controversies, genre categorization provides a common vocabulary which can be used to discuss musical categories. Additionally, users are already accustomed to browsing music collection by genres, and this approach is proved to be at least reasonably effective [11]. Although one may argue that generating ground truth is a serious issue that needs to be handled, manually labeling growing music collections is a much greater challenge. Therefore, contin-

SIGIR'11, July 24–28, 2011, Beijing, China.

uing efforts in automatic genre classification have much to offer. While previous approaches are concerned with learning from a set of music pieces that are each associated with a single label, it has been observed that a music piece could belong to multiple genres. Furthermore, different portions of a music piece might be classified as different genres which stand in contrast to each other [17]. Therefore, it is desirable that automatic genre classification be modeled as a multi-label process.

In our recent studies, we have identified a set of multi-label classification algorithms that perform well on a selection of music datasets. We believe that, due to the diversity of the datasets used and the comprehensibility of our experiments, our results are representative and can be further utilized for algorithmic improvements on genre classification. Toward this end, we propose a set of ensemble techniques, which are specific to the task of multi-label genre classification. In addition, we also investigate some existing ensemble techniques from machine learning. To the best of our knowledge, our work is the first to apply ensemble techniques to multi-label music genre classification. It is important to note that, it is commonly accepted that music genres may depend on cultural extrinsic habits. However, in our work, we assume that there are intrinsic properties of the music that can be used for automatic genre classification.

The paper is organized as follows. Section 2 introduces related works in multi-label classification of music while Section 3 discusses the multi-label classification algorithms and their evaluation metrics in our experiments. Section 4 presents our proposed ensemble techniques along with existing ones. Experiment setup is discussed in Section 5 and results are presented and analyzed in Section 6. Finally, Section 7 concludes our presentation with some future work.

2. PREVIOUS WORK

Multi-label classification has been used to categorize music into different emotions. Wieczorkowska *et al.* [25] address the problem of multi-label classification of emotions using a modified k-NN algorithm. A set of 875 audio samples, 30 seconds each, manually labeled into 13 classes of emotion are used for their experiment. The modified k-NN algorithm aims at taking multiple labels into account. Therefore, the algorithm returns a set of labels for each neighbor of a test instance. In addition, Trohidis *et al.* [19] evaluate and compare four multi-label classification algorithms for the purpose of detecting emotions in music. Experiments are conducted on a set of 593 samples, from which a 30-second excerpt is extracted and annotated with a set of emotions. It is claimed that the overall predictive performance is high and encourages further investigation of multi-label classification.

Multi-label classification has also been used for the purpose of automatic tag annotation of music. These tags can be any semantically meaningful words and can represent a variety of different concepts, including genre, instrumentation, emotions, geographic origins, social conditions, etc. Automatic tag annotation of music learns a relationship between acoustic features and words from a dataset of labeled audio tracks [12]. The resulting trained model can retrieve audio samples based on lists of tags and annotate unlabeled ones. For example, Wang *et al.* [24] study the problem of combining user-generated tags and music content for artistic style classification. They investigate the effectiveness of using tags and audio content separately for clustering and propose a novel language model that makes use of them. Results show that tag features are more effective than music content for artistic style clustering, and the proposed model can marginally improve clustering performance by combining tags and music content.

Despite the volume of previous results on the application of multi-label techniques, to the best of our knowledge, there has been limited work on the application of them to music genre classification. Lukashevich *et al.* [10] present a two-dimensional approach for genre classification. The multi-label classification problem is decomposed into multiple single-class problems. The novelty of the approach lies in the combination of segment-wise and domain-specific genre classification. The music collection used for testing is comprised of 430 full-length music pieces from 16 world genres. However, as described by Zhang and Zhou [26], decomposing multi-label problems into multiple binary classifications does not consider the correlation between the labels of each instance. Therefore, the expressive power of such an approach can be limited.

3. MULTI-LABEL CLASSIFICATION ALGORITHMS

Multi-label classification deals with problems where an object may belong to one or multiple classes simultaneously. These algorithms can be grouped into two categories as proposed in [20]: (1) *problem transformation methods*, and (2) *algorithm adaptation methods*. Problem transformation methods transform a multi-label classification problem into one or more single-label classification problems and offer the flexibility of using any single-label base classifier. Moreover, algorithm adaptation methods extend traditional single-label classifiers to handle multiple labels directly.

Multi-label Classifier	Base Classifier
RAkEL	DT
CLR	SVM
ML-kNN	N/A
HOMER	SVM
IBLR	N/A

Table 1: Multi-label classifiers along with the associated base classifier, where applicable.

Based on our recent studies with multi-label genre classification, in this work we select and combine the following algorithms using a set of ensemble techniques: *Random k-Labelsets* (*RAkEL*), *Calibrated Label Ranking* (*CLR*), *Multi-label k-Nearest Neighbor* (*ML-kNN*), *Hierarchy of Multi-label Classifiers* (*HOMER*), and *Instance Based Logistic Regression* (*IBLR*). A *Decision Tree* (*DT*) is used as a base classifier for RAkEL while a *Support Vector Machine* (*SVM*) is used for CLR and HOMER. Table 1 presents the multi-label classification algorithms derived for our study. The details of them can be found in [21].

3.1 Evaluation Metrics

In order to evaluate the performance of multi-label classification algorithms, a selection of evaluation metrics are employed. These metrics can be categorized into three groups: example-based, label-based and rank-based. The first two groups are based on a bipartition vectors while the third group derives ranking information from a score vector and conducts evaluations accordingly. Furthermore, different classification algorithms perform better under different evaluation metrics. Therefore, it is desirable that multiple and contrasting metrics are used in any multi-label classification experiment. We consider the following evaluation metrics for each group.

Example-based: Hamming Loss (*HL*), Accuracy (*Accu.*), Recall, F-Measure (F_1) and Precision (*Prec.*);

Label-based: Micro Precision (*MicroP*), Micro F-Measure (*MicroF*$_1$), Micro Recall (*MicroR*), Macro Precision (*MacroP*), Macro F-Measure (*MacroF*$_1$) and Macro Recall (*MacroR*);

Rank-based: Average Precision (AP), Coverage (CO), Ranking Loss (RL), and One-Error (OE).

For the sake of space and due to the nature of our work, we will not digress into the details of these evaluation metrics. The interested reader is referred to [20, 21].

4. ENSEMBLE TECHNIQUES

In this section, we discuss and propose a set of ensemble techniques for improving multi-label music genre classification.

Despite extensive work in multi-label classification, there exist two major challenges. The first challenge is that in many situations, we can have highly imbalanced datasets, due to the availability of instances for some labels. The second is related to our limited knowledge regarding the correlation among class labels for a given dataset. Surprisingly, most multi-label classification algorithms are designed to focus mainly on the second problem and limited work has been devoted to handling imbalanced datasets [18].

One approach to these problems is an ensemble of multi-label classifiers, which consists of a set of individually trained classifiers whose predictions are combined when classifying new instances. This approach is generally more accurate and achieves greater predictive performance than any of the individual classifiers [4].

Ensembles can be homogeneous, where each individual classifier is constructed using the same algorithm, or heterogeneous, where each classifier is constructed from a different algorithm [4, 18]. Some multi-label classification algorithms directly use homogeneous or heterogeneous ensemble techniques internally to improve overall performance. For example, Instance Based Logistic Regression [5] uses a combination of Logistic Regression and Nearest Neighbor classifiers.

Tahir *et al.* [18] present a first study, as claimed, on combining the outputs of multi-label classification algorithms. They propose two heterogeneous ensemble techniques and apply them to publicly available datasets using several evaluation metrics. The results show that these approaches provide significant performance improvements when compared with individual multi-label classifiers.

The goal of our work is to use a heterogeneous ensemble of existing multi-label classification algorithms to improve music genre classification. In the following, we introduce a set of ensemble techniques that combine multiple classifiers for the purpose of music genre classification. We first introduce some notation. Let D denote a set of music pieces and let $L = \{l_1, l_2, ...l_N\}$ be the finite set of labels. Given a training set $D_s = \{(x_1, Y_1), (x_2, Y_2), \cdots, (x_m, Y_m)\}$, where $x_i \in D$ is a single music piece and $Y_i \subseteq L$ is the label set associated with x_i. We attempt to design a multi-label classifier that predicts a set of labels for an unseen music piece from a test set $D_t = \{(x_1, Y_1), (x_2, Y_2), \cdots, (x_n, Y_n)\}$.

An *ensemble of multi-label classifiers* (*EML*) trains q multi-label classifiers $H_1, H_2, ...H_q$. In our work, all classifiers are likely to be unique and be able to generate different multi-label predictions. For an unseen instance x_j, classifier H_k produces two N-dimensional vectors: a score vector $P_k^j = [p_{1,k}^j, p_{2,k}^j, \cdots, p_{N,k}^j]$, where the value $p_{b,k}^j$ is the confidence of the class label l_b assigned by classifier H_k being correct, and a bipartition vector $V_k^j = [v_{1,k}^j, v_{2,k}^j, \cdots, v_{N,k}^j]$ where $v_{b,k}^j$ is 1 if the class label l_b is predicted by classifier H_k and 0 otherwise.

We denote by H_{eml} the classifier obtained after applying an ensemble technique to the q classifiers. We use $P_{eml}^j = [p_{1,eml}^j, p_{2,eml}^j, \cdots, p_{N,eml}^j]$ to represent the resulting score vector for the unseen instance y_j and use $V_{eml}^j = [v_{1,eml}^j, v_{2,eml}^j, \cdots, v_{N,eml}^j]$ to represent the corresponding binary vector.

There are many techniques to combine the outputs of these q classifiers. In this work, we consider two sets of combiners based on the output of the classifiers. The first set is based on the bipartition vector while the second set is based on the score vector. These techniques are discussed below. It is important to note that, multi-label classification algorithms may only output a score vector. These classifiers can employ a thresholding method to produce bipartitions [7]. In our experiments, we assume that all of the classifiers output a score vector and bipartition vector.

4.1 Bipartition-based Ensemble

4.1.1 Intersection Rule

The *Intersection rule* (EML_I) calculates the intersection of the bipartition vectors from the q classifiers using $v_{i,eml}^j = min_s(v_{i,s}^j)$, for $i = 1, 2, \cdots, N$, i.e., the binary values for each label in all vectors are combined using the logical AND operator. The set of output labels common to all classifiers result in an ensemble decision. We propose this naive method to emphasize the common labels output by all individual classifiers.

4.1.2 Union Rule

The *Union rule* (EML_U) calculates the union of the binary vectors from the q classifiers using $v_{i,eml}^j = max_s(v_{i,s}^j)$, for $i = 1, 2, \cdots, N$, i.e., the binary values for each label in all vectors are combined using the logical OR operator. An ensemble decision is constructed by computing, for each label, the union of outputs from the q classifiers. We propose this method to optimistically select a label for the ensemble if it is selected by any of the individual classifiers.

4.1.3 Majority Vote Rule

The *Majority Vote rule* (EML_{MV}) counts how many times a label appears in the q classifiers. It is one of the most frequently used ways for combining label outputs [8].

$$v_{i,eml}^j = \begin{cases} 1 & \text{if } \sum_{s=1}^{q} v_{i,s}^j / q \geq 0.5 \\ 0 & \text{otherwise} \end{cases}$$

where $i = 1, 2, \cdots, N$.

4.2 Score-based Ensemble

4.2.1 Minimum Rule

The *Minimum rule* [8, 18](EML_{Min}) represents a pessimistic view of the scores from the q classifiers and only considers the smallest score for each class label. We calculate the minimum score as shown in the following equation,

$$p^j_{i,eml} = min_s(p^j_{i,s}),\ i = 1, 2, \cdots, N.$$

4.2.2 Maximum Rule

The *Maximum rule* [8, 18] (EML_{Max}) represents an optimistic view of the scores from the q classifiers and only considers the largest score for each class label. We calculate the maximum score as shown in the following equation,

$$p^j_{i,eml} = max_s(p^j_{i,s}),\ i = 1, 2, \cdots, N.$$

4.2.3 Mean Rule

The *Mean rule* [8, 18] (EML_{Mean}) considers the scores from the q classifiers for a class label. We calculate the mean score as shown in the following equation,

$$p^j_{i,eml} = \sum_{s=1}^{q} p^j_{i,s}/q,\ i = 1, 2, \cdots, N.$$

4.2.4 Top-k Rule

We propose a *Top-k rule* (denote as EML_{Topk}), which is a combination of the Maximum and Mean rules. It selects the top k largest scores and averages them. We use the following equation to calculate $p^j_{i,eml}$. Constant k is a user-selected parameter. This method represents our desire to have a degree of certainty when calculating the score for H_{eml}.

$$p^j_{i,eml} = avg(topk(p^j_{i,1}, p^j_{i,2}, \cdots, p^j_{i,q}))$$

where $i = 1, 2, \cdots, N$, function $topk(\cdot)$ picks the largest k elements from a set and function $avg(\cdot)$ averages them.

4.3 Score-based Label Selection

In addition, we propose a score-based label selection technique wherein we first consider the output score from each classifier and select the top n scores and the corresponding labels. Then, we merge the results from all the classifiers, from which we select the top k labels that appear the most, where $n \geq k$. If there is a tie, we arbitrarily select one. For each of these k labels, we set the corresponding entry to be "1" in the bipartition vector for the final ensemble H_{eml}. For the other labels, we set the respective entries to be "0". In this proposed technique, since we first select the top n scores and then select the top k class labels accordingly, we refer to it as $EML_{C_n L_k}$ in the following discussions. We note that, this technique produces a bipartition vector and will be compared to the bipartition-based ensemble techniques in our experiments.

4.4 Hierarchical Label Substitution

We propose a label substitution technique that utilizes taxonomy information of music genres to improve multi-label genre classification. We call this technique *Hierarchical Label Substitution* (*HLS*). The technique reduces the number of labels using a substitution method. A set of multi-label classifiers are trained and the resulting output is combined using one of the bipartition-based techniques described above. A set of labels in the ensemble decision are then substituted based on a local genre hierarchy, represented as a *taxonomy*. For our experiments, we derive our local genre hierarchy based on the taxonomy of music genres developed by Allmusic[1]. Figure 1 depicts a small portion of the local genre hierarchy.

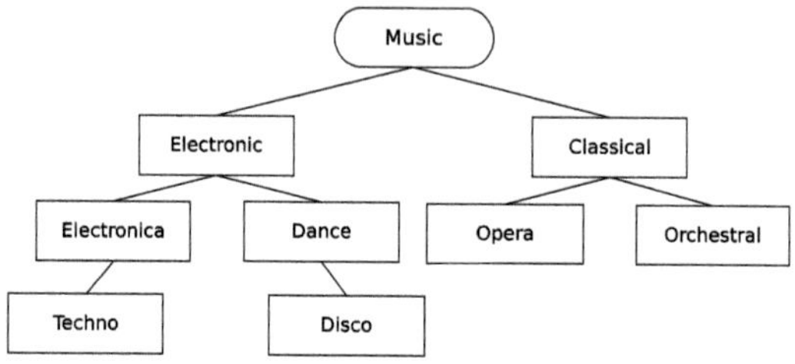

Figure 1: Example genre taxonomy used for Hierarchical Label Substitution.

Our hierarchy is constructed to only contain music genres in our datasets and consists of top level nodes referred to as "meta genres" [14], as shown in Figure 1. These should represent main musical genres, such as *Classical*, *Rock*, *Jazz*, etc. The hierarchy is further defined to consist of children nodes, i.e., *sub-genres*, which can be conceptualized as specific genres derived from a parent genre and become more concrete as the depth increases. For example, from Figure 1, *Techno* is considered as a sub-genre of *Electronica*. It is important to emphasize that our taxonomy is by no means authoritative but our substitution technique is applicable to any other genre taxonomy.

We define a *depth d* for label substitution, where all labels below d are substituted with their parent label at this level. For example, for sub-genre *Dance*, at $d = 2$, any occurrence of labels in the resulting classifier output below level d will be replaced with their parent label, e.g., *Disco* would be replaced with *Dance* and *Techno* with *Electronica*. It is easy to see that, as d decreases, the resulting label set shrinks.

Although our label substitution technique produces a smaller label set, the usefulness lies in its ability to simplify the label space by reducing the number of possible "overlapping" genres. Moreover it has been shown [1] that there is little consensus between the genre labels used by individuals. Simplification to a common set of high-level genres may provide a remedy to this.

5. EXPERIMENT SETUP

In this section we describe the preparation for our experiments. We apply the ensemble techniques discussed above to the multi-label classifiers in Table 1 and evaluate their performance. The evaluation is conducted using 10-fold cross validation. The Mulan [22] open source library for multi-label learning is used to train and evaluate each of the classifiers using default parameters, e.g., the number of neighbors is set to 10 for ML-kNN and IBLR, the SVM is trained with a linear kernel, etc.

5.1 Datasets

There are a variety of benchmark datasets available for multi-label classification in various domains. However, no dataset exists specifically for the task of multi-label music

[1]http://www.allmusic.com.

genre classification. Current datasets used in the evaluation of genre classification are comprised of music pieces annotated with a single genre. Therefore, for the purpose of our experiment, we derive three multi-genre datasets from the *Magnatagatune* collection [9].

Magnatagatune is a collection of approximately 21,000 music clips, each annotated with a combination of 188 different tags. The annotations are collected through an on-line game, referred to as "TagATune", developed to collect tags for music and sound clips. Each clip, 29 seconds in length and sampled at 16kHz, is an excerpt of a music piece published by Magnatune. All of the tags in the dataset have been verified, i.e., a tag is associated with a clip only if it is generated independently by more than two players. Moreover, only those tags that are associated with more than 50 clips are included in the collection.

For our experiment, we are only interested in those clips annotated with musical genres. A set of 22 genre tags, denoted as L, are identified and used to create a subset of the Magnatagatune collection, which is referred to as D_s in our following discussions. D_s is created by filtering the Magnatagatune collection to contain only clips annotated with the set of selected genre tags. The following three datasets are further derived from D_s and discussed further in Section 6.4.

The *Random* dataset, denoted D_{Ra}, consists of 1000 clips chosen at random from D_s. No other selection criteria are used in the creation of the dataset.

The *UniqueArtist* dataset, denoted D_{Ar}, consists of 198 clips derived from D_s. The dataset is created by randomly selecting a single clip from each artist in D_s. The use of an artist filter is recommended as it ensures that the artists in the test set are not present in the training set during classification [2].

The *UniqueAlbum* dataset, denoted as D_{Al}, consists of 375 clips derived from D_s. The dataset is created by randomly selecting a single clip from each album in D_s. Similar to the artist filter, the use of an album filter ensures that clips from the same album are not present in the training and testing sets simultaneously.

Dataset (D)	$\|D\|$	$\|L\|$	LC
D_{Ra}	1000	22	2.278
D_{Ar}	198	22	2.166
D_{Al}	375	22	2.212

Table 2: Multi-genre music datasets and their statistics.

Table 2 displays the datasets and their associated statistics. The *label cardinality* (LC) of a dataset D is the average number of labels each instance has in D and is used to indicate the number of alternative labels that characterize the instances in a multi-label training dataset [20].

5.2 Audio Parameters

Prior to classification, the music pieces must be parameterized based on a set of features and their changes over time. However, there is no accepted criteria as which features are best for music classification [3]. Therefore, we use the following set of features which are commonly used for genre classification: MFCC, ZCR, Spectral Centroid, Rolloff, Spectral Flux, and Chroma. The Marsyas[2] audio processing framework is used for the computation of the features.

Following a general practice in MIR, we consider a bag-of-frames approach based on the aforementioned features [15]. This approach consists of modeling the audio signal as the statistical distribution of audio features computed on individual, short segments. This process yields a large number of feature vectors. Therefore, the feature vectors are then aggregated together using statistical methods. Although more elaborate representations have been proposed in the literature, the simplicity of using a single vector for classification is appealing [12]. Frame-level features in our experiment are compressed into a single set of song-level features by computing the mean across the feature vectors [12].

Furthermore, we explore the effects of frame size on multi-label classification. For each <*dataset, classifier*> pair, we plot the classification performance as we adjust the frame size, f_r, represented as the number of samples collected during a certain time period. Each pair is evaluated using $f_r \in \{256, 340, 512, 1024, 2048, 3200, 4096\}$. In the following, we only report results for $f_r = 340$, corresponding to approximately 23 milliseconds. This frame size has been commonly used in the MIR literature for classification tasks. For instance, Tzanetakis and Cook [23] use a frame size of 23 milliseconds for automatic genre classification. We discuss the effects of frame size on classification performance in Section 6.4.

5.3 Ensemble Parameters

We use the following ensemble parameters in our experiments. For hierarchical label substitution (HLS), we set $d = 1$, i.e., sub-genres are replaced with their respective "meta genre". In addition, we set $k = 3$ for EML_{Topk}, that is, we select the top 3 largest scores and average them. For score-based label selection ($EML_{C_n L_k}$), we set $n = 3$ and $k = 2$. More specifically, we first select the top 3 scores from each classifier and then select the top 2 class labels accordingly. We provide more discussions on these parameters in Section 6.4.

6. RESULTS AND DISCUSSIONS

In this section, we present the results from our experiments. Each ensemble technique is compared with the individual multi-label classifiers to determine its performance.

6.1 Random Dataset

Table 3 shows the comparison of the bipartition-based ensemble techniques with the individual multi-label classifiers for D_{Ra} using example-based evaluation metrics; the best result for each metric is shown in bold face. Note that in the Table 3, (↓) indicates better performance when the value is smaller while (↑) indicates better performance when the value is bigger. When the individual multi-label classifiers are compared with each other, we find that CLR and HOMER demonstrate the best performance for different example-based metrics. Furthermore, when we compare the classifiers using label-based metrics, presented in Table 4, we find that CLR performs well for MicroP, MacroP,

[2]http://marsyas.sness.net.

	HL ↓	Accu. ↑	Recall ↑	F_1 ↑	Prec. ↑
CLR	0.0567	0.5697	0.5959	0.8098	0.8255
IBLR	0.0586	0.6045	0.6481	0.8040	0.7715
MLKNN	0.0576	0.6042	0.6354	0.8120	0.7764
RAkEL	0.0620	0.5918	0.6648	0.7739	0.7357
HOMER	0.0635	0.6255	0.6949	0.7867	0.7299
EML_U	0.0710	0.6239	0.7893	0.7568	0.6861
EML_I	0.0607	0.4828	0.4936	0.8008	0.8853
EML_{MV}	0.0544	0.6233	0.6559	0.8123	0.7958
HLS(EML_U)	0.0402	0.7001	**0.8435**	0.8177	0.7652
HLS(EML_I)	0.0337	0.6198	0.6198	**0.9180**	**0.9453**
HLS(EML_{MV})	**0.0304**	**0.7322**	0.7491	0.8978	0.8741
$EML_{C_nL_k}$	0.0601	0.6277	0.6731	0.7843	0.7390

Table 3: Comparison of bipartition-based ensembles for D_{Ra} using example-based metrics.

	MicroP ↑	MicroF_1 ↑	MicroR ↑	MacroP ↑	MacroF_1 ↑	MacroR ↑
CLR	0.8273	0.6759	0.5721	0.8141	**0.8088**	0.2613
IBLR	0.7661	0.6886	0.6259	0.6190	0.6438	0.3277
MLKNN	0.7841	0.6874	0.6125	0.7910	0.6622	0.2857
RAkEL	0.7255	0.6829	0.6453	0.6490	0.6507	0.3317
HOMER	0.7039	0.6877	0.6737	0.6347	0.7110	0.3175
EML_U	0.6294	0.6918	**0.7688**	0.4677	0.6513	**0.4221**
EML_I	0.8904	0.6171	0.4728	0.9196	0.7637	0.2201
EML_{MV}	0.8011	0.7065	0.6322	0.8124	0.6816	0.2905
HLS(EML_U)	0.6623	0.7081	0.7626	0.4731	0.6206	0.3864
HLS(EML_I)	**0.9453**	0.6560	0.5031	**0.9549**	0.7956	0.1788
HLS(EML_{MV})	0.8566	**0.7262**	0.6312	0.8363	0.6735	0.2333
$EML_{C_nL_k}$	0.7390	0.6911	0.6494	0.7493	0.6543	0.3258

Table 4: Comparison of bipartition-based ensembles for D_{Ra} using label-based metrics.

and MacroF_1, while IBLR, HOMER, and RA*k*EL perform well for MicroF_1, MicroR, and MacroR respectively. However, by using ensemble techniques, significant performance gains have been observed for a majority of example-based and label-based metrics. Specifically, HLS outperforms the individual multi-label classification algorithms and the EML techniques for example-based metrics and also offers an improvement in classification performance for various label-based metrics. If we exclude HLS from our analysis and compare the remaining ensemble techniques, we find that a selection of them perform better for a majority of the evaluation metrics. However, we find that there is little consistency between the techniques making it difficult to select one that performs the best overall.

	AP ↑	CO ↓	RL ↓	OE ↓
CLR	0.8080	3.2160	0.0569	0.1940
IBLR	0.8067	3.4510	0.0649	0.2050
MLKNN	0.8094	3.4420	0.0637	0.1980
RAkEL	0.7747	5.5360	0.1129	0.2140
HOMER	0.7240	7.2170	0.1617	0.2440
EML_{Max}	0.7905	3.243	0.0592	0.2530
EML_{Min}	0.7584	7.181	0.1556	0.1860
EML_{Mean}	**0.8195**	3.206	0.0556	0.1840
EML_{Topk}	**0.8195**	**3.1690**	**0.0550**	**0.1820**

Table 5: Comparison of score-based ensembles for D_{Ra} using rank-based metrics.

Table 5 presents the comparison of score-based ensemble techniques with the individual classifiers for D_{Ra} using rank-based evaluation metrics. First, when the individual classifiers are compared with each other, we find that CLR delivers the best performance for all of the metrics. We find this interesting as CLR does not outperform the other multi-label classifiers for the example-based and label-based metrics. Further investigation is needed into this result. As before, the fusion of multi-label classifiers has improved the overall performance for rank-based metrics. We observe that EML_{Topk} makes an impact on the performance in comparison to the other EML techniques and multi-label classifiers. Moreover, it offers the best performance for all of the rank-based metrics for D_{Ra}.

We find that the largest performance improvements are offered by HLS for bipartition-based ensembles and EML_{Topk} for score-based ensembles, respectively. It should be noted that, the performance gain observed for HLS is predictable as the label space is simplified by reducing the number of possible "overlapping" genres. This is further discussed in Section 6.4.

6.2 UniqueArtist Dataset

Table 6 shows the comparison of the bipartition-based ensembles with the individual multi-label classifiers for D_{Ar} using example-based evaluation metrics. We find it interesting that for this data set, when the individual multi-label classifiers are compared with each other, we find a similar trend to the results reported in Table 3. That is, CLR and HOMER perform well for a selection of evaluation metrics. When we compare the individual classifiers using label-based metrics, presented in Table 7, we find that CLR performs well for MicroP, MicroF_1, MacroP, and MacroF_1, while HOMER and RA*k*EL perform well for MicroR, and MacroR, respectively. This is similar to the results reported in Table 4. As before, using the proposed ensemble of multi-

	HL ↓	Accu. ↑	Recall ↑	F_1 ↑	Prec. ↑
CLR	0.0618	0.4641	0.4833	0.7390	0.8314
IBLR	0.0966	0.3811	0.4684	0.6723	0.5691
MLKNN	0.0750	0.3765	0.3965	0.6801	0.7418
RAkEL	0.0798	0.4500	0.5234	0.6932	0.6498
HOMER	0.0818	0.4900	0.5706	0.6984	0.6478
EML_U	0.1149	0.4647	0.7210	0.6297	0.5139
EML_I	0.0749	0.2671	0.2680	0.6865	0.9291
EML_{MV}	0.0646	0.4719	0.4934	0.7311	0.7843
HLS(EML_U)	0.0763	0.5146	**0.7908**	0.6753	0.5631
HLS(EML_I)	0.0485	0.4134	0.4134	**0.8517**	**0.9401**
HLS(EML_{MV})	**0.0432**	**0.6064**	0.6273	0.8465	0.8201
$EML_{C_nL_k}$	0.0779	0.5053	0.5735	0.7078	0.6133

Table 6: Comparison of bipartition-based ensembles for D_{Ar} using example-based metrics.

	MicroP ↑	MicroF_1 ↑	MicroR ↑	MacroP ↑	MacroF_1 ↑	MacroR ↑
CLR	0.8164	0.5995	0.4775	0.7903	0.7590	0.2987
IBLR	0.5159	0.4847	0.4603	0.3592	0.6399	0.3440
MLKNN	0.7229	0.5025	0.3892	0.6971	0.6920	0.2476
RAkEL	0.6127	0.5595	0.5182	0.5298	0.6665	0.3448
HOMER	0.5951	0.5759	0.5637	0.5184	0.6760	0.3723
EML_U	0.4514	0.5528	0.7194	0.3221	0.6463	**0.5386**
EML_I	0.9227	0.4034	0.2610	0.9137	0.6463	0.1638
EML_{MV}	0.7741	0.5946	0.4847	0.7402	0.7530	0.3058
HLS(EML_U)	0.4786	0.5744	**0.7241**	0.3342	0.6415	0.5217
HLS(EML_I)	**0.9401**	0.4962	0.3409	**0.9402**	0.6588	0.2014
HLS(EML_{MV})	0.7979	**0.6338**	0.5276	0.7781	**0.8005**	0.3062
$EML_{C_nL_k}$	0.6133	0.5890	0.5671	0.5815	0.7141	0.3658

Table 7: Comparison of bipartition-based ensembles for D_{Ar} using label-based metrics.

label classifiers has improved the overall performance for example-based and label-based metrics, i.e., HLS(EML_I), HLS(EML_U), and HLS(EML_{MV}) deliver improvements for a selected set of example-based and label-based metrics. Furthermore, if we exclude HLS from our analysis and compare the remaining ensembles, we find that for a majority of the evaluation metrics, a selection of the ensembles demonstrate the best performance. However, analogous to D_{Ra}, we find it difficult to select one that performs the best overall.

	AP ↑	CO ↓	RL ↓	OE ↓
CLR	0.7386	**4.1342**	**0.0895**	0.2526
IBLR	0.6218	5.7395	0.1412	0.4453
MLKNN	0.6907	4.8618	0.1100	0.2926
RAkEL	0.6579	8.0492	0.1951	0.2995
HOMER	0.6591	7.4418	0.1762	0.3089
EML_{Max}	0.6910	4.3029	0.0978	0.3695
EML_{Min}	0.6574	8.7550	0.2165	0.2534
EML_{Mean}	0.7372	4.2997	0.0923	0.2482
EML_{Topk}	**0.7430**	4.3258	0.0929	**0.2179**

Table 8: Comparison of score-based ensembles for D_{Ar} using rank-based metrics.

Table 8 presents the comparison of score-based ensembles with the individual classifiers for D_{Ar} using rank-based evaluation metrics. When the individual multi-label classifiers are compared with each other, we find that CLR performs the best for all of the metrics. However, the combination of multi-label classifiers offers improvements for different evaluation metrics. For example, performance gains are observed for the evaluation metrics AP and OE with an ensemble using the Top-k rule (EML_{Topk}). We also observe that CLR outperforms all of the proposed ensemble techniques for the evaluation metrics CO and RL. Note the difference in CO for CLR and EML_{Mean}. This will be discussed further in Section 6.4.

We find it interesting that for this dataset the average classification performance of each multi-label classifier and ensemble is lower than the performance on D_{Ra}. These results are expected as classification accuracy can be lower if an artist filter is used since an artist is restricted from appearing in both the training and testing sets [16]. This will be discussed further in Section 6.4.

6.3 UniqueAlbum Dataset

Finally, Table 9 shows the comparison of the bipartition-based ensembles with the individual multi-label classifiers for D_{Al} using example-based evaluation metrics. It is easy to see that the results for the individual classifiers are similar to those observed for D_{Ra} and D_{Ar}. Specifically, we find that CLR performs well for HL, F_1 and Prec. while HOMER delivers the best performance for Accu. and Recall. Moreover, when we compare the individual classifiers using label-based metrics, presented in Table 10, we find that CLR and HOMER perform well for various evaluation metrics. However, using the proposed ensemble techniques improves classification performance. Once again, we observe that HLS outperforms the other ensembles and classifiers for the majority of the evaluation metrics. If we exclude HLS from our analysis, we find that the performance of the remaining ensembles is similar to those reported on D_{Ra} and D_{Ar}, i.e., the ensembles demonstrate the best performance for a majority of the evaluation metrics. However, there is

	HL ↓	Accu. ↑	Recall ↑	F_1 ↑	Prec. ↑
CLR	0.0690	0.4240	0.4438	0.7726	0.7915
IBLR	0.0843	0.4327	0.5075	0.7008	0.6239
MLKNN	0.0765	0.3893	0.4105	0.7160	0.7189
RAkEL	0.0844	0.4364	0.5193	0.6830	0.6097
HOMER	0.0837	0.4964	0.5896	0.7077	0.6208
EML_U	0.1071	0.4795	0.7246	0.6465	0.5289
EML_I	0.0788	0.2661	0.2705	0.7156	0.8560
EML_{MV}	0.0687	0.4685	0.4932	0.7551	0.7376
HLS(EML_U)	0.0722	0.5309	**0.7950**	0.6898	0.5778
HLS(EML_I)	0.0505	0.4106	0.4106	**0.9001**	**0.8925**
HLS(EML_{MV})	**0.0444**	**0.5891**	0.6084	0.8479	0.8034
$\text{EML}_{C_n L_k}$	0.0774	0.5115	0.5803	0.7078	0.6272

Table 9: Comparison of bipartition-based ensembles for D_{Al} using example-based metrics.

	MicroP ↑	MicroF_1 ↑	MicroR ↑	MacroP ↑	MacroF_1 ↑	MacroR ↑
CLR	0.7905	0.5522	0.4276	0.7645	0.6965	0.2408
IBLR	0.5977	0.5425	0.4976	0.3931	0.6262	0.3296
MLKNN	0.7206	0.5090	0.3960	0.6664	0.6498	0.2220
RAkEL	0.5942	0.5479	0.5094	0.4929	0.6156	0.3079
HOMER	0.5884	0.5801	0.5753	0.5282	0.6702	0.3394
EML_U	0.4788	0.5739	0.7180	0.3176	0.6098	**0.4924**
EML_I	0.8626	0.3923	0.2558	0.8269	0.5679	0.1400
EML_{MV}	0.7468	0.5822	0.4786	0.7075	0.7246	0.2630
HLS(EML_U)	0.4887	0.5821	**0.7227**	0.2983	0.5937	0.4760
HLS(EML_I)	**0.8925**	0.4613	0.3135	**0.8993**	0.6222	0.1615
HLS(EML_{MV})	0.7852	**0.6102**	0.5004	0.7204	**0.7495**	0.2458
$\text{EML}_{C_n L_k}$	0.6272	0.5956	0.5672	0.6308	0.6484	0.3301

Table 10: Comparison of bipartition-based ensembles for D_{Al} using label-based metrics.

little consistency between the techniques making it difficult to select one that performs the best overall.

	AP ↑	CO ↓	RL ↓	OE ↓
CLR	0.7276	**4.1210**	**0.0872**	0.3052
IBLR	0.6719	4.9301	0.1144	0.3977
MLKNN	0.7134	4.4022	0.0957	0.2916
RAkEL	0.6572	7.2234	0.1725	0.3275
HOMER	0.6341	8.1062	0.1988	0.3527
EML_{Max}	0.6892	4.2461	0.0939	0.3834
EML_{Min}	0.6506	8.7422	0.2130	0.2994
EML_{Mean}	**0.7388**	4.1885	**0.0872**	0.2658
EML_{Topk}	0.7369	4.1936	0.0882	**0.2576**

Table 11: Comparison of score-based ensembles for D_{Al} using rank-based metrics.

Table 11 presents the comparison of score-based ensembles with the individual classifiers for D_{Al} using rank-based evaluation metrics. With regard to the individual multi-label classifiers, we observe that CLR performs the best for all of the metrics. This is analogous to the results presented for D_{Ra} and D_{Ar}. As before, improvements are observed by using the proposed ensemble of multi-label classifiers. Specifically, EML_{Mean} demonstrates the best performance of the proposed ensembles while EML_{Topk} follows shortly behind. Furthermore, we observe that CLR outperforms the other proposed ensemble techniques for Coverage. However, we note that the difference is marginal.

6.4 Discussions

The results in our experiments show the merits of combining multi-label classification algorithms for music genre classification. For all three datasets, we observe improvements to classification performance when using heterogeneous ensemble techniques. However, this performance gain is at the expense of inherent computational cost as individual classifiers need to be trained and combined. Additionally, some of the proposed ensemble techniques provide no improvement and it would be interesting to further explore them. It is important to note that all of the processing and experiments performed in this work are conducted off-line. Therefore, we are not primarily concerned with the inherent computational cost incurred. In the following, we discuss some other related issues.

Frame Size As discussed in Section 5, to capture the fine-timescale structures of music, features are typically extracted from short audio frames. We present a brief systematic exploration of the effects of frame size on multi-label genre classification. We examine the classification performance of each classifier and EML as we adjust the frame size, f_r, represented as the number of samples collected during a certain time period. Each classifier and ensemble is evaluated using $f_r \in \{256, 340, 512, 1024, 2048, 3200, 4096\}$, corresponding to approximately 16ms, 21ms, 32ms, 64ms, 128ms, 200ms, and 256ms, respectively.

For the sake of space, we only present the performance of the proposed ensembles along with two individual classification algorithms for comparison using D_{Ra}. Figure 2 shows the classification performance of the proposed bipartition-based ensembles along with CLR and HOMER using the evaluation metric HL. Moreover, Figure 3 shows the classification performance of the proposed score-based ensembles using the evaluation metric AP. We observe that the pro-

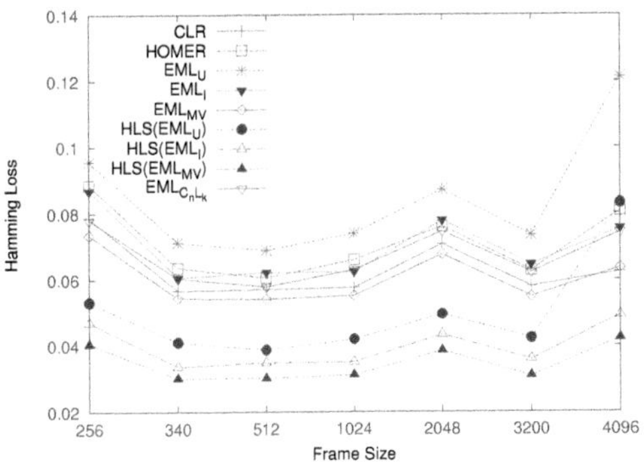

Figure 2: Bipartition-based ensemble performance using D_{Ra} for various frame sizes.

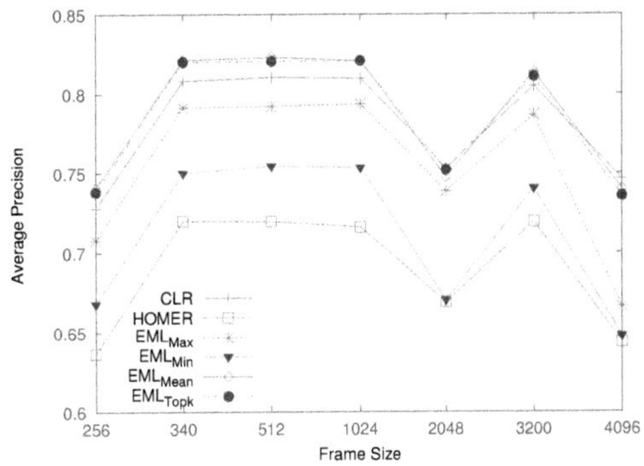

Figure 3: Score-based ensemble performance using D_{Ra} for various frame sizes.

posed ensembles tend to perform well when $f_r = \{340, 512, 1024, 3200\}$. However, we note a decrease in performance when $f_r = \{2048, 4096\}$. These results are consistently observed for the other evaluation metrics and datasets with the exception that classification performance increases for D_{Al} when $f_r = 4096$. These results lend support to the notion of using a frame size of 23ms, as proposed by various other works.

k	AP ↑	CO ↓	RL ↓	OE ↓
2	0.8118	3.2420	0.0575	0.1950
3	**0.8195**	**3.1690**	**0.0550**	0.1820
4	0.8194	3.2000	0.0559	**0.1760**
5	0.8100	**3.1690**	0.0553	0.1900

Table 12: Classification performance of EML_{Topk} for different k.

Top-k rule: The Top-k rule (EML_{Topk}) selects the top k largest scores and averages them, where k is a user-selected parameter. To determine this value, we perform a series of experiments on D_{Ra} and examine the performance as we adjust k. Table 12 shows the classification performance of EML_{Topk} where $k \in \{2, 3, 4, 5\}$ using the evaluation metrics AP, CO, RL, and OE. We observe that EML_{Topk} demonstrates good achievement on D_{Ra} when $k = 3$ for the majority of evaluation metrics. We note that when k is set to the number of classifiers in the ensemble, the result will be the same as the one obtained using the Mean rule.

Score-based Label Selection: Similar to the Top-k rule, we perform a series of experiments on D_{Ra} to determine the values of n and k for $EML_{C_nL_k}$. Recall that in this ensemble, we first select the top n scores and then select the top k class labels accordingly. Table 13 shows the classification performance of $EML_{C_nL_k}$ using the evaluation metrics HLoss, Accu., Recall, F_1, and Prec. We observe that as both values of n and k increase, classification performance tends to decrease for the evaluation metrics. We can see that $EML_{C_nL_k}$ performs best when $n = 3$ and $k = 2$. This could be plausibly explained by the label cardinality which is between 2 and 3 for each instance in our datasets, as shown in Table 2. It is important to note that we examine a wide range of values for n and k. However, due to space limitations, we only report a subset of the results.

Hierarchical Label Substitution: From the results presented above, we observe that Hierarchical Label Substitution (HLS) outperforms the bipartition-based ensemble techniques for a majority of the evaluation metrics. Moreover, significant performance gains are observed for all of the dataset when HLS is used with one of the proposed bipartition-based ensemble techniques. For example, there is a 14.51% increase in Prec. for D_{Ra} when compared to CLR. These results are attributed to the simplification of the label space by reducing the number of possible "overlapping" genres. We believe this ensemble produces a common set of high-level genres which is closer to the human experience.

	HLoss ↓	Accu. ↑	Recall ↑	F_1 ↑	Prec. ↑
n=3, k=2	**0.0603**	**0.6255**	0.6725	**0.7799**	**0.7380**
n=4, k=2	0.0674	0.5799	0.6366	0.7422	0.6990
n=5, k=2	0.0681	0.5786	0.6328	0.7484	0.6950
n=5, k=3	0.0820	0.5339	0.7825	0.7034	0.5790
n=5, k=5	0.1483	0.3902	**0.8934**	0.5611	0.4016
n=10, k=3	0.1398	0.3006	0.4876	0.5230	0.3670

Table 13: Classification performance of $EML_{C_nL_k}$ for different n and k.

Data Selection We observe, on average, that D_{Ra} achieves the best dataset performance as shown in Tables 3, 4, and 5. Moreover, classification performance on D_{Ar} is lower than D_{Ra} and D_{Al}. The artist filter limits performance by restricting artists from appearing in both the training and testing sets. In addition, D_{Al} employs an album filter to exclude music pieces from the same album appearing in both training and testing sets. However, this does not exclude artists from appearing in them. For this reason, we observe that the classification performance on D_{Al} is better than D_{Ar} but worse than D_{Ra}. We also notice a larger difference in the performance of the multi-label classifiers and ensemble techniques between D_{Ar} and D_{Al}. For example, if we examine the evaluation metric CO for CLR and EML_{Mean} we find that the difference between them in D_{Ar} (see Table 8) is larger than the difference between them in D_{Al} (see Table 11). This is due to the data selection as there is some possible overlap in D_{Al}, as discussed above.

7. CONCLUSION

In this work, we propose a set of ensemble techniques that not only improve upon individual multi-label classification algorithms, but also overcomes their limitations as aforementioned. For all of the datasets, we observe improvements to classification performance when using ensemble techniques. To the best of our knowledge, this is the first study that aims to combine heterogeneous multi-label classification algorithms for music genre classification.

To improve the impact of this work, we plan to use more multi-label classification algorithms and investigate other ensemble techniques. From our study, we observe that some of the proposed ensemble techniques provide no improvements and it would be interesting to further explore them. A wealth of work exists surrounding the area of ensemble methods and may offer some insight. Moreover, further investigation is needed into the selection of classifier parameters. Finally, while we focus on the computational classification of music genres, it would be interesting to investigate how to combine our conclusions here with human perception of music. We believe that this could further improve music genre prediction.

8. REFERENCES

[1] J. J. Aucouturier and F. Pachet. Representing musical genre: A state of the art. *J. New Music Research*, 32(1):83–93, 2003.

[2] J. J. Aucouturier and F. Pachet. Improving timbre similarity: How high is the sky? *J, of Negative Results in Speech and Audio Sciences*, 1(1), 2004.

[3] J. Bergstra, N. Casagrande, D. Erhan, D. Eck, and B. Kgl. Aggregate features and AdaBoost for music classification. *Machine Learning: Special Issue on Machine Learning in Music*, 65(2-3):2–3, 2006.

[4] N. V. Chawla and J. Sylvester. Exploiting diversity in ensembles: improving the performance on unbalanced datasets. In *Proc. Int'l Conf. on Multiple Classifier Systems*, pages 397–406, 2007.

[5] W. Cheng and E. Hullermeier. Combining instance-based learning and logistic regression for multilabel classification. *Machine Learning*, 76(2-3):211–225, 2009.

[6] J. Futrelle and J. S. Downie. Interdisciplinary communities and research issues in music information retrieval. In *Proc. Int'l Conf. Music Information Retrieval*, pages 121–131, 2002.

[7] M. Ioannou, G. Sakkas, G. Tsoumakas, and I. Vlahavas. Obtaining bipartitions from score vectors for Multi-Label classification. In *Proc. Int'l Conf. Tools with Artificial Intelligence*, pages 409–416, 2010.

[8] L. Kuncheva. *Combining Pattern Classifiers: Methods and Algorithms*. Wiley-Interscience, 2004.

[9] E. Law and L. von Ahn. Input-agreement: a new mechanism for collecting data using human computation games. In *Proc. Int'l Conf. Human Factors in Computing Systems*, pages 1197–1206, 2009.

[10] H. Lukashevich, J. Abeßer, C. Dittmar, and H. Grossmann. From multi-labeling to multi-domain-labeling: A novel two-dimensional approach to music genre classification. In *Proc. Int'l Conf. Music Information Retrieval*, pages 459–464, 2009.

[11] C. McKay and I. Fujinaga. Musical genre classification: Is it worth pursuing and how can it be improved? In *Proc. Int'l Conf. Music Information Retrieval*, pages 101–106, 2006.

[12] S. R. Ness, A. Theocharis, G. Tzanetakis, and L. G. Martins. Improving automatic music tag annotation using stacked generalization of probabilistic svm outputs. In *Proc. ACM Int'l Conf. Multimedia*, pages 705–708, 2009.

[13] F. Pachet. Content management for electronic music distribution: The real issues. *Comm. of the ACM*, 46(4):71–75, 2003.

[14] F. Pachet and D. Cazaly. A taxonomy of musical genres. In *Proc. Content-Based Multimedia Information Access*, 2000.

[15] F. Pachet and P. Roy. Improving multi-label analysis of music titles: A large-scale validation of the correction hypothesis. *IEEE Trans. on Audio, Speech & Language Processing*, 17(2):335–343, 2009.

[16] E. Pampalk, A. Flexer, and G. Widmer. Improvements of audio-based music similarity and genre classification. In *Proc. Int'l Conf. Music Information Retrieval*, pages 628–633, 2005.

[17] C. Sanden, C. R. Befus, and J. Z. Zhang. Perception based multi-label genre classification on music data. In *Proc. Int'l Computer Music Conf.*, pages 9–15, 2010.

[18] M. Tahir, J. Kittler, K. Mikolajczyk, and F. Yan. Improving multilabel classification performance by using ensemble of multi-label classifiers. In *Multiple Classifier Systems*, volume 5997, chapter 2, pages 11–21. Springer Berlin Heidelberg, 2010.

[19] K. Trohidis, G. Tsoumakas, G. Kalliris, and I. Vlahavas. Multilabel classification of music into emotions. In *Proc. Int'l Conf. Music Information Retrieval*, pages 325–330, 2008.

[20] G. Tsoumakas and I. Katakis. Multi-label classification: An overview. *Int'l J. Data Warehousing and Mining*, 3(3):1–13, 2007.

[21] G. Tsoumakas, I. Katakis, and I. Vlahavas. Mining multi-label data. *Data Mining and Knowledge Discovery Handbook*, 2010.

[22] G. Tsoumakas, J. Vilcek, E. Spyromitros, and I. Vlahavas. Mulan: A Java library for multi-label learning. *J. Machine Learning Research, Accepted*, 2010.

[23] G. Tzanetakis and P. Cook. Musical genre classification of audio signals. In *IEEE Trans. on Speech and Audio Processing*, pages 293–302, 2002.

[24] D. Wang, T. Li, and M. Ogihara. Are tags better than audio? The effect of joint use of tags and audio content features for artistic style clustering. In *Proc. Int'l Conf. Music Information Retrieval*, pages 57–62, 2010.

[25] A. Wieczorkowska, P. Synak, and R. Zbigniew. Multi-label classification of emotions in music. In *Intelligent Information Processing and Web Mining*, Advances in Soft Computing, pages 307–315. 2006.

[26] M. L. Zhang and Z. H. Zhou. ML-*k*NN: A lazy learning approach to multi-label learning. *Pattern Recognition*, 40(7):2038–2048, 2007.

PICASSO – To Sing you must Close Your Eyes and Draw *

Aleksandar Stupar
Saarland University
Saarbrücken, Germany
astupar@mmci.uni-saarland.de

Sebastian Michel
Saarland University
Saarbrücken, Germany
smichel@mmci.uni-saarland.de

ABSTRACT

We study the problem of automatically assigning appropriate music pieces to a picture or, in general, series of pictures. This task, commonly referred to as soundtrack suggestion, is non-trivial as it requires a lot of human attention and a good deal of experience, with master pieces distinguished, e.g., with the Academy Award for Best Original Score. We put forward PICASSO to solve this task in a fully automated way. PICASSO makes use of genuine samples obtained from first-class contemporary movies. Hence, the training set can be arbitrarily large and is also inexpensive to obtain but still provides an excellent source of information. At query time, PICASSO employs a three-level algorithm. First, it selects for a given query image a ranking of the most similar screenshots taken, and subsequently, selects for each screenshot the most similar songs to the music played in the movie when the screenshot was taken. Last, it issues a top-K aggregation algorithm to find the overall best suitable songs available. We have created a large training set consisting of over 40,000 image/soundtrack samples obtained from 28 movies and evaluated the suitability of PICASSO by means of a user study.

Categories and Subject Descriptors

H.3.1 [**Content Analysis and Indexing**]: [abstracting methods, indexing methods]; H.3.3 [**Information Search and Retrieval**]: [search process, selection process]; H.5.5 [**Sound and Music Computing**]: [methodologies and techniques]; I.4 [**Image Processing and Computer Vision**]: Applications

General Terms

Algorithms, Experimentation, Human Factors

Keywords

Automatic Music Selection, Background Music, Slide Show, Soundtrack Recommendation

1. INTRODUCTION

Presenting the most impressive pictures from the last vacation on a Greek island can be spiced up with a well chosen background music that underpins the beauty and ease of life enjoyed in the last summer. Being faced with these problems from time to time, unfortunately not often enough with pictures of Greek islands, we experience that choosing the right music is everything but trivial. A good solution to this problem must have a big repository of music to choose from to allow for a high level of diversity to avoid playing the same old "born to be wild" song for all pictures somehow related to motorbikes, for instance. While the requirement of having many songs is relatively easy to fulfill, and in fact is fulfilled already with the amount of, and often also diverse, songs on the personal mp3 players, the challenge of selecting the right song, out of hundreds or even thousands of songs, becomes difficult. To tackle the problem, we have devised a fully automated approach, coined PICASSO, which is not only the name of the famous painter, Pablo Picasso, but also an acronym for *PIcture CAtegorization for Suggesting SOundtracks*. PICASSO makes use of training data obtained by sampling screenshot/soundtrack pairs from popular common movies, to learn an appropriate mapping from images to music at first hand, given the expertise of professional movie directors.

Sketch of the approach: Given a set of movies, we take random samples of them. For a given sample point, we investigate if the corresponding sound surrounding the sample by a couple of seconds resembles a piece of music. If so, we take the screenshot and the music piece and consider it as training data to our approach. We do this for very many samples, for dozens of movies. The set of considered movies should be large enough and also diverse such that the training base is big enough and also the resulting categorization captures all (or almost all) situations appearing in pictures people take.

At query time, we obtain an image, uploaded to our Web application, and, roughly speaking, in a naïve approach, find first the most similar screenshots taken (in the training phase) and then pick the most similar music piece in

*The original quote "To draw you must close your eyes and sing" by Pablo Picasso has been reverted to become the main theme of our approach.
This work has been supported by the Excellence Cluster on Multimodal Computing and Interaction (MMCI).

SIGIR'11, July 24–28, 2011, Beijing, China.

our song database compared the soundtrack at the time the screenshot was taken.

Admittedly, we tamper a bit with Pablo Picasso's quote *"To draw you must close your eyes and sing."*, trying to figure out if the inverse holds, too, namely, if we manage to find music (singing) by looking at pictures (drawings).

1.1 Contribution and Outline

With this paper we make the following contributions:

(i) We present an algorithm for soundtrack recommendation for an arbitrary wide range of user generated images as input.

(ii) We show how a training dataset to achieve this goal can easily be extracted out of popular common movies, capturing the knowledge of experienced movie directors.

(iii) Two cases of soundtrack recommendation, for single image and for multiple images, with grouping of multiple images, are described.

(iv) We report on the results of a user study evaluating the suitability of our approach.

This paper is organized as follows. Section 2 gives an overview of the related work. Section 3 presents our framework and briefly recaps basic techniques and similarity measures used in our approach. Section 4 presents the core concepts of PICASSO. Section 5 shows experiments results. Section 6 concludes the paper and gives an outlook on ongoing work.

2. RELATED WORK

Although the problem of soundtrack suggestion has been addressed in a couple of recent publications, it received relatively low attention. This is surprising given the vast amount of potential users, in particular with the increasing number of digital cameras and the big success of portals like Youtube [30] and Flickr [9].

Approaches based on language models, built for both the image and the soundtrack (song), are proposed in [29, 3]. By design, these approaches are only applicable to the songs with known lyrics, hence, ignore a huge area of classical music and all other instrumental music pieces. In addition, these approaches are limited in the way the language models are created, as the initial dataset of image annotations is very sparse. While the approach in [3] is able to recommend only images obtained from web, using publicly available image search engines, the approach in [29] is able to infer image annotations to personal images using an image similarity measure based on low level features. However, none of these approaches address the problem of recommending the soundtrack to a given image(s), instead, they start with the given soundtrack and then find the set of images to accompany the soundtrack.

The problem of recommending a soundtrack for a set of images and combining them into a slide show is addressed in [15]. This work focuses on impressionism paintings, matching the emotions in soundtracks with the emotions in a given painting, hence, does not address a general set of images (e.g., photographs). Emotions are discovered using a trained classifier on low level features for both the paintings and the music.

The approach in [5] considers the problem of suggesting music, generated from midi files, to car drivers, given a video of the scenery, taken by a camera installed in the car. The correlation, learned from a set of documentary movies, between a limited number of features (three for videos and three for music pieces) using only three quantization levels for each of the features, were explored and used later on for the recommendation. In contrast to their work, we aim at supporting a larger variety of images and aim at providing music suggestions based on arbitrary music collections, such as the users' personal mp3 collection.

Research on automatic video generation systems has been presented in [12, 13, 28]. The main focus of these works is on aligning the video transitions with the transitions in a given music piece. Although the ultimate aim of the proposed work is different to ours, the similarity with our work comes from a fact that both video (image) and audio content are explored for purpose of alignment (recommendation). Our approach could serve as a way to generate input to this automatic video generation, as recommended soundtracks can be feed into these systems for alignment and video generation.

We base our approach on low level features for both image-to-image and song-to-song similarity measures. The best proven low level features for image similarity used in object recognition are SIFT local image features [16]. However, the extraction of these features result in a large number of feature vectors per image and their comparison for image similarity is computationally more demanding than methods based on global image features (e.g., MPEG-7). Concerning this and the fact that we wanted to capture the "global" feeling of the image rather than individual localized features, we use standardized MPEG-7 [18, 4] color and texture low level features for computing the image-to-image similarity.

For the song-to-song similarity measure, we use both the spectral shape and temporal low level features. The spectral decomposition representation based on mel scale of human auditory system, named MFCC, has been used extensively in speech recognition [20], music genre classification [26], artist identification [17], etc. Beside MFCC, we use Chroma features [7], which represent the song's spectrum in intensity measures of each of twelve semitones of the musical scale. We also used spectral centroid, spectral rolloff, spectral flux, and time domain zero crossings music features described in [26]. All music low level features are extracted using the open source software framework Marsyas [27].

3. FRAMEWORK

PICASSO is based on the expertise of movie directors to select appropriate songs for specific scenes in their movies. This knowledge is made public, naturally, when movies are presented in cinemas, TV, or DVD, generating a huge knowledge base that perfectly fits our goal. We extract samples of screenshot/soundtrack pairs from a certain amount of these movies and feed them to our framework.

As a final training dataset we aim at having, for each of the screenshots taken, a list of songs (for instance, the user's private mp3 collection), which are available for recommendation, in decreasing order of likelihood to be recommended for a specific screenshot. Building this dataset is done in the following steps:

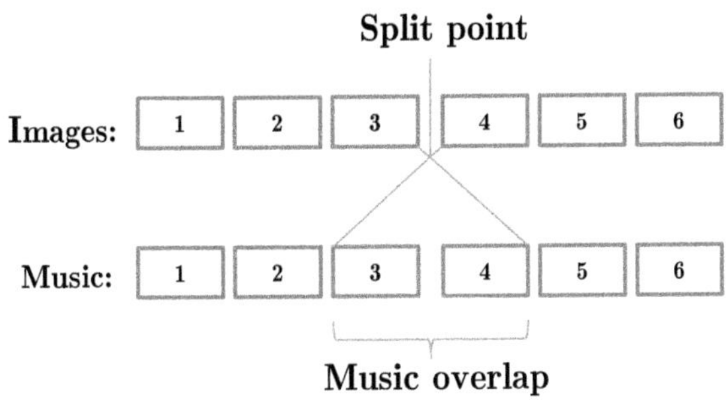

Figure 1: Splitting of the long scene

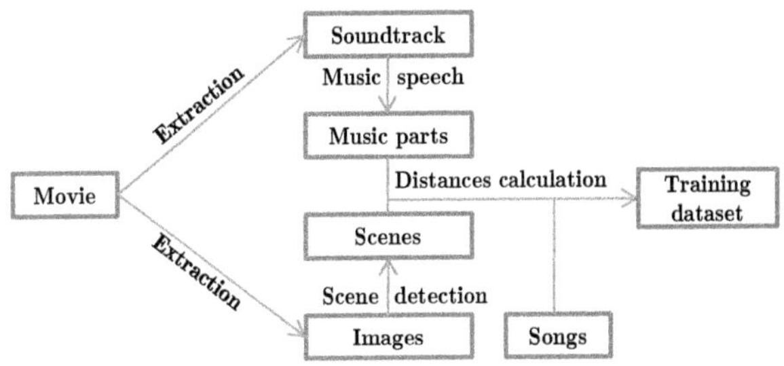

Figure 2: Training dataset building process

(i) the soundtrack of the movie is extracted
(ii) music/speech classification is done on the soundtrack
(ii) speech parts are discarded
(iv) screenshots, during the musical part, are taken
(v) parts of the same scene are detected
(vi) soundtrack is split according to the scenes
(vii) for each soundtrack part the distance to all songs is calculated
(viii) the song lists are sorted in increasing order of distance, resulting in our training set

Soundtrack and image extraction, from the movies, are easily achievable using one of many available tools and will not be covered here in greater depth. However, music/speech classification is not straight forward. For this task, we use the Naive Bayes [22] classifier, trained using the labeled dataset available at [19]. This training dataset for music/speech classification contains 64 speech samples, in different languages, and also 64 music samples of different genres. The already mentioned low level features (i.e., MFCC, Chroma, spectral centroid, spectral rolloff, spectral flux and time domain zero crossing) are used to train the classifier and for the later classification task. The Marsyas [27] tool is used for both the features extraction and the classification. The output of the classifier for a given soundtrack is a label (i.e., "music" or "speech") for each second of the soundtrack together with a confidence value. To be sure to use only the musical parts of the soundtrack, all parts that are classified as a music with the confidence value less than 95% and all speech parts are discarded. Musical parts of the soundtrack with length shorter than five seconds are also discarded, as they do not contain enough information to make the similarity measurement with the songs appropriate.

Screenshots are taken from the movies at each second of the remaining musical parts and, to obtain a more logical grouping, we divide these musical parts further into scenes. The scene detection is implemented by splitting the sequence of screenshots on positions where the image-to-image distance, measured as described in Section 3.1, is larger than a given threshold. The sequence of the screenshots from one split to the second one is considered a scene. This approach may not lead to exact movie scenes but, as we are only interested in image-to-image similarities for the further processing, it provides a reasonable grouping of similar images. To eliminate abrupt scene changes, for the same reason, we have eliminated short musical parts, i.e., we filter out and discard detected scenes whose length is shorter than 5 seconds.

Additionally, very long musical themes can cause problems as a too large amount of information can render them too specific and, hence, would not match to any parts of the available songs. This is why scenes, that are longer than 10 seconds, are split in multiple parts. Splitting these long scenes in multiple parts also improves the locality connection between the soundtrack part and the taken screenshot. To split the long scenes into smaller parts and to make musical parts of approximately the same length, we split the long scenes so that screenshots sequences are disjunctive, but with the possibility of having overlap between the music parts as illustrated in Figure 1. Screenshots together with links to theirs corresponding music parts are then saved for further processing.

After the musical parts are cut, first based on the music/speech classification and then based on scene detection, the distances between each of the musical parts of the soundtrack and all of the songs are calculated. The distance measure between the musical parts and the songs is described in Section 3.2. Songs are then ordered in increasing order of distance for each of the musical parts.

These ordered lists of songs together with the links from the taken screenshots represent our training dataset, which is later used for soundtrack recommendation, c.f., Figure 3 for an illustration. Each screenshot taken from the movie has a link to the part of the accompanying soundtrack which has a list of songs ordered by their distance to the soundtrack. The complete process of building the training dataset, from soundtrack extraction to song distance calculation, is illustrated in Figure 2.

3.1 Image Similarity Measure

For the image-to-image similarity measurement *we use the following MPEG-7 feature vectors* extracted from the images: scalable color, color structure, color layout, and edge histogram.

Scalable color describes all the colors found in the image by aggregating them in a color histogram. Each bin of the histogram represent one level of the color quantization. To lower the memory space needed for the histogram, the Haar transform [11, 25] is used for encoding. The standard defines three possible values for the number of Haar coefficients used: 128, 64, and 32.

The **color structure** descriptor is represented also by a histogram, where each bin represents the quantization of the color space and the value of the bin is a counter for the structuring elements, of 8×8 size, in which the respective color appears. Counting of color appearances is done while sliding the structural element over the whole image. The number of color quantization levels is a parameter for this descriptor and can by 184, 120, 64, and 32 as defined by the standard.

The **color layout** descriptor tries to summarize the distribution of colors in a given image, using YCbCr color space. First, the image is divided into 64 (8×8) equal sized parts and, in a second step, the average color for each of the parts is calculated. Discrete cosine transform (DCT) is performed on these 64 parts and only low frequency coefficients, for each component, are used.

The **edge histogram** descriptor is used for the spatial representation of the edges in the image. The image is divided into 16 (4×4) equal sized parts and the local edge histogram for each part is calculated. Each histogram has 5 bins representing 4 orientation directions and one used for non orientation specific edges. Concatenation of the local histograms with the histogram levels quantization produces the final descriptor.

In this work, we use common configurations of the MPEG-7 image descriptor coefficients, with 64 Haar coefficients for scalable color descriptor, 64 color quantization levels for color structure descriptor and 6 coefficients for Y component, 3 for Cr component and 3 for Cb component of the color layout descriptor.

After the distance calculation, for each of the descriptors, we need to combine them in one distance measurement for further comparison. We do this by first calculating the *standard score (z-score)* for each of the descriptors and then summing up all of the standard scores into a single score. The standard score is calculated by Formula 1, where μ is the expected value (mean) of the distances for the given descriptor and σ is the standard deviation of the distances for the same descriptor.

$$z = \frac{x - \mu}{\sigma} \quad (1)$$

The mean μ and the standard deviation σ for the descriptors are approximated from the training dataset. The distances between each pair of the images, for each of the descriptors, are calculated, and then the mean and the standard deviation for the descriptor are approximated by the estimated mean and standard deviation of this set of calculated distances.

3.2 Music Similarity Measure

For the music similarity measures, the following low level musical descriptors are used: *MFCC*, *Chroma*, *spectral centroid*, *spectral rolloff*, *spectral flux*, and *time domain zero crossing*.

Most of the musical low level descriptors are based on the spectral representation of a given musical signal. The spectral representation is given by employing a short time Fourier transform on the signal. Each descriptor uses different characteristics of the spectral representations to emphasize certain features of a musical signal.

The **Mel Frequency Cepstral Coefficients (MFCC)** [20, 26, 17]descriptor is based on the mel scale, model of the human auditory system, emphasizing the spectral distribution of a signal in the manner perceived by humans. First,

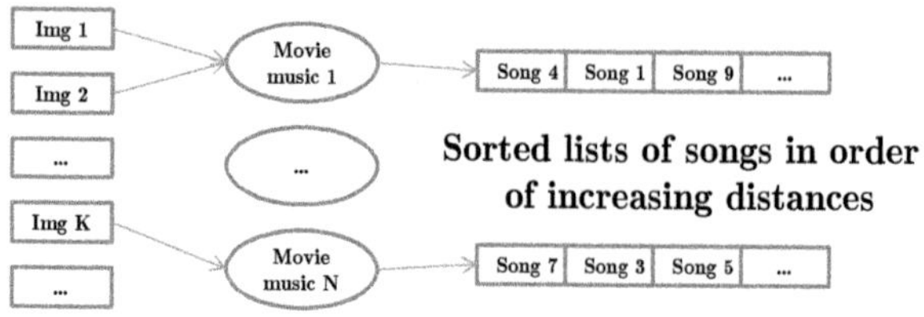

Figure 3: Training dataset structure

the spectral representation of a musical signal is transformed by the model and then the coefficients of the discrete cosine transform (DCT) are used as features. The DCT coefficients are used to lower the space requirement and save as much of the uncorrelated information as possible.

As the western music is based on a musical scales containing a subset of twelve basic musical semitones, the **Chroma descriptor** [7] represents the intensity of each of twelve semitones in the analyzed music part. It is a very valuable descriptor, used for musical similarity measurement, as it highly emphasizes melodical and harmonical characteristics of the analyzed musical piece.

The **spectral centroid** is defined as a center of gravity of a musical signal's spectral representation, while the **spectral rolloff** represents the frequency under which 85% of the signal's magnitude is located. The local spectral change, in the time domain, is represented by the **spectral flux** which is calculated as a squared difference between two successive spectral distributions. The **time domain zero crossing**, describing the noisiness of the signal, is defined as a number of times a musical signal crosses between positive and negative values in the time domain.

To calculate the similarity between two songs first the feature vectors of each of the descriptors are extracted for every 23.25 milliseconds of the song, resulting in 43 feature vectors per second (the default configuration for the Marsyas tool). Then, the pairwise similarity between the feature vectors is calculated and combined. The combination of distances of different descriptors into one distance measurement is done also using the sum of standard scores for each descriptor, as described in Section 3.1. The mean and the standard deviation for the standard scores are approximated using the mean and the standard deviation of the pairwise distances between the songs in the training dataset.

Calculating only pairwise distances between feature vectors is not enough as music also has a time dimension. One option to handle the time dimension is to calculate the sum of successive pairwise distances. As this option results in rigid comparison in time dimension, we use a more flexible option called Dynamic Time Warping [23]. **Dynamic Time Warping (DTW)** enables sequence matching with the variations in speed, making it possible to compare songs that are similar in content but with different speed measures. As speed change can be beneficial for the flexibility it also has to be limited such that the similarity between songs with different speed measures is less than between the songs with the same speed measure. This is also achievable using DTW by specifying the slope constrained condition and by specifying *Weighting Coefficient* for the case of speed change (time warp) and the case of no speed change (no time warp). In this work we use symetric variant of DTW with slope con-

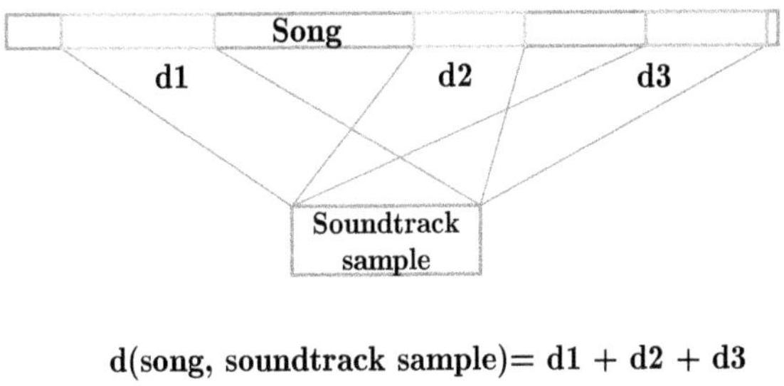

Figure 4: Song to soundtrack sample distance

strained condition set to 1, and with the value of $\sqrt{2}$ for the *Weighting Coefficient* in case of speed change and value 1 for the case of no speed change.

Beside giving us a distance, as a result, DWT also gives us a part of the song that matches the best to the other song. Because soundtrack samples are a lot shorter than the songs in general, we use DWT to find *three* positions in the song that are most similar to the soundtrack sample. The sum of distances between the soundtrack sample and these three positions in the song is used as the resulting distance between the song and the soundtrack sample, as illustrated in Figure 4.

4. APPROACH

Once the training dataset is extracted we can use it for soundtrack recommendation. We consider two types of recommendations, single image recommendation and multiple images recommendation.

- In the single image recommendation, one image is submitted as a query and a list of songs is returned, in decreasing order of their suitability to the query image.

- In case of multiple images, we consider the images as the input for the slide show generation and try to recommend a grouping of the images together with the songs recommended for each of the groups. We base the grouping of the images on the similarity between the lists of recommended songs for each of the image.

They key idea of finding the most suitable song for a query image is to employ two phases of K-nearest neighbor searches, first, in the image domain, and second, between musical pieces. Selecting the K-Nearest Neighbors (KNN) means that in a multi-dimensional feature space, for a given feature vector the K nearest feature vectors are selected (cf., [24] for an overview).

Phase 1: When the query image is submitted, its distance to each of the images in training dataset is calculated. The images in the training dataset are then ordered in increasing order of distances to the query image and only the top-K images (i.e., the K-nearest neighbors) are used for the further recommendation process. We focus only on the effectiveness in this task and omit any optimizations or approximations of the K-Nearest Neighbors search to speed up the overall runtime. However, once runtime becomes an issue, we can benefit from the rich literature on the KNN problem, which has been extensively studied (cf., e.g., [2, 10, 1, 6]).

Phase 2: After the top-K images are found, the list of the songs together with their score for each image is retrieved. First, the name of the soundtrack sample for each image is retrieved and then the list of songs, ordered in increasing order of distance to the soundtrack sample, is retrieved for that soundtrack sample. As a result, each image, retrieved from the training set, has a list of songs in decreasing score order to that image. To avoid a negative impact of outliers to the recommendation process, smoothing is applied on the top-K retrieved songs for each of the top-K retrieved images.

For smoothing purposes, we first assign the score to each of the top-K retrieved images based on the similarity. The score is normalized to the $[0.1, 1]$ interval by Formula 2, where d is the distance of the image to the query image, m is the distance to the most similar image (i.e., the smallest distance), and M is the distance to the least similar image (i.e., the largest distance). Each of the image scores is then further assigned to the top-K songs in the list of corresponding images. An average score for each song is then calculated and used to reorder the songs. The ordered list of songs, by their new calculated score, is returned as the final list of recommendations.

$$z = 1 - 0.9 * \frac{d - m}{M - m} \tag{2}$$

For each of the K images we get K songs, leading to a final number of songs between K (in case of heavy redundancy) and K^2 (in case of no redundancy), which, after duplicate elimination and a final ranking, assembles the final result list. In our experimental evaluation, we use $K = 10$.

While a fully automated process requires only one suggestion, in a semi automated approach we could easily return many results to let users do the final assignment. To show that the ranking is meaningful, i.e., the rank 1 is preferred over lower ranks, we also evaluate the performance at rank K.

4.1 The Case of Multiple Images

When multiple images are given as input, we group these images using a clustering algorithm and recommend a soundtrack for each of the groups. To achieve this, we first perform the recommendation for each of the images. This results in the list of recommended soundtracks for each input image. The similarity between these recommendation lists is then used as the grouping criteria and is computed using a slightly modified Spearman's footrule distance measure [8], as follows.

First, we find the length of the shortest list as the length of the list depends on the number of unique songs in the top-K songs for each of the top-K similar images from the dataset. The lists are cut at the length of the shortest list to make the pairwise similarity measure comparable. The similarity between two lists l_1 and l_2 is calculated by Formula 3, where L is the length of the lists, and pos_1 and pos_2 are positions where the song s is located in each of the lists. If a song is found in only one of the lists, score is left unchanged, as specified by the formula.

As we can see, this kind of similarity measure takes into account not only the overlap between the lists but also an ordering of songs in the lists, imposing that the lists with the same ordering will be more similar than the ones with the same overlap but different ordering. As the Spearman's footrule distance is defined over full (i.e., complete) rankings, we adjust it to be used also for our partial rankings (top-K lists) (cf., [8]) by ignoring the songs not present in one of the lists. Also, the list length L is added to the formula with subtracted $L1$ distance, turning the measure into a similarity measure.

$$sim(l_1, l_2) = \sum_{s \in l_1 \wedge s \in l_2} L - |pos_1 - pos_2| \quad (3)$$

The similarity matrix, containing all pairwise similarities between the lists, is calculated and used for a *bottom-up hierarchical clustering* which produces a grouping of images as a result. We use a hierarchical clustering with the explicit number of clusters and the maximum cluster size specified. The process of clustering begins with creating a cluster for each image instance (i.e., list) and then iteratively merging the clusters until the required number of clusters is achieved. In each step, all pairs of clusters, except those whose cumulative size becomes larger than the specified cluster size limit, are considered for merging. Two clusters whose pairwise similarity is smallest, compared to other cluster pairs, are merged. The pairwise similarity between clusters is defined as the average pairwise similarity between their instances as shown in Formula 4, where c_1 and c_2 are clusters, i_1 and i_2 are their instances respectively. Cluster sizes, represented by $|c_1|$ and $|c_2|$, are defined as the number of instances in each of the clusters.

$$sim(c_1, c_2) = \frac{1}{|c_1| \cdot |c_2|} \sum_{i_1 \in c_1 \wedge i_2 \in c_2} sim(i_1, i_2) \quad (4)$$

In our experiments, we use the floor of the number of input images divided by 5 for the number of clusters, aiming at the clusters with average size of 5 images, and we use 7 as the specified cluster size maximum.

After the grouping of the images is finished a soundtrack needs to be recommended for each of the groups. We use two approaches for group recommendation, *average position* and *least misery*. First, we find all the songs that are present in all of the lists for a specific group. If there are no songs present in all of the lists, we find all of the songs present in $n-1$ lists, where n is the number of the lists. If there are no songs present in $n-1$ lists, we find the songs present in $n-2$ lists, and so on.

- For the **average position** approach, we calculate the average position for each song found in the previous step. Songs are then reordered based on their average position in increasing order and the song with the smallest average position (best average ranking) is recommended for that group. The average ranking can sometimes be misleading for a group recommendation, as some group members can be highly disappointed by the recommendation but the average satisfaction is still high because of the high satisfaction of other group members.

- The **least misery** approach is used in group recommendation with intention to circumvent this problem. In least misery approach group recommendation is valued as a value gained by the group member who likes the recommendation the least. In our case, we find the maximum position (lowest rank) for each of the songs found in previous step and use this position as a score for recommendation. Like for the average ranking approach, songs are reordered on their new score in increasing order, and the song with the smallest score is recommended for that group.

5. EXPERIMENTAL EVALUATION

The training dataset used for the experiments is distilled, as described in Section 3, out of 28 movies of different genres. The movies were selected to have a high variance in content, with the intention to provide a high coverage of the training dataset, without having to process very many (random) movies. Processing these 28 movies resulted in 46,594 screenshots taken, with approximately 13 hours of accompanying soundtrack music.

We use 275 songs as potential soundtrack recommendations. As these songs are played to the users during the performed user study, we had to make sure to use only copyright free material. We obtained this dataset by downloading songs from the music2ten site [21], a site which contains only music given away by its creators for free use, as stated on the site: "All the music selections at music2ten.com are MP3s that are given away free with the artists' blessings.". As our songs dataset contains fairly unknown material, i.e., artists are not promoted by the big labels, it assures that there is no bias in users' assessments towards more popular songs.

5.1 Evaluation Set Up

To obtain a meaningful evaluation in absence of a publicly available benchmark, we conducted a user study for both cases of recommendation, the single image recommendation and the recommendation for the case of multiple images. We have asked users from our university environment to grade the suitability (aka., relevance, appropriateness) of a suggested soundtrack w.r.t. a given image or to the given slide show, in case of multiple images. Users were provided with the following options: "fits very good", "fits good", "fits ok", "does not fit" and "total miss". We assign grades from 5 to 1 for each of the option for the further numerical analysis of the results. Grade 5 is assigned to "fits very good", 4 to "fits good", and so on, having grade 1 for "total miss".

We include a random recommendation to the user study to help us interpreting the results. Additionally, to be able to see how much the ranking of the recommended soundtracks make sense, we include also the recommended soundtrack at rank 10 in the evaluation of the single image case. That means, during the evaluation, users were asked to grade the first ranked, the tenth ranked, and a randomly recommended soundtrack for each query image. To get consistent results for the random recommendation, a song was randomly chosen for every query image and then used consistently throughout the whole study (i.e., for all users).

The evaluation is performed using an online tool which we have developed, shown in Figure 5. This tool enables users to play three recommended songs for each query image, and to choose how well each song fits to the query. The user judgment on how well some soundtrack fits to the query may be influenced by the previously heard recommended soundtrack. That is why the evaluation tool places the songs on the web page in random order. The order of songs in which

	Average position	Least misery	Random
Average	3.69	3.31	2.38
Std. Dev.	0.95	0.95	1.26
With aggrement	3.90	3.49	1.89

Table 1: Multiple images grades

	First rec.	Tenth rec.	Random
Average	3.21	3.08	2.97
Std. Dev.	1.21	1.20	1.32
With aggrement	3.32	3.17	3.05

Table 2: Single image grades

they were placed on the web page is kept for the current session so that users are not confused with the new ordering when the web page is reloaded.

The evaluation for the single image recommendation is done on the following 12 pictures, shown in Table 4: (1) boats on the sea, (2) skeleton with a headache, (3) man with two guns, (4) formula one pit stop, (5) queue of four men, (6) red rock mountain, (7) satellite dish with stormy weather, (8) futuristic city buildings, (9) monks in orange dresses, (10) palm tree in front of the blue ocean, (11) stop sign on a crossing, and (12) stars in a galaxy. These pictures were selected to be very different in content, as we want to evaluate how well the recommendation performs in the general case, rather than in one or a few specific cases. We had to limit the number of query images to 12, as each user was asked to assess the suitability of 3 recommended soundtracks, for each of the query images, resulting in a tedious and time consuming task of listening to 36 different songs.

For the case of multiple images, we also add a random recommendation to the evaluation, together with the evaluation of the average position and the least misery approaches. We use 36 images taken indoors and outdoors, on various locations all around the world, for the slide show creation. The grouping of the images is done using hierarchical clustering, as described in Section 4.1. Three slide show videos are made with the recommended soundtracks: by average position approach, by least misery approach, and by the random selection of the songs as a soundtrack. The slide show videos are made with a light "dissolve" transitions between the images, inside the groups, and with the heavier "page fold" transition between the images from different groups. Each image is shown for five seconds, resulting in the total length of three minutes for each of the slide shows. The transition between the songs is done with the fade out effect on the end of each song and with the fade in effect on the beginning of each of the songs. The users are asked to rate how well the soundtrack fits to the slide show, for each of the three cases. This evaluation is also done with our online tool, where the slide shows were played and graded by the users. The placement of the slide shows on the web page is also in random order, for the same reason as for the song placement in the single image case.

5.2 Evaluation Results

A total of 13 users participated in the evaluation of the generated slide shows, i.e., the multiple images case. The aggregated results of the evaluation are shown in Table 1 where each option for the soundtrack's suitability was assigned a grade, as already explained in the previous Section. As we can see, the average grade for the average position approach is lot higher than the random soundtrack recommendation. The least misery approach has an average grade a lot higher than random, but slightly lower than the average position approach, indicating that users tend to grade the appropriateness of the soundtrack to a group of images on average rather than on the minimum suitability.

Besides having just a good average grade for the recommendation, it is also very important that people actually agree on how well the soundtrack fits to the image (or the set of images). The agreement between users is very important as high average grades could still have users with high disappointment, what we want to avoid. The agreement on the suitability of the recommended soundtrack is represented in Table 1 by the standard deviation of the results. The lower the standard deviation the larger the level of agreement between users. We see from the standard deviation that users agree more for the soundtracks recommended by our two approaches compared to the random recommendation.

For an easier comparison, a score that takes into account both the relevance measure and the agreement is constructed as a ratio between the average grade (the mean) and the standard deviation, aiming at giving higher grades to the evaluation on which people agree, and a lower score to the one on which people disagree. This combined score is presented in the last row of the Table 1. We see that the combined score for both of our approaches is a lot higher than the one for the randomly recommended songs.

Table 2 summarizes the results of the single image evaluation. Again, 13 users participated in the evaluation, but not all of them have evaluated the soundtracks for all of the 12 images. Each image is evaluated 10.83 times in average. We can see that the average grade for the first recommended song is higher than the random recommended song and that the tenth recommended is graded in between the first recommended and the random, showing that our ranking is indeed in line with the users' perceived ranking. As we can also observe, the difference in average score between the first recommended and the random one is lot smaller than the difference between the average position approach and the random one in case of multiple images evaluation. This kind of result is well expected as the slide show contains multiple images, accumulating the users perceived soundtrack relevance over all of the images.

For the case of single images the average agreement over all 12 tests, in terms of standard deviation, is better for the first recommended and tenth recommended song than for the random one. This shows that not only the first ranked and ten ranked recommended soundtrack have higher score but that users also agree more on these scores compared to randomly recommended song. The score, combining the relevance with the agreement, averaged over all 12 tests is shown in the last row of Table 2. We can see that the combined score for all three cases is slightly increased, compared to the average grade, but yields no significant impact.

Runtime & Scalability

Although we did not focus on the efficiency when designing PICASSO, we measured the runtime of the query processing

Thread(s)	4	3	2	1
Runtime (sec.)	86.13	99.19	132.09	213.84
Queries/sec.	9.75	8.46	6.35	3.92

Table 3: Scalability measurements

task to show that this approach can be used in real-time environments.

The average runtime for the 12 single image queries is 0.629 seconds per query image, with a standard deviation of 0.728. As the K-nearest neighbor search was done completely in main memory, it is yielding a very low runtime. Most of the running time was spent on extracting the image features for the query images, as these were not precomputed. The recommendation for the multiple image case was done in 14.933 seconds for our case of 36 input images. Here, again, most of the runtime was spent on the features extraction of each of the 36 images.

As all required indices, in total less than 500MB Java VM memory (in our setup with 28 movies), are kept in main memory, the runtime is CPU bound due to the feature extraction task. Given this small amount of required memory that nowadays every simple commodity PC provides, the indices can be replicated over many such PCs for scalability reasons. Additionally, the indices are read-only, creating even on a single machine with multiple cores no conflicts between memory accesses , rendering the approach "embarrassingly scalable", a common term for these kinds of parallelization. To show the scalability of the approach on a single machine, we measure the running times and the throughput (i.e., images per second), varying the number of threads used, for 840 query images, shown in Table 3. The measurements were done on the single machine with single four core processor. We did not measure the case of parallelizing the tasks on several separate machine, as the scale-up in throughput is obvious.

Once the memory consumption hits the limit of available memory, we can partition the indices on a per-movie basis. Then, for each machine, we obtain recommendations based only on a subset of all movies. These "local" results can get, however, easily merged by their similarity score in a final aggregation step (i.e., a very simple list merging task). We did not investigate this further. In a real world deployment one would install the approach directly in the cloud to benefit from the provided elasticity in terms of required computing power.

5.3 Lessons Learned

The lessons learned from the evaluation presented above can be put in the following statements. Naturally, in most cases these are not hard facts being universally true, rather reflecting the first insights obtained throughout developing and evaluating our approach.

- Publicly available movies contain expert knowledge on matching the soundtrack to the given images

- It is possible to extract that knowledge and use it for soundtrack recommendation

- Fairly simple methods for recommendation, in conjunction with the extracted training dataset, work quit well

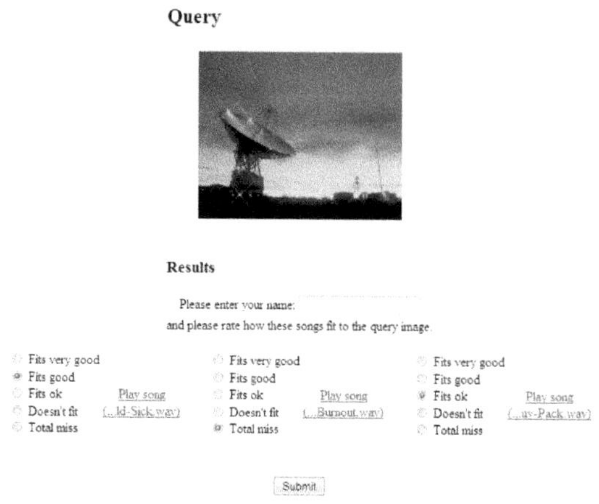

Figure 5: Screenshot of our evaluation tool

- Users find that the recommendation of the soundtracks, for single image or set of images, works well

- Users agree on the ranking of the recommended soundtracks

- The approach is scalable

6. CONCLUSION

We have presented PICASSO, an automated approach to recommend a soundtrack for a picture or a series of pictures. The main focus of the approach is the extraction of knowledge from popular, publicly available, common movies and how these information can be used for our specific task. We have shown how images and music can be matched together by identifying pairs of the most similar screenshots of the movies and the surrounding soundtrack music. PICASSO is based on the usage of low level features for similarity comparison between images and between songs, rendering it applicable for all cases of image/soundtrack matching problems as these features are always available. We have demonstrated the applicability of PICASSO by reporting on the results of a study involving user generated feedback.

As part of our ongoing and future work, we plan to address the problem of integrating user preferences, in terms of music and movie taste, to our approach. We believe that this can lead to an even higher level of user satisfaction. Potentially, we can benefit from existing information in Web portals, such as imdb [14] or youtube [30], to model user preferences.

7. REFERENCES

[1] Stefan Berchtold, Christian Böhm, and Hans-Peter Kriegel. The pyramid-technique: Towards breaking the curse of dimensionality. In *SIGMOD Conference*, 1998.

[2] Kevin S. Beyer, Jonathan Goldstein, Raghu Ramakrishnan, and Uri Shaft. When is "nearest neighbor" meaningful? In *ICDT*, 1999.

[3] Rui Cai, Lei Zhang, Feng Jing, Wei Lai, and Wei-Ying Ma. Automated music video generation using web image resource. In *ICASSP*, 2007.

Table 4: The 12 query images used in our user study.

[4] Shih-Fu Chang, T. Sikora, and A. Puri. Overview of the mpeg-7 standard. In *IEEE Trans. Circuits Syst. Video Techn.*, June 2001.

[5] Marco Cristani, Anna Pesarin, Carlo Drioli, Vittorio Murino, Antonio Rodà, Michele Grapulin, and Nicu Sebe. Toward an automatically generated soundtrack from low-level cross-modal correlations for automotive scenarios. In *ACM Multimedia*, 2010.

[6] Mayur Datar, Nicole Immorlica, Piotr Indyk, and Vahab S. Mirrokni. Locality-sensitive hashing scheme based on p-stable distributions. In *Symposium on Computational Geometry*, 2004.

[7] D.P.W. Ellis and G.E. Poliner. Identifying 'cover songs' with chroma features and dynamic programming beat tracking. In *ICASSP*, 2007.

[8] Ronald Fagin, Ravi Kumar, Mohammad Mahdian, D. Sivakumar, and Erik Vee. Comparing partial rankings. In *SIAM J. Discrete Math.*, 2006.

[9] Flickr. `http://www.flickr.com/`.

[10] Aristides Gionis, Piotr Indyk, and Rajeev Motwani. Similarity search in high dimensions via hashing. In *VLDB*, 1999.

[11] Alfred Haar. *Zur Theorie der orthogonalen Funktionensysteme. Mathematische Annalen, 69.* 1910.

[12] Xian-Sheng Hua, Lie Lu, and HongJiang Zhang. Automatic music video generation based on temporal pattern analysis. In *ACM Multimedia*, 2004.

[13] Xian-Sheng Hua, Lie Lu, and HongJiang Zhang. Optimization-based automated home video editing system. In *IEEE Trans. Circuits Syst. Video Techn.*, 2004.

[14] Internet movie database. `http://www.imdb.com`.

[15] Cheng-Te Li and Man-Kwan Shan. Emotion-based impressionism slideshow with automatic music accompaniment. In *ACM Multimedia*, 2007.

[16] David G. Lowe. Distinctive image features from scale-invariant keypoints. In *International Journal of Computer Vision*, 2004.

[17] Michael I. Mandel and Dan Ellis. Song-level features and support vector machines for music classification. In *ISMIR*, 2005.

[18] B. S. Manjunath, Jens-Rainer Ohm, Vinod V. Vasudevan, and Akio Yamada. Color and texture descriptors. In *IEEE Trans. Circuits Syst. Video Techn.*, 2001.

[19] Marsyas - music/speech dataset. `http://marsyas.info/download/data_sets`.

[20] A. Martin, D. Charlet, and L. Mauuary. Robust speech/non-speech detection using lda applied to mfcc. In *ICASSP*, 2001.

[21] Music2ten. `http://music2ten.com`.

[22] Irina Rish. An empirical study of the naive Bayes classifier. In *IJCAI-01 workshop on "Empirical Methods in AI"*, 2001.

[23] H. Sakoe and S. Chiba. Dynamic programming algorithm optimization for spoken word recognition. In *IEEE Transactions on Acoustics, Speech and Signal Processing*, February 1978.

[24] Hanan Samet. *Foundations of Multidimensional and Metric Data Structures*. Morgan Kaufmann, 2006.

[25] Zbigniew R. Struzik and Arno Siebes. The haar wavelet transform in the time series similarity paradigm. In *PKDD*, 1999.

[26] G. Tzanetakis and P. Cook. Musical genre classification of audio signals. In *IEEE Transactions on Speech and Audio Processing*, July 2002.

[27] George Tzanetakis. Music analysis, retrieval and synthesis of audio signals marsyas. In *ACM Multimedia*, 2009.

[28] Jinjun Wang, Changsheng Xu, Engsiong Chng, Lingyu Duan, Kongwah Wan, and Qi Tian. Automatic generation of personalized music sports video. In *ACM Multimedia*, 2005.

[29] Songhua Xu, Tao Jin, and Francis Chi-Moon Lau. Automatic generation of music slide show using personal photos. In *ISM*, 2008.

[30] Youtube. `http://www.youtube.com`.

Enhanced Results for Web Search

Kevin Haas
Microsoft
1065 La Avenida
Mountain View, CA 94043, US
kevin.haas@microsoft.com

Peter Mika
Yahoo! Research
Diagonal 177
08018 Barcelona, Spain
pmika@yahoo-inc.com

Paul Tarjan
Facebook
1601 S California Ave
Palo Alto, CA 94304, US
pt@fb.com

Roi Blanco
Yahoo! Research
Diagonal 177
08018 Barcelona, Spain
roi@yahoo-inc.com

ABSTRACT

"Ten blue links" have defined web search results for the last fifteen years – snippets of text combined with document titles and URLs. In this paper, we establish the notion of *enhanced search results* that extend web search results to include multimedia objects such as images and video, intent-specific key value pairs, and elements that allow the user to interact with the contents of a web page directly from the search results page. We show that users express a preference for enhanced results both explicitly, and when observed in their search behavior. We also demonstrate the effectiveness of enhanced results in helping users to assess the relevance of search results. Lastly, we show that we can efficiently generate enhanced results to cover a significant fraction of search result pages.

Categories and Subject Descriptors

H.3.3 [**Information Systems Applications**]: Information Search and Retrieval

General Terms

Design, Human Factors

Keywords

search results, user interfaces, web search, semantic web

1. INTRODUCTION

Ten blue links, along with document titles and approximately 100-character summaries (known as abstracts) have dominated Web search results for the last fifteen years. The goal of the abstract is to help users make a quick assessment of whether the Web document returned as a result is relevant to their query or not (see Figure 1). Extensive research has focused on effectively selecting the relevant parts of documents (the snippets) and generating a readable presentation (the abstract) in an efficient manner, e.g. [17, 18, 19, 21, 28, 30]. However, little has changed with the presentation of the search results and the type of data provided within the abstracts.

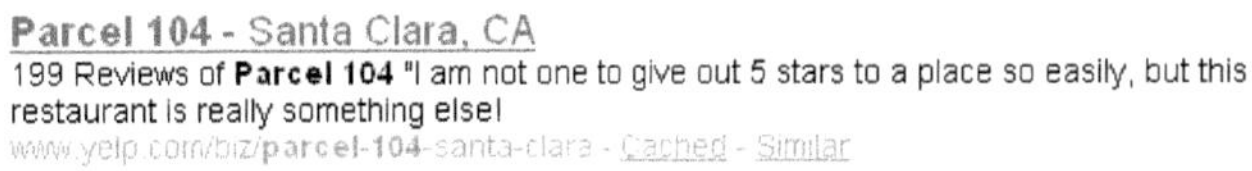

Figure 1: Example of an traditional search result

In this paper, we present a novel way of generating search abstracts based on structured data or *metadata* associated with Web documents. Structured representations of document content allow us to give more relevant and more compelling representations of search results, as well as to imbue them with entirely new interactive functionality. In short, a deeper understanding of Web content enables us to go well beyond the original concept of textual summarization of the document. This deeper understanding is enabled by two major streams of research: Information Extraction (IE) and the Semantic Web.

By now, the Semantic Web has reached a sufficient level of maturity in terms of defining standards (such as RDFa [1] and microformat markup[1]) that publishers can rely on to embed metadata in web pages. In addition, advances in automating extraction, element formalization within the HTML specification, commonalities between Web content management systems, and the increasing importance of head sites within Web search results (from the consumer perspective) allows search engines to leverage Information Extraction technologies at a wider scale. This enables the efficient extraction of structured data from Web documents that otherwise contain no semantic information about the content presented.

In our current work, we exploit both of these methods to go significantly beyond the expressive power of current textual abstracts, and propose the usage of *enhanced search results* that incorporate images, links, key-value pairs and

[1] www.microformats.org

SIGIR'11, July 24–28, 2011, Beijing, China.

Figure 2: Example of an enhanced search result

interactive elements (see Figure 2). We implemented metadata extraction in our web crawler to support information extraction from Web documents and to collect Semantic Web data necessary to generate enhanced results. Further, we created a system to efficiently develop, manage and execute the computer code necessary to translate structured data into search result presentations. This system is currently in production as part of our Web search engine where at least half of all search result pages currently served (October, 2010) contain at least one enhanced result. We evaluate our work by addressing the two foremost questions about enhanced search results.

- Do users have a preference for enhanced search results and are they helping them to find what they are looking for?
- Does the method for generating enhanced search results scale to the Web in terms of content coverage and user impressions?

Based on a side-by-side editorial evaluation and a comparative analysis of click-through rates on a fraction of real search traffic, we show that users both explicitly state their preference for enhanced results in a test scenario and find them more appealing in day-to-day search engine usage. We also measure the usefulness of enhanced results in helping users to distinguish relevant results from irrelevant ones, a crucial benefit for both publishers and search engine providers. Lastly, we show that generating enhanced results scales to a Web search scenario in terms of both content and query coverage.

2. MOTIVATION

The Web was originally designed for presenting information for human consumption. As a result, even though the website owners may put significant effort into modeling their data and managing it in structured forms such as relational tables, OO models or XML schemas, this structure is lost when formatted as text for human consumption. The Semantic Web provides the required standards for sharing structured data across the Web using a generic data model, the Resource Description Framework, or RDF, and for describing the schema of the data using expressive, logic-based languages such as the Web Ontology Language, or OWL.

The Semantic Web is increasingly being adopted in two settings. The Linking Open Data (LOD)[2] community projects use Semantic Web technology to directly expose public data sets in RDF, often for data that has previously not been accessible from the Web. The second main area of attention is the annotation of existing Web resources, in particular HTML documents. This appeals to the large majority of existing publishers who generate their web pages automatically and from an existing structured data source, since publishing data this way requires only minor modifications to the template that generates their pages. From the perspective of a Web search engine, this second area is also the one that holds immediate promise as it is closer to the traditional expectations of search engine processing. Collecting metadata embedded inside HTML pages requires minimal changes to the existing crawling infrastructure, whereas collecting Linked Data requires not only new crawling procedures but also additional mechanisms to establish and transfer trust from the network of HTML documents to the network of RDF data (or vice versa).[3] Allowing independent parties to provide metadata for sites which they do not own could have negative consequences, e.g. a manufacturer making statements about the price of a competing product.

There are several standards and conventions for embedding metadata inside (X)HTML documents. *RDFa* is a W3C recommendation for embedding RDF models inside (X)HTML documents as additional markup. *Microformats* are informally specified social conventions of encoding metadata about particular types of objects, e.g. persons or events. Loosely defined specifications make it easier to annotate using microformats, but microformats on the Web exhibit a more diverse application of the proposed syntax than RDFa.

We implemented support for RDFa and several popular microformats inside the indexer component of Yahoo Search, a major Web search engine. Figure 3 shows the growth in the percentage of indexed URLs with either RDFa or commonly supported microformats[4] in a collection of 12 billion Web documents.

We have argued in our previous work [23] that while similar figures are interesting to observe, what matters is whether this data is useful to satisfy the information needs of search users. In particular, we are interested in how often specific metadata formats would be surfaced by the search engine. To establish this, we replayed a random sample of 7117 queries of one month of Yahoo US query log and observed the returned results (see Table 1).[5] The last two columns show the total number of potential enhanced results and the average number of potential enhanced results per query within the top 10 results.

Based on this analysis, we know that despite having a relatively low percentage of URLs with metadata, on average every search result page features at least one result with page-based metadata, with the most popular hcard microformat returned once in every other search result page. By contrasting Table 1 and Figure 3 we can also see that our expectation is confirmed in that the most popular microformats (e.g. tagging) are not necessarily the ones appearing on pages that are most searched for.

We may note that not all forms of data are equally useful for presenting to the user, including the most popular tagging microformat originally invented for giving hints to the Technorati search engine for categorizing blog posts. RDFa

[2]`www.linkeddata.org`

[3]As an example, the website `http://dbpedia.org` provides RDF metadata that originates (and is extracted from) the website `http://www.wikipedia.org`. However, no formal connection exists between these domains in terms of ownership.

[4]with the exception of fb-img, which we denote as the Facebook Share format (`www.facebook.com/facebook-widgets/share.php`)

[5]The query log was sampled in January, 2009 and the experiment was run in January, 2010.

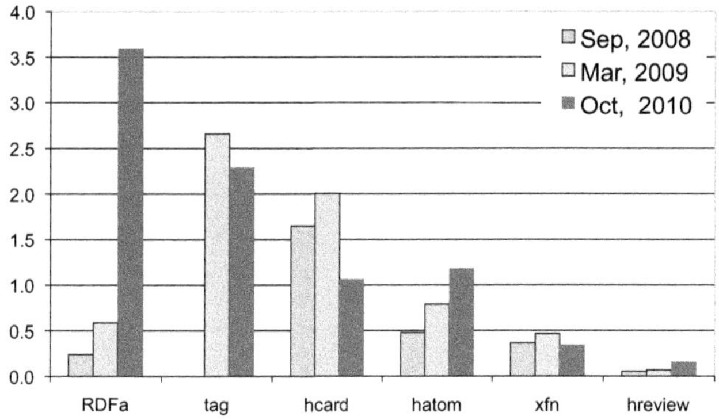

Figure 3: Percentage of Web pages with RDFa data and selected microformats.

Table 1: The number of queries that return zero to five results with various metadata within the first page of search results

format	0	1	2	3	4	5	Sum	Avg
hcard	4729	1702	483	145	38	8	3374	47.4%
license	5773	1294	47	3	0	0	1397	19.6%
adr	6090	714	193	72	19	9	1566	22.0%
hatom	6330	687	89	8	2	1	902	12.7%
fb-img	6379	640	76	14	6	0	872	12.3%
RDFa	6618	462	27	3	2	3	561	7.9%
xfn	6618	462	31	4	1	0	546	7.7%
geo	6716	351	46	4	0	0	455	6.4%
tag	6721	372	24	0	0	0	420	5.9%
ANY	2815	2175	1153	561	249	100	8072	113%

data itself contains information using a number of common and less common ontologies, making it hard to exploit efficiently. We will return to question of how much of this data can be successfully exploited in Section 5.2.

We also note that there are good reasons to move away from an average case analysis. Not only the amount of metadata varies by query category, but we may also attribute different value to different categories of queries, e.g. attributing smaller weight in evaluation to queries that are already "solved", e.g. navigational queries with near perfect results. One might also weight queries based on the possibility for monetization, but also by the value attributed by the users for solving the query. We leave these analysis for future work.

Our analysis above puts an upper bound on exploiting enhanced search results based on embedded metadata alone. The question then is how one could effectively increase the amount of data available for enhanced search results by information extraction. Despite the popular notion of the long tail of Web content, another set of analysis shows us that preferential treatment to "top sites" provides the opportunity for enhanced search results without needing metadata from the long tail. By running the same set of queries through the search engine, we observed that a relatively small number of sites have a disproportionate appearance on result pages compared to their size. For example, Wikipedia appeared in roughly 25% of all search results. Correlating this data with Table 2[6], we can see that despite its relatively small size Wikipedia alone is surfaced more often than even the most common microformats. These results tell us that one could effectively index the data of these top sites by creating wrappers, a fact that we exploit in our work. Such wrappers can be effectively hand-written by website owners or learned through wrapper induction from training data [20].

Table 2: The number of queries that return 0 to 2 results with pages from the top host names

host name	0	1	2	Sum	Avg
en.wikipedia.org	5321	1795	2	1797	25.2%
youtube.com	6691	426	0	426	6.0%
answers.com	6714	403	0	403	5.7%
amazon.com	6722	395	0	395	5.6%
local.yahoo.com	6739	378	0	378	5.3%
blog.360.yahoo.com	6846	271	0	271	3.8%
facebook.com	6867	250	0	250	3.5%
technorati.com	6883	234	0	234	3.3%
ehow.com	6889	228	0	228	3.2%

3. RELATED WORK

3.1 Search result summarization

Traditionally, Web search engines display a list of captions containing a title, an abstract and a URL. The importance of Web search result displays in helping users to determine the relevance of search results is firmly established. Clarke et al [6] explore how caption features influence Web search behavior. Their findings suggest that relatively simple text features like the readability of the snippet, and the length of the URL shown in the caption, can significantly influence users' Web search behavior.

Most improvements to search result presentation have come from advances in text summarization. Varadarajan and Hristidis [31] generate more relevant snippets from spanning trees built from a document graph and compare them to the ones generated by Google and MSN desktop search. Kanungo and Orr [19] describe a machine learned model for predicting the readability of search results by combining text readability measures and other features specific for Web search results (such as the presence of ellipses). With the exception of Cutrell and Guan [7] who investigated the influence of snippet length on Web search peformance using an eye-tracking study, most researchers in this area base their evaluation on user studies of some form. Although various measures exist for assessing the readability of natural language texts, e.g. the classic SMOG measure [22], these are not directly applicable to short runs of incomplete text. For example, in the above mentioned study, Kanungo and Orr train and test their model using human assessments of Web search results, where the judges evaluate readability on a 1-5 scale, from "Unreadable" to "Easy to read". They note that perfect agreement is fairly low (46.4%), though there is a near perfect agreement in 84.5% of the cases. There is no

[6] Note that in general Web search engines hide multiple results from the same host, unless the user explicitly triggers host-based search

standard user evaluation and a number of variations exist in the literature.

Few works have focused on improving the accessibility of Web search results by changing the form of search result displays. Dumais et al. [11] found that users perform search tasks faster if results are grouped by category in the interface. White et al. [33] evaluate techniques to promote user interaction with search results. In their work they treat the amount of time a user spends viewing a summary as an indicator of relevance. They presented three different solutions, based on the display of a summary, list of top-ranked relevant sentences of the results, and dynamic updates of the search result list using implicit feedback.

In our work, we propose new types of search result displays that represent a significant departure from the classical search abstracts in current Web search engines and therefore our first concern is user acceptance. For this reason, we first perform a user study to establish the users' choice for enhanced results using a binary, side-by-side evaluation that is easy to perform and results in higher agreement. We also perform a so-called bucket test, where we expose a fraction of our search traffic to enhanced results over an extended period of time and compare the user's interaction with the baseline. For enhanced results, we show an increase in Click-Through Rate (CTR), a metric commonly used in online advertizing, content and search engine optimization.

Despite the wide appeal of the CTR metric, more sophisticated models are required to consider effects such as the position bias, i.e. that a user may not get to examine certain search results. User interaction models have been developed in the past to explain observed user behavior in query logs [13, 3]. Interaction models have direct applications to ranking as a complement to editorial data but can also be used in comparative search engine evaluation [12, 16]. In our work, we extend Chapelle and Zhang's click model [3] and fit it to large-scale query log data to show that enhanced results are effectively helping users to distinguish relevant results from irrelevant ones. While clicks-through data has been used in improving text-based search result generation [28], to our knowledge this is the first time that interaction models are used in evaluating search result summaries.

3.2 Semantic Search

A number of end-to-end semantic search systems have been developed up to date, e.g. [10, 8, 4, 15, 24, 29, 32], although all of them are operated as academic demos and prototypes. Unlike web search engines, most of them focus on retrieving RDF resources directly instead of textual documents, while some engines perform hybrid retrieval on a collection of documents annotated with metadata, e.g. [34, 14]. With the exception of [24], semantic search engines that perform their own crawling only retrieve data published directly as RDF, and do not extract RDFa or microformats.

Although there is some experimentation in novel displays for Semantic Web search engines, publications on generating snippets in this context are few and far apart. In a Web search setting, Bai et al. worked on snippet generation for a semantic search engine (Sindice) that indexes instance data [2]. They divide the abstract in two parts: the first, static part showing statements related to the main topic of the document, and weighted by the importance of the predicate of the triple, while the second, dynamic part shows statements ranked by their relevance to the query. The evaluation considers the performance of the system, and compares various methods to identify the main topic of documents. Penin et al. [25] operate in the setting of a Semantic Web search engine that indexes only ontologies, and thus consider snippet generation as an ontology summarization problem. They posit that a succinct summary of the ontology should cover all main topics mentioned, and thus perform clustering on the RDF graph, selecting the most relevant statements from each cluster. Their evaluation centers around the effectiveness of clustering and performance, and provide only anecdotal evidence from end users. As in the case of text search results, these authors operating in the semantic search field do not have a standard evaluation methodology or benchmark to rely on.

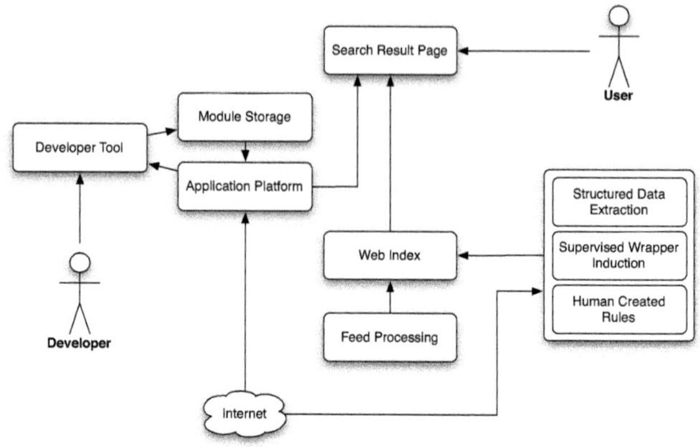

Figure 4: System Architecture

4. IMPLEMENTATION

Enhanced results can be implemented as an extension to a conventional inverted index based search engine, as shown in Figure 4.

In the offline indexing phase, metadata is extracted from Web documents by executing RDFa and microformat extraction, hand-written and machine-learned rules. The difference in RDFa and microformat extraction is that RDFa extraction needs to be implemented once, independent of the schema of the data, while microformat extraction needs to be coded separately for each format. In addition to the information coming from the indexed documents via extraction and markup, our system also admits data feeds submitted by website owners. Due to the potential exposure to spam injection, we allow only the website owner to provide annotations for a given page. As there is no standard format for RDF feeds, we developed our own format for this purpose [7]. Feeds are often preferred by publishers who would not like to make metadata publicly available.

All of the gathered data is stored internally in an RDF-based format. RDF was chosen over other options (such as XML) because of its flexibility: RDF can represent any graph structure, the data and the schema can be stored separately or intermixed, and publishers are free to combine multiple vocabularies if a single vocabulary doesn't match their needs.

[7] http://developer.yahoo.com/searchmonkey/smguide/datarss.h

When a user performs a query, the regular Web search engine retrieval process runs, returning the "ten blue links" and whatever structured data that was associated with them. For the pages that contain metadata, the search engine triggers one of the applicable plugins that can transform the data into the presentation. There are both default plug-ins enabled for all users, and plug-ins developed by external contributors, which require opting in. Note that we also call default plug-ins "object templates", because they only require the presence of particular data to appear, i.e. the data that gives the values for the presentation template. Such object templates exist for a number of popular objects types such business listings, products, video etc.

External plugins take precedence over default plugins. Further, the end user can add or remove both types of plugins via the search engine interface, i.e. there is a possibility for personalization. In order to develop new plug-ins, we have made available an online tool where a developer can

- Define which URLs they would like to change the appearance of (as a wildcard pattern)
- Optionally write custom extraction rules (in XSLT) to pull out any data that wasn't stored in the index already
- Select the sources of data that need to be present for the plug-in to trigger
- Create a translation from data to presentation in PHP
- Choose to list the application in the Application Gallery for other users to use

Although it would have been an option to define the presentation plug-ins using an RDF visual vocabulary such as Fresnel [26], we have opted for a solution where the transformation from data to presentation is described in a controlled subset of PHP. The advantage of choosing a fully-fledged programming language over a declarative mapping is that if/then checks and simple manipulations, such as converting number or date formats, can be still performed at this stage. In PHP, the data is queried by executing queries in a simple path expression language similar to Fresnel path expressions [26], which is more appropriate for this limited task of data selection then the SPARQL standard [27]. In particular, joins are not required. When developing any code in the developer tool, the results of the extraction or translation are shown immediately in a preview to help developers debug their code.

5. EVALUATION

In the evaluation of our work, we seek to answer the two basic questions we asked in Section 1: whether enhanced results bring clear benefits to users, and whether the method of generating them provides sufficient coverage of search results.

5.1 Explicit and Implicit User Feedback

To evaluate the effectiveness of enhanced results, we have first performed a user study to measure the explicit preference of users for these new types of results. Prior to deployment, we have also carried out a large-scale online evaluation using real search engine traffic, designed to measure implicit preference for enhanced results in terms of click-through. Lastly, by modeling user behavior using historical query-log data we show that enhanced results effectively help users to determine the relevance of search results.

5.1.1 Side-by-side editorial evaluation

As put forward in Section 3.1, no gold standard dataset or evaluation methodology exists to assess the quality of search abstracts. However, we can rely on a baseline for comparison, i.e. the existing presentation of search results. Although the methods of generating search result summaries vary by search engine, the appearance of search results are surprisingly uniform.

Using internal editorial resources, we ran side-by-side evaluations of enhanced search result templates and the traditional search result templates containing only textual summaries. Each template evaluation was performed independently using editorial teams ranging from three to fourteen assessors, depending on the number of results being reviewed. Each result pair was evaluated by three editors, and the overall preference was taken as the majority of the individual preferences.

Table 3 contains a subset of the data captured during these editorial reviews. Specific to the product template evaluation, we took 658 commonly-occurring URLs matching our "product" presentation template and asked the editorial team to evaluate the enhanced search result presentation versus the traditional presentation. Each editor was asked to judge which result was better as well as categorize the reason; additional comments could be recorded as feedback to the user experience teams.

Aggregating the data captured in Table 3 allows us to generate Table 4. The majority of results were deemed "better" by the reviewers when presented with an enhanced search result. When the traditional results were preferred, the most common complaints were the incorrectness of the data presented (e.g. incorrect prices) or irrelevance of images.

Table 4: Side-by-side product template analysis

Type	Enhanced	Traditional	No judgment
Preference	84%	3%	13%

5.1.2 Click-through rate analysis

In addition to our editorial user study, we performed a bucket test, a form of online experiment where a small fraction of search sessions is diverted to an alternate version of the search result page during a test period. In our case, the control group was shown a traditional, textual search result for all pages, and the test group was shown an enhanced local search result with the business's telephone number, address, and "curbside image" for websites with local metadata, with all other variables being constant. We used a 5% bucket of Yahoo Search search traffic in the United States and ran the experiment over a period of three months. Note that the sessions, and correspondingly the users are selected randomly from all sessions and users of the search engine, and therefore the query load is also representative of the total query load of the search engine.

We instrumented our search engine to collect CTR (click-through rate) data during the bucket test. CTR is a widely reported metric in search, content optimization and online

Template	URL	A/B	Reason	Comments
Product	#0	A	traditional doesn't convey as much info	
Product	#1	A	traditional doesn't convey as much info	slight preference to A because price is included in the result
Product	#2	-		inclusion of image does not help this result
Product	#3	A	traditional doesn't convey as much info	the price gives A the edge. The image is not particularly compelling.
...	...	...	...	...
Product	#657	B	bad data extraction	extracted price shown on SRP is wrong

Table 3: Subset of side-by-side results for the product template

advertizing. One important consideration in CTR measurement is being able to differentiate a "good click" from a "bad click." Good clicks include no further clicks from that search result or a long dwell time on the target page [9]. We considered a long dwell a time of 100 seconds or longer based on the results of the authors, who show that good clicks measured this way generally indicate a relevant result for the user, and a bad click indicates the search engine surfaced an irrelevant result. Our measure of CTR is thus defined as:

$$CTR = \frac{\#\text{ good clicks on the result}}{\#\text{ total views of the result}}$$

In Table 5, we show a subset of the data collected during this experiment.[8]

Table 5: Subset of bucket CTR data captured

Date	Template	Site	Bucket CTR
t0	Local	site 0	4.65%
t1	Local	site 0	4.97%
t2	Local	site 0	4.70%
t3	Local	site 0	4.54%
t4	Local	site 0	4.52%
...	...	...	...
t100	Person	site n	5.65%

We then generated the aggregation of the data by site and by template for the bucket period, as shown in Table 6.

Table 6: Bucket CTR analysis

Site	Template	Bucket CTR	Control CTR	Change
site 0	Local	5.3%	4.5%	17.8%
site 1	Local	5.8%	5.5%	5.8%
...	...	...	...	...
site n	Person	6.1%	6.0%	16.7%
ALL	ALL	4.6%	4.0%	15.0%

Comparing the CTRs we noticed that the enhanced search results showed an average increase of 15% CTR for all sites, with a maximum of 33% for an enhanced search result for a particular site. We consider this as a positive result, as negative rates might indicate that the result contained exactly the information that the user needed, and the user would not click through to the website itself. While great for a "task complete" metric, website owners would be less than happy with a search engine innovation that used data from their websites but reduced their referrals and the corresponding revenue opportunities.

[8]The data in Table 5 has been partly hidden, but we include this table as a representation of the data captured during the experiment.

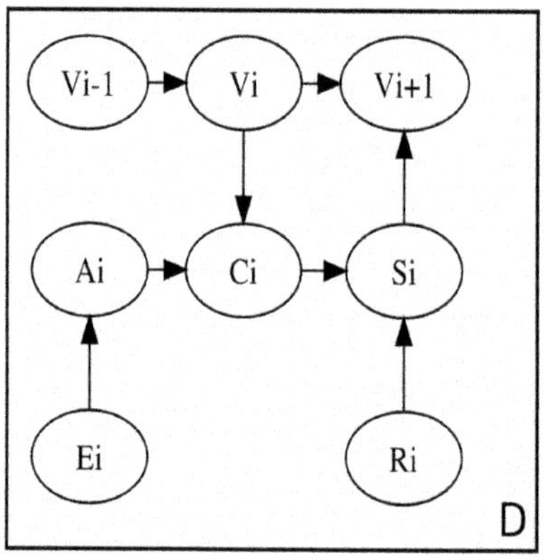

Figure 5: Click model

5.1.3 *User interaction model*

Click-through rate analysis reveals an implicit preference for enhanced results whenever such a result is displayed, but it can not show whether enhanced results are effective in helping the user to distinguish relevant results from irrelevant ones at the time of deciding on a click. In order to model how enhanced results impact user interaction, we extend Chapelle and Zhang's state-of-the-art click model [3] with the potential influence of enhancing a search result.

The resulting Dynamic Bayesian Network model is presented in Figure 5. The variables inside the plate are defined at a query-session level and define the possible interactions of the user. Snippets are placed in positions from 1 to 10 (denoted by i). All random variables are binary. C_i indicates whether there is a click at position i, V_i if the user has viewed the result, A_i if the user has been attracted by the result, S_i if the user was satisfied with the landing page, E_i indicates whether the result is an enhanced result or not, and R_i the relevance status of the document. The model is further characterized by the following equations [3]:

- $A_i = 1, V_i = 1 \Leftrightarrow C_i = 1$
- $C_i = 0 \Rightarrow S_i = 0$
- $S_i = 1 \Rightarrow V_{i+1} = 0$
- $p(V_{i+1}|V_i = 1, S_i = 0) = \gamma$
- $V_i = 0 \Rightarrow V_{i+1} = 0$

In the original model, only C_i is an observed variable, and R_i is estimated – in our case we will employ true relevance data from those URLs, and therefore R_i is an observed variable. Whether there is an enhanced result or not is also observed in our model, whereas the rest of the variables will be estimated by taking $\gamma = 0.9$, the value which provided the best estimation of relevance in [3]. We also assume that $C_i = 1, R_i = 1 \Rightarrow S_i = 1$.

In words, the assumption of the model is that upon submission of a query, there is a list of results displayed to a user (D). A user scans the result list from top to bottom, examining all the results in order. After viewing a result ($V_i = 1$), a user may get *attracted* by a result ($A_i = 1$), deciding to click on it ($C_i = 1$); if the user clicks on a result but she is not satisfied by the landing document, she examines the next result with probability γ. If the document is relevant we assume the user is satisfied and she stops the search process for the query ($V_{i+1} = 0$)

This model allows us to answer the following questions by probability estimation:

- What is the probability that an enhanced result is relevant *a priori*? That is, $p(R_i = 1|E_i = 1)$ compared to $p(R_i = 1|E_i = 0)$
- What is the probability that an enhanced result viewed by a user is relevant? That is, $p(A_i = 1|E_i = 1) = p(R_i = 1|V_i = 1, E_i = 1)$ compared to $p(R_i = 1|V_i = 1, E_i = 0)$
- What is the attractiveness of enhanced result when viewed by a user? That is, $p(C_i = 1|V_i = 1, E_i = 1)$ compared to $p(C_i = 1|V_i = 1, E_i = 0)$
- What is the probability that the enhanced result was useful? This is, $p(R_i = 1|C_i = 1, E_i = 1)$ compared to $p(R_i = 1|C_i = 1, E_i = 0)$

To compute the above transition probabilities, we took a sub-sample of 10 consecutive days of Yahoo US query log from October, 2010, collecting a total of 1.2M executions of queries for which the result page contained at least one enhanced snippet among the first ten results. Out of those queries we filtered out navigational sessions. Our definition of *navigational sessions* includes query executions that contain one relevant result in the first position, where the user clicked on that result and no further clicks were made. This helps us to clear out queries which are non-informative for the purpose of the experiment (like users issuing the query *twitter* and clicking on *www.twitter.com*). This resulted in 530K query sessions. Query and URL relevance was assesed by trained editors, as in previous experiments. The editors were asked to grade each pair on a 5-point scale (from *Not relevant* to *Perfect*); we consider a result relevant if its grade is higher than 2.

Table 7: Estimation of the different probabilities for the click model

Probability	Text Snippet	Enhanced	Change
$p(R\|E)$	0.320	0.417	+30.3%
$p(R\|V, E)$	0.376	0.468	+24.47%
$p(R\|C, E)$	0.286	0.533	+86.36%
$p(C\|V, E)$	0.051	0.019	-62.745%

Our model shows that on average a user examined 5.8 results per query and clicked on 1.5 results. Table 7 contains the different probabilities presented above. We compare the results of traditional textual snippets (column *text snippets*) with those of enhanced snippets (column *enhanced*). We assume that the random variables R (relevant), V (viewed), and C (click) are set to 1, whereas $E = 0$ for text snippets and $E = 1$ in the enhanced results column. The four rows thus correspond to one of each of the questions posed above.

Our results show that documents that trigger an enhanced snippet in the query sample, $p(R = 1|E = 1)$ are more likely to be relevant *a priori*, than traditional textual snippets $p(R = 1|E = 0)$, which is not surprising given that more enhanced results are generated for head sites than tail sites. The fact that enhanced results are relevant is also noticeable from the resuls displayed to the user: from all the results that the users have actually viewed, there is a 24.5% higher odds that result is relevant if it has an enhanced snippet $p(R = 1|V = 1, E = 1)$.

The most striking result is that even if non-enhanced results get a higher probability of clicking, $p(C = 1|V = 1, E = 0) > p(C = 1|V = 1, E = 1)$ as shown in the last row, the probability that users click on a relevant result, $p(R = 1|C = 1, E = 1)$, is 86.6% higher if the snippet contains an enhanced presentation. Please note that the probability of clicking is computed differently than the CTR of the previous experiment, where we only took into account *good* clicks, whereas this probability reflects all the clicks. In practice, this means that the enhanced results presentation was extremely useful in determining whether the document was relevant or not, and therefore likely to lower the overall search effort, lead to faster task completion and user satisfaction. This is a very positive finding.

5.2 Search result coverage

As alluded to in Section 2, there is a potential that a surprisingly small amount of metadata can power a large proportion of search results. Based on a sampling of the results generated by Yahoo search engine in November 2009, Table 8 shows a relatively small amount of data available. However, Table 9 proves that the majority of search results can contain at least one enhanced result with very little metadata in the crawled corpus.[9]

Table 8: Metadata availability within the Yahoo search corpus

Document type	% of corpus
All documents with metadata from any source	5.8%
All documents with RDFa- or microformat-based metadata	4.0%
All documents with enough metadata providing an enhanced result	2.3%

As called out in the side-by-side tests, improperly extracted key-value pairs have a profound impact on the usefulness of the data provided by enhanced results. To test the data, we exported 1000 URLs matching specific templates and asked internal editorial resources to evaluate the quality

[9]Recall from Section 2.1, Wikipedia can appear in over 25% of the search results

Table 9: Percentage of search result pages showing an enhanced search result

Template	Page views
Reference	28.2%
Product	8.4%
Person	5.9%
Video	5.5%
Local	4.3%
Event	1.1%
Other	0.3%

of extraction. To distinguish the two main sources of incorrect data, we asked evaluators to mark the data extracted data as either "correct" (extracted data matches the cached crawl content) or "bad" (extracted data does not match the cached crawl content).

As shown in Table 10, data source quality varies greatly by content contributor.[10] We found that feeds and general page markup had the greatest variance in data quality, and wrappers, page markup created specifically for SearchMonkey, and human-created extraction rules created for specific websites had the highest precision. During the analysis, we realized that the early results of data quality for generally available RDFa and microformat page markup was so low ($< 40\%$) that we terminated that analysis and excluded those sources from the remainder of the review process.

Table 10: Subset of source quality analysis

Template	Source Type	Source ID	Precision
Product	feed	0	59.2%
Product	human-created rule	1	92.8%
Product	wrapper	2	91.5%
Product	feed	3	86.9%
...	...	...	
Video	human-created	n	81.2%

Overall, the recommendation by the editorial reviewers was to consider the quality of metadata sources in the following order:

- page markup created specifically for our system SearchMonkey
- human-created extraction rule
- supervised wrapper induction
- partner feeds
- general page markup, such as RDFa and microformats

Precision was consistently high for markup created specifically for SearchMonkey. Wrapper-based entity extraction ($> 90\%$) also exhibits high quality on average, but with a larger variance. Some sites are very durable, and others frequently change their DOM structure often as a defense against page scrapers. However, this behavior is traceable and problematic sites can be removed from extraction.

[10]The data in Table 10 has been partly hidden, but we include this table as a representation of the data captured during the experiment.

In terms of reusing existing markup not specifically provided for our tool, we observed that popular microformats are often misused, while emerging, small microformats exhibit large variations in syntax. The hcard microformat is very popular on the Web, appearing in over 500M Web documents. Due to its popularity, hcard is often misused to represent data (such as news) for which its not intended. Due to the lack of extensibility of microformats, users also often abuse existing fields for representing information that could not be captured otherwise. Smaller microformats such as hrecipe and hproduct are problematic due to different versions being in use at the same time. Further, site owners often mark up data that is not representative of the main content of the page, e.g. an address that is within the template used to generate all pages of the site.

We have also found that relevant images improve the user's experience, but irrelevant images can actually lead to a negative experience in which no image would have been a better presentation. Consider various queries about Switzerland with the below presentation:

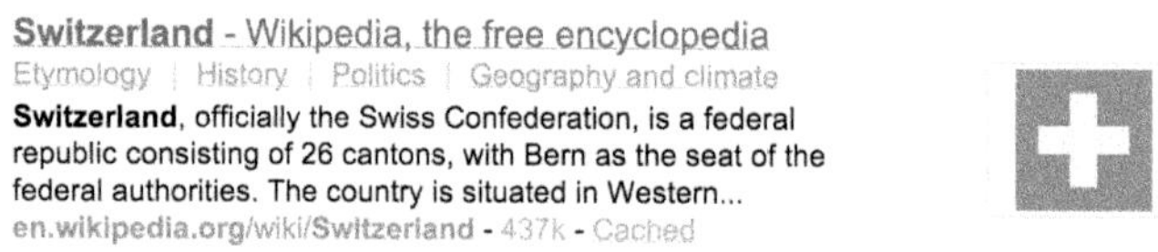

Figure 6: Example of an enhanced search result for "Switzerland"

- "Switzerland": the flag can provide a slightly positive or negative experience. Some users felt that the flag reinforces they are looking at the "right" Switzerland as the image confirmed the search engine found the right intent. Other users felt it was not helpful or possibly used space that could have provided better information from the snippet.

- "Switzerland flag": the flag is exactly what the user is looking for, providing a first result similar to what the user would receive using an image search engine

- "Switzerland map": the flag is irrelevant to the query intent, and opens the possibility that the search engine does not know the difference between a map and a flag

Likewise, the tolerance of adult content is lower for images than text, and can lead to interesting discussions whether visual content has a different threshold than textual content. Wikipedia, generally assumed to not be a source of adult rich media on the Web, does contain topics in which the textual summaries are not offensive by Yahoo editorial standards, but the image itself is offensive (or at least borderline). An example is the article on "pubic hair" which is considered generally acceptable when presented using a textual abstract. However, the article also contains graphic depictions, which are not considered appropriate. This discrepency between textual offensiveness scoring and image offensiveness scoring needs to be considered when generating enhanced results.

6. CONCLUSIONS

We have proposed the notion of enhanced search results as an extension of traditional search result display with images, key-value pairs, and other interactive elements. The generation of enhanced results is enabled by the standards and adoption of the Semantic Web and advances in Information Extraction. Based on this opportunity, we have implemented an extension to our search infrastructure that allows both users and search engine providers to easily define plugins that translate web page metadata into search result displays.

We conducted three major experiments to assess the effectiveness of enhanced results. In the context of a user study, we have shown that users prefer enhanced search results over the traditional search result by a large margin when explicitly asked to make a side-by-side comparison. We have also observed users under their normal search behavior in an online experiment that involved exposing part of our search traffic to an alternative search result page where enhanced results have been enabled. Compared to the activity on the baseline search result pages showing text-only abstracts, we have measured a higher CTR (excluding bad clicks) for enhanced results. This is a key finding because the CTR metric is widely used in search engine optimization, and higher CTRs may convince page owners to implement semantic markup, which in turn allows search engines to display enhanced results and provide other services.

By applying a more expressive user interaction model, we have also shown that enhanced results effectively guide the users to relevant content in general. This is a substantial finding that points to the effectiveness of enhanced results, as the enhancement of the snippet with structured data lowers the likelihood of bad clicks. It also provides ample motivation for publishers of web content to consider enhanced results as a way to avoid "bad clicks" and attract the searchers who would find their content relevant.

We have also shown in our fourth experiment that even though a relatively low number of web pages in our index contains explicit or extracted metadata, a large fraction of the search result pages feature enhanced results, due to the uneven distribution of user attention across content sources. This proves that despite the fragmentation of web content, we can generate enhanced results efficiently, and have a significant impact on the search experience of all users.

7. FUTURE WORK

Although enhanced results as described, implemented and evaluated in this paper are themselves radical departures from how search result abstracts are currently generated, there are a number of potential areas for further development.

As an example, existing studies show that structured data may play an even larger role in search from mobile devices, a growing area of both research and development. Church et. al [5] show that transactional and navigational queries are significantly more frequent in mobile usage compared to web search. Informational queries receive much less weight in mobile scenarios due to the amount of content that users can consume on the mobile: long running searches that require research, possibly using multiple sources, are typically missing. Instead, mobile search provides a larger role in getting information related to particular objects (places, events, schedules) near the user. The same study also shows an overwhelming dominance of adult queries due to the much more private sphere of mobile search. We expect that metadata-based search and result presentation will play a significant role in mobile search in the future.

User experience could be also further improved by allowing additional context to be taken into account in generating web search results. Although our current enhanced results are static, we foresee the possibility to modify the result presentation based on the query, or a structured interpretation of the query. For example, when the user is asking for the location of a restaurant, it makes sense to highlight location information in the result, if necessary by suppressing more generic information. Plug-ins may also take more than one result as input, leading to applications that can help the user aggregate information from multiple result documents. In fact, query aware applications may be triggered by the query itself, showing up dynamically as required.

8. ACKNOWLEDGEMENTS

We would like to acknowledge Amit Kumar, Micah Dubinko, Sara Golemon, Chris Lindsey, Weilin Ng and all other past and present members of the Yahoo! Search team who have helped us to realize SearchMonkey.

9. REFERENCES

[1] B. Adida, M. Birbeck, S. McCarron, and S. Pemberton. RDFa in XHTML: Syntax and Processing, October 2008. http://www.w3.org/TR/2008/REC-rdfa-syntax-20081014.

[2] X. Bai, R. Delbru, and G. Tummarello. RDF Snippets for Semantic Web Search Engines. In *OTM '08: Proceedings of the OTM 2008 Confederated International Conferences, CoopIS, DOA, GADA, IS, and ODBASE 2008. Part II on On the Move to Meaningful Internet Systems*, pages 1304–1318, Berlin, Heidelberg, 2008. Springer-Verlag.

[3] O. Chapelle and Y. Zhang. A dynamic bayesian network click model for web search ranking. In *Proceedings of the 18th international conference on the World Wide Web - WWW '09*, pages 1–10, New York, NY, USA, 2009. ACM.

[4] G. Cheng, W. Ge, and Y. Qu. Falcons: searching and browsing entities on the semantic web. In *Proceedings of the 17th international conference on the World Wide Web - WWW '08*, pages 1101–1102, New York, New York, USA, 2008. ACM Press.

[5] K. Church, B. Smyth, K. Bradley, and P. Cotter. A large scale study of European mobile search behaviour. In *MobileHCI '08: Proceedings of the 10th international conference on Human computer interaction with mobile devices and services*, pages 13–22, New York, NY, USA, 2008. ACM.

[6] C. L. A. Clarke, E. Agichtein, S. Dumais, and R. W. White. The influence of caption features on clickthrough patterns in web search. In *SIGIR '07*, pages 135–142, New York, NY, USA, 2007. ACM.

[7] E. Cutrell and Z. Guan. What are you looking for?: an eye-tracking study of information usage in web search. In *Proceedings of the SIGCHI conference on*

Human factors in computing systems, CHI '07, pages 407–416, New York, NY, USA, 2007. ACM.

[8] M. d'Aquin, C. Baldassarre, L. Gridinoc, S. Angeletou, M. Sabou, and E. Motta. Characterizing knowledge on the semantic web with watson. In *EON*, 2007.

[9] A. L. David Ciemiewicz, Tapas Kanungo and M. Stone. On the use of long dwell time clicks for measuring user satisfaction with application to web summarization. In *Yahoo! Research Technical Report*, 2010.

[10] L. Ding, T. Finin, A. Joshi, R. Pan, S. R. Cost, Y. Peng, P. Reddivari, V. Doshi, and J. Sachs. Swoogle: a search and metadata engine for the semantic web. In *CIKM '04: Proceedings of the thirteenth ACM conference on Information and knowledge management*, pages 652–659, New York, NY, USA, 2004. ACM Press.

[11] S. Dumais, E. Cutrell, and H. Chen. Optimizing search by showing results in context. In *Proceedings of the SIGCHI conference on Human factors in computing systems*, CHI '01, pages 277–284, New York, NY, USA, 2001. ACM.

[12] G. Dupret, V. Murdock, and B. Piwowarski. Web search engine evaluation using clickthrough data and a user model. In *Proceedings of the Workshop on Query Log Analysis*, 2007.

[13] G. E. Dupret and B. Piwowarski. A user browsing model to predict search engine click data from past observations. In *SIGIR '08*, page 331, New York, New York, USA, 2008. ACM Press.

[14] M. Fernandez, V. Lopez, M. Sabou, V. Uren, D. Vallet, E. Motta, and P. Castells. Semantic Search Meets the Web. In *IEEE Semantic Computing*, pages 253–260, 2008.

[15] A. Harth, J. Umbrich, A. Hogan, and S. Decker. YARS2: A Federated Repository for Querying Graph Structured Data from the Web. *The Semantic Web*, pages 211–224, 2008.

[16] J. He, C. Zhai, and X. Li. Evaluation of methods for relative comparison of retrieval systems based on clickthroughs. In *Proceedings of the 18th ACM conference on Information and knowledge management - CIKM '09*, page 2029, New York, New York, USA, 2009. ACM Press.

[17] Y. Huang, Z. Liu, and Y. Chen. Query biased snippet generation in XML search. In *SIGMOD '08: Proceedings of the 2008 ACM SIGMOD international conference on Management of data*, pages 315–326, New York, NY, USA, 2008. ACM.

[18] T. Kanungo, N. Ghamrawi, K. Y. Kim, and L. Wai. Web search result summarization: title selection algorithms and user satisfaction. In *CIKM '09: Proceeding of the 18th ACM conference on Information and knowledge management*, pages 1581–1584, New York, NY, USA, 2009. ACM.

[19] T. Kanungo and D. Orr. Predicting the readability of short web summaries. In *WSDM '09: Proceedings of the Second ACM International Conference on Web Search and Data Mining*, pages 202–211, New York, NY, USA, 2009. ACM.

[20] N. Kushmerick, D. S. Weld, and R. B. Doorenbos. Wrapper induction for information extraction. In *IJCAI*, pages 729–737, 1997.

[21] K. McKeown, R. J. Passonneau, D. K. Elson, A. Nenkova, and J. Hirschberg. Do summaries help? In *SIGIR '05*, pages 210–217, New York, NY, USA. ACM.

[22] G. H. McLaughlin. SMOG Grading-a New Readability Formula. *Journal of Reading*, 12(8):639–646, 1969.

[23] P. Mika, E. Meij, and H. Zaragoza. Investigating the semantic gap through query log analysis. In *Proceedings of the International Semantic Web Conference - ISWC '09*, volume 5823 of *Lecture Notes in Computer Science*, pages 441–455. Springer, 2009.

[24] E. Oren, R. Delbru, M. Catasta, R. Cyganiak, H. Stenzhorn, and G. Tummarello. Sindice.com: a document-oriented lookup index for open linked data. *IJMSO*, 3(1):37–52, 2008.

[25] T. Penin, H. Wang, T. Tran, and Y. Yu. Snippet Generation for Semantic Web Search Engines. In *ASWC '08: Proceedings of the 3rd Asian Semantic Web Conference on The Semantic Web*, pages 493–507, Berlin, Heidelberg, 2008. Springer-Verlag.

[26] E. Pietriga, C. Bizer, D. Karger, and R. Lee. Fresnel: A Browser-Independent Presentation Vocabulary for RDF. In *The Semantic Web - ISWC 2006*, pages 158–171, 2006.

[27] E. Prud'hommeaux and A. Seaborne. SPARQL Query Language for RDF, January 2008. http://www.w3.org/TR/2008/REC-rdf-sparql-query-20080115/.

[28] J.-T. Sun, D. Shen, H.-J. Zeng, Q. Yang, Y. Lu, and Z. Chen. Web-page summarization using clickthrough data. In R. A. Baeza-Yates, N. Ziviani, G. Marchionini, A. Moffat, and J. Tait, editors, *SIGIR'05*, pages 194–201. ACM, 2005.

[29] T. Tran, H. Wang, and P. Haase. SearchWebDB: Data Web Search on a Pay-As-You-Go Integration Infrastructure, 2008.

[30] A. Turpin, Y. Tsegay, D. Hawking, and H. E. Williams. Fast generation of result snippets in web search. In *SIGIR'07*, pages 127–134, 2007.

[31] R. Varadarajan and V. Hristidis. Structure-based query-specific document summarization. In *Proceedings of the 14th ACM international conference on Information and knowledge management*, CIKM '05, pages 231–232, New York, NY, USA, 2005. ACM.

[32] H. Wang, P. Haase, R. Studer, T. Penin, K. Xu, J. Chen, X. Sun, L. Fu, Q. Liu, Y. Yu, and T. Tran. Hermes: a travel through semantics on the data web. In *Proceedings of the 35th SIGMOD international conference on Management of data - SIGMOD '09*, page 1135. ACM Press, 2009.

[33] R. W. White, I. Ruthven, and J. M. Jose. Finding relevant documents using top ranking sentences: an evaluation of two alternative schemes. In *SIGIR'02*, pages 57–64, New York, NY, USA, 2002. ACM.

[34] L. Zhang, Q. Liu, J. Zhang, H. Wang, Y. Pan, and Y. Yu. Semplore: An ir approach to scalable hybrid query of semantic web data. In *In Proc. of the 7th Intl. Semantic Web Conference*, pages 652–665, 2008.

Summarizing the Differences in Multilingual News

Xiaojun Wan, Houping Jia, Shanshan Huang and Jianguo Xiao
Institute of Computer Science and Technology, Peking University, Beijing 100871, China
Key Laboratory of Computational Linguistics (Peking University), MOE, China
{wanxiaojun, jiahouping, huangshanshan, xiaojianguo}@icst.pku.edu.cn

ABSTRACT
There usually exist many news articles written in different languages about a hot news event. The news articles in different languages are written in different ways to reflect different standpoints. For example, the Chinese news agencies and the Western news agencies have published many articles to report the same news of "Liu Xiaobo's Nobel Prize" in Chinese and English languages, respectively. The Chinese news articles and the English news articles share something about the news fact in common, but they focus on different aspects in order to reflect different standpoints about the event. In this paper, we investigate the task of multilingual news summarization for the purpose of finding and summarizing the major differences between the news articles about the same event in the Chinese and English languages. We propose a novel constrained co-ranking (C-CoRank) method for addressing this special task. The C-CoRank method adds the constraints between the difference score and the common score of each sentence to the co-ranking process. Evaluation results on the manually labeled test set with 15 news topics show the effectiveness of our proposed method, and the constrained co-ranking method can outperform a few baselines and the typical co-ranking method.

Categories and Subject Descriptors
H.3.1 [**Information Storage and Retrieval**]: Content Analysis and Indexing – *abstracting methods*; I.2.7 [**Artificial Intelligence**]: Natural Language Processing – *text analysis*

General Terms
Algorithms, Experimentation, Design.

Keywords
Multi-document summarization, multilingual summarization, constrained co-ranking.

1. INTRODUCTION
With the advent of a hot news event, many news articles are written and published by different news agencies in different languages. The news articles in different languages are usually written in different ways. The contents in these news articles are overlapping with each other, but they usually cover a few different aspects about the event (or they have different focuses), because the agencies write the articles with different backgrounds, standpoints and purposes. For example, given the news of "Liu Xiaobo's Nobel Prize", in addition to the common content of event introduction, most Chinese news articles aim to reflect Chinese policies and standpoints about the event, but most English news articles aim to reflect the western countries' understanding about the event. The reading of only the news articles in a single language will be biased. The summary of the differences between the two sets of news articles in the two languages can be used to help people understand the event in a more comprehensive and unbiased way.

We focus on summarizing the major differences in multilingual news (Chinese vs. English) in this study. Given a Chinese document set and an English document set about the same event, a Chinese summary is required to be created to reflect the major differential aspects in the Chinese news articles, and an English summary is required to be created to reflect the major differential aspects in the English news articles. In other words, the content in the Chinese summary is not the focus of the English documents, and the content in the English summary is not the focus of the Chinese documents. Our task can be considered as an extension of the update summarization task [7] in the following two ways: 1) our task aims to simultaneously create two summaries for two document sets to reflect the major differences in the two sets, while the update summarization task aims to create a summary for one document set after reading the other document set; 2) our task is defined in a multilingual setting, while the update summarization task is defined in a monolingual setting.

In this study, we present two graph-based ranking methods for addressing this special summarization task. The first method is named CoRank, which can simultaneously extract a Chinese summary and an English summary from the two document sets in a unified graph-based ranking process. The second method is named Constrained CoRank (C-CoRank), which improves the CoRank method by introducing a new factor (common score) for each sentence and adding important constraints into the graph-based ranking process. We manually labeled the Chinese and English difference summaries for 15 news topics, and the experimental results on the data set show the effectiveness of our proposed method. The C-CoRank method can significantly outperform the baselines and the CoRank method.

The rest of this paper is organized as follows: Section 2 reviews related work. Our proposed method is presented in Section 3. Sections 4 and 5 show the experiments and results. Lastly, we conclude this paper in Section 6.

SIGIR'11, July 24–28, 2011, Beijing, China.

2. RELATED WORK

2.1 Generic Document Summarization

Document summarization methods can be extraction-based, abstraction-based or hybrid methods. We focus on extraction-based methods in this study, and the methods directly extract summary sentences from a document or document set by ranking the sentences in the document or document set.

In the task of single document summarization, various features have been investigated for ranking sentences in a document, including term frequency, sentence position, cue words, stigma words, and topic signature [16, 21]. Machine learning techniques have been used for sentence ranking [2, 13]. Litvak et al. [20] present a language-independent approach for extractive summarization based on the linear optimization of several sentence ranking measures using a genetic algorithm. In recent years, graph-based methods have been proposed for sentence ranking [9, 23]. Other methods include mutual reinforcement principle [33, 38].

In the task of multi-document summarization, the centroid-based method [28] ranks the sentences in a document set based on such features as cluster centroids, position and TFIDF. NeATS [17] makes use of new features such as topic signature to select important sentences. Machine Learning techniques have also been used for feature combining [37]. Themes (or topics, clusters) discovery in documents has been used for sentence selection [11]. Nenkova and Louis [26] investigate the influences of input difficulty on summarization performance. Celikyilmaz and Hakkani-Tur [6] formulate extractive summarization as a two-step learning problem by building a generative model for pattern discovery and a regression model for inference. Aker et al. [1] propose an A* search algorithm to find the best extractive summary up to a given length, and they propose a discriminative training algorithm for directly maximizing the quality of the best summary. Graph-based methods have also been used to rank sentences for multi-document summarization [24, 30, 32, 34].

2.2 Update Summarization

Update summarization is an emerging new summarization task in the very recent years. Piloted in DUC2007, the task aims to create a short summary of a set of news articles, under the assumption that the user has already read a given set of earlier articles [7]. The update summary is expected to be relevant to the given query or topic, and contain salient and new content in the current articles. Many existing multi-document summarization methods can be adapted for this task by considering the information in the earlier documents. For example, Fisher and Roark [10] present a supervised sentence ranking approach for extractive update summarization. Nastase et al. [25] present an update summarization technique based on query expansion with encyclopedic knowledge and activation spreading in a large document graph. Boudin et al. [3] revise the MMR criteria for update summarization. Li et al. [15] propose a novel graph-based sentence ranking algorithm named PNR^2 for update summarization, and it models both the positive and negative mutual reinforcement between sentences in the ranking process. Du et al. [8] propose a novel approach based on manifold ranking with sink points for update summarization. Wang and Li [2010] propose a new summarization method based on an incremental hierarchical clustering framework to update summaries when a new document arrives. In [36], the task is a little bit different from the above update summarization task, and it aims to address the problem of incremental summarization of a periodically updated document set in a timely way.

As mentioned earlier, the update summarization task is closely related to our task. Our task can be considered as an extension of the update summarization task by requiring creating difference summaries for two document sets in a multilingual setting.

2.3 Contrastive Summarization

Though there is no common definition for contrastive summarization, the general aim of the task is to create a comparative summary for two comparable document sets. Most previous work focuses on generating comparative summaries for opinionated texts, because the opinionated texts usually contain a few explicit comparable aspects. For example, Kim and Zhai [12] formulate the problem of contrastive opinion summarization as an optimization problem and present two general methods for generating a comparative summary using the framework. Paul et al. [27] present a two-stage approach with an unsupervised probabilistic model and Comparative LexRank to summarizing multiple contrastive viewpoints in opinionated text. The most closely related work is [22, 35]. Mani and Bloedorn [22] propose an approach based on term graph to highlight the similarities and differences in related documents. They first find the common and distinct terms and then pinpoint the similarities and differences based on the terms and align text extracts across documents. Wang et al. [35] study the problem of summarizing the differences between document groups in a monolingual setting. They propose a discriminative sentence selection method to extract the most discriminative sentences from each document group. Other related work includes correlated summarization [39], which aims to summarize the correlation or similarity for a pair of news articles.

2.4 Multilingual and Cross-Lingual Summarization

Multilingual summarization [19, 29] aims to create a summary in a specific language from multiple documents in multiple languages, which is very different from our task of summarizing the differences in multilingual documents.

Cross-lingual document summarization [5, 14, 31] aims to produce a summary in a different target language for a set of documents in a source language, which is also very different from our task. One popular method first translates the source documents into the corresponding documents in the target language, and then extracts summary sentences based on the information on the target side. The other popular method first extracts summary sentences from the source documents based on the information on the source side, and then translates the summary sentences into the corresponding summary sentences in the target language.

3. OUR PROPOSED METHOD

The task of summarizing the differences in multilingual news is defined as follows: Given a set of Chinese news articles and a set of English news articles about the same news topic, the task aims to extract a few sentences from the Chinese news articles to reflect the important but differential aspects about the topic, and also extract a few sentences from the English news articles to reflect the important but differential aspects about the topic. The content of the Chinese summary is not the focus of the English news articles, and the content of the English summary is not the focus of the Chinese news articles.

In order to address the above summarization task, we present a co-ranking method (CoRank) and a constrained co-ranking method (C-CoRank) within the graph-based ranking framework. The CoRank method is inspired by the recent graph-based ranking methods for document summarization [15, 30, 33], and it can extract the difference summaries from the two document sets in a unified ranking process. The C-CoRank method is an improvement of the CoRank method by incorporating a new factor into the graph model, and adding important constraints in the ranking process.

3.1 CoRank

In this method, the Chinese sentences and the English sentences are simultaneously ranked in a unified graph-based algorithm. We assign each sentence a difference score to indicate how much the sentence contains important but differential information. The difference score of each Chinese sentence relies not only on the Chinese sentences in the Chinese document set, but also on the English sentences in the English document set. Similarly, the difference score of each English sentence relies not only on the English sentences in the English document set, but also on the Chinese sentences in the Chinese document set. In particular, the CoRank method is based on the following four assumptions:

Assumption 1: The difference score of a Chinese sentence would be high if the sentence is heavily correlated with other Chinese sentences with high difference scores in the Chinese document set.

Assumption 2: The difference score of a Chinese sentence would be high if the sentence is very unrelated to the English sentences with high difference scores in the English document set.

Assumption 3: The difference score of an English sentence would be high if the sentence is heavily correlated with other English sentences with high difference scores in the English document set.

Assumption 4: The difference score of an English sentence would be high if the sentence is very unrelated to the Chinese sentences with high difference scores in the Chinese document set.

Formally, given an English document set D^{en} and a Chinese document set D^{cn}, let $G=(V^{en}, V^{cn}, E^{en}, E^{cn}, E^{encn})$ be an undirected graph for the sentences in the two document sets. $V^{en}=\{s^{en}_i \mid 1\le i\le m\}$ is the set of English sentences. $V^{cn}=\{s^{cn}_i \mid 1\le i\le n\}$ is the set of Chinese sentences. m, n are the sentence numbers in the two document sets, respectively. Each sentence is represented by a term vector in the VSM model[1]. The term weight is computed by TFIDF. E^{en} is the edge set to reflect the relationships between the English sentences in the English document set. E^{cn} is the edge set to reflect the relationships between the Chinese sentences in the Chinese document set. E^{encn} is the edge set to reflect the relationships between the English sentences and the Chinese sentences. Based on the graph representation, we compute the following matrices to reflect the three kinds of sentence relationships:

$\boldsymbol{M}^{en}=(M^{en}_{ij})_{m\times m}$: This matrix aims to reflect the similarity relationships between the English sentences. Each entry in the matrix corresponds to the cosine similarity between the two English sentences.

$$M^{en}_{ij}=\begin{cases} sim_{cosine}(s^{en}_i, s^{en}_j), & if\ i\neq j \\ 0, & otherwise \end{cases}$$

Then $\boldsymbol{M}^{en}$ is normalized to $\widetilde{\boldsymbol{M}}^{en}$ to make the sum of each row equal to 1.

$\boldsymbol{M}^{cn}=(M^{cn}_{ij})_{n\times n}$: This matrix aims to reflect the similarity relationships between the Chinese sentences. Each entry in the matrix corresponds to the cosine similarity between the two Chinese sentences.

$$M^{cn}_{ij}=\begin{cases} sim_{cosine}(s^{cn}_i, s^{cn}_j), & if\ i\neq j \\ 0, & otherwise \end{cases}$$

Then $\boldsymbol{M}^{cn}$ is normalized to $\widetilde{\boldsymbol{M}}^{cn}$ to make the sum of each row equal to 1.

$\boldsymbol{M}^{encn}=(M^{encn}_{ij})_{m\times n}$: This matrix aims to reflect the difference relationships between the English sentences and the Chinese sentences. Each entry M^{encn}_{ij} in the matrix corresponds to the distance between the English sentence s^{en}_i and the Chinese sentence s^{cn}_j. It is hard to directly compute the distance between the sentences in different languages. In this study, the distance value is computed by fusing the following two distance values: the normalized Euclidean distance between the English sentence s^{en}_i and the translated English sentence $s^{transen}_j$ for s^{cn}_j, and the normalized Euclidean distance between the translated Chinese sentence $s^{transcn}_i$ for s^{en}_i and the Chinese sentence s^{cn}_j [2]. We use the geometric mean of the two values as the difference weight.

$$M^{encn}_{ij}=\sqrt{Dis_{NEuclidean}(s^{en}_i, s^{transen}_j)\times Dis_{NEuclidean}(s^{transcn}_i, s^{cn}_j)}$$

The normalized Euclidean distance between two sentences (s_i and s_j) is computed by normalizing the Euclidean distance between the two term vectors ($\vec{s}_i$ and $\vec{s}_j$) by dividing the sum of the norms of the vectors.

$$Dis_{NEuclidean}(s_i, s_j)=\frac{\|\vec{s}_i-\vec{s}_j\|}{\|\vec{s}_i\|+\|\vec{s}_j\|}$$

Then $\boldsymbol{M}^{encn}$ is normalized to $\widetilde{\boldsymbol{M}}^{encn}$ to make the sum of each row equal to 1.

In addition, we use $\boldsymbol{M}^{cnen}=(M^{cnen}_{ij})_{n\times m}$ to denote the transpose of $\boldsymbol{M}^{encn}$, i.e., $\boldsymbol{M}^{cnen}=(\boldsymbol{M}^{encn})^{\mathrm{T}}$. Then $\boldsymbol{M}^{cnen}$ is normalized to $\widetilde{\boldsymbol{M}}^{cnen}$ to make the sum of each row equal to 1.

We use two column vectors $\boldsymbol{u}=[u(s^{cn}_i)]_{n\times 1}$ and $\boldsymbol{v}=[v(s^{en}_j)]_{m\times 1}$ to denote the difference scores of the Chinese sentences and the English sentences, respectively. The above four assumptions can be rendered as follows:

$$u(s^{cn}_i)\propto \sum_j \widetilde{M}^{cn}_{ji}u(s^{cn}_j)$$

$$v(s^{en}_j)\propto \sum_i \widetilde{M}^{en}_{ij}v(s^{en}_i)$$

[1] For Chinese sentences, a term means a Chinese word after applying Chinese word segmentation.

[2] We use the Google Translate service for automatic Chinese-to-English and English-to-Chinese sentence translation. The normalized Euclidean performs better than the cosine-based distance in our study.

$$u(s_i^{cn}) \propto \sum_j \widetilde{M}_{ji}^{encn} v(s_j^{en})$$

$$v(s_j^{en}) \propto \sum_i \widetilde{M}_{ij}^{cnen} u(s_i^{cn})$$

After fusing the above equations, we can obtain the following iterative forms:

$$u(s_i^{cn}) = \alpha \sum_j \widetilde{M}_{ji}^{cn} u(s_j^{cn}) + \beta \sum_j \widetilde{M}_{ji}^{encn} v(s_j^{en})$$

$$v(s_j^{en}) = \alpha \sum_i \widetilde{M}_{ij}^{en} v(s_i^{en}) + \beta \sum_i \widetilde{M}_{ij}^{cnen} u(s_i^{cn})$$

And the matrix form is:

$$\boldsymbol{u} = \alpha(\widetilde{\boldsymbol{M}}^{cn})^T \boldsymbol{u} + \beta(\widetilde{\boldsymbol{M}}^{encn})^T \boldsymbol{v}$$

$$\boldsymbol{v} = \alpha(\widetilde{\boldsymbol{M}}^{en})^T \boldsymbol{v} + \beta(\widetilde{\boldsymbol{M}}^{cnen})^T \boldsymbol{u}$$

where α and β specify the relative contributions to the final difference scores from the information in the same language and the information in the other language and we have $\alpha+\beta=1$.

For numerical computation of the scores, we can iteratively run the two equations until convergence. Usually the convergence of the iteration algorithm is achieved when the difference between the scores computed at two successive iterations for any sentences falls below a given threshold. In order to guarantee the convergence of the iterative form, $\boldsymbol{u}$ and $\boldsymbol{v}$ are normalized after each iteration.

After we obtain the difference scores $\boldsymbol{u}$ and $\boldsymbol{v}$ for the Chinese and English sentences, we apply the same greedy algorithm [34] for redundancy removing in each language. Finally, a few highly ranked Chinese sentences are selected as the difference summary for the Chinese document set, and a few highly ranked English sentences are selected as the difference summary for the English document set.

3.2 C-CoRank

This method improves the CoRank method by introducing a new factor for each sentence and adding strict constraints in the ranking process. In addition to the difference score, we introduce a common score for each sentence to indicate how much a sentence contains important and common information in the two document sets. Similarly, the common scores of the sentences can be computed based on the following four assumptions:

Assumption 5: The common score of a Chinese sentence would be high if the sentence is heavily correlated with other Chinese sentences with high common scores in the Chinese document set.

Assumption 6: The common score of an English sentence would be high if the sentence is heavily correlated with other English sentences with high common scores in the English document set.

Assumption 7: The common score of a Chinese sentence would be high if the sentence is heavily correlated with the English sentences with high common scores in the English document set.

Assumption 8: The common score of an English sentence would be high if the sentence is heavily correlated with the Chinese sentences with high common scores in the Chinese document set.

In addition to the above assumptions, we assume that the difference score and the common score of each sentence is mutually exclusive.

Assumption 9: The sum of the difference score and the common score of each sentence is fixed to a particular value.

The above assumption is reasonable because if a sentence is a good sentence to be selected into the difference summary, it is not suitable to be selected into the common summary, and vice versa. This assumption can be used to adjust the inappropriately assigned difference scores for some sentences.

In order to compute the common scores for the sentences, we need to compute the following new matrices:

$\boldsymbol{W}^{encn}=(W^{encn}_{ij})_{m\times n}$: This matrix aims to reflect the similarity relationships between the English sentences and the Chinese sentences. Each entry W^{encn}_{ij} in the matrix corresponds to the similarity value between the English sentence s^{en}_i and the Chinese sentence s^{cn}_j. Similarly, the similarity value is computed by fusing the following two values: the cosine similarity value between the English sentence s^{en}_i and the translated English sentence $s^{transen}_j$ for s^{cn}_j, and the cosine similarity value between the translated Chinese sentence $s^{transcn}_i$ for s^{en}_i and the Chinese sentence s^{cn}_j. We use the geometric mean of the two values as the affinity weight.

$$W_{ij}^{encn} = \sqrt{Sim_{cosine}(s_i^{en}, s_j^{transen}) \times Sim_{cosine}(s_i^{transcn}, s_j^{cn})}$$

Then $\boldsymbol{W}^{encn}$ is normalized to $\widetilde{\boldsymbol{W}}^{encn}$ to make the sum of each row equal to 1.

In addition, we use $\boldsymbol{W}^{cnen}=(W^{cnen}_{ij})_{n\times m}$ to denote the transpose of $\boldsymbol{W}^{encn}$, i.e., $\boldsymbol{W}^{cnen}= (\boldsymbol{W}^{encn})^T$. Then $\boldsymbol{W}^{cnen}$ is normalized to $\widetilde{\boldsymbol{W}}^{cnen}$ to make the sum of each row equal to 1.

We use two column vectors $\boldsymbol{y}=[y(s^{cn}_i)]_{n\times 1}$ and $\boldsymbol{z} =[z(s^{en}_j)]_{m\times 1}$ to denote the common scores of the Chinese sentences and the English sentences, respectively. Based on the assumptions 5-8, we can similarly obtain the following iterative forms:

$$y(s_i^{cn}) = \alpha \sum_j \widetilde{M}_{ji}^{cn} y(s_j^{cn}) + \beta \sum_j \widetilde{W}_{ji}^{encn} z(s_j^{en})$$

$$z(s_j^{en}) = \alpha \sum_i \widetilde{M}_{ij}^{en} z(s_i^{en}) + \beta \sum_i \widetilde{W}_{ij}^{cnen} y(s_i^{cn})$$

And the matrix form is:

$$\boldsymbol{y} = \alpha(\widetilde{\boldsymbol{M}}^{cn})^T \boldsymbol{y} + \beta(\widetilde{\boldsymbol{W}}^{encn})^T \boldsymbol{z}$$

$$\boldsymbol{z} = \alpha(\widetilde{\boldsymbol{M}}^{en})^T \boldsymbol{z} + \beta(\widetilde{\boldsymbol{W}}^{cnen})^T \boldsymbol{y}$$

In order to simplify the parameter tuning, we use the same parameters of α and β as in the CoRank algorithm, and we have $\alpha+\beta=1$.

Till now the common scores and the difference scores are computed by using the CoRank algorithm separately. Based on assumption 9, we can add the following constraints at each iteration:

$$u(s_i^{cn}) + y(s_i^{cn}) = \delta(s_i^{cn})$$

$$v(s_j^{en}) + z(s_j^{en}) = \delta(s_j^{en})$$

where $\delta(s^{cn}_i)$ and $\delta(s^{en}_j)$ are the specified constraint value for the sentences s^{cn}_i and s^{en}_j. It is obvious that the values for different sentences should be different, because not all sentences are equally important in the document sets. For example, the constraint value for a trivial sentence should be smaller than that for a salient sentence. In this study, we use the generic saliency score of each sentence as the constraint value for the sentence. The generic saliency score of a Chinese sentence is computed by using the basic graph-based ranking algorithm based on $\widetilde{M}^{cn}$ in the Chinese document set. It can be formulated in a recursive form as in the PageRank algorithm:

$$\delta(s_i^{cn}) = \mu \cdot \sum_{all\, j \neq i} \delta(s_j^{cn}) \cdot \widetilde{M}_{ji}^{cn} + \frac{(1-\mu)}{n}$$

where μ is the damping factor usually set to 0.85, as in the PageRank algorithm.

The generic saliency score of an English sentence is computed based on $\widetilde{M}^{en}$ in a similar way.

In order to add the constraints to the ranking process, all the difference and common scores are initialized to 1, and the following steps are iteratively performed:

1) Perform the following two equations to compute the difference scores of the sentences:

$$u^{(t+1)}(s_i^{cn}) = \alpha \sum_j \widetilde{M}_{ji}^{cn} u^{(t)}(s_j^{cn}) + \beta \sum_j \widetilde{M}_{ji}^{encn} v^{(t)}(s_j^{en})$$

$$v^{(t+1)}(s_j^{en}) = \alpha \sum_i \widetilde{M}_{ij}^{en} v^{(t)}(s_i^{en}) + \beta \sum_i \widetilde{M}_{ij}^{cnen} u^{(t)}(s_i^{cn})$$

$$\boldsymbol{u}^{(t+1)} = \boldsymbol{u}^{(t+1)} / \left\| \boldsymbol{u}^{(t+1)} \right\| \quad \boldsymbol{v}^{(t+1)} = \boldsymbol{v}^{(t+1)} / \left\| \boldsymbol{v}^{(t+1)} \right\|$$

2) Perform the following two equations to compute the common scores of the sentences:

$$y^{(t+1)}(s_i^{cn}) = \alpha \sum_j \widetilde{M}_{ji}^{cn} y^{(t)}(s_j^{cn}) + \beta \sum_j \widetilde{W}_{ji}^{encn} z^{(t)}(s_j^{en})$$

$$z^{(t+1)}(s_j^{en}) = \alpha \sum_i \widetilde{M}_{ij}^{en} z^{(t)}(s_i^{en}) + \beta \sum_i \widetilde{W}_{ij}^{cnen} y^{(t)}(s_i^{cn})$$

$$\boldsymbol{y}^{(t+1)} = \boldsymbol{y}^{(t+1)} / \left\| \boldsymbol{y}^{(t+1)} \right\| \quad \boldsymbol{z}^{(t+1)} = \boldsymbol{z}^{(t+1)} / \left\| \boldsymbol{z}^{(t+1)} \right\|$$

3) Normalize the difference score and the common score of each sentence to meet the constraints ($\boldsymbol{\eta}$, $\boldsymbol{\zeta}$ are temporary vectors):

$$\eta^{(t+1)}(s_i^{cn}) = u^{(t+1)}(s_i^{cn}) + y^{(t+1)}(s_i^{cn})$$

$$\xi^{(t+1)}(s_j^{en}) = v^{(t+1)}(s_j^{en}) + z^{(t+1)}(s_j^{en})$$

$$u^{(t+1)}(s_i^{cn}) = \delta(s_i^{cn}) \cdot \frac{u^{(t+1)}(s_i^{cn})}{\eta^{(t+1)}(s_i^{cn})}$$

$$y^{(t+1)}(s_i^{cn}) = \delta(s_i^{cn}) \cdot \frac{y^{(t+1)}(s_i^{cn})}{\eta^{(t+1)}(s_i^{cn})}$$

$$v^{(t+1)}(s_j^{en}) = \delta(s_j^{en}) \cdot \frac{v^{(t+1)}(s_j^{en})}{\xi^{(t+1)}(s_j^{en})}$$

$$z^{(t+1)}(s_j^{en}) = \delta(s_j^{en}) \cdot \frac{z^{(t+1)}(s_j^{en})}{\xi^{(t+1)}(s_j^{en})}$$

Note that the difference scores and the common scores are linearly normalized in the third step. For numerical computation of the scores, we can iteratively run the above steps until convergence or the iteration count reaches a preset number.

Finally, we obtain the difference scores $\boldsymbol{u}$ and $\boldsymbol{v}$ for the Chinese and English sentences, and we apply the same greedy algorithm [34] for redundancy removing in each language. The difference summaries in the two languages are produced by selecting the highly ranked sentences, respectively.

4. EVALUATION SETUP

4.1 Data Set

There is no benchmark dataset for difference summarization of multilingual news, so we built the evaluation dataset as follows:

We first selected 15 hot news topics (e.g. "G20 summit in 2010", "North Korea's attack on South Korea", "Liu Xiaobo's Nobel Prize", etc.), and then collected a few news articles about each topic in the Chinese and English languages by using both the Chinese and English versions of *Google News Search*[3]. For each topic, we selected the articles in the two languages within the same period. We collected the news articles published by major Chinese and Western news agencies. The statistics of the corpus are summarized in Table 1.

Table 1: Corpus statistics

	Average article number per topic	Average length per article
Chinese	36.3	498 words 885 characters
English	28.3	606 words

The articles were first split into sentences. The Chinese sentences were automatically translated into English sentences by using *Google Translate*[4], and the English sentences were automatically translated into Chinese sentences by using *Google Translate*. All the Chinese sentences (including the translated Chinese sentences) were segmented into words by using the Stanford Chinese Word Segmenter[5].

Two graduate students were employed to manually label the reference summaries for the 15 topics. Each student was asked to read both the Chinese and English documents for each topic, and then selected five Chinese sentences and five English sentences as reference difference summaries for the two document sets. The labeling process lasted two weeks. Finally, there were totally 30 Chinese reference summaries and 30 English reference summaries. The Chinese reference summaries were segmented into words by using the same word segmentation tool.

[3] The English Google News is http://news.google.com/
The Chinese Google News is http://news.google.com.hk/

[4] http://translate.google.com/

[5] http://nlp.stanford.edu/software/segmenter.shtml

4.2 Evaluation Metric

In the experiments, the summary length was fixed to five sentences in both languages. We used the ROUGE-1.5.5 [18] toolkit for comparing the system summaries with the reference summaries, which has been widely adopted by DUC and TAC for automatic summarization evaluation. It measured summary quality by counting overlapping units such as the n-gram, word sequences and word pairs between the candidate summary and the reference summary. We showed the most popular two ROUGE F-measure scores in the experimental results: ROUGE-2 (bigram-based) and ROUGE-SU4 (based on skip bigram with a maximum skip distance of 4). For Chinese summaries, we reported two types of ROUGE scores: character–based and word-based. Character-based ROUGE scores were computed based on Chinese characters, and word-based ROUGE scores were computed based on Chinese words after using word segmentation. Character-based evaluation will not be influenced by the word segmentation performance, but Chinese character is less meaningful than Chinese word.

5. EVALUATION RESULTS

The CoRank and C-CoRank methods are compared with the following three baselines:

Centroid: This baseline uses the centroid-based method [28] to compute the saliency scores of the sentences in each language separately. The saliency score of each sentence is computed by linearly combining the following three features: the cosine similarity between the sentence and the whole document set, the cosine similarity between the sentence and the first sentence within the same document, and the position-based weight. The highly ranked sentences are selected into the difference summary after removing redundancy. Note that this baseline does not make any use of the cross-lingual information between the two document sets.

Centroid++: This baseline is an improvement of the centroid-based method by integrating the feature of the similarity between each sentence and the sentences in the other language. The difference score of each sentence is the subtraction of the centroid-based weight and the cross-language similarity value.

MMR++: This baseline uses the update summarization method in [3]. It revises the MMR criteria [4] by incorporating the cross-language sentence similarity.

Table 2 shows the comparison results for Chinese difference summaries, and Table 3 shows the comparison results for English difference summaries. The parameter value of α for the CoRank and C-CoRank methods is simply set to 0.5 without tuning. We can see that both the CoRank and C-CoRank methods can significantly outperform the baselines methods over all metrics in both languages. The C-CoRank method can significantly outperform the CoRank method over most metrics. The results demonstrate the good effectiveness of the proposed C-CoRank method. The reason is that the introduction of the new factor of common score and the constraints can make the computation of the difference scores more reliable.

Table 2. Comparison results (F-measure) for Chinese difference summaries

	Word-Based		Character-Based	
	ROUGE -2	ROUGE -SU4	ROUGE -2	ROUGE -SU4
Centroid	0.01589	0.02676	0.08808	0.08372
Centroid++	0.01393	0.02943	0.07990	0.07823
MMR++	0.00959	0.02215	0.06364	0.07604
CoRank	0.03433*	0.04564*	0.17894*	0.17954*
C-CoRank	**0.04484*#**	**0.05314*#**	**0.18794*#**	**0.18578***

Table 3. Comparison results (F-measure) for English difference summaries

	ROUGE-2	ROUGE-SU4
Centroid	0.02568	0.04368
Centroid++	0.03079	0.04828
MMR++	0.01759	0.05342
CoRank	0.11505*	0.15421*
C-CoRank	**0.13193*#**	**0.16712*#**

(* indicates that the improvement over the three baselines are all statistically significant by using t-test. # indicates that the improvement over the CoRank method is statistically significant by using t-test.)

In order to show the influence of the parameter α on the performance of our proposed method, we present the performance curves of the CoRank and C-CoRank method over different metrics when α ranges from 0.1 to 0.9. Figures 1-4 show the performance curves for Chinese difference summaries. Figures 5-6 show the performance curves for English difference summaries.

Seen from the figures, the performance values of the CoRank method first increase with α, and then reach the peak values when α is set to a large value, and after that, the performance values almost do not change any more. The results demonstrate that the CoRank method relies more on the monolingual sentence links and the cross-language sentence links do not contribute much as expected. By analysis of the results, the CoRank method has the potential to select some sentences containing much common information into the summaries, which is not very appropriate for difference summarization.

However, the performance values of the C-CoRank method first increase with α, and then decease when α is set to a large value. The C-CoRank method can well incorporate both the monolingual information and cross-language information for the summarization task. Overall speaking, the C-CoRank method can outperform the CoRank method over almost all the metrics when α is set within a wide range. The results further demonstrate the robustness of the C-CoRank method. The use of the constraints in the C-CoRank method makes the difference score and the common score for each sentence mutually exclusive, and thus the difference score for a sentence containing much common information will not be high, when the common score for the sentence is high.

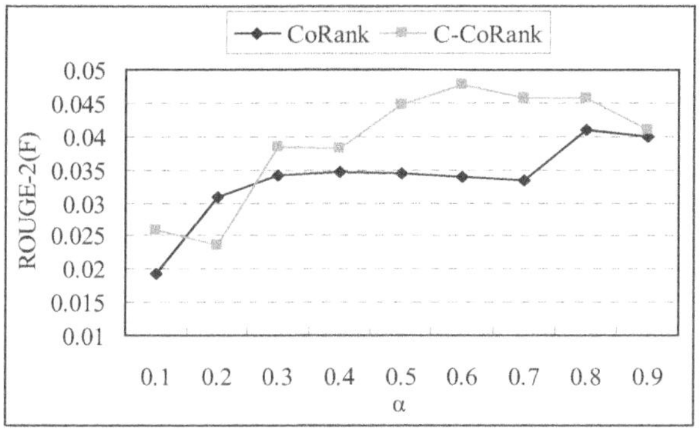

Fig.1. Word-based ROUGE-2(F-measure) vs. α for Chinese difference summaries

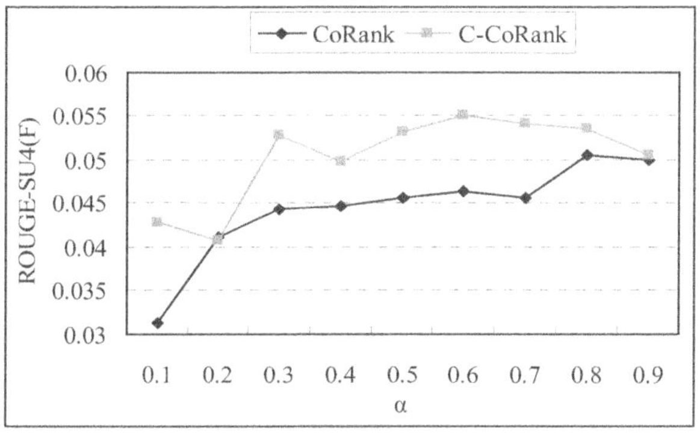

Fig.2. Word-based ROUGE-SU4(F-measure) vs. α for Chinese difference summaries

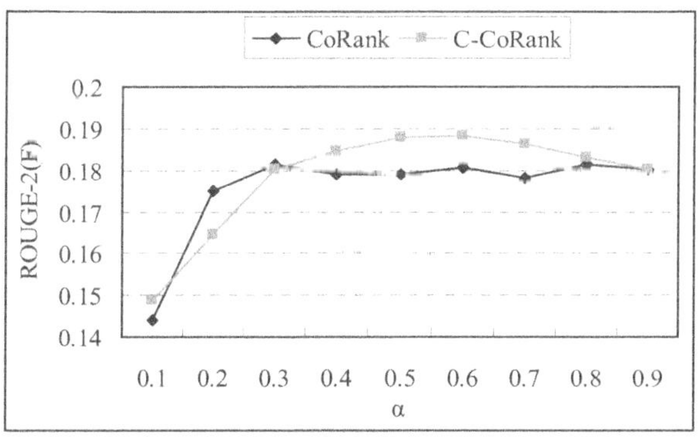

Fig.3. Character-based ROUGE-2(F-measure) vs. α for Chinese difference summaries

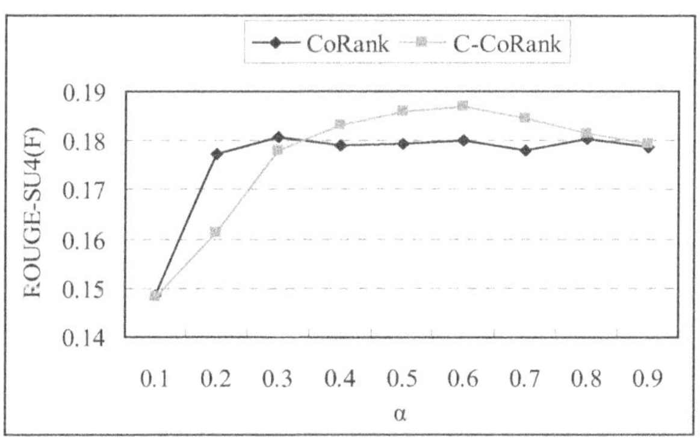

Fig.4. Character-based ROUGE-SU4(F-measure) vs. α for Chinese difference summaries

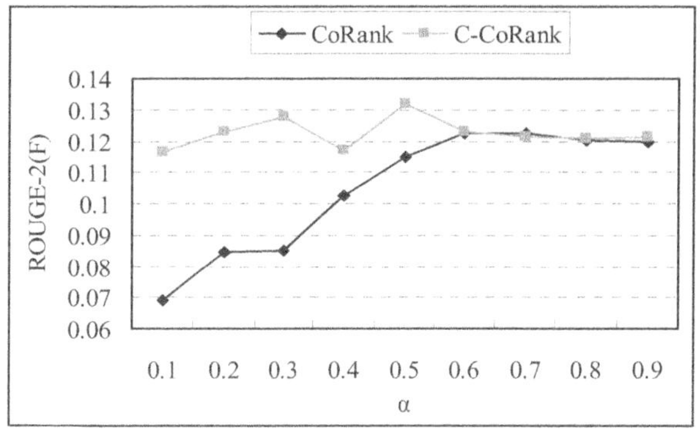

Fig.5. ROUGE-2(F-measure) vs. α for English difference summaries

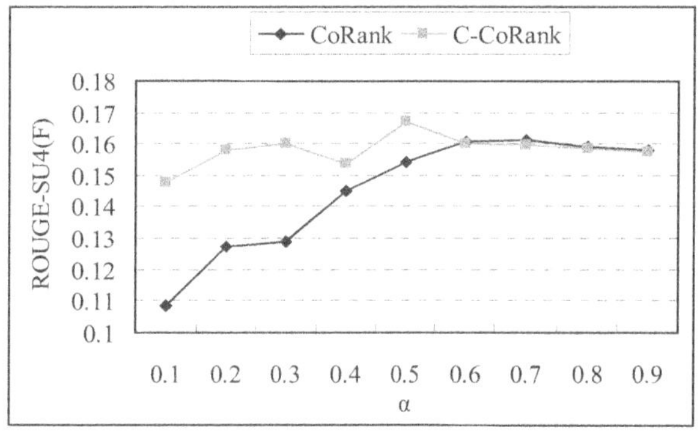

Fig.6. ROUGE-SU4(F-measure) vs. α for English difference summaries

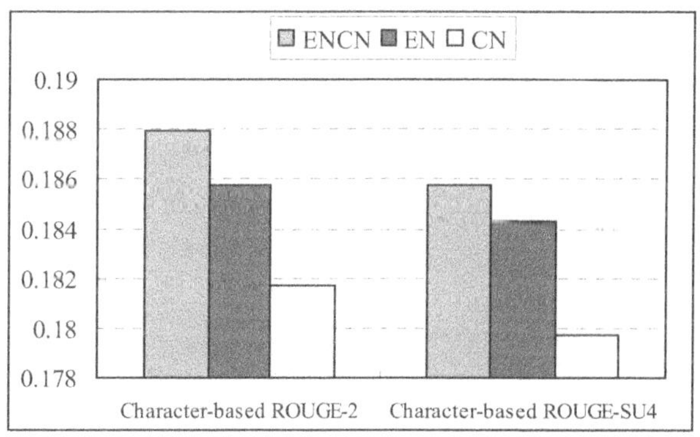

Fig.7. C-CoRank vs. Different cross-language sentence distance/similarity weights for Chinese difference summaries

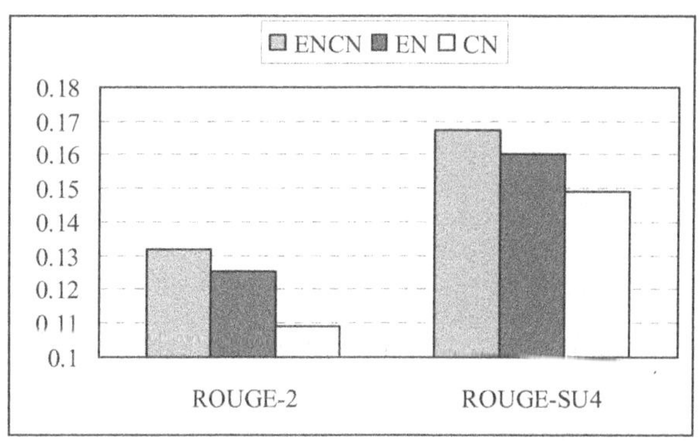

Fig.8. C-CoRank vs. Different cross-language sentence distance/similarity weights for English difference summaries

In the above experiments, the cross-language sentence distance weight in matrix $\boldsymbol{M}^{encn}$ and the cross-language sentence similarity weight in matrix $\boldsymbol{W}^{encn}$ in the C-CoRank method are computed based on the geometric mean of the Chinese-side value and the English-side value. In order to investigate whether the two values really contribute to the final performance, we compare the original weight computation method (**ENCN**) with the following two methods using only one-side value:

The first method (**EN**) uses only the English-side value, and the weights in the two matrices are computed as follows:

$$M_{ij}^{encn} = Dis_{NEuclidean}(s_i^{en}, s_j^{transen}) \quad W_{ij}^{encn} = Sim_{cosine}(s_i^{en}, s_j^{transen})$$

The second method (**CN**) uses only the Chinese-side value, and the weights in the two matrices are computed as follows:

$$M_{ij}^{encn} = Dis_{NEuclidean}(s_i^{transcn}, s_j^{cn}) \quad W_{ij}^{encn} = Sim_{cosine}(s_i^{transcn}, s_j^{cn})$$

The comparison results for the Chinese summaries and the English summaries are shown in Figures 7 and 8, respectively. We can see that the original weight computation method (ENCN) can outperform the two methods (EN and CN) using only one-side value, and both the Chinese-side information and the English-side information contribute to the final performance. We also observe that the English-side value is more reliable than the Chinese-side value for computing the cross-language sentence similarity or distance, and the reason lies in that the step of Chinese word segmentation may introduce some noise for the distance/similarity computation.

Finally, we show one running example for the topic of "Liu Xiaobo's Nobel Prize". The difference summaries produced by the C-CoRank method are given below. The manual English translation of the Chinese summary is also given. We can see that the Chinese summary focuses on the opposition and accuse of Liu Xiaobo's Nobel Prize, while the English summary focuses on the support of Liu Xiaobo's Nobel Prize and China's arrest of Liu Xiaobo. The difference summaries reflect the different standpoints of the Chinese news agencies and the Western news agencies.

The Chinese difference summary is as follows:

> 诺贝尔和平奖是西方给刘晓波的政治“犒赏”。挪威诺贝尔委员会将今年诺贝尔和平奖授予刘晓波，再次暴露了西方国家的双重标准. 诺贝尔委员会 8 日把今年的诺贝尔和平奖授予中国“异见人士”刘晓波。迄今诺贝尔和平奖授予过两个中国人，一个是达赖，另一个是刘晓波。挪威诺委会这个出于意识形态偏见和政治需要的决定，将诺贝尔和平奖沦为西方一些势力的政治工具，严重损害了诺贝尔和平奖的公信力，也玷污了诺贝尔先生的荣誉。
>
> (Nobel Peace Prize is a political "reward" to Liu Xiaobo by the West. Norwegian Nobel Committee awarded the Nobel Peace Prize to Liu Xiaobo in this year, which once again exposed the double standards of Western countries. Nobel Committee awarded this year's Nobel Peace Prize to the Chinese "dissident" - Liu Xiaobo on day 8. To date, the Nobel Peace Prize has been awarded to two Chinese persons: one is the Dalai Lama and the other is Liu Xiaobo. Norwegian Nobel Committee made the decision for ideological bias and political needs, and the Nobel Peace Prize will become a political tool of some Western forces, and it seriously undermined the credibility of the Nobel Peace Prize, but also tarnished the honor of Mr. Nobel.)

The English difference summary is as follows:

> As the West applauds Liu Xiaobo's Nobel, China sees another attempt to impose Western values on it. Norway's Nobel Peace Prize committee has done the right thing in awarding this year's prize to Chinese dissident Liu Xiaobo. Liu was represented at Friday's Nobel ceremony by an empty chair because China would not release him from prison - only the fifth time in the 109-year history of the prize that the winner was not in attendance. It tried to bully the Nobel committee into not awarding Mr. Liu this year's Nobel Peace Prize. China has prohibited Liu and his family members from leaving China to attend Friday's ceremony in Oslo. Two days after the prize was announced, Mr Liu's wife, Liu Xia, met with him at the prison in northeastern China where he is serving his sentence, but she was escorted back to Beijing and placed under house arrest, a human rights group said.

6. CONCLUSION AND FUTURE WORK

In this paper we address a novel summarization problem of summarizing the differences in multilingual news. We present the CoRank and the C-CoRank methods. In addition to the difference score of each sentence, the C-CoRank method incorporates the common score of each sentence into the ranking process by adding strict constraints. Evaluation results on the manually labeled test set demonstrate the effectiveness and robustness of the C-CoRank method.

In future work, we will adapt the proposed C-CoRank method for the update summarization task to further investigate its robustness. We will also summarize the differences between the news articles written by different news agencies in a monolingual setting. In addition to two languages, we will extend the summarization framework to summarize the differences in three or more languages.

7. ACKNOWLEDGMENTS

This work was supported by NSFC (60873155), Beijing Nova Program (2008B03) and NCET (NCET-08-0006). We thank the anonymous reviewers for their helpful comments.

8. REFERENCES

[1] A. Aker, T. Cohn, and R. Gaizauskas. Multi-document summarization using A* search and discriminative training. In Proceedings of EMNLP2010.

[2] M. R. Amini, P. Gallinari. The Use of Unlabeled Data to Improve Supervised Learning for Text Summarization. In Proceedings of SIGIR2002.

[3] F. Boudin, M. El-Bèze, J.-M. Torres-Moreno. The LIA update summarization systems at TAC-2008. In Proceedings of TAC2008.

[4] J. Carbonell and J. Goldstein. The use of MMR, diversity-based reranking for reordering documents and producing summaries. In Proceedings of SIGIR1998.

[5] G. de Chalendar, R. Besançon, O. Ferret, G. Grefenstette, and O. Mesnard. Crosslingual summarization with thematic extraction, syntactic sentence simplification, and bilingual generation. In Workshop on Crossing Barriers in Text Summarization Research, 5th International Conference on Recent Advances in Natural Language Processing (RANLP2005).

[6] A. Celikyilmaz and D. Hakkani-Tur. A hybrid hierarchical model for multi-document summarization. In Proceedings of ACL2010.

[7] H. T. Dang and K. Owczarzak. Overview of the TAC 2008 update summarization task. In Proceedings of TAC2008.

[8] P. Du, J. Guo, J. Zhang, X. Cheng. Manifold ranking with sink points for update summarization. In Proceedings of CIKM2010.

[9] G. ErKan, D. R. Radev. LexPageRank. Prestige in Multi-Document Text Summarization. In Proceedings of EMNLP2004.

[10] S. Fisher and B. Roark. Query-focused supervised sentence ranking for update summaries. In Proceeding of TAC2008.

[11] S. Harabagiu and F. Lacatusu. Topic themes for multi-document summarization. In Proceedings of SIGIR2005.

[12] H. D. Kim and C. Zhai. Generating comparative summaries of contradictory opinions in text. In Proceedings of CIKM2009.

[13] J. Kupiec, J. Pedersen, F. Chen. A.Trainable Document Summarizer. In Proceedings of SIGIR1995.

[14] A. Leuski, C.-Y. Lin, L. Zhou, U. Germann, F. J. Och, E. Hovy. Cross-lingual C*ST*RD: English access to Hindi information. ACM Transactions on Asian Language Information Processing, 2(3): 245-269, 2003.

[15] W. Li, F. Wei Q. Lu and Y. He. PNR^2: Ranking sentences with positive and negative reinforcement for query-oriented update summarization. In Proceedings of COLING2008.

[16] C. Y. Lin, E. Hovy. The Automated Acquisition of Topic Signatures for Text Summarization. In Proceedings of COLING2000.

[17] C..-Y. Lin and E.. H. Hovy. From Single to Multi-document Summarization: A Prototype System and its Evaluation. In Proceedings of ACL2002.

[18] C.-Y. Lin and E.H. Hovy. Automatic Evaluation of Summaries Using N-gram Co-occurrence Statistics. In Proceedings of HLT-NAACL -2003.

[19] C.-Y. Lin, L. Zhou, and E. Hovy. Multilingual summarization evaluation 2005: automatic evaluation report. In Proceedings of MSE (ACL2005 Workshop).

[20] M. Litvak, M. Last, and M. Friedman. A new approach to improving multilingual summarization using a genetic algorithm. In Proceedings of ACL2010.

[21] H. P. Luhn. The Automatic Creation of literature Abstracts. IBM Journal of Research and Development, 2(2), 1969.

[22] I. Mani and E. Bloedorn. Summarizing similarities and differences among related documents. Information Retrieval, 1: 35-67, 1999.

[23] R. Mihalcea, P. Tarau. TextRank: Bringing Order into Texts. In Proceedings of EMNLP2004.

[24] R. Mihalcea and P. Tarau. A language independent algorithm for single and multiple document summarization. In Proceedings of IJCNLP-2005.

[25] V. Nastase, K. Filippova, S. P. Ponzetto. Generating update summaries with spreading activation. In Proceedings of TAC2008.

[26] A. Nenkova and A. Louis. Can you summarize this? Identifying correlates of input difficulty for generic multi-document summarization. In Proceedings of ACL-2008:HLT.

[27] M. J. Paul, C. Zhai, and R. Girju. Summarizing contrastive viewpoints in opinionated text. In Proceedings of EMNLP2010.

[28] D. R. Radev, H. Y. Jing, M. Stys and D. Tam. Centroid-based summarization of multiple documents. Information Processing and Management, 40: 919-938, 2004.

[29] A. Siddharthan and K. McKeown. Improving multilingual summarization: using redundancy in the input to correct MT errors. In Proceedings of HLT/EMNLP-2005.

[30] X. Wan. Towards a unified approach to simultaneous single-document and multi-document summarizations. In Proceedings of COLING2010.

[31] X. Wan, H. Li and J. Xiao. Cross-language document summarization based on machine translation quality prediction. In Proceedings of ACL2010.

[32] X. Wan and J. Yang. Multi-document summarization using cluster-based link analysis. In Proceedings of SIGIR-2008.

[33] X. Wan, J. Yang and J. Xiao. Towards an Iterative Reinforcement Approach for Simultaneous Document Summarization and Keyword Extraction. In Proceedings of ACL2007.

[34] X. Wan, J. Yang and J. Xiao. Manifold-ranking based topic-focused multi-document summarization. In Proceedings of IJCAI-2007.

[35] D. Wang, S. Zhu, T. Li, and Y. Gong. Comparative document summarization via discriminative sentence selection. In Proceedings of CIKM2009.

[36] D. Wang, T. Li. Document update summarization using incremental hierarchical clustering. In Proceedings of CIKM2010.

[37] K.-F. Wong, M. Wu and W. Li. Extractive summarization using supervised and semi-supervised learning. In Proceedings of COLING-2008.

[38] H. Y. Zha. Generic Summarization and Keyphrase Extraction Using Mutual Reinforcement Principle and Sentence Clustering. In Proceedings of SIGIR2002.

[39] Y. Zhang, X. Ji, C.-H. Chu, and H. Zha. Correlating summarization of multi-source news with K-way graph bi-clustering. SIGKDD Explorations, 6(2), 2004.

Evolutionary Timeline Summarization: a Balanced Optimization Framework via Iterative Substitution

Rui Yan
Dept. of Computer Science
Peking University
Beijing 100871, P. R. China
r.yan@pku.edu.cn

Xiaojun Wan
Institute of Computer Science and Technology
Peking University
Beijing 100871, P. R. China
wanxiaojun@icst.pku.edu.cn

Jahna Otterbacher
Lewis Department of Humanities
Illinois Institute of Technology
Chicago IL 60616, USA
jotterba@iit.edu

Liang Kong
Dept. of Machine Intelligence
Peking University
Beijing 100871, P. R. China
kongliang@pku.edu.cn

Xiaoming Li
Dept. of Computer Science
Peking University
Beijing 100871, P. R. China
lxm@pku.edu.cn

Yan Zhang*
Dept. of Machine Intelligence
Peking University
Beijing 100871, P. R. China
zhy@cis.pku.edu.cn

ABSTRACT

Classic news summarization plays an important role with the exponential document growth on the Web. Many approaches are proposed to generate summaries but seldom simultaneously consider evolutionary characteristics of news plus to traditional summary elements. Therefore, we present a novel framework for the web mining problem named Evolutionary Timeline Summarization (ETS). Given the massive collection of time-stamped web documents related to a general news query, ETS aims to return the evolution trajectory along the timeline, consisting of individual but correlated summaries of each date, emphasizing *relevance*, *coverage*, *coherence* and *cross-date diversity*. ETS greatly facilitates fast news browsing and knowledge comprehension and hence is a necessity. We formally formulate the task as an optimization problem via iterative substitution from a set of sentences to a subset of sentences that satisfies the above requirements, balancing coherence/diversity measurement and local/global summary quality. The optimized substitution is iteratively conducted by incorporating several constraints until convergence. We develop experimental systems to evaluate on 6 instinctively different datasets which amount to 10251 documents. Performance comparisons between different system-generated timelines and manually created ones by human editors demonstrate the effectiveness of our proposed framework in terms of ROUGE metrics.

*Corresponding author.

Categories and Subject Descriptors

H.3.1 [**Information Storage and Retrieval**]: Content Analysis and Indexing—*Abstracting methods*; I.2.7 [**Artificial Intelligence**]: Natural Language Processing—*Text analysis*

General Terms

Algorithms, Experimentation, Performance

Keywords

Evolutionary summarization, timeline, optimization

1. INTRODUCTION

In the beginning, we will answer three possible questions.

Why timelines? The rapid growth of World Wide Web means that document floods spread throughout the Internet. Readers get drown in the sea of documents, wondering where to access. General search engines simply return webpages ranked by query relevance, but they are not quite capable of handling ambiguous intentioned queries, such as a query about evolving news "*Influenza A*". People may have the myriad of general interests about the beginning, the evolution or the most up to date situation, while IR techniques rank the returned webpages according to their understanding of relevance, which is insufficient.

In many cases, even if the ranked documents could be in a satisfying order, readers are tired of navigating every document in the overwhelming collection: they want to monitor the evolution trajectory of hot topics by simply browsing. Summarization is an ideal solution to provide a condensed, informative document reorganization for faster and better representation of news evolution. Timeline temporally summarizes evolutionary news as a series of *individual* but *correlated* component summaries and hence offers an option to understand the big picture of a developing situation.

Why not retrieve timelines created by editors? Manually generated timelines are concise, accurate and informative but require tremendous human labor of reading and the work is really energy consuming. Hence, it is impossible to generate timelines by hands for all queries from

Table 1: Part of human generated timeline about *Influenza A* outbreak in 2009 from Fox News website*.

February 2009
The first cases of an unusually aggressive cold are reported in the town of La Gloria in the Gulf coast state of Veracruz, Mexico.
April 2, 2009
The Veracruz government notifies authorities of a possible flu outbreak in the town of La Gloria. It is initially treated as a common respiratory illness.
April 25, 2009
The WHO announces that the world faces a swine flu pandemic.
April 27, 2009
The World Health Organization raises its pandemic alert status to Phase 4, meaning there is sustained human-to-human transmission of the virus causing outbreaks in at least one country.
April 29, 2009
The first U.S. death from swine flu is confirmed, a toddler from Mexico who traveled with family to Texas, where he died in the hospital on April 27. The WHO raises its pandemic alert status to Phase 5, meaning that a pandemic is imminent.
June 11, 2009
WHO declares the swine flu a pandemic, meaning that its spread is unstoppable.
July 21, 2009
The worldwide death toll passes 700, the WHO reports. An Australian pharmaceutical company says it will begin human trials of a swine flu vaccine.
Oct. 5, 2009
The first doses of swine flu vaccine, in nasal spray form, become available in the U.S. About 2.2 million doses are available.
Oct. 27, 2009
The CDC reports more than 22 million doses of swine flu vaccine are available.

*http://interactive.foxnews.com/health/swine-flu-timeline

users. Limited handcrafted timelines can be retrieved by search engines. Therefore, it is beneficial to automatically generate high-quality timelines from a collection of various news sources. The application can be embedded into search engines to improve users' retrieval experience. *Google News Timeline*[1] tries to provide such technique but it is coarse-grained, which merely clusters news articles into topic groups and sorts them chronologically [7]. Retrieved documents are neither summarized nor distinguished by their relevance, importance or informativeness.

Why not traditional summarization? A timeline is defined as a historical account of events ranged in chronological sequences. Unlike narratives, which select events in an interpretive context, timelines are more event-aware. Summarizing timelines is obviously different from traditional multi-document summarization (MDS). We first study a manual timeline of *Influenza A* epidemic spread trajectory in Table 1 from Fox News. We discover four prominent attributes from the timeline created by professional editors:

Relevance. As users issue queries for the news, they definitely need information relevant to what they query.

Coverage. To minimize the loss of main information, timelines should cover as many as possible important aspects during the news evolution, e.g. the first infected case, vaccine development, etc. illustrated in Table 1.

Coherence. Due to the dynamic nature of news over time, events on separate dates may share dependencies such as "follow-ups", "causes" or "consequences". The component summaries within the timeline capture such coherence to reflect the evolution trajectory, e.g. the escalated emergency, vaccine development from research to practical use, etc.

Diversity. Diversity has a double meaning: selected sentences tend to avoid information redundancy within a single date and a period of dates, namely cross-date diversity.

Unfortunately, traditional MDS neglects the significant temporal dimension for evolutionary summarization, nor does it incorporate news event characteristics into summarization, such as coherence, cross-date diversity and their balance by considering temporal proximity. Additionally, timeline consists several component summaries and the quality of these summaries should be optimized both locally, i.e., based on adjacent neighbors, and globally, i.e., based on the whole collection. Compared with traditional MDS without such concepts, timeline generation faces with new challenges.

We introduce a novel framework for the web mining service Evolutionary Timeline Summarization (ETS). Taking a general query issued by users and the returned collection as input, the system automatically outputs a timeline with items of component summaries which represent evolutionary trajectories on specific dates. According to the scores of timeline attributes, summaries are generated by ranking sentences in a balanced optimization framework through iterative substitution from a set of sentences to a subset of sentences under constraints. We build an experimental system on 6 real datasets to verify the effectiveness of our methods compared with 4 rivals. ETS addresses following challenges:

• The **1st challenge** for ETS is to model the the four attributes for component summaries: items are not assumed to be completely isolated because neighboring summaries are generated interdependently due to news characteristics over time. Diversity within an individual summary has been studied by others, but *cross-date diversity* has not previously been addressed. More importantly, *coherence* between component summaries has never been considered.

• We have global/local criteria to evaluate the qualities of component summaries. The **2nd challenge** is to formulate the task into a balanced optimization problem to generate summaries which satisfy double standards and above attributes. We propose an efficient framework via iterative substitution and enforce it through constraints construction.

• Due to ETS application scenario, the large-scale Web collection brings certain difficulties. Traditional MDS faces with a limited collection size (tens of documents) while ETS faces much larger corpora. A **3rd challenge** is to deal with significant corpus compression by filtering or pre-processing.

Our contributions are manifold by solving these challenges. In Section 2 we start by reviewing previous works. In Section 3 we formulate ETS task as an optimization problem and define calculation functions based on four attributes. We explain the balanced optimization solution in Section 4 and describe the experiments in Section 5, including experimental system, performance comparisons, result discussion and case studies. Finally we draw conclusions in Section 6.

2. RELATED WORK

• Multi-document Summarization (MDS)

MDS has drawn much attention all these years and gained emphasis in workshops and conferences (SIGIR, ACL, DUC, etc.). General MDS can either be extractive or abstractive. The former assigns salient scores to semantic units (e.g. sentences, paragraphs) of the documents indicating their importance and then extracts top ranked ones, while the latter de-

[1]www.newstimeline.googlelabs.com

mands information fusion, such as sentence compression and reformulation. In this study we focus on extractive summarization to chronicle important news for timeline generation.

Centroid-based method is one of the most popular extractive summarization method. MEAD [14] and NeATS [11] are such implementations, using position, term frequency and theme, etc. MMR [6] algorithm is used to remove redundancy. Most recently, the graph-based ranking methods have been proposed to rank sentences or passages based on the "votes" or "recommendations" between each other. TextRank [13] and LexPageRank [3] use algorithms similar to PageRank and HITS to compute sentence importance. Wan *et al.* improve the graph-ranking algorithm by differentiating intra-document and inter-document links between sentences [17]. Cluster information has been incorporated in the graph model to better evaluate sentences [16]. Li *et al.* use a structural SVM to learn for sentence selection in MDS [9]. However, all these approaches are for traditional MDS and they miss the temporal dimension.

Swan and Allan construct timelines by extracting clusters of noun phrases and named entities [15]. Later they build a system to provide timelines which consist of one sentence per date, considering usefulness and novelty [1]. Chieu *et al.* build a similar system in units of sentences with interest and burstiness [2]. None of these methods enriches timeline measurement nor involves the evolutionary characteristics of news mentioned above, so we fill in the gaps by generating component summaries which are not completely independent: they have influence on "neighbors". ETS is based on a balanced optimization framework via iterative substitution.

• **Understanding News**

Topic detection and tracking (TDT) in news streams is extensively studied in the literature and identifies nature of news. Lexical similarity, temporal proximity and query relevance are introduced for topic detection as a part of task initiative, which is later combined with improved clustering techniques to establish event linkage. Novelty detection [10] is an important research branch to docide candidate event sentences. News correlation is determined by causal, temporal and rich semantic relationships in [4] or hierarchical dependencies in [5]. Features such as named entities, date or place information, and domain knowledge are deeply analyzed [21]. In this study, we do not seek to cluster "topics" like in TDT or in topic models but to utilize evolutionary correlations of news coherence/diversity for summarization.

3. PROBLEM FORMULATION

We give a formal definition of ETS as follows:

Input: Given a general query $Q=\{q_1, q_2, \dots, q_{|Q|}\}$ from users where q_i is a query word, we obtain a sentence collection C from query related documents. We cluster the sentences into $\{C_1, C_2, \dots, C_{|T|}\}$ by associated publish dates $T=\{t_1, t_2, \dots, t_{|T|}\}$. t_i is the timestamp of sub-collection C_i.

Output: A evolutionary timeline which consists of a series of individual but correlated summary items, i.e. $I=\{I_1, I_2, \dots, I_{|T|}\}$, where I_i on date t_i is a subset of C_i ($I_i \subseteq C_i$).

According to our investigation, we observe that an effective summary should properly consider the following four key requirements: (1)*Relevance*. Users are more interested in sentences which are related to the given query, which is similarly defined as "*interest*" in [2]; (2)*Coverage*. The summary should keep alignment with the source collection, which is proved to be significant as proposed in [9]; (3)*Coherence*. News changes gradually as time elapses and evolution indicates consistency among component summaries. It is a novel insight never considered before; (4)*Diversity*. According to MMR principle [6] and its applications [17, 16], a good summary should be concise and contain as few redundant sentences as possible, i.e., two sentences providing similar information should not be both present. Under our scenario, we extend to measure *cross-date diversity* as penalization to balance "coherence" and "diversity". All requirements involve a measurement of similarity between two word distributions Θ_1 and Θ_2, which are measured by Kullback-Leibler divergence here. We introduce decreasing/increasing logistic functions, $\mathcal{L}_1(x) = 1/(1+e^x)$ and $\mathcal{L}_2(x) = e^x/(1+e^x)$, to map the distance into interval [0,1]. V is the vocabulary set and $p(w|\Theta) = \frac{tf(w,\Theta)}{\sum_{w'} tf(w',\Theta)}$ where *tf* denotes the term frequency for word w.

$$D_{KL}(\Theta_1||\Theta_2) = \sum_{k\in V} p(w|\Theta_1) log \frac{p(w|\Theta_1)}{p(w|\Theta_2)}$$

Relevance. Given query Q, users are more interested in query-relevant information, namely *relevance* measured by $\mathcal{F}_r(I_i)$. However, Θ_Q is too sparse to reflect essential word distribution. Query expansion is introduced by pseudo-relevance feedback to enlarge Q. We retrieve top-κ snippets (semantic units of our system described in Section 5.2) relevant to Q to build a language model $\Theta_{Q'}$ as a worthy approximation to Θ_Q. Larger distance between Θ_{I_i} and $\Theta_{Q'}$ is not desired:

$$\mathcal{F}_r(I_i) = \mathcal{L}_1(D_{KL}(\Theta_{I_i}||\Theta_{Q'})). \quad (1)$$

Coverage. Summary I_i focuses on minimizing the loss of main information from sub-collection C_i. As ETS requires double criteria of summary quality, a good component summary should represent global source C as well to avoid probable local bias caused by discordant distributions of C_i and C. Coverage $\mathcal{F}_{cv}(I_i)$ is merged by an aggregation function for global coverage $\mathcal{F}_G(I_i) = \mathcal{L}_1(D_{KL}(\Theta_{I_i}||\Theta_C))$ and local coverage $\mathcal{F}_L(I_i) = \mathcal{L}_1(D_{KL}(\Theta_{I_i}||\Theta_{C_i}))$. We use a Jelinek-Mercer (JM) interpolation controlled by parameter λ:

$$\mathcal{F}_{cv}(I_i) = \lambda \cdot \mathcal{F}_L(I_i) + (1-\lambda) \cdot \mathcal{F}_G(I_i). \quad (2)$$

Coherence. As mentioned above, a timeline consists of a series of individual but correlated summaries. News evolves over time and a good component summary is coherent with neighboring summaries so that a timeline tracks the gradual evolution trajectory for multiple correlative news rather than the development by leaps and bounds. Therefore, we use $\mathcal{F}_{ch}(I_i)$ to evaluate *coherence* to measure the distance between Θ_{I_i} and the word distribution Θ_{N_i} from I_i's neighboring summary sets N_i.

$$\mathcal{F}_{ch}(I_i) = \mathcal{L}_1(D_{KL}(\Theta_{I_i}||\Theta_{N_i})). \quad (3)$$

Due to the scrutinized study of temporal proximity in news streams, terms on different dates are not equally weighted. Exponential decay is usually utilized to measure temporal distance [20]. Given $dtf(w, I_j|t_i) = e^{-\alpha|t_j - t_i|} \times tf(w, I_j)$, the decayed word distribution is calculated by:

$$p(w|\Theta_{N_i}) = \frac{\sum_I dtf(w, I_j|t_i)}{\sum_I \sum_{w'\in I_j}^{V} dtf(w', I_j|t_i)}.$$

Diversity. Traditional MDS shows a uniform tolerance towards redundancy to all candidate sentences, while in ETS diversity is dynamic: the tolerance arises as temporal gap enlarges. Diversity measures the novelty degree of any of the sentence s compared with all other sentences not only within I_i, but also within other component summaries with decayed weights. Such *cross-date diversity* of an average novelty score $\mathcal{F}_d(I_i)$ is calculated by leaving out all sentences in I_i, one at a time. For diversity, larger distance is desired.

$$\mathcal{F}_d(I_i) = \frac{1}{|I_i|}\sum_{s \in I_i} \mathcal{L}_2(D_{KL}(\Theta_s||\Theta_{(N_i - s)})). \quad (4)$$

Utility. Given the source collection, the utility of an individual summary item I_i is evaluated based on the weighted combination of these requirements. All function values are between 0 and 1 and for simplicity, we let $\sum_k w_k = 1$.

$$\mathcal{U}(I_i) = w_1\mathcal{F}_r(I_i) + w_2\mathcal{F}_{cv}(I_i) + w_3\mathcal{F}_{ch}(I_i) + w_4\mathcal{F}_d(I_i) \quad (5)$$

Given the sentence set C_i and the compression rate ϕ_i on t_i, there are $\phi_i|C_i|$ out of $|C_i|$ possibilities to generate I_i. The ETS task is to predict the optimized sentence subset of I_i^* from the space of all combinations for all dates. The objective function is as follows:

$$I_i^* = \underset{I_i}{\mathrm{argmax}}\, \mathcal{U}(I_i). \quad (6)$$

As $\mathcal{U}(I_i)$ is measured by the neighboring summaries in the generated timeline in our framework, we generate I_i iteratively to approximate I_i^*, i.e, maximize $\mathcal{U}(I_i)$ based on the timeline generated in the last iteration.

4. OPTIMIZATION FRAMEWORK

4.1 Sentence Selection for Summaries

Based on the proposed metric of $\mathcal{U}(.)$, during each iteration the algorithm tends to highly score sentences which are more relevant to user interests, more aligned with source texts, more coherent with neighboring components generated in the last iteration and more diversified in the timeline. Hence top ranked sentences s according to $\mathcal{U}(s)$ are strong candidates for the target summaries.

Consider $I_i^{(n-1)}$ which consists of $\phi_i|C_i|$ sentences generated in the (n-*1*)-th iteration and the top $\phi_i|C_i|$ ranked sentences in the n-th iteration (denoted by $\mathcal{S}_i^{(n)}$), they have an intersection set of $\mathcal{Z}_i^{(n)} = I_i^{(n-1)} \cap \mathcal{S}_i^{(n)}$. There is a substitutable sentence set $\mathcal{X}_i^{(n)} = I_i^{(n-1)} - \mathcal{Z}_i^{(n)}$ and a new coming candidate sentence set $\mathcal{Y}_i^{(n)} = \mathcal{S}_i^{(n)} - \mathcal{Z}_i^{(n)}$. Under defined constraints, we substitute $\mathrm{x}_i^{(n)}$ sentences with $\mathrm{y}_i^{(n)}$, where $\mathrm{x}_i^{(n)} \subseteq \mathcal{X}_i^{(n)}$ and $\mathrm{y}_i^{(n)} \subseteq \mathcal{Y}_i^{(n)}$. During every iteration, our goal is to find a substitutive pair $< \mathrm{x}_i, \mathrm{y}_i >$ for I_i:

$$< \mathrm{x}_i, \mathrm{y}_i >: \mathcal{X}_i \times \mathcal{Y}_i \rightarrow \mathcal{R}_i.$$

To measure the performance of such substitution, a discriminant utility gain function

$$\begin{aligned} \Delta\mathcal{U}^{(n)}_{\mathrm{x}_i^{(n)},\mathrm{y}_i^{(n)}} &= \mathcal{U}(I_i^{(n)}) - \mathcal{U}(I_i^{(n-1)}) \\ &= \mathcal{U}((I_i^{(n-1)} - \mathrm{x}_i^{(n)}) \cup \mathrm{y}_i^{(n)}) - \mathcal{U}(I_i^{(n-1)}) \end{aligned} \quad (7)$$

is employed to quantify the penalty. Therefore, we can predict the substitutive pair by maximizing the gain function $\Delta\mathcal{U}_{\mathrm{x}_i,\mathrm{y}_i}$ over the state set $\mathcal{R}_i$, with a size of

$$\sum_{k=0}^{\mathcal{Y}_i} A^k_{\mathcal{X}_i} C^k_{\mathcal{Y}_i}$$

where $<\mathrm{x}_i, \mathrm{y}_i> \in \mathcal{R}_i$. Finally the objective function of Equation (6) changes into maximization of utility gain by substitute $\hat{\mathrm{x}}_i$ with $\hat{\mathrm{y}}_i$ during each iteration. Formally,

$$< \hat{\mathrm{x}}_i, \hat{\mathrm{y}}_i >= \underset{\mathrm{x}_i \subseteq \mathcal{X}_i, \mathrm{y}_i \subseteq \mathcal{Y}_i}{\mathrm{argmax}} \Delta\mathcal{U}_{\mathrm{x}_i,\mathrm{y}_i}. \quad (8)$$

4.2 Balanced Optimization

A well generated summary I_i should be evaluated highly within the global collection C, and also be optimized given the local set of C_i. However, the objectives of two optimizations are not always the same because the word distributions in these source sets C and C_i are different. The substitutive pair <x, y> may perform well based on the timeline globally while not on the neighboring set locally and vice versa. There is a tradeoff between the global optimization and local optimization and hence we need to balance both.

Recall the aggregation function of linear combination between local and global coverage in Equation (2). The utility for I_i can also be rewritten as an interpolation function from local utility $\mathcal{U}(I_i)|_{C_i}$ from sub-collection C_i and global utility $\mathcal{U}(I_i)|_C$ from the global collection C:

$$\mathcal{U}(I_i) = \lambda \cdot \mathcal{U}(I_i)|_{C_i} + (1 - \lambda) \cdot \mathcal{U}(I_i)|_C \quad (9)$$

The objective Equation (8) is actually to maximize $\Delta\mathcal{U}(I_i)$ from all possible substitutive pairs between two iterations to generate I_i. The algorithm is shown in Algorithm 1.

Algorithm 1 Interpolative Optimization

Input: $C_1, C_2, \ldots, C_{|T|}, \epsilon, \phi_i$
$I_i \leftarrow \{\}$ for i=1, 2, ..., $|T|$
repeat
  for $i = 1$ to $|T|$ **do**
    $\mathcal{U}'(I_i) = \mathcal{U}(I_i)$
    for all $s \in C_i$ **do**
      calculate $\mathcal{U}(s)$
    end for
    rank s with $\mathcal{U}(s)$
    $\mathcal{S}_i \leftarrow$ top $\phi_i|C_i|$ ranked sentences
    $\mathcal{Z}_i \leftarrow I_i \cap \mathcal{S}_i$
    $\mathcal{X}_i \leftarrow I_i - \mathcal{Z}_i$
    $\mathcal{Y}_i \leftarrow \mathcal{S}_i - \mathcal{Z}_i$
    for all $<\mathrm{x}_i, \mathrm{y}_i>$ pair where $\mathrm{x}_i \subseteq \mathcal{X}_i, \mathrm{y}_i \subseteq \mathcal{Y}_i$ **do**
      $\Delta\mathcal{U}_{\mathrm{x}_i,\mathrm{y}_i} = \mathcal{U}((I_i - \mathrm{x}_i) \cup \mathrm{y}_i) - \mathcal{U}'(I_i)$
    end for
    $< \hat{\mathrm{x}}_i, \hat{\mathrm{y}}_i >= \mathrm{argmax}\, \Delta\mathcal{U}_{\mathrm{x}_i,\mathrm{y}_i}$
    $I_i \leftarrow (I_i - \hat{\mathrm{x}}_i) \cup \hat{\mathrm{y}}_i$
    $\Delta\mathcal{U}_i = \mathcal{U}(I_i) - \mathcal{U}'(I_i)$
  end for
until $\forall\, \Delta\mathcal{U}_i < \epsilon$

The threshold ϵ is set at 0.0001 in this study. However, Algorithm 1 cannot avoid extreme situations. Significant rise in local utility which offsets much global utility loss still makes an available selection and vice versa. We seek to control such fluctuations to accelerate the convergence of the objective function. We choose the utility-maximized substitutive pairs under some constraints which are to ensure the overall utility is non-decreasing while finally both local and global optimizations are reached as iterations accumulate.

Local Optimization. The maximized substitutive pair should have utility improvement within sub-collection C_i. The local utility loss is not acceptable during the iterations.

Constraint 1.

$$\Delta\mathcal{U}_{x_i,y_i}|_{C_i} \geq 0 \quad (10)$$

Global Optimization. For each date, there can be a global utility loss for improvement in local utility, but with a borderline for such compromise. Global utility loss is acceptable for parts of the timeline but the loss from these dates should be offset by gains from the remaining dates. In other words, the sum of global utility is non-decreasing.

Constraint 2.

$$\sum_{I_i \in I} \Delta\mathcal{U}_{x_i,y_i}|_C \geq 0 \quad (11)$$

Constraint 3.

$$\Delta\mathcal{U}_{x_i,y_i}|_C > -\mu \qquad (\mu > 0) \quad (12)$$

μ is set as the maximum absolute value of $|(\Delta\mathcal{U}_{x_i,y_i}|_C)|$ from the last iteration and is initialized as positive infinity. Although allow utility compromises for parts of the timeline, we do not desire the situation of significant global utility gain for few dates along with slight utility loss for most others. Hence we set another constraint: for every iteration, the number of dates with global utility loss should not exceed m. In this study we let $m = \lfloor 0.8 \times |I| \rfloor$, which allows at most 80% dates with global utility loss.

Constraint 4.

$$|\{i|(\Delta\mathcal{U}_{x_i,y_i}|_C) < 0\}| < m \quad (13)$$

Optimization Problem. Considering the four types of constraints, we propose the balanced maximization framework enforcing both local and global optimization. Equation (8) can be rewritten as:

$$< \hat{x}_i, \hat{y}_i > = \underset{x_i \subseteq \mathcal{X}_i, y_i \subseteq \mathcal{Y}_i}{\operatorname{argmax}} \ \Delta\mathcal{U}_{x_i,y_i}, \quad (14)$$

subjected to:

$$(1)\Delta\mathcal{U}_{x_i,y_i}|_{C_i} \geq 0,$$

$$(2)\sum_{I_i \in I} \Delta\mathcal{U}_{x_i,y_i}|_C \geq 0,$$

$$(3)\Delta\mathcal{U}_{x_i,y_i}|_C > -\mu \quad (\mu > 0),$$

$$(4)|\{i|(\Delta\mathcal{U}_{x_i,y_i}|_C) < 0\}| < m.$$

Given results from Algorithm 1, suppose the size of the largest status space for a single date is $|H|$ within each iteration. We introduce a matrix $M_{|H|\times|T|}$ for all possible <x,y> pairs, where each element $M_{j,i}$ stands for a possible substitution. We calculate the global utility change $\Delta\mathcal{U}_{(M_{j,i})}|_C$, local utility change $\Delta\mathcal{U}_{(M_{j,i})}|_{C_i}$ and their linear combination $\Delta\mathcal{U}_{(M_{j,i})}$ for I_i. A **straightway understanding** is that we find a maximized overall utility $\Delta\mathcal{U}_{(M_{j,i})}$ at the j-th status space on date t_i, while at the same time global utility $\Delta\mathcal{U}_{(M_{j,i})}|_C$ and local utility $\Delta\mathcal{U}_{(M_{j,i})}|_{C_i}$ satisfy the four constraints. We select one element at each column by *Dynamic Programming*. After applying the substitution of $M_{j,i}$, a summary is hence generated within this iteration and the timeline is created by choosing a path in matrix $M_{|H|\times|T|}$.

We briefly describe the idea of dynamic programming and the details are left to Algorithm 2. Given matrix M, we sort all possible substitutions for I_i according to the overall utility change, i.e, $\Delta\mathcal{U}_{(M_{j,i})} > \Delta\mathcal{U}_{(M_{j+1,i})}$. We then split M into matrix M^L where elements $M^L_{j,i} = \Delta\mathcal{U}_{(M_{j,i})}|_{C_i}$ and matrix M^G where elements $M^G_{j,i} = \Delta\mathcal{U}_{(M_{j,i})}|_C$. In Algorithm 2 we set an array $\mathcal{A}[a][b][c]$= max $\{M_{j,a}\}$ where a is to record the processing column, b is to record how many $M^G_{j,i} < 0$ before column a on the path and c is to record the sum of $M^G_{j,i}$ before column a on the path. max $\{M_{j,a}\}$ denotes the maximum utility when specify a, b and c. Similar we set another array $\mathcal{P}[a][b][c]$ to record the path information. Details are illustrated in Algorithm 2. The worst time complexity is $O(|T| \times |H| \times m) \sim O(|T|^3)$ for Algorithm 2.

Algorithm 2 Dynamic programming with constraints

```
Input: Matrix M, M^L, M^G, m, μ
for a = 0 to |T| − 1 do
  for b = 0 to m do
    c_max = max(Σ_{i=0}^{a} M^G_{j,i})
    for c = −μm to c_max do
      dynamic programming given A[a][b][c], P[a][b][c]
      for l = 0 to |H| do
        if M^L_{l,a+1} > 0 && 0 > M^G_{l,a+1} > −μ then
          sn=1
        else if M^L_{l,a+1} > 0 && M^G_{l,a+1} > 0 then
          sn=0
        end if
        if A[a+1][b+sn][c+M^G_{l,a+1}]<A[a][b][c]+M_{l,a+1}
        then
          A[a+1][b+sn][c+M^G_{l,a+1}]=A[a][b][c]+M_{l,a+1}
          store path P[a+1][b+sn][c+M^G_{l,a+1}]=l_a
        end if
      end for
    end for
  end for
end for
for b = 0 to m do
  c_max = max(Σ_{i=0}^{|T|} M^G_{j,i})
  for c = 1 to c_max do
    find maximum A[|T|][b][c]
  end for
end for
trace way back by path P[|T|][b][c]
return l_{|T|}, ..., l_2, l_1
```

5. EXPERIMENTS AND EVALUATION

5.1 Datasets

Since there is no existing standard test set for ETS methods, we construct 6 test sets which consist of news datasets and golden standards to evaluate our proposed framework empirically. We downloaded 10251 news articles from 10 selected sources. As shown in Table 2, one of the sources is in China, three of them are in UK and the rest are in the US. We choose them because many of these websites provide timelines edited by professional editors, which serve as golden standards. 6 topics belong to different categories of Rule of Interpretation (ROI) [8]. Statistics are in Table 3.

5.2 Experimental System Setups

We present 2 practical systems for ETS, *off-line* and *online*. Given a topic related corpus, the systems return trajectory timelines automatically. Off-line system handles stabilized topics with no new occurring while on-line system can support incremental documents from topics still evolving.

Table 2: News sources of 6 datasets

News Sources	Nation	News Sources	Nation
BBC	UK	Fox News	US
Xinhua	China	MSNBC	US
CNN	US	Guardian	UK
ABC	US	New York Times	US
Reuters	UK	Washington Post	US

Table 3: Detailed basic information of 6 datasets.

Topics (Query Words)	#Docs	#GT	AL	Since
1.Influenza A (H1N1)	2557	5	83	2009
2.Financial Crisis	2894	2	118	2009
3.BP Oil Spill	1468	6	76	2010
4.Haiti Earthquake	247	2	32	2010
5.Michael Jackson Death	925	3	64	2010
6.Obama Presidency	2160	5	92	2010

GT: ground truth; AL: average length of GT measured in sentences.

• **Preprocessing.** As ETS faces with much larger corpus compared with traditional MDS, we apply further data compression besides stemming and stop-word removal. We extract *text snippets* representing atomic "events" from all these documents with a toolkit provided by Yan *et al.* [19]. After the snippet extraction procedure, we compress the corpora by discarding non-event texts and filtering those events non-relevant to any of the query words.

• **Compression Rate.** After preprocessing, we obtain numerous snippets, temporally tagged according to the publish time of their source documents, and then decompose them into temporally tagged sentences as the global collection C. We partition C according to timestamps of sentences, i.e., $C = C_1 \cup C_2 \cup \cdots \cup C_{|T|}$. I_i is generated from sub-collection C_i. The sizes of component summaries are not necessarily equal. Users specify the overall compression rate ϕ, and we extract more sentences for important dates while fewer sentences for others. The *importance* of dates is measured by the *burstiness* with probable significant occurrences [2]. The compression rate on t_i is set as $\phi_i = \frac{|C_i|}{|C|}$.

• **Off-line System vs. On-line System.** The difference between two systems is whether corpora are temporally updating or not. For stabilized corpus, component summaries are optimized based on neighboring summaries on dates before and after them. For evolving corpus, we cannot forecast futures sentence sets, so the on-line system is to consider neighboring summaries previously generated.

5.3 Algorithms for Comparison

We implement the following widely used multi-document summarization algorithms as the baseline systems. Some of the systems are designed for traditional summarization without temporal dimension. The first intuitive generation for such methods is a global summarization on collection C at a uniform compression rate ϕ and then distribute the selected sentences to their source dates. The other intuitive one is a local summarization on sub-collection C_i with a compression rate ϕ_i. To these methods we take the average score as their performance. For fairness we conduct the same preprocessing for all algorithms by compression or filtering.

Random: The method selects sentences randomly for each document collection.

Centroid: The method applies MEAD algorithm [14] to extract sentences according to the following parameters: centroid value, positional value, and first-sentence overlap.

GMDS: The Graph-based MDS proposed by Wan *et al.* [16] first constructs a sentence connectivity graph based on cosine similarity and then selects important sentences based on the concept of eigenvector centrality.

Chieu: Chieu *et al.* present a similar timeline system [2] with different goals and frameworks, utilizing *interest* and *burstiness* ranking but neglecting news evolution.

ETS: Our proposed algorithms with iterative substitution under constraints are tested as ETS_1 for the off-line system and ETS_2 for the on-line system.

5.4 Evaluation Metrics

To compare with the human timelines, we use ROUGE toolkit (version 1.5.5), which is officially applied by Document Understanding Conference (DUC) for document summarization performance evaluation [12]. The summarization quality is measured by counting the number of overlapping units, such as N-gram, word sequences, and word pairs between the candidate timeline set CT and the ground-truth timelines GT. Several automatic evaluation methods are implemented in ROUGE, such as ROUGE-N, ROUGE-L and ROUGE-W, each of which can generate three scores (recall, precision and F-measure). Take ROUGE-N as an example:

1. ROUGE-N-R is an N-gram recall metric as follows:

$$\text{ROUGE-N-R} = \frac{\sum\limits_{I\in GT}\sum\limits_{\text{N-gram}\in I}\text{Count}_{\text{match}}(\text{N-gram})}{\sum\limits_{I\in GT}\sum\limits_{\text{N-gram}\in I}\text{Count}\ (\text{N-gram})}$$

2. ROUGE-N-P is an N-gram precision metric as follows:

$$\text{ROUGE-N-P} = \frac{\sum\limits_{I\in CT}\sum\limits_{\text{N-gram}\in I}\text{Count}_{\text{match}}(\text{N-gram})}{\sum\limits_{I\in CT}\sum\limits_{\text{N-gram}\in I}\text{Count}\ (\text{N-gram})}$$

3. ROUGE-N-F is an N-gram F_1 metric as follows:

$$\text{ROUGE-N-F} = \frac{2\times\text{ROUGE-N-P}\times\text{ROUGE-N-R}}{\text{ROUGE-N-P}+\text{ROUGE-N-R}}$$

N in these metrics stands for the length of the N-gram and N-gram∈GT denotes the N-grams in the ground truth timeline while N-gram∈CT denotes the N-grams in the candidate timeline. $\text{Count}_{\text{match}}$(N-gram) is the maximum number of N-gram in the candidate summary and in the set of ground-truth summaries. $\text{Count}_{(\text{N-gram})}$ is the number of N-grams in the ground truth summaries or candidate summary.

Furthermore, as the timeline consists of a series of individual summaries which are not equally significant, we evaluate ROUGE F-score for the timeline by the weighted average ROUGE F-score of all summaries, weighted by ϕ_i:

$$\text{ROUGE-N-F(I)} = \frac{1}{|\text{I}|}\frac{\sum\limits_{I_i\in I}\phi_i\cdot\text{ROUGE-N-F}(\text{I}_\text{i})}{\sum\limits_{I_i\in I}\sum\limits_{I_k\in I}\phi_k\cdot\text{ROUGE-N-F}(\text{I}_\text{k})} \quad (15)$$

As we have similar conclusions in terms of any of the three scores, in this paper, we only report the average F-measure scores generated by unigram-based ROUGE-1, bigram-based ROUGE-2, and the weighted longest common subsequence based ROUGE-W to compare our proposed method with other implemented systems. These evaluation metrics have been shown to much agree with human judgments. The weight W is set to be 1.2 in our experiments. Intuitively, the higher the ROUGE scores, the similar the two summaries.

5.5 Overall Performance Comparison

We use a cross validation manner among 6 datasets, i.e., we train parameters on one topic set and examine the performance on the others. After 6 training-testing processes, we take the average F-score performance in terms of ROUGE-1, ROUGE-2, and ROUGE-W on all sets. The overall results are shown in Figure 1 and details are listed in Tables 4~6.

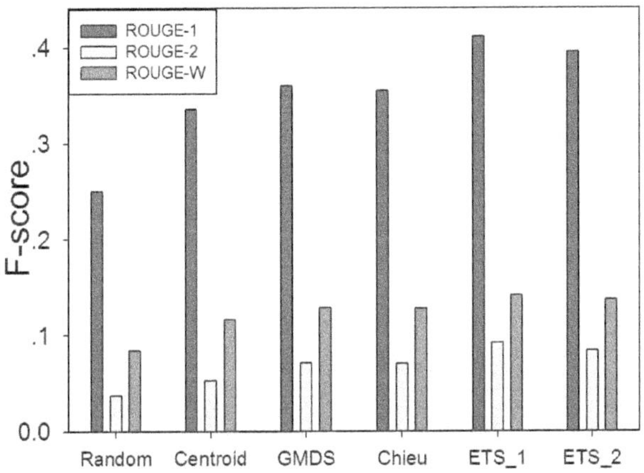

Figure 1: Overall performance on 6 datasets.

From the results, we have the following observations:

- Random has the worst performance as expected.
- The results of Centroid are better than those of Random. This is mainly because the Centroid based algorithm takes into account positional value and first-sentence overlap, which facilitates main aspects summarization.
- The GMDS system outperforms centroid-based summarization methods. This is due to the fact that PageRank-based framework ranks the sentence using eigenvector centrality which implicitly accounts for information subsumption among all sentences.

Traditional MDS only considers sentence selection from either the global or the local scope, and hence bias occurs. Many sentences are missed, which makes a low recall. Generally the performance of local priority summarization is better than global priority summarization. Probable bias is to some extent mitigated by searching for worthy sentence in every single date. However, precision drops due to excessive choice of local timeline-worthy sentences.

- In general, the result of Chieu's method is better than Centroid but unexpectedly, worse than GMDS. The reason in this case may be that Chieu's method does not capture sufficient timeline attributes. The "interest" modeled in their algorithms actually performs flat clustering-based summarization which is proved to be less useful [18]. GMDS utilizes sentence graph linkage, and partly captures "coherence".
- Both ETS_1 and ETS_2 under our proposed framework outperform baselines, indicating that the properties we use for timeline generation are beneficial. ETS_1 in off-line system performs better than ETS_2 in on-line system, indicating new coming documents do have influence on component summary generation within the timeline. ETS_2 is acceptable if on-line is required due to its advantage over baselines.

Table 4: Overall performance comparison on long lasting news. ROI* category: Science, Finance.

	1. Influenza A			2. Financial Crisis		
Systems	R-1	R-2	R-W	R-1	R-2	R-W
Random	0.257	0.039	0.081	0.230	0.030	0.071
Centroid	0.331	0.050	0.114	0.305	0.041	0.108
GMDS	0.364	0.062	0.130	0.327	0.054	0.110
Chieu	0.350	0.059	0.128	0.325	0.052	0.109
ETS_1	0.396	0.085	0.139	0.351	0.061	0.121
ETS_2	0.387	0.083	0.134	0.343	0.060	0.119

Table 5: Overall performance comparison on short breaking news. ROI category: Accidents, Disasters.

	3. BP Oil			4. Haiti Quake		
Systems	R-1	R-2	R-W	R-1	R-2	R-W
Random	0.262	0.041	0.096	0.266	0.043	0.093
Centroid	0.369	0.062	0.128	0.362	0.060	0.129
GMDS	0.389	0.084	0.139	0.380	0.106	0.137
Chieu	0.384	0.083	0.139	0.383	0.110	0.138
ETS_1	0.483	0.119	0.163	0.481	0.123	0.160
ETS_2	0.458	0.112	0.159	0.442	0.102	0.152

Table 6: Overall performance comparison on celebrities. ROI category: Legal Cases, Politics.

	5. Jackson Death			6. President Obama		
Systems	R-1	R-2	R-W	R-1	R-2	R-W
Random	0.232	0.033	0.080	0.254	0.039	0.084
Centroid	0.320	0.051	0.109	0.325	0.053	0.111
GMDS	0.341	0.059	0.127	0.359	0.061	0.129
Chieu	0.344	0.059	0.128	0.346	0.060	0.125
ETS_1	0.371	0.081	0.132	0.388	0.083	0.134
ETS_2	0.363	0.072	0.129	0.379	0.075	0.130

*ROI: news categorization defined by Linguistic Data Consortium. Available at http://www.ldc.upenn.edu/projects/tdt4/annotation

- The performance on intensive focused news within short time range (Topic 3, 4) is better than on long lasting news.

Having proved the effectiveness of our proposed methods, we carry the next move to identity how *relevance*, *coverage*, *coherence*, *diversity* and the 4 constraints take effects to enhance the quality of a summary in strategy selection.

5.6 Strategy Selection

Recall that utility $\mathcal{U}$ is the linear combination of local utility and global utility, both of which are the weighted sum of *relevance*, *coverage*, *coherence* and *diversity* under 4 constraints during the maximization process of $\mathcal{U}(I_i)$. Generally speaking, strategies can be sorted into two categories: parameter tuning and constraint selection. Each time, we tune one strategy while the other one is fixed.

5.6.1 Parameter Tuning

Keeping other parameters fixed, we vary one parameter at a time to examine the changes of its performance from all 6 datasets. The first group of key parameters in our framework is w_1, w_2 and w_3 where w_4=1-w_1-w_2-w_3. Experimental results indicate coherence and diversity facilitate ETS while relevance demonstrates a relatively weaker influence. Excessive use of these 3 attributes impairs performance, except coverage, showing its domination in text summariza-

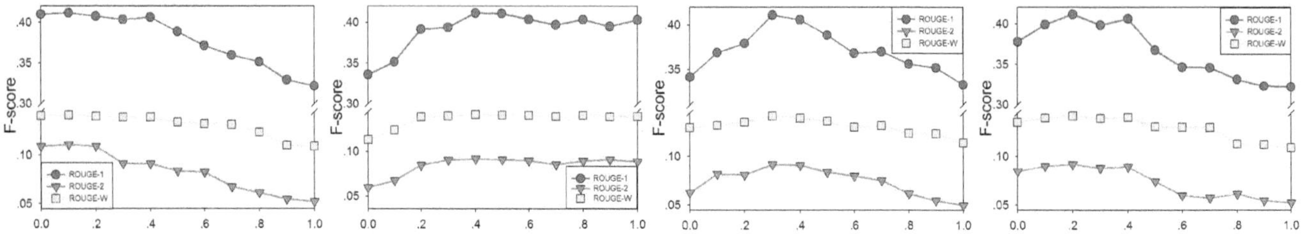

(a) w_1: effect of *relevance*. (b) w_2: effect of *coverage*. (c) w_3: effect of *coherence*. (d) w_4: effect of *diversity*.

Figure 2: Examine the performance of the four timeline-oriented attributes.

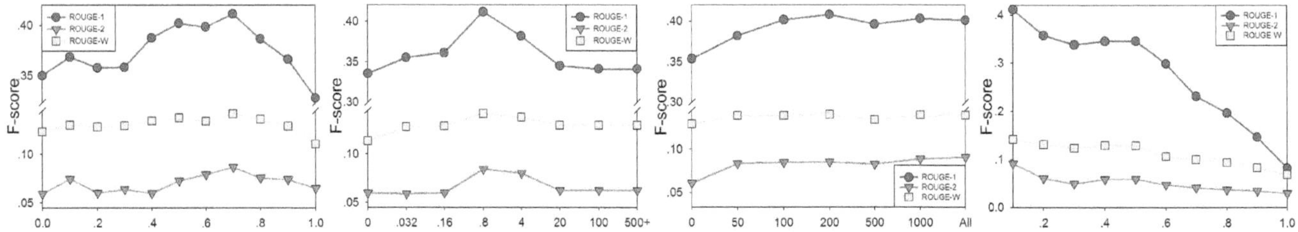

(e) λ: combine local/global balance. (f) α: control shape of decay. (g) κ: effect of pseudo-feedback. (h) ϕ: effect of compression rate.

Figure 3: Examine the performance of the experimental parameters.

tion. We set w_1=0.1, w_2=0.4, w_3=0.3 and hence w_4=0.2 in our experiments.

Another key parameter in our framework is λ in Equation (2) to measure the tradeoff between local and global collection. We gradually change λ from 0 to 1 at the step of 0.1 to examine the effect in Figure 3 (e). The combination of local and global utility outperforms the performance in isolation (λ=1 or 0). Furthermore, a larger λ (from 0.5 to 0.7) performs relatively better, but when λ exceeds 0.8, the extreme emphasis on global utility results in performance loss. We take λ=0.7 as the balance factor.

α controls the shape of the exponential decay and hence the size of influential neighboring window. We then examine the effect of neighboring summaries in ETS in Figure 3 (f). We vary α from 0 (all texts on timeline) to 500 (an approximation of $+\infty$, no neighbors considered). According to Figure 3 (f), the lines share a similar peak when $\alpha \in [0.8, 4]$. A moderate window size contributes to word distribution smoothing and reflects the trend for news evolution but too large a window introduces noise distribution as well. Therefore we choose α=0.8.

We then examine the results of different κ for pseudo-relevance feedback. According to Figure 3 (g), without any query expansion but simply compared with query Q, the performance is far from optimistic. Excessive document expansion impairs performance as well. κ=100 is shown large enough to smooth the word distribution in our experiments.

Finally we check the effect of overall compression rate ϕ which is usually designated by users. If the user would like to read more, he/she might favor a larger ϕ. We vary ϕ from 0.1 to 1 at the step of 0.1. Generally the lines are down-sloping as our ground-truth timelines are rather small compared with the huge global source collection. Recall is acceptable even when ϕ is small while precision drops accumulatively as ϕ increases.

5.6.2 Constraints Selection

To understand the effect of each proposed constraint, a series of experiments are conducted, illustrated in Figure 4, consisting all 2^4 combination tests of constraints C1$\sim$C4.

From Figure 4, we notice Constraint 1 and Constraint 2 are useful. Recall the description of these two constraints. They are to maximize local utility gain and global utility gain and therefore they benefit timeline generation. The effectiveness of Constraint 3 and Constraint 4 seems not obvious in Figure 4 (a). Constraint 3 is to restrict the global utility loss for a particular summary. However, these two constraints do help reduce iteration counts to convergence, shown in Figure 4 (b). As iteration accumulates, the change of utility $\Delta\mathcal{U}$ varies significantly from time to time. It is difficult to set a general borderline of global utility loss arbitrarily to balance the convergence rate and timeline quality: inappropriate choice of Constraint 3 may cause potential harm to timeline generation. Both Constraint 3 and Constraint 4 are beneficial in iteration count performance because they reduce the available search space and facilitate early pruning for state paths in Algorithm 2.

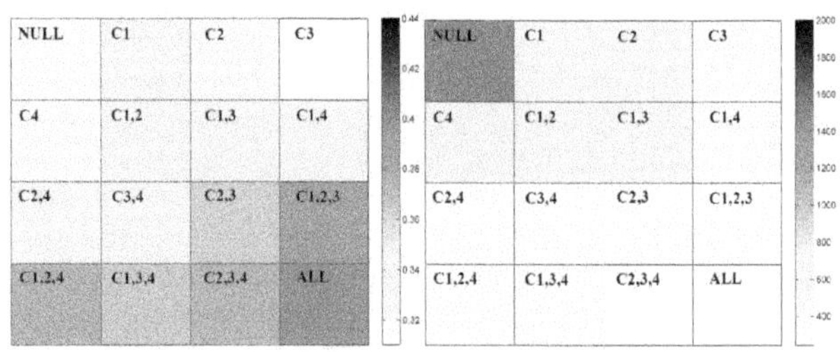

(a). ROUGE-F-score. (b). Iteration counts.

Figure 4: ROUGE-F and convergence performance comparison among all 16 constraint combinations.

6. CONCLUSION

In this paper we present a novel framework for the important web mining problem named Evolutionary Timeline Summarization (ETS), which generates trajectory timelines from massive data on the Internet. Given a query related news collection, ETS summarizes an evolution trajectory. We formally formulate ETS task as a balanced optimization problem via iterative substitution, measured on local sub-collections and the global collection. The objective function *Utility* is measured by four properties: *relevance*, *coverage*, *coherence* and *diversity*. We implement an off-/on-line system under such framework as experimental environment.

Abundant experiments are done on real web datasets. We compare numerous approaches, including two ways of implementation of 4 baselines and our proposed ETS_1, ETS_2. Through our experiments, we notice that among these properties, *coherence* plays an important role in timeline generation, indicating neighboring information is essential in evolutionary timeline trajectory: news evolves gradually. We also investigate the balance between local utility and global utility, and obtain the best combination coefficient at λ=0.7, meaning local utility weights slightly higher. We introduced four constraints, two of which ensure the local and global maximization, while the others ensure fast convergency. In case studies, our automatic timeline presents an informative document reorganization. However, as summaries generated by humans have potential biases, we will provide alternative evaluation metrics to measure ETS performance.

7. ACKNOWLEDGMENTS

We thank the anonymous reviewers for their valuable and constructive comments. This work is partially supported by NSFC Grant No.60933004, 61050009 and 61073081, and Xiaojun Wan is supported by NSFC Grant No.60873155.

8. REFERENCES

[1] J. Allan, R. Gupta, and V. Khandelwal. Temporal summaries of new topics. In *Proceedings of the 24th annual international ACM SIGIR conference on Research and development in information retrieval*, SIGIR '01, pages 10–18, 2001.

[2] H. L. Chieu and Y. K. Lee. Query based event extraction along a timeline. In *Proceedings of the 27th annual international ACM SIGIR conference on Research and development in information retrieval*, SIGIR '04, pages 425–432, 2004.

[3] G. Erkan and D. Radev. Lexpagerank: Prestige in multi-document text summarization. In *Proceedings of EMNLP*, volume 4, 2004.

[4] A. Feng and J. Allan. Finding and linking incidents in news. In *Proceedings of the sixteenth ACM conference on Conference on information and knowledge management*, CIKM '07, pages 821–830, 2007.

[5] G. P. C. Fung, J. X. Yu, H. Liu, and P. S. Yu. Time-dependent event hierarchy construction. In *Proceedings of the 13th ACM SIGKDD international conference on Knowledge discovery and data mining*, KDD '07, pages 300–309, 2007.

[6] J. Goldstein, M. Kantrowitz, V. Mittal, and J. Carbonell. Summarizing text documents: sentence selection and evaluation metrics. In *Proceedings of the 22nd SIGIR conference on Research and development in information retrieval*, pages 121–128, 1999.

[7] X. Jin, S. Spangler, R. Ma, and J. Han. Topic initiator detection on the world wide web. In *Proceedings of the 19th international conference on World wide web*, WWW '10, pages 481–490, 2010.

[8] G. Kumaran and J. Allan. Text classification and named entities for new event detection. In *Proceedings of the 27th annual international ACM SIGIR conference on Research and development in information retrieval*, SIGIR '04, pages 297–304, 2004.

[9] L. Li, K. Zhou, G.-R. Xue, H. Zha, and Y. Yu. Enhancing diversity, coverage and balance for summarization through structure learning. In *Proceedings of the 18th international conference on World wide web*, WWW '09, pages 71–80, 2009.

[10] X. Li and W. B. Croft. Improving novelty detection for general topics using sentence level information patterns. In *Proceedings of the 15th ACM international conference on Information and knowledge management*, CIKM '06, pages 238–247, 2006.

[11] C.-Y. Lin and E. Hovy. From single to multi-document summarization: a prototype system and its evaluation. In *Proceedings of the 40th Annual Meeting on Association for Computational Linguistics*, ACL '02, pages 457–464, 2002.

[12] C.-Y. Lin and E. Hovy. Automatic evaluation of summaries using n-gram co-occurrence statistics. In *Proceedings of NAACL'03*, pages 71–78, 2003.

[13] R. Mihalcea and P. Tarau. A language independent algorithm for single and multiple document summarization. In *Proceedings of IJCNLP*, 2005.

[14] D. Radev, H. Jing, M. Sty, and D. Tam. Centroid-based summarization of multiple documents. *Information Processing and Management*, 40(6):919–938, 2004.

[15] R. Swan and J. Allan. Automatic generation of overview timelines. In *Proceedings of the 23rd annual international ACM SIGIR conference on Research and development in information retrieval*, SIGIR '00, pages 49–56, 2000.

[16] X. Wan and J. Yang. Multi-document summarization using cluster-based link analysis. In *Proceedings of the 31st annual international ACM SIGIR conference on Research and development in information retrieval*, SIGIR '08, pages 299–306, 2008.

[17] X. Wan, J. Yang, and J. Xiao. Single document summarization with document expansion. In *AAAI*, pages 931–936, 2007.

[18] D. Wang and T. Li. Document update summarization using incremental hierarchical clustering. In *Proceedings of the 19th ACM international conference on Information and knowledge management*, CIKM '10, pages 279–288, 2010.

[19] R. Yan, Y. Li, Y. Zhang, and X. Li. Event recognition from news webpages through latent ingredients extraction. *Information Retrieval Technology*, pages 490–501, 2010.

[20] C. C. Yang and X. Shi. Discovering event evolution graphs from newswires. In *Proceedings of the 15th international conference on World Wide Web*, WWW '06, pages 945–946, 2006.

[21] K. Zhang, J. Zi, and L. G. Wu. New event detection based on indexing-tree and named entity. In *Proceedings of the 30th annual international ACM SIGIR conference on Research and development in information retrieval*, SIGIR '07, pages 215–222, 2007.

Table 7: Selected part of timeline generated by balanced ETS with optimization for *H1N1*.

April 23, 2009

s_1: The WHO makes its first report about the so-called Swine Influenza (A) H1N1.

s_2: In Mexico, more than a thousand people have been infected; WHO has sent a team of experts there to further study the outbreak.

April 25, 2009

s_1: WHO holds emergency meeting, says outbreak has potential to become a pandemic.

s_2: The Mexican Director-General declares Swine Influenza (A) H1N1 a public health emergency.

s_3: U.S. emergency departments step up efforts to control the virus should it surface.

s_4: More than 100 students are sick with flulike symptoms.

April 27, 2009

s_1: The World Health Organization raises the pandemic alert one level to phase 4, which is two steps short of declaring a full-blown pandemic.

s_2: A general practitioner considered swine flu a possible diagnosis, but specimens were not stored properly and a laboratory assessment could not confirm the case.

s_3: European Union's health commissioner warns Europeans to avoid nonessential travel to Mexico and the United States.

s_4: The World Bank in Washington, D.C., says a staff member who traveled to Mexico on business April 14-18 has been "preliminarily diagnosed" with swine flu.

s_5: 74 schools are closed, leaving students out of classes by swine flu.

April 29, 2009

s_1: President Obama asks Congress for $1.5 billion to fight the swine flu outbreak, build drug stockpiles and monitor future cases.

s_2: WHO's decision to raise the alert level helps mobilize pharmaceutical companies and governments to start manufacturing adequate antiviral drugs and speed up the creation of a vaccine.

s_3: For the first time, the World Health Organization raises the pandemic level to 5.

s_4: Egypt begins slaughtering the country's roughly 300,000 pigs as a precaution.

October 2, 2009

s_1: The US announces implementation of a massive campaign to vaccinate millions of Americans against swine flu, with the first 600,000 doses to be distributed in coming days.

s_2: The US ordered 979 million dollars worth of Fluviron H1N1 vaccine from Novaritis.

s_3: Spray vaccines will be the first to reach vaccination sites, one of the most vulnerable groups, pregnant women, will have to wait until later this month for the injection version.

October 5, 2009

s_1: UN officials warn that poor countries face "explosive outbreaks" of the global swine flu pandemic and need speedy financial assistance to access vaccines.

s_2: WHO said pharmaceutical firms can produce only 3 billion doses of H1N1 vaccines a year, covering less than half of the global population.

Table 8: Selected part of timeline generated by balanced ETS with optimization for *BP Oil*.

April 20, 2010

s_1: Explosion and fire on the BP-licensed Transocean drilling rig Deepwater Horizon in the Gulf of Mexico.

s_2: Deepwater Horizon oil rig fire leaves 11 missing.

s_3: The rig was drilling in about 5,000ft (1,525m) of water, pushing the boundaries of deepwater drilling technology.

s_4: A blowout preventer, intended to prevent release of crude oil, failed to activate.

April 22, 2010

s_1: The Deepwater Horizon sinks to the bottom of the Gulf after burning for 36 hours, raising concerns of a catastrophic oil spill.

s_2: Deepwater Horizon rig sinks in 5,000ft of water.

s_3: Reports of a five-mile-long oil slick. Search-and-rescue operations by the US National Response Team begin.

April 23, 2010

s_1: The US coast guard suspends the search for missing workers, who are all presumed dead.

s_2: The rig is found upside down about a quarter-mile from the blowout preventer.

s_3: The Coast Guard says it had no indication that oil was leaking from the well 5,000ft below the surface of the Gulf.

s_4: Underwater robots try to shut valves on the blowout preventer to stop the leak, but BP abandons that failed effort two weeks later.

s_5: Deepwater Horizon clean-up workers fight to prevent disaster.

April 24, 2010

s_1: Oil is found to be leaking from the well.

April 26, 2010

s_1: BP's shares fall 2% amid fears that the cost of cleanup and legal claims will hit the London-based company hard.

s_2: Roughly 15,000 gallons of dispersants and 21,000ft of containment boom are placed at the spill site.

April 27, 2010

s_1: The US departments of interior and homeland security announce plans for a joint investigation of the explosion and fire.

s_2: Oil spill to be set on fire to save US coast.

s_3: Minerals Management Service (MMS) approves a plan for two relief wells.

s_4: BP reports a rise in profits, due in large part to oil price increases, as shares rise again.

April 28, 2010

s_1: The US Coast Guard warns the oil leak could become the worst oil spill in US history.

s_2: The coast guard says the flow of oil is 5,000bpd, five times greater than first estimated, after a third leak is discovered.

s_3: Controlled burns begin on the giant oil slick.

s_4: BP's attempts to repair a hydraulic leak on the blowout preventer valve are unsuccessful.

Table 9: Selected part of timeline generated by balanced ETS with optimization for *Obama*.

January 15, 2010

s_1: US President Barack Obama spoke by telephone with Haitian President Rene Preval Friday morning, pledging full support of the United States in the ongoing earthquake relief effort.

s_2: US takes charge in Haiti with troops, rescue aid.

March 19, 2010

s_1: US President Barack Obama makes remarks on health care reform at George Mason University in Fairfax, Virginia.

March 21, 2010

s_1: Obama's presidency hinges on historic health care reform vote; If it passes, it's salvaged.

s_2: The United States House of Representatives will vote on President Barack Obama's healthcare reform bill, and either way, shockwaves will be heard throughout the globe.

March 23, 2010

s_1: Vice President Joe Biden introduces President Barack Obama on March 23, before the president signed the health care reform bill.

s_2: Doubted and deeply in need of a comeback, President Barack Obama had a political dream week: a historic remaking of America's health care system, an overhaul of how students pay for college and a groundbreaking deal with Russia to shrink nuclear arsenals.

s_3: Speaker Nancy Pelosi released the following statement today after President Barack Obama signed the Senate health insurance reform legislation into law.

June 26, 2010

s_1: The President holds separate bilateral meetings with Prime Minister David Cameron of the United Kingdom, President Lee Myung-bak of the Republic of Korea, President Hu Jintao of the People's Republic of China and attends the G20 Working Dinner.

November 2, 2010

s_1: WASHINGTON–President Obama holds a news conference in the White House to acknowledge that he and the Democratic party took a "shellacking" in the mid-term elections.

s_2: Republicans rolled to their greatest midterms gains in 80 years, recapturing the House of Representatives and cutting the Democrats' majority in the Senate.

s_3: Midterm election results show voters unhappy with President Obama's leadership.

November 12, 2010

s_1: The president and the first lady are in the midst of a 10-day visit to Asia, the longest foreign trip of the Obama presidency thus far.

s2: After what Mr. Obama termed a "shellacking," he pronounced himself ready to cooperate with Republicans.

December 3, 2010

s_1: (Reuters)-President Barack Obama makes a trip to Afghanistan to visit with US troops, and bad weather forced him to cancel a planned face-to-face meeting with Afghan President Hamid Karzai.

s_2: President Obama grants his first presidential pardons to 9 people.

Ranking Related News Predictions

Nattiya Kanhabua*
Dept. of Computer Science
Norwegian University of Science and Technology
Trondheim, Norway
nattiya@idi.ntnu.no

Roi Blanco
Yahoo! Research
Barcelona, Spain
roi@yahoo-inc.com

Michael Matthews
Yahoo! Research
Barcelona, Spain
mikemat@yahoo-inc.com

ABSTRACT

We estimate that nearly one third of news articles contain references to future events. While this information can prove crucial to understanding news stories and how events will develop for a given topic, there is currently no easy way to access this information. We propose a new task to address the problem of retrieving and ranking sentences that contain mentions to future events, which we call *ranking related news predictions*. In this paper, we formally define this task and propose a learning to rank approach based on 4 classes of features: term similarity, entity-based similarity, topic similarity, and temporal similarity. Through extensive evaluations using a corpus consisting of 1.8 millions news articles and 6,000 manually judged relevance pairs, we show that our approach is able to retrieve a significant number of relevant predictions related to a given topic.

Categories and Subject Descriptors

H.3.3 [**Information Storage and Retrieval**]: Information Search and Retrieval—*Retrieval models*; H.3.4 [**Information Storage and Retrieval**]: Systems and Software—*Performance evaluation (efficiency and effectiveness)*

General Terms

Algorithms, Experimentation, Performance

Keywords

News predictions, Future events, Sentence retrieval and ranking

1. INTRODUCTION

Predicting the future has long been the holy grail in the financial world. The leaders of large organizations need to analyze information related to the future in order to identify the key challenges that can directly affect their organizations. However, it is not just businesses that care about the future - all people have anticipation and curiosity about the future. Canton [8] describes the future trends that can influence our lives, our jobs, our businesses, and even our world. These include the energy crisis, the global financial crisis, politics, health care, science, securities, globalization, climate changes, and technologies. When people read news stories on any of these topics whether it is an article about war in the middle east or the latest health care plan, they are naturally curious about potential future events. How long will the war last? How much will it cost? What happens if we do nothing at all? This obsession with the future is also reflected in the news articles themselves - our analysis of one year worth of news from over 100 sources indicates that nearly one third of news articles contain at least one statement made about a future date.

Accessing this information in an intuitive way would greatly improve how people read and understand news. In this paper, we define a new task we call *ranking related news predictions* that directly addresses this problem by finding all predictions related to a news story in a news archive and ranking them according to their relevance to the news story. This task is motivated by the desire of news sites to increase user engagement by providing content that directly addresses the information needs of users. By providing links to relevant content, new sites can keep users on their site longer thus increasing the likelihood that users will click on revenue generating links and also improving user satisfaction. For a wide range of news events from natural disasters to political unrest in the middle east, the information need - the question most on people's minds - is what is going to happen next. This new task is a first step toward helping people answer this very question by finding and linking to predictions that are relevant to the user.

Our query is extracted from a news article currently read by a user, and is composed of a bag of *entities* or *terms*. Using an automatically-generated query, predictions are retrieved, ranked over the time dimension, and presented to the user. Note that there are a number of future-related information analyzing tools including *Recorded Future*[1], and *Time Explorer* [22]. *Recorded Future* extracts predictions from different sources (news publications, blogs, trade publications, government web sites, and financial databases). A user creates a query by selecting a topic of interest (e.g. a topic about "Financial Markets"), and then specifying an en-

*Work performed while intern at Yahoo! Research

[1] `https://www.recordedfuture.com/`

SIGIR'11, July 24–28, 2011, Beijing, China.

tity (people, companies, or organizations) from a set of "predefined" entities. The system will then retrieve predictions related to the selected topic and entity. A major difference with our system is that *Recorded Future* requires a query specified in advance, while our system automatically creates a query for the user based on the news article being read and it is not limited to "predefined" entities. *Time Explorer* is a search engine that allows users to see how topics have evolved over time and how they might continue to evolve in the future. The system extracts predictions from document collections and allows users to search for them using ad-hoc queries. However, neither *Time Explorer* nor *Recorded Future* provide details of how predictions are ranked nor do they evaluate performance in a formal setting as we do here.

The main contributions of this paper are: 1) the first formalization of the *ranking related news predictions* task, 2) an evaluation dataset with over 6000 relevance judgments from the New York Times Annotated Corpus[2] with queries that are selected from real-world future trends [8] 3) a learned ranking model incorporating four classes of features including term similarity, entity-based similarity, topic similarity, and temporal similarity 4) an in-depth analysis of feature selection to guide further research in the *ranking related news predictions* task.

The organization of the rest of the paper is as follows. In Section 2, we explain our system architecture, and outline the models for annotated documents, predictions as well as queries. In Section 3, we propose four classes of features used for learning a ranking model. In Section 4, we describe our ranking model. In Section 5, we evaluate the proposed ranking model. In Section 6, we give an overview of related work. Finally, in Section 7, we conclude and outline future work.

2. PROBLEM DEFINITION

In this section, we outline the system architecture, and give the formalization of the models for annotated documents, predictions, and queries.

2.1 System Architecture

Figure 1 depicts our system which retrieves a set of predictions (sentences containing future dates) related to a given news article. Predictions can be extracted from a temporal document collection – any collection that contains timestamped documents, e.g., personal emails, news archives, company websites and blogs. In this work, we automatically extract predictions from news archives using different annotation tools. Our *document annotation process* includes tokenization, sentence extraction, part-of-speech tagging, named entity recognition, and temporal expression extraction. The result of this process is a set of sentences annotated with named entities and temporal expressions, which will be indexed as *predictions* for further processing or retrieval.

A key component of the annotation process is the extraction of temporal expressions using a time and event recognition algorithm. The algorithm extracts temporal expressions mentioned in a document and normalizes them to dates so they can be anchored on a timeline. As explained in [1], there are three types of temporal expressions: explicit, implicit and relative. An explicit temporal expression mentioned in a document can be mapped directly to a time point or interval, such as, dates or years on the Gregorian calendar. For example, "July 04, 2010" or "January 01, 2011" are explicit temporal expressions. An implicit temporal expression is given in a document as an imprecise time point or interval. For example, "Independence Day 2010" or "New Year Day's 2011" are implicit expressions that can be mapped to "July 04, 2010" or "January 01, 2011" respectively. A relative temporal expression mentioned in a document can be resolved to a time point or interval using a time reference - either an explicit or implicit temporal expressions mentioned in a document or the publication date of the document itself. For example, the expressions "this Monday" or "next month" are relative expressions which we map to exact dates using the publication date of the document.

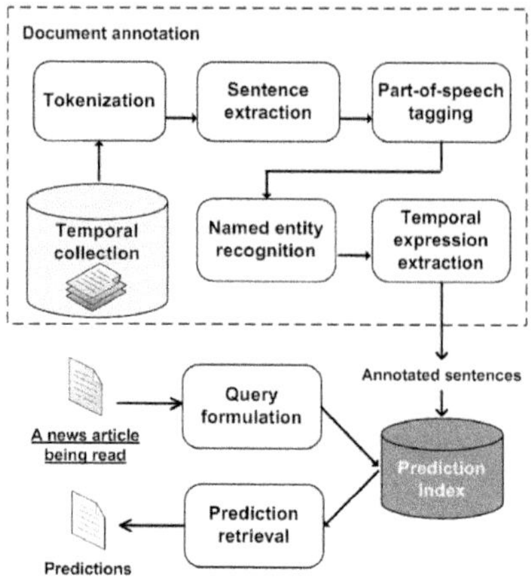

Figure 1: Prediction retrieval system architecture.

Instead of having an explicit information need provided, we automatically generate a query. In this case, we assume that the user's information needs lie in *the news article being read* by the user, and a query will be extracted from this news article (further details are given in Section 2.4). For a given news article, we retrieve predictions that are relevant to the news article, that is, relevant sentences containing future dates with respect to the publication date of the news article being read.

Retrieved predictions are ranked by the degree of relevance, where a prediction is "relevant" if it is future information about *the topics of the news article*. Note that we do not give any specific instructions about how the dates involved are related to relevance. Nevertheless, we hypothesize that predictions extracted from more recent documents are more relevant. In this paper, we use a machine learning approach [20] for learning the ranking model of predictions. This involves identifying different classes of features (see Section 3) to measure the relevance of a prediction with respect to the news article.

2.2 Annotated Document Model

Our document collection contains a number of news articles defined as $C = \{d_1, \ldots, d_n\}$. We treat each news article as a bag-of-words (an unordered list of terms, or features), $d = \{w_1, \ldots, w_n\}$. *time*(d) is a function given the creation or publication date of d. Some of our proposed features are extracted from annotated documents, which are defined

[2] http://www.ldc.upenn.edu/Catalog/docs/LDC2008T19/new_york_times_annotated_corpus.pdf

Table 1: Example of a prediction with field/value pairs.

Field	Value
ID	1136243_1
PARENT_ID	1136243
TITLE	*Gore Pledges A Health Plan For Every Child*
TEXT	*Vice President* **Al Gore** *proposed today to guarantee access to affordable health insurance for all children by* 2005, *expanding on a program enacted two years ago that he conceded had had limited success so far.*
CONTEXT	*Mr. Gore acknowledged that the number of Americans without health coverage had increased steadily since he and President Clinton took office.*
ENTITY	Al Gore
FUTURE_DATE	2005
PUB_DATE	1999/09/08

as follows. Each document d, has an associated annotated document $\hat{d}$, which will consist of three sets, $\hat{d}_e$, $\hat{d}_t$, $\hat{d}_s$: a set of named entities $\hat{d}_e = \{e_1, \ldots, e_n\}$, where each entity $e_i \in \mathcal{E}$ and $\mathcal{E}$ is the complete set of entities (typed as person, location, and organization) in the collection; a set of annotated temporal expressions $\hat{d}_t = \{t_1, \ldots, t_m\}$ and a set of sentences $\hat{d}_s = \{s_1, \ldots, s_z\}$

2.3 Prediction Model

A prediction p can be viewed as a sentence containing field/value pairs of annotation information and we define d^p as the *parent* document where p is extracted from. We define several fields for a prediction including ID, PARENT_ID, TITLE, ENTITY, FUTURE_DATE, PUB_DATE, TEXT, and CONTEXT. The field ID specifies a prediction's unique number, PARENTID and TITLE represent a unique number and the title of d^p respectively ENTITY contains a set of annotated entities $p_{entity} \subset \hat{d}_e$, FUTURE_DATE consists of "future" temporal expressions p_{future} annotated in p, PUB_DATE is the publication date of the *parent* document d^p and TEXT is a prediction's text p_{txt} or the sentence of p. Note that each prediction must contain at least one "future" temporal expression, that is, $p_{future} \neq \emptyset$. In addition, we explicitly model the context of the prediction p_{ctx}, represented by the field CONTEXT and defined as surrounding sentences of the main sentence [6]. In our work, we define the context p_{ctx} as the sentence immediately before and the one immediately after p_{txt}. Table 1 contains an example of a prediction with its field/value pairs.

2.4 Query Model

As mentioned earlier, a query q is automatically generated from a news article being read d^q; q is composed of two parts: keywords q_{text}, and the time of query q_{time}. The keywords q_{text} are extracted from d^q in three ways resulting in three different types of queries.

The first type of query is a bag of *entities*, noted as "entity query" or Q_E where its q_{text} is composed of the *top-m* entities (ranked by frequency) extracted from d^q. Intuitively, we want to know whether using only *key* entities frequently mentioned in the news article can retrieve relevant predictions with high precision or not. For example, given an actual document about "President Bush and the Iraq war", we extract Q_E with $q_{text} = \langle$*George Bush, Iraq, America*$\rangle$. At retrieval time, q_{text} will be matched with the ENTITY field of the predictions.

The second query is denoted "term query" or Q_T where its q_{text} is composed of *top-n* terms (ranked by term weighting, i.e., TF-IDF) extracted from d^q. Q_T is considered a bag of *terms* important to both d^q (locally) and the whole collection (globally). In contrast to the previous query type, Q_T aims at retrieving predictions related to the topics of news article, which can be represented as *a set of informative terms*. As an example, the Q_T with $q_{text} = \langle$*poll, bush, war, iraq*$\rangle$ is extracted from the same document used in the Q_E example above. In this case, q_{text} will be matched with the TEXT field of the predictions.

The last type is called "combined query" or Q_C where its q_{text} is a combination of both *top-m* entities and *top-n* terms formed by concatenating Q_E and Q_T. We discuss how we select *top-m* and *top-n* in Section 5.

The last component of the query is the *temporal criteria* or q_{time} used for retrieving predictions on the time dimension; q_{time} is composed of two different time constraints. The first constraint is specified in order to retrieve only predictions that are *future* relative to the publication date of query's parent article, or $time(d^q)$. The second constraint indicates that those predictions must belong to news articles published before $time(d^q)$. Both time constraints will be represented using a time interval, i.e., $[t_b, t_e]$, where t_b is a beginning time point and t_e is an ending time point, and $t_e > t_b$. In all cases, the first constraint is $(time(d^q), t_{max}]$, and the second constraint is $[t_{min}, time(d^q)]$, where $(time(d^q), t_{max}] = [time(d^q), t_{max}] - \{time(d^q)\}$, and t_{max} and t_{min} are the maximum time in the future and the minimum time in the past respectively. At retrieval time, the first constraint will be matched with the field FUTURE_DATE of predictions, whereas the second constraint will be matched with the field PUB_DATE of predictions.

3. FEATURES

In this section, we present features used for learning a ranking model for related news predictions. The model will be described in Section 4. We propose several classes of features to capture the similarity between a news article query q and a prediction p, i.e., term similarity, entity-based similarity, topic similarity, and temporal similarity. The detailed description of each class will be given next.

3.1 Term Similarity

Since a prediction is defined with multiple fields, we employ the fielded searching provided with Apache Lucene search engine. The first term similarity feature *retScore* is the default similarity scoring function[3] of Lucene, which is a variation of the tf-idf weighting scheme.

A disadvantage of *retScore* is that it will not retrieve any predictions that do not match the query terms. This issue is exacerbated in sentence retrieval by the fact that we have to retrieve short fragments of text which might refer to the query terms using anaphora or other linguistic phenomena. One technique to overcome this problem is to use query expansion/reformulation using synonyms or different words with very similar meanings. It has also been shown that

[3] http://lucene.apache.org/java/2_9_3/api/core/org/apache/lucene/search/Similarity.html

extending a sentence structure by its surrounding *context* sentences and weighting them using a field aware ranking function like bm25f consistently improves sentence retrieval [6]. Therefore, rather than reformulating a query, we will retrieve a prediction by looking at the CONTEXT and TITLE fields, in addition to the TEXT field. Thus, even if the TEXT field does not match exactly with a query term, p can receive a score if either the CONTEXT or TITLE field match the query term.

In our case, instead of weighting differently keyword matches in the title or body of a Web-page, we assign a different importance to matches in the sentence itself or its context. The second term similarity feature *bm25f* can be computed as follows.

$$\begin{aligned} bm25f(q,p,F) &= \sum_{w_i \in q} \frac{weight(w_i,p)}{k_1 + weight(w_i,p)} \cdot idf(w_i) \\ weight(w_i,p) &= \sum_{f \in F} \frac{freq(w_i,f) \cdot boost(f)}{(1-b_f) + b_f \cdot \frac{l_f}{avl_f}} \\ idf(w_i) &= \log \frac{N_P - n_{w_i} + 0.5}{n_{w_i} + 0.5} \end{aligned} \quad (1)$$

where l_f is the field length, avl_f is the average length for a field f, b_f is a constant related to the field length, k_1 is a free parameter and $boost(f)$ is the boost factor applied to a field f. N_P is the total number of predictions and n_{w_i} is the number of prediction containing w_i, and $F = \{\text{TEXT}, \text{CONTEXT}, \text{TITLE}\}$. We discuss parameter settings in Section 5.1.

3.2 Entity-based Similarity

This feature class is aimed at measuring the similarity between q and p by measuring the similarity of the entities they each contain. Note that, this class is only applicable for a query consisting of entities, that is, Q_E and Q_C, and it is ignored for Q_T. The first feature *entitySim* compares a string similarity between the entities of q and p_{entity} using the Jaccard coefficient, which can be computed as follows.

$$entitySim(q,p) = \frac{|q \cap p_{entity}|}{|q \cup p_{entity}|} \quad (2)$$

where p_{entity} is a set of entities, $|q \cap p_{entity}|$ and $|q \cup p_{entity}|$ are the size of intersection and union of entities of q and p.

Thus, the higher the overlap between the entities of a prediction and the query, the higher the prediction will be ranked for the query. We also want to rank predictions by using features that are commonly employed in an *entity ranking* task. For example, an entity is relevant if it appears in the title of a document, or it always occurs as a subject of sentence. We will employ *entity ranking* features by assuming that the more relevant entities a prediction contains, the more relevant it is. The entity-based features will be extracted and computed relative to the parent document of a prediction (d^p) or on the prediction itself (p).

Features extracted from documents are *title*, *titleSim*, *senPos*, *senLen*, *cntSenSubj*, *cntEvent*, *cntFuture*, *cntEventSubj*, *cntFutureSubj*, *timeDistEvent*, *timeDistFuture* and *tagSim*. Features extracted from predictions are *isSubj* and *timeDist*. The value of all features is normalized to range from 0 to 1, unless otherwise stated. First, the feature *title* indicates whether an entity e is in the title of d^p.

$$title(e,d^p) = isInTitle(e,d^p) \quad (3)$$

A value is 1 if e appears in the title of d^p, or 0 if otherwise. *titleSim* is a string similarity between e and the title.

$$titleSim(e,d^p) = \frac{|e \cap title(d^p)|}{|e \cup title(d^p)|} \quad (4)$$

senPos gives the position of the 1st sentence where e occurs in d^p.

$$senPos(e,d^p) = \frac{len(d^p) - pos(firstSen(e))}{len(d^p)} \quad (5)$$

where $len(d^p)$ gives the length of d^p in words. $pos(s_y)$ is the position of a sentence s_y in d^p. *senLen* gives the length of the first sentence of d that contains e.

$$senLen(e,d^p) = \frac{len(firstSen(e))}{\max_{s_y \in d^p} len(s_y)} \quad (6)$$

cntSenSubj is the number of sentences where e is a subject. We run a dependency parser over the sentences in order to determine whether an entity is a subject of not.

$$cntSenSubj(e,d^p) = \frac{1}{|\mathcal{S}_e|} \sum_{s_y \in \mathcal{S}_e} isSubj(e,s_y) \quad (7)$$

where $\mathcal{S}_e$ is a set of all sentences of e in d^p. $isSubj(e,s_y)$ is 1 if e is a subject of s_y. *cntEvent* is the number of event sentences (or sentences annotated with dates) of e.

$$cntEvent(e,d^p) = \frac{1}{|\mathcal{E}_d^p|} \sum_{s_z \in \mathcal{E}_d^p} \sum_{s_y \in \mathcal{S}_e} isEqual(s_z,s_y) \quad (8)$$

where $\mathcal{E}_d^p$ is a set of all event sentences in d^p. $isEqual(s_z,s_y)$ returns 1 if s_z equals to s_y. *cntFuture* is the number of sentences with a mention of a future date. *cntEventSubj* is the number of event sentences that e is a subject.

$$cntEventSubj(e,d^p) = \frac{1}{|\mathcal{E}_d^p|} \sum_{s_z \in \mathcal{E}_d^p} isSubj(e,s_z) \quad (9)$$

Similarly, *cntFutureSubj* is the number of future sentences that e is a subject. *timeDistEvent* is a measure of the distance between e and all dates in d^p.

$$timeDistEvent(e,d^p) = \frac{1}{|\mathcal{E}_e|} \sum_{s_z \in \mathcal{E}_e} avg(normist(e,s_z)) \quad (10)$$

where $normDist(e,s_z) = \frac{1}{|\mathcal{T}_{s_z}|} \sum_{t_k \in \mathcal{T}_{s_z}} \frac{maxDist(s_z) - dist(e,t_k)}{maxDist(s_z)}$. $dist(w_i,w_j) = |pos(w_i) - pos(w_i)| - 1$. $\mathcal{E}_e$ is a set of all event sentences of e, and $\mathcal{T}_{s_z}$ is a set of all temporal expressions in s_z. $dist(w_i,w_j)$ is a distance in words between terms w_i and w_j. $maxDist(s_z)$ is a maximum distance between terms in s_z. $timeDistFuture(e,d^p)$ is a distance of e and all future dates in d^p computed similarly to *timeDistEvent*. *tagSim* is a string similarity between e and an entity tagged in d^p.

$$tagSim(e,d^p) = \max_{e_n \in \mathcal{N}_d^p} \frac{|e \cap e_n|}{|e \cup e_n|} \quad (11)$$

where $\mathcal{N}_d^p$ is a set of all entities tagged in d^p. *tagSim* is only applicable for a collection provided with manually assigned tags (e.g., the New York Times Annotated Corpus).

$isSubj(e,p)$ is 1 if e is a subject with respect to a prediction p, and $timeDist(e,p)$ is a distance of e and all future dates in p computed similarly to *timeDistEvent*. All features in this class are parameter-free.

3.3 Topic Similarity

This class of features is aimed to compare the similarity between q and p on a higher level by representing them using topics. Examples of topics are "health care reform", "financial crisis", and "global warming". Several works [7, 32] have proposed to model a document with a low dimensionality, or to use topics rather than terms. We will use latent Dirichlet allocation (LDA) [7] to model a set of topics. LDA is based on a generative probabilistic model that models documents as mixtures over an underlying set of topic distributions. In general, topic modeling consists of two main steps. The first step is to learn topic models from training data. LDA requires the parameter N_z or the number of topics to be specified. After a model is trained, the next step is to infer topics from the learned topic model outputting a topic distribution for the prediction.

Wei and Croft [32] incorporated topic modeling for ad-hoc retrieval, and showed that linearly combining LDA with the query likelihood model outperformed non-topic models like the unigram model. We incorporate LDA into the retrieval process differently from Wei and Croft in two ways. First, instead of combining LDA scores with the original retrieval score, we represent q and p as vectors of topic distributions and compute the topic-based similarity using a cosine similarity between two vectors. Second, we explicitly take the time dimension into modeling topics because topics distributions can evolve over time. Intuitively, topics keep changing over time according to different trends.

We apply topic modeling to future retrieval in three main steps: 1) learning a topic model, 2) inferring topic models, and 3) measuring topic similarity.

Learning a topic model. We take into account the time dimension for learning topic models. As shown in Figure 2, we create training data by partitioning the document collection D_N into sub-collections (or document snapshots) with respect to time. In other words, we group documents by year of publication, and randomly select documents as training data, called a training data snapshot D_{train,t_k} at time t_k. Note that, we can also use more sophisticated approaches for modeling topics over time as presented in [31]. However, we will leave this study for future work.

Topic model inference. Using learned models from the previous step, we determine the topics for q and p from their contents. This process is called *topic inference*, which represents a query and a prediction by a distribution of topics (probabilities). For example, given a topic model ϕ, a prediction p can be represented as $p_\phi = p(z_1), \ldots, p(z_n)$, where $p(z)$ gives a probability of a topic z obtained from ϕ. Because our topic models are learned from different time periods, a question is which model snapshot we use for inference. Note that, q and p must be inferred from the same model snapshot in order to be comparable. We select a topic model for inferring in two ways. First, we select a topic model from a time snapshot $time(d^q)$ which corresponds to the publication date of the news article parent of q. Second, a topic model is selected from a time snapshot t which corresponds to the publication date of the news article making prediction p, or the $time(d^p)$. Moreover, a prediction p will be inferred in three different ways depending on the contents used: 1) only text p_{txt}, 2) both text p_{txt} and context p_{ctx}, and 3) the parent document d^p. For a query q, the contents of its parent document d^q will be used for inference.

In addition to using all N_z topics for inference, we will also select only top-k topics ranked by the importance. The idea is that measuring the topic similarity using too many topics may not be as accurate as using only the most important topics. We use *coverage* and *variation* proposed in [29] for ranking topics. A topic coverage $\mu(z)$ assumes that topics that cover a significant portion of the corpus content are more important than those covering little content, while a topic variation $\sigma(z)$ considers topics that appear in all the documents to be too generic to be interesting, although they have significant content coverage. $\mu(z)$ and $\sigma(z)$ are computed using a mean and a standard deviation over topic distributions, and the final score for ranking topic is a multiply of $\mu(z)$ and $\sigma(z)$. The calculation $\mu(z)$ and $\sigma(z)$ for a topic z at time t_k is given as:

$$\mu(z) = \frac{1}{\sum_{i=1}^{N_D} len(d_i)} \sum_{i=1}^{N_D} len(d_i) \cdot p_i(z) \tag{12}$$

$$\sigma(z) = \sqrt{\frac{1}{\sum_{i=1}^{N_D} len(d_i)} \sum_{i=1}^{N_D} len(d_i) \cdot (p_i(z) - \mu(z))^2} \tag{13}$$

where N_D is the number of documents in a training set at time t_k, or $|D_{train,t_k}|$. $p_i(z)$ gives a probability of a topic z in a document d_i and *len(d_i)* is the document length of d_i. A final score for ranking a topic z can be computed as:

$$rank(z) = \mu(z)^{\lambda_1} \cdot \sigma(z)^{\lambda_2} \tag{14}$$

where the parameters λ_1 and λ_2 indicate the importance of $\mu(z)$ and $\sigma(z)$. If $\lambda_1 = 1$ and $\lambda_2 = 0$, the ranking is determined purely by topic coverage. On the contrary, if $\lambda_1 = 0$ and $\lambda_2 = 1$, the ranking emphasizes topic variance.

Measuring topic similarity. Given a topic model ϕ, the topic similarity can be calculated using a cosine similarity between a topic distribution of query q_ϕ and a topic distribution of prediction p_ϕ as follows.

$$\begin{aligned} topicSim(q,p) &= \frac{q_\phi \cdot p_\phi}{||q_\phi|| \cdot ||p_\phi||} \\ &= \frac{\sum_{z \subset Z} q_{\phi_z} \cdot p_{\phi_z}}{\sqrt{\sum_{z \subset Z} q_{\phi_z}^2} \cdot \sqrt{\sum_{z \in Z} p_{\phi_z}^2}} \end{aligned} \tag{15}$$

We denote a topical feature using $LDA_{i,j,k}$, where i is one of the two different methods for selecting model snapshot: $i = 1$ for selecting a topic model from a time snapshot $time(d^q)$, and $i = 2$ for selecting from a time snapshot $time(d^p)$; j is one of the three different ways of using the contents for inference: p_{txt}, p_{ctx}, or d^p. Finally, k refers to whether we use *all* of only top-k of topics for inference. Thus, this results in 12 (=3*2*2) LDA-based features in total.

3.4 Temporal Similarity

As mentioned earlier, we explicitly exploit temporal expressions in ranking. To measure the temporal similarity between a query and a prediction, we employ two features proposed in previous work: *TSU* [16] and *FS* [15].

We will represent our model of time using a time interval $[b, e]$ having a begin point b and the end point e. The actual value of any time point, e.g., b or e in $[b, e]$, is an integer or the number of time units (e.g., milliseconds or days) passed (or to pass) a reference point of time (e.g., the UNIX epoch).

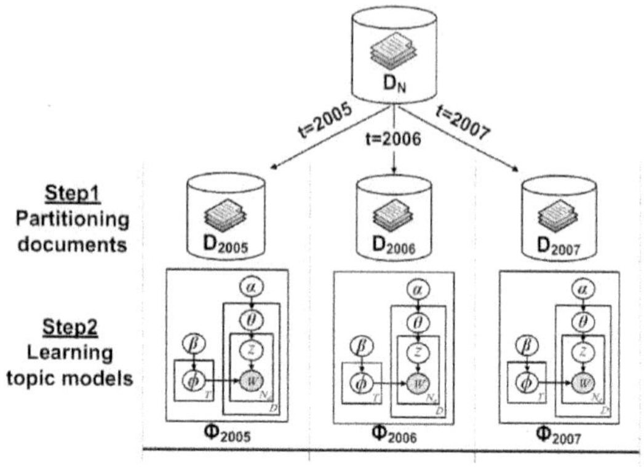

Figure 2: LDA topic snapshots based on time.

The first feature TSU is defined as the probability of generating the time of query q_{time} from the document creation date $time(d)$. TSU can be computed as follows.

$$TSU = DecayRate^{\lambda \cdot \frac{|q_{time} - time(d)|}{\mu}} \quad (16)$$

where $DecayRate$ and λ are constants, $0 < DecayRate < 1$ and $\lambda > 0$. μ is a unit of time distance. Intuitively, the probability obtained from this function decreases proportional to the distance between q_{time} and $time(d)$, that is, a document with its creation date closer to q_{time} will receive a higher probability than a document with its creation date farther from q_{time}.

We apply TSU for measuring the temporal similarity between q and p based on two assumptions. First, we assume that p is more likely to be relevant if its parent time $time(d^p)$ is closer to the time of query article $time(d^q)$. Our first temporal feature, denoted TSU_1, will be calculated similarly to Equation 16 resulting the following function.

$$TSU_1(q,p) = DecayRate^{\lambda \cdot \frac{|time(d^q) - time(d^p)|}{\mu}} \quad (17)$$

The second assumption, denoted TSU_2, is that a prediction is more likely to be relevant if its future dates p_{future} are closer to the publication date of query article $time(d^q)$. If there are more than one future dates associated to p, a final score will be averaged over scores of all future dates p_{future}. The temporal distance of TSU_2 of q and p is defined as follows.

$$TSU_2(q,p) = \frac{1}{N_f} \sum_{t_f \in p_{future}} DecayRate^{\lambda \cdot \frac{|time(d^q) - t_f|}{\mu}} \quad (18)$$

where t_f is a future date in p_{future} and N_f is the number of all future dates.

In addition to TSU_1 and TSU_2, we can measure the temporal similarity between q and p using a fuzzy membership function, which is originally proposed by Kalczynski and Chou [15].

We adapt the original fuzzy set function in [15] by using its parent time $time(d^p)$ and the time of query article $time(d^q)$. We denote this feature as FS_1, and it can be computed as follows.

$$FS_1(q,p) = \begin{cases} 0 & \text{if } time(d^p) < \alpha_1 \vee time(d^p) > time(d^q), \\ f_1(time(d^p)) & \text{if } time(d^p) \geq \alpha_1 \wedge time(d^p) < time(d^q), \\ 1 & \text{if } time(d^p) = time(d^q). \end{cases} \quad (19)$$

where $f_1(time(d^p))$ is equal to $\left(\frac{time(d^p)-\alpha_1}{time(d^q)-\alpha_1}\right)^n$ if $time(d^p) \neq time(d^q)$, or 1 if $time(d^p) = time(d^q)$.

We define the second temporal feature based on a fuzzy set by using the prediction's future dates p_{future} and the publication date of query article $time(d^q)$. Similarly, if a prediction p has more than one future date, a final score will be averaged over scores of all dates p_{future}. The second temporal feature FS_2 is defined as follows.

$$FS_2(q,p) = \frac{1}{N_f} \sum_{t_f \in p_{future}} \begin{cases} 0 & \text{if } t_f < time(d^q) \vee t_f > \alpha_2, \\ 1 & \text{if } t_f = time(d^q), \\ f_2(t_f) & \text{if } t_f > time(d^q) \wedge t_f \leq \alpha_2. \end{cases} \quad (20)$$

N_f is the number of all future dates in p_{future}, and t_f is a future date, i.e., $t_f \in p_{future}$. $f_2(t_f)$ is equal to $\left(\frac{\alpha_2 - t_f}{\alpha_2 - time(d^q)}\right)^m$ if $t_f \neq time(d^q)$, or 1 if $t_f = time(d^q)$. n and m are constants. α_1 and α_2 are the minimum and maximum time of reference with respect to q_{time}. α_1 is calculated by subtracting the time offset s_{min} from from q_{time} , and α_2 is calculated by adding the offset s_{max} to q_{time}.

4. RANKING MODEL

Given a query q, we will rank a prediction p using a ranking model obtained by training over a set of labeled query/prediction pairs using a learning algorithm. An unseen query/prediction pair (q,p) will be ranked according to a weighted sum of feature scores:

$$score(q,p) = \sum_{i=1}^{N} w_i \times x_i \quad (21)$$

where x_i are the different features extracted from p and q, N is the number of features, and w_i are the weighting coefficients. The goal of the algorithm is to learn the weights w_i using a training set of queries and predictions, in order to minimize a given loss function. Learning to rank algorithms can be categorized into three approaches: pointwise, pairwise, and listwise approaches [20]. The pointwise approach assumes that retrieved documents are independent, so it predicts a relevance judgment for each document and ignores the positions of documents in a ranked list. The pairwise approach considers a pair of documents, and relevance prediction is given as the relative order between them (i.e., pairwise preference). The listwise approach considers a whole set of retrieved documents, and predicts the relevance degrees among documents. For a more detailed description of each approach, please refer to [20].

We employ the listwise learning algorithm SVM^{MAP} [34]. The algorithm trains a classifier using support vector machines (SVM), and it determines the order of retrieved documents in order to directly optimize Mean Average Precision (MAP). In addition, we also experimented with other learned ranking algorithms: RankSVM [14], SGD-SVM [36], PegasosSVM [28], and PA-Perceptron [9]. However, these algorithms do not perform as well as SVM^{MAP} in our experiments. Thus, we will only discuss the results obtained from SVM^{MAP} in the next section.

Table 2: Examples of future-related topics.

Politics	Environment	Space
president election	global warming	Mars
Iraq war	energy efficiency	Moon
Science	**Physics**	**Health**
earthquake	particle Physics	bird flue
tsunami	Big Bang	influenza
Business	**Sport**	**Technology**
subprime	Olympics	Internet
financial crisis	World cup	search engine

5. EXPERIMENTS

In this section, we evaluate the retrieval effectiveness of our proposed ranking model using three different query formats. We will first describe the experimental settings followed by an explanation of the results and a detailed discussion.

5.1 Experimental Settings

Temporal document collection. We used the New York Times Annotated Corpus for our document collection, which contains 1.8 million documents covering the period from January 1987 to June 2007. In order to extract predictions and features, a series of language processing tools, including OpenNLP (for tokenization, sentence splitting and part-of-speech tagging, and shallow parsing), the SuperSense tagger (for named entity recognition) and TARSQI Toolkit (for extracting temporal expressions from documents). Given the importance of time to our system, we note that the temporal expression extraction of TARSQI has a reported performance of 0.81 F1 on the Time Expression Recognition and Normalization task[4].

We employed the Apache Lucene search engine for both indexing and retrieving predictions. The statistics of extracted data are as follows. There are 44,335,519 sentences and 548,491 are predictions. There are 939,455 future dates, and an average future date per prediction is 1.7 and the standard deviation is 0.92. Among 1.8 million documents, more than 25% of all documents contain at least one prediction (i.e., a reference to the future). In order to determine this percentage over a broader range of news sources, we performed the same analysis on 2.5 million documents from over 100 news sources from Yahoo! News for the one year period from July 2009 to July 2010 and found over 32% of the documents contained at least one prediction.

Future-related queries. There is no gold standard available to evaluate the task of ranking related news prediction. We manually selected 42 query news articles from the New York Times that cover the future-related topics shown in Table 2. The actual queries (Q_E, Q_T and Q_C) used for retrieving predictions are extracted from these news articles.

Relevance assessments. Human assessors were asked to evaluate query/prediction pairs (e.g., relevant or non-relevant) using 5 levels of relevance: 4 for *excellent* (very relevant prediction), 3 for *good* (relevant prediction), 2 for *fair* (related prediction), 1 for *bad* (non-relevant prediction), and 0 for *non prediction* (incorrect tagged date). The last option was presented because there are predictions incorrectly annotated with time (this is an error produced by the annotation tools). More precisely, an assessor was asked to give a relevance score $Grade(q,p,t)$ where (q,p,t) is a triple of a query q, a prediction p, and a future date t in p. Consider the following prediction about the topic "global warming" and the publication date of the news article is 2007/02/21:

> *Formal ratification of the pact – which commits the union to reduce emissions of "greenhouse gases" by 8 percent of 1990 levels during the five-year period from* **2008** *through* **2012** *– now goes to the European Council of heads of state and government, which could act as early as this month at the union summit in Barcelona.*

The prediction contains two future dates (as highlighted in bold). Hence, an assessor has to give judges to two triples corresponding to q, p and *both* future dates. A triple (q,p,t) is considered **relevant** if $Grade(q,p,t) \geq 3$, and it is considered non-relevant if $1 \leq Grade(q,p,t) \leq 2$. Relevance level 0 is not included in the evaluation[5]. These judgments are normalized by a query/prediction pair (q,p) since we are interested in presenting a prediction for all future dates, regardless of their number. That is, a query/prediction pair (q,p) is relevant if and only if there is at least one relevant triple (q,p,t), and a prediction is **non-relevant** if all triples are non-relevant. Our assumption is that predictions extracted from more recent documents are more relevant.

In total, assessors judged 52 queries and for each one of them we retrieved up to 100 sentences that contained predictions. On average 94 sentences with future mentions were retrieved, with an average of 1.2 future dates per prediction. Finally, assessors evaluated 4,888 query/prediction pairs (approximately 6,032 of triples)[6].

Our machine learning ranking models operate in a supervised manner, and as such, they need training data for learning. We created training data using cross validation by randomly partitioned query articles into N_F folds. We used $N_F - 1$ query/prediction from other folds for training a ranking mode and the remaining fold for testing. We removed queries with zero relevant results, and we obtained $N_F = 3, 4, 5$ for Q_E, Q_C, Q_T respectively.

Parameter setting. We set the boost factors on an independent experiment as $boost(\text{TEXT}) = 5.0$, $boost(\text{CONTEXT}) = 1.0$, and $boost(\text{TITLE}) = 2.0$. We use the recommended values for the constants $b = 0.75$ for all fields, and $k_1 = 1.2$ [26]. For LDA-based features, we trained a yearly model snapshot by selecting 4% of all documents in each year. For each document, we filtered out terms occurring in less than 15 documents and the 100 most common terms. We learn a topic model for each document snapshot by employing Stanford Topic Modeling Toolbox[7], and the number of topics for training LDA N_z is fixed to 500 and the number of topics for inference k is 200. A learning algorithm we use is the collapsed variational Bayes approximation to the LDA objective (CVB0LDA) [2]. All other parameters are default values of the topic modeling. Using CVB0LDA

[4] http://timex2.mitre.org/tern.html

[5] We are interested in assessing the performance of the ranking algorithm and not the annotation tools. However, we note the overall system will be impacted by the annotation errors.

[6] The evaluation collection we have created is available for download at http://www.idi.ntnu.no/~nattiya/data/sigir2011/futurepredictions.zip.

[7] http://nlp.stanford.edu/software/tmt/tmt-0.3/

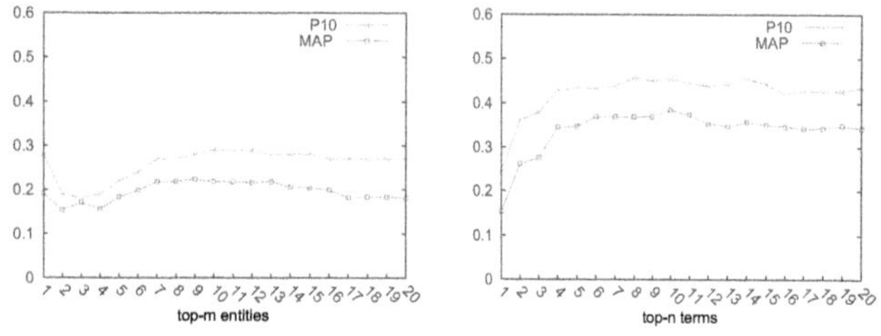

Figure 3: P@10 and MAP performance of Q_E (left) when varying top-m entities, and Q_C (right) when varying top-n terms.

Table 3: The effectiveness of each method when using all queries; †,∓ indicates statistical improvement over the corresponding simple methods using t-test with significant at $p < 0.1$,$p < 0.05$ respectively.

Method	P@1	P@3	P@10	MRR	MAP
Q_E	0.300	0.333	0.290	0.473	0.219
Q_T	0.643	0.579	0.455	0.760	0.385
Q_C	0.500	0.561	0.427	0.656	0.231
Re-Q_E	0.500	0.499	0.360	0.629	0.266
Re-Q_T	0.738†	0.619	0.462	0.831†	0.387
Re-Q_C	0.773∓	0.682∓	0.455	0.841∓	0.271

required high CPU and memory, but needed fewer iterations and had faster convergence rates than a collapsed Gibbs sampler [12], which requires less memory during training.

For both TSU_1 and TSU_2, $DecayRate = 0.5$, $\lambda = 0.5$ and $\mu = 2y$ are used where y the number of years. For both FS_1 and FS_2, $n = 2$, $m = 2$, $s_{min} = 4y$ and $s_{max} = 2y$ are used. So, $\alpha_1 = time(d^q) - 4y$ and $\alpha_2 = time(d^q) + 2y$.

Methods for comparison. We experiment with the three different ways of constructing the query Q_E, Q_T, and Q_C. The baseline for retrieval is Lucene's default ranking function and our queries incorporate two time constraints as explained in Section 2.4. We re-rank the baseline results using SVM^{MAP} yielding *Re-*Q_E, *Re-*Q_T and *Re-*Q_C. For the application of ranking related news predictions, we prefer top-precision retrieval performance metrics over recall-based metrics: a user will be typically interested in a few top predictions even though there are many predictions retrieved. Consequently, we envision a user interface that contains little space for displaying related predictions. Thus, we will measure the retrieval effectiveness by the precision at 1, 3 and 10 (P@1, P@3, and P@10 respectively), Mean Reciprocal Rank (MRR), and Mean Average Precision (MAP). We report the average performance over N_F folds to measure the overall performance, for each query type.

5.2 Experimental Results

The three types of queries (Q_E,Q_T, and Q_C) are composed of either *top-m* entities or *top-n* terms, or both. We first establish which are good m and n values for each one of the types. Instead of varying m and n in re-ranking, we select the m and n that give a reasonable improvement in a hold-out set (where we randomly divided queries into two folds). Therefore, we will use only one fixed version of m and n for the rest of our experiments. We select the values of m and n by performing a preliminary analysis as follows. First, by looking at P@10 and MAP, we select the value of m that yields the best performance using only Q_E to retrieve predictions for each varying m. As shown in Figure 3 (left), $9 \leq m \leq 12$ give almost no difference in terms of P@10. In spite of that, we choose the number of entities $m = 11$ because it is slightly better than the other values. Next, we find the optimal value of n by observing the performance of Q_C when m is fixed to 11 and the value of n is varied. As depicted in Figure 3(right), there is very slight difference in P@10 for $9 \leq n \leq 11$; We choose the number of terms $n = 10$ because it obtains the best in MAP among them.

The retrieval effectiveness of simple methods and their corresponding re-ranking methods are displayed in Table 3. These results are averaged over queries retrieving at least one relevant prediction. In general, Q_T gains the highest effectiveness in all measurements followed by Q_C and Q_E and the feature-based re-ranking approach improves the effectiveness for all query types. In addition, *Re-*Q_C has the highest effectiveness over other re-ranking methods for P@1 and P@3, while *Re-*Q_T gains the highest effectiveness for the rest of all metrics.

Q_E and Q_C pose a problem in not retrieving any relevant result of our judged pool among the first 100 for a large number of queries, which makes it impossible for the machine learning model to improve the ranking. However, we still want to compare the performance between the different variations of the query (Q_E, Q_C, Q_T). Therefore, we use a subset of queries that contained *at least* one relevant result among all the different methods. The results are shown in Table 4 where we compare all other methods against Q_E because we have observed that Q_E performs worst among them. As seen from the results of each re-ranking method, our proposed features improve the effectiveness for all corresponding simple methods. In particular, the re-ranking method *Re-*Q_C outperforms the simple method Q_E significantly. However, *Re-*Q_E did not provide a significant improvement over Q_E. The results show that, for the same set of queries, using entities alone are limited while terms alone are able to retrieve most of relevant predictions.

Interestingly, when looking at the same sub-set of queries with relevant predictions, the re-ranking approach *Re-*Q_C outperforms every other method, even if the plain retrieval Q_T is superior to Q_C. This is an indicator that entity-based features are able to produce higher quality results but only for a certain type of topics. We performed an error analysis to determine why Q_E is unable to retrieve relevant predictions. In general, Q_E fails for a topic that cannot be represented using only people, locations, or organizations. For example, for the topic about "the Europeans agreement of gas emissions", the top-5 Q_E is ⟨*European Union, Brussels, Finland, Germany, Hungary*⟩ and the top-5 Q_T is ⟨*european, emission, target, climate, brussels*⟩. In this case, Q_E is unable to represent the *key* terms "emission" and "climate", and thus fails to retrieve many relevant predictions that match those terms.

Similarly, for the query topic about "Clinton health care reform", Q_E is represented using the named entity *Clinton* (the terms "health care" and "reform" are not annotated as entities). When matching, all predictions containing the entity *Clinton* are matched which will return many documents that are not related to "health care" and "reform".

Table 4: The effectiveness of each method when using a subset of queries; †,∓,⋆ indicates statistical improvement over the method Q_E using t-test with significant at $p < 0.1$, $p < 0.05$, $p < 0.01$ respectively.

Method	P@1	P@3	P@10	MRR	MAP
Q_E	0.300	0.333	0.290	0.473	0.219
Q_T	0.500	0.533	0.430	0.638	0.219
Q_C	0.600†	0.533†	0.360	0.727†	0.163
Re-Q_E	0.500	0.499	0.360	0.629	0.266
Re-Q_T	0.700	0.600	0.410	0.762	0.236
Re-Q_C	1.000∓	0.714∓	0.443	1.000	0.303⋆

Table 5: Top-5 features with highest weights and lowest weights for each query type.

Q_E		Q_T		Q_C	
Feature	W_i	Feature	W_i	Feature	W_i
tagSim	1.00	*bm25f*	1.00	$LDA_{1,parent,k}$	1.00
FS_1	0.97	*retScore*	0.60	*retScore*	0.99
TSU_2	0.88	$LDA_{1,parent,k}$	0.55	$LDA_{1,parent,all}$	0.96
$LDA_{1,txt,k}$	0.87	$LDA_{2,parent,k}$	0.51	*bm25f*	0.93
$LDA_{1,txt,all}$	0.82	$LDA_{1,parent,all}$	0.49	*isSubj*	0.87
cntSenSubj	0.01	*timeDistEvent*	-0.03	*cntEventSen*	-0.02
cntEventSubj	0.01	*timeDistFuture*	-0.11	*querySim*	-0.05
isInTitle	0.00	*cntEventSen*	-0.12	*cntFutureSen*	-0.10
cntEventSen	0.00	*cntFutureSen*	-0.12	*timeDistFuture*	-0.14
querySim	-0.01	*senLen*	-0.16	*senLen*	-0.18

5.3 Feature Analysis

We analyzed feature weights obtained from the learning algorithm SVM^{MAP} in order to understand better what is the importance of the different features,. Note that, in order to compare the weights among different queries, we performed normalization by diving with the maximum value of all weights for each query. Column w_i in Table 5 displays the top-5 features with highest and lowest weights for each query type.

At least two topic based features of all query types are in the top-5 features with highest weight, and therefore topic-based features play an important role in the re-ranking model. Although *retScore* and *bm25f* measure the similarity on a term level, they help to re-rank predictions when incorporated into the machine learning model. as seen in the top-5 features for Q_T and Q_C. The feature that received the highest importance value for the Q_E type is *tagSim*, which measures the similarity between entities in a prediction and manually tagged entities. This indicates that tagged entities in a query document can precisely represent user information needs. The temporal features FS_1 and FS_1 also play an important role for Q_E.

Features in top-5 features with lowest weights are those from the entity-based class. Recall that these features are extracted in order to measure the importance of entities annotated in a prediction with respect to their respective parent documents. However, the results show that these features are not good enough for discriminating between relevant and non-relevant predictions.

6. RELATED WORK

Our related work includes sentence retrieval, entity ranking, temporal ranking, and domain-specific predictions.

Sentence retrieval is the task of retrieving a relevant sentence related to a query. Different application areas of sentence retrieval are mentioned in the book of Murdock [24] and references therein, including, for example, question answering [30], text summarization, and novelty detection. Surdeanu et al. [30] applied supervised learning to rank a set of short answers (sentences) matched a given question (query) by using different classes features. Li and Croft [19] proposed to detect novelty topics by analyzing sentence-level information (sentence lengths, named entities, and opinion patterns). Generally, because sentences are much smaller than documents and thus have limited content compared to documents, the effectiveness of the retrieval of sentences is significantly worse. To address this problem, Blanco and Zaragoza [6] proposed to use the context of sentences in order to improve the effectiveness of sentence retrieval.

There have been a number shared tasks with the goal of furthering research in the area of entity ranking. For instance, the TREC 2008 Enterprise track was created with the objective to find experts (or people) related to a given topic of interest. The INEX Entity Ranking track [10] was launched with the task of finding a list of relevant entities (represented by Wikipedia articles) for a given topic. Recently, the TREC 2009 Entity track was introduced, and the task is to find related entities (represented by homepages) given a topic (called a source entity). The difference between the TREC 2009 Entity and the previous tracks is that it allows a relation and a target entity type to be explicitly specified. There are various approaches to ranking entities by using language models [4], voting models [21], and entity-based graph models [35].

Many ranking models exploiting temporal information have been proposed, including [5, 11, 18, 23]. Li and Croft [18] experimented with time-based language models by assigning a document prior using an exponential decay function of its creation date, such that the more recent documents obtain the higher probabilities of relevance. Diaz and Jones [11] build a temporal profile of a query from the distribution of document publication dates. They use time dependent features derived from these profiles that improve the ranking of temporal queries.

Berberich et al. [5] integrated temporal expressions into query likelihood language modeling, which considers uncertainty inherent to temporal expressions in a query and in documents, i.e., two temporal expressions can refer to the same time interval even when they are not exactly equal. Metzler et al. [23] mined query logs to identify implicit temporal information needs and presented a time-dependent ranking model for certain types of queries.

There is much research in domain-specific predictions such as stock market predictions [27, 33] and recommender systems [17, 25]. The first aims at predicting stock price movements by analyzing financial news, while the latter applies collaborative filtering algorithms for recommending books, videos, movie, etc. based on users' interests.

The future retrieval problem was first presented by Baeza-Yates [3]. He proposed to extract temporal expressions from news, index news articles together with temporal expressions, and retrieve future information (composed of text and future dates) by using a probabilistic model. A document score is given as a multiplication of a *keyword* similarity and a time confidence, i.e., a probability that the document's events will actually happen. The limitation of this original work is that it is evaluated using a small data set and only a year granularity is used.

The more recent work on the future-related information retrieval is presented by Jatowt et al. [13]. In contrast to our work, they do not focus on relevance and ranking future-related information retrieval. They presented an analytical tool for extracting, summarizing and aggregating future-related events from news archives, but did not perform an extensive evaluation, only calculating averaged precision on a small set of generated results.

7. CONCLUSIONS AND FUTURE WORK

In this paper, we demonstrated that future related information is abundant in news stories and defined the task of *ranking related future predictions*. The main goal of this task is to improve user access to this information by selecting the predictions from a news archive that are most relevant to a given news article. We created an evaluation dataset with over 6000 relevance judgments and addressed this task using a learning to rank methodology incorporating four classes of features including term similarity, entity-based similarity, topic similarity, and temporal similarity that outperforms a strong baseline system. Finally, we performed an in-depth analysis of feature importance. Possible future work includes time-dependent query classification using query logs, combining multiple sources (Wikipedia, blogs, home pages, and tweets) of future-related information, sentimental analysis for future-related information and evaluating the effectiveness of the predictions in a real-world news application.

8. ACKNOWLEDGMENTS

We would like to thank Hugo Zaragoza for his help at the early stages of this paper. This work is partially supported by the EU Large Scale Integrated Project LivingKnowledge (contract no. 231126).

9. REFERENCES

[1] O. Alonso, M. Gertz, and R. Baeza-Yates. On the value of temporal information in information retrieval. *ACM SIGIR Forum*, 41(2):35–41, 2007.

[2] A. Asuncion, M. Welling, P. Smyth, and Y. W. Teh. On smoothing and inference for topic models. In *Proceedings of UAI'2009*, 2009.

[3] R. Baeza-Yates. Searching the future. In *Proceedings of ACM SIGIR workshop MF/IR 2005*, 2005.

[4] K. Balog, L. Azzopardi, and M. de Rijke. A language modeling framework for expert finding. *Inf. Process. Manage.*, 45(1):1–19, 2009.

[5] K. Berberich, S. Bedathur, O. Alonso, and G. Weikum. A language modeling approach for temporal information needs. In *Proceedings of ECIR'2010*, 2010.

[6] R. Blanco and H. Zaragoza. Finding support sentences for entities. In *Proceeding of SIGIR'2010*, 2010.

[7] D. M. Blei, A. Y. Ng, and M. I. Jordan. Latent dirichlet allocation. *J. Mach. Learn. Res.*, 3:993–1022, March 2003.

[8] J. Canton. *The Extreme Future: The Top Trends That Will Reshape the World in the Next 20 Years.* Plume, 2007.

[9] K. Crammer, O. Dekel, J. Keshet, S. Shalev-Shwartz, and Y. Singer. Online passive-aggressive algorithms. *J. Mach. Learn. Res.*, 7:551–585, 2006.

[10] G. Demartini, A. P. Vries, T. Iofciu, and J. Zhu. *Overview of the INEX 2008 Entity Ranking Track.* 2009.

[11] F. Diaz and R. Jones. Using temporal profiles of queries for precision prediction. In *Proceedings of SIGIR'2004*, 2004.

[12] T. L. Griffiths. Finding scientific topics. *Proceedings of the National Academy of Science*, 101:5228–5235, Jan. 2004.

[13] A. Jatowt, K. Kanazawa, S. Oyama, and K. Tanaka. Supporting analysis of future-related information in news archives and the web. In *Proceedings of JCDL'2009*, 2009.

[14] T. Joachims. Optimizing search engines using clickthrough data. In *Proceedings of KDD'2002*, 2002.

[15] P. J. Kalczynski and A. Chou. Temporal document retrieval model for business news archives. *Inf. Process. Manage.*, 41, 2005.

[16] N. Kanhabua and K. Nørvåg. Determining time of queries for re-ranking search results. In *Proceedings of ECDL'2010*, 2010.

[17] N. Lathia, S. Hailes, L. Capra, and X. Amatriain. Temporal diversity in recommender systems. In *Proceeding of SIGIR'2010*, 2010.

[18] X. Li and W. B. Croft. Time-based language models. In *Proceedings of CIKM'2003*, 2003.

[19] X. Li and W. B. Croft. Improving novelty detection for general topics using sentence level information patterns. In *Proceedings of CIKM'2006*, 2006.

[20] T.-Y. Liu. Learning to rank for information retrieval. *Found. Trends Inf. Retr.*, 3(3):225–331, 2009.

[21] C. Macdonald and I. Ounis. Searching for expertise: Experiments with the voting model. *Comput. J.*, 52(7):729–748, 2009.

[22] M. Matthews, P. Tolchinsky, R. Blanco, J. Atserias, P. Mika, and H. Zaragoza. Searching through time in the new york times. In *Bridging Human-Computer Interaction and Information Retrieval*, 2010.

[23] D. Metzler, R. Jones, F. Peng, and R. Zhang. Improving search relevance for implicitly temporal queries. In *Proceedings of SIGIR'2009*, 2009.

[24] V. Murdock. *Exploring Sentence Retrieval.* VDM Verlag Dr. Mueller e.K., 2008.

[25] M. J. Pazzani and D. Billsus. The adaptive web. pages 325–341, 2007.

[26] S. E. Robertson and S. Walker. Some simple effective approximations to the 2-poisson model for probabilistic weighted retrieval. In *Proceedings of SIGIR'1994*, 1994.

[27] R. P. Schumaker and H. Chen. Textual analysis of stock market prediction using breaking financial news: The azfin text system. *ACM Trans. Inf. Syst.*, 27:12:1–12:19, March 2009.

[28] S. Shalev-Shwartz, Y. Singer, and N. Srebro. Pegasos: Primal estimated sub-gradient solver for svm. In *Proceedings of ICML'2007*, 2007.

[29] Y. Song, S. Pan, S. Liu, M. X. Zhou, and W. Qian. Topic and keyword re-ranking for lda-based topic modeling. In *Proceeding of CIKM'2009*, 2009.

[30] M. Surdeanu, M. Ciaramita, and H. Zaragoza. Learning to rank answers on large online qa collections. In *Proceedings of ACL-08: HLT*, 2008.

[31] X. Wang and A. McCallum. Topics over time: a non-markov continuous-time model of topical trends. In *Proceedings of KDD'2006*, 2006.

[32] X. Wei and W. B. Croft. Lda-based document models for ad-hoc retrieval. In *Proceedings of SIGIR'2006*, 2006.

[33] D. Wu, G. P. C. Fung, J. X. Yu, and Q. Pan. Stock prediction: an event-driven approach based on bursty keywords. *Frontiers of Computer Science in China*, 3(2):145–157, 2009.

[34] Y. Yue, T. Finley, F. Radlinski, and T. Joachims. A support vector method for optimizing average precision. In *Proceedings of SIGIR'2007*, 2007.

[35] H. Zaragoza, H. Rode, P. Mika, J. Atserias, M. Ciaramita, and G. Attardi. Ranking very many typed entities on wikipedia. In *Proceedings of CIKM'2007*, 2007.

[36] T. Zhang. Solving large scale linear prediction problems using stochastic gradient descent algorithms. In *Proceedings of ICML'2004*, 2004.

Collective Entity Linking in Web Text: A Graph-Based Method

Xianpei Han
Institute of Software
Chinese Academy of Sciences
Beijing, China
xianpei@nfs.iscas.ac.cn

Le Sun
Institute of Software
Chinese Academy of Sciences
Beijing, China
sunle@nfs.iscas.ac.cn

Jun Zhao
National Laboratory of Pattern Recognition, Institute of Automation
Beijing, China
jzhao@nlpr.ia.ac.cn

ABSTRACT

Entity Linking (*EL*) is the task of linking name mentions in Web text with their referent entities in a knowledge base. Traditional EL methods usually link name mentions in a document by assuming them to be independent. However, there is often additional *interdependence* between different EL decisions, i.e., the entities in the same document should be semantically related to each other. In these cases, *Collective Entity Linking*, in which the name mentions in the same document are linked jointly by exploiting the interdependence between them, can improve the entity linking accuracy.

This paper proposes a graph-based collective EL method, which can model and exploit the *global* interdependence between different EL decisions. Specifically, we first propose a graph-based representation, called *Referent Graph*, which can model the global interdependence between different EL decisions. Then we propose a collective inference algorithm, which can jointly infer the referent entities of all name mentions by exploiting the interdependence captured in Referent Graph. The key benefit of our method comes from: 1) The *global* interdependence model of EL decisions; 2) The *purely collective* nature of the inference algorithm, in which evidence for related EL decisions can be reinforced into high-probability decisions. Experimental results show that our method can achieve significant performance improvement over the traditional EL methods.

Categories and Subject Descriptors

H.3.3 [**Information Systems**]: Information storage and retrieval – *Information Search and Retrieval.*

General Terms

Algorithms, Experimentation.

Keywords

Collective Entity Linking, Collective Entity Disambiguation, Graph-based Entity Linking.

SIGIR'11, July 24–28, 2011, Beijing, China.

1. INTRODUCTION

Recent years have witnessed a clear move from Web of information to Web of knowledge. For example, *Wikipedia* [1] provides a Web collaborative platform for knowledge sharing. The *Read the Web* project[2] is a research effort for the automatic knowledge base population from Web. The intended goal of such efforts is to create knowledge bases that contain rich knowledge about the world's entities, their semantic properties, and the semantic relations between them. One of the most notorious examples is *Wikipedia*: its 2010 English version contains more than 3 millions entities and 20 millions semantic relations (Milne et al. [15]). Such resources have often been used in tasks such as text understanding, word sense disambiguation, etc. They can also be used in IR to help better understand the texts and queries by bridging entity mentions in them with the entities in the knowledge base. There is a clear advantage to do this: it will be possible for a user to identify and explore the background knowledge of the searched item. For example, in Figure 1, by bridging the mentions in a web text with their referent entities *Michael Jordan*, *Chicago Bulls* and *Space Jam*, we can find and explore the related information about these entities in knowledge base, such as its textual descriptions, their entity types and the semantic relations between them(e.g., *Employer-of* and *Actor-of*).

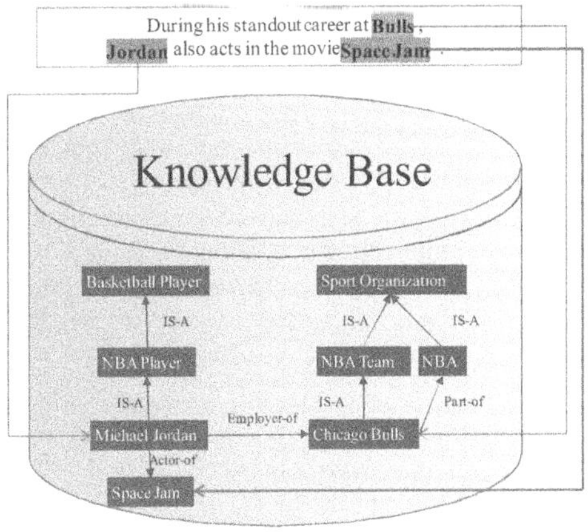

Figure 1. An illustration of entity linking

The key issue is to correctly link the name mentions in a document with their referent entities in the knowledge base, which is usually referred to as *Entity Linking* (*EL* for short). For example, in Figure 1 an entity linking system should link the

[1] http://www.wikipedia.org

[2] http://rtw.ml.cmu.edu/

name mentions "*Bulls*", "*Jordan*" and "*Space Jam*" to their corresponding referent entities *Chicago Bulls*, *Michael Jordan* and *Space Jam* in the knowledge base.

The entity linking, however, is not a trivial task due to the name ambiguity problem, i.e., a name may refer to different entities in different contexts. For instance, the name *Michael Jordan* can refer to more than 20 entities in Wikipedia, some of them are shown below:

- *Michael Jordan(NBA Player)*
- *Michael I. Jordan(Berkeley Professor)*
- *Michael B. Jordan(American Actor)*

To deal with this problem, conventional entity linking approaches have focused on making independent EL decisions using the local mention-to-entity compatibility ([1][3][4][5][6] [12][17][22][24]). The essential idea was to extract the discriminative features (e.g., the important words) from the description of a specific entity (e.g., the Wikipedia page about the entity), then link each name mention in a document by comparing the contextual similarity with each of its candidate referent entities. For example, the name mention "*Jordan*" in Figure 1 will be linked by comparing its contextual similarities with the entities *Michael Jordan*, *Michael I. Jordan* and *Michael B. Jordan*. As these approaches only exploit local features around each name mention, we call these approaches as *local compatibility-based approaches*.

The main drawback of the *local compatibility-based approaches* stems from the fact that they do not take into consideration the *interdependence* between different EL decisions. Specifically, the entities in a topical coherent document usually are semantically related to each other ([11]). For example, in Figure 1, the three entities contained in the document, the NBA player *Michael Jordan*, the NBA team *Chicago Bulls* and the Movie *Space Jam* are all related to each other. In such a case, figuring out the referent entity of one name mention may in turn give us useful information to link the other name mentions in the same document. For example, knowing the mention "*Bulls*" refers to the NBA team *Chicago Bulls* could help us link the mention "*Jordan*" to the basketball player *Michael Jordan* since only this candidate referent entity is semantically related to the *Chicago Bulls*. Similarly, knowing "*Jordan*" refers to the NBA player *Michael Jordan* could in turn help us figuring out the mention "*Bulls*" referring to the NBA team *Chicago Bulls*. These examples strongly suggest that the entity linking performance could be improved by resolving the entity linking problems in the same document jointly, rather than independently. We refer to this approach as *collective entity linking*.

Given a document, the key problem of collective entity linking is to correctly model and exploit the interdependence between the different EL decisions within it. Recent research work has proposed to model the interdependence in a *pair-wise* fashion (Medelyan et al. [16]; Milne & Witten [14]; Kulkarni et al. [11]). These methods model the interdependence between different name mentions as the sum of their *pair-wise* dependencies, and usually determine the referent entity of a name mention by comparing each of its candidate referents with other name mention's referent entities. For example, in Figure 1, the compatibility between the mention "*Jordan*" and the NBA player *Michael Jordan* is the average relatedness between (*Michael Jordan, Space Jam*) and between (*Michael Jordan, Chicago Bulls*). By leveraging the pair-wise dependency, these methods usually can make more accurate EL decisions than the local compatibility based methods, e.g., it can infer that the "*Jordan*" in this example refers to the NBA player *Michael Jordan* due to its relations with *Space Jam* and with *Chicago Bulls*.

However, these methods have a number of limitations: First, the *pair-wise* interdependence model cannot exploit the *global* interdependence between EL decisions, i.e., the structural properties of this interdependence. For instance, in Figure 1, the pair-wise dependence model cannot take into account the implicit dependency between the mention "*Bulls*" and the mention "*Space Jam*", since there is no direct relation between their referent entities *Chicago Bulls* and *Space Jam*. Second, by modeling the interdependence in the pair-wise fashion, the number of computation grows exponentially and the inference process is *NP-hard*, makes the pair-wise model too time-consuming to the real-world applications. Recent pair-wise model based methods ([11][14][16]) usually resolved the inference problem using approximate algorithms, which mostly cannot make the purely collective inference.

To overcome deficiencies of the traditional methods, this paper proposes a graph-based collective entity linking method, which can effectively and efficiently model and exploit the *global* (rather than the *pair-wise*) interdependence between different EL decisions. Specifically, we first propose a graph-based representation, called *Referent Graph*, which can model the global interdependence between different EL decisions as its graph structure. Then we propose a purely collective inference algorithm, which can jointly infer the referent entities of all name mentions in the same document by exploiting both the global interdependence between different EL decisions and the local mention-to-entity compatibility. We have evaluated our method on a standard EL dataset. The experimental results show that our method can achieve significant performance improvement over the traditional EL methods.

The main contributions of this paper are as follows:

1) We propose to model the *global* interdependence between different EL decisions, rather than the *pair-wise* interdependence between them. We also propose the effective *Referent Graph* representation, which can capture the global interdependence as its graph structure;
2) Based on the Referent Graph, we propose a *purely collective* EL algorithm, in which the EL evidence for related name mentions can be collectively reinforced into high-probability EL decisions. These allow us to achieve better performance than the traditional EL methods.

This paper is organized as follows. We first formulate the entity linking problem and briefly review the related work in Section 2. Section 3 describes how to capture the global interdependence between different EL decisions using the Referent Graph. Section 4 describes our method how to exploit the interdependence for collective entity linking. The experimental results are presented and discussed in Section 5. Finally, we conclude this paper and point to some future work in Section 6.

2. THE ENTITY LINKING PROBLEM AND RELATED WORK

In this section, we first formulate the Entity Linking (EL) problem, then compare and contrast the existing EL methods.

ENTITY LINKING (EL) PROBLEM: *Let* $M = \{m_1, m_2, ..., m_k\}$ *denote a collection of name mentions. Each name mention* **m** *in M is characterized by its name* **m.S**, *its local surrounding context* **m.C** *and the document containing it* **m.D**. *Given a knowledge base* **KB** *containing a set of entities* $\{e_1, e_2, ..., e_n\}$, *the objective of EL is to determine the referent entities in KB of the name mentions in M. Specifically, we use* **m.E** *to denote the referent entity of a mention m.*

As an example, consider the following EL problem – this will be our running example throughout the paper.

Example 1

NAME MENTIONS: $\{m_1$ = *Bulls*, m_2 = *Jordan*, m_3 = *Space Jam*$\}$

DOCUMENT: *During his standout career at Bulls, Jordan also acts in the movie Space Jam.*

KNOWLEDGE BASE: *Wikipedia*

Here, an EL system should identify the referent entities of the name mentions as $m_1.E$="*Chicago Bulls*", $m_2.E$="*Michael Jordan*" and $m_3.E$ = "*Space Jam*".

In recent years, much research work has focused on the EL problem. Depending on how they model and exploit the interdependence between EL decisions, the existing EL work can be classified into the following three broad categories:

• ***Local Compatibility Based Approaches***: Initial approaches to EL focused on the use of local compatibility based on some context features. As we stated earlier, the idea is to extract the discriminative features of an entity from its textual description, then link a name mention to the entity which has the highest contextual similarity with it. Mihalcea & Csomai [17] proposed a *Bag of Words* (*BoW*) based method, the compatibility between a name mention and an entity was the cosine similarity between them. Cucerzan [4], Bunescu & Pasca [3], Fader et al. [6] extended the *BoW* model by incorporating more entity knowledge such as its categories. Zhang et al. [22] and Mihalcea & Csomai [17] computed the compatibility using classification algorithms. Zheng et al. [23], Dredze et al. [5] and Zhou et al. [24] employed the learning-to-rank techniques, which can take into account the relative rank between the candidate entities. The main drawback of the local compatibility based approaches is that they do not take into account the interdependence between EL decisions.

• ***Simple Relational Approaches***: Observed that EL decisions in the same document are interdependent, Medelyan et al. [16] and Milne & Witten [14] have proposed to compute the mention-to-entity compatibility by leveraging the interdependence between EL decisions. The idea was that the referent entity of a name mention should be coherent with its unambiguous contextual entities. Medelyan et al. [16] determined the compatibility using the semantic relatedness between the candidate entity and the contextual entities. For example, in Example 1, using the only contextual entity *Space Jam*, the compatibility between the mention "*Jordan*" and the NBA player *Michael Jordan* is determined by the semantic relatedness between (*Michael Jordan*, *Space Jam*). Milne and Witten [14] extended the method of Medelyan et al. [16] by adopting learning-based techniques to balance the semantic relatedness, the commoness and the context quality. The drawbacks of these approaches are that they didn't make the collective entity linking, can only exploit the pair-wise interdependence between a name mention and its unambiguous contextual entities, which is usually limited in real world documents. For example, the simple relational approaches will still have difficulty to determine the referent entity *Chicago Bulls* for "*Bulls*" since *Chicago Bulls* is not semantically related to the *Space Jam* – the only unambiguous entity in the context.

• ***Pair-Wise Collective Approaches***: One recent approach proposed by Kulkarni et al. [11] can make collective entity linking, but which only model and exploit the *pair-wise* interdependence between EL decisions. Kulkarni et al. [11] proposed to resolve the collective EL as an optimization problem, where the interdependence between EL decisions is modeled as the sum of their *pair-wise* dependencies. Two approximation solutions were also proposed to resolve the *NP-hard* problem of their inference process.

From the above description, we can see that the interdependence between EL decisions can provide critical evidence for accurate EL decisions. However, all above approaches do not exploit the global interdependence. In the following sections, we demonstrate how the global interdependence can be modeled and exploited using our graph-based collective EL method.

3. THE REFERENT GRAPH

In this section, we propose a graph-based representation, *Referent Graph*, which can capture both the local mention-to-entity compatibility and the global interdependence structure between different EL decisions. In what follows, we first introduce how to model the mention-to-entity compatibility and the interdependence between two EL decisions in the *Referent Graph*, then define the *Referent Graph* in detail.

3.1 Local Mention-to-Entity Compatibility

The local mention-to-entity compatibility measures the likelihood of a name mention *m* referring to a specific entity *e*, based on its local context *m.C*. In this paper, the local context of *m* is the text window around *m*, and the window size is set to 50 according to the experiments in Pedersen et al. [18].

Traditionally, the compatibility between a name mention *m* and a specific entity *e* is determined by the term co-occurrences between the local context of *m* and the text description of *e*. Based on the same idea, in our *Referent Graph* we model the local compatibility as a *Compatible* relation between name mention and entity, and the strength of the *Compatible* relation (CP) is calculated based on the *Bag of Words* model:

$$CP(m,e)=\frac{m \cdot e}{|m||e|}$$

where the name mention *m* is represented as a vector of its context words, and the entity *e* is represented as a vector of its Wikipedia page's words. All words are weighted using the TFIDF schema.

3.2 Semantic Relation between Entities

As described in Section 1, the interdependence between two EL decisions in a document means that their referent entities should be semantically related to each other. Based on this observation, the *Referent Graph* models the dependency between two EL decisions as a *Semantic-Related* relation between their referent entities. We need a way to measure the strength of the semantic relation between entities, i.e., the semantic relatedness.

There has been several research which focused on computing the semantic relatedness between entities (Strube and Ponzetto [19]; Milne and Witten [9]). In this paper, we adopt the method proposed by Milne and Witten [9] to compute the semantic relatedness between entities, which computes the semantic relatedness as:

$$SR(a,b) = 1 - \frac{\log(\max(|A|,|B|)) - \log(|A \cap B|)}{\log(|W|) - \log(\min(|A|,|B|))}$$

where a and b are the two entities of interest, A and B are the sets of all entities that link to a and b in Wikipedia respectively, and W is the entire Wikipedia. We show an example of semantic relatedness between four selected entities in Table 1, where the semantic relatedness can reveal the semantic relations between *Michael Jordan* and *Space Jam*, and between *Michael Jordan* and *Chicago Bulls*.

	Space Jam	Chicago Bulls
Michael Jordan	*0.66*	*0.82*
Michael B. Jordan	*0.00*	*0.00*

Table 1. The relatedness table of four selected entities

3.3 The Referent Graph

Now we have two relations: the *Compatible* relation between name mention and entity and the *Semantic-Related* relation between entities. In this way, the interdependence between the EL decisions in a document can be best represented as a graph, which we refer to as *Referent Graph*. Concretely, the *Referent Graph* is defined as follows:

*A **Referent Graph** is a weighted graph **G=(V, E)**, where the node set **V** contains all name mentions in a document and all the possible referent entities of these name mentions, with each node representing a name mention or an entity; each edge between a name mention and an entity represents a **Compatible** relation between them; each edge between two entities represents a **Semantic-Related** relation between them.*

For illustration, Figure 2 shows the *Referent Graph* representation of the EL problem in Example 1.

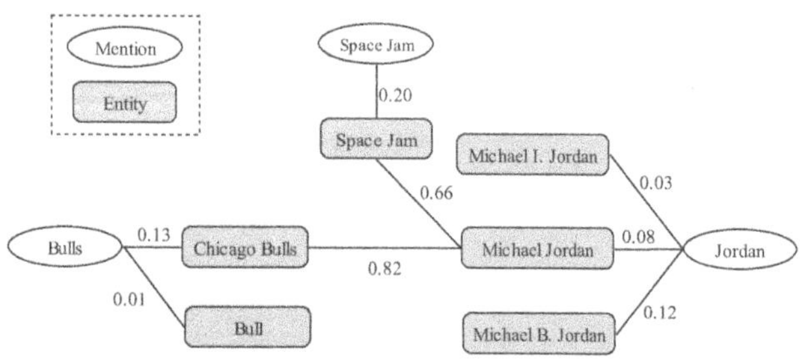

Figure 2. The *Referent Graph* of Example 1

By representing both the local mention-to-entity compatibility and the global entity relation as edges, two types of dependencies are captured in Referent Graph:

1) Local Dependency between name mention and entity.

In Referent Graph, the local dependency between a name mention and an entity is encoded as the edge between the nodes corresponding to them, with an edge weight indicates the strength of this dependency. For example, in Figure 2 the dependency between (*Bulls*, *Chicago Bulls*) is represented as an edge between them. Notice here the dependency between name mention and entity is *asymmetric*: only the entity depends on the name mention, but the name mention does not depend on the entity.

2) Global Interdependence between EL decisions.

By connecting candidate referent entities using the *Semantic-Related* relation, the interdependence between EL decisions is encoded as the graph structure of the Referent Graph. In this way, the referent graph allows us to deduce and use indirect and implicit dependencies, and can take the structural properties of the interdependence into consideration. For example, the name mention *Bulls* is related to the entity *Chicago Bulls*, which in turn is related successively to the entity *Michael Jordan*. An indirect relation between *Bulls* and *Michael Jordan* could be established and used in the EL when necessary. Such indirect relations cannot be identified using an approach based on pair-wise dependence modeling.

The Referent Graph Construction. Given a document, the construction of Referent Graph takes three steps: name mention identification, candidate entity selection and node connection. In this paper, we focus on the task of linking entities with Wikipedia, even though the proposed method can be applied to other knowledge bases. Thus we will only show how to construct the Referent Graph using Wikipedia:

1) **Name Mention Identification**. We first identify all name mentions in a document. Given a document, we gather all N-grams (up to 8 words) and match them to the anchor dictionary of Wikipedia (Medelyan et al. [16]). Not all matches are considered, because even stop words such as "*is*" and "*an*" may match to the anchor texts. We use Mihalcea and Csomai [2]'s *keyphraseness* feature to filter out the meaningless name mentions, and the retained name mentions will be represented in the graph.

2) **Candidate Entity Selection**. In this step, we select the candidate referent entities for each name mention detected in Step 1. We adopt the method described in Milne & Witten [14], where a name mention's candidate referent entities are the destination Wikipedia articles of the anchor text which are the same as this name mention.

3) **Node Connection.** In this step, we add the dependency edge to the Referent Graph. For each name mention, we add a *Compatible* edge between it and each of its candidate referent entities using the method in Section 3.1. For each pairs of entities in Referent Graph, if there is a *Semantic-Relation* between them, we add an edge between them using the method described in Section 3.2.

4. COLLECTIVE ENTITY LINKING

In this section, we propose a purely collective inference algorithm, which can jointly identify the referent entities of all name mentions in the same document. Given a Referent Graph representation, the goal of the collective EL is to use both the *Compatible* and the *Semantic-Related* relations simultaneously in EL decision making.

4.1 Problem Reformulation

As shown in Section 1, the referent entity of a name mention m should be both:

- Compatible with the name mention m;

- Topically coherent to the other referent entities in the same document.

With respect to the Referent Graph representation, the referent entity of a name mention m should be an entity node which has:

- A strong *Compatible* relation with the node corresponding to the name mention m;
- Many strong *Semantic-Related* relations with the nodes corresponding to the other referent entities.

To see how this can work, observe in Figure 2 that if we known the referent entities of "*Bulls*" and "*Space Jam*" is *Chicago Bulls* and *Space Jam*, then the *Semantic-Related* relation between (*Chicago Bulls*, *Michael Jordan*) and between (*Space Jam*, *Michael Jordan*) can provide more evidence for the entity *Michael Jordan* to be the referent entity of "*Jordan*". In contrast, the entity *Michael B. Jordan* lacks the *Semantic-Related* relations with *Chicago Bulls* and *Space Jam*, which suggests that it is not likely to be the referent entity of "*Jordan*", even if it has a stronger *Compatible* relation with the mention "*Jordan*".

But it seems that our method faces a 'chicken-and-egg' problem: The referent entity of a name mention depends on the other referent entities in the same document, and in turn the other referent entities depend on the referent entity of this name mention itself. So how we can resolve it?

In this paper, we resolve such a problem by making a purely collective inference:

1) Firstly, we collect the initial evidence for an entity to be the referent entity of a name mention;
2) Secondly, the evidence is simultaneously reinforced by propagating them between related EL decisions using the interdependence structure in Referent Graph;
3) Finally, our method makes the EL decisions that have the highest probability based on the reinforced EL evidence.

In the following sections, we describe these steps in detail.

4.2 Initial Evidence

Given a document, the initial evidence we used to decide whether an entity is a referent entity of this document is the name mentions in this document and the local compatibilities between these name mentions and their candidate referent entities. Notice that the local compatibility has been encoded as *Compatible* relation in Referent Graph, therefore we only use the name mentions in a document $M = \{m_1, m_2, \ldots, m_k\}$ as the initial evidence.

The Importance of Evidence. We observed that not all name mentions play equally important roles in the EL process. The referent entities of more important name mentions should provide more information than the referent entities of less important name mentions. For example, consider the following document:

"*The Hall of Fame opens its doors to Michael Jordan, the NBA's greatest player—Yahoo! News*"

The evidence of the name mention *Yahoo! News* should be less important than the evidence of the name mentions *The Hall of Fame*, *Michael Jordan* and *NBA*.

In order to measure the importance of the initial evidence, we assign a *prior* importance score to each name mention. Traditionally, the relative importance of a name mention (notice a name mention is also a phrase) in a document is determined by its TFIDF score. We do the same here: we assign a *prior* importance score to a name mention m according to its TFIDF score, and which is further normalized by the sum of TFIDF scores of all name mentions in the same document D:

$$\text{Importance}(m)=\frac{tfidf(m)}{\sum_{m\in D} tfidf(m)}$$

Using the above method, we can compute the prior importance of the three name mentions in Figure 2 as Importance(*Bulls*)=0.30, Importance(*Jordan*)=0.25 and Importance(*Space Jam*)=0.45.

4.3 Evidence Propagation

Given the initial evidence, the second step is to reinforce the evidence by propagating them according to the dependency structure captured in Referent Graph. Evidence can be propagated through the two types of edges in Referent Graph in the following way:

***Compatible* Edge**: By connecting a name mention and its candidate referent entities, the *Compatible* edge provides a way to propagate evidence from a name mention (i.e., the initial evidence) to its candidate referent entities. Intuitively, a name mention will only propagate evidence to the entity which has a *Compatible* link with it (i.e., will only propagate to its candidate referent entities), and will propagate more evidence to the entity which has a stronger *Compatible* link with it (i.e., has a larger local compatibility $CP(m, e)$ between them). Based on the above assumption, we define the evidence propagation ratio from a name mention m to an entity e as:

$$P(m \rightarrow e) = \frac{CP(m,e)}{\sum_{e\in N_m} CP(m,e)}$$

where N_m is the set of the neighbor entities of a name mention m. Notice that there is no evidence propagation from entity to name mention, as *Compatible* edges only go from a name mention to entities. Using this method, we can compute the evidence propagation ratio in Figure 2 as: *P(Space Jam* → Space Jam*)*=1.0, *P(Jordan*→Michael Jordan*)*=0.35 and *P(Jordan*→Michael B. Jordan*)*=0.52.

***Semantic-Related* Edge:** By connecting semantically related entities, the *Semantic-Related* edge provides a way to propagate evidence between two related EL decisions by propagating evidence between their referent entities. Intuitively, an entity will only propagate evidence to its neighbor entities, and will propagate more evidence to the entity which has stronger *Semantic-Related* relation with it. Based on the above assumption, we define the evidence propagation ratio from entity e_i to entity e_j as:

$$P(e_i \rightarrow e_j) = \frac{SR(e_i,e_j)}{\sum_{e\in N_{e_i}} SR(e_i,e)}$$

where N_e is the set of neighbor entities of an entity e. Using this method, we can compute the evidence propagation ratio between entities in Figure 2, e.g., *P*(Space Jam→Michael Jordan)=1.0 and *P*(Michael Jordan→Space Jam)=0.446.

4.4 Collective Inference

This section describes the collective inference algorithm of our EL method. Specifically, given a name mention m in a document d, we identify its referent entity as:

$$m.E = \underset{e}{\text{argmax}}\ CP(m,e) \times r_d(e)$$

where $CP(m,e)$ is the local compatibility between m and e, $r_d(e)$ is the evidence score for entity e to be a referent entity of the document d. In this way, the EL decision can combine the evidence from the name mention (i.e., the $CP(m,e)$) and the evidence from related EL decisions (i.e., the $r_d(e)$). Since $CP(m,e)$ is known in the Referent Graph, the only problem is to compute $r_d(e)$. Here we demonstrate how to jointly compute the $r_d(e)$ for all candidate referent entities of a document d, therefore collectively infer the referent entities of all name mentions in a document d.

To simplify the description of our algorithm, given a Referent Graph $\boldsymbol{G=(V, E)}$ contains $\boldsymbol{n}$ nodes (with $\boldsymbol{k}$ name mention nodes and $\boldsymbol{l}$ entity nodes) we assign each node an integer index from 1 to $|V|$ and use this index to represent the node, then we can write the adjacency matrix of the Referent Graph $\boldsymbol{G}$ as $\boldsymbol{A}$, where $\boldsymbol{A[i,j]}$ or $\boldsymbol{A_{ij}}$ is the edge weight between node i and node j. We introduce the follows three notations for our collective EL algorithm:

$\boldsymbol{s}$: The initial evidence vector, an $n \times 1$ vector where s_i=Importance(m) if i corresponds to a name mention m;

$\boldsymbol{r}$: The evidence vector, an $n\times 1$ vector where r_i is the evidence score for the node i to be an referent entity in document d (i.e., $r_d(e)$ if node i correspond to the entity e) or the evidence score contained in this node i (if node i corresponds to a name mention).

$\boldsymbol{T}$: The evidence propagation matrix, an $n\times n$ matrix where T_{ij} is the evidence propagation ratio from node j to node i. T_{ij} is computed using the method described in Section 4.3.

In this way, the initial evidence is encoded in the initial evidence vector $\boldsymbol{s}$ and the interdependence between EL decisions is encoded in the evidence propagation matrix $\boldsymbol{T}$, the problem is how to get the evidence vector $\boldsymbol{r}$.

To compute the evidence vector $\boldsymbol{r}$, we first set its initial value $\boldsymbol{r^0}$ as the initial evidence vector $\boldsymbol{s}$, i.e.,

$$r^0 = s$$

Then we can update the evidence vector by propagating them according to the interdependence between EL decisions, i.e., the evidence propagation matrix T. In this way, we can write the recursive form of the evidence vector as:

$$r^{t+1} = T \times r^t$$

where the $\boldsymbol{r^t}$ is the evidence vector we know at time t. One problem of the above formula is that some nodes in the Referent Graph without evidence outward edges, when the evidence propagates to this node it disappears. For example, in Figure 2 the entity node "*Michael I. Jordan*" cannot propagate any evidence to other nodes. To resolve this problem, we introduce a reallocate condition: at each step we reallocate a fraction of evidence to the initial evidence vector $\boldsymbol{s}$, then we can get the final recursive form of the evidence vector as:

$$r^{t+1} = (1-\lambda) \times T \times r^t + \lambda \times s$$

where $\lambda \in (0,1)$ is the fraction of the reallocation evidence at each step, which is set to the value *0.1* through a learning process in Section 5. By solving this equation, we can get the closed-form solution of evidence vector as:

$$r = \lambda(I - cT)^{-1}s$$

where $c = 1 - \lambda$ and I is the identity matrix. In this way, we can jointly infer the $r_d(e)$ value for each candidate referent entity in a document d. Observe the above formula, we can see that our collective inference algorithm can combine evidences from the interdependence between EL decisions ($\boldsymbol{T}$), the local compatibility between name mention and entities ($\boldsymbol{T}$) and the relative importance of name mentions ($\boldsymbol{s}$).

Using the above method, we can compute the evidence score for the entities in Figure 2 and the results are shown in Table 2. From Table 2 we can see that: ① our collective inference algorithm can effectively identify the referent entities of a document: the three referent entities *Space Jam*, *Chicago Bulls* and *Michael Jordan* all received a significantly higher evidence score than other candidate entities such as *Bull* and *Michael B. Jordan*; ② The interdependence between EL decisions is critical for the correct EL decision: although the compatibility between (*Jordan*, *Michael Jordan*) is lower than the compatibility between (*Jordan*, *Michael B. Jordan*), the interdependence information can still give the entity *Michael Jordan* a significantly higher evidence score.

Entity	**Space Jam**	**Chicago Bulls**	**Michael Jordan**
$r_d(e)$	*0.144*	*0.202*	*0.314*
Entity	**Bull**	**Michael I. Jordan**	**Michael B. Jordan**
$r_d(e)$	*0.0015*	*0.0045*	*0.018*

Table 2. The evidence scores for entities in Example 1

The Random Graph Walk Explanation of Our Algorithm. Notice that $\boldsymbol{s}$ is a normalized vector and T is a column normalized matrix, we can view the evidence propagation process as a random walk process in graph (Gbel & Jagers [8]), where $\boldsymbol{s}$ is the starting vector, $\boldsymbol{T}$ is the random transition probability matrix and $\boldsymbol{r}$ is the stationary probability of the nodes in Referent Graph. In this perspective, the collective inference algorithm of our method is the same as the *Random Walk with Restart* algorithm (Tong et al. [21]) in graph or the *Personalized PageRank* algorithm (Haveliwala [20]) in IR.

From the random graph walk perspective, we can explain $r_d(e)$ as the probability with which people who read the document d would be interested in the entity e. For example, using the $r_d(e)$ value, we may predict that 10% people who reading this paper will be interested in the research area *Entity Linking*, and only 0.01% people who will be interested in the NBA player *Michael Jordan*. Therefore, we can also view the entity linking task as the process of predicting which entities people will be interested by reading a document according to both the name mentions and the semantic relations between entities.

The *Posterior* Importance of Name Mention. For many applications such as the Wikification of Web page (Mihalcea & Csomai [17]), only the important name mentions in a document will be linked. Therefore, we need to assign an importance score to the name mentions in a document. In Section 4.2, we have assigned a *prior* importance score to name mention according to its TFIDF score. However, since we have known the referent entity of a name mention, we can update its *prior* importance score to its *posterior* importance score as follows:

$$\text{Importance}_{post}(m)=\text{Importance}(m)\times r_d(m.E)$$

5. Experiments

In this section, we assess the performance of our method and compare it with the traditional methods. As most of the earlier work, this paper evaluates the EL method on the task of *linking with Wikipedia*, even though the proposed method can be easily applied to other knowledge bases. In following, we first explain the experimental settings in Section 5.1, then evaluate and discuss the results in Section 5.2.

5.1 Experimental Settings

5.1.1 Knowledge Base

In our experiments, we use the Jan. 30, 2010 English version of Wikipedia[3] as the knowledge base. We prepared the Wikipedia data according to the method described in Hu et al. [25]. In total, the knowledge base we used contains:

- *Over 3,000,000 distinct entities;*
- *A name-to-entity dictionary which contains over 10,000,000 distinct entity names and the candidate referent entities of each name;*
- *Over 20,000,000 semantic relations between entities, which are used to compute the semantic relatedness.*

5.1.2 Data Set

Traditional methods usually used the Wikipedia articles as the ground truth entity linking results ([3][4][14][17]). However, as observed in Kulkarni et al.[11], Wikipedia articles are unsuitable to the evaluation of high-recall entity linking tasks because it annotates name mentions very sparsely (only the important name mentions are annotated). The recent Knowledge Base Population track in TAC 2009[4] (McNamee & Dang [12]) has provided a standard data set for the evaluation of entity linking task, but this data set focuses on individual EL tasks in different documents, and is unsuitable for our collective EL settings.

Due to the above reasons, we adopted the publicly available **IITB** data set[5] to evaluate the performance of our EL method, which is also the data set used in Kulkarni et al.[11]. The IITB data set contains a set of documents (107 documents in total) collected from the web sites belonging to a handful of domains. For each document, its name mentions' referent entities in Wikipedia are manually annotated to be as exhaustive as possible ([11]). In total, 17,200 name mentions are annotated, 161 name mentions per document on average. In our experiments, we evaluate the EL performance using only the name mentions whose referent entities are contained in Wikipedia.

5.1.3 Evaluation Criteria

This paper adopted the same performance metrics used in the Kulkarni et al.[11], which includes ***Recall***, ***Precision*** and ***F1***. Let M^* be the golden standard set of the linked name mentions, M be the set of linked name mentions outputed by an EL method, then these metrics are computed as:

$$Precision = \frac{|M \cap M^*|}{|M|}$$

$$Recall = \frac{|M \cap M^*|}{|M^*|}$$

Notice here that two name mentions are considered equal if and only if their names *m.S*, the documents containing them *m.D* and their referent entities *m.E* are all equal (Notice there is no guarantee that a method can achieve the *Recall* of 1.0). In the same way as in Kulkarni et al.[11], *Precision* and *Recall* are averaged across documents and overall *F1* is computed from average *Precision* and *Recall*. Because *Precision* and *Recall* are often negatively correlated, they do not always get their peaks at the same time. In this case, we used *F1* as the primary performance metric.

5.1.4 Baselines

We compare our method with four state-of-the-art baselines:

Wikify!. This is the same EL method described in Mihalcea & Csomai [17], which is a standard *Local Compatibility* based method. The *Wikify!* computes the local compatibility using the contextual overlap between the name mention and the dictionary definitions of the entity(in their method, its Wikipedia page).

Cucerzan. This is the same method described in Cucerzan [4]. This is also a *compatibility* based method, but the compatibility between a name mention *m* and a candidate referent entity *e* is determined by two factors: the standard local compatibility and the relatedness between *e* and all other name mentions' candidate referent entities in the same document.

M&W. This is the same EL method described in Milne & Witten [14], which is a state-of-the-art *simple relational method*. Given a name mention, *M&W* determines its referent entity by (mainly) comparing each of its candidate referent entity using the average relatedness between the entity and the name mention's unambiguous contextual entities.

CSAW. This is the same EL system described in Kulkarni et al.[11]. As described in Section 2, the *CSAW* is a collective EL method based on the *pair-wise* EL decision interdependence modeling.

Except for the *CSAW*, all other three baselines are designed only to link the important name mentions (i.e., key phrases) in a document. In our experiment, in order to compare the performances in a high recall, we push these systems' recalls by reducing their importance thresholds of linked name mentions.

5.2 Experimental Results

5.2.1 Overall Performance

We conduct experiments on the **IITB** data set with several methods: the baselines *Wikify!*, *Cucerzan*, *M&W* and *CSAW*, our method using only the local compatibility (i.e., the referent entity of a name mention is simply the entity which has the largest compatibility with this name mention)—which we denote as ***Our Method(LC)*** and the full model of our method—***Our Method***. For all methods, the parameters were configured through 10-fold

[3] It can be obtained from http://download.wikipedia.org for free research use

[4] http://projects.ldc.upenn.edu/kbp/data/

[5] http://www.cse.iitb.ac.in/~soumen/doc/QCQ/

cross validation. The overall performance results are shown in Table 3.

	Precision	Recall	F1
Wikify!	*0.55*	*0.28*	*0.37*
Cucerzan	*0.71*	*0.33*	*0.45*
M&W	*0.80*	*0.38*	*0.52*
CSAW	*0.65*	*0.73*	*0.69*
Our Method(LC)	***0.52***	***0.34***	***0.41***
Our Method	***0.69***	***0.76***	***0.73***

Table 3. The overall results on IITB data set

From the results in Table 3, we can make the following observations:

1) By modeling and exploiting the global interdependence between different EL tasks, our collective EL method can achieve significant performance improvements over the traditional methods: compared with the local compatibility based baseline *Wikify!*, our method can produce a 36% F1 improvement; compared with the simple relational baseline *M&W*, our method can produce a 21% F1 improvement; compared with the pair-wise based collective baseline *CSAW*, our method can produce a 4% F1 improvement.

2) The interdependence between the referent entities in the same document can provide critical evidence to the EL decision: □ By adding the relatedness between entities into the local compatibility, the *Cucerzan* can achieve a 8% F1 improvement over the local context based baseline *Wikify!*; ② By using only the relatedness between entities, the simple relational method *M&W* can achieve a 15% F1 improvement over the local context based baseline *Wikify!*.

3) By modeling and exploiting the interdependence between different EL tasks, the collective EL method can achieve significant performance improvement over the independent decision making based EL methods: ① Compared with the local compatiblity based baseline *Wikify!*, the two collective EL methods *CSAW* and *Our Method* can significantly improve the F1 measure by 32% and 36% respectively; ② Compared with the simple relational baseline *M&W*, the two collective EL methods *CSAW* and *Our Method* can significantly improve the F1 measure by 24% and 28% respectively; ③ By exploiting the interdependence and making the collective inference, *Our Method* can achieve a 32% F1 improvement over our local compatibility only system—*Our Method(LC)*.

4) By modeling and exploiting the global interdependence, our method can further improve the EL performance than the *pair-wise* interdependence model: compared with the pair-wise interdependence model based *CSAW* baseline, our method can achieve a 4% F1 improvement. We believe this is because our Referent Graph can encode more interdependence between EL tasks than the pair-wise based model, and our purely collective inferent algorithm can better exploit the global interdependence structure between different EL decisions, in particular, regarding indirect relations and mutual reinforcement.

5.2.2 *Disambiguation Precision*

For many EL applications such as the Wikification of Web pages and Wikipedia articles, the disambiguation precision plays a critical role. However, because precision and recall are strongly related, it is not straightforward to compare the disambiguation precision of different EL systems. Observed that in our experiments all EL systems can achieve a recall larger than 20%, we compare the disambiguation precision of different EL methods at the recall of 20%. The results are shown in Table 4.

	Precision
Wikify!	*0.60*
Cucerzan	*0.71*
M&W	*0.83*
CSAW	*0.87*
Our Method(LC)	***0.58***
Our Method	***0.87***

Table 4. The Precision results @20% Recall

From Table 4, we can make the following observations:

1) The local context typically is not enough to support a high disambiguation precision: even at the recall of 20%, the two local context based methods, *Wikify!* and *Our Method(LC)*, can only achieve precisions of 0.60 and 0.58.

2) The interdependence between referent entities is the better evidence for disambiguation than the local context of name mentions: all the three interdependence based methods (*M&W, CSAW* and *Our method*) can achieve a precision higher than 0.80 at the recall of 20%.

5.2.3 *Recall-Precision Tradeoff*

Usually, the disambiguation precision of an EL system is related to the recall of name mentions. To discuss the tradeoff between recall and precision, we show the precisions at different recalls of our method in Figure 3 (Notice that the highest *Recall* that can be achieved by *Our Method* and *Our Method(LC)* are correspondingly *0.83* and *0.32*). Furthermore, in order to intuitively demonstrate the EL result when pushing the recall into a higher value, Table 5 shows our method's results of the top 20% weighted and the last 20% weighted name mentions of the Wikipedia article *Michael I. Jordan*[6].

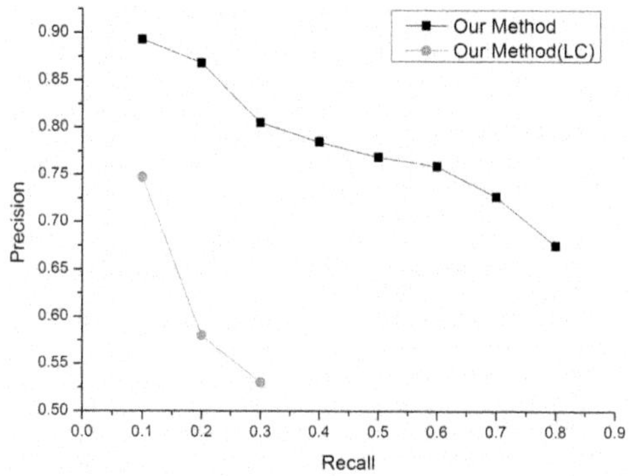

Figure 3. The Precisions vs. Recalls

[6] http://en.wikipedia.org/wiki/Michael_I._Jordan

	Name Mention	Referent Entity	Score
Top 20%	*Michael I. Jordan*	Michael I. Jordan	*0.0038*
	machine learning	Machine learning	*0.0033*
	formalisation	Formal system	*0.0029*
	cognitive	Cognitive science	*0.0025*
	statistics	Statistics	*0.0024*
	variational methods	Variational Bayesian methods	*0.0023*
	PhD	Doctor of Philosophy	*0.0022*
	Neural Networks	Neural network	*0.0019*
	EM	Expectation-maximization algorithm	*0.0019*
	artificial intelligence	Artificial intelligence	*0.0019*
	NSF	National Science Foundation	*0.0018*
	UC. Berkeley	University of California, Berkeley	*0.0014*
Last 20%	*paper*	Academic publishing	*7.92E-4*
	full professor	Professor	*7.29E-4*
	David E. Rumelhart	David Rumelhart	*6.47E-4*
	Zoubin Ghahramani	Zoubin Ghahramani	*6.25E-4*
	Presidential	President	*6.10E-4*
	application	Computer software	*5.99E-4*
	Pioneer Award	GLAAD Media Awards	*5.50E-4*
	R	R (programming language)	*4.89E-4*
	ACC	Atlantic Coast Conference	*4.50E-4*
	Investigator	Player character	*4.28E-4*
	Lawrence	D. H. Lawrence	*4.19E-4*
	American Control Conference	American Automatic Control Council	*3.67E-4*

Table 5. The EL results of the Wikipedia article of Berkeley professor *Michael I. Jordan*

From Figure 3 and Table 5, we can see that:

1) Our method can achieve high EL precision on the **important name mentions** of a document. Figure 3 showed that our method can achieve 0.90 precision at the recall of 0.1, and 0.87 precision at the recall of 0.2 (As shown in Section 4, when we push the recall of our method, we add the name mentions according to their relative importance in a document).

   We believe this is because important name mentions are more coherent to the topic of a document than less important name mentions, therefore the document contains more evidence for the EL decisions of these name mentions. For instance, in Table 5, the top 20% name mentions are all topical coherent to the topic of this document, i.e., the professor *Michael I. Jordan*, such as his research areas *machine learning* and *statistics*, his school *UC Berkeley*, etc. In contrast, the last 20% are less topical coherent to the topic, such as the name mentions *Presidential*, *application* and *R*.

2) Compared with the local compatibility based methods, the collective EL methods shows a greater advantage in linking less important name mentions in a document. Figure 3 shows that when we push the recall from 0.1 to 0.3, the performance improvement of Our Method increases from 15% to 18%. We believe this is because the EL method can capture more evidence than the local compatibility based methods: except for the local surrounding context, but also the interdependence between different EL decisions.

3) For real world usage, we must take the trade-off between precision and recall into consideration. For some applications like the identification of missing links in Wikipedia (Adafre & Rijke [1]) and the wikification of Web page (Mihalcea & Csomai [17]), the precision is critical, therefore we need to loose the recall to achieve a higher precision. For instance, we may only link the top 20% name mentions in Table 5 to hold a high entity linking precision. In contrast, for some applications where recall is critical like the topic indexing in IR (Medelyan et al. [16]) and web people search (Artiles et al. [2]), we need to loose the precision for a high recall.

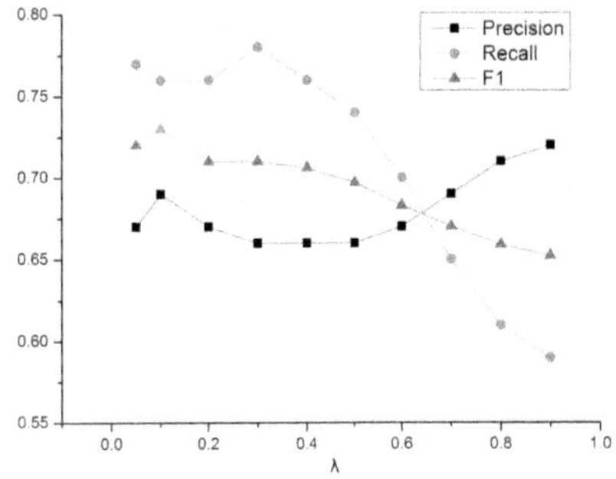

Figure 4. The Performance results vs. λ

5.2.4 *Optimizing Parameters*

Our method has only one parameter λ, which is the reallocation fraction of the evidence in every evidence propagation step. Intuitively, a larger λ will increase the importance of the initial evidence and the local compatibility in the collective EL decision; and at the same time decrease the importance of the interdependence between EL tasks. Figure 4 plots this trade-off. As shown in Figure 4, our method can achieve the best F1 performance when the value of λ is 0.1.

6. CONCLUSIONS AND FUTURE WORK

In this paper, we proposed a graph-based method to the entity linking task. This method can collectively infer the referent entities of all name mentions in the same document. By modeling and exploiting the global interdependence between different EL decisions, the proposed method can achieve competitive performance over the traditional methods.

In our method, we did not take into account the *NIL entity problem* of the EL task, i.e., the referent entity of a name mention may not be contained in the given knowledge base. For future work, we will resolve this aspect in our graph-based method by leading a pseudo NIL entity into our model. Furthermore, using the entity linking method, we want to develop a Web entity search and mining system by annotating billions of Web pages with their entity information.

7. ACKNOWLEDGMENTS

The work is supported by the National Natural Science Foundation of China under Grants no. 60773027, 60736044, 90920010, 61070106, 60875041 and 61003117, and the National High Technology Development 863 Program of China under Grants no. 2008AA01Z145. Moreover, we sincerely thank the reviewers for their valuable comments.

8. REFERENCES

[1] Adafre, S. F. & de Rijke, M. 2005. *Discovering missing links in Wikipedia.* In: Proceedings of the 3rd international workshop on Link discovery.

[2] Artiles, J., Sekine, S. & Gonzalo, J. 2008. *Web people search.* In: Proceedings of LREC, vol. 8.

[3] Bunescu, R. & Pasca, M. 2006. *Using encyclopedic knowledge for named entity disambiguation.* In: Proceedings of EACL, vol. 6.

[4] Cucerzan, S. 2007. *Large-scale named entity disambiguation based on Wikipedia data.* In: Proceedings of EMNLP-CoNLL.

[5] Dredze, M., McNamee, P., Rao, D., Gerber, A. & Finin, T. 2010. *Entity Disambiguation for Knowledge Base Population.* In: Proceedings of COLING.

[6] Fader, A., Soderland, S., Etzioni, O. & Center, T. 2009. *Scaling Wikipedia-based named entity disambiguation to arbitrary web text.* In: Proceedings of Wiki-AI at IJCAI.

[7] Gabrilovich, E. and Markovich, S. 2007. *Computing Semantic Relatedness using Wikipedia-based Explicit Semantic Analysis.* In: Proceedings of the IJCAI.

[8] Gbel, F. & Jagers, A. A. 1974. *Random walks on graphs.* In: Stochastic processes and their applications, vol. 2, no. 4, pp. 311-336.

[9] Han, X. & Zhao, J. 2009.*Named Entity Disambiguation by leveraging Wikipedia semantic knowledge.* In: Proceedings of CIKM.

[10] Han, X. & Zhao, J. 2010. *Structural semantic relatedness: a knowledge-based method to named entity disambiguation.* In: Proceedings of the 49th ACL.

[11] Kulkarni, S., Singh, A., Ramakrishnan, G. & Chakrabarti, S. 2009. *Collective annotation of Wikipedia entities in web text.* In: Proceedings of the 15th ACM SIGKDD.

[12] Li, X., Morie, P. & Roth, D. 2004. *Identification and tracing of ambiguous names: Discriminative and generative approaches.* In: Proceedings of AAAI, pp. 419-424.

[13] McNamee, P. & Dang, H. T. 2009. *Overview of the TAC 2009 Knowledge Base Population Track.* In: Proceeding of Text Analysis Conference.

[14] Milne, D. & Witten, I. H. 2008. *Learning to link with Wikipedia.* In: Proceedings of the 17th ACM CIKM.

[15] Milne, D., et al. 2006. *Mining Domain-Specific Thesauri from Wikipedia: A case study.* In: Proceedings of WI.

[16] Medelyan, O., Witten, I. H. & Milne, D. 2008. *Topic indexing with Wikipedia.* In: Proceedings of the AAAI WikiAI workshop.

[17] Mihalcea, R. & Csomai, A. 2007. *Wikify!: linking documents to encyclopedic knowledge.* In: Proceedings of the sixteenth ACM CIKM.

[18] Pedersen, T., Purandare, A. & Kulkarni, A. 2005. *Name discrimination by clustering similar contexts.* In: Proceedings of CICLing.

[19] Strube, M. and Ponzetto, S. P. 2006. *WikiRelate! Computing Semantic Relatedness Using Wikipedia.* In: Proceedings of AAAI.

[20] Taher H. Haveliwala. 2003. *Topic-Sensitive PageRank: A Context-Sensitive Ranking Algorithm for Web Search.* IEEE Transactions on Knowledge and Data Engineering.

[21] Tong, H., Faloutsos, C. & Pan, J. Y. 2007. *Fast random walk with restart and its applications, Data Mining.* In: Proceedings of ICDM.

[22] Zhang, W., Su, J., Tan, Chew Lim & Wang, W. T. 2010. *Entity Linking Leveraging Automatically Generated Annotation.* In: Proceedings of the 23rd COLING.

[23] Zheng, Z., Li, F., Huang, M. & Zhu, X. 2010. *Learning to Link Entities with Knowledge Base.* In: The Proceedings of NAACL.

[24] Zhou, Y., Nie, L., Rouhani-Kalleh, O., Vasile, F. & Gaffney, S. 2010. *Resolving Surface Forms to Wikipedia Topics.* In: Proceedings of the 23rd COLING.

[25] Hu, J., Fang, L., Cao, Y., et al. 2008. *Enhancing Text Clustering by Leveraging Wikipedia Semantics.* In Proceedings of SIGIR.

From One Tree to a Forest: a Unified Solution for Structured Web Data Extraction

Qiang Hao[†‡] [*] , Rui Cai[†], Yanwei Pang[‡], Lei Zhang[†]
[†]Microsoft Research Asia, Beijing 100080, P.R. China
[‡]Tianjin University, Tianjin 300072, P.R. China
[‡]{qhao, pyw}@tju.edu.cn, [†]{ruicai, leizhang}@microsoft.com

ABSTRACT

Structured data, in the form of entities and associated attributes, has been a rich web resource for search engines and knowledge databases. To efficiently extract structured data from enormous websites in various verticals (e.g., books, restaurants), much research effort has been attracted, but most existing approaches either require considerable human effort or rely on strong features that lack of flexibility. We consider an ambitious scenario – can we build a system that (1) *is general enough to handle any vertical without re-implementation* and (2) *requires only one labeled example site from each vertical for training to automatically deal with other sites in the same vertical*? In this paper, we propose a unified solution to demonstrate the feasibility of this scenario. Specifically, we design a set of weak but general features to characterize vertical knowledge (including attribute-specific semantics and inter-attribute layout relationships). Such features can be adopted in various verticals without redesign; meanwhile, they are weak enough to avoid overfitting of the learnt knowledge to seed sites. Given a new unseen site, the learnt knowledge is first applied to identify page level candidate attribute values, while inevitably involve false positives. To remove noise, site level information of the new site is then exploited to boost up the true values. The site-level information is derived in an unsupervised manner, without harm to the applicability of the solution. Promising experimental performance on 80 websites in 8 distinct verticals demonstrated the feasibility and flexibility of the proposed solution.

Categories and Subject Descriptors

H.3.3 [**Information Storage and Retrieval**]: Information Search and Retrieval - Information filtering; I.5.1 [**Pattern Recognition**]: Models - Statistical

*This work was performed at Microsoft Research, Asia.

General Terms

Algorithms, Experimentation, Performance

Keywords

Structured data, information extraction, vertical knowledge, site-level information

1. INTRODUCTION

With the development of search engines and knowledge databases [2], the target for indexing and retrieval goes beyond keywords to more concrete and comprehensive information, which is usually represented by structured data. Structured data is in the form of entities and associated attributes, *e.g.*, a `book` and its attributes {`title`, `author`, `publisher`}. Various categories of entities, called verticals, have been involved in a variety of applications. For example, for product search, it needs to collect product information for verticals like `Book`, `Auto`, and `Camera`. In addition, in each vertical, there are usually tens of thousands websites containing related structured data. To collect structured data from the Web, an industrial solution is desired to be *flexible* to handle various vertical, *scalable* to deal with numerous websites in each vertical, and *automatic* enough to lower down human effort.

Towards such a practical solution, we consider an ambitious scenario in this paper. That is, to build a system which (1) *is general enough to handle any vertical without re-implementation* and (2) *requires only one labeled example site from each vertical for training to automatically deal with other sites in the same vertical.*

However, it is a non-trivial task to extract structured data from unseen sites based on limited knowledge from only one labeled seed site. Consider the example shown in Fig. 1, where three verticals with associated attributes are listed to the left, as the target of structured data extraction. For each vertical, a seed site is labeled to indicate the occurrences of each attribute in its pages, based on which we aim to identify attribute values from web pages on other sites. The challenges in the task fall into three aspects:

– **Variation of attribute values.** Different sites usually deliver different values of the same attribute, leading to the difficulty in identifying unseen values. Essentially two reasons account for such inter-site variation. Firstly, some attributes (*e.g.*, `book-title`) correspond to numerous and diverse values which appear in different sites unevenly and can hardly be fully covered by a seed site. Secondly, attribute values may be presented using site-specific formats

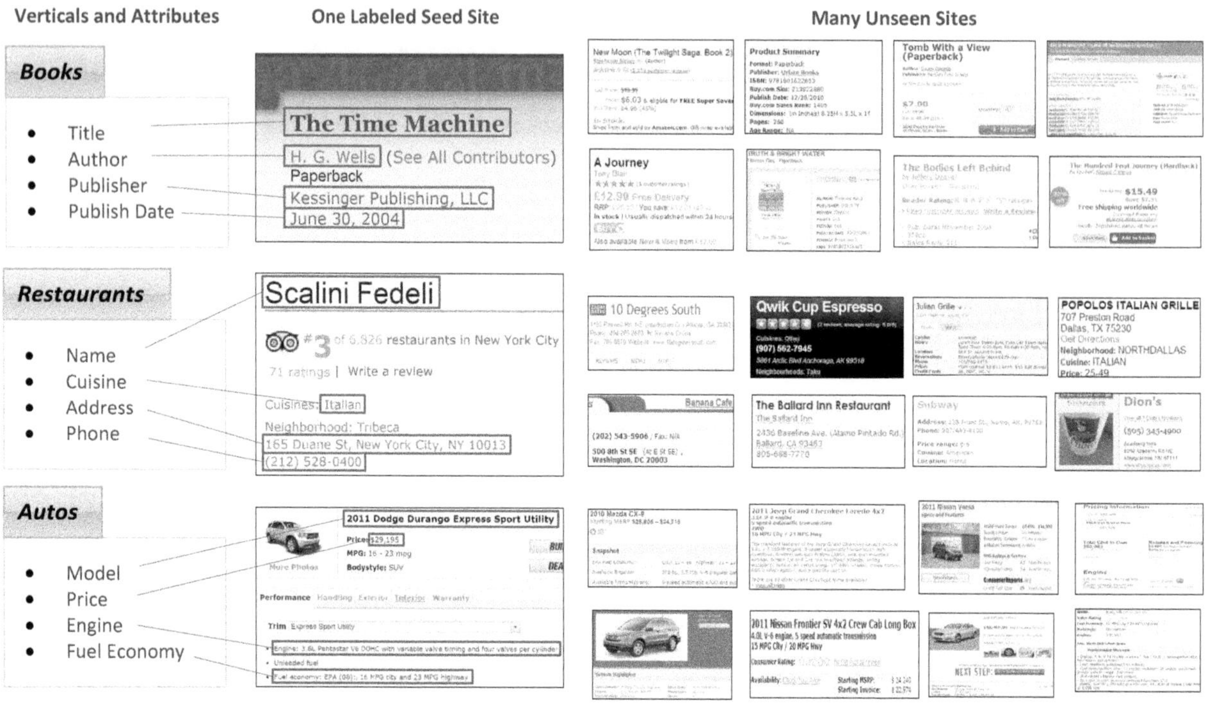

Figure 1: An illustration of the proposed scenario: automatically extracting structured data from websites based on one labeled seed site per vertical.

(*e.g.*, `book-author` can be presented as either abbreviated or full names).

- **Variation of layout.** In each vertical, the attributes are usually presented by different sites in various manners (*e.g.*, not necessarily in consistent positions or in well-formatted structures like tables), due to the various page layout structures across sites.
- **Noisy page content.** Web pages usually contain much noisy content intertwined with the target attribute values to be extracted. For instance, a book page may contain multiple date-type content besides the value of attribute `publish-date` we target on.

Related to the scenario we are concerned with, much research effort has been dedicated to extracting structured data from web pages. One popular category of methods relies on the DOM-tree representation of web pages [1], as well as the fact that many web pages are generated based on templates, which wrap data records in HTML tags. One early stream of such template-based work is wrapper induction [9, 11, 12, 18], which relies on manual annotation on example pages of a template and learns wrappers used for data extraction from other pages of that template. These methods can hardly scale up to large number of sites due to the considerable human effort required for both labeling unseen sites and maintaining wrappers of observed sites with periodically updated templates. To alleviate human labor, some unsupervised methods are proposed to extract structured data automatically, by deducing a template from a set of pages [4, 7] or by identifying repetitive patterns from a single page [6, 10, 17]. One major drawback of such methods lies in the disregard of semantics and consequent requirement for human effort to identify attribute values from all the extracted content.

Another category of methods further consider semantics during automatic data extraction by exploiting the content and page layout features (*e.g.*, positions, font sizes), other than HTML tags, of web pages in a unified manner. For instance, extensions of CRFs (conditional random fields) are proposed to predict semantics of web page elements based on individual elements and their interrelationships in two-dimensional [19] or hierarchical [20] layout structures. However, such CRF-based methods are not general enough to handle various verticals, but rather rely on carefully designed features specific to a target vertical. The semantic features adopted in [5] are more general to handle various verticals, but it still needs to train the model based on a number of example pages from various websites to avoid overfitting, leading to labor-intensive burden of preparing training data. Detailed comparisons of our method and [5] will be introduced in the experiments.

In this work, we aim to figure out a unified solution for structured web data extraction, with flexibility to various verticals and minimal human effort for labeling examples. To achieve this goal, we combine the information considered by above two categories of existing approaches, that is, to (a) exploit content and layout structures of pages and simultaneously (b) take advantage of interrelationships between template-generated pages. On one hand, we propose to derive relatively weak but general features from page content and layout structures. Such features keep capability of characterizing vertical knowledge learnt from a seed site to identify attribute values from new sites. In contrast to vertical-specific strong features, these features can be applied in various verticals without redesign; meanwhile, they are weak enough to avoid overfitting of the learnt knowledge to seed sites. On the other hand, to compensate the possible performance loss compared with solutions relying on strong features, we boost the preliminary page-level results by exploiting site-level information, based on the assumption that there are strong interrelationships between pages from the same website.

In general, site-level information leads to two main benefits as follows.

- **Providing useful features.** Based on site-level statistics, we can derive features useful to identify true attribute values and filter out noise. For instance, duplicate elements among pages can be identified by analyzing inter-page redundancy, and serve as contexts of their adjacent elements to provide semantic hints.
- **Boosting page-level attribute identification.** Site-level information can serve as inter-page constraints to boost page-level identification of attribute values. Because an incorrect decision on a page element could get revised by referring to the decisions made on many corresponding elements on other pages (*e.g.*, via a majority voting). In this way, occasionally identified false positives on some pages can get removed, while the true positives which receive sufficient supports from many pages are boosted up.

Moreover, such site-level information is derived in an unsupervised manner from each website, without involving burden of additional human labor.

Based on the above ideas, a unified solution is proposed in this paper for automatically extracting structured data for an arbitrary vertical and associated attributes. Specifically, we design a set of general features to characterize vertical knowledge, including attribute-specific semantics and inter-attribute layout relationships, derived from a seed site with labeled attribute values. For a given new site in the same vertical, the learnt vertical knowledge is first applied to identify candidate attribute values at the page level. As the knowledge is relatively weak, such page level results inevitably contain false positives. To further remove noise, site-level information of the new site is then exploited to boost up the true values in an unsupervised way. We evaluated the proposed solution on 80 websites in 8 distinct verticals and obtained promising results, verifying the feasibility and flexibility of the proposed solution.

The rest of this paper is organized as follows. We first refer to related work in Section 2, and outline the proposed solution in Section 3. The algorithm details are introduced from Section 4 to Section 6. Experimental results are reported in Section 7. In Section 8, we conclude the paper and discuss some future directions.

2. RELATED WORK

Extracting structured data from web pages has been studied extensively. An early stream of research focuses on wrapper induction [9, 11, 12], which relies on manually annotated examples to learn data extraction rules. A more recent work [18] further combines template detection with wrapper generation to improve extraction accuracy. Such approaches are semi-automatic and difficult to be scaled up, due to the human labor required for labeling pages of new sites. Another category of automatic approaches deduce templates from web pages sharing identical format. For instance, Roadrunner [7] generates a template by comparing the current template with more pages, while EXALG [4] deduces templates by analyzing co-occurrence of tokens across pages. One common limitation of these approaches is that they do not concern the semantics of extracted data; whereas we aim to extract structured data corresponding to specified semantics (i.e., vertical attributes).

To better leverage sematic information, a series of research efforts have been dedicated to content analysis of web pages. In [8], keyword distributions are learnt from an existing knowledge base and used to annotate web pages. Besides prior knowledge, machine learning techniques are also utilized. For instance, Zhu et al. [19, 20] propose CRF-based probability models to exploit the contents and page layout features of web pages for data record detection and semantic labeling. These methods rely on either existing vertical specific knowledge or abundant training data, and thus are not suitable for our scenario where flexibility for various verticals and minimal human effort are desired.

In recently years, some approaches are proposed to extract information within specific verticals. In [16], structured data in web forums is extracted by exploiting site-level knowledge, including interrelationships between homogeneous pages and linkages between heterogeneous pages. In [15], the authors present an unsupervised approach to extract information from online job advertisement documents in different domains. In contrast to these works, our work targets on a general solution for various verticals.

We also noticed that there is a very recent work [14] which addresses a similar scenario of learning wrappers from one website and adapting them to other sites. In [14], the authors focus on generative probabilistic model-based machine learning. By contrast, we are concerned more with the exploitation of site-level information and DOM structures than sophisticated learning models. Although our lightweight solution only adopts off-the-shelf learning techniques, the performance is still competitive with that reported in [14][1].

3. FRAMEWORK OVERVIEW

In our scenario, a specific task takes as input a vertical (*e.g.*, `book`) associated with a set of attributes and a labeled seed site, and aims to extract attribute values from an unseen site in the same vertical. By representing each web page as a DOM tree, the task is essentially to identify the *text nodes*, *i.e.*, leaf nodes with text-type values in DOM trees, that contain values of each target attribute.

The basic flowchart of the proposed solution is shown in Fig. 2. Given a labeled website as seed, we first extract features from its pages and learn vertical knowledge. Then, given a site previously unseen, we randomly sample a set of pages for the sake of efficiency in subsequent processing. After extracting features from these sample pages, the learnt knowledge is applied to the new site to identify attribute values. Such extraction results further serve as substitutes of manually labeled examples required in wrapper induction [18], to generate wrappers for structured data extraction from the entire page collection of the new site. Optionally, together with the extracted attribute values, the new site could serve as another "labeled" seed to provide additional vertical knowledge, in a bootstrapping manner.

[1]The extensive comparisons to the above state-of-the-art methods (*e.g.*, [14]) are in our future plan. It still needs considerable efforts to implement these algorithms.

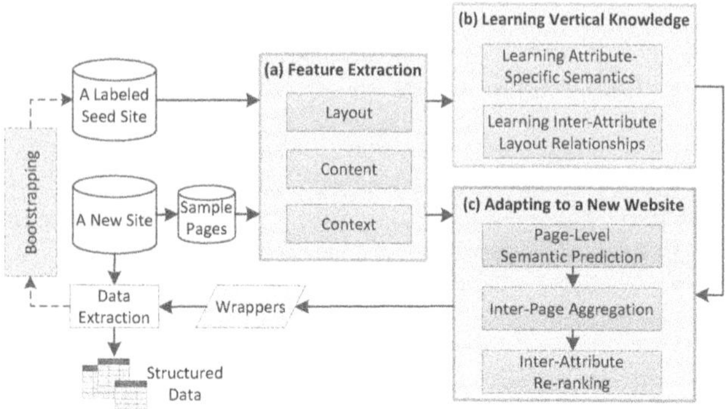

Figure 2: The flowchart of the proposed solution, which consists of three components: (a) feature extraction, (b) learning vertical knowledge, and (c) adapting to a new website.

As shown in Fig. 2, the algorithms of the solution are mainly distributed in three components, namely *feature extraction*, *learning vertical knowledge*, and *adapting to a new website*. These components are summarized as follows.

- **Feature extraction** takes multiple pages from a site as input and output a set of text nodes associated with ***content***, ***context***, and ***layout*** features. Details of this component are introduced in Section 4.
- **Learning vertical knowledge** learns two kinds of vertical knowledge from a seed site based on its attribute labels and extracted features. Knowledge of ***attribute-specific semantics*** is derived from *content* and *context* features for each attribute, while knowledge of ***inter-attribute layout*** is derived from *layout* features. Details of this part are presented in Section 5.
- **Adapting to a new website** exploits the learnt vertical knowledge to identify attribute values from a new site in three steps. In ***page-level semantic prediction***, the learnt *semantic* knowledge is applied to predict the semantics of text nodes in each page. In ***inter-page aggregation***, the page-level results are aggregated at the site level to get revised. In ***inter-attribute re-ranking***, the learnt *layout* knowledge is utilized to figure out the optimal results from both the semantic and layout perspectives. This component is described in Section 6.

4. FEATURE EXTRACTION

As described in Section 3, in this paper, we focus on identifying attribute values contained in text nodes. Other types of leaf nodes in DOM trees (*e.g.*, the image node representing rating score in Fig. 3 (a)) are out of our scope. For a set of pages from a given site, we parse them into DOM trees to obtain text nodes, from which three categories of features are extracted, including *layout features*, *content features* and *context features*. These features are described in the following three subsections, respectively.

4.1 Layout Features

Layout features describe the properties of a text node as a visual element on screen, when it is rendered via a web browser (*e.g.*, Internet Explorer). Layout information can help characterize both the intra-page and inter-page relationships between text nodes.

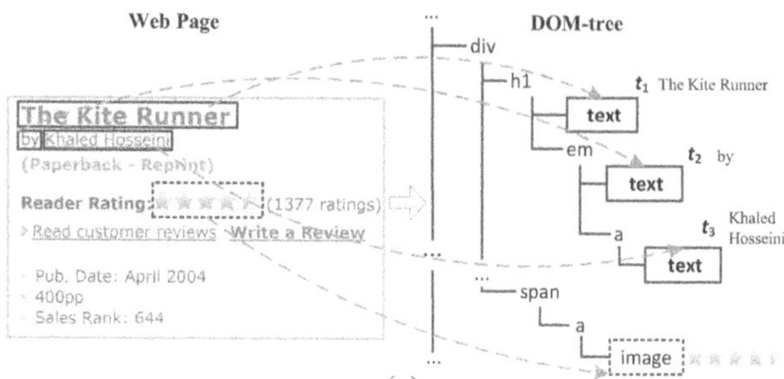

(a)

Node	Dom Path	Visual Size	Visual Position
t_1	/html/body/div/div/div/div/h1/text	(256, 32)	(0, 766)
t_2	/html/body/div/div/div/div/h1/em/text	(24, 16)	(0, 798)
t_3	/html/body/div/div/div/div/h1/em/a/text	(120, 16)	(24, 798)

(b)

Figure 3: Illustrations of (a) text nodes in a DOM tree and (b) layout features associated with a text node: DOM path, visual size and visual position.

In this paper, we leverage three types of layout features listed as follows.

- **DOM path** of a text node t, denoted by $dom(t)$, is its corresponding root-to-leaf tag path, which roughly characterizes its location in the DOM tree.
- **Visual size** of a text node t is a pair $\langle width(t), height(t) \rangle$ namely the width and height (in pixels) of its corresponding bounding box[2] on screen in web page rendering.
- **Visual position** of a text node t is the 2-D coordinates of the top-left vertex of its bounding box, denoted as another pair in pixels $\langle left(t), top(t) \rangle$.

For illustration, Fig. 3 (b) lists some example layout features of the text nodes in Fig. 3 (a).

4.2 Content Features

Content features correspond to the textual values contained in text nodes, and are very useful for characterizing the semantics of text nodes. In this paper, the value contained in a text node t is denoted by v_t, based on which five types of content features are extracted.

Unigram set. There are a number of attributes corresponding to values that come from a limited lexicon (*e.g.*, `NBA team`) or contain some representative terms with high frequencies (*e.g.*, the term "press" is very common in values of `book publisher`). Intuitively, pre-defined attribute-specific lexicons can help identify such kind of attributes, but it is labor-intensive to build lexicons manually for numerous attributes within various verticals. Instead, we leverage unigram as a general feature to characterize such information. Specifically, the *unigram set* of a text node t is defined as the set of tokens in v_t,

$$unigram(t) = \{w | w \in v_t\},$$

where v_t is split on whitespace into tokens $\{w\}$.

Token count. The values of many attributes consist of a relatively fixed number of tokens. For instance, `person`

[2]The bounding box of a DOM node can be retrieved using programming interfaces provided by web browsers, such as the APIs for Internet Explorer [3].

name usually contains 2 ∼ 4 terms. To enable learning of such knowledge from a labeled website, we define the *token count* of a text node t as a numerical feature,

$$token\_count(t) = |unigram(t)|.$$

Character count. It is observed that sometimes token-level granularity is still too coarse to distinguish between values of different attributes. For instance, both ISBN-13 and ISBN-10 of book contain only one token, while ISBN-13 has 13 digits and ISBN-10 has only 10. Hence, complementary to token count, a feature in a finer granularity is required to characterize the length of textual values. Here, we adopt the *character count* of a text node t,

$$char\_count(t) = \sum_{w \in unigram(t)} number\_of\_characters(w).$$

Character type. A variety of attributes correspond to values composed of specific types of characters. For example, values of price often contain digits and symbols (*e.g.*, \$, £). The occurrences of different character type are descriptive to such attributes, and are utilized by some existing work in a separate way (*e.g.*, directly using the occurrences of some specific characters as features). To be flexible to various attributes, we focus on three general character types (*i.e.*, *letter*, *digit*, and *symbol*) and define the *character type* of a text node t as a vector that encodes the proportion of each character type among all non-whitespace characters in v_t,

$$char\_type(t) = (c_t^{letter}, c_t^{digit}, c_t^{symbol}),$$

where c_t^* is the proportion of corresponding character type.

Page redundancy. We also observe that some attributes have distinct value redundancies. For instance, in the vertical restaurant, the attribute cuisine has very redundant values while name has almost unique values. Therefore, value redundancies of text nodes among pages are potentially helpful for predicting their semantics. Specifically, we define the *page redundancy* of a text node t as

$$page\_redundancy(t) = |\mathcal{P}_{v_t}| \,/\, |\mathcal{P}_{all}|,$$

where $\mathcal{P}_{v_t}$ is the set of pages that contain at least one text node with the value v_t, and $\mathcal{P}_{all}$ is the entire set of input pages. Note that the numerator is defined analogous to the document-frequency (DF) of a term in information retrieval, since what we concern is the inter-page redundancy rather than intra-page duplicates.

4.3 Context Features

In contrast to layout features and most content features, context features exploit site-level information to capture the surrounding text indicating semantics of text nodes. Actually, we have observed on many websites that the presented attribute values are preceded by some text that indicates their semantics (*e.g.*, "*Publisher:*" preceding to a book publisher value). This kind of text serves as site-level context to co-occur with corresponding attribute values extensively across pages, and thus can help identify values of such attributes if properly exploited.

Some existing approaches identify attribute values by seeking matches between handcrafted context lists and surrounding text of text nodes. However, these attribute-specific context lists require much human effort to create. Therefore, it is highly desired to design features that automatically capture such context as semantic clues. Besides, we also notice that the values of some attributes tend to contain common prefixes and/or suffixes, which potentially indicate and characterize the semantics of attribute values. Although such prefixes/suffixes are actually parts of text node values, we take them as a type of context because they serve as site-level semantic clues. Based on the above considerations, we propose two types of context features as described below.

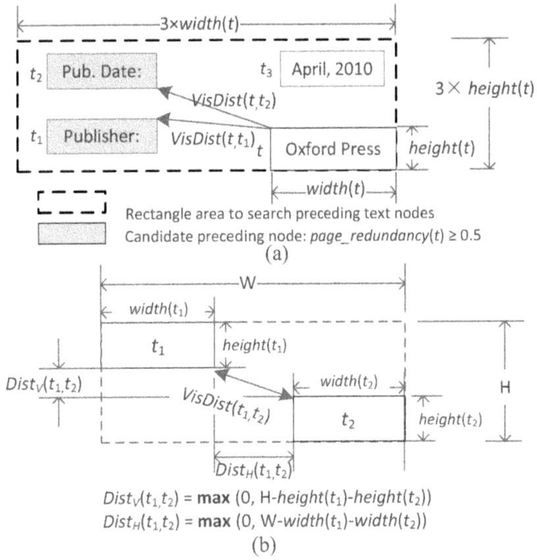

Figure 4: Illustrations of (a) identifying the preceding text of a text node t and (b) calculating the visual distance $VisDist(t_1, t_2)$ between two text nodes t_1 and t_2 when they are rendered on screen.

Preceding text of a text node t, denoted by *preceding*(t), is defined as the value of its preceding text node t^* that is constrained to be:

- located to the top-left of t and within a rectangle proportional to the visual size of t, as shown in Fig. 4 (a).
- associated with high *page_redundancy* (exceeding an empirical threshold such as 0.5). Here the preceding node is required to be sufficiently redundant among pages, because the context is expected to be static at the site level.
- more close to t than any other candidates that meet the previous two criteria (higher *page_redundancy* is preferred for the case of equal distance). As illustrated in Fig. 4 (b), the visual distance between two nodes is defined as

$$VisDist(t_1, t_2) = \sqrt{Dist_H(t_1, t_2)^2 + Dist_V(t_1, t_2)^2}.$$

For the example case in Fig. 4 (a), t_1 is determined to be the preceding node of t, yielding the preceding text "*Publisher:*" for the value "Oxford Press". When no preceding text node identified, *preceding*(t) is defined as null.

Prefix and Suffix of a text node t, denoted by $prefix(t)$ and $suffix(t)$, are defined as the beginning and ending substring (within its value v_t) commonly shared by lots of text nodes across pages. Given a set of text nodes coming from multiple pages, we extract their prefix and suffix features in three steps as follows.

1. Group values of text nodes in terms of rough formats, which are obtained by summarizing successive letters

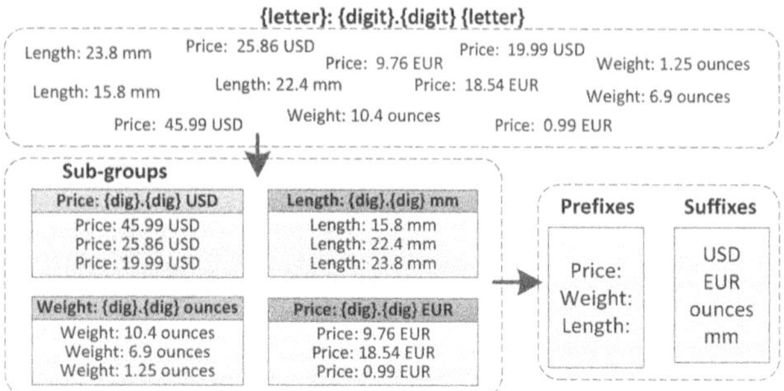

Figure 5: An illustration of identifying prefixes and suffixes. Text strings are grouped according to their formats, based on which popular sub-strings are discovered as prefixes or suffixes.

and digits with wildcards {letter} and {digit} (*e.g.*, the format of "2.36 cm" is "{digit}.{digit} {letter}").

2. For each group, further cluster text nodes according to their specific sub-strings.
3. Prefixes and suffixes are identified based on those sub-groups which contain text nodes from a sufficient proportion (*e.g.*, 50%) of pages.

As an example shown in Fig. 5, a set of values in the format "{letter}: {digit}.{digit} {letter}" are categorized into four sub-groups to extract prefixes and suffixes.

5. LEARNING VERTICAL KNOWLEDGE

In this section, we describe the detailed methods used to learn vertical knowledge from a seed site. Given a specified vertical and associated set of m attributes, denoted as $\mathcal{A} = \{a_1, \ldots, a_m\}$, we aim to learn two kinds of, namely *attribute-specific* and *inter-attribute*, vertical knowledge. For attribute-specific knowledge, we mainly focus on characterizing the semantics of each single attribute $a_j \in \mathcal{A}$ based on *content* and *context* features extracted from text nodes labeled with a_j. For inter-attribute knowledge, we target on characterizing the layout relationships between attribute based on the *layout* features of corresponding text nodes. The learning of such two kinds of knowledge is detailed in the following two subsections, respectively.

5.1 Learning Attribute-Specific Semantics

Given a set of text nodes from a labeled seed site, we learn the semantic knowledge of each attribute $a_j \in \mathcal{A}$ from a subset $\mathcal{T}_j$ of text nodes that are labeled as containing values of a_j. A straightforward idea is to combine all the features directly using a unified model. However, the *content* and *context* features have quite different behaviors – content features provide statistic evidences that can be adopted to evaluate any input text; while context features show indicative hints which are sufficient but not necessary. More specifically, matching of context features gives a strong confidence to acknowledging an attribute, but mismatching does not mean denying since context of an attribute may vary across websites. Therefore, we propose to exploit content and context features separately, to benefit from both of them.

For each attribute a_j, a classifier is trained to incorporate all the five types of content features described in Section 4.2. As different content features are heterogeneous and with different scales, each feature is first normalized into $[0, 1]$. For the *unigram set*, frequencies of tokens are first counted from $\{unigram(t) \mid t \in \mathcal{T}_j\}$, and then each unigram set is normalized based on the average frequency of its element token(s). For the *character type* with vector values, each feature value is converted to the cosine similarity to the mean of feature values in $\{char\_type(t) \mid t \in \mathcal{T}_j\}$. And for the other three content features with scalar values, the normalization is simply based on their maximums and minimums. After the normalization, an SVM classifier is built to learn a mapping from the content features of a text node t to an estimated probability, $ContentRel(t \mid a_j)$, that t is relevant to a_j.

For each attribute a_j, three lookup tables are respectively constructed for the *preceding text*, *prefix*, and *suffix* features described in Section 4.3. Each lookup table consists of feature values aggregated from text nodes in $\mathcal{T}_j$. For an unseen text node t, its context-based relevance to a_j, $ContextRel(t \mid a_j)$, is defined as the percentage of t's context features matching the corresponding lookup table of a_j. Here, exact match is adopted for the sake of efficiency, while more sophisticated measurements (*e.g.*, edit distance) are also feasible choices.

To combine the clues of both content and context features, the overall relevance of a text node t to an attribute a_j is estimated by

$$Rel_{TN}(t \mid a_j) = \max(ContentRel(t \mid a_j), ContextRel(t \mid a_j)).$$

The **max** operation is adopted here to properly leverage context features. As mentioned above, context features are sufficient but not necessary. Hence, we trust context features if the corresponding score is high enough; otherwise, the relevance estimation should rely only on content features.

5.2 Learning Inter-Attribute Layout

The power of page layout structures in identifying attribute values has been demonstrated by existing approaches such as [19]. In contrast to existing solutions that couple layout and semantic information together, we treat inter-attribute layout and attribute-specific semantics separately. This is because the attribute layout tends to vary across sites and should be exploited in a light-weighted manner.

In this paper, the inter-attribute layout is characterized just using pairwise visual distances. That is, given a set of m attributes and a seed site with attribute labels, an $m \times m$ layout matrix $\mathbf{A}$ is constructed, in which each element $\mathbf{A}_{ij}$ encodes the average visual distance between the attributes a_i and a_j, as

$$\mathbf{A}_{ij} = \frac{1}{w_{screen}} \cdot \frac{\sum VisDist(t_{a_i}, t_{a_j})}{|\mathcal{P}_{a_i \cap a_j}|},$$

where t_{a_i} and t_{a_j} are two text nodes labeled with a_i and a_j respectively on a page; $\mathcal{P}_{a_i \cap a_j}$ is the set of all pages containing values of both a_i and a_j; and $VisDist(\cdot, \cdot)$ is the same one defined in Section 4.3. To handle the inter-site variations of page size, the average distance is further normalized by the whole rendering width of a page, w_{screen}, which is almost consistent for every page in the same website.

An illustrative example is given in Fig. 6, where the inter-attribute layout matrices of five websites in the `book` vertical are visualized. From Fig. 6, it is clear that there are much consistence between layout matrices of these five websites (*e.g.*, `title` and `author` are closed to each other), despite some minor variations.

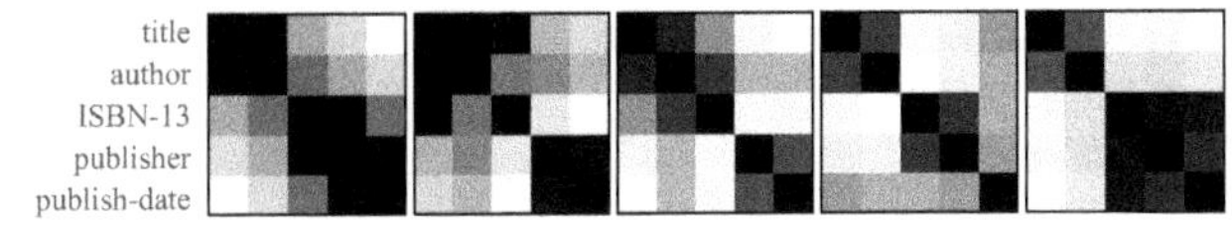

Figure 6: An illustration of the layout matrix A for five websites from the book vertical. The darker the matrix element, the closer the corresponding attributes in rendering.

6. ADAPTING TO A NEW WEBSITE

In this section, we introduce the details of adapting the learnt knowledge to extract structured data from an unseen website. As aforementioned, the learnt knowledge is weak and is just capable of indicating all possible candidate answers, a major part of which consists of noisy false positives. We will show in this section how the site-level statistics can help filter the candidates and boost the true answer. For the sake of efficiency, the adaptation is based on a set of pages $\mathcal{P}_{sample}$ randomly sampled from the new website.

6.1 Page-Level Semantic Prediction

Given a page $p \in \mathcal{P}_{sample}$, we extract its text nodes as well as the content and context features for each node. Following Section 5.1, each text node t is associated with an m-dimensional vector

$$(Rel_{TN}(t \,|\, a_1), \ldots, Rel_{TN}(t \,|\, a_m)),$$

which indicates its relevance scores to all the attributes. To determine the value of an attribute a_j on the page p, the simplest way is to assign it with the text node t_{a_j}

$$t_{a_j} = \arg\max_t Rel_{TN}(t \,|\, a_j).$$

6.2 Inter-Page Aggregation

The page-level results of semantic prediction are inevitably not accurate enough, due to the inter-site variations and weak features used to characterize vertical knowledge. Therefore, we resort to site-level information to boost these preliminary results, by exploiting inter-page dependencies on the new site. In other words, the semantics of some text nodes are highly consistent to some other text nodes in other pages, and thus we can get more accurate predictions by considering them simultaneously.

To leverage such inter-page dependencies, aligning text nodes in different pages is a crucial issue. A popular method is partial tree alignment [17], which performs partial matching between DOM trees. However, partial tree alignment is not appropriate for our task due to some reasons. First, the pairwise alignment of DOM trees is quite time-consuming, even for hundreds of sample pages. Furthermore, the alignment only considers information of HTML tags, and thus cannot differentiate between text nodes with distinct semantics but identical DOM paths[3]. Fig. 7 shows some statistics on 30 websites in three verticals. It is clear that DOM paths severely lack the ability to distinguish between text nodes.

Therefore, semantic information is required to distinguish between text nodes in different roles. Here, we propose to leverage the context features presented in Section 4.3. That is, two text nodes can be aligned if they have both the same DOM path and context features. From Fig. 7, it can be seen that context features could help lower down the risk of misalignment significantly. A set of aligned text nodes is called a *data field*, denoted as D. The detailed algorithm of aggregating text nodes into data fields is given in Algorithm 1.

[3]This is common in a table-like structure, where table cells share almost the same HTML tags but very likely have different content.

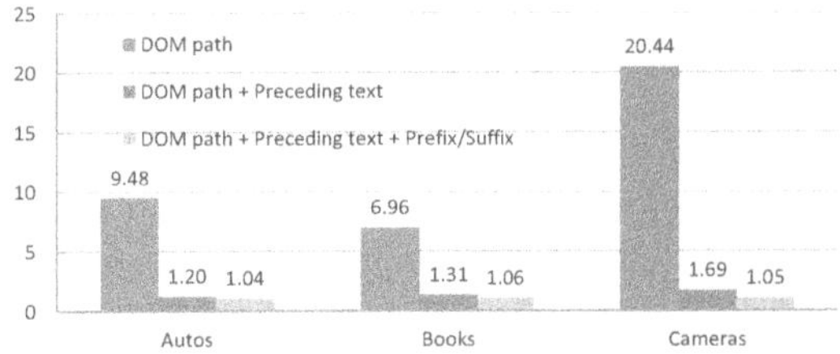

Figure 7: The average numbers (per page) of text nodes that have identical DOM path, DOM path+preceding text, and DOM path+preceding text+prefix/suffix, on websites in three example verticals.

To be statistically robust, the page-level relevance scores of text nodes can be aggregated to data fields. Specially, the attribute relevance vector of a data field D is computed by averaging over its member text nodes, as

$$(Rel_{DF}(D \,|\, a_1), \ldots, Rel_{DF}(D \,|\, a_m)),$$

where $Rel_{DF}(D \mid a_j) = \frac{1}{|D|} \sum_{t \in D} Rel_{TN}(t \mid a_j)$. Based on such relevance scores, each attribute a_j can be directly associated with the data field D_{a_j}

$$D_{a_j} = \arg\max_{D \in \mathbb{D}} Rel_{DF}(D \,|\, a_j).$$

The assembly

$$\mathbb{S}_{\mathcal{A}} = \{D_{a_1}, \ldots, D_{a_m}\}$$

is called a *solution* to the target attributes $\mathcal{A}$ on the new website. In practical, a threshold is set to remove data fields with low relevance scores in $\mathcal{S}_{\mathcal{A}}$, since some attributes may be unavailable in the new site.

6.3 Inter-Attribute Re-ranking

Aggregation to site-level data fields is noise-insensitive and more robust than page-level results. However, there are still difficult cases such as identifying `publish-date` from all date-type data fields in a book-seller site. As mentioned in Section 5.2, attribute layout is a good complement to semantics in such cases. For instance, the date-type data field being most close to `book-publisher` is likely to be the real `publish-date`. Therefore, it is natural to exploit characteristics of attribute layout to re-rank those possible solutions.

To generate more than one possible solutions, we need keep several candidate data fields for each attribute a_j. Specifically, data fields are first sorted in descending order according to $Rel_{DF}(D \mid a_j)$. Then the sorted list is truncated at the maximum drop point of the relevance score, yielding top-ranked data fields as candidates for a_j. Then, we enumerate every possible combination of attributes' data fields as a candidate solution to attributes $\mathcal{A}$.

From the perspective of semantics, the confidence of a candidate solution $\mathbb{S}^*_{\mathcal{A}}$ is defined as

$$Conf_{semantics}(\mathbb{S}^*_{\mathcal{A}}) = \sum_{j=1}^{m} Rel_{DF}(D_{a_j} \,|\, a_j), D_{a_j} \in \mathbb{S}^*_{\mathcal{A}}.$$

Algorithm 1 Aggregate-TextNodes-to-DataFields. Given a set of pages $\mathcal{P}_{sample}$, returns $\mathbb{D}$ consisting of all possible data fields in $\mathcal{P}_{sample}$.

$\mathbb{D} = \emptyset$
Initialize an empty hash-table $\mathcal{H}$
for all page $p \in \mathcal{P}_{sample}$ **do**
  for all text node t in p **do**
    $h = \text{GenHashValue}(dom(t), preceding(t), prefix(t), suffix(t))$
    if $\mathcal{H}$ contains the key h **then**
      Get the data field D associated with h from $\mathcal{H}$
      Add t to D
    else
      Create a new data field $D = \{t\}$
      Add to $\mathcal{H}$ the new key h associated with D
    end if
  end for
end for
for all $\langle h, D \rangle$ pair in $\mathcal{H}$ **do**
  if $|D| \geq 0.5|\mathcal{P}_{sample}|$ **then**
    Add D to $\mathbb{D}$
  end if
end for
return $\mathbb{D}$

To measure the confidence from the perspective of inter-attribute layout, we first compute the layout matrix $\mathbf{A}^*$ for $\mathbb{S}^*_{\mathcal{A}}$, following the algorithm in Section 5.2. Then, analogous to cosine similarity, the layout confidence of $\mathbb{S}^*_{\mathcal{A}}$ is defined as

$$Conf_{layout}(\mathbb{S}^*_{\mathcal{A}}) = \frac{\langle \mathbf{A}^*, \mathbf{A} \rangle}{\|\mathbf{A}^*\|_F, \|\mathbf{A}\|_F},$$

where the numerator denotes element-wise inner product, and $\|\cdot\|_F$ is Frobenius norm. Finally, the optimal solution $\mathbb{S}_{\mathcal{A}}$ is the one with highest overall confidence, as

$$\mathbb{S}_{\mathcal{A}} = \arg\max_{\mathbb{S}^*_{\mathcal{A}}}(Conf_{semantics}(\mathbb{S}^*_{\mathcal{A}}) \times Conf_{layout}(\mathbb{S}^*_{\mathcal{A}})),$$

where multiplication is adopted instead of addition because the layout confidence is essentially designed for punishment.

7. EVALUATION AND DISCUSSION

In this section, we report the evaluation results of the proposed solution on real-world structured data extraction tasks. Extensive experiments were performed on a variety of websites and verticals to verify the performance of both the component algorithms and the overall system.

7.1 Experimental Settings

7.1.1 Dataset

To evaluate both the effectiveness and flexibility of our solution, we constructed a dataset consisting of around 124K pages collected from 80 websites. These websites are related to 8 semantically diverse verticals, including `Autos`, `Books`, `Cameras`, `Jobs`, `Movies`, `NBA Players`, `Restaurants`, and `Universities`. For each vertical, 10 popular websites were identified by issuing queries to search engines and mining the search results. For each website, $200 \sim 2,000$ pages, each containing structured data of one entity, were downloaded following the deep crawl technology in [13], given a few manually selected pages as examples of crawling targets.

For each vertical, a set of $(3 \sim 5)$ common attributes were selected as the targets of structured data extraction. To label the ground-truth of each website, a few handcrafted regular expressions were carefully prepared, to tag corresponding attribute values on each page. An overview of the dataset is given in Table 1[4].

Table 1: Overview of the experimental dataset.

Vertical	#Sites	#Pages	Attributes
`Autos`	10	17,923	`model, price, engine, fuel-economy`
`Books`	10	20,000	`title, author, ISBN-13, publisher, publish-date`
`Cameras`	10	5,258	`model, price, manufacturer`
`Jobs`	10	20,000	`title, company, location, date`
`Movies`	10	20,000	`title, director, genre, rating`
`NBA Players`	10	4,405	`name, team, height, weight`
`Restaurants`	10	20,000	`name, address, phone, cuisine`
`Universities`	10	16,705	`name, phone, website, type`

7.1.2 Performance Metrics

For vertical knowledge learning, all the pages in a seed site were involved; when adapting to another website, 50% pages from the new site were randomly selected for the adaptation. For testing performance, the evaluations were based on all the pages except for those from the seed site.

Precision and recall, as well as the F-score, were adopted as performance metrics in the evaluation. For each attribute, *precision* of a method is the number of pages whose ground-truth attribute values are correctly extracted, called page hits, divided by the number of pages from which the method extracts values; while *recall* is the page hits divided by the number of pages containing ground-truth attribute values. F-score is the harmonic mean of precision and recall. As a side note, it is possible that a page contains more than one ground-truth values of an attribute (*e.g.*, co-authors of a book); while the current solution in this paper is designed to detect only one attribute value. For this case, an extracted value is considered to be correct if it matches any labeled value in the ground-truth.

7.2 From One Seed Site to a Vertical

First, the proposed solution was evaluated under the ambitious scenario "from one tree to a forest". That is to say, for each vertical, only one website was leveraged as seed for knowledge learning. To demonstrate the contributions of various component algorithms in the solution, we implemented three versions of the proposed system, as:

- **PL (page-level semantic prediction)** is the version which just outputs the page-level attribute values predicted following Section 6.1. In other words, only the weak vertical knowledge learnt from the seed site is utilized.
- **PL+IP (inter-page aggregation)** is the version which aggregates page-level results into data fields, to correct page-level results through site-level voting. This is actually the output of Section 6.2.
- **PL+IP+IA (inter-attribute re-ranking)** is the full version of the proposed solution which further re-ranks the possible solutions according to the layout distributions of attributes, following the details in Section 6.3.

In addition, we also implemented a state-of-the-art work, the **Stacked Skews Model** (SSM) [5], whose target scenario is similar to ours. Moreover, the **SSM** approach also leverages site-level information, through aggregating features

[4]The dataset with ground-truth information is publicly available at http://swde.codeplex.com/.

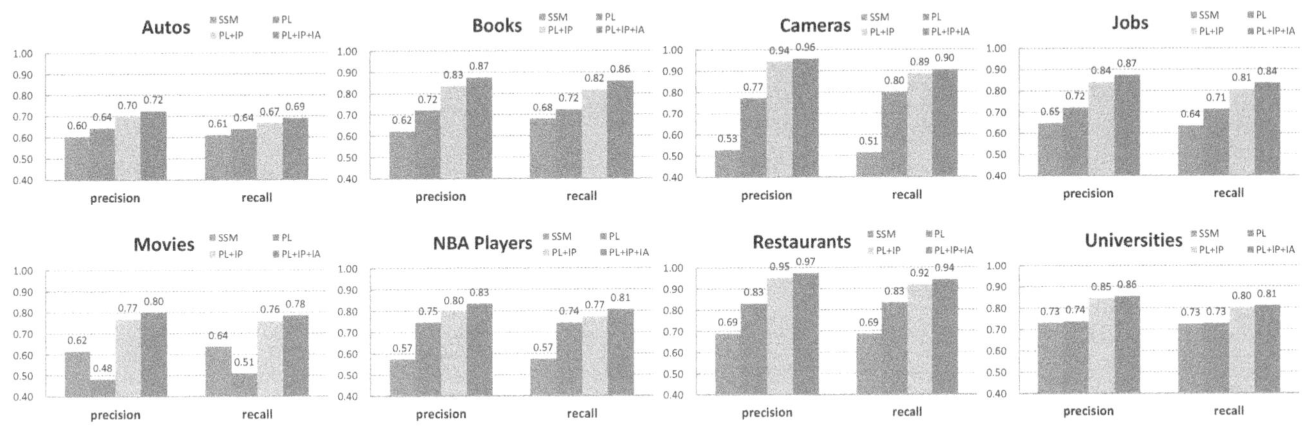

Figure 8: Comparisons of vertical-level performance of the stacked skews model (SSM) [5], PL (page-level semantic prediction), PL + IP (inter-page aggregation), and PL+IP+IA (inter-attribute re-ranking). The performance of each vertical is averaged over all its attributes and websites. The vertical knowledge was learnt based on only one seed site per vertical.

across a website. By contrast, our approach aggregates page-level extraction results rather than raw features.

For each vertical, all its 10 sites served as the seed site in turns to perform structured data extraction from the other 9 sites, yielding 90 runs of extraction in total. The vertical-level performance of each method was measured as the precision and recall averaged across all runs. Fig. 8 shows the overall results by vertical for each method, averaged across all the attributes in each vertical.

From Fig. 8, there are several observations. First, site-level information consistently and significantly boost the page-level results, for all the 8 verticals. Especially for the verticals `Cameras` and `Restaurants`, our solution can almost correctly identify values for all the attributes. The performance even exceeds our expectation as only one seed site was adopted for knowledge learning. Second, our performance is superior to that of the **SSM** approach, even the simplest **PL** version achieved better performance than **SSM** on 7 verticals. This is because **SSM** is designed for rich training data from multiple websites and is prone to overfit when training set is small (In Section 7.3 we will show the performance of **SSM** based on larger training set). Another reason is that the site-level feature aggregation is easy to be disturbed by misalignment, since precise tree-alignment is still an unsolved problem, as discussed in Section 6.2.

To show detailed evaluation results, we list the attribute-level performance of our system (**PL+IP+IA**) in Table 2. Although most results are very encouraging, there are still some attributes with unsatisfied performance. We analyzed some failure cases to diagnose the limitations of the current solution. For `height` of `NBA Players`, the main reason is its content format varies a lot (*e.g.*, 1.96m, 6 ft 5 in, 6'5", 6-5) across websites. The system has to rely on context features which are not always available. The `model` of `Autos` failed as there is no standard definition for this attribute. Different websites deliver different information for the `model` attribute. For instance, there are manufacturer, year, and even engine displacement listed under this attribute. The failure of `title` of `Movies` is due to multiple instances on a page. A page of a movie also contains other movies as "recommendation". Such recommendations tend to mislead the system away from the main entity of a page.

Table 2: Attribute-level performance of the proposed solution based on single seed site (averaged over different seed sites, in the form of "mean ± standard deviation").

Vertical	Attribute	Precision	Recall	F-score
Autos	model	0.46 ± 0.27	0.41 ± 0.26	0.43 ± 0.26
	price	0.80 ± 0.19	0.79 ± 0.19	0.80 ± 0.19
	engine	0.82 ± 0.14	0.82 ± 0.14	0.82 ± 0.14
	fuel-economy	0.81 ± 0.20	0.73 ± 0.18	0.77 ± 0.19
Books	title	0.89 ± 0.13	0.87 ± 0.14	0.88 ± 0.14
	author	0.95 ± 0.04	0.89 ± 0.04	0.92 ± 0.04
	ISBN 13	0.84 ± 0.19	0.84 ± 0.18	0.84 ± 0.18
	publisher	0.81 ± 0.06	0.81 ± 0.06	0.81 ± 0.06
	publish-date	0.88 ± 0.08	0.88 ± 0.08	0.88 ± 0.08
Cameras	model	0.93 ± 0.07	0.88 ± 0.06	0.90 ± 0.07
	price	0.98 ± 0.04	0.90 ± 0.05	0.94 ± 0.05
	manufacturer	0.96 ± 0.06	0.93 ± 0.06	0.94 ± 0.06
Jobs	title	0.99 ± 0.03	0.93 ± 0.04	0.95 ± 0.04
	company	0.84 ± 0.24	0.80 ± 0.22	0.82 ± 0.22
	location	0.87 ± 0.07	0.84 ± 0.07	0.85 ± 0.07
	date	0.79 ± 0.20	0.77 ± 0.19	0.78 ± 0.20
Movies	title	0.71 ± 0.25	0.68 ± 0.25	0.69 ± 0.25
	director	0.75 ± 0.11	0.80 ± 0.12	0.77 ± 0.12
	genre	0.96 ± 0.04	0.91 ± 0.04	0.93 ± 0.04
	rating	0.78 ± 0.23	0.75 ± 0.23	0.76 ± 0.23
NBA Players	name	0.84 ± 0.24	0.82 ± 0.23	0.83 ± 0.23
	team	0.82 ± 0.09	0.82 ± 0.09	0.82 ± 0.09
	height	0.76 ± 0.19	0.67 ± 0.17	0.71 ± 0.18
	weight	0.91 ± 0.10	0.91 ± 0.10	0.91 ± 0.10
Restaurants	name	0.95 ± 0.08	0.89 ± 0.07	0.92 ± 0.07
	address	0.97 ± 0.02	0.96 ± 0.02	0.96 ± 0.02
	phone	1.00 ± 0.00	0.98 ± 0.01	0.99 ± 0.00
	cuisine	0.98 ± 0.07	0.94 ± 0.06	0.96 ± 0.06
Universities	name	0.97 ± 0.05	0.95 ± 0.06	0.96 ± 0.06
	phone	0.79 ± 0.12	0.78 ± 0.12	0.79 ± 0.12
	website	0.96 ± 0.09	0.83 ± 0.08	0.89 ± 0.08
	type	0.70 ± 0.29	0.68 ± 0.27	0.69 ± 0.28

7.3 Multiple Seeds and Bootstrapping

The "one seed" scenario just proves that our solution has the ability to start with minimal human effort. Of course the solution can take multiple websites as seeds, as well as can accumulate vertical knowledge through bootstrapping. For bootstrapping, we simply keep those high-confidence extraction results of a website, and then consider the website as a new seed to the system. How to combine information from multiple seed sites is not a trivial task. Currently, we utilize a straightforward strategy without changing the sys-

Table 3: Average F-scores of the proposed solution based on multiple seed sites.

#Seeds	1	2	3	4	5
Our Solution	0.843	0.860	0.868	0.884	0.886
Our Solution (Bootstrap)	0.843	0.856	0.861	0.859	0.865
SSM	0.630	0.645	0.692	0.719	0.741

tem implementation too much. That is, an unseen website is evaluated based on each seed site independently, and the final solution is the one with the highest confidence score.

Table 3 shows the average F-scores of the proposed solution based on multiple seed sites. These seed sites can be manually labeled (*i.e.*, those in the ground-truth) or auto-tagged through bootstrapping. For comparison, we also trained the **SSM** model on multiple seeds manually labeled. From Table 3, we can see that the more websites involved in learning, the better the performance. When the seed sites were tagged through bootstrapping, the performance is a little worse than using manually labeled seeds. It is reasonable as the bootstrapping may introduce false examples into the learning process. Although the **SSM** method also benefits from more seed sites, its performance is still lower than the proposed solution. This again indicates the layout information (which was not fully adopted in **SSM**) is necessarily complementary to semantics to promote the performance.

8. CONCLUSIONS AND FUTURE WORK

In this paper, we propose a unified solution for extracting structured data from web sites based on one seed site given for a target vertical. The solution is general enough to tackle various verticals and relies on limited human effort to label one site for each vertical. A set of weak but general features are designed to characterize both semantic and layout knowledge of an arbitrary vertical. From a labeled seed site, we first extract features and learn vertical knowledge. Then, given a new site, the learnt knowledge is adapted to the site by exploiting site-level information, resulting in automatically identified attribute values for further wrapper induction. Experimental evaluations on 80 web sites in 8 diverse verticals showed promising results and demonstrated the feasibility and flexibility of the solution.

We consider several future directions to improve the proposed solution. First, a more principled strategy is desired to explicitly model and bridge the inter-site gaps in content and layout, with the number of observed sites increasing. Second, the solution could be combined with data record detection techniques to handle multiple entities in a page. From an experimental perspective, more extensive comparisons can be drawn to related approaches based on the published dataset. Moreover, it would be interesting to analyze the interactions among features, attributes, and seed sites, to get insight on feature design and seed site selection.

9. ACKNOWLEDGMENT

The first and third authors were partially supported by the National Natural Science Foundation of China (No. 60975001).

10. REFERENCES

[1] Document object model. http://en.wikipedia.org/wiki/Document_Object_Model.

[2] Freebase. http://www.freebase.com/.

[3] MSHTML reference. http://msdn.microsoft.com/en-us/library/aa741317(v=VS.85).aspx.

[4] A. Arasu and H. Garcia-Molina. Extracting structured data from web pages. In *Proc. SIGMOD*, pages 337–348, 2003.

[5] A. Carlson and C. Schafer. Bootstrapping information extraction from semi-structured web pages. In *Proc. ECML*, pages 195–210, 2008.

[6] C.-H. Chang and S.-C. Lui. Iepad: information extraction based on pattern discovery. In *Proc. WWW*, pages 681–688, 2001.

[7] V. Crescenzi, G. Mecca, and P. Merialdo. Roadrunner: Towards automatic data extraction from large web sites. In *Proc. VLDB*, pages 109–118, 2001.

[8] S. Dill, N. Eiron, D. Gibson, D. Gruhl, R. Guha, A. Jhingran, T. Kanungo, S. Rajagopalan, A. Tomkins, J. A. Tomlin, and J. Y. Zien. Semtag and seeker: bootstrapping the semantic web via automated semantic annotation. In *Proc. WWW*, pages 178–186, 2003.

[9] N. Kushmerick. *Wrapper induction for information extraction*. PhD thesis, 1997.

[10] B. Liu, R. Grossman, and Y. Zhai. Mining data records in web pages. In *Proc. KDD*, pages 601–606, 2003.

[11] I. Muslea, S. Minton, and C. Knoblock. A hierarchical approach to wrapper induction. In *Proc. AGENTS*, pages 190–197, 1999.

[12] S. Soderland. Learning information extraction rules for semi-structured and free text. *Mach. Learn.*, 34:233–272, 1999.

[13] M. L. A. Vidal, A. S. da Silva, E. S. de Moura, and J. M. B. Cavalcanti. Structure-driven crawler generation by example. In *Proc. SIGIR*, pages 292–299, 2006.

[14] T.-L. Wong and W. Lam. Learning to adapt web information extraction knowledge and discovering new attributes via a Bayesian approach. *TKDE*, 22:523–536, 2010.

[15] T.-L. Wong, W. Lam, and B. Chen. Mining employment market via text block detection and adaptive cross-domain information extraction. In *Proc. SIGIR*, pages 283–290, 2009.

[16] J.-M. Yang, R. Cai, Y. Wang, J. Zhu, L. Zhang, and W.-Y. Ma. Incorporating site-level knowledge to extract structured data from web forums. In *Proc. WWW*, pages 181–190, 2009.

[17] Y. Zhai and B. Liu. Web data extraction based on partial tree alignment. In *Proc. WWW*, pages 76–85, 2005.

[18] S. Zheng, R. Song, J.-R. Wen, and D. Wu. Joint optimization of wrapper generation and template detection. In *Proc. KDD*, pages 894–902, 2007.

[19] J. Zhu, Z. Nie, J.-R. Wen, B. Zhang, and W.-Y. Ma. 2d conditional random fields for web information extraction. In *Proc. ICML*, pages 1044–1051, 2005.

[20] J. Zhu, Z. Nie, J.-R. Wen, B. Zhang, and W.-Y. Ma. Simultaneous record detection and attribute labeling in web data extraction. In *Proc. KDD*, pages 494–503, 2006.

Improving Local Search Ranking through External Logs

Klaus Berberich
Max-Planck Institute for Informatics
Saarbrücken, Germany
kberberi@mpi-inf.mpg.de

Arnd Christian König, Dimitrios Lymberopoulos
Microsoft Research
Redmond, WA 98052
{chrisko,dlymper} @microsoft.com

Peixiang Zhao
Univ. of Illinois at Urbana-Champaign
Urbana, IL 61801, USA
pzhao4@illinois.edu

ABSTRACT

The signals used for ranking in local search are very different from web search: in addition to (textual) relevance, measures of (geographic) *distance* between the user and the search result, as well as measures of *popularity* of the result are important for effective ranking. Depending on the query and search result, different ways to quantify these factors exist – for example, it is possible to use customer ratings to quantify the popularity of restaurants, whereas different measures are more appropriate for other types of businesses. Hence, our approach is to capture the different notions of distance/popularity relevant via a number of external data sources (e.g., logs of customer ratings, driving-direction requests, or site accesses).

In this paper we will describe the relevant signal contained in a number of such data sources in detail and present methods to integrate these external data sources into the feature generation for local search ranking. In particular, we propose novel backoff methods to alleviate the impact of skew, noise or incomplete data in these logs in a systematic manner. We evaluate our techniques on both human-judged relevance data as well as click-through data from a commercial local search engine.

Categories and Subject Descriptors

H.3.3 [**Information Systems**]: Information Search and Retrieval

General Terms

Algorithms, Experimentation, Measurement

1. INTRODUCTION

Local search queries – which can be defined as queries which employ user location or geographic proximity (in addition to search keywords, a business category, or a product name) as a key factor in result quality – are becoming a more important part of (web) search. Specialized local search verticals are now part of all major web search engines and typically surface businesses, restaurants or points-of-interest relevant to search queries. Moreover, their results are also often integrated with "regular" web search results on the main search page when appropriate. Also, local search is a commonly used application on mobile devices.

Because of the importance of location and the different types of results (typically businesses, restaurants and points-of-interest as opposed to web pages) surfaced by local search engines, the signals used in ranking local search results are very different from the ones used in web search ranking. For example, consider the local search query [pizza], which is intended to surface restaurants selling pizza in the vicinity of the user. For this (type of) query, the keyword(s) in the query itself do very little for ranking, beyond eliminating businesses that do not feature pizza (in the text associated with them). Moreover, the businesses returned as local search results are often associated with significantly less text than web pages, giving traditional text-based measures of relevance less content to leverage. Instead, key signals used to rank results for such queries are (i) a measure of the *distance* between the result business and the user's location (or a measure of the effort to get there) and (ii) a measure of its *popularity*[1]. To assess these signals directly on the basis of click information derived from the local search vertical is very difficult, in part due to the position bias of the click signal [21]. Our approach therefore leverages external data sources such as logs of driving-direction requests to quantify these two signals.

In case of result *popularity*, the related notion of *preference* has been studied in the context of web search (e.g., [28]); however, techniques to infer preferences in this context are based on randomized swaps of results, which are not desirable in a production system, especially in the context of mobile devices which only display a small number of results at the same time. Other techniques used to quantify the *centrality* or *authority* of web pages (e.g., those based on their link structure) do not directly translate to the business listings surfaced by local search.

Instead, we look into data sources from which we can derive popularity measures specific to local search results; for example, one might use customer ratings, the number of accesses to the business web site in search logs, or – if available – data on business revenues or the number of customers. Depending on the type of business and query, different sources may yield the most informative signal. Customer ratings, for instance, are common for restaurants but rare for other types of businesses. Other types of businesses (e.g., plumbers) may often not have a web site, so that there is no information about users' access activity.

In case of result *distance*, it easy to compute the geographic distance between a user and a business once their locations are known. This number itself, however, does not really reflect the effort required for a user to travel to the business in question. For one, how sensitive a user is to the geographic distance is a function of the type of business that is being ranked: for example, users may be willing to drive 20 minutes for a furniture store, but not for a coffee shop. Moreover, if the travel is along roads or subways, certain locations may be much easier to reach for a given user than others, even though they have the same geographic distance; this can even lead to asymmetric notions of distance, where travel from point A

[1] Note that additional signals such as weather, time or personalization features (see [24]) can also be integrated into our overall framework.

SIGIR'11, July 24–28, 2011, Beijing, China.

to B is much easier than from B to A (e.g. due to traffic conditions) or simply much more common. We will provide concrete examples of such cases later.

Again, it is useful to employ external data sources to assess the correct notion of distance for a specific query: for example, one may use logs of driving-direction requests from map verticals – by computing the distribution of requests ending at specific businesses, one might assess what distances users are willing to travel for different types of businesses. Alternatively, one might use mobile search logs to assess the variation in popularity of a specific business for groups of users located in different zip codes. As before, the different logs may complement each other.

Challenges for integrating these external data sources stem from the fact that they are often *sparse* (i.e., cover only a subset of the relevant businesses), *skewed* (i.e., some businesses are covered in great detail, others in little detail or not at all) and *noisy* (e.g., contain outliers such as direction requests that span multiple states).

To illustrate why this poses a challenge, consider the following scenario: assume that we want to use logs of driving direction requests obtained from a map vertical to assess the average distance that users drive to a certain business. This average is then used in ranking to determine how much to penalize businesses that are farther away. Now, for some businesses we may have only few direction requests ending at the business in our logs, in which case the average distance may be unrepresentative and/or overly skewed by a single outlier. Moreover, for some businesses we may not have any log entries at all, meaning that we have to fall back on some default value. In both cases, we may consequently not rank the corresponding businesses accurately.

One approach to alleviate this issue is to model such statistical aggregates (i.e., the average driving distance in the example above) at multiple resolutions, which include progressively more "similar" objects or observations. While the coarser resolutions offer less coherent collections of objects, they yield more stable aggregates. When there is not enough information available about a specific object, one can then resort to the information aggregated at coarser levels, i.e., *back off* to successively larger collections of similar objects. Strategies of this nature have been used in different contexts, including click prediction for advertisements [2, 18, 29], collection selection [19], as well as language models in information retrieval [36] and speech recognition [22].

To give a concrete example, for the pizza scenario above we may want to expand the set of businesses based on which we compute the average driving distances to include businesses that (a) sell similar products/services and reside in the same area, (b) belong to the same chain (if applicable) and reside in different areas or (c) belong to the same type of business, regardless of location. All of the resulting averages can be used as separate features in the ranking process, with the ranker learning how to trade off between them.

Contributions: In this paper, we describe an approach to integrate and leverage external data sources in the feature generation process for local search ranking. First, we will describe different relevant external sources and examine which properties of user behavior/preferences they express. To capture the signals represented by these sources we propose a framework for feature generation which (a) allows us to integrate a wide range of external data sources into the feature generation for ranking, (b) addresses the issues of sparseness and skew via a flexible "multi-resolution approach" based on *backoff* techniques specific to our setting that extend to a variety of different distance functions, and (c) yields considerable improvements in ranking quality, which we will demonstrate through experiments on real-world data using both relevance judgements as well as click-through information.

2. RELATED WORK

We now put our work in context with existing prior research. The work that we deem related can be broadly classified as follows:

Backoff Methods and Smoothing. Katz [22], coining the notion of *backoff*, pioneered the idea of using observations about related objects (in his case N-grams) for statistical estimation in the context of language models; a number of competing techniques exist in this area. Similar concepts have been used in text database selection: Ipeirotis and Gravano [19] propose a approach to compute document synopses taking into account other documents from similar categories. This can be seen as a form of smoothing – a technique popular in language modeling [36]. Mei and Church [26], finally, study how effective a backoff based on IP-address prefixes can be for personalized search. In contrast to these approaches that determine related objects to consider based on rigid schemes, our approach is flexible by allowing for arbitrary distance functions to steer the backoff process.

Click-through Modeling and Estimation in computational advertising is also related to our work. Click-through data for ads suffers from a sparsity problem like our external data sources. Therefore, models proposed in the literature factor in information from related ads that are determined, for instance, based on term overlap [29], the ads' positions in a class taxonomy [2], or knowledge about the customer and her past campaigns [18].

External Data Sources (e.g., logs of user behavior) have proven useful in different applications. Selecting the right vertical (e.g., news or images) is one that was addressed in [4]. GPS traces, yet another kind of external data, were used in [10] to construct maps. Lane al. [24], most recently and closest to our work, used external data (including weather information) to improve relevance in mobile search.

Geographic Information Retrieval considers, for instance, rankings of documents that take into account geographic references – the problem addressed in [1, 5]. Queries, though, may not contain an explicit geographic reference (e.g., a city name) but have a "geo intent" nevertheless. Identifying such queries is orthogonal to our work and has been studied in [6, 25, 32, 35]. The issue of efficient index structures and query processing to support *spatial keyword queries* was studied in [14]. The problem addressed in this paper is to retrieve the k nearest results to a query location that contain all query keywords. The authors propose a dedicated index structure called *IR^2-Tree* for this task. Extension of their ideas to ranking functions that are a monotonic combination of textual similarity and spatial distance scores are described in [13] and [11]. A different data structure for queries with both textual as well as spatial filter conditions is introduced in [17]. Unlike all of these papers, our approach is not concerned with the indexing of the objects itself and is focused on a much more complex, machine-learning based ranking function incorporating a wide variety of features.

3. OUR APPROACH

In this section, we describe the overall architecture behind our approach. Our goal is an architecture to incorporate external data sources into the feature generation process for local search ranking. Examples of such data sources include logs of accesses to business web sites, customer ratings, GPS traces, and logs of driving-direction requests. Each of these logs is modeled as a set $\mathcal{O}$ of objects $\mathcal{O} = \{o_1, \ldots, o_k\}$. The different features that we consider in this paper are derived from these logs by means of (a) a *selection function* that selects an appropriate subset of objects and (b) an *aggregation function* that is applied to this subset to derive a single feature value.

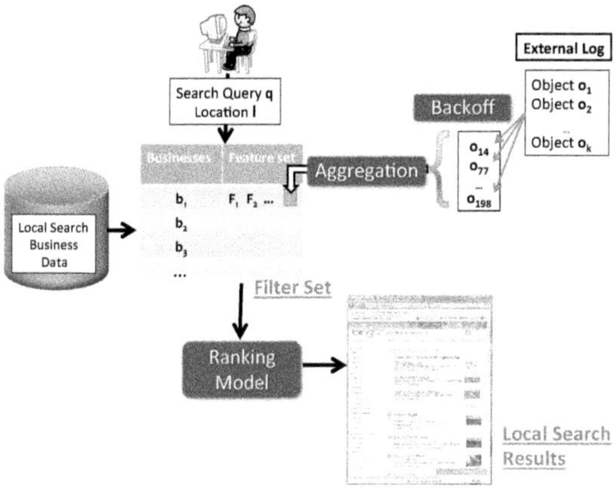

Figure 1: Our Architecture

For example, consider the running example of ranking a specific pizza restaurant and a log of driving direction requests; here, the selection function might select all log entries ending in the same location as the restaurant and the aggregation function might compute the average distance of the requests. We also refer to these features as *aggregate features* in the following.

Figure 1 depicts the overall architecture of our system. Initially, a query and location are sent as an input to the local search engine; this request can either come from a mobile device, from a query explicitly issued against a local search vertical, or a query posted against the web search engine for which local results shall be surfaced together with regular results. In the latter two cases, the relevant (user) location can be inferred using IP-to-location lookup tables or from the query itself (e.g., if it contains a city name). As a result, a local search produces a ranked list of entities from a local search business database; for ease of notation, we will refer to these entities as *businesses* in the following, as these are the most common form of local search results. However, local search may also return other entity types including sights and "points-of-interest".

Ranking in local search usually proceeds as a two-step approach: an initial "rough" filtering step eliminates obviously irrelevant or too distant businesses, thus producing a *filter set* of businesses, which are then ranked in a subsequent second step using a learned ranking model. Our *backoff methods* operate in an intermediate step, as illustrated in Figure 1, enriching businesses in the filter set with additional features aggregated from a suitable subset of objects in the external data source $\mathcal{O}$.

Given the current query q, user location l, and a specific business b from the filter set, the selection function first selects a subset of objects from the external data source $\mathcal{O}$, from which aggregate features are generated. We implement different levels of granularity in our backoff methods using different selection function; hence, we also refer to set of objects selected as the *backoff set*. The different selection functions are steered by a set of distance functions $d_1, \ldots d_m$ each of which captures a different notion of distance between the triple (q, l, b) (further referred to as *source object*) and an object o_i from the external data source. Examples of distance functions, that we consider later on, include geographic business distance (e.g., measured in kilometers) and categorical business distance that reflects how similar two businesses are in terms of their business purpose.

Unlike other backoff techniques (e.g., [26]), which only use single distance function, our approach does neither restrict the choice of distance functions nor their number. This in turn poses the challenge that the different distance functions must be combined or traded off when doing the backoff.

Our approach to do this is to expose aggregate features from a number of different backoff sets machine-learning based ranking model, each of which relaxed a different (combination) of distance function(s). This approach also has the advantage that we do not have to explicitly formulate a single scoring function that trades off between distance, popularity and other factors (as is done, for example, in [11] or [24] where this is realized through a metric embedding). Instead, the ranker can (learn to) trade off between the different features in different ways for different types of queries. As we will illustrate in the next section, the relative importance of distance, popularity, etc. can vary significantly for different types of business entities or queries, thereby making this flexibility essential for ranking.

4. LEVERAGING EXTERNAL SOURCES

We now describe the external data sources that we leverage using our architecture, give details on their characteristics, and explain why we consider them important for local search ranking.

4.1 Direction Requests

The first type of external data that we use for local search are logs of driving-direction requests, which could stem from map search verticals (e.g., **maps.google.com** or **www.bing.com/maps/**), web sites such as *Mapquest* or any number of GPS-enabled devices serving up driving directions. In particular, we focus on direction requests ending at a business that is present in our local search data. For these requests, we use both the (aggregated) driving distances (in miles) as well as the (aggregate) driving times (in minutes) to generate ranking features, as they represent two different aspects of how much "effort" is spent to reach a given business.

Data Preparation and Quality: Independent of whether the logs of direction requests record the actual addresses or latitude/longitude information, it is often not possible to tie an individual direction request to an individual business with certainty: in many cases (e.g., for a shopping mall) a single address or location is associated with multiple businesses and some businesses associate multiple addresses with a single store/location. Moreover, we found that in many cases users do not use their current location (or the location they start their trip from) as the starting location of the direction request, but rather only a city name (typically of a small town) or a freeway entrance. As a consequence, our techniques need to be able to deal with the underlying uncertainty; we use (additional) features associated with each business that encode how many other businesses are associated with the same physical location.

One important concern with location information is location privacy [23]; fortunately, our approach does not require any fine-grained data on the origin of a driving request and – because all features we describe in this paper are aggregates – they are also somewhat resilient to the types of obfuscation used in this context (see [23] for a more detailed description of the applicable techniques). In fact, any feature whose value is strongly dependent on the behavior of a single user is by default undesirable for our purposes, as we want to capture common behavior of large groups of users. We omit a more detailed discussion of privacy issues due to space limitations.

The Value of Direction Requests: The value of the direction request data stems from the fact that it allows us to much better quantify the impact of distance between a user and a local search result than mere geographic distance would. For one, the route length and estimated duration reflect the amount of "effort" required to get to a certain business much better than the geographic distance, since they take into account the existing infrastructure. Moreover, in aggregate, the direction requests can tell us something about which routes are more likely to be traveled than others even when the associated length/duration is identical.

Direction request data can also be used to assess popularity, as a direction request is typically a much stronger indicator of the intent to visit a location than an access to the corresponding web site would be. However, they do not convey reliable data on the likelihood of repeated visits as users are not very likely to request the same directions more than once. Also, directions to more popular or famous destinations are more likely to be known to users already.

Varying Distance Sensitivity: A hypothesis we mentioned in the introduction was that users' "sensitivity" regarding distance is a function of the type of business considered. In order to test this, we used a multi-level tree of business categories (containing paths such as `/Dining/Restaurants/Thai`); every business in the local search data was assigned to one or more nodes in this tree. We computed the average route length for driving requests in every category. The averages (normalized to the interval $[0, 1]$) for top-level categories are shown in Figure 2.

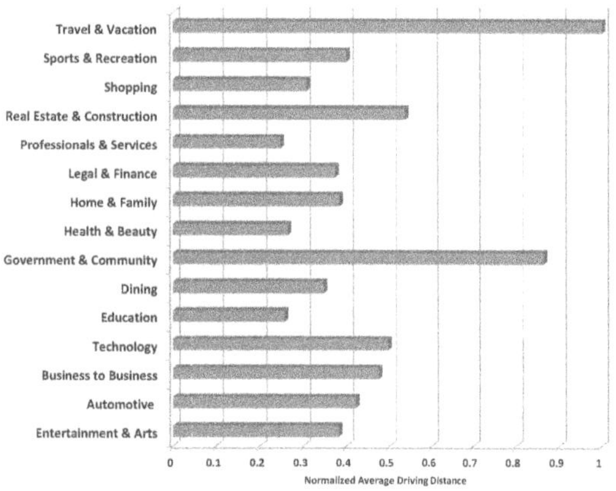

Figure 2: Average Driving Distance per Top-Level Category

As we can see, there are considerable differences between the average distances traveled to different types of businesses. Businesses associated with travel have the highest average, which is not at all surprising (the requests in this category are dominated by direction requests to hotels). While some of these numbers mainly reflect the density of businesses in categories where competition is not an issue (e.g., public institutions in the *Government & Community* category), larger averages in many cases also indicate a smaller "sensitivity" towards increased distances (e.g., entries in the fine dining category). To give one particular example, the (high) average driving distances to hotels are not at all a reflection of the density of distribution of hotels; approaches that seek to model distance sensitivity by retrieving the top-k closest distances to the user would fail for this scenario. As a consequence, we model *both* the distribution of driving distances for individual businesses as well as the "density" of alternatives around them in our features.

Distance Asymmetry: Some variation in the distance distribution of driving directions cannot be explained by the different business categories of the destinations themselves. To illustrate this, we plotted the starting points of driving directions to restaurants in Redmond and Bellevue (located east of Lake Washington) and of directions to restaurants in Seattle (west of Lake Washington) on the map in Figure 3 (larger circles denote more requests starting in the same vicinity). The figure shows that it is common for users from Redmond/Bellevue to drive to Seattle for dinner, but the converse does not hold. Hence, there appears to be a difference in the "distance sensitivity" for each group of users even though technically, the route lengths and durations are the same. While some of these effects can be explained by the greater density and (possibly quality) of restaurants in Seattle, a lot of the attraction of a large city lies in the additional businesses or entertainment offered.

Consequently, we either need to be able to incorporate distance models that are non-symmetric or be able to model the absolute location of a business (and the location's attractiveness) as part of our feature set. In the features proposed in this paper, we will opt for the second approach, explicitly modeling the popularity of areas (relative to a user's current location) as well as (the distance to) other attractions from the destination.

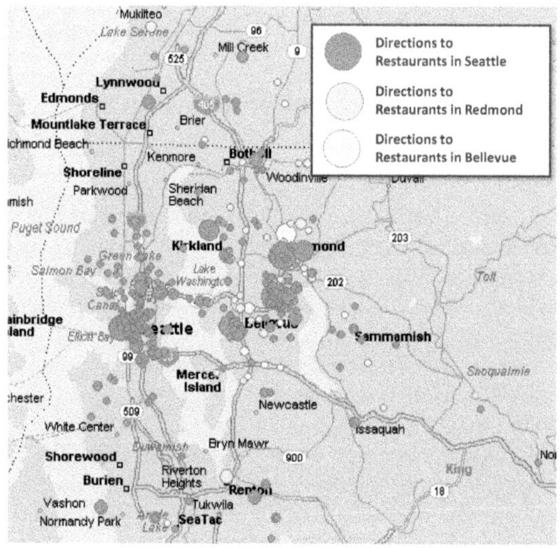

Figure 3: Distribution of a sample of starting points for driving direction requests to restaurants in Seattle, Bellevue and Redmond. This distribution is highly asymmetric: many users are willing to drive from Redmond or Bellevue to Seattle for dinner, but very few are willing to drive the opposite way, even though the driving times are similar.

4.2 Browsing Trail Logs

The second type of external data that we use are logs of *Browsing/Search Trails* [33]. These are logs of browsing activity collected with permission from a large number of users; each entry consists of (among other things) an anonymous user identifier, a timestamp and the URL of the visited web page (where we track only a subset of pages for privacy reasons[2]), as well as information on the IP address in use. A more detailed description of trail extraction can be found in [33].

Using these logs, we can now attempt to (partially) characterize the popularity of a specific business via the number of accesses we see to the web site associated with the business, by counting the number of distinct users, or the number of total accesses or even tracking popularity over time. In our experiments, we (similarly to [33]) break down the trails into sessions, and count repeated accesses to a single page within a session as one access. Note that our current approach does not make full use of the sequence information and dwell-times on contained in the trail log; we hope to further exploit this signal in future work.

Data Preparation and Quality: The main issue with tracking accesses here is how we define what precisely we count as an access to the web site stored with the business. For example, if the

[2] In the experiments in this paper we restrict this set to pages associated with the individual businesses in our databases, as well as a small set of referring sites (such as search engines, portals and review sites).

Rank	Business Web Site
1	**http://www.lwtc.edu/**
2	http://www.costco.com/
3	**http://bellevuecollege.edu/**
4	http://www.alaskaair.com/
5	http://www.windermere.com/
6	http://www.macys.com/
7	http://shop.nordstrom.com/
	...

Figure 4: The most frequently accessed business web sites in the Bellevue zip code in our browsing trail log data

site of a business according to our local search data is **www.joeyspizza.com/home/**, do we also count accesses to **www.joeyspizza.com/** or **www.joeyspizza.com/home/staff/** ? For simplicity, in this paper, we consider an access a match if the string formed by the union of *domain* and *path* of a browsed URL is a super-string of the domain + path stored in our local search data (we ignore the *port* and *query* part of the URL). Finding a better matching function than this for tracking accesses is actually an interesting engineering challenge, which is outside the scope of this work.

Similar to the issues we discussed earlier encountered with associating businesses with individual locations, we also face the issue that in our local search data, some web site URLs are associated with multiple businesses (typically, multiple instances of the same chain). To address this, we keep track of the total number of accesses as well as the number of businesses associated with a site and encode this information as a feature.

The Value of Trail Logs: We use the trail logs to derive features quantifying the *popularity* of businesses by tracking how often the corresponding sites are accessed over time. Here, the main advantage over search logs (local or otherwise) lies in the fact that trail logs allow us to account for accesses that originate from sites other than search engines (such as e.g., *Yelp* or *Citysearch*), which make up a very significant fraction of access for some types of businesses, especially smaller ones. Moreover, we can use the the notion of sessions, to avoid double-counting of repeated visits to a single site within a single session. Finally, using the IP information contained in the logs, we can (using appropriate lookup tables) determine the zip code the access originated from with high accuracy, thereby allowing us to break down the relative popularity of a business by zip codes. To illustrate this, consider Figure 4, which shows – for one month of data – the web sites associated with a business in our data that were most frequently accessed from the Bellevue zip code (98004), ranked by frequency. Both the top-ranked and 3rd-ranked site correspond to businesses (colleges) local to the Bellevue area; when comparing this to the adjacent Redmond zip code (98052), both of these web sites fail to make the top 20 of most frequently accessed sites; also, their relative order is reversed.

4.3 Mobile Search Logs

The final external data source that we use are logs of mobile search queries submitted to a commercial mobile search engine together with the resulting clicks from mobile users. The information recorded includes the GPS location from which the query was submitted, the query string submitted by the user, an identifier of the business(es) clicked in response to the query and a timestamp.

The Value of Mobile Search Logs: We use these logs to derive features relevant to both popularity (by counting the number of accesses to a given (type of) business or area) as well as to capture the distance sensitivity (by grouping these accesses by the location of the mobile device the query originated from). For this purpose, the mobile search logs differ from the other sources discussed previously in two important ways: first, they give a better representation of the "origin" of a trip to a business than non-mobile logs – in part due to the factors discussed above for direction requests (where the origin of the request is often not clear) and in part because these requests are more likely to be issued directly before taking action in response to a local search result (as the requester may already be on the move as opposed to in front of his PC). Second, mobile search logs contain significantly more accurate location information (e.g., via GPS, cell tower and/or wifi triangulation) compared to the reverse IP lookup-based approach used for desktop devices [27, 31].

5. DISTANCE-BASED BACKOFF

Having described our overall approach and the practical challenges associated with the external data sources that we want to leverage, we now introduce our approach to distance-based backoff. The importance of the resulting features is two-fold: first, the backoff method allows us to overcome issues like sparseness and outliers by yielding more robust aggregates; second, they help us express some of the properties of user preferences we have described in Section 4. For example, as illustrated previously, the relative importance of signals such as distance and popularity may vary tremendously across queries. Consequently, we do not want to propose a ranking model that uses a simple weighted combination of distance/popularity measures (with the weights computed from training data). Instead, the features generated from backoff sets allow us to detect behaviors specific to certain sets of retrieved objects dynamically – for example, using a backoff set that retrieves similar businesses (for driving direction logs) allows us to detect the relevant distance sensitivity (similar to Figure 2). Similarly, we can detect the popularity of regions (as discussed in Figure 3) by using a backoff set containing adjacent businesses.

Backoff Framework: As we already sketched in Section 3, our idea is to generate additional aggregate features for a concrete business in our filter set based on a subset of objects from the external data source. Selecting the subset of objects to consider is the task accomplished by a *backoff method*. Given a source object $s = (q, l, b)$ consisting of the user's query q, current location l, and the business b from our filter set, as well as an external data source $\mathcal{O}$, a backoff method thus determines a *backoff set* $B(s) \subsetneq \mathcal{O}$ of objects from the external data source.

Running Example: Consider an example user from Redmond (i.e., $l = (47.64, -122.14)$, when expressed as a pair of latitude and longitude) looking for a pizza restaurant (i.e., q = [pizza]) and a specific business (e.g., b = Joey's Pizza as a fictitious pizza restaurant located in Bellevue). Our external data source in the example is a log of direction requests where each individual entry, for simplicity, consists of a business, as the identified target of the direction request, and the corresponding route length.

Apart from that, we assume a set of distance functions $d_1, \ldots, d_m$ that capture different notions of distance between the source object $s = (q, l, b)$ and objects from the external data source. Example distance functions of interest in our running example could be:

- *geographic business distance* d_{geo} between the locations associated with businesses b and o, or
- *categorical business distance* capturing how similar the two businesses are in terms of their business purpose. Letting $Cat(s)$ and $Cat(o)$ denote the sets of business categories (e.g., `/Dining/Italian/Pizza`) that the businesses are associated with, a sensible definition based on the Jaccard coefficient would be

$$d_{cat}(s, o) = 1.0 - \frac{|Cat(s) \cap Cat(o)|}{|Cat(s) \cup Cat(o)|}$$

- *geographic user distance* which – when combined with logs that contain observations with a starting point (e.g., a current user location) and endpoint (e.g., a destination business) – measure the distance between the starting locations.

One baseline method is to include only objects in the backoff set for which all m distance functions report zero distance, i.e.,

$$B_{BL}(s) = \{\, o \in \mathcal{O} \mid \forall i : d_i(s,o) = 0 \,\} \ .$$

In our running example this only includes direction requests that have Joey's Pizza as a target location (assuming that there is no second pizza restaurant at exactly the same geographic location). Due to the sparseness of external data sources, though, this method produces empty backoff sets for many businesses.

To alleviate this, we have to relax the constraints that we put on our distance functions. For our running example, we could thus include other pizza restaurants in the vicinity by relaxing the geographic distance to $d_{geo}(s,o) \leq 2.5$, include other similar businesses (e.g., other restaurants) at the same location by relaxing $d_{cat} \leq 0.1$. Which choice is best, though, is not clear upfront and may depend on the business itself (e.g., whether Joey's Pizza is located in a shopping mall or at an out-of-town location). Furthermore, it is not easy to pick suitable combinations of threshold values for the distance functions involved, as the notions of distance introduced by each function are inherently different. We address the first issue by exposing (features based on) a number of different relaxations to the ranker, which can then pick and combine the most informative among them; regarding the second issue, we use a simple normalization scheme described in the following.

Distance Normalization: We address the issue of "incompatible" distance functions by re-normalizing them in a generic manner as

$$d_i^N(s,o) = \frac{|\{\, o' \in \mathcal{O} \mid d_i(s,o') < d_i(s,o) \,\}|}{|\mathcal{O}|} \ ,$$

so that the normalized distance $d_i^N(s,o)$ conveys the fraction of objects that have a smaller distance than o from the source object. Building on our distance normalization, we introduce an aggregated distance

$$d(s,o) = \sum_{i=1}^{m} d_i^N(s,o)$$

that captures the overall distance of object o.

5.1 Near-Neighbor Backoff

Our first method, coined near-neighbor backoff (NN), includes all objects in the backoff set that have an aggregated distance below a threshold α. Formally, the method produces the backoff set

$$B_{NN}(s,\alpha) = \{\, o \in \mathcal{O} \mid d(s,o) < \alpha \,\} \ .$$

Figure 5 illustrates near-neighbor backoff when applied to our running example. The determined backoff set contains all objects in the shaded triangle defined by $d(s,o) < 0.01$, i.e., only objects that are sufficiently *close* to the source object but none that are both geographically distant and of a very different business type (e.g., a Volvo dealer in Tacoma).

Computational Overhead: By its definition, near-neighbor backoff requires identifying all objects that have an aggregated distance below the specified threshold. If objects can be retrieved in ascending order of their distance, this can be done efficiently in practice. For instance, as an example optimization, once an object with distance $\alpha \leq d_i^N(s,o)$ has been seen, one can stop retrieving distances for the distance function d_i. Other optimizations, such as those proposed for efficient text retrieval [3] or top-k aggregation in databases [15], are also applicable in this case.

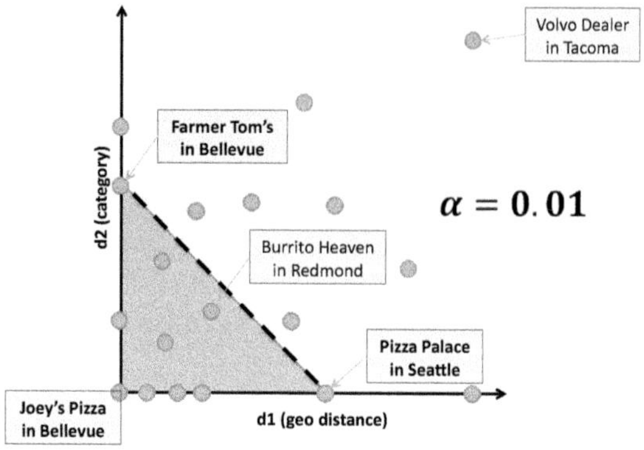

Figure 5: Near-Neighbor Backoff Illustrated

5.2 Pivot Backoff

Near-neighbor backoff, as explained above, ensures that all objects in the backoff set are individually close to the source object. Their distances according to the different distance functions, though, can be rather different, as can be seen from Figure 5 where we include Farmer Tom's in Bellevue (a fictitious supermarket) and Pizza Palace in Seattle, each of which is close to the source according to one but very distant according to the other distance function considered. As this demonstrates, near-neighbor backoff may produce a set of objects that, though individual objects are close to the source, is incoherent as a whole, which can be problematic when aggregating over them.

Pivot backoff, which we introduce next, addresses this issue and goes beyond near-neighbor backoff by not only ensuring that objects in the backoff set are individually close to the source object but also choosing a *coherent* set of objects. To this end, the method chooses the backoff set relative to a pivot object that has maximal distance, among the objects in the backoff set, for every distance function. The pivot thus serves as an extreme object and characterizes the determined backoff set – all objects in it are at most as distant as the pivot. While this ensures consistency among the objects in the backoff set, the choice of the pivot object now becomes critical. Since we are interested in determining reliable aggregate features in the end, we select the pivot object (among all pivot objects with aggregate distance less than α) that yields the largest backoff set, thereby creating an optimization problem. The backoff set is formally defined relative to a pivot object p as

$$B_P(s,\alpha) = \left\{\, o \in \mathcal{O} \mid \forall i :\ d_i^N(s,o) \leq d_i^N(s,p) \,\right\} \ .$$

The pivot object p is chosen so that the backoff set has maximal size, while ensuring that the pivot (and, in turn, all other objects in the backoff set) have aggregated distance below a specified threshold α. Formally, this can be cast into the optimization problem

$$\underset{p \in \mathcal{O}}{argmax} \left|\{\, o \in \mathcal{O} \mid \forall i : d_i^N(s,o) \leq d_i^N(s,p) \,\}\right|$$
$$\text{s.t. } d(s,p) < \alpha \ .$$

Figure 6 illustrates pivot backoff when applied to our running example. The method determines Burrito Heaven in Redmond as a pivot, thus producing a backoff set that contains the seven objects falling into the shaded rectangle.

Computational Overhead: It follows from our definition of pivot backoff that we only need to consider objects that have an aggregated distance $d(s,o) < \alpha$. These can be identified using techniques similar to the ones used in near-neighbor backoff. We now address the question of how a pivot object can be determined efficiently among these near neighbors. Note that our definition of

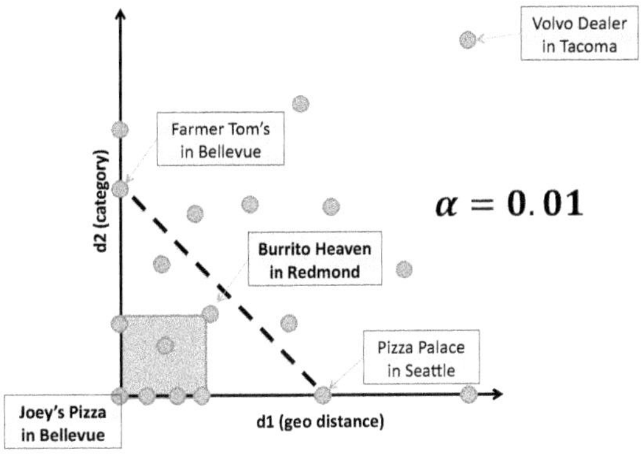

Figure 6: Pivot Backoff Illustrated

pivot backoff resembles skylines [7] that have been investigated in depth, for instance, in the database community. Algorithm 1 gives pseudo code for determining a pivot object, building on ideas from the sort-filter skyline computation described by Chomicki et al. [12]. Here, we exploit their idea that an object o can only be contained in the backoff set defined by the pivot p if $d(s,o) \leq d(s,p)$. For ease of explanation, we also assume that objects have distinct aggregate distances.

Input: `nearNeighbors` $= \{o \in \mathcal{O} \mid d(s,o) < \alpha\}$
sort `nearNeighbors` in descending $d(s,o)$ order
p^* = `nearNeighbors`.removeFirst()
`pivotCandidates` $= \{p^*\}$
for $o \in$ `nearNeighbors` **do**
  for $p \in$ `pivotCandidates` **do**
    if $\forall i : d_i^N(s,p) \leq d_i^N(s,o)$ **then**
      o.`containedIn`++;
      p.`contains`++;
      if p.`contains` $> p^*$.`contains` **then**
        $p^* = p$
      end if
    end if
    if o.`containedIn` $= 0$ **then**
      `pivotCandidates`.add(o)
    end if
  end for
end for
return p^*

Algorithm 1: Pivot Identification

The algorithm first sorts `nearNeighbors` in descending order of $d(s,o)$. The set of potential pivots, as those objects not contained in the set defined by another object, is maintained in `pivotCandidates`. When reading an object o from the sorted `nearNeighbors`, the algorithm tests whether the object is contained in the set of any potential pivot p. If so, it updates the count p.`contains` of objects in that set. Otherwise, if o is not contained in any such set, it is a potential pivot and thus added to `pivotCandidates`. As a side aspect, the algorithm maintains the currently best-known object p^* from `pivotCandidates` and finally returns it as the pivot. The algorithm has time complexity in $O(n^2)$ and space complexity in $O(n)$ where n denotes the number of near neighbors. The worst case occurs if every object defines a backoff set that contains only the object itself.

6. EXPERIMENTAL EVALUATION

In the following, we evaluate the effectiveness of our methods using two data sets. We first evaluate the improvement in ranking quality based on a set of 80K pairs of queries and local search results, which have been assigned relevance labels by human judges. While this data allows us to have clean relevance judgements rendered by experts, this type of "in-vitro" evaluation may not capture all real-life factors (e.g., the attractiveness of locations surrounding a business, or travel duration due to traffic) that impact local search result quality in practice. To capture these factors, we also evaluate our techniques using a data set of queries and click-through information from a commercial local search portal; for this data, we do not have human relevance judgements, so we instead we use the features in a click-predict setting and evaluate if the new features result in significant improvements in predicting result clicks.

6.1 Learning Model

The learning method for click prediction is based on *Multiple Additive Regression-Trees (MART)* [34]. MART is based on the *Stochastic Gradient Boosting* paradigm described in [16] which performs gradient descent optimization in the functional space. In our experiments on click prediction, we used the log-likelihood as the loss function (optimization criterion), used steepest-decent (gradient descent) as the optimization technique, and used binary decision trees as the fitting function.

To illustrate this in the context of our click-prediction experiments: at the beginning of every iteration, the click probabilities of the training data are computed using the current model. The click prediction is now compared with the actual click outcome to derive the errors (or residuals) for the current system, which is then used to fit a residue model – a function that approximates the errors – using *MSE* (Mean Square Error) criteria. In MART, we compute the derivatives of the log-loss for each training data point as the residual and use the regression tree as the approximation function-residual model. A regression tree is a binary decision tree, where each internal node splits the features space into two by comparing the value of a chosen feature with a pre-computed threshold; once a terminal node is reached, an optimal regression value is returned for all the data falling into the region. Finally, the residual model is added back to the existing model so that the overall training error is compensated for and reduced for this iteration. The new model – the current plus the residual model – will be used as the current model for the next boosting/training iteration. The final model after M boosting iterations is the sum of all M regression trees built.

Properties of MART: MART is *robust* in that it is able to handle the diverse sets of features proposed in the previous section. For one, it does not require transformations to normalize the inputs into zero mean and unit variance which is essential for other algorithms such as logistic regression or neural nets. More importantly, by its internal use of decision trees, which are able to "break" the domain of each feature arbitrarily, it is able to handle non-linear dependencies between the feature values and the output.

MART also computes the importance of a feature by summing the number of times it is used in splitting decisions weighted by the *MSE* gain this split has achieved. The relative importance of a feature is computed by normalizing its importance by the importance of the largest feature, i.e., the most important feature will have relative importance 1 and and other features will have relative importance between 0 and 1. These relative importances of input features makes the model interpretable – helping us gain an understanding of the input variables that are most influential.

For the experiments on relevance judgements, we use *Lambda-MART* [8], which is a state-of-the-art ranking algorithm based on a combination of boosted regression trees and *LambdaRank* [9], which has the same robustness and interpretability properties detailed above as MART. A detailed description of both LambdaMART as well as LambdaRank can be found in [8].

6.2 Feature Sets

In the following, we will describe the different feature sets used in our experiments. We begin by describing a "*baseline*" ranking feature set that does not make use of external information, subsequently define an "*aggregate*" feature set containing simple aggregate features derived from external sources, but not any of the backoff features. Finally, we add the features derived from the two types of backoff methods in Section 5 into the "*backoff*" feature set.

Baseline Features: in the *baseline* feature set, we characterize the location of the user and the local result using features encoding the latitude and longitude of both as well as their geographic distance (*DistanceInKM*). Also, if a query contains a reference to a city, state or zip code (e.g., [pizza in Miami] or [sushi near 98052]), we encode the location of the center of the mass of the polygon describing boundaries of the city/state/zip-code in question in two features (*Implicit_Latitude*, *Implicit_Longitude*) and encode the presence of a city/state/zip-code in the query in binary features. As before, we encode the geographic distance between this point and the location of the user (*Implicit_DistanceInKM*).

To characterize the textual relevance of a result, we use a feature (*Result_Relevance*) encoding the *BM25 score* [30] of the query and the text associated with the local search result.

Finally, we use some features to characterize the query itself: in addition to two features encoding the number of tokens and characters, we use two binary features that encode if (a) the query matches a business name exactly (e.g., [dunkin donuts]) and (b) if the query matches a business category in our category hierarchy (e.g., [pizza] or [mexican food]), as in these cases the expected ranking behavior is dramatically different: in case of the user specifying a business directly, this is a very strong indicator that the top-ranked result should be an instance of this business, even in spite of there being closer and more popular alternatives. In the case of categorical queries, we see the opposite behavior – the importance of matching the text in the query (e.g., in the business title) is low, whereas the other signals dominate the ranking.

In the click prediction experiment, we have additional information on the queries: first, and most importantly, the different results are displayed at different positions, which have a major impact on the click probabilities; we encode the position in a feature (*Result_Position*). Second, as shown in [24], time is an important factor in local search; hence, we use different features to encode the hour, day of the week and month each query was issued.

Aggregate Features: For this feature set, we used the *basic* features and add the following features derived from the external logs described in Section 4: first, as one way of measuring result popularity, we count the average number of accesses to a web site associated with a business in the trail logs (*ResultClickPopularity*). We use a log of 36M such requests for this purpose, limited to requests issued in the United States. To account for a web site being associated with multiple businesses, we also encode the total number of businesses associated with it (*WebsiteCohostedEntities*).

To model the distance sensitivity, we encode the average driving distance (*AvgDrivingDistance*) and average route length (as estimated by the direction provider) (*AvgRouteLength*) for the direction requests ending at the location of the result business; in order to assess the stability of these estimates, we also encode the number of such requests (which can also serve as a measure of popularity) (*NoDrivingDirectionRequests*) as well as the number of businesses located at the same location (*LocationCoLocatedEntities*).

Finally, we use the mobile search logs to model the overall popularity of the area a business is located in, given the area the user resides in. Because of the small size of the log we used, we use a relatively coarse "resolution" here, computing the fraction of accesses in the mobile search logs made from the current zip code of the user and accessing a business in the zip code of the result (*HitRateZip*).

In addition, as we discussed in Section 4.1, the attractiveness of a result may not only depend on the properties of the corresponding business, but also on the available shopping, parking, entertainment, etc. in its vicinity. To test this hypothesis, we experimented with features that measure the distance from the result to the nearest businesses of different types, with smaller distances being indicative of areas offering more attractions. In this feature set, we incorporate a single feature of this type, measuring the distance to the nearest coffee shop of a major chain (*DistanceToCoffee*). Note that in practice, this feature doesn't only reflect the availability of espresso, but serves as a proxy of how "urban" the area is where a business is located. Since urban areas contain – on average – more other "attractions" besides coffee shops, we can think of it as a very simple and crude heuristic to characterize the attractiveness of the surroundings of a business. A more detailed study of the effects of proximity of other businesses/attractions is an interesting area of study in its own right and beyond the scope of this paper.

Backoff Features: In our third feature set, we add features generated using the two backoff methods described in Section 5. In order to describe these, we first need to define the distance functions we use and the objects they operate on. As in Section 5, we define the *source object* $s = (q, l, b)$ for which we generate features as the 3-tuple formed by a query string q, the user's location l and the result business b. We use the two backoff methods on features generated from the logs of search trails (see Section 4.2) and logs of direction requests (see Section 4.1). Each observation o in one of these logs is characterized by its origin o_{orig} (which corresponds to the user location (inferred via the IP address) in the trail logs, or the starting point of the direction request) and its destination o_{dest} (corresponding to the location of the clicked business in the trail logs, or the end point of the direction request). Using these, we can now define the distance functions we use for backoff as:

Geographic Business Distance $d_{geo}(s, o)$, which is defined as the geographic distance between the location of b and the destination o_{dest} of an observation in the logs.

Categorical Business Distance: $d_{cat}(s, o)$, which is defined (see Section 5) as the overlap in business categories between b the destination o_{dest} of an observation.

Geographic User Distance: $d_{user}(s, o)$ which is defined as the geographic distance between the location of l of the user and the origin o_{orig} of an observation in the logs.

Using these distances, we now compute backoff features as follows: for a given source, we iterate over all combinations of distance functions and thresholds $\alpha \in \{0.001, 0.01, 0.025, 0.05\}$ and compute the corresponding backoff sets $B_{NN}(s, \alpha)$ and $B_P(s, \alpha)$ for both the direction request and the browsing/search trail logs. Now, for each of these, we use the following aggregate functions to compute the final features from each backoff set: (a) the *count* of objects in the backoff set, (b) for the driving direction log, we encode the *average* distance of the routes contained in the backoff set as well as the *variance* of the distances, and (c) for the trail log, we encode the *average* number of accesses for the businesses contained in the backoff set as well as their *variance*. Finally, for each entity b, we also compute the difference in average route length/time and number of accesses between b and (i) all other members in the backoff set and (ii) all other businesses in the filter set, and encode these as features.

6.3 Experiments using Relevance Judgements

Dataset: In this experiment, we use a set of 80K pairs of a query and a local search result, the quality of each of which has been judged by a human expert on a 5-level scale from 0 (the worst) to 4 (the highest). Note that we refer to these as quality scores and not as relevance scores, since they incorporate additional factors other than pure query relevance (e.g., distance). The queries were sampled at random from query log files of a commercial local search engine and the results correspond to businesses in our local search data; all queries are in English and contain up to 7 terms. To avoid any training/test contamination, we partition the data into training, test, and validation data, such that every query string is present only in one of these partitions. After this partitioning, we retain a set of 8K distinct queries for training, 1.7K queries in the validation set and 1.7K queries in the test set. We choose the parameters of LambdaMART based on the validation set, using 30 leaves in the LambdaMART decision trees, $M = 300$ iterations and using a random sample of 90% of the training data for each split.

Performance Measure: To evaluate the performance of the result ranking, we employ *Normalized Discounted Cumulative Gain* (nDCG) [20], which is defined as

$$nDCG_p = \frac{100}{Z} \sum_{r=1}^{p} \frac{2^{l(r)} - 1}{\log(1+r)}, \quad (1)$$

where $l(r) \in [0, 4]$ is the quality label of the local search result returned at rank position r and p is the cut-off level (i.e., maximal rank considered) at which we compute the nDCG, and Z is chosen such that the perfect ranking would result in $nDCG_p = 100$. We evaluate our results using the mean nDCG_{10}.

Results: We present the improvements in nDCG resulting from the different feature sets in Figure 7. As we can seen, the *aggregate* feature set yields a considerable improvement in nDCG. When using *backoff* features we observe a smaller improvement on top of that. We also evaluated the backoff feature set when using only features generated through either *near-neighbor* or *pivot* backoff. Interestingly, both of these perform as well as the full backoff set. To quantify the significance of the results, we performed signif icance tests, using paired t-tests. Both the gain of the aggregate features as well as the gain of the various backoff feature sets over the baseline are statistically significant at the 99% level.

	Baseline	Aggregate	Backoff	NN	Pivot
nDCG@10	76.80	77.25	77.79	77.79	77.79

Figure 7: nDCG@10

Feature Importance Analysis: As we described above, MART is able to assign meaningful feature-importance scores to the features used in ranking, allowing us to assess the relative importance of the different features. In this set of experiments, the most important features were (in order) the *DistanceInKM* between user and result business, the *ResultRelevance* and the *Implicit_DistanceInKM* between a business and the center of a city explicitly mentioned in the query. As expected, these very general measures of distance and relevance were the key factors in ranking – result *popularity* was less significant, which is in part a result of these experiments being done "in vitro": judges were not about to visit the result business and hence not influenced by its actual quality. For the same reason, the features characterizing average route length and driving duration for direction requests did also rank lower in feature importance, as "typical" user behavior is unlikely to be reflected via relevance judgements. Still, the aggregate features resulted in a noticeable improvement in nDCG, validating our use of external sources for ranking. The likely main reason for the additional improvement when adding the *backoff* features were features characterizing the differences (in route time/ length and popularity) between the business b to be ranked and the other businesses in the *filter set*, which ranked highest among the *backoff* features. Otherwise, few *backoff* features ($\leq 3\%$) were picked up by the classifier.

6.4 Experiments using Click Data

Dataset: Our second set of experiments uses logs of queries and displayed results from a commercial local search engine as well as click information. The motivation behind using this data is that it is able to capture additional real-life considerations (e.g., the attractiveness of the surroundings of a result, or the impact of time, etc.) that matter in (mobile) local search, but are hard to model through off-line relevance judgements.

The logs used were sampled at random (at the level on individual queries, for which we recorded the top-10 results and their clicks); in total, we recorded 352K impressions. We only considered queries for which there was at least one click on a result. All queries are in English and contain up to 6 query terms. Because we lack relevance judgements for this data, we instead use the features we generate for the task of predicting which of the results will receive clicks. Given the close relationship between the rate at which a result is clicked and its relevance, features that help us improve the accuracy of click prediction are also very likely to be beneficial for result ranking. We chose the MART parameters using the validation set, using 35 leaves in the MART regression trees, $M = 200$ iterations and a different 85% sample for each split.

Performance Measure: We report the error in click prediction (i.e., the 1 minus the *accuracy*) of the click-predictor.

Results and Discussion: For the purpose of evaluating our techniques, the most interesting results are seen when looking at the clicks for top-ranking results – for the lower results there is a high baseline probability that no click may occur. We present the performance for the different features sets defined above when predicting a click on the top result in Figure 8 (note that we are using the prediction error in this graph, so lower values are better). The fraction of clicks in the test data for this experiment is 47.13%, meaning that the accuracy of the click-predictor based on each feature set significantly improves upon this probability. As we can see, similar to the earlier ranking experiments, using the *aggregate* feature set results in a significant improvement over the *baseline* one. Unlike before, the improvement resulting from the *backoff* features is even more significant. It appears that these can capture various aspects of popularity and distance "sensitivity", which appear to make a noticeable difference regarding user clicks.

	Baseline	Aggregate	Backoff	NN	Pivot
Prediction Error	0.3245	0.3155	0.2894	0.2932	0.2938

Figure 8: Prediction error for clicks at rank-position 1

Feature Importance Analysis: The most important features for this experiment are shown in Figure 9. Here, the top-ranking feature (after the result rank itself) was *ResultRelevance*; however, unlike the earlier experiments, none of the various features encoding distance between user and business was among the top-5 features (most likely, because the result rank already reflected the distance to a large degree). Among the features in the *aggregate* set, the most important ones were the *WebsiteCohostedEntities* (which is a strong indicator of the overall success of a business, as the businesses with more than one location associated with a site are typically large, nation-wide chains), followed by the *DistanceToCoffee* (which is a proxy of the attractiveness of an area), both of which were among the 5 most important features. In addition to *DistanceToCoffee*, the feature *HitRateZip*, which encodes the attractiveness of an area using the mobile search logs, also ranks among the top 10 most important features, reflecting the importance of surroundings/location as opposed to the absolute distance of the business itself. Unlike the previous experiment, about 50% of the *backoff*

Feature Importance	Feature Name
1.0000	*Result_Relevance*
0.3945	*QueryMatchesEntityCategory*
0.3865	*WebsiteCohostedEntities*
0.3499	*DistanceToCoffee*
0.3320	*QueryMatchesEntityName*
0.2852	*DistanceInKM*
...	...
0.2117	*HitRateZip*
...	...

Figure 9: Feature Importance in Click Prediction

features are picked up by the model. Interestingly, the 10 most important *backoff* features all relax all three distance dimensions. This illustrates the value of our approach's ability to incorporate multiple, very different notions of distance and relax multiple of them in parallel. Also, most of these top-ranking *backoff* features have relatively large values α (8 of the top-10 features used the larger thresholds $\alpha \in \{0.025, 0.05\}$), which points to the value of coarser aggregates which trade off the coherence of objects for a larger number of observations from the external logs.

7. CONCLUSION

In this paper, we explored the benefits of additional signals derived from external logs for local search ranking. Here, we first described a number of logs and the type of user behavior captured by them in detail. Given that the logs can be sparse, skewed and noisy, we proposed an approach to alleviate these challenges through the use of a novel backoff framework that is highly customizable through different distance functions. We proposed two concrete backoff techniques, characterized their asymptotic overhead and evaluated the quality of the resulting features using human judged query-result pairs as well as click-through data from a commercial local search engine. Here, we showed that even without the backoff scheme, features derived from the external logs resulted in significant improvements in nDCG as well as click-prediction accuracy. Moreover, the aggregate features generated through the backoff approaches resulted in significant further improvements, especially in the experiments on real click data, which reflect a number of real-life factors that influence local search user behavior that are difficult to capture through human relevance judgements.

8. REFERENCES

[1] T. Abou-Assaleh and W. Gao. Geographic ranking for a local search engine. In *SIGIR* 2007.

[2] D. Agarwal, A. Z. Broder, D. Chakrabarti, D. Diklic, V. Josifovski, and M. Sayyadian. Estimating rates of rare events at multiple resolutions. In *SIGKDD* 2007.

[3] V. N. Anh and A. Moffat. Pruned query evaluation using pre-computed impacts. In *SIGIR* 2006.

[4] J. Arguello, F. Diaz, J. Callan, and J.-F. Crespo. Sources of Evidence for Vertical Selection. In *SIGIR* 2009.

[5] S. Asadi, X. Zhou, and G. Yang. Using local popularity of web resources for geo-ranking of search engine results. *World Wide Web*, 12(2), 2009.

[6] L. Backstrom, J. Kleinberg, R. Kumar, and J. Novak. Spatial variation in search engine queries. In *WWW* 2008.

[7] S. Börzsönyi, D. Kossmann, and K. Stocker. The skyline operator. In *ICDE* 2001.

[8] C. Burges. From ranknet to lambdarank to lambdamart: An overview. Technical report, Microsoft Research, 2010.

[9] C. J. C. Burges, R. Ragno, and Q. V. Le. Learning to rank with nonsmooth cost functions. In *NIPS* 2006.

[10] L. Cao and J. Krumm. From gps traces to a routable road map. In *GIS* 2009.

[11] Y.-Y. Chen, T. Suel, and A. Markowetz. Efficient query processing in geographic web search engines. In *SIGMOD* 2006.

[12] J. Chomicki, P. Godfrey, J. Gryz, and D. Liang. Skyline with presorting: Theory and optimizations. In *Intelligent Information Systems* 2005.

[13] G. Cong, C. S. Jensen, and D. Wu. Efficient retrieval of the top-k most relevant spatial web objects. *Proc. VLDB Endow.*, 2(1), 2009.

[14] I. De Felipe, V. Hristidis, and N. Rishe. Keyword search on spatial databases. In *ICDE* 2008.

[15] R. Fagin, A. Lotem, and M. Naor. Optimal aggregation algorithms for middleware. *J. Comput. Syst. Sci.*, 66(4), 2003.

[16] J. Friedman. Greedy Function Approximation: a Gradient Boosting Machine. *Annals of Statistics*, 29(5), 2001.

[17] R. Göbel, A. Henrich, R. Niemann, and D. Blank. A hybrid index structure for geo-textual searches. In *CIKM* 2009.

[18] D. Hillard, S. Schroedl, E. Manavoglu, H. Raghavan, and C. Leggetter. Improving ad relevance in sponsored search. In *WSDM* 2010.

[19] P. G. Ipeirotis and L. Gravano. When one sample is not enough: Improving text database selection using shrinkage. In *SIGMOD* 2004.

[20] K. Järvelin and J. Kekäläinen. Cumulated gain-based evaluation of ir techniques. *ACM TOIS*, 20(4), 2002.

[21] T. Joachims, L. Granka, B. Pan, H. Hembrooke, F. Radlinski, and G. Gay. Evaluating the accuracy of implicit feedback from clicks and query reformulations in web search. *ACM TOIS*, 25(2), 2007.

[22] S. Katz. Estimation of probabilities from sparse data for the language model component of a speech recognizer. *IEEE Transactions on Acoustics, Speech and Signal Processing*, 35(3), 1987.

[23] J. Krumm. A survey of computational location privacy. *Personal Ubiquitous Comput.*, 13(6), 2009.

[24] N. D. Lane, D. Lymberopoulos, F. Zhao, and A. T. Campbell. Hapori: Context-based Local Search for Mobile Phones using Community Behavioral Modeling and Similarity. In *Ubicomp* 2010.

[25] Y. Lu, F. Peng, X. Wei, and B. Dumoulin. Personalize web search results with user's location. In *SIGIR* 2010.

[26] Q. Mei and K. Church. Entropy of search logs: how hard is search? with personalization? with backoff? In *WSDM* 2008.

[27] J. Paek, J. Kim, and R. Govindan. Energy-efficient Rate-adaptive GPS-based Positioning for Smartphones. In *MobiSys* 2010.

[28] F. Radlinski and T. Joachims. Active exploration for learning rankings from clickthrough data. In *SIGKDD* 2007.

[29] M. Richardson, E. Dominowska, and R. Ragno. Predicting clicks: estimating the click-through rate for new ads. In *WWW* 2007.

[30] S. E. Robertson and S. Walker. Some simple effective approximations to the 2-poisson model for probabilistic weighted retrieval. In *SIGIR* 1994.

[31] G. Sun, J. Chen, W. Guo, and K. Liu. Signal processing techniques in network-aided positioning: a survey of state-of-the-art positioning designs. *IEEE Signal Processing Magazine*, 22(4), 2005.

[32] L. Wang, C. Wang, X. Xie, J. Forman, Y. Lu, W.-Y. Ma, and Y. Li. Detecting dominant locations from search queries. In *SIGIR* 2005.

[33] R. W. White, M. Bilenko, and S. Cucerzan. Studying the use of popular destinations to enhance web search interaction. In *SIGIR* 2007.

[34] Q. Wu, C. J. Burges, K. M. Svore, and J. Gao. Ranking, Boosting, and Model Adaptation. Technical report, Microsoft Research, 2008.

[35] X. Yi, H. Raghavan, and C. Leggetter. Discovering users' specific geo intention in web search. In *WWW* 2009.

[36] C. Zhai and J. D. Lafferty. A study of smoothing methods for language models applied to information retrieval. *ACM TOIS*, 22(2), 2004.

Query Suggestions in the Absence of Query Logs

Sumit Bhatia
Computer Science and Engineering
Pennsylvania State University
University Park, PA-16802, USA
sumit@cse.psu.edu

Debapriyo Majumdar
IBM Research India
Bengaluru-560045, India
debapriyo@in.ibm.com

Prasenjit Mitra
Information Science and Technology
Pennsylvania State University
University Park, PA-16802, USA
pmitra@ist.psu.edu

ABSTRACT

After an end-user has partially input a query, intelligent search engines can suggest possible completions of the partial query to help end-users quickly express their information needs. All major web-search engines and most proposed methods that suggest queries rely on search engine query logs to determine possible query suggestions. However, for customized search systems in the enterprise domain, intranet search, or personalized search such as email or desktop search or for infrequent queries, query logs are either not available or the user base and the number of past user queries is too small to learn appropriate models. We propose a probabilistic mechanism for generating query suggestions from the corpus without using query logs. We utilize the document corpus to extract a set of candidate phrases. As soon as a user starts typing a query, phrases that are highly correlated with the partial user query are selected as completions of the partial query and are offered as query suggestions. Our proposed approach is tested on a variety of datasets and is compared with state-of-the-art approaches. The experimental results clearly demonstrate the effectiveness of our approach in suggesting queries with higher quality.

Categories and Subject Descriptors

H.3.3 [**Information Storage and Retrieval**]: Information Search and Retrieval – Query formulation

General Terms

Algorithms, experimentation

Keywords

Query suggestion, query formulation, query completion, query log analysis, enterprise search.

1. INTRODUCTION

As users start typing a query in search engines' query boxes, most search engines assist users by providing a list of queries that have been proven to be effective in the past [26]. The user can quickly choose one of the suggested completions (in some cases, alternatives) and thus, does not have to type the whole query herself. Feuer et al. [15] analyzed more than 1.5 million queries from search logs of a commercial search engine and found that query suggestions accounted for roughly 30% of all the queries indicating the important role played by query suggestions in modern information retrieval systems. Furthermore, Kelly et al. [20] observed that the use of offered query suggestions is more for difficult topics, i.e., topics about which users have little knowledge to formulate good queries.

Most existing works on query suggestion utilize query logs to suggest queries [2, 4, 9, 10, 13, 18, 24, 25, 27]. Such query log based techniques are suitable for systems with a large user base. For example, web search engines have millions of users and if a user has some information need, almost always it turns out that some other users have searched for the same information before. The search engine can then utilize these large amounts of past usage data to offer possible query suggestions.

The scenario, however, is quite different for information retrieval systems that are not on the web or have a smaller user base, and thus, lack large amounts of query log data. For example, search engines built for customized applications in the enterprise domain are used by only a few hundreds or thousands of users. An effective query suggestion mechanism is required because the difference between users not finding some critical information and the users finding the information with ease may have a very significant business impact for the organization. The query logs of such systems are relatively much smaller, especially when a system is newly deployed for a small number of users, and even later on, the log seldom becomes as exhaustive as that of a web search engine. Even if a system can accumulate a relatively large query log over time, it would take a lot of time to be mature enough and most often that time is not affordable due to business needs. Furthermore, the data residing in these systems are also so customized that using a query log from another system is not a valid approach. However, the effectiveness of such enterprise search systems has significant business implications and even a small improvement can have a positive impact on the organization's business. Similarly, for personal data search systems, such as desktop search or personal email search, often there is only a single user resulting in very small query logs. Besides, query logs may not always be accessible in some applications due to privacy and legal constraints. Furthermore, even in the case of general-purpose web search engines, end-users sometimes pose queries that are not there in query logs or are not very frequent. *How to offer meaningful query suggestions to users in such scenarios* is thus, an interesting research problem, which we explore in this paper.

SIGIR'11, July 24–28, 2011, Beijing, China.

Effective query suggestion requires inferring a user's query intent and information needs and then suggesting queries that may help retrieve documents containing relevant information. Formulating such queries that can help information retrieval systems discriminate between relevant and irrelevant documents requires predicting and using words, phrases or their combinations that are present in relevant documents and absent in irrelevant documents, which is an extremely difficult task for an average end-user [8]. Cui et al. [14] have shown that in the term vector-space, a large gap exists between the terms used by users to formulate queries and terms that are present in relevant documents. The aim of a query suggestion mechanism then is to iteratively use the partial information about the user's need in the form of incomplete queries and to suggest to the end user queries that match the end-user's information needs and those for which the search engine knows good results. Inspired by this, we propose a *document-centric probabilistic mechanism* to generate query suggestions that does not depend on query logs and utilizes only the co-occurrence of terms in the corpus. The central idea of our approach is simple and intuitive. As soon as a user starts typing a query, phrases from the corpus that are highly related to the partial user-entered-query are selected as possible completions of the partial query and thus completed queries are offered as query suggestions.

We evaluated our proposed approach with a variety of datasets and compared the performance of our approach with that of the state-of-the-art approach [6] and that of one available in a widely used open-source enterprise search system [1]. The experimental results demonstrate the superiority of our method in its ability to *(i)* offer suggestions for a wide variety of queries, *(ii)* offer more contextually meaningful suggestions, and *(iii)* generate suggested queries with higher retrieval effectiveness when compared to the baselines.

As we discuss in Section 2, though there have been some works in the past that can be adopted for query suggestion without using query logs, but strictly speaking, to the best of our knowledge, this paper is the first to study the problem of *query suggestions in the absence of query logs*. Our approach is simple yet effective and powerful, and as discussed later in Section 6, it also opens up several aspects of improvements and future work aligned with the concept of facilitating user's search without the aid of query logs.

The rest of the paper is organized as follows. Section 2 provides a review of the previous work on query suggestion – both with and without query logs. In Section 3, we define the problem formally and describe the proposed probabilistic approach in detail. Experiments and results are described in Sections 4 and 5. Section 6 concludes the paper and offers directions for future work.

2. RELATED WORK

2.1 Relation With Interactive Query Expansion

Query suggestion differs from interactive query expansion (IQE) [16] in a fundamental way. In IQE, the user is offered a list of suggested terms from which she can select a few to *augment the original query*. However, users tend to prefer complete query suggestions to individual term suggestions because of the additional context provided by the complete query suggestion as opposed to an isolated term suggestion [20]. The Real Time Query Expansion (RTQE) technique as proposed by White and Marchionini [28] can also be seen as a means for providing real-time query expansions where a list of expansion terms is offered in real time that the user can select and expand the query. However, in addition to offering only single terms as suggestions, this method is limited by the fact that it requires the user to type complete query terms and can not offer suggestions for incomplete query terms as the goal here is to *refine the original query* so as to improve the retrieval performance. On the other hand, query suggestion mechanisms try to *suggest various possible completions* of the (incomplete) query the user is still typing so as to save time and cover various possible interpretations of the user's information needs.

2.2 Query Suggestion using Query Logs

Large scale web search engine logs contain real, user issued queries. Initial works on query suggestion focus on identifying past queries similar to the current user query. Baeza-Yates et al. [2] cluster queries present in search logs and given an initial query, similar queries from its cluster are identified based on vector similarity metrics and are then suggested to the user. Barouni-Ebrahimi and Ghorbani utilize phrases frequently occurring in queries submitted by past users as suggestions [4]. Gao et al. describe a query suggestion mechanism for cross lingual information retrieval where for queries issued in one language, queries in other languages can also be suggested [17].

In addition to user queries, query logs also contain valuable clickthrough data and session information. Many of the previous works on query suggestion, especially in the web domain, exploit this additional information. By utilizing clickthrough data and session information, Cao et al. propose a context aware query suggestion approach [10]. In order to deal with the data sparseness problem, they use *concept* based query suggestions where a *concept* is defined as a set of similar queries mined from the query-URL bi-partite graph. The user's *context* is defined as the sequence of concepts about which the user has issued queries before submitting the current query. Given this context information, queries that are asked frequently in a given context are mined from search logs and are suggested to the user. For a given user query, Ma et al. [24] utilize clickthrough data to identify semantically related queries from query logs. Song and He [27] combine information from clicked URLs as well as skipped URLs to identify suggestions for rare queries.

In a single search session, a user often modifies her initial query a few times in order to obtain the relevant information. Jones et al. [18] utilize such modifications made by previous users for suggesting queries to other users. Li et al. [22] describe a method to compute pairwise similarity scores between queries based on the hypothesis that queries that co-occur in a search session are related. Given a user query, most similar queries thus identified are used as suggestions. Cucerzan and White [13] utilize user *landing pages* (pages where users finally end up after post-query navigation) to generate query suggestions. For each landing page of a user submitted query, they identify queries from query logs that have these landing pages as one of their top ten results. These queries are then used as suggestions.

Boldi et al. [9] utilize *query flow graphs* for query suggestions. Nodes in a query flow graph are past user queries and an edge from q_i to q_j indicates that both queries are related to a similar information need. Short random walks on a query flow graph are then conducted to generate query suggestions. Baraglia et al. [3] however, note that the models based on query flow graphs suffer from an ageing effect and suggesting queries using the information extracted from them may not be possible over time.

Mei et al. [25] propose an algorithm based on hitting time on the Query-URL bipartite graph derived from search logs. Starting from a given initial query, a subgraph is extracted from the Query-URL bipartite using depth first search. A random walk is then conducted on this subgraph and hitting time is computed for all the query nodes. Queries with the smallest hitting time are then used as suggestions. Ma et al. [23] show how the hitting time analysis on Query-URL bipartite graph can be utilized to diversify suggestions.

2.3 Query Suggestion without Query Logs

Among the works where query logs are not used as the primary resource, Feuer et al. [15] describe a proximity search based system that suggests alternate queries if the initial query is highly specific (results in very few documents) or too broad (large number of search results). In case of underspecified queries, most frequent terms appearing in close proximity of the query terms in the corpus are added to the query to narrow down the search results. For specific queries, most frequent subphrases of the query are presented as possible modifications. Their work however is similar in principle to *query refinement* and is quite different from query suggestion where the objective is to present different possible queries to the user as soon as she starts typing in the query box. Furthermore, their approach is not real time and requires the user to type a complete query first.

Bast and Weber developed the CompleteSearch engine [6, 5], which is an efficient instant search system that computes and presents search results online and refreshes the results with each letter typed or modified by the user. It also offers real-time auto-completion of the last query term being typed by the user. These completions are extracted from the search results obtained by using the incomplete query (and the primary goal of their work is to use an efficient index to find those search results), in the order of decreasing frequency of the term's occurrence in the search results. When viewed as a query suggestion system, CompleteSearch is limited in the sense that it only offers completions of the last query word instead of suggesting complete queries related to the incomplete query. Moreover, it requires the user to type at least two characters of the last query term. Also, using frequency as the only criterion for ranking the completions is not an optimal choice as the most frequent completions of the last query word often are not related to the query terms already typed by the user. However, the auto-completion feature in their system can be viewed as a query suggestion system, and hence we consider this method as a baseline in our experiments.

3. PROPOSED APPROACH

3.1 Problem Setup and Solution Overview

Consider a user u who has an information need $\mathcal{I}$. She transforms the information need into a query Q and starts typing the query in the query box of a search engine. The user has some information need but is not sure what terms to use to formulate a query. Since the documents indexed by the search engine are not visible to the user, often the terms selected by the user to formulate the queries do not lead to good retrieval performance due to the gap between query-term space and document-term space [14]. To help the user, information retrieval system can search the query logs to identify queries similar to the user's query that have been successful in the past and can suggest such queries to the user. However, our goal is to offer query suggestions to the user even in scenarios where query logs are not available. In the absence of query logs, we adopt a document-centric approach by utilizing the documents in the corpus itself to generate query suggestions on the fly. We extract and index phrases from the document corpus and when the user starts typing a query, we utilize these phrases to complete the partial user query. The completed queries are then offered as suggestions to the user. In the remainder of this section, we first describe the phrase extraction process and then discuss how these phrases can be used to generate query suggestions.

3.2 Phrase Extraction

In order to create a database of phrases that can be used for completing partial user queries, we extract all N-grams of order 1, 2 and 3 (that is unigrams, bigrams and trigrams) from the document corpus. One can also extract higher order N-grams but the number of possible N-grams increases exponentially with the order N [19, Chapter 4] and hence, is not scalable for any real world corpus. Further, while extracting N-grams, we need to take special care of the stop words. Consider the phrase `president of usa`. Each of the possible bi-grams from this phrase (`president of`, `of usa`) starts or ends with a stop word and is thus, an *incomplete* phrase. Hence, they are not desired as the resulting query completions. One possible solution can be to remove all the stop-words from corpus before extracting N-grams. However, removing stop-words may also lead to loss of semantics and make the resulting suggestions harder to understand. For example, compare `president usa` with `president of usa` and `president in usa`. If we remove the stop-words, the second and third phrase will both reduce to the first phrase even though they mean different things. In order to avoid such difficulties, we use an idea similar to skip-grams [19, Chapter 4] from natural language processing. Instead of *skipping over* and *discarding* the adjacent words, whenever we encounter a stop-word we *jump over* to the next word and *retain* the stop-word so that the resulting phrases do not start or end with stop words. Thus, in the above example, we will only have *one* bi-gram (`president of usa`). Note that now the order of an N-gram is *not* the number of words in the N-gram but the number of *non stop-words*.

3.3 Probabilistic Model for Query Suggestion

Consider the time instant when the user has typed first k characters of the query, which we denote by Q_1^k. Note that these k characters can contain a space character and if it does that means the user has typed more than one query term. Let $\mathcal{P} = \{p_1, p_2, \ldots, p_n\}$ denote the set of extracted phrases that can be used for generating query suggestions and let $\mathcal{V}$ be the vocabulary of the corpus available to us. Given the incomplete query Q_1^k, $\mathcal{V}$ and $\mathcal{P}$ we wish to construct a set $\mathcal{S} \subset \mathcal{P}$ such that each $s \in \mathcal{S}$ is a possible completion for Q_1^k.

Ideally, we want to offer suggestions to the user such that the queries represent the information need of the user. However, the only information we have about the user is the incomplete query Q_1^k. Further, different users having different information needs can start with same Q_1^k. For example, the queries **linux in**`terview questions` and **linux in**`stallation` have the same prefix `linux in`. Thus, for a given partial query Q_1^k, our task is to select phrases that can be used for generating possible query suggestions. To solve this problem, we ask this question: *Given a partial query Q_1^k and a phrase $p_i \in \mathcal{P}$, what is the probability $P(p_i|Q_1^k)$, i.e., the probability that the user will eventually type p_i after typing Q_1^k?* Once we answer the above question, we can order the phrases by the probability of their being typed after Q_1^k and use the top ranked phrases for offering suggestions to the user. We now describe how to compute $P(p_i|Q_1^k)$.

We start by making the observation that at any given instant of time, Q_1^k can be decomposed as follows:

$$Q_1^k = Q_c + Q_t \qquad (1)$$

where, Q_c denotes the completed portion of the query, i.e., the set of words that the user has typed completely. Note that $|Q_c| \geq 0$.

Q_t is the last word of Q_1^k that the user is still typing. Note that it may be a complete word or a partial word. Further, $|Q_t| \in \{0, 1\}$.

Using Bayes' theorem, the probability $P(p_i|Q_1^k)$ can be written as:

$$P(p_i|Q_1^k) = \frac{P(p_i) \times P(Q_1^k|p_i)}{P(Q_1^k)} \quad (2)$$

Further, assuming that the query terms are conditionally independent, $P(Q_1^k|p_i)$ can be written as:

$$P(Q_1^k|p_i) = P(Q_t|p_i) \times P(Q_c|p_i) \quad (3)$$

Using equations 2 and 3, we have:

$$P(p_i|Q_1^k) = \frac{P(p_i) \times P(Q_t|p_i) \times P(Q_c|p_i)}{P(Q_1^k)} \quad (4)$$

where, Q_t and Q_c are as defined in equation (1).
By definition of joint probability, we have:

$$P(p_i)P(Q_t|p_i) = P(p_i, Q_t) = P(Q_t)P(p_i|Q_t). \quad (5)$$

Application of equation (4) to equation (5) yields:

$$P(p_i|Q_1^k) = \frac{P(Q_t)P(p_i|Q_t)P(Q_c|p_i)}{P(Q_1^k)} \quad (6)$$

Further, we note that Q_1^k and Q_t remain the same for all the phrases given a user submitted partial query. Therefore $P(Q_t)$ and $P(Q_1^k)$ are constants for a given user query and thus, can be safely ignored since we are interested only in the relative ordering of phrases. Taking these observations into account, equation (6) reduces to:

$$P(p_i|Q_1^k) \overset{rank}{=} \underbrace{P(p_i|Q_t)}_{\text{phrase selection probability}} \times \underbrace{P(Q_c|p_i)}_{\text{phrase-query correlation}} \quad (7)$$

The above equation summarizes our proposed model for query suggestion. The first component of equation (7) measures the probability that phrase p_i can be typed by the user given that he has already typed Q_t. The second component measures the correlation between p_i and component Q_c of the user query. We now describe how these two probabilities can be estimated.

3.4 Estimating Phrase Selection Probability

Selecting a candidate phrase given a partial word is a two step process. First find a completion of the partial word and then select a phrase that contains that completed word. Figure 1 illustrates this process in terms of a graphical model that can be used to estimate $P(p_i|Q_t)$. The root node corresponds to the event that the user has typed Q_t – a partial word. This partial word can be completed in m different ways where m is the number of words in vocabulary that start with Q_t. Let $\mathcal{C} = c_1, \ldots, c_m$ be the set of m such possible word completions represented by corresponding nodes in Figure 1. Let $\mathcal{P}_i = p_{i1}, \ldots, p_{in_i}$ be the set of n_i phrases that contain the completed word c_i. Given Q_t, each completion c_i has a probability $P(c_i|Q_t)$ of being selected. Once c_i is selected as a possible word completion, we select a phrase $p_{ij} \in P_i$ with the probability $P(p_{ij}|c_i)$. In this way, the probability of selecting a phrase given a partial word is expressed as follows.

$$P(p_{ij}|Q_t) = \underbrace{P(c_i|Q_t)}_{\text{term completion probability}} \times \underbrace{P(p_{ij}|c_i)}_{\text{term to phrase probability}} \quad (8)$$

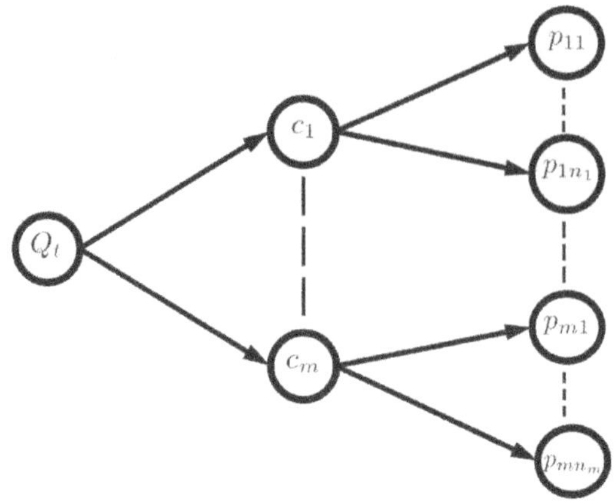

Figure 1: Graphical depiction of phrase selection process.

Since we have no other information about user's information need except for the partial word Q_t, we make a simplifying assumption. We assume that phrases in the corpus that are more important have a higher chance of being used by the user for formulating queries than the less important ones. One way to assess the importance of phrases is by using their occurrence frequencies in the corpus. However, this naïve approach has two serious shortcomings:

- In our formulation, the first step in phrase selection is to first find a completion c of the last query word Q_t with a probability $P(c|Q_t)$ and then select all phrases that contain that completion. If we use only raw frequencies to compute $P(c|Q_t)$, some of the important, but rare, completions will get suppressed. Hence, while computing $P(c_i|Q_t)$, we normalize the frequencies of different completions by their IDF values as follows.

$$P(c_i|Q_t) = \frac{freq(c_i) \times IDF(c_i)}{\sum_{i=1}^{m} freq(c_m) \times IDF(c_m)} \quad (9)$$

- In general, the frequency of unigrams in the corpus is much higher than the frequency of bigrams and trigrams. For the datasets used in this paper, we observe the average frequency of unigrams to be 15–25 times higher than the average bigram and trigram frequencies. Such large differences in frequency values suppresses the selection of bigrams and trigrams as compared to unigrams. Cui et al., [14] also faced similar problems and suggested using a constant multiplication factor to normalize the frequencies of bigrams and trigrams. Instead of using a constant factor for all phrases, we employed a normalization factor that normalizes raw frequencies of different order n-grams using the log ratio of their average frequencies as follows.

$$freq_{norm}(\text{order } m \text{ n-gram } p) = \frac{freq(p)}{log(avgFreq(m))} \quad (10)$$

where,
$avgFreq(m)$ is the average frequency of all n-grams of order m.

Using this formulation, the term to phrase probability can be computed as follows.

$$P(p_{ij}|c_i) = \frac{freq_{norm}(p_{ij})}{\sum_{k=1}^{n_i} freq_{norm}(p_{ki})} \quad (11)$$

3.5 Estimating Phrase-Query Correlation

The phrase selection component of equation (7) selects phrases on the basis of the last query word (Q_t) only. It does not take into account the context in which the user has typed Q_t. For example, consider following two partial queries: `bill gate` and `india gate`. The first query is related to Bill Gates and the second query is about a historical monument in India. For both these queries, the last word is same and therefore, we will end up with the same set of phrases for both these queries even though they represent very different information needs. Clearly, we require a mechanism to identify whether a given phrase is *contextually* important or not.

The second component of equation (7) takes into account such a relationship between a phrase and the user-submitted query. It represents the probability that the user has typed Q_c given that we know that the selected phrase p_i represents the completion of Q_c. In other words, given that p_i represents the latter half of the *complete query* we want to compute the probability that Q_c is the first half of the complete query.

By using the laws of probability, $P(Q_c|p_i)$ can be written as follows:

$$P(Q_c|p_i) = \frac{P(Q_c, p_i)}{P(p_i)} \quad (12)$$

Here, $P(Q_c, p_i)$ represents the probability of the joint occurrence of Q_c and p_i and $P(p_i)$ represents the probability of observing p_i alone. Both these probabilities can be estimated using the corpus as follows:

$$P(Q_c|p_i) = \frac{|D_{Q_c} \cap D_{p_i}|}{|D_{p_i}|} \quad (13)$$

Here, D_{p_i} and D_{Q_c} represent the sets of documents that contain phrase p_i and Q_c respectively. In order to find the set of documents containing a particular phrase p, we make a simplifying assumption and approximate D_p as the set of documents that contain all the constituent words in phrase p. Mathematically,

$$D_p \approx \bigcap_{w \in p} D_w \quad (14)$$

where D_w is the set of documents containing word w.

This approximation has two important advantages. First, it greatly simplifies finding the set D_p as all the required sets of documents containing the constituent words (i.e., D_w's in equation 14) are already available in the search engine's index in the form of postings lists of respective words. Second, it also helps overcome the data-sparseness problem. As an example, consider the following three search queries: `linux install firefox`, `install firefox linux` and `firefox install linux`. All these queries represent the same information need and are represented using the same set of terms. However, the ordering of the constituent terms is different in all three queries. Thus, it is possible that the phrases present in the corpus may have a different ordering than what the user has typed and thus, we will miss such phrases. Further, in the relevant documents these terms might not always appear together as a phrase. In Section 4, we show that the baseline method (SimSearch) that relies on such exact phrase matches performs poorly and is not able to offer any suggestions at all for many queries. Decomposing a phrase into its constituent terms avoids the above problems. By such a formulation, phrases that contain terms that co-occur frequently with the user query are given a higher weight. It also helps in making sure that the resulting query suggestions have good retrieval capability as the resulting query suggestions will consist of terms that frequently co-occur.

To summarize our approach, given a user query, the system first finds all the possible completions of the last query word. These completions are then used to identify a set of phrases that can be used for generating possible query suggestions. All the phrases in this candidate set are then assigned a probability score using equation 7. The top 10 highest scoring phrases are then presented to the user after appending to the Q_c portion of the user query.

		Ubuntu	TREC
No. of Documents		109,137	210,158
Avg Document Size (words)		378.02	374.26
N-Grams Extracted	**Unigrams**	114,702	191,123
	Bigrams	1,062,204	3,020,118
	Trigrams	888,492	2,677,026

Table 1: Different datasets used and their properties. These datasets differ in number of documents and average document length (measured in number of words). Number of words in a document was obtained by using the Unix wc command.

4. EXPERIMENTAL PROTOCOL

4.1 Data Description

We evaluated our proposed query suggestion mechanism using the following two datasets:

1. **TREC:** This dataset, available on TREC Disk4, consists of more than 200,000 news articles published in Financial Times between years 1991–1994.

2. **Ubuntu:** This dataset, used in previous research [7], consists of more than 100,000 discussion threads crawled from `ubuntuforums.org`, a set of 25 queries and relevance judgments. The documents contain discussions on various topics related to Linux and Ubuntu. One motivation for using this dataset was to test the robustness of the proposed approach as the text here is much more informal and noisy as compared to the TREC dataset.

For both the datasets, all the documents were pre-processed to remove punctuations and all the text was converted to lower case. N-Grams (order 1, 2 and 3) were extracted as described in Section 3. For extracting n-grams, stop words used came from a general stop word list of 429 words used in the Onix Test Retrieval Toolkit[1]. The number of N-Grams extracted for each dataset along with some other statistics are summarized in Table 1.

4.2 Baseline Methods

We compare our proposed approach with the following two baseline methods:

1. **Similarity based phrase search (SimSearch):** In this method, the phrase index is searched to find all the phrases that contain the user submitted partial query as a subphrase. The selected phrases are presented to the user in order of their

[1] http://www.lextek.com/manuals/onix/stopwords1.html

Dataset	Original Query	Type-A Query	Type-B Query
Ubuntu	automount hard drive partitions	automount	automount hard drive part
	virtualbox keyboard problem	virtualbox	virtualbox keyb
	wine microsoft office	wine	wine microso
TREC	falkland petroleum exploration	falkland	falkland petro
	encryption equipment export	encryption	encryption equip
	radioactive waste	radioactive	radioactive was

Table 2: Examples of queries used in experiments.

occurrence frequency. This method is used by the popular open source enterprise search server Solr[2].

2. **CompleteSearch (CompSearch):** This method refers to the query suggestion mechanism implemented in CompleteSearch search engine [6, 5] (as discussed in the section on related work).

We do not compare our system with any method that uses query logs because we strongly believe that such a comparison would essentially be comparing algorithms for totally different technical problems and would be unfair.

4.3 Test Queries

In order to compare our proposed approach with the baselines, we need a set of queries for which the suggestions can be generated. We evaluated our approach with a set of 40 test queries for each dataset. For the Ubuntu dataset, queries came from the 70 most searched for topics on ubuntu forums (provided by ubuntu forums) and for the TREC dataset, queries from TREC topics 351–400 (title field) were used. For each dataset, we removed stop words from each query, discarded all the single word queries and then randomly selected 20 queries from the remaining queries. Each such query was then used to generate two different partial queries as follows, leading to 40 partial test queries for each dataset.

- **Type-A Queries:** These queries were generated by retaining only the first keyword of each of the 20 queries.
- **Type-B Queries:** These queries were generated by retaining the first keyword of the query followed by the first k characters of the remaining query string ($2 \leq k \leq$ length of the remaining query string). The number k was selected at random for each query. Note that we use $k \geq 2$ because the CompSearch method requires users to type at least two characters as discussed in Section 2. The proposed method however, has no such restriction.

For example, the query correspinding to TREC topic 387 is `radioactive waste`. The type-A query for this query is `radioactive` and type-B query is `radioactive was`. This example also illustrates the main motivation behind generating two types of queries. Type-A queries are, in general, broader in scope than their type-B counterparts. For the query `radioactive`, all of `radioactive waste management`, `radioactive waste disposal` etc. could be valid query suggestions. However for `radioactive was`, the query suggestion mechanism should take into account the context in which the user is typing the last query word and ensure that queries such as `radioactive washington post` are not suggested. Some examples of queries used in our experiments are given in Table 2.

[2]`http://lucene.apache.org/solr/features.html#Query`

4.4 User Study

Due to the absence of standard test collections for the query suggestion task, we conducted a user study to measure the quality of the suggestions generated by different query suggestion methods. For each test query, we collected the top 10 suggestions generated by the three methods (SimSearch, CompSearch and our proposed method (Probabilistic)). Evaluation was performed with the help from 12 volunteers who were our colleagues and were not associated with the project. All the subjects were experienced users of search engines and used both web search engines as well as enterprise search engines on a daily basis. Each assessor was shown a randomly selected partial user query from the set of test queries and lists of query suggestions produced by the three methods. The order in which the suggestions produced by different methods were presented to the assessors was randomized for each query and each evaluator and the assessors did not know which set of suggestions was generated by which method. The suggestions produced by a particular method were presented in decreasing order of their respective scores. Each query was evaluated by three unique assessors and each provided evaluations for an equal number of test queries. For each query suggestion the subjects were asked to assign one rating from among the four possible options that are summarized in Table 3. The final rating for a suggestion was decided by a majority vote. By a *meaningful* (and hence relevant) suggestion for a partial query, we mean a query that represents *one possible prediction of the user's information need* as a valid search query, given the partial query typed by the user. Also, we do not desire almost duplicate suggestions, or malformed combination of words (which do not make sense) to appear in the list of suggestions. By designing the four options for rating each suggestion and by providing a clear guideline to the assessors, we made a best possible effort to convey the notion of a suggestion being *meaningful* to our assessors. The final judgments had to be subjective and we had to depend on our assessors as they are experienced users of several kinds of search engines and also the query suggestion features of web-search engines. In total, there were 1906 suggestions evaluated by the assessors and a majority decision (two out of three assessors assigned the same rating) was obtained for 91.45% (1743) of the suggestions. Further, 1147 suggestions were assigned a **Y**(meaningful) rating by the majority vote and out of these 915 suggestions were judged as **Y** by all the three assessors. These inter-assessor agreement results strongly indicate that the notion of suggestions being relevant or meaningful was considered very consistently among them.

A suggestion for which all the three assessors provided different ratings was assigned the rating of "Not Sure". For the purpose of comparing different query suggestion methods, we considered only suggestions marked as **Y** to be relevant and suggestions marked with any of the three remaining ratings were treated as non-

Rating	Meaning
Y	Yes, a meaningful suggestion
N	No, not a meaningful suggestion, or badly formed as a query
D	An (almost) duplicate suggestion, conveys no new information
??	Not sure

Table 3: Different rating options available to users and their meanings.

relevant. We use this information to compare success rates, precision etc. for the different methods in the following sub-sections.

4.5 Statistical Significance Tests

In order to assess the statistical significance of the results obtained, we used the paired two-sample one-tailed t-test. Statistically significant improvements over the SimSearch and CompSearch methods are indicated by **S** and **C**, respectively for $p < 0.01$ (99% confidence interval) whereas **s** and **c** indicate statistically significant improvements with $p < 0.05$ (95% confidence interval) over SimSearch and CompSearch, respectively.

5. RESULTS AND DISCUSSIONS

5.1 Success Rate of Different Methods

A popular metric to compare the performance of different query suggestion methods is *coverage*; it has been used previously to compare various query suggestion mechanisms [10, 18]. Coverage of a query suggestion method is defined as the fraction of queries for which the method is able to offer at least one query suggestion. However, we feel that coverage is, in general, a relaxed evaluation metric as it does not take into account the quality of the queries suggested. What if the queries suggested are not meaningful? As opposed to the query-log based query suggestion methods that generally offer frequent past *user queries* as suggestions, the query log oblivious methods evaluated in this paper *generate* suggestions by combining partial user query with terms/phrases derived from the corpus and hence, may not always generate meaningful queries. Also note that for a given partial query, in general, there will be *multiple* possible valid completions. We consider a query suggestion method successful for a given partial query if it is able to generate at least one meaningful suggestion for the partial query. The *Success Rate* for a query suggestion method is then defined as the fraction of queries for which the method was successful.

Table 4 summarizes success rates for different query suggestion methods on both the datasets. We show results separately for type-A queries, type-B queries and all queries considered together. We observe that the proposed method (Probabilistic) is able to generate at least one meaningful suggestion for all the queries in all cases. The CompSearch method fails to generate a meaningful suggestion for one type-B query for the TREC dataset. The SimSearch method on the other hand, performs worst and is not able to offer any meaningful suggestion for a large number of type-B queries. The improvements achieved by the Probabilistic and CompSearch methods over SimSearch were significant statistically. This is because the SimSearch method relies on finding phrases that contain the user-submitted partial query as a sub-phrase. However, as discussed in Section 3, this approach suffers from the data sparseness problem. Many times it happens that the query terms typed by the user are not present in the corpus as a phrase even though we may

	SimSearch	CompSearch	Probabilistic
Ubuntu			
Type-A	1.00	1.00	1.00
Type-B	0.75	1.00^{s}	1.00^{s}
Overall	0.875	1.00^{s}	1.00^{s}
TREC			
Type-A	1.00	1.00	1.00
Type-B	0.15	0.95^{S}	1.00^{S}
Overall	0.575	0.975^{S}	1.00^{S}

Table 4: Success Rate of different query suggestion methods for the two datasets. Superscripts s and S indicate statistically significant improvements over SimSearch with $p < 0.05$ and $p < 0.01$, respectively (one-tailed t-test).

have many documents in the corpus containing all the query terms. CompSearch and Probabilistic methods overcome the problem of data sparseness by using the last query word only to select a set of candidate phrases.

5.2 Quality of Suggestions

The user study described in a previous sub-section provided us with the information that whether a particular query suggestion was meaningful or not. By utilizing these relevance judgments, we now compare different query suggestion mechanisms for their ability to generate meaningful query suggestions. Some examples of suggestions generated by the different methods for some of the test queries are given in Table 5. The table illustrates some cases where the CompSearch and SimSearch methods failed to produce as many meaningful suggestions as our proposed approach. While for SimSearch failure to produce suggestions can be attributed to data sparseness as discussed before, poor performance of CompSearch is due to its limited scope as it only searches for most frequent completions of the last query word.

For a given query, the precision of a query suggestion method is defined as the fraction of suggestions generated that are meaningful. Note that since an exhaustive set of all possible suggestions for a given query is not available, recall cannot be computed. Also, for the query suggestion task, precision is a much more important metric than recall as the number of suggestions that can be offered is limited by the screen space. Hence high precision values at top ranks is favored for this task. Table 6 reports the MAP (mean average precision) values for different methods. The proposed method outperforms the two baseline methods, achieving statistically significant improvements in almost all the cases. We also show the precision values achieved by different methods at different ranks (rank 1 to 10) in Figure 2. We observe that the proposed method outperforms both the baselines methods in all the cases. The high MAP and precision values indicate that the proposed method is able to offer a larger number of meaningful suggestions in comparison to the baselines. Further, consistently high precision values at top ranks ($\approx 80\%$ till rank 3) indicate that in general, meaningful suggestions are presented at earlier ranks to the user, which is a very desirable characteristic. Also, the drop in precision values from rank one to last position is much less for the proposed approach in comparison to the baselines, illustrating the *consistency* of our proposed approach. The strengths of the proposed approach are displayed specifically by the results for type-B queries where it comprehensively outperforms both the baselines methods. These

Query = mount			Query = falkland		
SimSearch	**CompSearch**	**Prob**	**SimSearch**	**CompSearch**	**Prob**
mount	mount	mount	falklands	falklands	falklands
mounted	mounted	unable to mount	falkland	falkland	falklands war
mounting	mounting	mount point type	falkland islands	falklanders	falkland islands
mounts	mounts	sudo mount	falklands war		falklands conflict
sudo mount	mountpoint	able to mount	falklands conflict		1982 falklands
unable to mount	mountcifs	mountpoint	1982 falklands		1982 falklands conflict
system mount	mountable	try to mount	falkland islands government		falkland islands government
file system mount	mounter	mount the drive	1982 falklands conflict		falklands war in 1982
mount point type	mountunmount	mount the partition	falkland arms		1982 falklands war
system mount point type	mountpoints	file system mount	falklanders		invasion of the falklands
Query = screen resoluti			**Query = encryption equip**		
screen resolution	screen resolution	screen resolution	<No Suggestions Produced>	encryption equipment	encryption equipment
screen resolutions	screen resolutions	screen change the resolution			encryption digital equipment
preferences screen resolution	screen resolutionrefresh	screen native resolution			encryption office equipment
change screen resolution	screen resolutioni	screen set the resolution			encryption electronic equipment
screen resolution settings	screen resolutionbut	preferences screen resolution			encryption telephone equipment
login screen resolution	screen resolutio	screen correct resolution			encryption equipment and services
screen resolution hi	screen resolution1280	screen resolution and refresh			encryption video equipment
screen resolution issue	screen resolutionsrefresh	screen low resolution			encryption medical equipment
changing screen resolution	screen resolutionsize	screen monitor resolution			encryption transmission equipment
screen resolution preferences	screen resolutiondisplay	screen comparing resolution			encryption original equipment

Table 5: Examples of suggestions generated by different query suggestion methods.

Ubuntu			
	SimSearch	**CompSearch**	**Probabilistic**
Type-A	0.4597	0.1638	$\mathbf{0.5022}^{C}$
Type-B	0.2193	0.2309	$\mathbf{0.4746}^{SC}$
Overall	0.3395	0.1974	$\mathbf{0.4884}^{SC}$
TREC			
	SimSearch	**CompSearch**	**Probabilistic**
Type-A	0.5429	0.2709	$\mathbf{0.5697}^{C}$
Type-B	0.0614	0.2010	$\mathbf{0.3975}^{SC}$
Overall	0.3022	0.2359	$\mathbf{0.4836}^{SC}$

Table 6: Mean Average Precision (MAP) values achieved by different query suggestion methods for the two datasets. Superscripts S and C indicate statistically significant improvements over SimSearch and CompSearch methods, respectively (one tailed t-test, $p < 0.01$).

Ubuntu			
	SimSearch	**CompSearch**	**Probabilistic**
Type-A	3.4308	**3.7779**	3.5282^{s}
Type-B	2.8877	3.7118	$\mathbf{4.0856}^{Sc}$
Overall	3.1592	3.7448	$\mathbf{3.8069}^{S}$
TREC			
	SimSearch	**CompSearch**	**Probabilistic**
Type-A	4.7781	4.4922	$\mathbf{4.8323}^{c}$
Type-B	1.0497	4.9914	$\mathbf{5.5113}^{SC}$
Overall	2.9139	4.7418	$\mathbf{5.1718}^{SC}$

Table 7: Average clarity scores for queries generated by different query suggestion methods for the two datasets. Statistically significant improvements over SimSearch and CompSearch methods are indicated by superscripts S(s) and C(c), respectively using a one-tailed t-test with $p < 0.01$ ($p < 0.05$).

results assert the superiority of the proposed method in offering *contextually relevant* suggestions to the user.

5.3 Retrieval Effectiveness of Suggested Queries

One of the main motivation for query suggestion is to present users with queries that can lead to improved retrieval performance. What is the retrieval effectiveness of queries suggested by different methods and how do the different methods compare with each other? We try to find an answer to this question in this section.

We utilize *query clarity score* as proposed by Cronen-Townsend et al. [12] to measure the retrieval performance of suggested queries. Clarity score has been shown empirically to correlate positively with average precision [12] and is also used as a measure of ambiguity in a query with respect to a collection of documents [11,

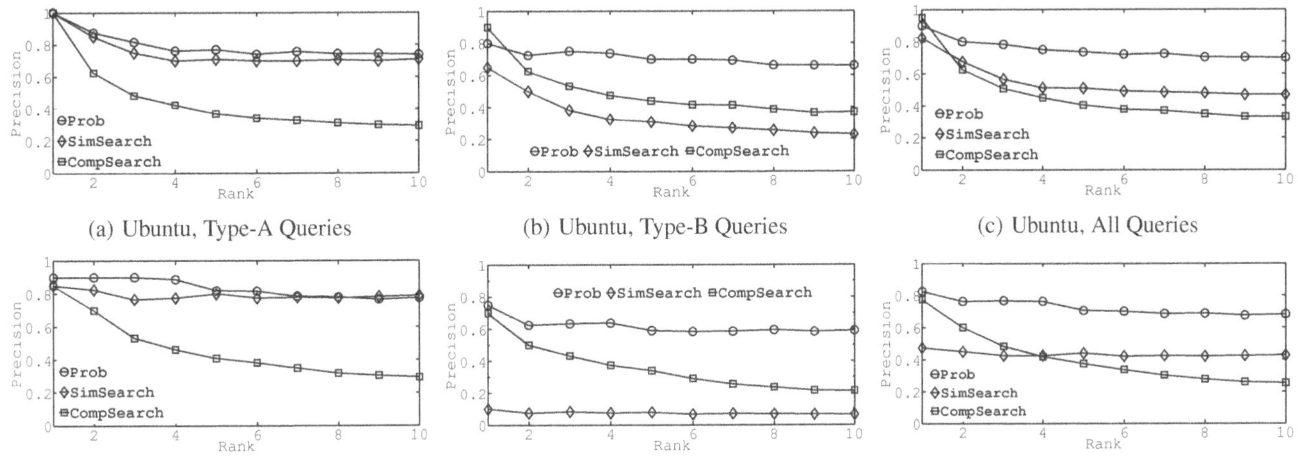

(a) Ubuntu, Type-A Queries (b) Ubuntu, Type-B Queries (c) Ubuntu, All Queries

(d) TREC, Type-A Queries (e) TREC, Type-B Queries (f) TREC, All Queries

Figure 2: Precision achieved by different query suggestion methods at different rank positions (rank 1 to rank 10) for Ubuntu and TREC datasets. First and second figures in each row show precision values for type-A and type-B queries respectively. The last figure in each row shows the precision values for all queries taken together. The proposed probabilistic method outperforms the two baseline methods in all cases. Also note that the drop in precision values for the proposed method is much less in comparison with the two baselines.

12]. Specifically, clarity score of a query increases if we add terms that reduce query ambiguity and it decreases on adding terms that make the query more ambiguous. Since we are generating suggestions by adding phrases to the partial user query, we expect the method that is able to select phrases related to the user query to have a higher clarity score. Note that for both the datasets used in this paper, relevance judgments are available only for *original queries* and not for the *suggested queries* that are generated by different query suggestion methods. Once we generate a partial query from an original topic, the suggested queries for that partial query can be different from the original topic (in fact diverse suggestions are desired). Therefore, retrieval effectiveness of the suggested queries cannot be measured by the available relevance judgments. Hence, the need for using a query performance predictor (clarity score).

Clarity score for a query is computed as the Kullback-Leibler divergence between the query language model and the collection language model. Mathematically, clarity score for a query q with respect to a collection of documents $\mathcal{C}$ is given by

$$\text{Clarity}(q, \mathcal{C}) = \sum_{v \in \mathcal{V}} P(v|q) \log_2 \frac{P(v|q)}{P(w|\mathcal{C})}, \qquad (15)$$

where $\mathcal{V}$ is the vocabulary of the collection.

For computing clarity score, we used the Lemur search engine toolkit[3]. The query language model was computed using the relevance model 1 as described by Lavrenko and Croft [21]. For each test query, we computed the clarity scores for all the suggestions generated by a particular query suggestion method and computed the average clarity value for resulting suggestions for the query. This computation is repeated for all the test queries and we report the mean average clarity values achieved by a query suggestion method. The results are summarized in Table 7.

From the table we observe that the proposed Probabilistic approach achieves statistically significant improvements over the baselines in all the cases except for CompSearch method with type-A queries for Ubuntu dataset. Here it is important to note that the SimSearch method failed to generate suggestions for many difficult queries and both the CompSearch and SimSearch methods generated less than 10 suggestions for many queries. On the other hand, the proposed method generated 10 suggestions for all the queries. Thus, the proposed method is able to offer suggestions for a variety of queries as well as it is able to generate suggestions without having an adverse effect on retrieval effectiveness of queries.

[3]`http://www.lemurproject.org/`

6. CONCLUSIONS AND FUTURE WORK

We have shown that meaningful query suggestions can be made in the absence of query logs with an unsupervised probabilistic approach using the occurrence of terms and phrases in a corpus of documents. Experimental results on two different datasets are encouraging and our proposed approach achieved statistically significant improvements over two state-of-the-art baselines. However, there are several aspects that have been out of the scope of this work and offer interesting future research directions, which we discuss below.

1. Our approach is essentially unsupervised and is limited to suggesting queries that are formed by combining a few related phrases from the corpus. Naturally, our system generates some suggestions that are badly formed and hence are not meaningful as search queries, although they may yield results as search queries. One possible future goal would be to ensure that the badly formed combination of phrases are eliminated from the suggestions.
2. Leveraging semantic and ontological information associated with the phrases would be another possible direction. Once the user has typed `hotel`, the system can try to consciously suggest queries such as `hotels in new york`, `hotels in bangalore`, etc. Use of synonyms and synonymous phrases to enable the system to suggest alternatives also needs to be explored.
3. Another interesting aspect that has been out of the scope of this paper is a systematic approach towards diversifying the suggested queries such that not only does the search engine suggest meaningful queries but it also suggests queries that cover a diverse range of concepts and thereby meets the information needs of a broad range of users.

4. In this work, we have primarily focused on the effectiveness of the queries suggested. The target systems for our approach typically have smaller scale datasets and so for that purpose, the efficiency of our algorithm is not critical, but it will be interesting to explore how we can produce similarly effective query suggestions more efficiently than we currently do so that our method can be applied to a relatively larger scale as well.

7. REFERENCES

[1] Solr–Enterprise Search Platform, `http://lucene.apache.org/solr/`.

[2] R. Baeza-Yates, C. Hurtado, and M. Mendoza. *Query Recommendation Using Query Logs in Search Engines*, volume 3268/2004 of *Lecture Notes in Computer Science*, pages 588–596. Springer Berlin / Heidelberg, November 2004.

[3] R. Baraglia, C. Castillo, D. Donato, F. M. Nardini, R. Perego, and F. Silvestri. Aging effects on query flow graphs for query suggestion. In *CIKM '09: Proceeding of the 18th ACM conference on Information and knowledge management*, pages 1947–1950, 2009.

[4] M. Barouni-Ebarhimi and A. A. Ghorbani. A novel approach for frequent phrase mining in web search engine query streams. In *CNSR '07: Proceedings of the Fifth Annual Conference on Communication Networks and Services Research*, pages 125–132, Washington, DC, USA, 2007. IEEE Computer Society.

[5] H. Bast and I. Weber. Type less, find more: Fast autocompletion search with a succinct index. In *SIGIR'06*, pages 364–371, 2006.

[6] H. Bast and I. Weber. The CompleteSearch Engine: Interactive, Efficient, and Towards IR& DB integration. In *CIDR'07*, pages 88–95, 2007.

[7] S. Bhatia and P. Mitra. Adopting inference networks for online thread retrieval. In *Proceedings of the Twenty-Fourth AAAI Conference on Artificial Intelligence*, pages 1300–1305, Atlanta, Georgia, USA, July 11-15 2010.

[8] D. C. Blair and M. E. Maron. An evaluation of retrieval effectiveness for a full-text document-retrieval system. *Commun. ACM*, 28(3):289–299, 1985.

[9] P. Boldi, F. Bonchi, C. Castillo, D. Donato, and S. Vigna. Query suggestions using query-flow graphs. In *WSCD '09: Proceedings of the 2009 workshop on Web Search Click Data*, pages 56–63, 2009.

[10] H. Cao, D. Jiang, J. Pei, Q. He, Z. Liao, E. Chen, and H. Li. Context-aware query suggestion by mining click-through and session data. In *KDD'08*, pages 875–883, 2008.

[11] S. Cronen-Townsend and W. B. Croft. Quantifying query ambiguity. In *Proceedings of the second international conference on Human Language Technology Research*, pages 104–109, San Francisco, CA, USA, 2002. Morgan Kaufmann Publishers Inc.

[12] S. Cronen-Townsend, Y. Zhou, and W. B. Croft. Predicting query performance. In *SIGIR '02: Proceedings of the 25th annual international ACM SIGIR conference on Research and development in information retrieval*, pages 299–306, 2002.

[13] S. Cucerzan and R. W. White. Query suggestion based on user landing pages. In *SIGIR '07: Proceedings of the 30th annual international ACM SIGIR conference on Research and development in information retrieval*, pages 875–876, 2007.

[14] H. Cui, J.-R. Wen, J.-Y. Nie, and W.-Y. Ma. Probabilistic query expansion using query logs. In *WWW '02: Proceedings of the 11th international conference on World Wide Web*, pages 325–332, 2002.

[15] A. Feuer, S. Savev, and J. A. Aslam. Evaluation of phrasal query suggestions. In *CIKM'07*, pages 841–848, 2007.

[16] B. M. Fonseca, P. B. Golgher, B. Pôssas, B. A. Ribeiro-Neto, and N. Ziviani. Concept-based interactive query expansion. In *CIKM'05*, pages 696–703, 2005.

[17] W. Gao, C. Niu, J.-Y. Nie, M. Zhou, J. Hu, K.-F. Wong, and H.-W. Hon. Cross-lingual query suggestion using query logs of different languages. In *SIGIR'07*, pages 463–470, 2007.

[18] R. Jones, B. Rey, O. Madani, and W. Greiner. Generating query substitutions. In *WWW '06: Proceedings of the 15th international conference on World Wide Web*, pages 387–396, 2006.

[19] D. Jurafsky and J. H. Martin. *Speech and Language Processing: An Introduction to Natural Language Processing, Speech Recognition, and Computational Linguistics*. Prentice-Hall, 2nd edition, 2009.

[20] D. Kelly, K. Gyllstrom, and E. W. Bailey. A comparison of query and term suggestion features for interactive searching. In *SIGIR '09: Proceedings of the 32nd international ACM SIGIR conference on Research and development in information retrieval*, pages 371–378, 2009.

[21] V. Lavrenko and W. B. Croft. Relevance based language models. In *SIGIR '01: Proceedings of the 24th annual international ACM SIGIR conference on Research and development in information retrieval*, pages 120–127, 2001.

[22] Y. Li, B. Wang, S. Xu, P. Li, and J. Li. Querytrans: Finding similar queries based on query trace graph. In *WI-IAT '09: Proceedings of the 2009 IEEE/WIC/ACM International Joint Conference on Web Intelligence and Intelligent Agent Technology*, pages 260–263, Washington, DC, USA, 2009. IEEE Computer Society.

[23] H. Ma, M. R. Lyu, and I. King. Diversifying query suggestion results. In *Proceedings of the Twenty-Fourth AAAI Conference on Artificial Intelligence, AAAI 2010, Atlanta, Georgia, USA, July 11-15, 2010*. AAAI Press, 2010.

[24] H. Ma, H. Yang, I. King, and M. R. Lyu. Learning latent semantic relations from clickthrough data for query suggestion. In *CIKM '08: Proceeding of the 17th ACM conference on Information and knowledge management*, pages 709–718, 2008.

[25] Q. Mei, D. Zhou, and K. Church. Query suggestion using hitting time. In *CIKM '08: Proceeding of the 17th ACM conference on Information and knowledge management*, pages 469–478, 2008.

[26] F. Silvestri. Mining query logs: Turning search usage data into knowledge. *Foundations and Trends in Information Retrieval*, 4(1–2):1–174, 2010.

[27] Y. Song and L. wei He. Optimal rare query suggestion with implicit user feedback. In *WWW '10: Proceedings of the 19th international conference on World wide web*, pages 901–910, 2010.

[28] R. W. White and G. Marchionini. Examining the effectiveness of real-time query expansion. *Inf. Process. Manage.*, 43(3):685–704, 2007.

Synthesizing High Utility Suggestions for Rare Web Search Queries

Alpa Jain
Yahoo! Labs
alpa@yahoo-inc.com

Umut Ozertem
Yahoo! Labs
umut@yahoo-inc.com

Emre Velipasaoglu
Yahoo! Labs
emrev@yahoo-inc.com

ABSTRACT

Search engines are continuously looking into methods to alleviate users' effort in finding desired information. For this, all major search engines employ query suggestions methods to facilitate effective query formulation and reformulation. Providing high quality query suggestions is a critical task for search engines and so far most research efforts have focused on tapping various information available in search query logs to identify potential suggestions. By relying on this single source of information, suggestion providing systems often restrict themselves to only previously observed query sessions. Therefore, a critical challenge faced by query suggestions provision mechanism is that of coverage, i.e., the number of unique queries for which users are provided with suggestions, while keeping the suggestion quality high. To address this problem, we propose a novel way of generating suggestions for user search queries by moving beyond the dependency on search query logs and providing synthetic suggestions for web search queries. The key challenges in providing synthetic suggestions include identifying important concepts in a query and systematically exploring related concepts while ensuring that the resulting suggestions are relevant to the user query and of high utility. We present an end-to end system to generate synthetic suggestions that builds upon novel query-level operations and combines information available from various textual sources. We evaluate our suggestion system over a large-scale real-world dataset of query logs and show that our methods increase the coverage of query-suggestion pairs by up to 39% without compromising suggestion quality or utility.

Categories and Subject Descriptors

H.3.3 [**Information Search and Retrieval**]: Query formulation

General Terms

Algorithms, Design, Experimentation, Measurement

Keywords

Query recommendations, search query logs, rare queries

1. INTRODUCTION

Search engines provide a variety of tools to assist users in better formulating their information needs. Examples include, suggestions for query completion, spell corrections and query reformulation. Among these, *post-submit query reformulation* suggestions, typically found in the left-column of a search engine's results page, focus on providing follow-up queries related to a user's original query. These suggestions can be categorized as: (1) *specializations* that expand the original query by adding terms, (2) *generalizations* that drop terms from the original query, and (3) *laterals* that suggest alternatives related to the original query and do not lexically overlap with the original query (e.g., suggesting 'myspace' to 'facebook').

Generating query suggestions has been the focus of several past research efforts [8, 13, 25, 29, 35] (see Section 7). Virtually all query suggestion techniques strictly depend on search query logs to discover query suggestions with sufficient statistics. Particularly, to mine lateral suggestions, the primary source of information is past *user sessions*, i.e., sequence of queries issued by a single user within a specific time window [4]. Unfortunately, relying on query session logs can restrict the coverage of queries for which post-submit suggestions are available: It is well known that the query distributions in web search are heavy tailed. To be more precise, in the query logs of a major search engine, we found that about 30% of unique queries that are observed in a given month are queries that were not seen within the past year before that month. User session logs are even further infrequent: in our experiments, we mined user session logs to derive lateral suggestions and over a random sample observed that 26.6% of unique queries have more than 5 suggestions, and 7.4% have between 1 and 4 suggestions, and the biggest portion is the queries with no suggestions that constitute 66% of the unique query traffic.

In this paper, we look into *building synthetic query reformulation suggestions*, i.e., suggestions that are not solely based on past user sessions. Our work is motivated by the following observation. Consider a simple query such as 'supercuts new jersey' for which no suggestions were provided by all major search engines. By appropriately tokenizing and relaxing this query, we may ascertain that 'supercuts' can be substituted by 'great clips' or 'fantastic sams' or 'cost cutters.' Further, by appending the context 'new jersey' from the original query, we can generate query suggestions such as 'great clips new jersey' or 'fantastic sams new jersey.' In line with this example, we are adding a forth category of suggestions which can be regarded as *partially lateral*, where we break the query into segments and make a lateral move of the parts, such as suggesting 'buca di beppo nutrition information' for 'macaroni grill nutrition information', or 'tampa bay fisheries' for 'tampa bay agriculture.'

The above example underscores several interesting challenges that need to be addressed. First, generating post-submit query suggestions differs from the task of query rewriting [3, 9, 16, 22, 26, 33, 34] which has mostly focused on rewriting queries to improve search results. Generating query suggestions differs from query rewriting in that we are now also interested in reformulations that are semantically related but not identical to the original query. For instance, for the user query 'tampa bay fisheries' we may provide 'tampa bay agriculture' as an interesting (lateral) query suggestion; however, this reformulation would not be considered for the task of improving search results since the latter query brings about different search results. Second, candidates for applying transformations need to be systematically identified. For instance, given the query 'supercuts new jersey' not all terms (e.g., 'new') can be substituted by related terms. Third, exploring synthetic queries can lead to suggestions that are not 'well-formed' or suggestions that are not semantically related to the user query. For instance, for the query 'tampa bay fisheries' we may generate 'tampa tribune fisheries' after identifying 'tampa bay' and 'tampa tribune' as related concepts. The resulting suggestion is however garbled and should be pruned. Finally, most query re-writing techniques consider query reformulation on a single query basis and do not account for the *utility* of the suggestion set as a whole. For instance, the query 'hawaii sunset pictures' could be reformulated as 'hawaii sunset photos' or 'hawaii sunset images'; while these suggestions are well-formed and relevant to the original query, they are less likely to differ in their result sets and thus in turn yield a low utility suggestion set. Note that this is not an issue when rewriting queries to improve search results.

To address these challenges, we develop an end-to-end system (see Figure 1) for synthesizing query suggestions. Our approach relies on a variety of query transformations over the original query in order to systematically explore candidates for query suggestions. As a key contribution, these generation methods do not solely rely on past user sessions but instead using query logs as a guide considers in concert several sources such as individual queries (i.e. queries not restricted by a session) in query logs, semantic information from web pages, and search results page. Given a set of candidate suggestions, we propose a holistic ranking mechanism which takes into account suggestion's (a) *well-formedness*, (b) *relevance* to the original query, and (c) *utility* to the user given other suggestions. In summary, our main contributions are as follows:

- A general framework for *synthesizing* suggestions for query reformulations that goes beyond query session logs.
- A variety of query transformations to systematically generate suggestion candidates (Sections 2 and 3).
- A holistic suggestion ranking technique that focuses on suggestion quality and utility (Section 4).
- An extensive experimental evaluation that includes user studies and real-world datasets (Section 5 and 6).

2. RELAXING USER QUERIES

Query suggestions is an assistance technique provided by search engines where given a user query q the search engine returns an ordered set S of suggestions for follow-up queries. For a large fraction of queries (e.g., tail queries), providing query suggestions is challenging since user session logs may not contain sufficient information. Our goal is to build for such queries an ordered set of S of useful suggestions for follow-up queries that are relevant to the user's original mission.

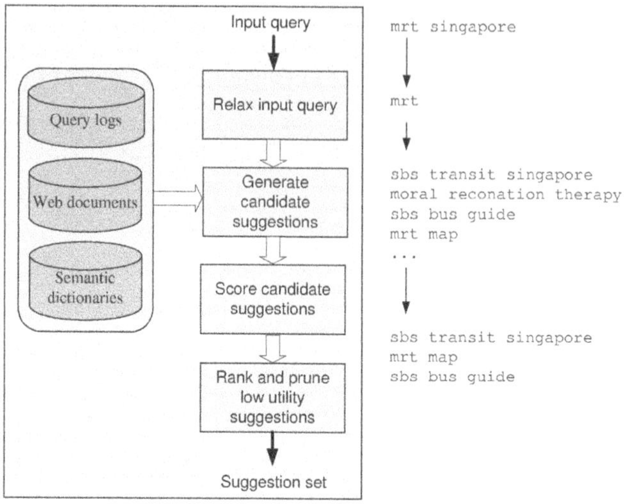

Figure 1: Stages of synthesizing query suggestions.

Given a query q, we begin by relaxing q to query q' by identifying and eliminating phrases in q that are not deemed important to the original information sought by the user. The intuition for this step is that rare queries often contain extraneous terms that are not critical to the underlying user intent. Such long queries thus suffer from the problem of insufficient query log information [22], and by eliminating unimportant terms we can derive the root query for which we may have richer information in the query logs or web pages. For example, the term "store" in the query "big lots furniture store" does not bring any significant information, hence we could relax this query to "big lots furniture" and further to "big lots."

We formulate the problem of identifying non-critical terms in a user query as a sequence labeling problem. More specifically, a user query q is treated as a sequence of tokens $\mathbf{x} = u_1 u_2 \cdots u_n$ which needs to be assigned a sequence of labels $\mathbf{y} = y_1 y_2 \cdots y_n$ such that $y_i \in \{C, D\}$. A label of C indicates a critical term whereas a label of D indicates a term that can be dropped from the original query. A promising approach for solving sequence labeling problems is Conditional Random Fields (CRFs) [23].

Training data: A practical challenge here is generating annotated data consisting of queries where each term in the query is labeled as C or D. Building large-scale annotated data that comprehensively covers a wide classes of queries is challenging and further such data is not readily available. To address this, we propose a method to automatically construct annotated data based on information available in search query logs. Our method is based on the observation that users often reformulate their queries when their original query did not lead to any interesting search results and furthermore, these reformulations contain important information regarding which terms may be replaced (i.e., dropped terms) and which terms may not be replaced (i.e., critical terms). Specifically, starting with user search queries, we split them into search sessions by considering all queries that occurred within a time frame of 15 minutes. Within a query session, we look at subsequent queries such that (a) the queries differ by one term, (b) the first query did not lead to clicks on any of the results, indicating an unsuccessful query or uninteresting search results page, (c) the second query led to at least one click on the results, indicating a potentially interesting search results page. Given a query pair q_1, q_2, we label all terms that are common to both queries as C and the terms that were removed from q_1 when generating q_2 as D.

Features: We used a combination of features including lexical-, query-logs-frequency-, and dictionary-based features derived from

description	source
frequency of t_i	query logs
standalone frequency of t_i	query logs
pairwise mutual information for (t_i, t_{i+1})	query logs
is first name	dictionary
is last name	dictionary
is location	dictionary
is stop word	dictionary
is wikipedia entry	wikipedia
has digit	lexical
has punctuations	lexical
position in query	lexical
length	lexical

Table 1: CRF features for each term t_i in a query $q = t_1, t_2, \cdots, t_n$.

various sources such as three months of query logs of a commercial search engine, Wikipedia, etc. Table 1 describes our feature set along with the sources used to derive them. In particular, given a query $q = t_1, t_2, \cdots t_n$ along with labels $l_1, l_2 \cdots l_n$ for each term, respectively, we compute the listed feature for each term t_i. Of the features shown in Table 1, the query-logs-based features, namely, standalone frequency and pairwise mutual information need further discussion.

The *standalone score* tries to capture whether a given term is an entity or a real-world concept or not: intuitively, a concept (e.g., california, ipod, madonna) should often occur in a standalone form among the search query logs. Therefore, among the query logs we must find queries of the form $Q == t_i$, capturing the fact that users are looking to learn more about the given concept. More formally, we compute the query-log-based standalone score as:

$$s(t_i) = \frac{|Q == t_i|}{|queries\ that\ contain\ t_i|} \tag{1}$$

The *pairwise mutual information (pmi)* score is computed for a pair of consecutive terms occurring in the query: intuitively, this score measures the "cohesiveness" of pairs of terms (e.g., 'san francisco' would have a high pmi score compared to 'drinking water'). More formally, we compute the pmi score for a pair (t_i, t_{i+1}) as:

$$pmi(t_i, t_{i+1}) = log\frac{C(t_i, t_{i+1})}{C(t_i) \cdot C(t_{i+1})} \tag{2}$$

where $C(x)$ is the number of queries that contain term x and $C(x, y)$ is the number of queries that contain ordered pair (x, y).

Upon eliminating terms that are labelled as non-critical, we use the resulting relaxed queries to generate candidates for query suggestions for the original query. Note that the set of relaxed queries themselves serves as suggestion candidates.

3. GENERATING SUGGESTION CANDIDATES

We now discuss a suite of algorithms to generate candidates for query suggestions for a query. Our algorithms *extend* information available in session logs utilizing information from query logs and web pages to simulate user sessions and derive suggestions.

3.1 Co-occurrence in query sessions

While searching for information, users usually issue related queries within a given session [4]. Sometimes they add or drop a term to their queries, or sometimes make a *lateral move* such as issuing "nikon d40" and "canon 50d". One rich source for generating suggestion candidates for a given query is to fetch the past session logs, and find queries that it is being manually formulated into [20, 29]. In practice, this rich reformulation data is typically available only for frequent queries and thus, we work with the root query obtained after query relaxation.

A simple approach to identify candidates would be to provide queries with high reformulation probability $p(q_n|q_c)$ as suggestions. This can simply be measured over the frequency counts in the session logs:

$$p(q_n|q_c) = \frac{f(q_n, q_c)}{f(q_c)} \tag{3}$$

where $f(q_n, q_c)$ is the frequency that these two queries are issued by the same user within a short time frame (will be referred as co-occurrence hereafter). The problem with using reformulation probability as the merit for suggestion candidate generation is that a query that is not dependent on q_c might have a high reformulation probability just because of its high marginal probability. To account for this, one can use pointwise mutual information (PMI) instead,

$$pmi(q_n, q_c) = log\left(\frac{f(q_n, q_c)}{f(q_c)f(q_n)}\right) \tag{4}$$

where $f(q_n)$ and $f(q_c)$ are individual marginal counts. The difference is that PMI normalizes the reformulation probability by a factor of $f(q_n)$; hence, it measures the dependency of these two queries. One weakness of PMI is that it might become very unstable for pairs of rare queries. As $f(q_c)$ and $f(q_n)$ get low, even a single coincidental co-occurrence might lead to a high PMI value. To account for this, one can use reformulation log-likelihood ratio (LLR) instead [20],

$$\begin{aligned} LLR(q_n, q_c) = p(q_n, q_c)\ pmi(q_n, q_c) + p(q_n, \overline{q}_c)\ pmi(q_n, \overline{q}_c) \\ +p(\overline{q}_n, q_c)\ pmi(\overline{q}_n, q_c) + p(\overline{q}_n, \overline{q}_c)\ pmi(\overline{q}_n, \overline{q}_c) \end{aligned}$$

where $\overline{q}_{next}$ denotes the set of all queries except q_n and similarly for q_c. LLR fixes the stability problem by taking the size of the all session data into account, and when the marginal query frequencies $f(q_n)$ and $f(q_c)$ get lower, other terms will start to dominate. We generate suggestion candidates using query reformulations with LLR above a certain threshold optimized empirically. (We will provide details about the session data later in Section 5). Additionally, we also apply various filters to guard against robots and spam details of which are out of scope of this paper.

As an example of applying this co-occurrence-based operator, for the query 'acoustic guitar strings', we obtain 'classical guitar' as a suggestion candidate after eliminating the term 'strings' from the original query. Or for 'cheap vegas hotels resorts', it gives 'las vegas specials' after dropping the term 'cheap'.

3.2 Semantic relations from web corpus

Our next method, explores candidates by replacing query terms by terms that are *distributionally similar* (i.e., synonyms, siblings, hypernyms, etc.) to them. We apply this transformation to both critical as well as the dropped query terms. This transformation relies on distributional similarity methods [24] that model the *Distributional Hypothesis* [14]: the distributional hypothesis links the meaning of words to their co-occurrences in text and states that *words that occur in similar contexts tend to have similar meanings*.

In practice, distributional similarity methods that capture this hypothesis are built by recording the surrounding contexts for each term in a large corpus and storing them in a *term-context matrix* [24]. Term-context matrix consist of weights for contexts with terms as rows and context as columns, and each cell x_{ij} is assigned a score to reflect the co-occurrence strength between the term i and context j. Methods differ in their definition of a context (e.g., text window or syntactic relations), or in their means to weigh contexts (e.g., frequency, tf-idf, pointwise mutual information), or ultimately in measuring the similarity between two context vectors (e.g., using Euclidean distance, Cosine, Dice). We build a term-context matrix as follows: we process a large corpus of text (e.g., web pages in our case) using a text chunker [24]. Terms are all noun phrase chunks with some modifiers removed; their contexts are defined as their rightmost and leftmost stemmed chunks. We weigh each context f using pointwise mutual information [7]. Specifically, we construct a pointwise mutual information vector $PMI(w)$ for each term w as: $PMI(w) = (pmi_{w1}, pmi_{w2}, \cdots, pmi_{wm})$, where pmi_{wf} is the pointwise mutual information between term w and feature f and is derived as:

$$pmi_{wf} = log\left(\frac{c_{wf} \cdot N}{\sum_{i=1}^{n} c_{if} \cdot \sum_{j=1}^{m} c_{wj}}\right) \quad (5)$$

where c_{wf} is the frequency of feature f occurring for term w, n is the number of unique terms, m is the number of contexts, and N is the total number of features for all terms. Finally, similarity scores between two terms are computed by computing a cosine similarity between their pmi context vectors [31]. As an example of applying the distributional similarity-based operator, for the query 'football hall of fame 2010 inductees' we generate 'football hall of fame 2010 award winners' since 'inductees' and 'award winners' are distributionally similar phrases.

3.3 Substitutions from co-clicked URL queries

Aside from co-occurrences, another dimensionality in the session logs that can bring additional valuable information is to consider the queries that lead to clicks to common URLs as in [29]. Query pairs with co-clicked URLs can be used to build a *substitutions dictionary*. This dictionary can be used to provide alternatives for the root query as well as for providing substitutions for the dropped terms *in a context-aware manner*, such that the term "turkey" can be substituted with "thanksgiving" in the context of "recipes" and with "turkish" in the context of "embassy" but not the opposites.

To build a substitutions dictionary, we build a query-URL bipartite graph with queries and urls as nodes and an edge $q \rightarrow u$ between a query node q and an url node u if a user clicked on url u after issuing query q. To eliminate outliers or noisy data, we only retain edges with clickthrough rate (i.e., clicks vs. views) above 0.01. Using this graph, we identify all pairs of queries that are connected to at least 2 and at most 10 common URLs[1]. There are two things that we have considered while constructing the query-URL bipartite graph:

- We removed URLs that are connected to more than 200 queries (most of which turn out to be very popular destination pages like `youtube.com`, `amazon.com` etc.). This prevents us from connecting vaguely related queries and bringing in irrelevant substitutables.
- For the URLs from tail domains, we used the domain-level information instead of the particular URL. If for a given domain, we have less than 30 unique queries leading to a click to a URL in that particular domain, we consider this a as a tail domain, and define the co-clicks over the domain, instead of the particular URLs. We found that this helps for enriching the suggestion sets for tail intents without losing the context.

When generating suggestion candidates, we simply look into the substitution dictionary for all possible substitutions. For example, for the query 'turkey recipes', if the relaxed query is 'turkey', we look at the substitutables of the dropped term 'recipes' to find 'roasting times', 'stuffing recipe' , 'how to roast' and many others, and generate the candidates 'turkey roasting times', 'turkey stuffing recipe' and 'how to roast turkey'[2].

3.4 Context from original query

After exploring suggestion candidates of the relaxed query, in many cases it is helpful to push the dropped term back into the query to generate a *partially lateral* move. Naturally, this context is only pushed to suggestions without the dropped terms or their substitutions. As an example, for the query 'acoustic guitar strings', we generated 'classical guitar' using the co-occurrence-based operator (Section 3.1) to which we push the term 'strings' to generate the suggestion 'classical guitar strings.' This operator re-inserts the original query context into the suggestions.

To summarize, we consider an expanded set of suggestions derived by relaxing the original query as well as using different combinations of operators discussed above.

4. RANKING SUGGESTIONS

While combining various information sources and text-based operations discussed in the previous section allow us to systematically construct candidates for query suggestions, they may also lead to erroneous query suggestions. Specifically, we may have at hand suggestions that are garbled; for example, in our experiments, for the query 'tampa bay fisheries' one of the suggestions generated using co-occurrence data and pushing the dropped term from the query was 'tampa tribune fisheries' (the original query was relaxed to generate 'tampa bay' for which session co-occurrence data produces 'tampa tribune' as a suggestion). Similarly, the candidate suggestions by applying various operators may not be relevant to the original query. To address these issues, we build a supervised ranking model to decide which candidate suggestions are valid.

The desiderata for ranking candidate suggestion for a given query include: (a) *well-formedness* of the suggestion (Section 4.1), (b) *relevance* to the query (Section 4.2, and (c) *utility* to users (Section 4.4). Additionally, we use a variety of lexical and syntactical features and train a gradient boosted decision tree (GBDT) [12] over this feature space for ranking candidate suggestions.

4.1 Well-formedness of a suggestion

In this step, our goal is to demote suggestions that are garbled, i.e., that do not conform to a real-world concept or language formulation. For instance, the suggestion 'tampa tribune fisheries' is not a a real-world concept and similarly 'marilyn monroe compendium' is a garbled suggestion. This is a critical in our setting since the suggestions are 'user-facing'; in contrast traditional query rewriting methods send rewritten queries to the search engine (i.e., backend) where the engine simply returns few or no results in case of poorly formed queries. To capture the well-formedness of a suggestion, we use *statistical language models* which is a probability distribution $P(s)$ over a sequence $w_1, w_2, \cdots w_m$ of words expressed as:$P(w_1, w_2, \cdots w_m) = \prod_{i=1}^{m} P(w_i|w_1, w_2, \cdots, w_{i-1})$. We use an n-gram model which computes the above probability based on "memory" of past (n-1) words given as:

$$P(w_1, w_2, \cdots w_m) \approx \prod_{i=1}^{m} P(w_i|w_{i-(n-1)} \cdots, w_{i-1})$$

In our experiments, we use a tri-gram model where

$$P(w_1, \cdots w_m) \approx \prod_{i=1}^{m} P(w_i|w_{i-2)}, w_{i-1})$$

which is estimated using a *maximum likelihood estimator* as:

[1]We decided to use an upper bound here as well, because with too many common URLs, the query pairs are starting to become synonymous with almost identical result sets, which provides almost no utility to the users. This will be detailed in Section 4.4.

[2]While generating the candidates we keep the structure of the co-clicked URL queries and do not put the placed term into the position of the dropped term (as it would end up with many garbled suggestions like 'turkey how to roast'

$$P(w_i|w_{i-2}, w_{i-1}) = \frac{C(w_{i-2}w_{i-1}w_i)}{w_{i-2}w_{i-1}} \quad (6)$$

where $C(w_{i-2}w_{i-1}w_i)$ is the relative frequency of observing the word w_i given that it is preceeded by the sequence $w_{i-2}w_{i-1}$.

A common problem in building language models is that of word sequences that do not occur in the training set used to compute quantities in the above equation. In such cases, $C(w_{i-2}w_{i-1}w_i)$ and therefore $P(w_i|w_{i-2}, w_{i-1})$ equals 0. To address this problem, several smoothing techniques have been proposed that appropriately discount the MLE estimates in (6) and use the left-over probability mass for sequences not observed in the training data. Several smoothing techniques have been proposed in the past and we use a commonly used method, namely, Kneser-Ney smoothing [21]. Kneser-Ney smoothing interpolates higher-order models with lower-order models based on the number of distinct *contexts* in which a term occurs instead of number of occurrences of a word. Formally,

$$P(w_3|w_1 w_2) = \frac{max\{C(w_1, w_2\} - D, 0}{C(w_1, w_2)} + \frac{D}{C(w_1, w_2)} N(w_2) P(w3|w_2) \quad (7)$$

where D is a discount factor [21] and $N(x)$ is the number of unique contexts following term x.

An important observation in our setting is that we are dealing with potentially valid suggestions that may not occur in the query logs. Specifically, since our suggestions are synthetically derived we want to incorporate sources other than query logs. With this in mind, we build and combine language models from query logs as well as web pages. We combine these models as:

$$P_C(w_3|w_1, w_2) = \lambda \cdot P_Q(w_3|w_1, w_2) + (1 - \lambda) P_W(w_3|w_1, w_2)$$

where λ is the interpolation weight optimized on a heldout training set. In the ranking step, we use P_C, P_Q and P_W as features that capture well-formedness of a candidate.

4.2 Relevance to original query

To assess the relevance of each suggestion candidate to the original query, we designed three types of features for each pair of query and its suggestion candidate. In this section, we discuss how we derive these features using query logs as well as search results.

4.2.1 *Click-vector similarity*

An obvious relevance feature along the lines with the co-clicked URL candidate generation method is to look at the overlap between the clicked URLs for each query pair. For a given query, consider the following document click-vector over the set of all documents $\mathbf{cl}(q) = [cl_1(q), cl_2(q), \ldots, cl_K(q)]$, where K is the number of clicked documents. We calculate the cosine similarity between the overlapping URLs in the click-vectors of each query and suggestion candidate pair as our first relevance feature,

$$Sim_{click} = \frac{\mathbf{cl}(q_1) \cdot \mathbf{cl}(q_2)}{\|\mathbf{cl}(q_1)\| \|\mathbf{cl}(q_2)\|} \quad (8)$$

This feature by definition is non-zero for the candidates that are coming from the co-clicked URL candidate generation method. On the other hand, the coverage over other candidate generation methods is quite low since we are working with synthetic suggestions not observed in the past. Note that although this feature relies on query logs, it does not require the query and suggestion to occur in the same session; later in this section, we derive features that are not derived from query logs.

4.2.2 *Context-vector similarity*

A relevance feature along the lines with the distributional hypothesis is to look at the similarity of the distribution of other terms

Require: Concept dictionary D, query q
Retrieve set R of top-k results for q
T = Terms from D contained in R
Eliminate from T terms in q
for term $t \in D$ **do**
  $d(t)$ = number of results that t appears
  $r(t)$ = total rank that t appears
  $R(t) = \frac{((k+1)\ d(t)) - r(t)}{d(t)\ k}$
  $S(t) = \frac{d(t)\ R(t)}{k}$
end for
Get the 20 terms with highest score $S(t)$

$$\mathbf{ab}(q) = [S(t_1), S(t_2), \ldots, S(t_{20})]$$

Algorithm 1: Algorithm to compute the aboutness vector.

that each query is searched along with. For example, consider two queries q_1 and q_2, and assume that in the session logs, the most frequent queries that include these two queries include "$\langle q_1 \rangle$ download", "$\langle q_2 \rangle$ download", "install $\langle q_1 \rangle$" and "install $\langle q_2 \rangle$". From the context with which the query is searched together with, it is clear that both queries are software related.

For a given query, consider the context vector as the frequencies of the terms that it is searched along with $\mathbf{co}(q) = [f_1, f_2, \ldots, f_L]$, where L is the number of co-queried terms in the session logs. Similar to above, we evaluate the cosine similarity for a pair of context-vectors of the overlapping context terms of each query - suggestion candidate pair as:

$$Sim_{context} = \frac{\mathbf{co}(q_1) \cdot \mathbf{co}(q_2)}{\|\mathbf{co}(q_1)\| \|\mathbf{co}(q_2)\|} \quad (9)$$

Although this is a useful feature for frequent queries, over a uniformly sampled query set the context-vector similarity has a very low coverage. In our experiments, many queries in our data set are rare (and long) queries that have a very low probability of being searched within other queries, and do not have a context vector. Furthermore, the suggestion candidates that are coming from substitutions from web corpus are not even guaranteed to be observed in the query logs, hence context is not defined.

4.2.3 *Web-based aboutness similarity*

So far, we discussed two features based on user query logs (i.e., observed data); however, of course, these features are sparse and will fail to assess the relevance of rare queries or queries that are *not* observed in the past. In the absence of session logs, one can use the search engine itself and look at the results to determine how related two queries are. Specifically, an earlier work by Raghavan and Sever [28] compares the ordered result sets returned for each query to measure query similarity. Their method requires ranking of all documents and $O(N^2)$ complexity, where N the number of documents, which is intractable for the web search scenario.

A subsequent approach is given by Fitzpatrick and Dent where they use the set overlap of the top k documents [10]. This is a tractable solution, however the result set overlap is only good at finding almost synonymous queries, and the overlap drops sharply when the queries are related but not (almost) identical. In the context of query suggestions, we are not interested in identifying nearly identical queries; instead, we need to assign reliable relevance scores to related query pairs as well. For example, although they are related and would make useful suggestions for each other, 'python' and 'ruby' have zero results in common in top 50. Thus, a measure simply based on the search results is insufficient and our next feature is captures what the results are *about*.

To assess a suggestion's relevance to the query, we build an *aboutness vector* [6] of the query and the suggestion and compute the similarity between these vectors. An aboutness vector succinctly describes a document and is represented as a set of salient *concepts* in the document along with their scores. Methods to build aboutness vectors differ in their definition of concepts (e.g., terms, named-entities, unigrams). In this work, we rely on a pre-built concept dictionary built using the method proposed in [2]. Our dictionary consist of 27 million phrasal concepts and named-entities obtained from a large web crawl as well as well as query logs and is intended to cover most "interesting" phrases on the web. (For steps to build the concept dictionary please refer to [2].)

Algorithm 1 describes our algorithm to compute the aboutness vector for a given a query q using the concept dictionary D. The final score $S(t)$ is a function of $d(t)$, the number of documents that the term t appears and, $R(t)$ the rank score. $R(t)$ gives higher weights to the terms that are contained in higher ranked documents; since documents that are ranked higher are more important than ones that rank lower, terms that are contained in higher ranked documents are more important. Given the aboutness vectors of the query q_1 and the suggestion candidate q_2, we calculate the cosine similarity between these two vectors to find the web-based aboutness similarity

$$Sim_{about} = \frac{\mathbf{ab}(q_1) \cdot \mathbf{ab}(q_2)}{\|\mathbf{ab}(q_1)\|\|\mathbf{ab}(q_2)\|} \quad (10)$$

We found that Sim_{about} is quite useful since it can assign reliable relevance scores to related queries. For example, for the above example, 'python' and 'ruby' have a Sim_{about} score of 0.29, with the aboutness terms 'download' 'programming language' and 'implementation' in common. This first may sound lower than expected, but note that this is a quite difficult comparison due to other meanings of the queries (snake and gemstone) that occupy some portion of the aboutness vector. Hence, 'python' vs 'boa snake' or 'ruby' vs 'saphire' also have non-zero Sim_{about} as well.

Another good thing about Sim_{about} is that it has full coverage. It can be computed as long as the query returns some results. Although it cannot be computed for zero-result queries, we still consider it as full coverage, since query suggestions with zero results cannot be relevant to the user by definition.

4.3 Suggestions ranker

In addition to the above, we also employ features that capture the lexical characteristics of a suggestion such as binary features which include, whether the suggestion contains a digit, punctuation, alphanumeric characters, as well as the length of the suggestion. Other family of features include the source that generated the suggestion. For instance, the feature `SRC.CO` is set to 1 when a suggestion is generated using the co-occurrence statistics. Finally, we also employ dictionary-based features that check if query terms that were dropped, inserted, or left intact belonged to any specific category. In particular, we use dictionaries to determine if these terms are locations (e.g., city, state, or country), wikipedia entities (e.g., surgery, alzheimer), or stop words (e.g., the, of, an).

We use Gradient Boosting Decision Tree (GBDT) as the learner [12], and pose the problem as a classification of good and bad queries. In this classification setting, for each test sample GBDT outputs the probability of good. We prune the test samples with probability of good less than $p(good) < 0.5$ and rank the remaining by this probability.

4.4 Suggestion utility

The final step is to filter out the low utility suggestions. Of all the pieces in the pipeline, there is nothing that ensures that utility of the suggestions, and thus the system may generate irrelevant suggestions, e.g., suggestions with no search results. Also, in all likelihood, the system can generate query suggestions that are synonymous to the original query, with an almost identical result set. We assert that a query suggestion should be presented only if it leads to a sufficiently different result set as compared to those of the original query and other presented suggestions. For this purpose, we define a measure of utility of the suggestion q_s conditioned on q_p, a query that is already presented to the user, $U(q_s|q_p)$.

Given q_s and q_p, let $URL_s = [u_{s1}, \ldots, u_{sN}]$ and $URL_p = [u_{p1}, \ldots, u_{pN}]$ be the result sets of these two queries. For the top 10 URLs in the result page of q_s, we define the examination probability of the URLs using the rank discounts in the commonly used DCG formula [18].

$$p(e(u_{si}) = 1|q_s) = d(u_{si}, q_s) = \frac{1}{\log_2(r_i + 1)} \quad (11)$$

where r is the rank of the URL and e is a binary random variable that shows whether the URL is examined or not. Again for each $u_{si} \in URL_s$, we also define the examination probability that the user will examine the URL in the result page of q_p as follows,

$$p(e(u_{si}) = 1|q_p) =$$

$$\begin{cases} 0 & : u_{si} \notin URL_p \\ 1 & : \begin{array}{c} u_{si} \in URL_p, \\ E\{d(q_p, u_{si})\} \geq E\{d(q_s, u_{si})\} \end{array} \\ \frac{E\{d(q_p, u_{si})\}}{E\{d(q_s, u_{si})\}} & : \begin{array}{c} u_{si} \in URL_p, \\ E\{d(q_p, u_{si})\} < E\{d(q_s, u_{si})\} \end{array} \end{cases} \quad (12)$$

In words,

- u_{si} cannot be observed via q_p, if it is not in the result set of q_p, hence the examination probability is zero.
- If q_p returns u_{si} at least as high as q_s does, the examination probability is 1
- If q_p returns u_{si} lower than q_s does, the examination probability of this URL is the ratio of the rank discounts of the two corresponding ranks.

We define the pairwise conditional utility $U(q_s|q_p)$ by combining (11) and (12) as

$$U(q_s|q_p) = 1 - \sum_{u \in URL_s} p(e(u) = 1|q_s)\, p(e(u) = 1|q_p) \quad (13)$$

Intuitively, the first term in the summation gives how important this particular URL is for the query q_s, and the second term gives how likely it is that the same user would examine this URL in q_p, with the assumption that the user would go as deep into the result set in q_p. Hence, $U(q_s|q_p)$ is, by definition is 0 if the results of the two queries are exactly the same or q_s has zero results. Also, $U(q_s|q_p)$ would be close to 0 for queries that share many URLs and rank them similarly. After defining $U(q_s|q_p)$, we use the following greedy approach to ensure that all suggestions are sufficiently different from the original query as well as each other.

- Get the ranked suggestion list with decreasing scores.
- For the first one in the ranked suggestion list, and put it into the final suggestion set if it satisfies $U(q_s|q_p) \geq \gamma$ where q_p is the original query.
- For all remaining queries, get the one with the highest score and put it into the final suggestion set if it satisfies $U(q_s|q_p) \geq \gamma$ for the original query and all queries in the final set.

User study to select the optimal γ value for the utility model is presented in Section 6.5.

Putting it all together, our end-to-end framework systematically explores candidate for query suggestions while allowing suggestions that may or may not lexically overlap with the original query. To this end, we proposed a supervised ranking algorithm to eliminate irrelevant or low utility suggestions. It is noteworthy that our pipeline is amenable to be incorporated in a web search engine since it can be run in an offline manner to generate a dictionary of queries and their suggestions.

5. EXPERIMENTAL SETUP

Query Set: We collected a random sample of 100,000 fully anonymized queries sent to Yahoo! search engine in the month of August, 2010 along with their frequency. Of these, we identified those for which the search engine does not present any suggestion and drew a random sample of 10,000 queries biased by their frequency (see Introduction for query suggestion distribution.) . Our goal was to capture queries from different quantiles of this distribution. Note that by nature the queries that the search engine cannot provide any suggestions are very likely to be tail queries of the overall query distribution. We perform 10-fold cross-validation over this dataset.

Distributional similarity filters: For this, we use a collection of 500 million web pages crawled by a commercial search engine crawl. We construct our distributional similarity database by adopting the methodology proposed in [27]. We POS-tagged our web corpus using Brill's tagger [5] and chunked it using a variant of the Abney chunker [1]. We built a distributional database from this chunked corpus using the method outlined in Section 3.2.

Clickthrough data: To generate the co-click graph and compute the co-occurrence log-likelihood ratio, we used 6 month of anonymized query clickthrough logs of Yahoo! search engine. The co-click graph consists of 2.7M unique queries and 55.6M unique URLs in total, with 167.3M edges in between them. The co-occurrence data has 4.3M unique (q_c, q_n) pairs for 913K unique q_c.

Compared methods: We are unaware of any existing system for synthetically generating suggestions from several candidate generation methods and blends them. However, several methods for generating suggestions have been proposed, which we use as sources for candidate suggestion generation [20, 29]. Therefore, we build baseline techniques for comparison using each candidate generation source:

- `CO+PS`:co-occurrence with pushing the dropped terms
- `CO` :co-occurrence
- `DS` :distributional similarity of the dropped term
- `Q+CK` :coclicks of the original query
- `R+CK` :coclicks of the relaxed query
- `DS+CK`:coclicks of `DS`
- `CO+CK`:coclicks of co-occurrence of relaxed query
- `HYB` :hybrid method that combines all

Note that we allow all the above methods to share the same query relaxation techniques and the ranking model.

User studies: All user studies and manual annotation tasks described were performed by a group of eight professional search engine quality evaluators experienced with assessing the quality of query suggestions and search results.

Evaluation method: Professional annotators provided binary judgments for the 10,000 queries we sampled, good, for the relevant and useful suggestions, and bad for the irrelevant, garbled, zero-result, or synonymous (hence useless) suggestions. Annotators were asked to input their judgments after looking at the results page and comparing those for the query and suggestion; this is important to capture the utility of a suggestion.

Evaluation metrics: We evaluate the performance of each system using information retrieval measures, namely, precision and recall defined as:

- **Precision:** Given a list L of suggestions for a query, we compute precision as $\frac{Number\ of\ correct\ suggestions\ in\ L}{|L|}$. We study the precision values at varying ranks averaged over queries with at least one suggestion.

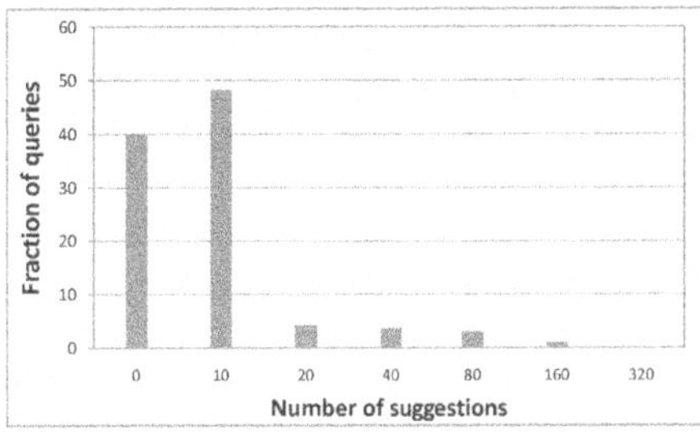

Figure 2: Distribution of number of suggestion candidates per query.

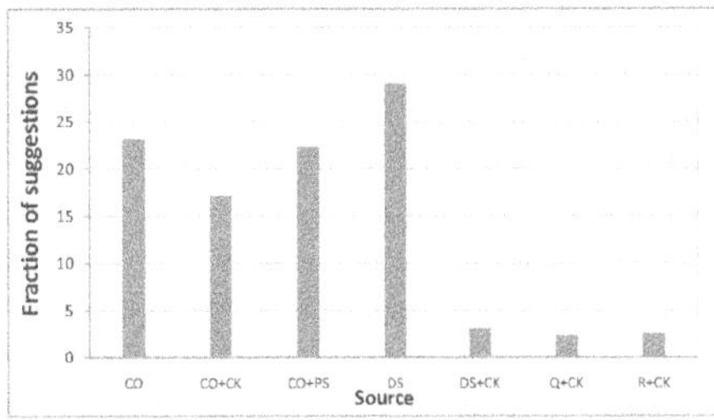

Figure 3: Distribution of number of suggestions for each candidate generation source.

- **Recall:** Given a list L of suggestions for a query, we compute recall as $\frac{|Number\ of\ correct\ suggestions\ in\ L|}{|All\ correct\ suggestions\ for\ query|}$ where all correct suggestions for query is the union of the correct suggestions across all methods.

6. EXPERIMENTAL RESULTS

6.1 Coverage of extended suggestion pool

Our main goal is to increase the coverage of the queries for which useful suggestions can be provided to the users. Thus, our first experiment studies the increase in this coverage along various directions. Note that our experiments consisted only of queries for which a commercial search engine does not provide *any* suggestions and therefore results reported in this section naturally translate to an increase in the coverage of queries with suggestions. (Implementation details of this suggestion service are proprietary and out of scope of this paper.) Figure 2 shows the distribution of the total number of suggestion candidates explored by our candidate generation methods per query. As we can see, our proposed query suggestion generation methods provide a large set of candidates. We further break down the suggestions by the source in Figure 3, and see that all methods have some substantial contributions, and some of them like `CO`, `CO+CK`, `CO+PS` and `DS` are contributing much more than the others.

To investigate the quality of the suggestion candidate pool, we look at the number of good suggestions per query in Figure 4. Before the pruning and ranking stage, 24% of the queries have at least one good suggestion candidate. This is encouraging since the query set was sampled from those with no suggestions, which constitutes 66% of the unique query traffic. We again break down the good suggestion distribution into individual sources. Among the most contributing sources there is the `CO` method, investigated earlier by Jones et al. [20], and three other candidate sources that we proposed in this paper provide good suggestions almost as much as that one. Also, all of the sources have some substantial contribution.

6.2 Quality of extended suggestions

We now evaluate the quality of the ranked lists for each source. Each list is run through the well-formedness, relevance, and utility

query	suggestions
free auto parts manual	auto body parts, discount auto parts, auto part stores
minneapolis days inn	minneapolis comfort inn, minneapolis motel 6, minneapolis super 8, minneapolis best western
muscular system diagram	human skeletal system diagram, circulatory system diagram, human muscular system, skeletal anatomy
puppy training 101	dog training basics, puppy housetraining, dog whisperer, puppy training tips
csi crime scene investigation cast	csi miami cast, csi new york cast, csi episode guide, cbs csi miami
honda insight review	ford fusion review, 2010 toyota prius, toyota prius review, honda civic hybrid
obsessive compulsive disorder symptoms	ocd test, ocd symptoms, causes of ocd, ocd treatment, symptoms of ocd

Table 2: Examples for query suggestion pairs

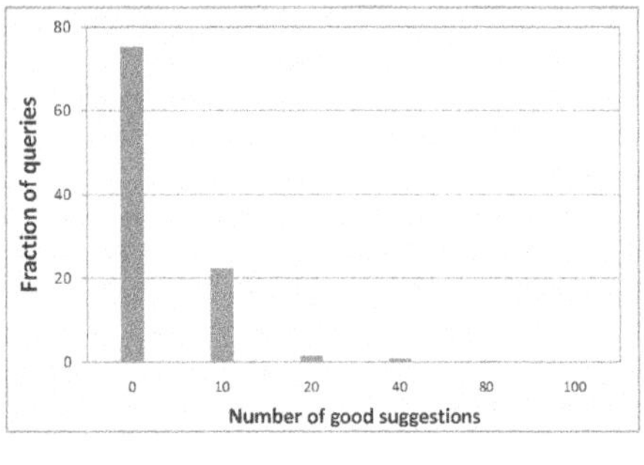

Figure 4: Number of good suggestions per query.

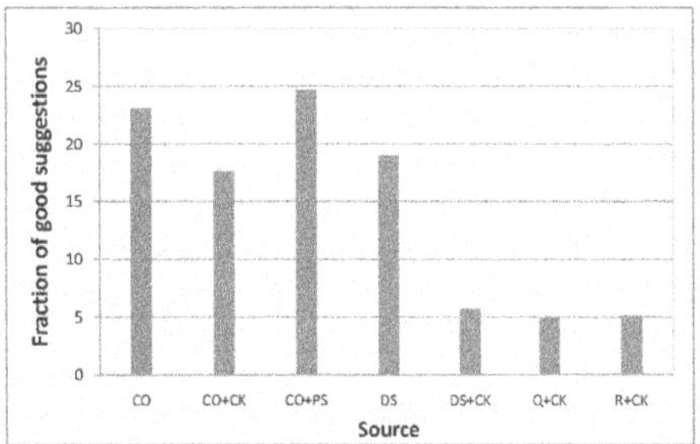

Figure 5: Distribution of good suggestions for each candidate generation source.

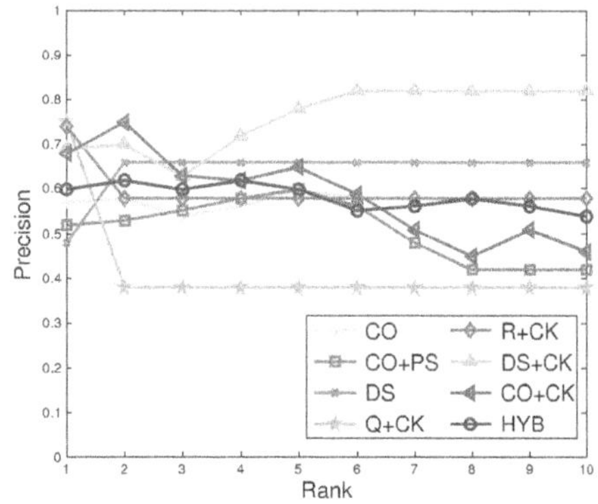

Figure 6: Mean precision at varying ranks.

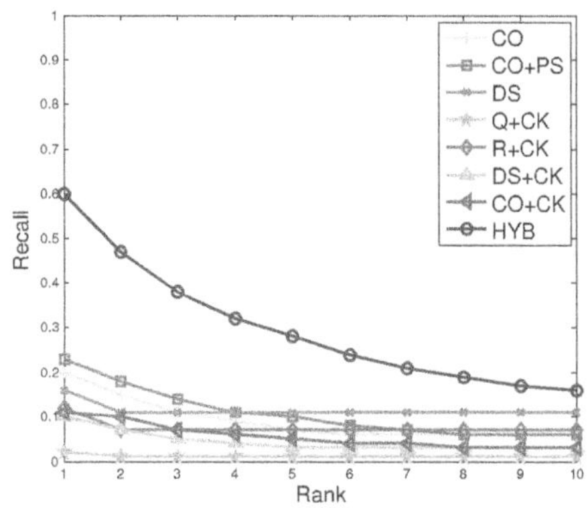

Figure 7: Average recall at varying ranks.

filters and for fairness, all sources share the same CRF relaxation, relevance thresholds.

Table 2 lists a few sample suggestions generated for our test queries. Figures 6 and 7 show the average precision and recall, respectively, of the ranked list produced by the GBDT model. We see that some of the sources like `Q+CK` are quite precise, but their recall as well as the depth of the ranked list is very low. `CO` and `CO+CK` are the ones with the highest recall, also they can provide up to 8-10 suggestions per query.

It is noteworthy that the precision for `HYB` is computed over more samples than those for the baseline since `HYB` produces the longest list of suggestions (see Figure 7). This, in turn, results in less variance of the precision values as compared to the baselines. In Figure 7, we observe that the recall for `HYB` is additive over the baselines, i.e., individual sources. The overlap between the suggestion candidates generated by each source is low with each source bringing in different and valuable candidates. Figure 8 gives the average f-measure over the suggestions set at each rank for all sources. As expected, `HYB` outperforms all individual sources including the earlier methods `CO` [20] and `Q+CK`, `R+CK` [29].

`HYB` in Figure 8 generates a relatively long list with 10 or more suggestions; in practice typically $k = 5$). If the desired size k is known a priori, one can tune the ranking stage to optimize for the precision and recall up to that k value. For example, if a deep list is not needed, the aim might be to *display a single suggestion per query, and increase the quality as much as possible.* This is perfectly reasonable. The exact number of suggestions to be displayed is a design choice: depending on where on the page they will be displayed, too many suggestions might distract the user. For this scenario, to optimize the f-measure at the top position, one can tune the GBDT confidence threshold, and compromise for the precision and recall at the lower ranks to improve the precision and recall at rank 1. See Figure 9 for a comparison of the f-measure for top 5 ranks for varying relevance confidence threshold levels. For example with the threshold 0.8, one can increase the f-measure at rank 1 very significantly to 0.82, by compromising the depth of the list; hence, the recall (and therefore the f-measure) decays much more sharply for increasing ranks as compared to the values with the threshold 0.5 -the black curve in Figure 8.

In summary, if a deep list is not needed, with a more strict relevance confidence threshold `HYB` can provide a ranking with 0.83 recall at rank 1, 0.56 recall at rank 2, 0.83 precision at rank 1, 0.85 precision at rank 2 and an average list length of 1.4. Precision value at rank two is 0.85, which is at the same level of quality of the suggestions that the search engine can provide for frequent queries via existing techniques -some of which we use as sources. Recall the distribution over the suggestion coverage provided in the Introduction section; 26.6% of unique queries have more than 5 suggestions, and 7.4% have between 1 and 4 suggestions, and 66% of the unique query distribution has no suggestions. It is remarkable that `HYB` with relevance threshold level 0.8 can increase the coverage of queries with at least one good suggestion from 34% to 47.2% of the unique query distribution, hence brings a coverage increase of 39% *without compromising precision.*

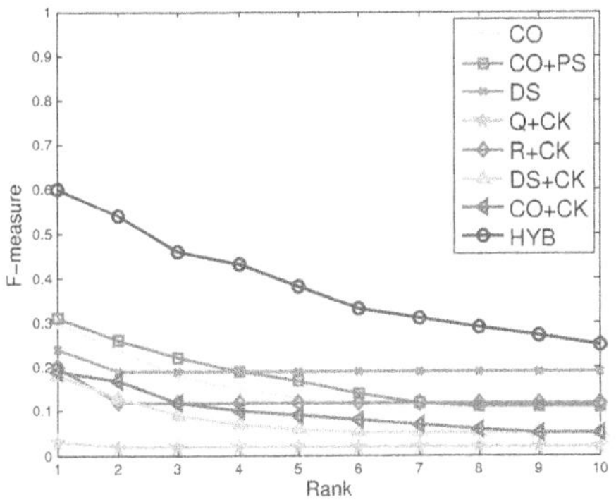

Figure 8: Average f-measure at varying ranks

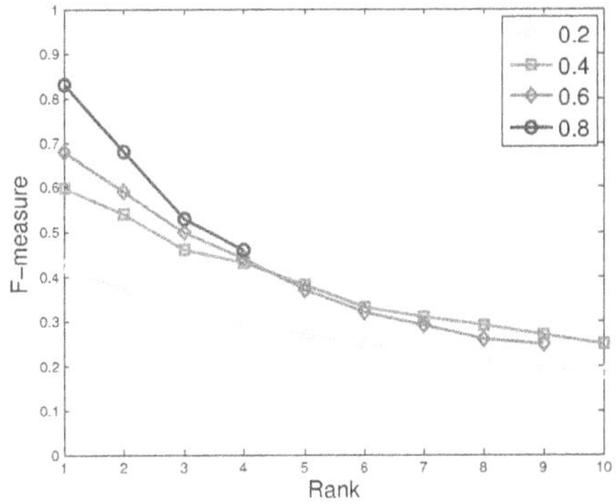

Figure 9: Average f-measure for varying relevance confidence threshold.

6.3 Query relaxation performance

After comparing each source, we now evaluate individual components in the pipeline starting with the CRF model from Section 2. Our evaluation of the proposed CRF model is two-fold. For our first evaluation, we ran 10-fold cross-validation and compared our model against a baseline method that eliminates the last term in the query. Table 6.3 compares these methods and shows that using a CRF model substantially improves the precision (15% gain) with a small amount of drop in recall (2%). Our second evaluation

method	precision	recall
CRF	0.82	0.87
Baseline	0.71	0.89

Table 3: Performance of query relaxation method.

involved a user study where annotators were provided the queries for which the CRF had dropped atleast one term. Annotators were asked to label (a) whether a query contained a non-critical term, (b) whether the CRF selected the correct term to drop. Of these queries 70% of queries did have a non-critical term, and for these queries CRF selects the correct term 81% of the time. Finally, a feature analysis of the model showed that the stand-alone ratio is consistently the most important feature in all 10 runs.

6.4 Feature analysis of suggestion ranker

To better understand the importance of various features used in our ranking model (Section 4.3), we examined for each feature the coverage as well as the importance ranking noted by the GBDT model. An encouraging result is that the GBDT feature importance ranking was consistent and thus stable across individual runs in our 10-fold cross-validation. Specifically, in all 10 runs Sim_{about} is the most important feature. Also, web and combined language model scores $P_{\mathcal{W}}$ and $P_{\mathcal{C}}$, and Sim_{click} are consistently among the top five most important features. Not surprisingly, the most important features are the ones with higher coverage, Sim_{about} with full coverage, combined (71%) and web (66.9%) language model scores. The one with the smallest coverage among the most important features is Sim_{click} with 17.5%. Also, lexical features seem more important than the source features overall.

6.5 Utility model performance

Finally, we discuss the performance of our utility model (Section 4.4). To select an optimal γ value, the threshold by which we decide to remove the query suggestion from the set due to redundancy, we carried out a user study where annotators were given 500 randomly selected pairs of queries and their suggestions. Annotators were asked if the suggestion is useful or redundant for the given query. Figure 10 shows $U(q_s|q_p)$ value versus the editor grade (a noise jitter is added into the editor grade for a better visualization), along with the precision-recall curve of $U(q_s|q_p)$ for varying γ values. For this model, we decided to use $\gamma = 0.70$, which corresponds to 0.94 precision and 0.67 recall on this dataset, as marked in Figure 10. In our experiments, the utility model removes low utility suggestions such as "cooking channel tv" → "cooking channel television", "tampa bay fisheries" → "tampa bay fishery".

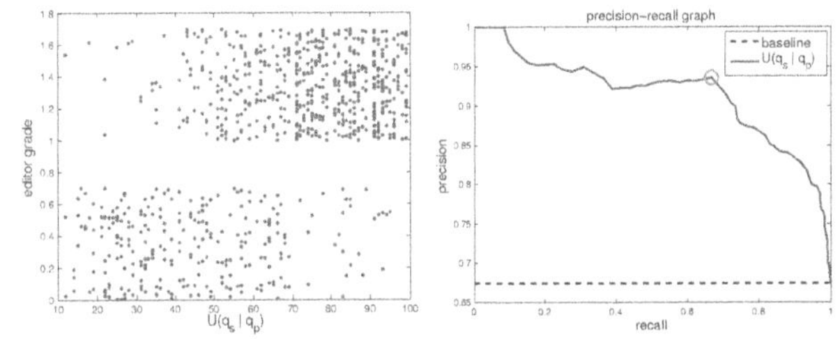

Figure 10: Utility estimate $U(q_s|q_p)$ versus the editor judgment (left), and precision recall curve of $U(q_s|q_p)$ with the operating point at $\gamma = 0.70$ and the precision recall curve of the baseline (majority) classifier.

7. RELATED WORK

Providing query suggestions: Research on query suggestion methods have largely relied on observed queries and developed similarity measures based on these observations. In [11] association rules are used to mine query recommendations from queries in individual users' search sessions which are defined as fixed length periods of interaction. In contrast, [36] builds a graph representation of the of the sequential search queries and combines it with a content based similarity method to account for the sparsity of the query logs. These methods simply mine query reformulations from observed queries. Other methods leverage the click information, as well. In [29], a query similarity measure is developed based on term-weight vector space representations of the queries and clicked URLs. Query term and click pattern overlap is used in [35] to develop query similarity measures in order to cluster user queries. Random walks on query-click graph is used by [8]. Slightly differently, Markov Random Field models are used over the query-click graph to generate bid terms in [13]. In [25], query-click graph based random walk techniques are further refined by considering the time to first visit to a query node. Main shortcoming of the query recommendation methods listed above is the limitation of suggestions to observed queries. This works fine for the frequent queries but not so well for the rare queries in the tail.

Earlier methods of generating alternative queries also included query expansion by pseudo-relevance feedback where additional query terms are obtained from the documents retrieved by the original query. These terms are used to expand the original query to retrieve more specific documents. Limitations of this method such as query drift are well documented [30]. Query term deletion has been tried in [19] but it leads to loss of specificity. In [32], query term substitution is considered using the retrieved documents, and in [2] user input is sought for selecting appropriate related terms, but these methods add an additional step to query reformulation. Automatic term substitution using query logs is considered in [20], however a non-contextual query segmentation is used leading to many marginally useful reformulation candidates. Their filtering method also lacks a language model, so it does not have the right information to separate well-formed queries from illegible ones. This is probably acceptable for bid term generation for ad matching but not so for query suggestions to be offered to a search user.

Earlier work has explored comparing information from query logs and other textual sources [15, 9]. Closest to our work is the method in [9] which examines anchor text in web pages solely for the task of query suggestions. Interestingly, Dang and Croft show that suggestions generated using anchor text are comparable to those generated using query logs. This work builds an alternative to query logs using web pages whereas our work uses web and additional textual information to *extend* query session logs, especially for rare queries. Further, our proposed method explicitly handle the case of lateral query reformulations. Recently, Szpektor et al˙ [17] showed how templates can be used to provide suggestions for rare queries; our work considers the generic problem of providing suggestions for *any* rare query.

Re-writing long queries To improve the performance of search engines on long queries (or tail queries), several prior research efforts have looked into query re-writing via term substitution or term reduction [3, 9, 16, 22, 26, 33, 34]. While these problems are well-studied and have shown significant improvements in performance on TREC data, their utility on web environment is not well understood. Long query re-writing is conceptually related to our candidate generation step; however, a critical difference is that we focus on generating query reformulations to be offered *as an ordered set* to the user instead of improving search results. In our setting, we need to consider non-lexically overlapping yet semantically related query reformulations as well as consider the quality and utility of a 'user-facing' suggestion set as a whole.

Identifying key concepts in queries: Finally, identifying key concepts in the context of search queries has also been extensively studied over TREC data and over search engine logs to some extent [3]. Conceptually, this is related to our query relaxation step, however our end-to-end approach considers the web search setting and uses complements such methods with algorithms to generate and rank candidate suggestions.

8. CONCLUSIONS

In this paper, we presented a supervised learning-based end-to-end framework to synthesize query suggestions offered to search engine users as follow-up queries. Our technique uses query logs as a guide to capture user search and intent behavior and leverages information available in web pages, search results, as well as click logs to derive suggestions. We systematically decompose a query and apply various transformations to automatically generate suggestion candidates and propose a ranking method that incorporates language models and other useful features to select high quality suggestions. We show that our system increases the coverage of unique queries with at least one good suggestion from 34% to 47.2%, leading to a 39% increase by high quality suggestions.

9. REFERENCES

[1] S. Abney and S. P. Abney. Parsing by chunks. In *Principle-Based Parsing*, 1991.

[2] P. Anick. Using terminological feedback for web search refinement: a log-based study. In *SIGIR '03*, 2003.

[3] M. Bendersky and B. Croft. Discovering key concepts in verbose queries. In *SIGIR '08*, 2008.

[4] P. Boldi, F. Bonchi, C. Castillo, D. Donato, A. Gionis, and S. Vigna. The query-flow graph: model and applications. In *CIKM '08*, 2008.

[5] E. Brill. Transformation-based error-driven learning and natural language processing: A case study in part-of-speech tagging. *Computational Linguistics*, 21(4), 1995.

[6] P. D. Bruza and T. W. Huibers. A study of aboutness in information retrieval. In *AI '96*, 1996.

[7] K. W. Church and P. Hanks. Word association norms, mutual information, and lexicography. In *ACL '89*, 1989.

[8] N. Craswell and M. Szummer. Random walks on the click graph. In *SIGIR '07*, 2007.

[9] V. Dang and B. Croft. Query reformulation using anchor text. In *WSDM '10*, 2010.

[10] L. Fitzpatrick and M. Dent. Automatic feedback using past queries: social searching? In *SIGIR '97*, 1997.

[11] B. M. Fonseca, P. B. Golgher, E. S. de Moura, and N. Ziviani. Using association rules to discover search engines related queries. In *LA-WEB '03*, 2003.

[12] J. H. Friedman. Greedy function approximation: A gradient boosting machine. *Annals of Statistics*, 29, 2000.

[13] A. Fuxman, P. Tsaparas, K. Achan, and R. Agrawal. Using the wisdom of the crowds for keyword generation. In *WWW '08*, 2008.

[14] Z. Harris. Distributional structure. *Word*, 10(23), 1954.

[15] J. Huang, J. Gao, J. Miao, X. Li, K. Wang, and F. Behr. Exploring web scale language models for search query processing. In *WWW '10*, 2010.

[16] S. Huston and B. Croft. Evaluating verbose query processing techniques. In *SIGIR '10*, 2010.

[17] Y. M. Idan Szpektor, Aristides Gionis. Improving recommendation for long-tail queries via templates. In *WWW '11*, 2011.

[18] K. Järvelin and J. Kekäläinen. Cumulated gain-based evaluation of IR techniques. *ACM Trans. Inf. Syst.*, 20, 2002.

[19] R. Jones and D. C. Fain. Query word deletion prediction. In *SIGIR '03*, 2003.

[20] R. Jones, B. Rey, O. Madani, and W. Greiner. Generating query substitutions. In *WWW '06*, 2006.

[21] R. Kneser and H. Ney. Improved backing-off for m-gram language modeling. *ICASSP 1995*, 1, 1995.

[22] G. Kumaran and V. R. Carvalho. Reducing long queries using query quality predictors. In *SIGIR '09*, 2009.

[23] J. D. Lafferty, A. McCallum, and F. C. N. Pereira. Conditional random fields: Probabilistic models for segmenting and labeling sequence data. In *ICML '01*, 2001.

[24] D. Lin. Automatic retrieval and clustering of similar words. In *COLING '98*, 1998.

[25] Q. Mei, D. Zhou, and K. Church. Query suggestion using hitting time. In *CIKM '08*, 2008.

[26] G. K. Niranjan Balasubramanian and V. R. Carvalho. Exploring reductions for long web queries. In *SIGIR '10*, 2010.

[27] P. Pantel, E. Crestan, A. Borkovsky, A.-M. Popescu, and V. Vyas. Web-scale distributional similarity and entity set expansion. In *EMNLP '09*, 2009.

[28] V. V. Raghavan and H. Sever. On the reuse of past optimal queries. In *SIGIR '95*, 1995.

[29] C. H. Ricardo Baeza-Yates and M. Mendoza. Query recommendation using query logs in search engines. In *Trends in Database Technology - EDBT 2004 Workshops*, 2005.

[30] I. Ruthven. Re-examining the potential effectiveness of interactive query expansion. In *SIGIR '03*, 2003.

[31] G. Salton. On the use of term associations in automatic information retrieval. In *COLING*, 1986.

[32] E. Terra and C. L. Clarke. Scoring missing terms in information retrieval tasks. In *CIKM '04*, 2004.

[33] M. B. Van Dang and W. B. Croft. Learning to rank query reformulations. In *SIGIR '10*, 2010.

[34] X. Wang and C. Zhai. Mining term association patterns from search logs for effective query reformulation. In *CIKM '08*, 2008.

[35] J.-R. Wen, J.-Y. Nie, and H.-J. Zhang. Clustering user queries of a search engine. In *WWW '01*, 2001.

[36] Z. Zhang and O. Nasraoui. Mining search engine query logs for query recommendation. In *WWW '06*, 2006.

Post-Ranking Query Suggestion by Diversifying Search Results

Yang Song, Dengyong Zhou, Li-wei He

Microsoft Research,
One Microsoft Way,
Redmond, WA 98052, USA
{yangsong, denzho, lhe}@microsoft.com

ABSTRACT

Query suggestion refers to the process of suggesting related queries to search engine users. Most existing researches have focused on improving the relevance of suggested queries. In this paper, we introduce the concept of diversifying the content of the search results from suggested queries while keeping the suggestion relevant. Our framework first retrieves a set of query candidates from search engine logs using random walk and other techniques. We then re-rank the suggested queries by ranking them in the order which maximizes the diversification function that measures the difference between the original search results and the results from suggested queries. The diversification function we proposed includes features like ODP category, URL and domain similarity and so on. One important outcome from our research which contradicts with most existing researches is that, with the increase of suggestion relevance, the similarity between the queries actually decreases. Experiments are conducted on a large set of human-labeled data, which is randomly sampled from a commercial search engine's log. Our experimental results indicate that the post-ranking framework significantly improves the relevance of suggested queries by comparing to existing models.

Categories and Subject Descriptors

H.3.3 [**Information Search and Retrieval**]: Text Mining

General Terms

Algorithms

Keywords

query suggestion, post-ranking re-ordering, learning-to-rank, random walk

SIGIR'11, July 24–28, 2011, Beijing, China.

1. INTRODUCTION

Query suggestion technique has been widely used in most commercially web search engines which facilitates the interaction between users and search engines. By its definition, a set of relevant queries are suggested to a user on the search engine result page (SERP) after the user submitted a query. If the user is not satisfied with the results shown on the page, he/she may choose to click on one of the suggested queries to refine the search. Research works have indicated that query suggestion greatly improves user satisfaction rate, especially for informational queries.

Previous efforts on improving the quality of query suggestion have mainly focused on discovering relevant queries from search engine logs. For example, leveraging co-clicked URLs and session information to identify relevant queries [2, 16, 3] have shown significant improvement over other methods. In the meantime, random-walk based models [17, 19] have been extensively studied due to their simplicity and scalability.

While many approaches have exhibited their effectiveness, most of them have failed to address an important issue, which is the *diversification* of the query suggestions. When a user clicks on a suggested query, he/she is expecting to gain additional information from a SERP with relevant topics to the original query. Therefore, we define the diversification between a query-suggestion pair to be *different but relevant of their contents*. Essentially, we try to find the optimal balancing point between the similarity and diversification between query-suggestion pairs. If the diversification factor is removed from our model, then the model should exhibit the same behavior as previous similarity-based approaches.

Since it is relatively difficult to measure the diversification directly by only looking at two query strings, we propose a query suggestion framework which leverages *post-ranking* features from search results. Specifically, post-ranking features are different from pre-ranking computation where all features are required to be computed before the ranked search results are returned to the users. Post-ranking features generally means the observable elements on the SERP, e.g., the titles, snippets and URLs of the results. Therefore, we define SERP diversification between two queries to be the difference between their top-returned search results. For example, Figure 1 shows an example where "delta air" is the user query and "Delta Airline" and "Delta Air Lines Jobs" are suggested queries. In this example, we treat "Delta Airline" as a bad suggestion since the top-3 results are almost identical to those of "delta air". On the other hand, "Delta Air Lines Jobs" is recognized as a good suggestion with diversified SERP results. The detailed diversification function will be discussed in our framework in Section 3.

The rest of the paper is organized as follows: Section 2 presents the related work of query suggestion; Section 3 introduces our post-ranking query suggestion framework; in Section 4 we conduct experiment to evaluate our proposal; we conclude this paper with future work in Section 5.

2. RELATED WORK

(Query Suggestion) Improving the performance and quality of query suggestion techniques have been extensively studied in the past decades. As a method mainly for interaction between search engines and users, query suggestion techniques usually cannot directly improve the relevance of the search results, but rather enhancing the entire user search experience within the same search intent. Most of the existing works rely on search engine server logs to suggest relevant queries to user inputs. Among all proposals, random walk-based methods [20, 17, 19] have exhibited noticeable performance improvement when comparing to other models. The basic idea behind random walk models is quite straightforward. Queries and URLs are represented as nodes in a bipartite graph where each edge connects one query with one URL, which indicates a click. A random walk model calculates the stable transition probability from one node to another and uses the probability to estimate the closeness between two nodes.

In [8], the authors used entropy to estimate the weight of edges instead of using the raw count. The model addressed the fact that various user clicks have different importance and therefore should be treated differently. For example, a click on a more specific URL is weighted higher than a click on a general (more common) URL. The authors introduced inverse query frequency (IQF) for edge weight estimation, which exhibited better performance than raw count-based random walk models.

The authors in [19] focused on a more difficult problem: suggest queries for rare queries. As rare queries often have very few or not click information, traditional click-based models are unable to perform well in this scenario. The authors therefore proposed to combine the information from clicked URLs and skipped URLs (URLs that are observed by the user who chose not to click) by constructing two bipartite graphs respectively. Two random walks are performed on each graph. Their results are combined optimally by minimizing the error function that calculates the correlation between URLs. Experiments suggested significant improvement over all other random walk models for rare queries.

(Diversify Query Suggestions) Recently, authors in [15] proposed a framework for diversifying query suggestion results. Their method leveraged Markov random walk model on the query-URL bipartite graph by calculating the query hitting time. The model was capable of encouraging diversities in the search results while keeping the queries semantically related. There are some key differences between our approach and theirs. First of all, we leverage the full SERP information which contains rich signals and features, while their approach only leveraged click information from log. Since it is well known that query-URL bipartite graph is often very sparse, the quality of suggestion may be impacted. Secondly, due to the sparseness of the query-URL graph, a rare query may not exist in the log and therefore the authors' method cannot work in this case, which has no impact on our framework. Finally, our framework is quite flexible and responsive. Given a set of suggestions, we are able to rank them in real-time and adjust to the change of SERP accordingly, while their approach worked on a static set of query-URL logs that needs to retrain itself very often.

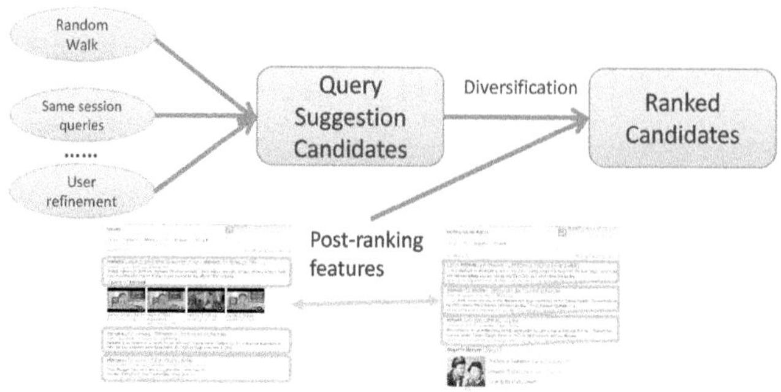

Figure 2: An illustration of our framework. Step 1 generates suggestion candidates. Step 2 rank the candidates by applying a diversification function.

(Diversify Search Results) There has been many researches that addressed the diversification of search results [1, 5, 25]. The basic idea is that search results should not only be relevant to the user query, but also relevant and different from each other. While resembles some of the techniques in this area, the objective of our research in this paper is quite different. Rather than focusing on improving the relevance of documents by re-ranking them, we aim at re-ranking suggested queries which help users refine their intent. Besides, previous researches mainly focused on *with-in query* document re-ranking for a particular query, while our approach handles *between-query* document list comparison–arguably a more challenging problem. One concern is that most of the existing works on diversifying search results only focused on ambiguous queries where those queries have more than one user intents, while our approach does not possess such limitation and can be generalized to all queries. In general, these two approaches are orthogonal to each other and can both be leveraged to improve user search experience without affecting each other.

(Post-ranking Relevance Improvement) To the best of our knowledge, there exists only a few techniques that leverage post-ranking or SERP features to improve the retrieval quality in real-time. In [22], the authors collect negative implicit feedbacks from users to improve ranking. Specifically, when a user clicks the next page button on SERP, the authors assume that all previous results are irrelevant. Given those top-N negative examples, the authors propose to re-rank the remaining U results in real-time. Consequently, the authors introduce two strategies for negative feedback: 1. modifies query directly given the negative feedback, and 2. combines scores from positive and negative feedbacks optimally. Improvements are observed on benchmark TREC data sets over traditional retrieval systems.

3. THE FRAMEWORK

Our framework is divided into primarily two steps. Dur-

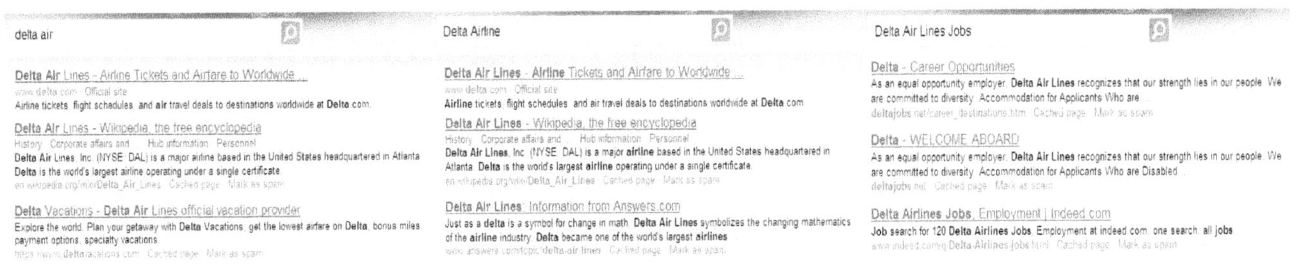

Figure 1: An example of SERP results for three queries. "Delta Airline" is a bad suggestion for query "delta air" due to identical search results. "Delta Airline Jobs" offers better diversification.

ing the first step, we generate query suggestion candidates from different sources based on log information. After that, we apply our diversification function to rank the candidates by leveraging post-ranking features. Figure 2 sketches the process.

3.1 Generating Suggestion Candidates

Step 1 of our process focuses on generating candidates from search logs. In this step we put emphasis on the recall of the suggestion, therefore a raw set of candidates from different sources are generated, regardless of their relevance, and to be ranked in the next step.

The first source of candidates we collect comes from random walk models. A basic random walk with restart (RWR) model is applied to the query-click logs due to its simplicity and scalability. For detail implementation of RWR, we refer interested users to [20].

User session is another important source for generating candidates. A user session is defined by search engines which often contains all user activities within a certain period of time. Search engines usually record user queries, clicks, timestamps and other information in the log. If the user becomes inactive for a while (e.g., 30 minutes), that user session ends. There exists much useful information that can be used to extract relevant queries. Specifically, we pay attention to user refined queries within the same user session. A user refined query is defined as the query reformulated by the user which followed immediately after a no-click query. For example, a user issued query "super bowl" but did not get the desired results. The user then reformulated the query to "super bowl 2011" and clicks on one of the results.

Note that there also exist many other sources that related queries can be discovered, which we do not explore in this paper. Since the focus of this paper is the diversification effect on query suggestion, this part only serves as a preliminary source that generates a set of query candidates, which could certainly be improved in the future work.

3.2 The Ranking Function

To achieve the diversification of search results while keep the suggested queries relevant, we introduce the following ranking function R:

$$R(Q_o, Q_s) = \mathcal{D}(Q_o, Q_s) + \lambda \mathcal{S}(Q_o, Q_s), \tag{1}$$

where Q_o denotes the original query and Q_s a suggested query. The first term on the right hand side of eq.(1) measures the SERP diversification between two queries, while the second term estimates the similarity between them. λ is a tuning parameter which balances the contributions of these two terms. This equation indicates that queries with high diversification score and high similarity with the original queries are likely to achieve high ranking scores (for $\lambda > 0$). Next, we discuss how the functions $\mathcal{D}$ and $\mathcal{S}$ are defined.

Since it is difficult to directly measure the diversification between two queries, we instead resort to post-ranking features, i.e., SERP features returned by search engines. Our assumption is similar to the traditional pseudo-relevance feedback strategy [11, 24] which treats all top results as relevant to the user queries. Specifically, the diversification of two queries is defined as the aggregated score over top N returned search results (SR):

$$\mathcal{D}(Q_o, Q_s) = \mathcal{D}(SR_{Q_o}, SR_{Q_s}), \tag{2}$$

where SR_{Q_o} indicates the ordered search results list for query Q_o. Furthermore, a set of features f is defined, where an adoption of a linear function for $\mathcal{D}$ that combines the scores from features is assumed.

$$\mathcal{D}(SR_{Q_o}, SR_{Q_s}) = \sum_k w_k f_k(SR_{Q_o}, SR_{Q_s}), \tag{3}$$

with w_k measuring the weight of the kth feature.

In Table 1, we list several features used in this paper. The first feature f_1 measures the similarity of the ODP categories between two URL sets SR_{Q_o} and SR_{Q_s}, which aggregates the similarity over each individual pairs of URLs. Specifically, the Open Directory Project (ODP) contains a repository of human-labeled URL categories with over 4 million URLs. A tree-based taxonomy is specified in ODP where lower levels indicate more specific categories, e.g., $/Sports/Baseball/International/$. To determine the category of URLs, we leverage a sophisticated content-based hierarchical classifier [4]. Algorithm 1 sketches the method to calculate the similarity between two hierarchical labels. Basically, two labels are more similar if their lowest common ancestor (LCA) is located at lower level. For example, as illustrated in Figure 3, label $/Sports/Football/NFL/$ has lower similarity with $/Sports/Baseball/International/$ than $/Sports/Baseball/Amateur/$.

Features f_2 and f_3 check the similarity between URL strings and domain names. The indicator function $\mathbb{I}$ equals to 1 if the two strings are the same and 0 otherwise. A discounted denominator is applied to address the importance of the URL position. Similar to the DCG [10] measurement, if URL_i and URL_j are the same with very high SERP positions (smaller values of i and j), they will be penalized a lot by the denominator.

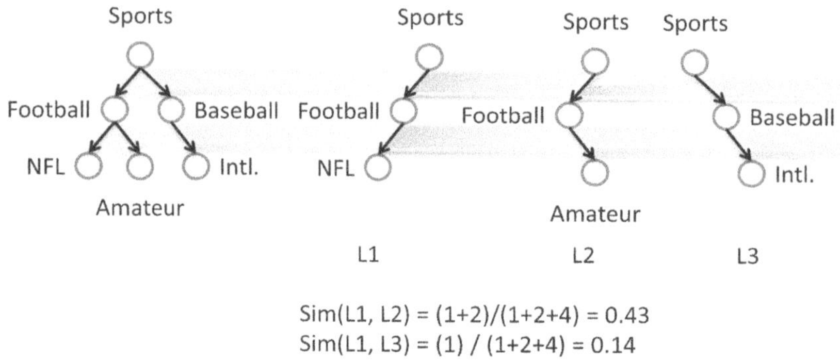

Figure 3: An example of calculating similarities between ODP categories. The left figure shows the subtree under node *Sports*. Tree $L1$ and $L2$ has higher similarity than $L3$ since their lowest common ancestor *Football* is closer to the leaf node. Here the similarity is calculated using $m = 2$.

Algorithm 1 URL Similarity Calculation

Input two URLs $\{URL_1, URL_2\}$, labels $\{lb_1, lb_2\}$, weight m $(m > 1)$
Initialize $base = 1$, $sim = 0$, $denominator = 0$
for each level i in the tree
  if $lb_1(i) = lb_2(i)$
    $sim = sim + base$
  end if
  $denominator = denominator + base$
  $base = base * m$
end for
$sim = \frac{sim}{denominator}$
Output sim

Feature f_4 uses Kendall τ rank correlation coefficient [12] to compute the correlation between two ordered SERP lists. A pair is said to be *concordant* if and only if both URLs are identical and ranked at the same position. Otherwise, they are *discordant*.

On the other hand, the second term $\mathcal{S}(Q_o, Q_s)$ in eq.(1) measures the string similarity between the query and a suggestion. A standard Levenshtein distance-based algorithm is applied here, with λ a free parameter controlling its relative weight. Algorithm 2 sketches the process. Note that there are lots of more sophisticated methods to calculate query similarity and arguably ours is an oversimplified one. However, since the focus of this paper is primarily on the diversification part, we leave this part for improvement in the future. Besides, as we shall see in the experiments, the query string similarity in general decreases with the increase of suggestion relevance. Nevertheless, even this oversimplified function leads to significant performance improvement when combined with several diversification features.

3.3 Learning The Ranking Function

Combining eq.(2) and eq.(3) into eq.(1), we have

$$R(Q_o, Q_s) = \sum_k w_k f_k(SR_{Q_o}, SR_{Q_s}) + \lambda \mathcal{S}(Q_o, Q_s), \quad (4)$$

which contains parameters λ and $w = \{w_1, ..., w_k\}$. We rename $\lambda = w_0$ and expand $w = \{w_0, w_1, ..., w_k\}$ to be the feature weights to learn. The objective is therefore to optimize these parameters given a set of labeled query-suggestion pairs. Similar to the learning-to-rank [14] framework, we use a supervised learning approach in our paper.

Algorithm 2 Query Similarity Calculation

Input two queries Q_o, Q_s, a list of stop words
max_length = max($len(Q_o)$, $len(Q_s)$)
word_distance = LevenshteinDistance(RemoveStopWords(Q_o), RemoveStopWOrds(Q_s))
query_similarity = word_distance / max_length
output query_similarity

3.3.1 Training Labels

We use human assessors to evaluate the relevance between query and suggestions. For each pair of query suggestions, the assessors are given the queries, their corresponding search result pages side-by-side, and asked to make a binary decision of whether these two queries are related. Every pair is given to three independent assessors. The final score is the number of assessors who labeled that pair as related. Therefore, the label is always between 0 and 3 with 3 being the most related and 0 unrelated.

It is important to notice that in the judgment guidelines, the assessors are only asked to label the pairs as related or not based on their impressions on the SERP. Because if the assessors are asked to judge the diversification of the page or the similarity between queries, then the judgment labels may not reflect the true relevance of the suggested query. The weight of the diversification function should be learnt from the labels rather than being used as a guideline for judgment, since diversifying the SERP may or may not lead to a higher click through rate (CTR) on the suggested queries, before we have the true relevance labels.

Besides the "related" label, we also ask assessors to judge if the two SERPs are totally identical on their top K ($K = 3$ in our guideline) results. If so, a "Duplicate" label becomes positive which overrides the related label to be zero.

3.4 Learning Algorithms

The general ranking function in eq. (4) presents us with opportunity to apply more than one categories of learning algorithms to the training data. Specifically, we learn the ranking function by using classification, linear regression, ordinal regression and learning-to-rank frameworks.

3.4.1 Classification

With four classes of labels ranging from 0 to 3, a multi-class Support Vector Machines (SVMs) classifier [21, 7] is applied to classify instances into one of the four classes. The objective of SVMs is to maximize the margin of the separation hyper plane while subject to minimizing the classification error rate. The output of SVMs is a probability distribution over the classes. Therefore, the final ranking of an instance is calculated as follows:

$$Rank(Q_t) = \sum_{c=0}^{3} cP(c). \tag{5}$$

For example, the instance with probability distribution of $\{0.1, 0.3, 0.2, 0.4\}$ has a higher rank (1.9) than the instance of $\{0.3, 0.1, 0.1, 0.5\}$ which has a rank of 1.8, even though both instances are classified into class 3. This approach has shown very effective ranking results in previous models [13].

3.4.2 Linear Regression

A linear regression model estimates the label (response) y_i as a continuous variable given a set of C independent variables $x_i = \{x_{i1}, ...x_{iC}\}$:

$$y_i = \beta_0 + \sum_{c=1}^{C} \beta_c x_{ic} + \epsilon_i, \tag{6}$$

with ϵ_i being the error term. Linear regression optimizes by minimizing the sum-of-squared residuals (SSE). The output is directly used as the final ranking of the queries.

3.4.3 Ordinal Regression

Ordinal regression is essentially an extension of the multinomial logistic regression, which is a regression model but generalizes logistic regression to discrete outputs. The shortcoming of logistic regression is due to its ignorance of the orders of categories. Instead, ordinal regression considers this situation by using a logit function in the model:

$$\begin{aligned} f(Z(x) &= \log \frac{Z(x)}{1 - Z(x)} \\ &= \log \frac{P(Y \leq y_i|X)}{P(Y > y_i|X)} \\ &= \alpha_i + \beta X, i = 1, ..., k-1 \\ where \quad Z(x) &= \frac{e^{(\alpha_i + \beta X)}}{1 + e^{(\alpha_i + \beta X)}}, \end{aligned} \tag{7}$$

The model is usually estimated using maximum likelihood method. Previous results have indicated its superiority over logistic regression [6].

3.4.4 Learning To Rank

Unlike all aforementioned algorithms, the learning-to-rank framework directly optimizes the ranking loss, i.e., it focuses on the relative order between two list items. Therefore, the objective of learning is to directly minimize the number of misclassified pairs. Out of all loss functions used in learning-to-rank, Normalized Discounted Cumulated Gain (NDCG) is most commonly used. Specifically, NDCG is defined as the DCG score of a ranking result, divided by the ideal DCG,

$$NDCG = \frac{DCG}{IDCG}, \tag{8}$$

Algorithm 3 The LambdaSMART algorithm

```
Input: N = # of queries, M = # of iterations,
       L = # of leaf nodes, v = the shrinkage parameter
for i = 1 to N
Initialize F_0(x_i) to be the base model
end for
for m = 1 to M
  for i = 1 to N
    y_i ← λ_i
    w_i ← ∂y_i / ∂F(x_i)
  end for
  Create L−terminal node tree {R_lm}_{l=1}^L
  for l = 0 to L
    r_lm ← (Σ_{x_i ∈ R_lm} y_i) / (Σ_{x_i ∈ R_lm} w_i)
  end for
  for i = 0 to N
    F_m(x_i) ← F_{m−1}(x_i) + v Σ_l r_lm 𝕀(x_i ∈ R_lm)
  end for
end for
```

where the DCG score is calculated by dividing the relevance score with the position of the ranking,

$$DCG = \sum_{i=1}^{M} \frac{2^{s(i)} - 1}{\log(1 + i)}, \tag{9}$$

where $s(i)$ is the relevance score assigned by human assessors. The higher the NDCG score is, the better the ranking result is assumed.

We choose the LambdaSMART [23] algorithm as our framework due to its superior ranking performance. The algorithm leverages the MART (multiple additive regression trees) boosting framework [9] to perform gradient descent at each iteration. Algorithm 3 sketches the framework.

4. EMPIRICAL ANALYSIS

This section presents experimental results on real-world data mined from a commercial Web search engine. We discuss how the diversification function affects the relevance of related queries, as well as the importance of individual features and their combinations.

4.1 Data Acquisition

From search engine server logs, we randomly sampled 13,421 queries between September 2010 and November 2010. These are queries that trigger at least one related search on the search result page. The search engine we use generates related queries from a combination of different resources, including but not limited to: random walk on the query-click graph, similar queries from the same user session, collaborative filtering from similar users and so on. Since generating query candidates is not the focus of this paper, we won't discuss in detail about this part. However, we will show the improvement of our approach by comparing to one of the techniques in later sections.

As mentioned above, the query-suggestion pairs are given to assessors for evaluation and assigned with a score between 0 and 3. Table 2 summarizes the statistics of the data set. In Table 3, we show several query-suggestion pairs and their judgment labels.

4.2 Parameter Initialization

We pre-define the following parameters in our experiments.

Label	Count
Unrelated (0)	1597
Somewhat related (1)	2099
Related (2)	2471
Closely related (3)	7254
Duplicate (0)	1875

Table 2: Statistics of data used in our experiment.

For comparing SERP difference, we choose the top-10 ($N = 10$) blue links returned by a major search engine. For the LambdaSMART algorithm, we choose $M = 500$ iterations and $v = 0.1$ the shrinkage parameter. These parameters are fixed since the algorithms are relatively robust to their changes, as shown in previous researches [23]. We show the sensitivity of the remaining parameters in later sections.

4.3 Feature Correlation

Figure 4 plots the boxplots of feature values vs. the human assigned labels. The first plot shows the query similarity vs. the labels, where the query similarity is used as a regularization factor in eq.(1). It can be observed that with the increase of relevance (from 0 to 3), the similarities between queries and suggestions generally decrease. This finding is contradictory to many existing researches that leveraged query similarity to find related queries, which strongly supports our introduction of the diversification metric. The second figure shows the ODP category similarity scores with the change of labels. We show that the most related query suggestions have higher category similarity than unrelated suggestions, which indicates that users are still interested in seeing more results from similar topics (categories), rather than switching to other intents.

The third and fourth figures plot the URL and domain similarity scores vs. labels. Both results demonstrate that the increase of relevance demands a decrease in result similarity. Comparatively, the decrease of URL similarity is more drastic than domain similarity, which makes sense since URLs within the same domain might still exhibit different topics which are potentially of interests to the users. The Kendall τ rank shows similar results as the domain similarity in Figure 5.

We further use Pearson's χ^2 test [18] to test the correlation significance between features and labels. Table 4 depicts the results of χ^2 as well as their corresponding p-values, where in general high χ^2 values with low p-value indicates higher significance (for a fixed degree of freedom). It can be observed that all five features have strong correlation with the labels, with statistically significance given p-values < 0.05.

4.4 Performance Analysis

In this section, we present the detailed results of the four learning algorithms. We separate the data into 60% training, 10% validation and 30% testing for tuning the parameters. For multi-class SVM, we use the linear kernel since it performed better than sigmoid and polynomial kernels for our data. The best balancing factor c is tuned using cross validation and found to be 0.85. For the LambdaSMART algorithm, we specify L the number of nodes in the leaf to be 2 (stump) and 20, respectively. The weight of a feature from LambdaSMART is calculated according to the number of times that feature is used to split the decision tree. Table 5 lists the feature weights learnt from all models. In general, the URL similarity and ODP category similarity features demonstrate the highest weights. The query similarity feature ranks second to the last, which indicates the importance of diversification features in overall performance.

Next, we compare the ranking performance of these algorithms. As illustrated in eq.(8) and eq.(9), NDCG is the most popular metric for retrieval performance which addresses both relevance and the position of the returned results. Since most of the time search engines return no more than six suggested queries, we will measure NDCG@5 and NDCG@1 in our experiments. For regression, the output is used directly to rank the suggestions. For SVM, eq. (5) is used to calculate the ranking based on the classification output. Figure 5 summarizes the results of NDCG@1 and NDCG@5. While linear regression shows the worst performance, the LambdaSMART algorithm significantly outperforms all others. In general, LambdaSMART achieves 0.79 and 0.74 for NDCG@1, with 20 and 2 leaf nodes respectively. For NDCG@5, it also performs well with 0.63 and 0.59 NDCG scores.

Furthermore, we illustrate the importance of individual features in retrieval performance. Specifically, we calculate the NDCG scores by using only one feature at a time, versus combining the only similarity feature (Query) with each individual diversification features. Since in our previous experiment, LambdaSMART demonstrated significantly better performance than all others, we will only use LambdaSMART for all our remaining experiments. Table 6 tabulates the results. In general, for individual feature comparison, ODP and URL similarity yield the highest NDCG scores. With the combination of similarity measurement and diversification criteria, we observe that Query+URL yields the best performance among all, whereas Query+ODP also shows competitive performance. Both combinations are very close to the optimal performance of LambdaSMART that uses all features, which suggests the usefulness of the similarity and diversification mixtures in real-world applications.

4.5 Performance for Different Query Types

Furthermore, we slice and dice the results to see how the proposed diversification measurement affects different types of queries. Statistically, in our data set, the average length of queries is 2.51, whereas the average length of suggestions

Query	Suggestion	Label
priceline.com	IMS Health	0
jet blue	Blue Jet Lightning	0
sign up for hotmail	Create Free Hotmail Account	1
inception	Dictionary Inception	1
youtube broadcast	YouTube Videos	2
broan	Home Depot	2
dessert	Dessert Recipes	3
yahoo maps	MapQuest Driving Directions	3
fun school	fun school kaboose	Dup
swa	Southwest Airlines	Dup

Table 3: Examples of query-suggestion pairs with their labels. Dup = 0 in our definition.

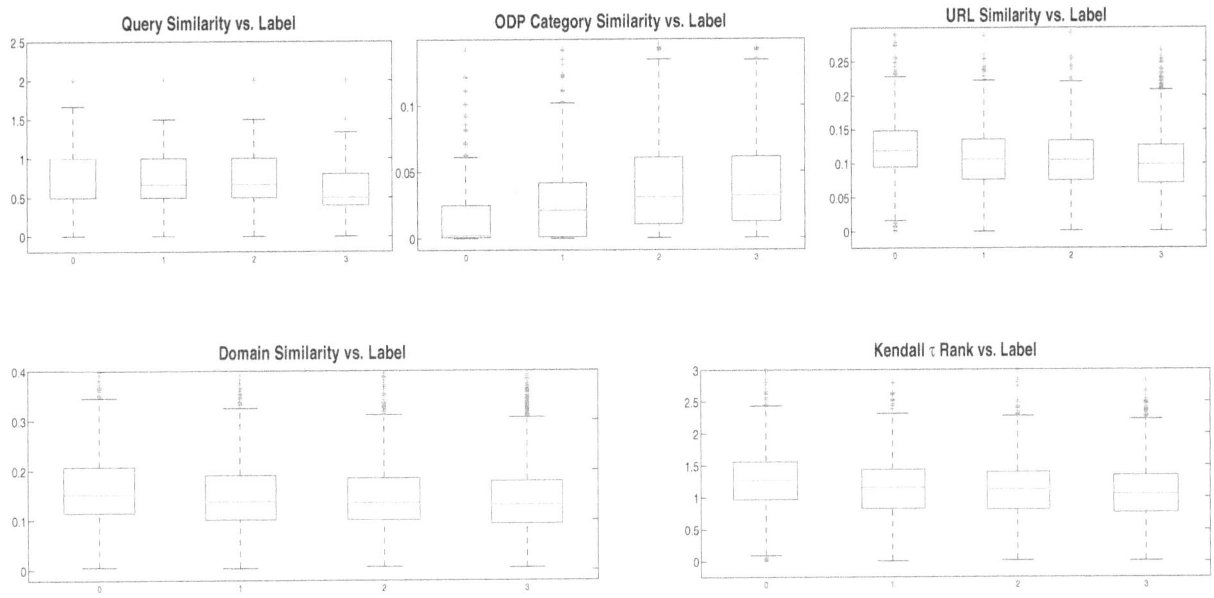

Figure 4: Boxplot of feature values vs. human-judged labels. Query similarity decreases with the increase of label relevance. The ODP category similarity increases when suggested queries are more related. All other diversification features indicate negative correlations with the labels.

Feature	χ^2	p-value
Query Similarity	22.0454	0.009098
ODP Category Similarity	27.4349	0.003289
URL Similarity	24.5443	0.005405
Domain Similarity	10.1814	0.012545
Kendall τ rank	18.5849	0.008500

Table 4: Pearson's χ^2 Test result with $df = 13,420$ and corresponding p-values.

Type	Query Length	Suggestion Length
Short	1	2.47
Medium	2.76	3.2
Long	4.87	3.7
Navigational	1.62	2.46
Informational	2.26	2.73
Overall	2.51	3.02

Table 7: Statistics of average query-suggestion lengths in several query types.

is 3.02. We break down the queries into Long ($length > 4$), Medium ($2 \leq length \leq 4$) and Short ($length < 2$). In total, there are 1350 long queries, 7551 medium queries, and 4283 short queries. On the other hand, we split queries into frequent queries and infrequent queries. Arguably, most frequent queries can be treated as navigational queries such as "facebook", while infrequent queries are mostly informational queries. Figure 6 shows the log-log plot of query length vs. query frequency. In our experiment, we specify the top 1% most frequent queries to be navigational, and the bottom 50% to be informational[1]. Table 7 summarizes the statistics.

In Figure 7, we report the comparison for different query types in terms of NDCG values, where the overall NDCG of all queries (the top bar) is measured against all query types. It is evident to observe that informational queries gain higher NDCG scores than navigational queries, whereas short queries gain lower NDCG scores than medium and long queries. As shown in Table 7, the average suggestion lengths for short and navigational queries are much higher than the queries themselves. In our opinion, users who issue navigational or short queries to search engines often have a quite clear intent in mind, and thus don't click on suggested queries very often. On the other hand, users who issue longer queries are less clear about their intent, and more likely to use related queries to reformulate their intent.

[1]Note that our cut-off threshold is not very strict, since the definition of navigational and informational are quite vague and varies from different data sets.

4.6 Comparison to Random Walk

Recall that our framework is essentially a ranking (or reranking) algorithm based on an existing set of query candidates. As discussed in Section 3.1, random walk techniques have shown noticeable performance on related search area. It is therefore important to see how much NDCG gain our framework can achieve by comparing to the results from random walks.

The underlying algorithm is quite straightforward which iteratively performs random walk on query-click bipartite graph until convergence. For details of using random walk on click graphs, we refer interested users to [20]. After random walk, each query and its related queries are represented in a vector, where each entry is a float point number indicating how close the suggestion is to the query. This number is naturally used to rank related queries.

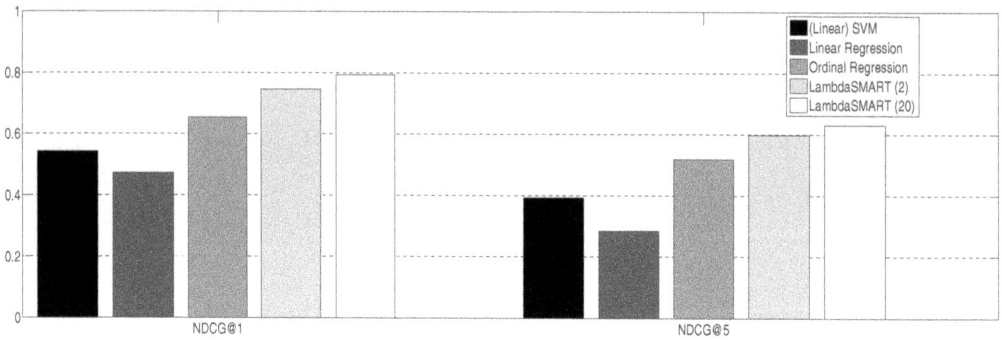

Figure 5: NDCG comparison of the four algorithms. Both NDCG@1 and NDCG@5 are shown. LambdaSMART demonstrates the best overall performance.

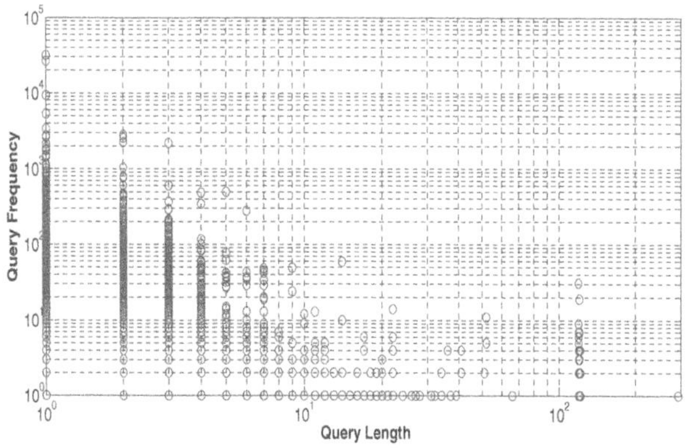

Figure 6: Log-log plot of query frequency vs. query length in our data set.

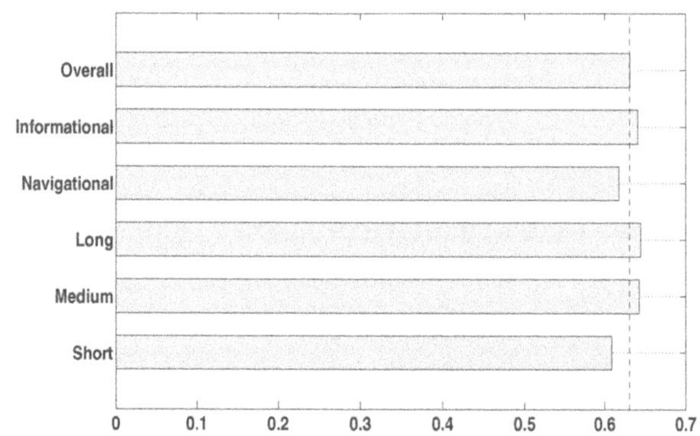

Figure 7: NDCG@5 performance on different query types. The overall performance is from LambdaSMART (20).

In addition, we also compare with the method (DQS) in [15] which essentially used random walk to find related queries and leveraged hitting time to measure their diversification qualities. All the parameters are set default as described in their paper.

Figure 8 compares the NDCG scores among four models. It is clearly that both our algorithms improve retrieval quality on the basis of random walk results. While linear regression gains 2.3% NDCG gain at position 1, LambdaSMART achieves more than 20% improvement against random walks. Both LambdaSMART and linear regression have relatively small standard deviation across all queries. On the other hand, the DQS algorithm has an overall performance close to the baseline algorithm. Although achieved a better NDCG score than baseline and linear regression for position 1 (0.5037), DQS exhibits the highest standard deviation among all algorithms and gradually loses the advantage over the baseline. Table 8 shows several examples of query-suggestion pairs, which demonstrates the effectiveness of re-ordering the related queries from random walk results.

5. CONCLUSION AND FUTURE WORK

In this work, we presented a novel way of improving the relevance of query suggestion by diversifying search engine results page. Specifically, our framework first gathered a set of suggestion candidates, and then ranked these suggestions in the descending order of their diversification scores. Our diversification function considered both the query similarity as well as several diversification features, including URL difference, domain difference, ODP category difference and Kendall τ coefficient rank. We randomly sampled a large set (over 10,000) of query-suggestion pairs from a commercial search engine, and asked human assessors to label their level of relevance. Given these labeled training data, we proposed to leverage different kinds of learning algorithms to optimize the ranking function, including SVM classifier, linear regression, ordinal regression and learning-to-rank algorithms. Experimental results indicated that the learning-to-rank algorithm – LambdaSMART – was able to achieve outstanding performance by outperforming all other learning algorithms, as well as two random walk-based algorithms, significantly. Our framework was able to improve the NDCG score from 0.45 to 0.79, for position 1 by comparing to random walk framework. Experimental results also demonstrated the importance of the diversification features which significantly improved the relevance of the suggested queries when combining with the query similarity feature.

An important discovery of this paper was that, with the increase of the suggestion relevance, the similarity between queries and suggested queries indeed drops. This is contra-

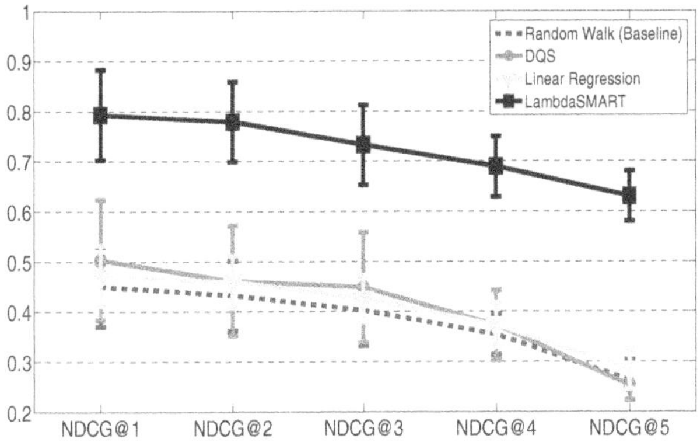

Figure 8: Comparison of NDCG between random walk results and two of our models: linear gression and LambdaSMART.

dictory to many existing researches with aimed at making suggestions based on query similarity solely. The human-judged labels indicated that users of search engines are more willing to click on suggestions that could potentially lead to more diversified search results, but still within the same user search intent. This fact is especially obvious for medium and long queries, as well as informational queries.

As a preliminary research towards the direction of using post-ranking features, there exists lots of room for improvement. In the future, we plan to explore more features and signals on the search result pages to improve the power of the diversification function. Another direction is to incorporate user behaviors into real-time suggestion re-ranking, including but not limited to, user clicked URLs, skipped URLs as well as behaviors from similar users.

6. REFERENCES

[1] R. Agrawal, S. Gollapudi, A. Halverson, and S. Ieong. Diversifying search results. In *Proceedings of WSDM '09*, pages 5–14, New York, NY, USA, 2009. ACM.

[2] R. Baeza-yates, C. Hurtado, and M. Mendoza. Query recommendation using query logs in search engines. In *In International Workshop on Clustering Information over the Web (ClustWeb, in conjunction with EDBT), Creete*, pages 588–596. Springer, 2004.

[3] R. Baeza-Yates and A. Tiberi. Extracting semantic relations from query logs. In *Proceedings of KDD '07*, pages 76–85, New York, NY, USA, 2007. ACM.

[4] P. N. Bennett and N. Nguyen. Refined experts: improving classification in large taxonomies. In *SIGIR '09*, pages 11–18, New York, NY, USA, 2009. ACM.

[5] J. Carbonell and J. Goldstein. The use of mmr, diversity-based reranking for reordering documents and producing summaries. In *Proceedings of SIGIR '98*, pages 335–336, New York, NY, USA, 1998. ACM.

[6] W. Chu and S. S. Keerthi. New approaches to support vector ordinal regression. In *Proceedings of ICML '05*, pages 145–152, New York, NY, USA, 2005. ACM.

[7] K. Crammer, Y. Singer, N. Cristianini, J. Shawe-taylor, and B. Williamson. On the algorithmic implementation of multiclass kernel-based vector machines. *Journal of Machine Learning Research*, 2:2001, 2001.

[8] H. Deng, I. King, and M. R. Lyu. Entropy-biased models for query representation on the click graph. In *SIGIR '09*, pages 339–346, New York, NY, USA, 2009. ACM.

[9] J. H. Friedman. Greedy function approximation: A gradient boosting machine. *Annals of Statistics*, 29:1189–1232, 2000.

[10] K. Järvelin and J. Kekäläinen. Cumulated gain-based evaluation of ir techniques. *ACM Trans. Inf. Syst.*, 20:422–446, October 2002.

[11] T. Joachims, L. Granka, B. Pan, H. Hembrooke, and G. Gay. Accurately interpreting clickthrough data as implicit feedback. In *SIGIR '05*, pages 154–161, New York, NY, USA, 2005. ACM.

[12] M. G. Kendall. A New Measure of Rank Correlation. *Biometrika*, 30(1/2):81–93, June 1938.

[13] P. Li, C. J. C. Burges, and Q. Wu. Mcrank: Learning to rank using multiple classification and gradient boosting. In J. C. Platt, D. Koller, Y. Singer, and S. T. Roweis, editors, *NIPS*. MIT Press, 2007.

[14] T.-Y. Liu. Learning to rank for information retrieval. *Found. Trends Inf. Retr.*, 3:225–331, March 2009.

[15] H. Ma, M. R. Lyu, and I. King. Diversifying query suggestion results. In *AAAI*, 2010.

[16] H. Ma, H. Yang, I. King, and M. R. Lyu. Learning latent semantic relations from clickthrough data for query suggestion. In *CIKM '08*, pages 709–718, New York, NY, USA, 2008. ACM.

[17] Q. Mei, D. Zhou, and K. Church. Query suggestion using hitting time. In *CIKM '08*, pages 469–478, New York, NY, USA, 2008. ACM.

[18] K. Pearson. On the criterion that a given system of deviations from the probable in the case of a correlated system of variables is such that it can be reasonably supposed to have arisen from random sampling. *Philosophical Magazine*, 302:157–175, 1900.

[19] Y. Song and L. He. Optimal rare query suggestion with implicit user feedback. In *WWW '10*, pages 901–910, New York, NY, USA, 2010. ACM.

[20] H. Tong, C. Faloutsos, and J.-Y. Pan. Random walk with restart: fast solutions and applications. *Knowl. Inf. Syst.*, 14:327–346, March 2008.

[21] I. Tsochantaridis. *Support vector machine learning for interdependent and structured output spaces.* PhD thesis, Providence, RI, USA, 2005. AAI3174684.

[22] X. Wang, H. Fang, and C. Zhai. Improve retrieval accuracy for difficult queries using negative feedback. In *CIKM '07*, pages 991–994, New York, NY, USA, 2007. ACM.

[23] Q. Wu, C. J. Burges, K. M. Svore, and J. Gao. Adapting boosting for information retrieval measures. *Inf. Retr.*, 13:254–270, June 2010.

[24] C. Zhai and J. Lafferty. Model-based feedback in the language modeling approach to information retrieval. In *CIKM '01*, pages 403–410, New York, NY, USA, 2001. ACM.

[25] C. Zhai and J. Lafferty. A risk minimization framework for information retrieval. *Inf. Process. Manage.*, 42:31–55, January 2006.

Feature	Description
$f_1(SR_{Q_o}, SR_{Q_s}) = Sim(ODP(SR_{Q_o}), ODP(SR_{Q_s}))$ $= \sum_i \sum_j Sim(ODP(SR^i_{Q_o}), ODP(SR^j_{Q_o}))$	The similarity of the ODP category between two URL sets
$f_2(SR_{Q_o}, SR_{Q_s}) = Sim(URL(SR_{Q_o}), URL(SR_{Q_s}))$ $= \sum_i \sum_j \mathbb{I}(URL(SR^i_{Q_o}) = URL(SR^j_{Q_o}))/\log_2(i+j)$	check if URL_i is the same as URL_j, discounted by the position of URL_i
$f_3(SR_{Q_o}, SR_{Q_s}) = Sim(DM(SR_{Q_o}), DM(SR_{Q_s}))$ $= \sum_i \sum_j \mathbb{I}(DM(SR^i_{Q_o}) = DM(SR^j_{Q_o}))/\log_2(i+j)$	check if the domain of URL_i is the same as URL_j, discounted by its position
$f_4(SR_{Q_o}, SR_{Q_s}) = \tau(SR_{Q_o}, SR_{Q_s})$ $= \{(\#\text{ concordant pairs}) - (\#\text{ discordant pairs})\}/0.5n(n-1)$	Kendall τ rank correlation coefficient for two ordered URL lists

Table 1: Features used to calculated diversification between two queries.

	Query Sim	ODP Sim	URL Sim	Domain Sim	Kendall τ Rank
(Linear) SVM	0.0145	0.0230	0.0783	0.0092	0.0110
Linear Regression	0.1341	0.1613	0.2935	0.2540	0.1755
Ordinal Regression	0.1758	0.2390	0.2406	0.1973	0.2055
LambdaSMART (2)	0.8391	0.8305	0.9512	0.9336	0.7795
LambdaSMART (20)	0.8214	0.9676	0.9827	0.7382	0.5882
Average	**0.39698**	**0.44428**	**0.50926**	**0.42646**	**0.35194**

Table 5: The weights of features from four learning algorithms. For SVM, linear kernel is applied. For LambdaSMART, we try both $L = 2$ and 20 for the number of leaf nodes.

	Query	ODP	URL	Domain	Kendall	Query+ODP	Query+URL	Query+Domain	Query+Kendall
NDCG@1	0.6466	0.6997	0.6606	0.5925	0.5641	0.7284	0.7245	0.6933	0.6873
NDCG@5	0.5728	0.6433	0.6082	0.5218	0.5039	0.6489	0.6407	0.6284	0.6177
Average	0.6097	0.6365	0.6694	0.5572	0.5340	0.6686	0.6826	0.6608	0.6525

Table 6: The NDCG scores of using individual features alone vs. combining similarity feature (Query) with individual diversification features. Results are measured using LambdaSMART algorithm.

Query	Random Walk Result	LambdaSMART Result	DCG_RW	DCG_Lambda	DCG Gain
delta airline	Delta Air Lines SkyMiles Alaska Airlines Delta Air Lines Credit Union Delta Airline Flight Delta Air Lines Reservations	Delta Airline Flight Delta Air Lines Reservations Delta Air Lines SkyMiles Alaska Airlines Delta Air Lines Credit Union	7.81	10.82	**+3.01**
sierra trading post	Sierra Equipment Sierra Trading Post Jobs Sierra Traders sierra club reviews Lands' End	Sierra Trading Post Jobs Lands' End Sierra Traders Sierra Equipment sierra club reviews	6.10	10.39	**+4.29**
old cars	cool cars Police Student oldsmobile cars antique cars old houses	antique cars cool cars oldsmobile cars old houses Police Student	6.51	9.39	**+2.88**

Table 8: Examples of query-suggestion pairs from random walk and re-ordered by LambdaSMART algorithm. DCG_RW is the DCG score achieved by random walk. DCG_Lambda is the score from LambdaSMART.

Automatic Boolean Query Suggestion for Professional Search

Youngho Kim
yhkim@cs.umass.edu

Jangwon Seo
jangwon@cs.umass.edu

W. Bruce Croft
croft@cs.umass.edu

Center for Intelligent Information Retrieval
Department of Computer Science
University of Massachusetts Amherst, MA 01003, USA

ABSTRACT

In professional search environments, such as patent search or legal search, search tasks have unique characteristics: 1) users interactively issue several queries for a topic, and 2) users are willing to examine many retrieval results, i.e., there is typically an emphasis on recall. Recent surveys have also verified that professional searchers continue to have a strong preference for Boolean queries because they provide a record of what documents were searched. To support this type of professional search, we propose a novel Boolean query suggestion technique. Specifically, we generate Boolean queries by exploiting decision trees learned from pseudo-labeled documents and rank the suggested queries using query quality predictors. We evaluate our algorithm in simulated patent and medical search environments. Compared with a recent effective query generation system, we demonstrate that our technique is effective and general.

Categories and Subject Descriptors

H.3.3 [**Information Storage and Retrieval**]: Information Search and Retrieval – Query Formulation, Search Process.

General Terms

Algorithms, Experimentation.

Keywords

Boolean query suggestion, prior-art search, patentability search.

1. INTRODUCTION

Query suggestion is an effective and practical way to help users formulate queries [15, 16]. While there have been many studies on how to provide alternative queries in general web search [15, 16], little work has been done about suggestion for domain-specific search, e.g., patent retrieval, legal search, and medical information search. Many of the users in such domains are search professionals, e.g., patent examiners and information specialists in companies and law firms, who perform specialized search tasks such as prior-art search and legal discovery. Query suggestion techniques should be designed for the unique search characteristics of these domains. For example, professional search is typically more recall-oriented than consumer search. In the patent validity task, for example, patent examiners formulate search queries from a new patent to validate its patentability, and generally spend about 12 hours to complete a single task by examining approximately about 100 patent documents retrieved by 15 different queries on average [1]. Another typical characteristic of professional search is the need to document the searches that are carried out.

For a number of reasons, both historic and technical, Boolean queries are particularly common in professional search. For example, in patent search, recent surveys [1, 2] revealed that the use of Boolean operators is one of the most important features to formulate effective queries from the perspective of patent professionals. Also, according to [2], most patent professionals who participated in the survey did not regard query term weighting and query expansion as important whereas 96.3% of participants agreed that Boolean operators are necessary. This is not because Boolean queries are the most effective. In fact, a number of studies over the years (e.g., [5, 6, 7, 9, 11]) have shown that "keyword" queries are often significantly more effective. Boolean queries, however, are easy for information professionals to manipulate and are essentially self-documenting in that they define precisely the set of documents that are retrieved.

Despite the importance of Boolean queries in professional search, there has not been much research on helping information professionals formulate those queries. Tseng and Wu [3] indicated that the provision of suggested search vocabulary would be helpful in patent search. Other studies on prior-art search that automatically generate queries from patent text (e.g., [6, 7]) did not investigate Boolean query suggestion. Current government or commercial patent search systems [1] used by information professionals all support Boolean queries but not query suggestion.

In this paper, we propose a method to suggest Boolean queries for professional search. We define a Boolean query as the sequence of terms associated by conjunction (AND) where each term can be prefixed by negation (NOT). Although the OR operator is often used by professionals to indicate synonym groups, the retrieval evidence shows that AND and NOT have much more impact on effectiveness in domains such as patent search with very detailed documents (e.g., [4]). Adding synonym structure is left for future work. Although the suggested Boolean queries can be generated and used with any search engine, we use a simple statistical Boolean retrieval model for our experiments (explained in Section 5). We do not adopt any additional query processing and term

SIGIR'11, July 24–28, 2011, Beijing, China.

[1]PATENT SCOPE (http://www.wipo.int/patentscope/), PatFT (http://patft.uspto.gov/), DELPHION (http://www.delphion.com/)

weighting because those features are not generally preferred by professionals and not supported by commercial search systems.

In order to suggest Boolean queries, we first focus on generating Boolean queries that describe the content of an initial set of retrieved documents. We then rank the generated queries to place effective (in terms of finding more relevant documents) queries at higher ranks. In other words, our system performs two sub-tasks: 1) Boolean Query Generation, and 2) Boolean Query Ranking. In the first task, we extract queries composed of Boolean operators and various terms, representing a pseudo-relevant document set, i.e., the top-*k* documents retrieved by a baseline system. To do this, we learn a decision tree from the pseudo-relevant documents so that the decision tree can determine whether a document is pseudo-relevant or not. Afterwards, each positive decision rule (i.e., a path from the root to a positive leaf node indicating pseudo-relevance) formulates a Boolean query. Our Boolean query generation process based on decision trees has two advantages: i) a (binary) decision tree can be equivalent to a Boolean function in terms of its expressiveness [20], and ii) decision trees naturally determine the number of query terms.

In the next step, among the many generated Boolean queries, we select the effective ones by ranking them. This is consistent with typical query suggestion techniques used in web search, where the "best" suggestions are presented to the user. We learn to rank the generated queries using various quality predictors proposed for adhoc retrieval [21, 22, 23, 24, 25] and several new features that consider unique properties of Boolean queries.

We show the effectiveness of our Boolean query suggestion system by verifying that the system is capable of generating effective Boolean queries at high ranks. Although our focus is on patent search, we show the generality of our approach through additional experiments with a medical literature database.

The rest of this paper is organized as follows. In Section 2, we outline previous work in query suggestion and generation, and describe the limitations of previous work. Section 3 defines the task of Boolean query suggestion for professional search, and we present the methods we used in Section 4. Section 5 contains the experimental results and discussion. Finally, we summarize the contributions of our research and future work in Section 6.

2. RELATED WORK AND LIMITATIONS

In this section, we explore previous work for query suggestion for web search and query generation.

Automatic query expansion [13] has been intensively researched to bridge the gap between users' queries and relevant documents. In particular, pseudo-relevance feedback [12] is known as one of the most effective techniques. Although many successful query expansion techniques have been proposed (e.g., [13, 14]), most of them are not easily applicable to our tasks because they are not able to generate Boolean queries required for professional search environments. However, the query expansion method proposed by Mitra et al. [13] is strongly related to our work because they addressed the effectiveness of Boolean filters to improve precision of automatic query expansion. Specifically, they manually formulate fuzzy Boolean operators (conjunction and disjunction) and select expanded terms from a set of pseudo-relevant documents refined by the Boolean filters. However, their work is limited in that the Boolean filters are manually constructed while we focus on automatic formulation. Moreover, they did not consider Boolean queries.

Jones et al. [17] proposed a query substitution system that suggests strongly related queries identified from user query sessions. In query reformulation, Wang and Zhai [18] discovered associated terms from query logs to substitute the original query terms or add new terms into an original query. Also, query recommendation techniques proposed in [16] provide alternatives by clustering related queries in query logs, and White et al. [15] studied types of query suggestions for web search preferred by users via a user study. While the query logs and session information that most previous techniques depend on are readily available for web search, such resources are mostly not available in domain-specific search environments that we address.

In patent search, although automatic query generation is crucial, most previous work has focused on improving a retrieval model. The participants in the patent retrieval task of NTCIR-6 [8] used terms from claim sections without term selection. Mase and Iwayama [9] added terms from abstract sections into claim-based queries and weighted the query terms by their TF-IDF scores in the query patent. Xue and Croft [6, 7] described a query generation technique for patent search. In [6], they generated a patent search query by selecting an effective section and extracting the top-ranked words from the section using TF-IDF weights. Their finding is that the "brief summary" section of patents can produce the most effective queries, while weighting query words by term frequencies is more effective than TF-IDF weighting. They also expanded search queries to incorporate noun phrases, but the improvement was not significant. In [7], they improved retrieval performance of queries generated from [6] by using a learning-to-rank model and various features. The queries generated by this approach, however, contain many terms that are weighted and have other constraints, making them unsuitable for query suggestion. Similar to the NTCIR workshop, TREC recently proposed the Chemical track. A sub-task of the track addresses search for chemical patents [10]. Though Gobeill et al. [11] considered query expansion and showed the best performance among the participants, their expansion technique is somewhat limited in that it depends on a concept identifier and external resources (PubChem[2]) which would not be applied to general patents.

The Boolean query suggestion approach is based on our previous work with professional searchers and studies such as Bache and Azzopardi [4]. They pointed out that patent searchers are in favor of exact-match models, i.e., traditional Boolean retrieval, because Boolean models can improve the retrievability of target documents. Accordingly, they proposed hybrid retrieval models in which target patents are ranked by TF-IDF or Okapi BM25 models and then filtered by conjunctive and disjunctive Boolean operators (AND and OR). Though their models are empirically effective, those are limited in using only two-word queries, i.e., two words are associated by conjunction or disjunction.

In the medical domain, Hashmi et al. [19] developed a system to generate context-specific queries from clinical guidelines, but they also used an external knowledge base to create query terms.

3. PROBLEM FORMULATION

In this section, we formulate the Boolean query suggestion problem for professional search and define associated terms.

---

[2] The database of compounds structure and description for chemical molecules (http://pubchem.ncbi.nlm.nih.gov/)

Definition 1 (Professional Search): *Professional search* is interactive information retrieval performed by professionals in a specific domain such as the patent or medical domain. The main difference of this task from adhoc retrieval (e.g., web search) is that professional search tends to be recall-oriented. The search behavior of professionals is quite different from that of general users. For example, since professionals tend to prefer finding more relevant documents to finding a small number of relevant documents at the top ranks, they examine more retrieval results than web search users. Accordingly, search processes are often long and repeatable, e.g., a patent examiner issues several queries until the obtained results are satisfactory.

Definition 2 (Topic): A *topic* is a subject for which queries against search engines are formed and the retrieval results are examined by professionals. For example, in prior-art search, a new patent to be validated can be a topic. In the medical domain, a description of patient symptoms can be a topic.

Definition 3 (Boolean Query): A *Boolean query* is a sequence of query terms all of which are connected by conjunction and each of which can be prefixed by negation, e.g., $aluminum \wedge \neg tartar \wedge casting\ mold$. In this work, as query term candidates, we consider bigrams as well as unigrams.

Definition 4 (Pseudo-Relevant Documents): *Pseudo-relevant documents* are the top k documents retrieved by a *baseline* system. The *baseline* system can handle a weighted or expanded query using a state-of-the-art retrieval model. We exploit the pseudo-relevant documents to formulate Boolean queries that are suggested to users.

Definition 5 (Boolean Query Generation): *Boolean query generation* is formulating Boolean queries from a set of query term candidates. Using terms appearing in a set of pseudo-relevant documents for topic, we formulate Boolean queries that consist of effective terms and Boolean operators (AND and NOT), where query term candidates can be unigrams or bigrams extracted from the pseudo-relevant documents.

Definition 6 (Boolean Query Ranking): *Boolean query ranking* is determining a preference among generated Boolean queries for a topic with respect to a recall metric, e.g., recall at 100 (R@100). This is necessary for suggesting a reasonable number of effective Boolean queries (e.g., 5~10) to users because many queries can be generated in the Boolean query generation phase. We produce a ranked list of generated Boolean queries where an effective Boolean query should be placed within the high ranks (e.g., top 10).

4. BOOLEAN QUERY SUGGESTION

In this section, we first propose a decision tree-based method for Boolean Query Generation, and then describe a Boolean Query Ranking model using various query quality predictors. Figure 1 demonstrates the overall process of our system. In Boolean Query Generation, we train decision trees using the baseline retrieval result (containing the top-*k* pseudo-relevant documents and beyond-*k* non-relevant documents) and formulate corresponding Boolean queries (BQs) (details in Section 4.1). In Boolean Query Ranking, the ranking model trained from sorted lists of BQs with respect to R@100 can rank the generated BQs by query quality predictors (details in Section 4.2). The top ranked queries are presented as suggestions.

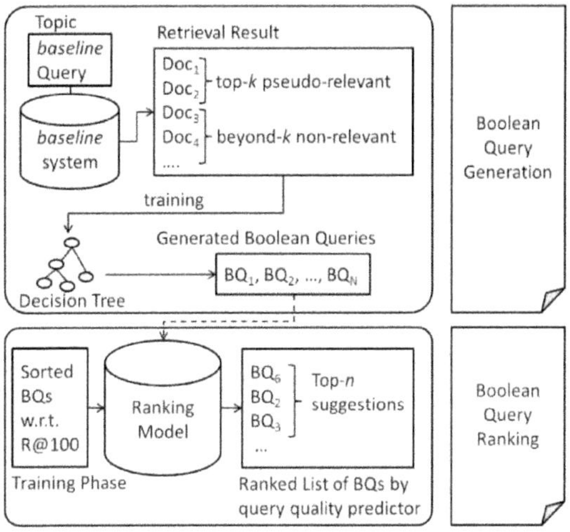

Figure 1: Boolean Query Suggestion System Workflow.

4.1 Decision Tree-based Boolean Query Generation

Binary decision trees are equivalent representations of Boolean functions [20]. If we could train a decision tree where a node corresponds to a term appearing in training documents in order to determine whether a document is relevant to a topic, the learned decision tree could imply a Boolean query representing a set of relevant documents. In addition, the length and query terms of a Boolean query are naturally determined by the depth and the nodes of the tree with reasonable accuracy. A problem, however, is that we do not have training data to learn a tree which can be generalized for every query because each query is associated with a different set of terms. So, instead of relevant documents, we use pseudo-relevant documents defined in Section 3 as training data. In other words, we learn a decision tree by using the top-*k* documents as positive examples. As negative examples, presumably non-relevant documents (ranked beyond-*k* in the baseline retrieval result) are used. Accordingly, Boolean queries generated from the positive nodes of the learned decision tree are expected to be as effective as the baseline query because the decision tree is learned from the pseudo-relevant documents.

Once we learn a decision tree from a topic, we identify a single path from a root to a positive leaf node in the decision tree and convert the rule (path) into a Boolean query. Accordingly, a decision tree produces as many Boolean queries as the number of positive leaf nodes. Figure 2 depicts how to generate Boolean queries from an example decision tree whose attributes (query term candidates) are *alloy*, *wheel*, and *steel*, and **True/False** values of each leaf node denotes a positive/negative decision for input documents. For example, a document including *alloy* and *wheel* is classified as **True** (or relevant) because a number of pseudo-relevant examples used for training include the two terms. That is, the path from *alloy* to the first **True** leaf can formulate query Q_1, which is expected to retrieve documents containing *alloy* and *wheel*. Since we concentrate on conjunction and negation, we generate two queries, Q_1 and Q_2, rather than a single unified query such as $(alloy \wedge wheel) \vee (\neg alloy \wedge steel)$ Note that AND and NOT have more impact on the effectiveness and Q_1 or Q_2 is empirically better than the unified query w.r.t R@100 that we use to evaluate a Boolean query.

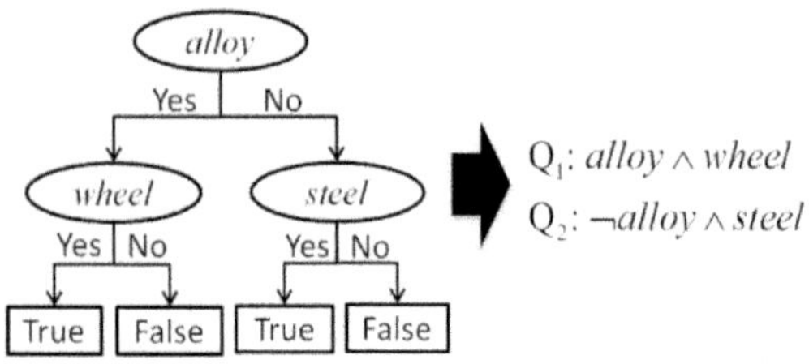

Figure 2: Decision Tree-based Boolean Query Generation.

We describe the Boolean Query Generation algorithm used for the example in the following. Figure 2 shows the process of generating Boolean queries from several sets of query term candidates (i.e., attributes), a set of pseudo-relevant documents (the top-k baseline retrieval results) and a set of non-relevant documents (the beyond-k baseline retrieval results). To produce a sufficient number of Boolean queries (among which we can find many effective Boolean queries), for each topic, we train several decision trees with different attributes, while all the trees are trained by the same training set. In this, the training set includes the k positive (pseudo-relevant) documents and an equal number of negative instances (non-relevant) for a topic. To obtain N sets of attributes, various approaches (e.g., thesaurus and concept identification) can be used. In this paper, we change the number of query term candidates in each set to get multiple attribute sets.

For the patent search experiments, in this paper, we select query term candidates from a unigram language model estimated from a topic patent (i.e., new patent) or its pseudo-relevant patent set. We first select unigrams which are likely to be generated from the following language models, assuming that terms are effective for retrieving pseudo-relevant patents if the terms frequently occur in the topic patent or pseudo-relevant patents.

$$P(w|D) \approx \frac{tf(w:D)}{|D|}$$

$$P(w|PRel) \approx \frac{\sum_{d_i \in PRel} tf(w:d_i)}{\sum_{d_i \in PRel} |d_i|}$$

where D is topic patent, $PRel$ is the set of pseudo-relevant patents for topic, $tf(w:d_i)$ indicates a term frequency of a word w in a document d_i, and $|d_i|$ denotes the length of d_i.

Stop-words[3] are removed. Using term probabilities, we can rank terms in a topic document or pseudo-relevant documents. We select the top-m terms as attributes for decision trees. In particular, to obtain multiple sets of attributes, we consider 20 different m's (in $\{5,10,\ldots,100\}$) , each of which makes an attribute set.

In addition, from an observation that patents contain many compound words that may help to improve the retrievability, we can add an equal number of bigrams into each set of selected unigrams. To rank bigrams, we estimate smoothed bigram language models for the topic patent and the pseudo-relevant patent set as follows:

$$P(w_{i-1}w_i|D) \approx (1-\lambda)\frac{tf(w_{i-1}w_i:D)}{|D|-1} + \lambda P(w_i|D)$$

[3] Stop-words contain articles, prepositions, acronyms (e.g., *fig.*), (relative) pronouns, and general nouns (e.g., *method*, *figure*, and *apparatus*), frequently appeared in patent documents (available at http://www.cs.umass.edu/~yhkim/).

ALGORITHM Boolean Query Generation
INPUT:
- N different sets of attributes s.t. $\{can_1, can_2, \ldots, can_N\}$ where can_i is a set of query term candidates
- The baseline retrieval results for a topic, B

OUTPUT: A set of Boolean queries, S
PROCESS:
- Initialize $S = \{\}$
- For $i = 1,\ldots,N$
    - Construct training data from B: the top-k documents (positive examples) and k documents randomly selected from the beyond-k (negative examples)
    - Train a decision tree using the training data and can_i as attributes.
    - Find paths from the root to every positive leaf node in the decision tree and formulate corresponding Boolean queries.
    - Append the Boolean queries to S.
- End For
- Return S

Figure 3: Boolean Query Generation Algorithm.

$$P(w_{i-1}, w_i|PRel) \approx (1-\lambda)\frac{\sum_{d_i \in PRel} tf(w_{i-1}w_i:d_i)}{\sum_{d_i \in PRel}|d_i| - 1} + \lambda P(w_i|PRel)$$

where λ is a bias to unigrams. We set λ to 0.7 and eliminate bigrams which contain any stop-word.

For the medical search experiments, we use the same setting except that we use only pseudo-relevant documents because topic documents are not usually given. In addition, since long Boolean queries may not return any retrieval results, we eliminate Boolean queries which contain more than 15 terms.

4.2 Boolean Query Ranking

To select a reasonable number of effective queries from a pool of generated Boolean queries, we propose a Boolean query ranking model and introduce features for the model.

4.2.1 Learning-to-Rank Boolean Queries

In order to rank generated Boolean queries, we learn a ranking function which predicts the preference between Boolean queries. That is, given a topic and generated Boolean queries, our ranking model produces a ranked list of the Boolean queries in descending order of recall at 100 (R@100). To do this, we use ranks by R@100's of the Boolean queries generated for each topic as target values to be predicted. The formal definition of this model is given as follows.

Suppose that $Y = \{r_1, r_2, \ldots, r_l\}$ is a set of ranks, where l denotes the number of ranks, and we can order the ranks $r_1 \succ r_2 \succ \cdots \succ r_l$ where $\succ$ indicates the preference between two ranks. For training, a set of topics $\boldsymbol{T} = \{T_1, T_2, \ldots, T_m\}$ is given and each topic T_i is associated with $\boldsymbol{BQ_i} = \{BQ_{i1}, BQ_{i2}, \ldots, BQ_{in(T_i)}\}$ a set of Boolean queries, where $n(T_i)$ means the number of generated Boolean queries for T_i and a list of labels $\boldsymbol{y_i} = \{y_{i1}, y_{i2}, \ldots, y_{in(T_i)}\}$ each of which $y_{ij} \in Y$ indicates the rank of each Boolean query, BQ_{ij}, in T_i. A feature vector $x_{ij} = \Psi(T_i, BQ_{ij}) \in \mathrm{X}$ is generated from each topic and Boolean query pair. We can represent a set of training examples as $S = \{(T_i, \boldsymbol{BQ_i}, \boldsymbol{y_i})\}_{i=1}^{m}$.

A ranking function $f: X \mapsto \Re$ maps a feature vector associated with a Boolean query to a score for the query. Specifically, this model generates a permutation of integers spanned in $[1, n(T_i)]$ for a topic, the corresponding Boolean query list, and the ranking function *f*. The permutation $\pi(T_i, \boldsymbol{BQ_i})$ is defined as a bijection from $\{1,2, \ldots, n(T_i)\}$ to itself where BQ_{ij} is identified by an integer of $[1, n(T_i)]$ and $\pi(j)$ denotes the position of BQ_{ij}. The model is learned to minimize a loss function which is defined by the disagreements between permutation $\pi(T_i, \boldsymbol{BQ_i})$ and rank list $\boldsymbol{y_i}$ for every training topic.

For learning, we use Ranking SVM [26]. In contrast to Boolean Query Generation where only pseudo-relevance is considered, we use real relevance judgments to compute R@100 of training examples for Boolean Query Ranking. This is because Boolean Query Ranking uses generalizable features while Boolean Query Generation uses terms which strongly depends on topics.

4.2.2 Features

In order to compose a feature vector for our query ranking model, we leverage features from previous studies for predicting query performance [21, 22, 23]. Previous studies (e.g., [24, 25]) proved that query quality predictors are effective for ranking sub-queries. Since generated Boolean queries also consist of subsets of terms in topic documents (e.g., query patents), we can expect those quality predictors also help to recognize effective Boolean queries. However, we additionally use more features specialized for our task because we observed that Boolean queries often show different characteristics from adhoc queries. Accordingly, we categorize our features into two groups, General Query Quality Predictor and Boolean Query Quality Predictor. Table 1 summarizes the features in each group.

General Query Quality Predictors contain features proposed by previous studies for quality prediction of adhoc queries. As shown in Table 1, these features include QCS, QS, SOQ, SCQ, IDF, and ICTF. Since Boolean queries show different aspects from adhoc queries for which those features have been proposed, we need to adjust the way these features are computed. For example, since adhoc queries do not contain negation (e.g., $\neg tartar$) in contrast to a Boolean query, we consider terms associated only with conjunctions. SOQ measures cosine similarity between a Boolean query and the baseline query while QS is computed only within pseudo-relevant documents, not within the whole collection because we aim to generate Boolean queries to retrieve pseudo-relevant documents. For IDF, ICTF, and SCQ, as [24] did, we calculate the sum, the standard deviation, the ratio of the maximum to the minimum, the maximum, the arithmetic mean, the geometric mean, the harmonic mean, and the coefficient of variation of each value of a query term. These modified rules are applied to both unigrams and bigrams.

Boolean Query Quality Predictors are features with the purpose of estimating Boolean query quality. All these features except BQTF are related to the retrieval results of a Boolean query because comparing a Boolean query result with the baseline result is a simple and effective way to predict Boolean query quality. BQCB is the ratio of the number of documents retrieved by both a Boolean query and the baseline system to the number of documents retrieved by the baseline system. This feature denotes how many of the documents retrieved by the baseline system can be found by a Boolean query. BQS is a measure of the number of pseudo-relevant documents retrieved by a Boolean query relative to the whole size of pseudo-relevant documents, i.e., *k*. This feature helps to assure the effectiveness of a Boolean query. LBQR measures the number of retrieved documents for a Boolean query. Since we found that an effective Boolean query sometimes returns a shorter result list containing highly relevant documents than the baseline result, we consider this feature as a signal to find such Boolean queries. BQTF counts the frequency of a conjunctive query term in pseudo-relevant documents, assuming that a frequent term in pseudo-relevant documents might be effective for retrieving the documents. Note that we do not consider negation terms because they rarely appear in pseudo-relevant documents. Besides, for BQTF, the same statistics as used for IDF are calculated.

Table 1: Two categories of Ranking Features.

General Query Quality Predictors	
QCS	Query Clarity Score [21]
QS	Query Scope [23] in pseudo-relevant patents
SOQ	Similarity to Original Query [24]
SCQ	Similarity Collection Query [22]
IDF	Inverse Document Frequency
ICTF	Inverse Collection Term Frequency [24]
Boolean Query Quality Predictor	
BQCB	Boolean Query result Coverage of Baseline retrieval results
BQS	Boolean Query Scope in pseudo-relevance
LBQR	Length of Boolean Query Result
BQTF	Boolean Query Term Frequency in pseudo-relevant documents

Overall, a feature vector contains 37 different feature values (from 10 different types).

5. EXPERIMENTS: Professional Search Simulation

We evaluate our Boolean query suggestion system by simulating professional search. We first describe how to set up experiments to simulate search processes and then provide experimental results and discussion with Boolean query examples.

5.1 Experimental Setup

To perform decision tree learning, the C4.5 algorithm[4] was used, with pruning turned on to obtain more accurate trees. For Boolean Query Ranking, SVM^{rank} [5] is used as a learning-to-rank algorithm, and 10-fold cross-validation is performed. Queries and documents are stemmed by the Krovetz stemmer. More details are provided as follows.

5.1.1 Search Tasks

We setup experiments for two different search tasks considering two domains of interest: the patent and medical domains. Our task for the patent domain is patentability search which aims to find prior patents which may conflict with a new patent. On the other hand, the search task for the medical domain is reference retrieval

[4] http://en.wikipedia.org/wiki/C4.5_algorithm

[5] http://www.cs.cornell.edu/People/tj/svm_light/svm_rank.html

upon the request of disease information that the patient is undertaking. Both tasks are known to be recall-oriented.

5.1.2 Assumptions for Simulation

We suggest Boolean queries to help professionals formulate queries. In order to demonstrate the practical effectiveness of our system, we test our system under the following assumptions. First, we assume that professionals directly use suggested Boolean queries without reformulation because we want to show the lower bound of performance that our system can achieve. In real environments, professionals may use our suggestions or formulate new Boolean queries based on the suggestions. Second, we assume that the searchers will examine a maximum of the top 100 of every Boolean query result since 100 patents on average are examined in real examination processes as reported in [1].

5.1.3 Collections

Experiments are conducted on two different collections, patents and medical documents. As a patent corpus, we use USPTO (United States Patent and Trademark Office) patents provided by NTCIR-6 [8]. The collection contains 981,948 patents published from 1993 to 2000. To develop topics (new patents), we randomly selected 100 patents published in 2000, ensuring that their citations list more than 20 patents and at least 90% of them are included in the test collection. As done in the TREC chemical track [10] and NTCIR-6 [8], we considered patents cited in each topic patent as "relevant". We call this collection USPAT. For a medical corpus, we used the OHSUMED collection [27] which consists of 348,566 medical references (documents) and 106 queries (topics). This test collection contains relevance judgments manually annotated using three relevance levels (*definitely relevant*, *possibly relevant*, and *not relevant*). We consider *definitely* and *possibly relevant* as "relevant."

5.1.4 Baseline system and statistical Boolean retrieval model

For collecting pseudo-relevant documents as well as comparing performance, we employ baseline systems. As a baseline system for the USPAT, we consider the prior-art query generation method proposed in [6]. We generate a prior-art query which includes 100 unigrams ranked by TF-IDF from the "brief summary" section of each topic patent. To formulate the queries, we used both unigrams and bigrams, with 100 unigrams showed the best performance in R@100. Each query term is weighted by its TF in the topic patent. In addition, as [6] used, we employ the Indri search engine [28] to run each baseline query. For example, a baseline query is formed as "*#weight* (15 *glyph* 20 *character* ...)". We consider the top 100 retrieved patents as pseudo-relevant. For OHSUMED, we consider all terms from the "Patient Information" and "Information Request" sections of each topic as a baseline query. The top 100 documents returned by the Indri search engine are regarded as pseudo-relevant.

To run Boolean queries, we use a statistical Boolean retrieval model. For each topic, we first find all documents satisfying the given Boolean function (i.e., Boolean query) and rank the documents by the generative probability of the query:

$$P(BQ|D) \approx \prod_{q \in BQ} P(q|D) \approx \prod_{q \in BQ} \frac{tf_{q,D} + \mu \cdot P(q|C)}{|D| + \mu}$$

where D is a target document satisfying a Boolean query BQ, q is the query term not associated with negation in BQ, $tf_{q,D}$ is the term frequency of q in D, $P(q|C)$ is the probability of q in the collection C, and μ is the Dirichlet smoothing parameter [29] set to 2000. Note that we do not use any query processing including query term weighting in this Boolean retrieval model. Since many current patent search systems (e.g., Patent Scope) are also based on these simple term statistics, query evaluation using this statistical Boolean retrieval model would be more practical and similar to real search environments than using other enhanced retrieval techniques (e.g., learning-to-rank or a dependency model) that are hard to integrate into current patent search systems.

5.1.5 Evaluation Measure

We use several metrics for evaluation. Since professional search is different from adhoc retrieval, and we are evaluating Boolean Query Suggestion, we employ new metrics in addition to conventional IR evaluation metrics.

Failure Rate measures the percentile ratio of "failure" Boolean queries to all generated ones for each topic. Boolean queries which failed to retrieve any target documents are considered as a "failure".

Success Rate measures the percentile ratio of "effective" Boolean queries to the all generated ones, where "effective" means a Boolean query performing identical to or better than the baseline query with regard to R@100. This metric denotes how many Boolean queries achieve the baseline performance.

Recall is a traditional IR evaluation metric; we use R@100 because every retrieval result is truncated at rank 100 according to the assumption for simulation. In order to evaluate our query ranking model, we use the best recall scores of the top-*n* Boolean queries for each topic because if the ranking model can place effective queries within top-*n* suggestions, they will be available to searchers.

F1 and F2 indicate weighted F-scores, both harmonic means of precision and recall, where F2 denotes double the weight on recall than F1. In particular, we compute F1@100 and F2@100 of the best performing query (with respect to R@100) from the top-*n* ranked queries. These metrics reflect the practical effectiveness of Boolean queries. Sometimes, the best Boolean query returns a short result list where many documents are relevant, which results in higher precision than the baseline results and expedites examination processes by professionals. F1 and F2 capture both recall and precision simultaneously, and help to measure search efficiency.

5.2 Results

5.2.1 Generation Performance

The first experiment is conducted to verify the effectiveness of Boolean Query Generation. We use the results of our baseline system as specified above and documents retrieved at ranks higher than 100 as non-relevant. In the USPAT, we generate 4 types of attribute sets; unigrams and unigrams+bigrams from a topic patent, and unigrams and unigrams+bigrams from the pseudo-relevant documents. For OHSUMED, only 2 types, unigrams and unigrams+bigrams from the pseudo-relevant set, are used because there is no topic document. Table 2 shows the performance of Boolean query generation. We report the average of each evaluation metric over all topics.

Table 2: Boolean Query Generation Performance. 'unigram' and 'bigram' indicate the Boolean queries generated from decision trees whose attributes are unigrams and bigrams, respectively. 'topic-doc' and 'prel-doc' denote that attributes are extracted from topic documents and a set of pseudo-relevant documents, respectively.

Metric	USPAT				OHSUMED	
	unigram (topic-doc)	uni+bigram (topic-doc)	unigram (prel-doc)	uni+bigram (prel-doc)	unigram (prel-doc)	uni+bigram (prel-doc)
Avg. # of Gen.	188.97	205.02	175.86	218.16	206.53	238.43
Avg. # of Fail.	17.25	15.06	11.97	13.28	16.37	18.22
Avg. Fail. Rate	9.47%	7.64%	6.98%	6.19%	7.93%	7.64%
Avg. # of Scc.	14.13	9.62	14.32	10.86	14.58	16.81
Avg. Scc. Rate	7.26%	4.56%	7.84%	4.63%	6.18%	5.85%

Table 3: Boolean Query Ranking Performance. A † indicates a significant difference from the baseline and a * denotes a significant difference of unigram results from unigram+bigram ('uni+bi') results in each row (the paired *t*-test is performed with $p < 0.05$). Significantly improved results on the baseline in each column are marked in bold. 'cut-off' indicates that all Boolean queries ranked within the cut-off ranks are examined. 'New Rel' and 'Missed Old Rel' denote the percentile ratio of new relevant documents (not retrieved by the baseline but discovered by the suggested Boolean query) and missed old relevant documents (which were retrieved by the baseline but missed by the suggested Boolean query) to all relevant documents, respectively.

	Metric	Recall@100		F1@100		F2@100		Missed Old Rel		New Rel	
USPTO	Baseline	0.2557		0.1184		0.1711		0.0%		0.0%	
	cut-off	unigram	uni+bi	unigram	uni+bi	unigram	uni+bi	unigram	uni+bi	unigram	uni+bi
	1	0.2227†	0.2174†	0.1062†	0.0969†	0.1515†	0.1421†	8.15%	9.60%	4.85%	5.21%
	2	0.2538	0.2445	0.1204	0.1096	0.1721	0.1604	6.49%	8.16%	6.30%	6.88%
	3	0.2670	0.2529	0.1264	0.1166	0.1808	0.1682	6.34%	7.65%	7.48%	7.36%
	4	0.2761	0.2535	0.1303	0.1169	0.1866*	0.1686	5.89%	7.65%	7.94%	7.42%
	5	0.2820	0.2592	**0.1330**$^{\dagger *}$	0.1191	**0.1905**$^{\dagger *}$	0.1721	5.58%	7.26%	8.21%	7.69%
	6	0.2852	0.2597	**0.1345**$^{\dagger *}$	0.1194	**0.1927**$^{\dagger *}$	0.1724	5.60%	7.20%	8.56%	7.69%
	7	**0.2883**$^{\dagger *}$	0.2622	**0.1359**$^{\dagger *}$	0.1209	**0.1947**$^{\dagger *}$	0.1745	5.53%	7.06%	8.79%	7.84%
	8	**0.2911**$^{\dagger *}$	0.2695	**0.1370**$^{\dagger *}$	0.1257	**0.1965**$^{\dagger *}$	0.1808	5.58%	6.98%	9.13%	8.46%
	9	**0.2952**$^{\dagger *}$	0.2710	**0.1388**†	0.1265	**0.1992**$^{\dagger *}$	0.1818	5.42%	6.88%	9.32%	8.66%
	10	**0.2991**$^{\dagger *}$	0.2722	**0.1402**†	0.1277	**0.2014**$^{\dagger *}$	0.1833	5.36%	6.83%	9.76%	8.91%
OHSUMED	Baseline	0.4377		0.2636		0.3462		0.0%		0.0%	
	cut-off	unigram	uni+bi	unigram	uni+bi	unigram	uni+bi	unigram	uni+bi	unigram	uni+bi
	1	0.3068†	0.3052†	0.2155†	0.2222†	0.2623†	0.2710†	15.02%	14.07%	6.20%	6.28%
	2	0.3618†	0.3611†	0.2490	0.2580	0.3063	0.3148	13.19%	13.09%	7.95%	7.88%
	3	0.3865†	0.3754†	0.2669	0.2774	0.3277	0.3382	12.48%	12.45%	7.89%	7.99%
	4	0.3970	0.3923†	0.2763	0.2874	0.3380	0.3493	11.17%	11.17%	8.18%	8.18%
	5	0.4009	0.4032	0.2836	0.2944	0.3440	0.3523	10.20%	10.56%	8.58%	8.58%
	6	0.4137	0.4082	0.2959	**0.3042**†	0.3569	0.3663	10.16%	10.11%	8.71%	8.58%
	7	0.4141	0.4106	**0.2961**†	**0.3045**†	0.3572	0.3676	10.11%	10.09%	8.76%	8.72%
	8	0.4143	0.4170	**0.2963**†	**0.3046**†	0.3573	0.3769	10.11%	10.04%	8.84%	8.84%
	9	0.4393	0.4232	**0.3076**†	**0.3169**†	0.3751	**0.3831**†	10.04%	9.63%	8.92%	9.84%
	10	0.4411	0.4232	**0.3089**†	**0.3185**†	0.3766	**0.3841**†	9.24%	9.41%	9.87%	9.84%

Table 4: Examples of the top-5 suggestions for Topic Patent titled as "compressor driving apparatus" 100+ indicates that the # of Retrieved documents is greater than 100. Each result is truncated at top-100. R is Recall@100 and F1 is F1@100.

n	unigram	R	F1	#Ret	unigram+bigram	R	F1	#Ret
1	inverter ∧ compressor	0.35	0.1167	100+	¬ inverter driving ∧ inverter ∧ compressor ∧ circuit	0.20	0.0748	87
2	inverter ∧ compressor ∧ circuit	0.55	0.1833	100+	inverter ∧ air conditioner ∧ circuit	0.50	0.1667	100+
3	inverter ∧ motor	0.05	0.0167	100+	¬ power unit ∧ air conditioner ∧ output ∧ inverter ∧ circuit	0.55	0.2500	68
4	¬ inrush ∧ ¬ metallic ∧ inverter ∧ compressor ∧ relay	0.10	0.0435	72	¬ relay driver ∧¬ compressor driving ∧ inverter ∧ circuit	0.05	0.0294	48
5	¬inrush ∧ ¬metallic ∧ ¬board ∧ circuit ∧ compressor ∧ supply ∧ inverter	0.25	0.1282	58	switching elements ∧ air conditioner	0.30	0.1000	100+

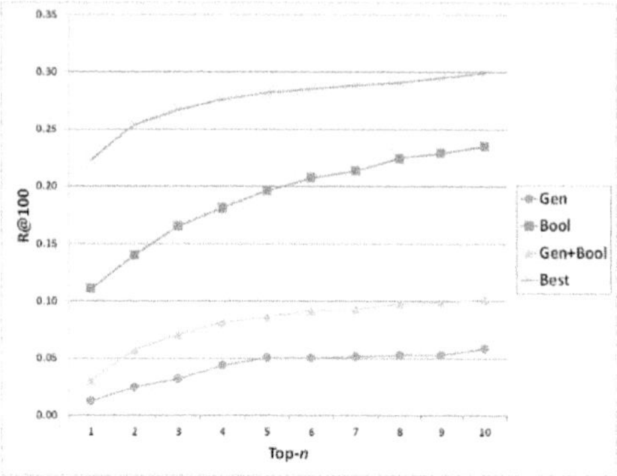

Figure 4: Recall of the best query within Top-*n* Boolean queries (unigram case in USPAT). 'Gen' and 'Bool' mean general query quality predictors and Boolean query quality predictors, respectively. 'Gen+Bool' uses all features, and 'Best' uses only selective features (QCS, SCQ, BQCB, and LBQR) achieving the best performance.

As shown in Table 2, our decision tree-based generation algorithm generates sufficiently many distinct Boolean queries. About 200 queries are generated for each topic, of which 6 ~ 9% fail to retrieve any target documents. In USPAT, pseudo-relevant documents are more reliable resources to generate Boolean queries than topic patents because of the smaller failure rate on average. Also, adding bigrams can lead decision trees to generate more queries, and the relative failure rate could drop. However, bigrams seems to be harmful in terms of the success rate. In addition, considering the number of "effective" Boolean queries (the number of successes), about 7% of queries show better or equal performance to the baseline system. Although this percentage may look low, we intend to obtain many effective queries via this generation process. Indeed, as you see from the number of successes, more than 10 effective queries are generated for each topic. If we can place these effective queries at top ranks using our Boolean query ranking method, professionals who examine these suggestions will find the effective queries. We address the performance of the query ranking technique in the following section.

5.2.2 Retrieval Performance

In the next series of experiments, we evaluate the effectiveness of Boolean Query Ranking by investigating if it succeeds in placing effective Boolean queries at high ranks, i.e., top 1 to 10. In training, generated queries for each topic are ordered by their R@100 scores. Also, in order to generate ground-truth ranked lists for training, we used Boolean queries from the topic-patent and pseudo-relevant patents in the USPTO, i.e., a ranked list contains unigram Boolean queries from the topic patent and pseudo-relevant patens and the other list includes unigram+bigram Boolean queries from the topic patent and pseudo-relevant patens. For the OHSUMED, we contain two ranked lists: unigram and unigram+bigram Boolean queries from pseudo-relevant documents. Creating a long ranked list by unifying unigram and unigram+bigram results is possible, but our scheme (handling unigram and unigram+bigram Boolean queries separately) empirically showed better performance. Overall, the training sets for the USPAT include 30,561 unigram and 38,034 unigram+bigram examples, and for OHSUMED contain 19,967 unigram and 23,122 unigram+bigram instances.

Prior to evaluating the performance of Boolean Query Ranking, we optimize the Ranking SVM by selecting optimal features. In order to obtain an optimal set, we tested several combinations of the proposed features (Section 4.2.2) using 10-fold cross-validation. To identify a better combination, we use the best recall scores of the top-1 to 10 ranked Boolean queries for each combination. We examine what features can help to produce better rankings. Figure 4 depicts the average recall of the best Boolean queries over all topics of unigram training set in the USPAT. **Gen** shows consistently the worst performance, and when combined with **Bool**, the performance of **Bool** is also degraded. The best combination (QCS, SCQ, BQCB, and LBQR) found via trials of several possible combinations that can outperform **Bool** only. This is consistent with what [25] found, i.e., SCQ and QCS are the most effective features for sub-query ranking. We additionally recognized that combining them with BQCB and LBQR is more effective because BQCB ensures that the Boolean query performs at least as well as the baseline and LBQR benefits effective Boolean queries returning a short result list. Experiments using the OHSUMED collection or unigram+bigram query terms showed similar tendencies.

With the optimal feature set, we now verify the effectiveness of our Boolean Query Ranking model by comparing with the baseline system. We calculate R@100, F1@100, and F2@100 of the best-performing query among the top-1 to 10 ranked queries.

Table 3 shows the retrieval results within the top-1 to 10 ranked Boolean queries by 10-fold cross validation. From the table, we can identify how many top-*n* Boolean queries need to be examined to find an "effective" one (i.e., performing as well as the baseline). In other words, results of the top-n queries which are not significantly different from the baseline result show that at least one effective Boolean query can be within the top-*n*.

In Table 3, we see that effective Boolean queries can be found within the top 2 or 4 suggestions in each corpus. In USPAT, an effective Boolean query is observed within the top 2 ranks in both unigram and unigram+bigram cases. Furthermore, in the unigram case, significantly improved results in terms of R@100 can be obtained by examining 7 or more Boolean queries. This is surprising to us because we expected Boolean queries to perform similar to the baseline. However, the result is a good indication that our system provides effective suggestions. In terms of F1 and F2, the top-5 unigram queries contain queries that outperform the baseline. These suggested queries retrieve about the same number of relevant documents as the baseline result, but with higher precision. That is, these Boolean queries may be more efficient in that they can allow professionals to examine fewer documents. On the other hand, effective queries are not successfully generated in case of unigram+bigram. For example, the number of generated effective queries in the unigram+bigram case is smaller than in the unigram case as seen in Table 2. Furthermore, many unigram results show statistically significant improvements over the unigram+bigram results, when comparing query performance at the same top-*n*.

In OHSUMED, more queries need to be examined to find effective Boolean queries compared to USPAT. For example, four query suggestions should be examined in the unigram case in the OHSUMED, while only two queries are needed in the USPAT. Furthermore, even more queries should be examined in the unigram+bigram case. In addition, we could not obtain significantly better Boolean queries with regard to R@100 in this domain. For F-scores, however, we also identify more efficient

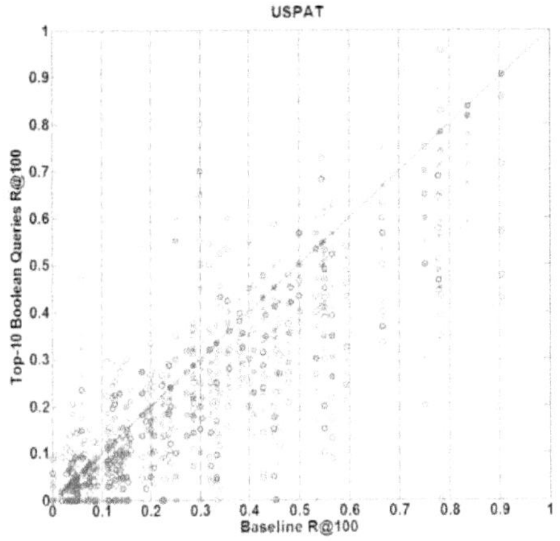

Figure 5: Scatter plot of the top-10 Boolean queries in USPAT. The x-axis represents R@100 of the baseline queries. A circle and a cross mean a unigram query and a unigram+bigram query, respectively.

Boolean queries by examining the top 6 or 7 queries. A critical difference between OHSUMED and USPTO is that there is little distinction between unigram and unigram+bigram results in the OHSUMED while unigram queries are consistently better than unigram+bigram queries in the USPTO. Overall, our ranking model is effective in placing "effective" Boolean query suggestions within the top 2 to 5 ranks.

In order to see how many new relevant documents (which were not retrieved by the baseline) are discovered and how many old relevant documents (which were retrieved by the baseline) are missed, by the best Boolean query within the top-n, we measure the ratios of the numbers of the new and missed old relevant documents to the number of all relevant documents (see "Missed Old Rel" and "New Rel" columns in Table 3). Generally, the more effective Boolean queries identified, the more new relevant documents are discovered while the less old relevant documents are missed. Specifically, for the best query in the top-10 suggestions, the number of newly discovered relevant documents is greater than that of missed old relevant documents. In addition, the difference between unigram and unigram+bigram queries is not significant.

Figures 5 and 6 depict scatter plots for the top-10 unigram and unigram+bigram Boolean queries in USPAT and OHSUMED, respectively. In Figure 5, the points on or above the diagonal line indicate effective Boolean queries (performing identical to or better than the baseline). The section from 0.0 to 0.1 in the x-axis contains many queries performing poorly. However, effective Boolean queries are also identified and some of them are superior to the low baseline. Also, there are many effective Boolean queries over the baseline performing moderately (0.1 ~ 0.7). In Figure 6, there are fewer poorly-performing queries (0.0 ~ 0.1), and most points are distributed between 0.1 and 0.9 in the x-axis. Along the diagonal line, effective queries in Figure 6 are more spread out than those of Figure 5. Although many Boolean queries underperform the baselines in both plots, our system is promising because effective queries can be identified by searchers in real environments.

Figure 7 depicts the accumulated length of the top-n query results which means the number of unique documents in all the results by the top-n queries. This is related to the efficiency of our system in the investigation, i.e., how long it takes to complete the task.

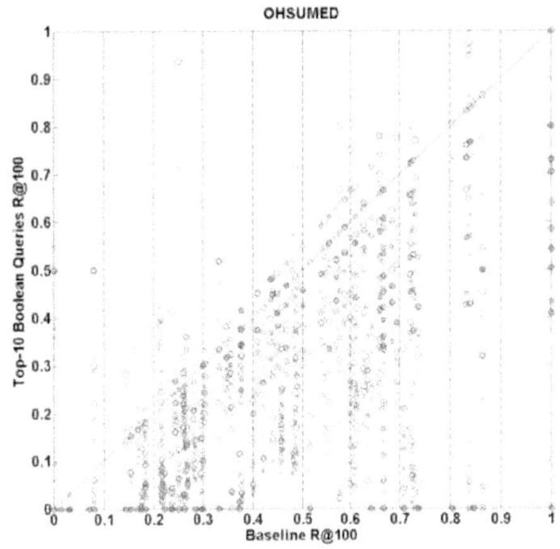

Figure 6: Scatter plot of the top-10 Boolean queries in OHSUMED. The x-axis represents R@100 of the baseline queries. A circle and a cross mean a unigram query and a unigram+bigram query, respectively.

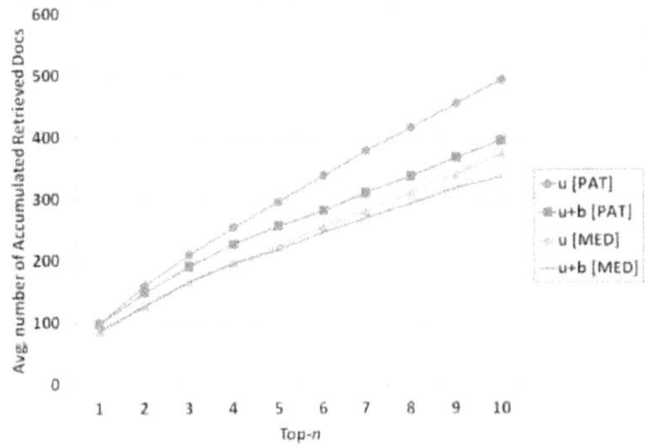

Figure 7: Average number of accumulated unique documents over the top-n Boolean queries. 'u' and 'b' indicate the results of unigram training examples and of bigram training examples, respectively. 'PAT' and 'MED' denote the USPAT and the OHSUMED collections, respectively.

Patent searchers generally examine maximally 600 patents to accomplish a single task (i.e., topic) [1]. In Figure 7, less than 500 unique documents accrue in the top-10 suggestions, which means that our suggestions can return a practical number of documents. Besides, since unigram+bigram queries return fewer documents than unigram queries, the coverage by unigram+bigram queries appears narrower.

5.2.3 Qualitative Analysis

We now provide a qualitative analysis of our system via real examples. Table 4 shows the top 5 Boolean queries suggested by our system, for a sample topic in USPAT. In this topic, the baseline system shows moderate performance (0.30 for R@100, 0.10 for F1@100), and some suggestions outperform the baseline. Many Boolean queries retrieve less than 100 documents, and some long suggestions (e.g., $\neg$power unit $\wedge$ air conditioner $\wedge$ output $\wedge$ inverter $\wedge$ circuit) can precisely retrieve relevant documents in the short result lists. Several suggestions return significantly more relevant documents. The suggested Boolean queries can provide reasonable query contexts. For example, "compressor" is often combined with "inverter", "supply", "circuit" in Table 4 because compressor driving apparatus can include power supply, inverter drivers and storage circuits. Also, looking at the negated terms, professional searchers can recognize where negation is applied in the provided context. For example, "power unit" is negated when it comes with "air conditioner", "output", "inverter", and "circuit" in Table 4. Since we found that past cited patents are dealing with inverters or circuits for air conditioners, power supplies can be considered less important.

6. CONCLUSION

We proposed a framework to automatically suggest Boolean queries to assist professional searchers. We defined professional search as recall-oriented interactive tasks performed by information professionals. In order to provide reasonable suggestions in this context, we first generate a sufficient number of Boolean queries by exploiting decision tree learning and pseudo-relevant documents. To provide a reasonable number of suggestions, we rank the generated queries by a query ranking model using query quality predictors. In experiments, we simulated professional search processes in the patent and medical domains with our suggestion system. We found that our system can not only generate many effective Boolean queries but also select highly effective queries for suggestion. For future work, we plan to conduct experiments on the legal domain (e.g., finding relevant cases). Also, we will consider adding synonym structure into the current suggestion framework.

7. ACKNOWLEDGMENTS

This work was supported in part by the Center for Intelligent Information Retrieval and in part by NSF CLUE IIS-0844226. Any opinions, findings and conclusions or recommendations expressed in this material are the authors' and do not necessarily reflect those of the sponsor.

8. REFERENCES

[1] H. Joho, L. Azzopardi, and W. Vanderbauwhede. A Survey of Patent Users: an analysis of tasks, behavior, search functionality and system requirement In *3rd Symposium on Information Interaction in Context*, 2010.

[2] L. Azzopardi, W. Vanderbauwhede, and H. Joho. Search System Requirements of Patent Analysts. In *SIGIR '10*, 2010.

[3] Y. Tseng and Y. Wu. A study of search tactics for patentability search: a case study on patent engineers. In *1st workshop on Patent Information Retrieval*, 2008.

[4] R. Bache and L. Azzopardi. Improving access to large patent corpora. *Transactions on Large-Scale Data and Knowledge-Centered Systems II* (LNCS), 2010.

[5] H. Turtle. Natural language vs. Boolean query evaluation: a comparison of retrieval performance. In *SIGIR '94, 1994.*

[6] X. Xue and W. B. Croft. Transforming patents into prior-art queries. In *SIGIR '09*, 2009.

[7] X. Xue and W. B. Croft. Automatic query generation for patent search. In *CIKM '09*, 2009.

[8] A. Fujii, M. Iwayama, and N. Kando. Overview of the patent retrieval task at the NTCIR-6 workshop. In *NTCIR-6*, 2007.

[9] H. Mase and M. Iwayama. NTCIR-6 Patent Retrieval Experiments at Hitach. In *NTCIR-6*, 2007.

[10] M. Lupu, F. Piroi, X. Huang, J. Zhu, and J. Tait. Overview of the TREC 2009 Chemical IR Track. In *TREC-18*, 2009.

[11] J. Gobeill, D. Teodor, E. Patsche, and P. Ruch. Report on the TREC 2009 Experiments: Chemical IR Track. In *TREC-18*, 2009.

[12] J. Rocchio. Relevance feedback in information retrieval. In *The Smart Retrieval System – Experiments in Automatic Document Processing*. Prentice-Hall, 1971.

[13] M. Mitra, A. Singhal, and C. Buckley. Improving automatic query expansion. In *SIGIR '98*, 1998.

[14] J. Xu. Improving the effectiveness of information retrieval with local context analysis. In *ACM Transactions on Information Systems*, 18(1), 2000.

[15] R. White, M. Bilenko, and S. Cucerzan. Studying the use of popular destinations to enhance web search interaction. In *SIGIR '07*, 2007.

[16] R. A. Baeza-Yates, C. A. Hurtado, and M. Mendoza. Query recommendation using query logs in search engines. In *EDBT workshops*, 2004.

[17] R. Jones, B. Rey, O. Madani, and W. Greiner. Generating query substitutions. In *WWW '06*, 2006.

[18] X. Wang and C. Zhai. Mining term association patterns from search logs for effective query reformulation. In *CIKM '08, 2008.*

[19] Z. Hashmi, T. Zrimec, and A. Hopkins. Automatic query generation from computerized clinical guidelines. *International Journal of Information Studies*, 1(4), 2009

[20] S. Russell and P. Norvig. Artificial Intelligence: A Modern Approach. Prentice Hall, 2010.

[21] S. Cronen-Townsend, Y. Zhou, and W. B. Croft. Predicting Query Performance. In *SIGIR '02*, 2002.

[22] Y. Zhao, F. Scholer, and Y. Tsegay. Effective Pre-retrieval Query Performance Prediction Using Similarity and Variability Evidence. In *ECIR '08*, 2008.

[23] B. He and I. Ounis. Inferring query performance using pre-retrieval predictors. In *18th Symposium on String Processing and Information Retrieval*, 2004.

[24] G. Kumaran and V. Carvalho. Reducing Long Queries Using Query Quality Predictors. In *SIGIR '09*, 2009.

[25] V. Dang, M. Bendersky and W. B. Croft. Learning to Rank Query Reformulations. In *SIGIR '10*, 2010.

[26] T. Joachims, Optimizing Search Engines Using Clickthrough Data In *KDD'02*, 2002.

[27] W. R. Hersh, C. Buckley, T. J. Leone, and D. H. Hickam. OHSUMED: an interactive retrieval evaluation and new large test collection for research. In *SIGIR '94*, 1994.

[28] T. Strohman, D. Metzler, H. Turtle, and W. B. Croft. Indri: a language-model based search engine for complex queries (extended version). *CIIR Technical Report*, 2005.

[29] C. Zhai and J. Lafferty. A study of smoothing methods for language models applied to adhoc information retrieval. In *SIGIR '01*, 2001.

Improved Video Categorization from Text Metadata and User Comments

Katja Filippova
Google Inc.
Brandschenkestr. 110
Zurich, Switzerland
katjaf@google.com

Keith B. Hall
Google Inc.
Brandschenkestr. 110
Zurich, Switzerland
kbhall@google.com

ABSTRACT

We consider the task of assigning categories (e.g., *howto/cooking*, *sports/basketball*, *pet/dogs*) to YouTube[1] videos from video and text signals. We show that two complementary views on the data – from the video and text perspectives – complement each other and refine predictions. The contributions of the paper are threefold: (1) we show that a text-based classifier trained on imperfect predictions of the weakly supervised video content-based classifier is not redundant; (2) we demonstrate that a simple model which combines the predictions made by the two classifiers outperforms each of them taken independently; (3) we analyse such sources of text information as video title, description, user tags and viewers' comments and show that each of them provides valuable clues to the topic of the video.

Categories and Subject Descriptors

H.3 [**Information Storage and Retrieval**]: Content Analysis and Indexing—*Linguistic processing*

General Terms

Algorithms, Experimentation

Keywords

Web video, video categorization, text analysis

1. INTRODUCTION

The amount of video content on the web has increased drastically in the recent years. Faster Internet connections, ubiquitous use of filming devices and the popularity of video blogging, all contribute to the steady growth of video content on the Internet. This trend requires more accurate video categorization to make the information searchable and hence more useful for users. Machine learning methods have been used extensively for video, image and text classification as they can handle thousands of features extracted from video and text. For videos, the former include signals computed from video frames. The latter are usually limited to what the uploader provided together with the video: the title and description, although these are not guaranteed to be informative. For example, it is not uncommon to find titles corresponding to file names, like *IMG_2309*, and the description is often left empty. Misspellings and the use of colloquial language make it more difficult to extract helpful features from text than it is in the case of news classification. This also implies that the feature space is larger as a word can be spelled in several ways (e.g., compare *loved* with *loooved, luved, luvd*).

Unlike video features which are universal in that they can be found in videos from any part of the world, text features are obviously language dependent. This makes it impossible to obtain a sufficiently large amount of human-labeled data to train a text-based classifier in a supervised way. Therefore, semi-supervised and unsupervised approaches become particularly attractive as they require no or very little labeled data.

In this paper we describe a way of overcoming the above mentioned difficulty of obtaining labeled data. We present a text-based classifier trained on imperfect predictions of a weakly supervised video content-based classifier [1] which acquires a complementary, text-based view on the data. The three main contributions of our work are as follows:

- Given a large collection of videos together with category predictions made by a weakly supervised video based classifier, we train a text based classifier on a complementary set of features in a supervised way. Surprisingly, the resulting classifier not only performs on par but is even more accurate than the original one, even for categories for which video-based predictions are very noisy.
- We use a simple method of combining predictions of the two classifiers and obtain a system which has higher overall accuracy than either of the two taken separately. We also observe that the two source models complement each other in making better predictions on certain classes of categories.
- We experiment with a very large set of features (hundreds of thousands) and show that a simple bag-of-words approach works well. Furthermore, we demonstrate that the performance improves when we add features from a noisy data source, the viewers' comments. We analyse the results and suggest reasons for why this is so.

The novelty of our work is that we show that integrating the viewers' perspective can be highly beneficial for video classification. Most of the previous work has centered around the information provided by the video (image) uploader only. However, we

[1] `http://www.youtube.com`

SIGIR'11, July 24–28, 2011, Beijing, China.

show in the related work review (Sec. 2), in the blog domain user comments have already proved to be a valuable data source which can be used to improve search, predict sentiment, opinion, popularity or trace the development of the blog story. Analysing video comments is a next step towards better understanding of online user interactions.

The paper is organized as follows: Section 2 gives an overview of related work. Section 3 explains how our study is different from previous work and poses new research questions. Sections 4 and 5 describe the general approach and the features we use. Finally, Section 6 presents the experimental results.

2. RELATED WORK

In this section we review video (image) classification work as well as studies which analysed the usefulness of user comments in the domain of weblogs.

2.1 Video and Image Classification

There has been a lot of research on image and video classification and video annotation [8]. In our brief overview we only focus on studies which considered text features.

Lin and Hauptmann [12] describe an approach where two sets of features – video and text – are used and two SVM classifiers are trained on those to predict whether a news video is a weather forecast or not. The paper introduces a novel way of combining predictions by training a meta-classifier.

Feng et al. [7] are perhaps the first to use co-training [3] for image annotation. They show that a smaller labeled set is required to achieve accuracy comparable with that of a supervised learner. They also address the problem of extracting relevant text features from HTML pages. The classification task they consider consists of assigning one of 15 non-abstract labels, such as *tiger, lion* or *cat* to images.

Cai et al. [4] consider the task of clustering image search results. The three kinds of features they use are extracted from text surrounding images, web page links and images themselves. First, the text and link features are used to identify groups of semantically similar images. After that, images within clusters are reorganized and clusters of visually similar images are formed.

Zhang et al. [20] classify videos with respect to five categories (*movies, music, fun, finance* and *news*) by using binary classifiers trained on two separated feature sets – meta-data (i.e., text) and content (i.e., visual). Their experiments demonstrated that category accuracy depends on the type of the classifier and therefore they take advantage of this prior knowledge by using a voting based category-dependent scheme. According to this scheme, the effectiveness of a classifier for predicting a certain category is estimated during the training phase and is later used during classification.

Yang et al. [17] present a study of video classification with respect to eleven categories (e.g., *animal, entertainment, news, sports, music*). They use four different feature sources: visual, audio, text and semantic. The latter can be expressed with video annotations or "visual words". The text features, which include video title, description and tags provided by the uploader, have *tf.idf* values. To amend the feature vector sparsity problem, Yang et al. use WordNet-based similarity measure to propagate the *tf.idf* among similar words. More than 10K human-labeled videos were used in the experiments. A binary classifier is trained for every category-feature combination. For predictions, scores from all the classifiers trained to recognize a certain category are fused to achieve a final confidence.

Cui et al. [5] classify YouTube videos in one of the 15 YouTube categories (e.g., *travel, news, game, people*) and learn from both text and video features. The novelty of their approach lies in that they use the content features during training only to define a better word similarity metric. This is motivated by the fact that computing video features is usually time and resource consuming. During the training phase, videos are clustered based on their video features. After that, a better word similarity metric is defined which assigns higher similarity to words from the same video cluster. For eleven out of 15 categories, the described method outperforms approaches which use only one of the feature sources, or which fuse the predictions of the two.

Huang et al. [11] analyse the effectiveness of a range of text features in detecting extremist videos on YouTube. Video title, description, tags as well as user comments, uploader's name and video category are used as feature sources. The features are broadly classified into lexical (character and word-based features), syntactic (function words and punctuation) and content-specific (word, character and part-of-speech ngrams). In their analysis they claim that all of the mentioned sources are useful because the features from their best model appear in any of the text source. However, it remains unclear whether any of the sources is indeed indispensable for video classification. Apart from that, extremist videos constitute a very special class and it is not guaranteed that the findings of the study generalize to videos from other categories.

Toderici et al. [16] describe a method for automatic tag recommendation system for YouTube videos where new tags are suggested based on a range of video content features. They also propose a method for assigning categories to videos. In an experiment with human raters they get the precision @5 of 70% for category predictions and tag relevance comparable with that of tags provided by uploaders.

2.2 User Comments Analysis

There has been some interest among researchers in the computational linguistics (CL) community in analysing user comments. Like weblog posts, user comments express personal opinion, and the variety found in the comments on a single post can help to identify controversy, sentiment and explain popularity of many topics. The CL research motivates us to look more closely at the comments left on videos and analyse their utility for video categorization.

Herring et al. [10] were the first to include user comments in their weblog analysis. In their study, they look at weblogs from the genre perspective and report comments on posts as one of the characteristic properties of weblogs; no further analysis of user comments is given.

Mishne and Glance [14] present a first in-depth analysis of weblog comments and consider the relationship between the post and the comments it gets. The questions they pose relate to the amount of comments, the post popularity and the use of comments for weblog search and content analysis. Their study indicates that, compared with posts themselves, user comments constitute a considerable data source on their own which is useful for weblog indexing and search. They also present an analysis of how comments account for controversy in the post and how they can help understand different opinions that the post provokes.

Yano and Smith [18, 19] consider the political blogs domain and aim at predicting which users are likely to respond to a post as well as the size (in the number of comments) and the topics of user responses. The unsupervised model they use is a variant of LDA which models the relationship between the post, the commenters and their responses [2, 6].

Recently, Popescu and Pennacchiotti [15] considered the task of discovering controversial events from Twitter. In their supervised

CATEGORY	SUBCATEGORIES
film	bollywood
	animation
	trailers
howto	bodybuilding
	cooking
	beauty_tips
music	arabic
	rap
	rock
news	elections
	documentary
	politics
sports	soccer
	basketball
	water_sports

Figure 1: Sample categories

approach two classifiers are trained to recognize whether a tweet is about an event and whether this event is controversial.

3. RESEARCH QUESTIONS

We consider the task of assigning categories to unrestricted web videos found on YouTube. Unlike the related research, our category set is large, comprising 75 two-level categories. Figure 1 gives an idea of what kind of categories we use in our study. The goal is to find a single most relevant two-level category for the video.

The research questions which have not been answered in previous studies and which we tackle here are as follows:

1. Given that it is prohibitively difficult to obtain a sufficient amount of human-labeled videos for a large set of classes and with a large, sparse feature space, can we learn from imperfect predictions of a classifier trained on a complementary feature set? Is the accuracy of the resulting classifier comparable with the accuracy of the original one? Can a combination of the two classifiers outperform either of the two taken on its own?

2. Which of the categories from our set can be predicted more reliably by the video resp. text-based classifier? Do they indeed capture different semantics of the data?

3. How useful is user-provided textual metadata (i.e., title, description, tags) for video category prediction? Which source of information is particularly helpful?

4. Can categories be reliably predicted from the viewers' comments on the video (comments are known to be extremely noisy)? Furthermore, does the viewers' perspective contribute useful features to improve the performance of the classifier trained on the metadata provided by the uploader? If so, how are the comment features different from those found in the video title, description and tags?

To our knowledge we are the first to use the approach of training a supervised system on noisy predictions of a weakly supervised classifier as previous work has explored co-training and supervised methods. Unlike previous work, our category set is large and includes 75 two-level categories.

4. METHODOLOGY

Our system builds on top of the predictions of a Video2Text classifier introduced by Aradhye et al. [1]. We use Video2Text for three reasons:

- it is weakly supervised and requires no labeled data other than video metadata (title, description) supplied by the user;
- it not only clusters similar videos but also generates a text label for each cluster;
- the resulting label set is comparatively large and is more suited for categorization of unrestricted video content found on YouTube.

Figure 2 describes the training procedure pipeline. Before we proceed with the details of our method, we first describe how Video2Text works.

4.1 Video2Text

Video2Text does not require labeled data to learn which categories to assign to a video. Furthermore, it does not need a predefined set of categories. Instead, it starts from a set of "weak" labels available in the form of video metadata, i.e., in the title, description and uploader-supplied tags. It further creates a vocabulary of concepts which are unigrams and bigrams found in the video metadata. Every concept in the vocabulary is associated with a binary classifier trained from a large set of audio and video signals extracted from the video. The positive instances are the videos which have the concept in their metadata; the negative instances are the videos which do not mention the concept. Initially the vocabulary contains all the possible unigrams and bigrams excluding very frequent and very infrequent ones. The following procedure is repeated until the vocabulary size does not change much or the maximum number of iterations has been reached:

1. A binary classifier is trained for every concept in the vocabulary. The accuracy of the classifier is assessed on a portion of a reserved validation set of videos. Each iteration uses a subset of yet unseen videos from the validation set. The classifier, and hence the concept, is retained only if both precision and recall are above a predefined threshold which is set to 0.7 in the paper.

2. The remaining classifiers are used to update the feature vectors of all videos – the scores assigned to those videos are appended as new features.

The idea behind this iterative procedure is that finer-grained concepts are being learned from concepts added at a previous iteration. E.g., the *video* category is soon discarded as uninformative; *anime* is learned from more general concepts like *cartoon* and *Japanese*. See the original paper by Aradhye et al. [1] for more details on the approach.

In our reimplementation of Video2Text we use the same parameter values as in the original paper. We limit the total number of binary classifiers (and therefore labels) to 75 by discarding those with lower precision or recall. We group together labels related to news, film, sports, howto, music, etc. and thus obtain the final set of 75 two-level categories.

4.2 Categorization with Video2Text

We use Video2Text to assign two-level categories to videos: since all the classifiers are binary, for every video we get a vector of 75 categories together with their likelihood. Figure 1 gives a few examples of the categories we consider. In Figure 2 the output of

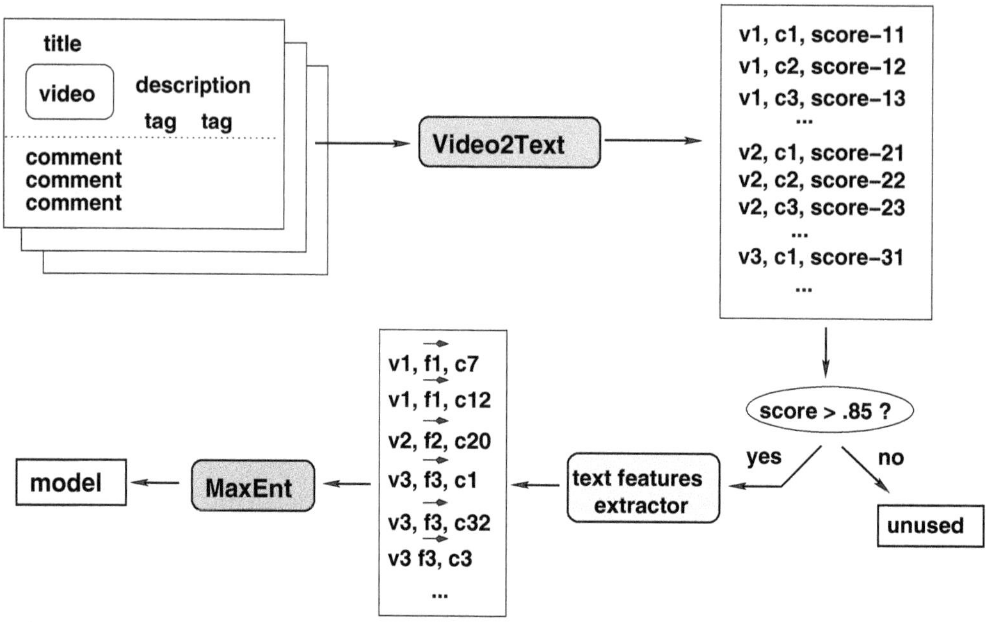

Figure 2: Training procedure pipeline

Video2Text is represented as a list of strings where each string is a sequence of video ID, one of the possible categories and a score which was assigned to this video-category pair – v_i, c_j, s_{ij}. Of course, there is no guarantee that every video would have a single high-scoring prediction.

To train a classifier from text features, we randomly extract approximately 15M videos which have a high-scoring prediction from the Video2Text classifier; in our experiment the threshold is set to 0.85. Videos which get a score smaller than 0.85 are filtered out. For the remaining videos we generate feature vectors, $\vec{f_i}$, from text data associated with them (i.e., title, description, tags, comments; see Sec. 5 for details). The resulting feature vectors and high-scoring categories $v_i, \vec{f_i}, c_j$ are used to train a model with a maximum entropy classifier.

The average number of categories assigned to a video is about 1.3. Based on a small evaluation with human raters, we found that the prediction precision varies across different categories. For example, the threshold of 0.85 results in 100% precision for animation but only 70% for documentary news. Unfortunately, the small size of the evaluation set does not allow us to tune the threshold for every category. However, this noisy setting makes it particularly interesting to see whether a useful model of a comparable quality can be trained from predictions which are known not to be very accurate.

4.3 Distributed MaxEnt

We explore very sparse models for classification where each example covers a very small fraction of the feature space. When combined with the large number of classes (75), the sparsity of a multi-class classification model requires large amounts of training data. The approach presented in this paper allows us to automatically generate training examples for the category classifier. We use a conditional maximum entropy (MaxEnt) optimization criteria to train the classifiers, resulting in a conditional probability model over the classes given the YouTube video:

$$c_i^* = \arg\max_{c \in \mathcal{C}} p_\theta(c|v_i) = \arg\max_{c \in \mathcal{C}} p_\theta(c|f_i)$$

where $c \in C$ is one of the 75 automatically discovered categories. We train the classifier to minimize an L1-regularized loss over the training data $D = ((v_1, c_1), \ldots, (v_m, c_m))$ (the automatically generated, high-precision predictions from the Video2Text classifier), where the loss is the negative log-likelihood of the training data: $L(D) = -\sum_{(f_i, c_i) \in D} \log p(c_i|f_i)$. This results in the following optimization objective function:

$$\theta^* = \arg\min_\theta ||\theta||_1 + \sum_i \log p_\theta(c_i|x_i)$$

In order to accommodate a large training set, we use a distributed training algorithm known as the Iterative Parameters Mixture update for stochastic gradient descent [13, 9]. This algorithms performs online gradient descent in parallel on subsets of the data, averaging the trained models after each iteration of training and then broadcasting the averaged models back to the parallel training processes. In the current experiments, we train from only 15 million YouTube videos; however, by using a distributed training approach, we are able to train on far larger datasets and can iterate over experimental conditions rapidly.

5. DATA AND MODELS

In this section we present the text-based feature sets and describe system configurations we use. We also introduce a model which predicts video category from the scored set of categories output by Video2Text and a text-based classifier.

5.1 Text Features

The text models we consider differ regarding the text sources from which features are extracted: title, description and user tags

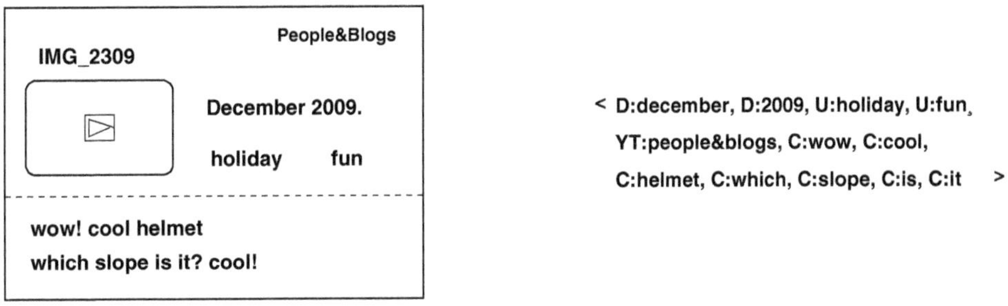

(a) Video with its metadata and comments

(b) Text-based features

Figure 3: An example video and its feature vector

are the metadata sources provided by the uploader (see the input box in Fig. 2). The video comments provide a viewers' perspective on the video. Finally, as an additional feature we add the YouTube category (one out of 15) which the uploader selected as a relevant one. Note that we are assigning a much more fine-grained classification of 75 categories and the YouTube category is only an indicator of which subset of categories might be relevant.

The features we use are all token-based. We do not use any linguistic preprocessing (e.g., stemming, part-of-speech tagging) other than lowercasing because the data is very noisy and we expect input in any language. To reduce the feature space, we filter out extremely infrequent tokens. Token frequencies are calculated over a set of 150K videos, 10K videos from each of the 15 YouTube categories. Similar to computing document frequency, we count every unique token only once per video. The threshold we use is set to 10 meaning that tokens which appeared in less than 10 videos from the 150K set are discarded.

To distinguish between tokens appearing in different text fields, every token is prefixed with the first letter of where it was extracted from (e.g., *T:xbox, D:xbox, U:xbox, C:xbox* – for the occurrences of *xbox* in the title, description, user tags and comments, respectively). Figure 3 gives an example video and the features extracted from its metadata and comments. The title of the video (*IMG_2309*) is the name of the corresponding file and is not sufficiently frequent to be included in the feature vector. The word *cool* occurs twice in the comment but is included only once as a feature.

Since the number of user comments varies considerably and can be as high as hundreds of thousands, we extract comment features from the 200 most recent comments for each video. We found that using token frequency results in lower accuracy: words from comments on videos with many comments may get extremely high value. However, using the inverted video frequency count as the value for comment features turns our to have a positive effect.

To address the question of which source of textual information is particularly useful, we try several system configurations. In what follows, we consider the following models which differ with respect to the feature sources they use. We train a classifier for each of the metadata sources – title (TITLE), description (DESCR), user tags (U-TAGS). We also look at the combination of all three (TDU) and at a model which is also informed about the YouTube category chosen by the video uploader (TDU+YT). Finally, we consider a model trained from the user comments on the video as the only feature source (COMM) and a model which profited from all five text sources (TDU+YT+C).

5.2 Combined Classifier

To see if the combination of the two views, video and text based, is beneficial, we consider a simple "meta" classifier which ranks video categories based on the predictions made by the two classifiers. The ranking is obtained by converting the video-based predictions into a probability distribution and multiplying it with the probability distribution returned by MaxEnt. Note that any of the text-based classifiers (e.g, TDU or C) can be used in the combination. This combination approach proved to be effective in our experiments, but may not be the optimal method. We do not explore optimizing the combination approach in this work as our goal is simply to support the hypothesis that the two models provide complimentary predictions. Figure 4 schematically represents how combining works for a single video (the normalization to a probability distribution step is omitted as it is not relevant).

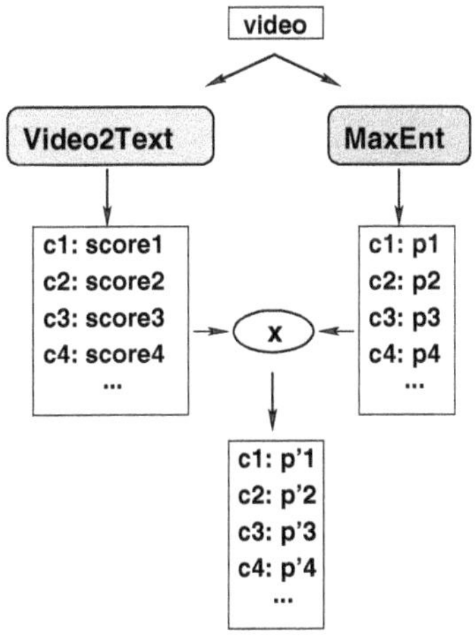

Figure 4: The combination procedure for a single video

The idea behind the multiplied combination is that each of the classifiers has veto power and can thus help rule out wrong categories. The final prediction of the combined classifier is the one with the highest product score. For example, the text-based classifier (MaxEnt) may distribute the total probability mass between two categories – *sports/winter_sports* and *sports/bikes* – because words related to both categories, like *helmet*, appear in the metadata. The video-based classifier (Video2Text) may assign a very low score to the former category (e.g., there is no snow in the video but fields and woods), a somewhat high score to *car/racing* and a high score to *animals/wild_animals*. The product of the two will then change the ranking so that only the category which is likely according to both models, *sports/bikes* gets the highest score.

Of course, the utility of the combined model presumes that the two models have complementary views on the data. In the experiments section we are going to show that this is indeed the case.

6. EXPERIMENTS

To test our hypotheses, we employ human raters and collect their judgments about the relevance of predicted categories. The three classes of models we want to compare are: (1) the Video2Text model, (2) the models trained on text features, and (3) the combination models, described in Section 5.2. Unfortunately, given the size of our category set and all the classes of text features we experiment with, it is prohibitively difficult to collect enough human judgments to compare all the text and the combined models: we would need to evaluate seven text-based models, Video2Text and at least one combined model over 75 categories. Therefore, we use a portion of automatically labeled data to get an idea as to which of the text models is likely to be the most accurate one. This "winner" model is further compared with the video classifier in an experiment with human raters. It is also the model used in combination with Video2Text. In this section, we first describe the results of the preliminary evaluation on the development set and then proceed with the results of the experiments with human raters.

6.1 Preliminary Evaluation of Text Models

As with out training data selection, we randomly collect about 100K videos which get a high-scoring prediction from the video model. A prediction is considered correct if it has a score of at least 0.85 from Video2Text. The average number of "correct" categories assigned to a video is 1.2, and for a video to count as correctly classified the text-based prediction has to be in the set of video-assigned categories. For evaluation we first consider videos which have at least one comment (1+), although we do not filter out cases when no sufficiently frequency feature can be extracted from the video. This restriction is applied to allow for a fair comparison of the models which use comment features. It also helps filter out videos with very little textual information because such videos are often uploaded for sharing with very few people and are not expected to be seen by many. To check whether more accurate predictions are made for videos with many comments, we measure accuracy on a subset of videos with at least ten comments (10+). Although less than 10% videos have ten comments or more, this is an important class of videos as they get considerably more views than those with very few comments. As with the training phase, the maximum number of comments we retrieve is 200.

Of course, the results on the development set (Table 1) should be taken with a grain of salt as predictions of Video2Text are not perfect and some videos may not have a correct label. However, we believe that significant differences are indicative of a better model.

Videos with at least one comment.

Concerning single text feature sources for videos with at least one comment (Accuracy 1+ in Table 1), user tags turned out to be particularly helpful, while comments and descriptions are the least useful sources. This is not surprising given that descriptions, unlike titles, can be left empty, and that a single comment like *lol* or *first* does not give any clue to the video category. Predictions made from user tags, which may be left blank, are more accurate because tags themselves constitute an open category set which the uploader selects as most relevant. However, a combination of all the features significantly improves the performance (TDU); providing YouTube category further refines the predictions (TDU+YT). The higher accuracy is largely due to the fact that in cases where user tags are missing, the title and possibly the description help predict the right category.

Videos with at least ten comments.

Interestingly, the accuracy numbers are much higher for all the models on videos with at least ten comments, even for models which do not use comments as a feature source. The reason is that those videos are of a better quality and have more informative titles and descriptions, which we believe is why they are viewed and commented on by more users. The boost in accuracy is particularly striking for the models using comments. Out of all the single-source models, the comments (COMM) model is the one which substantially outperforms all other models, including the combinations of all models (TDU and TDU+YT). This comes as a surprising result because it means that, given enough comment volume, the viewers can provide us with more helpful signals about video content than the uploaders themselves. The question of whether the uploader is often unable to give an adequate description to his video or whether he is not interested in it is left for future research.

For both evaluation sets (1+ and 10+), the best model is TDU+YT+C which combines all the text sources. It is this model whose performance we assess with human raters and which we use to combine with the video model.

6.2 Experiments with Human Raters

From the 100K videos in the development set, we extract the total of 750 videos equally from the 15 YouTube categories, 50 each. This way we aim at getting a balanced sample of the data with videos from all the possible categories. With the mentioned restriction on the maximum number of retrieved comments (200), the average number of comments and standard deviation in the evaluation set (1+) are 9.6 and 26, respectively. Thus, most videos have only very few comments.

A video and a category were presented to a human rater who was asked to rate it as either *fully correct (3), partially correct (2), somewhat related (1)*, or *off-topic (0)*. The instructions made clear that *partially correct* should be selected when only one of the two levels of the category is applicable. The raters did not see any meta information about the video or the comments. For every video-category pair we obtained exactly three ratings. 12% of the videos were excluded because they were no longer available for watching during the time of the experiment. The three ratings of a video were then converted into a single binary rating by summing the numeric values associated with them, normalizing the sum (i.e., dividing it over nine) and rounding the resulting score. A score of at least 0.5 makes a category count as a correct one. The accuracy we report in Table 2 is computed as $\frac{|correct|}{|total|}$. Note that our evaluation is very strict: for a category to count as correct, two raters must find it at least *partially correct* and the third rating cannot be *off-topic*. A category rated as *somewhat related* does not count as a correct one. A less strict evaluation would obviously result in higher accuracy numbers.

	VIDEO2TEXT	TDU+YT+C	COMBINED
Accuracy 1+	34.6%	38.5%	40.5%
Accuracy 10+	38.9%	43.5%	45.7%

Table 2: Accuracy on the set rated by humans

Video2Text vs. TDU+YT+C *vs. combination.*

The most remarkable result is that the text-based model performs not only on par with the video model it was trained from but is actually significantly better. Furthermore, the simple combination method we tried resulted in improved accuracy because, as we hypothesized, each of the models can help pruning wrong predictions. These findings allow us to answer the first group of questions posed

	TITLE	DESCR	U-TAGS	COMM	TDU	TDU+YT	TDU+YT+C
Accuracy 1+	39.4%	35%	42.4%	35.6%	48.1%	51%	53.2%
Accuracy 10+	44.8%	40.7%	49.2%	57.8%	54.7%	56.5%	62.8%

Table 1: Accuracy for different models on a set of videos with at least one or ten comments, respectively

in Section 3 affirmatively. The text-based classifier is not redundant but complementary to the video-based one. The complementarity explains the increased performance of the combination model.

Differences between the video and text based views. Having looked at the predictions made by the video and the text based models, we found that certain abstract categories which are difficult to recognize from video features (e.g., *news, finance* or *comedy*) were much more accurately predicted by the text model (more than 50% in precision). This is encouraging because it means that a competitive text-based classifier can be trained from very noisy predictions. However, certain categories are better predicted from video signals: *howto/dance* or *film/animation*. The combined model outperformed the source models across many categories; however, there are not specific categories in which it is consistently better. Thus, to answer the second group of questions from Section 3, the two views do capture different semantics of the data, the text classifier being more useful for abstract categories which do not have obvious visual features.

Performance on videos with many comments. We looked at the subset of videos in the rated set which had at least ten comments. 110 out of 660 videos satisfied this condition (10+ in Table 2). As in the preliminary evaluation on the development set, we found that the performance of all the models improves with the number of comments. However, the differences between the models' performance remain the same, the combined model being 6-7% better than the video-based one.

The improved performance on the 10+ subset is consistent with what we observed in our evaluation on the development set: that prediction accuracy increases with the number of comments. Apparently, a reasonable explanation is that more comment-based features can be generated for such videos, and this would allow us to see the comments stream as a valuable source of information about the video content. However, as we have seen in the previous subsection, on videos with many comments more accurate predictions are made even by the models which do not extract any features from the comments (e.g., TDU+YT). Therefore, an increase in accuracy can be expected also for comment-free models. To investigate the question of whether comments indeed provide helpful clues and why this is so we did one more experiment with human raters.

6.3 Impact of Comments

To address the final question in Section 3 and get an insight into why the model with comment features outperforms (at least on the development set) the one that lacks this feature source, we collected human ratings for videos which got different predictions from TDU+YT and TDU+YT+C. In our analysis we focused on three unrelated categories – *film/bollywood, music/arabic* and *howto/ bodybuilding* – and selected videos with at least ten comments to make the data set more informative. Thus, for each category c and each model m we extracted ten videos $v_1, ...v_{10}$ where m ranked c the highest and m' assigned some other c' the highest score. Pairs v_i, c and v_i, c' were rated by human experts.

Using the same instructions and approach as in the previous evaluation, we collected three ratings for the total of 120 ($3 \times 10 \times (2 + 2)$) video-category pairs. The average accuracy for the three selected categories as well as the overall accuracy on all the rated videos are presented in Table 3.

	TDU+YT	TDU+YT+C
bodybuilding	0%	22.2%
bollywood	14.3%	77.8%
arabic music	37.5%	100%
overall	26.1%	59.2%

Table 3: Results for the models with and without comment features

The difference between the two models is remarkable and indicates that comments do significantly improve prediction accuracy, provided that there are enough of them (e.g., at least ten). For almost all the videos where the two models got different ratings from the humans it was the comment-informed model whose prediction was correct. Having looked at the rated examples, we identified the following reasons for why viewers' comments were so helpful:

1. In some cases, there were no tags, and title and description were very short and provided little information about the content of the video. Some descriptions and titles contained words indicative of the correct category but they were misspelled, e.g., *boliwook* instead of *bollywood*. Here, comments became a **substitute** for a proper title / description.

2. Some videos had descriptions which could be applicable to many categories, e.g., *"Always playing this song, sorry for poor quality"*, *"This video has no meaning of life"* or *"From my favorite episode"*. The comments, on the other hand, referred to a particular scene and mentioned names of actors, players, characters or brands which made it clear that the video was from a (Bollywood) movie, a soccer game, a cartoon, or about a device. Here comments helped to further **disambiguate** the category.

3. Words from some titles and descriptions were misleading on their own and suggested a category unrelated to the video. E.g., *EZ, curls, pounds, girl* in the *People & Blogs* category made TDU+YT rank *howto/beauty_tips* as the most likely category. Comments like the following helped to **correct** wrong predictions: *"pancake chest, monstrous face, massive waist with mini gut, and weird, pencilish arms."* made it clear that the most relevant category is *howto/bodybuilding*.

Thus, our analysis on a subset of three unrelated categories demonstrates that the video comment stream should not be neglected as a feature source. It is noisy but the signals it provides us with are in many cases indispensable for video classification because the video title, description and tags are not always indicative of the most relevant category.

7. CONCLUSIONS

In this paper we presented a text-based approach to the task of assigning relevant categories to videos. We showed that a competitive classifier can be trained on high-scoring predictions made by a weakly supervised classifier learned from video features. We also showed that the two provide complementary views on the data and that a simple product model which combines two sets of predictions outperforms each of them taken on their own. The prediction rate of 41% is quite high given the unprecedentedly large size of our category set (75) and that we did not use any human-labeled data. Furthermore, for popular videos with at least ten comments we achieved an even higher accuracy of 46%.

We found that all of the text sources – title, description, tags and comments – are helpful for category predictions. A more significant result is that accurate predictions can be made from the users' comments, provided that there are enough of them. We analysed a set of video-category pairs rated by humans and suggested three reasons for why a model which also looks at the viewers' comments outperforms the one which lacks this information source.

Motivated by our findings as well as by recent research in the weblogs domain, in the future we are planning to investigate the usefulness of user comments for other tasks.

8. REFERENCES

[1] H. Aradhye, G. Toderici, and J. Yagnik. Video2Text: Learning to annotate video content. In *Proceedings of the 1st International Workshop on Internet Multimedia Mining,* Miami, Florida, December 6, 2009.

[2] D. M. Blei, A. Y. Ng, and M. I. Jordan. Latent Dirichlet allocation. *Journal of Machine Learning Research,* 3:993–1022, 2003.

[3] A. Blum and T. Mitchell. Combining labeled and unlabeled data with Co-Training. In *Proceedings of the 11th Annual Conference on Learning Theory,* Madison, Wisc., 24–26 July, 1998, pages 92–100, 1998.

[4] D. Cai, X. He, Z. Li, W.-Y. Ma, and J.-R. Wen. Hierarchical clustering of WWW image search results using visual, textual and link information. In *Proceedings of the 6th SIGMM ACM International Workshop on Multimedia Information Retrieval,* New-York, USA, 15-16 October, pages 952–959, 2004.

[5] B. Cui, C. Zhang, and G. Cong. Content-enriched classifier for web video classification. In *Proceedings of the 33rd Annual International ACM SIGIR Conference on Research and Development in Information Retrieval* Geneva, Switzerland, 19–23 July 2010, pages 619–626, 2010.

[6] E. Erosheva, S. Fienberg, and J. Lafferty. Mixed membership models of scientific publications. In *Proceedings of the National Academy of Sciences*, pages 5220–5227, 2004.

[7] H. Feng, R. Shi, and T.-S. Chua. A bootstrapping framework for annotating and retrieving WWW images. In *Proceedings of the 6th SIGMM ACM International Workshop on Multimedia Information Retrieval,* New-York, USA, 15-16 October, pages 55–62, 2004.

[8] S. Fischer, R. Lienhart, and W. Effelsberg. Automatic recognition of film genres. In *Proceedings of the 3rd ACM International Conference on Multimedia,* San Francisco, CA, 5-9 November, pages 295–304, 1995.

[9] K. Hall, S. Gilpin, and G. Mann. MapReduce/Bigtable for distributed optimization. In *Advances in Neural Information Processing Systems Workshop on Learning on Cores, Clusters and Clouds*, 2010.

[10] S. C. Herring, L. A. Scheidt, S. Bonus, and E. Wright. Bridging the gap: A genre analysis of weblogs. In *Proceedings of the 37th Annual Hawaii International Conference on System Sciences,* Hawaii, 5–8 January, 2004, 2004.

[11] C. Huang, T. Fu, and H. Chen. Text-based video content classification for online video-sharing sites. *Journal of the American Society for Information Science and Technology*, 61(5):891–906, 2010.

[12] W.-H. Lin and A. Hauptmann. News video classification using SVM-based multimodal classifiers and combination strategies. In *Proceedings of the ACM International Conference on Multimedia,* Huan-les-Pins, France, 1-6 December, pages 323–326, 2002.

[13] R. McDonald, K. Hall, and G. Mann. Distributed training strategies for the structured perceptron. In *Proceedings of Human Language Technologies Conference of the North American Chapter of the Association for Computational Linguistics,* Los Angeles, CA, 1–6 June 2010, pages 456–464, 2010.

[14] G. Mishne and N. Glance. Leave a reply: An analysis of weblog comments. In *Proceedings of the 3rd Annual Workshop on the Weblogging Ecosystem,* Edinburgh, Scotland, 23 May, 2006, 2006.

[15] A.-M. Popescu and M. Pennacchiotti. Detecting controversial events from Twitter. In *Proceedings of the ACM 19th Conference on Information and Knowledge Management (CIKM 2010),* Toronto, Canada, 26–30 October, 2010, pages 1873–1876, 2010.

[16] G. Toderici, H. Aradhye, M. Paşca, L. Sbaiz, and J. Yagnik. Finding meaning on YouTube: Tag recommendation and category discovery. In *Proceedings of the 23rd IEEE Conference on Computer Vision and Pattern Recognition,* San Francisco, CA, 13–18 June, 2010.

[17] L. Yang, J. Liu, X. Yang, and X.-S. Hua. Multi-modality web image categorization. In *Proceedings of the 8th ACM SIGMM International Workshop on Multimedia Information Retrieval,* Augsburg, Germany, 28-29 September, pages 265–274, 2007.

[18] T. Yano, W. W. Cohen, and N. A. Smith. Predicting response to political blog posts with topic models. In *Proceedings of Human Language Technologies Conference of the North American Chapter of the Association for Computational Linguistics,* Boulder, Colorado, 30 May – 5 June 2009, pages 477–485, 2009.

[19] T. Yano and N. A. Smith. What's worthy of comment? Content and comment volume in political blogs. In *Proceedings of the 4th International Conference on Weblogs and Social Media,* Washington, DC, USA, 23 – 26 May 2010, pages 359–362, 2010.

[20] R. Zhang, R. Sarukkai, J.-H. Chow, W. Dai, and Z. Zhang. Joint categorization of queries and clips for web-based video search. In *Proceedings of the 8th ACM SIGMM International Workshop on Multimedia Information Retrieval,* Santa-Barbara, CA, 26-27 October, pages 193–202, 2006.

Multifaceted Toponym Recognition for Streaming News*

Michael D. Lieberman Hanan Samet
Center for Automation Research, Institute for Advanced Computer Studies,
Department of Computer Science, University of Maryland
College Park, MD 20742
{codepoet, hjs}@cs.umd.edu

ABSTRACT

News sources on the Web generate constant streams of information, describing many aspects of the events that shape our world. In particular, geography plays a key role in the news, and enabling geographic retrieval of news articles involves recognizing the textual references to geographic locations (called *toponyms*) present in the articles, which can be difficult due to ambiguity in natural language. Toponym recognition in news is often accomplished with algorithms designed and tested around small corpora of news articles, but these static collections do not reflect the streaming nature of online news, as evidenced by poor performance in tests. In contrast, a method for toponym recognition is presented that is tuned for streaming news by leveraging a wide variety of recognition components, both rule-based and statistical. An evaluation of this method shows that it outperforms two prominent toponym recognition systems when tested on large datasets of streaming news, indicating its suitability for this domain.

Categories and Subject Descriptors

H.3.1 [**Information Storage and Retrieval**]: Content Analysis and Indexing

General Terms

Algorithms, Design, Performance

Keywords

Toponym recognition, geotagging, streaming news

1. INTRODUCTION

News plays a large role in today's information society. Thousands of newspapers all over the world publish a constant stream of many thousands of news articles every day to serve our need for news. The rise of the Internet has allowed their access from anywhere in the world through newspapers' online presence, and has fueled intense competition as evidenced by a swift and sometimes tempestuous news cycle. Blogs, tweets, and other social media have also expanded the realm of news to include citizen journalism. Our goal is to collect, analyze, and comprehend this streaming, ever-changing mass of information, to make it easily retrievable for humans. Specialized techniques are required to achieve this goal.

Importantly, news often has a strong geographic component. Newspapers often characterize their readership in terms of where their readers live, and include news articles describing events that are relevant to geographic locations of interest to their readers. Thus, in our database of news articles, we attempt to understand the geographic content present in each article, to enable retrieval queries with a geographic component. This process of understanding is known as *geotagging* of text, and amounts to identifying locations in natural language text, and assigning lat/long values to them. In this way, geotagging can be considered as enabling the spatial indexing of unstructured or semistructured text. This spatial indexing provides a way to execute both feature-based queries ("Where is X happening?") and location-based queries ("What is happening at location Y?") [4]. Systems using geotagging have recently flourished and have been implemented in a wide variety of domains, such as web pages [3, 16, 21], blogs [22], encyclopedia articles [8, 27], Twitter messages [26], spreadsheets [2, 11], the hidden Web [12], and of most relevance for us, news articles [5, 7, 13, 14, 23, 25, 28]. The methods in this paper were developed for the NewsStand system [28], which uses a geotagger to associate clusters of news articles with the geographic locations mentioned in them, thereby enabling users to explore the news visually on NewsStand's interactive map interface. In addition, commercial products for geotagging text are available, including MetaCarta's Geotagger[1], Thomson Reuters's OpenCalais[2], and Yahoo!'s Placemaker[3], the latter two of which we investigate here.

The process of geotagging consists of finding all textual references to geographic locations, known as *toponyms*, and then choosing the correct location interpretation for each toponym (i.e., assigning lat/long values). These two steps, known respectively as *toponym recognition* (which we investigate in this paper) and *toponym resolution* (also an important problem, but not discussed in this work), are dif-

*This work was supported in part by the National Science Foundation under Grants IIS-10-18475, IIS-09-48548, IIS-08-12377, CCF-08-30618, and IIS-07-13501.

SIGIR'11, July 24–28, 2011, Beijing, China.

[1] `http://metacarta.com`
[2] `http://opencalais.com`
[3] `http://developer.yahoo.com/geo/placemaker`

ficult because of several kinds of ambiguity present in location names. In particular, many names of places are also names of other type of entities, called *geo/non-geo ambiguity* (e.g., "Stanley Jordan", "Bristol Palin", and "Paris Hilton" are persons, while "Bristol", "Paris", and "Jordan" are also toponyms), and many different places have the same name, called *geo/geo ambiguity* (e.g., over 40, 50, and 60 places around the world named "Jordan", "Bristol", and "Paris", respectively). These examples and others proved problematic when testing OpenCalais and Placemaker in our experimental evaluation of toponym recognition (described in Section 4), and served as a motivation for our research.

Toponym recognition can be considered as a subset of a more general problem studied in natural language processing, called *named-entity recognition* (NER). Whereas toponym recognition involves finding entities in text that correspond to geographic location names, named-entity recognition involves finding locations, as well as entities of other types (e.g., names of people and organizations). In our example sentence "Jordan visited London last Friday", the output from a toponym recognizer would include the location "London", while correct output from a named-entity recognizer would also include "Jordan" as a person, and possibly "Friday" as a day of week. Sometimes evidence is stronger for a particular entity interpretation versus another interpretation. For example, in the pattern "X visited Y", the "visited" verb lends credence to X being a person and Y being a location, since locations are visited by people. Machine learning-based NER systems will often discover patterns like these from corpora of entity-annotated documents, and use them to build a language model by which entities and entity types can be predicted, given the linguistic context.

Given toponym recognition's status as a subproblem of NER, tools developed for the more general problem of NER can be used for toponym recognition. In this case, the general strategy is to take an input document, execute an off-the-shelf NER system on the document (e.g., LingPipe[4], Stanford NER[5], ANNIE[6]), and take the location entities. Once location entities are found, location interpretations are assigned from a gazetteer, and in the toponym resolution step, one of the interpretations is chosen for each toponym. However, this simple strategy is problematic. Because NER is a more general problem, systems developed for NER tend to be tuned for this more general problem, rather than specifically for locations, so they may be less accurate in detecting locations. Also, when evaluating NER systems on our domain of news articles (described in Section 4), we found that they were biased toward precision at the expense of recall. This may be due to the small size and homogeneity of corpora used in training NER systems, which do not capture the fast moving and ever changing nature of the news cycle. While this bias is not unacceptable for NER, it is problematic when used in a geotagging system, since toponym recognition upper-bounds recall for the entire geotagging process (i.e., toponym recognition and resolution). As a result, the low recall of these NER systems severely limits the entire geotagging process's recall, and thus we saw the need for more comprehensive techniques.

Bearing these considerations in mind, the toponym recognition process we designed for processing streaming news has a considerably more flexible architecture. Our multifaceted toponym recognition process uses standalone NER software as only one of many recognition methods, of potentially varying quality. We include rule-based recognition in the form of entity dictionary tables, cue word matching (e.g., "X County"), and toponym refactoring. In addition, we leverage statistical NLP tools in the form of NER software with postprocessing filters, and part-of-speech (POS) tagging with additional recognition rules. At the end of the entire procedure, we attempt to reconcile entity types, and establish groups of entities to be resolved concurrently, by grouping textually similar entities together. Essentially, we designed this multifaceted toponym recognition procedure in keeping with our goals to be flexible enough to capture variations that occur in streaming news, as well as to be as all-inclusive as possible when recognizing toponyms, in order to maximize the procedure's recall (i.e., to miss as few toponyms as possible). Our toponym resolution procedure, described by Lieberman et al. [14], serves to restore precision to the process by dropping supposed toponyms with no supporting evidence for any of their possible interpretations, as evidenced by the higher overall precision reported by Lieberman et al. [14].

In summary, our key contributions include:

- A comprehensive, multifaceted toponym recognition method designed for streaming news using many types of evidence, including:
  - A dictionary of entity names and cue words.
  - Statistical methods including POS tagging and NER, with appropriate postprocessing steps.
  - Rule-based toponym refactoring.
  - Grammar filters involving noun adjuncts and active verbs.
- A novel experimental evaluation of our methods tested on streaming news, showing sizable recall gains over OpenCalais and Placemaker.

Our recognition procedure can be broken into two stages. First, we generate an initial set of possible entities using many sources of evidence (Section 2). Second, we execute a variety of postprocessing filters that attempt to resolve entity types using additional forms of evidence (Section 3). We also incorporated our toponym recognition method into the NewsStand system and evaluated it by comparing it against two state-of-the-art competing systems (Section 4).

2. FINDING TOPONYMS

2.1 Entity Tables

Our first step is to look for a curated, small set of well-known locations and other entities appearing in the document's text, which serves as a convenient baseline for toponym recognition. This set of entities is gathered from several tables in our gazetteer, which is based on GeoNames[7], and is updated and kept current on a daily basis. In particular, we collect lists of continents, countries, and top-level administrative divisions (e.g., states, provinces), and search for them among the document's tokens. In addition, we search for common abbreviations for all of the above (e.g., "California" can be abbreviated as "Calif." or "CA"). We also search for *demonyms*, which are words used to refer

[4] `http://alias-i.com/lingpipe`

[5] `http://nlp.stanford.edu/ner`

[6] `http://gate.ac.uk/ie`

[7] `http://geonames.org`

to people from a particular place (e.g., "German", "Marylander"). Demonyms, while not locations proper, have some aspect of location that can be useful in recognizing and resolving toponyms, in that the location they represent can contribute to an overall sense of locality for the document. We iterate over the document's tokens, looking for groups of tokens that match an entry in an entity table, and if we find such a match, we create an entity of the corresponding type. For location entities, we also associate each entity with the proper location interpretation from the gazetteer.

2.2 Entity Dictionary

Next, we recognize additional entities of many and varied types by using an entity dictionary, containing names of entities that commonly appear in the news. We use this dictionary to recognize both toponyms and non-toponyms, because knowing that a particular entity strongly refers to a non-toponym is useful in resolving geo/non-geo ambiguities. For example, knowing that "Apple" is a famous brand name allows us to discount the possibility that "Apple" refers to a small city in Ohio, in the absence of strong evidence. In addition to particular instances of entities, the entity dictionary also contains many *cue word* patterns which serve as keywords to identify entities of various types. For example, the phrase "County of" strongly indicates that one or more following tokens corresponds to a location. We search for entities and cue words among the document's tokens, and collect matches as entities. For cue words in the dictionary, we search for adjacent capitalized tokens as the corresponding entity. Our entity dictionary was constructed by observing the output from our toponym recognition and resolution processes and checking for recognition errors, to discover which geo/non-geo ambiguities proved most problematic in our domain. The entity dictionary is by no means complete, but it serves as a useful starting point for a toponym recognition process in the news domain. In addition, as we discover new sources of ambiguity, the dictionary is updated with new classes of entities, so it is always evolving.

Table 1 contains a set of entity types and examples of entities and entity cue words present in the entity dictionary. All examples shown in the table are also names of various locations around the world, indicating the high degree of geo/non-geo ambiguity present in toponyms. In addition, we added many different forms of spatial cues to account for minor variations in how the cue words are used. For example, both "X Lake" and "Lake X" are common variants of the "Lake" cue. Universities are another special case because of the many ways in which they are specified in text, especially with multi-campus university systems. For example, "University of Maryland at College Park" might be written "University of Maryland, College Park", "University of Maryland in College Park", "University of Maryland—College Park", or other similar ways. Each of these variants are encoded into the entity dictionary's matching rules.

2.3 Proper Nouns

Next, we use a POS tagger to find proper noun phrases, which are useful in recognizing locations because locations tend to consist of proper nouns. We search for sequences of proper noun tokens, and consider them as locations. In addition, because our tokenizer considers possessive forms (i.e., "'s") and hyphens as distinct tokens, we include these elements in location names if they connect sequences of proper nouns as well. These are useful for capturing locations such as "Prince George's County", in which "'s" separates the proper noun sequences "Prince George" and "County". In addition, we also consider simple prepositional modifiers as proper noun separators, which will capture phrases such as "University of Texas at Arlington". For each proper noun phrase we find, we add an entity of type "proper noun phrase" to the entity pool for this document, since we cannot determine a more specific type using POS tags alone. We use TreeTagger[8], a decision tree-based POS tagger, trained on the Penn TreeBank corpus.

Obviously, not all proper noun phrases are locations, so this technique will be underprecise for toponym recognition in that it will capture many noun phrases that are not locations, such as names of people, organizations, and other entities. However, despite its lack of precision, finding proper noun phrases is consistent with our goal of high recall—that is, not missing any locations present in the document. At this stage of processing, we are not overly concerned with precision in location recognition, since that will be restored in the toponym resolution step, where erroneous location interpretations will be filtered.

2.4 Named-Entity Recognition

As a final toponym recognition method, we leverage tools developed to address the problem of *named-entity recognition* (NER). NER seeks to discover typed entities present in an input text, which usually includes at a minimum entities such as people, organizations, and importantly, locations. As noted earlier, NER methods have their limitations when used for toponym recognition, due to NER being a more general problem. However, in keeping with our philosophy of multifaceted toponym recognition, we include NER in our toponym recognition procedure. As an NER package, we use the Stanford NLP Group's NER and IE package, which is built around a conditional random field (CRF) classifier. We used the language model included with the Stanford NER distribution, a three-class classifier to find persons, organizations, and locations, which was obtained by training on a mixture of CoNLL, MUC-6 and MUC-7, and ACE corpora.

We feed the article text to the NER system, and save the person, organization, and location entities into our entity pool. To avoid frequently noisy output entities, we only keep the entities that have a minimum score of 0.95. One observation is that this NER method captured similar entities as found by collecting proper noun phrases (described in Section 2.3), a result which is not overly surprising as named entities tend to consist of proper nouns. However, using the NER system offers the benefit of determining entity types, in addition to simply finding entities. Knowing entity types helps to avoid geo/non-geo errors, as non-location entities can generally be disregarded.

Rather than simply using the output entities from the NER system directly, we perform a number of postprocessing steps that serve to avoid some common pitfalls with which the Stanford NER system has trouble. These postprocessing steps are executed sequentially and act as entity filters. For example, we found that some output entities were fragmented, in that the boundaries were chosen incorrectly, erroneously including or excluding nearby tokens, and we created filters to address this and other problems. Each filter is described below. Note that scores and score thresholds mentioned in each filter's description correspond to scores assigned by the Stanford NER package.

---

[8]`http://www.ims.uni-stuttgart.de/projekte/corplex/TreeTagger`

Table 1: Sample entity patterns and types from our entity dictionary. Cue word patterns are indicated with appropriate X and Y as necessary. Each non-cue example in the table is also the name of multiple locations present in our gazetteer, indicating the high level of geo/non-geo ambiguity in location names.

General entities	
Religion	Christian, Islam, Hindu
Season	Spring, Fall
Direction	South, Northeast, Midwest
Day	Monday, Friday
Month	March, August
Timezone	EST, WEST
Color	Gray, Navy, Lime
Organization entities	
Brand names	Apple, Coke, Toyota
News agencies	AP, UPI
Terror groups	Hamas, Taliban
Unions	NEA, PETA
Government orgs	Congress, Army
Postnominals	X Corp., Y Inc.

Spatial cues	
Populated regions	State of X
Populated places	Town of X, Y City
Comma groups	X and Y counties
Water features	Gulf of X, Y Lake
Spot features	X School, Mt. Y
Universities	University of X at Y
General	X-based, Y-area
Person entities	
Honorifics	Mr. X; Ms Y; Dr. Z
Generational suffixes	X, Jr.; Y III
Postnominals	X, KBE; Y, M.D.
Job titles	Sen. X; President Y; Sgt. Z
Declaratory words	X said; added Y
Common given names	John X; Jennifer Y

The following sections contain examples of entities presented within their textual context. For ease of presentation, we visually distinguish these entities using brackets. For example, in the text "In [LOC College Park], the mayor...", "[LOC College Park]" refers to the entity under consideration, while the surrounding text serves as context. Capturing the distinction between entity and context will be important for several filters described below.

2.4.1 *Boundary Expansion*

Oftentimes, the NER system will find an entity in the proper context, but select the entity boundaries incorrectly. For example, it may select "Equatorial [LOC Guinea]" rather than the correct "[LOC Equatorial Guinea]". In this example, the selected entity was correct, but the boundaries were not correct. Furthermore, the specific context in which an entity was found can effect how the NER system selects boundaries for the entity. In other words, the NER system may extract e_1 "[LOC Equatorial Guinea]" in one part of the document, and e_2 "Equatorial [LOC Guinea]" in another, simply due to the linguistic context in which e_1 and e_2 were found. This filter attempts to correct these fragmentation errors by expanding entity boundaries using other entities found in the text. In particular, we try to expand entities that are substrings of other entities. In our example, we can expand e_2 ("Guinea") to "Equatorial Guinea" because the e_2's preceding token, "Equatorial", matches the initial portion of e_1. Note that we do not expand across sentence boundaries.

In general, to accomplish this entity boundary expansion, we search for entities that are substrings of other entities. We say that an entity e_1 *dominates* another entity e_2 if e_2 is a substring of e_1. First, we group entities together based on domination, so that entities which are substrings of each other are grouped together. Algorithm 1 provides a pseudocode listing for this procedure, named GROUPENTITIES. The output for GROUPENTITIES is a set of entity buckets B, with each bucket b containing a set of entities, one of which dominates all entities in b and is designated b's *bucket head*, and is denoted HEAD(b). After initializing the set of output buckets B (line 2), we sort the entities in decreasing order of length (3). We iterate over each entity E_i and bucket B_k—note that initially, since $|B| = 0$, the inner loop is not entered when $i = 1$ (4–16). First, we check whether HEAD(B_k) dominates E_i, and if so, we add E_i to B_k (7).

Algorithm 1 Group entities according to dominance.

```
1: procedure GroupEntities(E)
     Input: List of entities E
     Output: Set of entity buckets B
2:   Initialize set of entity buckets B ← {}
3:   Sort entities E by decreasing length
4:   for i ← 1...|E| do
5:     for k ← 1...|B| do
6:       if HEAD(B_k) dominates E_i then
7:         B_k ← B_k ∪ E_i
8:         break to next i
9:       else if E_i dominates HEAD(B_k) then
10:        B_k ← B_k ∪ E_i
11:        HEAD(B_k) ← E_i
12:        break to next i
13:      end if
14:    end for
15:    Add new bucket b to B with HEAD(b) = E_i
16:  end for
17:  return B
18: end procedure
```

Otherwise, if E_i dominates HEAD(B_k), we add E_i to B_k, and set HEAD(B_k) $\leftarrow E_i$ (11), since the dominance property is transitive and hence E_i will also dominate all entities in B_k. If we find an appropriate bucket b for E_i, we continue with E_{i+1}; otherwise, we create a new bucket b with HEAD(B_k) $= E_i$, and add b to B (15). Eventually, all entities in E will have been placed into appropriate bucket.

Now that entities have been grouped into buckets based on dominance, we can attempt to expand entities within buckets. We implemented two strategies for entity expansion, which we term *strict* and *loose* expansion. Put simply, strict expansion means that we only expand entities in a bucket b if they contain enough nearby tokens so that they can be expanded to match HEAD(b). On the other hand, loose expansion attempts to expand each entity in b using other entities in b. In particular, we compare each entity $e \in b$ to each longer entity $e' \in b$ in order of decreasing length, and we expand e to e' if the proper nearby tokens exist that make it equivalent to e'.

The advantage of strict expansion is that it ensures greater accuracy for expanded entities, since if expansion succeeds, it is unlikely that the expanded entity is erroneous, due to the larger number of tokens required for a successful expansion. However, strict expansion's major drawback is that the head entity of each entity bucket may be unique in the document, affording no opportunity to correct fragmentation errors present in entities in the bucket. That is, simply because an entity is long does not make it very relevant for the document as a whole. For example, consider a document where the NER system collected entities e_1 "[$_{\text{LOC}}$ College Park]" (correct), e_2 "College [$_{\text{LOC}}$ Park]" (incorrect), and e_3 "[$_{\text{ORG}}$ College Park's Fire Department]" (correct). All these entities would be placed in the same entity bucket, with e_3 as the bucket head. Under strict expansion, each of e_1 and e_2 would be compared with e_3 only. Neither would be expanded, which is fine for e_1, but e_2 would remain unexpanded and erroneous, since it could not be expanded to match e_3. However, under loose expansion, in addition to a comparison with e_3, e_2 would be compared to e_1 and hence would be correctly expanded due to the appropriate preceding token "College". To capture more of these cases, we use loose expansion in our entity expansion filter.

2.4.2 *Entity Prefixes/Suffixes*

One problem with NER systems is that entity types may be chosen incorrectly—even for multiple instances of the same entity in the same document—due to differences in the way that entities are referred to. For example, an article may initially mention the person "Paul Washington", and simply "Washington" later, though both refer to the same person. While the first can easily be recognized as a person due to the presence of both a given name and surname, the second entity may be incorrectly typed as location because it only consists of a surname that is also a common location name. Articles can also refer to people by their given name alone, especially when mentioning childrens' names or the names of celebrities, since referring to a person by their given name reflects a higher level of familiarity or empathy. At times, organization names may also be typed incorrectly, as in "Kia Motor Cars" which is frequently referred to as simply "Kia". The former is more easily recognized as an organization than the latter, which may be mistaken for a person's name or even a location.

This filter attempts to correct these typing errors for fragments of larger entities found elsewhere in the document. The filter proceeds by selecting source entities from which entity types will be propagated. The selected entities include person entities consisting of at least two tokens (given name and surname), and organization entities consisting of at least three tokens. Furthermore, only entities with scores of above 0.90 are selected, ensuring high quality among the source entities. After selecting the source entities, the first and last tokens are taken from each entity and associated with the source from which they were taken. Finally, entity types are propagated to low scoring entities by searching for entities with scores below 0.60 and containing one of the tokens extracted above. If such an entity e contains one of the tokens t, e's type is set to the type of the entity from which t was taken. This procedure captures given names and surnames of person entities, as well as the primary portion of organization names. Because only the first and last tokens of each source entity are matched, the filter allows for partial matching of entities, which is useful given the NER system's penchant for entity fragmentation.

3. FILTERING TOPONYMS

After finding entities using a combination of the methods described above, we proceed with a sequence of filters that act as postprocessing to remove potential errors. Filters are applied in the order listed and are described in detail below.

Table 2: Entity names modified by the name refactoring filter. Cue words are expanded and shifted within the entity to generate new query names for each entity. Arrows indicate the match and action performed for each pattern.

First name		Second name
Co. *X*	⇒	County *X*
Dr. *X*	⇒	Doctor *X*
Ft. *X*	⇒	Fort *X*
Mt. *X*	⇒	Mount *X*
St. *X*	⇒	Saint *X*
X Co.	⇒	*X* County
X Twp.	⇒	*X* Township
X County	⇔	County *X*
X County	⇔	County of *X*
X Lake	⇔	Lake *X*
X Parish	⇔	Parish of *X*
X Township	⇔	Township of *X*
X SchType	⇒	*X SchType* School

3.1 Toponym Refactoring

Oftentimes, location names can be referred to in multiple ways. For example, locations of a particular type such as "county" often have the word "County" in their names. However, the position of "County" in the location name can vary by locale. For example, in the US, "County" often appears as a suffix, as in "Prince George's County". However, counties of Ireland often feature "County" as a prefix, as in "County Kildare". In addition, abbreviations of "County" such as "Co." are not uncommon in news articles. Furthermore, a specific type of spot location frequently mentioned in local newspapers are local public and private schools, and these may be written in any number of ways (e.g., "Walter Johnson HS", "Walter Johnson High"). This filter's purpose is to account for these entity name variations, and refactor entity names to generate extra query names that will be matched properly in our gazetteer. The filter contains a list of regular expressions to match against entity names, and if a match is made, suitable substitutions are performed.

Table 2 contains some of the entity name patterns that are refactored by this filter. The patterns fall into four main classes: prefix abbreviations, suffix abbreviations, suffix shifting, and school expansion. In prefix and suffix expansion, common abbreviations used in location names are expanded. For example, "Ft. Meade" would be expanded to "Fort Meade". For suffix shifting, location suffixes such as "County" are shifted before and after the main location name, so a location such as "County Kildare" would be expanded to "Kildare County" and "County of Kildare". Finally, school expansion searches for partial names of schools, which are indicated by a school name and a school type keyword, such as "Primary", "Middle", "MS", or "High". Note that the filter may erroneously match and expand query names for entities that are not locations. For example, "Co." is also a common abbreviation of "Company" and as such frequently appears in business names. Thus, "Ford Motor Co." will be incorrectly expanded to "Ford Motor County". However, this erroneous expansion will not be overly problematic as it is in keeping with our goal of high recall in toponym recognition. That is, having erroneous query names such as "Ford Motor County" will not cause problems because they will be corrected by the toponym resolution procedure, either by not being present in the gazetteer, or by having little evidence for such interpretations.

3.2 Active Verbs

To distinguish between toponyms and other types of entities, we note that many entities tend to be *active*, in that they perform actions (e.g., people, organizations), while locations tend to be *passive*, in that they do not. For example, it would make sense for a person to "say" something, while in general it would not for a location to "say" something. More generally, the grammatical subject of an active voice verb can be thought of as performing the action described by the verb. We can leverage the part of speech tags assigned by the POS tagger to find entities that perform actions, which in turn disqualifies them from being toponyms.

To find active entities, the filter searches for entities followed by an active voice verb, or by an adverb and an active voice verb. In this way, the method effectively performs a shallow parsing of the sentence. For each such entity of type "LOC" (location), the type is reset to "NNPP" (proper noun phrase). In other words, the entity is no longer considered as a location. Note that this method does not provide evidence for a particular entity type—e.g., determining whether such an entity is a person or organization. However, since we are primarily concerned with distinguishing between toponyms and non-toponyms, this lack of evidence can be overlooked.

One caveat with this method is that it does not properly account for *metonymy* associated with toponyms. Metonyms are a frequent occurrence in articles about, for example, local or international politics, where a government may be referred to by the city of its primary geographic presence. For example, "Washington", literally meaning "Washington, DC", is often used metonymically to refer to the US government, an organization which can be considered an active entity. As a result, in a sentence such as "Washington stated on Monday...", "Washington" would be disqualified as a toponym. However, we note that repeated instances of "Washington" would likely provide a means of correcting this error, as metonymic references are relatively uncommon in text [10]. As a result, additional instances of "Washington" would not likely be metonymic, and could be used to correct the earlier error through a voting scheme. Alternatively, we could incorporate a metonymy recognition method into this filter, such as that proposed by Leveling and Hartrumpf [10].

3.3 Noun Adjuncts

Sometimes, the correct interpretation of toponym evidence itself is in question. For example, consider a sentence beginning: "In Russia, U.S. officials..." In this sentence, both "Russia" and "U.S." refer to countries. However, consider that the form "Russia, U.S." might be mistaken for a particularly common form of evidence termed *object/container* evidence, which can be briefly described as a pair of toponyms, one of which contains the other in a geographic sense. Considering this evidence interpretation, we might erroneously think that the phrase "Russia, U.S." might refer to any of several populated places named Russia in the US in New York, New Jersey, or Ohio.

To help clear up this evidential ambiguity, we can use evidence by taking note of another grammatical concept, that of the *noun adjunct*. Noun adjuncts are nouns that function as adjectives by modifying other nearby nouns. In our example sentence, "U.S." is a proper noun adjunct that modifies the plain noun "officials". Because of its primary connection with "officials" through the noun adjunct relationship, using it in object/container evidence would not be warranted. By detecting noun adjuncts, we prevent toponyms acting as noun adjuncts from participating in other filters used in toponym resolution. We detect them by finding entities followed by a plain noun.

3.4 Type Propagation

Having grouped entities into equivalence classes in the previous step, we can now leverage these entity groups to improve the overall quality of entity and toponym recognition. Note that in a group of entities as determined above, some entities will have more specific types than others, due to the heterogeneous nature of our toponym recognition methods. For example, entities found using the POS tagger (i.e., selecting proper nouns, described in Section 2.3) will have an unknown type, while entities found using the NER system (described in Section 2.4) will have more specific types. We can propagate entity types within each group to make the types within a group consistent, in a similar fashion as was done for the NER system's postprocessing. Having consistent entity types is useful because though the entities in a group have the same referent, the context in which each entity reference appears differs. To propagate entity types, we examine entity types within each group. If a group g contains untyped entities as well as entities all of a single type t, we set the untyped entities to type t. However, if there are more than one type of entities in g, the types are not propagated. Compared with a simple type voting scheme (e.g., setting the types of all entities in a group to the most frequent entity type), this scheme ensures a high quality of type propagation, since conflicts disqualify type propagation.

4. EVALUATION

We incorporated our own toponym recognition methods into the NewsStand system [28], and compared with those of two prominent competitors: Thomson Reuters's OpenCalais and Yahoo!'s Placemaker. Although both OpenCalais and Placemaker are closed-source commercial products, and do not make public how they work, they provide public Web APIs which allow for automated geotagging of documents, with relatively liberal rate limits. As a result, they have been used extensively in state-of-the-art geotagging and entity recognition research (e.g., [1, 17, 22, 29, 31]). Placemaker provides a toponym recognition service, while OpenCalais performs recognition of toponyms, and recognition of other types of entities as well. In addition, both OpenCalais and Placemaker are full geotagging systems—that is, they perform toponym resolution as well. While toponym resolution is an important problem in its own right, in this work, we are only concerned with toponym recognition. As a result, even though OpenCalais and Placemaker assign lat/long values to each toponym reported as output, we disregard these lat/long values in our evaluation. In other words, we use OpenCalais and Placemaker in their toponym recognition capacity only, and do not include toponym resolution in their performance scores. Also note that at the time of writing, neither OpenCalais nor Placemaker offered a means of tuning the precision/recall balance, so we could not explore this aspect of the systems. From our experimental results described in Section 4.4, it appears that these systems are tuned for precision, but we could not verify this over a range of precision/recall values due to lack of tuning capability.

We continue with a description of existing geotagging corpora used in related work (Section 4.1). Next, we measure toponym statistics in a large collection of news gathered by NewsStand, as measured by our own toponym recognition method as well as OpenCalais and Placemaker (Section 4.2). Then, we describe a new corpus of hand-annotated news ar-

Table 3: Corpora used in geotagging-related research, showing sources, and document and toponym counts. Note that document and toponym counts refer to annotated counts, not total counts.

Work	Source	Docs	Topos	T / D
[3]	Web pages	600	7082	11.8
[5]	L'Adige	150	1042	6.9
[6]	GeoSemCor	186	1210	6.5
[7]	Gigaword	165	1275	7.7
[9]	RCV1	946	6980	7.4
[14]	LGL	588	4793	8.2
[15]	News	101	792	7.8
[19]	Wikipedia	1000	1395	1.4
[24]	ACE'05	369	5562	15.1
[30]	Reuters	250	?	?
	Average	436	3348	8.1

ticles created from NewsStand's constantly streaming news data (Section 4.3). We conclude with accuracy measurements for all three methods in two corpora of annotated news articles, as well as in streaming news (Section 4.4).

4.1 Existing Corpora

To get a sense of the corpora used in geotagging research, we present Table 3, which contains a listing of researchers and the corpora they used in their geotagging-related research. For each corpus, we give the source and total number of annotated documents and toponyms. In some cases, the exact numbers of documents and toponyms were difficult to determine due to lack of detail. Also note that the sources listed in the table were often used by multiple researchers, and here we present only an example usage of each source. The table reveals the relatively small sizes of annotated corpora used in geotagging research, with the number of annotated documents and annotated toponyms having averages of about 436 and 3348 and maxima near 1000 and 7000, respectively. These numbers stand in stark contrast to the huge volume of news retrieved by NewsStand in just a single day, which is roughly 40k documents and 250k toponyms. Furthermore, most corpora include articles from only one or two news sources, usually newswire, which amounts to a heavily biased sample, given the variety and number of news sources and writing styles all over the world.

However, one commonality that is apparent from the values in Table 3 is that the average number of toponyms in each article is remarkably consistent, with each article having 7–8 toponyms with few exceptions. This range is especially prevalent for corpora consisting of news articles, which is our domain of interest. One exception includes the Wikipedia corpus of Overell and Rüger [19], with an average of 1.4 toponyms per article. However, Overell and Rüger only considered toponyms in each article that also correspond to links to other Wikipedia pages; since generally only the first instance of an entity mentioned in an article is linked, this explains the seeming lack of toponyms. Another anomalous measure is the 15.1 toponyms per article reported by Roberts et al. [24], which are likely due to the consideration of locations nested within other entities as toponyms (e.g., "[$_{LOC}$ New York] Police Department"). Another, unfortunate commonality among the corpora used in geotagging research is that most are unavailable due to copyright restrictions, thereby making direct algorithmic comparisons on the same data generally not possible. In addition, a better measure for how frequently toponyms occur in text would be the ratio of toponyms to words, which would better account for variations in news article length. However, this data was not often presented by authors. Nonetheless, 7–8 toponyms serves as a useful rule of thumb for the number of toponyms expected in articles of reasonable length.

Table 4: Counts of articles, distinct sources, and geotagged toponyms for several days' worth of news, sampled at different time periods.

Date	Docs	Sources	Topos	T / D
02 Nov 2010	27591	2086	207110	7.5
06 Nov 2010	13355	1245	124430	9.3
10 Nov 2010	28795	2182	208366	7.2
15 Nov 2010	26052	1952	195669	7.5
19 Nov 2010	24193	2018	173630	7.2
23 Nov 2010	26937	2067	194804	7.2
28 Nov 2010	14245	1250	148996	10.5

4.2 Toponym Statistics

Now that we have characterized typical toponym counts in news articles, we wish to determine whether NewsStand's geotagger has performance that approaches our expectations in terms of toponym recall. To measure performance, we sampled seven days' worth of news from various days in November 2010, and executed NewsStand's geotagger on the news articles collected on each day. The days were chosen randomly, except we ensured that we had at least one of each day of the week, to account for the typically lower volume of news published on weekends. We collected articles from news feeds that published at least five articles on each sampling day, to ensure a measure of consistency among the collected data. Furthermore, we limited the sampling to articles with at least a word count of 300, which ensures a reasonable minimum length for the news articles and served to filter out erroneously-processed documents (e.g., articles that had been improperly extracted from their HTML source). Sampling in this fashion resulted in filtering out about half of each day's articles

For each set of sampled articles, we tabulated the total number of toponyms recognized by NewsStand's toponym recognition process. Table 4 reflects these counts. "Sources" indicates the number of sampled news sources from which sampled articles were taken. For each day, we include the total number of toponyms reported by our recognition method that have at least one interpretation in our gazetteer. The last column contains the toponym-document fraction—the number of toponyms with gazetteer interpretations over the number of sampled articles containing those toponyms.

We make several interesting observations from these statistics. First, and most importantly, we see that the majority of sampled days have toponym fractions between 7.2 and 7.5, which fall precisely in our expected range of 7–8 toponyms. The outliers of 9.3 and 10.5 are not totally unexpected given that they were measured on weekends which imply a different pattern of news publication. Overall, the measured toponym fractions are strong indications that our toponym recognition method identifies an appropriate number of toponyms. Next, in examining the number of articles and sources, the numbers show that our sampling resulted in a large number of articles from a variety of sources on each day, which demonstrates the extreme variety in our article samples. This stands in contrast to the small size and homogeneity of corpora used in previous geotagging-related research (described in Section 4.1), and the large number

Table 5: Corpora used in evaluating recognition accuracy.

	LGL	Clust
Articles	621	13327
News sources	114	1607
Annotated docs	621	1080
Annotated topos	4765	11564
Distinct topos	1177	2320
Median topos per doc	6	8
Location types:		
Total topos	4765	11564
City	2287	3837
$\geq$ 100k pop	756	2377
$<$ 100k pop	1531	1460
Country	911	3540
State	784	2487
County	525	519

and variety of articles lends weight to the credence of our measured toponym fractions.

This evaluation method can be easily applied to very large collections of articles, making it ideal for continual testing of performance on streaming and ever-changing collections of news. Of course, it says nothing of how many of the toponyms are correct, which is addressed in Section 4.4.

4.3 A New Corpus of Streaming News

We used two corpora in our evaluation. For the first corpus, we used *LGL*, introduced by Lieberman et al. [14], which consists of 621 articles from 114 local newspapers, with a total of 4765 annotated toponyms. The goal in creating LGL was to create a collection of news from smaller news sources, rather than the major news sources typically used in creating article corpora, since the former significantly outnumber the latter on the Web. As a result, LGL is useful for testing the accuracy of our toponym recognition method for a variety of smaller news sources. However, it does not capture the larger, major news stories that are often described and published in multiple news sources. Note that these major news stories naturally form clusters in NewsStand, and it is not unusual to have clusters of 100, 200, or even 1000 articles for especially major and ongoing news stories.

To capture these stories, we created another corpus consisting of sizable clusters of news articles found by NewsStand, and termed *Clust*. To create Clust, we selected clusters that had sizes of 5–100 articles, and contained articles from at least four unique news sources. The clusters were sampled between January and April 2010. This sampling strategy ensures reasonable cluster sizes which allows for enough variation among articles in the cluster. Furthermore, having multiple news sources ensures that different news sources are used, rather than many copies of the same article everywhere, which might result from erroneous preprocessing. In total, we sampled 1080 clusters containing a total of 13327 news articles, from 1607 distinct news sources. For each cluster, we randomly selected one article for manual annotation, resulting in 1080 annotated articles containing 11962 toponyms, with a median of 8 toponyms per article. Because multiple news sources and by extension their audiences are represented in each cluster, we expect the stories in Clust to have more journalistic impact, as well as a wider geographic significance, than the stories in LGL.

Table 5 summarizes and compares statistics for the LGL and Clust corpora. Clust has roughly twice as many annotated articles, and toponyms, as LGL. However, the most striking difference between LGL and Clust is the composition of toponym types in each corpus. Since LGL was created as a corpus of articles from smaller newspapers, and Clust as a corpus of larger news stories, we expect the toponyms in LGL to correspond to smaller places, and those in Clust to correspond to larger places. The type statistics in Table 5 reflect these expectations. Nearly half of annotated toponyms in LGL correspond to cities, and of those toponyms, two-thirds are cities under 100k population. On the other hand, Clust, consisting of larger news stories, has only 33% of toponyms corresponding to cities, and of those toponyms, nearly two-thirds are cities over 100k population. In addition, the fractions of country and state toponyms in Clust are larger than those in LGL, while the fraction of county toponyms in LGL is larger than those in Clust. These measurements reflect our motivations for using LGL and creating Clust, and show that these corpora, used together, allow for an effective evaluation on both smaller and larger news stories from a variety of news sources.

4.4 Toponym Accuracy

Having established the credibility of our two evaluation corpora, we are ready to examine our toponym recognition method's accuracy and compare its performance to that of OpenCalais and Placemaker. For each of NewsStand, OpenCalais, and Placemaker, we consider two versions of each method: the original algorithm, referred to as, e.g., "NS", and the original algorithm with a postprocessing filter that removes output toponyms if they have no interpretations in our gazetteer, denoted with a subscript $_{\text{G}}$, e.g., "NS_{G}". By doing so, we can determine the effect of using a gazetteer on toponym recognition, as well as characterize to some extent the gazetteers used by OpenCalais and Placemaker. To measure performance, we use the well-known measures *precision* and *recall*, which for a set of ground truth toponyms G and a set of system-generated toponyms S, are defined as

$$P(G,S) = \frac{|G \cap S|}{|S|}, R(G,S) = \frac{|G \cap S|}{|G|}.$$

In addition, we consider two different criteria for determining whether a ground truth toponym g matches a system-generated toponym s. The first, termed *exact* matching, states that g and s are equivalent if the starting and ending offsets of each are equal. The second, termed *overlap* matching, relaxes this criterion by allowing g and s to simply overlap in their offset ranges for them to match. Both are useful in characterizing the performance of toponym recognition. Exact matching could be considered the gold standard for measuring performance. However, overlap matching is sometimes necessary to avoid improper penalization due to gazetteer differences and other factors. For example, consider a ground truth toponym "[$_{\text{LOC}}$ New York state]" and system-generated "[$_{\text{LOC}}$ New York] state", which is correct, but is not an exact match and is an overlap match. Overlap matching serves a similar purpose as methods such as BLEU [20], in that partial matches are not overly penalized.

We measured all algorithms' performance over both the LGL and Clust corpora. Table 6 contains results for the LGL corpus. NewsStand, OpenCalais, and Placemaker are referred to as "NS", "OC", and "PM", respectively. In addition, for $|G \cap S|$, P, and R, exact and overlap matching are reported as two numbers in the table in "E/O" form ($|S|$ is unaffected by the matching method used). Comparing NewsStand against OpenCalais and Placemaker reveals that both NewsStand variants greatly outperform the com-

Table 6: Toponym recognition performance in the LGL corpus ($|G| = 4765$). In all cases, the NewsStand variants have highest toponym recall.

	$\|S\|$	$\|G \cap S\|$ (E/O)	P (E/O)	R (E/O)
NS	23345	3879/4645	0.166/0.199	**0.814/0.975**
NS_G	5960	3619/3738	0.607/0.627	**0.759/0.784**
OC	1959	1830/1871	0.934/0.955	0.384/0.393
OC_G	1873	1757/1791	0.938/0.956	0.369/0.376
PM	4593	3129/3683	0.681/0.802	0.657/0.773
PM_G	3796	3013/3112	0.794/0.820	0.632/0.653

Table 7: Toponym recognition performance in the Clust corpus ($|G| = 11564$). As with LGL, NewsStand had highest recall.

	$\|S\|$	$\|G \cap S\|$ (E/O)	P (E/O)	R (E/O)
NS	44184	10243/11330	0.232/0.256	**0.886/0.980**
NS_G	13589	9909/10036	0.729/0.739	**0.857/0.868**
OC	6452	6208/6326	0.962/0.980	0.537/0.547
OC_G	6060	5843/5941	0.964/0.980	0.505/0.514
PM	9796	6782/8549	0.692/0.873	0.586/0.739
PM_G	7466	6469/6593	0.866/0.883	0.559/0.570

petition in terms of toponym recall, having at least 0.10 and in some cases 0.20 or higher recall over OpenCalais and Placemaker, when measured using both exact and overlap matching. NewsStand's high recall comes at the expense of toponym precision; however, remember that in NewsStand, toponym recognition is only considered one stage of an integrated geotagging process, and toponym precision is restored by later stages of processing. The gazetteer postprocessing done for $NewsStand_G$ demonstrates this effect, dramatically improving precision with little corresponding decrease in recall. In addition, as mentioned earlier, our geotagging procedure is based on that of Lieberman et al. [14], who report a precision over 0.80 and correspondingly high recall for LGL, thus showing that precision is indeed restored.

Examining OpenCalais's and Placemaker's performance, we can see that these methods are much more biased toward toponym precision at the expense of recall, which is taken to the extreme in the case of OpenCalais (i.e., at least 50% less than NewsStand). Note that NewsStand and Placemaker are comparable in terms of F_1 scores (harmonic mean of precision and recall), while OpenCalais's is lower, illustrating the potential precision/recall tradeoff. Also, performing gazetteer postprocessing for $OpenCalais_G$ has little effect, while for $Placemaker_G$, a significant boost in precision is noted using exact matching, along with a significant decrease in recall when using overlap matching. These results seemingly indicate that Placemaker's toponym matching rules differ from our own. Examining differences between exact and overlap matching, we see that NewsStand and Placemaker are significantly affected by allowing overlap matches, while OpenCalais and all the gazetteer-filtered algorithms (i.e., $NewsStand_G$, $OpenCalais_G$, $Placemaker_G$) are mostly unaffected. For NewsStand, this is likely due to dropping many non-toponyms that were selected by NewsStand's filters (e.g., proper noun phrases not present in the gazetteer). Comparing $|S|$ of NewsStand and $NewsStand_G$, a very large number of toponyms were dropped by the gazetteer filtering, which accounts for the hefty precision increase. For Placemaker, gazetteer and matching differences can account for the performance difference.

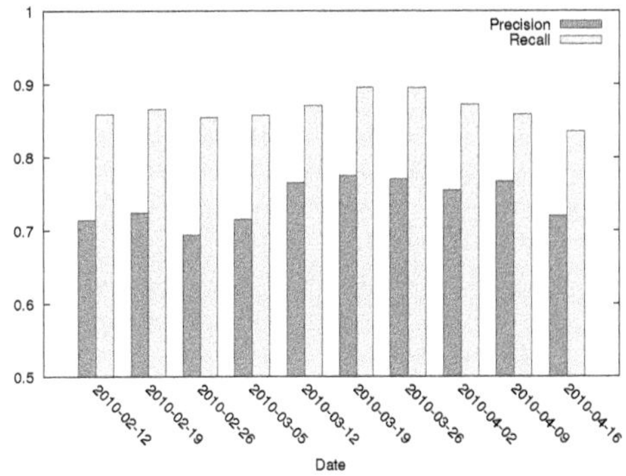

Figure 1: Toponym recognition performance on the Clust corpus measured over time.

Table 7 contains performance results for the Clust corpus. The NewsStand algorithms again outperform the competition in terms of recall, by an even larger margin than was seen for LGL, while OpenCalais and Placemaker are tuned for toponym precision. In addition, examining differences between LGL and Clust, we see that the performances scores for Clust are generally higher across all algorithms than the corresponding scores in LGL, with the only exception being Placemaker's recall. This difference indicates that in some sense, Clust's toponyms are easier to recognize than those of LGL, likely due to the greater presence of large, easily recognized toponyms such as country names.

4.5 Streaming Evaluation

We have shown that NewsStand's multifaceted toponym recognition procedure has a high recall for articles from both small, local news sources (LGL) as well as larger, better-known sources (Clust). However, measuring performance over an entire static corpus does not well reflect day-to-day toponym recognition performance on a constant stream of news data. To better characterize day-to-day performance, we split the Clust corpus into weekly samples of articles, and measured precision and recall for $NewsStand_G$ using overlap matching over each sample. Effectively, this test determines whether the NewsStand method would perform well if executed within that time range.

Figure 1 shows the performance of our toponym recognition procedure on the Clust corpus, measured over time. Performance in terms of both precision and recall is relatively consistent over all time periods tested, with a mean of 0.739 precision and 0.868 recall. In addition, the standard deviations of precision and recall are 0.029 and 0.018, which serve as further evidence of the method's performance stability. These results indicate that the NewsStand toponym recognition process is well suited for streaming news.

5. CONCLUSION

We have introduced a multifaceted toponym recognition method that is especially suited for the streaming news domain, which poses special challenges. In particular, streaming news is constantly in motion and ever-changing, which advises against the sole use of methods based on static corpora of news. Our recognition method involves many sources of evidence, and in our evaluation, was shown to outperform the competition in terms of toponym recall, the crucial measure of success. In future work, we plan to perform a more in-depth investigation of the individual components of toponym recognition used in our procedure, to determine their overall utility, as well as their performance for specific classes of toponyms. We also plan to investigate our heuristics' use within machine learning techniques such as coreference analysis [18] to determine their suitability in this domain. As more news sources move online, algorithms like ours which are tailored for streaming news will be vital to handle the resulting data deluge.

6. REFERENCES

[1] R. Abascal-Mena and E. López-Ornelas. Geo information extraction and processing from travel narratives. In *Proc. ELPUB*, pages 363–373, Helsinki, Finland, June 2010.

[2] M. D. Adelfio, M. D. Lieberman, H. Samet, and K. A. Firozvi. Ontuition: Intuitive data exploration via ontology navigation. In *Proc. GIS*, pages 540–541, San Jose, CA, Nov. 2010.

[3] E. Amitay, N. Har'El, R. Sivan, and A. Soffer. Web-a-Where: Geotagging web content. In *Proc. SIGIR*, pages 273–280, Sheffield, UK, July 2004.

[4] W. G. Aref and H. Samet. Efficient processing of window queries in the pyramid data structure. In *Proc. PODS*, pages 265–272, Nashville, TN, Apr. 1990.

[5] D. Buscaldi and B. Magnini. Grounding toponyms in an Italian local news corpus. In *Proc. GIR*, Zurich, Switzerland, Feb. 2010.

[6] D. Buscaldi and P. Rosso. A conceptual density-based approach for the disambiguation of toponyms. *IJGIS*, 22(3):301–313, Mar. 2008.

[7] E. Garbin and I. Mani. Disambiguating toponyms in news. In *Proc. HLT/EMNLP*, pages 363–370, Vancouver, Canada, Oct. 2005.

[8] W. Kienreich, M. Granitzer, and M. Lux. Geospatial anchoring of encyclopedia articles. In *Proc. IV*, pages 211–215, London, July 2006.

[9] J. L. Leidner. An evaluation dataset for the toponym resolution task. *CEUS*, 30(4):400–417, July 2006.

[10] J. Leveling and S. Hartrumpf. On metonymy recognition for geographic information retrieval. *IJGIS*, 22(3): 289–299, Mar. 2008.

[11] M. D. Lieberman and J. Lin. You are where you edit: Locating Wikipedia users through edit histories. In *Proc. ICWSM*, pages 106–113, San Jose, CA, May 2009.

[12] M. D. Lieberman, H. Samet, J. Sankaranarayanan, and J. Sperling. STEWARD: Architecture of a spatio-textual search engine. In *Proc. GIS*, pages 186–193, Seattle, WA, Nov. 2007.

[13] M. D. Lieberman, H. Samet, and J. Sankaranarayanan. Geotagging: Using proximity, sibling, and prominence clues to understand comma groups. In *Proc. GIR*, Zurich, Switzerland, Feb. 2010.

[14] M. D. Lieberman, H. Samet, and J. Sankaranarayanan. Geotagging with local lexicons to build indexes for textually-specified spatial data. In *Proc. ICDE*, pages 201–212, Long Beach, CA, Mar. 2010.

[15] D. Manov, A. Kiryakov, B. Popov, K. Bontcheva, D. Maynard, and H. Cunningham. Experiments with geographic knowledge for information extraction. In *Proc. AGR*, pages 1–9, Edmonton, Canada, May 2003.

[16] B. Martins, H. Manguinhas, and J. Borbinha. Extracting and exploring the geo-temporal semantics of textual resources. In *Proc. ICSC*, pages 1–9, Santa Clara, CA, Aug. 2008.

[17] B. Martins, I. Anastácio, and P. Calado. A machine learning approach for resolving place references in text. In *Proc. AGILE*, pages 221–236, Guimarães, Portugal, May 2010.

[18] A. McCallum and B. Wellner. Conditional models of identity uncertainty with application to noun coreference. In *Proc. NIPS*, Whistler, Canada, Dec. 2004.

[19] S. E. Overell and S. Rüger. Using co-occurrence models for placename disambiguation. *IJGIS*, 22(3):265–287, Mar. 2008.

[20] K. Papineni, S. Roukos, T. Ward, and W.-J. Zhu. BLEU: a method for automatic evaluation of machine translation. In *Proc. ACL'02*, pages 311–318, Philadelphia, PA, July 2002.

[21] R. S. Purves, P. Clough, C. B. Jones, A. Arampatzis, B. Bucher, D. Finch, G. Fu, H. Joho, A. K. Syed, S. Vaid, and B. Yang. The design and implementation of SPIRIT: a spatially aware search engine for information retrieval on the Internet. *IJGIS*, 21(7):717–745, Aug. 2007.

[22] T. Qin, R. Xiao, L. Fang, X. Xie, and L. Zhang. An efficient location extraction algorithm by leveraging web contextual information. In *Proc. GIS*, pages 53–60, San Jose, CA, Nov. 2010.

[23] G. Quercini, H. Samet, J. Sankaranarayanan, and M. D. Lieberman. Determining the spatial reader scopes of news sources using local lexicons. In *Proc. GIS*, pages 43–52, San Jose, CA, Nov. 2010.

[24] K. Roberts, C. A. Bejan, and S. Harabagiu. Toponym disambiguation using events. In *Proc. FLAIRS*, pages 271–276, Daytona Beach, FL, May 2010.

[25] H. Samet, B. E. Teitler, M. D. Adelfio, and M. D. Lieberman. Adapting a map query interface for a gesturing touch screen interface. In *Proc. WWW*, pages 257–260, Hyderabad, India, Mar. 2011.

[26] J. Sankaranarayanan, H. Samet, B. Teitler, M. D. Lieberman, and J. Sperling. TwitterStand: News in tweets. In *Proc. GIS*, pages 42–51, Seattle, WA, Nov. 2009.

[27] J. Strötgen, M. Gertz, and P. Popov. Extraction and exploration of spatio-temporal information in documents. In *Proc. GIR*, Zurich, Switzerland, Feb. 2010.

[28] B. E. Teitler, M. D. Lieberman, D. Panozzo, J. Sankaranarayanan, H. Samet, and J. Sperling. NewsStand: A new view on news. In *Proc. GIS*, pages 144–153, Irvine, CA, Nov. 2008.

[29] R. Tobin, C. Grover, K. Byrne, J. Reid, and J. Walsh. Evaluation of georeferencing. In *Proc. GIR*, Zurich, Switzerland, Feb. 2010.

[30] R. Volz, J. Kleb, and W. Mueller. Towards ontology-based disambiguation of geographical identifiers. In *Proc. I3*, Banff, Canada, May 2007.

[31] A. Weichselbraun. A utility centered approach for evaluating and optimizing geo-tagging. In *Proc. KDIR*, Madeira, Portugal, Oct. 2009.

Enriching Document Representation via Translation for Improved Monolingual Information Retrieval

Seung-Hoon Na
Department of Computer Science
National University of Singapore
nash@comp.nus.edu.sg

Hwee Tou Ng
Department of Computer Science
National University of Singapore
nght@comp.nus.edu.sg

ABSTRACT

Word ambiguity and vocabulary mismatch are critical problems in information retrieval. To deal with these problems, this paper proposes the use of translated words to enrich document representation, going beyond the words in the original source language to represent a document. In our approach, each original document is *automatically translated* into an *auxiliary language*, and the resulting translated document serves as a semantically enhanced representation for supplementing the original bag of words. The core of our translation representation is the *expected term frequency* of a word in a translated document, which is calculated by averaging the term frequencies over all possible translations, rather than focusing on the 1-best translation only. To achieve better efficiency of translation, we do not rely on full-fledged machine translation, but instead use *monotonic translation* by removing the time-consuming reordering component. Experiments carried out on standard TREC test collections show that our proposed translation representation leads to statistically significant improvements over using only the original language of the document collection.

Categories and Subject Descriptors

H.3.3 [**Information Storage and Retrieval**]: Information Search and Retrieval—*Retrieval models*; I.2.7 [**Artificial Intelligence**]: Natural Language Processing—*Machine translation*

General Terms

Algorithms, Experimentation, Performance, Theory

1. INTRODUCTION

Words, or stemmed words, are the most popular index terms used in modern information retrieval (IR) systems due to their high simplicity. However, there are critical challenges that retrieval systems face with the use of words, one of which is *word ambiguity* in a query and a document. The meaning of a word changes with its context. For example, the word *interest* may be used to mean "curiosity," or "a charge for borrowing money," depending on the surrounding context. Another challenge is *vocabulary mismatch* between a query and a document. Since there are many alternative ways to represent the same concept, such as using synonyms or paraphrases, a document may not contain a query word but may still be relevant to the query. For example, *find*, *observe*, or *detect* can possibly mean the same thing as *discover*.

To deal with these problems, many studies in IR have investigated *word sense disambiguation* (WSD) on queries and documents [20, 40, 34, 35, 13, 29, 36, 16], or have performed *query expansion* [15, 23, 43, 9, 10, 42, 2, 26] or *document expansion* [3, 24, 21] by appending semantically related words into the original query or document. Some of these approaches (e.g., pseudo-relevance feedback) have shown marked improvements in retrieval performance. However, most existing works in the literature are basically *monolingual approaches* which are restricted to the use of the original source language of the document collection, without taking advantage of potentially rich semantic information drawn from other languages. Through other languages, various ways of adding semantic information to a document could be available, thereby leading to potentially more improvements than using the original source language only.

Taking a step toward using other languages, we propose the use of *translation representation* by alternatively representing the original document content with the words of an additional language (i.e., an *auxiliary language*), one that is different from the language of a given collection (i.e., the source language). In our approach, each original document is "automatically translated" into an auxiliary language, and the resulting translated document serves as a semantically enhanced representation for supplementing the original bag of words. Specifically, the vocabularies of the source and auxiliary languages are connected in a many-to-many relation via translation, which could bring about important benefits in dealing with the two addressed problems. First, there are multiple candidate words in an auxiliary language that are translated to a source word. Therefore, the word ambiguity problem can be resolved, during the process of choosing a correct translation in a given context of a source word. Conversely, various different source words that refer to similar concepts or senses are translated into only a few words or a single word in an auxiliary language. Thus, the vocabulary mismatch problem in the source language is to

SIGIR'11, July 24–28, 2011, Beijing, China.

some extent ameliorated by using translated words in the auxiliary language.

To achieve better efficiency in translation, instead of relying on full-fledged machine translation (MT), we propose a simplified method of constructing the translation representation. Since there is no need for a full translation in our ad-hoc retrieval task, we only estimate the *expected term frequency* of a word in the translated document, by taking the average of the term frequencies of the word over all possible translated documents. Our core assumed setting is *monotonic translation* in which the word order in the source sentence is not changed after translation. This assumption enables us to exclude the time-consuming reordering module from the decoding process. In order to extensively apply monotonic translation into any pair of grammatically dissimilar languages (e.g., English and Chinese), we additionally employ a *distorted language model* for an auxiliary language in which the word order follows the grammatical order of the original source language, not of the auxiliary language. Based on these simplified settings for translation, the translation representation could be more efficiently constructed without relying on full-fledged MT.

Experimental results obtained on standard TREC collections show that the use of the proposed translation representation consistently outperforms baseline retrieval methods that use the collection language only. Our comparison is made against three different baselines – a commonly used baseline, query expansion based on pseudo-relevance feedback, and document expansion based on cluster-based retrieval.

2. RELATED WORK

2.1 Monolingual Retrieval

Word ambiguity has been extensively investigated in information retrieval using WSD. The initial research efforts on WSD for information retrieval were performed using manual sense annotation [20, 13], on artificially created pseudo-words [34], and on automatic sense disambiguation or clustering [40, 35, 29]. More recent work has scaled up the use of WSD to a large test collection [36] and two medium-size test collections [16], reporting improved retrieval performances using WSD compared to baseline word-based indexes.

Query expansion adds new expansion terms into the original query, which has been one of the most effective approaches to resolve the vocabulary mismatch problem. Expansion terms are selected from hand-crafted thesauri such as WordNet [10], co-occurrence based similarity thesauri [15], highly-ranked retrieved documents (i.e., pseudo-relevance feedback) [23, 43], highly-ranked retrieved passages [2, 26], or external collections such as the Web or Wikipedia [9, 42].

Document expansion has a similar motivation as query expansion, but expansion is applied to documents and not to the query [24, 21]. Expansion terms are selected from the cluster that a document belongs to [24], or from documents most similar to the given document [21].

An interesting work related to ours is Berger and Lafferty [3], which suggested the use of a translation model for the information retrieval task. However, no translation was applied between different languages. Instead, expansion was performed by adding words to a document, or reweighting words, so as to better match a given query. Their translation approach is therefore closer to document expansion.

Most approaches for monolingual retrieval tasks have been restricted to the use of the original collection language only, except for a few recent studies [12, 8]. As is the case with our study, they also utilized multilingual information by using an additional language in order to improve monolingual retrieval. However, they used an *external auxiliary language collection*, which is not automatically translated from the originally given collection. Gao et al. [12] expanded an original document by using similar documents from an external auxiliary language collection. Chinnakotla et al. [8] enriched the original expanded query by using additional expanded queries resulting from applying pseudo-relevance feedback on external auxiliary language collections, showing improved performances on CLEF test collections. Compared to our approach, these two methods are closer to monolingual-based approaches using *external* collections [9, 42] of the same language as the original collection. Unlike these approaches, we do not rely on an external collection but instead automatically create new translated documents, and thus our results are obtained *within* the given test collection only.

Recently, Trieschnigg et al. [39] used a *concept*-based representation in order to enrich the original word-based representation, thereby proposing the translation of the original word language to a *concept language*. While their use of concept language in part has a similar motivation to ours, their translation models are based solely on the use of translation at the lexical level (i.e., word-to-concept), and thus their method is very different from our context-dependent style of translation.

2.2 Cross-Lingual Retrieval

Cross-lingual information retrieval (CLIR) addresses the problem of retrieving documents written in a language different from the query language [30]. Even though a common approach in CLIR is to perform query translation (QT) using a bilingual dictionary [32], there were studies showing that combining both QT and document translation (DT) improved retrieval performance in CLIR by using bilingual representations in both the source and target language [28, 19, 7, 4]. McCarley [28] trained a statistical MT system from a parallel corpus, applied it to perform QT and DT, and showed that the combination of scores from QT and DT drastically improved either method alone. Similar results have been reported using either a full-fledged MT system [4] or a simple translation algorithm [7]. Kraaij et al. [19] used the translation model of IBM Model 1 [5], obtained from an automatically constructed parallel corpus from the web, and also reported that the combination of QT and DT improved either method alone.

These hybrid approaches in CLIR resemble ours in that we also use translated words of both queries and documents. The major difference, however, is that our goal is to improve monolingual IR and not CLIR. Furthermore, some of these approaches perform translation without taking into account the surrounding context of a source word [19, 7], while our proposed translation model is context-dependent and thus produces different translated words depending on the context of a source word.

To the best of our knowledge, the work most similar to ours is Franz and McCarley [11], who also applied auto-

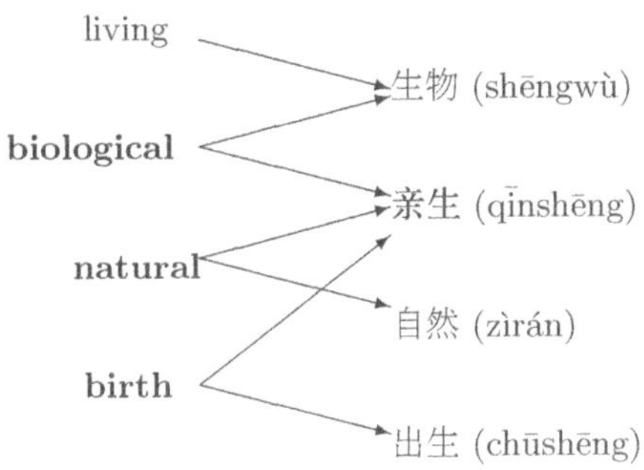

Figure 1: The word "*biological*" and its paraphrased or synonymous words, and their corresponding translated Chinese words.

matic translation for monolingual retrieval but using French as the auxiliary language. However, their method did not achieve any statistically significant improvement over a baseline retrieval that used monolingual representation. Moreover, they only considered the 1-best translation, while we use the expected frequency of a word computed from all possible translated representations.

3. AN ILLUSTRATING EXAMPLE

To illustrate why translation is helpful in handling the word ambiguity and vocabulary mismatch problems, consider the following TREC query Q335 "*Adoptive* ***Biological*** *Parents*", and focus on the ambiguous word "*biological*". The many-to-many translation relations for *biological* and its paraphrased or synonymous words between English and Chinese are depicted in Figure 1.

As shown in Figure 1, *biological* has two different Chinese translations, "生物(shēngwù)" and "亲生(qīnshēng)", which correspond to its two different senses in WordNet, respectively: (1) "pertaining to biology or to life and living things" ("生物": shēngwù), and (2) "of parents and children; related by blood; biological child" ("亲生": qīnshēng). Therefore, word ambiguity in the source language is dealt with during the process of selecting a correct translation between two candidates.

Moreover, the word *biological* in the query context can be equivalently replaced with *natural* or *birth*, (e.g., *natural parents*, *birth parents*) as paraphrased expressions, but the Chinese translation for all of them is only a single word, "亲生(qīnshēng)." This provides a good example to illustrate that the vocabulary mismatch problem in a source language can often be overcome if we use translated words in an auxiliary language.

4. OUR APPROACH: OVERVIEW

Our approach of using translation representation for a monolingual retrieval task is summarized in Figure 2. Each document in the source collection is translated using the proposed method of expected frequency estimation, producing bilingual document representations (Section 5). When a new test query is given, the query is translated using the same translation procedure, constituting bilingual query representations (Section 5). Next, initial retrieval on both representations is performed (Sections 6.1 and 6.2), and the two resulting relevance scores are combined to produce a ranked

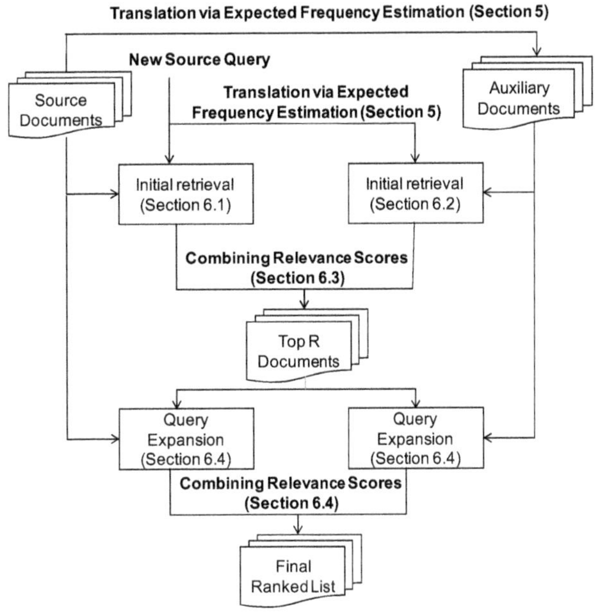

Figure 2: Overview of our approach of using translation representation.

list of retrieved documents (Section 6.3). Using the retrieved documents, pseudo-relevance feedback is performed for both representations, and the two resulting relevance scores of documents are again combined (Section 6.4). Furthermore, we also apply document expansion on bilingual representations, as an alternative option for the initial retrieval (Section 6.5).

5. CONSTRUCTION OF TRANSLATION REPRESENTATION

5.1 Expected Frequency of an Auxiliary Word

In this paper, *source language* refers to the language of a given document collection, and *auxiliary language* refers to an additional language used as the translation representation. Our translation model takes a *phrase* as translation unit, which refers to a contiguous sequence of words, conceptually including a single word. *Auxiliary word*, *auxiliary phrase*, and *auxiliary sentence* refer to a possible translation of a source word, phrase, and sentence, respectively.

Suppose that a source sentence is given by $\mathbf{e} = e_1^I = e_1 \cdots e_I$, where $|\mathbf{e}| = I$ is the length of the source sentence. We do not produce a full translation but instead use the expected frequency of a word in the translated auxiliary sentence for the given source sentence. The expected frequency is defined as follows.

Definition of expected frequency: Suppose $\mathbf{F}$ is a random variable, the range of which is $\mathcal{F}$, the set of all sentences of the auxiliary language. Given source sentence $\mathbf{e}$, the *expected frequency* of an auxiliary word w in the translation of $\mathbf{e}$ is the *conditional expectation* of $c(w, \mathbf{F})$ given the event $\mathbf{e}$, as follows:

$$E_{\mathbf{e}}[c(w, \mathbf{F})] = \sum_{\mathbf{f} \in \mathcal{F}} c(w, \mathbf{f}) P(\mathbf{f}|\mathbf{e}) \quad (1)$$

where $c(w, \mathbf{f})$ is the number of word occurrences of w in the auxiliary sentence $\mathbf{f}$, and $P(\mathbf{f}|\mathbf{e})$ is the sentence translation probability of $\mathbf{e}$ translating into $\mathbf{f}$ □.

5.2 Word-based Translation Model

Let us first describe a word-based model for computing the expected frequency of Eq. (1). We use simplified monotonic translation allowing only forward translation among possible translations in [38]. The word order is not changed during translation, and a source word at position i (i.e., e_i) is translated to an auxiliary word at the same position i. In this setting, the translation problem is exactly the same as the tagging problem of a hidden Markov model (HMM), where each state corresponds to an unknown auxiliary word and state translation is modeled by an n-gram language model. Thus, the expected frequency of Eq. (1) for the word-based model can be effectively calculated using the EM algorithm, which is based on the forward-backward algorithm of HMM.

5.3 Phrase-based Translation Model

We now generalize the word-based model to formulate a phrase-based translation model.

5.3.1 Word Lattice

A *word lattice* for a source sentence $\mathbf{e}$ is defined as a connected, directed acyclic graph $\mathcal{G}_\mathbf{e} = (\mathcal{V}_\mathbf{e}, \mathcal{E}_\mathbf{e})$ [27]. Here, $\mathcal{V}_\mathbf{e}$ is the set of vertices $\{0, 1, \cdots, I\}$ consisting of all source word positions, where 0 indicates a specialized *sentence-starting state* #, and $\mathcal{E}_\mathbf{e}$ is the set of edges. Each *edge* $\varepsilon \in \mathcal{E}_\mathbf{e}$ is labeled with a translated auxiliary phrase and it is denoted by $(i, j, \bar{f})$. i and j denote the starting and ending vertices of the source phrase $e_{i+1}^{j} = e_{i+1} \cdots e_j$, and $\bar{f}$ denotes an auxiliary phrase, that is, a translation of the source phrase e_{i+1}^{j}. The source and auxiliary phrases associated along the edge ε are referred to as $\bar{e}[\varepsilon]$ and $\bar{f}[\varepsilon]$, respectively. That is, for an edge $\varepsilon = (i, j, \bar{f})$, $\bar{e}[\varepsilon] = e_{i+1}^{j}$ and $\bar{f}[\varepsilon] = \bar{f}$.

A *translation path* $\boldsymbol{\pi}$ on $\mathcal{G}_\mathbf{e}$ is the sequence of edges $\boldsymbol{\pi} = \pi_1 \cdots \pi_{|\boldsymbol{\pi}|}$, where $|\boldsymbol{\pi}|$ is the number of edges in the path $\boldsymbol{\pi}$. Each edge π_i in the path immediately follows the previous edge π_{i-1}; the starting position of each edge π_i is equal to the ending position of the previous edge π_{i-1}. A path $\boldsymbol{\pi}$ is called a *complete translation path* on $\mathcal{G}_\mathbf{e}$ if $\boldsymbol{\pi}$ translates all source words $e_1 \cdots e_I$, so that the head of π_1 is 0 and the tail of $\pi_{|\boldsymbol{\pi}|}$ is I. The set of all complete translation paths is referred to as Φ. Given a path $\boldsymbol{\pi}$, the sequence of auxiliary phrases along the path is denoted by $\bar{\mathbf{f}}[\boldsymbol{\pi}]$ which means $\bar{f}[\pi_1], \cdots, \bar{f}[\pi_{|\boldsymbol{\pi}|}]$. Similarly, the sequence of source phrases on the path $\boldsymbol{\pi}$ is denoted by $\bar{\mathbf{e}}[\boldsymbol{\pi}]$ which means $\bar{e}[\pi_1], \cdots, \bar{e}[\pi_{|\boldsymbol{\pi}|}]$.

Word lattice example: Figure 3 shows an example of a word lattice, where the source language is English and the auxiliary language is German. There are 7 edges consisting of $\varepsilon_1, \cdots, \varepsilon_7$, and their source and auxiliary phrases are as follows: $\bar{e}[\varepsilon_1]$ = "*he*" and $\bar{f}[\varepsilon_1]$ = "*er*", and $\bar{e}[\varepsilon_2]$ = "*he goes to*" and $\bar{f}[\varepsilon_2]$ = "*er geht nach*", and so on. This lattice contains five complete translation paths: $\Phi = \{\boldsymbol{\pi}_1, \cdots, \boldsymbol{\pi}_5\}$ where $\boldsymbol{\pi}_1 = \varepsilon_1\varepsilon_3\varepsilon_5\varepsilon_7$, $\boldsymbol{\pi}_2 = \varepsilon_1\varepsilon_4\varepsilon_5\varepsilon_7$, $\boldsymbol{\pi}_3 = \varepsilon_1\varepsilon_3\varepsilon_6$, $\boldsymbol{\pi}_4 = \varepsilon_1\varepsilon_4\varepsilon_6$, and $\boldsymbol{\pi}_5 = \varepsilon_2\varepsilon_7$. Among these paths, source phrases and auxiliary phrases of $\boldsymbol{\pi}_1$ and $\boldsymbol{\pi}_3$ are $\bar{\mathbf{e}}[\boldsymbol{\pi}_1]$ = "*he*" "*goes*" "*to*" "*house*" and $\bar{\mathbf{f}}[\boldsymbol{\pi}_1]$ = "*er*" "*geht*" "*auf*" "*hause*", $\bar{\mathbf{e}}[\boldsymbol{\pi}_3]$ = "*he*" "*goes*" "*to house*" and $\bar{\mathbf{f}}[\boldsymbol{\pi}_3]$ = "*er*" "*geht*" "*zu haus*".

5.3.2 Path Probability

The *path probability* $p(\boldsymbol{\pi})$ is defined as the joint probability of the source phrases and auxiliary phrases along the path $\boldsymbol{\pi}$, denoted by $p(\bar{\mathbf{e}}[\boldsymbol{\pi}], \bar{\mathbf{f}}[\boldsymbol{\pi}])$. Applying the chain rule decomposes $p(\boldsymbol{\pi})$ into:

$$p(\boldsymbol{\pi}) \triangleq p(\bar{\mathbf{e}}[\boldsymbol{\pi}], \bar{\mathbf{f}}[\boldsymbol{\pi}]) = p(\bar{\mathbf{e}}[\boldsymbol{\pi}]|\bar{\mathbf{f}}[\boldsymbol{\pi}])p(\bar{\mathbf{f}}[\boldsymbol{\pi}]) \quad (2)$$

Note that $p(\boldsymbol{\pi})$ in Eq. (2) consists of two main parts – the *translation part* $p(\bar{\mathbf{e}}[\boldsymbol{\pi}]\,|\bar{\mathbf{f}}[\boldsymbol{\pi}])$, and the *language model part* $p(\bar{\mathbf{f}}[\boldsymbol{\pi}])$. First, the translation part, $p(\bar{\mathbf{e}}[\boldsymbol{\pi}]\,|\bar{\mathbf{f}}[\boldsymbol{\pi}])$ indicates the translation probability from the auxiliary phrases $\bar{\mathbf{f}}[\boldsymbol{\pi}]$ to the source phrases $\bar{\mathbf{e}}[\boldsymbol{\pi}]$, based on the phrase segmentation underlying the path $\boldsymbol{\pi}$. To estimate the translation probability, we make two simplifying assumptions. (1) Monotonic translation: As mentioned in the introduction, this ensures that the order of the auxiliary phrases in the translated sentence is the same as the original order of the source phrases. (2) Independent translation: Each source phrase is separately translated into an auxiliary phrase independent of the other source phrases. Based on these two assumptions, $p(\bar{\mathbf{e}}[\boldsymbol{\pi}]\,|\bar{\mathbf{f}}[\boldsymbol{\pi}])$ is simply decomposed to:

$$p(\bar{\mathbf{e}}[\boldsymbol{\pi}]|\bar{\mathbf{f}}[\boldsymbol{\pi}]) = \prod_{k=1}^{|\boldsymbol{\pi}|} p(\bar{e}[\pi_k]|\bar{f}[\pi_k])$$

Second, the language model part, $p(\bar{\mathbf{f}}[\boldsymbol{\pi}])$, denotes the probability that the auxiliary sentence $\bar{\mathbf{f}}[\boldsymbol{\pi}]$ along the path $\boldsymbol{\pi}$ is generated from the auxiliary language model. We utilize the trigram language model to estimate $p(\bar{\mathbf{f}}[\boldsymbol{\pi}])$, as it is widely used in statistical machine translation [17]. Let the auxiliary sentence of $\boldsymbol{\pi}$ be given by the word sequence $f_1, \cdots, f_J$. Then, $p(\bar{\mathbf{f}}[\boldsymbol{\pi}])$ is decomposed into trigram probabilities as follows:[1]

$$p(\bar{\mathbf{f}}[\boldsymbol{\pi}]) = \prod_{i=1}^{J} p(f_i|f_{i-2}, f_{i-1}) \quad (3)$$

5.3.3 Computing Expected Frequency

The part needed for computing the expected frequency defined by Eq. (1) is the sentence translation probability $p(\mathbf{f}|\mathbf{e})$. In this paper, $p(\mathbf{f}|\mathbf{e})$ is defined as the ratio of the probabilities of the paths generating $\mathbf{f}$ in the word lattice $\mathcal{G}_\mathbf{e}$ to the sum of all path probabilities in $\mathcal{G}_\mathbf{e}$, as follows:

$$p(\mathbf{f}|\mathbf{e}) = \frac{\sum_{\boldsymbol{\pi} \in \Phi(\mathbf{f})} p(\boldsymbol{\pi})}{\sum_{\boldsymbol{\pi} \in \Phi} p(\boldsymbol{\pi})}$$

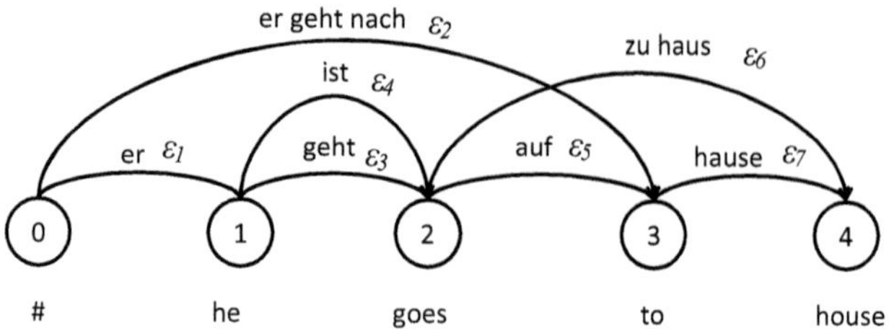

Figure 3: An example of a word lattice ($I = 4$), where the source language is English and the auxiliary language is German. Here, each ε_i is an edge, defined as $\varepsilon_1 = (0, 1,$ "*er*"$)$, $\varepsilon_2 = (0, 3,$ "*er geht nach*"$)$, $\varepsilon_3 = (1, 2,$ "*geht*'$)$, and so on.

[1] In Eq. (3) , we use the sentence-starting state # to define f_0 and f_{-1}. For example, $p(f_1|f_{-1}, f_0)$ and $p(f_2|f_0, f_1)$ indicate $p(f_1|\#, \#)$ and $p(f_2|\#, f_1)$, respectively.

where $\Phi(\mathbf{f}) \subseteq \Phi$ denotes the set of the complete translation paths, where each path generates $\mathbf{f}$.

A naive implementation to compute the expected frequency will be extremely inefficient, since the number of all possible translations is exponential with respect to the number of source words. To tractably estimate the expected frequency of Eq. (1), we compute the edge posterior $p(\varepsilon|\mathbf{e})$ for each edge ε in the lattice $\mathcal{G}_{\mathbf{e}}$:

$$p(\varepsilon|\mathbf{e}) = \frac{\sum_{\pi \in \Phi(\varepsilon)} p(\pi)}{\sum_{\pi \in \Phi} p(\pi)}$$

where $\Phi(\varepsilon) \subseteq \Phi$ denotes the subset of complete translation paths through the edge ε. The edge posterior is computed efficiently using a variant of the forward-backward algorithm, as presented in [41].

Finally, $E_{\mathbf{e}}[c(w, \mathbf{F})]$ is computed in terms of the edge posteriors as follows:

$$E_{\mathbf{e}}[c(w, \mathbf{F})] = \sum_{\varepsilon \in \mathcal{E}_{\mathbf{e}}} c(w, \bar{f}[\varepsilon]) p(\varepsilon|\mathbf{e})$$

where $c(w, \bar{f}[\varepsilon])$ is the number of word occurrences of w in the auxiliary phrase $\bar{f}[\varepsilon]$ labeled on the edge ε.

5.4 Distorted Language Model

The problem in using our simplified monotonic translation of Section 5.2 and Section 5.3 is that the word order of the trigram f_{i-2}, f_{i-1}, f_i is not consistent with the grammatical order of the auxiliary language. Therefore, our monotonic translation is acceptable only when the auxiliary language is grammatically similar to the source language.

In order to allow monotonic translation for a pair of grammatically dissimilar languages, we use a *distorted language model* for the auxiliary language, in which the auxiliary sentence follows the word order of the source language and not the auxiliary language. To estimate the distorted language model, we constructed a *reordered* auxiliary language corpus, by making the word order of each auxiliary sentence maximally consistent with the word order of the source language.

The details of the reordering procedure are given as follows. Suppose a pair of source and auxiliary sentences is given by $(\mathbf{e}, \mathbf{f})$ (i.e., (e_1^I, f_1^J)), a link (i, j) is a word alignment in which e_i is aligned to f_j, and $A = \{(i, j)\}$ is the set of word alignments for the given sentence pair. The outcome of the reordering procedure is the *reordered position* for f_j, denoted by b_j. To determine b_j, let B_j be $\{i|(i, j) \in A\}$, the set of all positions of source words that are aligned to f_j in the alignment set A. The reordered position b_j is then obtained as follows:

$$b_j = \begin{cases} \max B_j & \text{if } B_j \neq \emptyset \\ b_{a(j)} & \text{otherwise} \end{cases} \qquad (4)$$

where $a(j)$ is $\text{argmin}_k \{|j - k| \; |B_k \neq \emptyset\}$.

Once b_j is computed for all auxiliary words, we reorder each auxiliary sentence such that f_i precedes f_j if $b_i < b_j$. To ensure the uniqueness of reordering, when $b_i = b_j$, we make f_i precede f_j for $i < j$.

Example of reordering: Figure 4 shows an example of the reordering procedure. Each arrow denotes a word alignment from e_i to f_j. For f_2, f_3, and f_4, b_j is simply computed from the set of word alignments B_j. For instance, for the auxiliary word f_4, $B_4 = \{1, 2\}$, and b_4 is 2, according to Eq. (4). For another word f_1, however, B_1 is the empty set. To handle this case, the definition given by Eq. (4) states that we first find the nearest auxiliary word $f_{a(1)}$ to f_1 where $B_{a(1)}$ is not empty, and then use its reordered position $b_{a(1)}$ as b_1. In this example, the word $f_{a(1)}$ is f_2, resulting in $b_1 = b_2$.

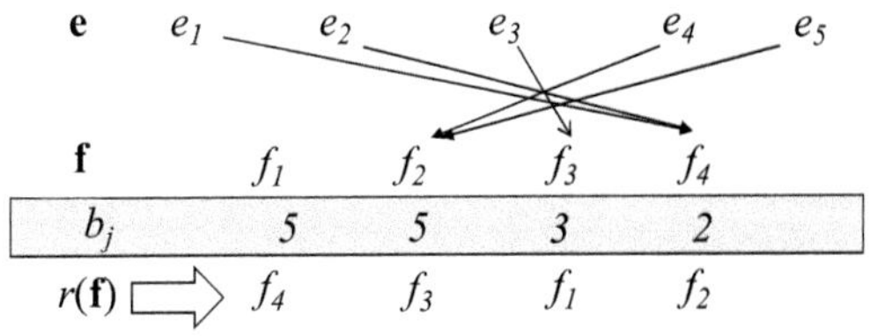

Figure 4: Example of the reordering procedure. $r(\mathbf{f})$ indicates the reordered auxiliary sentence for the given pair of aligned sentences $(\mathbf{e}, \mathbf{f})$.

5.5 Implementation Detail

We utilized the SRILM toolkit [37] with Kneser-Ney smoothing for estimating the auxiliary language models. Two types of translation probabilities $p(\bar{e}|\bar{f})$ for the word-based and phrase-based models were obtained from the word translation table of GIZA++ [31] and the phrase translation table of Moses [18], respectively. We used the word alignment output of GIZA++ to construct the reordered auxiliary language corpus described in Section 5.4. For the word-based model, we allowed null translation, and thus utilized a slightly modified version of the forward-backward procedure. For the phrase-based model, the maximum length of source phrases was fixed at 7. We only selected the top M auxiliary words (or phrases) for constructing the bilingual dictionaries obtained from GIZA++ and Moses for each source word (or phrase), ranked by the translation probability $P(\bar{f}|\bar{e})$.

We removed the translation candidates with very low probabilities at each word position j. To achieve this, we introduced $G(w, j) = \sum_{i<j} Q(w, i, j) / \sum_{\pi \in \Phi} p(\pi)$, which is the sum of the frequencies of word w, over all paths ending at position j, where $Q(w, i, j)$ is defined as follows:

$$Q(w, i, j) = \sum_{\substack{\varepsilon \in \mathcal{E}_{\mathbf{e}}: \\ \bar{e}[\varepsilon] = e_{i+1}^j}} \sum_{\pi \in \Phi(\varepsilon)} c(w, \bar{f}[\varepsilon]) p(\pi) \qquad (5)$$

which conceptually corresponds to the partial expected count of w in the case where the source phrase is restricted to e_{i+1}^j. We then applied the cut-off threshold θ to $G(w, j)$, below which it is excluded (i.e., $G(w, j) < \theta$) when computing the expected frequency of w. In addition, we kept only at most the top T values of $G(w, j)$ at each position j. In this paper, M, θ, and T were fixed at 10, 0.001, and 10, respectively.

6. MULTILINGUAL RETRIEVAL METHOD

6.1 Retrieval Model

We use the language modeling approach for the retrieval method. The language modeling approach ranks documents according to the likelihood that a query is generated from the document language model [33, 14], or more generally, the negative KL divergence between the query model $P(w|\mathbf{q})$

and document model $P(w|\mathbf{d})$ [22]:

$$Score(\mathbf{q}, \mathbf{d}) = \sum_{w} p(w|\mathbf{q}) log \frac{p(w|\mathbf{d})}{p(w|\mathbf{q})} \quad (6)$$

where $\mathbf{q}$ and $\mathbf{d}$ represent a query and a document, respectively.

We adopt Dirichlet-prior smoothing to estimate $p(w|\mathbf{d})$ as follows [43]:

$$p(w|\mathbf{d}) = \frac{c(w, \mathbf{d}) + \mu p(w|\mathcal{C})}{|\mathbf{d}| + \mu} \quad (7)$$

where $c(w, \mathbf{d})$ is the term frequency of w in document $\mathbf{d}$, $|\mathbf{d}|$ is the total number of words in $\mathbf{d}$, $p(w|\mathcal{C})$ is the background collection model, and μ is a smoothing parameter. The query model $p(w|\mathbf{q})$ is estimated by using MLE: $c(w, \mathbf{q})/|\mathbf{q}|$.

6.2 Retrieval Model for Translation Representation

We now extend the retrieval model described in Section 6.1 in order to support translation representation with expected frequencies. Let τ be the translation operator, $\tau(\mathbf{d})$ the translated representation resulting from applying the translation operator τ for a given document $\mathbf{d}$, and $Sent(\mathbf{d})$ the set of sentences in $\mathbf{d}$ obtained by sentence segmentation. The term frequency of word w in $\tau(\mathbf{d})$, denoted by $c(w, \tau(\mathbf{d}))$, is defined as follows:

$$c(w, \tau(\mathbf{d})) = \sum_{\mathbf{e} \in Sent(\mathbf{d})} E_{\mathbf{e}}[c(w, \mathbf{F})]$$

The length of $\tau(\mathbf{d})$, denoted by $|\tau(\mathbf{d})|$, is the expected length of the translated document, which is defined by $\sum_{w \in \mathcal{V}_F} c(w, \tau(\mathbf{d}))$, where $\mathcal{V}_F$ is the vocabulary of the auxiliary language.

By replacing $c(w, \mathbf{d})$ and $|\mathbf{d}|$ in Eq. (7) with $c(w, \tau(\mathbf{d}))$ and $|\tau(\mathbf{d})|$, we obtain the following smoothed model for $\tau(\mathbf{d})$:

$$p(w|\tau(\mathbf{d})) = \frac{c(w, \tau(\mathbf{d})) + \mu p(w|\tau(\mathcal{C}))}{|\tau(\mathbf{d})| + \mu} \quad (8)$$

where w is a word in $\mathcal{V}_F$, and $p(w|\tau(\mathcal{C}))$ is defined by

$$p(w|\tau(\mathcal{C})) = \frac{\sum_{\mathbf{d} \in \mathcal{C}} c(w, \tau(\mathbf{d}))}{\sum_{w \in \mathcal{V}_F} \sum_{\mathbf{d} \in \mathcal{C}} c(w, \tau(\mathbf{d}))} \quad (9)$$

where $\mathcal{C}$ refers to the set of documents in a given collection. Similar to $p(w|\tau(\mathbf{d}))$, we estimate the query model $p(w|\tau(\mathbf{q}))$ for the translation representation of the query $\mathbf{q}$ by using $c(w, \tau(\mathbf{q}))/|\tau(\mathbf{q})|$. Finally, we calculate the relevance score of document $\mathbf{d}$ with respect to query $\mathbf{q}$ using $Score(\tau(\mathbf{q}), \tau(\mathbf{d}))$ based on their translation representations.

6.3 Combining Relevance Scores for Multilingual Representation

To produce a single ranked list from two relevance scores using Eq. (6), that is, $Score(\mathbf{q}, \mathbf{d})$ on the source language and $Score(\tau(\mathbf{q}), \tau(\mathbf{d}))$ on the auxiliary language, we use the following linear combination:

$$Score_{E+F}(\mathbf{q}, \mathbf{d}) = \alpha \ Score(\mathbf{q}, \mathbf{d}) + (1 - \alpha) Score(\tau(\mathbf{q}), \tau(\mathbf{d})) \quad (10)$$

where α is an interpolation parameter.

6.4 Query Expansion for Multilingual Representation

We further apply query expansion for multilingual representations. We choose pseudo-relevance feedback, because it is one of the most effective query expansion approaches. The procedure is as follows:

1. Obtain an initial set of top R retrieved documents by applying $Score_{E+F}(\mathbf{q}, \mathbf{d})$.
2. Create expanded queries $\mathbf{q}'$ and $\tau(\mathbf{q}')$ by adding expansion terms from the top R documents of the source language and auxiliary language collections, respectively.
3. Re-score documents by $Score(\mathbf{q}', \mathbf{d})$ and $Score(\tau(\mathbf{q}'), \tau(\mathbf{d}))$ based on expanded queries $\mathbf{q}'$ and $\tau(\mathbf{q}')$ using Eq. (6) for both representations, respectively.
4. Combine the two relevance scores by using the linear interpolation $Score_{E+F}(\mathbf{q}', \mathbf{d})$, to obtain the final ranked list of documents as the outcome.

For pseudo-relevance feedback in step 2, we adopt RM3, a variant of the relevance language models of [23], which is one of the most effective and robust pseudo-relevance feedback methods in the language modeling framework [25]. To be more specific, suppose $\mathcal{D}_{init}$ is the set of the initially retrieved documents. Then, the expanded query model $P(w|\mathbf{q}')$ used by RM3 is estimated based on the following formula [25]:

$$P(w|\mathbf{q}') = \beta P(w|\mathbf{q}) + (1 - \beta) \sum_{\mathbf{d} \in \mathcal{D}_{init}} P(w|\mathbf{d}) P(\mathbf{d}|\mathbf{q}) \quad (11)$$

where β is an interpolation parameter for combining an original query with an expanded query, and $P(\mathbf{d}|\mathbf{q})$ is the posterior probability of $\mathbf{d}$, conditioned on having observed $\mathbf{q}$. The posterior probability $P(\mathbf{d}|\mathbf{q})$ can be rewritten in terms of $Score(\mathbf{q}, \mathbf{d})$ as follows:

$$P(\mathbf{d}|\mathbf{q}) = \frac{\exp(Score(\mathbf{q}, \mathbf{d}))}{\sum_{\mathbf{d}' \in \mathcal{D}_{init}} \exp(Score(\mathbf{q}, \mathbf{d}'))} \quad (12)$$

For re-scoring the documents in step 3, we re-apply Dirichlet-prior smoothing as described in Eq. (7).

6.5 Document Expansion for Multilingual Representation

Document expansion (or cluster-based retrieval) can also be applied to multilingual representation, where the representation of each document is enriched with a set of similar documents called a cluster [24, 21]. Suppose cluster $Clu_{\mathbf{d}}$ is a set of documents similar to $\mathbf{d}$, and $\mathbf{d}_{clu}$ is the cluster document representation of $\mathbf{d}$. Then, *cluster-term frequency* of $\mathbf{d}_{clu}$ for word w is defined as follows:

$$c(w, \mathbf{d}_{clu}) = \sum_{\mathbf{d}' \in Clu_{\mathbf{d}}} c(w, \mathbf{d}')$$

We now additionally introduce $\mathbf{d}'_{clu}$ to indicate the *cluster-enhanced document representation* of $\mathbf{d}$, which is the weighted representation of the original source document $\mathbf{d}$ and its cluster $\mathbf{d}_{clu}$ as follows:

$$c(w, \mathbf{d}'_{clu}) = c(w, \mathbf{d}) + \lambda_{clu} \cdot c(w, \mathbf{d}_{clu})$$

where λ_{clu} is the weight of document representation to cluster representation. To estimate the smoothed cluster language model, we adopt two-stage smoothing [24]: (1) The cluster-based model is first smoothed with the background

Table 1: Statistics for each test collection.

Statistic	ROBUST	WT2G	WT10G
NumDocs	528,156	247,491	1,692,096
NumWords	572,180	1,407,283	6,346,858
TopicSet	Q301–450 Q601–700	Q401–450	Q451–550

collection model. (2) The original document model is further smoothed by the smoothed cluster model. Starting from the basic form given by Eq. (7), two-stage smoothing is derived by replacing term frequencies $c(w, \mathbf{d})$ by the cluster-enhanced frequencies $c(w, \mathbf{d}'_{clu})$ as follows:

$$p(w|\mathbf{d}'_{clu}) = \frac{c(w, \mathbf{d}'_{clu}) + \mu p(w|\mathcal{C})}{|\mathbf{d}'_{clu}| + \mu} = \frac{c(w, \mathbf{d}) + \lambda_{clu} c(w, \mathbf{d}_{clu}) + \mu p(w|\mathcal{C})}{|\mathbf{d}| + \lambda_{clu}|\mathbf{d}_{clu}| + \mu} \quad (13)$$

where $|\mathbf{d}_{clu}|$ and $|\mathbf{d}'_{clu}|$ are the length of $\mathbf{d}_{clu}$ and $\mathbf{d}'_{clu}$, respectively.

Similarly, we could define the translation representation $\tau(\mathbf{d}'_{clu})$ for the cluster-enhanced document $\mathbf{d}'_{clu}$ by setting the term frequency $c(w, \tau(\mathbf{d}'_{clu}))$ of word w as follows:

$$c(w, \tau(\mathbf{d}'_{clu})) = c(w, \tau(\mathbf{d})) + \lambda_{clu} \cdot c(w, \tau(\mathbf{d}_{clu}))$$

with the following definition of $c(w, \tau(\mathbf{d}_{clu}))$:

$$c(w, \tau(\mathbf{d}_{clu})) = \sum_{\mathbf{d}' \in Clu_{\mathbf{d}}} c(w, \tau(\mathbf{d}'))$$

Given bilingual cluster-enhanced representations, we again use $Score_{E+F}(\mathbf{q}, \mathbf{d}'_{clu})$ for combining the two relevance scores obtained from the bilingual representations.

To define $Clu_{\mathbf{d}}$, we use the method suggested by [21], where $Clu_{\mathbf{d}}$ is a large virtual document comprising a concatenation of the k most similar documents to $\mathbf{d}$ ($\mathbf{d}$ itself can be included among the k documents). In this paper, k is fixed to 50. We apply Eq. (6) to find similar documents, with μ fixed to 1,500 and by taking the document as a query. Note that finding similar documents is only based on the source language, and thus $Clu_{\mathbf{d}}$ is shared by both the source and auxiliary language.

7. EXPERIMENTAL SETTING

For evaluation, we used three different standard TREC collections – ROBUST, WT2G, and WT10G. Table 1 shows the basic statistics for each test collection, where *NumDocs* is the number of documents, *NumWords* is the total number of word occurrences in each collection, and *TopicSet* is the range of topic numbers used for training and testing.

All experiments were based on the Lemur toolkit (version 4.12)[2]. When indexing English documents, we performed standard preprocessing on queries and documents by applying Porter's stemmer and removing stopwords using the standard INQUERY stoplist [1]. We used only the words in the "title field" of a query topic for all our evaluations. For translating English documents and queries, we used the Penn Treebank tokenizer to preprocess them[3].

MAP (mean average precision) was used as the evaluation measure. For each query, our evaluation was based on the top 1,000 retrieved documents. We reported statistical significance using paired t-test at 0.95 confidence level.

There are several parameters for each retrieval method: μ, λ_{clu}, α, and β. For ROBUST and WT10G, given a test set consisting of 50 queries, each parameter was selected by tuning on the other queries in the same test collection. For example, parameters for Q301–350 in ROBUST were tuned using Q351–450 and Q601–700 in the same ROBUST collection. For WT2G, we applied 5-fold cross validation, by dividing the 50 queries into 5 folds consisting of 10 queries each. For cluster-based retrieval, instead of directly tuning μ, we tuned μ' by setting $\mu = \mu'(\lambda_{clu} + 1)$, so that the final value for μ' is more similar to the value of μ used in the baseline retrieval.

For preparing the translation representation, we considered Chinese as the auxiliary language, and applied the proposed translation models from English to Chinese over the collection. To obtain the translation probabilities $p(\bar{e}|\bar{f})$, we used a subset of the parallel corpora used in [6], containing approximately 2.5M sentence pairs, 72M English tokens, and 65M Chinese characters. We removed long sentences containing more than 40 tokens when applying GIZA++ and Moses. Using the parallel corpus, we created two types of Chinese translation representations:

- Word: using the proposed word-based translation model (Section 5.2),
- Phrase: using the proposed phrase-based translation model (Section 5.3).

8. EXPERIMENTAL RESULTS

The major goal of our experiments is to examine whether the use of translation-enhanced document representation leads to improvements in retrieval performance, compared to using only the given collection language. Comparisons are made on three retrieval methods using the following language models:

- **LM** [43]: The commonly used baseline described in Section 6.1, which uses Dirichlet-prior smoothing described by Eq. (7) for computing $Score(\mathbf{q}, \mathbf{d})$;
- **RM3** [25]: The query expansion method described in Section 6.4, which is based on pseudo-relevance feedback RM3;
- **CLM** [21]: The document expansion method described in Section 6.5, which uses the cluster-based language model $P(w|\mathbf{d}'_{clu})$ described in Eq. (13) for the document model $P(w|\mathbf{d})$ of Eq. (6).

Throughout this section, we refer to the original source representation by E, and refer to the Chinese translation representation obtained from Word and Phrase by C_{Word} and C_{Phrase}, respectively.

8.1 Results

Table 2 shows a comparison of the results obtained using monolingual and bilingual representations on the setting of LM without query expansion and document expansion across three different collections. In Table 2, E denotes the baseline LM performed using Eq. (7), all of which used only the English queries and documents; C_X denotes the run of LM using Chinese translation representation, where X could be Word or Phrase; and E+C_X denotes the run of LM with the combination of monolingual and bilingual representation E and C_X.

[2]http://www.lemurproject.org

[3]http://www.cis.upenn.edu/~treebank/tokenizer.sed

Table 2: Comparison of bilingual representation with monolingual representation on the setting of LM. The mark * indicates statistical significance over E.

	ROBUST	WT2G	WT10G
E	0.2410	0.3067	0.1963
C_{Word}	0.2454	0.3021	0.1871
E+C_{Word}	0.2591*	0.3149	0.2036*
C_{Phrase}	0.2448	0.3164	0.1833
E+C_{Phrase}	**0.2684***	**0.3294***	**0.2054***

Table 3: Comparison of bilingual representation with monolingual representation on the setting of RM3. The symbols * and + indicate statistical significance over two baselines LM and RM3 using only English representation, respectively.

R		ROBUST	WT2G	WT10G
	E	0.2788*	0.3322*	0.2124*
5	E+C_{Word}	0.2910*+	0.3457*+	0.2252*+
	E+C_{Phrase}	**0.2998***+	**0.3586***+	**0.2294***+
	E	0.2750*	0.3314*	0.2150*
10	E+C_{Word}	0.2896*+	0.3493*+	0.2209*
	E+C_{Phrase}	**0.3012***+	**0.3594***+	**0.2287***+
	E	0.2794*	0.3441*	0.2161*
15	E+C_{Word}	0.2899*+	0.3556*+	0.2194*
	E+C_{Phrase}	**0.2982***+	**0.3643***	**0.2247***
	E	0.2780*	0.3328*	0.2063*
20	E+C_{Word}	0.2903*+	0.3526*+	0.2168*+
	E+C_{Phrase}	**0.2972***+	**0.3669***+	**0.2208***+
	E	0.2735*	0.3270*	0.2043
30	E+C_{Word}	0.2843*+	0.3485*+	0.2126*+
	E+C_{Phrase}	**0.2934***+	**0.3598***+	**0.2206***+

Our translation models (E+C_{Word} and E+C_{Phrase}) significantly improve the baseline E for most test collections. Comparing the two translation types Word and Phrase, we see that the phrase-based model (E+C_{Phrase}) gives the best results in combination for all test collections, and its improvements over E are statistically significant for all three test collections, especially achieving an increase of more than 2.5% in MAP on the ROBUST test collection. Interestingly, even our models using only the auxiliary language (C_{Phrase} and C_{Word}) often show better performances than E in ROBUST and WT2G for C_{Phrase}, and in ROBUST for C_{Word}.

8.2 Results with Query Expansion

Table 3 shows the comparison results of monolingual and bilingual representation on the setting of RM3 described in Section 6.4. In Table 3, E denotes the baseline RM3 using only the original English representation, and E+C_X denotes the run of RM3 based on the bilingual representation of E and C_X. The number of expanded terms for pseudo-relevance feedback in Section 6.4 was fixed to a maximum of 100. For the original English representation, the smoothing parameter μ used for computing Eq. (11) was fixed to 1,500. For Chinese translation representation, different values of μ were used for $P(w|\mathbf{d})$ and $P(\mathbf{d}|\mathbf{q})$ of Eq. (11), by fixing to 0 and 1,500, respectively.[4] The smoothing parameter μ at the second retrieval was fixed to 1,500 for both representations.

Applying RM3 alone without bilingual representation significantly improves the baseline E, which is also known from previous results on RM3 [25]. Importantly, further improvements over RM3 are obtained by utilizing the translation words, in both word and phrase translation types, and these improvements are statistically significant especially on ROBUST and often on WT2G and WT10G. Comparing the two translation types, the phrase-based model (E+C_{Phrase}) gives better retrieval performances than the word-based model (E+C_{Word}).

Table 4: Comparison of bilingual representation with monolingual representation on the setting of CLM. The symbols * and + indicate statistical significance over two baselines LM and CLM using only English representation, respectively.

	ROBUST	WT2G	WT10G
E	0.2699*	0.3091	0.2007
C_{Word}	0.2700*	0.3034	0.1866
E+C_{Word}	0.2783*+	0.3225*+	0.2068
C_{Phrase}	0.2743*	0.3166	0.1865
E+C_{Phrase}	**0.2909***+	**0.3321***+	**0.2119***+

8.3 Results with Document Expansion

Table 4 shows the comparison results of monolingual and bilingual representation on the setting of CLM using the document expansion method of Section 6.5. In Table 4, E denotes the baseline CLM using the original English representation only, and E+C_X denotes the run of CLM based on the bilingual representation of E and C_X.

Document expansion without translation representation (i.e., E in Table 4) is highly effective on the ROBUST collection, achieving more than 2.5% MAP increase over the baseline LM (i.e., E in Table 2), with statistical significance. However, its improvements on the other web test collections of WT2G and WT10G are insignificant. Additionally using the Chinese translation representation (E+C_X) achieves further improvements over CLM. Specifically, our phrase-based model (E+C_{Phrase}) achieves about 2% further increase of MAP over the baseline CLM (E) on ROBUST, finally leading to a noticeable increase of 4.5% MAP over the baseline LM. Even on the web collections of WT2G and WT10G, which are not improved by CLM, our phrase-based model (E+C_{Phrase}) leads to statistically significant improvements, achieving about 2% increase in MAP on WT2G and about 1.5% increase in MAP on WT10G.

8.4 Parameter Sensitivity of Combination

Figure 5 shows the curves of retrieval performances using our translation-enriched representations (E+C_{Word} and E+C_{Phrase}) with respect to the parameter α used in Eq. (10), across LM, CLM, and RM3. In Figure 5, we chose 1,500 for the smoothing parameter μ, fixed R to 10 for RM3, and used the best values for the other additional parameters for each test collection (λ_{clu} in CLM and the interpolation pa-

[4]Without this heuristic modification, since we do not remove any stopword for Chinese translation representation, the original RM3 of Eq. (11) gives common words unnecessarily high probabilities.

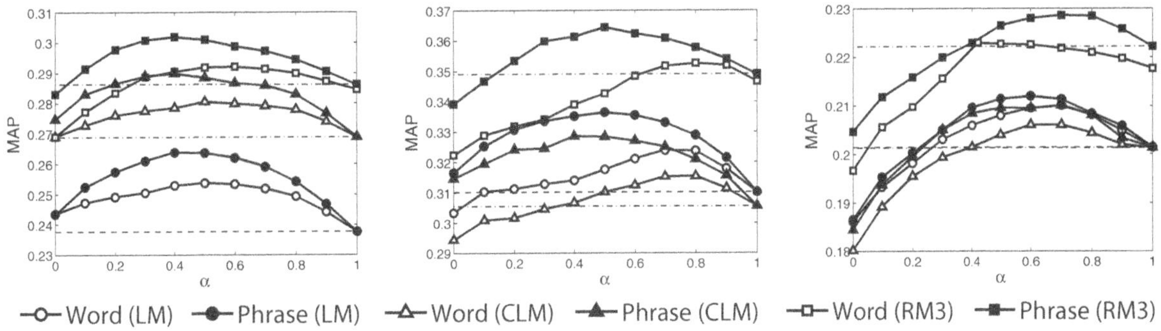

Figure 5: Performance curves of bilingual-based retrieval by using $\mu = 1,500$ (but using $\mu = 1,500 \times (\lambda_{clu} + 1)$ for CLM), varying α, on ROBUST (left), WT2G (middle), and WT10G (right). Performances of two single monolingual representations E and C_X are plotted at the points of α=1 and α=0, respectively.

Table 5: Comparison of our translation models (C_{Word} and C_{Phrase}) to full-fledged MT (C_{MT}) on the setting of LM, CLM, and RM3 on the ROBUST test collection. The symbols * and + indicate statistical significance over the baseline LM and the expansion-based baseline (CLM or RM3) using only English representation, respectively.

	E+C_{MT}	E+C_{Word}	E+C_{Phrase}
LM	0.2564*	0.2591*	**0.2684***
CLM	0.2814*+	0.2783*+	**0.2909*+**
RM3(R=5)	0.2964*+	0.2910*+	**0.2998*+**
RM3(R=10)	0.2952*+	0.2896*+	**0.3012*+**
RM3(R=15)	0.2956*+	0.2899*+	**0.2982*+**
RM3(R=20)	0.2939*+	0.2903*+	**0.2972*+**
RM3(R=30)	0.2896*+	0.2843*+	**0.2934*+**

rameter between the original query and in RM3, etc.). Two single monolingual representations E and C_X correspond to the case of α=1 and α=0, respectively.

We see that the best value of α depends on the performance difference between E and C_X for each retrieval method. The best value of α is larger when E produces a better performance than C_X. Despite the variations across different retrieval methods, the common range of the best α is between 0.4 and 0.8. In particular, the phrase-based model (E+C_{Phrase}) achieves in most cases the best improvements (at least the significant improvements) over the baseline (E) when α is around 0.4–0.6.

8.5 Comparison with Full-Fledged MT System

We now evaluate how different the results of our translation models are, compared to the results from a full-fledged MT system. To build a full-fledged MT system, we used Moses on the same parallel corpus in Section 7 based on the default feature weights without any development data set. For our evaluation, since applying our MT system to TREC collections requires substantial time, we only considered the ROBUST collection. We used the 1-best translation generated by Moses.

Table 5 shows comparison results of three bilingual representations on the setting of the bilingual-based retrieval (E+C_X) for LM, CLM, and RM3 on the ROBUST test collection. In Table 5, Chinese translation from the full-fledged MT system is referred to by C_{MT}. Full-fledged MT shows almost similar performances as the word-based model (E+C_{Word}) for all three retrieval methods of LM, CLM, and RM3. The phrase-based model (E+C_{Phrase}) achieves slightly better performances than the full-fledged MT model (E+C_{MT}) on the settings of LM and CLM. The general tendency is that as some expansion method (i.e., query or document expansion) is performed, the full-fledged MT model shows closer performance to that of the phrase-based translation models. This is because MT adopts the 1-best translation, in contrast to our translation models exploiting the N-best translations in calculating expected frequencies. That is, our models internally have the default expansion effect, whereas the full-fledged MT model does not, before performing query or document expansion. Without combining with the original representation, we also applied MT in the setting of the non-combined model (C_X) by setting $\alpha = 0$ in Eq. (10), and observed that the full-fledged MT model only achieved MAP of 0.1905 and 0.2305 in the case of LM and CLM, respectively. The performance is worse than that of our translation models in Table 2 and Table 4.

As a result, our proposed translation models perform at least as well as or better than the full-fledged MT system. However, there is one issue to be handled in estimating the distorted language model: the corpus used for learning the distorted language model is currently limited to only the auxiliary part of the available parallel corpus, and thus its size is far smaller than that for traditional MT. Resolving the corpus size limitation for estimating the distorted language model would be a subject worthy of further investigation.

9. CONCLUSION AND FUTURE WORK

In this paper, we proposed the use of translation representation, encouraged by the fact that a translated word in an auxiliary language can be taken in a disambiguated sense, or can act as a concept to capture various different expressions in the source language. We used a simplified translation model with monotonic translation to automatically translate all documents in the test collection, producing multilingual representations. Then, the relevance score of a document was calculated by combining multiple evidences derived from multilingual representations. Experimental results on standard TREC English test collections showed that by using English-to-Chinese translation, our approach achieves improvements over baseline monolingual retrieval, and the improvements are in many cases statistically significant.

For future work, we would like to extend the current experiments by considering other Western languages, for example, English-French, English-German, etc. We want to see how strongly the linguistic diversity between source and auxiliary languages affects retrieval performance.

Acknowledgments This research was done for CSIDM Project No. CSIDM-200804 partially funded by a grant from the National Research Foundation (NRF) administered by the Media Development Authority (MDA) of Singapore. We would like to thank the anonymous reviewers for their valuable comments.

10. REFERENCES

[1] J. Allan, M. E. Connell, W. B. Croft, F. Feng, D. Fisher, and X. Li. INQUERY and TREC-9. In *TREC-9*, 2000.

[2] M. Bendersky and O. Kurland. Utilizing passage-based language models for ad hoc document retrieval. *Information Retrieval*, 13, 2010.

[3] A. Berger and J. Lafferty. Information retrieval as statistical translation. In *SIGIR '99*, 1999.

[4] M. Braschler. Combination approaches for multilingual text retrieval. *Information Retrieval*, 7(1-2), 2004.

[5] P. F. Brown, V. J. D. Pietra, S. A. D. Pietra, and R. L. Mercer. The mathematics of statistical machine translation: parameter estimation. *Computational Linguistics*, 19, 1993.

[6] Y. S. Chan and H. T. Ng. Scaling up word sense disambiguation via parallel texts. In *AAAI'05*, 2005.

[7] A. Chen and F. C. Gey. Multilingual information retrieval using machine translation, relevance feedback and decompounding. *Information Retrieval*, 7(1-2), 2004.

[8] M. K. Chinnakotla, K. Raman, and P. Bhattacharyya. Multilingual PRF: English lends a helping hand. In *SIGIR '10*, 2010.

[9] F. Diaz and D. Metzler. Improving the estimation of relevance models using large external corpora. In *SIGIR '06*, 2006.

[10] H. Fang. A re-examination of query expansion using lexical resources. In *ACL-08: HLT*, 2008.

[11] M. Franz and J. S. McCarley. Machine translation and monolingual information retrieval. In *SIGIR '99*, 1999.

[12] W. Gao, J. Blitzer, M. Zhou, and K.-F. Wong. Exploiting bilingual information to improve web search. In *ACL-IJCNLP '09*, 2009.

[13] J. Gonzalo, F. Verdejo, I. Chugur, and J. Cigarran. Indexing with WordNet synsets can improve text retrieval. In *Proceedings of COLING-ACL '98 Workshop on Usage of WordNet in Natural Language Processing Systems*, 1998.

[14] D. Hiemstra. A linguistically motivated probabilistic model of information retrieval. In *ECDL '98*, 1998.

[15] Y. Jing and W. B. Croft. An association thesaurus for information retrieval. In *RIAO '94*, 1994.

[16] S.-B. Kim, H.-C. Seo, and H.-C. Rim. Information retrieval using word senses: root sense tagging approach. In *SIGIR '04*, 2004.

[17] P. Koehn. *Statistical Machine Translation*. Cambridge University Press, 2010.

[18] P. Koehn, H. Hoang, A. Birch, C. Callison-Burch, M. Federico, N. Bertoldi, B. Cowan, W. Shen, C. Moran, R. Zens, C. Dyer, O. Bojar, A. Constantin, and E. Herbst. Moses: Open source toolkit for statistical machine translation. In *ACL '07. Demonstration Session*, 2007.

[19] W. Kraaij, J.-Y. Nie, and M. Simard. Embedding web-based statistical translation models in cross-language information retrieval. *Computational Linguistics*, 29, 2003.

[20] R. Krovetz and W. B. Croft. Lexical ambiguity and information retrieval. *ACM Transactions on Information Systems*, 10(2), 1992.

[21] O. Kurland and L. Lee. Corpus structure, language models, and ad hoc information retrieval. In *SIGIR '04*, 2004.

[22] J. Lafferty and C. Zhai. Document language models, query models, and risk minimization for information retrieval. In *SIGIR '01*, 2001.

[23] V. Lavrenko and W. B. Croft. Relevance based language models. In *SIGIR '01*, 2001.

[24] X. Liu and W. B. Croft. Cluster-based retrieval using language models. In *SIGIR '04*, 2004.

[25] Y. Lv and C. Zhai. A comparative study of methods for estimating query language models with pseudo feedback. In *CIKM '09*, 2009.

[26] Y. Lv and C. Zhai. Positional relevance model for pseudo-relevance feedback. In *SIGIR '10*, 2010.

[27] W. Macherey, F. J. Och, I. Thayer, and J. Uszkoreit. Lattice-based minimum error rate training for statistical machine translation. In *EMNLP '08*, 2008.

[28] J. S. McCarley. Should we translate the documents or the queries in cross-language information retrieval? In *ACL '99*, 1999.

[29] R. Mihalcea and D. Moldovan. Semantic indexing using WordNet senses. In *Proceedings of the ACL Workshop on Recent Advances in Natural Language Processing and Information Retrieval*, 2000.

[30] D. W. Oard and B. J. Dorr. A survey of multilingual text retrieval. Technical report, 1996.

[31] F. J. Och and H. Ney. A systematic comparison of various statistical alignment models. *Computational Linguistics*, 29(1), 2003.

[32] A. Pirkola. The effects of query structure and dictionary setups in dictionary-based cross-language information retrieval. In *SIGIR '98*, 1998.

[33] J. M. Ponte and W. B. Croft. A language modeling approach to information retrieval. In *SIGIR '98*, 1998.

[34] M. Sanderson. Word sense disambiguation and information retrieval. In *SIGIR '94*, 1994.

[35] H. Schütze and J. Pedersen. Information retrieval based on word senses. In *Proceedings of the 4th Annual Symposium on Document Analysis and Information Retrieval*, 1995.

[36] C. Stokoe, M. P. Oakes, and J. Tait. Word sense disambiguation in information retrieval revisited. In *SIGIR '03*, 2003.

[37] A. Stolcke. SRILM - An extensible language modeling toolkit. In *ICSLP*, 2002.

[38] C. Tillmann, S. Vogel, H. Ney, and A. Zubiaga. A DP based search using monotone alignments in statistical translation. In *EACL '97*, 1997.

[39] D. Trieschnigg, D. Hiemstra, F. de Jong, and W. Kraaij. A cross-lingual framework for monolingual biomedical information retrieval. In *CIKM '10*, 2010.

[40] E. M. Voorhees. Using WordNet to disambiguate word senses for text retrieval. In *SIGIR '93*, 1993.

[41] F. Wessel, R. Schlüter, K. Macherey, and H. Ney. Confidence measures for large vocabulary continuous speech recognition. *IEEE Transactions on Speech and Audio Processing*, 9, 2001.

[42] Y. Xu, G. J. Jones, and B. Wang. Query dependent pseudo-relevance feedback based on Wikipedia. In *SIGIR '09*, 2009.

[43] C. Zhai and J. Lafferty. A study of smoothing methods for language models applied to ad hoc information retrieval. In *SIGIR '01*, 2001.

A Novel Corpus-Based Stemming Algorithm using Co-occurrence Statistics

Jiaul H. Paik
Indian Statistical Institute
Kolkata, India
jia.paik@gmail.com

Dipasree Pal
Indian Statistical Institute
Kolkata, India
dipasree.pal@gmail.com

Swapan K. Parui
Indian Statistical Institute
Kolkata, India
swapan@isical.ac.in

ABSTRACT

We present a stemming algorithm for text retrieval. The algorithm uses the statistics collected on the basis of certain corpus analysis based on the co-occurrence between two word variants. We use a very simple co-occurrence measure that reflects how often a pair of word variants occurs in a document as well as in the whole corpus. A graph is formed where the word variants are the nodes and two word variants form an edge if they co-occur. On the basis of the co-occurrence measure, a certain edge strength is defined for each of the edges. Finally, on the basis of the edge strengths, we propose a partition algorithm that groups the word variants based on their strongest neighbours, that is, the neighbours with largest strengths.

Our stemming algorithm has two static parameters and does not use any other information except the co-occurrence statistics from the corpus. The experiments on TREC, CLEF and FIRE data consisting of four European and two Asian languages show a significant improvement over no-stem strategy on all the languages. Also, the proposed algorithm significantly outperforms a number of strong stemmers including the rule-based ones on a number of languages. For highly inflectional languages, a relative improvement of about 50% is obtained compared to un-normalized words and a relative improvement ranging from 5% to 16% is obtained compared to the rule based stemmer for the concerned language.

Categories and Subject Descriptors

H.3.1 [**Information Systems**]: Content Analysis and Indexing - linguistic processing, indexing; H.3.3 [**Information Systems**]: Information Search and Retrieval

General Terms

Algorithm, Experimentation

Keywords

Stemming, Corpus analysis

SIGIR'11, July 24–28, 2011, Beijing, China.

1. INTRODUCTION

Vocabulary mismatch between queries and documents is a well known problem in an IR system. There are several forms of vocabulary mismatch, and the variation of words because of the morphological process (both derivational and inflectional) is such an instance. Stemming is a form of natural language processing that is commonly used in an IR system to address the aforementioned problem.

Stemming is a well studied technology and several stemmers of varying spirit and flavor exist in the literature. The most commonly used stemmers encode a set of language specific rules to group the morphologically related words. The potential danger of such stemmers is that they often produce aggressive conflation (for example, Porter stemmer conflates both execute and executive to the same term [22]).

The corpus based stemmers on the other hand do not use language specific rules and try to find groups from the ambient corpus. Depending upon the nature of the algorithm, corpus based stemmers can be classified into two broad categories. In one category, simply the lexicon (acquired from the corpus) is analyzed to find groups, and in other an additional evidence such as co-occurrence of word variants or the context of the words in which they appear are used. The former category of corpus based stemmers is found to give comparable performances with the rule based stemmers, whereas corpus analysis based stemmers with a background stemmers are much better alternatives, particularly in precision oriented systems such as web search [18].

Therefore, a solution to this problem of aggressive stemming is the usage of co-occurrence data that carries an additional evidence of their relatedness. Like Xu et. al [22], we hypothesize that, if two words co-occur in a document quite often then the likelihood of their proximity is high. We further advance our argument that words in a set are related if they co-occur as well as they form a community among themselves. Therefore, words which co-occur within a community are much better members to be grouped in a class rather than words which do not. In doing so, we might miss out some words which are actually morphological variations. But we believe such cases is either infrequent or cause less damage.

Several corpus based approaches [12, 22] exist for stemming which perform efficiently. For example, YASS, a method based on a string distance measure and complete linkage clustering algorithm, performs fairly well on languages like English, French, Bengali etc., but it is relatively ineffective on highly inflectional languages like Marathi and Hungarian.

The method developed by Xu et. al. [22] carries certain

weaknesses. First, the association measure depends on some parameter and therefore proper tuning is necessary. Second, two graph partition algorithms (connected component and optimal partition) used have different behaviors. The connected component algorithm creates chains [7] and the optimal partition algorithm is infeasible for complex languages where the morphologically related classes have large sizes. Obviously, the optimal partition algorithm can be used by first creating the classes using some background stemmer (as in case of English they used Porter and Krovetz stemmer), but that requires an additional constraint and may be difficult to apply on a language which does not have a background stemmer.

One important criterion of clustering algorithms is the determination of parameters that is used to form the clusters. For example, in partitional clustering algorithms (like k-means), the number of clusters needs to be specified beforehand. Also, in hierarchical clustering algorithms (like single linkage), a similarity threshold value is to be specified to determine the actual number of clusters. Both methods are crucially dependent on the parameter values. Parameters also depend on several factors like, the nature of the language, or the nature of the corpus, or the kind of similarity measure used etc. So a desirable property of a clustering algorithm is its insensitivity to parameters. Therefore, we take this argument into account in designing our algorithm and finally end up developing a clustering method which does not depend on any parameter.

Therefore, in the light of the above the purpose of our algorithm is three fold. The first aim is to see whether solely based on co-occurrence data we can design an effective language independent stemming method for mono-lingual retrieval. The second aim is to see whether it can act as a better alternative to stemmers based on extensive language specific rules. Thirdly, we want to develop a method for which the necessity of parameter fine tuning is limited thereby improving the robustness in performance.

The overview of our method is the following. We first collect the co-occurrence of words from the given corpus. Then the words sharing a common prefix of a given length are mapped in a graph with their edge weights equal to the value given by the co-occurrence metric. These strengths are then used to redefine the co-occurrence strength between words using their common co-occurring neighbours (words). Finally, this strength works as the basis of our grouping algorithm which proceeds as follows. First, it identifies some specially designated edges called strong edges and deletes all other edges which are not strong. Once this has been done, the next step finds the clusters of words simply by applying the connected component algorithm.

The organization of our article is as follows. In the next section, we discuss about the background work on various stemming strategies. Section 3 presents the proposed approach. The description about the data and the retrieval system is given in section 4. Experimental results are presented in section 5. In section 6 we discuss about possible merits and demerits of the baseline stemmers and the proposed stemmer. We conclude in section 7.

2. RELATED WORK

Stemming is a long studied technology and several stemmers of various principles and flavors exist in the literature. Broadly, they can be categorized into two classes, one category of stemmers relies on language specific rules and the other category is the corpus based approaches. The advantage of corpus based stemmers over the rule based methods is that they do not require knowledge of the specific languages. Additionally, corpus based stemmers reflect certain characteristics of the ambient corpus and therefore, are sometimes more effective compared to the rule based stemmers [22]. Corpus based stemmers can again be subdivided into mainly two types depending upon their principle. The one category simply analyzes the lexicon (words from a corpus) to understand the morphology of the concerned language. One category of corpus based methods, uses the context of the words to be stemmed or their co-occurrences in the particular corpus. For precision oriented systems, such analysis are reported to perform better than the blind rule based stemmers [22, 18]. Furthermore, corpus analysis can again be used to improve an already existing aggressive stemmer. Apart from the aforementioned methods, there are a number of works reporting the effectiveness of character n-gram tokenization for addressing the problem for alphabetic languages [14, 16]. In the rest of this section, we review some of these methods.

2.1 Language specif c methods

Perhaps the most widely used language specific stemmers used for English IR is the Porter [19] algorithm. A number of other language dependent methods exist such as Lovins [10] and Krovetz [8]. Lennon et. al. [9] compared the performance of Porter and Lovins stemmer on English queries and found little improvement. Harman [6] also experimented with English data using three stemmers without any positive outcomes. Nevertheless, subsequent studies [8, 22] demonstrated the usefulness of stemmers on simple language (like English) IR. The most notable advantage of these methods is their ease of use : rules once designed can be used on any corpus without further processing. Generally, these methods handle both derivational as well as inflectional morphology. But the obvious requirement to design such stemmers is the knowledge of the language.

A number of works have reported the effectiveness of light stemming approaches [20, 4] for a variety of languages both European and Asian. As opposed to the stemmers like Porter, light stemming methods focus on removing only inflectional variants from the end of a word.

2.2 Statistical methods

2.2.1 Lexicon analysis based approach

Majumder et al. [12] developed a language independent, clustering based unsupervised stemming algorithm (YASS) that is capable of handling a family of primarily suffixing languages. They defined a string distance measure between word pairs that reward long matching prefixes and penalize an early mismatch as follows.

Let the length of two strings X and Y be $n + 1$ (if strings are of unequal length, null characters are added at the end of the shorter string to make them equal), and let m denote the position of the first mismatch between X and Y (i.e. $x_0 = y_0$, $x_1 = y_1$, $\ldots$, $x_{m-1} = y_{m-1}$, but $x_m \neq y_m$). Now define D as follows:

$$D(X,Y) = \frac{n-m+1}{m} \times \sum_{i=m}^{n} \frac{1}{2^{i-m}} \text{ if } m > 0, \quad \infty \text{ otherwise} \tag{1}$$

First of all, such a string distance does not have the knowledge of whether one word is a morphological variation of the other. The string distance returns a high similarity simply because two words share a long prefix. Complete linkage clustering was used to discover groups of (presumably morphologically related) words. They concluded that in terms of retrieval effectiveness, this approach is comparable to rule based stemmers like Porter or Lovins for English. On Bengali and French test collections, YASS provides substantial performance improvement as compared to using no stemming.

Goldsmith [5] presented an unsupervised morphological analyzer based on minimum-description-length model. The frequency of stems and suffixes that result from every possible breakpoint in each term of a collection is examined. A breakpoint for each token is optimal if every instance of a token must have the same breakpoint and which minimizes the number of bits necessary to encode the collection. The underlying intuition is that breakpoints should be chosen in such a way that each token can be segmented into relatively common stems and common suffixes.

Bacchin et al. [2] described a language independent probabilistic model for stemmer generation which makes use of the mutual reinforcement relationship between stems and suffixes. From a finite collection of words they first generate a set of substrings (prefixes and suffixes) by splitting each word at all possible positions, except for those which generate empty substrings. Then they form a directed graph where a node implies a substring and a directed edge between node x and y exists if there is a word z in the collection such that $z = xy$. Now they estimate the prefix score and suffix score using HITS algorithm with the assumption that the *good prefixes point to good suffixes, and good suffixes are pointed to by good prefixes*. Once the prefix and suffix scores are estimated, the algorithm determines the most probable split (into prefix and suffix pair) for each word in the collection which maximizes the probability of the prefix and suffix pair.

Oard et al. [17] did suffix discovery statistically in a text collection and eliminated the word endings. They first counted the frequency of every one, two, three and four character suffix that would result in a stem of three or more characters for the first 500,000 words of the collection. Then they subtracted the frequency of the most common subsuming suffix of the next longer length from each suffix (for example, frequency of "-ing" from the the frequency of "-ng"). The adjusted frequencies were then used to sort all n-gram suffixes in descending order. In case of English, the count versus rank plot was found to be convex and so the rank at which the second derivative was maximum was chosen as the cutoff limit for the number of suffixes for each length.

2.2.2 Corpus analysis based approach

Xu and Croft [22] investigated the usefulness of corpus analysis in ad hoc retrieval. The basic assumption of their work is that word variants that should be conflated will occur in the same documents or, more specifically, in the same text window (they reported on 100 word text window). Based on this assumption, they devise a co-occurrence metric that measures the association of two words. The measure is given below.

$$em(a,b) = max\left(\frac{n_{ab} - En(a,b)}{n_a + n_b}, 0\right)$$

$$where \quad En(a,b) = kn_a n_b$$

where n_a, n_b are the number of occurrences of words a and b in the corpus, and n_{ab} is the number of times both a and b fall in the chosen window. Here k is a parameter and can be estimated from the corpus. Two graph partitioning algorithms (connected component, optimal partitioning) are then used to refine the initial equivalence classes of words that shares a number of characters in their common prefix or the classes generated by different rule based stemmers like Porter or Krovetz. This technique helps to identify the corpus dependent conflations and also minimizes the bad conflations (universal and university to the same class) made by a linguistic rule based stemmers. The reported results show that corpus analysis indeed improved the performance significantly on both English and Spanish corpora. Our method is similar in spirit with this approach, but varies in many respects. First, we use much simpler co-occurrence measure. Second, we introduce a re-weighting scheme that uses the initially calculated co-occurrence to respect their community affinity. Finally, the method for forming clusters here is different from connected component algorithm and is based on the nearest neighbour. Therefore, the nature of our proposed clustering algorithm provides us the liberty to ignore the tuning of parameters.

Recently Peng et. al [18] proposed a context sensitive stemming approach to web search. On the query side, they propose a statistical language modeling based approach to predict which word variants are better forms than the original word for search purpose and expanding the query with only those forms. In order to decide which morphological variants are better candidates to add to the original query, they use the bigrams to the left and right of a word as its context features by mining a large web corpus. At the same time on the document side, they propose a conservative context sensitive matching for the transformed word variants, only matching document occurrences in the context of other terms in the query. The method is found to perform effectively on web data. However, their method is not completely independent unlike others, since they determine the possible morphological variants using an already existing stemmer (such as porter).

2.2.3 Character N-gram based approach

Very recently, character n-gram tokenization [16] has been used to address the morphological variations in alphabetic languages. In contrast with the other methods presented in this section, n-gram method not only handles derivational and inflectional morphology, but also copes with the spelling variations as well as the word forms due to compounding. In particular, 4 and 5 grams provide substantial performance improvement on a wide variety of languages of different origins. One major pitfall with n-grams is the increase in the size of the inverted index. A passage of k characters contains $k - n + 1$ n-grams of length n, but only approximately $(k+1)/(l+1)$ words, where l is the average word length for the language [15]. As a consequence of index size expansion,

n-gram based indexing consumes 6 times disk space as opposed to plain word indexing and queries can take 8 times as long to execute.

3. PROPOSED WORK

The goal of the proposed method is to group the set of morphologically related words appearing in a corpus. The method takes a set of unique words and their co-occurrence information and returns a set of groups. We impose a necessary condition that the two words are morphologically related if they share a common prefix of given length. We follow here the same argument given by Xu et. al [22] (that if we choose too long common prefix the algorithm will fail to group words such as *cat* and *cats*) and consider only word pairs sharing first 3 characters (common prefix). This is the first static parameter (say, l_1).

The algorithm comprises of three main modules as follows.

1. Determine the co-occurrence strength of word pairs.
2. Re-calculate the co-occurrence strength using neighbours.
3. Group the words based on their new co-occurrence strength.

The words in each group are likely to be morphologically related. Certainly, such an algorithm does not guarantee that all words in a group are related or all morphological variations will be grouped together. However, we expect that such an approach will reduce the erroneous conflations.

The following explanation will help us to understand more clearly the usefulness of co-occurrence information. Let a and b be two words in a corpus and let $df(a)$ denotes the number of documents in that corpus that contain a. Now if we group a and b together, the effective df (denoted as edf) of each of the words will be the following.

$$edf(a) = edf(b) = df(a) + df(b) - df(a \wedge b)$$

Here, $df(a \wedge b)$ denotes the number of documents in which both a and b occur. Clearly, $df(a \wedge b) \leq min(df(a), df(b))$, and the values of $edf(a)$, $edf(b)$ will go up if $df(a \wedge b)$ is low (means a and b co-occurs infrequently). So a ranking function that uses inverse document frequency as a measure of importance of a query term, may influence the ranking heavily because of such merging (putting a and b together). Furthermore, it is more dangerous to group an infrequent term with a frequently occurring term and if such a case happens co-occurrence information controls the effect to some extent.

3.1 Measuring co-occurrence strength

The basic assumption of our method is that a document conveying a topic very often uses a term which is related to the original terms of the topic [23]. For example, a document discussing about *education* most likely uses the term *educate* or its variants. Furthermore, in the case of a document discussing about a person very frequently uses its inflectional variants. Since morphological variations are semantically closely related with the meaning of the original terms, their document level co-occurrence provides a very useful information which can be used to group them together.

We define the co-occurrence strength of two words a and b in a corpus C as follows.

$$CO(a,b) = \sum_{d \in C} min(tf_{a,d},\ tf_{b,d}) \quad (2)$$

where d and $tf_{p,q}$ represents the document and the term frequency of term p in the document q respectively. In other words, the quantity $CO(a,b)$ measures how often two words a, b occur in the same document of a given corpus C. Note that unlike the co-occurrence measure given by Xu et.al. [22], $CO(a,b)$ does not contain any parameter and therefore is much robust when the corpus or the language is changed.

3.2 Re-calculating co-occurrence strength

Once the co-occurrence strengths between words are computed, the words are then mapped in an undirected graph. A pair of words w_1 and w_2 is connected by an edge (w_1, w_2) if $CO(w_1, w_2) > 0$ and they have a common prefix of a given length (we chose 3) along with the suffixes (after truncating the longest common prefix) which are the residues (the ends after removal of longest common prefix) of more than one pair of co-occurring words with long common prefix (length larger than 5 which is the second static parameter, say, l_2). The second condition is used as a heuristic to predict a morphological variation. The edge (w_1, w_2) is assigned a weight $CO(w_1, w_2)$. Re-calculation of co-occurrence strength then operates on this graph and is motivated by the following principle.

Two co-occurring words will receive higher weight if both of them co-occur with other words.

With the document level co-occurrence strength in hand, we can re-weight the strengths by the following formula. Here we consider the word pairs (a,b) for which $CO(a,b) > 0$.

$$RCO(a,b) = CO(a,b) + \sum_{c \in N_{a,b}} min(CO(a,c), CO(c,b)) \times 0.5 \quad (3)$$

The notation $N_{a,b}$ denotes the set of common neighbours of a and b where a node w is a common neighbour of a and b if $CO(a,w) > 0$ and $CO(b,w) > 0$. Clearly, $RCO(a,b) \geq CO(a,b)$ and they are equal only if a and b have no common co-occurring words. The value of $RCO(a,b)$ depends on two factors given below.

1. The number of common co-occurring words of a and b. In other words, the value of $RCO(a,b)$ is more or less proportional to the size of $N_{a,b}$.
2. The strength in which they co-occur with the common co-occurring words, i.e, if two words co-occur frequently with a third word, the likelihood of their closeness would be high.

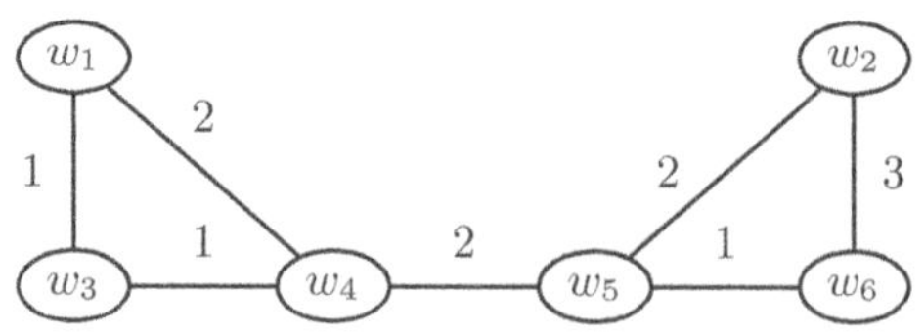

Figure 1: Before re-weighting

Figure 1 shows an motivating example underlying the role of co-occurring neighbours. The vertices represent the words and the edge weights represent their co-occurrence strength as computed by equation 2. A set of words is a better candidate to form a semantically related group if their co-occurring words form a community. It is, however, unlikely

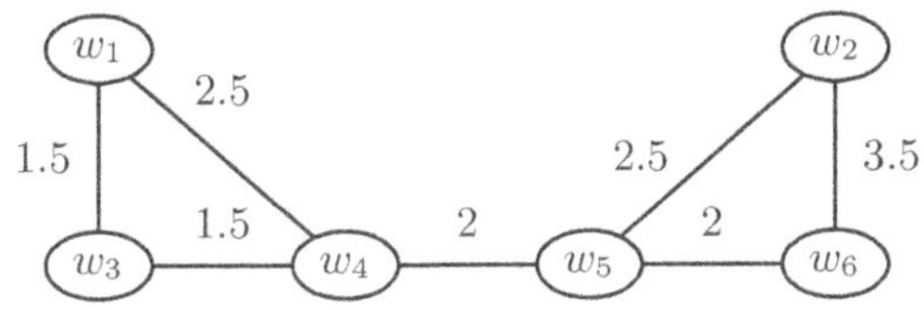

Figure 2: After re-weighting

that all the words in the group will co-occur with each other, but a word related with the theme of a group, is likely to co-occur with many members of the group. So the information embedded in the neighbourhood of two words are used to better infer the proximity of the word pairs.

As an example, consider graph given in Figure 1. Clearly, solely based on the co-occurrence strength it is hard to determine whether w_4 is to be grouped with w_1 or w_5, because both w_1 and w_5 have equal co-occurrence strength with w_4. But, since w_4 has more common neighbours with w_1, the chance is high that w_4 is semantically more related with w_1 than with w_5. The re-weighted graph in Figure 2 clears out the grouping dilemma using the measure given in equation 3.

3.3 Grouping the words

So far we have focused on measuring the co-occurrence strength between word pairs. Recall that our ultimate goal is to group morphologically related words. Here we present a simple algorithm based on the strongest neighbour of each word. The following principle is the key to our proposed algorithm.

A word (say w_1) will be grouped with another word (say w_2) if either w_1 is the strongest neighbour of w_2 or w_2 is the strongest neighbour of w_1.

The algorithm first identifies the strong edges from the given graph. A strong edge is an edge (u, v) if either of the following holds.

- $\underset{1 \le k \le n}{\text{argmax}}\ RCO(u, k)$ equals to v
- $\underset{1 \le k \le n}{\text{argmax}}\ RCO(v, k)$ equals to u

  n represents the number of vertices of the graph.

Upon doing this, the edges which are not strong are deleted from the graph. Finally, the clusters are formed by finding connected components. Each such cluster represents a morphologically related group. The complete stemming algorithm is given in Figure 3.

The clustering algorithm based on the above principle does not involve any parameter. The parameter free nature of the algorithm makes it more robust unlike other clustering algorithm such as single linkage algorithm, where a threshold is to be set to form the groups. The threshold selection is not a trivial task particularly in a multilingual set up where the parameters are very often language dependent as well as corpus dependent [12, 11].

Note that the proposed algorithm differs from the single linkage clustering algorithm in two respects. First parameter selection is not required and second, the algorithm does not create too many elongated clusters as elongation of clusters primarily depends on the value of the similarity threshold.

To better understand the difference between the proposed strongest neighbour based algorithm and single linkage clustering algorithm, consider the example graph of Figure 4. If single linkage clustering algorithm is used without any threshold the entire graph is returned as a cluster (Figure 5). On the contrary, the proposed strongest neighbour based algorithm automatically breaks the edge connecting w_3 and w_6 (Figure 6), since the nearest neighbours of w_3 and w_6 are w_2 and w_7 respectively (alternatively, the edge (w_3, w_6) is not a strong edge).

Input : A symmetric matrix $A = \{a_{ij}\}$ of order n, where $a_{ij} = CO(w_i, w_j)$.
Output : A set of clusters of words.

```
/* weights from neighbours */
for all i, j (1 ≤ i < j ≤ n) do
  if a_ij > 0 then
    let S = {m | a_im > 0 and a_jm > 0}
    b_ij ← Σ_{k∈S} min(a_ik, a_kj)
  end if
end for
/* adding the weights */
for all i, j (1 ≤ i < j ≤ n) do
  if a_ij > 0 then
    s_ij ← a_ij + b_ij/2
  end if
end for
let E_s = {φ} /* the set of strong edges */
/* clustering the vertices */
for all i (1 ≤ i ≤ n) do
  let p ← argmax_{1≤k≤n} s_ik
  E_s = E_s ∪ (i, p)
end for
Find the connected components considering only edges in E_s
Make each connected component a cluster
```

Figure 3: Stemming algorithm

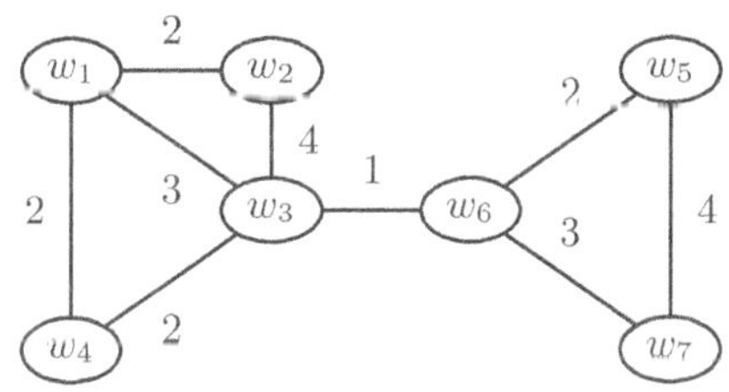

Figure 4: Input Graph

4. EVALUATION

In what follows, we describe an array of experiments for evaluating our proposed co-occurrence based stemmer on a number of languages. As part of our experiments we compare the performance of our method with a number of other stemmers (given in section 4.3).

In further explorations, we perform a deeper analysis to understand the impact of the proposed method on individual queries. In addition, we study the goodness of our method in improving precision at the top of the ranked list.

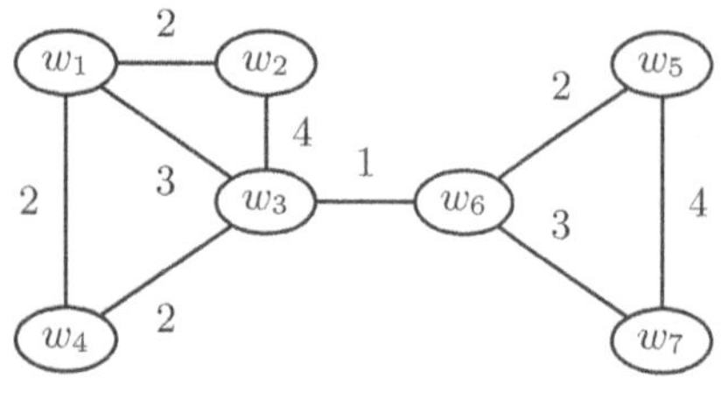

Figure 5: Output of single linkage clustering

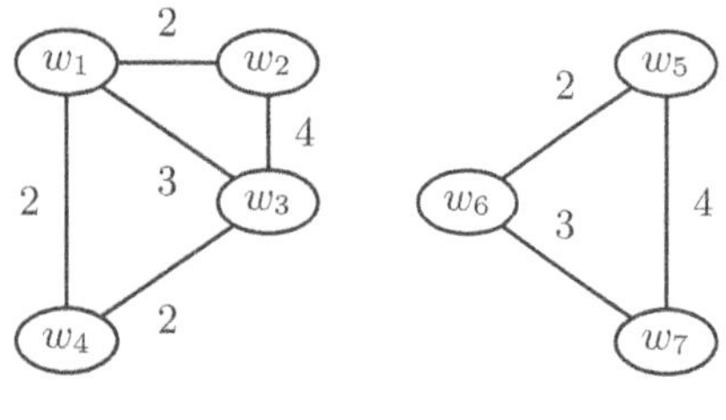

Figure 6: Output of proposed algorithm

4.1 Data

The details of our experimental test sets are as follows. We conducted our experiments on six languages of various origin and morphological complexity to evaluate our algorithm. Among the languages studied, Marathi and Hungarian are highly inflectional and agglutinative in nature whereas English is the least inflectional. Table 1 summarizes the corpora and queries used for evaluation. For the English experiments we used the TREC 6-7-8 queries and the document collection comprises of FBIS, Financial Times and Los Angles Times. Both Marathi and Bengali documents and topics have been taken from FIRE[1] 08 and FIRE 10. Bulgarian and Hungarian documents and topics are taken from CLEF 06 and CLEF 07 and the Czech test sets (queries and documents) are from CLEF 07. 2 topics from Hungarian and 12 topics from Marathi have no relevant documents in the recall base. Therefore, during experiments we removed those queries from our test set. The queries in each language have been formed using title and description fields of the experimental topics. Standard stopword lists are used to remove insignificant words from the documents and queries and no other preprocessing steps were applied.

Table 1: Test Collection

Language	Documents	Queries	Source
Bulgarian	87281	100	CLEF
Czech	81735	50	CLEF
Hungarian	49530	98	CLEF
Marathi	99362	88	FIRE
Bengali	123047	100	FIRE
English	472525	150	TREC

4.2 Evaluation Metrics and IR Model

We used MAP [13] as our primary evaluation metric and in addition we also report R-precision and precision at 10 in order to see the precision enhancing powers of the stemmers. In addition we also report the number of relevant document retrieved in each language. Statistical significance tests were performed using paired t-test based on the query wise MAP values at a 95% confidence interval. All experiments have been conducted using a probabilistic divergence from randomness based model called IFB2 [1]. We produce all our experimental results using TERRIER[2] retrieval system.

4.3 Baseline Stemmers

We compare the proposed method with three baselines stemmers and also against no stemming. Some recently developed rule based stemmers[3] were chosen to compare the performance of our algorithm. The stemmer developed by Dolamic et. al. [4] is chosen as the rule based approach for Marathi and Bengali. The Hungarian stemmer is by Savoy [21] and the Czech stemmer is by Dolamic et. al [3]. Porter stemmer was used as English rule based stemmer. The stemmer proposed by Xu et. al. [22] was used as a baseline corpus analysis based stemmer. The YASS was chosen as the other lexicon analysis based statistical stemmer. The experimental results of YASS are produced using the code[4] made available by the authors. We have implemented the stemmer proposed by Xu et. al. We did not implement the stemmer based on optimal partition technique, since that will be very inefficient for the kind of languages we are studying. Instead, we have implemented the algorithm based on connected component and trigram matching (the words sharing first three character).

Note that we have chosen the baseline stemmers which performs very well and also varies in their principle, since one of our goal is to see if the proposed method can be used as a better alternative to the existing stemmers. Some parameter needed to set for XU and YASS. XU depends on two parameters (namely k in em formula and the em score cut off value to determine the connected components) and YASS depends on similarity threshold value for cluster determination. We have chosen $k = 2.74 \times 10^{-6}$ and .01 as em cut off value for XU and for YASS we set the threshold to 1.5 as recommended by the respective authors.

5. RESULTS

In the tables we use the following abbreviations. NO means no stemming, RB for rule based stemmer, XU for the stemmer developed by [22] and PROP used for proposed method.

Table 2: Bulgarian

	NO	RB	XU	YASS	PROP
MAP	0.2166	0.2794	0.2450	0.3071	**0.3256**
R-Prec	0.2293	0.2930	0.2500	0.3161	**0.3289**
P@10	0.2570	0.3270	0.2750	0.3480	**0.3520**
Rel.Ret	1611	2003	1790	2085	**2101**
No. of Rel. doc : 2261					

The main experimental results are presented in Tables 2 to 7. Each table gives MAP, R-precision, precision at 10 and the number of relevant documents retrieved. From Table 2 it is clear that, on Bulgarian data all stemmers improved the MAP value. The MAP value achieved by the proposed

[1]http://www.isical.ac.in/~fire

[2]http://terrier.org/

[3]available at http://members.unine.ch/jacques.savoy/clef/index.h

[4]http://www.isical.ac.in/~clia/resources.html

algorithm is much better than that achieved by either of rule based stemmer or XU. However, the difference is not very large compared to the performance achieved by YASS. R-precision improved consistently with the improvement of MAP.

Table 3: Czech

	NO	RB	XU	YASS	PROP
MAP	0.2381	0.3409	0.2855	0.3415	**0.3624**
R-Prec	0.2611	0.3456	0.2868	0.3295	**0.3441**
p@10	0.2680	0.3480	0.3040	0.3400	**0.3700**
Rel.Ret	551	667	632	672	**681**
No. of Rel. doc : 762					

The trend is similar for the languages like Czech (Table 3), Hungarian (Table 4) and (Marathi Table 5). Marathi and Hungarian are two highly inflectional languages and therefore, a significant benefit is achieved. Figure 7 clearly demonstrates the improvement graphically. The experimental results once again validate the conclusions made by Savoy et. al. [21] and Majumder et. al. [11].

Table 4: Hungarian

	NO	RB	XU	YASS	PROP
MAP	0.2386	0.3132	0.2850	0.3060	**0.3588**
R-Prec	0.2518	0.3117	0.3019	0.3152	**0.3585**
P@10	0.3143	0.3990	0.3388	0.3837	**0.4224**
Rel.Ret	1367	1723	1803	1730	**1964**
No. of Rel. doc : 2219					

The experimental results obtained by using the proposed approach is noticeably better than XU on Czech (26.9%), Bulgarian (32.9%) and Hungarian (25.9%). Also, the performance differences between the proposed method and YASS are very large on both Marathi (24.6%) and Hungarian (17.3), whereas performance differences are relatively small for languages such as Czech and Bulgarian. The comparison between PROP and no stem reveals that PROP achieves more than 50% MAP on four languages (namely, Czech, Marathi, Bulgarian and Hungarian). On Bengali data this improvement is almost 20%. Although, English results improved through the application of PROP but not as much as other languages, which certainly confirms the previous reported results [12]. The relative percentage (MAP) improvement between the PROP and other methods is given in Table 8.

Table 5: Marathi

	NO	RB	XU	YASS	PROP
MAP	0.2918	0.3091	0.4097	0.3514	**0.4380**
R-Prec	0.3010	0.3114	0.4066	0.3472	**0.4190**
P@10	0.3273	0.3409	0.3864	0.3568	**0.3977**
Rel.Ret	1463	1472	1621	1546	**1653**
No. of Rel. doc : 1716					

The stemmer based on language dependent rules has successfully handled morphological variations from retrieval perspective. Porter stemmer is the best among all the stemmers studied on TREC 6-7-8 queries. But when the proposed co-occurrence based stemmer is applied on more inflectional languages, all languages achieve consistently better average precision than rule based stemmers. A particularly noticeable outcome is the performance of rule based stemmer on Marathi data. When all the languages have been benefited through the rule based stemmers significantly, Marathi results show very marginal improvement compared to no stemming. We suspect that there may be some error in the available code[5].

Table 6: Bengali

	NO	RB	XU	YASS	PROP
MAP	0.3611	0.4104	0.4073	0.4250	**0.4310**
R-Prec	0.3582	0.3923	0.3983	0.4024	**0.4153**
P@10	0.3960	0.4150	0.4060	0.4190	**0.4220**
Rel.Ret	2173	2264	**2279**	2272	2275
No. of Rel. doc : 2373					

Figure 8 shows the precision at 10 achieved by the chosen approaches on all data sets. The observation that can be made from the figure is that once again the precision at top for more inflectional languages is noticeably high when the proposed method is applied. Comparison between PROP and XU shows that on Hungarian, Czech and Bulgarian PROP is noticeably better than XU. However, the differences are relatively small on Marathi, Bengali and English. On English, Porter stemmer achieves the maximum p@10 which is slightly better than the others. Rule based stemmer also does fairly better (compared to no stem) on Bengali, Czech, Hungarian and English, but poorly performs on Marathi and Bulgarian.

We further study the recall enhancing ability of the various methods studied. In Figure 9 we show the number of relevant documents retrieved at 1000. Clearly, except Bulgarian XU retrieved almost an equal number of documents with PROP and even better in English. PROP retrieved maximum number of documents in Hungarian and also in Marathi.

Table 9 provides the percentage of query in which the proposed method achieves better MAP than the other methods including the un-stemmed runs on all six languages. More than 80% of Marathi and Hungarian queries have been benefited if the words are normalized using the proposed co-occurrence based method compare to the un-normalized case. Substantial amount (close to 80%) of Bulgarian and Czech queries also achieves better average precision due to the use of the proposed stemmer. However, stemming hurts many Bengali and English queries. Particularly, almost one-third English queries have been hurt for using the proposed method. When, we compare the query-wise performance, we observed that in all other languages (except English), the proposed method outperformed the other stemmers. Only in English, Porter stemmer performed marginally better than the proposed method.

The outcomes of statistical significance test is summarized in Table 10. A star (or a cross) symbol in a cell (x, y) means the proposed method performs statistically significantly better (or statistically equally) than the method y on language x. Clearly, the choice of the proposed method over no stemming is always significantly beneficial to an IR system. YASS and the proposed method performed statistically equally on Bengali and English data. Furthermore, no significant difference is found between the proposed approach

[5]http://members.unine.ch/jacques.savoy/clef/index.html

Table 7: TREC 6-7-8

	NO	RB	XU	YASS	PROP
MAP	0.2290	**0.2599**	0.2504	0.2499	0.2582
R-Prec	0.2733	**0.3008**	0.2934	0.2913	0.3001
P@10	0.4327	**0.4833**	0.4600	0.4633	0.4727
Rel.Ret	6812	**7751**	**7751**	7652	7638
No. of Rel. doc : 12848					

and both the Porter and XU stemmer on English data. But on all other languages the performance differences of the proposed method are statistically significant than the other methods (only exception is Czech where the performance difference between RB and PROP is not significant).

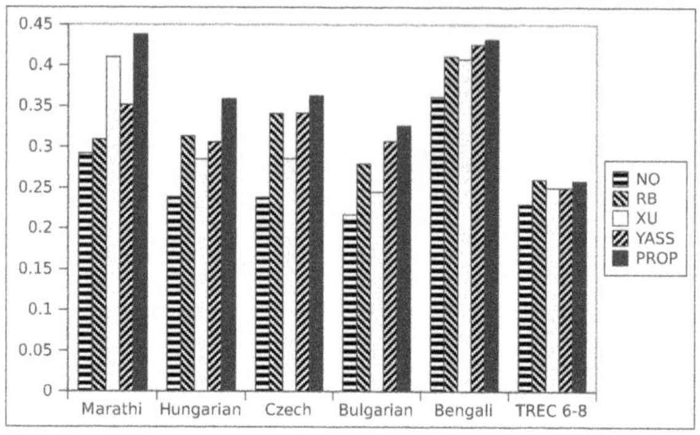

Figure 7: Mean average precision

Table 8: Better MAP (%) by PROP

	NO	RB	XU	YASS
Bulgarian	50.3	16.5	32.9	6.0
Czech	52.2	6.3	26.9	6.1
Hungarian	50.4	14.6	25.9	17.3
Marathi	50.1	41.7	6.9	24.6
Bengali	19.4	5.0	5.8	1.4
English	12.8	-0.7	3.1	3.3

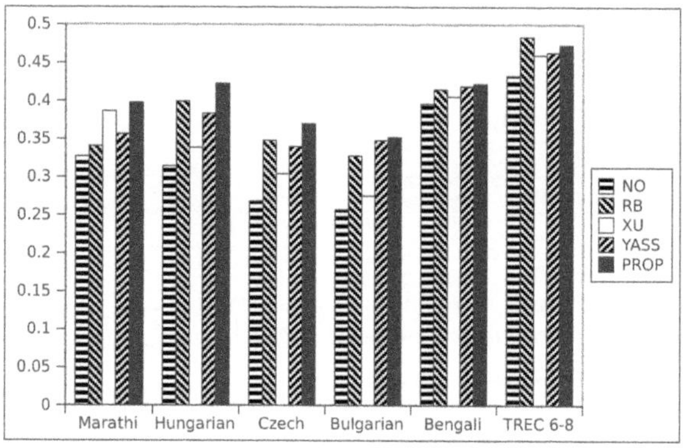

Figure 8: Precision at 10

Table 9: Query (%) better by PROP

	NO	RB	XU	YASS
Bulgarian	79	61	78	58
Czech	78	64	80	56
Hungarian	85	58	69	64
Marathi	81	74	56	68
Bengali	72	57	61	53
English	63	47	55	56

6. DISCUSSION

In the previous section we have reported the experimental results only. In this section we shed some light on the possible merits and demerits of each of the methods.

We have already pointed out some cases where the rule based stemmer falters for less morphologically complex languages like English. But such errors may be more detrimental for complex languages. Rule based stemmers generally remove some hand picked suffixes from word endings and in doing so it may commit serious mistake by removing a valid word ending treating it as a suffix. Sometimes, it also fails to conflate related terms. Therefore, co-occurrence analysis can be a choice to reduce such errors.

Now, consider the case of XU. Almost on all languages it performed quite well in terms of retrieving number of relevant documents. We believe this is because of the kind of graph partitioning technique used to group morphologically related words. The connected component algorithm used by XU, creates long classes and therefore, although it enhances recall but hurts the precision, which ultimately leads to the overall degradation of MAP values.

Turning to YASS, we have noticed that it performs very well on Bengali, Czech and Bulgarian but performs less effectively on Hungarian and Marathi. It does not suffer from

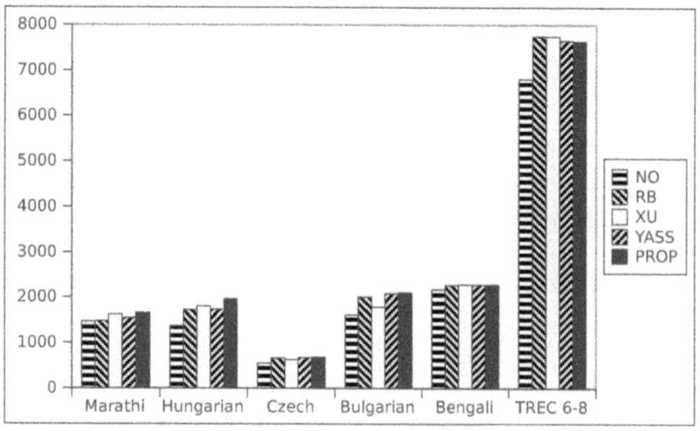

Figure 9: Relevant retrieved

Table 10: Statistical Significance

	NO	RB	XU	YASS
Bulgarian	⋆	⋆	⋆	⋆
Czech	⋆	×	⋆	⋆
Hungarian	⋆	⋆	⋆	⋆
Marathi	⋆	⋆	⋆	⋆
Bengali	⋆	⋆	⋆	×
English	⋆	×	×	×

Table 11: Re-weighting vs. no re-weighting

Language	No Reweight	Reweight
Bulgarian	0.3087	0.3256
Czech	0.3470	0.3624
Hungarian	0.3220	0.3588
Marathi	0.4122	0.4380
Bengali	0.4131	0.4310
English	0.2536	0.2586

the problem of chaining in creating clusters, but has some other limitations. First, the string distance measure falters when suffix lengths are long, which is very common in agglutinative languages (private and privatization are kept in separate groups because of the long suffix *ization* at the end of *privatization*). Secondly, the string distance measure returns the same similarity value for the word pairs like $\{cat, cats\}$ and $\{fat, fate\}$, which clearly is not right. In addition, complete linkage clustering produces different clusters of same objects if simply the objects are considered in different order, this erratically splits a valid cluster. Possibly, these are the main reasons why YASS is less effective on Marathi and Hungarian.

One important module of the proposed algorithm is the re-calculation of the initial co-occurrence strength. The re-calculated strength more clearly discriminates a word association from the other co-occurring word. The nearest neighbour based algorithm, coupled with the re-calculated weight, more accurately forms the clusters. Table 11 demonstrates the usability of re-weighting approach. Clearly, on all languages the re-calculated weights improved the performance of the algorithm.

The proposed method has two parameters, namely, l_1 and l_2. We conducted our initial experiments with English and Bengali by setting $l_1 = 3$ and $l_2 = 5$ and then extended our experiments with other four languages under the same settings. A noticeable loss is observed for a larger value of l_1, since a larger value of l_1 leads to fragmentation of some valid groups. On the other hand, $l_2 = 6, 7, 8$ led to marginal fluctuations in accuracy. For some languages, there was insignificant improvement while for the rest, there was insignificant loss. Finally, the choice of 0.5 in equation 3, was arbitrary and we did not experiment with any other value of this factor.

7. CONCLUSION

In this paper we have proposed a stemming algorithm based on co-occurrence of words in a corpus. One important characteristic of our algorithm is that its parameters are static. A set of experiments on several standard data sets shows that retrieval performance is significantly enhanced through the use of the method and in more than half of the languages the proposed approach outperformed the stemmers based on the language specific knowledge. Also, the method performed better than two other corpus based strong stemmers on all the languages. Further analysis reveals that the proposed stemmer outperforms the competing methods in large number of queries. Based on these results, we believe that the proposed method can be used as a better alternative to the rule based stemmers.

Acknowledgments

We are very grateful to Mandar Mitra for valuable discussions. We thank SIGIR and Singhal Family (Donald B. Crouch Travel Grant) for the student travel grant to the first author.

8. REFERENCES

[1] G. Amati and C. J. Van Rijsbergen. Probabilistic models of information retrieval based on measuring the divergence from randomness. *ACM Trans. Inf. Syst.*, 20(4):357–389, 2002.

[2] M. Bacchin, N. Ferro, and M. Melucci. A probabilistic model for stemmer generation. *Inf. Process. Manage.*, 41(1):121–137, 2005.

[3] L. Dolamic and J. Savoy. Indexing and stemming approaches for the czech language. *Inf. Process. Manage.*, 45(6):714–720, 2009.

[4] L. Dolamic and J. Savoy. Comparative study of indexing and search strategies for the hindi, marathi, and bengali languages. *ACM Trans. Asian Lang. Inf. Process.*, 9(3), 2010.

[5] J. Goldsmith. Unsupervised learning of the morphology of a natural language. *Comput. Linguist.*, 27(2):153–198, 2001.

[6] D. Harman. How effective is suffixing. *Journal of the American Society for Information Science*, 42:7–15, 1991.

[7] A. K. Jain, M. N. Murty, and P. J. Flynn. Data clustering: a review. *ACM Comput. Surv.*, 31:264–323, September 1999.

[8] R. Krovetz. Viewing morphology as an inference process. In *SIGIR '93: Proceedings of the 16th annual international ACM SIGIR conference on Research and development in information retrieval*, pages 191–202, New York, NY, USA, 1993. ACM.

[9] M. Lennon, D. S. Pierce, B. D. Tarry, and P. Willett. *An evaluation of some conflation algorithms for information retrieval*, pages 99–105. Taylor Graham Publishing, London, UK, UK, 1988.

[10] J. Lovins. Development of a stemming algorithm. *Mech. Tran. Comput. Linguistics*, pages 22–31, 1968.

[11] P. Majumder, M. Mitra, and D. Pal. Bulgarian, hungarian and czech stemming using yass. In *Advances in Multilingual and Multimodal Information Retrieval: 8th Workshop of the Cross-Language Evaluation Forum, CLEF 2007, Budapest, Hungary, September 19-21, 2007, Revised Selected Papers*, pages 49–56, Berlin, Heidelberg, 2008. Springer-Verlag.

[12] P. Majumder, M. Mitra, S. K. Parui, G. Kole, P. Mitra, and K. Datta. Yass: Yet another suffix stripper. *ACM Trans. Inf. Syst.*, 25(4):18, 2007.

[13] C. D. Manning, P. Raghavan, and H. Schutze. *Introduction to Information Retrieval.* Cambridge University Press, New York, NY, USA, 2008.

[14] J. Mayfield and P. McNamee. Single n-gram stemming. In *Proceedings of the 26th annual international ACM SIGIR conference on Research and development in informaion retrieval,* SIGIR '03, pages 415–416, New York, NY, USA, 2003. ACM.

[15] P. Mcnamee and J. Mayfield. Character n-gram tokenization for european language text retrieval. *Inf. Retr.*, 7(1-2):73–97, 2004.

[16] P. McNamee, C. K. Nicholas, and J. Mayfield. Addressing morphological variation in alphabetic languages. In *SIGIR*, pages 75–82, 2009.

[17] D. W. Oard, G.-A. Levow, and C. I. Cabezas. Clef experiments at maryland: Statistical stemming and backoff translation. In *CLEF*, pages 176–187, 2000.

[18] F. Peng, N. Ahmed, X. Li, and Y. Lu. Context sensitive stemming for web search. In *Proceedings of the 30th annual international ACM SIGIR conference on Research and development in information retrieval,* SIGIR '07, pages 639–646, New York, NY, USA, 2007. ACM.

[19] M. F. Porter. An algorithm for suffix stripping. pages 313–316, 1997.

[20] J. Savoy. Light stemming approaches for the french, portuguese, german and hungarian languages. In *Proceedings of the 2006 ACM symposium on Applied computing,* SAC '06, pages 1031–1035, New York, NY, USA, 2006. ACM.

[21] J. Savoy. Searching strategies for the hungarian language. *Inf. Process. Manage.*, 44(1):310–324, 2008.

[22] J. Xu and W. B. Croft. Corpus-based stemming using cooccurrence of word variants. *ACM Trans. Inf. Syst.*, 16(1):61–81, 1998.

[23] J. Xu and W. B. Croft. Improving the effectiveness of information retrieval with local context analysis. *ACM Trans. Inf. Syst.*, 18:79–112, January 2000.

Document Clustering with Universum

Dan Zhang
Computer Science Department
Purdue University,
West Lafayette, IN 47907, US
zhang168@cs.purdue.edu

Jingdong Wang
Microsoft Research Asia
Beijing, P.R. China, 100080
jingdw@microsoft.com

Luo Si
Computer Science Department
Purdue University,
West Lafayette, IN 47907, US
lsi@cs.purdue.edu

ABSTRACT

Document clustering is a popular research topic, which aims to partition documents into groups of similar objects (i.e., clusters), and has been widely used in many applications such as automatic topic extraction, document organization and filtering. As a recently proposed concept, Universum is a collection of "non-examples" that do not belong to any concept/cluster of interest. This paper proposes a novel document clustering technique – Document Clustering with Universum, which utilizes the Universum examples to improve the clustering performance. The intuition is that the Universum examples can serve as supervised information and help improve the performance of clustering, since they are known not belonging to any meaningful concepts/clusters in the target domain. In particular, a maximum margin clustering method is proposed to model both target examples and Universum examples for clustering. An extensive set of experiments is conducted to demonstrate the effectiveness and efficiency of the proposed algorithm.

Categories and Subject Descriptors

H.3.3 [**Information Storage and Retrieval**]: Information Search and Retrieval—*clustering*; I.2.6 [**Artificial Intelligence**]: Learning

General Terms

Algorithms, Performance, Experimentation

Keywords

Clustering, Universum, Maximum Margin Clustering, Constrained Concave-Convex Procedure (CCCP)

1. INTRODUCTION

Document clustering is a very important topic in information retrieval, and has received substantial attentions for unsupervised document organization, automatic topic extraction, etc (e.g. [1, 2, 7, 13, 15, 21, 23]). It aims to partition documents into groups of similar objects (i.e., clusters). From the information retrieval perspective, what document clustering does is to learn hidden patterns underlying the available documents, where these hidden patterns may contain some interesting concepts. A good clustering algorithm can automatically organize documents into a set of meaningful clusters for efficient browsing and navigation.

Current document clustering algorithms can be roughly divided into two categories (i.e., hierarchical methods and partitioning methods). The hierarchical methods divide the data into a hierarchical structure by employing bottom up or top down methods [6, 15, 18]. A typical algorithm for the hierarchical method is the hierarchical agglomerative clustering, which starts from taking each document as a single cluster, and then merges these documents gradually to build larger and larger clusters, until the whole dataset is merged as one single cluster. Partitioning methods divide the whole dataset into a fixed number of disjoint clusters [5]. A typical algorithm for the partitioning method is KMeans [5]. The basic motivation of KMeans is to find a set of clustering assignments such that the sum of distances between examples and their associated cluster centers can be minimized. Besides KMeans, some probabilistic methods such as Gaussian Mixture Model (GMM) [14] and Probabilistic Latent Semantic Analysis (PLSA) [8], as well as some graph based methods such as Normalized Cut (NCut) [19], have also shown promising results in clustering. However, one of the most significant drawbacks of these methods is that they only consider the target examples that need to be partitioned, but neglect other information that could be beneficial for clustering. It makes the clustering results only depend on the target examples. As shown in Fig.1(a), the traditional partitioning method wrongly groups one data point (square) into the other cluster, without employing any other prior knowledge.

Universum is a set of examples that do not belong to any concept/cluster of interest, which are different from the target examples that we need to cluster. Some previous work [4, 20, 28, 35] has demonstrated the benefits of treating these examples as prior knowledge imposed on the classification hyperplanes. However, there is no work on applying the Universum examples to the clustering problems. The major contribution of this paper is to show that Universum examples can be used to improve the performance of document clustering. The intuition is that Universum examples should not have a clear pattern, or meaningful concepts/clusters in

SIGIR'11, July 24–28, 2011, Beijing, China.

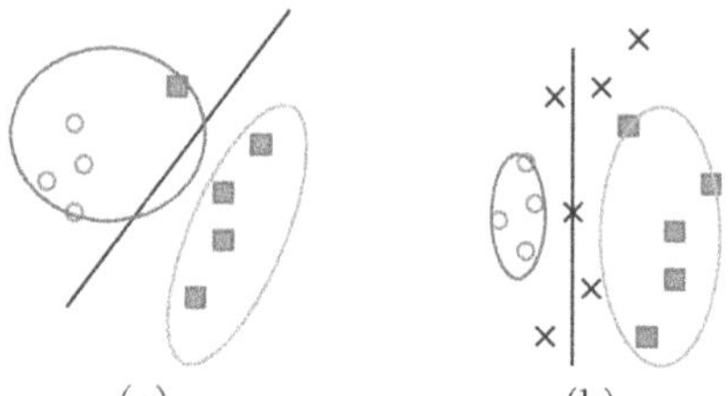

Figure 1: (a) An example clustering result of a typical clustering algorithm (partitioning) with two classes of examples (i.e., circles for class 1 and squares for class 2). It is clear that one square is misclassified; (b) An example clustering result with the guidance of Universum examples (i.e., check marks). Since Universum examples should not have a clear pattern/meaningful cluster to belong to, they should be distributed around the hyperplane, and provide some supervised information for the clustering problem. As can be seen from this picture, the previous misclassified example is now correctly classified.

the target domain. This intuition provides valuable guidance of the clustering process. As shown in Fig.1(b), since the Universum examples do not belong to any of the two clusters, it should only distribute around the hyperplane that separates these two clusters. With the guidance of these Universum examples, the square that was mis-clustered in Fig.1(a) can now be assigned to the right group.

This paper proposes a novel *Document Clustering with Universum* (*DCU*) problem, which utilizes Universum examples in document clustering. In particular, a formulation – *Maximum Margin Document Clustering with Universum* (*M*^{2}*DCU*) is presented to solve this problem. This formulation is based on Maximum Margin Clustering [30], and aims at finding desired hyperplanes that maximize the margins on the (target) examples that need to be partitioned, and minimize the margins on the Universum examples. The new formulation is not a convex optimization problem and therefore cannot be optimized directly. So, we first relax the original problem and then solve it by using *Constrained Concave-Convex Procedure* (*CCCP*) [26]. To accelerate the optimization speed for each sub optimization problem derived from CCCP, an extension of the *Cutting Plane* method [11] is designed. Our experiments on four real world datasets demonstrate the performance improvement brought by the Universum examples and show that the proposed method substantially outperforms state-of-the-art methods.

The rest of the paper is organized as: Section 2 introduces the related work. Section 3 puts forward the novel DCU problem. Section 4 proposes the M^{2}DCU algorithm. Section 5 presents the experimental results. Section 6 concludes this paper and points out some future research directions. The appendix proposes a novel optimization method to accelerate the optimization speed of the algorithm.

2. RELATED WORK

2.1 Universum

The concept of Universum was first proposed in solving classification problems, and was defined as a set of "non-examples" distributed in the same domain as the problem of interest, but known not belonging to any classes that need to be classified [28]. The channels of obtaining Universum examples are very diverse. In [28], three simple ways are suggested, i.e., the examples from some other categories that are known unlikely to belong to any of the target categories; the randomly generated examples; as well as the examples generated by randomly combining examples from different categories. Since they are not likely to belong to any of the target categories, when designing classifiers, these Universum examples should not be classified to any of the categories either.

Out of this motivation, in [28], Jeston et al. designed the first classification algorithm that utilizes Universum examples – $\mathscr{U}$-Support Vector Machines ($\mathscr{U}$-SVM). This work adds a penalty term on the Universum examples to the formulation of the traditional Support Vector Machines (SVM) [5] so that the output given by the classifier will minimize the empirical classification loss on the target examples, and will not give clear classification assignments for the Universum examples. This work is reasonable and performs better than SVM, as shown in an extensive set of experiments [28]. However, it can only deal with binary supervised classification problems. Inspired by this paper, in [35], Zhang et al. extended the Universum algorithm to solve multi-class classification problems and improved the performance of semi-supervised learning by using Universum examples. Later, Huang et al. proposed to use the Universum examples in a different way to solve the semi-supervised classification problems [9]. In [20], the authors analyzed some properties of $\mathscr{U}$-SVM. In [4], Chen et al. designed a method to choose the most useful Universum examples for classification.

All of the previous work has contributed a lot to the use of Universum examples in classification problems. However, there is no prior work on how to use Universum examples in clustering problems. In fact, in clustering, it is natural to consider the Universum examples as examples that do not belong to any of the clusters in the target domain. In this way, the Universum examples can be viewed as some supervised information in an unsupervised problem. It is also interesting to notice that in the toy experiments of [20], $\mathscr{U}$-SVM performs much better than SVM when the number of labeled examples is small. In a clustering problem, since no labeled example is given, we would also expect a great advantage over the traditional clustering algorithms by the utilization of the Universum examples.

2.2 Maximum Margin Clustering (MMC)

The proposed method M^{2}DCU is based on a recently developed algorithm – *Maximum Margin Clustering* (*MMC*). MMC was first proposed in [30]. In [30], the authors borrowed the idea of a standard machine learning principle - maximum margin principle, and used it for clustering. In particular, they tried to assign each of n instances to two classes $\{-1,+1\}$ so that the separation between the two classes can be as large as possible. It is formulated as:

$$\min_{\mathbf{y}\in\{-1,+1\}^n} \min_{\mathbf{w},b,\xi_i} \quad \frac{1}{2}\|\mathbf{w}\|^2 + \frac{C}{n}\sum_{i=1}^{n}\xi_i \tag{1}$$
$$s.t. \quad \forall i = 1,\ldots,n,\ y_i(\mathbf{w}^T\mathbf{x}_i + b) \geq 1 - \xi_i,$$
$$\xi_i \geq 0, -l \leq \mathbf{e}^T\mathbf{y} \leq l,$$

where $\sum_{i=1}^{n}\xi_i$ is divided by the number of examples to better capture how C scales with the data set size, where C is a trade-off parameter for the two parts of this formulation.

$l \geq 0$ is a constant controlling the class imbalance and $\mathbf{e}$ is an all-one vector [30]. The final clustering result is given by $\mathbf{y}$. It is clear that if we subsequently run an SVM with the clustering assignment obtained from MMC, the margin would be maximal among all possible labelings.

In this paper, we consider the distribution of Universum examples as prior knowledge in MMC. With similar motivations, in [29, 32], the authors propose to use some known similarity relationships (e.g., must-link, cannot-link and family/possible-link) between examples as the prior information in clustering. However, in their work, all the documents are still associated with some meaningful clusters, while this is not the case for clustering with Universum.

3. PROBLEM STATEMENTS

First of all, the new problem – Document Clustering with Universum (DCU) is formally proposed. Suppose we are given a set of documents/examples, represented by $\mathcal{X} = \{\mathbf{x}_1, \mathbf{x}_2, \ldots, \mathbf{x}_n\}$, $\mathbf{x}_i \in \mathbb{R}^d$, where n is the total number of documents. Besides these documents, some Universum documents/examples, which are in the same domain as $\mathcal{X}$, but known not belonging to any meaningful groups in $\mathcal{X}$, are also available, and denoted as $\mathcal{X}^* = \{\mathbf{x}_1^*, \mathbf{x}_2^*, \ldots, \mathbf{x}_N^*\}$, $\mathbf{x}_i^* \in \mathbb{R}^d$. N is the number of Universum examples. For convenience, throughout this paper, the examples in $\mathcal{X}$ are denoted as "**target examples/documents**", while the examples in $\mathcal{X}^*$ are referred to as "**Universum examples/documents**". The main objective of DCU is to divide the target examples into k clusters, with the help of Universum examples. A $1 \times n$ vector $\mathbf{y}$ is used here to denote the cluster assignment array, with y_i being the cluster assignment for $\mathbf{x}_i$.

4. MAXIMUM MARGIN DOCUMENT CLUSTERING WITH UNIVERSUM

4.1 Formulation

The proposed formulation tries to find a set of hyperplanes that can separate examples from different clusters, and minimize the confidence of assigning Universum examples to any category. To model these hyperplanes, for each cluster $p \in \{1, 2, \ldots, k\}$, we define a weight vector $\mathbf{w}_p$. For the target examples, we expect their cluster assignments to be as determined as possible. Therefore, M^{2}DCU intends to maximize the clustering margins/confidence on the target examples. For the Universum examples, since they should not be assigned to any one of the k clusters, we expect that the margins[1]/confidence on them should be small, which is expressed as:

$$\forall i = 1, \ldots, N, \quad \mathbf{w}_{u_i^*}^T \mathbf{x}_i^* - \mathbf{w}_{v_i^*}^T \mathbf{x}_i^* \leq \xi_i^* + \epsilon_1, \tag{2}$$

where ϵ_1 is a tolerance parameter, $u_i^* = \arg\max_p \mathbf{w}_p^T \mathbf{x}_i^*$, $v_i^* = \arg\max_{p \backslash u_i^*} \mathbf{w}_p^T \mathbf{x}_i^*$ [2]. ξ_i^* is the nonnegative hinge loss that needs to be optimized on the Universum examples. The concrete formulation of M^{2}DCU can be written as:

$$\min_{\mathbf{w}_p, \mathbf{y}, \xi_i \geq 0, \xi_i^* \geq 0} \quad \frac{1}{2}\sum_{p=1}^{k} \|\mathbf{w}_p\|^2 + \frac{C_l}{n}\sum_{i=1}^{n} \xi_i + \frac{C_u}{N}\sum_{i=1}^{N} \xi_i^* \tag{3}$$

$$s.t. \quad \forall i = 1, \ldots, n, r = 1, \ldots, k \tag{4}$$

$$\mathbf{w}_{y_i}^T \mathbf{x}_i + \delta_{y_i,r} - \mathbf{w}_r^T \mathbf{x}_i \geq 1 - \xi_i$$

$$\forall i = 1, \ldots, N, \quad \mathbf{w}_{u_i^*}^T \mathbf{x}_i^* - \mathbf{w}_{v_i^*}^T \mathbf{x}_i^* \leq \xi_i^* + \epsilon_1 \tag{5}$$

$$\forall p, q \in \{1, \ldots, k\}, \quad -l \leq \sum_{i=1}^{n} \mathbf{w}_p^T \mathbf{x}_i - \sum_{i=1}^{n} \mathbf{w}_q^T \mathbf{x}_i \leq l,$$

where $\delta_{y_i,r}$ is the indication function, which equals 1 if r equals y_i and otherwise 0. Constraint (4) is the large margin constraint on the target examples. Constraint (5) minimizes the margins on the Universum examples. l is a parameter that controls the cluster balance to avoid trivially "optimal" solutions, which may assign most of the examples to one cluster. It is clear that the proposed formulation tries to maximize the margins/confidence on the target examples, and minimize the margins/confidence on Universum examples simultaneously. By doing so, the maximum margin clustering procedure can be guided by the prior knowledge from the Universum examples.

Next we will show the number of variables involved in problem (3) can be reduced by n. In particular, Eq.(3) is equivalent to the following optimization problem:

$$\min_{\mathbf{w}_p, \xi_i \geq 0, \xi_i^* \geq 0} \quad \frac{1}{2}\sum_{p=1}^{k} \|\mathbf{w}_p\|^2 + \frac{C_l}{n}\sum_{i=1}^{n} \xi_i + \frac{C_u}{N}\sum_{i=1}^{N} \xi_i^* \tag{6}$$

$$s.t. \quad \forall i = 1, \ldots, n, \forall r = 1, \ldots, k \tag{7}$$

$$\mathbf{w}_{u_i}^T \mathbf{x}_i + \delta_{u_i,r} - \mathbf{w}_r^T \mathbf{x}_i \geq 1 - \xi_i$$

$$\forall i = 1, \ldots, N, \quad \mathbf{w}_{u_i^*}^T \mathbf{x}_i^* - \mathbf{w}_{v_i^*}^T \mathbf{x}_i^* \leq \xi_i^* + \epsilon_1 \tag{8}$$

$$\forall p, q \in \{1, \ldots, k\}, \quad -l \leq \sum_{i=1}^{n} \mathbf{w}_p^T \mathbf{x}_i - \sum_{i=1}^{n} \mathbf{w}_q^T \mathbf{x}_i \leq l,$$

where $u_i = \arg\max_p \mathbf{w}_p^T \mathbf{x}_i$, and the optimal y_i equals u_i. Furthermore, for the convenience of computation, three *concatenated* vectors are introduced:

$$\widetilde{\mathbf{w}} = [\mathbf{w}_1^T, \mathbf{w}_2^T, \cdots, \mathbf{w}_p^T, \cdots, \mathbf{w}_k^T]^T, \tag{9}$$

$$\mathbf{x}_{i(p)} = [\mathbf{0}, \cdots, \mathbf{x}_i^T, \cdots, \mathbf{0}]^T, \quad \mathbf{x}_{i(p)}^* = [\mathbf{0}, \cdots, \mathbf{x}_i^{*T}, \cdots, \mathbf{0}]^T,$$

where $\mathbf{0}$ is a $1 \times d$ zero vector. In $\mathbf{x}_{i(p)}$, only the $(p-1)d$ to pd-th elements are nonzero and equals $\mathbf{x}_i$ and it is clear that $\widetilde{\mathbf{w}}^T \mathbf{x}_{i(p)} = \mathbf{w}_p^T \mathbf{x}_i$. $\mathbf{x}_{i(p)}^*$ is defined similarly as $\mathbf{x}_{i(p)}$. We propose to absorb $\delta_{u_i,r}$ into ξ_i and use a separate variable ξ_{ir} for each constraint. The function $\mathbf{w}_{v_i^*}^T \mathbf{x}_i$ is nonconvex. To simplify the formulation, we relax this function by $mean_{t \backslash u_i^*}\{\widetilde{\mathbf{w}}^T \mathbf{x}_{i(t)}^*\}$. Here, the "*mean*" function calculates the average value of the input function with respect to the subscript variable. Then, Eq.(6) is rewritten as:

$$\min_{\widetilde{\mathbf{w}}, \xi_i^r \geq 0, \xi_i^* \geq 0} \quad \frac{1}{2}\|\widetilde{\mathbf{w}}\|^2 + \frac{C_l}{nk}\sum_{i=1}^{n}\sum_{r=1}^{k} \xi_{ir} + \frac{C_u}{N}\sum_{i=1}^{N} \xi_i^* \tag{10}$$

$$s.t. \quad \forall i = 1, \ldots, n, \forall r = 1, \ldots, k \tag{11}$$

$$\widetilde{\mathbf{w}}^T \mathbf{x}_{i(u_i)} - \widetilde{\mathbf{w}}^T \mathbf{x}_{i(r)} \geq 1 - \xi_{ir}$$

$$\forall i = 1, \ldots, N, \tag{12}$$

$$\frac{k}{k-1}(\widetilde{\mathbf{w}}^T \mathbf{x}_{i(u_i^*)}^* - mean_t\{\widetilde{\mathbf{w}}^T \mathbf{x}_{i(t)}^*\}) \leq \xi_i^* + \epsilon_1$$

$$\forall p, q \in \{1, 2, \ldots, k\}, \quad -l \leq \widetilde{\mathbf{w}}^T \sum_{i=1}^{n} (\mathbf{x}_{i(p)} - \mathbf{x}_{i(q)}) \leq l.$$

[1]It can also be considered as the difference between the largest output and the second largest output. As we shall see later, this kind of margin definition on Universum examples is also consistent with the margin defined on the target examples in Eq.(7).

[2]Throughout this paper, "\" means ruling out.

This formulation is reasonable, however, it is both nonconvex and nonsmooth. Therefore, it cannot be solved directly. We will show how to solve this problem by using CCCP in the following section.

4.2 CCCP Decomposition

The nonconvexity in problem (10) is caused by the constraint (11) and (12). However, it can be considered as the difference between two different convex functions[3]. Therefore the Constrained Concave-Convex Procedure (CCCP) can be employed to solve this problem.

Given an initial point $\tilde{\mathbf{w}}^0$, CCCP computes $\tilde{\mathbf{w}}^{(t+1)}$ [4] from $\tilde{\mathbf{w}}^{(t)}$ iteratively by replacing $\tilde{\mathbf{w}}^T\mathbf{x}_{i(u_i)}$ and $\tilde{\mathbf{w}}^T\mathbf{x}^*_{i(u_i^*)}$ in problem (10) with their corresponding first order Taylor expansions at $\tilde{\mathbf{w}}^{(t)}$ and solves the resulting quadratic programming problem, until convergence. Since $\tilde{\mathbf{w}}^T\mathbf{x}_{i(u_i)}$ and $\tilde{\mathbf{w}}^T\mathbf{x}^*_{i(u_i^*)}$ are non-smooth, their sub-gradients are used in their first order Taylor expansions. More precisely, for the t-th CCCP iteration, $\tilde{\mathbf{w}}^T\mathbf{x}_{i(u_i)}$ and $\tilde{\mathbf{w}}^T\mathbf{x}^*_{i(u_i^*)}$ are replaced by $\tilde{\mathbf{w}}^T\mathbf{x}_{i(u_i^{(t)})}$ and $\tilde{\mathbf{w}}^T\mathbf{x}^*_{i(u_i^{*(t)})}$, where $u_i^{(t)} = \arg\max_p(\tilde{\mathbf{w}}^{(t)})^T\mathbf{x}_{i(p)}$ and $u_i^{*(t)} = \arg\max_p(\tilde{\mathbf{w}}^{(t)})^T\mathbf{x}^*_{i(p)}$. In this way, problem (10) is decomposed into a set of convex subproblems and for the t-th CCCP iteration, the corresponding subproblem is:

$$\min_{\tilde{\mathbf{w}},\xi_{ir}\geq 0,\xi_i^*\geq 0} \quad \frac{1}{2}\|\tilde{\mathbf{w}}\|^2 + \frac{C_l}{nk}\sum_{i=1}^{n}\sum_{r=1}^{k}\xi_{ir} + \frac{C_u}{N}\sum_{i=1}^{N}\xi_i^* \quad (13)$$

$$\begin{aligned} s.t. \quad & \forall i = 1,\ldots,n, \forall r = 1,\ldots,k \\ & \tilde{\mathbf{w}}^T\mathbf{x}_{i(u_i^{(t)})} - \tilde{\mathbf{w}}^T\mathbf{x}_{i(r)} \geq 1 - \xi_{ir} \\ & \forall i = 1,\ldots,N, \\ & \frac{k}{k-1}(\tilde{\mathbf{w}}^T\mathbf{x}^*_{i(u_i^{*(t)})} - mean_b\{\tilde{\mathbf{w}}^T\mathbf{x}^*_{i(b)}\}) \leq \xi_i^* + \epsilon_1 \\ & \forall p,q \in \{1,2,\ldots,k\}, \quad -l \leq \tilde{\mathbf{w}}^T\sum_{i=1}^{n}(\mathbf{x}_{i(p)} - \mathbf{x}_{i(q)}) \leq l. \end{aligned}$$

It is clear that by using CCCP together with the subgradient, during each iteration, we are trying to maximize the clustering margin on the target examples, and minimize the margin on the Universum examples, based on the cluster assignments obtained in the previous iteration. It has been verified that CCCP decreases the objective function monotonically [26], and is guaranteed to find a local optimal solution in a relatively small number of iterations. The whole algorithm is then described in Table 1. Here, $J^{(t)} = \frac{1}{2}\|\tilde{\mathbf{w}}^{(t)}\|^2 + \frac{C_l}{nk}\sum_{i=1}^{n}\sum_{r=1}^{k}\xi_{ir}^{(t)} + \frac{C_u}{N}\sum_{i=1}^{N}\xi_i^{*(t)}$.

The proposed algorithm is straightforward. But if the number of target examples, as well as the Universum examples goes large, or/and if the data dimension is high, directly solving problem (13) in the primal form may be very time consuming, since it involves a lot of optimization variables and constraints. There are many optimization alternatives to solve this efficiency problem [10, 24]. In this paper, we suggest a novel optimization method, which is an extension of the cutting plane method [10], to solve problem (13). The detail of this optimization method is elaborated in the Appendix A.

[3]For constraint (11), $\tilde{\mathbf{w}}^T\mathbf{x}_{i(u_i)}$ is a convex and nonsmooth function, and $\tilde{\mathbf{w}}^T\mathbf{x}_{i(r)} - \xi_{ir}$ is convex and smooth. This constraint can be considered as the difference of these two convex functions, i.e., $(\tilde{\mathbf{w}}^T\mathbf{x}_{i(r)} - \xi_{ir}) - \tilde{\mathbf{w}}^T\mathbf{x}_{i(u_i)} \leq -1$. In the same way, constraint (12) can also be considered as the difference of two convex functions.

[4]The superscript t is used to denote that the result is obtained from the t-th CCCP iteration.

Algorithm: M^2DCU
Input:
1. A set of target documents: $\mathcal{X} = \{\mathbf{x}_1, ..., \mathbf{x}_n\}$
2. A set of Universum examples: $\mathcal{X}^* = \{\mathbf{x}_1^*, ..., \mathbf{x}_N^*\}$
2. parameters: regularization parameter C_l and C_u, tolerance parameter for Universum examples $\epsilon_1 = 0.5$, CCCP solution precision $\epsilon_2 = 0.01$, cluster number k, cluster size balance parameter l
Output:
The cluster assignment $\mathbf{y}$
CCCP Iterations:
1. Construct $\tilde{\mathcal{X}} = \{\mathbf{x}_{i(r)}\}$, $\tilde{\mathcal{X}}^* = \{\mathbf{x}^*_{i(r)}\}$
2. Initialize $\tilde{\mathbf{w}}^0$, t=0, $\Delta J = 10^3$, $J^{(-1)} = 10^3$
3. **while** $\Delta J/J^{(t-1)} > \epsilon_2$ **do**
4. Derive problem (13) by updating $u_i^{(t)} = \arg\max_p(\tilde{\mathbf{w}}^{(t)})^T\mathbf{x}_{i(p)}$ and $u_i^{*(t)} = \arg\max_p(\tilde{\mathbf{w}}^{(t)})^T\mathbf{x}^*_{i(p)}$.
5. $t = t + 1$
6. Get $(\tilde{\mathbf{w}}^{(t)}, J^{(t)})$ by solving problem (13).
7. $\Delta J = J^{(t-1)} - J^{(t)}$
8. **end while**
9. **Cluster Assignment**:
For $\mathbf{x}_i$, the corresponding cluster assignment $\mathbf{y}_i = \arg\max_p(\tilde{\mathbf{w}}^{(t)})^T\mathbf{x}_{i(p)}$.

Table 1: Algorithm description: M^2DCU

5. EXPERIMENTS

An extensive set of experiments is conducted to validate the effectiveness and the efficiency of the proposed method[5]. These experiments are conducted with Matlab r2008a on a 2.0GHZ Intel Quad Core computer with 4.0GB main memory.

5.1 Universum Examples

In practice, the Universum examples can be obtained easily. In this paper, three different ways are first employed to generate the Universum examples. A Universum selection method is then used to choose the most useful Universum examples.

$\mathscr{U}_{\text{rest}}$: some documents that are not included in the clustering tasks [28, 35]. We will elaborate $\mathscr{U}_{rest}$ for different clustering tasks when introducing datasets. Although this generation method sounds like needing category information, this is not necessary for a real application of clustering because it can obtain a separate set of documents that are not in categories in consideration. For example, we may be interested in clustering publications in some major computer science conferences (documents in major categories in their datasets), and we can assume $\mathscr{U}_{\text{rest}}$ consists of articles in a set of very specialized conferences on minority subject areas in computer science or even articles in another discipline.

$\mathscr{U}_{\text{rand}}$: Generate uniformly distributed features within the

[5]The code and data can be found on the author's homepage.

range of the min and max values on each dimension of the target examples [28, 35].

$\mathscr{U}_{\texttt{mean}}$: In [28], the authors designed some Universum examples which are combinations of different pictures from different categories. However, in a clustering problem, no label information is given. Therefore, an alternative method is used to design the Universum examples in the clustering problem. KMeans is first employed to pre-partition the whole dataset into k groups. $\frac{k(k-1)}{2}$ Universum examples are then generated by picking two clustering centers each time from the k groups and merging them together.

$\mathscr{U}_{\texttt{select}}$: In [4], the authors pointed out that the Universum examples that lie between different categories are the most helpful ones. Their basic motivation is reasonable. However, their method is only designed for classification problems, and is very time consuming. In this paper, we pick the most useful Universum examples for clustering in a different way. Our basic intuition is that the Universum examples that are closest to the target examples are the most useful ones for clustering. Although these Universum examples are close to the target examples, they do not belong to any of the clusters. So, they should have much higher impacts on the clustering results than the ones that lie far away. In order to measure the closeness of the Universum examples, a Gaussian Mixture Model is first trained on the target examples, with k being the number of gaussian models. Then, for each Universum example, we calculate the probability that it is generated by using this Gaussian Mixture Model. The Universum examples with the highest generation probabilities are then selected for use, and are referred to as $\mathscr{U}_{\texttt{select}}$. In our experiments, the top 10 percents of all the Universum examples are selected. As observed from these experiments, the selected proportions of $\mathscr{U}_{\texttt{rest}}$ and $\mathscr{U}_{\texttt{mean}}$ are much higher than that of $\mathscr{U}_{\texttt{rand}}$. This is because the randomly generated Universum often has a very low probability to be close to the target examples. But for $\mathscr{U}_{\texttt{rest}}$ and $\mathscr{U}_{\texttt{mean}}$, they are often closer to the target examples.

5.2 Datasets

We use four text datasets in our experiments.

20Newsgroup: This is a benchmark dataset[6], which contains four main categories, i.e., 'comp', 'rec', 'sci', 'talk', as well as some other categories with small number of examples, such as 'alt.atheism', 'misc.forsale', etc. The four main categories are used for clustering, while examples in the remaining categories are used as $\mathfrak{U}_{rest}$.

WebKB This dataset contains webpages from computer science departments at around four different universities[7]. They are divided into 7 categories (i.e., student, faculty, staff, course, project, department and other). We choose webpages from four categories as target examples for clustering (i.e., course, faculty, project, student), and the remaining 2 categories, i.e., "other" and "staff" will serve as $\mathfrak{U}_{rest}$.

Reuters-Volume I (ReutersV1): It is an archive of over 800,000 manually categorized newswire stories [12]. A subset of ReutersV1 is used. There are in total 126 topics in it. In the experiments, we choose examples from three categories "ECAT", "C151", and "M14" in this subset as target examples, and some examples from the remaining categories are randomly selected as $\mathfrak{U}_{rest}$. To avoid some overlap problems, the target examples with more than one label from these three categories are removed.

Reuters21578: This dataset contains documents collected from the Reuters newswire in 1987[8]. There are in total 135 categories in this dataset. In our experiments, we use two subsets of this data collection, i.e., Reuters21578-1 and Reuters21578-2. Reuters21578-1 contains 6 categories among these 135 topics. Similar to ReutersV1, the documents associated with more than one of these 6 categories are not used. Reuters21578-2 contains another 10 categories. And the documents associated with more than one of these 10 categories are not used. For both of these sub-datasets, $\mathfrak{U}_{rest}$ are randomly selected from examples in the remaining categories.

The basic information of these datasets is summarized in Table 2. For all of these documents, the tf-idf (normalized term frequency and log inverse document frequency) [15] features are extracted, with the stop words being removed and porter [15] as the stemmer. Furthermore, the most frequently appeared words are picked.

5.3 Methods

In experiments, the number of clusters k is set to be the true number of classes in target examples for all clustering algorithms. As described in Section 5.1, three different Universum methods are used in this paper. But we will not use them directly. The selection method mentioned previously is used to select the most useful Universum examples. $\mathscr{U}_{\texttt{select}}$ is then used for M^{2}DCU as selected Universum examples. The class imbalance parameter l is set by grid search from the grid $[0.001, 0.01, 0.1, 1, 10]$. The parameter C_l is searched from the exponential grid $2^{[1:1:6]}$ and the parameter C_u is searched through $[0.001, 0.01, 0.1, 1, 10]$. To measure the effect brought by the Universum examples, we further report the performance of M^{2}DCU-0, in which the C_u in problem (13) is set to be 0, and tune the other parameters using exactly the same way as we do for M^{2}DCU.

Several different kinds of clustering methods are used for comparison. It includes: the probability generative method – Gaussian Mixture Model (GMM) [14]; the methods based on matrix factorizations, such as Nonnegative Matrix Factorization (NMF) [31] and Probabilistic Latent Semantic Analysis (PLSA) [8]; spectral/graph based methods, such as Normalized Cut (Ncut) [33], Clustering with Local and Global Consistency (CLGR) [27] and KMeans; Maximum Margin based clustering, such as CPM3C [36]. For both KMeans and GMM, for each experiment, the result is summarized over 50 independent runs to avoid local optimal. For Ncut, its gaussian similarity is determined by local scaling [34]. The formulation of CPM3C [36] is similar to M^{2}DCU-0, but there is a significant difference in their optimization methods. The outer iteration of CPM3C is the cutting plane method and its inner iteration is CCCP. However, when using the cutting plane method to solve a nonconvex problem, the convergence property and optimality of the solution cannot be guaranteed. The parameters of CPM3C are tuned using exactly the same settings as M^{2}DCU-0.

[6] http://people.csail.mit.edu/jrennie/20Newsgroups/
[7] http://www.cs.cmu.edu/~webkb/
[8] http://www.daviddlewis.com/resources/testcollections/reuters21578/

5.4 Evaluation Metrics

5.4.1 Clustering Accuracy (Acc)

The clustering accuracy (Acc) [25, 30, 36] is used to evaluate the final clustering performance. Specifically, we first take a set of labeled examples, remove the labels of these examples and run the clustering algorithms, then we relabel these examples using the clustering assignments returned by the algorithms. Finally, we measure the percentage of correct classifications by comparing the true labels and the labels assigned by the clustering algorithms as follows:

$$Acc = \frac{1}{n}\sum_{i=1}^{n}\delta(y_i, map(c_i)),$$

where, $map(\cdot)$ is a function that maps each cluster index to a class label, which can be found by the Hungarian algorithm [16]. c_i and y_i are the cluster index of $\mathbf{x}_i$ and the true class label. $\delta(a,b)$ is a function that equals 1 when a equals b, and 0 otherwise.

5.4.2 Normalized Mutual Information (NMI)

Another evaluation metric we employed here is the Normalized Mutual Information (NMI) [22], which was originally a symmetric measure to quantify the statistical information shared between two distributions. More precisely, for two random variables X and Y, NMI is defined as:

$$NMI(X,Y) = \frac{I(X,Y)}{\sqrt{H(X)H(Y)}}. \tag{14}$$

Here, $I(X,Y)$ is mutual information between X and Y, while $H(X)$ and $H(Y)$ are entropies of X and Y. If there is a one to one correspondence between the distribution of X and that of Y, NMI equals one. From the perspective of information theory, it means all of the information encoded in X (sender) has already been correctly delivered to Y (receiver). Otherwise, if Y is merely a uniform distribution, NMI equals zero, which means no information would be transferred from X to Y. It is clear that $NMI(X,X) = 1$, which achieves the maximal possible value of NMI. Given two clustering results, we can consider the clustering assignments as distributions of random variables, and NMI in Eq.(14) can be estimated as:

$$NMI = \frac{\sum_{p=1}^{k}\sum_{q=1}^{k} n_{p,q} log(\frac{n\cdot n_{p,q}}{n_p \hat{n}_q})}{\sqrt{(\sum_{p=1}^{k} n_p log\frac{n_p}{n})(\sum_{q=1}^{k} \hat{n}_q log\frac{\hat{n}_q}{n})}}, \tag{15}$$

where n_p refers to the number of data contained in the p-th cluster, $\hat{n}_q$ is the number of data belonging to the q-th cluster, and $n_{p,q}$ denotes the number of data that are in the intersection between the p-th and the q-th clusters.

5.4.3 Rand Index (RandInd)

Suppose two clustering assignments, $\mathcal{I}$ and $\mathcal{L}$, are given. $\mathcal{I} = \{\mathcal{I}_1, \mathcal{I}_2, \ldots, \mathcal{I}_k\}$ represents the set of final clustering results and $\mathcal{I}_i$ is the i-th cluster. $\mathcal{L} = \{\mathcal{L}_1, \mathcal{L}_2, \ldots, \mathcal{L}_k\}$ denotes the set of true data classes such that $\mathcal{L}_i$ represents the i-th class.

The rand index measures the similarity between $\mathcal{I}$ and $\mathcal{L}$ as [17]: $R = \frac{a+b}{a+b+c+d}$, where a is the number of data pairs in $\mathcal{X}$ that are in both of these two clusters. b represents the number of data pairs in $\mathcal{X}$ that are in different sets in these two clusters. c is the number of data pairs that are in the same set in $\mathcal{I}$ but in the different sets in $\mathcal{L}$. d denotes the number of data pairs in $\mathcal{X}$ such that they are in different sets in $\mathcal{I}$ but the same set in $\mathcal{L}$. It is natural to consider $a+b$ as the number of agreements between $\mathcal{I}$ and $\mathcal{L}$, while $c+d$ represents the number of disagreements. If R equals 0, it means $\mathcal{I}$ and $\mathcal{L}$ are totally different, and if R equals 1, it means these two cluster assignments are exactly the same.

5.5 Clustering Results

The clustering results are reported from Table 3 to Table 5. In Table 6, the CPU running time of these different methods is also given.

From the clustering results, we can see that in all cases M^{2}DCU performs better than M^{2}DCU-0, which clearly demonstrates the benefits brought by the involvement of Universum examples. When compared with the probability generative methods, such as GMM, M^{2}DCU prevails in all cases. For the methods based on matrix factorizations, such as NMF and PLSA, their performances are good in some cases. As can be seen from Table 4, the NMI performance of M^{2}DCU on 20Newsgroup is worse than that of PLSA and NMF, and on Reuters21578-2, the Rand Index of NMF is also higher than M^{2}DCU. But it is clear that for the other clustering measurements on these datasets, the proposed method performs better than NMF and PLSA. For example, for the clustering accuracy and Rand Index measurements on 20Newsgroup, the performances of the proposed method are higher than NMF and PLSA. It is safe to say that in most cases, the proposed method performs much better than the matrix factorization based methods. Ncut, CLGR, and KMeans are spectral based methods, whose performances mainly rely on graph factorization. These methods are reasonable, which place the cluster boundaries in the low density regions of the dataset. However, they do not utilize the Universum examples to further guide the clustering process, and therefore, their performances are inferior to that of M^{2}DCU.

As a maximum margin clustering method, although the formulations of CPM3C and M^{2}DCU-0 are similar, CPM3C uses the cutting plane method to solve a non-convex optimization problem. As previously claimed, the cutting plane method is not originally designed to solve non-convex optimization problems, and therefore, the performance of CPM3C cannot be guaranteed. Different from CPM3C, M^{2}DCU uses the CCCP to solve the non-convex optimization problem, and the cutting plane method is suggested to solve the convex sub-problems derived from each CCCP iteration, and therefore it is theoretically much more elegant than CPM3C. As we shall see from experiments, in almost all cases, both M^{2}DCU and M^{2}DCU-0 perform better than CPM3C, which clearly validates our claims.

As for the CPU time, M^{2}DCU is ranked among the top three fastest algorithms in three of the five datasets. For the experiments on Reuters21578-1 and Reuters21578-2, the proposed method are seemingly slower than some other algorithms. However, it is clear that the corresponding clustering performances of the proposed method are much higher than those of the ones with faster CPU running times. We suspect that the lower efficiency of the proposed method on these two datasets is caused by the data distributions in these two datasets, which increases the number of convergence steps. It is interesting to notice that on WebKB dataset the CPU running time of M^{2}DCU is shorter than

Dataset	Categories	#Dim	# PCA Dim	#Documents	# $\mathscr{U}_{rest}$	# $\mathscr{U}_{rand}$	# $\mathscr{U}_{mean}$	# $\mathscr{U}_{selected}$
20Newsgroup	4	6600	1025	16060	2768	1000	6	378
WebKB	5	4560	700	3223	3660	1000	10	467
ReutersV1	3	8625	473	19619	7592	1000	3	860
Reuters21578-1	6	927	189	8050	2192	1000	15	321
Reuters21578-2	10	927	189	1689	4233	1000	45	528

Table 2: The detailed description of the datasets. # Dim represents the original data dimension, while #PCA Dim means the dimension after using Principal Component Analysis (PCA). For M^{2}DCU, KMeans, Ncut, GMM, CPM3C, CLGR, the datasets are processed by PCA to increase the efficiency and reduce some noise. But for NMF, PLSA, since they require that the features should be non-negative, the dataset processed by PCA cannot be used. So, we run these two algorithms in the original feature space. The Universum examples used in experiments are denoted as $\mathscr{U}_{selected}$, which are selected from $\mathscr{U}_{rest}$, $\mathscr{U}_{rand}$ and $\mathscr{U}_{mean}$.

	M^{2}DCU	M^{2}DCU-0	KMeans	NMF	Ncut	GMM	CPM3C	CLGR	PLSA
20Newsgroup	**69.0**	63.1	60.7	64.3	54.9	51.9	56.6	45.8	66.5
WebKB	**62.6**	59.2	48.3	47.8	47.2	60.4	51.4	48.9	52.7
ReutersV1	**95.7**	94.8	61.1	84.4	75.2	69.1	88.1	80.4	85.6
Reuters21578-1	**76.6**	73.2	45.6	57.4	62.6	59.4	60.6	47.6	48.7
Reuters21578-2	**53.2**	50.7	38.4	50.0	40.4	41.8	43.9	38.7	47.1

Table 3: Clustering Accuracy (%) comparisons. The results marked with black represent the best performances on the corresponding datasets. M^{2}DCU-0 represents the case when the weight of the Universum term C_u in Eq.(13) is set to be 0. It is clear that the Universum examples increase the maximum margin clustering performances dramatically. Although the formulations are similar, CPM3C and M^{2}DCU-0 differ in their optimization methods. For KMeans and GMM, the results are summarized over 50 independent runs.

	M^{2}DCU	M^{2}DCU-0	KMeans	NMF	Ncut	GMM	CPM3C	CLGR	PLSA
20Newsgroup	0.408	0.361	0.357	0.443	0.252	0.205	0.278	0.209	**0.476**
WebKB	**0.372**	0.340	0.283	0.342	0.181	0.333	0.307	0.242	0.335
ReutersV1	**0.827**	0.803	0.435	0.576	0.585	0.468	0.624	0.617	0.592
Reuters21578-1	**0.575**	0.536	0.442	0.517	0.448	0.508	0.412	0.275	0.497
Reuters21578-2	**0.503**	0.486	0.397	0.456	0.422	0.365	0.418	0.399	0.434

Table 4: Normalized Mutual Information (NMI) comparisons. The results marked with black represent the best performances on the corresponding datasets. M^{2}DCU-0 represents the case when the weight of the Universum term C_u in Eq.(13) is set to be 0. Although in 20Newsgroup, the NMI of M^{2}DCU is smaller than that of PLSA and NMF. But we can see that it improves the clustering results of M^{2}DCU-0 with the use of Universum examples. And as we shall see, on the other two corresponding clustering indices, i.e, clustering accuracy, and rand index, M^{2}DCU performs better than PLSA. For KMeans and GMM, the results are summarized over 50 independent runs.

	M^{2}DCU	M^{2}DCU-0	KMeans	NMF	Ncut	GMM	CPM3C	CLGR	PLSA
20Newsgroup	**0.802**	0.740	0.701	0.727	0.591	0.669	0.711	0.598	0.785
WebKB	**0.794**	0.698	0.654	0.740	0.643	0.689	0.667	0.609	0.737
ReutersV1	**0.952**	0.934	0.618	0.814	0.778	0.715	0.855	0.839	0.825
Reuters21578-1	**0.840**	0.799	0.741	0.778	0.673	0.784	0.691	0.614	0.759
Reuters21578-2	0.854	0.808	0.800	**0.860**	0.792	0.834	0.748	0.813	0.847

Table 5: Rand Index comparisons. The results marked with black represent the best performances on the corresponding datasets. M^{2}DCU-0 represents the case when the weight of the Universum term C_u in Eq.(13) is set to be 0. It is clear that M^{2}DCU shows the best performances on most of these datasets. For KMeans and GMM, the results are summarized over 50 independent runs.

	M^{2}DCU	M^{2}DCU-0	KMeans	NMF	Ncut	GMM	CPM3C	CLGR	PLSA
20Newsgroup	**801**	**789**	15204	35515	151760	105440	22838	207752	**10032**
WebKB	**232**	**307**	1940	3465	771	18373	**190**	821	682
ReutersV1	**576**	**304**	6303	32355	128810	21495	**2264**	162374	7551
Reuters21578-1	685	**662**	3449	4065	1094	11445	**382**	4203	**447**
Reuters21578-2	735	691	465	346	**99**	1550	256	**119**	**197**

Table 6: CPU Running Time (in seconds). For each dataset, the top 3 fastest algorithms are marked in black. M^{2}DCU-0 represents the case when the weight of the Universum term C_u in Eq.(13) is set to be 0. From this table, it is clear that the efficiency of M^{2}DCU is comparable with that of the other methods. Please note that the CPU running time for KMeans and GMM reported here are the results of 50 independent runs. It is interesting to note that in WebKB, M^{2}DCU is faster than M^{2}DCU-0, which indicates introducing the Universum examples may sometimes reduce the number of CCCP iterations.

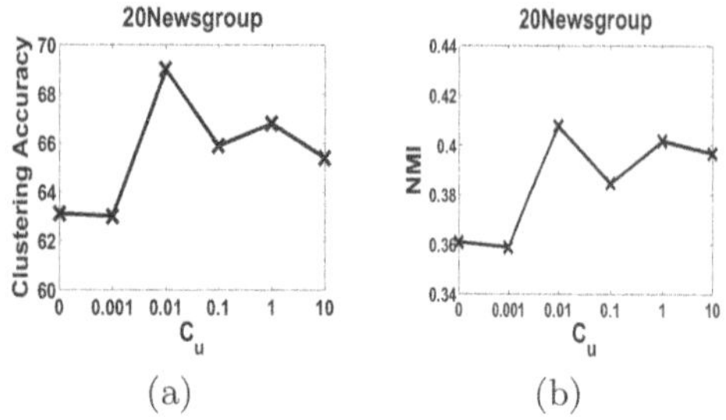

Figure 2: Parameter Sensibility on 20Newsgroup, with different C_u. It is clear that the performance is improved by incorporating the Universum examples.

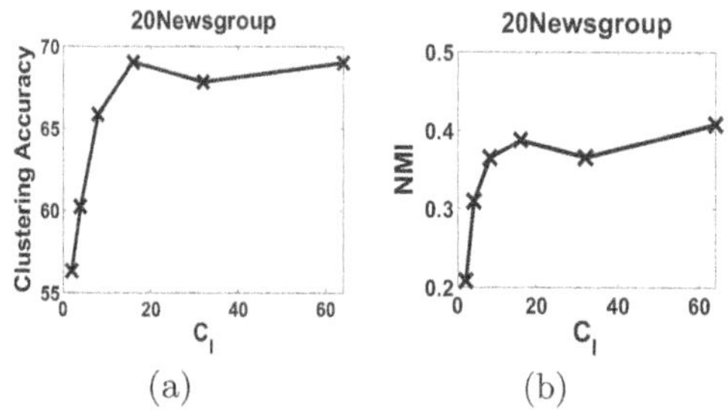

Figure 3: Parameter Sensibility on 20Newsgroup, with different C_l. From these two pictures, we can see that C_l is relatively stable in a very large range of the whole parameter space.

that of M^{2}DCU-0. We suspect that sometimes, introducing the Universum examples can reduce the number of CCCP iterations and therefore result in a shorter running time.

Besides these comparison experiments, we also measure the parameter sensibility of the proposed method for C_u, C_l, l. The experiments are conducted on 20Newsgroup. In these experiments, C_u is tuned and evaluated through the grid $[0.001, 0.01, 0.1, 1, 10]$. C_l is from the grid $2^{[1:1:6]}$. And l is from the grid $[0.001, 0.01, 0.1, 1, 10]$. The parameter sensitivity experiments are shown from Fig.2 to Fig.4. In Fig.2, the performances with different C_u values are evaluated. C_u reflects the involvement of the Universum examples, where $C_u = 0$ means no involvement for the Universum examples. As can be seen from the trend of the performances, we can conclude that M^{2}DCU benefits a lot by introducing the Universum examples. In Fig.3, it is shown that the performance of the proposed method increases with C_l at first, and is relatively stable within a very large range of the whole parameter space, especially after C_l reaches a relatively large value. And in Fig.4, we can see that the proposed method is relatively stable with respect to l. But the performance of the proposed method does decrease a little after a fixed l value. Therefore, a relatively small value of l is normally suggested. We have also observed similar behaviors on the other three datasets, i.e., WebKB, ReutersV1 and Reuters21578. But due to the limit of space, we cannot put these experimental results here.

6. CONCLUSIONS

Document clustering is an important research topic with

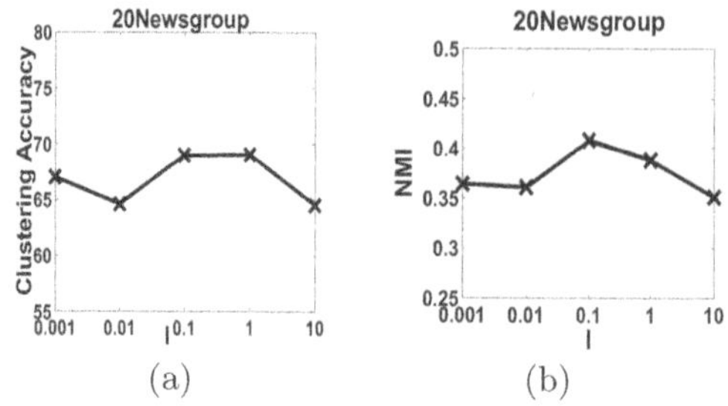

Figure 4: Parameter Sensibility on 20Newsgroup, with different l. The proposed method is relatively stable w.r.t l. But if l is too large, the performance will deteriorate. So, normally a relatively small value of l is suggested.

many practical applications. Previous document clustering methods only consider the examples that need to be clustered, but neglect the useful examples that can be obtained from some other sources. As a newly proposed concept, Universum, which is defined as a set of "non-examples" has been receiving more and more attentions. These examples can often be obtained easily and have already been shown the capability of improving the performances in classification problems. In this paper, we proposed a novel research problem – Document Clustering with Universum (DCU), which extends the idea of the utilization of Universum examples to document clustering problems, and suggest a method – Maximum Margin Document Clustering with Universum (M^{2}DCU) to solve this problem. The experimental results show that the Universum examples can be used to improve the performance of clustering under the framework of Maximum Margin Clustering, and the proposed method performs substantially better than state-of-the-art methods in most cases. In the future, we will further investigate: 1. how the Universum examples can be integrated to other clustering algorithms, such as KMeans, GMM, NMF; 2. how to design better ways to select Universum examples.

7. ACKNOWLEDGEMENT

We thank the anonymous reviewers for valuable comments. This research was partially supported by the NSF research grants IIS-0746830, CNS-1012208, IIS-1017837, CCF- 0939370.

References

[1] R. Bekkerman, H. Raghavan, J. Allan, and K. Eguchi. Interactive clustering of text collections according to a user-specified criterion. In *IJCAI*, pages 684–689, 2007.

[2] R. Bekkerman, S. Zilberstein, and J. Allan. Web page clustering using heuristic search in the web graph. In *IJCAI*, pages 2280–2285. IJCAI, 2006.

[3] S. Boyd and L. Vandenberghe. *Convex Optimization*. Cambridge University Press, March 2004.

[4] S. Chen and C. Zhang. Selecting informative universum sample for semi-supervised learning. In *IJCAI*, pages 1016–1021, 2009.

[5] R. O. Duda, P. E. Hart, and D. G. Stork. *Pattern Classification (2nd Edition)*. Wiley-Interscience, 2 edition, November 2001.

[6] J. Gong and D. W. Oard. Selecting hierarchical clustering cut points for web person-name disambiguation. In *Proceedings of the 32nd international ACM SIGIR conference on*

Research and development in information retrieval, SIGIR '09, pages 778–779, New York, NY, USA, 2009. ACM.
[7] J. He, E. J. Meij, and M. de Rijke. Result diversification based on query-specific cluster ranking. *Journal of the American Society of Information Science and Technology*, 2011. To appear.
[8] T. Hofmann. Probabilistic latent semantic indexing. In *SIGIR*, pages 50–57, 1999.
[9] K. Huang, Z. Xu, I. King, and M. R. Lyu. Semi-supervised learning from general unlabeled data. In *ICDM*, pages 273–282, 2008.
[10] T. Joachims. Training linear svms in linear time. In *KDD*, pages 217–226, 2006.
[11] J. Kelley Jr. The cutting-plane method for solving convex programs. *Journal of the SIAM*, pages 703–712, 1960.
[12] D. D. Lewis, Y. Yang, T. G. Rose, and F. Li. Rcv1: A new benchmark collection for text categorization research. *Journal of Machine Learning Research*, 5:361–397, 2004.
[13] Q. Li, B. M. Kim, and S.-H. Myaeng. Clustering for probabilistic model estimation for cf. In *WWW (Special interest tracks and posters)*, pages 1104–1105, 2005.
[14] X. Liu, Y. Gong, W. Xu, and S. Zhu. Document clustering with cluster refinement and model selection capabilities. In *SIGIR*, pages 191–198, 2002.
[15] C. D. Manning, P. Raghavan, and H. Schütze. *Introduction to Information Retrieval.* Cambridge University Press, 1 edition, July 2008.
[16] C. H. Papadimitriou and K. Steiglitz. *Combinatorial Optimization : Algorithms and Complexity.* Dover Publications, July 1998.
[17] W. M. Rand. Objective Criteria for the Evaluation of Clustering Methods. *Journal of the American Statistical Association*, 66(336):846–850, 1971.
[18] N. Sahoo, J. Callan, R. Krishnan, G. T. Duncan, and R. Padman. Incremental hierarchical clustering of text documents. In *CIKM*, pages 357–366, 2006.
[19] J. Shi and J. Malik. Normalized cuts and image segmentation. *IEEE Trans. Pattern Anal. Mach. Intell.*, 22(8):888–905, 2000.
[20] F. H. Sinz, O. Chapelle, A. Agarwal, and B. Schölkopf. An analysis of inference with the universum. In *NIPS*, 2007.
[21] M. Spitters and W. Kraaij. Unsupervised clustering in multilingual news streams. In *LREC 2002 workshoop: Event Modelling for Multilingual Document Linking*, pages 42–46, 2002.
[22] A. Strehl and J. Ghosh. Cluster ensembles — a knowledge reuse framework for combining multiple partitions. *Journal of Machine Learning Research*, 3:583–617, 2002.
[23] T. Tao and C. Zhai. A mixture clustering model for pseudo feedback in information retrieval. In *IFCS*, 2004.
[24] C. H. Teo, S. V. N. Vishwanathan, A. J. Smola, and Q. V. Le. Bundle methods for regularized risk minimization. *Journal of Machine Learning Research*, 11:311–365, 2010.
[25] H. Valizadegan and R. Jin. Generalized maximum margin clustering and unsupervised kernel learning. In *NIPS*, pages 1417–1424, 2006.
[26] A. S. Vishwanathan, A. J. Smola, and S. V. N. Vishwanathan. Kernel methods for missing variables. In *AISTAT*, pages 325–332, 2005.
[27] F. Wang, C. Zhang, and T. Li. Regularized clustering for documents. In *SIGIR*, pages 95–102, 2007.
[28] J. Weston, R. Collobert, F. H. Sinz, L. Bottou, and V. Vapnik. Inference with the universum. In *ICML*, pages 1009–1016, 2006.
[29] E. P. Xing, A. Y. Ng, M. I. Jordan, and S. J. Russell. Distance metric learning with application to clustering with side-information. In *NIPS*, pages 505–512, 2002.
[30] L. Xu, J. Neufeld, B. Larson, and D. Schuurmans. Maximum margin clustering. In *NIPS*, 2004.
[31] W. Xu, X. Liu, and Y. Gong. Document clustering based on non-negative matrix factorization. In *SIGIR*, pages 267–273, 2003.
[32] H. Yang and J. P. Callan. Near-duplicate detection by instance-level constrained clustering. In *SIGIR*, pages 421–428. ACM, 2006.
[33] S. X. Yu and J. Shi. Multiclass spectral clustering. In *ICCV*, pages 313–319, 2003.
[34] L. Zelnik-Manor and P. Perona. Self-tuning spectral clustering. In *NIPS*, 2004.
[35] D. Zhang, J. Wang, F. Wang, and C. Zhang. Semi-supervised classification with universum. In *SDM*, pages 323–333, 2008.
[36] B. Zhao, F. Wang, and C. Zhang. Efficient multiclass maximum margin clustering. In *ICML*, pages 1248–1255, 2008.

APPENDIX

A. EFFICIENT OPTIMIZATION

Formulation (13) is a standard quadratic programming subproblem for the t-th CCCP iteration. But if the number of constraints, i.e., the number of target examples and Universum examples, is huge, it would be very time consuming to solve this problem. Some of the previous large scale optimization methods can be adapted to solve this problem, such as [10] and [24]. In this section, inspired by [10], the cutting plane method [11], which has shown its effectiveness and efficiency in solving similar tasks, is suggested to solve this subproblem. But different from [10], which is mainly designed for optimization problems with only one set of constraints, in this paper, we propose a novel optimization method – Two-View Cutting Plane method that can be used to solve the optimization problem with two different sets of constrains, as is the case in problem (13).

Similar to [10], problem (13) is first transformed to the following equivalent form:

$$\min_{\tilde{\mathbf{w}},\xi\geq 0,\xi^*\geq 0} \quad \frac{1}{2}\|\tilde{\mathbf{w}}\|^2 + C_l\xi + C_u\xi^* \tag{16}$$

$$s.t. \quad \forall \mathbf{c} \in \{0,1\}^{n\times k}$$

$$\tilde{\mathbf{w}}^T \frac{1}{nk}\sum_{i=1}^{n}\sum_{r=1}^{k} \mathbf{c}_{ir}(\mathbf{x}_{i(u_i^{(t)})} - \mathbf{x}_{i(r)}) \geq \frac{1}{nk}\sum_{i=1}^{n}\sum_{r=1}^{k}\mathbf{c}_{ir} - \xi$$

$$\forall \mathbf{d} \in \{0,1\}^N$$

$$\frac{k}{N(k-1)}\sum_{i=1}^{N}\mathbf{d}_i(\tilde{\mathbf{w}}^T\mathbf{x}^*_{i(u_i^{*(t)})} - mean_b\{\tilde{\mathbf{w}}^T\mathbf{x}^*_{i(b)}\}) \leq \xi^* + \frac{\epsilon_1}{N}\sum_{i=1}^{N}\mathbf{d}_i$$

$$\forall p,q \in \{1,2,\ldots,k\}, \quad -l \leq \tilde{\mathbf{w}}^T\sum_{i=1}^{n}(\mathbf{x}_{i(p)} - \mathbf{x}_{i(q)}) \leq l$$

ξ and ξ^* are two newly introduced variables, where $\xi = \frac{1}{nk}\sum_{i=1}^{n}\sum_{r=1}^{k}\xi_{ir}$ and $\xi^* = \frac{1}{N}\sum_{i=1}^{N}\xi_i^*$. By doing this, the number of variables that need to be optimized is further reduced by $(n \times k + N - 2)$. However, it contains a large number of constraints. Fortunately, we don't need to take all of these constraints into account. to solve the problem, the cutting plane algorithm is adapted to find two polynomially sized subset of constraints Ω and Ω^* from the whole set of constraints $\{0,1\}^{n\times k}$ and $\{0,1\}^N$ respectively in problem (16). In particular, the constraint sets Ω and Ω^* are initially set to be empty, and are built step by step until the solution of the relaxed problem satisfies all the constraints up to the two cutting plane precisions ϵ_3 and ϵ_4, i.e., $\forall \mathbf{c} \in \{0,1\}^{n\times k}$,

$$\tilde{\mathbf{w}}^T \frac{1}{nk}\sum_{i=1}^{n}\sum_{r=1}^{k} \mathbf{c}_{ir}(\mathbf{x}_{i(u_i^{(t)})} - \mathbf{x}_{i(r)}) \geq \frac{1}{nk}\sum_{i=1}^{n}\sum_{r=1}^{k}\mathbf{c}_{ir} - (\xi + \epsilon_3) \tag{17}$$

and $\forall \mathbf{d} \in \{0,1\}^N$,

$$\frac{k}{N(k-1)} \sum_{i=1}^{N} \mathbf{d}_i(\widetilde{\mathbf{w}}^T \mathbf{x}^*_{i(u_i^{*(t)})} - mean_b\{\widetilde{\mathbf{w}}^T \mathbf{x}^*_{i(b)}\})$$
$$\leq \xi^* + \epsilon_4 + \frac{\epsilon_1}{N} \sum_{i=1}^{N} \mathbf{d}_i \tag{18}$$

It means, the remaining exponential number of the two sets of constraints will not be violated up to the precision ϵ_3 and ϵ_4 respectively. Therefore, we don't need to explicitly add them to Ω and Ω^*.

The cutting plane algorithm starts with two empty sets of constraints Ω and Ω^* as follows:

$$\min_{\widetilde{\mathbf{w}}, \xi \geq 0, \xi_i^* \geq 0} \quad \frac{1}{2}\|\widetilde{\mathbf{w}}\|^2 + C_l \xi + C_u \xi^* \tag{19}$$
$$s.t. \quad \forall p, q \in \{1, 2, \ldots, k\}$$
$$-l \leq \widetilde{\mathbf{w}}^T \sum_{i=1}^{n} (\mathbf{x}_{i(p)} - \mathbf{x}_{i(q)}) \leq l$$

After getting the solution $\widetilde{\mathbf{w}}^{(t_0)}$ [9] of the above optimization problem, the most violated constraints can be computed as:

$$\mathbf{c}_{ir}^{t_0} = \begin{cases} 1, & \texttt{if } (\widetilde{\mathbf{w}}^{t_0})^T \mathbf{x}_{i(u_i^{(t)})} - (\widetilde{\mathbf{w}}^{t_0})^T \mathbf{x}_{i(r)} \leq 1 \\ 0, & \texttt{otherwise} \end{cases} \tag{20}$$

and

$$\mathbf{d}_i^{t_0} = \begin{cases} 1, & \texttt{if } (\widetilde{\mathbf{w}}^{t_0})^T \mathbf{x}^*_{i(u_i^{*(t)})} - mean_b\{(\widetilde{\mathbf{w}}^{t_0})^T \mathbf{x}^*_{i(b)}\} \geq \epsilon_1 \\ 0, & \texttt{otherwise} \end{cases} \tag{21}$$

Then, $\mathbf{c}^{t_0}$ will be added to Ω if H^{t_0} is true, and $\mathbf{d}^{t_0}$ will be added to Ω^* if H^{*t_0} is true. Here, H^{t_s} is used to denote the condition $(\widetilde{\mathbf{w}}^{(t_s)})^T \frac{1}{nk} \sum_{i,r} \mathbf{c}_{ir}^{t_s}(\mathbf{x}_{i(u_i^{(t)})} - \mathbf{x}_{i(r)}) \leq \frac{1}{nk} \sum_{i,r} \mathbf{c}_{ir}^{t_s} - (\xi^{(t_s)} + \epsilon_3)$, and H^{*t_s} indicates whether $\frac{k}{N(k-1)} \sum_{i=1}^{N} \mathbf{d}_i^{t_s}(\widetilde{\mathbf{w}}^T \mathbf{x}^*_{i(u_i^{*(t)})} - mean_b\{\widetilde{\mathbf{w}}^T \mathbf{x}^*_{i(b)}\}) \geq \xi^{*(t_s)} + \epsilon_4 + \frac{\epsilon_1}{N} \sum_{i=1}^{N} \mathbf{d}_i^{t_s}$ holds or not. After updating Ω and Ω^*, the optimization problem becomes:

$$\min_{\widetilde{\mathbf{w}}, \xi \geq 0, \xi^* \geq 0} \quad \frac{1}{2}\|\widetilde{\mathbf{w}}\|^2 + C_l \xi + C_u \xi^* \tag{22}$$
$$s.t. \quad \forall \mathbf{c} \in \Omega,$$
$$\widetilde{\mathbf{w}}^T \frac{1}{nk} \sum_{i=1}^{n} \sum_{r=1}^{k} \mathbf{c}_{ir}(\mathbf{x}_{i(u_i^{(t)})} - \mathbf{x}_{i(r)}) \geq \frac{1}{nk} \sum_{i=1}^{n} \sum_{r=1}^{k} \mathbf{c}_{ir} - \xi$$
$$\forall \mathbf{d} \in \Omega^*,$$
$$\frac{k}{N(k-1)} \sum_{i=1}^{N} \mathbf{d}_i(\widetilde{\mathbf{w}}^T \mathbf{x}^*_{i(u_i^{*(t)})} - mean_b\{\widetilde{\mathbf{w}}^T \mathbf{x}^*_{i(b)}\})$$
$$\leq \xi^* + \frac{\epsilon_1}{N} \sum_{i=1}^{N} \mathbf{d}_i$$
$$\forall p, q \in \{1, 2, \ldots, k\}, \quad -l \leq \widetilde{\mathbf{w}}^T \sum_{i=1}^{n} (\mathbf{x}_{i(p)} - \mathbf{x}_{i(q)}) \leq l$$

[9]Throughout this paper, t_s is used to denote the s-th iteration of the cutting plane iteration for solving the problem derived from the t-th CCCP iteration.

Algorithm: Two-View Cutting Plane

Input:
1. Problem (13).
2. Cutting Plane precision for View 1: $\epsilon_3 = 0.01$, for View 2: $\epsilon_4 = 0.01$

Output:
The cluster hyperplane $\widetilde{\mathbf{w}}^{(t)}$ and the objective function value $J^{(t)}$

1. $s = -1$. $\Omega = \emptyset$, $\Omega^* = \emptyset$, $H^{t_s} =$ true, $H^{*t_s} =$ true
2. **while** $H^{t_s} | H^{*t_s}$ is true **do**
3. $\quad s = s + 1$
4. $\quad$ Get $(\widetilde{\mathbf{w}}^{(t_s)}, \xi^{(t_s)}, \xi^{*(t_s)})$ by solving (22) under Ω and Ω^*.
5. $\quad$ Compute the most violated constraints, i.e., $\mathbf{c}_{ir}^{t_s}$ and $\mathbf{d}_i^{t_s}$, by

$$\mathbf{c}_{ir}^{t_s} = \begin{cases} 1, \texttt{ if } (\widetilde{\mathbf{w}}^{(t_s)})^T \mathbf{x}_{i(u_i^{(t)})} - (\widetilde{\mathbf{w}}^{(t_s)})^T \mathbf{x}_{i(r)} \leq 1 \\ 0, \texttt{ otherwise} \end{cases}$$

and

$$\mathbf{d}_i^{t_s} = \begin{cases} 1, \texttt{ if } (\widetilde{\mathbf{w}}^{t_s})^T (\mathbf{x}^*_{i(u_i^{*(t)})} - mean_b\{\mathbf{x}^*_{i(b)}\}) \geq \epsilon_1 \\ 0, \texttt{ otherwise} \end{cases}$$

6. $\quad$ Update H^{t_s} and H^{*t_s}.
7. $\quad$ If H^{t_s} is true, then update the constraint set Ω by $\Omega = \Omega \bigcup \mathbf{c}^{t_s}$; If H^{*t_s} is true, then update the constraint set Ω^* by $\Omega^* = \Omega^* \bigcup \mathbf{d}^{t_s}$
8. **end while**
9. $\widetilde{\mathbf{w}}^{(t)} = \widetilde{\mathbf{w}}^{t_s}$
10. $J^{(t)} = \frac{1}{2}\|\widetilde{\mathbf{w}}^{(t)}\|^2 + C_l \xi^{(t_s)} + C_u \xi^{*(t_s)}$

Table 7: Algorithm description: Two-View Cutting Plane. It can be used to solve the step 6 in Table 1 efficiently.

Both Ω and Ω^* contain at most one constraint vector at this time. From this updated optimization problem, we can get the solution $\widetilde{\mathbf{w}}^{(t_1)}$. Then, the constraints $\mathbf{c}^{t_1}$ and $\mathbf{d}^{t_1}$ can be computed similarly as that in Eq.(20) and Eq.(21), where the only difference is that $\widetilde{\mathbf{w}}^{(t_0)}$ would be replaced by $\widetilde{\mathbf{w}}^{(t_1)}$. The procedure is repeated until all of the constraints satisfy the requirement in Eq.(17) and Eq.(18), i.e., both H^{t_s} and H^{*t_s} are false. In this way, a successive strengthening approximation series of the problem (13) can be constructed by the expanding number of cutting plane procedures that cut off the current optimal solution from the feasible set [11].

The concrete procedure is summarized in Table 7. In Step 4, the problem can also be solved efficiently through the dual form [3], since there are only a few constraints involved. Here, due to the limit of space, the concrete dual form is omitted.

It is clear that the Two-View Cutting Plane algorithm is an iterative method. One of the nice properties of employing this method is the guaranteed fast convergence rate as can be derived similar to that in [10]. So, the algorithm will converge with polynomial number of constraints in a linear time, and therefore is much faster than directly solving the optimization problem (13).

Identifying Points of Interest by Self-Tuning Clustering

Yiyang Yang [1] Zhiguo Gong [2] Leong Hou U [3]
Department of Computer and Information Science
University of Macau
Macau
[1]ya97405@umac.mo [2]fstzgg@umac.mo [3]ryanlhu@umac.mo

ABSTRACT

Deducing trip related information from web-scale datasets has received very large amounts of attention recently. Identifying points of interest (POIs) in geo-tagged photos is one of these problems. The problem can be viewed as a standard clustering problem of partitioning two dimensional objects. In this work, we study spectral clustering which is the first attempt for the POIs identification. However, there is no unified approach to assign the clustering parameters; especially the features of POIs are immensely varying in different metropolitans and locations. To address this, we are intent to study a self-tuning technique which can properly assign the parameters for the clustering needed.

Besides geographical information, web photos inherently store rich information. These information are mutually influenced each others and should be taken into trip related mining tasks. To address this, we study reinforcement which constructs the relationship over multiple sources by iterative learning. At last, we thoroughly demonstrate our findings by web scale datasets collected from Flickr.

Categories and Subject Descriptors

H.3.3 [**Information Search and Retrieval**]: Clustering; H.2.8 [**Database Applications**]: Data Mining, Image Databases, Spatial Databases and GIS

General Terms

Algorithms, Experimentation

Keywords

Web Images, Spectral Clustering

1. INTRODUCTION

In Web 2.0, people are easily to share diverse types of resources with other people. Web album is one example that people can share their photos with others. In many web album services, people not only share the photos, but also provide relevant information, such as tags, titles, description, taken time, and taken location. Such a large amount of user-contributed data constitutes spatial, temporal, textual, and visual information that can be used for different mining tasks. Deducing trip related information from web photos [3, 5, 7, 12, 13, 14, 19, 20, 21, 22] has been an active topic recently. These works include mapping the photos, identifying places of interest, predicting user travel behavior, and itineraries planning.

In this work, we consider the collection of geo- and time-tagged photos on Flickr. The geographical location was automatically captured by location aware camera, mobile phone, or manually input by some tool in Flickr. Also, the taken time was automatically recorded into the photo metadata. There are currently over 121 million geo-tagged photos on Flickr while there were only 40 million as reported by [13] in 2008. With the advent of more location aware devices, there is no doubt that the number of geo-tagged photos on Flickr and other sites grows rapidly. These involve in substantial research work for web scale mining process.

Our goal in this work is to identify high quality points of interest (POIs) using collections of geo- and time-tagged photos. In particular, point of interest is characterized by activities of photos based on the meta data, such as taken time and geographical location. Some results are recently reported in the community. Kennedy and Naaman [13] identify POIs in a city by applying k-means clustering on geotagged photos. The identified POIs are subsequently ranked by textual and visual features. Crandall et al. [7] study a similar problem on finding POIs in web scale datasets. The authors replace k-means with mean shift [6] that is a popular clustering approach in image segmentation. Mean shift clustering requires a *density radius* for clustering process instead of specifying the number of clusters in advance. In [7], the authors set the density radius to 100 meters by *subjective observation*. Nevertheless, we argue that such radius setting should not be set subjectively since the sizes of POIs could be immensely varying in different metropolitans and locations. For instance, the sizes of famous POIs, such as *Eiffel Tower*, *Musée du Louvre*, and *Arc de Triomphe*, in Paris are immensely varying as plotted in Figure 1. Besides k-means and mean shift clustering, Density-Based Spatial Clustering of Applications with Noise (DBSCAN) [8] is recently studied for POIs identification in [14]. However, the parameters in DBSCAN are not nature either. The detail of these clustering approaches are discussed in Section 2.

SIGIR'11, July 24–28, 2011, Beijing, China.
Copyright 2011 ACM 978-1-4503-0757-4/11/07 ...$10.00.

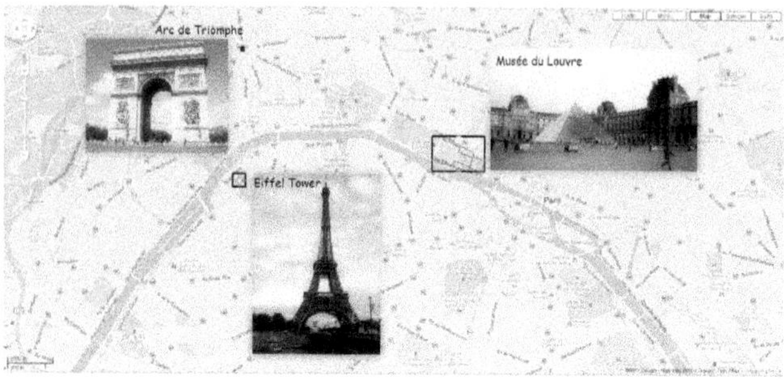

Figure 1: Famous POIs in Paris

Our first mission in this work is to remove *subjective* clustering parameters. Given a set of geo- and time-tagged photos, we propose a self-tuning clustering approach that can identify POIs neither knowing (1) the number of POIs, (2) the size of POIs, nor (3) the shape of POIs in advance. Our self-tuning clustering approach is based on *spectral* clustering [1, 23] which can be viewed as a grouping problem in graph theory. The set of objects in the features space are represented as a weighted undirected graph G, where the nodes are the objects and the edges are the relation between pairs of objects. In general, the weight on each edge is represented by the closeness in the features space. Spectral clustering then makes use of the spectrum of the graph similarity. It recursively seeks a bipartition of the dataset (i.e., done by various *cut* algorithms [1, 2, 4, 23, 24]) until all subsets fulfill the *termination criteria* (i.e., closeness of a dataset).

However, as discussed in the example (Figure 1), the sizes and densities of POIs are not necessarily identical in a city. There is no unified termination criteria for various POIs in different metropolitans or locations. We observe that the geo-tagged photos are Gaussian distributed in surrounding areas of an POI; and most likely the bi-partitions of the POI's photos follow the same distribution. Furthermore, we find that the costs to decompose a set of Gaussian distributed photos and its sub-sets are resembling. Therefore, if a cluster and its sub-clusters being created by spectral clustering have resembling costs, then the cluster is more likely an POI and should be preserved in the clustering result. The detail of our finding is introduced in Section 3.2.

Besides the parameters issues, the information being taken into the clustering process should be considered thoughtfully. Intuitively, web photos inherently have spatial and temporal information, such as taken location and time. Such information should be thoroughly participated in the clustering process. In this work, we attempt to integrate these information by *reinforcement* [15, 9] which is a well accepted method for analyzing richly structured data. In our reinforcement model, every pair of photos is appraised based on their distance (*spatial*), visit sequence (*temporal*), and region density (*spatial*). The detail of the model is discussed in Section 4.

We summarize our contributions as the following:

1. We attempt to identify POIs using non-subjective parameters. This is significant since the POIs features are immensely varying in different metropolitans and locations and there is no unified approaches to define the parameters appropriately.
2. We connect spatial and temporal information by reinforcement. Other types of information can be integrated into the reinforcement model after specific study.
3. We give a complete survey on POIs identification and thoroughly compare the state-of-the-art to our self-tuning approach by web scale datasets. In addition, we evaluate our reinforcement model and study its behavior in the experiments.

The rest of this paper is organized as follows. We first overview and compare the state of the art POIs identification in Section 2. Next, we discuss spectral clustering and our features similarity measurement in Section 3. Our reinforcement model is introduced in Section 4. It calculates the pairwise relationship of the photos based on their spatial and temporal features. Our approaches are thoroughly evaluated in Section 6 using web scale datasets collected from Flickr. Before we conclude our work and discuss possible future work in Section 8, we also introduce some related work in deducing trip related information in Section 7.

2. CLUSTERING TECHNIQUES FOR POIS IDENTIFICATION

Finding POIs from a collection of geo-tagged photos can be viewed as a clustering problem of identifying highly photographed locations. Kennedy and Naaman [13] use k-means clustering to identify famous locations using collections of geo-tagged photos. k-means clustering aims to partition n objects into k clusters such that each object belongs to the cluster with the nearest mean. The objective function can be formulated in the following equation.

$$minimize \sum_{1 \leq i \leq k} \sum_{o \in C_i} ||o - \mu_i||^2 \quad (1)$$

where C_i is one of the k clusters and μ_i is the centroid of C_i. Finding the exact solution of k-means is a NP-hard problem. The most common heuristic algorithm uses an interactive refinement technique. First the algorithm randomly selects k objects as initial means (i.e., the centroids of k clusters). Then the clustering proceeds by alternating between the following steps. (1) Every object is assigned to the closest mean. (2) Update the mean of each cluster to the centroid of the objects. The clustering process is terminated when the means no longer change. However, k-means clustering is a fixed-clustering approach which is problematic for POIs identification since the number and sizes of POIs are not known in advance. There is no appropriate rule to decide the value of k for different metropolitans and locations.

To address the problem of fixed-clustering approaches, Crandall et al. [7] study mean shift clustering [6] that supports arbitrary size and arbitrary number of clusters. Given a kernel function, mean shift locates the maxima by sampling discrete data from the function. It is a non-parametric feature-space technique since the clustering result depends on a kernel function other than some parameters. Broadly speaking, the mean shift clustering is an iterative process. At each iteration, every object o moves towards to a mean location where the mean is computed by a kernel function f_K and the nearby objects o_N. The kernel function f_K could be a typical Uniform kernel (i.e., $f_U(o_N - o) = 1$) or Gaussian kernel (i.e., $f_G(o_N - o) = \frac{1}{\sqrt{2\pi\sigma^2}} e^{-\frac{\|o_N - o\|^2}{2\sigma^2}}$). Accordingly, the mean is estimated by

$$\mu = \frac{\sum_{o_N \in N(o)} f_K(o_N - o) o_N}{\sum_{o_N \in N(o)} f_K(o_N - o)} \quad (2)$$

where $N(o)$ is the neighborhood of o and μ is the new mean estimated by the kernel function. We replace o by μ and iteratively do the mean estimation until μ converges to o. Finally, the objects share the same converge point should be grouped into a cluster.

However, mean shift is not completely parametric free while there is a bandwidth parameter for locating neighborhood (i.e., $N(o)$). The neighborhood of o is a set of objects for which k nearest objects (Uniform kernel) or $\|o_N - o\| \leq \eta$ (Gaussian kernel), where k and η are the neighborhood bandwidth. The clustering quality is substantially affected by the bandwidth which can be viewed as the *influential area* of an object. Every object moves towards the mean in the influential area at each iteration.

Both k-means and mean shift are *mean*-based clustering approaches since they share the same thesis behind. The only difference is that k-means has fixed number of means; while the number is varying on the kernel function and the corresponding influential area in mean shift. Their differences are demonstrated in Figure 2. Suppose k is set to 2 and the initial locations of μ_1 and μ_2 are shown in Figure 2(a). The changes of μ_1 and μ_2 are illustrated by the arcs. Two clusters ($\{a, b, c\}$ and $\{d, e, f\}$) are formed based on the converge locations of μ_1 and μ_2. In contrast to k-means, mean shift does not know the number of means in advance. Every object is moved towards to the mean according to the objects in their influential area, e.g., the influential area of object c is illustrated by a dash circle in Figure 2(b). In this example, all objects are converged to μ and grouped into one cluster.

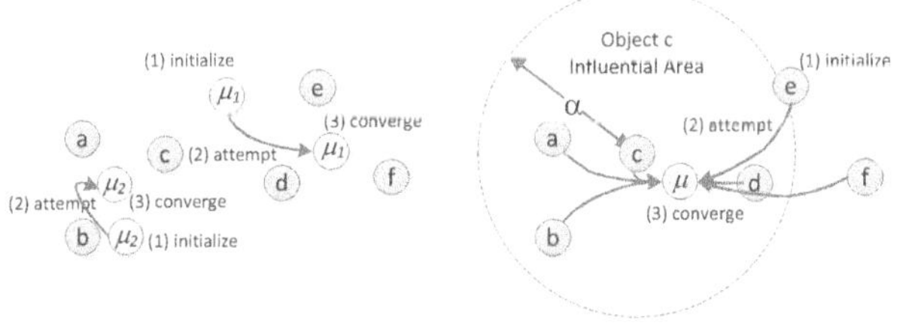

(a) k-means (b) Mean shift

Figure 2: k-means versus mean shift

Besides mean-based clustering approaches, Density-Based Spatial Clustering of Applications with Noise (DBSCAN) [8] is another popular clustering technique. Kisilevich et al. [14] recently analyze places and events in a collection of geo-tagged photos using DBSCAN. Basically, DBSCAN is based on notion of density reachability. An object o is *directly* density reachable from another object o' if it is not farther away than a given density radius ε and o' is surrounded more than θ objects. o is called density reachable from o'' if there is a directly density reachable sequence of objects from o to o''. Consequently, the objects are grouped into a cluster if they are density reachable.

A common DBSCAN algorithm is demonstrated by Figure 3(a). First, the algorithm randomly selects an object and form a range search with radius ε. In this example, object c is selected and objects a, b, and d are discovered by the range search. Suppose θ is set to 2, only d is directly density reachable from c. Consequently, we form a range search for d and iteratively discover subsequent density reachable objects. In this example, only one cluster is formed since all objects are density reachable from object c.

DBSCAN clustering works with generic points having a unified density threshold for all clusters; however, POIs may have varying sizes and density as discussed in Section 1. Kisilevich et al. [14] figure out this problem and propose P-DBSCAN where an adaptive density technique is added into the directly density reachable definition. In P-DBSCAN, an object o is directly density reachable from another object o' if it is not farther away than a given density radius ε and the ratio of surrounding objects between o and o' must be less than a density ratio ω.

P-DBSCAN is demonstrated by Figure 3(b). Suppose θ and ω are set to 2 and 0.3, respectively, object c is the first selected object to construct a cluster. According to the revised definition, object d is no longer directly density reachable from c since the ratio of the surrounding objects between c and d is higher than ω, i.e., $|(2-3)/3| \approx 0.33 \geq \omega$. The cluster constitutes only $\{a, b, c, d\}$. Next, the algorithm selects another object (i.e., k) and iteratively find density reachable objects. For instance, object h is directly density reachable from k, i.e., $|(6-5)/5| = 0.2 < \omega$. Accordingly, objects $\{g, h, i, j, k, l, m\}$ are grouped into the second cluster. In this example, P-DBSCAN forms better clusters since it takes local density into account. However, the effect of parameters ε, θ, and ω is never studied for POIs identification.

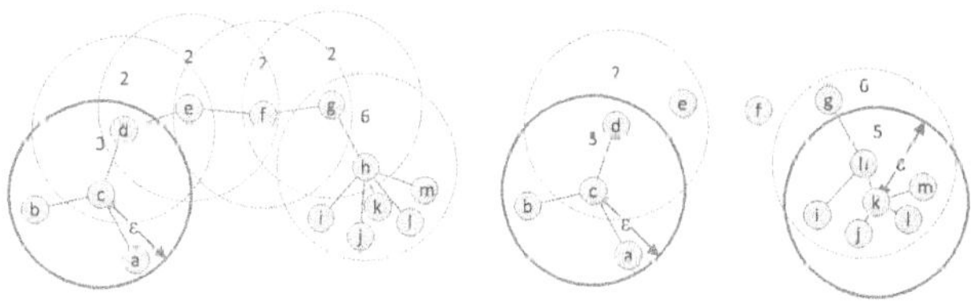

(a) DBSCAN (b) P-DBSCAN

Figure 3: DBSCAN versus P-DBSCAN

3. CUT TECHNIQUES FOR POIS IDENTIFICATION

In recent years, spectral clustering [1, 2, 4, 23] has evolved into one of the most common clustering methods and has been widely applied in many applications. However, it has not yet developed for POIs identification. Roughly speaking, spectral clustering is a hierarchical clustering technique which iteratively seeks a bipartition of a set of objects until all sub-partitions fulfill the termination criteria. The bipartition can be computed by various *cut* techniques, such as ratio cut [24], normalized cut [11, 23], and Cheeger cut [1, 2].

In graph theory, a *cut* is to remove some edges from a graph such that the graph is isolated into two subgraphs subject to an objective function. Let $G = (V, E)$ be an undirected graph with edge weight w_{ij} for edges e_{ij}. For $V_s, \bar{V_s} \subset V$, let $C(V_s, \bar{V_s})$ be the weight sum of edges between V_s and $\bar{V_s}$, i.e., $\sum_{i \in V_s, j \in \bar{V_s}} w_{ij}$. The objective and complexity of the *cut* techniques are summarized in Table 1.

Table 1: List of *cut* techniques

Name	Objective	Complexity
Ratio cut	$\min_{V_s \subset V} \frac{C(V_s, \bar{V_s})}{\lvert V_s \rvert}$	NP-hard
Normalized cut	$\min_{V_s \subset V} \frac{C(V_s, \bar{V_s})}{C(V_s, V)} + \frac{C(V_s, \bar{V_s})}{C(\bar{V_s}, V)}$	NP-hard
Cheeger cut	$\min_{V_s \subset V} \frac{C(V_s, \bar{V_s})}{\min\{C(V_s, V), C(\bar{V_s}, V)\}}$	NP-hard

The *cut* problem is known to be equivalent to a quadratic discrete optimization problem, *Rayleigh* problem, where the optimization objective is shown in Equation 3.

$$\min_{y^T Q 1 = 0, y_i \in \{-b, 1\}} \frac{y^T \mathcal{L} y}{y^T Q y} \tag{3}$$

where y is a vector having n variables, $\mathcal{L} = W^D - W$ is referred as the *Laplacian* of the graph, W is referred as the weight matrix of the graph, W^D is a diagonal matrix with $W^D_{ii} = \sum_{(i,j) \in E} w_{ij}$, and Q is a diagonal non-negative matrix which is set differently according to the *cut* technique. For example, Q is set to I in ratio cut and is set to W^D in normalized cut.

In general, *Rayleigh's* optimization is an NP-hard problem. A common approach to solve such optimization is to relax the integral constraints, such as replacing $y_i \in \{-b, 1\}$ by $y_i \in [-b, 1]$. In spectral clustering, the relaxation is done by solving an eigenvector problem which is a looser relaxation than relaxing the integrality requirement. For each *cut* technique, there is a corresponding eigenvector problem for the relaxation. Due to the page limitation, we only introduce the normalized cut in the paper.

Algorithm 1 is a general normalized cut clustering framework. After we construct all necessary matrices in the first two steps, the second smallest eigenvalue λ and the corresponding eigenvector $\mathcal{V}$ can be computed by Lanczos algorithm [10] in step 3. Note that this is the only step to be replaced if we change the cut technique. Based on the previous study [23], the second smallest eigenvalue λ can be viewed as the minimum *cost* to decompose the graph subject to the corresponding objective function. The graph is decomposed into two if the cost λ is smaller than the threshold δ. The decomposition is done by picking a value v (e.g., medium) in the corresponding eigenvector $\mathcal{V}$. The elements in the eigenvector are accordingly split into two groups where the first group contains all elements having better value than v and the second group contains the remaining elements. Note that the selection of v is substantial to the decomposition. Thereby, we try multiple v and pick the best one (i.e., maximize the objective function) such that the decomposition is optimized. Even though spectral clustering is widely used and shown good result in many applications, it does not fulfill the requirement of POIs identification due to the subjective threshold δ.

The input of spectral clustering is a weight matrix W. In general, we can construct W by Euclidean distances of photos. However, we observe that the photos are not uniformly distributed especially inside an POI. Figure 4(a) and 4(b) plot the photos distribution for *Eiffel Tower* and *Musée du Louvre*. In these examples, the photos are more likely in Gaussian distribution.

Algorithm 1 Spectral Clustering by Normalized Cut

Algorithm $SC_{NC}(W$:the weight matrix of the graph)
1: compute diagonal matrix W^D
2: compute Laplacian matrix $\mathcal{L}$ by W and W^D
3: **compute the second smallest eigenvalue** λ **and the corresponding eigenvector** $\mathcal{V}$ **of eigenvector problem** $\mathcal{L}y = \lambda D y$
4: **if** the eigenvalue λ is smaller than threshold δ **then**
5: decompose the graph into W_l and W_h according to $\mathcal{V}$
6: call $SC_{NC}(W_l)$ and $SC_{NC}(W_h)$

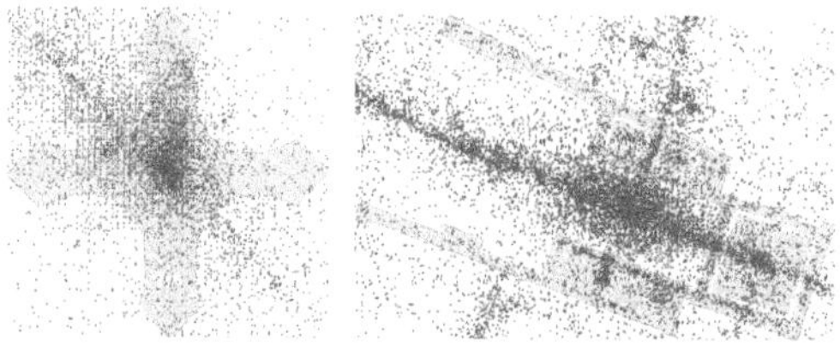

(a) Eiffel Tower (b) Musée du Louvre

Figure 4: Visualization of photos distribution

We denote the distance relationship as $D = [D_{ij}]_{n \times n}$, where i and j are two different photos. According to above discussion, D_{ij} is defined by a Gaussian equation as shown in Equation 4.

$$D_{ij} = \frac{1}{\sqrt{2\pi\sigma^2}} e^{-\frac{\|i-j\|^2}{2\sigma^2}} \tag{4}$$

where σ^2 is the variance of the Gaussian function.

3.1 Comparison of Variant Clustering

In this section, we demonstrate the parametric issues using a real dataset collected by Flickr API.[1] The dataset is a Paris photos collection having 216,092 geo-tagged photos in total. The detail of our data preparation can be found in Section 6. All figures are generated by our modified version of Java OpenStreetMap Editor [2] which is a map editor for OpenStreetMap [3] written in Java. For the ease of presentation, we highlight the clusters by different colors such that the size and shape of the clusters are clearly illustrated in the figures. Besides, we also plot the minimum bounding rectangles (MBRs) of tourist attractions for reference, where the tourist attractions are collected from the metadata of OpenStreetMap.

The parameters of k-means, mean shift, and P-DBSCAN are set to their default values as reported in the state-of-the-art [13, 7, 14]. For k-means, we set k to 100. For mean shift, we use Gaussian kernel with $\sigma^2 = 0.2$ and set η (influential area) to $100m$. Regarding P-DBSCAN, we set ω (density ratio), θ (minimum number of objects), and ε (density radius) to 0.1, 50, and $100m$, respectively. Also, we carefully study the effect of threshold δ for spectral clustering and set δ to the best value 0.6.

[1]http://www.flickr.com/services/api/
[2]http://josm.openstreetmap.de/
[3]http://www.openstreetmap.org/

The results are shown in Figure 5. Some attraction areas are precisely identified by these clustering approaches. For instance, the world famous POIs Eiffel Tower and Musée du Louvre are identified very well by P-DBSCAN in Figure 5(c) and spectral clustering in Figure 5(d), respectively. By carefully tuning these parameters, the clustering approaches could provide better identification. However, the tuning time might take very long and it is immensely varying in different metropolitans and locations. Besides the default values, we also illustrate other settings in Appendix. In summary, the parameters k (the number of clusters), η (influential area), ε (density radius), and δ (cut *cost* threshold) are quite significant and sensitive to the clustering quality of k-means, mean shift, DBSCAN, and spectral clustering, respectively.

3.2 Self-Tuning Spectral Clustering

To address the parameters issue, we develop a self-tuning technique that can eliminate the effect of threshold δ from spectral clustering. We attempt to refine spectral clustering since 1) the framework in Algorithm 1 is a hierarchical clustering so that each iteration is trackable and 2) the second smallest eigenvalue λ in each iteration can be viewed as the minimum *cost* to decompose the cluster. We do not have these properties in other clustering methods.

Consider the examples in Figure 4, the photos are Gaussian distributed in the POIs. Based on this observation, we create two sets of POI photos that are Gaussian distributed as shown in Figure 6(a). The photos are partitioned into 4 groups by spectral clustering and the *cuts* are shown by the solid and dash lines. We also show the hierarchical view of spectral clustering procedures in Figure 6(b).

Roughly speaking, the *cut* in spectral clustering seeks a balance decomposition subject to an objective function. Suppose that the solid line is the 1st cut in spectral clustering and the cut cost λ is 0.55 and δ is set to 0.5, the clustering procedure is terminated and perfectly identifies two POIs A and B. However, if δ is set to 0.85, then spectral clustering will execute two more cuts such that the photos are decomposed into 4 small clusters, A_1, A_2, B_1, and B_2. It is obvious that δ is substantial to spectral clustering. Besides, the cost to decompose A (λ=0.8) is similar to the cost to decompose A_1 (λ=0.85), but different from the cost to decompose $A \cup B$ (λ=0.55). It is because A and A_1 share resembling distribution. We summarize this finding in Observation 1.

OBSERVATION 1. *The cut costs of a cluster and its sub-clusters are resembling if the cluster is dense and Gaussian distributed.*

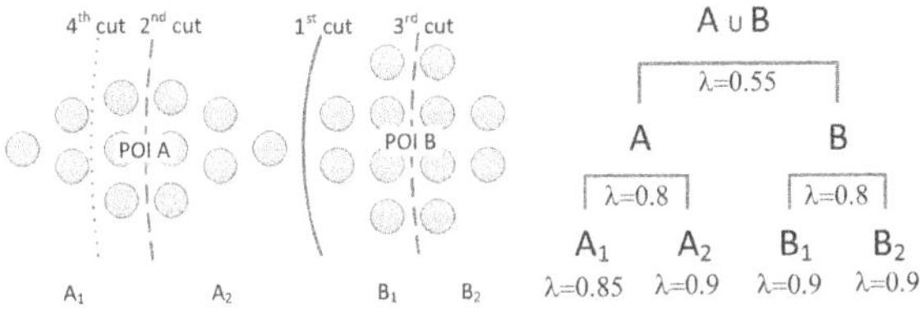

(a) Visualization of Cuts (b) Hierarchical View

Figure 6: Example of Spectral Clustering

We verify the observation using our Paris photos collection. Figure 7(a) shows the cut cost λ at different levels [4] of spectral clustering. The cut cost λ becomes very high (>1.8) and resembling after level 21. Also the costs drop a little bit after the peak due to the fluctuation of the cut costs of small clusters.

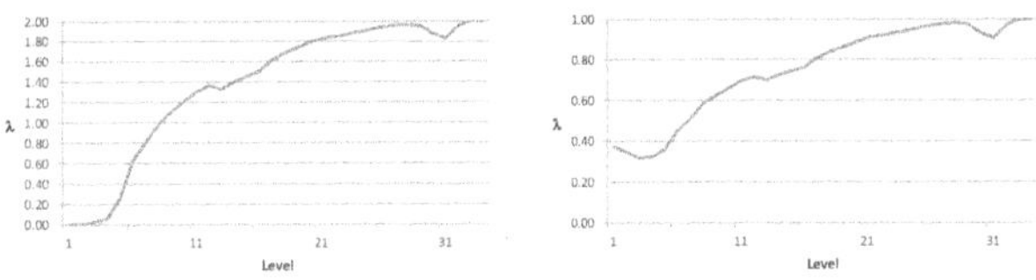

(a) Cut Cost, λ (b) Similarity

Figure 7: Statistics of Spectral Clustering

According to Observation 1, a cluster should be preserved in the result if the sub-clusters have resembling cut costs. Therefore, we propose a method to measure the costs similarity such that we can preserve the high quality clusters in the result. We first define a new concept, cut path p, in Definition 1.

DEFINITION 1 (CUT PATH). *Given the hierarchical structure of a spectral clustering, a cut path of a cluster C is the path from C to a leaf cluster.*

The cost of a cut path $cost(p)$ is the average cut cost among all nodes in the path which is denoted by Equation 5.

$$cost(p) = (\sum_{i \in p} i.\lambda)/size(p) \quad (5)$$

In Figure 6, the cost of cut path (A, A_1) is 0.825. Based on the cost of cut path, we define cut costs similarity in Definition 2.

DEFINITION 2 (CUT COSTS SIMILARITY). *Given the hierarchical structure of a spectral clustering, the similarity of a cluster C is defined in*

$$sim(C) = 1 - (\sum_{p \in P} |cost(p) - \mu_C|)/size(P) \quad (6)$$

where P is the set of cut paths of cluster C and μ_C is the mean cost of all cut paths in P.

In Figure 6, there are two paths from cluster A to the leave clusters which include $p_1 (= A \to A_1)$ and $p_2 (= A \to A_2)$. The average cost of these paths μ_A is $\frac{cost(p_1)+cost(p_2)}{2} =$ 0.8375. According to the equation in Definition 2, the cut cost similarity $sim(A)$ is 0.9875.

The value of the cut cost similarity $sim(C)$ can be viewed as the robustness of all sub-clusters under cluster C. Our strategy is to group the sub-clusters if $sim(C)$ is strong. We plot the average value of sim at different levels in Figure 7(b) as a reference. We observe that the similarity value drops after a local peak and the end levels are not stable due to the fluctuation of the cut costs of small clusters. Therefore, we identify the clusters using a top-down execution paradigm. Given a spectral clustering execution tree, a node is chosen

[4]The level is counted from top to bottom.

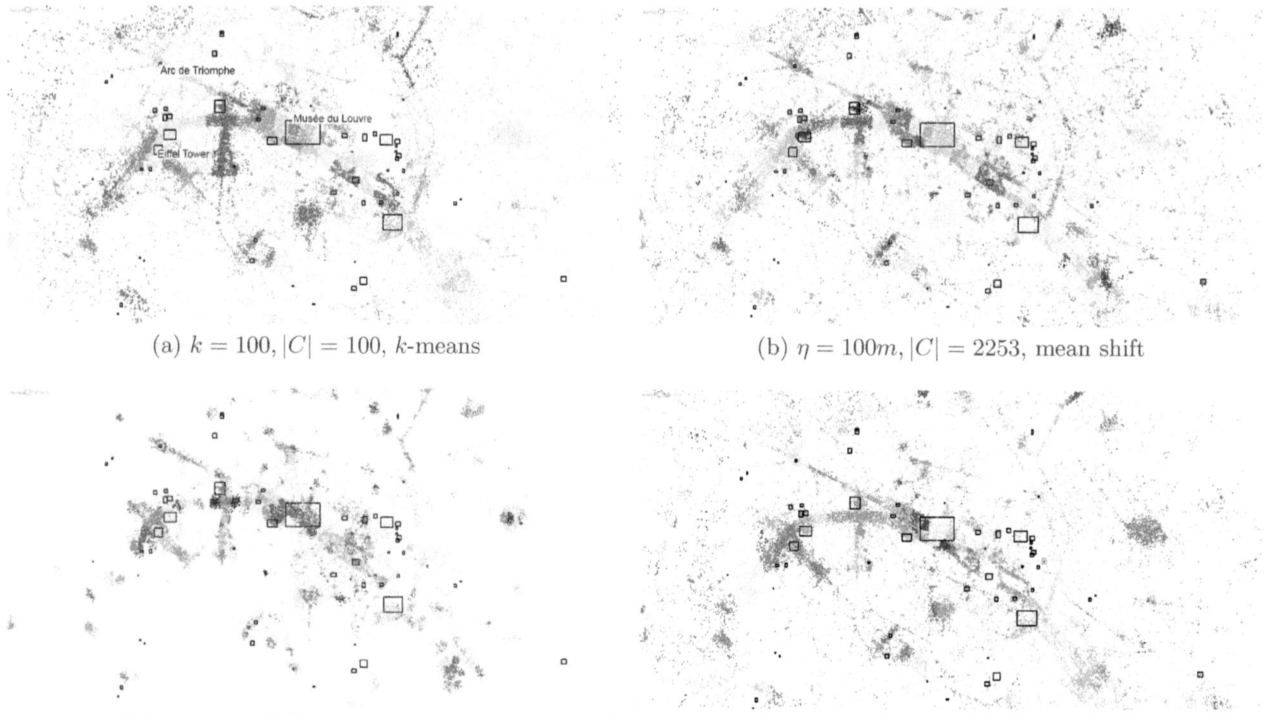

(a) $k = 100, |C| = 100$, k-means

(b) $\eta = 100m, |C| = 2253$, mean shift

(c) $\varepsilon = 100m, |C| = 528$, P-DBSCAN

(d) $\delta = 0.6, |C| = 1092$, normalized cut

Figure 5: Effect of default parameters in k-means, mean shift, P-DBSCAN, and normalized cut clustering

as a cluster result C if $sim(C)$ reaches to a good local peak. In this work, we simply set the local peak to the maximum value of the largest decreasing path. In other words, we group highly resembling sub-clusters into a larger cluster based on the similarity of their cut costs. The effectiveness of the self-tuning approach is shown in Section 6.

4. REINFORCEMENT

So far, the clustering approaches only take distance information into account. Apparently, there is room for improvement as web photos constitute rich information in spatial, temporal, textual, and visual aspects. However, there is no explicit guideline to connect these aspects. For POIs identification, the most common method is to perform clustering based on distance and subsequently refine the result by the information from other aspects [7, 13]. In other word, there are quite a lot affluent information not involved in the clustering process. This may affect the clustering quality as some trip related information (i.e., density and visit sequence are inherently recorded in web photos) are not involved in the clustering process. To be motivated by the discussion, we intend to study *reinforcement* which is a well accepted method for analyzing richly structured data [9, 25].

Consider the example in Figure 8, where we have 16 photos in the system. In Figure 8(a), we might form 2 clusters where the left cluster (in gray color) contains 12 photos and the right cluster (in white color) contains 4 photos if we only take pairwise distances information into account. If the temporal information are taken into account, we might have better result as demonstrated in Figure 8(b). The labels of the photos are represented the movement sequence of the photographers. For instance, the movement sequence of the photograph a is represented by four objects a_1, a_2, a_3, and a_4. By considering both pairwise distances and movement sequences, we might group left 8 photos into one cluster and group the remaining photos into another cluster as illustrated in Figure 8(b).

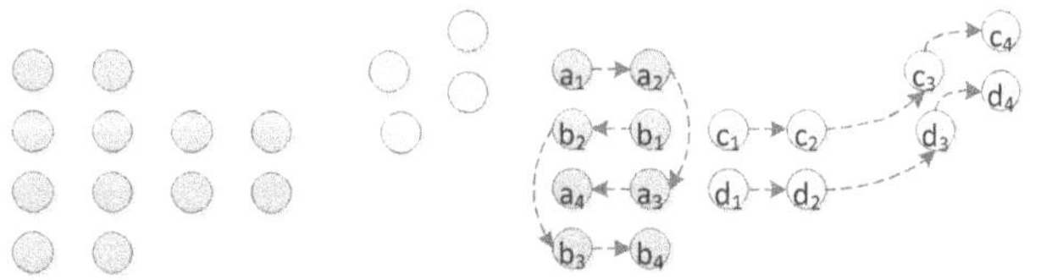

(a) Distances only (b) Distances + Visit Sequences

Figure 8: Effect of different trip information

In this work, we only attempt to connect spatial and temporal information by reinforcement. This can be viewed as a study to demonstrate the effectiveness of reinforcement for POIs identification. We add a note that other information (e.g., textual and visual) can be integrated well by reinforcement after specific study. In the following, we study the pairwise relationship construction for density (spatial) and visit sequence (temporal). The reinforcement algorithm will be discussed in next section.

Density Relationship Construction. As a crucial part in the density based clustering approaches (e.g., DBSCAN), density relationship should be thoughtfully considered in the reinforcement. Similar to DBSCAN, the density of a photo is counted by the number of surrounding photos within a range, which is indicated by e_i. We denote the density relationship as $E = [E_{ij}]_{n \times n}$. The value of E_{ij} represents the density similarity of two photos i and j. The formal definition is shown in Equation 7.

$$E_{ij} = \frac{\min\{e_i, e_j\}}{\max\{e_i, e_j\}} \cdot (e_i + e_j) \qquad (7)$$

where $\frac{\min\{e_i, e_j\}}{\max\{e_i, e_j\}}$ is the density similarity of two photos and we multiply it by the sum of their densities due to Observation 2 which is well accepted in density based clustering.

OBSERVATION 2. *Highly dense regions are more substantial to POIs identification.*

Visit Sequence Relationship Construction. Besides spatial aspect, the movement sequences of photographers are also substantial to POIs identification as discussed in the previous example in Figure 8. We denote the visit sequence relationship as $S = [S_{ij}]_{n \times n}$. In general, two consecutive photos are probably taken at the same POI. According to this, we define the visit sequence relationship between two photos in Equation 8.

$$S_{ij} = \begin{cases} 1/seq(i,j) & \text{if } seq(i,j) > 0 \\ 0 & \text{otherwise} \end{cases} \qquad (8)$$

where $seq(i,j)$ is the number of hops between photos i and j in the movement sequence of a photographer. $seq(i,j)$ is set to zero if the photos i and j are not taken by the same photographer. For instance, consider the example in Figure 8, $seq(c_1, c_3)$ and $seq(a_1, b_1)$ are set to 2 and zero, respectively.

4.1 Reinforcement Model

Heretofore, we obtain three feature matrices, D (distance based), E (density based), and S (visit sequence based), from both spatial and temporal aspects. In this section, we describe our iterative reinforcement model that constructs a robust structure between these information. Intuitively, these features mutually affect each others in the POIs identification. Updating the values of one feature will surely influence the values of other features. Consequently, we apply an iterative strategy for obtaining the robust features relationship. More importantly, clustering photos using the robust features potentially provides us better results.

Our reinforcement model is shown in Equation 9. It is a simple iterative model and can easily bias to a feature by tuning α, β, and γ accordingly. Initially, we set $D^{(0)}$, $E^{(0)}$, and $S^{(0)}$ to the original feature matrices respectively. $D^{(n)}$, $E^{(n)}$, and $S^{(n)}$ indicate the D, E, and S matrices at n^{th} iteration.

$$\begin{cases} D^{(n)} = \alpha D^{(0)} + (1-\alpha)E^{(n-1)} \\ E^{(n)} = \beta E^{(0)} + (1-\beta)S^{(n-1)} \\ S^{(n)} = \gamma S^{(0)} + (1-\gamma)D^{(n-1)} \end{cases} \qquad (9)$$

By iteratively executing Equation 9, the mutual influence of the features which include distance, density, and visit sequence is explored by the reinforcement model. Also, we normalize $D^{(n)}$, $E^{(n)}$, and $S^{(n)}$ at the end of each iteration to ensure reasonable reinforcements between them. After $D^{(n)}$ is convergent to $D^{(n-1)}$, we terminate the iterative process and normalize the values of $D^{(n)}$ by a Gaussian function as suggested in [25]. The effect of α, β, and γ will be evaluated in the experiments section.

5. IMPLEMENTATION DETAIL

In this section, we discuss the implementation detail for our approach. Obviously, constructing a complete feature matrix for web scale datasets is too expensive. For instance, we have 216,092 geo-tagged photos in our Paris collection. For the distance matrix D, it will consume approximate 173.96 GB space if all photo pairs are stored into D. It is definitely too large for present computer systems.

To address the space issues, we first group the photos by Hilbert curve grouping [16] based on their distances, where the Hilbert curve grouping is a popular multi-dimensional indexing techniques and well accepted by spatial databases. The grouping is shown to preserve very good quality to the original datasets, especially in low dimensionality. In this work, we carefully tune Hilbert curve parameters (e.g., maximum number of objects and grouping size) such that the photos collections are reduced to $\sim$ 10% of their original size.

After grouping, the group feature relationship X^G_{IJ} is set to the average feature relationship of the photos across the groups. This is shown in Equation 10.

$$X^G_{IJ} = \frac{\sum X_{ij}}{|X_{ij}|}, i \in I, j \in J \qquad (10)$$

where I and J are indicated two Hilbert curve groups of photos, respectively.

Furthermore, we should keep only substantial relations in the feature matrices. There are two reasons: 1) photos are generally grouped together into the cluster with strongest features similarity and 2) the weak features do not involve into the reinforcement process too much after normalization. One of the methods is to remove a distance relationship D^G_{IJ} from D^G if D^G_{IJ} is larger than 200m. The computational cost can be further reduced without much information loss.

6. EXPERIMENTS

In this section, we present several experiments to demonstrate the superiority of our findings. We first introduce our data preparation and evaluation measure in Section 6.1 and Section 6.2, respectively. We compare our self-tuning spectral clustering to other clustering approaches in Section 6.3. At last, we investigate the effect of parameters α, β, and γ for our reinforcement model.

6.1 Data Preparation

We collect three photos collections using Flickr API.[5]. For each photo collection, we fetch all geo-tagged photos using the city name as the search key by the Flickr API. We filter out the photos that are not located in the city (by latitude and longitude boundary as shown in Table 2) or have identical geo-location. The statistics of our photos collections are summarized in Table 2.

6.2 Evaluation Measure

We extract a set of tourist attractions in the metadata of OpenStreetMap. The total number of attractions for each city is shown in Table 2. The tourist attractions are represented by MBRs as shown in Figure 5. In the evaluation,

[5] http://www.flickr.com/services/api/

Table 2: List of photos collections

City	No. Photos	No. Clean Photos	Latitude and Longitude	No. MBRs
Paris	788,015	216,092	$\begin{bmatrix} 48.8151 & 48.9030 \\ 2.2232 & 2.4742 \end{bmatrix}$	92
Hong Kong, HK	191,565	43,294	$\begin{bmatrix} 22.17596 & 22.56773 \\ 113.79913 & 114.44252 \end{bmatrix}$	28
New York, NY	1,059,209	274,428	$\begin{bmatrix} 40.49866 & 40.93115 \\ -74.25797 & -73.71277 \end{bmatrix}$	62

the MBRs are enlarged to 150% of their original size since photos might be taken in the surrounding area as well. An POI is perfectly identified by a cluster if and only if all photos in the MBR are grouped into the cluster and their sizes are identical. In the evaluation, we filter out the clusters not intersect to any MBRs.

In IR community, a common way to interpretation of clustering is to view it as a series of decisions, one for each of the $N(N-1)/2$ pairs of photos in the collection. We classify these decisions by a simple binary classification. For instance, a true positive decision assigns two photos in the same MBR to the same cluster C and TP is indicated the total number of true positive decisions. We summarize other types of decisions in Table 3.

Table 3: Binary Classification

	P	N
T	C, MBR	¬C, ¬MBR
F	C, ¬MBR	¬C, MBR

In [17], the precision P, recall R, and F_β measure are defined by Equation 11. In this paper, we use F_1 measure as our evaluation measure. A large value of F_1 measure indicates a better clustering.

$$P = \frac{TP}{TP+FP}, R = \frac{TP}{TP+FN}, F_\beta = \frac{(\beta^2+1)PR}{\beta^2 P + R} \quad (11)$$

6.3 Performance Evaluation

Self-tuning Spectral Clustering. In this sub-section, we demonstrate the superiority of our self-tuning technique by Flickr photos collections. Figure 9 shows the effect of the parameter values to the corresponding clustering approach. For each experiment, we vary a single parameter for a clustering approach, while setting the others to their default values as listed in Table 4.

We first compare our self-tuning technique to k-means, mean-shift, P-DBSCAN, and spectral clustering using Paris photo collection. According to results in Figure 9, it is obvious that our self-tuning technique is superior. Without any parameters tuning, its F_1 measure is only worse than one case in mean shift ($\eta = 100m$) and one case in P-DBSCAN ($\varepsilon = 50m$). Surprisingly, our self-tuning method is better than spectral clustering for all tested parameters. It is because our approach can self-identify the dense region by the cut costs similarity instead of using a global threshold δ.

Note that our self-tuning approach might be worse than k-means, mean shift, P-DBSCAN, or spectral clustering in other parameter settings. However, as demonstrated by Figure 9, the self-tuning approach provides an acceptable quality without manual tuning. As a reference, we illustrate the snapshot of the self-tuning approach in Figure 10. This is not only valuable to the clustering problem (i.e., POIs identification) but also to other trip related mining problems.

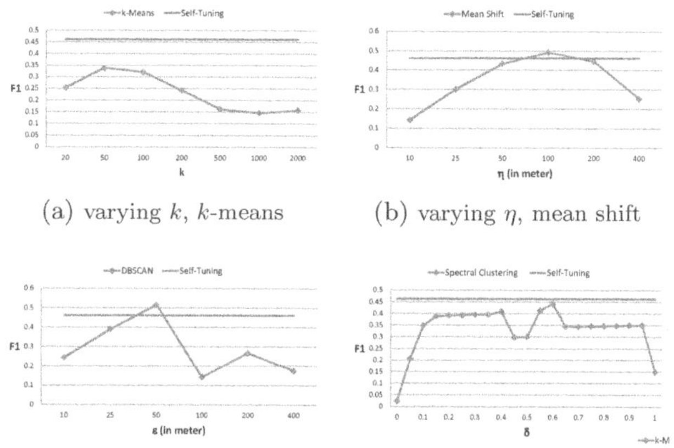

(a) varying k, k-means (b) varying η, mean shift

(c) varying ε, P-DBSCAN (d) varying δ, spectral clustering

Figure 9: F_1 measures for different clustering

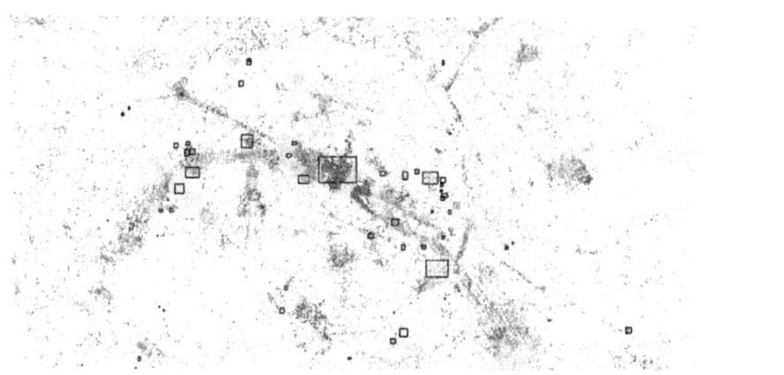

Figure 10: Self-tuning spectral clustering

Figure 11 compares the F_1 measures between spectral clustering and self-tuning approach for Hong Kong and New York photos collections. Again, our self-tuning technique outperforms spectral clustering for all tested δ values. The F_1 measures of Hong Kong collection are very small since the tourist attractions provided by OpenStreetMap are very limited and the sizes of attractions are also very small.

Reinforcement Model. In Equation 9, we can see that α, β, γ are three important parameters in the reinforcement model which control the degree of propagation. In this subsection, we evaluate their influences to the self-tuning performance. Due to space limitations, we fix α to 0.9 as the distance information involve the most in the clustering process. The effect of other parameters (β and γ) is shown in Figure 12. While setting $\alpha = 0.9$, $\beta = 0.9$, and $\gamma = 0.7$, the reinforcement model is 27% better than the distance based

Table 4: **Range of parameter values**

Clustering	Default Settings	Parameter	Values
k-means	-	k	20, 50, 100, 200, 500, 1000, 2000
mean shift	Gaussian kernel, $\sigma^2 = 0.2$	η (in meter)	10, 25, 50, 100, 200, 400
P-DBSCAN	$\theta = 50$, $\omega = 0.1$	ε (in meter)	10, 25, 50, 100, 200, 400
spectral clustering	-	δ	0, 0.05, 0.1, ..., 0.9, 0.95, 1

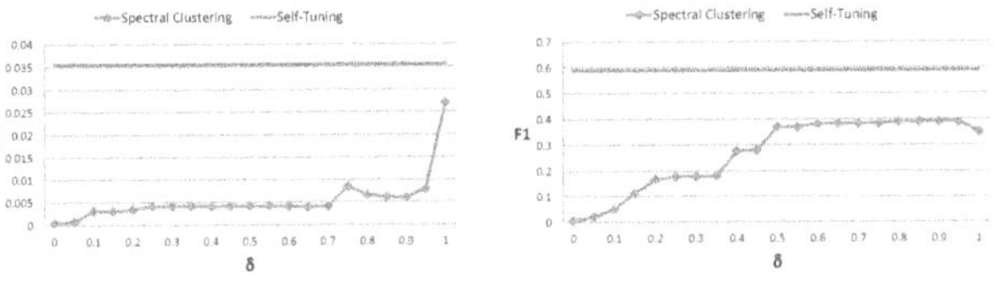

(a) spectral clustering, HK (b) spectral clustering, NY

Figure 11: Comparison between spectral clustering and self-tuning for Hong Kong and New York photos collections

model. Besides, our self-tuning technique is only 4.3% (in average) worse than the corresponding best spectral clustering result (by tuning δ) among all testings[6]. It shows the robustness of our self-tuning technique.

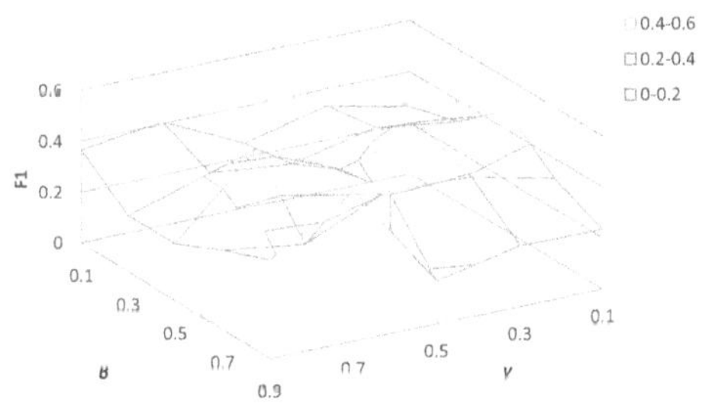

Figure 12: F_1 **vs.** β **and** γ **(setting** $\alpha = 0.9$**) on Paris photo collection**

7. RELATED WORK

Rattenbury et al. [21] is a prior work to discover the names of events and landmarks using geo-tagged and textual data of photos from Flickr. Kennedy and Naaman [13] and Crandall et al. [7] study a problem which can identify landmarks by applying clustering algorithms on geo-tagged photos. The result in [7] is used in many subsequent works being discussed shortly. The authors also propose a classification method to identify the taken location of a photo based on both visual and textual features. However, these works do not consider temporal information to improve the clustering quality.

Besides identifying POIs, there are many recent works that deduce trip information from web photos. Clements et al. [5] study a work that predicts travel interests for a user who had rich travel data in the past. Popescu and Grefenstette [19] attempt to deduce the typical visit duration for tourist attractions. The authors first study a heuristic filtering procedures to clean the photo collection. Then, an external coverage geographical gazetteer is used to map between the photos and POIs based on their textual and geotagged information. Other trip related information are extracted based on their result, such as maximum, minimum, and average duration time of the POIs. A similar work [20] is proposed by the same authors that extracts some day-tour information, such as people visit interests, visit time, and duration time. Their solution first identifies POIs by an external knowledge base, Wikipedia and then extracts the day-tour information based on the identified POIs.

Automatic tour planning from geo-tagged photos has been recently studied in [3, 12]. Choudhury et al. [3] constructs intra-city travel itineraries using spatio-temporal data from Flickr. Their solution first identifies a set of time paths and each time path is a sequence of POIs traversed by a user. The duration time and the transit time of POIs are subsequently extracted by the time paths. Antourage [12] automatically constructs tourist trip from the geo-tagged photos, by specifying a start location and maximum distance covered by the trip. A hexagonal grid overlay is used to map landmarks of a city. Each hexagonal cell is weighted by the number of photos taken inside. Therefore, the tour planning problem in their work becomes an optimization problem that maximizes the total weight of the selected cells where the total distance cannot exceed the given constraint.

Regarding self-tuning clustering, there are some results reported in machine learning [18, 26]. These methods aim at finding the best k in k means by statistical test or eigenvectors analysis. These algorithms typically determine all clusters at once which is different from our hierarchical clustering technique.

8. CONCLUSIONS

In this paper, we study spectral clustering which is the first attempt for POIs identification. In addition, we deeply compare the state of the art approaches and figure out the parametric issues. Therefore, we analyze spectral clustering procedures and propose a self-tuning approach based on the cut cost similarity so that the effect of the parameters is eliminated from spectral clustering. Furthermore, we study reinforcement that connects information from diverse aspects by iterative learning.

In the future works, we are intent to study the POIs ranking problems. In general, the POIs are ranked by simple observation (i.e., number of photos, number of users, or size). There is so much room for improvement. In addition, identifying POIs can be viewed as a module of other trip related mining tasks. We will investigate how these related tasks can get improved by our clustering framework. Moreover, we are highly interested in comparing different self-tuning clustering techniques for web scale photos collections.

[6]The details are omitted due to the space limitations.

Acknowledgments

This work was partially sponsored by Grant RG066/09-10S/11R/GZG/FST from University of Macau Research Committee.

9. REFERENCES

[1] T. Bühler and M. Hein. Spectral clustering based on the graph p-laplacian. In *ICML*, page 11, 2009.

[2] J. Cheeger. A lower bound for the smallest eigenvalue of the laplacian. *Problems in Analysis*, page 195, 1970.

[3] M. D. Choudhury, M. Feldman, S. Amer-Yahia, N. Golbandi, R. Lempel, and C. Yu. Constructing travel itineraries from tagged geo-temporal breadcrumbs. In *WWW*, pages 1083–1084, 2010.

[4] F. R. K. Chung. Spectral graph theory. *Regional Conference Series in Mathematics, American Mathematical Society*, 92:1–212, 1997.

[5] M. Clements, P. Serdyukov, A. P. de Vries, and M. J. T. Reinders. Using flickr geotags to predict user travel behaviour. In *SIGIR*, pages 851–852, 2010.

[6] D. Comaniciu and P. Meer. Mean shift: A robust approach toward feature space analysis. *IEEE Trans. Pattern Anal. Mach. Intell.*, 24(5):603–619, 2002.

[7] D. J. Crandall, L. Backstrom, D. P. Huttenlocher, and J. M. Kleinberg. Mapping the world's photos. In *WWW*, pages 761–770, 2009.

[8] M. Ester, H.-P. Kriegel, J. Sander, and X. Xu. A density-based algorithm for discovering clusters in large spatial databases with noise. In *KDD*, pages 226–231, 1996.

[9] L. Getoor. Link mining: a new data mining challenge. *SIGKDD Explorations*, 5(1):84–89, 2003.

[10] G. H. Golub and C. F. Van Loan. *Matrix computations (3rd ed.)*. Johns Hopkins University Press, Baltimore, MD, USA, 1996.

[11] D. S. Hochbaum. Polynomial time algorithms for ratio regions and a variant of normalized cut. *IEEE Trans. Pattern Anal. Mach. Intell.*, 32(5):889–898, 2010.

[12] S. Jain, S. Seufert, and S. J. Bedathur. Antourage: mining distance-constrained trips from flickr. In *WWW*, pages 1121–1122, 2010.

[13] L. S. Kennedy and M. Naaman. Generating diverse and representative image search results for landmarks. In *WWW*, pages 297–306, 2008.

[14] S. Kisilevich, F. Mansmann, and D. A. Keim. P-dbscan: a density based clustering algorithm for exploration and analysis of attractive areas using collections of geo-tagged photos. In *COM.Geo*, 2010.

[15] J. M. Kleinberg. Authoritative sources in a hyperlinked environment. *J. ACM*, 46(5):604–632, 1999.

[16] J. K. Lawder and P. J. H. King. Querying multi-dimensional data indexed using the hilbert space-filling curve. *SIGMOD Record*, 30(1):19–24, 2001.

[17] C. D. Manning, P. Raghavan, and H. Schtze. *Introduction to Information Retrieval*. Cambridge University Press, New York, NY, USA, 2008.

[18] D. Pelleg and A. W. Moore. X-means: Extending k-means with efficient estimation of the number of clusters. In *ICML*, pages 727–734, 2000.

[19] A. Popescu and G. Grefenstette. Deducing trip related information from flickr. In *WWW*, pages 1183–1184, 2009.

[20] A. Popescu, G. Grefenstette, and P.-A. Moëllic. Mining tourist information from user-supplied collections. In *CIKM*, pages 1713–1716, 2009.

[21] T. Rattenbury, N. Good, and M. Naaman. Towards automatic extraction of event and place semantics from flickr tags. In *SIGIR*, pages 103–110, 2007.

[22] P. Serdyukov, V. Murdock, and R. van Zwol. Placing flickr photos on a map. In *SIGIR*, pages 484–491, 2009.

[23] J. Shi and J. Malik. Normalized cuts and image segmentation. *IEEE Trans. Pattern Anal. Mach. Intell.*, 22(8):888–905, 2000.

[24] S. Wang and J. M. Siskind. Image segmentation with ratio cut. *IEEE Trans. Pattern Anal. Mach. Intell.*, 25(6):675–690, 2003.

[25] X.-J. Wang, W.-Y. Ma, L. Z. 0001, and X. Li. Iteratively clustering web images based on link and attribute reinforcements. In *ACM Multimedia*, pages 122–131, 2005.

[26] L. Zelnik-Manor and P. Perona. Self-tuning spectral clustering. In *NIPS*, 2004.

APPENDIX

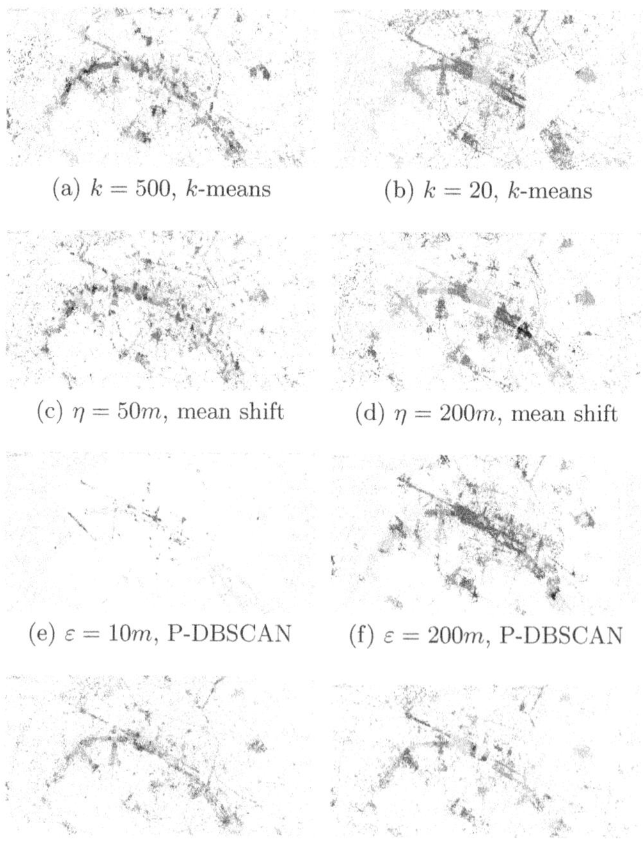

(a) $k = 500$, k-means (b) $k = 20$, k-means

(c) $\eta = 50m$, mean shift (d) $\eta = 200m$, mean shift

(e) $\varepsilon = 10m$, P-DBSCAN (f) $\varepsilon = 200m$, P-DBSCAN

(g) $\delta = 1.0$, normalized cut (h) $\delta = 0.5$, normalized cut

Figure 13: Effect of other parameters in k-means, mean shift, P-DBSCAN, and normalized cut clustering

Cluster-Based Fusion of Retrieved Lists

Anna Khudyak Kozorovitsky
annak@tx.technion.ac.il

Oren Kurland
kurland@ie.technion.ac.il

Faculty of Industrial Engineering and Management
Technion — Israel Institute of Technology
Haifa 32000, Israel

ABSTRACT

Methods for fusing document lists that were retrieved in response to a query often use retrieval scores (or ranks) of documents in the lists. We present a novel probabilistic fusion approach that utilizes an additional source of rich information, namely, inter-document similarities. Specifically, our model integrates information induced from clusters of similar documents created across the lists with that produced by *some* fusion method that relies on retrieval scores (ranks). Empirical evaluation shows that our approach is highly effective for fusion. For example, the performance of our model is consistently better than that of the standard (effective) fusion method that it integrates. The performance also transcends that of standard fusion of re-ranked lists, where list re-ranking is based on clusters created from documents in the list.

Categories and Subject Descriptors: H.3.3 [Information Search and Retrieval]: Retrieval models

General Terms: Algorithms, Experimentation

Keywords: ad hoc retrieval, fusion, cluster-based fusion

1. INTRODUCTION

Fusing document lists that were retrieved from a corpus in response to a query so as to compile a single result list is a long studied task [9]. The lists are often produced by using multiple query representations, document representations or ranking functions [9]. Many effective fusion methods are based on the premise that documents that are highly ranked in many of the lists are likely to be relevant [13, 23, 9, 12, 2, 29].

However, different retrieved lists can contain different relevant documents [10, 14, 5, 3]. Hence, fusion methods based on the premise just mentioned can fall short in such scenarios. A case in point, a relevant document that appears only in one list, and which is ranked low in this list, will be ranked low in the final result list. Nevertheless, if the document content is *similar* to that of other relevant documents — as implied by the *cluster hypothesis* [42] — and those are highly ranked in (many of) the lists, then the document can be "rewarded".

Accordingly, we present a novel probabilistic approach to fusion that lets similar documents across the lists provide relevance-status support to each other. Our model integrates information produced by *some* standard fusion method, which relies on retrieval scores (ranks) of documents in the lists, with that induced from *clusters* that are created from similar documents across the lists.

Empirical evaluation performed using TREC data demonstrates the effectiveness of our model. For example, the model posts performance that is consistently better than that of the standard fusion method that it integrates for three such effective fusion methods.

Our approach is also more effective than standard fusion of cluster-based re-ranked lists. In other words, re-ranking each list using clusters created from documents in the list so as to improve relevance estimates in the list [45, 25, 21]; and then, using standard fusion to aggregate the re-ranked lists, is shown to be less effective than our approach that uses clusters created from documents across the lists. We further demonstrate the merits of using across-list created clusters by showing that they can contain a (much) higher percentage of relevant documents than that in clusters created from each list separately.

Conceptually, our contributions are twofold. From a fusion perspective, we show that using information induced from clusters created from documents across the lists can help to substantially improve over methods that use only retrieval scores/rank information. From a cluster-based retrieval perspective, we address the multiple retrieved lists setting in which documents may appear in several lists with different retrieval scores. In contrast, previous work on cluster-based retrieval addressed the single retrieved list setting [45, 25, 21, 26, 46, 27, 18, 31].

2. FUSION FRAMEWORK

Let q, d, and $\mathcal{C}$ denote a query, a document, and a corpus of documents respectively. We assume that the document lists $L_1, \ldots, L_m$, each of which contains k documents, were retrieved in response to q by m retrievals performed over $\mathcal{C}$. The retrievals could be based, for example, on different representations of q, different document representations and/or different ranking functions [9]. We use $\mathcal{C}_L \stackrel{def}{=} \bigcup_i L_i$ to denote the *set* of documents that appear in the lists.

Our goal is to utilize information from the lists $L_1, \ldots, L_m$ so as to assign a positive *fusion* score, $F(d;q)$, to d ($\in \mathcal{C}_L$);

SIGIR'11, July 24–28, 2011, Beijing, China.

we set $F(d;q) \stackrel{def}{=} 0$ for $d \notin \mathcal{C}_L$. The score should reflect d's presumed relevance to the information need underlying q.

Standard fusion methods assign $F(d;q)$ based on the retrieval scores (or ranks) of d in the lists in which it appears [9]. Specifically, documents that are highly ranked in many of the lists are often "rewarded" [13]. For example, if $S_{L_i}(d)$ is d's positive retrieval score in L_i, and assuming that $S_{L_i}(d) \stackrel{def}{=} 0$ if $d \notin L_i$, then the **CombSUM** fusion method [13] scores d by the sum of its retrieval scores:

$$F_{CombSUM}(d;q) \stackrel{def}{=} \sum_{L_i} S_{L_i}(d).$$

The **CombMNZ** method [13, 22] further rewards documents that appear in many lists:

$$F_{CombMNZ}(d;q) \stackrel{def}{=} \#\{L_i : d \in L_i\} F_{CombSUM}(d;q).$$

The **Borda** method [47], on the other hand, considers only rank information. Specifically, d is scored by the number of documents not ranked higher than it in the lists:

$$F_{Borda}(d;q) \stackrel{def}{=} \sum_{L_i} \#\{d' \in L_i : S_{L_i}(d') <= S_{L_i}(d)\}.$$

2.1 Cluster-based fusion

A rich source of additional information that can be used to estimate d's relevance, and which is not utilized by standard fusion methods, is *inter-document similarities*. For example, suppose that d's content is highly similar to that of many documents that appear in the highest ranks of the lists. Presumably, then, d and these documents discuss the same topics/aspects. Hence, d should potentially be rewarded even if, in the extreme case, it appears in only one list in which it is ranked low. On the other hand, fusion methods that rely only on retrieval scores (ranks) will "penalize" d and rank it low in the final result list.

Thus, inspired by the *cluster hypothesis* [42], which states that "closely associated documents tend to be relevant to the same requests", we opt to devise a fusion method that lets similar documents across the lists provide relevance-status support to each other. To that end, we consider a set $Cl(\mathcal{C}_L)$ of document *clusters* created from $\mathcal{C}_L$ (the set of all documents in the lists) using *some* clustering algorithm; c will be used to denote a cluster. These clusters could potentially be viewed as representing query related "aspects", by the virtue of the way they are created, that is, from documents retrieved in response to the query. Hence, our goal becomes integrating cluster-based information with information used by standard fusion methods — retrieval scores and/or ranks of documents in the lists.

2.1.1 Using clusters as proxies for documents

Our goal is to estimate $p(d|q)$, the probability that d is relevant to the information need underlying q. Inspired by work on cluster-based retrieval in the language-modeling framework [20, 19], we use clusters as proxies for documents to estimate this probability. However, in contrast to these approaches [20, 19], which focus on a *single* retrieved list, we do not use language-model estimates for probabilities of the form $p(x|y)$ in the derivation to follow. Rather, we exploit the rich information provided by the occurrences and retrieval scores of documents in the lists to devise estimates. Thus, the resultant cluster-based fusion model that we derive is different — in the use of probabilities and in the formation of their estimates — from the single-list models by which its development was inspired.

Model derivation. We can write the probability for d's relevance as:

$$p(d|q) = \sum_{c \in Cl(\mathcal{C}_L)} p(d|c,q)p(c|q). \quad (1)$$

To estimate $p(d|c,q)$, we use a linear mixture governed by a free parameter λ: $\hat{p}(d|c,q) \stackrel{def}{=} (1-\lambda)p(d|q) + \lambda p(d|c)$ [20]; we use the notation $\hat{p}(\cdot)$, here and after, to denote estimates of (model) probabilities. Using $\hat{p}(d|c,q)$ in Equation 1, along with assuming that $p(c|q)$ is a probability distribution over $Cl(\mathcal{C}_L)$ — the universe of clusters that we consider, and then applying some probabilistic algebra, results in our **ClustFuse** algorithm:

$$F_{ClustFuse}(d;q) \stackrel{def}{=} (1-\lambda)p(d|q) + \lambda \sum_{c \in Cl(\mathcal{C}_L)} p(c|q)p(d|c). \quad (2)$$

ClustFuse uses a two component mixture model to score d. The first is the original probability of relevance, $p(d|q)$, from which we back off to using cluster-based information. The second component, which uses clusters as proxies for documents, "rewards" d if it is strongly associated with clusters c (as measured by $p(d|c)$) that presumably contain a high percentage of information pertaining to q (as measured by $p(c|q)$).

The remaining task for instantiating a specific algorithm from Equation 2 is deriving estimates for $p(d|q)$, $p(c|q)$, and $p(d|c)$. To that end, we assume *some* standard fusion method (e.g., one of those mentioned above, CombSUM, CombMNZ, or Borda) that assigns d with a score $F(d;q)$ that is based on d's retrieval scores (ranks) in the lists. The estimates we present are not committed to a specific standard fusion method.

Estimates. Using probability rules, we can write: $p(d|q) = \frac{p(q|d)p(d)}{p(q)}$; and, $p(q) = \sum_{d' \in C} p(q|d')p(d')$. Assuming a uniform prior distribution for documents ($p(d)$), we get that $p(d|q) = \frac{p(q|d)}{\sum_{d' \in C} p(q|d')}$. We use an estimate $\hat{p}(q|d) \propto F(d;q)$, where $F(d;q)$ is d's standard fusion score. Recall that $F(d;q)$ is by definition 0 for documents d not in $\mathcal{C}_L$. Thus, we get that

$$\hat{p}(d|q) \stackrel{def}{=} \frac{F(d;q)}{\sum_{d' \in \mathcal{C}_L} F(d';q)} \quad (3)$$

is d's normalized standard-fusion score. Note that $\hat{p}(d|q)$ is a probability distribution over the *entire* corpus.

Similarly, assuming a uniform prior for clusters, the probability that cluster c contains information pertaining to q can be written as: $p(c|q) = \frac{p(q|c)}{\sum_{c' \in Cl(\mathcal{C}_L)} p(q|c')}$. Now, we would like to exploit the fact that c contains documents that might have multiple appearances in the lists to be fused. Hence, we estimate $p(q|c)$ based on the standard-fusion scores of c's constituent documents. Recent work on representing sets of documents, specifically, clusters of similar documents, has demonstrated the merits of a product-based (geometric) representation [27, 31]. Such representation was advocated using arguments based on information geometry [31]. Accordingly, we set

$$\hat{p}(c|q) \stackrel{def}{=} \frac{\prod_{d \in c} F(d;q)}{\sum_{c' \in Cl(\mathcal{C}_L)} \prod_{d' \in c'} F(d';q)}; \qquad (4)$$

$\hat{p}(c|q)$ is a probability distribution over $Cl(\mathcal{C}_L)$. As all clusters we use in the evaluation in Section 4 contain the same number of documents, there is no bias incurred by using the product of fusion scores of documents in a cluster.[1]

To estimate $p(d|c)$, the document-cluster association strength, we, again, assume a uniform document prior. Thus, we get that $p(d|c) = \frac{p(c|d)}{\sum_{d_i \in c} p(c|d_i)}$. Now, to estimate $p(c|d)$, we set $\hat{p}(c|d) \stackrel{def}{=} 0$ for $d \notin \mathcal{C}_L$. That is, we assume no association between documents not in $\mathcal{C}_L$ and clusters of documents from $\mathcal{C}_L$. This assumption echoes those used in work on re-ranking a single retrieved list based on clusters of documents in the list [45, 25, 21]. (Refer to Section 3 for further details.) Our next task is then to estimate $p(c|d)$ for $d \in \mathcal{C}_L$. To that end, we use the mean inter-document-similarity between d and c's constituent documents: $\hat{p}(c|d) \propto \frac{1}{|c|} \sum_{d' \in c} sim(d', d)$; $|c|$ is the number of documents in c; $sim(\cdot, \cdot)$ is the inter-document-similarity estimate used to create the clusters. (See Section 4.1 for details). Thus, we arrive to:

$$\hat{p}(d|c) \stackrel{def}{=} \frac{\sum_{d' \in c} sim(d', d)}{\sum_{d_i \in \mathcal{C}_L} \sum_{d' \in c} sim(d', d_i)}, \qquad (5)$$

where $d \in \mathcal{C}_L$. As a result, $\hat{p}(d|c)$ is a probability distribution over the corpus.

It is important to note that d ($\in \mathcal{C}_L$) does not have to be a member of c to have a non-zero association strength, $\hat{p}(d|c)$, with c. Thus, even if we use a hard clustering technique, documents could be deemed associated (to some degree) with clusters to which they do not belong, yielding a soft clustering effect. The merits of such association approach were demonstrated in work on cluster-based retrieval [19].

ClustFuse in a nutshell. Using the estimates just described in Equation 2 yields the following fusion principle, which addresses the motivation for utilizing inter-document similarities. Document d is rewarded based on its: (i) standard-fusion score ($F(d;q)$), which reflects the extent to which d is highly ranked in (many of) the lists, and (ii) similarity ($\hat{p}(d|c)$) to clusters c that contain documents highly ranked in many of the lists (as measured by $\hat{p}(c|q)$).

We use **ClustFuseCombSUM**, **ClustFuseCombMNZ**, and **ClustFuseBorda** to denote the implementations of ClustFuse with the standard fusion methods described above. For $\lambda = 0$, ClustFuseCombSUM, ClustFuseCombMNZ, and ClustFuseBorda amount to CombSUM, CombMNZ, and Borda, respectively (see Equations 2 and 3); i.e., ClustFuse reduces to the standard fusion method that it utilizes. Higher values of λ result in more weight put on cluster-based information.

[1]We found that using the product of retrieval scores of documents in a cluster in Equation 4 yields fusion performance that is somewhat better than that of using the geometric mean of the scores. The performance is also superior to that of using the arithmetic mean (or sum) of the scores. The latter finding is in line with reports on using clusters from a single retrieved list to re-rank it [27, 31].

2.1.2 *Ranking clusters*

The ClustFuse method utilizes the estimate $\hat{p}(c|q)$ from Equation 4 for the probability that cluster c contains information pertaining to q. Naturally, the estimate should be high for clusters containing a high percentage of relevant documents. To study the extent to which $\hat{p}(c|q)$ reflects this percentage in c, we take an approach that was used in work on ranking clusters created from a single list [26, 21, 18].

We use $\hat{p}(c|q)$ to rank the clusters in $Cl(\mathcal{C}_L)$. Then, *all* δ documents of the *highest* ranked cluster are positioned at the top of the result list. (All clusters contain the same number, δ, of documents.) To neutralize within-cluster ordering effects, we only use the precision at δ measure (p@δ) to evaluate the resultant retrieval performance; this precision is the percentage of relevant documents in the highest ranked cluster. We use **ClustRank** to denote this retrieval approach, which, formally, scores d with 1 if d is a member of the highest ranked cluster, and with 0 otherwise; **ClustRankCombSUM**, **ClustRankCombMNZ**, and **ClustRankBorda** denote the implementations of ClustRank with the standard fusion methods.

3. RELATED WORK

Most fusion approaches utilize retrieval scores or ranks of documents but not the document content [13, 44, 23, 1, 9, 12, 2, 29, 24, 34]. Our ClustFuse method, which can incorporate these approaches, utilizes also information induced from clusters of similar documents. In Section 4.2 we show that ClustFuse outperforms the standard fusion method it incorporates; specifically, CombSUM, CombMNZ and Borda.

Clusters of documents can potentially be created based on document *snippets*, rather than the entire document content, if the content is not (quickly) available [48]. Document snippets, and other content-based features, were used for fusion [6, 41, 4, 30, 33], but inter-snippet (document) similarities were not utilized in these approaches.

Similarities between document titles were used for merging lists retrieved from non-overlapping corpora in response to a query [36]. In contrast to our approach, which operates on a single corpus, retrieval scores were not integrated with these similarities, and clusters were not utilized. Document clusters were also used for selecting terms for query expansion in federated search [35]. In contrast, ClustFuse uses clusters to rank documents based on the original query. Inter-document similarities were also used to re-rank a retrieved list using a second retrieved list [28]. However, clusters were not utilized. Furthermore, this asymmetric fusion (re-ranking) approach cannot be naturally extended to fusing several retrieved lists [28].

There is work studying the *potential* (e.g., for improving result interfaces) of using clusters created from documents retrieved from several collections [7]. Specifically, cluster-based and document-based retrieval are contrasted wherein the former is based on using clusters that are known to contain a high percentage of relevant documents. In Section 4.2 we present a similar study applied for the single corpus case that we address here. In contrast to our work, a specific document (or cluster) ranking method was not proposed [7].

There is recent work on using a graph-based approach for fusion that utilizes inter-document similarities [16]. In contrast to ClustFuse, document clusters were not used. In Section 4.2 we further discuss this work, and demonstrate the performance merits of ClustFuse with respect to the proposed graph-based method.

The clusters used by ClustFuse are *query specific* [45], as they are created from documents retrieved in response to the query. Previous work utilizing query-specific clusters has focused on re-ranking a single retrieved list using information induced from clusters of documents *within* the list [45, 25, 21, 26, 46, 27]. In contrast, ClustFuse fuses lists using information induced from clusters created from documents *across* the lists. Furthermore, ClustFuse also exploits the fact that documents might have multiple occurrences in the lists as is manifested in their standard-fusion scores.

We note that ClustFuse can, in fact, be used to re-rank a *single* retrieved list. The standard-fusion document score used by ClustFuse in this case is simply the retrieval score of the document in the list. This specific single list implementation echoes a previous cluster-based ranking method [20]. However, while this method [20] uses language-model-based estimates for the document-query and cluster-query "match", ClustFuse utilizes retrieval scores, however induced, for these estimates. Furthermore, we show in Section 4.2 that independently re-ranking each of the retrieved lists using this variant of ClustFuse, and then using standard fusion to merge the re-ranked lists, yields performance that is inferior to that of the original ClustFuse implementation, which exploits information induced from across-list clusters.

There has been some work on identifying clusters of documents from the same retrieved list that contain a high percentage of relevant documents [25, 21, 26, 27, 18, 31]. The estimate used by ClustFuse for the amount of query pertaining information in a cluster, which we explore as a cluster-based fusion method at its own right (ClustRank), is reminiscent of some of these methods [27, 18]; specifically, by the virtue of using the document-query "match" of the cluster's constituent documents. However, in contrast to previous methods, ClustFuse uses the standard-fusion score of documents rather than a retrieval score in a single list. Furthermore, while it was shown that there are clusters containing a high relevant-document percentage when created from a single retrieved list [15, 40, 32], we show in Section 4.2 that clusters created across multiple retrieved lists can contain a much higher relevant-document percentage.

4. EVALUATION

4.1 Experimental setup

We measure inter-document similarities using a previously proposed language-model-based estimate that was shown to be effective [20, 21]. Specifically, let $p_d^{[\mu]}(\cdot)$ denote the unigram, Dirichlet-smoothed, language model induced from document d; μ is the smoothing parameter which is set to 1000 [49]. The similarity between documents d_1 and d_2 is defined using the KL divergence:

$$sim(d_1, d_2) \stackrel{def}{=} \exp\left(-KL\left(p_{d_1}^{[0]}(\cdot) \,\middle|\middle|\, p_{d_2}^{[\mu]}(\cdot)\right)\right).$$

To cluster the *set* $\mathcal{C}_L$ of documents in the retrieved lists, we use a simple nearest-neighbors-based approach [14, 20, 21, 26, 39, 27]. Some previous work [19] demonstrated the merits of using this clustering approach with respect to other clustering methods for cluster-based document retrieval using a single retrieved list. For each d ($\in \mathcal{C}_L$) we define a cluster that contains d and the $\delta - 1$ documents d' in $\mathcal{C}_L$ ($d' \neq d$) that yield the highest $sim(d, d')$; note that the resultant clusters overlap. As relatively small clusters are known to be most effective for cluster-based retrieval [20, 21, 39, 27], we set $\delta = 10$, unless otherwise specified. (The performance of ClustFuse with $\delta = 5$ was inferior to that of using $\delta = 10$.)

We use TREC data for experiments: (i) the ad hoc track of trec3 (50 queries; 741,856 documents), which is based on news articles; (ii) the Web track of trec10 (50 queries; 1,692,096 documents); and, (iii) the robust track of trec12 (50 queries; 528,155 documents), which is a challenging benchmark [43]. We apply tokenization, Porter stemming, and stopword removal (using the INQUERY list) to documents using the Lemur toolkit[2], which is used for experiments.

Fusion methods are quite effective when the lists to be fused are relatively short [38, 41, 3]. Furthermore, utilizing similarities between top-retrieved documents is most effective when the number of documents considered is relatively small [11, 21]. Hence, to maintain the number of documents to be ranked ($|\mathcal{C}_L|$) relatively small, we fuse three lists, each of which is composed of the k (= 20) highest ranked documents in a submitted run in a track. In Section 4.2.3 we show that the resultant relative performance patterns are quite consistent for $k \in \{10, 20, 30, 40, 50\}$. The three runs to be fused, unless otherwise stated, are randomly selected from *all* submitted runs in a track (both automatic and manual). We use **run1**, **run2**, and **run3**, to denote the runs in descending order of MAP(@k) performance. We use 20 samples of randomly selected triplets of runs and report average performance over the samples. In Sections 4.2.6 and 4.2.7 we study the case of fusing the three most effective runs in a track.

The CombSUM and CombMNZ methods, utilized by the ClustFuse and ClustRank algorithms, require inter-list compatibility of retrieval scores. To that end, we normalize the retrieval score of a document in a list with respect to the sum of all retrieval scores in the list. If retrieval scores are negative, which is due to using logs, we use the exponent of a score for normalization,

To evaluate retrieval performance, we use MAP(@k) and the precision of the top 5 and 10 documents (p@5 and p@10, respectively). Statistically significant differences of performance are determined using the two-tailed paired t-test at a 95% confidence level [37].[3]

The ClustFuse method incorporates a single free parameter, λ. (ClustRank does not incorporate free parameters.) The value of λ ($\in \{0, 0.1, \ldots, 1\}$) is set using leave-one-out cross validation performed over the entire set of queries in a track; performance is optimized in the learning phase with respect to MAP. In other words, the performance for a query is that attained using a value of λ that maximizes MAP performance over all other queries in the track.

A note on efficiency. The computational overhead posted by our methods with respect to standard fusion approaches is not significant. The clustering of a few dozen documents from the retrieved lists can be performed quickly (e.g., based on document snippets) as was shown in work on clustering

[2]www.lemurproject.org

[3]A statistical significance test for a pair of methods in the case of 20 random samples of triplets of runs is employed upon the average (over the 20 samples) performance of the methods for the queries.

	trec3			trec10			trec12		
	MAP	p@5	p@10	MAP	p@5	p@10	MAP	p@5	p@10
run1	8.4	68.0	64.9	14.1	39.7	34.4	$\underline{25.2}$	48.4	42.2
run2	6.5	57.2	54.9	10.4	33.5	29.3	20.8	42.4	36.7
run3	4.3	41.7	40.7	6.3	22.5	19.9	13.2	29.7	25.2
CombSUM	7.4^{a}	65.3	60.8^{a}	12.3	38.9	33.9	22.7^{a}	46.9^{a}	39.9^{a}
ClustFuseCombSUM	$\underline{\mathbf{9.7}}^{a}_{f}$	$\underline{\mathbf{75.3}}^{a}_{f}$	$\underline{\mathbf{71.7}}^{a}_{f}$	$\mathbf{14.1}_{f}$	$\mathbf{42.4}_{f}$	$\mathbf{37.1}^{a}_{f}$	$\mathbf{25.0}_{f}$	$\mathbf{49.1}_{f}$	**43.2**
CombMNZ	7.4^{a}	65.4	60.9^{a}	12.7	40.1	34.2	22.7^{a}	46.9^{a}	39.9^{a}
ClustFuseCombMNZ	$\mathbf{9.6}^{a}_{f}$	$\mathbf{75.2}^{a}_{f}$	$\mathbf{71.1}^{a}_{f}$	$\underline{\mathbf{14.3}}_{f}$	$\mathbf{42.9}_{f}$	$\underline{\mathbf{37.8}}^{a}_{f}$	$\mathbf{24.5}_{f}$	**47.9**	$\mathbf{42.3}_{f}$
Borda	7.0^{a}	64.0^{a}	58.7^{a}	12.4	39.8	32.9	22.3^{a}	47.0^{a}	39.6^{a}
ClustFuseBorda	$\underline{\mathbf{9.7}}^{a}_{f}$	$\mathbf{74.1}^{a}_{f}$	$\mathbf{70.8}^{a}_{f}$	$\underline{\mathbf{14.3}}_{f}$	$\underline{\mathbf{43.5}}^{a}_{f}$	$\mathbf{37.1}^{a}_{f}$	$\mathbf{25.1}_{f}$	$\underline{\mathbf{49.8}}_{f}$	$\underline{\mathbf{44.0}}^{a}_{f}$

Table 1: Main result. Boldface marks the better performing between ClustFuseF and the standard fusion method F that it incorporates; a statistically significant difference between the two is marked with 'f'. Underline marks the best result per column; 'a' marks a statistically significant difference with run1. All performance differences between the fusion methods and run2 and run3 are statistically significant.

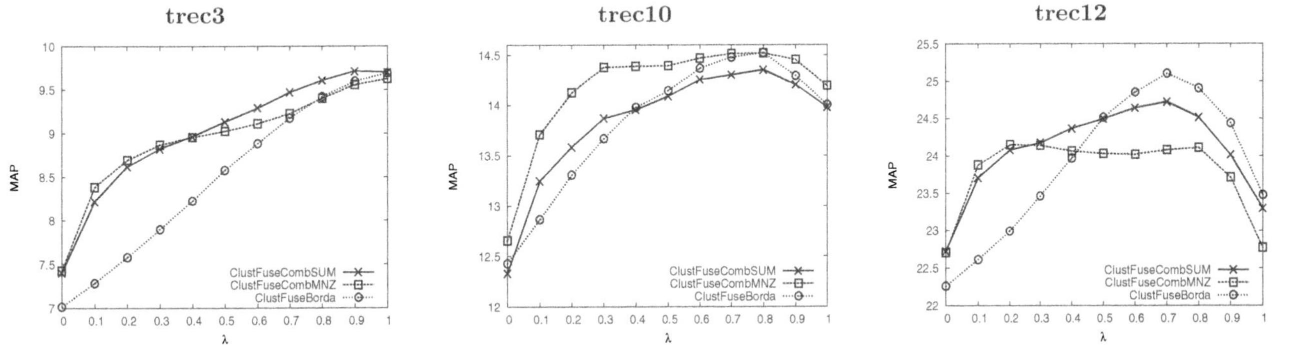

Figure 1: Effect of varying λ on the MAP performance of ClustFuse. For $\lambda = 0$, ClustFuseF amounts to F, the standard fusion method that it incorporates; higher value of λ corresponds to more weight put on cluster-based information. Note: figures are not to the same scale.

the results of Web search [48]; our methods are not committed to a specific clustering approach. Similar efficiency considerations were echoed in work on cluster-based re-ranking of a single document list [45, 25, 21]; and, in work on fusion based on document content [41, 36].

4.2 Experimental results

4.2.1 Main result

In Table 1 we present the performance numbers of ClustFuse. We can see that ClustFuse outperforms the standard fusion method that it incorporates in all relevant comparisons (track $\times$ evaluation measure). Many of these improvements are substantial and statistically significant. It is also worth noting that in many cases for trec10 the standard fusion methods underperform run1 (the most effective of the three runs), while ClustFuse almost always improves over run1 for trec10; sometimes, to a statistically significant degree. Moreover, in the very few cases that ClustFuse is outperformed by run1 (mainly, MAP for trec12), these performance differences are not statistically significant. The standard fusion methods, on the other hand, post in all cases for trec12 performance that is statistically significantly worse than that of run1. These findings attest to the merits of ClustFuse that integrates information induced from document clusters (created across the lists) with retrieval scores (or rank) information used by the standard fusion methods.

4.2.2 The effect of using cluster-based information

We next explore the effect of varying the value of λ on the performance of ClustFuse. (Refer back to Equation 2.) For $\lambda = 0$, ClustFuse amounts to the standard fusion method that it incorporates; higher values of λ correspond to more weight put on cluster-based information. For $\lambda > 0$ standard fusion scores of documents are used (also) for estimating the amount of query-pertaining information in a cluster. Figure 1 depicts the MAP-performance curves.

We see in Figure 1 that for $\lambda > 0$, and for all three tracks, the performance of ClustFuse is better than that of the standard fusion method that it incorporates, i.e., ClustFuse with $\lambda = 0$. Even for $\lambda = 0.1$, which amounts to assigning a relatively small weight to cluster-based information, some of the performance gains over not using this information ($\lambda = 0$) are substantial; furthermore, the improvements are quite large for $\lambda \in \{0.6, 0.7, 0.8\}$. Further increasing λ can result in performance decrease (e.g., for trec10 and trec12) that attests to the importance of integrating the standard fusion score assigned to the document with information induced from clusters to which it is similar.

4.2.3 The effect of list size

Insofar, we had our methods, and the reference comparisons, fuse lists of $k = 20$ documents each. We now turn to study the effect of the list size, k, on fusion performance. As noted above, fusion methods, so as methods that utilize inter-document similarities, are quite effective when operating over relatively short lists. In our case, the size of the

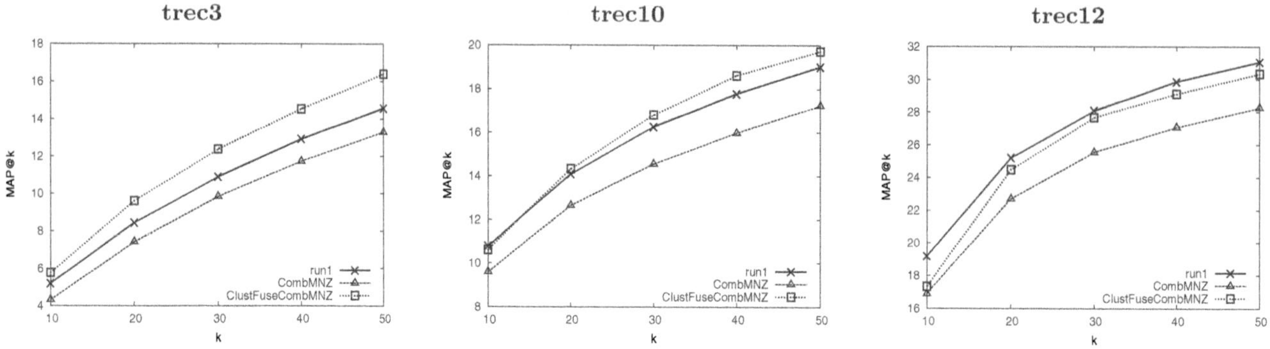

Figure 2: Effect of the size of the lists to be fused, k, on MAP@k. Note: figures are not to the same scale.

	trec3			trec10			trec12		
	MAP	p@5	p@10	MAP	p@5	p@10	MAP	p@5	p@10
run1	8.4	68.0	64.9	14.1	39.7	34.4	$\underline{25.2}$	48.4	42.2
Clust(run1)	8.8^{a}	72.2^{a}	68.2^{a}	14.1	40.6	36.1^{a}	24.6^{a}	47.6^{a}	42.0
run2	6.5	57.2	54.9	10.4	33.5	29.3	20.8	42.4	36.7
Clust(run2)	7.3^{b}	69.1^{b}	63.4^{b}	10.4	35.9^{b}	31.3^{b}	21.1	43.1	37.7^{b}
run3	4.3	41.7	40.7	6.3	22.5	19.9	13.2	29.7	25.2
Clust(run3)	5.1^{c}	54.3^{c}	49.7^{c}	6.5	24.5^{c}	21.1^{c}	13.7^{c}	31.8^{c}	27.0^{c}
CombSUM(Clust(run{i}))	8.2^{bc}	70.0^{bc}	64.9^{bc}	12.3^{bc}	41.3^{bc}	35.2^{bc}	22.4^{abc}	46.7^{abc}	40.0^{abc}
ClustFuseCombSUM	$\underline{\mathbf{9.7}}^{abc}_{s}$	$\underline{\mathbf{75.3}}^{abc}_{s}$	$\underline{\mathbf{71.7}}^{abc}_{s}$	$\mathbf{14.1}^{bc}_{s}$	$\mathbf{42.4}^{bc}$	$\mathbf{37.1}^{abc}_{s}$	$\mathbf{25.0}^{bc}_{s}$	$\mathbf{49.1}^{bc}_{s}$	$\mathbf{43.2}^{bc}$
CombMNZ(Clust(run{i}))	8.2^{bc}	69.4^{bc}	64.5^{bc}	12.7^{bc}	41.5^{bc}	35.4^{bc}	22.4^{abc}	46.8^{abc}	40.0^{abc}
ClustFuseCombMNZ	$\mathbf{9.6}^{abc}_{s}$	$\mathbf{75.2}^{abc}_{s}$	$\mathbf{71.1}^{abc}_{s}$	$\underline{\mathbf{14.3}}^{bc}_{s}$	$\mathbf{42.9}^{bc}$	$\underline{\mathbf{37.8}}^{abc}_{s}$	$\mathbf{24.5}^{bc}_{s}$	$\mathbf{47.9}^{bc}_{s}$	$\mathbf{42.3}^{bc}_{s}$
Borda(Clust(run{i}))	8.3^{bc}	69.8^{bc}	64.9^{bc}	12.4^{bc}	41.1^{bc}	34.4^{bc}	21.9^{abc}	46.8^{abc}	40.0^{abc}
ClustFuseBorda	$\underline{\mathbf{9.7}}^{abc}_{s}$	$\mathbf{74.1}^{abc}_{s}$	$\mathbf{70.8}^{abc}_{s}$	$\underline{\mathbf{14.3}}^{bc}_{s}$	$\underline{\mathbf{43.5}}^{abc}_{s}$	$\mathbf{37.1}^{abc}_{s}$	$\mathbf{25.1}^{bc}_{s}$	$\underline{\mathbf{49.8}}^{bc}_{s}$	$\underline{\mathbf{44.0}}^{abc}_{s}$

Table 2: Comparison of cluster-based fusion of runs (ClustFuseF) with standard fusion of cluster-based re-ranked runs (F(Clust(run{i}))); the performance of the better performing of the two is boldfaced, and 's' indicates that the difference is statistically significant. Underline marks the best result per column; 'a', 'b', and 'c' mark statistically significant differences with run1, run2, and run3, respectively.

document set to be ranked ($|\mathcal{C}_L|$) is determined by the number of lists to be fused (three), the number of documents in each list (k), and the overlap between the lists. In Figure 2 we present the MAP@k performance of ClustFuseCombMNZ, and that of the standard fusion method that it integrates (CombMNZ), where $k \in \{10, 20, 30, 40, 50\}$. (We use ClustFuseCombMNZ as a representative, as it is the focus of a comparison with some previous work on utilizing inter-document similarities for fusion that we present in Section 4.2.7.) For reference, we present the performance of run1 — the most MAP@k-effective run among the three to be fused.

As we can see in Figure 2, ClustFuseCombMNZ outperforms CombMNZ for all values of k over all three tracks; the relative improvements are often quite substantial. Furthermore, while CombMNZ underperforms (to quite a substantial degree) run1 for all values of k and for all three tracks, ClustFuseCombMNZ improves over run1 for trec3 and trec10 (but slightly underperforms it for trec12). These findings further attest to the benefits in using cluster-based information for fusion. We also note that the overall performance patterns are somewhat similar for $k \geq 20$; yet, the relative improvement of ClustFuseCombMNZ over CombMNZ for $k = 20$ can be somewhat lower than that for higher values of k (e.g., for trec10). Thus, we will continue to focus in the evaluation to follow on $k = 20$ so as to present a conservative picture of the performance our approach.

4.2.4 Cluster-based fusion vs. fusion of cluster-based re-ranked lists

Previous work on cluster-based retrieval has focused on the single retrieved list case. Specifically, there is much work on *re-ranking* a retrieved list using clusters of documents in the list [45, 25, 21, 46, 27, 19]. Our approach, on the other hand, fuses several retrieved lists using clusters created across the lists. Thus, we next explore the merits for fusion of using information induced from clusters created across the lists with respect to that induced from clusters created from each list. To that end, we study a fusion paradigm that is based, in spirit, on principles underlying the cluster-based re-ranking approaches just mentioned.

First, we cluster the documents in *each* run. Then, we use ClustFuse to *re-rank* a run using its clusters.[4] The motivation is to improve the relevance estimates in a run; the resultant re-ranking of run$i$ is denoted Clust(run$i$). The re-ranked runs are then fused using one of the standard fusion methods F ($\in$ {CombSUM,CombMNZ,Borda}); the fusion results are denoted F(Clust(run{i})). The resultant performance is compared with that of ClustFuseF — our original fusion methods that utilize clusters created across the runs. The performance numbers, all based on a leave-one-

[4]ClustFuse only requires a retrieval score for each document, $F(d;q)$, and information about clusters and inter-document similarities. When employed over a single list, ClustFuse echoes a previous cluster-based (re-)ranking method [20].

	trec3		trec10		trec12	
	p@5	p@10	p@5	p@10	p@5	p@10
OptCluster	93.6	86.4	64.4	50.7	72.8	58.1
run1	68.0	64.9	39.7	34.4	48.4	42.2
OptCluster(run1)	88.4^{a}	79.1^{a}	57.2^{a}	43.4^{a}	66.1^{a}	51.4^{a}
run2	57.2	54.9	33.5	29.3	42.4	36.7
OptCluster(run2)	83.3^{b}	71.9^{b}	50.3^{b}	37.5^{b}	60.0^{b}	45.5^{b}
run3	41.7	40.7	22.5	19.9	29.7	25.2
OptCluster(run3)	69.2^{c}	57.2^{c}	38.7^{c}	27.8^{c}	45.3^{c}	32.7^{c}
CombSUM	65.3^{bc}	60.8^{abc}	38.9^{bc}	33.9^{bc}	46.9^{abc}	39.9^{abc}
ClustRankCombSUM	68.3^{bc}_{f}	65.7^{bc}_{f}	40.6^{bc}	34.6^{abc}	46.8^{bc}	40.7^{bc}
ClustFuseCombSUM	$\mathbf{75.3}^{abc}_{f}$	$\mathbf{71.7}^{abc}_{f}$	$\mathbf{42.4}^{bc}_{f}$	$\mathbf{37.1}^{abc}_{f}$	$\mathbf{49.1}^{bc}_{f}$	$\mathbf{43.2}^{bc}_{f}$
CombMNZ	65.4^{bc}	60.9^{abc}	40.1^{bc}	34.2^{bc}	46.9^{abc}	39.9^{abc}
ClustRankCombMNZ	68.6^{bc}_{f}	65.9^{bc}_{f}	41.5^{bc}	35.2^{bc}	46.3^{abc}	40.5^{abc}
ClustFuseCombMNZ	$\mathbf{75.2}^{abc}_{f}$	$\mathbf{71.1}^{abc}_{f}$	$\mathbf{42.9}^{bc}_{f}$	$\mathbf{37.8}^{abc}_{f}$	$\mathbf{47.9}^{bc}$	$\mathbf{42.3}^{bc}_{f}$
Borda	64.0^{abc}	58.7^{abc}	39.8^{bc}	32.9^{bc}	47.0^{abc}	39.6^{abc}
ClustRankBorda	67.5^{bc}_{f}	65.7^{bc}_{f}	42.8^{abc}_{f}	35.0^{bc}_{f}	47.7^{bc}	42.1^{bc}_{f}
ClustFuseBorda	$\mathbf{74.1}^{abc}_{f}$	$\mathbf{70.8}^{abc}_{f}$	$\mathbf{43.5}^{abc}_{f}$	$\mathbf{37.1}^{abc}_{f}$	$\mathbf{49.8}^{bc}_{f}$	$\mathbf{44.0}^{abc}_{f}$

Table 3: The percentage of relevant documents in the cluster ranked highest by ClustRank. OptCluster and OptCluster(run*i*) are the clusters containing the highest relevant-document percentage among those created across the lists, and those created from run*i*, respectively. The performance of the fusion methods from Table 1 is presented for reference. Boldface marks the best performance in a block of methods. Statistically significant differences with run1, run2 and run3 and the standard fusion method (CombSUM, CombMNZ and Borda) are marked with 'a', 'b', 'c', and 'f', respectively.

out cross-validation performed for λ as described above, are presented in Table 2.

Our first observation based on Table 2 is that ClustFuse is somewhat effective in re-ranking a single list. Indeed, in a majority of the relevant comparisons, the performance of Clust(run$i$) is better than that of run$i$; sometimes, the differences are also statistically significant. Now, fusing the re-ranked runs with the standard fusion methods yields additional (often substantial) performance improvements with respect to run2 and run3, but not with respect to run1. (Refer to CombSUM(Clust(run$\{i\}$)), CombMNZ(Clust(run$\{i\}$)), and Borda(Clust(run$\{i\}$)).)

We can also see in Table 2 that the performance of fusing the cluster-based re-ranked runs is always worse — often, to a statistically significant degree — than that of our ClustFuse approach. (Compare CombSUM(Clust(run$\{i\}$)) with ClustFuseCombSUM, CombMNZ(Clust(run$\{i\}$)) with ClustFuseCombMNZ, and Borda(Clust(run$\{i\}$)) with ClustFuseBorda.) Furthermore, there are many cases wherein the ClustFuse-based methods improve over run1 (the best performing run among the three to be fused) in a statistically-significant manner, while fusion of re-ranked runs does not. These findings attest to the merits of utilizing clusters created across the runs as is done by ClustFuse.

4.2.5 Ranking clusters with ClustRank

The ClustFuse method, which was the focus of the evaluation insofar, utilizes an estimate for the presumed amount of query-pertaining information in a cluster. (Refer back to Equations 2 and 4.) The estimate is based on the standard-fusion scores of documents in the cluster. To evaluate the quality of this estimate, we devised ClustRank. This method ranks clusters based on the estimate, and positions the constituent documents of the highest ranked cluster at top of the result list. Hence, for clusters of δ documents the resultant precision at δ (p@δ) of ClustRank is the percentage of relevant documents in the highest ranked cluster. We study the performance of ClustRank with clusters of $\delta = 5$ and $\delta = 10$ documents in Table 3. For reference comparisons, we use **OptCluster** and **OptCluster(run*i*)**: the clusters that contain the highest percentage of relevant documents among those created across the lists, and among those created from run$i$, respectively. In addition, we present the p@δ performance of the standard fusion methods (CombSUM, CombMNZ and Borda) and the ClustFuse implementations.

We can see in Table 3 that the optimal clusters among those created across the lists (OptCluster) contain a very high percentage of relevant documents. If these clusters are automatically identified, then the resultant precision-at-top-ranks performance is by far better than that of all other methods considered. Furthermore, the percentage of relevant documents in these clusters is consistently higher than that in optimal clusters that are created from documents in a run (OptCluster(run$i$)). The latter finding further motivates the use of clusters created across the lists. Yet, identifying the optimal cluster in each run yields much better performance than that of the run, which is in accordance with previous reports on clustering a single retrieved list [18].

We can also see in Table 3 that ClustRank almost always outperforms — and in several cases, statistically significantly so — the standard fusion methods. Furthermore, the highest ranked cluster by ClustRank, which can be composed of documents from the three runs, often contains higher percentage of relevant documents than that in the optimal cluster for run3 (OptCluster(run3)); however, this percentage is still much lower than that in the optimal clusters for run2 and run1. In addition, while ClustRank almost always outperforms run1 for trec3 and trec10 (although statistically significantly so only in a single case), the reverse holds for trec12. As all other fusion methods, ClustRank outperforms run2 and run3 in a statistically significant manner.

Finally, as Table 3 shows, ClustRank is consistently less effective than ClustFuse. This is not surprising as ClustRank uses only the highest ranked cluster, while ClustFuse utilizes information from all clusters, and further integrates this information with standard fusion scores.

All in all, the conclusion rising from the analysis above is the following. While ClustRank is a relatively reasonable

	trec3			trec10			trec12		
	MAP	p@5	p@10	MAP	p@5	p@10	MAP	p@5	p@10
run1	10.4	74.4	72.2	30.7	63.2	58.8	28.8	51.1	44.8
run2	9.6	72.8	67.6	27.7	54.4	50.2	28.4	52.5	48.6
run3	9.5	76.0	71.2	21.6	55.6	46.8	28.1	51.5	45.2
CombSUM	10.9^{bc}	80.8^{ab}	74.6^{b}	37.2^{bc}	$\mathbf{71.2}^{abc}$	61.0^{bc}	30.3	53.7	$\underline{\mathbf{49.2}}^{ac}$
ClustFuseCombSUM	$\underline{\mathbf{11.6}}^{abc}$	$\mathbf{82.4}^{abc}$	$\underline{\mathbf{79.0}}^{abc}_{f}$	$\mathbf{37.3}^{bc}$	70.8^{abc}	$\mathbf{61.8}^{bc}$	$\underline{\mathbf{30.5}}$	**54.3**	49.1^{ac}
CombMNZ	10.9^{bc}	80.8^{ab}	74.6^{b}	37.2^{bc}	$\mathbf{71.2}^{abc}$	61.0^{bc}	30.3	53.9	$\underline{\mathbf{49.2}}^{ac}$
ClustFuseCombMNZ	$\mathbf{11.4}^{abc}$	$\underline{\mathbf{82.8}}^{abc}$	$\mathbf{77.2}^{bc}$	$\underline{\mathbf{38.3}}^{bc}$	70.8^{abc}	$\mathbf{61.8}^{bc}$	$\underline{\mathbf{30.5}}$	**54.1**	49.1^{ac}
Borda	10.7^{bc}	80.0^{b}	75.4^{b}	35.3^{bc}	$\underline{\mathbf{71.6}}^{abc}$	60.6^{bc}	**30.2**	$\underline{\mathbf{54.7}}^{c}$	48.3^{ac}
ClustFuseBorda	$\underline{\mathbf{11.6}}^{abc}$	$\mathbf{80.4}^{b}$	$\mathbf{78.6}^{abc}$	$\mathbf{36.5}^{bc}$	71.2^{abc}	$\underline{\mathbf{62.0}}^{bc}$	29.9	54.3	$\mathbf{48.8}^{ac}$

Table 4: Fusing the three best MAP-performing runs in a track. Boldface marks the better performing between ClustFuseF and the standard fusion method F that it incorporates; a statistically significant difference between the two is marked with 'f'. Underline marks the best result in a column. Statistically significant differences between the fusion methods and run1, run2, and run3 are marked with 'a', 'b', and 'c', respectively.

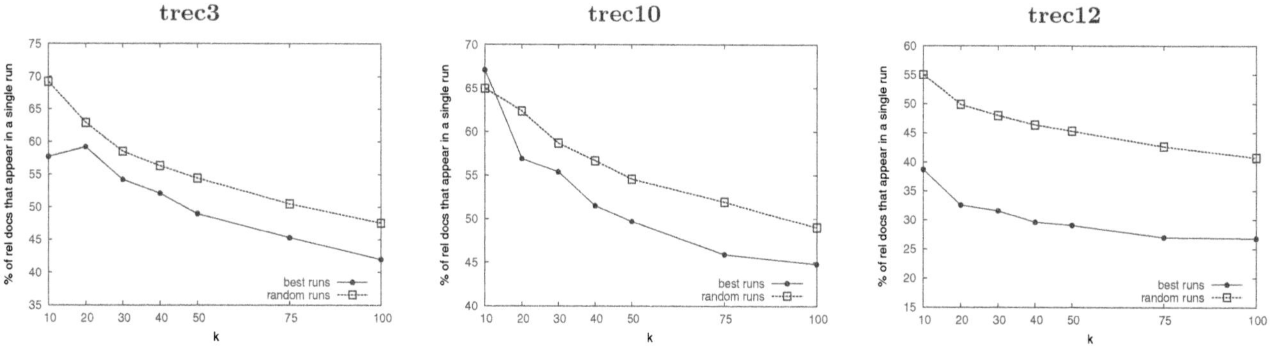

Figure 3: The percentage of relevant documents (of those that appear in the three runs) that appear in only one run as a function of the number of (top) documents considered for a run (k). We use either randomly selected runs, or the best (MAP@k) performing runs; for random runs, numbers represent averages over the 20 random samples of triplets of runs. Note: figures are not to the same scale.

method for ranking clusters based on the presumed percentage of relevant documents that they contain, more effective methods are called for. Evidently, the room for improvement, demonstrated by the numbers for the optimal clusters, is huge. We leave this challenge for future work; specifically, adapting estimates for the amount of within-cluster query-pertaining information that were proposed for the single-list setting to the multiple-lists setting that we address here. Using such estimates in ClustFuse can potentially help to improve its performance.

4.2.6 Fusing the best-performing runs in a track

Heretofore, the runs to be fused were randomly selected from all those available for a track. We now turn to study the effectiveness of ClustFuse in fusing the three most MAP(@k = 20)-effective runs in a track; these are denoted, in descending order of MAP performance, run1, run2 and run3. Naturally, this is not a realistic retrieval setting as in practice the quality of retrieval is not known. Nevertheless, this is a challenge for any fusion approach.

We can see in Table 4 that both the ClustFuse methods and the standard fusion approaches that they incorporate are effective in fusing the most effective runs in a track. Indeed, the performance transcends that of the three runs in almost all relevant comparisons (track $\times$ evaluation measure). Furthermore, in most relevant comparisons, ClustFuse outperforms the standard fusion method. While the performance differences are statistically significant for only a single relevant comparison, there are quite a few cases for trec3 in which ClustFuse improves over one of the runs in a statistically significant manner, and the standard fusion method does not; the reverse happens for a single relevant comparison in the table.

We also see that the relative improvements posted by ClustFuse over the standard fusion method when fusing the best performing runs are smaller than those posted for fusing random runs. (Compare Table 4 with Table 1). Furthermore, in a small number of cases ClustFuse is outperformed (although not to a statistically significant degree) by the standard fusion method when fusing the best performing runs, while this never happens for the random runs.

A possible explanation of these findings, following a recent report [17], can be made based on Figure 3. Figure 3 shows that the percentage of relevant documents, of those that appear in the three runs, that appear only in a single run is often higher for random runs than for the best runs; thus, the relevant-documents overlap is higher for the best runs than for the random runs. This finding can help explain the fact that the standard fusion methods that depend on this overlap are much more effective for the best runs than for the random runs — e.g., compare their performance with that of run1 in Tables 4 and 1; especially, for trec12 for which the difference in the percentages for random and best runs presented in Figure 3 (k = 20) is very high. Accordingly, our approach can improve over the standard fusion methods more for random runs than for the best runs as it

		trec3			trec10			trec12		
		MAP	p@5	p@10	MAP	p@5	p@10	MAP	p@5	p@10
Random runs	run1	8.4	68.0	64.9	14.0	39.5	34.2	25.2	48.4	42.2
	run2	6.5	57.2	54.9	10.7	34.0	29.7	20.8	42.4	36.7
	run3	4.3	41.7	40.7	6.6	23.2	20.2	13.2	29.7	25.2
	CombMNZ	7.4^{abc}	65.4^{bc}	60.9^{abc}	12.7^{bc}	40.1^{bc}	34.2^{bc}	22.7^{abc}	46.9^{abc}	39.9^{abc}
	GraphFuse	9.4^{abc}_{f}	72.7^{abc}_{f}	70.1^{abc}_{f}	$\mathbf{14.6}^{bc}$	41.8^{bc}	36.6^{bc}_{f}	$\mathbf{25.0}^{bc}_{f}$	$\mathbf{48.0}^{bc}$	$\mathbf{42.5}^{bc}_{f}$
	ClustFuseCombMNZ	$\mathbf{9.6}^{abc}_{fg}$	$\mathbf{75.2}^{abc}_{fg}$	$\mathbf{71.1}^{abc}_{fg}$	14.3^{bc}_{fg}	$\mathbf{42.9}_{fg}$	$\mathbf{37.8}^{abc}_{fg}$	24.5^{bc}_{f}	47.9^{bc}	42.3^{bc}_{f}
Best-performing runs	run1	10.4	74.4	72.2	30.7	63.2	58.8	28.8	51.1	44.8
	run2	9.6	72.8	67.6	27.7	54.4	50.2	28.4	52.5	48.6
	run3	9.5	76.0	71.2	21.6	55.6	46.8^{a}	28.1	51.5	45.2^{a}
	CombMNZ	10.9^{bc}	80.8^{ab}	74.6^{b}	37.2^{bc}	$\mathbf{71.2}^{abc}$	61.0^{bc}	30.3	53.9	$\mathbf{49.2}^{ac}$
	GraphFuse	11.0^{bc}	77.6	76.6^{b}	37.7^{bc}	70.4^{bc}	$\mathbf{62.0}^{bc}$	29.6_{f}	52.5_{f}	48.6^{ac}_{f}
	ClustFuseCombMNZ	$\mathbf{11.4}^{abc}$	$\mathbf{82.8}^{abc}$	$\mathbf{77.2}^{bc}$	$\mathbf{38.3}^{bc}$	70.8^{abc}	61.8^{bc}	**30.5**	**54.1**	49.1^{ac}

Table 5: Comparison with a graph-based fusion method (GraphFuse) [16]. Boldface marks the best result in a column per setup (random runs and best-performing runs). Statistically significant differences with run1, run2, run3, and CombMNZ are marked with 'a', 'b', 'c', and 'f' respectively; 'g' marks statistically significant differences between ClustFuseCombMNZ and GraphFuse.

can help address a low relevant-documents overlap by using inter-document similarities; and, since the standard fusion methods are already quite effective for the best runs.

Finally, we hasten to point out that in *both* settings (random runs and best runs) ClustFuse outperforms the standard fusion method that it incorporates in most relevant comparisons; and, posts more statistically significant improvements over the runs to be fused.

4.2.7 *Comparison with graph-based fusion*

As mentioned in Section 3, there is some recent work on utilizing inter-document similarities for fusion using a graph-based approach [16]. Specifically, a graph is constructed from document instances in the lists, and edge weights are based on inter-document similarities and retrieval scores of documents. The stationary distribution of a Markov chain defined over the graph is used to rank documents. The best performing graph-based method reported (BagDupMNZ) [16], which we refer to here as **GraphFuse**, amounts to CombMNZ if inter-document-similarities are not utilized. As our ClustFuseCombMNZ method also amounts to CombMNZ if inter-document-similarities are not utilized (i.e., cluster-based information is not used), we turn to compare the performance of ClustFuseCombMNZ with that of GraphFuse. As is the case for the λ parameter of ClustFuseCombMNZ, we use leave-one-out cross validation for setting the values of the two free parameters that GraphFuse incorporates (namely, graph out degree and edge weight smoothing factor); the search ranges for the parameter values are those originally reported [16]. The performance numbers for fusing randomly selected runs and the best-performing runs are presented in Table 5.[5]

We see in Table 5 that for the random-runs setting ClustFuseCombMNZ outperforms GraphFuse to a statistically significantly degree for 5 out of 9 relevant comparisons (track $\times$ evaluation measure), while the reverse holds for a single relevant comparison. (Refer to the 'g' marks.) Furthermore, for trec10 ClustFuseCombMNZ outperforms CombMNZ in a statistically significant manner for all three evaluation measures, while GraphFuse does so only for p@10. However, for trec12 GraphFuse is somewhat more effective than ClustFuseCombMNZ, although not statistically significantly so.

For the best-runs setup, ClustFuseCombMNZ outperforms GraphFuse in almost all relevant comparisons. Although the performance differences are not statistically significant, ClustFuseCombMNZ posts more statistically significant improvements over the runs, especially for trec3. Furthermore, for trec12, GraphFuse underperforms CombMNZ in a statistically significant manner for all three evaluation measures, while ClustFuseCombMNZ outperforms CombMNZ for two evaluation measures; moreover, in contrast to GraphFuse, ClustFuseCombMNZ is never outperformed by CombMNZ in a statistically significant manner.

All in all, we see that both ClustFuseCombMNZ and GraphFuse that utilize inter document-similarities, although using different approaches, are highly effective for fusion. Yet, ClustFuseCombMNZ is somewhat more effective — and robust, with respect to relative improvements over CombMNZ — than GraphFuse, which attests to the potential merits of using document clusters to exploit inter-document similarities. In addition, we note that an interesting venue for future work is using graph-based methods in ClustFuse. A case in point, a method similar in spirit to GraphFuse was used to find clusters containing a high percentage of relevant documents in the single retrieved list setting [18]. Adapting the method to the multiple lists setting, and integrating it in ClustFuse, is a challenge we plan to address.

5. CONCLUSIONS

We presented a novel approach to fusing document lists retrieved in response to a query. The approach is based on integrating information used by standard fusion methods (i.e., retrieval scores or ranks) with that induced from clusters of similar documents created across the lists. Specifically, our model, which can incorporate various standard fusion methods, lets similar documents across the lists provide relevance-status support to each other. Empirical evaluation shows that our model outperforms the standard fusion method that it integrates. In addition, we showed that our cluster-based fusion approach outperforms standard fusion of re-ranked lists, wherein list re-ranking is based on

[5]The performance numbers of GraphFuse that we present (for the best-runs setting) are different than those originally reported [16] for the following reasons. While we use leave-one-out cross validation to set free-parameter values (using MAP for the performance-optimization criterion), those were not learned in the original report. Rather, the best potential average performance with respect to free-parameter values (optimized for average p@5) was presented.

clusters of documents from the list. We also showed that clusters created from documents across the lists can contain a much higher percentage of relevant documents than that in clusters created from documents in a list — a finding which further motivates our approach.

Acknowledgments We thank the reviewers for their comments. This paper is based upon work supported in part by the Israel Science Foundation under grant no. 557/09, and by IBM's SUR award. Any opinions, findings and conclusions or recommendations expressed in this material are the authors' and do not necessarily reflect those of the sponsors.

6. REFERENCES

[1] C. C. V. ant Garrison W. Cottrell. Fusion via linear combination of scores. *Information Retrieval*, 1(3):151–173, 1999.

[2] J. A. Aslam and M. Montague. Models for metasearch. In *Proceedings of SIGIR*, pages 276–284, 2001.

[3] S. M. Beitzel, E. C. Jensen, A. Chowdhury, O. Frieder, D. A. Grossman, and N. Goharian. Disproving the fusion hypothesis: An analysis of data fusion via effective information retrieval strategies. In *Proceedings of SAC*, pages 823–827, 2003.

[4] S. M. Beitzel, E. C. Jensen, O. Frieder, A. Chowdhury, and G. Pass. Surrogate scoring for improved metasearch precision. In *Proceedings of SIGIR*, pages 583–584, 2005.

[5] A. Chowdhury, O. Frieder, D. A. Grossman, and M. C. McCabe. Analyses of multiple-evidence combinations for retrieval strategies. In *Proceedings of SIGIR*, pages 394–395, 2001. poster.

[6] N. Craswell, D. Hawking, and P. B. Thistlewaite. Merging results from isolated search engines. In *Proceedings of ADC*, pages 189–200, 1999.

[7] F. Crestani and S. Wu. Testing the cluster hypothesis in distributed information retrieval. *Information Processing and Management*, 42(5):1137–1150, 2006.

[8] W. B. Croft, editor. *Advances in Information Retrieval: Recent Research from the Center for Intelligent Information Retrieval.* Number 7 in The Kluwer International Series on Information Retrieval. Kluwer, 2000.

[9] W. B. Croft. Combining approaches to information retrieval. In Croft [8], chapter 1, pages 1–36.

[10] P. Das-Gupta and J. Katzer. A study of the overlap among document representations. In *Proceedgins of SIGIR*, pages 106–114, 1983.

[11] F. Diaz. Regularizing ad hoc retrieval scores. In *Proceedings of CIKM*, pages 672–679, 2005.

[12] C. Dwork, R. Kumar, M. Naor, and D. Sivakumar. Rank aggregation methods for the Web. In *Proceedings of WWW*, pages 613–622, Hong Kong, 2001.

[13] E. A. Fox and J. A. Shaw. Combination of multiple searches. In *Proceedings of TREC-2*, 1994.

[14] A. Griffiths, H. C. Luckhurst, and P. Willett. Using interdocument similarity information in document retrieval systems. *Journal of the American Society for Information Science (JASIS)*, 37(1):3–11, 1986.

[15] M. A. Hearst and J. O. Pedersen. Reexamining the cluster hypothesis: Scatter/Gather on retrieval results. In *Proceedings of SIGIR*, pages 76–84, 1996.

[16] A. K. Kozorovitzky and O. Kurland. From "identical" to "similar": Fusing retrieved lists based on inter-document similarities. In *Proceedings of ICTIR*, pages 212–223, 2009.

[17] A. K. Kozorovitzky and O. Kurland. From "identical" to "similar": Fusing retrieved lists based on inter-document similarities. *Journal of Artificial Intelligence Research*, 41, 2011. (To appear.).

[18] O. Kurland. The opposite of smoothing: A language model approach to ranking query-specific document clusters. In *Proceedings of SIGIR*, pages 171–178, 2008.

[19] O. Kurland. Re-ranking search results using language models of query-specific clusters. *Journal of Information Retrieval*, 12(4):437–460, August 2009.

[20] O. Kurland and L. Lee. Corpus structure, language models, and ad hoc information retrieval. In *Proceedings of SIGIR*, pages 194–201, 2004.

[21] O. Kurland and L. Lee. Respect my authority! HITS without hyperlinks utilizing cluster-based language models. In *Proceedings of SIGIR*, pages 83–90, 2006.

[22] J. H. Lee. Combining multiple evidence from different properties of weighting schemes. In *Proceedings of SIGIR*, pages 180–188, 1995.

[23] J. H. Lee. Analyses of multiple evidence combination. In *Proceedings of SIGIR*, pages 267–276, 1997.

[24] D. Lillis, F. Toolan, R. W. Collier, and J. Dunnion. Probfuse: a probabilistic approach to data fusion. In *Proceedings of SIGIR*, pages 139–146, 2006.

[25] X. Liu and W. B. Croft. Cluster-based retrieval using language models. In *Proceedings of SIGIR*, pages 186–193, 2004.

[26] X. Liu and W. B. Croft. Experiments on retrieval of optimal clusters. Technical Report IR-478, Center for Intelligent Information Retrieval (CIIR), University of Massachusetts, 2006.

[27] X. Liu and W. B. Croft. Evaluating text representations for retrieval of the best group of documents. In *Proceedings of ECIR*, pages 454–462, 2008.

[28] L. Meister, O. Kurland, and I. G. Kalmanovich. Re-ranking search results using an additional retrieved list. *Information Retrieval*, 2010.

[29] M. Montague and J. A. Aslam. Condorcet fusion for improved retrieval. In *Proceedings of CIKM*, pages 538–548, 2002.

[30] S. B. Selvadurai. Implementing a metasearch framework with content-directed result merging. Master's thesis, North Carolina State University, 2007.

[31] J. Seo and W. B. Croft. Geometric representations for multiple documents. In *Proceedings of SIGIR*, pages 251–258, 2010.

[32] J. G. Shanahan, J. Bennett, D. A. Evans, D. A. Hull, and J. Montgomery. Clairvoyance Corporation experiments in the TREC 2003. High accuracy retrieval from documents (HARD) track. In *Proceedings of TREC-12*, pages 152–160, 2003.

[33] D. Sheldon, M. Shokouhi, M. Szummer, and N. Craswell. Lambdamerge: merging the results of query reformulations. In *Proceedings of WSDM*, pages 795–804, 2011.

[34] M. Shokouhi. Segmentation of search engine results for effective data-fusion. In *Proceedings of ECIR*, pages 185–197, 2007.

[35] M. Shokouhi, L. Azzopardi, and P. Thomas. Effective query expansion for federated search. In *Proceedings of SIGIR*, pages 427–434, 2009.

[36] X. M. Shou and M. Sanderson. Experiments on data fusion using headline information. In *Proceedgins of SIGIR*, pages 413–414, 2002.

[37] M. D. Smucker, J. Allan, and B. Carterette. A comparison of statistical significance tests for information retrieval evaluation. In *Proceedings of CIKM*, pages 623–632, 2007.

[38] I. Soboroff, C. K. Nicholas, and P. Cahan. Ranking retrieval systems without relevance judgments. In *Proceedings of SIGIR*, pages 66–73, 2001.

[39] T. Tao, X. Wang, Q. Mei, and C. Zhai. Language model information retrieval with document expansion. In *Proceedings of HLT/NAACL*, pages 407–414, 2006.

[40] A. Tombros, R. Villa, and C. van Rijsbergen. The effectiveness of query-specific hierarchic clustering in information retrieval. *Information Processing and Management*, 38(4):559–582, 2002.

[41] T. Tsikrika and M. Lalmas. Merging techniques for performing data fusion on the web. In *Proceedings of CIKM*, pages 127–134, 2001.

[42] C. J. van Rijsbergen. *Information Retrieval.* Butterworths, second edition, 1979.

[43] E. M. Voorhees. Overview of the TREC 2005 robust retrieval task. In *Proceedings of TREC-14*, 2005.

[44] E. M. Voorhees, N. K. Gupta, and B. Johnson-Laird. The collection fusion problem. In *In Proceedings of TREC-3*, 1994.

[45] P. Willett. Query specific automatic document classification. *International Forum on Information and Documentation*, 10(2):28–32, 1985.

[46] L. Yang, D. Ji, G. Zhou, Y. Nie, and G. Xiao. Document re-ranking using cluster validation and label propagation. In *Proceedings of CIKM*, pages 690–697, 2006.

[47] H. P. Young. An axiomatization of Borda's rule. *Journal of Economic Theory*, 9:43–52, 1974.

[48] O. Zamir and O. Etzioni. Web document clustering: a feasibility demonstration. In *Proceedings of SIGIR*, pages 46–54, 1998.

[49] C. Zhai and J. D. Lafferty. A study of smoothing methods for language models applied to ad hoc information retrieval. In *Proceedings of SIGIR*, pages 334–342, 2001.

System Effectiveness, User Models, and User Utility: A Conceptual Framework for Investigation

Ben Carterette
Department of Computer & Information Sciences
University of Delaware, Newark, DE, USA 19716
carteret@cis.udel.edu

ABSTRACT

There is great interest in producing effectiveness measures that model user behavior in order to better model the utility of a system to its users. These measures are often formulated as a sum over the product of a discount function of ranks and a gain function mapping relevance assessments to numeric utility values. We develop a conceptual framework for analyzing such effectiveness measures based on classifying members of this broad family of measures into four distinct families, each of which reflects a different notion of system utility. Within this framework we can hypothesize about the properties that such a measure should have and test those hypotheses against user and system data. Along the way we present a collection of novel results about specific measures and relationships between them.

Categories and Subject Descriptors: H.3 [**Information Storage and Retrieval**]; H.3.4 [**Systems and Software**]: Performance Evaluation

General Terms: Experimentation, Measurement

Keywords: information retrieval, evaluation, user models

1. INTRODUCTION

There has always been interest in producing effectiveness measures that model user behavior for systems-based evaluations with test collections. These measures frequently involve summing over the product of a discount function of ranks and a gain function mapping relevance assessments to numeric utility values, i.e.

$$M = \sum_{k=1}^{K} gain(rel_k) \cdot discount(k)$$

The widely-used *discounted cumulative gain* (DCG) measure, for instance, is typically formulated with an exponential gain function and a log-harmonic discount [10], while *rank-biased precision* (RBP) uses binary relevance and a geometric discount [12]. *Expected reciprocal rank* (ERR) maps graded relevance judgments to probabilities and discounts dynamically according to the relevance judgments at previous ranks [6]. Many traditional measures can be interpreted this way as well [21].

The discount function is often viewed as modeling a user that scans down a ranked list, growing less interested with each successive rank; the gain function models the utility the user derives from each document. This interpretation hides a great deal of diversity in the choices one can make in such a measure. Some use a probability density function as the discount; others do not. Some discount dynamically depending on relevance; others use a static discount. Depending on these choices, the actual user model can vary in subtle ways. In this work we aim to formulate a *conceptual framework*—a way to organize and describe these choices so as to provide structure for reasoning about properties of these measures in general.

To illustrate this point, consider DCG and RBP: click log analysis has suggested that RBP matches "reality" (in the sense of being more closely correlated to observed click behavior) much closer than DCG [6, 20, 21]. Despite that, DCG continues to be far more widely-used in research and development. We may hypothesize why: inertia? familiarity? or is it possible that DCG is actually modeling something quite different than RBP, and what it measures as a result is more useful to developers? We lean towards the latter explanation, and with this work we hope to provide a framework within which to test it.

Though we use RBP and DCG as motivators, our interest is not specifically in them but in model-based measures in general. The primary contribution of this work is increased understanding of effectiveness measures based on explicit user models. We define our framework in Section 2; this framework generates many possible measures (Section 3). Given the measures generated by the framework, we formulate specific hypotheses about qualities such a measure should have and test them in data (Section 4). Finally, we explore differences in modeling document utility independently of rank discounting (Section 5). Along the way we prove a number of novel results about individual measures and relationships between them.

SIGIR'11, July 24–28, 2011, Beijing, China.

2. MODELS

We argue that model-based measures are actually composed from three distinct underlying models:

1. a *browsing model* that describes how a user interacts with results;

2. a model of *document utility*, describing how a user derives utility from individual relevant documents;
3. a *utility accumulation model* that describes how a user accumulates utility in the course of browsing.

Decisions about each component model can be made independently of the others. This establishes a framework for evaluating the outcomes of those decisions.

By far the most well-developed browsing model is that of a user scanning down ranked results one-by-one and stopping at some rank k. In this work we focus entirely on that model, comparing different ways of modeling the stopping rank. Similarly, binary and graded relevance are the two most common ways to model document utility. For simplicity, throughout this section and the next we only consider binary relevance. Graded relevance (and other types of relevance or utility judgments) can be included in measures in relatively straightforward ways discussed in Section 5 below.

Thus the scope of this section and the next is limited to describing four utility accumulation models that we see in existing measures, as well as looking at different choices in modeling the stopping rank k in the simple browsing model. While there are other, more accurate browsing models [20, 11, 2], we believe they can be studied within some framework similar to the one we present here.

2.1 Model 1: Expected utility

Consider a model of a user as progressing down a ranked list, looking at each document, and stopping at some rank k. The probabilistic component of the model is a distribution $P(k)$. Since a user can only stop at exactly one rank, $\sum_{i=1}^{\infty} P(i) = 1$. To model the cost of browsing, we usually constrain $P(k)$ so that $P(1) \geq P(2) \geq ... \geq P(n)$.

Given a probability distribution, a measure reflecting this model has the form:

$$M_1 : \sum_{k=1}^{n} rel_k P(k) \tag{1}$$

This expression can be understood as the expected relevance of the document at the stopping rank. This follows from the fact that the events of stopping at each rank k are mutually exclusive, and an expectation is computed as the sum of event probabilities times a numeric value of the event (in this case document relevance).

An exemplar for this model is *rank-biased precision* (RBP) [12], in which k is assumed to be geometrically distributed with "persistence" or "patience" parameter θ:[1]

$$P_{RBP}(k) = (1 - \theta)^{k-1}\theta$$

θ is a value between 0 and 1 reflecting the patience of users for progressing down the ranked list. It can be thought of as an *a priori* probability of quitting at any given rank; the probability that a user will stop at rank $k = 2$ is the probability that they do not stop at rank $k = 1$ times the probability that they do stop at rank $k = 2$: $(1 - \theta)\theta$.

2.2 Model 2: Expected total utility

The model above captures a user stopping at a particular rank, but not that the user looked at the documents above that rank. No matter where a user chooses to stop, they will see the first document with probability 1. They will only see the second if they do not stop at rank 1, so the probability of viewing document 2 is $1 - P(1)$. Continuing this way, it becomes apparent that the viewing probability at rank k is simply the cumulative probability of stopping at all ranks from k to n. Define this cumulative probability $F(k)$ as:

$$F(k) = \sum_{i=k}^{n} P(k)$$

Given a distribution, we can define a measure with the form:

$$M_2 : \sum_{k=1}^{n} rel_k F(k) = \sum_{k=1}^{n} rel_k \sum_{i=k}^{n} P(i) \tag{2}$$

The underlying user model becomes more apparent after algebraic manipulation. Arranging summands $rel_k P(i)$ in an $n \times n$ matrix, we obtain the following:

$$\begin{bmatrix} rel_1 P(1) & rel_1 P(2) & rel_1 P(3) & \cdots & rel_1 P(n) \\ & rel_2 P(2) & rel_2 P(3) & \cdots & rel_2 P(n) \\ & & rel_3 P(3) & \cdots & rel_3 P(n) \\ & & & \cdots & \cdots \\ & & & & rel_n P(n) \end{bmatrix}$$

Summing each row first, then summing the results, gives the expression above. Alternatively, summing each column first shows that:

$$\begin{aligned} M_2 : \sum_{k=1}^{n} rel_k \sum_{i=k}^{n} P(i) &= \sum_{k=1}^{n} P(k) \sum_{i=1}^{k} rel_i \\ &= \sum_{k=1}^{n} R_k P(k) \end{aligned}$$

where $R_k = \sum_{i=1}^{k} rel_i$, i.e. the number of relevant documents retrieved from rank 1 to rank k. This reveals an alternative user model: a user picks a stopping rank k, and then derives utility from *all* of the relevant documents from ranks 1 through k. The measure is the expected total utility.

We claim that *discounted cumulative gain* (DCG) [10] is an exemplar of this model, with $F(k) = 1/\log_2(k + 1)$. Define a stopping probability:

$$P_{DCG}(k) = \frac{1}{\log_2(k+1)} - \frac{1}{\log_2(k+2)}$$

Then:

$$\begin{aligned} \sum_{k=1}^{n} R_k P_{DCG}(k) &= \sum_{k=1}^{n} \left(\frac{1}{\log_2(k+1)} - \frac{1}{\log_2(k+2)} \right) \sum_{i=1}^{k} rel_i \\ &= \sum_{k=1}^{n} rel_k \sum_{i=k}^{n} \left(\frac{1}{\log_2(i+1)} - \frac{1}{\log_2(i+2)} \right) \\ &= \sum_{k=1}^{n} rel_k \left(\frac{1}{\log_2(k+1)} - \frac{1}{\log_2(n+2)} \right) \end{aligned}$$

For large enough n, $1/\log_2(n + 2)$ becomes negligible, and the expression reduces to:

$$\sum_{k=1}^{n} rel_k \frac{1}{\log_2(k+1)} = DCG@n$$

This means that DCG can be interpreted as modeling a user that picks a stopping rank k with probability $P_{DCG}(k)$,

[1]RBP was not originally defined as the expected relevance of one document, but it is a valid (and we argue more parsimonious) way to backfit to the expression. We discuss this further in Section 3.2.

then derives utility from all relevant documents to that rank. While others have treated DCG's discount as a viewing probability rather than a stopping probability [6], as far as we know this overall interpretation of DCG is novel, and clearly different from the usual interpretation which is closer to M_1 above. Furthermore, the stopping probability distribution is shaped similarly to the geometric distribution used by RBP (Fig. 1), meaning that DCG may encode a more realistic browsing model than previously thought.

2.3 Model 3: Expected effort

Rather than compute expected *utility*, as M_1 and M_2 do, we could compute the expected *effort* a user must put forth to achieve a particular amount of utility.

$$M_3 : \sum_{k=1}^{n} f(k)P(k) \qquad (3)$$

Here $P(k)$ is conditional on relevance judgments (the "gain times discount" formulation is recovered from the use of rel_i in $P(k)$). Unlike the previous two models, this is an expectation of effort modeled by rank rather than an expectation of relevance. If $f(k) = k$, it is the expected stopping rank; if $f(k) = 1/k$ it is the expected reciprocal stopping rank. The presumption is that $f(k)$ can be defined in a way that accurately reflects user effort.

The *expected reciprocal rank* (ERR) [6] measure is exemplar for this class. Let $f(k) = 1/k$ and

$$P_{ERR}(k) = \theta_{rel_k} \prod_{i=1}^{k-1} (1 - \theta_{rel_i})$$

Here θ_{rel_i} is a parameter indicating the probability that a document with relevance rel_i would be useful to the user. With binary relevance ($rel_i = 0$ or 1), and with $\theta_0 = 0$ and $\theta_1 = \theta$, this can be rewritten as:

$$P_{ERR}(k) = rel_k (1 - \theta)^{R_k - 1} \theta$$

revealing that P_{ERR} is geometric over total accumulated relevance, with non-zero probability only at ranks at which relevant documents appear. Here θ can still be understood as a patience parameter, as in RBP, but now the probability of stopping at a nonrelevant document is zero while the probability of stopping at a relevant document is θ. Thus we could reasonably re-express this model as:

$$M_3 : \sum_{R_k=1}^{R} f(k)P(R_k)$$

This makes explicit the idea of evaluating the effort the user expends to find R_k relevant documents (or in general to achieve a given amount of utility).

2.4 Model 4: Expected average utility

The final model combines the utility- or reward-based models M_1 and M_2 and the effort-based model M_3.

$$M_4 : \sum_{k=1}^{n} rel_k \sum_{i=k}^{n} f(i)P(i) \qquad (4)$$

Intuitively, this models a user that, after each relevant document, considers the expected effort of further browsing. As with M_2, the underlying user model becomes more transparent after algebraic manipulation:

$$\sum_{k=1}^{n} rel_k \sum_{i=k}^{n} f(i)P(i) = \sum_{k=1}^{n} f(k)P(k) \sum_{i=1}^{k} rel_i = \sum_{k=1}^{n} f(k) R_k P(k)$$

and if $f(k) = 1/k$,

$$\sum_{k=1}^{n} \frac{R_k}{k} P(k) = \sum_{k=1}^{n} prec@k \cdot P(k)$$

Thus the user model is based on average gain per document viewed: a user stops at a rank k and gains R_k total utility over k documents for an average of $prec@k$ each.

Average precision (AP) is the exemplar for this model (note the similarity to Robertson's AP model [13]). If

$$P_{AP}(k) = \frac{rel_k}{R}$$

where R is the total number of relevant documents in the corpus, we recover AP from the expression. Like $P_{ERR}(k)$, this models a user that will never stop at a nonrelevant document, but unlike any of our other distributions, it uses a simple uniform distribution over all possible stopping points. AP assumes knowledge of the complete set of relevant documents, but this is not required for measures in this family.

3. MEASURES

The previous section establishes our framework with four utility accumulation models for one common browsing model. Each accumulation model has a well-known exemplar measure, and those four measures have four different ways to model the stopping rank for browsing:

$$P_{RBP}(k) = (1 - \theta)^{k-1}\theta$$
$$P_{DCG}(k) = \frac{1}{\log_\theta(k + \theta - 1)} - \frac{1}{\log_\theta(k + \theta)}$$
$$P_{ERR}(k) = rel_k(1 - \theta)^{R_k - 1}\theta$$
$$P_{AP}(k) = \frac{rel_k}{R}$$

For compactness we will assume base $\theta = 2$ for P_{DCG}. For simplicity of exposition we still assume binary relevance, which is where the simplified P_{ERR} comes from. R_k is the total number of relevant documents retrieved at ranks 1 through k. We will add two more distributions to those:

$$P_{RR}(k) = \frac{1}{k(k+1)} \qquad P_{RRR}(k) = \frac{rel_k}{R_k(R_k + 1)}$$

These distributions are interesting because their cumulative forms are reciprocal ranks—hence the names P_{RR} (for reciprocal rank) and P_{RRR} (for reciprocal relevant rank)—and because they arise naturally as a mixture of the geometric distributions in both RBP and binary-ERR (Section 3.4).

The six distributions can be characterized by whether they are *static*, i.e. independent of relevance judgments, or *dynamic*, i.e. dependent on a specific ranking (cf. Yilmaz et al. [20]). P_{RBP}, P_{DCG}, and P_{RR} are static; P_{ERR}, P_{AP}, and P_{RRR} are dynamic.

All six distributions and their cumulative forms $F(k)$ are illustrated in Figure 1. The three static distributions have

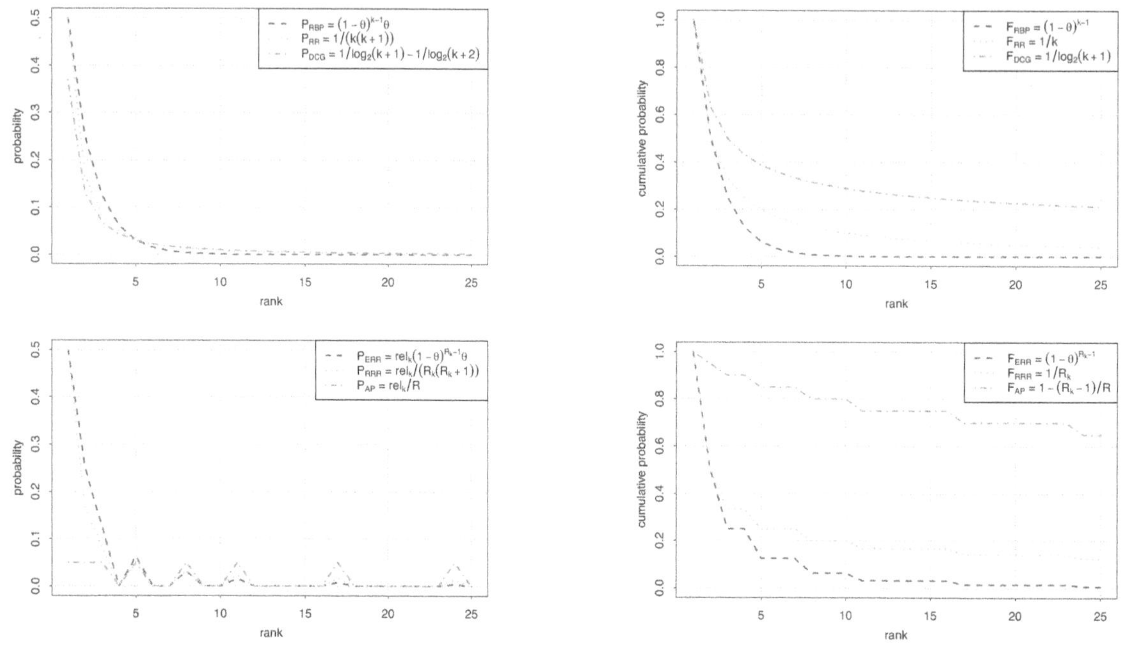

Figure 1: Comparison of stopping probability density functions. The left two plots compare stopping probabilities; the right two compare viewing probabilities (cumulative distributions of stopping probabilities). Upper left: static density functions; upper right: static cumulative density functions. Lower left: dynamic density functions (for a ranking with relevant documents at ranks 1, 2, 3, 5, 8, 11, 17, 24); lower right: dynamic cumulative density functions.

similar shape, but P_{DCG} and P_{RR} have much fatter tails than P_{RBP}—while this is difficult to see by inspection of Figure 1, it is very clear on a log-scale plot. Furthermore, P_{DCG} has a substantially fatter tail than P_{RR}, which becomes clear when looking at their cumulative densities. The dynamic distributions all give zero stopping probability to ranks at which nonrelevant documents appear. P_{ERR} and P_{RRR} have a similar shape over relevant documents, but P_{RRR} has a fatter tail (visible by inspection and very clear in the cumulative density). P_{AP} is uniform over relevant documents, so its cumulative density decreases slowly. For RBP and ERR, we used $\theta = 0.5$; these properties hold for other common values.

3.1 Alternative measures

The choice of a probability distribution produces up to four different measures, one for each model. We have mixed and matched models and distributions to produce eleven measures in addition to our four exemplars (Table 1). We have attempted to name them in a way that makes clear both the choice of model and distribution.

RBTR (rank biased total relevance, M_2 with P_{RBP}):

$$RBTR = \sum_{k=1}^{n} R_k(1-\theta)^{k-1}\theta = \sum_{k=1}^{n} rel_k(1-\theta)^{k-1}$$

RBAP (rank biased average precision, M_4 with P_{RBP}):

$$RBAP = \sum_{k=1}^{n} prec@k \cdot (1-\theta)^{k-1}\theta$$

CDG (cumulated discounted gain, M_1 with P_{DCG}):

$$CDG = \sum_{k=1}^{n} rel_k \left(\frac{1}{\log_2(k+1)} - \frac{1}{\log_2(k+2)}\right)$$

DAG (discounted average gain, M_4 with P_{DCG}):

$$DAG = \sum_{k=1}^{n} prec@k \left(\frac{1}{\log_2(k+1)} - \frac{1}{\log_2(k+2)}\right)$$

EPR (expected precision, M_4 with P_{ERR}):

$$EPR = \sum_{k=1}^{n} prec@k \cdot rel_k(1-\theta)^{R_k-1}\theta$$

ARR (average reciprocal rank, M_3 with P_{AP}):

$$ARR = \sum_{k=1}^{n} \frac{rel_k}{kR}$$

RRG (reciprocal rank gain, M_1 with P_{RR}):

$$RRG = \sum_{k=1}^{n} \frac{rel_k}{k(k+1)}$$

RR (reciprocal rank, M_2 with P_{RR}):

$$RR = \sum_{k=1}^{n} \frac{R_k}{k(k+1)} = \sum_{k=1}^{n} \frac{rel_k}{k}$$

RAP (reciprocal average precision, M_4 with P_{RR}):

$$RAP = \sum_{k=1}^{n} prec@k \cdot \frac{1}{k(k+1)}$$

type	$P(k\|\theta, rel_1...rel_n)$	$M_1: \sum rel_k P(k)$	$M_2: \sum R_k P(k)$	$M_3: \sum \frac{1}{k} P(k)$	$M_4: \sum prec@k P(k)$
static	$P_{RBP} = (1-\theta)^{k-1}\theta$	**RBP**	RBTR	–	RBAP
	$P_{DCG} = \frac{1}{\log(k+1)} - \frac{1}{\log(k+2)}$	CDG	**DCG**	–	DAG
	$P_{RR} = \frac{1}{k(k+1)}$	RRG	RR	–	RAP
dynamic	$P_{ERR} = rel_k(1-\theta)^{R_k-1}\theta$	–	–	**ERR**	EPR
	$P_{AP} = \frac{rel_k}{R}$	–	–	ARR	**AP**
	$P_{RRR} = \frac{rel_k}{R_k(R_k+1)}$	–	–	RRR	RRAP

Table 1: A model and a probability distribution together specify a measure, or possibly a family of measures parametrized by θ. Cells with – have been deemed uninteresting because they are either constant-valued or isomorphic to traditional recall or precision. Measures in bold font are the chosen exemplars for the model.

RRR (reciprocal relevant rank, M_3 with P_{RRR}):

$$RRR = \sum_{k=1}^{n} \frac{1}{k} \frac{rel_k}{R_k(R_k+1)}$$

RRAP (reciprocal relevant average precision, M_4 with P_{RRR}):

$$RRAP = \sum_{k=1}^{n} prec@k \frac{rel_k}{R_k(R_k+1)}$$

We do not claim that these measures are altogether new to IR—we know that some have been described before in various contexts (particularly our so-called RR, which has frequently been described as "DCG with a reciprocal rank discount"). Furthermore, there are other model-based measures that we do not discuss (e.g. the NCU family [16]). Our interest is less in developing or arguing for any particular measures than in using them to explore hypotheses about model-based measures in general.

3.2 Normalization

Some of the measures require normalization. The M_2 family in particular is heavily dependent on the total number of judged relevant documents for a topic. In addition, some of the probability distributions may not sum to one if the total number of relevant documents is low or if the ranking is truncated. Both of these are confounding effects that normalization helps resolve.

To normalize, we simply divide the value of the measure by the maximum possible value given the judged relevant documents, i.e. the value of the measure on a perfect ranking. This ensures that the maximum achievable value is 1 for all topics and all systems. This is of course a well-known normalization procedure, commonly used with DCG to produce nDCG [10]. We will apply it to all measures in the M_2 family, as well as a few other measures that do not naturally fall between 0 and 1 such as ARR.

Normalization is a somewhat thorny topic. In presenting RBP, Moffat and Zobel started with an unnormalized version that would fit in our M_2 family, but explicitly chose not to normalize by the maximum achievable effectiveness—instead normalizing by the expected number of documents viewed [12] and thereby moving the measure into the M_1 family. There is a tradeoff between preserving the user model and having a measure that can be averaged across topics, and it is not always clear how to resolve it.

3.3 Rank cut-offs

Some measures are calculated to a pre-specified rank cut-off rather than over the full ranking of n documents. This is particularly true of DCG. In the case of a rank cut-off $K \ll n$, the math in Section 2.2 does not work—K must be large enough that $1/\log_2(K+2)$ is close to zero, and that is certainly not the case for the usual values of K.

There is a simple resolution that fits with the user model, though. First, note that we can express DCG@K in terms of $P(k)$ and $F(K+1)$ with some simple algebraic manipulation:

$$\begin{aligned} DCG@K &= \sum_{k=1}^{K} rel_k \frac{1}{\log_2(k+1)} = \sum_{k=1}^{K} rel_k F_{DCG}(k) \\ &= \sum_{k=1}^{K} rel_k \sum_{i=k}^{n} P_{DCG}(i) \\ &= \sum_{k=1}^{K} rel_k \left(\sum_{i=k}^{K} P_{DCG}(i) + \sum_{i=K+1}^{n} P_{DCG}(i) \right) \\ &= \sum_{k=1}^{K} rel_k \left(\sum_{i=k}^{K} P_{DCG}(i) + F_{DCG}(K+1) \right) \\ &= \sum_{k=1}^{K} rel_k \sum_{i=k}^{K} P_{DCG}(i) + \sum_{k=1}^{K} rel_k F_{DCG}(K+1) \end{aligned}$$

We can then apply the same algebraic trick we used in Section 2.2 to complete the expression as:

$$DCG@K = \sum_{k=1}^{K} R_k P_{DCG}(k) + R_K F_{DCG}(K+1)$$

Note that $R_K F_{DCG}(K+1) = \sum_{k=K+1}^{n} R_K P_{DCG}(k)$. Thus the user model is exactly the same. The difference is that calculation of the measure now assumes the worst case for a user that chooses to stop beyond rank K—that the user will not find any new relevant documents, and therefore will only derive utility from those at ranks 1–K.

This argument generalizes to any M_2 measure.Therefore a rank cut-off K solves a problem with non-converging discounts by making a worst-case assumption about the effectiveness of the system below K.

3.4 Reciprocal rank distributions

Here we show how our P_{RR} and P_{RRR} distributions emerge from a mixture of geometric distributions, and that their cumulative forms are reciprocal ranks.

The geometric distribution has a parameter θ that requires the researcher/developer to specify a value *a priori*. Perhaps being unwilling to make any strong statements about user patience, one could instead use several different values of θ and average the results. Taken to the limit, they could obtain $P(k)$ by averaging geometric distributions over all possible values of θ:

$$P(k) = \int_0^1 P(k|\theta)p(\theta)d\theta = \int_0^1 (1-\theta)^{k-1}\theta p(\theta)d\theta$$

where $p(\theta)$ is uniform over the range $[0, 1]$. Since it is uniform, we can disregard it; then integration by parts gives:

$$P_{RR}(k) = \frac{1}{k(k+1)}$$

Thus P_{RR} can be seen as an average of infinitely many geometric distributions.

The cumulative distribution is:

$$F_{RR}(k) = \sum_{i=k}^{n} \frac{1}{i(i+1)} = \sum_{i=k}^{n} \frac{i+1-i}{i(i+1)} = \sum_{i=k}^{n} \left(\frac{1}{i} - \frac{1}{i+1}\right)$$
$$= \frac{1}{k} - \frac{1}{n+1}$$

As $n \to \infty$, $\frac{1}{n+1} \to 0$, so for large enough n this is approximated as reciprocal rank $1/k$. It does not require very large n for the effect to be negligible.

The same argument generalizes the binary-relevance version of P_{ERR} to P_{RRR} as an average of infinitely many geometric distributions over ranks of relevant documents.

4. ANALYSIS

We have presented a framework for classifying and generating measures that model system utility to a user. The benefit of a framework is that it poses questions and also provides a guide to answering them. Our goal is not to evaluate the new measures we propose, but to formulate specific hypotheses about model-based measures in general and answer them by appealing to our suite of measures.

Some of the questions the framework raises are:

1. Are utility-based models (M_1, M_2) better than effort-based models (M_3, M_4)? Our hypothesis is that there is no difference on average.

2. Are measures based on stopping probabilities (M_1, M_3) better than measures based on viewing probabilities (M_2, M_4)? Our hypothesis is that the latter are more robust to different sources of variance.

3. What properties should P have to produce a good measure? We hypothesize that it should have a fatter tail (within reason), and that static distributions are more robust than dynamic.

"Better" and "good" are of course qualitative words whose meaning depends on the retrieval task being studied, the users of the system, and a host of other factors. We will look at goodness-of-fit to user data and robustness of evaluation, though there are other ways to evaluate these questions.

4.1 Click logs

One possible definition of a "good" measure is one that more closely models user behavior. We compared our static stopping rank distributions to aggregated clicks from the 2006 AOL log. Of course, processing click log data is itself implicitly model-based. Comparing models to click logs should be seen not as comparing models to reality, but as comparing one model to another under all the assumptions that both models require. In this case we cannot know stopping ranks; we need to model them from recorded clicks.

We tried two different models. The first simply maps each recorded click to a stopping rank to estimate an empirical distribution of stopping ranks, with each rank mutually exclusive of the others. The implicit model is that every click is a new event for a new user/query pair, even if it is in not actually the last click by that user for that query. The second maps only the last recorded click for a user/query to a stopping rank. This may be more realistic, but it results in throwing out all clicks but the last. Other models are possible (e.g. the "gap" model of Zhang et al. [21]).

Both empirical distributions are shown in Figure 2 along with our static distributions. Among the distributions we are considering, P_{RR} is clearly the best fit to both models of the data. Previous work has suggested that DCG and reciprocal rank discounts do not adequately model users [20, 21, 6]. This analysis suggests they might model users well in some data, provided they are considered *cumulative* densities rather than probability densities.

4.1.1 *Critique of click log analysis*

While click log analysis can provide a guide for evaluating a probability distribution $P(k)$, it is not clear to us how it could be used to evaluate a model of utility accumulation. How can we use click log data to choose between M_1 (in which a user derives utility only from the document at the stopping rank) and M_2 (in which a user derives utility from all relevant documents from rank 1 to the stopping rank)? How can we use it to choose between M_1 and M_3 (in which a user expends a certain amount of effort to achieve a given total utility)? These decisions must be made on the basis of more than just user data.

Furthermore, even if only a small fraction of users are negatively affected by a poor model fit, the cost of not providing those users with the best possible system may be disproportionately large. Suppose that the probability of a user becoming frustrated and quitting the search engine altogether increases over ranks in a reverse geometric way up to rank K, so that

$$P(\text{quit engine}|k) = (1-\theta)^{K-k}$$

This is distinguished from

$$P(\text{stop current search at } k) = (1-\theta)^{k-1}\theta$$

Then:

$$P(\text{stop search and quit engine at } k)$$
$$= P(\text{quit engine}|k)P(\text{stop search at } k)$$
$$= (1-\theta)^{K-k}(1-\theta)^{k-1}\theta = (1-\theta)^{K-1}\theta$$

which is completely independent of rank! We may as well use a uniform stopping probability—leading us right back to traditional precision and recall.

We do not advocate that model; we only wish to point out the pitfalls in focusing on behavior evidenced in logs. This analysis suggests to us that fatter-tailed distributions are superior even if they do not fit behavior data, because those distributions are better-equipped for the risk of not satisfying users that are in the tail.

4.2 Robustness and stability

The previous section supposes that one purpose of an effectiveness measure is to model users in order to estimate the utility of the system. Another purpose of evaluation

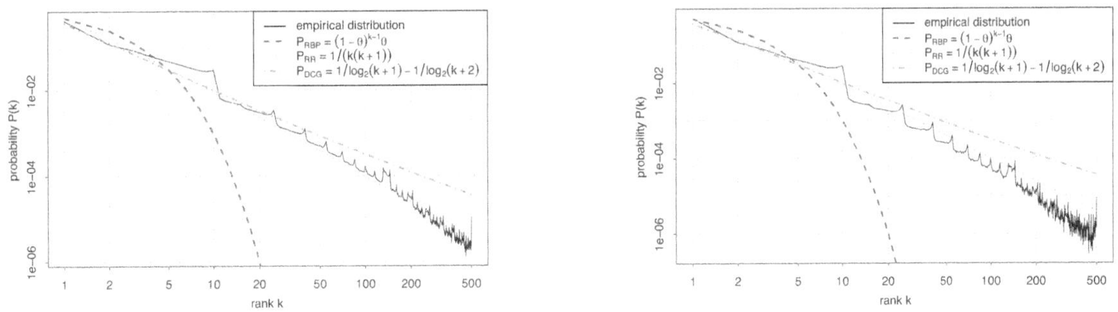

Figure 2: Comparison of empirical click probabilities to static stopping rank models. The left plot uses every recorded click; the right only uses the last recorded click for a user/query pair. It is clear that P_{RR} is the best fit to both distributions (though better fits are possible).

is to choose among different retrieval models, features, and system implementations. For that purpose we would like decisions to be roughly the same whether they are based on a few topics versus many, or extensive relevance judgments versus shallow pools, or one group of assessors versus another. The extent to which conclusions are different depending on differences in the data used to compute the measures reflects the *robustness* and *stability* of those measures. To investigate these properties we will look at how evaluation measure scores and relative rankings of systems change as the underlying data changes.

4.2.1 Data

Our primary data is the TREC-6 ad hoc data consisting of TREC topics 301–350, 72,270 total relevance judgments, and 74 submitted runs over a corpus of about 550,000 documents [18]. This is a small corpus, but its deep judgments make it useful for our study. Furthermore, there is an alternate set of relevance judgments from the University of Waterloo for these topics, allowing us to investigate the effect of assessor disagreement [9, 17].

We also used two more recent test collections:

- The named page retrieval task for the TREC 2006 Terabyte track [3]. This is a high-precision task: there are only a few relevant documents in the corpus. The data consists of TREC topics 901–1081, 2,361 total relevance judgments, and 43 submitted runs over the GOV2 corpus of some 25 million web pages.
- The ad hoc task for the TREC 2009 Web track (category A set) [7]. The data consists of TREC Web topics 1–50, 18,666 relevance judgments, and 37 submitted runs over the ClueWeb09 corpus of 1 billion web pages.

4.2.2 Evaluation

The approach is simple: we select some subset of the data (e.g. a subset of topics or a subset of judgments) and evaluate all systems with all 15 of our measures. We then use Kendall's τ rank correlation to compare the results to the "true" rankings using the full TREC data. Kendall's τ ranges from -1 to 1, with greater values indicating greater correlation. In practice, for meta-evaluation studies like this one Kendall's τ is nearly always over 0.6, and a value of 0.9 would be considered an effectively "perfect" correlation considering the presence of variance [17].

Since our hypotheses are about model families or distributions rather than individual measures, we average Kendall's τ results for each measure within a family or with a particular property. We use the averages to evaluate the hypothesis.

4.2.3 Results

The single clearest fact from the results is that measures in the M_2 family with fatter tails tend to be more robust. However, this is not true in all cases: when the judgment pool is shallow, models with distributions that put more weight on top-ranked documents tend to be more robust. For tasks with few relevant documents, tail fatness does not appear to matter. Detailed results follow below.

Varying assessors: We evaluated all 74 TREC-6 systems with all 15 of our measures over two different sets of relevance judgments. Table 2 shows the τ correlations for every measure between the rankings from the two judgment sets. The final column shows the mean τ for each stopping distribution; it is clear that the fatter-tail distributions P_{DCG} and P_{AP} are most robust w.r.t. assessor disagreement, while the slimmer-tail distributions P_{RBP} and P_{ERR} are least robust. Dynamic distributions actually appear to be more robust than static distributions on average, which we found surprising since they seem to have a greater dependence on which documents have been judged relevant.

The last row shows the mean τ for each model family; M_2 is more robust to assessor disagreement than the others. M_3 and M_4 are about equally robust, with M_3 taking the edge if the outlying fat-tailed P_{AP} is removed. M_1 is least robust to assessor disagreement.

Varying topic sample: We evaluated all 74 TREC-6 systems with all 15 of our measures over increasing topic sample sizes from $N = 5$ to 45. For each level of N, we performed 100 trials with a random subset of topics; each trial used the same topic sample to evaluate all 15 measures.

Figure 3 plots summary results for distribution model family (left) and tail type (right). Again we see that fatter tails result in more stable results, and M_2 provides more stable results than the other models. There are differences from the assessor disagreement results, however. M_3 appears to be least robust to varying the topic sample despite being more robust to assessor disagreement, while M_1 and M_4 look equally robust. The difference in robustness due to tail fatness is less pronounced, with a maximum difference

type	$P(k)$	M_1	M_2	M_3	M_4	mean
static	P_{RBP}	$\tau_{RBP} = 0.813$	$\tau_{RBTR} = 0.816$	–	$\tau_{RBAP} = 0.801$	0.810
	P_{DCG}	$\tau_{CDG} = 0.831$	$\tau_{DCG} = 0.920$	–	$\tau_{DAG} = 0.819$	0.857
	P_{RR}	$\tau_{RRG} = 0.819$	$\tau_{RR} = 0.859$	–	$\tau_{RAP} = 0.812$	0.830
dynamic	P_{ERR}	–	–	$\tau_{ERR} = 0.829$	$\tau_{EPR} = 0.836$	0.833
	P_{AP}	–	–	$\tau_{ARR} = 0.847$	$\tau_{AP} = 0.896$	0.872
	P_{RRR}	–	–	$\tau_{RRR} = 0.826$	$\tau_{RRAP} = 0.844$	0.835
mean		0.821	0.865	0.834	0.835	

Table 2: Kendall's τ correlation between TREC-6 relevance judgments and alternate judgments. The last column shows row means (mean τ for each $P(k)$); the last row shows column means (mean τ for each model).

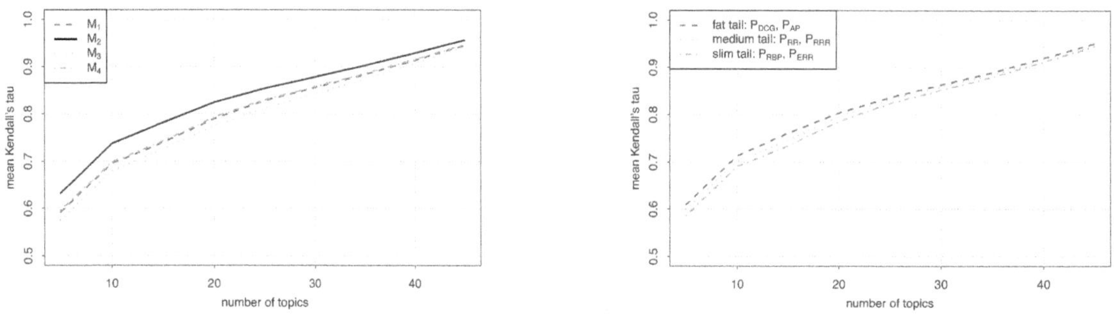

Figure 3: Kendall's τ correlations as topic sample size increases (averaged over 100 samples of size N). All differences are significant with $p < 10^4$. Fat-tailed distributions and the M_2 family clearly offer the greatest stability to topic set size.

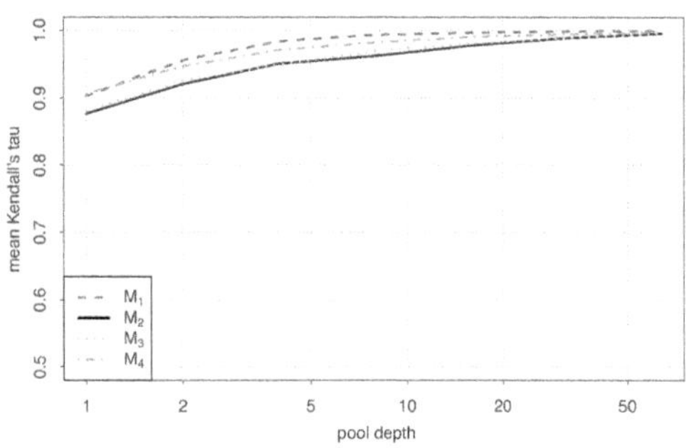

Figure 4: Kendall's τ correlations as pool depth increases. Correlation is already very good with a pool depth of just 1; this suggests that these systems are retrieving many common documents.

of 0.026 between any two points (though this is statistically significant).

Varying pool depth: We formed shallower judgment pools from the original TREC-6 qrels by iterating over systems and pooling only documents that appeared above a particular rank cutoff. For each of these pools we evaluated all 74 systems by all 15 measures and correlated the resulting ranking of systems to the "true" ranking using all judgments.

Figure 4 shows increasing τs for each of our models. The M_2 family is actually least robust to missing judgments, while the M_1 family is most robust. This makes sense, as the M_1 family places much more weight on the top-most documents than the others, and the top-ranked documents are the ones that are judged in both datasets. The M_4 family is more robust to missing judgments than the M_3 family, possibly because M_4 discounts lower-ranked documents more. Nevertheless, all four are quite robust on average, most likely because five of our six distributions weight the top-ranked documents very highly. Results for tail fatness are not shown, but here too there is a reversal: slim-tail distributions are more robust to shallow pools than fatter-tail ones. Again, this is most likely because the slimmer tails result in much more weight on the top-ranked documents.

Varying test collection: For our other two collections, we varied topic sample size and calculated τ correlations.

For the TREC 2006 Terabyte named page task—a high-precision task—the distribution does not appear to matter. There is almost no difference between τ correlations with fat- or slim-tailed distributions. M_2 measures are still more robust than other families, though M_3 is a very close second. This supports our intuition that M_3 is particularly useful for tasks where there are only a few highly-relevant documents.

For the TREC 2009 Web ad hoc task, M_3 measures with slim- or medium- tail distributions are most robust to varying topic sample. Fat-tail distributions are quite poor. M_2 measures are least robust, though not by much. This is most likely due to the challenge of evaluating an ad hoc retrieval task with sparse relevance judgments, but it may suggest that ERR is the best measure we have for web evaluation.

5. DOCUMENT UTILITY

To this point our discussion has focused on stopping probability distributions within a common browsing model and models of how users accumulate utility over documents. We simplified the idea of document utility itself to simple binary relevance, but we can investigate alternative models for that independently of stopping probabilities.

5.1 Graded judgments

Some documents are more useful than others. A common way to model this is with judgment grades, such as the ternary scale *nonrelevant, relevant, highly relevant* and the quinary scale *bad, fair, good, excellent, perfect*. A gain function maps grades to numeric values.

Though we have focused on binary judgments, graded judgments fit easily within our framework. DCG and ERR are, of course, explicitly designed with graded judgments in mind. AP can be adapted to graded judgments using a user-modeling distribution mapping grades to probabilities of relevance [14]. At any point where we use rel_k or R_k for binary judgments, we can substitute the mapping function $gain(rel_k)$ or the cumulative gain $CG_k = \sum_{i=1}^{k} gain(rel_i)$ respectively. In ERR, we can write $P(k)$ as:

$$P_{ERR}(k) = \prod_{g \in \text{grades}} (1-\theta_g)^{G_k - 1}\theta_g$$

where the product is over unique grades, θ_g is a patience parameter for grade g, and G_k is the total number of documents with grade g up to rank k. This is a slightly different formulation that originally presented by Chapelle et al. [6], but we feel it more clearly shows ERR as modeling cumulated gain up to rank k.

5.2 Preference judgments

Another way to model the idea that some documents are more useful is with preference judgments of the form "A is preferred to B for query q". When transitive, such judgments result in a total ordering of documents by utility [15]. Previous work has shown that preferences can be made easier and faster than graded judgments [5]. Kendall's τ rank correlation is based on preferences, and it can be extended to other measures for IR effectiveness [4].

Models M_2 and M_4 can be seen as instances of a more general family of preference-based measures. Consider the following stochastic process applied to a system ranking: sample a rank k with probability $P(k)$. Then sample one or more documents ranked above k. For each of those documents that was preferred by assessors to the document at k, increment a count of total concordant pairs.

Suppose we just have binary relevance and a preference relation stating that A is preferred to B if and only if A is judged relevant. If in the second sampling stage we sample only one document uniformly at random, the expectation of the process is exactly M_4 with $f(k) = 1/k$. If we use all documents above k, the expectation is exactly M_2.

For natural preference relations, uniform $P(k)$ results in the process having expectation proportional to Kendall's τ. This suggests that both M_2 and M_4 can be viewed as weighted versions of τ. This was already known for AP, our exemplar M_4 measure [19]; the fact that DCG can be viewed in this way is novel.

5.3 Novelty and diversity

In the novelty and diversity retrieval setting, document utility is a function of its relevance to different possible *user intents* as well as its redundancy with other documents in a ranking. The so-called "intent aware" (IA) family of measures uses a distribution of intents $P(i|q)$ for a given query q to compute a weighted average of a measure like AP or DCG computed with document judgments for each intent [1]. Any measure that fits in our framework can be turned into an intent aware variant by computing such a weighted average.

Redundancy can be penalized when computing total utility. Up to this point we have computed total utility as the number of retrieved relevant documents R_k. We could instead define the utility of the top k retrieved documents as:

$$U_k = \sum_{j=1}^{k} rel_j F(R_j)$$

where R_j is the number of relevant documents up to rank j and $F(R_j)$ is a redundancy discount taking the form of a cumulative probability density based on $P(R_j)$, the probability that the last relevant document a user would look at is the R_jth. The α-nDCG measure [8] uses $F(R_j) = \alpha^{R_j - 1}$; it is based on the same geometric penalty that ERR uses.

A full intent-aware, redundancy-penalizing novelty/diversity measure in the M_2 family could then be given as:

$$M = \sum_{i \in I_q} P(i|q) \sum_{k=1}^{n} U_{ik} P(k|i)$$

where I_q is the set of intents for query q and U_{ik} is defined as the utility to intent i (using relevance judgments distinguished by intent). Measures in the M_3 and M_4 families follow straightforwardly. Note that M_1 cannot truly model redundancy penalization in a natural way, since it does not model accumulated utility.

This suggests two directions for diversity evaluation:

- Consider the use of a stopping probability conditional on intent, i.e. $P(k|i)$. For an ambiguous query like "cardinals" for instance, some intents may be "navigational" (e.g. finding the home page for the St. Louis Cardinals baseball team) and others may be "informational" (e.g. finding information about Catholic cardinals). A user with the former need might be better modeled by a steeply-decreasing density function, while the latter might be better modeled by a more gentle decrease. Existing diversity measures assume that the same model will be used for all intents.
- Consider alternative models of decrease in utility due to redundancy. α-nDCG uses a geometric decrease. As we have seen in this work, a geometric discount by rank is quite harsh compared to user behavior; it may be a harsh penalty for redundancy as well. Our definition of U_k above allows a researcher or developer to plug in any probability density function to model the probability that information is still useful after having seen it R_j times.

6. DISCUSSION AND CONCLUSION

On one level this work is a collection of novel observations about common evaluation measures and user models. At that level, these observations emerge primarily from algebraic manipulation.

- The discounts in DCG and RBP are used for different purposes. RBP's is the probability of stopping at a particular rank, while DCG's is the probability of viewing a particular rank while progressing down. This leads to different interpretations of the two, as well as the understanding that their discounts are not directly comparable to each other. DCG's discount should instead be understood as arising from a stopping probability distribution that much more closely models user behavior.

- Nearly any measure that can be formulated in terms of a relevance gain times a rank discount can also be formulated in terms of a stopping probability distribution. The only constraint is that $disc(1) \geq disc(2) \geq \cdots \geq disc(n)$. Zhang et al. have shown that many traditional measures can be expressed this way [21].
- The reciprocal-rank discount arises naturally as the cumulative density of an infinite mixture of geometric discounts. It also fits user behavior better than other discounts when properly interpreted.
- M_2 measures with a rank cut-off are equivalent to using no rank cut-off, but making a worst-case assumption about relevance below a certain rank.
- DCG and other measures in both the M_2 and M_4 families can be understood as weighted rank correlations.
- Our measure families generalize to families of measures for novelty and diversity with new questions about modeling distributions.

At a deeper level, these observations all emerged from a conceptual framework in which we describe a measure in terms of its browsing model, specific attributes of its browsing model, and utility accumulation model. This alone shows the value of the framework: it led us to discover things that were not previously known about measures. We went further and used the framework to formulate specific hypotheses about models and measures. Some of our hypotheses turned out to be true in most cases: that fatter-tail distributions would be more robust; that measures in the M_2 family would be more robust. Others turned out to be wrong: that measures in the M_4 family would be more robust; that M_3 would not be significantly better than M_1; that dynamic distributions would be less robust than static distributions. These results open the door to additional hypotheses and discoveries about evaluation based on user models.

On a personal note, we will confess to beginning this study with an unease about DCG—we felt that the discount was perhaps too flat to model real users, that its user model was ad hoc, and that it was unclear what it really measured. We come out of it with a newfound appreciation of DCG. The stopping probability may still be ad hoc (it is not a formal probability distribution), but it is much more clear to us that the discount is not too flat and that it actually measures something very useful. Furthermore, it is a highly robust measure; within our framework, the fact that it uses M_2 and a fat-tail distribution predicts that it would be. To answer the question we posed in Section 1, perhaps this is why DCG has continued to find such wide use: not due to inertia or familiarity, but because it really is a useful user-centered measure of system effectiveness.

Acknowledgments

This work was supported in part by the National Science Foundation (NSF) under grant number IIS-1017026. Any opinions, findings and conclusions or recommendations expressed in this material are the author's and do not necessarily reflect those of the sponsor.

7. REFERENCES

[1] Rakesh Agrawal, Sreenivas Gollapudi, Halan Halverson, and Samuel Ieong. Diversifying search results. In *Proceedings of WSDM*, pages 5–14, 2009.

[2] Leif Azzopardi, Kalervo Jarvelin, Jaap Kamps, and Mark D. Smucker, editors. *Proceedings of the SIGIR 2010 Workshop on the Simulation of Interaction: Automated Evaluation of Interactive IR*, 2010.

[3] Stefan Buettcher, Charles L.A. Clarke, and Ian Soboroff. The TREC 2006 Terabyte Track. In *Proceedings of TREC*, 2006.

[4] Ben Carterette and Paul N. Bennett. Evaluation measures for preference judgments. In *Proceedings of SIGIR*, 2008. To appear.

[5] Ben Carterette, Paul N. Bennett, D. Maxwell Chickering, and Susan T. Dumais. Here or there: Preference judgments for relevance. In *Proceedings of ECIR*, pages 16–27, 2008.

[6] Olivier Chapelle, Donald Metzler, Ya Zhang, and Pierre Grinspan. Expceted reciprocal rank for graded relevance. In *Proceedings of CIKM*, 2009.

[7] Charles L. A. Clarke, Nick Craswell, and Ian Soboroff. Preliminary report on the trec 2009 web track. In *Proceedings of Text Retrieval Conference (TREC-2009)*, 2009.

[8] Charles L. A. Clarke, Maheedhar Kolla, Gordon V. Cormack, Olga Vechtomova, Azin Ashkan, Stefan Büttcher, and Ian MacKinnon. Novelty and diversity in information retrieval evaluation. In *Proceedings of SIGIR*, pages 659–666, 2008.

[9] Gordon V. Cormack, Christopher R. Palmer, and Charles L.A. Clarke. Efficient construction of large test collections. In *Proceedings of SIGIR*, pages 282–289, 1998.

[10] Kalervo Jarvelin and Jaana Kekalainen. Cumulated gain-based evaluation of ir techniques. *ACM Trans. Inf. Syst.*, 20(4):422–446, 2002.

[11] Evangelos Kanoulas, Ben Carterette, Paul D. Clough, and Mark Sanderson. Evaluation over multi-query sessions. In *Proceedings of SIGIR*, 2011. To appear.

[12] Alistair Moffat and Justin Zobel. Rank-biased precision for measurement of retrieval effectiveness. *ACM Trans. Info. Sys.*, 27(1):1–27, 2008.

[13] Stephen E. Robertson. A new interpretation of average precision. In *Proceedings of SIGIR*, pages 689–690, 2008.

[14] Stephen E. Robertson, Evangelos Kanoulas, and Emine Yilmaz. Extending average precision to graded relevance judgments. In *Proceedings of SIGIR*, pages 603–610, 2010.

[15] Mark E. Rorvig. The simple scalability of documents. *JASIS*, 41(8):590–598, 1990.

[16] Tetsuya Sakai and Stephen Robertson. Modelling a user population for designing information retrieval metrics. In *Proceedings of EVIA*, pages 30–41, 2008.

[17] Ellen Voorhees. Variations in relevance judgments and the measurement of retrieval effectiveness. In *Proceedings of SIGIR*, pages 315–323, 1998.

[18] Ellen M. Voorhees and Donna Harman. Overview of the Sixth Text REtrieval Conference (TREC-6). In *Proceedings of the Sixth Text REtrieval Conference (TREC-6)*, pages 1–24, 1997. NIST Special Publication 500-240.

[19] Emine Yilmaz, Javed A. Aslam, and Stephen Robertson. A new rank correlation coefficient for information retrieval. In *Proceedings of SIGIR*, pages 587–594, 2008.

[20] Emine Yilmaz, Milad Shokouhi, Nick Craswell, and Stephen Robertson. Expected browsing utility for web search evaluation. In *Proceedings of CIKM*, 2010. To appear.

[21] Yuye Zhang, Laurence A. Park, and Alistair Moffat. Click-based evidence for decaying weight distributions in search effectiveness metrics. *Inf. Retr.*, 13:46–69, February 2010.

Evaluating the Synergic Effect of Collaboration in Information Seeking

Chirag Shah
School of Communication & Information (SC&I)
Rutgers, The State University of New Jersey
4 Huntington St, New Brunswick, NJ 08901, USA
chirags@rutgers.edu

Roberto González-Ibáñez
School of Communication & Information (SC&I)
Rutgers, The State University of New Jersey
4 Huntington St, New Brunswick, NJ 08901, USA
rgonzal@eden.rutgers.edu

ABSTRACT
It is typically expected that when people work together, they can often accomplish goals that are difficult or even impossible for individuals. We consider this notion of the group achieving more than the sum of all individuals' achievements to be the synergic effect in collaboration. Similar expectation exists for people working in collaboration for information seeking tasks. We, however, lack a methodology and appropriate evaluation metrics for studying and measuring the synergic effect. In this paper we demonstrate how to evaluate this effect and discuss what it means to various collaborative information seeking (CIS) situations. We present a user study with four different conditions: single user, pair of users at the same computer, pair of users at different computers and co-located, and pair of users remotely located. Each of these individuals or pairs was given the same task of information seeking and usage for the same amount of time. We then combined the outputs of single independent users to form artificial pairs, and compared against the real pairs. Not surprisingly, participants using different computers (co-located or remotely located) were able to cover more information sources than those using a single computer (single user or a pair). But more interestingly, we found that real pairs with their own computers (co-located or remotely located) were able to cover more unique and useful information than that of the artificially created pairs. This indicates that those working in collaboration achieved something greater and better than what could be achieved by adding independent users, thus, demonstrating the synergic effect. Remotely located real teams were also able to formulate a wider range of queries than those pairs that were co-located or artificially created. This shows that the collaborators working remotely were able to achieve synergy while still being able to think and work independently. Through the experiments and measurements presented here, we have also contributed a unique methodology and an evaluation metric for CIS.

Categories and Subject Descriptors
H.3: INFORMATION STORAGE AND RETRIEVAL **H.3.3: Information Search and Retrieval**: *Search process*; **H.5.3 [Information Interfaces and Presentation]**: Group and Organization Interfaces—*Collaborative computing, Computer-supported cooperative work*

General Terms
Experimentation; Human Factors; Measurement

Keywords
Collaborative information seeking; Synergic effect; Evaluation.

1. INTRODUCTION
It is often argued that people should work together to solve hard problems (e.g., [1,2]). Information seeking is, mistakenly, not seen as a tough problem that could be effectively solved through collaboration [9,10]. Instead, IR researchers tend to spend their efforts on improving the systems that could boost an individual's search effectiveness. While this approach has achieved remarkable feat as evident by systems, theories, and their effects reported in the literature, including that of this forum, it is time to revisit the notion of collaboration and social/interactive elements of searching. In this paper we show how and why people working in collaboration for an information-seeking task could do far better than those working individually. More specifically, we look at the notion of synergy, where the whole becomes more than the sum of all, and demonstrate that an appropriate setup of collaborative information seeking (CIS) could lead to covering information that could otherwise not be discovered by individuals. We also show how remotely located collaborators achieve synergy by exercising independence and diversity.

In the next section, we review some of the relevant literature on CIS and collaboration in general focusing on two specific aspects: synergy and evaluation. Our specific research questions and hypotheses are also included in this section. To address these questions and specifically the hypotheses, we conducted a laboratory study with 10 single users, and 30 pairs of users in three different setups. The details of this study are given in Section 3. Following that, we describe what and how we evaluated in Section 4. Using these evaluation measures, we present the results and relevant discussion in Section 5. The paper is concluded in Section 6 with implications and directions for further research.

2. BACKGROUND

A brief overview of some of the related research is presented here to situate our work in the context of IR in general and CIS in particular. This review will also inform our research questions and hypotheses listed later in this section.

2.1 Related work

Synergy, from the Greek *synergos* (which means working together) is when two or more things, individuals, disciplines, etc. interact producing a result that is greater than the sum of the individual products of the involved parts [1]; this is commonly explained through the expression *1+1>2*. Synergy has been widely studied in a variety of contexts, which includes, chemistry, medicine, organizations, and education [1]. In the particular context of collaborative information seeking (CIS), little is known about the synergic effect and to what extent, if any, it affects users' behaviors, the processes, and the results produced by individuals searching information in collaboration, in comparison to those working individually. Furthermore, collaboration has been conceptually defined in different ways and to date there is no clear difference between it and related concepts such as cooperation [21]. Authors such as Fidel et al. [4]; Golovchinsky et al. [9], and Shah [21] have further defined and explored the conceptual implications of collaboration in order to have a more suitable definition for CIS.

Unlike the study of information seeking performed by single users, little is known about how users seek information in collaboration with others. During the past decade, some have explored different aspects of CIS in both naturalistic and experimental settings. The focus, however, has been on describing users' behaviors as well as the information seeking processes of teams. For example, Hyldegard [12, 13] studied the applicability of Kuhlthau's information search process [15] in the context of groups. Similarly, Shah & González-Ibáñez [22] attempted to map the stages in Kuhlthau's model to collaborative information seeking. Both studies revealed that even though some stages of this model may apply to CIS, they do not cover the social dimension of CIS.

More importantly, it has been recognized that collaborative search is a phenomenon widely present in social context where collaboration - in a more general sense - is required. For example, Morris [17] conducted a survey in a large company that revealed that workers engage in a variety of activities in which they collaborate searching for information. Through this survey, the author also identified obstacles that impact the collaborative information seeking process, different tasks that motivate collaborative search, and common methods that are employed to share search results during the process.

Specific studies have been conducted with the aim of comparing individual and collaborative search. For instance, Joho, Hannah, & Joemon [14] compared the search process of single users with collaborative-concurrent search. Through this study, the authors found that those working collaboratively were able to reduce overlapping in terms of the webpages covered during a recall-oriented search task; however, as the authors pointed out, this redundancy reduction did not improve the retrieval effectiveness. In a related study, Pickens et al. [19] and Shah et al. [23] found that collaborative search, with algorithmic mediation to enhance the collaboration process among participants, end up with better results than those obtained by merging of single users' results. Similarly, Foley [7] demonstrated that in order to enhance the performance in synchronous collaborative information retrieval (SCIR), it is necessary to have an appropriated division of labor and also a mediated support for sharing knowledge. On a more theoretical side, González-Ibáñez [10] proposed a conceptual map to study the behavior of users in the information seeking process of both individuals and collaborative teams. As the author suggested, such a map and the use of mixed methods would help to understand different dimensions involved in CIS, including the synergic effect of collaboration.

Though early studies have suggested the importance of providing support for collaboration in situations involving information search practices [25], and many have devised tools and technologies to facilitate CIS [16, 18, 26]; it has been recognized by several authors (e.g., [5, 20]) that there is a significant lack of theories and tools to investigate and support CIS. Moreover, to our knowledge, beyond the coverage of these and other works, none have studied specifically the synergic effect in collaborative information seeking, which is one of the core values and advantages of collaboration.

2.2 Research questions and hypotheses

From reviewing the literature, it is clear that (1) while collaboration is often considered a useful approach to solve a complex problem, it has been largely ignored when it comes to information seeking; (2) system-focused CIS works have primarily looked at creating algorithms and tools that provide improved effectiveness in collaboration, but ignore the actual user interaction and social component; and (3) interface-focused CIS works have predominantly studied various usability issues with the interface/system in a CIS situation. These explorations have not addressed some of the basic questions about working in collaboration, including the following that we are interested in investigating here.

1. How does collaborating with a shared workstation differ from that of working with individual computers?
2. How does the location of collaborators affect their interactions and effectiveness in a CIS task?
3. In a recall-oriented exploratory search task, can we simply combine the outputs of two independent users to achieve the same/similar results as a pair to produce the same results as users actually working together?
4. How can we measure the synergic effect in collaboration and what does it inform us?
5. To what extent, if any, does the cognitive load of collaborative teams working in a search task differs from the cognitive load of a single user working in the same task?

To narrow our investigation for better articulation of our goals and experiments, we propose the following hypotheses. Note that they are postulated for a recall-oriented exploratory search task.

1. Two collaborators working at the same computer will be able to accomplish as much as that of a single user.
2. Remotely located collaborators will be able to work more independently compared to those working co-located.
3. Real collaborative teams will accomplish more compared to artificially created teams by combining the outputs of two independent users.

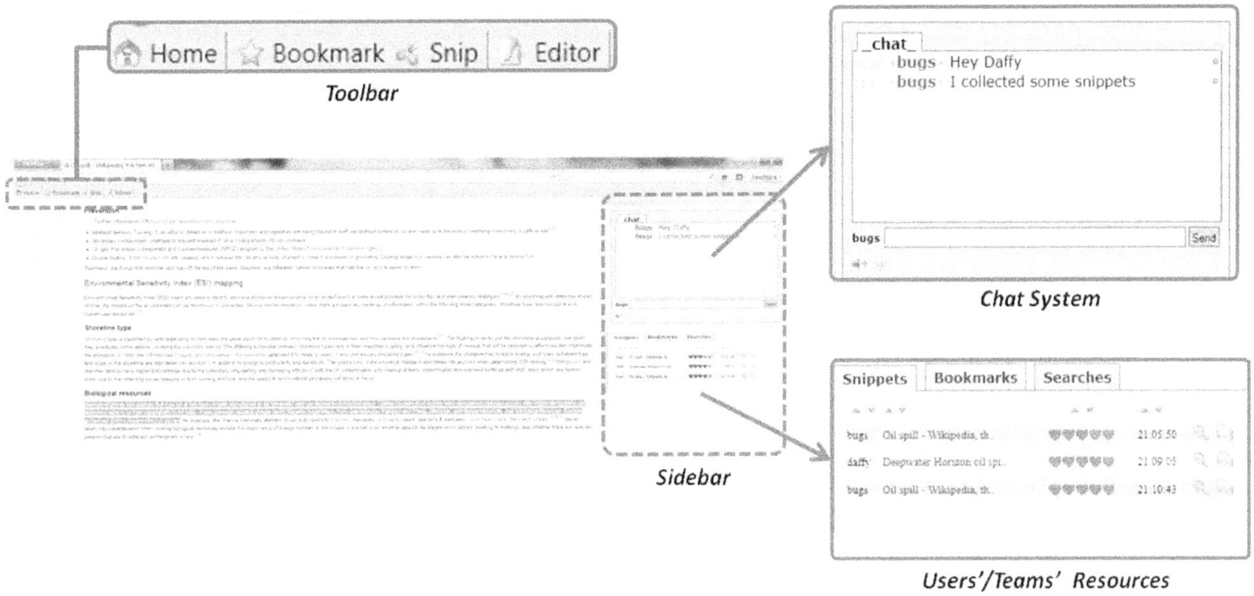

Figure 1: A snapshot of the experimental system with parts of it shown in details.

The following section describes a user study that we designed to test these hypotheses and address the research questions listed before.

3. METHOD

We conducted a laboratory study involving a total of 70 participants – 10 participants as single users, and 60 participants as collaborative teams. This section describes the study procedure, the subjects, the system, the task, and the experimental conditions.

3.1 Subjects

Participants in this study were asked to sign up in pairs with someone with whom they had previous experience collaborating. In addition, they were informed of their compensation for participating in the study, which consisted of $10 per person and the possibility to obtain additional prizes if they were among the three best performing teams ($50, $25, and $15 per person additionally) at the end of the study. Overall, 60 participants in 30 pairs, all of them students from Rutgers University, were recruited and randomly assigned to three experimental scenarios (Table 1). In addition, 10 more participants were recruited to work individually in the same search task performed by teams.

3.2 System

We developed a plugin for the Firefox web browser, called Coagmento,[1] which provided appropriate tools and support for the participants working in various conditions. A screenshot of this plugin within Firefox is shown in Figure 1. As shown, the plugin included a toolbar and a sidebar. The toolbar had the following buttons: (1) Home – for taking the participant to appropriate questionnaires, (2) Bookmark – for bookmarking a webpage, (3) Snip – for collecting a snippet using highlighted text from a webpage, and (4) Editor – for accessing a shared editor for writing the report.

The sidebar had two major components: a chat-box and a resources panel. The chat-box allowed the collaborators in a given team to communicate with each other. The researcher conducting the study also used it to provide instructions to the participants. The resources panel included tabs for bookmarks, saved snippets, and executed queries.

3.3 Session workflow

Each experimental session lasted less than an hour and was structured in six parts as depicted in Figure 2 and described below.

1. Participants were introduced to the study and asked to sign a consent form.
2. Participants watched a brief tutorial in order to learn the basic functionalities required during the task.
3. Participants individually filled out a set of pre-task questionnaires. In the case of two participants working at the same computer (condition later explained), the participants were separated for this phase.
4. Participants read the task description (given later).
5. Each participant/team worked for approximately 25 minutes on the given task that included searching for

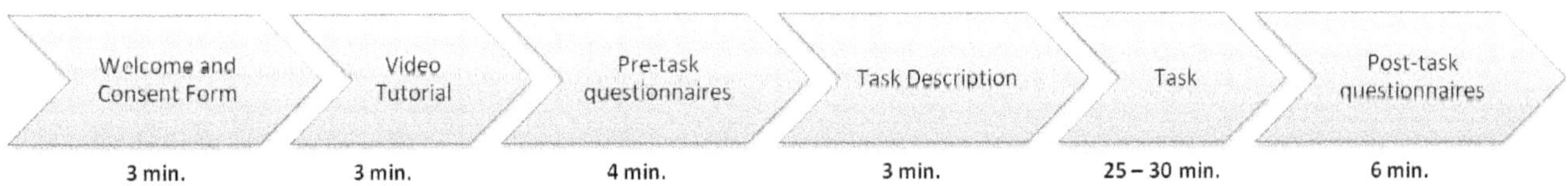

Figure 2: Study session workflow.

[1] Publicly available from http://www.coagmento.org.

relevant information, and using it to compose a report.

6. Participants filled out post-task questionnaires.

The researcher conducting the study communicated with the participants through the chat-box at different times during the study instructing them to start/stop the task or fill in a questionnaire.

3.4 Conditions

To study the difference between individual information seeking and CIS, as well as to understand how various CIS settings can affect a collaborative team's effectiveness in accomplishing an information-seeking task, we conducted experiments with four different conditions: single participants, two participants at the same computer, two participants in the same room but different computers, and two participants in different rooms with individual computers.

In order to have a baseline to study the synergic effect of collaboration, we artificially created pairs of users from C1 (single users). We generated all possible combinations of pairs in groups of 5, reaching a total of 49 groups and creating 245 artificial teams in total. This was done in order to cover all possible pairs of users while avoiding a given user appearing in more than one team within the same group of teams.

These five conditions are summarized in Table 1. Setups for four of these conditions are also depicted in Figure 3. Note that in the real experiment, those in C5 condition were located in different rooms separated by walls, and not just a partition. They could not see or talk to each other directly, and the only communication channel they had was the text-box provided with the system.

Table 1: Experimental conditions.

Cond.	Description
C1	Single participants
C2	Artificial team
C3	Co-located using the same computer
C4	Co-located using different computers
C5	Remotely located

3.5 Task

We chose "gulf oil spill" as the topic for this experimentation since it was quite popular and relevant at the time the study was being conducted. Our preliminary investigations, including a few pilot runs, indicated that there was a huge amount of material on this topic, and that the participants would find it interesting and challenging enough as an exploratory search task. Each participant was given the following task description.

"A leading newspaper has hired your team to create a comprehensive report on the causes, effects, and consequences of the recent gulf oil spill. As a part of your contract, you are required to collect all the relevant information from any available online sources that you can find.

To prepare this report, search and visit any website that you want and look for specific aspects as given in the guideline below. As you find useful information, highlight and save relevant snippets. Make sure you also rate a snippet to help you in ranking them based on their quality and usefulness. Later, you can use these snippets to compile your report, no longer than 200 lines, as instructed.

Your report on this topic should address the following issues: description of how the oil spill took place, reactions by BP as well as various government and other agencies, impact on economy and life (people and animals) in the gulf, attempts to fix the leaking well and to clean the waters, long-term implications and lessons learned."

The participants saw this description on the screen (phase 4 in the study), and were also given a printed copy to refer to during their session.

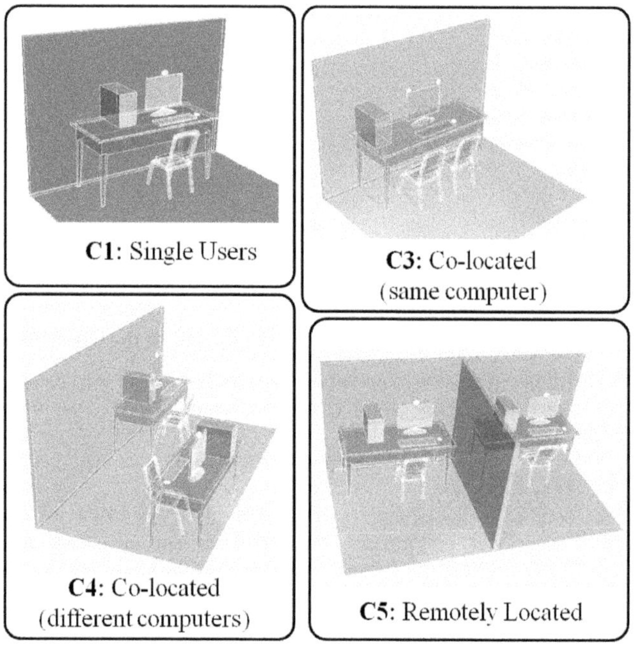

Figure 3: Experimental setups for four different conditions.

4. EVALUATION

In order to evaluate the effectiveness of the participants in various conditions, we employed a number of traditional and non-traditional evaluation measures, which are presented below. Here we also describe other useful constructs and definitions that will later be used while reporting and discussing the results.

4.1 Universe of webpages

In order to compute quantities such as coverage, we needed a universal set of webpages. Given that the search domain for our experiments was the open web, we needed a more confined set that we could use to compare with. We decided to take the union of all the webpages visited by all of our participants (total 70). In other words, the universe of webpages was defined by combining the visited webpages of each participant/team in every condition.

$$U = \bigcup_t Coverage(t) \quad \ldots (1)$$

Here, *Coverage(t)* is the coverage (webpages visited) by participant/team *t*.

4.2 Relevant webpages

This corresponds to the webpages that participants either bookmarked using the toolbar or from where one or more snippets were collected. Once again, we took the union of all such webpages by each participant/team to form a universe of relevant webpages.

$$U_r = \bigcup_t RelevantCoverage(t) \quad ... (2)$$

Here, *RelevantCoverage(t)* is the set of webpages that participant/team *t* visited and found as relevant.

4.3 Precision, recall, and F-measure

Two of the most common evaluation measures in IR are precision and recall, which for our purpose here, are defined as the following.

$$Precision(t) = \frac{RelevantCoverage(t)}{Coverage(t)} \quad ... (3)$$

$$Recall(t) = \frac{RelevantCoverage(t)}{U_r} \quad ... (4)$$

To combine precision and recall into one measure of effectiveness, we use the traditional formulation of F-measure as defined below.

$$F = \frac{2 \cdot Precision \cdot Recall}{Precision + Recall} \quad ... (5)$$

4.4 Coverage

We defined coverage of a given team/participant as the total number of distinct webpages visited within the universe of webpages.

$$Coverage(t) = \{wp_i : wp_i \, was \, visited \, by \, t \wedge wp_i \in U\} \quad ... (6)$$

We also considered a particular region of the coverage of teams/participants that was unique within the universe. We called such region unique coverage, which consists of all webpages within the coverage of a given team/participant *t* that were visited only by *t*.

$$UniqueCoverage(t) = Coverage(t) \setminus \bigcup_{t_i \in T \setminus \{t\}} Coverage(t_i) \quad (7)$$

4.5 Relevant coverage

We defined relevant coverage as the region of coverage of a given team/participant that intersects with the universe of relevant webpages.

$$RelevantCoverage(t) = Coverage(t) \cap U_r \quad ... (8)$$

In a similar way, we called unique relevant coverage to the set of webpages within the unique coverage of a given team/participant that intersects with the universe of all relevant webpages.

$$UniqueRelevantCoverage(t) = UniqueCoverage(t) \cap U_r \quad ... (9)$$

4.6 Useful webpages

In addition to relevance, we also studied the usefulness of webpages that teams/participants visited during the task. We used an implicit measure based on the dwell time on a webpage as described in [27], which is supported by previous findings [8]. As reported in these prior works, we considered a webpage to be useful if a team/user spent at least 30 seconds on it. Using the log data, we computed dwell time on a given webpage by a user, and if it was greater than or equal to 30 seconds, marked it as useful for that user. Note that we only considered content pages, discounting any search engine homepage or search engine results pages (SERPs).

4.7 Likelihood of discovery

To evaluate effectiveness of a team/participant in discovering hard to find information, we devised a new measured, called *likelihood of discovery*. We assume that webpages with a high likelihood are easier to find and are common among the majority of the users. On the other hand, those webpages with a low likelihood are difficult to reach and probably beyond the first results page of search engines. A participant/team finding these webpages are being more effective in discovering information that is not just relevant, but also diverse.

In order to operationalize this idea, we used a formulation similar to that of inverse document frequency (IDF). Using the frequency of each webpage in our log data, we computed its likelihood to be visited; in addition, we multiplied each webpage's likelihood by -1 in order to denote the IDF. As a result, each webpage was assigned with a normalized value between -1 and 0. In this sense, those webpages with a value close to 0 are rare (and even unique) to be reached by teams/participants, while those close to -1 are more likely to be visited.

4.8 Query diversity

In addition to the sources that teams/participants visited during the tasks, we also studied how they approached the task in terms of the queries they issued to find information. We studied how similar or different were the queries formulated by participants in real teams and artificial teams.

In order to evaluate query diversity, we used Lavenshtein distance to compute the distance between pairs of queries for each real team and also for all combinations of users in artificial teams. Based on the results of this computation, for a given pair of queries; the closer the distance to 0 the higher the similarity between them. On the other hand, the higher the distance between queries, more different (therefore diverse) were the queries formulated within a team.

4.9 Cognitive Load

To study if collaboration has some negative implications for users in terms of cognitive load experienced; we asked our participants to respond a questionnaire after finishing their task. This questionnaire was a simplified version of NASA's Task Load indeX (TLX) [6].[2] This instrument had the following questions.

1. *How mentally demanding was this task?*
2. *How physically demanding was this task?*
3. *How hurried or rushed was the pace of the task?*
4. *How hard did you have to work to accomplish your level of performance?*
5. *How insecure, discouraged, irritated, stressed, and annoyed were you?*

All these questions were responded using a 5-point Likert scale, where higher values in the responses indicate a more negative perception of the user with respect to of the areas considered in the above questions.

[2] Taken from http://www.cc.gatech.edu/classes/AY2005/cs7470 fall/papers/manual.pdf

5. RESULTS AND DISCUSSION

In this section we present our results and their related discussions. To facilitate this, we first provide a summary of all the universal sets used in Table 2. These sets were used to compute other constructs, such as precision, recall, and unique relevant coverage. Note that the numbers in this table represent the combined output of all the 70 participants.

Table 2: Summary of various universes used in our analysis.

	Total
Universe of all webpages (U)	562
Universe unique webpages	377
Universe all relevant webpages (U_r)	228
Universe unique relevant webpages	159

The analyses reported in this section were done using one-way ANOVA. We tested for homogeneity of variance and performed appropriate post-hoc tests to measure the difference between the conditions.

5.1 Precision, recall, and F-measure

To begin our analysis, we first looked at simple precision and recall for each condition as defined in the previous section. A summary of these measures is given in Table 3, with variance analysis in Table 4.

We found no difference between any of the conditions for precision. This is not surprising considering how it was computed and that it was relatively easy to find relevant results from the web, giving almost everyone a very high value for precision. This high precision was also due to the fact that the relevant set was constructed using the union of the relevance judgments provided by each participant.

Table 3: Relevance measures – means and standard deviations for each condition.

	Cond.	1	2	3	4	5
Precision	**Mean (s.d.)**	0.704 (0.293)	0.646 (0.233)	0.682 (0.141)	0.532 (0.132)	0.552 (0.163)
Recall	**Mean (s.d.)**	0.053 (0.032)	0.104 (0.046)	0.058 (0.032)	0.113 (0.038)	0.129 (0.040)
F-measure	**Mean (s.d.)**	0.092 (0.049)	0.165 (0.054)	0.106 (0.054)	0.182 (0.054)	0.202 (0.051)

We did, however, find differences among the conditions for recall. Not surprisingly, the single users (C1) had lower recall compared to every other condition except C3, where two collaborators used the same computer. Similarly, C3 had lower recall than C2, C4, or C5. In other words, teams with individual computers for their collaborators were able to achieve higher recall than those with a single or a shared computer. This was expected since the assigned task was recall-oriented and exploratory in nature, and given the limited amount of time, those with more resources achieved more results. If the task was non-dividable (e.g., brainstorming), we may not have found these differences.

Using F-measure, once again, we found that in real collaboration, those with individual computers (C4 and C5) outperformed those with shared computers (C3).

Table 4: Means differences between conditions (row-column). Bold values correspond to statistical significant difference at p≤.05 and italic bold values at p≤.01.

	Cond.	2	3	4	5
Precision	**1**	0.058	0.021	0.172	0.152
	2		-0.036	0.113	0.094
	3			0.150	0.131
	4				-0.019
Recall	**1**	***-0.051***	-0.005	**-0.059**	***-0.075***
	2		**0.046**	-0.008	-0.025
	3			**-0.054**	***-0.070***
	4				-0.016
F-measure	**1**	***-0.073***	-0.013	***-0.090***	***-0.109***
	2		***0.059***	-0.016	-0.036
	3			**-0.076**	***-0.096***
	4				-0.019

5.2 Coverage

While precision and recall correspond to relevance in traditional IR sense, they are not very appropriate in the present CIS setting given that the participants were searching the web, where a huge amount of information on the given topic existed, and that each participant/team was given the same amount of limited time, in which they could easily find a good amount of relevant information. Given this, a more important and interesting aspect to investigate here is coverage – a measure of the amount of information explored. Tables 5 and 6 report various kinds of coverage quantities, including the analysis of variance between different conditions. Just as recall, we found those with two people and two computers were able to cover more information than those with only one person and/or one workstation.

To extend our investigation for coverage, we looked at unique coverage for each individual/team, which is defined as the set of unique webpages that one covered and others did not. We found that C4 and C5 came out on the top with this measure, indicating their effectiveness in covering information that others could not. In fact, C5 outperformed not only C1 and C3, but also C2. In other words, when two real collaborators worked in remote CIS, they were able to cover more unique information than artificially created pairs of collaborators. Given that C2 and C4 had no difference, we can say that there is a value in remote collaboration when the task has clear independent components, and at the same time, having interactions that one finds in a real collaboration helps over completely working independently as C2 participants did.

We also looked at how much of the unique coverage was actually relevant, and found that C5 did better than C1 and C3. While we found no difference between C2 and C4 or C5, we can clearly see that those in C5 were able to get to the information that is not discovered by single users (C1), collaborators at the same computer (C3), or artificially created collaboration (C2). At the same time, the amount of unique relevant information that they discovered was found to be significantly more than what was found by C1 or C3. In other words, remotely located teams were able to leverage real interactions (as opposed to no interactions in artificial teams), and at the same time carry on independent exploration to achieve the synergic effect through collaboration.

Table 5: Coverage of information – means and standard deviations for each condition.

	Cond.	1	2	3	4	5
Coverage	Mean (s.d.)	8.50 (5.148)	16.57 (7.247)	9.30 (5.056)	17.90 (6.118)	20.50 (6.329)
Relevant Coverage	Mean (s.d.)	4.80 (2.098)	9.21 (2.323)	6.40 (3.658)	9.60 (4.377)	11.10 (4.458)
Unique Coverage	Mean (s.d.)	3.60 (3.062)	7.20 (4.707)	3.80 (3.225)	11.00 (3.712)	12.20 (5.007)
Unique Relevant Coverage	Mean (s.d.)	1.30 (1.418)	2.60 (1.766)	1.80 (1.687)	3.40 (1.506)	3.90 (1.729)

Figure 4 provides a depiction of various forms of coverage for C2, C3, C4, and C5. The figure is drawn to scale, with the area of a coverage region, proportional to the value of that kind of coverage for a given condition. Visually also, we could see that C5 has more coverage (total and unique), as well as more unique relevant coverage.

5.3 Usefulness

Moving beyond information exploration and relevancy, we looked at the usefulness of viewed information. As defined in the previous section, this referred to visiting webpages that one spends considerable amount of time (30 seconds or more).

We found (Tables 7 and 8) that C1 and C3 visited significantly fewer useful webpages than those by C4 and C5 participants. More importantly, real teams with individual computers (C4 and C5) outperformed artificial teams (C2) when it came to visiting useful webpages, including the webpages that were unique to a given team. In other words, with real collaboration, the teams were able to avoid overlapping their exploration and reach out to more sources of information. This is important for exploratory and recall-oriented search task like the one used for our study.

Table 6: Means differences between conditions (row-column). Bold values correspond to statistical significant difference at p≤.05 and italic bold values at p≤.01.

	Cond.	2	3	4	5
Coverage	1	***-8.067***	-0.8	**-9.4**	***-12.0***
	2		**7.267**	-1.333	-3.933
	3			**-8.6**	***-11.2***
	4				-2.6
Relevant Coverage	1	***-4.412***	-1.6	**-4.8**	***-6.3***
	2		2.812	-0.388	-1.888
	3			-3.2	-4.7
	4				-1.5
Unique Coverage	1	-3.6	-0.2	***-7.4***	***-8.6***
	2		3.4	-3.8	***-5.0***
	3			***-7.2***	***-8.4***
	4				-1.2
Unique Relevant Coverage	1	-1.3	-0.5	**-2.1**	***-2.6***
	2		0.8	-0.8	-1.3
	3			-1.6	**-2.1**
	4				-0.5

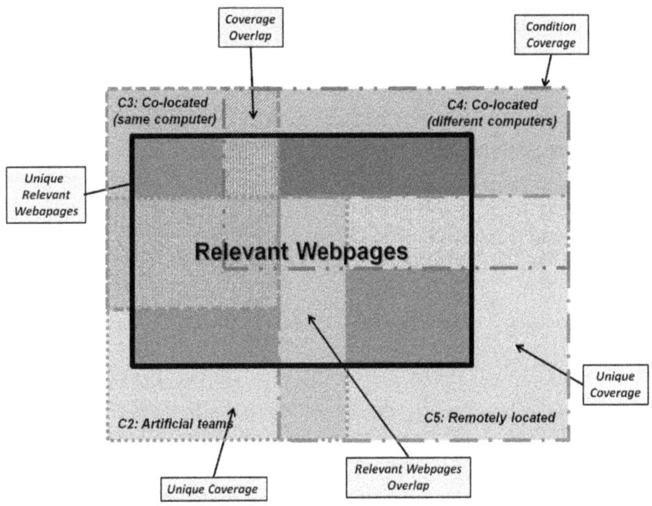

Figure 4: Depiction of coverage by various conditions (drawn to scale).

Table 7: Usefulness of explored information – means and standard deviations for each condition.

	Cond.	1	2	3	4	5
Useful Webpages	**Mean (s.d.)**	4.50 (2.593)	9.00 (3.726)	6.10 (3.315)	13.50 (4.007)	13.60 (2.914)
Unique Useful Webpages	**Mean (s.d.)**	1.90 (1.792)	3.80 (2.799)	2.10 (2.132)	7.50 (2.718)	7.30 (2.983)
Likelihood of discovery	**Mean (s.d.)**	-0.011 (0.005)	-0.008 (0.003)	-0.009 (0.006)	-0.006 (0.002)	-0.005 (0.001)

Table 8: Means differences between conditions (row-column). Bold values correspond to statistical significant difference at p≤.05 and italic bold values at p≤.01.

	Cond.	2	3	4	5
Useful Webpages	1	***-4.5***	-1.6	***-9.0***	***-9.1***
	2		2.9	***-4.5***	***-4.6***
	3			***-7.4***	***-7.5***
	4				-0.1
Unique Useful Webpages	1	-1.9	-0.2	***-5.6***	***-5.4***
	2		1.7	***-3.7***	***-3.5***
	3			***-5.4***	***-5.2***
	4				0.2
Likelihood of discovery	1	-0.0039	-0.0021	**-0.0056**	**-0.0064**
	2		-0.0017	-0.0017	**-0.0024**
	3			-0.0035	-0.0042
	4				-0.0007

In addition, we found that C4 and C5 participants visited many more difficult to reach (less likely visited) webpages than those in C1. This shows that collaboration, in this case, allowed a unit (a pair or users) get to the information that was otherwise ignored by those who worked alone. In fact, even when we combined two independent participants' explorations (C2), those who collaborated while remotely located (C5) could discover more information. Once again, C5 participants leveraged on the interactions through real collaboration while exercising their independence and exploring individual information trails.

5.4 Query diversity

To understand searching behavior of various individuals and teams, we looked at their querying effectiveness. Given that the assigned task was exploratory in nature, that there was plethora of useful information on the web, and that the time was limited, it was important that the participants construct a variety of queries and cover as large a ground as they could. To measure this, we computed query diversity for each participant/team as defined in the previous section (Table 9). A general overview of query distances for each condition is given in Figure 5. As we can see, those in C4 had more queries with higher distances among them. In other words, those in C5 tried more diverse queries.

Table 9: Query diversity – means and standard deviations for each condition.

	Cond.	2	4	5
Query Diversity	**Mean (s.d.)**	20.41 (9.205)	19.69 (8.863)	23.13 (8.465)

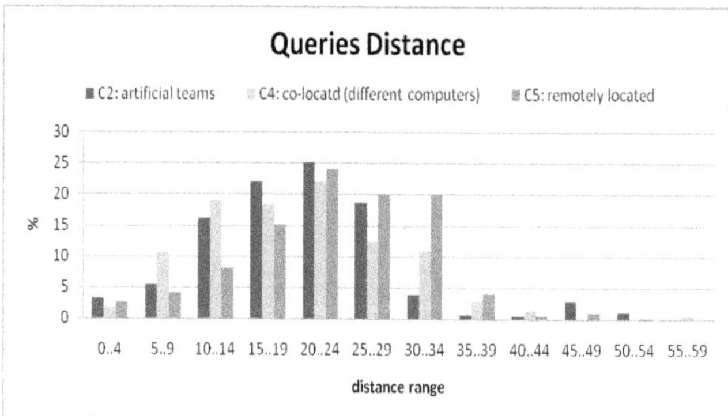

Figure 5: Query distance for C2, C4, and C5 using Lavenshtein algorithm.

Using ANOVA, we found (Table 10) that those in real collaborations with individual computers and remotely located (C5) had higher diversity in their queries than those co-located using different computers (C4). C5 participants also exhibited a larger variety in their queries than those by artificially created teams (C2). Combining these two facts indicates that (1) participants remotely located were able to successfully divide the task up and explore unique information through different queries, and (2) these participants had a chance to work more independently than those in the same space.

We believe that query similarity for teams in C4 is due to space sharing, which may influence the way in which users formulated their queries. Even though most teams split up the task, the physical closeness of users could enable them to hear what their peers think aloud; or even have brief conversations (facilitated by face-to-face interaction). This may have influenced implicitly common queries between those participants.

Table 10: Means differences between conditions (row-column). Bold values correspond to statistical significant difference at p≤.05 and italic bold values at p≤.01.

	Cond.	2	3	4	5
Query Diversity	2			0.720	***-2.724***
	4				***-3.444***

On the other hand, we think that users working remotely located and using only text chat for communicating with each other (C5) were more able to generate different queries because they were less directly influenced by their peers during the task.

5.5 Cognitive Load

Fidel et al. [5] showed that collaboration induces additional cognitive load, what they referred to as the *collaborative load.* Often, this is the price to pay for gaining the advantages of collaborating. We used NASA's TLX instrument to measure user perceived cognitive load during the task (see the previous section). For analysis, we combined the responses obtained from six different questions and created an index, since these responses were found to be statistically reliable for this instrument. A summary of what we found for the four real conditions (C2 was artificially created) is given in Table 11.

Table 11: Cognitive load – means and standard deviations for each condition.

	Cond.	1	3	4	5
Cognitive Load	**Mean (s.d.)**	15.00 (2.449)	16.00 (2.714)	17.60 (3.050)	15.70 (3.028)

Table 12: Means differences between conditions (row-column). Bold values correspond to statistical significant difference at p≤.05 and italic bold values at p≤.01.

	Cond.	3	4	5
Cognitive Load	1	-1.00	-2.60	-0.70
	3		-1.60	0.30
	4			1.90

Using this index, we performed the ANOVA and found no difference between the four conditions (Table 12). This indicates that the participants who worked in collaboration (C3, C4, and C5) experienced no more cognitive load than what was reported by those in C1. In other words, the collaborators in our experiment (at least C4 and C5) were able to gain the advantages of creating synergy without additional mental load.

6. CONCLUSION

Collaboration is often a useful approach for solving a complex problem, but it has its costs and overheads [6]. One typically gets involved in collaboration if it has good benefit-to-cost ration, or if the given problem is too difficult to be solved without collaboration [21]. It is, however, difficult to measure if and how a collaborative endeavor would pay off. Traditional objective or quantitative approaches used in IR are insufficient, and subjective or qualitative approaches may be expensive or difficult to employ. In this paper we proposed and demonstrated a unique framework for evaluating various aspects of collaborative information seeking (CIS), especially the synergic effect.

Using a user study with 70 participants working on an information-seeking task in different setups, we showed how various evaluation measures could be defined and operationalized. Here we summarize our findings and link them back to the research questions (RQ) and hypotheses (HT) listed in Section 2.2.

We first argued that the traditional measures of evaluating relevance are not appropriate for such situations, and proposed either modified or new kinds of evaluations. These included coverage, usefulness, likelihood of discovery, and query diversity. We believe this itself is an important contribution to the community, helping the researchers evaluate and design CIS systems and interfaces (RQ4). The results of the experiments reported here indicated that in a recall-oriented exploratory search task, two collaborators working at the same computer achieve similar results to the individual users (RQ1, HT1). It also became clear that those in remote collaboration were able to work more independently than those that were co-located (HT2). Independence is considered an important characteristic of a successful collaboration [24, 21]. Our results also provided a strong support for synergic effect in remotely located collaborators. In particular, we showed that two people working in collaboration (C4 and C5) is not the same as having the outcomes of two completely independent individuals combined (C2); they do better in terms of discovering more and diverse information for an information-seeking task. Not only that, but the cognitive load in a real collaborative situation was found to be no more than what was perceived by those working individually (RQ5). Thus, the synergic effect of *the whole being greater than the sum of all* was demonstrated and evaluated (RQ3, HT3).

We also want to point out a few of the limitations of our experiments. The study reported here was conducted with synchronous CIS task. The findings may be impacted if the collaborators were working asynchronously. Due to the nature of the laboratory study, we also gave limited amount of time to the participants. It has been shown that collaborations lasting longer and done over multiple sessions may produce significantly different results and user experiences [21, 22]. Having more than two participants per team could also lead to different group dynamics, influencing the results. Despite these limitations, we believe the methodology and the evaluation measures proposed and demonstrated here could help us further investigations of CIS with different setups, including asynchronous, non-time bound, multi-session, and non-dividable tasks, as well as collaborations that involve more than two participants. These contributions could be helpful for not just CIS, but IR in general.

7. REFERENCES

[1] Buckminster Fuller, R. (1975). SYNERGETICS Explorations in the Geometry of Thinking. http://www.rwgrayprojects.com/synergetics/synergetics.html.

[2] Corning, P. A. (1995). Synergy and self-organization in the evolution of complex systems. *Systems Research 12*(2):89-121.

[3] Denning, P. J. (2007). Mastering the mess. *Communications of the ACM, 50*(4), 21-25.

[4] Denning, P. J., & Yaholkovsky, P. (2008). Getting to "We". *Communications of the ACM, 51*(4), 19-24.

[5] Fidel, R., Bruce, H., Pejtersen, A. M., Dumais, S. T., Grudin, J., & Poltrock, S. (2000). Collaborative Information Retrieval (CIR). *The New Review of Information Behaviour Research*, 235-247.

[6] Fidel, R., Mark Pejtersen, A., Cleal, B., & Bruce, H. (2004). A multidimensional approach to the study of human-information interaction: A case study of collaborative information retrieval. *Journal of the American Society for Information Science and Technology, 55*(11), 939-953. doi: 10.1002/asi.20041.

[7] Foley, C. (2008). Division of Labour and Sharing of Knowledge for Synchronous Collaborative Information Retrieval. PhD Thesis. School of Computing, Dublin City University.

[8] Fox, S., Karnawat, K., Mydland, M., Dumais, S., & White, T. (2005). Evaluating implicit measures to improve web search. ACM Transactions on Information Systems (TOIS). 23(2): 147-168.

[9] Golovchinsky, G., Pickens, J., & Back, M. (2008). A taxonomy of collaboration in online information seeking. *Proceedings of JCDL 2008 Workshop on Collaborative Exploratory Search*. Pittsburgh, PA.

[10] González-Ibáñez, R. (2010). A proposal for studying users' behaviors in collaborative information seeking through a convergence map. *GROUP 2010 Workshop on Collaborative Information Behavior*. Sanibel Island, Florida.

[11] Hart, S. G., & Staveland, L. E. (1988). Development of NASA-TLX (Task Load Index): Results of Empirical and Theoretical Research. In P. A. Hancock & N. Meshkati (Eds.), *Human Mental Workload* (pp. 239-250). North Holland Press.

[12] Hyldegard, J. (2006). Collaborative information behaviour - exploring Kuhlthau's Information Search Process model in a group-based educational setting. *Information Processing and Management, 42*, 276-298.

[13] Hyldegard, J. (2009). Beyond the search process - exploring group members' information behavior in context. *Information Processing and Management, 45*, 142-158.

[14] Joho, H., Hannah, D., & Joemon, J. M. (2008). Comparing collaborative and independent search in a recall-oriented task. *Proceedings of Information Interaction in Context*. London, UK.

[15] Kuhlthau, C. C. (1991). Inside the Search Process: Information Seeking from the User's Perspective. *Journal of the American Society for Information Science and Technology, 42*(5), 361-371.

[16] Morris, M. R., & Horvitz, E. (2007). SearchTogether: An Interface for Collaborative Web Search. *ACM Symposium on User Interface Software and Technology (UIST)* (pp. 3-12). Newport, RI.

[17] Morris, M. R. (2008). A survey of collaborative web search practices. *Proceeding of the twenty-sixth annual CHI conference on Human factors in computing systems - CHI '08*. 2008:1657.

[18] Morris, M. R., Teevan, J., & Bush, S. (2008). Enhancing Collaborative Web Search with Personalization: Groupization, Smart Splitting, and Group Hit-Highlighting. *Proceedings of Computer Supported Cooperative Work (CSCW)*. San Diego, CA.

[19] Pickens, J., Golovchinsky, G., Shah, C., Qvarfordt, P., & Back, M. (2008). Algorithmic Mediation for Collaborative Exploratory Search. *Proceedings of the Annual ACM Conference on Research and Development in Information Retrieval (SIGIR)*. Singapore.

[20] Shah, C. (2009). Lessons and Challenges for Collaborative Information Seeking (CIS) Systems Developers. *GROUP 2009 Workshop on Collaborative Information Behavior*. Sanibel Island, Florida.

[21] Shah, C. (2010). Working in Collaboration - What, Why, and How? *Proceedings of Collaborative Information Retrieval workshop at CSCW 2010*. Savannah, GA.

[22] Shah, C., & Gonzalez-Ibanez, R. (2010). Exploring Information Seeking Processes in Collaborative Search Tasks. *Annual Meeting of the American Society for Information Science*. Pittsburgh, PA.

[23] Shah, C., Pickens, J., & Golovchinsky, G. (2010). Role-based results redistribution for collaborative information retrieval. *Information Processing & Management, 46*(6), 773-781. doi: 10.1016/j.ipm.2009.10.002.

[24] Surowiecki, J. (2004). Wisdom of Crowds : Why the Many Are Smarter Than the Few and How Collective Wisdom Shapes Business, Economies, Societies and Nations. Doubleday Publishing.

[25] Twidale, M. B. T., Nichols, D. M. N., & Paice, C. D. (1997). Browsing is a Collaborative Process. *Information Processing and Management, 33*(6), 761-783.

[26] Twidale, M. B., & Nichols, D. M. (1996). Collaborative browsing and visualisation of the search process. *Proceedings of Aslib* (Vol. 48, pp. 177-182).

[27] White, R. W., & Huang, J. (2010). Assessing the scenic route: Measuring the value of search trails in web logs. *Proceedings of the Annual ACM Conference on Research and Development in Information Retrieval (SIGIR)*. Geneva, Switzerland.

Repeatable and Reliable Search System Evaluation using Crowdsourcing

Roi Blanco
Yahoo! Research
Diagonal 177
Barcelona, Spain
roi@yahoo-inc.com

Harry Halpin
University of Edinburgh
10 Crichton St.
Edinburgh, UK
H.Halpin@ed.ac.uk

Daniel M. Herzig
Institute AIFB
Karlsruhe Institute of Technology
76128 Karlsruhe, Germany
herzig@kit.edu

Peter Mika
Yahoo! Research
Diagonal 177
Barcelona, Spain
pmika@yahoo-inc.com

Jeffrey Pound
David R. Cheriton School of Computer Science
University of Waterloo
Waterloo, Canada
jpound@cs.uwaterloo.ca

Henry S. Thompson
University of Edinburgh
10 Crichton St.
Edinburgh, UK
ht@inf.ed.ac.uk

ABSTRACT

The primary problem confronting any new kind of search task is how to boot-strap a reliable and repeatable evaluation campaign, and a crowd-sourcing approach provides many advantages. However, can these crowd-sourced evaluations be repeated over long periods of time in a reliable manner? To demonstrate, we investigate creating an evaluation campaign for the semantic search task of keyword-based ad-hoc object retrieval. In contrast to traditional search over web-pages, object search aims at the retrieval of information from factual assertions about real-world objects rather than searching over web-pages with textual descriptions. Using the first large-scale evaluation campaign that specifically targets the task of ad-hoc Web object retrieval over a number of deployed systems, we demonstrate that crowd-sourced evaluation campaigns can be repeated over time and still maintain reliable results. Furthermore, we show how these results are comparable to expert judges when ranking systems and that the results hold over different evaluation and relevance metrics. This work provides empirical support for scalable, reliable, and repeatable search system evaluation using crowdsourcing.

Categories and Subject Descriptors

H.3.3 [**Information Storage Systems**]: Information Retrieval Systems

General Terms

Performance, Experimentation

Keywords

crowdsourcing, search engines, retrieval, evaluation

1. INTRODUCTION

Advances in information retrieval have long been driven by evaluation campaigns using standardized collections of data-sets, query workloads, and most importantly, result relevance judgments. TREC (Text REtrieval Conference) [20] is a forerunner in IR evaluations, but campaigns also take place in specialized forums like INEX (INitiative for the Evaluation of XML Retrieval) [12] and CLEF (Cross Language Evaluation Forum). The main premises of these campaigns is that a limited and controlled set of human *experts* decide the correctness of a given set of results, which will be used as a ground truth for evaluating the performance of different systems [20]. Early evaluation campaigns targeted relatively narrow domains and used small collections, where evaluations using a small number of queries provided robust results. Moving to the open domain of the Web resulted in significantly larger heterogeneity of data sources and an increase in the potential information needs (and so diverse tasks) that need to be evaluated. Current research in campaigns (like TREC) and information retrieval evaluation in general focus primarily on the following goals:

Repeatability - As observed by Harter [11], there can be substantial variation among different expert judges performing the same task. If evaluation is to drive the next generation of search technologies, it is important to validate that relevance assignment is a repeatable process. This fundamental requirement exacerbates the scalability problem, because the agreement between assessors needs to be tested not only for each new search task, but also for each set of judges that have been employed (Agreement is a measure of the extent to which judges are interchangeable). However, outsiders who would like to validate an experiment will typically not have access to the original judges (or those judges may not be available or willing to repeat experiments at later times).

Reliability - The expert judges employed by campaigns such as TREC are expected to be sufficiently reliable to produce a ground truth for evaluation. However, setting up new "tracks" for novel search tasks is often not feasible or expedient, due to the time and effort it takes to set up such tracks and the limited resources of the organizers. In such cases, researchers need to set up their own evaluation and seek replacements for experts, training others to be judges of their work, where training is often nothing more than providing a description of the task.

How can researchers create repeatable and reliable evaluation campaigns that scale over the number of new tasks brought about by the Web? An increasingly popular way of evaluating novel search tasks is the approach known as *crowdsourcing*. Crowdsourcing is a method of obtaining human input for a given task by distributing that task over a large population of unidentified human workers. In the case of building a search evaluation collection, crowdsourcing means distributing relevance judgments of pooled results over this crowd. The advantage of the crowd is that it is always available, it is accessible to most people at a relatively small cost, and the workforce scales elastically with increasing evaluation demands. Further, platforms such as Amazon Mechanical Turk[1] provide integrated frameworks for running crowdsourced tasks with minimal effort. We show how crowdsourcing can help execute an evaluation campaign for a search task that has not yet been sufficiently addressed to become part of a large evaluation effort such as TREC: ad-hoc Web object retrieval [17], for which we created a standard data set and queries for the task of object retrieval using real-world data, and the way we employed Mechanical Turk to elicit high quality judgments from the noise of unreliable workers in the crowd. The queries, index used, and results of the evaluation campaign are also publicly available for use in the evaluation of web-object retrieval systems[2].

There are two research questions that must be answered for crowdsourcing to be used systematically in evaluation campaigns. First, are evaluation campaigns with crowdsourced workers **repeatable**, such that the resulting ranking of systems is the same for different pools of crowdsourced judges over a period of time? Second, are crowdsourced workers **reliable**, such that differences between experts and crowdsourced workers do not change the resulting ranking of the systems? As our primary contribution, we experimentally demonstrate the repeatability of our search system evaluation experiment using crowdsourcing. We also test the reliability of judges who are not task or topic-experts, which has been questioned in previous work [3], as crowdsourced workers do not have access to the original information need and may lack specialized training or background knowledge possessed by experts. The case of Mechanical Turk provides an extreme where the judges are not only likely to be untrained and non-expert, but they also sign up for payment and so have an incentive to "cheat" in order to gain monetary reward. Therefore, we repeat our evaluation and assess whether the results from the original campaign can be reproduced after six months with a new set of crowdsourced judges, and whether those results correspond to what we would have obtained using a more traditional methodology employing expert judges. We also explore the effect of different numbers of judges per result on the quality of judgments. Finally, we analyse the robustness of three popular information retrieval metrics under crowdsourced judgments. The metrics studied are discounted cumulative gain (NDCG), mean average precision (MAP), and precision at k (P@k).

[1]`http://www.mturk.com`

[2]`http://anonymized.for.review`

To the best of our knowledge, we are the first to analyze the repeatability of crowdsourcing in a real-world evaluation campaign.

2. EVALUATING OBJECT RETRIEVAL

The broad class of search technologies that exploit semantic data encodings are often called *semantic search* systems [9]. Largely due to the Semantic Web and related efforts such as Linked Data,[3] there is an increasing amount of structured data on the Web about real-world objects and their relations, given in the RDF (Resource Description Framework) format. We focus in particular on the class of semantic search systems that apply traditional information retrieval techniques directly on Semantic Web data, so that we evaluate keyword search over data in RDF. We are motivated by the increasing need to locate particular information quickly and effectively and in a way that is accessible to non-expert users.

There are already a number of semantic search systems that crawl and index Semantic Web data such as [7, 16], and there is active research into algorithms for ranking in this setting [8]. Despite the growing interest, there has been no standardized evaluation campaign for semantic search. One of the principle reasons for the lack of a standardized evaluation campaign is the cost of creating a new and realistically sized "gold-standard" data-set and annual evaluation campaign was considered too high by the community. We believe crowdsourcing can solve this problem.

2.1 Ad-Hoc Object Retrieval

Arriving at a common evaluation methodology requires the definition of a shared task that is accepted by the community as the one that is most relevant to potential applications of the field. The definition of the task has also been a precondition for establishing a set of procedures and metrics for assessing performance on the task, with the eventual purpose of ranking systems [20]. For the field of text-based information retrieval, this task is the retrieval of a ranked list of (text) documents from a fixed corpus in response to free-form keyword queries, or what is known as the ad-hoc document retrieval (ADR) task.

For the field of semantic search, Pound et al. [17] defined the task of ad-hoc object retrieval (AOR), where the goal is to retrieve a ranked list of objects (resources in RDF parlance) from a collection of RDF documents in response to free-form keyword queries. The unit of retrieval is thus individual objects and not RDF documents, and so the task differs from classic textual information retrieval insofar as the primary unit is structured linked data rather than unstructured textual data. Pound et al. also proposed an evaluation protocol and tested a number of metrics for their stability and discriminating power. In our current work, we instantiate their methodology in the sense of creating a standard set of queries and data on which we execute the methodology using a crowdsourcing approach. As keyword search over RDF is broadly comparable to existing evaluation campaigns (such as keyword search over XML and textual ad-hoc document retrieval), so the general results of our research should hold over a variety of ad-hoc ranking tasks, especially if the information need is clearly specified about

[3]`http://linkeddata.org`

a single entity and the systems have significant performance differences.

2.2 Data Collection

Current semantic search engines have vastly different indices, with some specializing on only single data-sources with thousands of triples and others ranging over billions of triples crawled from the Web. Therefore, in order to have a generalized evaluation of the ranking of results, it is essential to normalize the index.

We required a data-set that would not bias the results towards any particular semantic search engine. The data-set that we wanted to use in the evaluation campaign needed to contain real data, sizeable enough to contain relevant information for the queries, yet not so large that its indexing would require computational resources outside the scope of most research groups. We have chosen the 'Billion Triples Challenge' 2009 data set, a data-set created for the Semantic Web Challenge[4] in 2009 and which is well-known in the community. The raw size of the data is 247GB uncompressed and it contains 1.4B triples describing 114 million objects. This data-set was composed by combining crawls of multiple semantic search engines. Therefore, it does not necessarily match the coverage of any particular search engine. We refer the readers to `http://vmlion25.deri.ie/` for more information on the data set and to `http://km.aifb.kit.edu/ws/semsearch10` for the details of the semantic search challenge.

2.3 Real-World Web Queries

As the kinds of queries used by semantic search engines vary dramatically (ranging from structured SPARQL queries to searching directly for URI-based identifiers), it was decided to focus first on keyword-based search. Keyword-based search is the most commonly used query paradigm, is supported by most semantic search engines, and often serves as the foundation for more complex searches and processing.

Clearly, the type of result expected, and thus the way to assess relevance depend on the type of the query. For example, a query such as *plumbers in mason ohio* is looking for instances of a class of objects, while a query like *parcel 104 santa clara* is looking for information for one particular object, in this case a certain restaurant. [17] proposed a classification of queries by expected result type, and for our first evaluation we have decided to focus on object-queries, i.e. queries demonstrated by the latter example, where the user is seeking information about a particular object. Note that for this type of queries there might be other objects mentioned in the query other than the main object, such as *santa clara* in the above case. However, it is clear that the focus of the query is the restaurant named *parcel 104*, and not the city of Santa Clara as a whole.

Our evaluation required a set of object-queries that would be unbiased towards any existing semantic search engine. First, although the search engine logs of various semantic search engines were gathered, it was determined that the kinds of queries varied quite a lot, with many of the query logs of semantic search engines revealing idiosyncratic research tests by robots rather than real-world queries by actual users. Since one of the claims of semantic search is that it can help general purpose ad-hoc information retrieval on the Semantic Web, we have decided to use queries from actual users of hypertext Web search engines. As these queries would be from hypertext Web search engines, they would not be biased towards any semantic search engine. We had initial concerns if within the scope of the data-set it would be possible to provide relevant results for each of the queries. However, this possible weakness also doubled as a strength, as the testing of a real query sample from actual users would determine whether or not a billion triples from the Semantic Web realistically could help answer the real-world information needs of ordinary users, as opposed to the research-driven queries in most semantic search query logs [10].

We used a sample of the publicly available *Yahoo! Search Query Log Tiny Sample v1.0*, released by Yahoo! as a part of their WebScope program[5], which contains 4,500 queries sampled from the company's United States query log from January, 2009. One constraint of this data-set is that it contains only queries that have been posed by at least three different (not necessarily authenticated) users, which removes some of the heterogeneity of the log, for example in terms of spelling mistakes. We expected a random sample of these queries to be realistic but difficult to satisfy. Given the well-known differences between the top of the power-law distribution of queries and the long-tail, we used an additional log of queries from the Microsoft Live Search containing queries that were repeated by at least 10 different users. We expected these queries to be easier to answer.

overeaters ananymous
imdb batman returns
aloha sol
the longest yard sale
sacred heart u
sagemont church houston tx
david suchet
NAACP Image Awards
mr rourke fantasy island
old winchester shotguns
la scala restaurant philadelphia
the quick lift

Table 1: Example queries from the Yahoo! log.

We have selected a sample of 42 entity-queries from the Yahoo! query log by classifying queries manually, which filtered for ambiguous queries. A sample of these queries are given in Table 1. We have selected a sample of 50 queries from the Microsoft log. In this case we have pre-filtered queries automatically with a named entity recognizer, a gazetteer and rule-based named-entity recognizer that has shown to have very high precision in competitions, but these queries were not filtered for ambiguity. Both sets were combined into a single, alphabetically ordered list, so that participants were not aware which queries belonged to which set, or in fact that there were two sources of queries. We distributed the final set of 92 queries to the participants two weeks before the submission deadline.

[4] `http://challenge.semanticweb.org`

[5] `http://webscope.sandbox.yahoo.com/`

3. CROWDSOURCING JUDGMENTS

In this Section, we report how we used Amazon Mechanical Turk to assess the relevance of search results and describe the different sets of assessments we obtained for the evaluation. Using Mechanical Turk, tasks - called Human Intelligence Tasks (HITS) - are presented to a pool of human judges known as 'workers' who do the task in return for very small payments. Amazon provides a web-based interface for the workers that keeps track of their decisions and their payments. Because *anyone* can sign up to be a worker, we had to present each result for judgement in a way comprehensible to non-expert human judges. It was not an option to present the data in the native syntactic format of RDF such as RDF/XML or N-Triples, because they are too complex for average users, especially with the use of URIs as opposed to natural language terms for identifiers in RDF. In practice, semantic search systems use widely varying presentations of search results, sometimes tailored to particular domains. However, the rendering of results could possibly affect the valuation given by a judge. Allowing each participant to provide their own rendering would make it difficult to separate the measurement of ranking performance from effects of presentation, and would also eliminate the ability to pool results which reduces the total number of judgments needed.

For the purpose of evaluation, we have created a rendering algorithm to present the results in a concise, yet human-readable manner without domain-dependent customizations (see Figure 1). First, for each subject URI, all properties and objects were retrieved. Then the last rightmost hierarchical component of the property URI was used as the label of the property after tokenization. For example, the property `http://www.w3.org/1999/02/22-rdf-syntax-ns/type` was presented to the judge simply as `type`. A maximum of twelve object properties were displayed to the judge, with a preference being given to a few well-known property types defined in the RDF and RDF Schema namespaces, followed by custom-defined properties presented in the order retrieved from the data-set. In order to keep the amount of information given constant across judges and facilitate timely completion of the task, the URIs were not clickable and the judges were instructed to assess using only the information rendered, as to make the task of ad-hoc object retrieval directly comparable to tasks such as ad-hoc document retrieval. During the evaluation, we encountered the problem that some of the retrieved URIs only appear as objects, resulting in an empty display. Of the 6,158 URIs, a small minority of URIs (372) had triples only in the object position. For the current evaluation, we have ignored these results. Workers were given three options to judge each result: "Excellent - describes the query target specifically and exclusively", "Not bad - mostly about the target", and "Poor - not about the target, or mentions it only in passing." Note that we used the human-friendly labels "Excellent", "Not bad" and "Poor" for relevant, somewhat relevant and irrelevant results. We did not provide instructions to emphasize any particular properties (such as the "categories" in Figure 1), leaving the judgment to be based on general purpose judgment combining background knowledge about the entities and all of the displayed information.

In order to ensure quality in the presence of possible low-quality workers, each HIT consisted of 12 query-result pairs for relevance judgments. Of the 12 results, 10 were real results drawn from the participants' submissions, and 2 were gold-standard results randomly placed in the list of results. These gold-standard results were results from queries distinct from those used by the workers and have been manually judged earlier by an expert in RDF and information retrieval as being obviously 'relevant' or 'irrelevant'. For each HIT, there was both a gold-standard relevant and gold-standard irrelevant result included. These gold-standard results enabled the detection of workers who were not properly doing their task, as can be done by monitoring the average performance of judges on the gold-standard results hidden in their HITs. It is a common occurrence when using paid crowdsourcing systems for bogus workers to try to 'game' the system in order to gain money quickly without investing effort in the task, either by using automated bots or simply answering uniformly or randomly. Note that while we chose our gold-standards manually since we were evaluating a new task, one could in future campaigns use result with high inter-annotator agreement as new gold standards. Amazon Mechanical Turk allows payment to be withheld at the discretion of the creator of the HIT if they believe the task has not been done properly.

Before publishing the final tasks, we had done small-scale experiments with varying rewards for the workers. Mason and Watts have already determined previously that increased financial incentives increase the quantity, but not the quality, of work performed by participants [14]. Thus our approach was to lower the payment to workers down to the price where the speed of picking up the published tasks was still acceptable. When our results were published via Amazon Mechanical Turk, workers were paid $0.20 per HIT. In the first experiment reported here 65 workers in total participated in judging a total of 579 HITs or 1737 assignments (3 assignments per HIT), covering 5786 submitted results and 1158 gold-standard checks. (Note that of these only a subset of 4209 results and 842 checks is relevant here, being those which were also evaluated in MT2 and EXP, see below). Three workers were detected to be answering uniformly or randomly, and their work (a total of 95 assignments) was rejected and their assignments returned to the pool for another worker to complete. Two minutes were allotted for completing each HIT. On average the HITs were completed in 1 minute, with only two complaints that the allotted time was too short. This means that workers could earn $6-$12 an hour by participating in the evaluation. The entire competition was judged within 2 days, for a total cost of $347.16. We consider this both fast and cost-effective.

To study repeatability of our evaluation campaign we have re-evaluated the relevance of the search results returned by our test systems using a second set of workers. This second experiment has been performed six months after the initial evaluation using the exact same procedure. In the following, we will refer to the original set of assessments as MT1 and the repeated set of assessments as MT2.For MT1 there were 64 judges in total. The top four judges did 131 HITs and did not differ from the experts on the gold-standard items, with the overall percentage of mistakes over the 2176 gold-standard items in those 1088 HITs was 3.2%. For MT2 there were 69 judges in total. The top five judges did 165 HITs and did not differ at all from experts on the gold-standard items, and the overall percentage of mistakes with regards the 1662 gold-standard items in those 831 HITs was 4.5%. For future

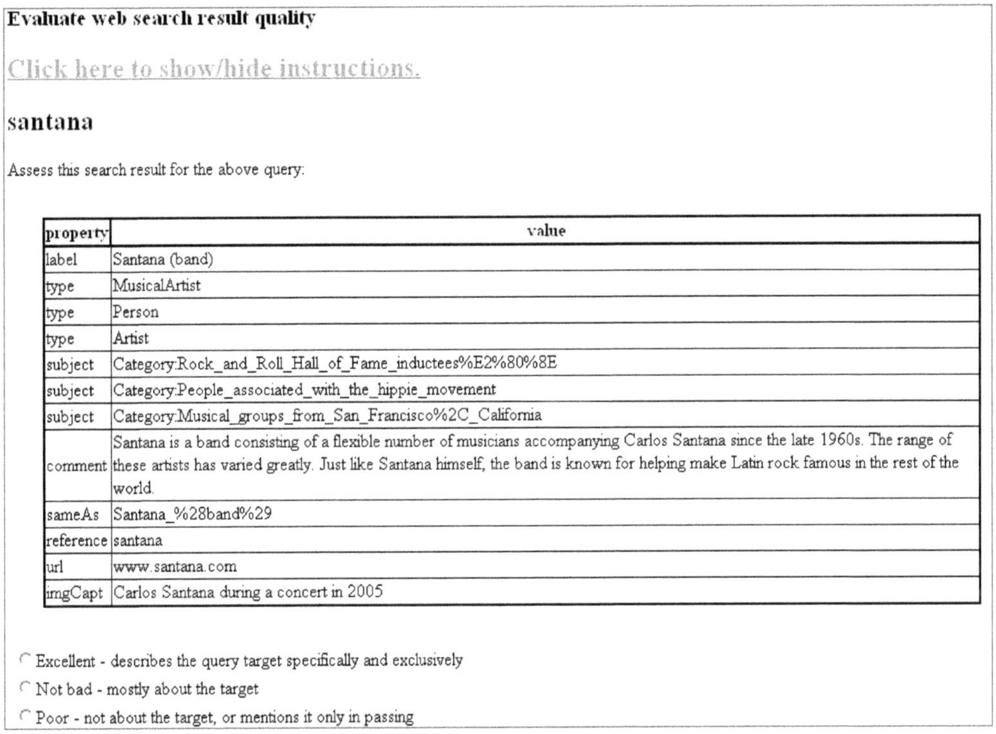

Figure 1: A sample HIT for semantic search evaluation.

campaigns items with a high inter-annotator reliability could be used to chose more gold-standard items.

To study the reliability of our crowdsourced judgments, we also created an "expert" set of relevance judgments over standard HITs that were not gold-standard items. Unlike repeatability, reliability concerns the ability of Mechanical Turk to reproduce a ground truth provided by experts. In our case, the authors of this paper have provided the ground truth by re-evaluating the same subset used in MT2. As this is a significant effort, we have used only one judge per HIT for re-evaluating the entire set of 4209 results, in 421 HITs of 10 results (leaving out the known-good and known-bad gold-standard check items). The resulting dataset is referred to as EXP herein.

For all of MT1, MT2, and EXP, we report here on the exact same set of queries and results. Some participants submitted more than one set of results (outputs from their system in differing configurations), of which we used the best submission of each of the competitor systems for testing repeatability. In total there were 6 competing systems with one submission each. Each result of every submission was judged by 3 crowdsourced workers, with systems results being judged to a depth of 10, given that it was a new unstudied task. We broke ties by taking the majority vote, except where the three judges each gave a different judgment, in which case we chose the middle, "Not Bad" assessment. In EXP, as mentioned above, each result was judged by a single expert, but a subset of 30 results were judged by three experts to determine intra-expert reliability.

Although the procedure for MT2 was the same as for MT1, the intervening six months appear to have seen a significant change in the worker pool: monitoring worker time-to-complete and performance on the known-good and known-bad gold-standard results revealed a total of 14 bogus workers for MT2, who completed a total of 1471 assignments between them before they were detected and blocked and their assignments returned to the pool. This change from 5% of assignments rejected in MT1 to 54% of assignments rejected in MT2 may indicate a significant increase in the number of bogus workers, and underlines the importance of including known-good and known-bad data in every HIT.

4. ANALYSIS OF RESULTS

We seek to answer the following in our experiments:

- **Repeatability** Are judges really inter-changeable?
  - Can we expect anonymous crowdsourced workers to agree on judgments?
  - Can we expect repeated experiments to produce the same results in terms of relevance metrics and the rank-order of the evaluated systems?

This requires also confirming previous results [2]:

- **Reliability** Can crowdsourced workers reliably reproduce the results we would have obtained if we were using expert judges?
  - Are the same items scored similarly by workers and experts?
  - Can worker evaluations produce the same results in terms of our relevance metrics and the rank-order of the evaluated systems?

We will use as parameters both the evaluation metric, the number of assessors per item and the relevance scale used. In particular, we would like to find out the following:

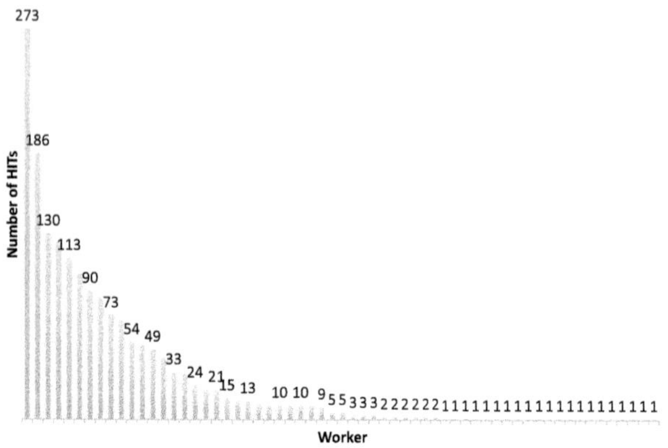

Figure 2: Workers ordered by decreasing number of items assessed.

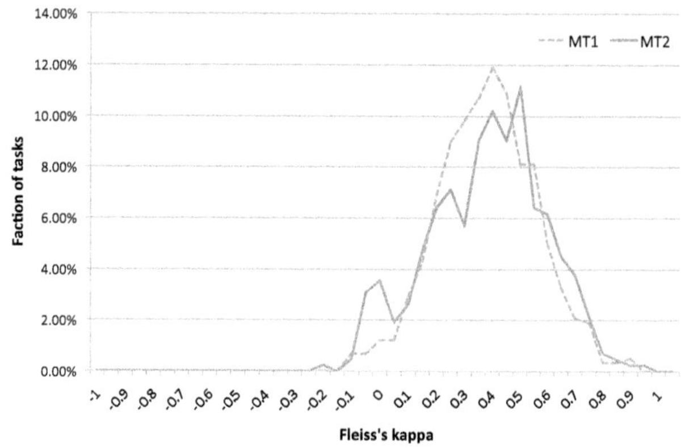

Figure 3: Agreement between workers.

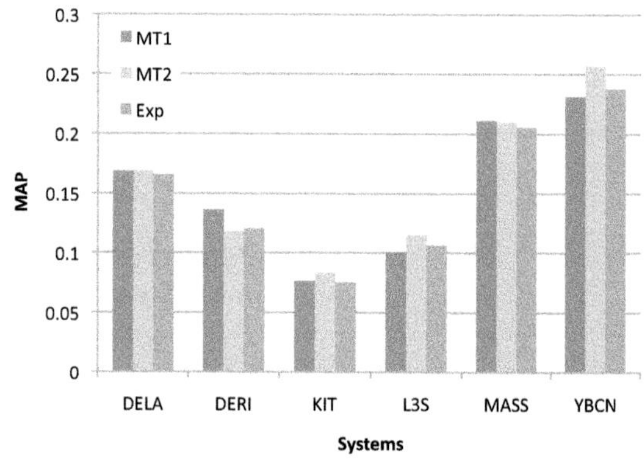

Figure 4: Mean average precision (MAP) for the systems using different test sets.

- Which of our three evaluation metrics (MAP, NDCG, P@10) are more robust to changing the pool of workers, and when replacing experts with workers?
- Do we obtain better results with increasing number of assessments per item?
- Do our results hold for both binary and ternary scale assessment?

4.1 Repeatability

As previously discussed, in IR evaluation the notion of repeatability is tied to measuring the extent to which judges are inter-changeable. The argumentation goes that if we show that judges from a particular pool of assessors are inter-changeable, the experiment can be repeated with any subset of judges from the pool: the judges will agree on the relevancy of items to be judged, which will be reflected in the metrics to be computed, and the eventual ranking of the competing systems.

The most common measures of inter-annotator agreement in IR evaluations are Cohen's κ for the case of two judges, and Fleiss's κ for the case of multiple judges, which has a free-marginal version [15]. While we report inter-annotator agreement, we note that the applicability of standard metrics to the case of crowdsourced workers can be questioned. The reason is that although we have a fixed number of workers for each HIT, in the crowdsourcing scenario the workers select the tasks, and thus they are not necessarily the *same* workers who assess each item. Figure 2 shows the number of items judged by each worker in our first experiment with Mechanical Turk. In the case of traditional expert-based evaluation, this distribution would be flat as each expert would assess the same items. In our case, each worker may assess a different number of the total set of HITs. Some workers assess a large number of HITs, with the most diligent worker going through 273 HITs, while a long tail of workers worked on a single task only. This long tail is especially problematic since there is much less data about these workers on which to base reliability tests.

Based on our knowledge of the related work, it seems that there is not yet consensus as to how to account for this deficiency [6] and the question of reliability is sometimes ignored altogether [8]. We believe the most prudent way to proceed is to report the distribution of Fleiss' κ values considering all HITs as individual assessments of a small number of 12 items. In Figure 3 we show this distribution for our first and second experiment. As the Figure shows, the level of agreement is very similar. The average and standard deviation are 0.36 ± 0.18 for the first experiment (MT1) versus 0.36 ± 0.21 for MT2. In fact, the difference between the average agreement appears at the fourth digit, strongly supporting the idea of a homogeneous pool of workers. We achieve slightly higher levels of agreement for binary relevance (with somewhat relevant and relevant judgments counted both as relevant), 0.44 ± 0.22 and 0.47 ± 0.25. There is thus no marked difference between a three-point scale and a binary scale, meaning that it was feasible to judge this task on a three-point scale.

Agreement numbers are not easy to interpret even in the context of related work, and agreement is only a proxy for a repeatable evaluation: what we are ultimately after is whether different pools of workers used in different experiments lead to the same results in terms of evaluation metrics, and ultimately the same ordering of the evaluated systems. Figure 4 shows Mean Average Precision (MAP) scores for the different systems using the two different evaluation sets obtained via Mechanical Turk (MT1 and MT2). The results are also included in Table 3. We can see that the scores are close in value, and in fact there is no change to the rank-order of the systems. The result holds for both binary and

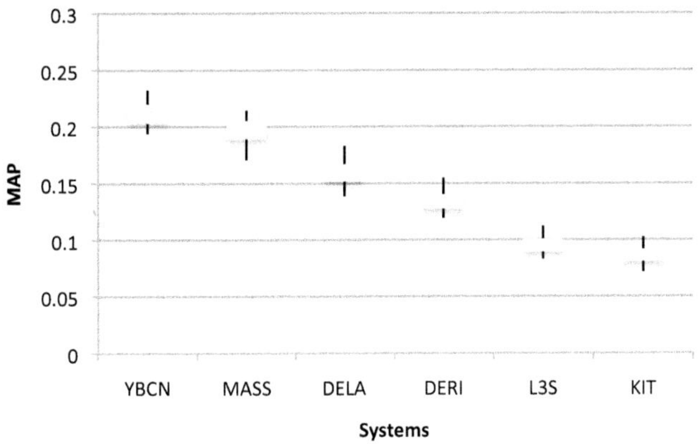

Figure 5: Mean average precision (MAP) for the systems using different test sets and a single worker.

ternary scale, and for both MAP, P@10 and NDCG. Broadly, this confirms our hypothesis that crowdsourced ad-hoc evaluation is repeatable. The relative change in scores across the two sets, for all systems in average, is 7.85% for MAP, 4.24% for NDCG and 6.87% for P@10. This gives us a first indication that two systems would need to be very close in performance in order to change places in the ranking produced by repeated experiments.

In fact, Mechanical Turk gives surprisingly robust results with just a single assessment per item. We have tested this by subsampling, i.e. selecting randomly a single assessment for each item from the six assessments we have collected in total. We have repeated this a 100 times and computed the min, max, mean and standard deviation of our metrics. Figure 5 shows the min, max, and the range of one standard deviation from the mean for each system, using MAP as the metric. This figure furthermore shows that even one standard deviation intervals provide different ranges for the different systems and effectively separate them. Though the score of a system in a particular sample may surpass the score of an overall inferior system, such cases would be rare. Note that there is a particular robustness to Mechanical Turk. Though conventional wisdom would certainly be against running an evaluation with a possibly unreliable single judge, in the case of crowdsourcing the assessments will come from not a single expert judge for all the results, but multiple workers. These workers may be individually unreliable, but each will judge a small number of items. When considering three judges, see Figure 6, the intervals around the mean get even tighter.

The decrease of standard deviation around the mean is also shown in Figure 7. This Figure shows the standard deviation on the y-axis, for different numbers of workers (x-axis), and using different metrics. We see that P@10 benefits the most from increasing the number of workers and that adding more workers decreases the standard deviation between workers.

4.2 Reliability

Repeatable evaluations require that each evaluation be reliable, and while work such as Alonso et al. [2] has shown that crowdsourced judges can be reliable in information retrieval tasks, we should show that this reliability holds over repeated experiments. We measured the agreement between expert judges on a subset of the items (30 HITs). In this case, the average and standard deviation of Fleiss's κ for the two- and three-point scales are 0.57 ± 0.18 and 0.56 ± 0.16, respectively. The level of agreement is thus higher for expert judges, with comparable deviation. For expert judges, there is practically no difference between the two- and three-point scales, meaning that expert judges had much less trouble using the middle judgment.

Set	Total items	Irrelevant	Somewhat R.	Relevant
MT1	4209	2593	970	646
MT2	4209	2497	975	737
EXP	4209	2847	640	722

Table 2: Scoring patterns in different evaluation sets.

The most basic statistic we can look at is the difference in scoring patterns of experts and non-experts. Moving on to comparing expert reliability with crowdsourced judgements from MT1 and MT2, Table 2 shows that again different sets of workers behave very similarly, though different from the experts on the whole. Fleiss's κ is similar with 0.412 between MT1 and experts, and 0.417 between MT2 and experts. In particular, experts are more pessimistic in their scoring, marking irrelevant many of the items that the workers would consider somewhat relevant.

This effect is also visible in Figure 8, which shows the assessments of the two worker sets compared to the assessments of the experts for the three assessment options. Whereas the two worker sets display similar behaviour compared to each to other, the difference towards more positive assessments compared to the experts can be observed. This may suggest that crowdsourced judgments cannot replace expert evaluations. Based on comments and the data, the source of this effect is likely the fact that experts understood "describes the query target specifically and exclusively" to be much of a more sharp distinction about objects than workers. An expert would note that the IMDB article about a movie featuring actor David Suchet would not be considered 'relevant', while workers would often judge that result as relevant if the query asked for David Suchet.

Looking at agreement rate in other settings, such a κ of 0.55 at TREC 2005 on sentence relevance at TREC 2004 Novelty Trac [18], our experts are clearly reliable, with agreement ratings of 0.57 (binary scale) and 0.56 (ternary scale). Yet then the reliability of non-expert crowdsourced judges of 0.36 in our experiment then appears to be less than ideal. However, does it change the ranking of the systems? This would be the ideal test of how far reliability has to degrade in order to impact an evaluation campaign.

Even if the level of agreement is higher amongst expert judges, if the ranking of the systems does not change when non-experts are employed, then a crowdsourcing approach is still reliable enough for the task (even if their reliability is strictly speaking relatively lower than expert judges). The relative change in scores when going from experts to workers (moving from EXP to three-samples of MT1 and MT2), for all systems in average, and using three judgments, is 1.8% for MAP, 3.5% for NDCG and 12.8% for P@10 (see also Table 3). These are comparable changes to what we have seen when moving from one worker set to another, but

	MAP			NDCG			P@10		
System	MT1	MT2	EXP	MT1	MT2	EXP	MT1	MT2	EXP
YBCN	0.23	0.26	0.24	0.35	0.38	0.33	0.48	0.54	0.45
MASS	0.21	0.21	0.21	0.34	0.34	0.33	0.48	0.51	0.40
DELA	0.17	0.17	0.17	0.29	0.27	0.28	0.41	0.43	0.35
DERI	0.14	0.12	0.12	0.24	0.24	0.22	0.39	0.36	0.30
L3S	0.10	0.11	0.11	0.20	0.21	0.20	0.28	0.30	0.24
KIT	0.08	0.08	0.08	0.15	0.14	0.15	0.26	0.28	0.23

Table 3: Evaluation results using different evaluation sets and metrics.

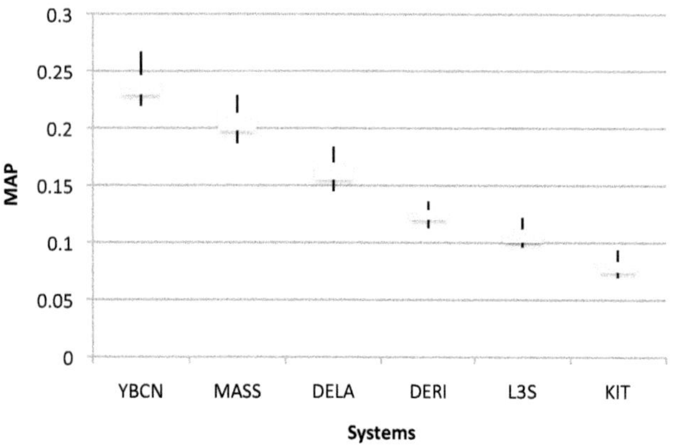

Figure 6: Mean average precision (MAP) for the systems using different test sets and three workers.

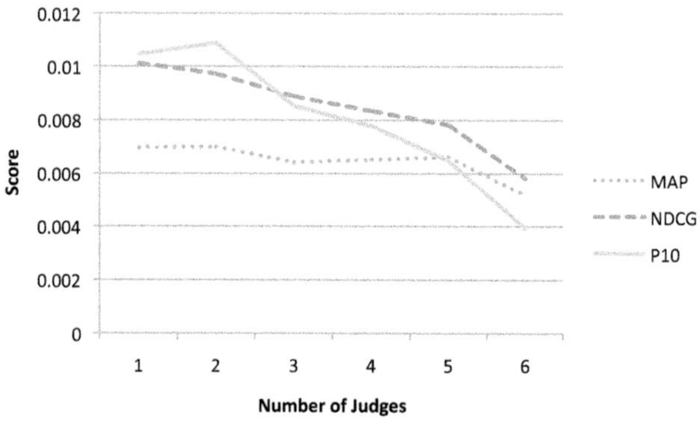

Figure 7: Average standard deviation around the mean for different numbers of workers and using different metrics.

the changes are mostly positive, with notable increases in P@10 when changing from experts to workers. In particular, the increase in somewhat relevant scores explains the increase of the binary P@10 measure. Somewhat relevant results (counted as relevant for the binary measures) that are coming in at lower ranks boost P@10 more than MAP and NDCG, which are less sensitive to changes in the lower ranks. While the reliability of non-expert judges is lower than expert judges, the reliability of non-expert judges is still sufficient for ranking systems in the evaluation.

Figure 4 illustrates visually the performance values for MAP for the different systems using the two MT evaluation sets and the expert judgments. The values are not only close, but in fact again the obtained values for the experts produce the same rank-order of the systems as with any of the MT evaluation sets.

As in the case of repeatability, we might ask whether crowdsourced assessments become more reliable when adding more judges. We have already shown in Figure 7 that increasing the number of workers decreases their standard deviation and increases the reliability of workers, and this trend seems to continue beyond 6 workers. Figure 9 shows the deviation resulting from using the workers' assessments instead of the expert assessments, in particular the average relative change in our metrics for subsamples, for different numbers of workers. We can see a clear benefit to using three workers instead of 1 or 2 workers, but there is comparatively less benefit from employing more than three judges. Figure 10 shows the same for MAP and NDCG using the average values of Kendall's τ between the subsamples of worker judgments and the expert assessments. This value of τ is already very close to one for three judges independent of the metric. While intra-worker reliability increases as the number of workers increase, adding more than three workers will lead to a higher number of disagreements with expert judges.

5. RELATED WORK

The main difference in using crowdsourcing to "gold standard" evaluation data-set creation in campaigns like TREC [4] is that human judges are no longer a relatively small group of professional expert judges who complete an equal-sized number of assessments, but large group of non-experts who may complete vastly differing numbers of assessments and may not actually have the required skill-set (such as command of English) to complete the task or be completing the task honestly. Earlier work in using crowdsourcing for information retrieval demonstrated quick turn-around times and the ability to have a much higher number of judges than previously thought possible [1]. This has led to a rapidly-expanding number of applications of crowdsourcing evaluation data sets to a wide range of information retrieval tasks such as XML-based retrieval [2]. Crowdsourcing has also been expanded successfully to related areas, such as machine translation [5].

In this vein, our primary contribution is in demonstrating the repeatability crowdsourcing judgments in creating evaluation data sets, even when entirely different sets of judges are used on the same task over long periods of time, a necessary feature for running large-scale campaigns for novel information retrieval tasks on an annual basis. Previous work

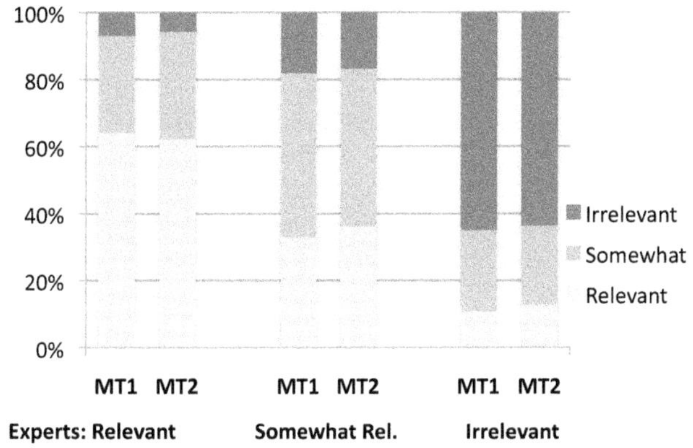

Figure 8: Assessments of the two workers sets compared to the experts' assessments for the three assessment options.

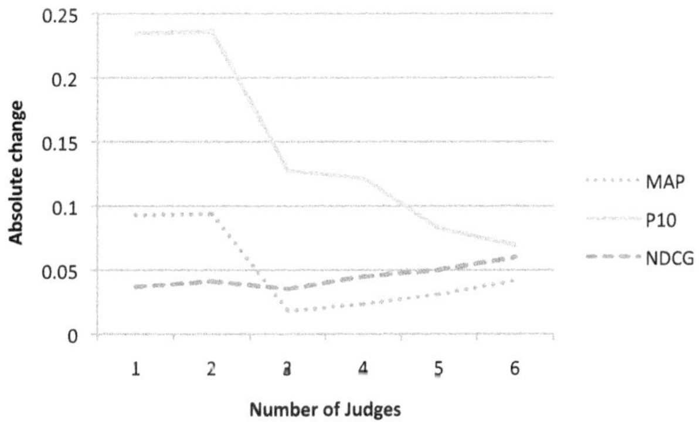

Figure 9: Average deviation of sample means from the expert assessments.

on crowdsourcing evaluation campaigns, such as work on replicating image labelling in ImageCLEF[15], has focused on determining the reliability of the judges over small subsets of the original campaign, but has not tested whether the evaluation campaign is repeatable over large time intervals (i.e., months or years), only inspecting differences over small amounts of time (4 days) and not comparing the judges performance over time to each other, but aggregating all judgments.

Previous work [1, 15] in general has focused on comparing crowdsourcing judgments to that of experts on existing campaigns with well-known "gold standards," not bootstrapping new evaluation campaigns for new search tasks where there are multiple competing but unevaluated search systems, such as in semantic search. Another goal of our work is to demonstrate the use of crowdsourcing for a large-scale evaluation campaign for a novel search task, which in our case is ad-hoc object retrieval over RDF. Many semantic search systems of this type, such as [9, 16, 19], have appeared in the past few years, but none have been evaluated against each other except on a very small scale. Semantic search systems are a subset of information retrieval systems, and thus it would be natural to apply existing IR benchmarks for their evaluation in a large-scale campaign.

There are two difficulties in applying the ad-hoc document retrieval methodology directly to our object retrieval problem as identified in [17]. The first and most apparent problem is that not all semantic search engines perform document retrieval, but rather retrieve knowledge that is already encoded in RDF, where factual answers may be found by aggregating or linking knowledge across RDF data. This is a clear difference to 'entity search' tracks such as the TREC Entity Track [4] or the INEX Entity Ranking Track [12]. With respect to addressing keyword retrieval on structured data, there is also existing work in the database literature (e.g., [13]), but this field of research has not produced a common evaluation methodology that we could have adapted. Second, in semantic search the unit of retrieval and thus the way to evaluate the results is dependent on the type of query. In turn, the types of queries supported may vary from search engine to search engine. By reducing the broad problem of semantic search to that of keyword-based ad-hoc object retrieval (i.e. retrieving objects given in RDF with relevant factual assertions connected as a property by a single link), we could invite multiple systems to our campaign, as most semantic search systems have this base-line feature. More complex query and result processing relies upon first retrieving a baseline of relevant RDF graphs, and so this baseline should be evaluated first.

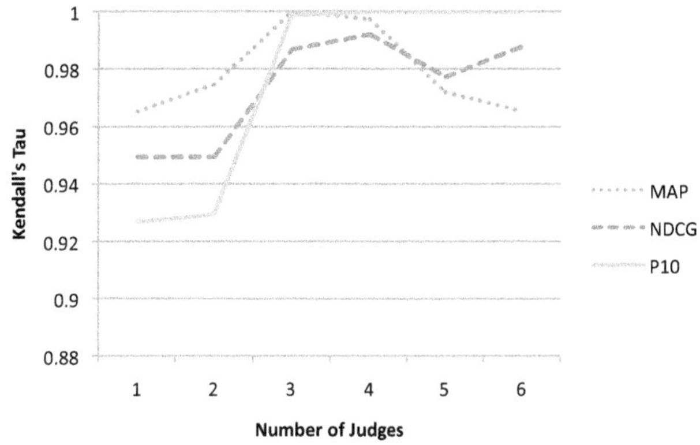

Figure 10: Kendall's Tau between workers and experts for different number of assessments per item.

6. CONCLUSIONS

With the advent of crowdsourcing platforms like Amazon Mechanical Turk, creating a "gold standard" evaluation data set of relevance judgments for new kinds of search tasks is now cheap, scalable, and easy to deploy. We have shown how to quickly boot-strap a repeatable evaluation campaign for a search task that has not previously been systematically evaluated, such as the object information retrieval task in semantic search, using Mechanical Turk. However, are such crowdsourced evaluation campaigns trustworthy? Are the relevance judgments of crowdsourced judges both reliable compared to experts and can such judgments be repeated with entirely different crowdsourced judges over time?

Regarding the **repeatability** of such crowdsourced judgments, we have shown that the level of agreement is the same for two pools of crowdsourced judges even when the evaluation is repeated after six months. Repeating an evaluation using crowdsourcing after six months led to the same result in evaluation metrics and the rank-order of the systems being unchanged. As regards the **reliability** of the crowdsourced judgments, while there were differences between expert judgments and crowdsourced judgments, with experts in general rating more results negative than crowdsourced judges. This is likely due to the object retrieval task and the time pressure on workers, as expert were more adept at discriminating between queries exclusively about an object to ones simply mentioning an object given time limits. However, the rank ordering of systems does not change when moving from experts to crowdsourced workers. Three judges seems to be a sufficient number and, surprisingly, increasing the number of crowdsourced judges has little effect unless the systems are particularly close. As regards evaluation metrics, *P@10* is more brittle than measures such as *MAP* and *nDCG* and so benefits most from collecting additional judgments.

We have successfully shown how a number of real-world and research semantic search systems can be evaluated in a repeatable and reliable manner via creating a new evaluation campaign using crowdsourcing. While the study here as focused on agreement between judges and workers over time and holding the items (queries and results) constant, future research needs to study the agreement between judges and workers on a per-item basis. So, for example, how does the ambiguity of entity queries effect reliability and repeatability? So the next study should also take into account if these results hold over different kinds of items, so the "Semantic Search" evaluation campaign will be broadened to deal with new kinds of semantic search tasks featuring different keyword queries and more expressive and complex queries beyond keywords. Of course, the methodology demonstrated in this work should be repeated for these new tasks if the task goes beyond object retrieval. Crowdsourced evaluation can lead to new tasks being evaluated quickly with reliable and repeatable evaluations. It also aids in having much larger corpora and query workloads for these campaigns. Most importantly, as the crowdsourced results are reliable and repeatable for this task at any time, evaluation campaigns can now run *continuously* (by using a standard community-driven evaluation web service) rather than annually. Our results support fast and scalable "just-in-time" evaluation of new search tasks, with empirically demonstrated repeatability and reliability.

7. ADDITIONAL AUTHORS

Thanh Tran Duc, Institute AIFB, Karlsruhe Institute of Technology, 76128 Karlsruhe, Germany ducthanh.tran@kit.edu

8. REFERENCES

[1] O. Alonso, D. E. Rose, and B. Stewart. Crowdsourcing for relevance evaluation. *SIGIR Forum*, 42(2):9–15, 2008.

[2] O. Alonso, R. Schenkel, and M. Theobald. Crowdsourcing assessments for XML ranked retrieval. In *ECIR*, pages 602–606, 2010.

[3] P. Bailey, N. Craswell, I. Soboroff, P. Thomas, A. P. de Vries, and E. Yilmaz. Relevance assessment: are judges exchangeable and does it matter. In *SIGIR*, pages 667–674, New York, NY, USA, 2008. ACM.

[4] K. Balog, A. P. de Vries, P. Serdyukov, P. Thomas, and T. Westerveld. Overview of the TREC 2009 Entity Track. In *NIST Special Publication: SP 500-278*, 2009.

[5] C. Callison-Burch. Fast, cheap, and creative: Evaluating translation quality using Amazon's Mechanical Turk. In *Proceedings of the 2009 Conference on Empirical Methods in Natural Language Processing*, pages 286–295, Singapore, August 2009. Association for Computational Linguistics.

[6] B. Carpenter. Multilevel bayesian models of categorical data annotation. technical report. Technical report, Alias-I, 2008. http://lingpipe.files.wordpress.com/2008/11/carp-bayesian-multilevel-annotation.pdf.

[7] L. Ding, T. Finin, A. Joshi, R. Pan, S. R. Cost, Y. Peng, P. Reddivari, V. Doshi, and J. Sachs. Swoogle: a search and metadata engine for the semantic web. In *CIKM*, pages 652–659, 2004.

[8] S. Elbassuoni, M. Ramanath, R. Schenkel, M. Sydow, and G. Weikum. Language-model-based Ranking for Queries on RDF-graphs. In *CIKM*, pages 977–986. ACM, 2009.

[9] R. Guha, R. McCool, and E. Miller. Semantic Search. In *WWW*, pages 700–709. ACM, 2003.

[10] H. Halpin. A query-driven characterization of linked data. In *Proceedings of the WWW Workshop on Linked Data on the Web*, Madrid, Spain, 2009.

[11] S. P. Harter. Variations in relevance assessments and the measurement of retrieval effectiveness. *J. Am. Soc. Inf. Sci.*, 47(1):37–49, 1996.

[12] J. Kamps, S. Geva, A. Trotman, A. Woodley, and M. Koolen. Overview of the INEX 2008 Ad Hoc Track. *Advances in Focused Retrieval: 7th International Workshop of the Initiative for the Evaluation of XML Retrieval, INEX 2008*, pages 1–28, 2009.

[13] Y. Luo, W. Wang, and X. Lin. SPARK: A Keyword Search Engine on Relational Databases. In *ICDE*, pages 1552–1555, 2008.

[14] W. Mason and D. J. Watts. Financial Incentives and the "Performance of Crowds". In *Human Computation Workshop (HComp2009)*, 2009.

[15] S. Nowak and S. M. Rüger. How reliable are annotations via crowdsourcing: a study about inter-annotator agreement for multi-label image annotation. In *Multimedia Information Retrieval*, pages 557–566, 2010.

[16] E. Oren, R. Delbru, M. Catasta, R. Cyganiak, H. Stenzhorn, and G. Tummarello. Sindice.com: a document-oriented lookup index for open linked data. *IJMSO*, 3(1):37–52, 2008.

[17] J. Pound, P. Mika, and H. Zaragoza. Ad-hoc Object Ranking in the Web of Data . In *Proceedings of the WWW*, pages 771–780, Raleigh, USA, 2010.

[18] I. Soboroff and D. Harman. Novelty detection: the trec experience. In *HLT '05*, USA, 2005. ACL.

[19] T. Tran, H. Wang, and P. Haase. SearchWebDB: Data Web Search on a Pay-As-You-Go Integration Infrastructure, 2008.

[20] E. Voorhees. The philosophy of information retrieval evaluation. In *In Proceedings of the The Second Workshop of the Cross-Language Evaluation Forum on Evaluation of Cross-Language Information Retrieval Systems*, pages 355–370. Springer-Verlag, 2001.

Cross-Language Web Page Classification via Dual Knowledge Transfer Using Nonnegative Matrix Tri-Factorization

Hua Wang
Department of Computer Science and Engineering
University of Texas at Arlington, TX 76019, USA
huawangcs@gmail.com

Heng Huang
Department of Computer Science and Engineering
University of Texas at Arlington, TX 76019, USA
heng@uta.edu

Feiping Nie
Department of Computer Science and Engineering
University of Texas at Arlington, TX 76019, USA
feipingnie@gmail.com

Chris Ding
Department of Computer Science and Engineering
University of Texas at Arlington, TX 76019, USA
chqding@uta.edu

ABSTRACT

The lack of sufficient labeled Web pages in many languages, especially for those uncommonly used ones, presents a great challenge to traditional supervised classification methods to achieve satisfactory Web page classification performance. To address this, we propose a novel Nonnegative Matrix Tri-factorization (NMTF) based Dual Knowledge Transfer (DKT) approach for cross-language Web page classification, which is based on the following two important observations. First, we observe that Web pages for a same topic from different languages usually share some common semantic patterns, though in different representation forms. Second, we also observe that the associations between word clusters and Web page classes are a more reliable carrier than raw words to transfer knowledge across languages. With these recognitions, we attempt to transfer knowledge from the auxiliary language, in which abundant labeled Web pages are available, to target languages, in which we want classify Web pages, through two different paths: word cluster approximations and the associations between word clusters and Web page classes. Due to the reinforcement between these two different knowledge transfer paths, our approach can achieve better classification accuracy. We evaluate the proposed approach in extensive experiments using a real world cross-language Web page data set. Promising results demonstrate the effectiveness of our approach that is consistent with our theoretical analyses.

SIGIR'11, July 24–28, 2011, Beijing, China.

Categories and Subject Descriptors

H.3.1 [**Information Storage and Retrieval**]: Content Analysis and Indexing

General Terms

Algorithms, Experimentation

Keywords

Cross-language Classification, Knowledge Transfer, Nonnegative Matrix Factorization

1. INTRODUCTION

With the rocketing growth of Internet in recent years, an ever-increasing number of Web pages are now available in many different languages. As of April 2011, over 131.1 million web sites are actively in operation[1], with billions of Web pages created in almost all human languages. As a result, cross-language information retrieval becomes unprecedentedly important for organizing and mining information stored in Web pages in various languages.

A potential problem in categorizing Web pages, especially for those written in uncommonly used languages, is the lack of sufficient labeled data. This prevents us from training an effective classification model, which usually requires a large amount of labeled data. Statistically speaking, the more labeled training data one can obtain, the more accurate and robust the classification model is. Fortunately, due to many reasons, there exists a lot of labeled Web pages in several most commonly used languages, such as English. It is hence useful and intriguing to make use of these labeled Web pages in one language, called as *auxiliary language*, to help to classify Web pages in another language, called as *target language*. This problem is called as *cross-language Web page classification* [15]. In this paper, we explore this important, yet challenging, problem by proposing a novel

[1] `http://www.domaintools.com/internet-statistics/`

Nonnegative Matrix Tri-factorization (NMTF) based Dual Knowledge Transfer (DKT) approach.

1.1 Challenges in Cross-Language Web Page Classification and Our Motivations

One of the most widely used strategy in cross-language Web page (text) classification is using language translation [15, 16, 18–21, 23]. One can either translate test data into the auxiliary language, or translate training data into the target language, and then train and classify the resulted data in one single language. Although this straightforward method may be feasible, it suffers from a number of critical problems that impede its practical use [15, 19, 20]. In this subsection, we examine the challenges in cross-language Web page classification and seek opportunities to overcome them, which motivate our approach.

Cultural discrepancy. The first difficulty in cross-language Web page classification is due to cultural discrepancies, which heavily impact the classification performance in spite of a perfect translation [15, 19]. Given that a language is the way of expression of a cultural and socially homogenous community, Web pages from a same category but different languages may concern very different topics. For example, we consider Web pages that report sports news in France (in French) and in USA (in English). While the former typically pays more attention to soccer, rugby and cricket, the latter is more interested in basketball and American football. From machine learning perspective of view, this corresponds to the situation where the training data and test data are drawn from different distributions, which makes it a challenge for traditional supervised and semi-supervised classification algorithms to achieve satisfactory Web pages classification performance.

Moreover, even we have sufficiently many labeled data in the target language, due to the differences of culture and social focus, they might not cover all the Web page categories. Consider that, for example [16], the English speakers tend to contribute more to some topics than their Czech counterparts (*e.g.*, to discuss "London" more than "Prague"), so that, having only data in English, we may expect them to do poorly at identifying topics like "Prague". Czech speakers, on the other hand, often talk about "Prague", so that by leveraging Czech data, we may expect to improve on detecting topic "Prague" in English Web pages.

To overcome this problem, instead of simply combining the data, we consider to transfer labeling information contained in Web pages in the auxiliary language to those in the target language [17]. Our approach is based on the observation that Web pages in different languages from a same category often share the same semantic information, although they are in different representation forms, *e.g.*, French words and English words [15]. Therefore, we may abstract the prior knowledge in the auxiliary language into semantic patterns, and make use of them to help to classify Web pages in the target language. To transfer knowledge across languages, the most natural carrier is the basic linguistic representation unit — words. We give an example to illustrate the usefulness of knowledge transfer by words in Web page classifications as in Figure 1.

Given a data set with four Web pages ($W1$, $W2$, $W3$ and $W4$) as shown in Figure 1(a), we represent them as a word-document matrix as shown in Figure 1(b). Because

W1: An Algorithm for Hyperlink Clustering　　**W3**: Texture Clustering Algorithms
W2: Algorithms for Webpage Classification　　**W4**: An Algorithm for Illumination Classification

(a) A synthetic data set of 4 Web pages in target language.

	Clustering	Classification	Illumination	Texture	Webpage	Hyperlink
W1	1	0	0	0	0	1
W2	0	1	0	0	1	0
W3	1	0	0	1	0	0
W4	0	1	1	0	0	0

(b) Original representation of the data set.

		Learning		Graphics		Web	
		Clustering	Classification	Illumination	Texture	Webpage	Hyperlink
IR	W1	1		0		1	
	W2	1		0		1	
Vision	W3	1		1		0	
	W4	1		1		0	

(c) Transformed representation of the data set by incorporating the prior knowledge learned from an auxiliary language, which leads to the meaningful clustering results.

Figure 1: An illustrative example to demonstrate the usefulness of leveraging the prior knowledge learned from an auxiliary language when clustering Web pages in a target language.

in practice we usually do not have labels for Web pages in the target language, we clusters them (the rows of the data matrix) based on cosine similarity, which results in two clusters, ($W1$ and $W3$) as a cluster and ($W2$ and $W4$) as a cluster. This result, however, is not meaningful. If we use the learned knowledge from the auxiliary language to guide this clustering process, we can transform the data matrix with 3 semantic features as in Figure 1(c). That is, "clustering" and "classification" belong to "learning", "illumination" and "texture" belong to "graphics", and "webpage" and "hyperlink" belong to "Web". Clustering on this new transformed data matrix, we obtain ($W1$ and $W2$) as a cluster and ($W3$ and $W4$) as a cluster. This is a very meaningful result, because the former is concerned with "information retrieval", while the latter is interested in "vision". More theoretical analysis for this example will be given later in Section 3.2.

In our approach, the first path to transfer knowledge across languages is by word cluster approximations, which is schematically shown by the red lines in Figure 2.

Translation ambiguity. In the process of language translation, the ambiguities introduced by dictionaries is another important challenge in cross-language Web page classification. For example, the word "阅读材料 (reading materials)" in Chinese Web pages could be reasonably translated as "textbooks", "required reading list", "reference" and so on. Since the linguistic habits in expressing a concept are different in different languages, the phrases for a same concept may have different probabilities in different languages. Therefore, transferring knowledge by the raw words sometimes are not reliable. However, the concept behind the phrases may have the same effect to indicate the class labels of the Web pages in different languages. In the same example, a Web page is more probable to be course-related if it contains the concept of "reading materials". In other words, only the concept behind raw words are stable in indicating taxonomy, and the association between word clusters and Web page categories is independent of languages [25]. Therefore, we use it as the second bridge to transfer knowl-

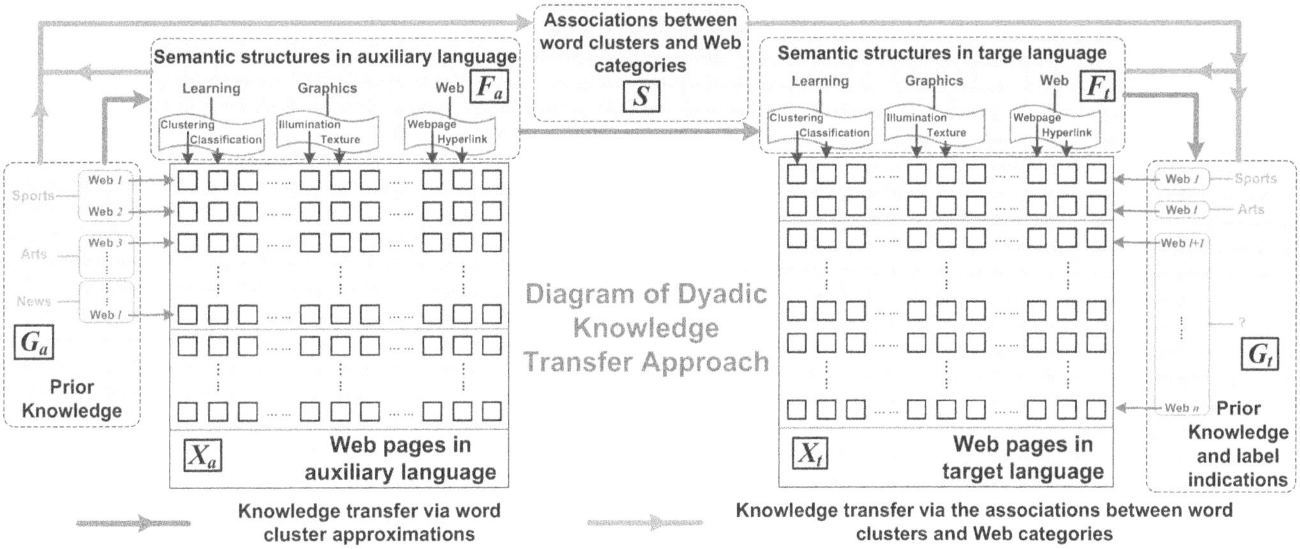

Figure 2: Diagram of the proposed Dual Knowledge Transfer (DKT) approach using NMTF. We transfer knowledge from auxiliary language to target language through two ways: *word cluster approximations* (F_a and F_t) and *the associations between word clusters and Web page categories* (S).

edge across different languages, which is illustrated by the green paths in Figure 2.

Data diversity. One more challenge in cross-language Web page classification is the data diversity. As illustrated in Figure 2, although we may have a lot of training Web pages in one language, usually not all of them are fully labeled. Similarly, even the labeled resources in the target language are scarce, we may still have a small number of Web pages in this language labeled by limited human effort. As a result, we can not rigidly assume the Web pages in the auxiliary language are always labeled and the Web pages in the target language are not labeled at all. Namely, model flexibility must be addressed to handle real world cross-language Web page classification tasks.

1.2 Our Contributions

Taking into account the three challenges in cross-language Web page classification, through a novel joint NMTF framework, we abstract the prior knowledge contained in Web pages in the auxiliary language, including both labeling information by human efforts and latent language structures, in two forms represented by the two factor matrices F_a and S of NMTF respectively, and then transfer them to the target language to guide the classification therein. The whole idea is summarized in Figure 2. Because we employ a two-way knowledge transfer, we call our proposed approach as *Dual Knowledge Transfer (DKT)* approach, which is interesting from a number of perspectives as following.

- In addressing the cross-language Web page classification problem, we observe the two possible paths to transfer knowledge across languages: the natural way by *word cluster approximations* and the reliable way by *associations between word clusters and Web page categories.* We propose a NMTF based DKT approach to make use of both of them.
- Through the general framework of the proposed approach, we consider a variety of conditions in cross-language Web page classification. Regardless the amount of labeled training data and locations where they are, either in auxiliary language or target language, or the both, our approach is always able to take advantage of the available labeling information.
- An efficient algorithm is presented to solve the proposed optimization objective, together with rigorous proof of its convergence.
- Extensive experiments on real world data sets demonstrate promising results that validate our approach.

2. A BRIEF REVIEW OF NMTF

In this section, we first briefly review NMTF and reveal how it transfers knowledge between data and features within a same data set, from which we will develop our approach.

Traditional Nonnegative Matrix Factorization (NMF) aims to find two nonnegative matrices whose product can well approximate the original nonnegative data matrix $X \in \mathbb{R}_+^{p\times n}$, *i.e.*, $X \approx FG^T$, where $F \in \mathbb{R}_+^{p\times k}$ and $G \in \mathbb{R}_+^{n\times k}$. The columns of X are data points and the rows of X are observations. An appropriate objective of NMF is to minimize [12]:

$$J_{\text{NMF}} = \|X - FG^T\|^2, \quad s.t. \quad F \geq 0, G \geq 0, \qquad (1)$$

where $\|\cdot\|$ denotes the Frobenius norm of a matrix. According to [5], NMF defined in Eq. (1) corresponds to simultaneous K-means clustering of the rows (features) and columns (data points) of X, where F can be considered as the clustering indictions for features and G can be considered as the clustering indications for data points. Because co-clustering the both sides of an input data matrix makes use of the interrelatedness between the data points and features, NMF based co-clustering methods usually report superior performance [5, 7]. In the context of Web page classification, the intrinsic linguistic structures of a language is described by X for a set of Web pages, and the prior knowledge by human efforts could be encoded in G, both of which are transformed into F as word (feature) clustering patterns through Eq. (1).

Because two-factor NMF in Eq. (1) is restrictive, which often gives a rather poor low-rank matrix approximation, we may introduce one more factor $S \in \mathbb{R}_+^{k_1 \times k_2}$ to absorb the different scales of X, F and G, which leads to NMTF [7] minimizing the following objective:

$$J_{\text{NMTF}} = \|X - FSG^T\|^2 \quad s.t. \quad F \geq 0, G \geq 0, S \geq 0, \quad (2)$$

where $F \in \mathbb{R}_+^{p \times k_1}$ and $G \in \mathbb{R}_+^{n \times k_2}$. S provides increased degrees of freedom such that the low-rank matrix representation remains accurate while F gives row clusters and G gives column clusters. Most importantly, S is a condensed view of X [13] and represents the associations between word clusters and Web page clusters [25].

Obviously, F and S convey two types of transformed knowledge, which we exactly expect to transfer across languages as outlined in Section 1. However, Eqs. (1–2) are both designed for one single data set, while in cross-language Web page classification we have two separate data sets, one in auxiliary language and the other in target language. Moreover, both of them are unsupervised where prior labeling knowledge is not utilized. Therefore, we further develop NMTF in Eq. (2) and propose a novel joint NMTF approach to transfer knowledge across languages to address the challenges in cross-language Web page classification to achieve improved classification performance.

3. DUAL KNOWLEDGE TRANSFER USING NMTF

In this section, we develop a novel NMTF based DKT approach for cross-language Web page classification, which transfers knowledge from the auxiliary language to the target one by two paths: (1) word cluster approximations and (2) the associations between word clusters and Web page classes. An efficient algorithm to solve the proposed objective with rigorous convergence proof is presented.

3.1 Problem Formalization

For a cross-language Web page classification problem, we have two Web page data sets, one in the auxiliary language $X_a = [\mathbf{x}_a^1, \ldots, \mathbf{x}_a^{n_a}] \in \mathbb{R}_+^{m \times n_a}$ and the other in the target language $X_t = [\mathbf{x}_t^1, \ldots, \mathbf{x}_t^{n_t}] \in \mathbb{R}_+^{m \times n_t}$, where $\mathbf{x}_a^i$ represents a Web page in the auxiliary language and $\mathbf{x}_t^i$ represents that in the target language. Thus X_a and X_t can be seen as the document-word co-occurrence matrices of the auxiliary data and target data respectively, or their *tf-idf* normalized counterparts. We assume that the both data sets are using a same vocabulary with m words: if the vocabularies differ, we may simply pad zeros in the feature vectors and re-express them under a same unified vocabulary so that the indices of the feature vectors from the both data sets correspond to the same word. Let $V \in \mathbb{R}^{m \times m}$ be a diagonal matrix with $V_{(ii)} = 1$ if the i-th word occurs in the both data sets, and $V_{(ii)} = 0$ otherwise.

Typically a large amount of Web pages in the auxiliary language are manually labeled, which can be described by an indication matrix $Y_a \in \mathbb{R}^{n_a \times k_2}$ such that $Y_{a(ik)} = 1$ if $\mathbf{x}_a^i$ belongs to the k-th class, and $Y_{a(ik)} = 0$ otherwise. Sometimes, though not always, we also have a limited number of labeled Web pages in target language. We similarly describe them using $Y_t \in \mathbb{R}^{n_t \times k_2}$ such that $Y_{t(ik)} = 1$ if $\mathbf{x}_t^i$ belongs to the k-th class, and $Y_{t(ik)} = 0$ otherwise. Again, we assume that the two data sets share a same set of classes. If not, we can pad the zero columns to Y_a or Y_t, or the both, such that the column indices of the both matrices correspond to the same classes. Our goal is to predict labels for the unlabeled Web pages in the target data set.

Throughout this paper, we denote the real number set as $\mathbb{R}$ and the nonnegative real number set as $\mathbb{R}_+$. The element at the i-th row and j-th column of a matrix M is denoted as $M_{(ij)}$. Frequently used notations are summarized in Table 1.

Table 1: Some frequently used notations.

X_a	data matrix of Web pages in auxiliary language
X_t	data matrix of Web pages in target language
n_a	number of Web pages in auxiliary language
n_t	number of Web pages in target language
F_a	word cluster indicator matrix of X_a
F_t	word cluster indicator matrix of X_t
S	the matrix associating word clusters and classes
G_a	class indicator matrix of Web pages in auxiliary language
G_t	class indicator matrix of Web pages in target language
Y_a	true label matrix of Web pages in auxiliary language
Y_t	true label matrix of Web pages in target language
V	word sharing indication matrix of the two data sets
C_a	label indication matrix of X_a
C_t	label indication matrix of X_t

3.2 Objective of the Proposed Approach

Given the Web page data X_a in auxiliary language and their labels Y_a, adopting the idea of NMTF, we may factorize X_a by minimizing the following objective [25]:

$$J_1 = \|X_a - F_a S_a G_a^T\|^2 + \alpha\, \mathbf{tr}\left[(G_a - Y_a)^T C_a (G_a - Y_a)\right],$$
$$s.t. \quad F_a \geq 0, S_a \geq 0, G_a \geq 0, \quad (3)$$

where $\mathbf{tr}(\cdot)$ denote the trace of a matrix. In Eq. (3), $\alpha > 0$ is a parameter that determines to which extent we enforce the prior labeling knowledge in the auxiliary language, *i.e.*, $G_a \approx Y_a$. $C_a \in \mathbb{R}^{n_a \times n_a}$ is a diagonal matrix with $C_{a(ii)} = 1$ if $\mathbf{x}_a^i$ is labeled by the i-th row of Y_a, and $C_{a(ii)} = 0$ otherwise. Note that, if $C = I$, all the Web pages in auxiliary language are completely labeled and specified by Y_a.

Transfer knowledge via word cluster approximations by F_a and F_t. Solving the optimization problem in Eq. (3), F_a and S_a contains information of the data in the auxiliary language which is to be transferred to those in the target language. We achieve this by minimizing:

$$J_2 = \|X_t - F_t S_t G_t^T\|^2 + \mathbf{tr}\left[\beta (G_t - Y_t)^T C_t (G_t - Y_t) + \gamma (F_t - F_a{}^*)^T V (F_t - F_a{}^*)\right], \quad (4)$$
$$s.t. \quad F_t \geq 0, S_t \geq 0, G_t \geq 0,$$

where $F_a{}^*$ is obtained by solving Eq. (3). The second term in Eq. (4) acts same as that in Eq. (3), which enforces labeling information in the target domain if it is available. Here, $\beta > 0$, and $C_t \in \mathbb{R}^{n_t \times n_t}$ is a diagonal matrix whose entry $C_{t(ii)} = 1$ if Web page $\mathbf{x}_t^i$ is labeled by the i-th row of Y_t, and $C_{t(ii)} = 0$ otherwise. When the labels for all the Web pages in target language are not available, we have $C_t = 0^{n_t \times n_t}$, which is a zero matrix. The key part is the third term. It enforces the constraint that word clusters in X_t is approximately close to F_a, learned from X_a. The extent of this approximation is determined by $\gamma > 0$. As a result, the label information contained G_a of X_a is transferred to the label assignments G_t in X_t via the semantic word structures F_a and F_t, which is schematically shown red paths in Figure 2.

In order to demonstrate the usefulness of knowledge transfer via word cluster approximations, we give more theoretical analysis on the example in Figure 1. Suppose the knowledge in auxiliary language is certain, we may set γ in Eq. (4) as ∞. In order to see the real effect of prior knowledge to improve classification performance, we temporarily ignore the training information in the target language by minimizing:

$$J_2' = \|X_t - F_a S_t G_t^T\|^2, \tag{5}$$

which is identical to the following problem [5,7]:

$$\max_{G_t} \mathbf{tr}\left(G_t^T X_t^T F_a F_a^T X_t G_t\right) . \tag{6}$$

By the equivalence between K-means clustering and principal component analysis (PCA) [4, 24], the clustering of Eq. (6) uses $X_t^T F_a F_a^T X_t$ as the pairwise similarity, whereas K-means clustering uses $X_t^T X_t$ as the pairwise similarity. For the example in Figure 1, we have

$$X_t^T X_t = \begin{bmatrix} 2 & 0 & 1 & 0 \\ 0 & 2 & 0 & 1 \\ 1 & 0 & 2 & 0 \\ 0 & 1 & 0 & 2 \end{bmatrix}, \tag{7}$$

and K-means clustering will produce (W1, W3) as a cluster and (W2, W4) as another cluster.

Now, with the knowledge F_a learned from auxiliary language, we have

$$X_t^T F_a F_a^T X_t = \begin{bmatrix} 1 & 1 & \frac{1}{2} & \frac{1}{2} \\ 1 & 1 & \frac{1}{2} & \frac{1}{2} \\ \frac{1}{2} & \frac{1}{2} & 1 & 1 \\ \frac{1}{2} & \frac{1}{2} & 1 & 1 \end{bmatrix}, \tag{8}$$

where we assume we already learned F_a from auxiliary language, which is

$$F_a^T = 2^{-1/2} \begin{bmatrix} 1 & 1 & 0 & 0 & 0 & 0 \\ 0 & 0 & 1 & 1 & 0 & 0 \\ 0 & 0 & 0 & 0 & 1 & 1 \end{bmatrix} . \tag{9}$$

Clearly, using the similarity in Eq. (8), K-means clustering will generate (W1, W2) as a cluster and (W3, W4) as another cluster, which is more meaningful as in Figure 1(c).

We may see more directly how knowledge in the word space from auxiliary language is transformed into the Web page space in target language. Let the square root of the semi-definite positive matrix be P: $F_a F_a^T = P^T P$. We have $X_t^T F_a F_a^T X_t = (PX)^T (PX)$ which means we cluster the Web pages using the transformed data $\tilde{X}_t = PX = \left(F_a F_a^T\right)^{1/2} X_t$.

For the example in Figure 1, we have

$$\tilde{X}_t = 2^{-1/2} \begin{bmatrix} 1 & 1 & 0 & 0 & 0 & 0 \\ 1 & 1 & 0 & 0 & 0 & 0 \\ 0 & 0 & 1 & 1 & 0 & 0 \\ 0 & 0 & 1 & 1 & 0 & 0 \\ 0 & 0 & 0 & 0 & 1 & 1 \\ 0 & 0 & 0 & 0 & 1 & 1 \end{bmatrix} X = 2^{-1/2} \begin{bmatrix} 1 & 1 & 1 & 1 \\ 1 & 1 & 1 & 1 \\ 0 & 0 & 1 & 1 \\ 0 & 0 & 1 & 1 \\ 1 & 1 & 0 & 0 \\ 1 & 1 & 0 & 0 \end{bmatrix} . \tag{10}$$

It is obvious that on this transformed data, W1 and W2 will be clustered into one cluster, W3 and W4 will be clustered into another cluster. This analysis shows how the knowledge in the word space learned from auxiliary language is transformed into the Web page space in target language.

Transfer knowledge via the association between the word clusters and Web page classes by S. As discussed earlier in Section 1, compared to words, the association between word clusters and Web pages classes are more reliable to convey semantic relationships across different languages. Formally, we achieve this by minimizing:

$$J_3 = \|X_t - F_t S_a{}^* G_t^T\|^2 \quad s.t. \quad F_t \geq 0, G_t \geq 0, \tag{11}$$

where $S_a{}^*$ is obtained by solving Eq. (3). As a result, $S_a{}^*$, learned from the auxiliary data set, is used as supervision to classify the target data. Namely, $S_a{}^*$ bridges the source and target languages such that prior labeling knowledge can be transferred from the former to the latter, which is schematically shown green paths in Figure 2.

Our optimization objective. Finally, we may combine the three optimization problems Eqs. (3–11) into a joint optimization objective to minimize:

$$\begin{aligned} J_{\mathrm{DKT}} &= \|X_a - F_a S G_a^T\|^2 + \|X_t - F_t S G_t^T\|^2 \qquad (12) \\ &+ \alpha\, \mathbf{tr}\left[(G_a - Y_a)^T C_a (G_a - Y_a)\right] \\ &+ \mathbf{tr}\left[\beta (G_t - Y_t)^T C_t (G_t - Y_t) + \gamma (F_t - F_a)^T V (F_t - F_a)\right], \\ &s.t. \quad F_a \geq 0, G_a \geq 0, S \geq 0, F_t \geq 0, G_t \geq 0 . \end{aligned}$$

In this formulation S is shared in the two matrix factorizations for both auxiliary and target data, which is used as a bridge to transfer knowledge between them. In addition, through the constraint in the last term, the two data sets are connected by F_a and F_t.

Note that, the last term of Eq. (4) only applies to the common words of X_a and X_t, which are encoded by V. When the auxiliary data set and the target data set do not share any word, *i.e.*, $V = 0^{m \times m}$ is a zero matrix, there will be no knowledge transfer through word cluster approximation path. Similarly, if the auxiliary data set and the target data set do not share common classes, there will be no knowledge transformation in the optimization problem of Eq. (11), because it is decoupled into two independent subproblems, one for auxiliary data and the other for target data. However, these two cases rarely happen simultaneously. As a result, our model is flexible and can always transfer knowledge in Eq. (12) through the either path, or the both.

Upon solving Eq. (12), the class label for the $\mathbf{x}_t^i$ in target language is determined by

$$\left(\mathbf{x}_t^i\right) = \arg\max_k G_{t(ik)} . \tag{13}$$

Solving Eq. (12) and assign labels to the unlabeled Web pages in the target language using Eq. (13), our cross-domain Web page classification approach is proposed. Because Eq. (12) transfers knowledge in two different paths, we call it as *Dual Knowledge Transfer (DKT)* approach.

3.3 Optimization Procedures

In the following, we derive the solution to Eq. (12) and present an alternating scheme to optimize the objective J_{DKT}.

Specifically, we will optimize one variable while fixing the rest variables. The procedure repeats until convergence.

First we expand the objective in Eq. (12) as follows,

$$\begin{aligned} J(F_a, G_a, S, F_t, G_t) &= \mathbf{tr}\Big(-2X_a^T F_a S G_a^T \\ &+ G_a S^T F_a^T F_a S G_a^T - 2X_t^T F_t S G_t^T + G_t S^T F_t^T F_t S G_t^T \\ &+ \alpha G_a^T C_a G_a - 2\alpha G_a^T C_a Y_a + \beta G_t^T C_t G_t - 2\beta G_t^T C_t Y_t \\ &+ \gamma F_t^T V F_t - 2\gamma F_t^T V F_a + \gamma F_a^T V F_a\Big), \end{aligned} \tag{14}$$

where constant terms are discarded.

Computation of F_a. For the constraint $F_a \geq 0$, following standard theory of constrained optimization, we introduce the Lagrangian multiplier $U \in \mathbb{R}^{m \times k_1}$, thus the Lagrangian function is

$$L(F_a) = J - \mathbf{tr}\left(U F_a^T\right) . \tag{15}$$

Setting $\partial L(F_a)/\partial F_a = 0$, we obtain

$$U = -2X_a G_a S^T + 2F_a S G_a^T G_a S^T - 2\gamma V F_t + 2\gamma V F_a . \tag{16}$$

Using Karush-Kuhn-Tucker condition $U_{(ij)} F_{a(ij)} = 0$, we get

$$\begin{aligned} &\Big(-2X_a G_a S^T + 2F_a S G_a^T G_a S^T \\ &- 2\gamma V F_t + 2\gamma V F_a\Big)_{(ij)} F_{a(ij)} = 0, \end{aligned} \tag{17}$$

which leads to the following updating formula:

$$F_{a(ij)} \leftarrow F_{a(ij)} \sqrt{\frac{(X_a G_a S^T + \gamma V F_t)_{(ij)}}{(F_a S G_a^T G_a S^T + \gamma V F_a)_{(ij)}}} . \tag{18}$$

Computation of G_a, S, F_t and G_t. Following the same derivations in Eqs. (15–18), we obtain the updating rules for the rest variables of J_{DKT} as following:

$$G_{a(ij)} \leftarrow G_{a(ij)} \sqrt{\frac{(X_a^T F_a S + \alpha C_a Y_a)_{(ij)}}{(G_a S^T F_a^T F_a S + \alpha C_a G_a)_{(ij)}}} \tag{19}$$

$$S_{(ij)} \leftarrow S_{(ij)} \sqrt{\frac{(F_a^T X_a G_a + F_t^T X_t G_t)_{(ij)}}{(F_a^T F_a S G_a^T G_a + F_t^T F_t S G_t^T G_t)_{(ij)}}} \tag{20}$$

$$F_{t(ij)} \leftarrow F_{t(ij)} \sqrt{\frac{(X_t G_t S^T + \gamma V F_a)_{(ij)}}{(F_t S G_t^T G_t S^T + \gamma V F_t)_{(ij)}}} \tag{21}$$

$$G_{t(ij)} \leftarrow G_{t(ij)} \sqrt{\frac{(X_t^T F_t S + \beta C_t Y_t)_{(ij)}}{(G_t S^T F_t^T F_t S + \beta C_t G_t)_{(ij)}}} \tag{22}$$

In summary, we present the iterative multiplicative updating algorithm of optimizing Eq. (12) in Algorithm 1.

3.4 Analysis of Algorithm Convergence

In this section, we will investigate the convergence of Algorithm 1. We use the auxiliary function approach [12] to prove the convergence of the algorithm.

LEMMA 1. *[12] $Z(h, h')$ is an auxiliary function of $F(h)$ if the conditions $Z(h, h') \geq F(h)$ and $Z(h, h') = F(h)$ are satisfied. [12] If Z is an auxiliary function for F, then F is non-increasing under the update $h^{(t+1)} = \arg\min_h Z(h, h')$.*

Algorithm 1: Algorithm to solve J_{DKT} in Eq. (12).

Input: 1. Data matrix X_a in auxiliary language,
2. data matrix X_t in target language,
3. labels of Web pages in auxiliary language Y_a,
4. optional labeling information Y_t in target data,
5. trade-off parameters α, β and γ.
Initialize F_a, G_a, S, F_t and G_t following [25];
while *not converge* **do**
  1. Update F_a using Eq. (18),
  2. Update G_a using Eq. (19),
  3. Update S using Eq. (20),
  4. Update F_t using Eq. (21),
  5. Update G_t using Eq. (22),
end
Predict labels for $\mathbf{x}_t^i$ using Eq. (13).
Output: Labels assigned to the unlabeled Web page $\mathbf{x}_t^i$ in target language.

LEMMA 2. *[7] For any matrices $A \in \mathbb{R}_+^{n \times n}$, $B \in \mathbb{R}_+^{k \times k}$, $S \in \mathbb{R}_+^{n \times k}$ and $S' \in \mathbb{R}_+^{n \times k}$, and A and B are symmetric, the following inequality holds*

$$\sum_{ip} \frac{(AS'B)_{ip} S_{ip}^2}{S'_{ip}} \geq \mathbf{tr}\left(S^T A S B\right) . \tag{23}$$

THEOREM 1. *Write J in Eq. (14) w.r.t. F_a, we have*

$$\begin{aligned} J(F_a) = \mathbf{tr}\Big(&-2X_a^T F_a S G_a^T + G_a S^T F_a^T F_a S G_a^T \\ &-2\gamma F_t^T V F_a + \gamma F_a^T V F_a\Big), \end{aligned} \tag{24}$$

then the following function

$$\begin{aligned} H(F_a, F_a') = &-2\sum_{ij}\left(X_a G_a S^T\right)_{(ij)} F'_{a(ij)}\left(1 + \log\frac{F_{a(ij)}}{F'_{a(ij)}}\right) \\ &+ \sum_{ij}\left(F'_a S G_a^T G_a S^T\right)_{(ij)} \frac{F_{a(ij)}^2}{F'_{a(ij)}} \\ &- 2\gamma\sum_{ij}(V F_t)_{(ij)} F'_{a(ij)}\left(1 + \log\frac{F_{a(ij)}}{F'_{a(ij)}}\right) \\ &+ \gamma\sum_{ij}(V F'_a)_{(ij)} \frac{F_{a(ij)}^2}{F'_{a(ij)}} \end{aligned} \tag{25}$$

is an auxiliary function for $J(F_a)$. Furthermore, it is a convex function in F_a and its global minimum is

$$F_{a(ij)} = F_{a(ij)} \sqrt{\frac{(X_a G_a S^T + \gamma V F_t)_{(ij)}}{(F_a S G_a^T G_a S^T + \gamma V F_a)_{(ij)}}} . \tag{26}$$

Proof. According to Lemma 2, we have

$$\mathbf{tr}\left(G_a S^T F_a^T F_a S G_a^T\right) \leq \sum_{ij}\left(F'_a S G_a^T G_a S^T\right)_{(ij)} \frac{F_{a(ij)}^2}{F'_{a(ij)}}, \tag{27}$$

$$\mathbf{tr}\left(F_a^T V F_a\right) \leq \sum_{ij}(V F'_a)_{(ij)} \frac{F_{a(ij)}^2}{F'_{a(ij)}} . \tag{28}$$

Because $z \leq 1 + \log z$, $\forall\ z > 0$, we have

$$\mathbf{tr}\left(X_a^T F_a S G_a^T\right) \geq \sum_{ij}\left(X_a G_a S^T\right)_{(ij)} F'_{a(ij)}\left(1 + \log\frac{F_{a(ij)}}{F'_{a(ij)}}\right), \tag{29}$$

$$\mathbf{tr}\left(F_t^T V F_a\right) \geq \sum_{ij} (VF_t)_{(ij)} F'_{a(ij)} \left(1 + \log \frac{F_{a(ij)}}{F'_{a(ij)}}\right). \tag{30}$$

Summing over all the bounds in Eqs. (27–30), we can obtain $H(F_a, F'_a)$, which clearly satisfies (1) $H(F_a, F'_a) \geq J(F_a)$ and (2) $H(F_a, F_a) = J(F_a)$.

Then, fixing F'_a, we minimize $H(F_a, F'_a)$.

$$\frac{\partial H(F_a, F'_a)}{\partial F_{a(ij)}} = -2\left[\left(X_a G_a S^T\right)_{(ij)} + \gamma (VF_t)_{(ij)}\right] \frac{F'_{a(ij)}}{F_{a(ij)}}$$
$$+ 2\left[\left(F'_a S G_a^T G_a S^T\right)_{(ij)} + \gamma \left(VF'_a\right)_{(ij)}\right] \frac{F_{a(ij)}}{F'_{a(ij)}} \tag{31}$$

and the Hessian matrix of $H(F_a, F'_a)$ is

$$\frac{\partial^2 H(F_a, F'_a)}{F_{a(ij)} F_{a(kl)}} = \delta_{ik}\delta_{jl} \left\{ 2\left[\left(X_a G_a S^T\right)_{(ij)} + \gamma (VF_t)_{(ij)}\right] \frac{F'_{a(ij)}}{F^2_{a(ij)}} \right.$$
$$\left. +2\left[\left(F'_a S G_a^T G_a S^T\right)_{(ij)} + \gamma \left(VF'_a\right)_{(ij)}\right] F'_{a(ij)} \right\}, \tag{32}$$

which is a diagonal matrix with positive diagonal elements. Therefore $H(F_a, F'_a)$ is a convex function of F_a, and we can obtain the global minimum of $H(F_a, F'_a)$ by setting $\partial H(F_a, F'_a)/\partial F_{a(ij)} = 0$ and solving for F_a, from which we get Eq. (26). This completes the proof of Theorem 1. □

THEOREM 2. *Using Algorithm 1 to update F_a, $J(F_a)$ in Eq. (24) will monotonically decreases.*

Proof. By Lemma 1 and Theorem 1, we can get that $J\left({F_a}^0\right) = H\left({F_a}^0, {F_a}^0\right) \geq H\left({F_a}^1, {F_a}^0\right) \geq J\left({F_a}^1\right) \ldots$ Therefore $J(F_a)$ is monotonically decreasing. □

THEOREM 3. *Using Algorithm 1 to update G_a, S, F_t and G_t, the respective objectives will monotonically decrease.*

Theorem 3 can be similarly proved as Theorems (1–2).

Because J in Eq. (12) is obviously lower bounded by 0, Algorithm 1 is guaranteed to converge by Theorems (2–3).

4. RELATED WORKS

In this section, we review several prior researches that are mostly related to our work, including transfer learning, cross-language classification and NMTF.

Transfer learning. From machine learning perspective of view, our work belongs to the topic of *transfer learning* (also called as *domain adaption* in some research papers), which deals with the case where training and test data are obtained from different resources thereby in different distributions [13–16, 18–21, 23, 25]. For a comprehensive survey of transfer learning, we refer readers to [17].

Cross-language classification. Cross-language Web page and document classification has attracted increased attention in recent years due to its importance in information retrieval. Bel *et al.* [1] studied English-Spanish cross-language classification problem. Two scenarios are considered in their work. One scenario assumes to have training documents in both languages, and the other is to learn a model from the text in one language and classify the data in another language by translation. Our work follows the first strategy. [16] employed a general probabilistic English-Czech dictionary to translate Czech text into English and then classified Czech documents using the classifier built on English training data. Ling *et al.* [15] classify Chinese Web pages using English data source by utilizing the information bottleneck theory. Other cross-language text classification researches include [23] (Chinese-English), [19] (English-Spanish-French), [20] (English-Chinese-French), *etc.*, to be mentioned.

NMTF. NMF is a useful learning method to approximate a nonnegative input data matrix by the product of factor matrices [11,12], which has been applied to solve many real world problems including dimensionality reduction, pattern recognition, clustering and classification [3,5–8,13,14,22,25]. Recently, Ding *et al.* extended NMF [7] to NMTF and explored its relationships to K-means/spectral clustering [5,7]. Due to its mathematical elegance and encouraging empirical results, NMTF method is further developed to address a variety of aspects of unsupervised and semi-supervised learning [3, 8, 13, 14, 22, 25], among which [13] and [25] are closely related to our work. The former investigated cross-domain sentiment classification, which transfers knowledge by sharing information of word clusters. This is similar to our approach to transfer knowledge through word cluster approximations. While they dealt with two separate tasks of matrix factorizations, first on the source domain and then on the target domain, our approach optimizes a combined and collaborative objective, which leads to extra values in classification as shown later in our experimental evaluations. In addition, they assume there exist no label information in target domain, which restricts its capability to solve real world problems. The latter considered the cross-domain document classification via transferring knowledge by the associations between word clusters and document classes, which, however, did not use the important information contained in words as both our approach and [13]. Again, they restrict that the data in the source domain are completely labeled while no data labeling information in the target domain. In summary, our approach has very close relationships to [13] and [25], but enjoys the advantages of both of them, with additional flexibilities to allow training data appearing in various forms.

Table 2: Description of testing data sets. English is used as auxiliary language in all the testing data sets.

Data	Target language	# Labeled auxiliary data	# Labeled target data
D1	German	3,500	0
D2	German	3,500	1,000
D3	French	3,500	0
D4	French	3,500	1,000
D5	Japanese	3,500	0
D6	Japanese	3,500	1,000

5. EXPERIMENTS

In this section, we evaluate the proposed Dual Knowledge Transfer (DKT) approach in cross-language Web page classification, and compare it with several state-of-the-art supervised, semi-supervised and transfer learning classifiers.

5.1 Data Preparation

We conduct our empirical evaluations on a publicly avail-

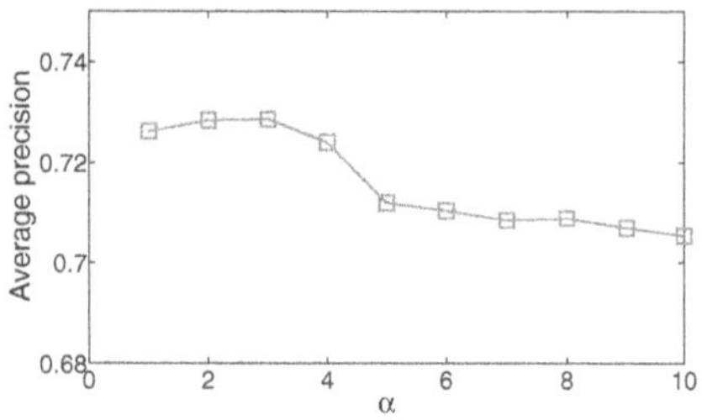

(a) α.

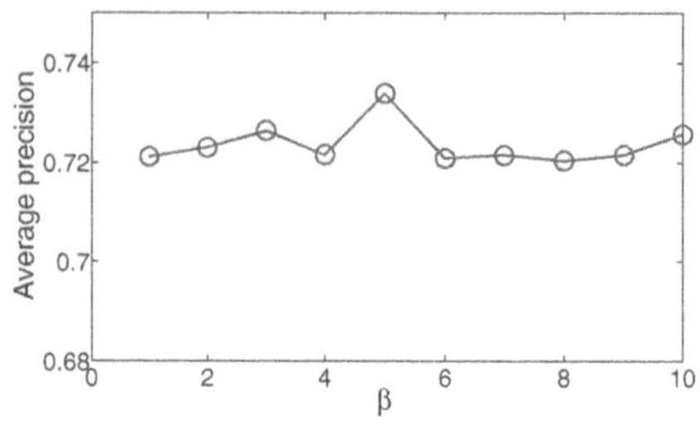

(b) β.

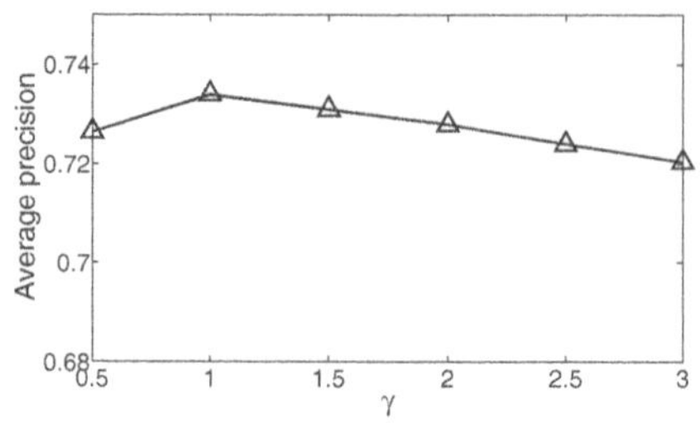

(c) γ.

Figure 3: Classification performance (measured by macro-average precision) with respect to different parameter settings of the proposed DKT approach on D2 data set, which show that our approach is stable with respect to a wide range of parameters settings.

able multi-lingual Web page data set — cross lingual sentiment corpus[2] [18]. This data set contains about 800,000 web pages from Amazon web site for product reviews in four languages: English, German, French and Japanese. The crawled part of the corpus contains more than 4 millions of Web pages in the three languages other than English from `amazon.{de|fr|co.jp}`. Besides the original Web pages, all the Web pages in German, French and Japanese are translated into English. The corpus is extended with English Web pages provided by Blitzer *et al.* [2]. All the Web pages in the corpus are divided into three categories upon the product they describe: books, DVDs and music.

In our experiments, we randomly pick up 5,000 Web pages from each language. Same as [18], we use English as auxiliary language and the rest three as target languages separately. Therefore we end up with three language pairs for testing: English-Germen, English-French, and English-Japanese. Because in real world applications not all the Web pages in auxiliary language are labeled, we randomly pick up 70% of English Web pages for each class as labeled data. On the other hand, because in real world applications the Web pages in target language are mostly unlabeled, we simulate two different cases: (1) no labeled Web pages in target languages and (2) we randomly pick up 20% Web pages from each class as labeled data in the concerned target language. As a result, we end up with six testing data sets, which are summarized in Table 2. For each testing data set, our task is to classify the unlabeled Web pages in the corresponding target language.

5.2 Performance Comparisons

We compare the proposed DKT approach against the supervised learning method (1) Support Vector Machine (SVM) method, and the semi-supervised learning method (2) Transductive SVM (TSVM) method [9] as baselines. We also compare to the two closely related cross-domain learning methods based on NMTF: (3) Knowledge Transformation by Words (KTW) method [13], (4) Matrix Tri-factorization based classification framework (MTrick) [25]; and a very recent cross-language Web classification method using information bottleneck theory (IB) [15].

5.2.1 Experimental Setups

SVM and TSVM methods can use either the labeled data in target language or the labeled data in both auxiliary and target language. We therefore refer to SVM_T, TSVM_T as the former case, and SVM_ST, TSVM_ST as the latter case. For the latter case, the data from the both auxiliary and target languages are used in a homogeneous way. This is equivalent to assume the Web pages from different laguanges are drawn from a same distribution, which, however, is not true in reality. Following previous works, for the both methods, we train one-versus-others classifiers, with the fixed regularization parameter $C = 1$. Gaussian kernel is used (*i.e.*, $\mathcal{K}(\mathbf{x}_i, \mathbf{x}_j) = \exp\left(-\gamma\|\mathbf{x}_i - \mathbf{x}_j\|^2\right)$) where γ is set as $1/m$. SVM and TSVM are implemented by SVM^{light} [10].

The parameters of KTW and MTrick are set as optimal following their original works [13,25]. The iteration number of IB method is set as 100.

For our approach, due to the nature of our optimization objective in Eq. (12), we always use S, *i.e.*, the associations between word clusters and Web page classes, to transfer knowledge. In order to test the flexibility of our approach, we consider two different cases of our approach for using words to transfer knowledge: (1) not use words transfer denoted as "DKT (S only)", *i.e.*, set $\gamma = 0$ in Eq. (12); and (2) use words transfer denoted as "DKT". Upon some preliminary test, for our appraoch we set the tradeoff parameters $\alpha = \beta = 1$, and $\gamma = 1.5$, the number of word clusters is set to same as Web page classes $k_1 = k_2 = 3$, the error threshold in Algorithm 1 to determine convergence is set $\varepsilon = 10^{-11}$, and the maximum iterating number is 100.

5.2.2 Evaluation Metrics

Two widely used classification performance metrics in statistical learning and information retrieval are used in our experiments: macro-average precision and F_1-measure. Let f be the function which maps from document d to its true class label $c = f(d)$, and h be the function which maps from document d to its prediction label $c = h(d)$ given by the classifiers. The macro-average precision P and recall R are defined as:

$$P = \frac{1}{\mathcal{C}} \sum_{c \in \mathcal{C}} \frac{\{d | d \in X_c \wedge h(d) = f(d) = c\}}{\{d | d \in X_c \wedge h(d) = c\}} \tag{33}$$

$$R = \frac{1}{\mathcal{C}} \sum_{c \in \mathcal{C}} \frac{\{d | d \in X_c \wedge h(d) = f(d) = c\}}{\{d | d \in X_c \wedge f(d) = c\}} \tag{34}$$

The F_1 measure is the harmonic mean of precision and recall, which is defined as follows:

$$F_1 = \frac{2PR}{P + R} \tag{35}$$

[2]`http://www.webis.de/research/corpora/`

5.2.3 *Experimental Results*

Table 3 presents the classification performances measured by macro-average precision and F_1 score of the compared methods on six different test data sets. From the results we have the following observations. First, the proposed DKT approach consistently outperforms the other compared methods. DKT (S only) method is always worse than DKT approach, which confirms the usefulness of the knowledge transfer path by word cluster approximations. Second, from the experimental results of SVM_ST and TSVM_ST methods, we can see that considering Web pages from different languages as homogenous typically leads to unsatisfactory classification performance. Because the cross-domain methods, including ours, are generally better than these two methods, knowledge transfer from the auxiliary language to the target one is important to improve the classification performance. Third, our DKT approach is able to transfer knowledge in two paths, *i.e.*, word cluster approximations and the associations between word clusters and Web page classes, thus it achieves encouraging classification performance on all the six test data sets. In contrast, KTW method can only transfer knowledge through word cluster approximations, and MTrick method only transfers knowledge through the associations between word clusters and Web page classes, their performances are generally not as good as other transfer learning methods. Last, but not least, our approach is able to exploit labeling information in both auxiliary and target data, whereas KTW method and MTrick method cannot benefit from labeling information in target domain, and SVM_T method and TSVM_T method cannot work with labeling information in auxiliary data. The more labeled data in target domain, the better classification performance our approach can achieve. In summary, all the above observations demonstrate the effectiveness of the proposed DKT approach in cross-language Web page classification.

5.3 Parameter Effect

The proposed DKT approach has three parameters α, β, γ in Eq. (12). Although it is tedious to seek an optimal combination of them, we can demonstrate that the performance of our DKT approach is not sensitive when the parameters are sampled in some value ranges. We bound the parameters in the ranges of $1 \leq \alpha \leq 10$, $1 \leq \beta \leq 10$ and $0.5 \leq \gamma \leq 3$ upon preliminary tests and evaluate them on data set D2 as it has labeled Web pages in both auxiliary language and target language.

From Figure 3 we can see that the average performance of all the parameter settings is almost the same as the results from the default parameters. Morever, the variance of all the parameter settings is small. It shows that the performance of our approach is stable with respect to the parameters in a considerably large range.

5.4 Algorithm Convergence

Because our DKT approach employs an iterative algorithm, an important issue is its convergence property. In Section 3.4, we have already theoretically proved the convergence of the algorithm. Here, we empirically check the convergence property of the proposed iterative algorithm. The classification accuracy in each iteration to classify D1 test data set is shown in Figure 4(a), where the x-axis represents the number of iterations, and the y-axis denote the macro-average precision. From the figure, it be can seen that DKT approach converges within about 10 iterations, which indicates that our algorithm is fast. In addition, the objective values of our algorithm in each iteration are plotted in Figure 4(b), which shows that the objective value of our algorithm keep to decrease along with iterative process, which is in accordance with our theoretical analysis.

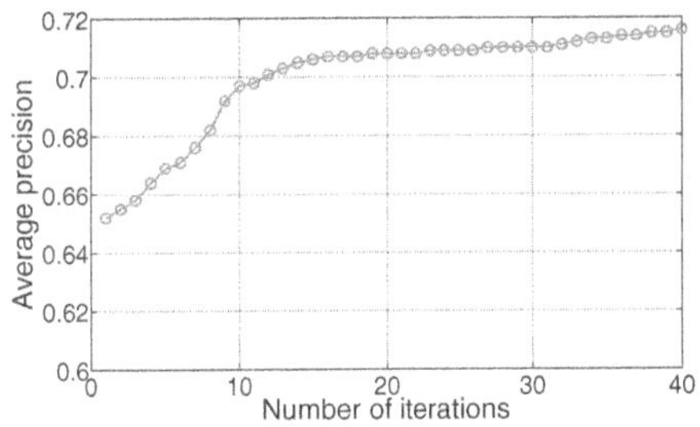

(a) Macro average precision.

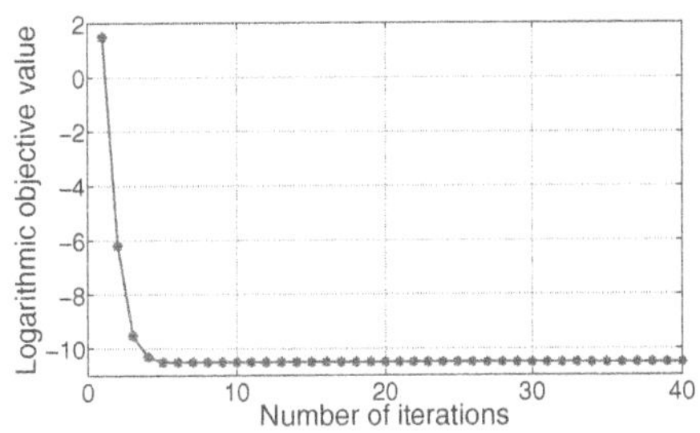

(b) Objective values.

Figure 4: Number of iterations *vs.* the performance of the proposed approach measured by macro-average precision and Objective Value.

6. CONCLUSIONS

In this paper, we proposed a novel NMTF based DKT approach for cross-language Web page classification. Our approach adopts the idea of transfer learning to pass knowledge across languages, instead of simply combining the Web page data from different languages. By carefully examine the cross-language Web page classification problem, we observed that common semantic patterns usually exist in Web pages for a same topic from different languages. Moreover, we also observed that the associations between word clusters and Web page classes are more reliable to transfer knowledge than using raw words. With these recognitions, our approach is designed to transfer knowledge across languages through two different paths: word cluster approximations and the associations between word clusters and Web pages classes. With this enhanced knowledge transfer, our approach is able to address the main challenges in cross-language Web page classification: cultural discrepancies, translation ambiguities and data diversity. Extensive experiments using a real world cross-language Web page data set demonstrated encouraging results from a number of aspects that validate our approach.

Acknowledgments

This research was supported by NSF-CNS 0923494, NSF-IIS 1041637, NSF-CNS 1035913.

Table 3: Macro-average precision and F_1 measure for each classifiers on each test data sets. The results demonstrate the advantage of the proposed DKT approach.

Data	Metrics	Compared methods								
		SVM_T	SVM_TS	TSVM_T	TSVM_TS	KTW	MTrick	IB	DKT (S only)	DKT
D1	Precision	–	0.682	–	0.689	0.673	0.695	0.691	0.697	0.716
	F_1	–	0.479	–	0.483	0.481	0.490	0.492	0.495	0.508
D2	Precision	0.679	0.692	0.682	0.701	0.675	0.699	0.703	0.718	0.730
	F_1	0.468	0.481	0.475	0.489	0.483	0.492	0.501	0.505	0.510
D3	Precision	–	0.670	–	0.675	0.663	0.682	0.680	0.683	0.701
	F_1	–	0.470	–	0.475	0.470	0.481	0.480	0.483	0.498
D4	Precision	0.663	0.682	0.670	0.687	0.669	0.681	0.690	0.702	0.718
	F_1	0.452	0.469	0.461	0.472	0.471	0.481	0.486	0.492	0.501
D5	Precision	–	0.662	–	0.668	0.656	0.674	0.672	0.679	0.688
	F_1	–	0.463	–	0.468	0.462	0.472	0.470	0.477	0.485
D6	Precision	0.651	0.676	0.663	0.676	0.658	0.672	0.681	0.695	0.707
	F_1	0.447	0.460	0.456	0.467	0.463	0.475	0.478	0.486	0.493

7. REFERENCES

[1] N. Bel, C. Koster, and M. Villegas. Cross-lingual text categorization. *Research and Advanced Technology for Digital Libraries*, pages 126–139, 2004.

[2] J. Blitzer, R. McDonald, and F. Pereira. Domain adaptation with structural correspondence learning. In *EMNLP*, 2006.

[3] G. Chen, F. Wang, and C. Zhang. Collaborative filtering using orthogonal nonnegative matrix tri-factorization. *Information Processing and Management*, 45(3):368–379, 2009.

[4] C. Ding and X. He. K-means clustering via principal component analysis. In *ICML*, 2004.

[5] C. Ding, X. He, and H. Simon. On the equivalence of nonnegative matrix factorization and spectral clustering. In *SDM*, 2005.

[6] C. Ding, T. Li, and M. Jordan. Convex and semi-nonnegative matrix factorizations. *TPAMI*, 32(1):45–55, 2010.

[7] C. Ding, T. Li, W. Peng, and H. Park. Orthogonal nonnegative matrix t-factorizations for clustering. In *SIGKDD*, 2006.

[8] Q. Gu and J. Zhou. Co-clustering on manifolds. In *SIGKDD*, 2009.

[9] T. Joachims. Transductive inference for text classification using support vector machines. In *ICML*, pages 200–209.

[10] T. Joachims. SVMLight: Support Vector Machine. `http://svmlight.joachims.org/`, 1999.

[11] D. Lee and H. Seung. Learning the parts of objects by non-negative matrix factorization. *Nature*, 401(6755):788–791, 1999.

[12] D. Lee and H. Seung. Algorithms for non-negative matrix factorization. In *NIPS*, 2001.

[13] T. Li, V. Sindhwani, C. Ding, and Y. Zhang. Knowledge transformation for cross-domain sentiment classification. In *SIGIR*, 2009.

[14] T. Li, V. Sindhwani, C. Ding, and Y. Zhang. Bridging Domains with Words: Opinion Analysis with Matrix Tri-factorizations. In *SDM*, 2010.

[15] X. Ling, G. Xue, W. Dai, Y. Jiang, Q. Yang, and Y. Yu. Can Chinese web pages be classified with English data source? In *WWW*, 2008.

[16] J. Olsson, D. Oard, and J. Hajič. Cross-language text classification. In *SIGIR*, 2005.

[17] S. Pan and Q. Yang. A survey on transfer learning. *IEEE TKDE*, 2009.

[18] P. Prettenhofer and B. Stein. Cross-language text classification using structural correspondence learning. In *ACL*, 2010.

[19] G. Ramírez-de-la Rosa, M. Montes-y Gómez, L. Villaseñor Pineda, D. Pinto-Avendaño, and T. Solorio. Using information from the target language to improve crosslingual text classification. In *Proceedings of the 7th international conference on Advances in natural language processing*, 2010.

[20] L. Shi, R. Mihalcea, and M. Tian. Cross language text classification by model translation and semi-supervised learning. In *EMNLP*, 2010.

[21] X. Wan. Co-training for cross-lingual sentiment classification. In *ACL*, 2009.

[22] F. Wang, T. Li, and C. Zhang. Semi-supervised clustering via matrix factorization. In *SDM*, 2008.

[23] K. Wu and B. Lu. A refinement framework for cross language text categorization. In *AIRS*, 2008.

[24] H. Zha, X. He, C. Ding, H. Simon, and M. Gu. Spectral relaxation for k-means clustering. In *NIPS*, 2001.

[25] F. Zhuang, P. Luo, H. Xiong, Q. He, Y. Xiong, and Z. Shi. Exploiting associations between word clusters and document classes for cross-domain text categorization. In *SDM*, 2010.

No Free Lunch: Brute Force vs. Locality-Sensitive Hashing for Cross-lingual Pairwise Similarity

Ferhan Ture[1], Tamer Elsayed[2], Jimmy Lin[1,3]

[1]Dept. of Computer Science, [3]The iSchool
University of Maryland

[2]Mathematical and Computer Sciences and Engineering Division
King Abdullah University of Science and Technology (KAUST)

fture@cs.umd.edu, tamer.elsayedaly@kaust.edu.sa, jimmylin@umd.edu

ABSTRACT

This work explores the problem of cross-lingual pairwise similarity, where the task is to extract similar pairs of documents *across* two different languages. Solutions to this problem are of general interest for text mining in the multilingual context and have specific applications in statistical machine translation. Our approach takes advantage of cross-language information retrieval (CLIR) techniques to project feature vectors from one language into another, and then uses locality-sensitive hashing (LSH) to extract similar pairs. We show that effective cross-lingual pairwise similarity requires working with similarity thresholds that are much lower than in typical monolingual applications, making the problem quite challenging. We present a parallel, scalable MapReduce implementation of the sort-based sliding window algorithm, which is compared to a brute-force approach on German and English Wikipedia collections. Our central finding can be summarized as "no free lunch": there is no single optimal solution. Instead, we characterize effectiveness-efficiency tradeoffs in the solution space, which can guide the developer to locate a desirable operating point based on application- and resource-specific constraints.

Categories and Subject Descriptors: H.3.3 [Information Storage and Retrieval]: Information Search and Retrieval

General Terms: Algorithms, Performance

Keywords: LSH, machine translation, Wikipedia

1. INTRODUCTION

In its most general form, pairwise similarity computation deals with finding pairs of objects in a large dataset that are similar according to some measure. This problem is frequently encountered in text processing applications, for example, clustering for unsupervised learning [28, 26], generation of similarity lists for "more-like-this" queries [18], and near-duplicate detection in the web context. Instances of this problem are encountered in other domains such as bioinformatics as well [22].

This work focuses on pairwise similarity in text collections, but introduces a new twist—we wish to mine similar pairs of documents that are in *different* languages. At a high level, this problem is driven by an evolution toward more multi-lingual societies, which makes the ability to communicate across language barriers increasingly important. Machine translation (MT) is one technological solution, and modern systems are heavily driven by statistical methods dependent on large amounts of training data [16]. Traditionally, algorithms have required texts that are mutual translations of each other—called *parallel* corpora—but there has also been work on exploiting *comparable* corpora—or texts in different languages that are similar, but not necessarily mutual translations [21, 29, 24, 31]. In our view, parallel and comparable corpora lie on a continuum of similarity, and solutions to the cross-lingual pairwise similarity problem can unlock new sources of training data for MT systems.

The specific application we focus on is automatically generating links between Wikipedia articles in different languages (so-called "interwiki" language links). In addition to contributing to the overall goal of data mining for machine translation, we believe the task is independently interesting. For example, there presently exists a link between the article "Friedensnobelpreis" in German and "Nobel Peace Prize" in English. However, as far as we know, these links are manually created, and therefore suffers from many shortcomings: link creation requires volunteers who know *both* languages and is a labor-intensive, error-prone endeavor. As a result, link coverage is relatively sparse. A cross-lingual pairwise similarity algorithm may help: its output can feed into a manual verification process that improves both speed and accuracy (e.g., perhaps aided by crowdsourcing).

Our approach uses locality-sensitive hashing (LSH) [4, 5, 2], which represents documents as bit-signatures, such that two similar documents are likely to have similar signatures. A sort-based sliding window algorithm on permutations of bit signatures is used to extract similar pairs. LSH provides a tradeoff between efficiency and effectiveness by user-controlled parameters, and can be straightforwardly parallelized since multiple randomizations run independently.

Although LSH is a well-explored solution to the pairwise similarity problem, this work has several contributions.

SIGIR'11, July 24–28, 2011, Beijing, China.

First, we introduce and motivate the cross-lingual variant of the pairwise similarity problem, which has received little attention in the literature. Second, we demonstrate that the cross-lingual variant of the problem is considerably more challenging since it requires mining document pairs that have low similarities, far lower than thresholds typically used in monolingual solutions. Third, we describe a scalable MapReduce [10] implementation of the sort-based sliding window LSH algorithm for solving the problem. The solution exhibits linear scalability and a high degree of parallelism that makes it suitable for large collections. Finally, we present an analytical and empirical analysis of our approach across a wide range of parameter settings, using the brute-force N^2 approach as a baseline. Our central finding can be summarized as "no free lunch": there is no single optimal solution to the cross-lingual pairwise similarity problem. Instead, we characterize effectiveness-efficiency tradeoffs within the solution space, which can guide the developer to locate a desirable operating point based on application- and resource-specific constraints. This characterization addresses a weakness of LSH approaches in general, in that they present a bewildering number of parameters that need to be set, and provide little guidance for an application developer approaching new problems. To this end, we show that the efficiency and the effectiveness of our algorithm can be analytically estimated, thus allowing the developer to characterize the tradeoff space for a particular problem without actually needing to run any experiments.

The remainder of the paper is organized as follows. We begin with related work in Section 2. A formal definition of the cross-lingual pairwise similarity problem is provided in Section 3. Our LSH-based approach is detailed in Section 4, followed by an analytical model in Section 5. Experimental results are presented in Section 6 before concluding.

2. RELATED WORK

The problem of efficiently computing pairwise similarity has been extensively studied by text processing and data mining researchers; in the database community, this is better known as the "set similarity join" problem [12, 33]. Another variant that has received attention is computing pairwise "functional" computations (not necessarily similarities) between elements in large datasets [23, 15].

In general, two approaches to the problem exist: the *index-based* approach focuses on building an inverted index and pruning it to achieve efficient similarity computations [3, 12, 32, 33]; and the *signature-based* approach that transforms the data into a more compact representation for performing similarity comparisons. The LSH [4, 5, 2] techniques we adopt exemplifies the second approach.

There is also extensive work on near-duplicate detection of web pages, which can be viewed as a special case that aims to detect highly-similar pairs, sometimes without a predefined similarity threshold or even a similarity measure. Both index-based [32, 35] and signature-based [6, 20, 17, 13, 14] approaches have been proposed to address this problem.

All of the above focus on monolingual or homogeneous similarity, either similarity within one language or similarity within a homogeneous collection of objects. We are aware of some work that attempts to solve the cross-lingual version of the problem, but in a slightly different setting. Anderka et al. [1] concluded that both signature-based and index-based approaches require at least a linear scan of the collection due to the low similarity thresholds. However, the authors do not describe an algorithm or show any experimental results. In another recent paper, Platt et al. [27] described techniques for projecting multi-lingual documents into a single vector space: training "encourages" comparable document pairs to have similar vector representations. This and other work on extracting parallel sentences [24, 31] focus primarily on representational issues and do not explicitly address questions of scale. Thus, these techniques can be viewed as complementary to our own.

Our work takes advantage of Hadoop, the open-source implementation of MapReduce [10], which has recently emerged as a popular model for large-scale data processing. The problem of pairwise similarity computation has been studied in MapReduce previously [18, 11, 33]. However, these algorithms adopt an index-based approach, which stands in contrast to our signature-based approach.

3. CROSS-LINGUAL SIMILARITY

Assuming a "bag of words" model, where a document d is represented as a vector of term weights $w_{t,d}$, one for each term t in the vocabulary space V, similarity between two document vectors u and v is computed via cosine similarity: $\text{Sim}(u, v) = \cos(\theta(u, v))$. There are, of course, many possible weighting schemes for $w_{t,d}$; here, we adopt BM25 [30], which has been shown to be effective for many retrieval tasks. In this scheme, each weight is a function of document frequency (df) and term frequency (tf) values.

The pairwise similarity problem is that of finding all pairs of documents (u, v) with cosine similarities above a certain threshold τ. In *cross-lingual* pairwise similarity, we additionally stipulate that the document vectors represent documents in different languages, thus introducing additional complexity. Due to different vocabulary spaces, document vectors in different languages are not directly comparable.

3.1 Matching Vocabulary Spaces

We experimented with two different solutions to overcome vocabulary mismatch: translation and vector projection.

The first approach is to *translate* documents from one language into the other using an off-the-shelf machine translation system. If we are working with German and English as the language pair, we could translate all German documents into English, and then perform pairwise similarity in the English vocabulary space. The advantage of this approach is that modern machine translation systems produce quite reasonable results, especially for European languages. The downside, however, is that machine translation is typically time-consuming and resource-intensive.

The second approach is to *project* document vectors from one language into another using cross-language information retrieval (CLIR) techniques. Adopting the approach proposed by Darwish and Oard [8], a document vector v in some foreign language F can be translated into a document vector v^* in the target language E by computing df^* and tf^* values for every term $e \in E$ as follows:

$$df^*(e) = \sum_{f \in F} p(f|e) \cdot df(f)$$

$$tf^*(e) = \sum_{f \in F} p(f|e) \cdot tf(f)$$

where we assume df and tf values are represented in v. Since

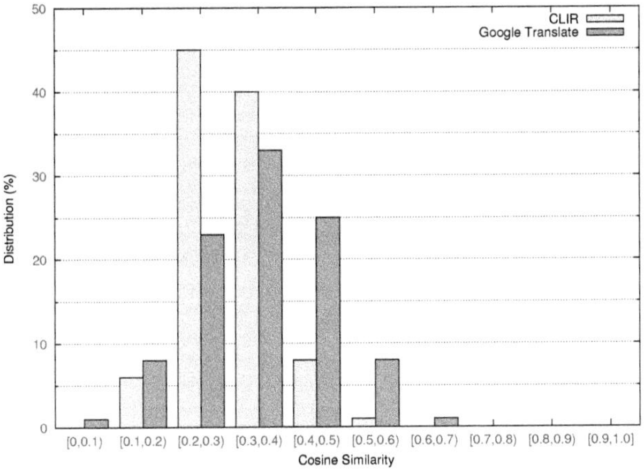

Figure 1: Histogram of cosine similarities from 505 semantically similar documents in German and English, comparing Google Translate with CLIR.

term weight is a function of df^* and tf^* values, this information is sufficient to construct the vector v^*. The quantity $p(f|e)$ is the conditional probability of a foreign language word f being the translation of a target language word e; this distribution captures lexical translation ambiguities—the fact that words in one language can translate to multiple words in another language. This distribution can be estimated from parallel corpora using unsupervised techniques, as the output of the word alignment problem [34, 25]. Solutions to this problem are well understood, and there exist multiple off-the-shelf implementations.

3.2 Implications

Typical instances of the monolingual pairwise similarity problem involve extracting pairs with high cosine similarities (e.g., 0.9 or higher). For the cross-lingual case, we expect similar documents in different languages to have lower similarities, since the translation process is noisy.

To empirically determine appropriate similarity thresholds for the cross-lingual case, we experimented with the German and English portions of the Europarl corpus, which contains proceedings from the European Parliament (1996–2009). We constructed artificial "documents" by concatenating every 10 consecutive sentences into a single document. In this manner, we sampled 505 document pairs that are mutual translations of each other (and therefore semantically similar by construction). This provides ground truth to evaluate the effectiveness of the two translation approaches discussed above: machine translation (in this case, we used Google Translate[1]) and direct vector projection using the CLIR approach. In the first case, we translated each German document into English and then processed the resulting translated English document into vector form. In the second case, we first processed the German document into vector form, and then projected the vector over into English. We then computed the cosine similarities of the document pairs, under both conditions.

The distribution of the cosine similarities is shown in Figure 1, binned in 0.1 intervals. We make two important observations. First, the cosine similarities are surprisingly low, and we expect even lower values in practice, since these are artificially created perfect document translations. This implies that in order to mine semantically similar document pairs in different languages, we need to extract documents that have low cosine similarities. Second, cosine similarity scores are higher for Google Translate, but vector projection seems reasonably competitive, especially considering the computational tradeoff: running an MT system on millions of documents is computationally expensive. For this reason, the remainder of this paper uses the CLIR vector projection technique.

[1]http://translate.google.com

4. SIMILARITY COMPUTATIONS

Our approach, which is based on LSH [4, 5, 2], consists of three steps. First, all documents are preprocessed into document vectors (Section 4.1). Second, document signatures are generated from document vectors (Section 4.2). Finally, a sliding window algorithm applied to the signatures finds all cross-lingual pairs above a similarity threshold (Section 4.3).

4.1 Preprocessing Documents

In the preprocessing step, documents from both languages are parsed, tokenized, and represented as weighted document vectors. All terms that occur only once in the collection are removed and each remaining term is converted into an integer for efficiency reasons. Document vectors of the foreign language (i.e., German) are projected into the target language (English) by the CLIR approach explained in Section 3. Thus, the collections in two languages are converted into a single collection of document vectors in the target language. Since we are only interested in cross-lingual pairs, we use document identifiers (docids) to determine the original language of a document vector.

4.2 Generating Document Signatures

At the core of any pairwise similarity algorithm is the similarity calculation between pairs of documents. The major drawback of cosine similarity is that the calculation requires a number of floating point operations linear to the number of terms in u and v, which is computationally expensive. Although it is possible to accurately approximate floating point values with integers using quantization methods, the similarity calculation still remains a bottleneck when dealing with many documents and large vocabularies.

Signatures are an efficient and effective way of representing large feature spaces. We explore three well-known methods to generate signatures from document vectors: random projection [5], Simhash [20], and Minhash [7].

Random projection (RP) signatures [5] use a series of random hyperplanes as hash functions to encode document vectors as fixed-size bit vectors. Let us assume a collection with vocabulary V, so that each document vector is from the domain $\mathbb{R}^{|V|}$. To obtain a signature of D bits using this approach, D randomly generated real-valued vectors of length $|V|$ are used to map each document vector u onto a RP signature $s_u \in [0,1]^D$. The ith bit of s_u is determined by an inner product of u and the ith random vector.

Given D random vectors $r_1, ..., r_D$, the signature s_u is computed as follows:

$$s_u[i] = h_{r_i}(u) = \begin{cases} 1 & \text{if } r_i \cdot u \geq 0 \\ 0 & \text{if } r_i \cdot u < 0 \end{cases} \quad (1)$$

The cosine similarity between two documents can be computed via hamming distance between their signatures, according to the following relationship [5]:

$$\text{Sim}(u, v) = \cos\left[\left(\frac{\pi}{D}\right) \text{hamming}(s_u, s_v)\right] \quad (2)$$

Simhash signatures are essentially a "hash" of the document vector. This approach relies on a hash function that generates hash values for every term in the document vector. Given a document vector u and a hash function h that maps string terms to D-bit hash values, we generate a D-bit signature s as follows:

$$s[i] = \begin{cases} 1 & \text{if } \sum_{(t,w)\in u} (2h(t)[i] - 1)w > 0 \\ 0 & \text{otherwise} \end{cases}$$

where every term-weight pair (t, w) in u contributes $+w$ to $s[i]$ if $h(t)[i] = 1$ and $-w$ otherwise. If the sum of contributions to $s[i]$ is greater than 0, then $s[i]$ is set to 1, otherwise, it is set to 0.

For this approach, signature quality depends on the quality of the hash function, which also dictates the signature length (which cannot be set arbitrarily). In this work, we use the hash function in Manku et al. [20], where it was applied to detect near-duplicate web pages. We leave exploration of more recent methods along similar lines, such as self-taught hashing [36] for future work.

Minhash signature for a document vector u requires K random orderings of terms in u. Given a hash function, terms can be ordered by their hash value, or alternatively, terms can be ordered by a random permutation on the vocabulary. For each of the K orderings, the term in a document that has lowest order is picked as the "minimum hash" of that document. The probability that two documents u and v have the same "minimum hash" term for a given ordering is $\frac{|u \cap v|}{|u \cup v|}$ (i.e., Jaccard similarity). This procedure is repeated for K different randomly selected orderings to reduce the risk of false positives; thus, the *Minhash* signature of a document vector consists of all K "minimum hash" terms. The cosine similarity between u and v is approximated by the proportion of terms they share. Chum et al. [7] showed its effectiveness on near-duplicate image detection.

In order to compare the precision of these three signature generation techniques, we selected a sample of 1064 document vectors from German Wikipedia. For every pair of document vectors, we computed the true cosine similarity and estimated values using each of the three signature methods and varying signature lengths. In each case, we computed the average absolute difference between the true and estimated cosine similarity value, shown in Table 1. For comparison, the last column shows the average time (in milliseconds) taken to generate one signature on a laptop with an Intel Core 2 Duo 2.26 GHz processor.

Simhash signatures generated by the approach in Manku et al. [20] are 64 bits. Since Minhash signatures are represented as a list of integers (corresponding to term ids), they take up 32 times more space than a Simhash or RP signature of the same length. We included 2-term (64 bits) and 32-term (992 bits) Minhash signatures in the comparison.

We performed three sets of experiments: First, we computed error for all possible pairs, then filtered out pairs with cosine similarity less than 0.1, and finally less than 0.2. Precision at very low similarities is not very important because relevant documents usually have values higher than 0.2 (based on Figure 1). We noticed that Minhash signatures perform worse as we filter out low-similarity pairs because it simply predicts 0.0 for many pairs. In contrast, RP signatures are more accurate when the cosine similarity is higher, an indicator of the robustness of the method.

Method	Bits	Avg. Absolute Error			Time (ms)
		> 0.0	> 0.1	> 0.2	
Minhash	64	0.061	0.168	0.215	0.28
Simhash	64	0.236	0.299	0.273	0.25
RP	64	0.154	0.152	0.123	1.17
RP	100	0.124	0.122	0.101	2.03
RP	200	0.088	0.086	0.069	4.52
RP	500	0.056	0.055	0.045	10.93
RP	1000	0.040	0.039	0.033	20.91
Minhash	992	0.050	0.056	0.075	1.82

Table 1: Average cosine similarity error per signature with different methods

In all cases, 64-bit RP signatures are more precise than Simhash signatures, and this becomes more apparent once the low-similarity pairs are filtered out. The only drawback of RP signatures is the amount of time necessary to generate them: an inner product is needed to determine every bit. The average time to create a 64-bit RP signature is about 5 times slower than other methods with the same number of bits and generating 1000-bit RP signatures is more than 10 times slower than 32-term Minhash signatures. However, the running time of the signature construction step is relatively brief compared to the actual pairwise similarity algorithm. Based on this analysis, we selected 1000-bit RP signatures for our experiments.

4.3 Sliding Window Algorithm

The sliding window algorithm [5] is a probabilistic method which uses randomization and approximation heuristics to provide a tradeoff between efficiency and effectiveness. In this section, we first describe a straightforward parallel implementation of the original version of this algorithm in MapReduce (Figure 2). Then, we discuss modifications to exploit the framework and take advantage of greater parallelism (Figures 3 and 4). For space considerations, we assume that the reader has at least passing familiarity with the sliding window algorithm, as it is a well-known LSH technique. We further assume that the reader is already familiar with the MapReduce programming model.

4.3.1 Basic Algorithm

In the sliding window algorithm, Q random permutation functions $p_1, ..., p_Q$ are created as a preprocessing step.[2] Input is the sequence of (docid, signature) pairs for the entire collection. Each mapper takes a docid n and signature s as input, and emits an intermediate key-value pair $(\langle i, s^i\rangle, n)$ for each permutation function $p_i, i = 1...Q$.[3]

Each key sent to a reducer is a pair of the permutation group number p and the signature s (denoted as $\langle p, s\rangle$) and the values are docids sharing that pair. The reduce step is designed so that all keys with the same permutation group number are sent to the same reducer (by appropriately partitioning the key space), and they are sorted according to the

[2] A permutation function is basically a permuted list of the integers $[1 \ldots D]$, where D is the signature size.

[3] We denote s^i as the permutation of s with respect to the permutation function p_i.

```
Mapper
1: method Map(docid n, signature s)
2:     for all permute func p_i ∈ [p_1, p_2, ..., p_Q] do
3:         Emit(⟨i, s.Permute(p_i)⟩, n)
Reducer
4: method Initialize
5:     docids ← new Queue(B)
6:     sigs ← new Queue(B)
7: method Reduce(⟨permno p, sig s⟩, docids [n_1, n_2, ...])
8:     for all docid n ∈ [n_1, n_2, ...] do
9:         for i = 1 to sigs.Size() do
10:            distance ← s.Distance(sigs.get(i))
11:            if distance ≤ T then
12:                Emit(⟨docids.get(i), n⟩, distance)
13:        sigs.Enqueue(s)
14:        docids.Enqueue(n)
15:        if sigs.Size() > B then
16:            sigs.Dequeue()
17:            docids.Dequeue()
```

Figure 2: Pseudo-code of the initial version of the sliding window algorithm.

signature bits (comparison of two signatures is from most significant to least significant bit). Therefore, each of the Q reducers receive a sorted list of permuted signatures, paired with respective docids, which we call a "table".

Based on LSH, more similar documents have higher probabilities of being closer in a table. Given a large enough Q and B, it can be shown that signatures of similar documents will be at most B positions apart in at least one table with high probability. Since sorted order depends on the positions of bits, having multiple permutations of the same signature increases the chance of retrieving a similar pair.

A queue of size B is used to implement the idea above (Reduce method in Figure 2): in each table, we compare all signatures that are at most B positions away from each other. The reducer iterates over the signatures and keeps the last B in the queue (lines 13–17). At each iteration, the current signature is compared to all signatures in the queue, and hamming distances are emitted as output (lines 8–12).

4.3.2 Improved Algorithm

A drawback of the basic algorithm is the inability to increase the number of reducers, because each reduce group processes a single permuted list of all the signatures in the collection. In other words, in the reduce phase, only Q reducers can operate in parallel, which may be an underutilization in very large clusters that are commonly used for MapReduce. In this case, being able to increase the number of reducers arbitrarily can help the algorithm better scale.

We achieved this by modifying the previous algorithm in the following way. The map function is exactly the same, but the reduce step divides each table into an arbitrary number of consecutive blocks (Figure 3). Each of the Q reducers iterates over sorted signatures, stores them in a list (lines 9–11), and outputs the list when its size reaches a pre-specified size, M (lines 12–14). We denote each of these M-sized lists as a *chunk*, and refer to this as the *chunk generation* phase. The actual comparison and similarity computation is performed in an additional map-only MapReduce task (Figure 4), called the *detection* phase, where the input is the chunks and each mapper finds all similar pairs in one chunk.

```
Mapper
1: method Map(docid n, signature s)
2:     for all permute func p_i ∈ [p_1, p_2, ..., p_Q] do
3:         Emit(⟨i, s.Permute(p_i)⟩, n)
Reducer
4: method Initialize
5:     docids ← new List
6:     sigs ← new List
7:     chunk ← new SignatureChunk
8: method Reduce(⟨permno p, sig s⟩, docids [n_1, n_2, ...])
9:     for all docno n ∈ [n_1, n_2, ...] do
10:        sigs.Add(s)
11:        docids.Add(n)
12:        if sigs.Size() = M then
13:            chunk.Set(sigs, docids)
14:            Emit(p, chunk)
15:            sigs ← sigs.SubList(M − B + 1, M)
16:            docids ← docids.SubList(M − B + 1, M)
17: method Close
18:     chunk.Set(sigs, docids)
19:     Emit(p, chunk)
```

Figure 3: Pseudo-code of the *chunk generation* phase of the sliding window algorithm.

Only pairs that have a distance less than the threshold T are emitted by the algorithm. We use the docids to make sure only cross-lingual pairs are included in the output. In this phase, there can be as many mappers as there are chunks, which allows full utilization of computational resources.

Note that some comparisons will be missed at the boundary of chunks (e.g., the last element of a chunk is not compared to the first element of the next chunk). We solve this problem by appending the last B signatures of the previous chunk at the beginning of the current chunk (Figure 3, lines 15–16). This results in redundancy in the chunks emitted to disk (the last B signatures of a chunk are the same as the first B signatures of the next one), but the redundancy is negligible especially since $B \ll M$.

5. ANALYTICAL MODEL

In this section, we provide a theoretical analysis of our LSH algorithm, which provides a model for estimating effectiveness analytically. The starting point is Equation 1, which shows how random vectors are used to generate bit signatures. For any two vectors u and v, the probability that a single random projection h_r collides is

$$\Pr[h_r(u) = h_r(v)] = 1 - \frac{\theta(u,v)}{\pi} \quad (3)$$

The proof can be found in [5], which we omit here. The intuition is that the hyperplane defined by the random vector divides our collection of vectors into two disjoint sets, and the probability that any two vectors will land in the same set is determined by the angle θ between them, according to the relation above.

Let $S_0 = \{u | h_r(u) = 0\}$ and $S_1 = \{u | h_r(u) = 1\}$, corresponding to the subsets of our collection of vectors that share the same hash value. Given a vector u, we can compute $h_r(u)$ and perform a linear scan in the corresponding set to find similar vectors. Given that vectors u and v have

Mapper

```
method Map(permno p, signatureChunk chunk)
    for i = 1 to (chunk.Size() − B) do                                      ▷ B is the size of the sliding window
        for j = (i + 1) to (i + B) do                            ▷ check that i and j are from different languages
            distance ← chunk.Signature(i).Distance(chunk.Signature(j))
            if distance ≤ T then                       ▷ detects similar pairs, where T is the distance threshold
                Emit(⟨chunk.DocId(j), chunk.DocId(i)⟩, distance)
```

Figure 4: Pseudo-code of the *detection* phase of the sliding window algorithm.

cosine similarity t, the probability that they are in the same subset is given by $1 - \cos^{-1}(t)/\pi$.

We can extend this basic approach by selecting n random vectors $\{r_1, r_2, ...r_n\}$ and construct corresponding hash functions $\{h_{r_1}(u), h_{r_2}(u), ...h_{r_n}(u)\}$. Using these hash functions we can divide up the collection into 2^n disjoint sets:

$$
\begin{aligned}
S_{000...0} &= \{u | h_{r_1}(u) = 0 \wedge h_{r_2}(u) = 0 \wedge ...h_{r_n}(u) = 0\} \\
S_{000...1} &= \{u | h_{r_1}(u) = 0 \wedge h_{r_2}(u) = 0 \wedge ...h_{r_n}(u) = 1\} \\
&... \\
S_{111...1} &= \{u | h_{r_1}(u) = 1 \wedge h_{r_2}(u) = 1 \wedge ...h_{r_n}(u) = 1\}
\end{aligned}
$$

Suppose we wish to find document vectors that are similar to u: we can apply the hash functions to determine the correct candidate set of vectors, and then perform a linear scan through all those candidates to compute the actual dot product. With n random projections, the probability that we'll find similar vectors becomes $(1 - \cos^{-1}(t)/\pi)^n$. More random projections reduce the number of comparisons we must make, but at the cost of compounding the error introduced by each random projection.

To alleviate this issue, we can repeat the entire process m times using m sets of n different random projections. The probability that we'll identify a valid similar pair becomes:

$$
\Pr[u, v \text{ in same set in at least one trial} \mid \cos(u, v) = t]
$$

$$
= 1 - \left[1 - \left[1 - \frac{\cos^{-1}(t)}{\pi}\right]^n\right]^m \tag{4}
$$

The above equation quantifies the error when searching for similar vectors using LSH. The second source of error is the hamming distance computation. As shown in Section 4.2, cosine similarity can be estimated from the hamming distance with Equation 2.

We use this similarity estimate to efficiently decide which documents to return during the linear scan of the candidate set. For a given vector u and similarity threshold τ, we calculate the corresponding hamming distance threshold T using Equation 2 and return all candidates with hamming distance less than or equal to T. The precision of this decision is given by the following:

$$
\Pr[\text{hamming}(u, v) \leq T | \cos(u, v) = t \wedge u, v \text{ share } n\text{-bit prefix}]
$$

$$
= \sum_{i=0}^{T} \binom{D-n}{i} \rho^i (1-\rho)^{D-n-i}, \text{ where } \rho = \frac{\cos^{-1}(t)}{\pi} \tag{5}
$$

How does this relate to our sliding window algorithm? Let us first consider a variation of our algorithm. Suppose instead of applying a sliding window B over the sorted bit signatures, we performed a pairwise N^2 comparison of all bit signatures that share n prefix bits. Another way to think about this is to dynamically adjust B so that it encompasses only those signatures that share the prefix. In this case, the expected probability of extracting a pair of vectors with similarity t (hamming distance $\leq T$) is quantified by the product of Equations 4 and 5 above. The number of tables (permutations) is equal to the number of trials m and the prefix length is equal to the number of random projections n in the above analysis. The probability of successfully extracting a similar pair has contributions from two sources: LSH (the two documents sharing the same signature prefix) and accuracy of hamming distance.

In actuality, we scan a fixed window B. However, we approximate n to be between $\lfloor \log_2(C/B) \rfloor$ and $\lceil \log_2(C/B) \rceil$, where C is the total number of vectors in the collection. We use both estimates to obtain a range of the estimated recall values. Although this is merely a rough model, it provides us with a basis for analytically estimating effectiveness, which we demonstrate later.

6. EXPERIMENTAL EVALUATION

We evaluated our cross-lingual pairwise similarity algorithm on English and German Wikipedia, selected because they are the largest Wikipedia collections available and because significant amounts of parallel corpora exist for the language pair. We used the German Wikipedia dump from 1/31/2011, which contains 2.41m articles totaling 8.5 GB. We used the English Wikipedia dump from 1/15/2011, which contains 10.86m articles totaling 30.6 GB. For both collections we discarded redirect pages and stub articles.

Our system is implemented on top of Ivory, an open-source Hadoop toolkit for web-scale information retrieval [19]. German articles were projected into English document vectors, as described in Section 3. For translation probabilities, we trained a word alignment using the Berkeley Aligner[4] on the Europarl German-English corpus, containing 1.08m sentence pairs from European parliament speeches. For tokenization, we used the Java-based OpenNLP toolkit.[5] After projection, document vectors containing fewer than five terms were discarded. We arrived at 1.47m German articles and 3.44m English articles. In the next step, RP signatures were generated from document vectors. Finally, we ran the improved sliding window algorithm (Section 4.3.2) to extract all document pairs with cosine similarity above a specified threshold. We only output pairs in which one document is from German Wikipedia and the other is from English Wikipedia.

All experiments were conducted on a Hadoop cluster (running Cloudera's distribution, version 0.20.2+320) with 16 nodes, each having 2 quad-core 2.2 GHz Intel Nehalem Processors, 24 GB RAM, and three 2 TB drives.

6.1 Effectiveness vs. Efficiency

The parameters in our algorithm are: the length in bits of each signature (D), the number of tables (Q), the chunk size (M), the window size (B), and the hamming distance threshold (T). We fixed D to 1000 based on the discussion

[4]http://code.google.com/p/berkeleyaligner

[5]http://opennlp.sourceforge.net

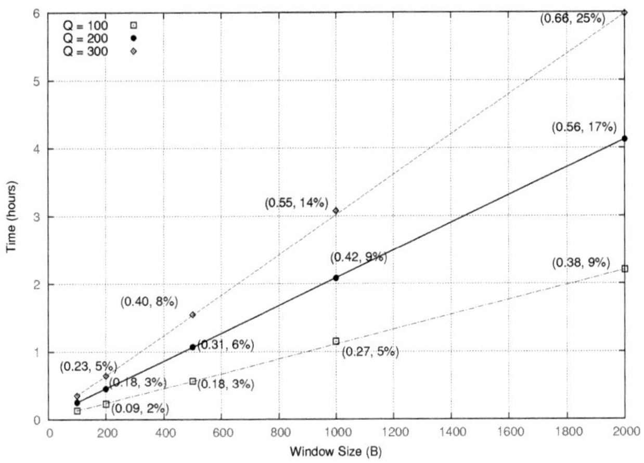

Figure 5: Running times of the detection phase of the sliding window LSH algorithm for $\tau = 0.3$, using 1000-bit signatures. Data points are annotated with recall and relative cost.

in Section 4.2, and fixed M to 0.49m so that each table is split into 10 chunks. For the rest of the parameters, we explored a number of choices and observed the changes in efficiency and effectiveness. Note that we need to run the preprocessing step and signature generation step only once for these experiments (this takes 1.67 hours). The *chunk generation* phase of the sliding window algorithm must be executed once for every value of Q (this takes 0.28, 0.53, and 0.75 hours, respectively, for $Q = 100, 200, 300$). The *detection* phase needs to be run for every different set of the remaining parameters, for which running times on the entire German-English Wikipedia collection are plotted in Figure 5 (varying window sizes for each value of Q). The regression lines clearly show that the algorithm scales linearly as Q and B increase ($R^2 > 0.999$ in all three cases). Note that the hamming distance threshold T does not affect the running time, but only determines which pairs are extracted; therefore, it is not included in this figure.

To assess effectiveness, we selected a sample of 1064 German Wikipedia articles. For every article, we calculated its true cosine similarity with all other documents in English Wikipedia and retained all pairs above threshold $\tau = 0.3$ to serve as the ground truth, informed by the similarity distribution in Figure 1. This corresponds to a hamming distance threshold of $T = 400$ for 1000-bit signatures, since $\cos(400\pi/1000) \sim 0.3$. Note that a hamming distance of 500 corresponds to no similarity at all, so we are looking for documents that may be very dissimilar. From this, we are able to measure the quality of the pairs extracted by our algorithm. We argue that recall is the most salient evaluation metric, i.e., the fraction of pairs in the ground truth set that are actually extracted, since the task is recall-oriented by definition. If precision is desired, one could always filter the extracted pairs and discard results that fall below the similarity threshold—the time necessary for this is negligible compared to the time for extracting the pairs to begin with. For instance, with parameters $Q = 300, B = 2000$, the number of extracted pairs is 64 million, 0.0013% of all possible cross-lingual pairs in the collection. This gives an idea of how much of the search space is filtered by the algorithm. Moreover, from an application point of view, it may not even be necessary to filter, since our τ threshold of 0.3 is somewhat arbitrary, and pairs with lower similarity scores may nevertheless be useful (see Figure 1).

The data points in Figure 5 are annotated with recall and a measure we call *relative cost*, defined as follows: for each condition, we can analytically compute the total number of similarity comparisons (i.e., in terms of hamming distance) necessary over the entire run. We can express this as a percentage of the total number of comparisons that a brute-force approach would require, which is the product of the size of the two collections: with 3.44m English articles and 1.47m German articles, this equals 5.05 trillion comparisons. The cost of the chunk generation process is also taken into account in these calculations (by translating that time into an equivalent in terms of number of comparisons). A relative cost lower than 100% means we're "saving work" by not considering pairs unlikely to be similar—the entire point of LSH. In essence, each pair in the graph delineates a point in the tradeoff space: the level of recall and efficiency that can be expected for a particular parameter setting.

To better understand these results, it is necessary to quantify the upper bound on effectiveness. Note that our algorithm has two sources of error: those introduced by the bit signatures (cf. Table 1) and those introduced by the sliding window algorithm (i.e., failure to find similar pairs within B). We can isolate the error introduced by the sliding window and compute an effectiveness upper bound by repeating the procedure that generated the ground truth, but using signatures instead. For every sample document's signature, we computed the hamming distance with all other signatures in English Wikipedia and extracted all pairs that have a distance less than $T = 400$. We then compared those pairs to the ground truth set and obtained 0.76 recall.[6] We see that the 0.04 absolute error in cosine similarity (cf. Table 1) introduced by 1000-bit random projections, which is negligible for other tasks that adopt high similarity thresholds (e.g., [28]), has a large impact for our task. Another way to understand this is that absolute error has an increasing impact as the similarity threshold is lowered (i.e., 0.04 absolute error is equal to 13% relative error when we are dealing with cosine similarity values of 0.3). The conclusion to draw from this analysis is that the upper bound on recall for our sliding window algorithm is not 1.0, but a more modest 0.76.

The adage "no free lunch" best characterizes our experimental results. There does not appear to be a single optimal solution to the cross-lingual pairwise similarity problem using LSH. Gains in efficiency inevitably come at a cost in effectiveness, and the extent to which it is worthwhile to trade off one for the other depends on application- and resource-specific constraints: i.e., how much recall is necessary, how much computational resources are available, etc. We provide a guide that helps the application developer locate a desirable operating point in the solution space.

We additionally explored the impact on upper bound effectiveness of different representations. Increasing the number of random projections produces longer and therefore more precise signatures, at the cost of linearly increasing running times. This is shown in Table 2, where we repeated the same experiment for 2000- and 3000-bit signatures and show the average time (in ns) to process a single pair. Increasing signature length, however, does not appear

[6]Based on micro-averaging, where the denominator is the sum of ground truth pairs across *all* topics.

Representation	Time (ns)	Precision	Recall
1000-bit	28	0.59	0.76
2000-bit	52	0.74	0.81
3000-bit	84	0.86	0.78
Doc Vector	450	-	-

Table 2: Comparing different representations: average time for a similarity comparison and the level of effectiveness achieved.

to have much of an impact on recall. As a reference, we also show results with the original document vector. Even with 3000 bits, hamming distance calculations are still more than 5 times faster than computing similarity directly on document vectors (which require floating point operations). Once again, there's no free lunch: representations that support faster similarity comparisons sacrifice fidelity.

6.2 Parameter Exploration

It would be desirable to more exhaustively explore the parameter space, beyond the experiments in Figure 5. The major impediment, however, is the long running times of the experiments. Nevertheless, it is possible to separately evaluate effectiveness and efficiency in a meaningful way. The amount of work required by our sliding window algorithm can be quantified by the number of comparisons required. This measure is convenient since it can be computed analytically without actually running experiments, and in some sense is better than (wall clock) running time since it abstracts over hardware differences and other natural variations. Since the results in Figure 5 confirm that our algorithm scales linearly, we can derive a straightforward mapping from number of comparisons to actual running time. To compute effectiveness, we can greatly speed up the experiments by considering only documents in the test set.

The results of separately evaluating effectiveness and efficiency are shown in Figure 6, where we vary the number of tables Q for $B = 200, 500, 1000$. Once again, this characterizes the tradeoff space by showing the recall and relative cost (labeled on the points) that is realized by a particular parameter setting.

Figure 6 also shows recall estimates based on our analytical model from Section 5. As previously discussed, we bound n by $\lfloor \log_2(C/B) \rfloor$ and $\lceil \log_2(C/B) \rceil$, where C is the total number of vectors in the collection: these are shown in the figure as dotted lines (but note overlaps). Despite the simplifications made in that model, we see that the estimates are fairly good. This rough model allows the application developer to tackle arbitrary collections, and *without performing any actual experiments*, estimate the effectiveness that can be achieved with different parameter settings. Combined with the ability to compute efficiency analytically, as we have shown above, the developer can characterize the tradeoff space with minimal effort. Such an analysis addresses a general weakness of LSH approaches: they present a bewildering number of parameters that need to be set, and provide little guidance for a developer approaching new problems. The ability to quantify efficiency and analytically estimate effectiveness provides a powerful tool for tackling the pairwise similarity problem.

In Figure 7, we push our analysis even further with a wider setting of parameters, enabled by separating effectiveness and efficiency measures as above. Each data point is annotated with actual recall achieved. The thick horizontal

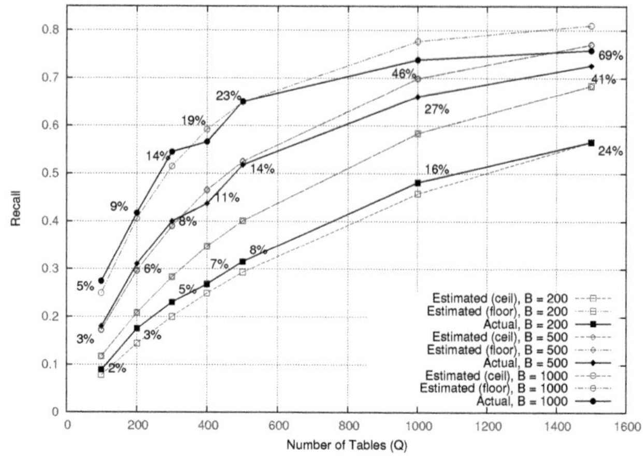

Figure 6: Effectiveness-efficiency tradeoffs of the sliding window LSH algorithm for $\tau = 0.3$, using 1000-bit signatures.

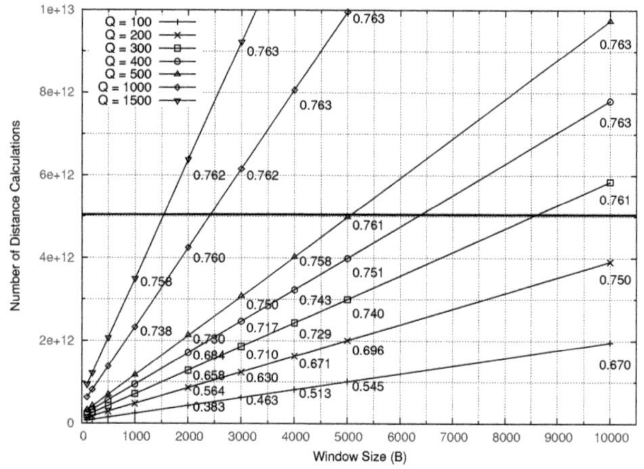

Figure 7: Number of distance calculations and corresponding recall values.

line indicates the number of comparisons required for the brute-force approach. This particular analysis holds important implications for the type of underlying hardware that can be used to run our algorithm. Since the number of tables Q dictates the amount of parallelism that can be extracted, this suggests that larger clusters with more processing capacity may benefit from larger values of Q to increase cluster utilization. On the other hand, a smaller cluster with faster processors might benefit from larger values of B, since the size of the sliding window determines how fast an individual chunk is processed. Once again, there is no one-size-fits-all solution: the most optimal operating point in the tradeoff space will depend on the specifics of a particular application and the computational resources at hand.

One interesting observation is that the brute-force solution should not be so readily dismissed. In fact, to achieve very high levels of recall, the brute-force approach actually requires less work. This is shown in Figure 8: the x-axis plots relative cost, while on the y-axis we normalize effectiveness with respect to the recall upper bound to obtain a relative effectiveness measure. Each of the lines corresponds to a different setting of Q under different settings of B. This

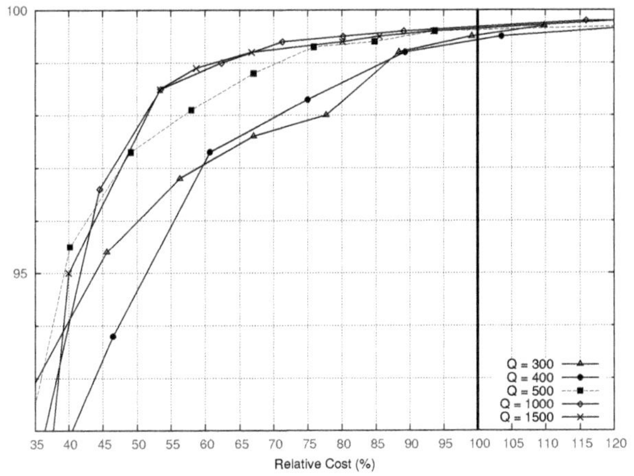

Figure 8: Relative effectiveness vs. relative cost of the sliding window algorithm

shows that if a relative effectiveness of greater than 99.5% is desired, it is more efficient to simply use the brute-force approach. On the other hand, the cost can be reduced significantly by trading off effectiveness. For instance, only 35% of the cost is required to achieve close to 93% relative effectiveness. The algorithm obtains 95% and 98% relative effectiveness with a cost about 60% and 50% less than the brute force approach, respectively. This analysis shows that $Q = 1000$ appears to be a good setting—but once again, there are many practical concerns that need to be taken into account. But inevitably, there is no free lunch, as efficiency can only be gained at the cost of effectiveness.

6.3 Error Analysis

Finally, we analyze the benefits and drawbacks of our end-to-end system, on the task of matching relevant cross lingual documents in Wikipedia. This can be done quantitatively by comparing the algorithm's output to "interwiki" language links. These links are created manually by users, and are supposed to connect pages about the same entity across languages. However, there has been some work showing that these links are inaccurate [9]. Therefore, we find these links unsuitable for use as ground truth, and present the following results with this strong caveat.

To establish a reference on output quality, for each sample German article, we extracted the English article with the highest cosine similarity (using document vectors). The actual "interwiki" links are available from the source of each Wikipedia page, but only 401 of the sample articles had one listed in our downloaded version of Wikipedia. Among those links, our algorithm identified 130 of them (33%) as the most similar article.

A deeper, qualitative analysis shows that our proposed links are generally helpful, and in many cases they are more comprehensive than the existing Wikipedia links. Table 3 shows examples of article pairs that were assigned a cosine score above 0.3. For the German article titled "Metadaten", the algorithm correctly puts "Metadata" at the top of the list and includes two other related articles: "Semantic Web" and "File format". Although "Pierre Curie", "Marie Curie" and "Hélène Langevin-Joliot" are all physicists from the same family, and therefore similar, the algorithm places Marie above Pierre in terms of similarity for the German version. This may be due to the richer content of the article about Marie Curie. For the German article "Kirgisistan", 10 articles about recent events in Kyrgyzstan, its leaders and neighbors are in the output (we show the top five matching articles in Table 3). In short, linking cross-lingual articles via similarity has the potential to discover related articles, not just articles on exactly the same entity.

German article	Top similar articles in English
Metadaten	1. Metadata
	2. Semantic Web
	3. File format
Pierre Curie	1. Marie Curie
	2. Pierre Curie
	3. Hélène Langevin-Joliot
Kirgisistan	1. Kyrgyzstan
	2. Tulip Revolution
	3. 2010 Kyrgyzstani uprising
	4. 2010 South Kyrgyzstan riots
	5. Uzbekistan

Table 3: Examples of relevant German–English article pairs found by our algorithm.

It is interesting that our system was not able to return any similar article for 571 of the 1064 sample German articles. For the remainder, it may simply be the case that a similar article does not exist. This is true especially for articles about specific locations in Germany (e.g., "Dortmund-Aplerbeck"). After analyzing some of these cases by hand, we discovered that there are two common situations where the algorithm struggles. The first is when there is a large gap between the document lengths and contents of the articles in different languages. For instance, the German version of the article about the music show on German TV channel ZDF ("ZDF-Hitparade") is far more comprehensive than the English version. Since cosine similarity measures how similar documents are, it falls below 0.3 in cases like this. Secondly, our system has difficulty matching highly technical articles (e.g., "Farbeindringprüfung", English "Dye penetrant testing"), due to out-of-domain vocabulary; the vector projection has difficulty matching technical terms across languages. This could be solved with more data or special processing of named entities. We will address these issues as part of future work.

7. CONCLUSION AND FUTURE WORK

The cross-lingual pairwise similarity problem requires extracting pairs that have low cosine similarity values—a requirement imposed by the nature of the task. In this work, we explored an LSH-based approach to the problem and analyzed two different components of the solution: the signature generation process and the sliding window algorithm for extracting similar pairs. We showed that 1000-bit signature vectors with random projections are not sufficient to achieve anywhere close to perfect recall but this is the cost of a representation that is significantly faster to process. Our solution is implemented as a parallel, scalable MapReduce algorithm and demonstrated to scale linearly on the two largest Wikipedia collections. We experimentally and analytically quantified the effectiveness-efficiency tradeoff of the sliding window approach with respect to a multitude of parameters. This characterization provides a guide to the application developer in selecting the best operating point for a specific situation. A somewhat surprisingly finding is that a brute-force approach should not be readily dismissed as a viable solution, especially when high recall is desired.

Part of our future work is to improve the representation and translation of documents by including named entity recognition and using broader and larger vocabularies, as well as techniques from natural language processing. German word translations may be very noisy due to compounding and other morphological phenomena, so we plan on experimenting with other language pairs. Using learning methods to find better random projections has been shown to work well [27] and we are interested in adapting that approach to our system. As a logical next step, we would like to go beyond cross-lingual pairwise similarity at the document level to directly extract bilingual sentence pairs, and then use these as an additional source for training machine translation systems. Finally, we hope to show the scalability of our algorithm on even larger datasets.

8. ACKNOWLEDGMENTS

This work has been supported in part by DARPA contract HR0011-06-2-0001 (GALE); NSF under awards IIS-0836560, IIS-0916043, and CCF-1018625. Any opinions, findings, conclusions, or recommendations expressed are the authors' and do not necessarily reflect those of the sponsors. The last author is grateful to Esther and Kiri for their loving support and dedicates this work to Joshua and Jacob.

9. REFERENCES

[1] M. Anderka, B. Stein, and M. Potthast. Cross-language high similarity search. *ECIR*, 2010.

[2] A. Andoni and P. Indyk. Near-optimal hashing algorithms for approximate nearest neighbor in high dimensions. *CACM*, 51(1):117–122, 2008.

[3] R. Bayardo, Y. Ma, and R. Srikant. Scaling up all pairs similarity search. *WWW*, 2007.

[4] A. Broder. On the resemblance and containment of documents. *SEQUENCES*, 1997.

[5] M. Charikar. Similarity estimation techniques from rounding algorithms. *STOC*, 2002.

[6] A. Chowdhury, O. Frieder, D. Grossman, and M. McCabe. Collection statistics for fast duplicate document detection. *ACM TOIS*, 20(2):171–191, 2002.

[7] O. Chum, J. Philbin, and A. Zisserman. Near Duplicate Image Detection: min-Hash and tf-idf Weighting. *British Machine Vision Conference*, 2008.

[8] K. Darwish and D. Oard. Probabilistic structured query methods. *SIGIR*, 2003.

[9] G. de Melo and G. Weikum. Untangling the cross-lingual link structure of Wikipedia. *ACL*, 2010.

[10] J. Dean and S. Ghemawat. MapReduce: Simplified data processing on large clusters. *OSDI*, 2004.

[11] T. Elsayed, J. Lin, and D. Oard. Pairwise document similarity in large collections with MapReduce. *HLT*, 2008.

[12] M. Hadjieleftheriou, A. Chandel, N. Koudas, and D. Srivastava. Fast indexes and algorithms for set similarity selection queries. *ICDE*, 2008.

[13] M. Henzinger. Finding near-duplicate web pages: a large-scale evaluation of algorithms. *SIGIR*, 2006.

[14] L. Huang, L. Wang, and X. Li. Achieving both high precision and high recall in near-duplicate detection. *CIKM*, 2008.

[15] T. Kiefer, P. Volk, and W. Lehner. Pairwise element computation with MapReduce. *HPDC*, 2010.

[16] P. Koehn. *Statistical Machine Translation*. Cambridge University Press, 2010.

[17] A. Kolcz, A. Chowdhury, and J. Alspector. Improved robustness of signature-based near-replica detection via lexicon randomization. *KDD*, 2004.

[18] J. Lin. Brute force and indexed approaches to pairwise document similarity comparisons with MapReduce. *SIGIR*, 2009.

[19] J. Lin, D. Metzler, T. Elsayed, and L. Wang. Of Ivory and Smurfs: Loxodontan MapReduce experiments for web search. *TREC*, 2009.

[20] G. Manku, A. Jain, and A. Das Sarma. Detecting near-duplicates for web crawling. *WWW*, 2007.

[21] H. Masuichi, R. Flournoy, S. Kaufmann, and S. Peters. A bootstrapping method for extracting bilingual text pairs. *COLING*, 2000.

[22] S. Matthews and T. Williams. MrsRF: An efficient MapReduce algorithm for analyzing large collections of evolutionary trees. *BMC Bioinformatics*, 11(Suppl 1):S15, 2010.

[23] C. Moretti, J. Bulosan, D. Thain, and P. Flynn. All-Pairs: An abstraction for data-intensive cloud computing. *IPDPS*, 2008.

[24] D. Munteanu and D. Marcu. Improving machine translation performance by exploiting non-parallel corpora. *Comp. Ling.*, 31(4):477–504, 2005.

[25] F. Och and H. Ney. A systematic comparison of various statistical alignment models. *Comp. Ling.*, 29(1):19–51, 2003.

[26] P. Pantel, E. Crestan, A. Borkovsky, A.-M. Popescu, and V. Vyas. Web-scale distributional similarity and entity set expansion. *EMNLP*, 2009.

[27] J. Platt, K. Toutanova, and W.-t. Yih. Translingual document representations from discriminative projections. *EMNLP*, 2010.

[28] D. Ravichandran, P. Pantel, and E. Hovy. Randomized algorithms and NLP: Using locality sensitive hash functions for high speed noun clustering. *ACL*, 2005.

[29] P. Resnik and N. Smith. The web as a parallel corpus. *Comp. Ling.*, 29(3):349–380, 2003.

[30] S. Robertson, S. Walker, S. Jones, M. Hancock-Beaulieu, and M. Gatford. Okapi at TREC-3. *TREC-3*, 1994.

[31] J. Smith, C. Quirk, and K. Toutanova. Extracting parallel sentences from comparable corpora using document level alignment. *HLT*, 2010.

[32] M. Theobald, J. Siddharth, and A. Paepcke. SpotSigs: robust and efficient near duplicate detection in large web collections. *SIGIR*, 2008.

[33] R. Vernica, M. Carey, and C. Li. Efficient parallel set-similarity joins using MapReduce. *SIGMOD*, 2010.

[34] S. Vogel, H. Ney, and C. Tillmann. HMM-based word alignment in statistical translation. *COLING*, 1996.

[35] H. Yang and J. Callan. Near-duplicate detection by instance-level constrained clustering. *SIGIR*, 2006.

[36] D. Zhang, J. Wang, D. Cai, and J. Lu. Self-taught hashing for fast similarity search. *SIGIR*, 2010.

An Event-centric Model for Multilingual Document Similarity

Jannik Strötgen
Institute of Computer Science
Heidelberg University
Heidelberg, Germany
stroetgen@uni-hd.de

Michael Gertz
Institute of Computer Science
Heidelberg University
Heidelberg, Germany
gertz@uni-hd.de

Conny Junghans
Institute of Computer Science
Heidelberg University
Heidelberg, Germany
cj@uni-hd.de

ABSTRACT

Document similarity measures play an important role in many document retrieval and exploration tasks. Over the past decades, several models and techniques have been developed to determine a ranked list of documents similar to a given query document. Interestingly, the proposed approaches typically rely on extensions to the vector space model and are rarely suited for multilingual corpora.

In this paper, we present a novel document similarity measure that is based on events extracted from documents. An event is solely described by nearby occurrences of temporal and geographic expressions in a document's text. Thus, a document is modeled as a set of events that can be compared and ranked using temporal and geographic hierarchies. A key feature of our model is that it is term- and language-independent as temporal and geographic expressions mentioned in texts are normalized to a standard format. This also allows to determine similar documents across languages, an important feature in the context of document exploration. Our approach proves to be quite effective, including the discovery of new similarities, as our experiments using different (multilingual) corpora demonstrate.

Categories and Subject Descriptors

I.5 [**Pattern Recognition**]: Clustering—*Similarity measures*; I.2.7 [**Artificial Intelligence**]: Natural Language Processing—*Language models, Text analysis*

General Terms

Algorithms, Languages

1. INTRODUCTION

When are two documents similar? This is the question essential to tasks such as document classification, clustering, or topic detection and tracking. To address this often subjective and application specific question, over the past decades several approaches for modeling the similarity of text documents have been developed (see, e.g., [12]). Respective approaches range from extensions to the vector space model, such as latent semantic analysis [6], to techniques that employ explicit knowledge representation schemes such as ontologies to estimate semantic relatedness (e.g., [9]). In general, documents can be similar according to the words they contain, their structure, the topic they address, or the semantic concepts that have been associated with the documents. This plethora of different similarity aspects clearly does not lead to a single, universally applicable document similarity measure. Instead, different measures may lead to new insights into document similarity that cannot be captured by just one single approach.

In this paper, we present a novel similarity approach that is based on an event-centric document model. Loosely speaking, an event is something that happens at a specific place and time. Our claim is that for many categories of documents, events are essential to describe a topic or theme. This holds, among others, for historical works or biographies, an aspect we will elaborate on later in this paper. Our approach is based on a simple characterization of an event: it is solely described by nearby occurrences of a temporal expression and a geographic expression in a document's text. We thus do not rely on complex statistical NLP-based techniques or rich ontology-based frameworks for extracting event descriptions from documents. In particular, the proposed model leads to a small footprint for documents as only sets of events extracted from documents need to be managed and used for the proposed document similarity measure.

There are two key aspects to temporal and geographic expressions describing events. First, both can be normalized in an explicit way. No matter what original expressions are used in the documents, they can be normalized to the same value represented in a standard date notation (for a temporal expression) or as a coordinate (for a geographic/location expression). Grounding our event-centric model on such types of information makes the model term- and language-independent. The model therefore allows to compare documents written in different languages. Second, with both temporal and location information simple concept hierarchies are associated that specify a containment relationship. For example, the granularity of temporal information (as part of an event) can be of type day, like '2011-01-14', or type month, like in '2011-01', with the former being contained in the latter. Similarly, different granularities can be associated with geographic information, such as city, county, country, etc. Exploiting the different levels of granularity for event specifications provides for an interesting technique to compare events extracted from documents. Thus, two documents may still be similar in terms of the events they contain even though the documents do not describe exactly the same events. Exploring event-based similarities among documents may also lead to new information that was not explicit before. For example, even though two documents talk about completely different topics, they both may mention the same event. This new information then can be used to investigate and establish new cross-document references.

In summary, the paper's main contributions are as follows:

- We describe a concise and succinct way to represent event information extracted from documents in the form of so-called document event profiles.
- We incrementally develop and present a model for an event-based document similarity measure that is term- and language-independent. The measure is based on normalized temporal and geographic expressions that can be compared using simple hierarchies for temporal and geographic concepts, respectively.
- We demonstrate the effectiveness of our new approach using different evaluations. For this, we investigate bilingual corpora (English and German) to show that our model identifies new document similarities across languages and topics, which are usually not detected by term-based methods.

The remainder of the paper is structured as follows. After a review of related work, we detail the extraction and representation of event information in documents in Section 3. In Section 4, we outline a similarity measure for pairs of events and extend this approach in Section 5 to compare event sets extracted from documents. In Section 6, we present a comprehensive evaluation of the proposed approach using different (multilingual) corpora. We conclude our paper in Section 7.

2. RELATED WORK

There are many approaches to the computation of document similarity in different IR related tasks such as document classification and clustering. In standard information retrieval, documents are typically represented as vectors, as are the queries [2, 14]. These vectors consisting of weights, such as tf-idf, for all terms in the documents are then used to calculate the similarity between a query and a document or two documents. There are numerous approaches to improve this standard similarity measure, e.g., by using (probabilistic) latent semantic analysis to analyze conceptual contents [4, 6]. Chim and Deng use phrase-based document similarity for clustering and show that feature vectors of phrase terms can be seen as expanded feature vectors for single-word terms [5]. Because of the large footprint of the vector space model for documents, the MapReduce framework was recently applied to large corpora for calculating document similarity [8].

An interesting empirical evaluation of models for text document similarity was conducted by Lee et al. [12]. They conclude that many automatic models have very good precision, but poor recall. That is, they detect only a subset of highly semantically similar document pairs. This observation is a motivation for our approach, because we do not want to replace existing similarity measures, but we do want to provide a measure for non-standard document similarity to identify new information, that is, event-based similarity relationships between documents.

An area related to our approach is topic clustering and in particular topic detection and tracking (TDT) where items of a document stream (e.g., a news stream) are analyzed. The goals of these approaches are to detect new unreported news events, and to track topics by assigning documents to already detected events [1]. There is a lot of research dealing with TDT for which the identification of events is necessary. Often, the similarity measures use information of named entity recognition, for example, locations, temporal expressions, or person and organization names mentioned in the documents [13, 27]. In contrast to our work, however, TDT systems try to identify a main event that can be associated with documents. Our goal, on the other hand, is to identify as many events in documents as possible, and to use the identified events for calculating document similarity.

Similar to our approach of applying concept hierarchies to temporal and geographic information, Lakkaraju et al. [11] use general concept trees to classify documents according to a taxonomy. Our concept hierarchies, however, are very small (less than 20 concepts in total) and specific to (standard) temporal and geographic aspects. There is also related research on similarities for event identification in social media [3]. In this work, however, they study general types of events and are not specifically concerned with temporal and geographic information. Some work combining geographic and temporal information extracted from documents for search and exploration tasks has been studied in [15, 20] but without focusing on document similarity.

As already pointed out, our model for document similarity is based on a combination of geographic and temporal information to identify events. We need to clarify that we do not consider events in the same way as it is done in linguistics, e.g., in TimeML, the standard markup language for temporal annotations [24]. Instead, we consider something to be an event if it is described by a temporal and a geographic expression. In the area of cross-language information retrieval, similarities are calculated on multilingual corpora. These calculations are usually based on translations while our approach uses normalized, language-independent information. There is only very few work on multilingual, translation-independent document similarity. One approach that makes use of a multilingual thesaurus for computing similarities has been proposed by Steinberger et al. in [18].

3. GEOGRAPHIC AND TEMPORAL INFORMATION IN DOCUMENTS

In contrast to most other works where a single temporal value (the document timestamp) and no geographic value are associated with a document, we use all geographic and temporal information mentioned in documents to form events. Therefore, we need to extract and normalize all geographic and temporal expressions using a geo-tagger and a temporal tagger. These named entity recognition and normalization tasks are outlined in the following Sections 3.1 and 3.2. In addition, we describe how the granularities of geographic and temporal expressions can be used for comparing expressions of different granularities. In Section 3.3, we combine geographic and temporal information into so-called document event profiles, which form the basis for our analysis of event-based document similarity.

3.1 Temporal Information

Temporal expressions can be grouped into four types, as done in the standard meta language for temporal annotations, TimeML [21]: *date*, *time*, *duration*, and *set*. In this paper, we only consider expressions of type *date*, although our method is suitable to support other types as well. Dates are anchored in a timeline, and a date's position in a timeline is referred to as its normalized value. It is important to note that the normalized value of a temporal expression, called *chronon*, is independent of the language used in the according document. Thus, this representation is perfectly suited for multilingual analysis tasks.

Normalization is done assuming a discrete representation of time, based on the Gregorian Calendar. Temporal expressions can be of different granularities, such as day, week, month, year, or decade. For the representation of these granularities, we assume different timelines, e.g., T_{day} for days and T_{month} for months. For example, 'March 19, 1999' can be anchored in T_{day} while 'May 2010' can be anchored in T_{month}. Timelines can be ordered into a hierarchy, which is a crucial point for our analysis of event-based similarities between documents. A hierarchy of temporal information granularities is given in Figure 1(a). Although there are other possible timelines (finer ones like hours or coarser ones like centuries), we use the following timelines for our hierarchy: $\mathcal{T} = \{T_{day}, T_{month}, T_{year}, T_{decade}\}$. A mapping can be performed from a value of a finer granularity to a coarser granularity, since months consist of days, years consist of months, and decades consist of years. The mapping from one timeline to the next coarser one is defined as one *temporal mapping step* α_t. For example, α_t('1999-03-19') ='1999-03' and $\alpha_t(\alpha_t$('1999-03-19')) = '1999'.

For the extraction and normalization of temporal expressions in documents, so-called *temporal taggers* are employed. Examples include GUTime, which is part of the Tarsqi toolkit [23], or HeidelTime [19], which was the best performing system for identifying and normalizing English temporal expressions in the TempEval 2010 challenge [24]. Using such temporal taggers, the following information about temporal expressions is extracted and used for further analysis: the offset (start and end position) of the expression in the document, the type (date, time, etc.), and chronon (normalized value). In Section 6, we give more details about the specific document processing pipeline employed in our approach.

3.2 Geographic Information

In the same way temporal expressions like dates refer to a point in time, geographic expressions refer to locations. We assume that with each geographic expression a geometry can be associated, which is represented as a latitude/longitude value pair. For the extraction and normalization of geographic expressions in documents, named entity recognition (NER) tools for locations can be used. Such *geo-taggers* usually use gazetteers and context information for the disambiguation of location names. Examples of such tools are MetaCarta [16] and Yahoo Placemaker [26]. Note that normalized location information is language-independent in the same way as temporal information.

Usually, geo-taggers only assign point geometry information to a location, regardless of the actual geographic extent of the location. Nevertheless, containment information, e.g., that a city is in a state or country, is often associated with an extracted expression. For example, the normalized con-

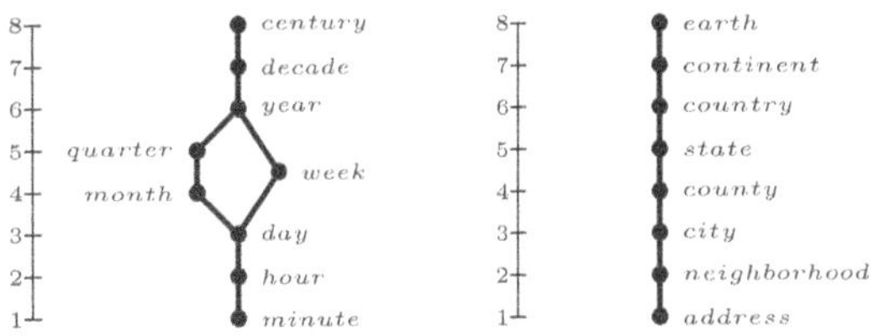

(a) Temporal hierarchy. (b) Geographic hierarchy.

Figure 1: Concept hierarchies for geographic and temporal information.

tainment information about 'New York City', which can be referred to by expressions such as 'New York, NY, US', 'New York', 'NYC', or 'Big Apple', is 'New York, NY, US'. This containment relationship is very important for geographic information and can be used directly and formalized in the following way: If a location g_i is contained in a location g_j, the relationship is denoted $g_i \subset_G g_j$. For example, the fact that a city g_1 is contained in a country g_2 can be expressed as $g_1 \subset_G g_2$.

Similar to the hierarchy of timelines for temporal expressions, the hierarchy of locations is crucial for our similarity measure. A general overview of the hierarchy of geographic information is depicted in Figure 1(b). Although there are many other levels (finer ones like addresses or coarser ones like continents), we use the following granularities for our hierarchy: city, state, and country. The mapping from one granularity to the next coarser one is defined as one *geographic mapping step* α_g. For example, α_g('San Diego, CA, USA') ='CA, USA'.

3.3 Document Event Profiles

As mentioned in Section 1, events in our scenario are co-occurrences of geographic and temporal expressions in a document. While there are several ways to form events from such expressions found in documents, we consider a pair of a geographic and a temporal expression to form an event if the two expressions occur in the same sentence. This method is much more precise than forming events from the cross-product of all pairs of geographic and temporal expressions in a document, which results in many false positives. Also, our method is much more efficient than a complete linguistic analysis of the documents, which is infeasible for large corpora.

We summarize the information about the geographic and the temporal dimension of all events in a given document d in a *document event profile*, denoted *dep*(d). The idea behind document profiles is to describe the information textually mentioned in a document in a concise manner and to make it accessible for further analysis. More precisely, a document event profile *dep*(d) contains a set of pairs $\langle(t_i, c_i, p(t)_i),$ $(g_i, v_i, p(g)_i)\rangle$ with (1) t_i and g_i being the temporal and geographic expressions occurring at the sentence level, (2) c_i and v_i being their normalized temporal (chronon) and geographic values, and (3) $p(t)_i$ and $p(g)_i$ being the offset of both expressions in document d. Instead of just recording the latitude/longitude information, we include the normalized containment information as the normalized geographic value v_i, since our similarity measure exploits this information. Note that events can be of different geographic granularities and timelines. Nevertheless, they can be compared using geographic and temporal mappings α_t and α_g, which were described in the previous paragraphs.

To summarize, in our approach, a document is solely described by an event profile. Compared to a vector space representation, our event-centric document model leads to a small amount of information that is used to compute the document similarity based on events. This computation and underlying similarity measure will be discussed next.

4. EVENT SIMILARITY

In this section, we introduce the fundamental step for calculating event-centric document similarity, which is the comparison of two arbitrary events. Specifically, we first describe the problem setting for computing the similarity of two events by specifying the requirements for such a similarity function in Section 4.1. In Section 4.2, we develop the similarity function and verify that all requirements are fulfilled. The similarity of pairs of events is then used in our new approach for calculating event-based document similarities, which will be detailed in Section 5.

4.1 Event Similarity Function Requirements

For comparing any two events, we use the normalized values of their temporal and geographic information as described in Section 3. Thus, an event is described by a chronon c and a normalized geographic value v. We call c and v the *dimensions* of an event $e = \langle c, v \rangle$. Both dimensions can be mapped to coarser granularities using the temporal and geographic mapping steps α_t and α_g introduced in Sections 3.1 and 3.2, respectively.

In order to define the requirements for the similarity function for events, denoted sim_e, we first list all possible similarity cases that can occur. In the listed cases, we do not distinguish the number of granularity mapping steps that have to be applied for one dimension, but use c^* for c and v^* for v being mapped to any coarser granularity. Given two events $e_1 = \langle c_1, v_1 \rangle$ and $e_2 = \langle c_2, v_2 \rangle$, the following similarities can occur:

1. Values of both dimensions of the events are identical.
   (1.1) $c_1 = c_2$ and $v_1 = v_2$
2. The values of one dimension have to be mapped to a coarser granularity.
   (2.1) $c_1^* = c_2$ and $v_1 = v_2$ (2.3) $c_1 = c_2$ and $v_1^* = v_2$
   (2.2) $c_1^* = c_2^*$ and $v_1 = v_2$ (2.4) $c_1 = c_2$ and $v_1^* = v_2^*$
3. The values of both dimensions have to be mapped to a coarser granularity.
   (3.1) $c_1^* = c_2$ and $v_1^* = v_2$ (3.4) $c_1^* = c_2$ and $v_1^* = v_2^*$
   (3.2) $c_1^* = c_2$ and $v_1 = v_2^*$ (3.5) $c_1^* = c_2^*$ and $v_1^* = v_2^*$
   (3.3) $c_1^* = c_2^*$ and $v_1^* = v_2$
4. It is not possible to map the values of one dimension to a coarser granularity to achieve equality.
   (4.1) $c_1^* \neq c_2^*$ and $v_1 = v_2$ (4.4) $c_1 = c_2$ and $v_1^* \neq v_2^*$
   (4.2) $c_1^* \neq c_2^*$ and $v_1^* = v_2$ (4.5) $c_1^* = c_2$ and $v_1^* \neq v_2^*$
   (4.3) $c_1^* \neq c_2^*$ and $v_1^* = v_2^*$ (4.6) $c_1^* = c_2^*$ and $v_1^* \neq v_2^*$
5. It is not possible to map the values of both dimensions to a coarser granularity to achieve equality.
   (5.1) $c_1^* \neq c_2^*$ and $v_1^* \neq v_2^*$

Using the listed set of possible cases, we now detail the requirements for the similarity function sim_e. For this, we state requirements followed by their detailed description.

R1: The more similar e_1 and e_2, the higher sim_e.

The more similar two events e_1 and e_2 are, the higher should be their similarity $sim_e(e_1, e_2)$, with $sim_e(e_1, e_2)$ being maximal if both events are identical. In (1.1), the events are identical and thus should have the highest possible similarity value.

R2: The fewer values of the same dimension need to be mapped, the higher sim_e.

In the second group, either at least one of the chronons has to be mapped to a coarser timeline (2.1 and 2.2) or at least one normalized geographic value has to be mapped to a coarser granularity (2.3 and 2.4). If only one value has to be mapped (2.1 and 2.3), the similarity score should be higher than if both values have to be mapped (2.2 and 2.4). This reflects the fact that the former ones can be correct (although described in an imprecise way) while the latter ones cannot be correct. For example, the sentences *he visits NYC in May 2010* and *he visits NYC on May 4, 2010* can talk about the same event. In contrast, the sentences *he visits NYC in May 2010* and *he visits NYC in April 2010* cannot talk about the same event. Nevertheless, there still is a similarity between e_1 and e_2 in the latter example, since both events happened at the same location and temporally close to each other (both in 2010). Consequently, sim_e should be higher for (2.1) and (2.3) and penalize (2.2) and (2.4).

The same cases occur in the third group: If only one value of each dimension has to be mapped (3.1, 3.2), the similarity score should be higher than if both values of the same dimension are involved (3.3, 3.4, and 3.5).

R3: If mapping leads to no equality, sim_e should be 0.

In the fourth group, either the chronons or the normalized geographic expressions cannot be mapped to a coarser granularity to achieve equality. In the fifth group both types of normalized values cannot be mapped sufficiently. Note that whether such cases can occur depends on the used hierarchies for geographic and temporal mappings (cf. Figure 1). For example, if 'Earth' is used as the top level of the geographic hierarchy, then every geographic expression can be mapped to the top of the hierarchy. However, if 'country' is at the top level, then, e.g., cities located in different countries cannot be mapped to a coarser granularity to achieve equality. Thus, if no sufficient mapping can be found, the assigned similarity score sim_e is 0, even though there may be a temporal or geographic similarity when using a different hierarchy. Instead, such unmatched events influence the aggregated similarity score when comparing two documents, as detailed in Section 5.

R4: The fewer mapping steps are needed, the higher sim_e.

The similarity score additionally depends on the differences of granularity between either c and c^* or v and v^*. The granularities are defined in Sections 3.1 and 3.2, and are represented by the timelines for temporal information and by the containment hierarchy for geographic expressions. The larger the differences, the less precise the information.

R5: The finer the granularities, the higher sim_e.

So far, the original granularities of the values, i.e., before they are mapped to coarser granularities, are not taken into account. For example, if there are two events $e_1 = \langle(2006), (\text{Germany})\rangle$ and $e_2 = \langle(2006\text{-}07\text{-}09), (\text{Berlin,Germany})\rangle$, then

$sim_e(e_1, e_1)$ should not equal $sim_e(e_2, e_2)$, as the similarity score should be sensitive to the original granularities of the events in the documents. An event that is mentioned more fine-grained in the document should be weighted higher than a coarser one, i.e., $sim_e(e_1, e_1) < sim_e(e_2, e_2)$ should hold.

4.2 Event Similarity Function

Having defined the requirements for a similarity measure for pairs of events, we now formalize a function $sim_e(e_1, e_2)$ that fulfills these requirements. As stated above, $sim_e(e_1, e_2) > 0$ only holds if equality of two events $e_1 = \langle c_1, v_1 \rangle$ and $e_2 = \langle c_2, v_2 \rangle$ can be achieved, namely by applying a certain number of mapping steps to the geographic and temporal dimensions of the events. We define $\alpha = \alpha_t + \alpha_g$ as the number of mapping steps that are needed to achieve equality for events e_1 and e_2 in both dimensions. Specifically, α_t is the sum of the number of temporal mapping steps that need to be applied to c_1 and c_2, respectively, in order to achieve equality in the temporal dimension. α_g is the corresponding sum of the number of mapping steps applied to v_1 and v_2 in the geographic dimension. That is, $\alpha \in \{0, \ldots, 2k\}$ with k being the total number of possible geographic and temporal mapping steps. Furthermore, we define β to be the maximum of the number of values per dimension that are involved in the mapping, thus $\beta \in \{0, 1, 2\}$. We tentatively define the event-centric similarity $sim_e(e_1, e_2)$ to be calculated in the following way:

$$sim_e(e_1, e_2) = \frac{1}{(1+\alpha)^\beta} \qquad (1)$$

While α is used to moderately decrease $sim_e(e_1, e_2)$, β increases the denominator exponentially, thus penalizing the similarity score stronger than α. This is motivated by requirement R2 that e_1 and e_2 can refer to the same event if $\beta = 1$, but cannot if $\beta = 2$ – no matter how large α is.

Equation 1 fulfills requirements R1 through R4 as will be shown below. However, it does not yet support R5 (the finer the original granularities, the higher sim_e). Thus, we additionally consider a parameter α_{poss}, which is the number of mapping steps (both temporal and geographic) that are still possible for e_1 and e_2 after both events have been mapped to be of equal granularity in both dimensions. That is, for example, if e_1 and e_2 were mapped to both represent $\langle (c = \text{2006-06}, v = \text{Germany}) \rangle$, then $\alpha_{poss} = 2$, as no further mapping step is possible for v and two more mapping steps are possible for c (year and decade). By weighting sim_e with $\alpha_{poss} + 1$, R5 is supported by our similarity function. Adding 1 to α_{poss} is necessary as the similarity of the coarsest granularity would be 0 otherwise.

$$sim_e(e_1, e_2) = \frac{1}{(1+\alpha)^\beta} \times (\alpha_{poss} + 1) \qquad (2)$$

Equation 2 fulfills all requirements R1 through R5, and can thus be used for calculating the similarity of two events. To exemplarily verify this, we calculate the similarity scores between four events (Table 1) and show that all five requirements are met. For better readability, we demonstrate this example using only the granularities day, month, and year for the temporal dimension, and city and country for the geographic dimension.

Although R1 (the more similar e_1 and e_2, the higher sim_e) is a subjective formulation, there are some examples in Table 1 for which this formulation is obvious, e.g., e_4 is more similar to e_3 than to e_1. This example shows that sim_e is calculated correctly with respect to R1, since $sim_e(e_3, e_4) > sim_e(e_1, e_4)$. R4 (the fewer mapping steps are needed, the higher sim_e) is considered by sim_e since, e.g., $sim_e(e_3, e_4)$ (one mapping step is needed) is higher than $sim_e(e_1, e_4)$ (three mapping steps are needed). The fact that R2 is taken into account can be shown directly using Equation 2. If zero, one, or two values of the same dimension need to be mapped, then β equals 0, 1, or 2, respectively. For $\beta = 0$, the denominator of Equation 2 equals 1. If $\beta > 0$, then $\alpha > 0$ and thus, $(1+\alpha) < (1+\alpha)^2$, i.e., R2 is fulfilled since $sim_e(\beta = 1) > sim_e(\beta = 2)$. The consideration of R5 (the finer the granularities, the higher sim_e) is already achieved by the modification from Equation 1 to Equation 2. Finally, if no equality can be achieved with any number of mappings, Equation 2 is defined as $sim_e(e_1, e_2) = 0$, i.e., R4 is fulfilled.

id	events
(e_1)	$\langle$(2006),(Germany)$\rangle$
(e_2)	$\langle$(2006-07),(Stuttgart,Germany)$\rangle$
(e_3)	$\langle$(2006-06),(Berlin,Germany)$\rangle$
(e_4)	$\langle$(2006-06-09),(Berlin,Germany)$\rangle$

	e_1	e_2	e_3	e_4
e_1	1	0.33	0.33	0.25
e_2		3	0.04	0.03
e_3			3	1.5
e_4				4

Table 1: Events (left) and similarity scores between them calculated using Equation 2 (right).

5. EVENT-CENTRIC DOCUMENT SIMILARITY

Defining the similarity of just two events is already not trivial and many requirements need to be satisfied by the similarity function, as discussed in the previous section. However, aggregating the similarity of two sets of events in a meaningful way is even more challenging. Therefore, before defining how to calculate a respective aggregation, we first give the problem statement and define some requirements for this aggregation in Section 5.1. Then, an event-based document similarity model satisfying these requirements is incrementally developed in Section 5.2.

5.1 Problem Statement

Informally, the problem of computing the event-centric document similarity can be stated as follows: Given two documents d_1 and d_2 represented through their document event profiles $dep(d_1)$ and $dep(d_2)$, with each profile describing a multiset of events. Using the profiles, compute the event-centric document similarity $sim_e(d_1, d_2)$ in a concise and meaningful way.

To be able to specify a suitable similarity function, we first formalize some requirements for the aggregation of event similarities that need to be fulfilled:

A1: the more matching events are in d_1 and d_2, the higher $sim_e(d_1, d_2)$

A2: the more non-matching events are in d_1 and d_2, the more $sim_e(d_1, d_2)$ should be penalized

A3: if only one document contains additional events, this should not be penalized as much as if both documents contain additional non-matching events

In addition, all the requirements formulated for event similarities apply here, too. That is, requirements R1 to R5 described in Section 4.1 can be summarized as:

A4: the more similar the events in d_1 and d_2, the higher $sim_e(d_1, d_2)$

5.2 Aggregation of Event Similarities

Given a document, the objective now is to determine a ranked list of most similar documents using the information given by their document event profiles. The simplest way to calculate this similarity is to view all events as terms. For every document, these terms then form a vector so that the similarity between two documents can be calculated by comparing their vectors with, e.g., the cosine similarity function. This simple approach satisfies A1. However, other requirements are not fulfilled, in particular A4 is not taken into account. Therefore, we base our model on the similarity function between events introduced in Section 4.2 (Equation 2). For this, we use the following methods:

- *granularity mapping* (M): both dimensions of an event are mapped to all coarser granularities to enable the comparison between two different events
- *granularity weighting* (W): two matching events are weighted according to their granularities

To satisfy A1 and A3, we furthermore utilize

- *quantity normalization* (N): the similarity score calculated for two documents is normalized with respect to the number of events in their document event profiles

For realizing these methods, the vector approach is not applicable since not only exact matches are considered but matches between events after granularity mapping. Therefore, instead of comparing vectors, we perform event alignment by building the cross-product of the document event profiles to compare all event pairs. If two events are not equal, they will be mapped to coarser granularities until equality is reached or no further mapping is possible. The similarity score for every pair is calculated according to $sim_e(e_1, e_2)$ (cf. Equation 2) and aggregated to $sim_e(d_1, d_2)$.

However, requirement A2 is not fulfilled so far. Therefore, we have to normalize $sim_e(d_1, d_2)$ according to the number of events in the documents. For two documents d_1 and d_2 containing n and m events, respectively, using the sum $n+m$ violates A3. Thus, we use $min(n, m)$ for normalization and $sim_e(d_1, d_2)$ is thus calculated as follows:

$$sim_e(d_1, d_2) = \frac{\sum_{i=0}^{n} \sum_{j=0}^{m} sim_e(e_i, e_j)}{min(n, m)} \quad (3)$$

This equation together with the methods M, W, and N represents our full document similarity model (FM). To analyze the influence of the different methods, we use three further models in our evaluation: a model without granularity mapping (FM-M), a model without granularity mapping and granularity weighting (FM-MW), and additionally a model without normalization (FM-MWN).

To calculate $sim_e(d_1, d_2)$ efficiently, we map and materialize the events to all coarser granularities before comparing pairs of events. This way, the mapping does not have to be done every time an event is compared with another one. An example showing how the granularities are used for the calculation is given in Table 2. At the top of Table 2(a) and 2(b), the original events of document d_1 and document d_2 are given. Below them, the original events and their mappings are grouped by α_{poss} since two events with different α_{poss} values cannot be equal, and thus do not have to be compared. Note that for better clarity, we only use day, month and year, and city and country as temporal and geographic concepts in the hierarchies, respectively. In Table 2(c), we show the steps for comparing some events.

Algorithm 1 CalculateSimE($dep1$, $dep2$)

```
1: sim = 0
2: aposs = (3, 2, 1, 0) {allowed mapping steps}
3: mappings1 = create_mappings(dep1)
4: mappings2 = create_mappings(dep2)
5: for all e1 in dep1 do
6:    for all e2 in dep2 do
7:       todo.add(e1.id_e2.id) {store ids in a hash set}
8: for all poss in aposs do
9:    for all e1 in mappings1(poss) do
10:      for all e2 in mappings2(poss) do
11:         if e1.term = e2.term then
12:            for all id1 in e1.getidset do
13:               for all id2 in e2.getidset do
14:                  if todo(id1_id2) then
15:                     todo.remove(id1_id2)
16:                     sim += get_sim(id1.t, id1.g, id2.t, id2.g, poss)
17:                     if todo.length = 0 then
18:                        return sim/min(dep1.length, dep2.length)
19: return sim/min(dep1.length, dep2.length)
```

The pseudocode for computing the similarity of two documents represented by their event profiles $dep1$ and $dep2$ is shown in Algorithm 1. In line 2, all values of α_{poss} are listed in descending sort order, with 3 being the highest value in our example. In lines 3 and 4, the possible mappings of all events in the document event profiles of d_1 and d_2 are precalculated. This results in the mappings grouped by α_{poss} as shown in Table 2(a) and 2(b). Using the ids of the events, the cross-product is calculated in lines 5 to 7 and stored in the hash set *todo*. Then, the real calculation starts with iterating over the sorted α_{poss} and the events contained in the mappings of the respective α_{poss}. If two events match (line 11), all ids of the events are combined by iterating over the events' ids (lines 12-13). In the example (Table 2), four event pairs are compared for $\alpha_{poss} = 3$ with one matching pair (a,f). Once $\alpha_{poss} = 0$, one event pair is left containing several ids for each document. However, not all event pairs are still in *todo*, i.e., their similarity might already have been calculated (e.g., for a,f). If the id pair is still in *todo* (line 14), the pair is removed from the hash set (line 15) and the event similarity score is added to the total score *sim* (line 16). The method *get_sim* calculates the similarity between two events according to Equation 2 (Section 4.2). Method *get_sim* accesses values α_t and α_g of events through their ids, e.g., *c.t* represents the value of α_t for event *c*. For better efficiency, the results can directly be stored in a hash map, since they are limited to the combinations of *id1.t*, *id1.g*, *id2.t*, *id2.g*, and *poss*. Finally, if the *todo* hash set is empty (lines 17-18) or if all α_{poss} are processed (line 19), the similarity score is normalized by dividing *sim* by the minimum of the lengths of *dep1* and *dep2* and returned. In the example, the aggregated similarity score is divided by 3, i.e., the number of events extracted from document *d2*.

In summary, using the above approach, a document similarity measure can effectively be computed solely based on document event profiles. Several optimizations can be applied to this computation (e.g., binning of events based on some granularity such as year and then only computing cross-products for same-year bins). Due to space constraints and to allow for a concise representation of our approach, these optimizations are not discussed in this paper. In the next section, we demonstrate that this new event-based similarity measure for documents is meaningful and also applies to multilingual corpora.

(a) Document d_1.

Original Events		
a	2006-07-09	Berlin, Germany
b	2006-06-09	Munich, Germany
c	2006-06	Germany
d	2006	Germany

Mappings of events		
$\alpha_{poss} = 3$		
$a_{0,0}$	2006-07-09	Berlin, Germany
$b_{0,0}$	2006-06-09	Munich, Germany
$\alpha_{poss} = 2$		
$a_{1,0}$	2006-07	Berlin, Germany
$b_{1,0}$	2006-06	Munich, Germany
$a_{0,1}$	2006-07-09	Germany
$b_{0,1}$	2006-06-09	Germany
$\alpha_{poss} = 1$		
$a_{2,0}$	2006	Berlin, Germany
$b_{2,0}$	2006	Munich, Germany
$a_{1,1}$	2006-07	Germany
$b_{1,1}$, $c_{0,0}$	2006-06	Germany
$\alpha_{poss} = 0$		
$a_{2,1}$, $b_{2,1}$, $c_{1,0}$, $d_{0,0}$	2006	Germany

(b) Document d_2.

Original Events		
e	2006-07-08	Bonn, Germany
f	2006-07-09	Berlin, Germany
g	2006	Germany

Mappings of events		
$\alpha_{poss} = 3$		
$e_{0,0}$	2006-07-08	Bonn, Germany
$f_{0,0}$	2006-07-09	Berlin, Germany
$\alpha_{poss} = 2$		
$e_{1,0}$	2006-06	Bonn, Germany
$f_{1,0}$	2006-07	Berlin, Germany
$e_{0,1}$	2006-06-09	Germany
$f_{0,1}$	2006-07-09	Germany
$\alpha_{poss} = 1$		
$e_{2,0}$	2006	Bonn, Germany
$f_{2,0}$	2006	Berlin, Germany
$e_{1,1}$, $f_{1,1}$	2006-07	Germany
$\alpha_{poss} = 0$		
$e_{2,1}$, $f_{2,1}$, $g_{0,0}$	2006	Germany

(c) Similarity Calculation.

pair	match	α	β	α_{poss}
a, e	$a_{1,1}$, $e_{1,1}$	4	2	1
a, f	$a_{0,0}$, $f_{0,0}$	0	0	3
a, g	$a_{2,1}$, $g_{0,0}$	3	1	0
...				
c, g	$c_{1,0}$, $g_{0,0}$	1	1	0
...				
d, g	$d_{0,0}$, $g_{0,0}$	0	0	0

Single similarities:

$$sim_e(a,e) = 0.08$$
$$sim_e(a,f) = 4$$
$$sim_e(a,g) = 0.25$$
$$\dots$$
$$sim_e(c,g) = 0.5$$
$$\dots$$
$$sim_e(d,g) = 1$$

Aggregated similarity:

$$sim_e(d_1, d_2) = \frac{\sum_i \sum_j sim_e(e_i, e_j)}{min(n,m)}$$
$$= \frac{0.08+4+0.25+\dots+0.5+\dots+1}{3}$$
$$= 2.23$$

Table 2: The calculation of $sim_e(d_1, d_2)$ for two example documents. Original events and their mappings contained in d_1 (Table (a)) and d_2 (Table (b)) are grouped by α_{poss}. Indices of event ids represent α_t and α_g. In Table (c) some examples for matching events and the similarity calculation are shown.

6. EVALUATION

In this section, we first discuss the evaluation objectives and scenarios followed by a description of the corpora used for evaluation and our document processing pipeline. Then, we present the evaluation results and compare event-centric document similarity to a simple term-based similarity measure, namely tf-idf combined with cosine similarity.

6.1 Objectives and Scenarios

Manual Evaluation. Evaluating event-centric similarity is a challenging task since no adequate gold standard is available. We cannot use standard similarity evaluation corpora as our goal is not to identify documents as similar that talk about the same topic in general, but only documents that contain similar events. Although there are evaluation corpora for related tasks such as topic detection and tracking (TDT), these are not suitable due to the different goals of TDT and our similarity model. While TDT systems associate a main event with documents and cluster incoming news articles according to these events, we take into account all events extracted from documents to calculate event-centric similarity scores. Thus, a straightforward way to evaluate our model is to use a corpus, calculate the similarities between all documents and manually check whether two documents are similar or not. However, this scenario is very labor-intensive and can only be done for a small subset of documents. The results of such a manual evaluation are presented in Section 6.6.

Cross-language Evaluation. Another way to evaluate our model is based on a multilingual corpus containing cross-language links between related documents from different languages. Intuitively, documents written in different languages having the same content (e.g., about the same person) can be assumed to be similar in an event-centric way. For example, the English and the German version of a biography can obviously be regarded as similar with respect to the mentioned events (e.g., birth, death, travels) – no matter whether or not the two documents are (partial) translations of each other. Using a multilingual corpus containing cross-language links, we can evaluate how often cross-language linked documents are the top-k most similar documents for each other. Note that the cross-language links are only used for evaluation purposes, and not considered for calculating the similarities. This evaluation scenario allows for a large-scale evaluation, and the results are described in Section 6.4.

6.2 Corpora Description

We created two corpora for our evaluation. The smaller corpus contains the English Wikipedia featured articles [25] and the corresponding German articles linked to the English ones through cross-language links. This corpus contains 3,124 English and 1,825 German articles. Note that the German articles are not necessarily featured. The reasons for choosing the Wikipedia featured articles are that (i) they are determined by the editors to be of high quality, and (ii) they are grouped into 30 categories and 13 biography subcategories. The latter fact allows for a detailed analysis which documents contain many events and for which topics our similarity model is particularly suitable. Table 3 shows some numbers for the categories. Topics such as history, warfare, or biographies tend to contain many events on average. We expect to achieve better results for them compared to categories containing only few events, such as computing or physics. The differing numbers for English and German can be explained by the different length of the documents. Featured articles tend to be very long.

As a second test set, we built a larger corpus to evaluate our model with more documents taken into account. We used the publicly available Wikipedia XML Corpus [7], containing Wikipedia articles as XML files. We selected the main collections of English and German articles consisting of 659,388 and 305,099 articles, respectively, and created a subset of all document pairs for which the English and the German article are available, resulting in 94,348 pairs.

Category	English Documents	English Events	German Documents	German Events
geography, places	178 (-/-)	198	114 (15/26)	31
history	115 (-/2)	186	57 (8/16)	30
education	37 (-/-)	140	15 (0/4)	8
sport, recreation	151 (-/3)	138	65 (7/16)	38
warfare	254 (-/3)	119	147 (14/51)	20
transport	107 (2/3)	115	32 (5/12)	21
all biographies	717 (2/11)	105	496 (47/81)	23
...				
video gaming	128 (12/32)	21	81 (24/33)	9
computing	18 (2/3)	17	15 (8/11)	2
physics, astronomy	92 (11/24)	14	81 (38/54)	2

Table 3: Statistics of the featured articles corpus grouped by category. In parentheses are the numbers of documents with no/less than 3 events.

	Featured articles			Wiki XML		
	English	German	Pairs	English	German	Pairs
Docs	3124	1825	1825	94348	94348	94348
Events	87	17		9	5	
$e \geq 1$	3059	1455	1447	59404	52843	44109
$e \geq 3$	2953	1173	1157	43516	35671	26909
$e \geq 5$	2868	985	972	34198	26280	18244
$e \geq 10$	2690	669	660	21054	14784	8518

Table 4: Statistics of both corpora with $e \geq x$ being the number of documents with at least x events.

Some details on both corpora, which will be of interest in the result sections, are given in Table 4. The large differences in the number of average events per document can mainly be explained by the different lengths of the documents. The featured articles tend to be much longer than other articles. In addition, the Wiki XML corpus contains several very short documents with just a couple of sentences. For both corpora, we only use the main parts of the articles, i.e., reference sections are ignored. These sections often contain bibliographic information including publication date and place, which are not relevant for the article itself.

6.3 Document Processing Pipeline

For the evaluation, we built a UIMA-based text mining pipeline [22]. We developed collection readers to access both corpora. Linguistic preprocessing, i.e., sentence splitting, tokenization, and part of speech tagging is done using components of the DKPro repository [10] and the Tree Tagger [17]. As temporal tagger, we chose HeidelTime [19] due to its best performance in the TempEval-2 challenge [24] for the extraction and normalization of temporal expressions from English documents. For identifying locations, we run Yahoo Placemaker [26] since it returns detailed containment information about extracted locations, which is crucial in terms of using the geographic hierarchy. While Yahoo Placemaker directly handles English and German documents, we had to develop a rule set for the temporal tagger to process German documents. Finally, we identify events by extracting co-occurrences based on the annotations of the temporal tagger, the geo-tagger and the sentence splitter. By applying our document processing pipeline, we obtain all the needed information to create document event profiles and thus to perform our event-centric document similarity analysis.

6.4 Cross-language Evaluation

The hypothesis for the cross-language evaluation is that two documents linked by a cross-language link are similar in an event-centric way. Although we do not expect the linked documents to be the most similar ones for each other in all cases, we assume that they are among the most similar ones. We compare the four models introduced in Section 5.2, i.e., our full model (FM) to the model without granularity mapping (FM-M), to the model without granularity mapping and weighting (FM-MW), and to the one additionally without normalization according to the number of events (FM-MWN). For every document, its similarity to each other document in the corpus is calculated. Obviously, if one document does not contain any events, no similarity score can be calculated for this document. In such cases, the score is set to zero. In addition, the similarity score can be zero if no similarity between the events of two documents is identified after the mapping process. For all models, given one document, we determine if its cross-language linked document belongs to the x most similar ones. We set x to 1, 3, 5, 10, 50 and 100. In addition, we set x to 10% of all compared documents.

Figure 2 shows the results for the Wikipedia featured articles corpus (2(a)) and for the Wiki XML corpus (2(b)). For both corpora, we show results for document pairs where both documents contain at least 1 event (bars) and at least 3 events (points). In addition, we group the results for the Wikipedia featured articles by the category of the documents (2(c)) using only the full model.

For the featured articles corpus, using the simplest model FM-MWN already results in 26% (29%) precision that a cross-language linked document is the most similar one if both documents contain at least 1 (3) events. This indicates that, in general, events can be helpful for identifying similar documents. Adding the event-occurrences normalization, weighting of different granularities, and the mapping of fine grained events to coarser granularities significantly improves the results in all cases. The full model achieves a precision of 36%, 54%, 62%, and 69% (top 1, 3, 5, and 10, respectively) for document pairs containing at least 3 events. A further advantage of the full model is that due to the mapping of the events to coarser granularities, more similarities can be calculated. While the full model identifies similarities for cross-language linked document pairs in 86% and 94% of the cases, the other three models identify only 67% and 76% for pairs containing at least 1 and 3 events, respectively.

In Figure 2(b), the results for the Wiki XML corpus are given. Note that due to the much larger number of documents in the corpus, the chance for a cross-language linked document to be within the x most similar documents decreases. In addition, there may be more documents in the corpus being very similar in an event-centric way. This explains the lower precision results for the Wiki XML corpus compared to the smaller corpus. Nevertheless, using the full model (FM) for documents with at least three events, in 15% (28%, 34%, 51%, 62%, 68%, 86%) of the cases cross-language linked documents are within the top x most similar documents, with x being 1, 3, 5, 10, 50, 100, and 10%, respectively. In addition, the results show that the full model outperforms the other models significantly. Especially the mapping of events to coarser granularities provides a substantial feature to discover new similarities.

Figure 2(c) shows the results grouped by the categories of the documents. Categories rich in events clearly outperform categories containing just few events (cf. Table 3), with biographies performing best with 69% (77%) for the cross-language linked documents being within the top 5 (top 10) most similar documents for each other.

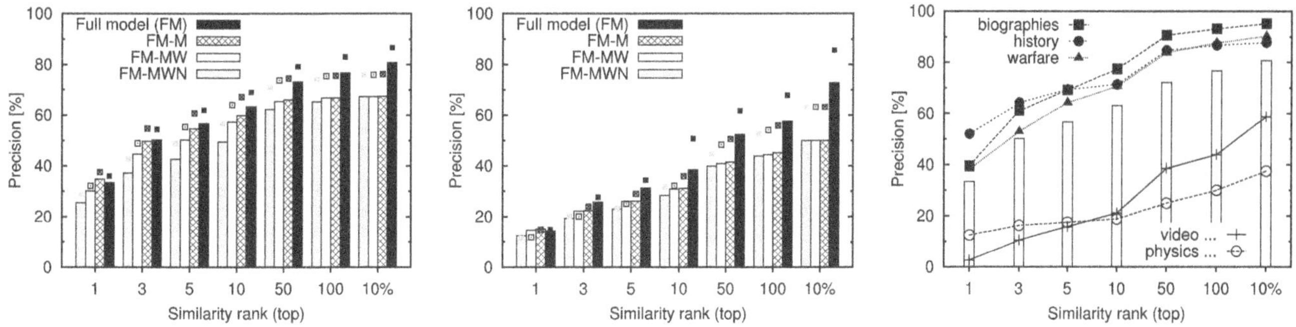

(a) Featured articles corpus. (b) Wiki XML corpus. (c) Results grouped by category.

Figure 2: Results of the cross-language evaluation. Figures (a) and (b) show results of the four models for documents containing at least one event (bars) and at least three events (points). Figure (c) shows the results of the full model for different categories (points) with average results for all categories (bars).

6.5 Comparison with Term-based Similarity

Although there are several advanced approaches to calculate document similarities as pointed out in Section 2, most of them are extensions to the vector space model and thus term-based. In comparison, our model is based on the document event profiles described in Section 3.3. Hence, we expect to find other kinds of documents to be similar compared to term-based models. Therefore, for comparison with term-based models, we do not have to use highly sophisticated methods such as latent semantic analysis, but can choose a simple model as representative for all term-based approaches. For this, we select the tf-idf measure combined with the cosine similarity denoted sim_t.

To evaluate the differences between sim_e and sim_t, we analyze pairs of documents (d_1, d_2) according to their rank for both similarity scores. This results in four categories:

c1. (d_1,d_2) is similar for both scores

c2. (d_1,d_2) is similar for sim_e, but not for sim_t

c3. (d_1,d_2) is similar for sim_t, but not for sim_e

c4. (d_1,d_2) is not similar for either scores

This evaluation is performed using the Wikipedia featured articles corpus. We use the top-n ranked documents for sim_e, with $n \in \{1, 3, 5, 10\}$, i.e., $rank_e(d_1, d_2) \leq n$ and calculate the ratio of documents that are similar using sim_t, i.e., for which $rank_t(d_1, d_2) \leq m$, with $m \in \{1, 3, 5, 10, 100, 1000\}$. As Figure 3 indicates, about 48% (56%) of the top-5 (top-10) ranked documents using sim_e are within the top-10 ranked documents using sim_t, and the best ranked document is the same for both measures in about 15% of the cases. This indicates that using sim_e leads to the discovery of new similarity relationships, which are hidden in the geographic and temporal information in documents. These cannot be discovered using standard similarity measures.

To demonstrate that the identification of similarities with both measures is still valuable, we give examples for pairs of documents for the categories (c1) to (c3). As the reference document d_1 for which similar documents are analyzed, we use the featured article '7 World Trade Center'. A document d_2 for which $rank_t(d_1, d_2) < 10$ and $rank_e(d_1, d_2) \gg rank_t(d_1, d_2)$, i.e., category (c3), is 'Tower of London'. Obviously, both documents do not talk about same events, but are similar with respect to the content, namely the topic of both documents is a tall building, its construction and design. A document for which $rank_t(d_1, d_2) < 10$ and $rank_e(d_1, d_2) < 10$, is 'American Airlines Flight 11'. Both documents are similar with respect to the topic of the terror attack and thus talk about same events, too. Finally, the article 'Ian Thorpe' is said to be similar in terms of mentioned events, i.e., $rank_e(d_1, d_2) < 10$ (with $rank_t \gg rank_e$). This surprising result is valid, as the article states that Ian Thorpe *was present at the World Trade Center on the morning of 11 September 2001, having stopped there on his jog, before returning to his hotel after forgetting his camera.*

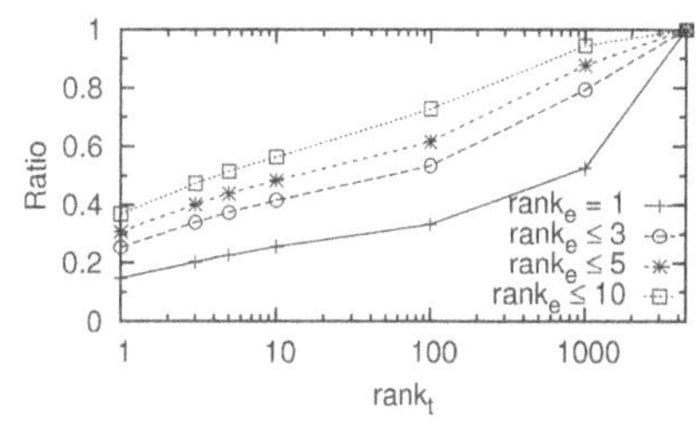

Figure 3: Ratio of documents that are ranked top n according to sim_t for different $rank_e$ values.

For further validation of the utility of sim_e, we perform a manual evaluation, which is described next.

6.6 Manual Evaluation

The objective of the manual evaluation is to validate the precision of the event-centric similarity model. For this, we use the Wikipedia featured articles corpus and randomly select 40 articles from the categories history, warfare, and biographies as source documents. These categories are especially suitable for event-centric document similarity as the cross-language evaluation showed since their documents contain many events (c.f. Table 3). We select the five most similar documents for each source document and evaluate whether they contain exactly the same events, belong to the same category, have a similar main topic, and are written in the same language.

The precision at 1, 3, and 5 for a document to be similar is 65%, 70%, and 64%, respectively. As expected, the results are independent of the language since 53% of the similar documents are not in the language of the source document.

Although there were many documents belonging to the same category (69%) and having a similar main topic (78%), there were several examples showing that sim_e identifies similarities across topics as well.

An error analysis showed that documents were wrongly identified to be similar mainly in the following cases: (i) one of the documents contains person names that were wrongly tagged as locations by the geo-tagger, and (ii) the source document contains no fine-grained events. While the first reason can be faced by using a high confidence value of the geo-tagger, the second one indicates that documents containing only coarse grained events are less suitable for our similarity model than documents with fine-grained events.

7. CONCLUSIONS AND ONGOING WORK

In this paper, we presented a novel model for the event-centric computation of document similarity. The model uses normalized event information, that is, pairs of temporal and geographic expressions extracted from documents to determine document similarity solely on the basis of events. Using this approach, it is possible to identify documents as being similar if they contain similar events although they might be different in other aspects, e.g., the main topic of the documents. In particular, because of the normalization of temporal and geographic expressions, including their containment relationships based on concept hierarchies, our model is applicable to multilingual corpora, an important feature not supported by other document similarity models.

We are currently extending our framework to include more languages, with a focus on Spanish and French, and to extend our corpora for evaluations correspondingly. We are also investigating structural aspects in terms of the order in which events are mentioned in a document. Such an order is obvious, for example, for the biography of a person written in two languages but might also lead to other interesting new information for other categories of documents. Finally, we are extending the types of events we consider by non-trivial events, such as names of holidays and their normalized temporal values.

8. REFERENCES

[1] J. Allan (Ed.). *Topic Detection and Tracking: Event-based Information Organization.* Kluwer Academic Publishers, USA, 2002.

[2] R. A. Baeza-Yates and B. Ribeiro-Neto. *Modern Information Retrieval.* Addison-Wesley, USA, 1999.

[3] H. Becker, M. Naaman, and L. Gravano. Learning Similarity Metrics for Event Identification in Social Media. In *WSDM '10*, 291–300, 2010.

[4] T. Brants and R. Stolle. Finding Similar Documents in Document Collections. In *Proc. LREC-2002 Workshop on Using Semantics for Information Retrieval and Filtering*, 2002.

[5] H. Chim and X. Deng. Efficient Phrase-based Document Similarity for Clustering. *IEEE Trans. on Knowledge and Data Eng.*, 20(9):1217–1229, 2008.

[6] S. Deerwester, S. Dumais, G. Furnas, T. Landauer, and R. Harshman. Indexing by Latent Semantic Analysis. *J. American Society for Information Science*, 41:391–407, 1990.

[7] L. Denoyer and P. Gallinari. The Wikipedia XML Corpus. *SIGIR Forum*, 40(1):64–69, 2006.

[8] T. Elsayed, J. Lin, and D. W. Oard. Pairwise Document Similarity in Large Collections with MapReduce. In *ACL-HLT '08*, 265–268, 2008.

[9] E. Gabrilovich and S. Markovitch. Computing Semantic Relatedness Using Wikipedia-based Explicit Semantic Analysis. In *Proc. Int. Joint Conf. on Artificial Intelligence*, 1606–1611, 2007.

[10] I. Gurevych, M. Mühlhäuser, C. Müller, J. Steimle, M. Weimer, and T. Zesch. Darmstadt Knowledge Processing Repository Based on UIMA. In *Proc. 1st Workshop on UIMA, Biannual Conf. Society for Comp. Ling. and Lang. Techn.*, 2007.

[11] P. Lakkaraju, S. Gauch, and M. Speretta. Document Similarity Based on Concept Tree Distance. In *Proc. ACM Conference on Hypertext and Hypermedia*, 127–132, 2008.

[12] M. D. Lee, B. Pincombe, and M. Welsh. An Empirical Evaluation of Models of Text Document Similarity, In *Proc. Annual Conf. Cognitive Science Society*, 1254–1259, 2005.

[13] J. Makkonen, H. Ahonen-Myka, and M. Salmenkivi. Topic Detection and Tracking with Spatio-Temporal Evidence. In *ECIR'03*, 251–265, 2003.

[14] C. D. Manning, P. Raghavan, and H. Schütze. *Introduction to Information Retrieval.* Cambridge University Press, USA, 2008.

[15] B. Martins, H. Manguinhas, and J. Borbinha. Extracting and Exploring the Geo-Temporal Semantics of Textual Resources. In *Proc. International Conference on Semantic Computing*, 2008.

[16] MetaCarta Inc. `http://www.metacarta.com/`.

[17] H. Schmid. Probabilistic Part-of-Speech Tagging Using Decision Trees. In *Proc. International Conference on New Methods in Language Processing*, 1994.

[18] R. Steinberger, B. Pouliquen, and J. Hagman. Cross-lingual Document Similarity Calculation Using the Multilingual Thesaurus EUROVOC. In *3rd Int. Conf. on Computational Linguistics and Intelligent Text Processing*, 415–424, 2002.

[19] J. Strötgen and M. Gertz. HeidelTime: High Quality Rule-based Extraction and Normalization of Temporal Expressions. In *SemEval'10*, 321–324, 2010.

[20] J. Strötgen, M. Gertz, and P. Popov. Extraction and Exploration of Spatio-Temporal Information in Documents. In *Proc. 6th Workshop on Geographic Information Retrieval*, 2010.

[21] TimeML. `http://www.timeml.org/`.

[22] UIMA. `http://uima.apache.org`.

[23] M. Verhagen and J. Pustejovsky. Temporal Processing with the TARSQI Toolkit. In *Coling 2008: Companion volume: Demonstrations*, 189–192, 2008.

[24] M. Verhagen, R. Sauri, T. Caselli, and J. Pustejovsky. SemEval-2010 Task 13: TempEval-2. In *SemEval'10*, 57–62, 2010.

[25] Wikipedia Featured Articles. `http://en.wikipedia.org/wiki/Wikipedia:Featured_articles`.

[26] Yahoo Placemaker. `http://developer.yahoo.com/geo/placemaker/`.

[27] K. Zhang, J. Zi, and L. G. Wu. New Event Detection Based on Indexing-tree and Named Entity. In *SIGIR '07*, 215–222, 2007.

Posting List Intersection on Multicore Architectures

Shirish Tatikonda
IBM Almaden Research
San Jose, CA, USA
statiko@us.ibm.com

B. Barla Cambazoglu
Yahoo! Research
Barcelona, Spain
barla@yahoo-inc.com

Flavio P. Junqueira
Yahoo! Research
Barcelona, Spain
fpj@yahoo-inc.com

ABSTRACT

In current commercial Web search engines, queries are processed in the conjunctive mode, which requires the search engine to compute the intersection of a number of posting lists to determine the documents matching all query terms. In practice, the intersection operation takes a significant fraction of the query processing time, for some queries dominating the total query latency. Hence, efficient posting list intersection is critical for achieving short query latencies. In this work, we focus on improving the performance of posting list intersection by leveraging the compute capabilities of recent multicore systems. To this end, we consider various coarse-grained and fine-grained parallelization models for list intersection. Specifically, we present an algorithm that partitions the work associated with a given query into a number of small and independent tasks that are subsequently processed in parallel. Through a detailed empirical analysis of these alternative models, we demonstrate that exploiting parallelism at the finest-level of granularity is critical to achieve the best performance on multicore systems. On an eight-core system, the fine-grained parallelization method is able to achieve more than five times reduction in average query processing time while still exploiting the parallelism for high query throughput.

Categories and Subject Descriptors

H.3.3 [**Information Storage Systems**]: Information Retrieval Systems

General Terms

Algorithms, Design, Performance, Experimentation

Keywords

Web search engines, multicore architectures, query processing, posting list intersection, intra-query parallelism

SIGIR'11, July 24–28, 2011, Beijing, China.

1. INTRODUCTION

Large-scale Web search engines run under strict performance constraints: they must operate at a high target peak throughput and achieve a short response time (i.e., query latency) for each query [8]. Given the size and extent of the Web, these tight constraints must be obtained by exploiting parallelism over very large search clusters. The Web collection is document-based partitioned, and each node in a cluster stores a subset of the collection and the corresponding index. Queries are processed in parallel, i.e., the same query is evaluated concurrently over all local indexes.

To increase the peak throughput, one may replicate resources of the search engine. Replicas of a search cluster serve different queries independent of each other, increasing the number of queries that can be concurrently processed [8, 12]. High throughput, however, is not the only indicator of the performance of a search engine; a low query latency is also important. Recently, it has been empirically shown that high query latencies not only degrade user satisfaction but may also lead to losses in revenues of a search engine [26]. Hence, it is critical to carefully devise optimizations to improve query latencies. If the time constraint cannot be satisfied, queries may have to be processed in a degraded mode, i.e., only partial search results are returned [14]. Degradation causes the quality of search results to drop.

Typically, the response time of a search node to a query is engineered to be under one hundred milliseconds. In order to keep processing times within these bounds, a number of optimizations are employed in the search nodes. These include caching [4, 20], multi-threading [11], index compression [2, 32], and early termination of processing [1, 13, 15, 23, 29]. Emerging multicore architectures provide a new opportunity to decrease query latencies further. Multicores, primarily motivated by energy and power constraints, pack two or more cores on a single die. They typically share an on-chip L2 cache as well as the front-side bus to main memory. As these systems become more popular, the general trend has been from single-core to many-core: from dual-, quad-, eight-core chips to the ones with tens of cores. So far, however, very little has been done to exploit the full potential of these chips in our context.

In this paper, we focus on the posting list intersection problem, where the objective is to identify the set of documents that appear in all posting lists corresponding to the query terms, as efficiently as possible. We consider various coarse-grained and fine-grained parallelization strategies for improving the efficiency of list intersection on multicore systems. While there has been some efforts in parallel query processing, existing strategies fail to exploit the fine-grained parallelism, which is critical to achieve good performance on multicore systems. To this end, we propose a framework, based on the producer-consumer model, that generates fine-grained processing tasks to achieve some form of intra-query parallelism so that the same query can be concurrently processed on multiple cores. For task generation, we propose an algorithm that uses the skip information in the lists to create a set of intersection tasks. We evaluate our techniques on a system with eight cores, using a large document collection and a query log obtained from AltaVista Web search engine. When compared to the baseline approach that runs on a single core, we are able to speed up the intersection operation by up to a factor of 5.75 while keeping the throughput degradation to be as small as 3.3% – previous approaches experience at least 36% degradation.

This paper is organized as follows. Section 2 gives an overview of query processing on a typical search node. In Section 3, we describe different models for parallelizing the list intersection process on multicore architectures. In Section 4, experimental results are presented. Section 5 summarizes the related work. We finish the paper with the conclusions in Section 6.

2. BACKGROUND

In this section, we summarize the basic steps of query evaluation in a search engine, illustrating alternative options. Due to the embarrassingly parallel nature of query processing in search clusters [8], we restrict the discussion to an individual search node. Interested readers may refer to previous work in the literature on parallelization at the level of a search cluster [24, 25].

Query processing in a search node typically contains two phases [15]. In the first phase, the posting lists that correspond to the terms in the query are intersected to identify the documents that contain all query terms. Identified documents are ranked by means of a simple yet effective scoring function, such as a linear combination of the BM25 score with a query-independent score (e.g., a link analysis metric). In the second phase, a subset of the documents that are top-ranked by the first phase are re-ranked by a more accurate, but costly ranking function (e.g., a machine-learned ranker). Depending on the properties of the query, either of these phases may dominate the query processing time.

In this work, we focus on the efficiency of the first phase ranking and, in particular, posting list intersection, which dominates the processing cost, compared to the cost of scoring. The main reason search engines compute the first phase document scores using the intersection of posting lists (i.e., conjunction), instead of the union of the lists (i.e., disjunction), is that intersection leads to shorter query latencies as the document collections in Web search are fairly large. Moreover, intersection leads to higher result quality as most Web queries are very short. We note that, herein, we omit a discussion on relevance as it is out of scope. We also omit discussions on some optimization techniques (e.g., document id reassignment, list processing order) as they are not directly related and they complement our work.

A typical posting list is composed of a sequence of postings, each keeping some useful information about a document that contains the respective term for the list. In its simplest form, this information contains the document identifier and the frequency of the term in the document. Although there are other options, postings in a list are typically sorted by decreasing frequency or increasing document id. The first option enables early-termination optimizations [1, 13, 23, 29], some of which speeds up processing while preserving the result quality for the top k results. The second option enables compression of postings based on d-gaps. Compressing posting lists [2, 32] leads to higher cache hit rates and fewer disk accesses, in exchange of increasing processing costs due to decompression overheads. A technique used to speed up processing of compressed posting lists is to place skip pointers at regular intervals between postings [28]. This provides a form of random access to postings in the list, which is not possible, otherwise, due to compression.

In our work, we assume that posting lists are compressed and contain skip information, and that the postings within lists are sorted by increasing document id. Typically, large-scale search engines dedicate significant portions of server memory to cache most frequently and/or recently accessed posting lists to prevent expensive disk accesses [32]. Hence, we assume that disk accesses do not form a bottleneck. Note that none of these assumptions are enforced by the proposed techniques as our methods are quite general. Selection of this particular setting is mainly because it reflects the current design practices in Web search.

3. QUERY PROCESSING ON MULTICORE ARCHITECTURES

Multicore systems constitute an important opportunity for developing efficient and scalable applications. The key to realize true benefits of these parallel systems lies in effective fine-grained parallelization of workloads. We now present various models for parallelizing the list intersection process (see Fig. 1). We consider two important metrics to compare these alternative models: *throughput* and *average query latency*. Throughput is measured as the number of queries processed per unit of time. Average latency is measured as the average time a query spends in the entire system. The latency of a query is defined as the difference between the time it arrives at the system and the time its processing is complete. Since all queries have to wait in the entry queue (associated with the search node) until their processing starts, the query latency includes both the waiting time in the queue and the processing time. Formally, we compute the latency $\ell(q)$ of query q by

$$\begin{aligned}\ell(q) &= \text{wait\_time}(q) + \text{processing\_time}(q)\\ &= (s(q) - a(q)) + (f(q) - s(q)) = f(q) - a(q),\end{aligned}$$

where $a(q)$ denotes the time q arrives at the system while $s(q)$ and $f(q)$ are the times at which processing of q is started and finished, respectively. Given a query workload W, the throughput $T(W)$ and the average query latency $L(W)$ under W are given respectively by:

$$T(W) = \frac{|W|}{t(W)},$$

$$L(W) = \frac{\sum_{q \in W} \ell(q)}{|W|}.$$

where $|W|$ is the number of queries processed, and $t(W)$ is the total wall-clock time spent in processing W.

Web search engines are typically hosted on systems comprising a number of clusters, where each cluster node is pos-

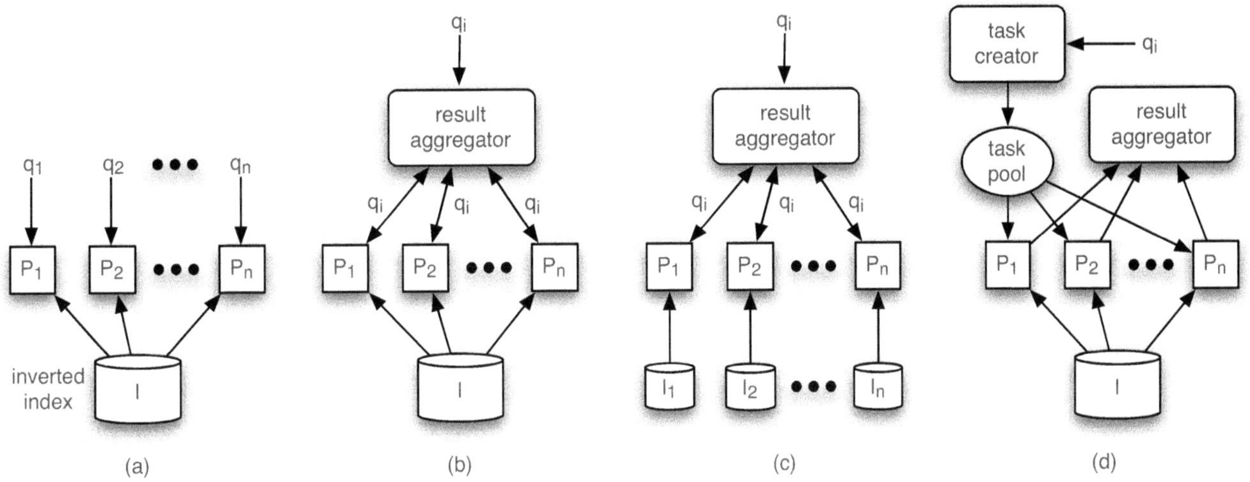

Figure 1: Parallel Models for List Intersection: (a) Inter-query, (b) DOCP-UI, (c) DOCP-PI, (d) FGQP

Algorithm 1 THREADFN(W, L)

Require: Query workload W
Require: Set of posting lists L
{Each core executes this function in parallel}
1: **while** W is not empty **do**
2: $q =$ GETNEXTQUERY(W)
3: $D =$ PROCESS(q, L)
4: $R =$ SCORE(q, D)
5: OUTPUT(R)
6: **end while**

sibly a multicore system. Here, we primarily focus on leveraging the parallelism *within a single cluster node*. Next, we present two paradigms for parallel list intersection: *inter-query* and *intra-query*. While the former exploits the parallelism *across different queries*, the latter focuses on the parallelism that is present *within a single query*.

3.1 Inter-query Processing

The simplest way to leverage multicore systems is to partition the query workload across different cores. Each incoming query is scheduled for execution on the next available processing core. All cores are kept busy by dispatching the queries from the entry queue to different processors using a simple first-come-first-serve strategy. This model explores the parallelism present among different queries. It relies on the fact that all queries are independent of each other in the sense that the output of one query does not affect the processing of any other query. Hence, we refer to this model as the inter-query processing model. This model is shown in Figure 1a – P_i's in the figure refer to different processing cores present in the multicore system; and I denotes the inverted index that hosts all the posting lists.

Algorithm 1 illustrate the way queries are processed in the inter-query-parallel model. In this model, all threads execute the function THREADFN in parallel. Each thread picks up a query from the workload W (or from a stream of queries), processes it using the posting lists L, and outputs a result set R. We process P lists to compute their intersection using a modified version of the Small Adaptive algorithm, proposed by Demaine et al. [17]. An eliminator e is initially set as the first item (document id) of the first list. The algorithm then repeatedly cycles through all lists searching for the eliminator. If e is present in all lists then its relevance score is computed, and the next eliminator is then chosen from the first list. If e is not present in some list L then the algorithm selects the smallest item from L that is larger than e as the next eliminator.

In a real-world scenario, the loop at line 1 is an infinite loop because the query stream is typically unbounded as queries continuously arrive at the system. For the parallel implementation, only the function call at line 2 forms a critical section, which requires synchronization. At any given time point, only one thread can exist in the GETNEXTQUERY method. Since the critical section is very small, the parallelization overhead incurred in this model is minimal. It is likely that this model achieves good parallel efficiency, resulting in high system throughput as the number of cores in the system is increased.

3.2 Intra-query Processing

Although the inter-query model improves the number of queries answered in a given time period, the time it takes to process an individual query does not change irrespective of the number of processing units in the system. This is because a query is always processed by a single core. However, as mentioned earlier, most commercial search engines are typically driven by the query latency, and improving this is critical for user satisfaction. We next describe three different models that leverages the intra-query parallelism present within a single query.

3.2.1 Document Partitioning (DOCP)

This strategy partitions the document collection present on the search node equally among all processing cores. Each core is responsible for identifying matching documents for the given query in the allocated partition of documents. To form the final answer, we aggregate the partial sets of results produced, one from each core. Recall that the search nodes summarize the information about all documents in the form of an inverted index. Hence, this strategy corresponds to partitioning the accesses over different parts of the index. The partitioning can be done in two ways – *logical* and *physi-*

cal. According to logical partitioning, all cores share a single unified index but each core accesses a different portion of the index. Such a strategy is shown as *DOCP-UI* in Figure 1b. Each processing core P_1 to P_n gets a *copy* of the query q_i, and they process the query against disjoint portions of the index I. The partial results produced by each core are then combined in the *result aggregator*, which is typically implemented as a shared data structure. *DOCP-UI* method of parallelization has been suggested by Frachtenberg [19].

The alternative choice to implement the DOCP is to *physically partition the index* I into n equal parts I_1 to I_n, where n is equal to the number of cores. This strategy is shown as *DOCP-PI* in Figure 1c. As it is evident from the figure, both *DOCP-UI* and *DOCP-PI* differ only in the way index is partitioned and used among processing cores.

For a simpler design, we implement these strategies using a master-slave model. The master (a designated core) is responsible for several tasks – to fetch the next query from the query stream; to send a copy of the query to all the other cores; to process the query against the allocated index partition; and to send the combined results out of the search node. While more decentralized methods are plausible, they introduce various control overheads. It is important to note that these document partitioning based parallel strategies require some form of *barrier synchronization* at the end of processing each query.

3.2.2 Fine-Grained Query Partitioning (FGQP)

Both DOCP-UI and DOCP-PI strategies divide the index accesses into n parts where n is equal to the number of cores. These coarse-grained strategies suffer from load imbalance, and they often provide suboptimal performance. Several earlier studies [30] have also shown that it is imperative to leverage the fine-grained parallelism to achieve good performance on multicore systems. We now present a mechanism that divides the work associated with a single query into several *small* and *independent* tasks (see Fig. 1(d)). These tasks are then processed in parallel to produce the result set. Small-sized tasks allow us to exploit the fine-grained parallelism within the query, and as a result, they enable mechanisms that guarantee good load balance among threads. It must be noted that very small tasks increase the parallelization overhead incurred in creating and managing these tasks. Independent tasks, on the other hand, reduce the need for synchronization and thereby help in realizing better parallel efficiency.

The framework of our intra-query model is shown in Fig. 2. This framework adopts a producer-consumer model, where one of the threads acts as the producer and remaining threads act as consumers. The producer takes a query from the entry queue, fetches associated posting lists, and produces multiple, independent posting list intersection tasks. Generated tasks are pushed into an intersection task pool. Each consumer thread iteratively obtains a task from this intersection task pool and processes its task. Processing a task mainly involves decompression and intersection of posting lists. Documents that are common in all lists are added to the scoring task pool. They are later picked up by different threads for scoring in order to produce the final, ranked result set. The producer thread also participates in processing of intersection and scoring tasks, whenever possible. In contrast to the producer-consumer model, one can consider a setup where all threads are capable of both producing and consuming tasks. Such a decentralized approach, however, requires complex synchronization methods, and it is likely to incur higher control overhead.

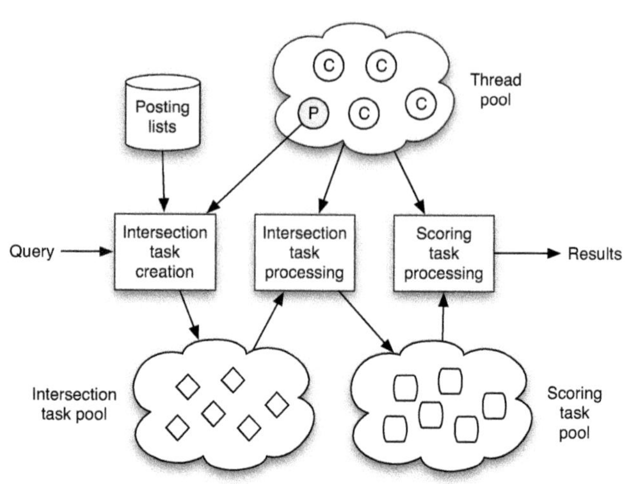

Figure 2: Framework of the intra-query model.

Algorithm 2 PRODUCER(W, P)

Require: Query workload W
Require: Set of posting lists P
Require: Intersection task pool ITP
Require: Scoring task pool STP
Require: Pool threshold θ
1: **while** W is not empty **do**
2:   **while** $|ITP| \leq \theta$ **do**
3:     q = GETNEXTQUERY(W)
4:     T = CREATETASKS(q, P)
5:     $ITP = ITP \cup T$
6:     NOTIFYCONSUMERS()
7:   **end while**
8:   {Act as a consumer}
9:   **while** $|ITP| > \theta$ **do**
10:     t = GETNEXTTASK(ITP)
11:     D = PROCESSTASK(t)
12:     $STP = STP \cup \{D\}$
13:   **end while**
14: **end while**

The scoring phase requires the threads to iteratively pop a document from the scoring task pool and compute a score, which is then used to rank the document. Evidently, the scoring step is an embarrassingly parallel problem that requires a simple data-parallel implementation.

Algorithms 2 and 3 show the steps of producer and consumer threads in the intra-query model, respectively. By Algorithm 2 (lines 2–7), the producer can choose to temporarily pause the task creation process and act as a consumer. If the size of the task pool is smaller than a threshold θ (line 9), the producer resumes the task creation duty. The producer relies on the pool threshold θ to decide whether or not to generate tasks for new queries. Higher values of θ delays the task generation, and generated tasks are likely to spend more time in the task pool before they get picked up for processing. Further discussion on the impact of θ is presented in Section 4.2. Note that only the producer process is responsible for task creation in this approach. Other decentralized variants are possible, but they are likely to incur high control overhead.

Algorithm 3 CONSUMER()

Require: Intersection task pool ITP
Require: Scoring task pool STP
1: **while** ITP is not empty **do**
2: $\quad t = \text{GETNEXTTASK}(ITP)$
3: $\quad D = \text{PROCESSTASK}(t)$
4: $\quad STP = STP \cup \{D\}$
5: **end while**

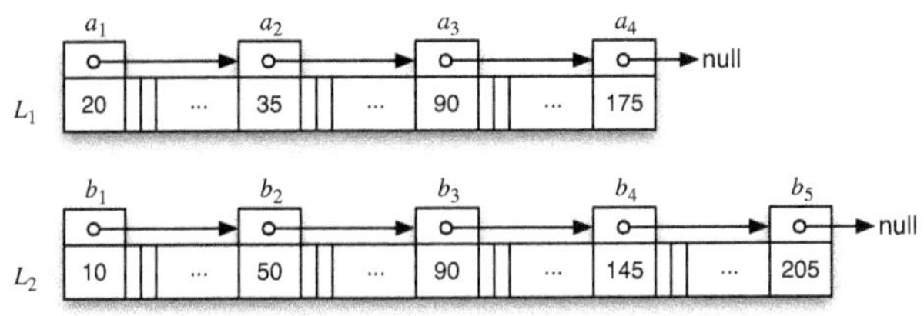

Tasks: $t_1 = (a_1, a_2) \otimes (b_1, b_2)$, $t_2 = (a_2, a_3) \otimes (b_1, b_3)$, $t_3 = (a_3, a_4) \otimes (b_3, b_5)$

Figure 3: Example skip lists

3.2.3 Task Creation

The producer thread receives a new query from the workload and partitions the work associated with the query into tasks by using the posting lists required by the query (lines 3–5 in Algorithm 2). We partition posting lists so that each task is responsible for intersecting some portion of the lists. Unfortunately, posting lists are stored in compressed format to save space and this limits the ability to perform random accesses required while creating tasks. To facilitate effective work partitioning while retaining the benefits of compression, we store postings in the form of skip lists. A skip list is a sorted list of document identifiers (also referred to as items), denoted using a linked list that connects sparse subsequences of items [22]. Each pointer in the list forms a link $i \rightarrow j$ between two non-consecutive items i and j. The number of items skipped between two skips[1] i and j is referred to as the skip block size or skip size. Two example skip lists are shown in Fig. 3, where a_i's and b_j's are the skips in lists L_1 and L_2, respectively.

We compress all document ids between a pair of skips, but store the skips without compression. For example, in L_1 of Fig. 3, the ids 20, 35, 90, and 175 are stored as uncompressed values, but the ids between these skips are compressed. For convenience, we also store the highest document id in the list as a separate skip pointing to null. More formally, the posting list for a query term a is denoted as $L(a) = (S_a, C_a)$, where S_a is the sequence of skips in the skip list and C_a is the sequence of document ids in compressed format.

The producer thread generates tasks by operating on these compressed skip lists. Without loss of generality, we assume that the lists are sorted in increasing order of their size. The main idea is, for each skip block in the first (or the shortest) list, to find the relevant skip blocks from the remaining lists. A task is then formed by the sequence of skips obtained from all lists in the query. The total number of tasks generated for a given query is equal to the number of skip blocks present in the shortest posting list.

Consider a query q with two terms a and b, whose posting lists are $L(a) = (S_a, C_a)$ and $L(b) = (S_b, C_b)$ with $|S_a| \leq |S_b|$. For each skip pointer in $L(a)$, we create a task with one

[1]We use the term "skip" interchangeably to indicate a link or the end points of a link.

Algorithm 4 CREATETASK()

Require: Set of posting lists P
Require: Intersection task pool ITP
Require: Query $q = (q_1, q_2, \ldots, q_m)$ {Assume that query terms are sorted in increasing order of posting list size}
1: $n = |S(q_1)|$ {The number of skips in $L(q_1)$}
2: **for** $i = 1$ to $n - 1$ **do**
3: $\quad \text{INITTASK}(t)$
4: $\quad d_1 = d[L(q_1), i]$
5: $\quad d_2 = d[L(q_1), i + 1]$
6: $\quad$ add $(i, i + 1)$ to t
7: $\quad$ **for** $r = 2$ to m **do**
8: $\quad\quad$ find j and k in $L(q_r) = (S_{q_r}, C_{q_r})$ s.t. $i \leq j < k \leq |S_{q_r}|$, $d_1 \geq d[L(q_r), j]$, and $d_2 \leq d[L(q_r), k]$
9: $\quad\quad$ add (j, k) to t
10: $\quad$ **end for**
11: $\quad ITP = ITP \cup \{t\}$
12: **end for**

or more skips from $L(b)$. We generate a set of independent tasks $\{t_1, t_2, \ldots, t_{|S_a|}\}$, where

$$t_i = [(s_i, s_{i+1}), (s_j, s_k)],$$
$$s_i, s_{i+1} \in S_a, \text{ for } 1 \leq i \leq |S_a|, \text{ and}$$
$$s_j, s_k \in S_b, \text{ for } 1 \leq j \leq k \leq |S_b|.$$

Note that s_{i+1} is undefined for $i = |S_a|$. Moreover, for a given s_i and s_{i+1} in $L(a)$, the skips from $L(b)$ are chosen such that $s_i \geq s_j$ and $s_{i+1} \leq s_k$. In other words, all documents in $L(a)$ within a skip pointer $s_i \rightarrow s_{i+1}$ fall in the id interval given by $[s_j, s_k]$ in $L(b)$. If the query contains more than two terms, for each skip block in the shortest list, a sequence of skips is found from all remaining lists. The entire procedure is summarized in Algorithm 4 for the general case of a query with m terms. Here, $d[L(a), i]$ denotes the document id at the ith skip in $L(a)$. The skips j and k in line 7 can be found either by a linear scan or by a binary search. Each task t that is generated by the algorithm has the following form:

$$t = [(s^1_{i_1}, s^1_{1+i_1}), (s^2_{i_2}, s^2_{i_{2'}}), \ldots, (s^m_{i_m}, s^m_{i_{m'}})], \quad (1)$$

where $m = |q|$ and s^j_k indicates the kth skip in the jth posting list. It is important to note that each task encapsulates the *complete* information required to intersect the relevant portions of all posting lists. Hence, a processor can *independently process a task* without requiring any information about other tasks. For the skip lists in Fig. 3, Algorithm 4 produces three tasks by considering the sequence of skips in L_1 and in L_2.

3.2.4 Task Processing

All threads iteratively dequeue tasks from the task pool and process them to determine the common documents. Every entry (s^j_k, s^j_ℓ), for $1 \leq j \leq m$, in a task can be treated as a sublist having a sequence of skips (s^j_k, s^j_ℓ) and the corresponding compressed skip blocks, as seen in Eq. (1). The problem of processing a task with m entries is then reduced to that of intersecting m sublists. Hence, any of the existing list intersection algorithms [5, 6, 7, 16, 17] can be used. As mentioned in Section 3.1, we use a modified version of the Small Adaptive algorithm [17] to intersect all sublists in a given task. Our task processing algorithm first decompresses a single skip block from all sublists. The intersection process is initiated on these decompressed blocks. Whenever the search for an eliminator overshoots the current block, the next skip block from the sublist is decompressed. This process is terminated either when there are no skip blocks for decompression or after all items in the shortest sublist are considered by the intersection process.

4. EMPIRICAL EVALUATION

4.1 Dataset and Setup

We evaluate different parallel query processing models using a subset of the AltaVista query log (about a quarter million queries).[2] Posting lists are obtained from a large crawl of the UK domain, obtained in May 2006.[3] All lists are compressed with skip list information as described in Section 3.2.3. Skip blocks are compressed using the PForDelta [33] algorithm, which is recently shown to be efficient in terms of both compression quality and decompression time [32]. The default skip block size is set to 512, but is varied in some experiments. We assume that all posting lists are loaded into the main memory before the queries are processed. In other words, we do not account for the time spent in disk I/O while evaluating our models (see the discussion in Section 2).

In our experiments, we consider that the query arrival process follows a Poisson distribution with an intensity of λ query/sec. We evaluate our models using the two metrics defined in Section 3: *query throughput* and *average query latency*. The parallel performance of our models is evaluated by considering the fastest sequential version as the baseline. This baseline is given by the inter-query model that runs on a single processor (denoted as `INTER-1`), where the queries are processed one after the other, on a first-come-first-serve basis. Therefore, the data points that correspond to running intra-query models on a single core are not shown in any of our performance plots.

All experiments are conducted on a multicore system with dual quad-core Clovertown E5345 2.33GHz processor (essentially, a total of eight cores) with 6GB main memory. The system has 8MB aggregated L2 cache space that is shared among eight cores. The parallel code is implemented in C++ using the *pthreads* library.

4.2 Performance Comparison

The performance differences between the two parallel query processing paradigms are shown in Figs. 4(a) and 4(b). We measure how throughput and average query latency vary with the number of cores used for query processing. For `FGQP`, we show two trends that differ in the value of pool threshold θ. Recall from Section 3.2.2 that the value of θ affects the producer process in generating tasks for new queries. The throughput achieved by `INTER` and `FGQP` models increases almost linearly with the number of cores. This indicates that these models effectively make use of the available computational resources. When using eight cores, the `INTER` is able to serve 850 query/sec while the `FGQP` (θ=150) model is able to serve up to 826 query/sec. The marginal throughput difference between `INTER` and `FGQP` is primarily due to additional parallelization overhead incurred in `FGQP`. This includes the time spent in creating and managing tasks, and aggregating partial results from individual cores. On the other hand, the overhead incurred in `INTER` is minimal since each core operates independently on a different query, and thereby reduces the need for synchronization – see Section 4.5 for further details on parallelization overhead.

When compared to `FGQP`, the query throughput achieved by other intra-query models that rely on document partitioning is small across the chart. This is mainly because `DOCP-UI` and `DOCP-PI` target *coarse-grained* parallelism among *large* document partitions, whereas `FGQP` exploits *fine-grained* parallelism among *small-sized* tasks. For a given query, the skew among the finish times of different cores is very high in `DOCP-UI` and `DOCP-PI` when compared to that in `FGQP`. Consequently, document partitioning based strategies suffer from load imbalance, and as a result, they deliver poor parallel efficiency. When compared to the sequential baseline (`inter` on a single core), `INTER` and `FGQP` (θ=150) improve the throughput by a factor of 7.9 and 7.6 when all eight cores in the system are used. In contrast, `DOCP-UI` and `DOCP-PI` models are able to improve it only by a factor of 5.1 and 4.8, respectively.

In terms of average query latency (see Fig. 4(b)), the inter-query model is unable to leverage extra processing capabilities in the multicore system to reduce latency. In fact, the average query latency achieved by `INTER` is almost constant across the board since queries are always executed on a single core irrespective of the number of available processing units. On the other hand, strategies that leverage intra-query parallelism are able to reduce the query latency since any given query is processed by multiple cores, in parallel. Note, however, that the reduction is not linear with the number of cores. For example, the average query latency from the sequential baseline `INTER-1` is about 9.27ms. In contrast, the latency achieved by `DOCP-UI` and `DOCP-PI` models has improved from 5.4ms to 1.9ms as the number of cores increases from 2 to 8. Similarly, the latency of `FGQP`(θ=5) has reduced from 5.4ms to 1.61ms. When compared to `INTER-1`, this amounts to an improvement by a factor of 5.75.

To summarize, `INTER` model gives the best query throughput as the parallelization overhead is minimal but it does not offer any improvement in query latency. The performance of both document partitioning based strategies (`DOCP-UI` and `DOCP-PI`) are very similar to each other. While they provide good improvements in query latency, their query throughput is significantly affected by load imbalance issues from coarse-grained parallelism. In contrast, `FGQP` leverages a fine-grained intra-query parallelism, and it delivers query throughput that is very close to `INTER` while providing excellent latency improvements that are similar to document partitioning strategies.

The performance of `FGQP`, however, depends on the value of pool threshold θ, which is illustrated in Fig. 4(c). We consider two metrics as we vary the value of θ: percent degradation in query throughput (*PDTP*) and improvement in average query latency (*IAQL*) due to task-based intra-query processing. These metrics are computed, respectively, as

$$PDTP = ((TP_{\texttt{INTER-1}} - TP_{\texttt{FGQP}})/TP_{\texttt{INTER-1}}) \times 100, \text{ and}$$
$$IAQL = T_{\texttt{INTER-1}}/T_{\texttt{FGQP}},$$

where $TP_{(\cdot)}$ and $T_{(\cdot)}$ refer to the realized query throughput and total wall-clock time spent in processing the entire query workload, respectively. We would like the throughput degradation to be as small as possible and the latency

[2]There are a total of 47,278 unique query terms.

[3]Available from the University of Milan: `http://law.dsi.unimi.it/webdata/uk-2006-05/`.

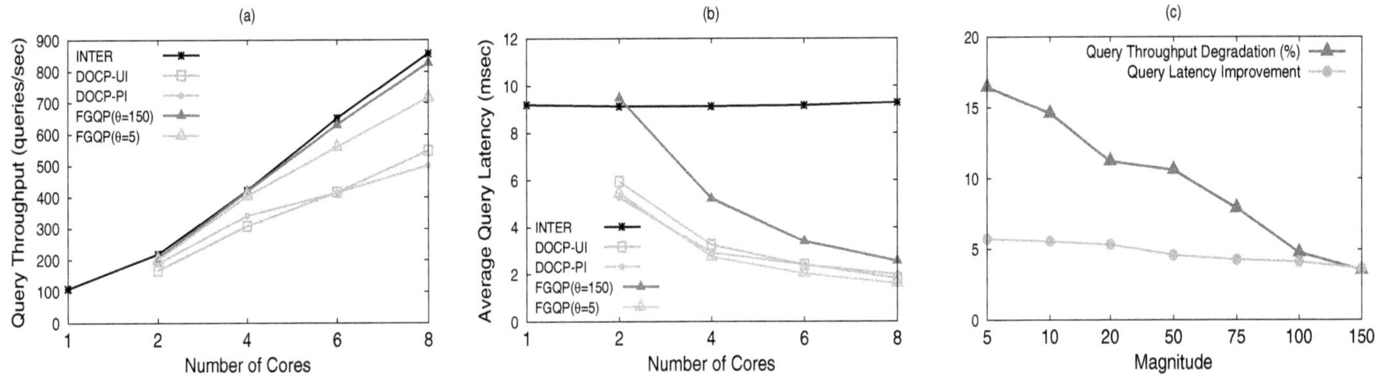

Figure 4: (a, b) Comparison of different parallelization models, and (c) impact of θ on FGQP.

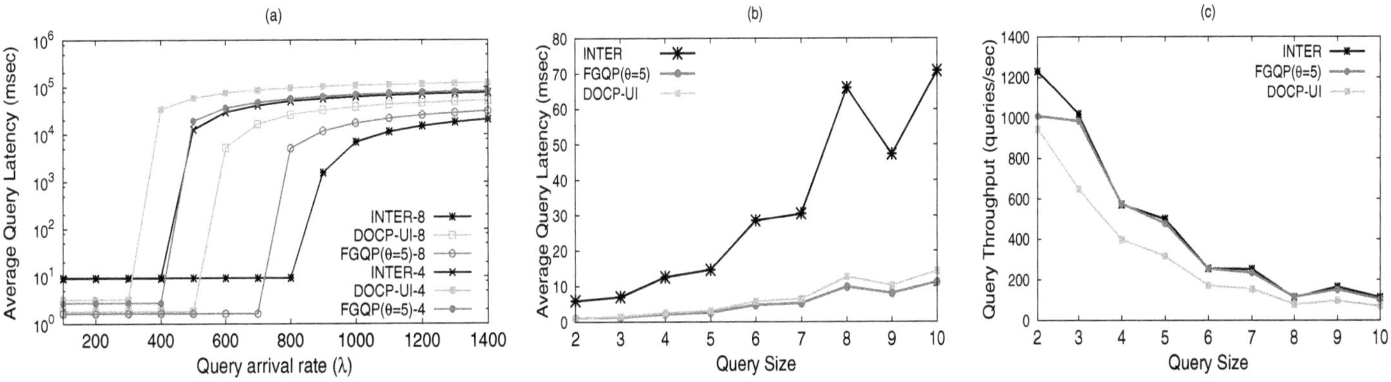

Figure 5: (a) Impact of λ on average query latency, and (b, c) performance as the query length varies.

improvement to be as high as possible. As the value of θ increases, the producer process creates new tasks more aggressively. This increases the average query latency as tasks spend more time in the task pool before they are consumed for processing. Aggressive task generation also reduces the chance of encountering an empty task pool. This increases the query throughput since the consumer processes are always kept busy processing the tasks. Therefore, higher θ values result in higher query throughputs and higher query latencies, and lower θ values give lower query throughputs and lower query latencies. Such a trade-off between throughput degradation and latency improvement is evident in Fig. 4(c). As the value of θ is increased from 5 to 150, the degradation in throughput (when compared to INTER-1) drops from 16% to 3.3%, while the latency improvements drop from 5.75-fold to 3.7-fold. As a comparison, we observed the degradation in throughput for DOCP-UI and DOCP-PI when running on eight cores to be 36% and 41%, respectively.

The value of θ can be tuned based on the performance requirements set by end applications. For a given upper bound on the query latency, the value θ can be adjusted to maximize the query throughput while keeping the latency within the given limit. On both extremes, we observed the best query throughput at $\theta = 150$, and similarly the average query latency can be improved by as much as 5.75-times by setting $\theta = 5$. The rest of the results in this section, unless otherwise mentioned, are obtained with $\theta = 5$.

4.3 Effect of System Load

To investigate the effect of system load, we model a Web search engine as a queue with λ queries arriving and μ queries getting served per second.[4] The system will be in a stable state as long as $\lambda \leq \mu$. When $\lambda > \mu$, the average number of queries present in the system (both waiting and in processing) will increase over time. In this experiment, we analyze the performance in such overloaded conditions by measuring how the average query latency varies as we increase the query arrival rate λ. The service rate μ, i.e., the rate at which queries are processed is directly proportional to the throughput of the system, which in turn relies on the number of cores used to process the queries.

We now consider a system with a fixed number of cores (equivalent to a fixed μ) and analyze the effect of increasing the query load (see Fig. 5(a)). We vary the value of λ from 100 query/sec up to 1400 query/sec and observe the change in the average query latency. As λ increases, the latency stays constant until the system saturates, after which the latency increases steeply with λ. The saturation point of the system is a point beyond which the arrival rate dominates the service rate. In case of INTER running on four cores (denoted as INTER-4), the system saturates around 400 query/sec. Any further increase in λ beyond 400 query/sec results in up to three orders of magnitude increase in query latency. In the figure, it can also be observed that the saturation point shifts towards the right as the number of cores increases (INTER-8 saturates around 800 query/sec). This highlights the fact that a system that is provisioned ith more computational resources can serve more requests without saturating. This is a significant result given the architectural trend that promises an increasing number of cores in

[4]The service rate μ in our models is primarily determined by the number of cores that are used in query processing.

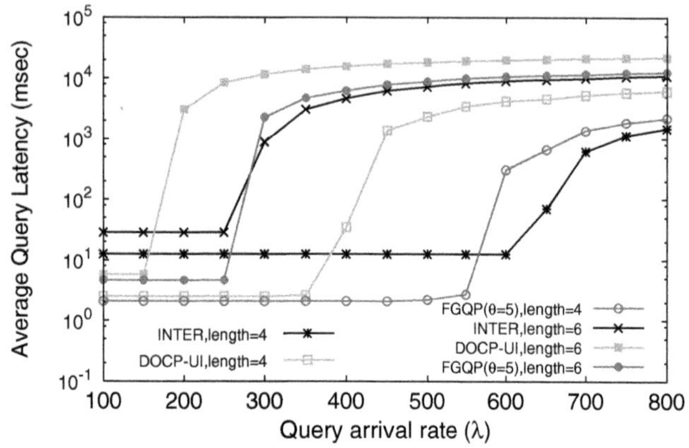

Figure 6: Performance with varying query arrival rate and query length.

future multicore server systems. We also observed similar trends for models that leverage intra-query parallelism. Furthermore, the performance of DOCP-PI is very similar to the one of DOCP-UI, and hence we do not include DOCP-PI in rest of the experiments.

While INTER and FGQP saturate around the same value of λ, the saturation point of DOCP-UI is notably much smaller. This can be attributed to the fact that document partitioning based strategies provide lower query throughputs (see Section 4.2). At small values of λ when the system is not saturated, the performance of FGQP is superior to that of INTER due to its task-level parallel processing. However, in a saturated system, this difference is small because the benefit from task-level processing is overshadowed by large queuing times experienced by the queries.

4.4 Effect of Query Length

Query length is known to be positively correlated with the performance of a search task [9]. A recent study showed that, in the past year, there has been a 22% growth in the number of queries with eight or more terms.[5] There are also estimations that the average query length has a tendency to increase over time.[6] Moreover, search backends are more likely to receive long queries as most short queries are caught by the result cache [27]. Given these observations, we conduct experiments to analyze the performance of our models as the query length is varied. For this experiment, we separate the AltaVista query log into nine bins according to query length (lengths are between two and ten). Each bin contains 10,000 queries of a particular length. This experiment is conducted on eight compute cores.

As shown in Fig. 5(b), the query length directly affects the average query latency, and it is indirectly related to the system throughput. Longer queries involve intersection of a larger number of lists, and hence they lead to higher query processing times. The average latency of queries with ten terms is approximately an order of magnitude greater than that of queries with only two terms. This accounts for a 11-fold drop in system throughput when processing longer queries. The intra-query models consistently provide better query latencies when compared to INTER, and FGQP performs marginally better than DOCP-UI. Fig. 5(c) indicates that the throughput of DOCP-UI is consistently lower than that of INTER and FGQP, and the difference between INTER and FGQP is only marginal. An interesting observation here is that the throughput difference among different models is higher when the queries are short. This is because the parallelization overhead is relatively significant when compared to the actual time spent in query processing.

The combined effect of query arrival rate λ and query length on the performance is studied in Fig. 6. We consider queries of length 4 and 6 in the experiment, and we change query arrival rate from 100 to 800 query/sec. For a given number of cores, the saturation limit is indirectly correlated to the query length – longer queries lead to earlier saturation. For a given query length, the trends are similar to those observed earlier in Fig. 5(a). In a saturated system, the queries suffer from large latencies, accounting for an increased waiting time spent in the queue. The amount of change in latency increases with the query length. It can again be noticed that DOCP-UI saturates prior to INTER and it experiences marginally higher latency at high values of λ. On the other hand, FGQP has a lower latency than INTER when the system is not saturated. They both saturate around the same value of λ, and beyond which they behave approximately in a similar manner.

4.5 Task Creation Overhead in FGQP

In this experiment, we measure the overhead incurred in FGQP model due to task-level processing. The task size not only affects the processing time but also affects the amount of synchronization that is required among cores. The synchronization overhead (due to accumulation, accessing the task pool etc.) is high when a given query is partitioned into a large number of tasks. We measure this overhead by defining two quantities: S_{avg} and O_{avg}. While S_{avg} is the average number of skips per list per task, O_{avg} measures the average number of overlapped skips per list, per task. They indirectly indicate the amount of work required and the amount of work that is repeated per task.

Recall that a task is denoted as the sequence of skips from each posting list involved in the query. For a query with m terms, a task t can be denoted as shown in Eq. (1). The average number S_t of skips in task t can be computed as

$$S_t = \frac{1 + (i_{2'} - i_2) + \cdots + (i_{m'} - i_m)}{m}.$$

The overall S_{avg} is computed as

$$S_{\text{avg}} = \frac{\sum_{\forall t \in T} S_t}{|T|},$$

where T is the set of all tasks generated for the entire workload of queries. Due to the way the tasks are generated, it is possible for two consecutive tasks t_1 and t_2 to share at most one skip per list. We quantify this overlap as follows:

$$t_1 = [(s^1_{i_1}, s^1_{1+i_1}), (s^2_{i_2}, s^2_{i_{2'}}), \ldots, (s^m_{i_m}, s^m_{i_{m'}})],$$
$$t_2 = [(s^1_{j_1}, s^1_{1+j_1}), (s^2_{j_2}, s^2_{j_{2'}}), \ldots, (s^m_{j_m}, s^m_{j_{m'}})],$$

where $j_1 = 1 + i_1$ and

$$O_{t_2} = \frac{\sum_{1<k\leq m} (j_k - i_{k'} + 1)^+}{m-1},$$

where $(\cdot)^+$ indicates that the entry is retained only if the

[5] http://www.itfacts.biz/average-us-query-size-in-january-2009/12782

[6] http://www.beussery.com/blog/index.php/2008/02/google-average-number-of-words-per-query-have-increased/

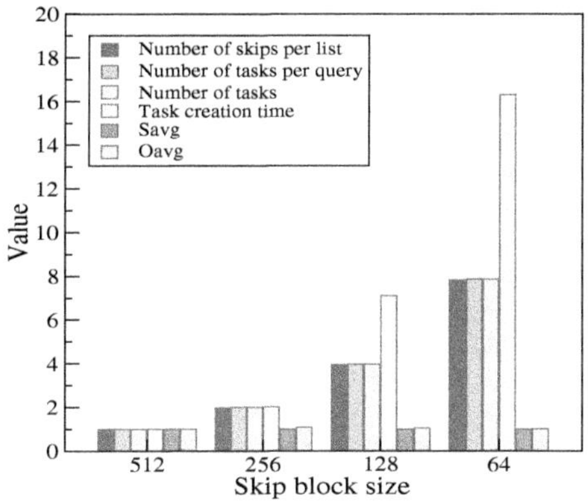

Figure 7: Overhead in task creation (8 cores).

argument is positive. Then, the quantity O_{avg} is computed as the average taken over all tasks in the workload.

$$O_{avg} = \frac{\sum_{\forall t \in T} O_t}{|T|}$$

Note that the first task that is generated for every query does not contribute to the summation.

Fig. 7 shows different quantities for various skip block sizes (B) by considering the values for $B = 512$ as the baseline. As B is reduced by half, both the number of skips per list and tasks per query double. Also, the amount of time spent in generating the tasks increases significantly as the value of B is decreased. Surprisingly, the values of S_{avg} and O_{avg} remain almost constant across the board. For each value of B, we observe S_{avg} and O_{avg} to be equal to 10.2 and 0.97, respectively, i.e., out of 10.2 skips/list/task, 0.97 skips overlap with the previous task. In other words, approximately 10% of the skips are processed twice. Overall, we observed that the time spent in task creation is only 2% of the total wall clock execution time. The overhead due to task creation is therefore very small when compared to the actual amount of work that is needed for posting list intersection.

5. RELATED WORK

In the literature, there are various techniques for parallel query processing on distributed architectures [3, 21, 24, 25], where the inverted index is partitioned over a number of nodes in a search cluster. These techniques are a form of high-level intra-query parallelism because parallelization is at the cluster-level and a query is processed concurrently by many index servers. Our work is complementary to these in that intra-query parallelism is employed further in every search node at the level of cores.

The problem of intersecting sorted lists has also attracted some attention [5, 6, 7, 16, 17]. Most of the proposed algorithms assume that the lists are already sorted. Typically, one of the lists is used as an eliminator and some random-access lookups are performed (via binary search, galloping search, or interpolation search) in the remaining lists for a target element in the eliminator list. Due to random accesses, these algorithms are not applicable to compressed posting lists unless skips are employed.

So far, the only work that considers the list intersection problem on multicore architectures is that of Tsirogiannis et al. [31]. The authors propose two algorithms called Dynamic Probes and Quantile-based. The idea in the first algorithm is to restrict the search space by using a micro-index that keeps a history of previous lookups. The second algorithm statically partitions the posting lists for the sake of improved load balancing, by using summaries of lists obtained via order statistics. Both algorithms require random accesses to the lists. The partitioning overhead is observed to become a bottleneck for high number of cores if the cache is not shared between all cores (see Figs. 11 and 12 in [31]).

Ding et al. [18] propose a framework for query processing on graphics processors (GPUs). Queries are first preprocessed on a CPU and then selectively scheduled on the GPU. Performance of their list decompression and intersection techniques developed for GPUs provide only marginal improvements over CPU-based implementations (see Table 2 in [18]). This is because the accesses to main memory from GPUs incur significant overhead, and more importantly, the way they parallelize the workload does not match the access pattern best suited to GPUs (sequential scans starting from some aligned memory locations).

Bonacic et al. [11] use a strategy similar to *Inter* that groups queries into batches and processes them sequentially on multicores. While their method is targeted at increasing query throughput, we focus also on reducing query latencies by exploiting the intra-query parallelism. Strohman and Croft [28] present a preliminary evaluation of in-memory query processing techniques on multicore systems. Their techniques exhibit modest performance improvements on a four-core system. Frachtenberg [19] also explores the performance differences between inter-query and document partitioning based strategies. In fact, the best approach suggested by Frachtenberg (referred to as FGMT in [19]) is same as `DOCP-UI` in Fig. 1(b). This work assumes that hits on document ids are evenly distributed. However, in practice, hits have a skewed distribution due to reassignment of document ids [10]. Our fine-grained `FGQP` model is immune to these kinds of biases in posting lists as intersection tasks are dynamically created. Moreover, compared to [19], we provide experimental results on a broader set of parameters.

6. CONCLUSION

We explored two different paradigms for parallel posting list intersection on multicore systems. While the inter-query model can scale system throughput with the number of cores by executing independent queries in parallel, the intra-query models are able to scale system throughput and reduce the average latency as we increase the number of cores. Our key contribution is in the design of a work partitioning strategy that divides a single query into multiple *small and independent tasks*, to enable *fine-grained parallelism* that is critical for effective parallel performance on multicores. When compared to the baseline approach that runs on a single core, this approach is able to speed up the intersection operation by up to a factor of 5.75 while keeping the throughput degradation to be as small as 3.3% – previous approaches experience at least 36% degradation. We also evaluated the influence of query length and arrival rate on latency and throughput, showing that the fine-grained intra-query model does not introduce any unexpected behavior compared to the inter-query approach. Finally, our analysis of skip block size indicated that smaller skip blocks increase the number of tasks and hence the overhead to create tasks. However, the fraction of redundantly processed skip blocks per task is almost constant irrespective of the skip block size.

We considered a hybrid strategy that switches between

intra-query and inter-query approaches according to query traffic. Our preliminary results did not show much improvement, and we are currently analyzing them carefully. As part of future work, we would like to investigate methods that leverage our parallel query processing models for improving the search quality, effective server resource provisioning, and designing *power-aware* algorithms that adaptively adjust the performance to stay within the budgeted power envelopes.

7. ACKNOWLEDGMENTS

This work has been partially supported by the COAST Project (ICT-248036), funded by the European Community.

8. REFERENCES

[1] V. N. Anh, O. Kretser, and A. Moffat. Vector-space ranking with effective early termination. In *Proc. 24th Int'l ACM SIGIR Conf. Research and Development in Information Retrieval*, pages 35–42, 2001.

[2] V. N. Anh and A. Moffat. Compressed inverted files with reduced decoding overheads. In *Proc. 21th Int'l ACM SIGIR Conf. Research and Development in Information Retrieval*, pages 290–297, 1998.

[3] C. Badue, R. Baeza-Yates, B. Ribeiro-Neto, and N. Ziviani. Distributed query processing using partitioned inverted files. In *Proc. 8th Symp. String Processing and Information Retrieval*, pages 10–20, 2001.

[4] R. Baeza-Yates, A. Gionis, F. Junqueira, V. Murdock, V. Plachouras, and F. Silvestri. The impact of caching on search engines. In *Proc. 30th Int'l ACM SIGIR Conf. Research and Development in Information Retrieval*, pages 183–190, 2007.

[5] R. A. Baeza-Yates. A fast set intersection algorithm for sorted sequences. In *Proc. 15th Annual Symp. Combinatorial Pattern Matching*, pages 400–408, 2004.

[6] J. Barbay. Optimality of randomized algorithms for the intersection problem. In *Proc. 2nd Int'l Symp. Stochastic Algorithms: Foundations and Applications*, pages 26–38, 2003.

[7] J. Barbay, A. López-Ortiz, and T. Lu. Faster adaptive set intersections for text searching. In *Proc. 5th Int'l Workshop on Experimental Algorithms*, pages 146–157, 2006.

[8] L.A. Barroso, J. Dean, and U. Holzle. Web search for a planet: the Google cluster architecture. *IEEE Micro*, 23(2):22–28, 2003.

[9] N.J. Belkin, D. Kelly, G. Kim, J.Y. Kim, H.J. Lee, G. Muresan, M.C. Tang, X.J. Yuan, and C. Cool. Query length in interactive information retrieval. In *Proc. 26th Int'l ACM SIGIR Conf. Research and Development in Information Retrieval*, pages 205–212. ACM New York, NY, USA, 2003.

[10] R. Blanco. *Index compression for information retrieval systems.* PhD thesis, University of A Coruña, 2008.

[11] C. Bonacic, C. Garcia, M. Marin, M. Prieto, F. Tirado, and C. Vicente. Improving search engines performance on multithreading processors. In *Proc. 8th Int'l Conf. High Performance Computing for Computational Science*, pages 201–213, 2008.

[12] Eric A. Brewer. Lessons from giant-scale services. *IEEE Internet Computing*, 5(4):46–55, 2001.

[13] C. Buckley and A. Lewit. Optimizations of inverted vector searches. In *Proc. 8th Int'l ACM SIGIR Conf. Research and Development in Information Retrieval*, pages 97–110, 1985.

[14] B.B. Cambazoglu, F.P. Junqueira, V. Plachouras, S. Banachowski, B. Cui, S. Lim, and B. Bridge. A refreshing perspective of search engine caching. In *Proc. 19th Int'l Conf. World Wide Web*, pages 181–190, 2010.

[15] B.B. Cambazoglu, H. Zaragoza, O. Chapelle, J. Chen, C. Liao, Z. Zheng, and J. Degenhardt. Early exit optimizations for additive machine learned ranking systems. In *Proc. 3rd ACM Int'l Conf. Web Search and Data Mining*, pages 411–420, 2010.

[16] E. Demaine, A. López-Ortiz, and J. I. Munro. Adaptive set intersections, unions, and differences. In *Proc. 11th ACM-SIAM Symp. Discrete Algorithms*, pages 743–752, 2000.

[17] E. Demaine, A. López-Ortiz, and J. I. Munro. Experiments on adaptive set intersections for text retrieval systems. *Lect. Notes Comput. Sc.*, 2153:91–104, 2001.

[18] S. Ding, J. He, H. Yan, and T. Suel. Using graphics processors for high performance IR query processing. In *Proc. 18th Int'l Conf. World Wide Web*, pages 421–430, 2009.

[19] E. Frachtenberg. Reducing query latencies in web search using fine-grained parallelism. *World Wide Web*, 12(4):441–460, 2009.

[20] Q. Gan and T. Suel. Improved techniques for result caching in web search engines. In *Proc. 18th Int'l Conf. World Wide Web*, pages 431–440, 2009.

[21] A. Moffat, W. Webber, J. Zobel, and R. Baeza-Yates. A pipelined architecture for distributed text query evaluation. *Inf. Retr.*, 10(3):205–231, 2007.

[22] A. Moffat and J. Zobel. Self-indexing inverted files for fast text retrieval. *ACM Trans. Inf. Syst.*, 14(4):349–379, 1996.

[23] M. Persin, J. Zobel, and R. Sacks-Davis. Filtered document retrieval with frequency-sorted indexes. *J. Am. Soc. Inf. Sci.*, 47(10):749–764, 1996.

[24] D. Puppin, F. Silvestri, and D. Laforenza. Query-driven document partitioning and collection selection. In *Proc. 1st Int'l Conf. Scalable Information Systems*, 2006.

[25] B. Ribeiro-Neto and R. A. Barbosa. Query performance for tightly coupled distributed digital libraries. In *Proc. 3rd ACM Conf. Digital Libraries*, pages 182–190, 1998.

[26] E. Schurman and J. Brutlag. Performance related changes and their user impact. *Velocity – Web Performance and Operations Conf.*, 2009.

[27] Gleb Skobeltsyn, Flavio Junqueira, Vassilis Plachouras, and Ricardo Baeza-Yates. ResIn: a combination of results caching and index pruning for high-performance web search engines. In *Proc. 31st Int'l ACM SIGIR Conf. Research and Development in Information Retrieval*, pages 131–138, 2008.

[28] T. Strohman and W. Croft. Efficient document retrieval in main memory. In *Proc. 30th Int'l ACM SIGIR Conf. Research and Development in Information Retrieval*, pages 175–182, 2007.

[29] T. Strohman, H. Turtle, and W. B. Croft. Optimization strategies for complex queries. In *Proc. 28th Int'l ACM SIGIR Conf. Research and Development in Information Retrieval*, pages 219–225, 2005.

[30] S. Tatikonda and S. Parthasarathy. Mining tree-structured data on multicore systems. *Proc. VLDB Endow.*, 2(1):694–705, 2009.

[31] D. Tsirogiannis, S. Guha, and N. Koudas. Improving the performance of list intersection. In *Proc. 35th Int'l Conf. Very Large Data Bases*, pages 838–849, 2009.

[32] J. Zhang, X. Long, and T. Suel. Performance of compressed inverted list caching in search engines. In *Proc. 17th Int'l Conf. World Wide Web*, pages 387–396, 2008.

[33] M. Zukowski, S. Heman, N. Nes, and P. Boncz. Super-scalar RAM-CPU cache compression. In *Proc. 22nd Int'l Conf. Data Engineering*, 2006.

Timestamp-based Result Cache Invalidation for Web Search Engines

Sadiye Alici
Computer Engineering Dept.
Bilkent University, Turkey
sadiye@cs.bilkent.edu.tr

Ismail Sengor Altingovde*
L3S Research Center
Hannover, Germany
altingovde@l3s.de

Rifat Ozcan
Computer Engineering Dept.
Bilkent University, Turkey
rozcan@cs.bilkent.edu.tr

B. Barla Cambazoglu
Yahoo! Research
Barcelona, Spain
barla@yahoo-inc.com

Özgür Ulusoy
Computer Engineering Dept.
Bilkent University, Turkey
oulusoy@cs.bilkent.edu.tr

ABSTRACT

The result cache is a vital component for efficiency of large-scale web search engines, and maintaining the freshness of cached query results is the current research challenge. As a remedy to this problem, our work proposes a new mechanism to identify queries whose cached results are stale. The basic idea behind our mechanism is to maintain and compare generation time of query results with update times of posting lists and documents to decide on staleness of query results. The proposed technique is evaluated using a Wikipedia document collection with real update information and a real-life query log. We show that our technique has good prediction accuracy, relative to a baseline based on the time-to-live mechanism. Moreover, it is easy to implement and incurs less processing overhead on the system relative to a recently proposed, more sophisticated invalidation mechanism.

Categories and Subject Descriptors

H.3.3 [**Information Storage and Retrieval**]: Information Search and Retrieval

General Terms

Design, Experimentation, Performance

Keywords

Web search, result cache, cache invalidation, freshness

1. INTRODUCTION

Large-scale web search engines maintain a cache of previously computed search results [5]. Successive occurrences of a query are served by the cache, decreasing the average query response latency as well as the amount of query traffic hitting the backend search servers. So far, most works in literature addressed issues related to cache eviction [23], admission [6], and prefetching [18], assuming limited capacity caches and a static web index. In practice, however, search engine caches are stored on disk and hence can be very large, resembling a cache with almost infinite capacity [10]. Moreover, the web index is not static; it is continuously updated due to new document additions, deletions, or modifications.

It has been recently shown that, when an incrementally updated web index is coupled with a very large result cache, the staleness of cache entries becomes an issue since cache hits may result in stale search results to be served [8, 10], potentially degrading user satisfaction. A simple solution to this problem is to associate with every cache entry a time-to-live (TTL) value so that the validity of an entry is expired after some time, i.e., hits on expired cache entries are considered misses and lead to reevaluation of the query. The TTL solution can be coupled with proactive refreshing of stale entries, i.e., recomputing cached results when backend servers have low user query traffic [10]. An alternative is to couple the TTL solution with cache invalidation mechanisms, where the cache entries whose results are predicted to change due to index updates are detected and invalidated [8].

This paper introduces a new mechanism, which utilizes timestamps to facilitate invalidation decisions. The proposed mechanism maintains a separate timestamp for each document in the collection and posting list in the index. Timestamps indicate the last time a document or posting list became stale, decided based on an update policy. Similarly, every query result in the cache is time-stamped with its generation time. In case of a cache hit, the invalidation mechanism compares the timestamp of the query result with timestamps of associated posting lists and documents to decide whether the query result is stale or not, based on a certain invalidation policy.

The proposed approach does not involve blind decisions, as in the case of TTL-based invalidation [10], or techniques that are computationally expensive [8]. In terms of computation, the proposed approach incurs little overhead on the system. Moreover, our approach can be easily integrated into a real search engine, due to its distributed nature. Finally, its accuracy in identifying stale queries and its suc-

*Work done while the author was at Bilkent University.

cess in reducing redundant query executions at the backend search system is better than that of TTL and reasonably close to that of a sophisticated mechanism [8]. In addition to the proposed invalidation mechanism, our work provides a detailed study of the cache invalidation problem, with several important parameters, such as query length, query frequency, result update frequency, and query execution cost, as real life query streams exhibit different characteristics for different applications (e.g., query results containing news pages may become stale more often than others).

The rest of the paper is organized as follows. Section 2 provides some preliminaries. The proposed cache invalidation framework and policies are presented in Section 3. We discuss our experimental setup in Section 4. Experimental results are presented in Section 5. Section 6 provides a cost analysis for the overhead incurred on the search system. Section 7 provides a survey of related work. We conclude and point to future research directions in Section 8.

2. PRELIMINARIES

2.1 Incremental Indexing Framework

We assume that every search node is responsible for storing and indexing a subset of documents in the collection as well as processing queries over its index (i.e., document-based partitioning). Mapping of documents to search nodes is through hashing of document ids into search node ids. Future modifications in the original document collection (i.e., document addition, deletion, and updates) are communicated to search nodes by the crawler, which continuously monitors the changes in the Web. Search nodes incrementally reflect these changes to their local indexes. We model updates on already indexed documents as the deletion of the old version succeeded by an addition of the new version.

In an ideal incremental indexing setup, changes on the document repository are immediately reflected to local indexes in search nodes. In practice, depending on the freshness requirements, the changes can be accumulated for a small time period and then reflected to index at once [8]. If the majority of the entire index is kept in main memory [13], this update process does not require a strict locking mechanism, i.e., updates can be applied on copies of inverted lists and do not affect queries that are concurrently processed on the lists. After all lists of a particular update are processed, the index pointers are set to point to the new lists. Document properties (such as length, link and content scores, etc.) are also updated accordingly. In our setup, we also maintain and update some timestamp values for affected documents and terms, as we will discuss in Section 3.

In Fig. 1, we illustrate a simplified version of the search system architecture we consider in this work. Typically, a result cache is placed within a broker machine. If the query is found in the cache, the answer is immediately served by the cache; otherwise, the query is processed at the backend search system. Note that, in the incremental indexing framework described above, the underlying index may be modified after query results are generated and stored in the cache. In this paper, we introduce mechanisms to detect and invalidate such stale query result entries in the cache.

2.2 Root Cause Analysis of Staleness

Before discussing our invalidation mechanism, we take a closer look at the causes that make a result in the cache

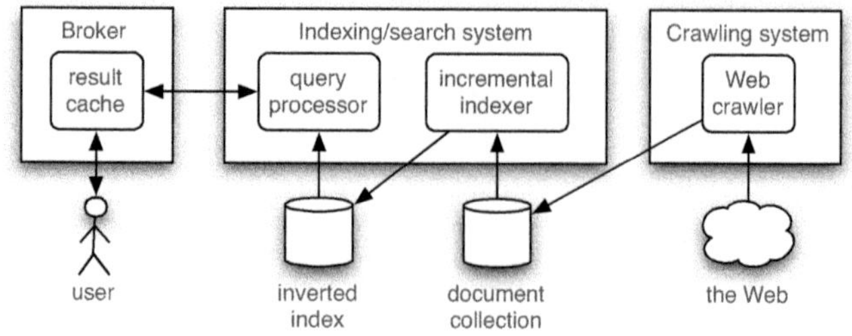

Figure 1: Architecture of the search system.

stale. We consider a query result stale if there is a change in the ids or the order of documents in the result [8]. In this respect, we claim that at least one of the following cases should hold to make the cached result R of a query q stale:

Case (i). At least one document d that was initially in R is either deleted, or revised in such a way that its rank in R is changed. In the latter case, some query terms that were previously found in d could have been deleted, their frequency could have been modified (i.e., by an increase or decrease), or document length could have been changed (i.e., terms that are not in q can be added to or deleted from d, or their frequency in d can be modified).

Case (ii). At least one document d that was not previously in R can qualify to enter R. In this case, a new document including all query terms (and yielding a high-enough score) could have been added to the collection, or an existing document could have been revised in such a way that its new score qualifies for R. In such an update, some query terms that were not previously in d could have been added to d, the frequency of query terms that appear in d could have been modified or, as in the previous item, the document length could have been changed due to modifications in other terms that are not in q.

We note that our discussion assumes a ranking function that is essentially based on basic document and collection statistics (e.g., TF-IDF, BM25). In practice, a revision on a document can also change the term distances within the text and subsequently, the document score, if a proximity-based scoring function is employed [24]. Similarly, changes on the graph-based features of a document (such as its PageRank score) may also change its overall score. In this paper, we assume a basic scoring function while evaluating the proposed timestamp-based invalidation framework to keep our experimental setup tractable (as in [8]). However, throughout the discussions, we point to possible extensions to our policies to cover more sophisticated ranking functions.

For handling case (i), the primary source of required information is the query result R (in addition to deleted and revised documents). However, handling case (ii) requires some knowledge of documents that are not in R, i.e., all other candidate documents for q in the collection. Obviously, this constraint is harder to satisfy. In the following section, we introduce our timestamp-based invalidation framework (TIF), which involves various policies that attempt to detect if one of the above cases hold for a cached query result. Note that, since it is not always possible to guarantee if any of these cases really occurred (without reexecuting the query), all invalidation prediction approaches involve a factor of uncertainty, and subsequently, a trade-off between prediction accuracy and efficiency. Hence, while tailoring our policies, our focus is on both keeping them practical and efficient to be employed in a real system and as good as the approaches in the literature in terms of prediction accuracy.

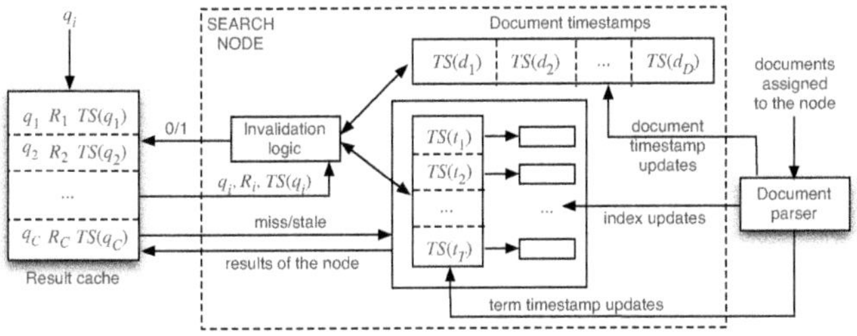

Figure 2: Proposed cache invalidation architecture.

3. INVALIDATION FRAMEWORK

Our framework has an offline (i.e., indexing time) and an online (i.e, query time) component (see Fig. 2). The offline component is responsible for reflecting document updates on the index and deciding on stale terms and documents. To this end, each term t in the vocabulary and each document d in the collection are associated with timestamps $TS(t)$ and $TS(d)$, respectively. The value of a timestamp shows the last time a term (or document) is deemed to be stale. The staleness decision for terms and documents are given based on the policies discussed in Section 3.1.

The online component is responsible for deciding on staleness of a query result. Each query q in the result cache is associated with a timestamp $TS(q)$, showing the last time the query results are computed at the backend. Our invalidation policy (Section 3.2) aims to predict whether any one of the cases discussed in Section 2.2 hold for a cached result. In a nutshell, we compare documents' TS values to query's TS value to identify the documents that are deleted or updated after the query result was generated, and can render the cached result invalid. To predict results that became stale due to the second reason, we compare query terms' TS values to query's TS value to identify queries whose terms start to appear in some new documents.

3.1 Timestamp Update Policies

Updating document timestamps. In Fig. 2, for the sake of simplicity and saving space, we present the data stored at a single node in the search cluster. At each index node, in addition to the inverted index and other auxiliary data structures that are typically used for query processing, we keep timestamp values for documents and terms.

We set the timestamp of newly added documents to the current date. For all deleted documents, we set TS to a predefined infinite value.[1] Finally, for a revised document, we compare the old and new versions of the document and set the timestamp to the new version's date only if their lengths (the total number of terms) differ by more than a fixed percentage L (this is similar to [8]). This parameter is intended to allow a level of flexibility in when a document can be considered as updated. When L is set to 0, every single modification of document would cause a TS update.

For document revisions, it is also possible to consider other features relevant to the underlying score function while determining the new TS. For instance, when the DOM structure or PageRank of an existing document changes (e.g., more than a predefined threshold), the document TS can also be updated. We leave exploring alternative score functions and their impact on invalidation as a future work.

Since each document is assigned to a certain index node via a hash function, we store a document's TS value only on the associated index node. That is, keeping track of document TS values is a simple operation and since its cost would be amortized during the in-place index update it would yield almost no additional burden on the system.

Updating term timestamps. For each term in the index (again, on a certain node), we update the timestamp value when a term's list is significantly modified in a time period. Analogous to the document TS case, our decision is guided by the amount of change in the length of a posting list. Furthermore, for terms, we can not only keep track of the number of modifications (addition and deletion of postings) but also estimate which of these modifications are more important in terms of the ranking score. In this respect, we describe two alternative policies, as follows.

i) Frequency-based update: In this policy, we keep an update counter that is incremented whenever the term's posting list is modified by addition or deletion of postings. Here, we only take into account the modifications due to postings that are newly added to a term's list (due to our anticipation that deletions from a revised document may less often make a result stale, in comparison to the addition of new content). When the value of a term's update counter exceeds a certain fraction (F) of its initial posting list length, the term is said to be stale. Then, a new timestamp is assigned to the term, and its update counter is set to zero.

ii) Score-based update: For each term's posting list, we initially sort the postings (in descending order) using the ranking function of the search system and store the score threshold, i.e., the score of posting at rank P ($S@P$). The parameter P can be set to a constant value (such as 10), or adaptively determined for each term as some percentage of the term's posting list length. At each modification to a list, we compute the score of the newly added posting, S_{new}. If $S_{new} > S@P$ for this list, we assign a new TS to the term, and recompute $S@P$.

In some sense, the latter policy resembles the posting list pruning method proposed by Carmel et al. [11]. In [11], posting lists are again sorted based on their ranking scores; and those postings with scores smaller than the score of the Pth postings are decided to be less worthy, i.e., can be pruned safely. Here, conversely, we imply that only those postings that can enter among the top-P postings of a term are valuable enough to update this term's timestamp.

Note that, both of these timestamp-update polices require only an additional field to be stored per index term, which a very modest requirement. Clearly, the score-based policy is more expensive than the frequency-based one as the former requires ranking of the postings in a list at each timestamp update for that term. In return to its higher cost, we anticipate that the score-based policy may identify those update operations that can change query results more accurately. This expectation is experimentally justified in Section 5.

It is possible to reduce the cost of the score-based update policy by employing a hybrid approach. For instance, it is possible to apply the score-based policy only for terms that appear in the most frequent queries (as can be obtained from previous query logs), whereas the frequency-based policy can be applied to other terms. Alternatively, the terms

[1]This choice simply allows a uniform presentation of our invalidation policy in the next section. In practice, it is also possible to set the timestamp value of a deleted document to a null value, or the deletion can be inferred by the system if it can not be found in the document TS data structure.

to apply the score-based policy can be determined based on the collection frequency or update frequency. These promising ideas are not evaluated in this work due to lack of space, and left as a future work.

3.2 Query Result Invalidation Policies

As seen in Fig. 2, the result cache stores the query string q, result R and timestamp value $TS(q)$.[2] For each cache hit, the triplet $\langle q, R, TS(q)\rangle$ is sent to index servers. Each node, in parallel, predicts whether the cached result is stale or not, using the term and document timestamps and the triplet $\langle q, R, TS(q)\rangle$ for the query in question. A node decides that a result is stale if one of the two conditions holds:

- C_1: If $\exists d \in R$, s.t. $TS(d) > TS(q)$ (i.e., document is deleted or revised after the generation of the query result), or
- C_2: If $\forall t \in q$, s.t. $TS(t) > TS(q)$ (i.e., each query term appeared in some new documents after generation of the query result)

Each node sends its prediction to the result cache, located in the broker. If at least one index server returns a stale decision, the query is re-executed at the index nodes, and R and $TS(q)$ information are updated in the cache; otherwise, the result in the cache is served to the user.

Note that the first condition of our policy can correctly detect all stale results due to deletion of documents in R. For result documents whose scores may have changed due to a revision, we adopt a conservative approach. If a document in R is found to have a larger TS value than the query's TS value, we assume that its rank in R would most probably change and we decide that the result would be stale. We also propose to relax this latter case by introducing a parameter M, which is a threshold for the number of revised documents to be in R to predict its staleness. That is, we predict a query result as stale if at least M documents in R is found to have a larger TS values than the query's TS value.

The second condition is intended to (partially) handle the stale results that are caused by a newly added document or a revised document (e.g., after addition of query terms), which was not in R but now qualifies to enter. For this case, we again take a conservative approach and decide that a query is stale if each one of its terms now appear in a sufficiently large number of new documents.

We note that the first condition, C_1 may cause some false positives (i.e., predict some results as stale that are, in reality, not), however does not yield any stale results to be served (when $L = 0$ and $M = 1$). That is, all stale results caused by the first case discussed in Section 2.2 would be caught. On the other hand, the second condition, C_2, can yield both false positives and stale results to be served, as it cannot fully cover the second case discussed in the previous section. For instance, assume a document that includes all terms of a particular query but its score does not qualify for top-10 results. Then, during a revision, if some terms that are irrelevant to the query are deleted from this document (so that it is significantly shortened), its score can now qualify for top-10. Clearly, this situation cannot be deduced by either conditions of our invalidation policy. We anticipate that such cases would be rather rare in practice. Nevertheless, to handle such cases and prevent accumulation of stale results in the cache, we adapt the practice in [8] and augment our policy with an invalidation scheme based on TTL.

[2]Snippets are omitted as they are irrelevant to this problem.

Thus, in case of a cache hit, a query TS is first compared to a fixed TTL value, and if expired, it is reexecuted; otherwise, our timestamp-based invalidation policy is applied.

4. EXPERIMENTAL SETUP

For the sake of comparability, we use the simulation setup introduced in [8] as blueprint and strictly follow that setup in terms of the dataset and query set selection as well as the simulation logic. In what follows, we discuss the details of our experimental setup.

Data. We obtain a public dump of the English Wikipedia site. This dump[3] includes all Wikipedia articles along with their revision history starting from Jan 1, 2006 to April, 2007. We omitted certain pages (e.g., help, user, image, and category pages) from our data as they are not useful for our experiments. The remaining data includes 3.5 million unique pages and their revision information. Since the information about deleted pages is not available, we construct the list of deleted pages on each day by querying Wikipedia using the MediaWiki API.[4]

Simulation setup. We consider all modifications on the collection (additions, deletions and updates) for the first 30 days following Jan 1, 2006. The initial snapshot on that date includes almost one million unique pages. For our dataset, the average number of page additions, revisions and deletions per day are 2,050 (0.2% of the initial dataset), 41,000 (4.1%) and 167 (0.02%), respectively. These numbers are similar to those reported in [8].

Following the practice in [8] (also to reduce the complexity of the simulation setup), we assume that all modifications on the collection are applied as a batch separately for each day. Thus, we create an index for each day by reflecting all changes of a particular day on top of the index constructed for the previous day. We used the open source Lucene library[5] for creating the index files and processing queries.

Query set. As the query set, we sample 10,000 queries from the AOL query log [28] such that each query has at least one clicked answer from Wikipedia.[6] The queries span a period of 2 weeks, and 8,673 of them are unique. We also verify that the query frequency distribution of our sample follows a power-law, which is typical for the Web.

We assume that, in each day, the set of queries is submitted to the search system. Using a fixed set of queries in each day allows evaluating the invalidation approaches in a way independent from other cache parameters (e.g., size, replacement policies, etc.), as discussed in [8]. Therefore, for each day in our simulation, we execute the query set on the current day's index and retrieve top-10 results per query, which constitutes the ground truth set. During query processing, we enforce the conjunctive query processing semantics.

Evaluation metrics. Each invalidation strategy predicts whether a query result in the cache is stale for each day within our evaluation period and accordingly decides either to return the cached result or reexecute the query. As defined in [8, Table 2], we evaluate cache invalidation strategies in terms of the stale traffic (ST) ratio (i.e., the percentage of stale query results served by the system) versus the false positive (FP) ratio (i.e., the percentage of redundant query

[3]`http://www.archive.org/details/enwiki-20070402`
[4]`http://www.mediawiki.org/wiki/API.`
[5]`http://lucene.apache.org/`
[6]`http://en.wikipedia.org`

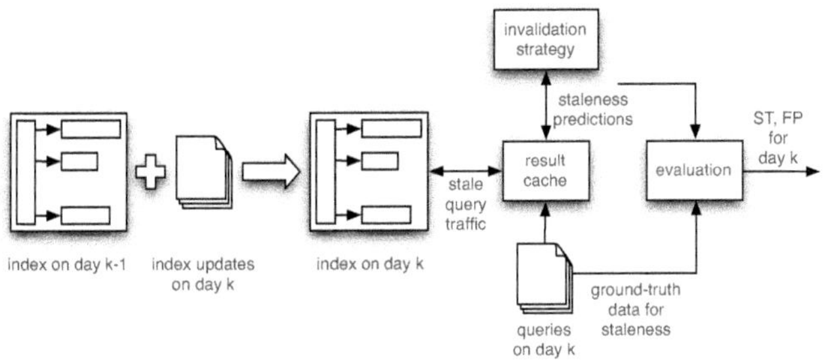

Figure 3: The simulation framework used.

executions). If the returned query result for a particular day differs from that day's ground truth in terms of the listed documents or their order, it is said to be stale. The entire simulation framework is illustrated in Fig. 3. All reported results are averages over the evaluation period.

Note that we do not present results with respect to the false negative (FN) ratio metric, which is also defined in [8], since we consider the ST ratio, which takes into account the frequency of the stale results that are served and stale results accumulated in the cache, as a more realistic metric to evaluate the success of an invalidation approach. Nevertheless, we also obtain plots with the FN ratio and when compared to plots with the ST ratio, we observe almost the same trends reported in [8]. These plots are discarded to make space for our presumably more interesting findings.

Baseline strategies. We compare our timestamp-based invalidation framework (TIF) to two baseline approaches in the literature. The most-straightforward baseline is assigning a fixed time-to-live (TTL) value to each cached query. As a stronger baseline, we implement the cache invalidation predictor (CIP) with its best-case parameters (i.e., using complete documents and score thresholding) [8, Fig. 6].

In our adaptation of the CIP strategy, a cached result is deemed to be stale if it includes at least one deleted document in a particular day (similar to the first case of our result invalidation policy discussed in Section 3.2). While handling additions, first all cached queries that match to the document at hand are determined, using conjunctive query processing semantics. Next, the score of the document with respect to each such query is computed, and if this score exceeds the score of the top-10th document in the cached result, the query result is marked as stale. For each day, we assume that collection statistics (such as inverse document frequency (IDF)) from the previous day are available to CIP.

5. EXPERIMENTAL RESULTS

In Table 1, we summarize the invalidation approaches and related parameters that are investigated in the following experiments. In the baseline TTL strategy each query result is associated with an expiration period (τ), and the result is decided to be stale at the end of this period. Since our simulation setup reflects all updates to the index in batch, each day, the $\tau = 1$ case simply corresponds to no caching at all, i.e., each query is executed everyday. This means that there is no stale traffic, however a very high fraction of queries are executed redundantly (i.e., about 86% in this setup). Not surprisingly, with increasing values of τ, the ST ratio increases while FP ratio decreases.

For the other baseline, CIP, we have two relevant parameters. We employ the document length parameter L in the same way as it is used for our timestamp-based policies; i.e.,

Table 1: Invalidation approaches and parameters

Approach	Parameter	Value range
TTL	τ	$1-5$
CIP [8]	τ	$2-5$
	L	0%, 1%, or 2.5%
TIF	τ	$2-5$
	L	0%, 1%, or 2.5%
	F	10%
	P	top-10
	M	1 or 2

a revised document is considered for invalidation only if its older and newer versions differ more than L% in terms of the number of terms contained. This is similar to the document modification threshold used in the CIP setup [8]. We also augment the CIP policy with the TTL strategy such that each cached query is also associated with τ.

Finally, our timestamp-based invalidation framework (TIF) uses the following parameters. For the document TS update policy, we experiment with L values of 0% (i.e., all revisions to a document causes an update on TS values), 1%, and 2.5%. For updating term timestamps, we use either the frequency-based or score-based TS update policy, as discussed in Section 3.1. For the former case, we set F to 10% (i.e., a term is assigned a new TS when the number of newly added postings exceed 10% of the initial count). For the latter case, we set P to 10 indicating that a term is assigned a new TS if a new posting has a score that can enter the top-10 postings of its list. Recall that, while computing posting scores, we can safely use the statistics from the previous day since the computation actually takes place at the index nodes and during the incremental index update process. Finally, the parameter M takes the values 1 or 2, indicating that a query result R at a particular day is predicted to be stale if it includes either one or two documents updated on that day (see Section 3.2). Our strategy is also augmented with TTL, i.e., the parameter τ is again associated with cached queries.

In Fig. 4(a), we compare the performance of TIF that uses a frequency-based term TS update policy (with L ranging from 0% to 2.5% and $M = 1$) to those of the baselines strategies. The figure reveals that our invalidation approach is considerably better than the baseline TTL strategy. In particular, for each TTL point, we have a better ST ratio with the same or lower FP ratio, and vice versa. For instance, when τ is set to 2 for TTL policy, an ST ratio of 7% is obtained while causing an FP ratio of 37%. Our policy halves this ST ratio (i.e., to less than 4%) for an FP ratio of 36%. Similarly, for τ values 3 and 4, we again provide ST ratio values that are relatively 31% and 38% lower than those of the TTL policy at the same or similar FP ratios.

In Fig. 4(b), we compare the performance of TIF that uses a score-based term TS update policy (with L ranging from 0% to 2.5% and $M = 1$) to those of the baselines strategies. A quick comparison of Figs. 4(a) and (b) reveals that TIF performs better when term update decision are given based on the scores, as expected. In this case, TIF yields about a half of the ST ratio values produced by TTL for the corresponding FP ratios for all values of τ. For instance, TIF yields around an ST ratio of 6% for an FP ratio of 23%, whereas TTL causes an ST ratio of 13% for almost the same number of false positives, i.e., at 22%.

While TIF can significantly outperform TTL baseline, its

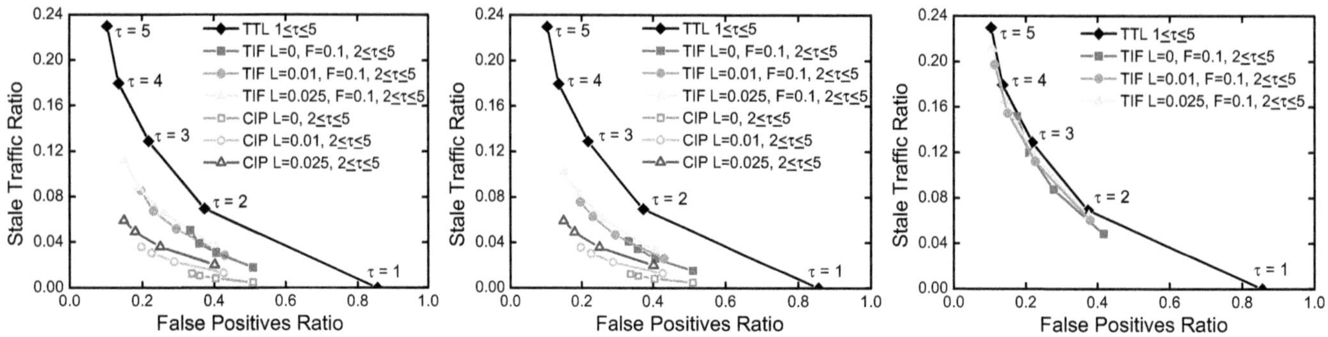

(a) (b) (c)

Figure 4: ST vs. FP for TIF: (a) frequency-based, (b) score-based, and (c) frequency-based ($M = 2$).

performance is inferior to CIP, although with a smaller margin at the smaller ST ratios. Our implementation of CIP is quite successful for reducing ST ratio; and it is even about 30% better than the best case reported in [8], which might be due to minor variations in the setup or other factors. However, this accuracy does not come for free, as CIP also involves some efficiency and practicality issues (of which discussion is deferred to Section 6). On the other hand, our approach is tailored to provide a compromise between prediction accuracy and efficiency, and not surprisingly, placed between TTL and CIP strategies in Figs. 4(a) and (b). In the following experiments, we also present cases where the gaps between TIF and CIP are further narrowed.

Impact of M. In Fig. 4(c), we report results with $M = 2$ for the case corresponding to Fig. 4(a). As expected, a higher value of M yields smaller false positive predictions but causes higher ST ratios. Surprisingly, even such a slight increase in M drastically affects the performance of TIF, rendering it almost same as the TTL strategy. This indicates that, document revisions are the most important causes of stale results, at least in our setup.

In the rest of this section, we analyze the performance of TIF regarding other aspects such as the query length, frequency, result update frequency and query processing cost.

Impact of query length. Previous works show that queries that are repeatedly submitted to a search engine have smaller lengths and, indeed, single-term queries constitute a large portion of them(e.g., see [32]). Therefore, it would be valuable to investigate the performance of cache invalidation approaches for single-term queries.

In Fig. 5(a), we compare the performance of TIF with the frequency-based TS update policy to TTL and CIP for single-term queries. As a quick comparison of Fig. 4(a) and Fig. 5(a) reveals, all strategies are more successful for single-term queries, as the absolute values of ST ratios drop. It also seems that the relative gain of our TIF over TTL is slightly improved for this case. For instance, in Figure 4(a), the ST ratios are around 9% and 13% for TIF and TTL for an FP ratio around 22%, respectively. Thus, the relative improvement of TIF over TTL is 31%. For the same FP ratio, Fig. 5(a) reveals ST ratios of 10% to 5%, for TTL and TIF, respectively, indicating a relative improvement of 50%.

For TIF with the score-based TS update policy, performance relative to baseline strategies are even better. In this case, TIF is not only superior to TTL, but it also performs very closely to the CIP strategy, as shown in Fig. 5(b). As the TIF approach employed in this experiment takes into account the changes in top-10 postings per each term, it can more accurately predict the changes in the results of single-term queries. Nevertheless, this experiment implies that for a real-life search engine where a significant amount of repeated queries include a single-term, the achievements of all invalidation strategies would be better and our TIF would provide better prediction accuracy.

Impact of query frequency. The simulation setting that we adapted from [8] involves several simplifications to be able to cope with the dynamicity and complexity of the overall system. One such simplification is for the query set, which is assumed to be repeated everyday. In fact, among 10,000 sampled queries used in our experiments, only 610 of them are repeated more than once in the original log (within the sampling period of two weeks). So, in a separate experiment, we investigated the performance of invalidation strategies for these queries that are more amenable to be repeated in the future. This is important, as repeated queries have different characteristics than those submitted only once [32]; i.e., they are shorter, may include more popular terms, etc.

We find that the performance trends are similar to those of single-term queries for all cases and therefore omit a graphical presentation of the results. The similarity of trends means that most of the frequent queries may involve only a single-term and we found that the fraction of single-term queries in queries repeated more than once reaches to 43%, whereas it is only 20% for our original query set. Again, this is an encouraging result indicating that the performance of invalidation polices would be better in more realistic settings, and the gains of TIF would be even more emphasized.

Impact of result update frequency. Depending on the collection change dynamics and the content of the queries, results of some queries may change rapidly (e.g., for a query about an event in news) while the results of some others may remain the same for a much longer time. We investigate the effects of the result update frequency on the invalidation policies. To this end, for each query, we computed the number of times the query result changes within our evaluation period (see Fig. 6(a)), and obtained their average, which is 4.32. In Figs. 6(b) and (c), we report the performance for queries that have higher or lower update frequency than this average value, respectively. In the former case, for all invalidation approaches, ST ratios significantly increase for frequently changing query results (see Fig. 6 (b)). This is an interesting finding, and it implies that more intelligent mechanisms should be developed for such queries. We also note that, while TTL gets considerably worse in this setup (e.g., for $\tau = 2$, ST ratio rises from 7% to 12%, a relative increase of 70%) , the drop in the performance of TIF is more

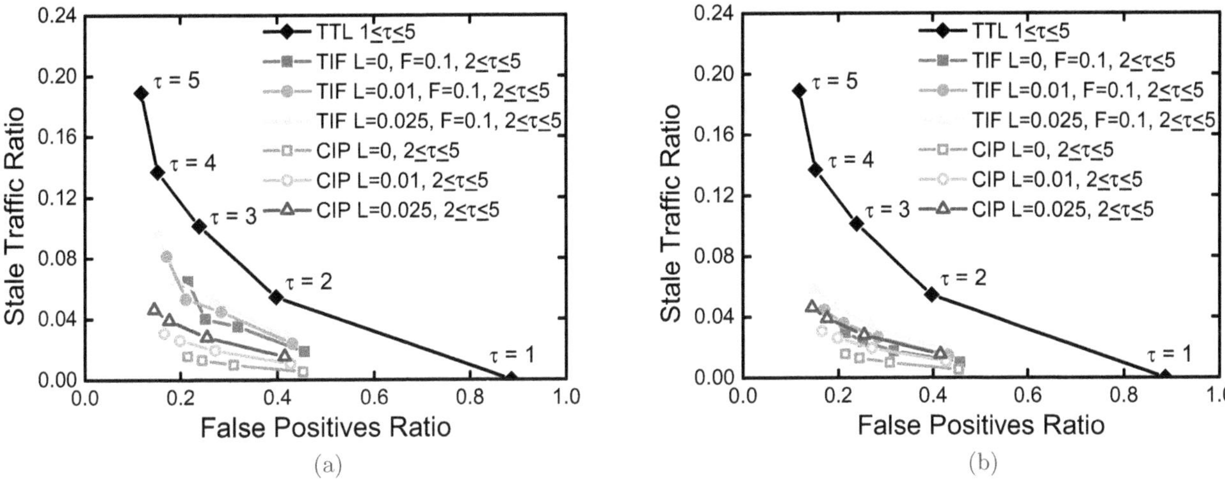

Figure 5: ST vs. FP for $|q|=1$ and TIF: (a) frequency-based and (b) score-based.

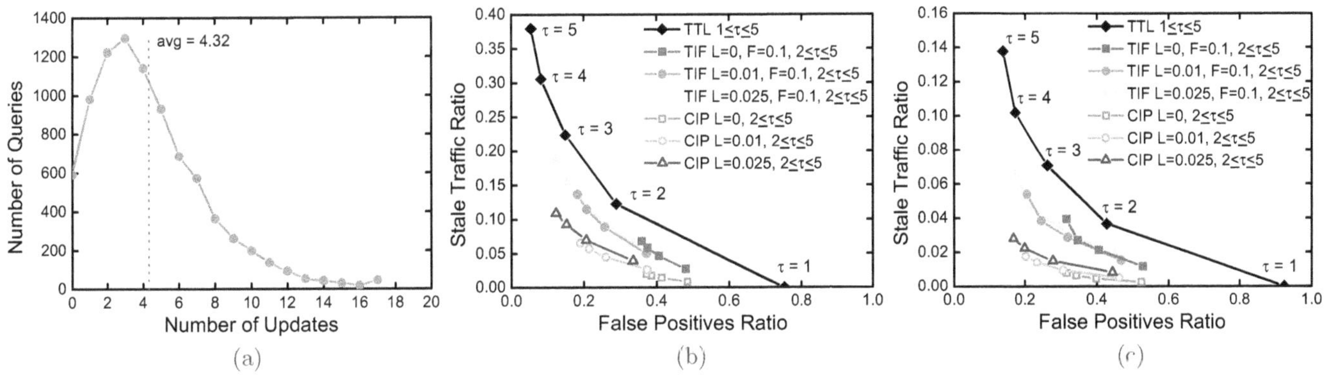

Figure 6: (a) Update frequency of queries (30 days), (b) ST vs. FP for $updateFreq > avg$, and (c) ST vs. FP for $updateFreq < avg$ (TIF with the frequency-based TS update policy).

reasonable, as TIF gets closer to CIP for small ST ratios, which would be more preferable in practice. Conversely, for query results that change less frequently, a comparison of Figs. 6(b) and 4(a) shows that all invalidation strategies perform better in this case (i.e., absolute ST ratios drop).

Effects of the query cost. In all experiments up to this point, we report false positive ratio, which is basically the fraction of queries that are executed redundantly. However, not all such queries have the same processing costs, and invalidation strategies may make different choices which may result in the same FP ratio but different processing burden on the search cluster. We investigate whether this phenomenon exists by modeling the processing cost of each query as the sum of its terms' posting list lengths (as in [16]) and repeating our experiments. In Fig. 7, we report FP-cost ratio vs. stale traffic ratio. A comparison of Fig. 4(a) to Fig. 7 reveals that the FP and FP-cost ratios are positively correlated for most cases. Therefore, integrating query costs into the decision mechanisms of the invalidation mechanisms may not yield significant improvements.

6. COST ANALYSIS

Since our timestamp-based invalidation framework and the CIP approach [8] share common underlying assumptions (i.e., most importantly, an incremental index update scheme) and have similar experimental setups, it is natural

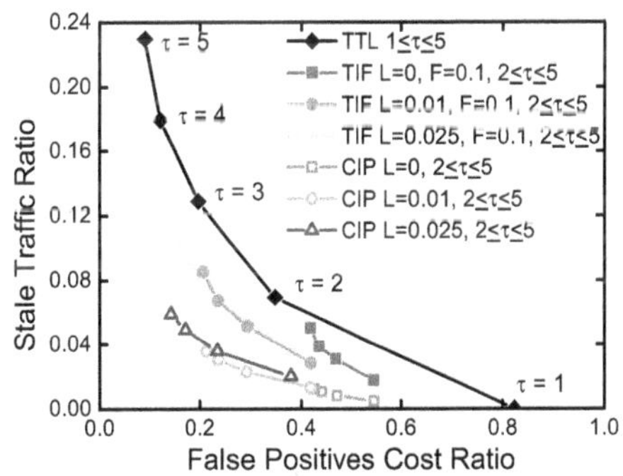

Figure 7: ST vs. FP-cost ratio (TIF with the frequency-based TS update policy)

to compare their efficiency. Recall that, our aim in this study is tailoring an efficient and practical invalidation strategy while providing prediction accuracies higher than the basic TTL scheme and close to that of the CIP. In the previous section, we showed that the latter goal is attainable, i.e., although CIP is generally superior to TIF, there are certain cases (especially for low ST values) where the prediction accuracy of TIF gets close to CIP. Here, we turn our attention to the cost of making invalidation decisions and compare TIF and CIP in terms of practicality and efficiency.

A major difference between the two approaches is the underlying architecture. Our invalidation framework is distributed, i.e., each index node updates document and term timestamps for its own subset of collection (offline) and checks staleness of results in case of a cache-hit (online). In contrast, CIP involves one or more centralized modules that find all matching queries in the cache to every modified (added or updated) document (offline), which may cause a bottleneck in the system. In this respect, we envision that our approach is more practical to fit in a real search engine. Moreover, our architecture allows the changes on the underlying index to affect further staleness predictions as soon as they are reflected. In contrast, CIP should match each document synopsis to the cached queries; and since it may not be possible to process all of the arriving synopses concurrently at a CIP module (especially if the collection changes are accumulated and propagated to CIP in batches), some queries might be served stale until all predictions are completed.

To evaluate efficiency, we formalize the cost of TIF and CIP in terms of the communication volume they cause on the network and the number of comparisons they need to make a prediction. We also provide a back-of-the-envelope calculation using some representative values of involved parameters in cost formulas, as described in Table 2.

i) Communication volume: The network cost of our policy involves the transfer of $\langle q, R, TS(q)\rangle$ triplets between the cache and index nodes for each cache hit. On the other hand, for CIP, the indexer should create a synopsis[7] for each change on the collection (i.e., added or updated document) and propagate it to the CIP module. We assume that the synopses include the term string, its frequency in the document and IDF value [8]. Note that the information in the synopses is needed to compute scores with matching queries in the CIP module. Moreover, the CIP module needs to transfer all cached queries and their results, so that it can make invalidation predictions and then forward its prediction for each query to the cache. In the formulas in Table 3, we neglected these latter costs for simplicity and only consider the cost of transmitting synopses.

ii) Number of comparisons during prediction: Another metric for comparing TIF and CIP is the number of in-memory operations to make a prediction. TIF (with the frequency-based TS update policy) simply compares query term timestamps and result document timestamps to the query timestamp, which is a negligible number of comparisons in the order of $r(q)+u(q)$. In contrast, the CIP module should make expensive score computations between all document synopses and matching queries in the cache. This computation requires an inverted index on the cached queries and accessing the posting list of each term in a synopsis.

As a further complication, invalidating queries with deleted result documents would indeed requires another inverted index on the cached results, i.e., an index mapping document ids to queries. This is not considered in cost formulas as its complexity would be similar to the score computation stage discussed above.

In Table 3, we provide the corresponding formulas for each cost metric discussed above. For a better comparison of TIF and CIP, we also consider a numerical example using the representative values provided in Table 2. We believe that the values presented in the table reflect the state-of-the-art for a large scale search engine. In particular, we consider

[7]We assume the synopsis is created for the entire document content since it yields the best prediction accuracy [8].

Table 2: The parameters and representative values for a large-scale search engine

	Parameter	Value
D	no. of documents in the collection	50 billion
N	no. of index servers	5K
Q	no. of queries per day	100M
C	no. of changed documents in D per day	$0.003\times D$
H	no. of cache-hits per day	$0.5\times Q$
$u(d)$	no. of unique terms in document d	500
$u(q)$	no. of unique terms in query q	2
$l(q)$	length of query q (in bytes)	20
$r(q)$	no. of cached results for query q	10
$p(t)$	posting list length of a term t (in the index over the cache)	10
$l(r)$	length of a unique result identifier (in bytes)	8
$l(p)$	length of a posting (in bytes)	8
$l(s)$	length of a timestamp (in bytes)	4
$l(t)$	length of a term (in bytes)	8

a collection size of 50 billion documents that is distributed over 5,000 index nodes. For simplicity, we assume that the textual part (after excluding mark-up etc.) of a document includes 500 unique terms and a query includes 2 unique terms, on the average.

Two key parameters in Table 2 are the collection change-rate and cache hit-rate per day, as they essentially determine the cost of CIP and TIF strategies, respectively. The former is hard to determine and there are several works reporting different rates of change for different subsets obtained from the Web (e.g., see [15, 1, 25]). Among these, the largest scale study of Web change has been conducted by Fetterly et al. [15], which reports that almost 3% of all Web documents change weekly. Relying on this finding, we set the daily change-rate of Web documents as 0.3% of the entire collection. That is, for a collection of 50 billion documents, we assume the number of page additions, deletions and revisions add up to 150M per day, which seems like a reasonable -or, even conservative- estimation (e.g., we anticipate that even the news sites all over the world can be adding millions of new pages in a daily basis). For the cache-hit rate, most works in the literature report a value around 50% depending on the cache parameters (e.g., see [5]), so we also rely on this value. Thus, for a daily load of 100M queries, which is, again, a reasonable assumption for state-of-the-art search engines, 50M queries result in as cache-hits. Finally, for the inverted index constructed over the cached query results in CIP, we assume average posting list length is 10; i.e., a term appears in 10 different queries, on the average.

When we plug the numbers of Table 2 into the formulas presented in Table 3, we see that CIP is more efficient than TIF in terms of the communication volume metric. The daily bandwidth usage of CIP is 5% of that of TIF. The disadvantage of TIF is caused since result triplets are sent to each of the N index nodes. However, in practice, the updates in the collection can be accumulated for a short time period and reflected to the index in batch (as discussed in Section 2). In this case, it is not necessary to resend the queries that occur frequently within a short time (such as "wikipedia") to the index nodes if the query timestamp is larger than the last batch's update time. We anticipate that this would significantly reduce the bandwidth usage of TIF in practice. Moreover, our calculation favors CIP as we as-

Table 3: The cost formulas for CIP and TIF

Cost Metric (per day)	CIP	TIF (with freq.-based TS update)
Communication volume (bytes)	$C \times (l(t) + l(p)) \times u(d)$	$H \times N \times (l(q) + r(q) \times l(r) + l(s))$
No. of comparison operations	$C \times \sum_{t \in d} p(t)$	$H \times (r(q) + u(q))$

sume just a single dedicated server for this purpose. In practice, there maybe several CIP servers in the system, which makes the bandwidth usage of both approaches comparable.

In terms of the number of comparison operations for invalidation predictions, TIF is a clear winner over CIP. In this latter case, CIP makes 1500 times more daily comparisons (i.e., by traversing the posting lists of the index over the cached queries) than TIF, which makes only a constant number of TS comparisons (e.g., 12 comparisons per cache hit according to Tables 2 and 3).

Finally, note that, although we assume a daily load of 100M queries, a search engine may cache a much larger number of queries, maybe all queries seen within a month, mimicking an infinite cache as discussed before. In this case, TIF performance would remain the same, as it only depends on the daily hit rate, but not the queries stored in the cache. In contrast, CIP has to access all cached queries to be able to invalidate them, which may further complicate the synchronization with cache servers and increase the costs.

Our analysis and example calculations show that although TIF causes a higher bandwidth usage, its prediction mechanism is very fast. CIP (at a single server) has lower bandwidth requirements, but actual prediction is much slower, which would be a bottleneck if the change-rate of the collections is high. Furthermore, TIF can be applied on top of a distributed search setup without additional burden, whereas CIP needs to synchronize CIP and cache servers. Hence, we conclude that TIF is a more practical and efficient policy than CIP, while providing better accuracy than TTL strategy, and a reasonably good accuracy in comparison to CIP.

7. RELATED WORK

Index updates. There are three basic approaches to keep a Web index fresh [20]. In the first approach, a new web index is periodically built from scratch over the current document collection and replaces the existing index. For mostly static document collections, this is the preferred approach. In the second approach, newly discovered documents are maintained in a so-called delta index [19]. Queries are processed over both main and delta indexes. Once the delta index is large enough, it is merged with the main index and a new delta index is grown. In the third approach, all modifications are performed on the main index [12, 31]. Modifications may be accumulated and performed in batches [33]. This approach requires maintaining some unused free space at the end of inverted lists, and the efficiency of update operations is important. It is preferred mainly for indexing document collections that are frequently updated. A hybrid strategy between the last two techniques is also possible [9].

Result caching. The first work on result caching in the context of search engines is [23], which provides a comparison between static and dynamic result caching approaches. A probabilistic caching algorithm is introduced in [18]. A two-level cache architecture that combines result and posting list caching is presented in [30]. A similar idea is discussed in [7], in the context of static result caching. A three-level cache architecture, which incorporates a cache for intersection of posting lists besides result and list caches, is proposed in [21]. A few recent works propose cache architectures that combine multiple item types [17, 22, 27]. A hybrid architecture, which combines static and dynamic result caches is discussed in [14]. Many issues in static and dynamic caching are covered by [5]. Several works [26, 3, 4, 16] consider query execution costs in caching. An incremental result cache is proposed in [29] for collection selection.

Staleness of result caches. We are aware of two recent works dealing with staleness of result caches in search engines. A TTL-based invalidation mechanism is presented in [10]. The same work also proposed proactively refreshing cached query results that are predicted to be stale by the TTL mechanism, before they are reissued by the users. Unfortunately, the impact of almost blindly reissuing queries to the backend servers on financial costs is unclear. This work is very different from ours in that it does not take into account the updates on the index when making staleness decisions. The closest work to ours is that in [8], which proposes an invalidation mechanism based on index updates. That work proposes identifying all stale queries by building an inverted index on the queries in the result cache and evaluating updated documents on this index.

In our work, we do not use a sophisticated invalidation mechanisms as proposed in [8]. Instead, our invalidation mechanism relies on very simple heuristics using timestamps assigned to queries, terms, and documents. Yet, we show that reasonable accuracies can be achieved by this mechanism, which incurs less overhead on the system and is much easier to implement. More detailed comparisons to this earlier work is provided in previous sections.

Finally, we have reported some preliminary findings in [2]. This paper extends our previous study in several ways. First, we introduce a new and effective score-based term TS update policy. Second, we investigate the performance of our approach for several parameters, such as query length and frequency, result update frequency, and query execution cost. Third, we implement and compare another closely related invalidation strategy, namely CIP [8], from the literature. Finally, we provide a detailed cost analysis and comparison of our timestamp based invalidation framework and CIP.

8. CONCLUSION

We investigated the trade-off between a cheap-but-inaccurate time-to-live based (TTL) strategy and a recently proposed accurate-but-expensive strategy [8] for invalidating stale results in a web search engine cache. To this end, we presented a simple yet effective approach that maintains timestamps for posting lists and documents, indicating their last revision times, which are compared with the generation time of cached query results to give invalidation decisions. Through a realistic and detailed simulation setup, we verified that the invalidation accuracy of our approach is better than TTL and reasonably close to that of the sophisticated invalidation strategy. Moreover, our approach is easier to implement and incurs less overhead on the system, rendering sophisticated invalidation strategies less attractive.

Result cache invalidation is a recent and active area of research, open to significant improvements. Existing works so far only concentrate on the accuracy of staleness decisions, ignoring other factors, such as the financial cost of these decisions on the search engine company or the satisfaction of users. As a future work, we plan to work on a unified invalidation framework that takes into account all these factors.

9. ACKNOWLEDGMENTS

This work is partially supported by The Scientific and Technological Research Council of Turkey (TÜBİTAK) under grant no. 110E135, FP7 EU Project LivingKnowledge (contract no. 231126) and the European Community funded project COAST-ICT-248036.

10. REFERENCES

[1] E. Adar, J. Teevan, S. T. Dumais, and J. L. Elsas. The Web changes everything: understanding the dynamics of web content. In *Proc. 2nd ACM Int'l Conf. Web Search and Data Mining*, pages 282–291, 2009.

[2] S. Alici, I. S. Altingovde, R. Ozcan, B. B. Cambazoglu, and Ö. Ulusoy. Timestamp-based cache invalidation for search engines. In *Proc. 20th Int'l Conf. World Wide Web (Companion Volume)*, pages 3–4, 2011.

[3] I. S. Altingovde, R. Ozcan, B. B. Cambazoglu, and Ö. Ulusoy. Second chance: A hybrid approach for dynamic result caching in search engines. In *Proc. 33rd European Conference IR Research*, pages 510–516, 2011.

[4] I. S. Altingovde, R. Ozcan, and Ö. Ulusoy. A cost-aware strategy for query result caching in web search engines. In *Proc. 31th European Conference on IR Research*, pages 628–636, 2009.

[5] R. Baeza-Yates, A. Gionis, F. Junqueira, V. Murdock, V. Plachouras, and F. Silvestri. The impact of caching on search engines. In *Proc. 30th Int'l ACM SIGIR Conf. Research and Development in Information Retrieval*, pages 183–190, 2007.

[6] R. Baeza-Yates, F. Junqueira, V. Plachouras, and H. Witschel. Admission policies for caches of search engine results. In *Proc. 14th Int'l Symposium on String Processing and Information Retrieval*, pages 74–85. 2007.

[7] R. Baeza-Yates and F. Saint-Jean. A three level search engine index based in query log distribution. In *Proc. 10th Int'l Symposium on String Processing and Information Retrieval*, pages 56–65. 2003.

[8] R. Blanco, E. Bortnikov, F. Junqueira, R. Lempel, L. Telloli, and H. Zaragoza. Caching search engine results over incremental indices. In *Proc. 33rd Int'l ACM SIGIR Conf. Research and Development in Information Retrieval*, pages 82–89, 2010.

[9] S. Büttcher, C. L. A. Clarke, and B. Lushman. Hybrid index maintenance for growing text collections. In *Proc. 29th Int'l ACM SIGIR Conf. Research and Development in Information Retrieval*, pages 356–363, 2006.

[10] B. B. Cambazoglu, F. P. Junqueira, V. Plachouras, S. Banachowski, B. Cui, S. Lim, and B. Bridge. A refreshing perspective of search engine caching. In *Proc. 19th Int'l Conf. World Wide Web*, pages 181–190, 2010.

[11] D. Carmel, D. Cohen, R. Fagin, E. Farchi, M. Herscovici, Y. S. Maarek, and A. Soffer. Static index pruning for information retrieval systems. In *Proc. 24th Int'l ACM SIGIR Conf. Research and Development in Information Retrieval*, pages 43–50, 2001.

[12] D. Cutting and J. Pedersen. Optimization for dynamic inverted index maintenance. In *Proc. 13th Int'l ACM SIGIR Conf. Research and Development in Information Retrieval*, pages 405–411, 1990.

[13] J. Dean. Challenges in building large-scale information retrieval systems. In *Proc. 2nd ACM Int'l Conf. Web Search and Data Mining*, page 1, 2009.

[14] T. Fagni, R. Perego, F. Silvestri, and S. Orlando. Boosting the performance of Web search engines: Caching and prefetching query results by exploiting historical usage data. *ACM Trans. Inf. Syst.*, 24(1):51–78, 2006.

[15] D. Fetterly, M. Manasse, M. Najork, and J. Wiener. A large-scale study of the evolution of web pages. In *Proc. 12th Int'l Conf. World Wide Web*, pages 669–678, 2003.

[16] Q. Gan and T. Suel. Improved techniques for result caching in web search engines. In *Proc. 18th Int'l Conf. World Wide Web*, pages 431–440, 2009.

[17] S. Garcia. *Search engine optimisation using past queries.* PhD thesis, RMIT University, 2007.

[18] R. Lempel and S. Moran. Predictive caching and prefetching of query results in search engines. In *Proc. 12th Int'l Conf. World Wide Web*, pages 19–28, 2003.

[19] N. Lester, A. Moffat, and J. Zobel. Efficient online index construction for text databases. *ACM Trans. Database Syst.*, 33(3):1–33, 2008.

[20] N. Lester, J. Zobel, and H. E. Williams. In-place versus re-build versus re-merge: index maintenance strategies for text retrieval systems. In *Proc. 27th Australasian Conf. Computer Science*, pages 15–23, 2004.

[21] X. Long and T. Suel. Three-level caching for efficient query processing in large web search engines. In *Proc. 14th Int'l Conf. World Wide Web*, pages 257–266, 2005.

[22] M. Marin, V. Gil-Costa, and C. Gomez-Pantoja. New caching techniques for web search engines. In *Proc. 19th ACM Int'l Symp. High Performance Distributed Computing*, pages 215–226, 2010.

[23] E. P. Markatos. On caching search engine query results. *Comput. Commun.*, 24(2):137–143, 2001.

[24] D. Metzler and W. B. Croft. A Markov random field model for term dependencies. In *Proc. 28th Int'l ACM SIGIR Conf. Research and Development in Information Retrieval*, pages 472–479, 2005.

[25] A. Ntoulas, J. Cho, and C. Olston. What's new on the Web?: the evolution of the Web from a search engine perspective. In *Proc. 13th Int'l Conf. World Wide Web*, pages 1–12, 2004.

[26] R. Ozcan, I. S. Altingovde, and Ö. Ulusoy. Cost-aware strategies for query result caching in web search engines. *ACM Trans. Web*, 5(2):9:1–9:25, May 2011.

[27] R. Ozcan, I. S. Altingovde, B. B. Cambazoglu, F. P. Junqueira, and Ö. Ulusoy. A five-level static cache architecture for web search engines. *Information Processing & Management*, in press, 2011.

[28] G. Pass, A. Chowdhury, and C. Torgeson. A picture of search. In *Proc. 1st Int'l Conf. Scalable Information Systems*, 2006.

[29] D. Puppin, F. Silvestri, R. Perego, and R. Baeza-Yates. Tuning the capacity of search engines: load-driven routing and incremental caching to reduce and balance the load. *ACM Trans. Inf. Syst.*, 28(2):1–36, 2010.

[30] P. C. Saraiva, E. Silva de Moura, N. Ziviani, W. Meira, R. Fonseca, and B. Riberio-Neto. Rank-preserving two-level caching for scalable search engines. In *Proc. 24th Int'l ACM SIGIR Conf. Research and Development in Information Retrieval*, pages 51–58, 2001.

[31] W.-Y. Shieh and C.-P. Chung. A statistics-based approach to incrementally update inverted files. *Inf. Process. Manage.*, 41(2):275–288, 2005.

[32] G. Skobeltsyn, F. Junqueira, V. Plachouras, and R. Baeza-Yates. Resin: a combination of results caching and index pruning for high-performance web search engines. In *Proc. 31st Int'l ACM SIGIR Conf. Research and Development in Information Retrieval*, pages 131–138, 2008.

[33] A. Tomasic, H. García-Molina, and K. Shoens. Incremental updates of inverted lists for text document retrieval. In *Proc. 1994 ACM SIGMOD Int'l Conf. on Management of Data*, pages 289–300, 1994.

Energy-Price-Driven Query Processing in Multi-center Web Search Engines

Enver Kayaaslan
Bilkent University
Ankara, Turkey
enver@cs.bilkent.edu.tr

B. Barla Cambazoglu
Yahoo! Research
Barcelona, Spain
barla@yahoo-inc.com

Roi Blanco
Yahoo! Research
Barcelona, Spain
roi@yahoo-inc.com

Flavio P. Junqueira
Yahoo! Research
Barcelona, Spain
fpj@yahoo-inc.com

Cevdet Aykanat
Bilkent University
Ankara, Turkey
aykanat@cs.bilkent.edu.tr

ABSTRACT

Concurrently processing thousands of web queries, each with a response time under a fraction of a second, necessitates maintaining and operating massive data centers. For large-scale web search engines, this translates into high energy consumption and a huge electric bill. This work takes the challenge to reduce the electric bill of commercial web search engines operating on data centers that are geographically far apart. Based on the observation that energy prices and query workloads show high spatio-temporal variation, we propose a technique that dynamically shifts the query workload of a search engine between its data centers to reduce the electric bill. Experiments on real-life query workloads obtained from a commercial search engine show that significant financial savings can be achieved by this technique.

Categories and Subject Descriptors

H.3.3 [**Information Storage Systems**]: Information Retrieval Systems

General Terms

Algorithms, Economics, Experimentation, Performance

Keywords

Web search engine, data center, query processing, energy

1. INTRODUCTION

A major challenge in front of web search engines is to cope with the growth of the Web and the increase in user query traffic volumes while maintaining query response times under a fraction of a second. The efficiency becomes an even more critical issue as user expectations about the quality of search results and the competitive nature of the search market enforce the use of more sophisticated and costly processing techniques. Consequently, satisfying the efficiency constraints in web search necessitates the use of large compute infrastructures as well as highly efficient software platforms.

The current solution to the efficiency problem is to carry out the web search business over massive data centers, containing tens of thousands of computers [3]. Due to space and power requirements, large-scale search engines spread their infrastructures and operations across several, geographically distant data centers. The key operations in a search engine involve web crawling, indexing, and query processing. In practice, a very large index is built over the crawled web documents. Each data center maintains a replica of the most recent version of this index. Queries issued by users are processed on the index replica in the closest available data center, yielding reductions in query response latencies.

As a consequence of their massive scale, search data centers incur significant financial overheads in the forms of depreciation costs, maintenance overheads, and operational expenses, taking away a large slice of the profit made through sponsored search. Among the operational expenses, an important cost is due to high energy consumption [2]. Most standard search engine tasks (e.g., query processing, crawling, indexing, text processing, link mining) are parallelized on many computers, consuming lots of energy. This, in turn, implies high electric bills for search engine companies.

In this work, we make an early attempt to reduce the electric bills of large-scale, multi-center search engines. Our work is mainly motivated by the following two observations:

- Energy prices show high spatio-temporal variation, i.e., they differ across countries and change in time [15].
- Query workloads of search data centers show spatio-temporal variation as well, i.e., the workload of a data center varies during the day [6] and some data centers may be under high traffic while others are mostly idle.

Based on these observations, we develop a technique that shifts the query workload from search data centers with higher energy prices to those with lower prices, to reduce the total energy cost. Although the idea of shifting the workload between data centers is simple, there are two constraints that complicate the problem in the context of web search engines. First, in practice, each data center has a fixed amount of hardware resources, i.e., a data center can handle only a certain amount of query volume, at any given

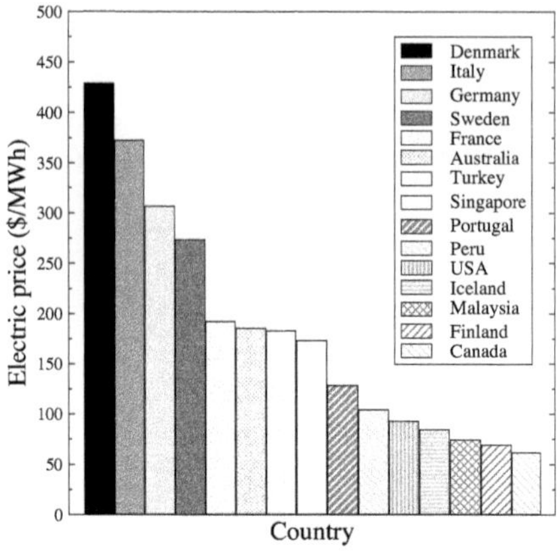

Figure 1: Electric prices in a representative set of countries in the world (source: Wikipedia).

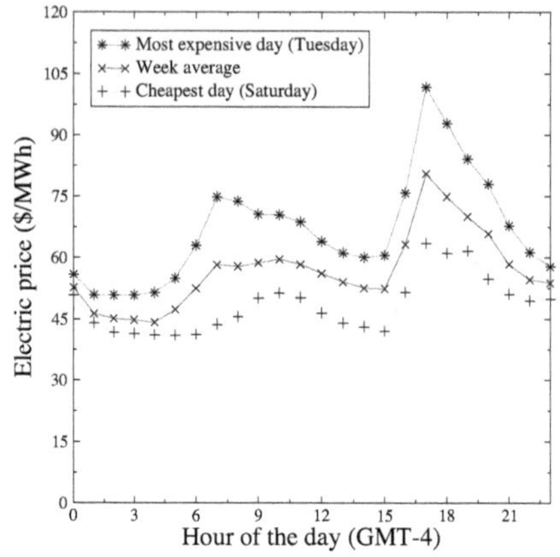

Figure 2: Hourly prices obtained over 15 different zones in the East Coast of the US (source: NYSIO).

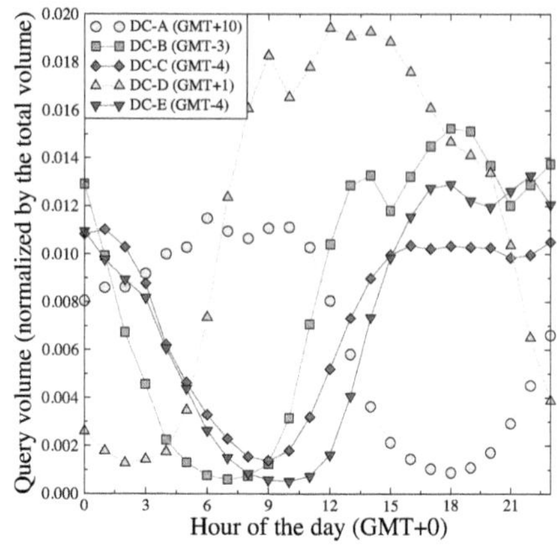

Figure 3: Hourly query traffic volumes observed on search front-ends of a commercial search engine.

time. Hence, it is not always feasible to redirect the entire search traffic volume to the data center with the cheapest electricity. Second, in web search, query response times are bounded. Hence, a query can be transferred from one data center to another only if the network latency between the data centers does not violate a query response time constraint. Our problem formulation captures both constraints.

The following summarizes our contributions. We discuss the energy-price-driven query processing problem in the context of multi-center web search engines. As a solution, we propose a probabilistic algorithm that dynamically shifts query workloads between data centers. We evaluate the proposed algorithm via simulations over a realistic search engine setting, using user queries obtained from a commercial web search engine, actual search front-ends, a large Web index, and real-life electric price data. Our results indicate significant financial savings for large-scale web search engines.

The rest of the paper is organized as follows. Section 2 motivates the idea of query workload shifting. In Section 3, we present the energy-price-driven query processing problem, together with the involved issues and performance metrics. The proposed solution is described in Section 4. We discuss, in Section 5, the details of our experimental setup. Section 6 provides the experimental results. A discussion on further issues is available in Section 7. Related literature is surveyed in Section 8. Finally, Section 9 concludes the paper.

2. MOTIVATION

Search data centers. Multi-center web search engines are known to have advantages over centralized search engines in terms of scalability and performance [7]. In practice, to further increase these benefits, the number and location of data centers should be carefully selected. The decision about data center locations is influenced by many factors, such as branding, user bases, energy prices and availability, climate, tax rates, and the political stability of countries. An important factor among these is industrial energy prices. A typical commercial web search data center consumes significant amounts of energy, which translates to an electric bill with many zeros for the search engine company.[1] Hence, there is a tendency to build data centers in countries where the energy is cheap (without completely ignoring other factors).

Variation in electric prices. Electric prices vary depending on geographical location. Fig. 1 shows the electric prices in a representative set of countries.[2] According to the figure, there is no apparent correlation between energy prices and the spatial distribution of countries. The price ratio between the most expensive (Denmark) and the cheapest (Canada) countries is about seven. Even if data center locations are restricted to the five cheapest countries, the price ratio is about 1.5. These numbers demonstrate the potential for financial savings in shifting query workloads from locations having high electric prices to cheaper locations.

Electric prices also vary in time, depending on factors such as supply/demand, capacity of transmission lines, and seasonal effects. The reader may refer to [15] for an analysis on the temporal behavior of electric prices in a wide range of markets in the US. Herein, we restrict our focus to hourly price variation within a day. As an illustrative case, we obtain the hourly electric prices from the day-ahead market of a power supplier, serving 15 zones in the East Coast of the US, and compute the hourly prices, averaged over all zones, for seven consecutive days in a week of December 2010.[3]

Fig. 2 shows the hourly electric prices for the cheapest and most expensive days, together with the average prices of the week. In general, there is high correlation across the days in terms of hourly price distribution. Prices make a peak early in the morning and late in the afternoon. Although web queries are online tasks, i.e., the processing of a user query cannot be delayed until the prices fall, temporal price variation provides further flexibility for workload shifting.

Variation in query traffic. The spatio-temporal variation in the query traffic volume provides another motivation to shift query workloads of data centers. Due to differences in time zones, some search data centers may operate under heavy workloads while others are underutilized. Moreover, the query traffic volume fluctuates throughout the day [6].

Fig. 3 shows the hourly query traffic volumes observed on five different front-ends of a commercial search engine,

[1]Some back-of-the-envelope calculations in a recent work estimate Google's annual electric bill to be $38 million [15].

[2]Wikipedia – Electricity pricing, visited on Dec. 28, 2010: `http://en.wikipedia.org/wiki/Electricity_pricing`.

[3]New York Independent System Operator, visited on Dec. 28, 2010: `http://www.nyiso.com/public/index.jsp`.

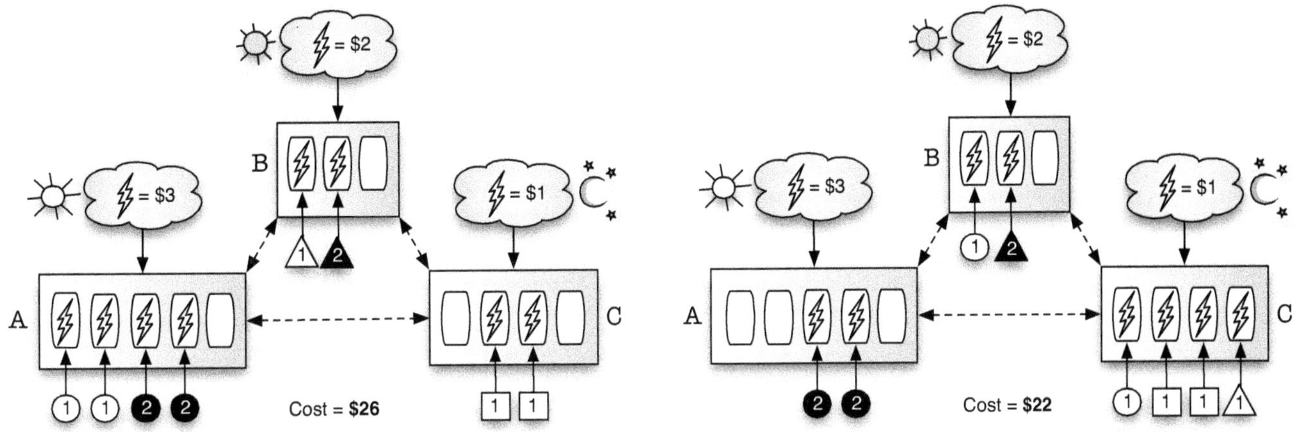

Figure 4: A sample query workload (left) is shifted between data centers to reduce the electric cost (right).

during the same 24-hour period. Query traffic volumes are observed to correlate with the local time. Typically, the volumes are higher during the day and lower during the night. As the time zone difference between two front-ends increases, the difference in their query volumes tends to increase.

Example. We informally describe our problem over the multi-center search engine setting depicted in Fig. 4. The example involves three data centers (A, B, and C), located in time zones that are sufficiently far apart. Data centers are connected through a wide area network. For simplicity, we assume that each data center maintains a number of homogeneous search clusters having the same compute power. In our example, data centers A, B, and C possess processing powers to concurrently process 5, 3, and 4 queries, respectively. In the figure, small triangles, circles, and squares represent queries issued to individual data centers at a particular instant in time. To further simplify the scenario, we assume that queries are either cheap or expensive, consuming 1 or 2 units of electricity, respectively. We also assume that expensive queries cannot be transferred between data centers due to the high overhead of network transfer, without exceeding a given hard limit on query response time. Finally, we assume that, at the instant of our example, each data center is charged a fixed cost for consuming one unit of electricity ($3, $2, and $1 for A, B, and C, respectively).

Given these assumptions, the initial setup on the left, where queries are processed in their local data centers, results in an electric cost of $26. By finding a better query-to-center mapping, this cost can be reduced. For example, in one extreme, if all queries are processed in C, which has the cheapest electricity, the total cost becomes $11. However, this is not feasible as the processing capacity of C can handle at most four concurrent queries. In practice, excess workload may cause intolerable delays in response time. Hence, in our work, we use data center capacities as a constraint. Moreover, we constrain response times of queries. A query is forwarded to a non-local data center only if its processing can be completed under a given time bound. In our example (on the right), two queries (one from A and one from B) are forwarded to C, and A further forwards one of its queries to B. However, although B has the capacity to process one more query, A cannot forward one of its expensive queries to B. The query-to-center mapping on the right yields the lowest possible cost ($22), without violating the constraints.

3. PROBLEM FORMULATION

The objective of the energy-price-driven query processing problem is to find a query-to-center mapping that minimizes the total electric cost incurred by a stream of web search queries. Our constraints are to keep query response times under a given time bound and to keep workloads of data centers under their capacities. Before formally specifying our problem, we introduce some notation and definitions.

Definitions. We are given a set $\mathcal{D}=\{D_1,\ldots,D_m\}$ of m data centers, a set $\mathcal{Q}=\{q_1,\ldots,q_n\}$ of n queries, and a continuous timeline T. Each data center $D_k \in \mathcal{D}$ is associated with a fixed query processing capacity C_k, which denotes the highest constant query traffic rate under which $\mathcal{D}_k$ can continue to process its queries before its waiting query queue starts infinitely growing, i.e., the capacity refers to the peak query processing throughput that can be sustained by the data center. Each query $q_i \in \mathcal{Q}$ is associated with a local data center $\hat{D}_i \in \mathcal{D}$, a time point $t_i \in T$ at which q_i is issued by the user, its processing time c_i, and the amount of energy e_i consumed while processing the query in a data center.[4]

We are given a response time limit r that sets an upper bound on the response time of a query, i.e., r is the maximum response time that can be tolerated by users. We are also given a function $\ell_{\text{uD}} : \mathcal{Q}\times\mathcal{D}\rightarrow\mathbb{R}$, where $\ell_{\text{uD}}(q_i, D_k)$ denotes the network latency between data center D_k and the user who issued query q_i, and a function $\ell_{\text{DD}} : \mathcal{D}\times\mathcal{D}\rightarrow\mathbb{R}$, where $\ell_{\text{DD}}(D_k, D_{k'})$ denotes the network latency between data centers D_k and $D_{k'}$.[5] Moreover, we define an energy price function $\pi : \mathcal{D}\times T \rightarrow \mathbb{R}$, where $\pi(D_k, t)$ denotes the financial cost of consuming a unit of energy in data center D_k at time point t. We also define a mapping $\Phi : \mathcal{Q} \rightarrow \mathcal{D}$ that assigns each query q_i to a unique data center $D_k \in \mathcal{D}$.

We now give three definitions that are used in our problem specification. First, we define the financial cost $\psi(q_i, D_k)$ of a query q_i processed in a data center D_k (at time t) as

$$\psi(q_i, D_k) = e_i\,\pi(D_k, t). \tag{1}$$

Second, the response time $\varrho(q_i, D_k)$ for a query q_i that is eventually processed on data center D_k is estimated as

$$\varrho(q_i, D_k) = 2 \times (\ell_{\text{uD}}(q_i, \hat{D}_i) + \ell_{\text{DD}}(\hat{D}_i, D_k)) + c_i. \tag{2}$$

[4]We assume that processing a query over the full web index consumes the same amount of energy in all data centers.
[5]Note that $\ell_{\text{DD}}(D_k, D_{k'})=0$ if and only if $D_k = D_{k'}$.

Finally, the workload $\omega(D_k, t, \Phi)$ of a data center D_k (at time t) for a given query-to-center mapping Φ is defined as

$$\omega(D_k, t, \Phi) = |\{q_i : \Phi(q_i) = D_k, t \in [s_{ik}, s_{ik}+c_i]\}|, \quad (3)$$

where s_{ik} denotes the time point that q_i is received by the data center D_k, i.e., $s_{ik} = t_i + \ell_{\mathrm{uD}}(q_i, \hat{D}_i) + \ell_{\mathrm{DD}}(\widehat{D}_i, D_k)$.

Problem definition. The energy-price-driven query processing problem is to find a query-to-center mapping Φ that minimizes the total energy cost $\chi(\Phi)$ incurred when processing a stream $\mathcal{Q}$ of queries under the mapping imposed by Φ, without violating performance constraints, i.e., to minimize

$$\chi(\Phi) = \sum_{q_i \in \mathcal{Q}} \psi(q_i, \Phi(q_i)) \quad (4)$$

while maintaining the response time of each query q_i below the given upper-bound r on query response time, i.e.,

$$\varrho(q_i, \Phi(q_i)) \le r, \quad (5)$$

and enforcing that the workload of no data center D_k exceeds its capacity C_k at no time point $t \in T$, i.e.,

$$\omega(D_k, t, \Phi) \le C_k. \quad (6)$$

Issues. There are three issues that complicate finding a solution to our problem. First, the estimated query response time ϱ of some queries may exceed the response time limit r, i.e., it may not be possible to find a feasible solution to the problem for any given input query stream. In practice, search engines have the freedom to fully process their queries or terminate their processing early so that the response time does not exceed r. While the first approach may lead to response times not tolerable by users, the second approach may yield degraded (low quality) search results [6]. Herein, we adopt the second approach and limit the query response time to r for all queries. This way, we can always satisfy the constraint in (5) at the expense of some degraded queries.

Second, search engines do not have a control on the incoming query traffic rate, i.e., the workload of a data center is an external, uncontrollable parameter. This may prevent finding a feasible solution to our problem, as the constraint in (6) may be violated. In practice, when the user query traffic rate exceeds the peak sustainable throughput rate of the search engine, a fraction of user queries (herein, referred to as overflow queries) are dropped without any processing or processed in degraded mode, spending little time.[6] Herein, we adopt a practical scenario and assume that the overflow queries are not processed by the search engine. This way, the constraint in (6) is always satisfied at the expense of some queries that are dropped without being processed.

Third, the query stream is not available from the start. Hence, an online algorithm is required to solve the problem at hand. This implies that the decisions made by the algorithm at some point may later turn out to be suboptimal.

Metrics. We have three different performance metrics. The first metric is the objective function given in (4), i.e., the total energy cost incurred by the query mapping Φ. This is our primary metric for evaluating the quality of a solution. The second metric is the rate R_{d} of queries that are degraded to prevent the violation of the constraint in (5), i.e.,

$$R_{\mathrm{d}}(\Phi) = \frac{|\{q_i \in \mathcal{Q} : \varrho(q_i, \Phi) > r\}|}{|\mathcal{Q}|}. \quad (7)$$

[6]Note that forwarding of queries may lead to constraint violations as well. We will take this into account in our solution.

Algorithm 1 MAPQUERYTODATACENTER(q_i, t)

Require: A user query q_i
Require: Time t at which the mapping decision is made

$\mathcal{W} \leftarrow$ ESTIMATEWORKLOADS(t)
$\mathcal{P} \leftarrow$ GENERATEPROBABILITIES$(\mathcal{W}, q_i, t)$
Select $D_k \in \mathcal{D}$ with probability $p_k \in \mathcal{P}$
$\Phi(q_i) \leftarrow D_k$
if $\varrho(q_i, \Phi(q_i)) > r$ **then**
  $\Phi(q_i) \leftarrow \widehat{D}_i$
end if

The third metric is the rate R_{o} of overflow queries that are dropped to prevent the violation of the constraint in (6), i.e.,

$$R_{\mathrm{o}}(\Phi) = \frac{|\{q_i \in \mathcal{Q} : |w'(s_{ik}, D_k, \Phi)| \ge C_k\}|}{|\mathcal{Q}|}, \quad (8)$$

where $w'(t, D_k, \Phi)$ represents the set of queries being processed on data center D_k at time instant t, i.e., the set $\{q_i \in \mathcal{Q} : \Phi(q_i) = D_k, t \in (s_{ik}, s_{ik}+c_i], w'(s_{ik}, D_k, \Phi) < C_k\}$, where overflow queries are not included in the workload.

4. WORKLOAD SHIFTING ALGORITHM

Overview. In this section, we present an online algorithm to solve our problem, taking into account the issues mentioned in Section 3. For every given query q_i, the algorithm decides on the data center $\Phi(q_i)$ at which q_i should be processed. Steps of the algorithm are as follows. First, the query workload of each data center is estimated by the local data center, at time t. Second, estimated data center workloads are used to compute a set $\mathcal{P}$ of probabilities, where p_k denotes the probability with which q_i should be processed on D_k. Finally, the data center $\Phi(q_i)$, which will process q_i, is selected based on the discrete probability distribution implied by $\mathcal{P}$. If the estimated query response time exceeds the response time limit, the query is mapped to the local data center. Algorithm 1 provides an overview of these steps.

Estimating workloads. We assume that data centers exchange messages at regular time intervals to let others know about their current workloads. We approximate the workload of a non-local data center at a certain time by using past workload values, sampled over a period of time, from its recent workload history. In Algorithm 1, $\mathcal{W}$ denotes the set of data center workloads estimated at time t. We assume that workloads and electric prices do not significantly vary while queries are being forwarded. Hence, the workload estimated for a data center is a close approximation for the workload the data center actually has while it processes q_i.

Generating probabilities. The basic idea is to forward queries to data centers that consume cheaper electricity with higher probability, also taking the capacities and current workloads of data centers into account. We note that, in practice, it is difficult to accurately determine the actual data center workloads when deciding whether to forward a given query or not. Hence, we resort to a probabilistic approach that spreads queries across data centers to prevent workload concentration in a single data center. Given a query q_i and the set $\mathcal{W}$ of estimated data center workloads, a local data center computes (at time t) the forwarding probabilities among all data centers as follows (see Algorithm 2). Initially, for every data center D_k, the current workload L_k of D_k is set to its estimated workload W_k. The algorithm

Algorithm 2 GENERATEPROBABILITIES($\mathcal{W}, q_i, t$)

Require: Set $\mathcal{W}$ of estimated data center workloads
Require: A user query q_i
Require: Time t at which the mapping decision is made

1: **for each** $D_k \in \mathcal{D}$ **do**
2: $\quad L_k \leftarrow W_k$
3: $\quad p_k \leftarrow 0$
4: **end for**
5: **for each** $D_k \in \mathcal{D}$ in increasing order of $\pi(D_k, t)$ **do**
6: $\quad$ **if** $D_k = \widehat{D}_i$ **then**
7: $\quad\quad p_k \leftarrow \widehat{L}_i / \widehat{W}_i$
8: $\quad\quad$ **return** $\mathcal{P} = \{p_k : D_k \in \mathcal{D}\}$
9: $\quad$ **end if**
10: $\quad$ **if** $L_k < C_k$ **then**
11: $\quad\quad \mathcal{D}' \leftarrow \{D_\ell : \pi(D_\ell, t) > \pi(D_k, t)\}$
12: $\quad\quad$ **while** $\mathcal{D}' \neq \emptyset$ **do**
13: $\quad\quad\quad \ell \leftarrow \arg\min_p \{L_p : D_p \in \mathcal{D}'\}$
14: $\quad\quad\quad s \leftarrow \min\{L_\ell, (C_k - L_k)/|\mathcal{D}'|\}$
15: $\quad\quad\quad L_k \leftarrow L_k + s$
16: $\quad\quad\quad L_\ell \leftarrow L_\ell - s$
17: $\quad\quad\quad \mathcal{D}' \leftarrow \mathcal{D}' - \{D_\ell\}$
18: $\quad\quad\quad$ **if** $D_\ell = \widehat{D}_i$ **then**
19: $\quad\quad\quad\quad p_k \leftarrow s / \widehat{W}_i$
20: $\quad\quad\quad$ **end if**
21: $\quad\quad$ **end while**
22: $\quad$ **end if**
23: **end for**

then iterates on all data centers where the unit energy consumption cost is lower than that of the local data center $\widehat{D}_i$ (in increasing order of prices). At each iteration, the algorithm picks a data center D_k and simulates forwarding decisions from remaining data centers to D_k. First, the current workload L_k of D_k is compared with its capacity C_k to make sure that there is available capacity for additional queries. If there is unused capacity, a set $\mathcal{D}'$ of data centers whose unit energy consumption costs are higher than that of D_k is constructed. Then, until $\mathcal{D}'$ becomes empty, the data center $D_\ell \in \mathcal{D}'$ with the lowest workload is picked and removed from $\mathcal{D}'$. At each iteration on $\mathcal{D}'$, the available capacity of D_k is evenly shared among the data centers remaining in $\mathcal{D}'$. Hence, the forwarding rate s, from D_ℓ to D_k, is computed as the minimum of the current workload L_ℓ of D_ℓ and an even share of the available capacity at D_k. Subsequently, current workloads of D_k and D_ℓ are updated. If the picked data center is the local data center $\widehat{D}_i$, the probability p_k of forwarding to D_k is set to the ratio of the forwarding rate s to the estimated workload $\widehat{W}_i$. The probability that q_i is locally processed is computed as the ratio of the remaining workload $\widehat{L}_i$ of $\widehat{D}_i$ to the estimated workload $\widehat{W}_i$.

The probability generation algorithm satisfies two invariants. First, the sum of the probabilities in $\mathcal{P}$ equals to one (line 8), i.e., there is at least one data center with non-zero probability. Second, if data centers conservatively estimate the workloads of others, then no data center becomes overloaded due to forwarded queries. When simulating workloads (lines 10–22), every data center conservatively assumes that the unused capacity of a candidate center will be evenly shared among centers with higher energy prices (line 14) and only forwards as many queries as its share allows.

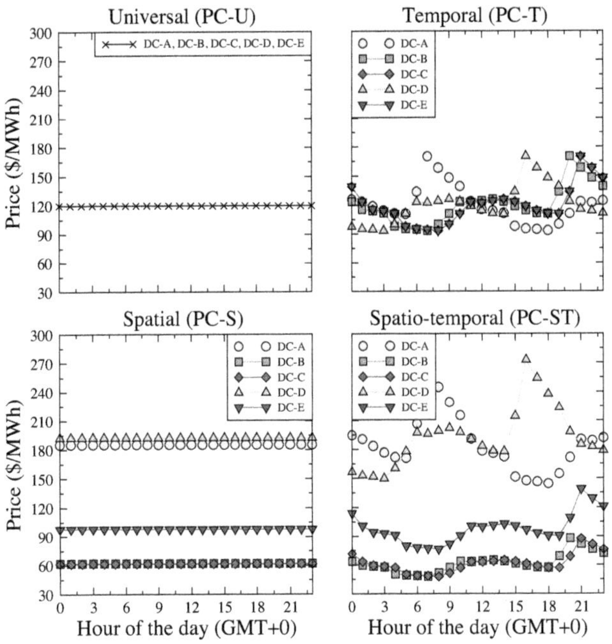

Figure 5: Electric price configurations used in the experiments: universal (PC-U), spatial (PC-S), temporal (PC-T), and spatio-temporal (PC-ST).

5. EXPERIMENTAL SETUP

Search data centers. We simulate a web search engine with five data centers, denoted as DC-A, DC-B, DC-C, DC-D, and DC-E. Data centers are assumed to be located in capital cities of five geographically distant countries, which are not disclosed due to the risk of revealing financially sensitive information about query traffic volumes. Network latencies between data centers as well as those between users and data centers are estimated by applying the technique described in [8]. We assume that the building blocks of data centers are identical, homogeneous search clusters. In our simulations, we determine the number of nodes in a search cluster such that each node serves about three million web documents. The number of search clusters in a data center is determined based on the query traffic volume received by the data center, i.e., each data center is associated with a separate peak sustainable query throughput value.

Result caching. We assume the presence of a query result cache with infinite capacity [6] in every data center. The result cache of a data center maintains results of queries issued by users as well as results of queries forwarded by other data centers. A time-to-live mechanism is not implemented as the performance is evaluated on a single day of queries. We assume that the time cost and energy consumption of looking up queries in the result cache are both negligible.

Electric price configurations. We generate four different price configurations (Fig. 5) based on the daily electric price distribution given in Fig. 2 and the mean of that distribution (about $120): universal (PC-U), temporal (PC-T), spatial (PC-S), and spatio-temporal (PC-ST). PC-U assumes that the price of electricity is fixed during the day and across all data center locations. In this configuration, all queries are locally processed since no cost saving can be achieved by workload shifting. PC-T assumes that prices vary during the day but not across data centers. Price distributions of data centers are identical to those in PC-U (but, they are shifted in time). PC-S assumes that prices do not vary during the day. However, there is spatial variability based on location. We obtain the spatial price variability by shifting the mean of the original price distribution by the real-life electric prices in the countries where data centers are located (using the data in Fig. 1). PC-ST is the most diverse, yet realistic configuration, where price distributions are computed by assuming both spatial and temporal price variations.

Data. We sample about 38 million queries from five different front-ends of the Yahoo! web search engine during four consecutive days (query sets S_1, S_2, S_3, and S_4). Queries in S_4 are used to evaluate our workload shifting algorithm. Those in S_2 and S_3 are used for parameter tuning purposes (see Section 6). Each set S_i is used to warm up the result cache before an experiment using the query set of day $i+1$. As the document collection, we obtain 200 million pages sampled from the Web. To prevent a mismatch between queries and the collection, we use only the documents whose predicted region matches one of the five data center locations. A proprietary region classifier is used to filter the pages.

Parameters. Each query is associated with a fixed preprocessing cost (e.g., query rewriting, spell checking), set to 20 ms. Queries are assumed to be processed over the full web index. Our algorithm is independent of the underlying ranking technique and has no impact on the search quality. The processing cost of a query is assumed to be correlated with the sum of its terms' inverted list sizes (i.e., the total number of postings) [11]. The total time needed to process a query is estimated by multiplying this cost with a per posting processing cost of 200 ns, which is an empirical value obtained from the Terrier search engine [14]. We try to keep the overflow query rate under a satisfactory value, set to 0.005 in our work (this requires the tuning described in the next section). As the query response time limit, we try several different values ($r \in \{100, 200, 400, 800, \infty\}$, in ms).

Baseline. Our baseline is the scenario in which all queries are processed in their local data centers, i.e., no query workload is shifted between data centers. We assume that a query is forwarded to non-local data center only if some reduction in the electric cost is forecasted. Ideally, some workload could have been shifted to reduce the overflow query rate even though there is no cost saving. We refrain from this kind of shifting as the primary objective of our work is to reduce the electric cost, not the overflow query rate.

6. EXPERIMENTAL RESULTS

Tuning data center capacities. In practice, data centers are given fixed compute resources, based on the query traffic volumes they receive. If the compute capacity of a data center is not carefully tuned, it may be underutilized or the overflow query rate may be too high. Hence, herein, we first perform such a tuning and assign each data center compute resources proportional with the peak query traffic volume it typically receives. When tuning, we assume that queries are not forwarded. In particular, we assign to a data center the least amount of compute resources sufficient to keep the overflow query traffic volume below a threshold.

In our setup, as shown in Fig. 6 (obtained with S_2), as data centers are given more resources, i.e., their peak sustainable throughput (PST) is increased, the overflow query rate almost linearly decreases. In our simulations, we set the PST values of a data center to the lowest value at which the overflow query rate remains below a threshold of 0.005. At this rate, the PST values we obtain are 31, 39, 34, 47, and 35 queries/sec, for the five data centers (listed in alphabetical order). In the presence of a result cache, the PST values we obtain are 13, 14, 14, 16, and 12 queries/sec. Note that lower PST values are sufficient in the latter case because a large fraction of queries are served by the cache. We use these two sets of PST values in the rest of our experiments.

Estimating data center workloads. A critical issue is to accurately estimate workloads of non-local data centers. We assume that each data center sends messages (every second) to other data centers to inform them about its current workload. The workload of a data center at a certain time is estimated by using its most recent workload history over a period of time, referred to as the window. In particular, we approximate the workload of a data center by the maximum observed workload value in its window. Note that taking the average is less conservative than using the maximum of sample workload values as it results in relatively lower workload estimates and thus higher overflow query rates. Hence, our choice of using the maximum sample value is reasonable.

In practice, the window size should be selected such that the workload estimates are as accurate as possible. Small windows may not have enough sample data while large windows may not capture the recent query traffic behavior, resulting in over-estimated workloads and hence low forwarding rates. In our work, we set the window size to the minimum possible value at which the total overflow query rate observed on the training query set (S_3) remains under the threshold we set before (i.e., 0.005). As shown in Fig. 7, when the window size is less than 10 seconds, overflow query rates are high as too many queries are forwarded to highly loaded data centers due to inaccurate workload estimates. In remaining experiments, for all data centers, we set the window size to 10 seconds for PC-T and to 16 seconds for PC-S and PC-ST. When caching is considered, we use 6, 7, and 7 seconds for PC-T, PC-S, and PC-ST, respectively.

Dissection of queries. We classify queries under degraded, overflow, non-local, and local classes. Degraded queries are those whose processing is early terminated due to the query response time limit. Overflow queries are those that are dropped as the data center does not have enough capacity. Non-local and local queries are processed in non-degraded mode at non-local or local data centers, respectively. This and remaining experiments use the test set S_4.

As seen in Fig. 8, the response time limit has a strong impact on the degraded query rate. Reasonable degraded query rates are obtained when the response time limit is larger than 400 ms. We note that the degraded query rate is independent of forwarding and is the same for all price configurations. The overflow query rate, on the other hand, is affected by these factors. However, due to the careful resource tuning mentioned before, this rate is kept under a satisfactory value in all possible scenarios (typically, 0.005, which is the permitted overflow query rate). Since the query response time limit is relaxed, there is more opportunity to forward queries between data centers. As mentioned before, no queries can be forwarded in the PC-U setup.

Impact of result caching. On aggregate, about 63% of the query traffic volume is served by the result cache. Fig. 9 shows the dissection of queries for the "miss" query traffic volume hitting the backend search systems. In general, caching reduces the degraded query rate. However, since

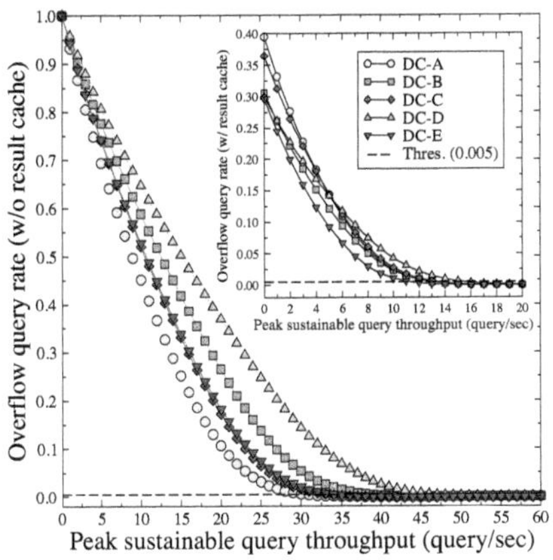

Figure 6: Overflow query rate versus peak sustainable query throughput of data centers.

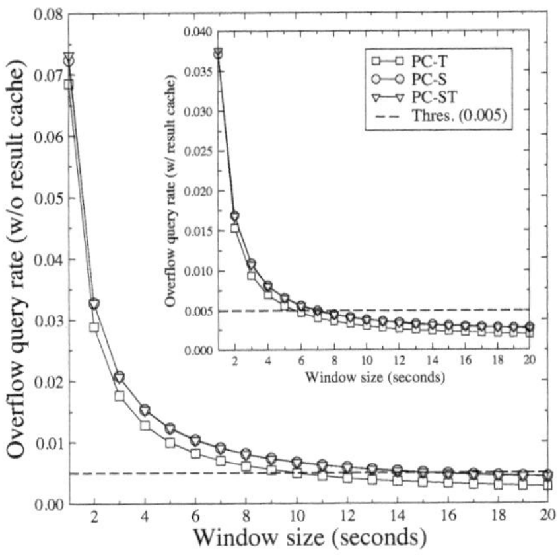

Figure 7: Overflow query rate as the window size varies.

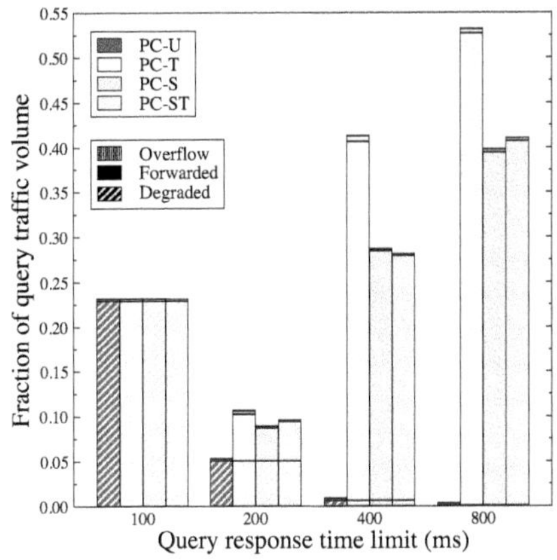

Figure 8: Degraded, forwarded, and overflow query rates (without result caching).

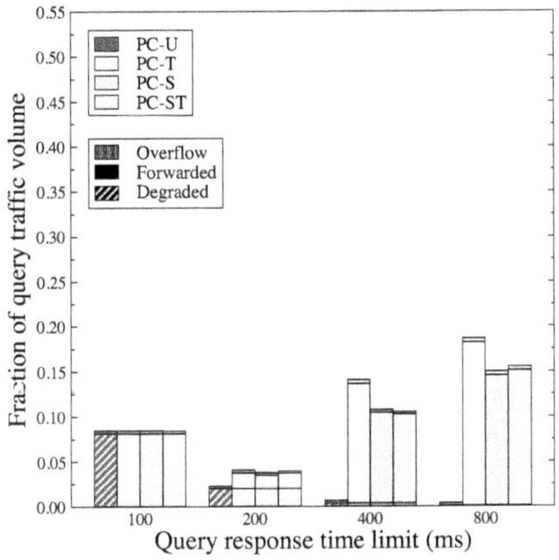

Figure 9: Degraded, forwarded, and overflow query rates (with result caching).

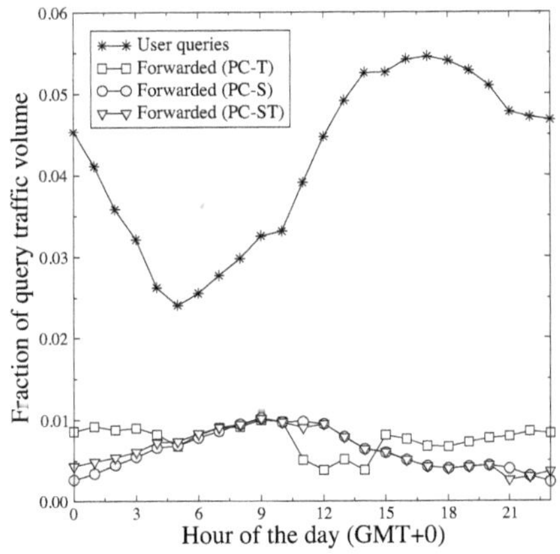

Figure 10: The rate of forwarded queries as the user query traffic volume varies ($r = 800$).

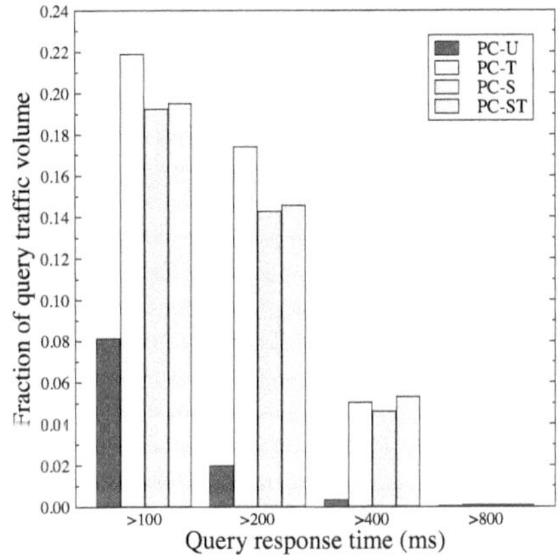

Figure 11: The rate of queries that are responded beyond a certain time delay ($r = \infty$).

data center capacities are separately tuned for the caching scenario, it has no impact on the overflow query rate, which remains around 0.005. In the rest of our experiments, we consider only the case in which a result cache is present.

Query forwarding rates. Fig. 10 shows the aggregate hourly query forwarding rate of data centers for different price setups and the variation of the hourly user query traffic volume (w.r.t. GMT+0). The reported forwarding rates are relative to the total user query traffic volume and include overflow queries, which may also be forwarded to non-local data centers. Intuitively, having more user queries implies a higher query forwarding rate. Interestingly, however, we observe that forwarding rates may drop as the user query traffic volume increases. This is because data centers have increased workloads and hence the solution space of our workload shifting algorithm is restricted. In general, the forwarding rate is more stable for the PC-T setup as price variation is lower relative to PC-S and PC-ST. We also observe that PC-ST highly correlates with PC-S, as forwarding decisions depend on the ordinal ranking of data centers according to their unit energy consumption costs, instead of the actual costs, and as electric price differences across countries are more dominant than intra-day price volatility.

Query response times. Fig. 11 shows the fraction of queries that cannot be answered under a specific amount of time, assuming there is no bound on the response time limit. According to the figure, almost all queries can be processed under 800 ms. In general, the PC-T, PC-S, and PC-ST scenarios result in higher query response times (on average, 109 ms, 103 ms, and 105 ms, respectively), relative to the average response time of the PC-U scenario (66 ms), where all queries are processed in their local data centers. Nevertheless, around only 5% of the query volume cannot be processed under 400 ms, which is a satisfactory result for the web search engine standards. This implies that, despite the large network latencies between data centers, forwarding of queries and hence reduction in electric costs is possible.

Saving in the electric cost. Fig. 12 shows our most striking result. Depending on the price setup, significant savings are achieved in electric costs relative to the respective baselines in which no workload is shifted. The largest saving (about 35% when $r = \infty$) is possible with the PC-ST scenario, which has the largest variation in electric prices.

Temporal effects. In general, the saving in the electric cost due to workload shifting is affected by the forwarding rate, which depends on the query traffic volume and electric

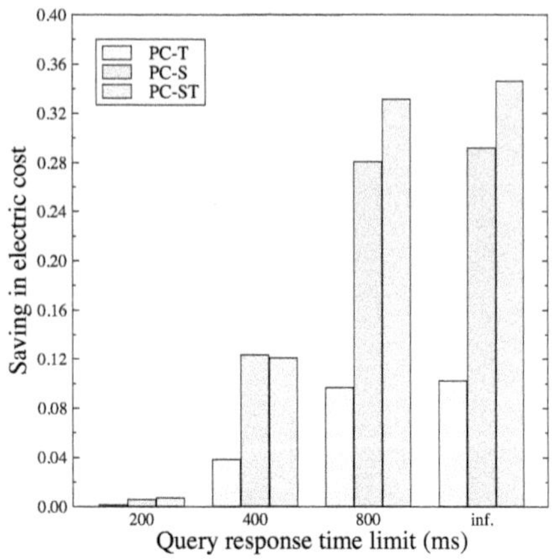

Figure 12: Saving in electric costs for different price configurations.

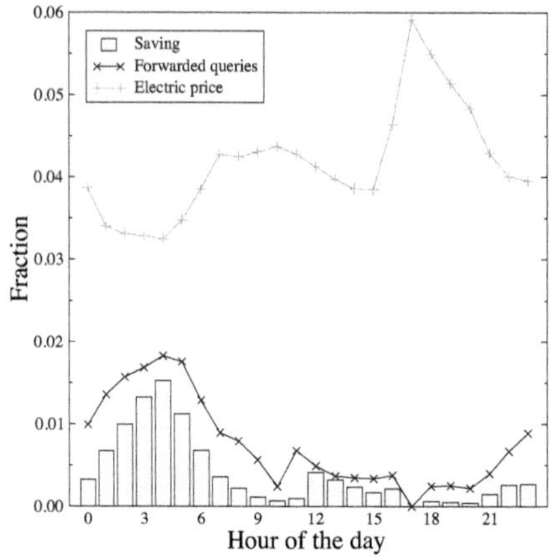

Figure 13: Temporal distribution of the cost saving (PC-T, $r = 800$).

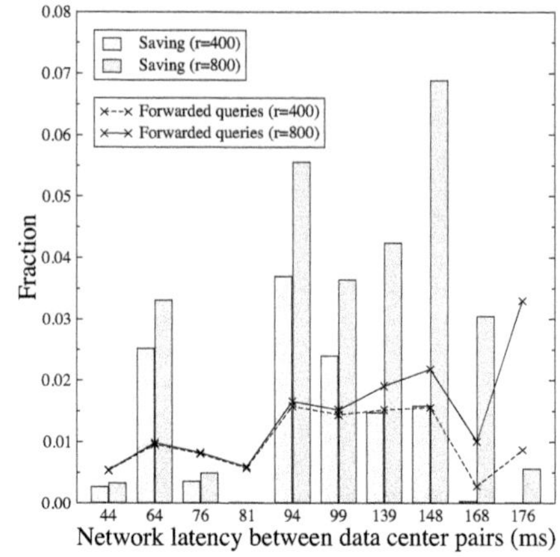

Figure 14: Spatial distribution of the cost saving (PC-S).

prices. Fig. 13 shows the distribution of the saving for the PC-T price setup, as the query forwarding rates and electric prices vary (for $r = 800$ and w.r.t the local time of the data center where the query is processed). As seen in the figure, there is a high correlation between the query forwarding rate and the saving. This implies a negative correlation between the electric price and cost saving, i.e., fewer queries are forwarded when electric prices are high. It is interesting to note that, at 17:00 PM, the query forwarding rate falls to zero. At this hour of the day, the price of electricity consumed by data centers reaches the global maximum and no queries can be forwarded to a data center operating at this hour.

Spatial effects. Fig. 14 shows the distribution of the saving for the PC-S setup, as the query forwarding rate varies (the x axis shows the network latencies between data center pairs, for all possible pairs). Although not very strong, we observe some positive correlation between query forwarding rates and network latencies between data centers. This is somewhat surprising as one may expect more queries to be forwarded when the latency between two data centers is low. In practice, however, data centers with low latencies tend to be located in nearby time zones. This implies that their hourly query traffic volumes follow a similar pattern, rendering forwarding of queries more difficult. The price of electricity consumed by data centers forms another factor. As an example, consider data centers DC-D and DC-A, which consume the most expensive electricity (see Fig. 5). Although they are geographically very close (the network latency is 81 ms, in Fig. 14), these two data centers almost never forward queries to each other, as they prefer forwarding their queries to other data centers. We note that, in the PC-S setup, the entire forwarded query traffic volume between two data centers is generated by the data center that consumes cheaper energy, whereas forwarding of queries can be bidirectional in the PC-T and PC-ST setups. In general, most of the saving is obtained from data centers located in far-away time zones with a large difference in electric prices. Finally, we note that, although the network latency is not dominantly decisive in query forwarding rates, it becomes more decisive as the response time limit is reduced. In Fig. 14, we observe that, when $r = 800$, a significant fraction of the cost saving is achieved due to forwarding of queries between far apart data centers. When $r = 400$, however, some distant pairs of data centers are unable to exchange their workloads.

7. DISCUSSION

Impact of server utilization. The energy consumption of modern servers depends on their utilization level [4]. Shifting query workloads between data centers may have an impact on the utilization of compute servers in data centers and, in turn, affect their energy consumption. In our setup, the utilization distribution we observe when no queries are forwarded (see Fig. 15) is comparable to that reported for Google servers [5, p. 55]. However, when the workload is shifted, we obtain a quite different distribution (shown in the figure for the PC-ST scenario). We observe that data centers now have significantly more idle cycles and, in the mean time, their utilization is shifted towards higher levels.

We analyze the impact of this shift in utilization levels on the cost saving, analytically, via representative functions that map a utilization level u to a value c, indicating the energy consumption at level u relative to the consumption at peak utilization. Following [5], we evaluate functions of the form $c(u,p) = (1+u^p)/2$, where p is a free parameter ($p \in \{0.25, 0.5, 1, 2, 4\}$). Here, increasing values of p increase the energy-efficiency of compute resources running at low utilization levels. For convenience, the evaluated functions are plotted in Fig. 16.[7] The linear function $c(u,1)$ is typical for today's servers while the rest are hypothetical.

In Fig. 17, we report the respective cost savings for the above-mentioned functions. For $r = 800$, we observe that workload shifting highly benefits from increasing energy efficiency of servers. We note that the increase in idle cycles lets workload shifting benefit from power saving techniques (e.g., shutting down servers or putting them in sleep mode).

Unified cost model. Shifting workloads is not only useful for reducing the energy cost, but also for increasing data centers' availability, performance, and service quality. Ideally, all these factors should be combined under a unified cost model. In the particular case of search engines, financial implications of search result quality and search efficiency should be quantified and incorporated into this cost model.

Electric prices. We assumed that the amount of workload shifted is not significant enough to alter electric prices. However, given that important financial savings are possible,

[7]Ideally, servers would consume no energy in the absence of load. Modern servers, however, draw an idle power that is about 50% of the peak consumption [4].

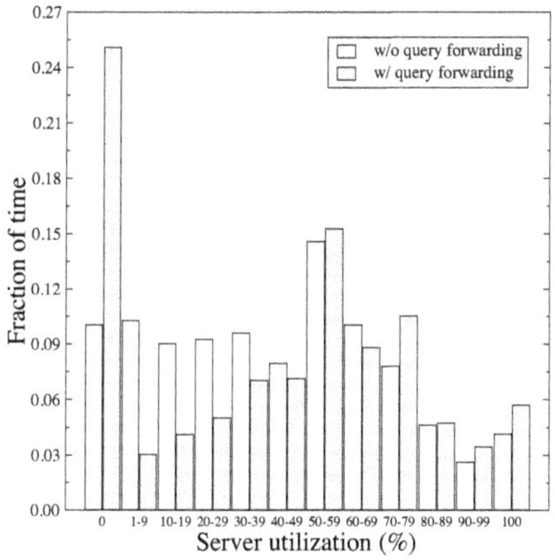

Figure 15: Fraction of time data centers run at a certain utilization level (PC-ST, $r = 800$).

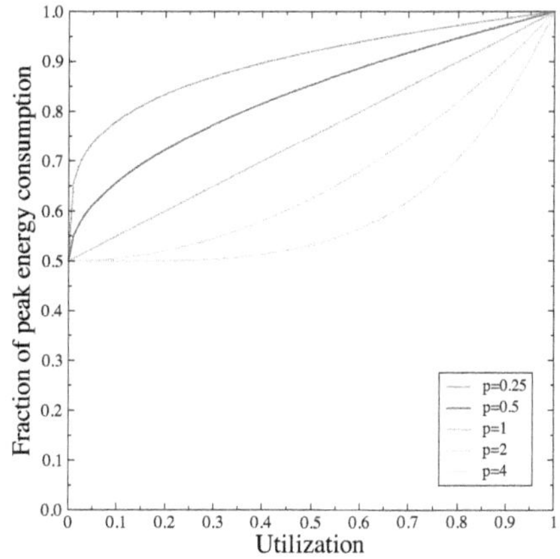

Figure 16: Mappings from utilization level (u) to energy consumption (c) (we use $c(u,p) = (1+u^p)/2$).

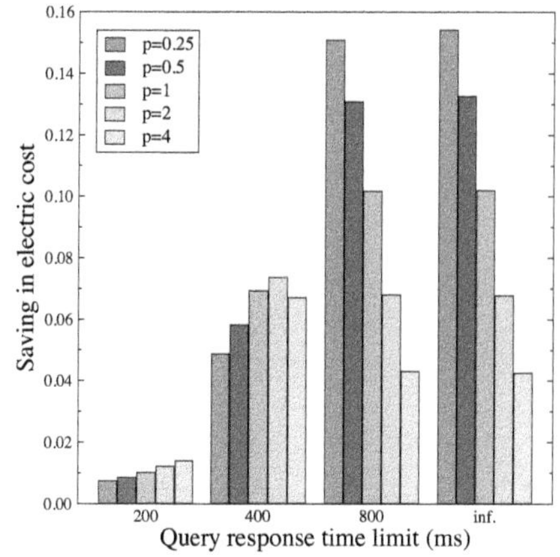

Figure 17: Saving in the electric cost for functions with varying p values (PC-ST).

many large-scale Internet services can be expected to start using similar workload shifting techniques. This may lead to an increase in prices at energy-cheap locations and vice versa, eventually converging prices to an equilibrium, which may render the technique less profitable. We also assumed a fixed electric cost model and a passive market participation strategy. A different approach is direct renegotiation of the electric price, rather than reacting to price-spotting. The reaction time to price changes has an influence on the final savings [15]. A few works [15, 17, 18] try to spot the electric price at a certain time in different electricity markets.

Environmental impact. The electric price model used by our work is rather general, allowing for different cost functions. As pointed out in [15] and [12], we may aim at reducing the environmental impact of data centers. In practice, this implies modeling the impact as a cost function (e.g., the carbon footprint of the energy the data center consumes) so that the system could decide to shift its workload to places that use renewable energy. The cost function may be time-dependent, i.e., seasonal, weekly, or even hourly.

Energy consumption. Data centers need adequate energy elasticity to achieve high cost savings when shifting their workload to data centers with cheaper energy. Some ongoing proposals to build more energy-elastic compute clusters include energy-proportional servers [4] and dynamic server provisioning techniques [13]. Another factor that might influence energy consumption is weather differentials. Cooling systems account for a significant fraction of the total energy consumption of data centers [5]. The energy consumption of chillers can be drastically reduced when the ambient temperature is low. This implies that the workload can be shifted to cooler regions that might reduce not only the energy price but also the consumption, as it is easier to cool down the heat dissipated from data centers.

8. RELATED WORK

Multi-center web search. A few works investigate the performance of multi-center web search engines [1, 7, 8]. Cambazoglu et al. [7] try to quantify performance benefits of such search engines. Baeza-Yates et al. [1] describe a multi-site search engine architecture, where the index is partitioned among data centers, also allowing partial replication of documents. Their work provides an algorithm for forwarding queries between data centers to maintain the quality of search results, relative to that of a centralized system. Cambazoglu et al. [8] propose an improved query forwarding algorithm, using linear programming. Both works have indirect consequences on reducing the energy cost, as they reduce the number of data centers involved in query processing. However, they do not directly tackle the financial aspect of the problem as they do not consider energy prices.

Workload shifting. Wang et al. [20] explore strategies to balance the load and locality in distributed systems, finding that, although algorithms that shift the workload across data centers are imperfect, using a content distribution net work may provide capacity increases ranging from 60% to 90%. Along the same line, Ranjan et al. [16] show that redirecting requests to geographically distant but lightly loaded centers can reduce the response time to about a half.

Minimizing the energy cost. Wang et al. [21] try to optimize the workload, power, and cooling management of a single data center. Shah and Krishnan [19] perform an in-depth analysis of environmental and economic costs of a large-scale technology warehouse and the potential energy saving achievable when the workload is distributed across data centers. They optimize thermal workloads based on local weather, showing that the environmental burden can be reduced by up to 30%. Due to space limitations, for more related work on the topic, we refer the reader to [5]. Herein, we discuss two works that are more related to ours [12, 15].

Qureshi et al. [15] characterize the variation in electric prices and argue that data centers could exploit this for economic gains. They quantify possible gains via simulations using workloads obtained from a content provider. Our work differs from [15] in three ways. First, we provide a formal optimization framework specific to web search engines (more suitable to throughput-intensive tasks), whereas [15] provides an informal study for general-purpose Internet services (more suitable to compute-intensive tasks). Second, the algorithm in [15] is deterministic and greedy, i.e., it does not consider the issues that motivate our probabilistic approach. Third, their problem employs a bandwidth constraint, whereas ours have a query response time constraint.

Le et al. [12] propose an optimization framework for green-aware Internet services. They try to cap the brown-energy consumption via a linear-programming-based algorithm, trying to incur the least increase in costs while satisfying some service-level agreements. Our work differs from [12] in three ways. First, our optimization problem is to directly reduce the electric bill, rather than reducing financial losses since some energy caps are respected. Second, we consider the problem in a search engine setting, taking into account degraded and overflow query rates, and propose a probabilistic solution. Third, we use a detailed setup with realistic price data, real-life query workloads, real search front-ends, result caching, a large web index, and network latencies.

9. CONCLUSION

We have provided an optimization framework and a practical algorithm, based on shifting query workloads between search data centers, in order to reduce the electric bills of multi-center web search engines. We evaluated potential savings via realistic simulations. The results demonstrate that, depending on electric price distribution, electric costs of search engines can be significantly reduced by shifting their query workloads to energy-cheap data centers.

We note that, when computing the savings in electric cost, we were quite conservative in some of our assumptions. We assumed very tight capacities for data centers [10], estimated based on past query traffic volumes. In practice, data centers allow for a certain amount of slackness in their capacities (typically, about 20%), which may allow more queries to be forwarded. Moreover, we assumed that user queries are forwarded between data centers. In practice, however, search engines make use of geographically scattered request schedulers [9], which may directly identify the best data centers to contact. This may result in lower query response latencies, which implies more forwarded queries. These practical aspects should be considered as a part of future work.

Finally, we emphasize that our work has implications for many other tasks in multi-center web search engines. Primarily, electric cost optimization frameworks similar to ours should be developed for multi-site web crawling and distributed indexing tasks. In particular, it may be interesting to devise an energy-price-aware result caching framework, where invalidation predictions are made for stale cache entries based on a combination of parameters (e.g., energy cost, backend workload, age and degradedness of search results) so that the financial cost of cache misses is reduced.

10. ACKNOWLEDGMENTS

This publication is based on work performed in the framework of the Project COAST-ICT-248036, funded by the European Community. The last author of the paper is partially supported by The Scientific and Technological Research Council of Turkey under grant EEEAG-109E019.

11. REFERENCES

[1] R. Baeza-Yates, A. Gionis, F. Junqueira, V. Plachouras, and L. Telloli. On the feasibility of multi-site web search engines. In *Proc. 18th ACM Conf. Information and Knowledge Management*, pages 425–434, 2009.

[2] L. A. Barroso. The price of performance. *Queue*, 3:48–53, 2005.

[3] L. A. Barroso, J. Dean, and U. Hölzle. Web search for a planet: the Google cluster architecture. *IEEE Micro*, 23(2):22–28, 2003.

[4] L. A. Barroso and U. Hölzle. The case for energy-proportional computing. *Computer*, 40(12):33–37, 2007.

[5] L. A. Barroso and U. Hölzle. *The Datacenter as a Computer: An Introduction to the Design of Warehouse-Scale Machines*. Morgan and Claypool Publishers, 1st edition, 2009.

[6] B. B. Cambazoglu, F. P. Junqueira, V. Plachouras, S. Banachowski, B. Cui, S. Lim, and B. Bridge. A refreshing perspective of search engine caching. In *Proc. 19th Int'l Conf. World Wide Web*, pages 181–190, 2010.

[7] B. B. Cambazoglu, V. Plachouras, and R. Baeza-Yates. Quantifying performance and quality gains in distributed web search engines. In *Proc. 32nd Annual Int'l ACM SIGIR Conf. Research and Development in Information Retrieval*, pages 411–418, 2009.

[8] B. B. Cambazoglu, E. Varol, E. Kayaaslan, C. Aykanat, and R. Baeza-Yates. Query forwarding in geographically distributed search engines. In *Proc. 33rd Annual Int'l ACM SIGIR Conf. Research and Development in Information Retrieval*, pages 90–97, 2010.

[9] V. Cardellini, M. Colajanni, and P. S. Yu. Dynamic load balancing on web-server systems. *IEEE Internet Comput.*, 3(3):28–39, 1999.

[10] A. Chowdhury and G. Pass. Operational requirements for scalable search systems. In *Proc. 12th Int'l Conf. Information and Knowledge Management*, pages 435–442, 2003.

[11] Q. Gan and T. Suel. Improved techniques for result caching in web search engines. In *Proc. 18th Int'l Conf. World Wide Web*, pages 431–440, 2009.

[12] K. Le, R. Bianchini, T. D. Nguyen, O. Bildir, and M. Martonosi. Capping the brown energy consumption of Internet services at low cost. In *Proc. 1st Int'l Green Computing Conf.*, pages 3–14, 2010.

[13] D. Meisner, B. T. Gold, and T. F. Wenisch. PowerNap: eliminating server idle power. In *Proc. 14th Int'l Conf. Architectural Support for Programming Languages and Operating Systems*, pages 205–216, 2009.

[14] I. Ounis, G. Amati, V. Plachouras, B. He, C. Macdonald, and D. Johnson. Terrier information retrieval platform. In *Advances in Information Retrieval*, volume 3408 of *Lect. Notes Comput. Sc.*, pages 517–519. Springer Berlin / Heidelberg, 2005.

[15] A. Qureshi, R. Weber, H. Balakrishnan, J. Guttag, and B. Maggs. Cutting the electric bill for Internet-scale systems. In *Proc. ACM SIGCOMM 2009 Conf. Data Communication*, pages 123–134, 2009.

[16] S. Ranjan, R. Karrer, and E. Knightly. Wide area redirection of dynamic content by Internet data centers. In *Proc. 23rd Annual Joint Conf. IEEE Computer and Communications Societies*, volume 2, pages 816–826, 2004.

[17] L. Rao, X. Liu, M. Ilic, and J. Liu. MEC-IDC: joint load balancing and power control for distributed Internet data centers. In *Proc. 1st ACM/IEEE Int'l Conf. Cyber-Physical Systems*, pages 188–197, 2010.

[18] L. Rao, X. Liu, L. Xie, and W. Liu. Minimizing electricity cost: optimization of distributed Internet data centers in a multi-electricity-market environment. In *Proc. 29th Conf. Information Communications*, pages 1145–1153, 2010.

[19] A. J. Shah and N. Krishnan. Optimization of global data center thermal management workload for minimal environmental and economic burden. *IEEE Trans. Compon. Packag. Technol.*, 31(1):39–45, 2008.

[20] L. Wang, V. Pai, and L. Peterson. The effectiveness of request redirection on CDN robustness. *SIGOPS Oper. Syst. Rev.*, 36:345–360, 2002.

[21] Z. Wang, N. Tolia, and C. Bash. Opportunities and challenges to unify workload, power, and cooling management in data centers. *SIGOPS Oper. Syst. Rev.*, 44:41–46, 2010.

Faster Top-k Document Retrieval Using Block-Max Indexes

Shuai Ding
Polytechnic Institute of NYU
Brooklyn, New York, USA
sding@cis.poly.edu

Torsten Suel
Polytechnic Institute of NYU
Brooklyn, New York, USA
suel@poly.edu

ABSTRACT

Large search engines process thousands of queries per second over billions of documents, making query processing a major performance bottleneck. An important class of optimization techniques called *early termination* achieves faster query processing by avoiding the scoring of documents that are unlikely to be in the top results. We study new algorithms for early termination that outperform previous methods. In particular, we focus on safe techniques for disjunctive queries, which return the same result as an exhaustive evaluation over the disjunction of the query terms. The current state-of-the-art methods for this case, the WAND algorithm by Broder et al. [11] and the approach of Strohman and Croft [30], achieve great benefits but still leave a large performance gap between disjunctive and (even non-early terminated) conjunctive queries.

We propose a new set of algorithms by introducing a simple augmented inverted index structure called a *block-max index*. Essentially, this is a structure that stores the maximum impact score for each block of a compressed inverted list in uncompressed form, thus enabling us to skip large parts of the lists. We show how to integrate this structure into the WAND approach, leading to considerable performance gains. We then describe extensions to a layered index organization, and to indexes with reassigned document IDs, that achieve additional gains that narrow the gap between disjunctive and conjunctive top k query processing.

Categories and Subject Descriptors

H.3.3 [**INFORMATION STORAGE AND RETRIEVAL**]: Information Search and Retrieval.

General Terms

Algorithms, Performance.

Keywords

IR query processing, top-k query processing, early termination, inverted index.

SIGIR'11, July 24–28, 2011, Beijing, China.

1. INTRODUCTION

Due to the rapid growth of the web, more and more people are relying on search engines to locate useful information. As a result, an increasing share of the world's computational resources is spent on search-related tasks. Current large-scale search engines have to be able to answer hundreds of millions of queries per day on tens of billions of web pages. Thus, highly optimized methods are needed to efficiently process all these queries.

One major bottleneck in query processing is the length of the inverted list index structures (described in the next section), which can easily grow to hundreds of MBs or even GBs for common terms (roughly linear in the size of the data set). Given that search engines need to answer user queries within fractions of a second, naively traversing this basic index structure, which could take hundreds of milliseconds or more for common terms, is not acceptable.

This basic problem has long been recognized by researchers, and has motivated a lot of work on optimization techniques including distributed computation [29, 5, 24], index compression [37], caching [7, 22], and early termination [31, 12] (also called pruning or optimized top-k processing). In this paper we focus on early termination, which in a nutshell means returning the best $k = 10$ or 100 results without an exhaustive traversal of the relevant index structures. In particular, we propose to augment the index by adding additional information. Essentially, we add to each compressed block in the inverted lists one value, the maximum impact score. While this is a simple idea, we are not aware of any previous work that stores such information for better query processing. We call this modified index structure a *Block-Max Index*. We also propose a new set of algorithms based on the WAND approach [11] for safe early termination (where exactly the same results as in the naive baseline are returned) using our block-max index structure. One interesting property of our algorithms is that they performs *document-at-a-time (DAAT)* index traversal, based on either document-sorted or impact-layered index structures.

2. BACKGROUND

In this section, we provide background on inverted index structures, query processing, and early termination.

2.1 Inverted Indexes and Index Compression

Current search engines perform query processing based on an inverted index, which is a simple and efficient data structure that allows us to find documents that contain a particular term [37]. Given a collection of N documents, we assume that each document is identified by a unique *document ID* (docID) between 0 and $N-1$. An inverted index consists of many inverted lists, where each inverted list L_w is a list of postings describing all places where term w occurs in the collection. More precisely, each posting contains the docID of a document that contains the term w, the number of occurrences of w in the document (called *frequency*), and sometimes the exact locations of these occurrences in the document (called *positions*), plus maybe other context such as font size etc. Postings in an inverted list are typically sorted by docID, or sometimes by some other measure (described later). Thus, in the case where we store docIDs and frequencies, each posting is of the form (d_i, f_i). We focus on this case in this paper, but all our techniques also apply to cases where positions, context information, or precomputed quantized impact scores are stored.

The inverted lists of common query terms may consist of many millions or even billions of postings. To allow faster access to lists on disk, and limit the memory needed, search engines use sophisticated compression techniques that significantly reduce the size of each inverted list [37]. Compression is crucial for search engine performance [14, 36], and there are many compression techniques in the literature; see [36, 35, 27]. In this paper we use the New-PFD compression method, which was shown to perform well in [35], but our ideas also apply to other compression techniques.

As the lists for common terms could be very long, we want to be able to skip most parts of the lists during query processing. To do so, inverted lists are often split into blocks of, say, 64 or 128 docIDs, such that each block can be decompressed separately. To do so, we have an extra table, which stores for each block the uncompressed maximum (or minimum) docID and the block size in this table. The size of this extra table is small compared to the size of the inverted index. Thus, 64 or 128 postings are grouped together as a block where we store 64 or 128 compressed docIDs, followed by the corresponding compressed frequencies.

2.2 Query Processing

Given the inverted index structure mentioned above, the most basic form of query processing is called *Boolean query processing*. A query **(apple AND orange) OR pear** for all documents containing both words **apple** and **orange**, or the word **pear**, can be implemented by first intersecting the docIDs in the inverted lists for **apple** and **orange**, and then merging the result with the inverted list for **pear**.

Search engines use *ranked query processing*, where a ranking function is used to compute a score for each document passing a simple Boolean filter, and then the k top-scoring documents are finally returned. This ranking function should be efficiently computable from the information in the inverted lists (i.e., the frequencies and maybe positions) plus a limited amount of other statistics stored outside the inverted index (e.g., document lengths or global scores such as Pagerank). Many classes of functions similar to BM25 or Cosine have been studied; see [6] for more details.

Current web search engines use ranking functions based on hundreds of features. Such functions are quite complicated and fairly little has been published about how to efficiently execute them on large collections. One "folklore" approach separates ranking into two phases. In the first phase, a simple and fast ranking function such as BM25 is used to get, say, the top 100 or 1000 documents. Then in the second phase a more involved ranking function with hundreds of features is applied to the top documents returned from the first phase. As the second phase only examines a small number of top candidates, a significant amount of the computation time is still spent on the first phase. In this paper we focus on executing such a simple first-phase function, say BM25, a problem that has been extensively studied in the literature.

Recall that ranked query processing consists of a Boolean filter followed by scoring and ranking the documents that pass this filter. The most commonly used Boolean filters are conjunctive (AND) and disjunctive (OR). In general, disjunctive queries have traditionally been used in the IR community while web search engines have often tried to employ conjunctive queries as much as possible. One reason is that disjunctive queries tend to be significantly (by about an order of magnitude for exhaustive query processing) more expensive than conjunctive queries, as they have to evaluate many more documents.

To traverse the index structure, there are two basic techniques, Document-At-A-Time (*DAAT*) and Term-At-A-Time (*TAAT*) [32]: For conjunctive queries, DAAT is often preferred, while many optimized approaches for disjunctive queries use TAAT.

2.3 Early Termination Algorithms

As discussed before, one bottleneck in query processing is the length of the inverted lists. Early termination is one important technique that addresses this problem. We say that a query processing algorithm is *exhaustive* if it fully evaluates all documents that satisfy the Boolean filter condition. Any non-exhaustive algorithm is considered to use *early termination (ET)*. There are four ways in which early termination often happens:

- **Stop early**: In this case, the postings are usually arranged such that the most promising documents appear early. Then we stop the traversal of the index as soon as we (may) have the *top-k* results. Well-known examples are the TA, FA, and NRA algorithms of Fagin [21]; see [8] for a highly optimized implementation of some of these algorithms.
- **Skip within lists**: When the postings in each list are sorted by docIDs, the promising documents are spread out throughout the inverted lists, and thus the standard intuition for "*stop early*" does not apply. There are few published works on early termination techniques under this scenario. An exception is the WAND algorithm in [11], which uses a smart pointer movement technique to skip many documents that would be evaluated by an exhaustive algorithm. More details are provided further below.
- **Omit lists**: One or more lists for the query terms are completely ignored, if they do not affect the final results by much.
- **Score only partially**: We partially evaluate a document by computing only some term scores, or by computing approximate scores. When we find that the document cannot be in the top results, we stop evaluation; an example is [33].

Note that our definition of ET is very general and includes other techniques such as static pruning [10, 19] and tiering [16]. In this paper we focus on *safe early termination* [30], which means we want exactly the same results as in the naive baseline, i.e., the same set of documents in the same order with the same scores. We will ignore other techniques, which try to return search results that are somehow similar, or of similar quality. Also, we focus on memory-based indexes, as for example considered in [30, 17], or at least on the case where disk is not the main bottleneck.

2.4 Index Organizations

Many existing techniques for early termination from the DB and IR communities are based on the idea of reorganizing the inverted index such that the most promising documents appear early in the inverted lists. This can be done by either reordering the postings in each list, or partitioning the index into several layers or tiers. In particular, we can distinguish among the following widely used index organizations:

- **Document-Sorted Indexes**: This is the standard approach for basic exhaustive query processing, where the postings in each inverted list are sorted by document ID.

- **Impact-Sorted Indexes**: Postings in each list are sorted by their impact, that is, their contribution to the score of a document. Postings with the same impact are sorted by document ID. Note that this assumes that the ranking function is decomposable (i.e., a sum or other simple combination of per-term scores), which is true for Cosine, BM25, and many other functions in the literature.
- **Impact-Layered Indexes**: We partition the postings in each list into a number of layers, such that all postings in layer i have a higher impact than those in layer $i + 1$, and then sort the postings in each layer by docID.

Impact-sorted and impact-layered indexes are very popular index organizations for early termination techniques, as they place the most promising postings close to the start of the lists [25, 21, 3, 4, 8, 30, 23, 32]. A problem with impact-sorted indexes is that compression could suffer as docID gaps in the inverted lists may be very large. In this case, an impact-layered index that uses a small number of appropriately chosen layers may provide a better alternative. However, impact-sorted indexes are useful when the number of distinct impact scores is small, or frequencies are used as proxies for impacts.

In contrast, document-sorted indexes tend to be less studied for early termination techniques, and only few algorithms use them (e.g., [11]).

2.5 Index Traversal Techniques

For index traversal, the two most commonly used techniques are:

- **Document-At-A-Time (DAAT)** : In DAAT query processing, each list has a pointer that points to a "current" posting in the list. All the pointers move forward in parallel as the query is being processed.
- **Term-At-A-Time (TAAT)**: In TAAT query processing, we first access one term, or one layer from one term, and then move to the next term, or the next layer from the same term or a different term. We use a temporary data structure to keep track of currently active top-k candidates.

Note that TAAT requires additional data structures to store promising candidates seen in some but not all of the lists; this is one of the main differences to DAAT. In this paper we use **TAAT** to refer to any techniques that use nontrivial data structures to keep track of promising candidates (beyond the simple heap structure used for the current top-k results), and thus this includes the original Term-At-A-Time technique [13] as well as Score-At-A-Time in [3].

For *conjunctive* and exhaustive query execution, DAAT is very fast and considered state of the art (at least for queries with a moderate number of queries terms), whereas TAAT-type methods are often bottlenecked by the nontrivial data structures. However, for *disjunctive* queries it is hard to integrate early termination and exploit layered indexes with DAAT. Thus, for this case most early termination algorithms in the literature are based on TAAT that use impact-sorted or layered indexes. In this paper we challenge this assumption and suggest DAAT algorithms may actually do better for early termination even in the case of disjunctive queries. We note that DAAT does have a significant advantage by not having any expensive temporary data structures.

2.6 Two State-of-the-Art Techniques

For disjunctive queries, the fastest existing safe early termination techniques appear to be the approach by Strohman and Croft (SC) in [30] (based on earlier work in [3, 2]), and the WAND approach by Broder et al [11]. Both approaches are safe in that they return exactly the same *top-k* results as the baseline in the same order and with the same score (actually, the original SC algorithm may not return the same scores, but is easily extended to do so).

The approach by Strohman and Croft (SC) uses impact-sorted indexes and assumes a ranking function proposed in [3], where all impacts have one of 8 distinct values; however, it can be extended to ranking functions such as BM25 using an impact-layered index organization. The approach then uses a variation of Term-At-A-Time (TAAT) query processing where we first access the higher layers of the lists and then move to the lower layers with smaller impact scores; when we are guaranteed to have a set containing the top-k results, we will switch from OR mode to AND mode, by only searching for the docIDs already stored in the structure among the remaining layers, to find the final correct results. Figure 1 shows one example of the index layout for SC, with equal-size layers. Note that the original SC applies a different ranking technique, so the size of each layer varies. We explore this and find that it does not make a big difference whether we use variable-size or equal-size layers; we will explain this further below. In SC, a sorted array is used to keep track of candidate documents that have been seen in some but not all term lists. After processing each layer, an extra phase is used to "filter out" candidates that can not make into the top-k. Thus, this approach requires temporary data structures (arrays) to keep track of promising candidates.

The WAND approach, on the other hand, uses a standard document-sorted index, and can thus employ a Document-At-A-Time (DAAT) approach that does not require additional temporary data structures (apart from the small top-k heap used by all methods). The downside is that the promising documents are spread out throughout the inverted lists, and thus the standard intuition for early termination does not apply. Instead, WAND uses an ingenious pointer movement strategy based on *pivoting* that allows it to skip many documents that would be evaluated by an exhaustive algorithm. More precisely, in DAAT query processing each list has a pointer that points to a "current" posting in the list, and that moves forward as the query is being processed. Thus any posting to the left of the pointers have already been processed. Throughout the algorithm, WAND keeps the terms sorted in increasing order by their current docIDs. Assume that at some point during a query "*dog, cat, kangaroo, monkey*", the current docIDs are 609, 273, 9007, and 4866, respectively, as shown in Figure 2, where the lists are arranged from top to bottom according to these docIDs. Suppose also that we know the maximum impact score for each list, and that a total document score of at least 6.8 (the threshold) is needed in order to make it into the current *top-k* results. We now sum up the maximum scores of the lists from top to bottom until we reach a score no smaller than 6.8. In Figure 2, this happens at the third list from the top ($2.3 + 1.8 + 3.3 > 6.8$). We can now claim that the smallest docID that can make it into the *top-k* is 4866. Thus, we can move the top two pointers forward to the first postings in their lists with docIDs at least 4866, enabling skipping in these lists. If docID 4866 appears in both the first two lists then we evaluate this docID. Otherwise, we sort the lists according to the current docIDs and *pivot* again. Thus, WAND achieves early termination by enabling skips over postings that cannot make into the top results. For the threshold value, we use the lowest score in the heap that contains the top-k results found thusfar. Note that WAND also stores one maximum impact score for each list, which could be kept in the term dictionary of the index.

These two methods are different in interesting ways – index organization and index traversal choices: WAND uses a document-sorted index and DAAT as index traversal technique, whereas SC uses an impact-ordered or layered index and TAAT, using an additional data structure to keep the candidates. For disjunctive queries SC seems to outperform WAND, although the numbers for SC that we report are not as fast as those in [30], due to our use of BM25 as the ranking function and due to us keeping stopwords and removing 1-term queries. WAND is of interest to us as it will form the basis of our improved approaches.

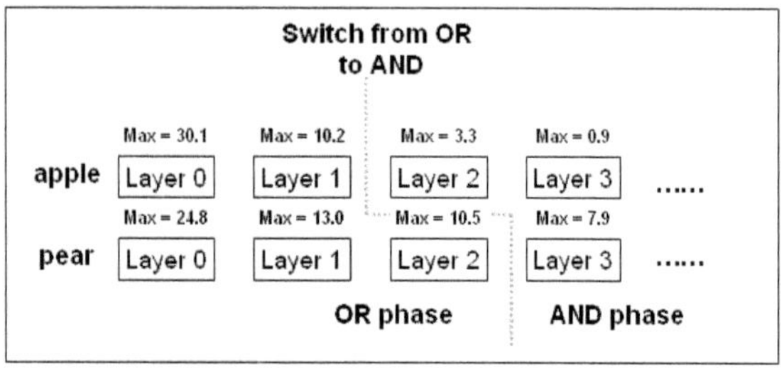

Figure 1: The index layout for SC. The layers are processed in descending order by their maximum impact scores. Inside each layer, postings are sorted by docIDs.

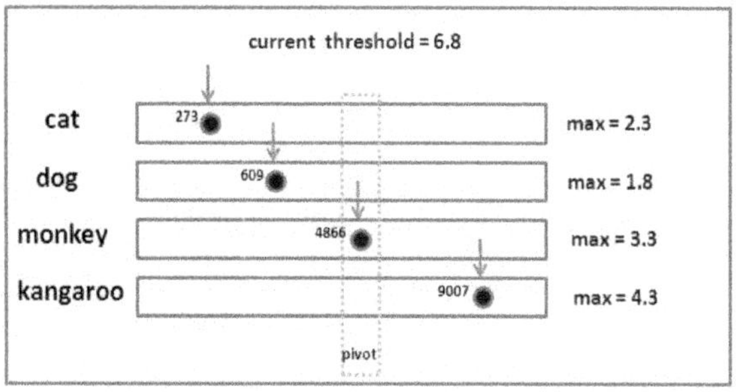

Figure 2: A scenario during the processing of a 4-term query, where the current pointers point to docIDs 273, 609, 4866, and 9007. WAND selects the third list as a pivot, and moves earlier pointers to docID 4866. Then all lists are sorted again according to their current docIDs.

3. OUR CONTRIBUTION

In this paper, we propose new early termination algorithms by building on the WAND approach [11]. Recall that WAND stores the maximum impact for each inverted list. Our initial insight is that skipping in WAND is limited because it uses the maximum impact scores over the entire lists, which can be much larger than average. Recall that we have an extra table to store information allowing us to skip blocks. We propose to augment the index structure by also storing in this table the maximum impact value for each block. We call such an index a *Block-Max Index*. In this way, we get a piece-wise upper-bound approximation of the impact scores in the lists, as shown in Figure 3. This approximation hides the detailed scores, shown in Figure 3 for one block in the kangaroo list, which can only be obtained by decompressing the block. This idea is very simple and easy to implement. As we will see later, this gives many optimization opportunities and leads to large performance gains.

After this slight change to the index structure, resulting in only a small increase in index size, we have to adapt the WAND algorithm to work with it. One obvious idea is to just use the local maximum value for the current block, instead of the global one, in the pivoting phase. Unfortunately, this does not guarantee correctness. To see this, let us look at the example in Figure 4. Looking only at the max scores for the blocks containing the current pointers (i.e., score

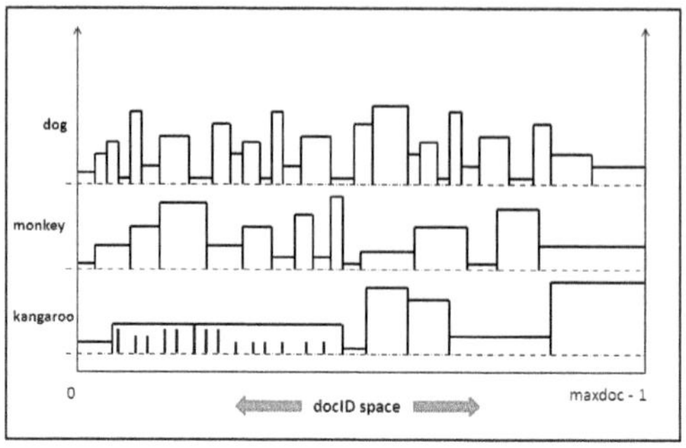

Figure 3: Three inverted lists where lists are piecewise upper-bounded by the maximum scores in each block. As shown for one block in the bottom list, inside each block we have various values, including many (implied) zero values, that can be retrieved by decompressing the block.

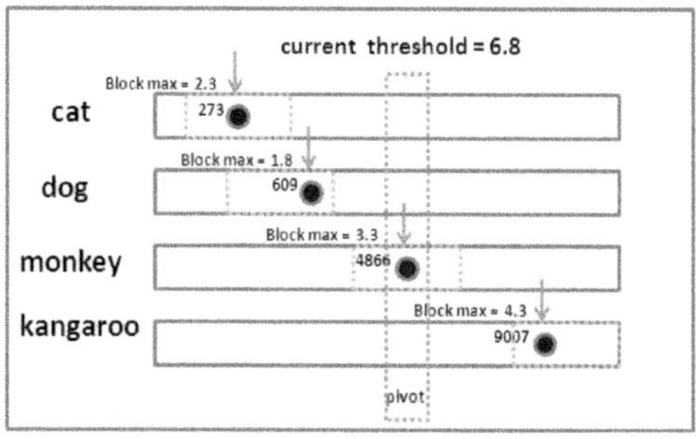

Figure 4: An example showing why directly using block max scores does not work.

2.3 for the first list, and so on), we cannot conclude that 4866 is the smallest docID that can make into it the *top-k*, because it is possible that the next block after docID 273 in the first list (but with docIDs smaller than 4866) has a much higher maximum impact score. Thus, directly applying the local max value does not work. We will describe how to modify the algorithm in later sections.

Overall, we make the following main contributions in this paper:

1. We propose a modified index structure, the Block-Max Index, which only slightly increases the index size. We then study improved techniques for safe early termination based on this index structure and the WAND approach in [11].
2. We show how to extend our techniques to layered indexes, reordered indexes, and conjunctive query processing.
3. We evaluate our techniques on the TREC GOV2 collection of 25.2 million documents, and demonstrate considerable improvements compared to the state-of-the-art techniques.
4. We discuss some interesting open questions resulting from our work.

4. RELATED WORK

Previous work on early termination (ET) techniques can be divided into two fairly disjoint sets of literature. In the IR community, researchers have studied ET techniques for the fast evaluation of vector space queries since the 1980s; some early work appears in [13, 32, 33]. There have been a large number of papers in recent years. Most relevant to us, several recent papers have focused on how to use impact-sorted indexes [2, 3, 30] for early termination, resulting in highly efficient methods for disjunctive queries.

There has also been a lot of work on early termination in the database community; see [21] for a survey and [20] for a formal analysis. Stated in IR terms, the algorithms also assume that postings in the inverted lists are sorted by their contributions and accessed in sorted order. However, the application scenarios are somewhat different, and many (but not all) of the algorithms assume that once a document is found in one inverted list, we can efficiently evaluate it by performing lookups into the other inverted lists. Such random lookups are highly undesirable in most IR scenarios.

Early termination techniques also differ in terms of their assumptions about result quality. We can distinguish between safe (or reliable) early termination techniques that return exactly the same top-k results as the baseline [30, 20], techniques that return mostly the same results, and those that just return results of equivalent quality, as determined by suitable IR measures. We focus on safe early termination of disjunctive queries, where the most relevant previous techniques are the approach of Strohman and Croft [30] and the WAND approach of Broder et al. in [11].

Two other recent ideas in IR query processing are also relevant to our work. First, a number of recent papers show how to decrease inverted index size and query processing costs by optimizing the assignment of docIDs to the documents in the collection [26, 9]. Intuitively, if we assign consecutive docIDs to very similar pages, for example by sorting pages by URL [28] or clustering by textual similarity, we obtain runs of small docIDs gaps that allow better index compression with suitable techniques. Moreover, as shown in [35], reordering significantly increases the speed of conjunctive queries. Our work here shows that, somewhat surprising to us, reordering can help even more for disjunctive queries.

The second relevant idea is that of two-level indexes proposed in [1]. The idea is to cluster documents by similarity and then in the first level only index the clusters (i.e., whether a cluster contains a term), while the second level says which documents in the cluster actually contain the term. Thus the first level basically approximates the overall index, similar to the way in which we use the maximum impact scores in each block to approximate the distribution of impact scores in a list.

Finally, we note that very recently, and independent of our work, Kaushik et al [15] have proposed an index structure very similar to the Block-Max Index in this paper, which also stores maximum impact information for blocks. Their algorithm for disjunctive queries first performs preprocessing to split blocks into intervals with aligned boundaries and to discard intervals that cannot contain any top results. Then a version of the maxScore technique [32] is applied to the remaining intervals. While their and our algorithms are different, they both achieve significant performance improvements based on similar underlying ideas.

5. BLOCK-MAX WAND ALGORITHM

In this section we give our basic algorithm, *Block-Max WAND (BMW)*, which is an extension of WAND to our Block-Max Index.

5.1 The Basic Idea

As described in Section 2, naively using the maximum impact score for each block in the "pivoting" phase will not work, and thus we need to add some additional ideas. In the traditional DAAT query processing, one core function is called *Next(d,list(i))* or *NextGEQ(d, list(i))* [11]; this function receives a docID d and an inverted list *list(i)* as inputs and returns the first docID after the current docID in *list(i)* that is equal to or greater than d. The call to this particular function usually involves a decompression of one block in *list(i)*. We call this a **deep pointer movement** due to the reason that it usually involves a block decompression. As we have the max score for each block, we design another function called *NextShallow(d,list(i))* which only moves the current pointer to the corresponding block without decompression (using d and information about the block boundaries in the table). We call this a **shallow pointer movement**. We use two main ideas in our modified algorithm: (i) we use the global maximum scores to determine a candidate pivot, as in WAND, but then use the block maximum scores to check if the candidate pivot is a real pivot, and (ii) we use shallow instead of deep pointer movements whenever possible.

5.2 The Algorithm

The detailed algorithm is shown in Algorithm 1, and we refer to it as **Block-Max WAND (BMW)**. Note that in BMW we still also keep the maximum score for the whole list as in WAND.

```
Initialize();
repeat
    /* sort the lists by current docIDs */
    Sort(lists);
    /* same "pivoting" as in WAND using the max
    impact for the whole lists, use p to denote
    the pivot */
    p = Pivoting(lists, θ);
    d = lists[p] → curDoc;
    if (d == MAXDOC) then
        break;
    end
    for i = 0 ... p + 1 do
        NextShallow(d, list(i));
    end
    flag = CheckBlockMax(θ, p);
    if (flag == true) then
        if ( lists[0] → curDoc == d ) then
            EvaluatePartial(d , p);
            Move all pointers from lists[0] to lists[p] by calling
            Next(list, d + 1)
        end
        else
            Choose one list from the lists before lists[p] with the
            largest IDF, move it by calling Next(list, d + 1)
        end
    end
    else
        d' = GetNewCandidate();
        Choose one list from the lists before and including lists[p]
        with the largest IDF, move it by calling Next(list, d')
    end
until Stop;
```

Algorithm 1: Block-Max WAND for disjunctive query processing based on local max values.

As shown in Algorithm 1, the main difference compared with WAND is that before we evaluate one docID, we will first move shallow pointers to check if we indeed have to evaluate this docID or not, based on the maximum scores for blocks. By doing this we filter out most of the candidates and achieve much faster query processing. Also, when the check fails, we can skip further forward using *GetNewCandidate()*, as described later in detail.

The two functions used in Algorithm 1, *NextShallow()* and *CheckBlockMax()*, are listed in Algorithm 2 and Algorithm 3. They are fairly obvious from the context. In *EvaluatePartial()*, we evaluate the document by summing up the scores from *list[0]* until *list[pivot+1]*. As soon as we find that the document can not make it into the top results, we stop the evaluation.

Another important improvement happens when *CheckBlockMax()* returns false, which means the current document d can not make it into the top results. Instead of picking one list (usually the one with the largest IDF) and moving it forward to at least $d + 1$, we

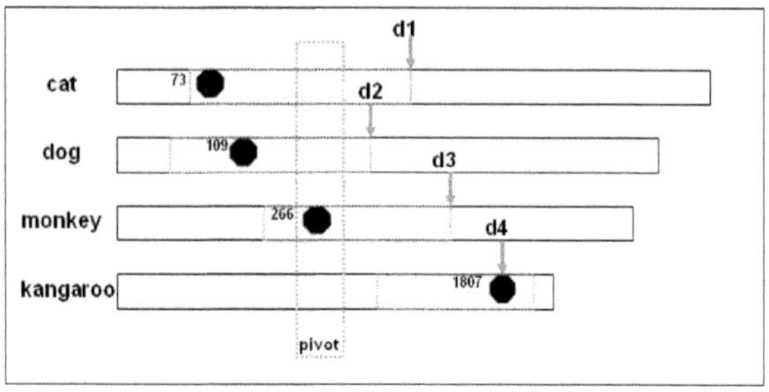

Figure 5: An example showing how *GetNewCandidate()* works. Assume 266 is the pivot and it fails to make it into the top results. In this case, we enable better skipping by choosing min($d1, d2, d3, d4$) as the next possible candidate, instead of $266 + 1$

will use the d' returned by *GetNewCandidate()*. The reason is that since the current document was ruled out based on the block maxima, we should skip at least beyond the end of one of the current blocks. This idea behind *GetNewCandidate()* is shown in Figure 5. Assume docID 266 is the pivot; when it fails the *CheckBlockMax()* check, instead of moving one of the first three lists to $266 + 1$, we will move it to $d' = min(d1, d2, d3, d4)$ where $d1, d2, d3$ are the block boundaries plus one of the first three lists, and $d4$ is the current docID in the forth list (equal to 1807 in this case). By doing this, skipping is greatly improved compared to using $d + 1$, while still guaranteeing a *safe* result. The proof should be obvious.

```
while did > list-> blockboundary[current_block] do
 | current_block++;
end
```

Algorithm 2: NextShallow(list, did)

```
maxposs = 0.0f;
for i = 0 ... pivot + 1 do
 | maxposs+ = list[i]-> blockmax[current_block];
end
if ( maxposs > threshold ) then
 | return true;
end
else
 | return false;
end
```

Algorithm 3: CheckBlockMax(threshold, pivot)

6. EXPERIMENTS

In this section, we provide a first set of experimental results.

6.1 Experimental Setup

We evaluate our methods on the TREC GOV2 collection. The GOV2 collection consists of 25.2 million web pages crawled from the gov Internet domain. The uncompressed size of these web pages is 426GB. We compress the inverted index using the NewPFD version of PForDelta as described in [35], with 64 docIDs and frequencies in each block.(We also tried other block sizes, but this one gave the best results.) The compressed index consumes 8759MB and the extra information for the Max-Block Index (the maximum score for each block) adds about 400MB (using 32 bits for each score though this could be reduced).

We randomly picked 1000 queries from the TREC 2006 Efficiency queries, and 1000 queries from the TREC 2005 Efficiency

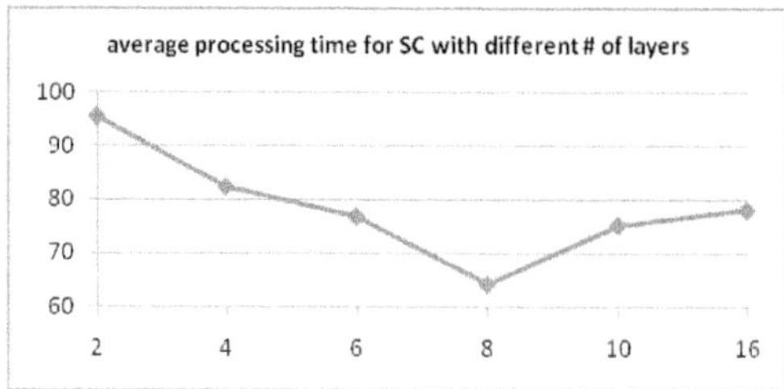

Figure 6: Processing time in ms for different number of layers in SC.

queries as our testing sets. The average numbers of postings per query are 4.67M and 6.07M using 2006 and 2005 set, respectively. We use BM25 as our ranking function. In all our runs, we load the inverted index completely into main memory. Unless stated otherwise, we return top-10 results. Runs are performed on a single core of a 2.27GHz Intel(R) Xeon CPU. All the codes are available by contacting the first author.

6.2 Results

In this section we compare our algorithm BMW with exhaustive OR (using DAAT), WAND, and SC on disjunctive queries. We measure the performance by three criteria – time (average time per query in ms), decoded integers per query and evaluated docIDs (docIDs that are completely scored against all query terms) per query. These criteria are also used in previous work [30, 11].

We reimplemented the SC algorithm based on the code available at http://repo.or.cz/w/galago.git, with BM25 as the ranking function. The original SC has four phases–*OR, AND, Refine, and Ignore*. In this paper we focus on getting safe results; thus we do not have an *Ignore* phase in our implementation (as we need the exact scores). Most of the time is spend in the *OR* phase, so this does not change the query processing time by much.

We partitioned each list into 8 equal-sized layers. Note that in the original SC algorithm in [30], a different ranking function was used that has only 8 distinct impact scores, with each layer dealing with one score, and thus the layers were of different sizes. We also tried different combinations of variable-sized layers We found that equal-sized layers usually did at least as well as the other heuristics, though in principle there is still room for better approaches. Our explanation is that in SC, there is a "switching point", where we are guaranteed to have encountered the docIDs of all the corrects top-k results in at least one list. At this point, we can switch from OR mode (TAAT) to AND mode before starting the next layer. Most of the computation time in SC is spend in OR mode, and things become much faster afterwards. While this "switching point" depends on how we partition the lists into layers, the switching point cannot happen before the point where the *threshold condition* is satisfied in the well-known TA algorithm of Fagin. The optimal partitioning would make a cut right after the threshold condition is satisfied for a query, but since this depends on the query one good choice is to spread out cuts evenly over the lists so that the next cut is never far away.

We also experimented with different numbers of layers. Figure 6 shows SC performance for different numbers of layers for equal-size layers, justifying the use of 8 layers.

Table 1 shows the query processing time using different algorithms. All runs in this paper exclude single-term queries, and no stopwords were removed (changing these assumptions would result in even better times). We observe that for TREC 2006, the effect of removing single-term queries is small, while for TREC 2005 the difference is significant as there are many such queries in the

TREC 2006						
	avg	2	3	4	5	> 5
exhaustive OR	225.7	60	159.2	261.4	376	646.4
WAND	77.6	23.0	42.5	89.9	141.2	251.6
SC	64.3	12.2	36.7	75.6	117.2	226.3
BMW	27.9	4.07	11.52	33.6	54.5	114.2
exhaustive AND	11.4	10.3	10.8	14.0	15.4	15.2
TREC 2005						
	avg	2	3	4	5	> 5
exhaustive OR	369.3	62.1	238.9	515.2	778.3	1501.4
WAND	64.4	23.5	43.7	73.4	98.9	265.9
SC	63.5	14.2	37.5	119.7	172.9	316.9
BMW	21.2	3.5	12.7	25.2	39	104
exhaustive AND	6.86	6.4	7.3	9.2	4.7	5.9

Table 1: Average query processing time in ms for different numbers of query terms, using different algorithms on the TREC 2006 and 2005 query logs. Exhaustive OR, WAND, SC, and BMW are for disjunctive queries, while Exhaustive AND is for conjunctive queries.

log. (But note that most single-term queries are resolved by result caching in real search engines.)

From Table 1 we can see that our *BMW* algorithm improves query processing performance. This is mainly due to the superiority of the DAAT index traversal over TAAT and the large amount of skipping. Also, our implementation for SC is not as fast as the numbers reported in [30], especially on *TREC 2005 query log*. This is because we remove single-term queries but do not remove stopwords as in [30], and also due to the use of BM25 as our ranking function. Still, SC outperforms basic WAND, as also reported in previous work. Overall, our basic *BMW* algorithm achieves much faster query processing but is still much slower than *exhaustive AND* using standard DAAT.

Table 2 shows the other two criteria for different methods on the *TREC 2006 query log* (we omit the 2005 data due to space constraints). We also include the number of deep pointer movements and shallow pointer movements. As these measures are only meaningful for DAAT index traversal, we ignore the numbers for SC which uses TAAT traversal. Note that we did not include numbers for SC for evaluated docIDs, mainly because SC adopts TAAT-like query processing and the definition of evaluated docIDs will be misleading. Also, in BMW each partial evaluation is counted as an evaluated docID, no matter whether it stops early or not.

From Table 2, we see that all techniques improve greatly over exhaustive OR. WAND only evaluates 4.6% of the docIDs compared to exhaustive OR, which approximately matches the numbers in [11]. BMW evaluates even fewer docIDs. This means that BMW should perform even better when we have a more expensive scoring function than BM25, such as the one mentioned in [11]. Another interesting point is that SC decodes less integers compared with the fastest method, BMW, which means that assigning promising docIDs to the first layers does help a lot. However, SC uses an additional data structure to temporarily store candidates, and this is the main drawback for SC and many other TAAT-based techniques.

6.3 Document ID Reassignment

In this section we show results after document ID reassignment. The idea for document ID reassignment is to assign docIDs to documents so that similar pages have close IDs. This idea is extensively explored in [28, 35, 18] and it is shown that after the reassignment, both compressed index size and query processing speed under exhaustive AND are significantly improved.

One natural question is whether reassignment can also help processing speeds for disjunctive query processing. For exhaustive OR, the intuition is that the improvement should be tiny because we fully evaluate the documents in all the lists anyway, no matter how the docIDs are assigned. For SC, the improvement should also be modest because in SC we will assign the postings such that the postings with higher impact scores appear earlier in the list. However, for WAND and BMW, reassignment of docIDs might give some benefits, as the distribution of impact values within each block should become more even, helping both WAND and BMW.

	evaluated docs	decoded ints	dpm	spm
exhaustive OR	3815676	9356032	15.9M	–
WAND	178391	6274432	1.18M	–
SC	–	965248	–	–
BMW	21921	2642752	0.42M	0.76M
exhaustive AND	20026	1939584	0.25M	–

Table 2: The average number of evaluated docIDs, decoded integers, deep pointer movements (dpm), and shallow pointer movements (spm) for different methods on the TREC 2006 query log. Exhaustive OR, WAND, SC, and BMW are for disjunctive queries, while Exhaustive AND is for conjunctive queries.

TREC 2006						
	avg	2	3	4	5	> 5
exhaustive OR	210.6	55.3	156.6	245.9	354.2	583.9
WAND	50.1	17.2	28.7	57.5	94.9	168.9
SC	69.3	14.1	40	80.9	126.7	239.9
BMW	8.89	1.4	3.6	10.2	16.9	37.8
exhaustive AND	6.56	5.5	5.3	7.1	10.8	8.4
TREC 2005						
	avg	2	3	4	5	> 5
exhaustive OR	349.7	56.4	226	495.8	743.1	1411.9
WAND	42.4	18.1	29.4	47.4	64.5	163.3
SC	76.4	12.6	52.9	112.2	162.8	288.9
BMW	7.2	1.3	3.7	8.9	13.5	35.8
exhaustive AND	4.5	4.3	4.7	5.9	2.7	4.1

Table 3: Average query processing times in ms for different numbers of query terms after docID reassignment, on the TREC 2006 and 2005 query logs.

Table 3 shows the query processing times for the different techniques after docID reassignment. In particular, we assign docIDs according to the alphabetical ordering used in [28, 35]. From the table, we see that query processing performance is greatly improved for WAND and especially for BMW. In fact, the gaps between disjunctive and conjunctive queries are significantly narrowed. This means that reassignment succeeds in making the scores inside the blocks block much smoother, thus improving skipping.

Query processing performance is also slightly improved for exhaustive OR. This is mainly because reassignment reduces the compressed size of the inverted index, thus reducing the cost of main memory accesses; see also [14] for more discussion of this issue.

Table 4 shows the corresponding results for evaluated docIDs and decoded integers on the *TREC 2006 query log*. We observe similar trends as in the query processing time, with significant reductions for WAND and BMW.

7. EXTENSIONS

In this section we give some extensions to our BMW algorithm.

7.1 A Layered Version of BMW

As shown in previous section, BMW achieved the best query processing performance for disjunctive queries, and significantly

	evaluated docs	decoded ints	dpm	spm
exhaustive OR	3815676	9356032	15.9M	–
WAND	221926	3472704	0.74M	–
SC	–	715776	–	–
BMW	9308	1181760	0.126M	0.22M
exhaustive AND	20026	951744	0.10M	–

Table 4: The average number of evaluated docIDs, average decoded integers, deep pointer movements (dpm), and shallow pointer movements (spm) for different methods, after docID reassignment on the TREC 2006 query log.

narrowed the performance gap between disjunctive and conjunctive queries. The main advantage for BMW seems to be that it uses DAAT index traversal, and thus does not have to use an expensive data structure to keep track of promising candidate documents.

On the other hand, SC achieves pretty good early termination performance (note from the previous section that SC actually decodes fewer integers than the other algorithms), by using an impact-layered index and assigning the most promising documents to the first layers. This means that the intuition for SC, putting top-scoring documents early in the lists to stop early, does have a lot of merit. A natural question is if we can combine this idea of a layered index with our BMW algorithm and its DAAT traversal mechanism. We now show how to do this. Our basic algorithm is very simple: For each inverted list, we split it into N layers. Then we *treat each layer just as a separate term*. In this case we directly apply the BMW algorithm on the impact-layered index.

The intuition behind this idea is that after we pick out the top-scoring documents from each list, the scores for the remaining docIDs are much smoother. So when we store the maximum impact score for each block, it is less likely that this score will be much larger than the others in the block. It's not difficult to understand that such spiky values are bad for BMW: If two two spikes are in two separate blocks, we probably have to decode both blocks, but if they are in one block we may only need to decode and access that one block. have to decode the two blocks. We call the new algorithm *N-layer BMW* where N is the number of layers. The disadvantage of doing this is that we will have a larger number of terms for each query. To minimize this disadvantage, we only split each list into 2 layers, a *fancy* layer and a *normal* layer, and each list is split only when it has more than α postings. We put the top-scoring β postings in each list into the fancy layer. After some experiments, we set $\alpha = 50K$ and $\beta = 2\%$, which seems to work well (getting the best possible parameters is left for future work).

Thus, in our *2-layer BMW*, we just treat the layers from one list as separate lists, and the different layers from the same list do not know the existence of each other. We also design a version where the layers from the same list know the existence of the others. The observation is that one document ID can only exist in one, if any, of the layers from the same list. In this case, in the "*pivoting*" phase of the BMW algorithm, we can do better by choosing the maximum score of the layers from the same list (instead of the sum of the scores). We experimented with this idea and found that it moderately decreases pointer movements and decoded integers, but not the actual running time, due to the overhead of tracking layers belonging to the same term during pivoting. For space reason we omit the results of these experiments, though future work may lead to more practical variants based on this idea.

Table 5 shows the query processing performance for *2-layer BMW* without and with docID reassignment. As we can see, *2-layer BMW* obtains improved running times over basic BMW. We also show the query processing time for queries with different numbers of terms in Table 6.

before reassignment	time (ms)	evaluated docs	decoded ints
BMW	27.9	21921	2642752
2-layer BMW	22.9	7435	1731264
after reassignment	time (ms)	evaluated docs	decoded ints
BMW	8.89	9308	1181760
2-layer BMW	7.4	4196	790464

Table 5: Query processing performance after combining layered index and BMW, before and after docID reassignment, on the TREC 2006 query log. All numbers are averaged per query.

before reassignment	avg	2	3	4	5	>5
BMW	27.9	4.07	11.52	33.6	54.5	114.2
2-layer BMW	22.9	2.9	10	30.8	46.3	98.2
after reassignment	avg	2	3	4	5	>5
BMW	8.89	1.4	3.6	10.2	16.9	37.8
2-layer BMW	7.4	1.1	3.3	8.5	15.0	31.4

Table 6: Average query processing time in ms for different number of query terms for BMW and 2-layer BMW, before and after docID reassignment, on the TREC 2006 query log.

7.2 Increasing Top-k

As mentioned, one commonly used ranking technique in current web search engines is based on a two-phase approach, where we first get the, say, top-1000 documents according to a simple ranking function such as BM25, and then compute the exact score according to a more complicated ranking function only for these 1000. An example appears in [34] for a ranking function that uses position information in addition to BM25. Of course, in these scenarios we usually need much larger values of k than $k = 10$, e.g., a few hundred or few thousand results.

In Figure 7 we show the performance as we increase k, with reassigned docIDs. We find that the performance for the naive *exhaustive OR algorithm* is quite stable as it decodes and evaluates all the postings anyway. For other algorithms, the query processing time increases. For SC, we observe a huge performance degradation. This is mainly because the performance of the temporal data structure degrades more and more as we store more candidates. We also see that *BMW* and *2-layer BMW* perform quite well even when k is equal to 1000, and that the increase in time is fairly moderate.

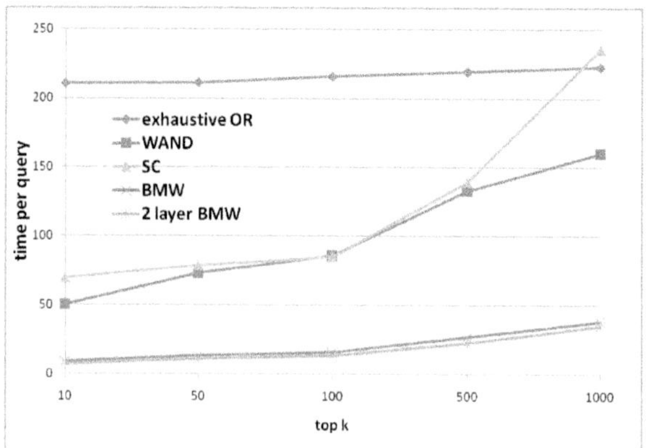

Figure 7: Query processing times for different techniques with docID reassignment, on the TREC 2006 query log. The X-axis is the value for k, while the Y-axis is the average processing time.

7.3 Block-Max AND

One advantage of BMW is that the idea can also be applied to *conjunctive* query processing using standard DAAT index traversal. For conjunctive query processing, *standard AND* starts from the shortest list, and then tries to find the corresponding docID in the longer lists. It is a natural extension to integrate the Block-Max Index structure and add shallow pointers in DAAT for conjunctive query processing. The improved DAAT algorithm is shown in Algorithm 4; it is called *Block-Max AND* (BMA).

```
Sort the lists from shortest to longest;
d = 0;
repeat
    d = NextGEQ(list[0], d);
    for i = 1 . . . n do
        NextShallow(d, list(i));
    end
    flag = CheckBlockMax(θ, n);
    if flag == true then
        search d in the rest lists, if found evaluate, otherwise
        d = d + 1
    end
    else
        d = GetNewCandidate();
        continue;
    end
until Stop;
```

Algorithm 4: Block-Max AND for conjunctive queries with n terms.

As we see we only have to slightly adapt the standard AND algorithm to get the BMA algorithm. In particular, we use three routines from BMW – *NextShallow()*, *CheckBlockMax()* and *GetNewCandidate()*. The processing cost for BMA is shown in Table 7. We observe that the BMA works better for queries with smaller numbers of terms (otherwise the shallow pointer movements will become expensive). So we also propose one *hybrid* algorithm: Apply BMA when the number of terms in the query is less than T; otherwise use exhaustive AND. We use $T = 4$ in this paper.

Table 8 shows the performance using BMA and the *hybrid* BMA, before and after docID reassignment. We can see significant improvements over an exhaustive AND. Note that *BMW* and *BMA* algorithms use the same index structure; thus the Block-Max Index can support both types of queries.

8. OPEN QUESTIONS

Our results in this paper raise several interesting open questions.

A Cleaner Algorithm and Analysis: While the described methods already achieve large benefits, we are not yet convinced that we have really found *the optimal algorithm*. It would also be interesting to provide some analysis, say of the optimal number of pointer movements and document evaluations under our approach.

Other Applications of Block-Max Indexes: The basic idea behind our augmented index structure could also be applied to other scenarios. For example, it would be natural to try to integrate local maximum scores into the two-level index structure in [1].

before reassignment	avg	2	3	4	5	> 5
exhaustive AND	11.4	10.8	10	12.5	11.57	9.94
BMA	9.89	3.96	7.92	13.2	14.08	14.63
after reassignment	avg	2	3	4	5	> 5
exhaustive AND	6.56	6.93	6.11	7.06	6.84	5.57
BMA	5.12	1.69	4.02	7.03	7.33	9.06

Table 7: Average query processing times in ms for different numbers of query terms, using exhaustive AND and BMA, before and after docID reassignment, on TREC 2006.

before reassignment	time	evaluated docs	decoded ints
exhaustive AND	11.4	20026	1939584
BMA	9.89	5725	1460992
Hybrid	9.4	6594	1568704
after reassignment	time	evaluated docs	decoded ints
exhaustive AND	6.56	20026	951744
BMA	5.12	3108	607680
Hybrid	4.53	3673	641344

Table 8: Average query processing times in ms, numbers of evaluated docIDs per query and average decoded integers per query for conjunctive queries, before and after docID reassignment, on TREC 2006.

	no reassignment	with reassignment
BMW	27.9	8.89
Clairvoyant BMW	23.0	7.2

Table 9: Average query processing times in ms for BMW versus Clairvoyant BMW, for top-10 results, on the Trec 2006 query log.

Estimating Top-k Thresholds: Our methods could be further improved if we somehow had a good a-priori estimate of what score is needed to make it into the top k results. Currently, we start with a threshold of zero, and then update the value as results are discovered. Thus, the algorithm starts slow and then speeds up. This motivates the following algorithmic problem that also has other applications, for example in distributed IR: Given an inverted index, a query, and a number k, how do we quickly estimate the score of the k-th best result (possibly using some small auxiliary structures), or conversely, given a threshold t how do we estimate the number of results with score higher than t.

For motivation, we show in Table 9 that a clairvoyant algorithm that knows the score of the k-th best result would get a circa 20% reduction in query processing costs.

Query Processing with Score Approximations: Another interesting more general question is how to best approximate the impact scores in inverted lists, and how to best use such approximations during query processing. Consider the scenario in Figure 3, where we have a long, sparse, array of impact values that is upper-bounded by some block-wise approximation. What is the best approximation for a given array of values? Does it make sense to have a multi-level structure (similar to wavelet trees) that provides upper bounds for progressively smaller block sizes as we descend to lower levels? Are there statistical measures other than the maximum impact, say the skew of the values, that are useful?

9. CONCLUSION

In this paper, we have described and evaluated improved safe early termination for disjunctive queries. This was achieved by an augmented index structure called a Block-Max Index, which stores maximum impacts for blocks of postings. We then showed how to integrate this structure into the WAND approach. Finally, we extended it to the impact-layered indexes, indexes with reassigned docIDs, and conjunctive queries, leading to additional improvements. Our results also lead to a number of interesting opportunities for future research, as discussed in Section 8.

Acknowledgments

This research was supported by NSF Grant IIS-0803605, "Efficient and Effective Search Services over Archival Webs", and by a grant from Google.

10. REFERENCES

[1] Ismail Sengor Altingovde, Engin Demir, Fazli Can, and Ozgur Ulusoy. Incremental cluster-based retrieval using compressed cluster-skipping inverted files. *ACM Transactions on Information Systems*, 26(3):1–36, 2008.

[2] V. Anh and A. Moffat. Simplified similarity scoring using term ranks. In *Proceedings of the 28th Annual International ACM SIGIR Conference on Research and Development in Information Retrieval*, pages 226–233, 2005.

[3] V. Anh and A. Moffat. Pruned query evaluation using pre-computed impacts. In *Proceedings of the 29th Annual International ACM SIGIR Conference on Research and Development in Information Retrieval*, pages 372–379, 2006.

[4] Vo Ngoc Anh, Owen de Kretser, and Alistair Moffat. Vector-space ranking with effective early termination. In *Proceedings of the 24th Annual International ACM SIGIR Conference on Research and Development in Information Retrieval*, 2001.

[5] C. Badue, R. Baeza-Yates, B. Ribeiro-Neto, and N. Ziviani. Distributed query processing using partitioned inverted files. In *Proceedings of the 9th String Processing and Information Retrieval Symposium*, 2002.

[6] R. Baeza-Yates and B. Ribeiro-Neto. *Modern Information Retrieval*. Addision Wesley, 1999.

[7] Ricardo Baeza-Yates, Aristides Gionis, Flavio Junqueira, Vanessa Murdock, Vassilis Plachouras, and Fabrizio Silvestri. The impact of caching on search engines. In *Proceedings of the 30th Annual International ACM SIGIR Conference on Research and Development in Information Retrieval*, 2007.

[8] Holger Bast, Debapriyo Majumdar, Ralf Schenkel, Martin Theobald, and Gerhard Weikum. IO-Top-K: Index-access optimized top-k query processing. In *Proceedings of the 32th International Conference on Very Large Data Bases*, 2006.

[9] Roi Blanco and Álvaro Barreiro. TSP and cluster-based solutions to the reassignment of document identifiers. *Information Retrieval*, 9(4):499–517, 2006.

[10] Roi Blanco and Alvaro Barreiro. Probabilistic static pruning of inverted files. *ACM Transactions on Information Systems*, 28(1), January 2010.

[11] Andrei Z. Broder, David Carmel, Michael Herscovici, Aya Soffer, and Jason Zien. Efficient query evaluation using a two-level retrieval process. In *Proceedings of the 12th ACM Conference on Information and Knowledge Management*, 2003.

[12] N. Bruno, L. Gravano, and A. Marian. Evaluating top-k queries over web-accessible databases. In *Proceedings of the 18th Annual International Conference on Data Engineering*, 2002.

[13] C. Buckley and A. F. Lewit. Optimization of inverted vector searches. In *Proceedings of the 8th Annual International ACM SIGIR Conference on Research and Development in Information Retrieval*, 1985.

[14] Stefan Buttcher and Charles L. A. Clarke. Index compression is good, especially for random access. In *Proceedings of the 16th ACM Conference on Information and Knowledge Management*, 2007.

[15] Kaushik Chakrabarti, Surajit Chaudhuri, and Venkatesh Ganti. Interval-based pruning for top-k processing over compressed lists. In *Proceedings of the 27th IEEE International Conference on Data Engineering (ICDE)*, 2011.

[16] J. Cho and A. Ntoulas. Pruning policies for two-tiered inverted index with correctness guarantee. In *Proceedings of the 30th Annual International ACM SIGIR Conference on Research and Development in Information Retrieval*, 2007.

[17] Jeffrey Dean. Challenges in building large-scale information retrieval systems. In *Proceedings of the Second ACM International Conference on Web Search and Data Mining*, 2009.

[18] S. Ding, J. Attenberg, and T. Suel. Scalable techniques for document identifier assignment in inverted indexes. In *Proceedings of the 19th International Conference on World Wide Web*, 2010.

[19] R. Fagin, D. Carmel, D. Cohen, E. Farchi, M. Herscovici, Y. Maarek, and A. Soffer. Static index pruning for information retrieval systems. In *Proceedings of the 24th Annual International ACM SIGIR Conference on Research and Development in Information Retrieval*, 2001.

[20] R. Fagin, A. Lotem, and M. Naor. Optimal aggregation algorithms for middleware. In *Proceedings of the ACM Symp. on Principles of Database Systems*, 2001.

[21] Ronald Fagin. Combining fuzzy information: an overview. *SIGMOD Record*, 31:2002, 2002.

[22] R. Lempel and S. Moran. Optimizing result prefetching in web search engines with segmented indices. In *Proceedings of the 28th International Conference on Very Large Data Bases*, 2002.

[23] X. Long and T. Suel. Optimized query execution in large search engines with global page ordering. In *Proceedings of the 29th International Conference on Very Large Data Bases*, 2003.

[24] S. Melnik, S. Raghavan, B. Yang, and H. Garcia-Molina. Building a distributed full-text index for the web. In *Proceedings of the 10th International Conference on World Wide Web*, 2000.

[25] Michael Persin, Justin Zobel, and Ron Sacks-davis. Filtered document retrieval with frequency-sorted indexes. *Journal of the American Society for Information Science*, 47:749–764, 1996.

[26] W. Shieh, T. Chen, J. Shann, and C. Chung. Inverted file compression through document identifier reassignment. *Information Processing and Management*, 39(1):117–131, 2003.

[27] F. Silvestri and R. Venturini. Vsencoding: efficient coding and fast decoding of integer lists via dynamic programming. In *Proceedings of the 19th ACM Conference on Information and Knowledge Management*, 2010.

[28] Fabrizio Silvestri. Sorting out the document identifier assignment problem. In *Proceedings of 29th European Conference on IR Research*, pages 101–112, 2007.

[29] Fabrizio Silvestri and Domenico LaForenza. Query-driven document partitioning and collection selection. In *Proceedings of the First International Conference on Scalable Information Systems*, 2006.

[30] T. Strohman and W. Bruce Croft. Efficient document retrieval in main memory. In *Proceedings of the 30th Annual International ACM SIGIR Conference on Research and Development in Information Retrieval*, 2007.

[31] Trevor Strohman, Howard Turtle, and Bruce W. Croft. Optimization strategies for complex queries. In *Proceedings of the 28th Annual International ACM SIGIR Conference on Research and Development in Information Retrieval*, 2005.

[32] H. Turtle and J. Flood. Query evaluation: strategies and optimizations. *Information Processing and Management*, 31(6):831–850, November 1995.

[33] HW. Wong and D. Lee. Implementations of partial document ranking using inverted files. *Information Processing and Management*, 29(5):647–669, 1993.

[34] Hao Yan, Shuai Ding, and Torsten Suel. Compressing term positions in web indexes. In *Proceedings of the 32th Annual International ACM SIGIR Conference on Research and Development in Information Retrieval*, 2009.

[35] Hao Yan, Shuai Ding, and Torsten Suel. Inverted index compression and query processing with optimized document ordering. In *Proceedings of the 18th International Conference on World Wide Web*, 2009.

[36] J. Zhang, X. Long, and T. Suel. Performance of compressed inverted list caching in search engines. In *Proceedings of the 17th International Conference on World Wide Web*, 2008.

[37] J. Zobel and A. Moffat. Inverted files for text search engines. *ACM Computing Surveys*, 38(2), 2006.

Utilizing Marginal Net Utility for Recommendation in E-commerce

Jian Wang and Yi Zhang
Department of Computer Science
University of California, Santa Cruz
Santa Cruz, CA 95060 USA
{jwang30, yiz}@soe.ucsc.edu

ABSTRACT

Traditional recommendation algorithms often select products with the highest predicted ratings to recommend. However, earlier research in economics and marketing indicates that a consumer usually makes purchase decision(s) based on the product's marginal net utility (i.e., the marginal utility minus the product price). Utility is defined as the satisfaction or pleasure user u gets when purchasing the corresponding product. A rational consumer chooses the product to purchase in order to maximize the total net utility. In contrast to the predicted rating, the marginal utility of a product depends on the user's purchase history and changes over time. According to the Law of Diminishing Marginal Utility, many products have the decreasing marginal utility with the increase of purchase count, such as cell phones, computers, and so on. Users are not likely to purchase the same or similar product again in a short time if they already purchased it before. On the other hand, some products, such as pet food, baby diapers, would be purchased again and again.

To better match users' purchase decisions in the real world, this paper explores how to recommend products with the highest marginal net utility in e-commerce sites. Inspired by the Cobb-Douglas utility function in consumer behavior theory, we propose a novel utility-based recommendation framework. The framework can be utilized to revamp a family of existing recommendation algorithms. To demonstrate the idea, we use Singular Value Decomposition (SVD) as an example and revamp it with the framework. We evaluate the proposed algorithm on an e-commerce (shop.com) data set. The new algorithm significantly improves the base algorithm, largely due to its ability to recommend both products that are new to the user and products that the user is likely to re-purchase.

Categories and Subject Descriptors

H.3.3 [**Information Storage and Retrieval**]: Information Search and Retrieval

General Terms

Algorithms, Design, Experimentation

Keywords

Recommender System, E-commerce, Consumer Utility Function

1. INTRODUCTION

With ever increasing e-commerce websites and online shoppers, the recommender system is becoming popular among internet users. It helps consumers to make purchase decisions, mainly by gathering information from other users. In the short term, it saves users' time and effort to find what they are looking for. In the long term, it helps to increase users' satisfaction rate and loyalty to the site.

In the literature, the satisfaction or pleasure a user gets when purchasing/consuming a product is called the marginal utility. According to consumer behavior theory, a rational consumer chooses the product with the highest marginal net utility, i.e., a product's marginal utility minus the price. A product's marginal utility is dependent on the user's previous purchase history. A product with the higher marginal net utility is more likely to be purchased. Some products have the diminishing marginal utility. For example, the utility of purchasing a second computer is less than that of purchasing the first computer. For these products, users are not likely to purchase them again and again in a short time period. This is called the Law of Diminishing Marginal Utility in economics. On the other hand, some products (pet food, baby diapers, etc.) are likely to be purchased again and again. We call it the "re-purchase" behavior in this paper.

In order to match users' purchase decision(s), the recommender system should choose products with the highest marginal net utilities to recommend. Such a system is able to capture characteristics of both types of products and makes recommendations accordingly. Unfortunately, most of existing recommendation algorithms are not based on the marginal net utility optimization and cannot model the above two different products well. Most existing algorithms select products with the highest predicted ratings to recommend, assuming that the value/utility of a product for a user does not change over time.

This paper introduces the concept of marginal net utility to develop recommendation algorithms. Inspired by the Cobb-Douglas function in consumer behavior theory, we propose a utility function for the recommender system in e-commerce sites. The new function contains a factor to control the product's marginal utility diminishing rate. Assuming that a user's purchasing decision depends on the marginal net utility, the rate can be learned from the purchase history of all users. The function can be applied on a family of existing recommender algorithms, which we call base algorithms. In this work, we choose SVD as our base algorithm. Applying our utility function to SVD leads to a new utility function SVD_{util} in this paper.

We evaluate our algorithm on the purchase history from an e-commerce website shop.com. The experimental results show that our approach can improve the base algorithm significantly with better precision, recall and conversion rates. If the user purchased what he/she purchased before, the product is denoted as a **re-purchase product**. Otherwise, if the user purchased a product that he/she never purchased before, the product is denoted as a **new product**. The recommended list generated by our proposed algorithm contains both new products and re-purchase products. Or we can add a filter on top of the recommender system to recommend only re-purchase products or only new products for specific recommendation tasks.

The major contributions of this paper include the following:

- Introduce the idea of utilizing the marginal net utility in the recommender system of e-commerce sites. Adapt the utility function from the Cobb-Douglas function to apply in a general framework.
- Apply the new utility function on SVD algorithm, denoted as SVD_{util}. The new algorithm achieves significant improvement in precision, recall and conversion rates.
- The new algorithm $SVD^{0.7}_{util}$ performs significantly better in the re-purchase product recommendation task, the new product recommendation task, and the long-tail product recommendation task.

The rest of this paper is organized as follows: Section 2 discusses the related work. Section 3 introduces basic utility functions in economics and marketing research. Then we propose a new utility-based recommendation framework, motivated by these basic utility functions. Section 4 applies the new framework to revamp the well-known SVD algorithm. Section 5 first introduces the experimental design to evaluate and understand the new algorithm. Then it presents experimental results and further analysis. In the end, Section 6 concludes the work and discusses some future work.

2. RELATED WORK

A major task of the recommender system is to present recommendations to the user. The task is usually conducted by first predicting a user's ratings (or probability of purchasing) for each item and then ranking all items in descending order. There are different information sources to find the relevant recommendation, including item's content, user's behavior history, user's demographical information, so on and so forth. There are two major recommendation approaches: content-based filtering and collaborative filtering.

The content-based recommendation is based on the assumption that descriptive features of an item (meta data, words in description, price, tags, etc.) tell much about a user's preferences to the item. Thus a recommender system makes a decision for a user based on the descriptive features of other items the user likes or dislikes. Usually, the system recommends items that are similar to what the user likes before. A user profile contains his/her previous transaction history, such as what he/she viewed or purchased before. How to determine the similarity between a product and the profile is the key challenge. Cosine similarity with TF.IDF term weights, the language modeling approach, Bayesian classifiers, clustering, etc., have been proposed [23, 24]. Largely influenced by the TREC filtering track, most of the early research on content-based filtering is about filtering text documents. In e-commerce systems, products usually have very limited description (title, user reviews, etc.). The effectiveness of content-based approaches is limited. Thus a content-based approach is usually not used by itself in e-commerce sites. It is used as part of a hybrid recommendation strategy [6]. In this work, we do not assume that a user likes things similar to what he/she likes before. Instead, we utilize the product's metadata to find similar products in order to determine the product's marginal net utility. As a result, a user may like or dislike an item that is similar to what he/she purchased in our model.

In the collaborative filtering approach, user behavior history is utilized to make recommendations. This approach is based on the assumption that users with similar tastes on some items may also have similar preferences on other items. Thus the main idea is to utilize the behavior history from other like-minded users to provide the current user with good recommendations. This approach usually operates on a user-item matrix, in which each row is a user vector and each column is an item vector. User-based methods find similar users to the current user, and fall into the category of **memory-based** approach in the literature [26, 5, 12]. However, these methods suffer from the poor quality and scalability issues. Item-based methods directly find items that are similar to the items a user has rated/purchased [25, 10]. Various similarity measures, such as cosine similarity, Pearson correlation coefficient, conditional probability-based similarity, have been proposed to find all neighbors. In addition, a group of model-based approaches have been developed in recent years. Model-based approaches use the collection of user behavior (ratings, purchases, etc.) to learn a model, and make predictions based on the learned model. Examples are Probabilistic Latent Semantic Indexing (PLSI) [14], Flexible Mixture Models [30], Decoupled Models [16], Multiple Multiplicative Factor Model [21], etc.

Research on collaborative filtering algorithms has reached a peak due to the 1 million dollar Netflix movie recommendation competition [4]. Factorization-based collaborative filtering approaches, such as the regularized Singular Value Decomposition, perform well on this competition, significantly better than the Netflix own well-tuned Pearson correlation coefficient (nearest neighbors) algorithm. A common characteristic of these models is to introduce user latent factors or/and product latent factors to solve the data sparsity issue. In this paper, we use SVD as our base algorithm, since it represents a family of factorization-based methods that work well on the Netflix dataset [4]. There are many extensions (AsySVD, SVD++, etc.) to the basic SVD in the literature [9, 18]. The approach proposed in this work can be applied to all these methods in the future.

In contrast to our work, most of the existing collaborative filtering methods assume that the utility of a product for a user does not change over time. Utility is typically represented by the rating. Although some work captures the temporal variations of a user's ratings [19], they cannot capture the economic behavior behind products' diminishing return and re-purchase characteristic.

Besides content based filtering and collaborative filtering approaches, other approaches such as *Graph-based methods* [1], *Bayesian network* [5], *association rules* [22], and *MDP-based methods* (Markov decision process) [29] were developed. Though it is not straightforward to use our proposed technique to revamp these filtering approaches, the basic idea of considering the marginal net utility, the diminishing return and the re-purchase behavior could be used to further improve these algorithms in the future.

Recommendation in the e-commerce domain is a topic that has been studied in the IR community [26, 28, 17, 11]. Several methods have been studied in this domain, including neighborhood-based method [26], graph models [15], MDP-based methods [29], multi attribute utility theory based methods [20] and so on. Existing research in economics and marketing can also be applied to model user behavior in e-commerce sites. This paper focuses on modeling users' purchase decisions based on the marginal net utility of products.

3. ALGORITHM DESIGN

In this section, we first define some basic notations to be used in the rest of this paper. Then we review two representative consumer utility functions. After proposing a new utility function for our problem, we describe how it can be used in a general framework to revamp some existing recommendation algorithms.

3.1 Notations

The following notations are used in the problem definition and analysis.

$u = 1, ..., M$: the index of a user. M is the number of unique users in the system.

i or $j = 1, ..., N$: the index of a product. N is the number of unique products in the system.

t: time.

c_i: the price of product i. We assume that this value is given. Making this value time dependent (i.e., replacing it with $c_{i,t}$) won't affect any analysis in the rest of this paper.

$P_{M \times N}$: user-product matrix. Depending on the context, each entry $P_{u,i}$ could be user u's rating of product i, user u's purchase count of product i, or a unary/binary value indicating whether user u has purchased product i or not.

The goal of our system is to provide a ranked list of personalized recommendations to user u. In this paper, each user's budget is not taken into consideration. The optimal purchase rule [3] indicates that a rational consumer purchases the product to maximize the marginal net utility. Accordingly the algorithm should choose the product with the maximum marginal net utility at each recommendation time point. Since the product price is given, the core problem of a recommender system is to determine the marginal utility for each product.

3.2 Marginal Utility

The utility of a product for a user depends on the user's purchase history. Marginal utility is used in economics and marketing research to represent the additional utility the consumer gets when consuming an additional unit of a product. The **Law Of Diminishing Marginal Utility** states that the marginal utility of a product drops while the consumption of the product increases. For example, for user u, the utility of consuming the first "iPhone 4" might be 10, the utility of consuming the second one might be 5, while the utility of consuming a third one might be only 1.

It is worth mentioning that the standard definition of the **Law Of Diminishing Marginal Utility** assumes continuity. It means that all units of a product are purchased one after another, without time gaps between any two purchases. However this assumption might not hold in an e-commerce site, where there are time gaps and purchases of other products between most re-purchases. For example, the user might purchase some pet food on Friday evening, then some books on the following Monday morning, and some pet food again after two weeks. Although the continuity assumption no longer holds in our e-commerce domain, we can still use the concept of marginal utility. Utility functions in economics can be adapted to our problem. This enables us to make recommendations based on the different diminishing return rate of different products.

3.2.1 Linear Utility Function

Linear utility function is one of the simplest functions in consumer behavior theory, as shown in Equation 1.

$$U(X) = \sum_j \alpha_j x_j \quad (1)$$

where X is the set of products the user consumed, and x_j is the consumption quantity of product j. α_j is the basic utility of product j, indicating the purchasing intention for product j. $U(X)$ is the utility of the entire purchase list X.

We can calculate the marginal utility $\Delta U(X,i)$ of purchasing one additional unit of product i in the following equation.

$$\Delta U(X,i) = U(X,i) - U(X) = \alpha_i$$

where $U(X,i) = \sum_{j:j \neq i} \alpha_j x_j + \alpha_i x'_i$ is the utility of the entire purchase list with one additional product i. $x'_i = x_i + 1$ is the updated quantity of product i.

The linear utility does not capture the diminishing return characteristic. From the deduction, we can see that the previous purchase count x_i of product i does not affect the marginal utility of purchasing one additional unit of product i. If product i's basic utility α_i is high, the system will recommend it regardless of previous purchase(s) of the same product.

In most existing recommender systems, products with the highest predicted values are recommended to the users. If these products include both re-purchase ones and new products, the approach follows the linear utility assumption. If only products that were never purchased are recommended, the following utility function is used:

$$U(X) = \sum_j \alpha_j \quad (2)$$

However, both of these two underlying utility functions do

not match how users make purchase decisions in the real world.

3.2.2 Cobb-Douglas Utility Function

Another representative utility function is the Cobb-Douglas utility function [8]. This function is widely used due to its attractive mathematical characteristic: the ability of modeling the diminishing marginal return. The functional form is:

$$U(X) = \sum_j \alpha_j log(x_j) \quad (3)$$

where the definitions of x_j and α_j are the same as before. The marginal utility of purchasing one additional unit of product i is:

$$\Delta U(X,i) = U(X,i) - U(X) = \alpha_i(log(x_i') - log(x_i)) \quad (4)$$
$$= \alpha_i(log(x_i+1) - log(x_i))$$

The above equation shows that the marginal utility of product i decreases as the consumption quantity of product i increases. The diminishing return rate is $log(x_i+1)-log(x_i)$.

3.3 New Marginal Utility Function for E-Commerce Sites

Diminishing marginal utility is a widely recognized consumer behavior which we intend to model in the design of a recommender system for e-commerce sites. This motivates us to utilize the Cobb-Douglas utility function in our algorithm design.

However, Equation 4 shows two major drawbacks of the Cobb-Douglas utility function. First, the marginal utility of different products has the same diminishing return rate $log(x_i + 1) - log(x_i)$. It does not differentiate two types of products: products that the user would not purchase many times vs. products that the user would purchase again and again. Second, the basic utility α_i of a product i does not depend on the particular user, which contradicts with the goal of a personalized recommender system.

A real-world e-commerce system could collect a large amount of consumer purchase data. This enables us to handle these drawbacks of the Cobb-Douglas utility function. We can learn the product-specific diminishing return rate and the user-specific basic utility from the data. Now we describe how to modify the Cobb-Douglas utility function to achieve this goal.

We propose a new marginal utility function as follows:

$$\Delta U_{u,t}(X,i) = \alpha_{u,i}((x_{u,i,t}+1)^{\gamma_i} - x_{u,i,t}^{\gamma_i}) \quad (5)$$

where $x_{u,i,t}$ is user u's consumption quantity of product j by time t.

There are four major differences between Equation 5 and Equation 4. First, we substitute $log(x_j)$ with x_j for the mathematical convenience. This simplification is motivated by the well-known **Constant elasticity of substitution (CES)** utility function in Equation 6 [31]:

$$U(X) = \sum_j \alpha_j x_j^{\gamma} \quad (6)$$

Second, x_i is substituted by $x_{u,i,t}$, so that it depends on the product, the user and the time. Third, α_i is substituted by $\alpha_{u,i}$, so that it is personalized to each individual user. Fourth, we introduce γ_i as a parameter to capture the diminishing return rate of product i.

One important question is how to determine $x_{u,i,t}$. The original definition of $x_{u,i,t}$ is user u's purchase count of product i by time t. We make two major modifications while calculating $x_{u,i,t}$ in the e-commerce domain. First, we define the purchase count as the number of purchase orders the current user made. Each order is counted once for the same product, regardless of the product quantity in the order. For example, if the user purchases 4 window panels in one order, the purchase count of window panel is 1. Second, we assume that the marginal utility is affected not only by previous purchase(s) of the same product, but also by previous purchase(s) of similar products. For example, the previous purchase of "iPhone 3" has effect on the marginal utility of the current purchase of "iPhone 4". We first find products that are similar to product i based on the metadata, such as the product title. Then let $x_{u,i,t}$ be the total similarity between these similar products and the current product i for user u at time t.

$$x_{u,i,t} = \sum_{j:sim(i,j)\geq\theta} C_{u,j,t} \times sim(i,j)$$

where $C_{u,j,t}$ is user u's purchase count of product j by time t, and $sim(i,j)$ is the similarity between product i and product j. θ is a similarity threshold, which will be estimated by the cross-validation in our experiments.

It is worth mentioning that the utility over a sequence of purchases can be calculated based on the definition of the above marginal utility (Equation 5). However, the utility of an unordered set of products is not defined. The only exception is when $\theta = 1$, in which case only the same product will influence the marginal utility. Under such circumstance, the utility over a sequence is independent of the sequential order of products. Then the utility can be used for an unordered set of products. With some derivation, we can get the definition of a user u's utility over an unordered set of products X at time t in this special case as follows:

$$U_{u,t}(X) = \sum_j \alpha_{u,j} x_{u,j,t}^{\gamma_j} \quad (7)$$

It is similar to the Constant Elasticity of Substitution utility function in Equation 6. However, the meaning of γ_i in Equation 7 is different from γ in Equation 6. γ is the parameter to tune the elasticity of substitution [1] and is the same for different products. In our new utility function (Equation 7), γ_i is a parameter to tune the diminishing return rate. It is product-specific and can be learned based on the purchase history of each product. Linear and Cobb-Douglas utilities can be viewed as special cases of our utility function. That is, in the limit as all γ_i approach 1, we get the linear utility; as all γ_i approach 0, we get the Cobb-Douglas utility.

3.4 Revamp Existing Algorithms with the New Marginal Utility Function

In most cases, we can view an existing recommendation algorithm as a function $f(u,i)$ to estimate the value of product i for user u without considering the diminishing return or the cost of a product. To reflect a user's true decision

[1] More information of CES utility function can be found in the reference [31].

behavior in reality, we model $v_{u,i,t}$, the marginal net utility of product i for user u at time t, as follows:

$$v_{u,i,t} = f(u,i)[(x_{u,i,t}+1)^{\gamma_i} - (x_{u,i,t})^{\gamma_i}] - c_i \quad (8)$$

Whether product i is likely to be purchased is dependent on the product's basic utility, its diminishing return rate, as well as the product's price. Comparing Equation 8 and Equation 5, we notice that $\alpha_{u,i}$ is replaced by $f(u,i)$. In other words, we propose to use an existing recommendation algorithm $f(u,i)$ to estimate $\alpha_{u,i}$, the basic utility of product i for user u.

At each decision point t, a higher marginal net utility $v_{u,i,t}$ indicates that user u is more likely to purchase product i. The following logistic function can be used to capture this intuition and model the conditional probability of making the purchase.

$$Pr(r_{u,i,t}|v_{u,i,t}) = \frac{1}{1+e^{-v_{u,i,t}\cdot r_{u,i,t}}} \quad (9)$$

where $r_{u,i,t} = 1$ if user u purchases i at time t. Otherwise $r_{u,i,t} = -1$.

Assume that the cost c_i of product i is given, the parameters of the above model include γ_i and parameters of function f. To learn these parameters, we can order the entire user purchase history by the purchase time. At each time point t, user u's purchase decision of product i is considered as a training point. If user u purchased the product, it is a positive training point with $r_{u,i,t} = 1$. Otherwise, it is a negative training point with $r_{u,i,t} = -1$.

When a new recommended list is needed, the system can estimate each product's marginal net utility based on Equation 8 and rank them accordingly. For email-based or message-based marketing/recommendation applications, the system can predict how likely a user will purchase an item using Equation 9 and decide whether to recommend an item to the user accordingly (as in TREC adaptive filtering tasks).

4. APPLY NEW MARGINAL UTILITY FUNCTION ON SVD

In this section, we choose a popular recommendation algorithm SVD as an example. The algorithm in Section 3.4 is used to revamp it. This leads to a new recommendation algorithm, which we call SVD_{util}.

4.1 SVD

In this work, we choose SVD as an example because it is a popular recommendation algorithm with a decent performance. It is the basis of several recommendation algorithms based on latent factors, which have been proven to work well on benchmark recommendation datasets including the Netflix dataset [4].

Following [9, 18], we represent SVD as a matrix factorization approach. The basic SVD algorithm operates over a user-product matrix $P_{M\times N}$. It assumes that each entry $P_{u,i}$ in the matrix P can be estimated using the following form:

$$\hat{P}_{u,i} = q_i^T p_u \quad (10)$$

where q_i and p_u are vectors, which are the hidden representation of product i and user u. These vectors can be estimated based on all given entries in $P_{M\times N}$.

The value of $P_{u,i}$ in the observed matrix $P_{M\times N}$ is determined by the user purchase history. In the e-commerce domain, $P_{u,i}$ is usually set to be a unary value that indicates whether user u purchased product i or not [13]. Existing work finds that unary value is more suitable than numerical value, i.e., the number of times the user purchased the product [27]. Our piloting experiment compares these two types of values and reaches the same conclusion.

When a recommender system ranks all products by their estimated $\hat{P}_{u,i}$ values and selects the top ones to recommend, it is equivalent to maximizing the linear utility.

4.2 SVD$_{util}$: Revamp SVD

In this section, we apply the technique in Section 3.4 to revamp SVD. To do so, we set the basic utility $\alpha_{u,i} = f(u,i) = q_i^T p_u$. Based on Equation 8, the marginal net utility is:

$$v_{u,i,t} = q_i^T p_u[(x_{u,i,t}+1)^{\gamma_i} - (x_{u,i,t})^{\gamma_i}] - c_i \quad (11)$$

For simplicity and as commonly done in the literature, we assume that prior distributions of user vector p_u and item vector q_i are Gaussian distributions. $Pr(p_u)$ and $Pr(q_i)$ have mean zero and variance $1/\lambda_1$. We assume that the prior distribution of γ_i is a Gaussian distribution with mean γ_0 and variance $1/\lambda_2$. We treat each purchase order made by a user as a decision point. The purchase history of all users can be viewed as the training data $D = (r_{u,i,t}, c_i, u, t)$. The joint probability (likelihood) of all parameters and the training data is:

$$L = \prod_u Pr(p_u) \prod_i Pr(q_i) \prod_i Pr(\gamma_i) \prod_{u,i,t} Pr(r_{u,i,t}|v_{u,i,t}) \quad (12)$$

4.3 Parameter Estimation

The model parameters can be found by maximizing the joint probability of all parameters and the training data. According to Equation 12 and Equation 9, this is equivalent to minimizing the negative log likelihood of the data as follows:

$$\begin{aligned}(p_u, q_i, \gamma_i) &= argmin\ [-logL] \\ &= argmin\ \frac{1}{2}\lambda_1 \sum_u ||p_u||^2 + \frac{1}{2}\lambda_1 \sum_i ||q_i||^2 + \frac{1}{2}\lambda_2 \sum_i (\gamma_i - \gamma_0)^2 \\ &+ \sum_{u,i,t} log(1+e^{-v_{u,i,t}\cdot r_{u,i,t}})\end{aligned}$$

λ_* can also be viewed as regularization factors to avoid the overfitting problem.

The first order derivatives are:

$$\begin{aligned}\frac{\partial(-logL)}{\partial q_i} &= \lambda_1 q_i + g_{u,i,t}\cdot[p_u \cdot d_{u,i,t}] \\ \frac{\partial(-logL)}{\partial p_u} &= \lambda_1 p_u + g_{u,i,t}\cdot[q_i \cdot d_{u,i,t}] \\ \frac{\partial(-logL)}{\partial \gamma_i} &= \lambda_2 \gamma_i + g_{u,i,t}\cdot[q_i^T p_u \cdot ((x_{u,i,t}+1)^{\gamma_i} \\ &\cdot log(x_{u,i,t}+1) - (x_{u,i,t})^{\gamma_i} \cdot log(x_{u,i,t}))]\end{aligned}$$

where

$$d_{u,i,t} = [(x_{u,i,t}+1)^{\gamma_i} - (x_{u,i,t})^{\gamma_i}]$$
$$v_{u,i,t} = q_i^T p_u d_{u,i,t} - c_i$$
$$g_{u,i,t} = \frac{\partial(log(1+e^{-v_{u,i,t}\cdot r_{u,i,t}}))}{\partial v_{u,i,t}}$$
$$= \frac{e^{-v_{u,i,t}\cdot r_{u,i,t}}}{1+e^{-v_{u,i,t}\cdot r_{u,i,t}}} \cdot (-r_{u,i,t})$$

Based on the above derivation, we can use the stochastic gradient descent method to find the optimal parameters. Following the standard stochastic gradient descent method, update rules at each iteration are shown in the following equations. The algorithm stops when the change in an iteration is small enough.

$$p_u = p_u - \beta_1 \cdot \frac{\partial(-logL)}{\partial p_u}$$
$$q_i = q_i - \beta_1 \cdot \frac{\partial(-logL)}{\partial q_i}$$
$$\gamma_i = \gamma_i - \beta_2 \cdot \frac{\partial(-logL)}{\partial \gamma_i}$$

where β_* controls the learning rate at each iteration. β_* and λ_* can be set by the cross-validation.

5. EXPERIMENTAL DESIGN AND RESULT

Since this paper focuses on the recommendation in e-commerce sites, we collect a dataset from a typical e-commerce website, shop.com, for our experiments. This dataset contains the purchase history from 2004-01-01 to 2009-03-08. Since our algorithm is dependent on users' previous purchase history, we sort all history by the purchase time. The first 90% of data is the training data, and the last 10% is the testing data. Tail users that made less than 5 unique product purchases are filtered out in the training data. The remaining training data contains 10,399 users and 65,551 products. There are 102,915 unique (user, product) pairs. As we can see, the user-product matrix for SVD is quite sparse, with only 0.015% density. There are 55,539 unique (user u, order time t) pairs and 119,322 unique (user u, product i, order time t) tuples. All products are kept in the training process. In the evaluation step, $user^{n>0}$ are returning users with at least one purchase in the training data. $product^{n>0}$ are products with at least one purchase in the training data. In following sections, we report the performance for returning users that purchased from: 1) all products and 2) $product^{n>0}$.

We first split the training data, using the last 10% of the training data as the validation data to set $(\beta_*, \lambda_*, \gamma_0, \theta)$. We have $\beta_1 = 0.015, \beta_2 = 0.035, \lambda_1 = 0.05, \lambda_2 = 0.01$ for positive training points, $\lambda_2 = 0.001$ for negative training points, $\gamma_0 = 1$, and $\theta = 0.7$. Instead of using all negative training points, we randomly sampled 1% from missing entries as negative training points in SVD_{util}. The sample percentage is determined by cross-validation. Both positive and negative training datas are used to learn model parameters. Finally the model is used to generate the recommendation list in the testing stage. For every decision point t in the testing data, all products are ranked by the marginal net utility $v_{u,i,t}$ (Equation 11). The top ranked products are recommended to the user.

We set the dimension of the user vector and the product vector to be 50. Product titles are used to calculate products' similarity. All stop words are removed. [2]

Some researchers have tried to fit SVD model parameters to the entire matrix P by replacing the missing entries with a base value such as 0. They found that such methods perform better for ranking metrics, such as recall and precision [9]. Their experiment results are performed on the movie data (Movielens and Netflix) with matrix density being 4.26% and 1.18% respectively. The matrix density on an e-commerce data set is usually much lower [13] (0.015% in our dataset). To train SVD, we randomly sample 0.1% missing entries and set them to 0, where percentage is determined by the cross-validation. The method is denoted as SVD_{matrix}.

5.1 Evaluation Metrics

There are several metrics to evaluate recommender algorithms in the literature [13]. Considering the usage scenario in a typical e-commerce web site, the ranking of all recommendations is more important than the rating prediction. Instead of using some common rating prediction accuracy measures (Root Mean Square Error, etc.), we evaluate all algorithms in the context of a ranking task [9].

- Each order $D_{u,t}$ corresponds to a testing point, which is uniquely identified by a (user, order time) pair. Let $S_{purchased}$ be the set that contains all products in this purchase order.
- Rank all products according to their predicted marginal net utility for user u at time t. Let $S_{K,recommended}$ be the set that contains the top K products.

Then we have:

$$recall@K = \frac{|S_{purchased} \cap S_{K,recommended}|}{|S_{purchased}|} \quad (13)$$

$$precision@K = \frac{|S_{purchased} \cap S_{K,recommended}|}{K} \quad (14)$$

Conversion rate, a commonly-used metric in e-commerce, is used as an additional evaluation metric in our experiments. If the user purchased at least one product from the recommended top K list, we consider that the user has converted from a browser into a buyer. The calculation of conversion rate for one testing point is shown in the following equation.

$$conversion\ rate@K = \begin{cases} 1 & S_{purchased} \cap S_{K,recommended} \neq \emptyset \\ 0 & otherwise \end{cases} \quad (15)$$

Conversion rate reflects whether a user receives at least one good recommendation. The average value of all testing points will be used to compare among different algorithms. Statistical significant tests are used when comparing two methods.

5.2 General Analysis

In this section, we intend to answer the following questions with the general analysis:

[2]Other metadata information, such as user's review to the product, product's limited description, can be used in the future.

Table 1: **Conversion rate performance for the general recommendation task. Value* is significantly better than the baseline SVD_{matrix} and TopPop.**

Method	K=1	K=2	K=3	K=4	K=5
for $user^{n>0}$ and all products					
TopPop	0.0002	0.0004	0.0006	0.0006	0.0011
SVD_{matrix}	0.0102	0.0194	0.0287	0.0363	0.0438
SVD_{util}^{same}	0.0266*	0.0425*	0.0542*	0.0575*	0.0607*
$SVD_{util}^{0.7}$	0.0190*	0.0324*	0.0432*	0.0499*	0.0536*
for $user^{n>0}$ and $product^{n>0}$					
TopPop	0.0005	0.0010	0.0015	0.0015	0.0025
SVD_{matrix}	0.0238	0.0456	0.0673	0.0851	0.1028
SVD_{util}^{same}	0.0623*	0.0997*	0.1271*	0.1347*	0.1423*
$SVD_{util}^{0.7}$	0.0446*	0.0759*	0.1013*	0.1170*	0.1256*

- **How does SVD_{util} perform?** We compare it with SVD_{matrix} and a naive method $TopPop$. The $TopPop$ method recommends the most popular products. It is a simple non-personalized recommendation algorithm that is commonly used in real world applications. Prior research has shown that it outperforms some common recommendation approaches and almost matches the accuracy of sophisticated algorithms in top-N recommendation task [9].

- **Does considering similar products help the performance compared to using the exact same product?** We compare SVD_{util} with different similarity thresholds: $\theta = 0.7$ vs. $\theta = 1.0$. When $\theta = 1.0$, only the purchase(s) of the same product influences the diminishing return. When $\theta = 0.7$, the purchase(s) of similar products also influences the diminishing return. In the analysis, we represent the model with $\theta = 0.7$ as $SVD_{util}^{0.7}$, and the model with $\theta = 1.0$ as SVD_{util}^{same}.

The conversion rate performance of all methods is shown in Table 1. It is clear that all personalized methods are significantly better than the non-personalized method $TopPop$. Although the precision and recall are not reported here, we have similar observations when evaluating with these two metrics.

Comparing $SVD_{util}^{0.7}$ and SVD_{util}^{same} with SVD_{matrix}, we can see that our proposed marginal utility function helps. Both $SVD_{util}^{0.7}$ and SVD_{util}^{same} are significantly better than SVD_{matrix} for all evaluation metrics.

Between two methods with the new utility function, the performance of SVD_{util}^{same} is significantly better than $SVD_{util}^{0.7}$. The method SVD_{util}^{same} only utilizes the same product to learn the diminishing return rate and estimate the marginal utility. Thus it might catch re-purchase behavior with the higher accuracy. This will be further analyzed in the next section.

5.3 Further Analysis: Re-purchase Product Recommendation and New Product Recommendation

In the previous section, we generate a recommended list by ranking all products, including both re-purchase products and new products. Besides the general recommendation task, there are more specific tasks in e-commerce sites. Now we perform further analysis to compare these recommendation algorithms in two different recommendation tasks.

One task is to recommend products for a user to re-purchase. In the testing data, 13.79% of the purchase orders from returning users contain re-purchase products, i.e., products that were purchased by the user before. To successfully recommend products for the user to re-purchase could save a consumer much time and effort, and might be able to increase sales.[3] The challenge is how to rank products the user has purchased before. For all re-purchase products in the testing data, we plot the the histogram of their previous purchase count (Figure 1). We observe that the majority of re-purchase products were purchased only once or twice in the training data. Thus it is hard to use the previous purchase count to rank. In Section 5.3.1, we compare all methods' performance in ranking products that were purchased before. Only re purchase products in each testing order are used to evaluate all methods' performance.

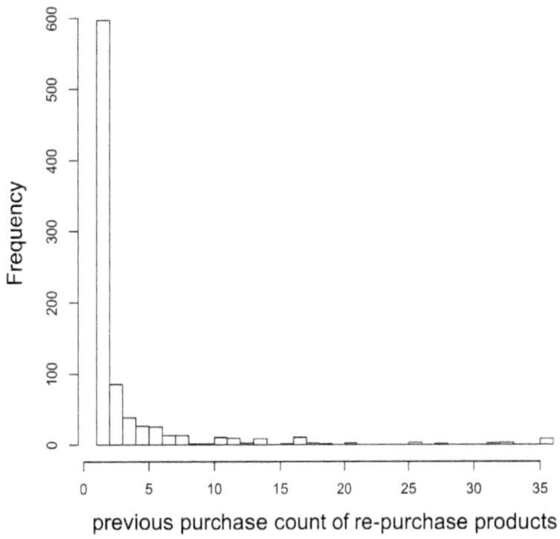

Figure 1: Histogram of the previous purchase count in the training data of all re-purchase products. If a product in the testing data was purchased before, it is a re-purchase product.

A second task is to recommend new products that a user has never purchased before. In the testing data, 90.64% in the dataset of all purchase orders from returning users contain new products. The new product recommendation task is much harder and more interesting than the re-purchase recommendation task. The recommendation candidates include all products that were not purchased by the current user before. Only new products in each testing order are used to evaluate all methods' performance.

In this section, we intend to answer the following questions:

- **How does SVD_{util} perform in the re-purchase product recommendation task?**

  The methods in general recommendation task, including $TopPop, SVD_{matrix}, SVD_{util}^{0.7}$ and SVD_{util}^{same}, recommend both new products and re-purchase products. We add a filter on top of them, so that only products that were purchased before are recommended. The method with filter is denoted as $method.Previous$. For testing, we use only orders that contain product(s) that the user has purchased.

[3]This is why amazon.com is providing subscribing service with discount to encourage re-purchase.

Table 2: Conversion rate@K for the re-purchase recommendation task. Value* is significantly better than the baseline SVD_{matrix} and TopPop.

Method	K=1	K=2	K=3	K=4	K=5
for $user^{n>0}$ and all products (13.79% orders contain repurchase purchase)					
TopPop	0.0	0.0013	0.0013	0.0013	0.0026
SVD_{matrix}	0.0609	0.1179	0.1735	0.2199	0.2662
SVD_{util}^{same}	0.1629*	0.2609*	0.3325*	0.3523*	0.3709*
$SVD_{util}^{0.7}$	0.1126*	0.1934*	0.2543*	0.2954*	0.3179*
for $user^{n>0}$ and $products^{n>0}$ (31.69% orders contain repurchase purchase)					
TopPop	0.0	0.0016	0.0016	0.0016	0.0032
SVD_{matrix}	0.0735	0.1422	0.2093	0.2652	0.3211
SVD_{util}^{same}	0.1965*	0.3147*	0.4010*	0.4249*	0.4473*
$SVD_{util}^{0.7}$	0.1358*	0.2332*	0.3067*	0.3562*	0.3834*
TopPop.Previous	0.1390	0.2476	0.3498	0.4249	0.4840
$SVD_{matrix}.Previous$	0.1230	0.2252	0.3243	0.3866	0.4553
$SVD_{util}^{same}.Previous$	0.1981*	0.3243*	0.4201*	0.4553*	0.4952*
$SVD_{util}^{0.7}.Previous$	0.2061*	0.3658*	0.4840*	0.5591*	0.6342*

- **How does SVD_{util} perform in the new product recommendation task?**

  Similarly, we add a filter to recommend only new products. The method with the filter is denoted as $method.New$. For testing, we use only orders that contain product(s) that the user has never purchased.

5.3.1 Re-purchase Product Recommendation Task

The conversion rate for the re-purchase product recommendation task is shown in Table 2.

Before the filter is applied, $SVD_{util}^{0.7}$ and SVD_{util}^{same} perform significantly better than baseline methods. This is as expected, since the new algorithm is expected to capture the re-purchase behavior.

SVD_{util}^{same} is better than $SVD_{util}^{0.7}$ before adding the filter, probably because using similar products introduces some noise into the model. However, it is worth mentioning that $SVD_{util}^{0.7}$ is able to catch some re-purchase behavior ignored by SVD_{util}^{same}. Some product was not purchased again and again in the training data, yet it is similar to the user's previous purchase. If such product is purchased in the testing data, the re-purchase behavior can only be captured by $SVD_{util}^{0.7}$ yet not SVD_{util}^{same}. For methods with filter, $SVD_{util}^{0.7}.Previous$ performs the best.

Here is one example. Table 3 shows product 2426's entire order history in the training data. Table 4 shows the product title of product 2426 and some of its similar products. 2426 was purchased only once by each of the five users. In this case, SVD_{util}^{same} cannot learn that it is a potential repurchase product. Yet user u_{2613} purchased two products (2365 and 1329) before, which are similar to product 2426. With this information, $SVD_{util}^{0.7}$ learns that product 2426 is likely to be purchased again after a user purchases a similar product or itself. In the testing data, $SVD_{util}^{0.7}$ recommends product 2426 to user u_{2857} at timestamp 12/1/08,17:52. It was purchased by user u_{2857} at that time, which is a repurchase behavior.

Table 3: Product 2426's purchase history in the training data. The table is used in Section 5.3.1.

userID	order time
u_{1916}	12/14/06 6:44
u_{2694}	12/16/07 19:34
u_{2613}	6/10/08 16:11
u_{2857}	8/6/08 20:11
u_{2863}	8/23/08 8:58

Table 4: Product title of Product 2426 and two similar products. The table is used in Section 5.3.1.

ProductID	Product Title
2426	Obsession by Calvin Klein TESTER for Women Eau de Parfum Spray 3.4 oz
2365	Eternity by Calvin Klein for Women Eau de Parfum Spray 1.7 oz
1329	Eternity by Calvin Klein for Women Eau de Parfum Spray 3.4 oz

5.3.2 New Product Recommendation Task

Table 5 compares the conversion rate of all methods in recommending new products.

Before using the filter, $SVD_{util}^{0.7}$ achieves better performance than the baseline SVD_{matrix} and TopPop. On the other hand, SVD_{util}^{same} does not help recommending new products. In this task, $SVD_{util}^{0.7}$ performs better than SVD_{util}^{same} since it learns from similar products' purchase behavior with $\theta < 1$. Recommending good and new products makes $SVD_{util}^{0.7}$ more attractive in e-commerce sites since it adds more serendipity to the user.

To better understand how the proposed method works, Table 6 shows user u_{3007}'s order and Table 7 shows the corresponding recommended lists generated by different methods.

User u_{3007} purchased product 915 in the training data. In the SVD_{util}^{same} method, only the marginal (net) utility of the exact same product 915 will be changed. Since product 915 was purchased by the other user(s) for many times, it is recommended to user u_{3007} by SVD_{util}^{same}. In the $SVD_{util}^{0.7}$ method, the marginal (net) utility of similar products will also be changed, including product 914. Its estimation shows that product 914 has a higher marginal net utility. Thus it appears in the top position of $SVD_{util}^{0.7}$ recommended list, which was actually purchased by the user in the testing

Table 5: Conversion rate@K for the new product recommendation task. Value* is significantly better than the baseline SVD_{matrix} and TopPop.

Method	K=1	K=2	K=3	K=4	K=5
for $user^{n>0}$ and all products (90.64% orders contain new purchase)					
TopPop	0.0002	0.0002	0.0005	0.0005	0.0007
SVD_{matrix}	0.0002	0.0002	0.0007	0.0007	0.0010
SVD_{util}^{same}	0	0	0	0	0.0002
$SVD_{util}^{0.7}$	0.0007	0.001	0.0024	0.0026	0.0026
for $user^{n>0}$ and $products^{n>0}$ (76.20% orders contain new purchase)					
TopPop	0.0007	0.0007	0.0013	0.0013	0.0020
SVD_{matrix}	0.0007	0.0007	0.0020	0.0020	0.0027
SVD_{util}^{same}	0	0	0	0	0.0007
$SVD_{util}^{0.7}$	0.0020	0.0027	0.0066*	0.0073*	0.0073*
TopPop.Previous	0.0007	0.0007	0.0013	0.0013	0.0020
$SVD_{matrix}.New$	0.0020	0.0020	0.0027	0.0027	0.0027
$SVD_{util}^{same}.New$	0.0007	0.0020	0.0020	0.0020	0.0027
$SVD_{util}^{0.7}.New$	0.0047	0.0073*	0.0086*	0.0100*	0.0113*

Table 6: user u_{3007}'s purchase order

times	productID	product title
In the training data		
9/28/08 0:20	915	Frontline Top Spot DOG up to 22lb (3 pack)
	1049	Pet Bio Guard Shampoo
	1033	Frontline Top Spot DOG 89-132lb. (3 pack)
In the testing data		
10/23/08 8:37	914	Frontline Top Spot DOG 45-88lb. (3 pack)
	293	Frontline PLUS - Dog (23 to 44 Lbs) 3-Pack

Table 7: Top 5 recommendation for user u_{3007} at time 10/23/08 8:37

Method	ProductID	Product title
TopPop	165	Frontline PLUS - Dog (45-88 Lbs)
	166	Frontline PLUS - Cat 3-Pack
	322	Pet Solid Compressed Rawhide Bone - 5"
	1611	Frontline PLUS - Dog up to 88 lbs. (6-Pack)
	1924	9" x 12" Colorations Heavyweight Construction Paper
SVD_{matrix}	165	Frontline PLUS - Dog (45-88 Lbs)
	1611	Frontline PLUS - Dog up to 88 lbs. (6-Pack)
	166	Frontline PLUS - Cat 3-Pack
	1593	Frontline PLUS - For Cats (6-Pack)
	2028	Colorations Simply Washable Tempera Paint
SVD_{util}^{same}	915	Frontline Top Spot DOG up to 22lb (3 pack)
	1033	Frontline Top Spot DOG 89-132lb. (3 pack)
	1049	Pet Bio Guard Shampoo
	2978	Nasal Aspirator
	2678	Brother LC51BK Compatible Black Ink Cartridge
$SVD_{util}^{0.7}$	914	**Frontline Top Spot DOG 45-88lb. (3 pack)**
	1033	Frontline Top Spot DOG 89-132lb. (3 pack)
	1610	Frontline Top Spot DOG up to 22lb (6 pack)
	915	Frontline Top Spot DOG up to 22lb (3 pack)
	30	Frontline Top Spot CAT (3 pack)

data. With these examples in the data, we discover that it is worthwhile to model the purchase decision based on the product's marginal net utility. The utility function can capture much information from consumer behavior.

After a filter is applied, $SVD_{util}^{0.7}.New$ performs better than the baseline SVD_{matrix} and the difference is significant.

5.4 Long-tail Product Recommendation Task

It is well known that the number of rated items follows a long-tail distribution, i.e., a small fraction of the most popular ones receive the majority of ratings (or purchase counts) [2]. Figure 2 plots the popularity (purchase count) of all products, reflecting that the majority of products were purchased by a few times (≤ 5). The 80:20 rule [7] is commonly used to divide between long-tail products and popular ones. In shop.com dataset, the short-head (20%) involves 0.814% of popular products. All the rest are long-tail products.

As mentioned in [9], to recommend popular products is easier yet more trivial. On the other hand, to recommend long-tail products adds more novelty yet it is also a harder task, due to the data sparsity issue. Though our algorithm is not targeted for recommending long-tail products, we would like to see how $SVD_{util}^{0.7}$ and SVD_{util}^{same} perform from this perspective. 96.09% of purchase orders in the testing data contain long-tail products. Only long-tail products in these testing orders are used to evaluate all methods' performance.

Table 8 shows the conversion rate of all methods for long-tail products. As expected, $TopPop$ cannot recommend any long-tail products. By maximizing the marginal net utility, $SVD_{util}^{0.7}$ and SVD_{util}^{same} can improve the baseline significantly. As long as the marginal net utility factor can be learned, the improvement is achieved for long-tail products.

Figure 2: Popularity (purchase count) of all products in the training data

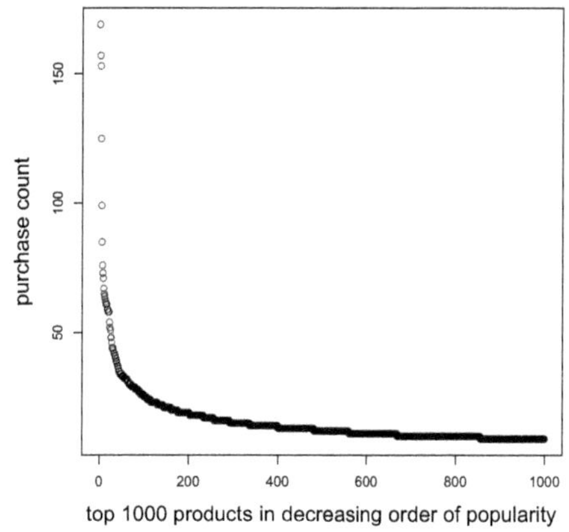

Table 8: Conversion rate@K for the long-tail product recommendation task(96.09% of all testing points). Value* is significantly better than the baseline SVD_{matrix} and TopPop.

Method	K=1	K=2	K=3	K=4	K=5
for $user^{n>0}$ and all products					
TopPop	0	0	0	0	0
SVD_{matrix}	0.0052	0.0108	0.0187	0.0225	0.0292
SVD_{util}^{same}	0.0148*	0.0267*	0.0364*	0.0396*	0.0416*
$SVD_{util}^{0.7}$	0.0108*	0.0200*	0.0272*	0.0335*	0.0360*

6. CONCLUSION AND FUTURE WORK

Inspired by the utility function in consumer behavior theory, we design a general framework to revamp existing recommendation algorithms for e-commerce sites. We apply it to SVD, which leads to a new algorithm SVD_{util}. We evaluate two special cases of the new algorithm: $SVD_{util}^{0.7}$ and SVD_{util}^{same}. The former one utilizes similar products in estimating the marginal utility while the latter one utilizes only the same product. These two methods use each purchase decision point in the data sequentially for the parameter estimation. On shop.com data, the new methods perform significantly better than baselines because they can better capture the re-purchase behavior as well as the diminishing return of the marginal utility. When comparing between these two cases, we found that SVD_{util}^{same} performs better in the re-purchase product recommendation task. $SVD_{util}^{0.7}$ is more useful in recommending new products, which is a harder task and generates more interesting result to the user.

This is just the first step towards revamping recommendation algorithms based on the concept of marginal net utility. In this work, the marginal utility diminishing rate only depends on each product. In the future, we plan to do more research to explore its dependency on each user, different time, or other features. Besides, the latent vectors and products' diminishing return rate are not updated online in the current work. In the future, online updating and online testing would be implemented to reflect real-world scenario. In addition, the rich implicit data can also be utilized to train our model better.

Acknowledgments

We would like to thank shop.com for sharing the data. This work was funded by National Science Foundation IIS-0713111 and IIS-0953908. Any opinions, findings, conclusions or recommendations expressed in this paper are the authors, and do not necessarily reflect those of the sponsors.

7. REFERENCES

[1] C. C. Aggarwal, J. L. Wolf, K. lung Wu, and P. S. Yu. Horting hatches an egg: A new graph-theoretic approach to collaborative filtering. In *Proceedings of the Fifth ACM SIGKDD*, 1999.

[2] C. Anderson. *The Long Tail: Why the Future of Business Is Selling Less of More.* Hyperion, 2006.

[3] W. J. Baumol and A. S. Blinder. *Microeconomics: Principles and Policy.* South-Western College Pub, 11 edition, July 2008.

[4] J. Bennett and S. Lanning. The netflix prize. 2007.

[5] J. S. Breese, D. Heckerman, and C. Kadie. Empirical analysis of predictive algorithms for collaborative filtering. pages 43–52. Morgan Kaufmann, 1998.

[6] R. Burke. Hybrid recommender systems: Survey and experiments. *User Modeling and User-Adapted Interaction*, 12:331–370, 2002.

[7] Y. Chen, P. P. Chong, and Y. Tong. Theoretical foundation of the 80/20 rule. *Scientometrics*, 28(2):183–204, October 1993.

[8] C. Cobb and P. Douglas. A theory of production. *American Economic Review*, 18:139 – 165, 1928.

[9] P. Cremonesi, Y. Koren, and R. Turrin. Performance of recommender algorithms on top-n recommendation tasks. In *Proceedings of the fourth ACM conference on Recommender systems*, pages 39–46, New York, NY, USA, 2010. ACM.

[10] M. Deshpande and G. Karypis. Item-based top-n recommendation algorithms. *ACM Trans. Inf. Syst.*, 22(1):143–177, 2004.

[11] D. Fleder and K. Hosanagar. Blockbuster culture's next rise or fall: The impact of recommender systems on sales diversity. *Manage. Sci.*, 55:697–712, May 2009.

[12] J. L. Herlocker, J. A. Konstan, A. Borchers, and J. Riedl. An algorithmic framework for performing collaborative filtering. In *Proceedings of the 22nd annual international ACM SIGIR*, pages 230–237, New York, NY, USA, 1999. ACM.

[13] J. L. Herlocker, J. A. Konstan, L. G. Terveen, and J. T. Riedl. Evaluating collaborative filtering recommender systems. *ACM Trans. Inf. Syst.*, 22:5–53, January 2004.

[14] T. Hofmann. Latent semantic models for collaborative filtering. *ACM Trans. Inf. Syst.*, 22(1):89–115, 2004.

[15] Z. Huang, W. Chung, and H. Chen. A graph model for e-commerce recommender systems. *J. Am. Soc. Inf. Sci. Technol.*, 55:259–274, February 2004.

[16] R. Jin, L. Si, C. Zhai, and J. Callan. Collaborative filtering with decoupled models for preferences and ratings. In *Proceedings of the twelfth CIKM*, pages 309–316, New York, NY, USA, 2003. ACM.

[17] Y. S. Kim, B.-J. Yum, J. Song, and S. M. Kim. Development of a recommender system based on navigational and behavioral patterns of customers in e-commerce sites. *Expert Syst. Appl.*, 28:381–393, February 2005.

[18] Y. Koren. Factorization meets the neighborhood: a multifaceted collaborative filtering model. In *Proceeding of the 14th ACM SIGKDD international conference on Knowledge discovery and data mining*, KDD '08, pages 426–434, New York, NY, USA, 2008. ACM.

[19] Y. Koren. Collaborative filtering with temporal dynamics. In *KDD '09: Proceedings of the 15th ACM*, pages 447–456, New York, NY, USA, 2009. ACM.

[20] S. li Huang. Designing utility-based recommender systems for e-commerce: Evaluation of preference-elicitation methods. *Electronic Commerce Research and Applications*, In Press, Corrected Proof:–, 2010.

[21] B. Marlin and R. S. Zemel. The multiple multiplicative factor model for collaborative filtering. In *ICML '04: Proceedings of the twenty-first international conference on Machine learning*, page 73, New York, NY, USA, 2004. ACM.

[22] B. Mobasher, R. Cooley, and J. Srivastava. Automatic personalization based on web usage mining. *Commun. ACM*, 43(8):142–151, 2000.

[23] R. J. Mooney and L. Roy. Content-based book recommending using learning for text categorization. In *DL '00*, pages 195–204, New York, NY, USA, 2000. ACM.

[24] M. Pazzani, D. Billsus, S. Michalski, and J. Wnek. Learning and revising user profiles: The identification of interesting web sites. In *Machine Learning*, pages 313–331, 1997.

[25] B. Sarwar, G. Karypis, J. Konstan, and J. Reidl. Item-based collaborative filtering recommendation algorithms. In *Proceedings of the 10th WWW conference*, pages 285–295, New York, NY, USA, 2001. ACM.

[26] B. Sarwar, G. Karypis, J. Konstan, and J. Riedl. Analysis of recommendation algorithms for e-commerce. In *Proceedings of the 2nd ACM conference on Electronic commerce*, pages 158–167, New York, NY, USA, 2000. ACM.

[27] B. M. Sarwar, G. Karypis, J. A. Konstan, and J. T. Riedl. Application of dimensionality reduction in recommender system – a case study. In *IN ACM WEBKDD WORKSHOP*, 2000.

[28] J. B. Schafer, J. A. Konstan, and J. Riedl. E-commerce recommendation applications. *Data Min. Knowl. Discov.*, 5:115–153, January 2001.

[29] G. Shani, D. Heckerman, and R. I. Brafman. An mdp-based recommender system. *J. Mach. Learn. Res.*, 6:1265–1295, 2005.

[30] L. Si and R. Jin. Flexible mixture model for collaborative filtering. In *Proc. of ICML*, pages 704–711. AAAI Press, 2003.

[31] H. Uzawa. Production functions with constant elasticities of substituion. *Review of Economic Studies*, 29(4):291–299, Oct 1962.

Recommending Ephemeral Items at Web Scale

Ye Chen*
Microsoft Corporation
Mountain View, CA 94086 USA
yec@microsoft.com

John F. Canny
University of California, Berkeley
Berkeley, CA 94720 USA
jfc@cs.berkeley.edu

ABSTRACT

We describe an innovative and scalable recommendation system successfully deployed at eBay. To build recommenders for long-tail marketplaces requires projection of volatile items into a persistent space of latent products. We first present a generative clustering model for collections of unstructured, heterogeneous, and ephemeral item data, under the assumption that items are generated from latent products. An item is represented as a vector of independently and distinctly distributed variables, while a latent product is characterized as a vector of probability distributions, respectively. The probability distributions are chosen as natural stochastic models for different types of data. The learning objective is to maximize the total intra-cluster coherence measured by the sum of log likelihoods of items under such a generative process. In the space of latent products, robust recommendations can then be derived using naïve Bayes for ranking, from historical transactional data. Item-based recommendations are achieved by inferring latent products from unseen items. In particular, we develop a probabilistic scoring function of recommended items, which takes into account item-product membership, product purchase probability, and the important auction-end-time factor. With the holistic probabilistic measure of a prospective item purchase, one can further maximize the expected revenue and the more subjective user satisfaction as well. We evaluated the latent product clustering and recommendation ranking models using real-world e-commerce data from eBay, in both forms of offline simulation and online A/B testing. In the recent production launch, our system yielded 3-5 folds improvement over the existing production system in click-through, purchase-through and gross merchandising value; thus now driving 100% related recommendation traffic with billions of items at eBay. We believe that this work provides a practical yet principled framework for recommendation in the domains with affluent user self-input data.

*This work was mainly conducted when the authors were affiliated with eBay Inc.

SIGIR'11, July 24–28, 2011, Beijing, China.

Categories and Subject Descriptors

H.3.3 [**Information Search and Retrieval**]: Clustering, Information filtering.

General Terms

Algorithms, Experimentation, Performance

Keywords

Recommender systems, collaborative filtering, generative models, clustering, Bayesian methods, evaluation

1. INTRODUCTION

Recommendation for online marketplaces such as eBay raises several unique challenges. First, a majority of items are ad hoc listings not covered by any predefined product or catalog taxonomy. This can be partially attributed to the nature of the inventory under study, which features a very long tail of item types and, not uncommon, "one-of-a-kind" inventory. Besides, to maintain such a catalog so to capture a highly dynamic and diverse inventory can be a daunting task. We approach this challenge by deliberately reducing volatile and noisy item data to persistent and robust latent products [6]. The latent products shall discover statistical structure underlying the item data, and may not necessarily have bearings on physical products. The projection space should be ultimately optimized for the effectiveness of recommendation or other information retrieval and filtering tasks.

Second, the historical transactional data at the user level is very sparse. For example, over a three-month period of time at eBay, each buyer on average made 17.31 bids and won 5.63 of them. The publicized Netflix user-movie rating data, on the other hand, has 208.33 ratings on average for each user [3], i.e., more than 30-fold sparser for purchases and 10-fold sparser for bids with the eBay transactional data. User-item ratings are not available in eBay's dataset[1], nor this kind of ratings are appropriate or calibrated preference measure for such a diverse inventory. We argue that historical purchases are at least no worse than rating-based collaborative filtering (CF) data, since purchases reflect monetary commitments. However, given the sparsity of historical transactions or bid attempts, the state-of-the-art CF approaches, devised for rating-based datasets,

[1]There does exist a feedback score from a buyer towards a seller with regard to an item purchase, but this cannot be used as user-item rating due to the significant role played by the seller.

such as latent factor models [17] may not be directly applicable or work as well. From the data perspective, we need to incorporate more implicit preference data such as search queries and results, item views, personalized saved searches and tracked items, bids and purchases. From the method perspective, we apply naïve Bayes to recognize co-preference or sequential-preference patterns [7]. The compactness of naïve Bayes is especially desired for such a sparse and noisy dataset, and it provides a probabilistic preference score for each candidate item. Recommendations can then be made by ranking and filtering candidates.

2. FROM ITEMS TO PRODUCTS

Deriving robust product concepts from item descriptions is an important first step for subsequent delivery of auction suggestions. Since most items are unique, typical modeling methods cannot be applied to user behavior since there is no link between user behaviors with the same or similar items. Items are defined by about 10 title words, possibly attribute values, a leaf category, price, and otherwise by behavioral data such as user views, bids and purchases. Our goal is to map each item ID to a more general product ID, i.e., to derive a map $f : I \to P$, where I is the space of possible item features, and P is the set of product labels. so the problem is a clustering problem. In many similar cases such as movie and book recommendation, ad targeting or even text clustering, a projection map g would be applied from I to a lower dimensional space before clustering is applied. However, that approach is not suitable here for several reasons. Instead we apply model-based clustering directly to the item data such as a bag-of-words feature vector for title text. The reasons are as follows:

First of all, title descriptions are extremely sparse having only about 10 terms on average in the case of eBay items. By contrast, movie data, texts for document clustering, or user history for targeting have hundreds or thousands of events. These events are highly correlated (e.g., users have similar ratings of similar movies) and projection serves to normalize dependencies (i.e., SVD creates a spherical Gaussian distribution in the low-dimensional space) and, most importantly, to robustly estimate the coordinates in the projection space. For such estimate to be accurate, the number of parameters in a typical record should be much larger than the dimension of the projection space. In the examples above, a good ratio of data parameters to dimension is 10:1. If the projection space dimension is too high, there is little or no value to the projection step. The variance is normalized, but this could equally well be achieved by normalizing the metric used in the original space. However, there is no "cleaning" of the data accomplished in such a projection. In practice, performance is very poor as the projection dimension approaches the number of item parameters in all the examples above.

More importantly, the statistical dependencies between title words in eBay items are very different from the other examples above. In the first place, they are already quite independent. Users consciously try to describe the important features of their item in relatively few words. In many cases, words are genuine attributes or product category names. What dependencies remain are highly localized and product specific. For instance, the term "red" has high co-occurrence with products that come in a red version (e.g., iPods), but zero co-occurrence with products that do not come in red (e.g., iPhones). All other attributes have similar properties. Thus dependencies are entirely local in the product space, and it does not make sense to look for a global map from the title word space to a latent space. This differs from the other examples above where there are global dependencies based on user preference or document topic. Finally, by using a generative clustering method, we can accurately model these dependencies in the original parameter space. This opportunity is lost after a global projection.

3. A LATENT PRODUCT MODEL

In this section we formally describe the generative clustering model for learning latent products. An item $\mathbf{x}$ is the basic unit of transaction, embodied by a set of unstructured and heterogeneous data including auction title, description, attribute name-value pairs, price, among others. The item data can be categorized into three types: (1) binary variables for term occurrences in textual data such as auction title and description, i.e., $\mathbf{b} = (b_1, b_2, \ldots, b_V)$ where V is the size of vocabulary; (2) categorical variables for indexed attribute values such as brand and color, i.e., $\mathbf{c} = (c_1, c_2, \ldots, c_U)$ where U is the number of attributes; and (3) continuous variables for numerical data such as price, i.e., $\mathbf{g} = (g_1, g_2, \ldots, g_S)$ where S is the dimension of numerical feature space. A dense representation of an item thus becomes a 3-tuple of vectors: $\mathbf{x} = (\mathbf{b}, \mathbf{c}, \mathbf{g})$.

A latent product $\mathbf{z}$ is the persistent concept underlying items. We use a binomial distribution $\text{Binom}(p)$ to model each binary variable, a multinomial distribution $\text{Mult}(\theta)$ for each categorical variable, and a Gaussian distribution $\mathcal{N}(\mu, \sigma^2)$ for each continuous variable, possibly after log transformation. Notice that we only allow one trial for each binomial and multinomial process per item, i.e., Bernoulli and categorical distributions, respectively. The one-trial specialization is appropriate for the item data, since sellers tend to use concise words for listing items and repeated terms are less relevant. A categorical attribute's values are mutually exclusive, hence an item has exactly one value. We further assume the variance σ^2 of a continuous variable is a constant w.r.t. a collection of items. A latent product is then represented as a vector of Bernoulli success probabilities, multinomial parameters, and Gaussian means: $\mathbf{z} = (p_1, p_2, \ldots, p_V, \theta_1, \theta_2, \ldots, \theta_U, \mu_1, \mu_2, \ldots, \mu_S)$. The belongingness of an item to a latent product is stochastically modeled as the following generative process:

1. For binary variables: $b_v \sim \text{Binom}(p_v), \forall v \in \{1, \ldots, V\}$;
2. For categorical variables: $c_u \sim \text{Mult}(\theta_u), \forall u \in \{1, \ldots, U\}$;
3. For continuous variables: $g_s \sim \mathcal{N}(\mu_s, \sigma^2), \forall s \in \{1, \ldots, S\}$.

Given a latent product $\mathbf{z}_k$, the likelihood of an item $\mathbf{x}_i$ is:

$$p(\mathbf{x}_i|\mathbf{z}_k) = \prod_{v:b_{iv}=1} p_{kv} \prod_{v:b_{iv}=0} (1 - p_{kv}) \prod_u \theta_{ku} \times \prod_s \frac{1}{\sqrt{2\pi\sigma^2}} \exp\left(-\frac{(g_{is} - \mu_{ks})^2}{2\sigma^2}\right), \quad (1)$$

where θ_{ku} is the multinomial probability corresponding to the outcome c_{iu}. The log likelihood is then:

$$\ell(\mathbf{x}_i|\mathbf{z}_k) \propto \sum_{v:b_{iv}=1} \log(p_{kv}) + \sum_{v:b_{iv}=0} \log(1 - p_{kv}) + \sum_u \log(\theta_{ku}) - \frac{1}{2\sigma^2} \sum_s (g_{is} - \mu_{ks})^2. \quad (2)$$

3.1 Parameter Estimation

Given a set of items $I = \{\mathbf{x}_i\}_{i=1}^n$, we wish to learn a smaller set of latent products $P = \{\mathbf{z}_k\}_{k=1}^m$ and derive assignments of items $\mathbf{x}_i$ to latent products $\mathbf{z}_k$ with maximum likelihood, such that the total intra-product log likelihood of the item data I is maximized.

$$(\mathbf{z}_1^*, \dots, \mathbf{z}_m^*) = \underset{(\mathbf{z}_1, \dots, \mathbf{z}_m)}{\operatorname{argmax}} \sum_k \sum_i \gamma_{ik} \ell(\mathbf{x}_i | \mathbf{z}_k), \tag{3}$$

where γ_{ik} is an indicator variable for item-product membership.

The latent product vectors $(\mathbf{z}_1, \dots, \mathbf{z}_m)$ are the only model parameters to be estimated, while γ_{ik} can be viewed as hidden variables. The hard product membership assumption directly yields the maximum likelihood estimate (MLE) of γ_{ik} with $\mathbf{z}_k \forall k$ fixed. Since we use binomial, multinomial and Gaussian distributions to model item generation, the MLE of the latent product parameters $\mathbf{z}_k$ are simply given by the means of the item random vectors belonging to that product. We thus derive the following EM algorithm:

$$\text{E-step:} \quad \gamma_{ik} \leftarrow \begin{cases} 1 & k = \underset{k'}{\operatorname{argmax}}\, \ell(\mathbf{x}_i | \mathbf{z}_{k'}), \\ 0 & \text{otherwise.} \end{cases} \tag{4}$$

$$\text{M-step:} \quad \mathbf{z}_k \leftarrow \mathbb{E}(\mathbf{x}_i | \gamma_{ik} = 1). \tag{5}$$

In a standard EM algorithm, the E-step would compute the expectation of hidden variables. In our formulation however, the expected value of γ_{ik} is deterministically given by its MLE. This approach is referred to as a variant of the generalized EM, or essentially an alternating coordinate ascent [20]. The model so far is quite similar to k-means clustering. However, there are significant differences in distance metric and cluster assignment. As we show later in the experiments, our probabilistic distance outperforms traditional metrics such as Euclidean and cosine similarity. More importantly, the probabilistic item-product belongingness allows us to derive a probabilistic item preference score for recommendation purpose.

The initialization of $(\mathbf{z}_1, \dots, \mathbf{z}_m)$ is obtained by first uniformly randomly sampling m groups of items and then performing a M-step assuming that these groups represent m latent products, respectively. To address the sparsity and possible noise of such initialization, we further smooth the local parameters $\mathbf{z}_k$ by the background probabilities $\mathbf{q}$, i.e., the Jelinek-Mercer method [16]:

$$\mathbf{z}_k \leftarrow (1 - \lambda)\mathbf{z}_k + \lambda \mathbf{q}, \tag{6}$$

where the background probabilities $\mathbf{q}$ are obtained by performing a M-step assuming that the entire set of items are generated from a single global latent product, and λ is the smoothing factor with a relatively small value, e.g., $\lambda = 0.01$. It is also desired to perform smoothing after each iteration of EM for the same reason of sparsity, especially at the early stage. A Bayesian smoothing method would impose a conjugate prior for $\mathbf{z}_k$ [23]. We choose the interpolation form mainly for computational efficiency, as elaborated in Section 3.2.

It is important to note that item clustering is an intermediate step towards recommendation learning, its primary goal is a mild entropy reduction or data cleaning. Our choice of the hard item-product membership has serious advantages in production in space and time. The current production implementation writes belonging latent products to the item search indexing system; hence allowing for two latent products for each item would double the precious production storage, as well as the item scoring and ranking time.

3.2 Efficient Inference

The inferential task given a model trained is to assign an unseen item $\mathbf{x}'$ to a derived latent product with maximum log likelihood:

$$k^* = \underset{k}{\operatorname{argmax}}\, \ell(\mathbf{x}' | \mathbf{z}_k), \tag{7}$$

which is identical to a final E-step. The same calculation (E-step) is performed iteratively during clustering, and dominates the run-time of training with a complexity of $\mathcal{O}(nmV)$ for a naïve dense implementation. Therefore the key to the performance is an efficient method to evaluate Eq. (2). For clarity, we will describe a method for the Bernoulli terms only, which are very numerous and sparse. Since the method involves only association of indices, the generalization to multinomial and Gaussian scores should be obvious. There should be only a few multinomial and Gaussian parameters and they are assumed to be dense. The simplified score after smoothing becomes:

$$\begin{aligned} \ell(\mathbf{x}_i | \mathbf{z}_k) = & \sum_{v: b_{iv}=1} \log\left((1-\lambda)p_{kv} + \lambda q_v\right) \\ & + \sum_{v: b_{iv}=0} \log\left(1 - (1-\lambda)p_{kv} - \lambda q_v\right). \end{aligned} \tag{8}$$

Let us define $p_a = (1-\lambda)p_{kv} + \lambda q_v$ and $p_b = \lambda q_v$, and further split the right-hand side of the above according to whether p_{kv} is zero or not:

$$\begin{aligned} \ell(\mathbf{x}_i | \mathbf{z}_k) = & \sum_{v: p_{kv}>0, b_{iv}=1} \log(p_a) \\ & + \sum_{v: p_{kv}>0, b_{iv}=0} \log(1 - p_a) \\ & + \sum_{v: p_{kv}=0, b_{iv}=1} \log(p_b) \\ & + \sum_{v: p_{kv}=0, b_{iv}=0} \log(1 - p_b), \end{aligned} \tag{9}$$

which can be rewritten by pre-computing dense $b_{iv} = 0$ terms as default:

$$\begin{aligned} \ell(\mathbf{x}_i | \mathbf{z}_k) = & \sum_{v: p_{kv}>0, b_{iv}=1} \log\left(\frac{p_a}{1 - p_a}\right) \\ & + \sum_{v: p_{kv}>0} \log(1 - p_a) \\ & + \sum_{v: p_{kv}=0, b_{iv}=1} \log\left(\frac{p_b}{1 - p_b}\right) \\ & + \sum_{v: p_{kv}=0} \log(1 - p_b), \end{aligned} \tag{10}$$

and we can push this idea one step further by assuming

$p_{kv} = 0$ in a densified pre-computation:

$$\ell(\mathbf{x}_i|\mathbf{z}_k) = \sum_{v:p_{kv}>0, b_{iv}=1} \log\left(\frac{p_a(1-p_b)}{(1-p_a)p_b}\right) + \sum_{v:p_{kv}>0} \log\left(\frac{1-p_a}{1-p_b}\right) + \sum_v \log(1-p_b) + \sum_{v:b_{iv}=1} \log\left(\frac{p_b}{1-p_b}\right). \quad (11)$$

We notice that of these four right-hand side terms, only the first depends on both the cluster k and the item i. It comprises only terms which are shared between both the item, and the nonzero components of p_{kv}. By pre-computing the item-independent sparse vectors $a_{kv} = (\log(p_a) - \log(1-p_a) - \log(p_b) + \log(1-p_b))$ only at nonzeros of p_{kv}, we can evaluate this first sum with a sparse matrix product $\sum_v a_{kv} b_{iv}$. The second and third right-hand side sums have been made independent of the item data, and so can be computed only once for each cluster, where the third term is in fact constant across all clusters. The fourth sum depends on the item data and p_b. But p_b depends only on the background probability, and not cluster data. There is no need to compute this term when deciding how to assign an item since it is fixed for that item. Therefore if we define

$$e_k = \sum_{v:p_{kv}>0} \log\left(\frac{1-p_a}{1-p_b}\right) + \sum_v \log(1-p_b), \quad (12)$$

then to assign an item to a cluster, we only need compute the partial score:

$$\ell(\mathbf{x}_i|\mathbf{z}_k) \propto \sum_v a_{kv} b_{iv} + e_k, \quad (13)$$

while the complete score including cluster-independent terms is:

$$\ell(\mathbf{x}_i|\mathbf{z}_k) = \sum_v a_{kv} b_{iv} + e_k + \sum_v f_v b_{iv}, \quad (14)$$

where $f_v = \log(p_b) - \log(1-p_b)$.

On typical data (cluster size around 20, several million items), there is only one overlapping term between a random item and a random cluster. With a straightforward sparse matrix multiplication implementation, one item-cluster comparison takes about 4 nanoseconds on a 3GHz single processor machine. For existing items which should account for the majority of inventory, we perform an offline batch final E-step to build an item-to-product (I2P) map, which is a sparse matrix for latent products lookup from query items. Since recommendations are derived at the latent product level, we also need to store a product-to-item (P2I) map, where $\text{P2I} = \text{I2P}^\top$, to lookup items from recommended latent products.

It is important to emphasize that the efficient inference described above generalizes to standard clustering and other problem domains with high-dimensional sparse data [12], such as language models for information retrieval [23]. A similar decomposition as Eq. (11) can be readily derived for k-means with squared Euclidean distance by pre-computing instance-independent and non-linear (quadratic) terms, while in our case log terms are pre-computed. The complexity of E-step now reduces to $\mathcal{O}(nm * \text{nnz}_\mathbf{x})$, where $\text{nnz}_\mathbf{x}$ is the average number of nonzeros per item. Given a typical vocabulary size of 100K and item size of 10, the speed-up is 10K times.

3.3 Cluster Management

The number of latent products m, as in other clustering methods, is an input parameter to the algorithm. The choice of m depends on domain requirements, particularly the desired granularity level of latent products. Accurate recommendations require fine-grained latent products, but too fine granularity may suffer noisy and unreliable recommendations. This is yet another instance of precision-recall trade-off, and the optimization objective in our case is to maximize the effectiveness of recommendations.

We wish to learn a relatively large number of latent products with high intra-product uniformity to make precise recommendations, while keeping the size of each product cluster above a certain threshold to maintain an acceptable recall level. Hence we use the following heuristics for cluster management:

1. Given n input item examples, initialize $m = \lfloor n/d \rfloor$ centroids as generating latent products by random sampling described in Section 3.1. Here d is the target average size of a cluster, e.g., $d = 20$.

2. After each EM iteration, specifically the M-step, dissolve clusters with a size less than a threshold (too noisy), i.e., $|\mathbf{z}_k| < \epsilon$. Here ϵ is the minimum cluster size we want to maintain, e.g., $\epsilon = 5$.

3. After every even EM iteration, break clusters with a size above a threshold (too diverse), i.e.,

$$|\mathbf{z}_k| \geq \exp(\mu(\log(|\mathbf{z}|)) + \delta\sigma(\log(|\mathbf{z}|))), \quad (15)$$

   where $\mu(\cdot)$ and $\sigma(\cdot)$ denote the mean and standard deviation of log cluster size respectively; and δ gives δ-sigma threshold, e.g., $\delta = 3$. We then randomly sample a subset of items in dissolved clusters as new centroids, using the same d as item-product ratio.

3.4 Related Models

Mixture models have been widely used for clustering, where each cluster is represented as a parametric distribution, e.g., a mixture of multinomial for document clustering [21]. Under a mixture model for learning latent products, the likelihood of an item $\mathbf{x}_i$ is:

$$p(\mathbf{x}_i) = \sum_k p(\mathbf{z}_k) p(\mathbf{x}_i|\mathbf{z}_k), \quad (16)$$

where an item $\mathbf{x}_i$ is modeled as a convex combination of m latent product distributions $p(\mathbf{x}_i|\mathbf{z}_k)$ with mixture proportions $p(\mathbf{z}_k)$. The mixture model assumes soft product membership of items, i.e., an item-level mixture; and model parameters can be estimated by using the standard EM algorithm. The mixture approach is more statistically sound for semantically rich data such as documents and images, but less so for the item datasets that we are investigating for recommendation. An ordinary document often exhibits multiple topics, but an item is physically associated with exactly one product. In other words, soft membership is not well-motivated for item-to-product projection. Instead, we want to impose very sparse per-item latent product mixture proportions.

Latent variable models, such as pLSI [14], LDA [4] and recent adaptation for recommendation [1, 2, 15, 22], allow even greater model expressiveness, i.e., a word-level topic mixture. However, these models do not serve the specific purpose of learning latent products, that is, a mild entropy reduction (e.g., 10-fold) with high within-cluster coherence (i.e., intra-product likelihood) in order to subsequently derive robust recommendations.

Finally, we shall note that our method is a heterogeneous generalization of the multivariate Bernoulli model originated from text classification [19, 24]. As we showed in Section 3, the same centroid-based generative approach shall work for any heterogeneous combination of parametric distributions, as long as the MLE of model parameters can be obtained as the expectation of feature vectors.

4. NAÏVE BAYES RECOMMENDER

Now that we have inferential machinery mapping volatile items to persistent latent products, we can perform recommendation by using the following naïve Bayes for ranking:

$$y^* = \operatorname*{argmax}_y p(y|x) \propto \operatorname*{argmax}_y p(x, y), \tag{17}$$

where x denotes a contextual or historical transaction of a latent product which will be used as the input to the recommender, e.g., a buyer's last purchase; and y indexes the recommended product for next purchase.

4.1 Product-level Recommendation Model

Given the objective of a recommender is to maximize sales, it is desired to compute $p(x, y)$ in Eq. (17) as the joint probability of purchasing both x and y. However, purchase data is extremely sparse[2], which makes the estimate noisy. Thus we smooth the pure purchase probability with other less sparse behaviors yet indicative of user preference, including clicks (i.e., clicking on a search result and landing to a view item page) and bids. Furthermore, it is unrealistic to assume a user is exposed to the entire inventory, so a normalized preference score should be made conditional on views (i.e., viewing search results). Finally, even the click or bid co-occurrence data can still be sparse, thus we further smooth the co-preference probability with a unigram popularity score dependent only on the candidate product y using Laplace smoothing.

Formally, let C be an $m \times m$ matrix of co-occurrences, where a subscript pair index the co-occurring latent products and a superscript pair encode the behavioral types respectively. For example, C^{vb}_{yx} is the number of users who bid on x and viewed y. We consider four types of co-occurrence patterns: (1) bid-bid (bb), (2) purchase-purchase (pp), (3) click-bid (cb), and (4) view-bid (vb). The product-to-product preference probability is:

$$p(y|x) = \frac{\alpha_1 C^{\text{bb}}_{yx} + \alpha_2 C^{\text{pp}}_{yx} + \alpha_3 C^{\text{cb}}_{yx} + \zeta}{C^{\text{vb}}_{yx} + \zeta / p(y)}, \tag{18}$$

where $(\alpha_1, \alpha_2, \alpha_3)$ are coefficients for a convex combination of the three co-preference patterns, ζ is the smoothing factor, and $p(y)$ is the baseline popularity of y:

$$p(y) = \frac{\beta_1 C^{\text{p}}_y + \beta_2 C^{\text{b}}_y + \beta_3 C^{\text{c}}_y}{\max(C^{\text{v}}_y, \varepsilon)}, \tag{19}$$

where $(\beta_1, \beta_2, \beta_3)$ are mixture weights and ε is a small value for numerical protection, e.g., $\varepsilon = 1.0 \times 10^{-8}$. Here C with a single subscript denotes a unigram count (for one latent product only) of a behavioral type encoded in a superscript. For instance, C^{v}_y is the number of users who viewed y.

4.2 Counting Co-occurrences

To compute the product-to-product co-preference probability in Eq. (18) mainly involves counting co-occurring events, which is the computational bottleneck in offline training. Of the four co-occurrence matrices in Eq. (18), the view-bid matrix C^{vb} is the least sparse. We now use C^{vb} as an example to discuss several important design issues for a sound and scalable implementation.

It turns out that one can leverage efficient sparse matrix operations to obtain the co-occurrence matrices. Since we count events in terms of users, we first form product-user count matrices, one for each relevant event type, by scanning the transactional data once and performing the inference in Eq. (7). Let D_v be an $m \times l$ product-user matrix of view counts, D_b be a bid counts matrix with the same dimensions, and both use sparse representation. The co-occurrence matrix C^{vb} is then obtained by a sparse matrix multiplication $D_\text{v} D_\text{b}^\top$. Furthermore, one only needs to count C^{vb} entries when at least one of the three numerator terms C^{bb}, C^{pp}, and C^{cb} has a nonzero corresponding entry. A dominant user behavioral conversion flow is: view $\rightarrow$ click $\rightarrow$ bid $\rightarrow$ purchase, and view events are typically an order of magnitude denser than non-view events; thus to leverage the data sparsity further we only count C^{vb} entries when the corresponding C^{cb} count is nonzero:

$$C^{\text{vb}} = D_\text{v} D_\text{b}^\top, \forall (x, y) \text{ where } C^{\text{cb}}_{yx} > 0. \tag{20}$$

The time period over which the co-occurrence matrices are defined (counted) is important, since the association between co-occurring events becomes noisier as they are spaced farther apart. Thus we only count co-occurring events if they happened within a relatively short overlapping time window. On the other hand, if the length of an overlapping window gets too short, there will be very few co-occurrences collected. We use a $t \times w$ sliding window to count co-occurrences, which works as follows. Along the time axis, we increment w-day transactional data into a $t \times w$-day sliding window, and over which perform one iteration of counting. The $t \times w$-day sliding window thus moves forward by w-day per iteration until the entire training period is exhausted. This design asserts that one pair of events co-occurred within a small w-day window casts t times as many counts as were the pair happened $t \times w$-day apart. Our experiments showed that a 3×7-day sliding window gives optimal recommendations, as illustrated in Figure 1.

A typical user first issues a search query, then views the search results, and potentially clicks some result landing to an item page. Since this voluntary user conversion course can be considered as a Markov chain and starts with click-through, i.e., view $\rightarrow$ click, it is critical to model the click-through process in a principled manner. It is known that the presentational position or rank of a result link in a search result page has significant impact on click-through

[2]Over a two-month period in one of the most popular categories at eBay (Clothing, Shoes & Accessories), above 50% of users only made one item purchase.

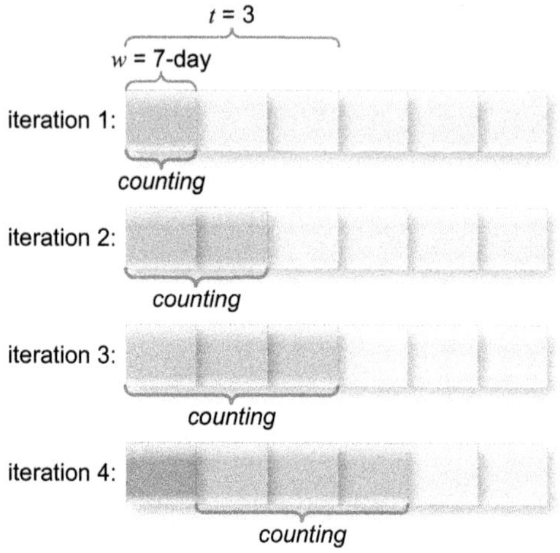

Figure 1: $t \times w$-day sliding window.

rate (CTR) [5, 11]. We adopt the position-bias model developed in [8], which imposes a positional prior to normalize (multiply) view count. A bottom position will have a lower prior probability than those higher up in a search result page, where a positional prior can be interpreted as the probability of a user physically viewing the link. Thus a result link showing at a lower position will only have a fraction of one normalized view count. From the click-through perspective, a user clicking lower-position item links effectively casts more preference votes (to Eq. (18)) than were these links shown at higher positions. We use an empirical positional prior distribution as follows,

$$p(r; \eta, \phi) = \frac{1}{Z_1} r^{-\eta}, r = 1, 2, \ldots, \phi. \tag{21}$$

Here η is a positive real number implying the rate at which a prior decreases as the positional rank r moves down in a search result page, ϕ is the lowest rank the prior covers, and $Z_1 = \sum_{r=1}^{\phi} r^{-\eta}$ is a normalizing constant. A default eBay search result page shows 50 item links and almost all clicks are from the first page, hence it is not only practically sufficient but also computationally efficient to define the prior over a discrete and finite range [1, 50]. When $\eta = 0.5$, there is a 7-fold *a priori* difference in CTR between the top and bottom positions, which fits well to the eBay search click-through data and is aligned with other similar domains such as sponsored search [8].

Counting events in number of unique users provides one level of robot filtering mechanism, since each user can only vote once w.r.t. one co-occurrence. In addition, we apply another level of data-driven robot filtering by removing users whose total number of activities during a w-day window is above a certain threshold, e.g., $\text{thres}_{\text{7-day}} = 2000$.

4.3 Item-level Ranking Model

In online recommendation, a triggering event is an item transaction (e.g., previous purchase), one then retrieves a candidate set of items and ranks them to recommend top N items. More formally, let i be a seed item and j be a candidate item. We wish to have a probabilistic scoring function to perform recommendation:

$$j^* = \operatorname*{argmax}_j p(j|i). \tag{22}$$

Recall that both the latent product clustering and product-level recommendation models are derived in a statistically rigorous manner, and hence provide probabilistic measures. The item-to-item recommendation score can be factorized as the following Markov chain:

$$\begin{aligned} p(j|i) &= \sum_{x,y} p(j|y)p(y|x)p(x|i) \\ &= p(j|y(j))p(y(j)|x(i))p(x(i)|i), \end{aligned} \tag{23}$$

where x and y denote input and recommended latent products, respectively. Under the hard membership assumption, marginalizing over latent variables x, y reduces to the belonging products $x(i), y(j)$, and the first link $p(x(i)|i)$ is deterministic. From here onwards, for simplicity we will shortcut $x(i), y(j)$ to x, y as the latent products corresponding to the items i, j respectively.

Additionally, there is one important factor to be incorporated in the scoring function, that is, the auction end time. User actions burst into the end time (within hours) of an auction; and the experience from search suggests that auction end time is one of the dominant factors in ranking items. We thus impose a time prior distribution biased towards ending-soon auction items. The final item-level scoring function becomes:

$$p(j, \Delta h(j)|i) = p(j|y)p(y|x)p(\Delta h(j)), \tag{24}$$

where $x = \operatorname{argmax}_{x'} \ell(i|x')$, and $\Delta h(j)$ is the time difference in hours from recommendation serving time to auction end time of item j. The product-to-product score $p(y|x)$ has been derived as Eq. (18) in Section 4.1, we now focus on the item-product membership score $p(j|y)$ and the time-dependent factor $p(\Delta h(j))$.

The inference step in Eq. (7) gives the MLE of latent product assignment, but even the likelihood cannot be directly used as membership score in Eq. (24) for the purpose of ranking items. The reason is that item likelihood is not well calibrated across latent products, and we typically need to retrieve multiple y's for a given x to surface a best candidate set of j's. For example, one latent product y_1 is more catalog-like and its items usually can be described in very few terms (some technological items). Another latent product y_2 is less structured and its items need more terms to be embodied (some clothing items). The item likelihoods in y_1 are then naturally higher than the ones in y_2; but this does not necessarily mean y_1 items are more coherent, nor should they be ranked higher. Within-product item log likelihood empirically appears Gaussian, from which we can transform to a standard Gaussian $\mathcal{N}(0, 1)$ to make it comparable across products. The calibrated item-product membership score is then:

$$p(j|y) = \frac{1}{Z_2} \exp\left(\frac{1}{\sigma}(\ell(j|y) - \bar{\ell}(\cdot|y))\right), \tag{25}$$

where $\bar{\ell}(\cdot|y)$ is the mean item log likelihood for a latent product, and σ is the standard deviation. Since σ serves as a normalization factor, we use a constant informed by data[3],

[3]For one major category "Clothing, Shoes & Accessories", the item log likelihood variable has mean −40.5, standard deviation 20.6, median −38.5, and mode −26.0.

e.g., $\sigma = 20$, for all y's. The normalization constant Z_2 is needed to preserve the probabilistic interpretation of $p(j|y)$.

The auction-end-time factor $p(\Delta h(j))$ can be interpreted as *a priori* purchase probability w.r.t. remaining auction time and made independent of any specific item content. We assume the time prior follows an exponential distribution over discrete hourly time windows traversing backwards from auction end time to the current time; and hence introduce a smoothed exponential decay function as the time-dependent score:

$$p(\Delta h(j)) = \frac{1}{Z_3} \max\left(\pi, \exp(-\lambda \Delta h(j))\right). \tag{26}$$

Here $\Delta h(j) = \lfloor (t_{\text{end}} - t_{\text{now}})/3600 \rfloor$, and λ is a positive decay constant. A two-day half-life gives $\lambda = \log(2)/47$. The smoothing factor π provides a minimum score; e.g., $\pi = 0.5$ enforces any items beyond half-life will still get a 0.5 time-dependent score. It turns out that this time score lower-bounding provides an important mechanism to mix up time-sensitive items (auction items) and time-insensitive items (fixed-price items). The normalization constant Z_3 makes $p(\Delta h(j))$ a distribution.

One fundamental advantage of the item ranking model derived so far stems from viewing the user conversion sequence as a stochastic process, and hence estimating the purchase probability as in Eq. (24). Ranking recommendations directly in purchase probability shall optimize number of purchases, but this statistical framework can be easily extended to maximize other business metrics as well, such as revenue and user satisfaction. User purchase is a Bernoulli process with a success probability estimated by Eq. (24), one can then multiply some utility function $f(u)$ by the purchase probability to obtain an estimate of the expected utility:

$$\mathbb{E}\left(f(u_j)\right) = f(u_j) p(j, \Delta h(j)|i), \tag{27}$$

where u_j is the unit price of the target item j, which is given for fixed-price items. For active auction items, the price can be estimated as the smoothed average price of closed items belonging to the same latent product:

$$\hat{u}(\cdot|y) = \frac{\sum_{j \in y} u_j + \rho}{\sum_{j \in y} 1 + \rho/u_0}, \tag{28}$$

where u_j is the winning bid amount of item j belonging to product y, ρ is a smoothing constant, and u_0 gives a default price. To optimize revenue, the utility function is essentially the pricing model or listing fee structure:

$$\begin{aligned} f_{\text{rev}}(u) &= a_1 \min(u, b_1) \\ &+ a_2 \max\left(0, (\min(u, b_2) - b_1)\right) \\ &+ a_3 \max\left(0, (u - b_2)\right), \end{aligned} \tag{29}$$

where (a_1, a_2, a_3) are the listing fees for three consecutive price intervals: $[0, b_1]$, $(b_1, b_2]$, and $(b_2, +\infty]$, respectively. The current values at eBay are: $(b_1, b_2) = (\$25, \$1000)$ and $(a_1, a_2, a_3) = (0.0875, 0.035, 0.015)$. User perceived utility or satisfaction is more subjective, and we use log-price as a surrogate for simplicity:

$$f_{\text{usr}}(u) = 1 + \log\left(\max(1, u)\right). \tag{30}$$

Finally, we apply several post-ranking filtering rules in compliance with domain-specific requirements: (1) items are active as of the time of delivery; (2) items with identical titles are de-duplicated; (3) current prices are below a threshold (e.g., \$5000 for clothing category) to avoid recommending excessively expensive items; and (4) items are from sellers with a trust score above a threshold (e.g., 99.99% positive feedbacks).

5. EXPERIMENTS

Both the latent product clustering and the item ranking models as a whole shall be evaluated by the quality of recommendation. Online A/B testing would evaluate how the new models perform against the current production system in a live environment, but requires a full-fledged production deployment and a fraction of revenue-sensitive live traffic. Offline evaluation thus becomes particularly valuable for a closed-loop exploration before going live [9]. We conducted both offline and online evaluation, where offline evaluation guides us towards a sensible objective function and online testing reports metrics of business significance, including CTR (click-through rate), BTR (bid-through rate), PTR (purchase-through rate), and GMB (gross merchandising bought).

5.1 Offline Evaluation

A common way to evaluate recommendation models is yet to be established. It is not fully satisfactory to use general estimations such as test data log likelihood and perplexity, since these metrics fail to emphasize the very important yet small head portion of view recall. Other metrics used in rating-based recommendation such as RMSE (root mean squared error) [18] is not suitable for click-through data in our case. We adapt for the recommendation problem the evaluation method established in other similar domains such as ad targeting [8, 10].

The quality of prediction is measured by two metrics: (1) the area under the click-view ROC curve (AUC), and (2) the relative CTR lift over a baseline predictor at a certain recall level of view. A click-view ROC curve plots the click recall vs. view recall, from the testing examples ranked in descending order of predicted score. The higher the AUC, the more accurate the predictor; and a random predictor would give an AUC of 0.5 (a diagonal ROC). Since view recall equals to click recall by random guess, each point on the ROC curve readily gives the relative CTR lift (click recall/view recall) over a baseline random predictor[4]. It is important to emphasize that in the context of recommendation, positive feedbacks include not only clicks, but also (and more so) bids, purchases, and even revenue. Therefore we use *click* and *CTR* in the above evaluation metrics in a generalized sense, which can also refer to other positive feedbacks.

We consider recommendation based on a contextual or historical transaction, e.g., a user who has purchased i would also likely purchase j. We first use the item and transactional data over a training period to learn the latent product and recommendation models; thus deriving a scoring function of co-preference item pairs (i, j) (Eq. (24) or (27)), where the temporal order of (i, j) is deliberately ignored for better coverage. For the transactional data over a testing period, we form a global event stream of sequential-preference

[4]The lift interpretation, besides easiness of implementation, motivates the use of click-view ROC for click-through data instead of traditional ROC. A traditional ROC plots true positive (TP) rate vs. false positive (FP) rate. For the click-view ROC in our case, we use (TP+FP) or all examples as the x-axis.

item pairs, where the temporal order is respected for faithful evaluation. We then apply the scoring function to score and rank test item pairs. Finally, we compare the ranked list against the ground-truth feedbacks to compute ROC curve and lift. The evaluation method using log-price utility for purchase feedback is formalized in Algorithm 1.

Algorithm 1: Offline evaluation

```
Data structure: Event
begin
    /* For non-view event types:  0:view, 1:click,
       2:bid, 3:bin, 4:watch, 8:winning bid.           */
    /* For view count:  position normalized.           */
    int u ;                                 /* user id */
    date t ;                             /* event time */
    int c ;                         /* non-view event type */
    float v ;          /* position-normalized view count */
    float a ;                            /* bid amount */
    int j ;                           /* event item id */
    int i ;             /* last winning item id, o/w 0 */
end
Input: Test event stream Event[e]
Output: ROC curve
begin
    Event[e] ← sort test event stream by (u, t);
    i[e] ← find most recent winning item by that user;
    /* To avoid stable sort artifacts                  */
    Event[e] ← RandomPermute(Event[e]);
    /* Score candidate item set                        */
    foreach j where i is nonzero do
        p(j, Δh(j)|i) ← p(j|y)p(y|x)p(Δh(j));
        E(f(a)) ← f_usr(a)p(j, Δh(j)|i);
        c ← c ≥ 8?1 : 0;
        v ← v where i is nonzero;
    end
    /* ROC curve                                       */
    curve ← ROC(E(f(a)),c,v);
end
```

We conducted experiments for one major category: "Clothing, Shoes & Accessories", which is representative of the unstructuredness, volatility, sparsity, and large scale characteristics of the domain. We used three-month worth of item and transactional data for training, and the following week for testing. For the recommendation modeling, the training data contains approximately 50M items, 1500M search events, and 600M down-streaming transactions. We sampled 50% search log for counting view-related co-occurrences. For the iterative clustering, the item data was down-sampled to 4M biased towards active ones (with at least one bid). After 10 EM iterations, 118,865 clusters converged with an average item log likelihood -14.68. With the learned latent products, we then performed an inference step to assign all items including those only seen in testing data to their MLE latent products, which yielded an average item log likelihood -29.47. All our experiments were run on a single node with $2\times$ Quad-Core 3.2GHz 64-bit processors and 8GB RAM, using a multi-core parallel implementation. It took about 4 hours to learn clusters, and 6 hours to assign 50M items. So one item assignment takes less than half a millisecond, which is sufficient for online real-time performance. The recommendation learning (offline for $p(y|x)$) used 14 hours. Our implementation achieved above 200 Mflops throughout, and hence highly efficient and scalable [8].

We experimented 10 variations in 2 scoring functions by 5 positive feedback types, as summarized in Table 1. For each type of positive feedback, we benchmarked the co-preference log-price utility scoring with the popularity baseline, with the only difference being that the $p(y|x)$ term in Eq. (27) is replaced with $p(y)$ for the popularity score. This shows the value added by contextual item. Varying in feedback types demonstrates how the proposed recommendation models optimize different key metrics. The ROC curves for the proposed co-preference scoring and the baseline popularity are plotted in Figures 2(a) and 2(b) respectively, and the lift curves are plotted in Figures 3(a) and 3(b). The numerical results of AUC and lifts are summarized in Table 2.

Table 1: Experimental Design

Label	Scoring function	Positive feedback
A	popularity	click ($c = 1$)
B	co-preference (Eq. (27))	click ($c = 1$)
C	popularity	bid, watch, purchase ($c > 1$)
D	co-preference (Eq. (27))	bid, watch, purchase ($c > 1$)
E	popularity	purchase ($c \geq 8$)
F	co-preference (Eq. (27))	purchase ($c \geq 8$)
G	popularity	revenue $((c \geq 8) * f_{\mathrm{rev}}(a))$
H	co-preference (Eq. (27))	revenue $((c \geq 8) * f_{\mathrm{rev}}(a))$
I	popularity	log-price $((c \geq 8) * f_{\mathrm{usr}}(a))$
J	co-preference (Eq. (27))	log-price $((c \geq 8) * f_{\mathrm{usr}}(a))$

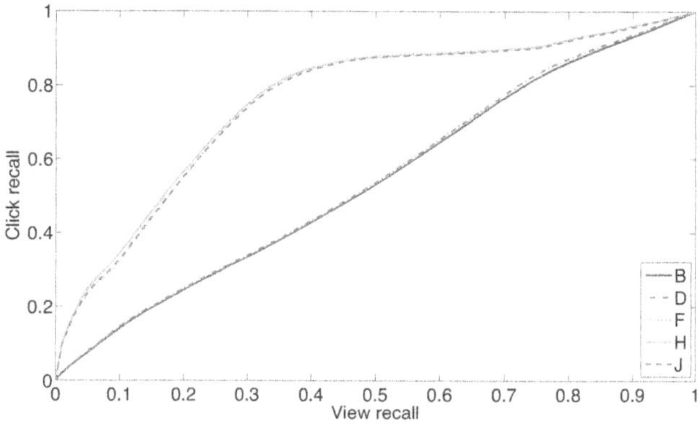

(a) Co-preference scoring.

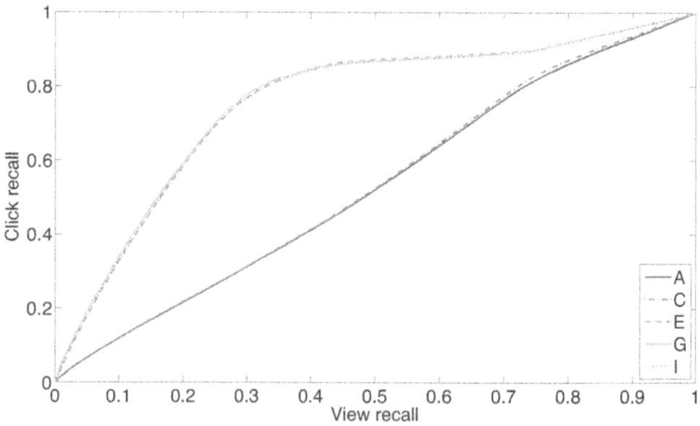

(b) Popularity scoring.

Figure 2: ROC of click-recall vs. view-recall.

As the results show, the log-price co-preference scoring outperforms the popularity baseline for all types of positive feedbacks. For the revenue feedback, the proposed recommendation model yields an AUC of 0.7595. The gain in lift

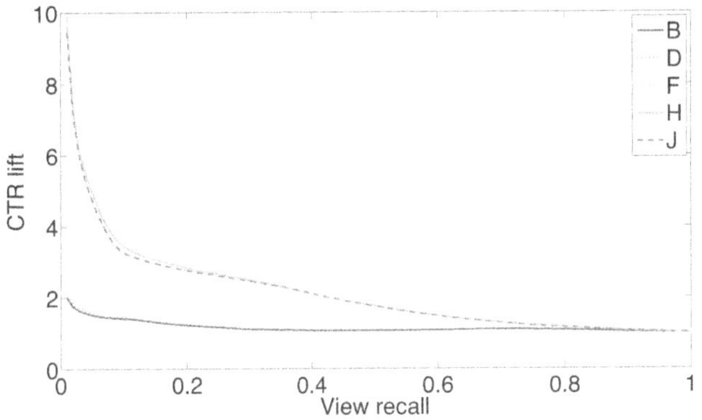

(a) Co-preference scoring.

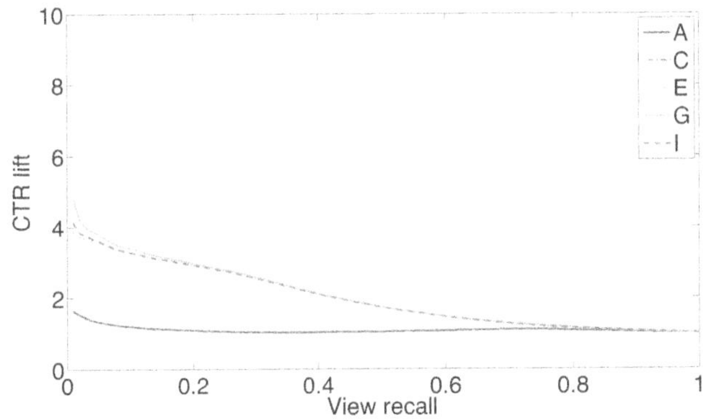

(b) Popularity scoring.

Figure 3: Lift in click-through.

Table 2: AUC's and Lifts at Top View Recalls

Label	AUC	Lift@1%	Lift@2%	Lift@5%	Lift@10%
A	0.5287	1.05	1.54	1.33	1.19
B	0.5397	2.00	1.74	1.51	1.41
C	0.5328	1.63	1.52	1.33	1.20
D	0.5452	2.07	1.81	1.56	1.45
E	0.7563	3.87	3.72	3.54	3.27
F	0.7562	9.63	7.11	4.69	3.24
G	0.7583	4.83	4.21	3.78	3.40
H	0.7595	9.92	7.28	4.94	3.45
I	0.7533	4.14	3.83	3.59	3.28
J	0.7536	9.47	7.06	4.72	3.28

is more pronounced. Our model obtains 9.92 times relative revenue lift at the 1% view recall, 3.5 times lift at the 10% view recall, and 2-3 folds better than the popularity baseline at the 1-2% view recall range. The proposed recommender optimizes key metrics very well including purchase, revenue and log-price; but interestingly and as desired, not as well for operational metrics including click-through and bid-through.

We also compared our generative clustering model with traditional k-means, specifically using squared Euclidean distance and cosine similarity in the tf-idf feature space. In terms of recommendation quality, the generative model is better than both conventional k-means. For log-price co-preference scoring against log-price feedback, generative clustering yields an AUC of 0.7536, while k-means gets 0.7488 with Euclidean distance and 0.7471 with cosine similarity. Most importantly, we prefer the generative model since it provides a probabilistic membership score $p(i|y)$ and naturally fits into the stochastic user conversion process as modeled in Eq. (24). With either distortion or cosine similarity, this nice probabilistic property is lost.

5.2 Online Testing

The proposed recommendation models were deployed to production. But before live traffic ramp-up, we conducted a longitudinal online A/B testing (the proposed model vs. the existing production system), lasting 4-6 months, explored the model space (positive event types and scoring functions), and tuned free parameters (event mixture weights α, β's, decaying factors η, λ's, and smoothing factors ζ, π's), on a daily basis. The final production model genuinely reflects an empirically optimal.

One of the major placements is check-out page, where a user just purchased an item and our recommender delivers 12 next-purchase prospects as one campaign impression to the user. The online testing was conducted for four major categories that exhibit a wide spectrum of domain characteristics: (1) Clothing, Shoes & Accessories (CSA), (2) Computers & Networking (Comp), (3) Electronics (Elec), and (4) Cell Phones & PDAs (Cell). The testing results over a one-week period are shown in Table 3. Our model substantially outperforms the current production recommender, which is a neighborhood-based collaborative filtering at the category level. For CSA, the historical CTR on check-out page was 2-3%, and PTR was about 1%. Thus our system would yield a 3-5 folds improvement should it go live. We also performed a paired t-test on the hourly pairwise performance metrics, and showed that all these performance differences were statistically significant at level $\alpha = 0.1\%$.

Table 3: Online Testing Results

Category	Impressions	CTR	BTR	PTR	GMB†
CSA	94,307	13.50%	8.93%	3.03%	4.9×
Comp	42,615	6.90%	3.28%	1.48%	2.6×
Elec	30,866	10.09%	5.72%	2.26%	2.4×
Cell	31,100	8.70%	4.05%	2.14%	3.8×

†Relative improvement over the current production system.

6. DISCUSSION

We have presented a generative clustering model to learn persistent latent products from otherwise unstructured and dynamic items, a probabilistic recommendation model to learn co-preference patterns from historical transactional data, and hence providing a comprehensive and statistically sound solution to recommendation for long-tail marketplaces such as eBay. The proposed methodology is, however, of much generality.

First, the generative clustering model is a simple yet principled way to capture hidden structure underlying volatile and heterogeneous data, and thus enables reasoning on such data for applications such as search and recommendation. There has been a remarkable trend of this type of data accumulating on the Web as social-networking sites (e.g., Facebook), video-sharing sites (e.g., YouTube), and micro-blogging services (e.g., Twitter) gain popularity. More importantly, we described a sparse and highly efficient inferential method to make the model scalable to large-scale real-world data. As future work, we shall evaluate soft item-product assignment to gauge whether the additional costs in terms of space and computational time could potentially result in additional gains in GMB.

Second, the recommendation model is learned by assuming the user conversion flow is a stochastic process and using the position-normalized view count as the denominator. This yields a probabilistic measure of preference, possibly conditioned on some previous transactions. Not only the probabilistic scoring function can be further used for optimizing other recommendation metrics of business interest, but also it can be leveraged by other important applications as a user preference feature, such as search results re-ranking by user click-through feedback or perceived relevance [13].

Finally, we have proposed an approach to offline evaluating item-based recommenders, particularly suitable for click-through data. The evaluation metrics, i.e., AUC and lift, are superior to other summary estimations such as test data log likelihood, since the former bears direct business significance. The closed-loop offline evaluation framework would considerably expedite exploration of much larger model and parameter spaces.

7. ACKNOWLEDGMENTS

The authors would like to thank the eBay merchandising team: Todd Forsyth, Petra Hofer, Jon Conradt, Helen Ye, Yan Huang; eBay Research Labs: Pavel Berkhin (now with Microsoft), Eric Brill, Neel Sundaresan, Dan Shen; eBay executive management: Mark Carges; and many other colleagues for making this work possible and successfully deployed.

8. REFERENCES

[1] D. Agarwal and B.-C. Chen. Regression-based latent factor models. *ACM Conference on Knowledge Discovery and Data Mining (KDD 2009)*, pages 19–28, 2009.

[2] D. Agarwal and B.-C. Chen. fLDA: Matrix factorization through latent Dirichlet allocation. *ACM International Conference on Web Search and Data Mining (WSDM 2010)*, 2010.

[3] J. Bennett and S. Lanning. The Netflix Prize. In *KDDCup'07: Proceedings of KDD Cup and Workshop 2007*, 2007.

[4] D. M. Blei, A. Y. Ng, and M. I. Jordan. Latent Dirichlet allocation. *Journal of Machine Learning Research*, 3:993–1022, 2003.

[5] O. Chapelle and Y. Zhang. A dynamic Bayesian network click model for web search ranking. *International World Wide Web Conference (WWW 2009)*, pages 1–10, 2009.

[6] Y. Chen and J. F. Canny. Probabilistic clustering of an item. *U.S. Patent Application 12/694,885*, filed: Jan, 2010.

[7] Y. Chen and J. F. Canny. Probabilistic recommendation of an item. *U.S. Patent Application 12/694,903*, filed: Jan, 2010.

[8] Y. Chen, M. Kapralov, D. Pavlov, and J. F. Canny. Factor modeling for advertisement targeting. *Advances in Neural Information Processing Systems (NIPS 2009)*, 2009.

[9] Y. Chen, D. Pavlov, P. Berkhin, A. Seetharaman, and A. Meltzer. Practical lessons of data mining at yahoo! *ACM Conference on Information and Knowledge Management (CIKM 2009)*, 2009.

[10] Y. Chen, D. Pavlov, and J. F. Canny. Large-scale behavioral targeting. *ACM Conference on Knowledge Discovery and Data Mining (KDD 2009)*, pages 209–218, 2009.

[11] N. Craswell, O. Zoeter, M. Taylor, and B. Ramsey. An experimental comparison of click position-bias models. *Web Search and Web Data Mining (WSDM 2008)*, pages 87–94, 2008.

[12] R. O. Duda, P. E. Hart, and D. G. Stork. *Pattern Classification*. Wiley-Interscience, 2nd Edition (October 2000), 2000.

[13] F. Guo, C. Liu, A. Kannan, T. Minka, M. Taylor, Y.-M. Wang, and C. Faloutsos. Click chain model in web search. *International World Wide Web Conference (WWW 2009)*, pages 11–20, 2009.

[14] T. Hofmann. Probabilistic latent semantic indexing. *ACM Conference on Information Retrieval (SIGIR 1999)*, pages 50–57, 1999.

[15] T. Hofmann and J. Puzicha. Latent class models for collaborative filtering. *International Joint Conference on Artificial Intelligence (IJCAI 1999)*, pages 688–693, 1999.

[16] F. Jelinek and R. L. Mercer. Interpolated estimation of Markov source parameters from sparse data. *Pattern Recognition in Practice*, pages 381–402, 1980.

[17] Y. Koren. Factorization meets the neighborhood: a multifaceted collaborative filtering model. *ACM Conference on Knowledge Discovery and Data Mining (KDD 2008)*, pages 426–434, 2008.

[18] Y. Koren. Collaborative filtering with temporal dynamics. *ACM Conference on Knowledge Discovery and Data Mining (KDD 2009)*, pages 447–456, 2009.

[19] A. Mccallum and K. Nigam. A comparison of event models for naïve Bayes text classification. *AAAI-98 Workshop on Learning for Text Categorization*, 1998.

[20] K. Nigam, A. K. McCallum, S. Thrun, and T. M. Mitchell. Text classification from labeled and unlabeled documents using EM. *Machine Learning*, 39(2):103–134, 2000.

[21] D. Pavlov, R. Balasubramanyan, B. Dom, S. Kapur, and J. Parikh. Document preprocessing for naïve Bayes classification and clustering with mixture of multinomials. *ACM Conference on Knowledge Discovery and Data Mining (KDD 2004)*, pages 829–834, 2004.

[22] L. Si and R. Jin. Flexible mixture model for collaborative filtering. *International Conference on Machine Learning (ICML 2003)*, pages 704–711, 2003.

[23] C. Zhai and J. Lafferty. A study of smoothing methods for language models applied to ad hoc information retrieval. *ACM Conference on Information Retrieval (SIGIR 2001)*, pages 343–348, 2001.

[24] S. Zhong and J. Ghosh. A comparative study of generative models for document clustering. *SIAM International Conference Data Mining Workshop on Clustering High Dimensional Data and Its Applications*, 2003.

A Unified Framework for Recommendations Based on Quaternary Semantic Analysis

Wei Chen Wynne Hsu Mong Li Lee
School of Computing, National University of Singapore, Singapore
{weichen,whsu,leeml}@comp.nus.edu.sg

ABSTRACT

Social network systems such as FaceBook and YouTube have played a significant role in capturing both explicit and implicit user preferences for different items in the form of ratings and tags. This forms a quaternary relationship among users, items, tags and ratings. Existing systems have utilized only ternary relationships such as users-items-ratings, or users-items-tags to derive their recommendations. In this paper, we show that ternary relationships are insufficient to provide accurate recommendations. Instead, we model the quaternary relationship among users, items, tags and ratings as a 4-order tensor and cast the recommendation problem as a multi-way latent semantic analysis problem. A unified framework for user recommendation, item recommendation, tag recommendation and item rating prediction is proposed. The results of extensive experiments performed on a real world dataset demonstrate that our unified framework outperforms the state-of-the-art techniques in all the four recommendation tasks.

Categories and Subject Descriptors

H.3.3 [**Information Search and Retrieval**]: [information filtering]

General Terms

Algorithms, Experimentation, Measurement, Performance

Keywords

Tensor factorization, Recommendation, Social tags, Personalization, Collaborative Tagging

1. INTRODUCTION

The amount of information on the Web is increasing at a lightning pace. In order to adequately cope with this information overload, recommendation systems are needed to bring the relevant resources to the attention of the users automatically. Recommendation systems are typically classified according to the type of tasks they are intended for, which include:

1. User recommendation - Here the task is to identify users with common interests so as to extend the connection among users with similar interests (e.g., Amazon [1] and Facebook [2]). Existing user recommendation systems (e.g., Amazon) determine users with common interests either through the fact that these users often give the same rating to similar resources, or they use similar tags to describe the resources.

2. Item recommendation - Instead of stopping at identifying users with common interests, this task goes one step further. Based on the identified set of users with common interests, the items that this set of users are interested in become the candidates for recommending to the target user (e.g., Amazon and YouTube [3]).

3. Tag recommendation - This task has emerged recently due to the popularity of social tagging activity. Users typically use an ubiquitous vocabulary as tags to reflect the semantics of the items from his/her point of view. In order to improve the selection of vocabulary to be used as tags, tag recommendation is now a hot research area which aims to provide users with a good set of tags to describe items (e.g., Amazon, Facebook and Flickr [4]). Most tag recommendation systems rely on identifying similar users and recommending the tags used by these similar users on similar resources.

4. Item rating prediction - Here, the task goes beyond just determining whether an item should be recommended to a user. Instead, the recommendation systems need to predict the degree of preference a user is likely to exhibit for an item (e.g., Netflix [5]).

Till now, most, if not all, recommendation systems utilize only ternary relationships in generating their recommendations. The collaborative filtering-based recommendation systems [8, 1, 12, 18] typically make use of the users-rating-items relationship to group users based on their ratings on

[1]http://www.amazon.com
[2]http://www.facebook.com
[3]http://www.youtube.com
[4]http://www.flickr.com
[5]http://www.netflix.com

SIGIR'11, July 24–28, 2011, Beijing, China.

items, whereas the tag-based recommendation systems utilize the users-tags-items relationship to perform the various tasks [20, 19, 15]. We argue that recommendations based on ternary relationships are not accurate as they would have missed out important associations.

Table 1: Ternary relations among user, rating and item

User	Rating	Item
U_1	like	Forrest Gump
U_1	like	Beautiful Mind
U_2	like	Forrest Gump
U_2	like	Groundhog Day
U_2	like	Groundhog Day
U_3	like	Forrest Gump
U_4	like	Forrest Gump
U_4	dislike	Toy Story
U_4	dislike	Toy Story
U_5	dislike	Forrest Gump
U_5	dislike	Groundhog Day

Let us consider the ternary relationship users-rating-items in Table 1. From this table, we conclude that users U_1, U_2, U_4 have common interests with U_3 since they all like the movie "*Forrest Gump*". Hence, these users will be highlighted to U_3 and the movies "*BeautifulMind*" and "*Groundhog Day*" will be recommended to U_3 because U_1 and U_2 also like "*Beautiful Mind*" and "*Groundhog Day*". Note that "*Toy Story*" is not recommended to U_3 since U_4 dislikes the movie.

Table 2: Ternary relations among user, tags, and item

User	Tag	Item
U_1	psychology	Forrest Gump
U_1	psychology	Beautiful Mind
U_2	comedy	Forrest Gump
U_2	excellent	Groundhog Day
U_2	comedy	Groundhog Day
U_3	comedy	Forrest Gump
U_4	comedy	Forrest Gump
U_4	overrated	Toy Story
U_4	comedy	Toy Story
U_5	comedy	Forrest Gump
U_5	overrated	Groundhog Day

Table 2 shows the ternary relationship users-tags-items. The users U_2, U_4 and U_5 are said to have common interests with U_3 because they all tag the movie "*Forrest Gump*" as "*comedy*". Thus, U_2, U_4 and U_5 will be highlighted to U_3. At the same time, the movies "*Groundhog Day*" and "*Toy story*" will be recommended to U_3 since U_2 and U_4 also tag "*Groundhog Day*" and "*Toy story*" as "*comedy*". In addition, suppose U_3 wants to tag the item "*Groundhog Day*", the set of tags {"*comedy*", "*excellent*", "*over rated*"} will be recommended to him/her as they have been used to tag "*Groundhog Day*" previously.

Now, instead of the two ternary relationships, we have the quaternary relationships among users, tags, ratings, and items as shown in Table 3. We note that only users U_2

Table 3: Quaternary relations among users, tags, ratings and items

User	Tag	Rating	Item
U_1	psychology	like	Forrest Gump
U_1	psychology	like	Beautiful Mind
U_2	comedy	like	Forrest Gump
U_2	excellent	like	Groundhog Day
U_2	comedy	like	Groundhog Day
U_3	comedy	like	Forrest Gump
U_4	comedy	like	Forrest Gump
U_4	overrated	dislike	Toy Story
U_4	comedy	dislike	Toy Story
U_5	comedy	dislike	Forrest Gump
U_5	overrated	dislike	Groundhog Day

and U_4 would be highlighted to U_3 and the only movie recommended to U_3 is "*Groundhog Day*". This is because even though U_1 is highlighted under the ternary relationship users-ratings-items, we realize from the quaternary relationship that U_1 likes "*Forrest Gump*" as a psychology movie, whereas U_3 likes the movie "*Forrest Gump*" as a comedy. Hence, U_1 does not share a common interest with U_3. As a result, U_1's item "*Beautiful Mind*" is also not recommended to U_3.

Similarly, under the ternary relationship users-tags-items, U_5 is highlighted to U_3 and the movie "*Toy Story*" is recommended to U_3. However, the quaternary relationship in Table 3 shows that U_5 dislikes the movie "*Forrest Gump*" although he/she tags it with "*comedy*". Since U_3 and U_5 have different opinions on "*ForrestGump*" even though they both use the tag "*comedy*", U_5 should not be considered as having common interests with U_3. At the same time, we observe that although U_4 tags "*Toy Story*" as "*comedy*", he/she does not like it. Hence "*Toy Story*" should not be recommended to U_3.

For tag recommendation, suppose U_3 wants to tag "*Groundhog Day*", a system based on the quaternary relationship would recommend the set of tags {"*comedy*", "*excellent*"}. Note that the tag "*overrated*", which is one of the tags recommended based on the ternary relationship users-tags-items, will not be recommended to U_3. This is because we are able to infer from the quaternary relationship that U_3 likes the movie "*Groundhog Day*" as it is a comedy. Since the tag "*overrated*" is associated with the rating "*dislike*", it is not a good tag to recommend for U_3.

The above examples clearly illustrates the need to consider the quaternary relationship among users, tags, ratings, and items together. The quaternary relationships can reveal semantics that cannot be obtained otherwise. This is reinforced by the following observations:

1. Users may use the same tag for an item but have different ratings for it. For example, users U_2 and U_4 both use the same tag "*comedy*" on item "*ForrestGump*". However, user U_2 likes the movie but U_4 does not. Hence using tag information alone is insufficient.

2. Items may have multiple tags indicating their different facets. This could give rise to varied ratings, depending on the facet considered by the user. For example, "*ForrestGump*" is tagged as a "*psychology*" movie by

user U_1 and a "*comedy*" by U_4. However, the movie may be not a good comedy movie as U_4 dislike it. Yet this movie could be an interesting psychology movie since user U_1 like it. In other words, rating information alone is insufficient.

3. Some tags may carry implicit semantics that can reveal the users' preferences. For example, user U_2 tags movie "*GroundhogDay*" with the tag "*excellent*" implying that U_2 likes the movie. Similarly, the tag "*overrated*" which is tagged by the user U_4 will imply that U_4 dislikes the movie "Toy Story". This observation tells us that the combination of tag and rating information gives extra insights into the users' preferences.

In order to capture the quaternary relationship among users, items, tags and ratings, we propose a model based on the 4-order tensor. We apply the Higher-Order Singular Value Decomposition (HOSVD) [11] in the 4-order tensor to reveal the latent semantic associations among users, items, tags and rating. With this model, we design a unified framework to perform item rating prediction as well as user, item and tag recommendations. We carry out experments on a real world dataset to demonstrate the effectiveness of our proposed approach. To the best of our knowledge, this is a first work to explore the use of the quaternary relationship among user, items, tags and ratings for recommendation tasks.

The rest of this paper is organized as follows. Section 2 provides the background on tensor operation and approximation. Section 3 presents the algorithm for quaternary semantic analysis. Section 4 describes the unified framework for user, item and tag recommendations as well as item rating prediction. Section 5 presents the experimental results. Related work is given in Section 6, and we conclude the paper in Section 7.

2. BACKGROUND

Tensor algebra and multilinear analysis have been applied successfully in many domains [9, 11]. In this section, we review the concepts and terminologies used in the paper.

A tensor is a multidimensional array. An N-order tensor $\boldsymbol{\mathcal{A}}$ is denoted as $\boldsymbol{\mathcal{A}} \in \mathbb{R}^{I_1 \times \cdots \times I_N}$ with elements $a_{i_1 \ldots i_n}$ and dimensions $I_1, I_2, \cdots I_N$.

For example, the corresponding 3-order tensor $\boldsymbol{\mathcal{A}}$ for the example dataset in Table 4 is:

$$\boldsymbol{\mathcal{A}}(:,:,1) = \begin{pmatrix} 1 & 0 & 0 \\ 0 & 0 & 0 \\ 1 & 0 & 0 \end{pmatrix}$$

$$\boldsymbol{\mathcal{A}}(:,:,2) = \begin{pmatrix} 0 & 1 & 0 \\ 0 & 0 & 0 \\ 0 & 0 & 0 \end{pmatrix}$$

$$\boldsymbol{\mathcal{A}}(:,:,3) = \begin{pmatrix} 0 & 0 & 0 \\ 0 & 0 & 1 \\ 0 & 0 & 0 \end{pmatrix}$$

Definition 1. *The **matrix unfolding** of an N-order tensor $\boldsymbol{\mathcal{A}} = \mathbb{R}^{I_1 \times \cdots \times I_N}$ along the dimension d are vectors obtained by keeping the index d fixed while varying the other indices.*

Table 4: Example dataset of a 3-order tensor

I_1	I_2	I_3	element value
1	1	1	1
1	2	2	1
2	3	3	1
3	1	1	1

The unfolding of our example 3-order tensor $\mathcal{A}$ along each dimension is:

$$\boldsymbol{A}_{(1)} = \begin{pmatrix} 1 & 0 & 0 & 0 & 1 & 0 & 0 & 0 & 0 \\ 0 & 0 & 0 & 0 & 0 & 0 & 0 & 0 & 1 \\ 1 & 0 & 0 & 0 & 0 & 0 & 0 & 0 & 0 \end{pmatrix}$$

$$\boldsymbol{A}_{(2)} = \begin{pmatrix} 1 & 0 & 1 & 0 & 0 & 0 & 0 & 0 & 0 \\ 0 & 0 & 0 & 1 & 0 & 0 & 0 & 0 & 0 \\ 0 & 0 & 0 & 0 & 0 & 0 & 0 & 1 & 0 \end{pmatrix}$$

$$\boldsymbol{A}_{(3)} = \begin{pmatrix} 1 & 0 & 0 & 0 & 0 & 0 & 1 & 0 & 0 \\ 0 & 1 & 0 & 0 & 0 & 0 & 0 & 0 & 0 \\ 0 & 0 & 0 & 0 & 0 & 1 & 0 & 0 & 0 \end{pmatrix}$$

Note that the definition of the matrix unfolding involves the tensor dimensions I_1, I_2, I_3 in a cyclic way. Hence, for the unfolding of dimension $I_c \times I_a I_b$, the index I_b varies more slowly than I_a.

Definition 2. *The **n-mode product** of a tensor $\mathcal{A} = \mathbb{R}^{I_1 \times \cdots \times I_N}$ by a matrix $U = \mathbb{R}^{J_n \times I_n}$, denoted by $\boldsymbol{\mathcal{A}} \times_n U$, is a $(I_1 \times I_2 \cdots I_{n-1} \times J_n \times I_{n+1} \cdots \times I_N)$-tensor where the entries are given by*

$$(\boldsymbol{\mathcal{A}} \times_n \boldsymbol{U})_{i_1 i_2 i_3 \cdots i_{n-1} j_n i_{n+1} \cdots i_N} = \sum_{i_n} a_{i_1 i_2 i_3 \cdots i_{n-1} i_n i_{n+1} \cdots i_N} \cdot u_{j_n i_n}$$

For example, the 1-mode product of a tensor $\boldsymbol{\mathcal{A}} = \mathbb{R}^{2 \times 3 \times 4}$ by a matrix $\boldsymbol{U} = \mathbb{R}^{5 \times 2}$, denoted as $\boldsymbol{\mathcal{A}} \times_1 \boldsymbol{U}$ is an $5 \times 3 \times 4$ tensor in which the entries are given by

$$(\boldsymbol{\mathcal{A}} \times_1 \boldsymbol{U})_{j i_2 i_3} = \sum_{k=1}^{2} a_{k i_2 i_3} \cdot u_{jk} \qquad 1 \leq j \leq 5$$

The Higher-Order Singular Value Decomposition (HOSVD) is a generalization of the Singular Value Decomposition (SVD) to higher-order tensors [11] and can be written as n-mode product:

$$\boldsymbol{\mathcal{A}} = \boldsymbol{\mathcal{S}} \times_1 \boldsymbol{U}^{(1)} \times_2 \boldsymbol{U}^{(2)} \cdots \times_N \boldsymbol{U}^{(N)}$$

where $\boldsymbol{U}^{(n)}$ contain the orthonormal vectors (or n-mode singular vectors) spanning the column space of the $\boldsymbol{\mathcal{A}}_{(n)}$ (n-mode matrix unfolding of $\boldsymbol{\mathcal{A}}$). $\boldsymbol{\mathcal{S}}$ is the core tensor and has the property of all orthogonality.

Consider our example tensor $\boldsymbol{\mathcal{A}}$ and its matrix unfolding $\boldsymbol{\mathcal{A}}_{(1)}$. We perform SVD on $\boldsymbol{\mathcal{A}}_{(1)}$ and obtain the resultant left singular matrix:

$$\boldsymbol{U}^{(1)} = \begin{pmatrix} -0.85 & 0 & 0.53 \\ 0 & -1 & 0 \\ -0.53 & 0 & -0.85 \end{pmatrix}$$

$$\boldsymbol{U}^{(2)} = \begin{pmatrix} 1 & 0 & 0 \\ 0 & 1 & 0 \\ 0 & 0 & 1 \end{pmatrix}$$

$$\boldsymbol{U}^{(3)} = \begin{pmatrix} 1 & 0 & 0 \\ 0 & 1 & 0 \\ 0 & 0 & 1 \end{pmatrix}$$

With this, the core tensor $\boldsymbol{\mathcal{S}} \in \mathbb{R}^{3\times3\times3}$ can be constructed as described in [11]. We have $\boldsymbol{\mathcal{S}} = \boldsymbol{\mathcal{A}} \times_1 (\boldsymbol{U}^{(1)})^T \times_2 (\boldsymbol{U}^{(2)})^T \times_3 (\boldsymbol{U}^{(3)})^T$ where

$$\boldsymbol{\mathcal{S}}(:,:,1) = \begin{pmatrix} -1.38 & 0 & 0 \\ 0 & 1 & 0 \\ -0.32 & 0 & 0 \end{pmatrix}$$

$$\boldsymbol{\mathcal{S}}(:,:,2) = \begin{pmatrix} 0 & -0.85 & 0 \\ 0 & 0 & 0 \\ 0 & -0.53 & 0 \end{pmatrix}$$

$$\boldsymbol{\mathcal{S}}(:,:,3) = \begin{pmatrix} 0 & 0 & 0 \\ 0 & 0 & -1 \\ 0 & 0 & 0 \end{pmatrix}$$

Definition 3. *The n-rank of tensor denoted by* $R_N = rank_n(\boldsymbol{\mathcal{A}})$*, is the dimension of the vector space spanned by the n-mode matrix We denote the rank of tensor* $\boldsymbol{\mathcal{A}}$ *as* $rank(\boldsymbol{\mathcal{A}}) = (rank_1(\boldsymbol{\mathcal{A}}) \cdots, rank_n(\boldsymbol{\mathcal{A}}))$

Definition 4. *Given a tensor* $\boldsymbol{\mathcal{A}} = R^{I_1\times\cdots\times I_N}$*, the RANK−*$(R_1 \cdots, R_N)$ *approximation* $\hat{\boldsymbol{\mathcal{A}}}$ *is defined as* $\min_{\boldsymbol{\mathcal{B}}\in\boldsymbol{\mathcal{S}}} ||\boldsymbol{\mathcal{A}} - \boldsymbol{\mathcal{B}}||_F^2$, $\boldsymbol{\mathcal{S}} = \{\boldsymbol{\mathcal{B}}||rank(\boldsymbol{\mathcal{B}}) \leq (R_1 \cdots, R_N)\}$ *where* $||\boldsymbol{\mathcal{A}} - \boldsymbol{\mathcal{B}}||_F^2$ *is the least-square cost.*[6]

Suppose we want to get the RANK-(2,3,3) approximation, we first retain the first c_i column of matrix $\boldsymbol{U}^{(i)}$ at mode i $(1 \leq i \leq 3)$ as follows:

$$\hat{\boldsymbol{U}}^{(1)} = \begin{pmatrix} -0.85 & 0 \\ 0 & -1 \\ -0.53 & 0 \end{pmatrix}$$

$$\hat{\boldsymbol{U}}^{(2)} = \begin{pmatrix} 1 & 0 & 0 \\ 0 & 1 & 0 \\ 0 & 0 & 1 \end{pmatrix}$$

$$\hat{\boldsymbol{U}}^{(3)} = \begin{pmatrix} 1 & 0 & 0 \\ 0 & 1 & 0 \\ 0 & 0 & 1 \end{pmatrix}$$

[6] the square frobenius norm is defined as $||\boldsymbol{\mathcal{A}}||_F^2 = \sum_{i_1=1}^{R_1} \cdots \sum_{i_N=1}^{R_N} \boldsymbol{\mathcal{A}}(i_1 \cdots, i_N)^2$

We can now construct the approximate core tensor $\hat{\boldsymbol{\mathcal{S}}} \in \mathbb{R}^{2\times3\times3}$ using $\boldsymbol{\mathcal{S}} = \boldsymbol{\mathcal{A}} \times_1 (\hat{\boldsymbol{U}}^{(1)})^T \times_2 (\hat{\boldsymbol{U}}^{(2)})^T \times_3 (\hat{\boldsymbol{U}}^{(3)})^T$:

$$\hat{\boldsymbol{\mathcal{S}}}(:,:,1) = \begin{pmatrix} -1.38 & 0 & 0 \\ 0 & 1 & 0 \end{pmatrix}$$

$$\hat{\boldsymbol{\mathcal{S}}}(:,:,2) = \begin{pmatrix} 0 & -0.85 & 0 \\ 0 & 0 & 0 \end{pmatrix}$$

$$\hat{\boldsymbol{\mathcal{S}}}(:,:,3) = \begin{pmatrix} 0 & 0 & 0 \\ 0 & 0 & -1 \end{pmatrix}$$

Finally, we obtain the RANK-(2,3,3) approximation $\hat{\boldsymbol{\mathcal{A}}} = \hat{\boldsymbol{\mathcal{S}}} \times_1 \hat{\boldsymbol{U}}^{(1)} \times_2 \hat{\boldsymbol{U}}^{(2)} \times_3 \hat{\boldsymbol{U}}^{(3)}$:

$$\hat{\boldsymbol{\mathcal{A}}}(:,:,1) = \begin{pmatrix} 1.2 & 0 & 0 \\ 0 & 1 & 0 \\ 0.72 & 0 & 0 \end{pmatrix}$$

$$\hat{\boldsymbol{\mathcal{A}}}(:,:,2) = \begin{pmatrix} 0 & 0.72 & 0 \\ 0 & 0 & 0 \\ 0 & 0.45 & 0 \end{pmatrix}$$

$$\hat{\boldsymbol{\mathcal{A}}}(:,:,3) = \begin{pmatrix} 0 & 0 & 0 \\ 0 & 0 & 1 \\ 0 & 0 & 0 \end{pmatrix}$$

where $||\boldsymbol{\mathcal{A}} - \hat{\boldsymbol{\mathcal{A}}}||_F^2$=0.618 which is minimized.

3. QUATENARY SEMANTIC ANALYSIS

The main idea behind the quaternary semantic analysis is to capture the underlying relationships among users-tags-items-ratings. Suppose we have a list of quadruples $<u,t,r,v>$ denoting that a user u will provide tag t to a movie v and give the rating r if he has watched v before. We first model this list of quadruples as a 4-order tensor $\boldsymbol{\mathcal{A}} \in U \times T \times R \times V$, where U is the set of all users, V the set of all items/resources, T the set of all tags and R the set of ratings. An entry $\boldsymbol{\mathcal{A}}(u,t,r,v)$ has a value 1 if the quadruple $<u,t,r,v>$ exists, otherwise it has a value of 0.

We reduce the rank of the original tensor to minimze the effect of noise on the underlying population and reduce spareness. This is achieved by approximating the tensor $\boldsymbol{\mathcal{A}}$ to a lower rank tensor. Given the dimensions of users, tags, ratings and items, namely, c_1, c_2, c_3, c_4, we want to obtain the RANK-(c_1, c_2, c_3, c_4) approximation of $\hat{\boldsymbol{\mathcal{A}}}$ such that the square frobenius norm defined as:

$$||\hat{\boldsymbol{\mathcal{A}}}||_F^2 = \sum_{i_1=1}^{I_1} \cdots \sum_{i_N=1}^{I_N} \hat{\boldsymbol{\mathcal{A}}}(i_1, \cdots, i_N)^2$$

is minimized.

In our experiments, we set c_1, c_2, c_3, c_4 to preserve 70%, 90%, 80%, 90% of the original tensor information in each dimension respectively (see Section 5.6).

3.1 Tensor Approximation Algorithm

Algorithm 1 shows the details for approximating a tensor. We first apply SVD on the four matrix unfoldings $\boldsymbol{A}_{(1)}, \boldsymbol{A}_{(2)}, \boldsymbol{A}_{(3)}$, and $\boldsymbol{A}_{(4)}$. Note that:

$$\boldsymbol{A}_{(i)} = \hat{\boldsymbol{U}}^{(i)} \cdot \boldsymbol{S}^{(i)} \cdot (\hat{\boldsymbol{V}}^{(i)})^T, \qquad 1 \le i \le 4 \tag{1}$$

In order to obtain the left matrix of the SVD, we first define a matrix $\boldsymbol{C}_i$ as follows:

$$\boldsymbol{C}_i = \boldsymbol{A}_i \cdot \boldsymbol{A}_i^T, \qquad 1 \le i \le 4, \tag{2}$$

Since each $\hat{\boldsymbol{U}}^{(i)}$ and $\hat{\boldsymbol{V}}^{(i)}$ are orthogonal and each $\boldsymbol{S}^{(i)}$ is diagonal, we substitute (1) into (2):

$$\begin{aligned} \boldsymbol{C}_i &= \boldsymbol{A}_i \boldsymbol{A}_i^T \\ &= (\hat{\boldsymbol{U}}^{(i)} \cdot \boldsymbol{S}^{(i)} \cdot (\hat{\boldsymbol{V}}^{(i)})^T) \cdot (\hat{\boldsymbol{U}}^{(i)} \cdot \boldsymbol{S}^{(i)} \cdot (\hat{\boldsymbol{V}}^{(i)})^T)^T \\ &= \hat{\boldsymbol{U}}^{(i)} (\boldsymbol{S}^{(i)})^2 (\hat{\boldsymbol{U}}^{(i)})^T \end{aligned}$$

Therefore, each required $\boldsymbol{U}^{(i)}$ can be computed by diagonalizing each $\boldsymbol{C}_i$ and taking its eigenvectors (Lines 3-4).

Algorithm 1 Quaternary Semantic Analysis

Input:

List of quadruples < users, tags, rating, items>;

Dimensions of users, tags, ratings and items $c1, c2, c3, c4$;

Output:

Approximate Tensor $\hat{\boldsymbol{\mathcal{A}}}$;

1: Initialization: From the quadruple (users, items tag and rating), we construct tensor $\boldsymbol{\mathcal{A}} \in \mathbb{R}^{|U|\times|T|\times|R|\times|V|}$, where $|U|, |V|, |T|$ and $|R|$ are the number of users, items and tags and rating respectively

2: Calculate the matrix unfolding $\boldsymbol{A}_{(1)}, \boldsymbol{A}_{(2)}, \boldsymbol{A}_{(3)}$, and $\boldsymbol{A}_{(4)}$ from tensor $\boldsymbol{\mathcal{A}}$.

3: Construct the variance matrix $\boldsymbol{C}_i = \boldsymbol{A}_{(i)} \boldsymbol{A}_{(i)}^T$ for each mode $1 \le i \le 4$

4: Compute $U^{(i)}$ by diagonalizing $\boldsymbol{C}_i, 1 \le i \le 4$

5: Remove the least significant rows $|U|-c_1, |V|-c_2, |T|-c_3$ and $|R|-c_4$ from $\boldsymbol{U}^{(1)}, \boldsymbol{U}^{(2)}, \boldsymbol{U}^{(3)}$, and $\boldsymbol{U}^{(4)}$, respectively. Denote the result as $\hat{\boldsymbol{U}}^{(1)}, \hat{\boldsymbol{U}}^{(2)}, \hat{\boldsymbol{U}}^{(3)}$, and $\hat{\boldsymbol{U}}^{(4)}$.

6: Calculate the approximate core tensor $\hat{\boldsymbol{\mathcal{S}}}$ as follows:

$$\hat{\boldsymbol{\mathcal{S}}} = \boldsymbol{\mathcal{A}} \times_1 (\hat{\boldsymbol{U}}^{(1)})^T \times_2 (\hat{\boldsymbol{U}}^{(2)})^T \times_3 (\hat{\boldsymbol{U}}^{(3)})^T \times_4 (\hat{\boldsymbol{U}}^{(4)})^T$$

7: Approximate the original tensor by:

$$\hat{\boldsymbol{\mathcal{A}}} = \hat{\boldsymbol{\mathcal{S}}} \times_1 \hat{\boldsymbol{U}}^{(1)} \times_2 \hat{\boldsymbol{U}}^{(2)} \times_3 \hat{\boldsymbol{U}}^{(3)} \times_4 \hat{\boldsymbol{U}}^{(4)}$$

Consider our example quaternary relations in Table 3. We initialize the the weights of the quadruples to 1, as shown in Table 5. A 4-order tensor $\boldsymbol{\mathcal{A}} \in \mathbb{R}^{5\times4\times4\times2}$ can be constructed from this table. For example, the first quadruple $< U_1, psychology, like, ForrestGump >$ will correspond to the entry $\boldsymbol{\mathcal{A}}(1,1,1,1)$=1.

For each matrix unfolding $A_{(i)}$, $1 \le i \le 4$, we compute $U^{(i)}$ as follows:

Table 5: Data of the tensor $\boldsymbol{\mathcal{A}}$

User	Tag	Rating	Item	Val
U_1	psychology	like	Forest Gump	1
U_1	psychology	like	Beautiful Mind	1
U_2	comedy	like	Forest Gump	1
U_2	excellent	like	Groundhog Day	1
U_2	comedy	like	Groundhog Day	1
U_3	comedy	like	Forest Gump	1
U_4	comedy	like	Forest Gump	1
U_4	comedy	dislike	Toy story	1
U_4	overrated	dislike	Toy story	1
U_5	comedy	dislike	Forest Gump	1
U_5	overrated	dislike	Groundhog Day	1

$$\boldsymbol{U}^{(1)} = \begin{pmatrix} -0.24 & 0.49 & 0 & -0.82 & 0.15 \\ -0.48 & -0.72 & 0 & -0.36 & -0.27 \\ -0.29 & -0.21 & 0 & 0.12 & 0.92 \\ -0.79 & 0.38 & 0 & 0.42 & -0.22 \\ 0 & 0 & 1 & 0 & 0 \end{pmatrix}$$

$$\boldsymbol{U}^{(2)} = \begin{pmatrix} -0.25 & 0.95 & -0.16 & -0.11 \\ -0.93 & -0.19 & 0.20 & 0.24 \\ -0.16 & -0.11 & 0.25 & -0.95 \\ -0.20 & -0.24 & 0.93 & -0.19 \end{pmatrix}$$

$$\boldsymbol{U}^{(3)} = \begin{pmatrix} -0.95 & 0.25 & 0 & 0.20 \\ -0.17 & 0.14 & 0 & -0.97 \\ -0.27 & -0.96 & 0 & -0.09 \\ 0 & 0 & 1 & 0 \end{pmatrix}$$

$$\boldsymbol{U}^{(4)} = \begin{pmatrix} 1 & 0 \\ 0 & 1 \end{pmatrix}$$

We maintain only a subset of the original dimensions in each of the four modes (Line 5). Here, we choose $c_1 = 4, c_2 = 4, c_3 = 4, c_4 = 2$. The resulting $\hat{U}^{(i)}$ are shown as follows:

$$\hat{\boldsymbol{U}}^{(1)} = \begin{pmatrix} -0.24 & 0.49 & 0 & -0.82 \\ -0.48 & -0.72 & 0 & -0.36 \\ -0.29 & -0.21 & 0 & 0.12 \\ -0.79 & 0.38 & 0 & 0.42 \\ 0 & 0 & 1 & 0 \end{pmatrix}$$

$$\hat{\boldsymbol{U}}^{(2)} = \begin{pmatrix} -0.25 & 0.95 & -0.16 & -0.11 \\ -0.93 & -0.19 & 0.20 & 0.24 \\ -0.16 & -0.11 & 0.25 & -0.95 \\ -0.20 & -0.24 & 0.93 & -0.19 \end{pmatrix}$$

$$\hat{\boldsymbol{U}}^{(3)} = \begin{pmatrix} -0.95 & 0.25 & 0 & 0.20 \\ -0.17 & 0.14 & 0 & -0.97 \\ -0.27 & -0.96 & 0 & -0.09 \\ 0 & 0 & 1 & 0 \end{pmatrix}$$

$$\hat{\boldsymbol{U}}^{(4)} = \begin{pmatrix} 1 & 0 \\ 0 & 1 \end{pmatrix}$$

Lines 6-7 computes the approximate tensor $\hat{\boldsymbol{\mathcal{A}}}$. The final weights of the quadruples are shown in Table 6. We observe that the algorithm has added the following four quadruples:

$<U_3$, *comedy, like, Groundhog Day*$>$
$<U_3$, *excellent, like, Groundhog Day*$>$
$<U_3$, *comedy, dislike, Toy story*$>$
$<U_3$, *overrated, dislike, Toy story*$>$

Note that user U_3 has not used the tag "*excellent*" previously, and there is no indication on which item should be recommend to U_3 based on the tags "*comedy*" and "*excellent*" in the original table (recall Table 5). However, the newly added quadruples indicate that the movie "*Groundhog Day*" is associated with user U_3 and tags "*comedy*" and "*excellent*" with a weight of 0.25. Hence, the movie "*Groundhog Day*" will be recommended to U_3.

Table 6: Output of the approximate tensor $\hat{\mathcal{A}}$

User	Tag	Rating	Item	Val
U_1	psychology	like	Forest Gump	1.01
U_1	psychology	like	Beautiful Mind	0.98
U_2	comedy	like	Forest Gump	1.1
U_2	excellent	like	Groundhog Day	0.92
U_2	comedy	like	Groundhog Day	0.92
U_3	comedy	like	Forest Gump	0.60
U_4	comedy	like	Forest Gump	1.1
U_4	comedy	dislike	Toy story	0.95
U_4	overrated	dislike	Toy story	0.95
U_5	comedy	dislike	Forest Gump	1
U_5	overrated	dislike	Groundhog Day	1
U_3	comedy	like	Groundhog Day	0.25
U_3	excellent	like	Groundhog Day	0.25
U_3	comedy	dislike	Toy story	0.21
U_3	overrated	dislike	Toy story	0.21

We observe that latent associations such as the newly added quadruples in Table 6 may not be found if the tensor data is sparse, that is, most of the entries are 0. This problem is particularly acute as we are working with the quaternary relationship. We overcome this problem by applying a smoothing technique to Line 1 in Algorithm 1. The smoothing method is based on the similarity between items. For each user $< u, r, t >$ in the tensor, let S_1 be the set of items that are rated and tagged by user u, and $S_2 = V$ - S_1 where V is the set of all items/resources. We assign $< u, r, t, v_j >$ with the overall similarly between item $v_j \in S_2$ and the items in S_1.

The overall similarity between item $v_j \in S_2$ and the items in S_1 can be calculated as follows:

$$SIM(v_j, S_1) = \frac{\sum_{v_i \in S_1} sim(v_i, v_j)}{|S_1|} \quad (3)$$

where $sim(v_i, v_j)$ is the cosine similarity between items v_i and v_j, assuming the items are represented by vectors of word weights.

The most time consuming steps in Algorithm 1 are the diagonalization of the unfolding matrices and the computation of the approximate core tensor. For real world applications involving large tensors, the work in [9] utilizes parallel architectures to optimize memory usage and reduce computation time. Note that the approximate tensor needs to be updated when we have new users, items, or tags. We adopt the methods described in [20] to incrementally update the approximate tensor.

4. FRAMEWORK FOR RECOMMENDATION AND PREDICTION

In this section, we describe how the proposed quaternary semantic analysis can provide a unified framework for the 4 common tasks: item recommendation, item rating prediction, user recommendation and tag recommendation.

- **User Recommendation.**

  This is achieved in the proposed framework as follows: We first initialize the set Q to be empty. For each quadruple $< u, r, t, i >$ involving the target user u, we find the set of quadruples that have the same r, t, and i values and add them to Q. Next, we group the quadruples in Q according to the user and aggregate the weights for each user. The top N users with the highest weights are recommended to u.

- **Item Recommendation.**

  Here, we assume that a user *likes* a movie if he/she has given a 5-star rating to the movie [10]. Let T_u be the set of tags that a user u has used to tag movies which s/he likes. For each item i in V, we compute its total weight

  $$w_i = \sum_{t \in T_u} \hat{\mathcal{A}}(u, t, r, i)$$

  Then we sort the items according to their w_i and return the top N items with the highest weights.

- **Tag Recommendation.**

  In our framework, the task of tag recommendation is reduced to examining the weights of the quadruples in the approximate tensor $\hat{\mathcal{A}}$ which indicate how likely a user u would use the tag t for an item i if he has given the rating r before. Hence, we sort the quadruples involving u, r and i according to their weights and return the top N tags.

- **Item Rating Prediction.**

  We use the approximate tensor $\hat{\mathcal{A}}$ to predict the item rating as follows. Let the rating scale be $[1, R_{max}]$. Let T_u be the set of tags that a user u has used to tag movies. The rating that a user u will give to an item i such as $r_{u,i}$ $(1 \leq r_{u,i} \leq 5)$ is given by:

  $$r_{u,i} = \frac{\sum_{j=1}^{R_{max}} \sum_{t \in T_u} j \cdot \hat{\mathcal{A}}(u, t, j, i)}{\sum_{j=1}^{R_{max}} \sum_{t \in T_u} \hat{\mathcal{A}}(u, t, j, i)}$$

5. PERFORMANCE STUDY

We conduct experiments to evaluate the effectiveness of our proposed framework for item recommendation, item rating prediction and tag recommendation. We implemented our framework in MATLAB and run the experiments on a 2.33Ghz Intel Core 2 CPU with 4GB RAM, running Windows 7-64 bit.

5.1 Experimental Dataset

We use the publicly available MovieLens dataset available at $http://www.grouplens.org/node/73$. This dataset comprises of two files. The first file contains users' tags on different movies. The second file contains users' ratings on different movies on a scale of 1 to 5, with 1 being bad and 5 being excellent. By joining these two files over user and movie, we obtain the quadruples $< user, movie, tag, rating >$. We have a total of 24563 quadruples with 2,026 users, 5,088 movies, and 9,078 tags. We pre-process these quadruples to generate a subset such that each user, movie and tag occur at least 10 times in the dataset. The resulting dataset has 11122 tuples with 201 users, 501 movies, and 404 tags. Table 7 shows the statistics of the users' ratings after preprocessing.

Table 7: Statistics of rating data

Statistics	Users	Movies
Min. # of ratings	5	1
Max. # of ratings	203	58
Mean. # of ratings	32.58 ± 35.61	13.06 ± 8.67

5.2 Experiments on Item Recommendation

We first evaluate the effectiveness of the proposed quaternary analysis model (**QSA**) for item recommendation. We compare our method with the following existing methods:

1. **UPCC** [16]. This method uses the Pearson's Correlation Coefficient to cluster similar users and recommend items based on these similar users.

2. **IPCC** [18]. This method uses the Pearson's Correlation Coefficient to cluster similar items for recommendation.

3. **Probabilistic Matrix Factorization (PMF)** [17]. This is a state-of-the art collaborative filtering algorithm that utilizes the ternary relationship among user, item and ratings.

4. **Ternary Semantic Analysis (TSA)** [20]. This method recommends items based on the ternary semantic analysis on users-items-tags.

We use the Hit Ratio [8] as the metric to evaluate the effectiveness of the various item recommendation methods. For each user $u \in U$, we randomly choose one item i that has a rating of 5 and withhold the quadruples involving u and i. Then we run the 5 methods to generate the top N items recommended for this user. If the item i is among the top N recommended items, then we say that a hit has occurred. The hit ratio of a method is given by:

$$HitRatio = \frac{Numberofhits}{|U|}$$

Figure 1 shows the hit ratio of the 5 methods as we vary N. We observe that the proposed QSA method has a higher hit ratio compared to the other methods. In particular, QSA outperforms TSA, PMF, IPCC and UPCC by more than 23%, 50%, 60% and 80% respectively. This is because QSA can find more accurate latent associations using quaternary relationships compared to ternary relationships of either users-items-ratings or users-items-tags. UPCC and IPCC find similar users or items (neighbors) by calculating Pearson correlation coefficient. If a user has few ratings for items, then it will be difficult for UPCC and IPCC to find neighbors. The PMF approach suffers from the data sparsity problem and is unable to extract sufficient feature information. On the other hand, TSA captures user's interest (topic) by using tag, but does not judge how much he likes these topics (rating). By utilizing quaternary relations, the proposed QSA overcomes the data sparsity problem and captures both users' opinions and interests with the rating and tagging information.

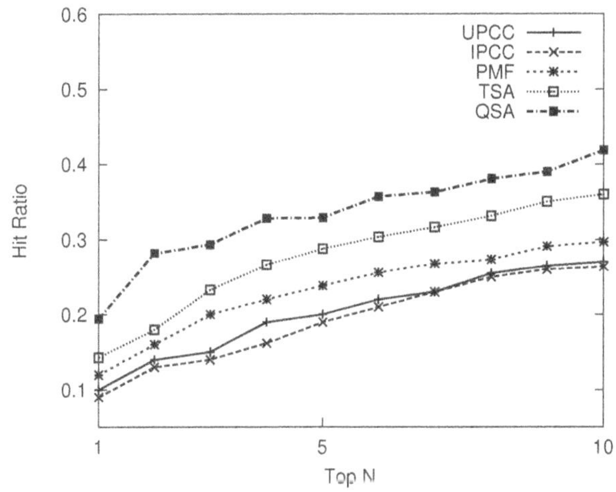

Figure 1: Hit ratio for Top N item recommendation

5.3 Experiments on User Recommendation

In order to evaluate the effectiveness of QSA in recommending interesting users, we determine the similarity of items among the recommended top N users [20] since users with shared interests are more likely to tag and rate similar items. We compute the item similarity as the average of the cosine similarity of their TF $\times$ IDF tag term vector [20] and cosine similarity of the rating vector [18].

Let NB_u be the set of top N users recommended to u. The intra-neighborhood similarity is given by the average cosine similarity of all items for the users in NB_u:

$$IntraSim(NB_u) = \frac{\sum_{w \in NB_u} \sum_{i \in I_u, j \in I_w} sim(i,j)}{\sum_{w \in NB_u} |I_u||I_w|}$$

where I_u and I_w are the sets of items tags by users u and w.

Let $Random_u$ be the set of N users randomly chosen from the set of users $U - \{u\}$. We can determine the inter-neighborhood similarity as follows:

$$InterSim(Random_u) = \frac{\sum_{w \in Random_u} \sum_{i \in I_u, j \in I_w} sim(i,j)}{\sum_{w \in Random_u} |I_v||I_w|}$$

where I_u and I_w are the sets of items tags by users u and w respectively.

Table 8: Comparison of intra- and inter- similarity between QSA and TSA

Method	*Intra − similarity*	*Inter − similarity*
TSA	0.10	0.08
QSA	**0.145**	**0.065**

Table 8 shows the intra-similarity and inter-similarity of QSA and TSA. We observe that the average intra-similarity is consistently higher than the average inter-similarity for both QSA and TSA. In particular, QSA outperforms TSA in intra-similarity indicating that more relevant users are found by QSA. Table 8 shows that the average of intra-similarity for QSA is about 0.15, while the average inter-similarity is only 0.065.

5.4 Experiments on Tag Recommendation

For the task of tag recommendation, we evaluate our algorithm QSA against the two state-of-the-art methods: TSA [20] and RTF [15]. For each user $u \in U$, we randomly choose one item i and remove all quadruples involving u and i from the dataset. Then we run the 3 methods to generate the top N tags recommended for this user.

We use the standard recall and precision measures to evaluate the results:

$$Precision = \frac{Number\ of\ Hits}{N}$$

$$Recall = \frac{Number\ of\ Hits}{|T_{u,i}|}$$

where $T_{u,i}$ is the set of tags used by user u on item i.

Figures 2(a) and 2(b) show the precision and recall of the 3 methods for varying values of N. It is clear that QSA is able to achieve a higher recall and precision compared to the other two methods.

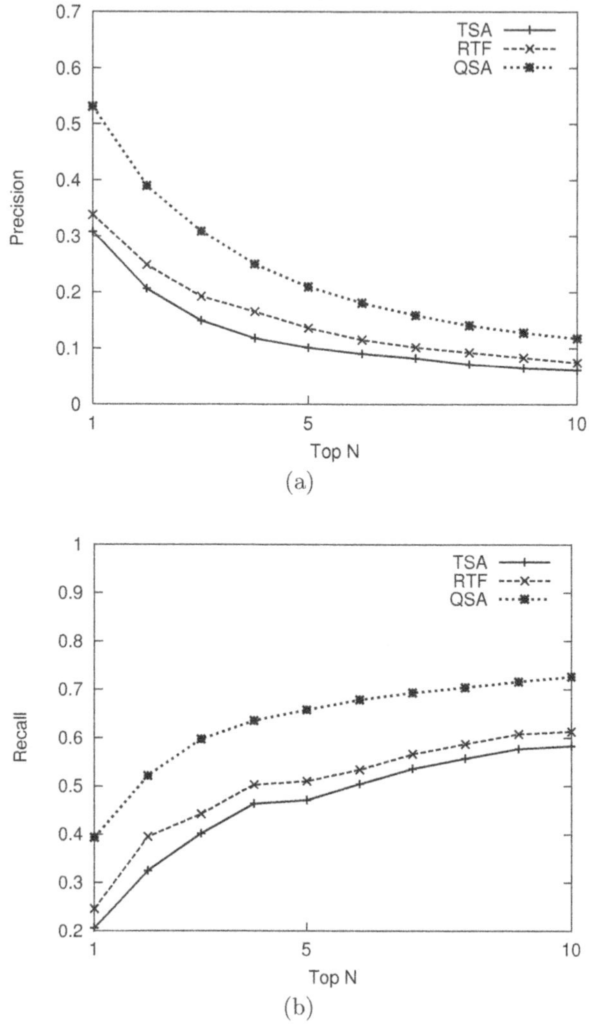

Figure 2: Precision and recall for tag recommendation

5.5 Experiments on Item Rating Prediction

In this set of experiments, we evaluate the predictive performance of QSA for item ratings. We compare QSA with UPCC, IPCC and PMF only because TSA is based on user-item-tag relationship and does not use rating information.

We use the Mean Absolute Error (MAE) and Coverage as the evaluation metrics [1]. Coverage refers to the fraction of items that an algorithm is able to give a predicted rating. The MAE is given by:

$$MAE = \frac{\sum_{t \in T} |r_{u,i} - \hat{r}_{u,i}|}{|D|}$$

where $r_{u,i}$ is the rating given by user u for item i, $\hat{r}_{u,i}$ is the predicted rating and D is the size of the testing dataset.

We use 80% of the dataset as training set and 20% as the testing set, and compute the MAE and coverage for different methods. The five-fold cross validation results are shown in Table 9. We observe that the coverage is not 100% for UPCC and IPCC, which confirms that these two methods are unable to deal with the problem of data sparsity effectively. On the other hand, QSA alleviates the data sparsity problem with the help of tagging information, thus achieving 100% coverage with a lower MAE.

To analyze the statistical significance of the results, we conduct a paired t-test. Let a_i, b_i, $i = 1, 2, \cdots, n$, be the MAE values obtained using methods A and B respectively. Let $d_i = a_i - b_i$ and $\bar{d}$ be the average value of d_i, $i = 1, 2, \cdots, n$. We set the null hypothesis as $\bar{d} = 0$. The *p-value* is computed using the t-statistics:

$$T = \frac{\bar{d}}{s/\sqrt{n}}$$

where s is the standard deviation of d. A *p-value* that is less than 0.01 indicates the existence of statistically significant evidence against the null hypothesis. We compare the results of QSA against UPCC, IPCC and PMF and obtain the p-values of 3.52E-06, 4.02E-06 and 1.70E-03 respectively. These results indicate that the improvement in the MAE values for QSA is statistically significant compared to UPCC, IPCC and PMF.

Table 9: MAE and Coverage

Method	*MAE*	*Coverage*
UPCC	0.7424	97.29%
IPCC	0.7458	98.05%
PMF	0.692	100%
QSA	**0.673**	**100%**

5.6 Effect of Tensor Dimensions on Item Recommendation

We also conduct experiments to study the effect of core tensor dimensions $c1, c2, c3$, and $c4$ on the performance of our algorithm QSA. We first vary each dimension to find the settings that give the best performance. This occurs when $c_1 = 45, c_2 = 125, c_3 = 165, c_4 = 4$.

For ease of visualization, we vary two of the four dimensions and keep the other two dimensions fixed at their optimal values. The results are shown in Figure 3. Figure 3(a) shows the effect on hit ratio as we vary c_1 and c_2 while keeping c_3 fixed at 165 and c_4 fixed at 4. Figure 3(b) shows the effect on hit ratio as we vary c_1 and c_3 while keeping c_2 fixed at 125 and c_4 fixed at 4. Figure 3(c) shows that results of varying $c2$ and $c3$ while $c1$ and c_4 are fixed at 45 and 4 respectively. From the figures, we observe that a good approximation of the original diagonal can be achieved by preserving 70%, 90%, 80%, 90% of the original tensor information in each dimension respectively, that is, $c_1 = 45, c_2 = 125, c_3 = 165, c_4 = 4$.

6. RELATED WORK

In this section, we review the related work in the various recommendation tasks.

Item recommendation. Existing systems for item recommendation can be roughly divided into two major categories. Content-based systems [2, 14] make use of explicitly stated profiles of users or products to characterize their nature. On the other hand, systems based on collaborative filtering (CF) [18, 17] do not exploit such explicit user profiles. Instead, they infer the user profiles through their past activities, such as their transaction history or product satisfaction expressed in ratings. These systems rely only on the associations between users, ratings, and items. They cannot be easily used to consider the the quaternary relationship among users, items, tags and ratings.

Recent work has focused on using tags to recommend items. The work in [21] proposed a generic method to incorporate tags to CF algorithms. This is done by decomposing the users-tags-items relationship into 3 binary relationships, namely, users-tags, tags-items, and user-items. A fusion method is then applied to perform item recommendation. [19] tries to infer tag preferences and recommend items to users based on their tag preferences. Recently, a ternary semantics analysis approach [20] has been proposed to utilize the ternary relationship users-items-tags for recommendation. None of these works have utilized the associations among users, items, tags and ratings.

User recommendation. Social networking sites have adopted the simple strategy of suggesting friends-of-friends to increase the connectivity among their users. Recently, content-based approaches [7] were proposed to match the content of user profiles and determine user similarities for recommendation. Research has also been done using known social network structures for recommendations. Groh et al. [4] generated user neighborhood information from known social network structures and demonstrated that collaborative filtering based on such neighborhoods outperforms classic collaborative filtering methods. The work in [20] proposed a ternary semantic analysis unified framework to perform user recommendation.

Tag recommendation. Personalized tag recommendation has attracted significant attention recently. The work in [6] provides a comprehensive evaluation and comparison of several state-of-the-art tag recommendation algorithms in three different real world datasets. Content-based collaborating filtering technique has been proposed in [13] to automate tag assignments to blogs. The works in [5, 20] have shown to generate high quality tag recommendations that outperform baseline methods such as the most-popular models and collaborative filtering [6].

Item rating prediction. There are three approaches to item rating prediction: user-based methods [12], item-based methods [18], and model-based methods [3, 17]. User-based methods search for similar users and utilize the ratings of these similar users to make prediction, while item-based methods search for similar items and utilize the ratings of these similar items to make prediction. Model-based methods try to learn a model from the data using statistical learning techniques. All these approaches are based on tenary relationships.

7. CONCLUSIONS

In this work, we have shown that quaternary semantic analysis can lead to more accurate recommendation. We have proposed using a 4-order tensor to model the four heterogenous entities: users, items, tags and ratings. We further employed the higher order singular value decomposition to reduce the dimensionality of the 4-order tensor, thereby casting the recommendation problem as a multiway latent semantic analysis problem. Extensive experiments have been conducted on a real world dataset for item recommendation, user recommendation, tag recommendation, and item rating prediction. The results demonstrated that quaternary semantic analysis outperforms state-of-the-art algorithms in all the four tasks.

8. REFERENCES

[1] X. Amatriain, N. Lathia, J. M. Pujol, H. Kwak, and N. Oliver. The wisdom of the few: a collaborative filtering approach based on expert opinions from the web. In *SIGIR*, pages 532–539. ACM, 2009.

[2] M. Balabanović and Y. Shoham. Fab: content-based, collaborative recommendation. *Communications of the ACM*, pages 66–72, March 1997.

[3] S. Funk. Netflix update: Try this at home.. sifter.org/simon/journal/20061211.html. 2006.

[4] G. Groh. Recommendations in taste related domains: Collaborative filtering vs. social filtering. In *In Proc ACM Group 07*, pages 127–136, 2007.

[5] A. Hotho, R. Jaschke, C. Schmitz, and G. Stumme. Folkrank: A ranking algorithm for folksonomies. In

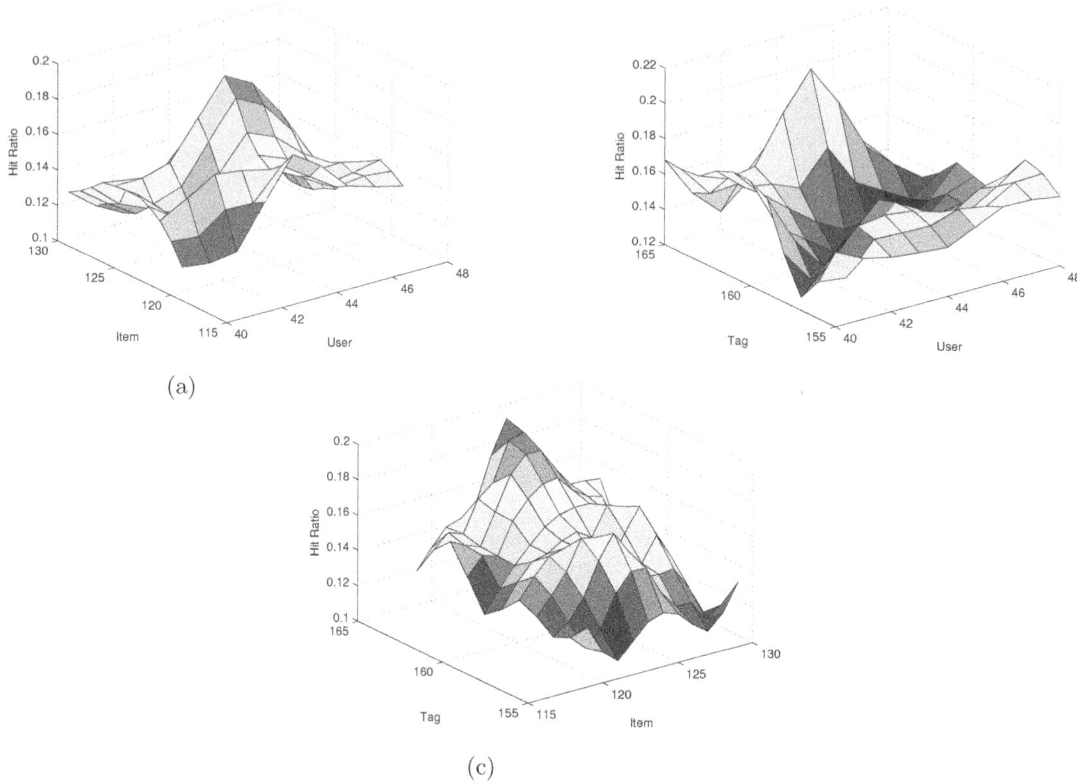

Figure 3: Effect of core tensor dimensions on hit ratio

University of Hildesheim, Institute of Computer Science, pages 111–114, 2006.

[6] R. Jäschke, L. Marinho, A. Hotho, S.-T. Lars, and S. Gerd. Tag recommendations in social bookmarking systems. *AI Commun.*, 21:231–247, December 2008.

[7] C. D. M. M. Jilin Chen, Werner Geyer and I. Guy.. Make new friends, but keep the old: recommending people on social networking sites. In *SIGCHI '09*, pages 201–210, 2009.

[8] G. Karypis. Evaluation of item-based top-n recommendation algorithms. In *CIKM*, pages 247–254, 2001.

[9] T. G. Kolda and J. Sun. Scalable tensor decompositions for multi-aspect data mining. In *ICDM*, pages 363–372, 2008.

[10] Y. Koren. Factorization meets the neighborhood: a multifaceted collaborative filtering model. In *KDD*, pages 426–434, 2008.

[11] L. D. Lathauwer, B. D. Moor, and J. Vandewalle. A multilinear singular value decomposition. *SIAM J. Matrix Anal. Appl.*, 21:1253–1278, March 2000.

[12] G. Linden, B. Smith, and J. York. Amazon.com recommendations: item-to-item collaborative filtering. volume 7, pages 76 – 80, jan/feb 2003.

[13] G. Mishne. Autotag: a collaborative approach to automated tag assignment for weblog posts. In *WWW '06*, pages 953–954, 2006.

[14] R. J. Mooney and L. Roy. Content-based book recommending using learning for text categorization. In *In Proceedings Of 5th ACM Conference On Digtal Libraries*, pages 195–204. ACM Press, 1999.

[15] S. Rendle, L. Balby Marinho, A. Nanopoulos, and S.-T. Lars. Learning optimal ranking with tensor factorization for tag recommendation. In *KDD*, pages 727–736, 2009.

[16] P. Resnick, N. Iacovou, M. Sushak, P. Bergstrom, and J. Riedl. Grouplens: An open architecture for collaborative filtering of netnews. In *ACM Conference on Computer Supported Collaborative Work Conference*, pages 175–186, 1994.

[17] R. Salakhutdinov and A. Mnih. Probabilistic matrix factorization. *Advances in Neural Information Processing Systems*, pages 1257–1264, 2008.

[18] B. Sarwar, G. Karypis, J. Konstan, and J. Reidl. Item-based collaborative filtering recommendation algorithms. In *WWW*, pages 285–295, 2001.

[19] S. Sen, J. Vig, and J. Riedl. Tagommenders: connecting users to items through tags. In *WWW*, pages 671–680, May 2009.

[20] P. Symeonidis, A. Nanopoulos, and Y. Manolopoulos. A unified framework for providing recommendations in social tagging systems based on ternary semantic analysis. *IEEE TKDE*, 22:179–192, February 2010.

[21] K. H. L. Tso-Sutter, L. B. Marinho, and L. Schmidt-Thieme. Tag-aware recommender systems by fusion of collaborative filtering algorithms. In *SAC*, pages 1995–1999, 2008.

Associative Tag Recommendation Exploiting Multiple Textual Features*

Fabiano Belém, Eder Martins, Tatiana Pontes, Jussara Almeida, Marcos Gonçalves
Computer Science Department
Universidade Federal de Minas Gerais, Brazil
{fmuniz, ederfm, tpontes, jussara, mgoncalv}@dcc.ufmg.br

ABSTRACT

This work addresses the task of recommending relevant tags to a target object by jointly exploiting three dimensions of the problem: (i) term co-occurrence with tags preassigned to the target object, (ii) terms extracted from multiple textual features, and (iii) several metrics of tag relevance. In particular, we propose several new heuristic methods, which extend state-of-the-art strategies by including new metrics that try to capture how accurately a candidate term describes the object's content. We also exploit two learning-to-rank (L2R) techniques, namely RankSVM and Genetic Programming, for the task of generating ranking functions that combine multiple metrics to accurately estimate the relevance of a tag to a given object. We evaluate all proposed methods in various scenarios for three popular Web 2.0 applications, namely, LastFM, YouTube and YahooVideo. We found that our new heuristics greatly outperform the methods on which they are based, producing gains in precision of up to 181%, as well as another state-of-the-art technique, with improvements in precision of up to 40% over the best baseline in any scenario. Further improvements can also be achieved with the new L2R strategies, which have the additional advantage of being quite flexible and extensible to exploit other aspects of the tag recommendation problem.

Categories and Subject Descriptors

H.3.1 [**Information Storage and Retrieval**]: Content Analysis and Indexing; H.3.5 [**Information Storage and Retrieval**]: Online Information Services

General Terms

Algorithms, Experimentation

Keywords

Tag Recommendation, Relevance Metrics

*This work is supported by the INWeb (grant 57.3871/2008-6) and by the authors grants from CNPq and FAPEMIG.

SIGIR'11, July 24–28, 2011, Beijing, China.

1. INTRODUCTION

The act of associating *tags* to objects has become paramount in Web 2.0 applications, mainly due to the strong stimuli and easiness for user participation in content creation. This content, typically multimedia (e.g., images and videos), brings challenges to current multimedia Information Retrieval (IR) methods, not only due to the scale of object collections and upload rate, but also due to the (usually) poor quality of user-generated material [5]. Tags, among other textual features such as title and description, commonly associated to Web 2.0 objects, offer a good alternative for supporting content organization, dissemination and retrieval services. In fact, recent studies have demonstrated that tags are one of the best textual features to be exploited by various IR services, such as automatic object classification [7].

In this context, tag recommendation services aim at improving the quality of the available content, and ultimately of information services that rely on them, by suggesting terms that are related to the content of a target object. Many existing strategies exploit term co-occurrence patterns in previous tag assignments in the collection, expanding an initial tag set $\mathcal{I}_o$ of a target object o with other tags that frequently co-occur together with the terms in $\mathcal{I}_o$ [11, 22, 9, 19]. Other methods do not assume the existence of such tags in the target object, using, instead, terms extracted from other textual features [16, 25]. However, various textual features, including tags, are created by the end users, and thus, may contain a lot of *noise* (e.g., misspellings or unrelated terms) [7, 14]. Thus, it is important to filter such terms out of the list of recommendations or reduce their importance, favoring terms that are more "relevant" for the target object. By relevant, we mean terms that are good descriptors of the object's content and/or that help discriminate it from others, for supporting services such as searching and classification which typically use tags as data sources. With that in mind, some previous methods [22, 16, 25, 4] exploit metrics of relevance, such as Term Frequency (TF), either to filter out irrelevant candidates or to boost candidates with more potential. In sum, many previous methods address the problem of recommending a tag for a target object by exploiting (i) term co-occurrences with tags pre-assigned to the object, (ii) terms extracted from multiple textual features, and (iii) metrics of relevance. However, to our knowledge, most of them exploit at most two of these three dimensions[1].

In contrast, we here address the task of recommending

[1]Other dimensions can also be exploited (e.g., user-object-tag relationships [10], and tag usage history [12]). Extending our methods to include them is left for the future.

tags for a given Web 2.0 object by jointly exploiting all three dimensions. In other words, we extend traditional tag co-occurrence based approaches to include not only tags that have been previously assigned to the objects (including the target object), but also terms contained in other textual features, such as title and description. The contents of these textual features are used to extract candidate terms. We also exploit several heuristic metrics to try to capture the *relevance* of each such term as a recommendation for the target object. Some of these metrics, to our knowledge, have never been applied to tag recommendation before. Our approach is to model the tag recommendation problem as a multiple term candidate *ranking* problem. That is, we develop functions to estimate the relevance of a candidate term as a tag recommendation for a given object, thus enabling us to rank the candidates according to such estimations and recommend the most relevant ones as tags for the object.

Specifically, we propose ten tag recommendations strategies. Eight of them are heuristics built as extensions of two state-of-the-art techniques that exploit tag co-occurrence and some metrics of relevance. Our heuristics extend these previous methods by including new metrics of relevance that try to capture how accurately a candidate term *describes* the object's content, and by exploiting multiple textual features. They are simple, easy to compute, and quite efficient, producing gains of up to 181% in precision over the original techniques on which they are based.

However, a number of heuristics can be devised to combine multiple metrics of relevance into a final tag recommendation function. Finding the "best" heuristic is not an easy task due to the potential large size of the search space, which, in our case, consists of all possible tag recommendation functions that can be built using the suggested metrics.

Thus, we also investigate the benefits of applying learning-to-rank (L2R) techniques for tag recommendation purposes, proposing two new strategies. One strategy exploits the traditional RankSVM method [13], whereas the other is based on Genetic Programming (GP) [3]. RankSVM and GP are here treated as *meta-heuristics* to generate ranking functions that combine all given metrics to accurately estimate the relevance of each given candidate term. Our motivation to use L2R methods are threefold: (1) they can effectively exploit many features in the generation of ranking functions, (2) they can be easily extended to include more features, and (3) there is a strong theoretical background on learning methods, which has been recently extended for ranking problems [27].

We evaluate the proposed tag recommendation functions, comparing them against three state-of-the-art techniques, namely Sum^+, the best function proposed in [22], which exploits co-occurrence of pre-assigned tags along with some document frequency statistics, $LATRE$ [19] a very recent, efficient and effective tag co-occurrence based method, and the winner of the ECML Discovery Challenge 2009 [16], referred to here as *Co-occurrence and Text-based Tag Recommender* (CTTR). CTTR exploits the contents of textual features associated with the target object along with one metric of relevance, but does not consider the tags previously assigned to the target object. Our evaluation is performed with real datasets collected from three popular Web 2.0 applications: the video sharing sites YouTube and YahooVideo, and the online radio station LastFM[2].

Our results indicate that our best heuristic outperforms the best baseline in any scenario by up to 40% in precision and 32% in recall. This heuristic extends the $LATRE$ baseline by incorporating a new metric that tries to capture the descriptive power of each candidate term and by exploiting multiple textual features. Moreover, some further improvements over our heuristics (up to 12% in precision) can also be achieved with our L2R based strategies, although the best of the two techniques depends on the dataset. Despite the somewhat modest improvements over our heuristics, the L2R based strategies provide a flexible framework that can be easily extended to include other metrics of relevance or to address other aspects of the tag recommendation problem.

The rest of this paper is organized as follows. Section 2 discusses related work, whereas Section 3 defines the problem and the main metrics used for tag recommendation. Section 4 introduces the methods we analyze here, while our experimental evaluation is presented in Section 5. Finally, conclusions and future work are offered in Section 6.

2. RELATED WORK

Many tag recommendation strategies exploit co-occurrence patterns computed over a history of tag assignments. In particular, some of them exploit tag co-occurrences to expand an initial set of tags $\mathcal{I}_o$ associated with an object o [22, 9, 11, 26, 15, 19]. For this purpose, Heymann *et al.* [11] use association rules, i.e., implications of the form $X \rightarrow y$, where the antecedent X is a set of tags, and the consequent y is a candidate tag for recommendation, restricting the rules by a confidence threshold. However, the authors do not provide a ranking of the recommended tags. Sigurbjornsson and Zwol [22], on the contrary, exploit simple global metrics of tag co-occurrence (e.g., confidence), applying them over all tags in the initial set to produce a final ranking of candidate tags. Some of the considered metrics, related to tag frequency, try to capture the "relevance" of each candidate. In comparison, we here consider a much richer set of metrics, including new metrics based on multiple textual features, which, as we shall see, are responsible for our largest improvements.

Due to efficiency issues, most of these strategies usually compute co-occurrences between only two tags (i.e., X contains only one tag), thus possibly missing important co-occurrence relationships. To address this problem, Menezes *et al.* [19] propose LATRE - Lazy Associative Tag Recommendation, which computes association rules in an on-demand manner, allowing an efficient generation of more complex and potentially better rules, and producing superior results in comparison with the best method in [22].

A few other efforts do not exploit tags previously assigned to the target object, focusing, rather, on other data sources [16, 25]. Lipczak *et al.* [16] extract terms from other textual features (e.g., title) of the target object, expanding them by association rules, and sorting the extracted terms by their usage as tags in a training set. Wang *et al.* [25] use the traditional $TF \times IDF$ metric to extract and rank the most important terms from the object's textual content.

In sum, these previous methods address the tag recommendation problem by exploiting (i) co-occurrence patterns

[2] http://www.youtube.com, http://www.yahoo.com/video, and http://www.last.fm, respectively

among previously assigned tags, (ii) multiple textual features, and (iii) metrics of relevance. However, to our knowledge, none of them jointly exploits all three dimensions. In contrast, in a very preliminary work [4], we investigated the benefits of combining all three approaches to perform tag recommendation, obtaining results that outperform those of some previous techniques. These preliminary findings motivated the present study, which greatly extends our prior work by proposing new metrics of relevance and several new recommendation strategies (including L2R based strategies), evaluating them on more recently collected and larger datasets, comparing them against more baselines, and reaching significantly better results.

In addition to co-occurrence and text based strategies, other approaches have also been exploited. For example, Wu *et al.* [26] add image content information to rank tags. Siersdorfer *et al.* [21] create a graph of videos based on content similarity, and make recommendations by propagating tags through its edges, whereas Song *et al.* [23] exploit a bipartite graph containing tags, documents and words. Other studies address the problem of *personalized recommendation*, often exploiting the history of per-user tag assignments. Collaborative filtering and *FolkRank* [12], as well as PITF - Pairwise Interactions Tensor Factorization [20] fall into this category. Other graph-based personalized recommendation strategies exploit social network relationships [10, 18]. We do not tackle personalization here, leaving the task of extending our strategies to address it for the future.

Finally, the only prior efforts to apply learning-to-rank techniques to recommend tags were pursued by Cao *et al.* [6], who exploited RankSVM, and by Wu *et al.* [26], who exploited RankBoost. However, the latter considered only metrics related to tag co-occurrences and image content, and did not exploit textual features, whereas the former considered only metrics related to tag frequency, disregarding tag co-occurrence metrics.

3. TAG RECOMMENDATION: PROBLEM STATEMENT AND METRICS

A Web 2.0 *object* refers to an instance of a media (text, audio, video, image) in a given Web 2.0 application. There are various sources of information related to an object, here referred to as its features. In particular, *textual features*, our main source of information, comprise the self-contained textual blocks that are associated with an object, usually with a well defined functionality [7]. The textual features here exploited are the object *tags*, *title* and *description*.

We define the recommendation problem as follows. Given a tag set $\mathcal{I}_o$ previously assigned to an object[3] o, and the set of textual features (other than tags) $\mathcal{F}_o = \{\mathcal{F}_o^1, \mathcal{F}_o^2, ..., \mathcal{F}_o^n\}$, where each element $\mathcal{F}_o^i$ is the set of terms in textual feature i associated with o, generate a candidate set $\mathcal{C}_o$ and recommend the k most relevant terms of this set.

Many tag recommendation strategies, and in particular the ones proposed here, exploit co-occurrence patterns by mining relations among tags assigned to the same object in an object collection. The process of learning such patterns is defined as follows. There is a training set $\mathcal{D} = \{\langle \mathcal{I}_d, \mathcal{F}_d \rangle\}$, where $\mathcal{I}_d$ ($\mathcal{I}_d \neq \emptyset$) contains all tags assigned to object d, and $\mathcal{F}_d$ contains the term sets of the other textual features associated with d. There is also a test set $\mathcal{O}$, which is a collection of objects $\{\langle \mathcal{I}_o, \mathcal{F}_o, \mathcal{Y}_o \rangle\}$, where both $\mathcal{I}_o$ and $\mathcal{Y}_o$ are sets of tags associated with object o. However, while tags in $\mathcal{I}_o$ are known (and given as input to the recommender), tags in $\mathcal{Y}_o$ are assumed to be unknown and are taken as the relevant recommendations to the target object o (i.e., the *expected answer*). Splitting the tags of each test object into these two subsets facilitates an automatic assessment of the recommendations, as performed in [9] and further discussed in Section 5.2. This evaluation simulates the recommendation of new tags ($\mathcal{Y}_o$) to an object that already has been annotated with $\mathcal{I}_o$. Similarly, there might be also a validation set $\mathcal{V}$ used for tuning parameters and "learning" recommendation functions (see Section 5.2). Thus, each object v in $\mathcal{V}$ also has its tag set split into input tags $\mathcal{I}_v$ and expected answer $\mathcal{Y}_v$.

Thus, we define associative and text based tag recommendation methods as algorithms that estimate the relevance of a tag candidate set relying on the elements described above. Next, we present several metrics that can be used to estimate the relevance of a candidate for tag recommendation. Some of them, like *Sum*, *Stability*, *TF* and *Entropy*, have been previously applied for recommending tags [22, 19, 11]. Others, such as *IFF* and *AFS*, were proposed in [7] for assessing the quality of textual features on the Web 2.0, and have not been exploited for tag recommendation yet.

3.1 Tag Co-occurrence

Tag recommendation approaches based on co-occurrence usually exploit association rules, that is, implications of type $X \rightarrow y$, where the antecedent X is a set of tags and the consequent y is a candidate tag for recommendation. The importance of an association rule is estimated based on **support** (σ), which is the number of co-occurrences of X and y in the training set, and **confidence** (θ), which is the conditional probability that y is assigned as a tag to an object $d \in \mathcal{D}$ given that all tags in X are also associated with d.

As the number of rules mined from $\mathcal{D}$ can be very large and some of them may not be useful for recommendation, minimum support and confidence thresholds (σ_{min} and θ_{min}, respectively) are used as lower bounds to select only the most frequent and/or reliable rules. This selection can improve both effectiveness and efficiency of the recommender.

At recommendation time, we select the rules whose antecedents are included in $\mathcal{I}_o$, the available tags in the target object o. For each term c appearing as consequent of any of the selected rules, we estimate its relevance as a tag for o as the sum of the confidences of all rules containing c, i.e.:

$$Sum(c, o, \ell) = \sum_{X \subseteq \mathcal{I}_o} \theta(X \rightarrow c), \quad (X \rightarrow c) \in \mathcal{R}, |X| \leq \ell \qquad (1)$$

where $\mathcal{R}$ is a set of association rules computed offline over the training set $\mathcal{D}$ given thresholds σ_{min} and θ_{min}, and ℓ is the size limit for the association rules' antecedents.

3.2 Discriminative Power

One may argue that recommending more infrequent terms (provided that they are not too rare) may be desirable, since they may better *discriminate* objects into different cate-

[3]We focus on cases in which there are a few available tags in the target object, and we want to recommend new (different) tags to it. However, our methods are also able to recommend relevant tags to an object with no initial tag by exploiting other textual features and metrics of relevance. We leave this for future work.

gories, topics, or levels of relevance, particularly considering that several services (e.g., classification, searching) often perform IR on multimedia content by using the associated tags as data sources. This aspect can be heuristically captured by the Inverse Feature Frequency (IFF) metric [7], an adaptation of the traditional Inverse Document Frequency (IDF) that considers the term frequency in a specific textual feature (in our case, tags). Given the number of objects in the training set $|\mathcal{D}|$, the IFF of a candidate c is defined as:

$$IFF(c) = \log \frac{|\mathcal{D}| + 1}{f_c^{tag} + 1} \quad (2)$$

where f_c^{tag} is the number of objects in $\mathcal{D}$ which contain c *attached as a tag*. Note that c may be extracted from other textual features. The value 1 is added to both numerator and denominator to deal with new terms that do not appear as tags in the training data. We note that this metric may privilege terms from other textual features that do not appear as tags in the training data. Nevertheless, this metric will be combined with the other metrics into a function, using learning-to-rank algorithms. Thus, its relative weight can be adjusted, as we describe in Section 4.

Along the same lines, one may consider that terms that are very common, such as "video" in a YouTube object collection, are too general, whereas very rare terms may be too specific or may represent noise (e.g., misspellings, neologisms and unknown words). In either case, such terms represent poor recommendations as they have very poor *discriminative power*. Sigurbjornsson *et al.* [22] propose the Stability ($Stab$) metric, which gives more importance to terms with intermediate frequency values:

$$Stab(c, k_s) = \frac{k_s}{k_s + |k_s - \log(f_c^{tag})|} \quad (3)$$

where k_s represents the "ideal frequency" of a term and must be adjusted to the data collection. We here also use $Stab$ to assess the relevance of a tag candidate, but, unlike [22], we apply it not only to tags but also to terms extracted from all textual features $\mathcal{F}_o$ associated with target object o.

3.3 Descriptive Power

We here exploit four heuristic metrics that try to capture, to some extent, the *descriptive power* of a candidate c. Two of them, Term Spread (TS) and Term Frequency (TF), were previously applied to tag recommendation. However, TS was exploited in a very preliminary study [4], whereas previous studies employing TF [25, 6] have not exploited it jointly with co-occurrence of pre-assigned tags, as we do here. The other metrics, derived from TS and TF, are applied here for the first time to tag recommendation.

We start by defining the *Term Spread* of a candidate c in an object o, $TS(c, o)$, as the number of textual features (except tags, in the present context)[4] of o that contain c [7]:

$$TS(c, o) = \sum_{\mathcal{F}_o^i \in \mathcal{F}_o} j, \text{ where } j = \begin{cases} 1 & \text{if } c \in \mathcal{F}_o^i \\ 0 & \text{otherwise} \end{cases} \quad (4)$$

The assumption behind $TS(c, o)$ is that the larger the number of features of o containing c, the more related c is to o's content. For example, if the term "Sting" appears in all features of a video, there is a high chance that the video is related to the famous singer. The maximum TS is given by the number of textual features, other than tags, considered. As we here consider title and description, $TS \leq 2$.

The *Term Frequency* of c in object o, $TF(c, o)$, is:

$$TF(c, o) = \sum_{\mathcal{F}_o^i \in \mathcal{F}_o} tf(c, \mathcal{F}_o^i), \quad (5)$$

where $tf(c, \mathcal{F}_o^i)$ is the number of occurrences of c in textual feature i of object o. Thus, TF considers all textual features of o as a single list of terms, counting all occurrences of c in it. In contrast, TS considers the structure of an object, composed by textual features, which are well-defined blocks of text, counting the number of blocks containing c.

Although both TS and TF try to capture how accurately a term describes an object's content, neither of them considers that different features may present, in general, different descriptive capacities. For example, the title may describe an object's content more accurately than other textual features [7]. Thus, we propose two other metrics, built on TF and TS, that weight a term based on the average descriptive powers of the textual features in which it appears.

The average descriptive power of a textual feature $\mathcal{F}^i$ is assessed by the Average Feature Spread (AFS) heuristic [7]. Let the *Feature Instance Spread* of a feature $\mathcal{F}_o^i$ associated with object o, $FIS(\mathcal{F}_o^i)$, be the average TS over all terms in $\mathcal{F}_o^i$. We define $AFS(\mathcal{F}^i)$ as the average $FIS(\mathcal{F}_o^i)$ over all instances of $\mathcal{F}^i$ associated with objects in the training set $\mathcal{D}$. We then define weighted TS and TF metrics as:

$$wTS(c, o) = \sum_{\mathcal{F}_o^i \in \mathcal{F}_o} j, \text{ where } j = \begin{cases} AFS(\mathcal{F}^i) & \text{if } c \in \mathcal{F}_o^i \\ 0 & \text{otherwise} \end{cases} \quad (6)$$

$$wTF(c, o) = \sum_{\mathcal{F}_o^i \in \mathcal{F}_o} tf(c, \mathcal{F}_o^i) \times AFS(\mathcal{F}^i) \quad (7)$$

3.4 Term Predictability

Another important aspect for tag recommendation is term predictability. Heymann *et al.* [11] measure this characteristic through the term's *entropy*. The entropy of term c in the tags feature, $H^{tags}(c)$, is defined as:

$$H^{tags}(c) = - \sum_{(c \to i) \in \mathcal{R}} \theta(c \to i) \log \theta(c \to i) \quad (8)$$

If a term occurs consistently with certain tags, it is more predictable, having lower entropy. Terms that occur indiscriminately with many other tags are less predictable, thus having higher entropy. In other words, $H^{tags}(c)$ measures the concentration of confidence values of all association rules whose antecedent is c. If a term is absent in the training set, it receives an arbitrarily high entropy, as, in this case, the result is not a real number. Term entropy can be useful particularly for breaking ties, as it is better to recommend more "consistent" or less "confusing" terms. Whereas term entropy was used in [11] only to evaluate recommendations, we here apply it as an input to the recommendation functions.

4. TAG RECOMMENDATION STRATEGIES

We now turn our attention to the analyzed tag recommendation strategies. We start by describing, in Section 4.1, the three baselines, which, as previously mentioned, exploit at most two of the following: term co-occurrence with

[4]We do not include tags to compute any of the descriptive power metrics, as it does not make sense to use tags previously assigned to the target object as candidates for recommendation.

pre-assigned tags, multiple textual features and metrics of relevance. Next, in Section 4.2, we introduce our new heuristics, which exploit these three dimensions and include novel relevance metrics. Our learning-to-rank based strategies, which also exploit the three dimensions as well as a larger set of relevance metrics, are presented in Section 4.3.

4.1 State-of-the-Art Baselines

Our first baseline is Sum^+, the best function proposed in [22], which exploits both tag co-occurrences and metrics of relevance. It extends the Sum metric (Eq. 1) by weighting the confidence values by the $Stability$ of the terms in the antecedent and consequent of the corresponding association rules, which are here generated by the *Apriori* algorithm [1]. Given a candidate c for an object o, Sum^+ is defined as:

$$Sum^+(c, o, k_x, k_c, k_r) = \sum_{x \in \mathcal{I}_o} \theta(x \rightarrow c) \times Stab(x, k_x) \times Stab(c, k_c) \times Rank(c, o, k_r) \quad (9)$$

where k_x, k_c and k_r are tuning parameters. $Rank(c, o, k_r)$ is equal to $k_r/(k_r + p(c, o))$, where $p(c, o)$ is the position of c in the ranking of candidates according to the confidence of the corresponding association rule. This factor is employed to make confidence values decay smoother.

Sum^+, as most co-occurrence based strategies [22, 9], restricts the size of the association rules to only one tag in the antecedent (i.e., ℓ=1) due to efficiency issues. In contrast, $LATRE$ - Lazy Associative Tag Recommender [19], our second baseline, is able to efficiently generate larger association rules by doing it *on demand*. This is in contrast to other strategies (e.g., *Apriori*), which compute all rules from the training set beforehand (i.e., offline), possibly including rules that might not be useful when recommending for objects in the test set. $LATRE$ ranks each candidate c by the sum of the confidences of all rules containing c. That is, it uses the Sum metric (Eq. 1) with $\ell \geq 1$, thus exploiting solely co-occurrence patterns. We note that two variations of $LATRE$, with and without calibration, are presented in [19]. We here consider the $LATRE$ without calibration since it has lower complexity and, according to [19], produces very similar results to those obtained with calibration, with no significant differences in most cases.

Our third baseline is *Co-occurrence and Text based Tag Recommender* (CTTR), which exploits terms extracted from other textual features and a metric of relevance, but does not consider tags previously assigned to the *target object*. CTTR is an adaptation of the winner of the ECML Discovery Challenge 2009 [16], which, in addition to both aforementioned aspects, also takes the user tag assignment history into account to provide personalized recommendations. We here do not include user statistics in CTTR as we aim at providing recommendations for a target object, thus leaving personalization for future work. We note however that, comparing our methods, which also consider terms extracted from other features, against CTTR allows us to assess the benefits of applying our metrics of relevance to such terms and to exploit co-occurrence of previously assigned tags.

In a nutshell, CTTR first extracts term candidates from the title and the description of the target object. For each such term c, it assigns a basic score, which is the fraction of objects containing c in the given textual feature (title or description) that also contain c as a tag. The authors then use a *leading precision rescorer* for weighting the different candidate sources, thus producing new scores for each term c. These new scores are then merged in a probabilistic sum. Terms extracted from the title (first step) as well as from the title-description merge are then expanded through association rules[5]. CTTR distinguishes two types of co-occurrences: (1) between tags, in which the antecedents are tags in the objects of the training set, and (2) between terms in the title of an object and its tags, in which the antecedents are terms in the titles of such objects. At recommendation time, the sets of rules related to the extracted terms are combined using corresponding scores. As a final step, the scores obtained from the association rules and from the title and description of the target objects are rescored once again, and merged, resulting in the final ranking. We omit a detailed description of CTTR due to space constraints.

4.2 Our New Heuristics

Our new heuristics extend the Sum^+ and $LATRE$ baselines to also include one of the four metrics of descriptive power, i.e., TF, TS, wTF or wTS (Section 3.3). We thus propose eight new ranking functions composed by a weighted linear combination of the output of Sum^+ (or of $LATRE$) and one of the four metrics. Let DP be the selected metric, and c be a candidate term for target object o. The proposed heuristics have the following general structures:

$$Sum^+DP(c, o, k_x, k_c, k_r, \alpha) = \alpha Sum^+(c, o, k_x, k_c, k_r) + (1 - \alpha)DP(c, o) \quad (10)$$

$$LATRE + DP(c, o, \ell, \alpha) = \alpha Sum(c, o, \ell) + (1 - \alpha)DP(c, o) \quad (11)$$

Parameter α ($0 \leq \alpha \leq 1$) is used as a weighting factor. Note that Sum^+ and Sum are computed only over candidates generated from the association rules, whereas DP (i.e., TS, TF, wTS or wTF) is computed for terms extracted from other textual features of target object o.

4.3 Learning-to-Rank Based Strategies

We here investigate the potential benefits of applying L2R techniques to the tag recommendation problem. The basic idea is to use such algorithms to "learn" a *good ranking function* based on a list $L_{metrics}$ of metrics of relevance. We here consider both the traditional RankSVM method (Section 4.3.1) and the Genetic Programming (GP) framework (Section 4.3.2). In both cases, $L_{metrics}$ includes Sum, IFF, $Stab$, TS, TF, wTS, wTF, H^{tags} and Sum^+, defined in Eqs. 1-9. In particular, we include Sum with ℓ=3, as used by the $LATRE$ baseline. We also include in $L_{metrics}$ two other functions, called $Vote$ and $Vote^+$, proposed in [22]. For a given candidate c and target object o, $Vote(c, o)$ is the number of association rules whose antecedent is a term in $\mathcal{I}_o$ and whose consequent is the candidate term c. $Vote^+$, like Sum^+, is built from $Vote$ by weighting each vote by the Stabilities of both antecedent and consequent. That is:

$$Vote(c, o) = \sum_{x \in \mathcal{I}_o} j, \text{ where } j = \begin{cases} 1, & \text{if}(x \rightarrow c) \in \mathcal{R} \\ 0, & otherwise \end{cases} \quad (12)$$

$$Vote^+(c, o, k_x, k_c, k_r) = \sum_{x \in \mathcal{I}_o} j \times Stab(x, k_x) \times Stab(c, k_c) \times Rank(c, x, k_r), \text{ where } j = \begin{cases} 1, & if \quad x \rightarrow c \in \mathcal{R} \\ 0, & otherwise \end{cases} \quad (13)$$

For both proposed strategies, the candidate tags $\mathcal{C}_o$ for each object o include all terms generated by $LATRE$ and

[5] We here apply the *Apriori* method.

all terms extracted from other textual features. For each candidate $c \in \mathcal{C}_o$, for each object o, we compute all metrics in $L_{metrics}$ using the training set $\mathcal{D}$ (e.g., for *Stab*, *IFF*) and the textual features associated with o. Each candidate c is then represented by a vector of metric values $M_c \in \mathbb{R}^m$, where m is the number of considered metrics. We also assign a binary label Y_c to each candidate c for each object v in validation set $\mathcal{V}$, indicating whether c is a relevant recommendation for v (Y_c=1) or not (Y_c=0), based on the contents of $\mathcal{Y}_v$. Note that we use training set $\mathcal{D}$ only to extract the association rules and to compute the metrics, relying on validation set $\mathcal{V}$ to learn the solutions (see discussion in Section 5.2). Thus, we only assign labels Y_c for objects in $\mathcal{V}$. The learned model, i.e., ranking function $f(M_c)$, is then applied to each candidate c for each object o in the test set. All reported results are based on the performance on the test sets. Next, we describe how we applied RankSVM and GP to the tag recommendation problem.

4.3.1 RankSVM Based Strategy

RankSVM is based on the state-of-the-art Support Vector Machine (SVM) classification method [13]. We use the SVM-rank tool[6] to learn a function $f(M_c)$=$f(W, M_c)$, where $W = <w_1, w_2, ...w_m>$ is a vector of weights associated with the considered metrics (i.e., $W \in \mathbb{R}^m$). W is learned by a maximum-margin optimization method that tries to find a hyperplane, defined by W, that best separates the "closest" candidate tags (represented by their metric vectors in $\mathbb{R}^m$) belonging to two different *levels of relevance* (i.e., relevant and irrelevant) assigned to each object-candidate pair in the training. They are employed to produce ranking statements (i.e., relevant tags must precede irrelevant ones), which in turn are used as input to the RankSVM learning process. At recommendation time, $f(M_c)$ is used to rank all candidates for target object o according to the their relative distances to the separating hyperplane.

RankSVM has two main parameters, namely, the type of kernel function, which indicates the structure of the solution function, and cost j, which controls the penalty given to classification errors in the training process. RankSVM is still a very competitive performer when considering average results across all collections in the LETOR 3.0 L2R benchmark[7], besides being readily available for experimentation, unlike other methods, which are proprietary.

4.3.2 GP Based Strategy

We apply GP to find a good ranking function $f(M_c)$ for tagging recommendation purposes. This is done through the evolution of a population in which each individual represents a different ranking function. This evolution is inspired on the biological mechanisms of natural selection and survival of the "strongest" or most "adapted" individuals. Next, we provide an overview of a GP algorithm, and introduce how we model the tag recommendation problem with it.

Overview of the GP Framework

Genetic Programming (GP) implements a global search mechanism. A GP algorithm evolves a population of tree-represented individuals (i.e., the solutions for the problem at hand), created from a set of terminals and functions related to the target problem. In each generation of the evolutionary process, individuals are evaluated according to a specific quality metric, calculated by a *Fitness* function. That is, the Fitness value is used as a criterion to select the best individuals, which will transmit their characteristics to the future generations through operations like crossover and mutation. We here implement the *tournament selection* method, which randomly chooses, with replacement, k individuals from the population and takes the one with highest Fitness value.

While the number of new individuals is smaller than the desired population size n, two individuals are picked through the adopted selection method, and, with probability p_c, have their "genetic material" exchanged in the *crossover* operation to generate a new individual. That is, we randomly choose one node of each of the two trees (the two individuals) and exchange the subtrees below them. The role of the crossover operation is to combine good solutions towards the most promising solutions in the search space. Moreover, with probability p_m, the *mutation* operation is performed to introduce new individuals (i.e., solutions) in the population, increasing its diversity. This is useful, for example, to avoid that the whole evolutionary process gets trapped in local minima during the search process. Here, the mutation of an individual (i.e., a tree) is performed by first randomly selecting one of its nodes, and then replacing it (and its corresponding subtree) by a new randomly generated subtree, without exceeding a maximum tree depth d.

The whole process is repeated until a target Fitness value f^{target} or a maximum number of generations g is reached. At the end, the individual with best fitness value, which usually belongs to the last generation in the evolutionary process, is chosen as the final solution for the problem.

GP is an effective non-linear method that has been successfully employed when there is a large search space and a goal to be optimized, having produced results close to the optimal in many applications [3]. Indeed, GP has been applied to various Information Retrieval tasks such as classification, search/ranking and image retrieval (e.g., [27]). However, to our knowledge, we are the first to apply it to tag recommendation. Our motivations are twofold. First, in comparison with RankSVM, GP exploits a different learning paradigm, which directly optimizes a target function (e.g., recommendation precision). Second, GP has been demonstrated to be competitive with other learning-to-rank techniques such as RankSVM itself and RankBoost [27, 8][8]. As we shall see, GP outperforms RankSVM in a few scenarios being statistically tied with it in many others.

GP Applied to Tag Recommendation

To apply GP to tag recommendation, we need to define the tree representation of an individual, which, in our case, is a tag ranking function, and a Fitness function. A tree is composed of terminals (leaves) and non-terminals (internal nodes). We choose the sum (+), subtraction (−), multiplication (×), division (/) and natural logarithm (*ln*) operations as non-terminals. The terminals are composed of variables and constants (uniformly distributed between 0 and 1). The variable set includes the (values of the) metrics in the given $L_{metrics}$ list, which, for a candidate c, is given by vector M_c. To ensure the closure property, we implement protected di-

[6] http://www.cs.cornell.edu/People/tj/svm_light/svm_rank.html

[7] http://research.microsoft.com/en-us/um/beijing/projects/letor

[8] In some initial tests with RankBoost and with an associative method for learning-to-rank [24], we found them to be very inefficient to train for the size of our collections.

vision and logarithm, such that these operators return the default value 0 when their inputs are out of their domains. As an example, a tree representing function $Sum+0.7\times TS$ contains operation "+" as root, with variable "Sum" and operation "×" as its children. Internal node "×", in turn, has constant "0.7" and variable "TS" as children.

The Fitness of an individual in this context represents the quality of the recommendations produced by the corresponding ranking function, which is here assessed in terms of the precision of the top-k terms in the ranking of recommended terms[9]. Given a ranking function $f(M_c)$, let $\mathcal{Y}_o$ be the set of relevant tags for an object o (identified by labels Y_c), $\mathcal{R}_o^f$ be the ranked recommendations produced by $f(M_c)$ for o, and $\mathcal{R}_{k,o}^f$ the top k elements of $\mathcal{R}_o^f$. The quality of the recommendations produced by f for o is measured as:

$$P@k(\mathcal{R}_o^f, \mathcal{Y}_o, f) = \frac{|\mathcal{R}_{k,o}^f \cap \mathcal{Y}_o|}{min(k, |\mathcal{Y}_o|)} \quad (14)$$

The Fitness (i.e., quality) of ranking function $f(M_c)$ is then computed as the average $P@k$ over all recommendations produced by $f(M_c)$ in a sample of objects of size s, extracted from validation set $\mathcal{V}$.

5. EXPERIMENTAL EVALUATION

In this section, we first present the data sets used to evaluate the tag recommendation strategies (Section 5.1) as well as our evaluation methodology (Section 5.2). We then describe how we parameterized each strategy (Section 5.3), and discuss a set of representative results (Section 5.4).

5.1 Data Collections

We evaluate the tag recommendation methods on three datasets, each containing the *title*, *tags* and *description* associated with real objects from LastFM, YouTube and YahooVideo. The LastFM and YouTube datasets were collected in August 2009, following a *snowball sampling*. That is, starting from a set of users (the most popular users) selected as seeds, the crawler recursively collects the objects posted by them and follows their social links to other users, collecting the objects posted by them. Our datasets include the textual features associated with 2,758,992 LastFM artists and with more than 9 million YouTube videos. The YahooVideo dataset was also gathered by snowball sampling, but using the most popular objects as seeds and following links of related videos[10]. It was gathered in October 2008, and contains the features of 160,228 objects. The YahooVideo dataset was the same used in [4], whereas the other two were collected more recently and are significantly larger than the collections analyzed in that work[11].

We considered only objects with textual features in English, and used the Porter Stemming algorithm[12] to remove the affixes of each word in each collected feature. Stemming was used to avoid trivial recommendations such simple variations of the same word (e.g., plural). We also removed stopwords and terms that are either too frequent (with more than 100,000 occurrences) or too rare (with fewer than 30 occurrences), as such terms are poor recommendations [22].

[9] We also experimented with other Fitness functions (e.g., Mean Average Precision - MAP) obtaining similar results.

[10] We adopted a slightly different sampling strategy for LastFM and YouTube, exploiting users and social links as opposed to videos and related video links, as we intend to use the collected datasets to evaluate personalized recommendation strategies in the future. As YahooVideo does not publish per-user information on tag assignment, we chose not to crawl that application again, thus relying on our previously gathered dataset.

[11] http://vod.dcc.ufmg.br/recc/

[12] http://tartarus.org/ martin/PorterStemmer/

Table 1: Object Subsets.

Dataset	Smallest Interval		Medium Interval		Largest Interval	
	#tags/ object	#objs	#tags/ object	#objs	#tags/ object	#objs
LastFM	2-4	63,973	5-6	93,080	7-507	78,439
Yahoo	2-6	43,353	7-11	54,143	12-52	49,372
YouTube	2-5	2.2mi	6-9	1.7mi	10-77	1.6mi

5.2 Evaluation Methodology

Similarly to [9, 20, 19, 10], we adopt a fully-automated evaluation methodology: we use a subset of the object's preassigned tags as an *expected answer* for the recommendation, that is, as the relevant tags for that object. As such, these tags are disregarded for the computation of metrics of relevance. This methodology was adopted because the manual evaluation of tag relevance is a very expensive process that may be affected by the subjectivity of human judgments. We note that the results obtained according to the proposed methodology represent lower bounds, as some of the recommended tags, although not in the expected answer, might still be considered relevant for the given object.

Following the proposed methodology, for each object $o = \langle \mathcal{I}_o, \mathcal{F}_o, \mathcal{Y}_o \rangle$ in the test and validation sets, we randomly select half of its tags to be included in $\mathcal{I}_o$. The other half are included in $\mathcal{Y}_o$, the expected answer for o. We also use title and description as textual features in $\mathcal{F}_o$, for each object o.

We use the $P@k$ metric (Eq. 14) with k=5 as the primary metric to evaluate all recommendation strategies. We also measure the *recall* and the *mean average precision (MAP)* of the recommendations. Recall is the fraction of the set of relevant tags for an object that were indeed recommended, whereas MAP considers the order in which tags are recommended, emphasizing ranking relevant tags higher [2].

We evaluate each recommendation method on each dataset in two scenarios. In the former, we divide each dataset into three object subsets based on the number of tags available in the object, so that each subset contains roughly the same number of objects, as shown in Table 1. We refer to the subsets as the *smallest*, *medium* or *largest* interval, referring to the range of number of tags per object in each of them. We evaluate each method separately for each subset, thus assessing its effectiveness under different amounts of training data. In a second, *mixed* scenario, we consider each dataset entirely, thus building a solution for a more heterogeneous object set. Thus, in the first scenario, we compute tag co-occurrence patterns and other metrics of relevance, "learn" solutions and perform parameter tuning for each subset separately, thus building more specialized recommendation functions. In the mixed scenario, a single function is built for all objects, with obviously lower cost.

For the first scenario, we randomly sample 50,000 objects from each subset (40,000 for YahooVideo). For the second scenario, we use a sample consisting of the combination of all three subset samples used in the first scenario. In both cases, each sample is divided into five equal-sized portions, which are used in a five-fold cross validation. That is, three

Table 2: **Selected Values for Subset of Parameters of Analyzed Recommendation Methods.**

Parameter	LastFM				YahooVideo				YouTube			
	Mixed	Smallest	Medium	Largest	Mixed	Smallest	Medium	Largest	Mixed	Smallest	Medium	Largest
σ_{min}	2	2	2	2	2	2	2	2	1	1	1	1
θ_{min}	0.2	0.01	0.1	0.4	0.2	0.01	0.2	0.3	0.1	0.01	0.1	0.2
$\alpha(Sum^{+}DP)$	0.95	0.95	0.95	0.95	0.8	0.8	0.8	0.7	0.8	0.8	0.8	0.7
$\alpha(LATRE{+}DP)$	0.99	0.95	0.95	0.99	0.9	0.8	0.9	0.95	0.9	0.7	0.8	0.95

portions are treated as training set ($\mathcal{D}$), which is used for extracting association rules and computing all metrics. A fourth portion is used as validation set $\mathcal{V}$, which, in turn, is used to "learn" the solutions (i.e., to compute the Fitness function in the GP evolutionary process, and to learn vector W in RankSVM) and to tune parameters of all recommendation methods (including the RankSVM based strategy, using cross-validation in $\mathcal{V}$). The last portion is used for testing.

Note that, our use of the 5-fold cross-validation process for both L2R based strategies is slightly different from the traditional use: we learn the ranking function and select parameter values in the validation set $\mathcal{V}$. We do so to avoid overfitting, which could occur if the solutions were learned in the same set from which association rules and metrics were extracted (i.e., training set $\mathcal{D}$), as metrics derived from the rules could be over-inflated[13]. We argue that our experimental design is fair because: 1) we do not use any privileged information from the test set in which results of all methods are reported; 2) all parameters are discovered in the same validation set; 3) our collections are large enough for effective learning, even when we conduct cross-validation in $\mathcal{V}$ for parameterization (e.g., results in these preliminaries experiments are basically identical to the ones reported in the test with the discovered parameters); and 4) the very tight confidence intervals reported in our results (Section 5.4) are evidence of low variation and thus learning convergence. Moreover, having a large amount of training data to generate the tag co-occurrence rules can help increasing the coverage of the rules (i.e., more co-occurrences can be potentially found), thus generating more candidates and more precise metric values. This benefits all methods.

5.3 Parameterization

Our evaluation starts with a series of experiments with the validation set $\mathcal{V}$ to find the best parameters of each method. The results of such experiments are omitted due to space constraints. In summary, we found that, for both Sum^{+} and $Sum^{+}DP$ (for DP equal to TS, TF, wTS and wTF), the best parameters are $k_r{=}k_x{=}k_c{=}5$. Best results for α varied between 0.7 and 1.0. We search for the aforementioned parameters sequentially, varying one of them at each time and fixing the others. For $LATRE$, $LATRE{+}DP$ and L2R based strategies, we set $\ell{=}3$, as in [19]. We also set k_s, parameter of the $Stab$ metric, equal to 5. Parameters σ_{min} and θ_{min} directly impact the number of association rules generated, thus affecting the processing time of the recommender. We look for a good trade off between processing time and recommendation precision. The lower σ_{min} (or θ_{min}), the larger the number of rules, thus, the longer the processing time. In most cases, precision decreases as σ_{min} and θ_{min} increase, particularly when fewer tags are provided, as the number of generated candidates is already small in this case.

[13]We did observe this overfitting problem in initial tests, with the learned solutions having lower generalization capabilities.

However, when the number of input tags is larger, the choice of thresholds can be more aggressive with no significant impact on precision. Thus, we chose σ_{min} and θ_{min} so that the precision loss, with respect to results for $\sigma_{min}{=}\theta_{min}{=}0$, is under 3%. Table 2 shows the selected values of some parameters. The chosen values for σ_{min} and θ_{min} are the same for all co-occurrence based methods.

For RankSVM, we tested two kernel functions, Linear and Radial Basis (RBF), choosing the former as the latter did not scale to our data sets. Using cross-validation in $\mathcal{V}$, we also varied cost j between 10^{-3} and 10^{3}, finding that the best choice was $j{=}100$, in most cases. We also tried different strategies to normalize our feature vectors, including L2-norm, z-score and the LETOR normalization procedure [17], with no improvements. Thus, the results reported here refer to non-normalized data. For the GP based strategy, we experimented, using $\mathcal{V}$, with population sizes n equal to 50, 100, and 200, selecting $n{=}200$, as the larger population allows a greater coverage of the solution space, leading to better results. For this population size, the algorithm converges (i.e., Fitness values stop improving) before 200 generations, value assigned to g. We fixed $k{=}2$, and set $d{=}7$, $p_c{=}0.6$ and $p_m{=}0.1$, as usually done in the literature [3]. Computing the Fitness during the evolutionary process over all validation objects can be infeasible. Thus, we used a sample of $s{=}500$ of those objects, as this was enough to learn functions that are more effective than our heuristics.

5.4 Representative Results

We now discuss the most relevant results of our new tag recommendation methods (8 heuristics and 2 L2R based strategies), comparing them against the 3 baselines. Table 3 shows $P@5$ results for all methods, datasets and scenarios. Recall and MAP results are omitted due to space constraints. We comment on them whenever appropriate.

All reported results are averages over 5 folds (test sets). For the GP-based strategy, which is stochastic, each experiment is repeated 5 times. Thus, results are averages over 25 runs (5 folds, 5 seeds). Table 3 also shows 95% confidence intervals, indicating that, with that confidence, results deviate from the reported means by up to 3%. For each dataset, the table is broken into 3 blocks: baselines, new heuristics and L2R based methods. Best results and statistical ties (according to a *2-sided t-test* with p-value < 0.05), within each block are shown as shaded entries. Best overall results (and statistical ties) are shown in bold.

We start with a general finding. The improvements obtained with our methods over the baselines are more modest in the LastFM dataset. This is possibly due to two factors: (1) there tends to be less overlap between the contents of title, description and tags associated with the same object on LastFM [7], which leads to a greater concentration of TS (and wTS) around small values, making it difficult to distinguish "good" from "bad" terms using these metrics; and (2) the number of tags per object tends to be smaller in our

LastFM dataset (e.g., 48% and 73% of our YahooVideo and YouTube objects have fewer than 10 tags, against 88% of LastFM objects). These factors limit the benefits from using TS and wTS and from exploiting co-occurrence patterns among pre-assigned tags in that dataset.

We now turn our attention to the relative performance of specific methods, starting with the baselines. Consistently with [19], we find that $LATRE$ outperforms Sum^+ (up to 25% in $P@5$, 33% in recall, and 31% in MAP) in most cases. However, $CTTR$ does appear as a good alternative to $LATRE$ in a few cases, particularly on YouTube (gains in $P@5$, recall and MAP of up to 111%, 63% and 75%).

Considering the best baseline in each scenario and dataset, we find that our heuristics produce gains in $P@5$ of as much as 40%, and in recall and MAP of up to 32% and 62%, respectively. Thus, introducing a metric of descriptive power can greatly improve recommendation effectiveness, particularly for objects with smaller number of tags (smallest interval). This is because fewer available tags restrict the benefits from exploiting tag co-occurrence. In such cases, our heuristics greatly benefit from also exploiting descriptive metrics.

Comparing each new heuristic with the original method on which it was based (Sum^+ or $LATRE$), we find that our heuristics provide gains of up to 181% in $P@5$, 116% in recall, and 186% in MAP (e.g, Sum^+wTS over Sum^+ on the smallest interval of YouTube). As discussed, the gains for LastFM are more modest (e.g., up to 4.6% in $P@5$). In comparison with $CTTR$, the gains in $P@5$, recall and MAP reach 98%, 32% and 96%, respectively, indicating great benefits from exploiting co-occurrences with tags previously assigned to the target object as well as descriptive metrics.

Among the new heuristics, the most promising one is $LATRE{+}wTS$, as it yields the best results in most cases. To reach this conclusion, we make two observations. First, for any given descriptive metric DP (i.e., TS, TF, wTS or wTF), $LATRE{+}DP$ outperforms Sum^+DP in most cases (up to 15% in $P@5$, 20% in recall, and 15% in MAP), confirming the benefits of exploiting more complex association rules. In the few cases where Sum^+DP outperforms $LATRE{+}DP$, the gains in $P@5$ are under 3%. This happens specifically in LastFM, where, in general, the differences between Sum^+DP and $LATRE{+}DP$ are smaller, possibly due to the smaller number of tags per object which restricts the number of more complex rules that can be mined. Conversely, the improvements of $LATRE{+}DP$ over Sum^+DP tend to be higher for objects with larger number of tags, particularly on YouTube and YahooVideo.

Our second observation is that, comparing all four descriptive metrics, wTS tends to yield the best results (or close to them), often followed by wTF, TS and TF. In particular, the use of wTS in $LATRE{+}wTS$, as opposed to the traditional TF metric, leads to gains of up to 8.3% in $P@5$. This is mainly because wTS considers that objects are composed of different features which may have different descriptive capacities. TF, in turn, tends to favor very frequent terms, even those appearing in a single feature, which are often less relevant than terms appearing in multiple features.

Turning our attention to the L2R based strategies, both methods provide some further improvements. For instance, the gains in $P@5$ and MAP obtained with the RankSVM based strategy over $LATRE{+}wTS$ can reach 4.8% and 3.2%, respectively. With the GP based strategy, corresponding gains reach 12% and 10% (e.g., largest interval on LastFM).

Table 3: Average P@5 Results and 95% Confidence Intervals: Best Results Within Each Block (Baselines, Heuristics, L2R based Strategies) in Shaded Entries. Best Overall Results in Bold.

LastFM

Strategy	Mixed	Smallest	Medium	Largest
Sum+	0.411±.001	.454±.003	.433±.004	.391±.001
LATRE	0.405±.001	.465±.004	.457±.005	.384±.004
CTTR	0.260±.001	.285±.003	.267±.002	.217±.002
Sum+TF	0.417±.001	.470±.004	.436±.004	.395±.001
Sum+TS	0.418±.002	.472±.005	.439±.004	.396±.001
Sum+wTF	0.417±.001	.470±.005	.436±.004	.395±.001
Sum+wTS	0.417±.002	.470±.005	.438±.004	.396±.001
LATRE+TF	0.408±.001	.479±.004	.459±.005	.385±.004
LATRE+TS	0.411±.001	.487±.005	.466±.005	.388±.003
LATRE+wTF	0.408±.001	.479±.004	.459±.005	.385±.004
LATRE+wTS	0.411±.001	.486±.005	.465±.005	.388±.003
GP-based	**0.433±.003**	**.500±.005**	**.476±.002**	**.434±.003**
SVM-based	0.411±.002	**.499±.007**	.450±.005	.393±.003

YahooVideo

Strategy	Mixed	Smallest	Medium	Largest
Sum+	0.484±.003	.453±.007	.511±.004	.615±.004
LATRE	0.608±.003	.525±.006	.619±.004	.731±.006
CTTR	0.465±.004	.649±.005	.407±.004	.394±.003
Sum+TF	0.643±.003	.755±.002	.597±.003	.663±.005
Sum+TS	0.674±.003	.764±.003	.631±.003	.714±.004
Sum+wTF	0.666±.002	.784±.003	.612±.003	.673±.004
Sum+wTS	0.707±.002	.795±.004	.660±.003	.721±.004
LATRE+TF	0.698±.002	.781±.002	.673±.004	.745±.007
LATRE+TS	0.716±.003	.785±.004	.710±.003	.778±.007
LATRE+wTF	0.729±.002	.821±.004	.706±.003	.754±.006
LATRE+wTS	0.733±.003	.818±.005	.729±.003	.780±.007
GP-based	**0.743±.007**	**.822±.004**	**.734±.003**	**.789±.006**
SVM-based	**0.752±.002**	**.826±.003**	.725±.003	**.800±.005**

YouTube

Strategy	Mixed	Smallest	Medium	Largest
Sum+	0.245±.002	.211±.006	.212±.003	.282±.004
LATRE	0.285±.004	.219±.005	.242±.005	.326±.006
CTTR	0.376±.002	.463±.005	.337±.004	.269±.002
Sum+TF	0.462±.001	.552±.004	.421±.006	.403±.003
Sum+TS	0.475±.002	.560±.004	.433±.005	.419±.004
Sum+wTF	0.490±.002	.583±.003	.451±.005	.416±.004
Sum+wTS	0.502±.003	.593±.003	.461±.005	.431±.004
LATRE+TF	0.472±.002	.557±.004	.436±.004	.425±.006
LATRE+TS	0.407±.003	.561±.004	.445±.004	.441±.007
LATRE+wTF	0.503±.003	**.596±.004**	.464±.004	.439±.005
LATRE+wTS	0.489±.003	.593±.003	.471±.005	.450±.007
GP-based	0.507±.001	**.595±.003**	.477±.002	**.462±.003**
SVM-based	**0.512±.002**	**.601±.005**	**.484±.005**	**.468±.003**

Thus, improvements are, in general, somewhat modest, although they can be more significant in a few specific cases. In terms of recall, results are the same as the three strategies generate the same candidates for each object.

Such overall modest improvements are due to the fact that both GP and RankSVM, in spite of receiving a list with several metrics, are mostly exploiting those used by $LATRE{+}wTS$. Indeed, we verified that the most frequent metric used by the best function produced by the GP process at its final generation is $Sum(c, o, 3)$ (also used by LATRE). Considering all datasets and scenarios, $Sum(c, o, 3)$ occurs in 95% of the generated functions. The next most frequent metric is wTS, which occurs in 74% of the functions. IFF comes next, occurring in 49% of the functions. All other metrics appear in less than 25% of the functions. Similarly, we also analyzed the weight vector W learned by RankSVM, finding that the largest weights, on average, are indeed associated with $Sum(c, o, 3)$ and wTS.

Although the L2R strategies yield only modest gains over our best heuristic, we note that they provide flexible frameworks that can be easily extended to incorporate new metrics and to exploit other aspects of the tag recommendation problem (e.g., personalization). We also note that, after the offline training step, the use of the functions generated by either GP or RankSVM, at recommendation time, does not incur in significant extra processing time in relation to the best heuristic. One possible source of delay for all of them is the on-demand generation of association rules by $LATRE$. However, as shown in [19], $LATRE$'s average processing time is well-suited for real-time recommendation.

The best L2R based strategy depends on the dataset. On LastFM, the GP based method leads to somewhat better results (up to 10% in $P@5$ for the largest interval), whereas on YahooVideo and YouTube, there is a statistical tie in most object sets with a slight advantage for either method over the other in a few cases. Comparing both solutions in terms of training time on our datasets, we also find that the most efficient technique depends on the dataset. For instance, the GP based method requires, on average, 63.5, 50.4 and 30.6 minutes to train on the LastFM, YouTube and YahooVideo datasets, respectively, running on an Intel 2.83GHz Quad-Core with 8GB RAM. Corresponding numbers for RankSVM are 100.8, 28.3 and (surprisingly) 0.81 minutes. We also note that, except on the YahooVideo dataset, RankSVM's training time exhibits a much higher variability across different folds than GP. We computed 95% confidence intervals for the training times measured over a fixed number of folds, and observed that GP training times deviate from the means by up to 10%, whereas RankSVM results deviate by as much as 48%. In other words, RankSVM's training time seems much more sensitive to the inherently difficulties of the input data.

6. CONCLUSIONS AND FUTURE WORK

In this paper, we proposed several new tag recommendation strategies that jointly exploit term co-occurrence with pre-assigned tags, multiple textual features and metrics of relevance. We proposed and evaluated eight new heuristics and two learning-to-rank based strategies, comparing them against three state-of-the-art techniques, in various datasets and scenarios. Our results indicate that our best heuristic, $LATRE{+}wTS$ provides gains of up to 40% in terms of precision, 32% in recall and 62% in MAP, over the best baseline in any analyzed scenario. Some further improvement (up to 12% in precision) can also be achieved with the RankSVM and GP based methods, although the best learning-to-rank strategy depends on the specific dataset. These results illustrate the benefits of jointly exploiting the three aforementioned dimensions, particularly metrics of descriptive power. Moreover, the use of learning-to-rank techniques arise as a promising solution, as they yield very competitive results while still being quite flexible, allowing the easy inclusion of new metrics and the extension of the scope of the problem.

Future work includes a manual evaluation of our solutions and extensions to address personalized recommendation.

7. REFERENCES

[1] R. Agrawal and R. Srikant. Fast Algorithms For Mining Association Rules. In *VLDB*, 1994.

[2] R. Baeza-Yate and B. Ribeiro-Neto. *Modern Information Retrieval*. Addison-Wesley, 1999.

[3] W. Banzhaf, P. Nordin, R. E. Keller, and F. D. Francone. *Genetic Programming – An Introduction On The Automatic Evolution Of Computer Programs And Its Applications*. Morgan Kaufmann, 1998.

[4] F. Belém, E. Martins, J. Almeida, M. Gonçalves, and G. Pappa. Exploiting Co-occurrence and Information Quality Metrics to Recommend Tags in Web 2.0 Applications. In *CIKM*, 2010.

[5] S. Boll. MultiTube–Where Web 2.0 And Multimedia Could Meet. *IEEE MultiMedia*, 14(1), 2007.

[6] H. Cao, M. Xie, L. Xue, C. Liu, F. Teng, and Y. Huang. Social Tag Prediction Based On Supervised Ranking Model. In *PKDD*, 2009.

[7] F. Figueiredo, F. Belem, H. Pinto, J. Almeida, M. Gonçalves, D. Fernandes, E. Moura, and M. Cristo. Evidence Of Quality Of Textual Features On The Web 2.0. In *CIKM*, 2009.

[8] Y. Freund, R. Iyer, R. E. Schapire, and Y. Singer. An Efficient Boosting Algorithm For Combining Preferences. *Journal Of Machine Learning Research*, 2003.

[9] N. Garg and I. Weber. Personalized, Interactive Tag Fecommendation For Flickr. In *RecSys*, 2008.

[10] Z. Guan, J. Bu, Q. Mei, C. Chen, and C. Wang. Personalized Tag Recommendation Using Graph-Based Ranking On Multi-Type Interrelated Objects. In *SIGIR*, 2009.

[11] P. Heymann, D. Ramage, and H. Garcia-Molina. Social Tag Prediction. In *SIGIR*, 2008.

[12] R. Jäschke, L. Marinho, A. Hotho, L. Schmidt - Thieme, and G. Stumme. Tag Recommendations In Folksonomies. In *PKDD*, 2007.

[13] T. Joachims. Training Linear SVMs In Linear Time. In *KDD*, 2006.

[14] G. Koutrika, F. A. Effendi, Z. Gyöngyi, P. Heymann, and H. Garcia-Molina. Combating Spam In Tagging Systems: An Evaluation. *ACM Trans. Web*, 2(4), 2008.

[15] R. Krestel, P. Fankhauser, and W. Nejdl. Latent Dirichlet Allocation For Tag Recommendation. In *RecSys*, 2009.

[16] M. Lipczak, Y. Hu, Y. Kollet, and E. Milios. Tag Sources For Recommendation In Collaborative Tagging Systems. In *PKDD*, volume 497, 2009.

[17] T. Liu, J. Xu, T. Qin, W. Xiong, and H. Li. Letor: Benchmark dataset for research on learning to rank for information retrieval. In *SIGIR*, 2007.

[18] H. Ma, I. King, and M. Lyu. Learning To Recommend With Social Trust Ensemble. In *SIGIR*, 2009.

[19] G. Menezes, J. Almeida, F. Belém, M. Gonçalves, A. Lacerda, E. Moura, G. Pappa, A. Veloso, and N. Ziviani. Demand-Driven Tag Recommendation. In *PKDD*, 2010.

[20] S. Rendle and S. Lars. Pairwise Interaction Tensor Factorization For Personalized Tag Recommendation. In *WSDM*, 2010.

[21] S. Siersdorfer, J. San Pedro, and M. Sanderson. Automatic Video Tagging Using Content Redundancy. In *SIGIR*, 2009.

[22] B Sigurbjornsson and R. van Zwol. Flickr Tag Recommendation Based On Collective Knowledge. In *WWW*, 2008.

[23] Y. Song, Z. Zhuang, H. Li, Q. Zhao, J. Li, W. Lee, and C. Giles. Real-Time Automatic Tag Recommendation. In *SIGIR*, 2008.

[24] A. Veloso, H. M. de Almeida, M. A. Gonçalves, and W. Meira Jr. Learning To Rank At Query-Time Using Association Rules. In *SIGIR*, 2008.

[25] J. Wang, L. Hong, and B. D. Davison. Tag Recommendation Using Keywords And Association Rules. In *PKDD*, 2009.

[26] L. Wu, L. Yang, N. Yu, and X. Hua. Learning To Tag. In *WWW*, 2009.

[27] J. Yeh, J. Lin, H. Ke, and W. Yang. Learning To Rank For Information Retrieval Using Genetic Programming. In *SIGIR 2007 Workshop: Learning To Rank For Information Retrieval*, 2007.

Evaluating Diversified Search Results Using Per-intent Graded Relevance

Tetsuya Sakai
Microsoft Research Asia, Beijing, P.R.C.
tetsuyasakai@acm.org

Ruihua Song
Microsoft Research Asia, Beijing, P.R.C.
Song.Ruihua@microsoft.com

ABSTRACT

Search queries are often ambiguous and/or underspecified. To accomodate different user needs, search result diversification has received attention in the past few years. Accordingly, several new metrics for evaluating diversification have been proposed, but their properties are little understood. We compare the properties of existing metrics given the premises that (1) queries may have multiple intents; (2) the likelihood of each intent given a query is available; and (3) graded relevance assessments are available for each intent. We compare a wide range of traditional and diversified IR metrics after adding graded relevance assessments to the TREC 2009 Web track diversity task test collection which originally had binary relevance assessments. Our primary criterion is discriminative power, which represents the reliability of a metric in an experiment. Our results show that diversified IR experiments with a given number of topics can be as reliable as traditional IR experiments with the same number of topics, provided that the right metrics are used. Moreover, we compare the intuitiveness of diversified IR metrics by closely examining the actual ranked lists from TREC. We show that a family of metrics called D♯-measures have several advantages over other metrics such as α-nDCG and Intent-Aware metrics.

Categories and Subject Descriptors

H.3.3 [**Information Storage and Retrieval**]: Information Search and Retrieval

General Terms

Experimentation

Keywords

ambiguity, diversity, evaluation, graded relevance, test collection

1. INTRODUCTION

Traditional information retrieval (IR) research has mostly focussed on satisfying clearly specified information needs. However, in Web search, queries are often *ambiguous* and/or *underspecified* [9]. When a search engine has no or little knowledge of the user, the best it can do may be to produce an output that reflects several *interpretations* (or *intents*) of such queries to accomodate a large population of users. In light of this, *search result diversification* is beginning to receive attention [1, 6, 10, 15, 24]. While modern search engines can display multiple blocks of information, some textual and others nontextual, a ranked list of URLs remains the primary output feature today. Hence how to appropriately evaluate a diversified list of URLs is an important research problem for advancing the state-of-the-art of search engines.

A popular method for evaluating *traditional* (i.e. non-diversified) IR is to use *normalised Discounted Cumulative Gain* (nDCG) [11] based on *graded relevance* assessments, taking into account the fact that some relevant documents are more relevant than others. Assuming that we can list up some possible intents for a given ambiguous or underspecified query in advance, a natural extension of the above evaluation framework would be to hire assessors to conduct graded relevance assessments *for each intent* of that query. For example, for the ambiguous query "apple," we should be able to collect documents that are highly/marginally relevant to the intent "Apple the Steve Jobs company," and those that are highly/marginally relevant to the intent "apple the fruit." Moreover, if we know that *some intents are more likely than others*, we should probably reflect that information in evaluating search engines. For example, if a search query log suggests that users are more likely to search for "Apple the company" than for "apple the fruit," the search engine may choose to return more URLs relevant to the former than ones relevant to the latter.

Recently, several evaluation metrics for handling search result diversification have been proposed. Surprisingly, however, not all of them accomodate *per-intent graded relevance* and *intent probabilities*. The objective of this study is to compare the reliability of diversified IR metrics as well as traditional IR metrics on which the diversity metrics are based. By reliability, we informally mean the ability of a metric to detect "real" performance differences as opposed to those observed by chance. As a measure of reliability, we use *discriminative power* [19] which has been used in several evaluation studies over the past five years [7, 17, 20, 25, 29]. In addition, we closely examine some actual ranked lists from TREC and discuss the intuitiveness of different diversified IR metrics.

To our knowledge, our work is the first to use a diversity test collection with per-intent graded relevance data for the purpose of comparing diversified IR metrics. This is somewhat surprising, as many of the existing diversity metrics can handle per-intent graded relevance. We first add graded relevance assessments to the TREC 2009 Web track diversity task test collection which originally had binary relevance assessments. We then examine a wide variety of metrics: six for traditional IR, and eleven for diversified IR. We show that a family of metrics called D♯-measures have several advantages over *α-nDCG* [8] and *Intent-Aware* metrics [1], including

SIGIR'11, July 24–28, 2011, Beijing, China.

high discriminative power and intuitiveness. We also show that the "best" diversified IR metrics can be as discriminative as the "best" traditional IR metrics, given the same number of topics.

The remainder of this paper is organised as follows. Section 2 discusses previous work related to the present study, and Section 3 formally defines the traditional and diversified IR metrics that we examine. Section 4 describes discriminative power, our primary criterion for choosing reliable metrics. Section 5 describes our test collections with per-intent graded relevance data, and Section 6 reports on our experiments. Finally, Section 7 concludes this paper.

2. RELATED WORK

Zhai, Cohen and Lafferty [31] used *subtopic recall* for evaluating *subtopic retrieval*. In the present study, we evaluate subtopic recall, but call it *intent recall*. Zhai, Cohen and Lafferty also defined *S-precision* and *WS-precision* at a given subtopic recall level, but the computation of these two metrics involves an NP-hard problem and an approximation is required. Carterette and Chandar [4] evaluated *faceted topic retrieval*, a task similar to subtopic retrieval. Their evaluation metric was subtopic recall at l_{min}, where l_{min} is the minimum rank at which perfect S-recall can be achieved. But they point out that computing l_{min} is NP-hard.

Clarke *et al.* [8] proposed a metric called α-nDCG for evaluating diversified search results. They view both intents and documents as sets of *nuggets*, and assume that the number of nuggets covered by a document determines the graded relevance of that document. Prior to discounting the *gain* of a document based on its rank (as traditional nDCG does [11]), α-nDCG discounts the gain based on "nuggets already seen." This metric was one of the official metrics used at the TREC 2009 Web track diversity task [6], and the present study uses the official α-nDCG values from TREC for computing its discriminative power.

Clarke, Kolla and Vechtomova [9] proposed *Novelty- and Rank-Biased Precision* (NRBP) by combining the ideas of α-nDCG and *Rank-Biased Precision* [13]. NRBP was used at the recent TREC 2010 Web track diversity task. However, Sakai *et al.* [20] argue that NRBP inherits the weaknesses of both α-nDCG and RBP: one practical weakness of (N)RBP is that it is heavily undernomalised for topics with few relevant documents and does not average well. Moreover, the advantage of NRBP over α-nDCG is not clear (at least in terms of discriminative power) in subsequent experiements reported by Clarke *et al.* [7]. We therefore do not consider NRBP.

Agrawal *et al.* [1] proposed *Intent-Aware* (IA) metrics for evaluating diversified search results. They were the first to explicitly incorporate intent probabilities in IR evaluation. Their approach is simple: compute a traditional metric *for each intent* and then finally take an expectation based on the intent probabilities. Clarke, Kolla and Vechtomova [9] have discussed the possibility of evaluation with IA versions of α-nDCG and NRBP.

Chapelle *et al.* [5] proposed *Expected Reciprocal Rank* (ERR) for traditional IR evaluation, and claimed that its IA version can handle diversified IR evaluation. *ERR-IA* was used at the TREC 2010 Web track diversity task. The essence of ERR is that relevant documents are discounted based on the number of *relevant* documents already seen rather than the absolute document ranks.

Robertson, Kanoulas and Yilmaz [17] recently proposed a metric for traditional IR evaluation called *Graded Average Precision* (GAP). GAP assumes that the user has a binary notion of relevance, but that different users have different thresholds over the relevance levels. The present study examines (for the first time) an IA version of GAP, as well as its normalised version.

Sakai *et al.* [20] proposed an alternative method for evaluating diversified search results. Their key idea is to define (global) graded relevance by combining intent probabilities and per-intent graded relevance. Based on an ideal ranked list thus defined, they introduced a family of metrics which we call *D-measures* and *D♯-measures*. Using the TREC 2009 Web diversity task data which have per-intent *binary* relevance assessments, they reported that D♯-measures perform at least as well as α-nDCG and intent recall in terms of discriminative power, while solving some shortcomings of α-nDCG and IA metrics.

Using the same TREC 2009 data set, Clarke *et al.* [7] also compared different diversified IR metrics (with and without "collection-dependent" normalisation) in terms of discriminative power. They pointed out that IA metrics do not necessarily reward high intent recall. Surprisingly, all of the diversified IR metrics they examined (including α-nDCG and NRBP) underperformed the simple intent recall in terms of discriminative power.

The present study is similar to the work by Sakai *et al.* [20] and Clarke *et al.* [7], but has the following new contributions: (a) It is the first to compare different diversified IR metrics *when per-intent graded relevance assessments are available*. (b) It examines the most extensive set of diversified IR metrics, including (normalised) GAP-IA which is being examined for the first time. All of these metrics can handle graded relevance: hence, in previous work, the full potential of these metrics for diversity evaluation has not been demonstrated. (c) While the previous two studies considered either a uniform [7] or non-uniform [20] intent probability distribution, this study considers both. (d) This study investigates the effect of measurement depth on discriminative power, in contrast to previous work which only considered a document cutoff of 10 [20] or 20 [7]. (e) It uses multiple test collections for evaluating *traditional* IR metrics on which our diversified IR metrics are based.

By employing Mechanical Turk users, Sanderson *et al.* [23] examined the *predictive power* of metrics: if a metric prefers one ranked list over another, does the user also prefer the same list? Using the same TREC 2009 Web diversity task data, they examined some traditional and diversified IR metrics. One of their findings was that diversified IR metrics agree reasonably well with human preferences. Clearly, discriminative power is not the only way to evaluate evaluation metrics (See Section 4), and other approaches, especially those that rely on human subjects (e.g. predictive power), should complement our work.

More recently, Brandt *et al.* [3] proposed a framework for presenting a tree of retrieved URLs dynamically, which includes an evaluation method that is a tree version of the IA approach. This probably deserves an investigation in terms of the user's physical and cognitive load when compared to our flat-list approach.

3. EVALUATION METRICS

3.1 Basic Metrics

First, we formally define some graded-relevance evaluation metrics that have been designed for *traditional* IR evaluation.

Our first premise is that we have relevance levels $\{0, \dots, h\}$, with 0 representing nonrelevance and h representing the highest level. Hence $h = 1$ implies a binary relevance environment. We say that a document is Lx-relevant if its relevance level is x ($0 < x \leq h$). Let R_x denote the number of Lx-relevant documents for a topic and let $R = \sum_x R_x$. Let $J(r) = 1$ if a document at rank r is Lx-relevant ($x > 0$) and $J(r) = 0$ otherwise. Let $C(r) = \sum_{k=1}^{r} J(k)$.

Let GV_x denote the *gain value* for retrieving an Lx-relevant document [11]. Let $g(r) = GV_x$ if a document at rank r is Lx-relevant and $g(r) = 0$ otherwise. Further, let $cg(r) = \sum_{k=1}^{r} g(k)$. We call $g(r)$ and $cg(r)$ the (cumulative) gain at rank r. Also, let

$g^*(r)$ and $cg^*(r)$ denote the (cumulative) gain at rank r in an *ideal ranked list*, obtained by exhaustively listing up Lx-relevant documents in descending order of relevance levels.

We define nDCG and *Q-measure* at document cutoff l as follows [20]:

$$nDCG@l = \frac{\sum_{r=1}^{l} g(r)/\log(r+1)}{\sum_{r=1}^{l} g^*(r)/\log(r+1)} \tag{1}$$

$$Q@l = \frac{1}{\min(l, R)} \sum_{r=1}^{l} J(r) \frac{C(r) + \beta cg(r)}{r + \beta cg^*(r)} \tag{2}$$

where β (≥ 0) is a user persistence parameter for Q. ($\beta = 0$ reduces Q to binary Average Precision.) We let $\beta = 1$ throughout this paper.

Next, we discuss Graded Average Precision (GAP) [17]. GAP assumes that the user considers only relevance levels $x, \ldots, h$ as relevant ($x > 0$) and the rest as nonrelevant with probability p_x, and that $\sum_{x=1}^{h} p_x = 1$. Following a recommendation by Robertson, Kanoulas and Yilmaz [17], we consider a uniform probability distribution: $p_x = 1/h$ for $x \geq 1$. In this particular case, GAP can be defined as follows.

Let $X(r) \in \{0, \ldots, h\}$ denote the relevance level of a document at rank r, and let $M(r,k) = \min(X(r), X(k))$ for any pair of ranks (r,k). Then the *Expected Precision* (EP) [17] at rank r is given by $EP(r) = \frac{1}{r}\sum_{k=1}^{r}\sum_{x=1}^{M(r,k)} p_x$. Under the uniformity assumption, it can be rewritten as:

$$EP(r) = \frac{1}{h\,r}\sum_{k=1}^{r}\sum_{x=1}^{M(r,k)} = \frac{1}{2h\,r}\sum_{k=1}^{r} M(r,k)(M(r,k)+1)\,. \tag{3}$$

Similarly, under the same assumption, the maximum possible value of cumulated EP is: $\sum_{x=1}^{h} R_x \sum_{y=1}^{x} p_y = \frac{1}{2h}\sum_{x=1}^{h} R_x\, x(x+1)$. Therefore, GAP can be expressed as:

$$GAP = \frac{\sum_{r=1}^{\infty} EP(r)}{\frac{1}{2h}\sum_{x=1}^{h} x(x+1)R_x} \tag{4}$$

$$= \frac{\sum_{r=1}^{\infty} \frac{1}{r}\sum_{k=1}^{r} M(r,k)(M(r,k)+1)}{\sum_{x=1}^{h} R_x\, x(x+1)}\,. \tag{5}$$

Note that the above denominator represents a summation over all Lx-relevant ($x > 0$) documents, and therefore can also be written as $\sum_{r=1}^{R} X^*(r)(X^*(r)+1)$, where $X^*(r)$ is the relevance level of a document at rank r in an ideal output. For the purpose of Web search evaluation where the number of documents to be evaluated is typically very small (e.g. $l = 10$), a division by the above sum over *all* relevant documents yields a heavily undernormalised metric. (It is usually impossible to list up all relevant documents if there is space for only 10 URLs.) Hence, we also define *normalised GAP* (nGAP) for evaluation with a small document cutoff:

$$nGAP@l = \frac{\sum_{r=1}^{l} \frac{1}{r}\sum_{k=1}^{r} M(r,k)(M(r,k)+1)}{\sum_{r=1}^{l} X^*(r)(X^*(r)+1)}\,. \tag{6}$$

Next, we define *Expected Reciprocal Rank* (ERR) [5]. Let $Pr(r)$ denote the relevance probability of a document at rank r. Let $dsat(r) = \prod_{k=1}^{r}(1 - Pr(k))$, which is interpreted as the probability that the user is dissatisfied with documents from ranks 1 to r. Then ERR is defined based on the expected probability that the user is finally satisfied at rank r:

$$ERR = \sum_{r=1}^{\infty} \frac{Pr(r)dsat(r-1)}{r}\,. \tag{7}$$

Following Chapelle *et al.* [5], we let $Pr(r) = (2^{X(r)} - 1)/2^h$. Note that this makes ERR a very top-heavy metric: any ranked list that has a document of the highest relevance level (h) at rank 1 receives an ERR of $(2^h - 1)/2^h$ or higher. Thus, if we have $h = 3$ relevance levels, the ERR is $7/8 = .875$ or higher; if $h = 4$, the ERR is .938 or higher. Also, in accordance with the above setting for ERR, we let $g(r) = 2^{X(r)} - 1$ for nDCG and Q. This gain value setting appears to be the *de facto* standard for nDCG[1].

Finally, for completeness, we also consider *normalised ERR* [7] for evaluation with a small document cutoff:

$$nERR@l = \frac{\sum_{r=1}^{l} Pr(r)dsat(r-1)/r}{\sum_{r=1}^{l} Pr^*(r)dsat^*(r-1)/r} \tag{8}$$

where $Pr^*(r)$ is the relevance probability of a document at rank r in an ideal ranked list and $dsat^*(r) = \prod_{k=1}^{r}(1 - Pr^*(k))$. However, we expect the impact of normalisation for ERR to be small since unnormalised ERR already tends to take very large values, as we have discussed earlier.

3.2 α-nDCG

Clarke *et al.* [8] proposed α-nDCG for evaluating diversified search results. They view information needs (i.e. intents) and documents as sets of *nuggets*. In their framework, the assessor judges whether each document contains a nugget or not (i.e. makes a binary decision). Let $J_n(r) = 1$ if a document at rank r is relevant to the n-th nugget and 0 otherwise; let $C_n(r) = \sum_{k=1}^{r} J_n(r)$, i.e. the number of documents observed within top r that contained the n-th nugget. Then *novelty-biased gain* $NG(r)$ is defined as:

$$NG(r) = \sum_{n=1}^{m} J_n(r)(1-\alpha)^{C_n(r-1)} \tag{9}$$

where m is the total number of nuggets for the query and $\alpha (< 1)$ is a parameter. Then α-nDCG can be defined by replacing the raw gain values $g(r)$ and $g^*(r)$ in Eq. 1 with the novelty-biased gains. Thus, α-nDCG discounts gains first based on "nuggets already seen," and then based on document ranks. Note that Eq. 9 defines graded relevance simply based on the number of nuggets that a document covers as well as nugget novelty.

Computing the ideal ranked list for α-nDCG is NP-complete [8] and an approximation is required. In this study, we simply use the official α-nDCG values reported at the TREC 2009 Web diversity task where $\alpha = .5$ [6]. Note that this setting of α corresponds to the assumption that the assessor "finds" a nonexistent nugget in a document 50% of the time but never misses an existing nugget, which is arguably counterintuitive [20].

3.3 Intent-Aware (IA) Metrics

Agrawal *et al.* [1] proposed a simple methodology for evaluating diversified search results. First, we assume that, given a query q with several different intents i, the probability of each intent $Pr(i|q)$ can be estimated, where $\sum_i Pr(i|q) = 1$. Second, we assume that document relevance assessments are available for each intent. Then, for example, nDCG for a particular intent i (nDCG$_i$) can be computed first, and finally *nDCG-IA* can be computed as:

$$nDCG\text{-}IA@l = \sum_i Pr(i|q)nDCG_i@l\,. \tag{10}$$

[1]GAP relies on a different notion of graded relevance and its graded relevance setting in our paper is not strictly equivalent to that we use for nDCG, Q and ERR. In the case of GAP with $h = 3$, for example, the uniform probability distribution implies that all users regard $L3$-relevant as relevant, while 67% of them regard $L2$-relevant as relevant, and only 33% regard $L1$-relevant as relevant [17].

Thus, unlike α-nDCG, IA metrics accomodate both intent probabilities and per-intent graded relevance[2]. Other IA metrics can be computed similarly: in the present study, we consider nDCG-IA, (n)GAP-IA and (n)ERR-IA.

One of the disadvantages of IA metrics is that their maximum value is not 1: a single ranked list is almost never ideal for every intent [20]. More importantly, IA metrics tend to be counterintuitive, in that they practically disregard minor intents (i.e. those with relatively low $Pr(i|q)$ values) [7, 20].

3.4 D-measures and D♯-measures

Sakai *et al.* [20] proposed an alternative way to evaluate diversified search results, given intent probabilities and per-intent graded relevance assessments. This solves the undernormalisation problem of IA metrics and also includes a mechanism for explictly boosting *intent recall*, i.e. number of intents covered by a ranked list.

Let us say that document d is relevant to q iff it is relevant to at least one of its intents ($\in \{i\}$). If we assume that the intents are *exclusive* (i.e. a user searching with q has exactly one intent), then the *Probability Ranking Principle* (PRP) [16] reduces to ranking documents by $\sum_i Pr(i|q)Pr(rel = 1|i, d)$, where $Pr(rel = 1|i, d)$ is the probability that document d is relevant to i. Note that relevance is a binary notion here. Let $GV_{i,d}$ denote a gain value for document d with respect to intent i. If we can assign these values so that $Pr(rel = 1|i, d) \propto GV_{i,d}$, then the PRP reduces to ranking documents by $\sum_i Pr(i|q)GV_{i,d}$. This defines a *globally ideal* ranked list, which retrieves documents that are highly relevant to major intents above those that are marginally relevant to minor intents. Based on this ideal list, cumulative-gain-based metrics such as nDCG and Q can be computed, by replacing the raw gain $g(r)$ discussed in Section 3.1 with the *global gain*:

$$GG(r) = \sum_i Pr(i|q)g_i(r) \quad (11)$$

where $g_i(r)$ is the gain value for document at rank r for intent i. Following Sakai *et al.*, we apply this idea to nDCG and Q, and call the resultant metrics *D-nDCG* and *D-Q* (D stands for diversity). Moreover, we collectively call such metrics *D-measures*.

Note that D-measures rely on a single ideal ranked list (in contrast to IA metrics which use multiple "locally ideal" lists), and that the relevance levels are defined more dynamically and implicitly than for traditional nDCG and Q. For example, suppose that we have three *local* (i.e. per-intent) relevance levels $L1$-$L3$. Then, for a topic with three intents, we will have at most $3*3 = 9$ *global* relevance levels. The number of global relevance levels will differ for other topics. Thus, an ideal list is defined not based on a discrete set of relevance levels (which is usually pre-defined over the entire test collection), but based on a sort by the global gain, defined per topic.

Apart from the fact that D-measures avoid the undernomalisation problem of IA metrics by relying on a single "globally ideal" list, these two metric families are quite similar. However, Sakai *et al.* [20] also proposed a simple method to explicitly encourage high intent recall in a search output within the D-measure framework. Let $I\text{-}rec@l$ denote the intent recall at document cutoff l. Then *D♯-measure* ("dee sharp measure") is defined as[3]

$$D\sharp\text{-}measure@l = \gamma I\text{-}rec@l + (1-\gamma)D\text{-}measure@l \quad (12)$$

where γ is a parameter. As Sakai *et al.* showed that the effect of the choice of γ on IR experiments is relatively small due to the fact that I-rec and D-measures are already highly correlated with each other (evidence will be given in Section 6.2), we let $\gamma = .5$ throughout this study. We examine *D♯-nDCG* and *D♯-Q* in this paper. Provided that the document cutoff l is larger or equal to the maximum number of intents, I-rec ranges between 0 and 1, and therefore D♯-measures also range between 0 and 1.

4. DISCRIMINATIVE POWER

Our primary method of comparing evaluation metrics is *discriminative power* [19]. We want metrics that are robust to variation across topics, so that the same conclusion can be reached as to which of two given systems is better, regardless of the choice of the topic set. More precisely, we measure discriminative power by conducting a statistical significance test for different pairs of runs, and counting the number of significantly different pairs. In this study, we randomly sample 20 runs from each test collection so 20*19/2=190 run pairs are tested in each case[4]. For significance testing, we use the two-tailed *paired bootstrap test*, with 1,000 bootstrap samples [19]. Note that this experiment is not about whether the metrics are right or wrong; it is about how metrics can be consistent across experiments and as a result how often differences between systems can be detected with high confidence. We regard high discriminative power as a necessary condition for a good evaluation metric, not as a sufficient condition. Later in this paper, we shall complement our discriminative power results by examining the actual ranked lists and comparing the intuitiveness of different diversity IR metrics.

It has been pointed out that discriminative power is not useful when, for example, the "metric" in question sorts systems alphabetically by the system name as this produces perfectly consistent judgments regardless of the data used [22, 29]. However, we are interested in metrics that are strictly functions of a ranked list of items (i.e. system output) and a set of judged items (i.e. right answers). We are not interested in a "metric" that *knows* that (say) one ranked list is from Google and that the other is from Bing, and *uses this knowledge* to say which is better than the other.

The discriminative power method also provides a natural estimate of the performance difference (Δ) between two systems required to achieve statistical significance. This is done by recording, for every run pair, the Δ that corresponds to the borderline between significance and nonsignificance among the 1,000 trials, and then by selecting the largest value among all run pairs (i.e. a conservative estimate). This is one of the advantages of using the bootstrap test, although other significance tests may be used just for computing discriminative power.

Other methods for evaluating evaluation metrics exist. The *swap method* proposed by Voorhees and Buckley [28] yields results similar to the discriminative power method but cannot directly examine the situation with the full topic set [19, 25]. The *maximum entropy method* [2, 17] can measure the informativeness of metrics but requires a mathematical derivation for each metric. Comparing the metrics with *user clicks* [5, 14] or with *user preferences* [23] should also be useful, and we expect these user-based approaches to complement our work.

[2]Clarke, Kolla and Vechtomova [9] have discussed the possibility of incorporating $Pr(i|q)$ into α-nDCG and NRBP.

[3]We call it D♯-measure because it "sharpens up" D-measure in terms of discriminative power, as we shall demonstrate later.

[4]Note that if we take the "top X% runs" from the run pool based on a metric, this may bias the metrics comparison results.

Table 1: Test collection statistics.

	(a) TREC 2009 Web Track Diversity Task Category A ("TR09DIV")	(b) NTCIR-6 CLIR Chinese ("NTCIR6C")
Documents	ClueWeb09 (approx. one billion Web pages) [6]	CIRB040r (901,446 Chinese news articles)
Topics	50 topics (12 ambiguous; 38 faceted) with 243 subtopics (177 informational; 66 navigational)	50
Intents	199 intents (i.e. subtopics with at least one relevant document). Max. #intents per topic: 6. Max. #intents per document: 5.	-
#relevant	across 50 topics: 4,942; across 199 intents: 6,499.	across 50 topics: 4,405 (1,807 $L1$, 1,519 $L2$ and 1,079 $L3$).

5. DATA

5.1 Adding Graded Relevance to TREC Data

Our experiments rely on the TREC2009 Web track diversity test collection with Category A runs [6], which we call TR09DIV. Some statistics are shown in Table 1(a). Unfortunately, TR09DIV contains neither the intent probabilities ($Pr(i|q)$) nor per-intent graded relevance assessments[5]. Hence, while this is a suitable situation for α-nDCG, it is difficult to demonstrate the advantages of other diversified IR metrics using TR09DIV.

Sakai *et al.* [20] compared D♯-measures, α-nDCG and nDCG-IA in terms of discriminative power and intuitiveness when the intent probability distribution is non-uniform. However, they did not use per-intent graded relevance. In contrast, this study fully utilises the capability of the diversified IR metrics to handle graded relevance, and considers both non-uniform and uniform distributions. To this end, we hired assessors to enrich the per-intent binary relevance data from TREC, as follows.

As Table 1(a) shows, we have 4,942 <topic, relevant document> pairs, or 6,499 <intent, relevant document> pairs. We assumed that all of these documents were judged as "partially relevant" by the TREC assessors[6]. Then, each intent-document pair was re-assessed by two assessors: only this time, each assessor had a choice between "relevant" (the document fully satisfies the information need expressed in the subtopic field) and "partially relevant" (the document only partially satisfies the information need). The assessors used an assessment tool on which the TREC description and subtopic fields as well as the document content were displayed. To URLs that no longer exist, the default assessment "partially relevant" was given. Finally, we defined a relevance level for each document based on the three assessments (including the original one from TREC): $L3$ (two relevants and one partially relevant); $L2$ (one relevant and two partially relevants); and $L1$ (three partially relevants). We call the resultant data set TR09DIV+gr, where "gr" stands for (per-intent) graded relevance. The inter-assessor agreement between the new graded assessments is 69.9% (Cohen's kappa: .325). In this way, we obtained 1,173 $L1$, 1,959 $L2$ and 3,367 $L3$ documents across intents. Note that we did not re-examine any documents that were judged nonrelevant at TREC.

As for the intent probability distribution, we considered "Non-uniform" and "Uniform". Uniform means that all intents are equally likely, and this is the assumption currently used at the TREC Web diversity task. As for Non-uniform, we followed Sakai *et al.* [20]: for each topic with n intents, and assumed that the j-th intent has the probability $2^{n-j+1}/\sum_{k=1}^{n} 2^k$. Methods for estimating intent probabilities exist [1, 26], but our focus is on the inherent property of different diversified IR metrics *given* these probabilities.

5.2 Reducing the Diversity Test Collection

In addition to evaluating diversified IR metrics using TR09DIV+gr, we evaluated *traditional* graded-relevance IR metrics on which the diversified IR metrics are based. Sanderson *et al.* [23] treated each intent (i.e. subtopic) from TR09DIV as an independent topic to study the predictive power of traditional metrics. However, we avoided this approach because (a) This means that the traditional version of the test collection has many more topics than the original diversity version, and makes our traditional/diversity comparison rather difficult; and (b) The topic set thus constructed probably violates the i.i.d. assumption.

Instead, we constructed traditional test collections in two ways. The first method reduces TR09DIV+gr, by taking the *maximum* relevance level across intents for each topic-document pair. For example, if a document is $L1$-relevant to intent i_1 and $L3$-relevant to intent i_2 for a topic that has these two intents, then we treat this document as $L3$-relevant *to this topic* in the new collection. We call the new collection TR09DIV+gr2T, where "2T" means "(converted) to traditional." TR09DIV+gr2T has 601 $L1$, 1,328 $L2$ and 3,013 $L3$ documents across topics.

For comparison, we also constructed another traditional test collection using the original TR09DIV, not TR09DIV+gr. This was accomplished by simply defining graded relevance in terms of how many intents a document covers. The resultant collection, which we call TR09DIV2T, has 3,622 $L1$, 1,113 $L2$, 178 $L3$, 28 $L4$ and 1 $L5$ documents across topics. (As shown in Table 1(a), the maximum number of intents covered by a document in TR09DIV is 5.) Note that TR09DIV2T does not rely on our per-intent graded relevance data.

5.3 Another Data Set: NTCIR6C

In general, it is dangerous to try to draw strong conclusions from experiments that rely on a single test collection. We therefore conduct an additional set of traditional IR experiments using another data set. Our choice is the NTCIR-6 CLIR Chinese data (NTCIR6C) [12]: Table 1(b) shows its statistics. We selected NTCIR6C because (a) It is radically different from the TREC data discussed above in that it is from outside TREC and outside Web search (The NTCIR-6 task was a newspaper search task); and yet (b) It is similar to our TREC data in that it also has 50 topics and comes with relevance levels $L1$-$L3$.

6. EXPERIMENTS

6.1 Evaluating Traditional Search

Using the three traditional graded-relevance IR test collections (NTCIR6C, TR09DIV+gr2T and TR09DIV2T), we evaluated nDCG, Q, (n)GAP and (n)ERR in terms of discriminative power, for document cutoffs $l = 1000$ and $l = 10$. The cutoff of 1,000 represents classical TREC, while 10 represents the more recent shallow-depth evaluation practices as exemplified by the TREC Web tracks.

Figure 1 shows the *Achieved Significance Level (ASL) curves* [19] for nDCG, Q, (n)GAP and (n)ERR for each experimental condition. (Note that normalisation does not affect GAP and ERR when $l = 1000$.) The x axis represents the 190 run pairs sorted by ASL, and the y axis represents the ASL (i.e. p-value). Metrics whose graphs are closer to the origin are more discriminative than others, i.e. they are able to detect more significant differences. Table 2 cuts these graphs in the middle (horizontally) to compare the discrimi-

[5] For the TREC 2010 Web track, a kind of graded relevance was introduced to the ad hoc task but not to the diversity task.

[6] TREC binary relevance assessments are known to be "liberal," at least for early collections [27].

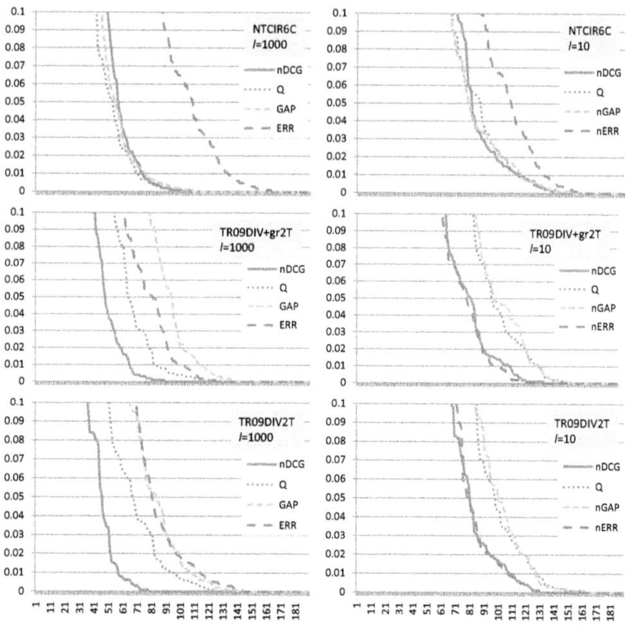

Figure 1: ASL curves for traditional metrics. The horizontal axes represent the 190 system pairs sorted by ASL; the vertical axes represent the ASL values.

native power at the .05 significance level. The table also shows the performance Δ that corresponds to a statistical significant difference. For example, with NTCIR6C at $l = 1000$, the discriminative power of Q-measure at the .05 level is $(137/190 =)72.1\%$, and if the Δ between two systems is 0.09 or larger, then that is usually statistically significant [19]. Figure 1 and Table 2 show that:

1. nDCG appears to be the most consistently discriminative metrics of all the traditional metrics for our data sets: Q does not perform as well as nDCG for the TREC data when $l = 10$; (n)GAP does not perform well for the TREC data when $l = 1000$ and when $l = 10$; (n)ERR doe not perform well for NTCIR6C, especially when $l = 1000$ as it suffers from its top-heaviness (i.e. virtually ignores all documents except for the very top ones).

2. Comparisons between $l = 1000$ and $l = 10$ show that, except for the top-heavy (n)ERR, using a small document cutoff (i.e. evaluating systems based on fewer data points) reduces discriminative power.

3. Comparisons across the three data sets with the same cutoff l show that the highest discriminative power achieved given 50 topics is similar: over 70% for $l = 1000$ and almost 60% for $l = 10$ at the .05 significance level. In particular, the results for TR09DIV+gr2T and TR09DIV2T are very similar, even though they have different number of relevance levels (up to $L3$ vs. up to $L5$). This suggests that the number of relevance levels and how they are obtained may not be major factors when comparing the discriminative power of metrics.

4. Normalisation improves the discriminative power of GAP, especially for NTCIR6C (Table 2(i), cutoff $l = 10$: the discriminative power goes up from 46.8% to 58.4%).

Table 2: Discriminative power of traditional metrics at $\alpha = .05$: Columns (a) and (b) show the discriminative power; (c) and (d) show the Δ required to achieve statistical significance.

cutoff $l = 1000$			cutoff $l = 10$		
	(a)	(b)		(c)	(d)
(i) NTCIR6C					
Q	72.1%	0.09	nGAP	58.4%	0.08
GAP	71.1%	0.07	nDCG	57.4%	0.11
nDCG	70.0%	0.11	Q	54.2%	0.09
ERR	42.6%	0.14	GAP	46.8%	0.04
			nERR	42.6%	0.16
			ERR	42.6%	0.15
(ii) TR09DIV+gr2T					
nDCG	74.7%	0.09	ERR	58.4%	0.17
Q	66.3%	0.05	nERR	57.9%	0.18
ERR	57.4%	0.15	nDCG	56.3%	0.11
GAP	50.5%	0.06	Q	48.4%	0.12
			nGAP	47.4%	0.13
			GAP	46.3%	0.02
(iii) TR09DIV2T					
nDCG	75.8%	0.07	nERR	58.4%	0.11
Q	64.7%	0.04	nDCG	57.9%	0.09
ERR	57.4%	0.04	ERR	50.0%	0.04
GAP	55.8%	0.05	Q	48.4%	0.08
			nGAP	47.4%	0.06
			GAP	43.2%	0.05

6.2 Evaluating Diversified Search

We now present our main results using TR09DIV+gr with per-intent graded relevance data. We evaluated I-rec, D($\sharp$)-nDCG, D($\sharp$)-Q, nDCG-IA, (n)GAP-IA, (n)ERR-IA as well as the official α-nDCG values at $l = 10$. As mentioned earlier, we considered both Non-uniform and Uniform intent probability distributions.

Figure 2 shows the ASL curves of the diversified IR metrics for four experimental conditions (two cutoffs $\times$ two intent probability distributions), and Table 3 compares the discriminative power at the .05 level. As α-nDCG and I-rec are not affected by intent probabilities, we show their results only in the Uniform results. Moreover, we do not consider I-rec (and therefore D$\sharp$-measures) when $l = 1000$ because I-rec is not useful with large document cutoffs: it would equal one most of the time. Also, we do not consider α-nDCG when $l = 1000$ as such values are not available from TREC. Figure 2 and Table 3 show that:

1. The Non-uniform and Uniform results are very similar. Thus, the intent probability distribution does not seem to have a major impact on discriminative power.

2. The most discriminative diversified IR metrics when $l = 1000$ are nDCG-IA and D-nDCG. The most discriminative when $l = 10$ are D$\sharp$-Q, α-nDCG, D$\sharp$-nDCG and I-rec.

3. The aforementioned "best" diversified IR metrics are at least as discriminative as the "best" traditional metrics: D-nDCG and nDCG-IA achieve well over 70% for $l = 1000$, while D$\sharp$-measures, α-nDCG and I-rec achieve well over 60% for $l = 10$ at the .05 level. (Hence, as in the traditional IR experiments, using a small document cutoff reduces discriminative power.)

4. In all four experimental conditions, (n)GAP-IA is substantially less discriminative than other metrics, and (n)ERR-IA is a middle-performer (it is as discriminative as nDCG-IA when $l = 10$, but less discriminative when $l = 1000$ due to its top-heaviness).

5. Normalisation improves the discriminative power of GAP-IA (Table 3, $l = 10$).

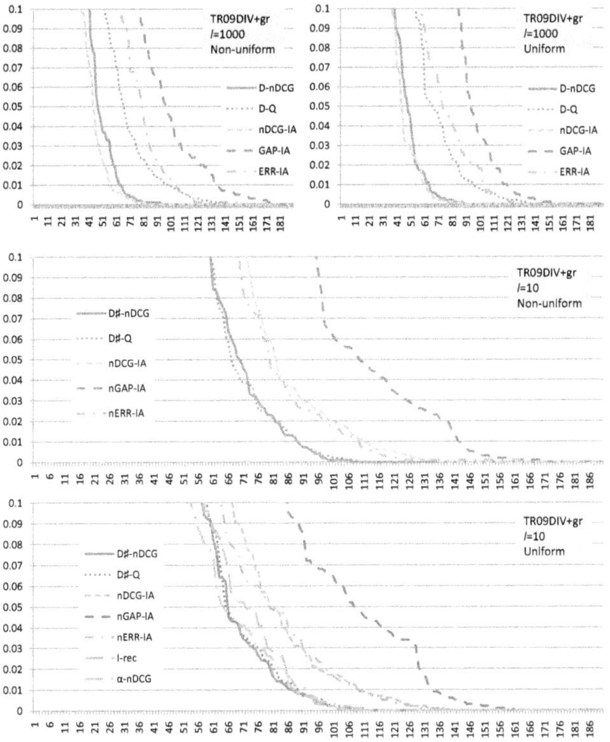

Figure 2: ASL curves for diversified IR metrics. The horizontal axes represent the 190 system pairs sorted by ASL; the vertical axes represent the ASL values.

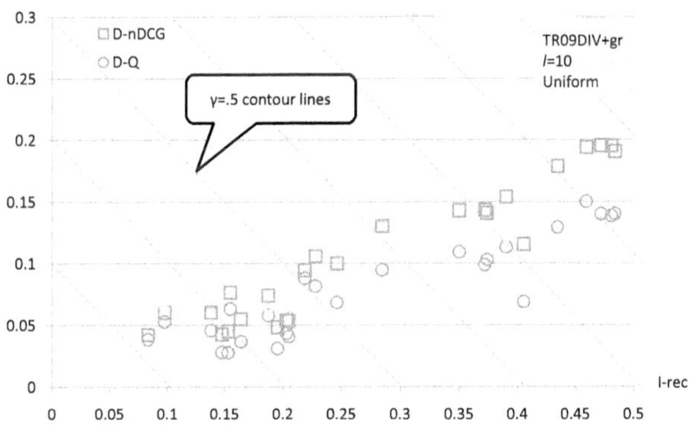

Figure 3: I-rec / D-measure graphs.

Note that the D♯-measures, which combine D-measures with I-rec, are slightly more discriminative than their components: for example, for the $l = 10$, Uniform case, the discriminative power of D-Q is 51.1%, that of I-rec is 62.6%, and that of D♯-Q is 66.3% at the .05 level (Table 3(ii)). Thus, D-measures and I-rec complement each other to achieve reliable evaluation results, by looking at a ranked list from two different (but not unrelated) angles. This generalises an observation by Sakai *et al.* [20].

Figure 3 plots all 25 runs for the TR09DIV+gr, $l = 10$, Uniform case with I-rec as the x axis and D-measure (i.e. D-nDCG or D-Q) as the y axis. The dotted lines represent the contour lines for a D♯-measure with $\gamma = .5$: if multiple runs lie on the same contour line, they are equally effective in terms of a D♯-measure. It can be observed that I-rec and D-measures are indeed already highly correlated with each other. A similar graph was shown by Sakai *et al.* [20] but they did not use per-intent graded relevance; the TREC 2009 overview paper [6] shows a similar graph for I-rec and the traditional *precision* metric.

Table 3: Discriminative power of diversified IR metrics at $\alpha = .05$: Columns (a) and (b) show the discriminative power; (c) and (d) show the Δ required to achieve statistical significance.

cutoff $l = 1000$			cutoff $l = 10$		
	(a)	(b)		(c)	(d)
(i) TR09DIV+gr; Non-uniform $P(i\|q)$					
nDCG-IA	77.4%	0.06	D♯-Q	65.3%	0.09
D-nDCG	75.3%	0.07	D♯-nDCG	63.7%	0.09
D-Q	61.1%	0.04	nERR-IA	58.4%	0.09
ERR-IA	58.4%	0.08	ERR-IA	57.9%	0.09
GAP-IA	48.9%	0.07	D-nDCG	57.4%	0.08
			nDCG-IA	57.4%	0.06
			D-Q	48.9%	0.09
			nGAP-IA	42.6%	0.07
			GAP-IA	24.2%	0.05
(ii) TR09DIV+gr; Uniform $P(i\|q)$					
nDCG-IA	76.8%	0.06	D♯-Q	66.3%	0.09
D-nDCG	75.3%	0.07	α-nDCG	66.3%	0.10
D-Q	63.2%	0.05	D♯-nDCG	65.8%	0.10
ERR-IA	61.6%	0.07	I-rec	62.6%	0.13
GAP-IA	50.5%	0.04	D-nDCG	60.5%	0.10
			nDCG-IA	58.4%	0.05
			nERR-IA	58.4%	0.08
			ERR-IA	57.9%	0.08
			D-Q	51.1%	0.10
			nGAP-IA	43.7%	0.04
			GAP-IA	35.3%	0.03

Table 4: τ and τ_{ap} (TR09DIV+gr; $l = 10$; Uniform).

	D♯-Q	D♯-nDCG	α-nDCG	nDCG-IA	nGAP-IA	nERR-IA
I-rec	.96/.97	.95/.86	.87/.74	.84/.84	.72/.70	.77/.63
D♯-Q	1/1	.97/.87	.87/.74	.88/.86	.74/.70	.79/.64
D♯-nDCG	-	1/1	.91/.87	.87/.76	.75/.62	.80/.76
α-nDCG	-	-	1/1	.84/.67	.74/.57	.90/.83
nDCG-IA	-	-	-	1/1	.85/.83	.86/.74
nGAP-IA	-	-	-	-	1/1	.78/.69

6.3 Examining Intuitiveness

Highly discriminative metrics, while desirable, may not necessarily measure what we want to measure. How do the different diversified IR metrics differ from one another, and which ones are more intuitive than others for the purpose of search result diversification?

Table 4 shows the Kendall's τ and τ_{ap} [30] values for different pairs of metrics, when the 20 runs are ranked in the TREC09DIV+gr, $l = 10$, Uniform setting. Kendall's τ is a monotonic function of the probability that a *randomly chosen* pair of ranked items is ordered identically in the two rankings. Hence a swap near the top of a ranked list and that near the bottom of the same list have an equal impact. Whereas, τ_{ap} is "top-heavy," in that it is a monotonic function of the probability that a randomly chosen item *and one ranked above it* are ordered identically in the two rankings. Like τ, τ_{ap} lies between -1 and 1, but unlike τ, it is not symmetrical: one of the input rankings is taken as the gold standard. When the errors (i.e. pairwise item swaps with respect to the gold standard) are uniformly distributed over the ranking being examined, τ_{ap} is equivalent to τ. For example, the τ between I-rec and D♯-Q is .96, while the τ_{ap} between the same pair of metrics is .97 when D♯-Q is taken as the ground truth. The main message Table 4 conveys is that all of these metrics (including the simple I-rec) are reasonably correlated with one another.

Based on the bootstrap test results used for our discriminative power experiments, Table 5 shows the *agreement* between metrics, focussing on I-rec, D♯-measures, α-nDCG and nDCG-IA in the $l = 10$, Uniform setting. Let A and B denote the sets of sigfinicantly different run pairs at the .05 level according to two metrics, respectively. We define agreement as $|A \cap B|/|A \cup B|$. For example, the agreement between D♯-nDCG and α-nDCG is 86%, as $|A - B| = 9$, $|A \cap B| = 116$ and $|B - A| = 10$ for these two

Table 5: Agreement of significant differences at the .05 level (TR09DIV+gr; $l = 10$; Uniform).

	D♯-Q	D♯-nDCG	α-nDCG	nDCG-IA
I-rec	4/115/11 (86%)	4/115/10 (89%)	9/110/16 (81%)	23/96/15 (72%)
D♯-Q	-	1/125/0 (99%)	9/117/9 (87%)	21/105/6 (80%)
D♯-nDCG	-	-	9/116/10 (86%)	21/104/7 (79%)
α-nDCG	-	-	-	20/106/5 (81%)

metrics. That is, for nine run pairs, D♯-nDCG says that they are significantly different while α-nDCG says they are not; the situation is reversed for another set of ten run pairs[7]. One observation from this table is that the agreement between I-rec and nDCG-IA is relatively low (72%): this supports the arguments by Sakai *et al.* [20] and Clarke *et al.* [7] that IA metrics do not necessarily reward high intent recall, i.e. diversification. (See also the relatively low rank correlation values between I-rec and the IA metrics in Table 4.) On the other hand, it can be observed that the D♯-measures, α-nDCG and nDCG-IA agree with one another for around 80% of the time or more. (D♯-Q is virtually identical to D♯-nDCG: the agreement between them is 99%.) The important question is: when do they disagree? Hereafter, we focus our attention on D♯-nDCG, α-nDCG and nDCG-IA, as our experiments suggest that nDCG is the most reliable traditional IR metric when the document cutoff is small, and as these three metrics represent three different approaches to diversified IR evaluation.

To examine how D♯-nDCG, α-nDCG and nDCG-IA differ from the viewpoint of intuitiveness, we selected ten pairs of actual ranked lists from TREC 2009 Web track diversity runs as follows. First, from the aforementioned nine run pairs which were significantly different with D♯-nDCG but not with α-nDCG (Table 5), we obtained five pairs of ranked lists (i.e. run pairs for a particular topic) with the largest per-topic Δ's in terms of D♯-nDCG, under the constraint that there is a disagreement among D♯-nDCG, α-nDCG and nDCG-IA as to which run is better. We refer to these five cases as **A-E**, as shown in Table 6. For example, **Case A** in this table represents two runs watd3 and Sab9wtBfDiv for Topic 47 which has two intents. The middle column shows which of the top 10 documents retrieved by each run are relevant to which intent (where $\mathbf{i}$ and i indicate informational and navigational intents according to the TREC diversity topic file, respectively); the last three columns show the per-topic Δ's (e.g. performance of watd3 minus that of Sab9wtBfDiv), and the arrows indicate which run is rated higher with each metric. Similarly, from the ten run pairs which were significantly different with α-nDCG but not with D♯-nDCG shown in Table 5, five cases with the largest per-topic Δ's in terms of α-nDCG were selected. These are shown as cases **F-J** in Table 6. In short, these ten cases are the ones that contributed most to the discrepancy (in terms of statistical significance) between D♯-nDCG and α-nDCG. We shall closely examine these cases below from the viewpoint of intuitiveness. Note that these results are from the Uniform setting: Sakai *et al.* [20] have already compared the intuitiveness of D♯-nDCG, α-nDCG and nDCG-IA when the intent probability distribution is Non-uniform, a situation which α-nDCG does not handle.

We examined the ten cases shown in Table 6 and categorised the results into the following four classes. The arguments below are somewhat subjective, as the right balance between diversity and relevance is hard to define. Nevertheless, we believe that they are useful for understanding the diversity metrics.

[7]In theory, *conflicts* can also occur, where one metric says that run X significantly outperforms run Y while another metric says that run Y significantly outperforms X. There was no such case in our experiments.

6.3.1 Only α-nDCG Prefers a Low-Relevance Run

In **Case B**, we argue that α-nDCG is counterintuitive. Both twCSodpRBB and MSDiv1 completely failed to diversify: they cover the fifth intent $\mathbf{i}_5$ only. However, twCSodpRBB has only one relevant document (though at rank 1), while MSDiv1 has eight, all of which are $L3$-relevant. Since $\mathbf{i}_5$ is *informational*, MSDiv1 should probably be preferred, since the two runs are equally poor in terms of diversity (i.e. intent recall) but MSDiv1 has much better overall relevance. The rightmost columns of Table 6 show that D♯-nDCG and nDCG-IA agree with this intuition, while α-nDCG does not. This counterintuitiveness of α-nDCG is precisely because of α, which tends to ignore repetition of relevant documents for the same intent. It should be remembered that, unless the intent is purely navigational, providing the user with multiple documents that are relevant to the same intent does not necessarily imply redundancy in practice: different relevant documents may carry different pieces of information. Of course, a smaller value of α may remedy this particular situation, but how to appropriately set α in advance is an open question.

On the other hand, α-nDCG may be the most intuitive for **Case C**, which is similar to **Case B** in that both runs failed to diversify but different in that the intent involved is *navigational* ("Go to the Alexian Brothers Health System homepage"). Thus, even though D♯-nDCG and nDCG-IA prefer MSDiv1 which returned three documents that are $L3$-relevant to i_1, the second and the third $L3$-relevant documents may not be useful in practice. In particular, D♯-nDCG appears to favour MSDiv1 perhaps too much (the difference is over .15). Note that the raw nDCG is inherently suitable for evaluation with informative queries. We will discuss this point further in Section 6.3.5.

6.3.2 α-nDCG and nDCG-IA Prefer a Non-diversified Run

Next, let us discuss **Case A**, **Case F** and **Case H**, where only informational intents are involved and D♯-nDCG disagreed with α-nDCG and nDCG-IA. It can be observed that, in all three cases, α-nDCG and nDCG-IA prefer the non-diversified run, even though they are supposed to reward diversified ranked lists. In contrast, D♯-nDCG (with $\gamma = 0.5$) consistenly favours a more diversified run, due to its explict intent recall component. However, as we have discussed earlier, the right balance between relevance and diversity (which in the case of D♯-nDCG is represented by the γ parameter) is hard to define.

6.3.3 Only α-nDCG Prefers a Poorly Diversifed Run

Next, we discuss **Case D** and **Case E**, where only informational intents are involved and α-nDCG disagreed with D♯-nDCG and nDCG-IA. In both cases, α-nDCG prefers the less diversified run which missed the fourth intent (but nevertheless returned a document relevant to two intents at rank 1).

6.3.4 Only nDCG-IA Prefers a Non-diversified Run

In **Case G**, nDCG-IA is *clearly* counterintuitive. It can be observed that THUIR09FuClu has a document $L2$-relevant to $\mathbf{i}_5$ at rank 2, and one $L2$-relevant to $\mathbf{i}_2$ at rank 3. (These two intents are informational.) On the other hand, MSRABASE has only a document $L2$-relevant to i_3 at rank 2. (This intent is navigational.) Thus, since we are examining the uniform intent probability setting,

Table 6: Ten ranked list pairs from TR09DIV+gr, l = 10, Uniform. 2nd column: topic IDs (number of intents). 3rd column: run IDs. 4th column: number of intents covered by each run. 5th column: relevance levels for each intent at ranks 1-10. The rightmost columns: performance differences in terms of each metric; arrows point to the preferred run.

				document rank (**i**: informational intents; i: navigational intents) 1	2	3	4	5	6	7	8	9	10	Δ in D♯-nDCG	Δ in α-nDCG	Δ in nDCG-IA
A	47 (2)	watd3	1	i_1L3	i_1L3	i_1L3			i_1L3					**−0.209** ⇓	0.018 ⇑	0.098 ⇑
		Sab9wtBfDiv	2		i_1L3 i_2L3					i_2L3						
B	21 (5)	twCSodpRBB	1	i_5L3										**−0.170** ⇓	0.023 ⇑	−0.084 ⇓
		MSDiv1	1			i_5L3	i_5L3	i_5L3	i_5L3	i_5L3	i_5L3	i_5L3	i_5L3			
C	46 (3)	twCSodpRBB	1		i_1L3		i_1L3							**−0.156** ⇓	0.010 ⇑	−0.031 ⇓
		MSDiv1	1						i_1L3		i_1L3		i_1L3			
D	26 (4)	watd3	2	i_1L2 i_3L1		i_1L1		i_1L2					i_1L1	**−0.141** ⇓	0.027 ⇑	−0.025 ⇓
		twCSodpRNB	3			i_1L1 i_3L2 i_4L1				i_1L2 i_3L3 i_4L2			i_1L2 i_3L1 i_4L2			
E	26 (4)	watd1	2	i_1L2 i_3L1	i_1L1			i_1L1		i_1L1		i_1L2		**−0.139** ⇓	0.042 ⇑	−0.023 ⇓
		twCSodpRNB	3			i_1L1 i_3L2 i_4L1				i_1L2 i_3L3 i_4L2			i_1L2 i_3L1 i_4L2			
F	50 (3)	Sab9wtBfDiv	1	i_3L2	i_3L2			i_3L2						−0.080 ⇓	**0.168** ⇑	0.116 ⇑
		spc	2					i_1L2 i_2L1								
G	20 (4)	THUIR09FuClu	2		i_5L2	i_2L2								0.220 ⇑	**0.150** ⇑	−0.092 ⇓
		MSRABASE	1		i_3L2											
H	14 (4)	Sab9wtBfDiv	1	i_2L1	i_2L1	i_2L1	i_2L1	i_2L1	i_2L1	i_2L1	i_2L1	i_2L1	i_2L1	−0.102 ⇓	**0.131** ⇑	0.028 ⇑
		spc	2				i_2L1						i_2L1 i_4L1			
I	50 (3)	MSRABASE	3	i_3L2	i_3L1				i_3L2	i_1L2 i_2L1				0.236 ⇑	**0.131** ⇑	−0.130 ⇓
		THUIR09FuClu	1	i_3L2	i_3L2	i_3L2	i_3L2	i_3L2		i_3L2	i_3L2	i_3L1	i_3L1			
J	38 (3)	Sab9wtBfDiv	2		i_1L2		i_3L3	i_1L2			i_1L3	i_1L2		0.141 ⇑	**0.130** ⇑	−0.019 ⇓
		Sab9wtBDiv1	1			i_1L3	i_1L2	i_1L3	i_1L3	i_1L2						

THUIR09FuClu should definitely be preferred over MSRABASE, and both D♯-nDCG and α-nDCG satisfy this requirement.

The above counterintuitive behaviour of nDCG-IA arises from the inherent property of IA metrics, namely that high IA metric values can be achieved by doing extremely well for a single intent. In **Case G**, MSRABASE did extremely well for i_3: this intent only has one relevant document ($L2$), and the run returned this document at rank 2. The gain value for an $L2$-document is $2^2 - 1 = 3$, and therefore $nDCG_3 = (3/\log(2+1))/(3/\log(1+1)) = \log 2/\log 3 = .631$. Thus, nDCG-IA, averaged over four intents, is $.631/4 = .158$. Whereas, THUIR09FuClu achieves only $nDCG_2 = .119$ and $nDCG_5 = .144$ for the two intents and therefore its nDCG-IA is only $(.119 + .144)/4 = .066$.

Case I and **Case J** are similar to **Case G** in that only nDCG-IA prefers a run that failed to diversify. (All intents involved are informational.) We argue that nDCG-IA is rather counterintuitive for these cases as well, as MSRABASE covers three intents in **Case I** and Sab9wtBfDiv covers two in **Case J**.

6.3.5 *Intuitiveness Summary*

To sum up the above analysis: while the right balance between relevance and diversity is difficult to define, D♯-nDCG consistently prefers the more diversified run compared to α-nDCG and nDCG-IA. If we want diversity more than we want high relevance, then D♯-nDCG would be the clear winner, as it explitly incorporates intent recall. This is in contrast to α-nDCG which tries to encourage high intent recall by discouraging retrieval of "redundant" documents. As for IA metrics, we have demonstrated that they can be clearly counterintuitive, as high IA metric values can be achieved by retrieving highly relevant documents for one (major) intent.

The only case where D♯-nDCG may be less intuitive than α-nDCG is **Case C**, where the intent was navigational and therefore retrieving multiple relevant documents may not be practically useful. For navigational intents, it may be better to use graded-relevance versions of Reciprocal Rank such as ERR and P^+ [18][8].

Finally, recall that the above analysis used our Uniform results. Given a non-uniform intent probability distribution, α-nDCG can be more counterintuitive as it disregards the probabilities [20]. Also, recall that α-nDCG completely disregards local relevance levels (e.g. $L1$ vs $L3$ in Table 6).

7. CONCLUSIONS

To our knowledge, our work is the first to have studied the properties of different diversity evaluation metrics using per-intent graded relevance data. Moreover, our experiments are more extensive than similar studies that have been reported recently [7, 20]. Our main findings from the discriminative power experiments are:

- Our traditional IR and diversified IR experiments suggest that (n)GAP and (n)ERR and their intent-aware versions are *not* the most discriminative of metrics[9];
- D♯-measures, α-nDCG and intent recall appear to be the most discriminative metrics for shallow-depth diversified IR eval-

[8]Q-measure, P$^+$ and ERR are all members of a family of metrics called *Normalised Cumulative Utiliy* (NCU) [21]. An NCU is defined in terms of a user's stopping probability distribution over ranks and a utility function at a given rank. Q-measure uses a uniform distribution over all relevant documents; P$^+$ uses a uniform distribution over all relevant documents retrieved within top r_p, where r_p is the rank of one of the most relevant documents in the ranked list. Whereas, ERR's stopping probability at a given rank depends on the relevance of previously seen documents.

[9]Recall, however, that we have only examined a version of GAP which uses a flat probability distribution over the relevance levels, a setting recommended by Robertson, Kanoulas and Yilmaz [17].

Table 7: Summary: properties of diversified IR metrics.

	α-nDCG	IA metrics	D♯-measures
Intent probabilities	NO	YES	YES
Pay attention to minor intents	YES	NO	YES
Per-intent graded relevance	NO	YES	YES
Max value guaranteed to be 1	NO	NO	YES
High discriminative power	YES	NO	YES

uation. Moreover, they are at least as discriminative as the most discriminative traditional metrics (e.g. nDCG).

The second finding suggests that diversified IR experiments with a given number of topics can be as reliable as traditional IR experiments with the same number of topics, provided that the aforementioned discriminative metrics are used. This is good news for IR test collection builders and users.

Moreover, our analysis showed that, while different diversified IR metrics are generally highly correlated with one another, D♯-nDCG is more intuitive than α-nDCG and nDCG-IA at least when high diversity is considered more important than high relevance.

Table 7 summarises the properties of diversified IR metrics examined in this study. The original α-nDCG (as used in TREC) can handle neither intent probabilities nor per-intent graded relevance; IA metrics tend to ignore minor intents; α-nDCG and IA metrics have normalisation issues. In contrast, D-measures range fully between 0 and 1, and so do D♯-measures provided that the measurement depth l is not smaller than the number of intents. In addition to these inherent differences, our present study showed that IA metrics have relatively low discriminative power, and that D♯-measures have strengths in terms of intuitiveness. (The latter observation is not included in Table 7 as it is somewhat subjective.) It is probably fair to say that the D♯-measures are promising for diversified IR evaluation. A practical recommendation for diversified IR evaluation would be to plot I-rec against D-nDCG as we have shown in Figure 3 and to discuss the contour lines that represent D♯-nDCG.

Our results on diversified IR metrics, however, rely solely on TR09DIV+gr (just as other studies [7, 20, 23] relied solely on TR09DIV). As future work, we plan to construct more diversity test collections (at the NTCIR "INTENT" task[10]) and strengthen our conclusions. We also plan to explore related questions such as: (1) how to seamlessly evaluate diversity and relevance for navigational and informational queries; and (2) how to evaluate diversity across verticals in aggregated search and across queries in a session, and formulate a unified, general framework for diversity evaluation.

8. REFERENCES

[1] R. Agrawal, S. Gollapudi, A. Halverson, and S. Leong. Diversifying search results. In *Proceedings of ACM WSDM 2009*, pages 5–14, 2009.

[2] J. A. Aslam, E. Yilmaz, and V. Pavlu. The maximum entropy method for analyzing retrieval measures. In *Proceedings of ACM SIGIR 2005*, pages 27–34, 2005.

[3] C. Brandt, T. Joachims, Y. Yue, and J. Bank. Dynamic ranked retrieval. In *Proceedings of WSDM 2011*, pages 247–256, 2011.

[4] B. Carterette and P. Chandar. Probabilistic models of novel document rankings for faceted topic retrieval. In *Proceedings of ACM CIKM 2009*, pages 1287–1296, 2009.

[5] O. Chapelle, D. Metzler, Y. Zhang, and P. Grinspan. Expected reciprocal rank for graded relevance. In *Proceedings of ACM CIKM 2009*, pages 621–630, 2009.

[6] C. L. Clarke, N. Craswell, and I. Soboroff. Overview of the TREC 2009 web track. In *Proceedings of TREC 2009*, 2010.

[7] C. L. Clarke, N. Craswell, I. Soboroff, and A. Ashkan. A comparative analysis of cascade measures for novelty and diversity. In *Proceedings of ACM WSDM 2011*, 2011.

[10] http://www.thuir.org/intent/ntcir9/

[8] C. L. Clarke, M. Kolla, G. V. Cormack, O. Vechtomova, A. Ashkan, S. Büttcher, and I. MacKinnon. Novelty and diversity in information retrieval evaluation. In *Proceedings of ACM SIGIR 2008*, pages 659–666, 2009.

[9] C. L. Clarke, M. Kolla, and O. Vechtomova. An effectiveness measure for ambiguous and underspecified queries. In *Advances in Information Retrieval Theory (ICTIR 2009), LNCS 5766*, pages 188–199, 2009.

[10] Z. Dou, S. Hu, K. Chen, R. Song, and J.-R. Wen. Multi-dimensional search result diversification. In *Proceedings of ACM WSDM 2011*, 2011.

[11] K. Järvelin and J. Kekäläinen. Cumulated gain-based evaluation of IR techniques. *ACM Transactions on Information Systems*, 20(4):422–446, 2002.

[12] K. Kishida, K. hua Chen, S. Lee, K. Kuriyama, N. Kando, and H.-H. Chen. Overview of CLIR task at the sixth NTCIR workshop. In *Proceedings of NTCIR-6*, 2007.

[13] A. Moffat and J. Zobel. Rank-biased precision for measurement of retrieval effectiveness. *ACM Transactions on Information Systems*, 27(1):Article No.2, 2008.

[14] F. Radlinski and N. Craswell. Comparing the sensitivity of information retrieval metrics. In *Proceedings of ACM SIGIR 2010*, pages 667–674, 2010.

[15] D. Rafiei, K. Bharat, and A. Shukla. Diversifying web search results. In *Proceedings of ACM WWW 2010*, pages 781–790, 2010.

[16] S. E. Robertson. The probability ranking principle in IR. *Journal of Documentation*, 33:130–137, 1977.

[17] S. E. Robertson, E. Kanoulas, and E. Yilmaz. Extending average precision to graded relevance judgments. In *Proceedings of ACM SIGIR 2010*, pages 603–610, 2010.

[18] T. Sakai. Bootstrap-based comparisons of IR metrics for finding one relevant document. In *Proceedings of AIRS 2006 (LNCS 4182)*, pages 374–389, 2006.

[19] T. Sakai. Evaluating evaluation metrics based on the bootstrap. In *Proceedings of ACM SIGIR 2006*, pages 525–532, 2006.

[20] T. Sakai, N. Craswell, R. Song, S. Robertson, Z. Dou, and C.-Y. Lin. Simple evaluation metrics for diversified search results. In *Proceedings of EVIA 2010*, pages 42–50, 2010.

[21] T. Sakai and S. Robertson. Modelling a user population for designing information retrieval metrics. In *Proceedings of EVIA 2008*, pages 30–41, 2008.

[22] M. Sanderson. Test collection based evaluation of information retrieval systems. *Foundations and Trends in Information Retrieval*, 4:247–375, 2010.

[23] M. Sanderson, M. L. Paramita, P. Clough, and E. Kanoulas. Do user preferences and evaluation measures line up? In *Proceedings of ACM SIGIR 2010*, pages 555–562, 2010.

[24] R. L. Santos, C. Macdonald, and I. Ounis. Selectively diversifying search results. In *Proceedings of ACM CIKM 2010*, 2010.

[25] I. Soboroff. Test collection diagnosis and treatment. In *Proceedings of EVIA 2010*, pages 34–41, 2010.

[26] R. Song, D. Qi, H. Liu, T. Sakai, J.-Y. Nie, H.-W. Hon, and Y. Yu. Constructing a test collection with multi-intent queries. In *Proceedings of EVIA 2010*, pages 51–59, 2010.

[27] E. Sormunen. Liberal relevance criteria of TREC: Counting on negligible documents? In *Proceedings of ACM SIGIR 2002*, pages 324–330, 2002.

[28] E. M. Voorhees and C. Buckley. The effect of topic set size on retrieval experiment error. In *Proceedings of ACM SIGIR 2002*, pages 316–323, 2002.

[29] W. Webber, A. Moffat, and J. Zobel. The effect of pooling and evaluation depth on metric stability. In *Proceedings of EVIA 2010*, pages 7–15, 2010.

[30] E. Yilmaz, J. A. Aslam, and S. Robertson. A new rank correlation coefficient for information retrieval. In *Proceedings of ACM SIGIR 2008*, pages 587–594, 2008.

[31] C. Zhai, W. W. Cohen, and J. Lafferty. Beyond independent relevance: Methods and evaluation metrics for subtopic retrieval. In *Proceedings of ACM SIGIR 2003*, pages 10–17, 2003.

Evaluating Multi-Query Sessions

Evangelos Kanoulas*, Ben Carterette†, Paul D. Clough*, Mark Sanderson‡
e.kanoulas@shef.ac.uk, carteret@cis.udel.edu,
p.d.clough@shef.ac.uk, mark.sanderson@rmit.edu.au
* Information School, University of Sheffield, Sheffield, UK
† Department of Computer & Information Sciences, University of Delaware, Newark, DE, USA
‡ School of Computer Science & Information Technology, RMIT, Melbourne, Australia

ABSTRACT

The standard system-based evaluation paradigm has focused on assessing the performance of retrieval systems in serving the best results for a single query. Real users, however, often begin an interaction with a search engine with a sufficiently under-specified query that they will need to reformulate before they find what they are looking for. In this work we consider the problem of evaluating retrieval systems over test collections of multi-query sessions. We propose two families of measures: a model-free family that makes no assumption about the user's behavior over a session, and a model-based family with a simple model of user interactions over the session. In both cases we generalize traditional evaluation metrics such as average precision to multi-query session evaluation. We demonstrate the behavior of the proposed metrics by using the new TREC 2010 Session track collection and simulations over the TREC-9 Query track collection.

Categories and Subject Descriptors: H.3.4 [Information Storage and Retrieval] Performance Evaluation

General Terms: Experimentation, Measurement

Keywords: information retrieval, test collections, evaluation, sessions

1. INTRODUCTION

Evaluation measures play a critical role in the development of retrieval systems, both as measures in comparative evaluation experiments and as objective functions for optimizing system effectiveness. The standard evaluation paradigm has focused on assessing the performance of retrieval systems in serving the best results for a single query, for varying definitions of "best": for ad hoc tasks, the most relevant results; for diversity tasks, the results that do the best job of covering a space of information needs; for known-item tasks, the single document the user is looking for. There are many test collections for repeatable experiments on these tasks, and dozens of evaluation measures assessing different aspects of task effectiveness.

Real users, however, often begin an interaction with a search engine with a query that they will need to reformulate one or more times before they find what they are looking for. Early studies on web search query logs showed that half of all Web users reformulated their initial query: 52% of the users in 1997 Excite data set, 45% of the users in the 2001 Excite dataset [15].

The standard evaluation paradigm of single-query test collections seems unable to assess the effectiveness of retrieval systems over sequences of query reformulations. Interactive evaluation has been employed as an alternative. In interactive evaluation the user is part of the evaluation cycle and freely interacts with the results of a retrieval system. Measures such as *instance recall* [11] and *session discounted cumulative gain* [6] have been proposed to capture the effectiveness of systems in these settings. Even though an interactive evaluation paradigm can better capture the actual user experience, it is both noisy due to the high degrees of freedom of user interactions and expensive due to its low reusability and need for many test subjects. Furthermore, conducting interactive comparative evaluation experiments is by no means an easy task.

The TREC 2010 Session track [7] proposed an experiment for the evaluation of retrieval systems over multi-query sessions. We defined a session as a sequence of reformulations in the service of satisfying a general information need, and constructed a test collection of two query reformulations (an initial and a follow-up query) for each of 150 information needs. This collection makes compromises for simplicity and tractability, but it provides a starting point for investigation of questions about test collection-based session evaluation.

In addition to a test collection, new evaluation measures are necessary as well. Traditional evaluation measures only capture per-query effectiveness; they are not necessarily appropriate for evaluating the effectiveness of a retrieval system over a multi-query session. While one could evaluate results for each query in the session in isolation, it may not be the case that the system is serving results for each query independently. Doing so would lose potentially valuable information about the ability of the system to provide results for the session as a unit, and thus reduce our ability to optimize system performance across sessions.

Due to the lack of appropriate measures Järvelin et al. [6] extended the normalized discounted cumulative gain (nDCG) measure to a measure that considers multi-query sessions. The measure—called *normalized session discounted cumula-*

SIGIR'11, July 24–28, 2011, Beijing, China.

tive gain (nsDCG)—discounts documents that appear lower in the ranked list for a given query as well as documents that appear after more query reformulations. In a sense the new model incorporates a cost for reformulating a query as well as scanning down a ranked list.

The nsDCG measure is computed as follows: for each query in a series of reformulations, DCG is computed in isolation of all other queries in the series. Each DCG is then discounted by a function of the position q of the query in the series. The measure can evaluate the effectiveness of retrieval systems over multiple queries in an interactive retrieval scenario, in which a user moves down a ranked list of documents and at some rank reformulates the query. Since the reformulation points are known (from observing the users), DCG is computed at those points for each query and at the stopping point for the last reformulation. In a test collection of static sessions, however, reformulation points are unknown. Using nsDCG requires the selection of a fixed reformulation cut-off, which clearly does not reflect the fact that different retrieval results may trigger different user behavior. Further, the measure does not model early abandonment of a query session; our TREC session collection comes with a fixed number of reformulations, but a user may choose to abandon the session before reaching the last reformulation (either due to satisfaction or due to frustration). A multi-query session measure should be able to model such behavior.

Yang and Lad [16] overcame the need to define a fixed reformulation point by defining a session measure as an expectation over a set of possible browsing paths. Based on this they proposed a measure of expected utility for a multi-query information distillation task. Given a series of m reformulations the proposed measure accounts for all possible browsing paths that end in the kth reformulation. Each path has a certain probability to be realized by a user. To define the probability of a user following a certain path Yang and Lad [16] follow the *rank biased precision* (RBP) framework [10], replacing RBP's stopping condition with a reformulation condition. The utility of each path is a function of the relevance and novelty of the returned documents being considered. The system effectiveness is then defined as the expected utility calculated over the aforementioned probabilistic space of browsing paths. Though the expected utility solves the problem of variable reformulation points, it still does not allow early abandonment of the query session.

In this work we consider the problem of evaluating retrieval systems over test collections of static multi-query sessions. We propose two families of measures: one that makes no assumptions about the user's behavior over a session, and another with a simple model of user interactions over the session. In the latter case we provide a general framework to accommodate different models of user interactions in the course of a session, avoiding predefined reformulation cut-offs and allowing early abandonment. In both cases we generalize traditional evaluation measures such as average precision to multi-query session evaluation.

2. MULTI-QUERY SESSION COLLECTION AND USER MODEL

We define a *session test collection* as one with a set of topics, each of which consist of a description of an information need and a static sequence of m title queries (an initial query and $m-1$ reformulations), and judgments of the relevance of documents to the topics. For simplicity, we assume that all reformulations are directed towards a single information need, so there is a global set of relevant documents of size R.[1] This definition is similar to those used by Järvelin et al. [6] and Yang & Lad [16], and it is essentially the definition used for the TREC 2010 Session track in the case of specification and generalization reformulations [7].

query $q_{1,1}$ ranking 1		query $q_{1,2}$ ranking 2		query $q_{1,3}$ ranking 3	
d_1	N	d'_1	R	d''_1	R
d_2	N	d'_2	R	d''_2	R
d_3	N	d'_3	R	d''_3	R
d_4	N	d'_4	R	d''_4	R
d_5	N	d'_5	R	d''_5	R
d_6	N	d'_6	N	d''_6	R
d_7	N	d'_7	N	d''_7	R
d_8	N	d'_8	N	d''_8	R
d_9	N	d'_9	N	d''_9	R
d_{10}	N	d'_{10}	N	d''_{10}	R
...	...	...	...	...	...

Table 1: Example rankings (document IDs and relevance judgments) for three queries $q_{1,1}, q_{1,2}, q_{1,3}$ in a session for topic number 1. Here we assume all documents are unique.

Following Cooper in his proposal for the *expected search length* measure [5], we assume a user stepping down the ranked list of results until some decision point. To this we add an additional possible action: the decision point can be either a stopping point for the search, or a point at which the user reformulates their query. Thus, a user experiences results by either moving down a ranking (i.e. moving from rank k to rank $k+1$ in ranking $\vec{r}_i$) or to the top of the next ranking by reformulating (i.e. moving from rank k in ranking $\vec{r}_i$ to rank 1 in ranking $\vec{r}_{i+1}$.).

Consider the example in Table 1. A user with a certain information need formulates a query and submits it to a retrieval system. The retrieval system returns a ranked list of documents, $\vec{r}_1 = (d_1, d_2, ..., d_{10}, ...)$. Suppose the user's first decision point occurs at document d_5. After seeing that document, the user decides to reformulate the original query and resubmit it to the retrieval system. The retrieval system responds with a second ranked list of documents, $\vec{r}_2 = (d'_1, d'_1, ..., d'_{10}, ...)$. The user reads the documents once again from top to bottom and abandons the session. If we only consider the documents the user has examined over the session of reformulations then a final composite ranked list, $\vec{cl}$, can be composed: $\vec{cl} = (d_1, d_2, \ldots, d_5, d'_1, d'_2, d'_3, \ldots)$.

Given the relevance of the documents in the composite ranked list $\vec{cl}$, any traditional evaluation measure can be calculated in the usual manner. We may require assumptions about the relevance of duplicates, e.g. if d_1 and d'_2 are the same relevant document, how they should count towards the evaluation measure; we will consider these in Section 5.

[1]In practice users' information needs may change during a search session and over time [1]; assuming it is fixed is a modeling assumption we make for tractability. Some of our measures require this assumption, but it can be relaxed for other measures.

2.1 Evaluation over paths

The composite list $\vec{cl}$ is the outcome of a series of decisions. We define a *path* ω through the results as a series of decisions to either move down a ranking, reformulate and start at the top of the next ranking, or abandon the search. We assume that at least one document—the first one—is viewed in each ranking. A *path of length* k is a path that results in k documents viewed. We denote the set of unique paths of length k as Ω_k, and the set of all unique paths as Ω. A path can be represented as a series of actions, e.g. $\omega = \{\text{down}, \text{down}, ..., \text{reformulate}, \text{down}, ..., \text{abandon}\}$; as a series of document IDs viewed, e.g. $\omega = \vec{cl}$ above; or as a series of ranks at which reformulations or abandonment occurred, e.g. $\omega = \{5, ...\}$. The three are equivalent in the sense of providing complete information about the series of decisions; the last, being most compact, is the one we will use.

Different paths result in different documents being seen, and in many cases different numbers of relevant documents. Precision after k documents viewed may result in very different values depending on the path chosen: a user that views 10 documents in $\vec{r}_1$ (the relevance of which is shown in Table 1), experiences 0 precision, while one that reformulates immediately after the first document in $\vec{r}_1$ and steps down $\vec{r}_2$ until rank 9 experiences precision of 5/10. In an interactive evaluation scenario where real users interact with the ranked list of documents returned by a retrieval system, the point at which a user decides either to reformulate their previous query or to abandon the search can be explicitly recorded by observation, or implicitly inferred by looking at (for instance) the last clicked document. In batch laboratory experiments with static sessions, however, the reformulation and stopping points are undefined—there is no user from which to record them. This presents a challenge for defining evaluation measures.

In this work we propose evaluating static sessions by summarizing evaluation results over *all* paths through the results. We will consider two directions: one a "model-free" approach inspired by interpolated precision and recall, the other a model-based approach that explicitly defines probabilities for certain actions, then averages over paths. In both approaches we would like to make as few assumptions as possible about the reasons a user reformulates.

2.2 Counting paths

The number of possible paths grows fairly fast. Consider a path of length k ending in reformulation number j. For example, the paths of length 4 ending at reformulation 2 are $\{d_1, d_2, d_3, d'_1\}$, $\{d_1, d_2, d'_1, d'_2\}$, and $\{d_1, d'_1, d'_2, d'_3\}$. For any given k and j, we can count the number of possible paths as follows: imagine a ranking as a list of k documents, then place $j-1$ reformulation points between any two documents in that list. The number of different places we can insert them is $\binom{k-1}{j-1}$, and this is therefore the number of paths of length k that end at reformulation j.

The total number of paths of length k is:

$$|\Omega_k| = \sum_{j=1}^{m} \binom{k-1}{j-1}$$

This is the definition of elements in the Bernoulli triangle. Its rate of growth is unknown, but it is $O(k^2)$ for $m = 2$ and approaches 2^{k-1} as m increases to k. The total number of paths of any length is $|\Omega| = \sum_{k=1}^{n} |\Omega_k| = O(2^n)$.

	$j=1$	$j=2$	$j=3$	...
$k=1$	$\{0\}$	–	–	
$k=2$	$\{0\}$	$\{1\}$	–	
$k=3$	$\{0\}$	$\{1,2\}$	$\{2\}$	
$k=4$	$\{0\}$	$\{1,2,3\}$	$\{2,3,3\}$	
$k=5$	$\{0\}$	$\{1,2,3,4\}$	$\{2,3,3,4,4,4\}$	
...				

Table 2: Relevant document counts for different paths of length k ending at ranking j from the example in Table 1.

On the other hand, if we only consider paths that end at reformulation j but continue down ranked list $\vec{r}_j$ indefinitely, the number is more manageable. We can enumerate these by simply iterating over stopping points $k_1 = 1...|\vec{r}_1|$, and for each of those over stopping points $k_2 = 1...|\vec{r}_2|$, and so on. Within the $(j-1)$st loop, $\omega = \{k_1, ..., k_{k-1}\}$ is the path to that point. This takes $|\vec{r}_1| \times |\vec{r}_2| \times \cdots \times |\vec{r}_{m-1}| = O(n^m)$ time, which, while not exactly fast, is at least manageable.

3. MODEL-FREE SESSION EVALUATION

Our first goal is to develop a method for evaluating the effectiveness of a system over a set of reformulations making no assumptions about when or why users reformulate. The approach is inspired by interpolated precision: there is no formal user model behind interpolated precision, but it reduces the full evaluation data (precision at every rank) to a manageable set while still providing useful intuition about system performance, particularly when plotted against recall values. Likewise, there is no formal user model behind these measures, but they give some intuition while greatly reducing the amount of evaluation data, which as we saw above grows exponentially.

Consider all paths of length k that end at reformulation j. On each of those paths the user will see a certain number of relevant documents. Let us define a set of relevant counts $\mathbf{rR}@j,k$ as the set of counts of relevant documents seen on all such paths.[2] In the example in Table 1, there is only one possible way for a user to see 4 documents without reformulating, and none of those documents are relevant; therefore $\mathbf{rR}@1,4 = \{0\}$. There are three ways for a user to see 4 documents over two queries: $\{d_1, d_2, d_3, d'_1\}$; $\{d_1, d_2, d'_1, d'_2\}$; $\{d_1, d'_1, d'_2, d'_3\}$. These paths have 1, 2, and 3 relevant documents respectively. Therefore $\mathbf{rR}@2,4 = \{1,2,3\}$. All sets $\mathbf{rR}$ for $j = 1..3$ and $k = 1..5$ are shown in Table 2; the size of a set is $\binom{k-1}{j-1}$ as described above.

We can then define session versions of precision and recall by dividing the relevant counts $\mathbf{rR}@j,k$ by k (for precision) or R (for recall). We will call these $\mathbf{rPC}@j,k$ and $\mathbf{rRC}@j,k$. This gives the session generalization to precision and recall: precision and recall for each possible path through the results. In traditional systems-based evaluation there is only one possible path of length k, and precision/recall for that path is identical to precision/recall at rank k.

Precision is sometimes interpolated to a particular recall point r by finding the first rank at which recall r is achieved, then taking the maximum of all precisions at that rank or deeper. Let us consider an analogous process for sessions by defining precision at a particular recall point in a particular

[2] We use boldface to denote sets and italics to denote scalars.

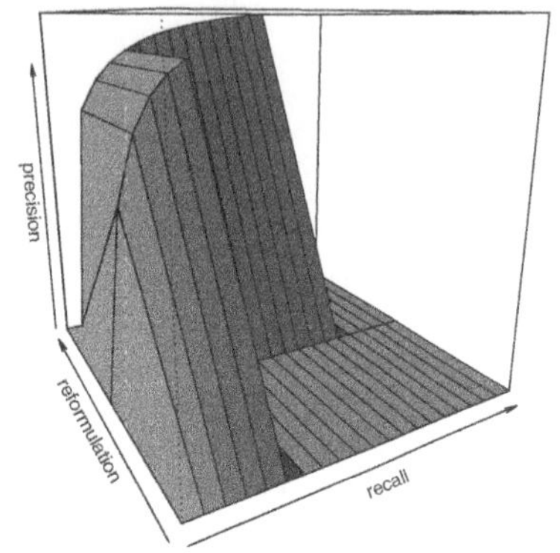

Figure 1: Reformulation precision-recall surface for the example in Table 1.

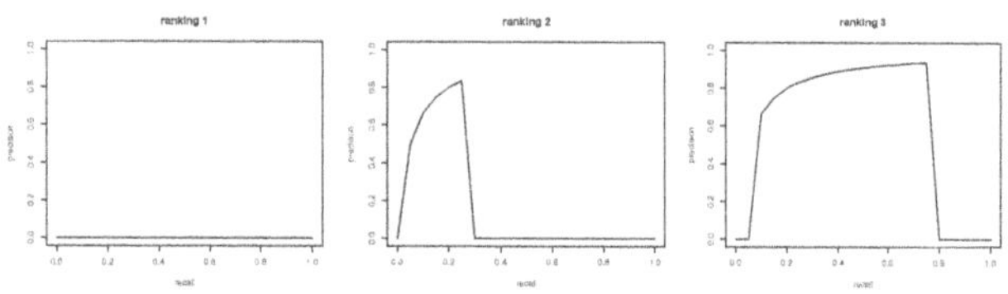

Figure 2: Reformulation precision-recall cross-sections of Figure 1 for the example in Table 1. Note that these are *not* precision-recall curves for the three rankings independently.

reformulation. At recall $1/R$ in $\vec{r}_2$, there is a set of possible precision values $\{1/2, 1/3, 1/4, ...\}$, each of which is achieved by a user looking at $k = 1, 2, 3, ...$ documents in ranking 1, then reformulating and looking at the first document in ranking 2. At recall $2/R$ in $\vec{r}_2$, the set is $\{2/3, 2/4, 2/5, ...\}$. Now we will define $sPC@r, j$ as the *maximum* value of the set of possible precisions at the first rank in $\vec{r}_j$ at which recall r is achieved. This reduces the amount of data to $m \cdot R$ precision values (with m being the number of queries in the static session) that reflect the best possible effectiveness a user could experience. Note that this is not interpolation in the traditional sense. $sPC@1/R, 2$ may still be less than $sPC@2/R, 2$, which is not possible in the usual definition.

Once we have computed $sPC@r, j$ for each r and j, we can plot a "precision-recall surface" over reformulations. Figure 1 shows the surface for the example in Table 1 with $R = 20$ under the assumption that all relevant documents in ranking 3 are unique (meaning there are five additional relevant documents that were not retrieved). We can see that precision increases with both recall and reformulation number, suggesting that the system is doing a better job with the later queries. (It may be easier to read cross-sections of the surface. They are shown in Figure 2.)

Finally, just as average precision is computed as the area under the precision-recall curve, we can define a model-free "session average precision" (sAP) as the the volume under

reformulation order	sAP
$\vec{r}_1, \vec{r}_2, \vec{r}_3$	0.261
$\vec{r}_1, \vec{r}_3, \vec{r}_2$	0.335
$\vec{r}_2, \vec{r}_1, \vec{r}_3$	0.344
$\vec{r}_2, \vec{r}_3, \vec{r}_1$	0.519
$\vec{r}_3, \vec{r}_1, \vec{r}_2$	0.502
$\vec{r}_3, \vec{r}_2, \vec{r}_1$	0.602

Table 3: Session average precisions for different permutations of the three ranked lists in Table 1. A system is rewarded for finding more relevant documents in earlier queries.

the precision-recall surface. An expression for sAP is:

$$sAP = \frac{1}{mR} \sum_{r=1}^{R} sPC@r/R, j$$

where $sPC@r, j$ is the max of the set of all possible precisions at the first point in $\vec{r}_j$ at which recall r is achieved. Computing $sPC@r, j$ can be done with the $O(n^m)$ approach described in Section 2.2:[3] within the jth loop, calculate precision and recall r over the documents on the path to that point; if precision is greater than the current known maximum for $sPC@r, j$, update $sPC@r, j$ to that precision.

In this example the volume under the surface is 0.261. To test whether sAP follows our intuition that it should be greater when more relevant documents are found for earlier queries, we calculate it for each permutation of the three rankings in our example. The results are shown in Table 3.

4. MODEL-BASED SESSION EVALUATION

In the previous section we extended three traditional evaluation measures to the case of multi-query session collections in a model-free fashion. The session-based system measures capture the optimal contribution of a system to answer an information need over an entire session. In this section we look at the problem from a user perspective.

Note that our definition of sPC in the previous section takes the maximum value of a set. We could instead take the *expected* value; this has the advantage of using all of the data as well as not assuming that a user will have the optimal experience with the system. However, taking such an expectation requires a probability distribution over paths; formulating such a distribution requires a user model[4].

To simplify the space of all possible browsing paths we follow the user model described in Section 2: a user steps down a ranked list of documents until some decision point. It is important that any realization of the distribution over possible paths allows for paths that end before the last reformulation in the static collection. Then, if Ω is the set of all possible browsing paths that follow the simple user model described earlier, $P(\omega)$ the probability of a certain path $\omega \in \Omega$, and M_ω a measure over the path ω, then we define a session based measure as the expectation

$$esM = \sum_{\omega \in \Omega} P(\omega) M_\omega$$

[3]There is also an $O(nm)$ dynamic programming approach, but we have not included it in this paper for reasons of space.
[4]A uniform distribution would not work, since most of the paths are very long and therefore have approximately zero precision.

4.1 Probability of browsing paths

As noted in Section 2, we can express a path ω as a set of reformulation points.Let us therefore formulate $P(\omega = \{k_1, k_2, ..., k_i\})$ as a joint probability distribution of a user abandoning the session at reformulation i, while reformulating at positions $\overrightarrow{\text{ref}} = \{k_1, k_2, ..., k_{i-1}\}$. Note that we do not include k_i, the abandonment cut-off at ranking i, in the probability. For the sake of generalizing traditional measures, we will assume that once the user arrives at the ith reformulation, they continue down that ranking as far as necessary to compute the measure.

We express the probability of a path ω as,

$$P(\omega) = P(r_i, \overrightarrow{\text{ref}}) = P(r_i) \cdot P(\overrightarrow{\text{ref}}|r_i)$$

Here we introduce a simplifying assumption: the reformulation position is independent across the ranked lists $1..r_i$. Then $P(\overrightarrow{\text{ref}}|r_i)$ can be expressed as,

$$P(\overrightarrow{\text{ref}}|r_i) = P(k_1|r_i)P(k_2|r_i) \cdots P(k_{i-1}|r_i)$$

In general, we could make each reformulation point dependent on the reformulation number and possibly even on the relevance of documents in the ranking; in this work we have elected to keep them independent for simplicity.

For the realization of the probability distribution over different browsing paths we follow Moffat and Zobel [10] in their definition of ranked biased precision and use two geometric distributions. The first gives the probability that the ith reformulation is the last; it has an adjustable parameter p_{reform} representing the probability that the user reformulates again from their current query. They will only arrive at reformulation i if they reformulate $i-1$ times, so:

$$P(r_i) = p_{\text{reform}}^{i-1}(1 - p_{\text{reform}})$$

Similarly, the second distribution gives the probability that the kth rank is a stopping or reformulation point with adjustable parameter p_{down}. A user will arrive at rank k only after deciding to progress down $k-1$ times, so:

$$P(k) = p_{\text{down}}^{k-1}(1 - p_{\text{down}})$$

The probability of a path is then

$$P(r_i, \overrightarrow{\text{ref}}) = p_{\text{reform}}^{i-1}(1 - p_{\text{reform}}) \prod_{j=1}^{i-1} p_{\text{down}}^{k_j - 1}(1 - p_{\text{down}})$$

$$= P(r_i) \prod_{j=1}^{i-1} P(k_j)$$

Our definition of $P(r_i)$ may give non-zero probability to a path that is not valid for a particular collection of static sessions, e.g. one that ends at some point past the last (mth) reformulation in the collection. To address this, we will truncate the distribution $P(r_i)$ and renormalize it to ensure that the probabilities to stop at different reformulations sum to 1. To do this we simply renormalize the probabilities from 1 to m by $Pr\{r \le r_i\} = 1 - p_{\text{reform}}^m$. That is,

$$P'(r_i) = \frac{p_{\text{reform}}^{i-1}(1 - p_{\text{reform}})}{1 - p_{\text{reform}}^m}$$

We could similarly truncate and renormalize $P(k_j)$. However, paths that extend beyond the last retrieved document for a reformulation (typically ranks beyond 1000) will have very low probability and thus they will not contribute in any significant way in the calculation of a measure.

4.2 Expectations over paths

Given a measure M_ω to be computed over the documents viewed on a particular path ω along with the probability distribution over all paths $\omega \in \Omega$, we can define a session measure as the expectation of M_ω over the probabilistic space of paths.

$$esM = E_\Omega[M] = \sum_{\omega \in \Omega} P(\omega) M_\omega$$

Let us consider a path-averaging generalization to precision at cut-off k. First define $PC@k(\omega)$ as the precision of the first k documents experienced on path ω. Then:

$$esPC@k = \sum_{\omega \in \Omega} P(\omega) PC@k(\omega)$$

$$= \sum_{\omega \in \Omega} PC@k(\omega) P'(r_i) \prod_{j=1}^{i-1} P(k_j)$$

$PC@k(\omega)$ is the total proportion of relevant documents at ranks $1..k_1$ in $\vec{r}_1$, $1..k_2$ in $\vec{r}_2$, and so on.

$$PC@k(\omega) = \frac{1}{k}\left(\sum_{j=1}^{k_1} rel_{1j} + \sum_{j=1}^{k_2} rel_{2j} + \cdots + \sum_{j=1}^{k_i} rel_{ij}\right)$$

where k_i, the abandonment cut-off at ranking i, is equal to $k - (k_1 + k_2 + \cdots + k_{i-1})$. Plugging that into the expression for $E[PC@k]$ completes the formula.

Similarly, the expectations of recall after k documents can be computed as

$$esRC@k = \frac{1}{R} \sum_{\omega \in \Omega} RC@k(\omega) P'(r_i) \prod_{j=1}^{i-1} P(k_j)$$

where

$$RC@k(\omega) = \frac{1}{R}\left(\sum_{j=1}^{k_1} rel_{1j} + \cdots + \sum_{j=1}^{k_i} rel_{ij}\right)$$

and k_i is defined as above.

A path-averaging generalization to average precision is:

$$esAP = \sum_{\omega \in \Omega} AP(\omega) P'(r_i) \prod_{j=1}^{i-1} P(k_j)$$

where $AP(\omega)$ is the average precision of the concatenated list of documents on path ω.

We can continue to define any measure this way. We will conclude with a path-averaging generalization to nDCG:

$$esnDCG@k = \sum_{\omega \in \Omega} nDCG@k(\omega) P'(r_i) \prod_{j=1}^{i-1} P(k_j)$$

where $nDCG@k(\omega)$ is the nDCG@k of the concatenated list.

All of the above formulations involve summing over paths ω. In general, summing a function $f(\omega)$ over all paths can be expressed in a brute-force way as:

$$\sum_{\omega \in \Omega} f(\omega) = \sum_{k_1=1}^{|r_1|} \sum_{k_2=1}^{|r_2|} \cdots \sum_{k_{i-1}=1}^{|r_{i-1}|} f(\{k_1, k_2, ..., k_{i-1}\})$$

Note that computing it involves on the order of $|r_1| \times |r_2| \times \cdots \times |r_{m-1}| = O(n^m)$ steps.

4.3 Monte Carlo estimation

A running time of $O(n^m)$ is manageable, but it is not fast, especially as m grows. Since our model for these measures is fully probabilistic, a faster alternative approach to estimating them uses simulation. A Monte Carlo simulation method allows the estimation of a measure via repeated random sampling. Running a Monte Carlo experiment requires defining a domain of possible inputs, generating inputs randomly from the domain using specific probability distributions, performing a deterministic computation using the inputs, and finally aggregating the results of the individual computations into the final result.

In the case of the user-model based measures proposed above, the input space is the ranking r_i at which the user abandons the query and the reformulation cut-offs at all previous queries $\{k_1, ..., k_{i-1}\}$.

Each of the above path-averaging measures can be thought as the expected outcome of the following random experiment:

1. Sample the last reformulation r_i from $P'(r_j)$.
2. Sample $(k_1, k_2, ..., k_{i-1})$ i.i.d. from $P(k_j)$ to form a path ω.
3. Create a ranked list of documents by concatenating ranks $1...k_1$ from r_1, $1...k_2$ from r_2, ..., $1...k_{i-1}$ from r_{i-1}, and $1...n$ from r_i. These are the documents seen along path ω.
4. Output measure M over that ranked list.

This random experiment defines one round of the Monte Carlo experiment. Executing the first two steps requires sampling from a geometric distribution. This can be easily performed assuming access to an algorithm that generates pseudo-random numbers uniformly distributed in the interval $(0, 1)$. Regarding the distribution of the last reformulation, since it is renormalized, we can first partition the interval $(0, 1)$ to $((0..P'(r_1)), (P'(r_1)..P'(r_1) + P'(r_2)), \cdots, (1 - P'(r_m)..1))$. We then use the random number generator to obtain a number in $(0, 1)$, and output j if this number is in the j-th partition. In the case of the cut-off distribution the same process can be followed. As mentioned earlier we did not renormalize this distribution and thus the last partition does not end in 1, however renormalization can be easily performed in the case of Monte Carlo by simply rejecting any sample larger than the upper bound of the last partition.

Repeating the process above B times and averaging the results gives an estimate of the expectation of measure M. For most purposes $B = 1000$ (which will usually be much less than n^m) should be sufficient; we explore the errors in estimates due to B in Section 6.

5. DUPLICATE DOCUMENTS

Our measures to this point make a strong assumption: that retrieval systems return unique documents for each query reformulation. Under this assumption, the concatenated ranked list of documents $\vec{cl}$ which corresponds to a certain browsing path ω resembles a typical ranked list of document in the standard evaluation paradigm. We certainly do not expect this assumption to hold in real systems; it is likely that documents retrieved for a second query will overlap with those retrieved for the first. When relaxing this assumption,we need to consider how these duplicate documents should be treated from the perspective of the evaluation measure.

The first question raised is whether documents repeated in ranked lists for subsequent reformulations have any value for a user. Järvelin et al. [6] noticed that in an empirical interactive search study conducted by Price et al. [12] searchers overlooked documents in early queries but recognized them in later reformulations. Due to this, the proposed sDCG measure does not give any special treatment to duplicate relevant documents; it considers them relevant regardless of the number of times they have been seen before.

But measures with a recall component (such as average precision or recall at k) cannot count duplicates in a sound way. Since there are multiple possible paths through the results, and these paths could have duplicate relevant documents, it is possible that more than R relevant documents could be observed along any given path. The computed measure may exceed the desired maximum value of 1.

We can instead consider duplicate documents nonrelevant in all cases. This has certain implications as well. For one, penalizing a retrieval system for returning duplicate documents may lead to systems that are less transparent to their users. Imagine a user that reformulates a query and expects to see previously observed relevant documents at higher ranks than before. If they are not there, the user may question whether the system can ever be useful to them.

Furthermore, by definition the expected measures reward a retrieval system that respond in an optimal way to a population of users. These different users may very well follow different browsing paths. In an actual retrieval setup, a system can infer whether a document has been observed by a user (e.g. by observing the users' clicks). In the case of a batch experiment, however, a certain document may be a duplicate for one user but not for another, depending on the browsing path each one of them has followed. This information is hidden in the parameters of the particular evaluation measure (which simulates the population of users). Taking these parameters into account a system could respond optimally by removing the expected duplicate documents. However, the need of such an inference process and a ranking function that accounts for the average browsing path is just an artifact of the batch nature of experiments. A retrieval system running in the real world will not need to employ such an algorithm.

Yang and Lad [16] take an approach in between the two extremes. Although they did not explicitly consider the problem of exact duplicates, the proposed measure is a measure of information novelty over multi-query sessions and thus it takes the typical approach other novelty measures take [4] by defining information nuggets and discounting documents[5] that contain the same relevant information nugget.

In this work we consider an alternative treatment of duplicates inspired by Sakai's compressed ranked lists [14] and Yilmaz & Aslam's inducedAP [17]. When considering a path ω out of the population of all paths, we construct the concatenated list $\vec{cl}$ that corresponds to this path. We then walk down the concatenated list and simply remove duplicate documents, effectively pushing subsequent documents

[5]The measure by Yang and Lad [16] was proposed for the task of information distillation and thus it operates over passages instead of documents; the same approach however could be used for the case of documents.

one rank up. This way, we neither penalize systems for repeating information possibly useful to the user, nor do we push unnecessary complexity to the retrieval system side. Further, the measures still reward the retrieval of new relevant documents. Note here that such an approach assumes that a system ranks documents independent of each other in a ranked list (probabilistic ranking principle [13]). If this is not true, i.e. if ranking a document depends on previously ranked documents and the retrieval system is agnostic to our removal policy then this may also lead to unsound evaluation.

6. EXPERIMENTS

In this section we demonstrate the behavior of the proposed measures. There is currently no "gold standard" for session evaluation measures; our goal in this section is to evaluate whether our measures provide information about system effectiveness over a session and whether they capture different attributes of performance in a similar way to traditional precision, recall, and average precision. We will compare our measures to the session nDCG measure proposed by Järvelin et al., though we consider none of these, nor any other measure, to be the one true session measure.

We use two collections towards these goals: (a) the TREC 2010 Session track collection [7], and (b) the TREC-8 (1999) Query track collection [2]. Though the latter is not a collection of multi-query sessions, we will find it useful to explore properties of our measures. Both of these collections are described in more detail below.

The instantiation of session nDCG@k we use is calculated as follows: we start by concatenating the top k results from each ranked list of results in the session. For each rank i in the concatenated list, we compute the discounted gain as

$$DG@i = \frac{2^{rel(i)-1}}{\log_b(i+(b-1))}$$

where b is a log base typically chosen to be 2. These are the summands of DCG as implemented by Burges et al. [3] and used by many others. We then apply an additional discount to documents retrieved for later reformulations. For rank i between 1 and k, there is no discount. For rank i between $k+1$ and $2k$, the discount is $1/\log_{bq}(2+(bq-1))$, where bq is the log base. In general, if the document at rank i came from the jth reformulation, then

$$sDG@i = \frac{1}{\log_{bq}(j+(bq-1))} DG@i$$

Session DCG is then the sum over $sDG@i$

$$sDCG@k = \sum_{i=1}^{mk} \frac{2^{rel(i)-1}}{\log_{bq}(j+(bq-1))\log_b(i+(b-1))}$$

with $j = \lfloor (i-1)/k \rfloor$, and m the length of the session. We use $bq = 4$. This implementation resolves a problem present in the original definition by Järvelin et al. [6] by which documents in top positions of an earlier ranked list are penalized more than documents in later ranked lists.

As with the standard definition of DCG, we can also compute an "ideal" score based on an optimal ranking of documents in decreasing order of relevance to the query and then normalize sDCG by that ideal score to obtain nsDCG@k.

nsDCG@k essentially assumes a specific browsing path: ranks 1 through k in each subsequent ranked list, thereby giving a path of length mk. Therefore, we set the cut-offs of our expected session measures to mk (with the exception of AP). For the computation of the expected session measures the parameter p_{down} is set to **0.8** following the recommendation by Zhang et al. [18]; in expectation, users stop at rank 5. The parameter p_{reform} is set arbitrarily to **0.5**. With $m = 2$ reformulations, the probability of a user stopping at the first reformulation is then 67% and moving to the next reformulation 33%, which is not far off the percentage of users reformulating their initial queries in the Excite logs [15].

6.1 Session track collection

The Session track collection consists of a set of 150 two-query sessions (initial query followed by one reformulation). Out of the 150 sessions, 136 were judged. The judged 136 topics include 47 for which the reformulation involves greater specification of the information need, 42 for which the reformulation involves more generalization, and 47 for which the information need "drifts" slightly. In the case of specification and generalization, both the initial query and its reformulation represent the same information need, while in the case of drifting the two queries in the session represent two different (but related) information needs. Given that some of the proposed session measures make the assumption of a single information need per session—these are the recall-based measures such as AP and recall at cutoff k—we drop the 47 drifting sessions from our experiments.

Each participating group submitted runs consisting of three ranked lists of documents:

RL1 ranked results for the initial query;

RL2 ranked results for the query reformulation independently of the initial query;

RL3 ranked results for the query reformulation when the initial query was taken into consideration.

Thus, each submission consists of two pairs of runs over the two-query session: RL1→RL2, and RL1→RL3. The document corpus was the ClueWeb09 collection. Judging was based on a shallow depth-10 pool from all submitted ranked lists. Kanoulas et al. detail the collection further [7].

Figure 3 shows example precision-recall surfaces for two submissions, CengageS10R3 [9] and RMITBase [8]. In both cases there is a moderate improvement in performance from the first query to the second. The decrease in precision is rapid in both, but slightly less so in RMITBase. As a result, though CengageS10R3 starts out with higher precisions at lower recalls, the model-free mean sAPs are close: 0.240 and 0.225 respectively. In general, these surfaces, like traditional precision-recall curves, provide a good sense of relative effectiveness differences between systems and where in the ranking they occur.

We use the submitted RL1 and RL2 runs (27 submissions in total) to compare the proposed model-based measures with normalized session DCG. nsDCG is computed at cut-off 10. We compute all measures in Section 2 with cut-off $2 \cdot 10 = 20$ (to ensure the same number of documents are used). Scatter plots of nsDCG@10 versus expected session nDCG@20 (esnDCG), PC@20 (esPC), RC@20 (esRC), and AP (esAP) are shown in Figure 4. Each point in the plot corresponds to a participant's RL1→RL2 submission; measures are averaged over 89 topics. The strongest correlation

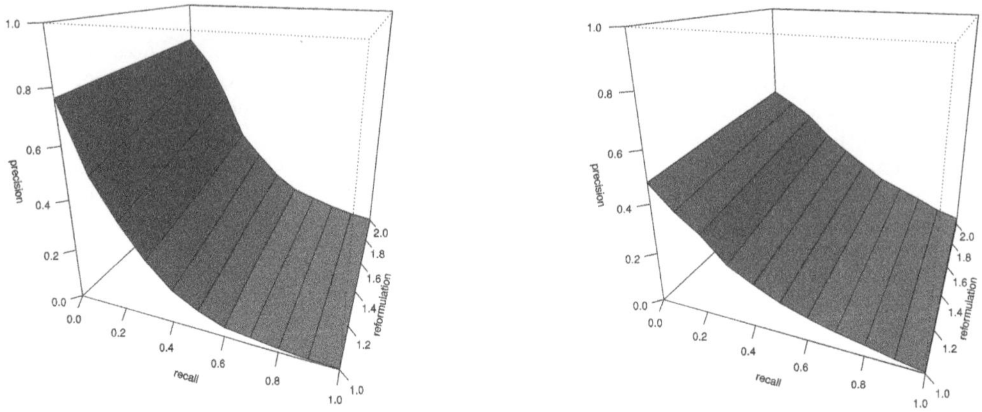

Figure 3: Precision-recall surfaces for CengageS10R3 and RMITBase.

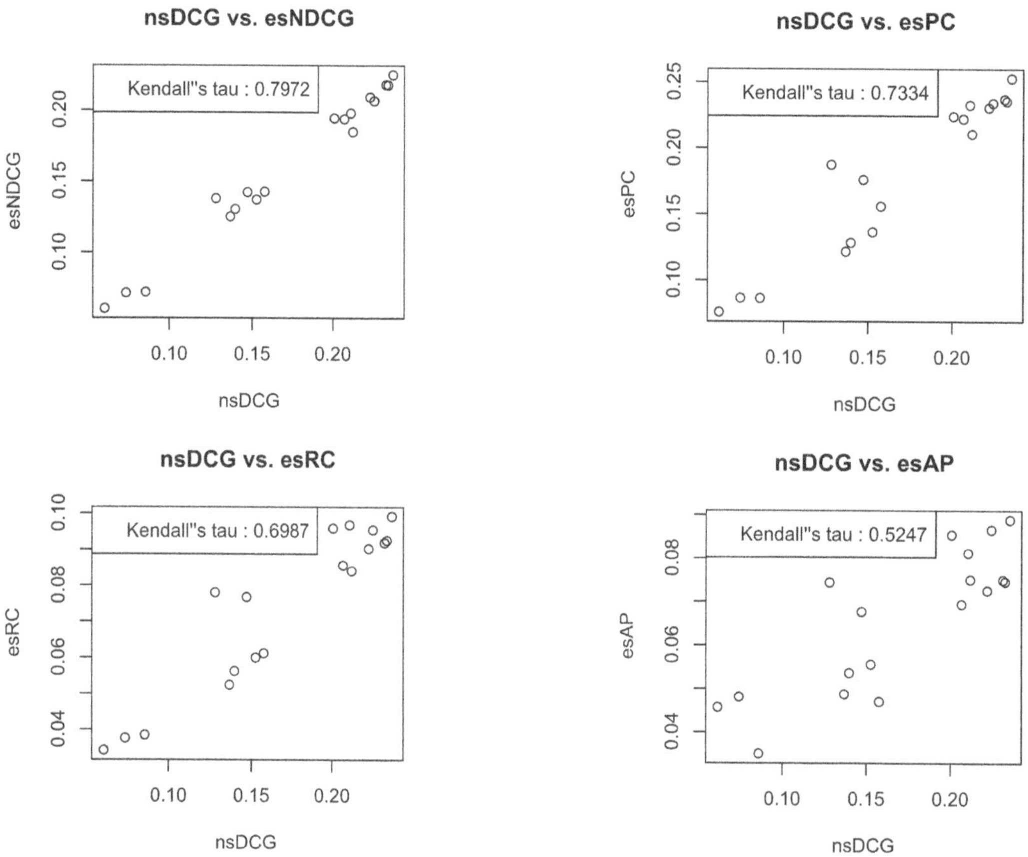

Figure 4: Scatter plots of the mean performance of systems in the Session track for the session RL1→RL2. The x-axis is sNDCG@10; the y-axis is expected session nDCG@20 (esnDCG), PC20 (esPC), RC@20 (esRC), and AP (esAP) for the four plots from left to right and top to bottom.

is between esnDCG and snDCG (as expected). Interestingly, esAP strongly disagrees with snDCG; this demonstrates that esAP measures different aspects of system effectiveness over sessions than snDCG. Table 4 shows τ correlations between all the expected measures as well as the model-free sAP; overall the correlations are within the range expected for these measures with a relatively small number of input systems. They are high relative to random orderings, but low enough that it is clear that all the measures are capturing different aspects of effectiveness. esAP and sAP do not correlate very well, but recall that sAP is based on maximums while esAP is based on averages.

6.2 Query track collection

The Query track [2] was an effort to understand the system-query-topic interaction often observed in IR experiments,

Kendall's tau correlation				
	esRC	esAP	esnDCG	sAP
esPC	0.88	0.79	0.93	0.78
esRC		0.80	0.84	0.87
esAP			0.72	0.78
esnDCG				0.74

Table 4: Kendall's tau correlation across the four expected session measures and sAP.

Average mean session measures			
	esMPC@20	esMRC@20	esMAP
"good"–"good"	0.378	0.036	0.122
"good"–"bad"	0.363	0.034	0.112
"bad"–"good"	0.271	0.023	0.083
"bad"–"bad"	0.254	0.022	0.073

Table 5: esPC@20, esRC@20, and esAP, each averaged over nine Query track systems simulating four session retrieval systems.

where certain systems perform well for certain queries but under-perform for others. A set of 50 topics (topics 51-100 from the TREC-1 collection) was provided to participants; they responded with a set of queries for each topic. The constructed queries were in one of the following forms, (a) very short: 2-4 words based on the topic and few relevance judgments; (b) sentences: 1-2 sentences using the topic and few relevant documents; (c) sentences+feedback: 1-2 sentences using only the relevant documents; and (d) weighted terms. Overall 23 query sets were produced, each consisting of 50 queries corresponding to the 50 topics of TREC-1. Participants ran their retrieval systems over each of the query sets and submitted results for each system for each query set. We use subsets of the 23 query sets and the submitted runs to simulate query sessions.

The goal of our first experiment is to empirically verify that the proposed measures reward early retrieval of relevant documents in the session. In this experiment we simulate four sets of session retrieval algorithms over 50 two-query sessions. The first simulated algorithm ("good"–"good") performs well on both the initial query and its reformulation in a hypothetical query session; the second ("good"–"bad") performs well on the initial query but not on its reformulation, the third ("bad"–"good") does not perform well on the initial query but does on its reformulation, and the last ("bad"–"bad") does not perform well on either queries.

To simulate these algorithms, we note that the systems participating in the Query track performed particularly well on short queries (with an average MAP of 0.227), while they did not perform well on the sentence-feedback queries (average MAP of 0.146) [2]. Taking this into consideration we simulate the best algorithm using runs over two short formulations of the same query. In particular, the nine runs over the query set named INQ1a with simulated reformulation results from the nine runs over query set INQ1b (with average MAP equal to 0.110 and 0.127 respectively, as computed by `trec_eval`) simulated a set of systems performing well both over the initial query of a hypothetical session and its reformulation. We simulate the worst system by runs over two sentence-feedback formulations. In particular the runs over query set INQ3a with reformulations being the runs over query set INQ3b (with average MAP 0.078 and 0.072 respectively) simulated a set of systems that performed well neither over the initial nor over the reformulated query. The other two combinations—INQ1a to INQ3b and INQ3a to INQ1b—simulated medium performance systems.[6]

What we expect to observe in this simulation is that session measures reward the "good"–"good" simulated systems the most, followed by the "good"–"bad", the "bad"–"good" and finally the "bad"–"bad" systems. Table 5 shows the average mean session scores produced by three of the expected session measures over the four simulated sets of retrieval algorithms. The results verify the behavior of the proposed measures. This is the exact same behavior we observed for the sAP measure in Table 3.

[6]The query sets INQ1a, INQ1b, INQ3a, INQ3b were manually constructed by students at UMass Amherst [2].

We conclude by testing the accuracy of the Monte Carlo method in computing the expected session measures. We simulated a two-query session by randomly selecting two sets of query formulations and their corresponding runs and forming a session from those. We run our $O(n^m)$ exact algorithm along with the Monte Carlo method. For the latter we use $B = 10$, $B = 100$ and $B = 1000$ trials. The results are illustrated in the left-hand plot in Figure 5, showing the high accuracy of the Monte Carlo simulation even with as few as 10 repetitions. Obviously, the accuracy of the method depends on the length of the session together with the set parameters p_{down} and p_{reform}. We did not test for different parameters, however we did repeat the same process over 3-query sessions. The results are illustrated at the right-hand side plot in Figure 5. There is somewhat more variance but even with $B = 10$ the results are very accurate.

7. CONCLUSIONS

In this work we considered the problem of evaluating retrieval systems over static query sessions. In our effort to make as few assumptions about user behavior over a session as possible, we proposed two families of measures: a model-free family inspired by interpolated precision, and a model-based family with a simple model of user interaction described by paths through ranked results. With a novel session test collection and a session collection simulated from existing data, we showed that the measure behaviors correspond to our intuitions about their traditional counterparts as well as our intuitions about systems that are able to find more relevant documents for queries earlier in the session. The measures capture different aspects of system performance, and also capture different aspects than what is captured by the primary alternative, snDCG.

They are surely other ways to generalize traditional evaluation measures and paradigms to session evaluation than those we have presented. Our goal with this work is to define measures as intuitively as possible while keeping models of user behavior simple. In the future we will want to consider explicit models of when and why users reformulate: is it based on the relevance of the documents they see? Does it depend on how many times they have already reformulated? Are they willing to go deeper down the ranking for a later reformulation than an earlier one?

There are many cases we have not explicitly considered. "Drifting" information needs, which were part of the TREC 2010 Session track, may require special treatment for eval-

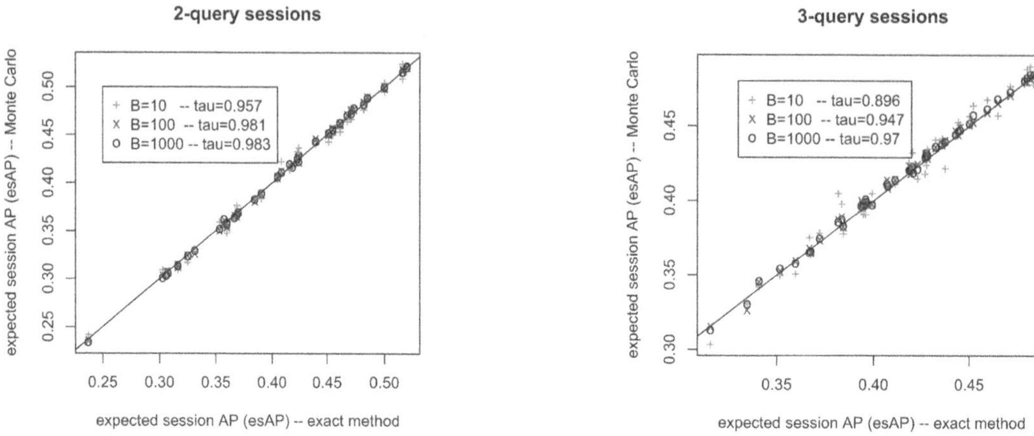

Figure 5: Exact method versus Monte Carlo in the computation of expected session AP (esAP) for $B = 10$, $B = 100$ and $B = 1000$, for 2 and 3 query sessions.

uation since the set of relevant documents can change as the need drifts. Furthermore, there are many examples of sessions in which a query and its results serve to guide the user in selecting future queries rather than immediately provide relevant documents; while we can apply our measures to these types of sessions, they are clearly not designed to measure a system's effectiveness at completing them.

Deeper understanding of session measures and their relationship to the user experience will come from future work on session test collections, application to "real" sessions in query log data, and extensive experimentation and analysis. We plan to continue all these lines of research in the future.

8. ACKNOWLEDGMENTS

We gratefully acknowledge the support provided by the European Commission grant FP7-PEOPLE-2009-IIF-254562 and FP7/2007-2013-270082 and by the University of Delaware Research Foundation (UDRF).

9. REFERENCES

[1] M. J. Bates. The design of browsing and berrypicking techniques for the online search interface. *Online review*, 13(5):407–431, 1989.

[2] C. Buckley and J. A. Walz. The trec-8 query track. In *The Eighth Text REtrieval Conference Proceedings (TREC 1999)*, 1999.

[3] C. J. C. Burges, R. Ragno, and Q. V. Le. Learning to rank with nonsmooth cost functions. In B. Schölkopf, J. C. Platt, T. Hoffman, B. Schölkopf, J. C. Platt, and T. Hoffman, editors, *NIPS*, pages 193–200. MIT Press, 2006.

[4] C. L. Clarke, M. Kolla, G. V. Cormack, O. Vechtomova, A. Ashkan, S. Büttcher, and I. MacKinnon. Novelty and diversity in information retrieval evaluation. In *SIGIR '08: Proceedings of the 31st annual international ACM SIGIR conference on Research and development in information retrieval*, pages 659–666, New York, NY, USA, 2008. ACM.

[5] W. S. Cooper. Expected search length: a single measure of retrieval effectiveness based on the weak ordering action of retrieval systems. *American Documentation*, 19:30–41, 1968.

[6] K. Järvelin, S. L. Price, L. M. L. Delcambre, and M. L. Nielsen. Discounted cumulated gain based evaluation of multiple-query ir sessions. In *ECIR*, pages 4–15, 2008.

[7] E. Kanoulas, B. Carterette, P. Clough, and M. Sanderson. Session track overview. In *The Nineteenth Text REtrieval Conference Notebook Proceedings (TREC 2010)*, December 2010.

[8] S. Kharazmi, F. Scholer, and M. Wu. RMIT University at TREC 2010: Session track. In *Proceedings of TREC*, 2010.

[9] B. King and I. Provalov. Cengage learning at the TREC 2010 Session track. In *Proceedings of TREC*, 2010.

[10] A. Moffat and J. Zobel. Rank-biased precision for measurement of retrieval effectiveness. *ACM Trans. Inf. Syst.*, 27(1):1–27, 2008.

[11] P. Over. Trec-7 interactive track report. In *The Seventh Text REtrieval Conference Proceedings (TREC 1998)*, pages 33–39, 1998.

[12] S. Price, M. L. Nielsen, L. M. L. Delcambre, and P. Vedsted. Semantic components enhance retrieval of domain-specific documents. In M. J. Silva, A. H. F. Laender, R. A. Baeza-Yates, D. L. McGuinness, B. Olstad, Ø. H. Olsen, and A. O. Falcão, editors, *CIKM*, pages 429–438. ACM, 2007.

[13] S. E. Robertson. The probability ranking principle in IR. *Journal of Documentation*, 33(4):294–304, 1977.

[14] T. Sakai. Alternatives to bpref. In *SIGIR '07: Proceedings of the 30th annual international ACM SIGIR conference on Research and development in information retrieval*, pages 71–78, New York, NY, USA, 2007. ACM.

[15] D. Wolfram, A. Spink, B. J. Jansen, and T. Saracevic. Vox populi: The public searching of the web. *JASIST*, 52(12):1073–1074, 2001.

[16] Y. Yang and A. Lad. Modeling expected utility of multi-session information distillation. In L. Azzopardi, G. Kazai, S. E. Robertson, S. M. Rüger, M. Shokouhi, D. Song, and E. Yilmaz, editors, *ICTIR*, pages 164–175, 2009.

[17] E. Yilmaz and J. A. Aslam. Estimating average precision with incomplete and imperfect judgments. In P. S. Yu, V. Tsotras, E. Fox, and B. Liu, editors, *Proceedings of the Fifteenth ACM International Conference on Information and Knowledge Management*, pages 102–111. ACM Press, November 2006.

[18] Y. Zhang, L. A. Park, and A. Moffat. Click-based evidence for decaying weight distributions in search effectiveness metrics. *Inf. Retr.*, 13:46–69, February 2010.

Quantifying Test Collection Quality Based on the Consistency of Relevance Judgements

Falk Scholer
School of Computer Science & Information Technology
RMIT University
Melbourne, Australia
falk.scholer@rmit.edu.au

Andrew Turpin
Dept of Computer Science & Software Engineering
University of Melbourne
Melbourne, Australia
aturpin@unimelb.edu.au

Mark Sanderson
School of Computer Science & Information Technology
RMIT University
Melbourne, Australia
mark.sanderson@rmit.edu.au

ABSTRACT

Relevance assessments are a key component for test collection-based evaluation of information retrieval systems. This paper reports on a feature of such collections that is used as a form of ground truth data to allow analysis of human assessment error. A wide range of test collections are retrospectively examined to determine how accurately assessors judge the relevance of documents. Our results demonstrate a high level of inconsistency across the collections studied. The level of irregularity is shown to vary across topics, with some showing a very high level of assessment error.

We investigate possible influences on the error, and demonstrate that inconsistency in judging increases with time. While the level of detail in a topic specification does not appear to influence the errors that assessors make, judgements are significantly affected by the decisions made on previously seen similar documents. Assessors also display an assessment inertia. Alternate approaches to generating relevance judgements appear to reduce errors. A further investigation of the way that retrieval systems are ranked using sets of relevance judgements produced early and late in the judgement process reveals a consistent influence measured across the majority of examined test collections.

We conclude that there is a clear value in examining, even inserting, ground truth data in test collections, and propose ways to help minimise the sources of inconsistency when creating future test collections.

Categories and Subject Descriptors

H.3.4 [**Information Storage and Retrieval**]: Systems and Software—*Performance evaluation (effectiveness)*

General Terms

Experimentation, Measurement, Performance

A preliminary version of this paper appeared at the 2010 Australasian Document Computing Symposium [14].

Keywords

Search engines, information retrieval evaluation

1. INTRODUCTION

The most common approach for evaluating an information retrieval system is through the use of a *test collection* using a standardized set of documents, topics, and human-generated relevance assessments, known as *qrels*. Test collections originate in the work of Thorne [17] and Gull [9] which inspired Cleverdon to create his Cranfield collections, defining the style of IR evaluation for decades [6]. Almost as soon as researchers described this evaluation approach, a number of criticisms were raised, many of which focused on the quality of the *qrels* and whether assessors would be able to reliably judge the relevance of documents to topics.

Over the nearly six decades that test collections have been used, many studies examined the impact of assessor mistakes on the quality of test collections. The format of these studies almost without exception used multiple assessors to calculate overlaps in judgements relative to each other. The studies showed that despite notable levels of disagreement, by and large, such noise did not affect the accuracy of test collections. These studies did not attempt to objectively calculate accuracy; neither did they try to measure an assessor's consistency across a set of judgements.

With the rise of crowd sourced relevance assessments, studies emerged measuring the accuracy of such judgments and, recently, there was work proposing models of assessor error with simulations of how such errors might impact on test collection based measurement. These recent studies highlighted that there has been no work to try to determine the levels of error made by traditional (and supposedly more trusted) test collection assessors; neither has there been an attempt to understand the nature of such errors. It is in this context that we conducted our research. The research questions that we investigate in this work are:

- Can one devise objective means of measuring assessor error?
- Are errors made by test collection assessors due simply to chance or are there discernible influences behind the mistakes?
- Are there alternate approaches to gathering relevance judgements that might reduce any measured error?

- Are there other consistent influences present in the relevance judgements of test collections that appear to affect the way that IR systems are evaluated?

The rest of this paper continues with a review of past work in this area. This is followed by a description of the data sets and methods used in our analysis. Next the results of a series of experiments on assessor error are presented. Experiments on other influences in relevance judgements are detailed after. Finally conclusions are drawn and future work is outlined.

2. RELATED WORK

Ever since the use of test collections became widely known, criticisms of the approach were described in the literature. In 1968, Katter [12] wrote that "a recurring finding from studies involving relevance judgments is that the inter- and intra-judge reliability of relevance judgments is not very high". Early test collection proponents, Cleverdon [7] and Lesk (with Salton) [13] both published studies comparing judgements by different assessors. They each concluded that despite a high level of disagreement between the assessors, the relative ranking of IR systems was largely unaffected by which set of judgements was used. These studies were repeated on a larger scale in a later study by Voorhees [19], in general drawing broadly similar conclusions, although Bailey et al. [2] showed that poor assessment can affect some aspects of measuring IR systems accurately.

The modern "standard" approach for gathering relevance assessments was established by TREC in the early 1990s [10]. A pooled set of documents are sorted by their document ID number (*DocID*) and judged in that order. The aim of such an approach is to minimise any influences on the assessors, who are unaware of how many retrieval systems returned a particular document or whether it was ranked high or low [10]. Other approaches to presenting pooled documents to assessors were proposed and their potential value discussed [24, 8]. When evaluated, the new methods were compared relative to the standard DocID sorting approach. However, these works did not consider the question of whether there is a way to determine if one approach is better than the other.

More recently, creating test collections using crowd sourcing (such as Mechanical Turk) grew in interest. Because workers in such approaches can be unreliable, there has been an increased focus on the potential of errors in relevance judgements. Alonso studied how best to obtain accurate judgements from workers using Mechanical Turk [1]. Carterette and Soboroff [4] suggested models of behavior in crowd sourced workers, simulating the impact of their posited patterns of mistakes on retrieval evaluation. A common approach to detecting errors by crowd sourced workers is to insert *ground truth* data (for which answers are already known) into the stream of items to be judged. If workers fail to mark up such data correctly, their inputs on other items can reasonably be assumed to be similarly mistaken. When building test collections, putting processes in place to check relevance assessors isn't common practice when non-crowd sourced assessors are used.

When researching the presence of duplicate documents in web collections, Bernstein and Zobel [3] pointed out that a number of duplicates in two web test collections (TREC's GOV1 and GOV2) had been "inconsistently classified" by relevance assessors. In effect, the duplicates were a form of ground truth data against which individual assessors could be tested. The extent to which assessors were examined in the paper was limited to calculating the fraction of inconsistently judged documents in the two collections studied.

The question of how to quantify assessor error has been considered in the context of e-discovery in the legal domain. The TREC Legal track interactive task simulates the process of reviewing documents in response to a request for production in civil litigation. In such a process, the relevance of a document (that is, whether the document should be considered to have a bearing on the case) is determined by a judge, called a *topic authority* in the TREC track [11]. It is therefore possible to objectively measure the rate at which relevance assessors make mistakes, by comparing their judgements against those of the topic authority [22]. However, despite a more objective notion of the "correctness" of relevance assessments, such comparisons are in essence still inter-assessor evaluations. Moreover, it is likely that the topic authority's own conception of relevance is subject to change over time.

From the review, it can be seen that examining the duplicates in test collections provides a means of determining the level of error made by relevance assessors, comparing different collections and different topics within collections. It potentially also enables comparisons to be made between different approaches for ordering *qrels*. As will be shown in the following section, the possible reasons for the inconsistent judgements made by assessors can also be explored.

3. METHODS AND DATA SETS

In this section we describe the test collections used and explain the methods that were applied to determine duplicate documents.

3.1 Test Collections

Collections from the Text REtrieval Conference (TREC) were chosen for our experiments for two reasons. First, the TREC approach to gathering relevance assessments is well documented and remained constant for many years. Second it has become a standard that many other collection formation methods are compared to. It was also realized by the authors of this paper that TREC files of *qrels* store the order that documents were shown to assessors. One can infer that the distance between two documents (for the same topic) in a TREC *qrels* file is proportional to the time between the two judgements being made.

This feature of the *qrels* was confirmed to us in a personal communication with Ellen Voorhees and Ian Soboroff at NIST, though with certain caveats. We are taking a simplified view of how distance equates to a difference in judgment time. Carterette and Soboroff [5] observed that more time is spent judging relevant documents than irrelevant documents. We experimented with counting relevant documents twice in the calculation of distance between two documents, assuming they take double the time to judge [5], but the results were consistent with simple counting, and so are not reported in detail. Another limitation of our assumption is that any breaks that may have been taken by assessors while judging documents for a particular topic are not reflected in the *qrels*. While it is theoretically possible that an assessor took an extended break from judging between every disagreeing pair of documents, this is highly unlikely, given the high number of disagreeing pairs per topic.

To analyse assessor behaviour, we examined relevance judgments over eight years of TREC, covering the early ad hoc test collections using mainly newswire and newspaper articles (TREC-1, 2, 3, 6, 7, 8) through to the more recent web collections (WT10G and GOV2). The ad hoc collections were grouped into three blocks, the first three years (labelled T123 in this paper), TREC-6 (T6, separated for reasons discussed later), and the final two years of TREC ad hoc (T78). Particular years were brought together if the collections used the same sets of documents.

3.2 Duplicate Documents

To identify pairs of highly similar documents that were both judged, a straight-forward document similarity approach was used. For each topic in a *qrels* file, all documents that have an entry (that is, an explicit relevance judgement) were indexed using the Zettair open-source search engine,[1] giving a *judged topic collection*. Next, each document with a judgement was submitted as a query to the previously created topic collection, with document similarities being calculated using the cosine measure [23]. The output of this step is a ranked list, ordering documents that have an explicit relevance judgment for a topic by decreasing similarity with the "query" document.

Manual inspection of duplicate documents from the collections showed that, almost without exception, documents retrieved with a similarity threshold of 0.9 or higher were very similar, near, or exact duplicate documents that a human assessor would be expected to judge consistently. Specifically, in the WT10G collection 58 duplicate documents were examined, 2 (~3%) were found not to be duplicates. In T78, 400 randomly selected pairs of documents were examined producing similar level of incorrectly identified pairs. In the web collections (WT10G and GOV2), duplicate documents commonly arose due to mirrored web sites. In the news-based TREC collections, the duplicates were due to newswire sources that were either repeating the release of documents, or sending updates of stories as they developed. Because the 0.9 threshold was found to be a reliable identifier of duplicates, it was used throughout our experiments.

As will be seen in the next section, the number of duplicate documents present in the *qrels* of test collections varied substantially, which for some collections limited the number of tests that could be run. However, the aim of this work was to examine the feasibility of using duplicate documents as ground truth data. In future test collections, duplicates or near duplicate documents could be inserted into *qrels* to allow measurment of assessors.

4. RESULTS

The examination of the data covered a number of aspects, each of which is detailed in the following sub-sections.

4.1 Fraction of Inconsistently Judged Duplicates

We first measure the number of duplicates present in each of the collections studied, and compute the fraction of duplicates that were judged inconsistently by the assessors, as shown in Table 1. Only duplicates where at least one document was judged relevant are included in this analysis; that is, assessor consistency in judging non-relevant documents was not considered. The two web collections (WT10G and GOV2) have three levels of relevance judgements: highly relevant, partially relevant, and not relevant. Results for the trinary judgements, and for judgements converted to binary (folding the highly relevant and partially relevant judgements into one category) are shown separately. Two outlier topics were found in the collections: in T123, topic 056 had over 4,800 pairs of duplicate documents in its qrels; in GOV2, topic 775 had over 13,000 duplicate pairs. In both collections the statistics for those topics would have dominated the collection micro-averages, and were therefore removed.

Collection	Consistent	Inconsistent	(% of Total)
T123	689	120	15%
T6	228	45	16%
T78	308	71	19%
WT10G-binary	1413	293	17%
GOV2-binary	10138	2346	19%
WT10G-trinary	1374	332	19%
GOV2-trinary	9504	2980	24%

Table 1: Consistency of relevance judgments across TREC collections. The columns show a count of the number of pairs of duplicate documents that were judged consistently and inconsistently, followed by the percentage proportion of inconsistent pairs. Only duplicates where at least one document was judged to be relevant are included.

As can be seen, the total number of duplicates varied substantially across the collections, with earlier newswire collections (T123, T6, and T78) showing few duplicates in the *qrels*, WT10G an order of magnitude more, and GOV2, an order of magnitude more again. The fraction of duplicates that were judged inconsistently was relatively similar across the collections, although for the trinary judgements in the web collections, the number of inconsistencies increased.

Past studies on assessor consistency focused on comparisons between assessors (*inter-assessor* consistency). Using the duplicate ground truth approach shows that such comparisons were not just finding disagreements on the nature of relevance between assessors with, there was also a striking level of internal disagreement by the assessors of these test collections.

It is worth remembering that although the absolute numbers of errors in the second column of Table 1 are small, there is no reason to think that the measured inconsistency is limited to duplicates. Semantically similar documents in the *qrels* are just as likely to be at least as inconsistently judged.

Topic length

One reason for studying the early TREC collections, T123, was that the first 100 topics were particularly long, with 60.1 words per topic on average, compared to around 20-30 words per topic in later TREC collections. The fraction of inconsistently judged duplicates in the first 100 topics was examined and found to be slightly lower (13%) than the fractions for the other newswire collections. However the

[1] www.seg.rmit.edu.au/zettair

Judgement of Pair	WT10G	GOV2
0–1	271	2142
0–2	22	204
1–1	1297	8441
1–2	39	634
2–2	77	1063

Table 2: Number of duplicate documents judged consistently and inconsistently (highlighted in bold) across the different trinary judgement combinations of document pairs, measured in the two web collections.

difference wasn't judged large enough to be attributable to the longer topics.

While it may be that extremely long topics do reduce assessor inconsistency somewhat, there is insufficient evidence of such an effect for the data studied here.

Examining Disagreements on Graded Judgements

As noted above, the web collections WT10G and GOV2 were judged with three levels of relevance: not relevant (0), partially relevant (1), and highly relevant (2). We examined the numbers of each possible combination of document pairs in the two collections. As can be seen in Table 2 there is a strong commonality in the results. The number of pairs where assessors are consistent is largest for partially relevant, and lowest for highly relevant. Inconsistencies between not relevant and partially relevant are the most common, followed by partially relevant with highly relevant. The smallest number of pairs is for documents which assessors once thought weren't relevant and then later judged them highly relevant.

The frequency of inconsistent pairs is strongly skewed across the classes 0–1, 0–2 and 1–2: making a judgement call between non relevant and partially relevant documents contributed the great majority of inconsistent judgements, at 82% and 72% for the WT10G and GOV2 collections, respectively. Where trinary relevance assessments are being made in the construction of a test collection, the judgments assigned to partially relevant documents appear to require extra scrutiny.

Topic Effects

The two outlier topics (056 & 775) showed that there was variation in the number of duplicates across the test collection topics. For each topic, t, there is a set of consistent and inconsistent pairs, and for each pair, the fraction of inconsistent pairs was examined. For analysis to be carried out, a sufficient number of duplicates need to be present in the collections. We therefore use the WT10G and GOV2 collections; the other collections have fewer duplicate pairs than topics, making it unlikely that any meaningful analysis would be possible from examining these collections further.

To ensure that calculations were not affected by small numbers, only topics with at least 10 duplicate pairs were considered, and relevance judgements were converted to binary. To compute which topics had a fraction larger than might be normally expected, the data was compared to a random distribution of duplicate pairs across the topics. Any topics with a fraction of inconsistently judged pairs

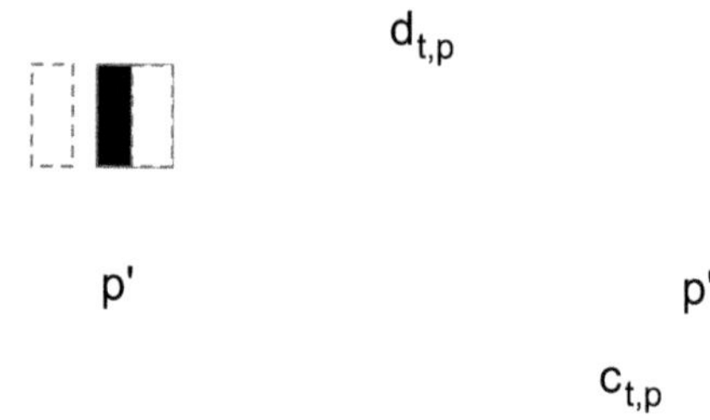

Figure 1: A hypothetical *qrels* file for a particular collection and topic. Each rectangle represents a document, in original *qrels* order. The two members of a pair of duplicates p are shaded in black and labeled p' and p''. The number of documents between these is $d_{t,p}$, 8 in this case. Intermediate documents that are highly similar to p' are shaded in light grey. The count of these, 3, is denoted by $s_{t,p}$ in the text. The number of documents between p'' and the closest similar document when moving back through the *qrels* is $c_{t,p}$, 1 in the example.

larger than three standard deviations from the mean of the randomly distributed fractions were noted.

In the GOV2 collection, 26% of the topics that were measured had a significantly higher number of inconsistently judged documents than would be expected by chance; in WT10G the corresponding number was 25%. Across all topics in both collections, the fraction of document pairs that were inconsistently judged ranged between 36% and 79%, substantially higher than the overall percentages of 17% and 19% reported in Table 1. Again, it seems reasonable to assume that this level of assessor inconsistency was not just found in the duplicate pairs, but also in other documents judged for these topics. With such high levels of error, one might question the value of including such topics in a test collection. Equally, one might view such levels of error as a warning sign about the quality of outputs from the assessors who judged these topics.

4.2 Distance

Having established that there are a notable number of inconsistent judgements, we now consider the properties of the duplicates, starting with the distance between them. For each pair of documents, p, found for a topic, t, let $d_{t,p}$ be the total number of documents judged between the *first* and *second* of each pair (that is, the distance between the pair in the *qrels* file, see Figure 1). Remembering that *qrels* order can be reasonably interpreted as being proportional to the temporal order in which documents were presented, $d_{t,p}$ is used as a measure of time between the assessor judging the first and second documents of the pair.

We examined if the relevance assessors were more likely to judge duplicate documents inconsistently when those documents were seen further apart (that is, when there was a greater amount of time between seeing the documents). The average $d_{t,p}$ was computed for all p that were consistently judged, and then again for all p that were inconsistently judged. These values were then averaged across all topics in the test collections (that is, macro-averaged). The results of this calculation are shown in Table 3.

Collection	Inconsistent	Consistent	p-value
T123	79.3	63.6	insignificant
T6	133.3	32.0	p<0.01
T78	83.4	60.8	insignificant
WT10G	457.1	206.9	p<0.01
GOV2	213.0	131.2	p<0.01

Table 3: The average distance $d_{t,p}$ between inconsistently and consistently judged pairs of documents.

As can be seen, the distance between disagreeing pairs was always greater than the distance between agreeing pairs. Using a randomization test computed for each collection [16], it was found that the difference in distances was significant for every collection except T123 and T78. For the remaining test collections, the results show that the distance in the *qrels* between duplicate documents influenced the likelihood that they would be judged consistently. It would appear that assessors were not always clear on the criteria used to judge a document and that such criteria were either forgotten, or alternatively that an assessor's view of what constituted relevance shifted over time as the documents were judged.

4.3 Other Factors Affecting Judgements

Given that identical or near identical documents were being judged inconsistently at different times in the assessment process, we next examine the agreeing and disagreeing pairs in the GOV2 and WT10G collections in more detail, to identify factors that might influence a change in judgement.

Reminder Documents

It seems reasonable to assume that when an assessor encountered a duplicate of a previously judged document, but gave a different judgement than previously, that they forgot their previous judgement, and perhaps even forgot the document itself. Where other, similar documents are present between the two, the intervening documents could serve as "reminders" of the original duplicate, and thus lead to a consistent judgement of the second in a pair.

This indeed seems to be the case. For each topic, t, there is a set of consistent and inconsistent pairs, and for each pair, p, let $s_{t,p}$ be the number of documents that was *similar* to the first document, and occurred between the first and second in judgement order (see Figure 1). We continue to use $d_{t,p}$ to represent the total number of documents judged (the *distance*) between the first and second of each pair. Figure 2 shows the mean difference, for each topic, of the ratio $s_{t,p}/d_{t,p}$ for consistent pairs and inconsistent pairs. A high value indicates that there are more similar documents between consistent pairs than for inconsistent pairs for that topic. Fifty-nine topics from GOV2 and WT10G have a mean ratio greater than zero, and thirty-one have a ratio less than zero, with the mean difference being 0.091. It seems clear that having a high number of similar documents between a pair means that the pair is more likely to be consistently judged.

Given that the distance between similar documents that were judged inconsistently was greater than the distance between consistent pairs, perhaps this wasn't too surprising. Assuming that $s_{t,p}$ was small for most topics and pairs, and the previous section demonstrates that $d_{t,p}$ was larger for inconsistent pairs, then naturally the ratio $s_{t,p}/d_{t,p}$ will be smaller for such pairs. Define $c_{t,p}$ to be the number of documents between the second of pair p and its nearest similar document, in judgement order, towards the first document in pair p. That is, $c_{t,p}$ is the distance to the *closest* "reminder" document to the second document in p (see Figure 1). If the presence of reminders has the effect that it is more likely to lead to consistency between the first and second judgements of p, then $c_{t,p}/d_{t,p}$ should be smaller for consistent pairs than for inconsistent pairs.

Again, this intuition is supported. Figure 3 shows the mean over all pairs p for each topic t of $c_{t,p}/d_{t,p}$ for consistent pairs, minus the same for inconsistent pairs. Fifty-five topics have a similar document closer for consistent pairs than inconsistent pairs (a negative difference in the ratio) and thirty-three have the opposite. As the mean was less than zero (t-test, $p = 0.008$), we conclude that consistent pairs were more likely to have a document, close to the second, that was similar to the first of the pair, in judgement order. This close document is likely to have served as a reminder of the first document to the assessor, thus leading to the judgement of the second document agreeing with the first.

Inertia

A further possible factor that may affect relevance judgments is that assessors simply prefer to continue assigning the same value to documents. For example, Carterette and Soboroff [5] showed that autocorrelation exists in their judgement data from the TREC Million Query track: immediately after judging a document relevant, the probability of the next judgement also being relevant is significantly higher than the simple probability of a relevant judgement occurring independently of the previous judgement.

This *inertia effect* is present in the GOV2 and WT10G qrels, with the probability of a relevant judgement following a relevant judgement being 42% and 29% respectively, while the unconditional chance of judging a document relevant is 20% and 4%, respectively. Similarly, the conditional probability of judging a document irrelevant given that the previous was judged irrelevant is 86% and 97%, compared with the unconditional 80% and 96%. All four conditional probabilities are higher than the unconditional using a test on proportions ($p < 0.001$). These simple calculations from the qrels files, however, might reflect a clustering of documents in the collection, rather than a genuine bias in judging.

An alternative way to test the hypothesis that inertia exists can be carried out using the pairs of similar documents that were used in previous sections. In particular, if the second document in a similar pair was judged independently of the rest of the documents, it should have the same relevance score as the first document in the pair. We know that this is not the case for *inconsistent* pairs, however, so there must be factors other than document content influencing the judgement of the second document, one of which could be the judgement immediately preceding the judging of the second document.

Table 4 shows the probabilities involved, derived from counting data in the GOV2 collection. There are only a handful of disagreeing pairs for the WT10G collection, and while the trends are the same as those reported for GOV2, there is too little data to draw any firm conclusion from that collection. Clearly, the probability of judging the

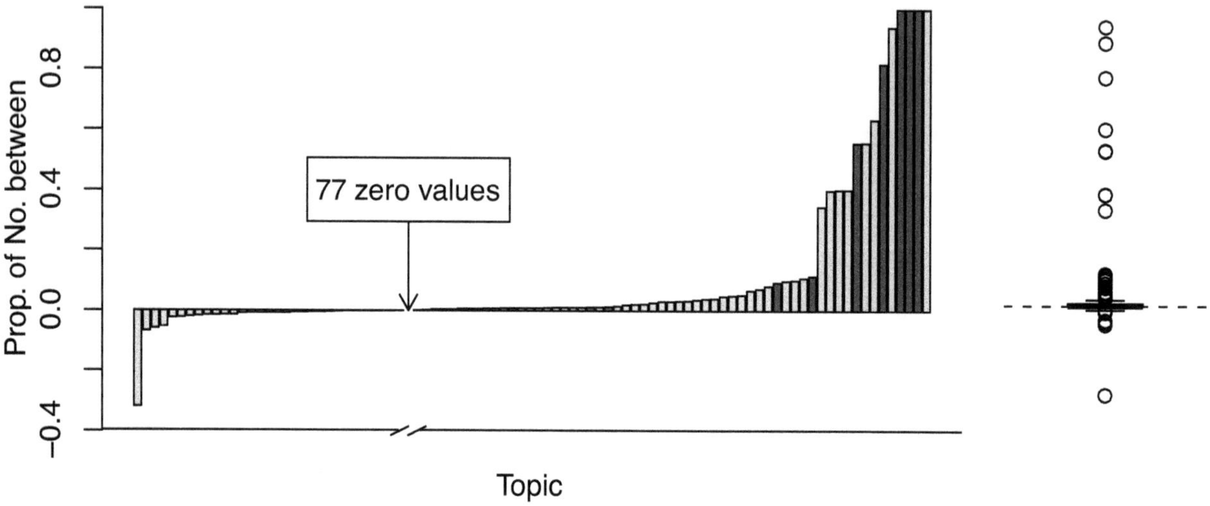

Figure 2: The difference between the mean number of documents similar to the first of a *consistent* pair that occurred between the first and second of the pair, as a proportion of the total number of documents between the pair, minus the corresponding quantity for *inconsistent* pairs. Topics that had no pairs with similar documents between were excluded (82 of 249 topics), and topics with a mean ratio of zero were not plotted in the barplot, but were included in the boxplot and statistics. Dark bars are topics from WT10G and light from GOV2. The boxplot on the right summarizes the values. The mean value is 0.058, which is different from zero (t-test, $p = 0.0003$).

Prob[Irrel.]	10.6%
Prob[Irrel. | preceding doc is Irrel.]	13.5%
	$p = 0.015$
Prob[Rel.]	3.0%
Prob[Rel. | preceding doc is Rel.]	8.0%
	$p < 0.001$

Table 4: Probability, derived from counting pairs of similar documents in the GOV2 collection, of judging the second document of a disagreeing pair either independently of the preceding document's judgement (rows 1 and 4), or conditional on the preceding judgement (rows 2 and 5). In both cases, the conditional probability was significantly higher (proportion test with p values as shown).

second document in a pair is conditioned on the previous judgement.

Testing Another Approach for Producing Qrels

In the TREC test collections, documents were presented to assessors in a consistent DocID sorted linear order. However, other orderings could be used; one example is an alternate set of *qrels* from Cormack et al. [8], whose work on an Interactive Search and Judge (ISJ) approach to assessment produced a set of *qrels* for the TREC-6 (T6) topics. Here, assessors searched for relevant documents for a particular topic by submitting multiple queries to an IR system. The authors of the paper kindly provided their ISJ *qrels* for us to examine. From this we computed the fraction of duplicate documents that were inconsistently judged and compared this to the numbers presented in Table 1. Note that the *qrels* produced by these two methods covered a different range of judged documents, which resulted in the different numbers of consistent and inconsistent judgements. As can be seen in Table 5, although the numbers are small, the fraction of inconsistently judged pairs is substantially smaller for the ISJ *qrels* than the DocID sorting method. A randomization test shows that the differences in percentages is statistically significant.

In the ISJ approach, the documents to be judged were presented to assessors as a series of ranked document lists. Since these are retrieved based on a similarity function, one would expect that duplicate documents occurred close to each other in such lists. This suggests that the time period between seeing duplicates was lower than in the linear presentation case, and so inconsistency rates were also likely to be lower. Similar, but non-duplicate, documents were also likely to be found close to each other in the rankings produced by the ISJ approach. From this result, we conclude that an ISJ approach to gathering *qrels* is potentially a more accurate approach compared to the DocID sorting method.

4.4 Correlations of System Performance

In addition to investigating the consistency of assessors at an individual judgment level, a further consideration is whether the demonstrated inconsistencies appear to impact significantly on system evaluation.

Computing the Tau of System Ranks

Measurement of an IR system using a test collection is in general only meaningful in the context of that collection,

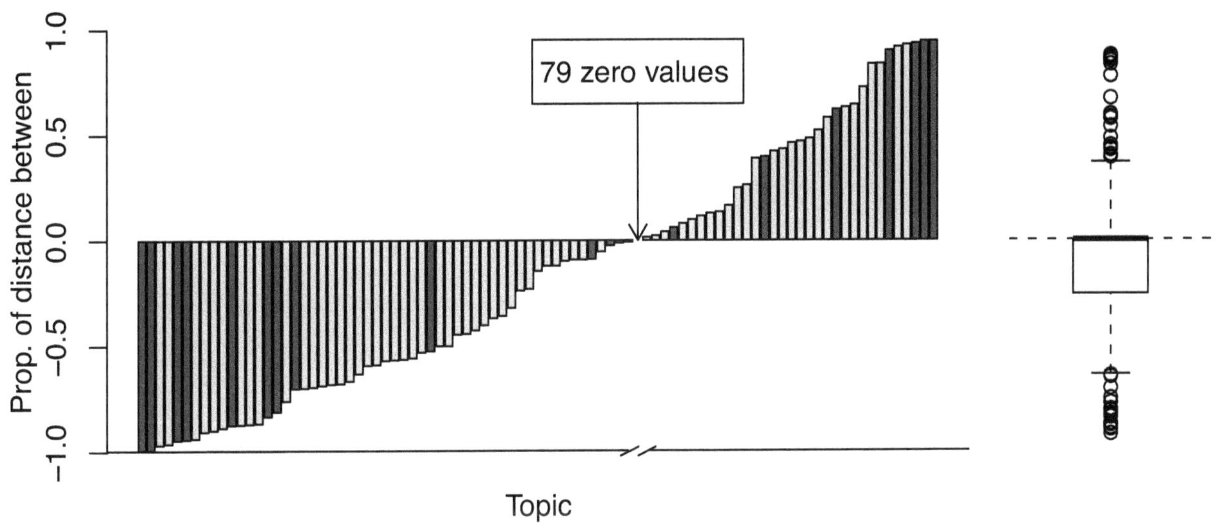

Figure 3: For a pair of duplicate documents, $c_{t,p}$ is the distance of the closest highly similar document that occurs between the pair in a *qrels* file. The figure plots the ratio of $c_{t,p}$ to the total distance between the duplicate documents for *consistent* pairs, minus the same ratio for *inconsistent* pairs. Details are as for Figure 2. The mean value is -0.09, which is different from zero (t-test, $p = 0.008$).

Collection	Consistent	Inconsistent	(% of Total)
T6-DocID	228	45	16%
T6-ISJ	417	35	8%

Table 5: The percentage of duplicate documents judged consistently and inconsistently. The final columns shows the number of inconsistent pairs as a proportion of the total number of pairs. Only duplicates where at least one document was judged relevant were considered.

and is not comparable for searches across different sets of documents [21]. For this reason, the focus of batch evaluation has been on *relative* system performance, rather than absolute. Where a set of queries has been run across a collection using a number of different search systems, the averaged effectiveness measures give an ordering of systems. When the same search systems are deployed on a different document collection, or with a different set of test queries, then even though the absolute scores are not directly comparable, a new relative ordering of system performance is obtained and these rankings can be compared.

A variety of measures are available to calculate such comparisons: Kendall's tau (τ) is commonly used in IR for this purpose. Tau measures the agreement between two ordered lists, and corresponds to the number of pairwise swaps that are needed to transform one ordering of one list to the other [15]. The value of tau is normalised to the range $-1 \le \tau \le +1$, with the extremes indicating perfect (inverse) agreement, and a value of zero indicating no association between the two lists.

Previous work on assessor consistency considered the level of agreement between system orderings when evaluation measures were calculated based on relevance judgements from different assessors. Voorhees [18] analysed this inter-assessor consistency by comparing system rankings based on *qrels* from different judges: TREC assessors and the ISJ approach of Cormack et al. [8]. She found that the average tau was 0.9, showing a relatively high level of agreement. This level is therefore representative of the kind of disagreement that might be expected when comparing *qrels* from different sets of people.

Given that it was shown that there is a DocID ordering to the *qrels* of many test collections, we focus on consistency across these ordered judgements sets. If there were systematic variations, they would warrant further investigation. We therefore proceeded as follows. First, the *ordered qrels* file was split in half, so that for each topic the first half of relevant documents were placed into an *early* partition, while relevant items that occur in the second half are placed into a *late* partition.

For retrieval systems, we used the official *runs* submitted to TREC for the ad hoc search tasks in TREC 2, 3, 6, 7 and 8; the Web tracks in TREC 9 and 10 (WT10G); and the Terabyte track in TREC 2006 (GOV2). Each set of runs represents a variety of different retrieval approaches, including both automatic (based only on a retrieval system) and manual (including human intervention) approaches. Because manual approaches often display strongly different characteristics, and in some cases reflect the ability of humans rather than the performance of search systems, we use only automatic runs in our analysis. Moreover, because submitted runs were from experimental systems, some submissions may include errors or unexpected behaviour; as a result, we follow standard practice and discard the bottom 25% of runs based on the MAP measure [20]. Finally, for the GOV2 collection, we note that the crawl of documents was carried out such that initially documents of type HTML were favoured, while later there was a bias

Collection	Tau	*p*-value	Overlap
TREC 2006	0.609	<0.001	0.667
TREC 10	0.628	0.047	0.333
TREC 9	0.702	0.273	0.538
TREC 8	0.396	<0.001	0.176
TREC 7	0.664	<0.001	0.667
TREC 6	0.466	<0.001	0.333
TREC 3	0.587	<0.001	0.429
TREC 2	0.456	<0.001	0.250

Table 6: Kendall's tau value between system orderings obtained when splitting the *ordered qrels*. The *p*-value indicates the result of a permutation test comparing the *ordered* and *random* split *qrels*. Overlap shows the change in the top 10 ranked systems when evaluated using the two halves of the *ordered qrels* (intersection divided by union).

towards PDF documents. To preclude possible interaction from this systematic variation in document types, we only used judgments for HTML documents in the analysis of this collection.

The level of Kendall's tau between system orderings based on the early and late partitions of the *qrels* files gives measures of agreement between system orderings, which can be compared to the 0.9 inter-assessor threshold.

We conducted a further comparison by partitioning the *qrels* into halves *randomly*. If there was a systematic change in relevance judgements that was related to judging order, then the tau score obtained by comparing the ordered partitioning would be lower than that obtained through random partitioning. In our experiments, we created 1000 random partitions of the *qrels*. These were used as a permutation test, to assess the significance of differences between the ordered and random levels of tau.

Results

The Kendall's tau correlation between system orderings based on the different partitions are shown for three TREC collections in Figure 4. For the GOV2 collection, shown in the left-most panel, the tau score for the *ordered* split qrels was 0.609, showing a relatively low level of agreement, especially in relation to earlier work on inter-assessor comparisons that resulted in a mean tau of 0.9 [18]. Moreover, the 1000 *random* split *qrels* led to tau values in the range from 0.764 to 0.946. Based on a permutation test, the intra-assessor effect is statistically significant ($p < 0.001$).

The tau scores, and *p*-values for a permutation test between the *ordered* and *random* split *qrels*, for the other TREC collections are shown in the first two columns of Table 6. As can be seen, results for the TREC 2, 3, 6, 7 and 8 collections were similar to those for GOV2: the tau scores between the two halves of the *ordered qrels* were substantially lower than the inter-assessor threshold of 0.9; and there was a statistically significant difference between the *ordered* and *random* split *qrels* ($p < 0.001$).

The only exception to this was the results for the TREC 9 and 10 Web track collections, as shown in the middle and right-hand panels of Figure 4. While still much lower than the 0.9 threshold, for TREC 9 the tau values for the *ordered* split were not significantly different from those obtained using *random* splits ($p = 0.273$) while for TREC 10 the difference was only slightly below the commonly used threshold for significance ($p = 0.047$). A possible explanation for this difference would be that the relevance judgments for the WT10G collection have a lower proportion of duplicate documents that are inconsistently judged; however, from Table 1 it can be seen that this is not the case. We also investigated whether there is a difference in the proportion of pairs that cross the "midpoint" at which the *ordered qrels* files are split for different collections, but again there appears to be no substantial variation.

Tau scores measure the agreement between two ranked orderings, taking the whole list into account. From a system evaluation perspective, however, we may be more interested in the top-ranked systems. It is therefore informative to consider the extent to which the set of the top 10 ranked systems changes when evaluation is carried out using the early or late halves of the *ordered qrels*. The right-most column of Table 6 reports the overlap between the two sets, measured as the intersection of the sets normalised by their union. For example, an overlap value of 0.333 indicates that 5 systems out of the top 10 are the same for both sets. The number of consistent systems in the top 10 sets ranges from 8 (overlap of 0.667 for TREC 2006 and TREC 7) to just 3 (overlap of 0.176, TREC 8). In particular, even the TREC 9 and 10 Web track collections show variation in the top 10 ranked systems (overlap of 0.538 and 0.333, respectively), despite showing less substantial variation in tau scores for the *ordered* versus *random* splits.

As can be seen from the analysis above, there appears to be substantial systematic variation in the way that retrieval systems are ranked between the early and later stages of the assessment process, leading to differences in the measured effectiveness of evaluation systems.

One possible source of such variation could be due to the inconsistency of relevance judgements, which are greater for judgements made further apart from each other. However, there are other plausible effects that are likely to also be contributing to the variation. In the earlier TREC test collections, DocID sorting of *qrels* has the unintended effect of grouping the documents by the news source they originated from. Therefore, the documents in the early partition will be from news sources, starting with letters early in the alphabet, such as the AP or Federal Register; documents in the later partition will more likely be from sources such as LA Times or Zipf. There should not be any influence of the source of an article on the relevance judgement or on the way that an IR system ranks that article. However, it would appear that such an effect is clearly present in the data shown here.

The order of documents in the *qrels* of the web collections appears to reflect the order in which the documents were crawled. The reason why an ordering effect exists in the GOV2 collection, beyond the document type effect discussed previously, is not as yet clear. We plan to investigate such factors in future work.

5. CONCLUSIONS AND FUTURE WORK

Relevance judgements are the key component for collection-based evaluation of IR systems. While there have been a number of studies examining the consistency of judgements made by different assessors, in this paper we examined the

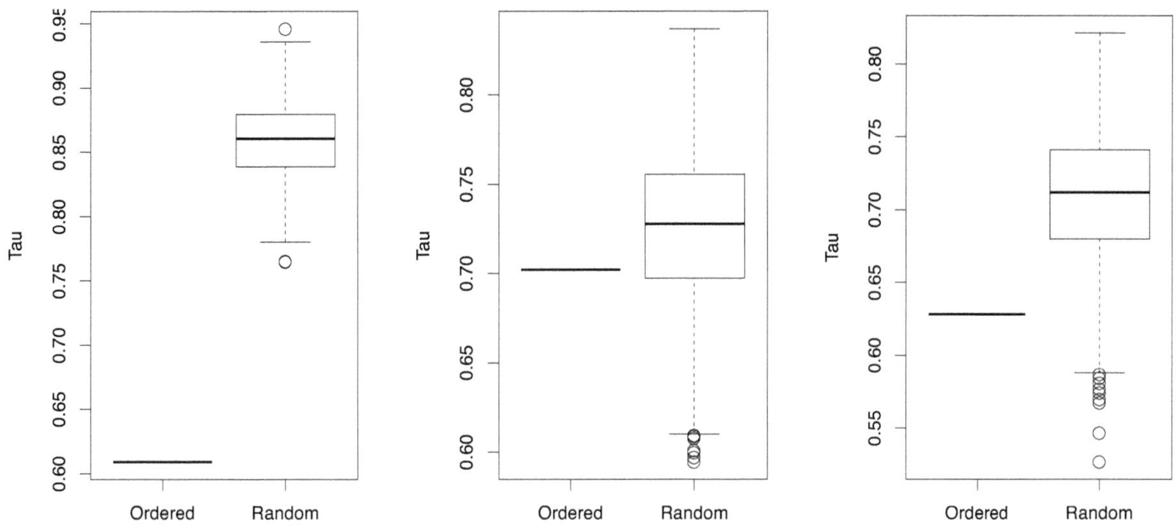

Figure 4: Kendall's tau correlation between system orderings when evaluated using the *ordered* and *random* split *qrels*. The three graphs show results for TREC 2006, TREC 9 and TREC 10, respectively. Corresponding statistics and data for the other TREC collections are presented in Table 6.

much less considered, but potentially more valuable, intra-assessor consistency.

Our first research question was how to objectively measure assessor error. By examining the inconsistent judging of duplicate documents in *qrels*, we demonstrated that one can measure a notable level of intra-assessor error in test collections. These error rates should be viewed as a lower bound, as it is expected that many more documents in the *qrels* will be subject to at least the same inconsistent assessment. Partially relevant documents were found to contribute disproportionately to assessor inconsistency. Means to identify problematic topics were described. Such a process can be used to guide test collection creation; for example, topics with high levels of inconsistency could be removed, or the work of the assessors judging these topics could be more carefully examined.

We next investigated whether the errors that were made by test collection assessors were simply due to chance, or if factors contribute to assessment mistakes. First, our analysis showed that the errors were impacted by the amount of time that passed between judgements being made on documents; it appears that assessors either forgot their criteria for judging the relevance of documents, or that their criteria changed over time. Second, assessors appear to have a judgement inertia: given a judgement on one document, assessors were predisposed to assign the next document with the same relevance value. A possible explanation for the inertia previously observed in qrels [5] was that relevant documents were clustered in the collection when viewed in *qrels* order, and so it is a feature of the collection, not the judges. However, our analysis in Section 4.3 showed that this was not the case in the GOV2 and WT10G collections; inertia existed for similar pairs that were not together in the collection. Third, judgements were shown to be influenced by the number of similar documents seen prior to judging a document. When similar documents were seen, these improved the consistency of judgments, serving as a reminder of the assessor's relevance criteria.

We investigated whether alternate approaches to gathering relevance judgements might reduce the measured error. An alternative set of *qrels*, built through an interactive searching and judging, process was obtained. The lower level of measured error in judging duplicates demonstrated that alternative methods for gathering judgments have the potential to significantly reduce the number of inconsistent judgements in a test collection.

Finally, we examined the impact of the ordering of *qrels* on the evaluation of IR systems. We calculated the correlation between system rankings obtained using judgements made early or late in the assessment process. The results indicated that there are significant, consistent and substantial differences in the way that retrieval systems are ranked when *qrels* are split based on the order in which those *qrels* are stored.

Although there have been a large number of studies on correlations between assessors, there has been little analysis of intra-assessor consistency. Neither have there been many examinations of problematic assessment on a per-topic basis. Overall, the results of this paper show that there can be great value in analysing the consistency of ground truth data. Our analysis and proposed diagnostic approach involved the examination of duplicate documents; however, in some collections, the occurrence of duplicates was a rare event. When building a test collection with few duplicates, one approach would be to manually insert duplicate documents at critical points of the judging process. We will examine such an approach in future work. We also plan to examine other types of duplicate or related documents that can be either found or inserted into collections. In particular, the data used in this paper is based on document-level relevance assessments. It would be illuminating to work with more fine-grained relevance data, where the specific sections of documents that are judged to be relevant are known. We will also examine the factors that are causing the low correlations in the system rankings from early and later splits in *qrels*.

It is rare for test collection creators to set up processes

to check the quality of their assessors, or to try to identify poorly judged topics. Our analysis has shown that even in carefully run test collection exercises, notable levels of error are present. However, this simple analysis allows such errors to be identified and reduced. We hope that the practical outcomes of this work will be to encourage use of this analysis method, which can further enhance the quality of collection-based evaluation of IR systems.

6. ACKNOWLEDGMENTS

We thank Ian Soboroff and William Webber for helpful discussions, and Gordon Cormack and Charlie Clarke for providing the set of alternative *qrels* for the TREC 8 data. Andrew Turpin was supported by ARC Grant FT0991326.

7. REFERENCES

[1] O. Alonso and S. Mizzaro. Can we get rid of TREC assessors? Using mechanical turk for relevance assessment. In *Proceedings of the SIGIR 2009 Workshop on the Future of IR Evaluation*, pages 15–16, 2009.

[2] P. Bailey, N. Craswell, I. Soboroff, P. Thomas, A. P. de Vries, and E. Yilmaz. Relevance assessment: are judges exchangeable and does it matter. In *Proceedings of the ACM SIGIR international conference on Research and development in information retrieval*, pages 667–674, 2008.

[3] Y. Bernstein and J. Zobel. Redundant documents and search effectiveness. In *Proceedings of the ACM CIKM international conference on Information and knowledge management*, pages 736–743, 2005.

[4] B. Carterette and I. Soboroff. The effect of assessor error on IR system evaluation. In *Proceedings of the ACM SIGIR international conference on Research and development in information retrieval*, pages 539–546, 2010.

[5] B. Carterette and I. Soboroff. The effect of assessor error on ir system evaluation. In *Proceedings of the ACM SIGIR International Conference on Research and Development in Information Retrieval*, pages 539–546, 2010.

[6] C. Cleverdon. The evaluation of systems used in information retrieval (1958: Washington). In *Proceedings of the International Conference on Scientific Information - Two Volumes*, pages 687–698. Washington : National Academy of Sciences, National Research Council, 1959.

[7] C. W. Cleverdon. The effect of variations in relevance assessments in comparative experimental tests of index languages. Cranfield Library Report 3, Cranfield Institute of Technology, 1970.

[8] G. V. Cormack, C. R. Palmer, and C. L. A. Clarke. Efficient construction of large test collections. In *Proceedings of the ACM SIGIR international conference on Research and development in information retrieval*, pages 282–289, 1998.

[9] C. D. Gull. Seven years of work on the organization of materials in the special library. *American Documentation*, 7(4):320–329, 1956.

[10] D. K. Harman. The TREC test collection. In E. M. Voorhees and D. K. Harman, editors, *TREC: experiment and evaluation in information retrieval.* MIT Press, 2005.

[11] B. Hedin, D. Oard, S. Tomlinson, and J. Baron. Overview of the TREC 2009 legal track. In *Proceedings of the 18th Text REtrieval Conference*, pages 4:1–40, 2010.

[12] R. V. Katter. The influence of scale form on relevance judgments. *Information Storage and Retrieval*, 4(1):1–11, 1968.

[13] M. Lesk and G. Salton. Relevance assessments and retrieval system evaluation. *Information storage and retrieval*, 4(4):343–359, 1968.

[14] M. Sanderson, F. Scholer, and A. Turpin. Relatively relevant: Assessor shift in document judgements. In *Proceedings of the Australasian Document Computing Symposium*, pages 60–67, Melbourne, Australia, 2010.

[15] D. Sheskin. *Handbook of parametric and nonparametric statistical procedures, 4th ed.* CRC Press, 2007.

[16] M. D. Smucker, J. Allan, and B. Carterette. A comparison of statistical significance tests for information retrieval evaluation. In *Proceedings of the ACMCIKM international conference on information and knowledge management*, pages 623–632, 2007.

[17] R. Thorne. The efficiency of subject catalogues and the cost of information searches. *Journal of documentation*, 11:130–148, 1955.

[18] E. M. Voorhees. Variations in relevance judgements and the measurement of retrieval effectiveness. *Information Processing and Management*, 36(5):697–716, 2000.

[19] E. M. Voorhees. Variations in relevance judgments and the measurement of retrieval effectiveness. *Information Processing and Management*, 36(5):697–716, 2000.

[20] E. M. Voorhees and C. Buckley. The effect of topic set size on retrieval experiment error. In *Proceedings of the ACM SIGIR International Conference on Research and Development in Information Retrieval*, pages 316–323, Tampere, Finland, 2002.

[21] W. Webber, A. Moffat, and J. Zobel. Statistical power in retrieval experimentation. In *Proceedings of the ACM CIKM International Conference on Information and Knowledge Management*, pages 571–580, Napa Valley, California, USA, 2008.

[22] W. Webber, D. Oard, F. Scholer, and B. Hedin. Assessor error in stratified evaluation. In *Proceedings of the ACM CIKM International Conference on Information and Knowledge Management*, pages 571–580, Toronto, Canada, 2010.

[23] I. Witten, A. Moffat, and T. Bell. *Managing Gigabytes: Compressing and Indexing Documents and Images.* Morgan Kaufmann Publishers, 2nd edition, 1999.

[24] J. Zobel. How reliable are the results of large-scale information retrieval experiments? In *Proceedings of the ACM SIGIR international conference on Research and development in information retrieval*, pages 307–314, 1998.

Pseudo Test Collections for Learning Web Search Ranking Functions

Nima Asadi[1], Donald Metzler[2], Tamer Elsayed[3], Jimmy Lin[1]
[1]University of Maryland, College Park
[2]Information Sciences Institute, University of Southern California
[3]King Abdullah University of Science and Technology (KAUST)
nima@cs.umd.edu, metzler@isi.edu, tamer.elsayedaly@kaust.edu.sa, jimmylin@umd.edu

ABSTRACT

Test collections are the primary drivers of progress in information retrieval. They provide yardsticks for assessing the effectiveness of ranking functions in an automatic, rapid, and repeatable fashion and serve as training data for learning to rank models. However, manual construction of test collections tends to be slow, labor-intensive, and expensive. This paper examines the feasibility of constructing web search test collections in a completely unsupervised manner given only a large web corpus as input. Within our proposed framework, anchor text extracted from the web graph is treated as a pseudo query log from which pseudo queries are sampled. For each pseudo query, a set of relevant and non-relevant documents are selected using a variety of web-specific features, including spam and aggregated anchor text weights. The automatically mined queries and judgments form a pseudo test collection that can be used for training ranking functions. Experiments carried out on TREC web track data show that learning to rank models trained using pseudo test collections outperform an unsupervised ranking function and are statistically indistinguishable from a model trained using manual judgments, demonstrating the usefulness of our approach in extracting reasonable quality training data "for free".

Categories and Subject Descriptors: H.3.3 [Information Storage and Retrieval]: Information Search and Retrieval

General Terms: Algorithms, Performance

Keywords: web, anchor text, hyperlinks, evaluation

1. INTRODUCTION

Reusable test collections play a central role in information retrieval (IR) research. A test collection consists of three components: a *corpus* of documents; a set of *queries* representing users' information needs (i.e., *topics*); and *relevance judgments*, which enumerate documents that are relevant (and not relevant) to a particular information need. These resources are critical to the development of ranking functions, one of the central problems in information retrieval research. Given a query and a corpus,[1] the task is to develop a ranking function that returns a ranked list of documents that maximizes the relevance of the retrieved documents with respect to the query. In this research framework, test collections serve two purposes: First, they provide a yardstick for assessing the effectiveness of ranking functions in an automatic, rapid, and repeatable fashion. Second, they provide training data for learning to rank models [19, 23, 33, 4, 30]. It would not be an exaggeration to say that test collections are the primary drivers of progress in IR today.

Academic researchers have access to only a small handful of test collections because they are very expensive to create. Traditionally, test collections are created as the byproduct of community-wide evaluations such as the NIST-organized Text REtrieval Conferences (TRECs). Using a process known as pooling [21, 37], NIST samples results from participating systems and coordinates a manual assessment process—this is a slow, labor intensive, and expensive proposition. As a result, typical test collections contain perhaps a few dozen queries. Over time, yearly community-wide evaluations accumulate sufficient queries and relevance judgments to be useful for evaluation and learning to rank. However, if the underlying document corpus changes (for example, as when the field moved from newswire articles to web pages in the last decade), existing relevance judgments become mostly useless since they are corpus-specific. Thus, to some extent, the academic IR community suffers from the phenomenon of searching in the dark only under the lamp post, since that is where the test collections are.

In contrast, researchers in industry (i.e., at search engine companies) are able to circumvent these challenges primarily in two ways. First, such companies typically possess the financial resources to gather a large amount of human editorial judgments. Second, researchers at search engine companies have access to a variety of data resources, including query logs, click logs, and toolbar data. Such resources provide a rich source of implicit relevance judgments [24, 1, 35, 20]. Both of these avenues are mostly closed off to academic researchers.

This paper explores the feasibility of constructing web search test collections automatically given only a large web

SIGIR'11, July 24–28, 2011, Beijing, China.

[1]To reduce confusion in terminology (i.e., document collection vs. test collection), we use corpus to refer to the documents over which search is performed.

corpus. In particular, we propose novel approaches for extracting queries and relevance judgments using the web graph in an unsupervised manner. Since the queries and judgments extracted have not been vetted by humans, we call these *pseudo test collections*. If successful, automatic methods for distilling test collections would have several key benefits. From the academic perspective, such methods would provide the means for gathering a large amount of relevance information using minimal resources. The methods would also likely be useful within industrial research settings, providing a way for search engine companies to augment their human judgments and implicit behavioral-based judgments with a novel source of relevance information.

This paper has three primary contributions. First, we describe a general framework for constructing pseudo test collections. The framework includes components for sampling pseudo queries and distilling pseudo relevance judgments for the queries. As far as we know, this is the first attempt to develop a general-purpose methodology for automatically constructing test collections that can be used for evaluation and learning to rank. Second, we describe a specific instantiation of the framework for constructing web search pseudo test collections. The approach exploits the fact that anchor text serves as a strong implicit relevance signal. Various schemes that aggregate anchor text weights are introduced and used for sampling web search queries and generating relevance judgments. Finally, we evaluate the quality of a web search pseudo test collection in the context of learning to rank. We show that learning to rank models trained using the unsupervised pseudo test collection are more effective than a standard unsupervised model and are statistically indistinguishable from a model trained using manual judgments.

The remainder of this paper is laid out as follows. First, Section 2 describes related research. Section 3 outlines our proposed framework for generating pseudo test collections, and Section 4 describes a specific instantiation for web search. Section 5 provides details of our experimental evaluation. Finally, Section 6 concludes the paper and describes several possible directions for future work.

2. RELATED WORK

There are two steps involved in constructing pseudo test collections—sampling pseudo queries and inferring pseudo relevance judgments for the queries. A number of previous studies have explored work along these lines, described below. However, we are not aware of previous work that combines these two threads within a single framework for automatically constructing test collections.

Sampling Pseudo Queries. Previous research has investigated methods for extracting implicit queries for contextual advertising [3, 27, 39] and the automatic generation of titles and quick-links for web pages [12, 13]. The goal of both tasks is to extract short phrases that are relevant to a given web page. Such approaches extract important phrases from various sources, including high *tf.idf* terms within a page, titles, anchor text, and query logs. Although these tasks are closely related to sampling pseudo queries, our work focuses on using implicit queries to automatically construct pseudo test collections, rather than solving advertising or user interface-related tasks. Of course, our work builds on these ideas.

Other related work has shown anchor text to be a reasonable surrogate to query logs for query reformulation [16]. We leverage this finding when constructing pseudo test collections for web search.

Generating Pseudo Judgments. The other step of the pseudo test collection construction process identifies a set of relevant (and non-relevant) documents for the sampled pseudo queries. A great deal of effort within the information retrieval community has been devoted to solving this problem. A key factor that differentiates our proposed approach from previous work is that all of our analysis and computation is performed *offline* using *global* information. Learning to rank systems often use a large number of features that are computed at runtime, typically based on evidence from a single document or a small set of top ranked documents. Our framework provides the ability to extract considerably more complex features that would likely be too costly (either in terms of space or in terms of computation) to use at runtime within a practical search engine. In this way, our approach can be thought of as computing relevance scores for a large set of query-document pairs offline using a wide variety of (potentially expensive) relevance signals. Similar approaches have been explored in the past, but almost exclusively in the context of leveraging implicit behavioral signals as pseudo judgments [23, 24, 17]. Our work instead focuses on using implicit corpus-based relevance signals to distill pseudo judgments.

One related line of research deals with methods for inferring the relevance of unjudged documents when computing retrieval metrics [36, 5, 7, 10, 9]. These approaches take as input a ranked list of documents retrieved in response to a query. Some of the documents have been judged, while the rest have not. The goal is then to estimate the relevance of the unjudged documents. This research has been shown to be useful for obtaining better estimates of retrieval system effectiveness in the presence of incomplete judgments. However, it should be clear that this task is easier than pseudo test collection construction, because it is assumed that documents, one or more queries, and some judgments are provided as evidence, whereas our framework relies only on having a corpus.

Finally, it is important to note that our work differs from semi-supervised learning to rank approaches [18, 28, 29]. Although such approaches are designed to learn highly effective ranking models, it is not straightforward to adapt them to constructing test collections. Our goal is to build test collections that can be used for a variety of tasks, and to do so in a completely unsupervised manner. In contrast, semi-supervised approaches assume that at least *some* labeled data are available.

3. PSEUDO TEST COLLECTIONS

As previously mentioned, information retrieval test collections consist of a document corpus, queries, and relevance judgments. It is often the case that researchers, when developing search technologies for a new task or domain, do not have access to all three components: in most cases, only a document corpus is available. Unfortunately, a corpus in isolation has limited utility; without queries and relevance judgments it would be very difficult to learn effective ranking functions (e.g., by learning to rank) or to evaluate the quality of a retrieval system built on the corpus. Even for tasks for which test collections already exist, there is never enough queries nor relevance judgments, since as with many machine learning tasks, algorithmic effectiveness increases with the amount of available training data.

Obtaining queries and relevance judgments is a labor-intensive and costly task. Commercial search engines are able to address this problem with data, in the form of query and click logs, and money, which can be used to hire large teams of humans to manually assess the relevance of documents. However, in resource-constrained academic settings, these options are not available, making it difficult to undertake research on new document corpora, new tasks, or work with machine learning algorithms that require lots of training data. This has led researchers to pursue low cost strategies for constructing *manual test collections*. Two emerging evaluation paradigms are minimal test collections [8, 7, 6] and crowdsourcing [2]. Both of these strategies are useful for low-cost *one-time* evaluations. However, they suffer from issues related to reusability [11, 9].

To overcome these issues, we propose to automatically construct test collections with minimal human effort. Given nothing but a document corpus $\mathcal{D}$, our goal is to automatically construct a high quality, reusable test collection that can be used to evaluate and train ranking functions over $\mathcal{D}$. Since the mined queries and relevance judgments are automatically *inferred*, we refer to the resulting test collections as pseudo test collections.

It is important to note that the goal of pseudo test collections is not to produce manual-quality test collections, but rather to minimize costs by automatically distilling *surrogate* test collections. It is assumed (and expected) that pseudo test collections will be noisy (i.e., have incorrect relevance assessments). However, this is not overly problematic, since recently-developed evaluation methodologies and learning to rank models are robust enough to handle certain amounts of missing or incorrect data. Indeed, as we will show in our experiments, even simple learning to rank approaches can be used with (noisy) pseudo test collections to learn effective ranking functions.

We propose constructing pseudo test collections by mimicking the process used to build manual test collections, which typically begins with a corpus. After a corpus has been obtained, a set of queries is chosen. The queries are either sampled from query logs or manually generated. Each query is then issued to one or more retrieval systems, which returns candidate documents that are then judged, either via pooling [21, 37], the minimal test collection paradigm [8, 7, 6], or crowdsourcing [2].

Our general pseudo test collection framework follows a similar process. The three primary steps are as follows:

1. **Corpus acquisition.** The only input to our proposed framework is a corpus of documents (e.g., a large web crawl, an archive of news articles, a collection of books, etc.). Automatic corpus acquisition and corpus expansion are beyond the scope of this paper. We assume that a corpus, generated in some way, is available. Since the corpus is the only input to the framework, it should be chosen with some care. Corpora that contain a large amount of potentially noisy implicit relevance information (e.g., anchor text, click information, user ratings, tags, metadata, etc.) are the most amenable to pseudo test collection construction.

2. **Pseudo query generation.** Given the corpus, we will then automatically generate a set of pseudo queries in a completely unsupervised manner. It is important that the pseudo queries are diverse, in terms of difficulty, topical coverage, user intent, etc. It is also important that the queries be "well-formed" and represent a realistic sample of information needs that can be addressed by documents in the corpus.

3. **Pseudo judgment generation.** For every sampled pseudo query, the final task is to assign automatically-generated relevance labels (e.g., "relevant" and "non-relevant") to some set of documents found in the corpus. Unlike the pooling method, this set of documents does not necessarily need to be the output of a retrieval system. Instead, it can be *any* subset of documents that can be accurately and reliably labeled in an unsupervised manner. It is also desirable, but not necessary, for each label to have a confidence score assigned to it. Such scores reflect the uncertainty in the automatically-generated label and may be informative for the purpose of evaluation or learning to rank.

Therefore, to instantiate this framework, methods for generating pseudo queries and pseudo judgments must be defined. These methods will vary depending on a number of factors, including the corpus, the search task, and the sources of implicit relevance signals that are available. Naturally, generating pseudo test collections for certain tasks will be substantially easier than others. In the following section, we propose a methodology for constructing pseudo test collections for web search. This serves as the first instantiation of our proposed framework to illustrate its utility.

4. AUTOMATIC CONSTRUCTION OF WEB SEARCH TEST COLLECTIONS

This section describes a specific instantiation of our general pseudo test collection framework whose output can be used to train learning to rank models for web search. Web search is a particularly interesting domain for our framework since the web graph encodes a great deal of implicit relevance information, in the form of links and anchor text. This is evidenced by the fact that anchor text and link analysis features (e.g., PageRank [34], HITS [25], and SALSA [26]) are known to be important for web search. As we will show, the web graph can be leveraged to extract high quality pseudo queries and pseudo judgments.

4.1 Implicit Relevance Signals

Starting from only a collection of web pages, anchor text provides a potentially high quality description of target documents. This implicit signal serves as a strong source from which relatively high quality pseudo queries can be sampled. In addition, given a line of anchor text, its target documents (i.e., the set of documents the anchor text points to) are reasonable candidates for relevant pseudo judgments. However, there is always a level of noise in this relevance signal which, if sampled naïvely, could yield poor results. Examples of poor anchor text-target document pairs include common web terminology (e.g. "privacy policy" and "homepage"), ambiguous anchor text, links from spam pages, and links that serve as citations for a piece of information (e.g. "born in X" which points to a biography as a reference).

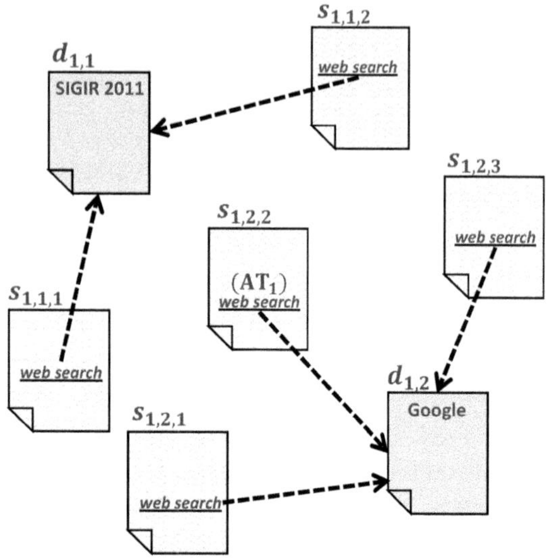

Figure 1: A sample structure of anchor text. In this figure, "web search" is a line of anchor text (AT_1) that points to two target documents $d_{1,1}$ and $d_{1,2}$. For each target document, anchor text originates from a number of source pages. For instance, $s_{1,1,1}$ and $s_{1,1,2}$ point to document $d_{1,1}$ with anchor text "web search".

Therefore, additional factors must be considered when using anchor text for constructing pseudo test collections.

In order to reduce the effect of noise and to sample higher-quality pseudo queries and pseudo judgments, a combination of strategies can be used, for example: excluding intra-domain links (also called internal anchor text), measuring the quality of each unique line of anchor text as well as its target documents, and designing effective sampling techniques. We adopt all three strategies. In this paper, we only consider external anchor text (inter-domain links) as our source for pseudo queries. In addition, we assign weights to every anchor text-target document (henceforth, anchor-document) pair based on a number of factors. These weights can be thought of as confidence scores for relevance pairs. Finally, a score is computed for each unique line of anchor text to capture its quality.

In what follows, we introduce a number of different weighting schemes to compute weights for anchor-document pairs. An aggregation function is then defined to estimate the quality of lines of anchor text.

4.1.1 Anchor-Document Weighting Schemes

Figure 1 illustrates the general structure of anchor text within the web graph. In general, anchor text AT_k points to $d_{k,i}$ documents (for $1 \leq i \leq n_k$). For each of the target documents $d_{k,i}$, the anchor text originates from a set of source pages $s_{k,i,j}$ for $1 \leq j \leq m_{k,i}$. From this structure, we extract a great deal of information about the anchor text, such as the set of all target documents, the set of sources that point at those documents, the URI of each of the documents, etc. Given this information, our goal is to design a suitable weighting scheme $w(\text{Anchor Text}, \text{Target Document}) \rightarrow \mathbb{R}$, that takes an anchor-document pair (e.g., $<AT_1, d_{1,2}>$ in Figure 1) as input and returns a real number as a confidence score. This score can later be used for extracting high quality pseudo queries and pseudo relevance judgments.

We propose the following four weighting schemes; some are novel, others have been used by researchers in the past. In the following, $0 \leq \text{PR}(d) \leq 1$ is the PageRank score of document d, while $1 \leq \text{HAM}(d) \leq 100$ is the "ham" score (i.e., $100 - \text{SPAM}(d)$, where $0 \leq \text{SPAM}(d) \leq 99$).

Spam. Spam pages by definition contain low quality content. As a result, a line of anchor text that describes a spam page should not be trusted. This weighting scheme measures the confidence of an anchor-document pair solely on the basis of the ham score of the target document:

$$w(AT_k, d_{k,i}) = \log\left[\text{HAM}(d_{k,i})\right] \quad (1)$$

SrcSpam. While the level of "spamminess" of a target document is important, the quality of sources from which a line of anchor text originates tells us how trustworthy that anchor text is as a descriptive phrase for the target document. This weighting scheme follows the intuition that if an anchor text originates from a reliable set of sources, then that anchor text is likely to accurately describe the target document. Since anchor text can originate from multiple source pages, we need to define an aggregation function. In this weighting scheme, we aggregate the reliability of the sources using a harmonic mean:

$$w(AT_k, d_{k,i}) = \log\left[\frac{\text{HAM}(d_{k,i}) \cdot m_{k,i}}{\sum_{j=1}^{m_{k,i}} [\text{HAM}(s_{k,i,j})]^{-1}}\right] \quad (2)$$

PageRank. PageRank scores indicate the importance of a particular page based on global link structure: A page is important if other important pages point to it. This weighting scheme sets the quality score of a document based on its PageRank score and ham score:

$$w(AT_k, d_{k,i}) = \log\left[\text{PR}(d_{k,i}) \times \text{HAM}(d_{k,i})\right] \quad (3)$$

Anchor. The validity of anchor text can be measured based on the number of unique domains it originates from and the number of times it is used to point to a particular target document. This is the basis for the following weighting scheme that is a variant of the weighted scheme originally described by Metzler et al. [32]:

$$w(AT_k, d_{k,i}) = \text{HAM}(d_{k,i}) \sum_{s \in S(d_{k,i})} \frac{\delta(AT_k, d_{k,i}, s)}{|\text{ANCHORS}(d_{k,i}, s)|} \quad (4)$$

where $S(d_{k,i})$ denotes sites that link to $d_{k,i}$, $\delta(AT_k, d_{k,i}, s)$ is 1 if and only if anchor text AT_k links to $d_{k,i}$ from some page within site s, and $|\text{ANCHORS}(d_{k,i}, s)|$ is the total number of unique anchors originating from site s that links to $d_{k,i}$.

4.1.2 Anchor Text Quality Score

In order to measure how well a line of anchor text describes its target document, we assign weights to each anchor-document pair according to different weighting schemes as explained in the previous section. Next, we must define a function $w(\text{Anchor Text}) \rightarrow \mathbb{R}$ that computes a quality score for a line of anchor text.

A simple approach is to make use of anchor-document weights in order to estimate the quality of a line of anchor text. However, a line of anchor text can have multiple target documents and therefore can be present in multiple anchor-document pairs. Hence, the quality of a line of anchor text can be estimated by an aggregation function over the weights of individual anchor-document pairs for that particular anchor text.

In this paper, we use a simple arithmetic mean to combine the weights of individual anchor-document pairs as follows:

$$w(\text{AT}_k) = \frac{1}{n_k} \sum_{i=1}^{n_k} w(\text{AT}_k, d_{k,i})$$

where $w(\text{AT}_k, d_{k,i})$ is the weight associated with anchor text AT_k and its target document $d_{k,i}$, and n_k is the number of target documents AT_k points to. This weight can be interpreted as the quality of a unique line of anchor text.

4.2 Pseudo Queries

As we described previously, pseudo test collections consist of pseudo queries and associated pseudo relevance judgments. We begin by describing how anchor text can be used for constructing a high quality set of pseudo queries. Note that a naïve approach to extracting pseudo queries would be to rank all anchor text according to their weights and take the top Q as pseudo queries. However, there are other factors that need to be considered.

Based on our observations, the number of target documents a unique line of anchor text points to, can, to some extent, verify whether an anchor text is of high quality or not. Anchor text that have very few target documents often contain misspellings or otherwise are overly-specific topics. On the other hand, anchor text that have a large number of target documents are often broader topics and, in essence, very ambiguous. Examples of this are phrases such as "privacy policy" and "homepage". We would like to avoid both extremes and thus favor anchor text that have an average number of target documents.

To accomplish this goal, we partition lines of anchor text based on the number of target documents they point to: a line of anchor text with n target documents falls into partition P_n. Since we want to favor lines of anchor text that have an average number of target documents, we are interested in partitions with an index that is neither too small nor too large. We can define a probability distribution over indices n to satisfy this criterion—in our case, we selected a normal distribution $N(\mu, \sigma^2)$. To sample pseudo queries, we first sample a partition according to the normal distribution, and then extract the highest weighted line of anchor text, weighted according to $w(\text{AT}_k)$ from the partition.

4.3 Pseudo Judgments

The final step of our proposed pseudo test collection framework is the automatic generation of relevance judgments, which we refer to as pseudo judgments.

While there has been a great deal of effort devoted to accurately estimating the probability of relevance, many of them, especially learning to rank approaches, are only effective when trained using a large set of manual judgments. Therefore, many of these approaches are not directly applicable to our problem. Instead, we rely on unsupervised methods for estimating the relevance of query-document pairs.

Positive Judgments. As we mentioned earlier, anchor text provides an implicit relevance signal which can be used to extract positive judgments. Since pseudo queries are simply lines of anchor text, each pseudo query has a set of documents that it points to. These target documents serve as a reasonable set of potentially relevant documents. Assuming that the relevance of each document can be reliably estimated with respect to the anchor text, we can assert that the documents with the highest scores are relevant. We rely on the weighting schemes introduced earlier in this section to estimate the relevance of a document with respect to a pseudo query. For each pseudo query, we sort its target documents according to their anchor-document weight and select the top d_p documents as positive judgments.

Negative Judgments. For a pseudo test collection to be complete, a set of negative judgments for each pseudo query is also essential. Negative judgments must not only be non-relevant with respect to the query, but also must contain a diverse set of documents. Despite the utility of anchor text for extracting pseudo queries and positive judgments, they do not appear to be a good source for negative judgments based on our experience.

Classic approaches to information retrieval such as BM25 or language modeling, on the other hand, define a content-based scoring function that measures the relevance of a given document with respect to a query. Documents that appear deep in the ranked list are likely to be "barely relevant" or "non-relevant". As a result, we retrieve a ranked list of R documents for each pseudo query using a simple ranking function (e.g., language modeling) and sample d_n documents from the bottom of that list to serve as negative judgments.

5. EXPERIMENTAL EVALUATION

This section describes the details of our experimental evaluation comparing the quality of learning to rank models trained using web search pseudo test collections and standard manually-constructed TREC test collections.

5.1 Data and Methodology

We performed our experiments on ClueWeb09, a best-first web crawl completed by Carnegie Mellon University in early 2009. The collection contains one billion pages in ten languages totaling around 25 TB. Of those, about 500 million pages are in English, divided into ten roughly equally-sized segments. Our experiments specifically focused on the first English segment, which contains 50 million documents (totaling 1.53 TB uncompressed, 247 GB compressed). The first segment of the English portion of the ClueWeb09 dataset contains approximately 7.5 million unique lines of external (i.e., inter-domain) anchor text, on which we applied our proposed methods to generate pseudo queries and pseudo judgments. For evaluation purposes, we used the set of 50 queries and their corresponding judgments from the TREC 2009 web track.

The criterion for determining if our proposed approach is successful or not is whether a learning to rank model trained using an automatically constructed pseudo web test collection can achieve higher effectiveness than alternative models. If this is the case, then we have shown that our pseudo test collections can be used to effectively extract implicit relevance signals without human judgments.

We compare our proposed approach against two models. The first is BM25, which is one of the most effective and widely used unsupervised retrieval models available. Most unsupervised models consist of a (semi-)heuristic combination of basic statistics, such as term frequency, inverse document frequency, and document length. We do not know of any existing retrieval models that can learn how to combine

	Query	Page Title Keywords	
Anchor	tax deductible	Gifts and Car Expenses	R
		Tax Deduct.-Wikipedia	R
		Hospitals...of charity	NR
		Mortgage Tax Calculator	NR
	google labs	Google Labs	R
		Google Labs-Wikipedia	R
		Info. Management	NR
		Blogger - Wikipedia	NR
	ny public library	NYPL Print Collection	R
		NYPL Photography Collection	R
		New York Law	NR
		Libraries and Schools	NR
	avoid plagiarism	Academic Integrity	R
		Citing Sources and Avoiding Plagiarism	R
		Research and Teaching Tools	NR
		How to use Google Alerts	NR
	shipping tips	FedEx - Service Guide	R
		Sportube Shipping Tips	R
		eBay Tools	NR
		Merchandise Coupon Codes	NR
	knee pain	Knee Pain - MayoClinic.com	R
		Knee Pain Symptoms	R
		Joint Replacement	NR
		Discussing Knee Pain	NR

	Query	Page Title Keywords	
PageRank	download realplayer	RealPlayer ... audio	R
		RealPlayer	R
		Sports games Download	NR
		Apple iPod...	NR
	yahoo privacy policy	Yahoo! Privacy Policy	R
		Yahoo! Store Privacy Po.	R
		download yahoo msngr	NR
		AltaVista-Privacy Policy	NR
	united states copyright office	US Copyright Office	R
		Copyright law of the US	R
		Justia Regulation Trackers	NR
		Sources and Notes	NR
	bbc weather	BBC Homepage	R
		BBC Weather Center	R
		Pippa Greenwood	NR
		BBC News	NR
	free hit counters	Rapid Counter	R
		Easy Counter	R
		Web Site Design	NR
		Jewelry and Watches	NR
	iphone sdk	Apple iPhone	R
		iPhone Developer Connection	R
		Google IO - Android	NR
		Gps - iPhone Buzz	NR

Table 1: Examples of pseudo queries and pseudo judgments extracted using the Anchor and PageRank weighting schemes. In the last column, R indicates "relevant" and NR indicates "not relevant".

an arbitrary set of features in a completely unsupervised manner. The second approach that we compare against is an upper bound, or "cheating" model, that is trained using the manual judgments from the TREC 2009 web track and then tested on the *same training set* (hence the "cheating" name). This is meant to approximate the effectiveness of a highly effective supervised learning to rank model trained over the same set of features using the same learning algorithm. For evaluation, all models are tested on TREC 2009 web track data.

Our pseudo query sampling strategy requires a mean and a variance for the underlying normal distribution $N(\mu, \sigma^2)$. Based on our observation, we found that anchor text pointing to ≤ 5 target documents are generally of low quality. These make up a large portion of the extracted anchor text from our corpus, totaling about 7 million unique lines. To ensure quality, we eliminate those anchor text that have 5 or fewer target documents, thereby reducing the size of potential pseudo queries to only 6 percent of the original set. We set the mean of the normal distribution, μ, based upon statistics gathered from the remaining collection. The filtered collection of anchor text has a median of 10 target documents, which we used for μ in the sampler. The value for σ^2 was set (arbitrarily) to 5. We used the Waterloo spam scores [15], computed for every document in the English portion of the ClueWeb09 dataset and freely available.[2]

Unless otherwise specified, we set the total number of sampled pseudo queries (Q) to 400, and the average number of pseudo positive (d_p) and negative judgments (d_n) for each query to 10 and 20, respectively, keeping the ratio of positive to negative judgments at 0.5. Pseudo negative judgments are sampled from the bottom of a ranked list of a thousand retrieved documents (R) using the language modeling query likelihood scoring function. To evaluate the effectiveness of our models, we report NDCG@20 [22] and ERR@20 [14], which are commonly used to evaluate the effectiveness of web search tasks. A one-side paired t-test (with $p = 0.05$) is used to determine statistical significance.

5.2 Illustrative Examples

Table 1 shows selected examples of pseudo queries and their corresponding pseudo judgments extracted using the Anchor and PageRank weighting schemes.

The PageRank weighting scheme favors anchor text that point to popular pages. Popular pages with high PageRank values are likely to be website entry pages. Consequently, associated anchor text are navigational in nature, which yields many navigational pseudo queries. As shown in the examples, queries such as "download realplayer" and "yahoo privacy policy" as well as other navigational queries like "wiki help", "yahoo myweb", and "metawiki" are extracted with the PageRank weighting scheme.

On the other hand, pseudo queries extracted using the Anchor weighting scheme consist of navigational as well as informational phrases, as illustrated in the examples. Other examples include "weather maps", "landscapes scenery", "free hit counter code", "national center health statistics nchs", and "passport services".

Of course, pseudo queries and pseudo judgments are noisy. For instance, a query such as "help forum" that was extracted using the Anchor weighting scheme seems like a poor query due to its ambiguity. Examining the results, we observe many judgments that humans are not likely to consider relevant. Despite the presence of noise, experimental evidence provided later illustrates that our pseudo test collections are nevertheless *useful*.

5.3 Learning to Rank Model

We make use of a relatively straightforward learning to rank model in our experiments. Recall that we need to learn two models—one from an automatically constructed pseudo test collection and another from manual judgments. To support a fair comparison, both models use the same features and the same learning algorithm.

[2] `http://plg.uwaterloo.ca/~gvcormac/clueweb09spam/`

Weighting Scheme	NDCG@20	ERR@20
BM25	0.291	0.135
Cheating	0.292	0.141
Anchor	0.298	0.149
SrcSpam	0.298	0.149
Spam	0.298	0.146
PageRank	0.110	0.062

Table 2: Evaluation of different ranking models on TREC 2009 web track data, comparing BM25, a "cheating" greedy feature selection model, and the same greedy feature selection model trained on pseudo test collections generated using different weighting schemes.

We learn a simple linear ranking function using a standard suite of features consisting of basic information retrieval scores (e.g., language modeling and BM25 scores), term proximity features (exact phrases, ordered windows, unordered windows, etc.), and query-independent features (e.g., PageRank). There are a total of 45 features. The parameters of the linear model are learned using a greedy feature selection approach [31]. The model is iteratively constructed by adding features to the model, one at a time, according to a greedy selection criterion. During each iteration, the feature that provides the biggest gain in effectiveness (as measured by ERR@20 [14], which is also our primary evaluation metric) after being added to the existing model is selected. This yields a sequence of one-dimensional optimizations that can easily be solved using line search techniques. The algorithm stops when the difference in ERR between successive iterations drops below a given tolerance (10^{-4}). This training procedure is simple, fast, and yields a model with minimal correlation/redundancy between features. We also explored the use of AdaRank [38], an effective learning to rank approach, but found the results to be consistently worse than the simple greedy feature selection algorithm with these features for this task.

5.4 Results

This section describes the results of our experimental evaluation. We first describe our basic findings and then provide a more in-depth analysis.

5.4.1 Basic Results

We begin by comparing the effectiveness of learning to rank models trained using pseudo test collections against BM25 and the cheating model. Table 2 shows the effectiveness for the different weighting schemes proposed in Section 4.1.1. All models are tested with TREC 2009 web track data. It is important to reiterate that the models trained with pseudo test collections do not require *any* manual intervention and are completely unsupervised.

As the results suggest, the PageRank weighting scheme leads to a less effective ranking model. This finding is not unexpected since the PageRank weighting scheme estimates the quality of anchor text based solely on the quality of its target documents, regardless of the quality of its sources. Furthermore, this weighting scheme suffers from the issues already discussed in Section 5.2. The extracted pseudo queries and pseudo judgments are low in quality, and hence it is not possible to learn an effective ranker.

On the other hand, the Anchor weighting scheme makes use of the sources from which anchor text originates. It takes into consideration the number of unique domains that use the same line of anchor text to point to a target document. In addition, it factors in the number of unique lines of anchor text that points to a target document, which approximates the breadth and ambiguity of topics within the document. These counts nicely capture the quality of a given anchor-document pair. As a result, the pseudo test collection generated using this weighting scheme contains higher quality pseudo queries and pseudo judgments, and therefore yields a more effective ranking model.

Results show that a learning to rank model trained using a pseudo test collection generated using the Anchor weighting scheme is more effective than baseline BM25, both in terms of NDCG@20 and ERR@20. Interestingly, all weighting schemes except for PageRank outperform the cheating experiment according to both metrics. Although the differences are not statistically significant, this suggests that our pseudo test collections, although noisy, provide valuable training data for learning to rank, compared to the "moderate" amount of TREC manual training data. We speculate that the cheating model is only slightly better than BM25 in NDCG due to the fact that all models were optimized for ERR@20. This may simply be a case of so-called metric divergence. For this reason, the ERR@20 numbers provide a more reliable comparison.

Finally, it is important to note that our learning to rank model does not include any spam features. If we were to include spam features in the "cheating" condition, it achieves an ERR@20 of 0.161. However, if the spam feature were also included in the models trained from the pseudo test collections, the results are no more effective than the results reported in Table 2. This suggests that the strategy we use for sampling non-relevant documents does not contain enough spam documents to allow the models to learn the importance of the spam feature.

This raises an important issue related to our pseudo test collection framework. The strategies used for generating positive and negative judgments run the risk of significantly biasing results in unexpected ways. To minimize this risk, it is beneficial to select a *diverse* set of relevant and non-relevant documents based on a wide variety of features and selection strategies. This is an important issue that should be better studied in the future. Nevertheless, the conclusion appears clear: learning to rank models trained in a completely unsupervised fashion outperform BM25 and are just as good as a model trained with manual judgments. In other words, we are able to exploit implicit relevance signals to improve ranking effectiveness in web search, and this improvement comes basically "for free".

5.4.2 Analysis of Learned Models

Analysis of the ranking models themselves shed some insight on feature selection. Table 3 shows the model learned using the pseudo test collection built with Anchor weighting, while Table 4 shows the cheating model learned using manual judgments.

The models are markedly different. For example, in the cheating model, bm25-term, the BM25 score on query unigrams, is assigned a high weight, while the same feature is assigned a low weight in the other model. This is likely the result of biases in both the pseudo test collection and the manual test collection. The pseudo test collection appears to be biased towards *phrase* features, which may stem from

Feature	Weight
lm-phrase	1.553
bm25-term	0.014
bm25-proximity	-0.567

Table 3: Ranking model trained on a pseudo test collection extracted using the Anchor weighting scheme.

Feature	Weight
lm-term	-0.0309
bm25-term	0.8911
bm25-phrase	0.1398

Table 4: Ranking model trained using TREC 2009 web track data.

the fact that the page a piece of anchor text points to is likely to contain the anchor text itself as a phrase. On the other hand, TREC judgments are collected via pooling, and it is known that such pools are biased towards BM25, since many TREC participants utilize that ranking function. Therefore, regardless of the source of judgments, it is difficult to avoid inherent biases.

We see that both models include the same feature types (i.e., term, phrase, and proximity), but their relative weights are different. It is interesting that the proximity score in the model trained using the pseudo test collection has a large negative weight. It is likely that the phrase feature is too large and the proximity feature is simply offsetting it.

5.4.3 *Pseudo Collection Size*

The number of pseudo queries and pseudo judgments together determine the size of a pseudo collection. Larger collections provide more training data. However, deeper sampling will draw in pseudo queries and pseudo judgments with lower quality scores, yielding nosier data. The tradeoff between these two factors needs to be studied.

In previous experiments, the number of sampled pseudo queries and positive/negative pseudo judgments were kept constant. Here, we present results from altering these parameters. However, to avoid an exhaustive search over all possible parameter and weighting scheme combinations, we focused on the Anchor weighting scheme, based on the results in Table 2. To further simplify the presentation, we only change the average number of pseudo negative judgments (d_n). This serves two purposes: first, by altering the number of negative judgments we are changing the size of the resulting pseudo collection. Second, this alters the ratio of positive to negative judgments.

Table 5 shows the effect of these changes for the Anchor weighting scheme for a small subspace of parameters Q and d_n. The table suggests that extracting more pseudo queries improves the resulting models slightly. In addition, lowering the ratio of positive to negative judgments (i.e., increasing d_n) adds more noise to the training data and results in slightly less effective models. The last row and last column in Table 5 show averages over the respective conditions.

Q / d_n	5	10	20	30	40	Avg.
200	0.112	0.111	0.111	0.113	0.111	0.112
400	0.150	0.148	0.149	0.146	0.147	0.148
800	0.150	0.152	0.152	0.146	0.147	0.149
1600	0.152	0.152	0.147	0.147	0.147	0.149
Avg.	0.141	0.141	0.139	0.138	0.138	

Table 5: Effects of varying the number of sampled queries and the number of negative judgments (Anchor weighting scheme, average number of positive judgments set to 10).

6. CONCLUSIONS AND FUTURE WORK

Motivated by the fact that although test collections are essential for information retrieval research, they remain labor-intensive and expensive to manually construct, this paper proposes an unsupervised framework for constructing high quality test collections given nothing but a corpus. The resulting pseudo test collections, which consist of a set of pseudo queries and pseudo relevance judgments, can be used to evaluate and train learning to rank models. We describe an instantiation of the proposed framework for web search that leverages anchor text as a source of implicit relevance signals. Our pseudo test collections are used to train simple learning to rank models. Experiments on TREC 2009 data illustrate that the resulting models outperform BM25 and are statistically indistinguishable from equivalent models trained using manual judgments. This illustrates the utility of our approach in being able to extract reasonable training data "for free".

There are several possible directions for future work. First, we would like to develop a better understanding of the weighting schemes within the current instantiation of the framework. Second, we would like to explore alternative methods for extracting relevance judgments, particularly negative judgments. In addition, we would like to study other sources of implicit relevance signals such as page titles and terms with high term frequencies. Finally, it would be interesting to use our pseudo test collections for evaluation purposes, comparing with alternatives such as pooling, minimal test collections, or crowdsourcing. We are particularly interested in the reusability of pseudo test collections and their ability to discriminate the effectiveness of ranking algorithms. Overall, we believe that this work opens up many future directions in information retrieval research.

7. ACKNOWLEDGMENTS

This work has been supported in part by NSF awards IIS-0836560, IIS-0916043, and CCF-1018625. Any opinions, findings, conclusions, or recommendations expressed are the authors' and do not necessarily reflect those of the sponsors. The first author's deepest gratitude goes to Katherine, for her invaluable encouragement and wholehearted support. The last author is grateful to Esther and Kiri for their loving support and dedicates this work to Joshua and Jacob.

8. REFERENCES

[1] E. Agichtein, E. Brill, S. Dumais, and R. Ragno. Learning user interaction models for predicting web search result preferences. *SIGIR*, pp. 3–10, Seattle, Washington, 2006.

[2] O. Alonso, D. E. Rose, and B. Stewart. Crowdsourcing for relevance evaluation. *SIGIR Forum*, 42(2):9–15, 2008.

[3] A. Broder, M. Fontoura, V. Josifovski, and L. Riedel. A semantic approach to contextual advertising. *SIGIR*, pp. 559–566, Amsterdam, The Netherlands, 2007.

[4] C. Burges, T. Shaked, E. Renshaw, A. Lazier, M. Deeds, N. Hamilton, and G. Hullender. Learning to rank using gradient descent. *ICML*, pp. 89–96, Bonn, Germany, 2005.

[5] S. Büttcher, C. L. A. Clarke, P. C. K. Yeung, and I. Soboroff. Reliable information retrieval evaluation with incomplete and biased judgements. *SIGIR*, pp. 63–70, Amsterdam, The Netherlands, 2007.

[6] B. Carterette. *Low-Cost and Robust Evaluation of Information Retrieval Systems.* PhD thesis, University of Massachuetts, Amherst, Massachusetts, 2008.

[7] B. Carterette and J. Allan. Semiautomatic evaluation of retrieval systems using document similarities. *CIKM*, pp. 873–876, Lisbon, Portugal, 2007.

[8] B. Carterette, J. Allan, and R. Sitaraman. Minimal test collections for retrieval evaluation. *SIGIR*, pp. 268–275, Seattle, Washington, 2006.

[9] B. Carterette, E. Gabrilovich, V. Josifovski, and D. Metzler. Measuring the reusability of test collections. *WSDM*, pp. 231–240, New York, 2010.

[10] B. Carterette and R. Jones. Evaluating search engines by modeling the relationship between relevance and clicks. *NIPS*, pp. 217–224, Vancouver, British Columbia, Canada, 2008.

[11] B. Carterette, E. Kanoulas, V. Pavlu, and H. Fang. Reusable test collections through experimental design. *SIGIR*, pp. 547–554, Geneva, Switzerland, 2010.

[12] D. Chakrabarti, R. Kumar, and K. Punera. Generating succinct titles for web URLs. *KDD*, pp. 79–87, Las Vegas, Nevada, 2008.

[13] D. Chakrabarti, R. Kumar, and K. Punera. Quicklink selection for navigational query results. *WWW*, pp. 391–400, Madrid, Spain, 2009.

[14] O. Chapelle, D. Metzler, Y. Zhang, and P. Grinspan. Expected reciprocal rank for graded relevance. *CIKM*, pp. 621–630, Hong Kong, China, 2009.

[15] G. V. Cormack, M. D. Smucker, and C. L. A. Clarke. Efficient and effective spam filtering and re-ranking for large web datasets. *CoRR*, abs/1004.5168, 2010.

[16] V. Dang and W. B. Croft. Query reformulation using anchor text. *WSDM*, pp. 41–50, New York, 2010.

[17] F. Diaz, D. Metzler, and S. Amer-Yahia. Relevance and ranking in online dating systems. *SIGIR*, SIGIR, pp. 66–73, Geneva, Switzerland, 2010.

[18] K. Duh and K. Kirchhoff. Learning to rank with partially-labeled data. *SIGIR*, pp. 251–258, Singapore, 2008.

[19] F. C. Gey. Inferring probability of relevance using the method of logistic regression. *SIGIR*, pp. 222–231, Dublin, Ireland, 1994.

[20] Q. Guo and E. Agichtein. Exploring mouse movements for inferring query intent. *SIGIR*, pp. 707–708, Singapore, 2008.

[21] D. K. Harman. The TREC test collections. In E. M. Voorhees and D. K. Harman, editors, *TREC: Experiment and Evaluation in Information Retrieval*, pp. 21–52. MIT Press, 2005.

[22] K. Järvelin and J. Kekäläinen. Cumulative gain-based evaluation of IR techniques. *ACM Transactions on Information Systems*, 20(4):422–446, 2002.

[23] T. Joachims. Optimizing search engines using clickthrough data. *KDD*, pp. 133–142, Edmonton, Alberta, Canada, 2002.

[24] T. Joachims, L. Granka, B. Pang, H. Hembrooke, and G. Gay. Accurately interpreting clickthrough data as implicit feedback. *SIGIR*, pp. 154–161, Salvador, Brazil, 2005.

[25] J. Kleinberg. Authoritative sources in a hyperlinked environment. *J. of the ACM*, 46(5):604–632, 1999.

[26] R. Lempel and S. Moran. The stochastic approach for link-structure analysis (SALSA) and the TKC effect. *Computer Networks*, 33(1-6):387–401, 2000.

[27] H. Li, D. Zhang, J. Hu, H.-J. Zeng, and Z. Chen. Finding keyword from online broadcasting content for targeted advertising. *The 1st International Workshop on Data Mining and Audience Intelligence for Advertising*, pp. 55–62, San Jose, California, 2007.

[28] M. Li, H. Li, and Z.-H. Zhou. Semi-supervised document retrieval. *Information Processing and Management*, 45:341–355, May 2009.

[29] Y. Lin, H. Lin, Z. Yang, and S. Su. A boosting approach for learning to rank using SVD with partially labeled data. *The 5th Asia Information Retrieval Symposium on Information Retrieval Technology*, pp. 330–338, Sapporo, Japan, 2009.

[30] T.-Y. Liu. Learning to rank for information retrieval. *Foundations and Trends in Information Retrieval*, 3(3):225–331, 2009.

[31] D. Metzler. Automatic feature selection in the Markov random field model for information retrieval. *CIKM*, pp. 253–262, Lisbon, Portugal, 2007.

[32] D. Metzler, J. Novak, H. Cui, and S. Reddy. Building enriched document representations using aggregated anchor text. *SIGIR*, pp. 219–226, Boston, Massachusetts, 2009.

[33] R. Nallapati. Discriminative models for information retrieval. *SIGIR*, pp. 64–71, Sheffield, United Kingdom, 2004.

[34] L. Page, S. Brin, R. Motwani, and T. Winograd. The PageRank citation ranking: Bringing order to the Web. Stanford Digital Library Working Paper SIDL-WP-1999-0120, Stanford University, 1999.

[35] F. Radlinski and T. Joachims. Query chains: Learning to rank from implicit feedback. *KDD*, pp. 239–248, Chicago, Illinois, 2005.

[36] I. Soboroff, C. Nicholas, and P. Cahan. Ranking retrieval systems without relevance judgments. *SIGIR*, pp. 66–73, New Orleans, Louisiana, 2001.

[37] K. Spärck Jones and C. J. van Rijsbergen. Information retrieval test collections. *J. of Documentation*, 32(1):59–75, 1976.

[38] J. Xu and H. Li. AdaRank: A boosting algorithm for information retrieval. *SIGIR*, pp. 391–398, Amsterdam, The Netherlands, 2007.

[39] W.-t. Yih, J. Goodman, and V. R. Carvalho. Finding advertising keywords on web pages. *WWW*, pp. 213–222, Edinburgh, Scotland, 2006.

Parallel Learning to Rank for Information Retrieval

Shuaiqiang Wang*
Shandong University of Finance, Jinan, China
wangsq@sdf .edu.cn

Byron J. Gao
Texas State University, San Marcos, TX, USA
bgao@txstate.edu

Ke Wang
Simon Fraser University, Burnaby, BC, Canada
wangk@cs.sfu.ca

Hady W. Lauw
Institute for Infocomm Research, Singapore
hwlauw@i2r.a-star.edu.sg

ABSTRACT

Learning to rank represents a category of effective ranking methods for information retrieval. While the primary concern of existing research has been accuracy, learning efficiency is becoming an important issue due to the unprecedented availability of large-scale training data and the need for continuous update of ranking functions. In this paper, we investigate parallel learning to rank, targeting simultaneous improvement in accuracy and efficiency.

Categories and Subject Descriptors: I.2.6 [Artificial Intelligence]: Learning; H.3.3 [Information Storage and Retrieval]: Information Search and Retrieval

General Terms: Algorithms, Performance.

Keywords: Learning to rank, Parallel algorithms, Cooperative coevolution, MapReduce, Information retrieval.

1. INTRODUCTION

Learning to rank represents a category of effective ranking methods for information retrieval (IR) systems. Given training data, in the form of a set of queries each associated with a list of search results labeled by relevance degree, learning to rank returns a ranking function that can be used to order search results for future queries [7].

While learning accuracy has thus far been the primary concern, learning efficiency is increasingly a crucial issue [1]. Due to the diversity of queries and documents, learning to rank involves increasingly larger training data with many features. For example, the CSearch dataset used in ListNet [1] contains ~25 million query-document pairs with 600 features. In addition, due to the rapid growth of the Web, ranking functions need to be re-learned repeatedly. Thus, it is important for learning to rank to achieve high efficiency through parallelization while maintaining accuracy.

Many learning to rank approaches have been proposed, e.g., ListNet [1], RankBoost [4] and RankSVM [6]. However, these studies were mainly concerned with accuracy and did not seek for improvement in learning efficiency through parallelization. Many parallel machine learning frameworks have been introduced, e.g., IBM Parallel Machine Learning Toolbox (www.alphaworks.ibm.com/tech/pml/) and cooperative coevolution (CC) [9]. However, none of these parallel machine learning methods have been applied to learning to rank.

In this paper, we investigate parallel learning to rank for information retrieval. In particular, we propose CCRank, an CC-based parallel learning to rank framework targeting simultaneous improvement in accuracy and efficiency. We also discuss other ways of achieving parallelization for learning to rank, such as MapReduce [3].

*This work was done while the first author was a postdoctoral fellow at Texas State University.

SIGIR'11, July 24–28, 2011, Beijing, China.
ACM 978-1-4503-0757-4/11/07..

2. PARALLEL LEARNING TO RANK

2.1 The CCRank Framework

Overview. Evolutionary algorithms (EAs) are stochastic search methods mimicking the metaphor of natural biological evolution. They operate on a population of potential solutions, called *individuals*, applying the principle of survival of the fittest to produce better and better approximations to the optimal solution.

Cooperative coevolution (CC) is a framework advantageous in solving problems with exceptionally large search space and complex structures [9]. In CC, a collection of EAs co-evolve simultaneously, where the EAs interact with one another in a cooperative manner. The fitness of an individual is based on how well it cooperates with other interacting individuals. CC follows a divide-and-conquer strategy, decomposing a problem into sub-problems and combining sub-solutions in the end to form a complete solution. The nature of CC allows easy parallelization.

CCRank adapts parallel CC to learning to rank. It starts with problem *decomposition*, followed by a parallel iterative *coevolution* process. At the end of each generation, parallel execution is suspended and a complete candidate solution is produced by *combination*. CCRank returns the best solution selected from all the candidates.

Decomposition and combination. Each complete solution is decomposed into a collection of individuals. Initially L solutions are generated randomly from the full feature space. Then, each solution is decomposed into N sub-individuals, resulting in N populations, each having L individuals. Each population will be assigned an EA to evolve. Combination is a reverse process of decomposition, which assemblies individuals into a complete solution.

Coevolution. Coevolution proceeds iteratively, where N populations co-evolve *in parallel* from generation to generation. Each population $\mathcal{P}_j$ maintains a collection of individ-

Algorithm 1: CCRank Framework

Input : Training set $\mathcal{T}$, number of generations G, number of populations N

Output: Ranking function f

1 $\mathcal{P}^{(0)}_{1,\ldots,N} \leftarrow$ `Initialize ()` // decomposition

2 **for** $g \leftarrow 1$ **to** G **do**

3 $\quad \mathcal{P}^{(g)}_{1,\ldots,N} \leftarrow$ `Evolve` $(\mathcal{P}^{(g-1)}_{1,\ldots,N})$ // coevolution

4 $\quad f^{(g)} \leftarrow$ `Combine` $(w_{1,\ldots,N})$ // combination

5 $\quad \mathcal{C} \leftarrow \mathcal{C} \cup \{f^{(g)}\}$

uals and a *winner* w_j, the best individual with the highest fitness score. Under the CC framework, fitness of individuals is based on how well they cooperate with other populations. First, individual i_j from $\mathcal{P}_j$ and winners of *other* populations selected in the *previous* generation are combined into a solution. Then, the evaluation measure, e.g., MAP, for the combined solution is calculated using the training data, and the resulting score is assigned to i_j as its fitness score.

Pseudocode. Algorithm 1 summarizes the CCRank framework. Line 1 performs initialization. Lines 2–6 show the entire evolution process from generation to generation.

2.2 Discussion

Parallel learning to rank. It is possible, but non-trivial, to adapt parallel machine learning algorithms to learning to rank. Some of such algorithms are included in IBM Parallel Machine Learning Toolbox. In addition, Proximal SVM [2] and Cascade SVM [5] are recent parallel SVMs that have demonstrated promising performance. On the other hand, MapReduce [3] provides a simple and unified parallel framework that has been widely applied in various domains. In the following we discuss how to adapt it to learning to rank.

Adapting MapReduce to learning to rank. MapReduce [3] is based on two fundamental functions, `Map` and `Reduce`. The `Map` function takes an input key/value pair and produces a set of intermediate key/value pairs. The MapReduce library groups together all intermediate values associated with the same intermediate key and passes them to the `Reduce` function. The `Reduce` function accepts an intermediate key and a list of intermediate values, and merges these values to form a value for the same key.

To adapt MapReduce to learning to rank, it is desirable to incorporate many existing learning to rank algorithms. However, since MapReduce achieves parallelism by dividing processes of algorithms, it is infeasible to have a unifying framework incorporating all learning to rank algorithms that have different processes. We propose an framework that is able to incorporate an important category of learning to rank algorithms by identifying and parallelizing some common and time-consuming operations.

This category of algorithms perform direct optimization of evaluation measures. They use ranking measures such as MAP and $NDCG$, or some measure-based formulae, as their loss functions directly. A common, time-consuming, and repeating key operation for these algorithms is evaluation of loss functions, which requires ranking of all associated documents for each query. We propose to parallelize this operation. In particular, each process of `Map` evaluates the ranking measure m_q of each query q for candidate ranking function f, and emits the key/value pair (f, m_q) to `Reduce`. Then, each process of `Reduce` calculates the value m of the loss function for f with measures $m_{q_1}, \ldots, m_{q_{|Q|}}$ of each query from different `Map` processes, and emits m.

3. EXPERIMENTS

We implemented CCRank based on RankIP [8]. $N = 8$ EAs are maintained, each containing $L = 70$ individuals that co-evolve up to $G = 30$ generations. The depth of the complete solution is $d = 8$.

For datasets, we used MQ2007 and MQ2008, a collection of benchmarks released in 2009 by Microsoft Research Asia (research.microsoft.com/en-us/um/beijing/projects/letor/). For comparison partners, we used state-of-the-art algorithms AdaRank [10], RankBoost [4], RankSVM [6] and ListNet [1].

We used the Map measure for accuracy comparison. For MQ2007, CCRank and RankBoost share the best performance. For MQ2008, CCRank outperformed all other algorithms, gaining 1.13%, 0.901%, 2.60% and 0.901% respectively. Note that the best and worst performances from those comparison partners differ by merely 1.67%.

To demonstrate the gain in efficiency by parallel evolution, we extracted 25%, 50%, and 100% portions of MQ2008 and generated 3 datasets, which have 3,803, 7,606, and 15,211 instances respectively. Then we ran CCRank on these datasets varying the number of processors (1, 2, 4, 8, and 16).

From the execution time analysis, we can see that parallel evolution leads to significant speed-up in CCRank. Comparing to the case of 1 processor, the averaged relative speed-ups are 173%, 299%, 486%, and 736% respectively, for the cases of 2, 4, 8, and 16 processors.

4. REFERENCES

[1] Z. Cao, T. Qin, T.-Y. Liu, M.-F. Tsai, and H. Li. Learning to rank: from pairwise approach to listwise approach. In *ICML*, 2007.

[2] R. Collobert, Y. Bengio, and S. Bengio. A parallel mixture of svms for very large scale problems. In *NIPS*, 2004.

[3] J. Dean and S. Ghemawat. MapReduce: Simplified data processing on large clusters. In *OSDI*, 2004.

[4] Y. Freund, R. Iyer, R. E. Schapire, and Y. Singer. An efficient boosting algorithm for combining preferences. *J. Mach. Learning Res.*, 4(1):933–969, 2003.

[5] H. P. Graf, E. Cosatto, L. Bottou, I. Durdanovic, and V. Vapnik. Parallel support vector machines: The cascade SVM. In *NIPS*, 2004.

[6] T. Joachims. Optimizing search engines using clickthrough data. In *KDD*, 2002.

[7] T.-Y. Liu. Learning to rank for information retrieval. In *WWW*, 2009.

[8] S. Wang, J. Ma, and J. Liu. Learning to rank using evolutionary computation: Immune programming or genetic programming? In *CIKM*, 2009.

[9] R. P. Wiegand. *An Analysis of Cooperative Coevolutionary Algorithms*. PhD thesis, George Mason University, 2004.

[10] J. Xu and H. Li. AdaRank: a boosting algorithm for information retrieval. In *SIGIR*, 2007.

Learning Features through Feedback for Blog Distillation

Dehong Gao, Renxian Zhang, Wenjie Li, Yiu Keung Lau†, Kam Fai Wong‡
Department of Computing, The Hong Kong Polytechnic University, Hong Kong
†City University of Hong Kong, Hong Kong, ‡The Chinese University of Hong Kong, Hong Kong
{csdgao, csrzhang, cswjli}@comp.polyu.edu.hk, raylau@cityu.edu.hk, kfwong@se.cuhk.edu.hk

Abstract

The paper is focused on blogosphere research based on the TREC blog distillation task, and aims to explore unbiased and significant features automatically and efficiently. Feedback from faceted feeds is introduced to harvest relevant features and information gain is used to select discriminative features. The evaluation result shows that the selected feedback features can greatly improve the performance and adapt well to the terabyte data.

Categories and Subject Descriptors

H.3.3 [**Information Storage and Retrieval**]: Information Search and Retrieval-Search Process

General Terms

Design, Experimentation

Keywords

Blog Distillation, Faceted Distillation, Feedback

1. Introduction

With the accelerated growth of social network, both organizations and individuals have shown great interest in conveying or exchanging ideas and opinions. The blogosphere provides an ideal platform for communication. According to the statistics of Blogpulse (*blogpulse.com*) in Jan. 2011, more than 152 million blogs have been published (more than 47,000 blog posts per day). One interesting issue related to the massive blogs is to automatically explore authors' behaviors from their blog posts.

Focusing on this issue, TREC introduces the blog distillation track in 2009 with two subtasks: baseline distillation and faceted distillation. The purpose of the former is to retrieve all the relevant feeds corresponding to given topics without any consideration of facets. The latter aims to rerank the baseline feeds according to specific facets [1].

At present, most published work deals with the two subtasks in sequence. Retrieving the relevant feeds according to given queries is regarded as a common IR task. For faceted distillation, several methods have been attempted. In [3], SVM and ME classifiers are introduced to predict the faceted inclinations of each feed according to pre-trained models. In [2], feed faceted scores are heuristically given to re-rank feeds. For classification as well as re-ranking, the challenge is to select the features related to each inclination. Most work above focuses on exploring heuristic features like permalink numbers or comment numbers. However, we observe that for some facets these features are far from enough. In view of this, we first discover more (non-heuristic) feature candidates with faceted feedback information. Then, a feature selection approach is employed to select discriminative features. Furthermore, we take some flexible processing to adapt to the massive dataset. In a word, we believe this can help us to explore the significant features automatically and efficiently. In the remainder of this paper, more details of our approach are given in Section 2; then the evaluation of baseline and faceted distillations is presented in Section 3; Section 4 concludes the whole paper.

SIGIR11, July 24-28, 2011, Beijing, China.
ACM 978-1-4503-0757-4/11/07.

2. Blog Distillation

Since the faceted blog distillation is based on the baseline distillation, we briefly introduce the latter first. To enhance efficiency in the face of the huge and noisy raw data (2.3TB), we implemented a distributed system and adopted the Indri tool (*www.lemurproject.org*) for our purpose, with its default language model and related toolkits. With the help of these tools, the top related feeds can be retrieved according to given topics in the baseline distillation.

Based on the ranking of the baseline distillation, we then focus on the **faceted blog distillation** subtask. The TREC 2010 task specifies three inclination pairs: opinionated vs. factual, personal vs. official, and in-depth vs. shallow, for operational simplicity [1]. According to those inclinations, the baseline feeds are to be re-ranked. The key issue is to discover the relevant and discriminative features for each faceted inclination, and determine the weight of each feature.

To solve the issue above, our approach explores features from three orientations: heuristic features, available lexicons, and corpora. Heuristic features, which have been used in some existing work, include Average Permalink/Sentence Length, Comment number, Organization Numbers, Opinion Rule, etc, which can be helpful for distinguishing some inclinations. In our method, besides these heuristic features we also use the statistics of the presence of Cyber Words and Cyber Emoticons (like '*LOL*' and '☺') in feeds, which provides clues to personal and official feeds. To discover the lexicon features, the SentiWordNet (*sentiwordnet.isti.cnr.it*) and Wilson Lexicon are used to manually select about 1500 opinion words as our own opinion lexicon. These two lexicons are vital in identifying the opinionated inclination feeds. However, most of these features suit the opinionated inclination and may not work well in other inclinations, and may introduce noise for other inclinations, especially for the factual and shallow inclinations. Thus, in order to discover more relevant features, we take the effort to explore some useful features from corpora.

Here, we propose a feature expansion approach by learning more feature candidates through feedback information of faceted feeds. Since TREC has released some faceted feeds for each topic, we can select some faceted-related word unigrams in the top ranking faceted feeds as new feature candidates according to the official release. These features are mainly opinion-independent words and unbiased for particular inclinations, resulting in more balanced feature structure.

A byproduct of feature expansion is that the unprocessed feature candidates contain too much useless information, which not only wastes computing resources but also harms the performance.

Therefore, we need to select the top discriminative features with feature selection methods. For fast and efficient handling of large and noisy data, the filter approach, rather than wrapper approaches is adopted [4].

With lexicon-based features and feedback features, an unanswered question is how to determine the weight of both features. Though each opinion word has a polarity weight and a feature selection measure is assigned to each feedback term, these weights are not in the same scale. To unitize the weights of selected features, for each inclination we conduct a SVM classifier with a linear kernel and calculate the weight of a support vector from the trained model that corresponds to a feature. The feeds are re-ranked with the summation of the products of the feature values and their weights.

3. Evaluation

Our experiment is conducted on the blog08 collection crawled over 14 weeks. It contains permalinks, feeds, and related information. The size of the blog08 collection is up to 2.3TB. In order to efficiently handle the terabyte dataset and reduce noise, the raw dataset is first cleaned and filtered by several regular expression rules, which reduce the size to 30%. Then, Indri is used to index the cleaned blog08 collection, and fetch the top 2000 related blog posts according to the 50 topics provided in TREC2009. Since feeds are what the task is concerned with, we rank the feeds by summing the relevance scores of retrieved blog posts corresponding to the same feed number. The top 100 relevant feeds are obtained and evaluated in table 1, and TREC provides four measures: the mean average precision (MAP), R-Precision (rPrec), binary Preference (bPref) and Precision at 10 documents (P@10), among which MAP is the primary measure for evaluating the retrieval performance [1].

Table 1: Evaluation of baseline distillation and comparison with official best, median and worst

Baseline Distillation	MAP	R-Prec	P@10	B-Pref
Language model	0.2494	**0.3047**	**0.3590**	0.2611
Official best	**0.2756**	0.2767	0.3206	**0.3821**
Official median	0.1752	0.1986	0.2447	0.3282
Official worst	0.0624	0.0742	0.0980	0.1410

As shown in table 1, our Indri-based language model run ranks competitively against official submissions. Based on our baseline feed ranking, we conduct the faceted distillation.

We first collect the lexicon features and the feedback features from the top ranking five feeds as feature candidates for feature selection. There are several commonly used feature selection approaches, and according to [4], information gain (IG) selects some negative features, but also has a bias for positive features. Thus, in our experiment IG is used to select features, and the formula is as follows:

$$IG(Ex, a) = H(Ex) - H(Ex|a)$$

where Ex is the set of all training examples; $H(x)$ represents the entropy; $a \in Attr$, the set of all attributes. Instead of using all instances in the official released answers, we calculate $H(Ex|a)$ using the top five feeds in our experiment. The change can greatly reduce the complexity of computing and make our approach more adaptable for the massive data collection. The top five feeds are a good surrogate for the whole feed set as they are statistically found to contain an approximately equal number of faceted and non-faceted feeds. More importantly, this "shortcut approach" adapts very well to the large dataset. We select the top 2,000 features (about 10% features in all feature candidates). To determine the weights of these features, an SVM classifier is conducted with these features for each inclination. We use the same strategy to randomly divide the top five feeds into training and testing datasets (ratio 4:1). Then, the weights of support vectors are calculated from trained models as the weights of these features for facet re-ranking. With selected features and their weights, feeds are re-ranked according to each inclination, and for comparison, ranking without feedback features (W/O Feedback) are evaluated as well.

Table 2: Evaluation against each inclination

Faced Distillation	MAP						
	All	Opin	Fact	Pers	Offi	Indp	Shal
Best 09	0.1261	0.1259	**0.1350**	0.1855	**0.1965**	0.1489	**0.1298**
W/O Feedback	0.1022	0.1340	0.0222	0.1754	0.1143	0.1859	0.0701
Feedback+IG	**0.1521**	**0.1596**	0.1275	**0.2360**	0.1702	**0.2159**	0.0554

From the evaluation (Table 2), compared with re-ranking without feedback features (W/O Feedback), re-ranking with feedback features (Feedback+IG) achieves a significant improvement, and outperforms the best of official runs. From the evaluation against each inclination, we can find that great improvements are observed for factual, personal and official identification. It is thus plausible that those inclinations may be more amenable to the usage of words rather than some heuristic features. One exception is the degradation of the shallow inclination performance, which may suggest that information gain is not suitable for selecting discriminative features and thus introduces noise for shallow inclination.

In the last experiment, comparisons are made to investigate the influence of different numbers of features selected.

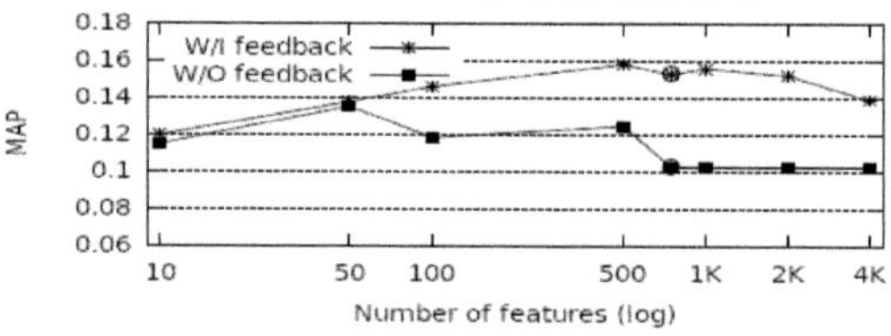

Figure 1: Re-ranking with different number of features

Figure 1 shows that the with-feedback (W/I feedback) and without-feedback (W/O feedback) approaches peak at 500 features and 50 features, respectively. The flat tail of without-feedback approach can be explained by the fact that only about 750 out of the 1500 features (shown by the points in the circle) are present in the features. The bottom line shown in this figure is that re-ranking with feedback feature outperforms the performance of that without feedback. Thus, this proves that feedback features are obviously efficient in faceted blog distillation.

4. Conclusion

To sum up, feedback feature expansion coupled with feature selection is effective and efficient for faceted blog distillation and adapts well to the terabyte dataset. It helps to automatically discover relevant and discriminative features. In the future, besides expanding features with unigrams, a possible extension is to learn some term combinations from unigrams.

Acknowledgements

The work presented in this paper is supported by a Hong Kong RGC project (No. PolyU 5230/08E).

5. References

[1] http://ir.dcs.gla.ac.uk/wiki/TREC-BLOG.

[2] Mostafa Keikha, Mark Carman, et al 2009. University of Lugano at TREC2009 Blog Track. *Proceeding of TREC09*. Lugano, Swiss.

[3] Richard McCreadie, Craig Macdonald, Iadh Ounis, et al 2009. University of Glasgow at TREC2009: Experiments with Terrier. *Proceeding of TREC2009*. Glasgow, Scotland, UK.

[4] Hua Liu, Hiroshi Motoda 2007. Computational Methods of Feature Selection. *Chapman&Hall/CRC*, P257-268, London.

Time-based Relevance Models

Mostafa Keikha
Faculty of Informatics
University of Lugano
Switzerland
mostafa.keikha@usi.ch

Shima Gerani
Faculty of Informatics
University of Lugano
Switzerland
shima.gerani@usi.ch

Fabio Crestani
Faculty of Informatics
University of Lugano
Switzerland
fabio.crestani@usi.ch

ABSTRACT

This paper addresses blog feed retrieval where the goal is to retrieve the most relevant blog feeds for a given user query. Since the retrieval unit is a blog, as a collection of posts, performing relevance feedback techniques and selecting the most appropriate documents for query expansion becomes challenging. By assuming time as an effective parameter on the blog posts content, we propose a time-based query expansion method. In this method, we select terms for expansion using most relevant days for the query, as opposed to most relevant documents. This provide us with more trustable terms for expansion. Our preliminary experiments on Blog08 collection shows that this method can outperform state of the art relevance feedback methods in blog retrieval.

Categories and Subject Descriptors

H.3.3 [**Information Storage and Retrieval**]: Information Search and Retrieval

General Terms

Algorithms

1. INTRODUCTION

Blog search users often wish to identify and subscribe to blogs that regularly write about a given topic. The goal of blog feed search, also called blog distillation, is to provide users with such blogs [6]. It is different from traditional ad-hoc search since the retrieval unit is a blog (a collection of the posts), not a single document.

One of the open challenges in blog retrieval is relevance feedback and employing the most appropriate documents for query expansion. It has been shown that traditional pseudo relevance feedback methods can not achieve any significant improvement in blog retrieval [2]. Using the top retrieved posts can not cover all the aspects of the query, and using the top retrieved feeds would add noise because not all the posts in them are relevant [4]. State of the art methods, use the top posts in the top retrieved feeds in order to have both coverage and relevance in the selected terms [4].

One of the main properties of blogs is their temporal behaviour. On one hand, content of blogs can change over time. On the other hand, topics can evolve over time and different aspects of the topic might be discussed in different time intervals. This effect of time on the blogs content provides us with a new generative model in blogosphere. In this new model, we assume that for a given topic, first we select a date and then for the given date and topic we generate a term. Based on this new model, we select new terms to expand the query with.

SIGIR'11, July 24–28, 2011, Beijing, China.
ACM 978-1-4503-0757-4/11/07.

2. TIME-BASED RELEVANCE MODELS

2.1 Relevance Models

The goal of relevance model is to select the most appropriate terms from initially retrieved documents to expand the original query [3]. Terms are selected based on their relevance to the query:

$$P(w|Q) \propto \sum_{\theta_D} P(w|\theta_D)P(\theta_D)\prod_{i}^{m} P(q_i|\theta_D) \qquad (1)$$

In order to improve the performance, relevance model can be smoothed with the original query model [5]:

$$P(w|\theta'_Q) = (1-\alpha)P(w|\theta_Q) + \alpha P(w|Q) \qquad (2)$$

α is the parameter and in our experiments is set to be 0.5 which has been shown to be effective in different models [5].

2.2 Relevance Feedback Methods in Blogs

When we want to use relevance models in blog retrieval, we should decide about documents to be used in the expansion. While one can use top retrieved posts or blogs as the source of expansion, they have been shown to be not effective in improving the performance of a blog retrieval system [2]. Different methods have been used before which can be summarized as follows :

- Top Feeds: Uses all the posts of the top retrieved feeds for the query expansion. This model has two parameters including the number of the selected feeds and the number of the terms in the expanded query [2, 4].
- Top Posts: Uses the top retrieved posts for the query expansion. The number of the selected posts and the number of the terms to use for expansion are the parameters of this model [2, 4].
- FFBS: Uses the top posts in the top retrieved feeds as the source for selecting new terms. The number of the selected posts from each feed is fixed among different feeds. This model has three parameters; the number of the selected feeds, the number of the selected posts in each feed and the number of the selected terms for the expansion [4].

- WFBS: Works the same as FFBS. The only difference is that number of selected posts for each feed depends on the feed rank in the initial list, such that more relevant feeds contribute more in generating the new query. Like FFBS, WFBS has also three parameters that are the number of the selected feeds, the total number of the posts to be used in the expansion and the number of the selected terms [4].

Among the mentioned methods, the "Top Feeds" method has the possibility to expand the query with non-relevant terms. The reason is that all the posts in a top retrieved feed are not necessarily relevant to the topic. On the other hand, the "Top Posts" method might not have enough coverage on all the sub-topics of the query, because the top retrieved posts might be mainly relevant to some dominant aspect of the query. FFBS and WFBS methods were originally proposed in order to have more coverage than the "Top Posts" method while selecting more relevant terms than the "Top Feeds" method [4].

2.3 Time-based Relevance Models

We propose a time-based relevance model where we assume that the date has effect on the terms written for a specific topic. In other word, we assume that the generative model of the query first selects a date and then select a term based on the date and the query:

$$P(w|Q) = \sum_{day} P(w|day, Q)P(day|Q) \tag{3}$$

where $P(w|day, Q)$ shows the importance of the term in a given day for the query and $P(day|Q)$ shows the importance of a day for the query. These probabilities are estimated as follows:

$$P(w|day, Q) = \sum_{p \in day} P(w|p)P(p|day, Q) \tag{4}$$

$$P(day|Q) = \frac{\sum_{p \in day} score(p, Q)}{\sum_{day'} \sum_{p \in day'} score(p, Q)} \tag{5}$$

where p shows a post and $p \in day$ means the post is published in the specified day. $P(p|day, Q)$ is set to be uniform for all the posts in each day. $score(p, Q)$ defines the similarity score of the post for the given query and in our experiments is calculated using language modeling technique with Dirichlet smoothing.

The assumption is that selecting the expansion terms based on time would provide us with a better coverage over subtopics than the Top Posts method. On the other hand, since we use the top retrieved posts in the expansion phase, we add less irrelevant terms than the Top Feeds method. This model has two parameters including the number of the posts considered in the expansion phase and the number of the terms selected for expansion.

3. EXPERIMENTAL RESULTS

To evaluate our methods we use the TREC Blog08 data collection that is a collection of about 1 million blogs crawled over a year [6]. We use only the permalinks component of the data which consist of approximately 28.4 million documents in the collection. We use the Terrier Information Retrieval system[1] to index the collection.

[1]http://ir.dcs.gla.ac.uk/terrier/

Table 1: Evaluation results for the implemented models over TREC09 data set.

Model	MAP	P@10	Bpref
BloggerModel	0.2745	0.3974	0.2867
TopBlogs	0.2777	0.4128	0.2973
TopPosts	0.2848	0.4282	0.3064
FFBS	0.2857	0.4256	0.3031
WFBS	0.2882	0.4256	0.3072
TemporalRM	**0.2931** $\star\dagger$	**0.4308**	**0.3116** $\star\dagger$

We employ the Blogger Model method for the initial ranking of the blogs [1] . All the parameters of the models are tuned by 5-fold cross validation technique. These parameters, depending on the system, include number of the posts and blogs used in the expansion and number of the terms selected for expansion.

Table 1 summarizes retrieval performance of Blogger Model and the baseline query expansion methods along with time-based relevance model on the TREC 2009 data set. As we can see in this table, the temporal relevance model outperforms all the baseline techniques in all the evaluation measures. Statistical significant tests are performed using Paired T-test at 0.05 level of significance. It can be seen that Temporal Relevance model has statistically significant improvements over the Blogger model and the Top Blogs model which is shown by $\star$ and $\dagger$ respectively.

The experimental results confirm our intuition that using the temporal information as a source for selecting terms can lead us to a better expanded query.

4. CONCLUSION

Relevance Feedback is known to be effective in information retrieval, however in the blog retrieval it is hard to select good terms for expansion. We showed that using temporal information for improving the coverage of the new query over all the subtopics can be useful and improve the performance of the retrieval system.

5. REFERENCES

[1] K. Balog, M. de Rijke, and W. Weerkamp. Bloggers as experts: feed distillation using expert retrieval models. In *Proceedings of SIGIR 2008*, pages 753–754, 2008.

[2] J. L. Elsas, J. Arguello, J. Callan, and J. G. Carbonell. Retrieval and feedback models for blog feed search. In *Proceedings of SIGIR 2008*, pages 347–354, 2008.

[3] V. Lavrenko and W. B. Croft. Relevance-based language models. In *In Proceedings of SIGIR 2001*, pages 120–127, 2001.

[4] Y. Lee, S.-H. Na, and J.-H. Lee. An improved feedback approach using relevant local posts for blog feed retrieval. In *Proceedings of CIKM 2009*, pages 1971–1974, 2009.

[5] Y. Lv and C. Zhai. Positional language models for information retrieval. In *Proceedings SIGIR '09*, pages 299–306, 2009.

[6] C. MacDonald, I. Ounis, and I. Soboroff. Overview of the TREC-2009 Blog Track. In *Proceedings of TREC 2009*, 2009.

Improved Query Performance Prediction Using Standard Deviation

Ronan Cummins
School of Computing Science
University of Glasgow
Scotland
ronan.cummins@nuigalway.ie

Joemon M. Jose
School of Computing Science
University of Glasgow
Scotland
jj@dcs.gla.ac.uk

Colm O'Riordan
Department of IT
National University of Ireland, Galway
colmor@it.nuigalway.ie

ABSTRACT

Query performance prediction (QPP) is an important task in information retrieval (IR). In this paper, we (1) develop a new predictor based on the standard deviation of scores in a variable length ranked list, and (2) we show that this new predictor outperforms state-of-the-art approaches without the need for tuning.

Categories and Subject Descriptors: H.3.3 [Information Storage and Retrieval]: Information Search and Retrieval: Query formulation

General Terms: Experimentation, Measurement, Performance

Keywords: Information Retrieval, Query Performance Prediction

1. INTRODUCTION

Query performance prediction (QPP) has been a vibrant area of IR research over the last decade [2, 4, 3]. The motivation for QPP is that, if we can predict the performance of a query for a given system, we can automatically develop different strategies for dealing with these different queries. Predictors for this task are usually divided into two classes: *pre-retrieval* and *post-retrieval*. Pre-retrieval predictors are usually computationally less expensive but suffer from poor performance. Post-retrieval predictors are more computationally expensive as they use the ranked output (and/or scores) of a system, but achieve a higher performance than their counterparts. In general, the effectiveness a predictor is usually measured by calculating the correlation between the output of the predictor and the actual performance (i.e. average precision) of the queries on a system. Pearson's (r) and Spearman's (ρ) are two common correlation coefficient's used.

2. TEST COLLECTIONS

The data used in this paper consists of a number of TREC collections and a considerably large number of topics available for those collections. The *title* field was used as a short query for each of the collections, while the *desc* field was used as another set of queries[1].Table 1 shows details of the data that consists of over 500 different topics.

Table 1: News (top) and Web (bottom) Collections

Collection	Documents	Topic Range	# Topics	length	
				title	desc
AP	242,918	051-200	149	2.4	7.5
FBIS	130,471	301-450	116	2.4	7.6
FT	210,158	250-450	188	2.5	7.6
WSJ	130,837	051-200	150	2.4	7.5
LA	131896	301-450	143	2.4	7.6
OHSU	293,856	001-63	63	-	6.7
WT2G	221,066	401-450	50	2.4	6.5
WT10G	1,692,096	451-550	100	2.4	6.5

3. STANDARD DEVIATION FOR QPP

Recent research has shown that the standard deviation (σ) of scores in a ranked list is a good predictor of query performance [4]. The intuition is that, a good query is one for which the scores of documents at the head of the ranked-list are highly dispersed (i.e. the user has chosen good query terms that enhance the signal of a certain number of topical documents compared to the noise of the collection). Some standard approaches [4] have shown that the standard deviation at fixed cut-off points (e.g. 100 documents) is correlated with query performance. It has also been shown [4] that even better prediction can be obtained if a variable cut-off point is used (i.e. a different cut-off point for each query) using a tuning parameter. We adopt this idea and derive a simple, yet intuitive, method of automatically determining the cut-off value for each query.

Table 2: Correlation of $\sigma_{x\%}$ with average precision

AP (title)	$\sigma_{90\%}$	$\sigma_{75\%}$	$\sigma_{60\%}$	$\sigma_{50\%}$	$\sigma_{40\%}$	$\sigma_{25\%}$	$n(\sigma_{50\%})$
Pearson (r)	0.352	0.421	0.535	**0.624**	0.617	0.505	0.672
Spearman (ρ)	0.312	0.348	0.500	0.602	**0.617**	0.542	0.650
OHSU (desc)	$\sigma_{90\%}$	$\sigma_{75\%}$	$\sigma_{60\%}$	$\sigma_{50\%}$	$\sigma_{40\%}$	$\sigma_{25\%}$	$n(\sigma_{50\%})$
Pearson (r)	0.232	0.328	0.481	**0.570**	0.516	0.299	0.622
Spearman (ρ)	0.323	0.335	0.475	**0.535**	0.534	0.347	0.538
WT2G (title)	$\sigma_{90\%}$	$\sigma_{75\%}$	$\sigma_{60\%}$	$\sigma_{50\%}$	$\sigma_{40\%}$	$\sigma_{25\%}$	$n(\sigma_{50\%})$
Pearson (r)	0.071	0.343	0.433	0.536	**0.621**	0.359	0.590
Spearman (ρ)	0.045	0.373	0.380	**0.526**	0.525	0.331	0.556

As it is the head of the retrieval list that is important, we calculate the standard deviation of the scores of the first N documents, where N is the number of documents that

[1]For the OHSUMED collection only the *desc* was used, as it is the actual information need for the topic

SIGIR'11, July 24–28, 2011, Beijing, China.
ACM 978-1-4503-0757-4/11/07.

Table 3: Natural tendency for longer queries to return increased σ of scores without an increase in performance (MAP)

	title		desc	
	MAP	$avg(\sigma_{50\%})$	MAP	$avg(\sigma_{50\%})$
AP	0.159	1.811	0.151	2.597
FBIS	0.225	1.839	0.202	2.567
FT	0.228	1.983	0.219	2.739
WSJ	0.221	1.924	0.209	2.796
WT2G	0.224	1.847	0.227	2.626

are assigned a score greater than a certain percentage (x) of the top score. For example, if we choose $x = 90\%$, all documents that have a score of at least 90% of the top score are included in the standard deviation calculation. Table 2 shows the performance of this approach on three of the collections for a $BM25$ system. We can see that performance (i.e. correlation) is optimised at $x = 50\%$ (i.e. all document scores that are at least 50% of the top score for a given query are are included in the standard deviation calculation). Results on all other collections used in this work (not included due to space limitations) report a similar trend. This simple method means that a varying number of documents are included in the standard deviation calculation, and that these documents are of a certain quality (as determined by the system itself).

Furthermore, we also determined that there is a natural tendency for longer queries to produce ranked lists with a higher deviation of document score, although these longer queries might not produce a higher performance. Table 3 outlines this phenomenon. Therefore, we normalised the standard deviation with respect to query length. Thus, our new normalised query performance predictor is $n(\sigma_{50\%}) = \frac{\sigma_{50\%}}{sqrt(ql)}$ where ql is the query length. The last column of Table 2 confirms that this new normalised predictor outperforms the unnormalised version on the collections. Furthermore, both new predictors ($\sigma_{50\%}$ and $n(\sigma_{50\%})$) are significantly correlated with average precision. Now that we have developed a new predictor we compare it against some state-of-the-art approaches.

4. EXPERIMENTS

In these experiments, we use a $BM25$ system and compare the performance of a number of state-of-the-art predictors against our newly developed predictor. The best pre-retrieval predictors from the literature are the simplified clarity score (*scs*), the average *idf* of query terms (idf_{avg}), and the maximum *idf* of the query terms (idf_{max}). The best post-retrieval predictors from the literature are query clarity (*clarity*) [1], *ncq* [5], standard deviation at 100 documents (σ_{100}), the maximum standard deviation in the ranked-list (σ_{max}), and a variable cut-off point (k) approach [4] (σ_k) which includes a tuning parameter λ which we set to 5.

4.1 Performance Comparison

Table 4 shows the performance of the predictors averaged over the News collections for each query type (*title* and *desc*). Firstly, we can see that while pre-retrieval predictors are useful for short queries, they are poor on longer queries. The clarity score achieves steady performance across the collections and query types. However, the predictors based on standard deviation are generally more highly correlated with query performance. Table 5 shows the best predictors on larger Web collections. There is a significant correlation with average precision on all the individual collections for the post-retrieval predictors which is mainly due to the large number of queries we use for each collection. The new predictor $n(\sigma_{50\%})$ outperforms the other predictors consistently over all query types and collections. Simply to outline the consistency of the increases over a good baseline, we performed a paired Wilcoxon test on the 15 (7 *title* sets and 8 *desc* sets) ρ coefficients of $n(\sigma_{50\%})$ compared to ncq and determined that the p-value was 0.012.

Table 4: Correlation coefficients (r and ρ) averaged for the News collections for title and desc queries

	title		desc	
Predictor	$avg(r)$	$avg(\rho)$	$avg(r)$	$avg(\rho)$
scs	0.374	0.307	0.205	0.172
idf_{max}	0.332	0.295	0.191	0.208
idf_{avg}	0.423	0.344	0.250	0.221
$clarity$	0.381	0.417	0.345	0.379
σ_{100}	0.456	0.442	0.499	0.504
σ_{max}	0.475	0.493	0.404	0.406
σ_{k5}	0.448	0.338	0.281	0.254
ncq	0.523	0.429	0.527	0.506
$\sigma_{50\%}$	0.501	0.487	0.535	0.525
$n(\sigma_{50\%})$	**0.569**	**0.538**	**0.604**	**0.588**

Table 5: Spearman correlation (ρ) for best predictors on Web collections

Collection	$clarity$	σ_{100}	ncq	$\sigma_{50\%}$	$n(\sigma_{50\%})$
WT2G (title)	0.352	0.445	0.411	0.502	**0.531**
WT2G (desc)	0.321	0.585	0.593	0.567	**0.606**
WT10G (title)	0.358	0.356	0.342	**0.447**	0.423
WT10G (desc)	0.401	0.502	0.492	0.550	**0.566**

5. CONCLUSION

In this paper, we have developed a new post-retrieval predictor for query performance, that needs no tuning to achieve a high correlation with average precision. The new predictor outperforms state-of-the-art predictors on a number of test collections for both short and medium length queries. The predictor is intuitively simple and less computationally expensive than some other approaches, such as the *clarity* score.

Acknowledgments

The first author is funded by the Irish Research Council for Science, Engineering and Technology (IRCSET), co-funded by Marie Curie Actions under FP7.

6. REFERENCES

[1] Steve Cronen-Townsend, Yun Zhou, and W. Bruce Croft. Predicting query performance. In *SIGIR '02*, pages 299–306, New York, NY, USA, 2002. ACM.

[2] Claudia Hauff, Djoerd Hiemstra, and Franciska de Jong. A survey of pre-retrieval query performance predictors. In *CIKM*, pages 1419–1420, 2008.

[3] Ben He and Iadh Ounis. Inferring query performance using pre-retrieval predictors. In *SPIRE*, pages 43–54, 2004.

[4] Joaquín Pérez-Iglesias and Lourdes Araujo. Standard deviation as a query hardness estimator. In *SPIRE*, pages 207–212, 2010.

[5] Anna Shtok, Oren Kurland, and David Carmel. Predicting query performance by query-drift estimation. In *ICTIR*, pages 305–312, 2009.

Learning to Rank Using Query-Level Regression

Jiajin Wu, Zhihao Yang, Yuan Lin, Hongfei Lin, Zheng Ye, Kan Xu
School of Computer Science and Technology, Dalian University of Technology
No. 2, LingGong Road, GanJingZi District DaLian, China 116024
wujiajin@mail.dlut.edu.cn, yangzh@dlut.edu.cn, yuanlin@mail.dlut.edu.cn, hflin@dlut.edu.cn, zye@mail.dlut.edu.cn, xukan@dlut.edu.cn

ABSTRACT
In this paper, we use query-level regression as the loss function. The regression loss function has been used in pointwise methods, however pointwise methods ignore the query boundaries and treat the data equally across queries, and thus the effectiveness is limited. We show that regression is an effective loss function for learning to rank when used in query-level. We propose a method, namely ListReg, to use neural network to model the ranking function and gradient descent for optimization. Experimental results show that ListReg significantly outperforms pointwise Regression and the state-of-the-art listwise method in most cases.

Categories and Subject Descriptors
H.3.3 [**Information Search and Retrieval**]: Retrieval Models

General Terms
Algorithms, Experimentation, Performance.

Keywords
Learning to Rank, Loss Function, Query-Level, Regression.

1. INTRODUCTION
Learning to rank [3] methods can be categorized into the following three groups: pointwise, pairwise and listwise approaches according to their different input spaces. The listwise approaches have been paid more and more attention for that all IR evaluation measures are defined at the query level. Listwise approaches can be divided into two types: using query-level loss function and directly optimizing evaluation measures. In this paper, we propose a novel listwise approach based on the first type.

In prior work, Cao et al [1] proposed to use *Top k Probability* based on *Plackett-Luce* model [5] to represent the listwise instances. Assuming there are n_q documents for a given query q, the number of permutation elements of the model is of order of $O(\frac{n!}{(n-k)!})$. They used *cross entropy* loss to measure the difference of distribution and gradient descent as optimization algorithm proposing ListNet. Similarly, Xia et al [3] used *likelihood* loss based on *Plackett-Luce* model proposing ListMLE. Qin et al [4] proposed RankCosine using boosting algorithm to optimize *cosine* loss.

To train a good ranking model, a robust loss function is needed. In this paper, we show how to use a robust and effective loss function of order $O(n)$ to improve the retrieval performance.

2. METHODOLOGY
2.1 Query-level Regression
Lan et al. [2] proposed a query-level ranking framework, within which the query-level loss is defined. In the listwise approach, each query is represented by a group of documents and their ground truth labels, and queries are assumed to be i.i.d. random variables.

Let $\mathbb{X}^m$ be the input space and $\mathbb{Y}$ be the output space, then $(\boldsymbol{x}, \pi_y)$ can be regarded as a random variable sampled from the space $\mathbb{X}^m \times \mathbb{Y}$ according to an unknown probability distribution. The query-level (also named listwise) loss is defined as follows:

$$L(f;q) = L(f;\boldsymbol{x},\pi_y) \quad (1)$$

Here f is the objective ranking function, q is the current query, and π_y is the permutation of $\boldsymbol{x}$ given according to their ground truth relevance. In our approach, we use the query-level regression (specifically square loss) as listwise loss function. Regression has been used in pointwise approach, in which the loss on a single sample $(\boldsymbol{x}, y)$ is given by $(f(\boldsymbol{x}) - y)^2$, and the training goal is to minimize the total losses of all samples in which the queries boundaries are obviously ignored. The query-level regression loss for query is given as follows:

$$L(f;q) = \sum_{i=1}^{n_q}[y_i - f(\boldsymbol{x}_i)]^2 \quad (2)$$

Here we assume that there are n_q documents for query q, and the ground truth label for document i is y_i. We denote the output for document i given by ranking function f is $f(\boldsymbol{x}_i)$.

2.2 The Learning Approach
The objective ranking function can be obtained by optimizing the query-level regression:

$$f(x) \equiv \min_{f \in F} \sum_{i=1}^{n_q}[y_i - f(\boldsymbol{x}_i)]^2 \quad (3)$$

here we use neural network as model and choose linear ranking i.e. $f(\boldsymbol{x}) = \boldsymbol{\omega} \cdot \boldsymbol{x}$ which in practice is a s-dimension function and s is the features number of document $\boldsymbol{x}$. We use gradient descent for optimization and refer our method as ListReg. The gradient $\nabla\omega$ of the loss function $L(f;q)$ with respect to parameter ω can be calculated as follows:

$$\nabla\omega = 2\sum_{i=1}^{n_q}[y_i - f(\boldsymbol{x}_i)] * \frac{\partial f(\boldsymbol{x}_i)}{\partial\omega} \quad (4)$$

where if we denote ω_t the *t*-th weight of ω and $\boldsymbol{x}_{i,t}$. Eq. 4 is then used in Gradient Descent for updating weight vector $\boldsymbol{\omega}$. Algorithm 1 shows the learning algorithm of ListReg.

Table 1. Ranking accuracies on LETOR3.0. Here we use N@k to denote NDCG@k for short. * and † indicate significant improvement to Regression and ListNet of our approach ("ListReg") respectively according to the LETOR3.0 t-test at the 0.05 level. Best result in each metric on each dataset is marked in bold. Note that ListReg outperforms Regression and ListNet in most cases.

Dataset	Method	P@1	P@2	P@3	P@4	P@5	MAP	N@1	N@2	N@3	N@4	N@5
OHSUMED	Regression	0.5965	0.6006	0.5768	0.5605	0.5337	0.4220	0.4456	0.4532	0.4426	0.4368	0.4278
	ListNet	0.6524	0.6093	0.6016	0.5745	0.5502	**0.4457**	0.5326	0.4810	0.4732	0.4561	0.4432
	ListReg	**0.7081***†	**0.6684***†	**0.6273***	**0.6064***†	**0.5938***†	0.4376	**0.5810***†	**0.5447***†	**0.5127***†	**0.4961***†	**0.4913***†
TD2003	Regression	0.3200	0.3000	0.2600	0.2450	0.2160	0.2409	0.3200	0.3200	0.3071	0.3082	0.2984
	ListNet	0.4000	**0.3300**	**0.2933**	0.2550	**0.2520**	0.2753	0.4000	0.3400	0.3365	0.3254	0.3393
	ListReg	**0.4044***	0.3233*	0.2911*	**0.2589***	0.2316*	**0.2837***	**0.4067***	**0.3644***	**0.3495***	**0.3504***†	**0.3540***
TD2004	Regression	0.3600	0.3400	0.3333	0.3200	0.3120	0.2231	0.3600	0.3467	0.3573	0.3469	0.3325
	ListNet	0.3600	0.3467	0.3600	**0.3367**	**0.3067**	0.2231	0.3600	0.3467	0.3573	0.3469	0.3325
	ListReg	**0.4800***†	**0.4400***†	**0.3733***	0.3333	0.3013	**0.2356***†	**0.4800***†	**0.4400***†	**0.3920***†	**0.3663***†	**0.3474**

Algorithms 1 Learning Algorithms of ListReg

Input: training instances $\{(x^{(1)},y^{(1)}),(x^{(2)},y^{(2)}),\dots,(x^{(m)},y^{(m)})\}$
Parameter: number of iterations T, initial learning rate η
Initialize parameter ω_0
Output: Neural Network model ω
for $t = 1$ **to** T **do**
  for $i = 1$ **to** m **do**
    Input $x^{(i)}$ of query $q^{(i)}$ to Neural Network and compute score list $z^{(i)}(f_\omega)$ with current $\boldsymbol{\omega}$
    Compute gradient $\nabla\boldsymbol{\omega}_t$ using Eq. 4
    Update $\boldsymbol{\omega}_{t+1} = \boldsymbol{\omega}_t - \eta \times \nabla\boldsymbol{\omega}_t$
  end for
end for

The query-level loss of query $q^{(i)}$ is a sum of n_q objects' regression losses, the time complexity is of order $O(n)$. Also note that the calculation of $\nabla\omega$ in ListReg is much simpler than that of ListNet, for more detail, [1] can be referred.

3. EXPERIMENTAL RESULTS

3.1 Experiments Settings

We use three datasets published in LETOR3.0 [4] package: OHSUMED, TD2003 and TD2004 and use Regression and ListNet as baselines. We perform 5-fold cross validation experiments, where in each fold 3/5 is used for training, 1/5 for testing, and the left 1/5 for validation. Models are trained using the training set, tuned on the validation set and tested on the testing set. For evaluation purpose, we use three widely used IR evaluation measures: precision (P@k) and normalized discounted cumulative gain (NDCG@k) and mean-average precision (MAP). The initial learning rate of ListReg is set to be 1E-4 on OHSUMED and 1E-5 on TD2003 and TD2004 respectively, and the dropping rate is set to be 0.5 on all datasets in the experiment.

3.2 Experimental Results

It can be observed from Table 1 that our method ListReg significantly outperforms Regression on all metrics on all three datasets except in terms of P@5 on TD2004 (which is comparative nevertheless). The reason is that there are great diversities between different queries, but Regression is of pointwise style, whose loss function is based on document, treating different queries equally, however, ListReg is a query-level method (of listwise style), and it can capture the characteristics of different queries. Accordingly ListNet also outperforms Regression in most cases.

It can also be observed that ListReg outperforms ListNet in most cases, especially on the top P@k and NDCG@k categories. For example, ListReg outperforms ListNet with 8.5% in terms of P@1 on OHSUMED and with 33.3% in terms of NDCG@1 on TD2004. This is quite meaningful in the scenario of real search engine where users usually care more about the top-most retrieved documents. Furthermore, the query-level regression loss function is much simpler than cross entropy, and the training time consumption for ListReg is less than ListNet.

4. CONCLUSION

In this paper, we have proposed a $O(n)$ complexity listwise approach using query-level regression as the loss function and gradient descent as the optimization algorithm. Experimental results show that by considering regression at query-level, ListReg significantly outperforms both the pointwise approach Regression and the listwise approach ListNet. In the future, we will investigate other loss functions in query-level style; we hope to find more appropriate loss functions both in time complexity and performance for information retrieval.

5. REFERENCES

[1] Z. Cao, T. Qin, and T. Y. Liu, et al. Learning to rank: From pairwise approach to listwise approach. In *Proc. of the ICML*, pages 129-136, 2007.

[2] Y. Y. Lan, T. Y. Liu, and T. Q, et al. Query-Level Stability and Generalization in Learning to Rank. In *Proc. of the ICML*, pages 512-519, 2008.

[3] T. Y. Liu. Learning to rank for information retrieval. Foundations and Trends in Information Retrieval, 3(3): pages 225-331, 2009.

[4] T. Y. Liu, J. Xu, and T. Qin, et al. Letor: Benchmark dataset for research on learning to rank for information retrieval. In *Proc. of the Learning to Rank workshop in SIGIR*, pages 3-10, 2007.

[5] R. L. Plackett. The analysis of permutations. *Applied Statics*, 24(2): pages 193-202, 1975.

[6] T. Qin, X. D. Zhang, and M. F. Tsai, et al. Query-level loss functions for information retrieval. In IP & M, (44): 838-855, 2008.

[7] F. Xia, T. Y. Liu, and J. Wang, et al. Listwise Approach to Learning to Rank – Theory and Algorithm. In *Proc. of the ICML*, pages 1192-1199, 2008.

Diversifying Product Search Results

Xiangru Chen, Haofen Wang, Xinruo Sun, Junfeng Pan and Yong Yu
Apex Data & Knowledge Management Lab
Shanghai Jiao Tong University
Shanghai, 200240, China
{xrchen, whfcarter, xrsun, panjf, yyu}@apex.sjtu.edu.cn

ABSTRACT

In recent years, online shopping is becoming more and more popular. Users type keyword queries on product search systems to find relevant products, accessories, and even related products. However, existing product search systems always return very similar products on the first several pages instead of taking diversity into consideration. In this paper, we propose a novel approach to address the diversity issue in the context of product search. We transform search result diversification into a combination of diversifying product categories and diversifying product attribute values within each category. The two sub-problems are optimization problems which can be reduced into well-known NP-hard problems respectively. We further leverage greedy-based approximation algorithms for efficient product search results re-ranking.

Categories and Subject Descriptors

H.3.3 [**Information Storage and Retrieval**]: Retrieval Models

General Terms

Algorithm

Keywords

Product Search, Result Diversification

1. INTRODUCTION

Nowadays, online shopping has become the first choice of a large group of users. Facing so many different kinds of products, product search systems are always the main entrance for most people to begin online shopping. Similar to searching Web documents, users type keyword queries to those product search systems and get a list of relevant products. Within the results, users wish to find products of different types or brands, products with different attribute values (like color, model, size) and their accessories on the first several pages. However, like Web search engines [2], existing product search systems perform poorly on result diversification and usually return very similar products.

To address the diversity issue, we propose a simple but effective approach with special considerations on the features of product data. Different from Web documents, products on the Web are usually semi-structured. Each product is described by a set of attributes (e.g., product name, color and model). It also belongs to one or several categories predefined in a taxonomy. According to the above observation of product features, the result diversification is composed of two parts: (1) diversifying product categories enables returning products of different types as well as product accessories; (2) diversifying attribute values of products within each category allows to return products of different attributes or particular attribute values. Both aspects ensure more diverse products are returned.

Like diversification approaches widely used in Web document search, our approach re-ranks relevant results provided by some general search engine. In other words, while finding diverse product results on the first pages, we also preserve the high relevance of top returned products. We define the two sub tasks as optimization problems in which both relevance scores and diversity of products are included in the objective functions. The optimization problems are further reduced to two well-known NP-hard problems and we use greedy approximation algorithms to produce diversified but relevant results efficiently.

Product result diversification is different from that in database search. When searching database with keyword queries, people usually focus on query translation for diversified structured queries. On the other hand, compared with result diversification for Web documents, we provide more dedicated algorithms by utilizing the structural features of product data. To the best of our knowledge, this is the first work to address the diversity issue in the context of product search.

SIGIR'11, July 24–28, 2011, Beijing, China.
ACM 978-1-4503-0757-4/11/07.

2. IMPLEMENTATION DETAILS

In order to diversify products, we re-rank the search results (with their relevance score) returned by some existing product search systems or general search engines. We first group product search results according to their categories. In each category, we re-rank products according to a newly defined score function called *attribute diversity score*. Then we merge the items from different categories according to another newly defined score function called *category diversity score*.

2.1 Attribute Diversification

For a keyword query q and a category c, we fetch all relevant items from the underlying search engine. The objective of attribute diversification is to present as many `<attribute, value>` pairs as possible in the top items while preserving the relevance of these items.

Suppose $L(q, c)$ is the result list of query q under category c. Let

$$g(L, i) = w(L_i) + \lambda_a \left| A(L_i) \backslash \bigcup_{j<i} A(L_j) \right| \quad (1)$$

be the *attribute diversity score* of the i-th item in list L, where L_i is the i-th item in list L, and $A(\cdot)$ is the set of attribute-value pairs of a product. The formula is composed of two parts. The former one $w(L_i)$ stands for the relevance of L_i while the latter one counts the contribution of attribute-value pairs of L_i which are not included in any previous items. Note λ_a is a parameter that adjusts the weight between relevance and diversity.

Given the number of returned products as k, the objective function for re-ranking within one category is defined as:

$$f_a(L, k) = \sum_{i=1}^{k} g(L, i) = \sum_{i=1}^{k} w(L_i) + \lambda_a \left| \bigcup_{i=1}^{k} A(L_i) \right| \quad (2)$$

Through mapping each product u to a set of all of its attribute-value pairs (each weighted by λ_a) and the product itself (weighted by $w(u)$), we reduce the re-ranking problem to the *weighted maximum coverage problem*. Since the problem is NP-hard, we employ a greedy $\frac{e}{e-1}$-approximation algorithm to make the re-ranking process practical. In each step, we add the item with the maximum attribute diversity score among the remaining items to the result list.

2.2 Category Diversification

We get the final result list by merging different result lists of diversified categories.

While a product might belong to more than one category, we can pick up a *dominant category* which shares the largest number of attribute schemata with the product. We denote the dominant category of a product u as $c(u)$.

Suppose u is the l-th element of $L(q, c(u))$, we define g_u as $g(L(q, c(u)), l)$. Let $\mathcal{L}$ be the final result list. Inspired by [3], we define the objective function as follow:

$$f_c(\mathcal{L}, k) = (k-1) \sum_{i=1}^{k} g_{\mathcal{L}_i} + 2\lambda_c \sum_{1 \le i,j \le k} \text{dist}(c(\mathcal{L}_i), c(\mathcal{L}_j)) \quad (3)$$

where $\text{dist}(\cdot, \cdot)$ is the *category diversity score* function which defines the node distance on a taxonomy tree, and λ_c is an adjusting parameter.

We further reduce the optimization problem to the *facility dispersion problem* by defining a distance function between two items u and v:

$$d'(u, v) = g_u + g_v + 2\lambda_c \text{dist}(c(u), c(v)) \quad (4)$$

The facility dispersion problem is also NP-hard, we employ a 2-approximation algorithm. In each step, we choose the pair of products with the maximum pairwise distance among the unselected items. Since the result list of each category is ordered non-increasingly by the product attribute diversity score, at each selection stage, we only need to consider the top two unselected items in each category's result list to make $d'(\cdot, \cdot)$ maximized, which yields a fast solution.

3. EVALUATION

The experiments were carried out on a product data set exported from a famous online shopping site. There exist 17,480,804 products in the data set. Each product has

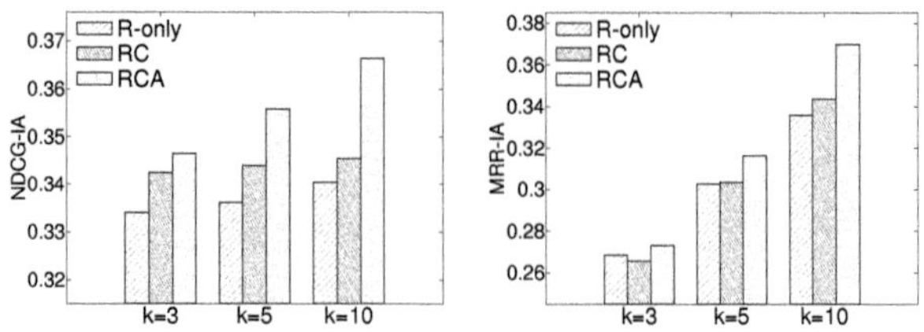

Figure 1: NDCG-IA scores and MRR-IA scores

18.55 attributes on average. These products belong to 712 categories which form a taxonomy tree.

We use *NDCG-IA* (intent-aware normalized discounted cumulative gain) and *MRR-IA* (intent-aware mean reciprocal rank) as the evaluation metrics which have been proposed in [1]. Since this is the first work of product result diversification, we use Lucene as our baseline to return the initial the result list by only considering relevance.

Since we do not own real product query logs, in order to reflect real user information needs, we selected 30 keyword queries covering different domains like IT, Office, Clothes, Mechanics, Food, Music and so on. The number of categories associated with these queries ranges from 2 to 4.

The search results of each query were labeled by our colleagues who are not involved in this project. The NDCG-IA scores and MRR-IA scores under different k are shown in Figure 1. The baseline system is marked as `R-only`. `RC` represents the system considering category diversification only, and `RCA` is the system further diversifies attributes within each category. As shown in the figure, we can notice with the increase of k, the NDCG-IA scores and MRR-IA scores of all three systems increase accordingly. In most cases, `RC` performs slightly better than the baseline. When further considering the attribute diversification, the performance gain becomes significantly large. Moreover, `RCA` performs consistently better than the other two systems no matter what k is with respective to both metrics.

Finally, we discuss the influence of the two parameters λ_a and λ_c. When λ_a increases, we prefer products with more attributes or different attribute values within one category. When λ_c increases, we prefer products belonging to more different categories. In both cases, we lower the importance of relevance contribution in the top products. In this paper, we adjusted the two parameters ($\lambda_c = 1$ and $\lambda_a = 1.5$) to reflect a balanced consideration of relevance and diversity.

4. CONCLUSION AND FUTURE WORK

In this paper, we proposed a simple but effective approach which tries to diversify search results for product data. The diversification is done through re-ranking products in one category and merging result lists from different categories. In the future, we plan to try other features in the calculation and carry out more extensive experiments on real query logs.

5. REFERENCES

[1] R. Agrawal, S. Gollapudi, A. Halverson, and S. Ieong. Diversifying Search Results. In *WSDM '09*. ACM, 2009.

[2] J. Carbonell and J. Goldstein. The Use of MMR, Diversity-Based Reranking for Reordering Documents and Producing Summaries. In *SIGIR '98*. ACM, 1998.

[3] S. Gollapudi and A. Sharma. An Axiomatic Approach for Result Diversification. In *WWW '09*. ACM, 2009.

Ad Hoc IR - Not Much Room for Improvement

Andrew Trotman
Department of Computer Science
University of Otago
Dunedin, New Zealand
andrew@cs.otago.ac.nz

David Keeler
Department of Computer Science
University of Otago
Dunedin, New Zealand
dkeeler@cs.otago.ac.nz

ABSTRACT
Ranking function performance reached a plateau in 1994. The reason for this is investigated. First the performance of BM25 is measured as the proportion of queries satisfied on the first page of 10 results – it performs well. The performance is then compared to human performance. They perform comparably. The conclusion is there isn't much room for ranking function improvement.

Categories and Subject Descriptors
H.3.3 [**Information Storage and Retrieval**]: Information Search and Retrieval – *Search process.*

General Terms
Measurement, Performance, Experimentation, Human Factors.

Keywords
Relevance Ranking, Document Retrieval.

1. INTRODUCTION
Armstrong et al. [2, 3] investigate the magnitude of the improvements in ad hoc searching seen on the TREC collections since 1994. They find "no discernible upward trend in Ad-Hoc scores over time" and find the results "reported in 2008 generally indistinguishable from those reported in 1999". In 2009 the best ad hoc relevance-in-context run submitted to INEX did not use structure in ranking [5]. A better ranking function and new features that improve ranking have remained elusive.

As a rule of thumb, the best ranking algorithms all perform at about the same level. BM25 with two tuning parameters performs comparably to language models with one and Divergence From Randomness [1] with none. Ranking performance has plateaued.

This plateau could be crossed if we knew the cause. Buckley [4] investigates the reasons why search engines fail and concludes that significant improvement may be seen if we could identify the cases where we incorrectly emphasized some aspect of the query. Query performance prediction research has not been fruitful.

We ask: *Is there room for improvement in ad hoc ranking?*

We explore this question by comparing stemmed BM25 performance to human performance (language models might equally be used). To do this we take all the TREC and INEX test collections that were multiply assessed and generate synthetic human runs. Comparing the performance of these runs to a search engine suggests that *there is little room for improvement*. We validate this by comparing manual and automatic runs submitted to TREC and again see the same result.

SIGIR'11, July 24-28, 2011, Beijing, China.
ACM 978-1-4503-0757-4/11/07.

2. DOCUMENT COLLECTION
Two TREC and four INEX ad hoc collections were multiple assessed. The TREC 4 collection is 567,529 documents with 49 queries. The TREC 6 collection is 556,077 documents with 50 queries. After TREC 4 assessment, up-to 200 relevant and 200 non-relevant documents were randomly chosen for reassessment by two alternate assessors. At TREC 6 the University of Waterloo submitted a manual run of documents thought to be relevant for each topic. For TREC experiments we trained on TREC 3.

The INEX 2002-2004 IEEE collection contains 12,107 academic articles, extended to 16,819 in 2005. The INEX 2006-2008 collection contains 659,388 Wikipedia articles and the INEX 2009-2010 collection has 2,666,190 Wikipedia articles. Between 2002 and 2010 the topic sets contained 24, 32, 34, 29, 114, 107, 70, 68, and 51 topics respectively. INEX topic pools were double assessed in parallel by participants who did not know their topic was chosen for reassessment. 5 topics were double assessed in 2004, 4 in 2005, and 15 in 2006. For our INEX experiments assessments were converted to whole document binary assessments by considering a document relevant if any part of it was relevant. The <title> field of the Content-Only (CO) topics were used (those without structural hints). Training was on INEX 2008.

The TREC and INEX designation of original and alternative assessor is maintained throughout these experiments.

3. EXPERIMENT 1:HOW GOOD IS IR?
Mean un-interpolated Average Precision (MAP) has been criticized for being recall oriented [7] and so a precision metric is used; success at n, S@n, the proportion of queries for which a relevant document is found at or before position n in the results.

The performance of the search engine for all topics in the sets was measured at each position on the first page of 10 results. The first page was chosen because clicking to a subsequent page is infrequent [6]. The results are in Figure 1 which shows that a relevant document is returned at position 1 between 56% and 86% of the time with TREC 6 being the outlier. By the end of the first page satisfaction levels are in excess of 96%, 88%, and 84% respectively for the Wikipedia, IEEE and TREC sets. Search engines are very effective at putting a relevant result high in the results list.

4. EXPERIMENT 2:HOW GOOD ARE WE?
Despite MAP criticism, it is important to ground this work in well understood metrics. The MAP of the search engine is compared against possible scores for the alternate assessor by constructing a synthetic best, typical (expected) and worst run for the assessor.

If all relevant documents are equally relevant then all permutations of relevant documents are equally good (to the alternate assessor). The highest scoring, however, starts with those documents both assessors consider relevant. The lowest has those the alternate assessor considers relevant and the original assessor does not, followed by those they both agree are relevant. These lists are the upper and lower bound on human performance, but it is important to compute the *expected* performance.

For each topic, 10,000 random permutations of the alternate assessor's relevant documents were generated and Average Precision (AP) computed for each. The average of these APs is the *expected* AP. The mean over all topics is the *expected* MAP.

The *expected* MAP scores were compared to those of the search engine. In Figure 2 the line represents the range of human scores (highest to lowest) with a tick at the *expected* score. The bar is the search engine. For TREC 4 the score of the 2 alternate assessors are designated alt1 and alt2. For TREC 6 the designation is alt; but also included is the original assessor's performance measured against the alternate assessor's ground truth (designated org).

Manual and automatic runs were submitted to TREC 4 and 6. The best, worst, and mean MAP of these runs is presented in the last two columns of Figure 2. The line is the range of manual runs (the tick is the mean). The bar is the best automatic run.

It can be seen that the search engine often performs inside the human range and sometimes better than *expected.* The notable exception is TREC 4. This, we believe, is because the alternate assessors were given a small and biased pool and were not asked to assess the original pool (they were unlikely to find new relevant documents). We also note that where there were more than 200 relevant documents for a topic those that were not reassessed were added to the alternate assessor's results (artificially inflating MAP). The runs submitted to TREC 4 are a better performance indicator – and the figure shows that by TREC 4 (1995) manual and automatic runs were performing comparably.

Although of questionable utility for the INEX collection (with few topics), a paired 2-tailed *t*-test was conducted. The results are presented in Table 1 where it can be seen that with TREC 6 and INEX IEEE, there is no statistically significant difference between the performance of the alternate assessor and the search engine.

Table 1: *t*-test scores, search engine against assessor

	2004	2005	2006	T4 alt 1	T4 alt 2	T6 alt	T6 org
Upper	0.19	0.54	0.00	0.00	0.00	0.00	0.00
Expected	0.06	0.32	0.03	0.00	0.00	0.08	0.01
Lower	0.01	0.13	0.51	0.00	0.00	0.63	0.58

5. DISCUSSION AND CONCLUSIONS

It is pertinent to ask whether this result is consequence of the methodology and search engine training. The high performance of the alternate assessors at TREC 4 is discussed in the previous section. In 1995 at TREC 4 and in 1997 at TREC 6 the manual and automatic runs performed at comparable levels. At INEX the number of multiple assessed topics is low which is likely reflected in the *t*-test results. None the less, it is reasonable to conclude that search engine performance is comparable to human performance.

To examine training, EXPERIMENT 1 was re-conducted on the INEX 2006 double-assessed topics. The nonparametric Divergence from Randomness (I(ne)B2), TF.IDF (inner product), and BM25 functions were used. The results are presented in Figure 3 from where it can be seen that when BM25 was introduced (circa 1994) there was room for improvement on TF.IDF. It can also be seen that the non-parametric I(ne)B2 function performs comparably to BM25 and the assessor.

Recent ranking functions are a substantial improvement on TF.IDF but there remains very little room for improvement in ad hoc search. In future work we will examine this result using graded relevance assessments and in known-entity searching where preliminary results suggests improvements can be made.

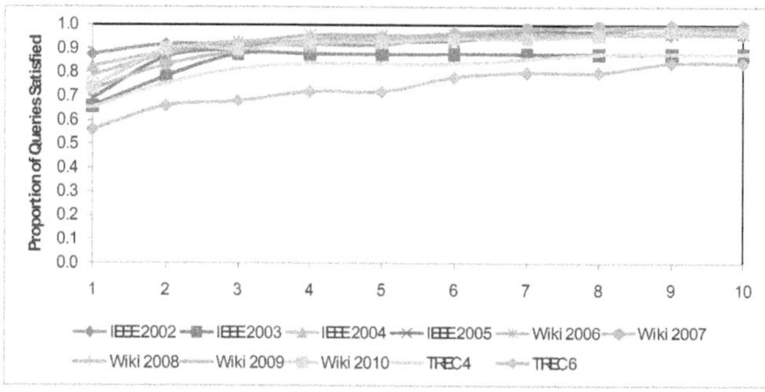

Figure 1: S@N of BM25 on the TREC and INEX collections

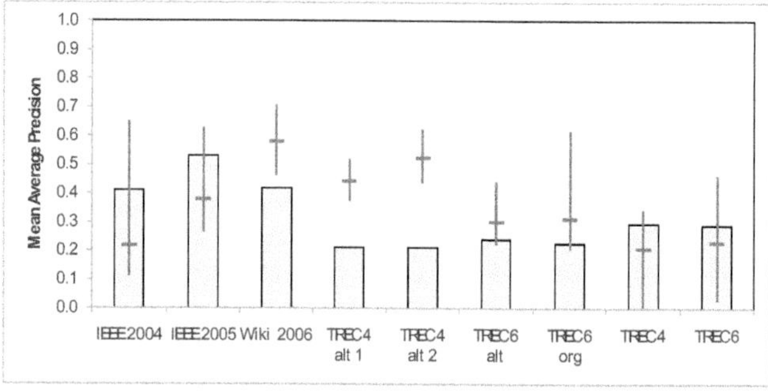

Figure 2: MAP of assessor (line) and search engine (box)

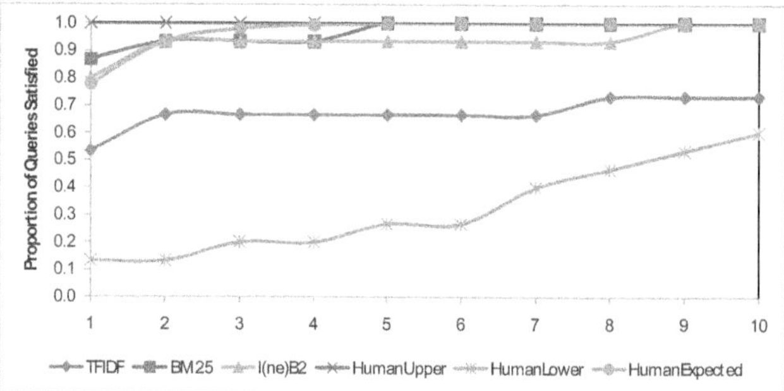

Figure 3:S@N of assessor and different ranking functions

REFERENCES

[1] Amati, G., van Rijsbergen, C.J. (2002) Probabilistic Models of Information Retrieval Based on Measuring the Divergence from Randomness, TOIS 20(4):357-389

[2] Armstrong, T., Moffat, A., Webber, W., Zobel, J. (2009) Has adhoc retrieval improved since 1994? SIGIR 2009:692-693

[3] Armstrong, T., Moffat, A., Webber, W., Zobel, J. (2009) Improvements that don't add up: ad-hoc retrieval results since 1998, CIKM 2009:601-610

[4] Buckley, C. (2009) Why current IR engines fail, Inf. Retr. 12(6):652-665

[5] Trotman, A., Jia, X.-F., Geva, S. (2009) Fast and Effective Focused Retrieval, Proceedings of INEX 2009:229-241

[6] Zhang, Y., Moffat, A. (2006) Some observations on user search behavior, ADCS 2006:1-8

[7] Zobel, J., Moffat, A., Park, L. (2009). Against recall: is it persistence, cardinality, density, coverage, or totality? SIGIR Forum 43:1:3-8

Image Annotation Based on Recommendation Model

Zijia Lin
School of Software, Tsinghua University
1 Tsinghua Park
Beijing, 100084, P.R.China
linzj07@mails.tsinghua.edu.cn

Guiguang Ding
School of Software, Tsinghua University
1 Tsinghua Park
Beijing, 100084, P.R.China
dinggg@tsinghua.edu.cn

Jianmin Wang
School of Software, Tsinghua University
1 Tsinghua Park
Beijing, 100084, P.R.China
jimwang@tsinghua.edu.cn

ABSTRACT
In this paper, a novel approach based on recommendation model is proposed for automatic image annotation. For any to-be-annotated image, we first select some related images with tags from training dataset according to their visual similarity. And then we estimate the initial ratings for tags of the training images based on tag ranking method and construct a rating matrix. We also construct a trust matrix based on visual similarity with a k-NN strategy. Then a recommendation model is built on both matrices to rank candidate tags for the target image. The proposed approach is evaluated using two benchmark image datasets, and experimental results have indicated its effectiveness.

Categories and Subject Descriptors
H.3.1 [**Information Storage and Retrieval**]: Content Analysis and Indexing

General Terms
Algorithms, Experimentation, Verification

Keywords
image annotation, recommendation model, TrustWalker, retrieval

1. INTRODUCTION
The exponential growth of Web images has created a compelling need for innovative methods to retrieve and manage them. As one of the promising solutions, automatic image annotation has recently attracted numerous research attentions, whose ambition is to find several tags that can well represent the visual content when given a to-be-annotated image with no or few tags. Though many effective algorithms and models have been proposed for this challenge, e.g. *JEC* [4], automatic image annotation is still far from practical and needs further research.

In this paper, image annotation problem is transformed into personal item recommendation problem, where images are modeled as users and tags as items. Then the process of image annotation is to recommend tags for to-be-annotated images.

To apply any recommendation model, the so-called "cold start" problem must be firstly taken into consideration, because to-be-annotated images have no or few tags. Here we adopt a trust-based and item-based recommendation model named *TrustWalker* [2] as our basic model, which recommends tags mostly according to the trust between images, without requiring that the to-be-annotated image should have any existing tags. Furthermore, the initial ratings for tags of each training image, and the trust between images, need to be estimated. Then a model developed from *TrustWalker* can be applied to recommend tags for to-be-annotated images. The whole process of our proposed approach, *IARM* for short, is shown in **Figure 1**, and it can be roughly separated into Rating Estimation and Recommendation Model.

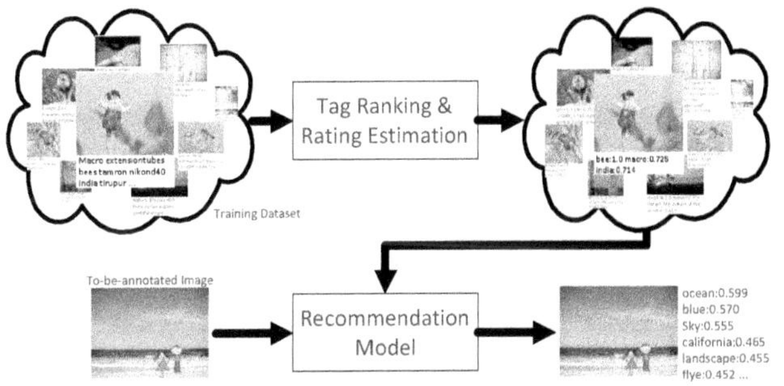

Figure 1: Process of our proposed *IARM*

2. RATING ESTIMATION
To estimate the initial ratings for tags of any training image, first we adopt the tag ranking method proposed by D. Liu [1], hoping to rank higher the tags that can better represent the visual content. The tag ranking method firstly employs a probability model to estimate a relevance score for each tag of image $\boldsymbol{v}$. Then a tag graph is constructed, where the edge weight is calculated with the exemplar similarity and semantic similarity between tags. Finally, a random walk is performed over the tag graph for obtaining stable tag scores, according to which all tags are ranked.

Inspired by the performance evaluation measurement named *NDCG* [1], the rating of any image $\boldsymbol{v}$ on tag $\boldsymbol{j}$, is initially estimated as $r_{v,j} = \frac{log\left(\frac{N}{N_j}\right)+1}{log_2(rk_{v,j}+1)}$, where $\boldsymbol{rk_{v,j}}$ is the rank position of the tag, $\boldsymbol{N}$ is the number of all images and $\boldsymbol{N_j}$ is the number of images containing tag $\boldsymbol{j}$. Here the numerator is the inverse image frequency of tag $\boldsymbol{j}$, which is introduced for punishing frequent but meaningless tags, e.g. "image". Furthermore, since existing tags are mostly relevant with visual content, mapping to higher ratings in recommendation model, we finally modify $\boldsymbol{r_{v,j}}$ into:

$$r_{v,j} = N_v \frac{log\left(\frac{N}{N_j}\right)+1}{log_2(rk_j+1)} + 0.5 \quad (1)$$

where $\boldsymbol{N_v}$ is a normalizing factor to map all ratings into [0, 1.0], and 0.5 acts as a score base. Then a rating matrix $\boldsymbol{R}$ can be constructed with all estimated ratings.

3. RECOMMENDATION MODEL
In basic *TrustWalker* model [2], to predict the rating of user $\boldsymbol{u_0}$ on item $\boldsymbol{i_0}$, the algorithm will firstly search the trust set of $\boldsymbol{u_0}$. If some trusted users have rated the target item, their ratings will be directly returned. As for those having not rated $\boldsymbol{i_0}$, the algorithm may return their ratings on some similar item, or further search their trust sets and return other users' ratings on $\boldsymbol{i_0}$ or similar items. Then all returned ratings are merged to be the predicted

SIGIR'11, July 24-28, 2011, Beijing, China.
ACM 978-1-4503-0757-4/11/07.

rating. The process of searching and selecting ratings can be simulated with several random walks, the step of which is equivalent to the depth of searching. Candidate items then are ranked according to their predicted ratings, and the top $\mathcal{K}$ will be recommended for u_0.

To better fit the challenge of automatic image annotation, we have made some improvements from basic *TrustWalker*, including restraint on the search range, introduction of real-valued trust degree, etc. When annotating a given image I_0, firstly we select $\mathcal{N}$ related images with tags from training dataset based on visual similarity, acting as a restricted search range and their tags being candidates. Such a restriction helps to reduce tag noise and computing complexity. Then the trust degree tr_{I_m,I_n} from image I_m to image I_n is calculated with the Gaussian kernel function [1]. That is, $tr_{I_m,I_n} = exp\,(-\frac{||I_m - I_n||^2}{\sigma^2})$, where $||I_m - I_n||$ is the visual distance, and σ is a radius parameter. Then each of the $(\mathcal{N}+1)$ images can respectively construct its own trust set with $\mathcal{M}$ of its most trusted images within the $\mathcal{N}$ related images. Finally a trust matrix $Tr_{(\mathcal{N}+1)\times(\mathcal{N}+1)}$ consisting of real-valued trust degree can be constructed. To predict the rating $\check{r}_{I_0,t_k}$ of image I_0 on candidate tag t_k, several random walks over the trust matrix are performed, as in basic *TrustWalker*. By calculating and merging the probability for rating selection, we can finally get the probability for the random walk to stop at image v and return its rating on tag j, namely, $P(v,j)$. Then $\check{r}_{I_0,t_k}$ can be calculated as:

$$\check{r}_{I_0,t_k} = \sum_{\{(v,j)|B_{v,j}\ \&\ j \in Top3\}} P(v,j) r_{v,j} \tag{2}$$

where $B_{v,j}$ is a boolean variable denoting whether image v owns tag j, $r_{v,j}$ is the tag rating, and $j \in Top3$ means that for any related image, we just merge the returned ratings of the top 3 most similar tags, hoping to reduce the negative effects of dissimilar tags. Then we rank all candidate tags based on their corresponding predicted ratings, and take the top $\mathcal{K}$ as annotating result.

4. EXPERIMENT

Our proposed approach, *IARM*, is evaluated with two benchmark image datasets, namely, Ground Truth Database of University of Washington (*UW*) [5] and the real-world *MIRFlickr* [6]. In *UW*, there are quite few noisy tags, and many similar images are of the same scene in different views. In *MIRFlickr*, however, the existing tags are fairly noisy, including much metadata and many meaningless tags, and the images are quite distinct from each other. In both datasets, we respectively take 1/10th of the images to form our test sets and the remaining are used as training datasets. And all tags in training datasets are pre-processed with WordNet, for stemming and kicking out strange words.

As for baselines, we take the *LNP* proposed by Wang [3] and the baseline *JEC* proposed by Makadia [4]. Moreover, we extract six kinds of features for each image, that is, ColorLayout, Gabor, Sift, ScalableColor, EdgeHistogram and Tamura. When calculating visual distance between images, we normalize and merge distances of different features with equal weights. As for experimental parameters, the threshold for random walk is set as 0.001, and σ in Gaussian kernel function is set as the average visual distance. In *UW*, we set $\mathcal{N}$ as 20, $\mathcal{M}$ as 5, while in *MIRFlickr*, both are respectively set as 40 and 10. And in *UW*, the top 5 tags of each algorithm are selected as its annotating result, while top 10 in *MIRFlickr*. The performances of all three approaches are measured with *top N precision rate* [7], which measures the correctness of the top *N* annotations for an image. *Top N precision rate* is defined as: $p(N) = \frac{1}{M}\sum_{i \in I_t} \frac{correct\_i(N)}{N}$, where I_t is the test image set, M is the size of I_t, and $correct\_i(N)$ is the number of correct annotations in the top *N* annotations for image i. For *UW*, the original tags of each test image act as the judging standard, while for *MIRFlickr*, volunteers fluent at English are asked to determine the correctness of each annotation, without knowing which algorithm it comes from.

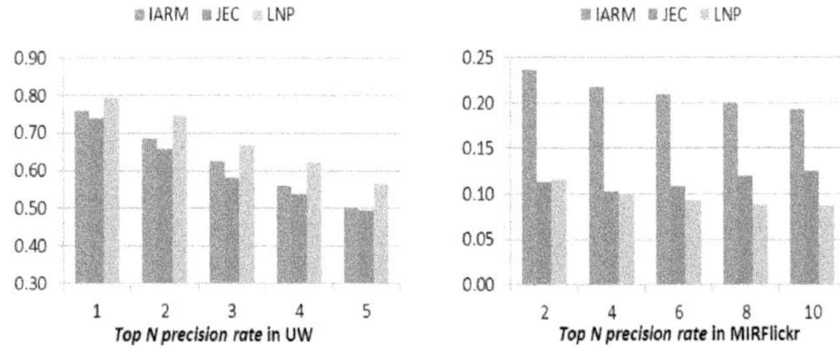

Figure 2: *Top N Precision Rate* in dataset *UW* and *MIRFlickr*

As shown in **Figure 2**, in dataset *UW*, *LNP* achieves the best performance, and our proposed *IARM* achieves the second, while *JEC* the worst. However, in dataset *MIRFlickr*, *IARM* performs much better than the other two, while *LNP* achieves the worst performance. Moreover, because of the considerable frequent noisy tags and the distinct images, all three algorithms that adopt the k-NN strategy perform much worse in *MIRFlickr*. By comparing the performances on both datasets, we can draw following conclusions: (1) Our proposed *IARM* is effective and relatively more robust; (2) Automatic image annotation is far from practical, as illustrated by performances in real-world *MIRFlickr*.

5. CONCLUSION

In this paper, we propose a novel approach *IARM* based on recommendation model for automatic image annotation. The proposed *IARM* is evaluated using two benchmark image datasets and experimental results have indicated its effectiveness, which suggests that other mature theories in recommendation problem may worth further research for being applied in image annotation.

6. ACKNOWLEDGMENTS

This research was supported by the National Natural Science Foundation of China (Grant No. 60972096, 90924003, 61005045)

7. REFERENCES

[1] D. Liu, X. Hua, L. Yang, M. Wang, H. Zhang. 2009. Tag Ranking. *ACM WWW'09.*

[2] M. Jamali, M. Ester. 2009. TrustWalker: A Random Walk Model for Combining Trust-based and Item-based Recommendation. *ACM SIGKDD '09.*

[3] F. Wang, C. Zhang. 2008. Label Propagation through Linear Neighborhoods. *IEEE TKDE.*

[4] A. Makadia, V. Pavlovic, S. Kumar. 2008. A New Baseline for Image Annotation. *ECCV'08.*

[5] http://www.cs.washington.edu/research/imagedatabase/

[6] M. J. Huiskes, M. S. Lew. 2008. The MIR Flickr Retrieval Evaluation. *ACM MIR'08.*

[7] X. Rui, M. Li, Z. Li, W. Ma, N. Yu. 2007. Bipartite graph reinforcement model for web image annotation. *ACM MM'07*

Utilizing Minimal Relevance Feedback for Ad Hoc Retrieval

Eyal Krikon
krikon@tx.technion.ac.il

Oren Kurland
kurland@ie.technion.ac.il

Faculty of Industrial Engineering and Management
Technion — Israel Institute of Technology
Haifa 32000, Israel

ABSTRACT

Using relevance feedback can significantly improve (ad hoc) retrieval effectiveness. Yet, if little feedback is available, effectively exploiting it is a challenge. To that end, we present a novel approach that utilizes document *passages*. Empirical evaluation demonstrates the merits of the approach.

Categories and Subject Descriptors: H.3.3 [Information Search and Retrieval]: Retrieval models; Relevance feedback

General Terms: Algorithms, Experimentation

Keywords: language models, passages, relevance feedback

1. INTRODUCTION

The effectiveness of ad hoc (query-based) retrieval can significantly improve if relevance feedback is available and exploited. Often, terms that are common in the relevant documents — but not very common in the corpus — are used for query expansion [7]. Since a document can be deemed relevant even if only a small part of it contains query-pertaining information, utilizing the commonalities between relevant documents is important. Indeed, using very few relevant documents, which reflects practical settings wherein relevance judgments are scarce, can sometimes fall short [8].

We present a novel retrieval method that addresses the challenge of utilizing very little relevance feedback; specifically, a single relevant document. This is a *query-by-example* task performed in a query-dependent context. We tackle the uncertainty about what makes the document relevant, and more specifically, which terms can represent the underlying information need, by using document *passages* in two capacities. First, rather than treat the relevant document as one unit, its passages are used so as to better focus on the document parts that presumably contain query-pertaining information. Second, to enrich the basis for performing query expansion, passages from documents in an initially retrieved list that are similar to the relevant document (and to its passages) are used as pseudo relevant units. Empirical evaluation demonstrates the merits of our method with respect to various reference comparisons.

2. RETRIEVAL FRAMEWORK

Suppose that some search algorithm is employed in response to query q so as to rank documents d in corpus $\mathcal{D}$ by their presumed relevance to information need I expressed by q. Let $\mathcal{D}_{\text{init}}$ denote the list of documents that are the highest ranked by the induced initial ranking (**initial** in short), and d_{rel} denote the highest ranked relevant document in $\mathcal{D}_{\text{init}}$.

Naturally, we can employ a relevance-feedback-based (**RF**) method using q and d_{rel} to create an expanded query form [7]. Since only a single relevant document is available, we opt to enrich the basis for creating this form; e.g., by employing a pseudo-feedback-based (**PRF**) approach that regards all documents in $\mathcal{D}_{\text{init}}$ as pseudo relevant. Indeed, recent work [6, 10] has demonstrated the potential merits of integrating true and pseudo relevance feedback (**RF+PRF**).

A potential drawback of such approaches is that they often treat a document as one unit. For example, it could be that all the information in the relevant document d_{rel} that pertains to I is confined to a single short *passage* g of d_{rel}. Moreover, the terms in g need not be the most dominant (e.g., frequent) in d_{rel}, and hence, might not be assigned with high enough weight by the relevance-feedback-based method. The same observations hold for documents in $\mathcal{D}_{\text{init}} \setminus \{d_{rel}\}$ for which no (positive) feedback is available. Thus, we use the passages in documents in $\mathcal{D}_{\text{init}}$ (the set of which is denoted G) as pseudo relevant units for performing query expansion. To that end, we estimate $p(g|I)$, the probability that passage g ($\in G$) contains information pertaining to I.

As q and d_{rel} are the only "signals" about I, we estimate $p(g|I)$ by $\lambda p(g|d_{rel}) + (1-\lambda)p(g|q)$; λ is a free parameter. Assuming a uniform prior for passages, we can score g by $\lambda \frac{p(d_{rel}|g)}{\sum_{g' \in G} p(d_{rel}|g')} + (1-\lambda)\frac{p(q|g)}{\sum_{g' \in G} p(q|g')}$. In addition, $\sum_{g'' \in d_{rel}} p(q|g'')p(g''|g)$ is used as an estimate for $p(q|g)$. The goal of using this estimate is addressing the potential vocabulary mismatch between passage g (which could be part of d_{rel}) that pertains to I and q by using d_{rel}'s passages (g'') as proxies for g; the impact of g'' is based on its "direct match" with q, which potentially reflects to some extent the likelihood that g'' contains information pertaining to I as it is part of d_{rel}.[1] Using the estimates just described results in our **PsgF** method that scores g ($\in G$) by:

$$S(g) \stackrel{def}{=} \frac{\lambda p(d_{rel}|g)}{\sum_{g' \in G} p(d_{rel}|g')} + \frac{(1-\lambda)\sum_{g'' \in d_{rel}} p(q|g'')p(g''|g)}{\sum_{g' \in G}\sum_{g'' \in d_{rel}} p(q|g'')p(g''|g')}. \quad (1)$$

The highest scoring passages are used for query expansion.

3. EVALUATION

[1]Inter-passage relations were also utilized, for example, for text summarization [3], finding documents similar to a given document [9], and re-ranking search results [4].

SIGIR'11, July 24–28, 2011, Beijing, China.
ACM 978-1-4503-0757-4/11/07.

Experiments were conducted with TREC corpora (disks, queries): AP (1-3, 51-150), TREC8 (4-5, 401-450), WSJ (1-2, 151-200), WT10G (WT10G, 451-550). Titles of TREC topics served for queries. Tokenization, Porter stemming and language model induction were performed using the Lemur toolkit (www.lemurproject.org). Half overlapping 150-terms windows in documents serve for passages [4].

We use $\exp\left(-D\left(p_x^{Dir[0]}(\cdot)\ \middle|\middle|\ p_y^{Dir[\mu]}(\cdot)\right)\right)$ [4] for $p(x|y)$ in Equation 1; D is the KL divergence; $p_z^{Dir[\mu]}(\cdot)$ is the Dirichlet-smoothed unigram language model induced from z with smoothing parameter μ.

The initial list, $\mathcal{D}_{\text{init}}$, is set to the 50 highest ranked documents d in the corpus by $p(q|d)$ with μ set to optimize MAP (at 1000) so as to have an initial list of reasonable quality.

We use relevance model number 3 (RM3) [1] as a query expansion method that assigns the probability $\beta p_q^{JM[0]}(t) + (1-\beta)\sum_{x\in X} p_x^{JM[\alpha]}(t)\, W(x)$ to term t; X is a set of passages or documents; $p_x^{JM[\alpha]}(\cdot)$ is the Jelinek-Mercer smoothed language model induced from x with smoothing parameter α; β is a free parameter; and, $W(x)$ is x's weight ($\sum_{x\in X} W(x) = 1$). Methods that use d_{rel} assign it with either a weight 1 (RF) or ρ (RF+PRF), which is a free parameter; in the latter case, the weight $(1-\rho)$ is distributed among the pseudo-relevant documents. For any method, except PsgF, that uses pseudo-relevant units f $(\in F \subseteq X)$, $\frac{p(q|f)}{\sum_{f'\in F} p(q|f')}$ serves as f's relative weight; for PsgF the (normalized) scores assigned in Equation 1 are used. The set X in RM3 is set to (i) d_{rel} for RF, (ii) k highest ranked documents in $\mathcal{D}_{\text{init}}$ for PRF, (iii) d_{rel} and the $k-1$ highest ranked documents d in $\mathcal{D}_{\text{init}}$ $(d \neq d_{rel})$ for RF+PRF, and (iv) the k highest ranked passages by Equation 1 for PsgF.

We use two additional passage-based baselines that utilize RM3. **TopPDrel** sets $X \stackrel{def}{=} \{g^*\}$ ($W(g^*) \stackrel{def}{=} 1$); g^* is d_{rel}'s passage with the highest $p(q|g)$ [2]. **AllPDrel** uses all d_{rel}'s passages ($X \stackrel{def}{=} \{g | g \in d_{rel}\}$) as pseudo relevant units.

For evaluation, d_{rel} is not considered (i.e., the residual corpus approach is employed); MAP(@1000) and p@5 are reported. The two-tailed paired t-test (95% confidence level) serves for determining statistically significant differences.

The following free-parameter-values' ranges are used: $\mu = 2000$ except in $p_d^{Dir[\mu]}(q)$ where we use the value used to create $\mathcal{D}_{\text{init}}$ to maintain consistency with the initial ranking; $k \in \{5, 10, 20, 30, 40, 50\}$; $\lambda \in \{0, 0.1, \ldots, 1\}$; $\rho \in \{0.2, 0.4, 0.6, 0.8\}$; the number of terms used by RM3 is set to $\{25, 50, 75, 100, 500, 1000, 5000, ALL\}$ ("ALL": all terms in the vocabulary); $\alpha \in \{0, 0.1, 0.3, 0.5, 0.7, 0.9\}$; $\beta \in \{0, 0.1, \ldots, 0.9\}$. To give the "best chance" to the reference comparisons RF, PRF, TopPDrel and AllPDrel, their free-parameter values are set to optimize MAP over all queries per corpus. For RF+PRF and PsgF, RM3's parameters are set to the values used by RF and AllPDrel, respectively; the other free parameters are set using leave-one-out cross validation performed over queries (MAP is the optimization criterion).

Results, conclusions, and future work. Table 1 shows that all methods outperform the initial ranking used to create $\mathcal{D}_{\text{init}}$. (Most of these improvements are statistically significant; hence, they are not marked to avoid cluttering.) The MAP performance of our PsgF method is superior (often, statistically significantly so) for most corpora to that of the reference comparisons. Specifically, PsgF always MAP-outperforms RF (often, statistically significantly), which is the standard approach of using d_{rel} as a whole unit. PsgF also outperforms RF+PRF in most relevant comparisons. As both methods integrate true and pseudo feedback, we see that using passages (by PsgF as opposed to RF+PRF) is of merit. We also see that TopPDrel is often inferior to AllPDrel and PsgF, which suggests that using several (weighted) passages rather than a single one is beneficial. Finally, except for WT10G, PsgF is MAP-superior to AllPDrel and posts more statistically significant MAP improvements over the other methods than AllPDrel does. This implies that using passages not in, as well as in, d_{rel} can be more effective than using just those in d_{rel}. However, in terms of p@5, PsgF is often outperformed by AllPDrel. Thus, integrating these two methods, along with utilizing term-proximity models [6, 5], is an interesting future venue.

	AP		TREC8		WSJ		WT10G	
	MAP	p@5	MAP	p@5	MAP	p@5	MAP	p@5
initial	21.8	40.9	23.0	40.8	27.2	43.2	15.6	25.1
RF	32.3	61.1	26.2	54.7	35.3	58.4	23.2	41.3
PRF	30.0	50.8^{r}	26.2	44.9^{r}	33.8	50.4	18.0^{r}	29.2^{r}
RF+PRF	32.9^{p}	$\mathbf{63.4}^{rp}$	26.0	53.5^{p}	35.6	57.2	22.6^{p}	41.5^{p}
TopPDrel	29.3^{r+}	59.4^{p+}	25.2	54.7^{p}	34.8	$\mathbf{58.8}^{p}$	21.9^{p}	42.0^{p}
AllPDrel	32.3_{t}	63.0_{t}^{rp}	26.3_{t}	$\mathbf{55.5}^{p}$	35.5	56.8	$\mathbf{23.8}_{+t}^{rp}$	$\mathbf{43.3}^{p}$
PsgF	$\mathbf{33.4}_{ta}^{rp}$	61.9^{p}	$\mathbf{27.4}_{t}^{r+}$	55.1^{p}	$\mathbf{36.5}_{t}^{r}$	56.8	23.4_{t}^{p}	42.0^{p}

Table 1: Performance numbers; 'r', 'p', '+', 't' and 'a' mark statistically significant differences with RF, PRF, RF+PRF, TopPDrel and AllPDrel respectively. The best result in a column is boldfaced.

Acknowledgments This paper is based upon work supported in part by the ISF under grant no. 557/09, and by IBM's SUR award. Any opinions, findings and conclusions or recommendations expressed here are the authors' and do not necessarily reflect those of the sponsors.

4. REFERENCES

[1] N. Abdul-Jaleel, J. Allan, W. B. Croft, F. Diaz, L. Larkey, X. Li, M. D. Smucker, and C. Wade. UMASS at TREC 2004 — novelty and hard. In *Proceedings of TREC-13*, 2004.

[2] J. Allan. Relevance feedback with too much data. In *Proceedings of SIGIR*, pages 337–343, 1995.

[3] G. Erkan and D. R. Radev. LexPageRank: Prestige in multi-document text summarization. In *Proceedings of EMNLP*, pages 365–371, 2004. Poster.

[4] E. Krikon, O. Kurland, and M. Bendersky. Utilizing inter-passage and inter-document similarities for reranking search results. *ACM Transactions on Infortmation Systems*, 29(1):3, 2010.

[5] H. Lang, D. Metzler, B. Wang, and J.-T. Li. Improved latent concept expansion using hierarchical markov random fields. In *Proceedings of CIKM*, pages 249–258, 2010.

[6] M. Lease. Incorporating relevance and pseudo-relevance feedback in the markov random field model. In *Proceedings of TREC 2008*, 2008.

[7] J. J. Rocchio. Relevance feedback in information retrieval. In G. Salton, editor, *The SMART Retrieval System: Experiments in Automatic Document Processing*, pages 313–323. Prentice Hall, 1971.

[8] E. L. Terra and R. Warren. Poison pills: harmful relevant documents in feedback. In *Proceedgins of CIKM*, pages 319–320, 2005.

[9] X. Wan, J. Yang, and J. Xiao. Towards a unified approach to document similarity search using manifold-ranking of blocks. *Information Processing and Management*, 44(3):1032–1048, 2008.

[10] L. Zhao, C. Liang, and J. Callan. Extending relevance model for relevance feedback. In *Proceedings of TREC 2008*, 2008.

Sense Discrimination for Physics Retrieval

Christina Lioma
Institute for Natural Language Processing
Stuttgart University, Germany
liomaca@ims.uni-stuttgart.de

Alok Kothari
Institute for Natural Language Processing
Stuttgart University, Germany
kotharak@ims.uni-stuttgart.de

Hinrich Schütze
Institute for Natural Language Processing
Stuttgart University, Germany
hs999@ifnlp.org

ABSTRACT

Information Retrieval in technical domains like physics is characterised by long and precise queries, whose meaning is strongly influenced by term context and domain. We treat this as a disambiguation problem, and present initial findings of a retrieval model that posits a higher probability of relevance for documents matching disambiguated query terms. Preliminary evaluation on a real-life physics test collection shows promising performance improvement.

Categories and Subject Descriptors

H.3.3 [**Information Systems**]: Information Search and Retrieval

General Terms

Algorithms, Experimentation, Performance

Keywords

Information Retrieval, Sense Discrimination

1. INTRODUCTION

User queries in technical domains like physics tend to be long and precise, e.g. `I am looking for a general expression for the heat transfer coefficient in a liquid solid interface`. For such queries, standard bag of word approaches may fail to capture the dependence between the query constituents, or the modification relationships of their components. For a shorter query this may not harm retrieval, and often the collocation of the query terms in the collection suffices. However, for longer queries, a similiar approach would result in notably more collocations in the collection, causing accidental matches with nonrelevant documents. An additional problem of technical domains like physics is that words may acquire special domain-specific meanings, e.g. in the query above, `expression` denotes a formula. This sense is not only different to other senses that `expression` may convey, but also central to the user need.

We present initial findings of a retrieval model that posits a higher prior probability of relevance for documents matching disambiguated query terms. Disambiguation is realised with Schütze & Pedersen's [3] unsupervised approach that disambiguates query terms by considering their context representations in the retrieval collection. This approach outputs a disambiguated sense for a query term, and a cluster of documents that contain the query term in its disambiguated sense. We treat this output as evidence of relevance of those documents to the query, and we embed it into the retrieval model as a prior probability. Initial findings on a real-life physics test collection are presented.

SIGIR'11, July 24–28, 2011, Beijing, China.
ACM 978-1-4503-0757-4/11/07.

2. SENSE DISCRIMINATION MODEL

Let t' be a query term that we wish to disambiguate. We use Schütze & Pedersen's [3] algorithm to build a context vector for each occurrence of t' in the collection and in the query. This context vector consists of features occurring within $n = 10$ words of t' (following [3]), and uses as features sequences of alphanumeric characters. Context vectors are weighted using inverse context frequency and cosine-normalised: $v_{ij} = \frac{\delta(i,j)\log\frac{N}{N(j)}}{\sqrt{\sum_k(\delta(i,k)\log\frac{N}{N(k)})^2}}$, where v_{ij} is component j of context vector $\vec{v}_i$ of term t'; $\delta(i,j)$ is 1 if feature j occurs in context i, 0 otherwise; $N(j)$ is the number of contexts of t' in which feature j occurs; and N is the total number of contexts of t'. The weighted context vectors in the collection are then clustered into $k = 20$ *sense clusters* using k-means clustering. Disambiguating t' consists of assigning the query context vector t' to the closest centroid of the sense clusters computed for t' in the collection.

The single sense cluster assigned to t' consists of contexts that occur in documents in the collection. These documents are deemed by our method to contain t' with the same sense as used in the query. Hence, boosting the ranking of these documents may benefit retrieval performance. We implement this boosting as a prior probability that these documents are relevant, which we incorporate into the basic query likelihood model used for retrieval.

Given a query Q and a document D, the query likelihood model [1] ranks D by $P(D|Q)$. By Bayes rule, $P(D|Q) \propto P(Q|D)P(D)$, where $P(Q|D)$ is the probability that D generates Q, and $P(D)$ is the document's prior probability. There are several ways of estimating $P(Q|D)$, for instance using Jelinek-Mercer or Dirichlet smoothing. $P(D)$ is usually assumed to be uniform, in which case documents are ranked solely by $P(Q|D)$. Alternatively, $P(D)$ can be viewed as prior knowledge about the relevance of D [4]. Various types of prior evidence about document relevance have been implemented as $P(D)$, e.g. document quality [4]. In this work, we measure the degree of match between the sense of

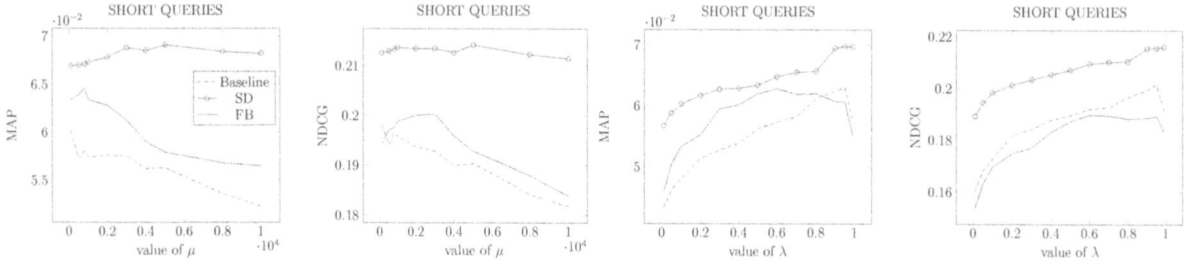

Figure 1: Retrieval performance vs. parameter μ (Dirichlet)/λ (Jelinek-Mercer) for short queries.

a term in the document with its sense used in the query, and we implement it as $P(D)$.

The value of $P(D)$ is typically derived from measurements about the evidence being modelled as the document prior. In this work we choose a fixed value ($P(D) = 0.5$) to boost those documents that disambiguate query terms. The performance of our approach reported in this work may further improve if prior values are tuned, however, at this stage, our aim is to test whether our approach is beneficial to retrieval, and not to optimise its performance.

	SHORT QUERIES			LONG QUERIES		
	MAP	BPREF	NDCG	MAP	BPREF	NDCG
Dir	0.0601	0.1954	0.1980	0.0552	0.1813	0.1892
JM	0.0630	0.1944	0.2017	0.0579	0.1844	0.1920
Dir+SD	**0.0691***	**0.1965***	**0.2141***	**0.0682***	**0.1874**	**0.2086**
JM+SD	**0.0698**	**0.1945**	**0.2161**	**0.0708**	**0.1855**	**0.2106**
Dir+FB	**0.0646**	**0.1959**	**0.2003**	**0.0585**	0.1802	0.1780
JM+FB	**0.0628**	0.1936	0.1896	**0.0610**	0.1819	0.1846

Table 1: Retrieval performance. * = stat. significance at $p < 0.05$ (2-tailed t-test). Bold = better than the baseline.

3. EVALUATION

We use the iSearch real-life physics test collection [2], which contains approx. half a million physics documents and 65 queries with graded relevance assessments, created by physicists. Queries contain 5 fields: *1. information need, 2. task, 3. background, 4. ideal answer, 5. keywords.* We use Indri for indexing and retrieval without removing stopwords or stemming, because these settings give the highest baseline performance. Our baseline runs use the Kullback-Leibler language model [1] with Dirichlet and Jelinek-Mercer smoothing (Dir, JM resp.). Our sense disambiguation (SD) runs use Dir & JM, enhanced with the SD priors presented above. We also include runs with pseudo-relevance feedback (FB) using Indri's default implementation, in order to compare our method to a more competitive approach. We use short queries (fields 1&5)[1] and long queries (all fields), to check the effect of query length on SD. We measure performance with: mean average precision (MAP), binary preference (BPREF), and normalised discounted cumulative gain (NDCG). For each measure, we tune: (for Dir) $\mu \in \{100, 500, 800, 1000, 2000, 3000, 4000, 5000, 8000, 10000\}$; (for JM) $\lambda \in \{0.01, 0.05, 0.1, 0.2, 0.3, 0.4, 0.5, 0.6, 0.7, 0.8, 0.9, 0.95, 0.99\}$; (for FB) the number of feedback documents $fbD \in \{1, 2, 5, 10, 20\}$ and the number of feedback terms $fbT \in \{3, 5, 10, 20, 40\}$.

Table 1 shows that for MAP & NDCG, SD performs the best, with large relative improvements over the baseline and FB. Note that MAP uses binary relevance, whereas NDCG uses graded relevance; SD is shown superior on both of these measures at all times, which is a good indication of its usefulness to IR. For BPREF, the improvement of SD over the baseline and FB is not large, but the best run for both types of queries is again a SD run. This result may be affected by a bias in iSearch: its relevance assessments contain a much larger proportion of documents judged as nonrelevant than of documents judged as relevant [2]. BPREF is affected by this because it depends heavily on the number of judged non-relevant documents that are retrieved at higher ranks than relevant documents (whereas MAP & NDCG do not distinguish between non-relevant and non-judged documents). Regarding query length, the longer the query, the higher the improvement brought by SD, most likely because longer queries have lower baseline scores, so there is more room for improvement. The improvement of SD is not heavily reliant on smoothing optimisation, as Figure 1 shows (the plots of long queries and BPREF are similar to these): the improvement of SD is more stable across different parameter values than the baseline and FB, especially for short queries.

4. CONCLUSION

This poster presented initial work on a retrieval model that includes a word sense disambiguation component, the output of which is embedded into the ranking function as a prior probability. The motivation was to improve retrieval performance for technical domains like physics, where words often have domain-specific senses. Preliminary experiments on a real-life physics test collection gave positive findings; more testing on other technical collections are needed to further explore our so-far promising approach.

5. REFERENCES

[1] W. B. Croft and J. Lafferty. *Language Modeling for Information Retrieval.* Kluwer, 2003.

[2] M. Lykke, B. Larsen, H. Lund, and P. Ingwersen. Developing a test collection for the evaluation of integrated search. In *ECIR*, pages 627–630, 2010.

[3] H. Schütze and J. O. Pedersen. Information retrieval based on word senses. In *SDAIR*, pages 161–175, 1995.

[4] Y. Zhou and W. B. Croft. Document quality models for web ad hoc retrieval. In *CIKM*, pages 331–332, 2005.

[1]We use fields 1&5 because they give higher baseline performance than field 5 alone.

When Documents Are Very Long, BM25 Fails!

Yuanhua Lv
Department of Computer Science
University of Illinois at Urbana-Champaign
Urbana, IL 61801
ylv2@uiuc.edu

ChengXiang Zhai
Department of Computer Science
University of Illinois at Urbana-Champaign
Urbana, IL 61801
czhai@cs.uiuc.edu

ABSTRACT

We reveal that the Okapi BM25 retrieval function tends to *overly penalize very long documents.* To address this problem, we present a simple yet effective extension of BM25, namely **BM25L**, which "shifts" the term frequency normalization formula to boost scores of very long documents. Our experiments show that BM25L, with the same computation cost, is more effective and robust than the standard BM25.

Categories and Subject Descriptors

H.3.3 [**Information Search and Retrieval**]: Retrieval models

General Terms

Algorithms

Keywords

BM25, BM25L, term frequency, very long documents

1. MOTIVATION

The Okapi BM25 retrieval function [2, 3] has been the state-of-the-art for nearly two decades. BM25 scores a document D with respect to query Q as follows:

$$\sum_{q \in Q \cap D} \frac{(k_3+1)c(q,Q)}{k_3+c(q,Q)} \cdot f(q,D) \cdot \log \frac{N+1}{df(q)+0.5} \qquad (1)$$

where $c(q, Q)$ is the count of q in Q, N is the total number of documents, $df(q)$ is the document frequency of q, and k_3 is a parameter. Following [1], we use a modified IDF formula in BM25 to avoid its problem of possibly negative IDF values.

A key component of BM25 contributing to its success is its sub-linear term frequency (TF) normalization formula:

$$f(q,D) = \frac{(k_1+1)c(q,D)}{k_1\left(1-b+b\frac{|D|}{avdl}\right)+c(q,D)} = \frac{(k_1+1)c'(q,D)}{k_1+c'(q,D)} \qquad (2)$$

where $|D|$ represents document length, $avdl$ stands for average document length, $c(q, D)$ is the raw TF of q in D, and b and k_1 are two parameters. $c'(q, D)$ is the normalized TF by document length using pivoted length normalization [4].

$$c'(q,D) = \frac{c(q,D)}{1-b+b\frac{|D|}{avdl}} \qquad (3)$$

SIGIR'11, July 24–28, 2011, Beijing, China.
ACM 978-1-4503-0757-4/11/07.

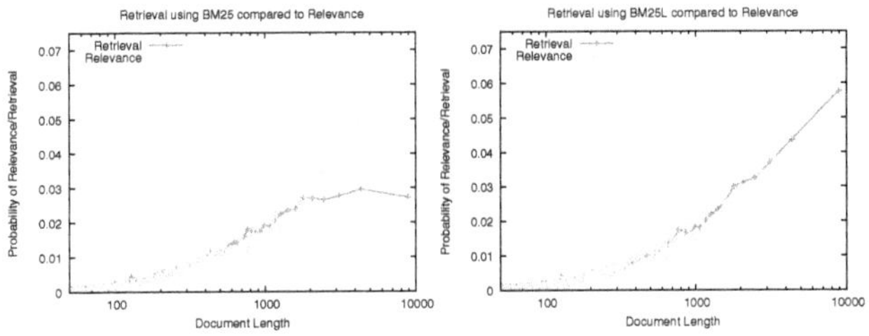

Figure 1: Comparison of retrieval and relevance probabilities against all document lengths.

When a document is very long, we can see that $c'(q, D)$ could be very small and approach 0. Consequently, $f(q, D)$ will also approach 0 as if q did not occur in D. That is, the presence of q in a very long document D fails to differentiate D clearly from other documents where q is absent. This suggests that the occurrences of a query term in very long documents may not be rewarded properly by BM25, and thus those very long documents can be overly penalized. (See Figure 1 for empirical evidence of this problem.)

2. BOOSTING VERY LONG DOCUMENTS

In order to avoid overly-penalizing very long documents, we need to add a constraint in TF normalization to make sure that the "score gap" of $f(q, D)$ between $c'(q, D) = 0$ and $c'(q, D) > 0$ be sufficiently large. However, we do not want that the addition of this new constraint violates those existing properties of BM25 [2], which have been shown to work quite well. Thus what we want is an improved sub-linear TF normalization formula $f'(q, D)$ that has all the following characteristics: (I) It is zero for $c'(q, D) = 0$; (II) it increases monotonically as $c'(q, D)$ increases but to an asymptotic maximum; (III) it decreases monotonically as $c'(q, D) > 0$ decreases but to *an asymptotic minimum that is sufficiently large.* Here (I) and (II) are characteristics of the TF normalization formula of the original BM25 [2].

One heuristic way to achieve this goal is to define $f'(q, D)$ as follows:

$$f'(q,D) = \begin{cases} \frac{(k_1+1)\cdot[c'(q,D)+\delta]}{k_1+[c'(q,D)+\delta]} & \text{if } c'(q,D) > 0 \\ 0 & \text{otherwise} \end{cases} \qquad (4)$$

which is essentially a shifted version of $f(q, D)$ by addition of a shift parameter $\delta > 0$. It is easy to verify that $f'(q, D)$ still satisfies both properties (I) and (II). Moreover, $f'(q, D)$ has a *positive* lower bound $(k_1 + 1)\delta/(k_1 + \delta)$ for $c'(q, D) > 0$. In this sub-linear function $f'(q, D)$, the score increase from the addition of δ is decreasing as $c'(q, D)$ increases. Therefore,

Method	Terabyte		WT10G		WT2G		Robust04		TREC8		AP8889	
	MAP	P@10	MAP	P@10	MAP	P@10	MAP	P@10	MAP	P@10	MAP	P@10
BM25	0.2942	0.5703	0.2099	0.3031	0.3198	0.4620	0.2543	0.4345	0.2557	0.4580	0.2631	0.4071
BM25L	**0.2999**	0.5703	**0.2154**	0.3072	**0.3260**	0.4780	0.2553	0.4390	0.2571	0.4560	0.2650	0.4152

Table 1: Comparison of optimal performance. δ is fixed to 0.5 in BM25L. Bold font indicates that the corresponding MAP improvement is statistically significant using the Wilcoxon test ($p < 0.05$).

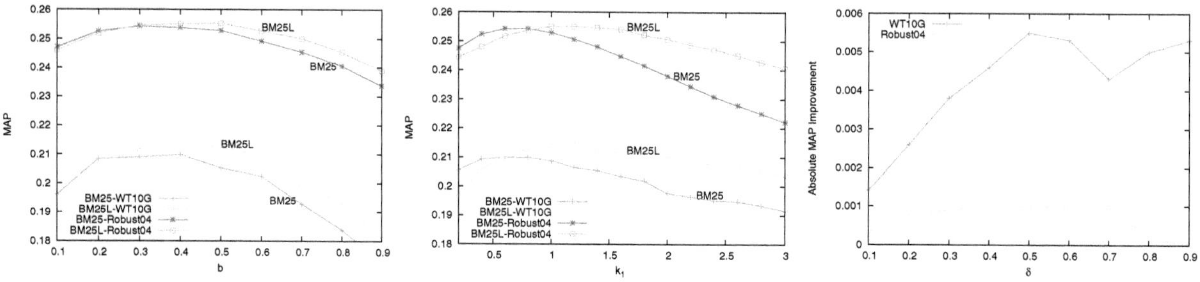

Figure 2: Performance Sensitivity to b (left), k_1 (middle), and δ (right).

$f'(q, D)$ tends to favor small $c'(q, D)$ values more, which would intuitively boost very long documents.

Finally, substituting $f'(q, D)$ into Equation 1 to replace $f(q, D)$, we obtain a new retrieval function, namely **BM25L**.

3. EXPERIMENTS

We compared BM25L with BM25 using six TREC collections: Terabyte, WT10G, and WT2G are web datasets with queries 701-850, 451-550, and 401-450 respectively; Robust04, TREC8, and AP8889 represent news datasets with queries 301-450&601-700, 401-450, and 51-150 respectively. The preprocessing included Porter stemming and removal of standard InQuery stopwords. For both BM25 and BM25L, we set $k_3 = 1000$ and tuned $b \in [0.1, 0.9]$ and $k_1 \in [0.2, 3.0]$ to optimize MAP. The parameter δ in BM25L was empirically set to **0.5** unless otherwise specified.

3.1 Retrieval Pattern VS. Relevance Pattern

Inspired by Singhal et al.'s finding that a good retrieval function should retrieve documents of all lengths with similar chances as their likelihood of relevance [4], we also compare the retrieval pattern of BM25 with the relevance pattern. We follow the binning analysis strategy proposed in [4] and plot the two patterns against all document lengths on WT10G in Figure 1 (left). It confirms our previous analysis that *BM25 retrieves very long documents with chances much lower than their likelihood of relevance.*

We also plot the retrieval and relevance patterns for BM25L in Figure 1 (right). As expected, BM25L indeed alleviates the problem of over-penalizing very long documents clearly.

3.2 Experimental Results

We first compare the optimal performance of BM25 and BM25L in Table 1. We observe that BM25L outperforms the well-tuned BM25 consistently in both MAP and P@10. Besides, BM25L works better on web collections than on news collections. This is likely because there are generally more very long documents in web collections, where the problem of BM25, i.e., overly-penalizing very long documents, would presumably be more severe.

Parameter b controls the influence of document length in TF normalization. We draw the sensitivity curves of BM25 and BM25L to b on WT10G and Robust04 in Figure 2 (left), where k_1 is optimized for each method. It shows that BM25L is more robust than BM25; if we increase b, the MAP of BM25 drops more quickly than BM25L. It intuitively makes sense in that, increasing b in BM25 would overly penalize very long documents even more. Overall, BM25L works effectively with $b \in [0.3, 0.6]$.

We also draw in Figure 2 (middle) the sensitivity curves of BM25 and BM25L through varying k_1, where b is optimized for each method. We can see that BM25 drops dramatically when increasing k_1, while BM25L appears more stable. This observation is expected: according to Formula 2, for a small $c'(q, D)$ in very long documents, the larger k_1 is, the smaller $f(q, D)$ will be; as a result, increasing k_1 would exacerbate the problem of BM25. However, the $f'(q, D)$ of BM25L is guaranteed to have a document-independent lower bound $(k_1 + 1)\delta/(k_1 + \delta)$ to avoid overly penalizing very long documents. Additionally, the optimal k_1 of BM25L is also larger than that of BM25 due to the effect of "shifting"; setting $k_1 \in [1.0, 2.0]$ usually works well for BM25L.

In previous experiments, we empirically set the shift parameter $\delta = 0.5$ in BM25L. To examine how δ affects the performance of BM25L, we plot the absolute MAP improvements against different values of δ in Figure 2 (right). It shows that the simple shifting strategy can successfully improve performance steadily and setting $\delta = 0.5$ works well for both web and news datasets. Besides, it confirms our finding that BM25L works more effectively on web data.

4. CONCLUSIONS

We proposed BM25L, a simple yet effective extension of BM25, to overcome the problem of BM25 which tends to over-penalize very long documents. Our experiments show that BM25L, with the same computation cost, is more effective and robust than BM25. BM25L can potentially replace the standard BM25 in all retrieval applications.

5. REFERENCES

[1] H. Fang, T. Tao, and C. Zhai. A formal study of information retrieval heuristics. In *SIGIR '04*, pages 49–56, 2004.

[2] S. E. Robertson and S. Walker. Some simple effective approximations to the 2-poisson model for probabilistic weighted retrieval. In *SIGIR '94*, pages 232–241, 1994.

[3] S. E. Robertson, S. Walker, S. Jones, M. Hancock-Beaulieu, and M. Gatford. Okapi at trec-3. In *TREC '94*, pages 109–126, 1994.

[4] A. Singhal, C. Buckley, and M. Mitra. Pivoted document length normalization. In *SIGIR '96*, pages 21–29, 1996.

Location and Timeliness of Information Sources During News Events

Elad Yom-Tov
Yahoo Research
111 W 41st st.
New York, NY 10018, USA
eladyt@yahoo-inc.com

Fernando Diaz
Yahoo Research
111 W 41st st.
New York, NY 10018, USA
diazf@yahoo-inc.com

ABSTRACT

People nowadays can obtain information on current news events through media outlets, social media, and by actively seeking information using search engines. In this paper we investigate the temporal relationship between news coverage by media outlets, social media, and query logs and show that social media frequently precedes other information sources. Additionally, we demonstrate that there is strong negative correlation between the probability for reporting of an event and the distance of the information source from the event.

Categories and Subject Descriptors

H.3.3 [**Information Search and Retrieval**]: Search process; H.4.3 [**Communications Applications**]: Information browsers

General Terms

Algorithms

Keywords

social,physical,distance,information,need

1. INTRODUCTION

The information people can receive of news events comes from diverse sources, including media outlets (TV, newspapers, media sites on the web), social media (Twitter, Facebook, etc), and active seeking of information using search engines on the web. These news sources assign importance to events (as manifested by the likelihood and extensiveness they will report on them) based on attributes of the event and on features of the news source itself.

Coverage of news is known to be influenced by the physical distance of consumers from the location of the event. As [2] showed, the distance of an event from the USA is one of the most predictive attributes for its media coverage. Furthermore, Wu [5] showed that the volume of media related to news events in Canada and Mexico by USA-based news channels is partially explained by the distance of the events from the closest USA border.

Historically, news outlets were the source of many people's information of world events. More recently, social media has emerged as a timely source of information. For example, almost immediate detection of earthquakes in Japan can be performed with very high confidence by tracking the micro-blogging service Twitter [4]. Active information seeking by users, through search engine queries, is another important way by which users can acquire information. This is exemplified by the work of Backstrom et al. [1], who developed a model for pinpointing events based on the location of people querying about them. Both [1] and [4] found that the closer people are to an event, the more likely they are to seek information about the event or to report about it.

In this paper, we investigate the relationship between the volume of information as a function of location and time during unusual news events. We show that social media frequently precedes other information sources, and that the probability to report an event has a high negative correlation with the location of the information source.

SIGIR'11, July 24–28, 2011, Beijing, China.
ACM 978-1-4503-0757-4/11/07.

2. DATA

In this paper we analyze three events, which are briefly described below (for more details, see [6]):

1. **San Bruno event**: On September 9th, 2010 a large pipe carrying natural gas exploded in the city of San Bruno (near San Francisco), California. The explosion killed eight people and destroyed 38 houses.
2. **New York storm**: A violent storm passed through New York city on the 16th September 2010, killing one person and causing widespread damage to property.
3. **Alaska elections**: The elections for representatives from Alaska to the USA Senate on the 2nd November 2010 drew significant attention because of a three-way race, which was won by an independent candidate.

These events were chosen because they were physically localized in their scope and thus have a clear epicenter. Therefore, the physical distance of users from the event are clearly defined for these events. Furthermore, because they are temporally limited, they act as an impulse to the system, and thus create high levels of interest for a relatively short and clearly-defined period.

We used three types of data in our study: First, we extracted query-log data (text, time, and an identification of the user who posted them) of the Yahoo search engine from several days before the event (one day for the first two events, and 10 for the last), until 8 days after the event.

The query log was parsed to identify those queries which were likely relevant to the event, using a term-matching scheme. This was done by manually generating a list of

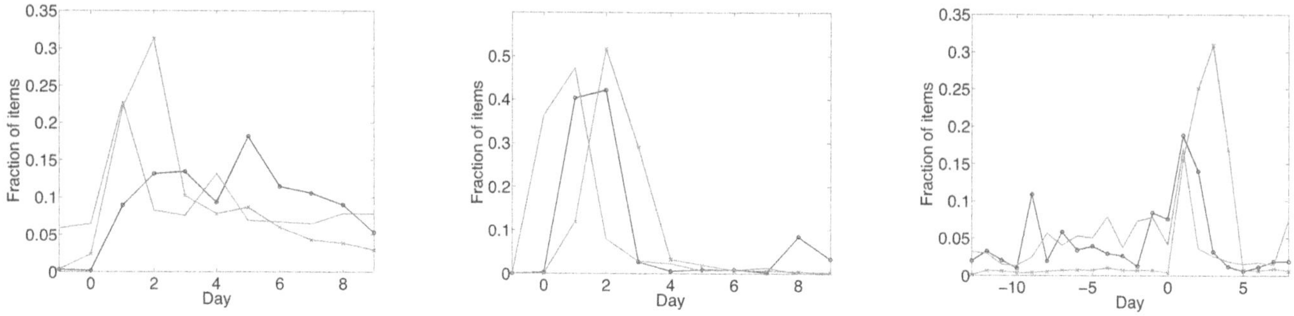

Figure 1: Fraction of media outlet items (blue, circles), social media items (red) and queries (green, crosses) posted in response to the San Bruno (left), New York (middle), and Alaska (right) events over time.

keywords for each event. The keywords were drawn from several categories such as where the event took place, who was involved in the event, and what happened at the event. We also generated a list of excluded words. Queries and keywords were stemmed using a Porter stemmer. A query was considered relevant to the event if keywords from at least two categories were used in the query, and none of the excluded words appearing in it.

We encode data at the granularity of a day in order to remove diurnal effects. The zip-code given by users at the time of registration with Yahoo was used to identify their approximate location. We computed the physical distance of each user to the event using the Haversine formula.

Daily media volume of news outlets related to an event was quantified by counting the number of document found on Yahoo News (`news.yahoo.com`) every day, which contained all the words used in any of the 50 most popular queries. Similarly, the volume of social media was measured via the number of Twitter messages which contained the words used in these queries.

3. RESULTS

Figure 1 shows the media and query volume related to the three events. Note the similarities in shapes between the different information sources, i.e. the spike on day 5 of the San Bruno event which is observed in both the query volume and general media volume. In general, the peak in social media volume precedes both general news media and query volume, and decays first. In the New York and Alaska events, query volume peaked and decayed later than media volume. San Bruno was unusual in that general media attention decayed more slowly than query volume. The cross-correlation of media volume with the number of queries per day, shown in Table 1, quantifies these findings and shows that news media and social media (Twitter) have a relatively strong correlation, as was also found by [3].

We binned the information sources according to their physical distance from the event, on a logarithmical-spaced axis, and computed the fraction of event-related items from the total items generated at this distance. Table 2 shows the Spearman correlation between the physical distance and the fraction of event-related items. The correlation is extremely high, validating the findings of [5] and extending them to social media and query volume.

Event	News-Queries	Twitter-Queries	Twitter-News
San Bruno	0.81 (-1)	0.87 (0)	0.87 (+1)
New York	0.93 (+1)	0.97 (+2)	0.98 (+1)
Alaska	0.84 (+2)	0.69 (+2)	0.82 (0)

Table 1: Maximum cross-correlation between media volume and the number of queries per day, for each of the three events. The number in parenthesis is the delay in days at which the maximum is reached, where a positive sign indicates that the first time series precedes the second time series.

Event	Queries	News	Twitter
San Bruno	-0.97	-0.97	-0.97
New York	-0.86	-0.95	-0.90
Alaska	-0.69	-0.91	-0.52

Table 2: Spearman correlation between physical distance and the fraction of media items and relevant queries, for each of the three events. All correlations are statistically significant at $p < 0.05$.

4. REFERENCES

[1] Lars Backstrom, Jon Kleinberg, Ravi Kumar, and Jasmine Novak. Spatial variation in search engine queries. In *Proceeding of the 17th international conference on World Wide Web*, WWW '08, pages 357–366. ACM, 2008.

[2] Tsan-Kuo Chang, Pamela J. Shoemaker, and Nancy Brendlinger. Determinants of international news coverage in the U.S. media. *Communications research*, 14(4):396–414, 1987.

[3] Jure Leskovec, Lars Backstrom, and Jon Kleinberg. Meme-tracking and the dynamics of the news cycle. In *Proceedings of the 15th ACM SIGKDD International Conference on Knowledge Discovery and Data Mining*, 2009.

[4] Takeshi Sakaki, Makoto Okazaki, and Yutaka Matsuo. Earthquake shakes Twitter users: real-time event detection by social sensors. In *Proceedings of the 19th international conference on World wide web*, WWW '10, pages 851–860. ACM, 2010.

[5] Haoming Denis Wu. Geographic distance and US newspaper coverage of Canada and Mexico. *International Communication Gazette*, 60(3):253–263, 1998.

[6] Elad Yom-Tov and Fernando Diaz. Out of sight, not out of mind: On the effect of social and physical detachment on information need. In *Proceedings of the 34th annual international ACM SIGIR conference on Research and development in information retrieval*, SIGIR '11. ACM, 2011.

What Deliberately Degrading Search Quality Tells Us About Discount Functions

Paul Thomas
CSIRO
Canberra, Australia
paul.thomas@csiro.au

Timothy Jones
Australian National University
Canberra, Australia
tim.jones@anu.edu.au

David Hawking
Funnelback Pty Ltd and
Australian National University
Canberra, Australia
david.hawking@acm.org

ABSTRACT

Deliberate degradation of search results is a common tool in user experiments. We degrade high-quality search results by inserting non-relevant documents at different ranks. The effect of these manipulations, on a number of commonly-used metrics, is counter-intuitive: the discount functions implicit in P@k, MRR, NDCG, and others do not account for the true relationship between rank and value to the user. We propose an alternative, based on visibility data.

Categories and Subject Descriptors: H.3.4 [**Information Storage and Retrieval**]: Systems and Software—*Performance evaluation*
General Terms: Measurement
Keywords: Metrics; result set manipulation

1. INTRODUCTION

There is considerable interest in the ability of IR evaluation metrics to predict user performance on search tasks. Similarly, there is interest in rating and comparing retrieval systems on the basis of implicit measures derived from user behaviour. Empirical exploration of these questions would benefit from the ability to generate search result lists with a particular expected score on a chosen measure. For example, it would be useful to produce result lists with expected NDCG scores of 0.2, 0.4, 0.6 and 0.8.

In previous work [5] this has been achieved by artificially constructing result lists from lists of known relevant and irrelevant documents. A major drawback of this approach is the need to constrain subjects to use queries from a predefined set for which judgments are available and to rely on third-party judgments. In our work we wanted to achieve controlled degradation of an initial high quality ranking, in the absence of "canned" queries and judgments.

2. DEGRADATION MODEL

We assume a retrieval system which produces a ranking $\langle d_1, \ldots, d_M \rangle$ to a depth M. These results are presented in pages of p results each, of which the first v are visible without scrolling (*above the fold*). A user of the system views results to a maximum rank V where V is usually less than M, may be less than p and varies with the user, the task and the results viewed earlier in the ranking. We also assume that we have a large set $\mathcal{N}$ of documents which are known (with high probability) to be non-relevant to the present topic.

A document from $\mathcal{N}$ can degrade a ranking $\langle d_1, \ldots, d_M \rangle$ by insertion at position $r \leq M$. As a result of the insertion the lowest ranked document d_M becomes invisible[1].

A *degradation* consists of an ordered set $\mathcal{I} = \{r_1, \ldots, r_m\}$ of insertions, in which the r_i represent the ranks at which insertions are made. The effect of a degradation depends upon both the metric and the ranking.

3. METRIC-DEPENDENT EFFECTS

Clearly, each of the metrics is affected in a different way by a particular degradation applied to a ranking. For example, all degradations which make the same number of relevant documents invisible will cause the same drop in P@k, regardless of where non-relevant documents are inserted. The effect of a degradation on MRR depends upon how many of the $r_1, \ldots, r_m$ are less than or equal to the rank of the first relevant document. If none, there is no drop in score. For P@k, MRR, AP, RBP [4] and the Microsoft variant of NDCG [1] which we use here, it is possible to calculate for a given ranking the score drops associated with all $2^M - 1$ possible degradations.

We took the four top-scoring runs from the TREC-13 web track [2] and all 75 topic distillation queries. We took result lists for each of these 300 run/topic pairs, using TREC qrels, and computed each of the metrics above. Then, letting $M = 10$, we applied all 1023 degradations to all 300 rankings and computed the resulting change in each metric.

The most dramatic $|\mathcal{I}| = 1$ degradation is obviously when we insert a non-relevant document at the highest rank: $\mathcal{I} = \{1\}$. We designate other degradations as *1-equivalent* if they cause the same change in score as insert-at-rank-1-only. Looking at the 300 changes for each of the 1023 degradations for the TREC data, we used a paired t test, $\alpha = 0.05$, to find all those degradations which are 1-equivalent.

By way of example, Figure 1 shows the changes in NDCG scores for a small number of 1-equivalent degradations. The 1-equivalent sets are different for different metrics.

Examining the 1-equivalent degradations in the figure gives pause for thought. Is it really the case that inserting non-relevant documents at ranks 5, 6, 7, 9, and 10 has equivalent effect to inserting a single non-relevant document at rank

[1] An alternative degradation would be that the nonrelevant document could replace d_i, but this would sometimes mean that the single best answer for a query (e.g. a homepage) originally ranked 1 might disappear entirely. We consider only insertions.

SIGIR'11, July 24–28, 2011, Beijing, China.
ACM 978-1-4503-0757-4/11/07.

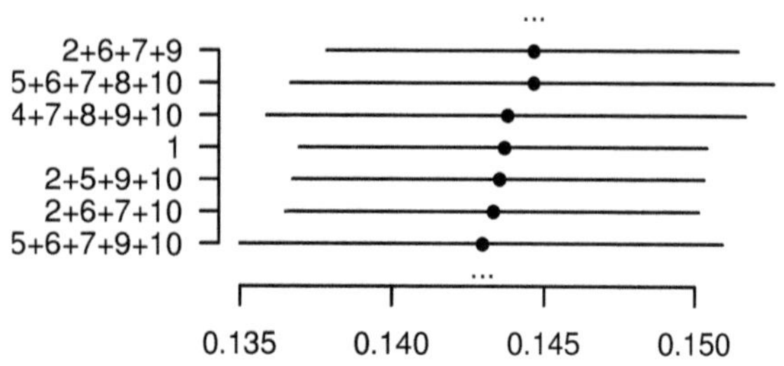

Figure 1: Changes in NDCG for some 1-equivalent degradations. Shown are mean change ± standard error.

one? What is NDCG measuring if this is the case? Would it still be equivalent if $v < 5$ as might be the case for search results presented on a mobile phone, i.e. none of the inserted documents are visible without scrolling, or if $p < 10$?

As a further example, under MAP the degradations $\{1\}$ and $\{4, 5, 6, 7, 8\}$ produce equivalent effects; under MRR there are 151 1-equivalent degradations (of 1023 possible degradations) including those with the insertion of only two documents and those which insert eight, leaving only two documents from the original ranking. Should a manipulation which leaves original documents only at ranks two and nine, say, be considered equivalent to one which includes a single insertion at high rank?

4. DISCOUNT FUNCTIONS

From the definition of a particular metric we can infer a user model, if we assume that scores are intended to reflect user satisfaction or performance. Of particular interest here is the relationship between the value (gain) attributed to a retrieved relevant document and the rank at which it is retrieved: Järvelin and Kekäläinen's "discount function" [3]. Figure 2 shows the striking differences between the discount functions inferred from several commonly used metrics.

Considering the effect of insertions of non-relevant documents on user performance or behaviour, it is clear that insertions beyond rank V can have no effect at all on user behaviour because the user never sees them. Insertions beyond rank v on a displayed page have less effect on users than those above because there is a less than unity probability that the user scrolls to see them. Finally, the effect of insertions beyond rank p is further diminished by the low probability that the user will click on the next-page button.

It is clear that if an IR metric is to predict user satisfaction or performance, the discount function implicit in the metric must attempt to more accurately model the dependence of view-probability on rank. Rank-biased precision (RBP) [4] explicitly models probability-of-view but does not take into account the discontinuities in probability which surely occur after ranks $p, 2p, 3p, \ldots$ and at $v, p + v, 2p + v, 3p + v, \ldots$.

Discount functions can easily be extended to accommodate these discontinuities. The plot labelled "RBP-visible" in Figure 2 illustrates such a modification, here of RBP, where the base probability of viewing the next result is normally 0.75 but drops to 0.5 at each fold ($v = 5$) and after each page ($p = 10$). The parameter values in the plot were arbitrarily chosen, but browser interaction logging and/or eye-gaze tracking can determine appropriate values for the

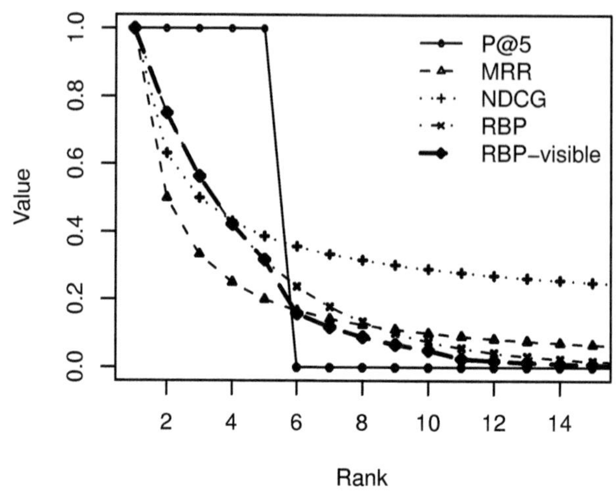

Figure 2: Discount functions implicit in some illustrative evaluation metrics. "RBP-visible" is discussed in the text. (Connecting lines shown only for clarity.)

constants in particular search scenarios. We are presently carrying out such studies.

5. SUMMARY AND CONCLUSIONS

In our user experiments, our attempts to artificially degrade search results to achieve specified quality levels have encountered a number of difficulties. Since we could not assume canned queries or prior relevance judgments, we inserted known non-relevant documents at chosen points in the ranking. The effect of degradation operations consisting of such insertions is highly dependent upon the metric chosen but all commonly used metrics showed counter-intuitive properties. We concluded that the discount functions implicit in metrics such as P@k, AP, MRR, NDCG and RBP do not model the true relationship between rank and visibility/value to the user. We propose an alternative shape of discount function for empirical confirmation, which is introduced for RBP but perfectly consistent with multiple relevance levels and NDCG. We suggest determining parameter values for this shape using browser instrumentation and eye-gaze tracking.

6. REFERENCES

[1] C. Burges, T. Shaked, E. Renshaw, A. Lazier, M. Deeds, N. Hamilton, and G. Hullender. Learning to rank using gradient descent. In *Proc. Int. Conf. on Machine Learning*, 2005.

[2] N. Craswell and D. Hawking. Overview of the TREC-2004 Web Track. In *Proc. TREC*, 2004.

[3] K. Järvelin and J. Kekäläinen. Cumulated gain-based evaluation of IR techniques. *ACM Trans. Inf. Syst.*, 20(4), 2002.

[4] A. Moffat and J. Zobel. Rank-biased precision for measurement of retrieval effectiveness. *ACM Trans. Inf. Syst.*, 27(1), 2008.

[5] A. Turpin and F. Scholer. User performance versus precision measures for simple search tasks. In *Proc. SIGIR*, 2006.

Collective Topic Modeling for Heterogeneous Networks

Hongbo Deng
Dept. of Computer Science
University of Illinois at Urbana-Champaign
Urbana, IL 61801
hbdeng@uiuc.edu

Bo Zhao
Dept. of Computer Science
University of Illinois at Urbana-Champaign
Urbana, IL 61801
bozhao3@uiuc.edu

Jiawei Han
Dept. of Computer Science
University of Illinois at Urbana-Champaign
Urbana, IL 61801
hanj@cs.uiuc.edu

ABSTRACT

In this paper, we propose a joint probabilistic topic model for simultaneously modeling the contents of multi-typed objects of a heterogeneous information network. The intuition behind our model is that different objects of the heterogeneous network share a common set of latent topics so as to adjust the multinomial distributions over topics for different objects collectively. Experimental results demonstrate the effectiveness of our approach for the tasks of topic modeling and object clustering.

Categories and Subject Descriptors:
H.3.3 [**Information Storage and Retrieval**]: Information Search and Retrieval—*text mining, clustering*

General Terms: Algorithms, Experimentation

Keywords: Topic modeling, heterogeneous network

1. INTRODUCTION

In the age of Web 2.0, various kinds of textual documents, blogs, papers, and other user-generated content are published online and connected with users and other objects, leading to a heterogeneous information network with multi-typed objects. Many topic models, such as PLSA [2] and LDA [1], have been proposed and shown to be useful for document analysis. However, very little research has been conducted on modeling the topics of documents as well as their associated objects simultaneously in heterogeneous networks. Although there are several extensions of the topic model proposed to consider the relationships between objects, including the Author-Topic model [3] and Author-Conference-Topic model [5], these models are designed specifically for academic networks, which cannot deal with many more general cases. Generally, the interactions among multi-typed objects play a key role at disclosing the rich semantics of the network. Taking bibliographic data as an example, papers are highly related to their authors and associated venues, because an author can be characterized based on his published papers while a venue consists of various papers in a specific research area. Therefore, it is reasonable to assume there is a common set of latent topics for different objects in a heterogeneous network. Inspired by this intuition, we propose a collective topic model by considering both the textual information of documents and the relations between different objects, which could improve the performance of both topic modeling and object clustering.

2. MODEL FORMULATION

Let $G = (V, E)$ denote a bibliographic heterogeneous network consisting of three types of object sets: a document set $\mathcal{D} = \{d_1, d_2, ..., d_{|D|}\}$, an author set $\mathcal{A} = \{a_1, a_2, ..., a_{|A|}\}$ and a venue (conference) set $\mathcal{C} = \{c_1, c_2, ..., c_{|C|}\}$. We represent a document d with a bag of words $\{w_1, w_2, ..., w_{|d|}\}$, and use N to denote the term-document matrix where N_{ij} is the co-occurrences of word w_i in d_j. In such a heterogeneous network, documents are linked with authors and venues based on the authorship and publish relationship, so it is reasonable to build a 'virtual document' for each author and venue by aggregating their associated documents. Then we obtain the term-author matrix A and the term-venue matrix C. In this way, the associations between different objects in the heterogeneous network are indirectly modeled through the content. The basic idea of topic models is to model documents with a finite mixture model of K latent topics and estimate the model parameters by fitting the data with the model. Documents, authors and venues are generally composed of words, so each of them can be decomposed by topic models, such as PLSA [2], respectively.

Rather than applying each separately, it is reasonable to merge them into a joint probabilistic model with a common set of underlying topics as shown in Fig. 1. Based on PLSA, one can define the following joint model for predicting terms in different objects: $P(w_i|d_j) = \sum_k P(w_i|z_k)P(z_k|d_j)$, $P(w_i|a_l) = \sum_k P(w_i|z_k)P(z_k|a_l)$ and $P(w_i|v_m) = \sum_k P(w_i|z_k)P(z_k|v_m)$. Notice that all the decompositions share the same latent topics $P(w_i|z_k)$. Thus the learned topics must be consistent across multi-typed objects. In this way, the relationships between different objects of the heterogeneous network are indirectly modeled in the proposed collective topic modeling. In general, we propose maximizing the following joint log-likelihood function with relative weights α, β and γ

$$\begin{aligned}\mathcal{L} = \; & \sum_i \Big(\alpha \sum_j N_{ij} \log \sum_{k=1}^K P(w_i|z_k)P(z_k|d_j) \\ & +\beta \sum_l A_{il} \log \sum_{k=1}^K P(w_i|z_k)P(z_k|a_l) \\ & +\gamma \sum_m C_{im} \log \sum_{k=1}^K P(w_i|z_k)P(z_k|v_m)\Big) .\end{aligned} \quad (1)$$

This model can be easily extended to handle general cases, e.g., news articles and their associated entities.

Following the EM approach it is straightforward to derive a set of re-estimation equations. For the E-step, the posterior probabilities of the latent variables associated with each observation are formulated as follows

$$\begin{aligned}P(z_k|w_i, d_j) &= \frac{P(w_i|z_k)P(z_k|d_j)}{P(w_i|d_j)}, \\ P(z_k|w_i, a_l) &= \frac{P(w_i|z_k)P(z_k|a_l)}{P(w_i|a_l)}, \\ P(z_k|w_i, v_m) &= \frac{P(w_i|z_k)P(z_k|v_m)}{P(w_i|v_m)}.\end{aligned} \quad (2)$$

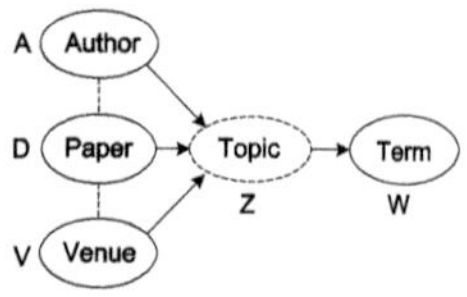

Figure 1: An illustration of collective topic model.

The multinomial distributions over topics are recomputed in the M-step according to

$$\begin{aligned} P(z_k|d_j) &= \frac{\sum_i N_{ij} P(z_k|w_i,d_j)}{\sum_{i'} N_{i'j}}, \\ P(z_k|a_l) &= \frac{\sum_i A_{il} P(z_k|w_i,a_l)}{\sum_{i'} A_{i'l}}, \\ P(z_k|v_m) &= \frac{\sum_i C_{im} P(z_k|w_i,v_m)}{\sum_{i'} C_{i'm}}, \end{aligned} \tag{3}$$

along with the mixing latent topics

$$\begin{aligned} P(w_i|z_k) \propto\ & \alpha \frac{\sum_j N_{ij} P(z_k|w_i,d_j)}{\sum_i \sum_j N_{ij} P(z_k|w_i,d_j)} \\ & + \beta \frac{\sum_l A_{il} P(z_k|w_i,a_l)}{\sum_i \sum_l A_{il} P(z_k|w_i,a_l)} + \gamma \frac{\sum_m C_{im} P(z_k|w_i,v_m)}{\sum_i \sum_m C_{im} P(z_k|w_i,v_m)}. \end{aligned} \tag{4}$$

For simplicity, we set $\alpha = \beta = \gamma = 1$. With an initial random guess of $\{P(w_i|z_k), P(z_k|d_j), P(z_k|a_l), P(z_k|v_m)\}$, the collective topic model (CTM) applies the E-step and M-step equations until a termination condition is met.

3. EXPERIMENTS

In this experiment, we use a subset of the DBLP records that belongs to four areas: database, data mining, information retrieval and artificial intelligence, and contains 28,569 documents, 28,702 authors and 20 conferences. The abstract is collected for representing each document, and this data collection has 11,771 unique terms. Moreover, we use a labeled data set [4] with 4057 authors, 100 papers and all 20 conferences for quantitative accuracy evaluation. For more details about the labeled data set, please refer to [4].

In order to visualize the hidden topics and compare different approaches, we extract topics from the data using both PLSA and CTM. Since the testing data is a mixture of four areas, it is interesting to see whether the extracted topics could automatically reveal this mixture. Therefore, in both PLSA and CTM, we predefine the number of topics to be 4. To make the comparison fair, we use the same starting points for PLSA and CTM. The most representative terms generated by CTM and PLSA are shown in Table 1. For the first three topics, although different algorithms select slightly different terms, all these terms can describe the corresponding topic to some extent. For Topic 4 (AI), the top keywords like "learning, based, knowledge" derived from CTM is obviously more telling than "problem, algorithm, paper" derived by PLSA. Similar subtle differences can be observed for Topic 3 (IR) as well. Intuitively, CTM selects more related terms for each topic than PLSA, which shows the better performance of CTM.

Now we give a quantitative evaluation of these models on object clustering. The hidden topics extracted by the topic modeling approaches can be regarded as clusters. The estimated conditional probability, e.g., $P(z_k|d_i)$ and $P(z_k|a_l)$, can be used to infer the cluster label for each object. In this experiment, we investigate the use of topic modeling approach for object clustering. To demonstrate how the multi-typed object clustering performance can be improved by collective topic modeling, we compared with the following state-of-the-art clustering algorithms.

- PLSA [2]: Performing on each object separatively.
- Author-Topic Model (ATM) [3].
- NetClus [4]: We implemented a topic based NetClus which utilizes the topic distribution instead of the word distribution for each document.

Table 1: The most representative terms generated by our CTM model and the PLSA model. The terms are selected according to the probability $P(w|z)$.

Topic 1 (DB)	Topic 2 (DM)	Topic 3 (IR)	Topic 4 (AI)
Collective Topic Model (CTM)			
data	data	web	learning
database	mining	information	based
query	learning	retrieval	knowledge
databases	based	search	system
queries	clustering	based	reasoning
systems	algorithm	text	systems
system	classification	document	problem
management	analysis	user	logic
xml	approach	query	model
PLSA			
data	data	information	problem
database	mining	retrieval	algorithm
systems	learning	web	paper
query	based	based	reasoning
system	clustering	*learning*	logic
databases	classification	knowledge	based
management	algorithm	text	time
distributed	*image*	search	algorithms
queries	analysis	system	*search*

Table 2: Clustering results of different methods.

	Accuracy(%)			NMI (%)		
Method	conf	paper	author	conf	paper	author
PLSA	81.00	57.80	80.29	77.84	30.69	54.39
ATM	-	**77.00**	74.13	-	52.21	40.67
NetClus	79.75	65.00	70.82	76.69	40.96	47.43
CTM	**85.25**	76.65	**83.55**	**80.01**	**52.83**	**59.98**

Table 2 reports the evaluation results of different methods using two metrics, the accuracy and the normalized mutual information (NMI). The final performance scores were obtained by averaging the scores from 20 tests. As we can see, our CTM approach gets the best performance. Moreover, the improvement of CTM over PLSA and NetClus is more significant on the results of papers than other two objects. Although ATM obtains comparable performance to CTM in terms of papers, our CTM approach can obtain significant improvements in terms of authors. This shows that CTM model could mutually enhance topic modeling across different objects by considering both the content and relations of multi-typed objects collectively.

As future work, instead of modeling the associations between different objects through the content indirectly, we aim at adopting topic propagation techniques to directly integrate the content with relations for collective topic modeling of heterogeneous networks.

Acknowledgements

The work was supported in part by the NSF IIS-09-05215, U.S. Air Force Office of Scientific Research MURI award FA9550-08-1-0265, and by the U.S. Army Research Laboratory under Cooperative Agreement No. W911NF-09-2-0053 (NS-CTA).

4. REFERENCES

[1] D. M. Blei, A. Y. Ng, and M. I. Jordan. Latent dirichlet allocation. *JMLR*, 3:993–1022, 2003.

[2] T. Hofmann. Probabilistic latent semantic indexing. In *SIGIR*, pages 50–57, 1999.

[3] M. Steyvers, P. Smyth, M. Rosen-Zvi, and T. L. Griffiths. Probabilistic author-topic models for information discovery. In *KDD*, pages 306–315, 2004.

[4] Y. Sun, Y. Yu, and J. Han. Ranking-based clustering of heterogeneous information networks with star network schema. In *KDD*, pages 797–806, 2009.

[5] J. Tang, J. Zhang, L. Yao, J. Li, L. Zhang, and Z. Su. Arnetminer: extraction and mining of academic social networks. In *KDD*, pages 990–998, 2008.

Graph-Cut based Tag Enrichment

Xueming Qian
Xi'an Jiaotong University
Xi'an 710049, P. R. China
qianxm@mail.xjtu.edu.cn

Xian-Sheng Hua
Microsoft Research Asia
Beijing 100080, P. R. China
xshua@microsoft.com

ABSTRACT
In this paper, a graph cut based tag enrichment approach is proposed. We build a graph for each image with its initial tags. The graph is with two terminals. Nodes of the graph are full connected with each other. Min-cut/max-flow algorithm is utilized to find the relevant tags for the image. Experiments on Flickr dataset demonstrate the effectiveness of the proposed graph-cut based tag enrichment approach.

Categories and Subject Descriptors
H.3.1 [**Information Storage and Retrieval Languages**]: Content Analysis and Indexing.

General Terms
Algorithms, Performance, Experimentation

Keywords: Tag enrichment, graph cut, Flickr, tag ranking, Min-cut/Max-flow.

1. INTRODUCTION
In recent years, social networks (e.g. Picasa, Flickr, YouTube) are very popular for people to share their photos. With the rapid advance in the technology of digital imaging, there is an explosive growth in the amount of available image data in social media sharing networks. Social media repositories allow users to upload their personal media data and provide several descriptive keywords for their metadata. The descriptive keywords are called tags [1]. Tag is one of the most important textual information on social media networks. They made the social networks are easy to management and better accessible to the users. Image tags have certain consistent with its visual content. Thus tag based image retrieval is very popular and practical in the searching engines such as Flickr. However, due to the noise, imprecise and incompleteness of user labeled tags, the performance of tag based application is inevitably influenced by the tag quality.

Extensive research has been dedicated to the tag enrichment for social images. Liu et al. [1] proposed to rank the original tags of the images using random walk model by taking both the textual and visual similarities of tags into account. The random walk model promotes the tag with many close neighbors and weakens the tags with fewer neighbors. Li et al propose a neighbor voting algorithm for tag relevance learning [2]. This approach is based on the fact that different users label visually similar images using the same tags. The relevance of a tag with respect to an image can be inferred from tags of visual similar images. In this paper, we view the tag enrichment as a combinational optimization problem. And graph-cut is utilized to find relevant tag list for the image.

SIGIR'11, July 25–29, 2011, Beijing, China.
ACM 978-1-4503-0757-4/11/07.

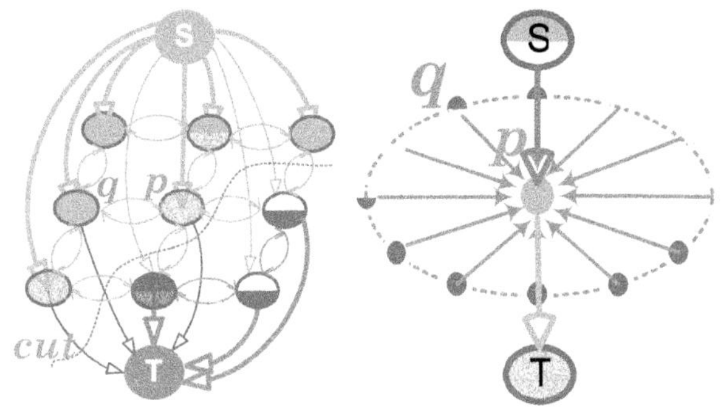

(a) (b)

Figure 1. (a) Example of graph cut based application in vision. (b) Example of the sub-structure of the tag graph.

2. GRAPH CUT BASED TAG ENRICH
For a given image I and its initial tags $\varphi = \{t_1, \cdots, t_n\}$, we utilize graph-cut based approach to determine the relevant tag set to the image.

A tag graph $G=<V,E>$ consists of a set of nodes V and a set of edge E. Each node corresponds to a tag. And E is the set of edges connecting each of two nodes. The tag graph contains two additional special nodes that called terminals [3]: the source s and the sink t. There are two types of edges in the tag graph: n-links and t-links. N-links connect each of two tags (nodes) and t-links connect tags (nodes) to the terminals. Graph based tag enrichment is exactly to find a cut on a graph that partitioning the tags (nodes) into two disjoint two subsets S and T, such that the source s in S and the sink t in T.

Fig.1 (a) shows a graph cut based applications in vision [3]. Nodes (pixels) are connected with the nodes in its four-neighbors. A cut departs the nodes into two disjoint sets. However, in the proposed graph based tag enrichment, each tag is full connected with the other tags by n-link and with terminal by t-links. Fig.1 (b) shows a substructure of a tag graph. Thus, the edge connection structure is complex than those utilized in vision based applications [3].Each tag is connected with the other tags. The weights of n-links can be viewed as tag to tag similarity. The tag enrichment can be viewed as assigning each tag a label (s or t). The label of a tag is assigned s if it is relevant to the image; otherwise its label is assigned t. How many tags are relevant to the image is a combinational optimization problem, which can be formulated by graph.

The energy function of graph cut based tag enrichment is determined as follows

$$E(L) = E_{smooth}(L) + E_{data}(L) \quad (1)$$

where $L = \{L_p \mid p \in \Omega\}$ is a labeling of the whole tags Ω . E_{smooth} measures the cost of departing the tags into two sets S and T

$$E_{smooth}(L) = \sum_{\{p,q\} \in \Omega, p \neq q} V_{p,q}(L_p, L_q) \quad (2)$$

$$V_{p,q}(L_p, L_q) = \begin{cases} \exp(-d(p,q)) & \text{if } L_p = L_q \\ 1-\exp(-d(p,q)) & \text{otherwise} \end{cases} \quad (3)$$

where $d(p,q)$ is the distance of tag p and q. In this paper we utilize Google distance is to measure the distance of two tags [1].

In Eq.(1), $E_{data}(L)$ measures the cost of the assignments of the tags relevant/irrelevant to the image.

$$E_{data}(L) = \sum_{\tau\in\Omega} D_\tau(L_\tau) \quad (4)$$

The cost is expressed as follows

$$D_\tau(L_\tau) = \begin{cases} S(\tau), & \text{if } L_\tau = s \\ 1-S(\tau), & \text{if } L_\tau = t \end{cases} \quad (5)$$

where $S(\tau)$ measure the score of a the tag τ to the image and initial tags list φ. $S(\tau)$ comes from the tag to tag similarity and the tag to image similarity

$$S(\tau) = \alpha W_I(\tau, I) + (1-\alpha)W_T(\tau,\varphi), \alpha \in [0,1] \quad (6)$$

$W_T(\tau,\varphi)$ is the similarity of the tag τ to the initial tags φ.

$$W_T(\tau,\varphi) = \sum_{t\in\varphi} \exp\left(-d(\tau,t)\right) \quad (7)$$

And $W_I(\tau, I)$ measures the similarity of tag τ to the image I.

$$W_I(\tau, I) = \frac{1}{|\Theta_\tau|} \sum_{x\in\Theta_\tau} \exp\left(-\|F_I - F_x\|^2 / \sigma^2\right) \quad (8)$$

where Θ_τ denote the image set that contains tag τ, the image number in this set is $|\Theta_\tau|$. σ^2 is set to be the median value of all the pair wise Euclidean distances between images [1]. F_I and F_x are the visual features of images I and x. Correspondingly, we utilize Min-cut/Max-flow algorithm to find the relevant tags for each image [3].

3. EXPERIMENTAL RESULTS

In this Section, we evaluate our approach on social images that are collected from Flickr. We select 25 queries, including *alcedoatthis*, *apple*, *beach*, *bear*, *butterfly*, *cherry*, *deer*, *eagle*, *forest*, *highway*, *jeep*, *lavender*, *lotus*, *orange*, *peacock*, *rose*, *sailship*, *sea*, *sky*, *strawberry*, *sun*, *sunflower*, *tiger*, *tower*, and *zebra*, then perform tag-based image search with "ranking by interestingness" option. The top 5000 returned images for each query are collected together with their associated information, including tags, uploading time, user identifier, etc. In this way, we obtain a social image collection consisting of 52,418 images.

For each image, we extract 470-dimensional features, including 225-dimensional block-wise color moment features generated from 5-by-5 fixed partition of the image, 170-dimensional hierarchical wavelet packet features [4], and 75-dimensional edge distribution histogram features.

We use NDCG as the performance evaluation measure [1]. 500 images are randomly selected from our Flickr set for labeling by five persons. For each image, each of its tags is labeled as one of the five levels: Most Relevant (score 5), Relevant (score 4), Partially Relevant (score 3), Weakly Relevant (score 2), and Irrelevant (score 1). After computing the NDCG measures of each image's tag list, we can average them to obtain an overall performance evaluation of the tag enrichment method.

The NDCG scores of initial tags (denoted INIT), tag enrichment results of random walk (denoted RANK [1]), and graph cut based approach (denoted Graph) under NDCG depths 1, 5, 10 and 20 (denoted @1, @5, @10 and @20) are shown in Fig.2 respectively. The improvement of our approach over RANK, and INIT are 3.1% and 11.3% respectively under @5.

Graph-cut based tag enrichment approach can adaptively determine the relevant tags according to the visual information and hints of initial tags. Table 1 shows the corresponding tag enrichment results of RANK and Graph based on the visual information and initial tags of the photos. From the above comparisons, we find that the graph cut based tag enrichment approach is satisfactory.

4. ACKNOWLEDGMENTS

This work is partly supported by foundations of national nature science foundation of China (NSFC) No.60903121 and Microsoft Research Asia FY11-RES-THEME-052.

5. REFERENCES

[1] D. Liu, X. Hua, L. Yang, M. Wang, and H. Zhang, "Tag ranking", in Proc. WWW, 2009.

[2] X. Li, C. Snoek, and M. Worring, "Learning Social Tag Relevance by Neighbor Voting", IEEE Trans. Multimedia, vol.11, no.7, 2009, pp. 1310-1322.

[3] Y. Boykov, and V. Kolmogorov, "An Experimental Comparison of Min-Cut/Max-Flow Algorithms for Energy Minimization in Vision", IEEE Trans. Pattern Anal. Mach. Intell, vol.26, no.9, pp. 1124-1137, 2004.

[4] X. Qian, G. Liu, D. Guo, Z. Li, Z. Wang, and H. Wang, "Object Categorization using Hierarchical Wavelet Packet Texture Descriptors," in Proc. ISM 2009, pp.44-51.

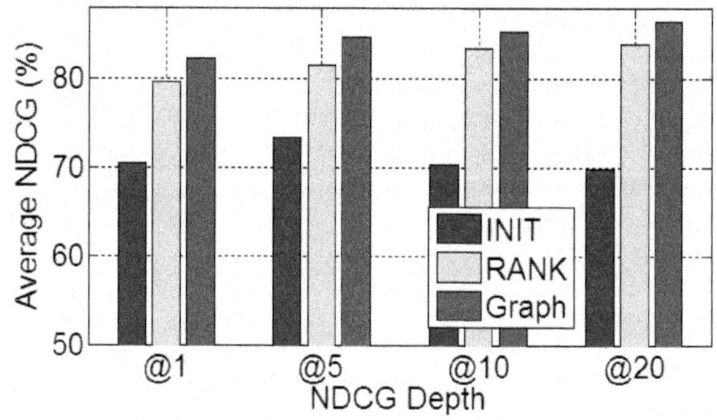

Figure 2. The performances of different tagging approaches Initial tag of Flickr (INIT), tag enrichment results of random walk (RANK) and Graph-cut (Graph).

Table 1. Initial tags (INIT), and tag enrichment results of RANK and the proposed graph cut based approach (Graph)

Photo	INIT	RANK	Graph
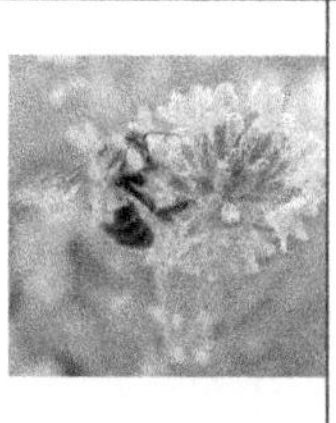	insect lavender bee pollen	pollen plant garden bee insect flower green yellow bokeh color nature flora purple beauty colorful	bee insect pollen nectar bumblebee honey lavender wing garden plant stamen shrub purple flower bokeh
	beach child tennessee	beach sand water sea ocean playa child sun	beach child tennessee family water wish action life

Personalized Social Query Expansion Using Social Bookmarking Systems

Mohamed Reda Bouadjenek[1,2], Hakim Hacid[1],
Mokrane Bouzeghoub[2], Johann Daigremont[1]
[1]Bell Labs France, Centre de Villarceaux, 91620, Nozay
[2]Laboratoire PRiSM, Université de Versailles , 45 Avenue des États Unis, 78035, Versailles France
[1]FirstName.LastName@alcatel-lucent.com, [2]FirstName.LastName@prism.uvsq.fr

ABSTRACT

We propose a new approach for social and personalized query expansion using social structures in the Web 2.0. While focusing on social tagging systems, the proposed approach considers (i) the semantic similarity between tags composing a query, (ii) a social proximity between the query and the user profile, and (iii) on the fly, a strategy for expanding user queries. The proposed approach has been evaluated using a large dataset crawled from *del.icio.us*.

Categories and Subject Descriptors: H.3.3 [Information Systems]: Information Storage and Retrieval, Information Search and Retrieval

General Terms: Algorithms, Experimentation.

Keywords: Personalization, Social Information Retrieval, Social networks.

1. INTRODUCTION

Nowadays, social networking sites, collaborative tagging, and micro-blogging sites are certainly the most representative and the most adopted applications in this new era of Web 2.0 for interacting with peers, exchanging messages, sharing resources like photos and videos, commenting on news, creating and updating profiles, etc. Valuable information is generally exchanged on these platforms but is not necessarily leveraged due to the dynamics of the ecosystem, the huge amount of information, information volatility, etc. In this context, it is natural that finding relevant pieces of information is a recurrent need for users. However, finding such relevant information becomes harder for end-users since: (i) by definition, the user doesn't necessarily know what she is looking for until she finds it, and (ii) even if the user knows what she is looking for, she doesn't necessarily know how to formulate the right query.

Query expansion comes then as a means to reduce the impacts of such problems. It enriches the user's initial query with additional information that could be relevant to the initial query so that the system may propose suitable results that better satisfy the user's needs. We consider in this work social bookmarking systems, also called *folksonomies*, which are generally modeled as a tripartite social graph with three types of entities: users, documents, and tags. We propose a new approach to query expansion through the combination of semantic and social information to reduce some of the limitations of the existing approaches, e.g., personalization.

The problem we are addressing can be formalized as follows: *For a given user u who issued a query* $Q = \{t_1, t_2, ..., t_m\}$, *how to provide for each* $t_i \in Q$ *a ranked list of its related terms* $\{t_{i1}, t_{i2}, ..., t_{ik}\}$, *such that the gap between user's expectations and system's offerings is minimized.* We translate this by the fact that the ranking function needs to take into account the semantic link between t_i and t_{ij} $(1 \leq j \leq k)$, and the social link between t_{ij} and u, which translates the closeness of the user firing the query with other users in the system. Thus, the objective is to transform Q into a new query Q' such that: (i) Q is necessarily included in Q', (ii) the results of Q are included in those of Q', and (iii) the obtained results with Q' should increase the accuracy of the results and doesn't decrease the user's satisfaction.

2. METHOD

To provide social and personalized expansions of a query term t with related term t_j, we propose to take into account two main features: (i) the similarity between t and t_j, i.e., the semantic strength between the two terms, and (ii) the similarity between t_j and the user profile expressing the extent to which a tag t_j is likely to be interesting to the considered user. We define a user profile as a weighted vector $\vec{p_u} = \{w_{t_1}, w_{t_2}, ..., w_{t_n}\}$, where w_{t_i} is the *user term frequency, inverse user frequency (utf-iuf)* that evaluates how important a term is to a user inside a set of users, i.e., similar to the tf-idf measure.

Once these two similarities are computed, a merge operation is necessary to obtain a final ranking value that indicates the similarity of t_j with t w.r.t. the user u. For this, we choose the *Weighted Borda Fuse (WBF)* as summarized in Equation 1, where $0 \leq \gamma \leq 1$ is a parameter that controls the strength of the semantic and the social parts.

$$Rank_t^u(t_i) = \overbrace{\gamma \times Sim(t, t_i)}^{\text{Semantic Part (i)}} + \underbrace{(1-\gamma) \times \frac{\sum_{t_j \in p_u}^{m} Sim(t_i, t_j) \times w_{t_j}}{m}}_{\text{Social Part (ii)}} \quad (1)$$

where $Sim(t, t_i)$ is a similarity computed between the query term t and t_i, m the profile's length, and w_{t_j} the weight of t_j in the user profile. In order to consider specific constraints in our approach, we propose a similarity measure that takes into account the credibility of entities in a folksonomy based on their popularity obtained using SPR [3], where the credibility of an entity e (i.e., user, document, or tag) is given by $-log(SPR(e)$. Then, we reduce into three bipartite graphs,

SIGIR'11, July 24–28, 2011, Beijing, China.
ACM 978-1-4503-0757-4/11/07.

i.e., User-Tag, User-Document, and Tag-Document, where we consider only the User-Tag graph (see [4]), to compute the similarity between tags inspired from the *Jaccard similarity* using Formula 2.

$$Sim(t_i,t_j)=\frac{\sum_{u\in N(t_i)\cap N(t_j)} Min(\omega(t_i,u),\omega(t_j,u))\times(-log(SPR(u)))}{\sum_{u\in N(t_i)\cup N(t_j)} Min(\omega(t_i,u),\omega(t_j,u))\times(-log(SPR(u)))} \quad (2)$$

Where $N(t_i)$ is the set of users that are the direct neighbors of t_i (resp. t_j) in the bipartite graph User-Tag, and $\omega(t_i, u)$ the number of times t_i interacts with u obtained by their aggregation over documents. Finally, we reduce the bipartite graph to obtain a graph of tags G_{tag}, which represents similarity between tags computed with Formula 2.

Algorithm 1 *Effective Social Query Expansion SoQuES*

Require: A Social folksonomy Graph G; u : a User; Q : a Query;

```
1: P_u[m] ← extract profile of u from G
2: for all t_i ∈ Q do
3:     l ← list of neighbor of t_i in tag graph G_tag
4:     for all t_j ∈ l do
5:         t_j.Value ← Rank^u_{t_i}(t_j)
6:     Sort l w.r.t. to t_j.Value and let only the top k terms in l
7:     Make a logical OR (∨) between t_i and all terms of l,
8:     Update Q'
9: return Q'
```

After getting the user's profile as explained above (Line 1), the purpose is to enrich each term t_i of Q with related terms (Line 2). Then, the objective is to get all the neighboring tags t_j of t_i in the tag graph G_{tag} (Line 3). After that, in Line 4, we compute for each t_j, the ranking value that indicates its similarity with t_i w.r.t. the user u (Line 5). Next, the neighborhood list has to be sorted according to the value of $Rank[t_j]$ and keep only the k top tags (Line 6). Finally, t_i and its remaining neighbors must be linked with the OR ($\vee$) logical connector (Line 7) and updated in Q'. *As an example, if a user u issues a query $Q = t_1 \wedge t_2 \wedge ... \wedge t_m$, it will be expanded to become Q'=($t_1\vee$ $t_{11}\vee$ ...$\vee$ t_{1l}) $\wedge$ ($t_2\vee$ $t_{21}\vee$ ...$\vee$ t_{2k}) $\wedge$ ...$\wedge$ ($t_m\vee$ $t_{m1}\vee$ ...$\vee$ t_{mr}).*

3. EVALUATIONS

The evaluation has been performed on data crawled from *del.icio.us* on September 2010, which consist of about 150×10^3 bookmarks. We have used the same evaluation protocol like in [1], which consists of: *the relevant documents for a personalized query $Q = (u, t)$ fired by user u with query term t are those tagged by u with t.* Q is enriched and transformed into Q', and documents that are indexed with tags of Q' are retrieved, ranked and sorted according to two IR model: (i) using the *cosine* similarity measure between Q' and each document d_j (Vectorial model), with values of Equation 1 as weights of Q'; or (ii) using the *Okapi BM25* similarity measure (probabilistic model). This is made on *1000* couples (u,t), over which we compute the *Mean Average Precision (MAP)*. We first begin by computing the optimal values of γ and the number of terms added to the queries (Figure 1).

We choose to fix $\gamma = 0.5$ for giving the same importance to the semantic similarity between terms, and to the social proximity with the user profile, and the query size = 6 per query term to compare with other approaches.

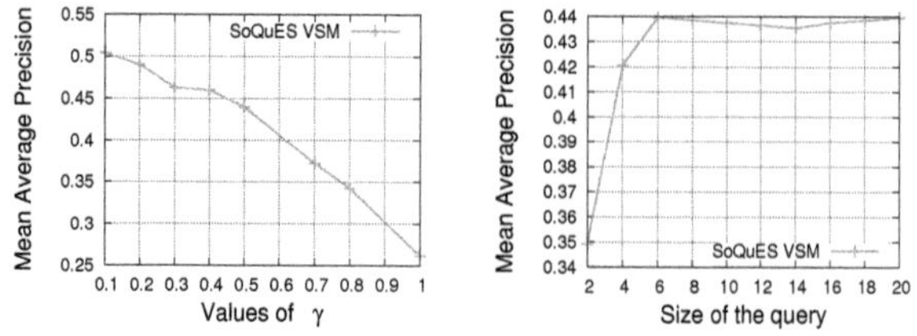

(a) MAP over different values of γ (size query=6) (b) MAP over different values of query size ($\gamma = 0.5$)

Figure 1: MAP for different values of γ, and query size, averaged over 1000 queries, using the VSM.

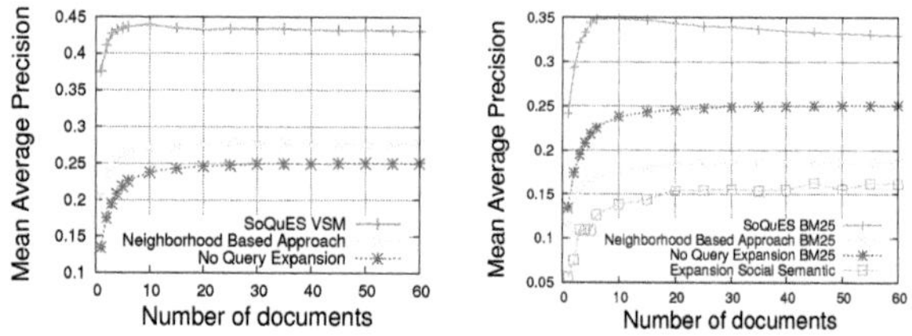

(a) Comparison with approaches based on the VSM. (b) Comparison with approach based on the Okapi BM25.

Figure 2: Comparison of the proposed approach, while fixing $\gamma = 0.5$ and query size to 6.

The comparison with other approaches is made while using the *Vectorial Model*, and the probabilistic model based on *Okapi BM25*. The results for our method are illustrated as *SoQuES VSM* and *SoQuES BM25* in Figure 2(a) and 2(b) respectively. These approaches are: (i) **Non expanded queries** based on VSM and BM25, (ii) **Neighborhood based approach**, which consists of enriching the query Q with the most related terms to t_i without considering the user profile, based on VSM and BM25, and (iii) **Expansion Social Semantic**, an approach proposed in [2], where documents are ranked using BM25 and tag similarity scores. We implemented this strategy and evaluated it over our *del.icio.us* dataset.

4. CONCLUSION

We described in this paper a new query expansion approach based on social personalization to transform an initial query Q to another query Q' enriched with close terms that are mostly used by a given user and her social relatives. A formal evaluation of the quality of the results, using datasets crawled from *del.icio.us*, has shown the benefits of this approach in comparison to other approaches. Reinforce the evaluation by including real users, improve the execution time, and combine our approach with existing techniques are among our plans for future work.

5. REFERENCES

[1] David Carmel et al. Personalized social search based on the user's social network. In *CIKM*, 2009.

[2] Matthias Bender et al. Exploiting social relations for query expansion and result ranking. In *ICDE Workshops*, 2008.

[3] Shenghua Bao et al. Optimizing web search using social annotations. In *WWW*, pages 501–510, 2007.

[4] Peter Mika. Ontologies are us: A unified model of social networks and semantics. *Web Semant.*, 5(1):5–15, 2007.

What are the Real Differences of Children's and Adults' Web Search?

Tatiana Gossen, Thomas Low, Andreas Nürnberger
Faculty of Computer Science,
University of Magdeburg, Germany
{tatiana.gossen,thomas.low,andreas.nuernberger}@ovgu.de

ABSTRACT

We present first results of a logfile analysis on web search engines for children. The aim of this research is to analyse fundamental facts about how children's web search behaviour differs from that of adults. We show differences to previous results, which are often based on small lab experiments. Our large-scale analysis suggests that children search queries are more information-oriented and shorter on average. Children indeed make a lot of spelling errors and often repeat searches and revisit web pages.

Categories and Subject Descriptors

H.3.3 [**Information Storage and Retrieval**]: Information Search and Retrieval

General Terms

Experimentation, Measurement

Keywords

children information retrieval, web log analysis, web search

1. INTRODUCTION

Internet usage nowadays knows no real age limits. Many children have access to the Internet and explore the web from a young age. Unfortunately, the web adapts slowly to the needs of children. There are many good techniques in IR for adults, but still not much scientific insights on how to design search engines for kids in terms of both user interfaces and underlying algorithms. Thus, the research on children web search is very important. Previous research shows a difference between kids and adults in their search behaviour [1]. However, these findings were based on small user studies with lab experiments and may not show real life behaviour. Only one research group previously attempted to identify children's queries in a large-scale query log [6]. Here, all queries where the user selected a search result whose domain is listed in the *DMOZ's kids&teens* directory were regarded as child queries. However, there is a significant chance that such pages were clicked by adults by accident. They also define a children session as one that contains at least one children query entry, which we do not consider as a good threshold. Additionally, AOL is a common search engine. To our knowledge, this is the first large-scale log study of search behaviour on children web search engines.

SIGIR'11, July 24–28, 2011, Beijing, China.
ACM 978-1-4503-0757-4/11/07.

2. DATASET

For our analysis we used logfiles of the three major german search engines, whose main target group are kids from 6 to 13: *Blinde-Kuh.de*, *FragFinn.de*, *Helles-Koepfchen.de*. The strength of these search engines lies in the retrieval of web documents containing only *child-appropriate* content, which means the kids are able to understand the content and have no access to "adult" web sites. The dataset is composed of 2.5 million requests gathered over one week in January 2011.

The logs contain both *searching interaction* and *click-through* records [8]. We specify a query log as the set:

$$Log = \langle \langle u_i, s_i, t_i, q_i, c_i \rangle \mid 1 \leq i \leq n \rangle \quad (1)$$

where u_i, s_i, t_i, q_i, c_i refer to the user information (user agent, geographic information), session ID, time of interaction, submitted query and its details (correction suggestions, total number of hits, list of result URLs with ranking), click-throughs (URL, referrer). Thus, the logs provide insight into interactions with the search engines' user interface: queries, navigation, pages visited before and/or after entering the query and viewings of result pages. Although the logs already contained session data, the session definition was not consistent among all three search engines. We refined the sessions by splitting those which had gaps of more than 15 min between session log entries. This is the common approach in logfile analysis, except for some variation of the chosen temporal cutoff parameter (5 to 120 min) [9]. The collected data contains a total of 608,162 sessions.

3. RESULTS

Search engine queries provide an insight into children's infomation needs. We analysed a total of 725,846 (226,387 unique) queries. Using the *Google Insights for Search* service[1], we compared the most frequent children queries to the most frequent queries by adults. We retrieved the latter for the same time period and the same location. The most frequent children and adults queries (translated from German) are shown in Table 1.

The results indicate that the information need (in terms of the *Broder taxonomy* [3]) of children differs from that of adults. The children's queries have a more informational intention. The purpose of *informational queries* is to find information about a topic assumed to be available on the web, in order to read about it. Meanwhile, the adults most frequent queries are *navigational* or *transactional*, with the immediate intent to reach a particular website that the user

[1]http://www.google.com/insights/search/

Table 1: **Most frequent queries from our logs (left) and from Google Insights (right) during the same period**

1. games	4. animals in winter	7. dogs
2. sex	5. squirrel	8. animals
3. electricity	6. whale	9. egypt

1. facebook	4. ebay	7. amazon
2. youtube	5. you	8. web.de
3. google	6. weather	9. gmx

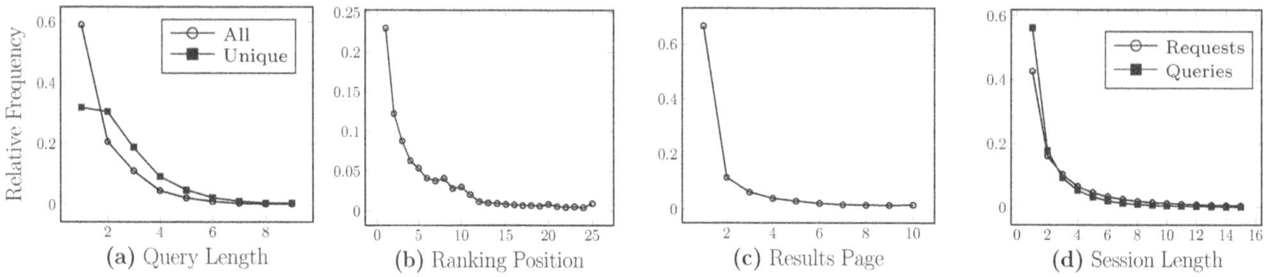

Figure 1: Distributions of relative frequencies of (a) the length of queries in number of words, (b) the ranking position of a clicked result, (c) the number of viewed results' page, and (d) the length of session in both number of all page requests (including queries) and queries only.

has in mind, or even further carry out some transactions, e.g. purchasing a product. Since children may also use the search engines for homework, queries like "egypt" could reflect the curriculum of their schools.

Figure 1(a) presents the distribution of query length. Note that the three search engines do not provide query string auto-completion. Queries contain on average 1.8 terms (2.4 for unique queries), whereas queries by adults have between 2.4 and 2.7 terms [10, 7]. Thus, our results contradict previous findings [1, 6] that children would use longer queries on average.

The three search engines combine textual links to search results with images, which also lead to the result web page. This is mainly done due to the belief that pictures attract children more than text. However, our results indicate that the kids click on a picture only slightly more often (52%) than on text (48%).

Figures 1(b), 1(c) illustrate how often a query result with rank n is clicked and how often the m_{th} results' page is viewed. The search engines provide 10 results per page. Only a few results (2–4) can be seen without scrolling. We found, that most children visited only the first results' page and looked at the first three results. These findings indicate similarity with adult click-through behaviour. More than 70% of the time, adults only view the top ten results [10].

The average session, ignoring identical queries, included about 1.8 queries. Adult studies found that most web search engine users searched one query per session and an average session included about 1.6 queries [10]. We found it similar to children web search behaviour (Figure 1(d)).

Earlier children studies discovered that kids have a *loopy* browsing style, whereas adults' browsing style is *linear* or *systematic* [1]. Children are supposed to click, repeat searches and revisit the same result web page more often than adults. We found evidence for this behaviour in the percentage of repeated URL clicks within a session given the same query (16.6%) and the percentage of repeated queries within a session (20.5%). Adults repeat roughly 12.4% of queries [4].

Another well known fact is that children have difficulty with spelling [2]. About 25% (using *Lingua-DE-Wortschatz*[2]), 21% (based on small random sampling and manual checking), 40% (with *GNU aspell* dictionary) of all queries contained at least one spelling error, which is signifcantly more than around 10-15% errors of adults [5].

[2]http://wortschatz.uni-leipzig.de/Webservices/

4. CONCLUSIONS AND FUTURE WORK

This paper presents first results of a large-scale logfile analysis of children's behaviour on targeted web search engines. We compared our findings with previous results about adults' behaviour on common search engines. We found that children tend to formulate informational queries while the adults' most frequent queries are navigational. In contrast to earlier findings, our results show that on average children formulate shorter queries than adults. We did not see any differences in click-through behaviour between kids and adults. We also did several statistics on the "loopy" browsing style of children and spelling errors in queries. We plan to analyse more complex patterns of children search behaviour, such as term co-occurrences and query reformulation.

5. ACKNOWLEDGEMENTS

This research is based on data collected by the German Youth Institute.

6. REFERENCES

[1] D. Bilal and J. Kirby. Differences and similarities in information seeking: children and adults as Web users. *Information Processing & Management*, 38(5):649–670, 2002.

[2] C. Borgman et al. Children's searching behavior on browsing and keyword online catalogs: the Science Library Catalog project. *J. Am. Soc. Inf. Sci.*, 46(9):663–684, 1995.

[3] A. Broder. A taxonomy of web search. In *ACM Sigir forum*, volume 36, pages 3–10. ACM, 2002.

[4] M. Chau et al. Analysis of the query logs of a web site search engine. *J. Am. Soc. Inf. Sci. Technol.*, 56(13):1363–1376, 2005.

[5] S. Cucerzan and E. Brill. Spelling correction as an iterative process that exploits the collective knowledge of web users. In *Proceedings of EMNLP*, volume 4, pages 293–300, 2004.

[6] S. Duarte Torres et al. Query log analysis in the context of information retrieval for children. In *Proc. 33rd Ann. Int. ACM SIGIR Conf.*, pages 847–848. ACM, 2010.

[7] E. Gabrilovich et al. Classifying search queries using the web as a source of knowledge. *ACM Trans. on the Web*, 3(2):1–28, 2009.

[8] B. Jansen. Search log analysis: What it is, what's been done, how to do it. *Libr. & Inf. Sci. Research*, 28(3):407–432, 2006.

[9] B. Jansen et al. Defining a session on Web search engines. *J. Am. Soc. Inf. Sci. Technol.*, 58(6):862–871, 2007.

[10] A. Spink and B. Jansen. A study of web search trends. *Webology*, 1(2):4, 2004.

Cognitive Coordinating Behaviors in Multitasking Web Search

Jia Tina Du
School of Computer and Information Science, University of South Australia
GPO BOX 2471, Mawson Lakes Campus, Adelaide, SA 5001, Australia
tina.du@unisa.edu.au

ABSTRACT

This paper investigates how users cognitively coordinate multitasking Web search across different information search problems. The analysis suggests that (1) multitasking is a prevalent Web search behavior including both sequential multitasking (31%) and parallel multitasking (69%); (2) multitasking is performed through a task switching process; and (3) such a process is supported and underpinned by cognitive coordination mechanisms and strategy coordination.

Categories and Subject Descriptors

H.3.3 [**Information Storage and Retrieval**]: Information Search and Retrieval – *relevance feedback, search process.*

General Terms: Human Factors, Performance, Theory.

Keywords: Cognitive coordination, Information problem, Multitasking, Task switching, Web search.

1. INTRODUCTION

Discovering the *multitasking* behavior of Web users is a growing research area. Recent Web query log studies show that multitask searching is a common human information retrieval behavior. Many users conduct information searching on multiple related or unrelated topics and also switch between the topics, with a mean of 2.1 topic changes per search session [5]. Buzikashvili's multitasking study based on the automatic task session detection procedure further reported that more than 98% search sessions were sequential execution, during which a searcher executed tasks one-by-one. This is in contrast to only 1% parallel execution, during which a user interrupted one task, started and completed the second task, and returned to the interrupted task later [1].

Unfortunately, previous multitasking Web search studies did not examine the type and complexity of multiple search tasks switching in detail. Existing research limits findings to information tasks level. The literature of psychology and cognitive sciences, however demonstrates that multitasking behavior is correlated closely to humans' cognitive processing and coordination capabilities [2]. The cognitive executive control systems govern processes including the selection, initiation, execution and termination of each task [4]. People could consciously trade-off performing one task for the other stemmed from their coordination capability. *Cognitive coordination* allows humans to manage the dependencies among tasks and the resources available [3]. The research presented in this poster is part of an investigation of multitasking and coordination behavior in Web search. This poster examines the following research questions: (1) what are characteristics of multitasking and task switching during Web search? and (2) how do users cognitively coordinate between multiple information search problems?

SIGIR'11, July 24–28, 2011, Beijing, China.
ACM 978-1-4503-0757-4/11/07.

2. METHODOGLY

An empirical study was conducted in a controlled lab environment to explore characteristics of multitasking behavior and the underlying cognitive coordination process during multitasking Web searches. The study participants were 42 graduate students (24 males and 18 females), with an average age of 29 years. They came from diverse disciplinary programs, ranging from Science and Technology, Business, Engineering, Education, and Health.

Different from search queries, information problems are of importance to interactive information retrieval because they provide a context implying users' motivations, constraints, searching scope, and affecting query formulation and relevance judgments. In order to investigate multitasking behavior, each study participant was asked to search on three individual information problems from their real work and life during a one-hour search period. These planned information problems were called original information problems (OIP). In total 126 OIPs across 15 various topic areas were observed over the Web searches, amounting to approximately 35 hours. Study participants were required to verbalize their thoughts, motivations/reasons, and actions as they were searching on the Web. The search logs and think-aloud audio data were recorded by Camtasia screen software. The analysis unit was each information search problem instead of search query.

3. RESULTS AND DISCUSSION

3.1 Characteristics of Multitasking and Task Switching during Web Search

Table 1 shows characteristics of multitasking Web search sessions based on quantitative analysis of the search logs. Beyond three OIPs planned beforehand, almost 71% of the study participants developed evolving information problems (EIP) during the process of the current Web searches. An EIP was detected by topic shifts. Compared to an OIP, an EIP was represented as changed or totally new problems. The number of EIPs ranged from zero to eight, with a mean number of 2 per search. That is, each study participant searched on 5 information problems (OIP + EIP) on average.

Table 1. Characteristics of multitasking behavior

Multitasking search sessions	Total	Min.	Max.	Mean
OIP identification	126	3	3	3
EIP generation	95	0	8	2
Total information problems (OIP+EIP)	221	3	11	5
Searching task switches	275	2	15	6
Search query	742	4	39	18
Search system	75	1	10	4
Windows/tabs browsing	730	3	39	17

Table 2. Multitasking as task switching during Web search

Out of 42 searches	No.	%	Mean time per task	Description	Example	Reasons for task switching (%)
Sequential multitasking	13	31	12min	Task switching from searching on one information problem to another and without iteration.	SOIP1 —①→ SOIP2 —②→ SEIP1 —③→ SOIP3 (SP37)	Coordination mechanism (45) Strategy coordination (17) Interest shift (0) Visual cues (0)
Parallel multitasking	29	69	8 min	Task switching from searching on one information problem to another and jumping back and forth.	SOIP1 —①→ SOIP2; SOIP2 —②→ SEIP1; SEIP1 —③→ SOIP2; SOIP2 —④→ SEIP2; SEIP2 —⑤→ SEIP3 —⑥→ SOIP3; SOIP3 —⑦→ SEIP4; SEIP4 —⑧→ SOIP3 (SP13)	Coordination mechanism (95) Strategy coordination (45) Interest shift (5) Visual cues (5)

In multitasking Web search, the number of submitted search queries varied from 4 to 39, with a mean of 18; the number of employed Web search systems varied from 1 to 10, with a mean of 4; and the mean number of browsed windows/tabs was 17 (Table 1). The results show the complexity of multitasking behavior involving users' interactions with Web technologies.

The study participants were found to switch between searching on original information problems (SOIP) and searching on evolving information problems (SEIP). A process of 275 searching task switches over the 42 Web searches was identified, with 6 task switches per multitasking search. People handled the demands of multiple tasks sequentially or interleaving through task switching, namely, sequential multitasking or parallel multitasking (Table 2), accounting for 31% and 69% of Web searches, respectively. For sequential multitasking, study participants spent an average of 12 minutes per task before switching to another task. In contrast, parallel multitasking study participants spent an average of only 8 minutes on one task before switching to another.

3.2 Cognitive Coordination during Multitasking Web Search

Based on the content analysis of search-utterance segments (combining search logs and transcribed think-aloud audio data), we found that the occurrence of cognitive coordination played an active role in multitasking and task switching activities. Multitasking and task switching were underpinned and supported by cognitive coordination processes including coordination mechanism and strategy coordination.

Coordination mechanism involved a conscious reasoning and judging process – most of these were content relevance feedback of making relevance judgments on the returned results, and self-learning and regulating process of making sense of the gathered information. Coordination mechanism was identified as the most important reason for users' task switching behavior (Table 2 last column, 45% for sequential multitasking and 95% for parallel multitasking). Multitasking Web search was cognitively constructed as users learned with information attainment during the process. Evidence can be elicited from study participants' utterance, such as "I have found enough related information, I'd move on to next information problem" (SP37), "I did not think the information was useful, I might change the keywords" (SP13), and "since this problem [OIP3] is about a tour available in Malaysia, I just quickly check the visitor visa [EIP1]" (SP8).

Strategy coordination was a strategic plan for solving multiple information problems within the resources available. Strategy coordination was viewed as the second most important reason for users' task switching behavior (Table 2 last column, 17% for sequential multitasking and 45% for parallel multitasking). Two types of strategies were identified: problem specific strategy (PSS) and global strategy (GS). The PSS was the collection of tactics on usable Web searching tools for each information search problem, including the selection of Web search systems and the adoption of search queries, etc. The GS was an overall plan guiding the whole searching process and was presented as users' decisions on the allocation of searching time between multiple information search problems. For instance, "still 40 minutes left, I'd like to back to find out more detailed information on my first information problem" (SP6).

Other two minor reasons for parallel multitasking and task switching were interest shift (5%) and visual cues (5%). Users switched from one searching task to another due to being bored with the current information problem, or just "followed his or her nose" unconsciously.

4. CONCLUSIONS

Multitasking Web search not only takes place at the physical task level, but also at the cognitive coordination level. It is a behavior associated closely with humans' cognitive processing including relevance judgment, self-learning and regulating process, and cognitive strategy of time allocation. Multitasking and coordination processes could be supported by different combinations of various retrieval techniques. Future studies will make use of these findings in Web search systems design.

5. REFERENCES

[1] Buzikashvili, N. 2006. An exploratory Web log study of multitasking. *Proceedings of the ACM SIGIR'06,* 623-624.

[2] Just, M. A., Carpenter, P. A., Keller, T. A., Emery, L., Zajac, H., and Thulborn, K. R. 2001. Interdependence of non-overlapping cortical systems in dual cognitive tasks. *Neuroimage,* 14, 417-426.

[3] Miyata, Y. and Norman, D. A. 1986. Psychological issues in support of multiple activities. In D. A. Norman & S. W. Draper (Eds.), *User Centered Design* (pp. 265-284) NJ: Lawrence Erlbaum.

[4] Rubinstein, J. S., Meyer, D. E., and Evans, J. E. 2001. Executive control of cognitive processes in task switching. *Journal of Experimental Psychology: Human Perception and Performance,* 27(4), 763-797.

[5] Spink, A., Park, M., Jansen, B. J., and Pedersen, J. 2006. Multitasking during Web search sessions. *Information Processing & Management,* 42(1), 264–275.

Optimizing Multimodal Reranking for Web Image Search

Hao Li
Inst. of Computing Technology
Chinese Academy of Sciences
lihao@ict.ac.cn

Meng Wang
National Univ. of Singapore
eric.mengwang@gmail.com

Zhisheng Li
National Univ. of Singapore
lizs@comp.nus.edu.sg

Zheng-Jun Zha
National Univ. of Singapore
zhazj@comp.nus.edu.sg

Jialie Shen
Singapore Management Univ.
jlshen@smu.edu.sg

ABSTRACT

In this poster, we introduce a web image search reranking approach with exploring multiple modalities. Different from the conventional methods that build graph with one feature set for reranking, our approach integrates multiple feature sets that describe visual content from different aspects. We simultaneously integrate the learning of relevance scores, the weighting of different feature sets, the distance metric and the scaling for each feature set into a unified scheme. Experimental results on a large data set that contains more than 1,100 queries and 1 million images demonstrate the effectiveness of our approach.

Categories and Subject Descriptors

H.3.3 [**Information Search and Retrieval**]: Retrieval models

General Terms

Algorithms, Experimentation, Performance

Keywords

Image Search; Reranking; Graph-based Learning

1. INTRODUCTION

Commercial image search engines, such as Google, Yahoo and Bing, usually index web images using textual information, such as images' titles and ALT text and the surrounding texts on web pages. However, frequently the text information does not describe the content of images, and it can severely degrade the web image search performance. Reranking is an approach to boosting image search performance by adjusting search results based on images' visual information [1][2][4][5][6]. Typically, image search reranking is based on two assumptions: (1) the results after reranking should not change too much from the initial ranking list; and (2) visually similar images should be close in ranking lists. These two assumption usually can be formulated as a graph-based learning scheme, where vertices are images and edges indicate the pairwise similarities [1][2][5].

Although many different reranking algorithms have been proposed, existing results show that reranking is not guaranteed to improve performance. In fact, in several cases search performance may even degrade after reranking. One reason is that the second assumption does not hold for the employed feature space. Actually the effective features should vary across queries.

In this work, we propose a web image search reranking approach with multiple modalities. Here a modality is regarded as a description of images, i.e., a feature set. Our proposed scheme integrates multiple modalities in a graph-based learning framework. It simultaneously learns the relevance scores, the weighting of different modalities, the distance metric and the scaling for each modality. The effects of different modalities can be adaptively modulated for each query. Although multiple modalities are involved, there are only two parameters in our algorithm.

2. MULTIMODAL RERANKING

2.1 Formulation

Generally, graph-based reranking can be formulated as a regularization framework as follows

$$\mathbf{r}^* = \min_{\mathbf{r}} Q(\mathbf{r}, \bar{\mathbf{r}}, \mathbf{X}) = \min_{\mathbf{r}} R(\mathbf{r}, \mathbf{X}) + \lambda L(\mathbf{r}, \bar{\mathbf{r}}) \quad (1)$$

where $\mathbf{r} = [r_1, r_2, \ldots, r_N]^T$ is the ranking scores corresponding to a sample set $\mathbf{X} = [\mathbf{x}_1, \mathbf{x}_2, \ldots, \mathbf{x}_N]^T$. Here the term $R(.)$ is the regularization term that models the assumption that visually similar images should be close, and the term $L(.)$ is a loss term that estimates the difference between $\mathbf{r}$ and $\bar{\mathbf{r}}$. For the first term, it is usually formulated as

$$R(\mathbf{r}, \mathbf{X}) = \sum_{i,j} w_{i,j} \left\| \frac{r_i}{d_{ii}} - \frac{r_j}{d_{jj}} \right\|^2 \quad (2)$$

where $\mathbf{W}$ is a similarity matrix in which w_{ij} indicates the visually similarity of $\mathbf{x}_i$ and $\mathbf{x}_j$, and d_{ii} indicates the sum of the i-th row of $\mathbf{W}$.

Now we extend the scheme to obtain our algorithm. First, considering using one modality, we use Mahalanobis distance metric instead of the Euclidean distance metric

$$w_{ij} = \exp(-(\mathbf{x}_i - \mathbf{x}_j)^T \mathbf{M} (\mathbf{x}_i - \mathbf{x}_j)) = \exp(-||\mathbf{A}(\mathbf{x}_i - \mathbf{x}_j)||^2) \quad (3)$$

Then we consider there are K modalities. Here we linearly combine the regularizer terms, i.e.,

$$R(\mathbf{r}, \mathbf{A}_1, \ldots, \mathbf{A}_K, \alpha) = \sum_{k=1}^{K} \sum_{i,j} \alpha_k w_{k,ij} \left\| \frac{r_i}{d_{k,ii}} - \frac{r_j}{d_{k,jj}} \right\|^2 \quad (4)$$

SIGIR'11, July 24–28, 2011, Beijing, China.
ACM 978-1-4503-0757-4/11/07.

where $w_{k,ij} = \exp(-\|\mathbf{A}_k(\mathbf{x}_i - \mathbf{x}_j)\|^2)$ and α_k is the weight for k-th modality that satisfies $0 \le \alpha_k \le 1$ and $\sum_{k=1}^{K} \alpha_k = 1$. As previously mentioned, we integrate the learning of the weights into our regularization framework in order to adaptively modulate the impacts of different modalities. Therefore, the regularizer term turns to

$$R(\mathbf{r}, \mathbf{A}_1, \ldots, \mathbf{A}_K, \alpha) = \sum_{k=1}^{K} \sum_{i,j} \alpha_k w_{k,ij} \left\| \frac{r_i}{d_{k,ii}} - \frac{r_j}{d_{k,jj}} \right\|^2 + \xi \|\alpha\|^2 \quad (5)$$

For the loss term, usually it estimates the difference between two ranking lists. Here we directly use the square loss. Therefore, our algorithm can be formulated as the following optimization problem

$$\min_{\mathbf{r}, \mathbf{A}_1, \ldots, \mathbf{A}_K, \alpha} \sum_{k=1}^{K} \sum_{i,j} \alpha_k w_{k,ij} \left\| \frac{r_i}{d_{k,ii}} - \frac{r_j}{d_{k,jj}} \right\|^2 + \lambda \|\mathbf{r} - \bar{\mathbf{r}}\|^2 + \xi \|\alpha\|^2$$

$$\text{s.t. } 0 \le \alpha_k \le 1, \sum_{k=1}^{K} \alpha_k = 1 \quad (6)$$

We can see that this optimization framework involves the following variables: (1) $\mathbf{r}$, the ranking scores to be estimated; (2) α, the weights for combining K modalities; and (3) $\mathbf{A}_k, (1 \le k \le K)$, the transform matrices for K modalities.

2.2 Solution

We adopt alternating optimization to solve the problem.

First, we consider α and $\mathbf{A}_k (k = 1, 2, ..., K)$ are fixed, then $\mathbf{r}$ can be solved with a closed-form solution.

Second, we consider $\mathbf{r}$, α, and $\mathbf{A}_1, \ldots, \mathbf{A}_{k-1}, \mathbf{A}_{k+1}, \ldots, \mathbf{A}_K$ are fixed, then we derive the derivative of Q with respect to $\mathbf{A}_k$. It can be derived that

$$\frac{\partial}{\partial \mathbf{A}_k} Q(\mathbf{r}, \alpha, \mathbf{A}_1, \ldots, \mathbf{A}_K)$$

$$= \alpha_k \sum_{i,j} (h_{ij}^2 \frac{\partial w_{k,ij}}{\partial \mathbf{A}_k} - w_{k,ij}^T h_{ij} (\frac{r_i}{\sqrt{d_{k,ii}^3}} \frac{\partial d_{k,ii}}{\partial \mathbf{A}_k} - \frac{r_j}{\sqrt{d_{k,jj}^3}} \frac{\partial d_{k,jj}}{\partial \mathbf{A}_k}))$$

where $h_{ij} = \frac{r_i}{d_{k,ii}} - \frac{r_j}{d_{k,jj}}$, $\frac{\partial d_{k,ij}}{\partial \mathbf{A}_k} = \sum_{j=1}^{N} \frac{\partial W_{k,ij}}{\partial \mathbf{A}_k}$, $\frac{\partial w_{k,ij}}{\partial \mathbf{A}_k} = -2 w_{k,ij} \mathbf{A}_k (\mathbf{x}_i^{(k)} - \mathbf{x}_j^{(k)})^T (\mathbf{x}_i^{(k)} - \mathbf{x}_j^{(k)})$ Thus, $\mathbf{A}_k$ can be optimized with gradient descent method.

Finally, considering $\mathbf{r}$ and $\mathbf{A}_k (k = 1, 2, \ldots, K)$ are fixed, then Eq.6 becomes:

$$\min_{\alpha} \sum_{k=1}^{K} \sum_{i,j} a_k w_{k,ij} \| \frac{r_i}{d_{k,ii}} - \frac{r_j}{d_{k,jj}} \|^2 + \xi \|\alpha\|^2 \quad (7)$$

$$\text{s.t. } 0 \le \alpha_k \le 1, \sum_{k=1}^{K} \alpha_k = 1$$

We can employ coordinate descent method to solve Eq.7.

We can iterate the optimization of $\mathbf{r}, \mathbf{A}_1, \mathbf{A}_2, \ldots, \mathbf{A}_K$ and α. Since each step decreases the objective in Eq.6 and the value of the objective function is lower bounded by 0, the whole process is guaranteed to converge.

3. EXPERIMENTS AND CONCLUSION

We evaluate our approach with several existing methods on the large-scale image search dataset, MSRA-MM Version 2.0[3], that contains the search results (1,011,738 images in total) of 1,165 queries from Microsoft Bing image search engine. In [3], the queries are manually classified into 10 categories, and each image is labeled with 3 relevance levels (0, 1, and 2). There are 7 feature sets are extracted. We compare the following methods:

(1) Bayesian rerankingBayesianReranking[5]. We concatenate all features into a long vector and then perform the preference strength based method in [5].

(2) Graph-based reranking with concatenated features. That is, we concatenate all the features into a long vector and then perform graph-based reranking.

(3) Proposed multimodal reranking algorithm. For the initial relevance score of i-th ranking position, we estimate it by averaging the ground truth scores at the i-th position of all 1,165 queries.

The methods are denoted as "Bayesian", "Concatenation" and "Multimodal", respectively. For all the involved parameters, we tune them to their optimal values on the 68 queries in of *Ver1* with the performance evaluation metric of average NDCG@100, and then these parameters are fixed in the processing of all queries.

Table 1: Average NDCG@100 comparison for each category of different reranking methods and the original search results. Here *Ver1*, *Animal*, *Cartoon*, *Event*, *Person*, *Object*, *People*, *Scene*, *Time08* and *Misc* are the 10 query categories in MSRA-MM dataset.

	Baseline	Bayesian	Concatenation	Multimodal
Ver1	0.544	0.542	0.556	**0.568**
Animal	0.734	0.775	0.758	**0.791**
Cartoon	0.807	0.859	0.842	**0.865**
Event	0.788	0.779	0.797	**0.811**
Person	0.908	0.916	0.926	**0.940**
Object	0.703	0.723	0.722	**0.745**
People	0.714	0.703	0.718	**0.742**
Scene	0.702	0.766	0.735	**0.792**
Time08	0.830	0.844	0.863	**0.870**
Misc	0.736	0.760	0.771	**0.790**
Mean	0.747	0.770	0.773	**0.795**

Table 1 illustrates the average NDCG@100 measurements of the queries in each category after reranking. We also demonstrate the performance of original search results without reranking. From the table we can see that, in average, all the reranking methods can improve the original search results. Our method performs the best for all categories. Its superiority over the "Concatenation" method demonstrates the effectiveness of our approach of integrating multiple modalities. All the experimental results clearly demonstrate the effectiveness of our approach.

4. REFERENCES

[1] W. H. Hsu, L. S. Kennedy, and S.-F. Chang. Video search reranking through random walk over document-level context graph. In *ACM MM*, 2007.

[2] M. Wang, K. Yang, X.-S. Hua, and H.-J. Zhang. Towards Relevant and Diverse Search of Social Images. *IEEE Trans. on Multimedia*, vol. 12, no. 8, 2010.

[3] H. Li, M. Wang, and X.-S. Hua. Msra-mm 2.0: A large-scale web multimedia dataset. In *IEEE ICDM Workshops*, 2009.

[4] M. Wang, X.-S. Hua, J. Tang,and R. Hong. Beyond Distance Measurement: Constructing Neighborhood Similarity for Video Annotation. In *IEEE Trans. on Multimedia*, vol. 11, no. 3, 2009.

[5] X. Tian, L. Yang, J. Wang, Y. Yang, X. Wu, and X.-S. Hua. Bayesian video search reranking. In *ACM MM*, 2008.

[6] M. Wang, X.-S. Hua, R. Hong, J. Tang, G.-J. Qi and Y. Song. Unified Video Annotation Via Multi-Graph Learning. In *Trans. on CSVT*, vol. 19, no. 5, 2009.

Multi-Layer Graph-Based Semi-Supervised Learning for Large-Scale Image Datasets Using MapReduce

Wen-Yu Lee†, Liang-Chi Hsieh†, Guan-Long Wu†, Winston Hsu†, and Ya-Fan Su‡
National Taiwan University†, Chunghwa Telecom Co., Ltd.‡, Taipei, Taiwan

ABSTRACT

Semi-supervised learning is to exploit the vast amount of unlabeled data in the world. This paper proposes a scalable graph-based technique leveraging the distributed computing power of the MapReduce programming model. For a higher quality of learning, the paper also presents a multi-layer learning structure to unify both visual and textual information of image data during the learning process. Experimental results show the effectiveness of the proposed methods.

Categories and Subject Descriptors

H.3.3 [**Information Storage and Retrieval**]: Information Search and Retrieval—*Retrieval models*

General Terms

Algorithms, Experimentation

Keywords

Image Retrieval, MapReduce, Semi-Supervised Learning

1. INTRODUCTION

Semi-supervised learning (SSL) is to automatically exploit lots of unlabeled data in the presence of a small amount of labeled data. Among the SSL methods, graph-based methods are quite popular where both labeled and unlabeled data are modeled as vertices followed by adding a weighted edge between any two vertices. This paper focuses on image data, where most previous works concentrated on the *visual* information of image contents only and then weighted each edge with the visual similarity between two image data (vertices). Previous work in [5] indicated that it is desirable to consider both *visual* and *textual* information for the learning quality improvement. As a result, (ad-hoc) early- and late-fusion methods, which fuse visual and textual information before or after learning, were proposed accordingly. On the other hand, learning on a *large-scale* dataset poses new challenges for the graph construction and the learning process, while most existing methods scale poorly with the data size [3]. In summary, this paper has three main contributions: (1) we propose a multi-layer learning structure to fuse image graphs seamlessly, (2) we combine distributed computation and a graph-based learning method with a distributed graph-based labeling algorithm, and (3) we test the proposed methods on a large-scale image dataset to validate its applicability.

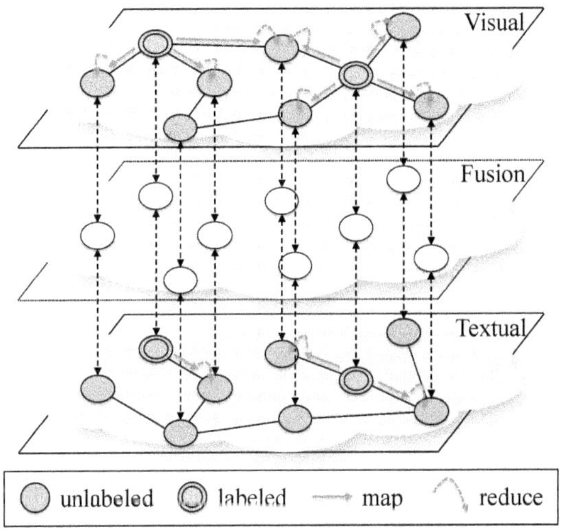

Figure 1: Multi-layer learning structure.

2. MULTI-LAYER SEMI-SUPERVISED LEARNING

2.1 Multi-Layer Learning Structure

Given an image dataset, we construct a visual graph and a textual graph. The visual (textual) graph is a complete graph where each vertex denotes an image, and the weight of an edge between two images shows the visual (textual) similarity of the two image contents. Note that in practical implementation, we do not work on complete graphs, but on sparse graphs in which lots of edges are removed to eliminate the spurious connections on dissimilar vertices. More details about the construction of a sparse graph can be found in [3].

The proposed multi-layer learning structure is sketched in Figure 1, where the top, middle, bottom layers are a visual graph, an abstract fusion layer, and a textual graph, respectively. Note that the given initial labels are shown in double circles. Our multi-layer SSL algorithm is an iterative process. Each iteration consists of two inferring processes and one fusion process. All of them are distributed algorithms based on the MapReduce programming model [1]. Note that the two inferring processes are the same but on different graphs: one is for the visual graph, and the other is for the textual graph. Take the visual graph as an example. As shown in the top layer, an inferring process is first activated to propagate the label information (e.g., a value) from each labeled vertex to its adjacent vertices. More precisely, the *map* procedure weights the (label) value on each labeled vertex while the *reduce* procedure collects the weighted value(s) for the unlabeled vertices. After the inferring processes, the fusion process is activated. The fusion process fuses every two vertices in the different graphs but referring to the same image, in a weighted fashion with a user-specified parameter $\beta \in (0, 1)$ (*cf.* Eq. (2), e.g., $\beta = 0.5$ for averaging) so that the two graphs can communicate with each other. Finally, both visual and textual graphs are updated by assigning each fused value back to the two corresponding vertices. The overall learning process is iterated until convergence.

2.2 Proposed Multi-Layer SSL Algorithm

This section details our multi-layer SSL algorithm, extended from [7], targeting at large-scale datasets. As space is limited, we shall concentrate on the operations in the visual graph, and shall not mention those in the textual graph. For simplicity, we assume each vertex in a visual graph contains a single label (i.e., value). However, our work can be extended to multiple labeling problems.

In the sequel, let G be the *sparse* visual graph with vertex set $\mathcal{X} = \{x_1, ..., x_n\}$, where n is the vertex number; let $W \in \mathbb{R}^{n \times n}$ be the similarity matrix of G, where W_{ij} denotes the edge weight between vertices x_i and x_j; let $D \in \mathbb{R}^{n \times n}$ be a diagonal matrix with D_{ii} equaling the inverse square root of the sum of the i-row of W; let $\mathcal{L} = \{1, ..., c\}$ be the label set of G; let $Y \in \mathbb{R}^{n \times c}$ be a matrix with $Y_{ij} = 1$ if x_i is initially labeled as j, and $Y_{ij} = 0$ otherwise; let $F \in \mathbb{R}^{n \times c}$ be a classification matrix, where each vertex x_i will be marked as a label $y_i = argmax_{j \leq c} F_{ij}$; let $\alpha \in (0, 1)$ be a user-specified parameter. Without loss of generality, assuming that initially the first l (typically, $l \ll n$) vertices $\{x_1, ..., x_l\}$ are individually labeled as $\{y_1, ..., y_l\} \in \mathcal{L}$, and the other $(n - l)$ vertices $\{x_{(l+1)}, ..., x_n\}$ are unlabeled. Our objective is to predict the labels of the unlabeled vertices.

Initially, we assign Y to F. Then we create a normalized weight matrix S, which equals the product of D times W times D. Next, we iteratively perform the following two operations (for inferring labels and fusing two graphs).

$$F^{((t+1),vis)} = \alpha S \times F^{(t,vis)} + (1 - \alpha) Y, \quad (1)$$

$$F^{((t+1),vis)} = \beta F^{((t+1),vis)} + (1 - \beta) F^{((t+1),txt)}, \quad (2)$$

where the meaning of a matrix with the superscript "(t, vis)" is twofold: obtained in the t-th iteration, and used for learning on the *visual* graph (i.e., $F^{(0,vis)} = F$). Similarly, $F^{((t+1),txt)}$ is the classification matrix for the *textual* graph obtained in the $(t+1)$-th iteration. Note that β is the fused parameter (*cf.* Section 2.1). Note that fusion (Eq. (2)) in the t-th iteration can only be done after inferring labels (Eq. (1)) in both of the visual graph and textual graphs in the t-th iteration. The iterative process is repeated until a certain condition is met. Finally, following the definition, given a classification matrix, we assign the labels of the unlabeled vertices accordingly (i.e., $y_i = argmax_{j \leq c} F_{ij}, 1 \leq i \leq n$).

Note that all of the (sparse) matrix operations above are implemented based on the MapReduce programming model. It is worth noting that the rationale behind matrix multiplication is to distribute the multiplication task into n partitions and work on several servers.

Table 1: Mean average precision comparison.

	VisualOnly	TextualOnly	EarlyFusion	LateFusion	MultiLayer
Flickr11k	0.374	0.411	0.442	0.488	0.521 (39%)
Flickr550k	0.239	0.326	0.341	0.356	0.374 (56%)

3. EXPERIMENTS

We implemented our algorithms using the Java programming language on a Hadoop cluster (version 0.20.2) consisting of 24 commodity machines. Empirically, parameters α and β were set to 0.9 and 0.5, respectively. The termination condition of our iterative process is a pre-defined number of iterations, 1,000. All of the experiments were based on two image datasets: Flickr11k [2] and Flickr550k [6]. The former contains 11,277 medium resolution (500×360) images while the latter contains 540,321 images. Each image is represented in both visual and textual high-dimensional features. Each dataset contains 1,282 ground truth images in seven query categories, including colosseum, eiffel tower, golden, torre pendente di pisa, starbucks, tower bridge, and triomphe.

We extracted the visual and textual features in the following ways.We took *visual word* as visual features for similarity computation. For visual word generation, we adopted the difference-of-Gaussian approach to detect feature points followed by describing them with scale invariant feature transform (or SIFT). The detected descriptors were then quantized into $10k$ clusters using k-means clustering, where each cluster defined a visual word containing the feature descriptors (feature points) in this cluster. For the textural features, we adopted the expanded Google snippet from the Google search engine to perform query expansion to represent associated (noisy) tags in textual feature in 91,004 dimensions.

For the comparative studies, Table 1 compares the visual graph only, textual graph only, early-fusion [5], late-fusion [5], and our multi-layer learning methods, where all of the them were implemented based on our SSL method (see Section 2.2). The percentages (%'s) are the improvement ratios between the visual graph only and the multi-layer methods. As revealed in the table, our multi-layer method can significantly improve the baselines by aggregating visual and textual contexts during message passing among the graphs.

4. CONCLUSION

We have presented a graph-based multi-layer SSL algorithm to unify the visual and textual information on large-scale image datasets. Experimental results have shown that our algorithm can work on a large-scale image dataset while effectively predict the image labels.

5. REFERENCES

[1] J. Dean and S. Ghemawat, "MapReduce: simplified data processing on large clusters," *ACM CACM*, 2008.

[2] Y.-H. Kuo, K.-T. Chen, and *et al.*, "Query expansion for hash-based image object retrieval," *ACM MM*, 2009.

[3] W. Liu, J. He, and S.-F. Chang, "Large graph construction for scalable semi-supervised learning," *ICML*, 2010.

[4] D. Rao and D. Yarowsky, "Ranking and semi-supervised classification on large scale graphs using map-reduce," *TextGraphs*, 2009.

[5] M. Wang, X.-S. Hua, and *et al.*, "Optimizing multi-graph learning: towards a unified video annotation scheme," *ACM MM*, 2007.

[6] Y.-H. Yang, P.-T. Wu, and *et al.*, "ContextSeer: context search and recommendation at query time for shared consumer photos," *ACM MM*, 2008.

[7] D. Zhou, Q. Bousquet, and *et al.*, "Learning with local and global consistency," *NIPS 16*, 2004.

Tackling Class Imbalance and Data Scarcity in Literature-Based Gene Function Annotation

Mathieu Blondel
Kobe University
1-1 Rokkodai, Nada, Kobe
657-8501, Japan
mblondel@ai.cs.kobe-u.ac.jp

Kazuhiro Seki
Kobe University
1-1 Rokkodai, Nada, Kobe
657-8501, Japan
seki@cs.kobe-u.ac.jp

Kuniaki Uehara
Kobe University
1-1 Rokkodai, Nada, Kobe
657-8501, Japan
uehara@kobe-u.ac.jp

ABSTRACT

In recent years, a number of machine learning approaches to literature-based gene function annotation have been proposed. However, due to issues such as lack of labeled data, class imbalance and computational cost, they have usually been unable to surpass simpler approaches based on string-matching. In this paper, we propose a principled machine learning approach based on kernel classifiers. We show that kernels can address the task's inherent data scarcity by embedding additional knowledge and we propose a simple yet effective solution to deal with class imbalance. From experiments on the TREC Genomics Track data, our approach achieves better F_1-score than two state-of-the-art approaches based on string-matching and cross-species information.

Categories and Subject Descriptors

H.4 [**Information Systems Applications**]: Miscellaneous; I.2.7 [**Artificial Intelligence**]: Natural Language Processing—*Text analysis*

General Terms

Algorithm, Experimentation

Keywords

Text Classification, Kernel Methods

1. INTRODUCTION

Since the completion of the Human Genome Project, a large number of studies have been conducted to identify the role of individual genes. However, the active research in the domain has been producing numerous publications. As a result, it is extremely labor-intensive for biomedical researchers alone to collect the information relevant to their need, since obtaining such information requires intensive reading. To remedy this problem, a number of organizations have been working on annotating each gene of model organisms with a controlled vocabulary organized as a Directed Acyclic Graph, called Gene Ontology (GO) terms, based on the contents of the published scientific articles. However, the annotation requires trained human experts with extensive domain knowledge. With limited human resources and the ever-growing literature, it was reported that it would never be completed at the current rate of production.

To alleviate the burden, TREC 2004 Genomics Track and BioCreative targeted automatic GO domain/term annotation. Overall, participants from the Genomics Track reported the effectiveness of supervised classification techniques while participants from BioCreative mainly adopted string-matching techniques. These different strategies can be attributed to the fact that Genomics Track only considered the three top-level GO terms (called GO domains) while BioCreative targeted all GO terms, which can amount to up to 30,000.

In this paper, we propose a a principled machine learning approach based on kernel classifiers. Kernel are computationally efficient and allow us to address the data scarcity issue by embedding additional knowledge. Moreover, existing methods for automatic GO annotation usually neglect the so-called class imbalance problem. We propose a simple but effective method to deal with the problem. From experiments on the Genomics Track data, our approach outperforms two existing state-of-the-art methods based on string-matching and cross-species information.

2. PROPOSED METHOD

2.1 System overview

The goal of this research is to design a system that can leverage annotated articles from the scientific literature in order to *learn* how to automatically map the function of genes mentioned in new articles to appropriate GO terms. More precisely, for a new non-annotated article, we would like to be able to answer the question: does the article contain supporting evidence that gene X has GO term Y? Our system is divided into a learning phase and a prediction phase, as depicted in Figure 1. In the information extraction step, articles are represented by concatenating three kinds of textual evidence: article title, abstract and relevant text fragments extracted by gene mention matching. In the learning step, since GO annotation is a multi-label task (i.e., one article can be associated with zero, one or more GO terms), we use a one-vs-all scheme, which consists in learning one binary classifier per GO term. In the post-processing step, we remove illogical GO term predictions based on the DAG structure.

2.2 Class imbalance

To deal with class imbalance (the number of annotated articles varies quite a lot from a GO term to another), we

SIGIR'11, July 24–28, 2011, Beijing, China.
ACM 978-1-4503-0757-4/11/07.

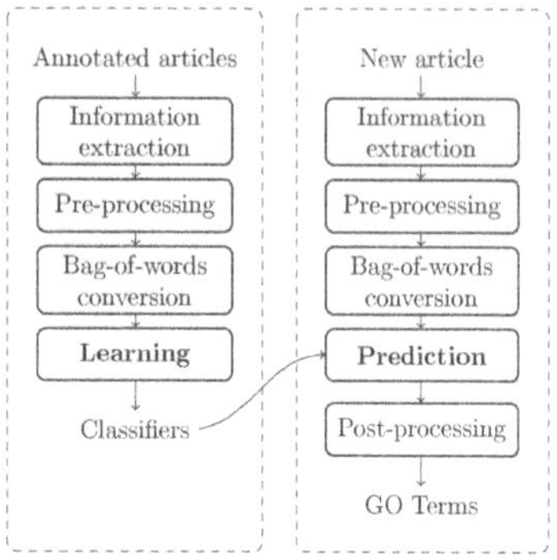

Figure 1: System overview: the learning (left) and prediction (right) phases.

employ a simple technique inspired by Osuna et al. [2] which consists in applying a stronger weight to positive examples than to negative examples. When learning the classifier for the cth GO term, we set the soft-margin SVM parameter C to $\lambda(n_{\neg c}/n_c)$ when an article is associated with this GO term and to λ otherwise. Here, we defined $n_{\neg c}$ as the number of articles which are not labeled with the cth GO term and n_c as the number of articles which are. λ is optimized by stratified cross-validation. Since $n_{\neg c} > n_c$, this consists in assigning a stronger weight to positive examples than to negative examples. This simple heuristic produced better results than other techniques such as negative example downsampling.

2.3 Data scarcity

In this research, vectors (bag of words) are very sparse and contain on average less than 300 unique words. We can therefore reasonably expect potentially discriminative words to be either absent or underrepresented in the vectors. For this reason, we propose to use the probabilistic Latent Semantic Analysis (pLSA) kernels [1]. Since they are estimated from all the articles, we can expect the latent topics used in these kernels to smooth the probability of words based on their semantic context. This is especially useful for GO terms which are annotated with only few articles.

3. EXPERIMENTS

For evaluation, we used the test dataset provided for the TREC 2004 Genomics Track and supplemented it by GO term information. The resulting dataset consists of 863 test instances. Each instance is a pair, represented by a PubMed ID and a gene mentioned in the article. For training data, we used the Genomics Track training dataset (1418 instances with full text available) supplemented with GO terms in the same way and MGD database (6750 instances with abstract only). These datasets are dealing with mouse genes only. We performed the usual document preprocessing: stop-word, punctuation and long-word (> 50 characters) removal, stemming and lowercase conversion. As an evaluation metric, we used the F_1 score for direct comparison with the previous work.

We used SVM as our classifier and compared three different kernels: $\mathcal{K}_{linear}$, $\mathcal{K}_{polynomial}$ and $\mathcal{K}_{plsa}$. A summary of the results is reported in Table 1. $\mathcal{K}_{plsa}$ (+U) corresponds to the results obtained when an additional 10,000 unlabeled abstracts from the MGD database were used to learn the pLSA model (semi-supervised learning). $\mathcal{K}_{plsa}$ (+U + T) corresponds to the results obtained when the test set was also used to learn the pLSA model, thereby tailoring the classifiers to the task of interest (transductive learning).

Table 1: Performance comparison.

Kernel	Precision	Recall	F_1-score
$\mathcal{K}_{linear}$	0.36	0.20	0.26
$\mathcal{K}_{polymial}$ $(d=2)$	0.35	0.19	0.25
$\mathcal{K}_{plsa}$	0.38	0.20	0.26
$\mathcal{K}_{plsa}$ (+U)	0.39	0.22	0.28
$\mathcal{K}_{plsa}$ (+U + T)	0.38	0.24	0.29
$\mathcal{K}_{plsa}$ (+U + T +O)	**0.42**	0.23	**0.30**
Stoica & Hearst	0.19	**0.46**	0.27
Seki et al.	0.26	0.27	0.26

For direct comparison, Table 1 provides the results of the methods of Stoica and Hearst [4] (re-implementation by the authors) and Seki et al. [3] (results taken from their paper). Our method achieves the highest precision and F_1 score. On the other hand, Stoica and Hearst accomplish the highest recall. This is because they perform string matching using the entirety of the GO term descriptors but eliminate inconsistent candidates using cross-species constraints. $\mathcal{K}_{plsa}$ (+U + T +O) are our results when cross-species constraints were also used in post-processing. Based on the t-test, the difference between our best method and the method of Stoica and Hearst was found statistically significant at the 0.05 significance level ($p = 0.03$).

4. CONCLUSION

This study proposed an approach to GO term annotation based on kernel classifiers. From the experiments on the Genomics Track data, we observed that 1) our system exhibits high precision and performs better in terms of F_1-score than two state-of-the-art methods based on string-matching and cross-species information 2) latent topics can be advantageously embedded into kernels and are a promising way to address the inherent data scarcity in GO term annotation 3) per-class regularization is a simple yet effective way to deal with the class imbalance problem.

5. REFERENCES

[1] T. Hofmann. Learning the similarity of documents: An information-geometric approach to document retrieval and categorization. In S. A. Solla, T. K. Leen, and K.-R. Müller, editors, *Advances in Neural Information Processing Systems 12*, pages 914–920, 1999.

[2] E. E. Osuna, R. Freund, and F. Girosi. Support vector machines: Training and applications. Technical report, Massachusetts Institute of Technology, 1997.

[3] K. Seki, Y. Kino, and K. Uehara. Gene functional annotation with dynamic hierarchical classification guided by orthologs. In *Proc. of Discovery Science*, volume 5808, pages 425–432, 2009.

[4] E. Stoica and M. Hearst. Predicting gene functions from text using a cross-species approach. In *Proc. of Pacific Biocomputing Symposium*, volume 11, pages 88–99, 2006.

Bootstrapping Subjectivity Detection

Valentin Jijkoun*
ISLA, University of Amsterdam
jijkoun@uva.nl

Maarten de Rijke
ISLA, University of Amsterdam
derijke@uva.nl

ABSTRACT

We describe a method for automatically generating subjectivity clues for a specific topic and a set of (relevant) document, evaluating it on the task of classifying sentences w.r.t. subjectivity, with improvements over previous work.

Categories and Subject Descriptors

H.3.1 [**Information Storage and Retrieval**]: Content Analysis and Indexing—*Linguistic processing*

General Terms

Experimentation, Measurement

Keywords

Subjectivity, sentiment retrieval

1. INTRODUCTION

We address the task of detecting on-topic subjectivity in text. Specifically, we want to (1) tell whether a textual document expresses an attitude (positive or negative) towards a specific topic, and moreover, (2) to find where exactly in the document it is expressed (up to a phrase or at least a sentence). The first task is in the area of *sentiment retrieval*. The simplest approach here consist of two stages: first, we find texts that are on topic, then we filter out (or, rank low) those without attitude [3]. A more elaborate approach is based on the assumption that documents are mixtures of two generative components, one "topical" and one "subjective" [4]. In practice, however, these components are not independent: a word that is neutral w.r.t. one topic can be a good subjectivity clue for another (e.g., compare *hard copy* and *hard problem*). Noticing this, Na et al. [6] generate a topic-specific list of possible clues, based on top relevant documents, and use this list for subjectivity filtering (reranking). Furthermore, Jijkoun et al. [1] argue that such clues are specific not only to the topic, but to the exact target they refer to, e.g., when looking for opinions about a sportsman, *solid* is a good subjectivity clue in the phrase *solid performance* but not in *solid color*.

Jijkoun et al. [1] describe a method for learning such pairs (clue, target) for a given topic in an unsupervised manner, using syntactic dependencies between clues and targets. Kim et al. [2] also use syntactic relations to bootstrap a set of topic-specific clues and use them for detecting sentences containing on-topic sentiment. Note that the methods in [1, 2] also address the second task introduced above: finding the exact location of sentiment in documents.

We go beyond the subjectivity lexicon generation methods from [1, 2], with the goal of improving subjectivity spotting. We extend the method of [1] using bootstrapping (similarly to [2]). Unlike [1], we directly evaluate the performance on the task of detecting on-topic subjectivity at the sentence level, not on sentiment retrieval with entire documents. Unlike [2], our method does not use a seed set for a given topic: we only need a general purpose subjectivity lexicon, a topic and a set of (presumably) relevant documents.

2. METHOD

We start with a topic T (a textual description) and a set $R = \{d_1, \ldots, d_N\}$ of documents deemed relevant to T. The method uses a general-purpose list of subjectivity clues L (in our experiments, the well-known MPQA lexicon [9]). We will also use a large background corpus BG of documents of a similar genre, covering many topics beside T. We use the Stanford syntactic parser to extract dependency relations in all sentences in all documents. Our method outputs a set of triples $\{(c_i, r_i, t_i)\}$, where c_i is a subjective clue, t_i a subjectivity target and r_i a dependency relation between the two words. We interpret an occurrence of such a triple in a document as an indication of sentiment relevant to T, specifically directed at t_i.

Our method operationalizes a number of intuitions. First, we assume that a given topic can be associated with a number of related targets (e.g., opinions about a sportsman may cover such targets as *performance, reaction, serve,* etc.) and each target has a number of possible clues expressing attitude towards it (e.g., *solid performance*). We assume that clues and targets are typically syntactically related (e.g., the target *serve* can be a direct object of clue *to like*), and every clue has syntactic relations connecting it to possible targets (e.g., for *to like* only the direct object can be a target, but not the subject, a adverbial modifier, etc.).

Step 1: Initial clue scoring. For every possible clue $c \in L$ and every type of syntactic relation r that can originate from it in the background corpus, we compute a *clue score* $s_{clue}(c, r)$ as the entropy of words at the other endpoint of r in BG (normalized between 0 and 1 for all c and r). The clue score gives an initial estimate of how well (c, r) may work as a subjectivity clue. Here, we follow the intuition of [1]: targets are more diverse than other syntactic neighbours of clues.

Step 2: Target scoring. For every word $t \in R$ we determine its target score that tells us how likely t is an opinion target related to topic T. Our main intuition here is that targets are words that occur unusually often in subjective contexts in relevant documents. First, we compute $C_R(t) = \sum s_{clue}(c, r)$ for all occurrences of the syntactic relation r between words c and t in corpus R. Sim-

*Current affiliation: Textkernel BV, Amsterdam.

SIGIR'11, July 24–28, 2011, Beijing, China.
ACM 978-1-4503-0757-4/11/07.

Method				P	R	F_1
method of [1]				0.23	0.31	0.26
R	K	N	M			
$r+100$	4	10	50	0.42	0.13	0.20
$r+100$	4	20	50	0.45	0.17	0.25
$r+100$	4	30	50	0.35	0.26	0.28
$r+100$	4	40	50	0.32	0.29	0.30
$r+100$	4	50	50	0.20	0.30	0.24
$r+100$	4	60	50	0.19	0.32	0.24
$r+100$	4	70	50	0.14	0.35	0.20
$r+100$	4	40	30	0.32	0.21	0.25
$r+100$	4	40	40	0.32	0.23	0.27
$r+100$	4	40	50	0.32	0.29	0.30
$r+100$	4	40	60	0.30	0.29	0.29
$r+100$	4	40	70	0.29	0.30	0.29
$r+100$	4	40	50	0.32	0.29	0.30
100	4	40	50	0.27	0.22	0.24
r	4	40	50	0.21	0.17	0.19

ilarly, we compute $C_{BG}(t)$ for the background corpus BG. We view $C_R(\cdot)$ and $C_{BG}(\cdot)$ as (weighted) counts, and compute a parsimonious language model $p_R(\cdot)$ using a simple EM algorithm [5]. We also compute a language model $p_BG(\cdot)$ from counts $C_{BG}(\cdot)$ by simple normalization. Finally, we define the target score of a word t as the likelihood that the occurrence of t in R comes from $p_R(\cdot)$ rather than $p_BG(\cdot)$:

$$s_{tgt}(t) = \frac{\gamma \cdot p_{tgt}(t)}{\gamma \cdot p_{tgt}(t) + (1-\gamma) \cdot p_{BG}(t)}.$$

Step 3: Clue scoring. Mirroring Step 2, we now use target scores to compute better estimates for clue scores. Here, our intuition is that good subjectivity clues are those that occur unusually often near possible opinion targets for a given topic. The computation is similar to Step 2, with $s_{clue}(c, r)$ and $s_tgt(t)$ interchanged: we compute weighted counts, a parsimonious model and, finally, the updated $s_{clue}(c, r)$. Now, we iterate Step 2 and Step 3, each time updating $s_{tgt}(\cdot)$ and $s_{clue}(\cdot, \cdot)$, respectively, based on the values at the previous iteration. After K iterations we select N targets and M pairs (clue, relation) with the highest scores. We check which of the N targets co-occur with which of the M clues in R.

3. EXPERIMENTS AND RESULTS

We evaluate different versions of our method on the following sentence classification task: for a given topic and a list of documents relevant to the topic, we need to identify sentences that express opinions relevant the topic. We compute precision, recall and F-score for detection of relevant opinionated sentences.

In our experiments, we use the NTCIR-6 [7] and NTCIR-7 [8] Opinion Analysis datasets, containing judgements for 45 queries and 12,000 sentences.

In order to understand how the quality of relevant documents affects the performance of the method, we selected R to be (1) R_{100}: top 100 document retrieved from the NTCIR-6/7 English collection using Lucene, (2) R_r: only documents with at least one relevant (not necessarily opinionated) sentence as identified by NTCIR annotators, and (3) R_{r+100} the union of (1) and (3).

We also ran the method with different numbers of iterations (K), different number of selected targets (N) and selected clues (M). In all settings, the overall performance stabilizes at $K \leq 5$. Table 3 shows the evaluation results:

As one might expect, we see that reducing the number of selected targets (N) improves precision but harms recall. Changing the number of selected clues (M) has little effect on precision: since for detecting opinionatedness we combine clues with targets, noise in clues does not necessarily lead to drop in precision.

Overall, we notice that with in the best setting ($K = 4$, $N = 40$, $M = 50$) the method outperforms [1] (significantly, at p=0.05, using t-test). Performance of the method varies substantially per topic (F_1 between 0.13 and 0.48), but the optimal values for parameters are stable for high-performing topics (with $F_1 > 0.26$).

4. CONCLUSIONS

We have described a method for automatically generating subjectivity clues for a specific topic and a set of (relevant) document, evaluating it on the task of classification of sentences w.r.t. subjectivity, demonstrating improvements over previous work. We plan to incorporate more complex syntactic patterns in our clues (going beyond word-word relations) and study the effect of user feedback (which extracted targets are correct? which clues are indeed subjective?) with the view of implementing an interactive system.

Acknowledgements

This research was partially supported by the European Union's ICT Policy Support Programme as part of the Competitiveness and Innovation Framework Programme, CIP ICT-PSP under grant agreement nr 250430, the PROMISE Network of Excellence co-funded by the 7th Framework Programme of the European Commission, grant agreement no. 258191, the DuOMAn project carried out within the STEVIN programme which is funded by the Dutch and Flemish Governments under project nr STE-09-12, the Netherlands Organisation for Scientific Research (NWO) under project nrs 612.-061.814, 612.061.815, 640.004.802, 380-70-011, the Center for Creation, Content and Technology (CCCT), the Hyperlocal Service Platform project funded by the Service Innovation & ICT program, the WAHSP project funded by the CLARIN-nl program, and under COMMIT project Infiniti.

REFERENCES

[1] V. Jijkoun, M. de Rijke, and W. Weerkamp. Generating focused topic-specific sentiment lexicons. In *ACL '10*, 2010.

[2] Y. Kim, Y. Choi, and S.-H. Myaeng. Generating domain-specific clues using news corpus for sentiment classification. In *ICWSM '10*, 2010.

[3] Y. Lee, S.-H. Na, J. Kim, S.-H. Nam, H.-Y. Jung, and J.-H. Lee. KLE at TREC 2008 Blog Track: Blog Post and Feed Retrieval. In *Proceedings of TREC 2008*, 2008.

[4] Q. Mei, X. Ling, M. Wondra, H. Su, and C. Zhai. Topic sentiment mixture: modeling facets and opinions in weblogs. In *WWW '07*, pages 171–180, 2007.

[5] E. Meij, W. Weerkamp, K. Balog, and M. de Rijke. Parsimonious relevance models. In *SIGIR '08*, 2008.

[6] S.-H. Na, Y. Lee, S.-H. Nam, and J.-H. Lee. Improving opinion retrieval based on query-specific sentiment lexicon. In *ECIR '09*, 2009.

[7] Y. Seki, D. K. Evans, L.-W. Ku, H.-H. Chen, N. Kando, and C.-Y. Lin. Overview of opinion analysis pilot task at NTCIR-6. In *Proceedings of NTCIR-6*, 2007.

[8] Y. Seki, D. K. Evans, L.-W. Ku, L. Sun, H.-H. Chen, and N. Kando. Overview of multilingual opinion analysis task at NTCIR-7. In *Proceedings of NTCIR-7*, 2008.

[9] J. Wiebe, T. Wilson, and C. Cardie. Annotating expressions of opinions and emotions in language. *Language Resources and Evaluation*, 39:165–210, 2005.

The Effects of Choice in Routing Relevance Judgments

Edith Law
Carnegie Mellon University
Pittsburgh, USA
elaw@cs.cmu.edu

Paul N. Bennett
Microsoft Research
Redmond, USA
pauben@microsoft.com

Eric Horvitz
Microsoft Research
Redmond, USA
horvitz@microsoft.com

ABSTRACT

The emergence of human computation systems, including Mechanical Turk and games with a purpose, has made it feasible to distribute relevance judgment tasks to workers over the Web. Most human computation systems assign tasks to individuals randomly, and such assignments may match workers with tasks that they may be unqualified or unmotivated to perform. We compare two groups of workers, those given a choice of queries to judge versus those who are not, in terms of their self-rated competence and their actual performance. Results show that when given a choice of task, workers choose ones for which they have greater expertise, interests, confidence, and understanding.

Categories and Subject Descriptors

H.1.2 [**User/Machine Systems**]: Human Information Processing; H.3.3 [**Information Search and Retrieval**]: Relevance Feedback

General Terms

Design, Experimentation, Human Factors

Keywords

Task Routing, Human Computation, Relevance Judgments

1. INTRODUCTION

Human computation systems have become an increasingly popular platform for distributing tasks, including search relevance judgments. To date, tasks are routed to individual workers in a random manner. Yet, judging the relevance of webpages is a knowledge-intensive task, requiring workers to not only understand the meaning of search queries, but also the different possible intentions that led searchers to issue the queries. We explore the use of a relevance judgment system to improve the match of judgment tasks to workers' interests and capabilities.

Obtaining relevance judgments to guide the evaluation, design, and optimization of retrieval methods has been a long-standing challenge in information retrieval [4]. These challenges include among others, obtaining quality judgments [3], controlling the cost of judgments [2], and collecting a sufficient number of judgments [8]. Studies have shown poor agreement among judges about the intentions behind queries [6,7]. Several efforts have focused specifically on the expertise of judges, showing that expertise can vary widely, and that there is poor agreement among judges with different levels of expertise [1]. In other related work, Russell & Grimes [5] concluded that users conducting searches for information were more engaged when choosing their own task, issuing fewer queries per task but engaging in longer search sessions. They hypothesized that self-selected tasks are clearer in the minds of searchers and noted that participants who provided input have a better preconceived notion of the task as they demonstrate a smaller range of possible alternate queries.

2. EXPERIMENT

We conducted an experiment with 26 subjects to investigate the effectiveness of routing relevance judgment tasks *by choice* to workers. In the *choice* condition, subjects are given a choice of five search queries, of which they choose one query to judge. Each set of queries are selected from a log of queries, input by real-world users to a major search engine. Note that unlike TREC, queries drawn from a log do not have a description of query intent. Mitigating such ambiguity has been discussed in other work [3]. The queries are balanced for length, difficulty (in terms of ambiguity as measured by click entropy, a metric capturing the variation of pages clicked on following a query), and topics. Thus, task distribution in the choice routing condition is aimed at providing a balanced set of queries leaving expertise and interests as the deciding factors for choosing a query. In the *yoked* condition, each participant is assigned exactly the same queries that a particular choice subject has selected. Pairing the yoked and choice subjects allows us to compare the two user groups using the same set of queries to control for query variance.

The participants performed 15 relevance judgment tasks in total (one task=one query). In each task, participants judge the relevance of five webpages (image captures) returned for a particular search query, rated using a 5-point scale: "perfect," "excellent," "fair," "good," and "bad."

For each query, before seeing and judging the webpages, subjects are given a pre-judgment questionnaire about the query, which asks the following: (1) Specify up to three intentions behind the search query (i.e., what the user was looking for?) and mark the most likely; (2) How confident are you that the most likely intention is the user's goal? (3) How knowledgeable are you in the topic of the search query? and (4) How interested are you in the topic of the search query? The latter three questions are assessed on a four-point scale.

After judging the relevance of results for a query, participants are given an identical post-judgment questionnaire, on which they can report any modifications to their previous answers, based on the knowledge they may have gained from reviewing the webpages.

We sought answers to two questions. First, does the routing of relevance judgment tasks to people by allowing them to choose (choice condition) result in a set of judges who see themselves as having higher expertise, interests, and confidence in the tasks than those who cannot choose tasks (yoked condition)? Second, beyond self-rated expertise and confidence, is there evidence that the choice subjects have a better understanding of the search query than the yoked subjects? We now discuss the results.

SIGIR'11, July 24–28, 2011, Beijing, China.
ACM 978-1-4503-0757-4/11/07.

2.1 Expertise, Interests and Confidence

Figure 1 summarizes the differences in self-ratings of expertise, interests, and confidence of choice subjects versus yoked subjects.

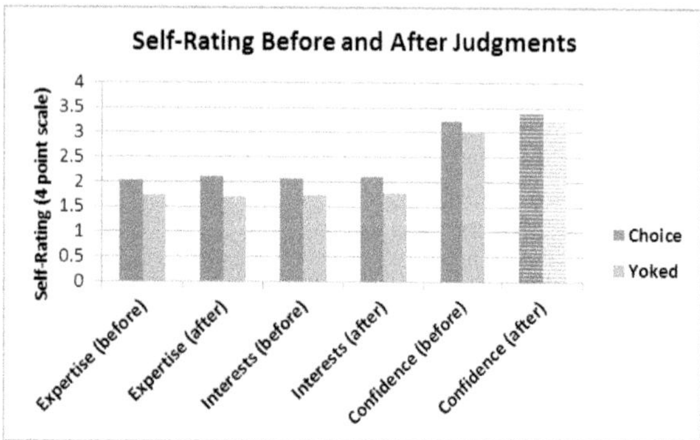

Figure 1. Results before and after judging webpages. Groups with solid bars indicate a statistically significant difference.

Results show that the choice subjects have higher self-rated expertise (difference before judging = 0.30, $p < 0.006$; difference after judging = 0.41, $p < 0.0003$), interests (difference before judging = 0.33, $p < 0.003$; difference after judging = 0.33, $p < 0.004$) and confidence in the intention of the search query (difference before judging 0.23, $p < 0.013$; difference after judging = 0.12, $p < 0.20$) than the yoked subjects. All differences are statistically significant by the paired *t*-test, except for the confidence in the intention behind the search query assessed *after* judging webpages, perhaps because both choice and yoked subjects gained an understanding about the meaning of the search query following review of the candidate webpages.

2.2 Understanding

Although self-rating may be a useful in routing, it only reveals the workers' *perception* of their own competence with solving a task and not necessarily their actual performance. For example, it is possible that by being granted a choice, workers feel more confident, regardless of *which* choice they made. One way to confirm that choice subjects have a deeper understanding of the task at hand than the yoked subjects, is to compare the number of modifications each group makes to their assessed intentions for the search query *after* judging the webpages, i.e., the differences in answers to Question 1 of the pre-judgment and post-judgment questionnaires. We assume that subjects who do not understand a query are more likely to make changes to the intentions that they had originally specified when they receive additional information.

We measured the percentage of queries for which modifications (addition, deletion, or revision) were made to (i) any of the intentions, and (ii) the most likely intention in the post-judgment questionnaire. Intentions were inspected by hand to remove superficial changes (e.g., re-wording, or spelling corrections). In both cases, the yoked subjects modified the intentions more often (29.23% of any intentions, and 19.85% of the most likely intention) than the choice subjects (15.38% of any intentions, and 14.50% of the most likely intention). This suggests that the yoked subjects are not as certain as the choice subjects about the meaning of the search query prior to reviewing the webpages.

Table 1 displays several examples of selected and unselected queries by choice subjects, providing additional support that people tend to select queries they understand. We note that this

Commonly Selected	Not Selected
weather vienna austria 10 day (3/3)	usb-uart controller nokia 6610i (0/8)
soccer (4/7)	th50px500u (0/7)
36 weeks pregnant baby size (2/3)	Webtender (0/7)

Table 1. Examples of commonly selected and non-selected queries and ratio of selected vs. presented.

does not indicate that people select queries that are *universally* understood (i.e. non-ambiguous), as in such a case, yoked subjects judging the chosen queries would be expected to have similar performance rather than the differences observed in Figure 1. Table 1 also suggests, that the number and proportion of times a query is selected are measures of query-understanding and interest (e.g. "soccer" is easily understood with a high number of selections but not all judges have an interest in the query); a potential future task routing system using the number of times a query has not been selected as part of the balance criterion may lead to more uniform completion rates for all queries as well as higher quality judgments. Verifying this is an area of future work.

3. CONCLUSION

Using relevance judgment of webpages as a case study, we investigate whether task routing by choice can lead to work being done by workers with greater self-rated expertise, interests, confidence, and understanding of the search queries. When given the option of selecting queries participants provided higher ratings for their expertise, interests, and confidence about the intentions behind queries. The choice cohort also modified assessments of intentions less than yoked subjects following review of additional information, suggesting they have greater expertise and confidence in their knowledge. We introduce statistics on the modification of intent assessment as a proxy for expertise on a relevance judgment task. We believe such statistics warrant additional study as potential signals of expertise. Overall, we view task routing systems and policies that take into account expertise as promising directions for crowdsourcing relevance.

4. REFERENCES

[1] Bailey, P., Craswell, N., Soboroff, I., Thomas, P., de Vries, A. and Yilmaz, E. Relevance assessment: are judges exchangeable and does it matter? In *SIGIR 2008*.

[2] Carterette, B., Allan, J., & Sitaraman, R. Minimal Test Collections for Retrieval Evaluation. In *SIGIR 2006*.

[3] Carterette, B., Bennett, P. N., Chickering, D. M., & Dumais, S. T. Here or there: preference judgments for relevance. In *ECIR 2008*.

[4] Cleverdon, C. The cranfield tests on index language devices. *Readings in IR*, Morgan Kaufmann, 1997.

[5] Russell, D. and C. Grimes. Assigned tasks are not the same as self-chosen web search tasks. In *HICSS 2007*.

[6] Teevan, J., Dumais, S. and Horvitz, E. Characterizing the Value of Personalizing Search. In SIGIR 2007

[7] Teevan, J., Morris, M. and Bush, S. Discovering and Using Groups to Improve Personalized Search. In *WSDM 2009*.

[8] Yilmaz, E. and Aslam, J. Estimating average precision with incomplete and imperfect judgments. In *CIKM 2006*.

Statistical Feature Extraction for Cross-Language Web Content Quality Assessment

Guang-Gang Geng, Xiao-Dong Li, Li-Ming Wang, Wei Wang, Shuo Shen
China Internet Network Information Center
Computer Network Information Center
Chinese Academy of Sciences
Beijing 100190, P. R. China
{gengguanggang, lee, wangliming, wangwei, shenshuo}@cnnic.cn

ABSTRACT

Web content quality assessment is a typical static ranking problem. Heuristic content and TFIDF features based statistical systems have proven effective for Web content quality assessment. But they are all language dependent features, which are not suitable for cross-language ranking. In this paper, we fuse a series of language-independent features including hostname features, domain registration features, two-layer hyperlink analysis features and third-party Web service features to assess the Web content quality. The experiments on ECML/PKDD 2010 Discovery Challenge cross-language datasets show that the assessment is effective.

Categories and Subject Descriptors

H.3.3 [**Information Storage and Retrieval**]: Information Search and Retrieval; I.2.6 [**Artificial Intelligence**]: Learning

General Terms

Measurement, Experimentation, Algorithms

Keywords

Quality Assessment, Feature Extraction, Machine Learning

1. INTRODUCTION

Web content quality assessment is a typical static ranking (query-independent ranking) problem [1], which is crucial to search engine, Web archiving and Internet directory, etc. Web quality assessment can also be applied to domain abuse detection to reduce false positive rate of the detection model.

In 2010, András A. et al [2] released a dataset for Web quality assessment; based on the dataset, ECML/PKDD 2010 Discovery Challenge(DC2010) was held. As multilingualism is imperative on the Web, the DC2010 involves a multilingual task and expects language-independent features to be used to classify the French and German language test sets. How to extract effective features to train a model for multi-language Web content quality prediction is a challenge and interesting topic. In DC2010, NLP, hyperlink, content and TFIDF features were used, among them heuristical content features and TFIDF features have proven the most effective features for English quality assessment [3] [5]. Yet, as language dependent features, content and TFIDF features are unfit for cross-language quality assessment.

Richardson M. et al [1] proposed *Feature Based Static Ranking* and claimed that they outperformed PageRank. In their work, most features are heuristic content attributes, such as *page* and *anchor text*; and the *popularity* feature is impracticable for most of researchers, as it is the commercial service data; also, they do not take Web spam into account, which severely distorts search engines' ranking results.

In the following of this paper, we will extract a series of language-independent features to assess the Web content quality and carry out contrast experiments on DC2010 dataset to demonstrate the effectiveness of these features.

2. FEATURES EXTRACTION

In this section, we will describe features used for learning an automatic cross-language Web content assessment model. The extracted features include hostname features, domain registration features, page and host level hyperlink analysis features, and third-party Web service features.

2.1 Hostnames Features

Hostname is usually a combination of local name with its parent domain name, which is a visiting card of various Web services. We will investigate whether the local name length, the hostname length, number of digits, ".", "-" , "year" substring in a hostname, and the top-level domain of a hostname are effective indicators of quality assessment.

2.2 Registration Features

To an approximate degree, registration features can describe "where" a site is registered, "who" owns it, and "when" it is changed. We can get the information of a domain name by WHOIS service. Then, we can map the features of a domain name to the corresponded host. The registration features include: creation date, updated date, expiration date, number of name servers, registrant and registrar, etc.

2.3 Third-party Features

Quite a few Internet services are available today, such as Yahoo! Site Explore (https://siteexplorer.search.yahoo.com), Alexa (http://www.alexa.com) and PageRank (http://toolbarqueries.google.com). We can get certain information that describes a host. For example, PageRank is one of the most famous link analysis algorithms, which reflects the importance of Web pages; although PageRank becomes unreliable

SIGIR'11, July 24–28, 2011, Beijing, China.
ACM 978-1-4503-0757-4/11/07.

as a quality measure due to the growing prevalence of link spam [4] [6], it should still be a useful measure for the Web content quality.

For a *host*, the third-party features include: PageRank and Alexa ranking of the *host*'s corresponded domain, number of inlinks gathered by Yahoo and Alexa, and number of pages indexed by Google and Yahoo.

2.4 Page Level Link Features

The page level hyperlink features used here are provided by the ECML/PKDD 2010 Discovery Challenge organization committee, i.e. link-based features [2]. Given that the transformed feature, such as TrustRank/PageRank, is meaningless for nonlinear classification algorithms, we do not use them in this paper.

2.5 Host Level HyperLink Analysis Features

Based on the common sense that benign sites tend to link to other high quality sites and malicious nodes are mainly linked by low quality nodes, we will extract a series of host level link analysis features to mine the quality relations from the Web topology dependency.

Truncated PageRank ($t = 1, 2, 3, 4$) [4] (spam detection), HostRank (static ranking) and Estimation of supporters ($d = 1, 2, 3, 4$) [4] (spam detection) are extracted. Considering the topological dependencies of low and high quality nodes, we also compute their neighbors' weighted mean values just as our previous work [3]. The neighbor relation include inlinks and outlinks, etc. We treat the $domainPR$ used in [3] as a third-party feature.

3. EXPERIMENTS

3.1 Learning Method and Evaluation

In DC2010, modeling via weighted probabilities of samples has proven one of the most effective assessment methods [3]. We adopt this strategy in the following experiments and use the same learning algorithm, i.e. bagging with C4.5. So we can focus on the effectiveness of the extracted features and compare with the DC2010 best results. The iterations of bagging is 90 in our experiments.

NDCG is used as our evaluation criterion, which is also used to evaluate the submissions of DC2010 [2].

3.2 Data Set and Feature Fusion

DC2010 data set consists of 23,808,829 pages, 600 million hyperlinks and 191,388 different hosts [2]. We use the labeled English training data for multilingual Web content quality assessment task (German and French).

We extract 11 $HostName$ features (N), 3 *Registration* features (R), 6 *Third-Party* features (T), 45 *Host Level Link* features (H) and 79 *Page Level Link* features (P)[1]. Conducting feature selection with information gain (IG) algorithm on the aforementioned features, we get the *Fusion* features (F). That is, $F = IG(N \bigcup R \bigcup T \bigcup H \bigcup P)$. In our experiments, the dimension of the *Fusion* features is 35.

[1]We queried the WHOIS and third-party services 2 months after DC2010 release, when some domains had expired. Given that domains with high reputation usually renew in advance, it should not quite affect the assessment results. The registration features include create date, update date and number of name servers.

3.3 Experiment Results

Table 1 gives the comparison of Web content quality assessment performance of different scale features and fusion features for cross language tasks.

Table 1: Comparisons of Web content quality assessment performance with different features (NDCG)

Features	German(DE)	French(FR)	Average
Page Level Link	0.8047	0.8051	0.8049
HostName	0.7998	0.8252	0.8125
Third-Party	0.8361	0.8345	0.8363
Host Level Link	0.8340	0.8332	0.8336
Registration	0.8354	0.8257	0.8305
Fusion	0.8736	0.8532	0.8634

We can see that all the features from different scales have assessment ability. Among them, the registration features, third party features and host level link features are more effective for cross-language tasks. We get the best result with fusing all the features. From the Table 1 we can find that the features extracted from different views can be complementary for cross-language Web content quality assessment.

In aforementioned experiments, the labeled German and French samples are not used for training the assessment models. Thus, we only employed the labeled English samples to validate the effectiveness of the extracted features for cross-language static ranking. Even so, the results with fusion features outperform all the final submissions in DC2010, where the best results are DE (0.8545) and FR (0.8362) [5].

4. CONCLUSIONS

In this paper, we have extracted a series of language-independent features. The experiments show that the proposed method is effective for cross-language assessment.

5. ACKNOWLEDGMENTS

This paper is supported by projects NSFC (No.61005029, No.61070039) and BJNSF (No.4112062).

6. REFERENCES

[1] Richardson, M. and Prakash, A. and Brill, E. Beyond PageRank: Machine Learning for Static Ranking. In *WWW'06*. ACM, New York, NY, USA, 707-715, 2006

[2] András B.,Carlos C.,Julien M.,Michael M.,Miklós E.,Zoltán G. ECML/PKDD 2010 Discovery Challenge data set. Crawled by European Archive Foundation.

[3] Geng, G., Xiao, B., Zhang, X., and Zhang, D. Evaluating Web Content Quality via Multi-scale Features. In *ECML/PKDD Discovery Challenge*, September 20th, 2010, Barcelona, Spain.

[4] Becchetti, L. and Castillo, C. and Donato, D. and Baeza-Yates, R. and Leonardi, S. Link analysis for web spam detection. *ACM Trans. Web* 2, 1, March 2008.

[5] Andras B., Carlos C., Zoltán G., and Julien M. Overview of the ECML/PKDD Discovery Challenge 2010 on Web Quality. In *ECML/PKDD Discovery Challenge*, September 20th, 2010, Barcelona, Spain.

[6] C. Castillo, D. Donato, A. Gionis, V. Murdock, and F. Silvestri. Know Your Neighbors: Web Spam Detection Using the Web Topology. ACM *SIGIR*, 423-430, 2007.

Exploiting Endorsement Information and Social Influence for Item Recommendation

Cheng-Te Li[1], Shou-De Lin[1], Man-Kwan Shan[2]
[1] Graduate Institute of Networking and Multimedia, National Taiwan University, Taipei, Taiwan
[2] Department of Computer Science, National Chengchi University, Taipei, Taiwan
{d98944005, sdlin}@csie.ntu.edu.tw, mkshan@cs.nccu.edu.tw

ABSTRACT

Social networking services possess two features: (1) capturing the social relationships among people, represented by the social network, and (2) allowing users to express their preferences on different kinds of items (e.g. photo, celebrity, pages) through endorsing buttons, represented by a kind of endorsement bipartite graph. In this work, using such information, we propose a novel recommendation method, which leverages the viral marketing in the social network and the wisdom of crowds from endorsement network. Our recommendation consists of two parts. First, given some query terms describing user's preference, we find a set of targeted influencers who have the maximum activation probability on those nodes related to the query terms in the social network. Second, based on the derived targeted influencers as key experts, we recommend items via the endorsement network. We conduct the experiments on DBLP co-authorship social network with author-reference data as the endorsement network. The results show our method can achieve effective recommendations.

Categories and Subject Descriptors: H.3.3 [**Information Systems**]: Information Search and Retrieval.

General Terms: Algorithms, Performance, Design.

Keywords: Social Network, Endorsement Network, Social Influence, Recommendation.

1. INTRODUCTION

In current social networking services (SNS), like Facebook and Twitter, an important characteristic is allowing users to express their favorites on different kinds of items by *endorsing* them. For example, in Facebook, users can "Like" pages, photos, celebrities, videos, and etc. In Twitter, users utilize "Favorite" or "Retweet" to show their preferences. Such endorsement information between users and items can be regarded as a kind of novel source for recommendation. A recent study on such endorsing data is to recommend items which not only relate to the user-given query of tags but also share a significant number of common endorsers [2]. However, in their proposal, they assume individuals in SNS are independent with each other. The social relationships (e.g. friendships) among users, which capture the knowledge about how people interact among different items, are ignored. Some studies use user-item interactions for recommendation. I. Konstas et al. [1] and I. Guy et al. [4] propose diverse modeling approaches to represent the interactions among users, items, and tags as a unified graph and perform different random walk-based methods to recommend items for specific users. On the other hand, in SNS, social network is a crucial medium for the spreading of influence and information. People who adopt a new idea or buy a new item could be affected by the trusts and decisions of their friends. Kempt et al. [3] investigate the behaviors of information diffusion and the *word-of-mouth* effect. They try to find influential individuals who can trigger maximum cascades of influence in a network, for *viral marketing*.

In this work, we propose a novel recommender system, which use the endorsement information and the influence propagation in a social network. Our central idea is to find topical influencers as the recommenders to recommend items via the endorsement information. Specifically, given query terms describing user's preference, we aim to find some individuals (termed *targeted influencers*) who have maximum influence potentials on some persons related to the query. We regard these targeted influencers as authoritative roles w.r.t. user's interests. And then using the endorsing information, we recommend the items which are commonly and effectively endorsed by the targeted influencers. Our method has two characteristics: (1) recommending items by the targeted influencers can be more explainable and convincing. (2) The social endorsement is a kind of the wisdom of crowds, and thus recommendation combining targeted influencers and such endorsing information can be regarded as crowdsourcing from key players.

Preliminary. First, the input of our recommendation is a set of query terms which represents user's preferences. The set of nodes whose interests satisfy the query terms is denoted by Q. Second, we represent the relationships among users in a SNS as a social network $G = (V, E, P)$, where V is the user set, E is the set of relationships between users, and each edge is associated with an influence probability $p(u,v) \in [0,1]$ as weight. Each node i is associated with a set of labels L_i describing his/her preferences. Third, we formulate the endorsement information as a bipartite graph $H = (V, U, E_H)$, where V is the user set, U is the item set, and E_H is the set of endorsing edges. Note that the set of user nodes in H could contain the user set in G. Fourth, we propose the *Collective Influence* (*CI*) model for query-based influence propagation in a social network. The *CI* model starts from an initial set of active nodes A_0, and proceeds by the following rules in discrete time rounds. In round r, each active node u has a single chance to activate each of its active or inactive neighbors v with the pre-determined influence probability $p(u,v)$. If u successfully activates v and v is inactive, v will become active at round $(r+1)$. If u successfully activates v and v is active, v will keep active at round $(r+1)$. This procedure will be terminated until no activations are possible. Fifth, given a source node $s \in V$ as a candidate targeted influencer, and a target node $t \in Q$ $(s \neq t)$, we define the *propagation path* $P_{s\to t} = \langle s = v_1, v_2, \dots, v_m = t\rangle$, where $v_1, v_2, \dots, v_m$ are active, as the highest probabilistic path from source s to target t. We also define the *activation probability* $ap(s,t) = \prod_{i=1}^{m-1} p(v_i, v_{i+1})$ as the chance that s successfully affects t. If s and t are disconnected, $ap(s,t) = 0$. In addition, for the set of nodes with query terms Q and the set of candidate targeted influencers S, we define the *average activation probability* as

$$R(Q,S) = \left(\textstyle\sum_{t\in Q} max_{s\in S}\{ap(s,t)\}\right)/|Q|.$$

Problem Statement. Given (a) a social network G, (b) a set of nodes with query terms: Q, (c) the endorsement bipartite network $H = (V, U, E_H)$, and (d) the number of targeted influencers k_s and the number of recommended items k_r, using the proposed Collective Influence model, we aim to (1) find a set of k_s targeted influencers S in G such that the objective function of average activation probability $R(Q,S)$ is maximized. (2) Recommend a ranked list of k_r items in H based on the set of targeted influencers S.

2. THE PROPOSED METHOD

Finding Targeted Influencers. This part contains two stages: (1) grouping nodes based on query terms, and (2) a greedy method to maximize the objective function for finding targeted influencers. We

SIGIR 2011, July 24 – 28, 2011, Beijing, China.

first assume nodes with query terms form several components in the social network. We identify such small groups, where each group contains only nodes with query terms, and obtain the corresponding induced subgraphs $\{G'_1, G'_2, \ldots, G'_m\}$, where m is the number of groups. This grouping will reduce the graph space and allow the search to be more efficiently. And then our goal is to distribute the set k_s nodes S as targeted influencers over these m subgraphs such that the determination of k_s nodes can maximize the average activation probability $R(Q,S)$. We first explain our objective $R(Q,S)$ satisfies the submodularity property, and then use such property to devise a greedy algorithm to maximize $R(Q,S)$.

First, R is *nondecreasing* $R(Q, X \cup \{v\}) \geq R(Q,X)$: adding a node to a set will not decrease R. Second, R is *submodular* (i.e., satisfies the diminishing returns) $R(Q, X \cup \{v\}) - R(Q,X) \geq R(Q, Y \cup \{v\}) - R(Q,Y)$: the *marginal gain* of adding a node v to a set X is higher than or equal to the marginal gain of adding v to X's superset Y ($X \subseteq Y$) for any nodes $v \in V \setminus Y$. That is, let $R(Q, \emptyset) = 0$ in the initial state, in t^{th} round, a targeted influencer v is determined and added into the set S_t, the marginal gain of the average activation probability $R(Q, S_t \cup \{v\}) - R(Q, S_t)$ is less than or equal to that of the $(t\text{-}1)^{\text{th}}$ round $R(Q, S_{t-1} \cup \{u\}) - R(Q, S_{t-1})$, where $S_t = S_{t-1} \cup \{u\}$.

To find the set of targeted influencers S, we use the submodularity to devise a greedy algorithm. The algorithm starts from initializing the set $S_0 = \emptyset$, and then iteratively adds a node s into S_t in the following t^{th} round (t>0) such that s maximizes the marginal gain

$$S_t = argmax_{s \in V \setminus S_{t-1}} \{R(Q, S_{t-1} \cup \{s\}) - R(Q, S_{t-1})\}.$$

The greedy algorithm will continue to add nodes into S_t until $t = k_s$, where we reach the budget of selecting targeted influencers.

Item Recommendation. Based on the derived targeted influencers, we use the *Random Walk with Restart* algorithm (*RWR*) [5] in the endorsement bipartite graph for the item recommendation. RWR is capable of predicting the preference or affinity of items for some indicated users. We set the targeted influencers as the designated restarting nodes and apply RWR to compute the proximity scores for all items in the bipartite graph. The restarting probability is set to 0.25 in this work. A ranked list with k_r items of highest scores will be returned as the recommended items.

3. EXPERIMENTAL RESULTS

To evaluate the effectiveness of the proposed method, we compile the DBLP bibliography data to a connected co-authorship social network containing 5,095 nodes and 11,800 edges in some premier conferences, including SIGIR, WWW, CIKM, WSDM, JCDL, KDD, ICDM, SDM, PAKDD, PKDD, VLDB, SIGMOD, and ICDE. The edges are constructed if two authors co-work more than 3 papers. The set of labels L_i associated with each author i are the textual terms occurring in at least 3 paper titles that he/she ever participated. And the probabilistic weights on edges are determined by $p(u,v) = |L_u \cap L_v| / \min\{|L_u|, |L_v|\}$. For the endorsement network, it consists of authors and papers as nodes. If an author v ever referenced to a paper u, we connect v to u. in the endorsing graph. Totally there are 18,357 nodes and 147,392 papers. Note that we only include the papers occur in mentioned conferences. We also compile two sets of query terms from two areas: information retrieval (IR-Query) and social network (SN-Query). For each query set, we manually find 20 authors as testing influencers, where each author must publish at least 5 related papers and serve as PC in at least 5 proceedings of our used conferences. The details about the queries are shown in Table 1.

The first experiment is computing the average activation probability $R(Q,S)$ for the proposed method of finding targeted influencers S (k_s is varied from 1 to 20.). We compare our method to the random selection as baseline and three heuristic methods: degree, closeness, and betweenness centralities, which aim to find different kinds of important nodes in a social network. The experimental results are shown in Figure 1. We can find our method outperforms the other five heuristics for both IR-Query and SN-Query.

Table 1. Query terms and testing authors for IR and SN queries.

	IR-Query	SN-Query
Query terms	retrieval, text, ranking	social, network(s), mining
Testing Authors	Wei-Ying Ma, Tat-Seng Chua, W. Bruce Croft, Chris H. Q. Ding, Susan T. Dumais, James Allan, Ji-Rong Wen, Charles L. A. Clarke, Chris Buckley, Jian-Yun Nie, and et al. (totally 20)	Jure Leskovec, Ee-Peng Lim, Evimaria Terzi, Jimeng Sun, Jon M. Kleinberg, Jie Tang, Hari Sundaram, Lise Getoor, Yutaka Matsuo, Tina Eliassi-Rad, and et al. (totally 20)

The second experiment is to test whether the top-k recommended papers are referenced by compiled productive authors. We define an accuracy measure *author hit rate* $HitRate_k = AuthorHit_k / N_{test}$, where $AuthorHit_k$ is the number of authors referencing to any of top-k returned papers and N_{test} (=20) is the total testing authors. We compare our method with the approach of pure Random Walk with Restart [5] considering all nodes with query terms as the restarting ones. We set k_s=10 and k_r=10. The experimental results are shown in Figure 2. For IR-query, we can find ours outperforms the RandomWalk approach as the k_r increases. This implies ours provides influential recommendations in IR domain. For SN-query, we find the effectiveness of ours is more distinguished over all k returned. After studying the recommended papers (that is not shown here for space limit), we find that ours precisely suggest social-networked papers while pure RandomWalk is prone to return papers that mix the areas of social network and sensor network mining.

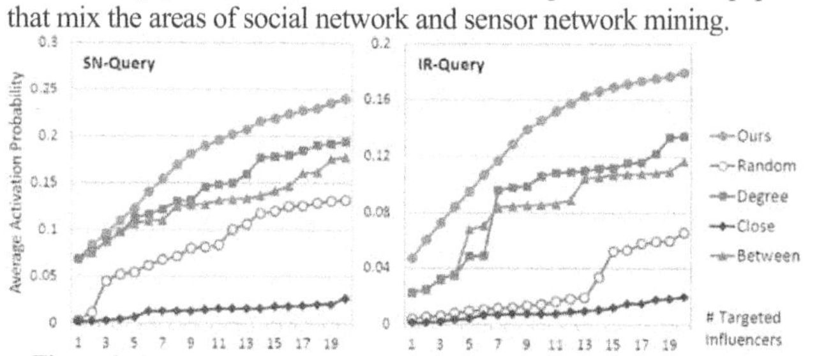

Figure 1. Average activation probability for SN-Query and IR-Query.

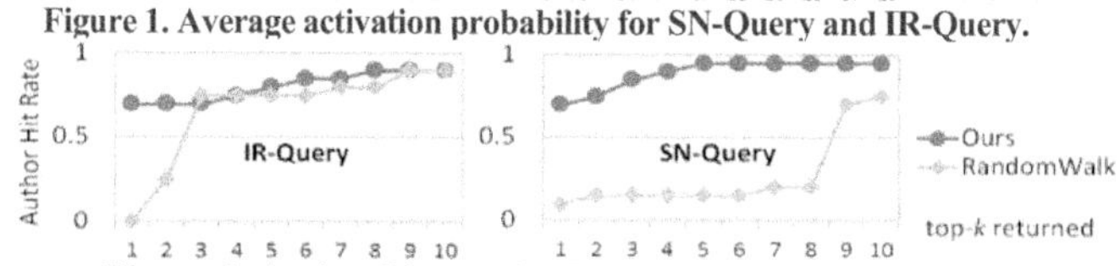

Figure 2. Author hit rate for IR-query and SN-Query.

4. CONCLUSION

We develop a novel recommender, which exploits the information of social and endorsement networks. The central idea is to leverage the concepts of viral marketing and the wisdom of crowds for item recommendation. We devise a greedy method which maximizes a submodular objective function to find the targeted influencers who can effectively activate nodes with query terms in the social network. And then we use the random walk mechanism to recommend items based on the targeted influencers in the endorsement network. Evaluations on academic data show promising results.

5. REFERENCES

[1] I. Guy, N. Zwerdling, L. Ronen, D. Carmel, and E. Uziel. Social Media Recommendation based on People and Tags. In *ACM SIGIR* 2010.

[2] T. Lappas and D. Gunopulos. Interactive Recommendations in Social Endorsement Networks. In *ACM Recommender System* 2010.

[3] D. Kempe, J. Kleinberg, and E. Tardos. Maximizing the Spread of Influence through a Social Network. In *ACM SIGKDD* 2003.

[4] I. Konstas, V. Stathopoulos, and J. M. Jose. On Social Networks and Collaborative Recommendation. In *ACM SIGIR* 2009.

[5] H. Tong, C. Faloutsos, and J. Y. Pan. Fast Random Walk with Restart and Its Applications. In *IEEE ICDM* 2006.

Modeling Subset Distributions for Verbose Queries

Xiaobing Xue W. Bruce Croft
Center for Intelligent Information Retrieval
Computer Science Department
University of Massachusetts, Amherst, MA,
01003, USA
{xuexb,croft}@cs.umass.edu

ABSTRACT

Improving verbose (or long) queries poses a new challenge for search systems. Previous techniques mainly focused on two aspects, weighting the important words or phrases and selecting the best subset query. The former does not consider how words and phrases are used in actual subset queries, while the latter ignores alternative subset queries. Recently, a novel reformulation framework has been proposed to transform the original query as a distribution of reformulated queries, which overcomes the disadvantages of previous techniques. In this paper, we apply this framework to verbose queries, where a reformulated query is specified as a subset query. Experiments on TREC collections show that the query distribution based framework outperforms the state-of-the-art techniques

Categories and Subject Descriptors
H.3.3 [Information Storage and Retrieval]: Information Search and Retrieval

General Terms
Algorithms, Experimentation, Performance

Keywords
Verbose Query, Query Distribution, Query Reformulation

1. INTRODUCTION

Verbose (or long) queries have attracted much attention recently, since they allow users to express their information need using natural languages. However, current search systems can not deal with the verbose query well due to its complexity. Thus, improving verbose queries poses a new challenge for the development of search systems.

Previous techniques on improving verbose queries can be roughly divided into two categories. The first category emphasizes important words and phrases of the original query [6][3][2]. The methods from this category do not consider how those important words and phrases are used together to form actual subset queries therefore missing important relationships between words and phrases. The second category attempts to select the best subset query [5][1]. The methods of this category indeed consider a subset query as a whole, but they mainly focus on picking the best subset query and ignore alternative subset queries.

Recently, a general reformulation framework has been proposed to transform the original query into a distribution of reformulated queries [9]. This framework addresses the disadvantages of previous techniques mentioned above. On one hand, a reformulated query is explicitly modeled in this framework, which helps capture the dependencies between words and phrases that are imposed by actual queries. On the other hand, this framework considers not only the best reformulated query but also other alternatives. In this paper, we apply this general framework to improve verbose queries, where the original verbose query is reformulated as a distribution of subset queries.

Modeling the subset distribution for a verbose query has been first studied by Xue et al [10]. However, they used a fixed parameter to combine the original query with the generated subset distribution. Thus, a principled method that can effectively incorporate the original query and its subset queries within the same distribution is still missing.

2. MODELING SUBSET DISTRIBUTION

In this section, we describe how to model the subset distribution for a verbose query. Formally, given the original verbose query Q, we first construct a set of subset queries $V_{Q_s} = \{Q_s\}$, where Q_s is a subset query extracted from Q. Note that Q also belongs to V_{Q_s}. Then, Q is reformulated as a distribution over V_{Q_s}, i.e. $\mathbf{P}_{Q_s} = \{(P(Q_s|Q)\ Q_s)\}$, where $P(Q_s|Q)$ is the probability assigned to Q_s in the distribution $\mathbf{P}_{Q_s}$. We will describe the generation of V_{Q_s} and the estimation of $P(Q_s|Q)$, respectively.

Following Kumaran and Carvalho [5], only subset queries with the length between three to six words are considered. In addition, we also consider two special subset queries, one is the original query and the other is the key concept discovered in previous work [2]. Furthermore, since the subset queries generated will be finally used for retrieval, it is necessary to indicate the retrieval model used. In this paper, we consider two types of retrieval models, the Query Likelihood Model (QL) [8] and the Sequential Dependency Model (DM) [7].

In order to estimate the probability for each Q_s, we assume $P(Q_s|Q)$ is a linear combination of a variety of query features. These features characterize a subset query as a whole therefore capturing the relationships between words and phrases. Examples of features include various query quality predictors, the number of passages where a subset query has been observed in target corpus and the language model probability returned by Microsoft Web NGram Service. In order to learn the combination parameter for each query feature, we generate the corresponding retrieval feature by calculating the sum of the retrieval scores of using all subset queries weighted by their query feature values. Then, a learning to rank method is used to learn the parameters

SIGIR'11, July 24–28, 2011, Beijing, China.
ACM 978-1-4503-0757-4/11/07.

Table 1: **Example of the subset distribution. For "subset query (n)", n indicates the length.**

Original Query (Q): remedies treatments given lessen stop effects ovarian cancer		AP: 13.53
QDist-QL		AP: 21.02
$P(Q_s\|Q)$	Subset Query(Q_s)	Subset Query Type
0.153	remedies treatments given lessen stop effects ovarian cancer	original query
0.099	remedies treatments ovarian cancer	subset query (4) & key concept
0.046	ovarian cancer	key concept
0.007	remedies treatments stop ovarian cancer	subset query (5)

Table 2: Results of different models.^{q,d,s,k} denotes significantly different with QL (^{q}), DM (^{d}), SRank (^{s}) and KeyConcept (^{k}), respectively.

	Gov2		Robust04	
	MAP	P@10	MAP	P@10
QL	25.43	52.21	25.49	43.13
DM	27.85	54.03	26.83	44.94
SRank	24.99	50.74	24.78	41.57
KeyConcept	27.52	53.83	25.97	41.65
QL+SubQL	26.76	53.15	26.20	43.21
DM+SubQL	28.70	55.37	27.37	**45.14**
QDist-QL	27.41^{qs}	53.42^{s}	26.07^{s}	42.69
QDist-DM	**29.59**^{qdsk}	**55.84**^{qs}	**27.55**^{qsk}	44.94^{qsk}

of these generated retrieval features and these parameters finally serve as the combination parameters of query features. In this paper, a ListNet [4] is used as the learning method.

3. EXPERIMENTS

Two TREC collections (Gov2 and Robust04) are used for experiments. For each collection, the index is built using Indri with Porter Stemmer. For each topic, the description part is used as the query after stopword removal. Mean average precision (MAP) and precision at 10 (P@10) are used to measure the retrieval performance. The two tailed t-test measures significance. The query set is split into a training set and a test set. Ten-fold cross validation is conducted. Two types of subset query distributions are implemented, one uses QL as the retrieval model (QDist-QL) and the other uses DM (QDist-DM). Table 1 shows an example of the subset distribution learned for QDist-QL, which significantly outperforms the original query.

The baselines used include QL, DM, SRank [5], KeyConcept [2] and two methods from Xue et al [10] (QL+SubQL and DM+SubQL). The retrieval performance is displayed in Table 2. The best performance is bolded.

Table 2 shows that QDist-QL is comparable with DM, SRank and KeyConcept, i.e., the state-of-the-art techniques on improving verbose queries. Moreover, QDist-DM significantly outperforms most of the baseline methods and achieves the best performance on both collections. Then, QL+SubQL and DM+SubQL are compared with QDist-QL and QDist-DM, respectively. The difference is that the former uses a fixed parameter to combine the original query with the generated subset distribution, while the latter learns a unified distribution including both the original query and the subset queries. The latter method outperforms the former one on Gov2 and they are comparable on Robust04.

The current subset distribution consists of queries with the mixed length from three to six. It is interesting to explore the fixed-length subset distribution. Table 3 shows the performance of using the fixed-length subset distribution from three to six. "mix" denotes the distribution mixing queries with different lengths.

Table 3 shows that the performance of the fixed-length subset distributions is close to and sometimes even better

Table 3: Retrieval performance of fixed-length subset query distribution.

	Gov2		Robust04	
length	MAP	P@10	MAP	P@10
3	27.39	53.56	26.10	42.65
4	27.33	53.96	25.97	42.33
5	27.09	53.36	25.97	42.09
6	27.21	53.62	26.01	42.09
mix	27.41	53.42	26.07	42.69

than the mixed-length distribution and the length itself does not have much influence. Thus, we can replace the mixed-length subset distribution with the fixed-length distribution, which significantly reduces the number of subset queries in the distribution therefore improving efficiency.

4. CONCLUSION

Modeling the subset distribution for a verbose query helps overcome the disadvantages of previous techniques. A recently proposed framework is used in this paper to learn a unified subset distribution. Experiments on TREC collections show the effectiveness of this method.

Acknowledgments

This work was supported in part by the Center for Intelligent Information Retrieval and in part by ARRA NSF IIS-9014442. Any opinions, findings and conclusions or recommendations expressed in this material are the author's and do not necessarily reflect those of the sponsor.

5. REFERENCES

[1] N. Balasubramanian, G. Kumaran, and V. R. Carvalho. Exploring reductions for long web queries. In *SIGIR10*, pages 571–578.

[2] M. Bendersky and W. B. Croft. Discovering key concepts in verbose queries. In *SIGIR08*, pages 491–498.

[3] M. Bendersky, D. Metzler, and W. B. Croft. Learning concept importance using a weighted dependence model. In *WSDM10*.

[4] Z. Cao, T. Qin, T.-Y. Liu, M.-F. Tsai, and H. Li. Learning to rank: from pairwise approach to listwise approach. In *ICML07*, pages 129–136.

[5] G. Kumaran and V. R. Carvalho. Reducing long queries using query quality predictors. In *SIGIR09*, pages 564–571.

[6] M. Lease, J. Allan, and W. B. Croft. Regression rank: learning to meet the oppotunity of descriptive queries. In *ECIR09*, pages 472–479.

[7] D. Metzler and W. B. Croft. A Markov random field model for term dependencies. In *SIGIR05*, pages 472–479.

[8] J. M. Ponte and W. B. Croft. A language modeling approach to information retrieval. In *SIGIR98*, pages 275–281.

[9] X. Xue and W. B. Croft. Representing queries as distributions. In *SIGIR10 Workshop on Query Representation and Understanding*, pages 9–12.

[10] X. Xue, S. Huston, and W. B. Croft. Improving verbose queries using subset distribution. In *CIKM10*, pages 1059–1068.

Domain Expert Topic Familiarity and Search Behavior

Sarvnaz Karimi
NICTA and Dept of CSSE
The University of Melbourne
skarimi@unimelb.edu.au

Falk Scholer
RMIT University
Melbourne, Australia
falk.scholer@rmit.edu.au

Adam Clark
Alfred Health
Melbourne, Australia
a.clark@alfred.org.au

Sadegh Kharazmi
RMIT University and NICTA
Melbourne, Australia
sadegh.kharazmi@rmit.edu.au

ABSTRACT

Users of information retrieval systems employ a variety of strategies when searching for information. One factor that can directly influence how searchers go about their information finding task is the *level of familiarity* with a search topic. We investigate how the search behavior of domain experts changes based on their previous level of familiarity with a search topic, reporting on a user study of biomedical experts searching for a range of domain-specific material. The results of our study show that topic familiarity can influence the number of queries that are employed to complete a task, the types of queries that are entered, and the overall number of query terms. Our findings suggest that biomedical search systems should enable searching through a variety of querying modes, to support the different search strategies that users were found to employ depending on their familiarity with the information that they are searching for.

Categories and Subject Descriptors

H.3.4 [**Information Storage and Retrieval**]: Systems and Software *Performance evaluation (effectiveness)*

General Terms

Experimentation, Measurement, Performance

Keywords

Search engines, biomedical search, evaluation.

1. INTRODUCTION

Users of biomedical information retrieval systems employ a variety of strategies when searching for documents to satisfy an information need. Search behavior is affected by many different criteria such as topic of the search, the domain within which the search takes place, or the depth of the information need (for example, the user may be looking for comprehensive information on a topic, such as for systematic reviewing, or only looking for a brief answer).

We investigate the impact of *level of topic familiarity* on the search behavior of experts in the biomedical domain. In a controlled user study, 38 participants carried out a series of six search tasks. Our subjects were *experts* that had an educational background in biomedical sciences and related domains. For each task, users were asked to specify their prior familiarity with the topic. Based on this, we analyze how users differed in their formulation of specific queries.

Previous work on the relationship between topic familiarity and search behavior has established that when users are more familiar with a topic, they spend less time on search tasks, and are likely to find a higher number of relevant documents as a proportion of documents viewed [1], users who are more familiar with a topic are also likely to use a more controlled vocabulary when querying [2], search behavior changes when domain knowledge increases [4], and the level of expertise of the user can have a substantial impact on how their searches are conducted when carrying out searches in the biomedical domain [3]. White *et al.* [3] carried out a large-scale log-analysis where users were divided into expert and non-expert groups. In our study, all the users were experts in the domain, but their degree of familiarity with topics — explicitly collected from our subjects — varied based on their occupation or educational background.

2. EXPERIMENTAL DESIGN

To investigate the impact of topic familiarity on search behavior, we carried out a user study. Participants were recruited through advertisements in the staff and student mailing lists of Alfred Hospital, and Melbourne University. All were experts in the biomedical domain, from a variety of backgrounds. All participants had prior experience in carrying out electronic searches for information, although the frequency of this varied; more than half of the participants reported carrying out searches on at least a weekly basis.

Participants were asked to carry out informational searches for a series of six provided information needs. The search topics were all in the biomedical domain, and selected from a list of search tasks that had previously been referred to health librarians in the library of Alfred Hospital. Each task involved a complex relationship, for example "exercise therapy for cystic fibrosis". The searches were framed in a task scenario, with participants being asked to imagine that they needed to write a short report about each given topic, their goal being to carry out searches to find useful articles that they would want to read in order to prepare their report.

Searches were conducted using an in-house biomedical retrieval system, modeled on the interface of PubMed. All searches were run over the MEDLINE collection of biomedical journal article citations, as published by the US National Library of Medicine. Citations which did not contain an abstract were excluded from the experiments.

SIGIR'11, July 24–28, 2011, Beijing, China.
ACM 978-1-4503-0757-4/11/07.

	Tasks	Queries entered	Ranked queries	Boolean queries	Complex Boolean	Total query terms	Result pages viewed	Items saved
Not familiar	147	438 (2.98)	154 (1.05)	271 (1.84)	13 (0.09)	1840 (13.24)	494 (3.36)	999 (6.80)
Familiar	71	204 (2.87)	51 (0.72)	148 (2.08)	5 (0.07)	960 (15.92)	253 (3.56)	425 (5.99)
Very familiar	10	14 (1.40)	5 (0.50)	9 (0.90)	0 (0.00)	92 (9.20)	28 (2.80)	57 (5.70)
χ^2		8.1	7.65	6.8	1.02	13.8	2.5	5.8
p-value		0.0172	0.0184	0.0334	0.6511	0.001	0.2801	0.0535

Table 1: Difference in search behavior by familiarity with task. The table shows the sum for each category, with the mean indicated in parentheses. Reported p-values are for a χ^2 goodness-of-fit test (calculated by Monte Carlo simulation for categories that have ≤ 5 observations).

3. FAMILIARITY AND SEARCH BEHAVIOR

The 38 participants in our user study carried out six search tasks each, giving a total of 228 tasks. After being presented with a topic, but before carrying out any searches, each participant was asked to indicate their prior familiarity with the topic on a 3 point scale: not familiar; familiar; or very familiar. As shown in the first column of Table 1, the level of familiarity across topics and participants is skewed, with 147 instances where there was no prior familiarity, and 10 instances of the topic being very familiar. These proportions therefore give a baseline against which other aspects of search behavior can be analyzed. Since the aspects of behavior to be analyzed are in the form of count data, a χ^2 goodness-of-fit test is used to evaluate the statistical significance of observed differences. To make the trends easier to interpret, we also report the mean values for each category.

The number of queries that users entered when carrying out a search session varied with their level of topic familiarity, as shown in column 2 of Table 1: for topics with a very high level of familiarity, users entered 1.4 queries on average, while topics with which users were not familiar led to an average of 3 queries ($p = 0.0172$).

Queries were also analyzed by the *mode* employed by users: ranked queries (a list of keywords with no special operators); Boolean queries (single line queries that employed at least one of the AND, OR and NOT operators); and complex Boolean queries (which made use of multi-line Boolean expressions, or employed advanced operators provided by many biomedical search systems such as specifying the field of a citation in which a term must occur). The number of ranked or Boolean queries employed by searchers varies significantly with the level of familiarity; note, however, that the relative popularity of query modes also varies, for example, for very familiar topics, a ranked query is only used for every second search topic, on average. Complex Boolean queries were very rarely used.

The total number of query terms used to carry out a search task also varies significantly with the level of topic familiarity, as shown in column six of the table. For very familiar topics, users employ fewer query terms across a search session, compared with topics for which they are only somewhat familiar or unfamiliar.

The number of individual search result pages viewed by users is shown in column seven (the experimental search system displayed 10 answers per page, with users being able to navigate through the larger answer set). There was no significant relationship between prior familiarity and the number of result pages viewed.

Task success can be measured by the number of items that a user selected as being useful for the information need (in the context of the user study, these are documents that the user would have liked to read in full before writing their report on the search topic). The differences in the number of items saved does not vary significantly with topic familiarity.

4. DISCUSSION

Users of search systems in the biomedical domain differ in their searching behavior depending on their prior familiarity with a search topic. Users enter substantially fewer queries during a search session when they are more familiar with a topic. These trends hold across both ranked and Boolean query types. However, the relative popularity for Boolean queries is highest when users are at least somewhat familiar with the topic, while for ranked queries the maximum occurs when the topic is not familiar. The total number of query terms that users submit in a search session also varies significantly with their level of prior topic familiarity; substantially fewer query terms are entered when a user is highly familiar with a topic. On the other hand, the number of results pages that are viewed does not vary significantly with familiarity; users are prepared to look through similar numbers of results, but require fewer queries to find them when they are more familiar with the topic area.

Even when people are experts within a domain, their level of familiarity with individual topics can vary. Our results indicate that topic familiarity can substantially impact on the search behavior of users of biomedical search systems, both in the number of queries and query terms entered, but also in the preferred querying mode that is employed.

Acknowledgements: NICTA is funded by the Australian government as represented by Department of Broadband, Communication and Digital Economy, and the Australian Research Council through the ICT centre of Excellence programme. We thank A. Bromage, L. Cavedon, D. Newman, S. Pohl, and L. Yencken for their scientific input and technical support.

5. REFERENCES

[1] D. Kelly and C. Cool. The effects of topic familiarity on information search behavior. In *JCDL*, pages 74–75, Portland, Oregon, 2002.

[2] A. Shiri. Topic familiarity and its effects on term selection and browsing in a thesaurus-enhanced search environment. *Library Review*, 54(9):514–518, 2005.

[3] R. W. White, S. T. Dumais, and J. Teevan. Characterizing the influence of domain expertise on web search behavior. In *WSDM*, pages 132–141, Barcelona, Spain, 2009.

[4] B. Wildemuth. The effects of domain knowledge on search tactic formulation. *JASIST*, 55(3):246–258, 2004.

Sample Selection for Dictionary-Based Corpus Compression

Christopher Hoobin, Simon Puglisi
School of Computer Science & Information Technology
RMIT University, Australia
firstname.lastname@rmit.edu.au

Justin Zobel
Department of Computer Science & Software Engineering
University of Melbourne, Australia
jzobel@unimelb.edu.au

ABSTRACT

Compression of large text corpora has the potential to drastically reduce both storage requirements and per-document access costs. Adaptive methods used for general-purpose compression are ineffective for this application, and historically the most successful methods have been based on word-based dictionaries, which allow use of global properties of the text. However, these are dependent on the text complying with assumptions about content and lead to dictionaries of unpredictable size. In recent work we have described an LZ-like approach in which sampled blocks of a corpus are used as a dictionary against which the complete corpus is compressed, giving compression twice as effective than that of *zlib*. Here we explore how pre-processing can be used to eliminate redundancy in our sampled dictionary. Our experiments show that dictionary size can be reduced by 50% or more (less than 0.1% of the collection size) with no significant effect on compression or access speed.

Categories and Subject Descriptors

E.4 [**Data**]: Coding and Information Theory – *data compaction and compression*; H.3.3 [**Information Storage and Retrieval**]: Information Search and Retrieval – *search process*

General Terms

Algorithms, Performance

Keywords

Dictionary Compression, Random Access, Document Retrieval, Sampling

1. BACKGROUND

Corpus compression can dramatically improve the efficiency of an information retrieval system, first by reducing storage and second by reducing the cost of disk seek and read operations. There are further benefits in improved bandwidth between levels of the memory hierarchy and more effective caching [6]. Key features of an effective algorithm are that the compression model needs to be determined globally (that is, is the same for all documents in the corpus) and that documents can be independently decoded.

A traditional approach is to use a semistatic model, where symbols are words that are assigned codes based on their probability distribution [5]. With natural language texts, use of words as symbols and of word–non-word alternation gives good compression, but depends on a definition of "word" that does not lead to excessive numbers of low-value symbols (such as strings of markup) and identifies "words" in the text that have a sufficiently skew distribution. Also, the map of symbols to codeword can easily grow larger than physical memory and the symbol set may be dominated by long arbitrary strings.

The most widely used general-purpose compression methods use adaptive LZ-based algorithms such as *deflate*, *zlib*, or *lzma* [2]. These exploit local duplication in a text through the use of a sliding window that acts a dictionary, with replacement of substrings by pointers to previous occurrences in the dictionary. These approaches require that decompression commence only at the start of the text or at synchronization points, with a trade-off between access speed and compression effectiveness. No use is made of global properties of the corpus. However, these kinds of methods are used by Lucene and Indri, and a similar method is described for Google's distributed storage system Bigtable [1].

In recent work we have described how to use LZ-like coding, but with a fixed external dictionary rather than a sliding window [3, 4]. The Lempel-Ziv factorization of a string x relative to a dictionary d is a factorization, $x = w_1 w_2 \dots w_k$, such that each w_i is either the longest matching substring in d, or a character c that does not occur in d. Each w_i is represented as a pair (p_i, l_i), where p_i specifies a offset to a position in d and l_i denotes the length of the factor in d. If $l_i = 0$, p_i contains a character c that does not occur in d. Well-known methods can be used to efficiently represent the $\langle p_i, l_i \rangle$ pairs. We have shown this technique to be highly effective for compressing collections of related genomes [4] and large web collections [3], outperforming all other methods tested. As our experiments focus on document retrieval, our RLZ implementation is designed to stop factorization at document boundaries.

2. REDUNDANCY ELIMINATION

Key to the effectiveness of such a method is that the dictionary be a representative sample of a collection. The aim is to capture global repetition across a collection that adaptive compression algorithms do not detect. We used an ex-

SIGIR'11, July 24–28, 2011, Beijing, China.
ACM 978-1-4503-0757-4/11/07.

tremely simple approach in which we treated a collection as a single string and took samples of lengths s (say 1024 bytes) at evenly-sized intervals across the collection (with m of say 0.5 Gb or 1.0 Gb). That is, we take m/s samples from $n/(m/s)$ locations, on the assumption (which our experiments confirmed) that any sufficiently frequent material in the corpus would be captured in this process.

However, although compression effectiveness was high, we observed that a significant percentage of the dictionaries was unused. There was a strong skew in the samples that were used, and, even amongst these, there was redundancy as some samples contained repeated material.

Such redundancy can be removed in a pre-processing phase, either to reduce memory footprint or to replace samples. For each encoded RLZ pair we incremented a counter corresponding to the sample the factor occurred in. Once the pairs have been processed we sorted the samples by frequency and generated a new dictionary comprised of the most frequently used entries, stopping when we reached a specific usage threshold or byte limit. Such an approach, although simple, gives explicit control of memory use and should maximize compression effectiveness for a given number of samples.

Results are shown in the tables. Dictionaries were generated from Clueweb09 256 Gb Wikipedia corpus. We generated samples as discussed above, and then pruned them to give a fixed-size dictionary. As can be seen, halving dictionary size led to a small increase in encoding size.

Even at a ten-fold reduction in dictionary size, compression and document access was still better than with *zlib*. We observed consistent access speeds of over 100 documents per second simulating document requests for a typical IR system. These requests were generated from ranked listings using the first 5000 queries of TREC's MQ09 query-log. The top 20 ranked documents were used for each query. This is more than double the speed of access to uncompressed documents, or to documents compressed with *zlib* and *lzma* in block groups of varied size. Sequential decompression runs at around 10,000 documents per second, a significant increase in access speed compared to our two baseline implementations.

Experiments were conducted on a 3.0 GHz Intel Xeon processor with 4Gb RAM running a Linux Kernel 2.6.18 and compiled with GCC 4.1.2 using full optimizations. Caches were dropped between each run. All timing results were recorded as wall clock time. Compressed collections used for evaluation are significantly larger than internal memory, so our timings account for disk seek and read latency as they are the dominant cost in document retrieval.

Our earlier results showed that RLZ is the method of choice for compressing a large corpus. It gives excellent compression, fast retrieval, and can be easily modified for a dynamic environment. In this work we have shown that the dictionary size can be substantially reduced without loss of efficiency.

3. REFERENCES

[1] F. Chang, J. Dean, S. Ghemawat, W. C. Hsieh, D. A. Wallach, M. Burrows, T. Chandra, A. Fikes, and R. E. Gruber. Bigtable: A distributed storage system for structured data. *ACM Transactions Computer Systems*, 26(2):1–26, June 2008.

Table 1: Sequential and Query-log results in documents/second for levels of redundancy elimination with 0.5 Gb, 1.0 Gb and 2.0 Gb RLZ dictionaries, using 1 Kb samples on a 256 Gb Wikipedia corpus.

Orig. (GB)	New. (GB)	Enc. (%)	Sequential	Query log
0.5	-	12.74	10406.33	120.38
0.5	0.4	12.78	9820.51	118.04
0.5	0.2	14.63	8613.01	120.86
0.5	0.1	18.02	7519.87	114.50
1.0	-	11.04	11540.16	123.51
1.0	0.5	12.02	10603.05	121.99
1.0	0.2	16.28	7334.68	113.78
1.0	0.1	19.30	6653.83	109.40
2.0	-	9.47	14602.09	123.54
2.0	1.0	10.04	12220.75	125.00
2.0	0.5	13.19	9384.42	112.52
2.0	0.2	17.00	7235.04	110.43
2.0	0.1	19.58	6362.05	112.53

Table 2: Sequential and Query-log results in documents/second for baseline ASCII and blocked LZ runs on a 256 Gb Wikipedia corpus. A block size of 0.0 denotes that a single document was stored in each block.

Alg.	Block (MB)	Enc. (%)	Sequential	Query Log
ascii	-	100.00	2093.22	50.44
zlib	0.0	24.13	2610.56	98.48
zlib	0.1	20.54	1690.13	90.00
zlib	0.2	19.38	902.98	80.24
zlib	0.5	18.66	355.73	64.35
zlib	1.0	18.43	172.56	48.63
lzma	0.0	22.33	604.53	93.19
lzma	0.1	17.24	437.68	86.90
lzma	0.2	14.29	271.41	79.36
lzma	0.5	11.92	123.67	55.12
lzma	1.0	10.81	65.62	32.76

[2] P. Ferragina and G. Manzini. On compressing the textual web. In *Proc. 3rd ACM International Conference on Web Search and Data Mining (WSDM'10)*, pages 391–400, New York, NY, USA, 2010. ACM.

[3] C. Hoobin, S. Puglisi, and J. Zobel. Relative Lempel-Ziv compression for fast random access (manuscript).

[4] S. Kuruppu, S. Puglisi, and J. Zobel. Relative Lempel-Ziv compression of genomes for large-scale storage and retrieval. In *Proc. 17th Symposium on String Processing and Information Retrieval (SPIRE'10)*, pages 201–206. Springer, 2010.

[5] I. H. Witten, A. Moffat, and T. C. Bell. *Managing Gigabytes: Compressing and Indexing Documents and Images, Second Edition.* Morgan Kaufmann, 1999.

[6] N. Ziviani, E. S. de Moura, G. Navarro, and R. Baeza-Yates. Compression: A key for next-generation text retrieval systems. *Computer*, 33:37–44, 2000.

Evaluating Medical Information Retrieval

Bevan Koopman*
Australian e-Health Research Centre, CSIRO
bevan.koopman@csiro.au

Peter Bruza
Queensland University of Technology
p.bruza@qut.edu.au

Laurianne Sitbon
Queensland University of Technology
sitbon@qut.edu.au

Michael Lawley
Australian e-Health Research Centre, CSIRO
michael.lawley@csiro.au

ABSTRACT

This paper presents a framework for evaluating information retrieval of medical records. We use the BLULab corpus, a large collection of real-world de-identified medical records. The collection has been hand coded by clinical terminologists using the ICD-9 medical classification system. The ICD codes are used to devise queries and relevance judgements for this collection. Results of initial test runs using a baseline IR system show that there is room for improvement in medical information retrieval. Queries and relevance judgements are made available at `http://aehrc.com/med_eval`.

Categories and Subject Descriptors

H.3 [**Information Storage and Retrieval**]: H.3.3 Information Search and Retrieval

General Terms

Experimentation, Measurement

Keywords

Medical Information Retrieval, Evaluation

1. INTRODUCTION

With the advent of electronic medical records and the continued increase of medical documents online (e.g. MEDLINE) there is an increasing need for information retrieval systems tailored to searching medical free-text [1]. Searching medical records presents some specific challenges. For example the presence of an organism in a laboratory test might lead a human being to conclude a certain disease, even though this is not stated explicitly. Furthermore, a user formulating a query might specify the active ingredient of a pharmaceutical, whereas the patient record might only state the brand name of a drug containing that ingredient [2]. We require IR systems capable of bridging the 'semantic gap' – overcoming the mismatch between the terms found in documents and the terms used in queries.

*Also Queensland University of Technology.

Another challenge for medical IR is empirical evaluation. To our knowledge no standardised evaluation framework exists. There is no test collection with associated queries and relevance judgements specific to medical records. Although there are biomedical test collections (e.g. TREC Genomics Track), these differ from medical records in that they focus specifically on identifying genes and associated diseases.

Our contributions to medical information retrieval are: (i) development of an evaluation framework using real world (de-identified) medical records (ii) collection of queries extracted from the medical records using the standard ICD-9 medical code terminology (iii) relevance judgements devised from human classified ICD-9 medical records (iv) results of initial test runs on the collection using a baseline state-of-the-art IR system.

2. MEDICAL CORPUS & HUMAN TAGGING

Our test corpus is the BLULab NLP repository[1], a collection of 81,617 de-identified clinical records from multiple U.S. hospitals during 2007. The collection is available to the community for research purposes. A number of different medical record types are provided, including: History and Physical Exams, Progress Notes, Consultation Reports, Radiology Reports, Emergency Department Reports, Discharge Summaries, Operative Reports, Cardiology Reports.

Each record has been coded by professional clinical terminologists using the ICD-9 classification system. ICD (International Statistical Classification of Diseases and Related Health Problems) is a coding of diseases, symptoms, abnormal findings, complaints, social circumstances and external causes of injury, as classified by the World Health Organisation. These ICD codes are used to extract queries and relevance judgements.

3. EVALUATION ARCHITECTURE

The process for developing a test set of queries and relevance judgements is illustrated in Figure 1. The steps required are:

❶ For each medical record (document) we extract the ICD codes assigned to that record;
❷ Each ICD code is considered an individual query, the

[1]BLULab provided by University of Pittsburgh, available online: `http://nlp.dbmi.pitt.edu/nlprepository.html`

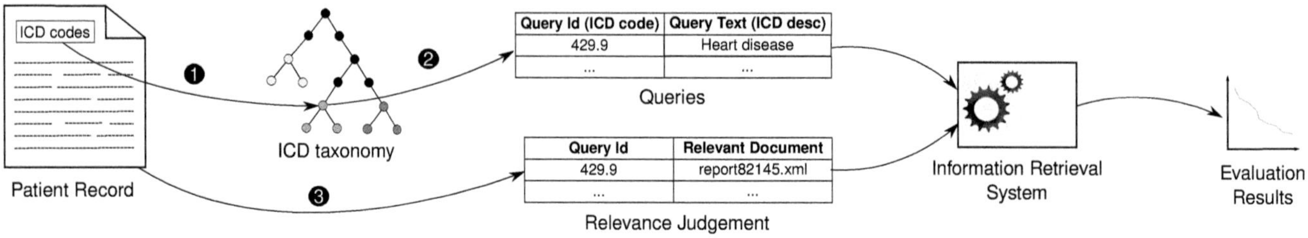

Figure 1: Evaluation architecture for BLULab collection.

Run	Documents used	Docs	Queries	MAP	Precision @5	Precision @10	Precision @20
A	All.	89268	3500	0.0485	0.1249	**0.1085**	**0.0918**
B	Discharge Summaries, History & Physical Exams, Emergency Department Reports. No laboratory based reports.	33671	3434	0.0817	0.1263	0.1072	0.0877
C	Discharge Summaries.	7837	2841	0.1322	0.1234	0.0983	0.0766
D	Discharge Summaries (excluding non-clinical queries).	7837	2420	**0.1445**	**0.1347**	0.1074	0.0834
E	Discharge Summaries, queries mapped to SNOMED CT.	7837	2489	0.1123	0.1075	0.0873	0.0697

Table 1: Experimental retrieval results for the BLULab NLP collection using ICD codes as gold standard.

query id is the ICD code id and the query text is the ICD code description as defined in the ICD taxonomy;

❸ The ICD code and record filename are then added to the relevance judgement file.

Queries length ranged from 1 to 98 words with an average of 18 words. Each query had on average 231 relevance judgements. Average document length was 365 words.

The ICD terminology is primarily used by hospitals for administrative and billing purposes. Consequently, there were initially a number of limitations as a result of both the characteristics of the ICD terminology and the manner in which terminologists assign codes to documents:

Granularity of coding Choice of ICD code is highly dependent on the diseases being described. For example general respiratory diagnoses codes are typically used rather than a more specific code, even though one exists. Conversely, certain high level codes such as "Kidney" (`198.0`) are hardly used as the terminologist would favour the use of a code specific to a disease. This affects the quality of relevance judgements.

ICD term hierarchy ICD codes in the form `XXX.XX` can only be understood in the context of their parent, e.g. "Septicemia" (`038`) has a child "Other" (`038.49`). "Other" obviously cannot be used as the query text for our evaluation so in these cases the query is formed by concatenation of the parent and child, thus forming "Septicemia Other".

4. INITIAL RESULTS

Using the evaluation framework described we provide the results of a number of baseline experiments on the BLULab corpus. Experiments were conducted on the entire corpus and on a number of subsets. The results presented in Table 1 were obtained with the Indri search engine, Porter stemmer and tf-idf term weighting, which performed better in comparison to a state-of-the-art BM25 system.

Run A, using all the documents, resulted in very low performance. This can be attributed in part to the many laboratory reports which contain little or no natural language. Excluding these documents in Run B improved results. Run C used only Discharge Summaries which represent a good overview of the patient encounter, using only these documents again improved performance. Run D excluded ICD codes of type "E" and "V" which are administrative rather than clinical in nature. Run E mapped ICD codes to SNOMED CT, a formal ontology for medical knowledge. This was done to determine whether SNOMED CT had better concept descriptions for use as query text.

In short, our framework provides a meaningful evaluation of medical IR. The low performance prompted some manual review which reaffirmed the challenges in medical IR, specifically the 'semantic gap' that exists between queries and documents. Bridging this gap involves more than matching keywords, it requires inference. The results also show plenty of scope for future work and strong motivation for a semantic search approach to medical information retrieval.

5. CONCLUSIONS

An evaluation framework for medical IR is provided using a human classified corpus of de-identified medical records. Queries and relevance judgements are devised from the human assigned ICD-9 codes. Initial results from test runs using a state-of-art baseline IR system show there is room for improvement and future work. Our queries and relevance judgements are available for other researches in medical information retrieval at `http://aehrc.com/med_eval`.

6. REFERENCES

[1] W. Hersh. *Information retrieval: a health and biomedical perspective.* Springer Verlag, New York, 2009.

[2] C. Patel, J. Cimino, J. Dolby, A. Fokoue, A. Kalyanpur, A. Kershenbaum, L. Ma, E. Schonberg, and K. Srinivasclass. Matching patient records to clinical trials using ontologies. *The Semantic Web*, 4825:816–829, 2007.

Region-Based Landmark Discovery by Crowdsourcing Geo-Referenced Photos

Yen-Ta Huang†, An-Jung Cheng†, Liang-Chi Hsieh†, Winston Hsu†, Kuo-Wei Chang‡

†National Taiwan University, Taipei, Taiwan ‡Chunghwa Telecom Co., Ltd., Taipei, Taiwan

ABSTRACT

We propose a novel model for landmark discovery that locates region-based landmarks on map in contrast to the traditional point-based landmarks. The proposed method preserves more information and automatically identifies candidate regions on map by crowdsourcing geo-referenced photos. Gaussian kernel convolution is applied to remove noises and generate detected region. We adopt F1 measure to evaluate discovered landmarks and manually check the association between tags and regions. The experiment results show that more than 90% of attractions in the selected city can be correctly located by this method.

Categories and Subject Descriptors

H.3.3 [**Information Storage and Retrieval**]: Information Search and Retrieval – *Information filtering*

General Terms

Experimentation, Human Factors.

Keywords

Region-based, crowdsourcing, geo-referenced photo.

1. INTRODUCTION

It is well observed that photo-sharing on Internet became a common behavior. These users upload photos with associated extra information (e.g. tags, geo-tags) to social websites such as Flickr. Recently many researchers leverage such freely available community-contributed photos to devise novel applications such as photo annotation and travel recommendation.

Related works such as [1] propose to locate landmarks on map with a point-based model which denotes a landmark as a circle or a point. For example, Fig. 1-b shows the famous landmark "Central Park" in Manhattan by several points. Such point-based model is limited since sampling by fixed (sometimes noisy) points.

In this work, we propose a novel region-based model for landmark discovery that locates landmarks with estimated regions on maps as Fig. 1(a). Compared with [1] which uses mean-shift (clustering) method and mines descriptive terms for landmarks from photo tags, our method uses the landmark candidate tags (e.g. "central park," mined automatically) to retrieve geo-referenced photos attached with these tags, and then estimates landmark boundaries. We can further associate the candidate tags with the automatically discovered regions (cf. Fig. 1(a)).

The basic assumption is that photos taken in the landmark can approximate the landmark region. To prove this assumption, we investigate the association between tags and locations. We found that the majority of photos in the cities are tagged with the names (or synonyms) of landmarks, but surely we also have to trim the

SIGIR'11, July 24–28, 2011, Beijing, China.
ACM 978-1-4503-0757-4/11/07.

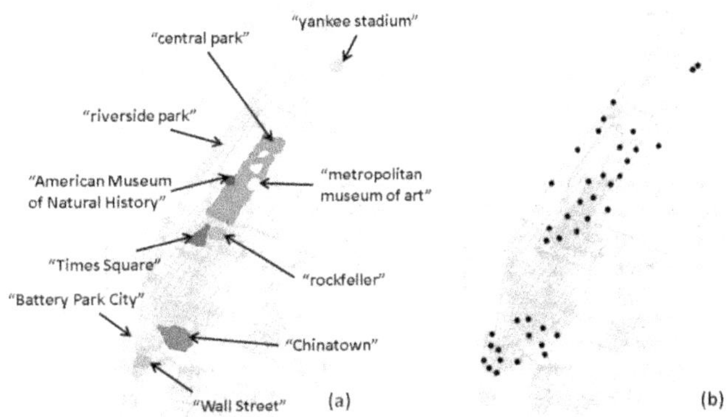

Figure 1: Region-based vs. point-based method. (a) The 10 major landmark regions and associated tags automatically discovered by the proposed method. (b) Point-based landmarks by mean-shift clustering suggested in prior work (e.g. [1]). Take "Central Park" and "Riverside Park" as examples. The two are rectangular and long-strip but identified correctly in our system, while are several random points in (b). Note that both results are based on the same geo-referenced photo collection.

wrongly tagged photos. To remove these noises, we use a Gaussian kernel, and set a cutting threshold as a filter. After filtering, we can automatically estimate the landmark region. Our evaluation shows that this method works well on landmark discovery, especially for large-region landmarks. For New York City and Taipei, more than 90% of the attractions can be found within the right place. Because the detected region depends on crowdsourcing tags, it can also give the reference boundaries of non-rigid attractions, such as trails, night markets, and those boundaries are difficult to define with point-based methods.

2. METHODS AND MATERIALS

2.1 Dataset

Our dataset is consisted of geo-tagged photos retrieved using Flickr API for the major cities including Manhattan, Taipei, Tokyo, London, Paris, Berlin, and San Francisco. We locate and download the photos, along with their metadata (e.g. tags, geo-tag, timestamp, and photographer), whose geo-locations are within the boundaries of these cities. Each city region can be determined by Geoname website and then treated as *city map* (cf. Fig. 2).

2.2 Methodology

Gaussian Kernel Our system retrieves the photo set whose tags contain the names of candidates which can be either given by users or mined from tags. We illustrate those retrieved photos as points with their corresponding coordinates in the *city map* as Fig. 2 shows (before convolution); there are one or more dense areas and some noises. Next we apply Gaussian kernel convolution to remove the noises. The kernel is 2-D by Gaussian distribution. K_{size} (kernel is a $K_{size} \times K_{size}$ matrix) and σ (standard deviation) are the parameters of kernel. We have conducted the sensitivity

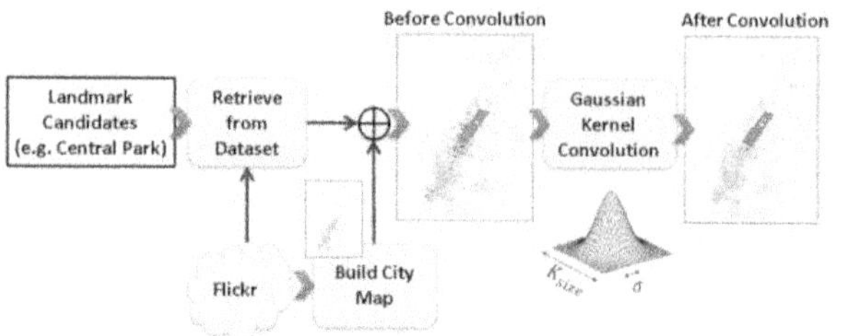

Figure 2: System Diagram

test for the parameters on some landmark attractions. We find that large kernel size is better for large regions, and vice versa.

Region Segmentation The next step is to decide the region threshold to locate the estimated regions, seeded with the retrieved geo-referenced photos. Define $threshold_{cut} = \alpha_t \times MAX(I_g)$, where I_g is the city map pixel value after convolution; we suggest α_t as $1/(K_{size} - 1)$, which considers region connectivity for optimizing segmentation. The detected region is the area with pixel values greater than the threshold. For sensitivity test, we use full-search method, and see how region detection score varies with parameters. σ affects scores limitedly compared with K_{size}. The best kernel size depends on the shape of region that we want to locate, but it is not practical to assume what the shape is. As we find in the experiments, this method works better on large landmark regions, because it can detect more precise boundaries with more geo-referenced photos provided within the regions.

For boosting detection performance, we also include region segmentation algorithms such as graph cut and even consider Google map image coherences. However, the further adopted methods do not further improve the performance.

Candidate Tag Selection We locate landmark candidate terms from the noisy tags associated with geo-referenced photos by two-step method. The first step is a weak filter in combination of date, frequency, and author number. The second step is the boundary information mentioned as above. Assume that salient landmarks should satisfy two conditions: (a) the number of detected regions should only be few; (b) these detected regions should not be dispersed. Therefore, we reject the false landmark terms by the number of detected regions. We divide the city map into grids. The grids associated with the detected regions should be located within 8-neighbor to satisfy the condition (b). We find about 80% of mined candidates is exact the name of attractions. The other 20% are events, abbreviations, and characteristics of the landmark.

3. EXPERIMENTAL EVALUATION

574K photos for Manhattan and 227K photos for Taipei from Flickr. To evaluate the results, it is necessary to define the ground-truth region, which is from Wikimapia with manually annotated regions by amateurs. We also apply the region images on Google Map to verify the results. Measure terms are defined as:

$$Recall = \frac{R_d \cap R_g}{R_d}; Precision = \frac{R_d \cap R_g}{R_g}; F1 = \frac{2 \times Recall \times Precision}{(Recall + Precision)}$$

R_d is the detected region; R_g is the ground-truth region, and $\cap$ is intersection operator. Top10 attractions come from Yahoo! Travel.

Because we cannot estimate precision and recall for point-based method (c.f. Fig. 1-b), we do not compare it with our method. Using circles with points as the centers in order to denote regions on maps is not practical as it is difficult to decide the proper radius for those circles. We even find some points of point-based method are not in the correct regions due to unstable clustering.

Table 1: Top 10 Landmarks in Manhattan and segmentation accuracy (by F1 measure).

Landmarks	F1	Landmarks	F1
Times Square	0.5380	Central Park	0.8436
St. Patrick's Cathedral	0.2857	Statue of Liberty	N/A*
Metropolitan Museum of Art	0.5266	Greenwich Village	0.7293
Yankee Stadium	0.6055	Brooklyn Bridge	0.1081
Chinatown	0.5351	Chrysler Building	0.1579

Table 2: Top 10 Landmarks in Taipei. For both tables, the major landmarks are with satisfying segmentation accuracy (F1 >0.5).

Landmarks	F1	Landmarks	F1
Taipei 101	0.2157	Tamshui Ferry Terminal	N/A*
Martyrs' Shrine	0.4554	Democracy Memorial Hall	0.8546
Yangming Park	N/A*	Sun Yat Sen Memorial Hall	0.8414
Shilin Night Market	0.5667	SOGO Taipei Store	0.5714
Tavern	?	Taipei City Zoo	0.6181

The experiment results are shown in Table 1. The "Statue of Liberty" is out of our city map. There are some landmarks in Table 1 with low F1. The main reason is the photographing behavior. People usually take photos of landmark "Brooklyn Bridge" when standing on the next bridge called "Manhattan Bridge." Another case is "Chrysler Building," a skyscraper. This kind of landmark can be seen from everywhere in the city. Besides, there is no large plaza existing in front of "St. Patrick's Cathedral," so people like to take photos of it across the street.

The results for Taipei are shown in Table 2. "Tamshui Ferry Terminal" and "Yangming Park" are not in the range of the investigated city map. We found that the ground-truth of "Tavern" is wrong. We check the Google Map by human and confirm that the estimated region by our method is correct. "Taipei 101" is a skyscraper too and thus suffers from a low F1 measure.

Observed from Table 1 and 2, we know that the association between region and attraction name is 100% in accuracy. Because if the association is wrong, the recall should be 0 (i.e., F1=0). It shows that our system can associate landmarks with correct tags.

Next, we want to justify the number of attractions that our system can locate, so we crawl attraction lists from Wiki-travel. We obtain 54 attractions for Manhattan, and 46 attractions for Taipei. 94% (51 of 54) from Manhattan can be found in the identified landmarks; 91% (42 of 46) from Taipei.

4. FUTURE WORK AND CONCLUSION

Compared with Wikimapia which is labor-intensive on tagging locations, our system can automatically and dynamically detect quality regions of interesting locations based on the freely available geo-referenced photos, Meanwhile, more than 90% of popular attractions can still be found within the right places by the proposed method. Such boundary information is very helpful for related applications such as tag mining, auto annotation, tour guide or recommendation. We also identify certain ways to improve, these emerging methods such as dealing with the photos taken inside buildings, photos of tall buildings, and the locations people cannot approach to take photos..

5. REFERENCES

[1] Crandall et al. Mapping the World's Photos. WWW 2009.

[2] Zhang et al. Tour the world: Building a web-scale landmark recognition engine. CVPR 2009.

[3] Singh et al. Social Pixels: Genesis and Evaluation. ACM MM 2010.

Towards Effective Short Text Deep Classification

Xinruo Sun
Apex Data & Knowledge Management Lab
Shanghai Jiao Tong University
Shanghai, China
xrsun@apex.sjtu.edu.cn

Haofen Wang
Apex Data & Knowledge Management Lab
Shanghai Jiao Tong University
Shanghai, China
whfcarter@apex.sjtu.edu.cn

Yong Yu
Apex Data & Knowledge Management Lab
Shanghai Jiao Tong University
Shanghai, China
yyu@apex.sjtu.edu.cn

ABSTRACT

Recently, more and more short texts (e.g., ads, tweets) appear on the Web. Classifying short texts into a large taxonomy like ODP or Wikipedia category system has become an important mining task to improve the performance of many applications such as contextual advertising and topic detection for micro-blogging. In this paper, we propose a novel multi-stage classification approach to solve the problem. First, explicit semantic analysis is used to add more features for both short texts and categories. Second, we leverage information retrieval technologies to fetch the most relevant categories for an input short text from thousands of candidates. Finally, a SVM classifier is applied on only a few selected categories to return the final answer. Our experimental results show that the proposed method achieved significant improvements on classification accuracy compared with several existing state of art approaches.

Categories and Subject Descriptors

H.3.3 [**Information Storage and Retrieval**]: Retrieval Models

General Terms

Algorithm

Keywords

short text, classification, large scale hierarchy

1. INTRODUCTION

In recent years, with the emergence of the Social Web, more and more short texts such as ads, tags and tweets are generated and consumed by web applications and users. Classifying short texts into a large taxonomy like ODP or Wikipedia category system has become an important mining task to improve the performance of many applications such as contextual advertising and topic detection for micro-blogging. However, this task faces two main challenges. Firstly, the information is expressed in very short text, which results in feature sparseness. Secondly, categories at deep levels of a large taxonomy usually have too few documents to train a classifier with satisfactory performance using statistical learning.

SIGIR'11, July 24–28, 2011, Beijing, China.
ACM 978-1-4503-0757-4/11/07.

There are two categories of research work related to our task: short text classification and deep classification. The former tries to deal with the feature sparseness issue by leveraging feature expansion while it only proves its effectivess when on a limited number of categories. A repesentiative example[3] classifies tweets into News, Events, Opinions, Deals and Private Messages. The latter category aims at preserving acceptable accuracy when facing a large-scale taxonomy. As mentioned in a report of a recent competition on deep classification[2], all participants focused on large hierarchies instead of situations when the length of textual content is short or categories contain few documents inside. To the best of our knowledge, there is no previous work to solve the above two challenges in the context of short text deep classification.

In this paper, we propose a multi-stage approach for effective short text deep classification. The contributions are threefolds. First we leverage explicit semantic analysis to extract rich explicit concept information from Wikipedia for short text expansion to solve the sparsity issue. Second, documents from descendants of a category in the taxonomy are aggregated to further enrich features. Third, information retrieval techniques are employed to find a few most relevant categories to the input short text for further finer-grained classification, thus avoiding the poor performance of traditional classifiers over a large-scale taxonomy.

2. APPROACH DETAILS

Text documents are usually represented as feature vectors using a mapping function $\Phi : D \rightarrow \mathcal{R}^m$, where D represents a document collection, $\mathcal{R}$ denotes the real-value set, and m is the feature dimension. One common feature representation is tfidf weighting: $\Phi_{tfidf}(d) = (tfidf_d(t_1), \ldots, tfidf_d(t_m))$.

When the lengths of text snippets are very short with several words, the tfidf scheme suffers from feature sparseness. We employ *explicit semantic analysis* (ESA)[1] to tackle this issue. ESA maps natural language fragments into a set of relevant Wikipedia concepts. More precisely, denote the Wikipedia article collection as $W = \{a_1, \ldots, a_n\}$. ESA uses $\Phi_{esa}(d) = (as(d, a_1), \ldots, as(d, a_n))$, where the function as calculates the *association strength* of documents with concepts. A widely used choice is to select tfidf weighting as well: $as(d, a_i) = \sum_{w_j \in d} tf_d(w_j) \cdot tfidf_{a_i}(w_j)$.

We treat categories as virtual documents, thus using the same feature representation scheme as individual documents, by computing the centroids of these categories. Current deep classification methods compute *flat centroids* without considering documents belonging to its descendant categories.

Instead, we compute *descendant centroids* that aggregate data from descendants in the hierarchy.

Facing a large number of categories, the accuracy cannot be ensured by directly applying a state of the art classifier. Thus we employ information retrieval techniques to first search for the most relevant categories for an input short text. We apply the cosine similarity to calculate the k nearest categories.

As the result of the search stage, the number of candidate categories significantly reduced to a small amount. So finer-grained classification methods could be employed to achieve better performance. We choose SVM in this paper. For each candidate category, the documents belonging to it become training data. A SVM is trained on these categories. The classifier is then used to classify the test document.

The two kinds of features, tfidf and esa, sometimes result in different classification results. We use an *ensemble classifier* to make the best of both of them. Suppose the classifiers estimate the probability of test sample d being in category c are P_{tfidf} and P_{esa} respectively, a weighted sum is computed as a simple way to ensemble:

$$P_{ensemble} = P_{tfidf} + \alpha P_{esa}$$

In the formula, α is a parameter, which can be determined according to the actual dataset using linear regression.

3. EXPERIMENTS

We used Open Directory Project (ODP)[1] in the experiments. It is a large directory of web pages labeled using a hierarchical category system. We randomly sampled 11,000 pages to be our test collection, the remaining being the training collection containing 1,299,987 pages distributed among 137,489 categories. In the test collection, the titles and descriptions are concatenated to be the test documents. In order to evaluate how shortness of training data can affect different classifiers, we made two training datasets of different text lengths, LITTLE and SHORT. The content of the former is just the title and the latter is the concatenation of the title and the description.

dataset	description	average document length
LITTLE	title of the web pages	3.11
SHORT	title and short description	14.9

Figure 1: Description of training datasets

To construct the ESA index, we obtained the Wikipedia dump of Nov.15, 2010. We selected the Wikipedia articles representing concrete concepts using heuristics similar to [1], resulting in a collection of 1,333,355 concepts.

As mentioned in [2], direct deployment of big-bang approaches and top-down approaches suffers from high computational complexity and propagation errors. Instead, we choosed a two-stage approach as the baseline. First search for k nearest documents using tfidf weighting scheme. Then the same SVM learn-and-classify strategy is carried out.

As a preliminary experiment, we fixed $k = 15$ and $\alpha = 1$. We evaluated the classification performance using Mi-F1. First, we compare the performance between our approach and the baseline on both datasets. One can see in Figure 2 that the ensemble classifier achieves higher Mi-F1 scores than the baseline on almost all levels. Also note that the improvement is not as big on SHORT as on LITTLE. This is because SHORT can not benefit much by enriching features as it already contains quite rich features.

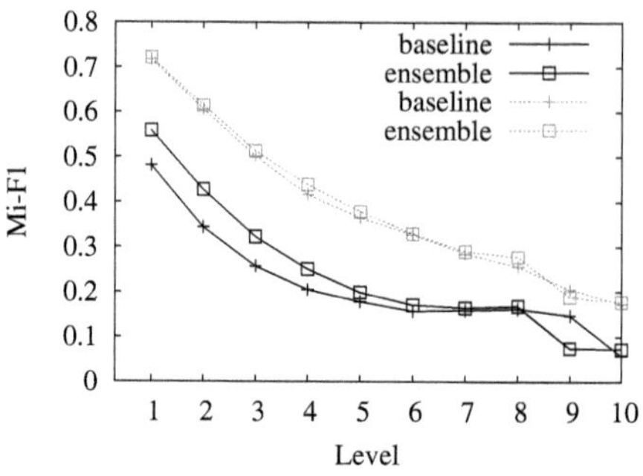

Figure 2: Ensemble classifier compared with baseline. Solid lines are of LITTLE, dotted lines are of SHORT.

Next, we compare the degree to which different features contribute to the performance. The result in Figure 3 shows that the ensemble classifier performs better than both single feature-based classifiers. The esa feature outperforms the ensemble classifier in the higher levels because we used the same α for all levels. This suggests an area of improvement by learning different αs for different levels.

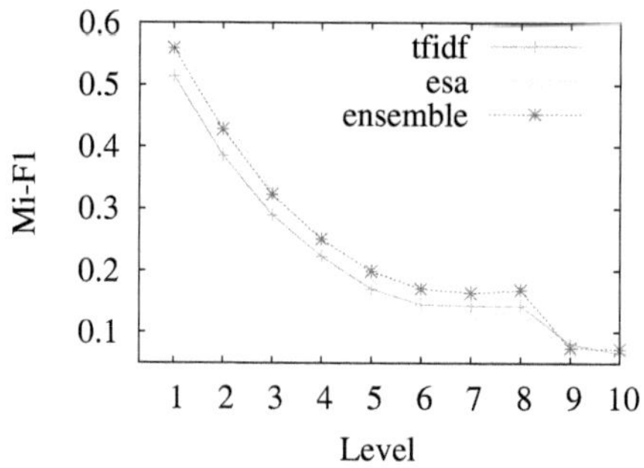

Figure 3: Both features compared with ensemble classifier on LITTLE

4. CONCLUSION AND FUTURE WORK

We conclude that our approach successfully improves the deep classification performance on short text. As of future work, we will try a more advanced ensemble method.

5. REFERENCES

[1] E. Gabrilovich and S. Markovitch. Computing semantic relatedness using wikipedia-based explicit semantic analysis. In *AAAI*, pages 6–12, 2007.

[2] A. Kosmopoulos, E. Gaussier, G. Paliouras, and S. Aseervatham. The ecir 2010 large scale hierarchical classification workshop. *SIGIR Forum*, 44:23–32, 2010.

[3] B. Sriram, D. Fuhry, E. Demir, H. Ferhatosmanoglu, and M. Demirbas. Short text classification in twitter to improve information filtering. In *SIGIR*, pages 841–842, 2010.

[1] http://www.dmoz.org

Temporal Latent Semantic Analysis for Collaboratively Generated Content: Preliminary Results

Yu Wang
Emory University
yu.wang@emory.edu

Eugene Agichtein
Emory University
eugene@mathcs.emory.edu

ABSTRACT

Latent semantic analysis (LSA) has been intensively studied because of its wide application to Information Retrieval and Natural Language Processing. Yet, traditional models such as LSA only examine one (current) version of the document. However, due to the recent proliferation of collaboratively generated content such as threads in online forums, Collaborative Question Answering archives, Wikipedia, and other versioned content, the document generation process is now directly observable. In this study, we explore how this additional temporal information about the document evolution could be used to enhance the identification of latent document topics. Specifically, we propose a novel hidden-topic modeling algorithm, temporal Latent Semantic Analysis (tLSA), which elegantly extends LSA to modeling document revision history using tensor decomposition. Our experiments show that tLSA outperforms LSA on word relatedness estimation using benchmark data, and explore applications of tLSA for other tasks.

Categories and Subject Descriptors

H.3.1 [**Content Analysis and Indexing**]: Indexing methods

General Terms

Algorithm, Experimentation

1. OVERVIEW

Mapping words to semantic concepts has been an active area of research in Information Retrieval (IR) and Natural Language Processing (NLP). Many approaches, such as LSA [3], pLSA, and LDA, have been introduced to identify semantic concepts by analyzing *static* documents. However, with the proliferation of Collaboratively Generated Content (CGC), such as the questions and answers posted in Yahoo Answers, blog posts and comments, as well as pages in Wikipedia, additional *temporal* information about the document evolution is available. This information has been shown to be helpful for fundamental IR and NLP tasks, such as ranking [1] and word similarity analysis [4]. It is then natural to ask, whether temporal document evolution information, such as revision history, can be used to enhance the identification of semantic concepts, by extending LSA to take advantage of the temporal document evolution.

We propose a new hidden-topic modeling algorithm, tLSA, to utilize the content authoring process of CGC. tLSA represents the collection as a *tensor*, with the dimensions corresponding to the documents, words, and time, respectively, and uses tensor decomposition to identify latent concepts in a process inspired by LSA. We show that incorporating temporal information in tLSA can be valuable for word similarity computation, which could in turn improve search quality over CGC. We also explore another application of tLSA, tracing the change of hidden-topic importance over time, which cannot be accomplished by static analysis.

Specifically, our contributions include: Introduction of a novel temporal latent semantic analysis method, tLSA (Section 2); Improved performance over LSA for predicting word relatedness, and an exploration of applying tLSA for temporal topic evolution analysis (Section 3).

SIGIR'11, July 24–28, 2011, Beijing, China.
ACM 978-1-4503-0757-4/11/07.

2. TEMPORAL LATENT SEMANTIC ANALYSIS WITH TENSOR DECOMPOSITION

Our tLSA algorithm extends LSA, which we briefly review, and use to provide intuition for our approach. A word-by-document matrix can be built to represent the collection of static documents. Matrix decomposition algorithms, such as Singular Value Decomposition (SVD) or Non-negative Matrix Factorization (NMF), can be performed onto the matrix to obtain semantic representation. By considering the generation process of the collection, we have time dimension upon the flat word-by-document matrix. Therefore, the matrix becomes a word-document-time cuboid, more precisely, an 3rd-order tensor (as shown in Figure 1). Intuitively, tensor decomposition algorithms could be applied to this 3rd-order tensor, with the goal of identifying important latent topics similar to the idea of LSA or SVD.

LSA decomposes the word-by-document matrix into the sum of rank-1 matrices, therefore captures the correlation/co-occurrence information between words. CANDECOMP/PARAFAC (CP) decomposition introduced in [2] decomposes a tensor in the same way. CP-decomposition factorizes word-document-time tensor into the sum of weighted rank-1 tensors. Each rank-1 tensor is associated with one hidden-topic and can be rewritten as the outer product of three vectors (word, document and time vector respectively). More formally, for CP-decomposition, we have:

$$T = \sum_{r=1}^{R} \delta_r \times (\mathbf{w}_r \circ \mathbf{d}_r \circ \mathbf{t}_r) \qquad (1)$$

T is the 3rd-order tensor, δ_r is the r-th "singular value", $\mathbf{w}_r$,$\mathbf{d}_r$ and $\mathbf{t}_r$ are the word, document and time vector respectively. R is the number of rank-1 tensors used to recover the original tensor T. We can also construct a matrix by aggregating the vectors, for example, $[\mathbf{t}_1, \mathbf{t}_2, \ldots, \mathbf{t}_R]$. This is illustrated in Figure 1. Tensor T is decomposed into three

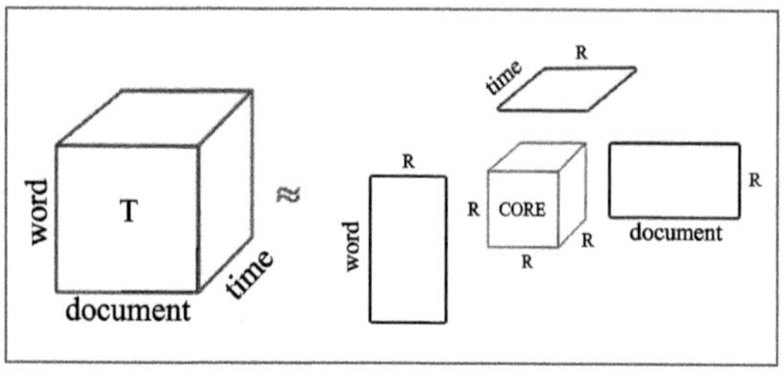

Figure 1: Tensor decomposition for the word-document-time tensor describing a CGC collection like Wikipedia.

matrices and a core tensor, the core tensor Λ is diagonal and the non-zero entries have the value of $\delta_1, \delta_2, \ldots, \delta_R$.

The original CP-decomposition could be done by iteratively solving a least square problem. However, we notice that the time dimension is different from document and word dimension. The continuity of time dimension should be considered when decomposing the tensor, while document and word dimension does not have this issue. Intuitively, two adjacent time slices in the tensor should have similar weights if we assume the weight of hidden-topic consistently changes over time. The loss function of time vector is redefined as:

$$L_{time}(\mathbf{t}) = \left\|T - \widetilde{T}\right\|_F^2 + \lambda_1 \mathbf{t} L \mathbf{t}^T + \lambda_2 \|\mathbf{t}\|^2 \quad (2)$$

Basically, loss function (2) adds regularization on time dimension when solving the least square problem, resulting in a smooth time vector. $\widetilde{T}$ is the recovered tensor as defined in (1). L is the Laplacian matrix which penalizes the difference between "neighborhoods" along the time vector $\mathbf{t}$.

3. EXPERIMENTAL RESULTS

We use WordSimilarity-353 (WS-353) benchmark dataset[1] to evaluate tLSA. To construct the tensor, we retrieve top 100 articles through Wikipedia default search engine for each word in WS-353 and 39183 articles in total are obtained. For each retrieved article, the revisions from Jan 1st, 2008 till Jan 31st, 2011 are collected. We take weekly snapshot for those articles since Jan 1st, 2008, resulting in 161 time slices. The baseline method, LSA, uses the last snapshot of this collection only. Word relatedness computed by LSA and tLSA are compared on WS-353. Pearson Correlation is employed here to estimate the performance of these models.

Algorithm	Pearson Correlation
LSA	0.4398
tLSA with time regularization	**0.4593 (+4.4%)**
tLSA without time regularization	0.3752

Table 1: Correlation with WS-353 word relatedness.

Table 1 shows that tLSA with time regularization performs better than LSA by 4.4% on word relatedness estimation. However, the words in the WS-353 dataset are relatively common, and primarily related to static concepts, such as "car" and "love". This may explain the relatively small absolute improvement of tLSA over LSA.

We now explore another application of tLSA - tracing hidden-topic evolution and importance over time (which is not possible with LSA or other static analysis methods). Furthermore, to show the applicability of tLSA, we run this algorithm on another corpus, 20-year New York Times articles. A section in this corpus is considered a "document", and all the articles of that section on a single day form a "revision" of this "document". This pseudo-document reflects the daily changing topics while these topics are connected by the theme of the section.

[1] http://www.cs.technion.ac.il/~gabr/resources/data/wordsim353/

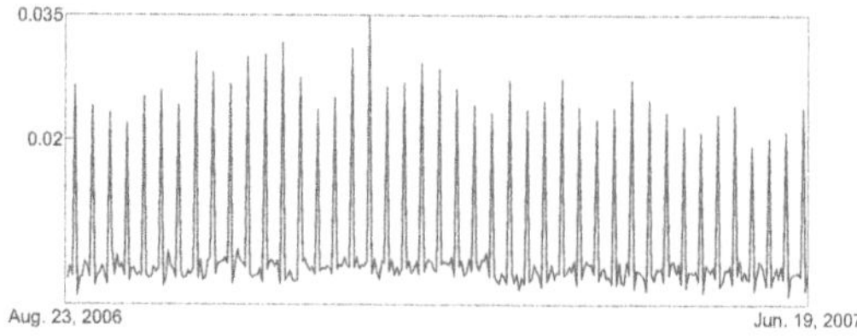

Figure 2: Periodic topic: A topic of weekly news associated with words *week*, *monday* and *church*.

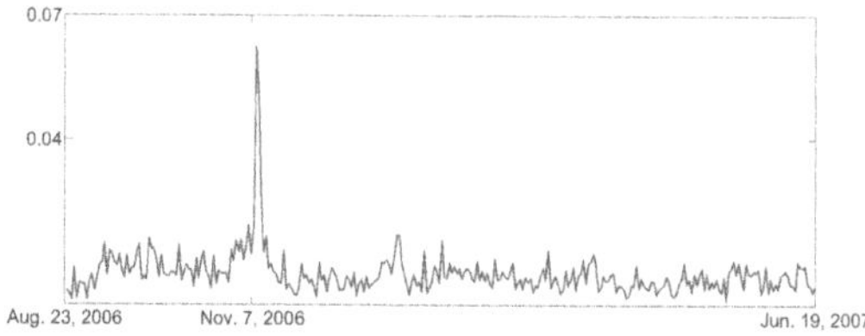

Figure 3: Event associated topic: A topic of U.S. Senate Election associated with words *senate* and *control*.

After the CP-decomposition, a time-by-topic matrix is obtained and the topic trend can be observed. We find two interesting patterns in the topic trend of New York Times corpus. One is periodic pattern as shown in Figure 2. The period of this topic is exact one week. The representative words for this topic are "week", "monday" and "church" etc. We can interpret this topic as weekly news, such as weekly report and weekly events. The other topic trend pattern is "event driven" topic as shown in Figure 3. Nov 7th, 2006 is the date of Unite States Senate Election and the Democrats regained control of the House. The top words for the topic in Figure 3 are "senate" and "control" etc.

4. CONCLUSION

In this study, we introduced a novel algorithm, tLSA, which extends latent semantic analysis by incorporating temporal information using tensor decomposition. The results of our preliminary experiments using tLSA for word relatedness estimation and for analyzing topic evolution in collections over time are encouraging and suggest promising directions for future work.

5. ACKNOWLEDGMENTS

This work was partially supported by the NSF grant IIS-1018321 and the Yahoo! Faculty Research Engagement Program.

6. REFERENCES

[1] A. Aji, Y. Wang, E. Agichtein, and E. Gabrilovich. Using the past to score the present: Extending term weighting models with revision history analysis. In *CIKM*, 2010.

[2] J. D. Carroll and J. J. Chang. Analysis of individual differences in multidimensional scaling via an n-way generalization of eckart-young decomposition. *Psychometrika*, 35:283–319, 1970.

[3] S. Deerwester, S. T. Dumais, G. Furnas, T. Landauer, and R. Harshman. Indexing by latent semantic analysis. In *JASIST*, 1990.

[4] K. Radinsky, E. Agichtein, E. Gabrilovich, and S. Markovitch. Word at a time: Computing word relatedness using temporal semantic analysis. In *WWW*, 2011.

Self-adjusting Hybrid Recommenders Based on Social Network Analysis

Alejandro Bellogín, Pablo Castells, Iván Cantador
Universidad Autónoma de Madrid, Escuela Politécnica Superior
Ciudad Universitaria de Cantoblanco, 28049 Madrid, Spain
{alejandro.bellogin, pablo.castells, ivan.cantador}@uam.es

ABSTRACT

Ensemble recommender systems successfully enhance recommendation accuracy by exploiting different sources of user preferences, such as ratings and social contacts. In linear ensembles, the optimal weight of each recommender strategy is commonly tuned empirically, with limited guarantee that such weights are optimal afterwards. We propose a self-adjusting hybrid recommendation approach that alleviates the social cold start situation by weighting the recommender combination dynamically at recommendation time, based on social network analysis algorithms. We show empirical results where our approach outperforms the best static combination for different hybrid recommenders.

Categories and Subject Descriptors: H.3.3 Information Search and Retrieval – *information filtering*.

General Terms: Algorithms, Performance, Experimentation.

Keywords: Hybrid recommender systems, social networks, graph theory, link analysis.

1. INTRODUCTION

Recommender Systems (RS) aim at automatically finding the most useful products or services for a particular user, providing a personalized list of items according to different input and attributes of users and items. State-of-the-art recommender systems are usually based on ratings and implicit feedback given by users about the items. Recently, due to the large number of social systems appearing in the so called Web 2.0, where friendship relations between people are explicit, "social contexts" exploitation has started to receive significant interest. In particular, social recommenders have started to be investigated that exploit social links between users in a community to suggest interesting items [2], [6]. On the other hand, Collaborative Filtering (CF) is one of the most popular strategies in RS [1], which makes use of explicit preferences to find similar-minded people according to the observed user interaction with the items, and presents suggestions on this basis.

Although social recommenders perform very well in some situations, they usually cannot provide any suggestion to users without a social context (social cold start). A solution to this problem is to exploit both sources of information, social and collaborative, by a hybrid ensemble recommendation approach. One of the most common forms of ensemble recommenders simply consists in a linear combination of recommenders. In this approach, the weights in the linear combination are generally the same for all users. However, not all users are equally active in terms of social connectivity. Thus, in this paper, we explore the adaptive adjustments of the ensemble coefficients on a user basis. More specifically, we explore a novel approach for self-adjusting the weight of each recommender by using social network analysis to balance the influence of each recommender. We report empirical results showing that our dynamic ensemble approach outperforms the best static combination in different hybrid recommenders.

SIGIR'11, July 24–28, 2011, Beijing, China.
2011 ACM 978-1-4503-0757-4/11/07.

2. SELF-ADJUSTING RECOMMENDERS

In [3], a detailed taxonomy is presented where hybrid recommenders are classified according to how they combine different recommendation techniques. In the following, we focus on the so called weighted hybrid recommenders, in which the scores of n individual techniques are aggregated by a linear combination. Without loss of generality, we focus on the case with $n = 2$, as follows:

$$s(u_m, i_n) = (1 - \lambda) \times s_1(u_m, i_n) + \lambda \times s_2(u_m, i_n)$$

with λ ranging between 0 and 1. This type of hybridization weights each recommender in a static way; i.e., once the value of λ is fixed, recommendations from each technique receive the same weight, independently of the target user. In this context, two main shortcomings arise. First, the optimal weight has to be found empirically by relying on current recommender performance, dataset characteristics, etc., which are subject to change [3]. Second, the optimal weight may not be the same for all users since the system gathers a different amount of information from each user, and thus, a recommender may be more useful than others in different situations.

In this paper, we explore a self-adjusting hybrid recommendation approach that makes use of adjusting factors to boost one of the combined recommenders for certain users. In our case, the value of λ is fixed at the user level, i.e. $\lambda = \lambda(u_m)$, aiming to promote the recommender that is expected to perform best for each particular user, e.g. because there is more meaningful available information for this recommender than for others. For this purpose, we analyze a particular hybrid configuration in which we combine social and CF recommenders. In this context, we propose to use graph-based measures as adjusting factors of the users' strength in the network, by balancing the influence of each recommender. More specifically, we apply these measures to set the weight of the social recommender, in such a way that when a user is very socially "active" (e.g., she plays a special role in the community), the recommendations from the social recommender are assumed to be more important than those from the CF recommender, and vice versa.

The adjusting factors used herein are based on vertex measures from graph theory. More specifically, we use user *degree*, i.e., the number of friends of each user in the network, *average neighbor degree*, and size of *two-hop neighborhood*, both described in [4]; *PageRank* and *HITS* scores, well-known measures of connectivity relevance within a social network; betweenness *centrality*, which is an indicator of whether a user can reach others on relatively short paths [5]; *clustering coefficient*, which measures the probability that the user's friends are friends themselves [8]; and *ego components size*, which is the number of connected components remaining when the user and her friends are removed [4].

3. EXPERIMENTS

We use the dataset provided in the social track of the CAMRa Challenge [7]. This dataset was gathered by the Filmtipset community, and contains social links between users, movie ratings, movie comments, and other attributes of users and movies. The set of users presented in the test set turns out to be very specific: every user has at least two friends, something not plausible in a real setting, where not every user has a social network. Because of that, we simulate a more realistic scenario to empirically compare social and CF recommenders in a fair environment where users with and without social contacts in their profiles are considered. We sampled randomly the same number of test users in the original test set (i.e., 439 users), but forcing them to have no friends, and include them in the new test set used in our experiments.

We evaluated a number of hybrid ensemble recommendation approaches combining CF and two different social recommenders. User-based CF [1] with a neighborhood size of 10 is denoted as *UB10*. One of the social recommenders is denoted as *PureSocial*. It is inspired by the approach presented in [6], and incorporates social information into the user-based CF model, by replacing the set of nearest neighbors with the active user's (explicit) friends. The other social recommender (denoted as *Personal*) is described in [2], where distances between users in the social graph are explicitly incorporated in the scoring formula as: $s(u_m, i_n) = \sum_{v \in X(u_m,L)} K^{-d(u_m,v)} rat(v, i_n)$. In this equation, $X(u_m, L)$ denotes the social tree of user u_m up to level L, and K is an attenuation coefficient of the social network that determines the extent of the effect of $d(u_m, v)$, i.e., the impact of the distance between two users in the social graph, weighted by the rating given by user v to item i_n, i.e., $rat(v, i_n)$. In our experiments, we used as distance d the one obtained by Dijkstra's algorithm, $K = 2$ and $L = 6$.

We evaluated three different recommender ensembles, depending on which social recommender was combined with *UB10*, and a threshold parameter in the number of common items required to decide when two users are considered neighbors. We denote the above hybrids as follows: H1 (*UB10* and *Personal*, with a threshold value of 2), H2 (*UB10* and *PureSocial*, threshold is 1), and H3 (the same as in H2 but with a threshold value of 2).

Table 1 shows the results obtained with the proposed self-adjusted hybridization technique, using the adjusting factors presented in the previous section. We only show P@5 and nDCG@5 results due to space constraints, but results are consistent for different cutoff values other than 5. In the table, we compare the results from the self-adjusted hybrid recommendations against those of the best statics, and a static with $\lambda = 0.5$, since this value is the natural choice (and best prior on average) in the absence of information about the recommender systems to be combined. We also include the performance for the extreme cases: $\lambda = 1$ (only social) and $\lambda = 0$ (collaborative).

In the table, we observe that the self-adjusted recommenders get a general advantage over the static configurations. For instance, the PageRank-based hybrid is better than statics in all cases (without statistical significance in H3 though), and all methods, except Centrality and Clustering on H3, improve over the 0.5 static –and the best posterior static in most cases. The improvements are less significant on the H3 ensemble. We hypothesize this can be due to the fact that the social algorithm in H3 performs significantly and systematically better than the CF, whereby any ensemble is suboptimal with respect to the best component (here, social). It is important to note that the best static is different for each ensemble (namely, $\lambda = 0.9$ for H1, 0.1 for H2, and 0.8 for H3), which further highlights the importance of this result, in that the best static is not actually a real configuration: a best static configuration would require a manual tuning of λ, and even so, the table shows the posterior best static, which a manually tuned λ would not guarantee. Nonetheless, although no self-adjusting hybrid method is significantly better in every situation, *PageRank*, *HITS*, and *ego components size* factors seem to be safe alternatives.

Table 1. Performance results for the three ensembles tested. The best absolute value is underlined. Improvements over the best static are shown in bold font, and over the static 0.5 with italics. Statistical significant (p<0.05) differences between self-adjusted hybrid recommenders and static 0.5, best static, and both are marked with *, †, and ‡, respectively.

	P@5			nDCG@5		
	H1	H2	H3	H1	H2	H3
Average Neigh Deg	**0.219***	**0.092***	*0.199*	**0.240***	**0.097***	*0.215*
Centrality	**0.222***	**0.106‡**	0.188†	**0.242***	**0.111‡**	0.204†
Clustering coef	*0.211**	**0.094***	0.188†	*0.231**	**0.100***	0.202†
Degree	**0.233‡**	**0.095***	*0.197*	**0.256‡**	**0.099***	*0.213*
Ego Comp Size	**0.227‡**	**0.096***	**0.201***	**0.249‡**	**0.101***	*0.215*
HITS	**0.225***	**0.110‡**	*0.197*	**0.248***	**0.114‡**	*0.212*
PageRank	**0.227‡**	**0.097***	**0.200**	**0.247***	**0.101***	***0.216***
Two Hop Neigh	**0.229‡**	**0.093***	*0.195*	**0.250‡**	**0.100***	*0.212*
Static 0.5	0.186	0.077	0.189	0.205	0.081	0.206
Best static	0.218	0.091	0.199	0.239	0.096	0.215
CF Component	0.076	0.043	0.076	0.082	0.047	0.082
Social component	0.372	0.055	0.270	0.409	0.053	0.298

Finally, it is worth noting that single approaches obtain lower accuracy values than hybrids on equal terms since they deal poorly with the social cold start situation if we measure the performance for all the users (the social component evaluated in this way is only able to recommend items for 55% of the test users, i.e., its "true" P@5 value for H1 should be 0.206). The empirical results thus suggest that significant improvements can be drawn from the proposed self-adjustment strategy based on graph-based social factors. The herein presented adjusting criteria only make use of social network structures; we shall explore alternative factors in the future, such as distributional properties of user ratings.

Acknowledgements. This work was supported by the Spanish Ministry of Science and Innovation (TIN2008-06566-C04-02), University Autónoma de Madrid and the Community of Madrid (CCG10-UAM/TIC-5877).

4. REFERENCES

[1] G. Adomavicius, A. Tuzhilin. Toward the next generation of recommender systems: a survey of the state-of-the-art and possible extensions. *IEEE TKDE*, **17**(6): 734–749, June 2005.

[2] D. Ben-Shimon, A. Tsikinovsky, L. Rokach, A. Meisles, G. Shani, L. Naamani. Recommender system from personal social networks. In *Proceedings of AWIC'2007*, 47–55, 2007.

[3] R. Burke. Hybrid recommender systems: survey and experiments. *UMUAI* **12**(4): 331–370, November 2002.

[4] M. De Choudhury, W. A. Mason, J. M. Hofman, D. J. Watts. Inferring relevant social networks from interpersonal communication. In *Proceedings of WWW'10*, 301–310, 2010.

[5] L.C. Freeman. A set of measures of centrality based on betweenness. *Sociometry* **40**(1), 35–41, 1977.

[6] F. Liu, H.J. Lee. Use of social network information to enhance collaborative filtering performance. *Expert Systems with Applications* **37**(7): 4772–4778, July 2010.

[7] A. Said, S. Berkovsky, E. W. De Luca. Putting things in context: challenge on context-aware movie recommendation. In *Proceedings of the RecSys'10 CAMRa Challenge*, 2–6, 2010.

[8] D. J. Watts, S. Strogatz. Collective dynamics of „small-world' networks. *Nature* **393**: 440–442, June 1998.

BlogCast Effect on Information Diffusion in a Blogosphere

Sang-Wook Kim
Dept. of Electronics and Computer Engineering
Hanyang University
Seoul, 133-791, Korea
swkim10@hanyang.ac.kr

Sang-Wook Kim
Dept. of Electronics and Computer Engineering
Hanyang University
Seoul, 133-791, Korea
wook@hanyang.ac.kr

Christos Faloutsos
Computer Science Department
Carnegie Mellon University
Pittsburgh, PA 15213, USA
christos@cs.cmu.edu

ABSTRACT

A blog service company provides a function named *BlogCast* that exposes quality posts on the blog main page to vitalize a blogosphere. This paper analyzes a new type of information diffusion via *BlogCast*. We show that there exists a strong *halo effect* in a blogosphere via thorough investigation on a huge volume of blog data.

Categories and Subject Descriptors: H.2.8 [**DATABASE MANAGEMENT**]: Database Applications—*Data mining*; J.4 [**SOCIAL AND BEHAVIORAL SCIENCES**]: Sociology

General Terms: Experimentation, Human Factors

Keywords: Blogosphere, Social Networks, Information Diffusion

1. INTRODUCTION

Owing to the recent advance of Internet technology, content development is being moved rapidly from offline to online. A *blog* is a personal website where individuals publish their thoughts in a post online. In a *blogosphere*, people write posts, exchange information, and establish relationships.

There have been a number of research efforts on information diffusion in a blogosphere. They model the blogosphere as a social network, and analyze the *network effect* on information diffusion [2][3]. A blog service company finds a small number of quality posts that deal with interesting topics and exposes them on the blog main page so that people easily access these posts. This function, referred to as *BlogCast*, significantly contributes to a vitalization of the blogosphere.

Information diffusion through *BlogCast* should show unique characteristics because the network effect does not occur anymore. To the best of the authors' knowledge, there is no such an analysis on information diffusion through broadcasting in a blogosphere. This paper analyzes this new type of information diffusion, and presents interesting implications.

2. TERMINOLOGY

Blog service companies provide useful functions to facilitate communications among bloggers. The *trackback* is putting links in related posts to each other in order to enable people to read them together. The *scrap*, unique in Korea, is copying someone else's post into one's own blog.

SIGIR'11, July 24–28, 2011, Beijing, China.
ACM 978-1-4503-0757-4/11/07.

The *blogroll* is maintaining a list of addresses of other blogs so that one easily visits them at any time.

Diffusion power (*DP*) is a measure that indicates how much a post (or a blogger) influences information diffusion in a blogosphere [2]. In this paper, we define the *DP of a post* simply as the total number of trackbacks and scraps that the post has received. Likewise, we define the *DP of a blog* as the sum of *DP*s of all the posts within the blog.

When a blogosphere is modeled as a network, a blog is represented as a node and a relationship between a pair of blogs is as an edge. Reference [2] regarded the space for the quality posts maintained by *BlogCast* as a special blog, and referred to this blog as a *super node*. In this paper, we call a post *SN-Post* if it has been exposed in a super node, and also call a blog *SN-Blog* if it has at least an *SN-Post*. We call the time when a post is added into a super node *SN-in* time, and the time when it is removed from a super node *SN-out* time.

3. RESULTS AND ANALYSES

For the analysis, we used anonymized blog data that was collected from blog.naver.com, one of the biggest blogospheres in Korea. The numbers of posts and blogs were about 14 millions and 700 thousands, respectively. Also, the numbers *SN-Posts* and *SN-Blogs* were 2,554 and 1,384 respectively.

In Experiment 1, we examined the the correlation between the number of posts in the *SN-Blog* and the average *DP* in the scatter plot. Figure 1 shows the result. The X-axis represents the number of posts in the *SN-Blog*, and the Y-axis represents the average *DP* of the posts in the *SN-Blog*. Generally, we expected that bloggers who write quality posts write a more number of posts and the post in a *SN-Blog* with more posts would have a higher *DP* on average. Contrary to our expectation, however, we found no correlation between the number of posts in the *SN-Blog* and the average DP of the posts in the *SN-Blog*. The Pearson coefficient is very low with -0.03.

In Experiment 2, we examined the tendency of the *DP* of *SN-Posts* over time. The *DP* of an individual *SN-Post* was shown to change quite differently depending on *SN-Posts*. So, we first grouped *SN-Posts* according to the month when they were added into the super node, aligned the time axis for the *SN-Posts* in the same month at the *SN-in* time, and computed the average *DP* of *SN-Posts* in each month for each day.

Figure 2 shows the results for two months. The results for the other months were shown similar, but omitted here due to space limitations. The X-axis represents the relative

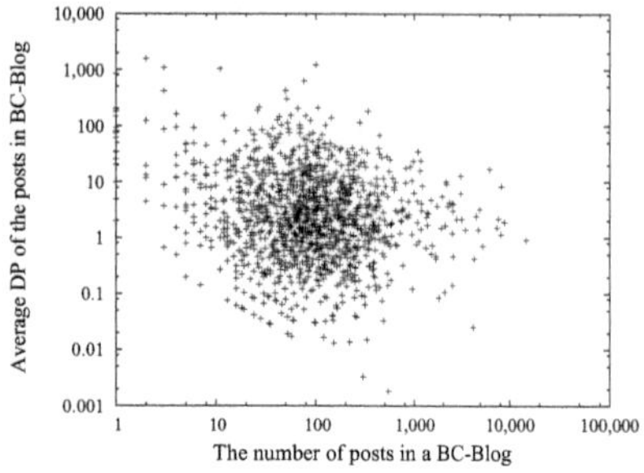

Figure 1: The correlation between the number and the average *DP* of the posts in the SN-Blog.

days before/after the *SN-in* time, and the Y-axis represents the average *DP* of *SN-Posts* in each day. The value of 0 on the X-axis indicates the *SN-in* time of each post. The inset depicts the tendency of the *DP after* the *SN-in* time in a log-log scale.

We see that the *DP* increases abruptly up to *several hundred times* in the day when it becomes an *SN-Post*. It also decreases drastically within one or two day(s) after the *SN-in* time. This is because an *SN-Post* is frequently replaced with other posts by a blog service company. As shown in the inset, we observe that the relaxation of the *DP* follows the well-known *power-law* distribution whose exponent is between -1.0 and -1.5. This coincides with the results found in a number of natural phenomena [1].

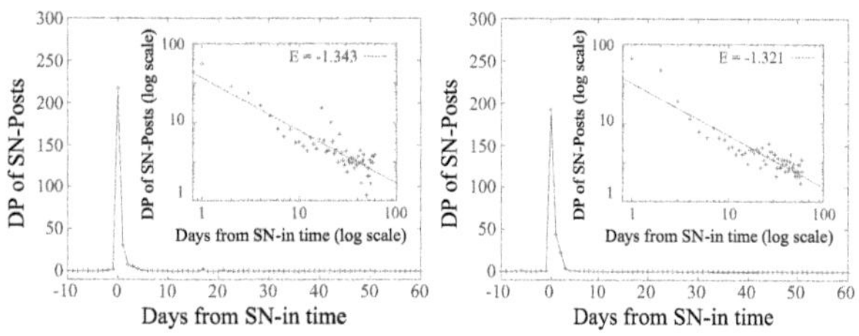

(a) June. (b) July.

Figure 2: *DP* of *SN-Posts*.

In Experiment 3, we examined the *DP* of *SN-Blogs* over time with the experimental settings and methods same as in Experiment 2. Because the *DP* of an *SN-Post* is dominant in an *SN-Blog*, for making the analysis clearer, we excluded the *DP* of *SN-Posts* when computing the *DP* of *SN-Blogs*. Figure 3 shows the results for the two months.

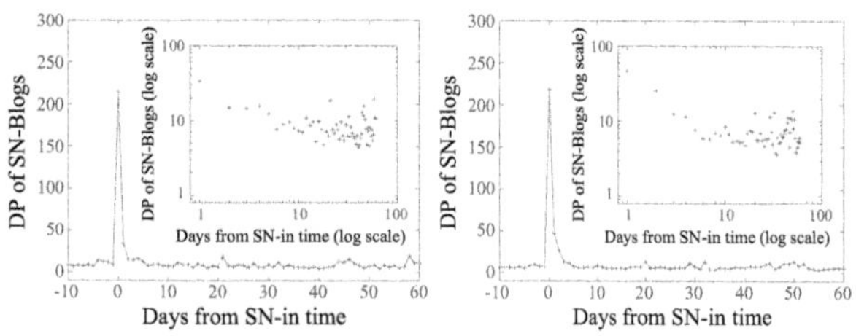

(a) June. (b) July.

Figure 3: *DP* of *SN-Blogs*.

The *DP* of *SN-Blogs* also dramatically increases up to *several hundred times* in the day when their post is selected as an *SN-Post*. As the *DP* of *SN-Posts* does, the *DP* of *SN-Blogs* shows rapid relaxation within one or two day(s) after the *SN-in* time.

The abrupt increase of the *DP* of *SN-Blogs* can be explained as follows (see Figure 4). When one reads the *SN-Post* via the super node (solid lines), she or he realizes that the *SN-Blog* has a number of quality posts inside (dashed lines). So, it is likely that she or he scraps or trackbacks those normal posts together. We call this phenomenon that the *DP* of *normal* posts within an *SN-Blog* significantly grows at the *SN-in* time due to the *SN-Post halo effect*.

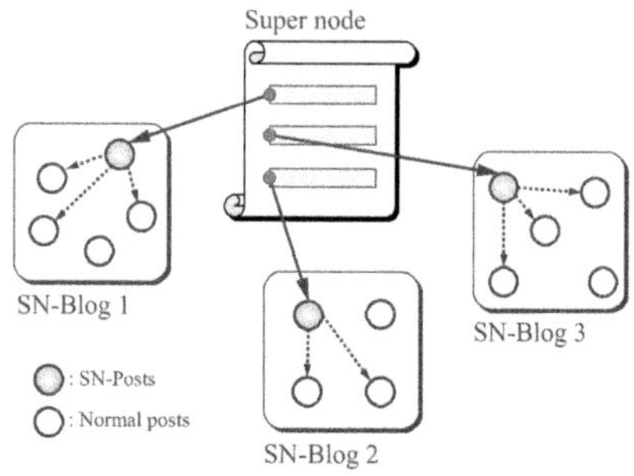

Figure 4: Halo effect.

4. CONCLUSIONS

This paper analyzed the *BlogCast* effect on information diffusion in the blogosphere: We discovered the *halo effect* that the *DP* of normal posts (and the relationships) within an *SN-Blog* dramatically grows at the *SN-in* time.

5. ADDITIONAL AUTHORS

Additional author: Jiwoon Ha (Dept. of Electronics and Computer Engineering, Hanyang University, Seoul, 133-791, Korea, email: `oneofus@agape.hanyang.ac.kr`)

6. ACKNOWLEDGEMENTS

This work was supported by NHN Corp. and the National Research Foundation of Korea(NRF) grant funded by the Korea government(MEST)(No. 2008-0061006) and the MKE(The Ministry of Knowledge Economy), Korea, under the Convergence-ITRC(Convergence Information Technology Research Center) support program(NIPA-2011-C6150-1101-0001) supervised by the NIPA(National IT Industry Promotion Agency). Any opinions, findings, and conclusions or recommendations expressed in this material are the authors' and do not necessarily reflect those of the sponsor.

7. REFERENCES

[1] A. Barabasi, "The Origin of Bursts and Heavy Tails in Human Dynamics," *Nature*, vol. 435, no. 7039, pp. 207-211, 2005.

[2] Y. Kwon, S. Kim, S. Park, S. Lim, and J. Lee, "The Information Diffusion Model in the Blog World," In *Proc. ACM KDD Workshop on Social Network Mining and Analysis*, pp. 1-9, ACM SNA-KDD, 2009.

[3] M. McGlohon, J. Leskovec, C. Faloutsos, M. Hurst, and N. Glance, "Finding Patterns in Blog Shapes and Blog Evolution," In *Proc. Int'l Conf. on Weblogs and Social Media*, ICWSM, 2007.

Product Comparison using Comparative Relations

Si Li[1,2], Zheng-Jun Zha[2], Zhaoyan Ming[2], Meng Wang[2],
Tat-Seng Chua[2], Jun Guo[1], Weiran Xu[1]
[1]School of Information and Communication Engineering, Beijing University of Posts and Telecommunications, China
[2]School of Computing, National University of Singapore, Singapore
{lisi,guojun,xuweiran}@bupt.edu.cn,{zhazj,mingzy,chuats}@comp.nus.edu.sg,
eric.mengwang@gmail.com

ABSTRACT

This paper proposes a novel Product Comparison approach. The comparative relations between products are first mined from both user reviews on multiple review websites and community-based question answering pairs containing product comparison information. A unified graph model is then developed to integrate the resultant comparative relations for product comparison. Experiments on popular electronic products show that the proposed approach outperforms the state-of-the-art methods.

Categories and Subject Descriptors

I.2.4 [**Knowledge Representation Formalisms and Methods**]: [Relation systems]

General Terms

Algorithms, Performance

Keywords

Product Comparison, Comparative Relations Graph

1. INTRODUCTION

When purchasing popular electronic products like mobile phones, consumers commonly compare several candidate products by seeking public opinions from online reviews before making purchase decision. However, this process is labor-intensive and time-consuming. To help consumer make purchase decision effortlessly, many review websites provide a simple product comparison functionality, which compares several candidate products in terms of various aspects. For each aspect, it scores each candidate by averaging the corresponding users' ratings within the website. However, this product comparison functionality is usually not effective due to the following limitations: (1) there are usually too few ratings to make the scores reliable for some products in a website; and (2) one website usually does not contain all the products that the consumer wants to compare. Meanwhile, it is not reasonable to simply integrate the comparison results from multiple websites, since different websites have different scoring strategies based on different user ratings.

Motivated by the above observations, in this paper we propose a novel Product Comparison (PC) approach based on the comparative relations between each pair of candidate products in four high-level product aspects: design, feature, performance and ease of use, which most consumers are concerned about. Our approach performs the product comparison task in two main steps: (1) The pairwise comparative relations on each high-level aspect are mined from both user reviews on major product review websites and community-based question answering (cQA) pairs containing comparative information between products. (2) For each aspect, a unified graph model is constructed to integrate the comparative relations from user reviews and cQA pairs. By performing graph propagation, each candidate product (i.e., each node in the graph) obtains a superiority score. The product having the largest score outperforms the others on the corresponding aspect. The contributions of this papers are two-fold. First, in order to generate reliable and comprehensive product comparison results, we integrate user reviews from multiple review websites and also incorporate the product-related cQA pairs as a new source of information to exploit the comparative relations between products. Second, a unified graph model is developed to fuse the comparative relations from the above two sources for product comparison. Some preliminary works have been dedicated to product comparison based on user reviews [3, 6]. However, they mainly make use of individual user ratings and neglect the product comparative relations expressed in review sentences and cQA pairs. Moreover, they all focus on low-level aspects, such as size and weight etc.

SIGIR'11, July 24–28, 2011, Beijing, China.
ACM 978-1-4503-0757-4/11/07.

2. THE APPROACH

2.1 Comparative Relations Mining

For each high-level aspect, we first group the review sentences and cQA pairs using K-means clustering method as proposed in [4]. We then employ Support Vector Machine (SVM) to classify the polarity [5] of the review sentences. As a result, the numbers of positive opinions (PS) and negative opinions (NS) from reviews are obtained for each product. Next, we identify the comparative sentences from the reviews and analyze them as in [1, 2]. We then summarize the comparative relations between products from the reviews. The number of opinions which indicate product A is better than B is marked as CP_A. Meanwhile, to mine the comparative relations from cQA pairs, we define a trigger lexicon containing the phrases that indicate the preferred product in the answers, such as 'I'd go with', etc. With the use of this lexicon, we adopt the reviews processing approach in [1, 2] to analyze the comparative relations in cQA to derive the relations between products A and B.

2.2 Graph based Product Comparison

In this section, we propose a graph-based product comparison approach, which consists of two graphs containing

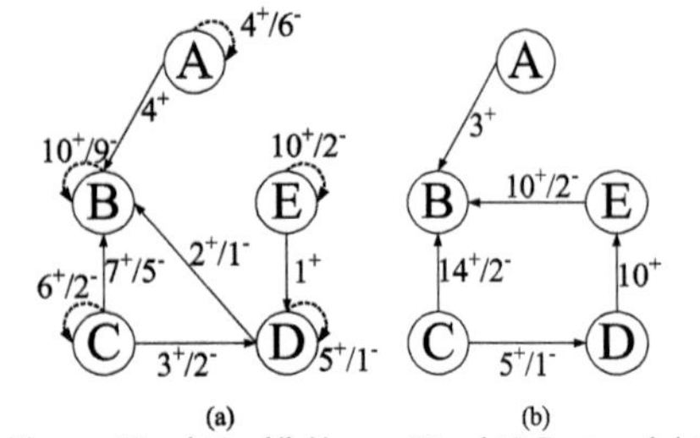

'+' means CP_j and PS_i, while '-' means CP_i and NS_i. For example in (a), PS_C=6 and NS_C=2 with an directed edge from C to C. CP_B=7 and CP_C=5 between B and C.

Figure 1: An illustration of $\mathcal{G}_{\mathcal{H}}$ incorporating pairwise comparative relations mined from user reviews (a) and cQA pairs (b), for five candidate products.

the comparative relations from the reviews and cQA pairs respectively. The graph for each high-level aspect $\mathcal{H}$ is defined as follows: $\mathcal{G}_{\mathcal{H}}$=($\mathcal{V}$,$\mathcal{E}$) where $\mathcal{V}$={p_i|p_i is a node that denotes a product, 0<$i \leq$ n}; $\mathcal{E}$={e_{ij}|e_{ij} is a directed edge from p_i to p_j and its weight is W_{ij}, 0<i,$j \leq$ n}; and n is the number of candidate products. The direction of e_{ij} is from p_i to p_j which means that CP_j is bigger than CP_i. In other words, it indicates that more users think product j is better than product i. The weight W_{ij} is defined as:

$$W_{ii} = (PS_i + NS_i) \times \frac{PS_i}{(NS_i + \lambda)} \tag{1}$$

$$W_{ij} = \begin{cases} (CP_j + CP_i) \times \frac{CP_j}{(CP_i+\lambda)} & i \neq j \\ \frac{W_{ij} - min\{W_{ii}\}}{max\{W_{ii}\} - min\{W_{ii}\}} & i = j \end{cases} \tag{2}$$

where the smoothing coefficient λ is set to 1 when NS_i or CP_i is 0; otherwise it is set to 0. Figure 1 shows an illustration of $\mathcal{G}_{\mathcal{H}}$ with the comparative relations derived from reviews (a) and cQA (b). Through performing graph propagation over the two graphs simultaneously, we integrate the comparative relations from the reviews and cQA pairs for product comparison as follows:

$$PCS(p_i)^{k+1} = (1-d) + d \sum_{m=1}^{2} \sum_{j=1}^{n} \mu_m \beta_m PCS_m(p_j)^k \times E_m(p_j p_i) \tag{3}$$

where $PCS(p_i)^{k+1}$ is the resultant superiority score for the product p_i; k is the number of iteration; d is the damping factor; $m \in \{1, 2\}$ indicates the comparative relations from the reviews or cQA; $\mu_m \in [0,1]$ is introduced to control the contribution of these two resources and $\sum_{m=1}^{2} \mu_m = 1$. If there is a directed edge from product p_j to p_i, β_m is set to 1; otherwise 0. $E_m(p_j p_i)$ is calculated as $\frac{W_{mji}}{\sum_{l=1}^{L} W_{mjl}}$, and L is the number of outbound links of product p_j.

3. EXPERIMENTS

We conducted experiments on six mobile phones and five MP3 players as shown in Table 1. We crawled 50,893 phone reviews and 3,604 MP3 reviews from multiple review websites, including Cnet, Amazon, Reevoo, Gsmarena(Gsm). We also downloaded 215 resolved cQA pairs, which contains the comparative information of products, from Yahoo! Answers. Each cQA pairs contains one question and its given best answer. In our experiments, d was empirically set to 0.85, μ_1 and μ_2 were set to 0.7 and 0.3, respectively.

We compared the proposed approach (PC_2) to the following three approaches: the product comparison functionality

Table 1: Candidate Products List

Phone	Apple Iphone 4, HTC Desire, Samsung Galaxy S, BlackBerry Bold 9700, Sony Ericsson Xperia X10 Mini, Nokia N97
MP3	Apple iPod Touch 4th Generation, Sandisk Sansa Clip+, Sony X-Series Walkman, Apple iPod Nano 6th Generation, Zune HD

Table 2: Four approaches' performance results

	Phone			
Aspect	Gsm	Reevoo	PC_1	PC_2
Design	0%	8.3%	41.7%	50%
Feature	0%	8.3%	41.7%	50%
Performance	8.3%	0%	8.3%	75%
Ease of use	0%	0%	0%	75%
Average	2.1%	4.2%	22.9%	62.5%

	MP3			
Aspect	Cnet	Reevoo	PC_1	PC_2
Design	41.7%	16.6%	0%	41.7%
Feature	33.3%	0%	8.3%	41.7%
Performance	8.3%	0%	8.3%	66.7%
Ease of use	0%	50%	0%	41.7%
Average	20.8%	16.7%	4.2%	48.0%

of two popular review websites (Gsm and Reevoo for mobile phone and Cnet and Reevoo for MP3.), and a simplified version of the proposed approach (PC_1), which only makes use of user reviews without cQA. Since it is laborious for human to summarize and rank the products by reading all the reviews, the manually created gold standard is not easy to obtain. Alternatively, we conducted user study to evaluate the comparison results from these four approaches. We invited 12 subjects who are electronics enthusiasts. For each aspect, each subject was asked to vote one result, which she prefers, from the four results, or 'none' if all the results are unsatisfactory. The evaluation results are summarized in Table 2. Each number indicates which percentage of subjects prefer the comparison result of the corresponding approach. From Table 2, the following observations can be obtained: (1) By comparing products using comparative relations from user reviews, the proposed approaches (PC_1 and PC_2) outperform the comparison functionality of review websites on most high-level aspects. (2) By further incorporating the comparative relations minded from cQA pairs, our PC_2 approach achieves the best overall performance and performs best on most aspects.

In summary, we have presented a novel product comparison approach using comparative relations derived from both the user reviews and cQA. The user study has demonstrated the effectiveness of our method.

ACKNOWLEDGEMENTS This work was supported by NSFC (No.60905017), Ministry of Science and Technology of China (No. 2011ZX03002-005-01), the 111 project(No. B08004), NExT Research Center funded by MDA (WBS:R-252-300-001-490) and the grand of No. 2011RC0122.

4. REFERENCES

[1] M. Ganapathibhotla and B. Liu. Mining opinions in comparative sentences. In *Proc. of Coling 2008*, 2008.

[2] N. Jindal and B. Liu. Identifying comparative sentences in text documents. In *Proc. of SIGIR 2006*, 2006.

[3] B. Liu and et al. Opinion observer: Analyzing and comparing opiniions on the web. In *Proc. of WWW 2005*, 2005.

[4] Y. Lu and et al. Rated aspect summarization of short comments. In *Proc. of WWW 2009*, 2009.

[5] B. Pang and et al. Thumbs up? sentiment classification using machine learning techniques. In *Proc. of EMNLP 2002*, 2002.

[6] K. Zhang and et al. Voice of the customers: Mining online customer reviews for product feature-based ranking. In *Proc. of WOSN'10*, 2010.

Collaborative Cyberporn Filtering with Collective Intelligence

Lung-Hao Lee and Hsin-Hsi Chen
Department of Computer Science and Information Engineering
National Taiwan University
Taipei, Taiwan
{d98922011, hhchen}@ntu.edu.tw

ABSTRACT
This paper presents a user intent method to generate blacklists for collaborative cyberporn filtering. A novel porn detection framework that finds new pornographic web pages by mining user search behaviors is proposed. It employs users' clicks in search query logs to select the suspected web pages without extra human efforts to label data for training, and determines their categories with the help of URL host name and path information, but without web page content. We adopt an MSN porn data set to explore the effectiveness of our method. This user intent approach achieves high precision, while maintaining favorably low false positive rate. In addition, real-life filtering simulation reveals that our user intent method with its accumulative update strategy achieves 43.36% of blocking rate, while maintaining a steadily less than 7% of over-blocking rate.

Categories and Subject Descriptors
H.3.3 [**Information Search and Retrieval**]: *Information filtering.*

General Terms
Experimentation, Human Factors

Keywords
Query log analysis, pornographic blacklists, searches-and-clicks.

1. INTRODUCTION
Filtering the wide spreading objectionable web content, e.g., pornography, violence, drug and gambling, has attracted intensive attention for child protection or anyone else from inappropriate materials. URL blocking relies on a blacklist to reject undesirable requests [2]. Content analysis selects features from text, image, and linking structure for training pornography classifier [1]. The URL-based features were empirically shown as an effective approach for correctly identifying pornographic websites [4]. Moreover, query-URL click pairs were also exploited for clustering the similar pornographic images [3].

Different from web content and structure mining in the past work, we only exploit implicit collective intelligence from query logs for web usage mining. Filtering cyberporn is challenging due to its variability. Traditional filtering techniques regard this problem as categorization with statically crawled data sets. Since it is difficult to know the actual changing trail of objectionable web content, we attempt to explore those successfully accessed in search query logs to keep up with the change of the web approximately. Our user intent model can capture the newly-appearing objectionable web content or the variants of the original ones for avoiding being filtered, if someone has visited them via searches-and-clicks.

SIGIR'11, July 24–28, 2011, Beijing, China.
ACM 978-1-4503-0757-4/11/07.

2. USER INTENT MODEL
Submitting queries to search engines and clicking search results, two common operations in daily life, provide implicit tagging on web pages. We employ click data in search query logs to classify web pages and generate a pornographic blacklist based on user intents. The algorithm is composed of 3 stages: (1) *query identification*, (2) *majority voting*, and (3) *category recognition*.

In *query identification* stage, the user intent model identifies suspected queries along with their clicked URLs from search query logs with a lexicon. The lexicon is constructed automatically as follows. We first select terms from the catalog of pornographic web sites as seed queries, and then regard any five seeds as a combination for term expansion by Google Sets. In total, there are 410 expanded terms and seeds in the lexicon for suspected query identification.

In *majority voting* stage, we count the clicks of a page for the same queries issued within a time period, e.g., one month, and identify the URL candidates which satisfy either one of the majority rules proposed as follows. (1) *Absolute majority rule*: A URL is selected if its total number of clicks is more than a half of total issues of a query. The physical meaning of this rule is: users' clicks on a URL show that the URL has similar intents in more than a half of query submissions. (2) *Relative majority rule*: A URL is selected if its total number of clicks is more than the average number of clicks among all URLs. The physical meaning of this rule is: a URL with higher tendency to be clicked than other URLs will be more related to the query.

In *category recognition* stage, we use words in hostname and path to tell out different intents. A candidate whose URL contains at least one categorical keyword will be proposed. A categorical keyword set is formulated automatically as follows. We first employ the blacklist released publicly in URLBlacklist.com to collect categorical keywords common used in URLs of pornographic web pages, then remove "http://" and "/" from URLs, further segment the remaining part of host name and path into all possible n-grams, and finally compose a 172-categorical-keyword set by consulting a pornographic dictionary.

Besides, we also propose an *accumulative update strategy*, i.e., to use all query logs up to now, to explore the change of collective intelligence and update the blacklist. The accumulative time periods imply that the same query can be issued at different time and different search results may be clicked by users with similar intents. The newborn objectionable web pages or the variants of the original ones for avoiding being filtered can be included in the updated blacklist if users have accessed them with similar intent.

3. EXPERIMENTS

3.1 Data Sets

The data set comes from the MSN 2006 RFP data. It consists of an MSN search query log excerpt with 15 million queries from US users during May 2006. Data made available include the issued queries, the clicked URLs and the time-stamps. We randomly selected 1% of MSN search query logs and removed those queries issued only once. After sampling, we manually labeled the pages as ground truth by examining their contents. Those pages which could not be accessed successfully at the labeling time were ignored. The numbers of unique queries issued in our testing data set are 43,198. Total 5,821 and 10,135 unique URLs are annotated in porn and non-porn categories, respectively.

3.2 Experimental Results

To examine the effects of the three stages in user intent model, i.e., (1) *query identification*, (2) *majority voting*, and (3) *category recognition*, we experiment different combinations of stages on the testing data set, where the time period is set to one month. Table 1 shows the experimental results. Strategy (1) achieves the highest recall, but a very bad false positive rate and precision. It reveals the category of queries does not always represent the category of web pages. Comparing Strategies (1)+(2) and (1)+(3), *category recognition* in URLs performs better than *majority voting*, due to clear categorical keywords of host names and paths in URLs. The disadvantage of *majority voting* is that even the same query was issued, different search results were proposed by search engines at different time.

The proposed *user intent* model, i.e., Strategy (1)+(2)+(3), performs the best. It achieves high precisions of 0.7418, while maintaining favorably low false positive rate 0.0707. We analyze the reason of lower recall, and find that the number of clicks will be distributed among different URLs of the same pornographic content. In such a case, the clicks cannot satisfy any majority voting rules. Because pornographic content is the major target for objectionable web content filtering, the content providers tend to create more hosts and redirections to avoid being filtered.

Table 1. Experimental results of MSN RFP data set

Strategy	Precision	Recall	False Positive Rate
(1)	0.5669	0.8505	0.3732
(1)+(2)	0.6057	0.4485	0.1677
(1)+(3)	0.6941	0.6628	0.1677
(1)+(2)+(3)	0.7418	0.3539	0.0707

Comparing Strategies (1) and (1)+(2)+(3), the former is an aggressive method for achieving a higher recall without concerning false positive rate; and the latter is a conservative method in which false positive rate is an important consideration. The *user intent* method achieves the lowest false positive rate of all the four methods. Obviously, this method is more proper to incorporate collective intelligence to search engines to mask pornographic search results before they are clicked.

We further evaluate the filtering effects by real-life simulation using query logs. Figure 1 shows the blocking rates of three update strategies when time period is set to one day. The *without update* strategy, i.e., query logs of the first time period are used to generate a blacklist, performs the worst. Its blocking rate decreases with the passage of the time. The *preceding update* strategy, which iteratively updates a blacklist with the query logs of the preceding time period, performs better than the *without update* strategy because similar search results will be reported for the same query with similar intent in the following day.

The *accumulative update* strategy achieves the macro-averaging blocking rate 43.36%, which is better than 28.44% and 20.56% with the *preceding update* and the *without update* strategies, respectively. In addition, its blocking rates vary between 40% and 50% with standard deviation 0.04. The over-blocking rate, which is the proportion of normal accesses incorrectly blocked as pornographic ones, of all the three strategies is less than 7%.

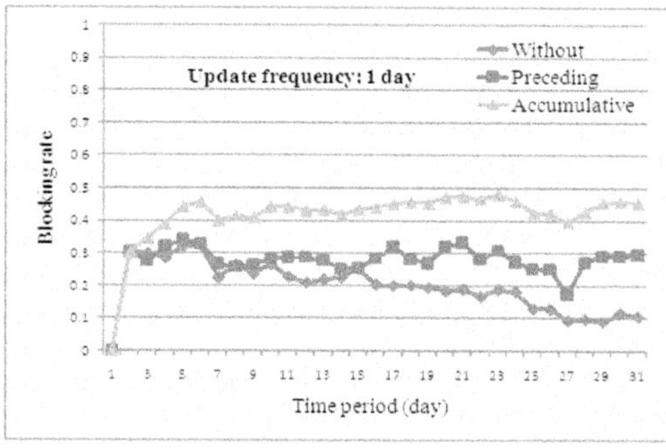

Figure 1. Blocking trend if update frequency is one day.

4. CONCLUSIONS AND FUTURE WORK

This paper proposes a simple but effective intent-based method for cyberporn filtering. Query ambiguity is a challenging issue for intent-based approach. Alternative suspected query identification methods such as considering a porn dictionary as seed queries will be investigated in the future for improving filtering performance.

5. ACKNOWLEDGEMENTS

This research was partially supported by National Science Council, Taiwan under grant NSC99-2221-E-002-167-MY3. We are also grateful to Microsoft Research Asia for the support of MSN Search Query Log excerpt.

6. REFERENCES

[1] Hammami, M., Chahir, Y., and Chen, L. 2006. WebGuard: a web filtering engine combining textual, structural, and visual content-based analysis. *IEEE Transactions on Knowledge and Data Engineering*, 18(2), 272-284.

[2] Lee, L.-H., and Luh, C.-J. 2008. Generation of pornographic blacklist and its incremental update using an inverse chi-square based method. *Information Processing and Management*, 44(5), 1698-1706.

[3] Szummer, M. and Craswell, N. 2008. Behavioral classification on the click graph. In *Proceedings of the 17th International World Wide Web Conference*, 1241-1242.

[4] Zhang, J., Qin, J., and Yan, Q. 2006. The role of URLs in objectionable web content categorization. In *Proceedings of the 2006 IEEE/WIC/ACM International Conference on Web Intelligence*, 277-283.

Do IR Models Satisfy the TDC Retrieval Constraint?

Stéphane Clinchant
Xerox Research Center Europe & Université Grenoble I, LIG
6, Chemin de Maupertuis
38240 Meylan, France
stephane.clinchant@xrce.xerox.com

Eric Gaussier
Université Grenoble I, LIG
BP 53 - 38041 Grenoble cedex 9
Grenoble, France
eric.gaussier@imag.fr

Categories and Subject Descriptors

H.3.3 [**Information Storage and Retrieval**]: Information Search and Retrieval

General Terms

Algorithms, Experimentation, Theory

Keywords

axiomatic constraint, TDC constraint

1. INTRODUCTION

Axiomatic methods were pioneered by Fang *et al.* [5] and used since then in several studies including [3, 2]. In a nutshell, axiomatic methods provide formal constraints that IR functions should satisfy in order to be valid, i.e. to perfom well on IR tasks. According to [2], the four main constraints for an IR function to be valid can be phrased as: the weighting function should (a) be increasing and (b) concave wrt term frequencies, (c) have an IDF effect and (d) penalize long documents. In addition to these four basic constraints, Fang *et al.* [5] introduced additional constraints to regulate the relative importance of different parameters, as TF and IDF for example.

The IDF effect mentioned above relates to the constraint referred to in [5] as the *TDC* constraint, which can be formulated as follows:

TDC: Let q be a query and $w1$, $w2$ be two query terms. Assume $l_{d1} = l_{d2}$, $c(w1, d1) + c(w2, d1) = c(w1, d2) + c(w2, d2)$. If $idf(w1) \geq idf(w2)$ and $c(w1, d1) \geq c(w1, d2)$, then $RSV(d1, q) \geq RSV(d2, q)$.

where $c(w, d)$ denotes the number of occurrences of w in d. This constraint aims at capturing the fact that, *ceteris paribus*, rarer terms (i.e. terms with a large IDF) should be preferred over more frequent ones. However, there are several ways to define the context (*ceteris paribus*) in which to place this constraint, and the study presented in [2] relies on a stricter context corresponding to a special case of the *TDC* constraint, where $w1$ only occurs in $d1$ and $w2$ only in $d2$. This constraint, referred to as *speTDC* can be formulated as:

speTDC: Let q be a query and $w1$, $w2$ two query terms. Assume $l_{d1} = l_{d2}$, $c(w1, d1) = c(w2, d2)$, $c(w2, d1) = c(w1, d2) = 0$. If $idf(w1) \geq idf(w2)$, then $RSV(d1, q) \geq RSV(d2, q)$.

SIGIR'11, July 24–28, 2011, Beijing, China.
ACM 978-1-4503-0757-4/11/07.

If it has been show in previous studies (as [5, 2]) that most IR models satisfy most IR constraints, the situation of the *TDC* constraint is unclear, and the goal of this short paper is to show that several state-of-the-art IR models indeed do not comply with the general *TDC* constraint, but do satisfy the *speTDC* one. We will review here the recently introduced log-logistic model [2], as well as the Jelinek-Mercer and Dirichlet language models.

2. IR MODELS AND THE TDC CONSTRAINT

The **log-logistic model** proposed in [2] is specified by:

$$t(w,d) = c(w,d)\log(1 + c\frac{avg(l_d)}{l_d})$$
$$r_w = \frac{N_w}{N}(-\frac{1}{\text{idf}(w)})$$
$$RSV(q,d) = \sum_{w \in q \cap d} c(w,q)(\log(r_w + t^d_w) - \log(r_w))$$

where N_w is the number of documents in the collection containing the term w and N the total number of documents in the collection; l_d is the length of document d, and $\text{avg}(l_d)$ the average document length in the collection.

Let us examine the *TDC* constraint for this model, and for that let us consider two documents d_1 and d_2 of equal length l; let $\gamma = \log(1 + c^{\frac{avg(l)}{l}})$. For simplification, we use a to denote w_1, b to denote w_b and a_1 (resp. a_2) for $c(a, d_1)$ (resp. $c(a, d_2)$). For a query q consisting of only a and b, the difference in score between d_1 and d_2 amounts to:

$$\Delta = RSV(q, d1) - RSV(q, d2) = \log(\frac{r_a + a_1\gamma}{r_a + a_2\gamma} \times \frac{r_b + b_1\gamma}{r_b + b_2\gamma})$$

Now, let us place ourselves in the conditions specified in the *TDC* constraint and let us assume that $r_a < r_b$, $a^1 > a^2$ and $a_1 + b_1 = a_2 + b_2$ (and thus $b_2 > b_1$). The TDC constraints stipulates in that case that $\Delta \geq 0$, that is:

$$\gamma(a_1b_1 - a_2b_2) + r_b(a_1 - a_2) + r_a(b_1 - b_2)) \quad > \quad 0$$

Setting: $a_1 = 7, b_1 = 4, a_2 = 6, b_2 = 5, r_a = 0.001$ and $r_b = 0.01$ shows that the above inequality is true *iff* $\gamma < 0.0045$. Hence, γ must be very small for the *TDC* constraint to be verified. Indeed, for documents of average length, $\gamma \approx \log(1 + c)$ and c should be chosen smaller to 0.005 for the above inequality to be satisfied.

We now provide a more formal proof that the log-logistic model does not comply with the *TDC* constraint. Let's first

Table 1: Pair of query terms (short query) below mean corpus language model

Collection	m	μ	$diff < m$
robust	0.0003	500	62.2 %
trec1-2	0.0005	1000	62.2 %

consider the following optimization problem:

$$\text{argmax}_{t_a \geq 0, t_b \geq 0} \quad \mathcal{A} = \sum_{w \in \{a,b\}} \log(r_w + t_w) - \log(r_w)$$

$$\text{subject to} \quad \sum_{w \in \{a,b\}} t_w = s$$

where s is a pre-defined, positive value. As the log is concave, the overall objective funciton is concave, and the solution to the above optimization problem correspond to the values maximizing the following Lagrangian:

$$\Lambda = \sum_{w \in \{a,b\}} \log(r_w + t_w) - \log(r_w) - \lambda(\sum_{w \in \{a,b\}} t_w - s)$$

for which the partial derivatives are defied as:

$$\frac{\partial \Lambda}{\partial t_w} = \frac{1}{r_w + t_w} - \lambda$$

Setting these derivatives to 0 leads to the following solution[1]:

$$t_a = \frac{s + r_b - r_a}{2}, \; t_b = \frac{s + r_a - r_b}{2}$$

Now let us consider a query q with two words (a and b) occurring only once, and let d_1 a,d d_2 be two documents of equal length. Let us furthermore assume that: idf(a) $= \frac{1}{r_a} \geq$ idf(b) $= \frac{1}{r_b}$, and:

$$t_a^{d_1} = \frac{s + r_b - r_a}{2} + \epsilon, \quad t_b^{d_1} = \frac{s+r_a-r_b}{2} - \epsilon$$

$$t_a^{d_2} = \frac{s + r_b - r_a}{2}, \quad t_b^{d_2} = \frac{s+r_a-r_b}{2}$$

for ϵ sufficiently small for all the quantities to be positive. In this case, all the conditions of the *TDC* constraint are verified, and thus one should observe that $RSV(q, d_1) \geq RSV(q, d_2)$, which is in contradiction with the fact that the values for d_2 are the ones that maximize $\mathcal{A}$ which corresponds in this case to the retrieval status value. This shows that the log-logistic model is not compliant with the *TDC* constraint. However, as shown in [2], the log-logistic model is compliant with the *speTDC* constraint, which represents a stricter version of the *TDC* constraint.

The situation for language models wrt the *TDC* and *speTDC* constraints is identical to the one of the log-logistic model. Indeed, it has been shown in [1] that the **Jelinek-Mercer model** could be seen as a special case of the log-logistic model. All the development made above in the context of the log-logistic model applies to the Jelinek-Mercer model, which is not compliant with the *TDC* constraint (it is however compliant with the *speTDC* constraint).

As shown in [5], and using the notations introduced previously, the **Dirichlet language model** agrees with the *TDC* constraint in the following case:

$$\mu \geq \frac{a_1 - b_2}{p(b|C) - p(a|C)} \quad (1)$$

[1]As $r_a \ll t_a$ and $r_b \ll t_b$, both t_a and t_b are ≥ 0.

where $p(a|C)$ represents the collection probability. Table 1 shows for several collections the mean value of $p(w|C)$ for query terms (denoted m), the optimal values obtained for the Dirichlet smoothing parameter μ and the percentage of pairs of query terms for which the corpus language model absolute difference ($|p(w'|C) - p(w|C)|$) is below m (denoted $diff < m$). As one can note, in almost two third of the cases, the numerator of equation 1 is very small. So, for the bound given in equation 1 to hold, one needs to rely on large values for μ (larger than 2,000 when the numerator is one). As shown in table 1, we are far from these values in practice, and the Dirichlet language model is in general not compliant with the *TDC* constraint. Furthermore, using the analytical formulation of the *speTDC* constraint proposed in [2], one can show that the Dirichlet language model is compliant with the *speTDC* constraint.

3. CONCLUSION

We have shown here that several state-of-the-art IR models do not satisfy the *TDC* retrieval constraint introduced in [5]. The IR models we have considered are the recently introduced log-logistic model, and two standard versions of the language model, namely the one based on Jelinek-Mercer smoothing, and the one based on Dirichlet smoothing. Furthermore, we have seen that all these models satisfy *speTDC*, a stricter version of the *TDC* constraint introduced in [2] to directly formalize the IDF effect. Because of the good behavior of the models we have reviewed, we believe that the above development suggests that the *TDC* constraint is not valid, and should be replaced with the *speTDC* one.

Directly assessing the validity of a particular retrieval constraint is not straightforward. The work presented in [4] shows that it is possible to experimentally assess whether a particular IR model complies or not with a given constraint. It is however not clear whether all constraints can be taken into account. We have followed here a different line, based on a theoretical analysis of the behavior orf IR models wrt a particular constraint.

4. REFERENCES

[1] S. Clinchant and E. Gaussier. Bridging language modeling and divergence from randomness models: A log-logistic model for ir. In *ICTIR*, pages 54–65, 2009.

[2] S. Clinchant and E. Gaussier. Information-based models for *ad hoc* IR. In *Proceeding of the 33rd international ACM SIGIR conference on Research and development in information retrieval*, SIGIR '10, pages 234–241, New York, NY, USA, 2010. ACM.

[3] R. Cummins and C. O'Riordan. An axiomatic comparison of learned term-weighting schemes in information retrieval: clarifications and extensions. *Artif. Intell. Rev.*, 28:51–68, June 2007.

[4] R. Cummins and C. O'Riordan. Measuring constraint violations in information retrieval. In *Proceedings of the 32nd international ACM SIGIR conference on Research and development in information retrieval*, SIGIR '09, pages 722–723, 2009.

[5] H. Fang, T. Tao, and C. Zhai. A formal study of information retrieval heuristics. In *SIGIR '04: Proceedings of the 27th annual international ACM SIGIR conference on Research and development in information retrieval*, 2004.

On Diversifying and Personalizing Web Search

David Vallet, Pablo Castells
Universidad Autónoma de Madrid
Cantoblanco, 28049 Madrid, Spain
{david.vallet, pablo.castells}@uam.es

ABSTRACT

Diversification and personalization methods are common approaches to deal with the one-size-fits-all paradigm of Web search engines. We performed a user study with 190 subjects where we analyzed the effects of diversification and personalization methods in a Web search engine. The obtained results suggest that our proposed combination of diversification and personalization factors may be a way to overcome the notion of intrusiveness in personalized approaches.

Categories and Subject Descriptors: H.3.3 Information Search and Retrieval – *retrieval models, information filtering.*

General Terms: Algorithms, Experimentation.

Keywords: Diversity, personalization, Web search

1. INTRODUCTION

With the ever increasing content made available on the Web, search systems struggle with finding the information required by users. The problem of selecting which results are relevant to a user is aggravated by two related characteristic of Web search systems: they follow a one-size-fits-all paradigm and represent the user's information need as a set of keywords. The latter characteristic results often in ambiguous or too broad search topics, which makes difficult to adopt the one-size-fits-all paradigm, as many different personal views of the topic have to be covered. Two different ways of overcoming these problems have been proposed in recent years: personalization and diversification approaches.

On the one hand, diversification techniques attempt to deal with ambiguous queries by presenting to the user a list of results that covers all the possible interpretations of the query. Thus, they try to maximize the probability that one of the presented interpretations is relevant to the user [1][4]. However, diversification models still follow a one-size-fits-all approach, which means that it may be that users with particular interests do not find their relevant results at the top of the result set. On the other hand, the field of personalization attempts a different way of overcoming the Web search problem: rather than adjusting to the one-size-fits-all approach, and trying to cover the different meanings of an ambiguous query, search results can be tailored to the particular meaning that is relevant to the user's interests [2]. However, the goal of personalization has yet to be met: user profiles are often not accurate enough and thus personalized results are often found to be intrusive by the user. This could be because personalization techniques take too much risk by only showing results related to the user profile representation.

In this paper we propose to meet halfway the above two approaches. We perform a user study in order to analyze if personalization and diversification techniques can be combined to overcome the one-size-fits-all paradigm and the intrusiveness felt from diversification and personalization techniques, respectively. Radlinski and Dumais [3] study the application of diversification techniques as a previous step to personalization. Their goal is to maximize the probability that a relevant result to the user is found in the diversified list. Still, their approach relies on an accurate representation of the user's interests. We suggest that this problem of inaccurate personalization approaches can be overcome by adding personalization components to a diversification approach.

SIGIR'11, July 24–28, 2011, Beijing, China.
ACM 978-1-4503-0757-4/11/07.

2. EVALUATED METHODS

In this section, we describe the different personalization and diversification approaches to be evaluated in our user study.

Personalization (Pers). As a pure personalization approach, we define a typical approach which represents interests of the user as a set of preferred topics and ranks documents with respect to their relation to each topic. This approach can be defined as a scoring function of a document related to a query and a user:

$$Pers(d|q,u) = \sum_c V(d|q,c)P(c|u,q)$$

where $V(d|q,c)$ is the quality (relevance) of the document given a query and a topic category and $P(c|u,q)$ is the relevance of the category to the user for the current query. The effect of this approach is that if the user has an interest towards only a single category related to a query, only documents related to this category will be shown to the user. If the user has multiple interests related to a query, the degree of interest to each topic will be used to decide the ranking of each document. Note that in our experiments this approach is applied over a diversified result list, and thus it can be considered an adaptation of the state of the art [3].

Intent Aware Select (IA-S). As a pure diversification algorithm, we implement the diversification approach by Agrawal et al [1], which finds a set S of documents of size k that maximizes:

$$P(S|q) = \sum_c P(c|q)\left(1 - \prod_{d\in S}(1 - V(d|q,c))\right)$$

where $P(c|q)$ is the distribution probability of a category belonging to the query, which can be supposed to be uniform if no other information is available.

Personalized Intent Aware Select (PIA-S). We propose to incorporate a personalized factor into the intent aware approach proposed by Agrawal et al. [1]. In our personalized intent aware approach, the probability distribution $P(c|q)$ in the objective function is substituted by the probability that the category is relevant to the user given a query, i.e. $P(c|u,q)$:

$$(S|q,u) = \sum_c P(c|u,q)\left(1 - \prod_{d\in S}(1 - V(d|q,c))\right)$$

The goal here is to promote those results that belong to a category related to the user's interests. However, the objective function still encourages including results from other categories with lower values. In this way, if the profile is not accurate enough, the users will be still able to find relevant results in the top positions.

Table 1: Average values for Likert scales

Question	Baseline	Pers	PIA-S	IA-S
Q1 (Topic)	3.805	4.304	4.209	3.813
Q2 (Interests)	3.117	4.216	3.973	3.219
Q3 (Overall)	3.305	4.272	3.899	3.284

3. EXPERIMENTS

In order to test our hypothesis, we performed a user centered study. Similar to Rafiei et al. [4] and Santos et al. [5], we identified possibly ambiguous queries from Wikipedia, and used the disambiguation pages to extract the possible related subtopics or categories. From each subtopic, we chose no less than 4 and no more than 7 related subtopics. In the case that more subtopics were presented in the disambiguation page, we chose those subtopics which returned a larger number of results. We used a well-known commercial search engine to obtain the results from each topic and subtopic. As Santos et al. [5] suggest, we use the subtopic definition from Wikipedia to obtain results related to each of the sub-topicalities of the query. In this way, we can suppose that if a Web page appears on the results of a subtopic, it is related to this subtopic related to the general topic. As we did not have access to the result scores, the relevance score of a document regarding a subtopic was computed using a rank-based normalization of the subtopic results. This score was computed as $V(d|q,c) = 1/n$, where n is the position of the document in the result set. This process resulted in 23 evaluation topics. The baseline of our evaluation is the set of results returned by the commercial search engine for the original topic query.

In order to evaluate the different approaches, we built a Web-based evaluation interface to perform a user-centered evaluation, with the following steps: 1) present a random topic to the subject, and show the possible subtopics related to the topic, as extracted from Wikipedia; 2) to obtain the interests of the subjects, we ask them to indicate a level of interest for each topic, which was used to estimate $P(c|u,q)$; 3) the topic and interest information is used as input of two of the evaluated approaches, chosen randomly; 4) the system presents an anonymized side-by-side comparison page with the two resulting search result pages (10 results per list).

We designed a small questionnaire to collect the subjects' opinions about the presented results. It consisted of three questions with 5-point liker scales: Q1) This result list is relevant to the topic (Topic); Q2 This result list adjusts to my interests (Interests); Q3) Overall, how would you rate this result list? (Overall) Additionally, users were asked to indicate which of the two result pages they preferred, if any. We performed the user experiment using a crowdsourcing service (http://crowdflower.com), collecting 351 side-by-side evaluations from 60 users.

3.1 Experiment Results

Table 1 shows the average Likert-scale values for each of the control questions. The obtained results indicate that users had a general preference for those approaches that had some personalization component over the baseline and the pure diversification approach (IA-S). Within the personalized approaches, users preferred the pure personalization approach (Pers) over those that included some diversity component (PIA-S, IA-S). These differences were statistically significant (Mann-Whitney U, $p < 0.05$). The side-by-side comparison also indicated a statistically significant preference of users for the personalized approaches (Wilcoxon signed ranked test, $p < 0.05$). We did not find any statistical evidence that users had a preference either over the baseline or over the IA-S approach, which suggests that the commercial search engine was effective at diversifying results – this was later confirmed with a visual inspection.

Table 2: Q3 (Overall) Likert values with noisy user profiles

Algorithm	Q3	Q3 (I = 1)	ΔQ3	Q3 (I = 2)	ΔQ3
Pers	4.27	3.92	-8.3%*	3.61	-15.5%*
PIA-S	3.90	3.81	-2.3%	3.71	-4.7%

So far, the obtained results indicate a better performance of classic personalization approaches (Pers) over diversified or a combination of both approaches. However, the preference feedback in the previous study was obtained explicitly form the user for each topic. This assumption is unrealistic in common scenarios, as this kind of explicit feedback requires an extra effort from users, which is usually not accepted. In other words, this aspect of the experimental setup introduces an artificial advantage in the Pers system. Personalization approaches usually rely on automatic (more imprecise) preference learning methodologies based on implicit user feedback, therefore resulting in less accurate representations of the user interests and lower performance. Hence, in order to complement our study, we simulate a situation in which we do not have such accurate user preference information: we modified the evaluation system to manipulate the user profiles in order to include a noise level of I, which indicates the number of category preferences $P(c|u,q)$ per user that are assigned a random value. We carried out two additional user evaluations with a level of noise of I=1 and I=2. We collected over 500 additional topic judgments from 130 distinct users.

Table 2 shows the results of this evaluation. The lambda differences with respect to the original Likert values indicate that, as expected, the pure personalization approach is penalized when using less accurate user profiles. These differences were statistically significant (Mann-Whitney U, $p < 0.05$). However, the PIA-S approach, which incorporates diversification factors, does not have such a negative impact due to noisy preferences. Moreover, at a noise level of $I = 2$, users preferred the PIA-S approach when compared to the Personalization approach (Wilcoxon, $p < 0.05$). These results suggest that our proposed approach, which combines personalization and diversification factors, is more robust to less accurate user preference representations.

To conclude, we performed a user study in order to inspect the preference of real Web search users towards personalization and diversification approaches. Our results suggest that in the idealistic case in which the user interests are highly accurate, a pure personalization approach is the best performing approach. However, in a more realistic scenario, where e.g. the users would not manually build their profiles, our proposed approach, PIA-S, which combines personalization and diversification factors, performed better.

Acknowledgments. This work is supported by the Spanish Government (TIN2008-06566-C04-02), and the Government of Madrid (S2009TIC-1542).

4. REFERENCES

[1] Agrawal, R., Gollapudi, S., Halverson, A., and Ieong, S. Diversifying search results. In *WSDM '09*, pages 5-14, 2009.

[2] Micarelli, A., Gasparetti, F., Sciarrone, F., and Gauch, S.. Personalized search on the World Wide Web. The Adaptive Web, pages 195-230, 2007

[3] Radlinski, F. and Dumais, S. Improving personalized web search using result diversification. In *SIGIR '06*, pages 691-692, 2006.

[4] Rafiei, D., Bharat, K., and Shukla, A. Diversifying web search results. In *WWW '10*, pages 781-790, 2010.

[5] Santos, R., Peng, J., Macdonald, C., and Ounis, I.. Explicit search result diversification through sub-queries. In *ECIR '10*, pages 87-99, 2010

Semantic Tag Recommendation Using Concept Model*

Chenliang Li, Anwitaman Datta, Aixin Sun
School of Computer Engineering, Nanyang Technological University, Singapore
{lich0020|anwitaman|axsun}@ntu.edu.sg

ABSTRACT

The common tags given by multiple users to a particular document are often semantically relevant to the document and each tag represents a specific topic. In this paper, we attempt to emulate human tagging behavior to recommend tags by considering the concepts contained in documents. Specifically, we represent each document using a few most relevant concepts contained in the document, where the concept space is derived from Wikipedia. Tags are then recommended based on the tag concept model derived from the annotated documents of each tag. Evaluated on a Delicious dataset of more than 53K documents, the proposed technique achieved comparable tag recommendation accuracy as the state-of-the-art, while yielding an order of magnitude speed-up.

Categories and Subject Descriptors

H.3.1 [**Information Systems**]: Information Search and Retrieval—*Content Analysis and Indexing*

General Terms

Algorithms, Experimentation

Keywords

Tag recommendation, Semantic tag, Concept model, Wikipedia

1. INTRODUCTION

Digital resources are increasingly being organized, summarized, shared and searched using tagging mechanisms. Consequently, there is immense research interest in efficient and effective tag recommendation techniques to boost manual tagging to cope with the continuously growing amount of digital data being produced.

In collaborative tagging, often, people emulate or share others' tagging behavior. As a result, semantically relevant tags emerge as the prominent tags with top frequency of occurrences, and a small set of common tags are typically reused to represent specific topics, which is known as *semantic tags* [2,5]. Semantic tags are normally common nouns and proper names (75.63% and 70.10% respectively), belonging mainly to the category of topic which describes what a tagged resource (*e.g.*, a document) is about [1]. Thus, it is reasonable to infer that a user subconsciously considers the concepts covered by a document when she is tagging that document.

*This work is partially supported by A-STAR grant 072 134 0055 and MOE AcRF Tier-1 Grant RG13/10, Singapore.

SIGIR'11, July 24–28, 2011, Beijing, China.
ACM 978-1-4503-0757-4/11/07.

In this paper, we attempt to emulate human tagging behavior, in that, people annotate semantic tags based on the concepts underlying a document and the semantic tags associated with these concepts. Specifically, we adopt a probabilistic framework to model a web document by its contained concepts and the likelihood of the semantic tags representing these concepts for tag recommendation. In our implementation, the concepts are derived from Wikipedia by taking each Wikipedia article as a concept.

Evaluated on a Delicious dataset containing more than 53K documents, our tag recommendation technique achieved comparable accuracy as state-of-the-art techniques, but yields a significant speed-up. This suggests that a small number of concepts contained in a document are effective in conveying the meaning of the document for meaningful tag recommendation. The concise concept-based representation against the commonly adopted uni-gram representation contributes to the speed-up.

2. CONCEPT MODEL

The key of the concept model is to represent a document using a small set of concepts contained in the document. In our implementation, the concept space is derived from Wikipedia, which is the largest knowledge repository. Each Wikipedia article (*i.e.*, article title) defines one concept.

Given a document, all keyphrases, each of which refers to at least one Wikipedia article, contained in the document are first identified through string matching. The extracted keyphrases are ranked by their *keyphraseness*, the priori probability that a keyphrase is used as anchor text of the wikilinks, no matter where it appears [4]. The lower-ranked keyphrases are then pruned for two reasons. First, the lower-ranked keyphrases are often not strongly related to any concepts, and hence are less effective in conveying the meaning of the document. Second, the pruning leads to a more concise representation of the document, enabling more efficient tag recommendation. The pruning is controlled by a parameter (*prune ratio*) set based on a validation set. Then, since a keyphrase may match multiple concepts, we apply word sense disambiguation [3] to derive the correct concepts under the context of the document of interest.

With concept based document representation, we adopt Equation 1 for semantic tag recommendation, where $P(t|d)$ is the likelihood that a tag t represents the meaning conveyed by document d, $P(t|c)$ is the likelihood that tag t represents concept c, and $P(c|d)$ denotes representativeness of concept c to document d.

$$P(t|d) = \sum_{c} P(t|c)P(c|d) \tag{1}$$

The tag recommendation problem is then to pick the top-k tags with the highest $P(t|d)$ values. We next discuss the estimation of $P(c|d)$ and $P(t|c)$ respectively.

Let $f(d,c)$ be the number of times concept c appears in document d. $P(c|d)$ is estimated by the concept's relative frequency with Jelinek-Mercer smoothing, shown in Equation 2. In this equation, $\lambda \in [0,1]$ is a smoothing parameter and $P(c|\mathcal{D})$ is the maximum likelihood estimate of concept c in the entire collection $\mathcal{D}$.

$$\hat{P}(c|d) = (1-\lambda)\frac{f(d,c)}{\sum_{c'} f(d,c')} + \lambda P(c|\mathcal{D}) \quad (2)$$

The probability $P(t|c)$ is estimated through the concept model of tag t (*i.e.*, $P(c|t)$) by Bayes' theorem: $P(t|c) = \frac{P(c|t)}{P(c)}P(t)$. While $P(c)$ and $P(t)$ can be easily estimated based on their corresponding frequencies in the collection, the estimation of $P(c|t)$ is not straightforward. Let D_t be the set of documents annotated by tag t. We build the concept model of tag t by a weighted concatenation of the concepts appearing in D_t, shown in Equation 3.

$$\hat{P}(c|t) = \frac{\sum_{d \in D_t} w(d,t) f(d,c)}{\sum_{c'} \sum_{d \in D_t} w(d,t) f(d,c')} \quad (3)$$

In this equation, $w(d,t)$ denotes the relevance or representativeness of document d towards tag t. Note that, many documents may carry the same tag, and a particular document may have multiple tags with varying frequencies given by multiple users (*e.g.*, Delicious).

Let T_d denote the set of tags assigned to document d, and $f(d,t)$ be the number of times tag $t \in T_d$ is assigned to d by (multiple) users. We consider four schemes to compute $w(d,t)$, summarized in Equation 4, where $f(t)$ is the frequency of tag t in the entire collection. The four schemes are: (i) Uniform Weighting (UW) where uniform weight of 1.0 is used, (ii) Document Perspective Weighting (DP) where $w(d,t)$ is the relative frequency of t assigned to d, (iii) Tag Perspective Weighting (TP) where $w(d,t)$ is the ratio of t being used to annotate d, and (iv) Document & Tag Perspective Weighting (DTP) which combines DP and TP.

$$w(d,t) = \begin{cases} 1.0 & \text{UW} \\ \frac{f(d,t)}{\max_{t' \in T_d} f(d,t')} & \text{DP} \\ \frac{f(d,t)}{f(t)} & \text{TP} \\ \frac{f(d,t)}{f(t)} \times \frac{f(d,t)}{\max_{t' \in T_d} f(d,t')} & \text{DTP} \end{cases} \quad (4)$$

3. EXPERIMENTS

Dataset. We evaluate the proposed concept based tag recommendation using Delicious dataset comprising 144,574 documents and 67,104 distinct tags [7]. After removing very short and unpopular documents (*i.e.*, less than 100 words and less than 50 users), the remaining 53,550 documents were randomly split into three sets: 49,550 for model training, 1,000 for parameter validation (*e.g.*, prune ratio, smoothing parameter), and 3,000 for performance evaluation. The concept space was derived from Wikipedia dump created on 12 March 2010.

Methods. Three baseline methods are compared in our experiments. The naïve baseline is to recommend the most popular tags (MPT) to all documents. The state-of-the-art baseline is the one based on language generative model (TPL) reported very recently in [6]. To evaluate the effectiveness of the notion of concept, another set of baseline methods are designed by replacing concept by uni-gram (*i.e.*, words) in the documents. Then Equation 1 is rewritten as $P(t|d) = \sum_w P(t|w)P(w|d)$. Coupled with the four weighting schemes in Equation 4, we use CM+{UW, DP, TP, DTP} and UM+{UW, DP, TP, DTP} to denote the four methods using concept model and uni-gram model respectively.

Performance Metrics. The recommendation accuracy is measured by *NDCG@N* and *Precision@N*. *NDCG@N* measures the consistency between the top-*N* recommended tag ranking and the ground truth tag ranking by users [5]. *Precision@N* (or *Prec@N*) is the ratio of tags indeed used by users among the top-*N* recommended tags. The execution time is also reported and all experiments were conducted on the same environment.

Table 1: Performance of methods, where * indicates the difference against the best performance is significant with $p < 0.01$

Methods	*NDCG@5*	*NDCG@10*	*Prec@5*	*Prec@10*
UM+UW	0.1778*	0.2323*	0.4009*	0.3485*
UM+TP	0.2383*	0.2946*	0.4462*	0.3758*
UM+DP	0.2357*	0.2914*	0.4461*	0.3733*
UM+DTP	0.2638*	0.3208*	0.4673*	0.3854*
CM+UW	0.3370*	0.4032*	0.5815*	0.4784*
CM+TP	0.4081*	0.4781*	0.6312*	0.5152*
CM+DP	0.4104*	0.4809*	0.6373*	0.5162*
CM+DTP	**0.4213**	**0.4915**	0.6355*	0.5151*
MPT	0.0900*	0.1196*	0.2753*	0.2412*
TPL	0.3983*	0.4843	**0.7055**	**0.5983**

Recommendation Accuracy. Table 1 reports the performance of all methods in terms of *NDCG@*{5, 10} and *Prec@*{5, 10}. For each metric, the best performing method is highlighted in boldface and the second best is underlined. Observe that: (i) unsurprisingly, the simple MPT performs the worst by all measures; (ii) all concept model based methods outperform uni-gram based methods significantly by all measures, regardless of weighting scheme used; (iii) among concept based methods, CM+DTP is the winner in terms of *NDCG@*{5, 10} and CM+UW performed the worst in both metrics. (iv) comparing with the state-of-the-art TPL, CM+DTP achieves better *NDCG@5* significantly and marginal improvement in *NDCG@10*. Although TPL yields better *Prec@*{5, 10}, a close investigation reveals that many tags recommended by TPL are of low frequency, which may only benefit a small group of users. This is also reflected by *NDCG@*{5, 10} as *NDCG* measures consider tag frequency in the evaluation and tags with higher frequencies are given more weights in the measure.

Execution Time. The average tagging time of UM+DTP, TPL and CM+DTP were 21.30, 22.23 & 2.50 seconds respectively. Note that the tagging time for CM+DTP includes concept detection time. That is, concept model based method incurs an order of magnitude computation cost reduction.

4. CONCLUSION

In this paper, we propose a semantic tag recommendation mechanism based on concept model. The concept model enables a concise representation of documents by considering only a few concepts most relevant to the documents. Comparing with the state-of-the-art, our method achieved comparable tag recommendation accuracy but yield a significant speed-up. Our future work is aimed at incorporating the concept model with other approaches for better tag recommendation accuracy.

5. REFERENCES

[1] K. Bischoff, C. S. Firan, W. Nejdl, and R. Paiu. Can all tags be used for search? In *Proc. CIKM*, 2008.

[2] H. Halpin, V. Robu, and H. Shepherd. The complex dynamics of collaborative tagging. In *Proc. WWW*, 2007.

[3] C. Li, A. Sun, and A. Datta. A generalized method for word sense disambiguation based on wikipedia. In *Proc. of ECIR*, 2011.

[4] D. Milne and I. H. Witten. Learning to link with wikipedia. In *Proc. of CIKM*, 2008.

[5] F. M. Suchanek, M. Vojnovic, and D. Gunawardena. Social tags: meaning and suggestions. In *Proc. CIKM*, 2008.

[6] D. Yin, Z. Xue, L. Hong, and B. D. Davison. A probabilistic model for personalized tag prediction. In *Proc. SIGKDD*, 2010.

[7] A. Zubiaga, A. P. García-Plaza, V. Fresno, and R. Martínez. Content-based clustering for tag cloud visualization. In *Proc. of ASONAM*, 2009.

Recommending Interesting Activity-Related Local Entities

Jie Tang
University of California, Berkeley
Berkeley, CA 94709
jietang@eecs.berkeley.edu

Ryen W. White
Microsoft Research
Redmond, WA 98052
ryenw@microsoft.com

Peter Bailey
Microsoft Bing
Bellevue, WA 98004
pbailey@microsoft.com

ABSTRACT
When searching for entities with a strong local character (e.g., a museum), people may also be interested in discovering proximal activity-related entities (e.g., a café). Geographical proximity is a necessary, but not sufficient, qualifier for recommending other entities such that they are related in a useful manner (e.g., interest in a fish market does not imply interest in nearby bookshops, but interest in other produce stores is more likely). We describe and evaluate methods to identify such activity-related local entities.

Categories and Subject Descriptors
H.3.3 [**Information Storage and Retrieval**]: Information Search and Retrieval – *search process, selection process.*

General Terms
Algorithms, Measurement, Experimentation.

Keywords
Local entities, entity resolution, entity-entity matching.

1. INTRODUCTION
People are frequently interested in finding out information about specific local entities, say the Museum of Modern Art (MOMA) in the city of New York, NY. They may be tourists and planning a trip, or residents exploring their city. In addition to retrieving Web documents matching users' search queries for the specific local entity, modern Web search engines may provide a rich and diverse results page with additional information related to the query. Understanding the local user intent behind such users' queries offers an opportunity to surface recommendations about other interesting activity-related local entities. For example, after visiting MOMA, a shopping trip or a visit to a local bar may be common activities. These relationships may not be commutative: an interest in a bar is unlikely to imply an interest in nearby cultural centers. Similarly, an interest in a cupcake shop may mean an interest in other nearby cupcake shops, not some different class of local entity. Lastly, as observed by Jones *et al.* [2], the nature of the entity and/or corresponding activity may imply a different willingness to travel. Thus for suggesting activity-related local entities, an interest in a major city attraction may indicate an interest in other city attractions several miles away, but an interest in a bar may only suggest interest in other nearby bars or cafés.

2. IDENTIFYING LOCAL ENTITIES
This work describes a procedure for identifying related local entities. Xiao *et al.* [6], similarly motivated about local *relatedness*, observed behavior in geographic (local map vertical) search logs and derived mechanisms to identify co-located queries at different geographic region resolutions. Our algorithms are unrelated to theirs, and we focus on identifying *entities*, not queries. Note that although we conduct our study in the context of Seattle, WA, the methods described could be applied to any city of reasonable size.

SIGIR'11, July 24–28, 2011, Beijing, China.
ACM 978-1-4503-0757-4/11/07.

2.1 Pre-processing and Geocoding
Unlike Wang *et al.*'s approach [4], which works to extract dominant locations (either explicit or implicit) associated with *queries*, we focused on identifying an *entity*'s location. The first step involves the identification of URLs that may be relevant to the location of interest. We obtained clickthrough logs from the Bing Web search engine and mined queries and the URLs that users clicked on for those queries, providing us with implicit associations between queries and URLs. We extracted URLs containing "seattle" in the associated query string, and identified address-based queries and their query-URL mapping. For example, the query [*pike place market, pike street, seattle*] could map to pikeplacemarket.org, describing the local entity Pike Place Market. To remove infrequently-visited sites, we also use browsing logs from a widely-distributed browser plugin, and retained URLs that appear in those logs and the clickthrough logs. This left us with a set of five to ten thousand URLs, potentially describing a local Seattle entity. To determine the physical location for each entity we use the Bing Maps Geocoding API (microsoft.com/maps/developers), which processes queries and returns their geocoded locations. Geocoding results over 100 miles from Seattle were removed from analysis.

2.2 Entity Resolution
We employ entity resolution to get from a URL to other URLs that refer to the same entity. Starting from every URL in the set created using the steps above we find the query which sends the most traffic to that URL (the canonical query). We then look at the top URLs by clickthrough rate for this query, and select those which attract more than 5% of the total click count. These URLs comprise an entity cluster, and we assign as the canonical entity the URL with the highest total click count of the set.

2.3 Entity Recommendation
Entities are represented by their canonical URL from Section 2.2. Entity-entity matching algorithms recommend related entities by processing entity information, location information, and clickthrough or session data, to generate an affinity matrix, $\boldsymbol{A}$. The matrix is $\boldsymbol{N} \times \boldsymbol{N}$, where $\boldsymbol{N}$ is the number of entities, and the entry $A_{\{i,j\}}$ determines the relatedness between entities i and j

Click graph: Search engine result-page clickthrough data from one year of Bing search logs are incorporated by using the canonical URLs as starting points and performing a two-step graph walk (URL to queries then back out to URLs) to obtain related URLs.

Search sessions: The frequency of URL co-occurrence in search sessions from one-week of browsing logs, comprising search engine queries and post-query navigation (as described in [5]), is used to compute the degree of relatedness between entities.

We also study a number of extensions to each of these methods:

Merged: We combine the two matrices using a convex weight.

Max-flow: We run a max-flow algorithm on the merged affinity matrix to generate a new affinity matrix A', where $A'_{\{i,j\}}$ corresponds to the maximum amount of flow that can be pushed from entity i to entity j [1]. For efficiency, this is restricted to a two-hop max-flow where flow can travel up to two edges.

Hitting time: We run a hitting time algorithm on the merged affinity matrix to create a new matrix A', where $A'_{\{i,j\}}$ is proportional to the expected time before a random walk from i reaches j [3].

3. JUDGING ENTITIES

Evaluating our entity resolution and recommendations requires ground truth data, preferably from human raters, who may be able to determine inter-entity relationships. To this end, we recruited judges from Amazon Mechanical Turk (*turkers*).

3.1 Selection

We generated sets of URL-URL pairs via a graph walk over A: for every canonical URL, we pull a few URLs from that cluster, a few URLs which are one hop away, two hops away, etc. to form the other half of the URL-URL pair. This ensures that we have pairs covering a spectrum from unrelated to exact matches to be judged.

3.2 Methodology

Judges considered the following scenario: *You are planning an outing in the city and you are searching for ideas for what to do. There are a few locations you have heard about or are already looking to visit, and you would like to find more attractions / restaurants / shopping / etc. to round out your day.* We presented people with URL-URL pairs for each of the suggested URLs in each cluster, and asked them to rate the relatedness between the entity associated with the recommended entity and the reference entity on a four-point scale: 1=*URLs are unrelated*, 2=*URLs are related*, 3=*URLs are obviously related*, and 4=*URLs are the same entity*. Distance data estimating the physical distance between the recommended entity and the reference entity were also provided. Three of the authors judged a set of 20 entities and cluster URLs to establish a gold standard data set that was used in selecting turkers. For example, for Seattle Art Museum (seattleartmuseum.org), visiting the Seattle Aquarium (seattleaquarium.org) may be a good related activity and received an average rating of three, whereas a visit to a local garden and stone company (lakeviewstone.com) received an average rating of one. The Fleiss's kappa (κ) between authors was 0.74, signifying substantial agreement and suggesting that the task was reasonable for remote judges.

We scaled out the study to turkers. To control for the quality of the ratings, we did two things. First, we assigned a qualification test drawn from our gold standard truth data, in which each of the volunteers had to attain over 50% correct to attempt any of our human intelligence tasks (HITs). Next, each HIT contained three questions, one drawn from our gold standard set and two novel questions. Each time a HIT was submitted we verified that the turker answer matched our ground truth. We used this to update the qualification score, taking a running average with a weight of 0.05. This continual assessment strategy was employed to ensure that turkers did not work hard to pass the initial qualification and then not devote similar effort to the post-qualification tasks, whose ratings were important for our study. Turkers with qualification below 50% had their ratings excluded from our test data.

3.3 Judgments

In total, we obtained 3,426 URL-URL rating pairs. These raw numbers include both duplicates and those which raters did not agree on. Fleiss's κ was 0.43, signifying moderate agreement between our raters. Each URL-URL pair rated by three separate turkers, and the rating was used only if all three turkers agreed. We had just over 800 questions where all three raters agreed. We use those questions for the evaluation of the performance of our entity resolution and entity-entity recommendations.

4. FINDINGS

4.1 Entity Resolution

Many different URLs can refer to the same local entity (e.g., for the local entity bethscafe.com, we may also return the yelp.com and citysearch.com pages for the same café). Recommending duplicates may create a poor user experience, and we did not want to reward an algorithm for finding duplicate entities. We use the method for resolving entities described in Section 2.2, and evaluate it using our human labeled data. Two URLs are regarded as the same entity iff the human rating is four. The F_1 score, the harmonic mean of precision and recall, was 0.63, suggesting that we can detect duplicate entities with reasonable accuracy.

4.2 Entity Recommendation

To evaluate entity recommendation, two entities are considered related if turkers assigned a rating of two or three, and unrelated if the rating was one. Any non-zero entry in A was counted as a classification. Table 1 shows the F_1 scores for each of the recommendation algorithms described earlier. We used F_1 since we wanted to weight precision and recall equally.

Table 1. F_1 scores for entity recommendation algorithms.

Algorithm	Click graph	Search sessions	Merged	Merged Max-flow	Merged Hitting
F_1-score	0.39	0.28	0.44	0.48	0.49

Merging the click-graph and search-sessions methods led to improved performance over either method alone (0.44 vs. 0.39/0.26). Enhancements to the merged model using max-flow and hitting time algorithms led to further improvements. One explanation for the poor performance of the search sessions is less data (one week of browsing versus one year of click logs). However, the fact that it can still obtain an F_1 score that is 72% of the click graph score with much less data suggests that sessions may be valuable.

5. CONCLUSIONS AND FUTURE WORK

We studied methods for identifying related local entities and identifying duplicate entities using search and browsing behavior. Our methods performed well in both tasks. Entity recommendations based on a combination of clicks and session data performed particularly well, especially when enhanced with max-flow and hitting time. Future work involves developing new and improved algorithms with more log data, evaluating models with a larger set of judgments, and scaling recommendations to multiple locations.

REFERENCES

[1] Ford, L.R. and Fulkerson, D.R. (1956). Maximal flow through a network. *Canadian Journal of Mathematics*, 399–404.

[2] Jones, R., Zhang, W.V., Rey, B., Jhala, P., and Stipp, E. (2008). Geographic intention and modification in Web search. *J. of Geographical Information Science*, 22(3): 229–246.

[3] Mei, Q., Zhou, D., and Church, K. (2008). Query suggestion using hitting time. *Proc. CIKM*, 469–478.

[4] Wang, L., Wang, C., Xie, X., Forman, J., Lu, Y., Ma, W-Y., and Li, Y. (2005). Detecting dominant locations from search queries. *Proc. SIGIR*, 424–431.

[5] White, R.W. and Drucker, S.M. (2007). Investigating behavioral variability in Web search. *Proc. WWW*, 21–30.

[6] Xiao, X., Wang, L., Xie, X., and Luo, Q. (2008). Discovering co-located queries in geographic search logs. *Proc. LOCWEB*, 77–84.

Cross-Corpus Relevance Projection

Nima Asadi
Dept. of Computer Science
University of Maryland
College Park, MD
nima@cs.umd.edu

Donald Metzler
Information Sciences Institute
Univ. of Southern California
Marina del Rey, CA
metzler@isi.edu

Jimmy Lin
The iSchool
University of Maryland
College Park, MD
jimmylin@umd.edu

Categories and Subject Descriptors: H.3.3 Information Storage and Retrieval: Information Search and Retrieval

General Terms: Algorithms, Experimentation

Keywords: test collections, learning to rank, web search

1. INTRODUCTION

Document corpora are key components of information retrieval test collections. However, for certain tasks, such as evaluating the effectiveness of a new retrieval technique or estimating the parameters of a learning to rank model, a corpus alone is not enough. For these tasks, queries and relevance judgments associated with the corpus are also necessary. However, researchers often find themselves in scenarios where they only have access to a corpus, in which case evaluation and learning to rank become challenging.

Document corpora are relatively straightforward to gather. On the other hand, obtaining queries and relevance judgments for a given corpus is costly. In production environments, it may be possible to obtain low-cost relevance information using query and click logs. However, in more constrained research environments these options are not available, and relevance judgments are usually provided by humans. To reduce the cost of this potentially expensive process, researchers have developed low-cost evaluation strategies, including minimal test collections [2] and crowdsourcing [1]. Despite the usefulness of these strategies, the resulting relevance judgments cannot easily be "ported" to a new or different corpus.

To overcome these issues, we propose a new method to reduce manual annotation costs by transferring relevance judgments across corpora. Assuming that a set of queries and relevance judgments have been manually constructed for a *source* document corpus $\mathcal{D}_s$, our goal is to automatically construct a test collection for a *target* document corpus $\mathcal{D}_t$ by *projecting* the existing test collection from $\mathcal{D}_s$ onto $\mathcal{D}_t$.

The goal of projecting test collections is not to produce manual quality test collections. In fact, it is assumed that projected test collections will contain noisy relevance judgments (i.e., ones which humans are unlikely to agree with). The important question, however, is whether these noisy projected judgments are *useful* for training ranking models in the target corpus.

SIGIR'11, July 24–28, 2011, Beijing, China.
ACM 978-1-4503-0757-4/11/07.

2. PROJECTED TEST COLLECTIONS

As mentioned earlier, the input to our proposed model consists of a source document corpus $\mathcal{D}_s$ along with a set of existing queries and relevance judgments for that corpus. It is assumed that these judgments are provided in the form of "relevance" (Q, D, R) tuples, i.e., (query, document, relevance). Our goal is to leverage the existing judgments for corpus $\mathcal{D}_s$ and create tuples of the same form for the target corpus $\mathcal{D}_t$ for the same set of queries. In this way, we use the same set of queries across test collections, but find new documents and estimate their relevance in the target corpus.

We group existing tuples based on their Q field and perform the procedure described below for each of the groups separately. In other words, we project the relevance judgments for each query separately.

Using a set of features extracted from existing relevance tuples for a query, we train what we refer to as a supervised "relevance classifier". This classifier is capable of predicting relevance scores for a given document with respect to the query for which the classifier is designed. It is important to note that the type of features used to train the classifiers as well as the learning model have a significant impact on the performance of the relevance classifiers. Therefore, it is important to choose an expressive set of features, such as those commonly used in learning to rank models.

Once a classifier is trained over the source corpus for a query, the next step is to find a set of documents from the target corpus that can be labeled by the relevance classifier. Unlike the pooling method, this set of documents does not necessarily have to be the output of a given retrieval system. However, for convenience, we use BM25 to retrieve 1000 candidate documents per query for automatic labeling.

The final task is to assign relevance labels to the set of documents found in the target corpus $\mathcal{D}_t$. Even though research has shown the usefulness of graded relevance judgments, it makes the most sense for our relevance classifiers to assign binary judgments (i.e., "relevant" and "non-relevant"). However, it might be desirable for each label to have an associated confidence score. These scores may be informative for evaluation or learning to rank.

After repeating the above steps for all queries from a source corpus, a complete set of relevance tuples is constructed for the target corpus. It is important to note that since projections are carried out per query, there is no restriction on the number of source corpora that can be used to construct test collections for a target corpus. That is to say, a set of relevance judgments can be constructed for a query, given the relevance classifier designed for that query,

		Target					
		Wt10g		Gov2		ClueWeb09	
		proj	*base*	*proj*	*base*	*proj*	*base*
Source	Wt10g	-	-	**.181**	.179	.097	**.098**
	Gov2	**.127**	.125	-	-	.087	.088
	ClueWeb09	.126*	.120	.168	.179	-	-

Table 1: Effectiveness (ERR@20) of training on the projected (*proj*) test collections versus the baseline models (*base*).

regardless of the source corpus. This provides a mechanism for accumulating projected judgments from different sources for a fixed target test collection.

3. EXPERIMENTAL EVALUATION

We performed experiments using three TREC datasets: Wt10g (1.6m pages, topics 451–550), Gov2 (25m pages, topics 701–850), and the first English segment of ClueWeb09 (50m pages, topics 1–100). Title queries are used in all cases.

Our relevance classifier uses a maximum entropy model and is trained on a feature set consisting of basic information retrieval scores (language modeling and BM25 scores), and term proximity features (exact phrases, ordered windows, unordered windows, etc.).

The criterion we use to determine if our proposed approach is successful or not is whether a learning to rank model trained using a projected test collection over the target corpus can achieve better performance than a learning to rank model trained on the source corpus and tested on the target corpus. If this is the case, then we have shown that our projection method can be used to effectively transfer judgments across corpora. The effectiveness of the learned models is measured using manual judgments from each TREC test collection described above, using Expected Reciprocal Rank (ERR). To determine if differences between the various models are statistically significant, we utilize a one-side paired t-test.

We use a relatively straightforward learning to rank model in our experiments: an iterative greedy feature selection strategy that directly optimizes ERR to produce a linear ranking function, similar to the one described by Metzler [3]. Note that our ranking model shares the same features as the relevance classifier. This is a deliberate choice, but the alternative approach (disjoint features) may also have merits.

Table 1 shows the effectiveness (ERR@20) of the models trained using the projected test collections. It also illustrates the effectiveness of the baseline systems across different corpora. As described previously, the baseline is a ranking model trained using manual judgments from the source corpus and evaluated using the target corpus—in other words, no domain adaptation (but otherwise using exactly the same features and same learning method). The differences are not statistically significant in most cases, which means that relevance projection provides little benefit. However, the projected conditions fared no worse either, which suggests that despite the noisy projection process, relevance signals from the source corpus are largely preserved in the target corpus.

However, an opportunity that our proposed method creates is the ability to project judgments from *multiple* sources onto a *single* target corpus. Table 2 shows the effectiveness of projecting from two different sources onto each target corpus. Here, the baseline is simply joining the feature vectors

Sources→Target	Baseline	Projection
(1) Gov2,Wt10g→ClueWeb09	0.091	**0.101***
(2) ClueWeb09,Wt10g→Gov2	0.174	**0.182***
(3) ClueWeb09,Gov2→Wt10g	0.122	**0.127**

Table 2: Effectiveness (ERR@20) of training on projections from multiple sources.

from the two source collections to train the model, and then testing on the target corpus.

Results show that the somewhat naïve baseline of taking the union of training data from the two sources works rather poorly—worse than simply training on the "better" of the two sources alone. However, it is important to note that in a real-world scenario, we wouldn't have access to test data in the target corpus, so there would be no way of knowing which source was "better".

We see that models learned by projecting from Gov2 and Wt10g onto ClueWeb09 (1) and from ClueWeb09 and Wt10g onto Gov2 (2) are significantly better than the baseline (as denoted by asterisks in Table 2). In the case of (1), the projection condition is significantly better than training on Gov2 alone and testing on ClueWeb09, but not true for Wt10g. In the case of (3), the projection condition is significantly better than training on ClueWeb09 alone and testing on Wt10g, but not true for Gov2.

Although the results are somewhat inconclusive, we find that our proposed approach for projecting relevance judgments yields reasonable quality training data in the target corpus. Our method also allows more than one source to be projected onto the same target, and hints that more, but possibly lower-quality, training data in some cases leads to significant improvements.

4. CONCLUSIONS AND FUTURE WORK

We proposed a classification-based approach to transfer existing relevance judgments from one or more source corpora to a target corpus. The resulting projected test collection, which contains the same queries as the source, can be used for evaluation and to train learning to rank models. Experimental evaluations show that when projecting multiple source corpora onto a target corpus, it is sometimes possible to obtain significant improvements. Although the results are somewhat inconclusive, this finding is nevertheless interesting, and encourages further study in a few directions: different classifiers, different feature sets, and a different set of candidate documents in the target corpus on which the classifier is applied.

5. REFERENCES

[1] O. Alonso, D. Rose, and B. Stewart. Crowdsourcing for relevance evaluation. *SIGIR Forum*, 42(2):9–15, 2008.

[2] B. Carterette. *Low-Cost and Robust Evaluation of Information Retrieval Systems.* PhD thesis, University of Massachuetts, 2008.

[3] D. Metzler. Automatic feature selection in the Markov random field model for information retrieval. In *CIKM 2007*, pages 253–262.

Location Disambiguation for Geo-tagged Images

Zhu Zhu, Lidan Shou, Kuang Mao, Gang Chen
Department of Computer Science, Zhejiang University, Hangzhou, China
{04jsjzz,should,mbill,cg}@zju.edu.cn

ABSTRACT

In this poster, we address the problem of location disambiguation for geotagged Web photo resources. We propose an approach for analyzing and partitioning large geotagged photo collections using geographic and semantic information. By organizing the dataset in a structural scheme, we resolve the location ambiguity and clutter problem yield by massive volume of geotagged photos.

Categories and Subject Descriptors

H.3.3 [**Information Systems**]: Information Retrieval

General Terms

Algorithms, Design

Keywords

Location Disambiguation, Geotagged Images

1. INTRODUCTION

The popularity of mapping mashup applications has enabled millions of users with GPS-equipped gadgets to upload, tag, and share diverse media resources by their geographic locations. The need to manipulate and retrieve such massive geotagged Web resources is faced by a serious ambiguity problem.

The *geotags* of a photo indicate its relevance to a certain location, while the *textual tags* describe the photo's content or user's interests in it. We define the location designated by the geotags of an image as its *Physical Location*. The physical location is in the form of longitude and latitude coordinates and typically indicates the place where the photo is taken. Then we define the location that the content of the image refers to as its *Semantic Location*, assuming this would be implied in the title or textual tags of the item. Thus, a *Geographic Semantic Gap* between the physical location and semantic location can be observed for many images, as photos taken at the same place may capture different semantic objects. Conversely, photos targeting at the same object may have different physical locations too.

A keyword search for "Big Ben" in the well-known Panoramio geo-image search engine exemplifies this ambiguity problem. The search results displayed on a 2D map contains many pictures of the Big Ben scattering around a certain area. All these items have coordinates close to the bell and a common tag "Big Ben" in their tags. However, in the midst of these photos there are ones about other landmarks too, such as London Eye and Thames River, which are located elsewhere. The ambiguity problem will subject the dataset in a *clutter*, leading to unpleasant geotag-based retrieval experiences.

In this work, we try to analyze the spatial and semantic aspects of geotagged photos in a systematic way. Our approach is based on two observations, which motivate the approach to an organization of image collections. On one hand, geotagged photos inherently reveal geographic relations between each other; on the other hand, the semantic content contained in textual tags provides effective information for location disambiguation within a limited geographic region. Thus we propose a two-level clustering scheme combining structural analysis on the *geotags* with content analysis on the *textual tags* to resolve the ambiguity problem. Such combination leads us to know the underlying correlation among image semantics. We believe this would be particularly useful in supporting keyword-based search for geotagged images. In addition, our work can also be utilized to discover interesting non-landmarks.

Prior work in [3] and [2] also use clustering methods to organize geo-photo collections by combining geotags with *visual features*, rather than *textual tags*. Therefore, our approach is expectedly more efficient when handling massive photos.

2. SOLUTION

In our solution, the physical and semantic aspects are considered to resolve location ambiguity. Our data model handles geotagged photo collections about landmarks. Each photo p in the dataset $\mathbb{P}$ is represented by a three-tuple (θ_p, l_p, T_p), where θ_p is the unique photo ID, l_p is the physical location marking the place where it was taken, and T_p denotes the tag set. We assume every image has some geo-related tags such as place name. This "place semantics" are treated as the semantic location of the photo.

Our solution mainly consists of two clustering phases, namely a *geo-clustering* phase and a *semantic clustering* phase. In the geo-clustering phase, we employ a density based method OPTICS [1] to roughly segment the image collection into a set of compact geo-clusters. For the semantic clustering step, a spectral clustering algorithm is performed on each geo-cluster generated previously. Since each

SIGIR'11, July 24–28, 2011, Beijing, China.
ACM 978-1-4503-0757-4/11/07.

geo-cluster has limited size, the computational cost for exploring its semantic meanings becomes reasonable. Besides, We also employ an intermediate *semantic enhancement* process to produce more precise results for semantic clustering. This process can not only capture the underlying surrounding context of images, but also eliminate the negative effects caused by some ill-formed tags. Another advantage of our solution is its ability to adapt to the granularity of geo-clustering, which make sense for location-skewed data.

Step 1. Geo-clustering

We perform OPTICS clustering in metric space $(\mathbb{P}, d_G)$, d_G is the geographic distance between any two points on a flat Earth surface. As a density-based algorithm, OPTICS does not impose any restriction to the shape of the resulting clusters. As well, it can discover clusters of varying density, which favors for multi-level 2D visualization of the clustered results.

Step 2. Semantic Enhancement

Since the textual tags provided by users are often brief and noisy, we cannot simply rely on the document proximity measure to calculate the similarity between tags. We leverage additional Web resources to enhance the image semantics. Treating the tag set as a query to the Google search engine, we take the snippets of search results, then select the words with high term frequency to form an *enhanced semantic vector* V_p for each photo.

Step 3. Semantic Clustering

The semantic clustering procedure is iteratively applied for each geo-cluster produced in step 1. We compute the *tf-idf* matrix with enhanced semantic context, and construct an undirected weighted graph whose weight is calculated by cosine similarity measure. Finally, we use spectral clustering algorithm to partition the graph into k subsets using the K-means algorithm.

To determine parameter k, we address a novel method to automatically estimate the value k. This method can adapt to the granularity of the previous geo-clustering. The intuitions behind our method is:

- The error bound of location ambiguity is limited, because a camera can only capture scenes within a certain distance.
- We assume each cluster generated in geo-clustering represent a meaningful landmark, since it corresponds to a dense area with a burst in number of photos.

Thus for each geo-cluster, we expand its margin with a certain error bound. The area will become larger in the map so that it may overlap with adjacent geo-clusters. We define the number of geo-clusters overlapping the expanded area as the *semantic uncertain degree*, denoted by d_u. This degree indicates the photos in this area might have d_u additional semantic locations, so the intended number of clusters is given by $k = d_u + 1$. Obviously, the value of d_u will increase as the granularity of geo-clustering refines, since the number of the overlapping clusters may increase as well, which is the way semantic clustering automatically adapt to the granularity of geo-clustering.

3. EXPERIMENTS

Our dataset contains more than 120,000 images crawled from Panoramio, covering several states of USA. We consider three location granularities during the geo-clustering phase. Each corresponds to different density neighborhood threshold. For semantic enhancement, we retrieve the top-20 search results and top-30 frequent-occurring words to form the enhanced semantic vector. During the semantic clustering, $L = L^{\frac{1}{2}} D L^{-\frac{1}{2}}$ is used for eigendecomposition of Laplacian matrix.

Preliminary results of the two clustering phases is presented below. Figure 1(a) shows part of the geo-clustering results. Here geo-clusters are plotted in different colors.

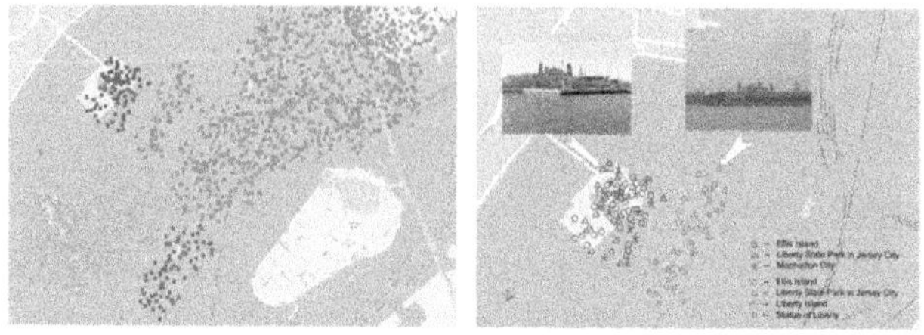

(a) Results of geo-clustering (b) Results of semantic clustering of 2 geo-clusters

Figure 1: Results of geo-clustering and semantic clustering.

Figure 1(b) illustrates the further semantic partitioning for two geo-clusters in the upper-left quadrant of Figure 1(a). The two geo-clusters (blue and pink) locate around Ellis Island in Jersey city. Different symbols are used to denote the subsequent semantic clusters generated from each geo-cluster.

4. CONCLUSION

In this poster, we address the problem of location disambiguation for geotagged photo collections. A two-level clustering scheme that exploits both the geographic and semantic features of photos has been proposed. We also propose a semantic enhancement technique and a method to determine the parameters for the semantic clustering phase. Our work provides a new standpoint for organization and manipulation of massive geotagged photos. Preliminary experiments confirm the effectiveness of our approach. We plan to conduct a comprehensive performance study on the proposed approach.

5. ACKNOWLEDGMENTS

This work is supported in part by the National Science Foundation of China (NSFC Grant No. 60803003, 60970124).

6. REFERENCES

[1] M. Ankerst, M. M. Breunig, H.-P. Kriegel, and J. Sander. Optics: Ordering points to identify the clustering structure. In *SIGMOD Conference*, pages 49–60, 1999.

[2] Y. S. Avrithis, Y. Kalantidis, G. Tolias, and E. Spyrou. Retrieving landmark and non-landmark images from community photo collections. In *ACM Multimedia*, pages 153–162, 2010.

[3] D. J. Crandall, L. Backstrom, D. P. Huttenlocher, and J. M. Kleinberg. Mapping the world's photos. In *WWW*, pages 761–770, 2009.

Towards an Indexing Method to Speed-Up Music Retrieval

Benjamin Martin, Pierre Hanna, Matthias Robine, Pascal Ferraro
Labri, University of Bordeaux
351, cours de la Libération
Talence, France
firstnam .name@labri.fr

ABSTRACT

Computations in most music retrieval systems strongly depend on the size of data compared. We propose to enhance performances of a music retrieval system, namely a harmonic similarity evaluation method, by first indexing relevant parts of music pieces. The indexing algorithm represents each audio piece exclusively by its *major repetition*, using harmonic descriptions and string matching techniques. Evaluations are performed in the context of a state-of-the-art retrieval method, namely cover songs identification, and results highlight the success of our indexing system in keeping similar results while yielding a substantial gain in computation time.

Categories and Subject Descriptors

H.3.1 [**Information Storage and Retrieval**]: Content Analysis and Indexing—*Indexing methods*

General Terms

Algorithms, Performance, Experimentation

1. INTRODUCTION

With the growing presence of large collections of musical content, methods for facilitating efficient browsing become more and more useful. The research field of Music Information Retrieval (MIR) aims at analysing and comparing music pieces on musical criteria, such as harmony, timbre, rhythm *etc.* Most MIR comparison systems are based on a common scheme to estimate similarity on audio material. One or several audio features are chosen and computed on signals segmented in small parts, or frames, thus providing feature sequences representing pieces. For instance, harmonic information is often used since it provides a good insight of the architecture of music pieces. Then, adapted algorithms, such as dynamic time warping or alignment techniques, are used to yield similarity scores between sequences. However, algorithms involved in such retrieval systems highly depend on the length of representative sequences. Harmonic sequences, for instance, are usually relatively long and induce a high computational cost to be compared. Hence, many works over the last decades focused on the detection of the most salient parts in musical sequences in order to speed-up music retrieval and analysis (see for instance [6]).

SIGIR'11, July 24–28, 2011, Beijing, China.
ACM 978-1-4503-0757-4/11/07.

In this study, we propose to reduce the size of musical sequences by selecting relevant parts in order to index data involved in retrieval tasks. Our indexing method uses harmonic representations analysed by string matching techniques to isolate specific parts. Then, our indexing process is evaluated in the context of harmonic similarity from a data reduction step preliminary to cover song identification.

2. INDEXING PROCESS

Audio pieces are represented by sequences using *Harmonic Pitch Class Profiles* (HPCP) [1], frequently used to describe harmonic information. The aim of the indexing step is to extract a specific part in each audio piece, namely the *major repetition*, that can roughly be described as the longest repeated part perceived in a piece. In western popular music, for instance, this repetition classically consists in the concatenation of a verse and a chorus. The motivation of such a selection is to reduce the audio representation to a summarized, less redundant version, that remains relevant to characterize properly the music piece. To isolate relevant parts, each harmonic sequence is analysed using string matching techniques by considering each HPCP feature as a symbol. We consider the polynomial algorithm proposed by Kannan *et al.* [2], that mainly relies on a local alignment algorithm [5] to detect approximate repetitions. In order to evaluate the alignment score of approximate repetitions, the latter technique requires scores for substituting each feature by another one and gap penalties. These scores are determined according to the *Optimal Transposition Index* (OTI) method [4], which ensures a higher robustness to musical variations. The Pearson correlation coefficient is used as a similarity measure for OTI evaluations. For a detailed description of the indexing process, please refer to [3].

3. HARMONIC SIMILARITY

The above process is evaluated as an indexing step for music retrieval, more specifically on harmonic content. One way to evaluate harmonic similarity retrieval systems is to identify cover songs, *i.e.*, every new recording, performance, or rendition of a previously recorded musical piece. In cover songs datasets, music pieces are divided into several classes, each one containing all the different covers of a track. Harmonic baselines of cover songs of a same piece are likely to remain very similar, even in presence of strong musical variations. For our experiments, we focus on a robust cover song identification method, proposed by Serrà *et al.* [4], and we compare its performances with and without the *major repetition* indexing step.

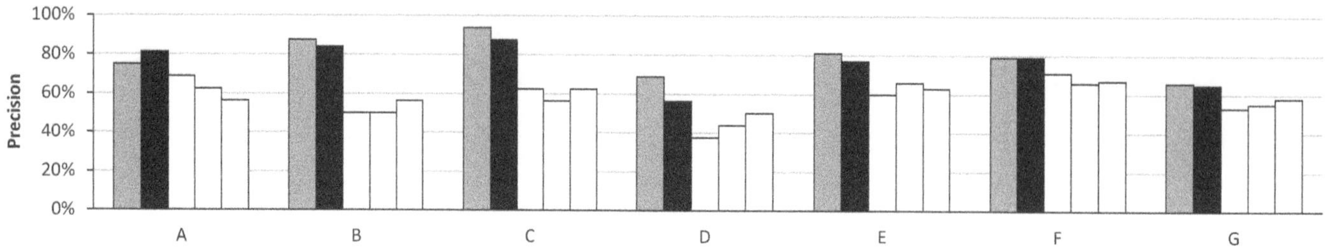

Figure 1: Distribution of cover identification results. Y-axis shows precision rates. Letters on X-axis correspond to different cover classes. Grey: retrieval without indexing; black: indexing by the *major repetition*; white: from left to right, naive indexing processes I1, I2, I3.

	None	MR	I1	I2	I3
Results (%)	78.7	**74.4**	57.5	57.1	59
Retrieval (min)	324	**41**	41	41	41
Indexing (min)	-	23	-	-	-

Table 1: Mean precision and computing durations for the retrieval system with each indexing method. MR stands for indexing by the *major repetition*.

We consider datasets chosen from personal music collections that incorporate 7 classes A to G containing each between 14 and 41 different covers songs (average of 32) of an original music piece, along with a "confusing songs" dataset incorporating 1000 songs of the same genres and artists. Each class was constituted as widely as possible, containing for instance an *a capella* performance, an orchestral version or an electronic remix of the same popular song, *Yesterday* from *The Beatles*.

Our method is compared to three naive indexing methods I1, I2 and I3. We denote by m the mean length of the indexed strings. I1 consists in indexing each sequence by its m first elements, I2 in indexing each sequence by its m' first elements, where m' denotes the length of the indexed string in the corresponding piece, and I3 in indexing each sequence by its m' consecutive elements from the central position in the piece. Note that these three indexing methods as well as our method reduce data size with the same rate. On the evaluation database, the indexing algorithm reduces the size of sequences by $k = 2.96$ on average on every cover classes. Since the local alignment techniques involved in [4] require $|u| \times |v|$ operations to compare two strings u and v, the overall number of operations performed by local alignment computations in cover song identifications is divided by k^2, *i.e.*, about 8.58 in our case. Tab. 1 summarizes the durations elapsed for each task. In our experimental framework, cover identification lasts 324 minutes without any indexing step, and 41 minutes with our indexing step pre-computed (23 minutes for the pre-computation).

For each cover class, the recall and precision rates of the retrieval process within the first N retrieved songs are computed, where N denotes the number of covers for the current class. Note that in this particular context, precision and recall values are identical. Overall results, presented in Tab. 1 show that the retrieval system correctly identifies cover songs with an average precision of 74.4% with our indexing step and 78.7% without. Hence, the deletion of information seems to slightly affect the accuracy of the system, which highlights a limit of the indexing step proposed. However, naive indexing methods having the same data reduction rate yield 15.4% to 17.3% significantly lower results, which confirms the relevance, for this application, of the parts identified by our method. Fig. 1 presents the distribution of precision scores over 7 cover classes. For each class, all the naive indexing methods (white bars) provide results 5% to 25% worse than the *major repetition* indexing method (black bars). For instance, the C cover class (38 cover songs) points out close values with our indexing system (88%) and without it (93%), although naive methods yield much poorer scores (63%, 56% and 63% resp. for I1, I2 and I3). This distribution is similar for every classes, with highest precisions for the non-indexed retrieval and with our process applied and significantly lower precisions with naive indexing methods.

4. CONCLUSION

The proposed method allows isolating in music pieces relevant parts, namely *major repetitions*, using harmonic features combined to string matching techniques. Indexing songs with these specific part in a music retrieval system based on harmonic similarity was tested in a cover song identification task. Results show that the application of our indexing method as a preliminary step to the harmonic similarity evaluation produces significant results, close to the non-indexed approach and much better than naive indexing methods, which highlights the relevance of the algorithm for indexing music retrieval systems. Experiments additionally show a significant gain in computing time, which gives the indexing step a substantial interest for computation issues, above all on large audio databases.

5. REFERENCES

[1] E. Gómez. *Tonal Description of Music Audio Signals.* PhD thesis, Univ. Pompeu Fabra, pp 63–100, 2006.

[2] S. Kannan and E.W. Myers. An algorithm for locating non-overlapping regions of maximum alignment score. *Proc. of CPM '93*, pp 74–86, London, UK, 1993.

[3] B. Martin, P. Hanna, M. Robine, and P. Ferraro. Indexing musical pieces using their major repetition. *Proc. of JCDL*, 2011.

[4] J. Serrà, E. Gómez, P. Herrera, and X. Serra. Chroma binary similarity and local alignment applied to cover song identification. *IEEE Trans. on Audio, Speech and Language Processing*, v 16, pp 1138–1151, 2008.

[5] T. F. Smith and M. S. Waterman. Identification of common molecular subsequences. *Journal of molecular biology*, v 147, pp 195–197, 1981.

[6] A. Uitdenbogerd and J. Zobel. Matching techniques for large music databases. *Proc. of ACM International Multimedia Conference*, pp 57–66, 1999.

An Investigation of Decompounding for Cross-Language Patent Search

Johannes Leveling, Walid Magdy and Gareth J. F. Jones
School of Computing, CNGL
Dublin City University
Dublin, Ireland
{jleveling, wmagdy, gjones}@computing.dcu.ie

ABSTRACT

Decompounding has been found to improve information retrieval (IR) effectiveness in general domains for languages such as German or Dutch. We investigate if cross-language patent retrieval can profit from decompounding. This poses two challenges: i) There may be few resources such as parallel corpora available for training an machine translation system for a compounding language. ii) Patents have a specific writing style and vocabulary ("patentese"), which may affect the performance of decompounding and translation methods. Experiments on data from the CLEF-IP 2010 task show that decompounding patents for translation can overcome out-of-vocabulary problems (OOV) and that decompounding improves IR performance significantly for small training corpora.

Categories and Subject Descriptors

H.3.3 [**INFORMATION STORAGE AND RETRIEVAL**]: Information Search and Retrieval—*Query formulation*; H.3.1 [**INFORMATION STORAGE AND RETRIEVAL**]: Content Analysis and Indexing—*Linguistic processing*

General Terms

Experimentation, Performance, Measurement

Keywords

Patent Retrieval, Decompounding

1. INTRODUCTION

Compounding languages such as German or Dutch allow combining simple words into complex words by concatenating them. In contrast to English, these compounds are written as single words. Splitting compounds into their constituent parts (i.e. decompounding) has been found to improve IR effectiveness, because it can overcome vocabulary mismatches [1, 2, 6].

An area of increasing interest in IR is prior art patent search, which is concerned with finding all relevant patents for a patent application. Since patents are often written in different languages, cross-language information retrieval (CLIR) is usually an essential component of effective patent search. For patent search in compounding languages, the CLIR effectiveness is usually lower than for other language pairs [3, 7]. This can be attributed to the presence of compounds, which leads to higher rates of OOV compound terms. OOV terms cannot be translated, which results in missing some portion of the query text and degrades IR effectiveness.

In this paper we apply decompounding on German patent topics in the cross-language patent search task from the CLEF-IP 2010 track and investigate machine translation (MT) quality by examining retrieval performance. The results show that decompounding improves retrieval performance significantly for small training corpora, or for corpora with high OOV rates.

SIGIR'11, July 24–28, 2011, Beijing, China.
ACM 978-1-4503-0757-4/11/07.

2. THE DECOMPOUNDING APPROACH

There has been little research on decompounding for patent search and for training MT systems. Koehn and Knight [4] train decompounding for MT using knowledge from parallel corpora, preventing incorrect decompounding when there is a one-to-one correspondence between two words in different languages. Jochim et al. [3] apply dictionary-based translation for cross-language patent search and expand monolingual queries with their translations. They conclude that translation could help patent retrieval, but not always.

In this paper, decompounding German words is realized by an approach which has been employed in domain-specific CLIR [2]. The decompounding is based on selecting the decomposition with the smallest number of words and the highest decomposition probability. A decomposition probability is defined as the product of constituent probabilities, which are estimated by the collection frequency of a word divided by the number of all words in a training collection. The training collection contains the English 3M sentence corpus from the Leipzig corpora list[1] and a random sample of 800k sentences from German patents in the CLEF-IP collection.

We evaluated the decompounding based on a gold standard corpus (GSC) of 2000 random sentences extracted from German patents. The GSC was manually annotated with the correct decomposition of words. It contains 27,932 unique words and 318k words in total. We found that spelling errors in the patent texts occur frequently, possibly resulting from the OCR source of documents. Spelling errors have also been manually decompounded in the GSC. In addition, 12.7% of the word forms in the annotated corpus are chemical formulas or substance names, which indicates the domain-specific nature of patents. In the GSC, chemical formulas are decompounded only when the head noun is a German word. For example, *Methylrest* (methyl radical) has the head noun *Rest* (radical).

This decompounding method achieves 95.0% accuracy (the percentage of correctly decompounded words) measured over all words in the annotated GSC and 81.4% accuracy for unique words. Decompounding the GSC increases the total number of words by 16.3%, while the number of hapax legomena (words occurring only once)

[1] http://corpora.uni-leipzig.de/

Table 1: Patent retrieval results for corpora.

	No decompounding		Decompounding	
MT Corpus Size	PRES	OOV	PRES	OOV
500K	0.486	10.2%	0.476	1.1%
50K	0.444	20.9%	0.479	3.7%
5K	0.360	40.8%	0.450	12.6%

is reduced by 48.8%, compared to the original GSC. This illustrates that compounding is a productive process in German.

3. EXPERIMENTS AND RESULTS

The cross-language search task in CLEF-IP 2010 is adapted for our patent retrieval experiments [7]. The main objective is to find patents in an English collection that are relevant to patent applications filed in German. The collection consists of 1.35M patents from the European Patent Office with 69% of them exclusively in English and 31% in German and French. The German and French patents in the collections often have sections manually translated into English, including the patent title, abstract, and claims. For our experiments, all the English text of the collection was indexed to create a monolingual index.

For the translation process, the MaTrEx MT system[2] was used to translate the 89 German patent topics from the small topic set (300 topics in English, French, and German) provided by the CLEF-IP 2010. A random set of parallel sentences in English and German from the title and claims sections of patents was extracted to train MaTrEx. Different sizes of a training corpus, namely 500k, 50k, and 5k parallel sentences, were used to investigate the effect of a training corpus on the translation quality which can be indirectly observed by retrieval effectiveness. For comparison, the German sentences in the three training corpora were decompounded to create another three training corpora, which creates a total of 6 translation models for the MT system. For the German topics, decompounding was applied too to create a decompounded version of the topics to be translated with the decompounded translation models.

Translated patent topics were processed to form queries by adding terms occurring more than twice in the title, abstract, description, and claims sections combined and all bigrams that occur more than three times, using the term frequency as a weight for these terms [7]. The INDRI[3] toolkit was used to index and search the patents.

Table 1 shows PRES results [5] and OOV for cross-language patent search for different MT training corpus sizes, using the 89 German patent topics. PRES scores increase when larger MT corpora are used which are not decompounded. However, significance tests (t-test, $p < 0.5$) show that the PRES scores using the decompounded model for 500k or 5k are not significantly different and that results for the 5k and 50k model are significantly better for the respective decompounded version (see Table 1).

Unexpectedly, results are significantly indistinguishable for the decompounded and the original 500k training corpus. To find an explanation, we investigated several topics for which PRES has decreased using MT with decompounding. We illustrate our findings on topic PAC-199, for which PRES decreases from 0.843 to 0.691 (mean average precision decreases from 0.414 to 0.158). The word *schwerbrennbar* (flame retardant or flame resistant) is incorrectly translated as heavy combustible, which results in matching non-relevant documents, compared to no additional non-relevant matches when the word is not translated at all. More importantly, the chemical formula *Methylvinylsiloxan* (term frequency 35 vs. 0) is split into the constituents *Methyl* (20 vs. 103), *Vinyl* (15 vs. 118), and *Siloxan* (7 vs. 43). The numbers in brackets show the changes in term frequency for the unprocessed topic versus the topic after decompounding (topics correspond to full patents). This indicates that splitting some compounds, especially highly frequent chemical formulas in patents, can result in performance loss. The high PRES scores for the 5k and 50k decompounded models can be at least partially explained by the lower OOV rate in the decompounded version (Table 1). For the 500k training model, the OOV rate decreases, but the positive effect of decompounding might be outweighed by over-splitting of some compounds.

[2] `http://www.openmatrex.org/`

[3] `http://www.lemurproject.org/indri/`

4. CONCLUSION

When using smaller MT training corpora or corpora with high OOV rates, decompounding shows higher performance compared to not decompounding. This effect is important for training MT systems for specific domains where only small parallel corpora are available for training MT systems, i.e. less training data is needed for good CLIR performance when decompounding is used to overcome OOV problems, and for training MT systems for languages with few linguistic resources.

The effect of incorrectly translating a constituent word of a compound is similar to a topic drift in blind relevance feedback, when adding query terms may result in a loss of precision. In patent search, where queries are formed by patent documents, incorrectly decompounded or incorrectly translated constituent words may result in a much higher query term frequency (and thus, a higher term weight in the query), causing a loss in retrieval effectiveness. This result is in line with observations made by Koehn and Knight [4], who conclude that "eager splitting fares abysmally".

Future work includes investigating methods to identify technical terms and chemical formulas in patents to treat them differently for decompounding and/or translation.

Acknowledgments

This research is supported by the Science Foundation of Ireland (grant 07/CE/I1142) as part of the Centre for Next Generation Localisation (`http://www.cngl.ie/`).

5. REFERENCES

[1] M. Braschler and B. Ripplinger. How effective is stemming and decompounding for German text retrieval? *Inf. Retr.*, 7(3-4):291–316, 2004.

[2] A. Chen and F. C. Gey. Multilingual information retrieval using machine translation, relevance feedback and decompounding. *Inf. Retr.*, 7(1–2):149–182, 2004.

[3] C. Jochim, H. Lioma, H. Schütze, S. Koch, and T. Ertl. Preliminary study into query translation for patent retrieval. In *PaIR '10*, Toronto, Canada, 2010.

[4] P. Koehn and K. Knight. Empirical methods for compound splitting. In *EACL '03*, pages 187–193, Stroudsburg, PA, USA, 2003. ACL.

[5] W. Magdy and G. J. F. Jones. PRES: a score metric for evaluating recall-oriented information retrieval applications. In *SIGIR 2010*, Geneva, Switzerland, 2010.

[6] C. Monz and M. de Rijke. Shallow morphological analysis in monolingual information retrieval for Dutch, German, and Italian. In *CLEF '01*, pages 262–277. Springer, 2002.

[7] F. Piroi. CLEF-IP 2010: Retrieval experiments in the intellectual property domain. In *CLEF 2010*, Padua, Italy, 2010.

Detecting Seasonal Queries by Time-Series Analysis

Milad Shokouhi
Microsoft Research
Cambridge, United Kingdom
milads@microsoft.com

ABSTRACT

Seasonal events such as Halloween and Christmas repeat every year and initiate several temporal information needs. The impact of such events on users is often reflected in search logs in form of seasonal *spikes* in the frequency of related queries (e.g. "halloween costumes", "where is santa"). Many seasonal queries such as "sigir conference" mainly target fresh pages (e.g. `sigir2011.org`) that have less usage data such as clicks and anchor-text compared to older alternatives (e.g. `sigir2009.org`). Thus, it is important for search engines to correctly identify seasonal queries and make sure that their results are temporally reordered if necessary.

In this poster, we focus on detecting seasonal queries using *time-series* analysis. We demonstrate that the seasonality of a query can be determined with high accuracy according to its historical frequency distribution.

Categories and Subject Descriptors

H.3.3 [**Information Storage and Retrieval**]: Information Search and Retrieval

General Terms

Algorithms, Performance

Keywords

Temporal Queries, Seasonal Query Classification

1. INTRODUCTION

Cyclic queries related to seasonal events have been estimated to account for more than 7% of search traffic [5]. The best result pages for many of these queries change every year, and in some cases such as "us open" the query itself becomes temporally ambiguous [4]. Therefore, it is important for search engines to detect – and predict – seasonal queries and respond to them with temporally relevant results.

Previous work has been mostly focused on identifying seasonal queries based on their reformulations, and the frequent occurrence of years in their words. For instance, Metzler et al. [5] define a query (e.g. "halloween") as *implicitly year qualified* if it frequently appears in the logs followed by years (e.g. "halloween 2009", "halloween 2010"). The authors rely on the number of unique years and their frequencies to classify query seasonality. Other related work includes modeling the temporal profile of queries based on the time-stamps of the documents they return [3]. Dong et al. [6] used a combination of reformulation and post-retrieval features to train a classifier for identifying seasonal queries.

We propose leveraging time-series decomposition techniques for measuring the seasonality of queries. In contrast to previous work, we do not rely on any information about previous query reformulations or document time-stamps.

2. TIME-SERIES AND QUERY HISTORY

A time-series [6] is referred to a group of data points at successive time spans with uniform intervals. The data points can represent any quantifiable such as sale records or temperature, and the interval can take any unit of time such as week or year. In the context of web search, one can generate a time-series for each query according to its past frequency at uniform intervals. That is, each data point in the time-series represents the query frequency at a time unit (e.g. day, or month). Having a time-series we can then apply different well-studied decomposition techniques such as STL [1] and HoltWinters [2] to analyze trends and seasonality. Figure 1 depicts how query frequency history at monthly intervals can be treated as time-series and decomposed by Holt-Winters additive exponential smoothing [2] into three main components; *level* ($\mathcal{L}$), *trend* ($\mathcal{T}$) and *season* ($\mathcal{S}$):

$$\begin{aligned}\mathcal{L}_t &= \alpha(\hat{X}_t - \mathcal{S}_{t-s}) + (1-\alpha)(\mathcal{L}_{t-1} + \mathcal{T}_{t-1})\\ \mathcal{T}_t &= \beta(\mathcal{L}_t - \mathcal{L}_{t-1}) + (1-\beta)\mathcal{T}_{t-1}\\ \mathcal{S}_t &= \gamma(\hat{X}_t - \mathcal{L}_t) + (1-\gamma)\mathcal{S}_{t-s}\end{aligned}$$

here α, β and γ are all between zero and one and can be set during the fitting process using standard techniques such as root mean square error. Parameter t denotes the current time-span, and s specifies the length of the seasonal cycle (12 in our experiments). $\hat{X}_t$ represents the value of the data point at time t (here, the monthly frequency of the query).

For seasonal queries, the *season* component ($\mathcal{S}$) is the most significant factor and noticeably resembles the distribution of the raw data. For instance in Figure 1, the *season* and *xhat* have very different distributions for query "britney spears", while they look remarkably similar for "us open".

Our seasonal query classifier is inspired by this observation; for a given query, we first convert its historical frequency into time-series with monthly splits. We then decompose the time-series by applying Holt-Winters additive

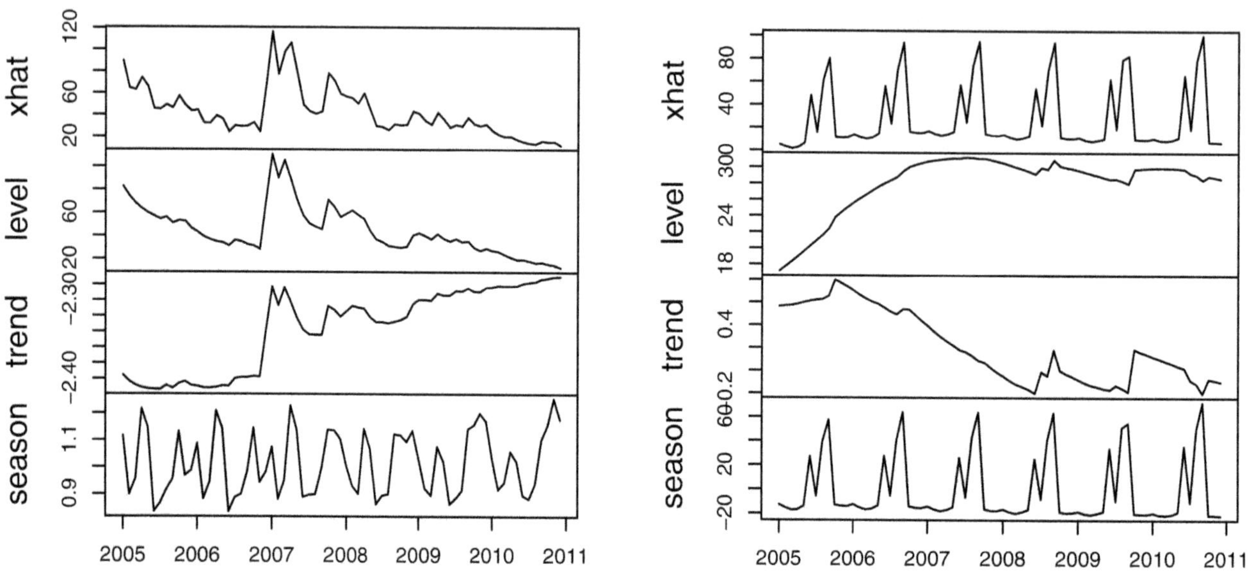

Figure 1: The Holt-Winters decomposition of time-series generated from monthly frequencies of "britney spears" (left), and "us open" (right). The xhat ($\hat{X}$) represents the raw monthly data, and is followed by the decomposed components in each plot. The raw data was collected from Google insight for search.

Table 1: The precision-recall changes in seasonal classification for different values of ω.

ω	.90	.80	.70	.60	.50	.40	.30	.20	.10
Precision	.78	.60	.47	.42	.38	.32	.32	.30	.30
Recall	.49	.68	.77	.81	.82	.84	.85	.89	.89

smoothing [2]. If the decomposed *season* component $\mathcal{S}$ and raw data $\hat{X}$ have similar distributions, we classify the query as seasonal. We use the Cosine similarity function to measure the similarity of the vectors for $\mathcal{S}$ and $\hat{X}$. That is,

$$\omega = \frac{\mathcal{S} \cdot \hat{X}}{\|\mathcal{S}\| \|\hat{X}\|}$$

The query is classified as seasonal if the similarity value ω is greater than a certain threshold. We require at least two spikes at seasonal peaks to reduce the chance of misclassification in cases where distributions are flat or similar due to reasons other than seasonality. Note that our approach is not restricted to any particular decomposition method and can work with other related techniques such as STL [1]. Similarly, we could use KL-Divergence or other appropriate functions for comparing the distributions of $\mathcal{S}$ and $\hat{X}$.

3. EXPERIMENTS

We evaluated our experiments on set of 259 queries annotated manually by professional editors as seasonal or normal (with respectively 74 and 185 queries in each group). We used the search logs of a commercial search engine to generate a time-series for each query according to its monthly frequency between 2006 and 2010 inclusive.

The results summarized in Table 1 suggest that our simple technique can classify half of seasonal queries with 78% precision. Our misclassification cases mainly included queries such as "miss world" that are cyclic but repeat at slightly different time of the year, and "powerball lottery results" that are related to repetitive events but at inconsistent intervals.

4. CONCLUSIONS

We proposed using time-series decomposition techniques for identifying seasonal queries. Our experiments showed that seasonal queries can be classified by (1) transforming the query frequency history into time-series and (2) comparing the decomposed seasonal factor of the time-series and the raw data distributions. Future work includes comparing the effectiveness of various decomposition and similarity functions for seasonal query classification.

5. REFERENCES

[1] R. Cleveland, W. Cleveland, J. Mcrae, and I. Terpenning. STL: A seasonal-trend decomposition procedure based on loess. *Journal of Official Statistics*, 6(1):3–73, 1990.

[2] P. Goodwin. The holt-winters approach to exponential smoothing: 50 years old and going strong. *Foresight: The International Journal of Applied Forecasting*, (19):30–33, 2010.

[3] R. Jones and F. Diaz. Temporal profiles of queries. *ACM Transactions Information Systems*, 25, July 2007.

[4] A. Kulkarni, J. Teevan, K. M. Svore, and S. T. Dumais. Understanding temporal query dynamics. In *Proceedings of WSDM conference*, pages 167–176, Hong Kong, China, 2011.

[5] D. Metzler, R. Jones, F. Peng, and R. Zhang. Improving search relevance for implicitly temporal queries. In *Proceedings of SIGIR conference*, pages 700–701, Boston, MA, 2009.

[6] R. Zhang, Y. Konda, A. Dong, P. Kolari, Y. Chang, and Z. Zheng. Learning recurrent event queries for web search. In *Proceeding of EMNLP conference*, pages 1129–1139, MIT, MA, 2010.

Learning to Rank under Tight Budget Constraints

Christian Pölitz
Saarland University
Campus E 1.7
Cluster of Excellence MMCI
66123 Saarbrücken
poelitz@mmci.uni-saarland.de,

Ralf Schenkel
Saarland University
Campus E 1.7
Cluster of Excellence MMCI
66123 Saarbrücken
schenkel@mmci.uni-saarland.de

ABSTRACT

This paper investigates the influence of pruning feature lists to keep a given budget for the evaluation of ranking methods. We learn from a given training set how important the individual prefixes are for the ranking quality. Based on there importance we choose the best prefixes to calculate the ranking while keeping the budget.

Categories and Subject Descriptors

H.3.3 [**Information Storage and Retrieval**]: Information Search and Retrieval

General Terms

Algorithms, Performance, Measurement

Keywords

Learning to Rank, Constraints

1. INTRODUCTION

Efficiently finding the best results for a query is an important issue in many precision-oriented, interactive tasks. Consequently, a large number of *top-k* or *dynamic pruning* algorithms have been proposed (see [2,6] for an overview). In many applications, results need to be provided within a controlled amount of time; however, only very few algorithms have been proposed that explicitly support execution under a limited budget of processing time or disk access costs. One of the few examples from the database community, proposed by Shmueli-Scheuer et al. [3], makes heuristic decisions at runtime based on the documents seen so far. A more fundamental approach that integrates budget constraints into a learning-to-rank framework was recently proposed by Wang et al. [5]; however, they focus on selecting features and do not consider evaluating features for some documents only, resulting rather long processing times of a few seconds per query.

We propose an algorithm that combines the best of both worlds: It selects, for each feature of the ranking function, a subset of documents to be evaluated before the actual query processing starts, extending the method of [5]. We demonstrate in experiments with TREC GOV2 and queries from the TREC Terabyte track that our method can achieve almost perfect precision while scoring only as few as 20% of the documents.

SIGIR'11, July 24–28, 2011, Beijing, China.
ACM 978-1-4503-0757-4/11/07.

2. SCORES

We focus on the family of linear ranking functions that come with a family of features–functions $F = \{f_1, \ldots, f_N\}$ assigning real values to (document,query) pairs–and model parameters $\Lambda = \{\lambda_1, \ldots, \lambda_N\}$. Our current work uses only unigram (i.e., term) features, but can be extended to bigram features. For simplicity, we assume that each term t_i corresponds to exactly one feature f_i, which can be its BM25 score (used in our experiments), a Dirichlet score, etc, and write $f_i(d)$ instead of $f_i(d, q)$; again, extension to multiple features per term is simple. The score of a document d with respect to a query $q = \{t_1, \ldots, t_n\}$ is computed as

$$score(d, q) = \sum_i \lambda_i f_i(d)$$

Following existing work [1], we define the feature weights as weighted sum of a number of document independent meta features (we use the unigram meta features from [5]), i.e., $\lambda_t = \sum_j \omega_j g_j(t)$, where the ω_i are learned from training queries.

3. BUDGET CONSTRAINTS

We assume that for each feature f_i, a corresponding inverted list L_i exists that provides all pairs $(d, f_i(d))$ of documents d with their feature values where $f_i(d) \neq 0$, and that is sorted by descending feature value. Processing a query q without budget constraints would read all entries from the lists for q and compute the top-k result documents. The problem considered in this paper is computing good approximate results for q when the budget, i.e., the aggregated number of entries read from all lists, is limited by B. Under the realistic assumption that documents with high feature values are more likely relevant than documents with low feature values, we will read only prefixes of lists. Representing by m_i the maximal feature value of any document in L_i, we denote by $L_i^{b_i} = \{(d, f_i(d)) \in L_i | f_i(d) > b_i \cdot m_i\}$ the prefix of L_i where the score is more than $b_i \cdot m_i$, for $b_i \in [0; 1)$. We denote by $|L|$ the number of entries in a list or a list prefix. We now want to compute an *access plan* $P \in [0; 1]^n$ that denotes, for each L_i, which prefix $L_i^{P_i}$ should be accessed. The execution cost of such an access plan is given as $|P| = \sum |L_i^{P_i}|$. Given such an access plan P, the score of a document now is

$$score_P(d,q) = \sum_{i:f_i(d)>P_i \cdot m_i} \lambda_i f_i(d)$$

Our goal is now to determine an access plan P for query q that keeps the given budget B, i.e., where $|P| \leq B$, and yields a good result quality. We leverage a general idea from [5] for selecting features under budget constraints: Intuitively, the weight λ_i of a feature indicates how important that feature is for the final ranking. We extend this approach by assigning a weight $\lambda_i^{b_i}$ to each prefix $L_i^{b_i}$, and select an access plan P^* that maximizes the sum of the prefix weights while keeping the budget:

$$P^* := argmax_{P\in[0;1]^n:|P|\leq B} \sum \lambda_i^{P_i}$$

This is an instance of the multiple-choice knapsack problem [4].For tractability, we restrict possible choices of P_i to a relatively small number of values (we use $\{0, 0.1, \ldots, 0.9\}$); this makes problem instances usually small enough to solve them exactly.

However, this just shifted the problem towards computing the $\lambda_i^{P_i}$. We believe that these weights should be derived from the weight λ_i of the corresponding list L_i in the unconstrained case, and examined the following two derivations (others could be possible as well):

- **relative cost**: Here, we assume that the usefulness of a prefix is proportional to its length:

$$\lambda_i^{P_i} := \frac{|L_i^{P_i}|}{|L_i|} \cdot \lambda_i$$

- **learning the weights**: W.r.t. [5] we determine weights that optimize the quality of results (in our case precision@20) over a set Q of training queries and over a set of budgets:

$$argmax_{\lambda_i^{P_i}} \frac{1}{|Q|} \sum_{q\in Q} \sum_{B} P@20(q, P^*(q,B)) \cdot P(B)$$

  Here, $P(B)$ denotes the probability that a query with budget B will occur, and $P^*(q,B)$ is the optimal access plan for query q and budget B. Instead of learning the $\lambda_i^{P_i}$ directly, we propose to derive them from the weight λ_i of list L_i in the unconstrained case, by setting $\lambda_i^{P_i} := \delta_{P_i} \cdot \lambda_i$.

4. EXPERIMENTS

We evaluate our method using the TREC GOV2 collection and topics from the TREC Terabyte tasks 2004–2006, which we split into training (100 topics from 2005+2006) and test (49 topics from 2004) topics. Our features are BM25 scores with $k_1 = 1.2$ and $b = 0.5$, and we use the same meta features used in [5]. We first learned optimal list weights (λ_i) on the training topics without budget constraints. We considered a set of relative budgets $\mathcal{B}= \{0.2, 0.25, \ldots, 1.0\}$, where a relative budget of 0.2 means the system can access at most 20% of the entries in all index lists for that query. We learned the δ_{P_i} on the training topics for precision@20 assuming uniform distribution of the budgets.

We then measured precision@20 for the test topics for the same selection $\mathcal{B}$ of relative budgets, solving the multiple-choice knapsack problem with the two different list prefix

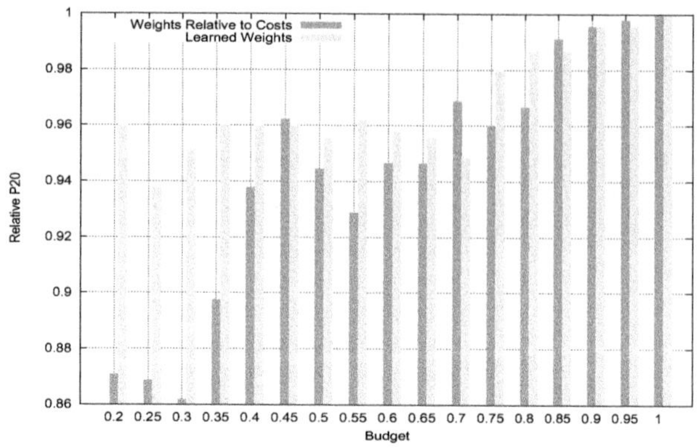

Figure 1: Precision@20 for different budgets, relative to unconstrained execution

weights introduced in the previous section. Figure 1 shows the result of this experiment, where we report relative precision compared to the precision with full feature lists. It is evident that both methods provide good results (relative precision >90%) over a large range of budgets. For small budgets below 35% of the full index lists, the learned weights outperform the simple cost-based weights, providing excellent performance even at 20% budget.

5. CONCLUSIONS AND FUTURE WORK

The results show the benefit of using the introduced prefixes when facing budget constraints. Under very tight constraints we could show that learning good prefix combinations can keep good ranking quality while skipping larger parts of the index lists. Here the effect to even tighter budgets will be examined in the future. A comparison to existing budget-aware top-k techniques, such as [3], will clarify if our proposed method is significantly better, while not requiring expensive bookkeeping at query execution time and additional statistics. Further we plan to additionally integrate multiple features per term and multi-term features to raise the ranking quality and better compare to [5].

6. REFERENCES

[1] Michael Bendersky, Donald Metzler, and W. Bruce Croft. Learning concept importance using a weighted dependence model. In *WSDM*, pages 31–40, 2010.

[2] Ihab F. Ilyas et al. A survey of top- query processing techniques in relational database systems. *ACM Comput. Surv.*, 40(4), 2008.

[3] Michal Shmueli-Scheuer et al. Best-effort top-k query processing under budgetary constraints. In *ICDE*, pages 928–939, 2009.

[4] Prabhakant Sinha and Andris A. Zoltners. The multiple-choice knapsack problem. *Operations Research*, 27(3):503–515, 1979.

[5] Lidan Wang, Donald Metzler, and Jimmy Lin. Ranking under temporal constraints. In *CIKM*, pages 79–88, 2010.

[6] Justin Zobel and Alistair Moffat. Inverted files for text search engines. *ACM Comput. Surv.*, 38(2), 2006.

A Novel Hybrid Index Structure for Efficient Text Retrieval

Andreas Broschart
Universitaet des Saarlandes and
Max-Planck-Institut fuer Informatik
Saarbruecken, Germany
abrosch@mmci.uni-saarland.de

Ralf Schenkel
Universitaet des Saarlandes and
Max-Planck-Institut fuer Informatik
Saarbruecken, Germany
schenkel@mmci.uni-saarland.de

ABSTRACT

Query processing with precomputed term pair lists can improve efficiency for some queries, but suffers from the quadratic number of index lists that need to be read. We present a novel hybrid index structure that aims at decreasing the number of index lists retrieved at query processing time, trading off a reduced number of index lists for an increased number of bytes to read. Our experiments demonstrate significant cold-cache performance gains of almost 25% on standard benchmark queries.

Categories and Subject Descriptors: H.3.1 [Content Analysis and Indexing]: Indexing methods

General Terms: Performance, Experimentation

Keywords: proximity scoring, efficiency

1. INTRODUCTION

Precomputed indexes for term pairs, not just single terms, have recently been proposed to improve not only quality of results, but also processing efficiency [4, 5]. While they can greatly improve performance for short queries, they are not that efficient for large queries or when lists are not available in a cache, but need to be read from disk. This disadvantage is rooted in the quadratic number of term pair lists that need to be accessed for every query. Especially with the pruning methods from [4] that store only a few thousand entries per pair list, query processing time is dominated by the time to locate and open index lists. Reducing the number of index lists for processing a query can therefore significantly improve efficiency, even if more data must be read from each list.

This paper introduces a novel hybrid index structure that decreases the number of index lists accessed at query processing time, trading it off for an increased number of bytes read from each list. Our experiments demonstrate significant performance gains for query processing on cold caches with our new index structure, using queries from TREC Terabyte and Efficiency Tracks.

2. BACKGROUND

We base on and extend the index framework for terms and term pairs presented in [4]. That paper proposes to use an index with TextLists (TL) that store, for each term, documents and their BM25 score for this term, and additional CombinedLists (CL) that store, for each pair of terms, a proximity-based score (a variant of the score proposed in [2]) for each document that contains both terms and additionally the document's BM25 scores for both terms. That paper proposes to sort TLs by score, CLs by proximity score, and runs a top-k algorithm to compute the best results for a query with early pruning. Experimental results indicated that it is enough to heuristically keep only the best few thousand entries in each list to achieve good result quality.

In earlier work [1], we pushed this setup to the limits by storing short prefixes of TLs and CLs in compressed form sorted by docid (applying delta encoding for docids and v-byte encoding for scores) and processing queries by a very efficient document-at-a-time algorithm, yielding average cold cache runtimes of about 59ms on GOV2 with about 10K bytes read.

3. HYBRID INDEX FRAMEWORK

For further improving this runtime, especially for medium-sized queries, it is necessary to reduce the number of lists accessed by each query. For a query with 5 terms, up to 10 term pair lists and 5 term lists need to be opened. The hybrid framework that we propose in this paper can reduce this to at most 10 lists in the best case, reducing the number of lists to open by 33%. We achieve this by combining the CL for a term pair (t_1, t_2) with the TLs for t_1 and t_2, yielding an *extended CombinedList* (CLExt) that now contains the best documents for both the term pair and the single terms. We can expect that many documents will be included in two or three of the lists, so that the number of entries in the resulting CLExt will be less than the aggregated number of entries of the three source lists. Within the CLExt, we store all entries in the same format, replacing unknown scores by 0, and sort all entries by their docid.

At query processing, only CLExt lists need to be read, reducing the number of index lists by n (for queries with n terms). For queries with 3 terms, the number of lists is only 3 compared to 6 in the existing approach. For queries with larger number of terms, the technique is less effective since there is still a relatively large number of CLExts to read, and information from one TL is now included in several CLExts, so some of the information read during query processing is not needed. We will see later that the break-even point is around 8 terms per query. Note that TLs need to be kept in the index for queries with just a single term.

4. REDUCING INDEX SIZE

If we build a hybrid index as we just explained, the size of that index will be a lot larger than the size of the index with just TLs and CLs. While this comes as a surprise at first view, it has a simple explanation: many pairs of terms hardly occur together in the same document, so the corresponding CL is very short, but they frequently occur in isolation, so the (prefix of the) TL of each term in the index is long. The CLExt for such pairs is therefore orders of magnitude larger than the CL for the same pair.

We can lower the required space for the hybrid index by using additional information on how frequently pairs are used, for exam-

SIGIR'11, July 24–28, 2011, Beijing, China.
ACM 978-1-4503-0757-4/11/07.

ple from a query log. We then build CLExt lists only for term pairs that are used frequently enough; for all other pairs we keep the old CL scheme. This drastically reduces the size of the hybrid index, while still providing reasonable performance improvements. With the TREC GOV2 collection, generating CLExt lists only for term pairs that occur at least once in the AOL query log reduced the on-disk size of the CLExt lists from over 3TB to 131.7GB; the on-disk size of all CL lists in the standard index was 93.2GB.

5. EXPERIMENTAL EVALUATION

We evaluated our proposed hybrid index with the well-known GOV2 collection, using the 150 adhoc topics from the TREC 2004–2006 Terabyte tracks and the first 10,000 queries from the Terabyte Efficiency Track (EffTrack) 2005 [3] as query loads. [1] elaborates on an index tuning approach that determines list pruning parameters under controlled result quality given a maximum index size. In this work, all TLs and CLs are pruned to at most 310 entries, and entries in CLs have a proximity score of at least 0.05; experiments in [1] have shown that this is enough to yield a similar quality for top-10 documents as produced by a BM25 score with unpruned index lists. We report average cold-cache runtimes (averaged over six independent runs) and access costs for top-10 retrieval with the original index (TL+CL) and the hybrid index with log-based pruning (TL+CLExt$_{Qlog}$); file-system caches were emptied *before running each query*, which is a very conservative setting. Note that runtimes and cost are largely independent of the number of retrieved results.

For the Terabyte queries, using the hybrid index improved runtime from 59ms to 49ms per query over the original index; for the EffTrack queries, the improvement was even better (55ms vs. 42ms per query). This clearly shows that our hybrid index can greatly improve cold-cache performance. We will now evaluate the impact for queries of different length, and the influence of log-based pruning.

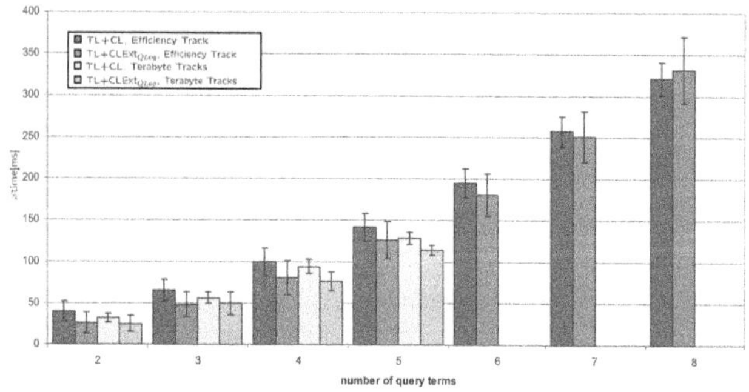

Figure 1: Average runtimes for Terabyte and EffTrack queries

Figure 1 reports average query times for the two query loads, grouped by number of terms per query. Improvements are best for short queries, but we see improvements up to 7 terms. The chart also indicates the standard deviations which are pretty low.

Figure 2 details the average number of bytes read per query for the EffTrack. The hybrid index reads up to twice as many bytes from disk, but is (as we saw before) still faster because it needs to open fewer lists (also depicted in this figure by triangles and diamonds).

Figure 3 shows the influence of log-based pruning on runtime. We computed, for each EffTrack query, the fraction of term pairs covered in the log, and grouped queries into five buckets from low coverage (0%-20%) to high coverage (80%-100%). Our method gives benefit only for queries with term pair coverage of at least

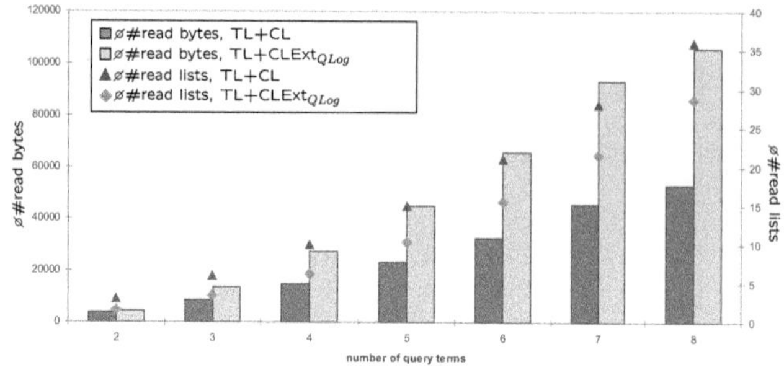

Figure 2: Average cost in bytes and average number of opened lists, for the EffTrack queries

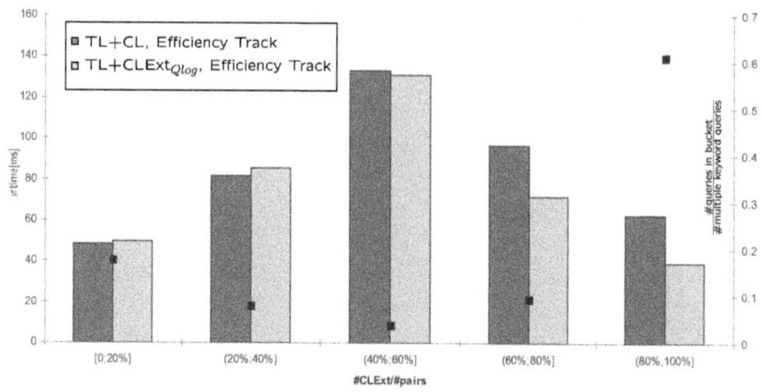

Figure 3: Effect of query term pair coverage in the AOL query log on runtime, for the EffTrack queries

60%; however, these are the most frequent queries in this load (indicated by the black dots). For the remaining queries, our method does not create a performance penalty.

6. CONCLUSIONS AND FUTURE WORK

We have demonstrated that our hybrid index structure significantly improves cold-cache query processing times by decreasing the number of fetched index lists, at the price of reading more from each list. Highest improvements are achieved for short queries. Our future work will therefore concentrate on improving performance for long queries, for example by precomputing lists for frequently used phrases.

7. REFERENCES

[1] A. Broschart and R. Schenkel. Real-time text queries with tunable term pair indexes. *MPI Technical Report MPI-I-2010-5-006*, 2010. Available at `http://www.mpi-inf.mpg.de/reports`.

[2] S. Büttcher, C. L. A. Clarke, and B. Lushman. Term proximity scoring for ad-hoc retrieval on very large text collections. In *SIGIR*, pages 621–622, 2006.

[3] C. L. A. Clarke, F. Scholer, and I. Soboroff. The trec 2005 terabyte track. In *TREC*, 2005.

[4] R. Schenkel, A. Broschart, S.-w. Hwang, M. Theobald, and G. Weikum. Efficient text proximity search. In *SPIRE*, pages 287–299, 2007.

[5] H. Yan, S. Shi, F. Zhang, T. Suel, and J.-R. Wen. Efficient term proximity search with term-pair indexes. In *CIKM*, pages 1229–1238, 2010.

A Weighted Curve Fitting Method for Result Merging in Federated Search

Chuan He
Computer Department
Beijing University of Posts and Telecommunications
Haidian District, Beijing, China
hechuanbupt@gmail.com

Dzung Hong
Department of Computer Science
Purdue University
West Lafayette, IN 47907, USA
dthong@cs.purdue.edu

Luo Si
Department of Computer Science
Purdue University
West Lafayette, IN 47907, USA
lsi@cs.purdue.edu

ABSTRACT

Result merging is an important step in federated search to merge the documents returned from multiple source-specific ranked lists for a user query. Previous result merging methods such as Semi-Supervised Learning (SSL) and Sample-Agglomerate Fitting Estimate (SAFE) use regression methods to estimate global document scores from document ranks in individual ranked lists. SSL relies on overlapping documents that exist in both individual ranked lists and a centralized sample database. SAFE goes a step further by using both overlapping documents with accurate rank information and documents with estimated rank information for regression. However, existing methods do not distinguish the accurate rank information from the estimated information. Furthermore, all documents are assigned equal weights in regression while intuitively, documents in the top should carry higher weights. This paper proposes a weighted curve fitting method for result merging in federated search. The new method explicitly models the importance of information from overlapping documents over non-overlapping ones. It also weights documents at different positions differently. Empirically results on two datasets clearly demonstrate the advantage of the proposed algorithm.

Categories and Subject Descriptors

H.3 [**Information Storage and Retrieval**]: H3.3 Information Search and Retrieval; H.3.4 Systems and Software

General Terms

Algorithms, Design, Performance

Keywords

Federated Search, Result Merging, Curve Fitting

1. INTRODUCTION

Text information behind individual search engines of distributed information sources may not be easily crawled for building a centralized index because of data protection, copyrights or security. Federated text search has been proposed to search the distributed information in these environments. There are three basic problems of federated search: resource representation, resource selection and result merging. This paper focuses on result merging for generating a single ranked list of documents in different sources for a user query.

Existing result merging algorithms can be categorized into two groups. The first group assumes some level of collaboration of distributed information sources and use some statistics provided by those sources for merging [1, 3]. In non-cooperative environment, a semi-supervised learning (SSL) [5] method is a more practical approach. Basically, after the first step of query-based sampling [1], each information source is represented by a set of sample documents. The set of all sample documents is called *centralized sample database*. SSL utilizes overlapping documents in both individual ranked lists and centralized sample database to build a regression. Once regression is done, SSL can convert the rank of any document returned from an individual source to that document's centralized score. Those centralized scores are used as global scores to merge all documents.

The more recent Sample-Agglomerate Fitting Estimate (SAFE) method [4] relaxes the requirement of SSL for overlapping documents. It estimates document ranks based on the uniform sampling assumption, and uses those estimated ranks for regression. SAFE algorithm however, does not distinguish the contribution of overlapping documents with accurate ranks (i.e., existing in the source's returned list) and sample documents with estimated ranks for regression. Moreover, top ranked documents (in source-specific list) are probably more important for curve fitting because of the goal of high-precision, which is not considered in SAFE.

Based on the observation, we propose a novel result merging method called Weighted Curve Fitting (WCF) that combines the features of SSL and SAFE for result merging. The new method distinguishes accurate and estimated rank information. It also considers the importance of documents in different positions for regression. Section 2 proposes the algorithm and Section 3 presents the empirical results.

2. WEIGHTED CURVE FITTING RESULT MERGING

We describe the method of estimating document ranks in SAFE, which is now reused in WCF. Suppose that the sampling process is uniform, a centralized document of rank r in the individual sample source is estimated to have rank P in the corresponding remote source, where we define $P = r \cdot |c_k|/|\theta_k|$ ($|c_k|$ and $|\theta_k|$ are the number of documents in the

This research was partially supported by the NSF research grants IIS-0746830, CNS-1012208, IIS-1017837, and a research grant from Google Inc.

SIGIR'11, July 24–28, 2011, Beijing, China.
ACM 978-1-4503-0757-4/11/07.

source c_k and its sample θ_k). P is then used for regression if the document is unseen in the source's ranked list.

As mentioned before, SAFE does not differentiate the contribution of overlapping documents and non-overlapping ones in making regression. It is better to put more weights on overlapping documents, since their ranks are more accurate than those estimated. Moreover, by assuming that top documents are more representative than the others, documents on top of the returned ranked list should contribute to the regression more than documents at the bottom. Formally, given a query and a ranked list of documents that match the query in the centralized database, let S_j be the centralized relevance score of document d_j, and let r_j be the rank of d_j in the source's individual ranked list. Note that r_j could either be real or estimated, depending on whether d_j appears in the individual ranked list. Then both SSL and SAFE attempt to fit the curve $S_j = a \cdot f(r_j) + b$, where f is any function, and a, b are the learning parameters. We fit the curve by minimizing the quadratic loss function:

$$G_{SSL} = min \sum_j ||S_j - (a \cdot f(r_j) + b)||^2$$

Now we add two more parameters for the new model:

$$G_{WCF} = min \sum_j \frac{1}{\varphi_e^2(d_j)} \cdot \frac{1}{\psi_p^2(d_j)} \left|\left| S_j - (a \cdot f(r_j) + b) \right|\right|^2$$

where φ_e is a function that gives larger value for the document with an estimated rank than a document with a true rank. ψ_p is a function depending on the position of document d_j in the centralized ranked list. In this paper, we choose a linear function for ψ_p, i.e. $\psi_p(d_j) = r_j$. We also choose a two-level function for φ_e:

$$\varphi_e(d_j) = \begin{cases} 1 & \text{if } d_j \text{ has true rank} \\ c(c > 1) & \text{if } d_j \text{ has estimated rank} \end{cases}$$

c is set to 16 in all the experiments, to indicate the penalized term for estimated ranks. We call this method Weighted Curve Fitting (WCF). Parameter estimation can be done by rewriting the objective function and solving the normal linear regression. Let $w_j = \varphi_e(d_j) * \psi_p(d_j)$, then

$$G_{WCF} = min \sum_j \left|\left| \frac{S_j}{w_j} - (\frac{a}{w_j} \cdot f(r_j) + \frac{b}{w_j}) \right|\right|^2$$

3. EXPERIMENTAL RESULTS

We conducted our experiments with two standard TREC datasets: trec123, which contains 100 collections of TREC CDs 1, 2 and 3 organized by publication sources; and trec4-kmeans, which contains 100 collections created from TREC4 by k-means clustering [1]. Each information source uses a different retrieval model among INQUERY [2], language modeling and vector space tf-idf. We sample 300 documents for each source, use CORI [1] to select the top 5 sources for each query and INQUERY for querying the centralized sample database. As for the function f, SAFE uses linear, log, square, power and hybrid functions. We follow the same approach, but only report and compare results of the hybrid choice, which was shown to obtain best results in [4].

Table 1 shows the precision results when top 20 documents returned from each source are merged. We also conduct experiments with top 50 and 100 documents selected from each source. The full result is shown in Figure 1.

Table 1: Document Precision on TREC123, TREC4 with Top 20 Documents of each Source

	TREC123				TREC4_kmeans			
P@n	@5	@10	@15	@20	@5	@10	@15	@20
SAFE	.32	.29	.27	.25	.27	.22	.19	.17
WCF	.34	.31	.29	.27	.31	.26	.24	.24

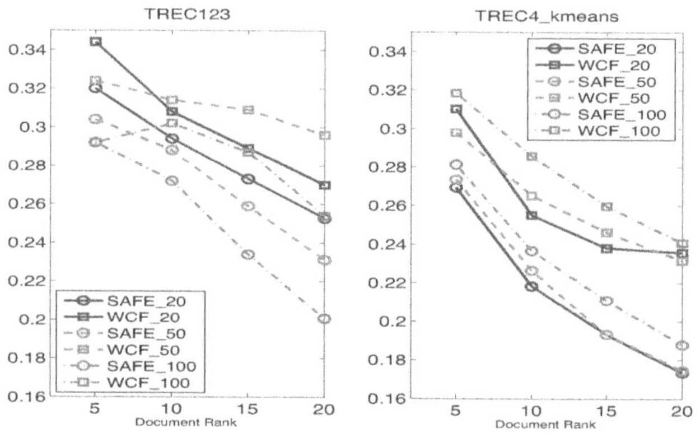

Figure 1: Document Precision with Top 20, 50, 100 Documents of each Source

In both datasets, the curves of the same color denote the performance of SAFE and WCF of the same setting. In general, WCF consistently outperforms SAFE. For trec4-kmeans, the precision is increasing when more documents from each source are merged. However, this is not the case with trec123. It may be argued that the algorithm has to deal with more noisy data when merging more documents, so a possible solution is to assign even smaller weight to documents along the tail of the returned list. The exploration of using other functions for ψ_p is reserved for the future work. In general, WCF works well without too much overhead.

4. CONCLUSION

This paper proposes a result merging algorithm for federated search. Similar to SAFE, the new method does not rely on overlapping documents. More importantly, the new method can accurately estimate global document scores for result merging by distinguishing accurate rank information and estimated rank information in regression. It also meets the high-precision criterion by putting more weights for documents in the top part of the ranked lists for curve-fitting. Empirical results on two datasets have shown the effectiveness of the proposed results merging algorithm.

5. REFERENCES

[1] J. Callan. Distributed information retrieval. *Advances in Information Retrieval*, pages 127–150, 2000.

[2] J. Callan, W. B. Croft, and S. M. Harding. The inquery retrieval system. In *Proceedings of the Third International Conference on Database and Expert Systems Applications*, 1992.

[3] S. Kirsch. Document retrieval over networks wherein ranking and relevance scores are computed at the client for multiple database documents, Aug. 19 2003.

[4] M. Shokouhi and J. Zobel. Robust result merging using sample-based score estimates. *ACM Transactions on Information Systems*, 27(3):1–29, 2009.

[5] L. Si and J. Callan. A semi-supervised learning method to merge search engine results. *ACM Transactions on Information Systems*, 21(4):457–491, 2003.

Effect of Different Docid Orderings on Dynamic Pruning Retrieval Strategies

Nicola Tonellotto
Information Science and Technologies Institute
National Research Council
Via G. Moruzzi 1, 56124 Pisa, Italy
nicola.tonellotto@isti.cnr.it

Craig Macdonald, Iadh Ounis
School of Computing Science
University of Glasgow
Glasgow, G12 8QQ, UK
{craig.macdonald,iadh.ounis}@glasgow.ac.uk

ABSTRACT

Document-at-a-time (DAAT) dynamic pruning strategies for information retrieval systems such as MAXSCORE and WAND can increase querying efficiency without decreasing effectiveness. Both work on posting lists sorted by ascending document identifier (docid). The order in which docids are assigned – and hence the order of postings in the posting lists – is known to have a noticeable impact on posting list compression. However, the resulting impact on dynamic pruning strategies is not well understood. In this poster, we examine the impact on the efficiency of these strategies across different docid orderings, by experimenting using the TREC ClueWeb09 corpus. We find that while the number of postings scored by dynamic pruning strategies do not markedly vary for different docid orderings, the ordering still has a marked impact on mean query response time. Moreover, when docids are assigned by lexicographical URL ordering, the benefit to response time for is more pronounced for WAND than for MAXSCORE.

Categories & Subject Descriptors: H.3.3 [Information Storage & Retrieval]: Information Search & Retrieval

General Terms: Performance, Experimentation

Keywords: Dynamic Pruning, Docid Ordering

1. INTRODUCTION

MAXSCORE [7] and WAND [2] are two document-at-a-time (DAAT) dynamic pruning strategies that can efficiently score documents without decreasing retrieval effectiveness at rank K, nor requiring impact-sorted posting lists. Instead, the postings for every term have the same global ordering, such that they can be read in parallel.

MAXSCORE achieves efficient retrieval by omitting the scoring of postings for documents that will not make the final retrieved ranking. In contrast, WAND takes a different approach, by repeatedly calculating a *pivot term*. The next document to contain the pivot term is called the *pivot document*, which will be the next document to be fully scored. A major benefit of WAND over MAXSCORE is that skipping [5] forward in posting lists is supported, which reduces posting list decompression overheads, and can reduce disk IO.

The ordering of index docids has been studied within the literature. In particular, as the posting lists typically record delta gaps between docids, ensuring that these gaps are as small as possible increases compression, while allowing efficient memory use at retrieval time. For instance, Blelloch and Blandford [1] argued that maximising the *clustering property* of posting lists so that documents with similar content should have similar docids resulted in smaller delta gaps. Silvestri [6] later showed that high clustering could be cheaply approximated by ordering docids according to the lexicographical order of their URLs.

Nevertheless, while URL docid ordering can attain highly compressed indices, there has been no published work examining the impact of docid orderings on the efficiency of dynamic pruning strategies. To address this, this work contributes a study of several dynamic pruning strategies using different docid orderings.

2. EXPERIMENTAL SETUP

Our investigation is conducted using the TREC ClueWeb09 (cat. B) collection, which comprises 50 million English Web documents, aimed to represent the first tier index of a commercial search engine. We index this collection using the Terrier information retrieval platform[1], with stemming and stopword removal. Each posting consists of only the Elias-Gamma encoded docid gap and the Elias-Unary encoded frequency. Skip points within the posting lists are placed in a separate file, with $L = 10,000$ [5].

For index orderings, we consider three alternatives, detailed below. Basically, the idea is to put documents sharing many common terms close to each other and assign identifiers accordingly. In this way the likelihood of having small gaps in posting lists is higher. Smaller gaps correspond to smaller (in terms of bit occupancy) codewords and, thus, smaller indexes.

Random ordering: As a baseline, we randomise the ordering of documents in our index, assigning identifiers to documents without any specific order.

Doclength ordering: Longer documents are more likely to share common terms. In this paper, we assign document identifiers by decreasing length of documents (i.e. the longest document takes docid 0), which has been shown to have a positive impact on the size of the resulting index [3].

URL ordering: Docids are assigned according to the lexicographical ordering of the URLs[2]. URL ordering is good for compression, as it approximates the clustering property [6].

By indexing ClueWeb09 with these different variants of docid ordering, we obtain several different inverted files. Statistics of the inverted files are detailed in Table 1. We

[1] `http://terrier.org`
[2] We would also liked to have used crawl ordering, however URL ordering is all that is available for ClueWeb09.

SIGIR'11, July 24–28, 2011, Beijing, China.
ACM 978-1-4503-0757-4/11/07.

Ordering	Inverted File Size	
Random	22.4 GB	100%
Doclength	19.6 GB	87.5%
URL	14.7 GB	65.6%

Table 1: Statistics of the created inverted files.

note that URL ordering gives the highest compression, followed by doclength. As expected, a random ordering increases the delta gaps in the posting lists, resulting in the largest inverted file size.

In the following experiments, we compare the MAXSCORE and WAND DAAT dynamic pruning strategies, as well as an exhaustive "Full" DAAT strategy, which scores all postings for each query term. For testing retrieval efficiency, we extract streams of user queries from a real search engine log [4]. In particular, we select the first 1,000 queries of the query log, applying stemming and stopwords removal (empty and no-match queries are removed). Two experiments are performed ranking documents using BM25, namely to evaluate the query average response time and the number of postings fully scored by each strategy. The number of documents retrieved for each query is set to the TREC standard value of $K = 1,000$. All experiments are made using a dual quad-core Intel Xeon 2.6GHz, with 8GB RAM and a 2TB SATA2 disk containing the index. Note that, as MAXSCORE and WAND do not impact on retrieval effectiveness to rank K, there is no need to compare effectiveness using measures such as NDCG.

		Ordering						
		random		doclength		URL		
postings	Full	3,973	100%	3,973	100%	3,973	100%	
	MAXSCORE	1,717	43.2%	1,871	47.0%	1,732	43.6%	
	WAND	428	10.8%	572	14.4%	436	10.9%	
times	Full	1.36	100%	1.36	100%	1.32	100%	97.1%
	MAXSCORE	1.24	91.1%	1.24	91.1%	1.17	88.6%	94.4%
	WAND	0.96	70.5%	0.96	70.5%	0.84	63.6%	87.5%

Table 2: Total number of postings scored in millions (top) and mean query response time in seconds (bottom), for 1,000 queries. Relative percentages compared to Full are reported. Relative percentages for URL ordered response time compared to random are reported on right.

3. RESULTS

Table 2 reports the results of our experiments in terms of both millions of postings scored and mean query response time for the 1,000 queries.

We first compare different docid orderings. In general, we note that response times are lower for URL ordering, while random and doclength are approximately the same. This is in marked contrast to Table 1, where the random baseline ordering resulted in a markedly larger inverted file than doclength, and hence a larger response time would be expected for the random ordering. In fact, the number of postings scored for the random index are actually the lowest. This suggests that even if less time is spent decoding and processing less postings, this is counter-balanced by more time spent by the operating system in managing IO operations for the larger random posting lists. On the other hand, while URL ordering does not markedly decrease the number of postings scored, it markedly benefits query response time, particularly for the WAND strategy.

With respect to dynamic pruning strategies, MAXSCORE scores 43-47% of all postings, while WAND scores 11-15%. This difference is also reflected, although with less strength, in the mean response times, where MAXSCORE and WAND respectively take about 90% and 63-70% of the response time of the exhaustive Full strategy. Once again, this can be explained by the fact that larger inverted files require more IO operations, which counter-act the benefits given by the reduced decoding and processing of postings.

Of all results, we note with particular interest that, while URL ordering scores more postings than random, the response time benefit is larger for WAND (87.5%) than for the other strategies. We hypothesise that by applying URL ordering, not only is the average gap between docids reduced, but the postings for the retrieved documents are placed closer together, which benefits the skipping used by WAND. To confirm this, for the 1,000 queries, we examined the mean standard deviation of the docids for the retrieved documents. On average, the URL ordered index had a smaller mean standard deviation (245k postings) than random (382k postings) and doclength (359k postings). The lower mean standard deviation suggests that the retrieved documents are more likely to be clustered within the URL ordered posting lists. As a consequence, the response time of WAND is enhanced by this URL ordering, as more clustered results permit more skipping (with the associated benefit of avoiding unnecessary posting decompression).

4. CONCLUSIONS

This paper is the first examination of index ordering in the context of DAAT dynamic pruning strategies. Our results show that the number of postings scored does not markedly vary for different index orders when applying the MAXSCORE and WAND pruning strategies. However, mean query response time does exhibit marked reductions, and comparably more for the dynamic pruning strategies than for an exhaustive Full DAAT strategy. These results show the value in URL docid ordering for both increasing inverted file compression and enhancing the efficiency of dynamic pruning strategies. Moreover the clustering property of posting lists benefits both query processing time (particularly when using skipping) and index compression. Finally, we note that, with 50 million documents, our experiments are carried out at a larger scale than previous works – for instance, 100 times as many documents than [1], and 10 times as many as [6].

5. REFERENCES

[1] D. Blandford and G. Blelloch. Index compression through document reordering. In *Proceedings of the Data Compression Conference 2002*.

[2] A. Z. Broder, D. Carmel, M. Herscovici, A. Soffer, and J. Zien. Efficient query evaluation using a two-level retrieval process. In *Proceedings of CIKM 2006*, 426–434.

[3] S. Büttcher, C. L. A. Clarke, and G. V. Cormack. Information retrieval: implementing and evaluating search engines. MIT Press, 2010.

[4] N. Craswell, R. Jone, G. Dupret, and E. Viegas. *Proceedings of the 2009 workshop on Web Search Click Data*. ACM Press.

[5] A. Moffat and J. Zobel. Self-indexing inverted files for fast text retrieval. *Transactions on Information Systems*, 14(4):349–379, 1996.

[6] F. Silvestri. Sorting out the document identifier assignment problem. In *Proceedings of ECIR 2007*, 101–112.

[7] H. Turtle and J. Flood. Query evaluation: strategies and optimizations. *Information Processing and Management*, 31(6):831–850, 1995.

Time-based Query Performance Predictors

Nattiya Kanhabua
Dept. of Computer Science
Norwegian University of Science and Technology
Trondheim, Norway
nattiya@idi.ntnu.no

Kjetil Nørvåg
Dept. of Computer Science
Norwegian University of Science and Technology
Trondheim, Norway
noervaag@idi.ntnu.no

ABSTRACT

Query performance prediction is aimed at predicting the retrieval effectiveness that a query will achieve with respect to a particular ranking model. In this paper, we study query performance prediction for a ranking model that explicitly incorporates the time dimension into ranking. Different time-based predictors are proposed as analogous to existing keyword-based predictors. In order to improve predicting performance, we combine different predictors using linear regression and neural networks. Extensive experiments are conducted using queries and relevance judgments obtained by crowdsourcing.

Categories and Subject Descriptors H.3.3 [Information Storage and Retrieval]: Information Search and Retrieval
General Terms Algorithms, Experimentation, Performance
Keywords Query performance prediction, Time-aware ranking

1. INTRODUCTION

In this paper we study the performance prediction of a query explicitly provided with time, for example, the eruptions of volcanoes in Iceland before 2010. The query is explicitly provided with *temporal information needs*, which means that a user wants to know about volcanic events in Iceland during the years before 2010. To determine query performance accurately, both textual and temporal information must be considered. If the query is predicted to perform very poorly, the system can help a user reformulate the query by performing "query suggestion" of *terms* and/or *time* relevant to the query, e.g., a list of all volcanic mountains and time periods of major eruptions in Iceland. On the other hand, if the query is predicted to be sufficiently *good*, it can gain further improvement by document re-ranking with *time-based pseudo-relevance feedback* [6].

2. PREDICTING TEMPORAL QUERY PERFORMANCE

Let q be a temporal query, D be a document collection, T be a set of all temporal expressions in D. N_D is the total number of documents in D and N_T is the number of all distinct temporal expressions in T. Temporal query performance prediction is aimed at predicting the retrieval effectiveness for q. Because q is strongly time-dependent, both the statistics of the document collection D and the set of temporal expressions T must be taken into account. Temporal query performance prediction is defined as $f(q, D, T) \rightarrow [0, 1]$, where f is a prediction function (so-called a predictor) giving a predicted score that can indicate the effectiveness of q. We are only interested in pre-retrieval predictors because they predict query performance independently from a ranking method as opposed to post-retrieval predictors. Temporal expressions and the publication date of a document is represented as a quadruple [1]: (tb_l, tb_u, te_l, te_u) where tb_l and tb_u are the lower bound and upper bound for the begin boundary of a time interval respectively. Similarly, te_l and te_u are the lower bound and upper bound for the end boundary of a time interval. A temporal query q is composed of keywords q_{text} and temporal expressions q_{time}. A document d consists of the textual part d_{text}, i.e., a bag of words, and the temporal part d_{time} composed of the publication date $PubTime(d)$, and temporal expressions mentioned in the document's contents $ContentTime(d)$ or $\{t_1, \ldots t_k\}$.

3. TIME-BASED PREDICTORS

We propose ten different *time-based* predictors analogous to *keyword-based* predictors, including *T-AvQL*, *T-AvIDF*, *T-MaxIDF*, *T-AvICTF*, *T-SCS*, *T-SumSCQ*, *T-SumVAR*, *T-AvVAR*, *T-AvPMI* and *T-MaxPMI*. The first time-based predictor *T-AvQL* is similar to the average length of a query in [7]. $T\text{-}AvQL = \frac{1}{|q_{time}|} \sum_{t \in q_{time}} \frac{(tb_l - te_l) + (tb_u - te_u)}{2}$ For example, a query's temporal expression July 2010 is more specific than 21st century, and the first query should perform better than the latter. Hence, the shorter the time span of query, the better it performs. *T-AvIDF* is determines the specificity of q by leveraging document frequencies as done in [4] and can be computed using the INQUERY *idf* formula.

$$T\text{-}AvIDF(q_{time}) = \frac{1}{|q_{time}|} \sum_{t \in q_{time}} \frac{\log(N_D + 0.5)/df(t)}{\log(N_D + 1)}$$

df(t) is the number of documents containing t. *T-MaxIDF* is the maximum value of *idf* scores. Similar to [4], the averaged inverse collection *time frequency* is measured as $T\text{-}AvICTF = \frac{1}{|q_{time}|} \sum_{t \in q_{time}} \log \frac{N_T}{tf(t)}$. $tf(t)$ is the total number of occurrences of t in T. The simplified (pre-retrieval) version of Clarity Score [2] is proposed in [4]. We incorporate time into the simplified Clarity Score given as *T-SCS*.

$$T\text{-}SCS(q_{time}) = \sum_{t \in q_{time}} P(t|q_{time}) \cdot \log \frac{P(t|q_{time})}{P(t)}$$
$$\approx \sum_{t \in q_{time}} \frac{1}{|q_{time}|} \cdot \log \frac{1}{|q_{time}|} \cdot \frac{N_T}{tf(t)}$$

T-SumSCQ is analogous to the summed collection query similarity [8], and it is aimed at capturing the similarity between q_{time} and all temporal expressions in T.

SIGIR'11, July 24–28, 2011, Beijing, China.
ACM 978-1-4503-0757-4/11/07.

$$T\text{-}SumSCQ(q_{time}) = \sum_{t \in q_{time}} (1 + \ln tf(t)) \cdot \ln(1 + \frac{N_T}{df(t)})$$

The sum of query weight deviation [8] estimates how difficult it is for the retrieval model to rank documents containing query terms by examining *term weights* e.g. TF-IDF. For a temporal query, *temporal weights* will be determined instead of *term weights*. In this paper, we employ the time-aware ranking method TSU [6] to measure *temporal weights*.

$$T\text{-}SumVAR(q_{time}) = \sum_{t \in q_{time}} \sqrt{\frac{1}{|D_t|} \times \sum_{d \in D_t} (TSU(t, PubTime(d)) - \overline{TSU}(t))^2}$$

where D_t are documents containing t and $|D_t|$ is the size of D_t, or $df(t)$. *T-AvVAR* is the averaged value of *T-SumVAR*. Time-based predictors above ignore the relationship between query terms and time. The query tsunami 2004 should perform better than tsunami 2002 because tsunami and 2004 co-occur in a collection more often than by chance, while tsunami and 2002 rarely occur together. PMI is used to determine the relationship between a query term $w \in q_{text}$ and time $t \in q_{time}$ [3]. *T-AvPMI* is the averaged value of all PMI scores. The maximum score *T-MaxPMI* is also considered in a case that the averaged PMI value is low but at least one pair of query term and time has a high PMI.

4. EXPERIMENTS

The New York Times Annotated Corpus is used and 40 queries and judgments from [1]. Queries with *day*, *month* or *year* are grouped into the category "short period" denoted *SP*, and queries with *decade*, *century* as "long period" queries denoted *LP*. There are two retrieval modes: 1) *inclusive* (both query terms and a temporal expression comprise a query q_{text}) and 2) *exclusive* (only query terms constitute q_{text} and a temporal expression is excluded from q_{text}). We use the time-aware ranking method TSU [6] for determining MAP. Parameters of TSU are an exponential decay rate $DecayRate = 0.5$, $\lambda = 0.5$, and $\mu = 6$ months. We use the Weka implementation to model simple linear regression for a single predictor, and linear regression and neural network for combining multiple predictors as done in [5]. The models are trained using cross-validation of 5 folds with 10 repetitions. The averaged values of correlation coefficient and root mean squared error (RMSE) of 5 folds are reported.

Table 1 shows the results of single predictors, where each predictor is statistically tested with the worst performed predictor (as underlined) using paired t-test with $p < 0.05$ (in bold). Because all queries in the dataset associate with one temporal expression, we omit the result of some predictors, e.g., the results of *T-MaxIDF* and *T-AvIDF* are the same, so we only report one of them. *AvQL* and *T-AvICTF* outperform other predictors for "short period", while *MaxIDF*, *SumSCQ* and *T-SumSCQ* perform best for "long period". RMSE shows similar results, that is, *AvQL* and *T-AvICTF* perform best (having the lowest RMSE) for "short period". *T-AvIDF* is the worst predictor for "long period", and its RMSE value unusually too high (=0.65). We found that the predicted scores of *T-AvIDF* for "long period" queries are very small yielding high RMSE values.

Table 2 shows the results of combination methods using linear regression† and neural networks∓. Each combined predictor is statistically tested with that of the best performing single predictors (that is, *AvQL* for "short period" and *T-SumSCQ* for "long period"). Each time-based predictor is combined with its corresponding keyword-based predictor. E.g., *T-AvQL*† denotes the combining of *T-AvQL* and its keyword-based predictor using linear regression. The combination of all predictors is denoted *ALL*. For "short period" and *inclusive*, both *T-AvQL*†, *T-AvQL*∓, *ALL*† and *T-MaxPMI*† outperform the best single predictor significantly. For "long period' the combined methods do not perform well since the correlation coefficient of *T-SumSCQ* is relatively high (though it is negative).

Table 1: Performance of single predictors.

Predictor	Correlation coefficient				RMSE			
	inclusive		*exclusive*		*inclusive*		*exclusive*	
	SP	*LP*	*SP*	*LP*	*SP*	*LP*	*SP*	*LP*
AvQL [7]	**0.36**	0.27	**0.39**	-0.02	**0.28**	**0.23**	**0.29**	**0.25**
AvIDF [2]	**-0.26**	<u>0.04</u>	-0.20	0.12	<u>0.30</u>	**0.24**	**0.29**	**0.24**
MaxIDF [4]	0.04	**-0.27**	-0.16	**-0.27**	0.29	**0.25**	0.30	**0.25**
AvICTF [4]	-0.13	0.19	-0.18	0.24	0.30	**0.22**	**0.29**	**0.23**
SCS [4]	-0.14	0.21	-0.14	0.24	0.30	**0.22**	**0.29**	**0.23**
SumSCQ [8]	-0.09	-0.05	**0.16**	**-0.45**	0.29	**0.24**	**0.29**	**0.24**
SumVAR [8]	-0.20	0.07	**-0.31**	0.19	0.30	**0.22**	<u>0.31</u>	**0.22**
AvVAR [8]	**-0.20**	0.23	**-0.35**	<u>0.00</u>	0.30	**0.23**	**0.30**	**0.23**
AvPMI [3]	**0.29**	-0.05	**0.28**	0.02	0.30	**0.24**	**0.28**	**0.24**
MaxPMI [3]	**0.32**	-0.06	**0.35**	-0.04	0.28	**0.24**	**0.28**	**0.24**
T-AvQL	**0.19**	0.05	**0.19**	0.05	**0.28**	**0.24**	**0.28**	**0.24**
T-AvIDF	**0.27**	-0.05	**0.27**	-0.05	0.29	<u>0.65</u>	**0.29**	<u>0.65</u>
T-AvICTF	**0.35**	0.08	**0.35**	0.08	**0.27**	**0.25**	**0.27**	**0.25**
T-SumSCQ	<u>-0.02</u>	**-0.59**	<u>-0.02</u>	**-0.59**	0.29	**0.32**	**0.29**	**0.32**
T-SumVAR	**0.21**	-0.07	**0.21**	-0.07	0.28	**0.24**	**0.28**	**0.24**
T-AvPMI	**0.15**	0.23	**0.28**	0.20	0.30	**0.22**	**0.27**	**0.23**
T-MaxPMI	0.02	0.08	0.13	0.08	**0.29**	**0.21**	0.27	**0.21**

Table 2: Performance of combined predictors.

Predictor	Correlation coefficient				RMSE			
	inclusive		*exclusive*		*inclusive*		*exclusive*	
	SP	*LP*	*SP*	*LP*	*SP*	*LP*	*SP*	*LP*
T-AvQL†	**0.50**	-0.07	0.33	-0.10	**0.26**	**0.25**	0.28	**0.24**
T-AvIDF†	-0.10	0.01	-0.05	0.01	0.30	**0.23**	0.30	**0.23**
T-AvICTF†	-0.02	-0.22	-0.02	-0.19	0.30	**0.26**	0.29	**0.26**
T-SCS†	-0.02	-0.16	-0.02	-0.19	0.29	**0.25**	0.29	**0.26**
T-SumSCQ†	-0.04	-0.16	-0.04	-0.19	0.29	**0.25**	0.29	0.32
T-SumVAR†	-0.07	-0.08	-0.07	-0.08	0.29	**0.23**	0.29	**0.23**
T-AvVAR†	-0.06	-0.07	-0.04	-0.07	0.30	**0.23**	0.29	**0.23**
T-AvPMI†	-0.10	0.03	0.41	0.03	0.33	**0.24**	**0.27**	**0.23**
T-MaxPMI†	**0.36**	-0.05	0.30	-0.10	**0.26**	**0.23**	0.28	**0.23**
ALL†	**0.43**	-0.04	0.29	-0.11	0.34	0.32	0.33	0.26
T-AvQL∓	**0.47**	0.13	**0.50**	-0.06	0.30	**0.27**	0.30	**0.26**
T-AvIDF∓	-0.02	-0.29	-0.05	-0.29	0.36	**0.27**	0.37	**0.27**
T-AvICTF∓	0.12	-0.17	0.22	0.01	0.33	**0.26**	0.30	**0.29**
T-SCS∓	0.13	-0.09	0.24	-0.07	0.33	**0.26**	0.31	0.30
T-SumSCQ∓	-0.06	-0.09	-0.11	-0.37	0.33	**0.26**	0.34	**0.24**
T-SumVAR∓	-0.09	-0.03	-0.14	0.03	0.35	**0.23**	0.37	**0.24**
T-AvVAR∓	-0.06	-0.05	-0.02	-0.10	0.34	**0.23**	0.35	**0.24**
T-AvPMI∓	0.11	0.16	0.41	0.16	0.36	**0.27**	0.30	**0.25**
T-MaxPMI∓	0.32	0.18	0.50	0.23	0.31	**0.23**	0.29	**0.23**
ALL∓	0.22	-0.09	0.17	0.00	0.38	0.45	0.44	0.42

5. CONCLUSIONS AND FUTURE WORK

To conclude, time-based single predictors outperform the baseline predictors significantly for "short period" queries, and the combined methods outperform single predictors significantly for most cases. Our planned future work are: 1) increase the number of temporal queries used for analysis, 2) consider time uncertainty as an indicator for predicting query performance, and 3) study post-retrieval prediction for temporal search.

6. REFERENCES

[1] K. Berberich, S. Bedathur, O. Alonso, and G. Weikum. A language modeling approach for temporal information needs. In *Proceedings of ECIR'2010*, 2010.

[2] S. Cronen-Townsend, Y. Zhou, and W. B. Croft. Predicting query performance. In *Proceedings of SIGIR'2002*, 2002.

[3] C. Hauff, L. Azzopardi, and D. Hiemstra. The combination and evaluation of query performance prediction methods. In *Proceedings of ECIR'2009*, 2009.

[4] B. He and I. Ounis. Inferring query performance using pre-retrieval predictors. In *Proceedings of SPIRE'2004*, 2004.

[5] R. Jones and F. Diaz. Temporal profiles of queries. *ACM Trans. Inf. Syst.*, 25, July 2007.

[6] N. Kanhabua and K. Nørvåg. Determining time of queries for re-ranking search results. In *Proceedings of ECDL'2010*, 2010.

[7] J. Mothe and L. Tanguy. Linguistic features to predict query difficulty. In *Proceedings of SIGIR Workshop*, 2005.

[8] Y. Zhao, F. Scholer, and Y. Tsegay. Effective pre-retrieval query performance prediction using similarity and variability evidence. In *Proceedings of ECIR'2008*, 2008.

Search Task Difficulty: The Expected vs. The Reflected

Jingjing Liu
Southern Connecticut State University
501 Crescent Street, New Haven, CT 06515
jliujingjing@gmail.com

Nicholas J. Belkin
Rutgers University
4 Huntington Street, New Brunswick, NJ 08901
belkin@rutgers.edu

ABSTRACT

We report findings on how the user's perception of task difficulty changes before and after searching for information to solve tasks. We found that while in one type of task, the dependent task, this did not change, in another, the parallel task, it did. The findings have implications on designing systems that can provide assistance to users with their search and task solving strategies.

Categories and Subject Descriptors

H.3.3 [**Information Storage and Retrieval**]: Information Search and Retrieval – *relevance feedback, search process*.

General Terms

Measurement, Performance, Experimentation, Human Factors.

Keywords

Task difficulty, predicted difficulty, reflected difficulty, task type

1. INTRODUCTION

Current search engines do a good job in returning answers with easy and simple tasks, e.g., "when is the poster submission deadline for SIGIR 2011?" One can simply type in Google (http://www.google.com) the keywords "SIGIR 2011 poster deadline" and find the answer from the snippet of the top ranked search result. However, search systems do not do as well with somewhat difficult tasks, e.g., "collect information that is helpful to make a 2-week tour plan to 3 cities in China: Xi'an, Shanghai, and Chengdu." The complexity nature of the task as well as the user's lack of knowledge with these cities and the Chinese culture could all make the task be difficult. Better search systems are needed that can help people more easily locate useful information and more effectively solve such difficult tasks.

Task difficulty has been attracting quite some research attention. It is defined as a subjective perception assessed by task doers [4], and could be formed both pre- and post-task [3]. Task difficulty has been found to be a significant factor influencing users' search behaviors and search performance. In difficult tasks, users are more likely to visit more web pages ([2][3][5]), issue more queries ([1][3][5]), and spend longer total time ([1][5]) and first dwell time [5] on search result pages. These findings in the relationship between users' behaviors and task difficulty suggest that it is possible to predict the difficulty level of a task from the users' search behaviors. Further, researchers have found that the relationship between search behaviors and task difficulty varies in different types of tasks such as in factual, interpretive, and exploratory [3], or in fact-finding and information gathering [5].

Even though a system can predict, from observing the user's behaviors, that he is having difficulty with his search, the system cannot help the user overcome the difficulty unless it has a further understanding on the nature of task difficulty. The following research questions need to be answered: 1) Does a user's perception of the level of task difficulty change along the search and task solving process? 2) Does this change of difficulty perception vary in different task types?

SIGIR'11, July 24–28, 2011, Beijing, China.
ACM 978-1-4503-0757-4/11/07.

2. METHOD

Data came from a 3-session lab experiment designed to examine users' behavioral and performance changes while searching for information to perform a task. A total of 24 college students participated, each coming 3 times in a 2-week period working on one assigned general task which had 3 sub-tasks. Each participant was asked to write a 3-section article on hybrid cars, each section being finished in one session based on one sub-task of his/her choice. Half of the participants worked on a parallel task (PT), which asked them to prepare an article comparing the Honda Civic, Nissan Altima and Toyota Camry hybrid cars. The 3 sub-tasks were parallel to each other. The other half worked on a dependent task (DT), which asked them to a) explore which car manufactures produce hybrid cars, b) identify 3 mid-priced hybrid cars, and c) compare the three cars' pros and cons. The accomplishment of some sub-tasks was assumed to be dependent upon that of others. Participants self-determined the order of the 3 sub-tasks in either task.

Both general tasks were in the same subject domain, had the same general requirements, and had the same levels of complexity (3 sub-tasks); their only difference is in task structure. At the beginning of the experiment, participants were asked to rate, on a 7-point scale (1=not, 7=very), how difficult they felt the task would be, i.e., their pre-task or expected task difficulty. At the end of the 3rd session, they were asked to rate how difficult the task was, i.e., their post-task or reflected task difficulty. In addition, in the beginning and the end of each session, each participant was also asked to rate the expected (pre-session) and reflected (post-session) sub-task difficulty.

3. RESULTS & DISCUSSION

3.1 Difficulty comparison of two general tasks

The difficulty ratings being not normally distributed, non-parametric Mann-Whitney U test was used to compare the difficulty of the two general tasks. Results (Table 1) show no significant difference in user ratings for the two tasks either before

Table 1. Pre- and post-task difficulty ratings in two tasks

Difficulty type	Mean (standard deviation)		U(p)
	Dependent task	Parallel task	
Pre-task	2.83 (1.34)	2.58 (0.90)	61.5 (0.551)
Post-task	2.92 (1.31)	2.08 (0.90)	43.5 (0.101)

or after they worked on them. This was reasonable given that both tasks were in the same domain and their general requirements were the same.

3.2 Expected vs. reflected general task difficulty

A non-parametric Wilcoxon test was used to compare users' expected and reflected general task difficulty. Results (Figure 1) show that in the DT, there was no significant difference between users' ratings on these two types of difficulty. However, in the PT, after working on the whole task, users felt that the general task was not as difficult as they expected in the beginning of the experiment (W(11)=4.5, p=.034). Since both tasks had multiple sub-tasks, it is reasonable to look at the sub-task difficulty for further analyses.

Figure 1. Pre- vs. post-task difficulty in individual tasks

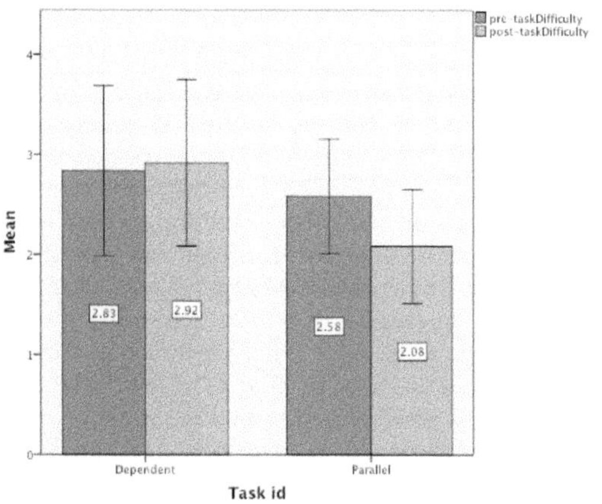

3.3 Expected vs. reflected sub-task difficulty

The Wilcoxon test was used to compare the expected vs. the reflected sub-task difficulty in individual sessions. Results show that in the DT, in any session, as well as in 3 sessions on average, the expected and the reflected sub-task difficulty were not significantly different.

Figure 2. Pre- vs. post-session sub-task difficulty in individual tasks

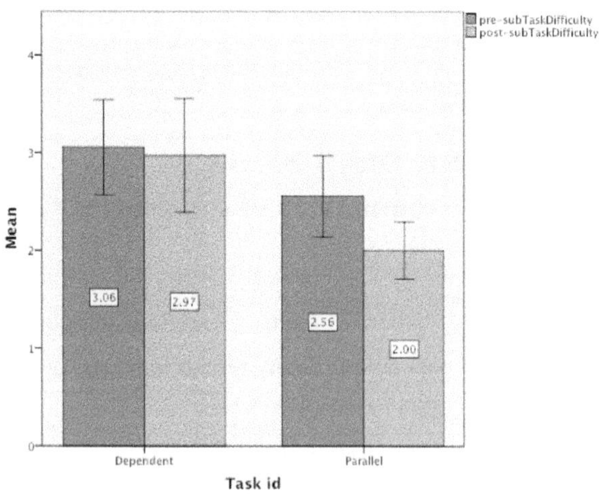

In the PT, no changes were found between users' expected and reflected difficulty of the sub-tasks in individual sessions. However, in all 3 sessions on average, Figure 2, users had a significantly lower rating on the sub-tasks' perceived difficulty than expected (W(35)=37.5, p=.015), meaning that they found the task less difficult after working on the sub-task than before. One reason could be that in the PT, although the topics of the sub-tasks were new each time, users found that the structure of the sub-task was similar, leading to a lower reflected difficulty rating. These results correspond with those in Section 3.2. It is possible that the users' perceptions of difficulty of the sub-tasks led to their perceptions of the difficulty of the general tasks.

4. CONCLUSIONS

Task difficulty requires in-depth understanding in order to build systems that can help users when they have difficult tasks to solve. We conducted analyses of users' ratings on the difficulty levels of the general multi-session tasks, as well as sub-tasks. Our results show that while the topics of two different types of tasks are the same, and their general task difficulty levels are comparable, users felt that one type of task, the PT, was in fact not as difficult as it looked like before they searched for information to solve the task. However, for the DT, users found it as difficult afterwards as before they worked on it. Further analysis shows that this corresponds to users' perceptions of sub-tasks' difficulty levels before and after they worked on the sub-tasks.

The findings of this study have implications for two aspects of search system design. First, the user's perception of a task's difficulty level could change along the way of searching for information to solve the task. In order for the systems to be able to provide help to users when they have difficulty, systems should be able to monitor this change along users' search process. Second, the above-mentioned change of the user's perception of a task's difficulty can be different in different task types. Systems could be designed to provide assistance for users in solving difficult tasks, not only by returning better results for queries and suggesting queries based on semantic meaning, but also by offering suggestions in their task solving strategies. Decomposing a task into several parallel sub-tasks rather than dependent sub-tasks could lead users to feel the task less difficult; systems could make query suggestions that help the users to solve a general task through parallel sub-tasks.

5. ACKNOWLEDGMENTS

This research was supported by IMLS grant LG-06-07-0105-07.

6. REFERENCES

[1] Aula, A., Khan, R. & Guan, Z. (2010). How does search behavior change as search becomes more difficult? *CHI '10*, 35-44.

[2] Gwizdka, J., Spence, I. (2006). What can searching behavior tell us about the difficulty of information tasks? A study of Web navigation. *ASIS&T '06*.

[3] Kim, J. (2006). Task difficulty as a predictor and indicator of web searching interaction. *CHI '06*, 959-964.

[4] Li, Y. & Belkin, N.J. (2008). A faceted approach to conceptualizing tasks in information seeking. *Information Processing & Management, 44*, 1822-1837.

[5] Liu, J., Gwizdka, J., Liu C., & Belkin, N.J. (2010). Predicting task difficulty for different task types. *ASIS&T '10*.

On the Suitability of Diversity Metrics for Learning-to-Rank for Diversity

Rodrygo L. T. Santos
rodrygo@dcs.gla.ac.uk

Craig Macdonald
craigm@dcs.gla.ac.uk

Iadh Ounis
ounis@dcs.gla.ac.uk

School of Computing Science
University of Glasgow
G12 8QQ Glasgow, UK

ABSTRACT

An optimally diverse ranking should achieve the maximum coverage of the aspects underlying an ambiguous or under-specified query, with minimum redundancy with respect to the covered aspects. Although evaluation metrics that reward coverage and penalise redundancy provide intuitive objective functions for learning a diverse ranking, it is unclear whether they are the most effective. In this paper, we contrast the suitability of relevance and diversity metrics as objective functions for learning a diverse ranking. Our results in the context of the diversity task of the TREC 2009 and 2010 Web tracks show that diversity metrics are not necessarily better suited for guiding a learning approach. Moreover, the suitability of these metrics is compromised as they try to penalise redundancy during the learning process.

Categories and Subject Descriptors: H.3.3 [Information Storage & Retrieval]: Information Search & Retrieval

General Terms: Experimentation, Performance

Keywords: Web Search, Learning-to-rank, Diversity

1. INTRODUCTION

An ambiguous query can pose additional difficulties for a search engine, since it may not be clear which *interpretations* or *aspects* underlying this query are of interest to the user [5]. An effective approach for tackling query ambiguity is to diversify the search results, in order to maximise the chance that different users will find at least one relevant result to their particular information need [3].

In this paper, we investigate whether a diverse ranking can be automatically learned from training data by optimising an evaluation metric that rewards diversity. In particular, an optimally diverse ranking should achieve the *maximum coverage* of the aspects underlying an ambiguous query, with *minimum redundancy* with respect to the covered aspects. Hence, it seems intuitive to guide a learning-to-rank algorithm by optimising an evaluation metric that directly accounts for both aspect coverage and redundancy. Although several such metrics have been proposed and shown to effectively reward diversity in the search results [1], it is not clear whether they are any better suited than traditional relevance-oriented metrics for learning a diverse ranking. To investigate this, we contrast two relevance-oriented metrics and their diversity counterparts as objective functions for learning-to-rank for search result diversification.

2. EXPERIMENTAL METHODOLOGY

Our investigation is conducted in the context of the diversity task of the TREC 2009 and 2010 Web tracks, henceforth WT09 and WT10 tasks, respectively. In particular, WT09 provides 50 queries, while WT10 provides 48 queries, all with relevance assessments at the sub-topic level. Our experiments are based on the TREC ClueWeb09 (cat. B) corpus, which comprises 50 million English documents, aimed to represent the first tier of the index of a commercial search engine. We index this collection using Terrier,[1] with Porter's weak stemmer and without removing stopwords.

For our learning setup, we produce a sample comprising the top 5,000 documents retrieved for each of the 98 considered queries, using the Divergence From Randomness DPH weighting model, as implemented in Terrier. Besides being effective, DPH is a parameter-free model, and hence requires no training. Based on this initial sample, we compute a total of 61 document features typically used in the learning-to-rank literature [2]. These include standard weighting models (e.g., DPH itself, BM25), field-based (e.g., BM25F) and dependence (e.g., Markov Random Fields) models, spam detection, URL and link analysis (e.g., PageRank) features.

To enable learning by directly optimising an evaluation metric, we use Metzler's Automatic Feature Selection (AFS) listwise learning-to-rank algorithm, which has been shown to perform effectively on a web setting [4]. As optimisation metrics, we consider two standard relevance-oriented metrics: expected reciprocal rank (ERR) and normalised discounted cumulative gain (nDCG). Additionally, we consider their diversity counterparts: ERR-IA and α-nDCG [1]. While ERR and nDCG are established metrics for web search evaluation, ERR-IA and α-nDCG are the primary evaluation metrics in the diversity task of the TREC 2010 Web track. Moreover, besides rewarding aspect coverage and penalising redundancy, both ERR-IA and α-nDCG allow for tuning how much redundancy should be penalised [1]. To assess how penalising redundancy impacts the learning outcome, we consider variants of these two metrics—called ERR-IA* and α-nDCG*, respectively—that do *not* penalise redundancy at all. To enable a deeper analysis, all optimisation metrics are computed at rank cutoffs 20 and 1000. Finally, we report the diversification performance attained by the learned models optimised to each of these metrics in

[1] `http://terrier.org`

SIGIR'11, July 24–28, 2011, Beijing, China.
ACM 978-1-4503-0757-4/11/07.

Optimisation Metric	Training Performance				Test Performance			
	WT09		WT10		WT09		WT10	
	ERR-IA @20	α-nDCG @20	ERR-IA @20	α-nDCG @20	ERR-IA @20	α-nDCG @20	ERR-IA @20	α-nDCG @20
ERR@20	0.1860	0.2940	0.2760	0.3569	0.1455	0.2377	$\underline{0.2777}$	$\underline{0.3880}$
ERR-IA@20	$0.2484^{\triangle}$	$0.3577^{\triangle}$	$0.3299^{=}$	$0.4204^{=}$	$0.1389^{=}$	$0.2318^{=}$	$0.2357^{=}$	$0.3442^{=}$
ERR-IA*@20	$\underline{0.2790}^{\blacktriangle\triangle}$	$\underline{0.3942}^{\blacktriangle=}$	$\underline{0.3410}^{\triangle=}$	$\underline{0.4423}^{\triangle\blacktriangle}$	$\underline{0.1747}^{=\blacktriangle}$	$\underline{0.2835}^{=\blacktriangle}$	$0.2373^{\triangledown=}$	$0.3467^{==}$
nDCG@20	0.2095	0.3272	0.3149	0.4305	$\underline{0.2014}$	$\underline{0.3028}$	0.2666	0.3760
α-nDCG@20	$\underline{0.2927}^{\blacktriangle}$	$\underline{0.4165}^{\blacktriangle}$	$\underline{0.3503}^{=}$	$\underline{0.4522}^{=}$	$0.1843^{=}$	$0.2889^{=}$	$\underline{0.2696}^{=}$	$\underline{0.3854}^{=}$
α-nDCG*@20	$0.2527^{\blacktriangle\blacktriangledown}$	$0.3729^{\triangle\blacktriangledown}$	$0.2902^{=\triangledown}$	$0.4012^{==}$	$0.1632^{==}$	$0.2622^{==}$	$0.2641^{==}$	$0.3728^{==}$
ERR@1000	0.1873	0.2944	0.2802	0.3729	0.1388	0.2176	$\underline{0.2749}$	0.3883
ERR-IA@1000	$\underline{0.2736}^{\blacktriangle}$	$\underline{0.3850}^{\blacktriangle}$	$0.3283^{=}$	$0.4130^{=}$	$0.1400^{=}$	$0.2400^{=}$	$0.2330^{\triangledown}$	$0.3481^{=}$
ERR-IA*@1000	$0.2727^{\blacktriangle=}$	$0.3799^{\blacktriangle=}$	$\underline{0.3347}^{\triangle\triangle}$	$\underline{0.4295}^{\triangle\triangle}$	$\underline{0.1614}^{=\triangle}$	$\underline{0.2673}^{\triangle\triangle}$	$0.2736^{==}$	$\underline{0.3895}^{==}$
nDCG@1000	0.2279	0.3460	0.3121	0.4247	0.2082	0.3290	0.2372	0.3535
α-nDCG@1000	$0.2601^{=}$	$0.3794^{=}$	$0.3423^{=}$	$0.4315^{=}$	$0.1511^{\blacktriangledown}$	$0.2580^{\blacktriangledown}$	$0.2223^{=}$	$0.3326^{=}$
α-nDCG*@1000	$\underline{0.2768}^{\blacktriangle=}$	$\underline{0.4024}^{\blacktriangle=}$	$\underline{0.3528}^{\triangle=}$	$\underline{0.4667}^{\blacktriangle=}$	$\underline{0.2338}^{\triangle\blacktriangle}$	$\underline{0.3568}^{\triangle\blacktriangle}$	$\underline{0.2496}^{==}$	$\underline{0.3662}^{=\triangle}$

Table 1: Training and test diversification performances of ranking models learned by optimising for relevance- (ERR, nDCG) or diversity-oriented (ERR-IA, α-nDCG, ERR-IA*, α-nDCG*) evaluation metrics.

terms of ERR-IA@20 and α-nDCG@20 under training and test scenarios. In particular, the latter scenario uses the WT09 and WT10 queries as separate training and test sets (i.e., we train on WT09 and test on WT10, and vice versa).

3. EXPERIMENTAL RESULTS

In this section, we investigate the suitability of relevance- and diversity-oriented metrics for guiding a listwise learning-to-rank approach in order to learn a diverse ranking. Table 1 shows the diversification performance of the models learned by AFS by optimising the previously described metrics. Statistical significance is verified using the Wilcoxon signed-rank test. The symbols $\blacktriangle$ ($\blacktriangledown$) and $\triangle$ ($\triangledown$) denote a significant increase (decrease) at the $p < 0.01$ and $p < 0.05$ levels, respectively, while = denotes no significant difference. A first instance of these symbols denotes the significance (or lack thereof) of ERR-IA and ERR-IA* compared to ERR, as well as of α-nDCG and α-nDCG* compared to nDCG. A second instance denotes the significance of ERR-IA* and α-nDCG* compared to ERR-IA and α-nDCG, respectively.

From the training results in Table 1 (left half), we observe that diversity-oriented metrics generally lead to an improved diversification performance compared to relevance metrics. However, these improvements are not always significant, particularly for metrics that penalise redundancy. Indeed, on the WT10 queries, neither ERR-IA nor α-nDCG can significantly outperform their relevance-oriented counterparts, and are generally worse than ERR-IA* and α-nDCG* (except for α-nDCG*@20), which do not penalise redundancy. These results show that, although models that promote diversity can be learned via listwise learning-to-rank, metrics that penalise redundancy do not seem to be particularly suited for guiding the learning process.

The test scenario in Table 1 (right half) complements these observations. In particular, the test performance attained by using ERR-IA and α-nDCG as optimisation metrics is not significantly better than that attained using ERR and nDCG, respectively. In fact, α-nDCG@1000 (for WT09) and ERR-IA@1000 (for WT10) significantly underperform compared to their relevance-oriented counterparts. On the other hand, when ERR-IA and α-nDCG are compared to their variants that do not penalise redundancy, we observe a significantly superior performance of the latter, particularly for ERR-IA*@1000 and α-nDCG*@1000. Nevertheless, although generalising better across different query sets in the test scenario, these variants still cannot consistently and significantly improve compared to relevance metrics.

4. CONCLUSIONS

We have investigated the suitability of diversity metrics as objective functions for learning effective models for search result diversification. Our results show that, contrarily to our intuition, deploying a diversity metric does not necessarily help produce learned models with superior diversification performance compared to those produced using standard relevance metrics as objective functions. This highlights the need to develop features that better indicate not only the relevance, but also the diversity of individual documents.

Our results also show that models learned by optimising for metrics that penalise redundancy seem to overfit to the training queries, with a poor generalisation across different query sets. This observation corroborates related research that shows that the target evaluation metric is not necessarily the best suited to guide a learning-to-rank approach [6]. Indeed, since standard listwise learning-to-rank approaches assume that the relevance of a document is independent of other documents, optimising for metrics sensitive to redundancy (i.e., metrics that consider the relevance of a particular document in light of the other documents) may actually introduce noise to the learning process.

5. REFERENCES

[1] C. L. A. Clarke, N. Craswell, I. Soboroff, and A. Ashkan. A comparative analysis of cascade measures for novelty and diversity. In *WSDM*, 2011.

[2] T.-Y. Liu. Learning to rank for information retrieval. *Found. Trends Inf. Retr.*, 3:225–331, 2009.

[3] R. L. T. Santos, C. Macdonald, and I. Ounis. Exploiting query reformulations for Web search result diversification. In *WWW*, pages 881–890, 2010.

[4] R. L. T. Santos, C. Macdonald, and I. Ounis. Intent-aware search result diversification. In *SIGIR*, 2011.

[5] K. Spärck-Jones, S. E. Robertson, and M. Sanderson. Ambiguous requests: Implications for retrieval tests, systems and theories. *SIGIR Forum*, 41(2):8–17, 2007.

[6] E. Yilmaz and S. E. Robertson. On the choice of effectiveness measures for learning to rank. *Inf. Retr.*, 13(3):271–290, 2010.

How Diverse are Web Search Results?

Rodrygo L. T. Santos
rodrygo@dcs.gla.ac.uk

Craig Macdonald
craigm@dcs.gla.ac.uk

Iadh Ounis
ounis@dcs.gla.ac.uk

School of Computing Science
University of Glasgow
G12 8QQ Glasgow, UK

ABSTRACT

Search result diversification has recently gained attention as a means to tackle ambiguous queries. While query ambiguity is of particular concern for the short queries commonly observed in a Web search scenario, it is unclear how much diversity is actually promoted by Web search engines (WSEs). In this paper, we assess the diversification performance of two leading WSEs in the context of the diversity task of the TREC 2009 and 2010 Web tracks. Our results show that these WSEs perform effectively for queries with multiple interpretations, but not for those open to multiple aspects related to a single interpretation. Moreover, by deploying a state-of-the-art diversification approach based on query suggestions from these WSEs themselves, we show that their diversification performance can be further improved.

Categories and Subject Descriptors: H.3.3 [Information Storage & Retrieval]: Information Search & Retrieval

General Terms: Experimentation, Performance

Keywords: Web Search, Search Engines, Diversity

1. INTRODUCTION

Queries submitted to a Web search engine (WSE) are typically short and often ambiguous [5]. In such a scenario, an effective approach is to diversify the search results. By doing so, the probability of satisfying potentially different information needs underlying an ambiguous query is maximised [3]. Although search result diversification is a naturally motivated approach in a Web search scenario, it is unclear how much diversity is actually promoted by existing WSEs.

In this paper, we assess the effectiveness of two leading WSEs in the context of the diversity task of the TREC 2009 and 2010 Web tracks [1, 2]. By breaking down this assessment over queries with different levels of ambiguity, we show that these WSEs perform effectively for queries open to multiple interpretations, but not for those open to multiple aspects of a single interpretation. In the latter case, we show that both WSEs can be further improved by leveraging evidence readily available to them—i.e., query suggestions—within a state-of-the-art diversification approach.

In the rest of this paper, Section 2 describes our methodology and the experimental setup that supports our investigations in Section 3. Our conclusions follow in Section 4.

SIGIR'11, July 24–28, 2011, Beijing, China.
ACM 978-1-4503-0757-4/11/07.

2. EXPERIMENTAL METHODOLOGY

Our investigations aim to answer two research questions:

1. How diverse are WSEs' search results?
2. Can we improve WSEs' diversification performance?

We investigate both questions in the context of the diversity task of the TREC 2009 and 2010 Web tracks [1, 2]. These tasks provide a total of 98 queries (50 from 2009, 48 from 2010), each classified by TREC assessors as either *ambiguous* (i.e., open to different *interpretations*) or *underspecified* (i.e., open to different *aspects* of a single interpretation) [3]. Moreover, each query comprises relevance assessments for 1 to 6 sub-topics, identified by TREC assessors as representing different interpretations or aspects of the query. Besides reporting average performance figures over all 98 queries, we break down our evaluation for queries with different types (ambiguous *vs.* underspecified) as well as with different number of sub-topics (1 to 6).

As WSEs, we consider Bing and Google, henceforth referred to as WSEs A and B, in no particular order, so as to preserve anonymity. In particular, for each of the considered 98 queries, we obtain up to 1000 results from these WSEs using their public APIs.[1] The URLs retrieved by each WSE are then normalised and matched against those in the TREC ClueWeb09 corpus. While this procedure is necessary to enable the reuse of the TREC Web track relevance assessments, the obtained rankings should be seen as a 'lower bound' of what these WSEs could have produced if they constrained themselves to the ClueWeb09 corpus. To provide an ample analysis, we consider both ClueWeb09 A, with 500 million English Web pages, and its first-tier subset, ClueWeb09 B, which comprises 50 million pages.

To investigate whether there is room for improving the diversification performance of these WSEs, we deploy a state-of-the-art diversification framework to re-rank their retrieved results. In particular, the xQuAD framework [4]—one of the top performers at the diversity task of the TREC 2009 and 2010 Web tracks [1, 2]—builds upon an explicit representation of the aspects underlying an ambiguous query. Following Santos et al. [4], we re-rank the results retrieved by each WSE using xQuAD, with query suggestions—provided by the WSE itself—representing different query aspects. As xQuAD requires an estimation of the relevance of each result for every query aspect, we score all the results retrieved for a query with respect to each query suggestion using BM25.

[1] Requests were sent anonymously to the US version of the WSEs, so as to isolate any customisation or localisation effects. All results were retrieved on February 7th, 2011.

				type		number of sub-topics					
			all	amb.	und.	1	2	3	4	5	6
	# queries		98	38	60	2	4	27	31	20	14
ClueWeb09 A	ERR-IA	WSE A	0.2712	0.2910	0.2586	0.0902	0.1828	0.3574	0.2643	0.2358	0.2217
		+xQuAD	0.2856$^{=}$	0.2647$^{=}$	0.2988$^{\blacktriangle}$	0.0515$^{=}$	0.2127$^{=}$	0.3584$^{=}$	0.2825$^{=}$	0.2266$^{=}$	0.2905$^{=}$
		WSE B	0.2997$^{\triangle}$	0.2867$^{=}$	0.3080$^{\triangle}$	0.1803$^{=}$	0.3204$^{=}$	0.3780$^{=}$	0.2889$^{=}$	0.2595$^{=}$	0.2412$^{=}$
		+xQuAD	0.3098$^{\triangle}$	0.2878$^{=}$	0.3237$^{=}$	0.0515$^{=}$	0.3983$^{=}$	0.3971$^{\blacktriangle}$	0.2807$^{=}$	0.2561$^{=}$	0.2943$^{\triangle}$
	α-nDCG	WSE A	0.3957	0.4235	0.3782	0.1637	0.2955	0.4971	0.3888	0.3386	0.3590
		+xQuAD	0.4096$^{=}$	0.3920$^{=}$	0.4208$^{\blacktriangle}$	0.1267$^{=}$	0.3123$^{=}$	0.4915$^{=}$	0.4131$^{=}$	0.3407$^{=}$	0.4107$^{=}$
		WSE B	0.4239$^{=}$	0.4195$^{=}$	0.4267$^{\triangle}$	0.2398$^{=}$	0.3983$^{=}$	0.5214$^{=}$	0.4038$^{=}$	0.3721$^{=}$	0.3881$^{=}$
		+xQuAD	0.4402$^{\triangle}$	0.4293$^{=}$	0.4471$^{=}$	0.1267$^{=}$	0.4796$^{=}$	0.5412$^{\triangle}$	0.4062$^{=}$	0.3792$^{=}$	0.4411$^{\blacktriangle}$
ClueWeb09 B	ERR-IA	WSE A	0.2776	0.2927	0.2681	0.1202	0.2258	0.3259	0.2905	0.2451	0.2398
		+xQuAD	0.3114$^{\blacktriangle}$	0.2859$^{=}$	0.3275$^{\blacktriangle}$	0.0721$^{=}$	0.2014$^{=}$	0.3541$^{=}$	0.3303$^{=}$	0.2663$^{=}$	0.3173$^{\triangle}$
		WSE B	0.3075$^{\blacktriangle}$	0.3106$^{\triangle}$	0.3055$^{=}$	0.1803$^{=}$	0.2546$^{=}$	0.3721$^{\triangle}$	0.3095$^{=}$	0.2773$^{\triangle}$	0.2547$^{=}$
		+xQuAD	0.3326$^{\blacktriangle}$	0.3027$^{=}$	0.3515$^{\blacktriangle}$	0.0902$^{=}$	0.3784$^{=}$	0.3917$^{\triangle}$	0.3084$^{=}$	0.3012$^{=}$	0.3381$^{\blacktriangle}$
	α-nDCG	WSE A	0.3977	0.4264	0.3795	0.1900	0.3023	0.4549	0.4129	0.3529	0.3746
		+xQuAD	0.4311$^{\blacktriangle}$	0.4204$^{=}$	0.4379$^{\blacktriangle}$	0.1470$^{=}$	0.2935$^{=}$	0.4767$^{=}$	0.4549$^{=}$	0.3797$^{\triangle}$	0.4439$^{=}$
		WSE B	0.4309$^{\triangle}$	0.4619$^{\triangle}$	0.4113$^{=}$	0.2398$^{=}$	0.3616$^{=}$	0.5005$^{=}$	0.4224$^{=}$	0.4037$^{\triangle}$	0.4016$^{=}$
		+xQuAD	0.4557$^{\blacktriangle}$	0.4560$^{=}$	0.4556$^{\blacktriangle}$	0.1637$^{=}$	0.4766$^{=}$	0.5119$^{=}$	0.4287$^{=}$	0.4286$^{=}$	0.4819$^{\blacktriangle}$

Table 1: Diversification performance (@20) of WSEs across queries of different type or number of sub-topics.

3. EXPERIMENTAL RESULTS

Clarke et al. [1, 2] have shown that rankings produced by a WSE outperform all systems in the diversity task of the TREC 2009 and 2010 Web tracks. While this result suggests that WSEs indeed seek to diversify their search results, it is unclear how much diversity they actually promote under different scenarios. To investigate this, Table 1 shows the diversification performance of WSEs A and B in contrast to each other and as input to the xQuAD diversification framework. In particular, we break down this evaluation across two orthogonal dimensions: document corpora and query ambiguity level. The first dimension covers a large sample of the Web (ClueWeb09 A) and a high-quality, first-tier subset of this sample (ClueWeb09 B). The second dimension groups all 98 available queries from the TREC 2009 and 2010 Web tracks according to their type (ambiguous or underspecified) or their number of sub-topics. Diversification performance is given by ERR-IA and α-nDCG, both at rank cutoff 20. Significance is verified for WSE B compared to WSE A, as well as for xQuAD compared to WSEs A and B, according to the Wilcoxon signed-rank test. In particular, the symbols $\blacktriangle$ ($\blacktriangledown$) and $\triangle$ ($\triangledown$) denote a significant increase (decrease) at the $p < 0.01$ and $p < 0.05$ levels, respectively, while the symbol $=$ denotes no significant difference.

Focusing on the ClueWeb09 A results, we note that WSE B outperforms WSE A on the whole set of 98 queries (significantly for ERR-IA). Looking at the breakdown by type, we observe that the higher performance of WSE A comes mostly from underspecified queries, for which it significantly outperforms WSE B. Indeed, when ambiguous queries are considered, the two WSEs do not differ significantly. In terms of the number of sub-topics underlying a query, WSE B consistently outperforms WSE A regardless of the number of sub-topics, although not significantly. When xQuAD is deployed on top of these WSEs (using each WSE's own query suggestions), no significant difference is observed for ambiguous queries. Regarding our first question, this suggests that Web search results are highly diverse, at least for ambiguous queries. For underspecified queries, however, both WSEs can be markedly improved (significantly for WSE A) with xQuAD. Regarding our second question, this shows that there is room for improving these WSEs' diversification performance, by leveraging their own query suggestions.

The results for ClueWeb09 B confirm these observations. In particular, WSE B significantly outperforms WSE A on the entire query set. Besides still markedly outperforming WSE A for underspecified queries, we observe that WSE B is now also significantly superior for ambiguous queries. Once again, the number of sub-topics does not play a significant role in explaining the relative performance of these two WSEs, with WSE B consistently outperforming WSE A. Lastly, we once more observe that xQuAD significantly improves both WSEs, with gains coming from underspecified queries, but not from ambiguous queries.

4. CONCLUSIONS

We have thoroughly investigated the diversification performance of two leading WSEs in the context of the diversity task of the TREC 2009 and 2010 Web tracks. Our results expand on initial observations from the literature by analysing how diverse Web search results are for queries with different ambiguity levels. In particular, we have shown that the considered WSEs are already very effective at diversifying the results for ambiguous queries. However, when underspecified queries are considered, we have shown that there is room for significantly improving these WSEs' performance by leveraging their own query suggestions.

5. REFERENCES

[1] C. L. A. Clarke, N. Craswell, and I. Soboroff. Overview of the TREC 2009 Web track. In *TREC*, 2009.

[2] C. L. A. Clarke, N. Craswell, I. Soboroff, and G. V. Cormack. Preliminary overview of the TREC 2010 Web track. In *TREC*, 2010.

[3] C. L. A. Clarke, M. Kolla, G. V. Cormack, O. Vechtomova, A. Ashkan, S. Büttcher, and I. MacKinnon. Novelty and diversity in information retrieval evaluation. In *SIGIR*, pages 659–666, 2008.

[4] R. L. T. Santos, C. Macdonald, and I. Ounis. Exploiting query reformulations for Web search result diversification. In *WWW*, pages 881–890, 2010.

[5] K. Spärck-Jones, S. E. Robertson, and M. Sanderson. Ambiguous requests: Implications for retrieval tests, systems and theories. *SIGIR Forum*, 41(2):8–17, 2007.

Analysis of An Expert Search Query Log

Yi Fang†, Naveen Somasundaram†, Luo Si†, Jeongwoo Ko‡, Aditya P. Mathur†
† Department of Computer Science, Purdue University, West Lafayette, IN 47907, USA
‡ Google Inc, Mountain View, CA 94043, USA
†{fangy, nsomasun, lsi, apm}@cs.purdue.edu; ‡jko@google.com

ABSTRACT

Expert search has made rapid progress in modeling, algorithms and evaluations in the recent years. However, there is very few work on analyzing how users interact with expert search systems. In this paper, we conduct analysis of an expert search query log. The aim is to understand the special characteristics of expert search usage. To the best of our knowledge, this is one of the earliest work on expert search query log analysis. We find that expert search users generally issue shorter queries, more common queries, and use more advanced search features, with fewer queries in a session, than general Web search users do. This study explores a new research direction in expert search by analyzing and exploiting query logs.

Categories and Subject Descriptors

H.3.3 [**Information Search and Retrieval**]: Query formulation

General Terms

Experimentation, Measurement

Keywords

Expert Search, Query Log Analysis

1. INTRODUCTION

As an important information retrieval application, expert search (also known as expert finding) has received substantial attention in the IR research community. Rapid progress has been made in modeling, algorithms and evaluations in the recent years [1] since the launch of TREC Enterprise track in 2005 [2], but we have very little understanding about how people actually use the expert search systems. On the other hand, query logs provide an excellent window for gaining valuable knowledge about how a search engine is used and what the users' interests and preferences are since they form a complete record of what users searched for in a given time frame. The past few years have seen an increased interest in the research of query log analysis. However, most of the related work is conducted on general Web search [5, 6] or with a special group of users on Web search such as children search [7]. There is no prior work on query log analysis for expert search. As expert search users have a specialized type of information need, it is desirable to understand their characteristics and to provide them with suitable IR systems. In this study, we collect a user query log of an expert search system and present an analysis of individual queries and sessions. Our findings support the conjecture that expert search users generally issue shorter queries, more common queries, and use more advanced search features, with fewer queries in a session, than general Web search (as well as children search) users do.

SIGIR'11, July 24–28, 2011, Beijing, China.
ACM 978-1-4503-0757-4/11/07.

2. AN EXPERT SEARCH QUERY LOG

The query log that we analyze is extracted from INDURE[1], which is an expert search system containing over 20,000 researchers from four universities in Indiana [3]. Besides the basic search function, INDURE also provides an advanced search interface[2] where users can refine their query by using filters or restrictions. The query log data is captured over a period of 90 days from October 19, 2010, to January 16, 2011 and it includes a series of requests. A request may consist of a new query or a new result screen for a previously submitted query or a click on one returned result. Each request includes the following fields: visitor IP, requested page, session ID, timestamp, and query terms. In the query log, the 6,434 unique visitors posted 14,503 queries with totally 104,030 requests. Among them, there are 851 empty queries and 2,923 unique queries of which 1,297 are advanced queries. The total number of sessions is 85,215.

3. FINDINGS

The analysis is carried out at the query level and at the session level, respectively. Query length and frequency are considered for the former, and session length and duration for the latter. The results are compared with those of Web search [5] and children search [7]. Table 1 presents the comparison with the statistics in [5] and [7] (other literatures such as [6] shows similar values of the statistics for Web search and children search).

3.1 Analysis of Queries

The number of terms in a query is an indicator of the complexity of the query and the difficulty of the user to express information needs using keywords. Figure 1 (a) shows the frequencies of queries with different length. As shown in Table 1, the average query length here is 1.96 which is lower

[1]https://www.indure.org/
[2]https://www.indure.org/search/advanced.cfm

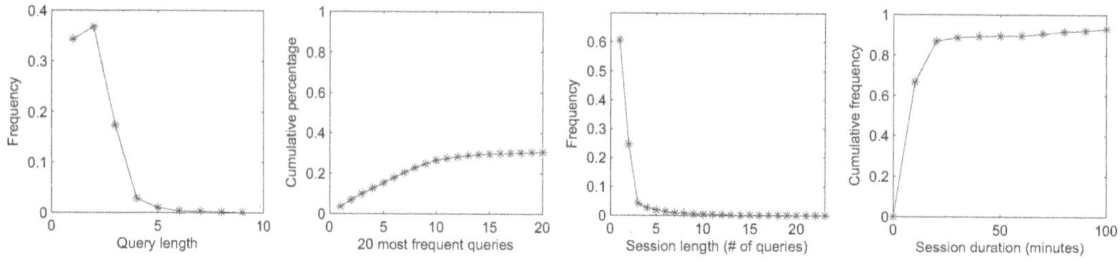

Figure 1: Statistics of the INDURE query log. (a) Query length frequency; (b) Cumulative percentage of frequent queries; (c) Session length frequency; (d) Cumulative percentage of session duration

Table 1: Comparison of statistics among Web search [5], children search [7] and the INDURE expert search. "N/A" means the statistics is not available in the reference

	Web	Children	Expert
Average query length	2.35	3.23	1.96
Average query frequency	3.97	N/A	5.65
Average session length	2.02	8.76	1.81
Average session duration	N/A	20.38	18.67

than that of Web search (2.35 words per query) and much lower than that of search used by children (3.23 words per query). On the other hand, out of 2,923 distinct queries, there are 1,297 advanced queries. This proportion (44.4%) is significantly higher than that in Web search (i.e., 21.4% of the distinct queries with operators [5]). This indicates that expert search users are more willing to use advanced search features to articulate their information needs.

Table 2 lists the 8 most frequent queries. Figure 1 (b) shows the cumulative percentage of the top 20 queries. The top 20 queries represent only 0.68% of all unique queries, yet they account for around 30% of all search queries as shown in Figure 1 (b). The average query frequency is 5.65 in INDURE and is 3.97 in Web search (Table 1). These statistics indicate that expert search users tend to use more common queries than Web search users do.

Table 2: 8 most frequent expert search queries

1) cancer	2) energy
3) electrical engineering	4) nanotechnology
5) engineering education	6) design
7) aerospace	8) biomedical engineering

3.2 Analysis of Sessions

A session is meant to capture a single user's attempt to fill a single information need. Figure 1 (c) shows the session length frequency (represented by the number of queries in a session). We can see that most sessions are short with over 80% of sessions consisting of only one or two queries. As shown in Table 1, the average session length is 1.81, which is shorter than Web search session (2.02) and much shorter than children session (8.76). The long average session length in children search can be explained by the nonlinear navigation style [7]. Considering the average session length in Web search is mostly between 2 and 3 [6], the gap between expert search and Web search is not insignificant. This may be explained by the fact that users in expert search know more exactly about what they search for and thus it is often easier for them to fulfill their information needs with shorter average session length.

Figure 1 (d) shows the distribution of session duration in minutes. The average session duration is 18.67 minutes, which is shorter than that of children search (20.38 minutes) while the difference is small. This may indicate that users require more time to explore and complete information needs associated to children content [7].

4. CONCLUSIONS AND FUTURE WORK

We present a query log analysis for expert search. To the best of our knowledge, this is one of the first query log analyses targeting on expert search. The findings can help improve user interface design for expert search. As a lot of work has been done on query log analysis for Web search, there is an abundance of research opportunities in the same analysis for expert search. In the future work, we will conduct deeper analysis of the expert search query log. We will also exploit the query log to develop ranking models for expert search by learning from the implicit user feedback [4].

5. ACKNOWLEDGMENT

We thank the anonymous reviewers for many valuable comments. This research was partially supported by the NSF research grants IIS-0746830, CNS-1012208, IIS-1017837, and a research grant from Google Inc. Any opinions, findings, conclusions, or recommendations expressed in this paper are the authors', and do not necessarily reflect those of the sponsors.

6. REFERENCES

[1] K. Balog. People search in the enterprise. In *PhD Thesis*. University of Amsterdam, 2008.

[2] N. Craswell, A. de Vries, and I. Soboroff. Overview of the trec-2005 enterprise track. In *TREC*, 2005.

[3] Y. Fang, L. Si, and A. Mathur. Discriminative probabilistic models for expert search in heterogeneous information sources. *Information Retrieval*, 14(2):158–177, 2010.

[4] C. Macdonald and R. White. Usefulness of click-through data in expert search. In *SIGIR*, pages 816–817, 2009.

[5] C. Silverstein, H. Marais, M. Henzinger, and M. Moricz. Analysis of a very large web search engine query log. In *SIGIR Forum*, pages 6–12, 1999.

[6] A. Spink, D. Wolfram, M. Jansen, and T. Saracevic. Searching the web: The public and their queries. *JASIST*, 52(3):226–234, 2001.

[7] S. Torres, D. Hiemstra, and P. Serdyukov. An analysis of queries intended to search information for children. In *Third Symposium on Information Interaction in Context*, pages 235–244. ACM, 2010.

A Model for Expert Finding in Social Networks

Elena Smirnova
INRIA Sophia Antipolis - Méditerranée, France
elena.smirnova@inria.fr

ABSTRACT

Expert finding is a task of finding knowledgeable people on a given topic. State-of-the-art expertise retrieval algorithms identify matching experts based on analysis of textual content of documents experts are associated with. While powerful, these models ignore social structure that might be available. In this paper, we develop a Bayesian hierarchical model for expert finding that accounts for both social relationships and content. The model assumes that social links are determined by expertise similarity between candidates. We demonstrate the improved retrieval performance of our model over the baseline on a realistic data set.

Categories and Subject Descriptors: H.3.3 [**Information Storage and Retrieval**]: Information Search and Retrieval

General Terms: Algorithms, Experimentation

1. INTRODUCTION

A large class of information needs requires a personal contact between a user and a knowledgeable person. These questions typically include details of background and context that are too specific to be addressed in existing documents [4]. In these cases, a user is looking for a person who can apply his knowledge on the topic to a special problem.

The task of identifying knowledgeable person on a given topic is known as expert finding task [3]. State-of-the-art expert finding algorithms model the knowledge areas of candidate experts from textual content of associated documents [1]. So far, social information was solely used to correct content-based expert scores [5]. In this work, we are interested in jointly modeling person's expertise and social network in a unified way. To this end, we develop a generative model for expert finding of both social links and content.

To model the text, we build on the previous work—Author-Topic (AT) model [6]—that models author's topics of expertise, called topical profile. We then assume that social links are generated based on similarity between topical profiles of persons. As a result, our model strengthens person's level of expertise in the topic that is also presented in the profiles of linked persons. Indeed, social networks demonstrate homogeneity with regard to many characteristics.

In the next section, we develop our model from the AT model. Then, we evaluate predictive performance of these models and compare their retrieval scores against the expert finding baseline with social network based smoothing [5].

2. THE MODEL

In this section we explain our model based on the AT model. The AT model extends latent Dirichlet allocation model by adding authorship information—see Figure 1 (Left). Specifically, it assumes the following generative process.

For each author $e_m, m = 1 \dots M$ and topic $t_k, k = 1 \dots K$:

1. Draw author's topic proportions $\theta_m|\alpha \sim \text{Dirichlet}(\alpha)$
2. Draw topic's word proportions $\beta_k|\mu \sim \text{Dirichlet}(\eta)$

For each document d, author set E_d and each word $w_{d,n}$:

3. Draw author $e_{d,n}|E_d \sim \text{Uniform}(E_d)$
4. Draw topic $z_{d,n}|e_{d,n}, \boldsymbol{\theta}_{1:M} \sim \text{Multinomial}(\theta_{e_{d,n}})$
5. Draw word $w_{d,n}|z_{d,n}, \boldsymbol{\beta}_{1:K} \sim \text{Multinomial}(\beta_{z_{d,n}})$

Our work further extends the AT model by adding social network between persons—see Figure 1 (Right). We assume that social links are generated based on similarity between topical profiles. This results in a profile strengthen effect: the model is more confident of person's expertise in the topic that is presented in profiles of linked persons. Formally, we define the link generation process as follows.

For each social link $y_{mm'} = 1$ between experts e_m and $e_{m'}$:

6. Draw social link $y_{mm'}|\mathbf{z}, \mathbf{e} \propto \exp(\bar{z}_m \cdot \bar{z}_{m'})$

The above link generation function is a composition of two: (i) the similarity measure between topical profiles, and (ii) the measure of the effect of this similarity on link formation. The former function is represented by the dot product of mean topic assignments, $\bar{z}_m \cdot \bar{z}_{m'}$, where mean topic assignment for topic t and expert e is defined as $\bar{z}_{e,t} = \frac{1}{D}\frac{1}{N_d}\sum_d \sum_n \mathbb{1}(z_{d,n} = t, e_{d,n} = e)$. The latter function is given by exponential function, proposed in [2]. It returns values that increase exponentially as topical profiles get closer.

With the model defined, we now turn to approximate posterior inference. We present a collapsed Gibbs sampling procedure that jointly samples an expert $e_{d,n}$ and a topic $z_{d,n}$ for the word $w_{d,n}$, given all other topic and expert assignments, denoted by $\boldsymbol{z}_{-(d,n)}$ and $\boldsymbol{e}_{-(d,n)}$:

$$p(z_{d,n} = t, e_{d,n} = e | w_{d,n} = w, \boldsymbol{z}_{-(d,n)}, \boldsymbol{e}_{-(d,n)}, \boldsymbol{w}, \boldsymbol{y}, E_d, \alpha, \eta) \propto$$
$$\frac{\eta_w + N^{WT}_{wt}}{\sum_{w'}(N^{WT}_{w't} + \eta_{w'})} \frac{\alpha_t + N^{TE}_{te}}{\sum_{t'}(N^{TE}_{t'e} + \alpha_{t'})} \exp\left(\frac{1}{N_e} \sum_{e' : y_{ee'}=1} \frac{N^{TE}_{te'}}{\sum_{t'} N^{TE}_{t'e'}}\right)$$

where N^{WT}, N^{TE} denote word-topic and topic-expert count matrices respectively, the sum under the exponent is taken over the set of experts linked to e and N_e is the size of

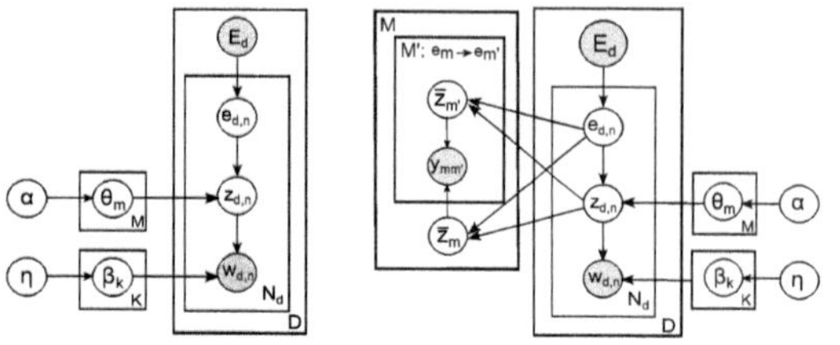

(a) AT model (b) This work

Figure 1: Graphical models. Shaded (unshaded) nodes represent observed (latent) random variables. Edges indicate conditional dependency between the variables.

this set. The last term differentiate our model from the AT model. It favors topic assignments to an expert that are also presented in counts of linked experts. We can view this term as a regularizer to topic model with social network. The posterior distributions on θ and β remain the same as in the AT model:

$$p(t|\theta_e) = \frac{\alpha_t + N_{te}^{TE}}{\sum_{t'}(N_{t'e}^{TE} + \alpha_{t'})}, \; p(w|\beta_t) = \frac{\eta_w + N_{wt}^{WT}}{\sum_{w'}(N_{w't}^{WT} + \eta_{w'})}$$

Finally, the probability of an expert e to be knowledgeable in query-topic q is the product of the probabilities of terms over the expert's topical profile:

$$p(e|q) = \prod_{w \in q} \sum_t p(w|\beta_t) p(t|\theta_e) \quad (1)$$

3. EXPERIMENTAL EVALUATION

We experimented on the English subset of the UvT Expert Collection [1], created from a publicly available database of employees involved in research or teaching at Tilburg University (UvT), The Netherlands. It contains heterogeneous information about 1,168 experts, namely 19,127 documents of four types: research descriptions, course descriptions, publications, and personal homepages. The UvT employees could select their expertise areas from a predefined set of 981 topics. These self-assigned topic labels are treated as relevance judgements. We extracted a social network based on the university hierarchy and researchers' publications included in the UvT collection. The resulted network links scientific collaborators and employees that belong to one department—in total 20,720 undirected connections.

From the data set we first investigate the validity of our assumption, i.e. social links positively correlate with similarity of persons' expertise. As a similarity score we calculated the Jaccard coefficient between sets of self-assigned expertise areas. In Figure 2 (Left), we show the density of positive similarity scores conditioned on whether there is a link between experts. We observe a larger similarity for linked experts on all examples.

Next, we trained the AT model and the proposed model using Gibbs sampling procedure. We set symmetric Dirichlet priors $\alpha = 50/K$ and $\eta = 0.01$, where K is the number of topics. For different K, we ran 10 different Markov chains for a fixed number of 500 iterations. We compare the models from two perspectives: as probabilistic models, where we evaluate their predictive distributions, and as retrieval models, where we compare retrieval scores.

We evaluated the predictive distributions of the models on the test set of held-out links and documents (10% of the data set). We measured how well the models predict the unseen links and words using perplexity [6] against different number

Table 1: Results of retrieval evaluation. $^{\dagger}(^{\ddagger})$ denote significant difference against the baseline at significance level $\alpha = 0.01(0.001)$ computed using two-tailed paired t-test.

	MAP	MRR	P@5
LM baseline	.2038	.3567	.1359
AT model	.2188†(+7%)	.3515	.1764‡(+23%)
This work	**.2763**‡(+35%)	**.3940**‡(+10%)	**.2143**‡(+57%)

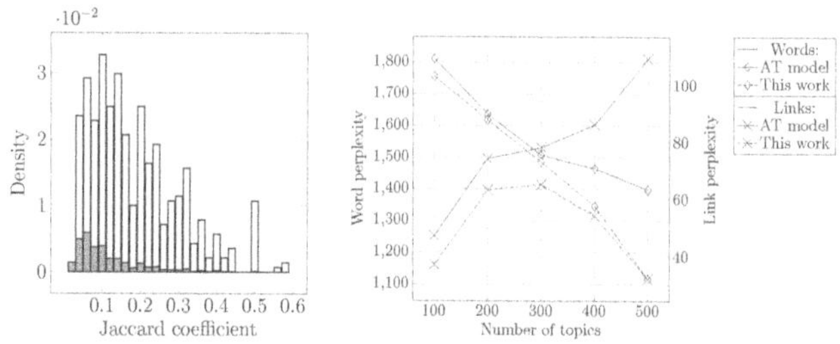

Figure 2: Left: Distributions of expertise similarity given the social link (white) or not (grey). Right: Word and link perplexity against the number of topics. Lower is better.

of topics—see Figure 2 (Right). Here lower values indicate better prediction. The proposed model outperforms the AT model in both tasks and thus, is able to better capture the joint structure of words and social links. Note that the word perplexity of the models decreases as the number of topics is increasing. In contrast, the link performance worsens for the AT model and generally improves for our model.

We performed retrieval evaluation of the AT model and the proposed model against the language modeling (LM) algorithm with smoothing over connected experts [5]—see Table 1. The weighting parameter of LM baseline was set to best reported value of 0.9. We evaluated the lists of persons ranked according to Eq. 1 for the best performing number of topics $K = 400$. The performance of the AT model is close to the LM baseline. At the same time, we see a notable improvement for our model over the baseline on all retrieval measures.

4. CONCLUSIONS

We presented a Bayesian hierarchical model for expert finding that jointly models content and social links between experts. Experiments showed that this model improves over the expert finding baseline. Future work is aimed at investigation of different link probability functions.

The author was supported by INRIA, CORDI fellowship and AxIS team via the EC funded Elliot project. Travel support was provided by SIGIR and Google Travel Grant.

5. REFERENCES

[1] K. Balog, T. Bogers, L. Azzopardi, M. de Rijke, and A. van den Bosch. Broad expertise retrieval in sparse data environments. In *SIGIR '07*, pages 551–558. ACM, 2007.

[2] J. Chang and D. Blei. Hierarchical relational models for document networks. *Annals of Applied Statistics*, 4(1):124–150, 2010.

[3] N. Craswell, A. P. de Vries, and I. Soboroff. Overview of the TREC-2005 Enterprise Track. In *TREC'06*, 2006.

[4] D. Horowitz and S. D. Kamvar. The anatomy of a large-scale social search engine. In *WWW '10*, pages 431–440. ACM, 2010.

[5] M. Karimzadehgan, R. W. White, and M. Richardson. Enhancing expert finding using organizational hierarchies. In *ECIR'09*, pages 177–188, 2009.

[6] M. Steyvers, P. Smyth, M. Rosen-Zvi, and T. Griffiths. Probabilistic author-topic models for information discovery. In *KDD'04*, pages 306–315, 2004.

Transductive Learning over Automatically Detected Themes for Multi-Document Summarization

Massih-Reza Amini
National Research Council Canada
Institute for Information Technology
283, boulevard Alexandre-Taché
Gatineau, QC J8X 3X7, Canada
Massih-Reza.Amini@nrc-cnrc.gc.ca

Nicolas Usunier
Université Pierre et Marie Curie
Laboratoire d'Informatique de Paris 6
4, Place de Jussieu
75252 Paris, cedex 05
Nicolas.Usunier@lip6.fr

ABSTRACT

We propose a new method for query-biased multi-document summarization, based on sentence extraction. The summary of multiple documents is created in two steps. Sentences are first clustered; where each cluster corresponds to one of the main themes present in the collection. Inside each theme, sentences are then ranked using a transductive learning-to-rank algorithm based on RankNet [2], in order to better identify those which are relevant to the query. The final summary contains the top-ranked sentences of each theme. Our approach is validated on DUC 2006 and DUC 2007 datasets.

Categories and Subject Descriptors

I.2.7 [**Artificial Intelligence**]: Natural Language Processing—*text analysis*

General Terms

Algorithms, Experimentation, Performance

Keywords

Mutli-document summarization, Learning to Rank

1. INTRODUCTION

Multi-document summarization (MDS) aims at reducing the information overload caused by the ever increasing number of documents on the same or similar topics, and hence has attracted significant research attention since the past decade. With the current web growth, there are increasingly more web-oriented summarization applications. MDS can be used with conventional search engines, for example to provide informative snippets to help users navigate through different parts of the result page [8]. It can also provide short summaries of documents initially clustered by e.g. a news aggregator to assist users in better understanding the different views presented in the news [5]. Another application is a Question & Answering system which, for each asked question, provides information about the answer in the form of a short extractive summary [3]. In this study, we consider query-biased MDS where we dispose of a set of queries and a set of relevant documents for each of these queries. For each query, an ideal multi-document summarizer consists in producing relevant information around key facets dealing with the query and which is present in the set of its relevant documents. A major issue for a MDS system is, therefore, to automatically detect these themes, and in each of these themes, to rank sentences relevant to the query.

This paper introduces a two-step method for query-biased MDS. Our approach first detects the main themes of the documents by clustering the sentences of all of the documents associated to a given query, where sentences are represented in a low-dimensional space obtained with LSI. For each cluster (or theme), the sentences are then ordered using a transductive learning-to-rank algorithm based on RankNet [2]. Experiments carried out on DUC 2006 and 2007 corpora show that we consistently improve over competing techniques.

2. THE PROPOSED MODEL

We consider a setting similar to the TAC competitions[1], where each query consists of a title and a question, and, for each query, we dispose of a set of relevant documents. Our algorithm operates in two steps.

Step 1 - Theme detection: For each query and its set of relevant documents, we suppose that each theme inside this set, provides a partial answer to the query. Our theme detection scheme indirectly takes into account the query through this assumption. To find these themes, we first group syntagmatic similar words by applying a word-clustering algorithm, proposed in one of the top performing systems at DUC 2007 for query expansion [1]. Sentences are then parsed and, adjectives and verbs are extended using word clusters found before. The augmented sentences are coded in the bag-of-words space with TF features, and the word-sentence matrix is reduced using SVD, a reduction technique similar to LSI. Under this reduced representation, sentence clustering is finally performed using X-means [7]. This clustering algorithm is an extension of the well-known K-means algorithm in which the optimal number of clusters is found at the same time than centroid locations. This clustering allows us to treat each theme independently, with the goal of finding the most relevant sentences to the query in each of them. At the end of this step, sentences are then ranked using their bag-of-words similarity with the query.

[1]http://www.nist.gov/tac/

SIGIR'11, July 24-28, 2011, Beijing, China.
ACM 978-1-4503-0757-4/11/07.

Step 2 - A transductive RankNet algorithm for MDS: As we shall see in the experiments, the ranking obtained at the end of the first step is rather crude. We propose to improve it with learning-to-rank techniques inspired by web search, adapted to the transductive setting. For each cluster, we first automatically define relevant (resp. irrelevant) sentences to the query by taking the top (resp. bottom) ranked sentences of the first step. This gives us a (artificially) labeled training set to initiate the learning process. By extracting a generic query for each theme defined as the most frequent terms of that theme, we then characterize sentences in the latter by taking 12 features used in the Letor datasets [6] as well as a feature produced by a bigram language model proposed in the top performing system at DUC 2006 [4]. Thus, for each theme, sentences have a representation that depends on the theme while the associated relevance judgment depends on the topic in hand. For each theme, we then iteratively train the RankNet algorithm [2] and assign pseudo-relevance judgments to sentences using the output of the learned ranking algorithm. With this new training set, we learn another ranking function using RankNet. This *transductive* learning scheme allows us to gradually improve the quality of the rankings.

For each topic, a summary is finally generated by taking the top ranked sentence given by different RankNet algorithms in each of the themes. The first top ranked sentence, of one of the themes, included in the summary is the one which appears in the most recent document of the set of documents associated to the topic. After including all the first ranked sentences, if the overall legnth of the summary does not exceed 250 words (as in DUC 2006 and DUC 2007 main task), we repeat the operation using the second ranked sentences until this summary length is reached.

3. EXPERIMENTAL RESULTS

We carried out experiments on DUC 2006 and DUC 2007 datasets[2]. DUC 2006 and DUC 2007 contain respectively 50 and 45 topics, each composed of a set of keywords (the title) and a question. Each topic is associated to 25 relevant documents from the AQUAINT corpus. For each topic, the dataset also has three reference summaries produced by human assessors. Since we do not need any *prior labeled* training data to run our algorithm, these reference summaries are only used for evaluation. In our experiments, we considered title keywords and non-stop words in the question as the query and employed the ROUGE toolkit applied by NIST for performance evaluation in DUC competitions. We compared our approach with two base-level summarizers, namely lead and random, and the top two performing systems in both competitions. The latter are those which achieved the highest ROUGE scores in that competition. In Table 1, these systems are denoted by system and their attributed numbers given in these competitions. The lead baseline returns all the leading sentences (up to 250 words) in the most recent document for each topic and the random baseline selects sentences in random. In order to show the contribution of each of the two steps; for each topic, we also generate summaries by extracting the most similar sentence to the topic question and title in each of the sentence clusters. The most similar sentences which appear in the most recent documents are added first. This strategy corresponds to our first step (before training) and is noted by step 1 in Table 1. We observe that on DUC 2006 and DUC 2007, the combination of step 1 and step 2, achieves the best results over other systems. These results indicate that the transductive approach is able to leverage from both the query dependent pseudo-relevance judgments and the theme dependent sentence representations to find an efficient combination of sentence features for the summary.

[2]http://www-nlpir.nist.gov/projects/duc/data.html

Table 1: Comparison results on DUC 2006 and DUC 2007.

	Method	ROUGE-2	ROUGE-L	ROUGE-SU4
DUC 2006	Random	0.04892	0.29384	0.10083
	Lead	0.05267	0.29726	0.10408
	Step 1	0.06842	0.31984	0.12454
	System 12	0.08990	0.37132	0.14753
	System 24	0.09513	0.37741	0.15478
	Step 1 + Step 2	**0.09855**	**0.38030**	**0.15739**
DUC 2007	Random	0.05968	0.30713	0.11001
	Lead	0.06490	0.31074	0.11278
	Step 1	0.08411	0.34001	0.13876
	System 15	0.12285	0.40561	0.17470
	System 24	0.11605	0.41033	0.17304
	Step 1 + Step 2	**0.12866**	**0.41897**	**0.17867**

4. CONCLUSION

We proposed a learning to rank approach for extractive summarization based on a transductive setting. Our approach allows to extract sentences from different themes of a document collection, which are relevant to the query. Our experiments on DUC 2006 and DUC 2007 show that our algorithm achieves the best results in terms of the ROUGE measures compared to state-of-the-art.

Acknowledgments

This work was supported in part by the IST Program of the EC, under the PASCAL2 Network of Excellence.

5. REFERENCES

[1] M.-R. Amini and N. Usunier. A contextual query expansion approach by term clustering for robust text summarization. In *Proceedings of DUC*, 2007.

[2] C. Burges, T. Shaked, E. Renshaw, A. Lazier, M. Deeds, N. Hamilton, and G. Hullender. Learning to rank using gradient descent. In Proceedings of ICML, pages 89–96, 2005.

[3] T. Hirao, Y. Sasaki, and H. Isozaki. An extrinsic evaluation for question-biased text summarization on QA tasks. In *Proceedings of the NAACL Workshop on Automatic Summarization*, pages 61–68, 2001.

[4] J. Jagarlamudi, P. Pingali, and V. Varma. Query Independent Sentence Scoring Approach to DUC 2006. In *Proceedings of DUC*, 2006.

[5] K. R. McKeown, R. J. Passonneau, D. K. Elson, A. Nenkova, and J. Hirschberg. Do summaries help? In *Proceedings of ACM SIGIR*, pages 210–217, 2005.

[6] T. Qin, T. Y. Liu, J. Xu, and H. Li. LETOR: A Benchmark Collection for Research on Learning to Rank for Information Retrieval. Information Retrieval Journal, 2010.

[7] D. Pelleg, and A. Moore. X-means: Extending K-means with Efficient Estimation of the Number of Clusters. In *Proceedings of ICML*, pages 727–734, 2000.

[8] A. Turpin, Y. Tsegay, D. Hawking, and H. E. Williams. Fast generation of result snippets in web search. In *Proceedings of ACM SIGIR*, pages 127–134, 2007.

Rating-based Collaborative Filtering Combined with Additional Regularization

Shu Wu and Shengrui Wang
Department of Computer Science, University of Sherbrooke
2500 Boul. de l'Universite, Sherbrooke, Quebec, Canada J1K 2R1
{Shu.Wu, Shengrui.Wang}@usherbrooke.ca

ABSTRACT

The collaborative filtering (CF) approach to recommender system has received much attention recently. However, previous work mainly focuses on improving the formula of rating prediction, e.g. by adding user and item biases, implicit feedback and time-aware factors, etc, to reach a better prediction by minimizing an objective function. However, little effort has been made on improving CF by incorporating additional regularization to the objective function. Regularization can further bound the searching range of predicted ratings. In this paper, we improve the conventional rating-based objective function by using ranking constraints as the supplementary regularization to restrict the searching of predicted ratings in smaller and more likely ranges, and develop a novel method, called RankSVD++, based on the SVD++ model. Experimental results show that RankSVD++ achieves better performance than existing main-streaming methods due to the addition of informative ranking-based regularization. The idea proposed here can also be easily incorporated to the other CF models.

Categories and Subject Descriptors

H.3.3 [**Information Storage and Retrieval**]: Information Search and Retrieval—*Information filtering*

General Terms

Algorithms, Experimentation

Keywords

Collaborative Filtering, Matrix Factorization

1. INTRODUCTION

A collaborative filtering (CF) [1] recommender system, primarily based on the neighborhood approach and the latent factor approach, produces personalized item recommendations to users by relying on past behaviors, e.g. ratings, transactions or even web click streams. A good CF system will not only enhance the satisfaction and loyalty of customers but also promote sales. Some e-commences and web service providers like Amazon and Netflix have adopted the CF-based recommendation to further their businesses.

Previous work on CF methods primarily focuses on improving the predicted function of rating. For instance, the factor models, e.g. SVD, SVD++ [3] and timeSVD++ [4], which are serial models originated from the basic Matrix Factorization (MF) model [1], are augmented by integrating user and item biases, implicit feedback of users, and temporal effects respectively in calculating predicted ratings. The Netflix Prize announced the success of these improvements.

To enhance the effectiveness of CF recommender, we propose to integrate the objective function with additional regularization. In this paper, we address optimization of the classic rating-based metric in combination with a ranking-based regularization. The rating-based metric in [1] receives reward for a predicted rating $\hat{r}$ close to the given rating value r and gets penalty for the predicted rating $\hat{r}$ far away from the given one. The rank-based regularization receives reward for predicting the same pairwise ordering $\hat{r}_i > \hat{r}_j$ as the given ordering $r_i > r_j$. The idea of this work is that a rating-based metric combined with extra ranking-based regularization helps to restrict the searching of predicted ratings in smaller and more likely ranges. The regularization factor depends on the difference between the given rating and the predicted rating to measure pairwise ranking. This measurement not only can be well unified with the loss function of rating but also make the new objective function a continuous function for convenient optimization.

	i_1	i_2	i_3	...	i_n
r	1	5	5	...	5
$\hat{r}_1$	5	5	5	...	5
$\hat{r}_2$	1.2	5	5	...	5

Figure 1: Given ratings r and predicted ratings $\hat{r}_1$, $\hat{r}_2$. The $\hat{r}_1$ is near-perfect for rating metric, but with bad ranking relation. The $\hat{r}_2$ is a near-perfect prediction of rating-based metric with an additional ranking-based regularization and is better than $\hat{r}_1$.

This work addresses the limitation of the conventional rating-based metric of CF. Since the perfect prediction of rating metric provides a perfect ranking scheme, one might think that a good prediction of rating would also provide a good ranking schema. That is not true. Consider the distribution of given ratings r in Fig. 1, there are $n-1$ ratings with highest value $r=5$ while just one with $r=1$. Judged according to the metric of rating, the prediction $\hat{r}_1$ provides excellent rating performance, however, it expresses a very poor ranking relation. When we impose the ranking-based regularization into the ranking metric, the new model is able to generate a near-perfect prediction $\hat{r}_2$ which is better than $\hat{r}_1$. In this work, we want to design such a model that exalts the performance of rating-based CF with added ranking-based regularization.

SIGIR'11, July 24–28, 2011, Beijing, China.
ACM 978-1-4503-0757-4/11/07.

2. RANKSVD++ METHOD

Let us assume a set of users $\mathcal{U}$ and a set of items $\mathcal{I}$ in a typical CF scenario. Each user u is associated with a set of items $\mathcal{I}_u$, which contains all the items that the user has rated. All known (u, i) pairs between $\mathcal{U}$ and $\mathcal{I}$ is denoted as a set $\mathcal{R}$. d_u and d_i indicate the deviations of user u and item i from the average rating μ of $\mathcal{R}$. f-dimension factor vectors $\mathbf{p}_u \in \mathbb{R}^f$ and $\mathbf{q}_i \in \mathbb{R}^f$ describe the latent characters of the user u and item i. A second vector $\mathbf{y}_i \in \mathbb{R}^f$ of item i is used to characterize users based on the set of items they rated as a implicit feedback. In SVD++ model [3], the function of predicted rating is written as $\hat{r}_{ui} = \mu + d_i + d_u + \mathbf{q}_i^T \mathbf{p}'_u$, where $\mathbf{p}'_u = \mathbf{p}_u + |\mathcal{I}_u|^{-0.5} \sum_{j \in \mathcal{I}_u} \mathbf{y}_j$.

Now we investigate the scenario of combining the metric of SVD++ with the supplementary ranking-based regularization. A simple and successful pairwise ranking [2] is involved in this work. Similar to other norm terms, we also use the Frobenius norm to calculate the regularization of pairwise ranking, i.e. $\|(r_i - r_j) - (\hat{r}_i - \hat{r}_j)\|^2$. To combine with the metric of rating, we calculate the sum of associated ranking-based regularization of items in $\mathcal{I}_u$ at each (u, i) pair and normalize the sum with coefficient $|\mathcal{I}_u|^{-0.5}$. Meanwhile, α is used to adjust the weight of ranking regularization. The model with the new objective function is learnt by minimizing the regularized least squares function. The objective function can be expressed as

$$\sum_{(u,i)\in\mathcal{R}} \overbrace{l\left(r_{ui}, \hat{r}_{ui}\right) + \|\mathbf{w}\|^2}^{SVD++} + \alpha|\mathcal{I}_u|^{-\frac{1}{2}} \sum_{j\in\mathcal{I}_u} \|(r_i - r_j) - (\hat{r}_i - \hat{r}_j)\|^2$$

where, the first two terms, i.e. the loss function of rating and regularized parameters of models in a (u, i) pair, compose the least square function of the SVD++ model [3]. The final term is the ranking-based regularization modeled by the loss between two given ratings and two predicted ratings. Finally, the objective function of our proposed RankSVD++ can be written as

$$\min_{b.,\mathbf{q}.,\mathbf{p}.,\mathbf{f}.} \sum_{(u,i)\in\mathcal{R}} \left(r_{ui} - \mu - d_i - d_u - \mathbf{q}_i^T {\mathbf{p}'}_u\right)^2 + \|\mathbf{w}\|^2 +$$

$$\alpha|I_u|^{-0.5} \sum_{j\in I_u} \left\| r_{ui} - r_{uj} - d_i + d_j - \mathbf{q}_i^T {\mathbf{p}'}_u + \mathbf{q}_j^T {\mathbf{p}'}_u \right\|^2$$

Since the criterion of RankSVD++ is composed of convex functions, it can be solved efficiently by the method of stochastic gradient descent [3]. We loop over all known ratings in $\mathcal{R}$, calculating:

$$\begin{aligned}
&d_u \leftarrow d_u + \gamma\left(e_{ui} - \lambda_1 d_u\right)\\
&d_i \leftarrow d_i + \gamma\left(e_{ui} - \lambda_1 d_u + \alpha|\mathcal{I}_u|^{-0.5} b_{ui}\right)\\
&\mathbf{q}_i \leftarrow \mathbf{q}_i + \gamma\left(e_{ui}\mathbf{p}'_u - \lambda_2 \mathbf{q}_i + \alpha|\mathcal{I}_u|^{-0.5} b_{ui}\mathbf{p}'_u\right)\\
&\mathbf{p}_u \leftarrow \mathbf{p}_u + \gamma\left(e_{ui}\mathbf{q}_i - \lambda_2 \mathbf{p}_u + \alpha|\mathcal{I}_u|^{-0.5}\mathbf{f}_{ui}\right)\\
&\forall j \in \mathcal{I}_u\\
&d_j \leftarrow d_j + \gamma\left(-\alpha|\mathcal{I}_u|^{-0.5} b_{ui}\right)\\
&\mathbf{q}_j \leftarrow \mathbf{q}_j + \gamma\left(-\alpha|\mathcal{I}_u|^{-0.5} b_{ui}\mathbf{p}'_u\right)\\
&\mathbf{y}_j \leftarrow \mathbf{y}_j + \gamma\left(e_{ui}|\mathcal{I}_u|^{-0.5}\mathbf{q}_i + \alpha|\mathcal{I}_u|^{-1}\mathbf{f}_{ui} - \lambda_2 \mathbf{y}_j\right)
\end{aligned}$$

where, to simplify the expression, some abbreviates are used such as $e_{ui} = r_{ui} - \hat{r}_{ui}$, $\mathbf{f}_{ui} = \sum_{j\in\mathcal{I}_u}(e_{ui} - e_{uj})(\mathbf{q}_i - \mathbf{q}_j)$, $b_{ui} = \sum_{j\in\mathcal{I}_u} e_{ui} - e_{uj}$. Learning rate is denoted as γ. Regularization factors λ_1, λ_2 and α are used to avoid overfitting.

3. EXPERIMENTAL RESULTS

For our experiments, we use the Yahoo Music rating data [5]. About 6.4 million ratings of 16,883 users and 2,676 songs between years 2002 and 2006 are chosen, where each user gives at least 20 ratings. Three ratings of each user are randomly chosen as test data, the remaining ones are treated as training data. The experiments are repeated 10 times by sampling new training and test data.

To illustrate the effectiveness of our model, we compare it with a number of factor models and neighborhood methods. The MF model is the basic SVD without the user and item biases. The SVD++ model improves SVD by integrating the implicit feedback of users. Since timeSVD++ needs time-aware factor as extra information, we did not implement it on this data. On the other hand, we implement two neighborhood methods, i.e. user-based and item-based methods, using the Pearson correlation to measure the similarity. The learning rate and hyperparameters of factor models are searched on the first training data. The quality of predictions is measured by the Root Mean Squared Error (RMSE)[1] (smaller is better). The average RMSEs of 10-time tests are listed in Fig. 2.

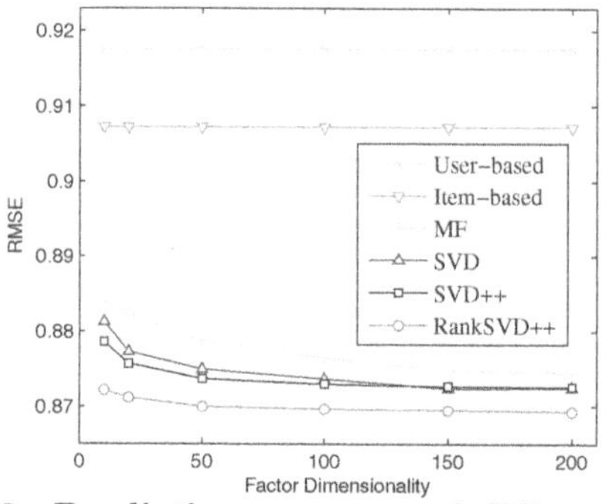

Figure 2: Prediction accuracy of different methods measured by RMSE for varying dimensionality f.

The empirical results indicate the factor models outperform two neighborhood models, and our RankSVD++ model performs the best among these factor models. All factor models benefit from the growing number of factor dimensions f, which can better express the latent characters of the users and items. The advantage delivered by RankSVD++ over SVD++ is consistently significant, due to the added constrains of ranking. Compared with the benefit brought by additional ranking regularization, the gain in accuracy by adding implicit feedback of users in SVD++ over SVD model is not as significant, and the gain decreases with the growing f. The gain in accuracy by integrating user and item biases in SVD over MF is smaller than the gain brought by ranking. Further evidence of the importance of combining ranking-based regularization is the fact that the RankSVD++ model at $f = 10$ is already more accurate than the other factor models at $f = 200$. The results show that RankSVD++ is a very effective single model.

4. REFERENCES

[1] F. Ricci, L. Rokach, B. Shapira and P.B. Kantor, Recommender Systems Handbook, *Springer*, 2011.

[2] C. Burges, T. Shaked, E. Renshaw, et al. Learning to rank using gradient descent, In *ICML '05*, 2005.

[3] Y. Koren, Factorization Meets the Neighborhood: a Multifaceted Collaborative Filtering Model, In *KDD '08*, 2008.

[4] Y. Koren, Collaborative Filtering with Temporal Dynamics, In *KDD '09*, 2009.

[5] Yahoo Music Data, http://webscope.sandbox.yahoo.com/

Words-of-Interest Selection based on Temporal Motion Coherence for Video Retrieval

Lei Wang[1], Dawei Song[1], Eyad Elyan[1]
[1]School of Computing, Robert Gordon University, United Kingdom
{l.wang4, d.song, e.elyan}@rgu.ac.uk

ABSTRACT

The "Bag of Visual Words" (BoW) framework has been widely used in query-by-example video retrieval to model the visual content by a set of quantized local feature descriptors. In this paper, we propose a novel technique to enhance BoW by the selection of Word-of-Interest (WoI) that utilizes the quantified temporal motion coherence of the visual words between the adjacent frames in the query example. Experiments carried out using TRECVID datasets show that our technique improves the retrieval performance of the classical BoW-based approach.

Categories and Subject Descriptors

H.3.3 [**Information Storage and Retrieval**]: Information search and Retrieval – *Multimedia Information Retrieval*

General Terms

Algorithms, Performance, Theory

Keywords

Bag of visual Words, Words-of-Interest, Video Retrieval, Temporal Motion Coherence

1. INTRODUCTION

Content-based video retrieval is an important and challenging task in multimedia information retrieval. We are especially interested in the case of query-by-example, i.e. copyright infringement detection, to find videos relevant to an example video issued by the user.

Inspired by the success in language modeling and text retrieval, visual content representation based on Bag of Visual Words (BoW) has been wildly investigated and has shown some impressive results in content-based video retrieval [2], image classification and object recognition. The BoW model is based on the assumption that all the visual words are generated independently, and the spatial-temporal relationships between the visual words are ignored to achieve better computational and representational efficiency. In the context of video understanding and retrieval, however, a single visual word contains only small amount of information, and the temporal relationships among the different words are sometimes critical to represent the visual information on how the objects behave.

Recently, several techniques have been proposed to address these limitations. Cao et al. [1] proposed a Spatial Coherence Latent Topic Model (Spatial-LTM) that groups visual words with respect to latent topics in order to improve the representative power. Liu and Chen [6] argued that spatial and temporal information could be used to extract the object of interest for video retrieval.

In this paper, we aim to discover the temporal relations between visual words and explore the possibility to enhance the BoW representation for video retrieval. Inspired by the method proposed by Wang et al. [5] which classifies the relative motion of visual words to represent the temporal patterns in a video, we propose to utilize relative motion to model the temporal relation of visual words.

According to [3], a subset of visual words is more descriptive for certain catalogue of objects than others. In context of query-by-example video retrieval, we believe that some selected visual words, called Words-of-Interest (WoI), are more related to the user's interest than others. The WoI should be given higher weights for similarity match between query and video data.

In this paper, we hypothesize that the WoI would appear and move in a relatively coherent manner in a video, while non-WoI occurs more singularly and randomly. Here, the *temporal motion coherence* can be defined as the degree to which a visual word moves coherently with other words on the temporally aligned frames in the query video.

The reminder of this paper is organized as follows. In section 2, our temporal motion coherence based WoI generation algorithms and the application in video retrieval are presented. The experimental results are discussed in Section 3. Finally, Section 4 concludes the paper and highlights some future research directions.

2. WoI Selection Based on Temporal Motion Coherence

In the BoW model, a number of local feature descriptors are automatically extracted, e.g., using the Speed Up Robust Feature algorithm (SURF) [4]. A visual vocabulary $\mathrm{Voc} = \{w_j\}, j = 1 \dots \mathrm{N_w}$ is generated by clustering a large amount of descriptors, e.g., by the K-means algorithm. Then a video V is represented as a set of key frames $\{f_c\}$ (sampling 1 key-frame per ten frames), where each f_c is a weighted vector of visual words, and the weight of each visual word is often its Term Frequency (TF) in the frame. Similarly, a given query example is also represented as a set of key frames $\{f_q\}$. The distance $|f_c - f_q|$ is computed for frame level similarity match.

2.1 Quantifying Temporal Motion Coherence

In this section, the temporal motion coherence defined in Section 1 is quantified by the relative motion between the visual words pair in the given query.

The motion of instances of a visual word can be extracted between every two neighboring frames by an algorithm based on L_2 norm [8] in the next frame. Specifically, for each instance p of a visual word w that can be successfully tracked, its motion $\boldsymbol{m_p} = (m_x, m_y)$ is calculated as a vector, where m_x and m_y identify the vertical and horizontal motion respectively. Each instance p is associated with a motion vector $\boldsymbol{m_p}$ and a visual word $w \in \mathrm{Voc}$.

To evaluate how coherently a pair of visual words moves in neighboring frames, we calculate a relative motion vector for them. The relative motion vector $\overline{m}_{i,j}$ of the visual words pair w_i and w_j in the query video is formulated as follows:

SIGIR'11, July 24–28, 2011, Beijing, China.
ACM 978-1-4503-0757-4/11/07.

$$\bar{m}_{i,j} = \frac{1}{N_i * N_j}\sum_{k=1}^{N_i}\sum_{n=1}^{N_j}(m_{p,i}{}^{k} - m_{p,j}{}^{n}) \quad (1)$$

where $m_{p,i}{}^{k}$ and $m_{p,j}{}^{n}$ are the motion vectors of the kth instance of w_i and the nth instance of w_j, and N_i and N_j indicate the number of instances of w_i and w_j respectively.

The smaller the relative motion vector, the higher the degree of motion coherence of the visual words pair. In order to quantify the temporal coherence of a visual word, a simplification is proposed. The relative motion vectors of a visual word with all other words are averaged as:

$$r_i = \sum_{j=1}^{N_w}|\bar{m}_{i,j}| * p(w_j)\ ,\ p(w_j) = \frac{tf_j}{N_q} \quad (2)$$

where $p(w_j)$ is the conditional probability that w_j occurs in the query q, tf_j is the term frequency of the visual word w_j and N_q is the number of instances of the visual words in q.

2.2 Selecting the WoI

Based on our hypothesis in Section 1, the WoI with high motion coherence can be selected when the corresponding r_i values are lower than an empirical threshold. However, a pre-fixed empirical threshold may not be suitable for every query. To tackle this problem, the EM algorithm [7] is used to classify the visual words based on temporal motion coherence adaptively.

More formally, each visual word w_i is associated with a hidden variable $z \in \{z_+ . z_-\}$. Here, z_+ denotes that w_i is WoI, and z_- denotes that w_i is out of user interest. Naturally, $p(z_+)$ represents the probability of a visual word belonging to WoI. The motion coherence of visual words is modeled as $p(r|z)$. We assume that $p(r|z_+)$ and $p(r|z_-)$ are both Gaussian distributions. From these definitions, the joint distribution of $p(z, r)$ is defined as $p(z,r) \equiv p(z)p(r|z)$, and we simplify the problem by assuming z and r are independent variables. All distributions are unknown yet, and the parameters should be estimated using the EM algorithm.

The steps of the EM algorithm for estimating the unknown distribution is given as follows:

Table 1: EM algorithm for WoI selection

E-step:

$p(\mathbf{z}|r) = c_1 p(\mathbf{z})p(r|\mathbf{z})$

$E_{p(z|r)}[\log p(r|\Phi)] = \prod_j \sum_i p(z_i)p(r_j|z_i)$

M-step:

$\Phi_{new} = argmax_{\Phi}(E_{p(z|r)}[\log p(r|\Phi)])$

where Φ is a set of parameters to be estimated, c_1 is the nominalization factor to guarantee that the sum of $p(\mathbf{z}|r)$ equals 1. The estimated $p(r|z_+)$ identifies the location of WoI in the temporal motion coherence space. We choose the visual words which are located within the standard deviation of the Gaussian distribution $p(r|z_+)$ as WoI: $WoI = \{w_j\}, j = id_1 \ldots id_k \ldots id_{N_{woi}}$.

The frame level similarity based on the WoI is measured by the distance:

$$\bar{D} = |f_c - f_q| + \alpha_{woi} \times |\acute{f}_c - \acute{f}_q| \quad (3)$$

where $\acute{f}_c$ represents the term frequency of WoI in the key frame of the video c and $\acute{f}_q$ represents the key frame of the query, and α_{woi} is an empirically selected weighting factor.

Finally, the videos with higher number of key frames similar to the key frames from the query are ranked higher in the results.

3. Experimental Results

To evaluate our temporal motion coherence based method, we select a dataset from TRECVID 2002, which consists of 3000 videos and 6 query topics. The evaluation is based on common criteria used in the information retrieval community: Precision, Recall and Mean Average Precision (MAP).

As shown in Figure 1, the WoI enhanced BoW model (denoted WoI) outperforms the classical BoW model for the query-by-example video retrieval task. Most points of the WoI curve are above the curve of classical BoW.

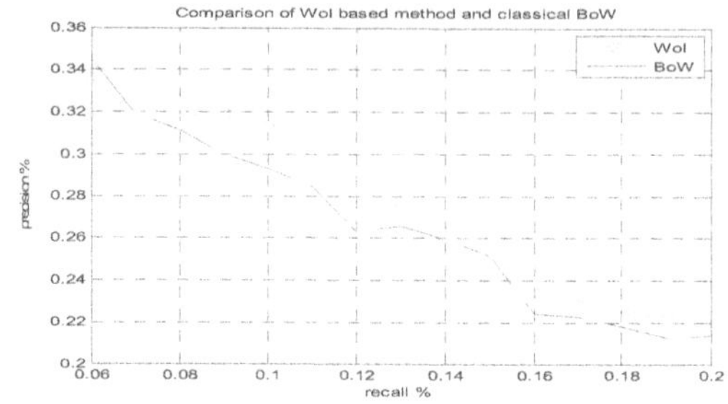

Figure 1: the performance comparison between WoI enhanced BoW model and classical BoW

Moreover, for 5 out of 6 topics, the WoI based method outperforms the classical BoW in term of Average Precision. The MAP (over all the 6 test topics) of WoI outperforms BoW by 2.3%, which is statistically significant (*P-value* = 0.02188).

This result demonstrates the feasibility of modeling the interest of a user by temporal motion coherence. We believe further improvement could be achieved by better quantification methods, as currently the approach in Section 2.1 may have over-simplified the motion coherence of visual words.

4. Conclusions and Future Work

In this paper, we propose a technique for WoI selection based on the quantified temporal motion coherence in the query video example. The experimental results show that the selection is effective and the generated WoI could improve query-by-example video retrieval based on classical BoW model.

Our future work will be focused on more descriptive user interest representation model which will incorporate spatial-temporal information.

5. References

[1] L. Cao and L. Fei-Fei. "Spatially coherent latent topic model for concurrent object segmentation and classification" Vol. 2. pp. 674-679 ICCV(2007)

[2] J. Sivic and A. Zisserman, "Efficient visual search for objects in videos," Proceedings of the IEEE, vol. 96, no. 4, pp. 548-566, 2008

[3] S. Zhang, Q. Tian, G. Hua, Q. Huang, S. Li, 'Descriptive Visual Words and Visual Phrases for Image Applications', in ACM MM, pp. 75-84 (2009)

[4] H. Bay, A. Ess, T. Tuytelaars, L. Van Gool, "SURF: Speeded Up Robust Features", CVIU, pp. 404-417 (2008)

[5] F. Wang, Y. Jiang, and C. Ngo. "Video event detection using motion relativity and visual relatedness", ACM MM, pp. 239-248 (2008).

[6] D. Liu and T. Chen. "Video retrieval based on object discovery". pp. 397-404 CVIU (2009)

[7] A. P. Dempster , N. M. Laird , D. B. Rubin. "Maximum likelihood from incomplete data via the EM algorithm", Journal Of The Royal Statistical Society, Series B Vol. 39, No. 1. (1977), pp. 1-38 (1977)

[8] B. D. Lucas and T. Kanade, "An Interative Image Registration Technique with an Application to Stero Vision", IJCAI, Vol. 2, pp. 674-679 (1981)

Aggregating Multiple Opinion Evidence in Proximity-Based Opinion Retrieval

Shima Gerani
University of Lugano
Faculty of Informatics
Lugano, Switzerland
shima.gerani@usi.ch

Mostafa Keikha
University of Lugano
Faculty of Informatics
Lugano, Switzerland
mostafa.keikha@usi.ch

Fabio Crestani
University of Lugano
Faculty of Informatics
Lugano, Switzerland
fabio.crestani@usi.ch

ABSTRACT

Blog post opinion retrieval is the problem of ranking blog posts according to the likelihood that the post is relevant to the query and that the author was expressing an opinion about the topic (of the query). A recent study has proposed a method for finding the opinion density at query term positions in a document which uses the proximity of query term and opinion term as an indicator of their relatedness. The maximum opinion density between different query positions was used as an opinion score of the whole document. In this paper we investigate the effect of exploiting multiple opinion evidence of a document. We propose using the ordered weighted averaging (OWA) operator in order to combine the opinion score of different query positions for a final score of a document, in the proximity-based opinion retrieval system.

Categories and Subject Descriptors

H.3.3 [**Information Storage and Retrieval**]: Information Search and Retrieval

General Terms

Experimentation, Performance

Keywords

Blog, Opinion Retrieval, Proximity, OWA

1. INTRODUCTION

Blog post opinion retrieval is the problem of finding blog posts that express opinion about a given query topic. This problem was introduced in the Text REtrieval Conference (TREC) 2006 blog track and continued to 2008 [3]. The main challenge in blog post opinion retrieval is assigning query-related opinion scores to documents. A basic method is to use the average opinion weights of terms in a document as an opinion score of the document. This method assumes that all opinion terms in a document are referring to the query topic while does not consider the fact that a document can be relevant to many different topics but express opinion about topics other than the query. A recent study [1] proposed a proximity-based method for scoring documents based on the relevant opinion expressions in them. The proximity-based method, estimates the opinion density at every position of a document. Then aggregates the opinion density at different query term positions to assign an opinion score to the document. Average and Maximum were employed in [1] to aggregate the opinion density at query term positions. While Maximum improved the opinion retrieval performance over the baselines, Average failed to achieve any improvement.

Although the maximum opinion density at query positions is the strongest opinion evidence, we believe that adding the opinion density of more query positions should not degrade the performance and can lead to great improvement in some cases. In this paper we investigate the effect of using the opinion density of more query term positions (as opposed to just the maximum value) in the proximity-based method. We show that better aggregation of these opinion evidence can improve the effectiveness of the system.

SIGIR'11, July 24–28, 2011, Beijing, China.
ACM 978-1-4503-0757-4/11/07.

2. PROXIMITY-BASED OPINION RETRIEVAL

Proximity-based method, uses the distance of an opinion term to the query term as a measure of their relatedness. It considers a proximity-based density kernel centered at each opinion term which favors the nearby positions. The kernel is weighed by the opinion probability of the opinion term. The opinion density at every position of the document is the accumulated opinion probability from different opinion terms to that position. Thus the probability of opinion at position i in the document is estimated as:

$$p(o|i,d) = \sum_{j=1}^{|d|} p(o|t_j)p(j|i,d) \tag{1}$$

where, $p(o|t)$ is the probability that term t is used to express an opinion (can be based on an opinion lexicon) and $p(j|i,d)$ is the probability that term at position j is referring to the term at position i and is estimated using density kernel k as follows:

$$p(j|i,d) = \frac{k(j,i)}{\sum_{j'=1}^{|d|} k(j',i)} \tag{2}$$

here $k(j,i)$, is the kernel function which determines the weight of propagated opinion from t_j to t_i.

The overall relevant opinion probability score, $p(o|d,q)$ can be calculated by aggregating opinion evidence at different query positions. In the original paper Max and Average has been applied. This aggregation step is the focus of this paper and will be discussed in the next section.

3. AGGREGATING MULTIPLE RELEVANT OPINION EVIDENCE

In this paper we explore and compare different possibilities of aggregating the opinion evidence at different query positions in a document. As our baseline we use the Max which has been used in the previous work:

$$p(o|q,d) = max_{i \in pos(q)} p(o|i,d) \qquad (3)$$

The drawback of the Max method is that it relies only on the highest opinion evidence of every document and misses other available evidence that might be useful.

As a more general aggregation method which takes into account more opinion evidence, we use ordered weighted averaging (OWA) operator, which was introduced by Yager [4]. OWA provides a parametrized class of mean type aggregation operators, that can generate OR operator (Max), AND operator (Min) and any other aggregation operator between them like $Mean$. An OWA operator of dimension K is a mapping $F : \mathbb{R}^K \to \mathbb{R}$ that has an associated weighting vector W,

$$W = [w_1, w_2, ..., w_K]^T$$

such that

$$\sum_{i=1}^{K} w_i = 1, \quad 0 \leq w_i \leq 1,$$

and where

$$OWA(a_1, ..., a_K) = \sum_{i=1}^{K} w_i a_{ind(i)} \qquad (4)$$

here $a_{ind(i)}$ is the ith largest element in the collection $a_1, ..., a_K$. OWA operators have different behaviours based on the weighting vector associated with them. Yager introduced two measure for characterizing OWA operator [4]. The first one is called *orness* which characterizes the degree to which the operator behaves like an OR operator (Max). The second measure is *dispersion* which measures the degree to which OWA operator takes into account all available information in the aggregation. To determine the weighting vector, we used the method proposed by O'Hagan[2]. He defines the problem as a constrained non-linear optimization problem. A predefined value of orness is the constraint for this problem and dispersion is its objective function to be maximized. It is worth noting that based on the weighting vector, we can produce different aggregation methods including the simple methods like Max. For example if we want to combine five values, the weighting vectors $[1,0,0,0,0]^T$, $[0,0,0,0,1]^T$ and $[1/5,1/5,1/5,1/5,1/5]^T$ will produce maximum, minimum and average of the values respectively (the *orness* value is 1, 0 and 0.5 respectively). In our opinion retrieval system, we consider the K query positions with highest opinion density as the operands of the OWA operator. The value of K and the degree of *orness* are the parameters of the model.

4. EXPERIMENTAL SETUP AND RESULTS

In order to compare the results with the proximity-based method, we followed the proposed setting and parameters in [1]. The extra parameters of our model are the value of K and the degree of *orness*. We tried K values of 2, 3, 4, 5 and 10 and also *orness* values between 0 and 1 with step size 0.1 over the training set of topics. We chose the parameters that maximize the MAP. Table 1 presents the results on the test set queries(1001-1050). From the table, we can compare the effect of using Maximum (proxMax) or OWA operator over multiple query positions (proxTopK) in the proximity-based opinion retrieval framework. It can be seen that the proposed method is consistently effective across all TREC baselines.

Table 1: Opinion retrieval performance on TREC 2008 topics over top 4 standard TREC baselines using different aggregation methods. A star(∗) and dagger(†) indicate statistically significant improvement at level 0.05 over the relevance and max-base proximity opinion retrieval baselines respectively.

	MAP	R-prec	bPref	p@10
baseline1	0.3239	0.3682	0.3514	0.5800
proxMax	0.3960∗	0.4369∗	0.4291∗	0.6860∗
proxTopK	**0.4394**∗†	**0.4669**∗†	**0.4662**∗†	**0.7444**∗†
baseline3	0.3564	0.3887	0.3677	0.5540
proxMax	0.3989∗	0.4369∗	0.4207∗	0.6600∗
proxTopK	**0.4003**∗	**0.4381**∗	**0.4214**∗	**0.6700**∗
baseline4	0.3822	0.4284	0.4112	0.6160
proxMax	0.4267∗	0.4545∗	0.4472∗	0.7080∗
proxTopK	**0.4322**∗†	**0.4640**∗	**0.4502**∗	**0.7100**∗
baseline5	0.2988	0.3524	0.3395	0.5300
proxMax	0.3188∗	0.3732	0.3698∗	0.6080∗
proxTopK	**0.3297**∗†	**0.3831**∗†	**0.3775**∗†	**0.6280**∗

5. CONCLUSION

In this paper, we investigated the effect of exploiting more opinion evidence compared to the maximum opinionated point in the proximity-based opinion retrieval method. OWA operator was used as an aggregator in our system. Experimental results over Blog06 collection showed the advantage of using multiple opinion query positions in comparing the opinion score of documents. In future, we plan to investigate the effect of adding other references to the query such as pronouns and use the opinion evidence in those positions.

6. ACKNOWLEDGMENTS

This research was partly funded by the "Secrétariat d'état à l'Éducation et à la Recherche (SER)" and COST IC0702 "Combining Soft Computing Techniques and Statistical Methods to Improve Data Analysis Solutions".

7. REFERENCES

[1] GERANI, S., CARMAN, M. J., AND CRESTANI, F. Proximity-based opinion retrieval. In *Proceedings of SIGIR '10* (2010), pp. 403–410.

[2] O'HAGAN, M. Aggregating template or rule antecedents in real-time expert systems with fuzzy set logic. In *Proceedings of Annual IEEE Conference on Signals, Systems, Computers* (1988), pp. 681–689.

[3] OUNIS, I., MACDONALD, C., AND SOBOROFF, I. Overview of the TREC-2008 blog track. In *Proceedings of TREC'08* (2008).

[4] YAGER, R. R. On ordered weighted averaging aggregation operators in multicriteria decision making. *IEEE Transactions on systems, Man, and Cybernetics 18*, 1 (1988), 183–190.

Enhancing Mobile Search Using Web Search Log Data

Yoshiyuki Inagaki, Jiang Bian, Yi Chang
Yahoo! Labs
Sunnyvale, CA 94089
{inagakiy, jbian, yichang}@yahoo-inc.com

Motoko Maki
Yahoo! Inc.
Sunnyvale, CA 94089
motoko@yahoo-inc.com

ABSTRACT

Mobile search is still in infancy compared with general purpose web search. With limited training data and weak relevance features, the ranking performance in mobile search is far from satisfactory. To address this problem, we propose to leverage the knowledge of web search to enhance the ranking of mobile search. In this paper, we first develop an equivalent page conversion between web search and mobile search, then we design a few novel ranking features, generated from the click-through data in web search, for estimating the relevance of mobile search. Large scale evaluations demonstrate that the knowledge from web search is quite effective for boosting the relevance of ranking on mobile search.

Categories and Subject Descriptors

H.3.3 [**Information Systems**]: Information Search and Retrieval - Retrieval functions

General Terms

Experiments, Measurements

Keywords

Mobile Search, Ranking, Ranking Features

1. INTRODUCTION

With rapid growth of mobile products in recent years, an increasing number of users become used to conducting search on mobile devices, therefore how to provide effective mobile search has become a critical research topic. Compared with traditional web search, there are a few unique characteristics for mobile search, which bring some new challenges. First, the texts in mobile pages are usually short and concise for the purpose of fitting in smaller screens of mobile devices. And, as Yamauchi et al. [5] pointed out, mobile users also prefer concise mobile content. This property of mobile search reduce the effectiveness of text matching features though they play an important role in web search. Second, anchor text features, which is another important category of features for web search, become not reliable in mobile search, because mobile pages contain much fewer anchor texts than Web pages. Moreover, click-through logs, known to be useful to estimate relevance in web search (e.g., [3]), is not rich enough in mobile search, partly due to *good abandonment* [4].

SIGIR'11, July 24–28, 2011, Beijing, China.
ACM 978-1-4503-0757-4/11/07.

As mobile search is still in its infancy, we propose to take advantage of the rich knowledge from web search to improve mobile search. Although mobile search is quite different from web search, there is still a strong connection between them: If a web page should be ranked at high position for query on web search, its equivalent mobile page should be similarly ranked at high position for the same query on mobile search. For example, for query,"Toyota", if `http://toyota.jp/` is ranked at the top position, its equivalent mobile page, `http://toyota.jp/mb/m/top`, should be ranked at top in mobile search.

As mobile search is growing fast, an increasing amount of web pages already have their mobile equivalence, such as many corporate official homepages and portals of online games and social network service (SNS). In order to use such equivalence to benefit mobile search, it is necessary to accurately convert Web host/URL names to mobile host/URL names so as to promote corresponding mobile pages in mobile search. As shown by a couple of examples in Table 1, there is no systematic way for the host name conversion, but the domain name conversion is less complicated. In this paper, we propose to use domain name matching to find equivalent mobile pages for traditional web pages and boost those mobile pages whose equivalence have high relevance in web search for the same query. In next section, we will describe in details about how to convert web page into mobile ones, followed by creating novel features based on knowledge from click-through in web search to benefit ranking relevance in mobile search.

Table 1: Example: Name conversion between web host names and mobile host names.

web host name	mobile host name
www.yahoo.co.jp	mobile.yahoo.co.jp
www.google.co.jp	m.google.co.jp
ja.wikipedia.org	mwkp.fresheye.com
www.grj.jp	www.grj-m.jp

2. TECHNICAL APPROACH

In this section, we first introduce our method for domain/URL conversion driven by click-through log in web search, then based on such conversion, we propose several new features that can be used to boost mobile search relevance.

To leverage knowledge from web search, we first accumulate a three-months click-through logs from a commercial web search. Then, we select a set of samples of ⟨`query, URL`⟩ pairs whose clicks are higher than a reasonable threshold values (which are to be empirically determined). From the selected `URLs`, domain names were extracted and converted into mobile domain names by looking up a domain name conversion dictionary whose entries look like examples in Table 1. If a web domain name does not match in the name conversion dictionary, we use the web domain name and slightly shortened domain name, e.g. `XXXX.jp` instead of `XXXX.co.jp`, as potential mobile domain names.

We then find all web search queries that have also been issued in mobile search. Each of these queries is stored in a *query-domain* dictionary together with correlated both web and mobile domain names and click-through data corresponding to the original web domains. When a query is issued to a mobile search engine, the system will look up the query-domain dictionary: if matched, the query is annotated with a list of domains retrieved from the dictionary for the query and sent to the mobile search engine. The search engine will try to match the domain name of a retrieved mobile page to the one in the list of domains annotating the query. If there is a name match, we propose to use additional novel ranking features to estimate relevance of this mobile page.

In particular, we propose two new ranking features as described below. Let $dmatch1(q, u)$ and $dmatch2(q, u)$ be the new domain name matching features for a query, q, and a mobile URL, u. Let $dom(q)$ be a set of domain names retrieved from the dictionary for q. Moreover, let d_u be the domain name of u.

Pseudo-Navigational Indicator:

$$dmatch1(q, u) = \begin{cases} 1/n & : \text{ if } d_u \in dom(q) \\ 0 & : \text{ otherwise} \end{cases} \quad (1)$$

where n is the number of clicked domain names retrieved from the dictionary for the query.

Query-Domain Level Percent of Click:

$$dmatch2(q, u) = \begin{cases} DPCTCLK(q, d_u) & : \text{ if } d_u \in dom(q) \\ 0 & : \text{ otherwise} \end{cases} \quad (2)$$

where $DPCTCLK(q, d_u)$ is a domain-level percent of click for the query-domain pair, (q, d_u).

The proposed new features are combined with other features in the machine learned framework for training a ranking algorithm. We employ a state-of-the-art algorithm Gradient Boosted Decision Tree [1] to learn the ranking function.

3. EXPERIMENTS

Since these two features are new and not available for ranking in the mobile products' setting, the experiments are purely based on evaluations on the offline data sets.

• **Feature Generation**

We gathered web search click-through logs from December, 2009, to February, 2010. And, training and testing data for mobile search were collected throughout the year 2009. We empirically set the minimum numbers of clicks and views of URLs for a query as 5 and 30 respectively to filter ⟨`query, URL`⟩ pairs, and generated the dictionary of clicked domains and feature values. The generated features covered about 5.0% of the training and holdout data sets that are 150K query-URL pairs with 11460 queries and the 27K query-URL pairs with 1005 queries, respectively.

• **Evaluation Metric**

In our experiments, we use Normalized Discounted Cumulative Gain (NDCG)[2] to evaluate ranking performance. In the following, we only report NDCG_5.

• **Results**

We compare the ranking model that trained using our new features with the baseline model trained without using any new features. Figure 1 shows NDCG_5 of the baseline model as well as NDCG_5's of three models that either used one of new features or used both.

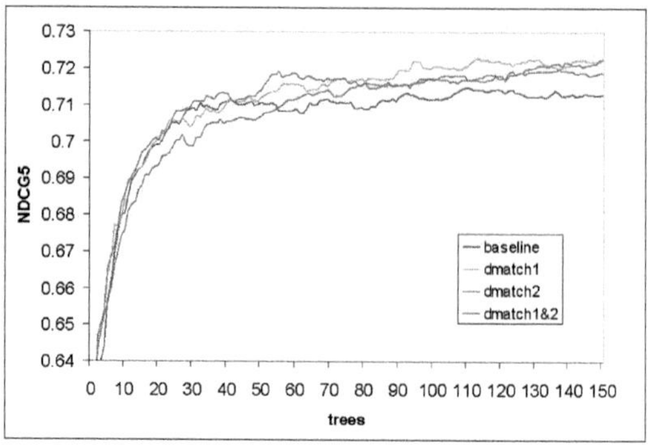

Figure 1: NDCG5 v.s. the number of trees in a machine learned model with mobile click feature.

Statistically significant NDCG_5 improvement was achieved if we use mobile click features that were generated from mobile click logs in the same manner as new features were generated (see Table 2). We will need to conduct online tests in order to see whether and how much new features will truly improve mobile search. It is usually the case that we introduce new rank features, new machine learned models often bring up new pages that have never been brought up.

Table 2: NDCG5 improvement over the baselines.

NDCG5	without mobile click	with mobile click
baseline	0.7087	0.7150
*dmatch*1	0.7124	0.7232
*dmatch*2	0.7146	0.7201
*dmatch*1&2	0.7137	**0.7226**

4. CONCLUSIONS AND FUTURE WORK

In this paper, we proposed and implemented rank features to enhance mobile search ranking by boosting the mobile pages equivalent to top ranked and well-clicked web pages. Our experiments show promising results on popular queries that are common to both web search and mobile search. However, due to the low coverage of such kind of queries, this method can not be extended to long tail queries. In future, we will investigate how to conduct search on long tail queries in mobile search by extending the idea of leveraging the knowledge from web search.

5. REFERENCES

[1] J. H. Friedman. Greedy function approximation: A gradient boosting machine. *Annals of Statistics*, 29(5):1189–1232, 2001.

[2] K. Jarvelin and J. Kekalainen. Cumulated gain-based evaluation of ir techniques. *ACM Transactions on Information Systems*, 20(4):422ÍC446, 2002.

[3] T. Joachims. Optimizing search engines using clickthrough data. In *Proceedings of the ACM Conference on Knowledge Discovery and Data Mining (KDD)*, 2002.

[4] J. Li, S. B. Huffman, and A. Tokuda. Good abandonment in mobile and pc internet search. *In Proceedings of the 32nd Annual ACM SIGIR Conference*, 2009.

[5] K. Yamauchi, W. Chen, and D. Wei. A study on japanese mobile phone market and its applications. *the 4th International Conference on Computer and Information Technology*, pages 875–878, 2004.

Award Prediction with Temporal Citation Network Analysis

Zaihan Yang Dawei Yin Brian D. Davison
Department of Computer Science and Engineering
Lehigh University
Bethlehem, PA, 18015 USA
{zay206 | day207 | davison}@cse.lehigh.edu

ABSTRACT

Each year many ACM SIG communities will recognize an outstanding researcher through an award in honor of his or her profound impact and numerous research contributions. This work is the first to investigate an automated mechanism to help in selecting future award winners. We approach the problem as a researchers' expertise ranking problem, and propose a temporal probabilistic ranking model which combines content with citation network analysis. Experimental results based on real-world citation data and historical awardees indicate that some kinds of SIG awards are well-modeled by this approach.

Categories and Subject Descriptors: H.3.3 [Information Storage and Retrieval]: Information Search and Retrieval

General Terms: Algorithms, Performance

Keywords: citation network, link analysis, temporal correlation

1. INTRODUCTION

Each year many ACM SIG communities will recognize an outstanding researcher through an award in honor of his or her profound impact and numerous research contributions. The most recent Salton award winner (year 2009) in the SIGIR community, for example, Dr. Susan Dumais, is widely acknowledged as an IR expert due to her contributions in both theoretical development and practical implementations of Latent Semantic Indexing and question-answering. Winning such an award is thus a particularly strong indication of expertise and prestige in a given field. Even though there has been research in evaluating scientists' reputation and thus finding experts in a certain field, no work has developed an automatic and efficient mechanism in selecting future award winners. This work takes the first step into this problem.

We approach the problem as a researchers' expertise ranking problem. In one direction of the approaches in evaluating the expertise of a researcher, different information probabilistic models have been provided, including language model [1], voting model [5], and discriminative model [3], which mainly emphasize evaluating the relevance between supporting documents and thus the corresponding authors with the query. Another direction of research, which is the research focus of this poster, takes use of social network analysis [2, 8] to boost ranking performance. However, in both of these approaches, one important factor has largely been ignored by previous research: temporal information. As the awards of a SIG community are often issued annually, the authority of a researcher varies over time. In this paper, we propose a novel temporal citation network analysis model to predict SIG-award winners.

SIGIR'11, July 24–28, 2011, Beijing, China.
ACM 978-1-4503-0757-4/11/07.

2. THE MODEL

Our weighted citation network can be represented as G=<A,E>, where A is a set of author nodes, and E is a set of edges. Two types of relationships (edges) between pairs of authors have been considered: coauthorship and citations. Thus, $(a_i, a_j) \in E$ if author a_i coauthored with author a_j or if at least one of the publications of author a_i cites a publication of a_j.

2.1 Temporal Factor

We introduce four temporal factors to represent an individual researcher's academic activity. 1) $CareerTime$: How long has a researcher been publishing papers? We assume that the longer the career time a researcher has, the higher authority he may have. 2) $LastRestTime$: How many years have passed since the last publication of a researcher? We assume that a long time without academic output will negatively affect a researcher's scholarly reputation. 3) $PubInterval$: How many years on average would a researcher take between every two consecutive publications? We assume that more frequent publication indicates more active academic participation. There is one other temporal factor which considers the long-lasting influence of a researcher's publication, and thus indirectly represents the influence of the researcher. We assume that if a paper continues to be cited a long time after its publication, it brings higher prestige to its author (e.g., the paper PageRank [6] is frequently and persistently cited by subsequent papers). To model this temporal factor, we first introduce a decay function to differentiate the weight between a pair of paper citations. If paper p_j published in year y_j cites another paper p_i published in year y_i $(y_j - y_i) \geq 0$, we define the *citation influence ratio* of paper p_j on p_i as: $CIR(p_{ji}) = \beta_1(1 - \beta_2^{y_j - y_i})$, where β_2 $(0 < \beta_2 < 1)$ is the decay base. We now define the *citation influence* between a pair of authors as: $CI(a_{ji}) = \sum CIR(p_{ji})$, where p_j is any paper of author a_j, p_i is any paper of a_i, and p_j cites p_i.

2.2 Temporal Authority Propagation Model

Based upon the discussion above, we define an *individual temporal importance* (ITI) to model the researcher's academic authority in terms of time. The ITI of author a_i can be expressed as: $ITI_i = CareerTime_i * (1/LastRestTime_i) * (1/PubInterval_i)$. The weight on an edge from a_i to a_j can then be defined as: $\omega(a_{ij}) = (NumCo(a_{ij}) + CI(a_{ij})) * ITI_j$, where $NumCo(a_{ij})$ is the number of times author a_i coauthored with a_j. We normalize the weights on edges over the whole network by defining the propagation probability from a_i to a_j as: $P(a_i, a_j) = \frac{\omega(a_i, a_j)}{\sum_{k:i \to k} \omega(a_i, a_k)}$. Under this definition, author a_i will propagate more authority to author a_j if they coauthored more often, if a_i has greater citation influence on a_j, or if a_j has greater individual temporal importance. Similar to the original PageRank

Table 1: Prediction performance across algorithms

	NumPub	NumCit	in-domain NumPub	in-domain NumCit	H-index	LM	CoRank	PR	TAP
NumTop10	28	30	25	31	13	2	20	30	**34**
NumTop20	38	40	38	40	18	2	28	36	**47**
MRR-All	0.1065	0.1189	0.0992	0.1183	0.0495	0.0080	0.1031	0.1053	**0.1291**

Table 2: Top20%: Individual SIG Award Prediction Results

SIGARCH	SIGSOFT	SIGPLAN	SIGKDD
0.35	0.40	0.21	0.71
SIGIR	SIGCOMM	SIGMOD	SIGCSE
0.60	0.17	0.65	0.45

[6] function, the propagation function in our model can be represented as: $PR(i) = (1-d)\sum_{j:j\rightarrow i} PR(j) * P(j,i) + d\frac{1}{N}$, where is N is the total number of author nodes.

3. EXPERIMENTAL WORK

From the ACM digital library[1], we crawled the descriptive web pages for published papers as our experimental dataset. For each publication, we extracted and recorded the information of its publishing year, authors, and citation references. We finally captured 170,897 authors and 172,890 papers. We retrieved for each year a time-based subset of all the papers and authors, which means if we aim to predict the award winners of 2009, we would first retrieve all the papers published before 2009, and their corresponding authors to build the graph.

3.1 Evaluation

In the portal website of Microsoft Academic Search[2] (a free computer science bibliography search engine), we found 23 categories covering the main disciplines of computer science research. For 6 of them, we collected the corresponding SIG awards in the ACM community. They are the awards for SIGCSE (20), SIGPLAN (19), SIGCOMM (18), SIGMOD (17), SIGARCH (17), SIGSOFT (15). We choose them because they have more examples of award winners. We furthermore collected the award winners for SIGKDD (7) and SIGIR (5) community for the sake of our interests. The number in the parenthesis indicates the number of award winners from 1990 to 2009 (our predicting period) that can be found in our dataset. As a result, we used these 8 categories as testing queries, and the 118 existing award winners as ground truth.

We further generate a profile for each author a by concatenating all of his publications in terms of title, abstract and ACM categories, and combine the citation network ranking results with the Okapi BM25 [7] ranking results as: $\lambda * rank_{BM25}(a) + (1-\lambda) * rank_{CitationNetwork}(a)$. λ is tuned between 0 and 1 to get the best outcome for each award winner. Three metrics have been used to evaluate the performance of an algorithm. 1) **NumTop10**: the total number of award winners that can be ranked within the Top 10. 2) **NumTop20**: the total number of award winners that can be ranked within the Top 20. 3) **MRR-All**: the average MRR score across all award winners.

3.2 Experimental Results

We compared our model with several existing algorithms previously used in citation network analysis work or expert-finding work. They include the ranking by 1) overall number of publications (NumPub), 2) overall number of citations (NumCit), 3) in-domain NumPub [8], 4) in-domain NumCit [8], 5) H-index [4], 6) Language-Model based approach as introduced in [1], and 7) CoRank algorithm as introduced in [9]. We also run a weighted PageRank (referred to as PR) on the network, where when compared with our Temporal Authority Propagation (referred to as TAP) model, no temporal information is considered. The weights on a edge from a_i to a_j would then be defined as: $\omega(a_{ij}) = NumCo(a_{ij}) + NumCit(a_{ij})$, where $NumCit(a_{ij})$ is the number of times author a_i cites a_j. We combined each baseline algorithm's (except 6) ranking results with the BM25 ranking results and tuned the λ to achieve the best performance for each award winner. Parameters β_1 and β_2 play important roles in our TAP model. Preliminary experiments show that the best performance of our model will be achieved when β_1 is set to 1, and β_2 is set to 0.9. As indicated in Table 1, our model can retrieve 47 award winners within Top 20, which is 39.8% of all the existing awards winners in our data set. NumCit and in-domain NumCit give the best performance in terms of NumTop20 among all non-temporal algorithms, while our algorithm improves their performance by 17.5%. We also investigated the influence of $NumCo$ and the four temporal factors and found that all were necessary to achieve the reported performance.

We are interested in finding out what fraction of all award winners in each SIG community can be ranked within Top 20. As indicated in Table 2, our model can make good predictions on several awards, such as SIGKDD, SIGMOD, and SIGIR, but comparatively worse on others, such as SIGCOMM and SIGPLAN.

Acknowledgments

This work was supported in part by a grant from the National Science Foundation under award IIS-0545875.

4. REFERENCES

[1] K. Balog, L. Azzopardi, and Rijke. Formal Models for Expert Finding in Enterprise Corpora. In *SIGIR*, pages 43–50, 2006.
[2] H. Chen, H. Shen, J. Xiong, S. Tan, and X. Cheng. Social network structure behind the mailing lists. In *TREC-14*, 2006.
[3] Y. Fang, S. Luo, and A. Mathur. Discriminative Models of Integrating Document Evidence and Document-Candidate Associations for Expert Search. In *SIGIR*, pages 683–690, 2010.
[4] J. E. Hirsch. Citation indexing: Its theory and application in science, technology, and humanities. In *Proceedings of National Academy of Sciences*. John Wiley and Sons, Inc., 2005.
[5] C. Macdonald and I. Ounis. Voting for candidates: adapting data fusion techniques for an expert search task. In *CIKM*, pages 387–396, 2006.
[6] L. Page, S. Brin, R. Motwani, and T. Winograd. The PageRank citation ranking: Bringing order to the Web. In *Stanford InfoLab, Technical Report 1999-66*, 1998.
[7] S. Robertson. Overview of okapi projects. *Journal of Documentation*, 53:3–7, 1997.
[8] Z. Yang, L. Hong, and B. D. Davison. Topic-driven Multi-type Citation Network Analysis. In *RIAO*, pages 24–31, 2010.
[9] D. Zhou, S. A. Orshanskiy, H. Zha, and C. Giles. Co-ranking authors and documents in a heterogeneous network. In *ICDM*, pages 739–744, 2007.

[1] http://portal.acm.org
[2] http://academic.research.microsoft.com

Rating Prediction using Feature Words Extracted from Customer Reviews

Masanao Ochi[1] Makoto Okabe[2] Rikio Onai[3]

The University of Electro-Communications[1,2,3], JST PRESTO[2]
1-5-1, Chofugaoka, Chofu, Tokyo, Japan[1,2,3]
{ochi, onai}@onailab.com[1,3] m.o@acm.org[2]

ABSTRACT

We developed a simple method of improving the accuracy of rating prediction using feature words extracted from customer reviews. Many rating predictors work well for a small and dense dataset of customer reviews. However, a practical dataset tends to be large and sparse, because it often includes too many products for each customer to buy and evaluate. Data sparseness reduces prediction accuracy. To improve accuracy, we reduced the dimension of the feature vector using feature words extracted by analyzing the relationship between ratings and accompanying review comments instead of using ratings. We applied our method to the Pranking algorithm and evaluated it on a corpus of golf course reviews supplied by a Japanese e-commerce company. We found that by successfully reducing data sparseness, our method improves prediction accuracy as measured using RankLoss.

Categories and Subject Descriptors

H.3.3 [**Information Storage and Retrieval**]: Information Search and Retrieval—*information filtering*

General Terms

Experimentation

Keywords

sentiment analysis, review mining, rating prediction

1. INTRODUCTION

Rating prediction is a practically important problem, because it enables the market to estimate how satisfied a customer will be with a service [1, 2, 5]. Given a dataset of customer reviews, rating predictors (like the Pranking algorithm [1]) can learn and predict the rating of a target customer. These algorithms work well for a small and dense dataset. However, the problem is that in practice a dataset is large and sparse, because it often includes too many products for each customer to buy and evaluate (Figure 1). The dimension of the feature vector increases as fast as the increase in the number of products. For example, the matrix of the EachMovie dataset is reportedly sparse (5% full) [5]. To address this problem, we developed a way to reduce the dimension of a feature vector using feature words extracted by analyzing the relationship between ratings and accompanying review comments. Figure 1 illustrates our approach. We reduced the dimension of the feature vector and increased the density of the matrix by extracting "delicious" and "terrible" as feature words. We extracted a word as a feature word when it appeared frequently and was accompanied with a polarized score. The words "delicious" and "terrible" appeared many times with high and low scores and therefore were selected as feature words. "Very" was not selected as a feature word; although it also appeared many times, its accompanying score varied. Our method of analyzing ratings and accompanying review comments is a simple but powerful way of extracting feature words that can capture a characteristic of each rating aspect well. This is often difficult to implement by relying only on natural language-processing techniques or other corpora such as WordNet [3, 4].

SIGIR'11, July 24–28, 2011, Beijing, China.
ACM 978-1-4503-0757-4/11/07.

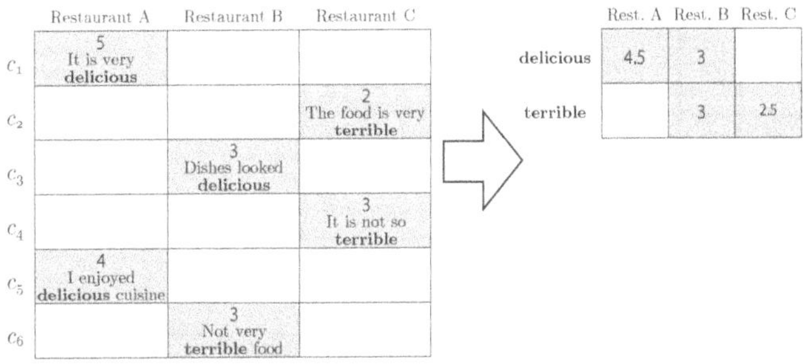

Figure 1: An illustration of our approach in the case of restaurant reviews. Left: The original dataset has ratings only in the blue cells and the whole matrix is sparse. Right: Instead of using customers, we use the feature vector of feature words extracted from the review comments. This reduces the dimension of the feature vector from 6 to 2, so the whole matrix becomes dense. The score of each cell is an average of the scores rated with each word.

2. EFFECT OF DATA DENSITY

As shown in Figure 1, the original dataset is often sparse. Crammer et al. proposed filling in blank cells with an intermediate score [1], which results in low prediction accuracy. We evaluated the relationship between data sparseness and the accuracy of the Pranking algorithm. Given a target customer and a product, the Pranking algorithm predicts the rating that the customer is likely to give the product by learning from the dataset how the customer has rated other products in the past. We used the Book-Crossing Dataset[1], which is a relatively dense dataset because of the

[1] http://www.informatik.uni-freiburg.de/~cziegler/BX/

Overall

word	average
great	4.6
Rope(golf course)	4.5
praise	4.5
splendid	4.4
mindful	4.4
beautiful	4.4
thoughtful	4.4
perfect	4.4
rich	4.4
thrilling	4.4

word	average
nasty	2.5
cheap	2.6
bad	2.7
asking	2.8
apology	2.8
anger	2.8
finally	2.8
embarrassingly	2.8
ass	2.9
dirty	2.9

Course

word	average
Inoue(name)	4.5
Seiichi(name)	4.5
great	4.4
skillful	4.4
Ishioka(golf course)	4.4
agitate	4.4
motivate	4.3
rarity	4.3
variety	4.3
championship	4.3

word	average
lack	3.0
nasty	3.0
cheap	3.0
weed	3.0
enforced	3.0
river	3.1
sand pit	3.1
monotone	3.1
gully	3.1
patchy	3.1

Cost performance

word	average
killer price	4.6
real cheap	4.6
performance	4.5
better	4.4
cost	4.4
CP	4.4
cheap	4.4
fire-sale	4.3
great	4.3
outclassing	4.3

word	average
relative expense	3.0
penny-wise	3.1
asking	3.2
terrible	3.2
apology	3.2
embarrassingly	3.3
arrogant	3.3
messy	3.3
ass	3.3
complaint	3.3

Figure 2: Feature words extracted from customer reviews. All reviews were written in Japanese, and we translated each extracted word into English.

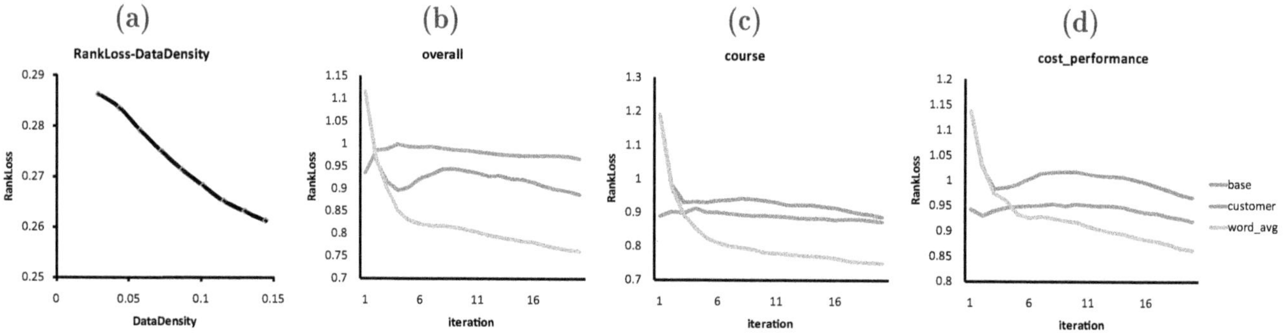

Figure 3: (a) The performance of a rating predictor depends on the data density. (b)-(d) The RankLoss for each aspect. Base means prediction of an intermediate score, 3 in this case. Customer means customer ratings are used as the feature vector. Word_avg means feature words are used as the feature vector.

nature of the service. The original matrix of this dataset is 15% full. We generated a sparse dataset by removing data from randomly selected cells and applied it to the Pranking algorithm. We evaluated prediction accuracy using RankLoss [1], $RankLoss = \sum_t^T \frac{|\hat{y}_t - y_t|}{T}$. T is the number of products, $\hat{y}_t$ is the t-th predicted output score, and y_t is the t-th desired output score. As shown in Figure 3 (a), the sparser the dataset becomes, the lower the prediction accuracy becomes. This result motivated us to solve the problem of data sparseness by reducing the dimension of the feature vector.

3. EXPERIMENT AND RESULTS

We applied our technique to the Pranking algorithm and evaluated it on a corpus of golf course reviews supplied by a Japanese e-commerce company[2]. Each review was accompanied by a set of three aspects, each on a scale of 1-5: overall experience, golf course, and cost performance. To extract feature words related to each aspect, we computed the score for each word as the average of all rated scores accompanied by a review comment that included the word. The score is shown as "average" in Figure 2. As a result, the score of a word irrelevant to the aspect was close to the total average score, and a word that captured the characteristic of the aspect had a high or low average score. Figure 2 shows that our method successfully extracts interesting feature words. Note that our method extracts not only positive and negative words but also words that explain the semantic context of the aspect. For example, "Inoue" and "Seiichi," shown in the Course table, refer to a famous golf course designer who has designed many golf courses in Japan. The negative side of the Course table includes words such as "weed," "river," and "sand pit," from which one learns that a customer's low rating is caused by complaints about the conditions of a golf course.

We used the extracted feature words as the feature vector of the Pranking algorithm and reduced the dimension to increase the density of the data. The original dataset had 85,000 customers and was sparse (0.5% full). We selected 100 feature words with high and low average scores, thereby reducing the dimension of the feature vector from 85,000 to 100. As a result, data density was increased (30% full). We evaluated the RankLoss (Figure 3 (b)-(d)), and our results outperformed the results of the original sparse dataset.

[2]http://rit.rakuten.co.jp/rdr/index.html

4. CONCLUSIONS

We have demonstrated that data density is important for prediction accuracy. We have developed a novel feature vector using feature words that successfully improves prediction accuracy as measured using RankLoss.

5. REFERENCES

[1] K. Crammer. Pranking with ranking. *NIPS'01*, pages 641–647, 2001.

[2] E. F. Harrington. Online ranking/collaborative filtering using the perceptron algorithm. *ICML'03*, pages 250–257, 2003.

[3] M. Hu and B. Liu. Mining and summarizing customer reviews. *KDD'04*, pages 168–177, 2004.

[4] J. Kamps, M. Marx, R. J. Mokken, and M. de Rijke. Using wordnet to measure semantic orientations of adjectives. *LREC'04*, pages 1115–11118, 2004.

[5] A. Sashua and A. Levin. Ranking with large margin principle: Two approaches. *NIPS'03*, pages 937–944, 2002.

Ranking Tags in Resource Collections

Dimitrios Skoutas
L3S Research Center
Hannover, Germany
skoutas@l3s.de

Mohammad Alrifai
L3S Research Center
Hannover, Germany
alrifai@l3s.de

ABSTRACT

We examine different tag ranking strategies for constructing tag clouds to represent collections of tagged objects. The proposed methods are based on random walk on graphs, diversification, and rank aggregation, and they are empirically evaluated on a data set of tagged images from Flickr.

Categories and Subject Descriptors: H.3 Information Storage And Retrieval: Information Search and Retrieval

General Terms: Algorithms

Keywords: tag clouds, tag ranking

1. INTRODUCTION

Assigning tags to Web resources, such as documents, images, videos or bookmarks, has become popular as a simple, easy and effective way to facilitate their retrieval and management. To reduce the cost and improve the effectiveness of tagging, several approaches have focused on (re-)ranking or suggesting tags for an *individual* resource, based on its content or the tags of other similar resources (e.g. [3]).

In this work, we consider instead the problem of selecting and ranking tags to describe *groups* of tagged resources. Typically, *tag clouds* are employed for this purpose. The goal of a tag cloud is to visualize the most relevant and important tags for the items in a group. In practice, the most frequently occurring tags are selected. We propose and examine alternative methods to select and rank tags in groups of tagged objects, based on tag co-occurance, diversification of tags, and rank aggregation. To compare these methods, we have conducted an experimental evaluation on a large real-world dataset containing groups of tagged photos obtained from Flickr. The comparison considers a set of proposed metrics, namely coverage, overlap and selectivity, that characterize the usefulness of a tag cloud for search and navigation. The results show that even though ranking tags based on their frequency performs well in most cases, more effective rankings can be obtained using other methods.

2. TAG SELECTION STRATEGIES

2.1 Based on Frequency

Frequency scoring. Let $fr(t, G)$ denote the frequency of tag t in the group G, i.e., the number of objects in the group containing t divided by the group size. A simple strategy, typically employed in practice, is to construct the tag cloud using the top-k most frequent tags.

TF.IDF scoring. An extension is to rank tags based on the same idea as $tf.idf$ scoring for document retrieval. This assigns a lower score to tags that also occur frequently in several other groups. Specifically, the score is modified as:

$$f(t) = fr(t, G) \cdot idf(t) \quad (1)$$

where the idf of a tag is defined analogously to the inverse document frequency of a term in a document collection.

Graph-based scoring. Another variation is to take into consideration co-occurrence of tags. For this purpose, we create a graph of the tags, where an edge between two tags t_i and t_j denotes that there is an object in G tagged with both t_i and t_j. The score of a tag is derived by performing a random walk on this graph. Initially, the score of each tag t is set to its frequency, i.e., $f_0(t) = fr(t, G)$. The transition probability from a tag t_i to a tag t_j is computed as

$$p(t_i, t_j) = \frac{sim(t_i, t_j)}{\sum_{t \in T(G)} sim(t_i, t)} \quad (2)$$

where the similarity $sim(t_i, t_j)$ between two tags can be computed based on the number of objects where these tags co-occur. After each iteration q, the score of each tag is updated according to:

$$f_q(t_i) = z \cdot \sum_{t_j \in T(G)} f_{q-1}(t_j) \cdot p(t_j, t_i) + (1 - z) \cdot f_0(t_i) \quad (3)$$

with z being a weight parameter. The process is repeated until the score of each tag t converges to a value $f(t)$.

2.2 Based on Diversity

This strategy increases the *diversity* [2] of the tags in the cloud to allow for more objects to be represented. We examine two variations.

Diversity. The goal is to select tags that are not only as frequent as possible but also as dissimilar as possible from each other, in the sense that they appear in different sets of objects. Therefore, the score of a tag t is defined as

$$f(t) = \lambda \cdot fr(t, G) + (1 - \lambda) \cdot (1 - \max_{t_i \in T_G} sim(t, t_i)) \quad (4)$$

where the parameter λ is used to weight the importance of frequency with respect to the factor of diversity. A greedy approximation algorithm can be used to select the top-k tags, similarly to the method described in [2].

SIGIR'11, July 24–28, 2011, Beijing, China.
ACM 978-1-4503-0757-4/11/07.

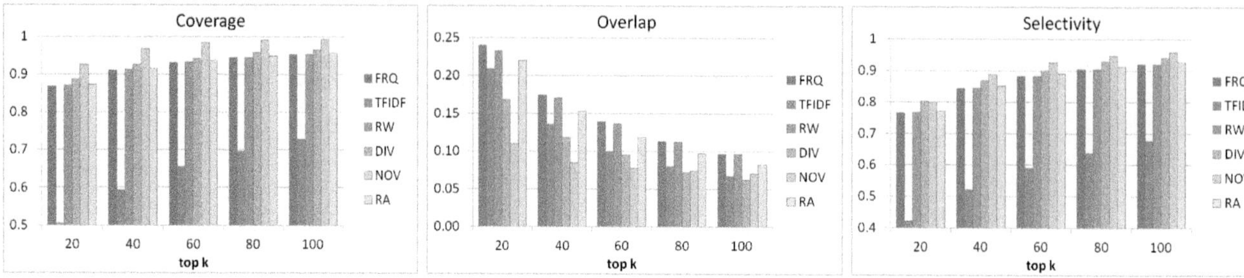

(a) coverage (b) overlap (c) selectivity

Figure 1: Evaluation results for the metrics (a) coverage (b) overlap and (c) selectivity.

Novelty. Alternatively, we can define the score of tags using the notion of *information nuggets*. We consider each object to constitute one information nugget. Selecting a tag t, provides a set of information nuggets $V(t)$ corresponding to the objects that this tag is assigned to. Let n_{v,T_G} be the number of times a nugget v appears in the tags currently contained in the cloud, and N_V the total number of information nuggets in the group. Given a tag t and the current contents of the tag cloud T_G, the score of t is defined as

$$f(t) = \frac{\sum_{v \in V(t)} \gamma(n_{v,T_G})}{N_V} \tag{5}$$

where $\gamma()$ is a discount function that reduces the contribution of each information nugget based on the number of times it has already been seen. As above, a greedy approximation algorithm can be used to select the top-k tags.

2.3 Based on Rank Aggregation

A different direction is to rank the tags of the group by aggregating their rankings in individual objects. The Borda Count method can be used for this purpose [1]. According to it, the score of a tag is computed as

$$f(t) = \frac{\sum_{u \in U(t)} \alpha(r_u(t))}{|G|} \tag{6}$$

where $r_u(t)$ is the position of the tag t in the list of tags assigned to object u and α a discount function as above.

3. EXPERIMENTAL EVALUATION

3.1 Dataset

We evaluated the different tag ranking methods on a data set comprising groups of tagged photos collected from Flickr. The data set contained in total 451 groups, 488,112 photos, and 112,514 tags, with each group having on average 1270 photos and 2707 distinct tags.

3.2 Metrics

We are interested in characteristics of a tag cloud that make it useful for search and navigation. For this purpose, we consider the three evaluation metrics described below.

Coverage. We define the coverage of a tag cloud T_G w.r.t. the group of objects G it represents as the portion of objects in G that have at least one tag appearing in T_G:

$$coverage(T_G) = \frac{|\{u \in G : T(u) \cap T_G \neq \emptyset\}|}{|G|} \tag{7}$$

Overlap. The overlap of two tags t_i and t_j is defined as the portion of objects tagged with both t_i and t_j, i.e., $|U(t_i) \cap U(t_j)| \,/\, |U(t_j)|$. Accordingly, the overlap of the tag cloud is defined as the average overlap between each pair of tags:

$$overlap(T_G) = \frac{\sum_{t_i, t_j \in T_G} \frac{|U(t_i) \cap U(t_j)|}{|U(t_j)|}}{|T_G| \cdot (|T_G| - 1)} \tag{8}$$

Selectivity. Assume a user is interested in object u and selects all the tags of u appearing in the cloud. The result will contain u and all other objects also having (at least) those tags, i.e., every $u_i \in G$ s.t. $T(u) \cap T_G \subseteq T(u_i)$. The goal is to maximize the number of filtered out objects. We call this the selectivity of u w.r.t. T_G. Thus, we measure the selectivity *sel* of the tag cloud by computing the average selectivity of the objects in the group:

$$sel(T_G) = \frac{\sum_{u \in G} \frac{|\{u_i \in G : (T(u) \cap T_G) \not\subseteq T(u_i)\}|}{|G|}}{|G|} \tag{9}$$

3.3 Results

We refer to the above methods using the abbreviations FRQ, TFIDF, RW, DIV, NOV, and RA, respectively. The presented results in Figure 1 are average values over all the 451 groups in the data set, for different tag cloud sizes.

FRQ performs reasonably well, mainly for coverage and selectivity, but less for overlap. RW and RA exhibit a similar performance to FRQ, with the latter outperforming the other two regarding overlap. In contrast, the performance of TFIDF is very low both for coverage and selectivity, but it outperforms all three previous approaches in overlap. Finally, DIV and NOV perform better than all other approaches. Especially for coverage, NOV achieves excellent results, ranging from 93% for top-k = 20 to 99% for top-k = 100. It also has good results for overlap for all values of k, although for $k > 60$ DIV becomes equally good or even better. As expected, increasing the size of the tag cloud improves the performance of all methods in all metrics.

4. REFERENCES

[1] J. A. Aslam and M. H. Montague. Models for metasearch. In *SIGIR*, pages 275–284, 2001.

[2] S. Gollapudi and A. Sharma. An axiomatic approach for result diversification. In *WWW*, pages 381–390, 2009.

[3] D. Liu, X.-S. Hua, L. Yang, M. Wang, and H.-J. Zhang. Tag ranking. In *WWW*, pages 351–360, 2009.

Identifying Similar People in Professional Social Networks with Discriminative Probabilistic Models *

Suleyman Cetintas†
Dept. of Computer Sciences
Purdue University
scetinta@cs.purdue.edu

Monica Rogati
LinkedIn Corp.
Mountain View, CA
monica@rogati.com

Luo Si, Yi Fang
Dept. of Computer Sciences
Purdue University
{lsi,fangy}@cs.purdue.edu

ABSTRACT

Identifying similar professionals is an important task for many core services in professional social networks. Information about users can be obtained from heterogeneous information sources, and different sources provide different insights on user similarity.

This paper proposes a discriminative probabilistic model that identifies latent content and graph classes for people with similar profile content and social graph similarity patterns, and learns a specialized similarity model for each latent class. To the best of our knowledge, this is the first work on identifying similar professionals in professional social networks, and the first work that identifies latent classes to learn a separate similarity model for each latent class. Experiments on a real-world dataset demonstrate the effectiveness of the proposed discriminative learning model.

Categories and Subject Descriptors: H.3.3 [**Information Search and Retrieval**]
General Terms: Experimentation, Performance, Theory
Keywords: Social Networks, Similar People, Discriminative Learning

1. INTRODUCTION

Professional social networks (PSNs) are business oriented social networks where many core services such as recruiting, job seeking, expert/profile search, item recommendation, ad-targeting, etc. rely on successful identification of similar people. Due to the variety of available activities in PSNs, information about their users can be obtained from many heterogeneous sources such as profile content (e.g., users' job titles, their industries, specialties/skills, etc.), social graph (e.g., connections, group memberships, etc.) and user activities on the website (e.g., search and profile viewing, news sharing, etc.). Different sources provide different insights on user similarity, therefore information coming from these sources needs to be weighted and combined carefully. For instance; for a pair who do not have similar profile content while having very similar connections (due to common friends, etc.), information from their profile content can be used to decrease the importance of the information from their connectivity for estimating the overall similarity.

To the best of our knowledge, there is no prior work on identifying similar people in professional social networks. Most existing research on identifying similar users or matching people (e.g., online dating systems [3]) either used information from a single/homogeneous source (e.g., user profile content [3]), or used information from heterogeneous sources, but did not differentiate the information from these sources in a principled way (e.g., [4]).

In this paper, we propose a discriminative probabilistic model to identify similar professionals in professional social networks. Unlike the prior work, the proposed model identifies latent content and graph classes for people with similar profile content and social graph similarity patterns, and learns a specialized similarity model for each latent class. Experiments on real-world proprietary data from LinkedIn show the effectiveness of the proposed discriminative model.

2. METHOD

In a PSN, similarity features indicating whether two people are similar or not can mainly be grouped into 3 heterogeneous categories: i) profile content features c; ii) social graph features g; iii) PSN usage features u. In particular, 5 content similarity features (comparing users' titles, industries, skills, specialties, associations), 3 social graph features (utilizing users' common connections, common groups, and whether their profiles are co-viewed or not), and 5 website usage features (utilizing the similarity in profile, search, inbox, news/sharing, accounts/settings page usage patterns) are used in this work. Given the set of similarity features f^v to denote all the similarity features of a people pair v, i.e., $f^v = \{c^v, g^v, u^v\}$, the proposed discriminative probabilistic model can be constructed as follows:

$$P(s^v = 1|f^v) = \sum_{t=1}^{N_t}\sum_{z=1}^{N_z} P(t|g^v)P(z|c^v)P(s^v|z,t,f^v) \quad (1)$$

where $s^v \in \{1, -1\}$ indicates whether the vth pair is similar or not, $P(z|c^v)$ and $P(t|g^v)$ denote the mixing coefficients which are the probabilities of choosing latent content and graph classes z and t given content and graph features c^v and g^v. N_z and N_t are the number of latent content and graph classes and are chosen to be 3 and 2 respectively by AIC [1]. $P(s^v|z,t,f^v)$ can be modeled by logistic function as $P(s^v|z,t,f^v) = \sigma(\sum_i \lambda_i f^v_{zti})$ where $\sigma(x) = 1/(1+\exp(-x))$ is the standard logistic function and λ_{zti}

*This research was partially supported by the NSF research grants IIS-0746830, CNS-1012208, and IIS-1017837.

†Part of this work was done when the first author was on a summer internship with LinkedIn.

SIGIR'11, July 24–28, 2011, Beijing, China.
ACM 978-1-4503-0757-4/11/07.

is the weight for the ith feature f_i^v under the latent classes z and t. The mixing proportions $P(z|c^v;\alpha)$ can be modeled by a soft-max function $\frac{1}{Z_{c^v}}\exp(\sum_j \alpha_{zj}c_j^v)$ where Z_{c^v} is the normalization factor that scales the exponential function to be a proper probability distribution (i.e., $Z_{c^v} = \sum_z \exp(\sum_j \alpha_{zj}c_j^v)$). $P(t|g^v;\beta)$ can also be modeled by a soft-max function $\frac{1}{Z_{g^v}}\exp(\sum_q \beta_{tq}g_q^v)$.

The parameters of the model in Eqn.(1) (λ, α, β) can be estimated by the EM algorithm [2]. The E-step can be derived by computing the posterior probability of z and t, i.e. $P(z,t|f^v)$. By optimizing the auxiliary Q-function, we can derive the following M-step update rules:

$$\lambda^*_{zt\cdot} = \arg\max_{\lambda_{zt\cdot}} \sum_v P(z,t|f^v)\log\Big(\sigma\big(\sum_i s^v\lambda_{zti}f_i^v\big)\Big) \quad (2)$$

$$\alpha^*_{z\cdot} = \arg\max_{\alpha_{z\cdot}} \sum_v\big(\sum_t P(z,t|f^v)\big)\log\Big(\frac{1}{Z_{c^v}}\exp\big(\sum_j \alpha_{zj}c_j^v\big)\Big) \quad (3)$$

The update rule for (β) can be achieved similarly with Eqn.(3). Eqns.(2,3) can be optimized by any gradient descent method. In particular, we use the Quasi-Newton method. The proposed discriminative probabilistic model that has latent content and social graph classes is referred as *Latent_CG_Mod*.

For better comparison, similar models that only model latent content or social graph classes (namely *Latent_C_Mod* and *Latent_G_Mod* respectively) are constructed (each with 3 classes chosen by AIC) as well. All of those discriminative models are compared to a baseline method without any latent class. The baseline method is modeled with logistic regression and is referred as *LogReg_Mod*.

3. EXPERIMENTS

We evaluate the effectiveness of the proposed models on proprietary data from LinkedIn. As the first step of creating a dataset of similar people, a set of 2200 key profiles (target people for whom similar people will be searched) are selected by intersecting two sets: a) profiles popular among recruiters, and b) profiles popular within general users (sets identified by mining the large-scale recruiter/user activity logs for a time period of 6 months). Next; using Lucene[1], public profiles in the PSN are indexed, and each key profile is used as a structured query to retrieve top 100 candidate profiles for the key profile. From these 100 profiles, 10 candidate profiles are selected under three strategies: i) top 10, ii) bottom 10; and iii) sampled 10 (i.e., between ranks 1-10, 91-100, and randomly). A total of 22000 profile pairs are identified for annotation. Finally, the CrowdFlower[2] crowdsourcing service is employed to annotate each people pair with a similarity rating from 1 (being the least similar) to 4 by three annotators. The final rating for each pair is calculated by the average rating weighted by annotator trust.

Pairs with a similarity rating > 2.5 are regarded as similar people (with a total of 4633 similar pairs). Due to the candidate profile selection strategy, all people pairs in the annotated dataset are above some similarity level, which introduces bias in the set of negative (dissimilar) data instances. Therefore, a set of 2419 pairs randomly selected from the set of annotated pairs with similarity rating ≤ 2, is combined with another set of 2373 (less similar) pairs randomly selected from the set of public member profiles. A total of 4792 pairs of profiles are collected as the set of dissimilar people, resulting in a dataset of 9425 profile pairs balanced between positive and negative examples. Two thirds of the data (6283 pairs) are used for training the models, and one third of the data (3142 pairs) is used for testing.

[1]lucene.apache.org
[2]www.crowdflower.com

Table 1: Experiment results of the proposed discriminative model. The † symbol indicates statistical significance with p-value < 0.1 (paired t-tests).

	F_1
LogReg_Mod	0.7720
Latent_G_Mod	0.7831
Latent_C_Mod	0.7859
Latent_CG_Mod	0.7921†

Experiments are conducted on the constructed dataset to evaluate the proposed model. The models are evaluated by the common F_1 measure as precision and recall are both important. It can be seen in Table 1 that both *Latent_C_Mod* & *Latent_G_Mod* achieve improvements over *LogReg_Mod*; and the improvement of *Latent_C_Mod* is comparable with *Latent_G_Mod* (while slightly better). This set of experiments shows that by having higher flexibility via introducing a latent class and allowing the combination weights vary accordingly, improvements can be achieved. Table 1 also shows that the proposed probabilistic discriminative model *Latent_CG_Mod* achieves the best performance by modeling the latent content and graph classes that provide more flexibility than *Latent_C_Mod* and *Latent_G_Mod* models, and much more flexibility than the *LogReg_Mod* model, leading to its superior performance. This explicitly shows that differentiating the pairs with different profile content and social graph similarity patterns, and specializing the similarity model for different pairs of people that share similar similarity patterns is important for achieving higher similarity accuracy.

4. CONCLUSIONS

Identifying similar people is an important task for professional social networks. Different people pairs have different profile content and social graph similarity patterns, and it is important to learn specialized similarity models for people with different similarity patterns. This paper proposes a discriminative probabilistic model that identifies latent content and graph classes for people with similar profile content and social graph similarity patterns, and learns a specialized similarity model for each latent class. Experiments on real-world data show the effectiveness of the proposed discriminative probabilistic model.

5. REFERENCES

[1] H. Akaike. A new look at the statistical model identification. *IEEE Trans. on Auto. Control*, 1974.

[2] A. Dempster, N. Laird, and D. Rubin. Maximum likelihood from incomplete data via the EM algorithm. *Journal of the Royal Statistical Society.*, 1977.

[3] F. Diaz, D. Metzler, and S. Amer-Yahia. Relevance and ranking in online dating systems. In *ACM SIGIR'10*.

[4] I. Guy, M. Jacovi, A. Perer, I. Ronen, and E. Uziel. Same places, same things, same people?: mining user similarity on social media. In *ACM CSCW'10*.

Intent-Oriented Diversity in Recommender Systems

Saúl Vargas, Pablo Castells and David Vallet
Universidad Autónoma de Madrid
Escuela Politécnica Superior, Departamento de Ingeniería Informática
{saul.vargas,pablo.castells,david.vallet}@uam.es

ABSTRACT
Diversity as a relevant dimension of retrieval quality is receiving increasing attention in the Information Retrieval and Recommender Systems (RS) fields. The problem has nonetheless been approached under different views and formulations in IR and RS respectively, giving rise to different models, methodologies, and metrics, with little convergence between both fields. In this poster we explore the adaptation of diversity metrics, techniques, and principles from ad-hoc IR to the recommendation task, by introducing the notion of *user profile aspect* as an analogue of query intent. As a particular approach, user aspects are automatically extracted from latent item features. Empirical results support the proposed approach and provide further insights.

Categories and Subject Descriptors: H.3.3 [Information Search and Retrieval] *Information filtering, Retrieval models*

General Terms: Algorithms, Measurement, Performance, Experimentation, Theory

Keywords: Diversity, recommender systems, user profiles, diversity metrics, query intent, profile aspects

1. INTRODUCTION
Search result diversity is being actively researched in the IR field as a means to address query ambiguity and underspecification in ad-hoc IR [1],[2],[3]. Recommendation diversity is also an active research topic in the Recommender Systems (RS) area [5],[6]. In general terms, and most particularly in common practical scenarios, recommendation can be seen as an IR task. Interestingly, the diversity issue has been stated and addressed quite differently in the research on the topic so far in RS and ad-hoc IR respectively. In particular, diversity has been studied under a quite specific motivation and precise problem definition(s) in the IR community –building around the problem of uncertainty in user queries– along with formally grounded and well understood diversity metrics, with a theoretical depth and a drive towards standardization (backed by a specific TREC diversity task) which are not presently found or equally emphasized in the RS literature on the topic. It seems therefore natural to wonder whether, as far as it were possible to draw models and principles from one area to the other, research on RS diversity might benefit from the insights and ongoing progress in search diversity –and vice-versa.

In this poster we explore the adaptation of diversity models, metrics, and methods from ad-hoc IR into a RS setting. Specifically, we propose the notion of *user profile aspect* as an analogue of query intent, upon which we adapt the IR diversity techniques and methodology to a recommendation task. We consider two scenarios that differ in the available information for the construction of user aspects in the diversification method. We propose an approach for the extraction of user aspects based on latent factors when the only available information relates to the interaction between users and items.

SIGIR'11, July 24–28, 2011, Beijing, China.
ACM 978-1-4503-0757-4/11/07

2. RECOMMENDATION DIVERSITY VS. SEARCH DIVERSITY
Diversity in RS is generally motivated as a means to reduce redundancy under the assumption that recommending too similar items is less profitable for the user –and the vendor– than offering a more varied experience. The rationale for diversity is often stated in association with the notion of novelty and surprisal, upon the understanding that recommendation value is to a significant extent related to discovery in the user experience. Looking back for a connection to diversity in ad-hoc IR, one finds that the issues of ambiguity and underspecification are generally absent from the problem statement in the RS literature. This may seem natural as far as there is no query in the recommendation task to begin with. However, there is certainly a user information need, expressed in the form of a user profile (ratings or item access records). This implicit information need expression arguably involves far more ambiguity and incompleteness than an explicit user query, whereby the uncertainty-oriented motivation would certainly hold for RS diversity. So does the principle of diversification as a means to minimize the risk of underperformance extremes, which is also common in the IR literature [1].

Query ambiguity and underspecification are modeled in terms of query interpretations, categories, aspects, nuggets, subtopics, and similar elements in ad-hoc IR. An analogy can be drawn in the RS setting by considering an equivalent notion of *user profile aspect*. This is in fact a natural idea, since a single user's interests have many different sides and subareas (e.g. professional, politics, movies, travel, etc.). Different user preference aspects can be relevant or totally irrelevant at different times therefore, similar to query intent, there is uncertainty at recommendation time about what area of user interest should play in the given context.

If one is able to give a consistent approximation to user interest aspects in the context of a RS, the theories and metrics in search diversity could be adapted to the recommendation task. This would bring benefits such as a) a new perspective and rationale for diversity in RS in terms of theory and models, and b) new diversity metrics for RS, such as the intent-aware metrics [1] or α-nDCG [3]. Additionally, such metrics would bring in several important properties currently lacking in RS diversity studies: a) the introduction of metrics that take into account the order of items when measuring the overall recommendation diversity (i.e. top positions are more important); b) the consideration of diversity only in the presence of relevance; c) related to this, the assessment of accuracy and diversity altogether by a single metric; and d) a step towards a shared consensus on common metrics and methodologies.

3. ASPECT-BASED RECOMMENDATION DIVERSIFICATION AND METRICS
In the proposed approach, we take a space of item features (or attributes) as the basis to extract the user profile aspects, taking user profiles as the equivalent of search queries. The space of item features fulfils here a similar role to the notion of categories in [1]. Based on this, we apply a greedy diversification algorithm, where a baseline ranking R is diversified into a re-ranked list S by itera-

tively picking the item $i \in R - S$ which maximizes an objective function. We adapt two objective functions from search diversity, based on IA-Select [1] and MMR [2] respectively. In the IA-Select scheme, we define the objective function as:

$$\sum_{f \in \mathcal{F}} p(f|u)\hat{r}_{\text{norm}}(u,i)p(f|i)\prod_{j \in S}\left(1 - p(f|j)\hat{r}_{\text{norm}}(u,j)\right)$$

where u is the target user and $\mathcal{F}$ is the feature space. The item quality component represented by $\hat{r}_{\text{norm}}(u,i)$ is a measure of user preference for items, given by the baseline RS being diversified, namely the scoring function returned by the system –typically a rating prediction– normalized to [0,1]. We estimate the distribution of features over user profiles and over items as:

$$p(f|u) \sim \frac{|\{i \in \mathbf{u} | f \in \mathbf{i}\}|}{\sum_{f' \in \mathcal{F}} |\{i \in \mathbf{u} | f' \in \mathbf{i}\}|} \qquad p(f|i) \sim \frac{\chi_{\mathbf{i}}(f)}{|\,\mathbf{i}\,|}$$

where $\mathbf{u}$ denotes the set of items in the profile of u, $\mathbf{i}$ denotes the set of feature values of item i, $\chi_{\mathbf{i}}(f) = 1$ if $f \in \mathbf{i}$, and 0 otherwise. In the MMR scheme, we define an objective function which combines a similarity and a diversity component, as follows:

$$(1 - \lambda)\,\hat{r}_{\text{norm}}(u,i) + \lambda \underset{j \in S}{avg}\left(1 - sim(i,j)\right)$$

The similarity component is, again, the baseline retrieval function. The diversity component is defined by the complement of a similarity function in terms of the shared features between two items. In our experiments we choose to compute similarity as the cosine of the respective feature vectors.

As mentioned earlier, we consider two scenarios in our approach. One in which the item feature data is explicit and known to the diversification method (e.g. movie genre, director, etc., in movie recommendation), and one in which it is not, and only the user-item preference data (e.g. item ratings by users) is available. In the former case, the feature distributions estimation, and the similarity function in MMR, are based on the known feature information (using binary feature vectors in MMR). In the latter case, we base the diversification on latent item features extracted by a matrix factorization approach [4]. For IA-Select, the feature weight is binarized as "present" / "not present" upon a threshold, and for MMR we keep the weights in the feature vectors. The factorization approach thus works as a form of automatic user aspect extraction.

To evaluate the quality of diversified recommendations we adapt measures such as the intent-aware metrics [1] and α-nDCG [3], where explicit item features are the analogue of categories (or subtopics), and user profiles play the part of queries. That is, for instance, given a user u, the intent-aware nDCG of the recommendation to u is defined as $\text{nDCG-IA} = \sum_{f \in \mathcal{F}} p(f|u)\text{nDCG}(u|f)$ where, analogously to [1], $\text{nDCG}(u|f)$ counts as relevant items only the ones that are relevant for u and have the feature f. In the evaluation of these metrics, the features $\mathcal{F}$ are always the explicit ones, regardless of what features –explicit or implicit– were used in the diversification method.

4. EXPERIMENTS

We have tested the behavior of the proposed approach on the MovieLens 100K dataset. We take as baselines two state of the art colaborative filtering algorithms: a common user-based nearest-neighbor (kNN) recommender, and a matrix factorization (MF) based algorithm [4]. As a simple feature space $\mathcal{F}$ for user interest aspects we take the set of movie genres. We test the two scenarios mentioned in the previous section, one in which the diversifier uses the known item genre data, and one in which it extracts latent user features as the space of user aspects in the diversification algorithm, using rating information only. The diversifiers re-rank the top 500 items returned by the baseline recommender for each user. We take the 80% training, 20% test data splits provided by the MovieLens distribution, with 5-fold cross-validation. For relevant judgments, we take as relevant (for each user) the items with a rating higher than 3 in the test set.

Table 1 shows the performance of the different configurations using three well known diversity metrics from ad-hoc IR, plus intra-list diversity (ILD) –based on the Jaccard similarity on genres–, a common metric used in RS diversity [6]. It can be seen that the proposed diversification methods work properly, consistently improving the non-diversified baselines (bottom row). The IA-Select approach performs overall significantly better than the MMR scheme on the three IR metrics. We believe this is because it builds upon a common formalization of diversity as do the metrics (after [1]). Somewhat surprisingly, diversification with latent features performs better than with explicit ones for IA-Select on kNN, and MMR on both. We attribute this to the fact that latent features provide a more dense representation of items, and also more significant in terms of explaining the differences in interests between users, and the similarity between items. On the ILD metric, MMR and IA-Select perform similarly, and explicit features work clearly better than latent. This is probably because ILD ignores relevance –with respect to which IA-Select and latent features seem to do better.

Table 1. Four diversity metrics (α = 0.5 in α-nDCG) on different diversification approaches: MMR (with λ=0.5) and IA-Select, combined with explicit and latent features, on two baseline RS, based on kNN and MF respectively. The best value of each column is underlined. All differences to baseline are statistically significant (p < 0.005, Wilcoxon), except values in parenthesis.

		α-nDCG@50		ERR-IA@50		nDCG-IA@50		ILD@50	
		kNN	MF	kNN	MF	kNN	MF	kNN	MF
IA-Sel	Explicit	0.1589	0.1838	0.0409	0.0516	0.0604	0.0755	0.8659	0.8734
	Latent	0.1596	0.1597	0.0465	0.0458	0.0618	0.0637	0.7951	0.7817
MMR	Explicit	0.1334	0.1652	(0.0367)	(0.0431)	0.0461	(0.0555)	0.8601	0.8761
	Latent	0.1320	0.1742	0.0373	0.0528	0.0492	0.0705	0.7906	0.7740
Baseline RS		0.1213	0.1451	0.0352	0.0425	0.0440	0.0561	0.7787	0.7655

We have carried out additional experiments with further configurations, using different baseline recommender systems, and different metric cutoffs, the results from which also confirm our findings. The results were similarly positive with movie director as the explicit feature space. We plan to further explore the relation between the feature space and the effectiveness of diversification, under the intuition that the effectiveness should benefit from a higher dependency between features and user interests.

5. ACKNOWLEDGMENTS

This work is supported by the Spanish Government (TIN2008-06566-C04-02), and the Government of Madrid (S2009TIC-1542).

6. REFERENCES

[1] Agrawal, A., Gollapudi, S., Halverson, A., and Ieong, S. Diversifying search results. *WSDM 2009*. Barcelona, Spain, 2009, 5-14.

[2] Carbonell, J. G., and Goldstein, J. The Use of MMR, Diversity-Based Reranking for Reordering Documents and Producing Summaries. *SIGIR 1998*. Melbourne, Australia, 1998, 335-336.

[3] Clarke, C. L. A. et al. Novelty and diversity in information retrieval evaluation. *SIGIR 2008*. Singapore, July 2008, 659-666.

[4] Koren, Y., Bell, R. M, Volinsky, C. Matrix Factorization Techniques for Recommender Systems. *IEEE Computer* 42(8):30-37, 2009.

[5] Zhang, M. and Hurley, N. Avoiding Monotony: Improving the Diversity of Recommendation Lists. *RecSys 2008*. Lausanne, Switzerland, October 2008, 123-130.

[6] Ziegler, C-N., McNee, S. M., Konstan, J. A., Lausen, G. Improving recommendation lists through topic diversification. *WWW 2005*. Chiba, Japan, May 2005, 22-32.

Disambiguating Biomedical Acronyms using EMIM

Nut Limsopatham, Rodrygo L. T. Santos, Craig Macdonald, and Iadh Ounis
{nutli,rodrygo,craigm,ounis}@dcs.gla.ac.uk
School of Computing Science
University of Glasgow
G12 8QQ, Glasgow, UK

ABSTRACT

Expanding a query with acronyms or their corresponding 'long-forms' has not been shown to provide consistent improvements in the biomedical IR literature. The major open issue with expanding acronyms in a query is their inherent ambiguity, as an acronym can refer to multiple long-forms. At the same time, a long-form identified in a query can be expanded with its acronym(s); however, some of these may be also ambiguous and lead to poor retrieval performance. In this work, we propose the use of the EMIM (Expected Mutual Information Measure) between a long-form and its abbreviated acronym to measure ambiguity. We experiment with expanding both acronyms and long-forms identified in the queries from the adhoc task of the TREC 2004 Genomics track. Our preliminary analysis shows the potential of both acronym and long-form expansions for biomedical IR.

Categories and Subject Descriptors: H.3.3 [Information Storage & Retrieval]: Information Search & Retrieval

General Terms: Experimentation, Performance

Keywords: Biomedical Retrieval, Acronym Expansion

1. INTRODUCTION

The frequent use of (non-standardised) acronyms is one of the major problems in biomedical information retrieval [1]. In particular, the terms of a 'long-form' that has been abbreviated with an acronym in a document will have lower term frequencies in that document, and hence the document will less likely be retrieved for a query with that long-form. Moreover, acronyms may have different meanings in different documents. For example, the acronym "AD" is often used in the biomedical context to refer to "Alzheimer's disease". However, according to the ADAM database of biomedical acronyms [5], "AD" can refer to 35 unique long-forms. Therefore, if a query containing "AD" is expanded with all of the corresponding long-forms, the other 34 unrelated long-forms would result in irrelevant documents being retrieved. Conversely, if another query containing "Alzheimer's disease" is expanded with "AD", the other 34 meanings of "AD" would result in irrelevant documents being retrieved as well.

These difficulties may explain the inconsistent conclusions in the literature for acronym expansion. For instance, Stokes et al. [3] used a pseudo-relevance feedback strategy to expand the query acronyms using the long-forms found in the retrieved documents. However, they reported that their approach was insufficient to deal with the ambiguity of acronyms. Similarly, Zhou et al. [6] used the ADAM acronym database to expand long-forms in the query with the corresponding acronyms as query concepts for their concept-based retrieval framework. Still, they encountered problems with the ambiguity of acronyms and gene names. In contrast, Büttcher et al. [1] were able to successfully improve retrieval performance by expanding acronyms in queries with their corresponding long-forms. However, their approach is based on a simple heuristic, which ignores the strength of the relationship between an acronym and its long-form.

To cope with acronym ambiguity, we propose to infer the ambiguity of acronyms during the expansion process. In particular, our proposed approach, described in Section 2, expands both the acronyms and long forms in a query, and uses EMIM to measure the ambiguity of the acronyms. In Section 3, we evaluate the proposed approach in the context of the adhoc task of the TREC 2004 Genomics track. Finally, conclusions are given in Section 4.

2. ACRONYM DISAMBIGUATION

Our approach comprises three steps. Firstly, following Schwartz and Hearst [2], we build a dictionary of acronym and long-form pairs automatically from the target corpus used in our investigations, as described in the next section. Table 1 shows the statistics of the generated dictionary.

total # of acronyms	89,052
total # of long-forms	300,905
avg. # of acronyms per long-form	0.2959
avg. # of long-forms per acronym	3.3790

Table 1: Statistics of the expansion dictionary.

Next, we use this dictionary to identify 'triggers' in a query. A trigger can be either an acronym or a long-form. For each trigger, we match 'candidate expansions' (either long-forms or acronyms, respectively) in the dictionary. As there may be multiple candidate expansions for a given trigger, we propose to weight different candidates based on their probability of co-occurring with the trigger in the target corpus. It is intuitive that the more an acronym and a long-form co-occur, the more likely that the acronym refers to the long-form exclusively, and hence can safely be used as an alternative for the long-form. In particular, van Rijsbergen [4] proposed to derive the level of dependence between terms from the distribution of co-occurrences in a document set, which can be measured by EMIM (Expected Mutual

SIGIR'11, July 24–28, 2011, Beijing, China.
ACM 978-1-4503-0757-4/11/07.

Candidate Expansion		Our approach	Min-occur [1]
Acronyms	Long-forms		
✔	✗	38	23
✗	✔	24	15
✔	✔	42	33

Table 2: Topics affected by acronym expansion.

Information Measure). Therefore, we use EMIM to measure the co-occurrence between a trigger and its candidate expansion in the corpus. EMIM is calculated as:

$$\text{EMIM}(tr, ce) = \log \frac{\text{P}(tr, ce)}{\text{P}(tr)\,\text{P}(ce)} \tag{1}$$

where tr is a trigger, and ce is a candidate expansion. P is the maximum likelihood estimation function, while $\text{P}(tr, ce)$ is the joint probability of tr and ce, estimated as the fraction of documents where they co-occur.

Finally, the calculated EMIM of each trigger and candidate expansion pair is integrated into the retrieval score of a document for a query as follows:

$$score(d, Q) = \sum_{t \in Q} score(d, t) + \lambda \cdot \sum_{\langle tr, ce\rangle \in matches(Q)} \text{EMIM}(tr, ce) \sum_{t' \in ce} score(d, t') \tag{2}$$

where λ is a parameter to weight the score of the expanded terms, $matches(Q)$ uses the dictionary to calculate a set of pairs $\langle tr, ce\rangle$, such that tr is a trigger in the query Q and ce is a corresponding (acronym or long-form) candidate expansion, and t' is a term of ce.

3. EXPERIMENTAL RESULTS

We evaluate our proposed acronym expansion approach using the 50 title-only topics from the adhoc task of the TREC 2004 Genomics track.[1] This task uses a corpus of 4.6M MEDLINE abstracts. We index this corpus using the Terrier[2] information retrieval platform, with Porter's stemming and removing stopwords. For retrieval, we use the Divergence From Randomness DLH weighting model. DLH is a parameter-free model, hence no training is required.

In Figure 1, we show the retrieval performance, in terms of mean average precision (MAP), of different acronym expansion approaches as we vary the expansion weight λ in Equation (2). In particular, we evaluate our approach using EMIM to add acronyms, long-forms, or both to the queries. As a baseline, we consider the approach of Büttcher et al. [1]—henceforth referred to as 'min-occur'—which expands the queries with long-forms that co-occur in at least five documents with the trigger acronyms. Additionally, as the min-occur approach only expands acronyms, we extend it to also expand long-forms with acronyms. Table 2 shows the number of queries impacted by the expansion approaches—in all cases, our approach expands more queries. In addition to the min-occur baseline, we consider a simple baseline that performs no expansion (i.e. λ=0).

From Figure 1, we first observe that our approach can substantially outperform the no-expansion and the min-occur expansion baselines for an appropriate setting of λ. Indeed, for acronym expansion, improvements are observed for λ in

[1]We do not consider the TREC 2005 Genomics collection, as its topics include both acronyms and long-forms.

[2]`http://terrier.org`

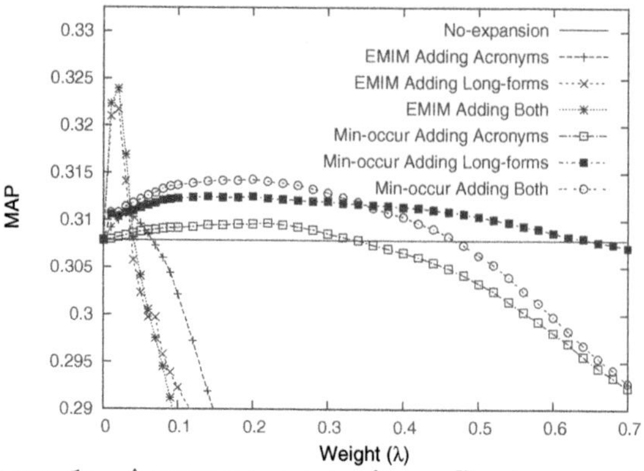

Figure 1: Acronym expansion effectiveness for a range of expansion weights (λ).

the range [0, 0.06], and are as high as 0.91% compared to no-expansion. In contrast, min-occur achieves an improvement of 0.58% in the same scenario. For long-form expansion, the ideal range for our approach is [0, 0.03], with gains up to 4.48% compared to no-expansion. In comparison, min-occur improves by 1.50 and 2.08% when adding long-forms or both acronyms and long-forms, respectively. Finally, while min-occur performs effectively for a wide range of λ values (particularly when adding long-forms), it can only improve over no-expansion by 2.08% in its best setting when expanding both acronyms and long-forms. In turn, for the same scenario, although our approach has a comparatively narrower range of effective λ values, its potential improvement is as high as 5.20%. Moreover, the effective range of λ values is stable across the three variants of our approach, which shows that it can be easily tuned in a deployment scenario.

4. CONCLUSIONS

We have proposed to improve acronym expansion for biomedical IR by disambiguating candidate expansions using EMIM. Our results show that the proposed approach can potentially outperform existing approaches in the literature, without requiring other techniques (e.g. synonym expansion, pseudo-relevance feedback) or external resources (e.g. ADAM). In the future, we plan to further investigate alternative mechanisms for estimating the probability of co-occurrence of acronyms and long-forms.

5. REFERENCES

[1] S. Büttcher, C. L. A. Clarke, and G. V. Cormack. Domain-specific synonym expansion and validation for biomedical information retrieval (MultiText experiments for TREC 2004). In *Proc. of TREC*, 2004.

[2] A. S. Schwartz and M. A. Hearst. A simple algorithm for identifying abbreviation definitions in biomedical text. In *Proc. of PSB*, pages 451–462, 2003.

[3] N. Stokes, Y. Li, L. Cavedon, and J. Zobel. Exploring abbreviation expansion for genomic information retrieval. In *Proc. of ALTW*, pages 100–108, 2007.

[4] C. J. van Rijsbergen. A theoretical basis for the use of co-occurrence data in information retrieval. *J. Documentation*, 33(2):106–199, 1977.

[5] W. Zhou, V. Torvik, and N. Smalheiser. ADAM: another database of abbreviations in MEDLINE. *Bioinformatics*, 22(22):2813–2818, 2006.

[6] W. Zhou, C. Yu, and W. Meng. A system for finding biological entities that satisfy certain conditions from texts. In *Proc. of CIKM*, pages 1281–1290, 2008.

Best Document Selection Based on Approximate Utility Optimization

Hungyu Henry Lin
University of California, Santa Cruz
hhlin@soe.ucsc.edu

Yi Zhang
University of California, Santa Cruz
yiz@soe.ucsc.edu

James Davis
University of California, Santa Cruz
davis@soe.ucsc.edu

1. INTRODUCTION

Selecting the best document from a set (i.e. Best document selection) is a common problem with many real world applications. On a news commenting web site like Digg.com, a major task is to promote one comment onto a highly-visible sidebar to entice visitors to participate in the discussion. On a web search engine like Google, a widely used functionality is the "I'm feeling lucky" button that leads user directly to the highest ranked URL. On a content web site like nytimes.com, a single ad needs to be selected and displayed on the banner for each visitor.

Best document selection is not a well studied problem by itself. One may think we can just cast it as a binary classification problem [1]. However, this approach lacks the ability to distinguish between multivariate levels of quality of the information. Another simple solution is just treat it as a ranking problem and use existing ranking algorithms to rank all documents (e.g. [2, 4], etc.). Then we can select only the first element from the sorted list. However, because ranking models optimize for all ranks, the model may sacrifice accuracy of the top rank for the sake of overall accuracy. This is an unnecessary trade-off.

We describe an alternative approach to handle the best document selection problem. We do this by first defining an appropriate objective function for the domain, then create a boosting algorithm that explicitly targets this function. Because of the comparative simplicity of the objective function and the special characteristics of the best document selection problem, we can use a stronger and tighter approximation to optimize the objective function than existing approximated ranking solutions. Based on experiments on a benchmark retrieval data set and Digg.com news commenting data set, we find that even a simple algorithm built for this specific problem gives better results than baseline algorithms that were designed for the more complicated ranking tasks.

Categories and Subject Descriptors: H.3.3 [Information Search and Retrieval]: Retrieval models
General Terms: Algorithms, Experimentation, Measurement
Keywords: Best Document Selection, Boosting, Learning to Rank

SIGIR'11, July 24–28, 2011, Beijing, China.
ACM 978-1-4503-0757-4/11/07.

2. OVERVIEW OF THE APPROACH

2.1 Utility Function

For the task of selecting the best document(s), we measure the utility as the average ratio between the selected document's relevance score and the best one:

$$U = \frac{1}{|Q|}\sum_{k=1}^{|Q|}\frac{r_{k,s}}{r_{k,o}} = \frac{1}{|Q|}\sum_{k=1}^{|Q|}\frac{1}{r_{k,o}}\sum_i r_{k,i}[d_{k,i} \textit{ is selected}] \tag{1}$$

where Q is the set of queries, and $r_{k,s}$ and $r_{k,o}$ are the relevance scores of the selected and optimal documents for the kth query, respectively. $d_{k,i}$ is a ith candidate document for the kth query, and $r_{k,i}$ is its relevance score. [] is the Iverson bracket that returns 1 for when the condition in the bracket is true, 0 otherwise. This measure is equivalent to Winner Take All (WTA), NDCG@1, and Precision@1 for binary labels. Otherwise, U can be seen as a multivariate case of Precision@1 as well as a non-exponentiated version of NDCG@1.

2.2 Approximate Objective Function

The utility measure in Equation 1 can not be optimized easily using gradient descent methods, since it is not differentiable. Similar to what people has done for optimizing ranking measures such as MAP or NDCG, we find an approximate solution by constructing a new approximate objective function that is differentiable. To do so, we approximate the Iverson bracket [] with a softmax function, which is commonly used in machine learning and statistics, for mathematical convenience. Thus the approximated objective function is:

$$\mathcal{M}(\vec{H}) = \frac{1}{|Q|}\sum_{k=1}^{|Q|}\frac{1}{r_{k,o}}\sum_i r_{k,i}\overbrace{\frac{\exp(\beta * H_{k,i})}{\sum_j \exp(\beta * H_{k,j})}}^{\approx[d_{k,i} \textit{ is selected}]} - \lambda * \underbrace{\sum_i \exp(\beta * H_{k,i})^2/(\sum_j \exp(\beta * H_{k,j}))^2}_{=l_2^2(\cdot)} \tag{2}$$

where H is the model (e.g. learner or hypothesis) to be learned, which can predict a relevance score for each document query pair, j is the index for candidate documents, $H_{k,i}$ is the retrieval score of document i for query k estimated by hypothesis H. β is a coefficient that controls the tightness of the approximation. Note that the function approaches the indicator as β approaches infinite. $l_2^2(\cdot)$ is introduced as a regularizer to control model complexity and avoid the overfitting problem, and λ is a pre-set parameter that controls the degree of regularization.

2.3 Algorithm: CommentBoost

The approximated objective function in Equation 2 can be optimized via gradient boosting. We employ a stage-wise gradient technique à la AdaBoost [3]. Its overview is presented in Fig. 1. We call this algorithm CommentBoost[1] or CBoost@1. It is a fast, list-wise boosting algorithm for best document selection.

CBoost@1 alternates between finding the gradient vector of the objective function given the current hypothesis, finding a weak learner that correlates well with the gradient vector, then finding an appropriate alpha coefficient.[2] If binary classifiers are used as weak learners, then this results in setting each label as $y_{k,i} = \texttt{sign}(\frac{\partial}{\partial H_{k,i}}\mathcal{M}(\vec{H}))$ and weights as $w_{k,i} = \texttt{abs}(\frac{\partial}{\partial H_{k,i}}\mathcal{M}(\vec{H}))$. However, any weak learners that may output real values (e.g. point-wise rankers) can be accepted as long as it is well correlated with the gradient.

Initialize: $H_{k,i} = 0$ for all document-query pairs.
$\beta \geq 0$ as a temperature parameter.
$\lambda \geq 0$ as a regularization parameter.

For $t = 1, ..., T$:

- For each document-query pair, compute

$$w_{k,i} = \frac{\partial}{\partial H_{k,i}}\mathcal{M}(\vec{H})$$

- Train a weak learner $h_t(d)$ that correlates well with $\vec{w}$ and get a weak ranking $h : d_{k,i} \rightarrow h_{k,i} \in \mathbb{R}$
- Compute:

$$\alpha_t = \frac{d}{d\gamma}\mathcal{M}(\vec{H} + \gamma\vec{h})|_{\gamma=0}$$

- Update hypotheses:

$$\vec{H} \leftarrow \vec{H} + \alpha_t\vec{h}$$

Output the final hypothesis: $H(d_{k,i}) = \sum_{t=1}^{T} \alpha_t h_t(d_{k,i})$

Figure 1: The CBoost@1 algorithm

3. EXPERIMENTS

The algorithm is tested on a user comments data set collected from Digg.com, where the best document selection problem is well motivated. Labels are gathered as the community's vote on each comment, and features are gathered from various lexical tests (e.g. word count, SMOG scores) as well as user profiles (account age, friend counts, etc.). Features are then query-level normalized. We also compared our algorithm against previously published baselines on the LETOR3.0 data set[3]. For CBoost@1, we use decision

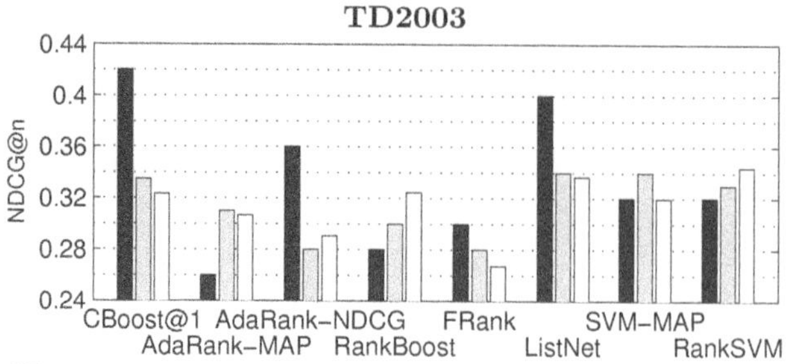

CBoost parameters are: $\beta = 1$, $\lambda = 0.4$, $T = 100$

Figure 2: Experiment results on TD2003.

stumps as our weak learners and selected the best parameters as rated against the validation set. For the purpose of comparison, we report NDCG figures instead of U on the Letor3.0 data set, and we report U on the Digg.com data set.

On both data sets, we see across-the-board improvements for NDCG@1 with our method. For NDCG@2 and beyond, our algorithm is comparable to the baselines, however, rarely improving upon them. On the Digg.com data set, our approach yields a utility score of 0.393, much better than a tuned svm_rank[4] (0.365).

4. CONCLUSIONS AND FUTURE WORK

This paper studies the problem of best document selection using a machine learning algorithm. Instead of using existing ranking algorithms, we propose a boosting algorithm that optimizes explicitly for the top rank. The strength of this approach is that it greatly simplifies the required objective function and allows us to use a tighter, more accurate approximation than before. We also demonstrate that our algorithm does out-performs a number of baselines on a benchmark ranking data set LETOR3.0 and a new Digg.com data set where best document selection problem is well motivated. As part of future work, we plan on investigating scalable, distributed best document selection algorithms.

5. REFERENCES

[1] Eugene Agichtein, Carlos Castillo, Debora Donato, Aristides Gionis, and Gilad Mishne. Finding high-quality content in social media. In *Proceedings of the international conference on Web search and web data mining*, WSDM '08, pages 183–194, New York, NY, USA, 2008. ACM.

[2] Yoav Freund, Raj Iyer, Robert E. Schapire, and Yoram Singer. An efficient boosting algorithm for combining preferences. *J. Mach. Learn. Res.*, 4:933–969, 2003.

[3] Yoav Freund and Robert E. Schapire. A decision-theoretic generalization of on-line learning and an application to boosting, 1995.

[4] Thorsten Joachims. Optimizing search engines using clickthrough data. In *Proceedings of the eighth ACM SIGKDD international conference on Knowledge discovery and data mining*, KDD '02, pages 133–142, New York, NY, USA, 2002. ACM.

[5] Ruslan Salakhutdinov, Sam Roweis, and Zoubin Ghahramani. On the convergence of bound optimization algorithms. In *in: Proc. 19th Conference in Uncertainty in Artificial Intelligence (UAI '03*, pages 509–516. Morgan Kaufmann, 2003.

[1]Because one major motivation for this algorithm is to select the best comment for users to discuss at Digg.com

[2]By taking $\frac{d}{d\alpha}\Psi(\alpha, \vec{\delta}, \vec{\Theta}) = -\alpha + \frac{\partial}{\partial\gamma}\mathcal{M}(\vec{\Theta} + \gamma * \vec{\delta})|_{\gamma=0}$, $\frac{d}{d\alpha}\Psi(\alpha, \vec{h}, \vec{H})$ is less than $\frac{d}{d\alpha}\mathcal{M}(\vec{H} + \alpha * \vec{h})$ when $\alpha < 0$ and greater than $\frac{d}{d\alpha}\mathcal{M}(\vec{H} + \alpha * \vec{h})$ when $\alpha > 0$. Thus there $\exists c \in \mathbb{R}$ s.t. $\Psi(0, \vec{h}, \vec{H}) + c = \mathcal{M}(\vec{H})$ and $\Psi(\alpha, \vec{h}, \vec{H}) + c \leq \mathcal{M}(\vec{H} + \alpha\vec{h})$ for all $\alpha \in \mathbb{R}$, satisfying properties for a lower bound whose optimal solution improves $\mathcal{M}$ (See [5]). Setting $\frac{d}{d\alpha}\Psi(\alpha, \vec{h}, \vec{H}) = 0$ and solving for α gives us our closed form solution.

[3]We only show TD2003 here due to space constraints; full results are reported in the full poster

Forecasting Counts of User Visits for Online Display Advertising with Probabilistic Latent Class Models *

Suleyman Cetintas
Dept. of Computer Sciences
Purdue University
scetinta@cs.purdue.edu

Datong Chen
Yahoo! Labs
Santa Clara, CA
datong@yahoo-inc.com

Luo Si, Bin Shen,
Zhanibek Datbayev
Purdue University
{lsi,bshen,zdatbaye}
@cs.purdue.edu

ABSTRACT

Display advertising is a multi-billion dollar industry where advertisers promote their products to users by having publishers display their advertisements on popular Web pages. An important problem in online advertising is how to forecast the number of user visits for a Web page during a particular period of time. Prior research addressed the problem by using traditional time-series forecasting techniques on historical data of user visits; (e.g., via a single regression model built for forecasting based on historical data for all Web pages) and did not fully explore the fact that different types of Web pages have different patterns of user visits.

In this paper we propose a probabilistic latent class model to automatically learn the underlying user visit patterns among multiple Web pages. Experiments carried out on real-world data demonstrate the advantage of using latent classes in forecasting online user visits.

Categories and Subject Descriptors: H.4 [**Information Systems Applications**]: Miscellaneous
General Terms: Experimentation, Performance, Theory
Keywords: Forecasting, User Visits, Display Advertising

1. INTRODUCTION

Online display advertising is a multi-billion dollar industry where advertisers buy user visits from publishers in order to promote their products by displaying advertisements (ads) on popular Web pages. An important problem in display advertising is forecasting the count of user visits for a Web page during a particular period of time (e.g., day, hour, etc.). Over-forecasting or under-forecasting leads to undesired ad delivery outcomes, such as missing an advertiser's goal or revenue loss due to unsold user visits [1].

Prior research has mainly adopted traditional time-series forecasting techniques [1, 3, 4]. Forecasting models are trained from historical user visits as a single regression model for all Web pages (assuming independence among different Web pages). In real online world, user visits among Web pages are not independent; and this results in groups of Web pages that have similar user visit patterns. For instance, one obvious factor shaping user visits is the physical structure of Web pages. A large proportion of users follow the navigation from a parent Web page, and visit the children Web pages step-by-step. Hence, some of the Web pages will have similar user visit patterns with each other, while having different user visit patterns than some other Web pages. To our best knowledge, prior research has not differentiated the groups of Web pages with similar user visit patterns.

In this paper, we learn user visit patterns hidden behind the online traffic of a large number of Web pages by using a novel probabilistic latent class model. In particular, different types/classes of Web pages that share similar patterns of user visits are automatically identified from historical data, and a regression model is built for each type/class of Web pages for making accurate prediction. The detailed formulation of the model is presented in Section 2. We then evaluate the performance of the model against typical traditional solutions using real-world data from Yahoo! in Section 3.

*This research was partially supported by the NSF research grants IIS-0746830, CNS-1012208, IIS-1017837, and a research grant from Yahoo!.

SIGIR'11, July 24–28, 2011, Beijing, China.
ACM 978-1-4503-0757-4/11/07.

2. METHOD

For forecasting user visit volume v_{st} for a Web page s (or bucket of web pages defined by a publisher) at time t, the proposed probabilistic latent class model can be described as follows:

$$P(s,t,v_{st}) = \sum_{z=1}^{N_z} P(s)P(z|s)P(v_{st}|z) \quad (1)$$

where $P(s)$ is assumed to be uniform distribution, $P(z|s)$ denotes the conditional probability of a latent class z given Web page s, and the N_z is the number of latent Web page classes that is empirically set to 5. The visit pattern in a class $P(v_{st}|z)$ can be modeled with a Laplace distribution as follows:

$$P(v_{st}|z, f^{st}, \lambda) = \frac{exp(-\frac{|v_{st}-\sum_i^K \lambda_{zi} f_i^{st}|}{\beta})}{2\beta} \quad (2)$$

where f_i^{st} is the ith feature for a Web page s and time t pair (more information about the features can be found in Section 3), λ_{zi} is the weight of latent class z for the ith feature, and K is the number of features.

The parameters of the model in Eqn.(1) ($P(z|s)$, λ) can be estimated by the EM algorithm [2]. The E-step can be derived by computing the posterior probability of z, i.e. $P(z|s,t,v_{st})$. By optimizing the auxiliary Q-function, we can derive the following M-step update rules:

$$P(z|s)^* \propto \sum_t P(z|s,t,v_{st}) \quad (3)$$

$$\lambda^*_{z\cdot} \propto \arg\max_{\lambda_{z\cdot}} \sum_{s,t} P(z|s)\Big(-|v_{st} - \sum_i^K \lambda_{zi} f_i^{st}|\Big) \quad (4)$$

Eqn.(4) is differentiable, and can be solved with gradient descent solvers. In particular, we use the Quasi-Newton method. An extreme case of the proposed latent class model, referred as *Latent_S_Mod*, is using only one latent class $N_z = 1$. In this case only the Laplace regression power is employed. We particularly report this case as *Laplace_Regr* in the experiments as one of the baselines. It should be noted that the *Latent_S_Mod* model and the *Laplace_Regr* model are run on the log-scaled (base-e) count data, and the estimated count is rescaled back for comparison with the raw user visit counts during evaluation.

3. EXPERIMENTS

Experiments are conducted on 1 month user visit logs of tens of millions users from Yahoo!. Data from the second and third weeks is used for training, and the last week is used for testing. Features are extracted for each Web page from its past week history. User visits in the same hour are aggregated together. Starting from the first hour of the second week, we extract the first 4 features as the average of visit volumes of the same hour-of-the-day in the past $1, 3, 5, 7$ days. For instance, the features for the hour, 9:00pm-9:59pm on Jan.10th, are extracted from the visits during 9pm-9:59pm on days between Jan.9th, 8th,..., Jan.3rd). Note that the first week data is only used while extracting this first set of features for the second week. We extract the second 4 features as the average number of visits in the past $1, 3, 6, 9$ hours. The number of user visits for the most visited i) 500, and ii) 1000 properties are computed (for each hour), and the corresponding datasets are referred as Top500Prop and Top1000Prop respectively. The Top500Prop and the Top1000Prop datasets have around $156K$ and $306K$ training, and $83K$ and $164K$ test data instances respectively.

The proposed model is compared to 3 types of baselines. The first baseline follows a simple forecasting approach that uses the average of past visit volume as the forecast of the coming hour. We use the 8 features as a set of 8 Web-page-independent baseline forecasts *B_LastNDay* for $N \in (1, 3, 5, 7)$ and *B_LastNHour* for $N \in (1, 3, 6, 9)$. The forecasting error is measured by the absolute percentage error between forecast and truth: $|v_{st}^{forecast} - v_{st}|/v_{st}$, where $v_{st}^{forecast}$ is the forecast and v_{st} is the actual visit count. In Table 1, we reported the average the forecasting error for all 8 baselines for the Top500Prop and Top1000Prop datasets. In order to protect the confidential information from the company, the actual errors are normalized with (i.e., divided by) the error of *B_Last1Hour* baseline on the Top1000Prop dataset (note that the actual error is in the range 0.5-1), and only the normalized errors are reported for relative comparison. It can be seen that *B_Last1Hour* is the best performing model out of all other 7 baselines, showing that the user visits in the last hour is the most relevant to the current hour, which is totally consistent with the common sense.

The second baseline of this work, namely *BB_PropSpec*, is similar to the first one, but allows each web page to have its own best model selected from the 8 features. The best feature is selected in the training data, and tested on the testing data. Interestingly, *BB_PropSpec* performs better than all other methods except *B_Last1Hour*. Selecting the best model for each Web page overfits the training data, and

Table 1: (Normalized) Results of the proposed probabilistic latent class model (i.e., Latent_S_Mod) in comparison to several baselines.

Methods	Top500Prop	Top1000Prop
B_Last7Days	2.293	2.385
B_Last5Days	2.288	2.451
B_Last3Days	2.091	2.318
B_Last1Day	1.195	1.794
B_Last9Hours	3.007	3.493
B_Last6Hours	2.116	2.577
B_Last3Hours	1.077	1.493
B_Last1Hour	0.614	1
BB_PropSpec	0.987	1.229
Laplace_Regr	0.545	0.893
Latent_S_Mod	0.499	0.829

generates more forecasting errors even in comparison to the simple baseline *B_Last1Hour*. Potential improvements can be achieved by following a direction between these two types of baseline approaches.

The third baseline is a traditional time-series regression model. We added a binary flag indicating weekends as an additional feature into the existing 8 features, and perform regression with Laplace distributions. This model is referred as *Laplace_Regr*. It can be seen in Table 1 that the *Laplace_Regr* outperforms all previously introduced approaches. This shows that combining the different information from past user visits intelligently is more effective than using only a specific type of information. Table 1 also shows that the proposed model (i.e., *Latent_S_Mod*) outperforms all the presented approaches by modeling the latent Web page classes that provide much higher modeling flexibility leading to its superior performance. This explicitly shows that differentiating the Web pages with different user visit patterns, and specializing the forecast model for different classes of Web pages that share similar patterns of user visits is important for achieving higher forecast accuracy.

4. CONCLUSIONS

Forecasting the number of user visits is an important task for display advertising. Different Web pages have different user visit trends, and it is important to learn specialized forecasting models for properties with different user visit trends. This paper proposes a probabilistic latent class model that identifies the latent classes for Web pages with similar user visit trends, and learns a separate forecasting model for each type/class of Web pages. Experiments on real-world data from a major internet company show the effectiveness of the proposed probabilistic latent class model.

5. REFERENCES

[1] D. Agarwal, D. Chen, L.-j. Lin, J. Shanmugasundaram, and E. Vee. Forecasting high-dimensional data. In ACM SIGMOD Conf., 2010.

[2] A. Dempster, N. Laird, and D. Rubin. Maximum likelihood from incomplete data via the EM algorithm. *Journal of the Royal Statistical Society.*, 1977.

[3] R. H. Shumway and D. S. Stoffer. *Time Series Analysis and Its Applications.* Springer, 2007.

[4] A. Zellner and J. Tobias. A note on aggregation, disaggregation and forecasting performance. *Journal of Forecasting*, 1999.

Knowledge Effects on Document Selection in Search Results Pages

Michael J. Cole[1]
m.cole@rutgers.edu

Xiangmin Zhang[2]
xiangminz@gmail.com

Chang Liu[1]
changl@eden.rutgers.edu

Nicholas J. Belkin[1]
belkin@rutgers.edu

Jacek Gwizdka[1]
sigir2011@gwizdka.com

[1]Rutgers, The State University of New Jersey
School of Communication and Information
New Brunswick, New Jersey 08901

[2]Wayne State University
School of Library and Information Science
Detroit, Michigan 80202

Click through events in search results pages (SERPs) are not reliable implicit indicators of document relevance. A user's task and domain knowledge are key factors in recognition and link selection and the most useful SERP document links may be those that best match the user's domain knowledge. User study participants rated their knowledge of genomics MeSH terms before conducting 2004 TREC Genomics Track tasks. Each participant's document knowledge was represented by their knowledge of the indexing MeSH terms. Results show high, intermediate, and low domain knowledge groups had similar document selection SERP rank distributions. SERP link selection distribution varied when participant knowledge of the available documents was analyzed. High domain knowledge participants usually selected a document with the highest personal knowledge rating. Low domain knowledge participants were reasonably successful at selecting available documents of which they had the most knowledge, while intermediate knowledge participants often failed to do so. This evidence for knowledge effects on SERP link selection may contribute to understanding the potential for personalization of search results ranking based on user domain knowledge.

Categories and Subject Descriptors

H.3.3 [**Information Storage and Retrieval**]: Information Search and Retrieval—*relevance feedback, search process*

General Terms

Performance, Design, Human Factors.

Keywords

knowledge effects, user study, personalization, information search behavior

1. INTRODUCTION AND RELATED WORK

Individual click through events in SERPs are not a reliable predictor of document relevance, due, in part, to user habitual rank selection bias [3, 2] which may be explained by user expectations of successful interpretation of their query. Alternatively, user SERP selection actions may be dominated by active evaluation of relevance hints in the links [4]. Domain knowledge or expertise has been shown to affect search behaviors [6, 7] and this work addresses the question of domain knowledge effects on click through.

2. METHODOLOGY

Undergraduate and graduate students (n=40) in biology-related programs rated their knowledge of 409 genomics-related MeSH terms (1–'No knowledge', 5–'Can explain to others'). They then performed four recall-oriented search tasks from the 2004 TREC Genomics Track using the Indri search system with Medline abstracts (n=1.85 million). Search interactions were recorded using a multi-source logging system [1]. Technical reasons prevented analysis of two participants.

The participant domain knowledge (PDK) was calculated as $PDK = \frac{\sum_{i=1}^{m}(k_i * t_i)}{5*m}$, where k_i is the term knowledge rating and i ranges over the terms. t_i is 1 if rated or 0 if not. The sum is normalized by a hypothetical expert who rated all terms as 'can explain to others'. Hierarchical clustering identified high domain knowledge (HDK) (n=5), intermediate domain knowledge (IDK) (n=21), and low domain knowledge (LDK) (n=12) groups.

For each document, the MeSH index terms were matched with the participant's self-reported term knowledge. We used the highest level of knowledge amongst the terms as the document knowledge representation. There is low coverage of participant-rated terms in the MeSH indexing space, so many document indexing terms could not be matched.

To reduce learning and knowledge interaction effects, only the first document selected in a SERP was considered. To reduce interface behavior effects, we analyzed cases where the first selected document was in the top five ranks that were available on the display without scrolling.

3. RESULTS

Figure 1 shows the rank distribution of selected documents by domain knowledge. There is little group variation.

Figure 2 shows the distribution of link selections by document knowledge representation. The actual selection distribution is contrasted with the distribution if the group

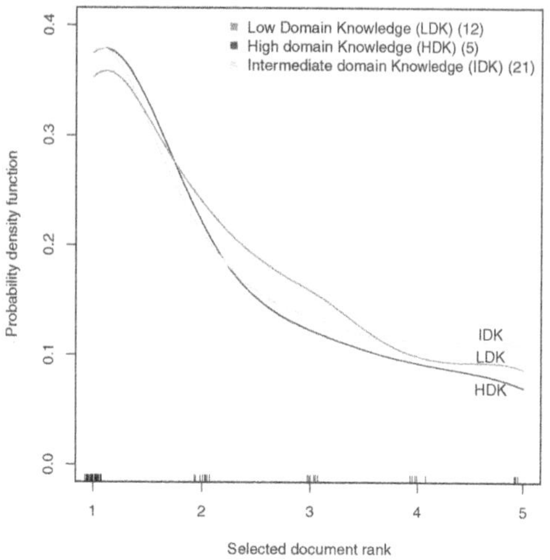

Figure 1: Domain knowledge and rank selection bias

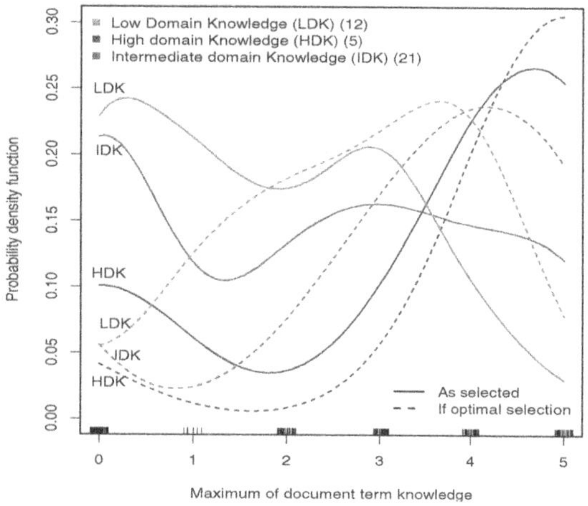

Figure 2: Link selection by indexing term knowledge

participants had always selected a document in the SERP containing the highest-rated indexing term.

The HDK group often selected a document that was the 'best' available. The LDK group was further from optimal. The IDK group was least likely to select the best available documents. Although the number of knowledge level 0 cases (no rated terms in any of the SERP documents) was similar for each group, and knowledge level 1 (highest rated term in all of the SERP documents was 'no knowledge') was similar for HDK and IDK, both the LDK and IDK groups selected one of these suboptimal documents relatively frequently.

4. DISCUSSION AND CONCLUSIONS

Assuming suitable topicality, documents of which a user has the greatest knowledge are the most likely to be accessible to them. These conceptually accessible documents represent better opportunities to extend user knowledge in ways that contribute to their task goal. That is, such documents are more likely to be *useful*. The observed differences between the 'as selected' and 'optimal selection' curves in figure 2 might be regarded as a measure of the potential for personalization of SERP results in the spirit of [5]. HDK participants were effective in such discrimination between document links. Despite a selection handicap for LDK users – there were few documents available with high knowledge indexing terms – they were rather effective for documents with highest term ratings of 2 ("vague idea") and 3 ("some knowledge"). This suggests some success for LDK users in discriminating amongst their choices. The IDK group was least successful in getting to the 'best' links.

The results provide evidence for knowledge effects in SERP link selection and suggest that high knowledge users are better able to discriminate between documents with different knowledge levels. The strong rank bias of high knowledge users may be explained by effective query formulation whose results were ranked by the user's knowledge of the links.

In many task sessions a user gains knowledge as they work towards their goal. These selection behavior observations on low, intermediate, and high domain knowledge groups may be considered from the perspective of changing factors affecting selection behavior for a single user within a task session. With respect to user knowledge, the potential for personalization of SERP link selection may therefore change over a session with the greatest potential in the earlier stages. Early possession of information about a user's knowledge might therefore be important to optimize interactive information retrieval performance. Unfortunately, this is hard to accomplish at the search server for several reasons. One solution may be client-side domain knowledge modeling and cooperation with a search service.

5. ACKNOWLEDGMENTS

IMLS grant LG-06-07-0105-07 supported this work.

6. REFERENCES

[1] Bierig, R., Cole, M. J., Gwizdka, J., and Belkin, N. J. A data analysis and modelling framework for the evaluation of interactive information retrieval. In *Proceedings of ECIR 2010, (Milton Keynes, UK 2010)* (2010), C. Gurrin et al., Eds., vol. 5993 of *Lecture Notes in Computer Science*, Springer, pp. 673–674.

[2] Joachims, T., Granka, L., Pan, B., Hembrooke, H., Radlinski, F., and Gay, G. Evaluating the accuracy of implicit feedback from clicks and query reformulations in web search. *TOIS 25*, 2 (2007), 7.

[3] Pan, B., Hembrooke, H., Joachims, T., Lorigo, L., Gay, G., and Granka, L. In Google we trust: Users decisions on rank, position, and relevance. *Journal of Computer-Mediated Communication 12*, 3 (2007), 801–823.

[4] Pirolli, P. *Information Foraging Theory*, 1st ed. Oxford University Press, New York, 2007.

[5] Teevan, J., Dumais, S. T., and Horvitz, E. Potential for personalization. *TOCHI 17*, 1 (March 2010), 1–31.

[6] White, R. W., Dumais, S. T., and Teevan, J. Characterizing the influence of domain expertise on web search behavior. In *Proceedings of WSDM* (2009), ACM New York, NY, USA, pp. 132–141.

[7] Zhang, X., Anghelescu, H., and Yuan, X. Domain knowledge, search behavior, and search effectiveness of engineering and science students: An exploratory study. *Information Research 10*, 2 (2005), 217.

Learning to Rank From a Noisy Crowd

Abhimanu Kumar
Department of Computer Science
University of Texas at Austin
abhimanu@cs.utexas.edu

Matthew Lease
School of Information
University of Texas at Austin
ml@ischool.utexas.edu

ABSTRACT

We study how to best use crowdsourced relevance judgments learning to rank [1, 7]. We integrate two lines of prior work: unreliable crowd-based binary annotation for binary classification [5, 3] and aggregating graded relevance judgments from reliable experts for ranking [7]. To model varying performance of the crowd, we simulate annotation noise with varying magnitude and distributional properties. Evaluation on three LETOR test collections reveals a striking trend contrary to prior studies: single labeling outperforms consensus methods in maximizing learner accuracy relative to annotator effort. We also see surprising consistency of the learning curve across noise distributions, as well as greater challenge with the adversarial case for multi-class labeling.[1]

Categories and Subject Descriptors

H.3.3 [**Information Search and Retrieval**]

General Terms

Algorithms, Design, Experimentation, Performance

Keywords

Crowdsourcing, learning to rank, active learning

1. INTRODUCTION

Crowdsourcing platforms like Amazon Mechanical Turk[2] are changing the dynamics of how we train our learners. While labeled data is no longer as difficult to obtain, individual labels tend to be noisier and require greater quality assurance, e.g. by requesting redundant labels from multiple annotators and resolving disagreements automatically via *consensus* [5, 3]. When annotation is noisy, how do we best utilize labeling effort to maximize learning? Do we label additional examples (improve coverage), or request more labels for already labeled examples to reduce label noise [5]? How should we compute consensus with such multi-labeling? For learning to rank [1, 7], how sensitive is the learner to different quanitities and distributions of label noise?

[1]Following acceptance to SIGIR'11, this paper underwent secondary review and was accepted to HCOMP 2011 [2] as a previously published work. The paper appears in the proceedings of SIGIR'11 only.

[2]`https://www.mturk.com`

SIGIR'11, July 24–28, 2011, Beijing, China.
ACM 978-1-4503-0757-4/11/07.

Prior work compares single labeling (**SL**) each example to multi-labeling for binary classification [5]. Given a fixed seed set of N singly-labeled examples and an infinite pool of unlabeled examples, SL grows this set of labeled examples with each new label (to increase example coverage), whereas multi-labeling requests additional labels for examples in the seed set (to increase label accuracy). With $2N$ labels, SL covers $2N$ examples with a single label while multi-labeling covers the N examples with two labels each in round-robin fashion. Simple majority vote (**MV**) is used for consensus.

Our prior work [3] on binary classification compared SL to multi-labeling with Naive Bayes (**NB**) [6] as well as MV. We studied effects of modeling vs. ignoring worker accuracy and saw across methods that modeling worker accuracy significantly improved classifier accuracy, indicating a limitation of the oft-used simple majority vote with noisy annotation. While a variety of crowd behaviors and noise may arise in practice, both prior studies [5, 3] assumed assumed uniform noise, as well as each label coming from a unique annotator. Other worker behaviors and noise characteristics may be observed in practice and could be usefully modeled.

Prior work by Yang et al. [7] studied learning to rank (with graded judgments) rather than binary classification, evaluating SL, MV, and other consensus algorithms for ranking with LambdaRank. They assumed labels come from reliable experts and provided limited analysis of the relationship between consensus method and the resulting learning curve.

This paper extends our earlier study from binary classification to learning to rank, and we consider learning under different noise quantities and distributions. We compare SL, MV, and NB for consensus, and we measure resulting ListNet [1] ranking accuracy on three LETOR [4] collections: `OHSUMED`, `MQ2007` and `MQ2008`. We observed similar results across all three and so present results on `OHSUMED` only due to space constraints. We respect LETOR's standard 5-fold partition with 3 training folds and the others for validation and testing. While training labels come entirely from the crowd, we make a significant assumption of having expert labels for the entire validation fold (≈ 3500 examples). Note this validation data is used only by ListNet, not by consensus methods. We also use expert labels as ground truth for evaluation. This reflects a scenario in which more costly expert annotation suffices for validation and testing, but larger volumes of more affordable data is desired for training.

We use a seed set size of $N = 800$ (potentially noisy) singly-labeled examples, reflecting a minimal training size to obtain stable results. The learning curve is then measured as a function of adding L additional labels. For each setting

L	0	800	1600	3200	6400	Avg
No noise (SL)	30.9	33.5	36.4	36.9	38.3	36.3

Distribution	L	SL	MV		NB	
		Rank	Rank	Label	Rank	Label
$\mathcal{N}(0.7, 0.2)$	0	21.2				
	800	23.5	27.6	61.8	25.2	62.3
	1600	29.0	27.3	63.6	28.6	75.3
	3200	33.0	27.0	70.2	30.6	90.6
	6400	35.3	26.4	77.0	30.4	96.9
	Average	30.2	27.1	68.1	28.7	81.2
$\mathcal{N}(0.5, 0.2)$	0	21.1				
	800	23.7	24.5	52.6	22.2	54.7
	1600	28.8	28.0	54.2	25.6	66.4
	3200	31.7	24.5	55.1	29.1	81.3
	6400	36.1	26.5	58.4	31.0	90.1
	Average	30.1	25.9	55.0	27.0	73.1
$\mathcal{N}(0.4, 0.2)$	0	17.0				
	800	19.5	22.6	46.8	22.9	49.0
	1600	25.8	24.0	44.7	23.9	61.4
	3200	30.4	22.7	44.4	28.4	76.1
	6400	34.0	21.9	39.5	27.0	85.7
	Average	27.4	22.8	43.85	25.6	68.0
$\ln\mathcal{N}(0.4, 0.2)$	0	18.4				
	800	21.1	22.3	40.6	21.7	41.1
	1600	26.9	23.4	40.1	22.2	40.0
	3200	27.9	19.8	35.8	21.7	37.1
	6400	28.6	19.7	30.5	21.8	36.7
	Average	26.1	21.3	36.7	21.8	38.7
$\mathcal{U}(0.2, 0.6)$	0	17.7				
	800	19.0	21.3	37.4	20.5	38.5
	1600	26.6	21.1	33.8	17.1	35.6
	3200	26.7	18.8	29.6	19.8	35.2
	6400	26.4	17.3	23.9	23.2	32.4
	Average	24.7	19.6	31.1	20.1	35.4

Table 1: Label accuracy and ListNet rank accuracy (%) achieved by SL vs. MV and NB consensus methods for varying L and quantity and distribution annotation noise (normal $\mathcal{N}(\mu, \sigma)$, log normal $\ln\mathcal{N}(\mu, \sigma)$, and uniform $\mathcal{U}(min, max)$. Expected label accuracy for SL is defined by noise parameters (mean μ or $\frac{min+max}{2}$; we report empirical accuracy for MV and NB. L additional labels are added to the seed set of $N = 800$ singly-labeled examples. We also report average accuracy of each method across $L = \{800, 1600, 3200, 6400\}$. We repeat experiments 5 times and average for stability.

of L, we compute consenus labels (no-op for single labeling) and then train ListNet using them. We report label accuracy achieved as well as the resultant ranking accuracy achived by ListNet. We measure this across different noise settings.

We simulate noisy annotation via a fixed-size pool of 100 annotators who select between $C = 3$ possible labels (ternary graded relevance classes: non-relevant, relevant, or highly relevant). Each annotator i has a unique parameter p_i denoting the probability he will produce the correct label for a given example. Otherwise he produces one of the other two possible labels (uniformly) at random. New labels are generated by selecting an annotator i from the pool at random and then generating a label according to p_i as just described.

Results without annotation noise and for five possible noise settings are shown in Table 1. Noiseless ranking accuracy with $N = 800$ $L = 0$ provides an approximate upper-bound for MV and NB consensus results across settings of L since perfect consensus would restore us to the noiseless condition. While level of noise clearly impacts the learning curve (Figure 1), we see relatively little impact of different noise distributions on ranking accuracy. Overall, it seems when average accuracy exceeds 50%, sufficient "good" annotators exist to overcome the noise of their less reliable peers.

Between $N = 800$ and $N = 1600$, **SL** begins to consistently outperform **NB** and **MV** across noise distributions, with greater example coverage apparently more important than label accuracy. Effects here may be task-specific or learner-specific, and having expert validation labels may benefit SL more than MV and NB since SL labeling accuracy on training examples is lowest. We aso see **NB** typically outperform **MV** across noise distributions.

We define an adversarial annotator for multi-class annotation with C classes as one whose $p_i < \frac{1}{C}$. In such cases, a simple way fix is to randomly pick one of the other $C - 1$ classes. We saw little benefit from doing so. Suppose an annotator has accuracy 0.2. Assuming a uniform prior over remaining classes, each has probability 0.4, so not much higher than the class originally labeled. We expect more benefit from handling adversarial labeling when accuracy is extremely low (i.e. strongly anti-correlated), or when we have a better prior for selecting between remaining classes.

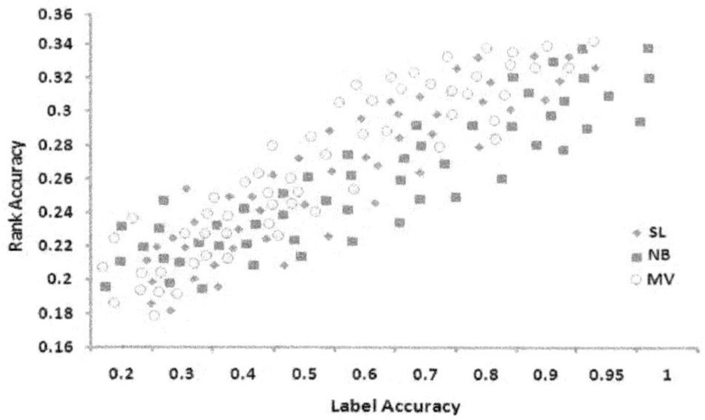

Figure 1: Consensus label accuracy vs. ranking accuracy of the ListNet learner shows a strong linear relationship across consensus methods and noise distributions considered (not shown). This suggests one can simply optimize for label accuracy with confidence of improving rank accuracy as a result.

Future work includes: a similar study with real crowd workers and data, developing more representative models for simulation, studying additional consensus methods and noise settings, and dynamic example selection for labeling.

Acknowledgments. We thank the anonymous reviewers for their valuable feedback. Eunho Yang provided the ListNet implementation. This work was partially supported by a John P. Commons Fellowship for the second author.

2. REFERENCES

[1] Z. Cao, T. Qin, T.-Y. Liu, M. Tsai, and H. Li. Learning to rank: from pairwise approach to listwise approach. In *ICML*, 2007.

[2] A. Kumar and M. Lease. Learning to rank from a noisy crowd. In *3rd Human Computation Workshop (HCOMP) at AAAI*, 2011.

[3] A. Kumar and M. Lease. Modeling annotator accuracies for supervised learning. In *WSDM Workshop on Crowdsourcing for Search and Data Mining*, 2011.

[4] T. Liu, J. Xu, T. Qin, W. Xiong, and H. Li. Letor: Benchmark dataset for research on learning to rank for information retrieval. In *SIGIR Learning to Rank Workshop*, 2007.

[5] V. S. Sheng, F. Provost, and P. G. Ipeirotis. Get another label? improving data quality and data mining using multiple, noisy labelers. In *KDD*, 2008.

[6] R. Snow, B. O'Connor, D. Jurafsky, and A. Y. Ng. Cheap and fast—but is it good? In *EMNLP*, 2008.

[7] H. Yang, A. Mityagin, K. Svore, and S. Markov. Collecting high quality overlapping labels at low cost. In *Proc. SIGIR*, 2010.

How to Count Thumb-Ups and Thumb-Downs?

An Information Retrieval Approach to User-Rating based Ranking of Items

Dell Zhang
Birkbeck, University of London
Malet Street
London WC1E 7HX, UK
dell.z@ieee.org

Robert Mao
Microsoft Research
1 Microsoft Way
Redmond, WA 98052, USA
robmao@microsoft.com

Haitao Li
Microsoft Corporation
1 Microsoft Way
Redmond, WA 98052, USA
lht1999@gmail.com

Joanne Mao
Hughes Network Systems
11717 Exploration Lane
Germantown, MD 20876, USA
zhijuan@gmail.com

ABSTRACT

It is a common practice among Web 2.0 services to allow users to rate items on their sites. In this paper, we first point out the flaws of the popular methods for user-rating based ranking of items, and then argue that two well-known Information Retrieval (IR) techniques, namely the Probability Ranking Principle and Statistical Language Modelling, provide a simple but effective solution to this problem.

Categories and Subject Descriptors:
H.3.3 [**Information Storage and Retrieval**]: Information Search and Retrieval — *retrieval models*

General Terms:
Human Factors, Measurement, Theory.

Keywords:
Web 2.0, Information Retrieval, Probability Ranking Principle, Statistical Language Modelling, Smoothing.

1. PROBLEM

Suppose that you are building a Web 2.0 service which allows users to rate items (such as commercial-products, photos, videos, songs, news-reports, and answers-to-questions) on your site, you probably want to sort items according to their user-ratings so that stuff "liked" by users would be ranked higher than those "disliked". How should you do that? What is the best way to count such thumb-ups and thumb-downs?

Let's focus on binary rating systems first and then generalise to graded rating systems later. Given an item i, let $n_\uparrow(i)$ denote the number of thumb-ups and $n_\downarrow(i)$ denote the number of thumb-downs. To sort the relevant items based on user-ratings, a score function $s(n_\uparrow, n_\downarrow) \in \mathbb{R}$ would need to be calculated for each of them.

2. POPULAR METHODS

There are currently three popular methods widely used in practice for this problem, each of which has some flaws.

SIGIR'11, July 24–28, 2011, Beijing, China.
ACM 978-1-4503-0757-4/11/07.

The first method is to use the *difference* between the number of thumb-ups and the number of thumb-downs as the score function, i.e.,

$$s(n_\uparrow, n_\downarrow) = n_\uparrow - n_\downarrow.$$

For example, Urban Dictionary, a web-based dictionary of slang words and phrases, uses this method. Assume that item i has 200 thumb-ups and 100 thumb-downs, while item j has 1,200 thumb-ups and 1,000 thumb-downs, this method would rank item i (whose score is 100) lower than item j (whose score is 200). However, this does not sound right, because item i has twice thumb-ups than thumb-downs, while item j has only slightly more thumb-ups than thumb-downs.

The second method is to use the *proportion* of thumb-ups in all user-ratings as the score function, i.e.,

$$s(n_\uparrow, n_\downarrow) = \frac{n_\uparrow}{n_\uparrow + n_\downarrow}.$$

For example, Amazon, the largest online retailer company in the United States, uses this method. Assume that item i has 200 thumb-ups and 1 thumb-down, while item j has 2 thumb-ups and 0 thumb-down, this method would rank item i (whose score is 0.995) lower than item j (whose score is 1.000). However, this does not sound right, because although both item i and item j have almost none thumb-down, item i has hundreds of thumb-ups, while item j has only a couple of thumb-ups.

The third method was advocated by Evan Miller's online article[1] on this topic to avoid the flaws of the above two simple methods. The idea is to treat the existing set of user-ratings as a statistical sampling of a hypothetical set of user-ratings from all users, and then use the *lower bound* of *Wilson score confidence interval* [3] for the proportion of thumb-ups as the score function, i.e.,

$$s(n_\uparrow, n_\downarrow) = \frac{\hat{p} + \frac{z_{1-\alpha/2}^2}{2n} - \sqrt{\frac{z_{1-\alpha/2}^2}{n}\left[\hat{p}(1-\hat{p}) + \frac{z_{1-\alpha/2}^2}{4n}\right]}}{1 + \frac{z_{1-\alpha/2}^2}{n}},$$

where $n = n_\uparrow + n_\downarrow$ is the total number of user-ratings, $\hat{p} = n_\uparrow/n$ is the observed proportion of thumb-ups, and

[1]http://www.evanmiller.org/how-not-to-sort-by-average-rating.html

$z_{1-\alpha/2}$ is the $(1-\alpha/2)$ quantile of the standard normal distribution. With the default parameter value $\alpha = 0.10$, the above score function estimates what the "real" proportion of thumb-ups at least is at 95% chance, therefore it balances the proportion of thumb-ups with the uncertainty due to a small number of observations. This method is considered as the current state of the art and thus adopted by many sites. For example, Reddit, a famous social news site, has mentioned in its official blog post[2] that this method is used for their ranking of comments. Nevertheless, this method is not well justified either. First, the above formula cannot be applied to calculate scores for the items that have not received any user-rating yet: the prevailing implementation assigns score 0 to such items, which is wrong since this implies that "no user-rating yet" is roughly same as "zero thumb-up vs. one billion thumb-downs". Second, as the lower bound is biased towards one side only, it always underestimates the "real" proportion of thumb-ups. Third, it is not clear how tight the lower bound is, i.e., how far it deviates away from the "real" proportion of thumb-ups. Fourth, the difference between the lower bound and the "real" proportion of thumb-ups are inconsistent for items with different number of user-ratings. Assume that item i has 1 thumb-up and 2 thumb-downs, while item j has 100 thumb-ups and 200 thumb-downs, this method would rank item i (whose score is 0.386) lower than item j (whose score is 0.575). However, this does not sound right, because while we are not really sure whether item i is good or bad, we have a lot of evidence that item j is bad, so we should rank item i higher than item j. For another example, using this method, we have $s(500, 501) > s(5, 1)$, which does not make much sense.

3. PROPOSED APPROACH

In this paper, we propose to address the problem of user-rating based ranking of items by formulating it as an extremely simple Information Retrieval (IR) [1] system: each user-rating — thumb-up or thumb-down — is considered as a *term*; each item is considered as a *document* that consists of a number of those two terms. Since users would like to find good items from the collection, the ranking of the items could be regarded as searching the collection with a virtual *query* of one term — thumb-up ($q = \uparrow$). The better ratings an item has received from users, the more *relevant* it is to the query thumb-up. According to the Probability Ranking Principle [2], we should rank documents by their probabilities of being relevant to the query, in our case, $\Pr[R = 1|i, \uparrow]$. This has been strictly proved to be the optimal retrieval strategy, in the sense that it minimises the expected loss (a.k.a. the Bayes risk) under 1/0 loss (i.e., you lose a point for either returning a non-relevant document or failing to return a relevant document). Making use of the Statistical Language Modelling [4] technique for retrieval, we treat each item i as a bag of user-ratings and construct a *unigram* model $M(i)$ for it, then the probability of an item being good (i.e., relevant to the query thumb-up) $\Pr[R = 1|i, \uparrow]$ can be calculated as the probability of the query being generated from its corresponding unigram model: $\Pr[\uparrow |M(i)]$. So the problem becomes how we can accurately estimate the probability $\Pr[\uparrow |M(i)]$ for each item i. Given only a small number of observed user-ratings, the maximum likelihood estimator using the proportion of thumb-ups (i.e., the second method mentioned in Section 2) does not work due to the limitation of its frequentist view of probabilities, which is a well-known fact in the Information Retrieval community. The solution is to move from frequentist inference to Bayesian inference. Before we see any user-rating for item i, we have a prior belief about the probability for it to get thumb-ups, e.g., $\Pr[\uparrow |M(i)] = 0.5$ if we do not have any reason to favour thumb-ups or thumb-downs. After we see a user-rating for item i, we should revise or update our belief accordingly, i.e., increase $\Pr[\uparrow |M(i)]$ when we see a thumb-up and decrease it otherwise. The above theoretical reasoning leads to the so-called *smoothing* technique in Statistical Language Modelling [4]. One of the simplest smoothing techniques is Laplace smoothing (a.k.a. Laplace's rule of succession), which assumes that every item "by default" has 1 thumb-up and 1 thumb-down (known as pseudo-counts). Although it avoids most flaws of those popular methods (such as getting zero-probability for unseen user-ratings), it probably puts too much weight on the prior. A better choice is its more generalised form, Lidstone smoothing, which assumes that every item "by default" has α thumb-ups and α thumb-downs, where $\alpha > 0$ is a parameter. Previous research studies have shown that the performance of Lidstone smoothing with $\alpha < 1$ is usually superior to $\alpha = 1$ (i.e., Laplace smoothing). From the Bayesian point of view, this essentially corresponds to the expected value of the posterior distribution of thumb-up probability, using beta distribution with parameter α as the prior and binomial distribution as the likelihood. To further account for the situation where users are risk-averse (e.g., in online shopping) or risk-loving, we could make it more general to use a non-uniform prior, i.e., assume that every item "by default" has α thumb-ups and β thumb-downs. In summary, we propose to use the following score function:

$$s(n_\uparrow, n_\downarrow) = \frac{n_\uparrow + \alpha}{(n_\uparrow + \alpha) + (n_\downarrow + \beta)},$$

where $0 < \alpha, \beta < 1$ are two parameters both of which have default values 0.5. It can be generalised to graded rating systems straightforwardly by taking each graded rating as multiple thumb-ups and thump-downs. For example, a 3-star rating in the 5-star scale system can be regarded as 3 thumb-ups and 5-3=2 thumb-downs. It can also be easily extended to take the ageing of user-ratings into account through Time-Sensitive Language Modelling techniques [5].

4. REFERENCES

[1] C. D. Manning, P. Raghavan, and H. Schütze. *Introduction to Information Retrieval*. Cambridge University Press, 2008.

[2] S. E. Robertson. *Readings in Information Retrieval*, chapter The Probability Ranking Principle in IR, pages 281–286. Morgan Kaufmann, 1997.

[3] E. B. Wilson. Probable inference, the law of succession, and statistical inference. *Journal of the American Statistical Association*, 22:209–212, 1927.

[4] C. Zhai. *Statistical Language Models for Information Retrieval*. Morgan and Claypool, 2008.

[5] D. Zhang, J. Lu, R. Mao, and J.-Y. Nie. Time-sensitive language modelling for online term recurrence prediction. In *In Proceedings of the 2nd International Conference on the Theory of Information Retrieval (ICTIR)*, pages 128–138, Cambridge, UK, 2009.

[2]http://blog.reddit.com/2009/10/reddits-new-comment-sorting-system.html

Predicting Users' Domain Knowledge from Search Behaviors

Xiangmin Zhang
Wayne State University
106 Kresge Library
Detroit, MI 48202
+1 877-263-2665
xiangminz@gmail.com

Michael Cole
Rutgers University,
4 Huntington Street
New Brunswick, NJ 80910
+1 732-932-7500
m.cole@rutgers.edu

Nicholas J. Belkin
Rutgers University
4 Huntington Street
New Brunswick, NJ 80910
+1 732-932-7500
belkin@rutgers.edu

ABSTRACT

This study uses regression modeling to predict a user's domain knowledge level (DK) from implicit evidence provided by certain search behaviors. A user study (n=35) with recall-oriented search tasks in the genomic domain was conducted.. A number of regression models of a person's DK, were generated using different behavior variable selection methods. The best model highlights three behavior variables as DK predictors: the number of documents saved, the average query length, and the average ranking position of documents opened. The model is validated using the split sampling method. Limitations and future research directions are discussed.

Categories and Subject Descriptors

H.3.4 [**Systems and Software**]: User profiles and alert services

General Terms

Measurement, Experimentation, Human Factors.

Keywords

User modeling, domain knowledge modeling, domain knowledge prediction, information retrieval, user studies

1 INTRODUCTION

Users of information retrieval (IR) systems have varying degrees of domain knowledge (DK). DK has been found to affect user search tactics and search performance [2], [5]. Automated prediction of DK is desirable and at least one algorithm has been reported using search log data to make binary classifiers (high or low DK) (White et. al. [4]). The current study develops a regression model for user DK from a rich data set of user behaviors collected in a controlled study. These behaviors are observable in computer interaction logs as they involve query properties, SERP link behavior and document use. Such behavior-based models can predict the user's DK level and permit systems to be personalized by adapting to the user's knowledge level. We treat DK as a continuous dependent variable to be predicted from distinct types of search behaviors and use multivariate regression modeling. Different variable selection methods are used to build alternative models for comparison.

2 RESEARCH DESIGN

2.1 Search system and collection

An IR system was implemented using the Indri search engine from the Lemur toolkit. The data set was the 2000-2004 portion of the TREC Genomics Track collection (n=1.85 million). Thirty five students, both graduate and undergraduate, from biology-related schools and departments participated in the study.

SIGIR'11, July 24–28, 2011, Beijing, China.
ACM 978-1-4503-0757-4/11/07.

2.2 Assessment of domain knowledge

The participants' DK was assessed in two ways:

a) Before any of the search sessions, participants rated their understanding of the MeSH terms in three genomics-related MeSH concept trees: Genetic processes (G05), genetic phenomena (G13), and genetic structures (G14). We used an anchored scale to capture knowledge judgments: 1 for "no knowledge", 2 for "vague idea", 3 for "some knowledge", 4 for "high knowledge", and 5 for "can explain to others".
b) Before each search task, after reading the task description participants were asked to rate both their expertise and familiarity with the search topic using a 7-point scale, from 1: 'not at all' to 7: 'extremely'. This scale was used to provide uniformity over all of the pre-task questions.

A participant's DK score is calculated as:

$$DK=((Z(\text{MeSH-rating}) + Z((\text{familiarity+expertise ratings})/2))/2$$

The mean of a participant's MeSH term ratings was calculated. Then the average of the participant's pre-task topic familiarity and expertise ratings was calculated. Since different scales were used for the MeSH and pre-task questionnaire ratings, the values were transformed to Z-scores. The mean of the two Z-scores provides the participant's DK score. This DK score is taken to represent a participant's task knowledge level.

2.3 Search tasks

Five search tasks were selected, based on their MeSH categories and the number of relevant documents available, from among 50 TREC Genomics Track topics. The topics and their corresponding MeSH categories are listed in Table 1.

Table 1. Search Topics/Tasks

Topic #	MeSH Category	Topic Keywords
2	Genetic structure	Generating transgenic mice
7	Genetic processes	DNA repair and oxidative stress
42	Genetic phenomena	Genes altered by chromosome translocations
45	Genetic phenomena	Mental Health Wellness-1
49	Genetic structure	Glyphosate tolerance gene sequence

2.4 User search behaviors

Three categories of search behaviors are considered in this study: querying behaviors; document selection/viewing behaviors, and the general task interaction behaviors, such as the number of actions per task, task completion time, and so on. More than 15 behavior variables were analyzed in this study.

2.5 Procedure

The user experiment was conducted in the work-task framework proposed by Borlund [1]. The participants were asked to rate the selected portion of MeSH terms first. Then they would complete the pre-task questionnaire, which was followed by conducting searches on the experimental system. Tasks were systematically-rotated in balanced blocks. Participants saved documents during the search and evaluated their level of relevance after completing the search. After evaluation of the documents for the search task, a post-task questionnaire was administered. The experiment was conducted in a human-computer interaction lab, and each participant was tested individually. The participant-system interaction was logged by computer software.

2.6 Multiple regression analysis

The collected user behavior data was analyzed using multiple regression analysis [3]. The generic multiple regression model is expressed as:

$$y=a + b1x1 + b2x2 + ... + bkxk \quad (1)$$

where y is the predicted value of the dependent variable, a the constant parameter, b coefficients, and $x_{1\text{-}k}$ are predicting variables. Both a and $b_1...b_k$ must be determined from the sample population data.

To predict DK from search behavior variables, we can use DK as y, and the distinct search behavior variables as x_1-x_x. The main research question is to identify the collection of behavior variables that do the best job of predicting the calculated task DK of the participants.

3 RESULTS

3.1 Variable selection

There are over 15 behavior variables involved in the study. We evaluated the meaningfulness of the variables used in the regression analysis using Pearson correlation analysis. First we looked at the relationship between these behavior variables and DK on the data set aggregated for all participants and all tasks. Eight significant behavior variables were identified (Table 3) and they were used as the candidate predictors in the multiple regression analysis.

3.2 The optimal model

Several standard techniques exist for selection of the most discriminative variables to include in a multiple regression model [3]. Using all candidate variables generated in 3.1, the stepwise estimation method and the backward elimination method were employed in analysis. In addition, we generated a model using all of the candidate variables as a standard for model comparison. Each method generated several models with different combinations of predictors.

Table 3. Behavior variables identified (n=140)

Behavior Variable	Variable Interpretation	Corr/Sig.
Q_length	mean query length (# of words)	.344/.000
Saved	# of documents saved	.357/.000
Viewed	# of documents viewed	.285/.001
Ratio	ratio of saved to viewed	.250/.003
numTaskActions	mean # of actions per task	.274/.001
numSerps	mean # of SERPs accessed	.201/.017
Task_T	mean task completion time (in second)	.174/.039
Rel_mean	mean ranking position of the docs opened in SERPs	.277/.001

We compared the models using model fit, model significance, and the contributions of individual predictors in each model. The stepwise model provided the best model, with an adjusted R^2 value of 0.265. This R^2 value is reasonably good for predicting human behaviors. This DK model fitted to the sample data is:

$$DK=-1.466+0.039Saved+0.147Q\_length+0.130Rel\_mean \quad (2)$$

This model suggests that a user's DK is indicated by the number of documents saved, the user's average query length, and the average SERP rank position of opened documents.

4 DISCUSSION

The stepwise model (equation 2) was validated by using the split sampling method. However, generalizability of the model needs to be further investigated because the data was collected in a controlled experiment and from only one domain. The contribution of this research is that it may enable real-time observation and prediction of a user's level of DK, supporting knowledge-based personalization of information retrieval systems.

5 ACKNOWLEDGMENTS

This research was supported by IMLS grant LG-06-07-0105-07.

6 REFERENCES

[1] Borlund, P. The IIR evaluation model: A framework for evaluation of interactive information retrieval systems. *Information Research*, 8(3), 152 (2003)

[2] Duggan, G.B. & Payne, S.J.: Knowledge in the head and on the web: Using topic expertise to aid search. In *Proceedings of SIGCHI*, 39-48 (2008)

[3] Hair, J. Jr., et al.: Multivariate Data Analysis, 5th ed. Prentice Hall, New Jersey (1998)

[4] White, R., Dumais, S.T., & Teevan, J.: Characterizing the influence of domain expertise on Web search behavior. In *Proceedings of WSDM 2009* (2009)

[5] Zhang, X., Anghelescu, H.G.B. & Yuan, X.: Domain knowledge, search behavior, and search effectiveness of engineering and science students. *Information Research*, 10(2), 217(2005).

The Interactive PRP for Diversifying Document Rankings

Guido Zuccon*, Leif Azzopardi, and C. J. "Keith" van Rijsbergen
{guido, leif, keith}@dcs.gla.ac.uk
School of Computing Science, University of Glasgow, Glasgow, UK

ABSTRACT

The assumptions underlying the Probability Ranking Principle (PRP) have led to a number of alternative approaches that cater or compensate for the PRP's limitations. In this poster we focus on the Interactive PRP (iPRP), which rejects the assumption of independence between documents made by the PRP. Although the theoretical framework of the iPRP is appealing, no instantiation has been proposed and investigated. In this poster, we propose a possible instantiation of the principle, performing the first empirical comparison of the iPRP against the PRP. For document diversification, our results show that the iPRP is significantly better than the PRP, and comparable to or better than other methods such as Modern Portfolio Theory.

Categories and Subject Descriptors: H.3.3 [Information Storage and Retrieval] - *Information Search and Retrieval - Retrieval Models*
General Terms: Algorithms, Theory.

1. INTRODUCTION

The PRP has played a central role in the development of Information Retrieval (IR); in the context of ad-hoc retrieval the PRP has underpinned the development of most formal models. This is because, if a system upholds the PRP then its response is guaranteed theoretically to be optimal given the query. In practice, this principle has largely stood the test of time, but it relies on a number of key assumptions which have been called into question [3, 5, 6]. In particular, the PRP has been criticised because of the *independence assumption*, which assumes only document and query are sufficient to determine whether a document is relevant, ignoring the influence of other documents in the ranking [3].

In non-traditional evaluation contexts such as subtopic retrieval, where dependencies between documents are considered, a number of ranking principles and strategies alternative to the PRP have been proposed. These include Maximal Marginal Relevance (MMR) [1] and Modern Portfolio Theory (MPT) [5], along with the recently proposed Quantum PRP (qPRP) [6], as well as the untested iPRP [2]. The latter provides a theoretical framework for extending the PRP to the context of interactive IR. However, the iPRP has not been empirically tested or validated; so it is unclear whether it performs better than other approaches, or not. In this poster, we compare the rankings that the iPRP would initially deliver to the user in the *first pass of retrieval*, against the rankings based on other approaches (and leave the interaction to future work).

*This author is supported by EPSRC EP/F014384/.

SIGIR'11, July 24–28, 2011, Beijing, China.
ACM 978-1-4503-0757-4/11/07.

2. THE INTERACTIVE PRP

In [2], Fuhr proposes a theoretical framework for extending the PRP to the context of interactive IR. In this framework, the independence assumption is rejected since relevance is assumed to depend upon the documents the user has previously examined. Search is then modelled as situation, called a list of choices, that are presented to the user. The user moves between situations by accepting one of the choices. Once a choice has been accepted, the retrieval system is required to produce a new list of choices depending upon the previous choice. The ranking principle strives to provide the optimum ordering of the choices presented in each situation, such that for each rank position i, documents under the iPRP are ranked as follows:

$$d_i = \arg\max_{d \in \mathcal{RE} \setminus RA} \left[e + P(d) \left(b_{d,i} Q(d) + g \left(1 - Q(d)\right) \right) \right]$$

where $Q(.)$ is the probability[1] that the user does not revise their choice of selecting document d; e is the effort of examining document d; g is the additional effort required for correction if the user judges a viewed document as irrelevant; and $b_{d,i}$ is the benefit of ranking document d if relevant.

The iPRP assumes that the user would examine each document in turn. Thus at each rank, the previous documents would influence the relevance of the subsequent documents. In order to obtain the ranking for the first pass of retrieval (i.e. before any actual user interaction has transpired), we can ignore the costs associated with the user or assume them constant. So both e and g are set to zero in the first pass. The probability $Q(.)$ of a user not revising their choice can be treated as constant for all the documents, and thus it is dropped for rank equivalence reasons.

This leaves one final choice to be made about the benefit of ranking a document d at rank i. Since this is dependent upon the documents that have been previously ranked, then a reasonable approximation of the benefit would be to determine how dissimilar the considered document is to all previous documents. This can be achieved through a summation over all previously ranked documents of a measure of dissimilarity or anti-correlation, i.e. we assume the possible benefit comes from novel information. If document d is

[1] i.e. the probability that the user does not change their mind about the relevance of the document d after examining it.

Table 1: Performances of PRP, MMR, MPT, iPRP and qPRP for subtopic retrieval. Significant better performances (measured by t-test) over the PRP are indicated with *. No statistically significant differences are calculated between runs in the TREC 6-8 dataset due to the limited amount of topics [4].

	TREC 6-8					TREC 18 (Clueweb09)				
Meas.	PRP	MMR	MPT	qPRP	iPRP	PRP	MMR	MPT	qPRP	iPRP
NRBP	0.127	**0.132** (+3.94%)	0.127 (0.00%)	0.134 (+5.51%)	**0.136** (+7.09%)	0.044	**0.074*** (+68.18%)	**0.074*** (+68.18%)	0.060* (+36.36%)	0.048 (+9.09%)
α-NDCG@10	0.426	0.457 (+7.28%)	0.426 (0.00%)	0.433 (+1.64%)	**0.461** (+8.22%)	0.097	0.137* (+41.24%)	**0.151*** (+55.67%)	0.144* (+48.45%)	0.132* (+36.08%)
IA-P@10	0.063	0.065 (+3.17%)	0.063 (0.00%)	0.065 (+3.17%)	**0.068** (+7.94%)	0.064	0.064 (0.00%)	**0.076*** (+18.75%)	0.074* (+15.63%)	0.070 (+9.38%)

similar to the previous documents, then the correlation will be low, or negative, leading to a low total benefit. Similar documents are then demoted in the ranking, while documents that are more diverse are promoted, giving rise to the following objective function:

$$d_i = \arg\max_{d \in \mathcal{RE} \setminus RA} (P(d) b_{d,i}) = \arg\max_{d \in \mathcal{RE} \setminus RA} \left(P(d) \frac{\sum_{d' \in RA} \rho_{d,d'}}{|RA|} \right)$$

Under the iPRP dependencies between documents are incorporated through multiplication, providing a completely different approach to alternative strategies. In contrast, MPT, MMR and qPRP combine relevance with diversity in an additive fashion.

3. EXPERIMENTS

In this paper we conducted an empirical study in the context of subtopic retrieval, with the aim of comparing the iPRP with previously proposed principles and strategies. In particular, we compare the empirical effectiveness of iPRP against those of PRP, MMR, MPT, and qPRP. We refer to [1, 5, 6] for the formulation of these approaches.

For this study, we employed the TREC 6-8 Interactive subtopic collection and the TREC 18 on the Clueweb09 (part B) dataset. Rankings are evaluated using IA-P[2], NRBP, and α-NDCG (with $\alpha = 0.5$). All approaches were implemented using Lemur[3]. Each collection was indexed where common stop-words were removed and Porter stemmer was applied. For each alternative ranking approach, re-ranking of the top[4] 100, 200, 500 and 1000 documents was performed. The Pearson's correlation between pairs of documents' term vectors was used to estimate dependencies between documents. Approaches were instantiated as follows.

PRP. The PRP is implemented employing Okapi BM25 scoring schema, where the model's parameters are set to standard values. Scores obtained by this method are used to generate the relevance estimates required by the other approaches, thus serving as baseline.

MMR. We investigated the effect on retrieval performances of MMR's parameter λ, varying λ in $[0, 1]$ with steps of 0.1.

MPT. No variance is associated with the relevance scores of Okapi BM25, and thus we resort to treat variance as adjunctive parameter, setting a constant variance value amongst documents. We investigated the optimal value of the variance σ_d^2 in the range $[10^{-10}, 10^{-1}]$ and combine it with the value of the parameter b, ranging in $[-10, 10]$.

[2]Where intents are considered to be equally important or probable.

[3] The Lemur Toolkit, http://www.lemurproject.org/

[4]We only report performances for re-rankings on the top 100 due to space limits. Performances were similar for alternative configurations.

qPRP. The implementation of the qPRP does not require extensive parameter tuning procedures. Without a method to estimate complex probability amplitudes, we resort to an approximation of phases by using Pearson's correlation between the two documents' term vectors, as suggested in [6].

Regarding parameters settings, here we present the performances of those runs that delivered the highest value of α-NDCG@10 over the whole topic set.

Results. The results of our empirical investigation are reported in Table 1. The best value of α-NDCG@10 on the TREC 6-8 for MPT is obtained when $\sigma_d^2 \leq 10^{-7}$, regardless of the value of b, and the obtained ranking is equivalent to that of PRP. This suggests that MPT's ranking formula reduces to the PRP one, when parameters are tuned so as to optimise α-NDCG@10 on the whole set of query topics for this collection. This is not the case however for TREC 18. The best performing model depends on the collection employed. For example, iPRP delivers the most effective ranking, with respect to α-NDCG@10, on the TREC 6-8 subtopics collection, while MPT delivers the best on TREC 18. Further analysis and testing are required to determine whether the differences depend upon the types of documents, needs, or number of subtopics.

4. CONCLUSIONS

In this poster, we have provided an initial attempt at instantiating the iPRP to provide the initial ranking of documents. This was evaluated in the context of subtopic retrieval. These findings suggest that the iPRP can be effective; significantly outperforming the PRP and providing comparable or better performance over other diversity approaches. While we have only considered one possible interpretation of the iPRP, further work will explore other possible instantiations, and in particular what happens when there is interaction.

5. REFERENCES

[1] J. Carbonell and J. Goldstein. The use of MMR, diversity-based reranking for reordering documents and producing summaries. In *SIGIR '98*, pages 335–336, 1998.

[2] N. Fuhr. A probability ranking principle for interactive information retrieval. *JIR*, 12(3):251–265, June 2008.

[3] M. D. Gordon and P. Lenk. When is the probability ranking principle suboptimal. *JASIS*, 43(1):1–14, 1999.

[4] C. J. van Rijsbergen. *Information Retrieval, 2nd Ed.* Butterworth, 1979.

[5] J. Wang and J. Zhu. Portfolio theory of information retrieval. In *SIGIR '09*, pages 115–122, 2009.

[6] G. Zuccon and L. Azzopardi. Using the quantum probability ranking principle to rank interdependent documents. In *ECIR '10*, pages 357–369, 2010.

Detecting Success in Mobile Search from Interaction

Qi Guo, Shuai Yuan, and Eugene Agichtein
Mathematics and Computer Science, Emory University, Atlanta, GA 30322, USA
{qguo3, syuan3, eugene}@mathcs.emory.edu

ABSTRACT

Predicting searcher success and satisfaction is a key problem in Web search, which is essential for automatic evaluating and improving search engine performance. This problem has been studied actively in the desktop search setting, but not specifically for *mobile search*, despite many known differences between the two modalities. As mobile devices become increasingly popular for searching the Web, improving the searcher experience on such devices is becoming crucially important. In this paper, we explore the possibility of predicting searcher success and satisfaction in mobile search with a smart phone. Specifically, we investigate client-side interaction signals, including the number of browsed pages, and touch screen-specific actions such as *zooming* and *sliding*. Exploiting this information with machine learning techniques results in nearly 80% accuracy for predicting searcher success – significantly outperforming the previous models.

Categories and Subject Descriptors

H.3.3 [**Information Storage and Retrieval**]: Information Search and Retrieval–*selection process, search process.*

General Terms

Algorithms, Experimentation, Human Factors, Measurement.

Keywords

Detecting success and satisfaction, mobile search behavior.

1. INTRODUCTION

Predicting searcher success and satisfaction is a key problem in Web search, which is essential for search engines to automatic evaluate and diagnose performance on a large-scale, as well as providing real-time intervention and assistance if dissatisfaction can be detected at an early stage [3]. Some previous research has attempted this problem [3][5][7] in a general Web search setting where computers were considered as the primary platform.

Recently, as mobile devices, such as smart phones, have become an increasingly popular platform for browsing and searching the Web, it is becoming crucial that the Web search experience on a mobile phone is satisfactory. However, to the best of our knowledge, no work has been done to understand how the behavioral patterns on a mobile device can reveal the success and satisfaction of a search task. There are many differences in the usage of computers and mobile devices [2] [8], and so it is unclear whether the models of searcher success in satisfaction developed for the desk-top setting (e.g., using fine-grained user signals, such as scrolling and mousing [1][4][6]) would translate to the mobile search setting.

As an attempt to close this gap, we present, as far as we know, the first study of automatically predicting *searcher success and satisfaction in mobile Web search* from behavior on mobile phones with touch screens, laying the groundwork for more extensive future research. In addition to previously studied behavioral signals of search success, we investigate *client-side interaction features*, including the number of pages browsed, zooming, scrolling/sliding, and orientation changing - increasingly common in modern smart phones - and show that these features significantly improve prediction accuracy.

SIGIR'11, July 24–28, 2011, Beijing, China.
ACM 978-1-4503-0757-4/11/07.

2. METHODOLOGY

We conducted a controlled user study to collect data with known search success outcome. Ten subjects were recruited (6 male, 4 female, average age 26.2 ± 3.2). All subjects were undergraduate and graduate students or staff at the Emory University, and had some experience with Web search and smart phones. We designed the search tasks (some examples are given in Table 1) for this study to be representative of common Web search tasks on mobile devices. The tasks have varying difficulty and topics, and highlight geographical intents that have been identified as a significant portion of mobile information needs [2].

Table 1. Example task descriptions *(initial queries)*

Task 2: Find the **MARTA routes and schedules** from Georgia Tech to Emory on Tuesdays after 7PM (marta schedules)
Task 5: Find the **closest zipcar location** to MathCS (zipcar locations)
Task 7: Find **the earliest show times** of "social network" after 7:00PM today in the closest movie theater (*social network*)

The user study proceeded as follows: before the tasks began, the participants were given a tutorial of using the phone, including opening bookmarks, clicking, zooming, scrolling, and changing the physical device orientation. Next, a warm-up task was given to each participant to familiarize them with the task procedure. To begin each task, the participants were presented a task description and an initial query. For each task, the participants were instructed to first open the bookmark with the Google search engine result page (SERP) of the initial query. Once they reached the SERP, they could click the search results and/or reformulate the query if needed until the information was found or it took too long than they would spend in reality. After each task, the participants were asked a few questions, including whether they have successfully completed the task and how satisfied they were about the search experience during the task. Following the warm-up, eight search tasks were given to each participant.

To capture the client-side interactions, including the number of browsed pages, zooming, and sliding, we developed a modified version of the Chrome browser application [1] for the Android phone. The events are encoded in a string and sent to the server as HTTP requests for analysis.

For each of the success and satisfaction dimensions, we formulate our prediction task as binary classification: that is, we classify each search task into two classes: successful/satisfied (user selected "very successful/ satisfied" in the post-task questionnaire) and unsuccessful/unsatisfied.

We then represented each search task as a feature vector, with values corresponding to the server-side features and client-side

[1] Available at http://ir.mathcs.emory.edu/intent/data/sigir2011/

features. The server-side features include the number of queries, clicks, clickthrough rate (CTR), average query length and task duration. The client-side features include the numbers of all browsed pages, search engine result pages (SERP), and non-SERP pages, as well as the event counts on these pages (e.g., scrolling, scaling). Additional details about the features are available on the project website referenced above.

Our intuition was that these client-side features can provide additional insights about the searcher success and satisfaction level. For example, a small number of queries and clicks with moderate task duration might indicate a successful search task, as it seems that the user did not need to spend too much time and effort to complete the task; however, if the user, during this task, browsed a large number of pages and had to intensively scroll and rescale on the browsed pages, she might be actually not satisfied and not even successful, since she actually spent a lot of efforts and was keeping searching without finding the relevant information.

We experimented with various classification algorithms, including Bayes Network (BN), Support Vector Machines (SVMs), decision trees, and others. We report classification results for BN only, as it performed best in this setup, even though other algorithms achieved similar performance.

3. RESULTS AND DISCUSSION

To simulate the real scenarios in mobile search, where searchers are less likely to attempt time-consuming and complex searches, we did not assign overly difficult tasks to our participants. As a result, the means of success and satisfaction ratings are 3.25 (std=1.0) and 3.0 (std=1.2) respectively, on a 5-point scale (i.e., 0 represents very unsuccessful/unsatisfied, 4 represents very successful/satisfied). Interestingly, success rating has a noticeably higher mean and the correlation between these two are high but not perfect (R=0.81), which makes sense since users might feel unsatisfied about the experience even if they end up finding the information successfully. Also, the noticeably higher variance of the satisfaction ratings for each task suggests higher subjectivity of making satisfaction judgments.

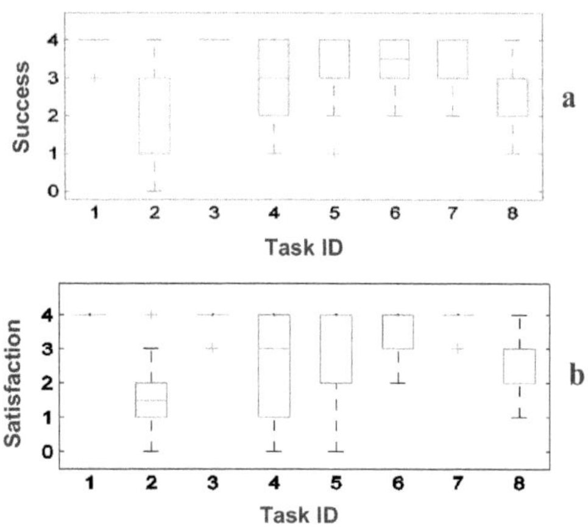

Figure 1. Success (a) and Satisfaction (b) by Task ID

As we can see in Figure 1, some tasks are better solved, while other tasks have more room for improvement. Interestingly, for easier tasks, the variance of both satisfaction and success ratings across users is smaller. In contrast, for more difficult tasks, the variance of both satisfaction and success ratings is larger, which suggests significant opportunities for personalization, or of exploiting successful "expert" mobile searchers to help unsuccessful "novice" mobile search users.

Table 2. Results of predicting success and satisfaction. Significance of differences is indicated between models and: Baseline: △ $p<.05$, ▲ $p<.01$; Server: ○ $p<.05$, ● $p<.01$.

Method	Both		Successful		Unsuccessful	
	Acc	F1	Prec	Recall	Prec	Recall
Baseline	57.5	36.5	57.5	100	0	0
Server	66.3	64.2▲	67.9▲	78.3△	63.0▲	50.0▲
Client	80.0△	79.2▲	80.0▲	87.0△	80.0▲	70.6▲
Full	78.8△	78.0▲	79.6▲	84.8△	77.4▲	70.6▲
Method	**Both**		**Satisfied**		**Unsatisfied**	
	Acc	F1	Prec	Recall	Prec	Recall
Baseline	53.8	35.0	53.8	100	0	0
Server	71.5▲	68.1▲	66.1▲	95.3	88.9▲	43.2▲
Client	76.3▲	75.6▲	74.0▲	86.0▲	80.0▲	64.8▲
Full	78.8▲	78.5▲○	78.3▲○	83.7▲○	79.4▲	73.0▲○

Ten-fold cross validation was used: in each fold, tasks of nine participants were used for training and the remaining tasks of the left-out participant were used for testing. We report the average of the results across the folds in Table 2. As we can see, the BN classifiers (our models) significantly outperformed the majority baselines, exhibiting the accuracy of 79% compared to the baseline system (accuracy of 54% for predicting satisfaction and 58% for predicting success). Interestingly, using client-side features achieved better performance than using server-side features, and combining the two achieved optimal performance for predicting search satisfaction, while clients-side achieved the best performance in predicting search success.

To understand the contributions of the various features, we computed the X^2 statistic for each feature with respect to the class. We found that the most significant features include the number of browsed pages, number of non-SERP events, task duration, clickthrough rate, number of clicks and average query length. Generally, the more effort a user spent on searching, the less likely she were to be satisfied or successful – which makes sense in a mobile setting, where the screen size is small, the bandwidth is limited, and each user interaction requires effort.

In summary, we explored the feasibility of predicting searcher success and satisfaction in mobile search. Our experiments show that we can predict search success and satisfaction with accuracy of nearly 80%, by incorporating additional client-side interactions. Our results support the feasibility of the automatic evaluation and improvement of the search engine performance for mobile search.

ACKNOWLEDGMENTS This work was partially supported by the NSF grant IIS-1018321 and the Yahoo! Faculty Research Engagement program.

4. REFERENCES

[1] Buscher G., van Elst, L., and G., Dengel A. Segment-level display time as implicit feedback: a comparison to eye tracking. In Proc. SIGIR 2009.

[2] Church, K., Smyth, B. Understanding the intent behind mobile information needs. In Proc. IUI 2009.

[3] Feild, H., Allan, J., and Jones, R. Predicting searcher frustration. In Proc. SIGIR 2010.

[4] Guo, Q., and Agichtein, E. Ready to buy or just browsing? Detecting web searcher goals from interaction data. In Proc. SIGIR 2010.

[5] Hassan, A., Jones, R., and Klinkner, K.L. Beyond DCG: user behavior as a predictor of a successful search. In Proc. WSDM 2010.

[6] Huang, J., White, R.W., and Dumais, S.T. No clicks, no problem: using cursor movements to understand and improve search. In Proc. CHI 2011.

[7] Liu, J., Liu C., Gwizdka, J., and Belkin N.J. Can search systems detect users' task difficulty? some behavioral signals. In Proc. SIGIR 2010.

[8] Kamvar, M., Kellar, M., Patel, R. and Xu, Y. Computers and iPhones and mobile phones, oh my! A logs-based comparison of search users on different devices. In Proc. WWW 2009.

Measuring Assessor Accuracy: A Comparison of NIST Assessors and User Study Participants

Mark D. Smucker
Department of Management Sciences
University of Waterloo
mark.smucker@uwaterloo.ca

Chandra Prakash Jethani
David R. Cheriton School of Computer Science
University of Waterloo
cpjethan@cs.uwaterloo.ca

ABSTRACT

In many situations, humans judging document relevance are forced to trade-off accuracy for speed. The development of better interactive retrieval systems and relevance assessing platforms requires the measurement of assessor accuracy, but to date the subjective nature of relevance has prevented such measurement. To quantify assessor performance, we define relevance to be a group's majority opinion, and demonstrate the value of this approach by comparing the performance of NIST assessors to a group of assessors representative of participants in many information retrieval user studies. Using data collected as part of a user study with 48 participants, we found that NIST assessors discriminate between relevant and non-relevant documents better than the average participant in our study, but that NIST assessors' true positive rate is no better than that of the study participants. In addition, we found NIST assessors to be conservative in their judgment of relevance compared to the average participant.

Categories and Subject Descriptors: H.3.3 [Information Storage and Retrieval]: Information Search and Retrieval

General Terms: Experimentation

Keywords: Relevance, assessors, signal detection theory

1. INTRODUCTION

Whether it is assessors judging the relevance of documents or users performing document triage in the midst of a search, humans are faced with a speed accuracy trade-off. When accuracy must be traded off for speed, relevant documents will be missed and judged non-relevant, and non-relevant documents will be judged to be relevant. Better user interfaces (UIs) will allow assessors and users to judge faster and more accurately than poorer interfaces.

To build better relevance assessing UIs, we need to be able to measure the performance of the users of these UIs. While it is easy to measure the rate at which assessors make judgments, the subjective nature of relevance makes measuring the quality of the judgments difficult.

To sidestep the issue caused by the subjective nature of relevance, and inspired by the work of Alonso and Mizzaro [1], we define relevance as the majority opinion of a group of qualified assessors. Alonso and Mizzaro [1] found that the majority vote of a group of 10 non-NIST assessors correctly judged the relevance of 28 of 29 documents for a single TREC topic, and that the non-NIST assessors discovered mistakes made by the NIST assessors. We expand on Alonso and Mizzaro's work by considering multiple topics and by using more than twice as many documents.

We demonstrate the usefulness of this approach by comparing NIST assessors to a group of user study participants and in doing so gain a better understanding of both groups.

SIGIR'11, July 24–28, 2011, Beijing, China.
ACM 978-1-4503-0757-4/11/07.

	Gold Standard Judgment	
Assessor	Relevant (Pos.)	Non-Relevant (Neg.)
Relevant	TP = True Pos.	FP = False Pos.
Non-Relevant	FN = False Neg.	TN = True Neg.

Table 1: Confusion Matrix. "Pos." and "Neg." stand for "Positive" and "Negative" respectively.

2. MATERIALS AND METHODS

We use a group's majority opinion to locate instances where NIST assessors may have made mistakes and establish a *gold standard* for a set of relevance judgments.

In making relevance assessments, an assessor has to make a classic signal detection yes/no decision. Once viewed as a signal detection task, it becomes clear that we should analyze the performance of assessors in terms of their true positive rate (TPR) and their false positive rate (FPR), where TPR = $|TP|/(|TP|+|FN|)$ and FPR = $|FP|/(|FP|+|TN|)$ (see Table 1).

Signal detection theory says that an assessor's relevance judging task may be modeled as two normal distributions and a criterion [2]. Given this model of the signal detection task, we can characterize the assessor's ability to discriminate as $d' = z(TPR) - z(FPR)$, and compute the assessor's criterion $c = -\frac{1}{2}(z(TPR) + z(FPR))$, where the function z is the inverse of the normal distribution function [2]. A positive c represents a conservative judging behavior where the assessor misses relevant documents to keep the false positive rate low, and a negative c is liberal, respectively.

As part of a study that we conducted [3], 48 participants judged the relevance of documents for 8 different topics. The topics were from the 2005 TREC Robust track, which used the AQUAINT collection of newswire documents. All the results here are based on phase 1 of the study.

An intentional by-product of our study was that we would obtain a large number of judgments on the same documents.

Topic	Docno	Participant R	Participant N	Participant %	NIST qrel	Gold qrel
336	NYT19980817.0234	10	1	91	N	R
336	NYT20000927.0154	8	4	67	N	R
362	NYT19990313.0150	11	1	92	N	R
362	NYT19980805.0250	9	1	90	N	R
362	XIE20000821.0238	2	8	20	R	N
383	NYT19991214.0159	7	5	58	N	R
427	NYT19990614.0216	5	7	42	R	R
436	XIE19980303.0229	7	4	64	N	R

Table 2: Documents on which participants disagreed with NIST assessors. R=relevant. N=non-relevant.

After conducting our study, we found that some documents were duplicates of each other. For both NIST assessors and study participants, we found cases where the same assessor had conflicting judgments for the same document.

After removing documents found to be duplicates, we had 71 documents with 10 or more judgments. There were 8 documents where the majority opinion of relevance differed from the NIST assessors' and 2 documents where there was a tie. For these 10 documents, we and an undergraduate assistant examined each document to determine whether the majority opinion or the NIST assessor was correct. We in effect acted as "swing votes" to determine the final majority in these few cases.

Both ties were from topic 426 and the NIST assessor had judged them relevant. At first, the relevance of these two documents was not obvious to us, but after looking at other examples of the topic's relevant documents, we set the gold standard judgment to agree with the NIST assessor.

For the remaining 8 of 10 documents, we determined that the majority opinion was correct in 7 of the 8 cases. Table 2 shows the 8 documents and the count of judgments by the participants. For each of the 6 documents judged non-relevant, we found relevant material in the document.

The one case where we found NIST assessors to have made a false positive mistake, it was because the on-topic document failed to describe a specific incident, which was required by the description of relevance for topic 362.

For the seemingly off-topic document where the majority was wrong, the final paragraph contained relevant content.

For both the computation of d' and c, a false positive or true positive rate of 0 or 1 will result in infinities. Rates of 0 and 1 are most often caused by these rates being estimated based on small samples. To better estimate the rates and avoid infinities, we employ a standard correction of adding a pseudo-document to the count of documents judged. Thus, the estimated TPR $= (|TP| + 0.5)/(|TP| + |FN| + 1)$ and the estimated FPR $= (|FP| + 0.5)/(|FP| + |TN| + 1)$.

Of the 8 total search topics, each study participant worked on different sets of 4 topics. As such, it is possible that one participant could have worked on easier topics or sets of documents than another participant. To correctly compare between participants and NIST assessors, we compute the NIST assessors' performance on 48 sets of documents. Each set of documents corresponds to the set of documents that a participant judged. We measure statistical significance using a paired, two-sided, Student's t-test. The measures for each participant are based on an average of 16.8 judgments.

Average	Participants	NIST Assessors	p-value
TPR	0.77	0.77	0.73
FPR	0.18	0.07	< 0.001
d'	1.9	2.3	< 0.001
c	0.10	0.37	< 0.001

Table 3: Results. Please see text for explanation.

3. RESULTS AND DISCUSSION

The averages reported in Table 3 all use estimated TPR and FPR. For the NIST assessors, we average performance over the 48 sets of documents determined by the 48 participants (see Section 2). The NIST performance on the 71 documents is similar with an overall TPR of 0.81 (26/32) and a FPR of 0.03 (1/39).

While our results are not based on a random sample of documents or topics, two observations stand out.

First, our study participants did as well as NIST assessors at judging relevant documents to be relevant. Both study participants and NIST assessors had an average a TPR of 0.77. We hypothesize that the TPR of human assessors is limited by the amount of time that can be devoted to searching a document for relevant material. Unless an assessor reads documents in their entirety, relevant material will be missed and a TPR of less than 1 will result.

Second, NIST assessors rarely judged non-relevant documents as relevant (a false positive). NIST assessors had a much lower FPR of 0.07 compared to the participants' 0.18. There are many possible reasons for this difference including different training, instructions, and user interfaces.

Taken together, the NIST assessors are better able to discriminate relevant from non-relevant documents than the study participants (d' of 2.3 vs. 1.9). While there is considerable variation in the criterion used by participants, on average the participants show little bias with a criterion $c = 0.10$. The NIST assessors were found to have a conservative bias with a $c = 0.37$.

4. CONCLUSION

By defining relevance to be a group's majority opinion, we were able to quantitatively compare the relevance judging performance of NIST assessors and user study participants. We found that while both groups effectively have the same true positive rate, NIST assessors have a significantly lower false positive rate.

5. ACKNOWLEDGMENTS

Special thanks to Gordon Cormack, Ian Soboroff, and Ellen Voorhees for their helpful feedback. As a URI, Michael Tatham did a preliminary analysis of this data. This work was supported in part by NSERC, in part by Amazon, and in part by the University of Waterloo.

6. REFERENCES

[1] O. Alonso and S. Mizzaro. Can we get rid of TREC assessors? Using Mechanical Turk for relevance assessment. In *Proc. SIGIR'09 FIRE Workshop*, pages 15–16, July 2009.

[2] N. Macmillan and C. Creelman. *Detection theory: a user's guide*. Lawrence Erlbaum Associates, 2005.

[3] M. D. Smucker and C. Jethani. Human performance and retrieval precision revisited. In *SIGIR'10*. ACM, 2010.

A Bipartite Graph Based Social Network Splicing Method for Person Name Disambiguation

Jintao Tang[1, 2], Qin Lu[1], Ting Wang[2], Ji Wang[3], Wenjie Li[1]

[1]Department of Computing, Hong Kong Polytechnic University, Hong Kong

[2]College of Computer, National University of Defense Technology, Changsha, P.R. China

[3]National Laboratory for Parallel and Distributed Processing, Changsha, P.R. China

{tangjintao, tingwang, wj}@nudt.edu.cn, {csluqin,cswjli}@comp.polyu.edu.hk

ABSTRACT

The key issue of person name disambiguation is to discover different namesakes in massive web documents rather than simply cluster documents by using textual features. In this paper, we describe a novel person name disambiguation method based on social networks to effectively identify namesakes. The social network snippets in each document are extracted. Then, the namesakes are identified via splicing the social networks of each namesake by using the snippets as a bipartite graph. Experimental results show that our method achieves better result than the top performance of WePS-2 in identifying different namesakes.

Categories and Subject Descriptors

H.3.3 [**Information Storage Retrieval**]: Information Search and Retrieval—*Clustering*; I.2.7 [**Artificial Intelligence**]: Natural Language Processing—*Text analysis*

General Terms

Algorithms, Experimentation

Keywords

Person name disambiguation, Social network, Bipartite graph.

1. INTRODUCTION

Name is not a unique identifier for a person. Normally, when you search for a person, say, "Andrew McCallum", a search engine will use it as a keyword and return pages relevant to any person with this name without distinguishing different "Andrew McCallum"s. Recently, person name disambiguation has become as an open challenge in many web-mining areas such as social network extraction, web people search and so on.

Recent works on person name disambiguation were reported at the WePS workshops [1]. The typical approach uses the set of webpages that contain the person name to cluster the pages based on the features contained in the pages [2]. However, we thought that the most important issue is to pinpoint each specific namesake based on the features that can uniquely identify them.

It is reasonable to assume that different namesakes have different social circles. Social network information can be a discriminative feature to identify the different namesakes. Existing works use social networks as common word co-occurrence features [3, 4]. However, there usually are millions of webpages mentioned the searched name n, so the names that co-occur with n in these webpages are high dimensional for the set, yet sparse in each document. The sparseness of feature in the aforementioned techniques is problematic. Since social networks are more like relational data, its network structure should be more useful to identify a specific person. This paper proposes a bipartite graph based person name disambiguation method using social network information directly. First, we represent each document by the social network snippet of a specific person. Then an effective bipartite graph based similarity measure is used to splice these snippets. As a result, different namesakes are identified and their social networks are generated. Experimental results show that the method has good ability of identify different namesakes.

2. Algorithm Design

Let n denotes a name entity. The set of webpages mentioned n, including its variants, is denoted by $D_n = \{d_1, d_2, \cdots, d_k\}$. All the names that co-occur with n in d_i, referred as its neighbors and denoted by s_j, forms the social network snippet for n as $d_i = \{s_1, s_2, \cdots, s_m\}$. Variants of s_i are also resolved and included to address the co-reference problem. The variants of n include abbreviated forms, last name and first name rotated forms, middle name initialized forms, middle name dropped forms, and combinations of them. From the relationship between n and its neighbors, we can construct a *candidate-neighbor* bipartite graph with the set of candidate nodes C_n and the set of neighbor nodes S_n as follows. A *candidate node* c_i is created for each possible specific namesake of n. First, each document d_i in D_n is considered as a *candidate node*. A *neighbor node* s_j is created for each name entity in the documents. A *social edge* e_{ij} is created between the *candidate node* c_i and a *neighbor node* s_j if s_j co-occur with n in the same paragraph in c_i. The weight w_{ij} of edge e_{ij} is the normalized frequency when both s_j and n occur in the same paragraph of d_i. **Figure 1** shows an example of a *candidate neighbor* graph.

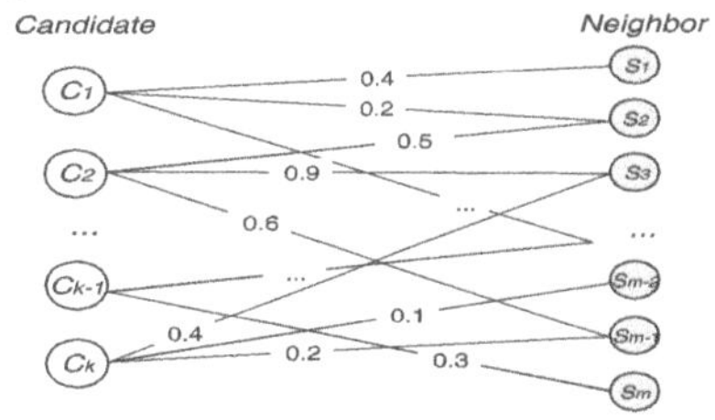

Figure 1. An Example of Candidate-Neighbor Bipartite.

Then we can cluster the bipartite graph to gradually merge similar *candidate nodes*. It is reasonable to assume that if two *candidates* share many *neighbors*, it is likely that they refer to the same person. So we propose a similarity measure based on the bipartite graph, and use a bottom-up method to cluster the *candidate nodes* for person name disambiguation. The distance between two *candidate nodes* c_i and c_j is,

$$dis(c_i, c_j) = \sqrt{\sum_{s_k \in S_n} (w_{ik} - w_{jk})^2} \quad (1)$$

According to this similarity measure, the normalized centroid

SIGIR'11, July 24–28, 2011, Beijing, China.

ACM 978-1-4503-0757-4/11/07.

method with dimension measures proposed in [5] is applied to clustering of the *candidate nodes*. The co-occurrence names in the million-scale webpages are high dimensional and sparse, which make the "curse of dimensionality" emerge as a great challenge. We use the *dimension array data structure* [5], to reduce clustering complexity effectively. Furthermore, we use the clusters as new candidate nodes to generate a new *candidate-neighbor* bipartite graph to gradually cluster the *candidate nodes* until the result is stable.

3. EXPERIMENTS

The WePS-2 task dataset [1] is used in our experiment. The WePS-2 test set consists of 30 names, each of which has 150 pages. A similarity threshold for the clustering algorithm to control the granularity of clusters is determined experimentally. Since our objective is to correctly identify different namesakes, we use the WePS-1 dataset to train the similarity threshold by appointing a strict correctness condition. Then, we test the webpages clustering performance of the proposed method by using the *B-Cubed* measure to compare with the *Top 3* systems reported in WePS-2. We also design a two-step clustering method based on [6] to incorporate the bipartite graph based method with textual features so the cluster result from our method is considered as a new document and then the textual features such as *URL, token, title* and *bigram* are used to compute the textural similarity among these documents.

Table 1. Clustering Results on WePS-2 Dataset

	BEP	BER	F1
WePS2 Top 1	0.87	0.79	0.82
WePS2 Top 2	.0.85	0.80	0.81
WePS2 Top 3	0.93	0.73	0.81
Bipartite Graph	**0.95**	0.53	0.68
Two-Step	0.90	0.78	**0.83**

Table 1 shows that the bipartite graph based clustering method is quite discriminative. The *B-Cubed precision* (BEP) of this method is the highest among all the compared systems. The reason is that the social circles differ a lot in different namesakes and the bipartite graph based method can catch the differences of the social networks. The two-step clustering method also shows high precision as it uses the bipartite graph based method as its first step. It gives the best *F1* value because the use of textual features obviously improves the recall for document clustering.

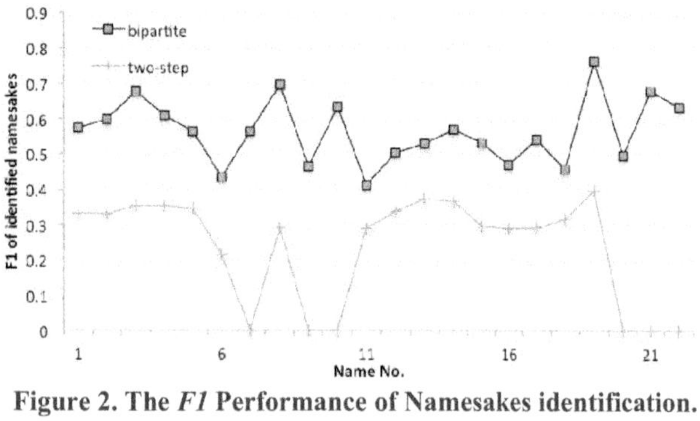

Figure 2. The *F1* Performance of Namesakes identification.

However, the *B-Cubed measures* are not designed for name entity disambiguation. When applied to namesakes being clustered, BEP does not penalize the same namesake being in separate clusters and BER does not penalize different namesakes being in the same cluster. So the criterion for namesakes clustering should be that a namesake is uniquely identified by a cluster. In other words, a cluster can identify a specific person if and only if the webpages in this cluster belong to this person. So, the *precision, recall* and *F1* on the clustering results to namesakes are examined. **Figure 2** shows the evaluation on our two proposed methods through the evaluation on namesakes' identification. Contrary to the result in **Table 1**, the namesake *F1* shows that the bipartite graph based method's average *F1* is 0.563 with standard deviation of 0.094, whereas for the two-step clustering method, its average *F1* is only 0.231 with standard deviation of 0.154. This means that the bipartite graph based method is better in its identification of unique namesakes as well as having less volatility. Since the testing data is a closed set, further investigation shows that some persons do not have social network information in these webpages. In these cases, the two-step clustering has better ability to use the additional textural feature to identify similarity of documents as indicated in **Table 1** to get better clustering performance. However, the additional textual features also introduce noises, which indeed affects its ability to uniquely identify namesakes.

4. CONCLUSION

A new algorithm for person name disambiguation is proposed to use social network information to identify different namesakes. A bipartite graph based method is used to effectively splice the social networks in the high dimensional and sparse data. As a result, different namesakes are identified and the social network of each specific person is generated. Experimental results show that our proposed method is discriminative to identify the namesakes and has better performance than the top performers in WePS-2.

5. ACKNOWLEDGEMENT

The research is supported by NSF of China (60873097, 60933005), the National Grand Fundamental Research Program of China (2011CB302603), and the Human Language Tech Lab, Dept. of Computing, Hong Kong Polytechnic University.

6. REFERENCES

[1] Amigó, E., Artiles, J., Gonzalo, J., et al. WePS-3 Evaluation Campaign: Overview of the Online Reputation Management Task. *In Proceedings of the 3rd Web People Search Evaluation Workshop* (Padova,Italy, 2010).

[2] Han, X., Zhao, J. Named entity disambiguation by leveraging wikipedia semantic knowledge. *Proceeding of the 18th ACM conference on Information and knowledge management* (Jan 1 2009), 215-224.

[3] Malin, B. Unsupervised name disambiguation via social network similarity. *SIAM SDM Workshop on Link Analysis, Counterterrorism and Security2005*, 93–102.

[4] Yoshida, M., Ikeda, M., Ono, S. et al. Person name disambiguation by bootstrapping. *Proceeding of the 33rd international ACM SIGIR conference on Research and development in information retrieval*(Jul 1 2010).

[5] Cao, H., Jiang, D., Pei, J. et al. Context-aware query suggestion by mining click-through and session data. *Proceeding of the 14th ACM SIGKDD international conference on Knowledge discovery and data mining*(2008).

[6] M. Ikeda, S. Ono, I. Sato, M. et al. Person Name Disambiguation on the Web by Two-Stage Clustering. *2nd Web People Search Evaluation Workshop* (WePS 2009).

Link Formation Analysis in Microblogs

Dawei Yin Liangjie Hong Xiong Xiong Brian D. Davison
Department of Computer Science & Engineering, Lehigh University
Bethlehem, PA, USA
{day207, lih307, xix209, davison}@cse.lehigh.edu

ABSTRACT

Unlike a traditional social network service, a microblogging network like Twitter is a hybrid network, combining aspects of both social networks and information networks. Understanding the structure of such hybrid networks and to predict new links are important for many tasks such as friend recommendation, community detection, and network growth models. In this paper, by analyzing data collected over time, we find that 90% of new links are to people just two hops away and dynamics of friend acquisition are also related to users' account age. Finally, we compare two popular sampling methods which are widely used for network analysis and find that ForestFire does not preserve properties required for the link prediction task.

Categories and Subject Descriptors: H.3.3 [Information Storage and Retrieval]: Information Search and Retrieval

General Terms: Algorithms, Experimentation, Performance

Keywords: link formation, link analysis, microblogs, link prediction

1. INTRODUCTION

The use of online social networks and social media in general has surged in recent years. In this work, we focus on the understanding of link formation of one particular type of social service—that of the microblogging network. In microblog services such as Twitter, Yammer and Google Buzz, participants form an explicit social network by "following" (subscribing to) another user. Unlike common online social networks such as Facebook, LinkedIn or Myspace, a followed user has the option but not the requirement to similarly follow back. Thus, relationships in these social networks may be asymmetric. Thus, User B in a microblog service can generate messages, and any followers of B, such as A, will automatically receive those messages along with messages generated by all other users that A follows. The combination of multiple message intentions and asymmetry of connections has led some to call microblogging services such as Twitter "hybrid networks" [4]. They are hybrid not just because they can carry multiple types of messages, but also because participants create links for multiple reasons—to be social (e.g., to connect online to existing offline social contacts) or to link to an information source [4].

Recently, Golder et al. [2] discuss prediction specifically in Twitter. They analyze several principles for link prediction, such as shared interests, shared followers, and mutuality. Romero and Kleinberg [4] also introduce the hybrid network concept and study the directed closure process in Twitter link formation. In this paper, by analyzing data collected over time, we will uncover more properties for the link formation in ego-centric networks.

SIGIR'11, July 24–28, 2011, Beijing, China.
ACM 978-1-4503-0757-4/11/07.

Type	Dynamic	Static	ForestFire
Unknown	0.08126	0.05939	0.90350
⇔⇔	**0.48712**	**0.49710**	0.00028
⇔⇒	0.03974	0.02341	0.00102
⇔⇐	0.04082	0.06068	0.00264
⇒⇔	0.01636	0.05391	0.00155
⇒⇒	0.03706	0.06889	**0.04457**
⇒⇐	0.01112	0.03830	0.01955
⇐⇔	0.17471	0.12875	0.00087
⇐⇒	0.02700	0.00869	0.00456
⇐⇐	0.08477	0.06084	0.02141

Table 1: The distribution of relationship types for new links.

2. DATASETS AND ANLYSIS

We randomly sampled 1000 users out of 9,026,165 users active between early February and the end of March 2010. Though users may appear multiple times in the public timeline, we sampled by name, not by tweet, so highly active users had no additional selection advantage. In the end, we had 979 users as our target users.[1] We monitored daily the changes in the selected users' ego-centric networks on Twitter. The number of immediate friends and followers of the 979 target users was nearly 200,000. The data we used in this paper is from April 5th to May 12th, 2010.[2]

2.1 New Links Analysis

By regularly monitoring changing networks, we can determine from where new links come. We examined the changes of ego-networks for each of the 979 users. We collected a total of 18,777 new friends for the 979 users. Most new users are friends of friends. In particular, 17,251 (91.78%) new friends were second level neighbors within the target user's ego-network and the remaining 781 ($P_{unknown} = 8.12\%$) new friends were of unknown relationship (i.e., more than two hops away). For each new friend, we further check its relationship type with the 979 target users.

Table 1 shows the distribution of relationship patterns for each new friend, prior to link creation. For example, ⇔⇔ means the new friend is the reciprocal friend of some reciprocal friend of the target users. Similarly, ⇒⇒ means the new friend is the following-only friend of some following-only friend of the target user. It is similar for other types. Based on the results shown in Table 1, if

[1]During monitoring, 21 users changed their privacy setting to "protect", preventing us from continuing to collect their information.
[2]The data is prior to the introduction of Twitter's friend recommendation system which may introduce a link formation bias.

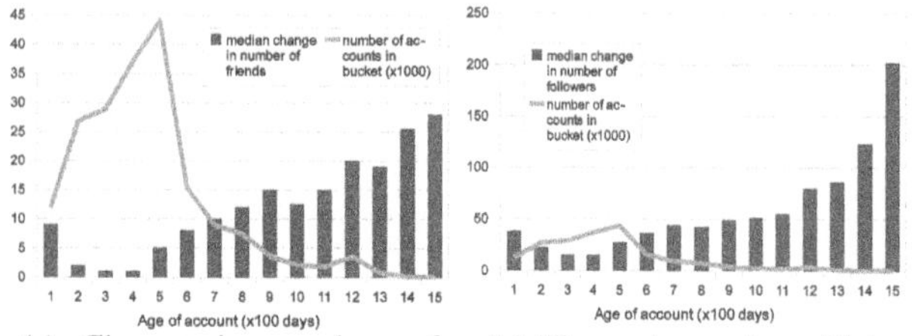

(a) Change in number of friends. (b) Change in number of followers.

Figure 1: From April to August 2010, the changes in the median number of neighbors as a function of account age.

we consider only two-hop neighbors in the ego-network as candidates to recommend as friends, we will only miss 8.12% of new friends. Another interesting result is that if the two users share an audience, it does not mean that they are interested in each other. Among two-hop users, most of the new friends have relationships $\Leftrightarrow\Leftrightarrow$, $\Leftarrow\Leftrightarrow$, $\Leftarrow\Leftarrow$. In contrast, Romero and Kleinberg [4] only find $\Rightarrow\Rightarrow$ to be a factor of link formation. We extend their observations and find $\Leftrightarrow\Leftrightarrow$ is by far the most important indicator for future link formation.

2.2 Age Analysis

We analyze the relationship between the changes in the size of a user's network and user's account age. We compare two snapshots (April 5th 2010 and August 20th 2010) of profiles of 200,000 users. The results are shown in Figure 1. The x-axis is the user's account age and y-axis is the median change in the number of neighbors. We find that in the very beginning (within 100 days), the users add many friends and then for the older users (100-400 days), their friends seem more stable. For much older users (more than 500 days), we find that their number of new friends is larger and larger, not as we might expect. For followers, Figure 1(b) shows a *rich get richer* pattern; the older the user, the larger the increase in followers. A more detailed analysis (not shown for space) reveals that young accounts (e.g., less than two years) have a larger (but decreasing over time) change in followers and friends, while more established accounts (from about two years on) have a more consistent relative growth rate.

3. COMPARING SAMPLING METHODS

Link prediction experiments are usually based on a sampled graph rather than the whole graph before deploying it on the real system. However, real dynamic data is often not available, in which case, artificial data is necessary. We study two methods. ForestFire [3] is a popular sampling method, preserving graph properties on the sampled graph, such as some static properties (e.g., degree distributions, clustering coefficients), temporal properties (e.g., shrinking diameters) and cascading properties (shown in [1]). We sample a graph by ForestFire, which contains 1,607,178 users, and remove 10% links at random as test data. Another data set is based on the April 5th snapshot of ego-centric networks. For 1000 egos, we remove 10% links at random as test data, which we call Static data. Treating those removed data as the new links, we perform the same analysis experiment as Section 2.1 to analyze whether the artificial data can retain properties consistent with real data. The results are also shown in Table 1. The Static data keeps consistent the distribution among all kinds of the two-hop relationships. For ForestFire, the properties are quite different from Dynamic: fewer than 10% of the candidates are found on the second hop, causing ego-network based structural methods, such as common neighbors and Jaccard's coefficient, to fail on such cases.

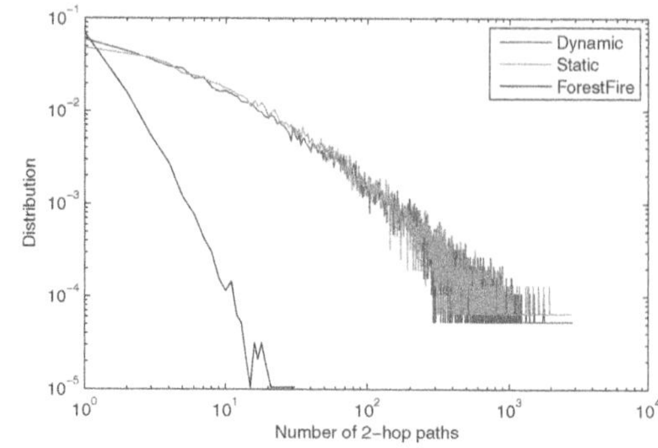

Figure 2: Distribution of links with exactly x 2-hop paths in the graph generated by each sampling method

Furthermore, the distribution of two-hop relationships are also changed in ForestFire. The fraction of $\Leftrightarrow\Leftrightarrow$ becomes very low and $\Rightarrow\Rightarrow$ becomes higher. We also draw the distribution of the number of 2-hop paths from the target users to the candidates. Figure 2 shows the distribution of three data sets. We can see that the distribution of Static data is very similar to the Dynamic data, but the distribution of ForestFire is considerably different from real Dynamic data. That means that even when we only use the candidates who are still available via two hops from the target users as our test data, the algorithms may still generate different performance, compared with the real Dynamic data. These experimental results suggests that for the link prediction task, the common evaluation method which is based on ForestFire sampled data may not produce the same the results as real data. Finally, we run a simple but popular method—Jaccard's coefficient—on the three data sets.[3] The results are 0.116 in Dynamic, 0.071 in Static, and 0.0013 in ForestFire data respectively. As we expect, it fails in the ForestFire data set and the performances on Dynamic and Static are somewhat similar.

4. CONCLUSION

By analyzing data collected over time, we find that 90% of new links are to people just two hops away and the dynamics of new link creation are affected by the user's account age. Based on these properties, we compare two methods of collecting network data—ForestFire and Ego-network sampling. The results show that ForestFire does not preserve important properties of the ego-network and is thus not suitable for the link prediction task.

Acknowledgments

This work was supported in part by a grant from the National Science Foundation under award IIS-0545875.

5. REFERENCES

[1] M. De Choudhury, Y.-R. Lin, H. Sundaram, K. S. Candan, L. Xie, and A. Kelliher. How Does the Data Sampling Strategy Impact the Discovery of Information Diffusion in Social Media? In *ICWSM 2010*.

[2] S. Golder and S. Yardi. Structural predictors of tie formation in Twitter: Transitivity and mutuality. In *SocialCom 2010*.

[3] J. Leskovec and C. Faloutsos. Sampling from large graphs. In *KDD 2006*, pages 631–636.

[4] D. Romero and J. Kleinberg. The directed closure process in hybrid social-information networks, with an analysis of link formation on twitter. In *ICWSM 2010*.

[3]We use the standard F_1-measure in the break even point.

Evolution of Web Search Results within Years

Ismail Sengor Altingovde[1]
L3S Research Center
Hannover, Germany
altingovde@l3s.de

Rifat Ozcan
Computer Eng., Bilkent University
Ankara, Turkey
rozcan@cs.bilkent.edu.tr

Özgür Ulusoy
Computer Eng., Bilkent University
Ankara, Turkey
oulusoy@cs.bilkent.edu.tr

ABSTRACT
We provide a first large-scale analysis of the evolution of query results obtained from a real search engine at two distant points in time, namely, in 2007 and 2010, for a set of 630,000 real queries.

Categories and Subject Descriptors
H.3.3 [**Information Storage and Retrieval**]: Information Search and Retrieval.

General Terms
Experimentation.

1. INTRODUCTION
The dynamicity of Web takes an increasing attention from the researchers as many studies investigating the changes in the Web content (e.g., [2]) and user queries (e.g., [7]) emerged in the last years. While these works provide quite valuable insight on the dynamics of Web search, another important dimension is usually overlooked: How do the real life search engines react to this dynamicity? That is, how the changes in the underlying collection and in the search engine's internal algorithms affect the query results presented to the end user? In this paper, we provide a first large-scale analysis of the evolution of query results obtained from a real search engine at two distant points in time, namely, in 2007 and 2010, for the same set of 630,000 real life queries.

To the best of our knowledge, only a few earlier works investigate the evolution of real search results. In one of the earliest studies, 25 queries are submitted daily to a number of search engines for a month to observe the stability of top-10 results [6]. A similar experiment with a larger set of 12,000 queries is reported in [3]. Bar-Ilan and Peritz monitor the change of a single topic, namely, "informetrics", for a period of 8 years [1]. Finally, McCown and Nelson investigate whether the application programming interfaces (APIs) provided by major search engines yield results synchronized with those retrieved from the Web interface [4]. In their experiments, 100 keyword queries are repeatedly submitted to different search APIs for five months. Nevertheless, our work differs from these in the following aspects: (i) Our queries are not synthetic, but taken from a real life query log, (ii) While the previous works involve a limited number of queries, we use a large set of 630,000 queries, (iii) We analyze real results retrieved by a commercial search engine in two points in time that are more than 3 years apart, and (iv) We focus on the properties of the results, rather than the evolution of the underlying collection.

Our analysis in this paper attempts to find answers to several high-level questions regarding the evolution of Web search results, such as: How is the growth in Web reflected to top-ranked query results? Do the query results totally change within time? Does higher number of Web documents lead to results that are located deeper in the Web site hierarchies? Do the result titles and extracted snippets exhibit any variation in time? We believe that this work, being the largest-scale longitudinal analysis of query results, would shed some light on these questions. We present our findings in the next section and summarize key results in Sec. 3.

2. EVOLUTION OF QUERY RESULTS
We used 630,000 unique queries that are randomly sampled from AOL Query Log [5]. For these queries, we obtained top-100 results from Web using Yahoo!'s public search API, twice: in June, 2007 and in December, 2010. Experiments spanned the entire month in each case, due to large number of queries. We identified a few Web sites that only listed all AOL query strings and removed them from the results as they are not real answers.

Number of query results. First, we simply compare the average number of results per query, as reported by the search engine. We are aware that these numbers are not completely reliable [4], but they still give a rough idea of how the result space has changed for our queries. We find that the average number of results per query is increased from 16.5M to 52.3M. This seems to be an expected result, as the Web has probably grown an order of magnitude from 2007 to 2010. Fig. 1(a) shows the distribution of queries based on the reported result counts in 2007 and 2010. Fig. 1(b) shows the percentage of queries whose result counts are increased or decreased in 2010 with respect to their result counts in 2007. For instance, 70% of the queries, which return at most 10 results in 2007, return more results in 2010. However, the increase percentage is lower for queries that have returned a small result set (i.e., less than 1000 results) in 2007. In contrast, queries with large number of results in 2007 can match to even larger number of results in 2010.

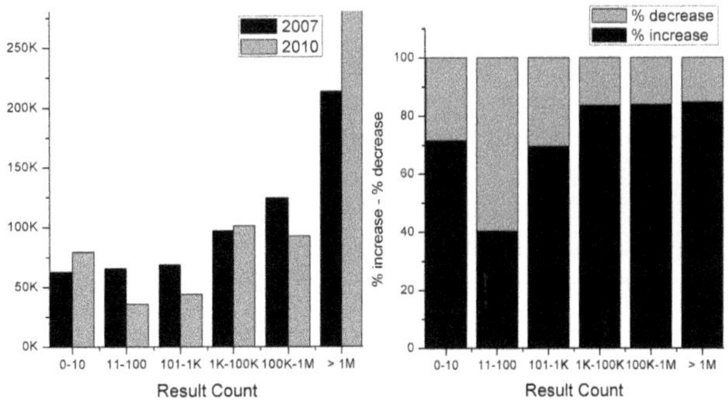

(a) Query count vs. result count (b) Result count change

Figure 1. Changes in the number of results in 2007 and 2010

[1] This work was done while the author was at Bilkent University.

SIGIR'11, July 24–28, 2011, Beijing, China.
ACM 978-1-4503-0757-4/11/07.

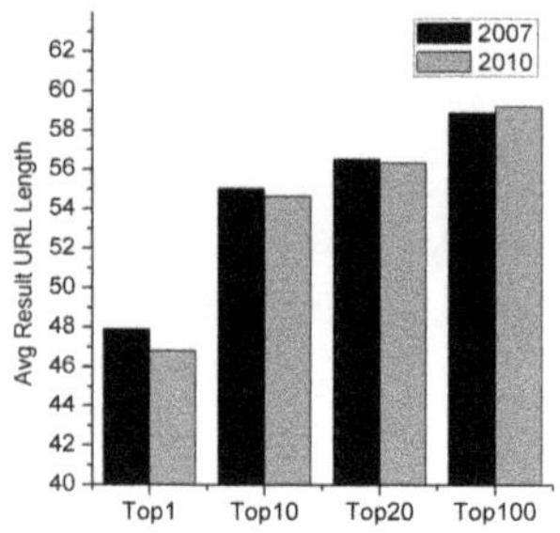

Figure 2. Result URL length

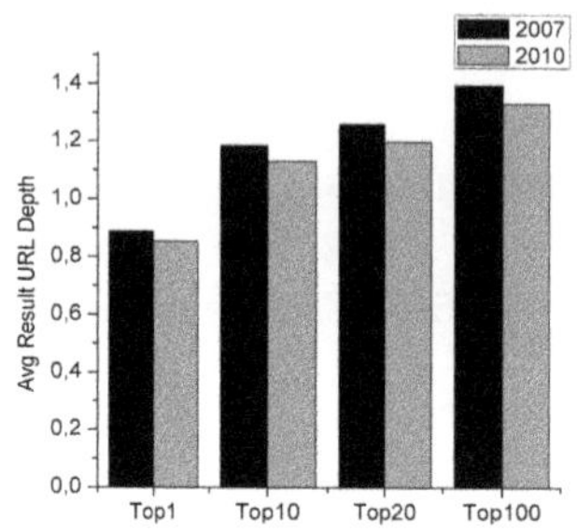

Figure 3. Result URL depth

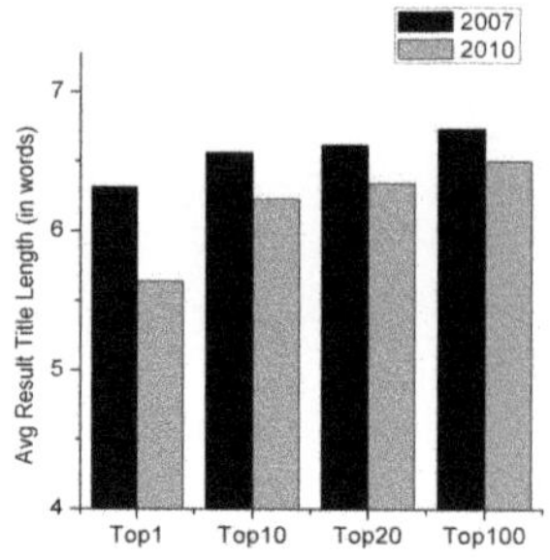

Figure 4. Result title length

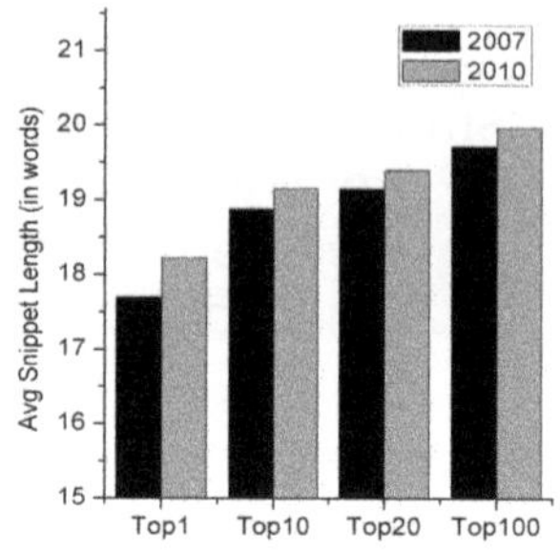

Figure 5. Snippet length

Table 1. Number of unique URLs in the query results.

	2007	2010	Overlap (% w.r.t 2010)
Top-1	475,860	437,483	87,248 (19.9%)
Top-10	4,377,299	4,456,026	476,649 (10.7%)
Top-20	8,330,692	8,737,776	836,125 (9.6%)
Top-100	34,576,357	39,437,931	3,384,122 (8.6%)

Length and depth of result URLs. In Figs. 2 and 3, we report the average length (in bytes) and depth of unique result URLs, respectively (The domain name is assumed to have a depth of 0.). We investigate whether the increase in the number of documents causes a search engine to retrieve pages that are located in a deeper position at a Web site. In contrary to this expectation, both URL length and depth decrease in 2010, which means that search engines prefer to retrieve pages at the top level of a domain most of the time. We also observe that the length and depth of URLs increase for those results that are ranked lower.

Number of unique URLs and domain names. In Table 1, we provide total number of unique URLs observed in top-*k* results ($k \in \{1, 10, 20, 100\}$) in 2007 and 2010. While this number slightly decreases for top-1 case, we observe a trend of increase with increasing values *k*. For top-100 results, the number of unique URLs increases by 14% in 2010 results. We also investigate the overlap in the retrieved URLs in 2007 and 2010. We find that 20% of the URLs returned at the highest rank in 2010 were at the same position in 2007. This implies that the "valuable" document space (i.e., documents that can answer real queries) does not grow in proportion with the entire Web.

Table 2. Number of unique domain names in query results.

	2007	2010	Overlap (% w.r.t 2010)
Top-1	230,464	242,859	90,040 (37.1%)
Top-10	1,065,881	1,362,538	373,811 (27.4%)
Top-20	1,678,452	2,249,991	599,280 (26.6%)
Top-100	4,462,468	6,599,437	1,705,899 (25.8%)

In Table 2, we make a similar analysis for unique domain names. The number of domains in top-*k* results is significantly smaller than the number of unique URLs, which implies that result documents share a smaller number of domains. The increase in unique domain names in 2010 is more emphasized in comparison to the increase in the number of unique URLs. For top-100 results, unique domains grow by a factor of 50% in 2010. On the other hand, the fraction of domains that have also appeared in the corresponding top-*k* list in 2007 is high, e.g., around 37% for top-1 results. This indicates that the domains that hosted query results in 2007 are successful for answering queries in 2010, as well.

Length of result titles and snippets. In Figs. 4 and 5, we present the average length of result title and snippet in terms of unique words. We see that, the both values increase for larger number of retrieved results. A comparison between 2007 and 2010 reveals that the search engine prefers to provide slightly shorter result titles and longer snippets in 2010. We guess that shorter titles aim to help the searcher to grasp the returned result more quickly, whereas the longer snippets possibly aim to be more informative.

3. KEY FINDINGS AND FUTURE WORK

Our key findings are: (i) we observe that although Web has probably grown significantly from mid-2007 to the end of 2010, this growth is mostly reflected to queries that already have rich results sets, but not to the other poor queries. (ii) A potentially high-quality set of URLs and domains appear in the query results of both 2007 and 2010. (iii) Result URL length and depth, as well as the title and snippet lengths, tend to increase at lower result ranks. The first three features are slightly smaller, whereas the last one, snippet length, is larger in 2010 in comparison to 2007.

In the future, we plan to make a query-wise analysis of our data.

4. ACKNOWLEDGMENTS

This work is partially supported by The Scientific and Technological Research Council of Turkey (TÜBİTAK) under grant no. 110E135 and FP7 EU Project LivingKnowledge (contract no. 231126).

5. REFERENCES

[1] Bar-Ilan, J., Peritz, B.C. The lifespan of "informetrics" on the Web: An eight year study (1998-2006). Scientometrics, 79(1), 7–25, 2009.

[2] Fetterly, D., Manasse, M., Najork, M., Wiener, J.L. A large-scale study of the evolution of web pages. In *Proc. of WWW*, 669–678, 2003.

[3] Kim, J., Carvalho, V.R. An analysis of time-instability in Web search results. In *Proc. of ECIR*, 466–478, 2011.

[4] McCown, F., Nelson, M.L. Search engines and their public interfaces: which apis are the most synchronized? In *Proc. of WWW*, 1197–1198, 2007.

[5] Pass, G., Chowdhury, A., Torgeson, C. A picture of search. In *Proc. of the 1st INFOSCALE*, 1, 2006.

[6] Selberg, E., Etzioni, O. On the Instability of Web Search Engines. In *Proc. of RIAO*, 223–236, 2000.

[7] Spink, A., Jansen, B.J. A Study of Web Search Trends. Webology 1(2), 2004.

Decayed DivRank: Capturing Relevance, Diversity and Prestige in Information Networks

Pan Du*, Jiafeng Guo, and Xue-Qi Cheng
Institute of Computing Technology, CAS
Beijing 100190, China
{dupan, guojiafeng}@software.ict.ac.cn, cxq@ict.ac.cn

ABSTRACT

Many network-based ranking approaches have been proposed to rank objects according to different criteria, including relevance, prestige and diversity. However, existing approaches either only aim at one or two of the criteria, or handle them with additional heuristics in multiple steps. Inspired by DivRank, we propose a unified ranking model, Decayed DivRank (DDRank), to meet the three criteria simultaneously. Empirical experiments on paper citation network show that DDRank can outperform existing algorithms in capturing relevance, diversity and prestige simultaneously in ranking.

Categories and Subject Descriptors

H.2.8 [**Database Applications**]: Data Mining

General Terms

Algorithms, Experimentation

Keywords

Diversity, Relevance, Prestige, Multi-objective Ranking

1. INTRODUCTION

Information networks are widely used to characterize the relationships between data objects. Ranking objects over information networks is a key problem in many real applications, where relevance, prestige and diversity are the three most recognized criteria. Two canonical approaches for network-based ranking are PageRank [1] and HITS [4], which mainly focus on the prestige of objects in ranking. Later, Personalized PageRank [3] was introduced to capture relevance as well as prestige. Recently, diversity in ranking has been widely studied [6] and different methods have been proposed, including GrassHopper [7], MRSP [2] and DivRank [5]. However, existing approaches either only aim at one or two of the three criteria, or handle them with additional heuristics (e.g. greedy vertex selection for diversity) in multiple steps.

In this paper, we propose a novel ranking model, Decayed DivRank (DDRank), to address relevance, prestige and diversity in a unified way. Our work is inspired by the model DivRank proposed by Moi et al. [5]. DivRank is basically a query independent ranking model, which balances prestige and diversity elegantly in ranking through a vertex-reinforced random walk process. One may turn DivRank into a query dependent model by simply introducing a query dependent prior. However, the reinforce process in DivRank essentially changes the structure of information network. In this way, the relevance between objects and the query, which is fully depend on the primitive network structure, may not be well captured. Different from DivRank, DDRank partially preserves the local relationship between objects around the query, and enhances the competitiveness of these objects in the process. The preserving and reinforcing operations over the network structure "cooperate" to acquire relevance and diversity simultaneously during the time-variant random walk process. Experiments conducted on paper citation network demonstrate the effectiveness of the proposed DDRank in capturing relevance, prestige and diversity simultaneously.

2. DECAYED DIVRANK

Before describing the DDRank approach, we first introduce the original DivRank. The iteration process of DivRank is described as equation 1:

$$f_{t+1}^T = \alpha f_t^T (P_0 N_t) D_t^{-1} + (1-\alpha) r^T, \ 0 \le \alpha \le 1 \quad (1)$$

where $P_0 = \beta P + (1-\beta) I$, $0 \le \beta \le 1$ and $D_t(i,i) = \sum_{j=1}^{n} P_0(i,j) N_t(j,j)$, f^T is the ranking score vector and r^T is the prior vector about relevance. P is the primitive transition matrix acquired from the adjacent relationship of a weighted network. P_0 is the new transition matrix on which the vertex-reinforced random walk depend. I is an identity matrix to forge self-links. The self-links in P_0 help to prevent the vertices from losing the profit already acquired during the reinforcement. N_t is a diagonal matrix with each diagonal element recording the visiting times of corresponding object. It acts as the reinforcing factor during the random walk process. Matrix D_t is to re-normalize PN_t into a transition matrix P_t, and to make sure the process will eventually converge.

We now describe our DDRank model, a query dependent ranking model where relevance, prestige and diversity are addressed simultaneously, To capture the relevance, we try to preserve the local structure around the query, and improve the competitiveness of these relevant objects during the DivRank process. For this purpose, we modify the DivRank algorithm by re-weighting the reinforcement on each object according to the relevance between the corresponding object and the query. In this way, we can achieve two goals: 1) If the object is more relevant to the query, it will be more competitive. 2) The competition between objects near the query is weaker than that away from it, which makes

*This work was supported by the National High-tech R&D Program of China under grant No.2010AA012500.

SIGIR'11, July 24–28, 2011, Beijing, China.
ACM 978-1-4503-0757-4/11/07.

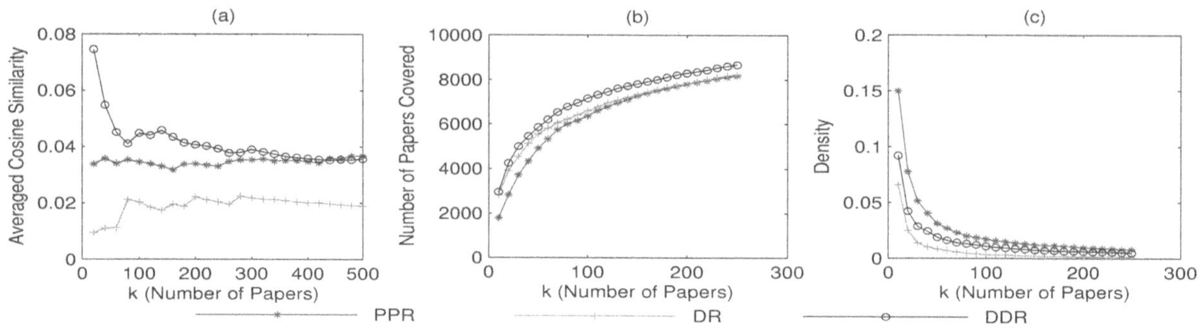

Figure 1: Performance comparison on relevance, prestige and diversity.

tradeoff between relevance and diversity. Therefore, we can balance relevance, prestige and diversity during the vertex-reinforced random walk.

Formally, the DDRank model can be described as follows:

$$f_{t+1}^T = \alpha f_t^T (P_0 N_t^{1-r}) D_t^{-1} + (1-\alpha) r^T,\ 0 \le \alpha \le 1 \quad (2)$$

where $P_0 = \beta P + (1-\beta) I,\ 0 \le \beta \le 1$ and $D_t(i,i) = \sum_{j=1}^{n} P_0(i,j) N_t(j,j)^{1-r}$. If the network is ergodic, after a sufficiently large t, the reinforced random walk defined by equation 2 also converges to a stationary distribution π. Then this distribution is used to rank the vertices in the information network by DDRank.

From equation 2 we can find that the ratio of N_t between a couple of neighbors (denoted as $\tilde{a} \approx \left[\frac{N_t(1)}{N_t(2)}\right]^{1-r} = a^{1-r}$) is suppressed according to their relevance r because the first order derivative form of $\tilde{a}$ on r is $\tilde{a}'_r = -ln(a)a^{1-r}$. We have $\tilde{a}'_r > 0$ if $a < 0$, and $\tilde{a}'_r < 0$ if $a > 0$. Similarly, the first order derivative form of reinforcement (denoted as $\tilde{e} = N_t^{(1-r)}$) on r is $\tilde{e}'_r = -ln(N_t)N_t^{1-r}$. Noting that $N_t \le 1$, we have $\tilde{e}'_r \ge 0$. This means the more relevant objects are attached more competitiveness than the less relevant ones in DDRank. Relevance r is approximated by the similarity between the query and others in our experiment.

3. EMPIRICAL RESULTS

In this section, we evaluate the effectiveness of DDRank empirically. Due to the space limitation, we only demonstrate the experiments conducted on a paper citation network. The paper citation network is known as the ACL Anthology Network (AAN)[1], which covers 11609 papers, with unit-weighted edges from each paper to the papers it cited. Given a paper, the task aims to find the most relevant, prestigious and diverse papers from the paper-citation network.

Ideally, the contents of the top-K selected papers should be relevant to that of the given paper. We leverages the average cosine similarity of the top-K papers' contents to evaluate the relevance performance. The assumption is that the relevant papers should be similar with each other, since they are all similar with the given paper. Hence, higher average cosine similarity implies good relevance of the top-K papers. Following [5], we use "impact coverage" of the top-K papers as the prestige measure. "Impact Coverage" counts the number of unique papers citing the top-K papers. The basic assumption is that the ideal top-K papers should be cited by as many unique papers as possible. One could notice that the "impact coverage" measure is not a pure prestige measure, where there is also an implicit notion of diversity.

[1] Downloadable at http://clair.si.umich.edu/clair/anthology/

Density measure evaluate the *inverse* diversity of the top-K papers. The density of a network is defined as the number of edges presenting in the network divided by the maximal possible number of edges in the network. Hence we can use the density of the subgraph $d(G_K)$ composed by the top-K papers as an inverse measure of diversity in top-K ranked papers. The assumption is that the smaller $d(G_K)$ is, the more independent the top-K papers are, thus higher diversity is contained by the top ranked papers.

We compare our method with personalized PageRank and DivRank with a simple prior, which records the cosine similarity of each paper with the given paper. The performance of relevance, prestige and diversity are demonstrated in Figure 1(a), 1(b) and 1(c) respectively. Personalized PageRank is denoted as PPR, DivRank as DR, and Decayed DivRank as DDR in the figures. From Figure 1, we can see that our approach outperforms Personalized PageRank and DivRank on relevance (as shown in Figure 1(a), the higher the better) and prestige (as shown in Figure 1(b), the higher the better). The performance on diversity (as shown in Figure 1(c), the lower the better) lies between personalized PageRank and DivRank, as can be expected.

In summary, experiments conducted on the paper citation network from AAN show that DDivRank balances the ranking criteria of relevance, diversity and prestige successfully in a unified way. We will perform more thorough theoretical analysis and empirical experiments to make the conclusion more convincing in our future work.

4. REFERENCES

[1] S. Brin and L. Page. The anatomy of a large-scale hypertextual web search engine. *Comput. Netw. ISDN Syst.*, 30(1-7):107–117, 1998.

[2] P. Du, J. Guo, J. Zhang, and X. Cheng. Manifold ranking with sink points for update summarization. In *Proceedings of the 19th ACM CIKM*, pages 1757–1760. ACM, 2010.

[3] T. H. Haveliwala. Topic-sensitive pagerank. In *Proceedings of WWW*, pages 517–526. ACM, 2002.

[4] J. M. Kleinberg. Authoritative sources in a hyperlinked environment. *J. ACM*, 46(5):604–632, 1999.

[5] Q. Mei, J. Guo, and D. Radev. Divrank: the interplay of prestige and diversity in information networks. In *Proceedings of the 16th ACM SIGKDD*, pages 1009–1018. ACM, 2010.

[6] F. Radlinski, P. N. Bennett, B. Carterette, and T. Joachims. Redundancy, diversity and interdependent document relevance. *SIGIR Forum*, 43:46–52, December 2009.

[7] X. Zhu, A. Goldberg, J. Van Gael, and D. Andrzejewski. Improving diversity in ranking using absorbing random walks. In *HLT 2007: NAACL*, pages 97–104. ACL, 2007.

Multi-Objective Optimization in Learning to Rank

Na Dai
Computer Sci. & Engr.
Lehigh University, USA
nad207@cse.lehigh.edu

Milad Shokouhi
Microsoft Research
Cambridge, UK
milads@microsoft.com

Brian D. Davison
Computer Sci. & Engr.
Lehigh University, USA
davison@cse.lehigh.edu

ABSTRACT

Supervised learning to rank algorithms typically optimize for high relevance and ignore other facets of search quality, such as freshness and diversity. Prior work on multi-objective ranking trained rankers focused on using *hybrid* labels that combine overall quality of documents, and implicitly incorporate multiple criteria into quantifying ranking risks. However, these hybrid scores are usually generated based on heuristics without considering potential correlations between individual facets (e.g., freshness versus relevance). In this poster, we empirically demonstrate that the correlation between objective facets in multi-criteria ranking optimization may significantly influence the effectiveness of trained rankers with respect to each objective.

Categories and Subject Descriptors: H.3.3 [Information Storage and Retrieval]: Information Search and Retrieval

General Terms: Algorithms, Performance

Keywords: multi-objective optimization, learning to rank

1 Introduction

To satisfy user information needs, retrieval systems consider several *facets* of search quality such as relevance, freshness and diversity in ranking documents. These facets may interact or correlate with each other in complex and query-dependent manners. For instance, previous research has demonstrated that relevance and freshness have high correlation for breaking news queries [2]. Similar scenarios exist in the information filtering and recommendation domains, where users' ratings on several aspects may correlate with each other depending on user profiles, and consequently affect the prediction models of user preferences on items [6].

Prior work that considered users' multi-criteria objectives in search or collaborative filtering have been mostly inspired by multi-criteria decision making (MCDM) theory from the operations research community [7]. The preference between different criteria is quantified by utility measures that affect optimization through preference model representation. The commonly used preference models for search or recommendation tasks include *value-focused* models [8, 9] and *outranking relations* models [3]. While these approaches exploit the search quality on each aspect (criterion-specific ratings) to enhance overall quality (measurement ratings), they ignore the inter-relationship between different objectives.

This poster explores the influence of interactions and correlations between multiple criteria for ranking optimization in the context of web search. As a preliminary step, we analyze the influence of bi-criteria inter-relationship on pairwise ranking models though the analysis can be generalized to other multi-criteria scenarios. While the definition of *measurement* utility is an open issue, we use the minimum relative ranking improvement on both criteria (denoted as *RelImp*) to measure the influence of bi-criteria optimization, emphasizing its relative benefits compared to optimizing for each single objective. We define $RelImp$ as follows:

$$RelImp = \min_{c,obj}[\text{perf}(c, bi\text{-}obj) - \text{perf}(c, obj)]/\text{perf}(c, obj) \quad (1)$$

where $\text{perf}(c, *)$ is the performance on criteria c when optimizing for objective "$*$". Our research explores the effect of correlation between two ranking criteria on the benefit of bi-objective ranking optimization, focusing on three main issues: (1) what is the correlation scale that can benefit *RelImp*? (2) how much benefit can it bring? and (3) what does a useful preference model look like under different correlation scales? We exploit a value-focused preference model implicitly for ranking optimization through minimizing bi-criteria ranking risk based on *hybrid* labels that combine the quality of documents on both aspects. We demonstrate that the correlation between multiple objectives (freshness and relevance in our case) may influence the outcome of multi-criteria ranking optimization.

2 Methodology

Given a query q and its associated documents $d_1,\ldots,d_n$, each query-document pair $<q,d_k>$ is rated based on its quality on each facet, i.e., $y^{(1)}_{q,d_k}$ and $y^{(2)}_{q,d_k}$. By exploiting *hybrid* labels to combine the overall quality, we average the score achieved on each aspect as the hybrid label for $<q,d_k>$, defined as:

$$\widetilde{y}_{q,d_k} = \Big(\frac{1}{n}\cdot\sum_{i=1}^{n}\big(y^{(i)}_{q,d_k}\big)^m\Big)^{\frac{1}{m}} \quad (2)$$

where $n = 2$ is the number of facets (e.g., freshness and relevance), and m determines the type of *hybrid* label function; quadratic mean (QM), arithmetic mean (AM), geometric mean (GM) and harmonic mean (HM) respectively for $m = 2, m = 1, m \to 0$ and $m = -1$. These variants reflect how sensitive the *hybrid* label is with respect to the lower (higher) rating scores on both aspects, assuming that the rating scores on two aspects fall into the same scale. We believe this perspective is reasonable since the criteria for judging query-document pair quality may vary from one person to another. We also include two extreme cases, i.e., MIN and MAX, representing the minimum and maximum rating scores on two aspects.

Pairwise ranking learning algorithms train a set of parameters ω by minimizing the ranking risk aggregated from loss of misclassified preferential query-document pairs based on relevance. By exploiting *hybrid* labels, we optimize model parameters by:

$$f^* = \arg\min_f \sum_{q\in\mathcal{Q}} \sum_{<d_i,d_j>\in\mathcal{D}_q} \mathcal{L}(\widehat{y}_{q,d_i}, \widehat{y}_{q,d_j}, \widetilde{y}_{q,d_i}, \widetilde{y}_{q,d_j}) \quad (3)$$

where $\mathcal{D}_q$ is the set of preferential query-document pairs for query q, and $\mathcal{L}$ is the loss function that penalizes $<d_i, d_j>$ if its predicted

SIGIR'11, July 24–28, 2011, Beijing, China.
ACM 978-1-4503-0757-4/11/07.

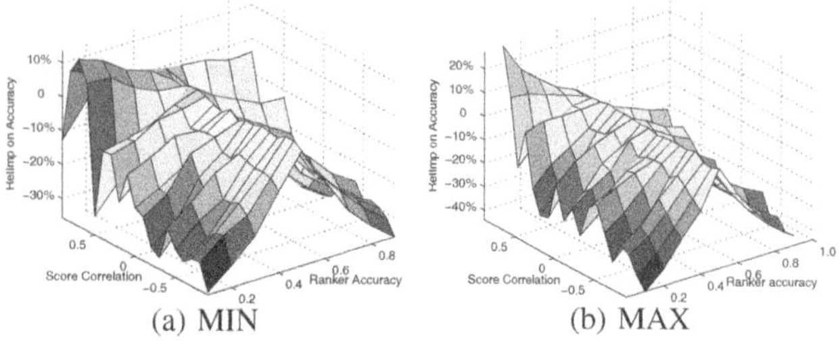

(a) MIN (b) MAX

Figure 1: The minimum relative ranking improvement on accuracy based on MIN and MAX *hybrid* labels under the variance of bi-criteria correlation and ranker accuracy.

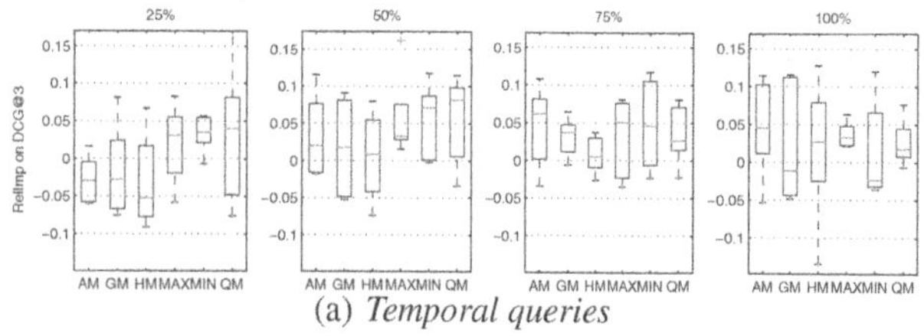

(a) *Temporal queries*

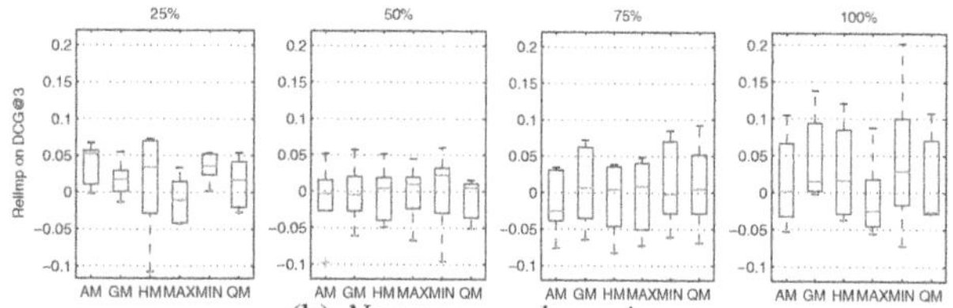

(b) *Non-temporal queries*

Figure 2: The average and standard deviation of *RelImp* on DCG@3 across five folds for the *temporal* (top) and *non-temporal* (bottom) query sets by using the top 25%, 50%, 75% and 100% (all) effective ranking features.

preferential relationship (based on $\widehat{y}_{q,d_i}$ and $\widehat{y}_{q,d_j}$) is discordant with groundtruth (based on $\widetilde{y}_{q,d_i}$ and $\widetilde{y}_{q,d_j}$). We use RankSVM [5] as our basic ranker. We note that the loss function defined on preferential query-document pairs is a linear combination of the loss on each criteria, with the coefficient depending on the actual rating scores on both criteria.[1]

3 Experiments

Our goal is to show how the gain of bi-criteria ranking optimization varies with the bi-criteria correlation and the optimization capability. To avoid data bias, we conduct experiments on two data sets.

We use syntactic data to simulate the process in which pairwise ranking models generate search results. Our dataset consists of 21 subsets, with each composed of 1000 simulated bi-criteria rating scores that have a fixed score correlation from -0.9 to 0.9 with a step size 0.1. Three pseudo-classifiers (i.e., simulated rankers) are used to generate preferential score pair relationships based on each aspect of bi-criteria (i.e., producing baseline results) and the *hybrid* labels in Section 2 respectively. To incorporate optimization capability variance, we exploit a probability threshold (ranging from [0.1,0.9] with step size 0.1) to control the chance that pseudo-classifiers generate correct pair relationships, denoted as *ranker accuracy*. For instance, if the *ranker accuracy* is 90%, the generated pair relationship has 90% chance to be consistent with the ground truth. The gain of bi-criteria ranking optimization is measured by *RelImp* based on the percentage of correctly classified preferential score pairs (i.e., *RelImp on accuracy*).

Figure 1 shows the minimum relative improvement on preferential pair classification accuracy for MIN and MAX as the bi-criteria correlation and *ranker accuracy* vary. Preliminary results demonstrate that the trends of others typically fall in between. The bi-criteria optimization brings benefits when the bi-criteria correlation is highly positive and *ranker accuracy* is low. When the ranker accuracy is high, bi-criteria optimization has negative impact on performance. It is not surprising given that it actually incorporates more inaccurate optimization objectives, and this can be mitigated with the increase of bi-criteria correlation.

To further investigate the effect of bi-criteria ranking optimization on real search scenarios, we use a learning to rank data set that is built on a large-scale archival web corpus [1]. The ranking criteria here are freshness and relevance. This data set contains 90 temporal queries manually selected from Google Trends and 90 non-temporal queries that are first randomly sampled from a 2006 MSN query log, and then filtered by a commercial temporal query classifier with high accuracy. An average of 71 documents (URLs) per query were judged by at least one worker of Amazon Mechanical Turk. Each URL is evaluated on a five point scale in terms of freshness and relevance with respect to a given query and a fixed time point (April 2007). The Pearson's correlation between freshness and relevance on temporal (nontemporal) query set is 0.912 ± 0.004 (0.429 ± 0.021). More details are provided in [1].

Figure 2 shows the average and standard deviation of RelImp on DCG@3 [4] across five fold cross-validation for *temporal* and *non-temporal* query sets. By using the different top $k\%$ effective ranking features that are selected by a reference model (a RankSVM model in this work) based on training data, we incorporate the influence of ranker effectiveness into the sensitivity study on the gain of bi-criteria ranking optimization. The results confirm our previous observations on simulated data and demonstrate that (1) RelImp is more sensitive to hybrid labels and ranker effectiveness when the correlation between relevance and freshness is highly positive (i.e., the *temporal* query set); and (2) bi-criteria ranking optimization can bring more benefits under highly positive bi-criteria correlation.

In summary, we showed that the gain from bi-criteria ranking optimization is sensitive to the bi-criteria correlation and the optimization capability. More benefits can be achieved when there exists a stronger positive correlation between the two criteria and the optimization capability is not strong. These observations reveal valuable insights towards better understanding multi-criteria ranking optimization and may provide hints about how we can exploit multi-criteria ranking optimization to improve search quality.

Acknowledgments

This work was supported in part by a grant from the National Science Foundation under award IIS-0803605.

4 References

[1] N. Dai, M. Shokouhi, and B. D. Davison. Learning to rank for freshness and relevance. In *Proc. 34th ACM SIGIR*, 2011.

[2] A. Dong, Y. Chang, Z. Zheng, G. Mishne, J. Bai, R. Zhang, K. Buchner, C. Liao, and F. Diaz. Towards recency ranking in web search. In *Proc. WSDM Conference*, pages 11–20, 2010.

[3] M. Farah and D. Vanderpooten. An outranking approach for rank aggregation in information retrieval. In *Proc. 30th ACM SIGIR*, pages 591–598, 2007.

[4] K. Jarvelin and J. Kekalainen. IR evaluation methods for retrieving highly relevant documents. In *Proc. 23rd ACM SIGIR*, pages 41–48, 2000.

[5] T. Joachims. Optimizing search engines using clickthrough data. In *Proc. SIGKDD*, pages 133–142, 2002.

[6] N. Manouselis and C. Costopoulou. Analysis and classification of multi-criteria recommender systems. *World Wide Web*, 10:415–441, December 2007.

[7] R. Steuer. *Multiple Criteria Optimization: Theory, Computation and Application*. John Wiley, 546 pp, 1986.

[8] L. Wang, J. Lin, and D. Metzler. Learning to efficiently rank. In *Proc. 33rd ACM SIGIR*, pages 138–145, 2010.

[9] S. R. Wolfe and Y. Zhang. User-centric multi-criteria information retrieval. In *Proc. 32nd ACM SIGIR*, pages 818–819, 2009.

[1] We omit the proof due to space limitations.

A Large-scale Study of the Effect of Training Set Characteristics over Learning-to-Rank Algorithms

Evangelos Kanoulas[*]; Stefan Savev[‡], Pavel Metrikov[‡], Virgil Pavlu[‡], Javed Aslam[‡]
e.kanoulas@shef.ac.uk, {savev, metpavel, vip, jaa}@ccs.neu.edu
[*] Information School, University of Sheffield, Sheffield, UK
[‡] College of Computer & Information Science, Northeastern University, Boston, MA, USA

ABSTRACT

In this work we describe the results of a large-scale study on the effect of the distribution of labels across the different grades of relevance in the training set on the performance of trained ranking functions. In a controlled experiment we generate a large number of training datasets wih different label distributions and employ three learning to rank algorithms over these datasets. We investigate the effect of these distributions on the accuracy of obtained ranking functions to give an insight into the manner training sets should be constructed.

Categories and Subject Descriptors: H. Information Systems; H.3 Information Storage and Retrieval; H.3.3 Information Search and Retrieval:Retrieval models

General Terms: Experimentation, Measurement, Theory

Keywords: Learning-to-Rank, Document Selection Methodologies

1. INTRODUCTION

Learning to rank has become one of the most prominent frameworks for constructing ranking functions. While much thought and research has been placed on the development of sophisticated learning to rank algorithms, relatively little research has been conducted on the construction of training datasets, nor on the effect of this on the effectiveness of learning to rank algorithms.

Aslam et al. [1] considered the problem of constructing effective training datasets with low cost by investigating a number of methods for selecting only a handful of documents to be labeled per query. A post-hoc analysis of the effectiveness versus the characteristics of the constructed datasets revealed that the ratio of relevant to non-relevant documents in the dataset was one of the most influential factors. The dataset used by Aslam et al. was based on TREC 6, 7 and 8 ad-hoc corpora. It contained 150 queries with binary labels and 22 features per query-document pair. Hence, even though this dataset allowed Aslam et al. to quantify performance as a function of the constructed training sets, the conclusions remain limited to small TREC collections and text-derived query features. Further, the construction methodology of the datasets did not allow Aslam et al to observe the performance of ranking functions over the entire range of relevant/non-relevant ratios.

In this work, we reconsider the effect of the distribution of "positive" and "negative" examples in the training set in a large-scale study. In a controlled experiment we construct a large number of training sets over the entire possible range of "positive" and "negative" instances and employ different learning to rank algorithms over these datasets. Understanding how the distribution of labels in the training set affects the quality of the trained ranking functions can provide a better insight into the manner researchers and practitioners should construct effective and efficient training data.

2. DATA AND METHODS

In this work we use the WEB30k dataset provided by Microsoft Research [1]. This dataset comprises more than 30,000 user-issued web queries. For each query-url pair 136 widely used in the research community features are provided. Relevance judgments (labels) are on a 5-grades scale, from 0 (completely irrelevant) to 4 (perfectly relevant). In order to control the distribution of "positive" and "negative" instances in the training set and given that the total number of labeled urls per query and the distribution of labels across the 5 relevance grades varies widely across the 30K queries we only select those queries that have at least k labeled urls in each of the relevance grades. Further, we combine the two highest relevance grades into a single one, since typically labels in these grades are sparse in the collection. For $k = 16$ there are 655 queries that have at least 16 judged urls in each of the four grades, while for $k = 8$ there are 3676 such queries and so on. For each one of these datasets we randomly select 3/5 of the queries to construct the training set, 1/5 the validation and 1/5 the test set. There is no further processing of the test set. For the training and validation sets we first select a total number of judgments per query n, with $n \leq k$. In the case of 655 queries ($k = 16$) $n \in \{4, 8, 16\}$. Then we generate as many training and validation sets as the possible distributions of the n judgments over the four grades (judgment sets). For instance, for $n = 8$, an example distribution would be (4,1,1,2) meaning that each query will have 4 completely irrelevant documents, 1 marginally relevant, 1 relevant and 2 highly/perfectly relevant.

Three learning-to-rank algorithms are run over the thousands of the aforementioned datasets, RankBoost [2], Lin-

[*]We gratefully acknowledge the support provided by the European Commission grant FP7- PEOPLE-2009-IIF-254562 and the NSF grant IIS-1017903.

[1]http://research.microsoft.com/en-us/projects/mslr

SIGIR'11, July 24–28, 2011, Beijing, China.
ACM 978-1-4503-0757-4/11/07.

ear Regression and Ranking SVM [3]. The performance of each of the algorithms is measured by nDCG at cut-off 10 (nDCG@10). We tuned the algorithms carefully by prior investigation of the effect of feature normalization and on the validation sets corresponding to each of our derived training sets. In the case of SVM we found prior to our study that feature normalization greatly affects the learning ability of SVM. We took the log of pagerank and similar static document features to put those features on the same scale as text-based (e.g. language model derived) features. Further, we applied zero-mean unit variance normalization in order to make the features scale-free. RankBoost was not sensitive to feature normalization and we ran it without transforming the features in any way.

3. RESULTS

To quantify the distribution of labels over the four relevance grades we use two summaries which were found to be particularly informative about the effectiveness of learning-to-rank algorithms as measured by nDCG@10, (a) the normalized cumulative gain of the judgment set, and (b) the variance over the judgment set.

Figure 1 demonstrates the interplay between the distribution of the labels over the different grades in the training sets and the three learning to rank algorithms. In Figure 1 (left column), the normalized cumulative gain of the grades of the labeled urls in the training set per query is computed. For instance, for the example distribution (4,1,1,2) above with 4 completely irrelevant documents, 1 marginally relevant etc., the cumulative gain is, $4^0 + 1^1 + 1^2 + 2^3$. The larger the normalized cumulative gain the more skewed is the distribution of labeled documents towards perfectly relevant documents; the smaller it is, the more it is skewed towards completely irrelevant ones. NCG values in the middle of x axis range indicate a balanced training set regarding the "positive" and "negative" instances. As it can be observed from all three plots on the left, the optimal performance is indeed reached when there is a balance of labels in the dataset. Note that this is not a contradiction to Aslam et al. who report a dropping performance when the ratio of "positive" to "negative" instances exceeds some threshold. In that work and due to the manner the datasets were constructed one can only view the right tail of what appears a bell-shape curve in the left-hand side plots of Figure 1.

Obviously, a number of different datasets can be constructed that have a level of balance in the labels. For instance, a uniform distribution is similarly balanced to an equal distribution of labels in the two middle grades (marginally relevant and relevant) or an equal distribution of labels in the two extreme grades (completely irrelevant and perfectly relevant). To distinguish these cases of balanced datasets we also compute the variance of the grades in the datasets. For instance, for the example distribution (4,1,1,2) above, the variance would be the variance of the flattened list of relevance grades: [[0,0,0,0], [1], [2], [3,3]]. The higher the variance the farther the labels are from the middle grades, while the smaller the variance the more uniform the distribution. The effectiveness of the learning algorithms as a function of variance is shown in Figure 1 (right column). As the figure demonstrates the higher the variance the more effective the algorithms are. Hence, optimal performance is reached when instances are mostly taken from the extreme grades of relevance.

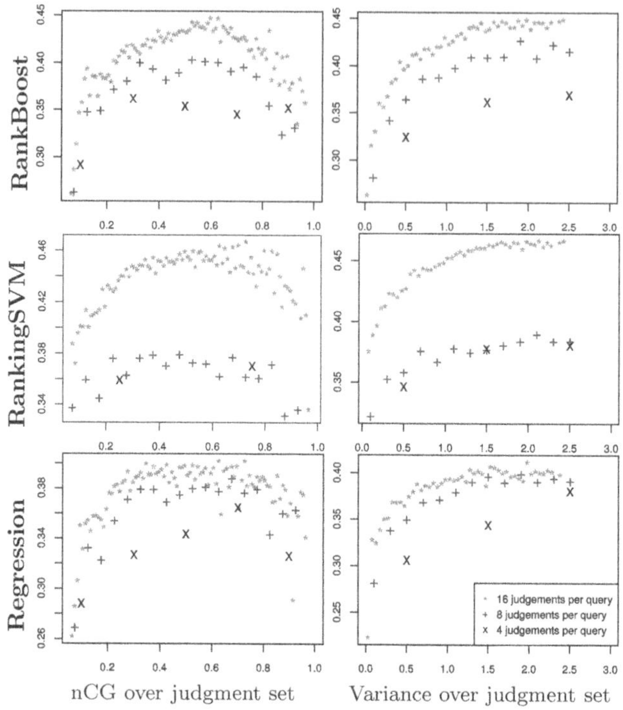

Figure 1: RankBoost, Ranking SVM, Regression performance (nDCG@10, y-axis) as a function of the normalized cumulative gain of the training dataset per query (x-axis, left) and the variance of the labels in the training dataset per query (x-axis, right).

4. CONCLUSION

In this paper we studied the effect of relevance grades distribution in training sets for a learning to rank task. We conclude that the relevance grade distribution in the training set is an important factor for the effectiveness of learning to rank algorithms. Based on our analysis, we can give qualitative advise about the construction of learning to rank datasets: distributions with a balance between the number of documents in the extreme grades are to be favored and that the middle relevance grades play less important role than the extreme ones. ANOVA studies not presented here due to space limitations confirm and quantify our findings.

5. REFERENCES

[1] J. A. Aslam, E. Kanoulas, V. Pavlu, S. Savev, and E. Yilmaz. Document selection methodologies for efficient and effective learning-to-rank. In *Proceedings of the 32nd ACM SIGIR*, pages 468–475. ACM Press, July 2009.

[2] Y. Freund, R. Iyer, R. E. Schapire, and Y. Singer. An efficient boosting algorithm for combining preferences. *J. Mach. Learn. Res.*, 4:933–969, December 2003.

[3] T. Joachims. Training linear svms in linear time. In *Proceedings of the 12th ACM SIGKDD*, KDD '06, pages 217–226, New York, NY, USA, 2006. ACM.

Exploring Term Temporality for Pseudo-Relevance Feedback

Stewart Whiting, Yashar Moshfeghi and Joemon M. Jose
School of Computing Science
University of Glasgow, UK
{stewh,yashar,jj}@dcs.gla.ac.uk

ABSTRACT

As digital collections expand, the importance of the temporal aspect of information has become increasingly apparent. The aim of this paper is to investigate the effect of using long-term temporal profiles of terms in information retrieval by enhancing the term selection process of pseudo-relevance feedback (PRF). For this purpose, two temporal PRF approaches were introduced considering only temporal aspect and temporal along with textual aspect. Experiments used the AP88-89 and WSJ87-92 test collections with TREC Ad-Hoc Topics 51-100. Term temporal profiles are extracted from the Google Books n-grams dataset. The results show that the long-term temporal aspects of terms are capable of enhancing retrieval effectiveness.

Categories and Subject Descriptors: H.3.3 [Information Storage and Retrieval] - *Information Search and Retrieval - Relevance Feedback*
Keywords: Temporal, Topic, Relevance Feedback, Retrieval

1. INTRODUCTION

The significance of time has been examined from a number of information retrieval (IR) perspectives including temporal document relevance [3], event detection in user-generated content, query log trend analysis and topic bursting in stream collections. However, work on temporally-sensitive retrieval has relied upon relatively short-term or otherwise limited time-stamped document collections such as those of the early TREC news or journal collections. Many documents without time-stamp information (e.g., web documents) still contain topics which are implicitly temporally-sensitive. Furthermore, such short-term collections have little coverage of long-term lexical dynamics [4] that could be used in a temporal relevance model. 'Culturomics' [5] quantitatively measures the rise and fall in terms of bursts and trends in the use of words and phrases over long periods as a consequence of changing political, economic, sociocultural and technological trends and events causing lexical evolution.

One of the aspects of IR for which temporal information could be of benefit is pseudo-relevance feedback (PRF). Users often submit short and simple queries. Likewise, many short queries may indicate significant temporal composition of the result sets [3]. The objective of PRF is to increase the effectiveness of retrieval by expanding the original query terms with frequent or distinctive terms from the top pseudo-relevant documents of the initial result set. As such, PRF effectiveness is highly dependent on the quality of both initially retrieved documents and the term selection techniques used. Much research has been dedicated to optimising term selection in PRF, however, correlation between terms based on a long-term temporal profile (see Section 2.1) has yet to be studied. In this work we propose using the long-term temporal profile correlation between terms from the pseudo-relevant documents and temporally significant query terms to improve PRF term selection.

SIGIR'11, July 24–28, 2011, Beijing, China.
ACM 978-1-4503-0757-4/11/07.

2. APPROACH

2.1 Temporal Pseudo-Relevance Feedback

With the effectiveness of PRF significantly depending on the quality of the selected terms from the pseudo-relevant documents [1], we propose two approaches in which the temporal aspect of the terms are taken into account. Unlike traditional PRF, which ranks possible expansion terms by their frequency (TF) in the retrieved documents, i.e. PRF(Text), our first approach, ignores TF and instead ranks terms by their temporal profile correlation with the most temporally significant term extracted from the query, i.e. PRF(Temporal). The temporal correlation (TC) is computed as the Pearson's correlation coefficient between each term's temporal profile (explained below). Our second approach, PRF(Text+Temporal), combines both techniques by ranking terms by $TC \times TF$.

The temporal profile of a term over a prolonged period could be mined from a large scale time-stamped collection, however not all collections include time-stamps, and those which do are not always accurate. We propose to use the Google Books (GB) n-gram dataset[1] [5] for obtaining temporal profiles. Whilst the temporal resolution is coarse (annual occurrence), books are likely to have good coverage of significant temporal words and phrases. To the best of our knowledge this is a first attempt to use this dataset for improving information retrieval.

To use the GB dataset, we have to extract descriptive n-grams from the query (in our case TREC topic title) and the pseudo-relevant documents. The Yahoo Term Extraction Service[2] was used for this purpose.

At this stage we consider the extracted topic title term

[1] This extensive dataset provides annual term usage statistics through the extraction of 1 (single word) to 5-gram (five word phrases) from the digitised Google Books corpus, containing over 5m books (4% of books ever published) and over 8bn English words and phrases.
[2] http://developer.yahoo.com/search/content/V1/termExtraction.html

Table 1: **Reporting MAP, P@30, Recall and IMP (based on MAP) values for LM (i.e. baseline), PRF(Temporal), PRF(Text), and PRF(Text+Temporal) using the AP88-89 and WSJ87-92 test collections and TREC Topics (51-100). Best performing approach for each metric is highlighted. Paired t-test statistical significance is denoted as * being $p < 0.05$ and ** being $p < 0.01$.**

AP88-89	LM	PRF(Temporal)		PRF(Text)		PRF(Text+Temporal)	
		Top 10 Terms	Top 20 Terms	Top 10 Terms	Top 20 Terms	Top 10 Terms	Top 20 Terms
MAP	0.274	0.286 (+4.4%)*	0.288 (+5.2%)**	0.303 (+10.4%)**	0.304 (+11.0%)**	**0.305 (+11.2%)****	0.304 (+11.0%)**
P@30	0.368	0.374 (+1.4%)	0.379 (+2.9%)*	**0.4 (+8.6%)***	0.395 (+7.4%)**	0.393 (+6.8%)**	0.395 (+7.2%)**
Recall	0.640	0.663 (+3.6%)	0.662 (+3.5%)**	0.696 (+8.8%)**	0.694 (+8.5%)**	**0.699 (+9.2%)****	0.694 (+8.5%)**
IMP		20	23	22	26	26	**28**

WSJ87-92	LM	PRF(Temporal)		PRF(Text)		PRF(Text+Temporal)	
		Top 10 Terms	Top 20 Terms	Top 10 Terms	Top 20 Terms	Top 10 Terms	Top 20 Terms
MAP	0.256	0.27 (+5.4%)**	0.27 (+5.1%)**	0.284 (+11.0%)**	0.283 (+10.6%)**	**0.286 (+11.7%)****	0.284 (+11.1%)**
P@30	0.373	0.384 (+3.1%)	0.387 (+3.9%)*	0.393 (+5.5%)*	0.395 (+5.9%)*	**0.399 (+6.9%)***	**0.399 (+6.9%)***
Recall	0.596	0.614 (+3.1%)**	0.617 (+3.6%)**	0.650 (+9.2%)**	0.652 (+9.4%)**	**0.652 (+9.6%)****	0.649 (+8.9%)**
IMP		24	26	31	33	34	**35**

with the highest kurtosis[3] as the primary clue of a topic's long-term temporality. We therefore select the topic n-gram with the highest kurtosis to temporally correlate with potential PRF terms found in pseudo-relevant documents. Pearson's correlation is used to calculate temporal similarity [2] between document and query term temporal profiles.

3. EXPERIMENT AND RESULTS

Implementation. Documents were indexed using Indri 5.0[4] with standard stop-word removal and Krovetz stemming applied. The top 1000 documents were retrieved for each topic using a unigram language model with Indri default Dirichlet smoothing ($\mu = 2500$). This run formed the baseline (identified as LM in Table 1) against which we compared three PRF approaches. For comparison, we also report the performance of PRF(Text) as a much stronger baseline. In each PRF approach, the top n temporally correlated or frequent terms (with n = 10, 20) in the top 10 retrieved documents were linearly-combined and used to expand the query[5]. To reduce query drift, the expanded query includes the original query terms weighted at 0.7, with possibly non-relevant PRF expansion terms weighted at 0.3.

The GB data was indexed, making n-grams case-insensitive. The temporal profile for each term from 1950-1994 was obtained from the GB index (aligning with test collection periods). Due to computational time and space limitations we only used 1 and 2-grams in this study.

Experiment Settings. Preliminary evaluation of the PRF technique is performed using the AP88-89 and WSJ87-92 test collections with TREC Ad-Hoc topics 51-100. We used a news collection at this stage as it is most likely to contain topics with long-term temporality. Mean average precision (MAP) for the top 1000 documents is used as the main effectiveness evaluation measure. Precision at 30 (P@30) and Recall have been included to observe whether PRF increases recall at the cost of precision [1]. We also include Improvement metric (IMP) [6] as the number of individual topics with improved MAP over the LM baseline, as to analyse per-topic variation.

Results. The results reported in Table 1 show that the temporal aspect of the terms can improve retrieval effectiveness. The temporal-based approach displays better performances than LM. We also observe that combining temporal and textual aspects of terms in PRF documents leads to the best performance (shown to be statistically significant), increasing over that of PRF(Text) alone. Thus, whilst effectiveness gains are marginal on average in this preliminary study, there is a case for using the long-term temporal correlation of terms in PRF term selection, particularly when considering individual topic improvements (i.e. IMP). Improvement gain across approaches is due to a significant variation in the selected terms as reflected by a per-topic average Spearman's ρ of 0.05 and 0.06 for AP88-89 and WSJ87-92 respectively.

4. DISCUSSION AND CONCLUSIONS

In this paper we investigated the effectiveness of using long-term temporal aspects of terms in PRF. The results are encouraging and show improvment when including temporal profile correlation in PRF term selection. This work is a foundation for future research on utilising long-term temporality in IR tasks. Future work will answer what the effect would be of such information if it is combined with textual features using more elaborate PRF models.

5. REFERENCES

[1] G. Cao, J.-Y. Nie, J. Gao, and S. Robertson. Selecting good expansion terms for pseudo-relevance feedback. In *SIGIR'08*, pages 243–250, 2008.

[2] T. R. Derrick, B. T. Bates, and J. S. Dufek. Evaluation of time-series data sets using the Pearson product-moment correlation coefficient. *Medicine & Science in Sports & Exercise*, 26(7):919–928, 1994.

[3] R. Jones and F. Diaz. Temporal profiles of queries. *ACM Trans. Inf. Syst.*, 25(3):14–es, 2007.

[4] R. Liebscher and R. K. Belew. Lexical dynamics and conceptual change : Analyses and implications for information retrieval. *Cognitive Science*, 1:46–57, 2003.

[5] J.-B. Michel, Y. K. Shen, A. P. Aiden, A. Veres, M. K. Gray, J. P. Pickett, D. Hoiberg, D. Clancy, P. Norvig, J. Orwant, S. Pinker, M. A. Nowak, and E. L. Aiden. Quantitative Analysis of Culture Using Millions of Digitized Books. *Science*, 331(6014):176–182, 2010.

[6] Y. Xu, G. J. Jones, and B. Wang. Query dependent pseudo-relevance feedback based on wikipedia. In *SIGIR '09*, pages 59–66, 2009.

[3] A statistical measure of the 'peakedness' of a time-series [3]

[4] http://www.lemurproject.org/indri

[5] Indri #combine query operators are used, therefore treating n-grams as multiple 1-gram terms.

MSSF: A Multi-Document Summarization Framework based on Submodularity

Jingxuan Li, Lei Li, Tao Li
School of Computing and Information Sciences
Florida International University
Miami, FL
{jli003,lli003,taoli}@cs.f u.edu

ABSTRACT

Multi-document summarization aims to distill the most representative information from a set of documents to generate a summary. Given a set of documents as input, most of existing multi-document summarization approaches utilize different sentence selection techniques to extract a set of sentences from the document set as the summary. The submodularity hidden in textual-unit similarity motivates us to incorporate this property into our solution to multi-document summarization tasks. In this poster, we propose a new principled and versatile framework for different multi-document summarization tasks using the submodular function [8].

Categories and Subject Descriptors: H.3.3 [Information Storage and Retrieval]: Information Search and Retrieval

General Terms: Algorithms, Performance

Keywords: Submodularity, Summarization, Framework

1. INTRODUCTION

Typical multi-document summarization tasks include generic and query-focused summarization. Recently, new summarization tasks such as update summarization [1] and comparative summarization [10] have also been proposed.

Lin et al. [5] proposed attacking generic summarization problem using submodularity along with a greedy algorithm. In this paper, we propose a new framework for ***M***ulti-document ***S***ummarization using the ***S***ubmodular ***F***unction (MSSF) which extends the submodularity to not only generic summarization, but also query-focused, update, and comparative summarization, and applies an improved greedy algorithm proposed by Minoux [6] (which is faster than the greedy algorithm in Lin et al. [5]) to generate summaries.

2. MSSF

In this section, first of all, the definition of submodularity is given since it is the core of MSSF. Then we explore how to map the summarization problem into a budgeted maximum coverage problem which is based on submodularity. Finally, the submodular functions for various summarization tasks performed by MSSF are presented.

2.1 Submodularity

Let E be a finite set and f be a real valued nondecreasing function defined on the subsets of E that satisfies

$$f(T \cup \{\varsigma\}) - f(T) \leqslant f(S \cup \{\varsigma\}) - f(S), \quad (1)$$

SIGIR'11, July 24–28, 2011, Beijing, China.
ACM 978-1-4503-0757-4/11/07.

Task	Submodular Function
Generic	$f(S) = \sum_{s_i \in D \setminus S} \sum_{s_j \in S} sim(s_i, s_j) - \sum_{s_i, s_j \in S, s_i \neq s_j} sim(s_i, s_j)$
Query-focused	$f(S, q) = f_G + \sum_{s_i \in S} sim(q, s_i)$
Update	$f(q, S_1, S_2) = f_G + \sum_{s_i \in S_2} sim(q, s_i) - \sum_{s_i \in S_2} \sum_{s_j \in S_1} sim(s_i, s_j)$
Comparative	$f(S) = f_G - \sum_{s_i \in S} \sum_{s_j \in OtherGroups} sim(s_i, s_j)$

Table 1: A quick summary of the submodular functions for different summarization tasks.

Notation	Meaning
D	Document Set
S	Summary
S_1	Summary for D_1
S_2	Summary for D_2
w_t	Weight of term t
s_i, s_j	Textual unit
sim	Similarity
q	Given query
f_G	General information coverage

Table 2: Notations.

where S and T are two subsets of E, $S \subseteq T$, and $\varsigma \in E \setminus T$, such a function f is called **submodular** function [8]. A key observation is that submodular functions are closed under nonnegative linear combinations [4].

2.2 Problem Formulation

The summarization can be modeled as a budgeted maximum coverage problem. The budgeted maximum coverage problem is described as: given a set of elements E where each element is associated with an influence and a cost defined over a domain of these elements and a budget B, the goal is to find out a subset of E which has the largest possible influence while the total cost does not exceed B. This problem is NP-hard [3]. However, Khuller et al. [3] proposed a greedy algorithm which sequentially picks up the element that increases the **largest possible** influence within the cost limit and it guarantees the influence of the result subset is $(1-1/e)$-approximation. It is easy to observe that submodularity resides in each "pick up" step.

Based on the definition of submodular function and the budgeted maximum coverage problem, we can derive the utilization of submodularity for multi-document summarization tasks.

The basic step of multi-document summarization is to extract a candidate sentence. If the budget B is the number of terms in the summary, the cost of each candidate sentence is the number of terms within it. A high quality summary should maximize the information coverage of the given document set, while minimize the redundancy. One of the most popular methods for serving these two purposes is MMR [2]. Hence, a MMR-similar definition for the quality of the current generated summary is given by

	DUC05	DUC06	TAC08 A	TAC08 B
Type of task	Query	Query	Query	Update
# of topics	50	50	48	48
# of docs per topic	25-50	25	10	10
Summary length (# of words)	250	250	100	100

Table 3: The brief description of the data sets.

$$f(S) = \sum_{s_i \in E \setminus S} \sum_{s_j \in S} sim(s_i, s_j) - \sum_{s_i, s_j \in S, s_i \neq s_j} sim(s_i, s_j), \quad (2)$$

where E is the whole sentence set, and $sim(s_i, s_j)$ is the similarity between the textual units s_i and s_j (the typical textual unit is sentence). Note that the first component of Eq.(2) is for information coverage and the second component is for redundancy removal. Both components are submodular, thus $f(S)$ is also submodular, since the linear combination of submodular functions is closed. The goal of multi-document summarization is to generate a summary which provides the largest possible quality within the budget. Hence, multi-document summarization problem can be modeled as a budgeted maximum coverage problem.

Eq.(2) has presented the submodular function for generic summarization task, thus we can define more submodular functions for different summarization tasks. All the submodular functions are shown in Table 1, and descriptions of the notations are given in Table 2. Notice that f_G can be presented by the functions for generic summarization. As we have obtained corresponding submodular function for each summarization task, the algorithm by Minoux [6] is utilized for extracting summaries which have the quality close to optimal.

3. EXPERIMENTS

Lin et al. [5] have already showed the feasibility of the generic summarization using submodularity. Thus, we conducted experiments on three new summarization tasks to evaluate our proposed MSSF based on submodular function.

3.1 Data sets

Table 3 shows the characteristics of all the datasets used for our experiments. All the tasks, except the comparative summarization, are evaluated by ROUGE, an widely used evaluation toolkit for document summarization.

	DUC05		DUC06	
	ROUGE-2	ROUGE-SU4	ROUGE-2	ROUGE-SU4
Average-Human	0.10236	0.16221	0.11249	0.1706
DUC Average	0.06024	0.11488	0.07543	0.13206
Random	0.04143	0.09066	0.04892	0.10083
LSA	0.04079	0.09352	0.05022	0.10226
SNMF	0.06043	0.12298	0.08549	0.13981
Qs-MRF	0.0779	0.1366	0.08917	0.14329
Wiki	0.07074	0.13002	0.08091	0.14022
MSSF	0.0731	0.12718	0.09193	0.14611

Table 4: Results on query-focused summarization.

3.2 Results

For the **query-focused summarization** task, we compared our method with some widely used and recently published methods: SNMF [9], Qs-MRF [11], and Wiki [7]. The empirical results are reported in Table 4. Our method achieves the best result.

For the **update summarization** task, Table 5 shows the comparative experimental results, "TAC Best" and "TAC Median" represent the best and median results from the participants of the TAC08 summarization track in the two tasks respectively according to the TAC08 report [1]. The experimental results demonstrate that MSSF leads to the competitive performance for update summarization.

For **comparative summarization**, we use the top three largest clusters of documents from TDT2 corpora to generate the summary by MSSF. From the summaries presented in Table 6, MSSF can extract discriminative sentences for all the topics.

	TAC08 A		TAC08 B	
	ROUGE-2	ROUGE-SU	ROUGE-2	ROUGE-SU
TAC Best	0.1114	0.14298	0.10108	0.13669
TAC Median	0.08123	0.11975	0.06927	0.11046
MSSF	0.08327	0.12109	0.09451	0.13180

Table 5: Results on update summarization.

Topic	MSSF
Iraq Issues	The arrival of U.S. Secretary of State Madeleine Albright could be an early test of **the accord iraq signed ten days ago with U.N. secretary-general Kofi Annan**.
Asia's economic crisis	Prueher addressed the army seminar in Manila and told delegates that **Asia's financial troubles** have affected **the United States' joint military activities with its Asian allies**.
Lewinsky scandal	In Washington, Ken Starr's grand jury continued its investigation of the **Monica Lewinsky matter**.

Table 6: A case study on comparative document summarization. The bold font is used to annotate the phrases that are highly related with the topics.

We also conduct experiments to evaluate the efficiency of the improved greedy algorithm used in MSSF. Compared with using general greedy algorithm, by applying the improved greedy algorithm, the running time of different summarization tasks is reduced by 10,000-100,000 milliseconds.

4. CONCLUSION

In this poster, we propose a principled and versatile framework for different multi-document summarization tasks including generic, query-focused, updated, and comparative summarization using the submodular function. In addition, it adopts an improved greedy algorithm which reduces the running time of generating the summary with the competitive summarization quality.

Acknowledgements

The work is partially supported by US National Science Foundation under grants IIS-0546280 and CCF-0830659.

5. REFERENCES

[1] H.T. Dang and K. Owczarzak. Overview of the TAC 2008 Update Summarization Task. In *Proc. of TAC*, 2008.

[2] J. Goldstein, V. Mittal, J. Carbonell, and M. Kantrowitz. Multi-document summarization by sentence extraction. In *NAACL-ANLP 2000 Workshop on Automatic summarization*, 2000.

[3] S. Khuller, A. Moss, and J.S. Naor. The budgeted maximum coverage problem. *Information Processing Letters*, 1999.

[4] A. Krause and C. Guestrin. Near-optimal observation selection using submodular functions. In *Proc. of AAAI*, 2007.

[5] H. Lin and J. Bilmes. Multi-document Summarization via Budgeted Maximization of Submodular Functions. In *NAACL/HLT*, 2010.

[6] M. Minoux. Accelerated greedy algorithms for maximizing submodular set functions. *Optimization Techniques*, 1978.

[7] V. Nastase. Topic-driven multi-document summarization with encyclopedic knowledge and spreading activation. In *Proc. of EMNLP*, 2008.

[8] GL Nemhauser, LA Wolsey, and ML Fisher. An analysis of approximations for maximizing submodular set functions. *Mathematical Programming*, 1978.

[9] D. Wang, T. Li, S. Zhu, and C. Ding. Multi-document summarization via sentence-level semantic analysis and symmetric matrix factorization. In *Proc. of SIGIR*, 2008.

[10] D. Wang, S. Zhu, T. Li, and Y. Gong. Comparative document summarization via discriminative sentence selection. In *Proc. of CIKM*, 2009.

[11] F. Wei, W. Li, Q. Lu, and Y. He. Query-sensitive mutual reinforcement chain and its application in query-oriented multi-document summarization. In *Proc. of SIGIR*, 2008.

SEJoin: an Optimized Algorithm towards Efficient Approximate String Searches

Junfeng Zhou, Ziyang Chen, Jingrong Zhang
School of Information Science and Engineering, Yanshan University
{zhoujf, zychen}@ysu.edu.cn; jr.zhang.zjr@gmail.com

ABSTRACT

We investigated the problem of finding from a collection of strings those similar to a given query string based on edit distance, for which the critical operation is merging inverted lists of grams generated from the collection of strings. We present an efficient algorithm to accelerate the merging operation.

Categories and Subject Descriptors

H.3.3 [**Information Systems**]: Search process

General Terms

Algorithms, Experimentation

Keywords

Approximate String Search

1. INTRODUCTION

Approximate string searching is very important and has attracted great attention with its ever increasing applications in Web service-based environment, such as data cleaning, query suggestion, spell checking, etc., where a prerequisite is supporting instant feedbacks to many users, and any improvements on the search algorithm will have a great impact on the overall system performance.

A query used for approximate string search finds from a collection of strings those similar to a given string. The similarity between two strings can be measured by different metrics such as edit distance, Jaccard similarity, and cosine similarity. In this paper, we focus on similarity search with edit distance thresholds. A broadly adopted method is using q-gram based strategy, which assumes that inverted lists of q-grams generated from the strings are built in advance [2–4], and works in two steps: (1) find from a set of lists the candidate strings; (2) apply the similarity function on the candidates to eliminate false positives. Similar to existing methods [2, 3], we aims at efficiently computing the set of candidates in the first step.

2. PRELIMINARIES

Let $\sum$ be an alphabet, for a string s consisting of the characters in $\sum$, "$|s|$" is used to denote the length of s, "$s[i, j]$ is the substring of s from the i-th to j-th character.

***Q*-Grams**: For a given positive integer q, a positional q-gram of a given string s is a pair (i, g), where g is the q-gram of s starting at the i-th character, that is $g = s[i, i + q - 1]$. For example, if $q = 2$, and s = sigir, we have the set of q-grams $G(s, q)$={(1,si),(2,ig),(3,gi),(4,ir)}. For simplicity, the positional information is omitted in the following discussion.

Approximate String Search: For two strings $s1$ and $s2$, the edit distance of $s1$ and $s2$ is the minimum number of edit operations (insertion, deletion, and substitution) on single character needed to transform $s1$ to $s2$, which is denoted as $ed(s1, s2)$ in our discussion. For example, ed("sigir", "sigmod") = 3. Let M be a collection of strings and Q the query string, the problem can be stated as: finding all $s \in M$ such that $ed(s, Q) \leq k$ for a given threshold k.

According to the result of [1], if for two strings $s1$ and $s2$, $ed(s1, s2) = k$, then they have at least t common grams, where $t = max(|s1|, |s2|) - q + 1 - qk$. Therefore for a given query string Q, the problem of computing candidate strings can be solved by finding the set of string ids that appear at least t times on the inverted lists of the grams of Q.

3. SWITCH-ELIMINATOR BASED JOIN

For a given string query Q with m grams $q_1, q_2, ..., q_m$, each q_i corresponds to a list L_i of sorted ids, L_i is associated with a cursor C_i pointing to some element of L_i. Henceforth, "C_i" or "element C_i" refers to the element C_i points to, when there is no ambiguity. The cursor can move to the element (if any) next to element C_i using $advance(C_i)$. Initially, all cursors point to the first elements of the corresponding lists.

Assume that for each list L_i, all elements before C_i have been processed, and without loss of generalization, we use $C_1(C_m)$ to denote the list with the minimum (maximum) cursor value, i.e., $C_1 \leq C_2 \leq ... \leq C_m$, then we have the following result.

LEMMA 1. *Assume that each cursor $C_i(1 \leq i \leq m)$ points to the first element of L_i, then any element e of list $L_j(1 \leq j \leq t-1)$ satisfying $C_1 \leq e < C_t$ is impossible to appear at least t times.*

PROOF. Since all cursors point to the first elements of the set of lists, e is impossible to appear in L_t since C_t is the first element of L_t. For the same reason, e would not appear in $L_j(t < j \leq m)$. Thus e will not appear in all lists at least t times. □

Lemma 1 tells us that all elements that are less than C_t can be safely discarded initially. Accordingly, the basic idea of our method is to use C_t as the eliminator to probe list $L_i(1 \leq i < t)$ until $C_i \geq C_t$. If C_t satisfies the requirements, output it as a candidate answer and move it to the next element.

SIGIR'11, July 24-28, 2011, Beijing, China.
ACM 978-1-4503-0757-4/11/07.

Algorithm 1: SEJoin$(t, L_1, L_2, ..., L_m)$

```
1  R ← ∅;
2  while (there are at least t lists not empty) do
3      Sort all cursors such that C_1 ≤ C_2 ≤ ... ≤ C_m;
4      k ← 0;
5      foreach(1 ≤ i ≤ m, i ≠ t) do
6          if(C_i > C_t) then break;
7          if(C_i < C_t) then
8              if(L_i[pos(C_i) + λ] < C_t) then
9                  indexLookup(L_i, C_t);
10             else sequencialScan(L_i, C_t);
11         endif
12         if (C_i = C_t) then
13             k ← k + 1; Move C_i to the next element;
14         endif
15     endfor
16     if(k ≥ t) then R ← R ∪ {C_t};
17     Move C_t to the next element;
18 endwhile
```

Function indexLookup(L_i, C_t)

```
1  nStart ← pos(C_i) + λ + 1;
2  nEnd ← |L_i|;
3  while (nEnd − nStart > λ) do
4      nMid ← (nStart + nEnd)/2;
5      if (L_i[nMid] = C_t) then
6          C_i ← L_i[nMid]; return;
7      else if(L_i[nMid] < C_t) then
8          nStart ← nMid + 1;
9      else nEnd ← nMid − 1;
10 endwhile
11 foreach(x ∈ [nStart, nEnd]) do
12     if (L_i[x] ≥ C_t) then
13         C_i ← L_i[x]; return;
14     else x ← x + 1;
15 endfor
```

As shown in Algorithm 1, in each iteration (line 2-18), we first sort all lists according to their cursor values (line 3), such that after the sort operation, we have $C_1 \leq C_2 \leq ... \leq C_m$. In line 5-15, we probe all lists in the direction from 1 to m, and increase the counter k by 1 if $C_i = C_t$ (line 12-13). Note that $pos(C_i)$ is used to get the position of C_i in L_i, seqentialScan() (line 10) is used to sequentially scan each element to make comparison with C_t, which is invoked only when the matched element[1] of C_t is located very close to C_i in L_i (less than λ elements). In our experiment, $\lambda = \lfloor \log |L_i| \rfloor$. If $L_i[pos(C_i) + \lambda] < C_t$, it means that the matched element of C_t in L_i is located far away from C_i, thus we use indexLookup() to find the matched element for C_t. According Lemma 1 and Algorithm 1, we have the following theorem, the correctness is obvious and we omit the proof for limited space.

THEOREM 1. *According to Algorithm 1, at any time, any element e of list $L_j (1 \leq j < t)$ satisfying $C_1 \leq e < C_t$ cannot be a candidate answer.*

Compared with existing methods [2,3], the difference lies in three aspects: (1) the eliminator element C_t that is used to conduct lookup operation on other lists is selected dynamically according to cursors values, not the length of lists, so as to skip more useless elements if possible; (2) before conducting lookup operation, we first check whether the matched element of C_t in L_i is located close to C_i so as to take advantage of the benefits of sequential scan operation (line 10 in Algorithm 1); (3) when finding the matched element by calling indexLookup(), unlike existing search methods, e.g., binary search, galloping search and interpolation search, that use a single strategy to reduce the search scope, our method uses binary search to quickly shrink the search interval (line 3-10 in Function indexLookup()) if its length is greater than λ; otherwise, we use sequential scan operation to complete the index lookup operation (line 11-15 in Function indexLookup()).

[1]For a given number n, the matched element n_i of n in list L_i is the first element that satisfies $n_i \geq n$.

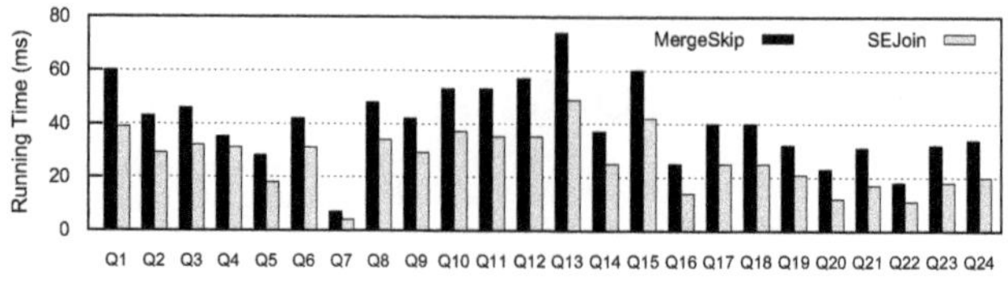

Figure 1: Comparison of running time.

4. EXPERIMENT

We have conducted experiments to verify the efficiency of SEJoin algorithm by comparing it with the MergeSkip [2] algorithm. We implement both the MergeSkip and SEJoin algorithms using Visual C++. We use DBLP dataset and generate lists of 2-grams for strings. We have compared 24 query strings containing 4 to 11 grams, of which the longest inverted list contains 115947 ids, and the shortest list contains 616 ids. In our experiment, $t = n - 2$, where n is the number of grams for a query string.

As shown in Figure 1, SEJoin is more efficient than MergeSkip algorithm for all queries. The reason lies in that the eliminator used to probe other lists comes from the tth list, and the index lookup operation used in our method will firstly check whether the matched id for the current eliminator is located close to the cursor of the probed list, so as to take advantage of the sequential scan operation.

5. CONCLUSIONS

In this paper, we presented a novel algorithm, namely SEJoin, for efficient processing of approximate string search. The experimental results verified the performance advantage of our method.

Acknowledgments: This research was partially supported by the grants from the National Natural Science Foundation of China (No.61073060, 61040023).

6. REFERENCES

[1] P. Jokinen and E. Ukkonen. Two algorithms for approximate string matching in static texts. In *MFCS*, pages 240–248, 1991.

[2] C. Li, J. Lu, and Y. Lu. Efficient merging and filtering algorithms for approximate string searches. In *ICDE*, pages 257–266, 2008.

[3] S. Sarawagi and A. Kirpal. Efficient set joins on similarity predicates. In *SIGMOD Conference*, pages 743–754, 2004.

[4] Z. Yang, J. Yu, and M. Kitsuregawa. Fast algorithms for top-k approximate string matching. In *AAAI*, 2010.

Bag-of-Visual-Words vs Global Image Descriptors on Two-Stage Multimodal Retrieval

Konstantinos Zagoris Savvas A. Chatzichristofis Avi Arampatzis
Department of Electrical and Computer Engineering
Democritus University of Thrace, Xanthi 67100, Greece
{kzagoris,schatzic,avi}@ee.duth.gr

ABSTRACT

The Bag-Of-Visual-Words (BOVW) paradigm is fast becoming a popular image representation for Content-Based Image Retrieval (CBIR), mainly because of its better retrieval effectiveness over global feature representations on collections with images being near-duplicate to queries. In this experimental study we demonstrate that this advantage of BOVW is diminished when visual diversity is enhanced by using a secondary modality, such as text, to pre-filter images. The TOP-SURF descriptor is evaluated against Compact Composite Descriptors on a two-stage image retrieval setup, which first uses a text modality to rank the collection and then perform CBIR only on the top-K items.

Categories and Subject Descriptors: H.3.3 [**Information Storage and Retrieval**]: Information Search and Retrieval—*retrieval models, search process*

General Terms: Measurement, Experimentation, Theory

Keywords: Image Retrieval, Bag-Of-Visual-Words, Two-Stage Retrieval

1. INTRODUCTION

In Content-Based Image Retrieval (CBIR) images are represented by either global or local features. Global features are capable of generalizing an entire image with a single vector, describing color, texture, or shape. Local features are computed at multiple points of interest on an image and are capable of recognizing objects.

Compact Composite Descriptors (CCDs) [4] are global image features capturing more than one type of information at the same time in a very compact representation. Their retrieval quality has so far been evaluated in several benchmarking databases and is found to be better than other descriptors such as the MPEG-7 descriptors.

SURF local features are among the best interest-point descriptors currently available. They have been shown to outperform other well-known methods based on interest points such as SIFT and GLOH. Nevertheless, in large-scale CBIR, it is clear that using the SURF descriptor is storage-wise infeasible [6].

Bag-Of-Visual-Words (BOVW) [5] is a representation of images which is built using a large set of local features. They are inspired by the bag-of-words models in text retrieval, where a document is represented by a set of distinct keywords. Analogously, in BOVW models, an image is represented by a set of distinct visual words derived from local features. The most modern implementation of BOVW suitable for a wide range of CBIR applications is the TOP-SURF [6] descriptor. TOP-SURF combines interest points with visual words, resulting in a high performance compact descriptor.

SIGIR'11, July 24–28, 2011, Beijing, China.
ACM 978-1-4503-0757-4/11/07.

The TOP-SURF descriptor initially extracts SURF local features from images and then groups them into a desired number of clusters. Each cluster can be seen as a visual word. All visual words are stored in a visual dictionary. Next, tf.idf weighting is applied in order to assign a score to all the visual words. The TOP-SURF image descriptor is created by choosing the top-scoring visual words.

Nowadays, information collections are multimodal and large (for example Wikipedia), where a single topic may be covered in several languages and include non-textual media such as image, audio, and video. In an image retrieval system where users are assumed to target visual similarity, all modalities beyond image can be considered as secondary; nevertheless, they can still provide useful information for improving CBIR.

In [2], we experimented with two-stage image retrieval from a large multimodal database, by first using a text modality to rank the collection and then perform CBIR only on the top-K items. The approach employed CCDs and was found to be significantly more effective than the text-only and image-only baselines when K was dynamically calculated with respect to the underlying query generality. Traditionally, the method that has been followed in order to deal with multimodal databases is to search the modalities separately and fuse their results. While fusion has been proven robust, we also found that two-stage is more effective than fusion [3]. Furthermore, a two-stage approach has an efficiency benefit: it cuts down greatly on expensive image operations.

The BOVW paradigm is fast becoming a widely used representation for CBIR, mainly because of its better retrieval effectiveness over global feature representations on collections with images being near-duplicate to queries. In this experimental study, we evaluate the performance of the BOVW approach in comparison to CCDs in a multistage multimodal setup. We intend to check whether the aforementioned reason holds also in such setups, where CBIR is performed on a pre-filtered set of images with a high probability of relevance. Given that the high relevance of such a subset is based on the text modality, it is likely to consist of more diverse images than the top-retrieved images of CBIR systems.

2. TOP-SURF VS CCDS

We experimented with the ImageCLEF 2010 Wikipedia test collection, which consists of 237,434 images associated with noisy and incomplete user-supplied textual annotations. There are 70 test topics, each one consisting of a textual and a visual part with one or more example images. The topics were assessed by visual similarity to the image examples. The collection is one of the largest benchmark image databases for today's standards. It is also highly heterogeneous, containing color natural images, graphics, grayscale images, etc., in a variety of sizes.

We indexed the images with two CCDs: the Joint Composite Descriptor (JCD) and the Spatial Color Distribution (SpCD) descriptor [4]. We also indexed the images with the TOP-SURF descriptor, employing two visual-word dictionaries: one with 10,000 and the other with 200,000 visual words. For CBIR we used the JCD, SpCD, and TOP-SURF, separately, as well as a late fusion setup of JCD and SpCD explained next.

Let i be the index running over example images ($i = 1, 2, \ldots$) and j running over the visual descriptors ($j \in \{1, 2\}$). Thus, DESC_{ji} is the score of a collection item against the ith example image for the jth descriptor. We normalize DESC_{ji} values with MinMax, taking the maximum score seen across example images per descriptor. Assuming that the descriptors capture orthogonal information, we add their scores per example image. Then, to take into account all example images, the natural combination is to assign to each collection image the maximum similarity seen from its comparisons to all example images; this can be interpreted as looking for images similar to *any* of the example images. Summarizing, the score s for a collection image against the topic, for the JCD/SpCD fused setup, is defined as:

$$s = \max_i \left(\sum_j \mathrm{MinMax}(\mathrm{DESC}_{ji}) \right) \tag{1}$$

With the same reasoning, the $\max_i$ is applied also in the TOP-SURF runs to handle multi-image topics.

For text indexing and retrieval, we employed the Lemur Toolkit V4.11 and Indri V2.11 with the tf.idf retrieval model. We used the default settings that come with these versions of the system except that we enabled Krovetz stemming. We indexed only the English annotations, and used only the English query of the topics.

First, the collection was ranked with the secondary text modality, and then the top-K results were re-ranked by the primary visual modality using CBIR methods based on the aforementioned descriptors. The threshold K was calculated dynamically per query using the Score-Distributional Threshold Optimization (SDTO) [1]. The method normalizes retrieval scores to probabilities of relevance (prels), enabling the the optimization of K by thresholding on prel. We report results for three prel thresholds, i.e. 0.800, 0.500, and 0.333; these were the best three performers in [2].

We evaluated on the top-1000 results with MAP, precision at 10 and 20. We tested the results for statistical significance against the text-only baseline; image retrieval based on the text queries and annotations was found to perform much better, with a wide margin, than CBIR-only in the same setup [2]. For measuring efficiency, we report the average matching time per topic. The results are presented in Table 1.

For all θ, the CCDs perform similarly (JCD) or significantly better (SpCD and JCD/SpCD) than the text-only baseline, while the TOP-SURF descriptor shows significant drops in effectiveness irrespective of dictionary size. The differences in effectiveness of CCDs and TOP-SURF are larger in early precision than in MAP. We also observe that the TOP-SURF effectiveness degrades with increased dictionary size. Furthermore, TOP-SURF is more sensitive to the choice of θ: as θ decreases (i.e. for larger Ks), effectiveness deteriorates faster than this of the CCDs.

Efficiency-wise, the experimental results show that although the TOP-SURF uses a speedy matching algorithm, it still cannot match the speed of the global descriptors.

3. CONCLUSIONS

We investigated the performance of BOVW models, specifically the TOP-SURF image descriptor, in a two-stage multimodal retrieval setup, in comparison to CCDs. We found that CCDs are more effective, as well as faster in matching speed, than TOP-SURF. Although BOVW models are currently trendy because of their ability to recognize objects and retrieve near-duplicate (to the query) images, this advantage over global features such as CCDs is diminished when visual diversity is enhanced by using a secondary modality, such as text, to pre-filter images. In practice this means that, applications like Google Goggles, where a user is querying an image in order to recognize a logo or a famous painting, BOVW models should be more effective. But in applications like Google Similar Images, where images are pre-filtered by text similarity, global features should be more suitable.

descriptor	θ	MAP	P@10	P@20	avg. time (sec.)
text-only	-	.1293	.3614	.3307	-
TOP-SURF (10,000)	.8000	.1156$^{\triangledown}$	.3743-	.3264-	.4359
	.5000	.0999$^{\blacktriangledown}$	.3200-	.2850$^{\triangledown}$	.7748
	.3333	.0893$^{\blacktriangledown}$	.2686$^{\triangledown}$	.2557$^{\triangledown}$	.7793
TOP-SURF (200,000)	.8000	.1149$^{\triangledown}$	.3300$^{\triangledown}$	.2979$^{\triangledown}$	.7714
	.5000	.1030$^{\blacktriangledown}$	.2857$^{\triangledown}$	.2579$^{\blacktriangledown}$	.6665
	.3333	.0956$^{\blacktriangledown}$	.2629$^{\triangledown}$	.2229$^{\blacktriangledown}$	.4185
JCD/SpCD	.8000	**.1428**$^{\vartriangle}$	**.4443**$^{\vartriangle}$	**.3857**$^{\vartriangle}$	.0360
	.5000	.1405$^{\vartriangle}$	.4357$^{\vartriangle}$	.3821$^{\vartriangle}$	.0432
	.3333	.1403$^{\vartriangle}$	.4357$^{\vartriangle}$	.3807$^{\vartriangle}$	.3632
JCD	.8000	.1348$^{\vartriangle}$	.4271$^{\vartriangle}$	.3743$^{\vartriangle}$	**.0095**
	.5000	.1305^{-}	.4171$^{\vartriangle}$	.3693$^{\vartriangle}$	.0110
	.3333	.1315^{-}	.4114^{-}	.3707^{-}	.2870
SpCD	.8000	.1342$^{\vartriangle}$	**.4443**$^{\vartriangle}$	.3771$^{\vartriangle}$	.0363
	.5000	.1302$^{\vartriangle}$	.4329$^{\vartriangle}$	.3693$^{\vartriangle}$	.0411
	.3333	.1307$^{\vartriangle}$	.4286$^{\vartriangle}$	.3743$^{\vartriangle}$	.0457

Table 1: Retrieval effectiveness and matching time. The best results per measure and retrieval type are in boldface. Significance-tested with a bootstrap test, one-tailed, at significance levels 0.05 ($^{\vartriangle\triangledown}$), 0.01 ($^{\vartriangle\triangledown}$), and 0.001 ($^{\blacktriangle\blacktriangledown}$), against the text-only baseline. Experiments contacted on a Pentium Dual-Core E2200 (2.4 GHz) with 4GB memory.

4. REFERENCES

[1] A. Arampatzis, J. Kamps, and S. Robertson. Where to stop reading a ranked list? Threshold optimization using truncated score distributions. In *SIGIR*, pages 524–531. ACM, 2009.

[2] A. Arampatzis, K. Zagoris, and S. A. Chatzichristofis. Dynamic two-stage image retrieval from large multimodal databases. In *ECIR*, volume 6611 of *Lecture Notes in Computer Science*, pages 326–337. Springer, 2011.

[3] A. Arampatzis, K. Zagoris, and S. A. Chatzichristofis. Fusion vs. two-stage for multimodal retrieval. In *ECIR*, volume 6611 of *Lecture Notes in Computer Science*, pages 759–762. Springer, 2011.

[4] S. A. Chatzichristofis, A. Arampatzis, and Y. S. Boutalis. Investigating the behavior of compact composite descriptors in early fusion, late fusion, and distributed image retrieval. *Radioengineering*, 19 (4):725–733, 2010.

[5] O. G. Cula and K. J. Dana. Compact representation of bidirectional texture functions. In *CVPR (1)*, pages 1041–1047, 2001.

[6] B. Thomee, E. M. Bakker, and M. S. Lew. Top-surf: a visual words toolkit. In *ACM Multimedia*, pages 1473–1476, 2010.

Query Term Ranking based on Search Results Overlap

Wei Song, Yu Zhang, Yubin Xie, Ting Liu, Sheng Li
Computer Science and Technology Department
Harbin Institute of Technology, China
{wsong, yzhang, ybxie, tliu, lisheng}@ir.hit.edu.cn

ABSTRACT

In this paper, we propose a method to rank and assign weights to query terms according to their impact on the topic of the query. We use *Search Result Overlap Ratio (SROR)* to quantify the overlap of the search results of the full query and a shorten query after removing one term. Intuitively, if the overlap is small, it indicates a big topic shift and the removed term should be discriminative and important. The *SROR* could be used for measuring query term importance with a search engine automatically. By this way, learning based models could be trained based on a large number of automatically labeled instances and make predictions for future queries efficiently.

Categories and Subject Descriptors

H.3.3 [**Information Systems**]: Information Search and Retrieval

General Terms

Algorithm, Experimentation, Performance

Keywords

Query Term Ranking, Query Reformulation, Search Results Overlap

1. INTRODUCTION

Query term ranking aims to assess query terms' importance and effectiveness. It has many potential applications. For example, it helps for formulating better queries by tuning term weights in retrieval models or removing ineffective terms. The important query terms or concepts also help for understanding a query's topic.

Recently, machine learning techniques have been adopted for similar tasks such as classification for key concepts identification [1], regression models for term ranking [3] and learning to rank for concept importance weighting [2]. Most of these approaches need manually labeled training data, either labeled key concepts or document relevance.

This paper proposes a simple approach based on *Search Result Overlap Ratio (SROR)*. The basic idea is to quantify a term's impact by considering the overlap of the search results of the full query and the shorten query leaving out the term. We assume the search results of a query represent its topic. If the overlap is small, it indicates the query's topic shifts a lot after removing the term. So the removed term plays an important role for determining the query's topic and should be discriminative. The experimental results on manually labeled queries showed that *SROR* based term ranking method had acceptable consistence with human judgement. This approach requires searching multiple times for a given query but the whole process can be done automatically with a search engine and does not need any human assistance. As a result, it could be used for automatically computing term weights for a large number of queries with a search engine beforehand. Learning based models could be trained using the statistical features extracted from these "labeled" instances. The learned models can make predictions for future queries efficiently. The experimental results on real web queries indicated the reformulated queries with *SROR* based weighting schemes improved the retrieval performance.

2. SEARCH RESULTS OVERLAP RATIO

For a given query $q=\{t_i\}$, we define the *Search Result Overlap Ratio (SROR)* for term $t_i \in q$ as

$$SROR(t_i) = \frac{\#(\varphi_N(q) \bigcap \varphi_N(q_{\neg t_i}))}{\#\varphi_N(q)} \quad (1)$$

where $\varphi_N(q)$ denotes the top N search results of query q returned by a search engine. $q_{\neg t_i}$ refers to the query after removing term t_i from query q. The sign # is used to count the size of a set. Heuristically, if $SROR(t_i)$ is large, it means t_i is not so important, because this term has little impact on the topic of query q. Otherwise, it indicates this term is discriminative for the full query. Based on $SROR(t_i)$, we assign weights to terms according to

$$Weight(t_i) = 1 - SROR(t_i) \quad (2)$$

$Weight$ can be used for both ranking and assigning weights to query terms. We demonstrate a query in Table 1. We can see the query term importance presented by normalized $Weight$ ($Weight(t_i)/\sum_{t_j \in q} Weight(t_j)$) is consistent with human intuition. Similar idea has been used for predicting query performance [5] by measuring the overlap of search results between using the full query and the individual query term. However, individual term may be not enough to indicate the query topic sometime. Instead, we borrow the idea from [3] they assume leaving out an important term results in decrease retrieval effectiveness. In our case, we assume removing an important term may lead to topic shift.

SIGIR'11, July 24–28, 2011, Beijing, China.
ACM 978-1-4503-0757-4/11/07.

Table 1: Terms' *SRORs* and normalized *Weights* of the query "movie free download website".

Query Terms	movie	free	download	website
SROR	0.0	0.8	0.3	0.5
Weight(Norm)	0.417	0.083	0.292	0.208

3. EXPERIMENTS

The experiments were conducted on real web queries and a web corpus. We used one month query log collected by Sogou[1] during June 2008 consisting of 5604251 unique queries and associated clicks. For 99.67% queries, the query length $l(q) \leq 10$. The web corpus containing 5 TB web pages was also crawled by Sogou during 2008. We used Indri [4] for indexing and searching this corpus. The top 30 search results of a input query returned by a search engine were used for computing *SROR*.

Term Ranking. We computed *SROR* using Sogou and Baidu[2] search engines respectively. To evaluate the ability of ranking terms using *SROR*, we accessed the agreement between the automatically generated rankings and human labelers. We sampled 120 queries, $3 \leq l(q) \leq 10$. Two labelers were asked to rank terms in each query according to the term importance for the full query. We computed Kendall's W coefficient[3], which ranges from 0 (no agreement) to 1 (complete agreement), between different rankings for each query. The average score over all queries is reported.

The agreement between using two search engines is consistent (0.77). It indicates *SROR* is stable across different search engines. The agreement between two labelers is 0.75. The average agreement between one *SROR* based ranking (using Sogou or Baidu) and one labeled ranking (by labeler 1 or labeler 2) is 0.64. The average agreement among one *SROR* based ranking and two labeled rankings is 0.57. Due to the difficulty of this task, there is a positive correlation.

Retrieval Effectiveness. For evaluating the retrieval effectiveness of the *SROR* based weighting schemes, we sampled test queries from the query log. Each query must have at least 5 associated clicked pages in the indexed corpus and $3 \leq l(q) \leq 10$. Finally, we collected 1538 test queries, 113 of which contained at least 7 terms. We viewed user clicked pages as relevant. The average MAP and p@10 over all queries were computed.

We could directly apply *Weight* for assigning weights to terms, noted as **WT**. This strategy has to search many times for a given query. For efficiency, we used *Weight* to automatically weight query terms for a large number of queries beforehand with a search engine. Then we trained a regression model based on statistical features extracted from the labeled instances. The learned model could predict weights for future queries efficiently at querying time. We trained this regression model based on 2000 queries automatically labeled by *Weight* using Baidu search engine, noted as **REG**. These queries contain 4 to 6 terms each. We do not use long queries for training, because the current search engines do not perform so well on such queries compared to shorter queries. The extracted features include *term index within a query, times the term occurs in query log as a whole query, average rank of associated clicks, corpus tf, corpus idf and mutual information among query terms.*

[1]http://www.sogou.com/

[2]http://www.baidu.com/

[3]http://en.wikipedia.org/wiki/Kendall's

Table 2: The retrieval effectiveness comparison of different weighting strategies on queries with different length.

%	MAP		p@10	
Length	[3,6]	[7,10]	[3,6]	[7,10]
UNF	9.84	4.51	8.95	1.96
WT	**10.23**	4.81	**9.23**	**2.23**
REG	10.02	4.86	9.02	2.06
IDF	9.37	**5.00**	7.92	2.05

Table 2 shows the retrieval effectiveness using different weighting methods on queries with different length. **UNF** denotes giving terms uniform weights. **IDF** denotes the corpus based IDF approach which solely depends on the term distribution within the corpus. We can see **WT** which directly uses *Weight* for term weighting outperforms other methods in most cases. It means *SROR* is a useful signal for query term ranking. The regression model **REG** performs better than **UNF** as well. It indicates the potential to use *SROR* for automatically labeling. **IDF** achieves good results when dealing with long queries but performs poorly on queries with moderate length in our experiments.

4. CONCLUSIONS

In this paper, we have proposed a simple approach to measure query term importance by examining the search results overlap ratio. The experiments showed *SROR* based weighting schemes improved the retrieval performance. We believe our method could be improved further if noun phrases or multi-term concepts are identified and used, because they explain the query topics better than individual terms. We also plan to incorporate more features for learning based on automatically labeled instances using *SROR*.

Acknowledgments

This research is supported by NSFC under Grant No. 60736044, 61073126 and 61073129, by HIT.KLOF.2009020.

5. REFERENCES

[1] M. Bendersky and W. B. Croft. Discovering key concepts in verbose queries. *In Proc. SIGIR 2008*, pages 491–498, 2008.

[2] M. Bendersky and W. B. Croft. Learning concept importance using a weighted dependence model. *In Proc. WSDM 2010*, pages 133–142, 2010.

[3] S.-H. K. Chia-Jung Lee, Ruey-Cheng Chen and P.-J. Cheng. A term dependency-based approach for query terms ranking. *In Proc. CIKM 2009*, pages 745–770, 2009.

[4] T. Strohman, D. Metzler, H. Turtle, and W. B. Croft. Indri: A language-model based search engine for complex queries (extended version). IR 407, University of Massachusetts, 2005.

[5] E. Yom-Tov, S. Fine, D. Carmel, and A. Darlow. Learning to estimate query difficulty: including applications to missing content detection and distributed information retrieval. In *In Proc. SIGIR 2005*, pages 512–519. ACM, 2005.

Tossing Coins to Trim Long Queries

Sudip Datta
Language Technologies Research Centre
International Institute of Information Technology
Hyderabad 500 032
sudip.datta@research.iiit.ac.in

Vasudeva Varma
Language Technologies Research Centre
International Institute of Information Technology
Hyderabad 500 032
vv@iiit.ac.in

ABSTRACT

Verbose web queries are often descriptive in nature where a term based search engine is unable to distinguish between the essential and noisy words, which can result in a drift from the user intent. We present a randomized query reduction technique that builds on an earlier learning to rank based approach. The proposed technique randomly picks only a small set of samples, instead of the exponentially many sub-queries, thus being fast enough to be useful for web search engines, while still covering wide sub-query space.

Categories and Subject Descriptors

H.3.3 [**Information Search and Retrieval**]: Query formulation

General Terms

Algorithms, Experimentation, Performance

Keywords

Verbose Queries, Randomized Algorithm

1. INTRODUCTION

Recent studies indicate a marked growth in the share of long queries[1] - containing more than 5 terms. Though, a user's intent might be well represented in a long query, 'bag of words' based search engines tend to fail on them, as they are unable to capture the complex structure of queries. This may result in query drift and consequent poor performance.

Existing approaches to address this problem can be classified into two categories. Query term weighing based techniques attempt to determine the importance of a term and associate a weight with each term in proportion to its perceived importance in the query. Query reduction techniques, on the other hand, focus on identifying the best performing sub-query of the original query by pruning away unimportant terms. The current work belongs to the latter category.

Kumaran et al. [5] (henceforth referred to as 'ExpRed') propose an approach that views identification of best representative sub-query as a ranking task and apply learning to rank approach using query quality predictors as features. Since an exponential number $2^n - 1$ of sub-queries can be generated from an n-word query, computationally it is very expensive to train a model and evaluate it on all sub-queries.

SIGIR'11, July 24–28, 2011, Beijing, China.
ACM 978-1-4503-0757-4/11/07.

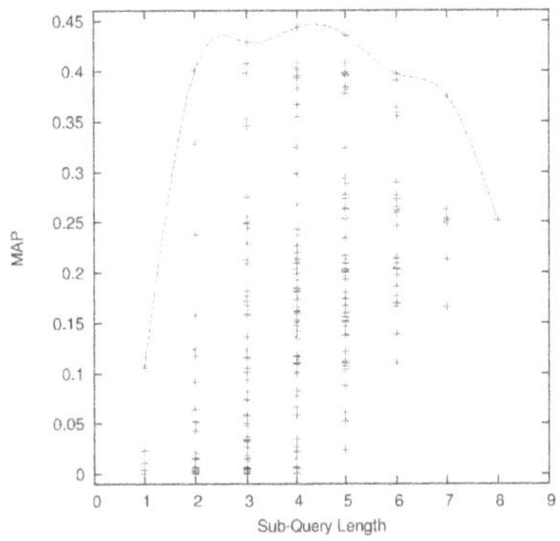

Figure 1: Sub-query scores for a typical query.

They propose a number of heuristics to reduce this set of sub-queries. Balasubramanian et al. [2] (henceforth referred to as 'SingleRed') extend this work by adopting regression based formulations and only consider sub-queries reduced by a single term from the original query, as candidates sub-queries, thus making their system web-scalable.

Our technique for query reduction uses a randomization mechanism to prune terms from original query and builds on Kumaran et al. [5] while considering only a small, configurable number of candidate sub-queries instead of the exponential number in baseline system. Our technique is web-scalable as it achieves substantial improvements over original query and the gains increase with larger samplings.

2. MOTIVATION

Performance improvement on verbose queries can be attained by removal of noisy terms such that the resultant shorter query performs better. Moreover, to be useful for web-search, the technique should minimise overhead on the retrieval process. ExpRed achieves the first objective by evaluation of all sub-queries, but is slow because of the exponential number $2^n - 1$ of sub-queries involved in an n word query. SingleRed trades off time for performance by confining the search to sub-queries with one fewer term than the original query. Figure 1, shows the performance of all sub-queries for a representative long query, where y-axis measures their Mean Average Precision (MAP) scores while x-axis indicates sub-query length. Thus, the original query, with largest number of terms is the sub-query with highest x co-ordinate (x_{max}) in this plot. It can be observed that maximum achievable performance (indicated by highest y score for an x value) increases till *optimal sub-query* and decreases on further addition of terms. As evident from the figure, employing SingleRed's choice of evaluating sub-queries with one fewer term than the original query, only sub-queries with $x = x_{max} - 1$ are considered, while the rest are ignored, leaving substantial scope for improvement. We propose an efficient method to explore this space. Another property of the curve is that it is steeper before it peaks while reducing slowly as the original query approaches. This indicates that removal of terms from optimal query, results in greater performance degradation than addition of extra terms. We employ this observation in our sampling technique.

3. OUR APPROACH

Since, evaluation of all sub-queries is infeasible in a web scenario, we propose a randomized reduction technique that samples only a small number of candidate sub-queries and yet efficiently explores the sub-query space. This method removes each query term of the original query, by an 'optimal query length' dependent probability. We argue that in small number of iterations of this sub-query generation method, with high probability, it is likely to pick at least one 'good' sub-query. Formally, to generate a sub-query from an n term query, a set of n random numbers $R[1..n]$ between 0.0 and 1.0 are generated. The kth term of this query is discarded if $R[k] > p$, where $p = l_{opt}/l_q$. Here, l_{opt} is the optimal length of queries and l_q is the length of query q in words.

Theoretically, this problem can be modeled as a geometric distribution where each new sample can be treated as a Bernoulli trial, where success is defined by selection of one 'good' query. Thus, if probability of a good sample being picked in a trial is m, then expected number of samples for an efficient sub-query to be picked is $1/m$ with a deviation of $\sqrt{(1-m)/(m^2)}$. As an illustrative example, among the 9 word queries in our corpus, 5.84% of their sub-queries scored within 10% of their best performing sub-query. Considering these sub-queries as 'good', 18 samples would be required to pick one efficient sample, with a standard deviation of 17.

Effectively, a learning to rank formulation is used, where each sub-query is represented by a set of query quality predictors and its MAP acts as the label. The proposed technique is used for generation of sub-queries on train and test data. The model is learned on a large number of candidate sub-queries. Testing requires generation of only a small number of sub-queries which are ranked according to their scores generated by the model and the top positioned version is used as representative of the original query. Unfortunately, the overall performance of our system is dependent not just on the ability to pick effective sub-queries as candidates, but also on the discriminative capabilities of the learning formulation. Despite this constraint, as show in Section 4, significant gains in performance were attained.

4. EXPERIMENTS

We use an experimental setup similar to [5]. Robust 2004 dataset consisting of around half million documents is used for experiments, with the 'description' field of topics acting as long queries. We use the definition of long query described in [3], $5 \geq l_q \geq 12$, where l_q is the length of query q. Thus, 184 of the 250 judged queries associated with this data, are used. A set of 30 query quality predictors such as mutual information, query clarity, query scope, are used to describe each sub-query. RankSVM implementation of SVM^{rank}[4] is used for ranking sub-queries.

The set of queries are partitioned into 4:1 split of train and test queries. At each iteration a set of twenty models, with different seeds, are learned from a large number of samples generated from the training set of queries. These models are used to predict rankings of an equal number of sets prepared from the test queries and the performance is averaged over the 20 sets. A linear 'multiplication factor' x determines the number of sub-queries generated for each query and is in proportion to its length. Since, according to [5] the optimal query length lies between 3 and 6, experiments were performed by varying l_{opt} between these values, for both train and test data.

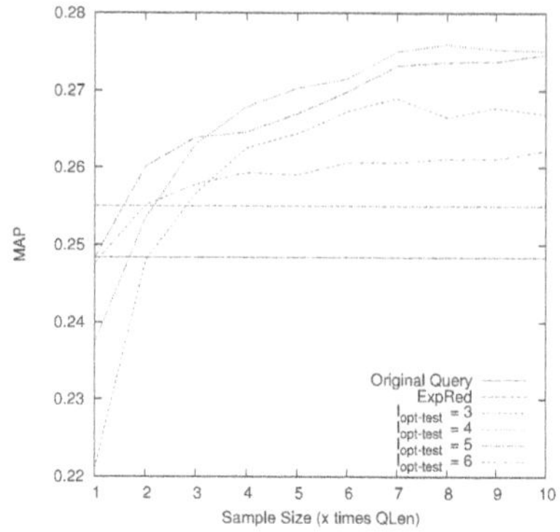

Figure 2: Random pruning with $l_{opt-train} = 6$

Due to space constraints, only the run with best results is depicted in Fig.2. For this run $l_{opt-train} = 6$ is used and plots for various $l_{opt-test}$ values with different 'multiplication factors' are shown. We believe that performance peaks for $l_{opt-train} = 6$ and $l_{opt-test} = 4$ because adequate training requires a large number of sub-queries with decent scores. Thus, as argued in Section 2, a higher average performance among candidate queries can be achieved with bias for longer queries. Testing, on the other hand, relies on a single 'good' sub-query and thus peaks closer to the true optimal length of 3.54. Overall, it is seen that irrespective of the choice of $l_{opt-test}$, performance gains over the original query and ExpRed are achieved with a sampling of just three times the query length. Moreover, a steady co-relation is observed between the number of samples drawn and the improved performance.

5. CONCLUSION

In this paper, we presented a randomization based sampling technique for reduction of long queries. We present results which confirm that this technique is more efficient than earlier techniques of selecting candidate queries during prediction. As future work, we plan to apply this sampling technique on more semantically rich units of information such as phrases and clauses.

6. REFERENCES

[1] `http://weblogs.hitwise.com/alan-long/2009/11/searches_getting_longer.html`.

[2] N. Balasubramanian, G. Kumaran, and V. R. Carvalho. Exploring reductions for long web queries. In *SIGIR'10*.

[3] M. Bendersky and W. B. Croft. Analysis of long queries in a large scale search log. WSCD '09.

[4] T. Joachims. Optimizing search engines using clickthrough data. In *KDD '02*.

[5] G. Kumaran and V. R. Carvalho. Reducing long queries using query quality predictors. In *SIGIR '09*.

A Comparison of Time-aware Ranking Methods

Nattiya Kanhabua
Dept. of Computer Science
Norwegian University of Science and Technology
Trondheim, Norway
nattiya@idi.ntnu.no

Kjetil Nørvåg
Dept. of Computer Science
Norwegian University of Science and Technology
Trondheim, Norway
noervaag@idi.ntnu.no

ABSTRACT

When searching a temporal document collection, e.g., news archives or blogs, the time dimension must be explicitly incorporated into a retrieval model in order to improve relevance ranking. Previous work has followed one of two main approaches: 1) a mixture model linearly combining textual similarity and temporal similarity, or 2) a probabilistic model generating a query from the textual and temporal part of a document independently. In this paper, we compare the effectiveness of different time-aware ranking methods by using a mixture model applied to all methods. Extensive evaluation is conducted using the New York Times Annotated Corpus, queries and relevance judgments obtained using the Amazon Mechanical Turk.

Categories and Subject Descriptors H.3.3 [Information Storage and Retrieval]: Information Search and Retrieval
General Terms Algorithms, Experimentation, Performance
Keywords Time-aware ranking, Temporal similarity

1. INTRODUCTION

We deal with a retrieval task that a query is explicitly provided with time, i.e., containing temporal information needs. In this case, the time dimension must be incorporated into a retrieval model in order to improve relevance ranking. Consider a query containing the temporal expression "Independence Day 2009", an existing retrieval model relying on term matching will fail to retrieve a document mentioning "July 4, 2009", although two temporal expressions refer to the same date. Hence, when dealing with the time dimension, *time uncertainty* should be taken into account because any two temporal expressions can be *relevant* even they are not equally written.

The previous time-aware ranking methods [1, 2, 3, 4, 5] are based on two main approaches: 1) a mixture model linearly combining textual and temporal similarity, or 2) a probabilistic model generating a query from the textual and temporal part of a document independently. It is shown that time-aware ranking performs better than keyword-based ranking. To the best of our knowledge, an empirical comparison of different time-aware ranking methods has never been done before. In this paper, we will evaluate the effectiveness of different time aware ranking methods: LMT [1], LMTU [1], TS [4], TSU [4], and FuzzySet [3] using the same dataset, and we will give a brief discussion of the evaluation.

SIGIR'11, July 24–28, 2011, Beijing, China.
ACM 978-1-4503-0757-4/11/07.

2. MODEL

A temporal expression or the publication date of a document is represented as a quadruple [1]: (tb_l, tb_u, te_l, te_u) where tb_l and tb_u are the lower bound and upper bound for the begin boundary of a time interval respectively. Similarly, te_l and te_u are the lower bound and upper bound for the end boundary of a time interval. A temporal query q is composed of keywords q_{text} and temporal expressions q_{time}. A document d consists of the textual part d_{text}, i.e., a bag of words, and the temporal part d_{time} composed of the publication date $PubTime(d)$, and temporal expressions mentioned in the document's contents $ContentTime(d)$ or $\{t_1, \ldots t_k\}$.

To be comparable, we apply a mixture model to linearly combine textual similarity and temporal similarity for all ranking methods. Given a temporal query q, a document d will be ranked according to a score computed as follows:

$$S(q,d) = (1-\alpha)\cdot S'(q_{word}, d_{word}) + \alpha \cdot S''(q_{time}, d_{time})$$

where the mixture parameter α indicates the importance of textual similarity $S'(q_{word}, d_{word})$ and temporal similarity $S''(q_{time}, d_{time})$. Both similarity scores must be normalized, e.g., divided by the maximum scores, in order to the final score $S(q,d)$. $S'(q_{word}, d_{word})$ can be measured using any of existing text-based weighting functions. $S''(q_{time}, d_{time})$ measure temporal similarity by assuming that a temporal expression $t_q \in q_{time}$ is generated independently from each other, and a two-step generative model was used [1]:

$$S''(q_{time}, d_{time}) = \prod_{t_q \in q_{time}} P(t_q|d_{time}) = \prod_{t_q \in q_{time}} \left(\frac{1}{|d_{time}|} \sum_{t_d \in d_{time}} P(t_q|t_d) \right)$$

Linear interpolation smoothing will be applied to give the probability $P(t_q|t_d)$ for an unseen query temporal expression t_q in d. In the next section, we will explain how to estimate $P(t_q|t_d)$ for different time-aware ranking methods.

3. TIME-AWARE RANKING METHODS

The time-aware ranking methods we study differ from each other in two main aspects: 1) whether or not time uncertainty is concerned, and 2) whether the publication time or the content time of a document is used in ranking. LMT ignores time uncertainty and it exploits the content time of d. LMT can be calculated as:

$$P(t_q|t_d)_{LMT} = \begin{cases} 0 & \text{if } t_q \neq t_d, \\ 1 & \text{if } t_q = t_d. \end{cases}$$

where $t_d \in ContentTime(d)$, and the score will be equal to 1 iff a temporal expression t_d is exactly equal to t_q. LMTU concerns time uncertainty by assuming equal likelihood for any time interval t'_q that t_q can refer to, that is, $t_q = \{t'_q | t'_q \in t_q\}$. The simplified calculation of $P(t_q|t_d)$ for LMTU is given as:

$$P(t_q|t_d)_{LMTU} = \frac{|t_q \cap t_d|}{|t_q| \cdot |t_d|}$$

where $t_d \in \mathit{ContentTime}(d)$. The detailed computation of $|t_q \cap t_d|$, $|t_q|$ and $|t_d|$ can be referred to [1].

TS ignores time uncertainty. $P(t_q|t_d)_{TS}$ can be computed similarly to $P(t_q|t_d)_{LMT}$, but t_d is corresponding to the publication time of d instead of the content time as computed for LMT. TSU exploits the publication time of d as done for TS, but it also takes time-uncertainty into account. $P(t_q|t_d)_{TSU}$ is defined using an exponential decay function:

$$P(t_q|t_d)_{TSU} = \mathit{DecayRate}^{\lambda \cdot \frac{|t_q - t_d|}{\mu}}$$

$$|t_q - t_d| = \frac{|tb_l^q - tb_l^d| + |tb_u^q - tb_u^d| + |te_l^q - te_l^d| + |te_u^q - te_u^d|}{4}$$

where $t_d = \mathit{PubTime}(d)$, $\mathit{DecayRate}$ and λ are constant, $0 < \mathit{DecayRate} < 1$ and $\lambda > 0$, and μ is a unit of time distance. The main idea is to give a score that decreases proportional to the time distance between t_q and t_d. The less time distance, the more temporally similar they are.

FuzzySet measures temporal similarity using a fuzzy membership function and it exploits the publication time of d for determining temporal similarity. $P(t_q|t_d)_{FuzzySet}$ is given as:

$$P(t_q|t_d)_{FuzzySet} = \begin{cases} 0 & \text{if } t_d < a_1, \\ f_1(t_d) & \text{if } t_d \geq a_1 \wedge t_d \leq a_2, \\ 1 & \text{if } t_d > a_2 \wedge t_d \leq a_3, \\ f_2(t_d) & \text{if } t_d > a_3 \wedge t_d \leq a_4, \\ 0 & \text{if } t_d > a_4. \end{cases}$$

where $t_d = \mathit{PubTime}(d)$. $f_1(t_d)$ is $\left(\frac{a_1 - t_d}{a_1 - a_2}\right)^n$ if $a_1 \neq a_2$, or 1 if $a_1 = a_2$. $f_2(t_d)$ is $\left(\frac{a_4 - t_d}{a_4 - a_3}\right)^m$ if $a_3 \neq a_4$, or 1 if $a_3 = a_4$. The parameters a_1, a_4, n, m are determined empirically.

4. EXPERIMENTS

The New York Times Annotated Corpus is used and 40 queries from [1] obtained using the Amazon Mechanical Turk. Note that, a standard dataset, e.g., TREC, is not applicable because queries are not time-related, and judgments are not targeted towards temporal information needs.

Documents are indexed and retrieved using the Apache Lucene version 2.9.3. There are two modes for retrieval [1]: 1) *inclusive* and 2) *exclusive*. For *inclusive*, both query terms and a temporal expression comprise a query q_{text}. For *exclusive*, only query terms constitute q_{text}, and a temporal expression is excluded from q_{text}. The baseline is the textual similarity $S'(q_{word}, d_{word})$, i.e., the Lucene's default weighting function, using *inclusive* mode denoted TFIDF-IN.

The smoothing parameter is set to 0.1. Parameters for TSU are $\mathit{DecayRate} = 0.5$, $\lambda = 0.5$, and $\mu = 6$ months. Parameters for FuzzySet are $n = 2$, $m = 2$, $a_1 = a_2 - (0.25 \times (a_3 - a_2))$, and $a_4 = a_3 + (0.50 \times (a_3 - a_2))$. The effectiveness is measured as the precision at 1, 5 and 10 documents (P@1, P@5 and P@10), mean average precision (MAP), and mean reciprocal rank (MRR). The sensitivity of the effectiveness to the mixture parameter α is depicted in Figure 1. The results show that the effectiveness of LMT and LMTU decreases when α is increased, whereas the effectiveness of all other methods slightly increases with the value of α.

Table 1 shows the best performing results of each method. In general, all time-aware ranking methods outperform the baseline significantly, except LMT. For each time-aware ranking, the effectiveness when retrieved using *exclusive* is better

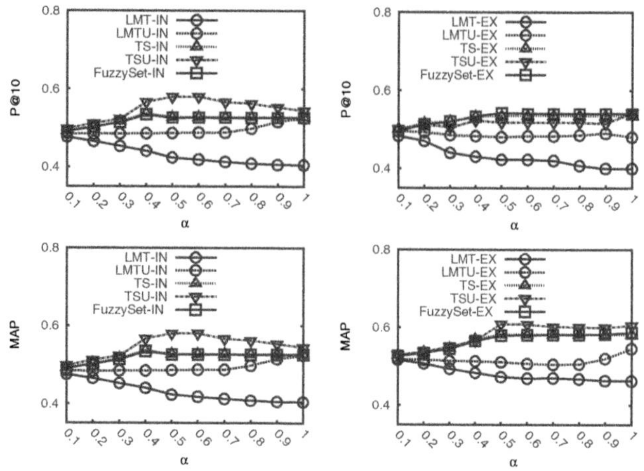

Figure 1: Sensitivity of P@10 and MAP to the mixture parameter α for both retrieval modes.

Table 1: Effectiveness of different ranking methods, in bold indicates statistically improvement over all other methods using t-test ($p < 0.05$).

Method	P@1	P@5	P@10	MAP	MRR
TFIDF-IN	.38	.43	.41	.49	.56
LMT-IN	.43	.41	.41	.48	.57
LMTU-IN	.48	.47	.45	.52	.68
TS-IN	.45	.49	.48	.54	.61
TSU-IN	**.65**	.51	.49	**.58**	**.76**
FuzzySet-IN	.45	.49	.48	.53	.61
LMT-EX	.38	.42	.48	.52	.55
LMTU-EX	.48	.48	.50	.55	.68
TS-EX	.48	.52	.53	.58	.63
TSU-EX	**.68**	.54	.54	**.61**	**.77**
FuzzySet-EX	.48	.53	.54	.59	.64

than *inclusive*. TSU performs best among all methods in both *inclusive* and *exclusive* modes, and it outperforms all other methods significantly for P@1, MAP and MRR.

5. CONCLUSIONS

Time-aware ranking methods show better performance compared to a method based on only keywords. When the time-uncertainty is taken into account, the effectiveness is improved significantly. Even though TSU gains the best performance among other methods, the usefulness of TSU is still limited for a document collection with no time metadata, i.e., the publication time of documents is not available. On the contrary, LMT and LMTU can be applied to any document collection without time metadata, but the extraction of temporal expressions is needed.

6. REFERENCES

[1] K. Berberich, S. Bedathur, O. Alonso, and G. Weikum. A language modeling approach for temporal information needs. In *Proceedings of ECIR'2010*, 2010.

[2] F. Diaz and R. Jones. Using temporal profiles of queries for precision prediction. In *Proceedings of SIGIR'2004*, 2004.

[3] P. J. Kalczynski and A. Chou. Temporal document retrieval model for business news archives. *Inf. Process. Manage.*, 2005.

[4] N. Kanhabua and K. Nørvåg. Determining time of queries for re-ranking search results. In *Proceedings of ECDL'2010*, 2010.

[5] X. Li and W. B. Croft. Time-based language models. In *Proceedings of CIKM'2003*, 2003.

Learning for Graphs with Annotated Edges

Fan Li
Yahoo! Labs
hustlfhustlf@gmail.com

ABSTRACT

Automatic classification with graphs containing annotated edges is an interesting problem and has many potential applications. We present a risk minimization formulation that exploits the annotated edges for classification tasks. One major advantage of our approach compared to other methods is that the weight of each edge in the graph structures in our model , including both positive and negative weights, can be learned automatically from training data based on edge features. The empirical results show that our approach can lead to significantly improved classification performance compared to several baseline approaches.

Categories and Subject Descriptors

H.4 [**Information Systems Applications**]: Miscellaneous

General Terms

Algorithms

Keywords

graph regularization, webpage categorization

1. INTRODUCTION

Automatic classification with graphs containing annotated edges is an interesting problem and has many potential applications. For example, in webpage categorization, the hyperlink structures among web-pages are very useful resources. The hyper-links can be thought as edges annotated by their associated anchor text and can be used to improve web-page classification performance. Many researcher have studied the problem of classification with graph structures. For example, [1] has exploited the web links using pagerank scores and combines these scores with local text features for webpage categorization tasks. [2] and [3] developed semisupervised learning methods to take advantage of graph structures in classification tasks.

While the above works successfully improved the classification performance using graph structures, they did not exploit the annotation information associated with the edges in the graph. For example, in [2], it is assumed that all the edges in hyperlink structures have the same positive weight. However, this assumption may not always yield the best result from a classification standpoint. The importance of these edges could be very different in terms of classification, depending on their associated anchor text. Furthermore, sometimes the edges in hyperlink structures may have negative weights. For example, in the catalog and product webpage classification task, the catalog pages often connect to product pages but seldom connect to other catalog pages.

One simple way to use annotation information is to pass edge annotations to node features. That is to treat the annotations of an edge as additional features of the two node connected by this edge. However, by doing this, we have merged the edge features into node features and lost part of the useful information. In this paper, we propose a novel objective function in the graph regularization framework to exploit the annotations on the edges. The general idea used in the paper is to create regularization for the graph with the assumption that the likellhood of two nodes to be in the same class can be estimated using annotations of the edge linking the two nodes.

There are other discriminative models that could learn edge weights in the graph automatically from the training data. For example, conditional random field (CRF) has been widely used for classification tasks on chain graphs. However, when the graph topology becomes more complex (which is always the case in hyper-link structures), the accurate solutions of such models will be very difficult to get. Our approach does not have such a problem.

2. METHOD

Consider the problem of predicting unknown labels for the testing examples based on their input vectors. In this paper, we are interested in the setting where we observe a training set $(\vec{x}_i, y_i)$ for $i = 1, ..., n$ and a test set $(\vec{x}_j)$ for $j = n+1, ..., m$. Here $\vec{x}_i$ is the input vector of the ith example and scalar $y_i \in \{-1, 1\}$ is the class label of the ith example. The true labels y_j for the test set $(\vec{x}_j)$ are unknown and to be predicted. We are interested in the case that in addition to the input vectors, a graph is also observed on the whole dataset (including both the training and the testing set). Each node in the graph corresponds to an example and each edge in the graph corresponds to some relationship between the two connected examples.

SIGIR'11, July 24–28, 2011, Beijing, China.
ACM 978-1-4503-0757-4/11/07.

The objective function we proposed is listed as formula 1,

$$\hat{f} = argmin_{f,\vec{\gamma}} \sum_{i=1}^{n} Loss(f_i, y_i) + \lambda f^T K^{-1} f$$
$$+\lambda' \sum_{(i,j)\in E} (f_i f_j - c_{ij})^2$$
$$\text{and set } c_{ij} = \vec{\gamma}\vec{a}_{ij} \tag{1}$$

Here $Loss()$ represents the loss function we defined on the training data. In our work, we will use the the least square loss function thus $loss(f, y) = (f - y)^2$. K is the $m \times m$ kernel matrix that is constructed only from the local text features. λ and λ' are regularization parameters that are treated as constants here. Notice that formula 1 will reduce to a standard ridge regression classifier when λ' is set to be zero. c_{ij} are the edge weights to be learned from the anchor text features. Vector $\vec{a}_{ij} = (a_{ij1}, \ldots, a_{ijp})$ represents the values of the p anchor text features associated with the hyperlink connecting web-page i and web-page j. Vector $\vec{\gamma} = (\gamma_1, \ldots, \gamma_p)^T$ consists of the parameters that represent the weights of anchor text features. Notice that we are using a least square loss function as $Loss(f_i, y_i)$ so that the values of $f_i f_j$ are encouraged to be similar to ± 1.

The intuition of formula 1 is clear. If we consider regularization of the form $(f_i f_j - c_{ij})^2$ with unknown annotation dependent parameter c_{ij}, then the proposed method seems the best way to use annotation information to optimize parameter c_{ij} because $c_{ij} = E(f_i f_j | \vec{a}_{ij})$. This has the desirable effect that if given the annotations, f_i and f_j are likely to have the same sign, then our objective function will strengthen this trend. When f_i and f_j are likely to have different signs given the annotations, formula 1 works in a similar pattern. In formula 1, each edge weight $c_{ij} = \vec{\gamma}\vec{a}_{ij}$ is assumed to be the sum of anchor text weights appeared in this hyperlink. Note that the f_i values for the training examples are encouraged to be close to y_i (either 1 or -1) by the first term of the above formula.

[2] has presented an efficient algorithm to solve the objective function with graph regularizers. In this paper, a similar algorithm with slight modifications is used to solve the objective function in formula 1.

Notice that formula 1 can be re-written as

$$\hat{f} = argmin_{f,\vec{\gamma},\vec{v},\vec{w}} \sum_{i=1}^{n} Loss(f_i, y_i) + \frac{\lambda}{2}(||\vec{w}||^2$$
$$+||\vec{v}||^2) + \lambda' \sum_{(i,j)\in E} (f_i f_j - \vec{\gamma}\vec{a}_{ij})^2$$
$$\text{s.t. } f_k = \vec{w}\vec{x}_k + v_k\sqrt{u} \quad (k = 1, ..., m) \tag{2}$$

Here u plays the role as a stabilizing parameter and we set it to be a small constant 0.1. It can be regarded as adding a feature $\sqrt{u}$ to each specific node. By reformulating the objective function as formula 2, the construction of the dense kernel matrix K is avoided. We can then solve the problem iteratively using the gradient descent algorithm. In each iteration, we first fix $\vec{\gamma}$ and solve $\vec{v}$ and $\vec{w}$. Then we fix $\vec{v}$ and $\vec{w}$ and solve $\vec{\gamma}$. This process is iterated until the algorithm converges. The initial values of these parameters are all set to be zero.

Table 1: The micor-F1 performance (mean $\pm$ std-dev %)

	Yahoo Directory Data	Webkb Data
Baseline	57.9 ± 0.5	86.5 ± 0.3
Baseline with anchor text	60.5 ± 0.4	87.6 ± 0.6
Our approach	64.8 ± 0.4	89.0 ± 0.5

Table 2: The macor-F1 performance (mean $\pm$ std-dev %

	Yahoo Directory Data	Webkb Data
Baseline	57.9 ± 0.4	77.2 ± 0.3
Baseline with anchortext	60.8 ± 0.4	82.6 ± 0.5
Our approach	65.1 ± 0.5	82.7 ± 0.3

3. EXPERIMENT

The two real hyperlinked collections used in our paper are WebKB data (http://www.cs.cmu.edu/webkb/) and Yahoo! Directory data (http://www.yahoo.com/). We constructed co-citation graphs on these two collections, in which two pages are connected by an undirected edge if both pages are linked to by a third page.

The WebKB dataset consists of 8275 web-pages crawled from university web sites. The vocabulary consists of 20000 most frequent words. Its co-citation graph has 1143716 edges. The Yahoo! Directory dataset consists of 22969 web pages. Each page of this collection belongs to one of the 13 top level topical directory categories (for example, arts, business and education). The vocabulary consists of 50000 most frequent words. The number of edges in its co-citation graph is 1170029. We randomly split the labeled data into two parts: 50 percent for training and another 50 percent for testing. We draw five runs and report test set averages and standard deviations.

The micro-F1 and macro-F1 performance of different approaches on multiple datasets with co-citation graphs are listed in table 1 and table 2. We use the graph regularization approach in [2] as our baseline approach and call it "Baseline" in the two tables. In order to be fair, we have also tried an extension of the baseline approach by putting the anchor text features associated with each edge into the body text of the two pages connected by this edge. We call this extension "Baseline with anchor text" in the following tables. The performance of our approach is shown in the last raw of the two tables. We can see that our approach has achieved significant improvement compared with the other two approaches.

4. CONCLUSION

This paper presents a novel risk minimization formulation for classification tasks with graphs containing annotated edges. The empirical results show that our approach can lead to improved classification performance, compared to several baseline approaches.

5. REFERENCES

[1] Z. Gyongyi, H. Garcia-Molina, and J. Pedersen. Web content categorization using link information. *Technical Report, standford University*, 2006.

[2] T. Zhang, A. Popescul, and B. Dom. Linear prediction models with graph regularization for web-page categorization. In *SIGKDD 2006*, 2006.

[3] X. Zhu, Z. Ghahramani, and J.Lafferty. Semi-supervised learning using gaussian fields and harmonic functions. In *ICML 2003*, 2003.

Formulating Effective Questions for Community-based Question Answering

Saori Suzuki
College of Knowledge and Library Sciences
University of Tsukuba
s0711607@u.tsukuba.ac.jp

Shin'ichi Nakayama
Graduate School of Library, Information and Media Studies
University of Tsukuba
nakayama@slis.tsukuba.ac.jp

Hideo Joho
Graduate School of Library, Information and Media Studies
University of Tsukuba
hideo@slis.tsukuba.ac.jp

ABSTRACT

Community-based Question Answering (CQA) services have become a major venue for people's information seeking on the Web. However, many studies on CQA have focused on the prediction of the best *answers* for a given question. This paper looks into the formulation of effective *questions* in the context of CQA. In particular, we looked at effect of contextual factors appended to a basic question on the performance of submitted answers. This study analysed a total of 930 answers returned in response to 266 questions that were formulated by 46 participants. The results show that adding a questionnaire's personal and social attribute to the question helped improve the perceptions of answers both in information seeking questions and opinion seeking questions.

Categories and Subject Descriptors

H.3.3 [**Information Search and Retrieval**]: Query formulation; H.3.5 [**On-line Information Services**]: Web-based services

General Terms

Experimentation, Human Factors

Keywords

Question formulation, context, CQA

1. INTRODUCTION

Taylor's 1968 model is perhaps one of the earliest work to point out that people's expression of their information needs can be compromised by a given environment [9]. Short queries frequently submitted to search engines show that Taylor's model is also evident on the Web. One goal of Information Retrieval (IR) research is to retrieve relevant information in response to such compromised expressions of people's information needs. In this regard, community-based Question Answering (CQA) sites are an interesting venue for information seeking on the Web, since the expression of information needs does not have to be compromised as much as typical search engine queries. People use natural language to formulate a query and it is common to use multiple sentences to elaborate the information needs in CQA services. Meanwhile, Yahoo! Answers alone are reported to have 200 million visitors worldwide in 2009[1], making CQA an important research area in IR. However, existing studies on CQA have been focused on the prediction of the best answers for a given question [1, 2, 8]. Investigations on how to formulate effective questions have been limited.

To address the problem, this paper examined effect of contextual factors in question formulation in the context of CQA. Appending a contextual factor has been shown to be effective in query formulation [7] in IR. Therefore, we hypothesised that appending a contextual factor to a basic question could improve the performance of submitted answers. To examine the hypothesis, we asked participants to formulate genuine questions with different contextual factors, submitted them to a CQA site, and assessed the answers responded to the questions.

SIGIR'11, July 24–28, 2011, Beijing, China.
ACM 978-1-4503-0757-4/11/07.

2. METHOD

2.1 Contextual Factors

The first task was to identify the contextual factors to be examined in our investigation. Our approach was two-fold. First, we revisited exiting context models proposed in IR. More specifically, we synthesised the context models proposed in Interactive IR [6], QE [7], and personalisation [3]. Second, we manually investigated a CQA archive to identify contextual factors that have been used in questions. We used the CQA data of Yahoo Japan Corporation which contains over 3 million questions posted during 2004 and 2005. 1,400 questions were randomly chosen from the data collection and manually analysed by one of the authors.

As a result of this process, we have identified five groups of contextual factors, namely, *task* (reasons, motivations, aims, and goals), *thought* (own thought, answer prediction), *situation* (circumstances, environment, experience, knowledge, and familiarity), *attribute* (personal attribute, social status), and *limit* (conditions on answers and answerers). The category of task, situation, and attribute had overlap with existing models in IR, while the category of thought and limit were found to be distinctive in CQA.

It should be noted that we appended only one contextual factor to basic questions once at a time in this study.

2.2 Question Types

We were also interested in how effect of contextual factors differed across the types of questions. We decided to look

[1] http://yanswersblog.com/index.php/archives/2009/12/14/yahoo-answers-hits-200-million-visitors-worldwide/

at two types of questions based on the investigations by [1, 5, 4]. One type was called information seeking questions while another type was called opinion seeking questions. As the name suggests, the former type was generally looking for information such as facts and methods, while the latter type was looking for opinions and suggestions.

2.3 User Study

46 participants (27 females and 19 males) were recruited for the study. The majority of participants were the undergraduate and postgraduate students of our institution, with varied backgrounds (e.g., Management, Physics, Mathematics, Linguistics, Engineering, Medicine, Cultural Study, Media Study, Computer Science, Information Science, Chemistry, Art, Robotics, Biology, etc).

Participants were asked to formulate six genuine questions. Three of them were information seeking questions while others were opinion seeking questions. Participants were asked to include one of the five contextual factors in their question formulation. The remaining question was formulated without any contextual factor. We rotated the order of contextual factors to append across participants.

The formulated questions were then submitted to one of the major CQA sites in Japan by the experimenter, and recorded any answers given to the questions for 7 days. Participants were called again and asked to assess the answers from eight perspectives. They were *Overall satisfaction*, *Topicality*, *Novelty*, *Situational relevance*, *Attitude*, *Trustiness*, *Promptness*, and *Length*. A 5-point Likert scale was used to capture participants' assessment of answers.

266 questions were formulated and 930 answers were collected and assessed by participants.

3. MAIN RESULTS

We examined effect of five contextual factors used in question formulation on the perception of answers, by comparing to the questions formulated without using contextual factors. This section reports only on a subset of analysis we carried out during this study.

First, we examined the number of answers submitted to the questions. Although opinion seeking questions tended to receive more answers than information seeking questions (3.9 vs. 2.9, $p \leq .005$ by T-test), there was no significant effect of contextual factors on the number of answers.

Second, we examined participants' perceptions on the answers. The result pattern differed across the question types. In information seeking questions, the questions with Attribute and Thought had a higher average score of Attitude of answers (Attribute: $p \leq .001$, Thought: $p \leq .003$, by T-test). In opinion seeking questions, the questions with Attribute had a higher average score of Novelty of answers ($p \leq .003$, by T-test). On the other hand, the factors such as Task and Situation had a negative impact on the perceptions of their answers.

Overall, we gained some evidence suggesting that appending a contextual factor is a promising way to formulate effective questions in a CQA site. At the same time, the results suggest that some contextual factors should be avoided in a CQA site. Also, our results suggest that effective contextual factors can differ across the question types. A comprehensive description of this study and analysis of the results will be reported elsewhere.

4. CONCLUSION

This paper explored effect of contextual factors as a means of formulating effective questions in the context of community-based question answering services. Genuine questions were formulated by our participants and some questions were presented with a contextual factor and others without. Based on the analysis of over 900 answers submitted to participants' questions, we gained evidence to support the following findings. First, including a contextual factor to the question can improve a questioner's assessment of the answers. Second, affective contextual factors can differ across the question type (information seeking and opinion seeking type). These findings can be a good starting point in guiding how beginners use CQA services to formulate their questions.

5. ACKNOWLEDGEMENTS

The authors thank to Yahoo JAPAN Corporation and National Institute of Informatics who gave us access to Yahoo! Chiebukuro Data (Version 1).

6. REFERENCES

[1] L. A. Adamic, J. Zhang, E. Bakshy, and M. S. Ackerman. Knowledge sharing and yahoo answers: everyone knows something. In *Proc. of the 17th international conference on WWW*, pages 665–674. ACM, 2008.

[2] E. Agichtein, Y. Liu, and J. Bian. Modeling information-seeker satisfaction in community question answering. *ACM Transactions on Knowledge Discovery from Data*, 3:10:1–10:27, 2009.

[3] A. Göker and H. I. Myrhaug. User context and personalisation. In *ECCBR Workshop on Case Based Reasoning and Personalisation, Aberdeen*, 2002.

[4] F. M. Harper, D. Moy, and J. A. Konstan. Facts or friends?: distinguishing informational and conversational questions in social q&a sites. In *Proceedings of the 27th international conference on Human factors in computing systems*, pages 759–768, New York, NY, USA, 2009. ACM.

[5] F. M. Harper, D. Raban, S. Rafaeli, and J. A. Konstan. Predictors of answer quality in online q&a sites. In *Proceeding of the twenty-sixth annual SIGCHI conference on Human factors in computing systems*, pages 865–874, New York, NY, USA, 2008. ACM.

[6] P. Ingwersen and K. Järvelin. *The turn: integration of information seeking and retrieval in context*. Springer, 2005.

[7] D. Kelly, V. D. Dollu, and X. Fu. The loquacious user: a document-independent source of terms for query expansion. In *Proc. of the 28th annual international ACM SIGIR conference*, pages 457–464, 2005.

[8] Y. Liu, J. Bian, and E. Agichtein. Predicting information seeker satisfaction in community question answering. In *Proc. of the 31st annual international ACM SIGIR conference*, pages 483–490, 2008.

[9] R. S. Taylor. Question-negotiation and information seeking in libraries. *College& Research Libraries*, 29(3):178–194, 1968.

ClusteringWiki: Personalized and Collaborative Clustering of Search Results

David C. Anastasiu
Texas State University-San Marcos
San Marcos, TX, USA
da1143@txstate.edu

Byron J. Gao
Texas State University-San Marcos
San Marcos, TX, USA
bgao@txstate.edu

David Buttler
Lawrence Livermore National Laboratory
Livermore, CA, USA
buttler1@llnl.gov

Categories and Subject Descriptors: H.3.3 [Information Storage and Retrieval]: Information Search and Retrieval – *Clustering*
General Terms: Algorithms, Design, Human Factors
Keywords: Personalized clustering, Search result clustering, Wiki, Mass collaboration, Web 2.0

1. EXTENDED ABSTRACT

How to organize and present search results plays a critical role in the utility of search engines. Queries are inherently ambiguous and search results are often diverse with multiple senses. The user has to sift through many irrelevant results to locate those relevant ones. Clustering divides a long list of disparate search results into a few topic-coherent clusters, allowing the user to quickly locate relevant results by topic navigation. There is good evidence that clustering improves user experience and search result quality [2].

Search result clustering is a highly user-centric task. Automatic algorithms often fail to fulfill the human factors in the objectives of search result clustering, generating meaningless, awkward or nonsense cluster labels [1]. In this demo, we explore a completely different direction in tackling the problem, utilizing the power of direct user intervention and mass-collaboration. In `ClusteringWiki` (dmlab.cs.txstate.edu/ClusteringWiki/), the user can edit and annotate the membership, structure and labels of clusters through a Wiki interface to personalize her search result presentation. Such edits and annotations can be implicitly shared among users as a mass-collaborative way of improving search result organization and search engine utility.

In collaborative tagging, tags can be used to collectively classify and find information. `ClusteringWiki` extends conventional tagging and allows tagging of structured objects, which are clusters of search results organized in a hierarchy.

Figure 1 shows a snapshot of `ClusteringWiki`. The left-hand *label panel* presents a hierarchy of cluster labels. The right-hand *result panel* presents search results for a chosen cluster label. A logged-in user can edit the current clusters by creating, deleting, modifying, moving or copying nodes in the cluster tree. Each edit will be validated against a set of predefined consistency constraints before being stored. Detailed descriptions of the framework and implementation can be found at dmlab.cs.txstate.edu/ClusteringWiki/pdf/cw.pdf.

Demonstration scenarios. After login, you are able to

Figure 1: Snapshot of `ClusteringWiki`.

personalize a cluster tree for a query, e.g. "Sergey Brin". You can edit the tree labels in the label panel by renaming, creating, copying, moving and deleting labels. You can also re-assign the cluster membership of search results by copy, move and delete operations. To reduce user editing effort, cluster edits in `ClusteringWiki` are available through context menus with pre-validated operations attached to labels and results. To perform a move/copy operation you can use cut/copy and paste or simply drag and drop a result or label.

To verify that `ClusteringWiki` retains personal preferences, you can log out, log in, and issue the same query. The resulting personalized cluster tree should allow you to explore the search results more effectively. To demonstrate aggregated clustering, `ClusteringWiki` lists the top 10 queries edited by the most users. You (without login) can choose some of these queries and observe how the aggregated trees differ from the initial trees. Aggregated trees reflect the collaborative effort and common preferences of many users.

Cluster editing takes user effort. `ClusteringWiki` attempts to reuse such effort.While preference aggregation can be considered sharing among users, preference transfer is sharing among queries. In `ClusteringWiki`, preference transfer is executed regardless of your login status. For example, you can issue a query "Sergey Brin" and edit the cluster tree. Then you can issue a similar query "Sergey M. Brin" and observe how those stored preferences for "Sergey Brin" are enforced in producing the cluster tree for "Sergey M. Brin".

Acknowledgments: This work (LLNL-CONF-461652) was performed under the auspices of the U.S. Department of Energy by Lawrence Livermore National Laboratory (contract DE-AC52-07NA27344).

2. REFERENCES

[1] C. Carpineto, S. Osiński, G. Romano, and D. Weiss. A survey of web clustering engines. *ACM Comput. Surv.*, 41(3):1–38, 2009.
[2] C. D. Manning, P. Raghavan, and H. Schtze. *Introduction to Information Retrieval.* Cambridge University Press, 2008.

SIGIR'11, July 24–28, 2011, Beijing, China.
ACM 978-1-4503-0757-4/11/07.

OrientSTS: Spatio-Temporal Sequence Searching in Flickr

Chunjie Zhou
School of Information
Renmin University of China
and Ludong University
Beijing, China
lucyzcj@ruc.edu.cn

Dongqi Liu
School of Information
Renmin University of China
Beijing, China
liudqq@gmail.com

Xiaofeng Meng
School of Information
Renmin University of China
Beijing, China
xfmeng@ruc.edu.cn

1. EXTENDED ABSTRACT

Nowadays, due to the increasing user requirements of efficient and personalized services, a perfect travel plan is urgently needed. However, at present it is hard for people to make a personalized traveling plan. Most of them follow other people's general travel trajectory. So only after finishing their travel, do they know which scene is their favorite, which is not, and what is the perfect order of visits.

In this research we propose a novel spatio-temporal sequence (STS) searching, which mainly includes two steps. Firstly, we propose a novel method to detect tourist features of every scene, and its difference in different seasons. Secondly, combined with personal profile and scene features, a set of interesting scenes will be chosen and each scene has a specific weight for each user. The goal of our research is to provide the traveler with the STS, which passes through as many chosen scenes as possible with the maximum weight and the minimum distance within his travel time.

However, the STS searching has not been addressed before. Zheng et al. [1] recorded GPS tracks of 107 users to determine the interestingness of tourist scenes. The authors of [2] also focused on mining similar traveling sequences from multiple users' GPS logs. None of these approaches considers scene features, user's profile and temporal information.

We propose a method based on topic model to detect scene features, and provide two approximate algorithms to mine STS: a local optimization algorithm and a global optimization algorithm. System evaluations have been conducted and the performance results show the efficiency.

Categories and Subject Descriptors

H.4 [**Information Systems Applications**]: prototyping

General Terms

Design

Keywords

spatio-temporal sequence, topic model, approximate

2. SYSTEM OVERVIEW

Figure 1 shows the interface of our prototype STS. It has five major components: profile-based scene choice, context-based algorithm choice, STS searching, parameter set, and photo gallery. *Profile-based scene choice* includes the choice of cities and scene categories based on user's profile. *Context-based algorithm choice* includes three different algorithms which are fit for different situations separately. If the user is more concern about the distance, the algorithm dLOA will be chosen; if he care more about the weight, the algorithm wLOA will be chosen; else, the algorithm GOA can be used, which considers both the distance and the weight of the sequence. After specifying a start point and an end point, clicking the button of *STS searching*, we will get a spatio-temporal sequence. *parameter set* includes the settings of map mode, the season, the profile, the balance factor and the total time. *photo gallery* shows the representative photos in the sequence.

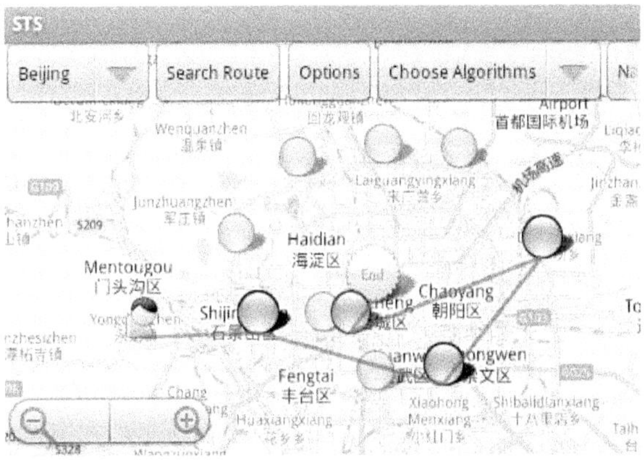

Figure 1: the Interface of STS

3. ACKNOWLEDGEMENTS

This research was partially supported by the grants from the Natural Science Foundation of China (No.60833005, 61070055, 61003205); the National High-Tech Research and Development Plan of China (No.2009AA011904).

4. REFERENCES

[1] Zheng, I., Zhang, L., Xie, X., Ma, WY.: Mining Interesting Locations and Travel Sequences from GPS Trajectories. Proceedings of the 18th International World Wide Web Conference (WWW). (2009)

[2] Gonotti, F., et al.: Trajectory Pattern Mining. Proceedings of the 13th ACM SIGKDD International Conference on Knowledge Discovery and Data Mining (KDD), pp. 330-339. (2007)

A Toolkit for Knowledge Base Population

Zheng Chen, Suzanne Tamang, Adam Lee, Heng Ji
Computer Science Department
Queens College and Graduate Center
City University of New York
New York, USA
zchen1@gc.cuny.edu,{suzanne.tamang,duo1123}@gmail.com,hengji@cs.qc.cuny.edu

ABSTRACT

The main goal of knowledge base population (KBP) is to distill entity information (e.g., facts of a person) from multiple unstructured and semi-structured data sources, and incorporate the information into a knowledge base (KB). In this work, we intend to release an open source KBP toolkit that is publicly available for research purposes.

Categories and Subject Descriptors: H.3.4 [Information Storage and Retrieval]: Systems and Software

General Terms: Experimentation

Keywords: knowledge base population, toolkit

1. INTRODUCTION

A knowledge base is a centralized repository for information. Automatic knowledge base population by extracting entity information from large-scale unstructured text data has been shown to be a very challenging task in the recent TAC KBP program[1]. In KBP2010, 45 teams registered but only 23 submitted results, most probably because some basic analysis components are not available. Therefore, we are distributing a toolkit based on our KBP system which achieved highly-competitive performance in KBP2010. The toolkit is able to not only set up a baseline KBP system for the default task defined in KBP2010 (extracting facts for pre-defined persons or organizations), but also facilitate the development of techniques and customization in distilling diversified new entity or attribute types (e.g., product KB for firms, medicine KB for pharmacies).

2. TOOLKIT OVERVIEW

Our toolkit aims to deal with the following challenges:

(1) **unstructured information extraction**, which requires to distill various entity facts (attribute-value pairs) from multiple unstructured and semi-structured data sources. In KBP2010, we developed three pipelines including pattern matching, supervised classification based Information Extraction (IE) and Question-Answering based [1]. We choose pattern matching as our baseline technique in the toolkit, because it can be easily customized to distill information for new types of entities and attributes. In contrast, the other two pipelines require domain-specific resources and domain knowledge, and we provide a general platform which allows developers to add or customize new functionalities.

(2)**entity integration**, which requires to resolve and merge references to the same real-world entity. There are two main difficulties, one is that entities can be referred to by multiple name variants (e.g., aliases, acronyms), and the other is that names can be ambiguous. For the former difficulty, we implemented a name expansion component which identifies name variants [1]; for the latter, we employed different strategies to disambiguate names.

(3)**scalability**, which requires easy integration of new components, reasonable processing speed with large-scale corpora. Keeping this in mind, the toolkit is implemented to be modular and configurable. The toolkit itself integrates many other useful IE and Wikipedia analysis tools.

[1]http://nlp.cs.qc.cuny.edu/kbp/2010/

SIGIR'11, July 24–28, 2011, Beijing, China.
ACM 978-1-4503-0757-4/11/07.

3. APPLICATION

To visualize the information stored in the KB, we demonstrate a web-based application which automatically augments recognized entities in a web page with links. As shown in Figure 1, if the user clicks the link of entity "Aaron Rodgers", a popup window will show the facts retrieved from KB.

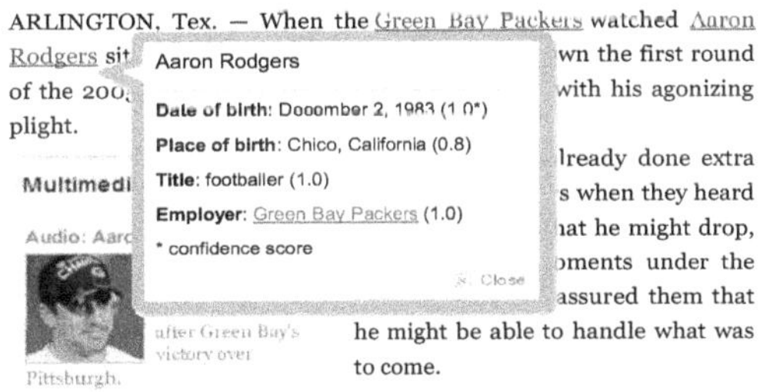

Figure 1: Snapshot of application

4. ACKNOWLEDGMENTS

This work was supported by the U.S. Army Research Laboratory under Cooperative Agreement Number W911NF-09-2-0053, the U.S. NSF CAREER Award under Grant IIS-0953149, PSC-CUNY Research Program.

5. REFERENCES

[1] Zheng Chen, Suzanne Tamang, Adam Lee, Xiang Li, Marissa Passantino, and Heng Ji. Top-down and bottom-up: A combined approach to slot filling. In *Proceedings of Asia Information Retrieval Societies Conference (AIRS2010)*, 2010.

iMecho: a Context-aware Desktop Search System

Jidong Chen *#, Hang Guo #
#EMC Research China, Beijing,China
{jidong.chen,hang.guo}@emc.com

Wentao Wu *, Wei Wang *
*Fudan University, Shanghai,China
{wentaowu,weiwang1}@fudan.edu.cn

ABSTRACT

In this demo, we present iMecho, a context-aware desktop search system to help users get more relevant results. Different from other desktop search engines, iMecho ranks results not only by the content of the query, but also the context of the query. It employs an Hidden Markov Model (HMM)-based user model, which is learned from user's activity logs, to estimate the query context when he submits the query. The results from keyword search are re-ranked by their relevances to the context with acceptable overhead.

Categories and Subject Descriptors: H.3.3 [Information Search and Retrieval]: Search process

General Terms: Algorithms, Design.

Keywords: Context-aware search, User model, Desktop search.

1. SYSTEM OVERVIEW

Searching personal data with keywords is becoming increasingly challenging as users create more and more personal data, e.g., large amounts of local files, emails or cached web pages in their PCs. Current desktop search systems such as Google Desktop only support keyword searches that rank results by their relevance to the query. One problem with keyword search is that the result set usually contains many unrelated documents. To solve it, we need to find out what the user really needs besides using keywords.

In most cases of desktop search, the user is more interested in documents related to his context. By "*context*" we mean the user's task when he submits the query. A task can be simply modeled as a set of documents accessed by the user for a specific purpose. A user constantly goes back to his previous tasks when he is using his PC. A user study [2] shows that about 40% tasks are re-opened by the user within a week. Another 23% tasks are re-opened within a month.

Following this observation, we develop a context-aware desktop search system called iMecho. The idea is to build a user behavior model based on the user's previous activities. When he submits a query, the model estimates his hidden task, i.e., the context of the query, and then the system refines the ranking results accordingly with reasonable overhead. iMecho employs the Hidden Markov Model (HMM) as the user model to estimate hidden tasks. In this model, a user keeps going from one task (a state of HMM) to another.

SIGIR'11, July 24–28, 2011, Beijing, China.
ACM 978-1-4503-0757-4/11/07.

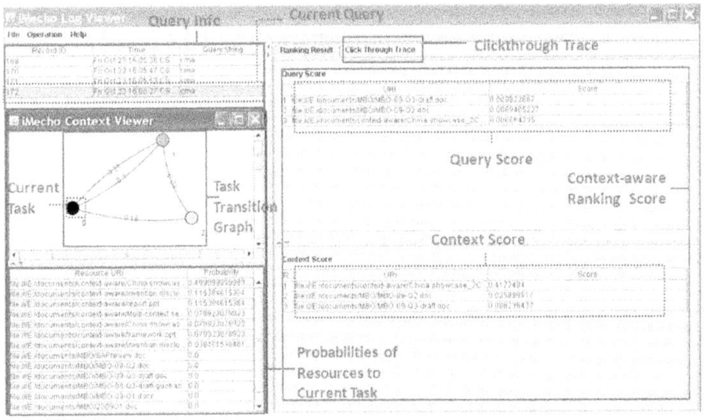

Figure 1: Interface of iMecho Query Viewer

Though a recent work [1] also applied HMM in context-aware search, it mainly focused on web searches and only provided context independent results for a particular user. iMecho can record the complete trace of user activities on his desktop and the query context of the specific user can be comprehensively modeled by the sequence of user activities with accepted cost. iMecho works as follows:

- The offline part: the user's click sequence is collected to build a user model. The model includes 1) the probabilities of a task sequence; 2) the probability that a document is related to a specific task.
- The online part: when the user submits a query, the latest user model is used to estimate his current task given real time click sequence. And the ranking score of each retrieved document is adjusted accordingly.

Figure 1 shows the interface of iMecho query viewer, which gives details of the user model, the transition of query contexts and query-related information (e.g. ranking scores and the clickthrough data) in the query time. We will demonstrate how to build the user model from user activity logs and how to apply the model to rank the results.

2. REFERENCES

[1] H. Cao, D. Jiang, J. Pei, E. Chen, and H. Li. Towards context-aware search by learning a very large variable length hidden markov model from search logs. In WWW 2009.

[2] D. Elsweiler and I. Ruthven. Towards task-based personal information management evaluations. In SIGIR 2007.

Visualizing and Querying Semantic Social Networks*

Aixin Sun†, Anwitaman Datta†, Ee-Peng Lim§, Kuiyu Chang†

†School of Computer Engineering, Nanyang Technological University, Singapore 639798

§School of Information Systems, Singapore Management University, Singapore 178902

{axsun,awitaman,askychang}@ntu.edu.sg eplim@smu.edu.sg

ABSTRACT

We demonstrate SSNetViz that is developed for integrating, visualizing and querying heterogeneous semantic social networks obtained from multiple information sources. A semantic social network refers to a social network graph with multi-typed nodes and links. We demonstrate various innovative features of SSNetViz with social networks from three information sources covering a similar set of entities and relationships in terrorism domain.

Categories and Subject Descriptors

H.3.4 [**Information Systems**]: Information Storage and Retrieval—*Systems and Software*

General Terms

Design

Keywords

Social network, Visualization, Integration, Search

1. INTRODUCTION

The increasing popularity of social network platforms has given opportunities to capture and understand the social structures among people and other types of entities on the Web. Nevertheless, the same users or entities may appear in different social networks where different sets of attributes and relationships are maintained. This calls for a tool to combine these social networks and conduct analysis on the combined network in a holistic manner.

SSNetViz offers a suite of functions to: (i) integrate multiple social networks through rule-based and manual matching approaches, (ii) visualize the integrated network with the ability of searching for a query relevant sub-network through entity name matching, free-text search of entity profiles, and path search, (iii) visualize the temporal evolution of the networks, and (iv) import/export the query relevant sub-network [2, 3]. The integration, free-text/path search and the sub-network import/export are the major features distinguishing our prototype from other similar systems [1, 4].

The main GUI of SSNetViz is shown in Figure 1. A query relevant sub-network can be defined based on the anchor nodes (*i.e.,* entities) selected by users in Panel 1, or node search results from Panel 4. The sub-network may also be determined from path search results which include all the intermediate nodes formulating the pathes between the source and target nodes. The sub-network visualized in Panel 3 is the integrated semantic social network where each node and link may be present in one or more individual social networks (*i.e.,* sources). The network visualizer uses color codes to distinguish the source(s) where a node and link is recorded. The source tabs with matching colors in Panel 2 present the detailed information about a selected node in Panel 3, known as node profile. By clicking multiple source tabs, a user gets the information about the same entity from multiple sources. Not shown in Figure 1, the network visualizer offers slider tools for controlling the number of neighboring nodes of anchor nodes to be displayed in the screen as well as the timeline control for social networks with timestamps to visualize their evolution over time and delta differences. Another set of GUIs is provided to enable both rule and manual based network integration and network import/expert.

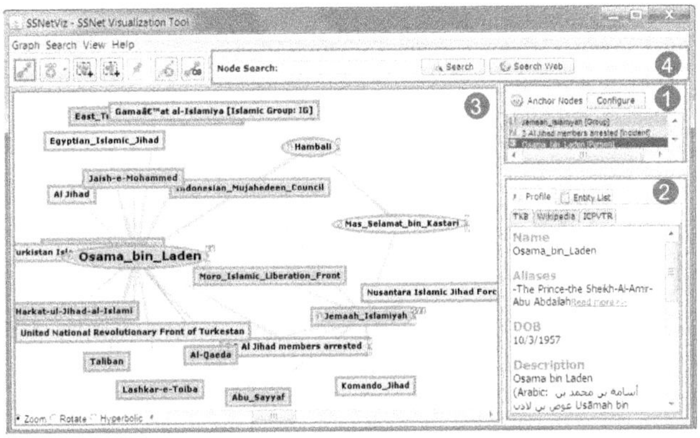

Figure 1: SSNetViz Main Graphical User Interface (GUI)

We will demonstrate how data can be integrated from multiple sources (using rule-based entity resolution as well as manually), and how a multi-dimensional network can be visualized, queried and manipulated. The demonstration will be loaded with three social networks in terrorism domain obtained from Terrorism Knowledge Base (TKB), Wikipedia, and a local research center.

2. REFERENCES

[1] J. Heer and D. Boyd. Vizster: Visualizing online social networks. In *IEEE Symposium on Information Visualization*, 2005.

[2] E.-P. Lim, A. T. Kwee, N. L. Ibrahim, A. Sun, A. Datta, K. Chang, and Maureen. Visualizing and exploring evolving information networks in wikipedia. In *Proc. ICADL*, pages 50–60, Gold Coast, 2010.

[3] E.-P. Lim, Maureen, N. L. Ibrahim, A. Sun, A. Datta, and K. Chang. Ssnetviz: a visualization engine for heterogeneous semantic social networks. In *Proc. ICEC*, pages 213–221, Taipei, 2009.

[4] Z. Shen, K.-L. Ma, and T. Eliassi-Rad. Visual analysis of large heterogeneous social networks by semantic and structural abstraction. *IEEE Trans. on VCG*, 12:1427–1439, 2006.

*This work was supported by Agency for Science, Technology and Research (A*STAR), Singapore, Project No. 062 101 0031.

SIGIR'11, July 24–28, 2011, Beijing, China.
ACM 978-1-4503-0757-4/11/07.

What-You-Retrieve-Is-What-You-See: A Preliminary Cyber-Physical Search Engine

Lidan Shou Ke Chen Gang Chen Chao Zhang Yi Ma Xian Zhang
College of Computer Science and Technology
Zhejiang University
Hangzhou, China
{should, chenk, cg, chaozhang, mayi}@zju.edu.cn lasiazhang@163.com

Categories and Subject Descriptors

H.3.3 [**Information Systems**]: Information Retrieval

General Terms

Design

Keywords

Cyber-Physical System, Visibility, Web Search

1. EXTENDED ABSTRACT

The cyber-physical systems (CPS) are envisioned as a class of real-time systems integrating the computing, communication and storage facilities with monitoring and control of the physical world. One interesting CPS application in the mobile Internet is to provide Web search "on the spot" regarding the physical world that a user sees, or literally *WYRIWYS* (What-You-Retrieve-Is-What-You-See).

WYRIWYS cannot be readily addressed by the existing location-based Web search (abbreviated LWS onwards) [1, 2] due to the following reasons. First, LWS retrieves objects and computes the query/object relevance by combining their content relevancy and geometric proximity. Therefore it is unaware of the visibility of the physical entities of the Web objects to the user. Objects spatially close to the user may always be retrieved whether they are being monitored by the user or not. Second, the data management scheme of LWS typically integrates spatial indexes with an inverted index. Search service built on such scheme is likely to ignore crucial cyber-physical events, for example change of user orientation, which are considered as useful feedback cues for interaction with the CPS.

The objective of our work is to develop server/browser software to support WYRIWYS search in our prototype cyber-physical search engine. A WYRIWYS search retrieves visible Web objects and ranks them by their cyber-physical relevances (term, visual, spatial, temporal etc.). The search server contains three key components: (1) A database of Web objects, where each object is associated with a set of highly correlated Web documents. (2) A term-visibility indexer which indexes the Web objects by keywords and viewing regions. The indexer also maintains the quantitative measures of the visibility of the Web objects with regard to different viewing regions. Given a set of keywords and a view point in the physical space, the indexer is able to efficiently find the relevant visible Web objects. (3) A C-P rank module which ranks the objects by cyber-physical relevance including keyword relevancy, document authority, visibility, and the temporal urgency that a user physically visits the object.

(a) 3D mode (b) 2D mode (c) List mode

Figure 1: Browser Interface

The browser runs on an Android phone and can support queries in both the 3D and 2D modes. Each query is issued by specifying a set of keywords and a physical setting, including the position, the orientation, and the speed of the user. The 3D-mode results are embedded into a real-time camera image. This provides an immersive cyber-physical experience during the search. Figure 1(a) shows the 3D search results displayed in clusters where each cluster corresponds to a semantic Web object. The 2D-mode provides a bird's-eye view of the surroundings, as figure 1(b) shows. Web objects that the user sees are shaded in green circles while those invisible are in red.

This work is distinguished from previous LWS as it provides quality Web search geared with the physical world. Compared to the LWS provided by Google, our prototype provides a brand new *immersive search* service for what the user sees in physical space. Therefore it suggests a very promising solution to cyber-physical Web search.

2. ACKNOWLEDGMENTS

The work is supported in part by the National Science Foundation of China(NSFC Grant No. 60803003, 60970124).

3. REFERENCES

[1] S. Asadi, X. Zhou, and G. Yang. Using local popularity of web resources for geo-ranking of search engine results. *World Wide Web*, 12(2):149–170, 2009.

[2] G. Cong, C. S. Jensen, and D. Wu. Efficient retrieval of the top-k most relevant spatial web objects. *Proc. VLDB Endow.*, 2:337–348, August 2009.

SIGIR'11, July 24–28, 2011, Beijing, China.
ACM 978-1-4503-0757-4/11/07.

QuickView: Advanced Search of Tweets

Xiaohua Liu [‡] [†], Long Jiang [†], Furu Wei [†], Ming Zhou [†], Microsoft QuickView Team [†]
[‡]School of Computer Science and Technology,Harbin Institute of Technology,Harbin,150001,China
[†]Microsoft Research Asia, No. 5, Dan Ling Street, Haidian District, Beijing, 100080, China
[†]{xiaoliu, longj, fuwei, mingzhou, qview}@microsoft.com

Categories and Subject Descriptors

H.3.1 [**Content Analysis and Indexing**]: Content Analysis and Indexing - indexing methods, linguistic processing; H.3.3 [**Information Search and Retrieval**]: Information Search and Retrieval - information filtering, retrieval models

General Terms

Algorithms, Design, Experimentation

1. EXTENDED ABSTRACT

With tweets being a comprehensive repository for super fresh information, tweet search becomes increasingly popular. However, existing tweet search services, e.g., Twitter [1], offer only simple keyword based search. Owing to the noisy and informal nature of tweets, the returned list does not contain meaningful information in many cases.

This demonstration introduces *QuickView*, an advanced tweet search service to address this issue. It adopts a series of natural language processing technologies to extract useful information from a large volume of tweets. Specifically, for each tweet, it first conducts tweet normalization, followed by named entity recognition(NER). Our NER component is a combination of a k-nearest neighbors(KNN) classifier (to collect global information across recently labeled tweets) with a Conditional Random Fields (CRF) labeler (to exploit information from a single tweet and the gazetteers). Then it extracts opinions (e.g., positive or negative comments about a product). After that it conducts semantic role labeling(SRL) to get predicate-argument structures(e.g.,verbs and their agents or patients), which are further converted into events (i.e., triples of who did what). We follow Liu et al. [1] to construct our SRL component. Next, tweets are classified into predefined categories. Finally, non-noisy tweets together with the mined information are indexed.

On top of the index, *QuickView* enables the following two brand new scenarios, allowing users to effectively access their interested tweets or fine-grained information mined from tweets.

Categorized Browsing. As illustrated in Figure 1(a), *QuickView* shows recent popular tweets, entities, events, opinions and so on, which are organized by categories. It also extracts and classifies URL links in tweets to allow users to check out popular links in a categorized way.

Advanced Search. As shown in Figure 1(b), *QuickView* provides four advanced search functions: 1) search results are clustered so that tweets about the same/similar topic are grouped together, and for each cluster only the informative tweets are kept; 2) when the query is a person or a company name, two bars are presented followed by the words that strongly suggest opinion polarity. The bar's width is proportional to the number of associated opinions; 3) similarly, the top 6 most frequent words that most clearly express event occurrences are presented; 4) users can search tweets with opinions or events, e.g., search tweets containing any positive/negative opinion about Obama or any event involving Obama.

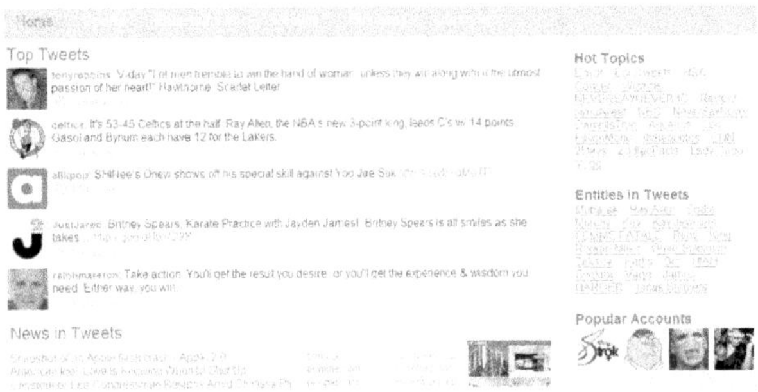

(a) A screenshot of the categorized browsing scenario.

(b) A screenshot of the advanced search scenario.

Figure 1: Two scenarios of *QuickView*.

[1]http://twitter.com/

SIGIR'11, July 24–28, 2011, Beijing, China.
ACM 978-1-4503-0757-4/11/07.

2. REFERENCES

[1] X. Liu, K. Li, B. Han, M. Zhou, L. Jiang, Z. Xiong, and C. Huang. Semantic role labeling for news tweets. In *Coling*, pages 698–706, 2010.

Personalized Video: Leanback online video consumption

Krishnan Ramanathan
HP Labs India
Bangalore, India
krishnan_ramanathan@hp.com

Yogesh Sankarasubramaniam
HP Labs India
Bangalore, India
yogesh@hp.com

Vidhya Govindaraju
HP Labs India
Bangalore, India
vidhya.govindaraju@hp.com

ABSTRACT

Current user interfaces for online video consumption are mostly browser based, lean forward, require constant interaction and provide a fragmented view of the total content available. For easier consumption, the user interface and interactions need to be redesigned for less interruptive and lean back experience. In this paper, we describe Personalized Video, an application that converts the online video experience into a personalized lean back experience. It has been implemented on the Windows platform and integrated with intuitive user interactions like gesture and face recognition. It also supports group personalization for concurrent users.

Categories and Subject Descriptors

H.4.3 [**Information Systems Applications**]: Communication Applications

General Terms

Algorithms, Human Factors

Keywords

Personalization, group recommendation, similar content, ranking

1. INTRODUCTION

Current user interfaces for online video suffer from a number of limitations. The interfaces are usually browser based and are modeled after a search metaphor. Users have to constantly interact with the online video website (e.g. YouTube) after each video and decide what the next video they should watch. Multiple websites host a fraction of the total content available, so users have to visit different content provider websites. The interfaces are mostly geared for English language users and do not have enough support for non-English videos and users. Finally, most interfaces today are geared to single users and do not cater to the group consumption habits that TV has encouraged.

2. PERSONALIZED VIDEO

We have created a Windows application that solves the interface and experience limitations mentioned above. We describe some of the technical innovations below.

Leanback online video consumption: The application aggregates videos from multiple online video providers using a topic based "channel" metaphor. A channel is any longstanding interest the user has. Videos are pushed into the channel without requiring users to make the same query again.

Personalization: This is accomplished by video recommendation based on user profiles, and using user feedback to prioritize videos within a channel. The video recommender constructs a user profile by extracting keyphrases from the video metadata (title, tags, description), weighted based on user rating, number of views

SIGIR'11, July 24–28, 2011, Beijing, China.
ACM 978-1-4503-0757-4/11/07.

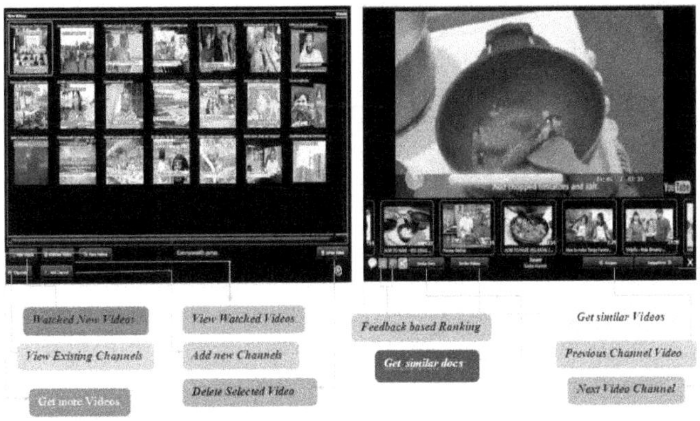

Figure 1. User interface elements (left) and technical innovations (right) in the Personalized Video application

etc. The recommender sources videos using this profile, and makes it available in the "Recommendations" channel. Within a channel, users are allowed to rate videos as "like" or "dislike". The video-keyphrase bipartite graph is then used to compute a rating on the unseen videos. The videos in the channel are then re-prioritized based on this predicted rating.

Similar content: Video keyphrases are also used to source similar videos and textual content. For e.g. a culinary video can point to the corresponding recipe, which the user can download or print. A user can also simply click on "Similar videos" to watch other videos related to the current one. Our solution works by first ranking the keyphrases, and then assessing the similarity of sourced content.

Group consumption of videos: We have built a group recommender to source and display content that is of interest to all the viewers. First, users are identified by a face recognizer. Then, a joint user profile is constructed as follows: individual interests are first expanded into representative topics (keyphrases from video metadata), and then a reciprocal rule is used to combine/discard topics, which has the effect of jointly satisfying all the users. Videos are then sourced based on the joint profile, and presented to the current set of users. Thus, our approach allows a strong discovery of joint interests, rather than merely identify matches in the individual profiles. A study on subgroups of 30 users indicated that the retrieval precision is around 70%; users are also very satisfied with the quality of recommendations.

Input methods: We have integrated the Gesture keyboard (developed at HP Labs India) that allows input in Indian language (e.g. Hindi). We have also implemented an application that allows a Symbian phone to be used for input at a distance (e.g. entering channel names). For video navigation, the application allows hand gesture navigation (in addition to touch). Users can provide feedback on the videos (like or dislike) with thumbs up/down gesture. We have also tested the user experience with the Logitech air mouse.

Integration with Facebook and Twitter: Users can share a video with friends on Facebook and Twitter with customized messages.

GreenMeter: A Tool for Assessing the Quality and Recommending Tags for Web 2.0 Applications*

Saulo Ricci, Dilson Guimarães, Fabiano Belém,
Jussara M. Almeida, Marcos A. Gonçalves, Raquel Prates
Universidade Federal de Minas Gerais, Belo Horizonte, Brazil
{saulomrr, dilsonag, fmuniz, jussara, mgoncalv, rprates}@dcc.ufmg.br

ABSTRACT

We present GreenMeter, a tool for assessing the quality and recommending tags for Web 2.0 content. Its goal is to improve tag quality and the effectiveness of various information services (e.g., search, content recommendation) that rely on tags as data sources. We demonstrate an implementation of GreenMeter for the popular Last.fm application.

Categories and Subject Descriptors: H.3.1 Information Storage and Retrieval: Content Analysis and Indexing

General Terms: Algorithms, Experimentation

Keywords: Tag Recommendation, Information Quality

1. SYSTEM OVERVIEW

The assignment of *tags* to describe and organize content is currently very popular on the Web 2.0. Indeed, being such content often multimedia, most current Information Retrieval (IR) services (e.g., searching, content recommendation) often rely on tags as one of the main data sources.

We here present GreenMeter, a tool for assessing tag *quality* and recommending tags for Web 2.0 objects. Tag quality is assessed from the perspective of supporting effective IR services, being thus related to how well the tag *describes* the object's content and/or *discriminates* it from other objects. We *estimate* tag quality by the combination of various *heuristic metrics* [1]. In particular, we use *Term Spread* (TS), which counts the number of textual features (e.g, title, description, comments, tags) associated with the object that contain a given candidate tag: the larger this number, the more related the tag is to the object's content and, thus, the higher its descriptive power (and its quality).

GreenMeter's tag recommendation method [1] extends existing tag co-occurrence based techniques [3] to include not only tags previously assigned to the objects (including the target of the recommendation), but also terms extracted from other textual features. It then applies the aforementioned heuristic metrics to rank candidate terms by their estimated quality, recommending the highly ranked terms. The proposed method greatly extends the state-of-the-art (e.g., [3, 2]) by combining tag co-occurrence and tag quality metrics, and by extracting candidates from multiple textual features. To perform such combination, we exploit both heuristic functions and machine learning techniques [1]. Moreover, GreenMeter's quality estimator is more sophisticated and realistic than simply favoring more popular tags, as performed by most applications, which can be easily target of malicious attacks (e.g., tag spamming).

Figure 1: Tag Cloud of "Miles Davis" on LastFM: original (left) and with GreenMeter (right).

We implemented GreenMeter in the LastFM online radio station. In LastFM, multiple users may assign the same tag to an object, as tags are mostly used for building personal collections. Figure 1(left) shows a snapshot of the LastFM tag cloud associated with the "Miles Davis" artist. Note that, like other applications, LastFM ranks tags by their popularity among users (more popular tags are shown in larger font sizes), and tends to recommend tags based on such metric. Figure 1(right) shows the use of GreenMeter on the same object. The color of each tag, in a red-to-green scale, represents its "quality": the greener, the higher its quality. The gauge indicates the quality of the tag cloud, computed as the average quality across all tags. The figure also shows the tags recommended by GreenMeter, "jazz", "funk", "psychedelic", "trumpet" and "fusion". In comparison with the tags recommended by LastFM (i.e., "jazz", "trumpet", "fusion", "bebop", and "blues"), such tags seem to better describe one of the Jazz Fusion's style precursors.

GreenMeter has two components. The *back-end* includes a data crawler, the tag quality estimator, and the tag recommender. The *front-end*, responsible for presentation, is built on top of the Greasemonkey Firefox add-on[1].

2. REFERENCES

[1] F. Belém et al. Associative Tag Recommendation Exploiting Multiple Textual Features. In *SIGIR*, 2011.

[2] G. Menezes et al. Demand-Driven Tag Recommendation. In *PKDD*, 2010.

[3] B. Sigurbjörnsson and R. Zwol. Flickr Tag Recommendation based on Collective Knowledge. In *WWW*, 2008.

*This work is supported by the INWeb (MCT/CNPq grant 57.3871/2008-6), and by the authors' grants from CNPq and FAPEMIG.

SIGIR'11, July 24–28, 2011, Beijing, China.
ACM 978-1-4503-0757-4/11/07.

[1]More information on GreenMeter can be found at http://sites.google.com/site/greenmeterdemo/

JuSe: A Picture Dictionary Query System for Children

Tamara Polajnar
School of Computing Science
University of Glasgow
United Kingdom
tamara@dcs.gla.ac.uk

Richard Glassey
School of Computing Science
University of Glasgow
United Kingdom
rjg@dcs.gla.ac.uk

Leif Azzopardi
School of Computing Science
University of Glasgow
United Kingdom
leif@dcs.gla.ac.uk

Categories and Subject Descriptors: H.3.3 [**Information Storage and Retrieval**]: Information Search and Retrieval - *Query Formulation*

General Terms: Design, Human Factors

Keywords: Information Retrieval, Children

EXTENDED ABSTRACT

As adults we take for granted our capacity to express our information needs verbally and textually. However, young children also have preferences and information needs, but are just learning to be able to express themselves effectively. Consequently they encounter many barriers when trying to spell, type, and communicate their needs to a 'faceless' search engine text box.

Junior Search (JuSe) is an interface that enables preschoolers and young children to search and find consumable online content (such as games for kids, videos, etc.) through adaptable picture dictionaries. Inspired by educational children's toys, rather than search engines designed for adults, JuSe incorporates a learning element by combining audio-visual and textual cues to improve written word recognition and vocabulary skills. JuSe provides an interactive learning environment that allows parents to introduce new words and concepts into the child's lexicon, as well as controlling the content and search queries.

The primary aim of JuSe is to stimulate information needs and enable children to formulate their queries in a manner that is congruous with their abilities:

A) Studies [1, 2, 4, 5, 6] have shown that children have difficulties using word-based queries due to problems with typing, spelling, and the appropriate selection of query words.

B) Children tend to revert to browsing when they encounter difficulties with the query formulation and they think that category browsing is an essential element of webpage design [5, 6]. However, [3] found that at the higher category levels there was a large mismatch in content expectations between the individual children and with the hierarchy produced by a community of adults.

To address the design concerns associated with browsing and query formulation (**A** and **B**), the interface combines browsing and picture query-based elements. Instead of the concentrating on document space, browsing occurs by the traversal of keyword categories. Children have a limited vocabulary of content words, mainly concentrated in the high-frequency categories associated with their needs: toys, characters, food, sports, occupations, animals, etc. The JuSe picture dictionary emulates books and television shows used for literacy education. This basic dictionary was compiled by studying lists of children's speech [7] and vocabulary lists of essential English words.

SIGIR'11, July 24–28, 2011, Beijing, China.
ACM 978-1-4503-0757-4/11/07.

Figure 1: The screenshot of the JuSe interface.

Acknowledgements: PuppyIR is funded by the EC's FP7 2007-2013 under grant agreement no. 231507.

REFERENCES

[1] D. Bilal. Children's information seeking and the design of digital interfaces in the affective paradigm. *Library Trends*, 54(3):197–208, 2005.

[2] D. Bilal and J. Kirby. Differences and similarities in information seeking: children and adults as Web users. *Information Processing & Management*, 38(5):649–670, 2002.

[3] D. Bilal and P. Wang. Children's conceptual structures of science categories and the design of web directories: Research articles. *J. Am. Soc. Inf. Sci. Technol.*, 56(12):1303–1313, 2005.

[4] A. Druin, E. Foss, H. Hutchinson, E. Golub, and L. Hatley. Children's roles using keyword search interfaces at home. In *CHI '10*, pages 413–422, New York, NY, USA, 2010. ACM.

[5] H. E. Jochmann-Mannak, T. W. C. Huibers, and T. J. M. Sanders. Children's information retrieval: beyond examining search strategies and interfaces. In *The 2nd BCS-IRSG Symposium*, pages 64–72, London, 2008. BCS.

[6] J. A. Large and J. Beheshti. Interface design, web portals, and children. *Library Trends*, 54(2):318–342, 2005.

[7] C. M. Tameron Morrison, A. D. Chappell, and W. Ellis. Age of acquisition norms for a large set of object names and their relation to adult estimates and other variables. *The Quarterly Journal of Experimental Psychology Section A: Human Experimental Psychology*, 50(3):528–559, 1997.

CrowdTracker: Enabling Community-Based Real-Time Web Monitoring

James Caverlee, Zhiyuan Cheng, Brian Eoff,
Chiao-Fang Hsu, Krishna Kamath, and Jeffrey McGee
Texas A&M University
College Station, TX 77843
{caverlee,zcheng,bde,drakihsu,kykamath,jeffamcgee}@cse.tamu.edu

ABSTRACT

CrowdTracker is a community-based web monitoring system optimized for real-time web streams like Twitter, Facebook, and Google Buzz. In this demo summary, we provide an overview of the system and architecture, and outline the demonstration plan.

Categories and Subject Descriptors: H.3.3 [Information Storage and Retrieval]: Information Search and Retrieval; H.3.4 [Information Storage and Retrieval]: Systems and Software

General Terms: Algorithms, Design, Experimentation

Keywords: community, crowd, real-time web, monitoring

1. INTRODUCTION

The real-time web is fast becoming an indispensable resource, opening up fresh opportunities for enabling a new generation of applications for monitoring, analyzing, and distilling information from the *prospective web* of real-time content that ref ects the current activity of the web's participants. As a step toward realizing this vision, we are investigating techniques and developing effective methods for automatically discovering and tracking the evolution of transient crowds from the massive scale of the real-time web. A transient crowd is an ad-hoc collection of users that ref ects the real-time interests and aff liations of users [2]. Unlike the more static and perhaps staler group-based membership offered on many social networks (e.g., members of the Texas A&M community, residents of Ohio), transient crowd discovery promises organic and highly-temporal group interest identif cation and provides a powerful mechanism for analyzing the topical, demographic, and social characteristics of crowds with respect to multiple spatial granularities. (e.g., neighborhood-based interests, city-based trends, statewide movements, etc.). Successful crowd monitoring can positively impact online event detection, content personalization, social information discovery, as well as lead to new crowd-based applications in areas like search, advertising, and emergency management.

2. SYSTEM OVERVIEW

The CrowdTracker system supports crowd-oriented web monitoring optimized for real-time web streams like Twitter, Facebook, and Google Buzz. Concretely, the system supports three overlapping crowd perspectives: (i) *communication-based*, ref ecting groups of users who are actively messaging each other, e.g., users coordinating a meeting; (ii) *location-based*, ref ecting groups of users who are geographically bounded, e.g., users posting messages from Houston, Texas [1]; and (iii) *interest-based*, ref ecting groups of users who share a common interest, e.g., users posting messages about a presidential debate. While each of these crowd perspectives can be monitored separately, in many cases it will be important to monitor cross-cutting crowds, e.g., users in Houston (location-based), messaging each other (messaging-based) about a local f re (interest-based). The crowd tracking prototype collects social media streams (primarily from Twitter for the purposes of this demo), and then passes these streams to the crowd tracking and trending component, including the three-layered crowd detection component (communication-based, geo-based, and topic-based).

Frontend: The frontend is designed to provide the user with a simple and f exible interface to maximize their options for exploring crowds. The primary display is a crowd display window, including both a global view panel and a personal workspace panel. The personal workspace panel is designed for exploration of a set of crowds marked by the user when exploring in the global view panel. Since each crowd may be associated with a starting and ending time, crowd participants, topics, messages, location data, and so on, we consider a timeline, list, and map format.

Backend: The backend relies on several modules, including a *crawler* for collecting information from real-time web streams; a *f lter* for removing unwanted spam messages and low-quality content encountered by the crawler; a *grouper* for identifying crowds from the data collecting and inserting them into a database; and *HTTP JSON RESTful APIs* for exposing an HTTP-based API that clients can query to return crowds, users, and their messages. Concretely, the backend relies on several tools including *Beanstalk*, a simple, fast work queue used to connect the crawlers, f lters, and groupers together; *Tornado*, a fast and scalable non-blocking web server; and *MongoDB*, a scalable, high-performance, open source, document-oriented database for storing discovered crowds.

3. DEMO PLAN

As part of the demonstration, attendees will be able to view signif cant crowds along a number of dimensions (e.g., by size, by growth rate), drill down for details on particular crowds (to view the timeline of the crowd, members of the crowd, and crowd-based themes), query for crowds that match simple keywords, and f lter crowds by geography (e.g., to view crowds based primarily in Texas).

4. REFERENCES

[1] Z. Cheng, J. Caverlee, and K. Lee. You are where you tweet: A content-based approach to geo-locating twitter users. In *CIKM*, 2010.

[2] K. Kamath and J. Caverlee. Transient crowd discovery on the real-time web. In *WSDM*, 2011.

SIGIR'11, July 24–28, 2011, Beijing, China.
ACM 978-1-4503-0757-4/11/07.

The *Meta-Dex* Suite: Generating and Analyzing Indexes and Meta-Indexes

Michael Huggett and Edie Rasmussen
University of British Columbia
Suite 470, 1961 East Mall
Vancouver, BC V6T 1Z1
(1-604) 827-5486
{m.huggett, edie.rasmussen}@ubc.ca

ABSTRACT

Our *Meta-dex* software suite extracts content and index text from a corpus of PDF files, and generates a *meta-index* that references entries across an entire domain. We provide tools to analyze the individual and integrated indexes, and visualize entries and books within the meta-index. The suite is scalable to very large data sets.

Categories and Subject Descriptors

H.5.2 **[Information Interfaces and Presentation]**: User Interfaces – *evaluation/methodology, prototyping*

General Terms

Algorithms, Measurement, Design.

Keywords

Digital collections, digital books, indexes, meta-indexes, visualization, user interfaces.

1. THE UTILITY OF META-INDEXES

Large-scale digitization projects such as the Gutenberg Project, and Google Books [1] have placed large amounts of text in the public domain. Scholars have long used back-of-book indexes (BoBIs) to find information in print [2]. BoBIs are compiled by professional indexers as a useful summary of content, and as indicators of important concepts. They also offer an alternative to keyword search for locating relevant information [3, 4].

The multiple indexes in a corpus contain a range of domain vocabulary. They reveal knowledge structures and provide entry points for navigation. With this in mind, our *Indexer's Legacy* project is investigating how BoBIs can add value to search. The *Meta-dex* suite is the product of this endeavour. To our knowledge no widely-available software exists to create meta-indexes from plain-text and PDF documents.

2. OVERVIEW OF THE PROTOTYPE

Meta-indexes are generated across several steps (Fig.1). At each step, summary statistics are calculated and saved to the database for later analysis. We will demonstrate the build process, and show visualizations of end products. The suite's components are:

Extractor. Plain-text files of content and index are generated from the book PDF.

OCR error filter. An enhanced editor highlights for correction terms that are likely to be OCR errors.

Expander. Each entry in an index is 'expanded' into fully-qualified entries from the main heading through each subheading to each individual page reference.

Compressor. The large sorted file is 'compressed' back into a tabbed index format, to compile references under similar headings. Index terms are generalized to reduce the effects of plurals, gerunds, etc. The entries from each book are tagged with the book's unique ID number. The result is a global domain index that references specific pages in specific books.

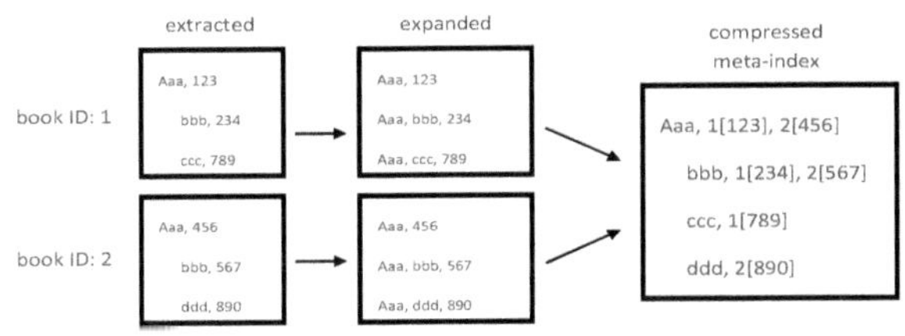

Figure 1: Building a meta-index

Analysis tools. During extraction, the number of lines, entries, sub-entries, parts-of-speech, etc. and term frequencies are saved to a database for later analysis. Basic proportions of most-representative books, 'singleton' entries, expansion and compression ratios, etc. are generated for comparison between domains. Language modeling is also used to gauge the coherence between index and content, both within books and across an entire domain. Visualization tools show entries and terms from personalized searches projected onto the domain meta-index, and will use interactive colour, zooming, and three-dimensional displays.

Suite components can be run locally, but can also be run on the cloud in order to accommodate users without adequate local computing power and storage. Our current implementation uses an Amazon EC2 server to read from and write to storage on S3.

3. REFERENCES

[1] Coyle, K. 2006. Mass digitization of books. *Journal of Academic Librarianship* 32,6, 641-645.

[2] Jörgensen, C. and Liddy, E.D. 1996. Information access or information anxiety?—an exploratory evaluation of book index features. *The Indexer* 20, 64-68.

[3] Abdullah, N. and Gibb, F. 2008. Using a task-based approach in evaluating the usability of BoBIs in an E-book environment. *ECDL 2008, LNCS* 4956, 246-257.

[4] Egan, D.E., Remde, J.R., Gomez, L.M., Landauer, T.K., Eberhardt, J. and Lochbaum, C.C. 1989. Formative design evaluation of Superbook. *ACM Transactions on Information Systems* 7(1), 30-57.

SIGIR'11, July 24–28, 2011, Beijing, China.
ACM 978-1-4503-0757-4/11/07.

Tulsa: Web Search for Writing Assistance

Duo Ding[1], Xingping Jiang[2], Matthew R. Scott[2], Ming Zhou[2], Yong Yu[1]
[1]Shanghai Jiao Tong University, Shanghai, 200240, P. R. China
[1]{dding, yyu}@apex.sjtu.edu.cn
[2]Microsoft Research Asia, Beijing, 100080, P. R. China
[2]{v-pjiang, mrscott, mingzhou}@microsoft.com

Categories and Subject Descriptors
H.3 Information Storage Retrieval: Online Information Services

General Terms
Management, Design, Human Factors, Language.

1. INTRODUCTION
Searching the web while authoring has become a common behavior for many users. Some search the web to research content, while others, especially those writing in a foreign language, search to learn if their usage is appropriate. Can we unify the experiences of search and writing to make authoring more productive? That's the central question of project Tulsa, which puts the web at writers' fingertips in a novel writing assistance experience based on implicit web search and natural language techniques. It provides assistance at three levels: word, phrase and paragraph. Tulsa offers web-mined, contextual reference information and suggestions for completing or revising words and phrases. Paragraph analysis is also provided which can detect outlier usage of language in larger chunks of text. Tulsa bases its suggestions and rankings on the Web as Corpus (WaC) through search engine queries, combined with a Support Vector Machine (SVM) trained on N gram language features of a web-scale language model

2. OVERVIEW
In our demo, Tulsa is realized as an add-in to a word processing application with three key features. "Sense" enables word and phrase contextual suggestions. "Analysis" examines the document text to suggest potential language errors. And "Bilingual Mode" makes writing in a foreign language easier.

Sense: The primary feature of Tulsa, "Sense," provides word and phrase completion in addition to revision suggestions which exploit writing context. "Sense" operates in three writing scenarios. The first is word complete, which occurs when the cursor is at the end of a word; Tulsa provides auto-completion results derived from a web-based dictionary. Second is the revision scenario, which occurs when the cursor is within a word; Tulsa suggests statistically more likely alternatives according to the context. To achieve this, a web-scale language model [1][2] is leveraged along with search engine hit numbers to train a SVM model. After training, each suggestion candidate is assigned a probability score for ranking the top N shown to the user (Figure 1). The third scenario is sentence complete, and occurs when the space key is entered after a word; Tulsa offers web-based suggestions to complete the phrase or sentence. Figure 2 shows the interface of Tulsa in the revision scenario.

SIGIR'11, July 25–29, 2011, Beijing, China.
ACM 978-1-4503-0757-4/11/07.

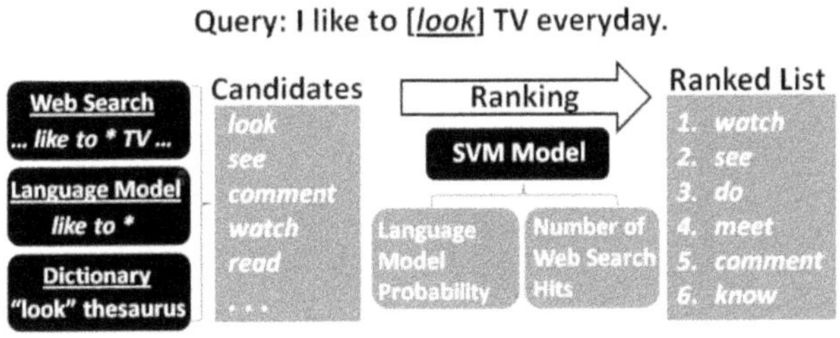

Figure 1: Tulsa high level design

Analysis: The "Analysis" feature of Tulsa helps users find language usage mistakes and semantic errors, including grammar and collocation problems. The method "touches-up" every tri-gram in the paragraph and calculates probability scores for them. In this way, it operates like a batch mode of the "Sense" feature. Additionally, we augment the "Analysis" feature with heuristic language rules to help detect writing quality mistakes. For example, when the same word or expression appears too often inside a paragraph, Tulsa will suggest the user to replace them with web-culled suggestions, synonyms or similar expressions.

Bilingual Mode: After turning "Bilingual Mode" on, web-mined translations of each suggestion will appear besides the results In the tooltip reference window that appears when hovering the mouse over suggestions; the definition, and sample sentences will appear in both the users' original language and target language, and highlighted using word-alignment techniques.

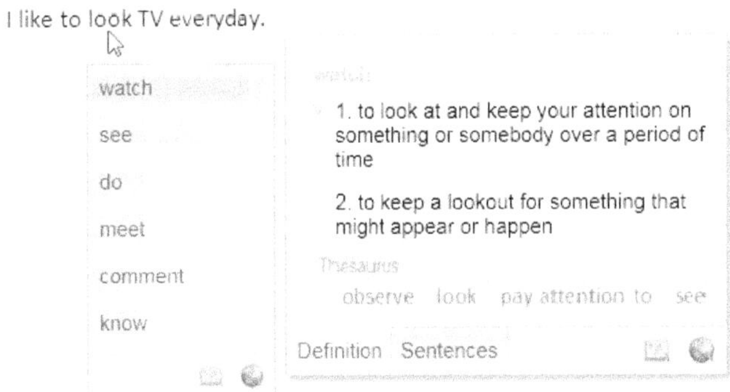

Figure 2: A screenshot of Tulsa providing suggestions.

3. REFERENCES
[1] Jian Huang, Jianfeng Gao, and etc. 2010. Exploring Web Scale Language Models for Search Query Processing. In *Proceeding of WWW 2010*, Raleigh, USA.

[2] Kuansan Wang, Christopher Thrasher and etc. 2010. An overview of Microsoft Web N-gram Corpus and Applications. In *Proceeding of the NAACL HLT 2010: Demonstration Session, pages 45-48.* Los Angeles, California, USA.

The TREC Files: The (Ground) Truth Is Out There

Savvas A. Chatzichristofis   Konstantinos Zagoris   Avi Arampatzis
Department of Electrical and Computer Engineering
Democritus University of Thrace, Xanthi 67100, Greece
{schatzic,kzagoris,avi}@ee.duth.gr

ABSTRACT

Traditional tools for information retrieval (IR) evaluation, such as TREC's `trec_eval`, have outdated command-line interfaces with many unused features, or 'switches', accumulated over the years. They are usually seen as cumbersome applications by new IR researchers, steepening the learning curve. We introduce a platform-independent application for IR evaluation with a graphical easy-to-use interface: the TREC_Files Evaluator. The application supports most of the standard measures used for evaluation in TREC, CLEF, and elsewhere, such as MAP, P10, P20, and bpref, as well as the Averaged Normalized Modified Retrieval Rank (ANMRR) proposed by MPEG for image retrieval evaluation. Additional features include a batch mode and statistical significance testing of the results against a pre-selected baseline.

Categories and Subject Descriptors: D.0 [**Software**]: General
General Terms: Experimentation, Measurement
Keywords: TREC files, Evaluation Measurements

1. THE TREC_FILES EVALUATOR

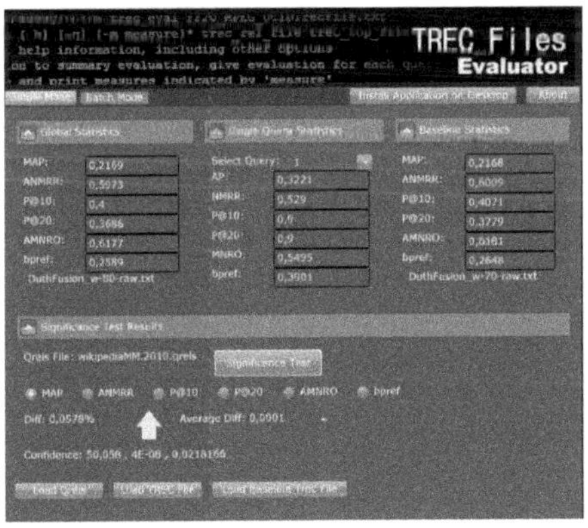

Figure 1: The TREC_Files Evaluator.

The program is developed in Silverlight technology which is an application framework for writing rich Internet applications. Its run-time environment is available for most browsers and it is compatible with Microsoft Windows, Mac OS X, Linux, FreeBSD, and other *nix open source platforms through the Moonlight plugin. The TREC_Files Evaluator (Fig. 1) is freely available at: `http://thetrecfiles.nonrelevant.net`

A user must first load the relevance assessments file (qrels), which represents the ground truth of the experiment. Next, the user loads the experimental results file. Both files must be in the standard TREC format. Then, all the available standard evaluation measures can be calculated with a press of button. All calculations are taking place locally, i.e. at the client side.

Figure 2: The output of the program in Batch Mode.

The *batch mode* (Fig. 2) allows a user to evaluate several TREC files together and calculate all the measures without manual intervention. At the same time, the system can check statistical significance against a selected baseline run, using a bootstrap, one-tailed test, at significance levels 0.05, 0.01, and 0.001. The results are presented in an interactive table and can be sorted on any measure. Additionally, the TREC_Files Evaluator can export the results in a LaTeX friendly format.

2. CONCLUSIONS

Given that MAP, P10, P20 and bpref constitute main evaluation criteria for the retrieval results in TREC, CLEF, and elsewhere, the TREC_Files Evaluator can be used in order to help either new researchers or organizers of multi-group controlled experiments to evaluate the submitted results more easily. Moreover, the inclusion of ANMRR evaluation metric [1] will encourage researchers from the image retrieval field to employ the standard TREC format for evaluating their experiments.

Future plans include the implementation of more evaluation metrics, such as R-prec and nDCG, as well as enabling users to plug in their custom implementation of metrics.

3. REFERENCES

[1] MPEG-7. *Subjective Evaluation of the MPEG-7 Retrieval Accuracy Measure (ANMRR)*. ISO/WG11, Doc. M6029, 2000.

SIGIR'11, July 24–28, 2011, Beijing, China.
ACM 978-1-4503-0757-4/11/07.

A Tool for Comparative IR Evaluation on Component Level

Thomas Wilhelm, Jens Kürsten, and Maximilian Eibl
Chemnitz University of Technology
Straße der Nationen 62, 09111 Chemnitz, Germany
{thomas.wilhelm, jens.kuersten, eibl}@cs.tu-chemnitz.de

Categories and Subject Descriptors
H.3.4 [**Information Storage and Retrieval**]: Systems and Software – performance evaluation

General Terms: Experimentation, Measurement, Performance

1. MOTIVATION

Experimental information retrieval (IR) evaluation is an important instrument to measure the effectiveness of novel methods. Although IR system complexity has grown over years, the general framework for evaluation remained unchanged since its first implementation in the 1960s. Test collections were growing from thousands to millions of documents. Regular reuse resulted in larger topic sets for evaluation. New business models for information access required novel interpretations of effectiveness measures. Nevertheless, most experimental evaluations still rely on an over 50 year old paradigm.

Participants of a SIGIR workshop in 2009 [1] discussed the implementation of new methodological standards for evaluation. But at the same time they worried about practicable ways to implement them. A review about recent publications containing experimental evaluations supports this concern [2]. The study also presented a web-based platform for longitudinal evaluation. In a similar way, data from the past decade of CLEF evaluations have been released through the DIRECT[1] system. While the operators of the latter system reported about 50 new users since the release of the data [3], no further contributions were recorded on the web-platform introduced in [2].

In our point of view archiving evaluation data for longitudinal analysis is a first important step. A next step is to develop a methodology that supports researchers in choosing appropriate baselines for comparison. This can be achieved by reporting evaluation results on component level [4] rather than on system level. An exemplary study was presented in [2], where the Indri system was tested with several components switched on or off. Following this idea, an approach to assess novel methods could be to compare to related components only. This would require the community to formally record details of system configurations in connection with experimental results. We suppose that transparent descriptions of system components used in experiments could help researchers in choosing appropriate baselines.

2. DEMONSTRATION

Our demo[2] aims to record and visualize the actual configuration of components used in modern IR systems. A flexible interface was developed for the import of experimental results. Visual presentation allows comparison on component level. Interactively selected configurations are provided for export. A large-scale experimental study on several test collections served as data source to introduce the concept. In contrast to the study presented in [2], numerous commonly used implementations of IR system components were tested here. The tool was applied to analyze relations and interactions of system components across test collections w.r.t. retrieval effectiveness.

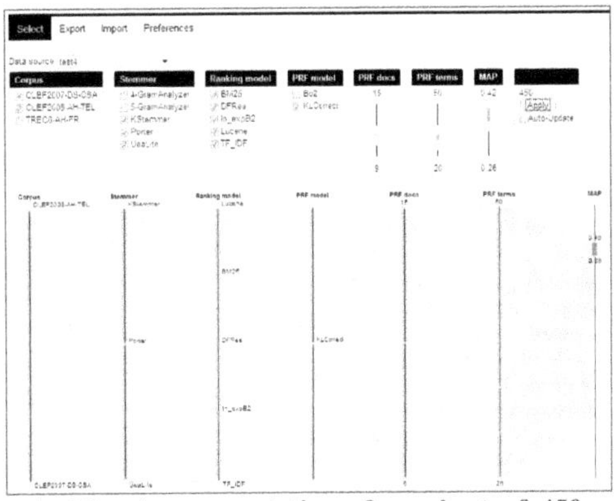

Figure 1: Visual representation of a subset of 450 experiment configurations evaluated on two document collections

Another intention of this demo is to stimulate the discussion of current issues and future directions in experimental evaluation:

- To what extent are common baselines needed?
- How and where to implement such baselines?
- How to persuade/convince IR researchers to use them?

We suggest that a simple but formal description of system components should be incorporated and archived at the level of evaluation campaigns. This could be presumably achieved by integrating this demo into existing evaluation platforms.

REFERENCES

[1] Jaap Kamps, Shlomo Geva, Carol Peters, Tetsuya Sakai, Andrew Trotman, and Ellen Voorhees. 2009. Report on the SIGIR 2009 workshop on the future of IR evaluation. *SIGIR Forum* 43, 2, pp. 13-23.

[2] Timothy G. Armstrong, Alistair Moffat, William Webber, and Justin Zobel. 2009. Improvements that don't add up: ad-hoc retrieval results since 1998. In *Proceedings of the 18th ACM CIKM conference*, pp. 601-610.

[3] Maristella Agosti, Giorgio Maria Di Nunzio, Marco Dussin, and Nicola Ferro. 2010. 10 years of CLEF data in DIRECT: Where we are and where we can go. In *Proceedings of the 3rd EVIA workshop*, pp. 16-24.

[4] Allan Hanbury and Henning Müller. 2010. Automated component-level evaluation: present and future. In *Proceedings of the 2010 international conference on Multilingual and multimodal information access evaluation.* Springer-Verlag, Berlin, Heidelberg, pp. 124-135.

[1] http://direct.dei.unipd.it/
[2] http://sachsmedia.tv/compeval

SIGIR'11, July 24–28, 2011, Beijing, China.
ACM 978-1-4503-0757-4/11/07.

Machine Learning for Information Retrieval

Luo Si
Department of Computer Science
Purdue University
lsi@cs.purdue.edu

Rong Jin
Department of Computer Science and Engineering
Michigan State University
rongjin@cse.msu.edu

ABSTRACT

In recent years, we have witnessed successful application of machine learning techniques to a wide range of information retrieval problems, including Web search engines, recommendation systems, online advertising, etc. It is thus critical for researchers in the information retrieval community to understand the core machine learning techniques. In order to accommodate audiences with different levels of understanding of machine learning, we divide this tutorial into two sessions: the first session will focus on basic machine learning concepts and tools; in the second session, we will introduce more advanced topics in machine learning, and will present recent developments in machine learning and its application to information retrieval. Each season is self-contained.

Session 1: Core Learning Technologies for Information Retrieval. This session of the tutorial will cover the core machine learning methods, basic optimization techniques and key information retrieval applications. In particular, it includes: 1). Core concepts in machine learning, such as supervised learning/unsupervised learning, bias and variance trade off, and probabilistic models; 2). Useful concepts and algorithms in optimization including the first and second order gradient methods, and Expectation and Maximization; 3). The application of machine learning methods to key information retrieval problems including text classification, collaborative filtering, clustering and learning to rank;

Session 2: Emerging Learning Technologies for Information Retrieval. This session will cover more advanced machine learning techniques that have started to be utilized in information retrieval applications. In particular, it will cover: 1). Advanced Optimization Techniques including stochastic optimization and smooth minimization; 2). Emerging Learning Techniques such as Multiple-Instance Learning, Active Learning and Semi-supervised Learning.

The tutorial will benefit a large body of audience in the information retrieval community, ranging from students who are new to machine learning to the seasoned researchers who would like to understand the recent advance in machine learning for information retrieval research. This tutorial will also benefit the practitioners who apply learning techniques to real-world information retrieval systems.

Categories and Subject Descriptors

H.3.3 [**Information Storage and Retrieval**]: Clustering, Information filtering, Retrieval models; I.2.6 [**Artificial Intelligence**]: Learning; I.5.2 [**Pattern Recognition**] Design Methodology; Classifier design and evaluation; G.1.6 [**Optimization**] Convex programming, gradient methods; G.3 [**Probability and Statistics**] Probabilistic algorithms

General Terms

Algorithms, Performance, Design, Experimentation, Theory.

Keywords

Information Retrieval Application, Machine Learning, Probabilistic Methods, Optimization

Bios

Si Bio: Dr. Si is an Assistant professor at Computer Science Department and Statistic Department (by courtesy) at Purdue University. Dr. Si's research interests include information retrieval, machine learning techniques and applications, and text mining techniques. Dr. Si is an associate editor of ACM Transactions on Information System and an editorial board member of Information Processing and Management. Dr. Si got NSF Career Award in 2008. Dr. Si got his Ph.D. degree from Carnegie Mellon University in 2006. Dr. Si has collaborated with industry companies such as Yahoo! and Google.

Jin Bio: Dr. Jin is an Associate professor of the Computer and Science Engineering Dept. of Michigan State University. He has been working in the areas of statistical machine learning and its application to information retrieval. Dr. Jin has extensive research experience in a variety of machine learning algorithms such as conditional exponential models, support vector machine, boosting and optimization for different applications including information retrieval. Dr. Jin is an associate editor of ACM Transactions on Knowledge Discovery from Data. Dr. Jin got NSF Career Award in 2006. Dr. Jin got his Ph.D. degree from Carnegie Mellon University in 2003. Dr. Jin has collaborated with industry companies such as Yahoo!, Intel and NEC.

SIGIR'11, July 24–28, 2011, Beijing, China.
ACM 978-1-4503-0757-4/11/07.

Enhancing Web Search by Mining Search and Browse Logs

Daxin Jiang
Microsoft Research Asia
No. 5 Danling Street
Haidian, Beijing, China
djiang@microsoft.com

Jian Pei
Simon Fraser University
8888 University Drive
Burnaby, BC, Canada
jpei@cs.sfu.ca

Hang Li
Microsoft Research Asia
No. 5 Danling Street
Haidian, Beijing, China
hangli@microsoft.com

ABSTRACT

Huge amounts of search log data have been accumulated in various search engines. Currently, a commercial search engine receives billions of queries and collects tera-bytes of log data on any single day. Other than search log data, browse logs can be collected by client-side browser plug-ins, which record the browse information if users' permissions are granted. Such massive amounts of search/browse log data, on the one hand, provide great opportunities to mine the wisdom of crowds and improve web search results. On the other hand, designing effective and efficient methods to clean, model, and process large scale log data also presents great challenges.

In this tutorial, we will focus on mining search and browse log data for search engines. We will start with an introduction of search and browse log data and an overview of frequently-used data summarization in log mining. We will then elaborate how log mining applications enhance the five major components of a search engine, namely, query understanding, document understanding, query-document matching, user understanding, and monitoring and feedbacks. For each aspect, we will survey the major tasks, fundamental principles, and state-of-the-art methods. Finally, we will discuss the challenges and future trends of log data mining.

The goal of this tutorial is to provide a systematic survey on large-scale search/browse log mining to the IR community. It may help IR researchers to get familiar with the core challenges and promising directions in log mining. At the same time, this tutorial may also serve the developers of web information retrieval systems as a comprehensive and in-depth reference to the advanced log mining techniques.

Categories and Subject Descriptors

H.2.8 [**Database Management**]: Database Applications—*Data Mining*; H.3.3 [**Information Search and Retrieval**]: Search process

General Terms

Algorithms, Experimentation

Keywords

Search and browse logs, log mining, search applications

SIGIR'11, July 24–28, 2011, Beijing, China.
ACM 978-1-4503-0757-4/11/07.

Presenter Bios

Daxin Jiang, Ph.D., Researcher, Microsoft Research Asia. Daxin Jiang's research focuses on information retrieval and log data mining. He received Ph.D. in computer science from the State University of New York at Buffalo. He has published extensively in prestigious conferences and journals, and served as a PC member of many conferences. He received the Best Application Paper Award of SIGKDD'08 and the Runner-up for Best Application Paper Award of SIGKDD'04. Daxin Jiang has been working on development of Microsoft search engines, including Live Search and Bing.

Jian Pei, Ph.D., Associate Professor, Associate Director, School of Computing Science, Simon Fraser University. Jian Pei's research focuses on data mining and analytic queries on various data repositories. With prolific publications in refereed journals and conferences, he is the recipient of several prestigious awards. He is the Associate Editor-in-Chief of IEEE Transactions on Knowledge and Data Engineering (TKDE), and an Associate Editor of 4 premier journals on data mining and analytics, including ACM Transactions on Knowledge Discovery from Data (TKDD). He has served regularly in the organization committees and the program committees of numerous international conferences and workshops, such as a PC co-chair of the ICDM 2011 conference. He is a senior member of both ACM and IEEE.

Hang Li, Ph.D., Senior Researcher and Research Manager, Microsoft Research Asia. Hang Li's research areas include natural language processing, information retrieval, statistical machine learning, and data mining. He graduated from Kyoto University and holds a PhD in computer science from the University of Tokyo. Hang has about 80 publications in international conferences and journals. He is associate editor of ACM Transaction on Asian Language Information Processing and area editor of Journal for Computer and Science Technology, etc. His recent academic activities include PC co-chair of WSDM 2011, senior PC member of WSDM 2010, senior PC member of KDD 2010, area chair of ACL 2010, and PC member of WWW 2010. Hang has been working on development of several products. These include NEC TopicScope, Microsoft SQL Server 2005, Microsoft Office 2007, Microsoft Live Search 2008, and Microsoft Bing 2009.

A New Look at Old Tricks: The Fertile Roots of Current Research

Paul B. Kantor
LIS and CS Rutgers University
4 Huntington St.
New Brunswick NJ 08901 USA
732-932-7500 x 8216
paul.kantor@rutgers.edu

ABSTRACT

As we face an explosion of potential new applications for the fundamental concepts and technologies of information retrieval, ranging from ad ranking to social media, from collaborative recommending to question answering systems, many researchers are spending unnecessary time reinventing ideas and relationships that are buried in the prehistory of information retrieval (which, for many researchers, means anything published before they entered graduate school). A lot of the ideas that surface as "new" in today's super-heated research environment have very firm roots in earlier developments in fields as diverse as citation analysis and pattern recognition. The purpose of this tutorial is to survey those roots, and their relation to the contemporary fruits on the tree of information retrieval, and to separate, as much as is possible in an era of increasing secrecy about methods, the problems to be solved, the algorithms for solving them, and the heuristics that are the bread and butter of a working operation.

While some might think that an examination of the roots is of merely historical interest, it has practical value as well. When you know which earlier research has provided the origins for the things that you are interested in, you can use that fact to trace its other descendents, and often find rich and rewarding ideas in a literature that you would not normally reach, because it was not considered important by your instructors when you were learning about the problems. In addition to pattern recognition and citation analysis, the tutorial will also expose and review some of the relations to the fields of statistics and operations research.

Participants will become familiar with roots in Pattern Analysis, Statistics, Information Science and other sources of key ideas that reappear in the current development of Information Retrieval as it applies to Search Engines, Social Media, and Collaborative Systems. They will be able to separate problems from algorithms, and algorithms from heuristics, in the application of these ideas to their own research and/or development activities. Course materials will be made available on a Web site two weeks prior to the tutorial. They will include links to relevant software; links to publications that will be discussed; and mechanisms for chat among the tutorial participants, before, during and after the tutorial.

Specific Topics will include: 1. The earliest "automated retrieval; 2. Vectors and Logarithms: their pragmatic origins; 3. Probabilistic approaches. A frequentist foundation; 4. The quest for a theoretical foundation; 5. Generative approaches; 6. Network approaches; 7. Binding approaches together.

Certain materials that are very hard to find, such as some papers by H.P. Luhn and I.J. Good will be scanned and placed on a web site for the tutorial. Since this will not be a public site, we will need some information on advance registration to add participants to the site.

Categories and Subject Descriptors
H.3.0 General; H.3.3 Information Search and Retrieval

General Terms
Algorithms, Measurement, Performance, Theory

Keywords
Foundations of Information Retrieval

SIGIR'11, July 24–28, 2011, Beijing, China.
ACM 978-1-4503-0757-4/11/07.

Crowdsourcing for Information Retrieval: Principles, Methods, and Applications

Omar Alonso
Microsoft Corp.
1056 La Avenida
Mountain View, CA 94043
omar.alonso@microsoft.com

Matthew Lease
School of Information
University of Texas at Austin
1616 Guadalupe Ste 5.202
Austin, TX 78701
ml@ischool.utexas.edu

ABSTRACT
Crowdsourcing has emerged in recent years as a promising new avenue for leveraging today's digitally-connected, diverse, distributed workforce. Generally speaking, crowdsourcing describes outsourcing of tasks to a large group of people instead of assigning such tasks to an in-house employee or contractor. Crowdsourcing platforms such as Amazon Mechanical Turk and CrowdFlower have gained particular attention as active online market places for reaching and tapping into this still largely under-utilized workforce. Crowdsourcing also offers intriguing new opportunities for accomplishing different kinds of tasks or achieving broader participation than previously possible, as well as completing standard tasks more accurately in less time and at lower cost. Unlocking the potential of crowdsourcing in practice, however, requires a tri-partite understanding of principles, platforms, and best practices. We will introduce the opportunities and challenges of crowdsourcing while discussing the three issues above. This will provide a basic foundation to begin crowdsourcing in the context of one's own particular tasks.

Categories and Subject Descriptors
H.3.4 [**Information Storage and Retrieval**]: Systems and software — performance evaluation

General Terms
Measurements, performance, experimentation, human factors

Keywords
Crowdsourcing, human computation.

1. Motivating Application: Search Evaluation
To motivate and ground general discussion of crowdsourcing, we will focus primarily upon applications to evaluating search accuracy (with other examples like blending automation with human computation for hybrid search). While search evaluation is an essential part of the development and maintenance of search engines and other information retrieval (IR) systems, current approaches for search evaluation face a variety of practical challenges. Many Web search engines reportedly use large editorial staffs to judge the relevance of web pages for queries in an evaluation set. This is expensive and has obvious scalability issues. Academic researchers, without access to such editors, often rely instead on small groups of student volunteers. Because of the students' limited time and availability, test sets are often smaller than desired, making it harder to detect statistically significant differences in performance by the experimental systems being tested. While behavioral data, such as obtained automatically from search engine logs of user activity, is much cheaper than the editorial method, it requires access to a large stream of data, something not always available to a researcher testing an experimental system. These challenges provide an ideal setting for demonstrating both the potential and practical challenges for the crowdsourcing paradigm.

SIGIR'11, July 24–28, 2011, Beijing, China.
ACM 978-1-4503-0757-4/11/07.

2. Target Audience
The tutorial is designed for those with little to intermediate familiarity with crowdsourcing who want to learn about the capabilities and limitations of crowdsourcing techniques for IR. The tutorial will highlight opportunities and challenges of the crowdsourcing paradigm, emphasize design and execution of experiments, provide practical "how to" knowledge on using existing platforms (Mechanical Turk and CrowdFlower), and present established best practices for achieving efficient, inexpensive, and accurate results with crowdsourcing. Recommended background includes basic familiarity with IR evaluation and experimentation.

3. Tutorial Outline
- Introduce crowdsourcing and human computation
- Survey recent "killer apps" of crowdsourcing principles
- Provide practical "how to" guidance for effectively using Amazon's Mechanical Turk's API and user interface
- Summarize recent surveys of crowd worker demographics
- Discuss a variety of incentive structures available to encourage quality and quantity of work
- Emphasize design and human-centric practices with statistical methods to maximize results
- Describe Summarize key best practices for achieving efficient, inexpensive, and accurate work
- Review current opportunities, untapped potential, and open challenges for IR crowdsourcing, particularly evaluation

Practical Online Retrieval Evaluation

Filip Radlinski
Microsoft
Vancouver, BC, Canada
filiprad@microsoft.com

Yisong Yue
H. John Heinz III College,
Carnegie Mellon University
Pittsburgh, PA, USA
yisongyue@cmu.edu

ABSTRACT

Online evaluation is amongst the few evaluation techniques available to the information retrieval community that is guaranteed to reflect how users actually respond to improvements developed by the community. Broadly speaking, online evaluation refers to any evaluation of retrieval quality conducted while observing user behavior in a natural context. However, it is rarely employed outside of large commercial search engines due primarily to a perception that it is impractical at small scales. The goal of this tutorial is to familiarize information retrieval researchers with state-of-the-art techniques in evaluating information retrieval systems based on natural user clicking behavior, as well as to show how such methods can be practically deployed. In particular, our focus will be on demonstrating how the Interleaving approach and other click based techniques contrast with traditional offline evaluation, and how these online methods can be effectively used in academic-scale research. In addition to lecture notes, we will also provide sample software and code walk-throughs to showcase the ease with which Interleaving and other click-based methods can be employed by students, academics and other researchers.

Categories and Subject Descriptors

H.3.3 [**Information Storage and Retrieal**]: Information Search and Retrieval

General Terms

Measurement, Experimentation

Keywords

Web Search, Online Evaluation, Interleaving, Clickthrough Data, Preference Judgments

SIGIR'11, July 24–28, 2011, Beijing, China.
ACM 978-1-4503-0757-4/11/07.

1. TUTORIAL OUTLINE

- Overview of online evaluation
- Collecting usage data: How to be their search engine (with code walk-through)
- The Interleaving approach for click-based evaluation
- Practical issues in deploying Interleaving experiments (with code walk-through)
- Analyzing and interpreting Interleaving results
- Quantitative comparison of Interleaving with other evaluation methods (both online and offline)
- Algorithmic subtleties, extensions, and limitations
- From evaluation to optimization: Deriving reliable training data from user feedback

2. PRESENTERS

Filip Radlinski is an applied researcher at Microsoft and a contributor to Bing, where he works on machine learning approaches to information retrieval. He completed his dissertation on learning to rank from implicit feedback at Cornell University in 2008. His recent research focuses on learning personalized rankings, measuring ambiguity in queries and user intents, and studying how to assess the quality of ranked lists of documents from the user perspective by using click information.

Yisong Yue is a postdoctoral researcher in the Machine Learning Department and the Heinz College at Carnegie Mellon University, where he works on machine learning approaches to information retrieval. He completed his dissertation on structured prediction and interactive approaches to learning to rank at Cornell University in 2010. His recent research focuses on machine learning approaches to leveraging user feedback, diversified retrieval, and interactive information retrieval.

Web Retrieval: The Role of Users

Ricardo Baeza-Yates
Yahoo! Research, Barcelona, Spain
rbaeza@acm.org

Yoelle Maarek
Yahoo! Research, Haifa, Israel
yoelle@ymail.com

ABSTRACT

Web retrieval methods have evolved through three major steps in the last decade or so. They started from standard document-centric IR in the early days of the Web, then made a major step forward by leveraging the structure of the Web, using link analysis techniques in both crawling and ranking challenges. A more recent, no less important but maybe more discrete step forward, has been to enter the user in this equation in two ways: (1) Implicitly, through the analysis of usage data captured by query logs, and session and click information in general; the goal here being to improve ranking as well as to measure user's happiness and engagement; (2) Explicitly, by offering novel interactive features; the goal here being to better answer users' needs. This half day tutorial covers the user-related challenges associated with the implicit and explicit role of users in Web retrieval. More specifically, we review and discuss challenges associated with:

- **Usage data analysis and metrics** - It is critical to monitor how users take advantage and interact with Web retrieval systems, as this implicit relevant feedback aggregated at a large scale, can provide insights on users' underlying intent as well as approximate quite accurately the level of success of a given feature. Here we have to consider not only clicks statistics, the sequences of queries, the time spent in a page, the number of actions per session, etc. This is the focus of the first part of the tutorial.
- **User interaction** - Given the intrinsic problems posed by the Web, the key challenge for the user is to conceive a good query to be submitted to the search system, one that leads to a manageable and relevant answer. The retrieval system must assist users during two key stages of interaction: efore the query is fully expressed and after the results are returned. After quite some stagnation on the front-end of Web retrieval, we have seen numerous novel interactive features appear in the last 3 to 4 years, as the leading commercial search engines seem to compete for users' attention. The second part of the tutorial will be dedicated to explicit user interaction. We will introduce novel material (as compared to previous versions of this tutorial that were given at SIGIR'2010, WSDM'2011 and ECIR'2011) in order to reflect recent Web search features such as Google Instant or Yahoo! Direct Search.

The goal of this tutorial is to teach the key principles and technologies behind the activities and challenges briefly outlined above, bring new understanding and insights to the attendees, and hopefully foster future research. A previous version of this tutorial was offered at the ACM SIGIR'2010, WSDM'2011 and ECIR'2011.

SIGIR'11, July 24-28, 2011, Beijing, China.
ACM 978-1-4503-0757-4/11/07.

Categories and Subject Descriptors

H.3.3 [Information Search and Retrieval]

General Terms

Algorithms, Human Factors

Keywords

Web Retrieval, User Interaction

BIOGRAPHIES OF PRESENTERS

Ricardo Baeza-Yates is VP of Yahoo! Research for Europe and Latin America. Until 2005, he was the director of the Center for Web Research at the Department of Computer Science of the Engineering School of the University of Chile, and ICREA Professor at the Dept. of Technology of University Pompeu Fabra in Barcelona, Spain. He is co-author of the book *Modern Information Retrieval*, whose 2nd edition appeared in 2011, as well as co-author of the 2nd edition of the *Handbook of Algorithms and Data Structures*, Addison- Wesley, 1991; and co-editor of *Information Retrieval: Algorithms and Data Structures,* Prentice-Hall, 1992, among more than 200 other publications. He has been PC Chair of the most important conferences in the field of Web Search and Web Mining. Most recently, he was one of the co-chairs WWW'2010 Web Search Track and PC co-chair of SIGIR'2011. He has received the organization of American States award for young researchers in exact sciences (1993) and with two Brazilian research articles (1997). In 2003 he was the first computer scientist to be elected to the Chilean Academy of Sciences. During 2007, he was awarded the Graham Medal for innovation in computing, given by the University of Waterloo to distinguished ex-alumni and in 2009 was named ACM Fellow.

Yoelle Maarek is a Senior Research Director at Yahoo! Labs and heads Yahoo! Research in Israel since 2009. Prior to this, Yoelle was the Director of Google Haifa Engineering Center, which she opened in 2006. There, she led the development of "Google Suggest", a query completion feature deployed on google.com and YouTube worldwide. Before this, Yoelle had been with IBM Research, first in the US, and then in Israel, where she led the search and collaboration department and became a Distinguished Engineer. She graduated from the ENPC in Paris, France, and received her DEA in CS from Paris VI University. Yoelle obtained her PhD in Computer Science from Technion, Israel Institute of Technology. Yoelle has published extensively in the Web and IR communities. Most recently, she has served as Program co-chair of WWW'2009, as senior PC member at several SIGIR and WWW conferences. She is also Program co-chair for WSDM'2012 and SIGIR'2012. Yoelle is a member of the Board of Governors of Technion, and was appointed ACM Distinguished Scientist in 2010.

Information Organization and Retrieval with Collaboratively Generated Content

Tutorial Abstract

Eugene Agichtein
Emory University
eugene@mathcs.emory.edu

Evgeniy Gabrilovich
Yahoo! Research
gabr@yahoo-inc.com

ABSTRACT

Proliferation of ubiquitous access to the Internet enables millions of Web users to collaborate online on a variety of activities. Many of these activities result in the construction of large repositories of knowledge, either as their primary aim (e.g., Wikipedia) or as a by-product (e.g., Yahoo! Answers). In this tutorial, we will discuss organizing and exploiting Collaboratively Generated Content (CGC) for information organization and retrieval. Specifically, we intend to cover two complementary areas of the problem: (1) using such content as a powerful enabling resource for knowledge-enriched, intelligent representations and new information retrieval algorithms, and (2) development of supporting technologies for extracting, filtering, and organizing collaboratively created content

The unprecedented amounts of information in CGC enable new, knowledge-rich approaches to information access, which are significantly more powerful than the conventional word-based methods. Considerable progress has been made in this direction over the last few years. Examples include explicit manipulation of human-defined concepts and their use to augment the bag of words (cf. Explicit Semantic Analysis), using large-scale taxonomies of topics from Wikipedia or the Open Directory Project to construct additional class-based features, or using Wikipedia for better word sense disambiguation.

However, the quality and comprehensiveness of collaboratively created content vary significantly, and in order for this resource to be useful, a significant amount of preprocessing, filtering, and organization is necessary. Consequently, new methods for analyzing CGC and corresponding user interactions are required to effectively harness the resulting knowledge. Thus, not only the content repositories can be used to improve IR methods, but the reverse pollination is also possible, as better information extraction methods can be used for automatically collecting more knowledge, or verifying the contributed content. This natural connection between modeling the generation process of CGC and effectively using the accumulated knowledge suggests covering both areas together in a single tutorial.

The intended audience of the tutorial includes IR researchers and graduate students, who would like to learn about the recent advances and research opportunities in working with collaboratively generated content. The emphasis of the tutorial is on comparing the existing approaches and presenting practical techniques that IR practitioners can use in their research. We also cover open research challenges, as well as survey available resources (software tools and data) for getting started in this research field.

Categories and Subject Descriptors

H.3.3 [**Information Storage and Retrieval**]: Information Search and Retrieval

General Terms

Experimentation, Human Factors

Keywords

Collaboratively generated content

Presenters' bios

Dr. Eugene Agichtein is an Assistant Professor in the Math & Computer Science Department at Emory University, where he founded and directs the Emory Intelligent Information Access Laboratory (IR Lab). His research interests are in information retrieval, text mining, and machine learning, and human computer interaction. Eugene's is a recipient of the "Best Student Paper" award at the ICDE 2003 conference, and the "Best Paper Award" at the SIGMOD 2006 conference. He is a Program Co-Chair of the WSDM 2012 conference, and served as a Senior PC member of SIGIR, ICWSM, ICDM, and ACL/HLT conferences. Eugene earned a Ph.D. in Computer Science from Columbia University, and a B.S. from The Cooper Union.
URL: `http://www.mathcs.emory.edu/~eugene/`

Dr. Evgeniy Gabrilovich is a Senior Research Scientist and Manager of the NLP & IR Group at Yahoo! Research. His research interests include information retrieval, machine learning, and computational linguistics. Evgeniy is a recipient of the 2010 Karen Spärck Jones Award for his contributions to natural language processing and information retrieval. He served as a Senior PC member or Area Chair at SIGIR, AAAI, IJCAI, WWW, WSDM, EMNLP, ICDM, and ICWSM. Evgeniy earned his PhD degree in Computer Science from the Technion - Israel Institute of Technology.
URL: `http://research.yahoo.com/~gabr`

SIGIR'11, July 24–28, 2011, Beijing, China.
ACM 978-1-4503-0757-4/11/07.

Persistence in the Ephemeral: Utilizing Repeat Behaviors for Multi-Session Personalized Search

Sarah K Tyler
University of California, Santa Cruz
Santa Cruz, CA, USA
skt@soe.ucsc.edu

1. ABSTRACT

As the abundance of information on the Internet grows, an increasing burden is placed on the user to specify his or her query precisely in order to avoid extraneous results that may be relevant, but not useful. At the same time, users have a tendency to repeat their search behaviors, seeking the same URL (re-finding)[2, 5] as well as issuing the same query (re-searching)[1, 3, 4]. These repeated actions reveal a form of user preference that the search engine can utilize to personalize the results.

In our approach, we personalize search results related to ongoing tasks, allowing for a different degree of *strength of interest*, and *diversity of interest* per task. We use both re-finding and re-searching to identify tasks, and user preference within the task. Such task based queries may be of higher value than non-task related queries, since they may be used again in the future.

Categories and Subject Descriptors

H.3.3 [**Information Systems**]: Information Search and Retrieval - Query formulation, Search process

General Terms

Human Factors, Algorithms

Keywords

Re-search, Re-finding, Query Log Analysis, Task Oriented Search

2. TASK ORIENTED MULTI-SESSION SEARCH

When a user re-finds within a task, he or she shows a strong interest in the particular URL, or the specific content from the URL. Within the same task, users also have a tendency to seek new information in terms of new URLs, and new content. This action is a form of diversity seeking. Some of these new found URLs may be related, revealing subtopics that are of interest to the user. When the user clicks on multiple related results, but does not re-find those results, he or she may be looking for new content within the subtopic. The goal of task oriented multi-session search is to support the dual need of personalized diversification, as well as the need to return to valuable information.

Consider an example of a user searching for colleges. She clicks on academic rankings frequently, occasionally clicking on athletics and fraternities while skipping over sites concerning campus dinning. As she continues her search over time, her often re-found URLs reveal her primary interests, but the clicks on athletics and fraternities show shallow interests in these areas. The search engine could filter out topics for which she shows no interest, provide greater diversification for her shallow interests and help her re-find her deep interests.

Users usually multi-task, and could be engaged in multiple tasks in any given session. If we consider the task to be the state the user is in, then each new query issued by the user is an observed variable indicating whether the user has transitioned to a new task. The transition probability could depend on all past tasks the user has previously been engaged in within the session, as well as where the user is in the session. A natural model for task identification would be a conditional random field.

Predicting whether a URL will be clicked depends on the probability of the URL to satisfy the user's need to re-find or find new information via diversification. The URL will satisfy a user's diversification needs if it is relevant to the subtopics the user is interested in. The probability to satisfy a user's re-finding needs depends on how often and when it was previously clicked. This concept is closely related to the constant elasticity of substitution property in economics, which models the relative gain of a repeated action. Thus we will explore using economics and probabilistic models to solve the task oriented multi-session search problem.

SIGIR'11, July 24–28, 2011, Beijing, China.
ACM 978-1-4503-0757-4/11/07.

3. REFERENCES

[1] A. Aula, N. Jhaveri, and M. Käki. Information search and re-access strategies of experienced web users. In *WWW*, 2005.

[2] H. Obendorf, H. Weinreich, E. Herder, and M. Mayer. Web page revisitation revisited: implications of a long-term click-stream study of browser usage. In *CHI*, 2007.

[3] M. Sanderson and S. Dumais. Examining repetition in user search behavior. In *ECIR*, 2007.

[4] J. Teevan, E. Adar, R. Jones, and M. A. S. Potts. Information re-retrieval: repeat queries in yahoo's logs. In *SIGIR*, 2007.

[5] S. K. Tyler and J. Teevan. Large scale query log analysis of re-finding. In *WSDM*, 2010.

Search Engines that Learn Online

Katja Hofmann
ISLA, University of Amsterdam
K.Hofmann@uva.nl

ABSTRACT

The goal of my research is to develop self-learning search engines, that can learn *online*, i.e., directly from interactions with actual users. Such systems can continuously adapt to user preferences throughout their lifetime, leading to better search performance in settings where expensive manual tuning is infeasible. Challenges that are addressed in my work include the development of effective *online learning to rank algorithms* for IR, *user aspects*, and *evaluation*.

Categories and Subject Descriptors

H.3 [**Information Storage and Retrieval**]: H.3.3 Information Search and Retrieval

General Terms

Algorithms, Experimentation

Keywords

Online learning to rank, Implicit feedback, Evaluation

1. INTRODUCTION

As search engines are becoming increasingly complex, and combine more and more sources of information, the question of how to tune these systems to optimize search results becomes essential. Current methods for optimizing ranking functions typically work *offline*, meaning that systems are tuned to a given data set before deployment. While offline methods are appropriate for many settings and can result in excellent search performance, there are limitations. Data needed for tuning is often created manually, and therefore expensive and error-prone.

We address the limitations of offline methods by working towards self-learning search engines, i.e., search engines that learn ranking functions *online*. Learning online means that there is no distinction between training and operating. Instead, the search engine observes users' natural interactions with the search interface (so-called *implicit feedback*, e.g., clicks on result documents), infers information from them, and improves its ranking function automatically. Because implicit feedback is used for learning, expensive data collection is not required, and the collected data matches the target users and the target setting.

2. RESEARCH QUESTIONS

Several steps have been taken to make online learning to rank for IR a reality, but many open challenges remain. My thesis work addresses the following questions.

SIGIR'11, July 24–28, 2011, Beijing, China.
ACM 978-1-4503-0757-4/11/07.

RQ 1 How can retrieval systems *learn effectively* from implicit feedback in an online settings?

Online learning to rank for IR differs from other learning to rank tasks, because of the characteristics of the implicit feedback available for learning. While correlated with relevance, it varies widely across tasks, users, and queries. As a result, only noisy, relative preferences can be inferred. Furthermore, the feedback that can be obtained is biased towards the top-ranked documents displayed.

Our first results to address these issues focused on the problem of balancing *exploration* and *exploitation*, meaning that result lists to be displayed to the user need to both satisfy the user's information need as much as possible (i.e., exploit what has already been learned), while also allowing to collect feedback that can provide as much new information as possible (i.e., explore new solutions). We found that such a balance can significantly improve the performance of online learning to rank systems [1].

RQ 2 What *user aspects* need to be considered?

Previous work in online learning to rank for IR has been grounded in user studies, but many open questions remain. Here, we investigate the relation between explicit and implicit feedback, and develop methods for inferring information from implicit feedback more reliably. Our first results include a new, probabilistic method for comparing rankers using click data, that is more accurate and more robust to noise than previous methods [2].

RQ 3 How can online learning to rank methods be *evaluated*?

Online learning to rank approaches for IR can be evaluated using live search engine traffic, lab studies, or log data. Each of these has advantages and limitations. Moving forward, we need to analyze the benefits and limitations of existing evaluation methods for assessing online learning to rank approaches, and to develop new approaches to address any identified limitations.

Some online learning to rank approaches have been evaluated on life traffic of large-scale web search engines. However, such a setup is not always accessible or feasible, especially when potentially risky new methods need to be evaluated, or when many comparisons under a wide range of settings are required. As an alternative to real-life experiments, we developed an evaluation setup that simulates user behavior at a sufficient level of detail, using learning to rank data sets and a model of click behavior [1]. In the future, we need to continue to assess and refine this methodology.

References

[1] K. Hofmann, S. Whiteson, and M. de Rijke. Balancing exploration and exploitation in learning to rank online. In *ECIR'11*, pages 251–263, 2011.

[2] K. Hofmann, S. Whiteson, and M. de Rijke. A probabilistic method for inferring preferences from clicks. Under review, 2011.

Query Expansion Based on a Semantic Graph Model*

Xue Jiang[1, 2]
jiangxue@nfs.iscas.ac.cn
[1] Institute of Software, Chinese Academy of Sciences
Beijing, China
[2] Graduate University of Chinese Academy of Sciences
Beijing, China

ABSTRACT

Query expansion is a classical topic in the field of information retrieval, which is proposed to bridge the gap between searchers' information needs and their queries. Previous researches usually expand queries based on document collections, or some external resources such as WordNet and Wikipedia [1, 2, 3, 4, 5]. However, it seems that independently using one of these resources has some defects, document collections lack semantic information of words, while WordNet and Wikipedia may not include domain-specific knowledge in certain document collection. Our work aims to combine these two kinds of resources to establish an expansion model which represents not only domain-specific information but also semantic information.

In our preliminary experiments, we construct a two-layer word graph and use Random-Walk algorithm to calculate the weights of each term in pseudo-relevance feedback documents, then select the highest weighted term to expand original query. The first layer of the word graph contains terms in related documents, while the second layer contains semantic senses corresponding to these terms. These terms and semantic senses are treated as vertices of the graph and connected with each other by all possible relationships, such as mutual information and semantic similarities. We utilized mutual information, semantic similarity and uniform distribution as the weight of term-term relation, sense-sense relation and word-sense relation respectively. Though these experiments show that our expansion outperform original queries, we are troubled with some difficult problems.

Given the framework of semantic graph model, we need more effort to find out an optimal graph to represent the relationships between terms and their semantic senses. We utilized a two-layer graph model in our preliminary research, where terms from different documents are treated equally. Maybe we can introduce the document as a third layer in future work, where we can differ the same terms in different documents according to document relevance and context.

Then we need appropriately represent initial weights of this words, senses and relationships. Various measures for weights of terms and term relations have been proved effective in other information retrieval tasks, such as TFIDF, mutual information (MI), but there is little research on weights for semantic senses and their relations. For polysemous words, we add all of their semantic senses to the graph and assume that these senses are uniformly distributed. Actually, it is not precise for a word in a specific document and query. As we know, a polysemous word may have only one or two senses in a document, and they are not uniformly distributed. Given a word, what we should do is to determine its word senses in a relevant document and estimate the distribution of these senses. Word sense disambiguation may help us in this problem. Then, there are many methods to compute word similarity according to WordNet, which we use to represent the weights of relationships between word senses. Varelas et al implemented some popular methods to compute semantic similarity by mapping terms to a ontology and examining their relationships in that ontology [4]. We also need to study which algorithm for semantic similarity is most suitable for our model.

Additional, WordNet is suitable to calculate word similarity but not suitable to measure word relevance. The inner hyperlinks of Wikipedia could help us to calculate word relevance. We wish to find an effective way to combine the similarity measure from WordNet and relevance measure from Wikipedia, which may completely reflect word relationships.

*Partially funded by NSFC (No. 60773027, 60736044, 90920010) and National Science and Technology Major Project (No. 2010ZX01037-001-002).

SIGIR'11, July 24–28, 2011, Beijing, China.
ACM 978-1-4503-0757-4/11/07.

Categories and Subject Descriptors

H.3.3 [**Information Storage and Retrieval**]: Information Search and Retrieval

General Terms

Algorithms, Design, Experimentation

Keywords

Query expansion, semantic network, word graph

REFERENCES

[1] D. Buscaldi, P. Rosso, E. S. Arnal. 2005. A WordNet-based Query Expansion method for Geographical Information Retrieval. Lecture Notes in Computer Science, Volume 4730/2007, 954-957.

[2] Zhiguo Gong, Chan Wa Cheang, Leong Hou U. 2005. Web Query Expansion by WordNet. In *Proceedings of DEXA'05.*

[3] C-C. Hsu, Y-T. Li, Y-W. Chen, and S-H. Wu. 2008. Query Expansion via Link Analysis of Wikipedia for CLIR. In *Proceedings of NTCIR-7.*

[4] G. Varelas, E. Voutsakis, P. Raftopoulou, E. G. M. Petrakis, E. E. Milios. 2005. Semantic Similarity Methods in WordNet and Their Application to Information Retrieval on the Web. In *Proceedings of the WIDM'05.*

[5] Y. Xu, Gareth J. F. Jones, B. Wang. 2009. Query Dependent Pseudo-Relevance Feedback based on Wikipedia. In *Proceedings of SIGIR'09.*

Descriptive Modelling of Text Classification and its Integration with other IR Tasks

Miguel Martinez-Alvarez
School of Electronic Engineering and Computer Science
Queen Mary, University of London
miguel@eecs.qmul.ac.uk

ABSTRACT

Nowadays, Information Retrieval (IR) systems have to deal with multiple sources of data available in different formats. Datasets can consist of complex and heterogeneous objects with relationships between them. In addition, information needs can vary wildly and they can include different tasks. As a result, the importance of flexibility in IR systems is rapidly growing [1]. This fact is specially important in environments where the information required at different moments is very different and its utility may be contingent on timely implementation. In these cases, how quickly a new problem is solved is as important as how well you solve it.

Current systems are usually developed for specific cases. It implies that too much engineering effort is needed to adapt them when new knowledge appears or there are changes in the requirements [2]. Furthermore, heterogeneous and linked data present greater challenges, as well as the simultaneous application of different tasks.

This research proposes the usage of descriptive approaches for three different purposes: the modelling of the specific task of Text Classification (TC), focusing on knowledge and complex data exploitation, the flexible application of models to different tasks; and the simultaneously application of different IR tasks. This investigation will contribute to the long-term goal of achieving a descriptive and composable IR technology that provides a modular framework that knowledge engineers can compose into a task-specific solution. The ultimate goal is to develop a flexible framework that offers classifiers, retrieval models, information extractors, and other functions [4]. In addition, those functional blocks could be customised to satisfy user needs.

Descriptive approaches allow a high-level definition of algorithms which are, in some cases, as compact as mathematical formulations. One of the expected benefits is to make the implementation clearer and the knowledge transfer easier. They allow models from different tasks to be defined as modules that can be "concatenated", processing the information as a pipeline where some of the outputs of one module are the input of the following one. This combination involves minimum engineering effort due to the paradigm's "Plug & Play" capabilities offered by its functional syntax. This solution provides the flexibility needed to customise and quickly combine different IR-tasks and/or models. Classification is a desired candidate for being part of a flexible IR framework because it can be required in several situations for different purposes. In particular, descriptive approaches will improve its modelling with complex and heterogeneous objects. Furthermore, we aim to show how this approach allows to apply TC models for *ad-hoc* retrieval (and *vice versa*) and their simultaneous application for complex information needs.

The main hypothesis of this research is that a seamless approach for modelling TC and its integration with other IR-tasks will provide a general framework for rapid prototyping and modelling of solutions for specific users. In addition, it will allow new complex models that take into account relationships [3] and inference from large ontologies. The importance of flexibility for information systems and the exploitation of complex information and knowledge from heterogeneous sources are the main points for discussion. The main challenges are expressiveness and scalability. Abstraction improves flexibility and maintainability. However, it limits the modelling power. A balance between abstraction and expressiveness has to be reached. On the other hand, scalability has been traditionally a challenge for descriptive modelling. Our goal is to prove the feasibility of our approach for real-scale environments.

Categories and Subject Descriptors

H.3.3 [**Information Storage and Retrieval**]: Information Search and Retrieval; I.2.4 [**Artificial Intelligence**]: Knowledge Representation Formalisms and Methods

General Terms

Design, Languages

Keywords

Descriptive Approach, Modelling, Text Classification

1. REFERENCES

[1] R. Cornacchia and A. P. de Vries. A parameterised search system. *ECIR*, pages 4–15, 2007.

[2] D. Hiemstra and V. Mihajlovic. A database approach to information retrieval: The remarkable relationship between language models and region models. *CoRR*, abs/1005.4752, 2010.

[3] L. D. Raedt, A. Kimmig, and H. Toivonen. ProbLog: a probabilistic Prolog and its application in link discovery. *IJCAI'07*, pages 2468–2473, 2007.

[4] T. Roelleke *et al.* Modelling retrieval models in a probabilistic relational algebra with a new operator: the relational Bayes. *The VLDB Journal*, 17(1):5–37, 2008.

SIGIR'11, July 24–28, 2011, Beijing, China.
ACM 978-1-4503-0757-4/11/07.

Efficient and Effective Solutions for Search Engines

Xiang-Fei Jia
Department of Computer Science
University of Otago
Dunedin, New Zealand
fei@cs.otago.ac.nz

Categories and Subject Descriptors

H.3.3 [**Information Storage and Retrieval**]: Information Search and Retrieval – Search process; H.3.4 [**Information Storage and Retrieval**]: Systems and Software – performance evaluation (efficiency and effectiveness)

General Terms

Algorithms, Experimentation, Performance

Keywords

Efficiency, Pruning, Impact-ordering

Abstract

Effectiveness and efficiency are two of the main issues in Information Retrieval (IR). IR efficiency is normally addressed in terms of accumulator initialisation, disk I/O, decompression, ranking and sorting. This research is about (1) identifying the bottlenecks in a search engine, (2) devising efficient and effective solutions to minimise or eliminate the bottlenecks and (2) adopting the solutions for distributed IR.

As shown previously [4], a large portion of the performance of the search engine is dominated by (1) slow disk read of dictionary terms and the corresponding postings lists, (2) CPU-intensive decompression of postings lists, (3) complex similarity ranking functions and (4) sorting a large number of possible candidate documents.

In order to speed up disk access, operating systems usually provide general-purpose buffer caching, prefetching and scheduling optimisation algorithms. However for special-purpose applications, it is better for application to bypass the general ones and deploy their own I/O optimisation algorithms. In Jia et al. [3], a number of application-specific I/O optimisation algorithms have been proposed and tested.

A number of static pruning algorithms have been deployed to minimise the runtime overhead of processing a vast number of postings and sorting a large number of accumulators [4, 2, 1]. The *topk* algorithm uses a special version of quick sort for fast sorting of the accumulators. Instead of explicitly sorting all accumulators, the improved *topk* algorithm keeps track of the current top documents during query evaluation. It requires two linear scans of the current top documents to swap out the minimum document among the top. This causes the performance of the improved *topk* algorithm to grow exponentially when there are large number of documents and postings to be processed. The *heapk* algorithm uses a minimum heap to efficiently keep track of the current top documents. In the case of swapping in a new candidate document, the first document in the minimum heap can be simply replaced.

Similarity scores are pre-computed at index time to eliminate the CPU cost of the complex similarity ranking function. Postings are impact ordered so that most important postings can be processed first and then less important ones can be pruned. Static pruning with impact ordering has shown to be very effective and efficient even when only a small portion of the postings has been processed.

Accumulator initialisation becomes the bottleneck when a small portion of postings are processing using the static pruning algorithms. An efficient accumulator initialisation has been proposed and tested [2]. Essentially, it converts the one dimension array of accumulators into a logical two dimensional table and only the required logical rows are initialised.

There are three areas of the research work to be addressed in the future. First, a comparison of the proposed pruning algorithms against other pruning algorithms will be conducted. Second, an efficient solution for dictionary compression has been designed and a formal analysis of the algorithm will be derived. Third, multi-core architectures bring two types of communication for distributed IR. One type is a fast communication between the cores on a single die and the other is the network communication between each node in the cluster. How can distributed IR address this new architecture?

1. REFERENCES

[1] X.-F. Jia, D. Alexander, V. Wood, and A. Trotman. University of otago at inex 2010. In *INEX '10: Pre-Proceedings of the INEX*. ACM, 2010.

[2] X.-F. Jia, A. Trotman, and R. O'keefe. Efficient accumulator initialisation. In *ADCS '10*, 2010.

[3] X.-F. Jia, A. Trotman, R. O'Keefe, and Z. Huang. Application-specific disk I/O optimisation for a search engine. In *PDCAT '08*, pages 399–404, 2008.

[4] A. Trotman, X.-F. Jia, and S. Geva. Fast and effective focused retrieval. volume 6203 of *Lecture Notes in Computer Science*, pages 229–241. 2010.

SIGIR'11, July 24–28, 2011, Beijing, China.
ACM 978-1-4503-0757-4/11/07.

Modeling Document Scores for Distributed Information Retrieval

Ilya Markov
Faculty of Informatics, University of Lugano
Lugano, Switzerland
ilya.markov@usi.ch

ABSTRACT

Distributed Information Retrieval (DIR), also known as Federated Search, integrates multiple searchable collections and provides direct access to them through a unified interface [3]. This is done by a centralized *broker*, that receives user queries, forwards them to appropriate collections and returns merged results to users.

In practice, most of federated resources do not cooperate with a broker and do not provide neither their content nor the statistics used for retrieval. This is known as *uncooperative* DIR. In this case a broker creates a *resource representation* by sending sample queries to a collection and analyzing retrieved documents. This process is called *query-based sampling*. The key issue here is the following:

1.1 *How many documents have to be retrieved from a resource in order to obtain a representative sample?*

Although there have been a number of attempts to address this issue it is still not solved appropriately.

For a given user query resources are ranked according to their similarity to the query or based on the number of relevant documents they contain. Since resource representations are usually incomplete, the similarity or the number of relevant documents cannot be calculated precisely. Resource selection algorithms proposed in the literature estimate these numbers based on incomplete samples. However these estimates are subjects to error. In practice, inaccurate estimates that have high error should be trusted less then the more accurate estimates with low error. Unfortunately none of the existing algorithms can make the calculation of the estimation errors possible. Therefore the following questions arise:

2.1 *How to estimate resource scores so that the estimation errors can be calculated?*

2.2 *How to use these errors in order to improve the resource selection performance?*

Existing results merging algorithms estimate normalized document scores based on scores of documents that appear both in a sample and in a result list. The problem similar to the resource selection one arises. The normalized document scores are only the estimates and are subjects to error. Inaccurate estimates should be trusted less then the more accurate ones. Again none of the existing algorithms provide a way for calculating these errors. Thus the two question to be address on the results merging phase are similar to the resource selection ones:

3.1 *How to estimate normalized document scores so that the estimation errors can be calculated?*

3.2 *How to use these errors in order to improve the results merging performance?*

In this work we address the above issues by applying score distribution models (SDM) to different phases of DIR [2]. In particular, we discuss the SDM-based resource selection technique that allows the calculation of resource score estimation errors and can be extended in order to calculate the number of documents to be sampled from each resource for a given query. We have performed initial experiments comparing the SDM-based resource selection technique to the state-of-the-art algorithms and we are currently experimenting with the SDM-based results merging method.

We plan to apply the existing score normalization techniques from meta-search to the DIR results merging problem [1]. However, the SDM-based results merging approaches require the relevance scores to be returned together with retrieved documents. It is not yet clear how to relax this strong assumption that does not always hold in practice.

Categories and Subject Descriptors

H.3.3 [**Information Storage and Retrieval**]: Information Search and Retrieval

General Terms

Algorithms

Keywords

Distributed Information Retrieval, Federated Search, Score Distribution Models

1. REFERENCES

[1] A. Arampatzis and J. Kamps. A signal-to-noise approach to score normalization. In *Proceedings of the ACM CIKM*, pages 797–806. ACM, 2009.

[2] A. Arampatzis and S. Robertson. Modeling score distributions in information retrieval. *Inf. Retr.*, 14(1):26–46, 2011.

[3] J. Callan. *Advances in Information Retrieval*, chapter Chapter 5. Distributed Information Retrieval, pages 127–150. Kluwer Academic Publishers, 2000.

SIGIR'11, July 24–28, 2011, Beijing, China.
ACM 978-1-4503-0757-4/11/07.

Improving Query and Result List Adaptation in Personalized Multilingual Information Retrieval

M. Rami Ghorab
Centre for Next Generation Localisation,
Knowledge & Data Engineering Group, Trinity College Dublin, Dublin 2, Ireland.
ghorabm@scss.tcd.ie

Categories and Subject Descriptors
H.3.3 [**Information Storage and Retrieval**]: Information Search and Retrieval.

General Terms
Algorithms, Experimentation, Languages.

Keywords
Personalized Multilingual Information Retrieval, User Modeling.

1. Extended Abstract
A general characteristic of Information Retrieval (IR) and Multilingual IR (MIR) [5] systems is that if the same query was submitted by different users, the system would yield the same results, regardless of the user. On the other hand, Adaptive Hypermedia (AH) systems operate in a personalized manner where the services are adapted to the user [1]. Personalized IR (PIR) is motivated by the success in both areas, IR and AH [4]. IR systems have the advantage of scalability and AH systems have the advantage of satisfying individual user needs. The majority of studies in PIR literature have focused on monolingual IR, and relatively little work has been done concerning multilingual IR.

This PhD research study aims to improve personalization in MIR systems, by improving the relevance of multilingual search results with respect to the user and not just the query. The study investigates how to model different aspects of a multilingual search user. Information about users can be demographic information, such as language and country, or information about the user's search interests. This information can be gathered explicitly by asking the user to supply the required information or implicitly by inferring the information from the user's search history. The study will then investigate how to exploit the modeled user information to personalize the user's multilingual search by performing query and result list adaptation. The main research questions that are addressed in this study are: how to improve the relevance of search results with respect to individual users in PMIR and how to construct profiles that represent aspects and interests of a multilingual search user.

So far, the work carried out for this study included: (1) a proposed framework for the delivery and evaluation of PMIR [3]; and (2) exploratory experiments with search history and collection (result) re-ranking on a dataset of multilingual search logs [2]. The next stage of experimentation will involve the investigation and development of algorithms for: (1) constructing multilingual user profiles; (2) pre-translation and post-translation query expansion based on terms from the user profile; and (3) result list re-ranking based on the user's interests, and preferred language.

Two types of experiments will be conducted in an *in-lab* setting, with a group of users from different linguistic backgrounds. In the first set of experiments, users will be asked to use a baseline web search system for their daily search activities over a period of time. The baseline system will be wrapped around one of the major search engines. Interactions with the system will be logged, and part of this information will be used for training the system (constructing user profiles from text of queries and clicked documents); the other part (remaining queries) will be used for testing the effectiveness of the query adaptation and result list adaptation algorithms, where the users will be asked to provide some personal relevance judgements. In the second set of experiments, the users will be asked to use the PMIR system to fulfill a number of defined search tasks.

Quantitative and qualitative techniques will be used to evaluate different aspects of the experiments, including: (1) retrieval effectiveness, which can be measured using standard IR metrics; (2) user's performance on search tasks, which can be measured in terms of time and number of actions needed to fulfill the tasks; (3) user profile accuracy, which can be assessed by questionnaires that indicate how well the user profile depicted the users' search interests; and (4) usability and user satisfaction, which can be assessed using standard system usability questionnaires.

SIGIR'11, July 24–28, 2011, Beijing, China.
ACM 978-1-4503-0757-4/11/07.

2. ACKNOWLEDGMENTS
This research is supported by the Science Foundation of Ireland (grant 07/CE/I1142) as part of the Centre for Next Generation Localisation (www.cngl.ie) at Trinity College, Dublin.

3. REFERENCES
[1] Brusilovsky, P., Kobsa, A. and Nejdl, W. (eds.). *The Adaptive Web - Methods and Strategies of Web Personalization*. Springer, 2007.

[2] Ghorab, M.R., Leveling, J., Zhou, D., Jones, G.J.F. and Wade, V. Identifying Common User Behaviour in Multilingual Search Logs. in Peters, C., Di Nunzio, G., Kurimo, M., Mandl, T., Mostefa, D., Peñas, A. and Roda, G. eds. *Lecture Notes in Computer Science (6241/2010), Multilingual Information Access Evaluation I*, Springer, 2010.

[3] Ghorab, M.R., Zhou, D., O'Connor, A. and Wade, V. A Framework for Cross-language Search Personalization *4th International Workshop on Semantic Media Adaptation and Personalization (SMAP)*, San Sebastian, Spain, 2009, 15-20.

[4] Micarelli, A., Gasparetti, F., Sciarrone, F. and Gauch, S. Personalized Search on the World Wide Web. in Brusilovsky, P., Kobsa, A. and Nejdl, W. eds. *The Adaptive Web*, Springer, 2007, 195-230.

[5] Oard, D.W. Multilingual Information Access. *Encyclopedia of Library and Information Sciences, 3rd Edition*. 3682 – 3687.

Using k-top Retrieved Web Snippets to Date Temporal Implicit Queries based on Web Content Analysis

Ricardo Nuno Taborda Campos
LIAAD – INESC Porto, LA, University of Porto, Portugal
Polytechnic Institute of Tomar, Portugal
ricardo.campos@ipt.pt

ABSTRACT

Temporal Information Retrieval (T-IR) has been a topic of great interest in recent years. Its purpose is to improve the information retrieval of documents by exploiting temporal information. However and despite the relative maturity of the area and an increasing involvement of the IR community in recent years, few works have fully used temporal information for exploration and search purposes [1], causing many queries not to be inferred by search engines. Such a lack lies in the fact that the used retrieval models continue to represent documents and queries simplistically, ignoring the underlying temporal semantics. Inferring the user intentions and the period he has in mind, may therefore play an extremely important role in the retrieval of the results. Our work goes in this direction.

We aim at introducing a temporal analysis framework for analyzing documents in a temporal dimension in order to identify and understand the temporal nature of any given query, namely implicit ones (e.g., *SIGIR*). Our analysis is not based on metadata, but on the exploitation of temporal information from the content itself. As referred by [2] this is an interesting future research direction, for which, there isn't still a clear solution. Specifically we aim at looking for temporal information within web snippets. In order to validate this approach we have already studied how large the temporal value of web snippets is related to the user's query. This preliminary research [3] showed us that web snippets, are interesting pieces of concentrated information, where time clues, especially years, often appear. Our intention is to develop a language-independent solution and to model the degree of relationship between the terms and dates identified. This is the core part of the framework and the basis for both temporal query understanding and search results exploration, such as temporal clustering. One of the challenges of our system, however, is how to deal with conceptually ambiguous queries, such as *Madagascar* (the country or the movie) or *Scorpions* (the rock band, the arachnid or the zodiac sign) which can have a different temporal dimension in each different meaning. We believe that inferring this knowledge is a very important step in the process of adding a temporal dimension to IR systems, thus disambiguating a large class of queries for which search engines continue to fail.

Motivated by this, we aim to contribute with 1) a model that takes into account both content importance and temporal distance within web snippets capable of understanding the query users' intents in order to identify not only relevant documents but also relevant time periods; 2) develop a classification system to classify a query both in the conceptual and temporal perspectives; 3) determine the most appropriate visualization interface: timelines, clusters or user-features, such as query expansion.

So far we have developed a rule-based model solution to automatically extract temporal information, namely dates expressed by numerical formats in the interval [1000..2099]. We have also formulated web snippet modeling by means of two vectors, a conceptual and a temporal one. Our next step is to model, somehow, the relations between encountered time stamps and terms in the web snippets. This will allow an improvement in the similarity between two documents. Given this representation we can then disambiguate the query in terms of concept and time by computing the similarity value between each of the snippets. We propose to do this by clustering the *k* top snippets retrieved from the execution of any given query. Based on the new representation of the web snippets and on the query issued, the system should be able to provide a temporal classification on the assumption that only clear concept queries (non-ambiguous in concept) can be valued in terms of temporal intent. Determining whether a query is temporal or not can thus be seen as a classification problem which categorizes any conceptually unambiguous query into one of three temporal categories introduced by [4]: 1. ATemporal, i.e. not sensitive to time (e.g., *make my trip*); 2. Temporal Unambiguous i.e. taking place at a specific period in time (e.g., *bp oil spill*); 3. Temporal Ambiguous i.e. with multiple instances over time (e.g., *oil spill*). We have already performed an experiment [3] over 176 clear concept queries individually analyzed upon real data observation. We conclude, contrary to the 7% presented by [5], that 25% of the queries have an implicit temporal nature. Predicting this temporal classification will then lead us to automatically customize the results and employ different visualization or query expansion solutions for the different kinds of queries: 1. list of documents; 2. timelines; 3. temporal or/and topic clusters; 4. query expansion.

Categories and Subject Descriptors

H.3.3 [**Information Storage and Retrieval**]: Information Search and Retrieval – Query Formulation, Search Process, Clustering

General Terms

Algorithms.

Keywords

Temporal Information Retrieval, Implicit Temporal Queries.

1. ACKNOWLEDGMENTS

This research is supervised by Gaël Dias and Alípio Jorge, and is partially funded by a Portuguese grant (SFRH/BD/63646/2009).

2. REFERENCES

[1] Alonso, O., Gertz, M., & Baeza-Yates, R. (2009). Clustering and Exploring Search Results using Timeline Constructions. *In CIKM*.

[2] Berberich, K., Bedathur, S., Alonso, O., & Weikum, G. (2010). A Language Modeling Approach for Temporal Information Needs. *In LNCS* (Vol. 5993/2010, pp. 13 - 25).

[3] Campos, R., Dias, G., & Jorge, A. M. (2011). What is the Temporal Value of Web Snippets? In TWAW2011 associated to WWW2011.

[4] Jones, R., & Diaz, F. (2007). Temporal Profiles of Queries. In TOIS: ACM Transactions on Information Systems , 25(3).

[5] Metzler, D., Jones, R., Peng, F., & Zhang, R. (2009). Improving Search Relevance for Implicitly Temporal Queries. In SIGIR 2009.

Domain-Specific Information Retrieval Using Recommenders

Wei Li
Centre for Next Generation Localization
School of Computing, Dublin City University
Dublin 9, Ireland
wli@computing.dcu.ie

ABSTRACT

The continuing increase in the volume of information available in our daily lives is creating ever greater challenges for people to find personally useful information. One approach used to addressing this problem is Personalized Information Retrieval (PIR). PIR systems collect a user's personal information from both implicit and explicit sources to build a user profile with the objective of giving retrieval results which better meet their individual user information needs than a standard Information Retrieval (IR) system. However, in many situations there may be no opportunity to learn about the specific interests of a user and build a personal model when this user is querying on a new topic, e.g. when a user visits a museum or exhibition which is unrelated to their normal search interests. Under this condition, the experiences and behaviours of other previous users, who have made similar queries, could be used to build a model of user behavior in this domain. My PhD proposes to focus on the development of new and innovative methods of domain-specific IR. My work seeks to combine recommender algorithms trained using previous search behaviours from different searchers with a standard ranked IR method to form a domain-specific IR model to improve the search effectiveness for a user entering a query without personal prior search history on this topic. The challenges for my work are: how to provide users better results; how to train and evaluate the methods proposed in my work.

Since there are no suitable data collections available to enable us to explore this proposal, simulation plays a key role in our research. We have conducted an initial experiment study incorporating a very simple simulation method. The details are as follows:

- The INEX 2009 Wikipedia document collection [2] was used, with 20 topics from INEX 2009 topic dataset for which relevance assessments were avaiable;
- !0 variants of each topic were made by randomly deleting one or two from the original topic;
- An extended SMART retrieval system [3] was used with each topic variant to the rank top 20 documents ;
- A user grating for each retrieval document was generated using the topic relevance assessment: 1 for relevant documents and 0 for other documents;
- Retrieved document rating values used to train a recommender for each topic using the weighted slope-one collaborative algorithm [1];
- The original topic statement was used as a test topic to retrieve a ranked list using extended SMART system. The retrieved documents were used to select the most similar recommender.
- The information in this recommender was used to predict ratings for retrieved documents;
- For each document j, a final ranking weight FW_j was calculated by linearly combining its score in initial ranked list from extended SMART system RW_j and its rating in the prediction list from recommender algorithm RW_j, where α in equation (1) is a scalar constant determining the contribution of each component.

$$FW_j = \alpha \cdot PW_j + (1-\alpha) \cdot RW_j \qquad (1)$$

The results of ranking retrieved results for each original topic using the extended SMART system are used as our baseline. The MAP increases from 0.0744 to 0.1178 (+58%). This initial experiment demonstrates the potential for utilizing recommender algorithms in IR. My current work is focusing on developing more realistic simulation models for the training environment, exploring the use of relevance feedback in combination with recommenders, automatically identifying topical domain of topics and automatically clustering topics for training recommenders, exploring the development of more suitable evaluation metrics, and exploiting other recommender algorithms to make this approach more effective.

Categories and Subject Descriptors

H.3.3 [**Information Search and Retrieval**]: Information Search and Retrieval, Information Filtering

General Terms

Recommender Algorithm, Simulation, Experimentation

Keywords

Domain-Specific IR, Recommender

1. ACKNOWLEDGMENTS

This research is supported by the Science Foundation Ireland (Grant 07/CE/I1142) as part of the Centre for Next Generation Localisation (CNGL) project.

2. REFERENCES

[1] Lemire, D. and Maclachlan, *A. Slope One Predictors for Online Rating-Based Collaborative Filtering*. In Proceedings of SIAM Data Mining (SDM), 2005

[2] Geva, S., Kamps, J., Lethonen, M. Schenkel, R., Thom, J.A., and Trotman, A. *Overview of the INEX 2009 Ad Hoc Track*, In Proceedings of INEX'2009

[3] Debasis Ganguly, *Implementing Language Modeling in SMART*, Indian Statistical Institute, Calcutta, India,July 2008

Understanding and Using Contextual Information in Recommender Systems

Licai Wang
Beijing Key Laboratory of Intelligent Telecommunications Software and Multimedia
Beijing University of Posts and Telecommunications, China
wiizane@gmail.com

Categories and Subject Descriptors

H.3.3 **[Information Storage and Retrieval]**: Information Search and Retrieval – *information filtering, retrieval models.*

General Terms: Algorithms, Experimentation.

Keywords: Recommender systems, Context, User preferences, HOSVD, Mood, Social network.

ABSTRACT

With the rapid development of information technology, the availability of huge amounts of online information makes retrieval a hard task for the average user. Recommender systems (RS) have been employed across several domains to ease this so-called "information overload" problem since the mid-1990s. Recently, context-aware recommender systems (CARS), aiming to further improve the performance accuracy and user satisfaction by fully utilizing contextual information (such as time, location, mood and company) into RS, has become one of the hottest topics [1]. Although a certain progress has been made, CARS still has to face to many challenges. This thesis investigates some key problems in CARS and then proposes some tested and untested approaches to mine the latent relationship among users, contextual information and items (such as movies, web pages and mobile services).

In this thesis, the first task is how to elicit contextual user preferences implicitly. All of the existing CARS are based on the assumption that there are available explicit contextual user ratings (e.g., "Sam × Avatar × Morning × Home→3"). However, it is hard to obtain sufficient contextual user preferences in practice. This thesis proposes a MAUT (multi attribute utility theory)-based approach to implicitly elicit contextual user preferences through analyzing contextual user behaviors. It considers every type of context as an attribute of items, elicit every unidimensional contextual user preferences based on a new context-based IF-IDF formula, and finally elicit multidimensional contextual user preferences after identifying different weights of different contexts. We design a personalized mobile services-oriented prototype system as a test bed to elicit contextual user preferences as well as generate contextual recommendations. I perform experimental comparison of this approach against the other baseline approaches, attaining significant improvements.

Secondly, how to alleviate the sparsity problem in CARS is a key challenge. The data sparsity exists in any traditional RS. While incorporating contextual information, the problem of sparse in CARS becomes even more serious. I propose a HOSVD-based contextual recommendation approach, called TensorCARS [2]. It first constructs an N-order tensor to represent multidimensional contextual user preferences and decomposes it into (N-2) 3-order tensors according to different contexts, then uses the HOSVD technique to predict unknown unidimensional contextual user preferences, and then calculates every contextual influence coefficient that each context factor influences user preferences, and finally constructs a new N-order tensor using weighted linearization method. I perform experimental comparison using the prototype system, showing TensorCARS can help alleviate the sparsity problem and increase the prediction accuracy.

Thirdly, I consider mood as an important context and design two mood-based hybrid collaborative filtering approaches. ACM CAMRa2010 [3] releases two datasets gathered by the Moviepilot and Filmtipset. I participate in the Moviepilot challenge track which addresses the contextual dimension related to a user's mood. I first propose a new mood-based user-based collaborative filtering approach based on the assumption that users with similar mood-preference patterns may have similar user preferences to items, and then propose two new hybrid ones through fusing the former presented approach and the traditional user-based CF (i.e., a multiple-step KNN similarity fusion and a weighted predicted rating fusion strategy respectively). Both hybrid CF approaches outperform the other user-based CF ones in terms of all three evaluation metrics (i.e., MAP, P@N (N=5, 10) and AUC).

Lastly, I focus on bring social network analysis into CARS in order to further improve recommendation accuracy. Intuitively, user needs are not only affected by his interests and environment, but also by many other factors such as social network relationship (due to the content and information contributed or distributed through the Social Web). Now I am designing a general model of social network-based context-aware recommender systems (SCRS) to search nearest neighbors in high dimensional spaces that contain both social networks and contextual user preferences data. I plan to perform experiments on the public Filmtipset dataset.

SIGIR'11, July 24–28, 2011, Beijing, China.
ACM 978-1-4503-0757-4/11/07.

ACKNOWLEDGMENTS

This study is supported by the National Natural Science Foundation of China under Grant No. 60872051.

REFERENCES

[1] G. Adomavicius and A. Tuzhilin. Context-aware recommender systems. *Recommender Systems Handbook*, Springer, 2011: 217-253.

[2] L. Wang, et al. Applying HOSVD to alleviate the sparsity problem in context-aware recommender systems. *Submitted.*

[3] L. Wang, et al. New approaches to mood-based hybrid collaborative filtering. *ACM CAMRa'10*, 2010: 28-33.

Multidimensional Search Result Diversification: Diverse Search Results for Diverse Users

Sumit Bhatia
Computer Science and Engineering
The Pennsylvania State University
University Park, PA-16802, USA
sumit@cse.psu.edu

Categories and Subject Descriptors

H.3.3 [**Information Storage and Retrieval**]: Retrieval models, Search process, Clustering.

General Terms

Algorithms, Theory, Human Factors, Experimentation.

Keywords

Search result diversification, diversity, query log analysis.

ABSTRACT

Hundreds of millions of people today rely on Web based Search Engines to satisfy their information needs. In order to meet the expectations of this vast and diverse user population, the search engine should present a list of results such that the probability of satisfying the *average user* is maximized [1]. This leads us to the problem of **Search Result Diversification**. Given a user submitted query, the search engine should include results that are relevant to the user query and at the same time, *diverse* enough to meet the expectations of diverse user populations. However, it is not clear in what respect the results should be diversified.

Much of the current work in diversity [1, 3] focuses on *ambiguous and underspecified queries* and tries to include results corresponding to diverse interpretations of the ambiguous query. This is not always sufficient. My analysis of a commercial web search engine's logs reveals that even for well-specified informational queries, click entropy is very high indicating that different users prefer different types of documents. Very recently, a diversification algorithm fine-tuned for such informational queries has been proposed [5]. Further, high click entropies were also observed for a large fraction of transactional queries. One major goal of my PhD thesis will then be to identify the various possible dimensions along which the search results can be diversified. Having such an information will enhance our understanding about the *expectations of an average user from the search engine*. By utilizing aggregate statistics about queries, users and their interaction with the search engine for different queries, more concrete evidences about diverse user preferences as well as relative importance of different diversity dimensions can be derived.

Once we know different diversity dimensions, the next natural question is: given a query, how can we determine the diversification requirement best suited for the query? For some queries sub-topic coverage may be more important while for others diversification with respect to document source or stylistics might be important. This problem is related to the problem of selective diversification [4] where the goal is to identify queries for which diversification techniques should be used. However, in addition, we are also interested in identifying different diversity classes a given query belongs to. Further, for some queries it may be required to diversify along multiple diversity dimensions. In such cases, it is also important to determine the relative importance of different diversity dimensions for the given query. By utilizing past user interaction data, query level features (like query clarity, entropy, lexical features etc.) and document level features (e.g. popularity, content quality, previous click history etc.), classifiers for diversification requirements can be developed.

Given a user query, once we know the type of diversity requirements for the user, an appropriate diversification technique is required. I would like to study the problem of simultaneously diversifying search results along multiple dimensions, as discussed above. One possible way here could be to build upon the *nugget* based framework introduced by Clarke et al. [2] where we represent each document as a set of nuggets, each nugget corresponding to a diversity dimension.

1. REFERENCES

[1] R. Agrawal, S. Gollapudi, A. Halverson, and S. Ieong. Diversifying search results. In *WSDM '09: Proceedings of the Second ACM International Conference on Web Search and Data Mining*, pages 5–14. ACM, 2009.

[2] C. L. Clarke, M. Kolla, G. V. Cormack, O. Vechtomova, A. Ashkan, S. Büttcher, and I. MacKinnon. Novelty and diversity in information retrieval evaluation. In *Proceedings of the 31st annual international ACM SIGIR conference on Research and development in information retrieval*, SIGIR '08, pages 659–666, New York, NY, USA, 2008. ACM.

[3] R. L. Santos, C. Macdonald, and I. Ounis. Exploiting query reformulations for web search result diversification. In *WWW '10: Proceedings of the 19th international conference on World wide web*, pages 881–890, New York, NY, USA, 2010. ACM.

[4] R. L. Santos, C. Macdonald, and I. Ounis. Selectively diversifying web search results. In *Proceedings of the 19th ACM international conference on Information and knowledge management*, CIKM '10, pages 1179–1188. ACM, 2010.

[5] M. J. Welch, J. Cho, and C. Olston. Search result diversity for informational queries. In *WWW '11: Proceedings of the 20th international conference on World wide web*, 2011.

SIGIR'11, July 24–28, 2011, Beijing, China.
ACM 978-1-4503-0757-4/11/07.

Sensor-Aided Mobile Information Management and Retrieval

Edward Y. Chang
Google Research
edchang@google.com

ABSTRACT

The number of "smart" mobile devices such as wireless phones and tablet computers has been rapidly growing. These mobile devices are equipped with a variety of sensors such as camera, gyroscope, accelerometer, compass, NFC, WiFi, GPS, etc. These sensors can be used to capture images and voice, detect motion patterns, and predict locations, to name just a few. This keynote depicts techniques in configuration, calibration, computation, and fusion for improving sensor performance and conserving power consumption. We also present novel mobile information management and retrieval applications that can benefit a great deal from enhanced sensor technologies.

Categories and Subject Descriptors

H.2.8 [**Database Management**]: Database applications – *Spatial databases and GIS.*

General Terms

Algorithms, Performance, Design, Experimentation, Theory.

Keywords

Inertial navigation system, location, mobile, sensor.

1. OVERVIEW

This keynote presents a signal-fusion architecture XINS, where X stands for a signal source that can calibrate a moving device's location as an external reference, and INS stands for inertial navigation system. An X can be GPS, WiFi, or location information of a nearby device transmitted over a P2P protocol. An INS can be, but is not limited to, an accelerometer, a gyroscope, and a magnetic sensor. Modern phones like Google Nexus S and iPhone are equipped with tiny and energy-efficient INS'. The design goals of XINS are (1) to fuse signals from Xs and INS' to predict the location of a moving device, and (2) to achieve so in a power-conserving way.

System architectures similar to XINS have been developed before, but with vastly different constraints and at much higher costs. For instance, aircrafts, guided missiles and submarines have been designed to compute positions and velocities using external references and inertial navigation systems. A mobile phone, though, while equipped with similar motion-sensing devices, cannot compute positions and velocities as accurately as the former due to several factors. Some factors include low manufacturing quality originating from cost constraints, environmental noise, and the dynamic motions of people carrying the devices (as opposed to an aircraft for example). Moreover, the power usage of acquiring X signals on a mobile phone is much higher as a percentage of total energy consumed compared to that used on e.g., a submarine. These factors make the design of XINS exceedingly challenging.

Inexpensive inertial navigation systems are notorious for producing errors due to misalignment, zero bias, and integration drift. A slightly inaccurate reading on linear acceleration (accelerometers) and angular velocity (gyroscopes) can be integrated into progressively (in time) large errors in velocity, which are compounded into greater errors in position. Worse yet, the motion of a mobile device is often "non-smooth" compared to an aircraft. For instance, different people can carry a mobile device at different time and in different manners. It is virtually impossible to tell true signals from noise. To eliminate noise, we have devised calibration schemes, and breakthrough signal processing algorithms using *Equipartition theorem* [1]. We further demonstrate that by using selected signals as primary sources and the others as constraints, signal fusion [2] can be performed both effectively and efficiently.

We enumerate applications that can benefit a great deal from XINS. Three examples are as follows:

1. XINS can predict indoor locations of mobile devices where GPS signal may be unavailable.
2. XINS can achieve location prediction in a power-conserving way by reducing sampling rates of primary signals and filling the gaps with power-conserving signals.
3. XINS can track the angle and the movement of a camera with high accuracy to enable smart image processing applications such as panoramas.

2. ACKNOWLEDGMENTS

My thanks to Google collaborators Qingxuan Yang, Yuan Gao, Guanfeng Li, and Chengu Wang, and Hang Qu.

3. REFERENCES

[1] XINS: The Anatomy of an Indoor Positioning and Navigation Architecture, Yuan Gao, Qingxuan Yang, Guanfeng Li, Edward Y. Chang, Dong Wang, Chengu Wang, Hang Qu, Pei Dong, Faen Zhang, Google Technical Report, April 2011

[2] Foundations of Large-Scale Multimedia Information Management and Retrieval, Mathematics of Perception, Edward Y. Chang, Springer, 2011

SIGIR'11, July 24–28, 2011, Beijing, China.
ACM 978-1-4503-0757-4/11/07.

Predicting eBay Listing Conversion

Ted Tao Yuan
eBay Inc.
2145 Hamilton Avenue
San Jose, California 95125 USA
1(408) 376-5477
teyuan@ebay.com

Zhaohui Chen
eBay Inc.
2145 Hamilton Avenue
San Jose, California 95125 USA
1(408) 376-6794
zhachen@ebay.com

Mike Mathieson
eBay Inc.
2145 Hamilton Avenue
San Jose, California 95125 USA
1(408) 376-5739
mike.mathieson@ebay.com

ABSTRACT

At eBay Market Place, listing conversion rate can be measured by number of items sold divided by number of items in a sample set. For a given item, conversion rate can also be treated as the probability of sale. By investigating eBay listings' transactional patterns, as well as item attributes and user click-through data, we developed conversion models that allow us to predict a live listing's probability of sale. In this paper, we discuss the design and implementation of such conversion models. These models are highly valuable in analysis of inventory quality and ranking. Our work reveals the uniqueness of sales-oriented search at eBay and its similarity to general web search problems.

Categories and Subject Descriptors

H.3.3 [**Information Storage and Retrieval**]: Information Search and Retrieval – *information filtering*

General Terms

Algorithms, Design.

Keywords

Online auction, ecommerce, predictive model, ranking.

1. INTRODUCTION

eBay's online inventory is a collection of listing pages that have short lifespan comparing to that of normal web pages, i.e., listings are generally for sale in days versus months or years availability of web pages. At present, the majority of eBay's search result pages (SRP) are item based with category navigation. In addition to query-item relevance, customer satisfaction is measured by how easily and quickly they can find items they are interested in, and sale transaction efficiency.

2. Design Consideration

eBay's search ranker is built on top of intermediate factor models; each targets a specific goal, and can be implemented at different stages of the business workflow. Predicted item conversion model is a lower-tier model and computationally intensive. We choose to run such model at listing stages, and append the model output to items as listing attributes. Runtime models are less computationally intensive but can achieve higher accuracy by incorporating observed user behavioral data.

SIGIR'11, July 24–28, 2011, Beijing, China.
ACM 978-1-4503-0757-4/11/07.

In this study, we averaged out queries that bring search impressions, item views that lead to sales, and focused on the intrinsic properties of a listing as well as market statistics. A runtime item conversion model is built to incorporate observed user demand measurements.

3. Predicting Item Conversion

3.1 Factor Exploration

Our conversion models rely on informative factors. We identified repetitive conversion patterns, and found that item price, clicks, listing category, duration, seller feedback, sale format such as auction or fixed price (Buy-It-Now) are crucial factors. We notice previous studies on predicting listings' final prices[1,2]. Our pricing model is to establish item's fair market price based on similar items sold on eBay. Statistics on sold similar items reveal important demand measurements such as past sales count, clicks and bids, etc.. They provide good normalization base for an active listing. For instance, the ratio of initial total price to the median total price of recently sold similar items is highly correlated with conversion (Figure 1). Seller past conversion rate is also a strong indicator. Low seller conversion rate tends to underestimate item conversion, but overestimates when it is at high end.

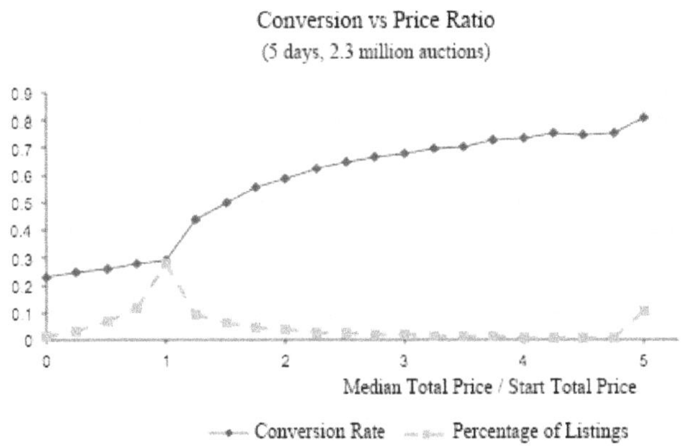

Figure 1. Item conversion and population versus price ratio

3.2 Training and Validation Sets

Training data were sampled from eBay's item database. They maintain the statistical distribution of eBay production listings, i.e., mix of sold/unsold, different products, formats, etc. Certain noises and outliers were removed. Both temporal and static factors are collected. Static factors are available at listing time, such as item features specified by sellers, seller historical metrics and other market priors. Dynamic or temporal factors such as item page views, watch and impression counts are also used in the final predictive model. Validation sets were sampled without overlapping with the training data.

3.3 Heuristic Model

We assumed that item conversion probability is a multiplication of supply quality and demand attractiveness. The heuristic model assumes independency of supply and demand, therefore it tends to underestimate the interaction or correlation among factors on both supply and demand sides. The binary classification model was implemented using curve fitting to capture information gain from predicting factors. Its accuracy is reported in Table 1.

3.4 Machine Learning Models

3.4.1 Gradient Boosted Decision Trees

Gradient boosted decision trees (GBDT) gain popularity in data mining and machine learning community in recent years[3]. GBDT has the reputation of working well for non-linear complex classification and regression models with large number of correlated factors. The result is stable even when some important factors are missing at runtime.

3.4.2 Listing Time Conversion Model

Our listing-time conversion prediction model uses only factors known at the listing start time. Several predictors from the heuristic model were also used. The binary regression decision trees compute score between 0 and 1 for each item, and the result is stored as item feature. When comparing with the heuristic model, we found GBDT model greatly improved the prediction result of item at listing start-time.

3.4.3 Runtime Conversion Model

To predict conversion dynamically at runtime, we combined the saved listing time prediction score with seller level priors, and a number of dynamic factors observed at listing end time, such as item's recorded impressions, page views, click through rate, etc. We chose to use logistic regression which is lighter in CPU cycles. By incorporating user behavioral information, the runtime model achieved higher prediction accuracy.

Comparisons of the prediction results are shown in Figure 2, 3 and Table 1.

4. ACKNOWLEDGMENTS

Our thanks go to eBay Search organization for continuous support.

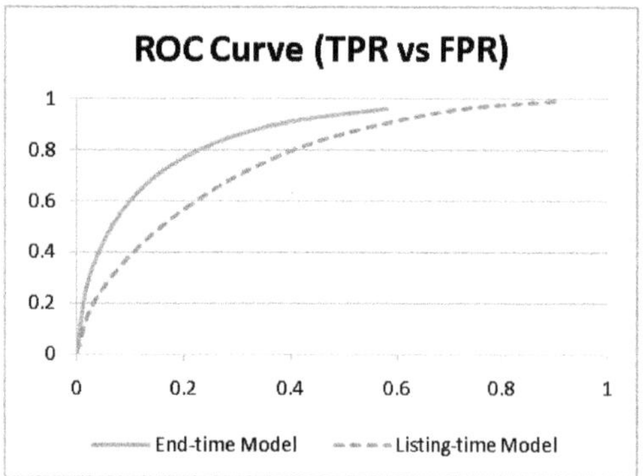

Figure 2. Comparison of two machine learned models

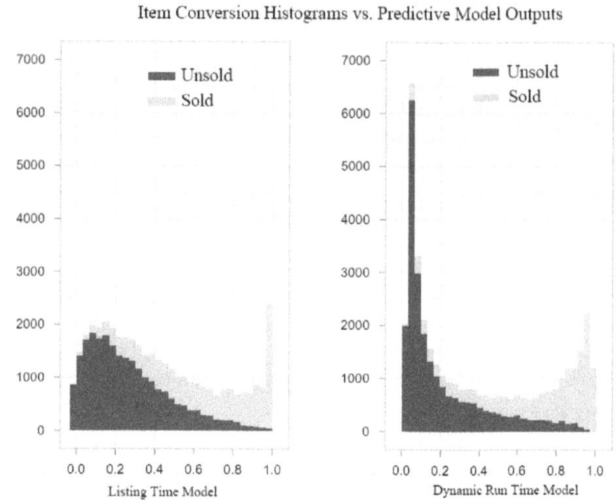

Figure 3. Stacked histograms of listing and runtime models

Table 1. Model Comparison

Model	Purpose	Detail	Accuracy
Heuristic	Predict item conversion	~20 factors, price, shipping, price history, seller quality, clicks, past demand data	64% (at listing time) 80% (with demand observations)
GBDT (50 trees, 50 leaf nodes)	Predict conversion at listing time	~100 factors, listing attributes, seller quality, duration, format, site category, recent similar sale price, sales count, views, impression	82%
Logistic Regression with GBDT result	Predict conversion at runtime	< 10 factors, GBDT result, CTR, clicks, seller past conversion	88%

5. REFERENCES

[1] Van Heijst, D., Potharst, R. and Van Wezel, M. 2008. A Support System for Predicting Ebay End Prices. *Decision Support Systems.* v44 i4, pp. 970-982, 2008. DOI= http://portal.acm.org/citation.cfm?id=1342702.

[2] Gregg, D.G. and Walczak, S.. Auction Advisor: An Agent-Based Online Auction Decision Support System. *Decision Support Systems.* v41 n2, pp. 449-471, 2004.

[3] Friedman, J. H. Greedy Function Approximation: A Gradient Boosting Machine.1999. DOI=http://www-stat.stanford.edu/~jhf/ftp/trebst.pdf.

A Large Scale Machine Learning System for Recommending Heterogeneous Content in Social Networks

Yanxin Shi
Facebook Inc.
1601 S. California Ave
Palo Alto, CA 94304
1-650-714-2189
yanxin@fb.com

David Ye
Facebook Inc.
1601 S. California Ave
Palo Alto, CA 94304
1-650-714-2189
dye@fb.com

Andrey Goder
Facebook Inc.
1601 S. California Ave
Palo Alto, CA 94304
1-650-714-2189
agoder@fb.com

Srinivas Narayanan
Facebook Inc.
1601 S. California Ave
Palo Alto, CA 94304
1-650-714-2189
srinivas@fb.com

ABSTRACT

The goal of the Facebook recommendation engine is to compare and rank heterogeneous types of content in order to find the most relevant recommendations based on user preference and page context. The challenges for such a recommendation engine include several aspects: 1) the online queries being processed are at very large scale; 2) with new content types and new user-generated content constantly added to the system, the candidate object set and underlying data distribution change rapidly; 3) different types of content usually have very distinct characteristics, which makes generic feature engineering difficult; and 4) unlike a search engine that can capture intention of users based on their search queries, our recommendation engine needs to focus more on users' profile and interests, past behaviors and current actions in order to infer their cognitive states. In this presentation, we would like to introduce an effective, scalable, online machine learning framework we developed in order to address the aforementioned challenges. We also want to discuss the insights, approaches and experiences we have accumulated during our research and development process.

Categories and Subject Descriptors

H.3.3 [**Information storage and retrieval**]: Information search and retrieval– *relevance feedback, retrieval models.*

General Terms

Algorithms, Performance.

Keywords

CTR prediction, Large scale system, Online learning

SIGIR'11, July 24–28, 2011, Beijing, China.
ACM 978-1-4503-0757-4/11/07.

With over 500 million active users, Facebook is the world largest social network giving people the power to connect with their friends and share their daily experiences. User growth and engagement are always important goals for Facebook. In line with these goals, the right hand column of Facebook page views is used for personalized recommendation of heterogeneous types of content, such as people you may know, pages you may like, friends' photos, and interesting articles from partner websites. Currently, there are nearly 100 different content types, and this number is still increasing.

The goal of the Facebook recommendation engine is to compare and rank these heterogeneous types of content in order to find the most relevant recommendations based on user preference and page context. There are four major challenges for such a recommendation engine. First, the online queries being processed are at very large scale. To illustrate, for each of the tens of billions of daily page views on Facebook, a query containing user information and page context is generated and sent to the engine, which will select the most relevant recommendations out of billions of indexed candidate objects (e.g., pages, photos, people, ads, etc.) within milliseconds. Second, with new content types and new user-generated content constantly added to the system, the candidate object set and underlying data distribution change rapidly. This makes the timeliness of model learning and updating very important. Third, different types of content usually have very distinct characteristics, which makes generic feature engineering difficult. In other words, an important feature for one content type might not be useful for another. For example, user-user interaction features can help achieve good people suggestions but not page suggestions. Finally, it is also fairly challenging to effectively model and retrieve a user's cognitive states in real time from multiple data sources, such as user profile and user behaviors. Unlike a search engine that can capture intention of users based on their search queries, our recommendation engine needs to focus more on users' profile and interests, past behaviors and current actions in order to infer their desires.

To solve the aforementioned challenges, we have devised and developed an effective, scalable, online machine learning framework. Using a generalized linear model which can contain millions of sparse features, this framework is able to process online queries at very large scale. For model learning and updating, it utilizes the user's behavior in real time as learning examples, and updates the production model in minutes to reflect any underlying data distribution change. This framework also enables us to easily add per content type sparse features such that we can effectively model different characteristics of various types of content. To understand a user's current cognitive state, we use a hierarchical model to predict the concepts of hundreds of millions of diverse and enriched user-generated content (such as status updates, likes, comments, etc). These predicted concepts are 1) fed into our machine learning model as features, and 2) used to retrieve recommendations closely related to a user action in real time (e.g., a "winter sports" page recommendation will be refreshed in immediately after a user posts "I like skiing", because winter sports matches the concept of skiing).

In summary, unlike traditional document search, the problem we face at Facebook is to consider user information and page context as query to retrieve the most relevant recommendations from heterogeneous types of content with distinct characteristics. How to effectively compare and rank these different types of content in order to optimize user experience raises several fairly challenging yet interesting questions, especially with the scale of the data and queries we are operating at. We address these questions by using modern machine learning and information retrieval technologies that are either developed in house or improved from existing literature. In our presentation, we would like to discuss and share the insights, approaches and experiences we have accumulated during our research and development process.

Review of MSR-Bing Web Scale Speller Challenge

Kuansan Wang Jan Pedersen
Microsoft Research and Bing
One Microsoft Way
Redmond, WA 98052, USA
+1(425) 882-8080
http://web-ngram.research.microsoft.com

ABSTRACT

In this paper, we provide an overview of the MSR-Bing Web Scale Speller Challenge of 2011. We describe the motivation and outline the algorithmic and engineering challenges posed by this activity. The design and the evaluation methods are also reviewed, and the online resources that will remain publicly available to the community are also described. The Challenge will culminate in a workshop after the time of the writing where the top prize winners will publish their approaches. The main findings and the lessons learned will be summarized and shared in the Industry Track presentation accompanying this paper.

Categories and Subject Descriptors

I.2.7 [**Artificial Intelligence**]: Natural Language Processing – *Language models*. H.3.3 [**Information Storage and Retrieval**]: Information Search and Retrieval – *query formulation*

General Terms

Algorithm, Measurement, Experimentation.

Keywords

Web search, Language model, Spelling Alteration, MSR-Bing Speller Challenge.

1. INTRODUCTION

As a follow-up to the invited talk in SIGIR 2010 on the critical role of query understanding for web search [2], Microsoft Research (MSR) and Bing jointly announced a public contest in December 2010 [3] to promote the algorithmic and engineering research in this area. The focus for the MSR-Bing Web Scale Speller Challenge is on an early stage of query understanding: spelling alteration. Spelling alteration has traditionally been studied in the field of natural language processing (NLP) [1]. As the web has dramatically democratized the content publishing business, it has been noted [4] that traditional NLP techniques that excel at handling editorial quality contents are no longer sufficient for processing the web contents. Specifically for web search, one often observes that search queries sometimes consist of segments from different languages that are difficult to detect using the conventional language identification techniques, and the term usages and the lexicon for the web are rapidly growing and changing over time. Popularized by the short message services and the conflated domain names commonly seen for online marketing, many terms are a mixture of alphabetical of numeral characters that do not follow conventional word boundaries, and even individual terms are well constructed the search queries are often expressed in a "pidgin" language that does not abide by normal linguistic rules. The notion of a "correct" spelling can vary with contexts, and it is not unusual that some relevant documents can themselves contain spelling errors that an overzealous speller in the query processing stage would prevent these documents from being retrieved and ranked high.

In addition to these algorithmic challenges, applications for web search typically need to process a large amount of data and complete the NLP task in a split second. Engineering quality plays as critical a role as algorithmic excellency. As such, a peculiar setting of the Speller Challenge is to require the participants to implement their entries as publicly accessible web services with a REST interface defined in [3], based on which the engineering quality, such as reliability and latency, can also be evaluated by the on-demand, web-based tools developed by MSR (Sec. 2). An intended side effect is the participating teams can easily replicate the results and learn from the submitted spellers among one another. The contest rules allow and encourage teams to pool their resources online and utilize social networks or other collaborative means to improve their spellers for a period of five months with a final entry deadline at noon on May 31, 2010. After the Challenge results are finalized, all the web-based tools and data resources will be reopened to the public so that future researchers can benchmark their systems against the participating entries at high fidelity with minimum effort.

2. SPELLER CHALLENGE FORMAT

The objective of spelling alteration is to produce plausible alternatives for a given query. As laid out in [2], the problem can be formulated as the noisy channel problem in information theory where the optimal solution is known to be

$$h_{opt} = argmax\, P(h|q) \tag{1}$$

where h and q denote a hypothesized alternative and the received queries, respectively. A realization of (1) is a spelling alternation task when the hypothesized alternatives are limited to lexical manipulations on the received query and no semantic revisions are considered.

In practice, spelling alteration is merely a subcomponent of the query understanding process where multiple spelling alternatives are often desirable and the respective posterior probabilities $P(h|q)$ serve as an invaluable cue for the optimization of the overall query processing. The Challenge therefore requires the submissions to not only produce a list of alternatives for each query but also estimate their posterior probabilities.

SIGIR'11, July 24–28, 2011, Beijing, China.
ACM 978-1-4503-0757-4/11/07.

2.1 Measurements

To take into account the posterior probabilities, the Challenge modified slightly the conventional definition of *F1* measure for evaluating the the algorithmic performance of a speller. First, the *Expected Precision* (*EP*) is defined as

$$EP = \frac{1}{|Q|} \sum_{q \in Q} \sum_{h \in H(q)} I[h \in S(q)]\, P(h|q) \qquad (2)$$

where $I(.)$ is the Boolean indicator function, Q is the full query set, and $H(q)$, $S(q)$ are the list of alternatives generated by the speller and the set of the desirable alterations for query $q \in Q$, respectively. The design is to favor spellers that do not over-generate alteration hypotheses because the total posterior probability must be distributed among all the hypotheses and summed up to 1. The corresponding *Expected Recall* (*ER*) is defined as

$$ER = \frac{1}{|Q|} \sum_{q \in Q} \sum_{a \in S(q)} I[a \in H(q)] P(a|q) \qquad (3)$$

For this Challenge, we only use manually annotated data that does not estimate the relative importance of each plausible alteration that $P(a|q) = 1/|S(q)|$ is used. It is hoped that in the future the proper distribution can be estimated for $P(a|q)$ either through the search behavioral data or cross-validations among a diverse collection of multiple spellers. Finally, the harmonic mean of *EP* and *ER*, called the *Expected F1* (*EF1*), is used as the main metric for the Challenge.

MSR maintains a web site [3] to accept the URI of a speller for evaluation. The evaluator sets a 60 second timeout for the speller to respond to each query, and treats the response as $H(q) = \emptyset$ if an HTTP 500 level error or timeout expiration is encountered. In addition to *EF1*, the average latency for each query is also computed as the potential tie-breaker for the Challenge.

2.2 Datasets

The Challenge uses search queries received by Bing in March 2010 as the final test set Q with $|Q| = 1500$. The queries are uniformly sampled from the tail section of the query log so that the uniform frequency assumptions intrinsically in both (2) and (3) are valid. The queries are manually annotated with spelling alterations, and are tokenized in the same fashion as described in [5]. After the award contest phase of the Challenge is completed, this dataset will continue to be used by the evaluator (Sec. 2.1) for researchers to benchmark future spelling alteration systems.

Three datasets are made available for the purpose of developing spelling alteration systems. First, the query set from TREC 2008 Million Query Track (1MQ) is annotated with spelling alterations using the same guidelines as the Bing test set and is made available for download [3]. The TREC dataset, with a size of more than 5500 queries, consists of search queries seeking public information published by US government websites. Roughly 10% of the queries contain typographical errors and, although the queries are collected in the EN-US region, the dataset contains a subset of queries in ES-US Spanish. These non-English queries are deliberately preserved because having rudimentary multi-lingual capability is a necessity for web search query processing. The frequencies of having non-English or spelling errors in TREC query set, however, are lower than the Bing dataset for the final evaluation of the Challenge.

The second dataset is the Microsoft Web N-gram service [5], available exclusively in the web service format. The dataset includes multiple statistical language models created from text resources on the web, including queries received by Bing over a 10 month period. In addition, the dataset includes language models built from the body, title, and the anchor text of the web documents indexed by Bing. Two snapshots from the Bing index are available: one from June 30, 2009 and April 30, 2010, respectively. These language models are provided as a reference resource for the speller developers to estimate the contextual probabilities of the alterations.

As misspelling is common in the web documents and the cut-off is set low in processing these snapshots, the web N-gram dataset appears to be a valuable resource to discover common patterns of misspelling in a large scale. To that end, the Challenge organizer made available a service to identify tokens appearing in the similar N-gram context that can be used as a supplement material to the TREC data in developing a speller.

3. PRESENT AND FUTURE

At the time of writing, the prize competition phase of the Challenge is still ongoing and there are 339 teams producing over 400 prototypes vying for the top 5 cash reward positions. The Challenge will consummate in July, 2011 when a workshop is held for the Challenge participants to discuss their work and exchange experience. The papers and discussion will be published in an electronic workshop proceedings, with summary shared in the SIGIR-2011 industry track presentation.

The dataset and the evaluation tools will continue to be available as web services at the Challenge web site [3]. It is the hope that researchers can utilize these resources to benchmark future improvements against the competition results.

4. ACKNOWLEDGMENTS

The authors would like to thank Mr. Christopher Thrasher, Nikolas Gloy and Amit Koul for their technical assistance in maintaining the online infrastructure for the Challenge. Drs. Bo-Jun "Paul" Hsu, Evelyne Viegas and Jianfeng Gao contributed to the design of the Challenge.

5. REFERENCES

[1] Gao, J., Li, X., Micol, D., Quirk, C., Sun, X. 2010. A large scale ranker-based system for search query spelling correction. In *Proc. 23rd International Conference on Computational Linguistics (COLING-2010),* Beijing, China, August, 358-366.

[2] Pedersen, J. 2010. Query Understanding at Bing. Invited talk at the 33rd Annual ACM SIGIR Conference (SIGIR-2010), Industry Track, Geneva, Switzerland, July.

[3] Speller Challenge, http://www.spellerchallenge.com, also at http://web-ngram.research.microsoft.com/spellerchallenge.

[4] Wang, K., Thrasher, C., Hsu, B.-J. 2011. Web scale NLP: A case study on URL word breaking. In *Proc. 20th International Conference on World Wide Web (WWW-2011),* Hyderabad, India, March, 357-366. DOI=http://doi.acm.org/10.1145/1963405.1963457

[5] Wang, K., Thrasher, C., Viegas, E., Li, X., Hsu, B.-J. 2010. An overview of Microsoft web N-gram corpus and applications. In *Proc. NAACL-HLT 2010,* Los Angeles, CA, May, 45-48. Also, http://web-ngram.research.microsoft.com.

Elsevier SIGIR 2011 Application Challenge

Jukka Valimaki, Remko Caprio
Elsevier
360 Park Ave S.
New York, NY 10010, USA
J.Valimaki@elsevier.com, R.Caprio@elsevier.com

Abstract

Elsevier SIGIR 2011 Application Challenge is an international competition that encourages software developers to create applications that run on Elsevier's SciVerse platform. The Challenge is open to all SIGIR 2011 Conference participants.

SciVerse Applications platform empowers the scientific community to build, find and use applications that enhance the research experience and are fully integrated with Elsevier content. Developers can create fee-based or free applications accessing a vast corpus of scientific content via web APIs. The Developers own the intellectual property of the application code, get access to Elsevier's 10 million full text article content base and will benefit from potentially reaching Elsevier's 15 million SciVerse users with their applications.

SciVerse is an implementation of OpenSocial. SciVerse applications access content and context via open APIs in SciVerse ScienceDirect and Scopus.

Registration is open in June 2011. SIGIR 2011 participants are eligible to participate individually or in teams. One representative of each team must be present in the SIGIR Conference on July 26th in Beijing, China. Submission deadline for applications is July 23rd and the winners will be announced on July 26th.

Winners receive VISA gift cards: First place – $1,500; Second place – $1,000; Third place – $500.

For more information, please visit developer.sciverse.com/SIGIR2011

Categories & Subject Descriptors: H.3.3 Information Search and Retrieval.

General Terms: Performance, Experimentation.

SIGIR'11, July 24–28, 2011, Beijing, China.
ACM 978-1-4503-0757-4/11/07.

Author Index

www.ingramcontent.com/pod-product-compliance
Ingram Content Group UK Ltd.
Pitfield, Milton Keynes, MK11 3LW, UK
UKHW051455290926
15471UKWH00008B/1216

9 781450 312523